45TH EDITION

KOVELS'
Antiques &
Collectibles
PRICE GUIDE 2013

BLACK DOG
& LEVENTHAL
PUBLISHERS
NEW YORK

Published by
Black Dog & Leventhal Publishers, Inc.
151 W. 19th Street
New York, NY 10011

Distributed by
Workman Publishing Company
225 Varick Street
New York, NY 10014

Designed by Sheila Hart Design, Inc.
Manufactured in the United States of America

ISBN-978-1-57912-915-6
Library of Congress Cataloging-in-Publication Data is available on file at
the offices of the publisher.

Paperback
b d f h g e c a

Front cover photographs, from top to bottom:
Webb, rose bowl, globe shape
Lamp, electric, Wilkinson, trumpet vine shade
Galle Pottery, figurine, cat

On the spine:
Weather vane, horse, running, full body, copper

Back cover photographs, from top to bottom:
Furniture, chair, rococo revival, walnut
Toy, car, jalopy, sedan, driver
Advertising, tin, Strong-Heart Coffee

Authors' photographs © Molly Nook (top) and Alex Montes de Oca (bottom)

BOOKS BY RALPH AND TERRY KOVEL

American Country Furniture, 1780–1875

A Directory of American Silver, Pewter, and Silver Plate

Kovels' Advertising Collectibles Price List

Kovels' American Antiques 1750–1900

Kovels' American Art Pottery

Kovels' American Collectibles 1900–2000

Kovels' American Silver Marks, 1650 to the Present

Kovels' Antiques & Collectibles Fix-It Source Book

Kovels' Antiques & Collectibles Price Guide

Kovels' Bid, Buy, and Sell Online

Kovels' Book of Antique Labels

Kovels' Bottles Price List

Kovels' Collector's Guide to American Art Pottery

Kovels' Collectors' Guide to Limited Editions

Kovels' Collectors' Source Book

Kovels' Depression Glass & Dinnerware Price List

Kovels' Dictionary of Marks—Pottery and Porcelain, 1650 to 1850

Kovels' Guide to Selling, Buying, and Fixing Your Antiques and Collectibles

Kovels' Guide to Selling Your Antiques & Collectibles

Kovels' Illustrated Price Guide to Royal Doulton

Kovels' Know Your Antiques

Kovels' Know Your Collectibles

Kovels' New Dictionary of Marks—Pottery and Porcelain, 1850 to the Present

Kovels' Organizer for Collectors

Kovels' Price Guide for Collector Plates, Figurines, Paperweights, and Other Limited Edition Items

Kovels' Quick Tips: 799 Helpful Hints on How to Care for Your Collectibles

Kovels' Yellow Pages: A Resource Guide for Collectors

The Label Made Me Buy It: From Aunt Jemima to Zonkers—The Best-Dressed Boxes, Bottles, and Cans from the Past

INTRODUCTION

This is the forty-fifth year *Kovels' Antiques & Collectibles Price Guide* has been published. It is also the 101st book we have had published. The past year, 2012, has been another year of the weak economy that started in 2008 (but this year prices are a little better than last) and another year of great changes in the way antiques are collected because of the Internet, cell phones, iPads and other electronic ways to buy and sell. Since 1953, the year we published our first book, the antiques world has gone from one or two antiques shows in a city per year to one almost every week. Auctions for expensive antiques used to be held in a few large cities; small towns had "farm auctions" often held outside a farmhouse. A local auctioneer who sold antiques often sold the stuff in the barn, too. There were no antiques malls and no Internet shops, sales, or auctions. Collectors went on antiquing trips to look for the furniture, pottery, or glass they collected in a few shops in each town, so buying was limited to a small area and a few items. Even research material was scarce. When we wrote our first book, it was one of just 60 titles about antiques announced that year. In 1969 there were maybe 200. Then several publishers started to offer picture-price books (with limited historical background) about a single type of collectible. Soon hundreds of books for collectors filled shelves at bookstores across the country. Now fewer books about collectibles are published each year but many new sources of information are written for the Internet. And much of the information found in old books, even old company catalogs or advertisements, can be found by searching the Internet. Our old newspaper columns, newsletters, special reports, books of marks, and other writings are now easily found via an Internet search.

Almost no one has noticed that we kept up with the times by changing the title of this book. It went from *The Complete Antiques Price List* to *The Kovels' Complete Antiques Price List* to *Kovels' Antiques Price List* to *Kovels' Antiques & Collectibles Price List* to, as of now, *Kovels' Antiques & Collectibles Price Guide*. The "list" became a "guide" because more people look online for a guide.

The economic problems that started with the stock market crash late in 2008 spread to other investments, including antiques. There is still a myth that if you buy antiques, they will go up in value every year and therefore are a good investment. That is only half true. If you buy the right antiques and sell at the right time, they sell for higher prices, even when you consider inflation. Consider this: Our first price book lists a Diamond Dye cabinet for $50. Last year two Diamond Dye cabinets were listed in the Advertising category, one at $540 and the other at $550, very low prices. This year the common Diamond Dye Cabinets in good condition were $407, $1,320, and $1,540. In the early months of 2008, the same cabinets sold for $1,112 and $2,633.

The ongoing worldwide recession is still affecting the value of antiques, but prices are starting to go up, show organizers are seeing better attendance, and there are many more auction bidders because most auctions today are online and international, so bids come from phones, computers, and those in the room. Final prices show that the average auction ends with many unsold lots, but the auction makes enough money to stay in business.

Prices for items offered by individuals on eBay are still low, and many do not sell at all. Prices have gone up for some things that have international appeal, like Chinese porcelain and ivory, and down for other things, like Hummel and Royal Doulton figurines, "country furniture" with peeling paint, and "brown furniture" like period Chippendale desks and 1890s oak dining tables with pedestal bases. Through it all, the malls, shows, and shops have seen fewer buyers and lower prices than they could get four years ago. But we talk to collectors and dealers, and most agree that "good stuff sells" and well-run shows, shops, and sales are doing "okay." Usable furniture in good condition and "smalls" are selling for expected prices and the "best" of every type of antique or collectible is still in demand. Auction prices are closer to retail than they were before because of the large, worldwide pool of bidders. One new influence in the market is the booming demand for Asian antiques. Jade, ivory, cloisonné, and ceramics made in China, Japan, Korea, and other Asian countries are selling for many times estimate. An auction that advertises top-quality Asian items often is visited by buyers and appraisers who travel to the United

States from China to see pieces at the preview before bidding way over estimated prices. Do Asian buyers know more than Americans do about the age and quality of these pieces? Or are they eager to bring their culture back home no matter what the price? A few items estimated to be worth thousands have sold for millions of dollars. Unfortunately, there is a growing problem with bids from China. Some bidders refuse to honor the bid and ask for a large reduction or just don't pick up the piece. Often this "sale" is reported at the time of the auction, but there is rarely a public announcement that the bid was not honored.

Kovels' Antiques and Collectibles Price Guide 2013 still has the same current, reliable information as always, plus two generations of Kovels editing the content. The book has 2,500 color photographs, 40,000 prices, dozens of facts of interest, and tips about care and repair. Each photograph is shown with a complete caption that includes the price. The book has color tabs and color-coded paragraphs that make it easy to find the listings you want and it has a modern, readable typestyle. There are more than 700 categories with introductory paragraphs that include company history. We make some changes in the paragraphs every year to indicate new owners, new distributors, or new information about production dates. This year we made over sixty changes to update the history told in the paragraphs, many of which tell of the sale or closing of a company. And, as always, all of the antiques and collectibles priced here were offered for sale during the past year, most of them in the American market. Almost all auction prices given include the buyer's premium because that is part of what the buyer paid. None include local sales tax.

READ THIS FIRST

This is a book for the collector. We check prices, visit shops, shows, and flea markets, read hundreds of publications and catalogs, check Internet sales and other online services, and decide which antiques and collectibles are of most interest to most collectors. We concentrate on the average pieces in any category. Sometimes high-priced items are included so you will realize that rarities are very valuable. This year several important collections sold at auction. These were collections assembled over the past 50 years that included rare pieces in close-to-mint condition. The toys and banks were often accompanied by their original boxes. Prices were very high because of the fame of the collectors and the great quality of the items. These collections included toy cars, toy boats, a collection of anything that pictured a fox, and the last sales of the Kaufman toy collection.

Some furniture, silver, Tiffany, art pottery, ivory, and other items may sell for more than $40,000; we list a few. Most listed pieces cost less than $10,000. The highest price in this book is $132,000 for a Tiffany glass window made in 1916 that pictures a river landscape, 38 ½ by 38 inches. The lowest price is $1 for a 144-page American Red Cross First Aid textbook. The smallest is a ⅜-inch plastic button shaped like a pair of dice that sold for $6. The largest, 15 by 13 feet, is a pharmacy divider that brought $5,166.

We also include the weird and the wonderful. This year we have a rare roll-top desk for a doctor patented in 1875. It is made of burled walnut and has a glass-enclosed top so the bottles of chemicals inside can be located. The desk sold for $9,500. Graniteware bowls in a holder were labeled soda, sand, and salt and sold for $400. The set was used when doing laundry. Other unusual entries include an American silver spoon that was the award in a pretty-baby contest. It was made in about 1900 and cost $191. A Doulton urn inscribed with the name and age of the deceased and his age was made in 1871. It sold for $96, empty. In Architecture, we list a jailhouse trap door, 76 by 27 inches. It was made of wood and iron in 1827 and sold this year for $384. A quack medical device called Dr. Scott's Electric Hairbrush No. 5 is embossed with the saying, "The germ of all life is electricity." The brush sold for $28. A brick embossed "Don't spit on the sidewalk" sold for $154. It was made during a health campaign to control the spread of tuberculosis. There is also a tin squirrel cage shaped like a church that sold for $770.

There are still bargains to be had, some that have been emerging over the last five years plus a few others. Most are in newer categories, like modernist jewelry and twentieth-century studio pottery. Big is still "big." Small sets of figurines or plates are very hard to sell. But large-scale accent pieces with colors and lines that blend in with modern furnishings— pieces like huge crocks, floor vases, centerpieces, and garden statuary—attract decorators as well as the owners of large homes. Orange and lavender are popular colors this year, so decorators are buying orange pottery and glass, especially Czechoslovakian. Anything from clothes and glass to ceramics and furniture that was in the newest style between the 1950s and the 1990s is hot. Also wanted are very large beige pots from the 1960s that can be displayed on the floor. And some old standbys, like toy cars, mechanical banks, and war and political memorabilia, are going up in price because they

are attracting new buyers. Interest in the presidential election in November 2012 has increased interest in all political things. Of major interest today are antique guns and ammunition. But costume jewelry is the most popular item we see selling at shows. Prices for pieces marked with important makers' names can sell for as much as $1,500. A few very popular collectibles of the past, like Roseville pottery and wicker furniture, have come down in price. The biggest change is silver tableware. The high meltdown price for sterling silver has made it more profitable to melt some pieces than to sell them as antiques. Hundreds of coin silver items, especially spoons, and no-name sterling serving dishes and flatware are also disappearing in the meltdown craze. But sterling by well-known companies or designers like Tiffany, Georg Jensen, or Paul Storr still get top dollar. Quality sells high—even with an uncertain economy, it retains its value.

This book seems to have gotten younger over the past forty-five years. Most items in our original book were made before 1860. Today we list pieces made as recently as 2000, and there is great interest in furniture, glass, and ceramics made since 1950.

The book is about 750 pages long and crammed full of prices and photographs. We try to have a balanced format—not too many glass, pottery, or collectible items; furniture from the eighteenth through the twentieth century; and not too many items that sell for over $5,000. We list a few very expensive pieces so you can realize that a great paperweight may cost $9,000 but an average one only $25. Nearly all the prices are from the American market for the American market. Few European sales are reported. We take the editorial privilege of not including prices we think result from "auction fever."

There is a computer generated index. Use it often. It includes categories and much more. For example, there is a category for Celluloid. Most celluloid will be there, but a toy made of celluloid will be listed under Toy and also indexed under Celluloid. There are also cross-references in the listings and in the paragraphs. But some searching must be done. For example, Barbie dolls are in the Doll category; there is no Barbie category. And when you look at "doll, Barbie," you find a note that "Barbie" is under "doll, Mattel, Barbie" because most dolls are listed by maker. Where possible, we list the maker at the beginning of an entry, and the size and age at the end.

All photographs and prices are new. Antiques and collectibles pictured are items that were offered for sale or sold for the amount listed in 2011–2012. Auction prices include the buyer's premium. Wherever we had extra space on a page, we filled it with tips about the care of collections and other useful information. Don't discard this book. Old Kovels' price guides should be saved for future reference and for tax, estate, and appraisal information.

The prices in this book are reports of the general antiques market. As we said, every price in the book is new. We do not estimate or "update" prices. Prices are either realized prices from auctions or completed sales or they're asking prices. We know that a buyer may have negotiated an asking price to a lower selling price, but we report asking prices. No price is an estimate. We do not pay dealers, collectors, or experts to estimate prices. Experience has shown us that estimated prices are usually high or low, but rarely an accurate report. If the price is from an auction, it includes the buyer's premium if one was charged; but like all the prices, it does not include sales tax. If a price range is given, at least two identical items were offered for sale at different prices. Price ranges are found only in categories like Pressed Glass, where identical items can be identified. Some prices in *Kovels' Antiques & Collectibles Price Guide* may seem high and some may seem low because of regional variations, but each price is one you could have paid for the object somewhere in the United States. Some Internet prices from sellers' ads or listings are avoided. Because so many non-collectors sell online but know little about the objects they are describing, there are often inaccuracies in descriptions. Sales from well-known Internet sites, shops, and sales, carefully edited, are included.

If you are selling your collection, do not expect to get retail value unless you are a dealer. Wholesale prices for antiques are usually 40 to 50 percent of retail prices. The antiques dealer must make a profit or go out of business. Internet auction prices are less predictable—because of an international audience and "auction fever," prices can be higher or lower than retail.

RECORD PRICES

Record prices for antiques and collectibles make news every year. We report those that relate to the entries in this book. We do not include record prices for works of art that are usually seen in museums, like oil paintings, antique sculptures, or very recent work by modern artists. It is a snapshot of the collectors' market. This year we include the prototype Coca-Cola bottle, a Lalique car mascot (hood ornament), a Hermès Birkin handbag, five separate records for comic books, a Stradivarius violin, a World Series program, and eight records for guns.

ADVERTISING

Rock Island Railroad sign: $71,500 for a Rock Island Railroad reverse-painted glass train sign, with original gilt frame, 1906, 99 x 24 in.

Coca-Cola prototype bottle: $240,000 for a 1915 prototype Coca-Cola bottle designed by Earl R. Dean in 1915, becoming the first bottle granted trademark status by the U.S. Patent Office.

DECOY

Decoy by Elmer Crowell: $241,500 for a one-of-a-kind standing redhead duck decoy, carved by Elmer Crowell (1862-1952).

Decoy by Charles Perdew: $207,400 for a sleeping mallard hen decoy by Charles Perdew.

Decoy by John English: $131,500 for a canvasback drake decoy by John English.

Curlew decoy by Charles Clark: $80,011 for a curlew decoy by Charles Clark.

Decoy by Charles Reeves: $22,483 for a green-winged teal duck decoy by Charles Reeves.

Decoy by D.K. Nichol: $18,515 for a hollow carved bluebill duck decoy by D.K. Nichol.

Carving by Oscar Peterson: $140,960 for a carved plaque by Oscar Peterson of 2 partridges in a pine tree, 15 x 24 in.

Perdew duck call: $17,739 for a rare transitional duck call by Charles Perdew.

John Cochran duck call: $19,176 for a duck call by John Cochran.

Benjon duck call: $6,814 for a duck call by "Benjon."

FURNITURE

Maloof rocking chair: $80,500 for a Sam Maloof rocking chair, walnut and ebony, signed "No. 31 1986/Sam Maloof facc©," inscribed dedication dated August 2002.

High chest of drawers: $3,554,500 for a Queen Anne high chest of drawers, figured mahogany, shell-carved, open talons, inscribed, John Townsend, Newport, Rhode Island, 1756, 88 ½ x 40 ¼ x 21 ⅛ in.

Josef Hoffmann furniture: $116,500 for a pair of Josef Hoffmann side chairs, Model 322, bent beechwood, leather upholstery, designed 1904-05, for Purkersdorf Sanatorium, marked "J. & J. Kohn, Wien, Austria," 38 ¾ x 17 in.

William Haines furniture: $31,250 for a pair of William Haines armchairs, lacquered wood, copper, vinyl upholstery, designed c.1950 (for Joan Crawford), 35 ½ x 27 in.

Settee: $422,500 for an Aesthetic Revival settee, designed by Louis Comfort Tiffany and Samuel Colman, double-arched crest decorated with peacocks in foliage, reeded spindle back, curved arms, padded seat on tapered reeded legs, claw and glass ball feet, c.1890-91, 33 ⅜ in. h. x 67 ¾ in. w.

GLASS & BOTTLES

Chinese snuff bottle: $3,328,400 for a famille rose enameled glass Chinese snuff bottle, made in the Imperial Palace workshops in Beijing, 1736–1795 (Qianlong period).

Lalique car mascot: $204,750 for the Lalique frosted glass fox car mascot, "Renard," in prowling position with long tail.

MISCELLANEOUS

Early motorcar: $4,620,000 for an 1884 De Dion Bouton et Trepardoux steam runabout (oldest running motorcar), with twin compound steam engines, "dos-a-dos" seating for four people, "spade handle" steering, solid front and rear axles with semi-elliptic springs, locomotive-style connecting-rod motion, and single-acting mechanical brakes, 43-in. wheelbase.

Handbag: $203,150 for a Hermès Diamond Birkin handbag, porosus crocodile, shiny red, with solid 18K white gold and diamond hardware, 12 x 8 x 6 in.

Tiffany Aztec dagger: $105,000 for a Tiffany "Aztec" presentation dagger made of sterling, ivory, and faceted obsidian, designed by G. Paulding Farnham in the early 1900s, 11 ½ x 2 in.

Saddle: $718,000 for the embroidered saddle that once belonged to Pancho Villa, with silver-wrapped threads over

leather stump work, silver conchas, silver stirrups carved with the initials of Francisco Villa (Villa's given name), saddle marked by the craftsmen.

Single penny: $1,150,000 for the United States experimental copper penny minted in 1792, pictures Lady Liberty, silver plug in the center (so legal requirements were met).

MUSIC

Les Paul guitar: $180,000 for a rare 1982 Gibson Les Paul prototype recording model guitar.

Stradivarius violin: $15,894,000 for the "Lady Blunt" Stradivarius violin of 1721.

PAINTINGS & PRINTS

American Folk Art portrait: $1,271,000 for an American School portrait of Abigail Rose, age 14, sitting in Queen Anne chair beside table with books and Battersea patch box, molded wood frame, 1786, 37 ¾ x 36 ¼ in.

Work of art at auction: $119,922,500 for the 1895 pastel-on-board version of The Scream, by Norwegian artist Edvard Munch, in its original frame, inscribed with an 1892 poem by Munch that inspired the work.

PAPER

Mahzor/Illuminated Hebrew manuscript: $2,401,422 for a fifteenth-century illuminated manuscript Mahzor on vellum, a festival prayer book written in Hebrew containing everyday customs, rituals, and practices of Jewish life, gold highlights, created in Tuscany, c.1490, over 400 pages.

Batman No. 1 comic book: $850,000 for the Batman No. 1 comic book that introduced the Joker & Catwoman, CGC-certified 9.2, off-white pages, originally sold for 10 cents when published in 1940.

The Avengers **No. 1 comic book:** $250,000 for *The Avengers* No. 1 comic book, featuring the first appearance of the superhero team, published in 1963, CGC-certified 9.6.

Journey into Mystery **No. 83 comic book:** $222,200 for *Journey into Mystery* No. 83 comic book, first appearance of Thor at Marvel Comics, August 1962, CGC-certified 9.2.

Single comic book: $2,160,000 for the first issue of Action Comics comic book, introducing Superman, 1938, CGC-certified 9.0.

POTTERY & PORCELAIN

American stoneware: $402,900 for an Absalom Stedman stoneware jug incised in cobalt blue with a spread-winged American eagle wearing a breast shield, holding an American flag in one talon and arrows in the other, a cloud-like banner coming from the eagle's beak is incised "Made by A. Stedman," c.1825-30, 19 ¼ in.

Anna Pottery "fair jug": $86,250 for an Anna Pottery salt glazed "fair jug," commemorating the Southern Illinois Anna Fair of 1884, incised tubular design, rows and columns of names of prominent fair officers, city and county officials, prominent citizens and U.S. presidential candidates, incised "C & W Kirkpatrick, Anna Pottery, Anna, Fair on August 26th, 27th & 28th, 1884," 22 x 13 in.

Anna Pottery Horace Greeley presentation pig flask: $25,875 for an Anna Pottery Horace Greeley presentation pig flask, Albany slip glaze, incised with political statements, drawings, and railroad guides.

Anna Pottery Snake jug: $80,500 for an Anna Pottery snake jug, salt glazed, commemorating the victory of Hayes over Tilden in the 1876 U.S. presidential election, twelve applied snakes with scales and "8 to 7" incised on rim, creamy yellow kaolin clay, 11 x 9 in.

SPORTS

Any item of sports memorabilia: $4,415,658 for the New York Yankees road jersey worn by Babe Ruth, c.1920.

World Series program: $241,500 for the 1903 World Series program for the game played in Exposition Park in Pittsburgh between the American League Boston Americans and the National League Pittsburgh Pirates.

Ty Cobb game-worn uniform: $358,500 for the Ty Cobb Detroit Tigers uniform worn during the 1922 season.

"Shoeless Joe" Jackson autographed baseball: $77,675 for a "Shoeless Joe" Jackson autographed baseball.

TEXTILE

Needlework sampler: $1,070,500 for a needlework sampler from Burlington County, New Jersey, worked in silk & painted paper on linen, picturing a house, trees, and animals, the name Mary Antrim and the year 1807 signed in ink in a crescent, 17 x 16 ¾ in.

WEAPONS

Single firearm: $1,142,500 for a Colt pocket revolver, Model No. 1849, Serial No. 63306, .31 caliber, gold inlay and deep relief on the frame of five different animals, 9 in.

U.S. Colt 1911 army pistol: $109,250 for a U.S. Colt semi-automatic pistol, Model 1911, Serial No. 33.

U.S. DWM Lugar pistol: $74,750 for a U.S. DWM Model 1902 American Eagle cartridge-counter Lugar pistol with holster.

World War II P38: $43,125 for a Walther prototype P38 semi-automatic pistol, Serial No. 1020.

U.S. Army test Lugar: $40,250 for a DWM U.S. Army Model 1900 test Lugar pistol with U.S. holster and accessories.

U.S. Warner & Swasey sniper rifle: $46,000 for a U.S. Model 1903 Springfield 1913 Warner & Swasey sniper rifle.

Colt Super 38 pistol: $32,625 for a Colt Super 38 pistol.

Record prices listed here were set by the following auction houses: Bonhams, Los Angeles; Christie's, New York; Clars Auction Gallery, Oakland, Calif.; Doyle New York; Guyette, Schmidt & Deeter, St. Michaels, Md.; Heritage Auctions, Dallas; High Noon Western Americana Auction, Mesa, Ari.; Hunt Auctions, Exton, Pa.; Julien's Auctions, Los Angeles; Metropolis Collectibles, New York; Pedigree Comics, Wellington, Fla.; Pook & Pook, Downingtown, Pa.; RM Auctions, Hershey, Pa.; Rock Island Auction Co., Rock Island, Ill.; SCP Auctions, Laguna Niguel, Calif.; Showtime Auction Services, Ann Arbor, Mich.; Skinner, Boston; Sotheby's, New York; Tarisio Fine Instruments & Bows, London; Wiederseim Associates, Glenmoore, Pa.

A NOTE TO COLLECTORS

You already know this is a great overall price guide for antiques and collectibles. Each entry is current, every photograph is new, and all prices are accurate. There is also another Kovel publication designed to keep you up-to-the-minute in the world of collecting. Things change quickly. Important sales produce new record prices. Fakes appear. Rarities are discovered. To keep up with developments, you can read *Kovels on Antiques and Collectibles*, our monthly newsletter. It is now available by subscription in two forms, a print edition that is mailed and an electronic format that is available in an online subscription at Kovels.com. Both have the identical current information and photos so useful to collectors. They are filled with color photographs, about forty per issue. The newsletter reports prices, trends, auction results, Internet sales, and other news for collectors as it happens.

Join the community of collectors at Kovels.com to keep up on more in the buy-sell world of antiques. Register; there is no charge for most of the information on the site, including our directory of services for collectors and dealers and thousands of searchable prices. Other information, including a database of pottery and porcelain marks and makers and another of silver marks and makers, is available for a fee.

HOW TO USE THIS BOOK

There are a few rules for using this book. Each listing is arranged in the following manner: CATEGORY (such as Pressed Glass), OBJECT (such as vase), DESCRIPTION (as much information as possible about size, age, color, and pattern). Some types of glass, pottery, and silver are exceptions to this rule. These are listed CATEGORY, PATTERN, OBJECT, DESCRIPTION. All items are presumed to be in good condition and undamaged, unless otherwise noted. In most sections, if a maker's name is easily recognized, like Gustav Stickley, we include it near the beginning of the entry. If the maker is obscure, the name may be near the end.

Many of the general glass entries are in special categories: Glass-Art, Glass-Blown, Glass-Bohemian, Glass-Contemporary, Glass-Midcentury, and Glass-Venetian. Major glass factories are listed under factory names. Well-

known types of glass, such as Cut, Pressed, Depression, Carnival, etc., can be found in their own categories. You will find silver flatware in either Silver Flatware Plated or Silver Flatware Sterling. There is also a section for Silver Plate, which includes coffeepots, trays, and other plated hollowware. Most solid or sterling silver is listed by country, so look for Silver-American, Silver-Danish, Silver-English, etc. Silver jewelry is listed under Jewelry. Most pottery and porcelain is listed by factory name, such as Weller; by item, such as Calendar Plate; in sections like Dinnerware or Kitchen; or in a special section, such as Pottery-Art, Pottery-Contemporary, Pottery-Midcentury, etc. This year there are two new categories, Porcelain-Asian and Scheier Pottery (art pottery, 1939-2007).

Sometimes we make arbitrary decisions. Fishing has its own category, but hunting is part of the larger category called Sports. We have omitted most guns except toy guns; these are listed in the Toy category. It is not legal to sell weapons without a special license, so guns are not part of the general antiques market but are often seen at auctions. Air guns, BB guns, rocket guns, and others are listed in the Toy section. Everything is listed according to the computer alphabetizing system. This means words such as "Mt." are alphabetized as "M-T," not as "M-O-U-N-T." All numerals are before all letters; thus "2" comes before "A." A space comes before a comma, so you will see "chair set" listed before "chair, Chippendale."

We have made several editorial decisions. A butter dish is a "butter." A salt dish is called a "salt" to differentiate it from a saltshaker. It is always "sugar and creamer," never "creamer and sugar." Political collectors often refer to "pinbacks," the round celluloid or tin pins decorated with candidates' names and faces. We use the word "button" instead of "pinback." The word "button" is also used when referring to fasteners on clothing. Where one dimension is given, it is the height; or if the object is round, it's the diameter. The height of a picture is listed before width. Glass is clear unless a color is indicated.

Entries are listed alphabetically, but idiosyncrasies of language remain. There is some confusion caused by words with more than one meaning, like iron (the metal) and iron (the pressing tool) or enamel (graniteware) and enamel (painted decoration on glass) and enamel (ground glass heated on metal to make an ashtray or piece of jewelry). We have indexed these so the appropriate pieces are listed together.

Some antiques terms, such as "Sheffield" or "Pratt," also have two meanings. Read the paragraph headings to know the definition being used. All category headings are based on the vocabulary of the average person, and we use terms like "mud figures" even if not technically correct.

This book does not include price listings for fine art paintings, antiquities, stamps, coins, or most types of books. Big Little Books and similar children's books are included. Comic books are listed only in special categories like Superman, but original comic art and cels are listed in their own categories.

Prices for items pictured can be found in the appropriate category. Look for the matching entry with the abbreviation "Illus." The photograph will be nearby.

Because of the computer, the book can be produced quickly. The last entries are added in June; the book is available in August. But human help finds prices and checks accuracy. We read everything at least five times, sometimes more. We edit more than 50,000 entries down to the 40,000 entries found here. We correct spelling, remove incorrect data, write category paragraphs, and decide on new categories. We proofread copy and prices many times, but there will always be some misspelled words and other errors. Information in the paragraphs is updated each year and this year more than fifty updates and additions were made.

Prices are reported from all parts of the United States, Canada, and Europe, converted to U.S. dollars at the time of the sale. The average rate of exchange in June 2012 was $1 U.S. to about $1.03 Canadian, €0.79 (Euro), and £0.64 (British Pound). Prices are from auctions, shops, Internet sales, and shows. Every price is checked for accuracy, but we are not responsible for errors.

We cannot answer your letters asking for price information, but please write if you have any requests for categories to be included in future editions or any corrections to the paragraphs or prices. You may find the answers to your questions at Kovels.com.

When you see us at shows auctions, house sales, and flea markets, please stop and say hello. Don't be surprised if we ask for your suggestions. You can write to us at P.O. Box 22192-K, Beachwood, Ohio 44122, or visit us on our website, www.Kovels.com.

TERRY KOVEL AND KIM KOVEL
July 2012

ACKNOWLEDGMENTS

The world of antiques and collectibles is filled with people who have answered our every request for help. Dealers, auction houses, and shops have given advice and opinions, supplied photographs and prices, and made suggestions for changes. Special thanks to all of them: Aleph-Bet Books, Allard Auctions, American Bottle Auctions, American Glass Gallery, Anderson Americana, Auction Team Breker, Bertoia Auctions, Bob Courtney Auctions, Bonhams & Butterfields, Brunk Auctions, Conestoga Auction Co., Cottone Auctions, Cowan's Auctions, DuMouchelles Art Gallery, Early American History Auctions, Early Auction Company, Fontaine's Auction Gallery, Fox Auctions, Garth's Auctions, Glass Works Auctions, Gray's Auctioneers, Hake's Americana & Collectibles, Humler & Nolan, Ivey-Selkirk Auctioneers, James D. Julia Inc., Jeffrey S. Evans & Associates, Lang's Sporting Collectibles, Leighton Galleries, Leland Little Auction, Leslie Hindman Auctioneers, Los Angeles Modern Auctions, Marbeth Schon Gallery, Martin Auction Co., Morphy Auctions, Neal Auction Co., New Orleans Auction Galleries, Noel Barrett Antiques & Auctions, Norman C. Heckler & Co., Northeast Auctions, Old Barn Auction, Past Tyme Pleasures, Philip Weiss Auctions, Potteries Specialist Auctions, Rago Arts and Auction Center, Rock Island Auction Co., Seeck Auctions, Serious Toyz, Showtime Auction Services, Skinner Inc., Sloans & Kenyon, Stein Auction Co., Strawser Auction Group, Theriault's Antique Doll Auctions, Tom Harris Auctions, Treadway and Toomey Galleries, Victorian Casino Antiques, William H. Bunch Auctions, William Morford Antiques, Willis Henry Auctions.

To the others who knowingly or unknowingly contributed to this book, we say thank you: Abby's Crate, Alderfer Auction, Antique Bottle & Glass Collector, Antiques & The Arts, Apple Tree Auction Center, Aspire Auctions, Auction Gallery of the Palm Beaches, Aunty Anne's Attic, Austin Auction Co., Belhorn Auction Services, British Bottle Review, Bottles & Extras, Bruhns Auction Gallery, Buffalo Bay Auction Co., Burchard Galleries, Capo Auction, Christie's, Clars Auction Gallery, Copake Auction, Copperton Lane Antiques and Collectibles, CRN Auctions, Crocker Farm, Dallas Auction Gallery, A Date in Time, Deco Dame, Dirk Soulis Auctions, Doe Run Antiques & Collectibles, Don Presley Auction, Doyle New York, Eldred's Auction Gallery, Emmelia's Attic, Fenton Art Glass Collectors of America, Flipside Collectors Mall, Forsythes' Auctions, Freeman's Auctioneers, Great Vintage Jewelry, Hatchett's Glass Treasures, Heisey Collectors of America, Heritage Auction Galleries, Hill House Wares, Hoosier Collectibles, Horst Auction, The Internet Antique Shop, Jackson's International Auctioneers, Jim Wroda Auction Service, Kamelot Auctions, Kaminski Auctions, Ken Farmer Auctions, Keno Auctions, L.H. Selman Ltd., Lone Star Antiques of San Francisco, Maine Antique Digest, Matthews Auctions, McCoy Lovers' NMXpress, McMasters Harris Auction Co., A Memory in Time, Michaan's Auctions, Morton Kuehnert Auctioneers, Mosby & Co. Auctions, National Toothpick Holder Collectors' Society, O'Gallerie Auctioneers, Ohio's Attic, Once Upon a Time Antiques, Paper & Advertising Collectors' Marketplace, Political Bandwagon, Pook & Pook, Purcell's Auction Gallery, Quinn's Auction Galleries, Rachel Davis Fine Arts, Richard Opfer Auctioneering, Rich Penn Auctions, Robert Edward Auctions, Ruby Lane, St. Charles Gallery, The Settings Place, Silver Magazine, Sotheby's, Southern Folk Pottery Collectors Society, Spring Brook Treasures, Stair Galleries, Stanton's Auctioneers, Susanin's Auctions, Tea Leaf Club International, Thomaston Place Auction Galleries, A Touch of Glass (Depression glass), Trader Fred's Antique Toys, Tradewinds Antiques & Auctions, Trocadero Directory, Tymes Remembered, Vintage and Modern, Vintage Jewelry Online, Watt Pottery Shop, Weschler's Auctioneers, William J. Jenack Auctioneers, Woody Auction Co., Ziegler Auction.

Our publisher, Black Dog & Leventhal, and its president, J.P. Leventhal, have continued to suggest and implement improvements to this book. There are also improvements in design and technology that add to the speed of production and ease of use. Thanks to J.P. Leventhal; Lisa Tenaglia, our editor; Pamela Schechter, production editor; Courtney Cullinan and Maureen Winter, sales; and Sally Feller, publicity. Mary Flower, Kelly Suzan Waggoner, and Robin Perlow did the job of copyediting and proofreading the entire book and found the tiniest of errors.

Thanks to Sheila Hart and her assistant, Mike Levay, who put all the prices, photographs, and paragraphs together and created the look and layout of *Kovels' Antiques & Collectibles Price Guide 2013*.

The details and hard work required to record prices, assemble photos and information, check accuracy and spelling, and solve many other problems are all done by our Kovels staff. We thank Carmie Amata, Mary Ellen Brennan, Grace DeFrancisco, Marcia Goldberg, Katie Karrick, Liz Lillis, Hamsy Mirre Lungha, Tina McBean, Mindy Reed, Renee McRitchie, Erika Risley, and Cherrie Smrekar. Special thanks to Lee Markley, who helped proofread the categories that include carnival glass. Photographs came from many sources, and they were all sized and digitally enhanced by our photo editor, Janet Dodrill, and her staff, Carolyn K. Lewis, Liz Blankschaen, and Stan Bujak. Gay Hunter, our in-house editor, always worries the most about the book. She kept detailed records and made sure all of us were on track and on schedule. She read and reviewed pages of prices, corrected our spelling errors, and handled computer problems. And during the final proofing and re-proofing, she kept finding minor errors. Together we updated paragraph information when a company closed or was purchased. Thanks to all of them. We have what we are sure is our best and most accurate book ever. We know that the book is possible only because of the group effort, even though it is our names that appear on the cover.

A. WALTER made pate-de-verre glass under contract at the Daum glassworks from 1908 to 1914. He decorated pottery during his early years in his studio in Sevres, where he also developed his formula for pale, translucent pate-de-verre. He started his own firm in Nancy, France, in 1919. Pieces made before 1914 are signed *Daum, Nancy* with a cross. After 1919 the signature is *A. Walter Nancy.*

Bowl, Bumblebee, Yellow Flowers, Mottled Ground, Signed, 3 ½ In. ....*illus*	2128.00
Box, Crab, c.1900, 2 x 3 x 4 In.	4400.00
Dish, 2 Scarabs, Dark Blue, Oval, Impressed, 6 ½ In....................................	1500.00
Dish, Applied Locust, Yellow, Brown, c.1920, 1 ¼ x 7 In..............................	1600.00
Dish, Lizard, On Leaf, Butterfly, Signed, c.1920, 2 ½ x 8 ¼ In.	1200.00
Dish, Lobster, Green, 5 x 6 In.	1800.00
Paperweight, Crab, Brown, 1 ¾ In..	850.00
Paperweight, Crayfish, Dark Blue, Black, 1 ¾ In...	950.00

ABC plates, or children's alphabet plates, were most popular from 1780 to 1860, but are still being made. The letters on the plate were meant as teaching aids for children learning to read. The plates were made of pottery, porcelain, metal, or glass. Mugs and other items were also made with alphabet decorations.

Clock, Rupert & Spot, Roman Numerals, Brownhills Pottery, c.1880, 7 ⅛ In.	425.00
Cup, Cats, Parrot, Garden Fence, Loop Handle, England, c.1890, 2 ¾ In.....................	450.00
Mug, Alphabet, I Is For Iceberg, J Is For Jackal, Applied Handle, Staffordshire, c.1840, 3 x 3 In.	350.00
Mug, Nursery Characters, Animals, Silver Plate, Loop Handle, c.1920, 2 ½ In.	100.00
Mug, Robinson Crusoe, Making Boat, Staffordshire, c.1880, 2 ⅞ In.	350.00
Mug, Tin, Flowers, Leaves, Applied Loop Handle, c.1860, 1 ¾ x 2 ¾ In.	225.00
Plate, Alphabet, Double, Sign Language, Dressed Cats, H. Aynsley, 6 ¼ In............... 121.00 to	450.00
Plate, Bible Scenes, Rebekah At Well, England, c.1880, 7 ½ In.	250.00
Plate, Ceramic, Bank, Vagrants Walking, Multicolor, c.1860, 8 In..............................	32.00
Plate, Chick, In Basket, Germany, c.1905, 6 ¼ In...	89.00
Plate, Children, Beehive, Bee Poem, Raised Rim...	85.00
Plate, Coney Island, Marine Railway Station, Manhatton Beach Hotel, 8 ¼ In. ....*illus*	24.00
Plate, Does Thou Love Life, Staffordshire, c.1825..	99.00
Plate, Dog In The Manger, Brownhills Pottery, c.1880, 8 In.	300.00
Plate, Dutch Kids Hugging, Goose, Aynsley Longton England, c.1875, 8 In..................	180.00
Plate, Gipsy Girl, Transfer, England, c.1840, 7 In..	150.00
Plate, Girls, Wearing Nightgowns, Doctor, Doll, Transferware, c.1875, 6 ¾ In.	125.00
Plate, Hey, Diddle Diddle, Brownhills Pottery, c.1880, 6 ½ In.	325.00
Plate, Hotel Brighton, Concourse, c.1860, 6 ¾ In..	50.00
Plate, Lamb, Crown Staffordshire, c.1900, 6 ¼ In..	115.00
Plate, Letter A, Staffordshire, c.1840, 6 ½ In..	225.00
Plate, Months Of The Year, November, Child, Bow, Horn, England, c.1840, 7 ½ In........	325.00
Plate, Mother, Child, Backyard, Elsmore & Forster, c.1860	180.00
Plate, Nations Of The World, Chinese, Brownhills Pottery, c.1880, 8 ⅛ In.	200.00
Plate, Niagara Falls, American Side, Raised Rim, 19th Century	95.00
Plate, Old Mother Hubbard, England, c.1880, 7 ½ In..	350.00
Plate, Old Mother Hubbard, Tunstall, Staffordshire Transfer, Alphabet Border, 7 ¼ In.	70.00
Plate, Pet Rabbit, Brown, Blue, England, c.1880, 6 ⅝ In.....................................	500.00
Plate, Sponge Bath, Dark Green, Brownhills Pottery, c.1860, 6 ⅛ In.	300.00
Plate, Steam Engine, Staffordshire, England, 7 ½ In..	40.00
Plate, The Walk, c.1800, 7 ⅞ In..	65.00
Plate, Tin Lithograph, Girl On Swing, Ohio Art Co., c.1920, 3 ½ In.........................	90.00
Plate, Tin, Embossed, Dragon Lion, 7 In..	50.00
Plate, Tin, Who Killed Cock Robin, c.1890, 7 ⅞ In..	125.00
Plate, Washington's Tomb, England, c.1880, 7 ⅜ In..	375.00
Plate, Woman, Gooseneck Bone Shaker Bicycle, Ironstone, 8 ½ In..........................	250.00
Plate, Women, Children, Cotton Field, Transferware, 19th Century...........................	65.00

ABINGDON POTTERY was established in 1908 by Raymond E. Bidwell as the Abingdon Sanitary Manufacturing Company. The company started making art pottery in 1934. The factory ceased production of art pottery in 1950.

Planter, Aqua, Marked, 10 x 7 x 2 In.	42.00
Planter, Star Shape, Aqua, 7 x 7 In..	38.00
Vase, Scalloped, Dusty Rose, Marked, c.1945, 11 x 2 In......................................	32.00
Vase, Transferware Figures, Gilt, Footed, Flared Rim, c.1942, 8 In., Pair....................	180.00

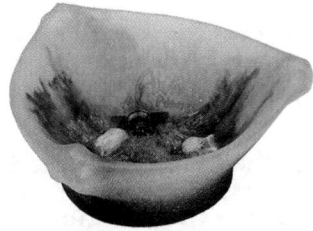

A.Walter, Bowl, Bumblebee, Yellow Flowers, Mottled Ground, Signed, 3 ½ In. $2128.00

James D. Julia Inc.

ABC, Plate, Coney Island, Marine Railway Station, Manhatton Beach Hotel, 8 ¼ In. $24.00

Conestoga Auction Co., Inc.

Adams, Plate, Adams' Rose, c.1820, 8 ½ In. $165.00

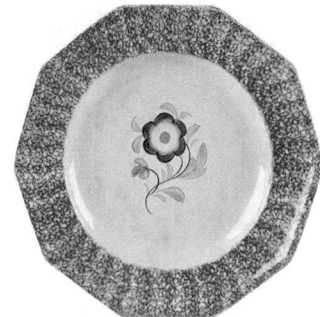

Morphy Auctions

Adams, Platter, Bologna, Purple Transfer, Scalloped Edge, Marked, 13 ¾ x 17 In. $147.00

Conestoga Auction Co., Inc.

Advertising, Banner, General Good, 5 Cent Hand Made Cigar, Linen, Globe Co., Akron, Oh., 34 In. $678.00

Showtime Auction Services

Advertising, Bell, Hotel, Apollinaris Brand Mineral Water, Bronze, Porcelain Top, 3 ½ x 3 In. $715.00

Wm Morford Antiques

Advertising, Bin, Standard Licorice Lozenges, Tin Lithograph, Glass Panel, 5 x 7 ½ x 5 In. $83.00

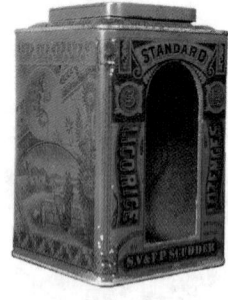

Showtime Auction Services

Advertising, Box, Boulevard Coffee, Automotive Street Scene, Cardboard, 10 x 5 ⅝ In. $143.00

Wm Morford Antiques

ADAMS china was made by William Adams and Sons of Staffordshire, England. The firm was founded in 1769 and became part of the Wedgwood Group in 1966. The name *Adams* appeared on various items through 1998. All types of tablewares and useful wares were made. Other pieces of Adams may be found listed under Flow Blue and Tea Leaf Ironstone.

Bowl, Cereal, Mandalay, Center Flowers, 6 ⅞ In.	67.00
Butter, Cover, White, c.1865	85.00
Cup & Saucer, Adams' Rose, Blue, Brown Ground, Handleless, c.1820	153.00
Cup & Saucer, Persimmon, Fruit, Branch	58.00
Mug, Stoneware, White, Metal Mount, c.1800, 7 ½ In.	136.00
Plate, Adams' Rose, c.1820, 8 ½ In. *illus*	165.00
Plate, Adams' Rose, Red & Blue, Rainbow Edge, c.1820, 7 ½ In.	59.00
Plate, Dinner, Anita, Divided Flower Border, 10 In.	55.00
Plate, Luncheon, Georgian, Flowers, Pale Green Ground, 9 ¾ In.	60.00
Plate, Rainbow, Rippled Edge, Concentric Circle Of Red, Blue, Green, Marked, 6 In.	118.00
Plate, Salad, Sprig Pink, Overall Flowers, 8 ¾ In.	40.00
Platter, Bologna, Purple Transfer, Scalloped Edge, Marked, 13 ¾ x 17 In. *illus*	147.00
Platter, Pink Sea Design, Scalloped Rim, Stamped, Staffordshire, 1800s, 14 x 17 In.	365.00
Platter, Tulip, Stick, 10 ¼ x 12 ¾ In.	28.00
Soup, Dish, Brentwood, Blue, White Rim, 7 In.	70.00

ADVERTISING containers and products sold in the old country store are now all collectibles. These stores, with the crackers in a barrel and a potbellied stove, are a symbol of an earlier, less hectic time. Listed here are many of the advertising items. Other similar pieces may be found under the product name, such as Planters Peanuts. We have tried to list items in the logical places, so enameled tin dishes will be found under Graniteware, paper items in the Paper category, etc. Store fixtures, cases, signs, and other items that have no advertising as part of the decoration are listed in the Store category. The early Dr Pepper logo included a period after "Dr," but it was dropped in 1950. We list all Dr Pepper items without a period so they alphabetize together. For more prices, go to kovels.com.

Apron, Wall Street Journal, It Brings You Business, Brown, Orange, 21 x 21 In.	127.00
Ashtray, Banquet Hall Bouquet Cigar, Metal, Orange Paint, Shaped, 2 Wells, 5 In.	45.00
Ashtray, Bishop Conklin, Paint Company, Elf, Paintbrush, Plaster, 1940s, 8 ½ In.	540.00
Ashtray, Dewar's Scotch, Globe, Base, Porcelain, c.1890, 5 In.	875.00
Ashtray, Dubble Bubble, 1 Cent, Pure, Seated Figure, Fleers, Plaster, Glass, 1930s, 7 In.	660.00
Ashtray, Master, World's Strongest Padlock, Muscular Man, Padlock Head, Plaster, 1930s, 7 ½ In.	510.00
Banner, Flint Glass Cutters, Meriden, Ct., Cloth, Gold, Blue, Fringe, 44 x 29 In.	5175.00
Banner, General Good, 5 Cent Hand Made Cigar, Linen, Globe Co., Akron, Oh., 34 In. *illus*	678.00
Banner, Ladies' Home Journal, Zane Grey, Bee Hunter, Canvas, 1925, 34 x 46 In.	1200.00
Banner, Peters Ammunition Heavy Paper, 1950s, 45 x 22 x 19 In.	66.00
Banner, Whistle, Thirsty?, Just Whistle, New Handy Bottle, Paper, c.1930, 28 x 70 In.	360.00
Bell, Hotel, Apollinaris Brand Mineral Water, Bronze, Porcelain Top, 3 ½ x 3 In. *illus*	715.00
Billhook, Aetna Mills Gold Dollar Flour, Flour Sack Shape, Cardboard, 1909, 5 x 3 In.	75.00
Bin, Beech-Nut, Chewing Tobacco, We Keep It Fresh, Flip Top, Blue, Red, 8 ¾ x 8 In.	450.00
Bin, Chase & Sandborn Coffee, Standard Java, Lithograph, Green & Black, 13 x 22 In.	207.00
Bin, Golden Rio Coffee, Green, Wood Top, Black Ground, Tin, c.1910, 28 x 19 ½ In.	148.00
Bin, King Bee Coffee, Dayton, Hinged Lid, Wood, 1800s, 32 x 22 In.	415.00
Bin, Mail Pouch Chewing Tobacco, Tin, 13 ½ x 11 x 10 In.	944.00
Bin, Standard Licorice Lozenges, Tin Lithograph, Glass Panel, 5 x 7 ½ x 5 In. *illus*	83.00
Blotter, Swans Down, Celluloid, Cake Flour On Front, Black, 1940s, 3 x 5 In.	110.00
Books may be included in the Paper category.	
Bottles are listed in their own category.	
Bottle Openers are listed in their own category.	
Bottle Topper, 7Up, Fresh Up, Turkey Dressed As Chef, Cardboard, 1948, 10 In.	65.00
Bottle Topper, Mission Beverages, Naturally Good, Fruit, Sun, Cutout, Cardboard, 10 x 9 In.	30.00
Bowl, Crawford Cooking Ranges, Flow Blue, 6 In.	88.00
Bowl, Reddy Kilowatt, Syracuse, 1957, 4 ⅞ In.	110.00
Box, see also Box category.	
Box Insert, Dupont Smokeless Shotgun Powder, 3 ¾ x 3 ¾ In.	56.00
Box, Albers Flapjack Flour, Trial Sample, Cardboard, 4 In.	90.00
Box, Boulevard Coffee, Automotive Street Scene, Cardboard, 10 x 5 ⅝ In. *illus*	143.00
Box, Columbia Catsup, Food Products, Shields, Red, Blue, Stenciling, Wood, 17 x 16 ¼ In.	390.00
Box, Display, Yucatan White's Chewing Gum, 6 ¾ x 4 ¾ In.	28.00
Box, Gum, Adams Spearmint, Chewing Gum, Square, Black & Green, 6 In.	780.00
Box, Gum, Yucatan, Square, Yellow, Red, Black, 6 In.	780.00
Box, Milky Way, Jack-O'-Lanterns, Orange Ground, 1950s, 6 x 8 In.	55.00
Box, North-Maid Rolled Oats, Girl, Red Dress, Cardboard, 9 ¾ x 5 ¼ In. *illus*	143.00

Box, Oatmeal, Poehler Rolled Oats, Polar Bear, Theo. Poehler Mercantile Co., 9 ½ In. .....*illus*	177.00
Box, Pigeon, E.D. Miller Lofts, Kings Carneau Modenas, Handle, 1800s, 23 x 16 In..................	444.00
Box, Royal Desserts Pudding, Warren Spahn, Blue Tint, 1950, 3 ½ In.............................	1645.00
Box, Van Ogden's Brand Ginger, Smiling Black Chef, Cardboard, 1930s, 4 In.................	95.00
Brochure, Buckeye Grain Drills, Sunbeam Cultivators, Color, 11 x 33 In.............................	345.00
Brush, Clothing, Williamsport Buick, Buick Logo, Celluloid, 1920s, 3 ¼ In.	115.00
Cabinet, DeLaval Cream Separators, Wood, Embossed, Tin Front, 17 x 26 In. ....*illus*	720.00
Cabinet, Diamond Dyes, Children With Balloon, Oak, Tin, Embossed, 24 ¼ x 15 In................	407.00
Cabinet, Diamond Dyes, Governess, Children With Ribbons & Balls, Oak, 29 ¾ x 23 In..........	1320.00
Cabinet, Diamond Dyes, Governess, Tin Lithograph, Walnut, 30 x 23 In.	1541.00
Cabinet, Diamond Dyes, Oak, Washer Woman, 23 x 30 In.	288.00
Cabinet, Diamond Dyes, Red-Headed Fairy, 10 Cent, Oak, c.1900, 30 ½ x 24 In......................	1920.00
Cabinet, Dr. Daniels' Veterinary Medicines, Remedies, Oak, Tin, 27 x 21 In.	3000.00
Cabinet, Dy-O-La Dye, Mahogany, Door, 17 x 13 ½ In...	243.00
Cabinet, German Household Dyes, Home Dyeing, Oak, 23 ½ x 14 In. ....*illus*	1018.00
Cabinet, Peerless Dyes, 10 Cents A Package, Peacock, Wood, 1900s, 31 x 23 In....................	2700.00
Cabinet, Peerless Dyes, Locomotive, Train Cars, Camels, Men, Wood, 30 ¼ x 23 In.............	7800.00
Cabinet, Pratts Veterinary Remedies, Stencils, Keys, Tin, 17 x 33 In. ....*illus*	6900.00
Cabinet, Putnam Fadeless Dyes, Tints, Tin, Monroe Chemical Co., Quincy, Ill., 19 x 15 In.......	374.00
Cabinet, Sirup De Goudron, Cod Liver Syrup, Fish, Wood Base, Porcelain, 24 x 11 In.	360.00
Cabinet, Spool, Belding Bros. & Co., 7 Drawers, 6 Glass Fronts, 21 x 19 In.	575.00
Cabinet, Spool, Clark's O.N.T. Spool Cotton, Ruby Glass, 29 x 22 x 3 In. ....*illus*	3300.00
Cabinet, Spool, Corticelli, Always Reliable, Silk Worm, Leaf, Oak, Tin, 20 ½ x 14 In............	1320.00
Cabinet, Spool, J. & P. Coats', 6 Drawer, Oval Wood Door Decals, 26 x 20 In.	863.00
Cabinet, Spool, J. & P. Coats', 6 Drawers, 29 x 23 In...	403.00
Cabinet, Spool, J. & P. Coats', 6 Glass Front Drawers, Oak, 21 x 27 In.............................	177.00
Cabinet, Spool, J. & P. Coats', Spool Cotton, Wool Top Opening, Oak, 24 x 31 In.	1320.00
Cabinet, Spool, Merrick's Cotton, Six Cord, Oak, 6 Drawers, Lift Top, 14 x 30 x 22 In............	339.00
Cabinet, Spool, Merrick's, Oak, Revolving, Hinged Door, c.1890, 22 x 18 In. ....*illus*	920.00
Cabinet, Spool, Merrick's, Six Cord, Spool Cotton, 4 Drawers, 30 x 22 In.........................	170.00
Cabinet, Spool, Royal Society, Oak, 12 Pullout Trays, 12 Sections, Glass Fronts, 36 x 18 In.	497.00
Cabinet, Spool, Willimantic, Six Cord, Spool Cotton, Oak, 4 Drawers, 14 ¾ x 24 ½ In............	178.00
Cabinet, West Hair Nets, Fine As A Fairy Web, West Electric, Dome Top, Tin, 18 x 13 In...........	300.00
Calendars are listed in their own category.	
Can, Nourse Kill 'Em Kwik Fly Spray, Fly Graphics, Metal, Flat, Pt..................................	51.00
Can, Winchester Gun Oil, Oiler Top, Oval, Metal, Pt..	51.00
Canisters, see introductory paragraph to Tins in this category.	
Cards are listed in the Card category.	
Cart, Homemade Bread, 1800s, 35 x 46 In..	425.00
Case, Display, Eveready Flashlight Batteries & Mazda Lamps, Tin, Glass, 1920s, 12 In............	288.00
Case, Display, Hickok Initial Belts, Wood, Pullout Tray, Fitted, Velvet, 1920, 13 In.................	173.00
Catalog, Jarman & Co., Tin Boxes, Tin Lithograph, Hinged Cover c.1900, 6 x 10 In. ....*illus*	489.00
Chair, Duke's Cameo Cigarettes, Girl's Image On Chair Back, Folding, Wood, 30 ½ In.....*illus*	1485.00
Change Receiver, see also Tip Tray in this category.	
Charger, Budweiser, Say When, Couple, Pouring & Stirring, Beer Bottles, c.1920, 16 In............	570.00
Charger, Robert Burns Cigar, Burns Bust, Tin, 24 In..	460.00
Cigar Cutter, Argo Club, Rigby's, Shield, Wood Base, Square Metal Handle, 4 ½ x 7 ¾ In........	90.00
Cigar Cutter, Artie, Best Cigar Of The Year, Man, On Crate, Iron, 10 In.	1200.00
Cigar Cutter, Champagne E. Mercier & Co., Brass, Mother-Of-Pearl, 2 In.	308.00
Cigar Cutter, Don Rosa, Highest Grade, Havana Cigars, Cast Iron, 6 ½ x 10 In.	840.00
Cigar Cutter, Straiton & Storm, New York Segars, Indian Figure, Pot Metal, 17 ¾ In.	1080.00
Clicker, Had Your Toddy Today?, Child Holding Glass, Tin Lithograph, 1930s, 2 In.................	114.00
Clicker, Jack & Jill, Instantly Prepared Gelatin Dessert, Tin Lithograph, 2 In. ....*illus*	40.00
Clicker, Prairie Rose, It's Real Butter, Yellow Child, Buttercup Hat, Tin Lithograph, 2 In.	114.00
Clocks are listed in their own category.	
Coat Rack, Whistle, Thirsty?, Golden Orange Refreshment, Elves, Wood, c.1940, 8 x 35 In......	330.00
Container, Bing Crosby Vanilla Ice Cream, Bing On Cover, 1940s, 4 x 3 In.	40.00
Cookie Cutter, Robin Hood Flower, Robin's Hat, Plastic, 4 x 2 In...................................	12.00
Cooler, Royal Crown Cola, Metal, 121 x 18 In.	678.00
Crock, Knickerbocker Catering Co., Genuine Boston Baked Beans, 1800s, 4 ½ In..................	138.00
Crock, Lowe & Husband, General Merchandise, Mt. Pleasant, Rolled Rim, 8 In.....................	292.00
Crock, Osage Rub For The Hair & Head, Swing Handle, M.E. Waite, N.Y., 10 x 7 In.................	797.00
Cuspidor, Redskin Brand, Chewing Tobacco, Indian, Headdress, Brass, 10 ½ In....................	60.00
Dispenser, Birchola, 5 Cents, Round, Spread Foot, Leaves, Ball Pump, c.1920, 16 In..............	1920.00
Dispenser, Cherry Julep, Bulbous, Red & White, Pump, Ceramic, c.1910, 15 In.	518.00
Dispenser, Cherry Smash, Fowler's, Porcelain, Silver Plate Pump, 1913, 15 In......................	1150.00

Advertising, Box, North-Maid Rolled Oats, Girl, Red Dress, Cardboard, 9 ¾ x 5 ¼ In.
$143.00

Wm Morford Antiques

Advertising, Box, Oatmeal, Poehler Rolled Oats, Polar Bear, Theo. Poehler Mercantile Co., 9 ½ In.
$177.00

Showtime Auction Services

Advertising, Cabinet, DeLaval Cream Separators, Wood, Embossed, Tin Front, 17 x 26 In.
$720.00

Victorian Casino Antique Auction

Advertising, Cabinet, German Household Dyes, Home Dyeing, Oak, 23 ½ x 14 In.
$1018.00

Wm Morford Antiques

Advertising, Cabinet, Pratts Veterinary
Remedies, Stencils, Keys, Tin, 17 x 33 In.
$6900.00

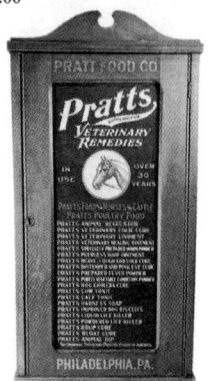

Showtime Auction Services

Advertising, Cabinet, Spool, Clark's
O.N.T. Spool Cotton, Ruby Glass,
29 x 22 x 3 In.
$3300.00

Showtime Auction Services

Advertising, Cabinet, Spool, Merrick's,
Oak, Revolving, Hinged Door, c.1890,
22 x 18 In.
$920.00

James D. Julia Inc.

Advertising, Catalog, Jarman & Co.,
Tin Boxes, Tin Lithograph, Hinged Cover
c.1900, 6 x 10 In.
$489.00

Bertoia Auctions

Dispenser, Cherry Smash, Our Nation's Beverage, Round, Pump, c.1900, 15 In.		2300.00
Dispenser, Cherry Smash, Syrup, Ruby Glass, Chrome, Clamp, 14 ¼ x 7 ¼ In.		230.00
Dispenser, Drink Hires, Milk Glass Globe, Marble Base, 35 In.		7975.00
Dispenser, Drink Hires, Pump, Counter	*illus*	480.00
Dispenser, Drink, Mission Orangeade, Spigot, Metal, Chrome Base, 16 In.		173.00
Dispenser, Eskimo Pie, Cylindrical, 3 Eskimo Shape Legs, Counter, c.1928, 16 In.		920.00
Dispenser, Mission Orange, Healthful, Refreshing, Black, Orange, c.1925, 27 In.		300.00
Dispenser, Orange Crush, Feel Fresh, Fiesta Style, Pear Shape, Handle, 8 ¾ In.		480.00
Dispenser, Toothpick, Sanitodis, Metal, Glass, 5 x 8 x 5 In.		113.00
Dispenser, Ward's Lime Crush, Lime Shape, Spout, Round Base, c.1920, 14 In.		3738.00
Dispenser, Ward's Orange Crush, Fruit Shape, Ceramic Ball Pump, c.1920, 14 In.		805.00
Dispenser, Ward's Orange Crush, Round, Multicolor, Impressed 3-24-1919, 14 ¾ In.		748.00
Display, Automatic Merchandizer Candy Bar Vending Machine, c.1910, 33 x 9 ½ In.		30.00
Display, Baker Figure, Daisy Donuts, Holding Donut, Stretched Arm, Papier-Mache, 26 In.		510.00
Display, Box, Cardorundum Niagara Scythe Stones, Wood, Dovetailed, c.1890, 6 x 14 In.		132.00
Display, Box, Fairy Soap, Fairbank's, Fairy Holding Banner, Wood, c.1900, 8 ½ x 17 In.		210.00
Display, Bryant Furnace, Bryant Pup, Papier-Mache, Cleve., Ohio, c.1927, 19 ½ x 10 In.		431.00
Display, Bunte Cough Drops, Give Positive Relief, Coughing Man, Tin, 10 ¼ In.		480.00
Display, Calso Water, Woman, Next To Bottle, Hands On Hips, Plaster, 1930s, 10 In.		480.00
Display, Caterpillar Tractor, Holt Fg. Co., Embossed, Iron, Gas Powered, 29 In.	*illus*	20700.00
Display, Chief Watta Pop, Indian Bust, Chalk, 8 ½ x 9 ½ x 5 In.	*illus*	201.00
Display, Chiquita Banana Figure, Dancing, Round Base, 1947, 3 ½ In.		660.00
Display, Chubby Man Figure, Men's Store, Sweater, Hat, Umbrella, Base, 1940s, 12 In.		960.00
Display, Clark's Teaberry Pepsin Gum, Teaberry Branch, Held 40 Packs, 1910		395.00
Display, Curlox, Oversize Hair Nets, Oak, 15 x 8 ½ In.		303.00
Display, Curtiss Candies, Baby Ruth, Butterfinger, Glass Doors, Slant Front, Decals, 17 x 20 In.		136.00
Display, Diamond Dyes, Hinged Lid, Tin Lithograph, Wood Base, Counter, 19 x 16 ½ In.		102.00
Display, Dunlop Man, Golf Ball Head, Carrying Golf Clubs, Composition, c.1950, 15 ½ In.		717.00
Display, Eberhard Faber, Wood Stand, 72 Pencil Holes, Turned Finials, 1920, 5 x 11 In.		209.00
Display, Edison Mazda Lamps, General Electric, Girl, Stand-Up Cardboard, 1920s, 34 x 22 In.	*illus*	1265.00
Display, Figural, Ice Cream Cone, Lyons' Pola Maid, Composition, 59 In., 2 Piece	*illus*	600.00
Display, G.H. Mumm Champagne, Bottle, Glass, 1950s, 19 ½ In.		158.00
Display, Gentleman, Milwaukee Beer, Light-Up, Counter, 6 ½ x 13 In.		367.00
Display, Gutta Percha Footwear, Perky Dog Of West Lodge, Plaster, 1930s, 9 ½ In.		390.00
Display, Heddon River Runtie Spook Lures, 11 Fly Rod Runties, Counter		1298.00
Display, Heinz Ketchup, Bottle Figure, Label & Cap, 1920s, 26 ¼ In.		570.00
Display, Hercules Powders, Cardboard, Trifold, Panel Design, Soldier, Dog, Hunter, 32 x 24 In.		1725.00
Display, Hills Bros. Coffee, Man, In Nightshirt, Drinking Coffee, Chalkware, c.1939, 12 x 10 In.		440.00
Display, Hires, Right Note For Home Refreshment, Girl, Red Dress, Cardboard, 1940s, 13 In.		120.00
Display, Hoffman Chocolates, Vaseline Glass, Embossed, 6 ½ x 9 ½ In.		45.00
Display, Holley Carburetor Co. Automotive Accessories, Counter, 11 x 14 In.		1074.00
Display, Hollywood Vassarette, Bras & Girdles, Woman, 1950s, 8 ½ In.		780.00
Display, Hoyt Water Heaters, Light-Up, Reverse Painted, 10 x 28 In.		254.00
Display, I Will Candy Bars, Cardboard, Sisco Hamilton Co., Box, 5 x 10 ½ x 3 In.		31.00
Display, Jockey Figure, Jockey Underwear, Rubber, Square Base, 1940s, 15 ¼ In.		360.00
Display, Just Call Me Squirt, Figural, Boy, Unopened Bottle, 12 In.	*illus*	300.00
Display, Keenes Plaster & Salve, Foot, Face On Sole, Papier-Mache, Canton, Oh., c.1900, 8 x 17 In.		7763.00
Display, Kool Cigarettes, Mr. Kool Penguin, Top Hat, Smoking, Papier-Mache, 14 In.		570.00
Display, Koveralls, Keep Kids Klean, Tin, Die Cut, Pat. June 8, 1918, 11 x 19 ½ In., Pair	*illus*	7150.00
Display, Lucky Strike Cigarette, 10 Packs, Counter, 12 x 12 In.		2938.00
Display, Mansfield's Pepsin Gum, Decals, Glass, Wood, 4 x 11 In.		2006.00
Display, Mautz Paint, Benny Moss Figure, Holding Brush, Papier-Mache, 1940s, 31 In.		5400.00
Display, McGregor Happy Foot, Molded Sock, Composition, 1930s, 6 x 10 x 16 In.	*illus*	923.00
Display, Miller High Life, Champagne Of Bottle Beer, Reverse Painted, Easel, 4 x 8 In.		254.00
Display, Milliken Talcum Powder, Celluloid, Hinged, Violets, White Ground, 6 x 5 ½ In.		236.00
Display, Miss Uptown Hosiery, Woman, Slip, Arm Up, Rubber, 1930s, 17 ½ In.		1440.00
Display, National Mazda Lamps, Light Bulbs, Tin, Counter	*illus*	660.00
Display, Nichol Kola, America's Taste Sensation!, Girl, Ship's Wheel, Sailboats, Cardboard, 19 x 11 In.		330.00
Display, Oakwood Taxi Co. All 7-Passenger Packard, No Cheaper Rates In Town, 8 x 9 In.		904.00
Display, Paris Garters, Wood, Decal, 5 ¼ x 13 ¾ In.		303.00
Display, Park & Tilford Candies, Santa, Child, Die Cut, Chromolithograph, 1900, 36 In.		459.00
Display, Peerless Amber Beer Of Good Cheer, Light-Up, 11 x 12 In.		198.00
Display, Pen & Pencil Set, Parker, 24 In., Pair	*illus*	1625.00
Display, Peter Rabbit Figure, Fine Shoes For Little Folks, Scarf, Cane, Plaster, 1940s, 16 In.		660.00
Display, PEZ Space Gun, 49 Cents, Cardboard, Easel, 6 Plastic Guns, 1950s, 9 x 13 In.		3163.00
Display, Phillip Morris, Johnny Figure, Doorman Uniform, Red & Black, Plaster, 1930s, 13 In.		1200.00

Display, Premier, All That The Name Implies, Vacuum Graphic, Counter, 11 x 12 In.	85.00
Display, Red Goose Shoes, Neon, Porcelain, c.1940, 39 x 36 In.	2070.00
Display, Red Jacket Coal Authorized Dealer, Indian Logo, Counter, 12 ½ x 9 In.	339.00
Display, Reddy Kilowatt, Your Electrical Servant, Lightning Bolt Body, Wood, 1930s, 32 In.	2400.00
Display, Reliable Seeds, Sioux City Seed Co., Seed Packs ....*illus*	649.00
Display, Robin Hood Figure, None So Good, Children's Shoes, Sword, Plaster, 1940s, 14 In.	210.00
Display, Sawyer's Crystal Laundry Soap, Mother Washing, Cardboard, Die Cut, Easel, 11 x 8 In.	577.00
Display, Schaefer Fine Beer, Light-Up, Counter, 8 x 12 In.	198.00
Display, Silver King Golf Balls, Figure, With Club, Golf Ball Head, Papier-Mache, 1920s, 14 ½ In.	4200.00
Display, Star Pepsin Gum, Tin, Painted, 8 ½ x 4 ½ In.	110.00
Display, Supersite Rear View Mirror, Mounted Mirrors, Wood Base, Counter, 1930s	495.00
Display, Ted Williams Creamy Root Beer, Yellow, Black, 1950s, 15 x 10 In.	529.00
Display, Texaco Home Lubricant, Metal, Painted, Counter	7425.00
Display, Tobacco, Elephant, Clockwork, Cardboard, Embossed, France, 17 x 12 ½ In.	413.00
Display, Towle's Log Cabin Syrup, Fold, Cardboard, Copyright 1914, 15 x 15 x 10 In. ......*illus*	523.00
Display, Wahl Eversharp, Fountain Pen, Etched Glass Top, Wood Back, 15 ½ x 3 ½ In.	339.00
Display, Western Union Telegraph, 9 x 12 In.	452.00
Display, Wrigley's Chewing Gum, Multicolor, c.1925, 18 x 14 In.	600.00
Display, Wrigley's, Metal & Celluloid, 4 Display Boxes, 1935	413.00
Display, Yankee Cigar, 5 Cents, Marching Girl, Top Hat, Rubber, 1930s, 16 ¾ In.	540.00
Dolls are listed in their own category.	
Door Push, Kayo Chocolate, Bottle, Delightful, Refreshing, Tin Litho, 1930s, 11 x 4 In.	162.00
Door Push, Orange Crush, 5 Cents, Thirsty?, Crushy, Tin, 1920s, 9 In.	510.00
Door Push, Polar Bear Tobacco, Always The Best, Bear, Red, Blue, Porcelain, 7 x 3 ½ In.	840.00
Door Push, Senate Beer, Beer Bottle, Yellow, Blue Band Top & Bottom, Tin, 3 ½ x 11 In.	96.00
Door Push, Squirt, Tin Lithograph, 9 x 4 In.	242.00
Door Push, Sunbeam Bread, Batter Whipped, Girl Eating Toast, 26 ¾ In.	330.00
Door Push, Vicks Vaporub, Salve, For All Cold Troubles, Porcelain, 1930s, 6 ½ x 3 ¾ In.	180.00
Fan Pull, Orange Crush, 2-Sided, Healthful Carbonated Drink, Cardboard, 1934, 9 x 8 In.	330.00
Fan, Moxie, Girl With Hair Bow, Dated 1916, 9 x 8 In.	157.00
Fans are also listed in their own category.	
Figure, American Furnace Company, AFCO, Man, Boots, Hair, Plaster, 1930s, 10 ½ In.	840.00
Figure, Big Boy, Holding Hamburger, Checkered Overalls, Molded, 55 x 43 In.	1242.00
Figure, Blatz Brewing Co., Girl On Barrel, Holding 8 Steins, Chalkware, 19 In.	226.00
Figure, Bust, Old Grand Dad, White, Gold Letters, Chalkware, 1940s, 7 x 3 In.	75.00
Figure, Clark Candy Bar Kid, Smiling, Blue & Orange Shirt, 1950s, 8 x 4 In.	115.00
Figure, Dog, RCA, Nipper, Keller's Music Room, Chalkware, Painted, 1930s, 4 ¼ In.	115.00
Figure, Dog, RCA, Nipper, Papier-Mache, 1950s, 34 In.	330.00
Figure, Donkey, Royal Corona Coffee, Plaster, 10 x 9 x 6 In.	193.00
Figure, Durofix, Dad, Where's The Boy, Holding Slingshot, Broken Vase, 1930s, 15 ½ In.	720.00
Figure, Fresh-Up Freddie, Woodpecker, Holding Bottle, Vinyl, 1950s, 9 ¼ In.	240.00
Figure, Heinz 57, Tomato Head Character, Rubbery Composition, 5 x 2 x 2 In.	770.00
Figure, Krantz Old Dutch Beer, We Serve The Good Beer, Man, Woman, Drinking Beer, 12 x 18 In.	660.00
Figure, Lenox Heating Systems, Lenny Lenox, Slide For Business Card, Rubber, 1940s, 9 In.	330.00
Figure, Manny, Pep Boys, Glasses, Cigar In Mouth, Waving, Bowtie, Plaster, 1930s, 15 ¾ In.	1680.00
Figure, McDonald's Hamburglar, 1976, 11 x 8 ½ In.	75.00
Figure, Nikolai Vodka, Russian Peasant Dancing, With 6-Sided Bottle, 1960s, 12 x 5 In.	169.00
Figure, Pola Cola, Polar Bear, Seated, Arms Up, Shaped Base, Rubber, 1930s, 11 ½ In.	450.00
Figure, Polar Ginger Ale, Seated Polar Bear, Round, Shaped, White, Blue, 1930s, 7 In.	300.00
Figure, Premier Cigarette, Young Boys, Smoking, Spelter, Ruffony, 5 ½ x 9 ½ In.	102.00
Figure, Saxon Slacks, Man, Standing, Holding Pipe, Rubber, 1940s, 15 ½ In.	480.00
Figure, Smiling Golfer, He Played A Penfold, Ellis Display, 1930s, 20 ½ In. ......*illus*	380.00
Figure, Wosley Ties, Bust, Man, Side-Glancing, Red, Headwrap, Plaster, 1930s, 9 In.	270.00
Firkin, Brick's Mince Meat, Lid, Bentwood Handle, Bands, Painted Green, Brown, 9 ½ In.	176.00
Flag, You Are Safe When You Buy Zig Zag, American Flag, Felt, 10 x 16 In.	450.00
Hairnet, Lorraine Human Hair Net, Dupont Nylon Co., Envelope, c.1945	10.95
Humidor, Benson & Hedges, Walnut, Brass, Engraved Cartouche, Tin Liner, c.1890, 7 x 14 In.	732.00
Humidor, Cremo Cigars, Always In Perfect Condition, Wood & Metal, Hinged, 28 x 17 In.	115.00
Jam Jar, Smokey Bear, Sitting, Prevent Forest Fires, Ceramic, Norcrest, 1960s, 5 In.	115.00
Jar, Heinz's Pickling Vinegar, Glass Lid, 11 x 4 ½ x 5 ½ In. ......*illus*	3630.00
Jar, Jergens Face Cream, Milk Glass, Sample, c.1941, 2 ½ x 2 ¾ In.	45.00
Jar, Lid, Heinz, Glass, Octagonal, Square Top Handle, c.1900, 11 ½ In.	90.00
Jar, Smokey Bear, Figural, Holding Shovel, Norcrest, Japan, 1960s, 9 ¾ In.	171.00
Jar, Water Paints, American Paint Maker, Tin Lithograph, Indian, Davoe & Raynolds, 8 x 2 In.	56.00
Jug, C.R. & Q. High Class Groceries, Denver, Cone Top, Blue Stencil, ½ Gal., 7 ½ x 6 In.	358.00
Key Chain, Flying A Texaco Dogs, Scottie, Mascots For Texaco Gas Stations, 1950s, 1 In.	45.00

Advertising, Chair, Duke's Cameo Cigarettes, Girl's Image On Chair Back, Folding, Wood, 30 ½ In.
$1485.00

Wm Morford Antiques

Advertising, Clicker, Jack & Jill, Instantly Prepared Gelatin Dessert, Tin Lithograph, 2 In.
$40.00

Hake's Americana & Collectibles

Advertising, Dispenser, Drink Hires, Pump, Counter
$480.00

Victorian Casino Antique Auction

Advertising, Display, Caterpillar Tractor, Holt Fg. Co., Embossed, Iron, Gas Powered, 29 In.
$20700.00

Bertoia Auctions

ADVERTISING

A

Advertising, Display, Chief Watta Pop, Indian Bust, Chalk, 8 ½ x 9 ½ x 5 In. $201.00

Showtime Auction Services

Advertising, Display, Edison Mazda Lamps, General Electric, Girl, Stand-Up Cardboard, 1920s, 34 x 22 In. $1265.00

Wm Morford Antiques

Advertising, Display, Figural, Ice Cream Cone, Lyons' Pola Maid, Composition, 59 In., 2 Piece $600.00

Victorian Casino Antique Auction

Advertising, Display, Just Call Me Squirt, Figural, Boy, Unopened Bottle, 12 In. $300.00

Victorian Casino Antique Auction

Label, Cigar Box, 55 Private Stock, Embossed, Gold Leaf, Syracuse, N.Y., 8 ⅜ x 6 ¼ In.	112.00
Label, Cigar Box, Ace Of Hearts, Card Suit Motif, 4 ¼ x 4 In.	168.00
Label, Cigar Box, American Belle, Gold Leaf, Embossed, Hoehle Litho Co., 1904, 4 ⅜ x 4 In. *illus*	90.00
Label, Cigar Box, Drummer Queen, Embossed, Gold Leaf, F. Heppenheimer's & Sons, 8 ½ x 5 ¾ In.	144.00
Label, Cigar Box, Eagles Toast, Embossed, Gold Leaf, Batesville, Ohio, 10 ¾ x 7 In.	252.00
Label, Cigar Box, El Valor, Embossed, Gold Leaf, Harris Litho Co., 8 ½ x 6 In.	252.00
Label, Cigar Box, Elita Flor Fina, Art Nouveau, Embossed, Gold Leaf, 10 x 6 In.	67.00
Label, Cigar Box, Fatty Felix, Otis Litho Co. Cleveland, Embossed, Gold Leaf, 7 x 5 In. *illus*	259.00
Label, Sunkist Fruit, Tom Cat Lemons, Black & White Cat On Front, 1920s, 12 x 8 In.	85.00
Label, Tobacco, Choctaw, Lorillard Co., American Indian, Fighting, 11 x 11 In. *illus*	990.00
Lamps are listed in the Lamp category.	
Lampshade, Old Dutch Cleanser, Blue, Picture Of Cleanser In Center, 1940s, 6 x 8 In.	295.00
Ledger Marker, Thos. Q. Seabrooke, Comic Opera Co., Man In Top Hat, 12 ¼ In.	540.00
Ledger Marker, Van Sicklen & Spaulding Grocers, Tree, Flowers, 12 ½ In.	900.00
Lunch Boxes are listed in their own category.	
Menu Board, 7Up, Shaped, Red, White, Green, Masonite & Wood, 1940-50s, 16 x 26 ½ In.	150.00
Menu Board, Bob's Big Boy Drive-In, Light-Up, Speaker Below, 2-Sided, 57 In.	243.00
Menu Board, Delaware Punch, Delicious, Not Carbonated, Tin, Chalkboard, 1960s, 24 x 18 In.	60.00
Menu Board, Gold-En Cola, Drink, Enjoy, Refreshing As A Cup Of Coffee, Tin, 1950s, 27 x 19 In.	90.00
Menu Board, Orange Crush, 5 Cents, Bottle, Oranges, Tin, 1933, 13 x 38 In.	510.00
Menu Board, Orange Crush, There Is Only One, Today's Special, Oranges, Tin, 1928, 19 x 27 In.	510.00
Menu Board, Royal Crown Cola, Bet By Taste Test, Bottle, Chalkboard, Tin, 1950s, 27 x 19 In.	90.00

Advertising mirrors of all sizes are listed here. Pocket mirrors range in size from 1 ½ to 5 inches in diameter. Most of these mirrors were given away as advertising promotions and include the name of the company in the design.

Mirror, Beautyskin, Woman, Chichester Chemical Co., Celluloid, 1 ½ x 2 ⅜ In.	230.00
Mirror, Columbia Flour, Miss Liberty, Celluloid, Bastian, 2 ⅛ In. *illus*	115.00
Mirror, Dunville's Whiskey, Reverse Painted, c.1880, 27 x 34 ½ In.	748.00
Mirror, Foxgirl, Gibson Girl Type Woman, Nurse Uniform, 1 ¾ x 2 ¾ In.	67.00
Mirror, I Use Red Cross Shoe Polishes, Celluloid, Woman, 2 ⅛ In.	56.00
Mirror, Kinne's Laundry, First Monday, Garden Of Eden Scene, Celluloid, Oval, 2 ¾ In.	127.00
Mirror, Kist, Thermometer, Barometer, White, Red, Gold, 1940s, 23 x 15 In.	150.00
Mirror, Liberty Mills Vanity Self-Rising Flour, Peacock, Celluloid, 3 x 2 In. *illus*	198.00
Mirror, Ondoca, Delicious Food Drink, Woman, Beach Ball, Celluloid, Oval, 2 ¾ In.	197.00
Mirror, Royal Cat's Eye, A Royal Chew Or Smoke, Tiger, Metal Frame, Flower Crest, 12 x 7 ½ In.	240.00
Mirror, San Fox, Woman, Nurse Uniform, Celluloid, 1 x 2 In.	67.00
Mirror, Sovereign Remedy Co., At Last!, Cure & Prevent Disease, Celluloid, 1900s, 2 In.	173.00
Mirror, The Invincible Junior, Woman Vacuuming, Pocket, Celluloid, 1 x 2 In.	45.00
Mixer, Horlick's Malted Milk, Glass, Pictures Lum & Abner From 1930s Radio, 9 In.	100.00
Mug, McDonald's, Good Morning, c.1960, 3 ½ In.	10.00
Noisemaker, Robin Hood Shoes, Robin, Green Metal, 1 ⅞ x 7 ⅞ In.	18.00
Opener, Cigar Box, Whitehead & Hoag Co., Flat Celluloid Panel, Metal Arrow, 4 ½ In.	200.00
Pails are also listed in the Lunch Box category.	
Pail, Buffalo Brand Peanut Butter, Metalware, R.M. Hoyt, Amesbury, Mass., 20 Lb.	269.00
Pail, Buffalo Brand Peanut Butter, Tin Lithograph, Berteis Metalware, Pa., 10 x 9 ½ In.	269.00
Pail, Central Union Tobacco, Woman's Face, Half Moon, Red, Square, Handle, 6 In.	60.00
Pail, Jackie Coogan Peanut Butter, Girl Eating, Multicolored, 3 ½ In.	510.00
Pail, Mayo's Tobacco, Cut Plug, Collapsible, Handle, Cobalt Blue, Gold, 5 ½ In.	60.00
Pail, Roach Doom, Death To Roaches, Edgar A. Murray Co., Detroit, Mich., 5 Lb.	330.00
Pail, Round Trip Smoking Tobacco, Cut Plug, Cruise Ship, Red, Handle, 3 ½ x 6 ½ In.	570.00
Pail, School Days Peanut Butter, Children Playing, 3 ¼ x 3 ¾ In. *illus*	253.00
Pail, Squirrel Peanut Butter, Tin, Pry Lid, Canada Nut Co., Vancouver, 48 Oz., 4 ¾ x 5 ⅛ In. *illus*	385.00
Pail, Star Meat Co., Lard, Tin, Bail Handle, 4 Lb.	236.00
Pail, Toyland Peanut Butter, Marching Band, Blue, Bail Handle, 2 Lb.	83.00
Patch, Dr Pepper, White On Red, Embroidered, 1960s, 3 x 2 In.	10.00
Pill Box, Chichester's Pills, Indispensable To Women, Celluloid, Brass, Folding, 2 In.	115.00
Pin Holder, Success Spreader, Fertilizes The Earth, Globe, Tin, 2-Sided, c.1905, 2 In.	86.00
Pin, Borden's Elsie The Cow, Off-White Plastic, 3-D, Garland Of Daisies, 1950s, 3 In.	45.00
Pin, Buy Camels By The Carton, Yellow, Black Letters, Bastian Bros., 1940s, 2 In.	52.00
Pin, Cogan's Hiking Shoes, Ee-Yah, Baseball Player Hughie Jennings, 1 ¼ In.	763.00
Pin, Dr Pepper, Drink A Bit To Eat, Hands Of Clock At 10, 2 & 4, 1930s	25.00
Pin, Hi, Skelly!, What Is Tailor-Making?, Lithograph, c.1935, 4 In.	52.00
Pin, International Dealer, Friendly Man, Red Bowtie, c.1910, 1 ¾ In.	82.00
Pin, International Shirt & Collar Co., Shriner, Camel, Fez, Troy, N.Y., 2 In.	230.00
Pin, J.I. Case Threshing Machine Co., Corn Palace, Mitchell, S.D., c.1921, 1 ¾ In.	86.00

Pin, Kirchner & Son, Farm Implements, Belleville, Ill., Ornate Letters, c.1905, 2 In.	82.00
Pin, New Idea Manure Spreader, At Work In The Fields, Farm Scene, c.1905, 1 In.	75.00
Pin, Omaha, Market Town, Indian Warrior, Peace Necklace, c.1910, 1 ¼ In.	75.00
Pin, P.B. Ale, Clown, Oh Be Jolly, Orange Ground, Boston, Mass., c.1900	52.00
Pin, Port Huron, The Only General Purpose, Steam Tractor, c.1905, 1 ½ In.	52.00
Pin, Samson Galvanized Steel Wind Mills, Windmill, c.1904, 1 ¼ In.	52.00
Pin, Spider-Man, WNEW-TV 5, 1970s, 3 In.	158.00
Pin, Stouffers Salutes, Apollo 11, Armstrong, Aldrin, Collins, Moon, 1969, 1 ½ In.	52.00
Pin, Sunday Boston Herald, Newsboy Holding Paper, Orange, 1 ¼ In.	75.00
Pin, Sunlight Soap, Makes Clothes Wear Longer, Scotsman, Canada, 1900, 1 ¼ In.	76.00
Pin, Welcome Back Johnny, Bellhop, Philip Morris, c.1945, 2 ½ In. .... *illus*	75.00
Plaque, Iroquois Brewing Co., Indian Head, Plastic, 1950s, 14 x 14 In.	56.00
Plaque, Tobacco, Carved Eagle, Pine, Crossed Flags, Stars, Shield, George Stapf, c.1910, 37 In.	7050.00
Plate Set, Color Wheel, Cooley's Powder Colors, Boston, Mass., 8 In., 10 Piece .... *illus*	1380.00
Plate, Paradise Cracker Co., Season's Greetings, Carnival Glass, Amethyst, 1900s, 6 In.	555.00
Pot Scraper, Sharples Tubular Cream Separator, Barn Scene, 2-Sided, 2 x 3 In.	78.00
Pot, Lid, Saponaceous Compound, T.H. Peters, Philadelphia, Pottery, c.1850, 4 x 2 In. ....*illus*	489.00
Rack, Mad Magazine, Metal, 40 x 13 In.	1582.00
Razor Blade Bank, Listerine, Donkey Shape, Ceramic, USA, c.1930, 2 x 2 In.	75.00
Ring, Green Hornet, Glow-In-The-Dark, Secret Compartment, Plastic, 1947	278.00
Rolling Pin, Polar Bear Flour, Porcelain, Tulsa Feed Store, 15 In.	660.00
Salt & Pepper Shakers are listed in their own category.	
Scales are listed in their own category.	
Scoop, Coffee, Woolson Spice Co., Red, Tin Lithograph, 12 ½ In.	248.00
Scoop, Polar Bear Flour, Tin, Celluloid Button On Handle, 6 ½ In.	56.00
Scorekeeper, Hires Root Beer, Put Out Route For Thirst, Man, Celluloid, c.1915, 3 In.	120.00
Shoehorn, Moe's Shoe Emporium, Woman, Brown Hair, Celluloid, 6 ½ In.	412.00
Sign, 5 Brothers Plug, Toothsome As Honey, 5 Bear Cubs, Tobacco Pack, Red, Black, Tin, 16 x 16 In.	3000.00
Sign, 7 Oaks Dairy, Tree, Porcelain, 30 In. Diam.	605.00
Sign, 7Up, Fresh Up With 7Up, Bottle, Square, Embossed, Tin, c.1949, 27 x 20 In.	236.00
Sign, 7Up, The Uncola, Sunrise, Peter Max Style, Metal, Enamel, c.1971, 12 x 24 In.	115.00
Sign, 7Up, You Like It-It Likes You, White, Green, Red, Tin, 8 x 10 ½ In.	198.00
Sign, A.W. Titus, Lion & Lamb Tavern, Paint, Pine Panel, Early 1800s, 23 x 37 In.	1896.00
Sign, AAA Approved Restaurant, 2-Sided, Porcelain, Oval, 23 x 30 In.	367.00
Sign, Adams Brushes, You Can Buy Them Here, Paint Brushes, Clown, Tin, Cardboard, 27 ¾ x 19 In...	570.00
Sign, Agrico A Better Lawn In Every Bag, Logos, Green, Red, Tin, 18 x 30 In.	113.00
Sign, Allen's Red Tame Cherry, 2 Children, Drinking, Tin, Die Cut, Easel, c.1900, 40 x 27 ¾ In.	28800.00
Sign, American Family Soap, Miss Liberty, Laundry, Cardboard, 30 ½ x 20 In. ....*illus*	2310.00
Sign, AMF Roadmaster, Bicycle, Porcelain, Flange, 22 x 15 ½ In.	358.00
Sign, Anheuser-Busch 100th Anniversary, Color, 1976, 36 x 36 In.	24.00
Sign, Anheuser-Busch, Girls Holding Big Bottle On Tray, Self-Framed, Tin, c.1900, 18 x 26 In.	460.00
Sign, Anheuser-Busch, Malt-Nutrine, Cardboard, Die Cut, Easel Back, 4 ½ x 6 In.	115.00
Sign, Apartments With Westinghouse Electric Refrigerators, Logo, Porcelain, 19 x 20 In.	452.00
Sign, Apparel, Zinc Letters, On Sheet Iron Band, Art Deco, 9 x 69 x 3 In.	1067.00
Sign, Arden Milk Boy, Metal, Die Cut, 18 x 48 In.	904.00
Sign, Armed By Fordson Tractors, Tin, Embossed, 14 x 19 In.	396.00
Sign, Armour Vegetable Shortening, Tin, Can Of Shortening & Donuts, 1930s, 19 x 13 In.......	190.00
Sign, Armour's Extract Of Beef, Happy Baby, Spoon, Stone Lithograph, 46 x 48 In.	2875.00
Sign, Atlantic, Metal, White Letters, Red Ground, 52 x 73 In.	338.00
Sign, Ayer's Pills, Dr. Bolus, Children, Cardboard, Die Cut, Easel, Glass, Frame, 7 x 11 ½ In. .... *illus*	248.00
Sign, Ayer's Sarsaparilla, Father Holding Daughter, Will Cure You, c.1905, 29 x 41 In.............	4313.00
Sign, Ballantine 3-R, On Tap, 3 Interlocked Circles, Pink, Blue, Neon, Metal Frame, 1950s, 16 ¼ In.	150.00
Sign, Baltimore Monument Wks., Wood, Green & White, 1900s, 96 x 12 In.	207.00
Sign, Bank Note Cigars 5 Cents, Cardboard, Easel Back, Cigar Box Image, 21 ½ x 13 ⅝ In. ......*illus*	231.00
Sign, Banner Milk, It Tastes Better, Red & White, 21 x 36 In.	91.00
Sign, Barker's Liniment, Men & Women, Riding In Buggy, Paper, Frame, c.1900, 25 x 20 In. ..	1680.00
Sign, Barrel, Drink Triple XXX Root Beer, Curved, Orange, Black, Red, 14 x 20 ½ In.	330.00
Sign, Bavarian's Old Style, Neon, White, Yellow, Blue, Green, Metal Frame, 1950s, 21 In.........	120.00
Sign, Bavis & Son Grocers, Boxed & Canned Goods, Wood, c.1875, 74 x 31 In.	4500.00
Sign, Beacon Coal, Lighthouse Logo, Tin, Round, 14 In.	311.00
Sign, Beech-Nut Chewing Tobacco, Porcelain, Red, White, Blue, c.1935, 22 x 10 ½ In.	226.00
Sign, Beech-Nut Gum, Woman, Holding Drum, Die Cut, Easel, 38 x 14 In.	633.00
Sign, Bell, Sheet Zinc, Medina, Ohio, c.1900, 39 In.	235.00
Sign, Big Chief Cigars, Always The Best, Indian, 7 x 11 In.	522.00
Sign, Big Giant Cola, 16 Oz., Bigger 'N Better, Bottle, Red, White, Blue, Tin, 1960s, 11 ½ x 29 ½ In.	60.00
Sign, Billiard, Painted Wood, Arched, Hanging Pool Balls, Black & Cream, 1900s, 69 In..........	2844.00

Advertising, Display, Koveralls, Keep Kids Klean, Tin, Die Cut, Pat. June 8, 1918, 11 x 19 ½ In., Pair
$7150.00

Showtime Auction Services

Advertising, Display, McGregor Happy Foot, Molded Sock, Composition, 1930s, 6 x 10 x 16 In.
$923.00

Hake's Americana & Collectibles

Advertising, Display, National Mazda Lamps, Light Bulbs, Tin, Counter
$660.00

Victorian Casino Antique Auction

Advertising, Display, Pen & Pencil Set, Parker, 24 In., Pair
$1625.00

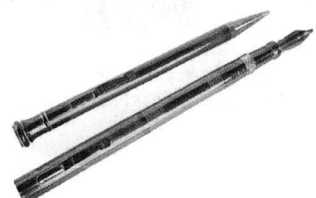

Bonhams & Butterfields

Peanut Butter Invented
The Kellogg Brothers were the first to invent peanut butter, but they failed to patent it.

Advertising, Display, Reliable Seeds, Sioux City Seed Co., Seed Packs
$649.00

Showtime Auction Services

Advertising, Display, Towle's Log Cabin Syrup, Fold, Cardboard, Copyright 1914, 15 x 15 x 10 In.
$523.00

Wm Morford Antiques

Advertising, Figure, Smiling Golfer, He Played A Penfold, Ellis Display, 1930s, 20 ½ In.
$380.00

Hake's Americana & Collectibles

Advertising, Jar, Heinz's Pickling Vinegar, Glass Lid, 11 x 4 ½ x 5 ½ In.
$3630.00

Wm Morford Antiques

Advertising, Label, Cigar Box, American Belle, Gold Leaf, Embossed, Hoehle Litho Co., 1904, 4 ⅜ x 4 In.
$90.00

Showtime Auction Services

Advertising, Label, Cigar Box, Fatty Felix, Otis Litho Co. Cleveland, Embossed, Gold Leaf, 7 x 5 In.
$259.00

Showtime Auction Services

Advertising, Label, Tobacco, Choctaw, Lorillard Co., American Indian, Fighting, 11 x 11 In.
$990.00

Wm Morford Antiques

Advertising, Mirror, Columbia Flour, Miss Liberty, Celluloid, Bastian, 2 ⅛ In.
$115.00

Hake's Americana & Collectibles

Advertising, Mirror, Liberty Mills Vanity Self-Rising Flour, Peacock, Celluloid, 3 x 2 In.
$198.00

Wm Morford Antiques

Advertising, Pail, School Days Peanut Butter, Children Playing, 3 ¼ x 3 ¾ In.
$253.00

Wm Morford Antiques

Advertising, Pail, Squirrel Peanut Butter, Tin, Pry Lid, Canada Nut Co., Vancouver, 48 Oz., 4 ¾ x 5 ⅛ In.
$385.00

Wm Morford Antiques

Advertising, Pin, Welcome Back Johnny, Bellhop, Philip Morris, c.1945, 2 ½ In.
$75.00

Hake's Americana & Collectibles

Sign, Bire-Ley's, Let's Sit This Out, Couple Sharing Bottle, Cardboard, 1948, 33 x 19 In.	90.00
Sign, Black & Gilt Relief Carved, Incised Characters, Chinese, 38 x 77 In.	91.00
Sign, Black Cat Cigarettes, Painted, Porcelain, 8 ¾ x 12 ½ In.	385.00
Sign, Black Horse Ale, Stylized Lone Ranger & Tonto, 1977, 25 x 18 In.	86.00
Sign, Black Minorcas Pratt's Poultry Food, 2 Roosters, Cardboard, 11 x 14 In.	45.00
Sign, Blackhawk Beer, Indian Chief, Red, Pink, Black, Neon, Glass Frame, 1940s, 22 ½ In.	570.00
Sign, Blair's Alloa, Ales, On Draught, In Bottles, Moose, Glass, Frame, 40 x 61 In.	283.00
Sign, Blatz Beer, Neon, Drink Blatz Beer, Red, Black, White, 96 x 38 In.	2475.00
Sign, Blatz Milwaukee, Woman, Victorian Dress, Holding 2 Bottles, Round, Tin, 12 In. Diam.	1920.00
Sign, Blatz, Draft-Brewed, Barrel, Motion, Unicyclist Rolls Around, Round, 1960s, 17 ¾ In.	300.00
Sign, Booth's Oysters, Oval Brand, 2-Sided, Cardboard, Frame, c.1900, 26 ¾ x 21 ¼ In.	120.00
Sign, Borax King Soap, Boy, Dressed As Cowboy, 20 Mule Team Package, 34 ½ x 23 ½ In.	120.00
Sign, Borden's Ice Cream, Elsie Logo, Tin, 1967, 12 x 24 In.	452.00
Sign, Borden's Ice Cream, Shaped Top, Cow, Flower, Tin, Red, Yellow, Blue, White, 1950s, 29 ¾ x 33 In.	570.00
Sign, Brazier's Chocolates, Chrysanthemum Girl, Tin, Cardboard, Self-Framed, c.1910, 12 x 14 In.	1120.00
Sign, Breyers Ice Cream, Leaf, Elongated, White, Red, Green, Tin, Oval, 51 x 32 In.	85.00
Sign, Briggs & Stratton Authorized Parts-Service, Light-Up, Plastic, 18 x 24 In.	339.00
Sign, Buck Cigar, King Of The Range, Buck's Head, Tin, 10 x 12 ⅛ In.	540.00
Sign, Budweiser, King Of Bottled Beer, Tin, Flange, c.1930, 17 ¾ x 13 In.	295.00
Sign, Burger Beer, Pink & Green, Neon, Metal Frame, 1940-50s, 15 ½ In.	120.00
Sign, Cameronia, Twin Screw Steamships, Anchor Line, c.1912, 38 x 25 In.	177.00
Sign, Canadian Cream Ale, It's Rich & Full Bodied, Green & Red, Neon, Back Lit Panel, 1940s, 25 ¼ In.	2040.00
Sign, Carter's Mucilage Glue, Man Pulling Another Man Who's Glued To Box, Tin, c.1890, 12 x 17 In.	4800.00
Sign, Cartridge Board, Winchester Repeating Arms, Cartridges, Oak Frame, 42 ½ x 29 ½ In.*illus*	56350.00
Sign, Cartridge Board, Winchester, Double-W, Bear Hunters, Oak Frame, 40 x 57 ½ In....*illus*	18800.00
Sign, Case Quality Machine For Profitable Farming, Eagle, Reflective Paint, Tin, 36 x 72 In.	3107.00
Sign, Castle Gate Coal, Orange Logo, Porcelain, 12 x 30 In.	593.00
Sign, Cat's Paw Non-Slip Rubber Heels, & Shoes, Light-Up, Reverse Sign, 8-Sided, 19 x 19 In.	141.00
Sign, Cattle Crossing, Red Rose Farm Feeds, Yellow, Blue & Red, Metal, 24 x 18 In.	11.00
Sign, Charge Accounts Of American Oil Honored Here, 2-Sided, Porcelain, 15 x 24 In.	254.00
Sign, Chas. S. Higgins' German Laundry Soap, Black Woman By Washtub, Die Cut, 11 x 6 In.	687.00
Sign, Cheap Cash Store, Painted, Wood, Early 1900s, 14 x 95 In.	711.00
Sign, Cheer Up, A Delightful Beverage, Owl, Bottle, Tin, Frame, 1940-50s, 15 x 48 In.	330.00
Sign, Chesapeake Bay Crab House, Carved Crab, Pine, Paint, c.1900, 43 x 59 In.	5750.00
Sign, Chesterfield Cigarettes, Pack, Buy Here, Tin, Embossed, 1950s, 18 In.	115.00
Sign, Chesterfield Cigarettes, Tin, Flange, 16 x 12 In.	141.00
Sign, Chew Early Bird Tobacco, Birds, Flowers, 2-Sided, Lithograph, c.1900, 6 x 13 In.	518.00
Sign, Chippewa Lake, Swim With Me, Girl Wearing Swimsuit, Die Cut, Wood, c.1930, 21 x 41 In. ...*illus*	944.00
Sign, Clark's Teaberry Gum, A Happy Thought!, Tin Lithograph, 1930s, 9 x 13 In.	153.00
Sign, Cleo Cola, Rich In Flavor, Bottle, Tin, 18 x 54 In.	120.00
Sign, Cleveland Baking Powder, Dish Of Biscuits, 1920s, 11 x 21 In.	90.00
Sign, Clockmaker, Pocket Watch, Bourisk, Zinc, 2-Sided, Gold, Black, White, 40 x 29 In.	940.00
Sign, Coats & Clarks, Quality Threads, Spools, Cardboard, Die Cut, 1950s, 12 ½ x 10 In.	90.00
Sign, Cogetama Cigares, Indian Smoking Cigar, Porcelain, Emaillerie Belge, c.1936, 29 x 37 In.	863.00
Sign, Colonial Club, 5 Cent Cigar, Woman, Wide Rim Straw Hat, 16 x 22 In.	805.00
Sign, Conibears Drug Store, Cartoon Cat, List Of Products, Black & White, 1900s, 49 x 37 In.	144.00
Sign, Country Creamery, Banana Split, Blue Ground, Paint, Steel, 49 x 96 In.	475.00
Sign, Crosley Radio & Home Appliances, Neon Lighted, Painted, 18 x 16 In.	170.00
Sign, Cuba Kola, 5 Cents, Bottle, Palm Trees, Red, White, Green, Tin, c.1940s, 43 x 12 In.	450.00
Sign, Curtis Davis & Co., Soap, Welcome, Woman In Window, Tin, Frame, c.1890, 31 x 23 In.	7200.00
Sign, Curtis' Pepsin Gum, Cardboard, Embossed, Die Cut, Matted Under Glass, Frame ...*illus*	413.00
Sign, Dargai Cigar, Marconi, 2-Sided, Tin, Geo. Kelly & Co., 9 ½ x 6 ½ In.	205.00
Sign, David's Prize Soap, Chinese Laundry Workers, Paper Litho, Frame, 24 x 19 In. ......*illus*	2310.00
Sign, Days Of 49 Whiskey, Gold Rush Wagon Train, Lithograph, Frame, 33 ½ x 21 ½ In.	2875.00
Sign, Deliciously Yours, Dad's Root Beer, Bottle Cap, Blue, Yellow, Tin, 1950s, 28 x 20 In.	120.00
Sign, Denver Post, Paper With Heart & Soul, Meek Co., Tin, Self-Framed, 13 x 20 In.	10638.00
Sign, Devlish Good Cigars 5 Cents, None Better, Tin, Embossed, Marked, 13 ¾ x 9 ¾ In.	96.00
Sign, Diamond Dyes, Busy Day In Dollville, Tin Lithograph, Gutmann, Frame, 11 x 17 In. ......*illus*	1670.00
Sign, Diamond Shirt, Victorian Wedding, Paper, Frame, Daniel Miller & Co., 27 x 21 In.	978.00
Sign, Dickens Dry Ale, Rocket, Blue, Green, Yellow, Neon, Glass Frame, 1940s, 29 In.	540.00
Sign, Dick's Beer, Black, White, Plastic, Neon, 16 x 71 In.	198.00
Sign, Dixcel, Milton Oil Co. Products, Orange, White, Black, Porcelain, 2-Sided, 42 In.	351.00
Sign, Dixon's Stove Polish, Victorian Parlor, Woman On Telephone, 13 x 29 In.	1840.00
Sign, Dodger Cola, Bottle Shape, Tin, Die Cut, Embossed, 15 x 66 In. ....*illus*	240.00
Sign, Don't Shiver Next Winter, Order Coal Now, Penguin, Shovel, 26 x 18 In., 1944	316.00

Advertising, Plate Set, Color Wheel, Cooley's Powder Colors, Boston, Mass., 8 In., 10 Piece
$1380.00

James D. Julia Inc.

Advertising, Pot, Lid, Saponaceous Compound, T.H. Peters, Philadelphia, Blue Transfer, Pottery, c.1850, 4 x 2 In.
$489.00

Glass Works Auctions

Advertising, Sign, American Family Soap, Miss Liberty, Laundry, Cardboard, 30 ½ x 20 In.
$2310.00

Wm Morford Antiques

Advertising, Sign, Ayer's Pills, Dr. Bolus, Children, Cardboard, Die Cut, Easel, Glass, Frame, 7 x 11 ½ In.
$248.00

Showtime Auction Services

Advertising, Sign, Bank Note Cigars
5 Cents, Cardboard, Easel Back, Cigar
Box Image, 21 ½ x 13 ⅝ In.
$231.00

Wm Morford Antiques

Advertising, Sign, Cartridge Board,
Winchester Repeating Arms,
Cartridges, Oak Frame, 42 ½ x 29 ½ In.
$56350.00

James D. Julia Inc.

Advertising, Sign, Cartridge Board,
Winchester, Double-W, Bear Hunters, Oak
Frame, 40 x 57 ½ In.
$18800.00

Garth's Auctions, Inc.

Advertising, Sign, Chippewa Lake, Swim
With Me, Girl Wearing Swimsuit, Die Cut,
Wood, c.1930, 21 x 41 In.
$944.00

Showtime Auction Services

Sign, Door, Orange Crush, Come In, Bottle, Orange, Black, Tin, Embossed, 1930-40s, 12 In....	330.00
Sign, Double Cola, Double Measure, Double Pleasure, Bottle, Glasses, Tin, 1949, 18 x 26 In.	300.00
Sign, Douglas Feed, Gluten Feed, Meal, Yellow, Red, Black, Tin, 24 x 36 In.	283.00
Sign, Dr Pepper, 10-2-4, Bottle Cap Shape, White, Red, Metal, 38 In.	297.00
Sign, Dr Pepper, Bottle, Men, Women, Shaped Wood Frame, Cardboard, 1940s, 33 ¾ x 16 ½ In.	840.00
Sign, Dr Pepper, Good For Life, Bottle, Brick Wall, Tin, 1940s, 18 x 54 In.	240.00
Sign, Dr. D. Jayne's Expectorant, Girl, Reverse Painted Scene, Wood Frame, c.1890, 14 x 12 In. *illus*	211.00
Sign, Dr. Daniels' Gall Cure, Nuf Sed, Cardboard, 10 ½ x 15 In.	605.00
Sign, Drink Certified Pure, Whistle, Orange, Navy, Porcelain, 1930s, 7 x 20 In.	300.00
Sign, Drink Dybala's Spring Beverages Bottle Only At The Spring, Tin, Embossed, 20 x 9 In....	158.00
Sign, Drink Frostie Root Beer, Frostie, Red Mittens, Thumbs Up, Plastic, Die Cut, 13 In.	70.00
Sign, Drink Hires In Bottles, Tin, Embossed, Bottle Cap Shape, 36 In.	367.00
Sign, Drink Lime-Julep, In Bottles, Green, White Letters, Tin, Embossed, 7 x 20 In.	70.00
Sign, Drink Moxie, Embossed, Tin Lithograph, Car, Horse & Rider, Self-Framed, 19 x 27 In.	690.00
Sign, Drink Nesbitt's, 5 Cents, California Orange, Bottle, Tin, 1940-50s, 49 x 16 In.	360.00
Sign, Drink Ski, Say Skee-E-E, Bottle Water Skiing, Yellow, Green, Tin, 1960s, 11 ¾ x 31 ¾ In.	330.00
Sign, Drummond Tobacco, American Beauty Tobacco, Woman, Roses, Lithograph, 1895, 22 x 28 In.	115.00
Sign, Dunlop Pneu Velo, Bike Rider Graphics, Tin, Die Cut, 21 x 23 In.	932.00
Sign, Dupont Powders, Grandfather, Boy, Dogs, Guns, Self-Framed, 1903, 23 x 33 In.	826.00
Sign, Dutch Boy White Lead, Painter Logo, Orange Ground, Tin, Embossed, 24 x 35 In.	254.00
Sign, E. Stearns, Bootmaker, Carved, Painted, Pine Panel, 2 Boots, 3 Shoes, c.1810, 20 x 54 In.	1715.00
Sign, Eastman Co., Kodak Camera, Blue & White, Porcelain, 16 x 20 In.	354.00
Sign, Ebbert Wagons, Man & Woman, Picking Apples, Tree, c.1906, 38 x 26 In.	1243.00
Sign, Eberhardt & Ober Brewing Co., Brewery & Buildings, Lithograph, Frame, 51 x 35 In.	875.00
Sign, Eichler's, Beer On Draught, Round, Tin, Eagle, Brown, Red, 19 ¼ In.	210.00
Sign, El Principe De Gales Havana, Celluloid, Frame, Easel Back, Tuscaloid Enamel, 8 x 10 In.	115.00
Sign, El Verso, Shelf Strip, Tin, Embossed, 14 ¾ x 2 ¾ In.	101.00
Sign, El-Bart Dry Gin, Woman, Raised Arms, Standing On Beach, Tin Lithograph, 23 x 36 In.	6195.00
Sign, Elk Lake, Boat Livery, Boats-Bait-Tackle, Tin, Wood, c.1900, 36 x 71 ½ In.	1062.00
Sign, Elongated Diamond Shape, Arrow, Porcelain, Blue, Yellow, Red, 22 ¼ x 18 ½ In.	390.00
Sign, Everybody Is Happy When They Buy Our Goods, Tin, Embossed, Winesburg, Oh., 28 x 10 In.	358.00
Sign, Eyeglasses, Optical, Eyeglass Shaped Metal, Light Bulbs, c.1900, 68 x 31 In.	10200.00
Sign, Farm Bureau Insurance Companies, 2-Sided, Tin, Round, 18 In.	113.00
Sign, Fat Tire, Neon Bicycle, 22 ½ x 28 In.	325.00
Sign, Fauerbach Beer, Red & Green, Neon, Glass Frame, 1940s, 30 ½ In.	300.00
Sign, Faultless Pepsin Chips Chewing Gum, Woman, Blue Dress, Paper, c.1900, 6 x 10 In.	345.00
Sign, Favorite Stoves & Ranges, Best In The World, 2-Sided, Porcelain, 24 x 18 In.	3107.00
Sign, Ferry Seeds, Jack & The Beanstalk, Jack Planting Magic Seeds, Frame, 21 x 21 In. *illus*	853.00
Sign, Fireman's Fund Insurance Company, San Francisco, Glass, Reverse Painted, Frame, 36 x 22 In.	96.00
Sign, Fly TWA, London, Queen's Guard, Big Ben, Airliner, Linen, 1950s, 25 x 16 In.	175.00
Sign, Fox Head 400, Beer Ale On Tap, Orange, Blue, Green, Neon, Glass Frame, 1940-50s, 28 In.	720.00
Sign, Fred's Radio Service, Radio Tube Shape, Wood, c.1924, 18 x 48 In.	236.00
Sign, Fresh Fish, Cutout Pine, Fish Shape, Gray & Black Paint, Wood, c.1950, 12 x 36 In.	356.00
Sign, Gail & Ax Navy Tobacco, 10 Cents, Sailor, Yellow, Blue, Frame, 41 ½ x 31 ½ In.	510.00
Sign, Garcia Grande Cigars, Woman In White, Hat, Cardboard, 30 x 35 In.	118.00
Sign, George Oakley & Sons, Wood, Painted, c.1875, 108 x 48 In.	4375.00
Sign, George, Supreme Master Of Magic, Owls, Bats & Devils, 1920s, 27 x 41 In.	588.00
Sign, Get Hep For Yourself, Soda Bottle, Flange, Tin, Oval, 13 ½ x 17 ¾ In.	300.00
Sign, Gibelin & L. Rubod, Centiane-Kola, Woman, Bottle, Scene, Tin, Embossed, 14 x 19 In.	288.00
Sign, Glenadaal Scotch Whiskies, Reverse Glass, Paper Sticker, Case & Co., 18 x 24 In.	3850.00
Sign, Gold-En Sun-Drop Goodness, Bottle Cap Shape, Tin, Embossed, 36 In. *illus*	330.00
Sign, Golden West Coffee, Drink More Good Coffee, Cardboard, 26 x 38 In.	138.00
Sign, Good Earth Health Store, 2-Sided, Wood, Wheat, U.S.A., c.1950s, 19 x 30 In.	51.00
Sign, Good Old Reading Beer, White, Brown, Porcelain, c.1935, 15 x 12 In.	213.00
Sign, Gottschalk & Co. Whiskies, Reverse On Glass, Eagle, Banner, Frame, 44 ½ x 32 In.	780.00
Sign, Grape Crush, Flapper Girl, Grapes, Purple, Yellow, Cardboard, Frame, c.1920, 16 x 13 In.	240.00
Sign, Green Spot Orange-Ade, Ice Cold, Bottle On Ice, Tin Litho, 1940s, 12 x 20 In.	126.00
Sign, Gretz Beer, Man On Bicycle, Pink & Blue, Neon, Glass Frame, 1940-50s, 20 In.	210.00
Sign, Greyhound Lines, Dog Logo, 2-Sided, Porcelain, Die Cut, 20 x 36 In.	622.00
Sign, Griesedieck Bros., Shield, Multicolor, Brown Ground, Tin, Germany, 50 x 48 In.	650.00
Sign, Hanger, Liz Cigars, Girl, Brownies Figure, Goat, Monkey, Tin, c.1920s, 13 ½ x 9 ½ In.	3000.00
Sign, Hanley Ale, Dog Shape, Green, Orange & Green Neon, 26 ¼ x 12 ¼ In.	1080.00
Sign, Harrison's, Fresh Fruit, Heart O' Orange, 5 Cents, 2 Oranges, Tin, c.1940, 11 ¾ x 20 ½ In.	240.00
Sign, Harry L. Stillwell Plumbing & Heating, Sheet Iron, Painted, c.1910, 32 x 45 In., Pair .... *illus*	1422.00
Sign, Hart Brand Fruits & Vegetables, Tin, Cardboard, 9 ¼ x 13 ¼ In. .... *illus*	770.00
Sign, Headquarters For Hyacinths, 15 Cents, All Colors, Dye, Tin, c.1920, 15 x 102 In.	150.00

Sign, Heatherwood Golden Guernsey, America's Table Milk, 2-Sided, Porcelain, 21 x 26 In.	480.00
Sign, Heirloom Beer, World's Finest, Yellow, Neon, In Metal Can, Glass, 1940-50s, 12 In.	960.00
Sign, Henry Clay Havana Cigars, Senator On Cover, 1905, 20 x 26 In.	645.00
Sign, Herrick's Saw Mill, Painted Wrought Iron Saw, Scroll, 1800s, 46 x 32 In.	429.00
Sign, Hershey's Chocolate Syrup, Can, Ice Cream Dish, c.1935, 46 x 30 In.	148.00
Sign, Hershey's Chocolate, Mild & Mellow Candy Bar, 1934, 45 ¾ x 29 ½ In.	148.00
Sign, Hershey's Cocoa, Steaming Mug, 1937, 45 ½ x 30 ¾ In.	148.00
Sign, Hinckel, Lager Beer, Brewing Company, Men, Boat, Uncle Sam, Frame, c.1890, 28 ¾ x 21 In.	3600.00
Sign, Hires Root Beer, It's High Time For Hires, Bottle, Tin, 30 x 11 ½ In.	113.00
Sign, Hires Root Beer, Young Boy, Goat Cart, Paper, Canvas, Frame, 1892, 27 x 41 In.	10350.00
Sign, Hollywood Orange, Soda Bottle, Tin, Embossed, 5 Cent, 20 x 9 In.	450.00
Sign, Hot Frankfurter, With Vienna Roll, 5 Cents, Reverse Paint, Black, Gold, Frame, 16 x 26 In.	326.00
Sign, Howdy, Orange Flavored Sugar Drink, 3 Kids, Party, Paper, Frame, 1920s, 14 In.	115.00
Sign, Howel's Root Beer, Bottle Shape, Tin, Springfield, Ohio, 57 x 15 In.	367.00
Sign, Humming Bird Pure Silk Hosiery, Oval, On Stand, 21 ½ In.	168.00
Sign, Illinois Springfield Watches, Man, Oil Can, Tin, Over Cardboard, c.1905, 13 x 19 In.	1035.00
Sign, Ingersoll Watches, Figural, Pocket Watch, Zinc, 25 x 35 In. ....*illus*	825.00
Sign, Interloc Tire Repair, Moulded To Fit, Permanent, Tin, Embossed, 19 x 13 In.	230.00
Sign, International McCormick, Logo, Die Cut, Porcelain, 32 x 47 In.	537.00
Sign, J.B. Stohler Axe Manufacturing, Pine, Penn., 1866, 14 ½ x 67 In.	2607.00
Sign, J.R. Anderson, Jeweler, Pocket Watch, Cast Iron, Zinc, Round, 2-Sided, c.1890, 40 x 30 In.	1041.00
Sign, Jackson Razors, Uncle Sam's Choice, Uncle Sam Shaving, 12 x 7 In.	1925.00
Sign, Jell-O, Die Cut, Cardboard, Easel Back, Genesee Pure Food Co., 24 ¼ x 15 ¾ In. ....*illus*	798.00
Sign, John Collins, Bottle Cap, Boy, Hat, Red, Yellow, Tin, Cutout, 39 ¼ In.	300.00
Sign, John Deere Quality Farm Implements, Deer Logo, Tin, Embossed, 12 x 23 In.	509.00
Sign, John Deere, Deer Logo, Green, Yellow, 38 x 42 In.	452.00
Sign, Johnson Halter, Horse's Head, Painted, Brown, White, Harness, Papier-Mache, 6 x 25 x 20 In.	4400.00
Sign, Johnson Oils, Time Tells, Hourglass, Wings, Porcelain, 29 x 24 In. ....*illus*	193.00
Sign, Johnson Sea-Horse Outboard Motors, Teal Duck, Cardboard, Die Cut, 9 x 8 In.	46.00
Sign, Johnston Candies, & Chocolates, Poster, Bell Hop, Holding Boxes, Paper, Frame, 40 x 55 In.	138.00
Sign, Jos. Doelger's Sons, Lager Beer, Hefty Man, Holding Beer Glass, Leaves, Tin, 27 x 19 In.	4800.00
Sign, Kaiserien Auguste Victoria, Steamship, Harbor, Hamburg-American Line, Tin, c.1910, 48 x 36 In.	575.00
Sign, Keepsake Diamond Rings, Neon, 24 ½ x 10 x 5 In. ....*illus*	248.00
Sign, Kellogg's Toasted Corn Flakes, Cardboard, Lithograph, 1920s, 20 ⅝ x 11 In. ....*illus*	908.00
Sign, Kis-Me Gum, Cardboard, Embossed, Die Cut, American Chicle Co., Frame, 9 ¾ x 14 ½ In.	708.00
Sign, Kis-Me Gum, Reclining Woman, Man, Man-In-The-Moon Frame, Embossed, Die Cut, 7 x 7 ½ In.	495.00
Sign, Kis-Me Gum, Woman, Cherry Border, Embossed, Die Cut, 10 x 16 In. ....*illus*	1100.00
Sign, Kist, Orange Kist & Other Kist Flavors, Bottle, Tin, Cardboard, c.1950, 13 ¼ x 6 In.	240.00
Sign, Kodak Developing Printer Enlarging, Logos, Hanging Bracket, 2-Sided, Tin, 17 x 17 In.	226.00
Sign, Kositos Cooked Maize, Farm Animals, Porcelain, 30 x 50 In.	237.00
Sign, Kotex, Nurse, Holding Box, Tin Litho, H.D Beach Co., 1920s, 8 ½ x 13 ¼ In. ....*illus*	173.00
Sign, La Flor De Don Jose Cigars, Habana, Embossed, Gold Gesso Frame, 1931, 26 x 34 In.	1036.00
Sign, Lash's Kidney & Liver Bitters, Tin, Scrolled Corners, Mayer & Lavenson, N.Y., 21 x 16 In. ..*illus*	819.00
Sign, Lee Riders Authentic Western Pants & Jackets, Cowboy Logo, Tin, 2-Sided, Round, 18 In. ...	452.00
Sign, Lewt. Lewis Co. Optometrist, Eye, Eyes Tested, Iron Bracket Case, 2-Sided, 24 x 26 ½ In.	4200.00
Sign, Lightning Freezer Saves Ice & Salt, Eagle, Spread Wing, Cardboard, Frame, 21 x 23 In..	400.00
Sign, Lightning Mouse Trap, Cardboard, Tin, Embossed, H.D. Beach Co., 9 ½ x 6 ⅜ In.	7188.00
Sign, Liqueurs Speciales, Cusenier, Woman, Frame, France, 1898, 59 ½ x 42 In. ....*illus*	1062.00
Sign, Lowe Brothers High Standard Paint, Porcelain, Flange, 20 x 13 In.	170.00
Sign, Lowe Brothers Paints Style Tested Colors, Yellow, Black, 2-Sided, Tin, Die Cut, 18 x 36 In.	85.00
Sign, Lucky Lager, X Shape, Blue, Red, Yellow, Neon, Glass Frame, 1950s, 19 ¼ In.	150.00
Sign, Mad About Moxie For Thanksgiving, Pilgrim, Indian, Paper, 9 x 23 In.	150.00
Sign, Magic Garden, 2-Sided, Light-Up, 34 x 36 In.	85.00
Sign, Make Mine Spiffy, A Swell Cola Drink, Freckle-Faced Boy, Tin, 1950s, 9 x 6 In.	115.00
Sign, Maple Lane Kennel, 2-Sided, Tin, Wood Frame, 36 x 72 In.	1195.00
Sign, Maple, Burts Dairy, Diamond Shape, Green, Paint, c.1875, 48 In.	723.00
Sign, Mayo's Plug Tobacco, Rooster Image, Canvas Paper, 17 x 29 ½ In.	269.00
Sign, Messett's Musical Entertainers, Black Gent, Horse Race, Hat Full Of Money, 13 x 42 In...	1150.00
Sign, Mikado, Oversize Pencil Shape, Eagle, Wood, 42 In.	390.00
Sign, Mil-Kay, Vitamin B1 Drink, Made With Real Oranges, Orange, Tin, 1950s, 35 x 14 In.	210.00
Sign, Miller, High Life, Peanut Shape, Pink, Green, Neon, Metal Frame, 1940s, 18 In.	210.00
Sign, Moose Beer, Reverse Glass, Metal, Duluth & Malting Brewing Co., 19 ½ x 3 In.	38500.00
Sign, Morse's Chocolate, Easter Greetings, Rabbit, Standing, Cardboard, Die Cut, 7 x 16 In......	28.00
Sign, Mountain Dew, Ya-Hooo!, It'll Tickle Yore Innards!, Man Holding Jug, Tin, 1965, 17 x 35 In.	570.00
Sign, Moxie, Distinctively Different, Man On Horseback, Car, Tin, Cardboard, c.1920, 12 ¾ x 18 ½ In...	1140.00
Sign, Moxie, Horsemobile, Candy, Soda, Cigars, Billboard, Tin, c.1933, 54 x 30 In.	2300.00

ADVERTISING

Advertising, Sign, Dr. D. Jayne's Expectorant, Girl, Reverse Painted Scene, Wood Frame, c.1890, 14 x 12 In. $211.00

Norman C. Heckler & Company

Advertising, Sign, Ferry Seeds, Jack & The Beanstalk, Jack Planting Magic Seeds, Frame, 21 x 21 In. $853.00

Wm Morford Antiques

Advertising, Sign, Gold-En Sun-Drop Goodness, Bottle Cap Shape, Tin, Embossed, 36 In. $330.00

Victorian Casino Antique Auction

Advertising, Sign, Harry L. Stillwell Plumbing & Heating, Sheet Iron, Painted, c.1910, 32 x 45 In., Pair $1422.00

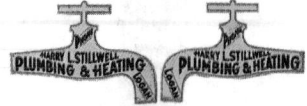

Skinner, Inc.

Sign, Moxie, Of Course You'll Have Some, Girl, Tin, Embossed, Frame, 23 x 31 In. ...illus	780.00
Sign, Moxie, Soda Syrups, Very Healthful, 5 Cents, Stained Glass, Multicolor, Tin, 19 x 13 ¼ In.	7800.00
Sign, Muehleback, Pilsener Beer, Since 1868, Clock, Bottle & Glass, Bubbler, Neon, 14 In.	210.00
Sign, Muffin 'N Breakfast From 80 Cents, Painted Wood, Red & White, 10 x 72 In.	46.00
Sign, Nesbitt's, California Orange Sold Here, 5 Cents, Bottle, Tin, Flange, 1940s, 13 x 18 In.	510.00
Sign, New Idea Quality Equipment, Logo, Porcelain, 30 x 72 In.	1695.00
Sign, New Yorker Beverages, Bottle, Wedding Couple, Yellow, Green, Red, Tin, 1940s, 32 x 56 In.	150.00
Sign, Nicodemus Ice Cream, White, Red Letters, Tin Litho, Parker Metal, Baltimore, 19 ¾ x 28 In.	51.00
Sign, Norwich Union Fire Insurance Society Norwich, England, Pressed, Victorian, 24 x 19 In.	115.00
Sign, NuGrape Soda, Everybody Likes A Change, Girl, Swimsuit, Cardboard, Frame, c.1950, 29 x 16 In.	60.00
Sign, NuGrape, Flavor You Can't Forget, Hand Holding Bottle, Tin, 36 x 14 In.	330.00
Sign, Nutmeg Beer, Meriden Brewing Co., Man & Woman, Having Glass Of Beer, Wood, 20 x 14 In.	480.00
Sign, O. Labossiere, Shoemaker, Boot, Harness, 19th Century, 44 In.	3100.00
Sign, Oak Leaf Soap, Premiums For Wrappers, Red, Green, White, Frame, Tin, 36 x 17 ¾ In.	330.00
Sign, OK Used Cars, 3-Color, Porcelain, Texlite Inc., 43 x 55 In.	7920.00
Sign, Old Dutch Beer, Red & Green Neon, Glass Rods, Round, 1940s, 17 ¼ In.	150.00
Sign, Old Dutch Beverages, Windmill, Tin, Blue & White, 18 x 35 In.	51.00
Sign, Old Tea Cup & Springfield Whiskey, Pretty Woman, Frame, 1906, 25 x 21 In.	392.00
Sign, Opia Cigar, 5 Cent, Smokers Dream, Woman, Flowers, Oval, 19 ¾ In.	15000.00
Sign, Orange Crush, Always On Ice, Meet Crushy, Oranges, Tin, 1929, 32 x 56 In.	480.00
Sign, Orange Crush, Bottle, Oranges, Cardboard, Metal Edge, c.1920, 20 x 40 In.	780.00
Sign, Orange Crush, Crushy, Orange, Navy, Glass, Round, 9 In.	240.00
Sign, Orange Crush, Ice Cold Carbonated Drink, 2 Bottles, Tin, 1930s, 13 x 38 In.	570.00
Sign, Orange Crush, There's Only One, Diamond Shape, Tin, 1941, 21 ¼ x 21 ¼ In.	270.00
Sign, Orange Crush, Thirst Aid Station, Crushy, Triangular, Yellow, Tin, 1930s, 13 x 12 In.	960.00
Sign, Orange Crush, Woman, Bouquet, Drinking, Feel Fresh, Die Cut, c.1940, 25 x 36 In.	578.00
Sign, Ortlieb's Beer, Oval, Neon, Red & Green, Glass Frame, 1940s, 21 In.	120.00
Sign, Pabst Blue Ribbon, Don't Just Sit There, Nag Your Husband, Wood, 1970s, 24 x 11 In.	35.00
Sign, Pabst Blue Ribbon, What'll You Have?, Ribbon Shape, Red, Blue, Neon, Frame, 20 ½ In.	210.00
Sign, Patrick Henry Beer, Green, Blue, Red, Neon, Metal Frame, 1940s, 36 In.	360.00
Sign, Peter Pan Bread, Slow School Zone, Policeman, Masonite, 48 x 24 In.	226.00
Sign, Peters Big Game Ammunition, Bull Elk, Standing On Rock, Mountains, 20 x 29 In.	1610.00
Sign, Peters Big Game Ammunition, Mother Bear, Cubs, Mountain, 19 x 28 In.	920.00
Sign, Peters Cartridge, Rustless, Long Horn Sheep, Rocky Cliff, Cardboard, 13 x 17 In.	1840.00
Sign, Peters Loaded Shells, Flock Of Mallard Ducks, c.1915, 19 x 29 In.	1725.00
Sign, Peters Referee Semi Smokeless Shells, Hanging Game Birds, Oak Frame, 30 x 14 ¾ In.	1840.00
Sign, Peters Weatherbird Shoes, Uncle Sam, Student, Birds, Cardboard, 24 x 15 In.	118.00
Sign, Philadelphia Life Insurance Co., Black & Yellow, 13 x 8 In.	79.00
Sign, Pioneer Corn, Corncob Shape, Tin Lithograph, Yellow & Black, 96 x 22 In.	226.00
Sign, Pix-Liquida Compound, Embossed, Die Cut, Cherub, Ivy Border, 9 x 9 ¼ In.	3850.00
Sign, Popsicle, Cardboard, 1932, 16 x 24 In.	190.00
Sign, Premier Coffee Mill, Cardboard, Bold Colors, 12 x 18 In.	245.00
Sign, Proctor's Photograph Rooms, Sewing Machines, Wood, Gilt, 32 x 62 In.	2070.00
Sign, Property Of United States Weather Bureau, Porcelain, c.1915, 8 x 2 In.	67.00
Sign, Punch & Judy, Cocktail, It Recuperates, Celluloid, 12 x 7 In.	3450.00
Sign, Puritan, Good Shoes Deserve, Leather Soles, Porcelain, Quaker, 20 x 30 In.	147.00
Sign, Py-Sicle Ice Cream, On A Stick, Boy, Dog, Joe Lowe Corp., 1938, 16 x 11 In.	75.00
Sign, Quail Cigar, Hunter, Dog, Quail, Cardboard, John T. Stier & Sons, c.1910, 11 ½ x 21 In.	374.00
Sign, RC Cola, Santa, Best Way To Wish Friends Merry Christmas, Paper, 28 In.	33.00
Sign, Recruit Cigars, Army Recruit, Field, Paper, 29 x 20 In.	518.00
Sign, Red Goose Shoes, For Boys & Girls, Tin Lithograph, 1950s, 13 x 19 In.	127.00
Sign, Red Top Flour, Boy, Holding Bag Of Flour, Fence, Red, Blue, Porcelain, 22 x 18 In.	300.00
Sign, Remington Rifles, Shotguns, Woman, Rifle, Cardboard, F.E. Getty, 1901, 10 ½ x 16 In. ...illus	220.00
Sign, Republic Truck Service, Logo, Red, White & Blue, 2-Sided, Porcelain, 13 x 20 In.	763.00
Sign, Rexall Drugs, Leaded Glass, Burlingame & Stahl, Wood Frame, 63 x 27 In.	550.00
Sign, Rhum Quinquina, Hair Tonic, 25 Cents, Application, Bottle, Cardboard, c.1900, 10 ¾ x 9 In.	180.00
Sign, Rice's Flower Seeds, Woman Holding Basket Of Blooms, Long Hair, 20 x 29 In.	2415.00
Sign, Rice's Seeds, Uncle Sam, International Characters, Food Basket, 27 x 21 In.	3910.00
Sign, RMS Lusitania, Cunard Steamship Line, Tin, Wavy, Self-Framed, c.1910, 39 x 27 In.	885.00
Sign, Robin Hood Flour, Porcelain, Red, White, Green, 24 x 48 In.	96.00
Sign, Rods Sports Guns, Transom Stenciled, Black & White, Early 1900s, 61 x 12 In.	148.00
Sign, Roxbury Rye, Uncle Sam, Bottle, Yellow Ground, Lithograph, 38 x 29 In.	575.00
Sign, Rumsey & Co. Trucks, Black Rural Figures, Frame, 20 x 14 ½ In.	295.00
Sign, S. & H. Green Stamps, Screen Painted, Sheet Steel, 2-Sided, 29 x 20 In. ...illus	130.00
Sign, S.D. Sollers & Co., Shoes, Children Making Pyramid Of Shoes, Frame, c.1890, 19 x 23 ¾ In.	1680.00
Sign, Sacco Fertilizers, Tin, Embossed, 19 x 13 In.	45.00

12

Sign, Sapolin Hot Pipe, Aluminum Enamel, Metal Toy Stove Model, 9 x 13 In.	424.00
Sign, Schell's Carbonated Mead, Pretty Woman, Peacock, August Schell Brewing, Frame, 16 x 32 In.	767.00
Sign, Schmidt's Brewing Co., Canvas, Hunters, Log Cabin, Frame, c.1905, 38 x 29 In.	826.00
Sign, Schorn Certainly Makes Fine Paint, Porcelain, Embossed, 44 x 42 In.	509.00
Sign, Schrafft's Chocolates, Christmas Theme, Die Cut, Easel Back, 11 ½ x 25 In.	58.00
Sign, Seal Test Eggnog, White Ground, Red Lettering, Get The Best, 24 x 20 In.	165.00
Sign, Sen-Sen Chewing Gum, Woman In Kimono, Cardboard, Die Cut, Easel, 8 x 15 In.	266.00
Sign, Shasta, Sparkling Beverages, It Hasta Be Shasta, Snowy Mountains, Tin, 1950s, 11 x 23 In.	360.00
Sign, Sherwin-Williams Paints, Cover The Earth Logo, Porcelain, Die Cut, 10 ½ x 24 In.	480.00
Sign, Simonds Saw, Crescent Ground, Lumberjack, Cardboard, 1880s, 9 x 12 ¾ In. ....*illus*	853.00
Sign, Singer Machines, Lady At Sewing Machine, Multicolor, Porcelain, France, 35 x 33 In.	509.00
Sign, Smoke Exmoor Hunt Mixture, Tobacco, Porcelain, Brown, White, 12 x 24 In.	85.00
Sign, Snug-Hug Slip, Woman In Pink Slip Bending Over, Cardboard, 13 x 9 In.	357.00
Sign, Socony Air-Craft Oils, Airplane Graphics, Porcelain, 20 x 30 In.	1130.00
Sign, Socony, Vacuum Oil, Pegasus, Tin, 1934, 40 x 40 In.	1950.00
Sign, Spanish Bull Fighting, Plaza De Toros Monumental, Woman, Fan, c.1928, 92 x 45 In.*...illus*	649.00
Sign, Sprite, Button, Dark Green, White, Tin, Germany, 1960s, 16 In. Diam.	360.00
Sign, Spur Cigarettes, Young Girl & Horse, Frame, 15 ½ x 21 ½ In.	57.00
Sign, Squire's, We Recommend, Pig, Seated, Oval, Tin, 24 x 19 ¾ In.	510.00
Sign, Squirrel Brand Peanuts, Cardboard, Die Cut, Easel Back, 20 x 30 In.	385.00
Sign, Squirt, New Taste Sensation, Best For Health, Tin Litho, Embossed, 1940s, 8 x 11 In.	140.00
Sign, Stanley Garage Door Holders, Tin, Garage, Doors Open, 48 x 54 In.	3520.00
Sign, Star Tobacco Sold Here, Porcelain, 12 x 24 In.	537.00
Sign, Stoddard Mfg. Co., Tiger Bicycle, Mountain Road, Bike, Figures, Litho, c.1890, 23 x 17 In.	460.00
Sign, Street, Flatbush Ave., Brooklyn, White, Blue, Porcelain, 2-Sided, 8 x 32 In.	600.00
Sign, Strouse & Holden, House Painter & Paper Hanger, c.1900, 28 x 43 In.	230.00
Sign, Sugar Cane, Pointed Cone Shape, Eagle, Wood & Iron, c.1880s, 29 In.	305.00
Sign, Sun Crest Soda, Cardboard, Boy With Bat & Glove, Bottle, 12 x 9 In.	88.00
Sign, Sun Drop Golden Cola Drink & Enjoy, Convex, Tin, Oval 29 x 43 In.	537.00
Sign, Sun Spot, Made With Real Orange Juice, Bottle, Green, Orange, Tin, 1947, 11 ¾ x 4 In. .	120.00
Sign, Sunkist Oranges, Golden Cross Brand, Cardboard, 10 x 13 In.	45.00
Sign, Sunrise, Refreshing Beverages, Orange, Leaves, Sun Sipping From Straw, Tin, 1950s, 28 x 12 In.	150.00
Sign, Sweet Nectar Cigarettes, Woman, Garden, Pond, Paper, Frame, F.W. Felgner & Sons, 23 x 17 In.	288.00
Sign, Sweet-Orr Overalls, Union Made, Men, Tug Of War, Porcelain, 17 x 14 In.	935.00
Sign, Tappan Zee Gin, Fisherman, Hudson River, Canvas, Lithograph, Frame, 21 x 17 In.	650.00
Sign, Tarrant's Seltzer Aperient, Woman Holding Banner, 50 x 32 In.	345.00
Sign, Tavern, Entertainment By W. Palmer, 2-Sided, Pine, Stenciled, Wrought Iron, c.1800, 42 x 30 In.	1145.00
Sign, Tea, Hovis Rule Of The Road, Wood, Scrolled Wrought Iron, England, 1900, 36 x 38 In.	1265.00
Sign, Texaco, Black T, Aviation Products, 2-Sided, Porcelain, Round, 24 In.	735.00
Sign, Thomas Moore Whiskey, Have A Little Moore, Bottle, Old Possum Hollow, Tin, 17 x 7 In.	330.00
Sign, Trailways National Systems Bus Depot, Virginia, Map, 2-Sided, Porcelain, 22 x 22 In.	339.00
Sign, Trinity Cement, State Of Texas, Rectangular, Blue, Yellow, Red, Porcelain, 26 x 30 In.	170.00
Sign, Try Our 5 Cent Win Rozensucker, Press Fiber Board, 14 x 11 ½ In.	56.00
Sign, Tuxedo Tobacco, T.A. Dorgan, Cardboard, c.1910, 11 x 21 In. ......*illus*	230.00
Sign, Tyler Davidson & Company, Folding Straight Razor, Wood, Metal, Black, Gold, c.1850, 45 In.	999.00
Sign, Uncle Green Cigars, Thinker's Smoke, Cardboard, Framed, 18 ½ x 42 In. ......*illus*	495.00
Sign, Uneeda Biscuit, Boy In Slicker, National Biscuit Company, Paper, Frame, 17 x 23 In. ...*illus*	354.00
Sign, Union 76, Outboard Fuel The Finest Mix, Round, 2-Sided, Porcelain, 42 In.	850.00
Sign, Union 7600 Marine Gasoline, Round, Pump Plate, Porcelain, 11 ½ In.	450.00
Sign, Van Camp's Pork & Beans, Boy, Girl, Tray Of Beans, Cardboard, c.1920, 16 x 19 In.	240.00
Sign, Van Merritt Beer, Windmill, Pink, Green, Orange, Neon, Glass Frame, 1940s, 28 In.	420.00
Sign, Velvet Tobacco, Paper, Woman, Riding Standing On 2 Black Horses, Frame, 21 x 31 In. .	605.00
Sign, Vernor's Ginger Ale, 5 Cents, Ice Cold, 2 Bottles, Yellow, Blue, c.1935, 48 x 16 ½ In.	330.00
Sign, Vernor's Ginger Ale, Winking Elf, Enameled Steel, 1940s, 10 x 30 In.	139.00
Sign, Vicente Protuondo, Cuban Hand Made, High Grade Cigars, Tin, c.1900, 10 x 13 ¾ In.	660.00
Sign, Vinolia Soap, Woman, Holding Basket Of Flowers, Paper, Frame, 26 ¾ x 20 ½ In.	180.00
Sign, Volvolutum, The World's Best Soap, Porcelain, 1920s, 15 x 48 In.	124.00
Sign, Walter Baker & Co.'s Chocolate, Broma & Cocoa, 1872, 31 x 27 In.	403.00
Sign, Ward's Lime Crush, Batter Up!, I'm All Set!, Die Cut, Frame ......*illus*	275.00
Sign, Warner's Safe Kidney & Liver Cure, President Garfield & Cabinet, Litho, 26 In.	3500.00
Sign, We Sell Atlantic Aviation Motor Oil, Plane Logo, Tin, Wood Frame, 44 x 15 In.	1130.00
Sign, We Serve Nehi Ice Cold, Soda Bottle, Tin, 1950s, 26 In.	250.00
Sign, Wentworth Golf Club, Member's Bar, Wood, Golfer, Swinging Club, 49 x 26 In.	63.00
Sign, Western Union Here, Porcelain, Flange, 10 x 17 In.	452.00
Sign, Whiskey, Pure Rye, Elephant, Reverse Glass, Silver, Copper, Brass Leaf, Frame, 36 x 32 In.	11000.00

Advertising, Sign, Hart Brand Fruits & Vegetables, Tin, Cardboard, 9 ¼ x 13 ¼ In.
$770.00

Advertising, Sign, Ingersoll Watches, Figural, Pocket Watch, Zinc, 25 x 35 In.
$825.00

Advertising, Sign, Jell-O, Die Cut, Cardboard, Easel Back, Genesee Pure Food Co., 24 ¼ x 15 ¾ In.
$798.00

Advertising, Sign, Johnson Oils, Time Tells, Hourglass, Wings, Porcelain, 29 x 24 In.
$193.00

ADVERTISING

Advertising, Sign, Keepsake Diamond Rings, Neon, 24 ½ x 10 x 5 In.
$248.00

Showtime Auction Services

Advertising, Sign, Kellogg's Toasted Corn Flakes, Cardboard, Lithograph, 1920s, 20 ⅝ x 11 In.
$908.00

Wm Morford Antiques

Advertising, Sign, Kis-Me Gum, Woman, Cherry Border, Embossed, Die Cut, 10 x 16 In.
$1100.00

Showtime Auction Services

Advertising, Sign, Kotex, Nurse, Holding Box, Tin Litho, H.D. Beach Co., 1920s, 8 ½ x 13 ¼ In.
173.00

Hake's Americana & Collectibles

Advertising, Sign, Lash's Kidney & Liver Bitters, Tin, Scrolled Corners, Mayer & Lavenson, N.Y., 21 x 16 In.
$819.00

Norman C. Heckler & Company

Advertising, Sign, Liqueurs Speciales, Cusenier, Woman, Frame, France, 1898, 59 ½ x 42 In.
$1062.00

Ivey-Selkirk Auctioneers

Advertising, Sign, Moxie, Of Course You'll Have Some, Girl, Tin, Embossed, Frame, 23 x 31 In.
$780.00

Victorian Casino Antique Auction

Advertising, Sign, Remington Rifles, Shotguns, Woman, Rifle, Cardboard, F.E. Getty, 1901, 10 ½ x 16 In.
$220.00

Showtime Auction Services

Advertising, Sign, S. & H. Green Stamps, Screen Painted, Sheet Steel, 2-Sided, 29 x 20 In.
$130.00

Conestoga Auction Co., Inc.

14

Sign, Whistle Soda, Die Cut, Cardboard, Boy Carrying Bottle, 13 x 26 In.	715.00
Sign, Whistle, Demand The Genuine, Hand Holding Bottle, Tin, Embossed, 7 x 10 In.	650.00
Sign, Whistle, Golden Orange Refreshment, Tin, Embossed, 4 x 21 In.	238.00
Sign, Wild Cherry Bitters, Reverse On Glass, Burgundy, Silver, c.1920, 15 ½ x 8 In.	300.00
Sign, Wilshire Tile Co., Porcelain, Diagonal, 1950s, 14 x 14 In.	55.00
Sign, Winchester Rifles, Shotguns & Ammunition, Metal, Frame, 10 x 13 In.	565.00
Sign, Window, Sunbeam Bread, Paper, Sunbeam Girl, Tricornered Hat, 1964, 11 x 21 In........	35.00
Sign, Wise Potato Chips, Santa Eating Chips In Front Of Fireplace, 1940s, 10 x 14 In.	150.00
Sign, Woodward's Peanut Butter Filled Candy, Boy, Girl, Cardboard, Die Cut, 10 x 14 In.	944.00
Sign, World's Greatest Flyer 5 Cent Cigar, Spirit Of St. Louis, New York, Paris, Tin, 19 x 8 In....	147.00
Sign, Wrigley's, Halloween Theme, Kids Dressed Up Holding Gum, 1930s, 12 x 8 In.	12.00
Sign, Yeast Foam, A Wise Choice, Cardboard, Die Cut, Frame, 12 x 18 In.	303.00
Sign, Yuengling Beer, Reverse Glass, Convex Oval Glass, 21 x 25 In...........................	4400.00
Sign, Yuengling Beer, Tin, Hand, Pouring Bottle, 1940s, 27 x 19 In.	300.00
Stickpin, Brownos, Cigar, Figural, Composition, Simulated Ash, c.1910, 1 ⅜ In.	123.00
Stickpin, Cat's Paw, Black Cat, I Like Rubber Heels, Celluloid, Heel Shape, 1 In.	52.00
Stickpin, Dr. Hyman, America's Greatest Painless Dentist, Flag Shape, Brass, 1 ½ In.	51.00
Stickpin, Hart-Parr 16-30, Tractor Shape, Goldtone Metal, 2 ⅛ In.	75.00
Stickpin, Sweeney's Iron Horse, Horse Shape, Silvertone Metal, 3 In.	127.00
Stringholder, Braun's Town Talk Bread, Favored By Folks, 1950s, 14 x 14 In.................	150.00
Stringholder, Chase & Sanborn Coffees & Teas, 2-Sided, Cardboard, 10 x 13 In.	355.00
Stringholder, Walker's King Of Soap, Beehive Shape, Cast Iron, 6 ½ x 5 In. ....*illus*	403.00
Stringholder, Who's Your Tailor?, Man, Stand, Round Foot, Tin, c.1900, 15 In.	450.00
Tablet, Memo, Novena Rye, America's Finest Whiskey, Celluloid, Bottle Shape, 1901.............	52.00
Tag, Member Patsy Doll Club, Effanbee Durable Dolls, Cord Holds Heart-Shaped Tag, 1 In.	40.00
Thermometers are listed in their own category.	

Advertising tin cans or canisters were first used commercially in the United States in 1819 and were called tins. Today the word *tin* is used by most collectors to describe many types of containers, including food tins, biscuit boxes, roly poly tobacco containers, gunpowder cans, talcum powder sprinkle-top cans, cigarette flat-fifty tins, and more. Beer Cans are listed in their own category. Things made of undecorated tin are listed under Tinware.

Tin, A.D.S. Talcum Powder, American Druggist Syndicate, Tin Litho Label, Embossed, 5 ¾ x 3 In.	45.00
Tin, American Eagle Chewing Tobacco, Painted, 6 x 4 In.	201.00
Tin, Bambino, Baseball Player, Tobacco, Red, Black, Vertical, Pocket, 4 ½ In.	1440.00
Tin, Beech-Nut Cigar, Proof Sheet, 6 x 4 ¾ In......................................	308.00
Tin, Big Ben, Clock Tower, Tobacco, Red, Yellow, Rounded Rectangular, 4 ½ In.	510.00
Tin, Biscuit, Carr's, Sheep In The Corn, Carlisle, England, 1910, 2 ¾ In.	236.00
Tin, Biscuit, English Toby, Cylindrical, Flared Rim, Multicolor, 7 In..........................	136.00
Tin, Biscuit, Hudson Scott, Toby Jug, England, 6 ¼ In.	142.00
Tin, Biscuit, Huntley & Palmers, Camera, Embossed Lens, Lithograph, c.1913, 3 ¾ x 4 In. ...*illus*	518.00
Tin, Biscuit, Huntley & Palmers, Chinese Vase, Paneled, 1928, 10 In.........................	224.00
Tin, Biscuit, Huntley & Palmers, Egg Stand, Hammered Aluminum, Handle, Eggcups, c.1910, 6 In. *illus*	403.00
Tin, Biscuit, Huntley & Palmers, Fire Brigade, 1892, 6 ¼ In.........................	885.00
Tin, Biscuit, Huntley & Palmers, Playmates, Fan Shape, Dogs, 1897, 9 In...................	354.00
Tin, Biscuit, Huntley & Palmers, Soldier, Box Shape, Red, White, Black, 9 In.................	51.00
Tin, Biscuit, Huntley & Palmers, Sundial, Cherubs, 1913, 8 In........................	142.00
Tin, Biscuit, Jacob Humming, Top Shape, 1928, 9 In.	560.00
Tin, Biscuit, Lucie Attwell Fairy House Biscuit & Money Box, Crawford, 1934, 8 In. ....*illus*	472.00
Tin, Biscuit, Macfarlane Lang, Violin Case Shape, Handle, 1903, 9 ½ In.	708.00
Tin, Biscuit, McVitie & Price, Bluebird, Bird's Head Lid, England, c.1911, 6 ½ In. ....*illus*	316.00
Tin, Biscuit, McVitie & Price, Bluebird, c.1910, 9 ½ In.	144.00
Tin, Biscuit, McVitie & Price, Cabinet, 1933, 8 ½ x 6 In.	177.00
Tin, Biscuit, Peek Frean, Little Red Riding Hood, Litho, Hinged, c.1930, 7 x 4 x 3 In............	225.00
Tin, Biscuit, Peek Frean, The Winner, Spinning, Paper Label, 1935, 5 ½ In.	189.00
Tin, Biscuit, Perrin's, Halifax To Vancouver, Bus, Tin Lithograph, Canada, c.1920, 10 In. *illus*	403.00
Tin, Biscuit, Stack Of Books Shape, Painted, England, c.1900, 6 x 6 In........................	237.00
Tin, Biscuit, W. Crawford & Sons, Fire Brigade, England, c.1920, 12 In. ....*illus*	6900.00
Tin, Biscuit, Wedj, Bekkers & Zoom, Airplane, Dutch, c.1930, 27-In. Wingspan ....*illus*	3450.00
Tin, Blue Bird Coffee, Bail Handle, 5 Lb., 6 x 7 ½ In. ....*illus*	330.00
Tin, Bulldog, Cut Plug, Tobacco, Red Dog, Metallic Blue, Gold, Pipes, Vertical, Pocket, 1910, 4 ½ In.	570.00
Tin, Cadette Talc For Mi-Lady, Soldier, Turquoise, White, Lithograph, 7 ⅜ x 2 ¼ In. ....*illus*	385.00
Tin, Camo Brand Fine Coffee, Camel, Water, Tin Lithograph, 5 Lb., 7 x 8 In......................	364.00
Tin, Cigar, Gobblers The Latest Smoke, Turkey, White, Red Letters, 5 x 5 In........................	1075.00

Advertising, Sign, Uneeda Biscuit, Boy In Slicker, National Biscuit Company, Paper, Frame, 17 x 23 In.
$354.00

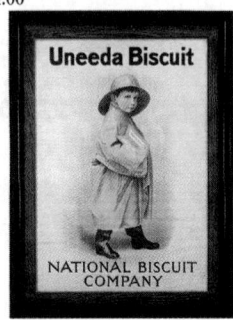

Showtime Auction Services

Advertising, Sign, Ward's Lime Crush, Batter Up!, I'm All Set!, Die Cut, Frame
$275.00

Showtime Auction Services

Advertising, Stringholder, Walker's King Of Soap, Beehive Shape, Cast Iron, 6 ½ x 5 In.
$403.00

Showtime Auction Services

Advertising, Tin, Biscuit, Huntley & Palmers, Camera, Embossed Lens, Lithograph, c.1913, 3 ¾ x 4 In.
$518.00

Bertoia Auctions

16

Tin, Cigarette, Ardath Brand, Flip Top, c.1900, 3 x 3 ⅜ In.	27.00
Tin, Coffee, Velvet, Cylindrical, Bail Handle, Cup & Saucer, Yellow, Blue, Gold, 8 ½ In.	480.00
Tin, Comfort Powder, Ideal Infant Powder, Unequaled, 3 ½ x 2 In.	196.00
Tin, Dan Patch Coffee, Bail Handle, Tennessee Coffee Co., 5 Lb., 11 ⅜ x 7 ¼ In. *illus*	2035.00
Tin, Dyer's Indian Herb Cough Drops, Maiden, Warriors, J. Dyer Taylor, Trenton, 1882, 5 x 8 In. *illus*	144.00
Tin, Eastman Kodak, Flash Cartridges, No. 2, 1 x 3 In.	45.00
Tin, Egret Cigars, G.A. Strobeck, Red Lion, Pa., 4 ¾ x 5 ½ In.	259.00
Tin, Elk Brand Spice, Elk On Front, Jellico, Tenn., 2 ¼ x 2 ¾ In.	235.00
Tin, English Pug Smoking Tobacco, Square Corner, Spaulding & Merrick, 4 ½ x 3 ¼ In.	252.00
Tin, Felix Cream Toffee, R.K. Confectionery, Felix The Cat, c.1920, 6 x 5 ¾ In. *illus*	1035.00
Tin, Forest & Stream Tobacco, Red, Fishermen In Canoe, Lithograph, Pocket, 4 ¼ x 3 In. *illus*	303.00
Tin, Four Roses, Smoking Tobacco, Roses, Tin Lithograph, Embossed, 3 x 3 x 1 In.	660.00
Tin, GB Coburn & Co., Girl, Flowers, c.1940, 3 ½ x 2 ¼ In.	18.00
Tin, Gobblers The Latest Smoke, Cigars, White With Red Letters, 50 Count, 5 x 5 In.	1075.00
Tin, Golf Girl Talcum Powder, Metal Top & Base, Paper Label, 5 ⅝ x 2 ½ In. *illus*	358.00
Tin, Goodhonest Coffee, Lewis De Groff Co., Abe Lincoln, 5 ⅝ x 4 ⅜ In. *illus*	303.00
Tin, Handsome Dan Tobacco, Granule Cut, 6 ½ x 2 ½ In.	303.00
Tin, Hash-Brown Tri Cut Blend Tobacco, Hookah, Falk Tobacco Co., Richmond, 1920s, 4 ⅜ x 3 ¼ In.	70.00
Tin, Hindoo, Tobacco, Seated Man, Turban, Cross-Legged, Blue, Yellow, Pocket, 3 ½ In.	420.00
Tin, Howard's Cough Drops, Green, Leaves, Scrolls, H.C. Howard Co., Mass., 6 ⅞ x 5 ⅛ In. *illus*	303.00
Tin, Ivins Cheese Flakes, Red, Yellow, Round, c.1920, 5 x 5 In.	32.00
Tin, Knock 'Em Dead Bed Bug Killer, Goulard & Olena, Gal.	196.00
Tin, La Nora Cigar, 25's, Ritter Mfg. Co., Skilled Union Labor	110.00
Tin, Lake View Spice, Cinnamon, Girl In Blue Bathing Suit, 1920s, 4 x 2 In.	175.00
Tin, Log Cabin Syrup, Frontier Inn, Horse, Men, Towle's Log Cabin Brand, 5 Lb., 6 ¼ x 6 ½ In. *illus*	110.00
Tin, Lucky Curve Pug Cut Tobacco, Lowell-Buffington Tobacco, 7 x 4 ½ In.	661.00
Tin, May Queen, Tobacco, J.G. Flint, Woman, Reclining, Flowers, Yellow, Black, 3 ¾ In.	420.00
Tin, Midget Pop Corn, Black, White, Hales Milling Co., 16 Oz.	55.00
Tin, Mission Brand Spice, Carmel Mission In California, Paper Label, 2 ½ x 3 ¾ In.	235.00
Tin, Monarch Teenie Weenie Toffies, Reid, Murdoch & Co., Chicago, 150 Pckgs. *illus*	472.00
Tin, Nash's Coffee, Red, White, Windup, c.1957, 3 ½ In.	45.00
Tin, Nut-Brown Coffee, Key Wind, Woman With Cup Of Coffee, 1930s, Lb.	75.00
Tin, Old Virginia Smoke Tobacco, Polk Miller & Chum Henry, c.1860, 4 x 2 ⅜ In.	288.00
Tin, Opera Man, US Marine Cut Plug Tobacco, 6 ½ In.	142.00
Tin, Peanuts, Buffalo Brand, Fancy Salted Peanuts, Buffalo, Red, Yellow, 9 ¾ In.	210.00
Tin, Peanuts, Giant Salted, Lid, Superior Peanut Co., Cleveland, O., 10 Lb. *illus*	236.00
Tin, Peanuts, Robinson Crusoe Salted Peanuts, H.A. Robinson Co., Inc., c.1900, 4 ½ In.	115.00
Tin, Perique Tobacco Mixture, Cream & Gray, 1883 Tax Stamp, 4 x 3 x 2 In.	440.00
Tin, Perla-Denta Tooth Powder, Penslar Co., Contents, Box, 4 ⅛ x 7 ¾ In. *illus*	330.00
Tin, Players Digger Flake Tobacco, John Player & Sons, Pocket, 3 ¼ x 2 In.	22.00
Tin, Poudre De Talc, Pompeia, Made In France, U.S.A., 3 x 4 In. *illus*	90.00
Tin, Pounce Powder, For Tracing Cloth, Keuffel & Esser Co., Hoboken, N.J., 5 In.	23.00
Tin, Radford's Roasted Nuts, Yellow, Red, Round, Hinged, 6 In.	10.00
Tin, Raleigh Plug Cut Tobacco, Cameron & Cameron, Richmond, 4 ½ x 3 ½ In. *illus*	144.00
Tin, Robertson Brothers, Chocolate, Golf Bag Shape, 1915, 11 In.	1298.00
Tin, Rock-Co Pure Cocoa, Waiter Serving Cocoa, Cardboard, Tin Lid, 9 x 4 ⅛ In. *illus*	55.00
Tin, Roly Poly, Dutchman, Mayo's Brand Tobacco, Lithograph, 6 ¾ x 6 In. *illus*	468.00
Tin, Roly Poly, Man In Blue Jacket, Mayo's Cut Plug, Smoking Pipe, 6 ½ In.	1020.00
Tin, Roly Poly, Man In Red Suit, Mayo's Cut Plug, Moustache & Pipe, 6 ½ In.	1080.00
Tin, Roly Poly, Mayo's Mammy, Pipe In Mouth, 6 ½ In.	1020.00
Tin, Roly Poly, Singing Waiter, Red Indian Brand Tobacco, Lithograph, 7 x 6 In. *illus*	440.00
Tin, Schepp's Coconut, Monkey Juggling Coconuts, 1878, 1 ¾ x 5 ½ In.	45.00
Tin, Sea Pilot, Trademark, General Coffee Co., Lb.	121.00
Tin, Spice, Columbia Brand, Cloves, Sutherland & McMillan, 1 ½ Oz., 3 x 1 ¼ In. *illus*	633.00
Tin, Stollwerck, Milk Cocoa, Gold Brand, Lithograph, c.1920, 4 ½ In. *illus*	259.00
Tin, Strong-Heart Coffee, Indian, Tin Litho, Charles Hewitt & Sons, Co., 1920s, 5 ¾ In. *illus*	432.00
Tin, Sunset Trail 5 Cent Cigar, Red, Lithograph, 25 Count, 5 ⅝ x 3 ⅝ In. *illus*	413.00
Tin, Tape, 3M Electrical, Scotch Plaid Design, Round, 3 ½ In.	6.00
Tin, Three Crow Mustard, Atlantic Spice Co., 3 Oz., 2 ½ x 4 In.	179.00
Tin, Tobacco, Bohemian Plug Mixture, Man, Camping Scouts, Lithograph, 5 x 6 In.	138.00
Tin, Towle's Log Cabin Syrup, Trading Post, Lithograph, 6 x 6 ½ x 4 In. *illus*	88.00
Tin, Towle's Log Cabin, Express Office, Cowboys, Stagecoach, 5 x 4 ¾ In. *illus*	66.00
Tin, Uncle Dan, Tobacco, Fine Cut Dark Pie, Red, 8 ¼ x 2 In.	198.00
Tin, United Bond Cigars, Lid, Round, 50 Cigars *illus*	550.00
Tin, Virginia Dare, Cut Plug Tobacco, 4 ⅜ x 3 ¼ In.	168.00
Tin, W.H.I. Hayes' Select Cut Smoking Tobacco, Square Corner, 4 ½ x 3 ⅜ In.	201.00
Tin, William Penn, Tobacco, Embossed, Hinged, 3 x 3 ¼ x ¼ In.	99.00

Advertising, Tin, Biscuit, Huntley & Palmers, Egg Stand, Hammered Aluminum, Handle, Eggcups, c.1910, 6 In.
$403.00

Advertising, Tin, Biscuit, Lucie Attwell Fairy House Biscuit & Money Box, Crawford, 1934, 8 In.
$472.00

Advertising, Tin, Biscuit, McVitie & Price, Bluebird, Bird's Head Lid, England, c.1911, 6 ½ In.
$316.00

Advertising, Tin, Biscuit, Perrin's, Halifax To Vancouver, Bus, Tin Lithograph, Canada, c.1920, 10 In.
$403.00

Advertising, Tin, Biscuit, W. Crawford & Sons, Fire Brigade, England, c.1920, 12 In.
$6900.00

Advertising, Tin, Biscuit, Wedj, Bekkers & Zoom, Airplane, Dutch, c.1930, 27-In. Wingspan
$3450.00

Advertising, Tin, Blue Bird Coffee, Bail Handle, 5 Lb., 6 x 7 ½ In.
$330.00

Advertising, Tin, Cadette Talc For Mi-Lady, Soldier, Turquoise, White, Lithograph, 7 ⅜ x 2 ¼ In.
$385.00

Advertising, Tin, Dan Patch Coffee, Bail Handle, Tennessee Coffee Co., 5 Lb., 11 ⅜ x 7 ¼ In.
$2035.00

Advertising, Tin, Dyer's Indian Herb Cough Drops, Maiden, Warriors, J. Dyer Taylor, Trenton, 1882, 5 x 8 In.
$144.00

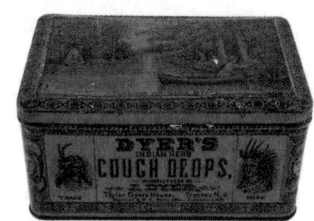

Advertising, Tin, Felix Cream Toffee, R.K. Confectionery, Felix The Cat, c.1920, 6 x 5 ¾ In.
$1035.00

Advertising, Tin, Forest & Stream Tobacco, Red, Fishermen In Canoe, Lithograph, Pocket, 4 ¼ x 3 In.
$303.00

A

Advertising, Tin, Golf Girl Talcum Powder, Metal Top & Base, Paper Label, 5 5/8 x 2 1/2 In.
$358.00

Wm Morford Antiques

Advertising, Tin, Goodhonest Coffee, Lewis De Groff Co., Abe Lincoln, 5 5/8 x 4 3/8 In.
$303.00

Wm Morford Antiques

Advertising, Tin, Howard's Cough Drops, Green, Leaves, Scrolls, H.C. Howard Co., Mass., 6 7/8 x 5 1/8 In.
$303.00

Wm Morford Antiques

Advertising, Tin, Log Cabin Syrup, Frontier Inn, Horse, Men, Towle's Log Cabin Brand, 5 Lb., 6 1/4 x 6 1/2 In.
$110.00

Wm Morford Antiques

Advertising tip trays are decorated metal trays less than 5 inches in diameter. They were placed on the table or counter to hold either the bill or the coins that were left as a tip. Change receivers could be made of glass, plastic, or metal. They were kept on the counter near the cash register and held the money passed back and forth by the cashier. Related items may be listed in the Advertising category under Change Receiver.

Tip Tray, Ballard's Obelisk, Louisville, Tin, 4 1/4 In.	83.00
Tip Tray, Bartholomay Brewery, Man On Running Horse, Tin Lithograph, 4 In.	392.00
Tip Tray, Chesterfield Cigarettes, Pack, 4 x 6 In. *illus*	295.00
Tip Tray, I Just Love Moxie Don't You, Tin Lithograph, H.D. Beach, c.1905, 6 In. *illus*	115.00
Tip Tray, Jenney Aero, Tin Lithograph, 4 1/4 In.	143.00
Tip Tray, King's Pure Malta, Nurse Holding Tray, 4 x 6 In.	56.00
Tip Tray, La Toco Havana Cigars, Tin, T. & O. Co., Tampa, Fl., 4 In.	101.00
Tip Tray, Moxie, I Like It, Girl Holding Glass, Cobalt Blue, Green, Gilt Rim, c.1910, 6 In.	720.00
Tip Tray, Red Raven Splits, For High Livers' Livers, 4 1/4 In. *illus*	177.00
Tip Tray, Red Raven, Ask The Man, Tin Lithograph, 4 1/4 In. *illus*	187.00
Tip Tray, Robert Burns Cigar, 4 In.	57.00
Tip Tray, Sparrows Chocolates, Imperial Chocolates Co., 4 3/8 In.	110.00
Tip Tray, Square Deal Bread, The Satisfaction Of Eating, Man Cutting Bread, 4 1/4 In.	270.00
Tip Tray, Stock Broker, Woman, Horse, Tin Lithograph, 4 1/4 In.	330.00
Tip Tray, Taka-Kola, Every Hour, 5 Cents, Take No Other, Girl Holding Bottle, c.1910, 4 1/4 In..	210.00
Tip Tray, Tam O'Shanter Ale, Man Holding Glass, Tin Lithograph, 4 In.	468.00 Tip
Tray, Tivoli Brewing Co., Altes Lager Bier, Factory, Bottle Label, 4 1/4 In.	67.00
Tray, Acme Beer, Cowgirl Pouring Beer, Pressed Aluminum Die Cut, c.1945, 17 x 9 In.	56.00
Tray, Anchor Brewery, Purity, c.1900, 16 1/2 x 13 1/2 In. *illus*	644.00
Tray, Anheuser-Busch Brewing Co., St. Louis, Factory, Hops & Grain, Oval, 18 In.	1375.00
Tray, Bartlett Spring Mineral Water, Bottle, Woman, Ruffled Dress, c.1900, 13 In.	180.00
Tray, Buffalo Brewing Co., Bohemian Beer, Chas. Ehlen, Cincinnati, 1905, 16 1/2 x 13 1/2 In. ..*illus*	1176.00
Tray, Buffalo Brewing Co., San Francisco Expo, Tin Lithograph, 1915, 12 In.	364.00
Tray, Bull Durham Smoking Tobacco, Bull, Woman, Tin Lithograph, Round, 24 In.	1395.00
Tray, Centennial Beer, Christ Diehl Brewing Co., Tin, 12 In.	374.00
Tray, Cremo Sparkling Ale, Girl Holding Glass, Tin, Round, 1940s, 13 In.	86.00
Tray, Crown Baking Powder, Tin Lithograph, Vienna Art Plate Style, Shonk Litho Co., 10 In. .... *illus*	385.00
Tray, Dixie Brewing Co., Beer That Speaks For Itself, New Orleans, c.1935, 13 In.	146.00
Tray, Dr Pepper, 10-2-4, Drink A Bite To Eat, Woman, Green Dress, 10 1/2 x 13 1/4 In.	236.00
Tray, Drink Dr Pepper, Pretty Girl, You'll Like It Too, 1940s, 13 1/4 x 10 1/2 In.	163.00
Tray, Drink Nehi, Cardboard, String Hung, 1930s, 13 x 21 In.	532.00
Tray, Ebling Brewing Co., Celebrated Beers, Factory Scene, 10 1/2 x 13 In.	1092.00
Tray, Edelweiss Beer, Pretty Girl, Tin Lithograph, 1913, 13 In.	504.00
Tray, Hires Root Beer, Young Girl Portrait, Self-Framed, Signed, Haskell Coffin ....*illus*	230.00
Tray, Janice, Woman, Holly, Thanks For Business, Meaderville, Montana, 1913, 16 In.	700.00
Tray, Pin, Dr Pepper, Boy, Watermelon, At All Soda Fountains, 5 Cents, Scalloped Edge, 3 In. ..	600.00
Tray, Popel-Giller Brewing Co., Evangeline, 1910, 13 x 10 1/2 In.	146.00
Tray, Purity Ice Cream, Has A Better Flavor, Mother, Children, Tin Litho, 10 x 13 In. ....*illus*	523.00
Tray, Remedy, Hicks Capudine, Liquid, For Headaches, 10-25 & 50 Cents A Bottle, Cupids, c.1900, 10 In.	360.00
Tray, Ruhstaller Brewing Co., Lager & Gilt Edge Steam Beer, 13 x 16 In.	420.00
Tray, Serving, Rainier Beer, Woman With Grizzly Bear, 1913, 13 In.	485.00
Tray, The Ware That Wears, Stransky & Co., N.Y., 24 x 19 1/2 In. *illus*	295.00
Tray, Union Cycle Co., Porcelain, Silver Plate Edge, Highlandville, Mass., 4 In.	90.00
Tray, Washington Brewery, 25 U.S. Presidents Through Theodore Roosevelt, c.1910-11, 12 x 17 In. *illus*	420.00
Tray, Wieland's Beer, 1909, 13 x 10 1/2 In.	308.00
Tray, Tip, see Tip Trays in this category.	
Urn, J.D. Iler, Kansas City, Samurai Warriors, Foo Dog Handles, Satsuma, 31 In.	8750.00
Whirligig, Pedaling Man, Spinning Blade, Bub's Beer Sign, Tin, Iron, Red, Blue Paint, 18 x 48 In.	840.00

AGATA glass was made by Joseph Locke of the New England Glass Company of Cambridge, Massachusetts, after 1885. A metallic stain was applied to New England Peachblow, which the company called Wild Rose, and the mottled design characteristic of agata appeared. There are a few known items made of opaque green with the mottled finish.

Vase, Pink To White, Blue Oil Spots, Gold Metallic Mottling, Lily Shape, Ruffled Rim, 8 In.	575.00
Vase, Pink, Morgan, Amber Resin Griffin Base, 10 In.	2100.00
Vase, Pink, Mottled Highlights, Trumpet Shape, 12 1/4 In.	850.00

AKRO AGATE glass was founded in Akron, Ohio, in 1911, and moved to Clarksburg, West Virginia, in 1914. The company made marbles and toys. In the 1930s it began making other products, including vases, lamps, flowerpots, candlesticks, and children's dishes. Most of the glass is marked with a crow flying through the letter *A*. The company was sold to Clarksburg Glass Co. in 1951. Akro Agate marbles are listed in this book in the Marble category.

Apothecary Jar, Black Amethyst, Pedestal, 3 ⅝ In.	19.00
Ashtray, Green, White, Marbleized, 1930s, 4 x 2 In.	38.00
Ashtray, Leaf Shape, Blue, Marbleized, 4 ⅛ In.	8.00
Ashtray, Oxblood, White, 2 Tabs, 4 ¾ In.	28.00
Basket, Double Handle, Basket Weave, Green, Yellow, Marbleized, 4 In.	12.00
Bell, Dark Forest Green, Hexagonal Handle, 5 ½ In.	595.00
Bowl, Cereal, Concentric Ring, Blue, White, Marbleized, 2 ⅜ In.	18.00
Candlestick, Ivory, 1940s, 3 ½ In.	89.00
Child's Set, Interior Panel, Amber, 12 Piece	249.00
Cornucopia, Blue, Marbleized, 3 ½ In.	14.00
Creamer, Stacked Disc, White, 2 Handles, 1 ⅛ In.	7.50
Cup & Saucer, Blue, White, Marbleized, Demitasse	28.00
Dish, Shell Shape, Green, Marbleized, 4 x 3 In.	12.00
Jardinere, Orange, Square Mouth, Scalloped Top	59.00
Planter, Jade Green, Oval, Ribs, Scalloped Rim, 6 x 3 x 2 In.	25.00
Planter, Orange, Yellow, Jonquils, Footed, 5 x 3 x 2 In.	25.00
Planter, Ribbed Band, Marbleized, 3 ¼ In.	22.00
Plate, Red, Yellow, Marbleized, Octagonal, 4 ¼ In.	20.00
Powder Jar, Colonial Woman, Green	489.00
Sugar & Creamer, Darts & Ribs, Yellow, Child's	10.00
Toothpick Holder, Urn Shape, Footed, Amber, 3 ¼ In.	16.00
Tumbler, Jade Green, Paneled, 2 In.	12.50
Urn, Red, White, Marbleized, Footed, Beaded Top, 3 ¼ In.	25.00
Vase, Lilies, Leaves, Footed, Green, White, 4 ¼ In.	16.00
Vase, Orange, Marbleized, 4 x 4 In.	189.00
Vase, Ribbed, Fluted, Cream, 3 In.	18.00

ALABASTER is a very soft form of gypsum, a stone that resembles marble. It was often carved into vases or statues in Victorian times. There are alabaster carvings being made even today.

Bowl, Pedestal, Gilt Bronze Fairy Support, Squat Bowl, Rolled Rim, 15 In.	688.00
Bowl, Round, 4 Bird Mounts, Square Foot, 12 In., Pair	427.00
Bust, Augustus Caesar, Light Brown, Black Socle, 10 ½ In.	1140.00
Bust, Gentleman, 1800s, 20 ½ In.	2252.00
Bust, Girl, Reeded Stem, Leaf Tip, Octagonal Base, Pedestal, Italy, c.1890, 49 x 15 In.	1041.00
Bust, Mignon, Renaissance Woman, Multicolor, Signed Prof. G. Bessi, c.1910, 14 ¼ In.	489.00
Bust, Mother's Joy, Child, Arms Around Mother's Neck, Signed P.E. Fiasche, Italy, c.1900, 10 ¾ In.	270.00
Bust, Napoleon, Socle Base, 11 In.	179.00
Bust, Nun, Head Scarf, Italy, c.1900, 10 ½ In.	207.00
Bust, Woman, Cap On Head, Italy, c.1900, 21 ½ In.	518.00
Bust, Woman, Hat, Flowers, Marble Stand, 67 x 17 In.	1187.00
Bust, Woman, Sideward Glancing, Torso, Italy, 18 In.	207.00
Bust, Woman, Victorian, Pierced Bonnet, Signed, c.1880, 24 x 13 ½ In.	633.00
Bust, Woman, Wearing Headscarf, White, Italy, 15 In.	207.00
Bust, Woman, Wide Brim Hat, Beveled Plinth, Signed Cipriani, 17 In.	230.00
Figurine, 2 Girls, Smiling, 1900s, 7 ½ In.	189.00
Figurine, Girl, Basket On Shoulders, c.1900, 15 In.	148.00
Figurine, Girl, Holding Jug, Base, Italian, c.1900, 15 ½ In.	590.00
Figurine, Napoleon, Standing, Reading, Carved, Thomas Ball, 1905, 11 ¼ In.	360.00
Figurine, Woman, Evening Dress, Seated On Rock, c.1890, 30 In.	62.00
Figurine, Woman, Semi-Clad, Gray Marble Base, 24 In.	374.00
Figurine, Woman, Standing, Carved, Italy, 1890, 31 ¾ In.	429.00
Font, Bowl, Seminude Nymph Supports, Carved, Veined Gray Pedestal, 27 x 12 In.	1989.00
Pedestal, Bronze Mounts, Column Shape, Stepped Base, 39 x 11 In.	622.00
Pedestal, Octangular Top & Base, Column Standard, Italy, c.1900, 28 In.	474.00
Pedestal, Square Top, Canted Corners, Ringed Column, Octagonal Base, c.1900, 30 x 14 In.	861.00
Plaque, Monk, Praying, Crosier, Parcel Giltwood Frame, Spanish School, 6 ¼ x 5 ½ In.	1298.00
Sculpture, Boy Feeding Goat, Seated, Round Rocky Base, 15 In.	403.00
Sculpture, Classical Maiden, Signed, Umberto Stiaccini, c.1900, 30 In. *illus*	2151.00
Sculpture, Couple, Embracing, Classical, 26 In.	1309.00
Sculpture, Crying Girl, In Bonnet, Holding Dead Bird, Marble Base, Signed, Italy, c.1900, 14 In.	173.00
Sculpture, Cupid, Psyche, Carved, Raised Base, 18 x 19 In.	403.00
Sculpture, Harlequin, With Mandolin, Seated, Square Base, Signed, Austria, 13 x 7 In.	863.00
Sculpture, Woman, Seated, Savonarola Chair, Tinted Base, Italy, 1800s, 18 ⅝ In.	3081.00
Urn, Cream, Blue Veined Body, Curved Handles, 12 ¼ In.	384.00
Urn, Louis XVI Style, Gilt Metal, Dome Lid, Rope Twist, Beaded, Scroll Handles, 16 x 6 In., Pair	1755.00

Advertising, Tin, Monarch Teenie Weenie Toffies, Reid, Murdoch & Co., Chicago, 150 Pckgs.
$472.00

Advertising, Tin, Peanuts, Giant Salted, Lid, Superior Peanut Co., Cleveland, O., 10 Lb.
$236.00

Advertising, Tin, Perla-Denta Tooth Powder, Penslar Co., Contents, Box, 4 ⅛ x 7 ¾ In.
$330.00

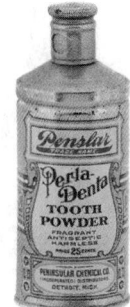

Advertising, Tin, Poudre De Talc, Pompeia, Made In France, U.S.A., 3 x 4 In.
$90.00

A

ALUMINUM was more expensive than gold or silver until the 1850s. Chemists learned how to refine bauxite to get aluminum. Jewelry and other small objects were made of the valuable metal until 1914, when an inexpensive smelting process was invented. The aluminum collected today dates from the 1930s through the 1950s. Hand-hammered pieces are the most popular.

Basket, Grapevine, Double Round Handle, Square Knot Top, Serrated Edge, 8 In.	35.00
Basket, Porcelain Center, Roses, Handle, Scroll Trim, Farber & Shlevin, 7 x 5 In.	15.00
Basket, Pressed, Flowers, Reticulated, Ruffled, Handle, 1960s, 7 x 7 In.	27.00
Bowl, Blue, Flared, Ruffled Edge, Flowers, 11 x 3 In.	68.00
Bowl, Cast, Flower & Scroll Pattern, Incised, Krischer, 8 x 13 In.	19.00
Bucket, Champagne, Spun, U-Shape, Ball Handles, On Stand, 8-In. Bucket, 30 In.	49.00
Bun Holder, Globular, Bentwood Handle, Finial, Interior Wirework, Russel Wright, 9 In.	59.00
Compote, Wild Rose, Hammered, Continental Silver Co., 4 ½ In.	28.00
Container, Grease, Bakelite Lid, Black, c.1965, 4 ¾ In.	12.95
Dish, Tulips, Hand Forged, Rodney Kent, c.1950, 12 x 7 In.	26.00
Lazy Susan, Embossed, Pressed, 1960s, 15 In. Diam.	35.00
Lazy Susan, Leaf, Pedestal, Gailstyn Mfg., 1950s, 17 In. Diam.	18.00
Mailbox, Cast, Flags, Eastern Star, Hasp, Remington Hardware, c.1930, 13 x 5 In.	135.00
Pitcher, Hammered, Ice Lip, Gailstyn, 1960s, 8 In.	30.00
Plaque, Virgin Mary, Tombstone Shape, 1940s, 3 x 5 In.	35.00
Pot, Double Boiler, Mirro, 1 ½ Qt.	18.00
Silent Butler, Bamboo Design, Hinged Lid, Everlast Metal, 1940s, 10 In.	40.00
Silent Butler, Hammered, Applied Rose, Continental, 1940s, 12 x 7 In.	32.00
Spurs, Leather, 1950s	55.00
Teapot, Black Knob, Cornered, Banner Stamping Works, 7 In.	16.00
Tray, Embossed, Everlast Forged, Handles, 11 x 11 In.	38.00
Tray, Fruit, Hammered, Handles, c.1945, 21 x 12 In.	85.00
Tray, Gazelles, Leaves, Fluted Edges, Cromwell, Curled Handles, 17 x 12 In.	10.00
Tray, Hammered, Central Well, 24 In.	55.00
Tray, Pomegranate, Twisted Handles, Crimped Rim, c.1960, 13 In. Diam.	9.50
Trivet, Hand Forged, Handle, Everlast, 4 x 5 In.	22.00
Umbrella Stand, Ettore Sottsass, Anodized, Rinovel, 1950s, 21 x 13 In.	6200.00

AMBER, *see Jewelry category.*

AMBER GLASS is the name of any glassware with the proper yellow-brown shading. It was a popular color just after the Civil War and many pressed glass pieces were made of amber glass. Depression glass of the 1930s–50s was also made in shades of amber glass. Other pieces may be found in the Depression Glass, Pressed Glass, and other glass categories. All types are being reproduced.

Bowl, Yellow To Amber, Globular, Flowers, Crimped Rim, Tripod Feet, Blue Lining, 4 ½ In.	177.00
Vase, Fan, Applied Yellow & Green Flower Spray, Footed, 7 ½ In. ......*illus*	59.00

AMBERINA, a two-toned glassware, was originally made from 1883 to about 1900. It was patented by Joseph Locke of the New England Glass Company, but was also made by other companies and is still being made. The glass shades from red to amber. Similar pieces of glass may be found in the Baccarat, Libbey, Plated Amberina, and other categories. Glass shaded from blue to amber is called *Blue Amberina* or *Bluerina.*

Biscuit Jar, Metal Lid, Amber To Rose, Desert Scene, Oasis, Opalescent, Mt. Washington, 8 In.	403.00
Biscuit Jar, Thumbprint, Silver Plated Lid, Bail Handle, 6 ½ In.	350.00
Bowl, Crimped, Pulled, Ruffled Edge, c.1955, 5 x 3 In.	22.00
Bowl, Murano Style, Controlled Bubbles, Applied Ridged Handles, 5 x 7 In.	30.00
Creamer, Squat, Applied Handle, 12 Protruding Ribs, 4 ½ In.	7000.00
Creamer, Thumbprint, Shades Of Amber, Ruby Rim, 4 ½ In.	150.00
Cruet, Coin Spot, 5 ½ In.	75.00
Decanter, Thumbprint, Faceted Stopper, Foot, Amber To Red, c.1900, 12 x 5 In.	259.00
Inkwell, Vertical Ribbing, Round, White Lining, Metal Collar, Hinged Lid, 3 ¾ In.	920.00
Jar, Sugar, Thumbprint Pattern, Silver Plate Spout, Lid, Pierced Handle, 8 In.	1035.00
Lamp, Oval, Leaf Shaped Feet, Dome Top, Ruby Shading, 9 In.	1725.00
Marmalade, Hobnail, Footed, Silver Plated Lid & Bail Handle, 5 ½ In.	225.00
Pitcher, 6 Tumblers, Coin Spot, Applied Amber Ribbed Handle, 8 In., 7 Piece	250.00
Pitcher, Amber To Red, Ribbed Design, Melon Shape, Loop Handle, c.1800s, 8 In.	89.00
Pitcher, Coin Spot, Ruffled Rim, 9 ½ In.	100.00
Pitcher, Crackle Glass, Clear Applied Handle, 4 In.	29.00
Pitcher, Thumbprint, Handle, 6 ½ In.	125.00
Pitcher, Thumbprint, Red To Amber, Clear Loop Handle, Baluster Shape, c.1900, 9 In.	59.00

Pitcher, Water, Bulbous, Melon Ribbed, Scalloped Rim, Amber Loop Handle, 8 In. 17250.00
Pitcher, Water, Coin Spot, Amber Handle, 9 In. 75.00
Pitcher, Water, Herringbone, Melon Ribbed, 8 In. 350.00
Pitcher, Water, Square Mouth Form, Lincoln Drape, Reeded Handle, 7 In. 175.00
Pitcher, Water, Swirl, 7 ¼ In. 225.00
Punch Cup, Diamond-Quilted, Handles, 10 Piece 100.00
Salt & Pepper, Stand, Ribbed, Metal Tops, Silver Plated Stand, Wilcox, c.1885, 7 In. 460.00
Sugar & Creamer, Rose Amber, Thumbprint Pattern, Applied Handle, 5 In. 500.00
Sugar, Ribbed, Spread Bottom, Amber To Rose, 2 Round Handles, 3 In. 1150.00
Syrup, Round, Silver Plated Embossed Collar, Flip Top, 6 In. 403.00
Tankard, Daisy & Button, Applied Handle, Star Cut Base, Scalloped Rim, 12 In. .... *illus* 345.00
Toothpick Holder, Diamond-Quilted, Cylindrical, 2 ¾ In. 100.00
Toothpick Holder, Diamond-Quilted, Cylindrical, Silver Plated Holder, 7 ½ In. 475.00
Toothpick Holder, Set, Diamond-Quilted, Silver Plated Holder, Figural Rabbit, 4 In. 225.00
Tumbler, Amber Ribs, Yellow, Cylinder, 3 ¾ In. 920.00
Tumbler, Cylindrical, Ribbed, Amber To Rose, 4 In. 1955.00
Vase, Applied Amber Rigoree, 8 In. 60.00
Vase, Bulbous, Stick Shape, Honeycomb Pattern, 10 In. 86.00
Vase, Diamond-Quilted, Asymmetrical Ruffled Rim, 10 ¼ In. 129.00
Vase, Optic Wave, Melon Ribbed, Ruffle Rim, Rope Twist Collar, Raspberry Prunt, 5 In. 345.00
Vase, Square Shape, Lobed, Pinched Neck, Ruffled Rim, Gold To Amber, 3 In. 69.00
Vase, Trifold Rim, Rigaree Collar, Bulbous, Flask Shape, 8 ½ In. .... *illus* 431.00

AMERICAN DINNERWARE, *see Dinnerware.*

AMERICAN ENCAUSTIC TILING COMPANY was founded in Zanesville, Ohio, in 1875. The company planned to make a variety of tiles to compete with the English tiles that were selling in the United States for use in fireplaces and other architectural designs. The first glazed tiles were made in 1880, embossed tiles in 1881, faience tiles in the 1920s. The firm closed in 1935 and reopened in 1937 as the Shawnee Pottery.

Tile, Fish, Swirls, Water Splashes, Green, White, Yellow, 6 In. 107.00
Tile, Flamingos, Pink, Blue, Green, Wood Frame, 4 In. 269.00
Tile, Frogs, Dancing, Green, Wood Frame, 8 ¾ In. 518.00
Tile, Stylized Flower, Multicolor, Art Nouveau, Frame, 10 x 13 In. 56.00
Tile, Turkey, Black Border, 4 ½ In. .... *illus* 58.00
Tile, Tuscan Geometric, Green, Brown Crystalline Glaze, Label, 6 x 6 In. .... 28.00 to 30.00

AMETHYST GLASS is any of the many glasswares made in the dark purple color of the gemstone amethyst. Included in this category are many pieces made in the nineteenth and twentieth centuries. Very dark pieces are called *black amethyst* and are listed under that heading.

Bowl, Lobed Body, Scalloped Rim, Hardwood Stand, Chinese, 10 ½ In. .... *illus* 1265.00
Figurine, Eagle, In Flight, Stand, 10 x 11 In. 244.00
Goblet, Clear Stem, 7 ½ In., 12 Piece 180.00
Goblet, Flint, Cone Shape, Bladed Knop Bottom, Button Knop, 5 In., 4 Piece 236.00
Vase, Diamond Design, Bronze Dore Frame, Applied Faun Heads, Handles, 8 x 6 In. 427.00

AMPHORA *pieces are listed in the Teplitz category.*

ANDIRONS *and related fireplace items are included in the Fireplace category.*

ANIMAL TROPHIES, such as stuffed animals, rugs made of animal skins, and other similar collectibles made from animal, fish, or bird parts, are listed in this category. Collectors should be aware of the endangered species laws that make it illegal to buy and sell some of these items. Any eagle feathers, many types of pelts or rugs (such as leopard), ivory, and many forms of tortoiseshell can be confiscated by the government. Related trophies may be found in the Fishing category. Ivory items may be found in the Scrimshaw or Ivory categories.

African Cape Buffalo, Shoulder Mount, c.1950, 38 x 40 In. 598.00
African Gemsbok, Antelope Head, Walnut Pedestal, Republic Of Namibia, 85 ¼ In. 345.00
African Jackal, Full Body Mount, Standing On Rock, 33 x 40 x 15 In. 472.00
African Nyala Antelope, Full Body Mount, Standing, Base, Republic Of Namibia, 69 x 74 In. 633.00
African Poku Antelope, Shoulder Mount, 35 x 9 x 16 In. 154.00
African Sable Antelope Head, c.1950, 49 In. 478.00
African Steenbok, Antelope, Full Wall Mount, Zimbabwe, 36 In. 259.00
African Zebra Head, Walnut Pedestal, Republic Of Namibia, 73 In. 1150.00
Alligator, Full Body Mount, On Grassy Base, 70 In. 353.00

Advertising, Tin, Spice, Columbia Brand, Cloves, Sutherland & McMillan, 1 ½ Oz., 3 x 1 ¼ In.
$633.00

Wm Morford Antiques

Advertising, Tin, Stollwerck, Milk Cocoa, Gold Brand, Lithograph, c.1920, 4 ½ In.
$259.00

Auction Team Breker

Advertising, Tin, Strong-Heart Coffee, Indian, Tin Litho, Charles Hewitt & Sons, Co., 1920s, 5 ¾ In.
$432.00

Hake's Americana & Collectibles

Advertising, Tin, Sunset Trail 5 Cent Cigar, Red, Lithograph, 25 Count, 5 ⅝ x 3 ⅝ In.
$413.00

Wm Morford Antiques

Advertising, Tin, Towle's Log Cabin Syrup, Trading Post, Lithograph, 6 x 6 ½ x 4 In.
$88.00

Wm Morford Antiques

Advertising, Tin, Towle's Log Cabin, Express Office, Cowboys, Stagecoach, 5 x 4 ¾ In.
$66.00

Wm Morford Antiques

Advertising, Tin, United Bond Cigars, Lid, Round, 50 Cigars
$550.00

Showtime Auction Services

Advertising, Tip Tray, Chesterfield Cigarettes, Pack, 4 x 6 In.
$295.00

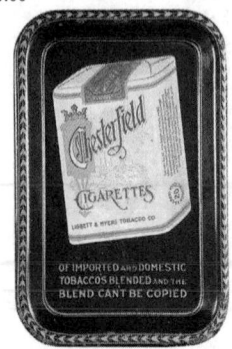

Showtime Auction Services

Antlers, Red Stag, 9-Point, Skull Cap, Wood Shield Shape Plaque, 27 x 26 In.	37.00
Bear, Black, Full Mount, Walking, Wheel Platform, Canada, 61 In.	978.00
Bear, Brown, Full Mount, Standing, Base, Alaska, 98 In.	2070.00
Bison, American Plains, Full Mount, Base, South Dakota, 84 x 101 In.	1265.00
Blesbok Antelope, Standing, Rectangular Landscape Base, Full Body Mount, S. Africa, 1997	863.00
Boar's Head, Tusks, Mount	122.00
Cape Buffalo Head, Tanzania, 78 In.	748.00
Coyote, Full Body Mount, On Rock & Log, 28 In.	1175.00
Deer Head, 10-Point Antlers, Wall Mount	92.00
Deer, 7-Point Antlers, Mounted On Shield Shape Plaque, Cast Zinc, c.1900, 30 x 27 In.	690.00
Diamondback, Full Body, 27 In.	206.00
Elephant Feet, Coffee Table, Glass Top, 3 Supports, c.1950, 19 x 72 In.	896.00
Gemsbok Head, 50 In.	441.00
Grizzly Bear, Full Body Mount, On Rock Shape Base, 65 In.	1645.00
Himalayan Tahr, Full Body Mount, Landscape Base, New Zealand, 1999, 46 In.	633.00
Javelina, Full Body Mount, 18 x 30 x 14 In.	472.00
Kechwe, Full Body Mount, Flat Base, 54 In.	999.00
Lion, African, Standing, Raised Front Paw, Open Mouth, Case, 67 x 97 In.	2585.00
Lion, Front Half, Full Mane, Artificial Rock Mount, 54 x 34 In.	1169.00
Lion, Male, Reclining, Full Body Mount, Tanzania, 1999, 71 In.	1725.00
Mallard Duck, In Flight, Wall Mount, 28 x 21 x 12 In.	74.00
Moose Antlers, 7-Point, 3 Brow Tines, Mount, Oak Plaque, 55 In.	633.00
Mule Deer, Shoulder Mount, 36 x 25 In.	236.00
Polar Bear, Full Body Mount, Ice Shape Base, 98 In.	7050.00
Red Fox, Full Body Mount, On Grass & Tree Trunk, 31 In.	999.00
Ringneck Rooster Pheasant, Standing Alert, 16 x 7 x 28 In.	123.00
Rug, African Zebra, Black Felt Backing, Tanzania, 10 ½ x 8 ½ Ft.	1380.00
Rug, Leopard Skin, Full Head, Black Felt Backing, c.1950, 97 x 68 In.	10158.00
Rug, Zebra Hide, Africa, c.1925, Full Size *illus*	176.00
Russian Boar, Shoulder Mount, 20 x 18 x 26 In. *illus*	210.00
Sailfish, Wall Mount, 29 x 81 x 5 In.	246.00
Serval Cat, Full Body Mount, Tanzania, 1999	403.00
Skull, African Crocodile, 26 ½ In.	316.00
Skull, Bison, Wall Mount, Painted Hunter On Forehead, 26-In. Horn Span	316.00
Skull, Longhorn, 22 x 46 x 7 In.	120.00
Steer Horns, Longhorn, Mounted, 58 In.	266.00
Stone Sheep Head, 26 In.	441.00
Walrus, Skull, Ivory Tusks, 17 In.	1793.00
Warthog Head, Wall Mount *illus*	275.00
Whitetail Deer Head, 10-Point, Shoulder Mount, 1964, 34 x 19 In.	369.00
Wild Boar, Black Russian, Shoulder Mount, 29 x 17 x 26 In.	295.00
Zebra Head, 25 In. *illus*	940.00

ANIMATION ART collectibles include cels that are painted drawings on celluloid needed to make animated cartoons shown in movie theaters or on TV. Hundreds of cels were made, then photographed in sequence to make a cartoon showing moving figures. Early examples made by the Walt Disney Studios are popular with collectors today. Original sketches used by the artists are also listed here. Modern animated cartoons are made using computer-generated pictures. Some of these are being produced as cels to be sold to collectors. Other cartoon art is listed in Comic Art and Disneyana.

Cel, Br'er Bear, Song Of The South, Disney, 1946, 4 ½ x 7 In.	2599.00
Cel, Bugs Bunny, Frame, Linda Jones, Warner Brothers, 1980, 12 x 9 ¾ In.	207.00
Cel, Bugs Bunny, Wrong Number, Lithographed Back, Virgil Ross, 16 x 13 In.	295.00
Cel, Cinderella & Prince, Disney, 9 ½ x 10 ½ In.	3658.00
Cel, Cogsworth, Lumiere, Mrs. Potts, Beauty & The Beast, Frame, 11 x 15 ½ In.	362.00
Cel, Dinah, Alice In Wonderland, Frame, Disney, 4 ¼ x 4 ½ In.	520.00
Cel, Donald Duck, Dressed As Pioneer, 3 ½ x 4 ¾ In.	40.00
Cel, Dopey, Snow White, 5 ½ x 5 ¾ In.	2596.00
Cel, Dumbo, Timothy The Mouse, Disney, 6 ½ x 8 In.	2596.00
Cel, Figaro, By The Window, Pinocchio, Disney, Frame, 1939, 15 x 17 In.	2300.00
Cel, Flintstones, Fred, Wilma, Pebbles On Dino The Dinosaur, Mat, 8 x 11 In.	119.00
Cel, George Jetson, Color Photography Background, Hanna-Barbera, 8 x 9 ¾ In.	35.00
Cel, Jessica Rabbit, Eddie Valiant, Black, White, Ground, Disney, 14 ½ x 9 ½ In.	520.00
Cel, Ludwig Von Drake, Holding Mother Goose Book, Mat, 1963, 11 x 14 In. *illus*	190.00
Cel, Mickey's Amateurs, Serigraph, Disney Studios, Frame, 13 ½ x 9 ½ In.	196.00
Cel, Mowgli, King Louis, Jungle Book, Disneyland Art Corner, 5 ½ x 8 ½ In.	520.00

Cel, Pearly Band, Mary Poppins, 1960s, 7 ½ x 11 In.	708.00
Cel, Pinocchio, Figaro, Geppetto's Apron Covered Legs, Frame, c.1940, 9 x 11 In. ....*illus*	1010.00
Cel, Pluto, Mickey, Checking In, Frame, 10 x 12 In.	203.00
Cel, Roger Rabbit, Black & White Background, 13 x 8 In.	354.00
Cel, Roger, Who Framed Roger Rabbit, Disney, 11 x 7 In.	328.00
Cel, Tramp, Bone In Mouth, Lady & The Tramp, Disney, Frame, 1955, 4 ½ x 5 ½ In.	452.00
Cel, Tramp, Professor, Lady & The Tramp, Disney, 1955, 7 ½ x 12 In.	960.00
Cel, Winnie The Pooh & Tigger Too, Tigger Tackle, Disney Studios, Frame, 1996, 14 x 11 In. ..	288.00
Cel, Winnie The Pooh, Disney, Frame, 1968, 22 x 20 In.	203.00
Cel, Wolf & The Three Little Wolves, 1936, 4 x 9 ½ In.	1475.00
Character Set Up, Beauty & The Beast, Hand Painted, Disney, 1994, 26 x 22 In.	384.00
Drawing, Baloo, Bagheera, Mowgli, Jungle Book, Pencil, 9 ½ x 16 In.	85.00
Drawing, Batman, Pencil, Signed Adam West, c.1977, 5 ½ x 5 In.	85.00
Drawing, Maleficent, Sleeping Beauty, Pencil, 1959, 15 ½ x 12 ½ In.	565.00
Drawing, Mickey Mouse, Playing Drums, Pencil, 1930s, 5 x 7 In.	622.00
Drawing, Pinocchio, Pencil, Disney, 1940, 4 ¼ x 3 ¼ In.	57.00
Drawing, Prince Philip, Sleeping Beauty, Pencil, Walt Disney, 1959, 5 x 9 ½ In.	249.00
Serigraph, Mickey Mouse, Pluto, Goofy, Disney, 7 x 7 ½ In.	124.00

ANNA POTTERY was started in Anna, Illinois, in 1859 by Cornwall and Wallace Kirkpatrick. They made many types of utilitarian wares, bricks, drain tiles, and giftware. The most collectible pieces made by the pottery are the pig-shaped bottles and jugs with special inscriptions, applied animals, and figures. The pottery closed in 1894.

Anna Pottery

Bottle, Pig, California & Black Hills Railroad Map, c.1884, 6 ½ In.	9775.00
Bottle, Pig, Incised Hooves, Pierced Ears, Inscription, Stoneware Railway, c.1880s, 8 In.	2703.00
Bottle, Pig, Incised Map, Mississippi River, St. Louis, Cincinnati, Chicago, 8 In. ....*illus*	14100.00
Bottle, Pig, Railroad & River Guide, Illinois Towns, Incised, 1882, 7 x 3 ¾ In.	12650.00
Bottle, Pig, Reclining, Applied Tail, Incised Features, Bristol Slip Glaze, c.1890, 5 In.	201.00
Churn, Salt Glaze, Gray, Cobalt Blue Quill Design, 4, Applied Lug Handles, 4 Gal.	1093.00
Crock, Salt Glaze, Cobalt Blue Quill Mark, Albany Slip Glaze Inside, 3 Gal., 11 x 10 In.	920.00
Flask, Pig, Good Old Rye, In A Hog's, Wallace & Cornwall Kirkpatrick, c.1880, 3 x 7 In.	2588.00
Flask, Pig, Horace Greeley Presidential Trap, Presentation Poem, Albany Slip Glaze	17250.00
Flask, Pig, Presentation, Greeley, Albany Slip Glaze, Rabbit Trap, Railroad Map, 4 x 8 In.	28875.00
Flask, Pig, Presentation, Railroad, River Guide, Albany Slip Glaze	8625.00
Flask, Pig, Pure Old Peach, In A Hog's, Incised, Wallace & Cornwall Kirkpatrick, 3 x 7 In.	863.00
Flask, Pig, Salt Glaze, Cobalt Blue Accents, 3 x 6 In.	1495.00
Flask, Pig, Union County, Illinois, Incised Map, c.1880	14100.00
Flask, Pig, Whiskey Distillers, Cobalt Blue Writing, Paducah, Ky., 1883.	18400.00
Flask, Sanford, Wells & Co., St. Louis, Incised Mississippi River, Rockingham Glaze, 7 ½ x 3 In.	4600.00
Flask, Shoo-Fly, Cobalt Blue, Cold Paint, Woman Holding Flask's Neck, Incised, Signed, 6 In..	14950.00
Flask, Sow Pig, Incised Eyes, Large Snout, Good Old Bourbon, 1860s, 3 x 7 In.	4313.00
Inkwell, Frog, Sitting On Clamshell, Albany Slip, Salt Glaze, Marked, 1881, 3 x 4 In.	14950.00
Inkwell, Presentation, J.S.R. Wedding, Attorney At Law, Albany Slip Glaze, 1896, 2 ¾ x 7 In.	575.00
Jar, Canning, Cobalt Blue Quill Design, Horizontal Stripes, Salt Glaze, Grooved Rim, 9 ½ x 4 In.	2070.00
Jug, Commemorating Southern Illinois 1884 Anna Pottery Fair, Salt Glaze, 1884, 22 In.	86250.00
Jug, Little Brown Jug, Albany Slip, Applied Strap Handle, Incised, Kirkpatrick, 4 x 3 ½ In.	2185.00
Jug, Little Brown Jug, Brachman, Massard Wines, Liquors, Cincinnati, Albany Slip, 5 x 4 In.	4313.00
Jug, Little Brown Jug, Bully Holden, Incised Stump, Coin Spot, Applied Strap Handle, 4 x 3 ½ In.	2875.00
Jug, Little Brown Jug, Incised, Albany Glaze Jug, Strap Handle, 1877, 4 x 3 x 3 ¼ In.	690.00
Jug, Little Brown Jug, Presentation, Jessie A. Palmer, Strap Applied Handle, Fluted Spout, 5 x 4 In.	4025.00
Jug, Snake, 8-7 Victory, Hayes, Tilden, 1876 Presidential Election, Salt Glaze, 11 x 9 In.	80500.00
Jug, Snake, High Water Flask, Incised Verse, Little Brown Jug, 1884, 8 x 6 ½ In.	34500.00
Mug, Frog, Albany Slip Glaze, Cylindrical, Strap Handle, St. Louis Swamp, c.1880, 2 ¾ In.	805.00
Mug, Frog, Brown Albany Slip Glaze, Applied Strap Handle, Frog In Base, 5 ½ x 2 ¾ In.	805.00
Pitcher, Frog, Monkey Handle, Bristol Slip Glaze, c.1880, 14 In.	1265.00
Pitcher, Salt Glaze, Cobalt Blue Quill Design, Applied Strap Handle	3163.00
Whistle, Owl, Night Operator, Glass Eyes, Salt Glaze, Incised, 1888, 5 x 3 ½ x 4 In. ....*illus*	17250.00

APPLE PEELERS *are listed in the Kitchen category under Peeler, Apple.*

ARABIA began producing ceramics in 1874. The pottery was established in Helsinki, Finland, by Rörstrand, a Swedish pottery that wanted to export porcelain, earthenware, and other pottery from Finland to Russia. Most of the early workers at Arabia were Swedish. Arabia started producing its own models of tiled stoves, vases, and tableware c.1900. Rörstrand sold its interest in Arabia in 1916. By the late 1930s, Arabia was the largest producer of porcelain in Europe. Most of its

ARABIA FINLAND

Advertising, Tip Tray, I Just Love Moxie Don't You, Tin Lithograph, H.D. Beach, c.1905, 6 In.
$115.00

Advertising, Tip Tray, Red Raven Splits, For High Livers' Livers, 4 ¼ In.
$177.00

Advertising, Tip Tray, Red Raven, Ask The Man, Tin Lithograph, 4 ¼ In.
$187.00

Advertising, Tray, Anchor Brewery, Purity, c.1900, 16 ½ x 13 ½ In.
$644.00

Advertising, Tray, Buffalo Brewing Co., Bohemian Beer, Chas. Ehlen, Cincinnati, 1905, 16 ½ x 13 ½ In. $1176.00

Past Tyme Pleasures

Advertising, Tray, Crown Baking Powder, Tin Lithograph, Vienna Art Plate Style, Shonk Litho Co., 10 In. $385.00

Wm Morford Antiques

Advertising, Tray, Hires Root Beer, Young Girl Portrait, Self-Framed, Signed, Haskell Coffin $230.00

Bertoia Auctions

Advertising, Tray, Purity Ice Cream, Has A Better Flavor, Mother, Children, Tin Litho, 10 x 13 In. $523.00

Wm Morford Antiques

products were exported. A line of stoneware was introduced in the 1960s. Arabia worked in cooperation with Rörstrand from 1975 to 1977. Arabia was bought by Hackman Group in 1990 and Hackman was bought by Iittala Group in 2004. Arabia is now a brand owned by Iittala Group.

Cup, Rice, 2 ¾ In.	40.00
Plate, Blue Rose Pattern, 9 ½ In.	30.00
Plate, Dinner, Faenza, Yellow, 10 ¼ In.	26.00
Plate, Teema, 7 ½ In.	25.00

ARCHITECTURAL antiques include a variety of collectibles, usually very large, that have been removed from buildings. Hardware, backbars, doors, paneling, and even old bathtubs are now wanted by collectors. Pieces of the Victorian, Art Nouveau, and Art Deco styles are in greatest demand.

Altar, Elm, Upturned Ends, 3 Drawers, 2 Hinged Doors, Brass Mounts, 35 x 86 In.	2390.00
Bathtub, White Enamel, Cast Iron, Ball & Claw Feet, c.1890, 16 x 31 In.	385.00
Block, Terra-Cotta, Chicago Stock Exchange Building, Louis Sullivan, c.1893, 21 x 12 In.	1440.00
Bracket, Beechwood, Carved, Paint, Draped Cherub, S-Scroll Surround, 1800s, 49 x 44 In.	32386.00
Bracket, Carved Cypress, Mounted, White Paint, 1900s, 14 x 12 In.	584.00
Bracket, Giltwood, Silver, Gesso, Grape Clusters, Carved, France, c.1800, 14 ½ In., Pair	1475.00
Bracket, Onyx Demilune Top, Silver Plate, Shell, Sea Life Base, Italy, 16 x 12 In., Pair	1845.00
Bracket, Regency Style, Parcel Gilt, Scalloped, Leaves, Scroll Support, Painted, 10 x 9 In., Pair	497.00
Bracket, Wrought Iron, Leaves, Scrolls, 20 x 23 In.	310.00
Brick, Don't Spit On Sidewalk, c.1910, 1 x 4 ½ x 8 ⅞ In.	154.00
Brick, Red Clay, Impressed, F.R. Brick Co., Albany, Ca, c.1910, 2 ¼ x 3 ¾ x 8 In.	66.00
Brick, Red Clay, Impressed, Graves B'Ham, Ala, c.1901, 3 ½ x 4 ¼ x 9 In.	77.00
Capital, Terra-Cotta, Figural, Ram's Head, Polychrome Glaze, 8 x 7 x 7 In., Pair	119.00
Ceiling Panel, Giltwood, Baroque Style, Oval, Pierced Leaves & Flowers, 10 x 42 In.	2574.00
Chimney Pot, Terra-Cotta, Crown Top, 9-Point, Horizontal Vents, Square Base, 43 In.	413.00
Chimney Pot, Terra-Cotta, Rocket Shape, Cone Top, Square Base, 47 In.	531.00
Chimney Pot, Terra-Cotta, Rocket Shape, Vertical Openings, Square Base, England, 1800s, 47 In.	236.00
Column, Carved, Flat Top, Spiral Shape, Fruit Bearing Branches, Acanthus, Gilt, 70 In.	1416.00
Column, Cut Corners, Marble, Bulbous Base, Octangular Plinth, Veining, c.1910, 41 x 11 In.	805.00
Column, Ebonized, Fruitwood Inlay, Square Top, Round Standard, Stepped Base, 48 In., Pair	551.00
Column, Fruitwood, Tower, Cherubs, Tree Trunk, Flowers, Grapes, Bowl, 96 In., Pair	17775.00
Column, Gilt, Carved, Twisted Grape Clusters, Vines, Multicolor, Italy, c.1700, 42 In. *illus*	598.00
Column, Marble, Rectangular, Top, Twist Standard, Octangular Base, Gray, Green, 32 x 15 In.	431.00
Column, Wood, Baroque, Painted, Stepped Base, Acanthus, Volutes, 97 In., Pair	1793.00
Column, Zinc, Flame Design, France, 1800s, 49 x 18 In., Pair	2500.00
Curtain Pins, Pressed Glass, Electric Blue, 6 Petals, Screw Extension, c.1870, 2 ⅝ In., Pair	104.00
Door Latch, Cast Iron, Duck Head, Pivoting, c.1900, 8 In.	542.00
Door Latch, Punch & Judy, c.1700	1700.00
Door Panel, Mahogany, 2 Panels, Eagle Emblem, U.S.A., Pelican, 80 x 36 In.	554.00
Door, Castle, Mixed Woods, Arched, Iron Mounts, England, 1800s, 117 x 65 In., Pair	3120.00
Door, Courtyard, 6 Vertical Panels, 3 Strap Panels, Geometric Bands, Saudi Arabia, 34 In.	239.00
Door, Elm, Pine, Open Fretwork Panel, Carved, Chinese, 27 x 121 In., 4 Piece	374.00
Door, French, Painted, Relief Detail, 94 x 24 In., Pair	246.00
Door, Horse Stable, Rectangular Windows, Slats, Late 1700s, Pa.	650.00
Door, Jailhouse, Plank, Iron, Trap Door Panel, Iron Nail Decoration, c.1827, 76 x 27 In.	384.00
Door, Oak, 2-Sided, Carved, Floral Panels, 80 x 32 In., Pair	345.00
Door, Oak, Carved, Gilded, Relief Panel, 80 x 32 In.	122.00
Door, Painted Flowers & Vase, Germany, 1812, 59 ½ x 57 In.	575.00
Door, Paneled, Grain Painted, White Distressed, 1800s, 76 x 25 ¾ In.	30.00
Door, Pine, Bamboo & Cranes, Japan, 72 x 39 In.	1240.00
Door, Pocket, Parcel Gilt, Faux Mahogany, Giltwood Molding, c.1890, 112 x 46 In., Pair	861.00
Door, Wood, Applied Chinoiserie Panels, Paint, France, c.1910, 96 x 53 In., Pair	800.00
Door, Wood, Mirrors, Victorian Streetscape Form, J. Dickinson, c.1972, 104 x 129 In., Pair	24800.00
Doorframe, Oak, Gothic Revival, Leaf Crest, Arched, Spires, c.1855, 117 x 54 In.	2091.00
Doorknob, Glass, Swirl, Brass	22.00
Doorknob, Paperweight, Millefleur, Amethyst, Cranberry Ground, Brass, 3 ⅜ In., 4 Piece	590.00
Doorknocker, Amish Man & Woman, Black Hair, Hat & Beard, Wilton, 1950s, 5 In., Pair	80.00
Doorknocker, Brass, Art Deco, Esmeralda, Crinoline Dress, Parasol, Marked, 1920s, 3 ½ In.	60.00
Doorknocker, Bronze, Patinated, Grotesque Masque Plate, Man, Woman, 21 x 11 In., Pair	3107.00
Doorknocker, Cast Brass, Lion's Mask, Ring, 10 ¼ In.	708.00
Doorknocker, Cast Iron, Girl Knocking, 3 ¾ In.	189.00
Doorknocker, Cast Iron, Morning Glory, Judd Co., 3 ¼ In. *illus*	118.00
Doorknocker, Cast Iron, Parrot, Multicolor, Creations Co., 3 ¾ In.	71.00

Doorknocker, Cast Iron, Ship, Hubley, 4 In.	83.00
Downspout, Copper, Figural, Lion's Head, c.1900, 20 In. ....*illus*	1645.00
Downspout, Sheet Copper, Lion's Head, c.1880, 20 In.	940.00
Eagle, Iron, Gilt Paint, 11 x 30 In.	2200.00
Entry Arch, Gate, Wrought Iron, Flower Crest, Fleur-De-Lis, Frame, c.1930, 91 x 60 In.	677.00
Entry Gate, Wrought Iron, Scroll Design, Applied Flowers, c.1890, 93 x 44 In., Pair	4920.00
Entryway, Bronze & Iron, Fleur-De-Lis Crest, Hapsburg Crest, c.1900, 98 x 66 In.	1968.00
Faucet Head, Cast Bronze, Swan, Taking Flight, Brass Handles, 12 x 9 In.	214.00
Finial, Copper, 2 Piece Ball Top, 8 Piece Radial Base, 11 In. ....*illus*	354.00
Finial, Giltwood, Fluted Flames, Urn On Pedestal Base, 24 x 8 In., Pair	1035.00
Finial, Zinc, Globe Shape, Urn & Sphere Top, Plinth, 28 In.	460.00
Fireboard, Flowers With Cabbage Roses & Tulips, Hand Painted	225.00
Fireboard, Pine, Paint, Stylized Fruit Tree, Grapevines, Ivory Ground, Conn., c.1800, 30 x 44 In.	9480.00
Fireboard, Pine, Stylized Fruit Tree, Grapevines, Conn., c.1800, 30 x 44 In.	9480.00
Fireboard, Trompe L'Oeil, Fireplace, Tongs, Ears Of Corn, Kitten In Boot, c.1890, 33 x 41 In..	940.00
Fireplace Surround, Brass, Shell Crest, Ribbons, Flowers, Directoire, France, 34 x 35 In.......	143.00
Fireplace Surround, Bronze, Verde Marble Mantle, Cast Figures, Flowers, 43 x 66 In.............	489.00
Fireplace Surround, Cast Bronze, Shaped Marble Mantel, Cast Flowers, Figures, 54 x 65 In.	460.00
Fireplace Surround, King Arthur's Tale Character Tiles, Iron Frame, France, 38 x 36 In.......	138.00
Fireplace Surround, Poplar, Gray, Faux Marble Cornice, Federal, 1800s, 68 x 84 In...........	1180.00
Fireplace Surround, Tiger Oak, Carved, Scrolling, Mirror, 110 x 77 In.....................	3245.00
Fireplace Surround, Variegated Marble, Carved Figures, George III Style, 49 x 60 In..........	1375.00
Fireplace Surround, White Marble, Baluster Columns, Neoclassical Style, 1900s, 43 x 55 In.	1645.00
Fireplace Surround, Wood, Dentil Molding, Beveled Mirror, Carved, Reeded Pilasters, 120 x 72 In.	1180.00
Fireplace Surround, Yellow Pine, Matchstick Frieze, Fluted Pilasters, Federal, 55 x 61 In. ...	161.00
Fireplace Surround, Yellow Pine, Overhang, Painted White, Greek Revival, 59 x 73 In........	863.00
Gate, Cast Iron, Cemetery, Open Scrollwork, Torch Of Life Design, Knob Latch, 32 x 48 In.	6325.00
Gate, Cast Iron, Central Circles, Scrolling, Latch, Josiah Bender, 1865, 41 x 39 In.	334.00
Gate, Enameled Wrought Iron, Art Deco, 2 Scrolled Doors, 1930s, 53 x 20 In................	248.00
Gate, Wrought Iron, Diamond & Circle Design, Bronze Accents, c.1910, 66 x 56 In.	1169.00
Gate, Wrought Iron, Grape Arbor Design, Arched, 60 x 79 In., Pair	7500.00
Gate, Wrought Iron, Twisted, Scrolled, c.1940, 60 x 42 In.	338.00
Gym Locker Storage Unit, Steel, Green Paint, 60 x 48 In., 8 Piece........................	590.00
Knocker, Brass, Eagle, 10 x 13 In..	350.00
Knocker, Bronze, Woman's Head, Masqueron, 1800s, 7 x 5 In.............................	201.00
Lantern, Portico, Victorian Style, Iron, Hexagonal, Leaf Bracket, Pendant, c.1900s, 38 x 15 In., Pair	738.00
Mailbox, Iron, Wall, Red, White, Blue Paint, 20 x 13 In.	450.00
Mantel, Cast Iron, Rococo, Inset Glass Panels, H. Tucker, 1850, 53 x 65 In...............	748.00
Mantel, Gray Marble, White Inset Flowers, c.1880, 62 x 43 In.	978.00
Mantel, Oak, Shaped Pilasters, 59 x 12 In..	102.00
Mantel, Pine, Classical, Painted Yellow, c.1810, 60 x 63 In.............................	235.00
Mantel, Pine, Federal, Reeded, Columns, Painted, Late 1700s, 62 x 76 In.................	1126.00
Mantel, Pine, Stepped Cornice, Reeded, Carved Fan, Medallion, Pilasters, 60 x 80 In..........	2242.00
Mantel, Walnut, Carved, Pan, Lion Heads, Cartouche Shield Crest, Griffins, c.1880, 9 x 6 Ft. ..	27500.00
Mantel, Yellow Pine, Blue Paint, North Carolina, 1800s, 37 x 47 In.	230.00
Model, Winged Staircase, Demilune Domed Bay, Renaissance Style, Fruitwood, Mahogany, 16 x 18 In.	861.00
Newel Post, Paperweight, Clichy Millefiori, Circles, Multicolor, Metal, 4 x 7 In.........................	10350.00
Newel Post, Paperweight, Perthshire, Millefiori, Metal, Signed Peter McDougall, 4 x 5 ½ In....	1121.00
Newel Post, Paperweight, St. Louis, Millefiori Sphere, Metal, Signed, 1995, 3 ½ x 7 In.	2013.00
Newel Post, Paperweight, St. Louis, Millefiori, Close Pack, Metal, Signed, 1974, 3 ½ x 7 In.....	805.00
Obelisk, Mirrored, Stepped Wood Base, 74 x 15 In.	1940.00
Obelisk, Verde Antico Marble, 54 x 13 ½ In., Pair	3346.00
Overmantel Mirror, 3 Plates, Classical Frieze Pediment, Columns, Ebonized, 35 x 56 In.......	2250.00
Overmantel Mirror, Blocked Cornice, 3-Part, Mirror Plate, Rope Twist Columns, 28 x 55 In.	717.00
Overmantel Mirror, Classical, Giltwood, Applied Half Columns, 3 Beveled Plates, 26 x 64 In.	161.00
Overmantel Mirror, Classical, Giltwood, Carved, Blocked Cornice, Panels, 29 x 55 In...........	1830.00
Overmantel Mirror, Creme Peinte, Gilt, Chariot, Lion Frieze, Oval, Columns, 42 x 56 In.......	598.00
Overmantel Mirror, Eastlake Style, Walnut, Shelves, High Crest, Carved, c.1975, 62 x 57 In..	184.00
Overmantel Mirror, Federal Style, Giltwood, Eagle Crest, Carved, 38 x 45 ½ In.	630.00
Overmantel Mirror, Federal Style, Giltwood, Fluted Frieze, Garlands, c.1910, 38 x 72 In.	225.00
Overmantel Mirror, Federal, Mahogany, Gilt Paint, Winged Eagle, 1900, 33 x 73 In.	300.00
Overmantel Mirror, Gilt, Gesso, Acanthus, Oak Leaf, Acorns, 1875, 48 x 63 In........................	403.00
Overmantel Mirror, Giltwood, 3-Part, Horizontal Plates, Gilt Pilasters, Rosettes, c.1845, 26 x 64 In.	553.00
Overmantel Mirror, Mahogany, Carved, Neptune On Crest, 1900s, 48 x 66 In........................	2185.00
Overmantel Mirror, Regency Style, Giltwood, Greek Fret Frieze, 3 Plates, 44 x 48 In.............	819.00
Overmantel Mirror, Renaissance Revival, Parcel Gilt, Ebonized Walnut, 67 x 48 In..............	1845.00

Advertising, Tray, The Ware That Wears, Stransky & Co., N.Y., 24 x 19 ½ In. $295.00

Conestoga Auction Co., Inc.

Advertising, Tray, Washington Brewery, 25 U.S. Presidents Through Theodore Roosevelt, c.1910-11, 12 x 17 In. $420.00

Past Tyme Pleasures

Alabaster, Sculpture, Classical Maiden, Signed, Umberto Stiaccini, c.1900, 30 In. $2151.00

Neal Auction Co.

Amber Glass, Vase, Fan, Applied Yellow & Green Flower Spray, Footed, 7 ½ In. $59.00

Ivey-Selkirk Auctioneers

As always, the edited listings in *Kovels' Antiques & Collectibles Price Guide* aren't available on any website, but readers should visit Kovels.com for information on trends, tips, reproductions, marks, old prices, and more!

25

A

Amberina, Tankard, Daisy & Button, Applied Handle, Star Cut Base, Scalloped Rim, 12 In.
$345.00

James D. Julia Inc

Amberina, Vase, Trifold Rim, Rigaree Collar, Bulbous, Flask Shape, 8 ½ In.
$431.00

Early Auction Co.

American Encaustic, Tile, Turkey, Black Border, 4 ½ In.
$58.00

Humler & Nolan

Amethyst Glass, Bowl, Lobed Body, Scalloped Rim, Hardwood Stand, Chinese, 10 ½ In.
$1265.00

Leland Little Auction

Overmantel Mirror, Victorian Style, Arched Crest, Carved, Molded, 72 x 32 In.	275.00
Panel, Antiqued, Lacquer, Wood, Jade, Stone Appliques, Fruit, Character, c.1900, 38 x 28 In.	799.00
Panel, Art Deco, Fer Forge, France, 1930, 28 ½ x 43 ½ In.	677.00
Panel, Art Deco, Fer Forge, Scrolls, Vertical Bars, France, c.1930, 68 x 20 ½ In.	923.00
Panel, Art Deco, Iron, Scroll, Screen Backing, France, c.1930, 37 x 57 In.	1107.00
Panel, Balcony, Art Deco, Brass, Rail, Circles, Lines, c.1930, 37 x 58 In.	461.00
Panel, Balcony, S-Scroll, Wrought Iron, Bronze, c.1910, 36 x 70 In., Pair	2952.00
Panel, Cement, Sea Dragon, c.1900, 20 ½ x 33 In.	186.00
Panel, Center Lozenge, Rosette, Scrolling Arabesque, Molded Field, c.1850, 55 x 57 In.	956.00
Panel, Iron, Face, Scrolls, c.1910, 33 x 90 In.	800.00
Panel, Iron, Scrolls, France, c.1920, 34 x 48 In.	338.00
Panel, Lacquer, Wood, Jade, Ivory, Stone, Insect, Quail, Flowers, Frame, Chinese, c.1900, 44 x 28 In.	4674.00
Panel, Louis XVI, Molded Cornice, Rope Twist Border, Flaming Urn, Vines, 1790, 58 x 43 In.	2689.00
Panel, Mixed Woods, Figures, Relief Carved, Pierced Metal Hangers, Chinese, 29 x 15 In.	236.00
Panel, Stained Glass, Heraldic Medallion, Crown, Keys, Multicolor, 72 x 18 In.	316.00
Panel, Teakwood, Quipar Marble, Carved, Exotic Scenes, 1800s, 72 x 35 ½ In.	144.00
Panel, Wrought Iron, Scrolls, c.1910, 70 x 26 In., Pair	215.00
Panels, Art Deco, Iron, Fer Forge, Stylized, Flared, Scrolling, c.1930, 65 x 42 In.	1169.00
Pedestal, Brass, White Onyx, Square Top, Octagonal Base, 36 x 12 In.	201.00
Pedestal, Carved Stone, Draped Urn, Fruit, Flowers, c.1920, 59 x 20 In.	738.00
Pediment, Oak, Broken Arch, Flowers, Heraldic Shield, c.1860, 9 x 34 In.	475.00
Pew, Church, Walnut, Shaped Sides, Celtic Shamrock Cross, c.1905, 36 x 55 In.	115.00
Pilaster, Giltwood, Lion's Head, Pendant, Leaves, Carved, Austria, 27 x 7 ¾ In., Pair	936.00
Pilaster, Oak, Carved, Figural, Woman, Seminude, 1900s, 65 x 22 In., Pair	20060.00
Plaque, Eagle, Carved, Gold Paint, c.1900, 47 ½ In.	1580.00
Plaque, Parcel Gilt, Flag, American, Tassel End, Scrolled, Carved, Painted, 66 x 14 In.	2925.00
Post Finial, Gilt, Swan, Long Neck, Bead Necklace, France, c.1800, 15 x 17 In., Pair	1599.00
Railing, Bronze, Gilt, Regency Style, 3 Geometric Panels, c.1920, 38 x 92 In., Pair	1968.00
Rondel, Lead, Eagle, Spread Wings, Crossed Arrows, Ribbon Wreath, 11 Ft. 8 In. x 5 Ft.	4972.00
Roof Crest, Pressed Glass, Amethyst, Pinwheels, Amber, Fleur-De-Lis, 8 x 10 In., 2 Piece	288.00
Roof Tile, Man Riding Horse, Pottery, Chinese, 11 ⅝ x 9 ¾ In.	354.00
Screens are also listed in the Fireplace and Furniture categories.	
Shelf Unit, Pine, Crescent Shape, 6 Shelves, Column Shape Supports, England, 61 x 80 In.	2360.00
Shelf, Baroque Style, Pottery, Glazed, Cherub, Gold Trim, Germany, 9 x 13 In.	173.00
Shelf, Onyx, Carved Carrera Marble Supports, 24 ½ x 23 In., Pair	1610.00
Shutters, Pine, Molded Raised Panels, Wrought Iron Strap Hinge, 58 x 15 In., 17 Pair	1380.00
Shutters, Wood, Interior, Mustard Grain Painted, c.1870, 33 ½ x 16 In., Pair	59.00
Surround, Brass, Reeded Balls, Double Rails, Rectangular Canted Base, 1800s, 11 ¾ x 48 In.	359.00
Surround, Federal, Painted, Faux Fan Design, Kentucky, 1800s, 45 ½ x 53 ¾ In. ....*illus*	1062.00
Surround, Neoclassical Style, Brass, Open Work, Leaves, Figures, Paw Feet, 10 x 51 In.	191.99
Surround, Victorian, Brass, Tan Leather Upholstery Seat, 54 In.	500.00
Tieback, Brass, Gilt Bronze, Le Roi Soleil, Lion's Head, Wreath, France, 7 ⅜ x 4 ¾ In., Pair	1281.00
Toilet, Porcelain, Back Inlet, High Tank, Embossed Scrolls, Pull Chain, 18 x 16 In.	1400.00
Trim, Indian, Stylized Feather Headdress, Fruit Garland, Zinc, Verdigris, c.1870, 33 In.	3819.00
Trim, Shell Shape, Giltwood, Painted, Carved, Italy, 1800s, 18 In.	690.00
Trim, Stylized Caryatid, Bronze Dore, France, 1800s, 25 ½ In.	388.00
Urn, Tin, Gilt, Openwork, Paint, Handles, South America, 32 In., Pair	385.00
Vent, Wood, Fan Shape, Radiating Slats, 1800s, 49 x 54 In.	844.00
Window, Leaded Glass, Multicolor Slag, Scrollwork, Wood Frame, 71 x 27 In., 6 Piece	4025.00

AREQUIPA POTTERY was produced from 1911 to 1918 by the patients of the Arequipa Sanatorium in Marin County, north of San Francisco. The patients were trained by Frederick Hurten Rhead, who had worked at the Roseville Pottery.

Vase, Green & Blue Matte Glaze, Bulbous, 1912, 5 x 7 ¾ In.	960.00
Vase, Squeezebag, Incised Mark, 3 ¾ x 4 In.	2604.00

ARGY-ROUSSEAU, *see G. Argy-Rousseau category.*

ARITA is a port in Japan. Porcelain was made there from about 1616. Many types of decorations were used, including the popular Imari designs, which are listed under Imari in this book.

Bowl, Cereal, Genesis, Mauve	12.00
Bowl, Fish, Aquatic Plants, Blue Underglaze, 1900s, 12 x 4 ⅛ In. ......*illus*	329.00
Brazier, Landscape, Blue Glaze, c.1900, 19 x 13 In.	276.00
Vase, Baluster, Blue & White, Dragon, Clouds, Marked, 1900s, 13 ¾ In.	148.00

ART DECO, or Art Moderne, a style started at the Paris Exposition of 1925, is characterized by linear, geometric designs. All types of furniture and decorative arts, jewelry, book bindings, and even games were designed in this style. Additional items may be found in the Furniture category or in various glass and pottery categories, etc.

Sculpture, Flapper, Base, 12 In.	153.00
Vase, Glass, Wide Rim, Bulbous, Round Narrow Foot, Wiener Werkstatte, Germany, c.1915, 8 In.	6875.00
Vase, Nickel Plate, France, c.1930, 7 x 10 In.	598.00

ART GLASS, *see Glass-Art category.*

ART NOUVEAU is a style of design that was at its most popular from 1895 to 1905. Famous designers, including Rene Lalique and Emile Galle, produced furniture, glass, silver, metalwork, and buildings in the new style. Ladies with long flowing hair and elongated bodies were among the more easily recognized design elements. Copies of this style are being made today. Many modern pieces of jewelry can be found. Additional Art Nouveau pieces may be found in Furniture or in various glass categories.

Vase, Blue Iridescent, Amber Serpent Coiled Around Stem, Austria, Marked, c.1900, 10 In. ...*illus*	796.00
Vase, Ceramic, Pewter Overlay, Tulips, Leaves, Trailing Stems, Marked, Orvit, c.1900, 9 ½ In. .....*illus*	1041.00

ART POTTERY, *see Pottery-Art category*

ARTS & CRAFTS was a design style popular in American decorative arts from 1894 to 1923. In the 1970s collectors began to rediscover Mission furniture, art pottery, metalwork, linens, and light fixtures from this period. The interest has continued. Today everything from this era is collectible, including jewelry, graphics, and silverware. Additional items may be found in the Furniture category and other categories.

Box, Cover, Wood, Pewter, Glass, Pottery, Flower Design, Oval Cabochon, c.1900, 2 x 6 ¾ In. ......*illus*	95.00
Desk Set, Brass, Art Nouveau Flowers In Relief, Arts & Crafts Shop, 1908, 6 Piece	148.00
Panel, Leaded Stained Glass, Castle In Landscape, 22 x 37 ½ In. .....*illus*	868.00
Plaque, Wood, Cabin Scene, Mica Window Panel Detail, Carved, 24 x 12 In.	420.00
Vase, Flared Rim, Blue, Cream, Chameleon Ware, Marked, 7 In.	106.00

AURENE, *see Steuben*

AUSTRIA *is a collecting term that covers pieces made by a wide variety of factories. They are listed in this book in categories such as Royal Dux or Porcelain.*

AUTO parts and accessories are collectors' items today. Gas pump globes and license plates are part of this specialty. Prices are determined by age, rarity, and condition. Signs and packaging related to automobiles may also be found in the Advertising category. Lalique hood ornaments will be listed in the Lalique category.

Ad, Magazine, Morgan & Wright Tires, Want To Ride In Good Tires, Frame, 24 x 19 In.	622.00
Ad, Willy's Overland Car, Sept. 1914, 12 x 17 In.	18.00
Air Meter, Eco Model 224, Water Dispensers, Red & White, 57 In.	1700.00
Air Pump, Eco, Stand, Cast Iron, Red, c.1930, 50 In.	1140.00
Ashtray, Michelin Tires, Michelin Man, Black & White, 1930s, 4 ½ In.	180.00
Ashtray, Pennsylvania Tires, Embossed, Glass, Tread, 1 ½ x 4 ½ In.	143.00
Ashtray, Pontiac Fine Car, Seated Indian, Ceramic, Green, White, 1940s, 6 In.	210.00
Badge, Colorado Licensed Driver, No. 1272, 1926, Silvered Brass, Embossed Scene, 2 In.	158.00
Banner, Sunoco Mercury Made Motor Oil, Cloth, 36 x 60 In.	339.00
Banner, Sunoco Mercury Made Motor Oil Prevents Power Killing Carbon, Cloth, 36 x 60 In.	452.00
Battery Charger, Exide, Metal, 7 ½ x 7 In.	198.00
Bottle, Motor Oil, Daniel Boone, B.O. Rhodes Manufacturing Co. Spout, Qt.	495.00
Bottle, Motor Oil, Mobiloil Filpruf, Gargoyle, Metal Spout, Wire Holder, Gal.	1375.00
Bottle, Motor Oil, Penn Joy, Cap, Imperial Qt.	248.00
Bottle, Motor Oil, Polarine, Green, Embossed, c.1909	495.00
Bottle, Motor Oil, Skelly Tagolene, Paper Label, Master Spout, Qt.	220.00
Bottle, Motor Oil, Standard Iso-Vis, Spout, Qt.	143.00
Bottle, Motor Oil, Texaco 574, Qt.	209.00
Bottle, Motor Oil, Viscoyl, Spout, Qt.	220.00
Cabinet, Trico 5-Ply Wiper Blades & Spring Pressed Wiper Rods, Woman, Car, Metal, 14 x 10 In.	198.00
Cabinet, Tung-Sol Fixed-Focus Auto Bulbs, Slogan, Metal, 18 x 12 In.	226.00
Can, Atlantic Dome Top, Metal, Cylindrical, 5 Gal.	68.00
Can, Carigas, Emergency Gasoline Tank, Under Seat, Gal.	57.00

Animal Trophy, Rug, Zebra Hide, Africa, c.1925, Full Size
$176.00

Garth's Auctions, Inc.

Animal Trophy, Russian Boar, Shoulder Mount, 20 x 18 x 26 In.
$210.00

DuMouchelles Art Gallery

Animal Trophy, Warthog Head, Wall Mount
$275.00

Victorian Casino Antique Auction

Animal Trophy, Zebra Head, 25 In.
$940.00

Garth's Auctions, Inc.

A

Animation Art, Cel, Ludwig Von Drake, Holding Mother Goose Book, Mat, 1963, 11 x 14 In.
$190.00

Hake's Americana & Collectibles

Animation Art, Cel, Pinocchio, Figaro, Geppetto's Apron Covered Legs, Frame, c.1940, 9 x 11 In.
$1010.00

Hake's Americana & Collectibles

Anna Pottery, Bottle, Pig, Incised Map, Mississippi River, St. Louis, Cincinnati, Chicago, 8 In.
$14100.00

Cowan's Auctions

Anna Pottery, Whistle, Owl, Night Operator, Glass Eyes, Salt Glaze, Incised, 1888, 5 x 3 ½ x 4 In.
$17250.00

Rock Island Auction Company

Can, Conoco Harvester Oil, Soldier Logo, Flat, Metal, ½ Gal.	1130.00
Can, Gas, Union Gasoline Carigas, Under Seat, Shield, Orange	200.00
Can, Husky Motor Oil, Yellow Ground, Round, Metal, Qt.	622.00
Can, Motor Oil, Texaco, 5 Gal.	57.00
Can, Nourse Motor Oil, Viking Logo, Cylindrical, 5 Qt.	226.00
Can, Nourse Spring Oil, Viking Logo, Metal, Pt.	57.00
Can, Oil, Gem Mfg. Co., 1900s, 14 In.	15.00
Can, Polarine Oil, Opening Touring Car, Yellow Ground, 1913, ½ Gal., 8 x 6 ¼ In.	138.00
Can, Red Indian Motor Oil, Round, Metal, Imperial, Qt.	180.00
Can, Richlube Motor Oil, Car On Shield, Cylindrical, Metal, 5 Qt.	678.00
Can, Ring-Free Drag Oil, Round, Composite, 1960s, Qt.	90.00
Can, Sage Oak Treatment For Automobiles, Indian Maiden Logo, Metal, Pt.	57.00
Can, Sinclair Extra Duty Motor Oil, Bail Handle, Cylindrical, Red, Green, White, c.1940, 16 In.	90.00
Can, Speedway Grease, Open Car Graphics, 5 Lb.	113.00
Can, Thoni Motor Oil, Round, Metal, Qt.	28.00
Can, Tiopet Motor Oil, Indian Logo, Round, Metal, Qt.	735.00
Can, Union Oil Of California, Aristo Motor, Flat, Metal, Green & Red, Gal.	200.00
Can, Vico Motor Oil, Flat, ½ Gal.	311.00
Can, Voco Vickers Oil Co., Flat, Metal, ½ Gal.	153.00
Can, Zerolene F For Fords, Logo, Flat, Metal, ½ Gal.	147.00
Car Topper, Flipje Raspberry Jam, Boy, Waving, Raspberry Bunch, Chef's Hat, Vinyl, 1950s, 19 In.	360.00
Clock, AC Spark Plugs, Multicolor, Coralox, Plastic Insert, 22 x 22 In.	250.00
Clock, Century Tires, Light-Up, Fletcher's Dualite Display, Inc., 15 x 15 In.	113.00
Clock, Champion Spark Plugs, America's Favorite, Light-Up, Art Deco, 16 x 26 In.	848.00
Clock, Dependable Champion Spark Plug, Plastic, Light-Up, 23 x 26 In.	311.00
Clock, Exide Batteries, Light-Up, Round, 15 In.	254.00
Clock, Fram Oil & Motor Cleaner, Light-Up, Round, 16 In.	170.00
Clock, Hester Batteries, Double Bubble Light, Round, 15 In.	480.00
Clock, Kendall 2000 Mile Oil, Hand Logo Spinner, Round, Neon, 20 In.	452.00
Clock, Marvel Mystery Oil, Yellow, Light-Up, 16 x 16 In.	283.00
Clock, Mohawk Tires, Logo, Octagon, Neon, 18 x 18 In.	565.00
Clock, Mopar Parts Accessories Chrysler Corp., Octagon, Neon, 18 x 18 In.	622.00
Clock, Phillips 66 Batteries, Double Bubble Light, Round, 15 In.	650.00
Clock, Phillips 66, Double Bubble, Red & White, Shield, Round, 16 In.	900.00
Clock, Super Kendall Motor Oil, Light-Up, Round, 15 In.	283.00
Cover, Switch, Restroom, Humble Oil & Refining, Cleanliness Notice, Porcelain, 4 ½ x 4 ½ In.	254.00
Display, Ask For AC Spark Plug 1075 For Fords, Metal Cabinet, 11 In.	622.00
Display, Bardahl, Try It!, Bardahl Man Logo, Tin, Rack Topper, 10 x 10 In.	283.00
Display, Buss Auto Fuses, Why Be Helpless When Fuses Blow, Counter, Metal, 1950s, 9 x 6 In.	85.00
Display, Champion Spark Plugs Box, Metal, 3 x 7 ½ In.	68.00
Display, Champion Spark Plugs, Slogan, Metal, 12 x 18 In.	904.00
Display, Edison Mazda Automobile Lamps, Name Your Car I'll Light It, Metal, 24 x 13 In.	508.00
Display, Eveready Radio Batteries, Cardboard Tube, Wood Lid, 1925, 31 x 13 In.	452.00
Display, Flying A Gasoline, Restroom, Light-Up, Metal, Glass, 7 x 10 In.	622.00
Display, Gilmer Super Service Moulder Rubber Fan Belt, Slogan, Metal, 22 x 17 In.	367.00
Display, Goodyear Tire Savers, Faux Wood Metal, 20 x 24 In.	1469.00
Display, Kerosene Oil Standard Oil Of New York, Elephant Graphics, Porcelain Flange, 18 x 24 In.	706.00
Display, Matchless Autolamps For Dependable Bright Light, Lady Holding Bulb, Metal, 17 x 14 In.	226.00
Display, Mazda Super Auto Lamps, Metal, Glass, 17 x 7 In.	848.00
Display, New Carr Chains Look Better & Last Longer, Cardboard, Stand-Up, 16 x 13 In.	791.00
Display, Outstanding Eveready Spotlight Electric Torch, Foldover, Cardboard, 14 x 15 In.	1356.00
Display, Texaco Havoline Racing Allison No. 28 Ford Thunderbird, Electric, 24 x 48 In.	876.00
Display, Texaco Home Lubricant, Painted Metal, 12 x 12 In.	7627.00
Display, Texaco Winter Wear May Make You Walk, Logo, Easel Back, Cardboard, 34 x 24 In.	198.00
Display, Whiz Radiator, Stop Leak, 1920s Car Scene, Cardboard Box, 4 Cans, 5 x 14 In.	1017.00
Door, Hansom Cab, Latch, Wood, Glass, 33 In.	60.00
Emergency Car Kit, Yankee Reflector Flare, Red Plastic Lens, 1940s, 8 x 3 ½ In.	52.00
Figure, Greeter Girl, Union 76, Mechanical, Head Turns, Arm Moves, 41 In.	565.00
Folder, 1931 Nash Automobile, The New Nash Six	9.00
Gas Pump Globe, American Gas, Glass Body, Wood Base, 13 ½ In.	480.00
Gas Pump Globe, American, Red, White, Blue, Glass Body, 12 ½ In.	198.00
Gas Pump Globe, Associated Aviation Ethyl, Logo, Metal, Lenses, 15 In.	1695.00
Gas Pump Globe, Blue Sunoco, Plastic, Metal, 15 In.	452.00
Gas Pump Globe, Chevron Supreme Gasoline, Plastic, Metal, Single Lens, 15 In.	678.00
Gas Pump Globe, Coastal Anti-Knock, Seagull Logo, Single Lens, 13 ½ In.	904.00
Gas Pump Globe, Crown, Opaque, White, Red, 15 x 16 In.	708.00

Gas Pump Globe, Dixie Ethyl, Logo, Capco Globe, 13 ½ In.	367.00
Gas Pump Globe, Falcon, Logo, White, Red, Single Lens, 13 ½ In.	1074.00
Gas Pump Globe, Flame, Red, Blue, Plastic, Light-Up, Wood Stand, 15 x 13 In.	124.00
Gas Pump Globe, Flying A Gasoline, 2-Sided, Letter A With Wings, Red, White, Plastic, 17 In.	270.00
Gas Pump Globe, Frontier Rarin' To Go, Cowboy, Horseback Silhouette, Lenses, 13 ½ In.	565.00
Gas Pump Globe, Gilmore Blue Green Gasoline, Metal, 15 In.	226.00
Gas Pump Globe, Gulf, Glass Body, Orange, Black, 12 ½ In.	198.00
Gas Pump Globe, Gulf, Orange, Black, Milk Glass Case, 13 ½ In.	791.00
Gas Pump Globe, Hayes, Glass Cylinder, Red, Star, 10 Gal.	1300.00
Gas Pump Globe, Hi-Power Gasoline, Ethyl Logo Lenses, Red Ripple Glass Body	2400.00
Gas Pump Globe, Hi-Power With Ethyl, Logo, 13 ½ In.	396.00
Gas Pump Globe, Mobilgas, Pegasus Logo, Plastic, Metal Case, 15 In.	226.00 to 339.00
Gas Pump Globe, Pan-Am Premium Gasoline, Plastic, Metal, 15 In.	283.00
Gas Pump Globe, Panhandle, Steer Horn Logo, Porcelain, Metal, 15 In.	3672.00
Gas Pump Globe, Perfect High Test, Plastic, Metal, 15 In.	452.00
Gas Pump Globe, Red Crown Gasoline, Metal Lenses, 15 In.	1921.00
Gas Pump Globe, Save More Regular System, Dollar Sign, Round, Glass	350.00
Gas Pump Globe, Sinclair Dino Supreme, New Capco Body, 13 ½ In.	141.00
Gas Pump Globe, Sinclair Gasoline, Glass Black & White, 17 ½ In.	1440.00
Gas Pump Globe, Sinclair, Power-X, Plastic, White, Red, Green, Dinosaur, 17 In.	210.00
Gas Pump Globe, Speed Wing 700, Oval, Capco Globe, 13 ½ In.	706.00
Gas Pump Globe, Standard Oil Gold Crown, Crown Shape, Gold & White, Milk Glass	400.00
Gas Pump Globe, Standard Oil Of California Gasoline, Crown, Metal Body, 15 In.	650.00
Gas Pump Globe, Sunoco, Single Lens, Metal, 15 In.	1469.00
Gas Pump Globe, Super Shell Ethyl, Shell Shape, Red & White, Milk Glass	900.00
Gas Pump Globe, Texaco Diesel Chief, Capco Body, 13 ½ In.	198.00
Gas Pump Globe, Texaco Ethyl, Black T, Star Logo, Glass, 1937, 13 ½ In.	791.00
Gas Pump Globe, Texaco Sky Chief, White T, Gill Lenses, Glass Screw Base Body, 13 ½ In.	509.00
Gas Pump Globe, Thoni Oil Company Magic Benzol Gasoline, Single Lens, Glass Hull, 13 ½ In.	1187.00
Gas Pump Globe, Thrifty Gas, Scottie Dog Logo, Red Capco Body, 13 ½ In.	904.00
Hood Ornament, Comet, Art Deco, Silver, Signed Andre-Vincent Becquerel, c.1925, 7 In.	3884.00
Hood Ornament, En Avant, Art Deco, Silvered Bronze, Frederick Bazin, c.1925, 5 ½ In.	777.00
Hood Ornament, Epsom, Horse, Frosted Glass, Glass Plinth, Red Ashay, c.1930, 8 In.	2390.00
Hood Ornament, Fraternal, Knights Of Columbus Emblem, Nickel Over Brass, 5 ⅝ In. *illus*	44.00
Hood Ornament, Frog, Leaping, Bronze, Marble Plinth, Signed Bertin, c.1915, 4 ½ In.	2151.00
Hood Ornament, Grasshopper, Art Deco, Silvered Bronze, Signed Demaniquet, c.1920, 6 ½ In.	4780.00
Hood Ornament, Grizzly Bear, Silver Bronze, Marble Plinth, Charles Paillet, c.1925, 5 ½ In.	956.00
Hood Ornament, Indian, Holding Das Badge, Silvered Bronze, Marble Plinth, Baluichon, 5 In.	1673.00
Hood Ornament, Lion, 1927 Franklin Car, Sterling Bronze, Co.	219.00
Hood Ornament, Lion, Art Deco, Silvered Bronze, Marble Plinth, Georges Poitvin, c.1925, 6 In.	7170.00
Hood Ornament, Old Doc Yac, Painted, Cast Iron, Arcade, 1911-17, 5 ½ In. *illus*	805.00
Hood Ornament, Pan, Silvered Bronze, Black Mark Base, c.1920, 7 ½ In.	2151.00
Hood Ornament, Pelican, Art Deco, Silvered Bronze, Signed Bourcart, c.1925, 4 ¾ In.	1434.00
Hood Ornament, Putto, On Turtle, Silvered Bronze, Signed, Antoine Bohill, c.1920, 5 ½ In.	1912.00
Hood Ornament, Racing Driver, Silvered Bronze, Dog Bone Cap, Signed H. Muller, c.1920, 8 In.	3346.00
Hood Ornament, Spirit Of Ecstasy, Rolls-Royce, Chrome, Radiator Cap, Charles Sykes, c.1930, 6 In.	2629.00
Horn, Brass, Rubber Bulb, Powell & Hammer, Birmingham, 19 ¼ In. *illus*	130.00
Kit, Sample, Panther Oil & Grease, Jars Inside, 10 x 20 In.	226.00
License Plate Attachment, Cities Service Koolmotor Gasoline, Reflective, 4 x 3 In.	141.00
License Plate Attachment, Flagler Chevrolet, Miami, Fla., Metal, 5 x 11 In.	339.00
License Plate Attachment, Goodyear Safety Equipped Lifeguards, Metal, 2 ½ x 10 In.	57.00
License Plate Attachment, Mobil Drive Safely, Tin, Die Cut, 5 ½ x 6 ½ In.	141.00
License Plate Attachment, Nealso Anti-Freeze, Eskimo, Metal, 7 x 4 In.	113.00
License Plate Attachment, Standard Oil Research Test Car, Wing Logo, Metal, 6 x 9 In.	198.00
License Plate, 1939 New York World's Fair, Embossed, Tin Lithograph, 4 ½ x 11 ½ In. *illus*	303.00
License Plate, California, 1937, Black, Orange Letters, 5S1431	125.00
License Plate, Illinois, 1914, Turquoise Letters, White Ground, 7 ½ x 14 In.	26.00
License Plate, Massachusetts, 1913, Enamel, Blue With White Numbers, Ingram Richardson	195.00
License Plate, Ohio, 1966, White, Red Ground	8.00
Mirror, Woods Motor Vehicle Co., Beveled, Pocket, 2 In. Diam.	523.00
Pedestal, Covered With Red, White & Blue Indiana License Plates, 1940s, 27 In.	450.00
Pin, Distributor Of Rambler & Ford Automobiles, Sioux City, Iowa, c.1905, 1 ½ In.	52.00
Pin, Ford-Mercury, Award Badge Style, 2 ½ In.	59.00
Poster, Cleveland Automobile Show, Paper, Otis Lithograph Co., Frame, 1915, 30 x 37 In. *illus*	7200.00
Poster, Ford, Red Car, 1942, 48 x 36 In.	100.00
Poster, Let Us Prepare Your Car For Winter, 1950s Car, Logo, 48 x 35 In.	254.00

Architectural, Column, Gilt, Carved, Twisted Grape Clusters, Vines, Multicolor, Italy, c.1700, 42 In.
$598.00

Neal Auction Co.

Architectural, Doorknocker, Cast Iron, Morning Glory, Judd Co., 3 ¼ In.
$118.00

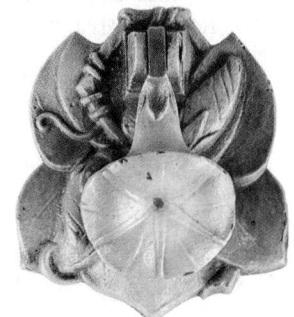

Morphy Auctions

Architectural, Downspout, Copper, Figural, Lion's Head, c.1900, 20 In.
$1645.00

Garth's Auctions, Inc.

Architectural, Finial, Copper, 2 Piece Ball Top, 8 Piece Radial Base, 11 In. $354.00

Conestoga Auction Co., Inc.

Architectural, Surround, Federal, Painted, Faux Fan Design, Kentucky, 1800s, 45 ½ x 53 ¾ In. $1062.00

Brunk Auctions

Arita, Bowl, Fish, Aquatic Plants, Blue Underglaze, 1900s, 12 x 4 ⅛ In. $329.00

Neal Auction Co.

Art Nouveau, Vase, Blue Iridescent, Amber Serpent Coiled Around Stem, Austria, Marked, c.1900, 10 In. $796.00

Skinner, Inc.

Poster, United Motors Authorized Service, Early Car, Big Wheel Bicycle, 31 x 41 In. 283.00
Pump Plate, Atlantic Hi-Arc, Red, White, Black, Porcelain, 17 x 13 In. 311.00
Pump Plate, Atlantic Premium, Porcelain, 11 x 13 In. 147.00
Pump Plate, Atlantic Premium, Flag Logo, Porcelain, 11 x 13 In. 170.00
Pump Plate, Atlantic, White Flash, Porcelain, 17 x 13 In. 254.00
Pump Plate, Blue Sunoco 200, Red Arrow, Yellow & Blue, Porcelain, Die Cut, 21 x 15 In. 200.00
Pump Plate, Blue Sunoco, Porcelain, Die Cut, 22 x 18 In. 452.00
Pump Plate, Blue Sunoco, Yellow Ground, Porcelain, 8 x 12 In. 339.00
Pump Plate, Conoco, Triangle Shape, Green, 9 x 10 In. 170.00
Pump Plate, Fill'Em Fast Gasoline, Red, Black, Yellow, Porcelain, 9 ½ x 16 In. 254.00
Pump Plate, Good Gasoline, Red, White, Porcelain, 8 ½ x 15 In. 170.00
Pump Plate, Husky Hi-Power Inc., Square, Porcelain, 15 x 14 In. 600.00
Pump Plate, Mobilgas, Pegasus Logo, Porcelain, 5-Point Shield, 1947, 12 x 12 In. 170.00
Pump Plate, Premium 100, Red & White, Porcelain, 12 x 11 In. 85.00
Pump Plate, Pride Of Oregon Regular, Logo, Porcelain, 24 x 14 In. 367.00
Pump Plate, Regular 94, Black & White, Porcelain, 12 x 11 In. 113.00
Pump Plate, Shamrock No. 2 Diesel, Porcelain, 13 x 11 In. 283.00
Pump Plate, Smith-O-Lene Gasoline Aviation Brand, Airplane Logo, Round, Porcelain, 10 In. 904.00
Pump Plate, Super Premium, Porcelain, Die Cut, 12 x 16 In. 198.00
Pump Plate, Texaco Diesel Chief, White T, Mounting Holes, Porcelain, 1952, 18 x 12 In......... 226.00
Pump Plate, Texaco Fire Chief Gasoline, White T, Helmet Logo, Porcelain, 1960, 18 x 12 In. . 113.00
Pump Plate, Texaco Sky Chief Gasoline Petrox, Red, Green, Porcelain, 22 x 12 In. 123.00
Pump Plate, Texaco Sky Chief Gasoline With Petrox, White T, Porcelain, 1958, 15 x 8 In. 1113.00
Pump Plate, Tidewater Premium, Porcelain, 12 x 10 In. 124.00
Pump Plate, Union 76 Regular Gasoline, Porcelain, Orange, Blue, 18 x 14 In. 170.00
Pump Sign, Texaco Fire Chief, White, Hat, Pole, Tin, 18 x 12 In. 311.00
Sign, AC Spark Plug Cleaning Station, Sparky Logo, Tin, Flange, 15 x 11 In. 1300.00
Sign, AC Spark Plug, Logo, Black, Red, Tin, 18 x 9 In. 283.00
Sign, Aeropel Gasoline, Propeller Logo, 2-Sided, Tin, Round, 36 In. 565.00
Sign, Aeroshell Huile Pour Motreurs, Winged Shell Logo, 2-Sided, Porcelain, Die Cut, 18 x 32 In. 1187.00
Sign, Aladdin Gasoline Lake Co. Farm Supply Co., Red, Black, Embossed Tin, 7 x 19 In. 339.00
Sign, Alco Oil American, Lubricants Co., Porcelain Flange, 10 x 14 In. 339.00
Sign, Alemite Motor Oil, Per 35 Qt., Round, Porcelain, 7 x 6 In. 198.00
Sign, American Brakeblok The Safety Lining, Dog Logo, Tin, 24 x 18 In. 141.00
Sign, Are You Putting Me On?, Seat Belt, Porcelain, 16 x 24 In. 180.00
Sign, Aristo Motor Oil, Union Co., California Best All Ways, Shield Shape, Porcelain, 18 x 18 In. 1187.00
Sign, Aristo Union Motor Best All Ways, Shield Shape, Green, Red, Porcelain, 18 x 21 In. 275.00
Sign, Ask For Gargoyle Mobiloil Authorized Service, Porcelain, 24 x 20 In. 424.00
Sign, Ask For Socony Motor Oil, Porcelain, Curved, 15 x 13 In. 170.00
Sign, Ask For Veedol Motor Oils 100 Percent Pennsylvania, 2-Sided, Porcelain, 28 x 22 In. 706.00
Sign, Ask For Veedol Motor Oils, Arched Shape, Black, Orange, Porcelain, 28 x 22 In. 1582.00
Sign, Atlantic Credit Card Honored Here, Tin, Wood Frame, 22 x 37 In. 283.00
Sign, Atlantic Imperial Motor Oil In A Class By Itself, Tin, 11 x 18 In......... 141.00
Sign, Atlantic Motor Oils Sold Here Keep Upkeep Down, Black, Red, Tin, Flange, 15 x 21 In. ... 565.00
Sign, Atlantic Refining Co. Automobile Gasoline For Sale Here, Porcelain Flange, 20 x 30 In.. 735.00
Sign, Atlantic Refining Company, Crossed Arrow Logo, Tin, Round, 10 ½ In. 283.00
Sign, Atlantic White Flash For Top Performance, Tin, Wood Frame, 1938, 32 x 73 In. 367.00
Sign, Atlantic White Flash Plus, 2-Sided, Porcelain, 30 In. 226.00
Sign, Autolite Batteries With Car Headlights On, Green, Red, Tin, 60 x 18 In. 904.00
Sign, Auto-Lite Spark Plugs, Embossed Tin, 24 x 12 In. 226.00
Sign, Bardahl Fights Grime Gang, Logo, Tin, For Wire Rack, 17 x 20 In. 70.00
Sign, Bear Wheels Alignment Service, Laughing Bear Logo, Tin, Die Cut, 54 x 36 In. 565.00
Sign, Bee Line Alignment Service, Bee Graphics, Tin, 2-Sided, 24 x 36 In. 226.00
Sign, Best In The Long Run, Marathon Running Man, Neon, Porcelain, Die Cut, 57 x 40 In... 3842.00
Sign, Blue Grass Axle Grease For Tired Wheels, Indian Refining Co., Embossed, Porcelain, 7 x 14 In. 678.00
Sign, Bosch Injector Pump, Tin, Germany, 1959, 20 x 12 In. 113.00
Sign, Briggs & Stratton, 4-Cycle Gasoline Engine, Plastic, Light-Up, 8 x 28 In. 226.00
Sign, Brown's-Oyl, For Fords, Brownie Trademark, Embossed, Tin, 20 x 14 In. 424.00
Sign, Buick Valve In Head, Porcelain, Round, 20 In. .... 367.00 to 565.00
Sign, Burd's Antique Cars, Tin, Reflective Paint, Red, Black, White, 24 x 36 In. 311.00
Sign, Buy On Universal Credit Ford Cars, Ford Trucks, Lincoln Zephyr, Mercury Eight, 9 x 20 In. 904.00
Sign, Cardinal Motor Oil With Logo, Tin, Tacker, 6 ½ x 6 ½ In. 424.00
Sign, Champion Dependable Spark Plugs, Hand Pointing To Plug, Tin, Cardboard Back, 13 x 19 In. 763.00
Sign, Champion Gasoline, Eagle, Spread Wing, 2-Sided, Porcelain, 60 x 36 In. 226.00
Sign, Champion Spark Plugs, Embossed, Yellow, Black, Tin, 14 x 30 In. 396.00
Sign, Champion World's Favorite Spark Plug, Plane Flying, Reverse Painted Glass, 15 x 13 In. 283.00
Sign, Chevrolet Logo, Bowtie Shape, Plastic, Light-Up, 26 x 54 In. 226.00

Sign, Chevrolet OK, Porcelain, Neon, Round, 24 In.	848.00
Sign, Chevron National Credit Cards Accepted, Porcelain, 2-Sided, 18 x 24 In.	565.00
Sign, Cities Kerosene Sold Here If It's Cities Service It Has To Be Good, Green, Tin, 12 x 22 In.	452.00
Sign, Cities Service Charge Cards Accepted Here, Tin, Flange. 12 x 20 In.	198.00
Sign, Cities Service Oil Once Always, Red Logo, 2-Sided, Porcelain, 42 In.	960.00
Sign, Conoco Gasoline, Ethyl Logo, Soldier, 15 In., Base 7 In.	1695.00
Sign, Conoco Germ Processed Motor Oil, Winter Grade, Summer Grade, Tin, 2-Sided, 25 x 38 In.	593.00
Sign, Crown Oil & Gas, Logo, Tin, 9 x 11 In.	113.00
Sign, Curb, Pennzoil Safe Lubrication, 2-Sided, Porcelain, Cast Iron Base, 21 In.	1017.00
Sign, Cycol Motor Oil Free From Destructive Sulpho Compounds, Tin Flange, 16 x 23 In.	960.00
Sign, Dearco Motor Oil Fortify Your Motor, Tin, Die Cut, 19 x 12 In.	180.00
Sign, Delco Batteries, 6 Volt Battery Logo, Tin, Wood Back, 1939, 70 x 19 In.	452.00
Sign, Delco Battery For Power With United Motor Service, Logo, Tin, 60 x 19 In.	622.00
Sign, Delco Battery, Hanging, Screen Print, Sheet Steel, Blue, Yellow, White, 18 x 24 In.	94.00
Sign, Dependable Dodge Service, Arrow, 2-Sided, Round, Porcelain, 42 In.	1978.00
Sign, Diamond Tires, Albion Auto Service, Porcelain, 28 x 59 In.	622.00
Sign, Dodge Plymouth 2-Sided, Porcelain, Flange Edges, 35 x 18 In.	2260.00
Sign, Douglas Gasoline Aviation Tested, Flying Heart Logo, Porcelain, 12 x 12 In.	565.00
Sign, Dreadnaught Chains, Always Grip Never Slip, Battleship, Tire, Cardboard, Easel, 19 x 13 In.	1695.00
Sign, Dunlop Authorized Dealer, Logo, Yellow, 2-Sided, Porcelain, 18 In.	113.00
Sign, Dunlop, Porcelain, Die Cut, 16 x 36 In.	283.00
Sign, Dupont Anti-Freeze Methanol Is Better!, Cardboard, Metal Frame, 30 x 21 In.	254.00
Sign, Eagle Service Vico, Oiling, Greasing Graphics, 2-Sided, Wood, Frame, 32 x 49 In.	735.00
Sign, Empire Tire, Brandon Inn Garage Repairs-Supplies, Tin, Wood Frame, 48 x 36 In.	339.00
Sign, En-Ar-Co Motor Oil, Boy Holding Slate, Round, 2-Sided, Tin, 40 In.	550.00
Sign, En-Ar-Co Motor Oil, Yellow, Red, Embossed, Tin, 7 x 20 In.	339.00
Sign, Esso Gas, Bottle Logo, Porcelain, 23 x 17 In.	790.00
Sign, Esso Motor Cleaner, Dirty Motors Need It, Light-Up, Reverse Painted Glass, 9 x 20 In.	311.00
Sign, Esso, Enamel On Tin, Square, Cutout Corners, Red, White, Blue, 27 x 30 In.	196.00
Sign, Esso, Light-Up, Plastic Front, Metal Can, 18 x 26 In.	198.00
Sign, Esso, To Keep Your Wife Happy Change To Esso, Eyes, 1 Black End, 21 x 27 In.	1500.00
Sign, Exide Batteries Service, Black & White, 2-Sided, Porcelain, 20 x 26 In.	339.00
Sign, Exide Batteries, Embossed Tin, 14 x 39 In.	424.00
Sign, Federal Tires, Good For A Long Safe Ride, Embossed, Self-Framed, 60 x 14 In.	170.00
Sign, Firestone Batteries, Porcelain, 7 x 24 In.	678.00
Sign, Firestone Gasoline Lubricants Tires Batteries Brake Lining, 2-Sided, Porcelain, 30 x 36 In.	537.00
Sign, Firestone One-Stop Service, Porcelain, 42 x 42 In.	396.00
Sign, Firestone, Tin, 71 x 15 In.	424.00
Sign, Fleet Motor Oil-Grease, Plane, Car Logo, Red, Black, Tin, 12 x 23 In.	339.00
Sign, Fleet Wing, Large Red Bird Graphics, Round, Porcelain, 48 In.	4240.00
Sign, Flying A Gasoline, Logo, Porcelain Pump Plate, 10 x 10 In.	254.00
Sign, Ford America's Favorite V-8, Crest Logo, Tin, 48 x 106 In.	226.00
Sign, Ford Crest, Porcelain, Die Cut, 35 x 34 In.	2034.00
Sign, Fort Pitt Motor Oil, 100 Percent Pure Pennsylvania, Porcelain, 18 x 22 In.	1074.00
Sign, Fred'k Gamash Automobiles, Newport, N.H., Embossed, Tin Litho, 13 x 19 In. ....*illus*	805.00
Sign, Frye Drop Gasoline Starts Quickly-Explodes Complete, Porcelain, 28 x 40 In.	1830.00
Sign, General Gasoline & Lubricants, Green, Black, Round, Porcelain, 30 In.	1470.00
Sign, General Petroleum Corp., Porcelain, 12 x 24 In.	85.00
Sign, Genuine Star Car Parts, Logo, Tin, Wood Frame, 31 x 37 In.	452.00
Sign, Glido Motor Oil American Lubricants Inc., Buffalo, 2-Sided, Tin, 18 x 24 In.	509.00
Sign, Globe Battery Station Sales & Service, Porcelain, 2-Sided, Round, 20 In.	396.00
Sign, Golden West Oil Company, Logo, Round, Yellow, Black, White, Porcelain, 10 In.	367.00
Sign, Goodrich Tires Silvertown Cords, Porcelain Flange, 19 x 23 In.	593.00
Sign, Goodrich Tires, G In Wreath, Porcelain, Self-Framed, 20 x 60 In.	351.00
Sign, Goodyear Fan Belt Hose, Tin, 9 ½ x 18 In.	113.00
Sign, Goodyear No-Rim Cut 10 Percent Oversize Tires, 2-Sided, Porcelain, 12 x 24 In.	424.00
Sign, Goodyear Radiator Hose, Fan Belts, Serviceman Graphics, Cardboard, Die Cut, 26 x 18 In.	960.00
Sign, Goodyear Service Station Goodyear Means Good Wear, Summit Garage, Tin, 12 x 22 In.	1808.00
Sign, Goodyear Spark Plugs Check Lazy Plugs-They're Gas Eaters, Cardboard, Die Cut, 26 x 20 In.	1074.00
Sign, Goodyear Tire & Battery Service, Tin, 1952, 18 x 72 In.	480.00
Sign, Goodyear Tire They Cost No More, Blue, Gold, Double Edge Porcelain, Die Cut, 10 x 20 In.	311.00
Sign, Goodyear Tires, Foot & Flag Logo, 2-Sided, Porcelain, Die Cut, 28 x 48 In.	791.00
Sign, Goodyear, Winged Foot Logo On Blimp, Porcelain, Die Cut, 2-Sided, 5 x 26 In.	1695.00
Sign, Grant Batteries 6 Volt, Battery Graphics, Red, White, Embossed, Tin, 13 x 39 In.	254.00
Sign, Gulf Quality, Porcelain, Round, 24 In.	85.00
Sign, Gulf, Super Marine, Logo, Navy & Orange, Square, Porcelain, 8 ½ x 11 ½ In.	325.00
Sign, Ha Dees Car Heater Can't Beat The Heat, Cardboard, Die Cut, 1933, 28 x 17 In.	1695.00

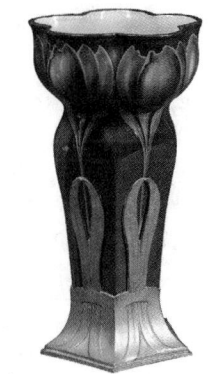

Art Nouveau, Vase, Ceramic, Pewter Overlay, Tulips, Leaves, Trailing Stems, Marked, Orvit, c.1900, 9 ½ In. $1041.00

Skinner, Inc.

Arts & Crafts, Box, Cover, Wood, Pewter, Glass, Pottery, Flower Design, Oval Cabochon, c.1900, 2 x 6 ¾ In. $95.00

Skinner, Inc.

Arts & Crafts, Panel, Leaded Stained Glass, Castle In Landscape, 22 x 37 ½ In. $868.00

Rago Arts & Auction Center

Auto, Hood Ornament, Fraternal, Knights Of Columbus Emblem, Nickel Over Brass, 5 ⅝ In. $44.00

Wm Morford Antiques

Auto, Hood Ornament, Old Doc Yac, Painted, Cast Iron, Arcade, 1911-17, 5 ½ In. $805.00

Bertoia Auctions

Auto, Horn, Brass, Rubber Bulb, Powell & Hammer, Birmingham, 19 ¼ In. $130.00

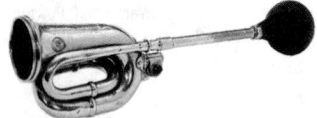

Auction Team Breker

Auto, License Plate, 1939 New York World's Fair, Embossed, Tin Lithograph, 4 ½ x 11 ½ In. $303.00

Wm Morford Antiques

Auto, Poster, Cleveland Automobile Show, Paper, Otis Lithograph Co., Frame, 1915, 30 x 37 In. $7200.00

Victorian Casino Antique Auction

Sign, Ha Dees Hot Water Car Heater, Devil Graphics, Cardboard, Die Cut, 1933, 18 x 11 In.	1582.00
Sign, Hanging, Colonial Gas & D.E. Copeland General Store, Metal, Paint, 48 x 56 In.	678.00
Sign, Havoline Motor Oil, Black, White, Porcelain, 2-Sided, c.1934, 21 ¼ x 10 ¾ In.	460.00
Sign, Havoline, The Power Oil, Indian Refining Company, Porcelain, 20 x 24 In.	848.00
Sign, Hood Tires Man, Saluting, Red, Black, White, 2-Sided, Porcelain, 32 x 36 In.	452.00
Sign, Humble Oil Company, Porcelain, Elongated Oval, 26 x 52 In.	124.00
Sign, Icy-Flo Motor Oil, The 30 Below Zero, Porcelain, Round, 24 In.	509.00
Sign, Iso-Vis Motor Oil Standard Oil, Indiana, Flame Logo, Round, Porcelain, 30 In.	1130.00
Sign, Jayhawks Oils, Bird Logo, Tin, 36 x 24 In.	283.00
Sign, Johnson Seahorse Outboard Motors, Seahorse Logo, Wood Mounted, 32 x 56 In.	3955.00
Sign, Kaiser Willys Approved Service, Red, White, 2-Sided, Porcelain, Round, 60 In.	678.00
Sign, Kanotex With Ethyl Logo, 2-Sided, Porcelain, 30 In.	396.00
Sign, Keeler's Garage Automobiles, Supplies, Repairs, Early Car Logo, Tin, 44 x 12 In.	763.00
Sign, Kelly-Springfield Automobile Tires, Consolidated Rubber Tire, Embossed, Tin, 14 x 20 In.	3277.00
Sign, Kelly-Springfield Tires Tubes, Logo, Tin, Reflective Paint, 18 x 72 In.	1243.00
Sign, Kelly-Springfield Tires, 2-Sided, Porcelain, 28 x 40 In.	424.00
Sign, Kendall 2000 Mile Oil, Hand, Tin, Die Cut, Flange, 14 x 18 In.	678.00
Sign, Kendall Motor Oil, Hand Logo, Red, White, 2-Sided, Tin, Round, 24 In.	141.00
Sign, Kendall Super B Motor Oil, 2-Sided, Tin, Arc Shape, 4 x 32 In.	57.00
Sign, Lafayette Nash Authorized Service, Fish Scale Logo, Porcelain, Die Cut, 41 x 22 In.	1582.00
Sign, Lark, Car, Banner, Red Satin, 52 x 41 In.	141.00
Sign, Lincoln Square Garage, Wood, Yellow, Black Paint, Red Arrow, Milford M., c.1950, 12 x 36 In.	178.00
Sign, Lubri-Gas Protects The Motor, Camel Logo, Tin, 19 x 28 In.	367.00
Sign, Lubri-Gas, The Correct Motor Fuel, Camel Logo, Tin, 20 x 28 In.	339.00
Sign, Macmillan Ring-Free Motor Oil, Thrifty Lubricant, Red, Black, Scotsman & Dime, 28 x 20 In.	24.00
Sign, Mapco Speedway Coil, Dependable Ignition, Better Motor Performance, Roadster, Tin, 13 x 9 In.	1695.00
Sign, Marathon Tires, Tin Lithograph, Self-Framed, Kaufman & Strauss, 23 x 20 In.	16520.00
Sign, Mercedes-Benz Service, Logo, Rolled Edge, Porcelain, 31 x 23 In.	1356.00
Sign, Mergraf Lubricant Oiler Than Oil, Logo, Tin, Die Cut, Flange, 18 x 18 In.	254.00
Sign, MFA Gasoline Motor Oil, 2-Sided, Porcelain, Round, 42 In.	961.00
Sign, Minute Man Service, Round, 2-Sided, Orange, Blue, Porcelain, 30 In.	11250.00
Sign, Mobil, Diesel, Pegasus, Shield Shape, Porcelain, 12 ⅛ x 12 ¼ In.	660.00
Sign, Mobil, Pegasus, Red, Blue Border, Porcelain, c.1930, 48 In.	1495.00
Sign, Mobilgas Restroom Pledge, Logo, Red, White, Porcelain, 5-Sided Shield Shape, 7 ½ x 8 In.	452.00
Sign, Mobilgas Socony-Vacuum, Pegasus Logo, 2-Sided, Porcelain, 72 x 72 In.	623.00
Sign, Mobilgas, Pegasus, Shield Shape, Navy, Orange, Pump Plate, Porcelain, 12 ½ x 12 ½ In.	140.00
Sign, Mobiloil E For Ford Cars, Gargoyle Logo, 2-Sided, Paddle, Porcelain, 11 x 9 In.	450.00
Sign, Mobiloil Socony-Vacuum, Pegasus, 2-Sided, Porcelain Logo, 5-Point Shield Shape, 32 x 32 In.	2825.00
Sign, Mohawk Tires, Indian Face, Feather, Tin Lithograph, c.1930, 18 ¼ x 72 In. ....*illus*	980.00
Sign, Mohawk Tires, Indian Logo, Tin, Die Cut, Donaldson Art Sign Co., Ky., 336 x 30 In.	1074.00
Sign, Mother Penn Motor Oil, Logo, Red, White, Black, Porcelain, 6 x 8 ½ In.	706.00
Sign, Motor Parts & Accessories, Red, Black, Embossed, Tin, 16 x 60 In.	650.00
Sign, Motorists Mutual Automobile Insurance, Hand, Torch, 2-Sided, Porcelain, Flange, 18 x 24 In.	254.00
Sign, NAPA Professional Automotive Refinishing, Early Car Graphics, Tin, 2-Sided, Hanger, 24 x 30 In.	85.00
Sign, National Battery Complete Service, Embossed Tin, 47 x 13 In.	509.00
Sign, National Tire Service, 2-Sided, Tin, Die Cut Arrow Shape, 72 x 24 In.	565.00
Sign, National Tire Service, Arrow, Tin, Die Cut, Metal Holder, 72 x 24 In.	1017.00
Sign, New Texaco Motor Oil Furfural Film Does It, Tin, 18 x 30 In.	311.00
Sign, New Texaco Motor Oil, Can Logo, 2-Sided, Tin, 30 x 30 In.	509.00
Sign, Northland Oils, 50th Anniversary, Red, White, Black, Tin, 12 x 24 In.	424.00
Sign, Nourse Guaranteed Motor Oil Business Is Good, Viking Logo, 2-Sided, Tin, 9 x 7 In.	1800.00
Sign, Nourse Lubricants Business Is Good, Viking Logo, Embossed Tin, 18 x 24 In.	311.00
Sign, Oak Motor Oil, Lollipop Shape, Porcelain, Green, Red, White, Black, 2-Sided, 122 x 14 In.	10350.00
Sign, Oakland Pontiac Service, 2-Sided, Porcelain, 24 x 36 In.	1243.00
Sign, Oilzum Automotive Choice Of Champions, Tin, 15 x 36 In.	113.00
Sign, Oilzum Motor Oil, Can Shape, Red, White, Tin, 48 x 33 In.	791.00
Sign, Oldfield Tires, Logo, Porcelain Flange, 16 x 20 In.	848.00
Sign, Oldsmobile Service, Crest Logo, Yellow Logo Ring, Single Lens, 13 ½ In.	3108.00
Sign, Penfield Motor Oil Finest From Pennsylvania Fields, Oil Derricks, Embossed Tin, 14 x 20 In.	339.00
Sign, Penn Drake Lubricants, Oil Derrick Logo, Gray, Black, Red, Tin Flange, 20 x 14 In.	763.00
Sign, Pennzoil Safe Lubrication, Brown Bell Logo, Porcelain, Round, 24 In.	791.00
Sign, Pennzoil Safe Lubrication, Oval, Curb, 2-Sided, Yellow, 19 x 31 In.	250.00
Sign, Pennzoil Sound Your Z, Yellow, Black, 2-Sided, Tin, Die Cut, 1948, 22 x 31 In.	480.00
Sign, Pennzoil Sound Your Z, Yellow, Red, Black, Painted, Metal, 2-Sided, 12 x 16 In.	130.00
Sign, Pennzoil Sound Your Z, Yellow, Red, Black, Tin, Flange, 17 x 23 In.	424.00
Sign, Perfect Circle Piston Rings Authorized Dealer, Wake Up Your Car, Tin, 2-Sided, 28 x 20 In.	509.00
Sign, Phillips 66 Battery Service, Red, Black Logo, Embossed, Tin, Wood Back, 72 x 18 In.	1074.00

Sign, Phillips 66 Motor Oil, Green Ground, Porcelain, 21 ½ In.	767.00
Sign, Phillips 66 Motor Oil, Red, Black, Embossed, Tin, Wood Back, 35 x 22 In.	960.00
Sign, Phillips 66 Philgas The All Purpose Fuel, Orange, Black, Tin, Wood Back, 34 x 70 In.	339.00
Sign, Phillips 66, Orange & Black, 2-Sided, Porcelain, Shield Shape, 1955, 30 x 30 In.	678.00
Sign, Pierce Oil Corp. Pennant Oils, Convex, Round, Red, White, Blue, Porcelain, 15 In.	593.00
Sign, Polarine Oil & Greases For Motor Car & Boat Lubrication, Tacker, Tin, 4 ½ x 20 In.	452.00
Sign, Power Lube Motor Oil, Smooth As The Tread Of A Tiger, Logo, 2-Sided, Porcelain, 20 x 38 In.	2147.00
Sign, Pride Of Oregon Ethyl, White Ground, Yellow, Red, Porcelain Pump Plate, 22 x 14 In.	367.00
Sign, Pump Plate, Indian Gasoline, Green, Blue, Porcelain, 18 x 12 In.	325.00
Sign, Pure-Pep Be Sure With Pure, Logo, Porcelain, 1952, 12 x 10 In.	102.00
Sign, Pure-Pep, Be Sure With Pure, Pump Plate, Porcelain, 12 x 10 In.	100.00
Sign, Purol Gasoline Product Of Pure Oil Co., U.S.A., Arrow Logo, Porcelain, 18 x 70 In.	480.00
Sign, Quaker State Motor Oil, Tombstone Shape, Green, White, 2-Sided, Porcelain, 29 x 27 In.	141.00
Sign, Raybestos Check Brakes, America's Biggest Selling Brake Lining, Logo, Tin, Flange, 19 x 26 In.	254.00
Sign, Red Crown Gasoline Power Service Economy, Porcelain, 28 x 60 In.	254.00
Sign, Red Crown Gasoline With Ethyl, Logo, 2-Sided, Porcelain, Round, 30 In.	537.00
Sign, Red Crown Gasoline, Crown Logo, 2-Sided, Porcelain, Flange, 26 x 26 In.	1074.00
Sign, Red Hat Motor Oil Gasoline, Hat Logo, Porcelain, Round, 32 In.	4520.00
Sign, Redseal Dry Battery, A Battery Suitable For Every Use, Porcelain Flange, 24 x 13 In.	1695.00
Sign, Refill With Cities Service Oils & Koolmotor, 2-Sided, Tin, 12 x 21 In.	1187.00
Sign, Replace With Delco Battery, Logo, Red, White, Black, Tin, 14 x 20 In.	311.00
Sign, Replace With Delco Battery, Red, White, Blue, Tin Flange, 18 x 22 In.	537.00
Sign, Richlube Motor Oil, Race Car Graphics, Yellow, Black, White, Round, Porcelain, 30 In.	2599.00
Sign, Richlube Safety Motor Oil, 100% Pure Pennsylvania, Round, 2-Sided, Porcelain, 24 In.	9605.00
Sign, Royal, Red, White, Triangular, Porcelain, Die Cut, 9 x 10 In.	367.00
Sign, Seaside Gasoline, Sea Gulls, Triangular, 2-Sided, Orange, Yellow, Porcelain, 38 x 38 In.	1100.00
Sign, Shell Motor Oil, Metal, Flange, Die Cut, 2-Sided, American Art Works, 1930s, 16 x 14 In.	336.00
Sign, Shell, Figural, Neon, 48 x 48 In. ....*illus*	1180.00
Sign, Shell, Logo Shape, Yellow, Red, Plastic, Wood Base, Light-Up, 2-Sided, c.1960, 25 x 23 In.	1017.00
Sign, Shell, Logo, Red, Yellow, Plastic, 58 x 55 In.	170.00
Sign, Shellubrication, The Motor Upkeep Service, 2-Sided, Octagonal, Porcelain, 36 x 36 In.	400.00
Sign, Signal Gasoline, Red Stoplight Logo, Porcelain Pump Plate, Round, 12 In.	367.00
Sign, Sinclair Clean Rest Room, Windshield Service, Porcelain, 2-Sided, 38 x 38 In.	283.00
Sign, Sinclair Clean Rest Rooms, 2-Sided, Porcelain, 38 x 30 In.	424.00
Sign, Sinclair Credit Cards Honored Here, Embossed, Tin, 13 x 19 In.	198.00
Sign, Sinclair H-C Gasoline, 2-Sided, Porcelain, Round, 24 In.	565.00
Sign, Sinclair Opaline Motor Oil, Can Logo, Porcelain, 20 x 48 In.	2373.00
Sign, Sinclair Opaline, Circle With Stripes, Porcelain, 12 x 12 In.	475.00
Sign, Sinclair Pennsylvania Motor Oil, Mellowed 100 Million Years, Porcelain, 11 In.	339.00 to 750.00
Sign, Sinclair, Dinosaur Logo, Die Cut, 44 x 60 In.	226.00
Sign, Sinclair, Service Will Not Be Rendered While Motors Are Running, Porcelain, 18 x 22 In.	311.00
Sign, Socony Motor Oil Lubester Paddle, Porcelain, 9 x 6 In.	565.00
Sign, Socony Motor Oil, Porcelain, Curved, 15 In.	283.00
Sign, Sovereign Coupon Accepted, Yellow, Black, 2-Sided, Tin, 18 x 24 In.	226.00
Sign, Sovereign Service, Logo, Yellow, Black, 2-Sided, Porcelain, Die Cut, 51 x 41 In.	254.00
Sign, Speedwell Motor Oil, Running Made Easy, Black Boy, Tiger, Porcelain Flange, 16 x 23 In.	1582.00
Sign, Spencer Axle & Drive Shafts, Oval, Black, Blue, Porcelain, 10 x 20 In.	198.00
Sign, Standard Motor Gasoline Polarine Oil, 2-Sided, Porcelain, Round, 30 In.	1469.00
Sign, Standard Oil Company Indiana, 1000.00 Reward, Porcelain, 12 x 5 In.	367.00
Sign, Standard Oil Of Indiana Red Crown, Square, Pump Plate, Porcelain, 14 x 12 In.	95.00
Sign, Stanley Garage Door Holders, Hold Your Doors Open, Tin, Cardboard, 26 x 34 In.	3616.00
Sign, Stop, Re-Line Your Brakes With Johns-Manville, Tin Flange, E.A. Shank Co., 20 x 12 In.	2260.00
Sign, Studebaker Authorized Service Parts, Logo, Masonite Sign, 9 ½ x 13 In.	480.00
Sign, Sunoco Charge Accounts Honored, 2-Sided, Porcelain, Flange Bracket, 14 x 18 In.	650.00
Sign, Sunoco Motor Oil, Can Graphics, Tin, 2-Sided, 11 x 14 In.	537.00
Sign, Sunoco Visible Gas Pump Pricer Box, Embossed Blue Sunoco, Porcelain, Flange, 12 x 18 In.	1921.00
Sign, Sunoco, 2-Fisted High Test Performance High Knockless Power, Tin, Die Cut, 1930s, 16 x 40 In.	904.00
Sign, Sunoco, Logo Arrow, Plastic, Light-Up, 32 x 48 In.	339.00
Sign, Sunray Oil Corp., Natural Power Oils, Logo, Red, Green, Yellow, White, Porcelain, 10 x 18 In.	367.00
Sign, Tankar, Logo, Single Lens, Globe Body, 13 ½ In.	2825.00
Sign, Taxi Light With Suction Cups, Electric Cord, 4 x 12 In.	85.00
Sign, Texaco Authorized Motor Tune-Up Service, White-T, Red, White, Tin, Embossed, 10 x 15 In.	678.00
Sign, Texaco Credit Card, Other Major Cards, 2-Sided, Tin, 32 x 16 In.	11.00
Sign, Texaco Eight Ball, Ethyl Logo, 2-Sided, Porcelain, Round, 30 In.	593.00
Sign, Texaco Fire Chief, Red Helmet, White Ground, Porcelain Pump Plate, 1962, 18 x 12 In.	136.00
Sign, Texaco Motor Oil, Clean Clear, Golden With Oil Pouring, Black Ground, Porcelain, 14 x 12 In.	1470.00
Sign, Texaco Motor Oil, Clean Golden, Pouring Can Logo, Tin, 16 x 16 In.	848.00

Auto, Sign, Fred'k Gamash Automobiles, Newport, N.H., Embossed, Tin Litho, 13 x 19 In.
$805.00

Bertoia Auctions

Auto, Sign, Mohawk Tires, Indian Face, Feather, Tin Lithograph, c.1930, 18 ¼ x 72 In.
$980.00

Hake's Americana & Collectibles

Auto, Sign, Shell, Figural, Neon, 48 x 48 In.
$1180.00

Showtime Auction Services

Baccarat, Biscuit Jar, Cameo, Textured Vaseline, Red Poppies, Gilt Fitting, Signed, 7 ¼ In.
$259.00

Early Auction Co.

Baccarat, Candelabrum, 3-Light, Prisms, Putti Support, Acid Etched Base, Signed, 21 x 11 In. $676.00

New Orleans Auction Galleries, Inc.

Baccarat, Perfume Bottle, Hexagonal, Opaque Pink, Silver Star, Step Cut Stopper, Stamped, 4 ⅜ In. $3105.00

Humler & Nolan

Bank, Bank Building, Capitol Treasury, Clock, Cast Iron, Gold Finish, Key, 10 ½ x 6 ⅜ In. $3738.00

Bertoia Auctions

Bank, Cottage, Tin, Stenciled Windows, Filigree Trim, George Brown, c.1870s, 5 ⅞ x 5 ⅜ In. $403.00

Bertoia Auctions

Sign, Texaco Motoroil, Insulated, 2-Sided, Tin, 11 x 22 In.	120.00
Sign, Texaco, Black T Star Logo, Porcelain, Round, 15 In.	339.00
Sign, Texaco, Fire Chief Gasoline, Curved, White, Orange, Pump Plate, Porcelain, 18 x 12 In.	175.00
Sign, Texaco, Sea Chief, Logo, Embossed, White, Gold, Red, Tin, 10 x 15 In.	424.00
Sign, Texaco, Sky Chief Gasoline, Logo, Green, Red, White, Porcelain, 18 x 12 In.	158.00
Sign, Texaco, Sky Chief Gasoline, Rectangular, Green, Orange, Pump Plate, Porcelain, 18 x 12 In.	100.00
Sign, The Luster Lasts, Mobo Auto Body Polish, Cardboard, Stand-Up, c.1930, 40 x 20 In.	2640.00
Sign, This Ranch Too Uses Seaside Gasoline, Aluminum, 28 x 30 In.	250.00
Sign, Time Premium Gasoline, Clock Logo, Red, White, Blue, Porcelain Pump Plate, 14 x 9 In.	790.00
Sign, Tiolene Motor Oil, Arrow Pure Oil Co., 2-Sided, Porcelain, Blue, White, Round, 26 In.	396.00
Sign, Tires By Dayton, Horse Logo, Vertical Embossed, Tin, 71 x 17 In.	622.00
Sign, Tires Repaired, Wood, Red & Black Paint, c.1905, 86 x 12 In.	368.00
Sign, Titan Storage Batteries Service Station, Little Man Batteries, Tin, 2-Sided, 28 x 40 In.	339.00
Sign, Trico Windshield Wipers, Tin Flange, 14 x 21 In.	311.00
Sign, Triton Motor Oil, 2-Sided, Porcelain, 24 x 21 In.	283.00
Sign, Truck Door, Sinclair, Dino Logo, Porcelain, Die Cut, 5 x 7 In.	763.00
Sign, Tydol, The Engineer Top Cylinder Oil In Every Gallon, Oil Can Man, Tin, 15 x 10 In.	311.00
Sign, U.S. Tires, Porcelain, Blue, White Letters, 72 x 18 In.	378.00
Sign, Union 76 Royal Gasoline, Orange, Blue, Pump Plate, Porcelain, 18 x 14 In.	100.00
Sign, Union 76 Triton, Extra Margin Of Safety, 2-Sided, Porcelain, Round, 30 In.	550.00
Sign, Union 76, No Dumping No Trespassing, Rectangular, 12 x 24 In.	350.00
Sign, Union Diesel, Diesel Fuel, Pump Plate, Porcelain, Round, 11 ½ In.	150.00
Sign, Union Ethyl Gasoline, Logo, 2-Sided, Curb, Base, Porcelain, Round, 30 In.	1100.00
Sign, Union Gasoline, Shield Logo, Red, White & Blue, 2-Sided, Porcelain, Round, 42 In.	275.00
Sign, Union Kerosene, A Cleaner Brighter Flame, Masonite, 15 x 30 In.	200.00
Sign, Union Oil Company, Credit Cards Honored Here, Shield Shape, Flange, Porcelain, 11 x 14 In.	500.00
Sign, Union, Women's Room, Woman With Powder Puff, Blue, Square, Porcelain, 12 x 12 In.	200.00
Sign, United Motors Service, Red, Blue, Oval, Neon, 42 x 72 In.	6497.00
Sign, United Motors Service, Touring Car Graphics, Oval, Hanger, Porcelain, 36 x 60 In.	1808.00
Sign, USL Batteries, Economical Dependable, Black, Red, Porcelain, 17 x 60 In.	3955.00
Sign, Valvoline Motor Oil, Light Medium, Round, Black, Yellow, 2-Sided, Paddle, Tin, 7 In.	225.00
Sign, Vanderbilt Tires, Leopard Logo, Yellow, Black, Self-Framed, Tin, 60 x 18 In.	424.00
Sign, Wagner's Brake Service, Light-Up, Plastic, 12 x 22 In.	170.00
Sign, Walker Oil Filter Service, Spinner, Wall Mount, 9 x 12 In.	339.00
Sign, We Recommend Diamond Motor Oil, 760 Motor Oil, Costs Less Per Mile, Tin, 18 x 60 In.	622.00
Sign, Weed Chains As Necessary As Gasoline, Tin, Wood Frame, 24 x 17 In.	1695.00
Sign, Welch Motor Oil, Oil Can Graphics, Yellow, Green, Tin, 9 x 24 In.	424.00
Sign, White Rose, Flower Logo, White, Red, Porcelain, Die Cut, 39 x 39 In.	1074.00
Sign, Wilco Wheel Alignment Cross Sight, Crosshair Logo, 2-Sided, Porcelain, Round, 30 In.	2147.00
Sign, Willard Battery, Red, Black, Tin, Die Cut Flange, 15 x 14 In.	480.00
Sign, Willshire Polly Men Restroom, Man Graphics, Blue, White, Porcelain Flange, 6 x 18 In.	848.00
Sign, Willshire Polly Women Restroom, Woman Graphics, Blue, White, Porcelain Flange, 6 x 18 In.	1695.00
Sign, Winker Garage, To Wildrose N.D., Embossed Tin, Die Cut, 6 ½ x 29 In.	904.00
Sign, Wix Oil Filters & Filterfills, Check Your Filter, Light-Up, Glass, 8 x 16 In.	565.00
Sign, Wolf's Head Motor Oil, Finest Of The Fine Since 1879, Tin Flange, 22 x 17 In.	198.00
Sign, Wolf's Head Motor Oil, Wolf Logo, Tin Flange, 22 x 17 In.	452.00
Sign, Yellow Knight Service, Shield Logo, Porcelain, Round, 30 In.	1356.00
Sign, Zerolene Oils & Greases, Polar Bear Logo, Porcelain Flange, 20 x 24 In.	1074.00
Thermometer, Champion Dependable Spark Plugs, Wood, Die Cut, 21 x 5 In.	480.00
Thermometer, Champion Spark Plugs, Insure More Power Speed, Tin, 15 x 7 In.	678.00
Thermometer, Fram Filter Service, Tin, 39 x 8 In.	678.00
Thermometer, Shaler Rislone, Tin, 26 x 10 In.	260.00
Thermometer, Use Trico Winter Blades, Car, Winter Graphics, Tin, 36 x 9 In.	509.00
Thermometer, Utoco, Plastic Pole, 7 In.	480.00
Thermometer, Vanderbilt Tires, Leopard Logo, Tin, 27 x 7 In.	311.00
Traffic Signal, Cast Metal Stand, Yellow, Black Paint, Econolite, 64 ½ x 17 In.	518.00
Traffic Signal, Double, Cast Metal Stand, Yellow, Black Paint, Econolite, 68 ¾ x 25 ¼ In.	345.00

AUTUMN LEAF pattern china was made for the Jewel Tea Company beginning in 1933. Hall China Company of East Liverpool, Ohio, Crooksville China Company of Crooksville, Ohio, Harker Potteries of Chester, West Virginia, and Paden City Pottery, Paden City, West Virginia, made dishes with this design. Autumn Leaf has remained popular and was made by Hall China Company until 1978. Some other pieces in the Autumn Leaf pattern are still being made. For more prices, go to kovels.com.

Bowl, Fruit, 5 ½ In.	5.00
Bowl, Nesting, Melon Ribbed, Gold Trim, 3 ⅜ x 6 In.	12.00
Butter, Cover, Gold Trim, c.1959, 8 ¾ x 5 ⅝ In.	149.00

Cake Plate, Gold Trim, 9 ½ In.	20.00
Cake Plate, Pedestal, Candlestick Base, 9 ½ x 3 ½ In.	149.00
Casserole, 1 Qt.	25.00
Casserole, Cover, Gold Trim, c.1935	28.00
Clock, Quartz, Square	100.00
Coffee Mug, Round Pedestal Foot, c.1966	90.00
Coffeepot	389.00
Coffeepot, Lid, Ribbing, Gold Trim, 10 x 8 ½ In.	55.00
Cookie Jar, Handles, Gold Trim, 9 x 9 ½ In.	248.00
Cookie Jar, Ribbed, Tab Handles	245.00
Cookie Jar, Ribbed, Tootsie	325.00
Cup & Saucer	9.00
Custard Cup, c.1933, 2 ¼ x 3 ½ In., 5 Piece	35.00
Custard Cup, Gold Trim, 2 x 3 ½ In.	10.00
Drip Jar, Cover, Gold Trim, c.1936, 3 ¾ x 5 In.	30.00
Jug, Ball Shape, Large	55.00
Jug, Ball, Gold Trim, c.1938-76, 5 ½ Pt.	60.00
Jug, Ball, Marked	155.00
Jug, Rayed, c.1937-76, 7 x 5 ¾ In.	40.00
Marmalade, Underplate, 1938, 3 ½ In.	120.00
Mixing Bowl, Gold Trim, 7 ½ In.	14.00
Mixing Bowl, Gold Trim, c.1930s, 4 ¾ x 8 ½ In.	20.00
Pitcher, Milk, Ribbed, Pinched Handle, 5 ¾ In.	30.00
Pitcher, Tilt Ball, Gold Trim, c.1930-60s, 7 ½ x 9 In.	52.00
Platter, Oval, 13 ½ In.	25.00
Ramekin, 4 ½ x 2 ½ In., Pair	19.00
Soup, Dish, 2 Handles	30.00
Syrup, Cover, Finial	115.00
Tablecloth, 1955-58, 54 x 54 In.	175.00
Teapot, Gilt, 6 Cup	185.00
Teapot, Lid, Aladdin Shape, 7 x 11 In.	60.00
Teapot, Nautilus, Lid, 5 ¾ In.	145.00
Teapot, Tea Ball, Paneled, Lid	175.00
Tidbit, 3 Tiers, 1954-69, 10 ½ In.	100.00
Tin, Candy, Lid, 5 ½ x 5 In.	29.00
Trivet, Cast Iron, Decal, Glazed	60.00
Tumbler, 5 ½ In.	25.00
Vase, Bulbous, Footed, Bud, 3 ¼ In.	60.00
Vase, Fluted, Ribbed, Footed, 6 ½ In.	45.00
Water Bottle, Vertical Ribs On Front & Back, 7 x 6 x 2 In.	75.00

AVON *bottles are listed in the Bottle category under Avon.*

AZALEA dinnerware was made for Larkin Company customers from 1918 to 1941. Larkin, the soap company, was in Buffalo, New York. The dishes were made by Noritake China Company of Japan. Each piece of the white china was decorated with pink azaleas.

Berry Bowl, Deep	129.00
Bowl, Cranberry, Gold Trim, 5 ¼ In.	48.00
Bowl, Grapefruit, Round Foot, Pedestal, Gold Trim, 4 ⅝ In.	199.00
Bowl, Thumbprint Design, Round, Shaped Handles, Green, Flowers, Round Foot, 3 x 10 In.	60.00
Bowl, Vegetable, Cover, Round, 2 Handles, c.1925, 10 x 5 In.	49.00
Butter Chip, 3 ½ In.	89.00
Butter Chip, Round, Gold Trim, c.1930-33	59.00
Compote, Gold Trim, Round Foot, Pedestal, 6 ½ In.	80.00
Dish, Lemon, Handle, Round, Gold Trim, 5 ½ In. Diam.	15.00
Dish, Mayonnaise, Ladle, Underplate, Gold Trim, c.1900, 2 x 4 ½ In.	32.00
Mustard, Lid, Spoon, Gold Trim, Cylindrical, Japan	40.00
Pitcher, Square Handle, Gold Trim, 5 ½ In.	89.00
Plate, Salad, Square Shape, Gold Trim, 7 ⅝ In.	50.00
Platter, Oval, Gold Accents, c.1925, 13 ¾ In.	39.00
Platter, Oval, Gold Trim, 11 ¾ In.	39.00
Salt & Pepper, Urn Shape, Gold Accents, c.1921, 3 In.	125.00
Spoon Holder, Caddy, Square Handles, Gold Trim, 8 In.	70.00
Sugar & Creamer, Cover, Gold Trim, Squared Handles, c.1920	135.00
Sugar & Creamer, Round, Gold Finial	149.00
Sugar Shaker, Slender, Round Foot, 6 ½ In.	137.00

Bank, Dog, Basset Hound, Cast Iron, Gold Paint, M 380, 3 ¼ In.
$748.00

Bertoia Auctions

Bank, Kitty Kat, White Paint, Blue Ribbon, Pink Nose, Hubley, M 349, 5 In.
$47.00

Conestoga Auction Co., Inc.

Bank, Mechanical, Boy On Trapeze, Boy Revolves, J. Barton & Smith Co., c.1891
$805.00

Bertoia Auctions

Bank, Mechanical, Confectionary, Saleswoman Gives Candy, Cast Iron, Kyser & Rex, c.1881
$4888.00

Bertoia Auctions

A

Bank, Mechanical, Frog On Round Base, Cast Iron, J. & E. Stevens, c.1870
$575.00

Bertoia Auctions

Bank, Mechanical, Hall's Excelsior, Red, White, Blue, J. & E. Stevens, c.1869
$920.00

Bertoia Auctions

Bank, Mechanical, Hall's Liliput, Man, Holding Tray, Cast Iron, J. & E. Stevens, 1870s, 4 ¼ In.
$306.00

Hake's Americana & Collectibles

Bank, Mechanical, Henry, Comic Strip Character, Stained, Painted, Pendulum, 9 x 9 In.
$649.00

Conestoga Auction Co., Inc.

Sugar, Cover, Handles, Gold Trim	20.00
Toothpick Holder, Square Shape, Pedestal Foot, Gold Trim, c.1930	74.00

BACCARAT glass was made in France by La Compagnie des Cristalleries de Baccarat, located 150 miles from Paris. The factory was started in 1765. The firm went bankrupt and began operating again about 1822. Cane and millefiori paperweights were made during the 1845 to 1880 period. The firm is still working near Paris making paperweights and glasswares.

Biscuit Jar, Cameo, Textured Vaseline, Red Poppies, Gilt Fitting, Signed, 7 ¼ In. ....*illus*	259.00
Bowl, Dessert Set, Massena, 2 x 4 ½ In., 12 Piece	590.00
Box, Frosted Glass, Brass Trim, Footed, Oval, 5 ½ x 8 ½ In.	1080.00
Candelabrum, 3-Light, Prisms, Putti Support, Acid Etched Base, Signed, 21 x 11 In. .....*illus*	676.00
Candelabrum, 5-Light, Baluster, Rope Twist, Flower Collar, Spread Foot, 1800s, 15 ¾ x 9 In., Pair	179.00
Candlestick, Spiral Pattern, Albert Prisms, France, c.1860, 18 ½ In., Pair	418.00
Chalice, 4 Millefiori Caned Panels, White Latticinio, Gilt Outline, Paperweight Foot, 6 ¾ In.	12650.00
Champagne Bucket, Crystal, Sterling Ring, Handles	340.00
Champagne Bucket, Octagonal, Ribbed, 2 Gilt Handles & Banding, 9 In.	777.00
Clock, Boy, Reading Books, Lion Heads, Clear, Frosted Glass, Gilt Bronze, Key Wind, c.1910, 16 In.	2478.00
Compote, Cover, Orb Knop, Footed, 6 ½ x 5 ½ In.	148.00
Decanter, Clear, Applied Fleur-De-Lis & Rigaree, Remy Mappin & Co., 12 In., Pair	153.00
Decanter, Paneled, Square-Shape Stopper, Narrow Neck, Perfection, Marked, 1900s, 10 In.	492.00
Decanter, Stopper, Clear Glass, 11 ½ In., Pair	159.00
Decanter, Stopper, Teardrop Shape, Acid Etched Design, 12 x 5 ½ In.	183.00
Decanter, Tapered, Bulbous Vertical Ribs, Stepped Stopper, 9 ½ x 5 In.	118.00
Decanter, Wine, Bottle Shape, Ball Stopper, Dionysus, Marked, 1900s, 14 In.	276.00
Fernery, Sarcophagus Shape, Footed, Signed, 5 x 11 In.	144.00
Figurine, Elephant, 3 x 3 In.	35.00
Figurine, Grog, 4 ½ In.	83.00
Figurine, Heart, Puffed, Ruby, 3 x 3 In.	127.00
Figurine, Hippo, Acid Etched Mark, 6 x 2 x 3 In.	196.00
Goblet, Blue To Clear, Etched, 5 ½ In., 8 Piece	714.00
Goblet, Champagne, Flute, 9 ½ In., 6 Piece	300.00
Goblet, Champagne, Flute, Harcourt, Signed, 7 In., 12 Piece	833.00
Goblet, Champagne, Flute, Massena, 8 ½ In., 6 Piece	767.00
Goblet, Water, Perfection, 7 In., 12 Piece	510.00
Inkwell, Crystal, Sterling Silver, Twisted Facets, Twist Cap, 5 x 3 ½ In.	1020.00
Jug, Stopper, Blown, Oval, Etched Insignia, 1900s, 11 In.	120.00
Lamp, Enameled, Brass Mounted, Opaline Glass, Classical Woman, Electrified, 18 In., Pair	1722.00
Obelisk, Prism Cut, Acid Stamp, 18 In.	338.00
Paperweight, 4-Leaf Clover, Etched Circular Stamp, 1 x 4 x 4 ½ In.	90.00
Paperweight, Blue, Purple Close Pack Millefiori, Zodiac Canes, Signed, 3 x 2 ⅜ In.	345.00
Paperweight, Bonsai, Black Pulled Glass, Green Leaves, Yellow Ground, 1987, 2 x 3 In.	283.00
Paperweight, Brown Basket Filled With Fruits, Clambroth Ground, Signed, 2 x 3 In.	345.00
Paperweight, Close Pack Millefiori, 6 Animal Canes, Signed, 1848, 3 ¾ x 2 ½ In.	6325.00
Paperweight, Close Pack Millefiori, Zodiac Canes, Signed 1973, 3 x 2 ½ In.	403.00
Paperweight, Concentric Millefiori Mushrooms, Red, White Overlay, 6 Facets, Signed, 1970, 3 x 2 In.	590.00
Paperweight, Deer Silhouette, Twisted Spokes, Marked, 3 In.	675.00
Paperweight, Mushroom, Close Millefiori, Blue, White Torsade, Star Cut Base, 3 x 2 In.	1035.00
Paperweight, Pansy, Clear Star Base, Flowers, Birds, Salamanders & Butterflies, 1850, 3 In.	900.00
Paperweight, Pink Pompon Flower, White Ground, White, Multicolor Cane Garland, 1992, 3 x 2 ¼ In.	633.00
Paperweight, Round, Faceted, Iris, Clear Overlay, Yellow, Basket Weave Design, 3 x 3 In.	688.00
Paperweight, Snake, Green Pulled Glass, Flower, Millefiori Center, Cobalt Blue, 1970, 2 x 3 In.	480.00
Paperweight, White Dahlia, Red, White Starburst Millefiori Circle, 2 ½ In.	1035.00
Perfume Bottle, Hexagonal, Opaque Pink, Silver Star, Step Cut Stopper, Stamped, 4 ⅜ In. ...*illus*	3105.00
Toothpick Holder, Frosted Figures, Young Girls, Holding Barrel, Dome Base, Beaded Border, 4 In.	173.00
Tumbler, Juice, Footed, Etched, 3 ¾ In., 8 Piece	207.00
Vase, Bud, Teardrop, Asymmetrical, 7 x 2 In.	72.00
Vase, Bulb Pattern, Globular, 5 In.	88.00
Vase, Cobalt Blue, Clear Cut Grid, 1900s, 7 In.	660.00
Vase, Cranberry To Green, Acid Cut Flowers, Gold Highlights, 5 In.	400.00
Vase, Globular Bottle Shape, Swirl Design, Cylindrical Neck, Flared Rim, Marked, 1900s, 7 In.	118.00
Vase, Panel Shaped, Stepped, Marked, France, 1900s, 10 In.	276.00
Vase, Spill, Etched Clear, Over Millefiori Base, Signed B 1848, 5 ¼ In.	4888.00
Wine Set, Cranberry To Clear, Etched, Scalloped Foot, Signed, 8 ¼ In., 12 Piece	3163.00
Wine, Green To Clear, 6 ½ In., 6 Piece	327.00
Wine, Yellowish Green To Clear, Intaglio Design, 7 ¾ In.	165.00

BADGES have been used since before the Civil War. Collectors search for examples of all types, including law enforcement and company identification badges. Well-known prison or law enforcement badges are most desirable. Most are made of nickel or brass. Many recent reproductions have been made.

12th Army Corp., Civil War, Star, Brass, 1 ½ In.	250.00
Barksdale Fire Department, Metal, Symbols, 1 ¾ x 1 ¾ In.	48.00
Bellboy, No. 4, Metal, 1940s, 1 ½ x 1 ¾ In.	35.00
Cable Car Operator, San Francisco, No. 4891, Brass, 1940s, Pair	45.00
Chauffeur, Iowa, No. 6499, 1934	85.00
Chauffeur, Minnesota, State Seal, No. 4390, 1926	30.00
Civil War Veteran, Nebraska, American Flag, Celluloid, c.1890	85.00
Fireman, Flushing, Ohio, Swivel Latch, Ladder, Hose, 1 ½ x 1 ½ In.	25.00
Fireman, Virginia State Fireman's Association, Silver, Ribbon, c.1897, 4 Piece	225.00
Fishing, California Fish & Game Protector, Metal, Pin, c.1938, 2 ½ x 1 ¾ In.	295.00
Fishing, Colorado Game Warden, Nickel Silver, Long Pin, 2 ¼ In.	200.00
Fishing, North Dakota Game Warden, D.J. Rutten, Nickel Plated Brass, Pin, 2 In.	165.00
Fishing, North Dakota Warden, No. 659, Nickel Plated Brass, 2 In.	295.00
Fishing, Pennsylvania Game Protector, No. 204, Brass Plate, Pin, 2 ¼ In.	354.00
GAR, Mourning, Post 222, Cedar Rapids, Iowa, Silk Ribbon, Celluloid, Tassels, c.1890, 8 In.	135.00
Insignia, Flaming Grenade Bomb Design, Hessian Grenadiers, Cast Bronze, c.1775, 2 ½ x 1 ½ In.	767.00
Security Enforcement Officer, No. 161, Gold Tone	95.00
Tarzan Radio Club, Bursley Coffees Premium, Metal, 1935, 1 ½ In.	288.00
U.S. Army Engineers, New York District, Copper, Insignia, 1940s, 2 x 1 In.	85.00

BANKS of metal have been made since 1868. There are still banks, mechanical banks, and registering banks (those that show the total money deposited on the face of the bank). 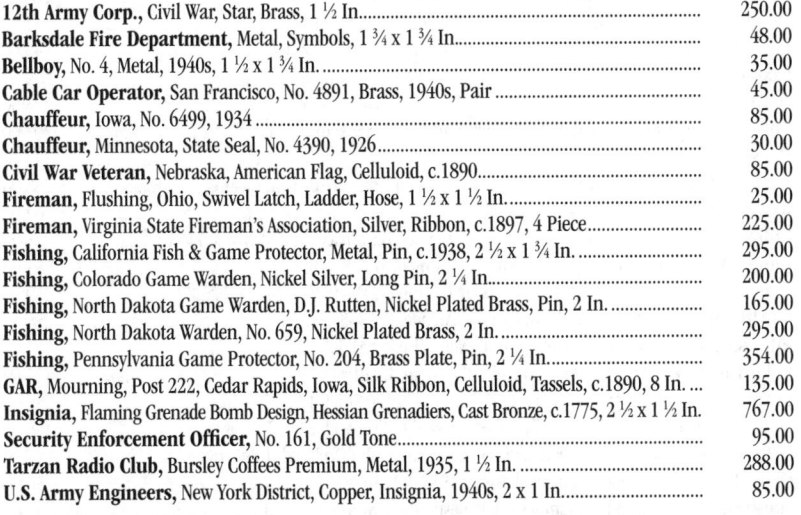 Many old iron or tin banks have been reproduced since the 1950s in iron or plastic. Some old reproductions marked *Book of Knowledge, John Wright,* or *Capron* may be listed. Pottery, glass, and plastic banks are also listed here. Mickey Mouse and other Disneyana banks are listed in Disneyana. We have added the M numbers based on *The Penny Bank Book: Collecting Still Banks* by Andy and Susan Moore and the R numbers based on *Coin Banks by Banthrico* by James L. Redwine.

Bank Building, Arched Windows, Cast Iron, 5 ¾ In.	79.00
Bank Building, Capitol Treasury, Clock, Cast Iron, Gold Finish, Key, 10 ½ x 6 ⅜ In. *illus*	3738.00
Bank Building, Cast Iron, White, Green, Orange, Paint, 4 ¼ In.	226.00
Bank Building, Flat Iron, Painted, Embossed, Kenton, c.1905, M 1159, 8 ¼ In.	489.00
Bank Building, Home Savings, Cast Iron, Paint, Blue, Red, M 1201, 11 x 7 In.	593.00
Bank Building, National Recording Bank, Iron, Pat. 1891, M 1062, 7 In.	104.00
Bank Building, Open Windows, Cast Iron, Finial, Kyser & Rex, c.1887, 5 ¾ In.	230.00
Bank Building, State Bank, Cast Iron, Gold Patina, M 1083, 4 x 3 x 2 In.	102.00
Bank Building, Triangular, Clock, Cast Iron, Hubley, 5 ¾ In.	690.00
Baseball Player, Holding Bat, Cast Iron, A.C. Williams, 5 ¾ In.	288.00
Baseball, Mobile Oil Premium, Pittsburgh Pirates, Pegasus, Glass, Steel Trap, 3 In.	125.00
Baseball, On 3 Bats, Nickeled Cast Iron, Hubley, M 1608, 5 ¼ In.	4888.00
Bayview Federal Savings, Premium, Dakin, 1976, 7 In.	75.00
Bear, Begging, Outstretched Paws, A.C. Williams, M 715, 5 ⅜ In.	69.00
Beehive, Bear Stealing Honey, Cast Iron, Japanned, Gold Highlights, England, 7 In.	230.00
Beehive, Registering Savings, Bees, Flowers, Nickeled Finish, c.1891, M 681, 5 x 6 In.	173.00
Big Aggie, On Tractor, WNAX Radio Station, Plaster, 1930s, 7 ½ In.	120.00
Boat, Battleship Maine, Cast Iron, Japanned, M 1440, 4 ½ In.	90.00
Boat, Oregon, J. & E. Stevens, Cast Iron, Guns On Deck, Japanned, M 1450, 4 ⅞ In.	86.00
Bob's Big Boy, Blue Shoes, Vinyl, 1990s, 8 In.	20.00
Buffalo Sled Co., Celluloid Over Metal, Wagon, 2-Sided, Round, 2 ½ x ½ In.	550.00
Building, Fort, Embossed, Round, Finial, Cast Iron, M 1172, 4 ⅛ In.	403.00
Building, Santa's Workshop, Lollipop, Tin, Blue Roof, 4 ⅜ In.	105.00
Building, Washington Monument, Cast Iron, Painted, A.C. Williams, M 1048, 6 In.	201.00
Calumet Baking Powder, Paper Label, Indian Chief, 2 x 5 In.	56.00
Cat, Cast Iron, Painted, 5 In.	147.00
Chest Of Drawers, Scroddleware, Claw Feet, England, 5 ½ x 6 ¼ In.	356.00
Church, Twigs, Shingle Back, Lunette, Pulls Out For Coin Slot, Door Opens, 32 x 16 In.	546.00
Clown, Hobo, Small Hat, Pottery Rockingham Glaze, c.1910, 6 In.	115.00
Cottage, Tin, Stenciled Windows, Filigree Trim, George Brown, c.1870s, 5 ⅞ x 5 ⅜ In. *illus*	403.00
Daily Dime, Tin, Clown & Circus, Square, Cut Corners, 2 ½ x 2 ½ In.	23.00
Devil, 2 Faces, Cast Iron, A.C. Williams, M 31, 4 ¼ In.	489.00
Dinner Pail, Tin, Handle, Key Lock Trap, c.1896, 2 ⅛ x 3 ⅛ In.	201.00
Dog, Basset Hound, Cast Iron, Gold Paint, M 380, 3 ¼ In. *illus*	748.00

Bank, Mechanical, Leap Frog, Shepard Hardware Co., c.1890
$3738.00

Bertoia Auctions

Bank, Mechanical, Mammy & Child, Red Dress, Kyser & Rex, c.1884
$8625.00

Bertoia Auctions

Bank, Mechanical, Merry-Go-Round, Bells Chime, Kyser & Rex, c.1885
$5750.00

Bertoia Auctions

Bank, Mechanical, Picture Gallery, Rotating Dial, Alphabet, Numbers, Iron, Shepard Hardware, c.1885
$5750.00

Bertoia Auctions

B

Bank, Mechanical, Pistol, Cast Iron, Pull Trigger, Coin Is Deposited In Handle, Elliot Co., Pat. 9/21/1909
$173.00

Bertoia Auctions

Bank, Mechanical, Santa Claus, Chimney, Shepard Hardware, Patent 10/15/1889
$863.00

Bertoia Auctions

Bank, Mechanical, Trenton Trust, 75th Anniversary, c.1950
$1093.00

Bertoia Auctions

Bank, Mechanical, World's Fair, Columbus, Indian Chief, J. & E. Stevens, Patent 10/10/1893
$489.00

Bertoia Auctions

Dog, Fido, Cast Iron, Black & White, Red Collar, Hubley, M 417, 5 In.	11.00
Dog, Nipper, RCA, White, Black, Porcelain, M 375, 6 ¼ In.	250.00
Dog, Shaggy, Sitting, Pacific First Bank, Seattle, Black & White, 6 ½ In.	58.00
Doghouse, Pug, Cardboard, Shells, Germany, 4 x 5 ½ In.	51.00
Duck, On Tub, Save For Rainy Day, Umbrella, Hubley, 1933, 5 ⅜ In.	185.00
Dutch Boy, On Barrel, Cast Iron, Hubley, Painted, M 180, 5 ¾ In.	11.00
Eagle Pure White Lead Paint, Tin Lithograph, Premium, 2 x 2 In.	45.00
Exxon Tiger, Vinyl, Humble Oil & Refining Co., 1960s, 8 ½ In.	79.00
Football Player, Football Under Arm, Cast Iron, A.C. Williams, N 11, 6 In.	173.00
Golliwog, Cast Iron, Painted, John Harper, England, M 85, 6 In.	201.00
Horse, Saddle, Cast Iron, A.C. Williams, M 523, 2 In.	144.00
Ice Cream Freezer, Cast Iron, Nickeled, Wire Turn Handle, Grey Iron Casting, 4 ¼ In.	288.00
Icee Polar Bear, Vinyl, 7 ½ In.	62.00
Indian, National Shawmut Bank Of Boston, Copper, Banthrico, M 220, 6 ½ x 4 ½ In.	125.00
Indian, With Tomahawk, Cast Iron, Hubley, Painted, M 228, 6 In.	51.00
Indian, With Tomahawk, Headdress, Cast Iron, Hubley, M 228, 5 ¾ In.	259.00
Kelvinator, Door Opens, Cast Iron, Painted, Arcade, M 1338, 3 ⅞ In.	288.00
Kitty Kat, White Paint, Blue Ribbon, Pink Nose, Hubley, M 349, 5 In. ....*illus*	47.00
Koko The Wise, Monkey, Sitting, Fez, Holding Coin, Banthrico, 5 ½ In.	125.00
Lennie, Lennox Furnace Co. Logo, Ceramic, Blond, Blue Shirt, 1949, 7 ¼ In.	245.00
Lichfield Cathedral, Cast Iron, Chamberlain & Hill, England, c.1903, M 968, 6 ½ In.	86.00
Little Three Arrows, Arrowhead Savings Bank, Vinyl, Slot On Head, 1980, 10 In.	45.00
Lucky Joe, Nash's Prepared Mustard, Glass, 1938, 4 ¾ In.	50.00
Mailbox, Air Mail, Cast Iron, Embossed, Pedestal Base, M 828, 6 x 2 In.	43.00
Mammy, Cast Iron, Red, White, M 176, 5 In.	34.00
Mammy, Red, Dress, White Apron, Hands On Hips, Cast Iron, Hubley, 5 In.	149.00

Mechanical banks were first made about 1870. Any bank with moving parts is considered mechanical. The metal banks made before World War I are the most desirable. Copies and new designs of mechanical banks have been made in metal or plastic since the 1920s. The condition of the paint on the old banks is important. Worn paint can lower a price by 90 percent.

Mechanical, Boat, Battleship Maine, Painted, Cast Iron, J. & E. Stevens, M 1439, 10 ¼ In.	920.00
Mechanical, Boy On Trapeze, Boy Revolves, J. Barton & Smith Co., c.1891 ....*illus*	805.00
Mechanical, Bulldog, Coin On Nose, Brown Paint, Cast Iron, J. & E. Stevens, 8 In.	767.00
Mechanical, Cabin, Black Man, Somersaults, Cast Iron, J. & E. Stevens, c.1890, 3 ¾ In.	354.00
Mechanical, Chief Big Moon, Cast Iron, Painted, J. & E. Stevens, 6 x 10 In.	1121.00 to 2034.00
Mechanical, China Man, Reclining, Holding 4 Aces, J. & E. Stevens, 8 In.	1416.00
Mechanical, Clown, On Globe, Spins, Painted, Cast Iron, J. & E. Stevens, c.1890, 9 x 11 In.	4800.00
Mechanical, Confectionary, Saleswoman Gives Candy, Cast Iron, Kyser & Rex, c.1881 .....*illus*	4888.00
Mechanical, Creedmoor, Soldier, Rifle, Painted, Cast Iron, J. & E. Stevens, 10 ¼ In....	177.00 to 460.00
Mechanical, Darktown Battery, Black Baseball Players, Painted, J. & E. Stevens, 9 ¾ In.	1416.00 to 5040.00
Mechanical, Eagle & Eaglets, Black, Cast Iron, J. & E. Stevens, 6 In.	237.00
Mechanical, Frog On Round Base, Cast Iron, J. & E. Stevens, c.1870 ....*illus*	575.00
Mechanical, Girl Skipping Rope, Painted, Cast Iron, J. & E. Stevens, 9 In.	12650.00
Mechanical, Hall's Excelsior, Red, White, Blue, J. & E. Stevens, c.1869 ....*illus*	920.00
Mechanical, Hall's Liliput, Man, Holding Tray, Cast Iron, J. & E. Stevens, 1870s, 4 ¼ In. ... *illus*	306.00
Mechanical, Henry, Comic Strip Character, Stained, Painted, Pendulum, 9 x 9 In. ....*illus*	649.00
Mechanical, Humpty Dumpty, Cast Iron, Red Hat, Shepard Hardware, 8 x 6 In.	848.00
Mechanical, I Always Did 'Spise A Mule, Boy On Bench, Cast Iron, J. & E. Stevens, 10 In.	575.00 to 3163.00
Mechanical, I Always Did 'Spise A Mule, Jockey, On Mule, Cast Iron, J. & E. Stevens, c.1895, 9 ½ In.	245.00
Mechanical, Jolly Nigger, Hand Raises, Eyes Roll, Tongue Moves, Cast Iron, c.1900, 6 x 5 In..	531.00
Mechanical, Leap Frog, Shepard Hardware Co., c.1890 ....*illus*	3738.00
Mechanical, Lion, 2 Monkeys, Kyser & Rex, 9 ½ In.	1416.00
Mechanical, Magician, Red Table, Cast Iron, J. & E. Stevens, 9 x 7 In.	2825.00
Mechanical, Mammy & Child, Red Dress, Kyser & Rex, c.1884 ....*illus*	8625.00
Mechanical, Mason, Bricklayers, Shepard Hardware Co., 7 ¼ In.	2300.00
Mechanical, Merry-Go-Round, Bells Chime, Kyser & Rex, c.1885 ....*illus*	5750.00
Mechanical, Monkey, Cast Iron, Hubley, Key, 7 ½ x 9 In.	1410.00
Mechanical, Novelty Bank, Cashier Swings Out, Red Roof, Cast Iron, J. & E. Stevens, 7 In.	354.00
Mechanical, Organ Bank, Boy & Girl, Monkey, Cast Iron, Kyser & Rex, 7 ¾ In.	767.00
Mechanical, Owl, Turns Head, Cast Iron, Painted, J. & E. Stevens, 7 ½ In.	354.00 to 830.00
Mechanical, Paddy & The Pig, Cast Iron, J. & E. Stevens, 7 ¾ In.	520.00
Mechanical, Penny Pineapple, Cast Iron, Box, Imswiller & Saylor, 1959, 9 In.	288.00
Mechanical, Picture Gallery, Rotating Dial, Alphabet, Numbers, Iron, Shepard Hardware, c.1885 *illus*	5750.00
Mechanical, Pistol, Cast Iron, Pull Trigger, Coin Is Deposited In Handle, Elliot Co., Pat. 9/21/1909 *illus*	173.00

Mechanical, Punch & Judy, Cast Iron, Shepard Hardware, 6 x 7 ½ In.	452.00 to 1074.00
Mechanical, Santa Claus, Chimney, Shepard Hardware, Patent 10/15/1889 ....*illus*	863.00
Mechanical, Speaking Dog, Girl, Pink Dress, Cast Iron, J. & E. Stevens, c.1890, 7 x 8 In.	1920.00
Mechanical, Stump Speaker, Black Man, Painted, Cast Iron, Shepard Hardware, 10 In.	920.00
Mechanical, Tammany, Boss Tweed, Seated, Coin In Pocket, Cast Iron, c.1890, 5 ¾ In.	531.00 to 674.00
Mechanical, Tammany, Gray Pants, Sliding Trap, J. & E. Stevens, 5 ¾ In.	950.00
Mechanical, Teddy & The Bear, Cast Iron, Gray Tree, 9 ½ x 7 In.	2034.00
Mechanical, Trenton Trust, 75th Anniversary, c.1950 ....*illus*	1093.00
Mechanical, Trick Dog, Clown, Hoop, Barrel, Hubley.	516.00
Mechanical, Trick Pony, Painted, Cast Iron, Shepard Hardware, 8 In.	652.00 to 805.00
Mechanical, William Tell, Cast Iron, J. & E. Stevens Co., 1896, 10 ½ In.	1200.00
Mechanical, William Tell, Paint, Cast Iron, J. & E. Stevens, Box, c.1900, 6 ¾ x 10 ½ In.	2880.00
Mechanical, World's Fair, Columbus, Indian Chief, J. & E. Stevens, Patent 10/10/1893 ..*illus*	489.00
Mulligan Policeman, Cast Iron, Holding Club, A.C. Williams, M 177, 5 ¾ In.	86.00 to 489.00
Owl, Pawtucket Institution, Bronze, Round Base, 6 ½ x 3 ½ In.	28.00
Penny, Clown Head, Soft Paste, Sculpted & Painted Features, France, c.1850, 4 In. ....*illus*	280.00
Piano, B. Dreher's Sons Co., Steel, Etched, Pat. 1904, 5 ⅛ x 5 ⅞ In.	288.00
Pig, Chicago Stockyards, Bronze, 5 x 9 In.	192.00
Pig, Pottery, Mottled Brown Glaze, 4 ¼ In.	23.00
Policeman, Cast Iron, Painted, 1920s, 5 ½ In.	209.00
Professor Pug Frog, Cast Iron, Painted, A.C. Williams, M 311, 3 ¼ In.	106.00
Puppo, Black & White, Painted, Cast Iron, Hubley, 5 In. ....*illus*	57.00
Rabbit, Standing, Cast Iron, A.C. Williams, M 574, 6 ¼ In.	575.00
Radio, Cast Iron, Kenton.	165.00
Radio, Majestic, Painted, Cast Iron, Steel Back, Arcade, c.1933, M 827, 4 ½ In. ....*illus*	158.00
Radio, Templetone, Painted, Cast Iron, Nickel Trap, Kenton, M 826, 4 In.	173.00
Reddy Kilowatt, Light Bulb Nose, Vinyl, Red, Yellow, White, Blue, 1960s, 5 ½ In.	840.00
Register, Dime, Jackie Robinson, Save & Win, Tin Lithograph, 2 ⅝ x 2 ⅝ In. ....*illus*	176.00
Register, Dime, Ten Dollars, Chein	150.00
Rooster, Cast Iron, Painted, Arcade, M 547, 4 ⅝ In.	316.00
Rooster, Redware, Glazed, Oval, Pedestal Base, 1800s, 10 In.	86.00
Roper Stove, Cast Iron, Burner Covers Lift Up, Arcade, M 1341, 4 In.	345.00
Safe, American Trust, Nickeled, Cast Iron, 2 Doors, Combination, Kenton.	1035.00
Safe, Bank Of Industry, Relief Design On Door, 4 x 5 x 3 ½ In.	62.00
Safe, Diamond, Cast Iron, Nickeled, Diamond Pattern, Key, 4 ½ x 3 ¾ In.	690.00
Safe, Document, Lithograph Paper Panels, Key, Cast Iron, Paint, J. & E. Stevens, 11 x 8 In.	805.00
Safe, Fidelity Trust Vault, Cast Iron, Clock, J. Barton Smith, M 903, 6 x 5 x 5 In.	452.00
Safe, Hexagon, Combination, Grill, Klotz Mfg. Co., 4 ⅜ In.	345.00
Safe, Horn Of Plenty, Cast Iron, Nickeled, E.M. Roche Novelty Co., 6 In. ....*illus*	1150.00
Safe, Ideal Safe Deposit, Cast Iron, Nickel Plated, Bolt Knob, 4 ½ In.	57.00
Safe, Ideal Safe Deposit, Combination, Nickel Plated, 4 In.	250.00
Safe, Pay Phone, Crank, Cast Iron, American Toll Tel. Co., 9 In.	1035.00
Safe, Royal, Combination, Painted, Cast Iron, 5 ⅞ In.	259.00
Safe, Time, Cast Iron, Nickel Finish, Eagle, E.M. Roche, M 895, 7 ⅛ In.	144.00
Safe, Tree Trunk Shape, Bronze, France, 34 ½ x 16 In., Pair.	1638.00
Safe, Ulysses S. Grant, Vault Base, Cast Iron, Turn Handle, J.M. Harper, M 115, 5 ¾ In.	1725.00 to 1955.00
Safe, Uncle Sam Security, Combination Dial, Cast Iron, Wing Mfg., 4 ⅞ In.	288.00
Safe, Young America, Cast Iron, Children Playing, J. & E. Stevens, 1890s, M 881, 4 In.	175.00
Sailor, Saluting, Oar, Cast Iron, M 28, 5 ½ In.	65.00
Sailor, Seamen's Bank For Savings, Sack Over Shoulder, McCoy, 6 In.	125.00
Santa Claus, Robe, Boots, Holding Tree, Cast Iron, Wing, 5 In.	173.00
Santa Claus, Tree, Cast Iron, Hubley, M 61, 5 ⅞ In. ....*illus*	1725.00
Save & Smile Money Box, Black Face, Red Hat Brim, Cast Iron, Chamberlain & Hill, 4 x 4 In. . *illus*	345.00
Sharecropper, Black, Gold, Cast Iron, M 173, 5 ¾ In.	51.00
Shmoo, Li'l Abner Character, Plastic, Blue, 8 x 5 In.	85.00
Soldier, Doughboy, Cast Iron, Grey Iron Casting Co., M 48, 7 In.	230.00
Squirrels, Chipmunks, Tin, Lithographed, c.1925, 4 x 1 x 3 In.	175.00
St. Louis Cardinals, Mascot Bird, Ceramic, Gibbs-Conner, c.1950, 7 ⅝ In. ....*illus*	144.00
Statue Of Liberty, Cast Iron, Painted, Kenton, M 1166, 9 ⅝ In.	230.00
Stork, Standing, Wearing Suit, Clock, Vinyl, Serfin, 1960s, 8 In.	45.00
Tally Ho, Horse's Head In Horseshoe, Chamberlain & Hill, M 535, 4 ½ x 4 ½ In.	68.00
Tower, John Brown Fort, Cast Iron, Japanned, Kyser & Rex, 1890, M 1185, 6 ⅞ In. ....*illus*	575.00
Turkey, Cast Iron, Painted, A.C. Williams, M 585, 4 In.	90.00
Water Wheel, Turns, Cast Iron, Pressed Steel, M 1606, 4 ½ In.	575.00
White City, Barrel, Puzzle No. 3, Electroplated, Paper Label, c.1893, M 916, 5 In.	518.00
Wise Pig, Thrifty, Tan, Yellow Base, Cast Iron, Hubley, M 609, 6 In.	57.00
Zeppelin Airship Dock, Duraluminum, Goodyear, 1930s, 7 ¼ In.	144.00

Bank, Penny, Clown Head, Soft Paste, Sculpted & Painted Features, France, c.1850, 4 In.
$280.00

Theriault's

Bank, Puppo, Black & White, Painted, Cast Iron, Hubley, 5 In.
$57.00

Conestoga Auction Co., Inc.

Bank, Radio, Majestic, Painted, Cast Iron, Steel Back, Arcade, c.1933, M 827, 4 ½ In.
$158.00

Hake's Americana & Collectibles

Bank, Register, Dime, Jackie Robinson, Save & Win, Tin Lithograph, 2 ⅝ x 2 ⅝ In.
$176.00

Wm Morford Antiques

Bank, Safe, Horn Of Plenty, Cast Iron, Nickeled, E.M. Roche Novelty Co., 6 In. $1150.00

Bertoia Auctions

Bank, Santa Claus, Tree, Cast Iron, Hubley, M 61, 5 ⅞ In. $1725.00

Bertoia Auctions

Bank, Save & Smile Money Box, Black Face, Red Hat Brim, Cast Iron, Chamberlain & Hill, 4 x 4 In. $345.00

Bertoia Auctions

Bank, St. Louis Cardinals, Mascot Bird, Ceramic, Gibbs-Conner, c.1950, 7 ⅝ In. $144.00

Hake's Americana & Collectibles

BARBER collectibles range from the popular red and white striped pole that used to be found in front of every shop to the small scissors and tools of the trade. Barber chairs are wanted, especially the older models with elaborate iron trim.

Backbar, Quartersawn Oak, 3 Station, Carved, Mirror Back, 189 x 104 In.	6900.00
Bowl, Birds, Feather, Green, Brown, Yellow, Pierced To Hang, Tin Glaze, Italy, c.1835, 10 ¼ In.	215.00
Cabinet, Wood, 3 Doors, Drawers, Waste Bin, Set Back Shape, Art Deco, c.1935	540.00
Chair, August Kern, B.C.S. St. Louis, Mo., Red Leather, Oak, 26 x 46 x 45 In. ....*illus*	1870.00
Chair, Child's, Horse Head, Painted, Leather Seat, Adjustable, Koken, c.1910, 44 ½ In. ...*illus*	2013.00
Chair, Harley-Davidson Motif, Paidar	48.00
Chair, Koken, Oak, Black Leather, Nickel Trim ....*illus*	8400.00
Chair, Oak, Cast Iron, Leather, Koken	961.00
Pole, Cast Iron, Milk Glass, Koken, Red, White, Blue, 81 In.	1650.00
Pole, Light-Up, Red, White, Blue, Wall Mount, 24 In.	385.00
Pole, Light-Up, Wall Mount, Red, White, Blue, Paidar Co., 38 In.	440.00
Pole, Painted Red, White, Blue, Pine, Turned, c.1900, 72 In.	1116.00
Pole, Pine, Painted, Red & White Stripe, Blue Ball Ends, Indiana, 1930s, 25 ¾ In. ....*illus*	1020.00
Pole, Red, White, Blue Stripes, Gold Round Finial, 63 In.	173.00
Pole, Red, White, Blue, Globe, Rose Supply Co., Wall Mount	396.00
Pole, Wood, Carved, Painted Red, White, Blue, South Carolina, c.1890, 36 In.	2160.00
Pole, Wood, Painted, Red, White Spiral Stripes, Blue Detail, Square Base, 78 x 17 In.	201.00
Pole, Wood, Painted, Red, White Spiral Stripes, Silver Ball Finial, 30 In.	550.00
Pole, Wood, Red, White, Blue, Painted Spiral, 54 ¼ In.	226.00
Pole, Wood, Turned, Paint, Stand, c.1910, 68 x 6 ½ In.	341.00
Pot Lid, Worsley's Saponaceous Shaving Compound, Philadelphia, Black Transfer, c.1870, 3 ⅞ In.	585.00
Sign, Barber Shops Ask For Wildroot, Tin, Embossed, 14 x 39 In.	565.00
Sign, Gibbs, Painted, Red, White, Blue, Porcelain, Flange, 2-Sided, 17 x 24 In.	531.00
Towel Steamer, Hygienic, Nickel Plated, Copper, Brass, Ideal Metal Works	1100.00
Towel Sterilizer, Globe Shape, Nickel Plated, Slide Door, Brass Plate, Theo. A. Kochs & Son, 36 In.	230.00
Vase, Shaving Paper, Green, Ribbed, Tennis Players, White Enamel, Polished Rim, 7 ¾ In.	403.00
Vase, Shaving Paper, Yellow Green, Coin Spot, Yellow, Orange, White Enamel, 7 ¼ In.	115.00

BAROMETERS are used to forecast the weather. Antique barometers with elaborate wooden cases and brass trim are the most desirable. Mercury column barometers are also popular with collectors. It is difficult to find someone to repair a broken one, so be sure your barometer is in working condition.

Banjo, George III, Mahogany, Steel Dial, Inscribed, 1800s, 47 In.	1000.00
Banjo, George III, Scrolled Border, Silver Dials, 40 In.	531.00
Banjo, Louis XVI Style, Bronze, Signed, Gliezes, Painted Flower Garland, Paris, 43 In.	374.00
Banjo, Mahogany, George III, Convex Mirror, Ebonized Surround, 38 ½ x 10 ½ In.	410.00
Banjo, Papier-Mache, Mother-Of-Pearl, Thermometer, Hygrometer, Level Indicator, c.1850, 38 In. *illus*	777.00
Banjo, Rosewood, Internal Mercury & Glass Tube, Dials, England, 1800s, 39 In.	127.00
Banjo, Thermometer, Mahogany Inlay, J. Somalvico & Son, Broken Pediment, England, 42 In.	2124.00
Banjo, Thermometer, Silvered Dial, Scrolled, Ireland, 1800s, 40 ¼ In.	830.00
Black Forest, Carved Lindenwood, Hound's Head, Birds, Enameled Backplate, 1900s, 28 x 12 In.	399.00
Flower, Musical Crest, Gilt, Carved, France, 36 x 21 In.	1476.00
Holosteric, Chelsea, Brass, 4 ¾ In.	147.00
Hydrometer, Fabric Testing, Celluloid Backed, Mahogany Case, Sikes, 8 ¼ In.	236.00
Louis XVI, Giltwood, Carved, Dials, Mirror, Signed Bourrassean Opt, 1772, 38 x 18 In.	936.00
Lyre Shape, Hexagonal Face, Giltwood, France, 1800s, 37 x 20 In.	1464.00
Mahogany Veneer, Inlaid Stick, Thin Bone, Mercury Tube, Brass Finial, F. Amadio, 39 In.	586.00
Mahogany, Convex Mirror, Negretti & Zambra, London, 38 In.	192.00
Mahogany, Regency, Scrolling Broken Arch, Scotland, c.1810, 40 x 11 In.	239.00
Nautical, Ship's, Mahogany, Brass Mounts, Steel Dials, Pivot Ring, Disc Support, 39 x 4 ½ In.	702.00
Stick, A. Abraham & Co., Mahogany, Glass Tube, Tombstone Shape Ivory Plaque, 1800s, 37 In.	1610.00
Stick, Georgian, Mahogany, Inlays, Broken Pediment, Silver Register, Scotland, 1800s, 38 In.	563.00
Stick, Griffin & George, Ltd., Brass, Mahogany Panel, c.1900, 43 In.	748.00
Stick, Mahogany, Arched Top, Ivory Face, Incised Standard, Victorian, 36 ½ x 3 ½ In.	374.00
Stick, Mahogany, Engraved Dial, Octagonal Base, A. Fantoine, 36 ½ x 4 ½ In.	351.00
Stick, Phil L. O'Grady Harness Horse Goods, Standard Thermometer & Barometer Mfg., 3 x 8 ¼ In.	295.00
Stick, Regency, Mahogany, Silvered Register, England, 1800s, 38 In.	1067.00
Stick, Thermometer, Brass, White Metal, Mahogany Plaque, Henry J. Green, N.Y., 1800s, 45 In.	177.00
Stick, Thermometer, Mother-Of-Pearl Knob, Arched Ivory Scale, Rosewood, 1800s, 38 In.	499.00
Stick, Thermometer, Silvered Dial, Pitched Pediment, Brass Finial, 39 In.	2607.00
Stick, Thermometer, Turned Maple, Acorn Finial, Curved Glass Cover, c.1860, 39 In.	652.00
Stick, Thermometer, Walnut, Victorian, Black Forest, Tree Trunk Shape, Leaves, c.1865, 45 ½ In.	1150.00

Stick, Walnut, Opaline Face, Signed, J.W., Philadelphia, c.1885, 36 ¾ x 4 ⅜ In. .... *illus*	1599.00
Thermometer, Empire Style, Wood, Gilt Eagle, Pendant Base, 1800s, 36 x 10 In......................	390.00
Thermometer, Hydrometer, Convex Round Mirror, Etched, L. Balerna, 1800s, 39 In.	266.00
Thermometer, Mahogany, Eglomise Panels, Eagle, Ball Finial, A. Leeuwarded, Holland, 51 x 8 In.	644.00
Thermometer, Turned Frame, Half Circle Top, Marked, D.R.G.M., 22 In.	345.00
Thermometer, Wheel, Gilt, Ebonized, Canted Top, Acorn Finial, Round Dial, France, 1700s, 42 In.	300.00
Walnut, France, Carved Volutes, Scrolls, France, 1800s, 27 x 11 In.	549.00
Wheel, Abraham & Co., Mahogany, Engraved Silvered Dial, Thermometer, Empire Case, 40 In. ...*illus*	1185.00
Wheel, Gilt Wood, Ribbon Shape Crest, Long Neck, Round Dial, Carved Leaves, 1900s, 41 In..	413.00
Wheel, Mahogany, Scrolling Pediment, Long Neck, 38 ¼ In.	325.00
Wheel, Mahogany, Veneer, Broken Arch Pediment, Brass Finial, c.1820, 39 x 10 In.	748.00
Wheel, Mahogany, Victorian, String Inlay, Shell, Flowers, Broken Arch Pediment, 1800s, 39 In.	345.00
Wheel, Thermometer, Walnut, Painted, Leafy Vine Border, England, 1800s, 37 In.	245.00
Wood, Glass, Signed Selon Toricelli, France, 39 ½ x 5 ½ In.	113.00

BASALT is a special type of ceramic invented by Josiah Wedgwood in the eighteenth century. It is a fine-grained, unglazed stoneware. Some pieces are listed in that section. The most common type is black, but many other colors were made. It was made by many factories. Some pieces are listed in the Wedgwood section.

Bowl, Fruit, Footed, Drapery Swags, Striped Engine Turned Body, Black, 1800s, 9 In. Diam.....	948.00
Candlestick, Triton, Seated, Among Rocks, Holding Cornucopia Sconce, Black, c.1800, 11 In.	474.00
Ewer, Wine, Bacchus, Seated, Holding Horns Of Ram, Grapevine Festoons, Black, 1800s, 15 In.	674.00
Figurine, Poodle, Glass Eyes, Black, c.1913, 3 In.	95.00
Jardiniere, Flower Border, Fruiting Grapevine Festoons, Lion Masks, Rings, Black, c.1900, 7 In.	415.00
Jug, Club, Enameled, Flowers, Leaves, Black, 1800s, 6 In...................................	356.00
Plaque, Rectangular, Hercules, Scantily Clad, Black, 1800s, 3 x 8 In.	1541.00
Tazza, Black, Marble Mosaic Inlaid Band, Pedestal Base, 8 ½ x 13 In.	173.00
Teapot, Cover, Squat Shape, Enamel Flower Sprays, Black, Late 1800s, 2 In.	326.00
Vase, Leaf Design, Trumpet Shape, Black, 1800s, 11 In...................................	326.00

BASEBALL COLLECTIBLES *are in the Sports category, except for baseball cards, which are listed under Baseball in the Card category.*

BASKETS of all types are popular with collectors. American Indian, Japanese, African, Shaker, and many other kinds of baskets can be found. Of course, baskets are still being made, so the collector must learn to tell the age and style of the basket to determine the value.

Berry, White Oak Splint, Red Dyed Bands, 19th Century, U.S.A., 5 x 6 ½ In.	367.00
Birch Bark, Quills, Moose On Lid, 5 x 2 ¼ In. ....*illus*	165.00
Buttocks, Ash Handle, Multicolor Stain, 11 ½ x 12 ½ In...	113.00
Buttocks, Blue Over Red Paint, Spoke Woven, Collar, Hoop Handle, 10 x 11 In.	254.00
Buttocks, Splint, Oak, Painted, Band Style, Handle, c.1880, 3 ½ x 3 ¾ In.	660.00
Carrying, Pierced Wood, Oval, Waisted, Handles, Peaches, Clouds, Wood Slats, Gilt Band, 18 In.	110.00
Carved Notched Handle, Square Bottom, Round Rim, Oak, 12 x 14 In.	28.00
Coil, Round, Stylized Animal & Bird Design, Strap Handle, 9 In................................	50.00
Crown Of Thorns, Puzzle Pieces Of Wood, Openwork, Handles, 4 ¾ x 13 In.	83.00
Feather, Splint, Ash, Oval, Cover, Cutouts For Handles, Painted White, c.1900, 24 x 15 In........	196.00
Feather, Woven, Bulbous, Vase Shape, Flared Rim, Brown Stain, 1800s, 27 ½ x 13 In.	288.00
Field, Oak, Square Bottom, Cutout Handles, Twisted Splint Foot, Oval, 12 x 29 In.	124.00
Field, Splint, Oak, Wrapped Rim, Cutout Handles, Square Bottom, Round Rim, 11 x 21 In.	57.00
Gathering, Black Ash, Wrapped Round Rim, Squared Bottom, Hoop Handle, c.1845, 9 x 12 ½ In.	3627.00
Gathering, Splint, Oak, Open Weave, Bentwood Handles, 11 ¾ x 23 In...................................	47.00
Gathering, Splint, Oak, Oval, Handle, 1880s, 12 ½ x 17 In...	193.00
Gathering, Splint, Oak, Round, Notched Handle, Wrapped Foot Ring, 10 x 11 In....................	147.00
Gathering, Splint, Oak, Tight Weave, Bentwood Handles, 13 ½ x 23 In.	106.00
Gathering, Splint, Round, Swing Handle, Woven Design, 1800s, 16 In............................	326.00
Gathering, Splint, White Oak, Oblong, Oval Rim, High Arch Handle, Varnished, 12 x 6 In......	207.00
Hamper, Rye Straw, Bentwood Handles, Lid, Turned Wood Finial, 1800s, 23 x 27 In.	8888.00
Ikebana, Bamboo, Handle, Japan, 7 ½ x 18 In.	360.00
Ikebana, Double Gourd, Root Wood Base, Bentwood Stand, Japan, 11 ¾ x 18 In. ....*illus*	563.00
Key, Leather, Plain Rim, Stitched, Arched Handle, Oblong, Virginia, 3 x 4 ½ In.................	374.00
Melon Shape, Splint, Oak, Oval, Spoke Woven Hoop Handle, 9 x 13 In.	147.00
Nantucket, Curved, Swing Handle, E. Geisner, c.1890, 3 x 6 ½ In.	518.00
Nantucket, Oval, Swinging Oak Handle, Signed, Jose Formoso, c.1950, 8 x 14 In.................	3450.00
Nantucket, Purse, Lightship, Oval, Lid, Eagle, Ivory Latch, Signed, Jose Formoso, 1971, 5 x 9 In.	5175.00
Nantucket, Round Swing Handle, Inscribed Marion C. Robbins, 1910, 4 x 7 ¼ In.	633.00

Bank, Tower, John Brown Fort, Cast Iron, Japanned, Kyser & Rex, 1890, M 1185, 6 ⅞ In.
$575.00

Bertoia Auctions

Barber, Chair, August Kern, B.C.S. St. Louis, Mo., Red Leather, Oak, 26 x 46 x 45 In.
$1870.00

Showtime Auction Services

Barber, Chair, Child's, Horse Head, Painted, Leather Seat, Adjustable, Koken, c.1910, 44 ½ In.
$2013.00

James D. Julia Inc.

B

Barber, Chair, Koken, Oak, Black Leather, Nickel Trim
$8400.00

Victorian Casino Antique Auction

Barber, Pole, Pine, Painted, Red & White Stripe, Blue Ball Ends, Indiana, 1930s, 25 ¾ In.
$1020.00

Cowan's Auctions

Nantucket, Round, Swing Handle, F. Sylvaro, c.1910, 3 ½ x 6 ½ In.	920.00
Nantucket, Round, Wrapped Rim, Round, Handle, c.1900, 9 In.	900.00
Nantucket, Turned Wood Bottom, Square Swing Handle, c.1905, 7 x 12 ¾ In.	863.00
Nantucket, Woven, Nut Brown Patina, Arched Handle, 8 ½ x 6 ½ In.	690.00
Oval, Woven Lid, 2 Swinging Bail Handles, c.1900, 19 x 14 In.	52.00
Picnic, Oak, Slat, Hinged Lid, Vintage, 14 x 9 x 7 In.	85.00
Rectangular, Painted, Green Weave, Square Handle, c.1900, 19 In.	29.00
River Cane, Tricolor, Oak Splint Handle, Square, 1900s, 8 ¾ In.	275.00
Rush Covered, Tight Weave, Reds, Yellows, Lid, Knob, 8 x 8 ½ In.	316.00
Rye, Openwork Border, Penn., 1800s, 3 ½ x 10 ¾ In.	237.00
Splint, Blue Paint, Woven, Deep Round, Flared Rim, Carved Upright Handle, Late 1800s, 15 In.	368.00
Splint, Circular, Woven, Bail Bentwood Handle, c.1900, 14 In.	35.00
Splint, Lid, Square, Weaved, Red Banding, New England, 10 x 14 In.	69.00
Splint, Oak, Bentwood Handle, Mary Causby, North Carolina, 8 ¼ In.	250.00
Splint, Oak, Dark Patina, Bentwood Frame, Shelton Sisters, North Carolina, c.1890, 6 In.	1800.00
Splint, Oak, Double Rim, Wire Handle Ears, Bail Handle, Disc Base, Painted, 6 ¼ x 10 In. ....*illus*	848.00
Splint, Oak, Oval, Round, c.1900, 3 ¾ In.	121.00
Splint, Oak, Paint, 1800s, 17 x 19 In.	237.00
Splint, Oak, Round, Carved Notched Handle, 12 x 14 In.	68.00
Splint, White Oak, Double Rim, Natural Finish, Green Splints, c.1910, 9 x 17 In.	104.00
Splint, White Oak, Painted Blue, Yellow, 2 Arched Handles, Page Co., Va., c.1880, 2 x 5 In.	3105.00
Splint, White Oak, Ribbed, Elongated Boat Shape, Ear Handles, Banded, Yellow, Black, 8 x 22 In.	196.00
Splint, White Oak, Round, Handles, Painted, Blue, Yellow Stripes, 2 x 5 In.	3105.00
Splint, Woven Oak, Yellow Patina, Bentwood Frame, Shelton Sister, North Carolina, c.1890, 6 In.	2400.00
Splint, Woven, Wool-Gathering, Footed, Round Over Square Shape, Handholds, 1800s, 19 x 24 In.	368.00
Tray, Sea Grass, Star, Round, c.1955, 14 In.	121.00
Trinket, Lid, Makah, Multicolor, Saudi Arabia, 4 x 3 ¾ In.	173.00
Twined, Lid, Natural, Geometric Design, Red, Olive, Purple Embroidery, Aleutian, 8 In. ...*illus*	1135.00
Utility, Oak Splint & Handle, Yellow Paint, 10 x 19 In.	452.00
Utility, Oak, Tapered Notch Carved Handle, 12 x 21 In.	68.00
Utility, Splint, Ash, Rectangular, Fixed Handle, 15 x 27 In.	45.00
Wedding, 3 Tiers, Cover, Angled Handle, Chinese, 26 In.	191.00
Wood Lathes, Rootwood Handle, Japan, c.1900, 18 ½ x 18 In.	267.00

BATCHELDER products are made from California clay. Ernest Batchelder established a tile studio in Pasadena, California, in 1909. He went into partnership with Frederick Brown in 1912 and the company became Batchelder and Brown. In 1920 he built a larger factory with a new partner. The Batchelder-Wilson Company made all types of architectural tiles, garden pots, and bookends. The plant closed in 1932. In 1936 Batchelder opened Batchelder Ceramics, also in Pasadena, and made bowls, vases, and earthenware pots. He retired in 1951 and died in 1957. Pieces are marked *Batchelder Pasadena* or *Batchelder Los Angeles*.

BATCHELDER LOS ANGELES

Bowl, Tan Glaze, Muted Green, Pasadena, c.1915, 15 x 1 In.	51.00
Tile, Bird, Diamond Outline, Heart Shape Leaves, Farmhouse, Brown, Blue, 3 x 3 In.	95.00
Tile, Birds, Facing Each Other, Diamond, Corner Vines, Brown, Blue, 3 x 3 In.	125.00
Tile, Boat, River, Tan, Blue, Wood Frame, Marked, 9 In.	157.00
Tile, Dog, Tree, Brown, Blue, c.1920, 5 x 5 In.	355.00
Tile, Man Riding Prancing Horse, Cape, Brown, Blue, c.1920, 3 x 3 In.	95.00
Tile, Prancing Buck, 3-Line Circle, Gray, 1920s, 5 x 5 In.	165.00
Tile, Sunflower, Mythical Creatures, Brown, Blue, 3 x 3 In.	65.00
Tile, Trees, Rolling Hills, Building, Reddish Brown, Blue, 3 x 3 In.	125.00
Tile, Tulip, Cartouche, Brown, Blue, c.1920, 5 x 5 In.	245.00
Tile, Urn, 3 Flowers, Checked Ground, Self-Framed Edge, Tan, 5 x 5 In.	180.00

BATMAN and Robin are characters from a comic strip by Bob Kane that started in 1939. In 1966, the characters became part of a popular television series. There have been radio and movie serials that featured the pair. The first full-length movie was made in 1989.

Action Figure, Batgirl, Removable Boots, Belt, Cowl & Cape, Mego Super Gals, 1973, 8 In.	880.00
Action Figure, Batman, Flex-A-Toy, On Card, Wonder Toys, 1966, 7 ½ In.	115.00
Action Figure, Batman, Posable, 1st Issue, Kresge Sticker, Card, Mego, 1973, 8 In.	1551.00
Action Figure, Batman, Superhero Costume, Shorts, Cape, Boots, Blister Card, Mego, 1973, 8 In.	1551.00
Action Figure, Catwoman, Suit With Tail, Removable Boots, Gloves, Mego Super Gals, 1973, 8 In.	2349.00
Action Figure, Joker, Posable, 1st Issue, Kresge Sticker, Card, Mego, 1973, 8 In.	2021.00
Action Figure, Penguin, Posable, Mego, Box, 1973, 8 In.	127.00
Action Figure, Riddler, Posable, Mego, Box, 1973, 8 In.	441.00
Action Figure, Robin, Posable, On Card, Mego, 1st Issue, Kresge Sticker, 1973, 8 In.	1606.00

Action Watch, Bat Shape Case, Plastic, Fabric Band, Gilbert, Plastic Case, 1966, 3 In.	538.00
Bank, Painted, National Periodical Publications, 1966, 7 In.	20.00
Cape, Action Boy Robin, Yellow, Buckle, Belt, Strap, Ideal, 1967	150.00
Car, Black Night, Batman, Robin, Battery Operated, Box, Japan, 11 ½ In.	1035.00
Doll, Removable Mask, Emblem On Front, Cape, Mego, 1972	100.00
Game, Batman & Robin Marble Maze, Tray, 2 Metal Balls, Box, Hasbro, 1966, 12 x 12 In.	443.00
Mask Menu, Paper, Unused Sample, Yogg & Co., 1968, 10 x 14 In.	115.00
Model Kit, Penguin, Sealed Box, NPP Inc., 13 x 5 In.	506.00
Mug, Batman, Robin, White, Red Image, Fire-King, 1960s	28.00
Pin, Enamel, Batman, Robin, Multicolor, c.1966, 3 x 1 ¼ & 2 ½ x 1 ½ In.	195.00
Poster, Movie, Adam West, Burt Ward, 20th Century Fox, 1966, 27 x 41 In.	310.00
Toy, Batman Climbing Figure, Cable, Glow-In-Dark Eyes & Spotlight, Remco, Box, 9 In.	221.00
Toy, Boy Robin's Green Gloves, Captain Action Figure, 1967	75.00
Toy, Helicopter, Plastic, Chinook Style, Dual Blade, Irwin, c.1966, 6 x 24 In.	173.00
Toy, Helmet & Cape Set, Molded Plastic, Vinyl, Batsymbol, Ideal, Box, 1966, 11 ½ In.	348.00
Toy, Jeep, Tin, Friction, Ichimura, Japan, c.1966, 5 In.	209.00
Toy, Pop Gun & Holster Set, Tin Gun, Lithograph, Vinyl, Aoshin Shoten, Japan, c.1966	3479.00
Toy, Radio Super-Micro Secret Bat With Earphone, Case, Display Box, Topp, 1966, 4 x 6 In.	1725.00
Toy, Top, Tin Lithograph, Plastic Stem, Japan, c.1966, 2 ½ In.	86.00
TV Magazine, Feb. 20-26, 1966, Adam West As Batman On Cover, Article, 7 ¼ In.	86.00

BATTERSEA enamels, which are enamels painted on copper, were made in the Battersea district of London from about 1750 to 1756. Many similar enamels are mistakenly called Battersea.

Box, Heart, Enameled, Hinged Lid, Love Birds, Take This For A Kiss, 1 ½ x 2 ½ In.	144.00
Box, Leopard, On Hunter, Yellow, Black, Green Ground, Metal Clasp, Oval, c.1750, 4 x 3 In.	2750.00
Card Stand, Enamel, Multicolor, Romantic Couple, Child, Rural Scene, c.1800, 4 x 5 In.	575.00
Scent Bottle, Bust Of Fashionable Woman, Flowers, White, Gold Trim, Flask, 3 ¼ In.	259.00
Snuffbox, Hound Head, 1 ¾ In.	504.00
Snuffbox, Hound Head, Pug, Polished Stone Head, 1800s, 2 ¾ In.	770.00

BAUER pottery is a California-made ware. J.A. Bauer bought Paducah Pottery in Paducah, Kentucky, in 1885. He moved the pottery to Los Angeles, California, in 1909. The company made art pottery after 1912 and introduced dinnerware marked *Bauer* in 1930. The factory went out of business in 1962 and the molds were destroyed. Since 1998, a new company, Bauer Pottery Company of Los Angeles, has been making Bauer pottery using molds made from original Bauer pieces. The pottery is now made in Highland, California. Pieces are marked *Bauer Pottery 2000 Highland USA.* Original pieces of Bauer pottery are listed here. See also the Russel Wright category.

Cal-Art, Jardiniere, Ivory, 6 ½ x 8 ¼ In.	125.00
Cal-Art, Planter, Oval, White, 15 x 9 x 3 In.	31.00
Cal-Art, Planter, Swan Shape, White, 6 x 4 x 3 In.	40.00
Candlestick, Green, Handle, Matt Carlton, 3 ¾ In.	91.00
Chop Plate, Pale Green, 12 ¾ In.	35.00
Flower Bowl, Glossy Green, 2 x 6 In.	175.00
Kitchenware, Batter Bowl, Brown, Handle, Spout, 11 ¾ In.	80.00
Kitchenware, Mixing Bowl, No. 18, Brown Gloss	55.00
Kitchenware, Mixing Bowl, No. 24, Green	95.00
Kitchenware, Mixing Bowl, No. 24, Ivory Gloss	40.00
Ring, Cookie Jar, Lime Green, 1940s, 9 ½ In.	28.00
Ring, Cookie Jar, Pink, 9 ½ In.	99.00
Ring, Cup & Saucer, Burgundy	75.00
Ring, Cup & Saucer, Yellow	20.00
Ring, Pitcher, Yellow, Banded, 4 ½ In.	17.00
Ring, Plate, Jade, Green, 1940s, 9 ½ In.	160.00
Ring, Sherbet, Cobalt Blue, Footed	125.00
Ring, Vase, Beehive, Yellow, 8 x 8 In.	40.00
Ring, Vase, Blue Shoulder, 9 ¾ In.	18.00
Ring, Vase, Cobalt Blue, Flared, Footed, Bud, 5 ½ In.	350.00
Ring, Vase, Red, 7 In.	40.00
Strawberry Pot, 8-Cup, Yellow, 9 ¼ In.	295.00
Vase, Fan Shape, Blue, Footed, 5 ¾ In.	25.00
Vase, Midcentury Modern, Muted Yellow, Signed, 5 In.	299.00
Vase, Swirled Ribs, Off-White, 6 In.	30.00
Vase, Yellow Semi High Glaze, Monumental Shape, Handles, 10 x 18 In.	1080.00

BAUER

B

Barometer, Banjo, Papier-Mache, Mother-Of-Pearl, Thermometer, Hygrometer, Level Indicator, c.1850, 38 In.
$777.00

Neal Auction Co.

Barometer, Stick, Walnut, Opaline Face, Signed, J.W., Philadelphia, c.1885, 36 ¾ x 4 ⅜ In.
$1599.00

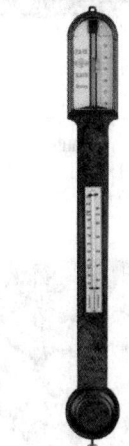

New Orleans Auction Galleries, Inc.

Barometer, Wheel, Abraham & Co., Mahogany, Engraved Silvered Dial, Thermometer, Empire Case, 40 In.
$1185.00

Skinner, Inc.

B

Basket, Birch Bark, Quills, Moose On Lid, 5 x 2 ¼ In.
$165.00

Old Barn Auction

Basket, Ikebana, Double Gourd, Root Wood Base, Bentwood Stand, Japan, 11 ¾ x 18 In.
$563.00

Skinner, Inc.

Basket, Splint, Oak, Double Rim, Wire Handle Ears, Bail Handle, Disc Base, Painted, 6 ¼ x 10 In.
$848.00

Conestoga Auction Co., Inc.

Basket, Twined, Lid, Natural, Geometric Design, Red, Olive, Purple Embroidery, Aleutian, 8 In.
$1135.00

Neal Auction Co.

BAVARIA is a region in Europe where many types of porcelain were made. In the nineteenth century, the mark often included the word *Bavaria*. After 1871, the words *Bavaria, Germany*, were used. Listed here are pieces that include the name *Bavaria* in some form, but major porcelain makers, such as Rosenthal, are listed in their own categories.

Bowl, Red Currants, Pearlized Luster Interior, Oval, Footed, Signed Polehow, 12 ½ In.	150.00
Charger, Portrait, Tiger, Cream, Signed Constance Pisha, 12 In.	200.00
Cheese Dish, Cover, Painted, Flowers, Marked, c.1880, 6 x 7 In.	40.00
Plate, Black Knight, Hohenberg Studios, Cobalt, Gilt Border, Flowers, 10 ½ In., 12 Piece	316.00
Plate, Raised Silver Border, Neoclassical Pattern, Ivory Ground, c.1945, 10 ¾ In., 12 Piece	799.00
Vase, Pink, Green, Pink Rose, Oval, Signed F. Wood, 10 ¾ In.	40.00

BEADED BAGS *are included in the Purse category.*

BEATLES collectors search for any items picturing the four members of the famous music group or any of their recordings. Because these items are so new, the condition is very important and top prices are paid only for items in mint condition. The Beatles first appeared on American network television in 1964. The group disbanded in 1971. Ringo Starr and Paul McCartney are still performing. John Lennon died in 1980. George Harrison died in 2001.

Bank Set, John, Paul, George, Ringo, Yellow Submarine, Pride Creations, 1968, 7 ¾ In., 4 Piece *. illus*	1668.00
Binder, Blue Vinyl, Portrait, Facsimile Signatures, 3-Ring, c.1964, 11 x 9 ½ In.	190.00
Button, I'm A Beatles Fan, Headshots, Red & White Ground, Lithograph, 4 In.	21.00
Clock, Alarm, Yellow Submarine, Metal, Round, Luminous Hands, 2 Bells, Sheffield, 4 In.	1113.00
Figure Set, Plastic, Instruments, Remco, 1964, 6 ½ In., 4 Piece	708.00
Figurine, Yellow Submarine, Cast Porcelain, Painted, Gartlan, U.S.A., Box, 11 Piece	149.00
Guitar, New Beat, Red Plastic, Photograph, Cardboard Box, Selcol, England, 1964, 33 In.	460.00
Handbill, Pete Best Autograph, Cavern Club Photo, 8 ½ x 11 In.	62.00
Invitation, Last American Concert, Paramount Theater, N.Y., Sept. 20, 1964, 5 x 7 In.	3078.00
Lunch Box, Brunch Bag, Blue Vinyl, Zipper, Portraits, Thermos, Aladdin, 1965, 4 x 8 x 8 In.	431.00
Lunch Box, Embossed Metal, Blue, Graphics, Thermos, Aladdin, 1965, 6 ½ x 8 In.	563.00
Overnight Case, Black Vinyl, White Portraits, Zipper, Round, Air Flite, 1964, 12 x 13 x 5 In.	325.00
Phonograph, Photographs On Cover, 4 Speeds, 1964, 10 x 17 x 6 In.	2910.00
Poster, John Lennon, At Piano, It's Here, Black & White, Red Letters, 1970, 32 x 22 In.	425.00
Poster, John Lennon, Yoko, Nude, Censored, Spread Happiness To The World, 1970, 29 x 23 In.	130.00
Poster, Movie, A Hard Day's Night, Half Photos, 1964, 27 x 41 In.	657.00 to 759.00
Program, Concert Tour, 4 Singers Color Cover, 32 Black & White Pages, 1964, 12 x 12 In.	57.00
Program, Last American Concert, Paramount Theater, N.Y., Sept. 20, 1964, 10 In.	1670.00
Purse, Clutch Bag, Tan Vinyl, Black Portraits, Letters, Cutout Handle, Brass Trim, 10 In.	430.00
Record Case, 45 RPM, Red Textured Paper Over Cardboard, Hinged Lid, 1964, 8 In.	173.00
Record Case, Disk-Go, 45 RPM, Brown Plastic, Round, String Tag, 1966, 8 ½ x 7 ½ In.	443.00
Record Case, LP, Photograph, Green Textured Paper Over Cardboard, Hinged Lid, 1964	230.00
Record, 1st Album, Capital Record, LP, c.1962	45.00
Record, Everywhere It's Christmas, 33 ⅓ RPM	200.00
Record, Help, Capital Record, LP Mono, 1965	70.00
Record, Pantomime, Premium To Fan Club Members, Flex-Disc, 33 ⅓ RPM, 1966	150.00
Record, Revolver, Capital EMI Record, LP Mono	70.00
Schoolbag, Beige Vinyl Coated Cardboard, Image Of All 4, Burnel Ltd., 1964, 12 x 9 In.	885.00
Soaky Bottle, Mild!, Wild!, Figural, Paul & Guitar, Ringo & Drum, Box, 1965, 7 In., 2 Piece	459.00
Tape, Sgt. Pepper, Reel To Reel, 4 Track, Box, 1968	40.00
Ticket Stub, D.C. Stadium, Aug. 15, 1966, Upper Deck, Photograph, 3 ¼ In.	949.00
Ticket Stub, Green, St. Louis Concert, August 21, 1966, 2 x 3 ½ In.	429.00
Ticket Stub, White, Back To School Concert, Houston, August 19, 1965, 3 x 4 ⅜ In.	192.00
Ticket, Concert, Indiana State Fair, September 3, 1964, Pink, Pictures	590.00
Tin, With The Beatles Talc, Tin Lithograph, Plastic Stopper, Margo Of Mayfair, 1964, 16 Oz.	348.00
Toy, Yellow Submarine, Corgi, Box, 1967	495.00

BEEHIVE, Austria, or Beehive, Vienna, are terms used in English-speaking countries to refer to the many types of decorated porcelain bearing a mark that looks like a beehive. The mark is actually a shield, viewed upside down. It was first used in 1744 by the Royal Porcelain Manufactory of Vienna. The firm made what collectors call Royal Vienna porcelains until it closed in 1864. Many other German, Austrian, and Japanese factories have reproduced Royal Vienna wares, complete with the original shield or beehive mark. This listing includes the expensive, original Royal Vienna porcelains and many other types of beehive porcelain. The Royal Vienna pieces include that name in the description.

Bowl, Portrait, Dancers, Pan, Man With Jug, Women, Red, Marked, Royal Vienna, c.1880, 9 ½ In.	345.00
Charger, 2 Women, Man, Multicolor, Gilt, Signed, Ed. Borschneider, 11 ½ In. Diam.	119.00

Item	Price
Compote, Round, Pedestal, Enameled, Birds, Leaves, White, Blue, Green, Orange, Gold, 9 x 5 In.	207.00
Cup, Saucer, Cover, Maroon Ground, Gilding, Apollo & Herse, Marked, 1800s, 3 ⅜ In.	504.00
Dresser Box, Lid, Flowers, Paint, Signed, R. Coulory, Royal Vienna, 10 ¾ x 5 ¼ In.	249.00
Ewer, Lavender, Yellow, Brown, Pink Roses, Gold Highlights, Pedestal, Royal Vienna, 9 ½ In.	100.00
Ewer, Reclining Woman & Cherubs In Cartouche, Cobalt Blue, Gilt, 9 In.	863.00
Ewer, Yellow, Brown, Daisies, Handles, Presentation, Royal Vienna, 1903, 8 ¼ In.	125.00
Fernery, Brown, Yellow, Pink Roses, Gold Highlights, Royal Vienna, 4 x 8 ½ In.	150.00
Figurine, Seminude Woman & Child, Birds, E.W., Bohemian, Royal Vienna, c.1870, 21 ½ In.	1464.00
Figurine, Seminude Woman, Standing, Dog, Pink, Green Robes, Impressed Vienna, 5 ½ In.	173.00
Plate, Emporer Henry IV, Leopold IV Of Austria, Soldiers, Gold Trim, Royal Vienna, 9 ½ In.	1121.00
Plate, Lisette, Young Woman, Candle, Royal Vienna, c.1895, 10 In.	748.00
Plate, Luna, Woman, Blond Hair, Pink Flowers, Green & Red Border, Royal Vienna, 10 In.	590.00
Plate, White Ground, Flower Bouquets, Gold Scalloped Rim, Royal Vienna, c.1800, 10 In., Pair	84.00
Plate, Young Maiden, Strumming Harp, Flowers In Hair, Leaves & Scroll Border, 9 ½ In.	1955.00
Urn, Classical Woman, Landscape, Blue Ground, Gilt, Beading, Royal Vienna, 11 In., Pair	595.00
Urn, Cobalt Blue Glaze, Gilt, Figures, Woodland Scene, 2 High Handles, Square Base, 1900s, 11 In.	110.00
Urn, Cover, Allegorical Scenes, Cobalt Ground, Gilt Highlights, Vienna, 38 In., Pair	2520.00
Urn, Cover, Classical Heaven Scene, Gold Ground, Cobalt Blue, Mark, Royal Vienna, 20 ½ In.	748.00
Urn, Cover, Converted To Lamp, Handles, Royal Vienna, 15 In.	360.00
Urn, Cover, Courting Scene, Maid Scenes, Handles, Square Stepped Base, Royal Vienna, 17 ½ In.	144.00
Urn, Cover, Dome, Acorn Finial, 2 Handles, Socle Foot, Ruby, Gilt, Nude Women, 1800s, 9 In., Pair	1900.00
Urn, Cover, Painted, Diana Bathing, Handles, C. Forster, Royal Vienna, 8 x 4 In.	708.00
Urn, Rectangular, 2 Handles, Romanesque Life, Gold Scrolling, Royal Vienna, 31 In.	500.00
Vase, Blue & Purple, Medallion Of Woman, Cylindrical, Marked, Royal Vienna, 6 In.	175.00
Vase, Bottle, Cupid & Venus, Blue Beehive Mark, Royal Vienna, 13 ¼ In.	115.00
Vase, Cobalt Blue Ground, Gilt Highlights, Figures, Bottle Shape, 1900s, 6 In.	148.00
Vase, Cover, Gilded Handles, Square Base, Spring, Autumn, Putti, Marked, 1800s, 30 In.	7500.00
Vase, Cover, Triumph Of Venus & Aurora, Hand Painted, Gilt, Marked, 1800s, 17 ½ In. *...illus*	919.00
Vase, Grecian Maiden, Sitting On Terrace, Cherubs, Gold Trim, Footed, Cylindrical, 7 In.	978.00
Vase, Outdoor Scenes, Gilt Handles, Multicolor, Royal Vienna, 10 x 5 ¾ In.	173.00
Vase, Portrait, Burgundy Ground, White Enamel, Gilt Flower Garlands, Cupid, Bow, Signed, 10 In.	424.00
Vase, Portrait, Woman, Gold Flowers, Brown Ground, Marked, Royal Vienna, 1809, 3 ¼ In.	575.00
Vase, Woman, Laurel Leaf Wreath, Burgundy, Gilt Trim, Handle, Marked, c.1900, 11 In. *...illus*	413.00

BEER BOTTLES *are listed in the Bottle category under Beer.*

BEER CANS are a twentieth-century idea. Beer was sold in kegs or returnable bottles until 1934. The first patent for a can was issued to the American Can Company in September of that year, and Gotfried Kruger Brewing Company, Newark, New Jersey, was the first to use the can. The cone-top can was first made in 1935, the aluminum pop-top in 1962. Collectors should look for cans in good condition, with no dents or rust. Serious collectors prefer cans that have been opened from the bottom.

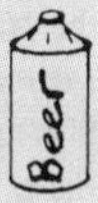

Item	Price
Alpine Lager, Blue, White, Jos. Huber Brewing Co.	7.50
Bock Beer, Yellow, Brown, Orange, 12 Oz.	6.00
Breunig's Lager, Blue, Gold, Rice Lake Brewing Co., 12 Oz.	5.00
Breunig's Lager, Flat Top, Rice Lake Brewing Co., Wis., 12 Oz.	15.00
Coors, Pull Top, Gold, Red Ribbon, Waterfall, Tigers, 12 Oz.	3.00
Falstaff Beer, Falstaff Brewing Co., 14 Oz.	15.00
Falstaff, Brown, Gold, 14 Oz.	15.00
Grain Belt Bock Beer, Grain Belt Breweries, Minn., 12 Oz.	6.00
Grain Belt Special Beer, Cone Top, 1940s, 6 In.	40.00
Grain Belt, Cone Top, Minneapolis Brewing Co., 6 In.	65.00
J.R. Beer, Dallas TV Wearing Character, Pearl Brewing Co., San Antonio, Texas, 1980	5.00
Premium Grain Belt, Cone Top, Minneapolis Brewing Co., 6 In.	65.00
Rhinelander, Pull Tab, Joseph Huber Brewing Co.	6.00
Schell's Beer, Flat Top, Schell Brewing Co., New Ulm, Minn., 12 Oz.	15.00
Schell's, It's A Grand Old Beer, 12 Oz.	15.00
Schmidt Beer, Tab Top, Lassie, Guarding Sheep, Jacob Schmidt, Minn., 12 Oz.	10.00
Schmidt, Dog, Flock Of Sheep, Valley, Pull Tab, 12 Oz.	10.00
Tennent's Girls Beer, Susan On Parade, Scotland, 15 ½ In.	12.50
Tennent's Girls Beer, Vicky In The Woods, Scotland, 15 ½ In.	12.50
Tennent's Girls, Flat Top, Susan On Parade, Scotland, 15 ½ In.	13.00
Tennent's Girls, Flat Top, Vicky In The Woods, 15 ½ In.	13.00
Walter's Beer, Flat Top, 12 Oz.	15.00
Walter's Beer, Red, White, 12 Oz.	15.00

Beatles, Bank Set, John, Paul, George, Ringo, Yellow Submarine, Pride Creations, 1968, 7 ¾ In., 4 Piece $1668.00

Hake's Americana & Collectibles

Beehive, Vase, Cover, Triumph Of Venus & Aurora, Hand Painted, Gilt, Marked, 1800s, 17 ½ In. $919.00

Skinner, Inc.

Beehive, Vase, Woman, Laurel Leaf Wreath, Burgundy, Gilt Trim, Handle, Marked, c.1900, 11 In. $413.00

Brunk Auctions

Bell, Cast Iron, Nickel Plate, Figure Turning Ship's Wheel, Footed Base, Deponirt, 7 ½ In. $354.00

Showtime Auction Services

Bell, Cast Iron, School, Labeled Steel Alloy School Bell, Clapper, Wheel, Wooden Base, c.1850
$1195.00

Neal Auction Co.

Bell, Hotel, Snail, Figural, Metal, Windup, Push Button For Long Ring, 2 ½ x 4 ⅝ In.
$633.00

Wm Morford Antiques

Bennington, Bottle, Toby On Barrel, Impressed, Lyman Fenton & Co., 1849, 10 ¾ In.
$830.00

Skinner, Inc.

Bennington, Figurine, Dog, Poodle, Basket In Mouth, Mottled Brown & Yellow Glaze, c.1850, 8 ½ x 9 ½ In.
$450.00

DuMouchelles Art Gallery

BELL collectors collect all types of bells. Favorites include glass bells, figural bells, school bells, and cowbells. Bells have been made of porcelain, china, or metal through the centuries.

Brass, 6 Ring Crown, No Clapper, Mears Co., London, 1864, 18 x 19 In.	1080.00
Brass, School, Wood, c.1900	35.00
Brass, Single Ring Crown, Iron Yoke, Leeds, England, 1800s, 12 x 12 In.	420.00
Brass, Single Ring Crown, No Clapper, Mears Co., London, 1964, 13 ½ x 13 In.	660.00
Brass, Squat Round Base, Drip Pan, Spanish Capstan, 1600s, 4 ¼ In.	863.00
Brass, Steam Locomotive, Iron Yoke, Arm & Cradle, c.1930, 25 x 14 In.	1920.00
Bronze, Ax Blade Shape, Engraved Finial, Burma, 1800s, 9 x 5 In.	59.00
Bronze, Barrel Shape, 2 Dragons Form Hanger, Clouds, Pearls, Scroll, Plaque, c.1749, 8 ¼ In.	49200.00
Bronze, Bow String Designs, Coiled Dragon Finial, Chinese, 1800s, 4 In.	237.00
Bronze, Figural, Indian Maid, Seated, Flowers, c.1910, 7 ½ In.	682.00
Bronze, Monkey, Seated, Forging Drum Shape, Hammer, Pull Tail, Oval Marble Base, 7 In.	980.00
Bronze, Stand, Archaic Style, Chinese, c.1900, 6 In.	207.00
Bronze, Temple, 8 Immortals, Dueling Dragons, Flowers, Incised, 18th Century, 9 ¼ In.	350.00
Cast Iron, Dinner, Yoke, Frederick Town Bell Co., No. 4	158.00
Cast Iron, Dinner, Yoke, Hibbard, Spencer, Bartlett & Co., Upright 188	113.00
Cast Iron, Farm, Marked Crystal Metal, Brace, c.1900, 10 In.	173.00
Cast Iron, Nickel Plate, Figure Turning Ship's Wheel, Footed Base, Deponirt, 7 ½ In. .....*illus*	354.00
Cast Iron, Plantation, Clapper, Wheel, Supports, Wood Base, Blymyer Bros. & Co., c.1890, 41 x 26 In.	4481.00
Cast Iron, School, Labeled Steel Alloy School Bell, Clapper, Wheel, Wooden Base, c.1850 .....*illus*	1195.00
Cast Iron, Trunnio, Seidle & Sherk, Lebanon, Pa., 16 x 20 In.	367.00
Glass, Cranberry, Swirled Ribs, Clear Clapper & Baluster Handle, c.1880, 11 ¼ In.	92.00
Glass, Ruby Cut To Clear, Whirling Star Design, 8 ½ In.	75.00
Glass, Ruby Flash, Thumbprint & Depressed Circles, Zippered Handle, 8 In.	120.00
Hotel, Snail, Figural, Metal, Windup, Push Button For Long Ring, 2 ½ x 4 ⅝ In. ......*illus*	633.00
Silver Plate, Jugendstil, Lute Player, Kidskin Hammer, WMF, Germany, c.1905, 10 In.	248.00
Silver, Double, Dinner, Flower Buds From Joined Stems, F. Ramierez, Mexico, c.1965, 6 In.	86.00
Silver, Table, George III, Shaped Handle, Ball Knop, Ball Finial, c.1798, 5 In.	1150.00
Sterling Silver, Dinner, Repousse, American, 1900, 4 ¾ In.	443.00
Wood, Carved, Barong Creature, Red, Black, Gold, Bali, Indonesia, 4 x 9 x 2 ½ In.	120.00

BELLEEK china was made in Ireland, other European countries, and the United States. The glaze is creamy yellow and appears wet. The first Belleek was made in 1857. All pieces listed here are Irish Belleek. The mark changed through the years. The first mark, black, dates from 1863 to 1890. The second mark, black, dates from 1891 to 1926 and includes the words *Co. Fermanagh, Ireland.* The third mark, black, dates from 1926 to 1946 and has the words *Deanta in Eirinn.* The fourth mark, same as the third mark but green, dates from 1946 to 1955. The fifth mark (second green mark) dates from 1955 to 1965 and has an R in a circle added in the upper right. The sixth mark (third green mark) dates from 1965 to 1981 and the words *Co. Fermanagh* have been omitted. The seventh mark, gold, was used from 1981 to 1992 and omits the words *Deanta in Eirinn.* The eighth mark, used from 1993 to 1996, is similar to the second mark but is printed in blue. The ninth mark, blue, includes the words *Est. 1857* and the words *Co. Fermanagh Ireland* are omitted. The tenth mark, black, is similar to the ninth mark but includes the words *Millennium 2000* and *Ireland.* It was used only in 2000. The eleventh mark, similar to the millennium mark but green, was introduced in 2001. The twelfth mark, black, is similar to the eleventh mark but has a banner above the mark with the words "Celebrating 150 Years." It was used in 2007. The thirteenth trademark, used from 2008 to 2010, is similar to the twelfth but is brown and has no banner. The fourteenth mark, the Classic Belleek trademark, is similar to the twelfth but includes Belleek's website address. The Belleek Living trademark was introduced in 2010 and is used on items from that giftware line. The word *Belleek* is now used only on the pieces made in Ireland even though earlier pieces from other countries were sometimes marked *Belleek.* These early pieces are listed by manufacturer, such as Ceramic Art Co., Haviland, Lenox, Ott & Brewer, and Willets.

Cup & Saucer, Shamrock, Basket Weave, Twisted Vine Handle, c.1900	230.00
Ice Pail, Cover, Putti, Dolphin, Seahorses, Coral, Mermaids, Pedestal, c.1875, 18 In.	10665.00
Pitcher, Flowers, Beading, Fluted Body, Shaped Spout, Scroll Handle, c.1900, 9 In., Pair	356.00
Teakettle, Cover, Thorn, Gilt, Branches, Blossoms, Octagonal, Branch Handle, Knop, c.1875, 6 In.	641.00
Teapot, Shell Shape Feet & Finial, Twisted, c.1900	850.00

BENNINGTON ware was the product of two factories working in Bennington, Vermont. Both the Norton Company and Lyman Fenton & Company were out of business by 1896. The wares include brown and yellow mottled pottery, Parian, scroddled ware, stoneware, graniteware, yellowware, and Staffordshire-type vases. The name is also a generic term for mottled brownware of the type made in Bennington.

Basin, Flint Enamel, 12-Sided, Reeded Rim, 1848-58, 4 x 14 In.	563.00

Bottle, Coachman, Flint Enamel, Rockingham Glaze, Brown Mottled, 11 x 4 In.	920.00
Bottle, Toby On Barrel, Impressed, Lyman Fenton & Co., 1849, 10 ¾ In. ....*illus*	830.00
Bottle, Toby, c.1850, 10 ½ In..	270.00
Bowl, Brown Drip Glaze, Flared, 8 ½ In...	5.15
Bread Tray, Wheat, Give Us This Day Our Daily Bread, 1800s, 12 x 10 In...........................	99.00
Candlestick, Flint Enamel, Rockingham Glaze, Brown Mottled, Blue, 6 ¾ x 4 In................	489.00
Creamer, Cow Shape, Cover, Brown Mottled, Oval Base, 5 ½ x 6 ¾ In.................................	104.00
Creamer, Figural, Cow, Looped Tail Handle, Oval Base, 7 In...	28.00
Curtain Tiebacks, Rockingham Glaze, Brown Mottled, 10-Point Star, 4 ¼ x 4 In..............	460.00
Doorknob, Flint Enamel, Rockingham Glaze, Brown Mottled, 2 x 2 ¼ In.............................	161.00
Figurine, Dog, Poodle, Basket In Mouth, Mottled Brown & Yellow Glaze, c.1850, 8 ½ x 9 ½ In. *illus*	450.00
Figurine, Lion, Coleslaw Mane, Paw On Ball, Brown Glaze, 7 ½ x 10 In., Pair......................	6440.00
Flask, Book, Rockingham Glaze, Brown Mottled, Green, Orange, 2 Qt., 10 ¾ x 3 ¾ In.	4313.00
Flask, Book, Rockingham Glaze, Brown Mottled, Titled Departed Spirits, Pt., 5 ¾ x 2 In.	173.00 to 368.00
Flask, Book, Titled Battle, Brown, Tan, Green, Mottled, 1840-80, 5 ⅝ In. ....*illus*	497.00
Frame, Rockingham Glaze, Brown Mottled, Oval, Grooved Shoulder, 8 ¼ x 9 ¾ In..............	1265.00
Jar, Lid, Rose, Branch, 2, Blue, Handles, J. Norton & Co., 11 ¼ In..	527.00
Jug, Flowers, Dotted Trails, Cobalt Blue, J. & E. Norton, 3 Gal., 13 ¼ In............................	489.00
Pitcher, 6 Panels, Molded Roses & Grapes, Leaves, Scrolls, 1845-47, 10 In.......................	237.00
Pitcher, 8 Panels, Flint Enamel, Lyman Fenton & Co., c.1850, 12 ½ In. ....*illus*	504.00
Pitcher, Boar & Stag Hunt, Tree & Twig Handle, Brown Glaze, 1860s, 10 In.......................	225.00
Pitcher, Diamond Pattern, Scalloped Rim, Wide Spout, Loop Handle, Flint Enamel, c.1850, 8 In.	385.00
Pitcher, Man, Trees, 6 ½ In...	95.00
Pitcher, Molded Raised Waterfall, Branch Handle, Parian, Impressed, 8 ⅜ In. ....*illus*	385.00
Pitcher, Rockingham Glaze, Flint Enamel, Brown Mottled, Green, 10 ½ x 7 ¾ In.................	345.00
Pitcher, Toby, General Stark, Glazed, 1850s, 6 ⅛ In..	1541.00
Pitcher, Toby, General Stark, Glazed, Scalloped Rim, 1800s, 6 In..	1541.00
Pitcher, Wild Rose Pattern, 8 Panel Molded Vessel, Rose Vine Design, 1853-58, 10 In.	245.00
Snuff Jar, Man's Head, Exaggerated Features, Brown Glaze, 4 ½ In.......................................	1208.00
Tobacco Jar, Flint Enamel, Rockingham Glaze, Alternate Rib Pattern, 7 x 5 ½ In.	259.00
Vase, Spill, Cow, Lying Down, Coleslaw Plants, Flint Enamel, Lyman Fenton & Co., 1949, 7 x 10 In. *illus*	5925.00

BERLIN, a German porcelain factory, was started in 1751 by Wilhelm Kaspar Wegely. In 1763, the factory was taken over by Frederick the Great and became the Royal Berlin Porcelain Manufactory. It is still in operation today. Pieces have been marked in a variety of ways.

Plaque, St. Cecilia, Paint, Standing, Holding Organ, Frame, c.1800s, 15 x 12 In.	2489.00
Urn, Cover, Painted Green, Scenic Reserves, Gold Trim, Figural Handles, c.1880, 15 x 13 In., Pair	960.00
Urn, Cover, Turquoise Ground, Painted Reserves, Woman's Head Handles, c.1880, 15 x 13 In., Pair	1080.00

BESWICK started making earthenware in Staffordshire, England, in 1936. The company is now part of Royal Doulton Tableware, Ltd. Figurines of animals, especially dogs and horses, Beatrix Potter animals, and other wares are still being made.

Ashtray, 3 Dogs Applied, Green, Brown, 4 x 2 ½ In.	30.00 to 35.00
Beatrix Potter, Figurine, Appley Dapple, BP 3B, 1975, 3 In.............................	99.00
Beatrix Potter, Figurine, Fierce Bad Rabbit, BP 3B, 1980, 4 ½ In..........................	95.00 to 103.00
Beatrix Potter, Figurine, Foxy, Hands Behind Back, BP 36, 1954, 5 In.	165.00
Beatrix Potter, Figurine, Ginger & Pickles, Box, Certificate, Limited Edition, Tableau ....*illus*	113.00
Beatrix Potter, Figurine, Hunca Munca, BP 2 Gold, 1955, 2 ¾ In.	52.00
Beatrix Potter, Figurine, Hunca Munca, Bunnies In Basket, BP 3C, 2 ½ In.	95.00
Beatrix Potter, Figurine, Jemima Puddle-Duck, BP 3B, 1970, 4 In........................	80.00 to 95.00
Beatrix Potter, Figurine, Lady Mouse, BP 3A, 1970, 4 In.	45.00 to 65.00
Beatrix Potter, Figurine, Lamp, Jemima Puddle-Duck, Tree, Shade, 1970, 16 In....................	89.00
Beatrix Potter, Figurine, Miss Moppet, BP 3B, 1980, 3 In.	49.00 to 55.00
Beatrix Potter, Figurine, Mr. Alderman Ptolemy, Turtle, BP 32, 1973, 3 ⅜ In.	55.00
Beatrix Potter, Figurine, Mr. Jackson, BP 3C, 1985, 3 In.	41.00
Beatrix Potter, Figurine, Mrs. Flopsy, BP 3B, 1965, 4 In.	55.00
Beatrix Potter, Figurine, Mrs. Rabbit, Holding Umbrella, 4 In.	70.00
Beatrix Potter, Figurine, Mrs. Tiggy Winkle Takes Tea, BP 3B, 1980, 3 In...........	50.00
Beatrix Potter, Figurine, Mrs. Tiggy Winkle, BP 3A, 1948, 3 In............................	110.00
Beatrix Potter, Figurine, Peter Rabbit, Anniversary, BP 7, 1993, 6 ¾ In...................	41.00
Beatrix Potter, Figurine, Pigling Bland, 3P 3B, 1956, 4 In.	250.00
Beatrix Potter, Figurine, Rebeccah Puddle-Duck, BP 3B, 1981, 3 ½ In..................	75.00
Beatrix Potter, Figurine, Sir Issac Newton, BP 3A, 1970, 3 ¾ In.	330.00
Beatrix Potter, Figurine, Squirrel Nutkin, BP 2A, 1948, 3 ½ In.	185.00
Beatrix Potter, Figurine, Thomasina Tittle Mouse, BP 3B, 1982, 3 ¼ In...............	57.00
Beatrix Potter, Figurine, Timmy Willie Sleeping, BP 6A, 1986, 1 ¾ In..................	85.00

Bennington, Flask, Book, Titled Battle, Brown, Tan, Green, Mottled, 1840-80, 5 ⅝ In.
$497.00

Norman C. Heckler & Company

Bennington, Pitcher, 8 Panels, Flint Enamel, Lyman Fenton & Co., c.1850, 12 ½ In.
$504.00

Skinner, Inc.

Bennington, Pitcher, Molded Raised Waterfall, Branch Handle, Parian, Impressed, 8 ⅜ In.
$385.00

Skinner, Inc.

Bennington, Vase, Spill, Cow, Lying Down, Coleslaw Plants, Flint Enamel, Lyman Fenton & Co., 1949, 7 x 10 In.
$5925.00

Skinner, Inc.

Beswick, Beatrix Potter, Figurine, Ginger & Pickles, Box, Certificate, Limited Edition, Tableau
$113.00

Potteries Specialist Auctions

Betty Boop, Chalk Figure, Standing, Yellow & Red Dress, Plaster, Painted, 1930s, 14 ¼ In.
$278.00

Hake's Americana & Collectibles

Betty Boop, Stringholder, Betty Head & Shoulders, Mouth Hole, Wire Hanger, Plaster, 1930s, 6 x 7 ¼ In.
$288.00

Hake's Americana & Collectibles

Beatrix Potter, Figurine, Timmy Willie, BP 3C, 1949, 2 ¾ In.	60.00
Beatrix Potter, Figurine, Tommy Brock, BP 1A, 1955, 3 ½ In.	225.00
Birds, Blue Jays, No. 925, 1950, 5 In.	30.00
Birds, Geese, No. 820, 1940, 4 In.	44.00
Celery Dish, Figural Shape, Green, Basket Weave Sides, No. 220, 1930s, 12 x 5 ¾ In.	30.00
Creamer, Mr. Micawber, Green Hat, No. 674, 1940s, 3 ¼ In.	40.00
Decanter, Golden Eagle, Beneagles Scotch Whiskey Decanter, 1969, 10 In.	95.00
Figurine, Bird, Bluetit, Yellow, Black, No. 992B, 2 ½ In.	42.00
Figurine, Bird, Bullfinch, Red, Black, No. 1042, 2 ½ In.	42.00
Figurine, Bird, Goldcrest, Green, Black, No. 2415, 2 ½ In.	45.00
Figurine, Bird, Greenfinch, Flower, 2105A, 1950, 3 In.	40.00
Figurine, Bird, Greenfinch, No. 2105B, 1973, 3 In.	79.00
Figurine, Bird, Wagtail, Gray, No. 1041B, 2 ½ In.	42.00
Figurine, Cat, Ginger, Seated, No. 1436, 1965, 3 ¼ In.	22.00
Figurine, Cat, Gray, No. 1436, 1965, 3 ¼ In.	24.00
Figurine, Cat, Kittens, Siamese, No. 1296, 1964, 2 ¾ In.	55.00 to 65.00
Figurine, Cat, Persian Kitten, No. 1886, 4 In.	38.00
Figurine, Cat, Persian, No. 1867, 1989, 5 In.	175.00
Figurine, Cat, Siamese, Lying On Side, No. 1558B, 7 ¼ In.	75.00
Figurine, Cat, Siamese, No. 2139, 1960, 13 ¾ In.	250.00
Figurine, Dog, Ball, Caught It, No. 2951, 1988, 2 ¾ In.	75.00
Figurine, Dog, Basset Hound, No. 2045B, 1965, 5 In.	51.00
Figurine, Dog, Boxer, Tan & White, No. 1852, 3 In.	56.00
Figurine, Dog, Bulldog, Bosun, No. 1731, 1960, 2 ½ In.	39.00
Figurine, Dog, Cocker Spaniel, Horseshoe Primula, No. 967, 5 ½ In.	81.00
Figurine, Dog, Collie, No. 1814, 1965, 3 ¼ In.	49.00
Figurine, Dog, Dachshund, Begging, No. 1461, 1970, 2 ½ In.	51.00
Figurine, Dog, Dachshund, Seated, No. 1460, 1956, 2 ¾ In.	95.00
Figurine, Dog, Dalmatian, No. 961, 1941, 5 ¾ In.	89.00
Figurine, Dog, Golden Retriever, Cabus Cadet, No. 2287, 1980, 5 ½ In.	52.00
Figurine, Dog, Pug, Standing, No. 1997, 5 In.	190.00
Figurine, Dog, Scamp, No. 1058, 4 ½ In.	69.00
Figurine, Dog, Springer Spaniel, No. 3135, 1999, 5 ½ In.	68.00
Figurine, Dog, Yorkshire Terrier, No. 3083, 1988, 5 ½ In.	65.00
Figurine, Foal, Glossy Brown, No. 1813, 1965, 4 ¾ In.	70.00
Figurine, Girl, Flowers, Yellow Hat, No. 2317, 1971, 4 ¾ In.	52.00
Figurine, Girl, Holding Doll, No. 2293, 1970, 4 ½ In.	41.00
Figurine, Horse, Palomino Galloping, No. 1374, 10 x 7 ½ In.	250.00
Figurine, Horse, Palomino, Prancing Arab, No. 1261, 1952, 6 ¾ In.	74.00
Figurine, Lamb, White, No. 936, 1940s, 3 ¼ In.	31.00
Figurine, Lamb, White, No. 937, 1960, 2 ¼ In.	24.00
Figurine, Mad Hatter, Alice Series, No. 2479, 1974, 4 ½ In.	31.00
Figurine, Mother Pig, Sitting, No. 832, 3 ¾ In.	49.00
Figurine, Old English Sheepdog, No. 2232, Glossy White & Gray, Protuding Tongue, 11 In.	250.00
Figurine, Parakeet, On Stump, No. 930, 1950, 6 In.	250.00
Figurine, Penguin, Red Umbrella, No. 802, 1940, 4 ¼ In.	41.00
Figurine, Pig & Piglet, No. 2746, 1990, 6 ½ In.	47.00
Figurine, Piglet, Running, No. 833, 1940, 1 ¾ In.	28.00
Figurine, Sheep, Black Face, No. 1765, 1964, 3 ¼ In.	41.00
Figurine, Winnie The Pooh, No. 2193, 1968, 2 ½ In.	50.00 to 89.00
Flask, Loch Ness Monster, No. 2051, 1969, 5 x 3 ½ In.	75.00
Jug, Character, Tony Weller, No. 281, 1973, 7 In.	99.00
Jug, Embossed Palm Tree, Cobalt Blue Ground, No. 1067, 11 In.	150.00
Jug, Romeo & Juliet, Multicolor, No. 1214, 8 In.	108.00
Plaque, Swallow, Blue, No. 757, 1945, 7 ½ In.	75.00
Plate, Christmas In England, Inside Scene, No. 2393, 1972, 8 x 8 In.	31.00
Plate, Christmas In Mexico, Group, Outside, No. 2419, 1973, 8 In.	31.00
Platter, Green Ground, Raised Purple, Yellow Flowers, Oblong, 1924, 11 ¼ x 5 ¾ In.	25.00
Teapot, Sairey Gamp, No. 691, 1940s, 5 In.	42.00
Vase, Fan, Sea Foam Green, White Flowers, No. 844-1, c.1940, 10 ½ In.	159.00
Vase, Green Glaze, Applied Flower Detail, 3 Handles, No. 95, 1934, 10 In.	75.00

BETTY BOOP, the cartoon figure, first appeared on the screen in 1931. Her face was modeled after the famous singer Helen Kane and her body after Mae West. In 1935, a comic strip was started. Her dog was named Bimbo. Although the Betty Boop cartoons ended by 1938, there was a revival of interest in the Betty Boop image in the 1980s and new pieces are being made.

Bank, Composition, Box Base, Germany, 8 ¼ In.	1495.00

Bookends, In Front Of Gold Screen, Resin, 7 ½ In.		54.00
Chalk Figure, Standing, Yellow & Red Dress, Plaster, Painted, 1930s, 14 ¼ In.	*illus*	278.00
Necklace, Golf Theme, Enameled, Brass, Segmented Chain, Cop. D.S. Fleischer, 1930s, 1 ½ x 1 In.		1323.00
Nodder, Celluloid, Box, 1930s, 7 In.		741.00
Nodder, Doll, Celluloid, Blue Tin Base, Heart Label, Fleischer Studios, 7 In.		354.00
Stringholder, Betty Head & Shoulders, Mouth Hole, Wire Hanger, Plaster, 1930s, 6 x 7 ¼ In.	*illus*	288.00

BICYCLES were invented in 1839. The first manufactured bicycle was made in 1861. Special ladies' bicycles were made after 1874. The modern safety bicycle was not produced until 1885. Collectors search for all types of bicycles and tricycles. Bicycle-related items are also listed here.

Airwing, Kool Kats, Orange Peel, Drum Brakes, Sissy Bar, Sachs 3-Speed Shifter	400.00
Cleveland, Model 96, Pneumatic, Troxel Tip Top Saddle, c.1895, 22 In. Frame	1000.00
Columbia, Model 39, Tall Boy, Split Frame, Cyclometer, c.1824, 34 In.	3500.00
Columbia, Syracuse, Front Hub Brake, Headlight, c.1950	250.00
Elgin, Twin Bar, 4-Star Deluxe, Twin Headlights, Allstate Whitewalls, 1939	2500.00
Gormully & Jeffery Rambler, Pneumatic, Woman's, c.1893, 20 ½-In. Frame	400.00
High Wheel, H.B. Smith Co., Pony Star, Rubber Tires, c.1885, 44 In.	5500.00
High Wheel, Rudge, Cow Horn Handlebars, 1880s, 51 In.	3100.00
Huffy, Wheel III, Muscle Bike, Shimano 3-Speed	1800.00
Irish Mail, Wood, Metal, c.1920, 22 x 38 ½ In.	267.00
J.C. Higgins, Red Whitewall Tires, Horn, White Tank Boys, 1959, 26 In.	500.00
Lock, Combination, Tyack, Pat. Dec. 31, 1895, Box	200.00
Mergomobile, Wood, Yo-Yo Drive, Hard Rubber Tires, New England, 19th Century	2800.00
Monark, Silver King, Aluminum, Woman's, 1940s, 24 In.	100.00
Nike, March Madness Is Spreading, Leather Seat, Front Emblem, 40 x 93 In.	288.00
Poster, Goodyear Bicycle Tires, Multicolor, 24 x 22 In.	45.00
Poster, Sterling Bicycle, 2 Girls On Beach, Bicycle, Lighthouse, Linen, 1897, 73 x 38 In.	4250.00
Raleigh, Grand Prix, 10-Speed, 1970s	70.00
Raleigh, Lucas, Head Lamp, 3-Speed, c.1935	175.00
Schwinn, Black Phantom, Blue, c.1949	660.00
Schwinn, Deluxe American, Springer, Westwind Tires, 1966	475.00
Schwinn, Phantom, Balloon Tires, 1952 Fresno California Plate, 1950s	625.00
Schwinn, Sting Ray, No. J-33, Tassels, Lime Green, Muscle Bike, 1965	500.00
Schwinn, Twinn Tandem, Stainless Fenders, 1970s	250.00
Scooter, Globe, Strap Steel, Rocker Drive, 1920s	35.00
Scooter, Tricycle, Kick-N-Go	60.00
Shelby Bicycle Co., Lindy, 1928.	5000.00
Stand, Cast Iron, Albert Farnell Branford, Adjustable, 19th Century, 16 x 15 x 17 In.	175.00
Tandem, Wolff American Sociable, Duplex, Spoon Brake, Tricycle, c.1896	3300.00
Tandem, Wolff American, Man, Woman, Wood Rims, c.1898	750.00
Tricycle, Anthony Bros., Cast Aluminum, 14-In. Front Wheel	10.00
Tricycle, Bloch, Red, Metal, Philadelphia, c.1910, 19 ½ x 25 In.	89.00
Tricycle, Cat Shape, Red Bow & Seat, Black Body, c.1925, 22 x 22 In.	119.00
Tricycle, Metal, c.1920, 26 ½ In.	148.00
Tricycle, Rambler, Metal, Steinfeld Inc., c.1910, 29 x 31 In.	213.00
Unicycle, c.1930, 65 In.	150.00
Velocipede, Boneshaker, Cast Iron, Wood, c.1860	2280.00
Velocipede, Tricycle, Wooden, Cast Iron Saddle, Star Logo, 1880s, 19-In. Front Wheel	875.00
Westfield, Chainless, Pneumatic, Draw Back Handles, c.1900	1900.00
Whizzer, Red, White, Restored, c.1950	1870.00

BING & GRONDAHL is a famous Danish factory making fine porcelains from 1853 to the present. Underglaze blue decoration was started in 1886. The annual Christmas plate series was introduced in 1895. Dinnerware, stoneware, and figurines are still being made today. The firm has used the initials *B & G* and a stylized castle as part of the mark since 1898. The company became part of Royal Copenhagen in 1987.

B&G
KJØBENHAVN
MADE IN
DENMARK

Figurine, Cat, Siamese, Sitting, No. 2308, 5 ½ In.	135.00
Figurine, Cat, Sitting, Gray, No. 1876, 5 In.	94.00
Figurine, Early Bird, White, Signed MCN, c.1890, 5 In.	160.00
Figurine, Frog, Green, No. 2476, 4 In.	130.00
Figurine, Girl, Hugging Boy, No. 1614, 7 In.	53.00
Figurine, Girl, Standing, Long Dress, Bonnet, Holding Doll, No. 1721, 7 ½ In. *illus*	60.00
Figurine, Kitten Sitting, No. 1553, 4 In.	125.00
Figurine, Meditation, Nude On Dish, No. 1532, 8 In.	118.00
Figurine, Merete, Girl Reading, Lying On Stomach, No. 2304, 8 In.	60.00
Figurine, Mother, Holding Child, Signed Felix Nylund, Sic, c.1920, 21 ½ In.	2500.00

Bing & Grondahl, Figurine, Girl, Standing, Long Dress, Bonnet, Holding Doll, No. 1721, 7 ½ In.
$60.00

DuMouchelles Art Gallery

Bing & Grondahl, Plate, Christmas 1899, Crows Enjoying Christmas, Dahl Jensen, 7 In.
$480.00

DuMouchelles Art Gallery

Birdcage, Cloisonne, Bird, Pedestal, Door, 2 Bowls, Scrolling Lotus, Marked, Chinese, 17 In.
$13475.00

Skinner, Inc.

Birdcage, Mahogany, Glass & Wire Panels, Inlay, Glass Water Bottles, Sliding Tray, 1800s, 16 ¾ x 10 ¾ In.
$235.00

Garth's Auctions, Inc.

Birdcage, Wire, Mixed Wood, Victorian Style, Cupola, Brown Paint, c.1900, 34 ½ In.
$499.00

Garth's Auctions, Inc.

Figurine, Red Cross Nurse, Seated, Hand To Chin, Book Open, No. 1866, 6 ¾ In.	1800.00
Figurine, Red Cross Nurse, Seated, Sewing, No. 1867, c.1930, 7 ¾ In.	2000.00
Plate Set, Dessert, White, Marked, c.1895, 8 ¼ In., 12 Piece	1000.00
Plate, Christmas 1899, Crows Enjoying Christmas, Dahl Jensen, 7 In. ....*illus*	480.00
Vase, Globular, White, Flowers, 6 In.	177.00

BINOCULARS of all types are wanted by collectors. Those made in the eighteenth and nineteenth centuries are favored by serious collectors. The small, attractive binoculars called opera glasses are listed in their own category.

Biascope Wollensak, Brass, Black Paint, 1920s, 3 ½ x 3 ¼ In.	30.00
Bigelow Kennard & Co., World War I, Leather Case, 3 ¼ x 4 ¼ In.	45.00
Brass, Dean St. Newcastle, E. Robson Optician	100.00
Chevalier, Leather, Cupped Eyepiece, France	195.00
Hensoldt Artillerie, World War II, Brown Leather Case	120.00
Lawrence & Mayo, Lynx, Brass, Integrated Compass, Hinged Lid, 4 x 2 x 3 In.	395.00
Le Jockey Club Sportiere, Black Leather, France, 19th Century	65.00
Marine, Brass, Box, c.1910, 5 x 5 x 2 In.	155.00
Metal, Scrolled Design, 3x, Occupied Japan, c.1940	39.00
Monocular, Brass, 2-Draws, c.1865, 4 ½ In.	395.00
Rodenstock, Germany, c.1917, 4 ½ x 4 ¾ x 2 In.	66.00
SPI Field, 8 x 25, Case, 4 x 5 ½ In.	65.00

BIRDCAGES are collected for use as homes for pet birds and as decorative objects of folk art. Elaborate wooden cages of the past centuries can still be found. The brass or wicker cages of the 1930s are popular with bird owners.

Brass, George III, Acorn Finial, Cross Suspension Bar, c.1950, 38 x 20 In.	461.00
Brass, Moorish, Domed Top, Cylindrical, Leaves, c.1915, 24 ½ x 12 In.	861.00
Brass, Square, Dome Top, 20 x 9 ½ In.	65.00
Brass, Stand, c.1915, 65 In.	150.00
Cloisonne, Bird, Pedestal, Door, 2 Bowls, Scrolling Lotus, Marked, Chinese, 17 In. ....*illus*	13475.00
Ivory, Domed, Key Fret Banding, Mask & Ring Handles, 3 Scrolling Feet, 15 In.	10980.00
Mahogany, Glass & Wire Panels, Inlay, Glass Water Bottles, Sliding Tray, 1800s, 16 ¾ x 10 ¾ In. *illus*	235.00
Metal, Painted, Victorian, 13 ¾ In.	94.00
Wire, Mixed Wood, Victorian Style, Cupola, Brown Paint, c.1900, 34 ½ In. ....*illus*	499.00
Wire, Victorian Style, House Shape, Painted Wood, 31 x 27 ½ In.	155.00
Wood, Pierced, Shaped, Metal Wires, Carved Feet, Art Nouveau, 37 x 23 In.	115.00
Wood, Red Paint, Perches, Drawers, Handle, 1800s, 30 x 17 In.	115.00
Wood, Wire, Red Paint, 5 Graduated Levels, Iron Stand, 8 ½ Ft. x 38 In.	207.00

BISQUE is an unglazed baked porcelain. Finished bisque has a slightly sandy texture with a dull finish. Some of it may be decorated with various colors. Bisque gained favor during the late Victorian era when thousands of bisque figurines were made. It is still being made. Additional bisque items may be listed under the factory name.

Bust, Young Woman, Floral Band In Hair, Signed Gregoire, 1800s, 16 x 11 In.	1003.00
Figurine, American Robin, On Branch, Michael Van Horyen, 7 x 8 In.	150.00
Figurine, Bathing Beauty, Reclining Under Turtle Shell, Molded Hair, Germany, 1910, 5 In.	399.00
Figurine, Bride & Groom, Painted, Lace Veil, Bouquet, Hertwig, Germany, c.1917, 7 ½ In., Pair	109.00
Figurine, George Washington, Shoulder Head, Painted Features, Germany, c.1880, 3 In.	143.00
Figurine, Man, Woman, Colonial Dress, Continental, Late 1800s, 27 In., Pair ....*illus*	3300.00
Figurine, Man, Woman, Multicolor, Enamel, Japan, 1900s, 21 ¼ In., Pair	1185.00
Figurine, Peasants Playing Tug Of War, Painted, Incised Popov, Russia, 1800s, 5 ½ x 7 ½ In.	3360.00
Figurine, Ring Neck Pheasant, Rudisill, 12 x 8 In.	295.00
Figurine, Woman On Tricycle, 19th Century, 3 ½ In.	225.00
Figurine, Woman, Seated, Seminude, Blanket In Lap, Sewing, Round Base, 12 In.	89.00
Figurine, Woman, Wearing Scarf, Holding Fan, Young Man, Wearing Cape, Beret, 17 In., Pair	295.00
Group, Mongol Warrior, Attacking Tiger, 8 ¾ x 10 ¾ In.	489.00
Holy Water Dispenser, Angel, Holding Shell, Gilt Trim, 16 In.	118.00

BLACK memorabilia has become an important area of collecting since the 1970s. The best material dates from past centuries, but many recent items are also of interest. F & F is the mark used on plastic made by Fiedler & Fiedler Mold & Die Works, Inc. in the 1930s and 1940s. Objects that picture a black person may also be listed in this book under Advertising, Sign; Bank; Bottle Opener; Cookie Jar; Doll; Salt & Pepper; Sheet Music; Toy; etc.

Ashtray, Boy, Alligator, Cast Iron, 4 ½ In.	203.00
Blackamoor, Man, Woman, Carrying Basket, 28 x 28 In., Pair	403.00

Blackamoor, Wood Carving, Standing, Turban, Green Robe, Marble Base, 64 In.	3438.00
Book, Golliwog's Bicycle Club, Cloth Backed, Longmans, 1896	600.00
Boot Scraper, Mammy, Cast Iron, 15 x 14 ½ In. ....*illus*	495.00
Broadside, Paper, Wood's Burlesque Troop, Friendship Hall Philadelphia, 1869, 23 x 9 In.	127.00
Caddy, Bellhop, White Uniform, Holding 10-In. Demilune Tray, Wood, Art Deco, 36 In.	230.00
Cigarette Case, Lighter, Black Bartender, Shaking Drink, Ronson Bar, 6 x 7 In.	1150.00
Clicker, Man With Monkey, Box, 4 In.	175.00
Cookie Jars are listed in the Cookie Jar category.	
Doll, Armand Marseille, Brown Bisque, Sleep Eyes, Composition, Baby Body, c.1925, 16 In.	285.00
Doll, Armand Marseille, Floradora, Bisque Head, Sleep Eyes, Open Mouth, Pink Dress, 9 In.	102.00
Doll, Ballerina, Dancing, Wooden, Articulated Limbs, 12 In.	850.00
Doll, Bisque, Simon & Halbig, No. 939, Brown Glass Eyes, Black Hair, Dress, Bonnet, 19 In.	1254.00
Doll, Celluloid, Jointed Limb, Painted Face, c.1900, 6 In.	112.00
Doll, Cloth, Silk Body, Head, Felt Lips, Applied Wig, Striped Dress, Apron, Bloomers, c.1910	299.00
Doll, Poured Wax, Muslin, Glass Upper-Glancing Eyes, Linen Uniform, Cap, c.1925, 17 In.	456.00
Doll, Woman, Knit Stocking, Embroidered Eyes, Mouth, Dress, Petticoat, Boots, c.1900, 16 In.	1304.00
Dolls, Amos 'n' Andy, Composition, Shoulder Head, Straw-Filled, Taxi Logo, c.1928, 17 In., Pair	912.00
Door, Restroom, Men Colored, Men White, Wood, Richmond, Va., 32 x 81 In., Pair	2350.00
Doorstop, Boy, Riding Alligator, Cast Iron, 10 In.	475.00
Figurine, Boy, Eating Watermelon, Bisque, Germany, Late 1800s, 3 ¼ x 4 In.	115.00
Figurine, Boy, Grass Shirt, Beating Drum, 4 In.	25.00
Figurine, Boy, Sitting, Eating Watermelon, 3 ½ In.	51.00
Gourd, Kids In Front Of Log Cabin, Man Playing Banjo, Painted, 1883, 8 In.	588.00
Kettle Holder, Figural, Man, Woman, Apron, Black Dress, Tuxedo, Hat, 6 ½ x 3 ½ In., Pair	295.00
Lighter, Cigar, Slave, Bronze, Claw Foot, 5 x 9 ½ In.	1092.00
Painting, 2 Black Men, Seated On Crate Playing Banjo, Dancing, S. Heller, 1900s, 30 x 24 In.	113.00
Pencil Sharpener, Sambo, Cast Metal, Painted, 1950s, 2 In.	65.00
Pin, Store Clerk, Aunt Jemima Breakfast Club, Adcraft, Chicago, 1950s, 4 In. ....*illus*	127.00
Postcard, Man Pulling Dog, E. Nash.	8.00
Program, Minstrel Review, East Palestine, Ohio, 1925	15.00
Saltshaker, Aunt Jemima, c.1925, 4 In.	25.00
Shadowbox, Man, Checkered Shirt, Hat, Expression Changes, Animated, c.1900, 21 x 26 In.	4025.00
Slave Tag, Charleston 1837, Copper, William Rouse, 2 ½ x 2 ¾ In.	4560.00
Slave Tag, Charleston 1849, Copper, William Rouse, 2 x 2 In.	4320.00
Slave Tag, Hire, Mechanic, No. 239, Diamond Shape, Charleston, S.C., c.1845, 2 x 2 In.	2596.00
Soap Dish, Mammy, Standing, Basket On Head, Red Dress, Yellow Shawl, Hubley, Cast Iron	85.00
Smoking Stand, Bellhop, Wood, Red, Wood Tray, Vaseline Glass Ashtray, 36 ½ In.	117.00
Smoking Stand, Butler, With Tray, Red Coat, Black Pants, Bowtie, 33 In.	385.00
Stringholder, Mammy, Multicolor, Red Head Scarf, Yellow Dress, Occupied Japan, 6 ¼ In.	120.00
Tin, Aunt Jemima, Pure Corn Oil, Tin Litho, 5 Gal., 9 x 13 ½ x 9 ½ In. ....*illus*	354.00
Tobacco Jar, Child's Head, Green Hat, Red Bowtie, 6 x 5 In.	472.00

BLACK AMETHYST glass appears black until it is held to the light, then a dark purple can be seen. It has been made in many factories from 1860 to the present.

Biscuit Jar, Tab Handles, Cover, 6 ½ In.	155.00
Bowl, Nut, Cut Rim, Center Handle, 5 ½ In.	23.00
Bowl, Oval, 4-Footed, 12 x 8 In.	95.00
Bowl, Scalloped Rim, Textured Fruit, Oval, 4-Footed, 12 x 8 x 4 In.	45.00
Candleholder, Open Braided Stem, Footed, 9 ½ In.	18.00
Change Tray, 7 ½ x 2 ¼ In.	65.00
Cup & Saucer, Scalloped Edge, Square Saucer, Ribbed Cup, 1920s	29.00
Dish, Lid, Enameled Flowers, Gilt Finial, Round, c.1880, 5 x 6 In.	210.00
Hat, Turned Up Brim, 3-Pinch Crown, c.1950, 11 x 10 x 4 In.	285.00
Pitcher, Applied Handle, 20th Century, 7 ½ In.	100.00
Plate, Square, Scalloped, Handles, 1920s, 10 In.	18.00
Vase, Art Deco Style, Ruffled Rim, Footed, 4 ½ In.	49.00
Vase, Sterling Overlay Panels, Flared, 12 In.	89.00
Vase, Triangular, Scalloped, 6 ¾ In.	58.00

BLENKO GLASS COMPANY is the 1930s successor to several glassworks founded by William John Blenko in Milton, West Virginia. In 1933, his son, William H. Blenko Sr., took charge. The company made tablewares and vases in classical shapes. In the late 1940s it hired talented designers and made innovative pieces. The company made a line of reproductions for Colonial Williamsburg. It is still in business and is best known today for its decorative wares and stained glass. All products are made to order.

Bottle, Tequila Sunrise, Bulbous, Stopper, 1960s, 18 In.	225.00

Bisque, Figurine, Man, Woman, Colonial Dress, Continental, Late 1800s, 27 In., Pair
$3300.00

DuMouchelles Art Gallery

Black, Boot Scraper, Mammy, Cast Iron, 15 x 14 ½ In.
$495.00

Showtime Auction Services

Black, Pin, Store Clerk, Aunt Jemima Breakfast Club, Adcraft, Chicago, 1950s, 4 In.
$127.00

Hake's Americana & Collectibles

Black, Tin, Aunt Jemima, Pure Corn Oil, Tin Litho, 5 Gal., 9 x 13 ½ x 9 ½ In. $354.00

Showtime Auction Services

Boehm, Woodcock, Signed, 10 In. $388.00

Sloans & Kenyon

Bookends, Book Slide, Coromandel, Plaque, Putto, Clouds, Betjemann's, Howell James & Co., 13 In. $579.00

Leslie Hindman Auctioneers

Bookends, Dog, Greyhound, Seated, Gilt Metal, Onyx, Art Deco, 10 ½ In. $210.00

DuMouchelles Art Gallery

Bowl, Square & Ribbed Center, Pontil, Foil Label, 1950s, 3 x 13 In.	89.00
Decanter, Flame Stopper, Tangerine Glass, Etched Signature, 25 ½ x 10 ¼ In.	279.00
Decanter, Frosted, Red, Clear, Charisma, Signed, 22 In.	300.00
Decanter, Green, Ribbed, Stopper, 23 In.	79.00
Decanter, Optic Turquoise Glass, 23 ½ x 9 In.	496.00
Decanter, Smoky Glass, 35 x 8 ½ In.	527.00
Decanter, Tangerine Glass, 35 ½ x 8 In.	558.00
Jug, Amber, Crackle, 6 In.	30.00
Paperweight, Top Shape, Foil Label, 3 x 4 In.	45.00
Pitcher, Amethyst, Optical Wave, Footed, 11 In.	75.00
Pitcher, Blue, Crackle, Indented, 9 In.	65.00
Pitcher, Crackle, Applied Ribbed Handle, Blue, c.1950, 3 ½ In.	29.00
Pitcher, Crackle, Blue, Applied Ribbed Handle, Hourglass Shape, c.1955, 3 ½ In.	39.00
Plaque, Partridges, Tree, White On Clear, Round.	69.00
Vase, Flattened, Oval, Green, Applied Medallion, 1955, 13 In.	695.00
Vase, Pinched Sides, Emerald Green, Foil Label, 11 In.	110.00
Vase, Rock, Don Shepherd, Oval, 11 In.	475.00
Vase, Rock, Globular, Don Shepherd, 6 x 7 In.	250.00
Vase, Ruby, Crackle, 10 In.	85.00

BLOWN GLASS, *see Glass-Blown category.*

BLUE GLASS, *see Cobalt Blue category.*

BLUE ONION, *see Onion category.*

BLUE WILLOW, *see Willow category.*

BOCH FRERES factory was founded in 1841 in La Louviere in eastern Belgium. The wares resemble the work of Villeroy & Boch. The factory closed in 1985. M.R.L. Boch took over the production of tableware, but went bankrupt in 1988. Le Hodey took over Boch Freres in 1989, using the name Royal Boch Manufacture S.A. It went bankrupt in 2009. A new managing director is now running the company.

Vase, Art Deco, Sgraffito, White Crackle Ground, Charles Catteau, 11 In.	138.00
Vase, Painted, Stylized Blue Roses, Gourd Shape, Marked, Signed, 5 x 7 ½ In.	180.00
Vase, Red, Gold Trim, Spiral From Rim To Base, Iridescent, Urn Shape, 12 ⅛ In.	115.00
Vase, Round, 12 Panels, Blue, Ocher, Turquoise Matte Glaze, Charles Catteau, 5 x 6 In.	541.00
Vase, Stylized Blue Roses, White Panels, Gourd Shape, Belgium, 5 x 7 ½ In.	165.00

BOEHM is the collector's name for the porcelains of Edward Marshall Boehm. In 1953 the Osso China Company was reorganized as Edward Marshall Boehm, Inc. The company is still working in England and New Jersey. In the early days of the factory, dishes were made, but the elaborate and lifelike bird figurines are the best-known ware. Edward Marshall Boehm, founder, died in 1969, but the firm has continued to design and produce porcelain. Today, the firm makes both limited and unlimited editions of figurines and plates.

American Avocet, 16 x 9 x 6 In.	1353.00
American Bald Eagle, 40th Presidential Inauguration, Brown, White, 1981, 8 ¾ x 11 In.	230.00
American Fox Hound, Reclining, 13 x 6 In.	431.00
Baby Blue Jay, 4 ½ x 3 ½ In.	123.00
Baby Bluebird, 4 In.	83.00
Baby Cardinal, 4 ½ x 3 x 5 In.	62.00
Baby Woodthrush, 5 x 3 ½ In.	49.00
Ballerina, Box, 4 x 6 In.	65.00
Blue-Throated Hummingbird, 4 ¾ In.	111.00
Bookends, Owl, Book Base, c.1950, 9 ¼ In.	118.00
Bowl, Iridescent, Bowl Rim Supported By Free-Form Draped Base, 6 ½ x 11 In.	115.00
Canada Goose, Painted, 4 In.	96.00
Catbird, Perched Next To Hyacinth Flowers, 14 In.	972.00
Crested Flycatcher, 18 ½ In.	401.00
Crested Flycatcher, Perched On Branch, Orange Leaves, 19 In.	770.00
Cymbidium Orchid, 7 In.	236.00
Downy Woodpeckers, 2 Baby Birds, Perched In Tree, Flowers, Leaves, 13 In.	533.00
Eagle, Wood Base, 13 In.	465.00
Eastern Bluebirds, 14 x 11 x 7 ½ In.	615.00
Eastern Meadowlark, 8 x 4 ½ x 7 In.	277.00

Family Of Bobwhite Quails, 4 Birds, 12 x 17 x 9 In.	738.00
Female Mute Swan, 20 x 10 x 17 In.	677.00
Fledgling Goldfinch, 4 x 3 x 3 In.	62.00
Fledgling Kingfisher, 6 x 4 In.	49.00
Forester's Tern, Marshall Boehm, 18 x 18 In.	920.00
Goddess Selket, Standing, Open Arms, Glancing Sideways, Headpiece, Square Base, 17 In.	374.00
Goldfinch, 2 Birds Perched On Leafy Plant, Ladybug, Round Base, 11 In.	385.00
Great Blue Heron, 1984, 30 x 25 x 17 In.	1353.00
Great Egret, Signed, Helen Boehm, 17 x 12 ½ In.	345.00
Harpooner, Egyptian, Holding Spear, Gilt, Rectangular Base, 17 x 17 In.	259.00
Horse, Stud, Standing, Yellow Saddle, Brown, Black Mane, Base, 14 In.	516.00
Irish Beauty Rose, 7 ½ x 11 x 5 ½ In.	277.00
King Tut Mask, Gilt, 12 x 9 ½ In.	489.00
Koala Cub, Holding Leaf, On Branch, 9 x 10 In.	238.00
La Pieta Madonna, Bust, Downward Glancing, Arms Folded, Marked, 9 ½ x 6 x 5 In.	120.00
Lizard, Sitting On Tree Stump, Mouth Slightly Open, Curled Tail, 3 ¼ In.	356.00
Long-Billed Marsh Wren, Rocky Base, 6 x 4 x 2 In.	123.00
Male Mute Swan, 22 x 18 x 19 In.	861.00
Meadowlark, 8 ½ x 7 In.	550.00
Mountain Bluebirds, 2 Perched On Flowering Branch, 12 In.	711.00
Mourning Dove, 16 x 10 x 12 In.	1107.00
Orchid, Pink, 6 In.	51.00
Parula Warblers, 16 In.	519.00
Patriotic Eagle, American Flag In Talons, 23 In.	620.00
Peach Rose With Daisies, 1980, 15 x 7 x 5 In.	185.00
Princess Diana Rose With Daffodils, 1984, 9 ½ x 15 x 6 In.	185.00
Prothonotary Warbler, Feeding Her Young, 6 x 6 x 5 ½ In.	74.00
Red-Shouldered Hawk, 27 x 23 In.	2952.00
Roadrunner, 9 x 17 x 12 In.	677.00
Robin, Butterfly In Beak, 4 ½ x 3 ½ In.	74.00
Sandpipers, In Flight, 1982, 12 x 10 In.	413.00
Song Thrush, Mushrooms On Base, 8 ½ x 8 x 4 In.	492.00
Tree Sparrow, 8 x 7 x 3 In.	98.00
Tufted Titmice, 2 Birds, Perched In Snow Covered Red Berry Branch, 13 ¼ In.	444.00
Tumbler Pigeon, Standing, Feathery Feet, White & Gray, 8 ½ In., Pair.	119.00
Verdins, 2 Birds Perched In Branches, Thorny, Round Base, 9 In.	119.00
Western Bluebirds, 17 x 18 In.	738.00
Wild Turkey, 36 ½ In.	5412.00
Woodcock, Signed, 10 In. *illus*	388.00

BOOKENDS have probably been used since books became inexpensive. Early libraries kept books in cupboards, not on open shelves. By the 1870s bookends appeared, especially homemade fret-carved wooden examples. Most bookends listed in this book date from the twentieth century. Bookends are also listed in other categories by manufacturer or material. All bookends listed here are pairs.

2 Kinds Of Pups, Metal, J.L. Drucklieb, 1940s, 6 ½ In.	115.00
Abraham Lincoln, Bust, Spelter, Marked, Bradley & Hubbard, c.1920, 6 x 8 In.	113.00
Abraham Lincoln, Metalware, Philadelphia Manufacturing Co., 6 In.	24.00
Book Slide, Coromandel, Plaque, Putto, Clouds, Betjemann's, Howell James & Co., 13 In. ...*illus*	579.00
Boy, Girl, Dog, Paint, Cast Iron, 5 In.	113.00
Brass, Leaf Design, Carence Crafters, 7 x 4 In.	270.00
Builder, Nude Man, Kneeling, Bronze Patinated, 7 ½ x 4 ½ In.	117.00
Cherub, Holding Butterfly & Book, Kneeling, Cattails, Metal, c.1924, 6 x 4 x 2 In.	185.00
Children Reading, Cast Iron, 5 ½ In.	177.00
Copper, Hammered, Fossilized Bone, Totems, Albert Berry, 6 ¼ x 5 x 4 ½ In.	2480.00
Corrugated, Branch, Holly Leaf, Berries, Green, Marked, 5 ¼ x 5 In.	68.00
Covered Wagon, 2-Horse Team, Casting, Hubley, 4 x 6 ½ In.	86.00
Cylindrical, Angled Top, Marble, Mounted Insects, 7 ½ In.	219.00
Dancer, Arabesque, Cast Iron, Hubley, 6 In.	575.00
Dog, Brown, Germany, 5 In.	47.00
Dog, Cast Iron, Painted, 7 x 7 In.	226.00
Dog, Greyhound, Seated, Gilt Metal, Onyx, Art Deco, 10 ½ In. ...*illus*	210.00
Dog, Scottie, Porcelain, White, Black, c.1930, 5 x 4 x 3 In.	80.00
Dog, Setter, Iron, Brass Finish, c.1925, 8 x 5 In.	165.00
Dog, Terrier, Bronze Finish, Cast Iron, Hubley, 5 x 6 In.	28.00

B

Bottle, Barber, Emerald Green, White & Orange Enamel, Tooled Mouth, Pontil, 8 ½ In.
$104.00

Glass Works Auctions

Bottle, Barber, Milk Glass, M.Y. Hendricks, Enameled Eye, Bible, Pewter Top, W.T. & Co., c.1900
$633.00

Glass Works Auctions

Bottle, Beer, D. Davis, 12-Sided, Cobalt Blue, Applied Tapered Collar, Lockport, N.Y., c.1860
$863.00

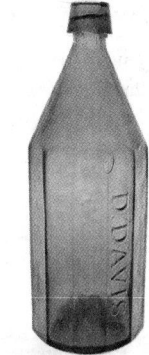

Glass Works Auctions

TIP
Keep your rare books away from children, food, and drinks.

BOOKENDS

Bottle, Beer, Engeman & Hubener, N.Y., Philadelphia XXX, Porter, 1861, Blue Green, c.1860, 6 ½ In.
$196.00

Glass Works Auctions

Bottle, Bitters, Dr. Fisch's, Figural, Fish, Yellow Amber, Tooled Collared Mouth, 1866-80, 11 ½ In.
$380.00

Norman C. Heckler & Company

Bottle, Bitters, Dr. Van Dyke's Holland, Patented Jun 2nd 1896, Tooled Mouth, Contents, c.1890-1910, 9 ⅞ In.
$196.00

Glass Works Auctions

Dog, Terrier, Cast Iron, Brown, White, Hubley, 5 x 5 In.	275.00
Dolly & Bobby, Cast Iron, Painted, Hubley, U.S.A., 5 x 4 In.	34.00
Eagle, Spread Wings, Metal, Virginia Metalcrafters, 1952, 4 x 7 In.	40.00
Elephant, Smiling, Brass, Concrete, 6 x 5 In.	75.00
Elk, Bust, Horns, Bronze, 6 ½ x 6 ¼ In.	575.00
Female Bust, Aesthetic Revival, Bronze, Cold Painted, 6 In.	351.00
Foo Dog, Cinnabar, 6 x 8 In.	200.00
Football Players, Yale, Cast Iron, 5 ½ In.	180.00
Frog, Crowned, Iron, Bronze Finish, Jan Barboglio, 4 x 3 x 4 In.	275.00
Hippopotamus, Open Mouth, Square Base, Black Glaze, 1933, 4 In.	1610.00
Horse Head, Walnut, Signed, Lead Interior, 8 In.	303.00
Horse, Grazing, Cast Iron, 5 ½ In.	50.00
Indian Chief, Full Headress, Stoneware, Salt Glaze 6 ½ x 5 In.	690.00
Indian, Horse, End Of Trail Pose, Bronze, c.1930, 6 x 4 In.	77.00
Lawn Jockey, Black Face, White, Green, Red Clothes, Cast Metal, c.1950, 10 ¼ x 5 In.	201.00
Leaves, Copper, Stamped Jarvie Shop, 4 ½ x 5 In.	10540.00
Lion, Ceramic, Base, 1965, 7 x 6 ½ In.	200.00
Lion, Reclining, Cast Iron, Helvetiorum Fidei Ac Virtutui, c.1890, 5 x 7 In.	288.00
Maids Reading Books, Red Hooded Attire, Art Deco, Paint, Chrome Base, 6 ¾ x 6 In.	288.00
Man & Woman, Heads Bowed, Pitchfork, Iron, 1928, 5 x 4 In.	89.00
Mantarani's Dante, Metal, Marked, c.1910, 6 x 6 In.	285.00
Mule, Ivory Matte Glaze, Standing, Square Base, 1936, 6 In.	1725.00
Native American Horseback Rider, Rifle, Bronze, A.H. Sanders, 1900s, 5 x 5 ¾ In.	411.00
Nymph, Winged, Dancing In Waves, Flowing Scarf, Cast Iron, Art Nouveau	285.00
Owl, Perched, White Matte Glaze, Square Base, 1948, 6 In.	104.00
Owls, Perched, Ivory Matte Glaze, Square Base, c.1940, 5 ¾ In.	207.00
Pierrot, Art Deco, c.1940	59.00
Pigeon, Art Deco, Spelter, Cold Painted, c.1940, 7 x 2 ½ In.	154.00
Pirate, Treasure Chest, Cast Brass, 6 In.	17.00
Poodle, Wearing Bow, On Tasseled Pillow, Syroco Wood, 6 x 7 In.	79.00
Quails, Cast Iron, Grass, Hubley	316.00
Rams, Bucking, Chrome Plated, Wood Base, Art Deco, 8 x 4 In.	395.00
School Of Fish, Bronze Finish, K & O Co., 5 x 4 x 3 In.	65.00
Seckatary Hawkins, Novel Character, Standing, Hands In Pocket, Square Base, 1920, 12 In.	518.00
Shell, Ribbed, Brass Plated, 6 In.	49.00
Ship, Cast Iron, Coral, Blue, Green, Gold, c.1930, 4 x 4 In.	45.00
Sitting Bull, Bronze, Marked, 7 x 5 In.	575.00
Smiling Native, Basket On Head, Multicolor, Chalkware, 1944, 6 x 5 In.	60.00
Squirrel, Eating A Nut, Bronze, Profile, Marble Base, Art Nouveau, France, 6 In.	326.00
St. Francis Of Assisi, Seated, Fox, By His Side, Brown, Gray, Blue, 1946, 7 ⅜ In.	690.00
Stone, Geode, Cobalt Blue, Inner White Crystal Core, Divided, Polished, 5 ½ x 4 ¼ In.	345.00
Thinker, Gold Tone, 1928, 3 x 4 In.	125.00
Warbler, Perched On Boughs, Circle Shape Behind, Square Base, Blue, 5 ⅜ In.	2990.00
Warrior, Holding Panther By Chain, Bronze Metal, Round Base, Art Deco	79.00
Woman Disrobing, Testing Water With Toe, Bronzed Metal, Art Nouveau, 1900s, 8 In.	337.00
Woman, At Well, Cast Iron, 5 ½ In.	40.00

BOOKMARKS were originally made of parchment, cloth, or leather. Soon woven silk ribbon, thin cardboard, celluloid, wood, silver, tortoiseshell, and metals were used. Examples made before 1850 are scarce, but there are many to be found dating before 1920.

Celluloid, Heron, Multicolor, 4 In.	31.00
Celluloid, Pacific Coast Steamship Co., Totem Pole On Reverse, 1915, 3 In.	69.00
Celluloid, Violets, Lord Bless Thee, Die Cut, Cross, 1900s, 4 x 2 In.	26.00
Embroidery, Oriental, Flowers, Butterfly, 2 ½ x 9 In.	7.00
Enamel, Butterfly, 5 ½ x 2 In.	12.00
Needlepoint, Remember Me, 1800s, 8 x 4 In.	16.00
Needlepoint, Thy Will Be Done, 8 x 2 In.	5.00
Punch Paper, Green Ribbon, Lavender Cross, 4 x 2 In.	20.00
Punch Paper, Hand Sewn, Chalice, Crucifix, Alphabet, 4 x 2 In.	65.00
Silk, Child Holding Cross, c.1880, 3 x 7 In.	14.00
Sterling Silver, Cherub, Howard Sterling Co., c.1890, 5 ¼ In.	183.00
Sterling Silver, Dagger, 2 ½ In.	25.00
Sterling Silver, Man In Moon, Star, 3 ½ In.	45.00
Sterling Silver, Shell Shape, Monogram, Reed & Barton, c.1950, 1 ½ x 1 In.	30.00
Sterling Silver, Toad, 2 ¾ In.	53.00

B

BOSSONS character wall masks (heads), plaques, figurines, and other decorative pieces were made by W.H. Bossons, Limited, of Congleton, England. The company was founded in 1946 and closed in 1996. Dates shown are the date the item was introduced.

Figurine, Briar Rose Donkey, 1970s, 7 x 5 In.	60.00
Plate, Old English Cottage, Beautiful Britain Series, Hand Painted, 1948, 14 In.	175.00
Wall Mask, Abduhl, 1960, 7 ½ x 5 ½ In.	60.00
Wall Mask, Abduhl, 1965, 7 ¾ In.	15.00
Wall Mask, Abduhl, c.1970, 7 ½ In.	135.00
Wall Mask, Boatman, 1962	13.00
Wall Mask, Boatman, 1967	85.00
Wall Mask, Boxer Dog, 4 In.	95.00
Wall Mask, Brettone Woman, c.1990, 6 x 5 In.	45.00
Wall Mask, Chef, c.1970	80.00
Wall Mask, Cocker Spaniel	20.00
Wall Mask, English Setter Spaniel, c.1969, 5 In.	95.00
Wall Mask, Eskimo, 1970, 8 In.	200.00
Wall Mask, Golden Lab Retriever, 4 In.	95.00
Wall Mask, Himalayan, c.1963	100.00
Wall Mask, Irish Man's Head, 5 In.	40.00
Wall Mask, Kurd, 1963, 5 x 4 In.	75.00
Wall Mask, Liechtensteiner, 1962, 5 ½ x 3 ½ In.	45.00
Wall Mask, Pancho, 1960, 7 ½ x 6 ½ In.	80.00
Wall Mask, Persian Man, 5 x 3 ½ In.	20.00
Wall Mask, Pirate, F. Wright, 1985	85.00
Wall Mask, Punjabi, 1964, 7 In.	15.00
Wall Mask, Rawhide, 1967, 6 ½ In.	59.00
Wall Mask, Saracen, 1959, 7 ¾ x 4 ¼ In.	47.00
Wall Mask, Saracen, 1960	50.00
Wall Mask, Sarah Gamp, Dickens Series, 1982, 6 In.	90.00
Wall Mask, Scrooge, 1981, 5 x 3 In.	40.00
Wall Mask, Sherlock Holmes, c.1987, 5 ¾ x 4 ¼ In.	65.00
Wall Mask, Sikh, c.1963	175.00
Wall Mask, Skipper, 6 x 3 ¾ In.	95.00
Wall Mask, Smuggler, No. 32, 1964, 5 ½ In.	50.00
Wall Mask, Uriah Heep, 1964, 5 ½ x 3 ⅜ In.	55.00
Wall Plaque, Anne Boleyn, 1986, 6 x 4 In.	175.00
Wall Plaque, Betsey Trotwood, Dickens Series, 1982, 6 In.	90.00
Wall Plaque, Blue Tits, Wildlife Series, 1968, 4 ¾ x 3 ¾ In.	85.00
Wall Plaque, Cavalier, c.1962, 8 In.	280.00
Wall Plaque, Cheyenne, Paper Tag, c.1967	22.00
Wall Plaque, Custer & Sitting Bull, 1989	249.00
Wall Plaque, Evzon, 6 x 3 In.	325.00
Wall Plaque, Koala, 10 In.	115.00
Wall Plaque, Mr. Bumble, Charles Dickens Series, 5 In.	130.00
Wall Plaque, Owl On Branch, 7 x 5 In.	35.00
Wall Plaque, Poodle, 1960s, 5 x 4 ¼ In.	36.00
Wall Plaque, Raccoon In Tree, 1963, 12 ¼ x 4 In.	65.00
Wall Plaque, Scottie Dog, 1969, 5 x 3 ¼ In.	75.00
Wall Plaque, Spring Flowers, Incised, 1958	70.00
Wall Plaque, Squirrel, 7 In.	30.00
Wall Plaque, Woodpecker, Baby Birds, 1968, 12 x 5 ¼ In.	75.00

BOSTON & SANDWICH CO. pieces may be found in the Sandwich Glass category.

BOTTLE collecting has become a major American hobby. There are several general categories of bottles, such as historic flasks, bitters, household, and figural. ABM means the bottle was made by an automatic bottle machine after 1903. Pyro is the shortened form of the word *pyroglaze*, an enameled lettering used on bottles after the mid-1930s. This form of decoration is also called ACL or applied color label. For more prices, go to kovels.com.

Avon started in 1886 as the California Perfume Company. It was not until 1929 that the name Avon was used. In 1939, it became Avon Products, Inc. Avon has made many figural bottles filled with cosmetic products. Ceramic, plastic, and glass bottles were made in limited editions.

Avon, American Schooner, 1972	15.00
Avon, Blacksmith Anvil, 1972	10.00

Bottle, Bitters, Drake's Plantation, 6 Log, Patented 1862, Strawberry Puce, c.1870, 10 In.
$748.00

Glass Works Auctions

Bottle, Bitters, E. Dexter Loveridge Wahoo, Patd DWD, Cabin, Yellow Amber, 1863
$4200.00

American Glass Gallery

TIP
To clean the inside of a bottle or a decanter wash in warm soapy water using a soft-bristle baby bottle brush. Dry, then put a rolled-up paper towel into the top of the bottle but leave a few inches sticking out. The towel will get the last bit of moisture out.

Bottle, Bitters, Fish, W.H. Ware, Patented 1866, Yellow Amber, c.1870, 11 ¾ In. $207.00

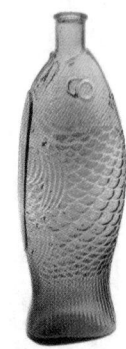

Glass Works Auctions

The First Bottle Club

The first organized bottle collectors club was probably the one formed by John Tibbitts in Sacramento, California, in the 1960s. It was the Antique Bottle Collectors Association and later was renamed the Federation of Historic Bottle Collectors (FOHBC). You can still join.

Bottle, Bitters, Herkules, Monogram, Grass Green, c.1900, 1 Qt., 7 ½ In. $1150.00

Glass Works Auctions

Bottle, Bitters, Kelly's Old Cabin, Patented 1863, Cabin, Deep Amber, c.1870, 9 ⅜ In. $3163.00

Glass Works Auctions

Avon, Butter, Cape Cod, Ruby, Wheaton Glass Co., 1975, 7 x 3 ½ In.	25.00
Avon, Chess Piece, Bishop I, 1974	20.00
Avon, Chess Piece, King II, 1975	20.00
Avon, Chess Piece, King, 1972	20.00
Avon, Chess Piece, King, White, 1971	25.00
Avon, Chess Piece, Pawn, 1974	20.00
Avon, Chess Piece, Rook, 1973	21.00
Avon, Creamer, Cape Cod, Footed, 5 ½ In.	15.00
Avon, Decanter, Cape Cod, Ruby Glass, 10 ½ In.	20.00
Avon, Dueling Pistol, 1780, 1973	15.00
Avon, Figurine, Dutch Girl, 1973	12.00
Avon, Harvest Time Spice Garden Candle, Wheat Stalks Shape, Gold, 1980, 6 In.	17.00
Avon, No Parking Fire Plug, 1975	10.00
Avon, Open Golf Cart, 1972	12.00
Avon, Pepperbox Pistol, 1850, 1979	12.00
Avon, Pipe, Bull Dog, 1972	12.00
Avon, Pipe, Corncob, 1974	10.00
Avon, Pony Post, 1972	16.00
Avon, Pony Post, Light Green, 1971	15.00
Avon, Side Wheeler, 1971	30.00
Avon, Soap, Sure Winner, 1973	20.00
Avon, Spirit Of St. Louis, 1970	25.00
Avon, Stein, Blacksmith, 1985	45.00
Avon, Stein, Football, 1982	55.00
Avon, Stein, Gold Rush, 1987	55.00
Avon, Stein, Iron Horse, 1982	45.00
Avon, Stein, Western Round-Up, 1980	35.00
Avon, Telephone, French, 1971	30.00
Avon, Telephone, La Belle, 1974	9.00
Avon, Treasure Turtle, 1971	6.00
Barber, Bay Rum, Milk Glass, Multicolor Enamel, Bird, Flowers, Tooled Lip, 11 In.	546.00
Barber, Cover, White, Lilac, Green, Grapevine Swags, Grapes, Flower Festoons, 1800s, 10 In.	2695.00
Barber, Cut Glass, Crosshatching, Sterling Silver Top, 9 In.	395.00
Barber, Emerald Green, White & Orange Enamel, Tooled Mouth, Pontil, 8 ½ In. *illus*	104.00
Barber, Hairbrush, Electric, Dr. Scott's, No. 5, Germ Of All Life Is Electricity, Embossed, 9 ½ In.	28.00
Barber, Klorofil Dandruff Cure, Enameled Label, Clear, 7 ¾ In.	176.00
Barber, Milk Glass, M.Y. Hendricks, Enameled Eye, Bible, Pewter Top, W.T. & Co., c.1900 *illus*	633.00
Barber, Milk Glass, Whitall Tatum & Co., Multicolor Enamel, Swans On Pond, W.T. & Co., c.1900	1035.00
Barber, Toilet Water, Amethyst, Ribbed, White Enamel Windmill, 7 ¾ In.	288.00
Barber, Turquoise, Ribbed, Multicolor Flowers, Tooled Lip, Open Pontil, 10 In.	207.00

Beam bottles were made to hold Kentucky Straight Bourbon, made by the James B. Beam Distilling Company. The Beam series of ceramic bottles began in 1953.

Beam, Cable Car, 1968, 3 x 5 x 7 In.	40.00
Beam, Centennial 1868-1968, B.P.O.E. Elks, 1968, 11 In.	9.00
Beam, Ponderosa Ranch, 7 x 9 x 3 In.	22.00
Beam, Reno, Nevada, 100th Anniversary, 9 x 5 x 2 In.	15.00
Beer, Canadian Ace Brand, Manhattan Brewing Co., Amber, Paper Label, c.1944, ½ Gal.	55.00
Beer, D. Davis, 12-Sided, Cobalt Blue, Applied Tapered Collar, Lockport, N.Y., c.1860 *illus*	863.00
Beer, Engeman & Hubener, N.Y., Philadelphia XXX, Porter, 1861, Blue Green, c.1860, 6 ½ In. *illus*	196.00
Beer, Gluek Fine Pilsner Beer, Paper Label, 1950s, 9 In., 12 Oz.	45.00
Beer, Grolsch, Porcelain Swing Bail Closure, Amber, 9 ⅜ In.	10.00
Beer, John Lyon & Co., Fluted, Dark Green, c.1900, 9 ¼ In.	30.00
Beer, Liebmann Brewery, Brooklyn, N.Y., Clear, c.1900, 9 ½ In.	10.00
Beer, McAvoy Beer, Brown, 8 In.	7.00
Beer, North Star, Jacob Schmidt Brewing Co., Paper Label, c.1960, 12 Oz.	15.00
Beer, NSW Bottle Co., Dark Brown, Australia, c.1930, 9 ¼ In.	22.00
Beer, Royal 58, Duluth Brewing, Duluth, Minn., Paper Label, Brown, 12 Oz.	12.00
Beer, Stegmaier Bottling, Embossed, Green, c.1900, 9 ¼ In.	20.00
Beer, Weber Waukesha Draft Beer, Wisconsin, 1940s, 64 Oz.	65.00
Beer, Weiss, Schroeder's B.W.B. Co., St. Louis, Mo., Porcelain Stopper, Wire Ball	110.00
Beer, Wisconsin Holiday Beer, Potosi, Brown, 7 Oz.	40.00
Beer, Wooden Hell, Flossmoor Station Restaurant & Brewery, 22 Oz.	415.00
Bininger, A.M. & Co., 19 Broad St., N.Y., Old Kentucky, Barrel, Double Ring Lip, 8 In.	250.00
Bininger, A.M. & Co., 338 Broadway, N.Y., Amber, Applied Top, Barrel, c.1850	430.00
Bininger, A.M. & Co., 338 Broadway, Old London Dock Gin, Olive, Square, 9 ½ In.	448.00

Bottle, Bitters, Lacour's Sarsapariphere, Amber, Applied Top, 1874-75, 9 ⅛ In. $4256.00

American Bottle Auctions

Bottle, Bitters, National, Ear Of Corn, Olive Yellow, Applied Sloping Collar, c.1870, 12 ¼ In. $2925.00

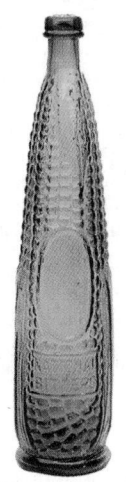

Norman C. Heckler & Company

Bottle, Bitters, National, Ear Of Corn, Patent 1867, Amber, Applied Mouth, c.1870, 12 ¾ In. $518.00

Glass Works Auctions

Bottle, Bitters, National, Ear Of Corn, Patent 1867, Yellow Amber Olive, Applied Mouth, 12 ½ In. $1840.00

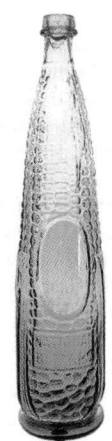

Glass Works Auctions

Bottle, Bitters, Pineapple, Golden Amber, Applied Mouth, 1860-75, 8 ⅞ In. $308.00

American Glass Gallery

Bottle, Bitters, Professor Geo. J. Byrne, Great Universal Compound Stomach, Amber, c.1875 10 ⅞ In. $4446.00

Norman C. Heckler & Company

Bottle, Bitters, Smyrna Stomach, Prolongs Life, Dayton, Ohio, Amber, Tooled Lip, c.1890, 9 In. $546.00

Glass Works Auctions

Bottle, Bitters, Sol Frank's Panacea, Lighthouse Shape, Golden Amber, Mouth Ring, 1860-80, 10 In. $2457.00

Norman C. Heckler & Company

Bottle, Cologne, White, Impressed Lion Panel, Scrolls, Opalescent Flared Mouth, Pontil, c.1850, 4 x 2 ¾ In. $2457.00

Norman C. Heckler & Company

Bottle, Decanter, 13 Vertical Ribs, Swirled To Right, Aqua, Applied Ring, Pontil, c.1820, 9 ½ In.
$728.00

American Bottle Auctions

Bottle, Decanter, Loaf Of Bread, Amber, 12 Post, Folded Lip, Pontil, 11 In.
$179.00

American Bottle Auctions

Bottle, Flask, Admiral Dewey, Canteen, Painted, String Tie, 5 In.
$728.00

American Bottle Auctions

Bottle, Flask, Byron & Scott, Yellow Olive, Sheared Mouth, Pontil, ½ Pt.
$351.00

Norman C. Heckler & Company

Bitters, Aromatic Orange Stomach, Semi-Cabin, Golden Amber, Sloping Collar, 10 In.	2576.00
Bitters, Baker's Orange Grove, Cabin, Apricot Topaz, Roped Corners, 9 ½ In.	1456.00
Bitters, Baker's Orange Grove, Cabin, Golden Amber, Shaded, Roped Corners, 9 ½ In.	532.00
Bitters, Barber's Indian Vegetable Jaundice, Providence, R.I.	198.00
Bitters, Bell's Cocktail, New York, Lady's Leg, Copper Puce, 10 ⅝ In.	532.00
Bitters, Bourbon Whiskey, Barrel, Apricot, Square Collar, 9 ¼ In.	784.00
Bitters, Bourbon Whiskey, Barrel, Strawberry Puce, Square Collar, 9 ¼ In.	420.00
Bitters, Brown's Castilian, Honey Amber, Bell Shape, Square Collar, 10 ⅝ In.	504.00
Bitters, Brown's Catalina, Golden Amber, Bell Shape, Square Collar, 10 ⅞ In.	364.00
Bitters, Brown's Celebrated Indian Herb, Patented Feb. 11 1868, Honey Amber, 12 In.	672.00
Bitters, Brown's Celebrated Indian Herb, Patented Feb. 11 1868, Yellow Amber, 12 ¼ In.	1680.00
Bitters, Bryant's Stomach, Green, 8-Sided, Lady's Leg, Applied Collar	2128.00
Bitters, Carpathian Herb, Hollander Drug Co., Braddock, Pa., Amber, 9 In.	148.00
Bitters, Davis' Kidney & Liver, Best Invigorator & Cathartic, Amber, Tooled Top	224.00
Bitters, Doctor Fisch's, Figural, Fish, Yellow Amber, Tooled Collared Mouth, 1866-80, 11 ½ In. *illus*	380.00
Bitters, Doctor Fisch's, Fish Shape, Amber	504.00
Bitters, Doctor Fisch's, Fish, Amber, 1866, 11 ⅝ In.	236.00
Bitters, Dr. A.S. Hopkins Union Stomach, Shaded Olive Yellow, Square, 9 ⅝ In.	616.00
Bitters, Dr. Bishop's Wa-Hoo, New Haven, Conn., Semi-Cabin, Yellow, 10 ⅛ In.	1120.00
Bitters, Dr. Bull's Superior Stomach, Saint Louis, Orange Amber, Square, 9 In.	235.00
Bitters, Dr. C.W. Roback's Stomach, Cincinnati, O, Barrel, Amber, Sloping Collar, 9 ¾ In. 258.00 to 948.00
Bitters, Dr. Caldwell's Herb, Great Tonic, Honey Amber, 3-Sided, 12 ⅝ In.	476.00
Bitters, Dr. Campbell's Scotch, Golden Yellow Amber, Strap Side Flask, ½ Pt., c.1890	259.00
Bitters, Dr. Gillmore's Laxative Kidney & Liver, Amber, Fluted Shoulder, Tooled Top	168.00
Bitters, Dr. Harters Wild Cherry, Amber, 7 ⅞ In.	85.00
Bitters, Dr. Henley's Wild Grape Root, IXL, Aqua, Applied Band	258.00
Bitters, Dr. J. Hostetter's Stomach, Dark Green, 9 ½ In.	392.00
Bitters, Dr. J. Hostetter's Stomach, Golden Amber, 9 ½ In.	672.00
Bitters, Dr. Loew's Celebrated Stomach & Nerve Tonic, Green, Roped Neck, Tooled Top, 9 In.	420.00
Bitters, Dr. Petzhold's Genuine German, Great Elixer Of Life, Golden Amber, Oval, 6 ¾ In.	213.00
Bitters, Dr. Renz's Herb, Light To Medium Amber, Applied Collar, 9 In.	616.00
Bitters, Dr. Soule's Hop Bitterine, 1872, Embossed Hops, Pink Topaz	1568.00
Bitters, Dr. Stephen Jewett's Celebrated Health Restoring, Amber, Square Collar, 7 In.	5265.00
Bitters, Dr. Van Dyke's Holland, Pat. Jun 2nd 1896, Tooled Mouth, Contents, c.1890-1910, 9 ⅞ In. *illus*	196.00
Bitters, Dr. Von Hopf's Curacoa, Amber, 7 ½ In.	95.00
Bitters, Drake's Plantation, 6 Log, Cherry Puce, 9 ½ In.	300.00
Bitters, Drake's Plantation, 6 Log, Golden Yellow Olive, 10 ¼ In.	840.00
Bitters, Drake's Plantation, 6 Log, Green, 1860	3584.00
Bitters, Drake's Plantation, 6 Log, Patented 1862, Strawberry Puce, c.1870, 10 In.	748.00
Bitters, Drake's Plantation, 6 Log, Peach Puce, 9 ¾ In.	4388.00
Bitters, Drake's Plantation, 6 Log, Smokey Saffron Yellow, Peach Tone, 9 ¾ In.	3218.00
Bitters, Drake's Plantation, 6 Log, Yellow Apricot, 9 ¾ In.	448.00
Bitters, Drake's Plantation, 6 Log, Yellow Olive Shaded To Chartreuse, 10 In.	1904.00
Bitters, Drake's Plantation, 6 Log, Yellow Olive, Sloping Collar, 9 ½ In.	1521.00
Bitters, Drake's Plantation, Patented 1862, 6 Log, Strawberry Puce, Applied Tapered Collar, 10 In.	489.00
Bitters, E. Dexter Loveridge Wahoo, Patd DWD, Cabin, Yellow Amber, 1863 *illus*	4200.00
Bitters, Edw Wilder's Stomach, Clear, House, Indented Sides, Tooled Lip	224.00
Bitters, Fish, Figural, Smokey Orange Puce, Applied Collar, 11 ½ In.	1112.00
Bitters, Fish, Fish Shape, W.H. Ware, Patented 1866, Golden Amber, 11 ¾ In.	115.00
Bitters, Fish, Fish Shape, Green	4480.00
Bitters, Fish, W.H. Ware, Amber, Applied Mouth, c.1863, 11 ½ In.	392.00
Bitters, Fish, W.H. Ware, Patented 1866, Amber, Ring Collar, 11 ⅝ In.	336.00
Bitters, Fish, W.H. Ware, Patented 1866, Yellow Amber, c.1870, 11 ¾ In. *illus*	207.00
Bitters, Geo. Benz & Sons Appetine, St. Paul, Minn., Amber, Square, Scrolls, 3 ½ In.	532.00
Bitters, Greeley's Bourbon, Barrel, Copper Puce, 9 ⅜ In. 500.00 to 1120.00
Bitters, Greeley's Bourbon, Barrel, Golden Ginger Ale, Topaz Tone, Square Collar, 9 In.	1872.00
Bitters, Greeley's Bourbon, Barrel, Olive Green, Barrel, Flattened Lip	2464.00
Bitters, H.P. Herb Wild Cherry, Reading, Pa., Tree, Cabin, Honey Amber, 9 ⅞ In.	616.00
Bitters, Herkules, Monogram, Grass Green, c.1900, 1 Qt., 7 ½ In. *illus*	1150.00
Bitters, Holtzermann's Patent Stomach, Cabin, Orange Amber, Sloping Collar	728.00
Bitters, John W. Steele's Niagara Star, 1864, Semi-Cabin, Amber, Sloping Collar, 10 In.	896.00
Bitters, Johnson's Calisaya, Burlington, Vt., Amber, Arched Panel Sides	280.00
Bitters, Kelly's Old Cabin, Patented 1863, Cabin, Deep Amber, c.1870, 9 ⅜ In. *illus*	3163.00
Bitters, Kimball's Jaundice, Yellow Olive, Beveled Corners, Sloping Collar, 8 In.	1404.00
Bitters, Lacour's Sarsapariphere, Amber, Applied Top, 1874-75, 9 ⅛ In. *illus*	4256.00
Bitters, Lediard's Morning Call, Forest Green, Cylindrical, Sloping Collar, 9 ⅝ In.	364.00

Bitters, Mishler's Herb, Yellow, Square, Indented Panels, Sloping Collar, 9 In.		187.00
Bitters, Mist Of The Morning, Barnett & Lumley, Barrel, Golden Olive Green, 10 In.		2950.00
Bitters, Morning Inceptum 5869, Star, Amber, 12 ¾ In.		532.00
Bitters, Moulton's Oloroso, Embossed Pineapple, Aqua		1344.00
Bitters, National, C.C Jerome & Co., Detroit, 1865, Black Amethyst, 3-Sided, 10 ½ In.		12880.00
Bitters, National, Ear Of Corn, Olive Yellow, Applied Sloping Collar, c.1870, 12 ¼ In. *illus*		2925.00
Bitters, National, Ear Of Corn, Patent 1867, Amber, Applied Mouth, c.1870, 12 ¾ In. *illus*		518.00
Bitters, National, Ear Of Corn, Patent 1867, Yellow Amber Olive, Applied Mouth, 12 ½ In. *illus*		1840.00
Bitters, National, Ear Of Corn, Patent 1867, Yellow Amber, Ringed Mouth, 12 ¼ In.		3105.00
Bitters, New York Hop, Embossed Flag, Aqua		246.00
Bitters, Normandy Herb & Root Stomach, Shaded Amber, Squared Lip, 8 In.		146.00
Bitters, OK Plantation, 1840, Olive Green, 3-Sided, Embossed, 1868, 11 In.		1888.00
Bitters, Old Homestead Wild Cherry, Cabin, Tobacco Amber, Sloping Collar		672.00
Bitters, Old Sachem & Wigwam Tonic, Barrel, Cherry Plum Red, Square Collar, 9 In.		936.00
Bitters, Old Sachem & Wigwam Tonic, Barrel, Yellow, Topaz Tone, Squared Collar, 9 ¼ In.		1638.00
Bitters, Pepsin, R.W. Davis Drug Co., Chicago, 7Up Green, Fluted Neck		280.00
Bitters, Pineapple, Amber, Figural, Sloping Collar, 9 In.		308.00
Bitters, Pineapple, Golden Amber, Applied Mouth, 1860-75, 8 ⅞ In. *illus*		308.00
Bitters, Pineapple, J.C. & Co., Amber, Double Ring Collar, 8 ⅜ In.		1232.00
Bitters, Pineapple, W & Co., N.Y., Dark Amber, Embossed, Double Collar, 8 ⅜ In.		224.00
Bitters, Professor Geo. J. Byrne, Great Universal Compound Stomach, Amber, c.1875, 10 ⅞ In. *illus*		4446.00
Bitters, Prune Stomach & Liver, Amber, Sloping Collar, Case Gin Shape		134.00
Bitters, Reed's, Lady's Leg, Amber, Applied Lip, 12 ¾ In.		364.00
Bitters, Romaine's Crimean, Patented 1863, Semi-Cabin, Golden Amber, 10 In.		840.00
Bitters, Sanborn's Kidney & Liver Vegetable Laxative, Amber		168.00
Bitters, Sazerac Aromatic, Lady's Leg, Amber, Applied Lip, 10 In.		1232.00
Bitters, Sazerac Aromatic, Lady's Leg, Milk Glass, Applied Ring, 12 ½ In.		784.00
Bitters, Schroeder's, Louisville, Ky., Lady's Leg, Amber, 8 ¾ In.		123.00
Bitters, Schroeder's, Louisville, Ky., Lady's Leg, Amber, 11 ½ In.		672.00
Bitters, Smyrna Stomach, Prolongs Life, Dayton, Ohio, Amber, Tooled Lip, c.1890, 9 In. *illus*		546.00
Bitters, Sol Frank's Panacea, Lighthouse Shape, Golden Amber, Mouth Ring, 1860-80, 10 In. *illus*		2457.00
Bitters, Sun Kidney & Liver, Vegetable Laxative Bowel Regulator, Blood Purifier, Amber		168.00
Bitters, Tippecanoe, H.H. Warner, Embossed Bark & Canoe, Amber, Log Shape Cork		476.00
Bitters, William Allen's Congress, Semi-Cabin, Blue Green, c.1870, 10 ¼ In.		3540.00
Bitters, Woodcock Pepsin, John Schroeder's, Red Amber, Ribbed Corners		90.00
Bitters, Zingari, F. Rahter, Lady's Leg, Apricot, Cylindrical, Flattened Lip, 12 In.		532.00
Black Glass, Cylindrical, Champagne, Olive Amber, Tapered, Sloping Collar, 11 ¾ In.		761.00
Black Glass, Cylindrical, Dark Root Beer Amber, Dip Mold, 11 ½ In.		10.00
Black Glass, Cylindrical, Olive, Embossed Pirate Cross On Base, 3-Piece Mold, 11 ¼ In.		85.00
Black Glass, Kidney, Squat, Deep Olive Amber, Collar, Pontil, 7 x 7 ¼ In.		761.00
Black Glass, Mallet, Olive Green, Applied String Lip, 1735-1745, 7 ½ In.		420.00
Black Glass, Onion, Olive Green, Painted Coat Of Arms, Wide Mouth, Pontil, 9 ⅝ In.		1064.00
Black Glass, Rectangular, Olive Green, Tombstone Shoulders, Double Collar, 5 ⅝ In.		308.00
Black Glass, Rum, Embossed Crown On Shoulder, 3-Piece Mold, 9 ¼ In.		15.00
Black Glass, Wine, Porter, Deep Forest Green, Long Neck, 9 In.		40.00
Blown, Bellows, Clear, Rigaree, Applied Prunts, 1820-1840, 8 ½ In.		224.00
Blown, Chestnut, Blue Green, Rolled Lip, c.1790, 8 ½ In.		728.00
Blown, Chestnut, Emerald Green, String Lip, 9 ¼ In.		2016.00
Blown, Chestnut, Olive Amber, Flattened Lip, Pontil, 8 ¼ In.		364.00
Blown, Chestnut, Straw Yellow, Olive Tone, String Lip, Pontil, 5 ⅜ In.		420.00
Blown, Chestnut, Yellow Olive, Applied Lip, c.1790, 8 In.		336.00
Blown, Globular, Emerald Green, Sloping Collar, 7 ½ In.		1456.00
Blown, Globular, Yellow Olive Amber, Flattened Base, Ring Collar, 10 ¼ In.		728.00
Coca-Cola bottles are listed in the Coca-Cola category.		
Cologne, 12 Lobes, Emerald Green, Faceted Stopper, 6 ½ In.		431.00
Cologne, 3 Panels, Malachite, Opaque, Mottled, Roses, Stopper, 5 In.		104.00
Cologne, 6 Panels, Ruby, Pinched Waist, Double Shoulder, Tapered Stopper, 8 In.		403.00
Cologne, 6-Sided, Diamond Point Panel, Yellow, Tapered Paneled Stopper, 4 In.		345.00
Cologne, 6-Sided, Panel & Rib, Peacock Green, Bulbous, Tapered Paneled Stopper, 7 In.		489.00
Cologne, 8 Panels, Electric Blue, Horizontal Ovals, Pinched Paneled Neck, Gold Trim, 6 In.		748.00
Cologne, 8-Sided, Elongated Loop, Bisecting Band, Amber, Stopper, 7 In.		460.00
Cologne, Cut Glass, 8 Panels, Pink Cut To Clear, White & Gold Scrolls, Tapered, 7 In.		374.00
Cologne, Cut Glass, 8-Sided, Blue Cut To Clear, 4-Step Neck, Star-Cut Base, 8 In.		633.00
Cologne, Cut Glass, 8-Sided, Ruby Cut To Clear, Stepped Shoulder, Stopper, 6 In.		316.00
Cologne, Cut Glass, Moorish Arches, Trefoil Tassels, White Cut To Green, Stopper, 7 In.		316.00
Cologne, Cut Glass, Pillar Molded, Bulbous, Knop, Tapered Neck, Yellow, Flame Stopper, 8 In.		345.00

Bottle, Flask, Chestnut, 10 Diamond, Aqua, Sheared, Tooled Mouth, Pontil, Zanesville, c.1825, 5 ⅛ In.
$316.00

Glass Works Auctions

Bottle, Flask, Corn For The World, Peacock Blue, Applied Mouth, Smooth Base, Baltimore, c.1860, Qt.
$3163.00

Glass Works Auctions

Bottle, Flask, Double Eagle, Olive Amber, Sheared & Tooled Lip, Open Pontil, c.1830, Pt.
$431.00

Glass Works Auctions

Bottle, Flask, Eagle & Grapes, Aqua, Qt.
$224.00

American Bottle Auctions

Bottle, Flask, Isabella, Anchor & Glasshouse, Blue Green, Sheared Mouth, Pontil, c.1850, ½ Pt.
$8190.00

Norman C. Heckler & Company

Bottle, Flask, Lafayette & Masonic, Green, Pontil, West Virginia, 1815-30, ½ Pt., 6 ½ In.
$15120.00

American Bottle Auctions

Cologne, Cut Glass, Punty & Panel, White Cut To Cranberry, Cylindrical, Ball Stopper, 5 In.	288.00
Cologne, Cut Glass Swirled Panels, Cobalt Cut To Clear, Squat, Mushroom Stopper, 6 In.	575.00
Cologne, Jenny Lind, Milk Glass, Fostoria, 8 In.	60.00
Cologne, Loop, Canary Yellow, Squat, Applied Collar, Stopper, 7 x 4 ¾ In.	288.00
Cologne, Overshot, Canary Yellow, Opal Cased, 6 Vertical Lobes, Gold Stripes, 7 ½ In.	196.00
Cologne, Pagoda Shape, 8-Sided, Blue, Gold Trim, Panel Cut Neck, Stopper, 5 ¾ x 3 In.	546.00
Cologne, Paneled Cane, Yellow, Square, Rounded Corners, Stopper, 6 In.	288.00
Cologne, Paneled Pebbles, Clambroth, Gold Trim, Ruffled Rim, Blue Stopper, 7 ½ x 5 ¾ In. ..	161.00
Cologne, Spiral Ribbons, Blue & White, Bell Shape, Blue Tapered Stopper, 8 In.	104.00
Cologne, Star Blocks, 5 Vertical Rows, Green, Tapered, Gold Trim, Steeple Stopper, 7 In.	184.00
Cologne, Translucent Starch Blue, Vertical Ribs, 3 Steps, Bulbous, Ribbed Stopper, 6 In.	161.00
Cologne, White, Impressed Lion Panel, Scrolls, Opalescent Flared Mouth, Pontil, c.1850, 4 x 2 ¾ In. *illus*	2457.00
Cordial, Wishart's Pine Tree Tar, Phila, 1859, Tree, Yellow Olive, Square, 9 ⅜ In. ... 1008.00 to 1232.00	
Cosmetic, A. Wanner & Co.'s Sepia Hair Dye, Orange Amber, Double Collar, 6 ¾ In.	616.00
Cosmetic, C. Heimstreet & Co., Troy, N.Y., Sapphire Blue, 8-Sided, Double Collar, 7 In.	224.00
Cosmetic, C.A.P. Mason Alpine Hair Balm, Providence, R.I., Yellow Olive, 6 ⅝ In.	3640.00
Cosmetic, Dodge Brothers Melanine Hair Tonic, Amber, Arched Panels, Ring Collar, 7 ½ In. ...	1008.00
Cosmetic, Dodge Brothers Melanine Hair Tonic, Plum Amethyst, Rectangular, 7 ½ In.	560.00
Cosmetic, Dr. Tebbett's Physiological Hair Regenerator, Puce, Indented Panels, 7 ¼ In.	322.00
Cosmetic, Kickapoo Sage Hair Tonic, Cobalt Blue, Cylindrical, Squat, Ring Collar, 4 ¼ In.	179.00
Cosmetic, Mrs. S.A. Allen's World's Hair Restorer, Amethyst, Flared Mouth, 7 ⅜ In.	234.00
Cosmetic, Mrs. S.A. Allen's World's Hair Restorer, Yellow Apricot, 7 ¼ In.	200.00
Cosmetic, St. Clair's Hair Lotion, Cobalt Blue, Arched Panels, Squared Lip, 7 ¼ In.	336.00
Cure, Alexander's Sure, Liver & Kidney Tonic, Akron, O., Amber, 7 ¾ In.	36.00
Cure, Ayers' Ague, Lowell, Mass., Pale Aqua, Indented Panels, Double Collar, 7 In.	78.00
Cure, Dr. Fenner's Kidney & Backache, Fredonia, N.Y., Amber, Oval, 10 ⅜ In.	65.00
Cure, River Swamp Chill & Fever, Augusta, Ga., Alligator, Amber, Tooled Top, 6 ½ In.	3136.00
Cure, Sanford's Radical, Cobalt Blue, Indented Panels, Squared Lip, 7 ½ In.	190. 00
Cure, Warner's Safe, Melbourne, London, Toronto, Rochester, Straw Yellow, Blob Top, 9 In.	190.00
Cure, Warner's Safe, Pressburg, Red Amber, Blob Top, Germany, 1888-1891, 9 ½ In.	448.00
Decanter, 13 Vertical Ribs, Swirled To Right, Aqua, Applied Ring, Pontil, c.1820, 9 ½ In. ...... *illus*	728.00
Decanter, Barrel, Yellow Olive, Hobnail & Fluted Bands, Sloping Collar, Pt.	1521.00
Decanter, Chestnut, Yellow Olive Amber, Striations, Sloping Collar, 9 In.	1568.00
Decanter, Cobalt Blue, Golf Scene, Sterling Overlay, Stopper, c.1940, 9 ¼ In.	192.00
Decanter, Diamond Thumbprint, Applied Double Collar, Pontil, 7 In.	196.00
Decanter, Loaf Of Bread, Amber, 12 Post, Folded Lip, Pontil, 11 In. .... *illus*	179.00
Decanter, Pillar Molded, Cobalt Blue, 10 Ribs, Bell Form, Flattened Lip, Mushroom Stopper, 7 ½ In.	345.00
Decanter, Pillar Molded, Cobalt Blue, 8 Ribs, Shouldered, Applied Ring, Squared Lip, 12 In...	431.00
Decanter, Pillar Molded, Cobalt Blue, Cone Shape, Ribs, Neck Ring, c.1860, 10 In.	920.00
Decanter, Pillar Molded, Sapphire Blue, 8 Ribs, Neck Ring, Bar Lip, Pt., 10 ½ In.	1725.00
Decanter, Pineapple, Yellow Green, Barrel, 3-Piece Mold, 8 ⅜ In.	3920.00
Decanter, Red Amber, Elongated Neck, 10 In.	336.00
Demijohn, Golden Amber, Heart Form, Sloping Collar, Pontil, Sample Size, c.1870, 3 In.	179.00
Demijohn, Loop Closure, 1 ½ Gal., 13 In.	400.00
Demijohn, Olive Amber, Globular, Sheared Mouth, Applied Ring, c.1800, 19 ⅝ In.	1904.00
Demijohn, Olive Green, Blown, Cone Shaped Neck, Applied Collar, Iron Banded Basket, 30 ½ In.	413.00
Demijohn, Tobacco Amber, Bulbous, Elongated Tapered Neck, Banded Collar, c.1840, 17 In. .	207.00
Figural, Cannon Barrel, Yellow Olive Amber, Sloping Collar, 13 In.	2688.00
Figural, Seashell, Blue, Green, Orange & Yellow Glaze, Prattware Type, 4 x 3 ⅝ In.	322.00
Flask, 10 Diamond, Butterscotch, Chestnut, Sheared, 5 In.	616.00
Flask, 18 Ribs, Swirled To Right, Plum Amethyst, Oval, Flared Neck, Sheared, 6 In.	235.00
Flask, 20 Vertical Ribs, Horizontal Rows Of Ovals, Grape Amethyst, 6 ¾ In.	840.00
Flask, 24 Vertical Ribs, Amber, Shaded, Chestnut, Sheared, Pontil, Pocket, 5 In.	336.00
Flask, 24 Vertical Ribs, Blue Aqua, Pontil, Midwest, 7 ⅝ In.	168.00
Flask, 24 Vertical Ribs, Golden Orange Amber, Sheared, Pontil, Pocket, 4 ½ In.	448.00
Flask, Admiral Dewey, Canteen, Painted, String Tie, 5 In. .... *illus*	728.00
Flask, Amethyst, Diamond & Daisy, Blown, 5 In.	5925.00
Flask, Amethyst, Diamond & Daisy, c.1780, 4 ½ In.	4740.00
Flask, Aqua, Blown, Opaque White Draping, Sheared Lip, Pontil, 7 ¼ In.	153.00
Flask, Byron & Scott, Yellow Olive Amber, Sheared Mouth, Pontil, ½ Pt.	336.00
Flask, Byron & Scott, Yellow Olive, Sheared Mouth, ½ Pt.	288.00
Flask, Byron & Scott, Yellow Olive, Sheared Mouth, Pontil, ½ Pt. .... *illus*	351.00
Flask, Cheatham & Kinney, Nashville, Tenn., Aqua, Ringed Mouth, ½ Pt.	2691.00
Flask, Chestnut, 10 Diamond, Aqua, Sheared, Tooled Mouth, Pontil, Zanesville, c.1825, 5 ⅛ In.... *illus*	316.00
Flask, Chestnut, Clear, Blue Cased Loopings, Opal Inside, Tooled Mouth, c.1870, 7 In.	196.00
Flask, Chestnut, Dark Green, Pulled Neck, Rolled Rim, Pontil, 5 In.	283.00

Flask, Chestnut, Free-Blown, Olive Green, Flattened Shape, Applied Rolled Mouth, c.1830, 8 ½ x 5 In..	748.00
Flask, Chestnut, Rows Of Diamonds, Aqua, Tooled Flared Lip, 4 ⅜ In.	69.00
Flask, Cobalt Blue, Strap Side, Double Collar, ½ Pt.	547.00
Flask, Coffin, Amber, Sloping Collar, Pt., 7 ¼ In.	90.00
Flask, Columbia & Eagle, Aqua, Sheared Mouth, Pontil, Pt.	728.00
Flask, Corn For The World, Peacock Blue, Applied Flattened Collar, Qt.	19890.00
Flask, Corn For The World, Peacock Blue, Applied Mouth, Smooth Base, Baltimore, c.1860, Qt. *illus*	3163.00
Flask, Cornucopia & Urn, Aqua, Pontil, ½ Pt.	224.00
Flask, Cornucopia & Urn, Blue Green, Sheared Mouth, ½ Pt.	259.00
Flask, Cornucopia & Urn, Medium Blue Green, Double Collar, Pontil, Pt., 6 ¾ In.	649.00
Flask, Cornucopia & Urn, Olive Green, Sheared Mouth, ½ Pt.	150.00
Flask, Cornucopia & Urn, Teal, Sheared Lip, Pontil, ½ Pt.	392.00
Flask, D.B. Lester, Grocer, Savannah, Ga., Amber, Strap Side, Double Collar, ½ Pt.	173.00
Flask, Diamond Daisy, Amethyst, Horseshoe Form, Sheared, Pontil, Pocket, 5 In.	5320.00
Flask, Double Eagle, Amber, Shaded, Applied Ringed Mouth, ½ Pt.	138.00
Flask, Double Eagle, Aqua Green, Neck Ring, Pt.	213.00
Flask, Double Eagle, Aqua, Sheared Mouth, Pontil, ½ Pt.	374.00
Flask, Double Eagle, Aqua, Sheared Mouth, Pontil, Qt.	420.00
Flask, Double Eagle, Blue Aqua, Sheared Mouth, Pontil, Pt.	308.00
Flask, Double Eagle, Grass Green, Tooled Lip, ½ Pt.	1232.00
Flask, Double Eagle, Olive Amber, Sheared & Tooled Lip, Open Pontil, c.1830, Pt. *illus*	431.00
Flask, Double Eagle, Yellow Amber, Olive Tone, Sheared, Pontil, ½ Pt.	202.00
Flask, Double Eagle, Yellow Olive, Qt.	1035.00
Flask, Double Eagle, Yellow Olive, Sheared Mouth, Pt.	439.00
Flask, Eagle & Banner, Calabash, 7Up Green, Sloping Collar, Qt.	246.00
Flask, Eagle & Cornucopia, Aqua, Rolled Lip, ½ Pt.	308.00
Flask, Eagle & Cornucopia, Olive Amber, Sheared, Pontil, Pt.	202.00
Flask, Eagle & Cornucopia, Olive Green, Sheared, Pontil, Pt.	213.00
Flask, Eagle & Cornucopia, Yellow Olive Amber, Sheared, Pontil, Pt.	235.00
Flask, Eagle & Grapes, Aqua, Qt. *illus*	224.00
Flask, Eagle & Louisville, Vertical Ribs, Blue Aqua, ½ Pt.	288.00
Flask, Eagle & Louisville, Vertical Ribs, Blue Aqua, Pt.	173.00
Flask, Eagle & Oak Tree, Deep Tobacco Amber, Pontil, ½ Pt.	3360.00
Flask, Eagle & Willington, Deep Yellow Olive, Double Collar, ½ Pt.	196.00
Flask, Eagle & Willington, Forest Green, Sheared Mouth, Pontil, Pt.	878.00
Flask, Eagle & Willington, Golden Amber, Double Collar, ½ Pt.	308.00
Flask, Eagle, Amber, Shaded, Tooled Mouth, ½ Pt.	207.00
Flask, Eagle, Blue Aqua, Tooled Mouth, ½ Pt.	127.00
Flask, Embossed U.S., President Taft, Label Under Glass, Rope Handle, Pocket, 5 In.	840.00
Flask, Emerald Green, Strap Side, Flattened Neck Ring, ½ Pt.	127.00
Flask, Eye Opener, Embossed, Enameled, 3 ½ x 5 ½ In.	575.00
Flask, For Pike's Peak, Prospector, Eagle, Blue Aqua, Ring Mouth, ½ Pt.	92.00
Flask, For Pike's Peak, Prospector, Hunter, Aqua, Sheared Mouth, Pt.	269.00
Flask, Franklin & Dyott, Aqua, Kensington Glass Works, Pt.	840.00
Flask, Franklin & Dyott, Where Liberty Dwells, Aqua, Sheared Mouth, 7 In.	531.00
Flask, Gemel, Opal Cased, Blue & Rose Loopings, Flattened, Pontil, c.1870, 7 ½ In.	138.00
Flask, Gemel, Sapphire Blue, Flattened Oval, Pontil, 7 In.	104.00
Flask, Girl On Bicycle & Eagle, Aqua, Applied Ring, Pt.	527.00
Flask, Granite Glass Co., Stoddard, N.H., Amber, Sheared Lip, Pontil	616.00
Flask, Granite Glass Co., Stoddard, N.H., Golden Amber, Double Collar, Pt.	672.00
Flask, Honeycomb Over Flutes, Grape Amethyst, Horseshoe Form, Pontil, 5 In.	3360.00
Flask, Hunter & Rifle, Grape & Vine, Cobalt Blue, Vertical Ribs, Flared Lip, Pontil, 7 In.	295.00
Flask, Isabella, Anchor & Glasshouse, Blue Green, Sheared Mouth, Pontil, c.1850, ½ Pt. *..illus*	8190.00
Flask, Jenny Lind & Glass House, Calabash, Green Aqua, Sloping Collar, Qt.	123.00
Flask, Jenny Lind, Calabash, Blue Green, Rolled Lip, Pontil, Ravenna Glassworks, 9 ¾ In.	316.00
Flask, Lafayette & Masonic, Green, Pontil, West Virginia, 1815-30, ½ Pt., 6 ½ In. *illus*	15120.00
Flask, Log Cabin & Flag, Cider Barrel & Plow, Aqua, Pontil, Pt.	5320.00
Flask, Marbrie Loop, Opal, Rose Loopings, Oval, Flattened, Tooled Mouth, c.1870, 7 ¼ In.	69.00
Flask, Marbrie Loop, Red, White & Blue Loopings, Oval, Flattened, Pontil, 7 ½ x 4 In.	219.00
Flask, Masonic & Eagle, Aqua, Sheared Mouth, Pontil, Pt.	336.00
Flask, Masonic & Eagle, Blue Green, Tooled Lip, Pontil, Pt.	819.00
Flask, Masonic & Eagle, Golden Amber, Orange Tone, Sheared, Pontil, Pt.	560.00
Flask, Masonic & Seeing Eye, Light Yellow Olive, Sheared Mouth, Pt.	585.00
Flask, Masonic, Clasped Hands & Eagle, Apple Green, Squared Collar, Qt.	1053.00
Flask, Masonic, Clasped Hands & Eagle, Blue Aqua, Pontil, ½ Pt.	92.00
Flask, Moon, Porcelain, Tea Dust Glaze, Round, Pinched Neck, 2 Handles, Chinese, 1900s, 13 In.	1304.00

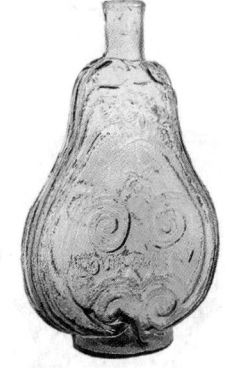

Bottle, Flask, Scroll, Olive Yellow, Louisville, Ky., Red Iron Pontil, Sheared & Tooled Lip, 1845-55, Qt.
$31050.00

Glass Works Auctions

Famous Bottle Collectors
Andrew Carnegie, Henry Ford, and President Carter collected bottles.

Bottle, Flask, Sheaf Of Grain & Star, Calabash, Root Beer Amber, Applied Collar, Iron Pontil, c.1850, Qt.
$199.00

Norman C. Heckler & Company

Bottle, Flask, Sunburst, Keen, P. & W., Yellow Amber, Tooled Lip, Open Pontil, c.1820, Pt.
$633.00

Glass Works Auctions

Bottle, Flask, Sunburst, M'Carty & Torreyson Mfr., Wellsburg, Va., Aqua, Pontil, c. 1850, 7 ¼ In.
$1344.00

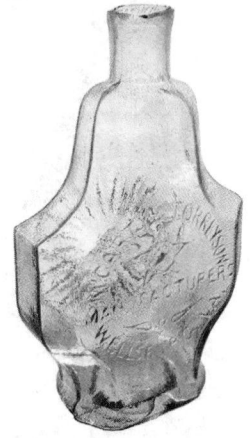

American Bottle Auctions

Bottle, Flask, Sunburst, Green, Sheared Mouth, Pontil, Keene Marlboro Street Glassworks, c.1820, Pt.
$1112.00

Norman C. Heckler & Company

Bottle, Flask, Washington & Taylor, Cobalt Blue, Applied Square Collared Mouth, Pontil, c.1850, Qt.
$1521.00

Norman C. Heckler & Company

Bottle, Flask, Washington & Tree, Calabash, Cobalt, Applied Sloping Collar, Tubular Pontil, c. 1850, Qt.
$28080.00

Norman C. Heckler & Company

Bottle, Fruit Jar, Lid, Iron Yoke Clamp, Hitall's Patent, Aqua, Millville Glass, 1860-80, ½ Pt.
$380.00

Norman C. Heckler & Company

Bottle, Fruit Jar, Mason's, Patent Nov. 30th 1858, Citron, Ground Lip, Zinc Screw Lid, c.1870-85, Qt.
$438.00

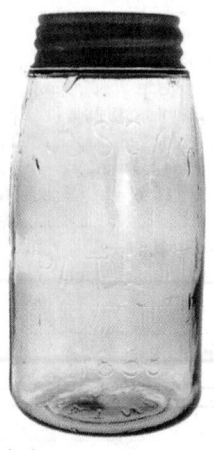

Glass Works Auctions

Bottle, Ink, Farley's, 8-Sided, Yellow Olive, Sheared Mouth, Pontil, 1 ¾ In.
$1053.00

Norman C. Heckler & Company

Bottle, Ink, Geometric, Olive Amber, Diamond Point, Ribbed Bottom, 1 ¾ In.
$308.00

American Bottle Auctions

Bottle, Ink, J. & I.E.M., Turtle, Blue Green, Sheared Lip, Embossed Base, c.1875, 1 ⅝ In.
$1232.00

American Glass Gallery

Bottle, Ink, Teakettle, Cobalt Blue, Ground Lip, Brass Neck Ring & Cap, c.1885, 2 In.
$403.00

Glass Works Auctions

Flask, Pitkin Type, 22 Melon Ribs, Yellow Green, Flattened, Sheared, 4 ½ In.	392.00
Flask, Pitkin Type, 32 Ribs, Swirled To Right, Blue Green, Inward Rolled Mouth, 6 ⅝ In.	936.00
Flask, Pitkin Type, 32 Ribs, Swirled To Right, Sea Green, Sheared Mouth, Pontil, 7 In.	702.00
Flask, Pitkin Type, 36 Broken Ribs, Root Beer Amber, Flattened Oval, Pontil, Pt.	690.00
Flask, Pitkin Type, 36 Ribs, Swirled To Right, Forest Green, Sheared Mouth, Pontil, 6 ½ In.	995.00
Flask, Pitkin Type, 36 Ribs, Swirled To Right, Olive Green, Rolled Rim, Pontil, 4 ⅞ In.	3218.00
Flask, Prospector & Eagle, Blue Aqua, Milky Striations, Applied Ringed Mouth, ½ Pt., 6 ¼ In.	115.00
Flask, Scroll, Aqua, Iron Pontil, Qt.	728.00
Flask, Scroll, Citron, Sheared Mouth, Pontil, Pt.	1120.00
Flask, Scroll, Golden Yellow, Sheared Mouth, Iron Pontil, Qt.	380.00
Flask, Scroll, Olive Yellow, Louisville, Ky., Red Iron Pontil, Sheared & Tooled Lip, 1845-55, Qt. *illus*	31050.00
Flask, Scroll, Root Beer Amber, Sheared Mouth, Pontil, Qt.	1568.00
Flask, Sheaf Of Grain & Star, Amber, Shaded, Rolled Collar, ½ Pt.	1265.00
Flask, Sheaf Of Grain & Star, Calabash, Root Beer Amber, Applied Collar, Iron Pontil, c.1850, Qt. *illus*	199.00
Flask, Sheaf Of Grain & Star, Deep Olive Green, Rolled Collar, ½ Pt.	150.00
Flask, Sheaf Of Grain & Star, Light To Medium Green, Double Collar, Pt.	351.00
Flask, Sheaf Of Grain, Westford Glass Co., Tobacco Amber, Collar, ½ Pt.	308.00
Flask, Sheaf Of Grain, Westford Glass Co., Yellow Olive, Sheared, ½ Pt.	1404.00
Flask, Smoky Tint, Enameled Rooster, 1819, Pocket	224.00
Flask, Soldier & Hound, Golden Red Amber, Neck Ring, Pontil, Qt.	936.00
Flask, Spring Garden & Anchor, Aqua, Pebbled, ½ Pt.	161.00
Flask, Spring Garden & Anchor, Aqua, Pt.	134.00
Flask, Success To The Railroad & Eagle With Stars, Olive Amber, Sheared, Pt.	532.00
Flask, Success To The Railroad, Yellow Amber, Sheared Mouth, Pontil, Pt.	819.00
Flask, Summer & Winter, Blue Aqua, Applied Collar, ½ Pt.	138.00
Flask, Summer & Winter, Blue Green, Sheared Mouth, Pontil, Qt.	761.00
Flask, Sunburst, Green, Sheared Mouth, Pontil, Keene Marlboro Street Glassworks, c.1820, Pt. *illus*	1112.00
Flask, Sunburst, Keen, P. & W., Yellow Amber, Tooled Lip, Open Pontil, c.1820, Pt. *illus*	633.00
Flask, Sunburst, M'Carty & Torreyson Mfr., Wellsburg, Va., Aqua, Pontil, 1850, 7 ¼ In. *illus*	1344.00
Flask, Sunburst, Medium To Dark Olive Green, Sheared Mouth, ½ Pt.	748.00
Flask, Sunburst, Olive Amber, Coffin Shape, Double Collar, Pontil, 7 ⅜ In.	995.00
Flask, Teardrop, 16 Ribs, Amethyst, Sheared Mouth, Pontil, Midwest, 6 ⅜ In.	761.00
Flask, Traveler's Companion & Sheaf Of Grain, Fork, Rake, Applied Mouth, c.1870, Qt., 9 In.	189.00
Flask, Traveler's Companion, Ravenna, Aqua, Rolled Collar, Pt.	138.00
Flask, Union, Clasped Hands & Cannon, Yellow Green, Flattened Ring, ½ Pt.	173.00
Flask, Union, Clasped Hands & Eagle, Amber, Ring Mouth, ½ Pt.	196.00
Flask, Union, Clasped Hands & Eagle, Citron, Ring Mouth, ½ Pt.	460.00
Flask, Union, Clasped Hands & Eagle, Shaded Citron, Ringed Mouth, ½ Pt.	1638.00
Flask, Union, Clasped Hands & Eagle, Yellow, Amber & Olive Tones, ½ Pt.	633.00
Flask, Washington & Eagle, Green Aqua, Sheared, Tooled Lip, Pittsburgh Glass Works, c.1835, Pt.	489.00
Flask, Washington & Eagle, Stars, Tooled Lip, Open Pontil, c.1830, Qt.	219.00
Flask, Washington & Monument, Copper, Apricot Tint, Sheared, Pontil, Pt.	8400.00
Flask, Washington & Taylor Never Surrenders, Teal Blue, Qt.	1495.00
Flask, Washington & Taylor, Blue Aqua, Sheared, Pontil, Pt.	364.00
Flask, Washington & Taylor, Cobalt Blue, Applied Square Collared Mouth, Pontil, c.1850, Qt. *illus*	1521.00
Flask, Washington & Taylor, Cornflower Blue, Sheared Mouth, Pontil, Qt.	1904.00
Flask, Washington & Taylor, Pink Lilac, Pontil, Pt.	20160.00
Flask, Washington & Tree, Calabash, Cobalt, Applied Sloping Collar, Tubular Pontil, c.1850, Qt. *illus*	28080.00
Flask, Washington, Father Of His Country, Aqua, Applied Mouth, Qt.	392.00
Flask, Washington, Father Of His Country, Pine Green, Applied Collar, Pontil, Qt.	1680.00
Food, Blueberry Preserves, Green, Cylindrical, Fluted Shoulders, Double Collar, 11 ⅜ In.	644.00
Food, Extract, Crosse & Blackwell, Cobalt Blue, 6 Petaled Sides, Swollen Neck, 4 In.	92.00
Food, Gilbert's Air-Tight Butter Jar, Square, Embossed Lid, Wire Cage, Bail Handle, 6 ½ In.	498.00
Food, Shriver's Oyster Ketchup, Baltimore, Green, Cylindrical, Sloping Collar, 7 ½ In.	1568.00
Food, Yellow Olive, Petaled Shoulders, Applied Collar, Midwest, Qt.	644.00
Fruit Jar, Ball Mason's, Patent Nov 30th, 1858, Blue, Zinc Lid, ½ Gal.	55.00
Fruit Jar, Flaccus Bros., Milk Glass, Pt.	350.00
Fruit Jar, Globe, Wide Mouth, Aqua, 3-Piece Iron Clamp, c.1900, Pt.	390.00
Fruit Jar, Lid, Iron Yoke Clamp, Hitall's Patent, Aqua, Millville Glass, 1860-80, ½ Pt. *illus*	380.00
Fruit Jar, Mason, Aqua, Wide Mouth, Insert, Pat. June 9 1863, Hemingray, Qt.	460.00
Fruit Jar, Mason, Black Amber, Lugged Zinc Cap, Hemingray Glass Co., 1877, Qt.	10350.00
Fruit Jar, Mason's CFJCo Patent Nov 30th 1858, Amber, Zinc Lid, Qt.	556.00
Fruit Jar, Mason's Cross Patent Nov 30th 1858, Aqua, Lid, Midget.	35.00
Fruit Jar, Mason's Keystone Patent Nov 30th 1858, 23 On Base, Amber, ½ Gal.	269.00
Fruit Jar, Mason's Patent Nov. 30th 1858, Citron, Ground Lip, Zinc Screw Lid, c.1870-85, Qt. *illus*	438.00
Fruit Jar, Mason's Patent Nov 30th 1858, Yellow Amber, Cylindrical, Zinc Lid, Midget, Pt.	878.00

Bottle, Ink, Teakettle, Lime Green, Sheared & Ground Lip, c.1880, 3 In. $518.00

Glass Works Auctions

Bottle, Ink, Umbrella, 8-Sided, Blue Green, M & P, New York, Lip, Pontil, c.1850, 2 ⅜ In. $896.00

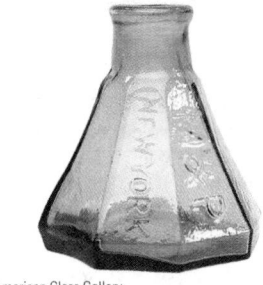

American Glass Gallery

Bottle, Ink, Umbrella, 8-Sided, Yellow Olive, Rolled Lip, Open Pontil, c.1850, 2 ½ In. $978.00

Glass Works Auctions

Bottle, Mineral Water, M.T. Crawford Hartford Ct., Slug Plate, Union Glass Works, Cobalt, c.1850, 7 ⅜ In. $690.00

Glass Works Auctions

B

Bottle, Pepper Sauce, Cathedral, Blue Green, Smooth Base, Applied Double Collar, c.1865-75, 8 ½ In.
$138.00

Glass Works Auctions

Bottle, Pepper Sauce, J. McCollick & Co., New York, Cathedral, Medium Blue, Applied Mouth, 8 ½ In.
$3360.00

American Bottle Auctions

Bottle, Pickle, Cathedral, Blue Green, Applied Mouth, 11 ¼ In.
$1232.00

American Bottle Auctions

Fruit Jar, Mason's Patent Nov. 30th 1858, Zinc & Glass Lid, Blue, 9 In.	5015.00
Fruit Jar, Melon, Dark Aqua, Ribbed, Hemingray, 1860s, Qt.	938.00
Fruit Jar, Sapphire Blue, Cylindrical, Sheared Wide Mouth, 3-Piece Mold, 6 x 4 In.	1638.00
Fruit Jar, Trademark Lightning, Citron, Glass Lid, Wire Bail, Qt.	497.00
Fruit Jar, Van Vliet Jar Of 1881, Aqua, Cylindrical, Glass Lid, Metal Yolk Clamp, Wire, Qt.	761.00
Gemel, Applied Eagles, Incised, Oval, Slip Glaze, Stoneware, Jacob Cone, Conn., c.1850, 6 ¾ In.	2070.00
Gin, Case, Blue Green, Pigeon Blood Striations, Embossed Geometrics, Flowers, 8 In.	644.00
Gin, Case, Green, Applied String Lip, c.1745, 16 In.	1456.00
Gin, Case, Olive Amber, Dip Mold, Pontil, c.1800, 13 ½ In.	672.00
Gin, Case, Yellow Green, Sheared Mouth, String Rim, 11 ⅜ In.	410.00
Ginger Beer, L. Werrbach, Milwaukee, Golden Amber, Mug Base, 7 ⅛ In.	224.00
Household, Crocker's Union Boot Polish, Light Green, Square, Rounded Shoulders, 4 In.	2340.00
Ink, 22 Vertical Ribs, Emerald Green, 3-Piece Mold	728.00
Ink, Carter's, Ma & Pa Carter, Stoppers, Germany, Pair	165.00
Ink, Cylindrical, Diamond Diaper Sides, Olive Green, Pontil, 2 x 2 ¼ In.	173.00
Ink, Davids & Black, New York, Blue Green, Cylindrical, Sloping Collar, Master, 6 In.	174.00
Ink, Diamond Panels Within Diamonds, Dark Olive Green, Cylindrical, 1 ½ x 2 In.	161.00
Ink, Dome, Clear, White & Pink Looping, Swirled To Right, Sandwich, c.1860, 2 x 3 In.	784.00
Ink, F. Kidder, Indelible Ink, Rectangular, Aqua, Inward Rolled Mouth, 2 ⅜ In.	280.00
Ink, Farley's, 8-Sided, Yellow Olive, Sheared Mouth, Pontil, 1 ¾ In. *illus*	1053.00
Ink, Geometric, 3-Piece Mold, Inset Tooled Mouth, Sandwich, c.1835, 2 x 2 In.	1064.00
Ink, Geometric, Honeycomb, Corset Waist, 3-Piece Mold, Sandwich, c.1830, 1 ¾ x 2 In.	6720.00
Ink, Geometric, Olive Amber, Diamond Point, Ribbed Bottom, 1 ¾ In. *illus*	308.00
Ink, Geometric, Sunburst Band, 3-Piece Mold, Pontil, Sandwich, c.1835, 2 ¼ In.	4480.00
Ink, Harrison's Columbian, Blue, Pontil, Gal.	5000.00
Ink, Harrison's Columbian, Sapphire Blue, Cylindrical, Inward Rolled Lip, 1 ⅞ In.	672.00
Ink, Hover, Phila., Yellow Green, Cylindrical, Ring Lip, Pontil, c.1850, Master, 5 ¾ In.	146.00
Ink, J. & I.E.M., Turtle, Blue Green, Sheared Lip, Embossed Base, c.1875, 1 ⅝ In. *illus*	1232.00
Ink, Pitkin Type, 36 Ribs, Swirled To Left, Yellow Green, Cylindrical, 1 ⅜ In.	1989.00
Ink, Teakettle, Cobalt Blue, Ground Lip, Brass Neck Ring & Cap, c.1885, 2 In. *illus*	403.00
Ink, Teakettle, Lime Green, Sheared & Ground Lip, c.1880, 3 In. *illus*	518.00
Ink, Teakettle, Milk Glass, Fiery Opalescent, Enameled Flowers, Sandwich, 3 ½ In.	560.00
Ink, Umbrella, 8-Sided, Blue Green, M & P, New York, Lip, Pontil, c.1850, 2 ⅜ In. *illus*	896.00
Ink, Umbrella, 8-Sided, Sapphire Blue, Violet Tone, Ring Lip, c.1875, 2 ½ In.	392.00
Ink, Umbrella, 8-Sided, Yellow Olive Amber, Sheared Mouth, c.1850, 2 ½ In.	364.00
Ink, Umbrella, 8-Sided, Yellow Olive, Pontil, 1845-1860, 2 ¼ In.	336.00
Ink, Umbrella, 8-Sided, Yellow Olive, Rolled Lip, Open Pontil, c.1850, 2 ½ In. *illus*	978.00
Ink, Umbrella, 16-Sided, Olive Amber, Sheared Mouth, Pontil, c.1850, 2 In.	392.00
Ink, Waters Ink, Troy, N.Y., Umbrella, 6-Sided, Melon Lobed, Aqua, 2 ⅝ In.	448.00
Jar, Blue, 5-Point Star, Zinc Screw Band, c.1875, ½ Gal.	92.00
Jar, Storage, Dark Aqua, Wax Sealer Mouth, Iron Pontil, Ravenna Glass Works, 1850s, Qt.	3155.00
Jar, Storage, Yellow Olive, Wide Neck, Flared Rim, Dip Mold, 9 ¼ In.	235.00
Medicine, A.B.L. Meyers, Rock Rose, New Haven, Blue Green, Indented, 9 ¼ In.	1989.00
Medicine, Apothecary, Glass, Enamel, Gilt Images, Gilt Lid, c.1900s, 13 In., Pair	353.00
Medicine, Apothecary, Pear Shape, Faceted Stopper, c.1900, 23 In.	529.00
Medicine, Apothecary, Porcelain, Flowers, Cobalt, Gilt, Labeled Cyanic, Opium, 1800s, 11 In., Pair	2350.00
Medicine, Apothecary, Teal, Cylindrical, Flared Mouth, Pontil, 11 ⅜ In.	179.00
Medicine, B.O. & G.C. Wilson Botanic Druggists, Boston, Aqua, Indented Panels, 9 ¼ In.	224.00
Medicine, Beekman's Pulmonic Syrup, New York, Yellow Olive, 8-Sided, 7 ¼ In.	49.00
Medicine, C. Brinkerhoff's Health Restorative, Price $1.00, New York, Yellow Olive, 7 In.	952.00
Medicine, Carter's Little Liver Pills, Glass Vial, Red, Cork Stopper, 2 ¼ In.	10.00
Medicine, Carter's Spanish Mixture, Yellow Olive, Cylindrical, Sloping Collar, 8 ¼ In.	439.00
Medicine, Clemen's Indian Tonic, Aqua, Oval, Rolled Lip, Pontil, Label, 5 ½ In.	476.00
Medicine, Clemen's Indian Tonic, Medicine Man, Aqua, Oval, Rolled Mouth, 5 ⅜ In.	702.00
Medicine, Compound Syrup Of Iceland Moss, J.C. Dubose, Light Aqua, Arched Sides, 6 In.	1120.00
Medicine, Dickey Chemist, S.F., Pioneer, 1850, Mortar, Sapphire Blue, Squared Lip	123.00
Medicine, Doctor Kennedy's, Prairie Weed, Roxbury, Mass., Iridescent Aqua, Paneled	112.00
Medicine, Dr. Davis's Depurative, Phila., Blue Green, Square, Beveled Corners, 9 ¾ In.	2240.00
Medicine, Dr. Hartshorn's, Golden Amber, Oval, Squared Collar, 6 In.	1404.00
Medicine, Dr. Jas. C. Kerr's Great System Renovator, Cincinnati, O, Amber, Square, 8 In.	112.00
Medicine, Dr. Larookahs Indian Vegetable Pulmonic Syrup, Aqua, 8 ¾ In.	80.00
Medicine, Dr. S.A. Weaver's Canker & Salt Rheum Syrup, Aqua, Oval, 9 ½ In.	157.00
Medicine, E.A. Buckhout's Dutch Liniment, Man With Pipe, Aqua, Rectangular, 4 ⅝ In.	252.00
Medicine, E.A. Buckhout's Dutch Liniment, Mechanicville, N.Y., Aqua, Rolled Rim, 5 In.	819.00
Medicine, Follansbee's Elixir Of Health, Blue Aqua, Square, Beveled Corners, 8 ¾ In.	2128.00
Medicine, G. Marsh, S.W. Pain Reliever, Cornflower Blue, Rectangular, Rolled Lip, 4 In.	1680.00

Medicine, G.W. Merchant, Lockport, N.Y., Blue Green, Rectangular, Sloping Collar, Pontil, 5 In.	241.00
Medicine, Gargling Oil, Lockport, N.Y., Green, Indented Panels, Sloping Collar, 5 ½ In.	190.00
Medicine, H.H. Warner & Co., Tippecanoe, Log, Yellow Olive, Mushroom Top, 9 In.	9520.00
Medicine, Hampton's V. Tincture, Balto., Puce, Oval, Squared Collar, 6 ¼ In.	410.00
Medicine, Hopkins' Chalybeate, Baltimore, Olive Amber, Cylindrical, 7 ¼ In.	439.00
Medicine, Houses Indian Tonic, Aqua, Oval, Rolled Lip, 1845-1850, 5 ¼ In.	1344.00
Medicine, Hyatt's Infallible Life Balsam, N.Y., Teal, Pontil, 9 ¾ In.	1800.00
Medicine, Hyatt's Infallible Life Balsam, N-Y, Green, Indented Panels, Sloping Collar, 9 ¾ In.	2016.00
Medicine, J. Doherty, Boston, Drug Store, Sacramento, Smoky Tint, Oval, Flared Lip, 5 ½ In.	78.00
Medicine, J.L. Leavitt, Boston, Olive Green, Cylindrical, Sloping Collar, 8 In.	308.00
Medicine, John J. Smith, Louisville, Ky., Blue Green, Cylindrical, Pontil, 5 ¾ In.	92.00
Medicine, Johnson's American Anodyne Liniment, Cylindrical, Flared Mouth, 4 ⅜ In.	380.00
Medicine, Kickapoo Sagwa Stomach Liver & Kidney Renovator, Aqua, 8 ½ In.	70.00
Medicine, Lewis & Fletchers New Vegetable Compound, Franklin, Ind., Aqua, Panels, 8 In.	1872.00
Medicine, Log Cabin Cough & Consumption Remedy, Golden Amber, Paneled, 6 ⅞ In.	112.00
Medicine, Madm M. Kyoulin Majestic Syrup, Green, Rectangular, Double Collar, 2 ½ In.	1872.00
Medicine, Maternal Friend, Light Green, Indented Panels, Flared Flattened Lip, 4 ¾ In.	392.00
Medicine, N. Wood, Portland, Me., Tobacco Amber, Rectangular, Beveled, 7 ⅛ In.	2016.00
Medicine, Nathan Jarvis', Orris Tooth Wash, Boston, Aqua, Rolled Lip, Pontil, 4 ¾ In.	202.00
Medicine, Olive Green, Shaded, Arched Shoulders, Sloping Collar, 6 In.	728.00
Medicine, Owl Drug Co., Owl In Mortar & Pestle, Cobalt Blue, Square, Beveled, 9 ¼ In.	392.00
Medicine, Phelps's Arcanum, Worcester, Mass., Yellow Olive, Cylindrical, Panels, 8 ½ In.	3510.00
Medicine, Prof. De Grath's Electric Oil, Philad., Aqua, Indented Panels, Lip, 5 ½ In.	476.00
Medicine, Rowler's Rheumatism, Prepared By Dr. J.R. Boyce, Sacramento, Green, 7 ¾ In.	336.00
Medicine, Rushton & Aspinwall, New York, Yellow Olive, Beveled, 6 ½ In.	4973.00
Medicine, Sanderson's Blood Renovator, Milton, Vt., Aqua, Oval, Collar, Pontil, 8 In.	1521.00
Medicine, Scott & Stewart Syrup, New York, Green, Rectangular, Sloping Collar, 3 ⅝ In.	3276.00
Medicine, Shaker Syrup, Enfield N.H., Indented Panels, Beveled Corners, 6 ½ In.	819.00
Medicine, Smith's Green Mountain Renovator, East Georgia, Vt., Cornflower Blue, Oval, 7 In.	151.00
Medicine, Swaim's Panacea, Philada, Olive Amber, Cylindrical, Panels, Sloping, 7 ¾ In.	761.00
Medicine, Swaim's Panacea, Philadelphia, Genuine, Aqua, Rectangular, Beveled, 7 ¾ In.	448.00
Medicine, Trafton's Buckthorn Syrup, For Scrofula, Aqua, Beveled Corners, 7 In.	1287.00
Medicine, U.S., Marine Hospital Service, 1798, Star, Caduceus, Anchor, Aqua, Cylindrical, 9 In.	364.00
Medicine, U.S.A. Hosp. Dept., Yellow Amber, Cylindrical, Double Collar, 9 ¼ In.	728.00
Medicine, West's Rheumatic Remedy, Aqua, 8 In.	45.00
Milk, A. Stone & Co., Aqua, Smooth Base, Applied Wax Seal Ring, 1865-70, ½ Pt.	978.00
Milk, Brooke, Farm & Dairy, Tooled Mouth, Lightning Wire Closure, Porcelain Stopper, 7 ¾ In.	173.00
Milk, Eversweet, American Pure Milk, Blob Top, Lightning Wire Closure, c.1895, 11 ½ In., 1 Qt.	173.00
Milk, Hinckley Dairy, Chicago Il., ¼ Pt.	24.00
Mineral Water, A.C. Evans, Wilmington, NC, Yellow Green, Sloping Collar, 7 ⅝ In.	4760.00
Mineral Water, Alex Eagle, Blue Green, Blob Top, 7 ⅛ In.	115.00
Mineral Water, Blount Springs, Natural Sulphur Water, Monogram, Cobalt Blue, 7 ⅜ In.	92.00
Mineral Water, Chase & Co., San Francisco, Green, Sloping Collar, Iron Pontil	308.00
Mineral Water, Congress & Empire Spring Co., Hotchkiss' Sons, C, Amber, Pt.	235.00
Mineral Water, Congress & Empire Spring Co., Hotchkiss' Sons, C, Lime Green, Pt. .	476.00 to 840.00
Mineral Water, Congress & Empire Spring Co., Hotchkiss' Sons, E, Emerald Green, Pt.	392.00
Mineral Water, Excelsior Spring, Teal, 8-Sided, Blob Top, Iron Pontil	364.00
Mineral Water, Highrock Congress Spring, 1767, Rock, Teal Blue, Pt.	532.00
Mineral Water, J. Boardman & Co., New York, Cobalt Blue, 8-Sided, Pontil, 7 ⅝ In.	784.00
Mineral Water, John Ryan, Excelsior, Savannah, Ga., Sapphire Blue, Blob Top, Pontil, 7 In.	173.00
Mineral Water, M.T. Crawford Hartford Ct., Slug Plate, Union Glass Works, Cobalt, c.1850, 7 ⅜ In. *illus*	690.00
Mineral Water, Olive Yellow, Chestnut, Crimped Collar, 7 ⅞ In.	280.00
Mineral Water, S & C, Elkton, Md., Blue Green, Shouldered, Sloping Collar, Slug Plate	1064.00
Mineral Water, Seitz & Bro., Premium, Easton, Pa., Sapphire Blue, Blob Top, 7 In.	288.00
Mineral Water, Southwick & Tupper, New York, Blue Green, 10-Sided, 7 ⅝ In.	392.00
Mineral Water, Stirlings Magnetic Spring, Eaton Rapids, Mich., Orange Amber, Qt.	157.00
Pepper Sauce, Cathedral, 2 Embossed Clocks On Shoulders, Teal, 11 In.	1904.00
Pepper Sauce, Cathedral, Aqua, Cohansey Glass Works, 8 ⅝ In.	168.00
Pepper Sauce, Cathedral, Blue Green, Smooth Base, Applied Double Collar, c.1865-75, 8 ½ In. *illus*	138.00
Pepper Sauce, Cathedral, Blue Green, Trefoils, Quatrefoils, Rolled Collar, 11 ½ In.	258.00
Pepper Sauce, Cathedral, Crosshatching, Light Green, 7 ⅜ In.	179.00
Pepper Sauce, Cathedral, Green Aqua, Cohansey Glass Works, 13 ½ In.	364.00
Pepper Sauce, Cathedral, Green Aqua, Outward Rolled Ring Collar, 11 ½ In.	190.00
Pepper Sauce, J. McCollick & Co., New York, Cathedral, Medium Blue, Applied Mouth, 8 ½ In. *illus*	3360.00
Pepper Sauce, P.D. Code & Co., S.F., Green, Tapered, 11 ¼ In.	1008.00
Perfume bottles are listed in their own category.	

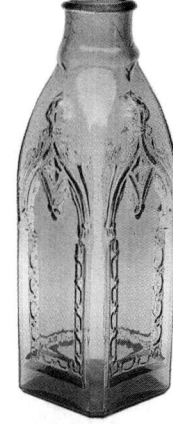

Bottle, Pickle, Cathedral, Yellow Green, Tooled Rolled Collared Mouth, Smooth Base, c.1865, 13 ¼ In.
$4973.00

Bottle, Pickle, Shaker Brand, E.D. Pettengill Co., Portland, Me., Label, Applied Lip, 1890s, 7 ¾ In.
$468.00

Bottle, Poison, Embossed Wasp, M.P., Cobalt Blue, Tooled Lip, England, c.1890, 5 ⅝ In.
$690.00

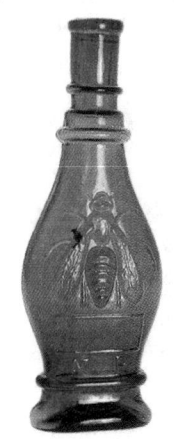

BOTTLE

Bottle, Sarsaparilla, Dr. Guysott's Yellow Doc & Sarsaparilla, Cincinnati, Oh., Aqua, Pontil, 9 ¾ In.
$476.00

American Bottle Auctions

Bottle, Seal, Wine, A.S.C.R., Black Glass, Applied String Lip, Dip Mold, Pontil, c.1775, 10 ½ In.
$374.00

Glass Works Auctions

Bottle, Snuff, Glass, Overlay, Ocher Over White, Antique Objects, Stopper, Chinese, c.1910, 2 ½ In.
$368.00

Skinner, Inc.

Pickle, Atmore's, Cathedral, Aqua, Squared Collar, 11 ½ In.	150.00
Pickle, Bunker Hill, Skilton Foot & Co., Aqua, Lighthouse, Sloping Collar, 8 In.	728.00
Pickle, Cathedral, Blue Green, Applied Mouth, 11 ¼ In. ...illus	1232.00
Pickle, Cathedral, Yellow Green, Tooled Rolled Collared Mouth, Smooth Base, c.1865, 13 ¼ In. ..illus	4973.00
Pickle, Shaker Brand, E.D. Pettengill Co., Portland, Me., Label, Applied Lip, 1890s, 7 ¾ In. illus	468.00
Poison, Bowman's Drug Store, Cobalt Blue, Raised Ribs, Flattened Lip, 4 In.	336.00
Poison, Brecklein, Cobalt Blue, 6-Sided, Raised Ribs On Sides, Flattened Lip, 7 ½ In.	560.00
Poison, Cobalt Blue, 6-Sided, Raised Ribs, Turquoise Blue, Square Collar, 1890-1910, 5 In.	308.00
Poison, Embossed Wasp, M.P., Cobalt Blue, Tooled Lip, England, c.1890, 5 ⅝ In. ...illus	690.00
Poison, Owl Drug Co., 1-Wing Owl, Cobalt Blue, 3 Arched Panels, 9 ½ In.	1120.00
Poison, Owl Drug Co., 1-Wing Owl, Cobalt Blue, 3 Arched Panels, Flattened Lip, 6 In.	364.00
Poison, Wm. Radam's Microbe Killer No. 3, Stoneware, Jug, Black Stencils	123.00
Sarsaparilla, Crowell, Crane & Brigham, Yellow Doc, Aqua, Open Pontil, 9 ¼ In.	3360.00
Sarsaparilla, Dr. Guysott's Yellow Doc & Sarsaparilla, Cincinnati, Oh., Aqua, Pontil, 9 ¾ In. ..illus	476.00
Sarsaparilla, Dr. Myers' Vegetable Extract, Wild Cherry Dandelion, Aqua, 8 ⅜ In.	1064.00
Sarsaparilla, Dr. Townsend's, Albany, N.Y., Blue Green, Square, Beveled, Pontil, 9 In.	448.00
Sarsaparilla, Dr. Townsend's, Albany, N.Y., Olive Green, Pontil, Sloping Collar, 9 ¼ In.	336.00
Sarsaparilla, Dr. Woodworth's, Birmingham, Ct., Aqua, Beveled Corners, Sloping Collar, 10 In.	497.00
Sarsaparilla, Hurd's, Aqua, Rectangular, Beveled Corners, Sloping Collar, 9 ¼ In.	878.00
Sarsaparilla, Old Dr. J. Townsend's, New York, Blue Green, Square, Sloping Collar, 9 In.	322.00
Sarsaparilla, Sand's, New York, Aqua, Sloping Collar, 6 In.	179.00
Scent, Amber, Flower, Hearts, Flattened Pear Shape, Footed, Pewter Collar, Screw Cap, 3 ½ In.	575.00
Scent, Amethyst, 2-Headed Eagle, Crown, Scrolling Flowers, Flattened Pear Shape, 3 ½ In.	3738.00
Scent, Cameo Glass, Flowers, Leaves, Green, Gold Trim, Frosted, Textured, Silver Domed Lid, 6 In.	1725.00
Scent, Carved Mineral, Silver Stopper & Foot, c.1900, 5 In.	59.00
Scent, Crackle Glass, Blue, Opaline, Bulbous, 19th Century, 6 ½ In.	450.00
Scent, Cut Glass, 8-Sided, Green To Clear, Squat, Medial Band, Flat Stopper, 4 ½ In.	518.00
Scent, Cut Glass, Spiral Ribbons, Multicolor, 3 ½ In.	226.00
Scent, Cut Glass, Thumbprint, Blue To Clear, Metal Fittings, 3 ¾ In.	219.00
Scent, Opalescent Glass, Hobnail, 1930s, 6 In.	39.00
Scent, Spiral Ribbons, Blue & Opal Cased, Ribbed, Gilt Metal Fittings, Laydown, 4 ½ In.	345.00
Scent, Translucent Starch Blue Glass, Cylindrical, Double End, Gilt Metal Fittings, 4 ¾ In.	219.00
Scent, Vaseline Glass, Faceted, Cylindrical, Double End, Gilt Metal Fittings, 6 In.	403.00
Seal, DVO 1724, Black Glass, Mallet, Olive Green, Rainbow Iridescence, String Lip, 7 In.	3920.00
Seal, G.N. 1817, Black Glass, Olive Yellow, Cylindrical, Squat, Double Collar, 11 ¼ In.	1568.00
Seal, WCG, Black Glass, Olive Amber, Cylindrical, String Lip, 10 ⅜ In.	448.00
Seal, Wine, A.S.C.R., Black Glass, Applied String Lip, Dip Mold, Pontil, c.1775, 10 ½ In. ..illus	374.00
Seltzer, Big Chief, Clear, Red, Indian Chief, Pump, 12 In.	90.00
Seltzer, New York Seltzer Water Co., Deposit 50¢, Woman Serving Drinks, Blue ACL, 12 In.	18.00
Snuff, Agate, Banded, Duck, Under Tree, White, Brown, Oval, Red Stopper, Chinese, 2 ½ In.	329.00
Snuff, Agate, Brown, Silver Stopper, Inset, Coral Stone Pewter Spoon, 1800s, 1 ½ x 2 ½ In.	330.00
Snuff, Agate, Carved, Bulbous, Coral & Turquoise Insets, Silver Filigree Stopper, 1700s, 2 x 3 In.	770.00
Snuff, Agate, Chi Dragon Under Clouds, Crane, Pine Tree, 1800s, 2 In.	175.00
Snuff, Agate, Eagle, Flowers, White, Russet, Flattened Oval, Stopper, Chinese, 3 In.	203.00
Snuff, Agate, Eagle, Pine Tree, Russet, Flattened Circle, Stopper, Chinese, c.1880, 2 ½ In.	448.00
Snuff, Agate, Figures, Pine Tree, Flowering Prunus, Pagoda, 3 ⅛ In.	478.00
Snuff, Agate, Fisherman, Outcrop, Russet Accents, Rounded Square, Stopper, Chinese, 2 ¼ In.	237.00
Snuff, Agate, Floater, Flattened Shape, Agate Top, 2 ⅜ In.	738.00
Snuff, Agate, Green Streaks, Rounded Body, White Jadeite Body, Chinese, 1800s, 2 ½ In.	593.00
Snuff, Agate, Horse & Rider, Pine Tree, Flattened Circle, Chocolate Color, Stopper, Chinese, 3 In.	299.00
Snuff, Agate, Immortals, Attendants, Smoky Gray, Amber, Red, Chinese, 1900s, 3 ¼ In., Pair	420.00
Snuff, Agate, Inset Coral & Jade, Pewter Stopper, Agate Spoon, 1800's, 2 x 2 ¾ In.	935.00
Snuff, Agate, Lotus Branches, Flattened Oval, Stopper, Chinese, 1800s, 3 In.	478.00
Snuff, Agate, Mottled Tan, Brown Relief Carved Cat, 2 ½ In.	266.00
Snuff, Agate, Relief Carved, Elders In Landscape, Spade Form, Gray Striations, Chinese, 3 In.	472.00
Snuff, Agate, Russet, Chocolate, Flattened Oval, Pierced Stopper, Chinese, 1800s	568.00
Snuff, Agate, Square, Coral, Turquoise, Silver Mount & Stopper, 19th Century, 4 ¾ In.	250.00
Snuff, Agate, Tan, Mustard, Bulbous, Metal, Green Stone Stopper, Ivory Spoon, 1800s, 2 x 3 In.	303.00
Snuff, Agate, Turquoise, Flowers, 3 In.	527.00
Snuff, Amber, Chi Dragons, Clouds, Pear Shape, 19th Century, 1 ½ In.	500.00
Snuff, Amber, Coral Stem Shape Stopper, 1700s, 1 ½ x 3 ½ In.	1320.00
Snuff, Amber, Flattened Oval, Foo Dog Handles, 1800s	1793.00
Snuff, Amber, God, Shoulao, Deer, Wave Ground, Domed Stopper, Flat Hu Shape, Chinese, 2 ¾ In.	415.00
Snuff, Amber, Pear Shape, Stem Shape Stopper, 1700s, 1 ½ x 3 ½ In.	1210.00
Snuff, Amethyst, Carp Shape, 19th Century, 2 ½ In.	225.00
Snuff, Amethyst, Chi Dragons, Domed Stopper, Chilong Finial, 1800s, 1 ⅞ In.	593.00

Snuff, Amethyst, Flowering Branches, Birds, Rockwork Base, Bird Stopper, 2 ⅝ In.....................	854.00
Snuff, Aquamarine, Carved Figures, Pine Trees, Chinese, 1800s, 2 ½ In.	10158.00
Snuff, Aquamarine, Carved Flowers, Lion Shape Stopper, 1 ⅞ In.	915.00
Snuff, Cameo Glass, Foo Dog, Brocade Ball, Mask Lugs, Red, White, Red Stopper, Chinese, 1800s, 2 In.	1007.00
Snuff, Camphor Glass, Red Overlay, Hydra Dragons, Sodalite Top, Chinese, 1800s, 3 In.	922.00
Snuff, Carnelian, Carved, Bamboo, Flying Goose, Jade Stopper, 2 ⅝ In.........................	930.00
Snuff, Carnelian, Carved, Rose Blossom, Butterfly Stopper, Chinese, 1900s, 3 In.	415.00
Snuff, Carnelian, White Overlay, Carved, Deer, Pine Tree, Chinese, 3 In........................	179.00
Snuff, Chalcedony Agate, Cylindrical Neck, Rectangular Foot, Inscribed, Stopper, 1800s, 3 In.	677.00
Snuff, Chalcedony Agate, Flattened Globular Body, Oval Foot, Carved, Stopper, 2 ⅝ In.	956.00
Snuff, Chicken Blood Stone, Fish Shape, Chinese, 3 ½ In.	359.00
Snuff, Cinnabar, Globular, Carved Design, 3 ⅛ In.	1037.00
Snuff, Cinnabar, Metal, Turquoise Inlay, Flask Shape, Round Foot, 6 In., Pair	744.00
Snuff, Cinnabar, Over Copper, Peach Tree, Bats, Pear Shape, 19th Century, 3 ¼ In.	300.00
Snuff, Cinnabar, Scholars, Landscape, Geometrics, Stopper, c.1895, 2 ½ In.	385.00
Snuff, Cloisonne Dragon, Pearl Wire Inlays, Purple, Hardstone Stopper, Mark, Chinese, c.1890, 2 In.	337.00
Snuff, Cloisonne, Birds, Flower Inlay Cartouches, Blue Scrolls, Yellow, Stopper, Chinese, c.1800, 3 In.	919.00
Snuff, Cloisonne, Flowers, Grasshopper, Elongated Pear Shape, Stopper, 3 ¼ In.	519.00
Snuff, Cloisonne, Phoenix, Flower Border, Dragon, Cloud Ground, Chinese, c.1800, 2 ¼ In....	7703.00
Snuff, Cloisonne, Rabbit, Mushrooms, Clouds, Turquoise Ground, Chinese, 1800s, 2 ½ In......	1067.00
Snuff, Coral, Pink, Flowering Peony Branch, Chinese, 3 In.	448.00
Snuff, Demuth's, Lancaster, Pa., 7 In.	283.00
Snuff, Famille Verte, Crab, Red Waves, Flattened Oval, Dragon Head Handles, 2 ¾ In..............	717.00
Snuff, Famille Verte, Scholars, Attendants, Blue, White Border, Chinese, 1800s, 3 In.	10073.00
Snuff, Glass, Amethyst, Bombe Shape, Red Stopper, Chinese, 1800s, 2 ½ In.	359.00
Snuff, Glass, Blue, Splashed Gold, Flattened Pear Shape, 1800s, 2 ⅝ In.	299.00
Snuff, Glass, Buddha's Hand, Opaque White, Red Stopper, Chinese, 19th Century, 2 In...........	717.00
Snuff, Glass, Double Gourd Shape, Squirrel On Top, Chinese, 2 ½ In.	738.00
Snuff, Glass, Enameled, Pheasant, Flowering Plants, Chinese, c.1900s, 2 ⅜ In.......................	521.00
Snuff, Glass, Flattened, Rounded Shoulders, Tourmaline Needles, Coral Stopper, Chinese, 2 ½ In.	399.00
Snuff, Glass, Orange, Red Streaks, Heart Shape, Dome Glass Stopper, Stand, Chinese, 1800s, 2 In.	1067.00
Snuff, Glass, Overlay, Aubergine Over White, Carved, Fish, 1800s, 2 ½ In.	598.00
Snuff, Glass, Overlay, Crane, Pavilion, Bat, Sunset, Waves, Pale Green, Flattened Disc, c.1800, 2 ⅛ In...	5124.00
Snuff, Glass, Overlay, Ocher Over White, Antique Objects, Stopper, Chinese, c.1910, 2 ½ In. ......*illus*	368.00
Snuff, Glass, Overlay, Peonies, Opaque White, Red, Green, Ruby, Blue, c.1860, 2 ½ In.	4063.00
Snuff, Glass, Overlay, Red Over Snowflake, King Charles IV Spanish Coin, Aventurine Stopper, 2 ⅜ In...	984.00
Snuff, Glass, Painted, 2 Beauties In Garden, Trees, Chinese, 3 In.	295.00
Snuff, Glass, Pink, White, Flat Hu Shape, Green Stopper, Chinese, 1800s, 2 ½ In......................	296.00
Snuff, Glass, Red & Green, Dragon Heads, Tiger's Eye Top, 1800s, Chinese, 2 ⅝ In.	259.00
Snuff, Glass, Red Cut To White, Carps, Peony Branches, Stopper, Chinese, c.1910, 2 ⅛ In. ....*illus*	1541.00
Snuff, Glass, Red, Tortoiseshell, Flattened Oval, Elongated Neck, White Jade Lid, 2 ½ x 1 ¾ In.	523.00
Snuff, Glass, Reverse Painted, Butterflies, Grass, Inscriptions, Stopper, Signed, 1900s, 2 ⅜ In.	4740.00
Snuff, Glass, Reverse Painted, Landscape, Figures, Jade Stopper, Chinese, 4 In.	207.00
Snuff, Glass, Snowflake, Green Overlay, Animals & Leaves, Elongated Oval, Stopper, Chinese, 3 In.	717.00
Snuff, Glass, Snowflake, Green Overlay, Squirrels, Vines, c.1810, 2 ⅞ In. ....*illus*	2684.00
Snuff, Glass, Snowflake, Red Overlay, Dragon, Ball Shape, Chinese, 1800s, 3 In.	627.00
Snuff, Glass, Translucent White, Oval, Chinese, 2 In.	474.00
Snuff, Glass, Yellow, Cottage, River, Calligraphy, Round, Green Glass Stopper, c.1900, 2 ¼ In..	3437.00
Snuff, Hair Crystal, Black Tourmaline Needles, Opaque White Elephant, Flattened Rectangle, 3 In.	1968.00
Snuff, Hardstone, Brown & White Swirls, Green Peking Glass & Metal Stopper, 1700s, 2 x 3 In.	1980.00
Snuff, Hardstone, Flask Shape, Flared Neck, 2 ¼ In.	372.00
Snuff, Honeycomb Basket, Oval, 19th Century, 2 In...	650.00
Snuff, Hornbill, Carved Figure, Lotus, Flattened Oval, Dragon Shape Handles, Stopper, 2 ½ In.	2390.00
Snuff, Hornbill, Cicada Shape, Red, Chinese, 3 In.	1912.00
Snuff, Hornbill, Fish Shape, Flowers, Chinese, 3 In.	2390.00
Snuff, Hornbill, Incised, Ink Characters, Carved Dragon, Ivory Base, Bakelite Disc, Chinese, 3 In. .*illus*	265.00
Snuff, Hornbill, Orange, Pagoda, Flowers, Flattened Square, Dome Stopper, Chinese, c.1800, 3 In.	944.00
Snuff, Hornbill, Tortoise, Dragon, Chinese, 2 ½ In.	2868.00
Snuff, Ivory, Black, Red Lacquer, Woman, Garden, Domed Stopper, Chinese, 1800s, 2 ½ In.....	770.00
Snuff, Ivory, Carved, Man, Boy, Willow Tree, Woman, Carriage, Round Foot, Stopper, Chinese, 3 In.	209.00
Snuff, Ivory, Children At Play, Vase Shape, Handles, 19th Century, 4 In.	425.00
Snuff, Ivory, Mother-Of-Pearl, 2 Dragons, Flaming Pearl, Lion Heads, Chinese, c.1800, 2 ¾ In.	2990.00
Snuff, Ivory, Relief Carved, Figures & Immortals, Tapered Oval, Chinese, 4 In....................	354.00
Snuff, Ivory, Relief Leaves, Pomegranate Form, Lobed, Stopper, Chinese, 2 ⅞ In.	236.00
Snuff, Ivory, Turtle Shape, Leaf Stopper, Marked, 19th Century, 3 In.	400.00
Snuff, Ivory, Woman, Flowers, Birds, Carved, Wood Stand, 5 ¼ In., Pair..........................	460.00

Bottle, Snuff, Glass, Red Cut To White, Carps, Peony Branches, Stopper, Chinese, c.1910, 2 ⅛ In.
$1541.00

Skinner, Inc.

Bottle, Snuff, Glass, Snowflake, Green Overlay, Squirrels, Vines, c.1810, 2 ⅞ In.
$2684.00

Leslie Hindman Auctioneers

Bottle, Snuff, Hornbill, Incised, Ink Characters, Carved Dragon, Ivory Base, Bakelite Disc, Chinese, 3 In.
$265.00

Ivey-Selkirk Auctioneers

Bottle, Snuff, Meriwether's Scotch, Clarksville, Tenn., Amber, Label, c.1900, 4 ⅛ In. $184.00

Glass Works Auctions

Bottle, Snuff, Porcelain, Boys At Play, Flattened, Coral Stopper, Marked, 18th Century, 2 In. $4880.00

Leslie Hindman Auctioneers

Bottle, Snuff, Porcelain, Dragon, Red Underglaze, Pink Glass Stopper, Chinese, c.1910, 3 ⅜ In. $490.00

Skinner, Inc.

TIP

To dry a small-necked bottle, give it a last rinse with alcohol.

Snuff, Ivory, Women, Bird, Flowers, Double Gourd Shape, Domed Stopper, Chinese, 1800s, 2 ½ In.	593.00
Snuff, Jade, 3-Legged Frog Shape, Pearl Eyes, Stopper In Mouth, 2 ½ In.	4392.00
Snuff, Jade, Amber, Fruit Shape, Animal On Top, Green Stopper, 4 In.	184.00
Snuff, Jade, Bat, Leafy Metal Neck, Oval, White, Russet Veining, Chinese, 1800s, 2 ¾ In.	5925.00
Snuff, Jade, Buddha Shape, Celadon, Red Stopper, Chinese, 1840-80, 3 In.	418.00
Snuff, Jade, Buddha's Hand Shape, Celadon, Multi-Arm Coral Stopper, 2 In.	793.00
Snuff, Jade, Buddha's Hand Shape, Citron, Green, Chinese, 1800s, 2 ½ In.	385.00
Snuff, Jade, Carp, Lotus Leaf, Pod, White, Green, Flattened Rounded Square, Stopper, Chinese, 2 In.	337.00
Snuff, Jade, Carved, Bat, Calligraphy, Round, Chinese, 2 ½ In.	299.00
Snuff, Jade, Cat Shape, 19th Century, 2 In.	425.00
Snuff, Jade, Celadon, Carved Green Cap, Chinese, 1800s, 3 ½ In.	20145.00
Snuff, Jade, Celadon, Russet, Rounded Rectangle, Coral Stopper, 3 In.	3904.00
Snuff, Jade, Crane, Pine Branches, White & Green, Russet Accents, Flattened Oval, Chinese, 2 ⅜ In.	356.00
Snuff, Jade, Figures, Zither, Boat, Yellow, Brown, Soapstone Stopper, Chinese, 1800s, 2 ¼ In.	3851.00
Snuff, Jade, Green, White, Metal & Amethyst Stopper, Round, 1800s, 2 ¼ x 2 ¾ In.	960.00
Snuff, Jade, Honey, Chocolate, Flattened Oval, Chinese, 1800s, 3 In.	598.00
Snuff, Jade, Immortal, Crane, Pine, Foo Dog Lugs, Ocher, Chinese, 1800s, 2 ½ In.	980.00
Snuff, Jade, Koi Fish Shape, Stopper, 19th Century, 2 ½ In.	375.00
Snuff, Jade, Lavender, Tapering Flask, Round Foot, Jade Stopper, 2 ½ In.	7930.00
Snuff, Jade, Medallion, Neck Lugs, Pear Shape, Flat Stopper, Emerald Green, Chinese, 2 In.	830.00
Snuff, Jade, Milky White, Green & Brass Cap, Chinese, 1800s, 3 In.	16590.00
Snuff, Jade, Milky White, Ribbed, Baluster Shape, Red, Black Cap, Chinese, 2 ¼ In.	3402.00
Snuff, Jade, Pale Green, Chilong Climbing, Round Flattened, 3 In.	366.00
Snuff, Jade, Rounded Square, Yellow, Russet, Silver & Orange Stopper, Chinese, 1800s, 3 In.	5333.00
Snuff, Jade, Scholars, Landscape, Green Glass Stopper, c.1890, 2 ½ In.	5206.00
Snuff, Jade, Tree, Flower, Carved, Oval, 19th Century, 2 ½ In.	175.00
Snuff, Jade, White, Spade Shape, High Shoulder, Coral Stopper, Chinese, 1800s, 3 In.	1464.00
Snuff, Lacquer, Pine Tree, Lotus Pond, Ducks, Compressed Flask Shape, Gilt, Jade Stopper, 2 ⅛ In.	671.00
Snuff, Lapis Lazuli, Rounded Rectangle, Red Glass Stopper, 3 In.	915.00
Snuff, Lapis Lazuli, Urn, Cover, Flowering Peonies, 3 x 2 ½ In.	97.00
Snuff, Leonard Appleby, Rail Road Mills, Amber, Rectangular, Outward Rolled Lip, 4 ⅜ In.	235.00
Snuff, Meriwether's Scotch, Clarksville, Tenn., Amber, Label, c.1900, 4 ⅛ In. ....*illus*	184.00
Snuff, Milk Glass, Cobalt Blue Overlay, Flattened Oval, Dragons, Flaming Pearl, Stopper, 2 ½ In.	4392.00
Snuff, Monk, Lohan Carved, Agate, Chinese, 1800s, 3 In.	1003.00
Snuff, Moss Agate, Foo Dog, Flattened Oval, Ring Handles, Stopper, Chinese	239.00
Snuff, Moss Agate, Rectangular, Rust, Brown, 2 ⅝ In.	458.00
Snuff, Mother-Of-Pearl, Spade Shape, Cylindrical Neck, Carved, Bat, Palm, Stopper, 2 ½ In.	956.00
Snuff, Porcelain, 18 Monks, Wavy Ground, White Glaze, Brass Stopper, Chinese, 1800s, 2 ¼ In.	415.00
Snuff, Porcelain, 9 Dragons, Multicolor, Enamel, Cylindrical, c.1800, 3 In.	356.00
Snuff, Porcelain, Blue Dragons, Round, Signed, 1700s, 2 ¼ x 2 ¾ In.	825.00
Snuff, Porcelain, Boys At Play, Flattened, Coral Stopper, Marked, 18th Century, 2 In. ......*illus*	4880.00
Snuff, Porcelain, Cabbage Form, Articulated Leaves, Natural Veins, Chinese, 3 In.	207.00
Snuff, Porcelain, Camel, Landscape, Blue, White, Red, Tapered, Cylindrical, Flat Stopper, Chinese, 3 In.	153.00
Snuff, Porcelain, Deer, Mushroom Sprig, Monkey, Pine Tree, Coral Stopper, Chinese, c.1820 2 In.	830.00
Snuff, Porcelain, Double Gourd, Reticulated, Blue, Green & Red Leaves, Shou Symbols, 3 In.	325.00
Snuff, Porcelain, Dragon Shape, Bulbous, Long Neck, Green Yellow Glaze, Chinese, 2 ¾ In.	153.00
Snuff, Porcelain, Dragon, Red Underglaze, Pink Glass Stopper, Chinese, c.1910, 3 ⅜ In. ..*illus*	490.00
Snuff, Porcelain, Dragons, Blue & White, Signed, 1700s, 2 ¼ x 2 ¾ In.	900.00
Snuff, Porcelain, Famille Rose, Quails, Flowers, Branches, Cobalt, Gilt, Pear Shape, Stopper, 3 In.	1315.00
Snuff, Porcelain, Flowers, Birds, Incised, Painted, Green Jade Stopper, 1 ¾ x 2 ¾ In.	330.00
Snuff, Porcelain, Lotus Scrolls, Blue & White, Cylindrical Stopper, Chinese, 2 ½ In.	119.00
Snuff, Porcelain, Red, Plants, Butterfly, Bird, Coral Stopper, Chinese, 1800s, 2 ¾ In. ......*illus*	295.00
Snuff, Quartz, Cameo, Deer, Under Tree, Rounded Rectangle, Faux Mask & Ring Handles, 2 ¾ In.	1240.00
Snuff, Relief Scrolls, Gold Trim, White Fade Florets, Flattened Double Gourd, Silver	443.00
Snuff, Rock Crystal, Crane, Pine Tree, Calligraphy, Rectangular, Chinese, 3 In.	984.00
Snuff, Rock Crystal, Figure, Trees, Flowers, Oval, Stopper	2750.00
Snuff, Rock Crystal, Seated Monkey, Fruit, Tiger's Eye, Turtle Shape Stopper, Chinese, 3 In.	413.00
Snuff, Rock Crystal, Tree, Flattened Pear Shape, Chinese, 2 ½ In.	448.00
Snuff, Ruby Glass, Snowflake, Red To White, Bats, Cloud Scrolls, Round, Stopper, c.1900, 2 ⅜ In.	2015.00
Snuff, Rutilated Quartz, Cranes, Trees, Fungus, Flattened Rectangle, Agate Stopper, 3 In.	793.00
Snuff, Shadow Agate, Landscape, Globular, Lapis Lazuli Stopper, 3 In.	519.00
Snuff, Silver, Dragon, Scroll Openwork, Flattened Circle, Stopper, 3 In.	295.00
Snuff, Silver, Enamel, Raised Wire, Stylized Bats, Apocryphal Seal Mark, Chinese, 2 ½ In.	277.00
Snuff, Stone, Russet & Brown Striations, Pebble Form, 19th Century, 3 In.	649.00
Snuff, Turquoise, Matrix, Figural Carving, Chinese, Stopper, 3 In.	207.00
Snuff, Turquoise, Warrior, Cherry Tree, Carved, c.1800, 3 ½ In.	155.00

Soda, A. Coffin & Co., Sapphire Blue, Blob Top, 7 ½ In.	150.00
Soda, A.P. Smith, Charleston, S.C., Sapphire Blue, Sloping Collar, Iron Pontil, 7 ⅜ In.	374.00
Soda, Allen & Richards, Horseshoe, Philada, Hutchinson	5.00
Soda, B & G, San Francisco, Blue, Paneled Mug Base, Blob Top	308.00
Soda, Classen & Co. Sparkling, Crossed Anchors, Aqua, Square Collar	101.00
Soda, Columbia Soda Works, S.F.C.C. Dall, Green Aqua, Blob Top	448.00
Soda, Compton Bottling Co., Sheridan, Wyo., 3-Leaf Clover, Light Green, Tooled Top	364.00
Soda, Cottle, Post & Co., Portland, Ogn., Phoenix Bird, Green Aqua, Blob Top	235.00
Soda, Crystal Palace Premium Soda Water, Teal, Blob Top, Iron Pontil, 7 In.	518.00
Soda, Crystal Soda Water Co., Green, Patented Nov. 12, 1872, Applied Blob Top, 7 ½ In. ....illus	336.00
Soda, D.T. Cox, Port Jervis, N.Y., Teal Green, Blob Top, 7 In.	196.00
Soda, Dyottville Glass Works, Philada., Forest Green, Sloping Collar, Pontil, 7 In.	161.00
Soda, E. Ottenville, Nashville, Cobalt Blue, Cylindrical, Blob Top, 6 ¾ In.	150.00
Soda, Emerald Green, Slug Plate, Spread-Wing Eagle Holding Arrows, Blob Top, 7 In.	345.00
Soda, F & L Schaum, Baltimore, Olive Amber, Iron Pontil, Sloping Collar	2688.00
Soda, Forbes & Bodine Bottlers, Evanston, Wyo., Light Green, Bubbles	392.00
Soda, H. Fitzgerald, Torpedo, Green Shaded To Clear, Sloping Collar	3584.00
Soda, Henry Kuck, Savannah, Green, Blob Top, 7 ¼ In.	75.00
Soda, Hollister & Co., Honolulu, Aqua Green, Blob Top, 7 ¼ In.	425.00
Soda, Hugh P. McFadden, South Bethlehem, Pa., Aqua, Hutchinson, 6 ½ In.	6.00
Soda, J.C. Parker & Son, New York, Teal, Iron Pontil, Blob Top	190.00
Soda, John Ryan, Savannah, Geo., 1859, Cobalt Blue, Blob Top, Pontil	225.00
Soda, Keach, Torpedo, Green, Shaded, Sloping Collar	1456.00
Soda, Lyman Astley, Cheyenne, Wyo., Light Green, Shaded, Tooled Top	123.00
Soda, Napa, Phil Caduc, Natural Mineral Water, Light Green, Striations, Blob Top	280.00
Soda, S.S. Knicker Bocker, Blue Green, Paneled, Sloping Collar, 7 ⅛ In.	784.00
Soda, Southwick & Tupper, New York, Green, Iridescent, Sloping Collar	616.00
Soda, Star Bottling Works, South Sharon, Pa., Aqua, Embossed Star, Hutchinson, 7 ¾ In.	7.00
Soda, Thompson's Premium Mineral Waters, San Francisco, Aqua, Ten Pin, Blob Top	448.00
Soda, W.H. Burt, San Francisco, Green, Blob Top, 1850s	476.00
Soda, XLCR Soda Works, 738 Broadway, S.F., Aqua Blue, 8-Sided, Blob Top, c.1864	1680.00
Stiegel Type, Flowers, Birds, Heart, 8-Sided, Pewter Cap, 7 ½ In.	367.00
Stiegel, Flowers, Mold Blown, 8 In.	118.00
Syrup, Grape Smash Soda, Enameled Label, Applied Lip, 11 ½ x 3 ⅜ In. ....illus	413.00
Target Ball, Amber, Hexagonal, Indented Panels, Sure Break Patent Apl'd For, c.1890, 2 ⅝ In.	7475.00
Target Ball, Bogardus, Amber, Raised Dots, Sheared Mouth, c.1890, 2 ⅝ In.	4025.00
Target Ball, Bogardus, Amethyst Shaded To Clear, Rough Sheared Lip, c.1877, 2 ⅝ In.	2300.00
Target Ball, Bogardus, Pat'd Apr 10 1877, Diamond Quilted, Deep Amber, 2 ⅝ In.	8960.00
Target Ball, Diamond, Man Shooting Inside Circle, Cobalt Blue, England, c.1890 ....illus	863.00
Target Ball, E.E. Sage & Co., Chicago, Illinois, Patented August 21st 1877, Golden Amber, 2 ⅝ In. .illus	6900.00
Target Ball, For Hockey's Patent Trap, Emerald Green, Fish Net, c.1890, 2 ⅜ In.	1150.00
Target Ball, Ira Paine's Filled Ball, Golden Yellow, Sheared Mouth, 2 ⅝ In.	308.00
Target Ball, Ira Paine's Filled Ball, Pat. Oct 23 1877, Golden Amber, Sheared Mouth, 2 ⅝ In. ..illus	527.00
Target Ball, Van Cutsem, A St Quentin, Striations, Diamonds, Cobalt Blue, 2 ¾ In.	127.00
Tonic, Columbia Tiger Hair Tonic, Label, Nude Woman On Reverse, 6 ¾ In.	633.00
Tonic, Harrison's Columbian Stimulant, Roof Shoulders, Pontil, Label, c.1850, 6 ⅜ In. ....illus	1287.00
Tonic, Rohrer's Expectoral Wild Cherry, Amber, Pyramidal, Sloping Collar, Rope Corners, 10 ⅝ In.	266.00
Tonic, Rohrer's Expectoral Wild Cherry, Honey Amber, Pyramid, 10 ½ In.	336.00
Utility, Olive Amber, Chestnut Form, Sloping Collar, Kick Up, 9 x 5 ½ In.	431.00
Whimsy, Ladder Back Chair In Bottle, Civil War Veteran, Confederate Flag, c.1900, 7 In.	206.00
Whiskey, AAA Old Valley, Embossed Cross, Amber, Flask, Roll Collar, Pt.	672.00
Whiskey, AAA Old Valley, Embossed Cross, Olive Green, Roll Collar, Pt.	2912.00
Whiskey, Backbar, Admiral Dewey, Battle Scene, Lady's Leg, Label Under Glass	448.00
Whiskey, Backbar, Morville Rye, 10-Sided, Enamel Letters, Double Ring	224.00
Whiskey, Backbar, Tod Sloan, Cut Glass Neck, Label Under Glass	2912.00
Whiskey, C.A. Richards, 99 Washington St., Boston, Mass., Amber, Square, 9 ⅝ In.	78.00
Whiskey, C.A. Richards, Boston, Mass., Tobacco Amber, Square, Beveled Corners, 9 ½ In.	235.00
Whiskey, Casper Co., Old N.C. Corn, Winston, N.C., Round, Flattened, Back Bar, 9 In.	431.00
Whiskey, Casper, Very Old Corn, Lowest Priced, Amethystine, Etched, 10 Panels, 11 In.	316.00
Whiskey, Casper's, Made By Honest North Carolina People, Cobalt Blue, Cylindrical, 12 In.	448.00
Whiskey, Casper's, Made By Honest North Carolina People, Cobalt Blue, Lady's Leg Neck, Qt.	560.00
Whiskey, Caspers, Made By Honest North Carolina People, Cobalt, Tooled Lip, 1895, 12 In. ..illus	489.00
Whiskey, Castle, Old Bourbon, F. Chevalier & Co. Sole Agents, Amber, Flask	4928.00
Whiskey, Castle, Swirled, Backbar	364.00
Whiskey, Chestnut Grove, C.W., Seal, Golden Honey, Chestnut, Handle, 8 ¾ In.	336.00
Whiskey, Choice Old Cabinet, Ky. Bourbon, Amber, Embossed Crown, Fifth	2128.00

Bottle, Snuff, Porcelain, Iron Red, Flowering Plants, Butterfly, Bird, Coral Stopper, Chinese, 1800s, 2 ¾ In. $295.00

Brunk Auctions

Bottle, Soda, Crystal Soda Water Co., Green, Patented Nov. 12, 1872, Applied Blob Top, 7 ½ In. $336.00

American Bottle Auctions

Bottle, Syrup, Grape Smash Soda, Enameled Label, Applied Lip, 11 ½ x 3 ⅜ In. $413.00

Wm Morford Antiques

69

Bottle, Target Ball, Diamond, Man Shooting Inside Circle, Cobalt Blue, England, c.1890
$863.00

Glass Works Auctions

Bottle, Target Ball, E.E. Sage & Co., Chicago, Illinois, Patented August 21st 1877, Golden Amber, 2 ⅝ In.
$6900.00

Glass Works Auctions

Bottle, Target Ball, Ira Paine's Filled Ball, Pat. Oct 23 1877, Golden Amber, Sheared Mouth, 2 ⅝ In.
$527.00

Norman C. Heckler & Company

Whiskey, Daniel Visser, Aromatic Schnapps, Schiedam, Black Glass, Square, 7 ¾ In.	35.00
Whiskey, E.G. Booz's Old Cabin, Cabin Shape, Yellow Amber, 1840, Sloping Collar, 8 In.	1003.00
Whiskey, Ernst Gerstenberg, Pretzel Flask, Pottery, Brown Glaze, c.1900, 3 ⅝ In. *illus*	690.00
Whiskey, Golden Amber, Cylindrical, Brooklyn Glass Works, Sloping Collar, Fifth	179.00
Whiskey, Griffith Hyatt & Co., Baltimore, Golden Amber, Pear Shape, Handle, 7 ¼ In.	672.00
Whiskey, Hamilton Glass Works, Emerald Green, Cylindrical, Sloping Collar, 10 ½ In.	152.00
Whiskey, Henry Chapman & Co., Montreal, Golden Amber, Flask, Teardrop, 6 In.	235.00
Whiskey, Hopatkong, J.C. Hess & Co., Phila., Cobalt Blue, 12-Sided Base, 10 ½ In.	1344.00
Whiskey, J.C. Herlihy, Bangor, Me., Golden Amber, Strap Side Flask, Double Collar, Pt.	644.00
Whiskey, J.F. Cutter Extra Old Bourbon, Star In Shield, Amber, Flask, Roll Collar, Pt.	952.00
Whiskey, J.F. Cutter Extra Old Bourbon, Star In Shield, Yellow Green, 1871-75 *illus*	4704.00
Whiskey, J.H. Cutter Old Bourbon, C.P. Moorman, Orange Amber, Coffin Flask, Pt.	364.00
Whiskey, J.H. Cutter Old Bourbon, E. Martin & Co., Crown, Amber, Flask, Pt.	5600.00
Whiskey, Lilienthal & Co., Amber, Crown, Teardrop Flask, Ground Lip, Metal Closure	840.00
Whiskey, Lilienthal & Co., Cincinnati, San Francisco & N.Y., Amber, Flask, Pt.	952.00
Whiskey, Louis Taussig & Co., 205 & 207 Battery Street, S.F., Amber, Slug Plate, Fifth	2240.00
Whiskey, Louis Taussig & Co., S.F., Shaded Amber, Flask, Double Collar, Pt.	616.00
Whiskey, McKenna's Nelson County Extra Kentucky Bourbon, Yellow Amber, Fifth	1560.00
Whiskey, N. Vanderbergen & Co. Gold Dust Kentucky Bourbon, Aqua, Fifth	728.00
Whiskey, N. Vanderbergen & Co. Gold Dust Kentucky Bourbon, Clear, Fifth	448.00
Whiskey, Old Bourbon, Pumpkinseed Flask, Clear, Stopper, Pt.	134.00
Whiskey, Our Choice Old Bourbon, Hencken & Schroder, Amber, Slug Plate, Fifth	308.00
Whiskey, P. Morville's AAA Old Bourbon, Clear, Label, Tooled Top, Stopper, Fifth	476.00
Whiskey, Phoenix Bourbon, Naber, Alfs & Brune, Lady's Leg, Amber, Kick Up, Fifth	728.00
Whiskey, R.T. Carroll & Co. Sole Agents, Amber, Slug Plate, Sloping Collar, Fifth	4256.00
Whiskey, Renz's Blackberry Brandy, Yellow Olive Amber, Slug Plate, Fifth	2240.00
Whiskey, Rosedale OK, Orange Amber, Sloping Collar, Fifth	896.00
Whiskey, Roth & Co., 214 & 216 Pine St., San Francisco, Flask, Amber, Roll Collar, ½ Pt.	179.00
Whiskey, Rum Punch, Label Under Glass, Curly-Haired Woman, Wicker Cover, Handle, Fifth	246.00
Whiskey, Standard Od Bourbon, Weil Bros, S.F. Agts., Amber, Slug Plate, Sloping Collar, Fifth	616.00
Whiskey, Thos. H. Jacobs & Co. Philadelphia, Yellow Olive, Cylindrical, 10 ½ In.	2211.00
Whiskey, Thos. Taylor & Co., For P. Vollmers Old Bourbon, Louisville, Ky., Amber, Fifth	616.00
Whiskey, Tobacco Amber, Cylindrical, 3-Piece Mold, Willington Glass Works, Fifth	364.00
Whiskey, Wm. Hakes Sour Mash, Label Under Glass, Bearded Man, Olive Amber, Wicker, Fifth	308.00
Whiskey, Wolters Bros. & Co., S.F., Golden Amber, Slug Plate, Fifth	2688.00
Wine, Black Glass, Olive Amber, Painted, Musicians, Globular, c.1740, 11 x 9 In.	4313.00
Wine, Carved, Joined Bamboo Sections, Sea Green, Stoneware, Red Markings, 11 In.	119.00
Wine, Celadon Glaze, Raised Design, Flowers, Butterflies, Black, White, Stoneware, 1900s, 15 In.	184.00
Zanesville, 24 Broken Ribs, Amber, Globular, Molded, c.1815-35, 6 ⅝ In. *illus*	5175.00
Zanesville, 24 Ribs, Swirled To Left, Aqua, Club Form, Rolled Collar, 7 ½ In.	202.00
Zanesville, 24 Ribs, Swirled To Right, Golden Honey Amber, Globular, 7 ¾ In.	560.00
Zanesville, 24 Ribs, Swirled To Right, Honey Amber, Rolled Lip, Pontil, 8 ½ In.	560.00

BOTTLE CAPS for milk bottles are the printed cardboard caps used since the 1920s. Crown caps, used after 1892 on soda bottles, are also popular collectibles. Unusual mottoes, graphics, and caps from bottlers that are out of business bring the highest prices.

Crown, Caravan Strawberry Soda, Plastic Lined	3.00
Crown, Clicquot Club Tom Collins, Green, White, Cork Lined	3.00
Crown, Crush Grapefruit Soda, Yellow, White, Cork Lined	3.00
Crown, Donald Duck, Ginger Ale, Green, Orange, Cork Lined	9.00
Happy Home Milk, Paper, Old Dairy, Iowa, 1 ½ In.	10.00
Kimberland Dairy, Paper, McDonald, Pa., 2 ¼ In.	10.00
Nichols Creamery, Paper, Morning Sun, Iowa, 1 ⅝ In.	10.00
Pennsylvania Railroad, Pasteurized Milk, Red, White Letters, Altoona, Pa.	18.00
Washington, Plastic, White, Art Deco, 4 ½ x 3 In.	13.00
Wellman Coop Creamery, Skim Milk, Iowa Dairy, 2 ¼ In.	10.00

BOTTLE OPENERS are needed to open many bottles. As soon as the commercial bottle was invented, the opener to be used with the new types of closures became a necessity. Many types of bottle openers can be found, most dating from the twentieth century. Collectors prize advertising and comic openers.

Black Man, Holding Metal Guitar Opener, Wood Cap, Japan, 7 In.	35.00
Camel, Metal, Standing On Pyramid, Metal, Israel, 6 x 2 ½ In.	24.00
Cowboy, Guitar, Cast Iron	68.00
Drunken Man, Leaning Forward, Corkscrew, Metal, 6 x 1 ¼ In.	24.00
Figural, Nude Woman, Brass, Marked, 1950s, 4 ¼ In.	78.00

Knight, Copper Tone, O'Keefe Bottle Opener, 5 ½ In. 24.00
Larry Costley Chevrolet, Miami, Florida, White, Red 15.00
Old Knickerbocker, Ruppert Beer, Metal, 1940s, 3 ¼ In. 15.00
Parrot, Metal, Corkscrew, 5 ½ x 2 In. 36.00
Parrot, On Perch, Green, Orange, Cast Iron, 1900s, 4 ¾ x 3 ½ In. 60.00
Rheingold Beer, Metal, 3 ¾ In. 5.00
Rooster, Brass, Black Paint, England, c.1950, 2 ¼ In. 75.00
Spoon, Cherry Stem, Handle Terminal Opener, Silver, Vaughn Chicago, 7 ¾ In. 25.00
Storz, Wood, c.1960, 10 In. 26.00
Sycro Pickwick, Syracuse Ornamental, c.1920, 6 x 2 ½ In. 62.00
Whale, Cast Iron, 1 ½ x 3 In. 70.00
Winking Man, Big Smile, WHAM-EE, 1900, 4 In. 75.00
Woman, Nude, Metal, 7 ¼ In. 39.00

BOXES of all kinds are collected. They were made of thin strips of inlaid wood, metal, tortoiseshell, embroidery, or other material. Additional boxes may be listed in other sections, such as Advertising, Battersea, Ivory, Shaker, Tinware, and various Porcelain categories. Tea Caddies are listed in their own category.

2-Finger, Pantry, Maple, Square Copper Tacks, Lap Joint Lid, 2 x 6 In. 147.00
Altar, Fruit Melon, Famille Rose, Divided Interior, Round, Green, Pink, Chinese, 5 ½ x 8 In. 175.00
Amber Glass, Bohemian, Flowers, Gilt Ribbons, Trunk Shape, Ormolu Mounted, Hinged 885.00
Apple, Wood, Hexagonal, Fluted Handle, Footed, Painted, c.1900 3000.00
Artist, Hardwood, Covered Case, Fitted Interior, Accessories, c.1900, 7 x 4 In. 236.00
Ballot, Clasped Hands, Mahogany, 1800s, 4 x 16 In. 533.00
Band, Blue Wavy Line, White Flowers, Ivory Ground, Lid, 1800s, 11 x 15 In. 110.00
Band, Cardboard, Lid, Volunteer Firemen Design, Hunters, Countryside, c.1835, 12 x 19 In. 362.00
Band, Cloth, Paper Lined, Painted, Lid With Napoleon, Horse, Village Scenes, c.1830, 8 x 14 In. *illus* 6463.00
Band, Oval, Leaf Wallpaper, Bentwood, Georgian Street Scenes, c.1855, 11 x 16 ¾ In. 230.00
Bentwood, Glued Seams, Painted, Flowers, Flourishes, Scandinavia, 3 ¾ x 9 ¾ In. 121.00
Betel, Mixed Metal, Inlaid Silver Leaves, 2 Loop Handles, 4 Lidded Sections, 3 ¾ x 8 In. 122.00
Bible, 2 Carved Tulips, England, c.1707, 9 ¾ x 29 In. 547.00
Bible, Oak, Carved, William & Mary, Hinged Lid, Late 1600s, 9 x 22 In. 334.00
Bible, Oak, Plank Top, Scroll Carved, Stand, Turned Legs, England, c.1700, 36 x 29 In. 488.00
Bible, Pine, Flame Graining, Staple Hinges, Molded Lid Edge, Dovetailed, 1800s, 21 x 15 In. 588.00
Bible, Pine, Painted, Ivory Escutcheon, Inscribed, 13 ½ x 10 ½ In. 316.00
Bible, Pine, Painted, Scandinavia, 1842, 18 x 13 In. 259.00
Bible, Walnut, Notch Edge, Scroll Carving, Lid, England, 1700s, 28 x 19 In. 690.00
Bible, Walnut, Queen Anne, Arched Apron, Phil., c.1750, 8 ½ x 23 ½ In. 1067.00
Bible, William & Mary, Inlaid Walnut, Date AM 1749, Bun Feet, 11 ¼ x 21 ¼ In. 49770.00
Bible, Wood, Open Sided, Painted Red, E. McVea, R. Waters, 1811, 16 x 12 In. 529.00
Bird Food, Stretched Canvas Top, Bluebird On Branch, Painted, Lift Lid, 1900s, 11 x 15 In. 127.00
Bird Shape, Round, Cover, Amber & Brown Splashes, 2 In. Diam. 1830.00
Bird's-Eye Maple, Hinged Lid, Ivory Escutcheon, 10-Point Star, Diamonds, 1800s, 6 x 14 In. 711.00
Black Silk, White Jade Inlay, Twisted Rope Shape, Chinese, 3 x 2 In. 533.00
Blue Paint, Red Cornucopia, Gold, Hinged Lid, Bootjack Ends, c.1820, 7 x 11 In. 5175.00
Book Shape, Bronze, Marble, Arts & Crafts, 5 In. 177.00
Book, Jackwood, Animal Finial, Hand Carved, Scrolls, Dome Lid, Bali, 1700s, 14 x 15 In. 375.00
Boxwood, Monkeys, Relief Carved, Inlaid Eyes, Lid, Signed, Japan, 3 ¼ In. *illus* 1778.00
Brass, Malachite, Cross, Lid, Square, Arts & Crafts, Signed, England, 1800s, 4 x 8 In. 431.00
Brass, Rectangular, Plaque, Peaches, Bat, Landscape, White Jade Lid, c.1885, 5 ½ In., Pair 5166.00
Bride's, Bentwood, Laced Seams, Painted Green, Tree, Oval, 8 x 18 In. 241.00
Bride's, Bentwood, Laced Seams, Painted Tulips, c.1850, 5 x 14 In. 264.00
Bride's, Bentwood, Laced Seams, Painted, Couple, Tulip Borders, Oval, Lid, 1820, 6 ½ x 19 In. 512.00
Bride's, Bentwood, Laced Seams, Painted, Tulips, Colonial Couple, 1800s, 8 x 18 In. 588.00
Bride's, Bentwood, Painted, Wedded Couple On Lid, Flowers, Oval, 1800s, 7 ¾ x 18 ¾ In. 558.00
Bride's, Bentwood, Turtledove, Flower, Oval, c.1820, 7 x 15 ½ In. 608.00
Bride's, Flowers, Painted, Oval, Scandinavia, 1800s, 4 ¾ x 11 In. 237.00
Bride's, Pennsylvania Dutch, Painted, Black, Flowers, Birds, Dome Lid, c.1800, 16 x 15 ½ In. 660.00
Bride's, Rosemaling, Painted, For Peter's Daughter, Norway, c.1884 750.00
Brocade, Book Shape, Fitted Interior, Chinese, 5 ¾ x 4 ½ In., Pair 533.00
Bronze Dore, F. Marjorell, Femme-Fleur, Hinged, Satin Lining, Signed, 5 x 9 In. 329.00
Bronze Dore, Repousse, Grape Harvesters, Hinged Lid, France, 1800s, 3 x 5 ¾ In. 385.00
Bronze, Casket, Boule Lacquer, Brass Inlay, Mask Corners, Ormolu, Paw Feet, Handles, 29 In. 5400.00
Bronze, Jade, Dome Plaque, Spinach Green, Phoenix Among Clouds, Lid, 4 In. 275.00
Bronze, Persimmon Shape, Japan, 1800s, 5 ½ In. 184.00
Brush, Porcelain, Blue & White, 2 Dragons, Wave Design, Lid, Chinese, 1800s, 8 x 4 In. 546.00

Bottle, Tonic, Harrison's Columbian Stimulant, Roof Shoulders, Pontil, Label, c.1850, 6 ⅜ In.
$1287.00

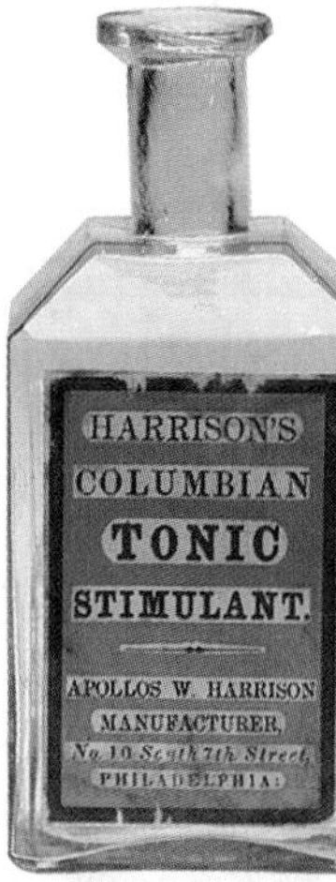

Norman C. Heckler & Company

Bottle, Whiskey, Caspers, Made By Honest North Carolina People, Cobalt, Tooled Lip, 1895, 12 In.
$489.00

Glass Works Auctions

Bottle, Whiskey, Ernst Gerstenberg, Pretzel Flask, Pottery, Brown Glaze, c.1900, 3 ⅝ In.
$690.00

Glass Works Auctions

Bottle, Whiskey, J.F. Cutter Extra Old Bourbon, Star In Shield, Yellow Green, 1871-75
$4704.00

American Bottle Auctions

Bottle, Zanesville, 24 Broken Ribs, Amber, Globular, Molded, c.1815-35, 6 ⅝ In.
$5175.00

Glass Works Auctions

Box, Band, Cloth, Paper Lined, Painted, Lid With Napoleon, Horse, Village Scenes, c.1830, 8 x 14 In.
$6463.00

Garth's Auctions, Inc.

Brush, Porcelain, Rose Medallion, Figures, Flowers, Lid, Chinese, 1800s, 7 In.	326.00
Burl Walnut, Brass Handles, Lock, England, 12 x 12 In.	406.00
Burl, Inlaid Brass, Mother-Of-Pearl, Signed Tahan Paris, 1800s, 3 x 7 ½ In.	584.00
Caddy, Ebonized Wood, Brass Inlay, Fitted Interior, Center Top Handle, 3 x 10 x 13 In.	108.00
Candle, Grain Painted, Chamfered Lid & Till, Rust Color, Compartment, 1800s, 12 ½ In.	489.00
Candle, Mahogany, Scalloped, Chip Carved, Compass, Octagonal, 1800s, 9 x 13 In.	413.00
Candle, Painted, Raised Panel Slide Lid, Finger Notch, Divided, Dovetailed, 7 x 8 x 14 In.	311.00
Candle, Pine, Green Paint, Pierced Arched Back, 11 x 7 In.	245.00
Candle, Pine, Painted, Slide Lid, Circular Designs, 1874, 7 x 11 In.	830.00
Candle, Poplar, Slide Lid, Red Swirl & Dot Decoration, c.1825, 2 x 7 x 4 In.	5925.00
Candle, Walnut, Slide Lid, Raised Panel, Finger Groove, Square Iron Nails, 5 ⅜ x 13 In.	177.00
Candle, Walnut, Wall, Dovetailed, Slide Lid, c.1875, 24 x 10 ½ x 4	345.00
Candle, Wood, Hinged Sloping Lid, Pierced Shaped Back Plate, Drawer, c.1800, 18 x 9 In.	148.00
Carnelian, Squat, Ribbed, Bail Handle, Wooden Base With Arch, Lid, 8 x 7 In.	598.00
Carved, Lotus Blossom, Leaves, Blue Glaze, Round, Lid, Footed, 5 ⅛ In.	3416.00
Casket, Bronze, Gilt, Oval, Acorn Finial, Leaf Base, Charles X, 6 ¼ x 6 ¼ In.	738.00
Casket, Enameled Glass, Gilt, Canted Corners, Flowers, Jeweled, Paw Feet, 6 In.	732.00
Casket, Jewelry, Gilt Bronze, Glass, Enameled Porcelain, Wreaths, Navette Shape, 6 x 4 In.	584.00
Casket, Porcelain, Figural, Woman, Kneeling In Prayer, c.1850, 11 ½ x 11 In.	1353.00
Ceramic, Butterflies, Birds, Flowers, Putti Finial, Shaped Feet, Lid, 1800s, 10 In.	2818.00
Ceramic, Village Scenes, Green, Glazed, Frog Finial, Lid, Seal Mark, Chinese, 5 In.	992.00
Champleve, Gilt Bronze, Sarcophagus Shape, Flowers, Scroll Feet, Hinged Lid, 10 In.	1778.00
Chippendale, Cherry, South Carolina, c.1780, 7 x 10 In.	5925.00
Cigarette, Bronze Sterling Overlay, Hunt Scene, Cedar, c.1920, 8 ½ x 3 ½ In.	375.00
Cinnabar, Lacquer, Brass, Carved Dragon, Carp, Figures, Stand, Chinese, 3 x 6 In., Pair	1560.00
Cloisonne, Lacquer, Chinese Drum Shape, Red, Black, 7 x 9 In.	450.00
Coffer, Needlepoint Tapestry, Nailhead Trim, Carved Oak Frame, England, 1800s, 23 x 27 In.	671.00
Copper, Hammered, Round, Rope Edge, Arts & Crafts, c.1910, 5 x 3 In.	420.00
Cosmetic, Gilt Silver, Round, Repousse, Peony Blossom, Leaves, Scrolling Lid, 4 ¾ In.	9760.00
Cosmetic, Rosewood, Mother-Of-Pearl & Ivory Inlay, Immortals, Brass, Chinese, c.1800, 13 x 10 In.	1593.00
Cosmetic, Rosewood, Mother-Of-Pearl Inlay, Brass, Birds, Flowers, Chinese, 1800s, 12 x 9 In.	1041.00
Cutlery, Curly Maple, Handle, Dovetailed, Branded, Eldred Wheeler, 17 x 7 In.	184.00
Cutlery, Mahogany, Serpentine Case, Angled Lid, Divided Interior, George III, 14 x 9 In.	325.00
Cutlery, Walnut, 2 Compartments, Dovetailed, Divider, Cutout Handle, Va., 8 x 14 In.	138.00
Cutlery, Wood, Green Paint, Splayed Sides, Center Divider, Pierced Handle, 16 x 11 In.	207.00
Desk, Inlay, Lacquered, Sloping, Folding, Gilt, Abalone, Flowers, Hinged Lid, Footed, 4 x 13 In.	115.00
Desk, Mahogany, Sarcophagus, Silver Plate, Hipped Lid, Liftout Tray, William IV, 7 x 16 In.	461.00
Desk, Marble, Silver Plated Edging, Hinge, Lined Interior, France, c.1900, 2 x 4 In.	110.00
Desk, Pine, Slant Lid, Lift Top, Interior Compartments, 10 x 29 x 19 In.	49.00
Desk, Rosewood, Banded, Diamond Pattern Inlay, Tunbridge Ware, Victorian, 5 x 10 In.	154.00
Desk, Rosewood, Marquetry Inlay, Elephant, Victorian, 5 ½ x 12 ¼ In.	276.00
Desk, Satinwood, Compartmented Interior, Liftout Center, Signed, India, 1800s	805.00
Desk, Walnut, Brass Mounted, Hinged Doors, Letter Holder, Inkstand, England, 1800s, 9 ⅝ x 7 ¼ In.	178.00
Desk, Walnut, Mother-Of-Pearl Inlay, Tunbridge Ware Bands, 1800s, 5 ½ x 9 ¾ In.	338.00
Document, Applied Stars, Diamond, Blue, Red, Gold Paint, Slant Lid, 1800s, 8 x 4 ¼ In.	1035.00
Document, Birch, Pine, Yellow Leaves, Crest, Isanna Smith, Hinged Lid, c.1800, 6 x 15 In.	3623.00
Document, Bird's-Eye Maple, Dovetailed Case, Brass Handle, Wallpaper Lining, 7 x 13 In.	176.00
Document, Black Paint, Flowers, Landscape, Dome Lid, 1800s, 5 x 10 In.	374.00
Document, Black, Blue Paint, Metal Latch, 14 x 8 In.	115.00
Document, Grain Painted, Yellow, Green, Hinged Lid, Leather Straps, c.1805, 6 ½ x 14 In.	690.00
Document, Lacquer, Tortoiseshell, Mother-Of-Pearl, Gold Seashells, Flowers, c.1900, 3 x 16 In.	153.00
Document, Leather, Gilt Embossed, Top Handle, 5 ¼ x 14 In.	504.00
Document, Painted, Swag, Red, Gold & White Bands, New England, 1800s, 5 x 9 x 14 In.	380.00
Document, Pine, Green, Red Compass, Cream, Dome Lid, Rosehead Nails, 8 x 18 In.	353.00
Document, Pine, Lock, Blue & Brown Over Yellow, Dovetailed, c.1830, 4 ¼ x 14 In.	382.00
Document, Pine, Painted Black, Red, Stencil, Fitted Interior, Brass Handle, c.1850, 15 x 10 In.	470.00
Document, Pine, Stencils, Fruit Compote, Border Design, Early 19th Century, 7 x 16 x 9 In.	489.00
Document, Regency, Mahogany, Coffin Shape, c.1825, 8 ¼ x 15 In.	246.00
Document, Sheet Iron, Red, Yellow Stripes, Bronze Stencil, Arched Lid, Wire Ring, 5 x 9 In.	59.00
Document, Tortoiseshell, Silver Inlay, Center Medallion, England, c.1800, 9 ½ x 3 In.	1422.00
Document, Walnut, Parquetry, Paper Lined Interior, Dome Lid, Germany, 9 x 19 In.	500.00
Document, Wood, Painted, Block Feet, Lid, Early 1800s, 17 x 24 In.	770.00
Document, Yellow Pine, Carved Corners, 1800s, 5 ½ x 10 In.	110.00
Dresser, 3 Veneered Drawers, Turned Knobs, 1800s, 11 x 21 In.	400.00
Dresser, Bird's-Eye Maple, Rosewood, Curly Walnut, Lock, Brass, 3 ¾ x 10 In.	41.00
Dresser, Decoupage, Horse, Figure, Birds, Bun Feet, Flip Lid, 1830, 6 x 14 In.	267.00

Dresser, Figure Holding Rifle, Keep Out, Carved, 5 Drawers, Lid, c.1900, 12 x 12 In.	1035.00
Dresser, Gilt Metal, Embossed, Pictorial, Portrait Of Woman, Garlands, Round, Lid, 4 In.	201.00
Dresser, Gilt Metal, Porcelain, Heart Shape, Princess Devonshire, Scrolling, Angel, 5 In.	288.00
Dresser, Glass, Metal, Egg Shape, Blue, Mottled, Enameled Butterfly, Flowers, Flip Lid, Footed, 8 In.	345.00
Dresser, Lapis Lazuli, Beveled Hinged Lid, Metal Bracket Feet, 2 x 4 x 3 In.	492.00
Dresser, Mahogany, Inlaid Compass Star, Hinged Lid, Lock, c.1830-40, 4 x 9 In.	176.00
Dresser, Mahogany, Veneer, Raised Panel Lid, Ball Feet, Ivory Key Escutcheon, 7 x 12 In.	57.00
Dresser, Maple, Walnut, Parquet, Greek Key, Checkerboard, 3 Trays, Padded Lid, 5 x 10 In.	28.00
Dresser, Ormolu, Glass, Strapwork, Flowers, Hinged Lid, Oval, c.1900, 3 ⅝ x 8 ⅜ In.	443.00
Dresser, Painted Ivory Tusk, Figures, Hills, Trees, Instruments, Oval, Lid, Persia, 3 x 7 In.	415.00
Dresser, Painted, Orange Ground, House, Trees, Birds, Flowers, Lid, Europe, 1842, 7 x 13 In.	356.00
Dresser, Parquet, 8-Point Stars, Geometric Shapes, Mirror, Tray, 8 x 12 x 9 In.	181.00
Dresser, Pine, Drawer, Green, Black, Yellow, Lift Lid, c.1850, 7 x 16 x 7 In.	1085.00
Dresser, Pine, Painted, Carved Geometric Design, Hinged Lid, 1842, 3 x 7 In.	326.00
Dresser, Poplar, Painted, Sun Design, Lid, c.1835, 3 x 14 In.	89.00
Dresser, Rosewood, Brass Inlay, Paper Interior, 3 Cut Glass Jars, Silver Plate, 11 x 8 In.	110.00
Dresser, Rosewood, String Inlaid, Ivory Escutcheon, Ivory Edging, Banded Lid, 8 x 14 x 8 In.	158.00
Empire, Rosewood, Satinwood, Loop Handles, Paw Feet, Shaped Lid, France, 4 x 6 In.	431.00
Enamel, Gold Wash Silver Mounts, Classical Scenes, Lid, H. Ratzerdorfer, Austria, c.1866, 4 x 3 In.	2252.00
Enameled Opaline, Oak Leaves, Acorns, Insect, Lid, 3 Oak Leaf Feet, 6 x 5 In.	281.00
Enameled, Birds, Flowers, Vermeil, Silver Stand, Egg Shape, France, 2 ½ x 3 In.	900.00
Enameled, Quail, Flowering Plants, Gilt Accents, Lid, Japan, 12 x 3 In.	427.00
Famille Rose, 2 Quails Perched On Rock, Multicolor, Lid, Chinese, Marked, 6 ½ In.	6573.00
Famille Rose, Calligraphy, Flowers, Yellow, Lid, Chinese, Character Mark, 5 In.	299.00
Figural, Silver, Bone, Musician On Stool, Playing Bass, Hinged, Ball Feet, c.1890, 4 ¾ In.	2726.00
Gilt Bronze, Porcelain, Art Nouveau, Painted, Flowers, Lounging Woman, c.1890, 10 x 16 In.	5060.00
Gilt Metal, Clamshell Shape, Mounted With Turquoise Points, Hinged, 1 ½ x 3 In.	295.00
Gilt Metal, Enamel, Portrait, Una Gitana, Lining, Oval, Hinged Lid, 1900s, 2 x 3 In.	276.00
Gilt Silver, Transfer, Painted Putti, Engraved, Hinged Enamel Lid, 1800s, 3 ¼ x 2 In.	826.00
Glass, Cobalt Blue, Gilt, Flowers, Cone Finial, Footed, Hinged Lid, 14 In., Pair	281.00
Grain Painted, 2 Drawers, Shaped Skirt, Porcelain Knobs, Lift Lid, 1800s, 11 x 16 In.	123.00
Hardstone, Gilt Mounts, Celadon Color, Rectangular, Elephant Finial, Lid, Footed, 3 In.	1488.00
Hardwood, Ebonized, Pietra Dura Design, Bird Perched On Branch, Lid, c.1800s, 3 x 9 In.	584.00
Hardwood, Mother-Of-Pearl, Scalloped, Inlaid Buddhist Emblems, Lid, Chinese, 8 In.	930.00
Hat, Faux Snakeskin Paper, 10 x 4 In.	18.00
Hat, Red Parchment, Brass Mount, Gilt, Flowers, Cylindrical, Chinese, 1900s, 21 In., Pair	881.00
Hinged, Wrought Iron, Carved Designs, 1677, 7 x 16 In.	468.00
House Shape, Combed Green Paint, Pitched Roof, Hinged Lid, 1800s, 37 x 41 In.	1150.00
Incense, Porcelain, Cover, Steel Blue Glaze, Dragons, c.1890	368.00
Ink, Porcelain, Blue & White, Scenic Black & White Reserve, Gilt Trim, 3 x 3 In.	840.00
Iron, Scrolled Openwork Flowers, Green Paint, Dome Lid, Russia, c.1800, 4 x 3 ¼ In.	533.00
Ivory, Figures, Landscape, Yellow Ground, Hinged, Cylindrical, Painted, Persian Signed, 4 In.	288.00
Jewelry, Agate, Shell Shape Lid, Hinged, Footed, 5 x 3 In.	59.00
Jewelry, Baroque, Mixed Woods, Fitted Interior, Relief Carved, Dome Lid, 8 x 20 In.	240.00
Jewelry, Biedermeier, Mahogany, Birch, Ebonized, Painted, Temple Shape, c.1830, 8 x 14 In.	5975.00
Jewelry, Brass, 3 Drawers, Cherubs, Music Symbols, Flowers, Scroll, c.1895, 7 x 8 ¼ In.	385.00
Jewelry, Brass, Padlock, Engraved, Semiprecious Stones, Ball Feet, Hinged Lid, 6 x 5 ½ In.	1888.00
Jewelry, Brass, The Guardian, Panel Dome Top, Pedestal Base, H. Christensen, 1975, 10 x 8 In.	2318.00
Jewelry, Bronze, Casket Shape, Gold Finish, Hinged, Tiffany, 3 x 4 x 8 In.	2013.00
Jewelry, Casket Shape, Flowers, Gilt Frame, Handles, Scroll Feet, Sevres Style, 7 ¾ x 13 In.	492.00
Jewelry, Casket Shape, Gilt, Pietra Dura, Birds, Flowers, Shaped Legs, Hinged Lid, 5 x 8 In.	750.00
Jewelry, Copper, Enamel, Blue, Lily Of The Valley, Gilt, Jewel Borders, Lid, Round, c.1900, 4 x 8 In.	295.00
Jewelry, Gilt Brass, Molded Leaves, Enameled Plaque, Courting Couple, Oval, 3 x 9 In.	1770.00
Jewelry, Gilt Bronze, Casket Shape, Geometric Border, Flowers, Hinged Lid, 6 x 8 In.	119.00
Jewelry, Gilt, Enameled Copper, Octagonal, Fluted, Woman's Portrait, c.1925, 4 In.	430.00
Jewelry, Gold, Pink Roses, Red Velveteen Lining, Japan, 1950s, 3 ¾ x 2 ¾ In.	55.00
Jewelry, Majolica, Pink Glaze, Raised Dots, Recessed Handle, Japan, 1930s, 4 ½ x 3 ¾ In.	35.00
Jewelry, Nakashima, Rosewood, 3 Drawers, Wood Knob Pulls, Japan, 1980s, 6 ½ x 13 In.	2480.00
Jewelry, Openwork, Roses, Swags, Panels, Velvet Lining, Glass Lid, 1950s, 3 ¾ x 2 ¾ In.	55.00
Jewelry, Pietra Dura, Ebony, Casket Shape, Flowers, Paw Feet, Hinged Lid, 1800s, 9 x 12 In.	1896.00
Jewelry, Puzzle, Wood, Amorphic, Carved C, Velvet Lining, 2 Compartments, 9 x 3 ½ In.	45.00
Jewelry, Quilted Design, 8-Point Star, Beaded Fringe, Cord Strap, Morocco, 10 x 7 In.	60.00
Jewelry, Silver, 2 Cherubs, Roundel, Flower & Husk Garland, Oval, Lid, c.1900, 8 In.	652.00
Jewelry, Silver, Enamel, Roundel, Cherub, Green Ground, Lid, Austria, c.1890, 4 ¼ x 3 ½ In.	919.00
Jewelry, Silver, Gold Washed, Enamel, Beaded, Plaque, Pagoda, Lid, c.1900, 3 ½ x 5 ½ In.	6221.00
Jewelry, Silver, Heart Shape, Mirrored, Rope Border, Lining, Dome Lid, Japan, c.1945, 3 x 1 ½ In.	40.00

Box, Boxwood, Monkeys, Relief Carved, Inlaid Eyes, Lid, Signed, Japan, 3 ¼ In.
$1778.00

Skinner, Inc.

Box, Knife, Georgian, Mahogany, Herringbone Inlay, Medallion, Compass Star, 14 x 9 ½ In.
$748.00

Leland Little Auction

Box, Knife, Mahogany, Serpentine, Inlay, Crossbanding, Bracket Feet, c.1785, 15 x 8 In.
$430.00

New Orleans Auction Galleries, Inc.

Box, Letter, Burl, Veneer, Chest Shape, Nailed Hardware, England, 1700s
$300.00

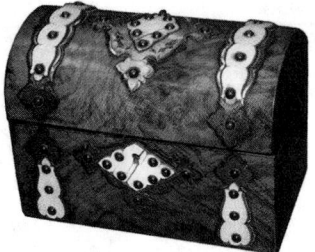

DuMouchelles Art Gallery

Box, Letter, Edwardian, White Oak, Fluted Column, Carved, Fabric Lining, c.1910, 24 ½ In.
$5900.00

Brunk Auctions

Box, Pine, Lid, Lapped Seam, Blue, Applied Carved Ebony Whale, 1800s, 2 ⅜ x 5 ⅛ In.
$4148.00

Skinner, Inc.

Box, Silver, Mixed Metal, Insect, Branch, Lid, Art Nouveau, Geo. W. Shiebler, 1 ¾ In.
$444.00

Skinner, Inc.

> **TIP**
>
> *Dust frequently if you live near the seashore. Salt air causes problems.*

Jewelry, Silver, Repousse, Chased Flowers, Foo Dog, Shaped Oval, Hinged Lid, 2 ¼ x 5 ¼ In....	118.00
Jewelry, Silver Plate, Casket Shape, Flared, Hinged Lid, Edward VII, 1905, 3 ⅝ x 4 ⅝ In.	948.00
Jewelry, Tortoiseshell, Ivory Inlay, Gadrooned, Silver, Pagoda Top, c.1830, 8 x 5 ½ In.	2963.00
Jewelry, Tortoiseshell, Regency, Casket Shape, Dome Top, Ebony Bun Feet, c.1825..................	1035.00
Jewelry, Tortoiseshell, Silver, Ivory Inlay, Hinged Lid, Ivory Trim & Feet, c.1800, 6 ¾ In.	711.00
Jewelry, Victorian Women, Flowers, Scrolling, Silver Finish, Lined, Footed, 5 x 4 In.	85.00
Jewelry, Walnut, Carved Flowers, Fitted Interior, Hinged Lid, Brass Feet, 1800s, 15 x 9 In.	948.00
Jewelry, Walnut, Mother-Of-Pearl Inlay, Interior Mirror, Banded Lid, Tray, Victorian, 6 x 9 In.	300.00
Jewelry, Wood, Black Forest, Birds, Figural Finial, 2 Birds, Round, 11 x 11 In..........................	604.00
Jewelry, Wood, Brass, Scrolled Lid, Sides, Loop Handles, Indo-Persian, c.1925, 3 x 3 ½ In.	98.00
Knife, Chippendale Style, Mahogany Veneer, Serpentine Front, Flame Veneer, England, 15 x 9 In.	437.00
Knife, Chippendale, Mahogany, Serpentine Front, Fitted Interior, England, 1800s, 15 x 8 In., Pair	1476.00
Knife, Federal, Mahogany Veneer, Conch Shell, Line Inlay, Star, Drawer, c.1800, 15 x 9 In.......	885.00
Knife, Federal, Mahogany, Shaped, Copper Inlay, Slant Lid, 14 ½ In., Pair	3600.00
Knife, Georgian, Mahogany, Herringbone Inlay, Medallion, Compass Star, 14 x 9 ½ In. ....*illus*	748.00
Knife, Georgian, Mahogany, Inlays, Compass Star Design, 14 ¾ x 11 ½ In..............................	575.00
Knife, Hepplewhite, Mahogany, Kingwood Inlay, Serpentine Front, Late 1700s, 15 x 9 In.........	460.00
Knife, Hepplewhite, Satinwood, Serpentine Front, Ring Handle, Eng., 12 x 8 In.	443.00
Knife, Mahogany, Herringbone Borders, Brass Paw Feet, c.1805, 15 ½ In...............................	236.00
Knife, Mahogany, Serpentine, Inlay, Crossbanding, Bracket Feet, c.1785, 15 x 8 In. ....*illus*	430.00
Knife, Pine, Blue Paint, Dovetailed, Cutout Handle, c.1850, 4 ½ x 15 In.................................	264.00
Knife, Satinwood, Mahogany, Serpentine, Hinged Lid, Conch Shell, 1700s, 15 x 9 In., Pair......	1880.00
Lacquer, Birds, Fruits, Flower, Red, Gold, Gray, Blue, Lobed, Round, Chinese, 17 ½ In............	161.00
Lacquer, Black Ground, Courtyard Scene, Brass Handles, Lock, Lid, 1800s, 19 x 28 In.............	1550.00
Lacquer, Black, Mother-Of-Pearl Inlay, Animals, Cranes, Prunus, Tortoises, 1800s, 5 x 11 ⅝ In.	2205.00
Lacquer, Black, Red Interior, Landscape, Figures, Lift Lid, Russia, 6 x 4 ½ In.	104.00
Lacquer, Chinoiserie Design, Green Ground, Hinged Lid, Gilt, 2 x 5 In.................................	444.00
Lacquer, Court Scene, Animals, Calligraphy, Lid, Octagonal, India, 6 x 2 In.	46.00
Lacquer, Fish Shape, Glass Eyes, Silver Accent Scales, Japan, 7 ⅛ In..................................	1464.00
Lacquer, Fitted, Bouquet, Tray, Drawers, Lock, Tassels, Lid, Japan, c.1855, 8 x 10 In..............	748.00
Lacquer, Gilt, Rectangular, Lid, 2 Men, Playing A Game, Phoenix, Japan, 4 In.	682.00
Lacquer, Gold, Cranes, Bamboo, Abalone Shell Inset, Brass Mounts, Japan, 1800s, 24 x 16 In.	858.00
Lacquer, Lobed, Red, Dragons, Clouds, Gold, Marked, Chinese, c.1890, 15 In. Diam.	7110.00
Lacquer, Mother-Of-Pearl Inlay, 2 Deer, Peach Tree, Japan, 1900s, 11 ⅜ x 8 ¾ In.	490.00
Lacquer, Rectangular, Mountain Landscape, Trees, Fence, Stream, Sparrow, Arched Lid, Footed, 16 In.	1722.00
Lacquer, Red & Black, Bird & Flowers, Rectangular, Rounded Corners, Chinese, 16 In............	687.00
Lacquer, Red Interior, Hand Painted Figures, 4-Footed, Hinged Lid, Russia, 7 x 5 In.	184.00
Lacquer, Square, Black, Gold, Silver, Morning Glory, Mimosa, Lid, c.1900, 5 ¾ x 6 In.............	1045.00
Lapis Lazuli, Brass, Hinges, Continental, 2 ½ x 1 ⅝ In...	553.00
Leather Cover, Tack, Covered Rope Handle, Iron, Brass, Lock, Lining, 7 x 15 In......................	47.00
Letter, Brass, Calamander Veneer, Gothic Style Mounts, Fitted Slots, England, 1800s, 8 ¾ In. .	296.00
Letter, Burl, Veneer, Chest Shape, Nailed Hardware, England, 1700s ....*illus*	300.00
Letter, Edwardian, White Oak, Fluted Column, Carved, Fabric Lining, c.1910, 24 ½ In. ....*illus*	5900.00
Letter, Gothic Style, Faux Grain Painted, Openwork Brass Mounts, Lined, 5 ½ x 8 ¾ In..........	236.00
Letter, Hotel, Oak, Tombstone Shape, Brass Plaque, Paneled Locking Door, c.1900, 14 x 8 In.	1150.00
Letter, Oak, Frieze Drawers, Cylindrical, Dome Lid, c.1880, 16 ½ x 8 ¾ In.	7763.00
Liquor, Ebonized Wood, Ormolu, Medallions, Couples, Doors, Gilt Finial, 1800s, 13 ½ x 13 In.	1416.00
Liquor, Mahogany, Roll Top, Desk Shape, Leaf Inlay, Gilt Highlights, 1800s, 9 x 10 In...........	767.00
Liquor, Regency, Satinwood, Inlaid Shell, Brass Handles, Hinged Lid, England, 9 x 12 In.......	1725.00
Lock, Walnut, Tulips, Birds, Houses, Carved, Inscribed Mrs. R.N. 1873, Pa., 6 x 12 In.	652.00
Mahogany, Cove Lid, Brass Handle, Ebonized, George III, c.1800, 5 x 9 ½ In........................	430.00
Mahogany, Finial, Red Stain, Turned Feet, Dovetailed, Slide Lid, c.1850, 7 ½ x 10 ½ In.	382.00
Mahogany, Inlay, Fitted Interior, Top Handle, Cove Molded Lid, England, 1800s, 6 x 11 In......	236.00
Mahogany, Nailed, Finger Notch, Slide Lid, 4 ⅜ x 16 In..	47.00
Mahogany, Satinwood Inlaid Star, Octagonal, Diamond Panels, 1800s, 5 x 10 In.	384.00
Metal, Dragon, Pearl, Cloud, Wave Repousse, Wood Lines, Chinese, 1900s, 4 x 5 In..............	246.00
Metal, Repousse Design, Inset Jewels, Wood Interior, Alfred Daguet, c.1902, 9 x 6 In............	5700.00
Mixed Wood, Pagoda Shape, Hexagonal, Footed, Hinged, c.1890, 11 ½ In...........................	354.00
Morning Glories, Pink Ground, Green Leaves, Round, Lid, 1938, 2 x 5 In............................	345.00
Neoclassical, Gilt Bronze, Relief Design, Initials, Velvet Lining, 6 ¼ x 4 ½ In.......................	207.00
Novelty, 2 Parts, Stacked Books Shape, Brocade Lids, Wooden Stand, 1900s, 5 ½ In..............	1107.00
Oak, Carved Side Figures, Petit Point Panel, Lift Lid, 9 ½ x 13 In.	115.00
Oak, Carved, Flowers, Geometric, Lock, 6 x 7 In...	40.00
Oak, Square Nail, Red, Black, Brown, Cream Ground, Dome Lid, c.1800, 4 ½ x 10 x 4 In.	323.00
Ottoman, Silver, Copper, Inlaid Brass, Arabic Calligraphy, 1800s, 8 x 4 In...........................	227.00
Painted, Chariot, Flags, Gilt Borders, Monograms, Flowers, Garland, Lift Lid, 1800s, 4 x 12 In.	385.00

Painted, Multicolor Flowers, Leaves, Scallops, Black, Leather Hinges, Dome Lid, c.1800, 5 x 9 In.	3555.00
Painted, Orange, Red, Black Leaves, Slide Lid, 1800s, 4 x 12 In.	474.00
Parquetry, Geometric Design, Stepped, Lift Lid, Late 1800s, 8 x 15 In.	104.00
Parquetry, Rectangular Shape, Painted Interior, 8 x 13 In.	488.00
Patch, Enamel, Painted, Flowers, Horse Rider In Countryside, 1700s, 3 ½ In.	210.00
Patch, Tortoiseshell, Rectangular, Silver Piping, Faceted Steel Beads, c.1800, 2 In.	276.00
Pie, Poplar, Painted, Bread Board Ends, Tin Panel, Punched Wheel Design, 15 x 21 In.	2185.00
Pill, Enamel, Painted, Pail Shape, Daisies, Ivory, Rope Twist Handle, Hinged, c.1900, 2 x 1 ¾ In.	575.00
Pin, Ceramic, Dresser Shape, 3 Dogs, Mirror, Blue, Orange, Gold, 4 ⅝ In.	45.00
Pine, Banded, Wood Staved Tub, Red Paint, Hinged Lid, 9 ¾ x 16 In.	770.00
Pine, Blue, White Flowers, Salmon Ground, Slide Lid, 4 x 10 ¾ In.	668.00
Pine, Finger Gouge, Painted Herringbone, Medallions, Scribes, Slide Lid, 1800s, 19 x 11 In.	955.00
Pine, Green & Red, Sponged Vinegar Design, Dovetailed, c.1850, 10 x 25 In.	588.00
Pine, Leather Straps, Brown, Gold Circles, Dome Lid, Feb. 4, 1821 Stencil, 8 x 15 ½ In.	805.00
Pine, Lid, Lapped Seam, Blue, Applied Carved Ebony Whale, 1800s, 2 ⅜ x 5 ⅛ In. ....*illus*	4148.00
Pine, Mahogany, Flame Grain Painted, Drawer, c.1850, 14 x 13 In.	1175.00
Pine, Molded Case, Block Feet, Hinged Lid, 11 x 21 In.	88.00
Pine, Molding, Paint, Flowers, Gilt Trim, Wreaths, Lift Lid, c.1850, 6 ¾ x 14 In.	1763.00
Pine, Multicolor Flowers, c.1800, 2 ¼ x 9 x 8 ¼ In.	5875.00
Pine, Multicolor Flowers, Tin Hasp, Dome Lid, Heinrich Bucher, c.1800, 5 x 10 ½ In.	1175.00
Pine, Oak, Desk Shape, Slant Lid, Scalloped Crest, Painted Black, Table Top, 10 x 16 In.	362.00
Pine, Painted Bittersweet, Lock, c.1850, 7 x 13 In.	206.00
Pine, Painted Blue, Green, White Flowers, Dome Lid, c.1880, 7 ½ x 12 In.	499.00
Pine, Painted, Carved Diamond Shape, Dovetailed, Hinged Lid, 1800s, 4 x 9 In.	385.00
Pine, Painted, Multicolor Flowers, Trunk Shape, Dome Hinged Lid, 1800s, 11 x 26 In.	1778.00
Pine, Painted, Multicolor Stylized Flowers, Yellow Leaves, Dome Hinged Lid, 11 x 28 In.	2320.00
Pine, Painted, Yellow, Green, Dovetailed, Hinged Lid, Early 1800s, 7 x 16 In.	593.00
Pine, Putty Painted, Brass Swing Handle, Iron Latch, Dovetailed, Dome Lid, Early 1800s, 8 x 16 In.	184.00
Pine, Red, Brown Grain Paint, Divided, Safrina Marble, Slide Lid, Maine, 4 x 10 In.	60.00
Pine, Salmon Paint, Slide Lid, c.1825, 10 x 21 ½ In.	441.00
Pine, Smoke Design, Putty Ground, Lock, Dovetailed, Wire Hinged Lid, 1800s, 6 x 12 In.	1067.00
Pine, White Washed, Carved, Inlaid Hearts, Diamonds, Initials, 4 Drawers, c.1860, 9 x 20 In.	176.00
Pipe, Mahogany, c.1800, 19 x 6 In.	237.00
Pipe, Pine, Red Paint, Lower Drawer, Pierced Arched Lid, Early 1800s, 20 x 6 In.	1007.00
Pipe, Pine, Rosehead Nails, Dovetailed Drawer, Shaped Top, Wall, c.1775, 20 In.	3525.00
Poplar, Grain Painted, Yellow Trim, Divided Interior, Slide Lid, c.1850, 12 x 28 In.	558.00
Poplar, Painted Yellow, Leaves, Marbleized Paper Liner, c.1870, 6 ½ x 24 In.	529.00
Poplar, Pine, Divided, Stenciled Fruit, Yellow Border, Slide Lid, 5 x 6 x 1 In.	452.00
Poplar, Red Flame Grain, Iron Handles, Lock, Dovetailed, Dome Top, c.1850, 12 x 30 In.	294.00
Porcelain, 3 Tiers, Blue, Flowers, Chinese, 1800s, 5 In.	184.00
Porcelain, Bronze, Blue, Gilded Cartouche, Bird, Flowers, Lid, 1800s, 4 x 6 In.	429.00
Porcelain, Gilt Brass, Octangular, Green Ground, Gilt, Napoleonic N, c.1890, 1 x 3 In.	276.00
Porcelain, Notched Corners, Blue, White, Dragons, Pearls, Seascape, Lid, Chinese, 1800s, 4 x 8 In.	1888.00
Porcelain, Woman, Basket, Flowers, Guinea Fowl, Feast, Molded Feet, Round, 1800s, 10 x 8 In.	276.00
Pottery, Green & Amber Spotted Glaze, Cover, Round, 3 In.	5124.00
Powder, Lead Glass, Swan, Pleated Base, Lid, Jeannette, 1950s, 4 ¾ x 4 ½ In.	45.00
Purple Stained Shell Veneer, Lid, 3 x 5 x 3 In.	122.00
Quartersawn Oak, Brass Corners & Handles, 31 x 17 x 7 ½ In.	193.00
Razor, Pine, Leather Strop, Red, Blue, Dovetailed, Slide Lid, 1800s, 2 ½ x 11 ½ In.	1116.00
Red Flowers, Birds, Blue Ground, Dome Lid, New England, c.1815, 12 x 33 In.	5103.00
Red Lacquer, Center Band, 4 Figures, 13 x 15 ½ In.	94.00
Red, White Flowers, Blue Ground, Dome Lid, Compass Artist, Penn., c.1810, 10 x 14 In.	42660.00
Regency, Rosewood, Coffin Shape, Divided, Scrolled Feet, Stepped Lid, c.1825, 3 ¾ x 7 ½ In.	369.00
Reliquary, Brass, Silvered Metal, Porcelain, Christ, Saints, Life Scenes, Repousse, 19 ¾ In.	563.00
Repousse Medallion Lid, Blue Cabochons, Boyer & Boyarina, Russia, c.1915, 7 ½ x 7 ½ In.	1020.00
Rosewood, 3 Stacked Trays, Humped Handle, Haunghuali, 8 ½ x 13 ½ In.	8260.00
Rosewood, Hardstone, Jade, Ivory, Lacquer, Figures, Goats, Garden, Chinese, 1800s, 8 x 11 In.	1599.00
Rosewood, Hardstone, Silver Filigree Inlay, Foo Dogs, Bird, Hexagonal Lid, 2 ¾ x 5 ¾ In.	357.00
Rosewood, Inlaid, Flowers, Carved, India, 6 x 3 In.	55.00
Rosewood, Mother-Of-Pearl Flower Inlays, Chinese, 1800s, 12 ½ x 7 In.	3063.00
Salt, Demilune, Yellow, Wall Mount, Wood Lid, 7 ½ x 5 ½ In.	71.00
Salt, Mahogany, Wall, Arch Shaped Top, Dovetailed, Hinged Slant Lid, 18 ¾ x 10 ⅝ In.	118.00
Scent, Mother-Of-Pearl, Ormolu, Triangular, Shells, Hinged Lid, 3-Footed, 3 Bottles, 5 In.	593.00
Scent, Porcelain, Ormolu, Egg Shape, Flowers, Round Alabaster Base, 2 Bottles, 6 In.	415.00
School, Pine, Divided, Molded, Grapes, Scrolling, Dovetailed, Lid, c.1800, 3 x 10 In.	235.00
Seed, Poplar, Yellow & Green Fan, Painted Drawers, Wall, 16 In.	23700.00

Boy Scout, Button, Newark Boy Scouts, Boy Saluting, Celluloid, W&H Back Paper, c.1915, 1 ¼ In. $141.00

Brass, Pitcher, Normandie, Chrome Plated, Peter Muller-Munk, Revere Copper & Brass, c.1935, 12 In. $2400.00

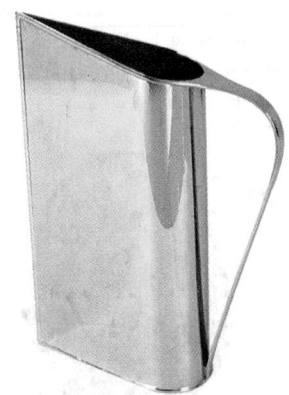

Bronze, Brazier, 6-Sided, Pierced Design, Jump Ring Handles, Chinese, 1800s, 5 x 4 ½ In. $214.00

As always, the edited listings in *Kovels' Antiques & Collectibles Price Guide* aren't available on any website, but readers should visit Kovels.com for information on trends, tips, reproductions, marks, old prices, and more!

Flea Market Tricks

Ever go to a flea market, buy something heavy, but not want to carry it around with you all day? Worried you will have trouble finding your way back to the booth? No problem. Ask the dealer to hold it and then pay for it. Take a picture with your phone of both the item and the number sign on the booth. You will have a way to find the booth again when it is time to pick up your purchase. Be sure the dealer's name is on your receipt as an added precaution.

Bronze, Bust, Bush, Elwyn, Marion Anderson, Wood Base, Signed, 1975, 13 ½ In.
$1200.00

Cowan's Auctions

TIP
Display groups of at least three of your collectibles to get decorating impact.

Silver, Engraved Azalea Flowers & Branches, Butterfly, Teakwood Lined, 2 x 6 x 4 In.		325.00
Silver, Gold Wash, Relief Enameled Flowers, Carved Jade Mount, 4 ½ In.		1150.00
Silver, Lions, Landscape, Birds, Engraved Lid, Middle East, c.1900, 6 x 3 ⅜ In.		533.00
Silver, Mixed Metal, Insect, Branch, Lid, Art Nouveau, Geo. W. Shiebler, 1 ¾ In.	*illus*	444.00
Silvered Bronze, Art Nouveau, Embossed Scrolls, Flowers, Domed Lid & Base, 9 In.		780.00
Softwood, Tulips, Hearts, Wire Staple Hinges, Iron Hasp Lock, Dome Lid, 5 ½ x 8 ½ In.		969.00
Soup, Enamel, Cylindrical, S-Scroll Handles, Birds, Flowers, Greek Key, Gilt, Lid, 1900s, 6 In.		3565.00
Stationery, Burl Walnut, Brass Mounts, Domed, Hinged Top, Victorian, 6 x 8 In.		205.00
Stationery, Engraved Bone Plaque, Drawer, Hinged, Waterlow & Sons, c.1890, 10 x 16 In.		325.00
Stationery, Mahogany, Shell, Compass Star Inlay, Brass Handles, c.1800, 13 x 9 In.		1016.00
Stationery, Rosewood, Marquetry, Banded, Horseman, Fitted Interior, Tray, Lid, 1800s, 5 x 12 In.		275.00
Stationery, Shackamaxon Treaty Elm, Astragal Molding, John C. Clark, c.1855, 14 x 8 In.		502.00
Storage, Brass Knob, Tacks, Marbled Paper, Leather, Initialed, Cover, 1800s, 6 x 6 In.		58.00
Storage, Footstool, Pine, Black Paint, Gilt, Leather Strap Handle, Hinged Lid, 1800s, 8 x 21 In.		582.00
Storage, Green Paint, Arched Handle, 6 Compartments, 1800s, 13 x 9 In.		98.00
Storage, Hexagonal, Lacquered Wood, Gilt Accents, Figures, Trees, Japan, 11 x 13 In.		250.00
Storage, Iron Strap Work, Handle, Paint, Blue, Flowers, Scrolls, c.1824, 9 x 23 In.		502.00
Storage, Lacquer, Porcelain, Gilt, Figures, Flowers, Rectangular, Oval Insert, Chinese, 10 In.		200.00
Storage, Lily, Trailing Vine, Paint, Lift Top, Lancaster Co., 1925, 13 ½ x 18 In.		122.00
Storage, Mother-Of-Pearl Inlay, Lacquered, Birds, Flowers, Hinged Lid, c.1900, 7 x 12 In.		266.00
Storage, Pine, Paint, Drawer, 2 Ovals, Scenic Views, Hinged Lid, c.1853, 11 x 17 In.		2607.00
Storage, Pine, Red Over Black Stipple Design, Dome Lid, Maine, 11 x 27 In.		374.00
Storage, Pine, Square, Ball Feet, Slide Lid, 1800s, 12 x 16 In.		148.00
Storage, Poplar, Cherry, Dovetailed Case, Painted Blue, 1800s, 8 x 18 ½ In.		411.00
Storage, Poplar, Painted, Red, Orange, Flip Lid, 1800s, 6 x 15 In.		182.00
Storage, Red & Gold Lacquer Pail, Carved, Chinese, c.1900, 12 x 13 In.		119.00
Storage, Red Lacquer, Mother-Of-Pearl, Double Gourds, Lid, Round, Chinese, 1900s, 16 In.		764.00
Storage, Rosewood, Black Lacquer, Fitted Interior, Hinged Lids, G. Myrstrand, Sweden, 20 x 18 In.		210.00
Storage, Walnut, Square, Hinged Lid, 1800s, 7 x 12 x 12 In.		30.00
Storage, Wood, Paint, Drop Front, c.1910, 22 x 37 In.		62.00
Strong, Cast Iron, Resting Lion Panels, Handles, Divided Interior, c.1820, 15 x 25 In.		598.00
Stumpwork, Pen Trays, Inkwells, Biblical Scenes, Camels, Mirror, Hinged Lid, 8 ⅜ x 11 ¾ In.		4740.00
Sugar, Maple, Interior Cutter, Slotted Base, Dovetailed, Hinged Lid, Scandinavia, 9 x 10 In.		127.00
Sugar, Wood, Red Paint, Stencil, Open Handle, Round, 19th Century, 7 In.		690.00
Tantalus, Ebonized, Inlaid, Serpentine, Fitted, 4 Cut Glass Decanters, Cordials, 10 x 13 In.		584.00
Tantalus, Gothic Revival, Coromandel, Brass, Lining, Fitted, Decanters, Glasses, c.1875, 14 In.		1541.00
Tantalus, Wood, Boulle, Lacquer, Brass Inlay, Serpentine Lift Lid, c.1875, 9 x 8 x 11 In.		216.00
Tiger's Eye, Gilt Metal, Hinged, 1 ¼ x 4 ½ x 3 ¼ In.		266.00
Tiger's Eye, Stone, Limestone Interior, Hinged Lid, Beveled Edges, 2 x 6 In.		246.00
Tin, Painted, White Bird, Flowers, Hinged Dome Lid, c.1800, 6 x 8 In.		613.00
Tobacco, Carved, Painted, Gothic Arches, Central Blossom, Flowers, Lift Lid, 1892, 4 x 7 In.		1185.00
Tobacco, Lead, Blackamoor Knob, Paper Label, Royalty, Octagonal, Harlequin Lid, 4 ¼ In.		130.00
Toilet, Federal, Walnut, Hinged Top, 4 Faux Graduated Drawers, c.1800s, 28 x 24 In.		239.00
Tortoiseshell, Bone Trim, Fitted, Lined Interior, 4 Bun Feet, c.1875, 2 x 6 ¾ In.		922.00
Tortoiseshell, Brass, Portrait, Young Woman En Venus, Tooled Edge, c.1790, 3 ½ In.		2271.00
Tortoiseshell, Inlaid Gold, Silver, Mother-Of-Pearl, Lunette Shape, Victorian, 2 x 4 In.		307.00
Traveling, Walnut, Mother-Of-Pearl, Ivory, Marquetry Inlays, Continental, 5 ½ x 12 In.		115.00
Traveling, Woman's, Rosewood, Fitted, Drawers, Leather Interior, 6 Jars, 1800s, 7 x 12 In.		230.00
Treasure, Hardwood, Painted, Woman, Red Top, Lock, Slide Lid, Square, c.1850, 13 ½ In.		177.00
Trinket, Cherry, Leaves, Green Ground, Dome Lid, c.1850, 3 x 5 x 2 In.		705.00
Trinket, Round, Blue & White, Flowers, Scrolling Leaves, Lid, Chinese, Marked, 5 In.		269.00
Trinket, Round, Blue, Amber, Cream Glaze, Flower Heads, Lid, 2 ½ In.		4148.00
Trinket, Enamel, Landscape Scenes, Courtiers, Dome Lid, 2 In. Diam.		385.00
Trinket, Faux Coral Veneer, Lid, 3 x 6 In.		122.00
Trinket, Gilt Brass, Portrait, Leaf & Dart Band, Painted, Miniature, c.1900, 3 ½ x 2 ¾ In.		369.00
Trinket, Gilt Metal, Casket Shape, Repousse, Putti, Hinged Lid, Marked, France, 1800s, 3 ½ x 12 In.		444.00
Trinket, Gilt Metal, Enamel, Coliseum, Flowers, Ball Feet, Oval, Hinged Lid, c.1915, 1 ¾ x 4 ½ In.		518.00
Trinket, Pine, Painted, Owl In A Tree, Lid, Stan Sparre, 4 x 11 In.		115.00
Trinket, Pine, Tulips, Yellow, White, Blue Ground, 2 x 3 ¾ x 2 ¼ In.		4994.00
Trinket, Tortoiseshell, Silver, Gold Inlay, Bouquet, Lid, c.1805, 3 ½ x 2 In.		652.00
Trinket, Wood, Carved, Flower Design, Leaves, Germany, 1900s, 4 x 8 In.		58.00
Vanity, Glass, Enamel, Round, Pink On Silver, Flowers, Domed Lid, 1900s, 2 ⅝ x 4 ½ In.		177.00
Vanity, Silver, Engraved Panels, Swag & Leaf, Oval, Lid, Japan, 1950s, 4 ½ x 4 ½ In.		65.00
Vanity, Victorian, Rosewood, Brass Mounts, Fitted Interior, c.1850, 5 ½ x 13 In.		575.00
Vinegar Grained, Dome Lid, Side Handles, New England, c.1802, 13 x 25 In.		178.00
Wall, Chestnut, Pine, Shaped Back, Base Molding, Gray, Ohio, c.1810, 9 x 13 In.		646.00
Wall, Open, Shaped Sides, Canted Front, Wood, 1800s, 14 x 9 In.		176.00

Wall, Painted, Stenciled Hearts & Diamonds, Nailed Corners, Hinged Slant Lid, 8 x 12 In.	254.00
Wall, Pine, Carved Crest, Lollipop Finial, Stars, Red Paint, U.S.A., c.1800, 19 x 11 In.	940.00
Wallpaper, Blue Flowers, Mauve Ground, Pa., c.1840, 4 ½ x 9 In.	1541.00
Wallpaper, Blue Flowers, Orange Ground, Pa., 2 ½ x 7 ½ In.	1304.00
Wallpaper, Green Flowers, Pennsylvania, 4 x 7 ½ In.	207.00
Wallpaper, Heart Shape, Pink Flowers, Blue Ground, c.1850, 4 x 6 ¾ In.	8295.00
Wallpaper, Orange Leaves, Blue Ground, c.1850, 3 ¾ x 6 In.	7703.00
Wallpaper, Orange Leaves, Blue Ground, Round, c.1850, 2 ½ x 3 ¼ In.	7110.00
Wallpaper, Orange Leaves, Blue Ground, Round, c.1850, 4 ¼ x 8 ¼ x 5 ¾ In.	4977.00
Wallpaper, Oval, Flowers, Green Ground, 2 ½ x 4 ½ In.	415.00
Wallpaper, Round, Flowers, Blue Ground, 3 ¾ x 4 ¾ In.	1007.00
Wallpaper, Yellow Pinwheels, Blue Ground, Penn., c.1840, 3 ¾ x 7 ¾ In.	948.00
Walnut, Brass Fitted, Domed, Etched Band, 4-Petal Decoration, Twill Lining, c.1880, 9 x 7 In.	388.00
Walnut, Inlaid Eagle, Spread Wings 12 Compartments, Early 1900s, 5 x 14 In.	230.00
Walnut, Inlaid, Front, Back Doors, Compartments, Hinge Slide Lids, 1800s, 12 x 11 In.	593.00
Walnut, Italian Baroque, Carved Cherub, Leaf Scrolls, Paw Feet, Hinged Lid, 12 x 21 In.	878.00
Walnut, Oval, Pennsylvania, 1800s, 3 ½ x 16 In.	2925.00
Wedding, Octagonal, Wood Handles, Brass Plate, 1900s	100.00
Wedding, Round, Flattened Dome, Black Lacquer, Mother-Of-Pearl Inlay, Flowers, 15 In. Diam.	207.00
White Pine, Double Slide Lids, Painted, c.1810, 7 x 11 x 9 In.	2200.00
Wood, Black, Diapered, Gold Accents, Cloisonne Enamel, Lid, 6 x 4 In.	173.00
Wood, Carved Flowers, Band Design, Flip Lid, Lock, c.1700, 12 x 22 In.	2430.00
Wood, Carved, Rectangular, Lid, Bamboo Shoots, Song Bird, Chinese, c.1895, 10 x 6 In.	354.00
Wood, Decorated, Painted, Canted Corners, Persia, c.1920, 2 x 6 x 5 In.	270.00
Wood, Flower & Vine Design, Lift Lid, East Indian, c.1900, 20 x 9 ¼ In.	115.00
Wood, Gothic Style, House Shape, Overall Tracery, Carved Shoe Feet, c.1890, 16 x 33 In.	1353.00
Wood, Iron Hardware, Carved, Painted, Hinged Lid, 3-Footed, Italy, 1700s, 9 ½ In.	1541.00
Wood, Painted Reserves, Whaling Scenes, 5 x 9 In.	210.00
Wood, Painted, Iron Hardware, Lock, 1800s, 9 x 29 In.	89.00
Wood, Red, Gold Accents, Scroll Case, Bail Handles, Hinged Dome Lid, Chinese, 6 x 23 In.	89.00
Wood, Sliding, Top Panel, Carved Sides, 20 x 17 In.	214.00
Wood, Vinegar Decorated, Brown & Mustard, Turned Foot, Lid, 6 In.	617.00
Wood, Wallpaper, Flowers, Gilt Border, Hinged Dome Lid, Brass Handle, 1800s, 2 x 3 In.	474.00
Wood, Zitan Lid, Cylindrical, Central Hole, Engraved, Chinese, 5 In.	2214.00
Writing, Burl, Boulle Work, Hinged, Fitted Interior, 1800s, 4 x 14 In.	186.00
Writing, Burl, Owl, Carved Pottery, Perched On Magnolia Branch, Square, 9 x 11 In.	18300.00
Writing, Marquetry, Sloped Lid, Barber Pole Inlay, Molding, Dutch, c.1800, 8 x 20 ½ In.	518.00
Writing, Rosewood, Rectangular, Drop Front, Scrollwork, Handles, c.1900, 12 x 8 In.	444.00
Writing, Victorian, Rosewood, Boulle, Abalone Shell, Hinged, Fitted Interior, 6 ¾ x 11 In.	431.00
Yellow Rosewood, 3 Stacked Trays, Fitted Frame, Handle, Chinese, c.1750, 8 ½ x 14 In.	5760.00
Zodiac, Bronze, Scroll Design, Marked, 1 x 5 In.	424.00

BOY SCOUT collectibles include any material related to scouting, including patches, manuals, and uniforms. The Boy Scout movement in the United States started in 1910. The first Jamboree was held in 1937. Girl Scout items are listed under their own heading.

Booklet, Published By Institute Of Life Insurance For Explorers, Fall 1963	5.00
Bugle, Brass, Leather Shoulder Strap, 9 ½ In.	385.00
Button, Newark Boy Scouts, Boy Saluting, Celluloid, W&H Back Paper, c.1915, 1 ¼ In. ....*illus*	141.00
Compass, Tin, Silva System, 1960s, 4 x 3 In.	22.00
Handbook, Norman Rockwell Drawing Cover, 1939	35.00
Hat, Scout Master, Stetson, Box, Chin Strap, 1940s, 13 ¾ In.	125.00
Pin, Campaign Worker, Red, White, Blue, Gold, Offset Gravure Back Paper, Celluloid, ⅞ In.	10.00
Poster, Jamboree, 25th Anniversary, On To Washington, D.C., 1935, 27 ½ x 42 In.	359.00
Symbol, Fiberglass, 1960s, 48 In.	695.00
Toy, Co. B, Wood, Paper, Lithographed, Die Cut Figures, Tents, Box, 21 x 11 In., 50 Piece	177.00
Troop Shield, Turtle Shell, Eagle, Be Prepared, Troop 1, Sanford, Me., c.1900, 23 x 22 In.	518.00

BRADLEY & HUBBARD is a name found on many metal objects. Walter Hubbard and his brother-in-law, Nathaniel Lyman Bradley, started making cast iron clocks, tables, frames, andirons, bookends, doorstops, lamps, chandeliers, sconces, and sewing birds in 1854 in Meriden, Connecticut. The company became Bradley & Hubbard Manufacturing Company in 1875. Charles Parker Company bought the firm in 1940. Bradley & Hubbard items may be found in other sections that include metal.

Cuspidor, Figural, Dragon, Iron	358.00
Figurine, Le Gamin, The Urchin, Spelter, 12 In.	170.00
Lamp, 8-Panel Shade, Organic Overlay, 15 x 19 In.	780.00

Bronze, Bust, Pohl, Adolph Joseph, Miner, Wearing Hat, Plaque, Base, Signed, 15 In.
$474.00

Skinner, Inc.

Bronze, Cabinet, Evans, P., Vertical Column, Doors, Signed, 1970, 78 x 24 In.
$11160.00

Rago Arts & Auction Center

Bronze, Candleholder, Nude Man, Holding Sconce, Patina, 6 ⅝ In. $444.00

Skinner, Inc.

Bronze, Scroll Weight, Dragon, Pearl In Mouth, Twisting Body, Chinese, 1700s, 4 ¾ In. $518.00

Leland Little Auction

Lamp, Bronze Patina, Caramel Slag Glass Shade, White Metal Base, 1900s, 18 x 19 In.	930.00
Lamp, Gone With The Wind, Glass Globe, Roses, Brass Base, Electric, 27 In.	184.00
Lamp, Metal Filigree Shade, 6 Panel, Linen, Textured Glass, Bronze Base, 19 x 24 In.	978.00
Lamp, Piano, Domed Shade, Goldfish, Aqua Water, Molded Fish Base, 18 In.	2655.00
Lamp, Pod, Bent Slag Glass, Bronze Finish, 14 ½ In.	650.00
Lamp, Stepped Pyramid Shade, Caramel, Green & Red Slag, Palm Base, 29 In.	4425.00

BRASS has been used for decorative pieces and useful tablewares since ancient times. It is an alloy of copper, zinc, and other metals. Additional brass items may be found under Bell, Candlestick, Tool, or Trivet.

Ashtray, Spinner, Panels, Cherubs, Push Knob, 1925, 4 ½ x 3 In.	55.00
Bar Dispenser, Nickel Plated, Agate Knob, 15 ½ In.	92.00
Basin, Pressed Body, Iron Handle, Riveted, Rolled Rim, 17 In.	62.00
Bed Warmer, Pierced Cover, Coat Of Arms, Latin Inscription, Turned Handle, c.1785, 42 In.	307.00
Bed Warmer, Queen Anne Style, Hinged Lid, Tulips & Sunflower Design, 1790, 42 ½ In.	1035.00
Bed Warmer, Round, Hinged Pierced Lid, Scrolling Flowers, Bird, Maple Handle, c.1800, 43 In.	230.00
Bed Warmer, Tooled Lid, Punched Initials, Wrought Iron Handle, 1800s, 42 In.	118.00
Bed Warmer, Turned Wooden Handle, Round, 42 In.	46.00
Beer Tap, Porcelain Handle, 15 x 4 ½ In., Pair	800.00
Belt Buckle, Chinese Dragon Head, 3 x 3 In.	76.00
Bookrack, Pine Cone Branches, Expandable, H. L. Judd Co., 1920s, 12 To 22 In.	175.00
Bookstand, Iron & Wood, John Cartier Literary Machine, 4-Footed, 44 In.	313.00
Bowl, See, Eye & Brow Inside, Round, Shaped Rim, H. Christensen, Denmark, 1982, 10 ½ In.	1339.00
Brushpot, Deer, Bamboo, Waisted Cylinder Shape, Tripod Feet, Chinese, 1800s, 5 ¼ In.	276.00
Bucket, Ecclesiastical Figure, Handles, Stylized Feet, 1900s, 8 In.	649.00
Bucket, Embossed Eagle, 3-Footed, Ring Handles, 10 x 14 In.	41.00
Bucket, Tinned Ears & Bale, 3 ½ x 4 ½ In.	23.00
Buckle, American Express, Imprinted	96.00
Bust, Victorian Woman, Upswept Hair, Grape Leaves, Square Base, 21 ½ x 10 In.	90.00
Cannon, Wood Carriage, Wheels, England, c.1850, 6 ½-In. Barrel	1062.00
Censer, Globe Shape, Foo Dog Masks, Rings, Reticulated Lid, Tripod Feet, Chinese, 1800s, 6 In.	1838.00
Censer, Lid, Foo Dog Finial, Pierced, Engraved, 2 Handles, 3-Footed, Chinese, 12 x 10 In.	150.00
Cross, Molded Base, 36 x 16 In.	335.00
Cross, Pierced, Engraved, Abyssinian Coptic, Ethiopia, 1800s, 24 ¼ In.	385.00
Cross, Silvered, Repousse Flowers, I.N.R.I. Inscribed, 33 ¾ In.	770.00
Cuspidor, Top Hat Shape, c.1890, 7 In.	189.00
Desk Set, Cast, Triangular Base, Urn Body Handle, Canisters, Hook, Pen Rest, 6 x 5 In.	106.00
Die Stamp, Numeral, Hammer Style, ½ To 0, Wood, Budde & Westermann, 12 x 6 In.	94.00
Disc, Engraved, Military Stand Of Arms, Waterloo, June, 1815	215.00
Diving Helmet, Wood Stand, Mid 1900s, 20 In.	316.00
Dog Collar, Engraved, England, c.1800	395.00
Doorknob, Bas-Relief Flowers, Scrollwork, Vine, c.1880	30.00
Eagle, Spread Wings, On Branch, Cast, 25 ½ x 34 In.	144.00
Easel, Aesthetic Revival, Scrolled, 72 x 29 In.	1170.00
Ewer, Grapes, Drunken Revelry, Putti Holding Goblets, Dionysus, 1800s, 21 x 9 In, Pair	922.00
Ewer, Jeweled, Bulbous, Spout, Ball Shape Neck, Cone Top, Spread Foot, Tibet, 1800s, 15 In.	598.00
Ewer, Swimming Duck Shape, Repousse, Korea, 1900s, 10 In.	237.00
Figurine, Buddha, Seated, Copper Plated, 13 ¾ In.	201.00
Figurine, Eagle, Spread Wings, Sideward Glancing, Holds Flag, c.1891, 32 x 10 In.	1840.00
Figurine, Pug Dog, Standing, Blue Flower Marble Base, Marked, 5 ¾ x 5 ¾ In.	90.00
Foot Warmer, Fretwork, Flowers, Handle, Chinese, 4 x 7 In.	234.00
Frame, Art Nouveau, Flowers, Leaves, Languishing Ladies, 11 ½ x 14 In.	805.00
Frame, Beveled Mirror, Cast, Leaves, Geometric, Urn Pediment, Dolphins, 15 In.	71.00
Girandole Set, Gilt Lacquer, Cut Glass, Longstockings, Cornelius & Co. 18 x 17 In., 3 Piece	215.00
Girandole, Patriot, Musket, Girl, Cut Glass Prisms, White Marble Base, 15 In., Pair	106.00
Girandole, Prisms, 3-Light &1-Light Sconce Pair, Dolphin Stem, Marble, c.1850, 16 x 17 In.	777.00
Handle, Twisted Stem, 3 x 9 ½ In., Pair	92.00
Helmet, Head Crest, Cannon Insignia, Chin Strap, France, c.1890	316.00
Helmet, Parade, Guard's, Lion Crest, Red Horsehair Plume, Nickel Veneer, England, c.1900	1150.00
Humidor, Composition, Raised Forest Scene, Holland, 7 x 4 In.	150.00
Incense Burner, 2-Headed Peacock, Standing, 2 Elephants, India, 1800s, 12 x 10 ¼ In.	356.00
Incense Burner, Egyptian Revival, Reclining Girl, Snake, Gilt, Multicolor, 1920s, 3 x 13 In.	60.00
Incense Burner, Reticulated Lid, Handle, Trees, Pagoda, Cloud Bands, Chinese, 1800s, 9 x 11 In.	3738.00
Jardiniere, Lion Mask Handles, Turned Pedestal Supports, Leaves, Ball Feet, Stand, 41 In.	413.00
Medal, St. Benedict, 1 In.	22.00
Medallion, General Lafayette, Portrait, Stamped, Paper Label, c.1830, 4 ½ In.	588.00

Milk Jug, Dovetailed, Flared Foot, Loop Handle, Copper Armorial, c.1735, 19 ½ x 16 In.	522.00
Music Stand, Scalloped Rim, Wood, Metal Tripart Base, 1922, 52 ½ In......................	104.00
Palm Tree, Segmented Trunk, Leaves, Hexagonal Base, 6-Footed, 1800s, 108 In.....................	10073.00
Pitcher, Baluster, Copper Handle, Banding, Pierced Trim, Rolled Rim, Signed, Russia, c.1901, 12 In.	460.00
Pitcher, Normandie, Chrome Plated, Peter Muller-Munk, Revere Copper & Brass, c.1935, 12 In.. *illus*	2400.00
Plaque, American Indian Head, 5 x 4 In.	132.00
Plaque, Motto, Jester, Arts & Crafts, Wharf-Eaton Co., Chicago, c.1902, 5 ¾ x 6 ¼ In.	330.00
Posy Ring, Engraved, Fear God, c.1650	295.00
Samovar, Urn Shape, Square Base, Scroll Handles, Russia, 11 In.	72.00
Sculpture, Egg, Oval, H. Christensen, 1974, 7 x 10 In.	1200.00
Sculpture, Last Leaf, John Risley, Rods, Wood Base, c.1972, 38 x 26 In.	2852.00
Sculpture, Puzzle, 16 Molded Pieces, Romeo E Giulietta, Miguel Berrocal, c.1967, 6 x 8 In.	3884.00
Sculpture, Tree Of Life, Copper Plated Steel, Curtis Jere, Artisan House, 1991, 42 x 33 In........	450.00
Shield, Family Crest, Crossed Swords, c.1900, 25 x 22 In...........	345.00
Shoehorn, Curved Handle, c.1760..........	185.00
Stand, Book, Pierced, Painted, Jeweled, 15 x 15 x 12 In.	270.00
Tankard, Dragon Handle, Upright Spout, Stylized, Chased, Engraved, Tibet, 1800s, 12 In.	259.00
Tray, Alms, Embossed Tulips, Script, Holland, 1600s, 16 ½ In...........	948.00
Vase, 2 Ring Handles, Middle East, c.1900, 20 x 23 In.........	124.00
Vase, Bulbous, Narrow Neck, Flared Mouth, Ring Handles, 16 x 14 In.	30.00
Vase, Cane Holder, Applied Flying Cranes, Birds, Lobed, Handles, Asia, c.1900, 30 In.	173.00
Vase, Floor, Hammered, Copper Straps, Stickley Bros., 8 x 31 In.........	240.00
Vase, Fluted Rim, Columnar Body, Pierced Scrollwork, Round Foot, Stamped, 15 In., Pair......	178.00
Vase, Trumpet Shape, Scrolling Saber Legs, 4-Footed, 14 x 14 ½ In., Pair	210.00
Wall Hanging, Eagle, Spread Wings, Talons Out, Beak Open, 20 x 36 In..................	420.00
Wall Sculpture, Mounted Metal Discs, Raindrops, Cluster Of Circles, Curtis Jere Style, 24 x 42 In.	180.00

BRASTOFF, *see Sascha Brastoff category.*

BREAD PLATE, *see various silver categories, porcelain factories, and pressed glass patterns.*

BRIDE'S BOWLS OR BASKETS were usually one-of-a-kind novelties made in American and European glass factories. They were especially popular about 1880 when the decorated basket was often given as a wedding gift. Cut glass baskets were popular after 1890. All bride's bowls lost favor about 1905. Bride's bowls and baskets may also be found in other glass sections. Check the index at the back of the book.

Art Glass, Crimped, Fluted, Silver Plate Stand, c.1875, 13 x 10 In..........................	250.00
Blue, Ruffled, Silver Mica Highlights, White Exterior, Tufts Silver Plated Frame, 11 x 8 In.	250.00
Clear, Poppies, Serpentine Edge, Silver, Bail Handle, Pierced, Hinged, Wallace, c.1890, 13 In..	830.00
Cranberry Glass, White Enamel Daisies, Silver Plate, Meriden, c.1870, 7 In.............	147.00
Cranberry, Enameled Thumbprint, Meriden Silver Plated Frame, 9 x 9 ½ In.	345.00
Frosted, Peppermint Glass, Pairpoint, Reed & Barton Medallion, Handle, 7 ¾ x 5 ½ In.	259.00
Glass, White, Pink Ruffled Rim, Shaped Handle, c.1900, 14 x 10 In.	177.00
Green Oil Spot, Iridescent Red Border, Ruffled, Middletown Silver Plated, 12 x 10 ½ In.	2500.00
Green, Maroon, Ruffled, White Exterior, Aurora Silver Plated Frame, 11 ½ x 10 ¼ In.........	175.00
Lilac Iridescent, Polished Pontil, Steuben, 1930s, 12 In.	450.00
Opaline, White, Ruffled Rim, Enameled Flowers, Raspberry Branches, Silver Plate, 11 In......	115.00
Opaque White Glass, Silver Plate, Pairpoint, c.1900, 13 x 11 In..........................	165.00
Pairpoint, Cranberry Glass, Ruffled Rim, Silver Plate, c.1900, 10 x 11 In.	89.00
Peachblow Ruffled Rim, Swirled Pattern, Wilcox Holder, New Martinsville, 11 In.	300.00
Pink Cased, Ribbed, Enamel Flowers, Lions, Silver Plated Frame, 10 x 14 In.	2800.00
Pink Cased, Ruffled Bowl, White, Square, Silver Plated Frame, 10 ½ In.........	180.00
Pink Cased, Silver Mica Highlights, Silver Plated Frame	250.00
Pink Glass, Ruffled, Scroll Fixed Handle, Pedestal Foot, Silver Plated Frame, 14 In.	316.00
Pink, White, Diamond Quilted, Ruffled, Napoleon Hat Shape Bowl, Silver Plate, 12 In.	400.00
Pink, White, Ruffled Bowl, Silver Plate, 11 In.........	195.00
Turquoise & White, Enamel Flowers, Ruffled, 3 ¾ x 12 In.	75.00
White, Pink Ruffled, Silver Plated Applied Bird Handles, Stand, 12 x 18 In.	366.00
Yellow & Pink Cased, Lacy Trim, Derby Silver Plated Base, Putti Supports, 13 ½ In.	1304.00

BRISTOL glass was made in Bristol, England, after the 1700s. The Bristol glass most often seen today is a Victorian, lightweight opaque glass that is often blue. Some of the glass was decorated with enamels.

Mug, Federal Eagle, Stars, Opalescent, Gold Rim, c.1810, 4 ½ In.........................	6950.00
Urn, Cover, Glass, Tall & Narrow, Round Foot, Green Flowers, Blue Bird, Gilt Trim, 1800s, 18 In.	81.00
Vase, Enameled, Opalescent, Ruffled Rim, Pink, Flowers, Elongated Oval, 1800s, 13 In., Pair..	173.00

Bronze, Sculpture, Asian Man, Woman, On Bench, Austria, c.1900, 1 ⅝ x 2 ⅝ x 1 ⅜ In.
$354.00

Brunk Auctions

Bronze, Sculpture, Barye, Antoine-Louis, Striding Lioness, Inscribed, 4 ¼ x 8 ¾ In.
$1342.00

Neal Auction Co.

Bronze, Sculpture, Bernhardt, Richard, Boy Smoking, Marble Base, c.1900, 8 ⅝ In.
$118.00

Brunk Auctions

Bronze, Sculpture, Bergman, Franz, Boy, Donkey, Reins & Saddle, Cold Painted, c.1900, 5 ¼ In.
$1041.00

Skinner, Inc.

Bronze, Sculpture, Buddha, Seated, Lotus Throne, Lacquered, Red, Gold, c.1800, 19 ½ In.
$15405.00

Skinner, Inc.

Vase, Overlay, Woman's Portrait, c.1780, 8 ½ In.	354.00
Vase, Pink, Milk Glass Portrait Medallion, Scalloped, 3 Curled Brass Feet, 13 In., Pair	207.00

BRITANNIA, *see Pewter category.*

BRONZE is an alloy of copper, tin, and other metals. It is used to make figurines, lamps, and other decorative objects. Bronze lamps are listed in the Lamp category. Pieces listed here date from the eighteenth, nineteenth, and twentieth centuries.

Amulet, Zodiac, Animal Symbols, Avenging Deity, Central Aperture, Chinese, 3 In.	805.00
Ashtray, Gilt, French Bulldog, Kneeling Over Tray, Ears Up, Signed, 4 In.	563.00
Ashtray, Louis XV, Farm Scene, French, c.1875	395.00
Basin, Concentric Bands, 2 Scroll Handles, Asia, 29 In.	236.00
Basket, Figural, 2 Maidens Emerging From Sea Handles, Locked In Kiss, c.1900, 7 x 14 In.	676.00
Bottle Stopper, Owl Shape, Japan, c.1920, 7 ¾ x 4 ½ In.	896.00
Bowl, Applied Cutout Sterling Flowers, Tapered, Art Metal Studios, c.1925, 8 ¾ x 3 ¼ In.	444.00
Bowl, Console, Marble, Lion Mask Handles, 2-Tier Pedestal, Putti, Dolphin, 12 x 17 In.	345.00
Bowl, Cover, Silvered, Heavenly Creatures, Repousse, Chinese, 1700s, 4 x 8 ½ In.	717.00
Bowl, Figural, 2 Blackamoor, Carrying Rectangular Bowl, Gilt, Patina, 6 ¾ x 11 In.	1896.00
Bowl, Lotus, Cast, Brown Patina, Inverted Base, 7 x 4 In.	230.00
Bowl, Sea Life, Dragons, Scalloped Rim, Round Foot, Engraved, Chinese, 1800s, 8 ½ x 6 In.	245.00
Box, Stamp, Growling Bear, Hinged Lid, 3 x 5 In.	125.00
Brazier, 6-Sided, Pierced Design, Jump Ring Handles, Chinese, 1800s, 5 x 4 ½ In. ....*illus*	214.00
Brush Holder, Trunk Shape, Gilt Inlaid Bamboo, Signed, c.1900, 9 ½ In.	177.00
Brush Rest, Mountain Shape, Hardwood Stand, 11 ¾ In.	4270.00
Buddha, Seated On Double Lotus Pedestal, Holding Vessel, Decorated Robes, Gilt, 11 In.	644.00
Buddha, Seated, 3-Tier Jeweled Throne, Gilt, Chinese, c.1900, 20 In.	1680.00
Buddha, Standing, Gilt, Wood Base, Thailand, 12 x 3 ½ In.	1888.00
Buddha, Standing, Left Hand Blessing, Cape, Stand, Thailand, 1800s, 22 In.	830.00
Bulb Planter, Geometric, Butterfly Design, Scroll, Cast Feet, Chinese, c.1910, 3 x 5 In.	144.00
Bust, Achilles, Sideward Glancing, Dark Brown Patina, Square White Marble Base, 10 In.	100.00
Bust, Alda, Villanis E., Woman, Mark, 4 ½ x 9 In.	660.00
Bust, Ayudthya, Square Marble Base, Thailand, 15 x 9 x 7 In.	2300.00
Bust, Buddha, Long Earlobes, Beaded Hat, Wood Stand, 4 In.	276.00
Bust, Buffalo Bill, Polished Geode Base, Signed, 12 x 10 In.	288.00
Bust, Burns, Susan B. Anthony, Marble Base, Signed 13 In.	115.00
Bust, Bush, Elwyn, Marion Anderson, Wood Base, Signed, 1975, 13 ½ In. ....*illus*	1200.00
Bust, Carpeaux, Jean-Baptiste, Anna Foucart, Curly Hair, Signed, c.1860, 20 ¼ In.	2242.00
Bust, Clark, Herbert W. Jr., Woman, Hollow Cast, Incised, New York, c.1909, 18 ½ In.	1200.00
Bust, Coudray, George, Young Woman With Hat, Brown Patina, France, c.1920, 11 ½ In.	450.00
Bust, Dancer With Headdress, Flared Round Head Piece, Bali, 16 ½ x 11 In.	360.00
Bust, De Rudder, Isidorre, Young Lady & Serpent, Belgium, 1870, 22 x 11 In.	2373.00
Bust, Dussart, Cavalier, Gilt Face, Green Base, Signed, 9 In.	296.00
Bust, Gasq, Paul, Diana, Dore, Black Socle, France, c.1920, 18 In.	1265.00
Bust, George Washington, 3-Quarter Profile, Tapering Square Base, 1903, 15 In.	875.00
Bust, Gruet, Prevost, Signed, Paris, 1883, 24 In.	536.00
Bust, Guanyin, Downcast Eyes, 19th Century, 9 ¾ In.	250.00
Bust, Hare, Long Ears, Glass Eyes, Oval Wooden Base, c.1900, 8 In.	1593.00
Bust, Jors-Concours, Moreau, Woman, Shawl, Silver Gilt, Base, Signed, Math, c.1900, 19 In. ..	978.00
Bust, Kauba, Carl, Woman, Art Nouveau, Signed, Austria, c.1880, 6 ¾ x 4 ½ In., Pair	1250.00
Bust, Lecompte, Marie Antoinette, Inscribed, 1800s, 34 In.	1560.00
Bust, Man, Profile, Marble Plaque Mount, American School, 1800s, 24 x 15 In.	288.00
Bust, Mineleas, Beard, Helmet, Embossed Military Scene, White, Round Base, 17 x 8 In.	1287.00
Bust, Moor, Beard, Turban, France, 1800s, 7 x 6 In.	2200.00
Bust, Mucha, A., Woman, Long Flowing Hair, Heart Shape Base, Flowers, Signed, 7 In.	500.00
Bust, Muller, H., Napoleon, Waisted Socle, Brown Patina, Incised, c.1900, 3 ¾ In.	385.00
Bust, Napoleon III, Field Dress, Patinated, Marble Base, 19 x 13 In.	246.00
Bust, Nelson A., Maiden, Art Nouveau, Flower Base, Brown Patina, Tiffany, c.1900, 30 In.	3851.00
Bust, Neoclassical Woman, Fluted, Rose Draped Pedestal, c.1900, 7 In., Pair	522.00
Bust, Pohl, Adolph Joseph, Miner, Wearing Hat, Plaque, Base, Signed, 15 In. ....*illus*	474.00
Bust, Salmson, Jean J., Woman, Gilded, France, 1873, 20 ½ In.	1800.00
Bust, Savage, Stylized Indian Warrior, Brown Patina, 10 x 5 In.	138.00
Bust, Seneca, Round Base, Continental, 16 In.	1625.00
Bust, Shoop, Buffalo Bill, Incised, 12 x 10 In.	288.00
Bust, Sir Peter Paul Rubens, Brown Patina, Base, France, c.1880, 8 ½ In.	300.00
Bust, Tsar Alexis Mikhailovich, F. Chopin Foundry, c.1867, 10 ¾ In.	2040.00
Bust, Van Rysselberghe, Theo, Man, Bald, Brown Patina, c.1900, 11 ½ In.	261.00

Bust, Van Rysselberghe, Theo, Woman, Hair In Bun, c.1900, 12 ¼ In.	1375.00
Bust, Victorian Woman, Grape Cluster On Shoulder, Sun Hat, 14 x 10 In.	161.00
Bust, Wein, Hagenauer, Woman, African, Stamp, 10 ½ x 14 ¼ In.	960.00
Bust, Woman, Orientalist Style, Signed, 15 ¼ x 8 ½ In.	260.00
Bust, Woman, Ruffle Sleeve, Hat, Draped Dress, Art Nouveau, Austria, Inscribed, 26 ¾ In.	1185.00
Cabinet, Evans, P., Vertical Column, Doors, Signed, 1970, 78 x 24 In. ....*illus*	11160.00
Candleholder, Nude Man, Holding Sconce, Patina, 6 ⅝ In. ....*illus*	444.00
Cassolette, Marble, Dancing Putti, Ram's Head Handles, 1900s, 21 x 8 ½ In., Pair	5676.00
Censer, 3 Foo Dog Supports, Dragon, Wave, Japan, c.1890	889.00
Censer, Animal Mask Handles, Pierced Rosewood Cover, Chinese, 1800s, 8 x 4 ½ In.	1541.00
Censer, Applied Dragons, Tripod Elephant Head Base, c.1910, 12 x 18 In.	460.00
Censer, Archaic Style, Taotie Mask Legs, Squat, Upright Handles, Chinese, 1800s, 11 In.	1541.00
Censer, Bow String, Tripod Feet, Chinese, 2 ½ In.	1715.00
Censer, Cylindrical, Flared Rim, Circles, Flowers Design, Foo Dog Feet, 1800s, 6 In.	770.00
Censer, Dome Lid, Bulbous, Figural Hinge, Bird Shape Spout, Ring Handle, 4 Legs, 10 x 12 In.	8625.00
Censer, Dome Lid, Foo Dog, Clouds, 2 Handles, Footed, Chinese, 1800s, 5 x 5 In.	1035.00
Censer, Dragon Handles, Flared Rim, Bulbous, Chinese, 1800s, 4 x 6 In.	245.00
Censer, Duck Shape, Open Slits, Chinese, 5 x 7 In.	1880.00
Censer, Elephant Shape Handles, Gold Flecks, Squat, 3-Footed, Signed, Chinese, 1800s, 2 x 6 In.	7480.00
Censer, Elephant, Holding Pagoda Shape, Chinese, 1800s, 9 In.	1164.00
Censer, Foo Dog Finial, Handles & Feet, Pierced Lid, Lotus Scrolls, Chinese, 12 x 12 In.	3081.00
Censer, Foo Dog Finial, Top Handles, Cloisonne, c.1800, 12 ½ In.	1094.00
Censer, Geometric Inlay, Elephant Shape Handles, Footed, Chinese, 14 ½ x 10 ½ In.	384.00
Censer, Gilt, Flowers, Punched Ground, Round Legs, Upright Handles, 1700s, 4 ¾ x 5 ¾ In.	1778.00
Censer, Gilt, Foo Dog Finial, Stilt Legs, Chinese, 7 x 4 In., Pair	183.00
Censer, Gilt, Tripod Base, Upright Handles, Japan, c.1900, 14 In. Diam.	1838.00
Censer, Hammer Shape, Rat Finial, Patina, Japan, 4 x 5 In.	406.00
Censer, Lid, Archaic Style, Bird Shape, Forward Facing, Chinese, 8 In.	244.00
Censer, Lion With Ball Finial, Pierced Lid, 2 Panels, Bird Scenes, Animal Handles, 11 In.	183.00
Censer, Lion's Head Handles, Footed Base, Chinese, 3 ½ x 5 ½ In.	288.00
Censer, Lotus Pad Stand, Pierced Lid, Round, Inverted Elephant Head Handles, 3-Footed, 10 In.	610.00
Censer, Pierced Lid, Foo Dog Finial, Flared Handles, Dragons, Flaming Pearl, 3-Footed, 11 In.	305.00
Censer, Pot Shape, 2 Round Handles, 3-Footed, Stand, Chinese, 6 x 3 In.	791.00
Censer, Round, Squat, 2 Foo Dog Handles, Foldover Flat Rim, Chinese, 8 In. Diam.	227.00
Censer, Rounded Corners, Animal Mask Handles, Squat, Chinese, 9 x 5 ½ In.	276.00
Censer, Silver Inlay, Masks, Lion Lugs, Dome Wood Cover, Tripod Feet, Chinese, 1800s, 6 ½ In.	3308.00
Censer, Spherical, Animal Shape Finial, Figural Scenes, 3 Squat Legs, 8 In.	147.00
Censer, Squat, Square, 2 Upright Square Handles, Footed, Chinese, 4 ½ In. Diam.	657.00
Censer, Squat, Wide Rim, Round Base, Engraved & Hammered, 2 Handles, 1900s, 7 x 18 In.	570.00
Censer, Stand, Pierced, Bamboo, Downturned Handles, Squat Bowl, Chinese, 1800s, 15 x 13 In.	5819.00
Censer, Steer Shape, Rope In Nostrils, Preparing To Buck, Chinese, 1800s, 5 x 8 In.	115.00
Centerpiece, Figural, Napoleon III, Silvered, Val St. Lambert Crystal Bowl, Christofle, 17 x 10 In.	1006.00
Centerpiece, Gilt, Wirework Basket, C-Scrolls, Flowers, Shell, Putti, Grapes, 1800s, 10 x 17 In.	1800.00
Cigar Cutter, Frog & Orb, Rocky Landscape, Patina, c.1900, 6 In.	230.00
Dish, Dore, Shaped Sides, Relief Design Rim, Stamped, 9 In.	293.00
Dish, Maurel, E., Flower Shape, Woman's Face In Center, Signed France, c.1890, 8 ½ In.	92.00
Ewer, Climbing Lion, Winged Cherub Handles, Round Foot, 1800s, 25 x 12 In., Pair	920.00
Ewer, Egyptian Revival, Scroll Handle, c.1895, 14 ½ x 5 In., Pair	657.00
Ewer, Gilt, Twisted Dragon Handle, Ram's Head, Sitting Satyrs, 1800s, 19 In., Pair	2585.00
Faucet Handle, Gamecock, Cast, Black Paint, 1800s, 18 x 7 In.	1422.00
Frame, Gilt, Beaded, Grouse, Oval, Hinged Easel, 11 ½ In., Pair	247.00
Garniture, Gilt, Love Allegory Clock Case, Putti Candlesticks, Oval Dome, c.1880, 10 x 15 In.	923.00
Garniture, Marble Base, Man, Woman, Swag & Tassel, c.1885, 7 ¾ x 4 ½ In., Pair	1045.00
Hand Warmer, Octagonal, Pierced Cover, Marked, Chinese, 4 ½ In.	837.00
Head, Male, Curly Beard, 1800s, 6 ½ In.	307.00
Hook, Elephant Head, Gilt Lacquered Backplate, Raised Trunk, Lower Scroll Hook, 7 In., Pair	1968.00
Humidor, Dog's Head, Bulldog, Pointed Ears, Studded Collar, Neck Opens, 1800s, 10 In.	3851.00
Incense Burner, Buddha Lion, Standing, Hinged Head, Open Mouth, Chinese, 1800s, 5 ¾ In.	676.00
Incense Burner, Cover, Claw Feet, Foo Dog, Dragon, Serpent Handles, 1800s, 9 x 11 In.	2478.00
Incense Burner, Cover, Old Man, Boy, Dragons, Birds, Border Handles, 4 Legs, Japan, 23 In.	2370.00
Incense Burner, Foo Dog Shape, Hinged Head, Open Mouth, Scroll Hocks, Chinese, 14 x 8 In.	708.00
Incense Burner, Old Man, Donkey, Chinese, 10 x 9 In., 2 Piece	345.00
Incense Burner, Pierced Cover, Shishi Handles, 3 Legs, Birds, Pine Trees, Lion Finial, 17 In.	307.00
Incense Holder, Leaf Design, Hexagonal, Footed, 5 ½ In., Pair	915.00
Jardiniere, Birds, Oval, Beaded Rim, Pierced Upper Band, Twin Swing Handles, 8 ½ x 17 In.	502.00
Jardiniere, Cylindrical, Elephant Masks, Japan, Late 1800s, 14 x 19 In.	4250.00

Bronze, Sculpture, Buddha, Shakyamuni, Seated, Lotus Throne, Gilt, Red Lacquer, Chinese, c.1900, 9 In. $2006.00

Brunk Auctions

Bronze, Sculpture, Bonheur, Isidore-Jules, Bull, Standing, Marble Base, France, 5 In. $444.00

Skinner, Inc.

Bronze, Sculpture, Child, Riding Turtle, 10 In. $1208.00

Early Auction Co.

B

To Clutter or Not to Clutter

Modern design is simple, uncluttered, and neat. But some need clutter in their lives, so old trunks as tables, a row of green vases, or old toys must be included. Several modern designers are taking pieces of old machinery or buildings and transforming them into new lamps and tables.

Bronze, Sculpture, Crane, Rocks, Leaves, Faux Bamboo Base, Japan, c.1900, 56 ¾ In.
$3200.00

Skinner, Inc.

Jardiniere, Dragon, Fretwork Panels, Lobed, Elephant Head Feet, Chinese, 10 x 14 In.	468.00
Jardiniere, Footed Base, Bamboo Shape Handles, Geometric Design, 1800s, 9 ½ x 11 ¾ In.	492.00
Jardiniere, Louis XV Style, Gilt, Relief Scrolling Leaves, Acanthus Handles, France, 14 ½ In.	593.00
Jardiniere, Louis XV Style, Navette Shape, Cartouches, Handles, Scroll Feet, c.1900, 7 x 22 In.	492.00
Jardiniere, Metal Inlaid Design, Crane Shape Handles, Japan, 14 In.	1037.00
Jardiniere, Napoleon III, 2 Black Men, Carrying Open Chest, Bamboo Staves, 1800s, 14 In.	2252.00
Jardiniere, Roundels, Shishi, Japan, c.1900, 18 In. Diam.	207.00
Jardiniere, Veiled Woman, Leaning On Handles, Painted, Signed, Austria, 33 In.	2390.00
Lecturn, St. Ambrose, Renaissance Attire, Oval Marble Stand, 7 x 5 ¾ In.	702.00
Letter Clip, Seesaw, 2 Children, Shaped Rectangular Base, 6 In.	296.00
Letter Holder, Dog Shape, Seated Retriever, Spring Hinged Jaw, Oval Base, 1800s, 9 In.	1304.00
Log Carrier, Baroque Style, Woven Sides, Flowers, Rope Twist Frame, c.1850, 18 x 24 In.	805.00
Magnifying Glass, Art Nouveau, 3 ½ x 6 ½ In.	207.00
Medallion, Warber, Olin, Sabina, Woman's Profile, Brown Patina, 1891, 5 ¾ In.	600.00
Mirror, Bevel Edge, Easel Stand, Nude Woman, Flowers, Mask Head, Ivy, c.1900, 18 x 13 In.	575.00
Mirror, Birds, Flowering Tree, Japan, 12 ½ In.	118.00
Mirror, Box, Buddha, Flowers, Japan, 1700s, 4 ½ In.	474.00
Mirror, Characters, Birds, Flowers, Bamboo Handle, Round, Japan, 11 ¼ x 7 ¾ In.	59.00
Mirror, Hand, Enamel Scene, Continental, Early 20th Century, 8 In.	47.00
Panel, 8 Figures, Chariot Scene, Fruits, Laurels, Walnut Frame, c.1910, 27 x 13 In.	1080.00
Paperweight, Scroll, Sinuous Dragon, 5 In.	3904.00
Pedestal, Marble Top, 2 Women, Draped Dresses, Feather, Square Base, 46 x 21 In.	489.00
Pedestal, Neoclassical Style, Round Top, Child Figure Supports, Scroll Ends, 53 x 20 In.	2390.00
Plaque, Angel, Sleeping, Round, 11 In.	268.00
Plaque, Classical Revival, Bust Of Woman, Oak Frame, 22 x 18 In.	400.00
Plaque, Face, Many Hands, Relief, Signed, Frame, 17 x 15 In.	1000.00
Plaque, Horse Head, 3-D, Wood Base, Signed, 1923, 7 x 5 In.	235.00
Plaque, Huntington, Anna H., Theodore Roosevelt, Round, Signed, c.1919, 9 ½ In.	920.00
Plaque, Laverne, Philip & Kelvin, Japanese Figures, Patina, Multicolor, 1960s, 48 x 24 In.	2108.00
Plaque, Napoleon, Bas-Relief, Gilded, 18 x 14 In.	327.00
Plaque, Rowland, Etosha, Moonscape, Relief Flamingoes, Signed, 5 ⅜ x 11 ⅜ In.	885.00
Pod, Lotus Seed, Round, 10 Movable Seeds, Makes Sounds, Hardwood Stand, 1700s, 3 In.	2990.00
Rain Drum, Cylindrical, Banded Design, Thailand, 1800s, 19 In.	764.00
Scroll Weight, Dragon, Pearl In Mouth, Twisting Body, Chinese, 1700s, 4 ¾ In. ....*illus*	518.00
Scroll Weight, Duck Shape Body, Loop Finial, 8 In.	366.00
Sculpture, 2 Birds, Perched On Branch, Tray, Marble Base, Austria, 1800s, 6 In.	499.00
Sculpture, 2 Boys, Feather Caps, Standing, Rectangular Base, c.1900, 13 In.	294.00
Sculpture, 2 Horses, Facing Each Other, Marble Base, France, c.1850, 15 x 21 In.	316.00
Sculpture, 2 Hounds, Sniffing Rocky Landscape, Oval Base, France, c.1850, 9 x 15 In.	2844.00
Sculpture, 2 Knights, Jousting, Marble Base, 1858, 29 ½ x 30 ½ In.	1046.00
Sculpture, 2 Sea Bass, Open Mouths, Oil Spot & Enamel, Round Marble Base, 24 In.	230.00
Sculpture, 2 Seated Hunting Dogs, Tied Together, Oval Base, 9 In.	2726.00
Sculpture, 2 Warrior Demons, Footed Base, Japan, c.1890, 13 x 9 ½ In.	956.00
Sculpture, 2 Wrestlers, Wood Base, Japan, c.1890, 13 x 8 ½ In.	956.00
Sculpture, 3 Cherubs, Holding Grapevine, Marble Base, 33 x 30 In.	863.00
Sculpture, 4 Fish, Leaping Out Of Water, Round Marble Base, 17 x 25 In.	259.00
Sculpture, 4 Horned Owls, Marked, c.1890, 2 x 2 In.	275.00
Sculpture, 4 Soldiers Riding Horses, Raised Guns, Marble Base, 41 x 33 In.	2952.00
Sculpture, Adam, Standing, Asp, Tree Trunk, Cape, Square Base, 14 ½ In.	385.00
Sculpture, African Altar Head, 2 Birds Perched On Headdress, Mask, Benin, 10 ½ x 4 ½ In.	240.00
Sculpture, African Boy, Reclining, Feeding Monkey, Cold Painted, Austria, c.1890, 4 ¼ In.	2000.00
Sculpture, African Vendor, Standing, Parrot On Wrist, Cold Painted, Austria, 1800s, 6 In.	1500.00
Sculpture, Aitken, Mother, Child, Brown Patina, Signed, 3 In.	356.00
Sculpture, Alexander Hamilton, Seated, Book, 9 x 11 In.	237.00
Sculpture, Allegorical Figure Of Science, Winged Woman, Gilt, Holding Olive Branch, Gilt, 11 In.	399.00
Sculpture, Allegrain, C.G., Venus Au Bain, Seminude, Signed, c.1760, 22 ½ In.	1610.00
Sculpture, American Indian, Archer, Square Marble Base, Signed, 1900s, 34 x 23 In.	1195.00
Sculpture, Apache, Man, Hand Over Eyes, Patina, Label V.H. Blackington Co., 1920s, 8 In.	173.00
Sculpture, Apollo, Nude, Hands Upraised, Marble Base, Berlin, 17 In.	863.00
Sculpture, Arab, Kneeling On Prayer Rug, Cold Painted, 2 ½ x 4 ¾ In.	207.00
Sculpture, Archangel Gabriel, Holding Branch, Mary Bible, Gothic Pedestal, 17 x 15 In.	3525.00
Sculpture, Arctic Explorer, Holding Pole, White Marble Arctic Ice Base, 14 In.	460.00
Sculpture, Asian Man, Woman, On Bench, Austria, c.1900, 1 ⅝ x 2 ⅝ x 1 ⅜ In. ....*illus*	354.00
Sculpture, Astra, Erte, Stepped Base, Multicolor, Incised Romain De Tirtoff, c.1930, 20 x 11 In.	1968.00
Sculpture, Athena, Goddess Of Wisdom, Books, Easel, 16 ½ x 18 In.	671.00
Sculpture, Atsuyoshi, Woman, Clam Digger, Standing, Basket, Clams, Signed, Japan, c.1900, 8 In.	307.00

Sculpture, Bacchante, Infant Faun, Nude Woman, Standing, Round Base, France, 1894, 33 In.	7687.00
Sculpture, Barraulte, B., Water Nymph, Gilt, France, c.1800, 19 In.	1680.00
Sculpture, Barye, A.L., Mountain Lion, Devouring A Hare, Signed, France, c.1800, 13 In.	805.00
Sculpture, Barye, Antoine-Louis, Cat, Standing, France, c.1850, 8 x 11 In.	2000.00
Sculpture, Barye, Antoine-Louis, Dog, Hunting, Pheasant, Rock Base, c.1850, 9 ¼ In.	345.00
Sculpture, Barye, Antoine-Louis, Striding Lioness, Inscribed, 4 ¼ x 8 ¾ In. *illus*	1342.00
Sculpture, Barye, Hare, Couching, Oval Base, Stamped, 2 x 3 In.	2990.00
Sculpture, Basset Hound, Stepped Rectangular Base, France, 12 In.	1778.00
Sculpture, Beach, Chester, Glint Of The Sea, Nude, Raised Arms, Marble Base, c.1950, 9 ½ In.	497.00
Sculpture, Bear, Seated In Chair, Smoking Pipe, Reading Book, Oval Base, 1900s, 12 In.	1896.00
Sculpture, Bear, Standing, Naturalistic Ground, Marble Base, Russia, 8 In.	976.00
Sculpture, Behn, Fritz, Panther, c.1950, 7 x 17 In.	1035.00
Sculpture, Bennett, Bob, Woman Sitting, Nude, Marble Base, Inscribed, 1977, 13 In.	288.00
Sculpture, Bergman, Franz, Boy, Donkey, Reins & Saddle, Cold Painted, c.1900, 5 ¼ In. *illus*	1041.00
Sculpture, Bergman, Man, Robed, Turban, Seated On Carpet, Open Book, c.1900, 6 x 4 In.	2032.00
Sculpture, Bernhardt, Richard, Boy Smoking, Marble Base, c.1900, 8 ⅝ In. *illus*	118.00
Sculpture, Bertoia, Harry, Cube On Cubes, 1970s, 5 x 4 In.	4960.00
Sculpture, Biggs, Electra W., Into The Sunset, Will Rogers, Horse, Wood Base, 1982, 12 x 9 ½ In.	2090.00
Sculpture, Bird, Hawk, Wood Base, c.1900, 11 x 17 ½ In.	9480.00
Sculpture, Bird, Ho Ho, Standing, Base, Gilt, France, 1800s, 7 In.	593.00
Sculpture, Birds On Branch, Budgies, Cold Painted, Vienna, 3 ¾ x 5 ¾ In.	575.00
Sculpture, Birds, Snuggling, Marble Base, Signed, Paris, 11 x 6 In.	475.00
Sculpture, Bodhisattva, 4 Arms, Seated, Holding Jewel, Topknot, Sino-Tibetan, 19 ¾ In.	1793.00
Sculpture, Bodhisattva, Seated, Lotus Base, Hand In Varada Mudra, c.1900, 7 In.	2655.00
Sculpture, Bodhisattva, Standing On Base, Chignon, Beaded Necklace, Celestial Scarf, 12 In.	538.00
Sculpture, Bolinger, Truman, Indian Brave, On Horse, Signed, 1971, 20 In.	863.00
Sculpture, Bonheur, Isidore-Jules, Bull, Standing, Marble Base, France, 5 In. *illus*	444.00
Sculpture, Bonheur, Rosa, Rooster, Gilt, Signed, Veined Black Marble, 6 x 4 In.	527.00
Sculpture, Bordini, Pietro, Knight, Armored Horse, Silvered, Signed, c.1890, 18 x 12 ¾ In.	1955.00
Sculpture, Boy, Acrobatic Pose, Standing On Stone Sphere, Round Base, Mask, Japan, 12 In.	1220.00
Sculpture, Boy, Benin Style, Standing, No Shirt, Necklace, Pair	369.00
Sculpture, Brothers, Seated, Arms Linked, Holding Box, Chinese, 1800s, 2 x 1 ¾ In.	600.00
Sculpture, Buckner, M., Pioneer Woman, Seated, Marble, Hardwood Base, 12 x 6 In.	316.00
Sculpture, Buddha, As Child, Raised Hand, Standing, Double Lotus Blossom Base, 8 In.	1952.00
Sculpture, Buddha, Seated On Lotus Flower Base, Crowned, Chinese, 10 In.	9560.00
Sculpture, Buddha, Seated, Double Lotus Blossom Base, 18 In.	1240.00
Sculpture, Buddha, Seated, Lotus Throne, Halo Scrolls, Parcel Gilt, Chinese, 10 In.	1348.00
Sculpture, Buddha, Seated, Lotus Throne, Lacquered, Red, Gold, c.1800, 19 ½ In. *illus*	15405.00
Sculpture, Buddha, Seated, Lotus Throne, Robes, Cross-Legged, Gilt, Headpiece, 6 In.	896.00
Sculpture, Buddha, Seated, Mudra, Double Lotus Blossom Base, Tibet, 7 ¼ In.	1952.00
Sculpture, Buddha, Seated, Robes, 2-Tiered Seat, Chinese, 9 In.	1016.00
Sculpture, Buddha, Seated, Throne, Helmet, Gilt, Sino-Tibetan, 19th Century, 14 In.	1035.00
Sculpture, Buddha, Shakyamuni, Seated, Lotus Throne, Gilt, Red Lacquer, Chinese, c.1900, 9 In. *illus*	2006.00
Sculpture, Buddha, Shakyamuni, Seated, Throne, Lions, Chinese, c.1900, 8 ¼ In.	4320.00
Sculpture, Buddha, Sitting, Base, Thailand, 19th Century, 14 ½ In.	850.00
Sculpture, Buddha, Standing, Hands Raised In Abhaya Mudra, Gilt, Thailand, c.1800, 28 In.	1912.00
Sculpture, Buddha, Standing, Headpiece, Robes, Round Base, Lacquered, Gilt, Chinese, 9 In.	1434.00
Sculpture, Buddha, Standing, Leaf Shape Back, Long Robes, Chinese, 4 In.	598.00
Sculpture, Buddhist Disciple, Patchwork Robe, Bats, Clouds, Cloisonne, Wood Stand, 6 In.	2196.00
Sculpture, Buffalo, Walking, Head Down, Marble Base, Early 1900s, 13 x 17 In.	549.00
Sculpture, Bull Elephant, Standing, Curled Trunk, Landscape Base, 24 In.	230.00
Sculpture, Bull, Head Down, Ready To Charge, France, Signed, 21 In.	1645.00
Sculpture, Bulldog, Chained & Straining, Attached To Post, c.1900, 3 x 6 In.	237.00
Sculpture, Bustamante, Sergio, Sun, On Stick, Cone Shape, Patina, Signed, 16 In.	354.00
Sculpture, Capitoline Lion, Resting, Patina, Gilt, Red Marble Base, c.1830, 5 x 9 ½ In., Pair	2091.00
Sculpture, Caravanniez, Alfred, Joan Of Arc, Silvered, Marble Base, c.1910, 21 ½ In.	2390.00
Sculpture, Cardoni, Flamenco Dancer, Signed, 1900s, 13 x 10 In.	236.00
Sculpture, Carrier-Belleuse, A., Nostradamus, Signed, c.1870, 17 ½ x 6 In.	1187.00
Sculpture, Carrier-Belleuse, A.E., Man, Holding Jug, Period Attire, 17 ¾ x 7 ½ In.	735.00
Sculpture, Cartier, E., Soldier, British, World War I, Standing, Rifle, Signed, 12 In.	1126.00
Sculpture, Cartier, E., Soldier, Striding, Gun, Signed, France, 8 1/14 In.	345.00
Sculpture, Caswell, Rip, Big Horn Sheep, Bust, Octagonal Wood Pedestal, c.1980, 15 x 13 In.	920.00
Sculpture, Chapirus, Temple Goddess, Headdress, Green, Yellow, 14 ½ In.	230.00
Sculpture, Cheetah, Dore, Black Stepped Base, 1 ¾ In.	144.00
Sculpture, Cherub, Cartier Et Cie, Marble Base, 22 ½ x 14 In.	1098.00
Sculpture, Cherub, Holding Birds, Bow & Arrow, 1800s, 5 ¾ In.	173.00

Bronze, Sculpture, Cupid, Bow & Arrow, Red Marble Base, c.1910, 21 ¾ In. $677.00

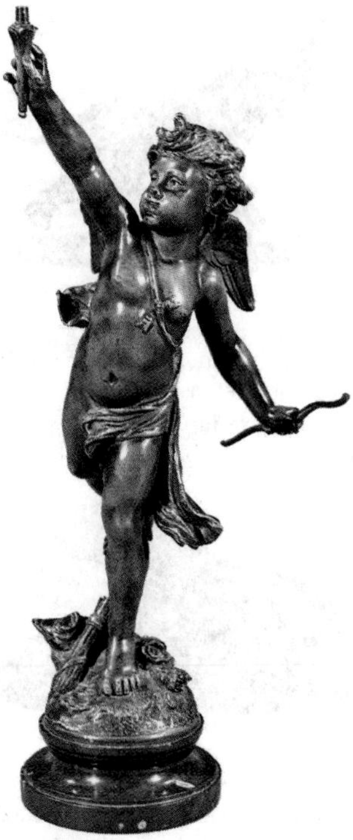

Neal Auction Co.

TIP

Restoring and reusing old things is the purest form of recycling.

Bronze, Sculpture, Ebi, Lobster, Articulated Legs, Tail & Antennae, Inscribed, Japan, c.1900, 15 ⅝ In. $732.00

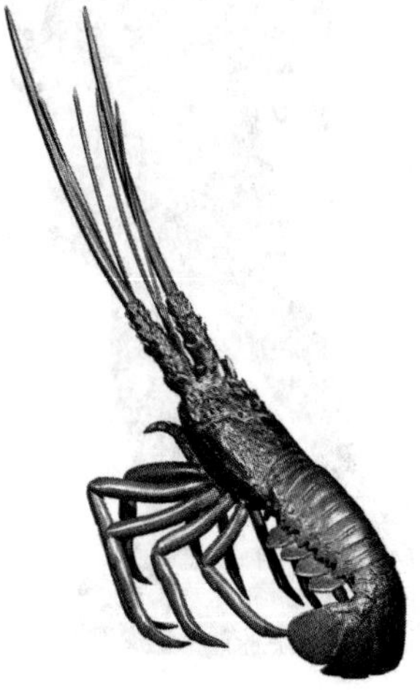

Neal Auction Co.

B

Bronze, Sculpture, Elephant, Running, Ivory Tusks, Stand, Japan, 1800s, 33 In. $7110.00

Skinner, Inc.

Bronze, Sculpture, Fremiet, Emmanuel, Chien Courant Couche, Lying Dog, Signed, 4 ½ x 9 In. $1298.00

Brunk Auctions

Bronze, Sculpture, Picault, Emile Louis, Warrior, Standing, Grasping Sword, Signed, 19 ¼ In. $1470.00

Skinner, Inc.

Sculpture, Cheyenne, Indian, Horse, Marble Base, 21 x 22 ½ In.	345.00
Sculpture, Child, Riding Turtle, 10 In. ....*illus*	1208.00
Sculpture, Classical Beauty, Reclining In Chair, Scroll, Lyre, Patina, 10 x 13 In.	357.00
Sculpture, Classical Figure, Leaning On Pedestal, Greek Key Border Robe, 19 x 10 In., Pair	2318.00
Sculpture, Classical, Man, Nude, Standing, Holding Tool, Marble Base, 9 ½ In.	207.00
Sculpture, Cockatiel, Cold Painted, Yellow Head, Gray, Pink, c.1900, 7 x 8 In.	593.00
Sculpture, Colinet, J.C., Young Dutch Man, France, 8 In.	230.00
Sculpture, Cornelius, Baker, Allegorical, Freedom, Bondage, Marble Base, 1800s, 23 In., Pair	1912.00
Sculpture, Cowboy, Horseback, Marble Base, 1900s, 22 ½ x 22 In.	259.00
Sculpture, Crane, Rocks, Leaves, Faux Bamboo Base, Japan, c.1900, 56 ¾ In. ....*illus*	3200.00
Sculpture, Cuccillato, V., Winged Victory, Marble Base, Patinated, c.1930, 35 ¼ In.	3107.00
Sculpture, Cumerworth, Charles, Mother & Child, Brown Patina, Inscribed, France, c.1875, 12 ½ In.	780.00
Sculpture, Cup Bearer, Nude, Holding Vessel, Patina, 13 ¾ In.	761.00
Sculpture, Cupid Forging An Arrow, Anvil, Oval Base, France, 1800s, 11 x 8 In.	173.00
Sculpture, Cupid, Bow & Arrow, Red Marble Base, c.1910, 21 ¾ In. ....*illus*	677.00
Sculpture, Cupid, Holding Bow, Quiver On Back, Slate Round Base, 1900s, 12 In.	646.00
Sculpture, Dancer, Nude Woman, Cylindrical Marble Pedestal, Austria, 1900s, 19 In.	1200.00
Sculpture, Dancer, Woman Leaning Back, Holding Orb, Draped Scarf	500.00
Sculpture, Dancer, Woman, Hinged Dress Reveals Her Nude, Marble Base, Erotica, 13 ¾ In.	3851.00
Sculpture, Dancing Shiva, 4 Arms, Standing On Dwarf, Circular, Rectangular Base, 13 x 15 In.	150.00
Sculpture, David, Holding Sword, Stepping On Head Of Goliath, France, 23 In.	919.00
Sculpture, De Blaquiere, C., Wrestlers, Tumbling, Signed, Black Marble Stand, 13 x 11 In.	9945.00
Sculpture, De Chemellier, George, Get Up, Circus Performer, Poodle, Signed, 15 ¼ In.	748.00
Sculpture, De Moncel De Perrin, A. Emmanuel, Woman, Carrying Buckets, Gilt, c.1900, 7 In.	399.00
Sculpture, De St. Marceaux, Rene, Harlequin, Arms Crossed, Paddle, Base, France, c.1900, 27 x 11 In.	2340.00
Sculpture, De Tavera, F.P., Girl, Seated, Inscribed, c.1900, 9 In.	2489.00
Sculpture, Deity, Seated, Double Lotus Throne, 8 Hands, Crown, 5 ½ In.	1315.00
Sculpture, Deity, Seated, Leaf Design, Flowing Scarves, Double Lotus Base, Gilt, Tibet, 5 In.	434.00
Sculpture, Deity, Vajrabhairava, 2 Heads, 10 Arms, Standing On Children, Base, 7 x 6 In.	1800.00
Sculpture, Deity, Woman, Standing, Fingers Pointing Down, Wide Robes, Chinese, 21 In.	1304.00
Sculpture, Delaplanche, E., La Musique, Woman, Violin, Laurel Wreath, France, c.1880, 33 In.	8925.00
Sculpture, Desert Tribesman, Standing, Robes, Holding Sword, 1880s, 38 In.	6274.00
Sculpture, Diana The Huntress, Pedestal Base, 32 In.	633.00
Sculpture, Diana The Huntress, Standing, Dog, Holding Bird, Slate Base, France, 22 In.	1610.00
Sculpture, Diana, Draped, Upswept Hair, Sideward Glancing, Pedestal Base, 1800s, 18 ½ In.	956.00
Sculpture, Diana, Seminude, Tiara, Stepped Stone Base, c.1915, 25 ½ x 11 In.	307.00
Sculpture, Dionysus, Mythological Figure, Standing, Nude, Pointing, Lotus Base, 1800s, 24 In.	1293.00
Sculpture, Dog, Great Dane, Cold Painted, Vienna, 7 x 3 In.	294.00
Sculpture, Dog, Great Dane, Seated, Cast, Patina, 27 x 48 In.	793.00
Sculpture, Dog, Greyhound, Hollow, Male, Female, 1900s, 32 x 34 In., Pair	837.00
Sculpture, Dog, Greyhound, Rabbit Pinned Under Paw, Gilt, Green Marble Base, 11 In.	889.00
Sculpture, Dog, Greyhound, Standing, Marble Stand, 7 ¾ x 7 ¼ In.	215.00
Sculpture, Dog, Hunting, Standing, Pointing, Oval Wood Base, 1900s, 8 x 9 In.	366.00
Sculpture, Dog, Looking Down At Turtle, Rounded Oval Base, France, Signed, 6 In.	1770.00
Sculpture, Dog, Pointer, Chocolate Brown, Base, Signature, 14 ½ In.	948.00
Sculpture, Douchoiselle, Indian Woman, In Canoe, Patina, Signed, France, c.1800s, 10 x 15 In.	288.00
Sculpture, Dragon, Rock, Serpentine Shape, Japan, 31 In.	2868.00
Sculpture, Dubois, Ernest, Harvest, Woman, Basket, c.1920, 26 In.	1093.00
Sculpture, Dubois, Ernest, Woman, Standing, Mask, Signed, France, c.1925, 26 In.	1150.00
Sculpture, Duck, Cold Painted, Austria, 9 In.	531.00
Sculpture, Ducks, Frog, Cold Painted, Austria, c.1925, 2 ¼ In.	444.00
Sculpture, Dying Warrior, Gloria Victus, Marble Base, France, 1900s, 27 ½ In.	1778.00
Sculpture, Eagle, Champleve, Spread Wings, Japan, 1800s, 19 x 25 In.	1840.00
Sculpture, Eagle, Spread Wings, On Granite, c.1900, 12 x 15 In.	2252.00
Sculpture, Eagle, Taking Flight, Tree Trunk Pedestal, Round Marble Base, 29 x 29 In.	288.00
Sculpture, Ebi, Lobster, Articulated Legs, Tail & Antennae, Inscribed, Japan, c.1900, 15 ⅝ In. *.illus*	732.00
Sculpture, Elephant & Rider, Bearded Man, Topknot, 1800s, 16 x 13 In.	805.00
Sculpture, Elephant, 2 Attacking Tigers, Patina, Japan, 6 ¾ In.	334.00
Sculpture, Elephant, Attacked By 3 Tigers, Glass Eyes, Rootwood Base, 39 In.	11160.00
Sculpture, Elephant, Baku, Inlaid Designs, Mixed Metals, Chinese, 5 ½ x 3 ½ In.	935.00
Sculpture, Elephant, On Rear Legs, Leaning On Books, 44 In.	805.00
Sculpture, Elephant, Running, Ivory Tusks, Stand, Japan, 1800s, 33 In. ....*illus*	7110.00
Sculpture, Elephant, Running, Oval Base, France, 8 x 3 In.	3200.00
Sculpture, Elephant, Tigers On Back, Tusk Raised, Japan, 8 ¾ x 10 In.	237.00
Sculpture, Elephant, Trunk Up, Attacked By 3 Tigers, Ivory Tusks, Signed, Japan, 30 In.	17080.00
Sculpture, Elephant, Trunk Up, Outspread Ears, Stride Position, Japan, c.1900, 11 In., Pair	460.00

Sculpture, Elephant, Walking, Dark Patina, 19 x 5 ½ In.	230.00
Sculpture, Elk, Marble Base, 1900s, 15 x 7 In.	372.00
Sculpture, Emperor Napoleon, On Horseback, Rectangular Base, France, c.1857, 25 In.	20315.00
Sculpture, Erte, Woman, Silver Robes, Stone Studded, Cold Painted, 1987, 18 ½ In.	3120.00
Sculpture, Falguiere, J., Diana, Nude, Incised, France, Thiebault Freres Stamp, c.1890, 32 In.	1840.00
Sculpture, Faun, Playing Flute, Nude, Square Column, Rectangular Base, c.1900, 10 In.	688.00
Sculpture, Fighting Bengals, Growling, Base, France, 11 x 19 In.	984.00
Sculpture, Flapper, Fur Trimmed, Ivory Face, Muff, Blowing Skirt, France, c.1925, 8 In.	3500.00
Sculpture, Fleisher, Max, Bird, Standing, Beak Down, Tail Up, Wood Base, 41 x 14 In.	940.00
Sculpture, Foo Dog, Foot On Orb, Chinese, 11 In.	598.00
Sculpture, Foo Dog, Lying Down, Chinese, 6 ¼ In.	239.00
Sculpture, Foo Dog, Seated, Guarding Position, Chinese, 19 In., Pair	472.00
Sculpture, Foo Dog, Sitting Up, Backward Glancing, Horn, Chinese, 11 x 10 In.	1195.00
Sculpture, Foo Dog, Standing, Pup, Ball, Rectangular Base, Pierced Panels, 9 In., Pair	732.00
Sculpture, Fremiet, Emmanuel, Chien Courant Couche, Lying Dog, Signed, 4 ½ x 9 In. ..*illus*	1298.00
Sculpture, Fremiet, Emmanuel, Hound, Seated, F. Barbedienne Fondeur, 5 x 6 In.	585.00
Sculpture, French General, Joseph Joffre, Standing, Arms Crossed, Holding Map, 12 In.	770.00
Sculpture, Frick, F., Smelter, Bare Chested, Tongs, Brick, Marble Stand, Signed, 18 x 9 In.	644.00
Sculpture, Frog, Leaping, Patina, 26 In.	344.00
Sculpture, Ganesha, Elephant Headed Deity, Seated On Lotus, 6 Arms, Indian, 16 In.	115.00
Sculpture, Ganesha, Seated, Elephant Head, Outstretched Hands, Crown, Footed Base, 6 In.	246.00
Sculpture, Garnier, Woman, Nude, Marble Base, Signed, 6 In.	452.00
Sculpture, Gaudez, Adrien-Etienne, Le Duo Difficle, 2 Baroque Musicians Practicing, c.1890, 27 ½ In.	10060.00
Sculpture, Gemignani, Alejandro Volta, Standing, Hand In Pocket, Square Base, c.1927, 21 In.	978.00
Sculpture, Ghiglieri, L., Stallion, Full Gallop, His Elegance, 1988, 30 x 21 In.	2588.00
Sculpture, Gilt, Woman Seated On Pedestal, France, Signed, 1800s, 19 In.	400.00
Sculpture, Giraffe, Standing, Reclining Pose, 15 In. & 29 In., Pair	161.00
Sculpture, Girl, Blindfolded, Square Marble Base, 7 ½ In.	138.00
Sculpture, Gladenbeck, O., David, Dark Brown Patina, Germany, c.1900, 13 In.	900.00
Sculpture, Goat, Reclining, Slate Base, 1900s, 6 x 3 In.	178.00
Sculpture, Goddess, Standing, Lotus Blossoms On Shoulders, Headpiece, Gilt, 28 In.	161.00
Sculpture, Goethe, Holding Top Hat & Cane, Marble Base, 14 In.	2205.00
Sculpture, Gompf, Floyd, Bed, Unmade Disheveled Blankets, Shelf, 1900s, 19 x 17 In.	313.00
Sculpture, Granlund, Paul, Draped Female, Nude, Incised, 1956, 7 ½ In.	230.00
Sculpture, Gregoir, J., Woman, Seated, Robed, 15 ½ In.	1020.00
Sculpture, Guanyin, Reclining, Gilt, Flowing Robes, Supporting Head In One Hand, 15 In.	310.00
Sculpture, Hagenauer, Female Tennis Player, 2 ½ x 6 ¾ In.	420.00
Sculpture, Hand, Fingers Pointed Upward, Wood Stand, Thailand, 20 In.	900.00
Sculpture, Harders, Johannes, Man, Playing Flute, Art Deco, c.1925, 11 ¾ x 8 In.	226.00
Sculpture, Harlequin, Playing Guitar, Marble Base, 5 ½ x 4 In.	124.00
Sculpture, Heikka, Earl, Horse, Rider, Blanket, Wide-Brimmed Hat, c.1929, 11 x 8 In.	403.00
Sculpture, Heron, Standing, Tree Stump, Bulrush, Frog, Jade Base, 1900s, 18 x 25 In.	950.00
Sculpture, Herzog, L., Bacchanalian Putti, Panther, Patina, Germany, 1909, 14 ¼ In.	1140.00
Sculpture, Hippo, Open Mouth, Standing, Cold Painted, Austria, c.1900, 3 x 6 In.	2006.00
Sculpture, Hoffman, Malvina, Cornell La Frileuse, Cast, Verdigris Patina, c.1912, 10 In.	1840.00
Sculpture, Hopkins, Mark, Panther, 13 In.	230.00
Sculpture, Horse, Cart, Barrels, Gilt, Silver, Cobblestone Base, c.1890, 11 In.	356.00
Sculpture, Horse, Head Down, Gilt, Chinese, Stand, Late 1800s, 6 x 3 ½ In.	1715.00
Sculpture, Horse, Running Pose, Tang Style, Chinese, 15 In.	443.00
Sculpture, Horse, Running, Woman Rider, Hair Flowing, Raised Arms, Chinese, 1939, 24 x 19 In.	3450.00
Sculpture, Horse, Snake, 1900s, 9 ½ x 12 ¾ In.	248.00
Sculpture, Hound, Oval Natural Base, Brown Patina, 8 ¾ x 4 ½ In.	980.00
Sculpture, Huber, D., The Critic, Horse, Head Down, Cowboy Sketching, 1900s, 11 ½ x 13 In.	1495.00
Sculpture, Huber, Dan, Herd Bull, Buffalo, Dark Brown Patina, 1988, 9 x 12 ½ In.	748.00
Sculpture, Humphriss, Charles, Indian, Dancing, 1911, 14 ½ In.	1800.00
Sculpture, Hunt, Child, Standing, Nude, Octangular Base, Inscribed, c.1900, 19 In.	1659.00
Sculpture, Indian Brave, Bow Hunter, Horse, Full Gallop, Marble Base, 1900s, 6 ½ x 12 ½ In.	339.00
Sculpture, Indian, Maiden, Brave, Canoe, Marble Base, Signed, France, 1800s, 12 In., Pair	881.00
Sculpture, Janensch, Gerhard A., Smelter, Pinchers, Marble Base, Signed, 1926, 19 x 8 In.	234.00
Sculpture, Jeager, G.A., Woman, Seated, Fan, Ivory, Marble Base, Inscribed, 10 In.	720.00
Sculpture, Jockey, On Horse, c.1950, 25 ½ x 27 In.	474.00
Sculpture, Jockey's Gear, Wood Horse, Feed, Water Buckets, Dog, Rat, c.1880, 6 x 8 In.	288.00
Sculpture, Jonchery, Charles Emile, Stealthy Cat, Gilt, Goldscheider, c.1900, 12 ¼ x 20 In.	3042.00
Sculpture, Kainz, Gebr., Man Using Scythe, Base, Inscribed, Austria, c.1900, 17 x 11 In.	2070.00
Sculpture, Kainzwon, G., Man, Sowing Seeds, Marble Base, Austria, c.1900, 19 x 10 In.	1840.00
Sculpture, Kauba, C., Indian, Holding Staff, Canoe, Cold Painted, c.1900, 6 x 10 In.	1356.00

Bronze, Sculpture, Vienna, Bedouin On Camelback, Cold Painted, Marked, Austria, 6 ¾ In.
$1470.00

Skinner, Inc.

Bronze, Vase, 3 Dragons Wrapped Around Center, Japan, 34 ½ In.
$5368.00

Leslie Hindman Auctioneers

TIP
Dust your bronze, then try the Chinese method of polishing. Rub the bronze with the palm of your hand. This puts a little oil on the metal.

Bronze, Vase, Boschetti, Benedetto, Gods & Heroes, Base, Handles, Signed, c.1850, 15 x 8 ½ In.
$2689.00

Neal Auction Co.

Bronze, Vase, Oriental Style, Lizard Handles, Green Patina, 20 x 7 In.
$210.00

DuMouchelles Art Gallery

Sculpture, Kelsey, Girl, Bareback On Pony, Rectangular Base, Signed, c.1946, 6 x 6 In.	690.00
Sculpture, Knight, Horseback, Spear, Chain Mail, France, c.1910, 12 ¾ x 12 ½ In.	430.00
Sculpture, Knight, Standing, Holding Pilum & Sword, Round Base, Germany, c.1884, 14 ⅜ In.	796.00
Sculpture, Koop, S., Bald Eagle, Spread Wings, Gilt, Tree Trunk Base, Signed, 32 x 46 In.	2070.00
Sculpture, Kouba, C., Bison, Signed, 1910, 6 ¾ In.	1500.00
Sculpture, Kracht, W., Blacksmith, Cap, Apron, Knife Anvil, Pink Marble Stand, Signed, 11 x 7 In.	439.00
Sculpture, Krafft, Cobbler, Standing, Holding Boots, Round Base, France, 1800s, 6 In.	593.00
Sculpture, Kwan Yin, Goddess Of Mercy, Wood Base, 20 In.	460.00
Sculpture, Lama, Seated, Lotus Throne, Robes, Peaked Hat, Gilt, Tibet, 1800s, 5 ½ In.	3081.00
Sculpture, Lanceray, Eugene, Horse Drawn Sled, Base, Stamped, 8 x 17 In.	5482.00
Sculpture, Larche, Raoul, Young Man, Vingt Ans, c.1900, 36 x 13 In.	2034.00
Sculpture, Larroux, Peasant Woman, Harvesting Grapes, Gilt, Signed, 1898, 17 In.	1680.00
Sculpture, Lasansky, William, Head Of A Sage, Raised On Stand, 1961, 10 ½ In.	1063.00
Sculpture, Laurent, E., Diana The Huntress, Slate Base, Signed France, c.1850, 22 In.	1610.00
Sculpture, Lavergne, Adolphe Jean, Woman, Fixing Hair, c.1885, 17 ½ In.	633.00
Sculpture, Lavroff, G., L'Elephant, Trunk Up, Patinated, Signed, Marble Base, 6 x 8 ½ In.	659.00
Sculpture, Le Penseur, Male, Nude, Seated Atop Rocky Mound, Marble Base, 21 In.	813.00
Sculpture, Learning Together, Brother, Sister, Open Book, 40 In.	374.00
Sculpture, Liberich, Nikolai I., Bear, On Hind Legs, Tree Trunk Base, Russia, 1800s, 21 In.	3776.00
Sculpture, Lion & The Serpent, Growling, Squatting, Black Marble Base, 14 x 15 x 8 In.	720.00
Sculpture, Lion, Guardian, Seated, Rectangular Base, 38 x 47 In., Pair	978.00
Sculpture, Lion, Guardian, Standing, 35 In., Pair	1495.00
Sculpture, Lion, Mouth Open, Ready To Strike, Green Glass Stand, Art Deco, c.1915, 5 x 6 In.	153.00
Sculpture, Lion, Reclining, Burl Stand, 1800s, Japan, 17 In.	1000.00
Sculpture, Lion, Standing, Curved Tail, Open Mouth, Japan, c.1910, 10 x 16 In.	922.00
Sculpture, Lion, Walking, Brown Patina, Wood Stand, Japan, c.1920, 4 x 7 In.	300.00
Sculpture, Lioness, Pierced By 2 Arrows, Open Mouth, France, c.1915, 11 x 18 In.	922.00
Sculpture, L'Isolee, Crouching Grieving Woman, On 1 Knee, Black Marble Base, 8 x 8 In.	9775.00
Sculpture, Lloyd, Tom, 3 Muses, Dancing, Marble Base, Signed, 1900s, 28 x 18 In.	316.00
Sculpture, Lorenzl, Josef, Dancer, Ivory, Green Onyx Base, Austria, 8 ½ In.	657.00
Sculpture, Lorkowski, J., Owl, Signed, c.1950, 12 In.	107.00
Sculpture, MacLean, Thomas, Classical Woman, Gilded, England, c.1870, 19 In.	1440.00
Sculpture, Maimon, I., Woman, At Vanity, Arms Up, Fixing Hair, Shaped Base, Signed, 17 In.	688.00
Sculpture, Malric, Charles L., Putto, Grapes, France, c.1930, 4 ¾ In.	413.00
Sculpture, Man With Broom, Stepped Pedestal, 24 ½ x 5 In.	585.00
Sculpture, Man, Draped Robe, 1800s, 8 x 5 ¼ In.	271.00
Sculpture, Man, Draped, Beaded Design, White Marble Stand, 14 x 5 In.	237.00
Sculpture, Man, Seminude, Holding Staves, Brown Patina, Marble Base, 1900s, 17 In.	403.00
Sculpture, Mandolin Player, Seated Woman, Marble Base, Signed, 8 ½ In.	288.00
Sculpture, Manjushri, Seated, On Lion, Lotus, Leaf Crown, Pillow Base, 19 In.	5975.00
Sculpture, Marguerite From Faust, 27 x 8 In.	735.00
Sculpture, Marioton, Eugene, Flute Player, 40 In.	4510.00
Sculpture, Market Seller, Painted, Outstretched Arms, Holding Ivory, Austria, 1900s, 9 In.	2000.00
Sculpture, Marley, Horse, Man Beside Horse, Slate Base, Bracket Feet, 9 In., Pair	580.00
Sculpture, Mascre, L., Musician, Pierrot A La Mandoline, Gilt, Base, France, c.1920, 12 In.	316.00
Sculpture, Masson, Clovis E., Wolfhound, Resting, Head Raised, Signed, 17 x 7 In.	763.00
Sculpture, McClure Kelly, May, Female Nude Holding Grapevine, Grapes, Gilt, c.1910, 12 In.	1440.00
Sculpture, McDonald, R., Jacques In The Box, White Face, Mime Series, 11 x 12 In.	7140.00
Sculpture, McVey, William Mozart, Old Grizzly, Brown Patina, Walnut Base, 9 x 8 In.	1524.00
Sculpture, Mene, P.J., Bullfighter, Standing, c.1850, 21 In.	1978.00
Sculpture, Mene, P.J., Stag, Attacked By 3 Hounds, Wood Base, Incised, France, 12 In.	1838.00
Sculpture, Mene, Pierre J., Horse, Head Down, Rectangular Base, France, Signed, 11 In.	2875.00
Sculpture, Mene, Pierre Jules, Setter, On The Scent, Signed, 6 ¼ x 13 In.	1404.00
Sculpture, Mene, Pierre, L'Accolade, Stallion, Mare, France, c.1859, 13 ½ x 20 ½ In.	6900.00
Sculpture, Mene, Pierre-Jules, Fauconnier Arabe A Cheval, Arab Falconer On Horse, 24 x 13 In.	2868.00
Sculpture, Mene, Pierre-Jules, Jockey & Horse, Patina, Signed, 9 ½ x 12 ½ In.	1534.00
Sculpture, Mephistopheles, Playing Mandolin, c.1880, 10 ½ In.	518.00
Sculpture, Mercury, Brown Patina, Green Marble Base, 19 ½ In.	674.00
Sculpture, Miriam & Infant Moses At River, Palm Tree, Child In Crib, c.1900, 15 x 13 In.	1000.00
Sculpture, Mival, C., Woman, Arms Up, Kneeling, Ormolu, Base, France, 1900s, 15 ¼ In.	940.00
Sculpture, Moigniez, A.J., Quail, With Chicks, Oval Base, Signed, 7 x 5 x 9 ½ In.	480.00
Sculpture, Molins, Woman, Dancing, Marble Base, Inscribed France, 17 ½ In.	748.00
Sculpture, Monk, Gilt, Standing, Holding Staff, Robes, Lotus Base, 16 In.	598.00
Sculpture, Monk, Kneeling, Hands Clasped At Front, Tibet, Chinese, 11 In.	580.00
Sculpture, Monk, Lohan, Kneeling On Rock, Holding Attribute, 7 In.	119.00
Sculpture, Moose, Standing, 1 Tan, 1 Red, Austria, c.1900, 6 x 6 In., Pair	2015.00
Sculpture, Moreau, A., Children With Baby Birds, France, c.1900, 22 ¾ In.	3600.00

Sculpture, Moreau, A., Girl On Vine-Covered Swing, Art Nouveau, 9 In.	399.00
Sculpture, Moreau, Auguste, Aurore, Marble Base, c.1900s, 25 In.	690.00
Sculpture, Moreau, Auguste, Dawn, Signed, c.1900, 16 x 8 In.	400.00
Sculpture, Moreau, Math, Nude Seated, Robe, Flowers, Marked, c.1900, 27 In.	1725.00
Sculpture, Moreau, Mathurin, Woman, Holding Wheat Bundle, Sickle, c.1900, 22 ½ In.	2390.00
Sculpture, Moreau, Nude, Leaning Against Tree, Gilt, Signed, 23 In.	800.00
Sculpture, Moses, Seated, Clutching 2 Tablets, Rectangular Base, Italy, 19 In.	1125.00
Sculpture, Mother Slicing Bread For Children, Standing, Holding Loaf, Round Base, 36 In.	3851.00
Sculpture, Mother, Child, Musical Instrument, Marble Base, England, c.1975, 16 x 22 In.	720.00
Sculpture, Mouse Nibbling Sugar, Alabaster, Marble Base, 4 In.	504.00
Sculpture, Mouse, Seated In Slipper, Wheat Stem In Mouth, Austria, c.1900, 3 ¾ In., Pair	1470.00
Sculpture, Mozart, Playing Violin, Brown & Verdigris Patina, Round Marble Base, 21 In.	104.00
Sculpture, Muller, Hans, Thirsty Reaper, Signature, Art Deco Marble Base, 1930s, 16 ½ In.	598.00
Sculpture, Muse, Seated, Leaning On Pipe Organ, Open Book, France, 15 ⅝ x 21 In.	2370.00
Sculpture, Muse, Standing, Draped Gown, Bare Feet, Sideways Glancing, Base, 20 In.	938.00
Sculpture, Narcissus, Standing, Nude, Round Base, Italy, 15 ¼ In.	615.00
Sculpture, Nicholas II, Alexandria, Standing, Silvered, c.1897, 14 ½ In.	18960.00
Sculpture, Nude Woman, Lying On Stomach, Holding Conch Shell, 12 x 4 In.	288.00
Sculpture, Nude Woman, On Leopard, Laurel Leaf, Draped Robe, 1900s, 9 In.	267.00
Sculpture, Nude Woman, Seated, Pierced Tray, Bacchic Figures, Marble Base, 56 In.	1830.00
Sculpture, Nymph, Rushes, Cattails, Patina, 102 x 25 In.	2091.00
Sculpture, Omerth, George, Gilt, Marble, Soldier, On Horseback, 15 x 11 In.	2633.00
Sculpture, Parsons, E.B., Lamb, Playing, Signed, Gorham, 3 ½ x 4 ½ In.	480.00
Sculpture, Phillips, Parrot, Sitting On Branch, Signed, 60 In.	863.00
Sculpture, Philomela, Standing, Nude, Arms Out, Wings, Round Base, 1970s, 11 ½ In.	8365.00
Sculpture, Picault, E., Soldier, Shield On His Back, Lion's Pelt, Inscribed, 1900s, 30 In.	144.00
Sculpture, Picault, Emile L., Don Cesar De Razon, Cavalier, Sword, c.1890, 32 x 15 In.	1342.00
Sculpture, Picault, Emile L., Man, Hermut Darmes, Standing, France, c.1900, 24 x 13 In.	1017.00
Sculpture, Picault, Emile Louis, Warrior, Standing, Grasping Sword, Signed, 19 ¼ In. *illus*	1470.00
Sculpture, Pig, Standing, Boar, Sow, Brown, Gilt Highlights, Chinese, 9 x 15 In., Pair	1045.00
Sculpture, Powell, Ace, Horse, Standing, Reins, c.1950, 11 x 12 In.	633.00
Sculpture, Quarry Laborer, Barefoot Man, Splitting Stone, Marble Base, 22 x 11 In.	1495.00
Sculpture, R.S., Horse, Standing, Scratching Head With Leg, Signed, 1900s, 3 In.	4025.00
Sculpture, Radbourg, Van, Young Boy, Holding Wheat, Jaunty Hat, 1800s, 21 x 9 In.	1320.00
Sculpture, Ram, Head Up, On Hind Legs, Front Legs In Air, Shaped Base, 22 x 20 In.	250.00
Sculpture, Rauch, Christian Daniel, Friedrich II The Great Of Prussia, 1800s, 11 x 7 In.	242.00
Sculpture, Rebecca, Carrying Water Jug On Head, Middle Eastern Attire, 29 In.	3125.00
Sculpture, Rhoden, John, Woman Combing Hair, c.1975, 4 x 5 x 9 ½ In.	3000.00
Sculpture, Riese, H., Athlete, Bending Stick, Marble Base, Signed, 1900s, 22 In.	767.00
Sculpture, Rigual, T.P., Cock Of The Walk, France, c.1910, 9 ½ In.	246.00
Sculpture, Rumsey, C.C., Puma, Resting, Signed, c.1900, 4 x 12 In.	1265.00
Sculpture, Satyr, In Flight, Woman On Shoulders, Stone Base, Signed, c.1925, 19 In.	6000.00
Sculpture, Scholar, Bearded Man, Seated, Wearing Robes, Triangular Hat, Wood Base, 8 x 8 In.	120.00
Sculpture, Scout, Crouched Behind Rock, Oval Marble Base, 1900s, 7 ¼ x 9 ¼ In.	399.00
Sculpture, Shelton, Sea Turtle, Rocks, Marble Swivel Base, Cold Painted, 1900s, 7 In.	1063.00
Sculpture, Shepherd Boy, Dog, Seated, Cane Handle, Rocky Mound, c.1900, 27 In.	3125.00
Sculpture, Shiva, Divinity, Lord Of Dance, Arms, Leg Raised, India, 1800s, 19 In.	1838.00
Sculpture, Silenus, Oil Lamp Base, Italy, c.1910, 23 ½ x 9 ½ In.	478.00
Sculpture, Simon, Paul, Le Jeune Elephant, Trunk Down, Patinated, Signed, 6 ½ x 8 ¼ In.	1298.00
Sculpture, Soldier, On Horseback, Confronting Tiger, 23 ½ In.	575.00
Sculpture, Stafford, James, Flight, Elk Bull, Running, Wood Stand, c.1945, 33 ½ In.	2070.00
Sculpture, Strada, P. Masulli, Man, Black Patina, Round Base, Inscribed, c.1864, 25 In.	949.00
Sculpture, Szczeblewski, V., Whistler, Hands In Pocket, Red Marble Base, Signed, 1889, 9 ¼ In.	748.00
Sculpture, Taoist Official, Standing, Beard, Robe, Lobed Cap, Holding Tablet, c.1800, 14 In.	1169.00
Sculpture, Taschner, I., Woman, On Bull, Black, Wood Pedestal, Germany, c.1900, 20 x 17 In.	9600.00
Sculpture, Terrier, Chained, Lunging, Post, Knocked Over Bucket, Oval Base, c.1900, 6 x 7 In.	770.00
Sculpture, Tiger, Crouching, Looking Back, Tail Raised, Silver Claws, Chinese, 5 In.	6100.00
Sculpture, Trail Boss, Horse, Trotting, Cowboy Rider, Hat Off, Rectangular Base, 1958, 25 In.	2318.00
Sculpture, Tschacbasov, Nahum, Abstract Head, Elongated Neck, Signed, Russia, 4 ¼ x 3 ¼ In.	230.00
Sculpture, Vairocana, Seated, Lotus Throne, 6 Arms, Ewer, Sword, Leaf Crown, Tibet, c.1800, 8 ½ In.	5819.00
Sculpture, Vajrasattva, Seated, Double Lotus Throne, Base Plate, Gilt, Tibet, 1700s, 7 In.	2695.00
Sculpture, Venus De Milo, Seminude, Standing Woman, Square Base, c.1900, 20 x 6 In.	598.00
Sculpture, Viani, Satyr, Dancing, Italy, Signed, 31 ½ x 13 In.	1912.00
Sculpture, Vienna, Bedouin On Camelback, Cold Painted, Marked, Austria, 6 ¾ In. *illus*	1470.00
Sculpture, Vienna, Bedouin, On Camel, Cold Painted, Amphora Mark, Austria, c.1905, 5 In.	900.00
Sculpture, Vienna, Indian, Running, Raised Hand, Feather Headdress, Marble Stand, 12 In.	1175.00
Sculpture, Vienna, Wolf, Cold Painted, Austria, c.1905, 2 ¾ x 5 ½ In.	770.00

Brownies, Biscuit Jar, Pinched, Gilt Fishnet, Metal Lid, Embossed Flowers, Butterfly, Napoli, 8 In.
$10350.00

Early Auction Co.

Brownies, Drawing, At The Zoo, Original Art, Pencil Caption, Palmer Cox, 5 ½ x 4 In.
$4250.00

Aleph-Bet Books

B

Brownies, Saltshaker, Enameled Beetle On Reverse Side, Metal Cap, Mt. Washington, Napoli, 3 In. $3680.00

James D. Julia Inc.

How a Bronze Is Made

Artists who create a bronze sculpture first sculpt the figure using clay or wax. Then the sculpture is taken to a foundry, where a rubber mold of the figure is made. Wax is poured in and sloshed around until a hollow wax model is made. A shell of ceramic coating is applied to the wax and the model is fired. The wax melts out. The ceramic shell that's left is filled with molten bronze. Then the shell is removed and the bronze sculpture is ground and polished.

Sculpture, Von Damnecker, Ariadne, On Panther, Seminude, Marble Base, c.1920, 23 x 21 ½ In.	1778.00
Sculpture, Vonnoh, Bessie Potter, Motherhood, Seated Mother, Child In Lap, c.1902, 11 In. ...	4720.00
Sculpture, Vonnoh, Bessie, Girl, Standing, Draped Robes, Square Base, 11 In.	1422.00
Sculpture, Vonnoh, Bessie, Mother & Child, Golden Brown Patina, 1902	4320.00
Sculpture, Vorsin, V., Lynx, Feasting, Patinated, Signed, 1935, 3 ¼ In.	518.00
Sculpture, Waagen, Arthur, Dog, Whippet, Signed, c.1870, 16 ½ x 21 In.	2242.00
Sculpture, Water Carrier, Woman, Standing, 2 Buckets, Yoke, Marble Base, c.1900, 12 In.	1007.00
Sculpture, Wenck, Ernst, Woman, Bent Over, Gilt, Marble, Signed, c.1900, 7 ½ x 9 ¼ In.	1356.00
Sculpture, Whale, Humpback, Round Marble Base, Signed, 1900s, 8 x 20 In.	1495.00
Sculpture, Whippet, Spaniel, Oval Marble Base, France, 1800s, 10 x 9 In.	489.00
Sculpture, Wicked Pony, Horse, Thrown Rider, Marble Base, 22 x 11 In.	366.00
Sculpture, Williams, C., Cowboy, On Horse, Rifle, Desperado, Wood Base, 12 x 16 In.	460.00
Sculpture, Winans, W., Show Horse, Brown Patina, Inscribed, 1907, 22 In.	2400.00
Sculpture, Winged Lion, Of St. Mark's Square, Paw On Book, Marble Base, c.1925, 3 x 4 In.	153.00
Sculpture, Woerffel, C.E., Soldier's Return, On Horseback, Hugging Girl, Marble, Incised, 10 ½ x 9 In.	4212.00
Sculpture, Wolf, Howling, Seated, Head Upwards, Square Marble Base, 10 x 20 In.	316.00
Sculpture, Woman Swimmer, Diving From Rocky Crag, Patina, c.1910, 17 In.	171.00
Sculpture, Woman, Dancer, Bended Knee, Arm Over Head, Onyx Base, 20 x 22 In.	1845.00
Sculpture, Woman, Dancer, Headdress, Tiered Marble Base, Art Nouveau, France, 15 x 6 In.	150.00
Sculpture, Woman, Holding Wineglass, Armchair, Removable Dress, c.1910, 3 In.	1416.00
Sculpture, Woman, Nude, Standing, Drinking From Bowl, Square Marble Base, 14 In.	1175.00
Sculpture, Woman, Rebecca At Well, Leaning, Ewer, Draped Headdress, 1876, 14 x 11 In.	799.00
Sculpture, Woman, Robed, Dore, Green Marble Base, c.1898, 8 ½ In.	896.00
Sculpture, Woman, Standing, Ivory Face, 2 Russian Borzoi, Art Nouveau, c.1914, 17 x 17 In.	18800.00
Ship Model, Ark Royal, Wood Base, 9 In.	480.00
Sphinx, Marble Base, 22 x 35 In., Pair	805.00
Tabernacle, Gothic Revival, 4 Columns, Spires, Velvet Base, France, c.1890, 38 x 16 ½ In.	1298.00
Tazza, Egyptian Revival, Caryatid Handles, Round Marble Base, France, 1800s, 9 In.	540.00
Tazza, Moigniez, J., Marble, Round Top, Hares, Stags, Birds, Fox Finial, Vulture, Signed, 12 x 11 In.	714.00
Tazza, Nudes, Cherubs, Winged Creatures, Rams, Head Supports, 1800s, 6 In.	83.00
Tazza, Scrolling Oak Branches, Boar, Dog Mask, Ivy Handles, Trumpet Foot, 1800s, 6 In.	207.00
Tazza, Venus & Cupid Shaft, 1800s, 7 In.	360.00
Teapot, Lid, Dragon Handle & Spout, Animals, Frog Finial, Raised, 3-Footed, 11 x 9 In.	196.00
Tray, Calling Card, 2 Stags, 17 x 9 x 9 In.	235.00
Tray, Mask Handles, Footed, 5 x 15 In.	214.00
Tray, Nude Woman, Seated, Gazing At Snail, Sinuous Base, c.1900, 9 In.	711.00
Tray, Shell Shape, Women, Dolphin, Mythical Landscape, Mark, c.1900, 13 x 16 In.	413.00
Urn, Art Nouveau, Ladybugs, Fruit, Marble Base, France, c.1895, 4 x 2 ¾ In., Pair	122.00
Urn, Baluster, Ribbed, Band, Figures, Scroll Handles, Masks, Marble Base, 1800s, 23 In., Pair	3750.00
Urn, Campagna, Swags, Cherubs On Lion Mask Handles, Patina, 31 x 30 In., Pair	1793.00
Urn, Chalice Shape, Neoclassical, Handles, Marble, Square Base, 8 In., Pair	682.00
Urn, Champleve, Flowers, Bamboo Shape Handles, Leaf C-Scroll Feet, France, 1800s, 8 In.	582.00
Urn, Charles X Style, Reeded, Scroll Arms, Gilt Metal, Marble Pedestal, 13 x 11 In., Pair	1638.00
Urn, Classical Figures Relief, Oval, Reeded, Raised Handles, Marble Base, 12 ½ x 6 In., Pair	702.00
Urn, Cover, Hexagonal Footed Pedestal, Bulbous, Ball Finial, 35 x 22 In.	173.00
Urn, Cover, Patina, Classical Scenes, Swan Shape Handles, Marble Base, 17 In., Pair	523.00
Urn, Footed, Campana, Grapevine Design, 2 Men Shaped Handles, 29 x 25 In.	288.00
Urn, Gadrooned, Round, Lion Ring Handles, Square Pedestal Foot, 24 ¾ x 32 In., Pair	575.00
Urn, Lid, Relief Cast Flowers, Masks, Footed, 33 In.	259.00
Urn, Neoclassical, Putto In Chariot, Drawn By Ram, Stepped Slate Base, 13 In., Pair	793.00
Urn, Ram's Head Handles, Raised Leaf Design, Round Pedestal Foot, 29 In.	196.00
Urn, Rococo, Lid, Putti, Masks, Flowers, Finial, Pedestal, Stepped Base, 66 In.	2151.00
Urn, Seated Winged Cherubs, Column Pedestal Base, 2 Handles, 55 x 27 In.	575.00
Urn, Snake Handles, Seated Putti, Round Foot, Oval, Warwick, 1800s, 15 x 18 In.	1035.00
Vase, 2 Birds, Bowling Pin Shape, Patina, c.1900, 2 ¾ x 9 ½ In.	600.00
Vase, 3 Dragons Wrapped Around Center, Japan, 34 ½ In. *illus*	5368.00
Vase, Animal Mask, Tiered Loose Rings, Chinese, 1800s, 15 ¼ In.	593.00
Vase, Applied Dragon, Signed, 12 In.	1062.00
Vase, Applied Flowers, Bird Flying, Reddish Brown, Gilt, Japan, 13 ½ In.	360.00
Vase, Art Nouveau, Winged Women, Ewer Shape, 16 x 8 In.	400.00
Vase, Baluster, Cranes In Flight, Cresting Waves, Gold Fretwork Borders, c.1900, 5 In., Pair	1045.00
Vase, Baluster, Deer, Landscape, Trees, Flared Rim, Early 1900s, 8 ½ In., Pair	150.00
Vase, Baluster, Dragon Handles, Landscape Scenes, Japan, 20 In., Pair	341.00
Vase, Baluster, Dragon Head Handles, Wave Design, Cloisonne Bands, Lotus, 1900s, 9 ½ In.	123.00
Vase, Baluster, Elongated, Inlaid Figures & Landscape, Wood Base, c.1900, 9 ¼ In.	354.00
Vase, Baluster, Gilded Joss Stick, Scrolling Cloud, Coiled Dragon, 1800s, 4 In.	550.00
Vase, Baluster, Leaves, Eagle, Pine Branch, Round Foot, Flared Rim, Late 1800s, 14 ½ In.	600.00

Vase, Baluster, Stick Neck, Gold, Copper & Silver Design, Flowering Branches, 6 In., Pair	465.00
Vase, Birds, Reed Pond Relief, Bulbous, Japan, Late 1800s, 8 ¾ In.	1422.00
Vase, Boschetti, Benedetto, Gods & Heroes, Base, Handles, Signed, c.1850, 15 x 8 ½ In. ...*illus*	2689.00
Vase, Bottle Shape, Dragon Wrapped Around Neck, Cranes, Japan, 7 ½ In.	413.00
Vase, Bottle Shape, Elongated Neck, Band Of Scrolls, Chinese, 9 In.	358.00
Vase, Brayer, G., Raven On Rim, Cone, Branch Applied To Side, Art Nouveau, Signed, 9 ¾ In. .	995.00
Vase, Brocade Panels, Wave Pattern, Neck Flange, Chinese, 1800s, 9 In.	356.00
Vase, Buddhist Symbols, Pedestal, Ear Shaped Handles, Rings, Chinese, 1800s, 7 ½ In.	267.00
Vase, Cartouche, Peacock, Waterfall, Birds, Tree, Scroll Border, Cylindrical, 1800s, 12 In.	345.00
Vase, Dragon Band, Cicada Blade Flared Mouth, Pedestal, Chinese, 1800s, 5 ½ In., Pair	398.00
Vase, Dragon Band, Cicada Neck Blades, Pedestal, Bulbous, Chinese, 1800s, 6 In., Pair	296.00
Vase, Dragon Bands, Animal Masks Lugs, Rings, Baluster, Flared, Chinese, 1800s, 13 In.	830.00
Vase, Dragon, Holding Crystal Pearl, Japan, 1800s, 12 ½ In.	388.00
Vase, Dragon, Wave Relief, Japan, 1800s, 16 x 5 In.	652.00
Vase, Dragons, Chasing Flaming Pearl, Bottle Shape, Footed, Chinese, 16 In.	239.00
Vase, Fish, Embossed, 8 ¾ x 7 In.	316.00
Vase, Flaring Neck, Encircled With Dragon, Peacock, Birds, Greek Key, Japan, 24 In., Pair	885.00
Vase, Flower, Butterfly Metal Inlays, Japan, 6 In.	374.00
Vase, Galleried Rim, Basket Weave Branch Handles, Eagle, Snake, Dragon, Frog, Japan, 22 ¾ In.	1178.00
Vase, Gilt, Cylindrical, Applied Blossoms & Bats, 1800s, 15 In., Pair	5500.00
Vase, Hexagonal Sides, Patterned Bands, Chinese, 1800s, 10 In.	504.00
Vase, Korschann, Climbing Figure, Embossed, Art Nouveau, Signed, Louchet Foundry, 5 x 3 ½ In.	620.00
Vase, Leaf Band, Centaurs Lid, Entwined Snake Handles, Gilt, France, c.1870, 16 In.	6000.00
Vase, Lid, Scrollwork Band, Tripod Base, Handle, Spout, Patina, Chinese, 9 In.	2975.00
Vase, Mask Band, Notched Flanges, Loop Handles, Wood Stand, Footed, Chinese, 1800s, 17 In.	613.00
Vase, Medallions, Flanges, Flared Top, Japan, 10 ¾ In.	153.00
Vase, Medallions, Monkeys, Trees, Gilt, Silver, Oval, 2 Mask Handles, Round Foot, 11 ⅛ In.	4720.00
Vase, Mythical Bird Band, Lobed Body, Pedestal Foot, Chinese, 1800s, 16 ¾ In.	948.00
Vase, Oriental Style, Lizard Handles, Green Patina, 20 x 7 In. ...*illus*	210.00
Vase, Raised Design, Mixed Metal, Baluster, Lacquered Accents, Japan, 13 In.	732.00
Vase, Sanglan E., Satyr, 2 Handles, Round Foot, Art Nouveau, Signed, 7 x 8 In.	325.00
Vase, Scroll, Panel, Waist Flange, Cylindrical Beaker Shape, Chinese, 1800s, 12 ½ In.	385.00
Vase, Spill, Tree Trunk Shape, Flowering Vines, Birds, Japan, 9 ½ In., Pair	1003.00
Vase, Square, Trumpet Top, Flared Bottom, Square Base, Chinese, 1800s, 6 In., Pair	388.00
Vase, Trumpet Neck, Phoenix Head Handles, Feathers, Spread Foot, Chinese, 1700s, 12 In.	2015.00

BROWNIES were first drawn in 1883 by Palmer Cox. They are characterized by large round eyes, downturned mouths, and skinny legs. Toys, books, dinnerware, and other objects were made with the Brownies as part of the design.

Band, 9 Figures, Lithographed Paper, Wood, Whitney Reed, 8 In., 10 Piece	944.00
Biscuit Jar, Pinched, Gilt Fishnet, Metal Lid, Embossed Flowers, Butterfly, Napoli, 8 In. ...*illus*	10350.00
Candleholder, Figural, 7 ½ In.	236.00
Candy Container, Papier-Mache, Wood, Cloth Hat, Egg Shape, Spindly Legs, 8 In.	472.00
Display, Millionaire Dude, Top Hat, Schoenhut, c.1910, 40 In.	6325.00
Drawing, At The Zoo, Original Art, Pencil Caption, Palmer Cox, 5 ½ x 4 In. ...*illus*	4250.00
Figurine, Uncle Sam, 9 In.	165.00
Napkin Ring, 6 Figures, Incised, Silver Luster Metal, 1 In.	75.00
Saltshaker, Enameled Beetle On Reverse Side, Metal Cap, Mt. Washington, Napoli, 3 In. ...*illus*	3680.00
Sign, If You Like Chocolate Soda Drink Brownie, Cardboard, 21 x 60 In. ...*illus*	330.00
Stickpin, Running, Hands Out, Looking Over Shoulder, Die Cut, Sterling Silver, 2 ½ In.	75.00
Tea Set, Decals, Highlights, China, Teapot, Sugar, Creamer, 5 Cups, Saucers, Plates, 4 ½ In.	354.00
Toy, Brownie On Horse Drawn Sulky, Cast Iron, Wilkens Hardware Co., c.1895, 5 ½ In.	147.00

BRUSH-MCCOY, see Brush category and related pieces in McCoy category.

BRUSH POTTERY was started in 1925. George Brush first worked in 1901 in Zanesville, Ohio. He started his own pottery in 1907, but it burned to the ground soon after. In 1909 he became manager of the J.W. McCoy Pottery. In 1911, Brush and J.W. McCoy formed the Brush-McCoy Pottery Co. After a series of name changes, the company became The Brush Pottery in 1925. It closed in 1982. Old Brush was marked with impressed letters or a palette-shaped mark. Some new pieces are being marked in raised letters or with a raised mark. Collectors favor the figural cookie jars made by this company. Because there was a company named Brush-McCoy, there is great confusion between Brush and Nelson McCoy pieces. See McCoy category for more information.

Cookie Jar, Cow, Back Is Cover, Brown, Tan, 8 ¼ In.	23.00
Figurine, Duck, Head Up, Satin Blue, 4 ½ In.	30.00
Figurine, Frog, Green, Black, 7 In.	84.00

Brownies, Sign, If You Like Chocolate Soda Drink Brownie, Cardboard, 21 x 60 In.
$330.00

Victorian Casino Antique Auction

Brush, Vase, Stoneart Jewel, Triangles, 3 In.
$196.00

Humler & Nolan

TIP
To remove wax from a Hanukkah menorah or another candleholder with small candle cups, run hot water in the holes or use a hair dryer to warm the metal, then remove the wax with cotton swabs.

Buck Rogers, Button, Buck Rogers Club Member, Shaw Mfg., Toronto, c.1937, 1 In.
$1739.00

Hake's Americana & Collectibles

Buck Rogers, Toy, Rocket Police Patrol, Tin Lithograph, Windup, Built-In Key, Marx, 1939, 12 In.
$421.00

Hake's Americana & Collectibles

Burmese, Cruet, Melon Ribbed, Stopper, 6 In.
$86.00

Early Auction Co.

Flower Frog, Green, Brown, 10 In.		90.00
Jardiniere & Pedestal, Greek Key Pattern, Blended Glaze, 25 ½ In.		184.00
Planter, Frog Shape, Green, Brown, Marked, 8 In.		17.00
Vase, Jewel Neck Band, Cobalt Blue Top & Base, 1900s, 9 ¾ In.		258.00
Vase, Stoneart Jewel, Triangles, 3 In.	*illus*	196.00

BUCK ROGERS was the first American science fiction comic strip. It started in 1929 and continued until 1967. Buck has also appeared in comic books, movies, and, in the 1980s, a television series. Any memorabilia connected with the character Buck Rogers is collectible.

Book, Pop-Up, A Dangerous Mission, Blue Ribbon, 1934, 3 ¾ x 5 In.		475.00
Book, Pop-Up, Calkins & Nowlan, 1935		158.00
Button, Buck Rogers Club Member, Shaw Mfg., Toronto, c.1937, 1 In.	*illus*	1739.00
Button, Strange World Adventures Club, Blue, Silver, 1939, 1 ¼ In.		1683.00
Comic Strip, Lost Planet Of Thor Series, 8-6-1949, Rick Yager, 17 x 5 ½ In.		316.00
Cutout Adventure Book, Uncut, Cocomalt Premium, 1933, 9 ¼ x 12 ¼ In.		949.00
Lunch Box, Space Adventure Series, Aladdin, 1979		125.00
Pencil Box, Characters, Spaceship, Cardboard, Snap Closure, 1935, 6 x 10 In.		115.00
Ring, Glow-In-Dark Ring Of Saturn, Luminous Plastic, White, Red, Corn Toasties, 1946		278.00
Ring, Initial H, Birthstone, Brass, Adjustable Band, Cocomalt		348.00
Ring, Portrait, Profile In Space Helmet, Brass, Paper, Plastic Top		345.00
Star Explorer Chart, Designed By Hayden Planetarium, Cream Of Wheat Premium, 1936		423.00
Toy, Rocket Police Patrol, Tin Lithograph, Windup, Built-In Key, Marx, 1939, 12 In.	*illus*	421.00
Toy, Rocket Ship, Rocket Police Patrol, Pings, Sparks, Tin Litho, Winup, Marx, 12 In.		575.00
Toy, Strato-Kite Kit, Jet-Propelled, Flies Like An Aeroplane, In Envelope, 1946, 19 In.		146.00

BUFFALO POTTERY was made in Buffalo, New York, after 1902. The company was established by the Larkin Company, famous manufacturers of soap. The wares are marked with a picture of a buffalo and the date of manufacture. Deldare ware is the most famous pottery made at the factory. It has either a khaki-colored or green background with hand-painted transfer designs.

BUFFALO POTTERY

Ashtray, Kippys, New York, White, Red Lettering, 5 ⅜ In.		7.00
Bowl, Restaurant, White, Burgundy Scroll, Scalloped Edge, 8 In., 3 Piece		21.00
Bowl, White, Green Bands, 5 ¼ x 1 ¾ In.		12.00
Chamber Pot, Chrysanthemum, Green, Fluted, Scalloped Handle, 1907, 5 ¼ x 9 In.		35.00
Chamber Pot, Lid, Flower Transfer, Pink, Yellow Roses, 9 x 11 In.		45.00
Cup & Saucer, Restaurant, White, Burgundy Scroll, 1960s		10.00
Cup, Restaurant, White, Red Flowers, Leaves, Scalloped Rim, 4 x 2 ¼ In.		6.00
Grillplate, Willow, Divided, Round		35.00
Pitcher & Bowl, Flower Transfer, Pink, Yellow Roses		175.00
Pitcher, Flower Transfer, 7 ½ In.		49.00
Pitcher, Geranium, Cobalt Blue, c.1910, 5 ½ x 6 ½ In.		345.00
Pitcher, Landing Of Roger Williams, Betsy Williams' Cottage, c.1906		575.00
Plate, Albino War, Sailing Ship, 1912		1159.00
Plate, Christmas Carol, Scrooge Buys A Turkey For The Cratchets, RIX Jennings, 1957		18.00
Plate, Country Gardens, 1920s, 11 ¼ In.		49.00
Plate, Dinner, Restaurant, White, Burgundy Scroll, 1960s, 9 ½ In., 4 Piece	16.00 to	19.00
Plate, Independence Hall, Teal		49.00
Plate, Mt. Vernon, Teal Transfer, Flower Bouquet Rim		59.00
Plate, Niagara Falls, Green, Early 1900s, 7 ½ In.		55.00
Plate, White House, Blue, c.1905, 10 In.		62.00
Platter, Willow, c.1906, 14 x 11 In.		196.00
Platter, Willow, c.1917, 18 x 14 ½ In.		365.00
Platter, Willow, c.1935, 9 ½ In.		55.00
Platter, Willow, Marked, c.1911, 14 x 11 In.		60.00
Soup, Dish, Willow, 9 In., Pair		30.00
Sugar & Creamer, Flower Transfer, 5 In.		25.00
Teapot, Lid, Tea Ball, Argyle, Blue & White		100.00

BUFFALO POTTERY DELDARE

Bowl, Fruit, Ye Village Tavern, 3 Men Drinking, c.1924, 9 In.	450.00 to	559.00
Bowl, Plate, Fallowfield Hunt, Death, c.1908, 9 In.		850.00
Bowl, Ye Village Tavern, Signed, c.1924, 3 ¾ In.		495.00
Calling Card Tray, Tavern, Signed E. Wayson, c.1908, 8 In.		350.00
Chop Plate, Evening At Ye Lion Inn, 13 ½ In.		350.00

Pitcher, Their Manner Of Telling Stories, Signed G. Mat., 1908, 6 In.	106.00
Pitcher, To Demand My Annual Rent, c.1909, 8 In.	595.00
Pitcher, With A Cane Of Superior Air, English Aristocrats, Octagonal, c.1909	452.00
Plate, Bread & Butter, Ye Lion Inn, Signed Lita Palmer, c.1908, 6 ¼ In.	225.00
Plate, Breaking Cover, 7 ½ In.	200.00
Plate, Ye Olden Times, Patriots, Walking Sticks, Signed K.P. Laird, c.1909, 9 ¼ In.	64.00
Plate, Ye Village Street, Men Walking, Signed G. Eaton, 7 ¼ In.	250.00

BUNNYKINS, *see Royal Doulton category.*

BURMESE GLASS was developed by Frederick Shirley at the Mt. Washington Glass Works in New Bedford, Massachusetts, in 1885. It is a two-toned glass, shading from peach to yellow. Some pieces have a pattern mold design. A few Burmese pieces were decorated with pictures or applied glass flowers of colored Burmese glass. Other factories made similar glass also called Burmese. Related items may be listed in the Fenton category, the Gundersen category, and under Webb Burmese.

Biscuit Jar, Flowers, Silver Plate Lid, Bail Handle, Mt. Washington, 7 In.	200.00
Creamer, Peach, Yellow, White Daisies, Squat, Loop Handle, 5 In.	460.00
Creamer, Satin Finish, Crimped Rim, Mt. Washington, 5 ½ In.	1900.00
Cruet, Melon Ribbed, Stopper, 6 In. ....*illus*	86.00
Cruet, Ribbed Pillar Body, Teardrop Stopper, Mt. Washington, 6 ¾ In.	345.00
Cruet, Yellow To Peach, Globular, Ribbed, Pointed Stopper, Loop Handle, 7 In.	546.00
Fairy Lamp, Berry Branches, Ruffled Rim Base, Shade, Clarke Insert, 6 ¼ In. ....*illus*	920.00
Fairy Lamp, Clear Insert, Mt. Washington, 5 ½ In.	200.00
Fairy Lamp, Dome Shape, Yellow To Pink, Glass Crystal Cup, Signed, 4 In.	115.00
Fairy Lamp, Double, Cricklite Holder, Clear Base, 19 x 14 In.	650.00
Fairy Lamp, Flower Clusters, Dome Shape, Rolled Rim, Clarke Insert, 6 ½ In. ....*illus*	6613.00
Pitcher, Egyptian, Bird, Flowers, Yellow Ground, 6 ¾ In.	345.00
Pitcher, Water, Red Rose, Green Leaves, Thomas Hood Verse, 7 In. ....*illus*	1265.00
Sugar & Creamer, Flowers, White Beaded Trim, Creamer 4 In.	575.00
Sugar & Creamer, Round, Yellow Loop Handles, Peach Ground, 3 In.	316.00
Syrup, Embossed Flip Lid, Flower Clusters, Daisies, 6 ½ In. ....*illus*	3105.00
Vase, Amber Shaded To Rose, Elephant Scene, Drivers, 13 ½ In. ....*illus*	20125.00
Vase, Ball Shape Ivy, Crimped Top, 3 In.	250.00
Vase, Bottle Shape, Green To Pink To Yellow, 9 ¼ In.	30.00
Vase, Bud, Footed, Satin Finished, 7 In.	100.00
Vase, Bulbous Stick Shape, Queen's Design, Amber Shaded To Pink, 10 In. ....*illus*	2875.00
Vase, Bulbous, Posy Form, Ruffled, Hawthorn Pattern, 4 In.	100.00
Vase, Bulbous, Red Berries, Branches, Cream To Peach, Scalloped Ruffle Rim, Signed, 4 In.	173.00
Vase, Bulbous, Square Rim, Enameled Ivy, Yellow To Peach, 3 In.	138.00
Vase, Bulbous, Stick, Amber To Pink, Spring Grapevine, 12 In.	3565.00
Vase, Cover, Raised Gold, Leaves, Flowers, Pink Ground, 8 ½ In.	5463.00
Vase, Gold, Red Flowers, Beaded Stamen, Curled Gilt Handles, 10 ½ In.	3680.00
Vase, Jack-In-The-Pulpit, Footed, Trumpet, Tight Crimped Rim, Yellow, Peach, 10 In.	213.00
Vase, Jack-In-The-Pulpit, Ruffled Rim, 10 In.	345.00
Vase, Lily, Footed Stick Form, Trifold Rim, Mt.Washington, 13 In.	225.00
Vase, Lily, Ruffled Rim, Slender Stem, Round Foot, Pale Green & Peach, Mt. Washington, 13 In.	403.00
Vase, Lily, Trifold Rims, 16 In.	600.00
Vase, Quadrafold Rim, Yellow To Pink, Mt. Washington, 4-Footed, 7 In.	400.00
Vase, Queen's Burmese, Tapestry Flowers, 9 ½ In.	1650.00
Vase, Ruffled Rim, Pedestal, 10 ½ In.	125.00
Vase, Stick Shape, Pinched Sided, Cascading Gilt Gingko Branches, 6 In., Pair	489.00
Vase, Trumpet, 24 In.	500.00
Vase, Trumpet, Blue Floral Blossoms, Decorated Foot, Mt. Washington, 10 In., Pair	1200.00
Vase, Trumpet, Star Crimped Top, 6 ½ In.	325.00
Wall Mounts, Scrolling Vines, Flowers, Leaves, Winged Beast Base, 38 In., Pair	1159.00

BUSTER BROWN, the comic strip, first appeared in color in 1902. Buster and his dog, Tige, remained a popular comic and soon became even more famous as the emblem for a shoe company, a textile firm, and other companies. The strip was discontinued in 1920. Buster Brown sponsored a radio show from 1943 to 1955 and a TV show from 1950 to 1956. The Buster Brown characters are still used by Brown Shoe Company, Buster Brown Apparel, Inc., and Gateway Hosiery.

Button, Buster, Tige, Celluloid, c.1900, ⅞ In.	12.00
Button, Vote For Buster Brown, 1 ¼ In.	11.00
Coin, Plastic, 50th Anniversary, 1954	7.00
Figure, Buster & Tige, Chalk, 19 x 11 In.	200.00

Burmese, Fairy Lamp, Berry Branches, Ruffled Rim Base, Shade, Clarke Insert, 6 ¼ In.
$920.00

Early Auction Co.

Burmese, Fairy Lamp, Flower Clusters, Dome Shape, Rolled Rim, Clarke Insert, 6 ½ In.
$6613.00

Early Auction Co.

TIP
Always wash antique china in a sink lined with a rubber mat or towels. This helps prevent chipping. Wash one piece at a time. Rinse and let it air dry. If you suspect a piece has been repaired, do not wash it. Clean with a soft brush dampened in a solution of ammonia and water.

Burmese, Pitcher, Water, Red Rose, Green Leaves, Thomas Hood Verse, 7 In. $1265.00

Early Auction Co.

Burmese, Syrup, Embossed Flip Lid, Flower Clusters, Daisies, 6 ½ In. $3105.00

Early Auction Co.

Burmese, Vase, Amber Shaded To Rose, Elephant Scene, Drivers, 13 ½ In. $20125.00

Early Auction Co.

Burmese, Vase, Bulbous Stick Shape, Queen's Design, Amber Shaded To Pink, 10 In. $2875.00

Early Auction Co.

Photograph, Boy, As Buster Brown, Dog Tige, Town Street, Frame, c.1900, 18 ¾ x 12 ¾ In.	150.00
Plate, Buster Brown, Tige, Teapot On Nose, Scalloped Rim, 8 In.	57.00
Puzzle Game, Hand Held, 1 ½ In.	17.00
Ruler, Wood, 12 In.	12.50
Shoe Inserts, Plastic, 1950s, 4 x 9 In.	70.00
Sign, Apples, Buster & Tige, Cardboard, String Hanger, Frame, 11 ⅜ x 12 In. *illus*	1540.00
Sign, Bread, Buster, Tige, Metal Lithograph, Die Cut Flange, 2-Sided, 13 x 8 In.	4950.00
Sign, Bread, Golden Sheaf Bakery, Buster Brown, Tige, Tin, 19 ¾ x 27 ¾ In.	210.00
Sign, Buster Brown Shoes, Advertised To The Nation, Buster & Tige, Tin, 20 x 14 ½ In.	420.00
Sign, Buster Brown Shoes, Neon, Porcelain, 2-Sided, Girl Winking, Dog, 54 x 54 In.	5888.00
Stickpin, Buster In Oval, Enameled Metal, 3 In.	115.00
Tin, Cinnamon, Buster & Tige, Glossy Paper Over Cardboard, Tin Lid, 5 ⅜ x 3 In. *illus*	165.00
Toy, Rolly Dolly, Papier-Mache, Painted, Weighted, Schoenhut, 9 ½ In.	266.00
Toy, Yo-Yo, Buster & Tige On Both Sides, Reverse Side Is Green, 1 x 2 In.	35.00
Toy, Yo-Yo, Buster Brown Shoes, Tin Lithograph, 1930s, 1 ¾ x ½ In. *illus*	82.00
Watch Fob, Buster & Tige, Cartoon On Reverse, Celluloid, 1 ¾ In.	144.00
Whistle, Buster Brown Bread, Worth Blowing About, Gartner Baking Co., Celluloid, 1 In.	52.00
Wristwatch, Buster, Tige, Combination, Chrome Case, Leather Band, Box, 1972	115.00

BUTTER MOLDS *are listed in the Kitchen category under Mold, Butter.*

BUTTON collecting has been popular since the nineteenth century. Buttons have been known throughout the centuries, and there are millions of styles. Gold, silver, or precious stones were used for the best buttons, but most were made of natural materials, like bone or shell, or from inexpensive metals. Only a few types are listed for comparison.

Bakelite, Carved Maltese Cross, Red, ⅞ In.	5.00
Bakelite, Carved, Woman's Head, Flowers, Black, c.1940, 1 ⅝ In.	25.00
Bakelite, Ruffled, Translucent, Green, ⅞ In.	4.00
Bakelite, Wheat Carved, Brown, 1 ¾ In., Pair	36.00
Brass, Roman Couple, Rope Border, ⅞ In.	6.50
Glass, Domed, Etched, Gold Luster, Triad Groves, Green, Marked Costumakers, ⅞ In.	4.00
Glass, Moonglow, Aqua, Gold Fern Border, Ribbed, ¾ In.	5.00
Glass, Moonglow, Lime Green, Gold Horizontal Detail, Marked Costumakers, ¾ In.	5.00
Glass, Moonglow, Navy, Contour Molded, 3 Luster Line Ovals, ¾ In.	5.00
Glass, Moonglow, Red, Gold Dotted Rays, ¾ In.	5.00
Glass, Painted Multicolor Lattice & Flowers, Yellow Ground, ¾ In.	4.00
Glass, Silver Edge, Ridged, Green, 1 In.	5.00
Glass, Star Shape, Ribbed, Clear, ¾ In.	4.00
Leather, Embossed Horse Head, ¾ In.	4.00
Lucite, Carved, Spiny Spider, Oblong, 1 In.	13.00
Lucite, Reverse Carved, Spiraled Leaves, Square, 1 ¾ In.	6.00
Metal & Stone, Arts & Crafts, Hull Ark, Guild Button, Birmingham, England	336.00
Metal, Arts & Crafts, Lapis Stone Center, Hallmark	347.00
Metal, Arts & Crafts, Marked A.R. Iona, Iona Celtic Arts, Hallmark	1120.00
Metal, Openwork, Glass Stones, Purple, 2 In.	18.00
Milk Glass, Blue Painted Seaside Symbols, ¾ In.	5.00
Mother-Of-Pearl, Exotic Bird, Flowering Branches, Gold, Art Nouveau, 1 In., Pair	474.00
Plastic, American Flag, Glossy, 1 ¼ In.	2.00
Plastic, Blue, Gold, 3 Snap-Together Pieces, ⅞ In.	4.00
Plastic, Carved Casein Leaf, Metal Loop Shank, ⅞ In.	3.00
Plastic, Deep-Cut Well, Peach Tone, ⅞ In.	4.50
Plastic, Dice, Square, Black, White, ⅜ In.	6.00
Plastic, Domed, Petals, Shelf Shank, Tan Buffed Brown, ⅝ In.	2.00
Plastic, Etched Well, Red Semimatte, 1 ⅛ In.	4.50
Plastic, Laser Etched, Black White, Flapper Face, Side-Glancing Eyes, ¾ In.	4.00
Plastic, Rays, Green, 1 ¾ In.	5.00
Plastic, Ringed, Black, Wire Shanks, 1 ⅜ In.	8.00
Plastic, Textured Dish, Orange Shades, 1960s, 1 ½ In.	4.50
Porcelain, Cuff, Painted, Rose Blossom, Green Ground, ⅝ In., Pair	25.00
Ruskin Pottery, Arts & Crafts, Ruskin Pottery, Impressed Mark	140.00
Satsuma, Bamboo, 1 In.	39.00
Shell, Iridescent, Geometric Cross, 4-Hole, 1 In.	6.00
Silver, Mexican, Peaked Malachite Stone, Square, ¾ In.	15.00
Stone, Carnelian, Oval, ⅞ In.	4.00
Wood, Angelfish Shape, 1 ¼ In.	3.00

BUTTONHOOKS have been a popular collectible in England for many years and are now gaining the attention of American collectors. The buttonhooks were made to help fasten the many buttons of the old-fashioned high-button shoes and other items of apparel.

Ivory, Victorian, Swollen Handle	45.00
Lion, Agate Ball, Edwardian, 4 In.	115.00
Mother-Of-Pearl, 5 In.	9.00
Mother-Of-Pearl, Carved, c.1890, 2 ¼ In.	66.00
Scalloped, Celluloid, c.1900, 6 ½ In.	22.00
Steel, Folding Handle, c.1900, 11 ¾ In.	17.00
Sterling Silver, Raised Flowers, c.1895, 7 In.	35.00

BYBEE POTTERY of Bybee, Kentucky, was started by Webster Cornelison. The company claims it started in 1809, although sales records were not kept until 1845. The pottery is still operated by members of the sixth generation of the Cornelison family. The handmade stoneware pottery is sold at the factory. Various marks were used, including the name Bybee, the name Cornelison, or the initials BB. Not all pieces are marked. A mark shaped like the state of Kentucky with the words "Genuine Bybee" and similar marks were also used by a different company, Bybee Pottery Company of Lexington, Kentucky. It was a distributor of various pottery lines from 1922 to 1929.

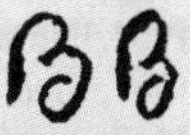

Batter Bowl, Brown, Handle, 7 ½ In.	18.00
Bowl, Tan Over Green, Crystalline Glaze, 2 Ear Shape Handles, 1927, 2 ⅝ In.	196.00
Dish, Oval, Blue Glaze, 8 In.	7.50
Figurine, Duck, Red, 3 ⅛ In.	9.00
Pitcher, Copper Crystalline Matte Glaze, Loop Handle, Narrow Spout, 1927, 4 ⅝ In.	184.00
Vase, Peachblow Like Glaze, Smokestack, 1927, 5 ⅞ In.	173.00

CALENDARS made to hang on the wall or to be displayed on a desk top have been popular since the last quarter of the nineteenth century. Many were printed with advertising as part of the artwork and were given away as premiums. Calendars with guns, gunpowder, or Coca-Cola advertising are most prized.

1895, Lord & Taylor, Stores, Delivery Wagon, String, 8 ½ x 5 ½ In.	125.00
1896, California Powder Works, Woman's Photograph, 15 x 19 In.	1736.00
1896, Snag-Proof Rubbers, Brownies, Lambertville Rubber Co., Full Pad, 5 ¼ x 7 In. *illus*	560.00
1899, Halbert Bros. Millinery Store, Die Cut, Sheridan, Frame, 6 x 8 ½ In.	90.00
1900, U.S. Naval Ships, Dupont, 14 x 28 In.	2875.00
1902, Laflin & Rand Powder Co., It's Infallible, 16 x 24 In.	1008.00
1904, Our Sailor Boy, Cannon, Lithograph, Embossed, Die Cut, Ernst Nister, 12 ½ x 10 In.	236.00
1904, S.S. Patterson, Blatz Brewing Co., Full Pad, Lithograph, 18 x 23 In.	367.00
1906, Peters Cartridge Co., Coming Out Ahead, Guide, Hunter, Moose Head, 26 In.	470.00
1907, Bridges & Shanks Drug Store, Child In Uniform, Flag, Embossed, Die Cut, 7 x 18 In.	275.00
1907, George Bauer Beer, Cardboard, Cutout, Mustache, Cap, Apron, Barrel, 9 ½ x 13 In.	240.00
1907, Miners' Pride Canned Goods, Crowded Streetcar, Die Cut, Embossed, 14 In.	375.00
1907, Wm. Delong, Dealer In Confectionery, Embossed, Die Cut, Girl, Lilacs, 5 x 8 In.	55.00
1908, Keystone Brand Overalls, Celluloid, Pocket, 2 ⅜ x 3 ¾ In.	120.00
1909, Jerome B. Rice Seed Co., Cambridge Valley Seed Gardens, N.Y., Mar.-Dec. Pad, 22 x 10 In. *illus*	143.00
1910, Woman Butcher, W.H. Scott, Fresh, Salt & Smoked Meats, Embossed, 9 ¾ x 15 ¾ In. *illus*	374.00
1911, Dupont Explosives, Just Look At 'Em, 15 x 27 In.	1625.00
1912, Emil Voegele Fine Groceries & Delicatessen, West Chester, N.Y., Full Pad, 11 x 15 In. *illus*	58.00
1912, Morris Gross Clothiers, Children Sledding, Die Cut, Full Pad, 6 x 13 In. *illus*	193.00
1913, Lambertville Boots, Snag Proof, Girl Golfer, 18 x 13 In.	303.00
1914, American Art Works, Dec. Page Only, B. Kichtman, Frame, 13 x 41 In.	358.00
1915, Federal Tires, Couple In Roadster, Lithograph, Frame, 31 ½ x 17 In. *illus*	2310.00
1917, Business Man, Man, Gun & Bird, Quotes, Parrish, Box, 6 x 8 In.	800.00
1926, Round Oak Stoves, Embossed, A.W. Schultz Hardware, Fox Lake, Wis., 10 ⅜ x 20 ⅝ In.	316.00
1927, Yard Long, Flappers, Stars, 10 x 37 In.	308.00
1936, Great Northern Railroad, Route Of The Empire Builder, Blackfeet Indian Boy	90.00
1941, Fuller Brush Company, Girl Brushing Doll's Hair, 7 x 12 In.	45.00
1941, Royal Crown Cola, Woman Drinking Pop, 11 x 23 In.	375.00
1943, Dr Pepper, Blond Woman, Green Purse, Earl Moran, 10-2-4 Bottle, Clock, 14 x 25 In.	144.00
1946, Alberto Varga Pinup Girl, December Page	20.00
1946, Warren S. Mitchell, Pinup, Majorette, All-American Girl, Rolf Armstrong, 22 x 34 In.	95.00
1948, Madonna & Child, 9 ½ x 15 In.	18.00
1954, Don't Commit Teenicide, Playing With Death, 29 x 23 In.	56.00
1954, Kemper-Thomas Co., Hy Hintermeister, 17 x 24 In.	45.00
1956, Marilyn Monroe, Nude, Golden Dreams, Full Pad, Tom Kelly, 11 x 24 In.	226.00
1958, Bireley's, Elizabeth Taylor, Soda Bottle, Frame, 25 ½ x 19 In.	270.00
Perpetual, Royal Tailors, Chicago, Putti, Boy & Girl, Clock Hands, 6 ⅜ x 6 ⅜ In. *illus*	66.00

Buster Brown, Sign, Apples, Buster & Tige, Cardboard, String Hanger, Frame, 11 ⅜ x 12 In.
$1540.00

Wm Morford Antiques

Buster Brown, Tin, Cinnamon, Buster & Tige, Glossy Paper Over Cardboard, Tin Lid, 5 ⅜ x 3 In.
$165.00

Wm Morford Antiques

Buster Brown, Toy, Yo-Yo, Buster Brown Shoes, Tin Lithograph, 1930s, 1 ¾ x ½ In.
$82.00

Hake's Americana & Collectibles

TIP

When the weather is bad, the auction will probably be good. Brave storms and cold and attend auctions in bad weather when the crowd is small and the prices low.

C

Calendar, 1896, Snag-Proof Rubbers, Brownies, Lambertville Rubber Co., Full Pad, 5 ¼ x 7 In.
$560.00

Showtime Auction Services

Calendar, 1909, Jerome B. Rice Seed Co., Cambridge Valley Seed Gardens, N.Y., Mar.-Dec. Pad, 22 x 10 In.
$143.00

Wm Morford Antiques

CALENDAR PLATES were popular in the United States as advertising giveaways from 1906 to 1929. Since then, a few plates have been made every year. A calendar and the name of a store, a picture of flowers, a girl, or a scene were featured on the plate.

1909, Compliments Of L.C. Roberts, Bird With Ribbon, 9 In.	9.99
1910, 4-Leaf Clover, Green, White, H.E. Carman, General Merchandise, Dresden, c.1910, 8 In.	45.00
1910, Carnation McNicol, Flower Border, Woman's Portrait, 8 ½ In.	40.00
1910, Cherubs, Striking Bell, Scalloped Edge, 10 In.	20.00
1910, White, Green, Pink, Shabby Rose, C.F. Company, 8 ¾ In.	95.00
1916, Eagle On Flag, World War I, Off-White Ground, Harker, 7 ½ In.	45.00
1953, 4 Seasons, Jubilee, Homer Laughlin, 10 In.	9.00
1953, Debutante, Homer Laughlin	25.00
1962, Horoscope, White, Gold, 9 ¼ In.	12.00
1962, Windmill, Gold Accents, 10 In.	13.00
1963, Pink Pebbleford, House, Hills, Taylor, Smith & Taylor, 10 In.	18.00
1965, Black On White, Gold Trim, Pink Flowers, 9 ¾ In.	15.00
1966, Zodiac, Green, Bell, Alfred Meakin	24.00
1968, 4 Sports, Scalloped Edge, 10 ¼ In.	14.00
1968, White, Gold Transfers, Eagle, Zodiac Signs, Swirled, Sheffield, 10 In.	21.00
1969, Green, Coupe, Currier & Ives, Royal China, 10 In.	30.00
1971, Cherubs, Zodiac Signs, Queen's Ware, Wedgwood, 10 In.	10.00
1972, Animal Carnival, Zodiac Signs, Wedgwood, 10 In.	19.00
1972, Zodiac Signs, Country House, Alfred Meakin, 10 In.	18.00
1973, Blue, Currier & Ives, Royal China, 10 In.	28.00
1973, Centennial, Boro Of Fleet, Pennsylvania, White, Yellow & Black, 10 ¾ In.	4.75
1973, Sports, Vine Border, Metal, 10 In.	10.00
1973, Zodiac, Log Cabins, God Bless Our Home, Staffordshire, 9 In.	16.00
1977, Blue, Currier & Ives, Royal China, 10 In.	28.00
1979, America The Beautiful, Red, White, Blue, Spencer Gifts, 9 In.	19.00
1980, Lincoln Memorial, Home Of The Free, Red, White, Blue	22.00
1981, Land Of Liberty, Red, White, Blue, Spencer Gifts, 9 In.	19.00
Land Of Liberty, Statue Of Liberty, Series VI, Months Border, Japan, 1981, 9 In.	25.00

CAMARK POTTERY started out as Camden Art Tile and Pottery Company in Camden, Arkansas. Jack Carnes founded the firm in 1926 in association with John Lessell, Stephen Sebaugh, and the Camden Chamber of Commerce. Many types of glazes and wares were made. The company was bought by Mary Daniel in the early 1960s. Production ended in 1983.

Basket, White, Handle, Crimped Edge, Impressed Mark, 4 x 5 ½ In.	34.00
Ewer, Iris, Pink, Elongated Shaped Spout, 13 ½ x 12 In.	27.00
Frog, Open Mouth, Aqua, 2 ¾ x 4 In.	48.00
Vase, Aqua Matte Glaze, Footed, Handles, Impressed Mark, 1930s, 6 x 4 In.	80.00
Vase, Drip Glaze, Oval, 3 ½ In.	125.00

CAMBRIDGE GLASS COMPANY was founded in 1901 in Cambridge, Ohio. The company closed in 1954, reopened briefly, and closed again in 1958. The firm made all types of glass. Its early wares included heavy pressed glass with the mark *Near Cut*. Later wares included Crown Tuscan, etched stemware, and clear and colored glass. The firm used a *C* in a triangle mark after 1920.

Aero Optic, Tumbler, Green, Footed, 6 Oz., 3 ¾ In.	12.00
Aero Optic, Tumbler, Pink, 4 ⅜ In.	18.00
Apple Blossom, Candelabrum, 3-Light, Keyhole	40.00
Azurite, Candlestick, Gold Trim, Square Base, 10 In., Pair	75.00
Azurite, Compote, Gold Trim, 10 ½ In.	125.00
Caprice, Bowl, 4-Footed, Crimped	35.00
Caprice, Bowl, Clear, Oval, 4-Footed, 2 Handles, 11 In.	36.00
Caprice, Bowl, Moonlight Blue, Crimped, 4-Footed, 11 ½ In.	95.00
Caprice, Cordial, Moonlight Blue, Stem, 1 Oz.	150.00
Caprice, Cup & Saucer, Mocha Amber	16.50
Caprice, Dish, Lemon, Clear, Tab Handles, c.1950, 5 x 5 In.	8.00
Caprice, Dish, Mayonnaise, 2 Sections, Footed, Blue	525.00
Caprice, Pitcher, Water, Tilt Ball, 80 Oz.	525.00
Caprice, Plate, Luncheon, Clear, 8 ½ In.	12.00
Caprice, Plate, Moonlight Blue, 6 In.	24.00
Caprice, Plate, Salad, Mocha Amber, 8 ¼ In.	15.00
Caprice, Relish, 3 Sections, 8 In.	18.00
Caprice, Sugar & Creamer, Amber	20.00
Caprice, Sugar & Creamer, Blue	20.00

Caprice, Sugar, Clear	12.00
Caprice, Wine, Moonlight Blue, Stem, 2 ½ Oz.	60.00
Cascade, Goblet, Water, Clear, 8 Oz., 5 ½ In.	15.00
Chantilly, Cornucopia, Sterling Silver Base	425.00
Chantilly, Goblet, 9 Oz., 8 In.	32.00
Cleo, Candlestick, Moonlight Blue, 1-Light, 3 ¾ In.	150.00
Cleo, Candy Dish, Pink, Footed, Cover	35.00
Decagon, Creamer, Pink	12.00
Decagon, Server, Ebony, Etched	75.00
Decagon, Sugar, Pink, Lightning Bolt Handles	16.00
Diane, Goblet, Water, Clear, 11 Oz., 7 ¼	32.00
Diane, Sherbet, Clear, 7 Oz., 6 ⅜ In.	25.00
Everglades, Plate, Clear, Cattail & Swan, 16 In.	65.00
Gloria, Bowl, Pink, 4-Toed, 12 In.	80.00
Lemonade Set, Rose, Engraved Gilt Design, Pitcher, 5 Glasses, 11 x 6 ¾ In., 6 Piece	115.00
Majestic, Dish, Mayonnaise, Moonlight Blue, Ladle	75.00
Martha Washington, Sugar, Amber, Footed, 2 Handles	20.00
Nautilus, Creamer, Amber, Clear Handle, 4 In.	35.00
Nautilus, Oil Bottle, Stopper, Clear	25.00
Pitcher, Leaf, Berries, Green Matte Glaze, Mark, 6 ⅛ In.	161.00
Portia, Candlestick, Green, Keyhole, 5 In., Pair	200.00
Pristine, Candy Dish, Clear, Cover, 3-Footed, Rose Finial, 6 In.	75.00
Rosalie, Flower Frog, Pink, 3 In.	95.00
Rose Point, Candleholder, 3-Light	45.00
Rose Point, Celery Dish, 3 Sections, Scalloped Edge, 12 x 8 In.	70.00
Rose Point, Plate, Salad, Clear, 7 ½ In.	20.00
Rose Point, Relish, Clear, 3 Sections, 12 In.	75.00
Tally-Ho, Candlestick, Carmen Red, 5 In.	45.00
Tally-Ho, Compote, Carmen Red, 6 ½ In.	55.00
Tally-Ho, Mug, Carmen Red, 14 Oz.	65.00
Tally-Ho, Relish, 3 Sections, 2 Handles, Clear, 8 In.	40.00
Wildflower, Compote, Green	75.00

CAMEO GLASS was made in much the same manner as a cameo in jewelry. Parts of the top layer of glass were cut away to reveal a different colored glass beneath. The most famous cameo glass was made during the nineteenth century. Signed cameo glass pieces are listed under the glasswork's name, such as Daum or Galle.

Biscuit Jar, Pink Textured, Flowers, Gilt Leaves, Embossed Collar, Rope Twist Handle, Cylindrical, 8 In.	316.00
Compote, Garances Pattern, Mottled Fuchsia, Purple Round Foot, Wide Bulbous Rim, 6 x 9 In.	1180.00
Finger Bowl, Underplate, Red, Morning Glory Vine, Oval, 8 In.	1150.00
Finger Bowl, Underplate, Sunshine Yellow, Stemmed Iris, 5 ½ In.	800.00
Iris, Leaves, Cranberry, Ruby, Green Ground, c.1905, 15 ¾ In.	1440.00
Perfume Bottle, Lay Down, Elongated Teardrop Form, Prussian Blue With White Gingko, 10 In.	2300.00
Perfume Bottle, Lay Down, Teardrop Form, Prussian Blue, White Butterflies, 10 In.	2300.00
Perfume Bottle, White Flowers, Square Body, Silver Screw Cap, Collar, England, 6 In.	1610.00
Pitcher, Bulbous, Cylindrical Neck, Loop Handle, Ruby, Frosted, Ship Cecelle, Waves, c.1900, 12 In.	4600.00
Rose Bowl, Globular Form, Brown Satin Glass, Cascading Raspberry Branch, 2 ½ In.	1050.00
Vase, Barrel Shape, Flower & Fern Design, Gilt Accents, Enamel, 10 In.	589.00
Vase, Bell Flowers, Red Shaded To Pink, Tapered, Pinched Neck, Footed, Charder, 15 In.	2006.00
Vase, Brown Flowers, Mottled Orange & Yellow Ground, Elongated Oval, Flared Lip, 12 In.	1725.00
Vase, Bulbous, Yellow With Thorny Branch, Fern & Butterfly, 8 In.	800.00
Vase, Cinnamon Color, Blooming Leafy Dogwood, 6 ½ In. ....*illus*	1265.00
Vase, Cylindrical, Raisin Colored Glass, Stemmed Fuchsia Leafy Branch, 5 In.	1300.00
Vase, Daturas Pattern, Flowers, Pink, Yellow, Orange, Mottled, Bulbous Round Foot, 8 In.	1298.00
Vase, Fan & Circle Design, Black, Red, 6 x 7 In.	259.00
Vase, Grape Design, Signed BW, 7 ¾ In.	115.00
Vase, Green Carved To Light Green, Branch, Leaves, White Flowers, Gold Trim, X Band, 7 ½ In.	173.00
Vase, Leafy Flowers, Stems, Crimson Brown, Baluster, Flared Rim, 5 In.	575.00
Vase, Mottled Blue Ground, Palm Trees, Wide Mouth, Charder, 6 ¾ In. ....*illus*	1896.00
Vase, Mt. Fuji Scene, Caramel, White, Asia, 7 x 3 ½ In.	90.00
Vase, Orange Flowers, Amber Leaves, Round Foot, Trumpet Shape, Intaglio Cut, 8 In.	115.00
Vase, Pale Yellow Flowers, Stem, Leaves, Globular, Swollen Neck, Wheel Carved, BS & Co., 8 x 7 In.	1955.00
Vase, Pheasant, Trees, Shrubs, Red, Frosted Ground, Tapered Cylindrical Shape, Signed, Harrach, 7 In.	431.00
Vase, Prussian Blue, Cascading Dogwood Branch, Butterfly, Pear Shape Bottom, 5 In.	1265.00
Vase, Purple Cherries, Purple Shaded Ground, Baluster, St. Louis, Nancy, 5 In.	708.00
Vase, Red Ground, White Flowers, Leaves, Banded Lip & Neck, Bulbous, Flared Lip, Round Foot, 5 In.	1035.00

C

Calendar, 1910, Woman Butcher, W.H. Scott, Fresh, Salt & Smoked Meats, Embossed, 9 ¾ x 15 ¾ In. $374.00

Showtime Auction Services

Calendar, 1912, Emil Voegele Fine Groceries & Delicatessen, West Chester, N.Y., Full Pad, 11 x 15 In. $58.00

Bertoia Auctions

Calendar, 1912, Morris Gross Clothiers, Children Sledding, Die Cut, Full Pad, 6 x 13 In. **$193.00**

Showtime Auction Services

Calendar, 1915, Federal Tires, Couple In Roadster, Lithograph, Frame, 31 ½ x 17 In. **$2310.00**

Wm Morford Antiques

Calendar, Perpetual, Royal Tailors, Chicago, Putti, Boy & Girl, Clock Hands, 6 ⅜ x 6 ⅜ In. **$66.00**

Wm Morford Antiques

Vase, Stick Form, Knopped Stem Design, Poppies & Bell Flowers, Butterfly, 7 In.	1200.00
Vase, Tapering Cylindrical, Wide Rim, Flowers, Leaves, Stems, Plum, Green, Gilt, 1900s, 15 In.	385.00
Vase, Urn Shape, Frosted Yellow, Leafy Flowers, Stemmed, Arrow Points Border, 8 In.	575.00
Vase, White Cut To Blue, Bamboo, Flowers, Perched Bird, Leaves, 5 ¼ In. *illus*	2128.00
Vase, Yellow, Morning Glory Vine, Flower Band, Globular, Stick Neck, 4 In.	1380.00

CAMPAIGN *memorabilia are listed in the Political category.*

CAMPBELL KIDS were first used as part of an advertisement for the Campbell Soup Company in 1904. The kids were created by Grace Drayton, a popular illustrator of the day. The kids were used in magazine and newspaper ads until about 1951. They were presented again in 1966; and in 1983, they were redesigned with a slimmer, more contemporary appearance.

Dish, White, Transfer, Mark, Buffalo Pottery, Child's, 7 ½ In.	20.00
Mug, Figural, Hard Plastic, 1960s	15.00
Sign, Kid, Bowl Of Soup, Red & White, Cardboard, 11 x 21 In. *illus*	770.00
Toy, Truck, Farm, Pull Toy, Fisher-Price, No. 854, 1954, 9 In.	124.00
Toy, Truck, Farm, Wood, Paper Lithograph, Pull, Fisher-Price, 1954, 8 x 6 In.	295.00

CANDELABRUM refers to a candleholder with more than one arm to hold many candles; a candlestick is designed to hold one candle. The eccentricity of the English language makes the plural of candelabrum into candelabra.

2-Light, Brass Socket Slides, Knobbed Standard, Raised Round Base, c.1700, 9 ½ In., Pair	3220.00
2-Light, Brass, Arts & Crafts, Round Base, Tapering Stem, 14 ½ In., Pair	118.00
2-Light, Brass, Omicron, Central Stem, 2 Torch-Type Holders, Signed, 10 ½ x 8 ½ In. *illus*	1860.00
2-Light, Bronze, Argente, Leaf Standard, Flame Finial, Dome Base, c.1920, 13 x 9 ½ In., Pair	799.00
2-Light, Bronze, Art Nouveau, Woman, Flowing Skirt, Patina, 15 ⅛ In. *illus*	1067.00
2-Light, Bronze, Gilt, Rock Crystal, Scroll Arms, Cut Glass Stem, 1800s, 11 ¾ In., Pair	504.00
2-Light, Bronze, Louis XVI Style, Urn On Pedestal, Scrolling Branches, 15 x 8 In., Pair	500.00
2-Light, Bronze, Male Demon, On 1 Foot, Holding Square Box In Each Hand, Japan, 11 In.	337.00
2-Light, Bronze, Marble, Louis XVI Style, Fluted Base, Acorn Finial, c.1885, 10 In., Pair	276.00
2-Light, Bronze, Robed Woman, Outstretched Arms, Sockets, Child Covers Eyes, 1911, 28 ½ In.	1722.00
2-Light, Bronze, Winged Figure, Holding Torches, Crystal & Gilt Pedestal Base, Pair	649.00
2-Light, Gilt Brass, Neoclassical, Spread Wing Eagle Shape, Scroll Arms, Torch, 18 In., Pair	415.00
2-Light, Pewter, Scantily Clad Nymph, Entwined Goldtone Stem, c.1900, 10 In., Pair	3200.00
2-Light, Sconce, Giltwood, Openwork Carved, Gilded, Mirror, c.1905, 26 x 18 In., Pair	230.00
2-Light, Silver, Bud, Scroll & Berry Design, Caldwell & Co., c.1900, 7 x 10 In., Pair	1080.00
2-Light, Silver, Rococo Scrolls, Shaped Oval Base, Round Bobeche, Peru, c.1965, 6 ⅛ x 8 ⅞ In.	276.00
2-Light, Sterling Silver, Weighted Base, Randahl Shop, c.1920, 5 x 10 In., Pair	359.00
3-Light, Brass, Central Urn, Artichoke Finial, c.1890, 18 ½ In., Pair	300.00
3-Light, Bronze, Empire Style, Column, Paw Feet, Pineapple Finial, 1800s, 20 In., Pair	448.00
3-Light, Bronze, Fluted Columns, Tripod Base, Scrolling Acanthus Leaves, 1800s, 24 In., Pair	184.00
3-Light, Bronze, Louis XVI Style, Leaf Arms, Cherubs On Ice Skates, Holding Torches, 11 In., Pair	774.00
3-Light, Bronze, Narrow Reeded Column, Tripod Paw Feet, Shaped Base, 18 x 7 x 7 In., Pair	240.00
3-Light, Bronze, Winged Maiden, Standing, Ball, Pedestal Base, Arms Up, 1900s, 26 x 10 In.	173.00
3-Light, Bronze, Winged Woman, Pedestal Base, 25 ½ x 9 ½ In.	173.00
3-Light, Cloisonne, 3 Entwined Dragons, Orb, Sconce In Mouth, 1800s, 21 In., Pair	10665.00
3-Light, Copper, Arts & Crafts, Hammered, 13 ½ x 9 In.	210.00
3-Light, Cut Glass Baluster, Silver, Leaf Arms, 4 Dolphins, Bun Feet, Germany, c.1900, 20 In., Pair	3525.00
3-Light, Cut Glass, Inverted Vase Shape, Rings, Hanging Spear Prisms, c.1850, 19 x 15 In., Pair.	2091.00
3-Light, Flemish Baroque, Oak Brass Mounts, Lion Paw Feet Base, 15 x 10 In., Pair	761.00
3-Light, Gilt Brass, Porcelain, Louis XVI Style, Flower Heads, Faux Candles, c.1935, 16 x 9 ¼ In., Pair	276.00
3-Light, Gilt Bronze, Alabaster, Hoof Footed Base, France, 12 In.	259.00
3-Light, Gilt Bronze, Cut Glass Vase, Greek Revival, Trumpet Shape, c.1890, 18 In., Pair	1230.00
3-Light, Gilt Bronze, Fluted, Tapered, Columnar Standard, Tripod Paw Feet, 1800s, 22 ⅝ In., Pair	415.00
3-Light, Gilt Bronze, Louis XVI, Hoof Feet, Acanthus Leaf, Wheat, 17 ¼ In., Pair	4248.00
3-Light, Gilt Bronze, Meissen Porcelain, Songbird, Branch Arms, 13 x 11 In., Pair	717.00
3-Light, Gilt Bronze, Turkish Man, Scroll Branches, Drum, Leaves, Marble Base, 25 x 13 In., Pair	1599.00
3-Light, Glass, Gilt, Gothic Revival, Ruffle Edge Bobeches, Hanging Pendants, c.1890, 23 In., Pair	1058.00
3-Light, Jacobean Revival, Dogs, Scrolled Support, Ring Turned Shaft, c.1920, 23 x 9 In., Pair	369.00
3-Light, Malachite, Gilt Bronze, Baluster, Toupee Feet, Scrolled Arms, c.1900, 13 x 9 In., Pair	2868.00
3-Light, Molded Glass, Crystal Prisms, 16 x 13 In., Pair	300.00
3-Light, Napoleon III, Bronze, Gilt, Torch Shape Standard, Trumpet Supports, 16 x 11 In., Pair	777.00
3-Light, Parcel Gilt, Painted, Marble Pedestal, 31 In., Pair	519.00
3-Light, Porcelain, Applied Flowers, Putti, Germany, 1900s, Pair	325.00
3-Light, Porcelain, Couple Embracing, Caged Bird, Flower Heads, Germany, 1800s, 19 In., Pair	250.00
3-Light, Sconce, Brass, Shield Back, Masks, Acanthus Arms, 16 x 10 x 14 In., Pair	151.00

3-Light, Silver Electroplate, 16 x 14 ½ In., Pair	120.00
3-Light, Silver Plate, 2 Scroll Branches, Twisting Arms, Stepped Round Base, 17 In., Pair	100.00
3-Light, Silver Plate, Baluster, Scroll Arms, Engraved Crest, 16 In., Pair	177.00
3-Light, Silver Plate, Baluster, Scroll Arms, Leaves, Stepped Base, Eng., c.1912, 14 In., Pair	179.00
3-Light, Silver Plate, Convertible, England, 19 x 17 In., Pair	207.00
3-Light, Silver Plate, Glass Stem, Glass Chimneys, Round Quilted Foot, 30 ½ In.	60.00
3-Light, Silver Plate, Regency Style, Baluster Stem, Round Stepped Foot, 19 In., Pair	354.00
3-Light, Silver Plate, Regency Style, Scroll Entwined Arms, Round Fluted Foot, 22 In., Pair	531.00
3-Light, Silver Plate, Removable Bobeches, Stepped Round Base, Beaded, Sheffield, 20 x 20 In., Pair	1912.00
3-Light, Silver Plate, Scroll Arms, Square Base, Baluster Stem, England, 18 x 15 In., Pair	125.00
3-Light, Silver Plate, Upswept, Reeded, Leaf & Shell Design, Old Sheffield, 13 In., Pair	650.00
3-Light, Silver, 3 Cylindrical Cups, Angled Base, Spherical Accents, Mexico, 11 In., Pair	915.00
3-Light, Silver, Asymmetrical, 3, Oval Base, Scroll Edge, Mexico, c.1935, 6 ¼ x 7 ¾ In.	369.00
3-Light, Silver, Baluster Standard, Reed & Barton, 11 In., Pair	220.00
3-Light, Silver, Baluster Standard, Scrolling Arms, Round Base, 15 In., Pair	976.00
3-Light, Silver, Convertible, Weighted, Gorham, 14 x 12 In., Pair	270.00
3-Light, Silver, Curved Arms, Gorham, 7 x 9 In.	120.00
3-Light, Silver, Curved Arms, Repousse, Interchangeable, Poole, 15 x 13 In., Pair	644.00
3-Light, Silver, Duchine, 7 ½ In.	120.00
3-Light, Silver, Gadrooned Rim, Intertwined Arms, Round Foot, 6 In., Pair	472.00
3-Light, Silver, Gadrooned Rim, Reeded Arms, Tapering Stem, Dome Foot, c.1950, 14 ½ In., Pair	593.00
3-Light, Silver, Looped Arms, S. Kirk & Son, 8 x 12 ½ In., Pair	403.00
3-Light, Silver, No. 676, Gorham, 9 x 4 ¼ In.	259.00
3-Light, Silver, Panel Knob Stem, Stepped Base, Continental, 1800s, 10 x 9 In., Set Of 4	1080.00
3-Light, Silver, Round Lobed Foot, Swollen Stem, Germany, c.1900, 14 ½ In., Pair	472.00
3-Light, Silver, Scroll Arms, Round Base, Gorham, 11 ½ In., Pair	510.00
3-Light, Silver, Scroll Arms, Round Foot, Converts To Candlestick, Gorham, Mid 1900s, 12 In., Pair	144.00
3-Light, Silver, Scrolled, 12 ½ In., Pair	230.00
3-Light, Silver, Scrolled, Columbia, 14 x 16 In., Pair	173.00
3-Light, Silver, Scrolled, Embossed, Friedman Silver Co., 1900s, 15 ¼ In., Pair	210.00
3-Light, Silver, Scrolled, Weighted, 6 ½ In., Pair	180.00
3-Light, Silver, Tapered, Gadrooned, Scroll Arms, Fisher, 14 x 14 In., Pair	584.00
3-Light, Silver, Twist Arms, Removable, Round Stepped Foot, Gorham, 1900s, 14 In., Pair	531.00
3-Light, Sterling, Scroll Arms, Round Reeded Base, Weighted, 6 x 10 In., Pair	156.00
3-Light, Wrought Iron, Scroll Arms & Feet, Rectangular Band, 1700s, 17 ½ x 13 ¾ In.	690.00
4-Light, Bronze, Curved Arms, Scroll, Pedestal Base, 22 In., Pair	345.00
4-Light, Bronze, Cut Glass, Tiered, Scroll, Amethyst & Amber Prisms, Grapes, c.1890, 21 ½ In., Pair	598.00
4-Light, Bronze, Empire Style, Dark Patina, Gold Trim, Tripart Base, 27 In., Pair	1265.00
4-Light, Bronze, Marble, Empire, Scrolling Arms, Tapering Shaft, Drops, c.1885, 23 In., Pair	236.00
4-Light, Bronze, Marble, Figural, Putti, Holding, Flower Arms, Gagneau, c.1895, 30 In., Pair	3450.00
4-Light, Bronze, Porcelain, Flower Stems, Cherubs, Kneeling, Plaques, France, c.1900, 16 3/8 In., Pair	3675.00
4-Light, Bronze, Porcelain, Winged Woman, Standing On Orb, Square Base, 30 x 11 In., Pair	780.00
4-Light, George III Style, Scroll Arms, Leaves, Round Base, Gorham, 14 In., Pair	475.00
4-Light, Gilt Brass, Porcelain, Scrolling, c.1900, 18 ½ In., Pair	432.00
4-Light, Gilt, Bronze, Figural, Scroll Arms, Boy, Playing Flute, c.1890, 15 In.	266.00
4-Light, Metal, Silvered, Scroll Arms, Maiden, Standing, Pierced Leaf Base, c.1900, 20 3/8 In., Pair	674.00
4-Light, Pine, Neoclassical, Scrolled, Half Urn Shape, Carved, Italy, 1800s, 14 x 13 ½ In., Pair	590.00
4-Light, Porcelain, Putto Support, Dresden, Germany, 15 ¾ In., Pair	173.00
4-Light, Silver Plate, Twisting Arms, Trumpet Shape Shaft, Gadrooned Base, c.1800s, 23 ¼ In., Pair	2868.00
4-Light, Silver Plate, Winding Branches, Leaves, Berries, Openwork Foot, 1800s, 20 In., Pair	720.00
4-Light, Silver, Weighted, Duncan, 9 ½ In.	180.00
4-Light, Silvered Metal, Flower Shape, Openwork Stem, Pierced Base, c.1906, 15 In., Pair	2813.00
4-Light, Wrought Iron, Hanging, Pagoda Shape Frame, 20 In.	115.00
5-Light, Brass, Neoclassical, Scroll Arms, Water Leaves, Clear Hanging Prisms, 18 ¼ In., Pair	826.00
5-Light, Brass, Squared Standard, Leaf Cast Candle Arms, Neoclassical, 24 In., Pair	732.00
5-Light, Bronze Dore Athlete Finial, Scroll Drops, Column, Marble Plinth, 44 In.	446.00
5-Light, Bronze Male Pedestal, Square Column, White Glass Shades, 16 ½ x 10 ½ In.	575.00
5-Light, Bronze, Acanthus Leaf Legs, Raised Base, c.1920, 24 x 17 In., Pair	215.00
5-Light, Bronze, Flower Arms, Seated Putti, Raised Base, France, 1800s, 31 ½ In., Pair	8888.00
5-Light, Bronze, Flowers & Leaves, Standing Cherub, Gilt, France, 1800s, 26 In.	521.00
5-Light, Bronze, Stork, Maiden, Flowers, Lion Heads, Paw Feet, Gilt, 1800s, 40 In., Pair	3075.00
5-Light, Bronze, Stylized Leaves, Winding Vines, Round Foot, 1900s, 19 In., Pair	764.00
5-Light, Bronze, Urn Central Nozzle, 4 Leaf Arms, Column Standard, Stepped Base, 28 x 13 In., Pair	1195.00
5-Light, Bronze, Urn Shape, Scrolling, Square Marble Base, 4-Footed, 20 x 6 ½ In., Pair	270.00
5-Light, Charles X Style, Gilt Bronze Cups, Mounts, Patinated Column, Marble Base, 28 x 12 In., Pair	1872.00
5-Light, Charles X Style, Gilt, Bronze, Cherubs, Holding Wreath, Scrolling Arms, 24 In., Pair	2460.00
5-Light, Gilt Brass, Art Nouveau, Wreath Base, Fluted Column, Serpentine Arms, 12 x 9 In.	460.00

Cameo Glass, Vase, Cinnamon Color, Blooming Leafy Dogwood, 6 ½ In.
$1265.00

Cameo Glass, Vase, Mottled Blue Ground, Palm Trees, Wide Mouth, Charder, 6 ¾ In.
$1896.00

Cameo Glass, Vase, White Cut To Blue, Bamboo, Flowers, Perched Bird, Leaves, 5 ¼ In.
$2128.00

Campbell Kids, Sign, Kid, Bowl Of Soup, Red & White, Cardboard, 11 x 21 In.
$770.00

Candelabrum, 2-Light, Brass, Omicron, Central Stem, 2 Torch-Type Holders, Signed, 10 ½ x 8 ½ In.
$1860.00

Rago Arts & Auction Center

Candelabrum, 2-Light, Bronze, Art Nouveau, Woman, Flowing Skirt, Patina, 15 ⅛ In.
$1067.00

Skinner, Inc.

Candelabrum, 6-Light, Silver, S-Scroll Form, Marked, A. Michelsen, Copenhagen, 9 ¾ In., Pair
$1830.00

Leslie Hindman Auctioneers

Candelabrum, 7-Light, Cast, Gilt Brass, 2nd Empire Style, Woman, Cornucopia Vases, c.1910, 32 ½ In., Pair
$2655.00

Ivey-Selkirk Auctioneers

5-Light, Gilt Bronze, Belle Epoque, Rococo Style, c.1880, 23 x 16 ½ In., Pair	1968.00
5-Light, Gilt Bronze, Cherub Stem, Scrolls, 20 In., Pair	1035.00
5-Light, Gilt Bronze, Flower Bouquet, Face Pedestals, Tripod, France, 1800s, 24 ½ In., Pair	413.00
5-Light, Gilt Bronze, Stylized Leaf Border, Scrolled, Tapered, Reeded, Sweden, 1800s, 25 ½ In., Pair	3220.00
5-Light, Gilt Bronze, Urn Shape, Flowers, Marble Base, Paw Feet, 24 In., Pair	1464.00
5-Light, Gilt Metal & Onyx, Victorian, Baluster Stem, Scrolling Arms & Feet, 19 In., Pair	305.00
5-Light, Gilt Metal, Intertwined Leaves, Ribbons, 22 In., Pair	176.00
5-Light, Gilt Metal, Palm Tree Shape, Leaf Shape Cup, Entwined Trunks, 24 In., Pair	6518.00
5-Light, Gilt, Flowering Roses, White Marble Urns, Ram's Head Handles, Festoons, 29 In., Pair	944.00
5-Light, Gilt-Bronze, Porcelain, Cherub, On Knee, Flowering Branches, 1800s, 23 In., Pair	1250.00
5-Light, Glass, Fairy, Classical Woman, Gold Robes, Burmese Shades, Clark's Cricklite, 34 In.	7475.00
5-Light, Louis XIV Style, Gilt Metal, Acanthus Leaves, Electrified, 29 x 10 ½ In., Pair	132.00
5-Light, Mixed Metal, Butterflies, Beetles, Dragonflies, Scroll Arms, Spear Prisms, 23 x 14 In.	861.00
5-Light, Renaissance Revival, Dore Bronze, Scroll Stems, Prisms, France, 17 ½ In., Pair	385.00
5-Light, Silver Plate, Baluster, Scrolled Arms, Leaves, Square Foot, 1900s, 20 ½ In., Pair	478.00
5-Light, Silver Plate, C-Scroll Arms, Baluster Standard, 16 In., Pair	62.00
5-Light, Silver Plate, Leaves, Acanthus Candle Cups, Scrolled Leafy Arms, 26 ½ In., Pair	1845.00
5-Light, Silver Plate, Scroll Arms, Leaves, Flowers, Elkington & Co., Birmingham, c.1900, 21 x 17 In.	184.00
5-Light, Silver Plate, Standing Woman, Supporting Scrolling Arm, 1800s, 21 In., Pair	3525.00
5-Light, Silver Plate, Victorian Style, Baluster Stem, Leaf Design Base, 1900s, 16 In., Pair	59.00
5-Light, Silver, 8-Sided Beaker Stem, Scrolled Arms, Germany, 14 x 14 In., Pair	1521.00
5-Light, Silver, Convertible, Gorham, 2 ¼ x 13 In., Pair	690.00
5-Light, Silver, Flute Shape, Different Heights, Wood Base, H. Christensen, Denmark, 1970, 17 x 14 In.	9000.00
5-Light, Silver, Hexagonal Stem, Scrolling Arms, Mexico, 11 In., Pair	4148.00
5-Light, Silver, Inverted Bell Nozzles, Scrolled, Tapered Stem, Conquistador, Mexico, 1900s, 16 ¾ In.	1896.00
5-Light, Silver, Louis XV, Scrolls, Flowers, Gorham, 15 x 15 In., Pair	1955.00
5-Light, Silver, Twisted, Reeded, J.E. Caldwell, 13 ¼ In., Pair	920.00
5-Light, Silver, Urn Shape, Griffin Head Ring Handles, Belle Epoque, Gilt, 1800s, 20 In., Pair	1722.00
5-Light, Tin, Knockers, Petal Stems, Round Punch Base, 2 Half Circle Design, 1800s, 9 ¾ x 10 In.	345.00
5-Light, Wood, Carved, Painted, Gilt, Urn Shape, Flowers, Swags, Hung Prisms, 46 In., Pair	310.00
6-Light, Bronze, Gilt, Leaves, Cobalt Blue, Portraits, Maidens, Flowers, Sevres, 1800s, 33 In., Pair	7350.00
6-Light, Bronze, Gilt, Tiered Arms, Bouquet Finial, Putto, Plaques, Sevres, 1800s, 25 x 9 In., Pair	2689.00
6-Light, Bronze, Marble Base, 28 x 10 In., Pair	565.00
6-Light, Bronze, Slate, Child, Turned Socle, Octagonal Base, Scroll Arms, 25 In., Pair	1062.00
6-Light, Gilt Bronze, Louis XVI, Putti, Faun, Basket, Grapes, Urn, Hoof Feet, 1700s, 28 In., Pair	2700.00
6-Light, Gilt Bronze, Patinated Putto Support, Burgundy Marble Base, 35 x 15 In., Pair	4802.00
6-Light, Louis Phillipe, Gilt, Bronze, Winged Victory, Stepped Plinth, c.1840, 34 x 11 In., Pair	7170.00
6-Light, Louis XVI, Putto Supporting Cornucopia, Scrolling Branches, Gilt, 31 In., Pair	4160.00
6-Light, Silver, S-Scroll Form, Marked, A. Michelsen, Copenhagen, 9 ¾ In., Pair *illus*	1830.00
7-Light, Bronze Dore, Marble, Louis XV Style Urn, Scrolling Leafy Arms, France, 34 In., Pair	1315.00
7-Light, Bronze, Figures, Flowers, Grapes, Birds, Ornate, Tripod Base, 26 ½ In.	518.00
7-Light, Cast, Gilt Brass, 2nd Empire Style, Woman, Cornucopia Vases, c.1910, 32 ½ In., Pair *illus*	2655.00
7-Light, Empire Style, Gilt Metal, France, c.1890, 32 x 22 In., Pair	472.00
7-Light, Gilded, Lilies, Sheaves Of White, Ivy, Vase Shape Standard, Cross, Pierced Handles, 44 In., Pair	738.00
7-Light, Gilt Brass, Renaissance Revival Style, Scrolled Leafy Arms, 31 ½ In. *illus*	244.00
7-Light, Gilt Bronze, Intertwined Maidens, Grape Clusters, Flowers, Pedestal, c.1835, 31 ¼ In., Pair	4575.00
7-Light, Gilt Bronze, Marble, Classical Women, Scrolled Arms, Base, c.1800s, 18 In., Pair	4880.00
7-Light, Gilt Bronze, Scrolling Leaf Arms, Triangular Base, 1800s, 41 x 14 In., Pair	10000.00
7-Light, Gilt Metal, Rococo, Twisted Vines, Scrolls, c.1910, 29 x 15 In.	519.00
7-Light, Glass, Bronze, Scrolled Leaves, Fluted Stem, White, Turquoise, Gilding, 1800s, 29 ½ In., Pair	2370.00
7-Light, Silver, Central Sconce, Acanthus Arms, Domed Foot, Germany, c.1910, 24 ¼ In., Pair *illus*	7963.00
9-Light, Gilt Metal, George II, Archangel, Scroll Candle Arms, Tripod Base, 33 ½ In., Pair	504.00
9-Light, Wrought Iron, 3 Tiers, Black Paint, Floor, 71 ¼ In.	403.00
10-Light, Gilt Bronze, Marble, Louis XVI, Urn Shape, Putto Mounts, Bow, Torch Finial, 42 In.	1220.00
13-Light, Torchere, Bronze, Greek Goddess Stem, Gilt, Paint Base, 102 x 22 In., Pair	12200.00
Bronze, Man, Seminude, Supporting Nozzle, Fruits, Flowers, Pierced Base, 1900s, 11 ½ In., Pair	490.00
Girandole, Czech Glass, Red, Scalloped Rim, Prisms, 12 ¾ In.	129.00

CANDLESTICKS were made of brass, pewter, glass, sterling silver, plated silver, and all types of pottery and porcelain. The earliest candlesticks, dating from the sixteenth century, held the candle on a pricket (sharp pointed spike). These lost favor because in times of strife the large church candlesticks with prickets became formidable weapons, so the socket was mandated. Candlesticks changed in style through the centuries, and designs range from Classical to Rococo to Art Nouveau to Art Deco.

Altar, Bronze, Columnar, Raised On 3 Shaped Supports, Ring Base, Japan, 14 In., Pair	868.00
Altar, Wood, Carved, Gesso, Gilt, Tin Bobeche, Iron Spindle, Venetian, 20 In., Pair	864.00

Asian Warrior, Sword, Bronze, Candleholder Torch, c.1900, 9 ½ In.	115.00
Bone China, Royal Aves Design, Gold Birds & Leaves, Crown Derby, 11 In., Pair	267.00
Brass, 2-Tone, Acanthus Leaf, Tripod Plinth, 12 ½ x 5 In., Pair	923.00
Brass, Baluster Post, Drip Plates, 3-Footed, Russia, 1800s, 9 In., Pair	295.00
Brass, Chimney Shade, Ruby Stained Flowers, Rim, Gilt Crest, Russia, 1800s, 21 x 13 In., Pair	863.00
Brass, Cobra Shape, Hood Spread, Ready To Strike, Flower Shape Cup, 8 In., Pair	326.00
Brass, Dome Base, Baluster Stem, c.1725, 7 ½ In.	558.00
Brass, Egyptian Revival, Egyptian Woman Pedestal, Urn Shape Candle Cup, 1800s, 8 In., Pair	175.00
Brass, Flared Cup, Ring Knob, Tapered Stem, Domed Base, Polished, c.1800, 10 In., Pair	118.00
Brass, Flared Drip Pan, Candles Ejector, c.1790, 7 ¼ In., Pair	489.00
Brass, Flared Socles, Fluted Tapered Body, Square Stepped Base, 1700s, 10 In., Pair	374.00
Brass, Jesters, Collar Shape Trays, Jingle Bells, Ring, Trumpet Shape Base, 10 In., Pair	652.00
Brass, Louis XVI, Scalloped Base, Armorials, Tripartite Standard, c.1785, 10 In., Pair	461.00
Brass, Mother-Of-Pearl, Fused Shells Stem, Round Base, Signed, Christian Dior, 9 In., Pair	306.00
Brass, Octagonal Cup, Knobbed Faceted Stem, Stepped Base, France, 1700s, 9 In., Pair	295.00
Brass, Octagonal, Spool Shape Cup, Knobbed Stem, Stepped Base, Shaped Rim, France, c.1800, 8 In.	89.00
Brass, Owl, Holding Flower Stem With Candle Cup, 6 ¾ In., Pair ....*illus*	490.00
Brass, Paneled, Seamed Construction, Octagonal Base, Threaded Posts, 1700s, 10 In., Pair	499.00
Brass, Pewter Finish, Repousse Base, Holland Brass Works, 39 In.	96.00
Brass, Pierced Baluster, Raised Drip Pan, Domed Base, Heemskirk, Dutch, 1600s, 10 In.	805.00
Brass, Princess Diamond, c.1895, 11 In., Pair	89.00
Brass, Queen Anne, Square Base, Cut Corners, Turned, Vase Shape Stem, 1800s, 6 In., Pair	403.00
Brass, Scalloped Bobeches, Shouldered Knobbed Stems, Petal Shape Base, 9 In., Pair	1003.00
Brass, Scalloped Cup, Cylindrical Shaft, Flower Shape Base, 10 In.	89.00
Brass, Silvered, Terrier, Sitting On Hind Legs, Paws Around Baluster Stem, 9 In., Pair	326.00
Brass, Soldered, Hexagonal Foot, Inverted Beehive Shape Shaft, 8 ¾ In., Pair	35.00
Brass, Tapered Shaft, Leaf, Stem Borders, France, c.1810, 5 ¼ In., Pair	354.00
Brass, Tavern, Banded Handle, Round Stepped Base, 20 In., Pair	717.00
Bronze, Art Nouveau, Flowers Form Top, Fluted Columns, Stylized Base, 13 ¼ In., Pair	288.00
Bronze, Art Nouveau, Young Boy, Young Girl, Standing On Spheres, McCartan, 17 In., Pair	3585.00
Bronze, Baluster Shape Stem, Tripod Base, 1700s, 15 In., Pair	184.00
Bronze, Cherub Shape, Holding Socle, Continental, 1800s, 13 ½ In., Pair	920.00
Bronze, Cherub, Holding Flower Shape Torch, Neoclassical Base, Cast, 9 ¼ x 4 In.	368.00
Bronze, Cherub, Supporting Torch & Bow, 13 In., Pair	537.00
Bronze, Crane, Cup On Beak, Parcel Gilt, Patinated, Waisted Base, 10 In., Pair	1800.00
Bronze, Dore, Art Nouveau, Flower Shape, 10 ¼ In., Pair	465.00
Bronze, Dore, Fluted Shaft, Leaf Collar, Triangular Plinth, France, 12 In., Pair	478.00
Bronze, Dore, Reticulated, 3 Women's Heads Stem, Lobed Round Base, France, 1800s, 7 x 5 In.	244.00
Bronze, Enamel, Spherule, Pink Heart Design, Turquoise Accents, France, 1800s, 7 ¾ In., Pair	521.00
Bronze, Figural, Bacchanalian Putto, Lily Socket, Scrolled Pedestal, France, 20 In.	450.00
Bronze, Figural, Boy, Holding Lotus, Chinese, 1800s, 9 ¾ In., Pair	2489.00
Bronze, Figural, Classical Woman, Marble Base, c.1835, 19 ¾ In., Pair	800.00
Bronze, Figural, Devil Supporting 2 Demons, Cauldron Shape Cup, 9 In., Pair	1185.00
Bronze, Figural, Nude Boy, Dolphin, Leafy Tripod Pedestal, Scrolled Feet, 17 In.	59.00
Bronze, Figural, Woman, Silver Gilt Flower Robe, Holding Bowl, 63 In., Pair	1093.00
Bronze, Girl Standing On Globe, Water Jug Socket, Marble Base, 17 In.	1304.00
Bronze, Lacquer, Gilt, Restauration, Fluted, Tripod Base, Paw Feet, Plinth, c.1850, 13 In., Pair	1722.00
Bronze, Leaf Design, Columnar Shape, Descending Lizard, 3-Part Paw Base, 12 In.	366.00
Bronze, Leaf Nozzle, Cherub, Scrolled Pierced Base, France, 1800s, 9 ⅞ In., Pair	674.00
Bronze, Marble, Louis XV Style, Putto, Urn Shape Nozzle, Round Base, 1800s, 7 ½ In., Pair	269.00
Bronze, Marble, Napoleon III, Putto, Holding Trumpet, Octagonal Fluted Base, c.1870, 14 ½ In., Pair	677.00
Bronze, Nude Boy, Standing On Sphere, Holding Vase Candleholder, Marble Base, 17 In.	69.00
Bronze, Oil Lamp Shape, Seated Elephant Support, Peacocks, 8 In.	184.00
Bronze, Rococo, Green Glazed Porcelain, Continental, 1700s, 10 In., Pair ....*illus*	1121.00
Bronze, Seahorse, Round Plate Base, c.1905, 6 ¾ In.	431.00
Bronze, Theta, Signed Jarvie, 13 ½ x 6 In.	2604.00
Cast Metal, Prince Of Wales Feather Plume, Fluted Glass Shaft, Round Lucite Base, 26 In., Pair	184.00
Chamber, Brass, Adjustable, Toile Shade, Marked, France, 1800s, 15 ¾ In., Pair ....*illus*	353.00
Chamber, Patinated Iron, Tooled, Stamped Coberg, Germany, c.1900, 7 ¾ In.	108.00
Chamber, Silver, Gadrooned Rim, Flower Capped Thumbpiece, 3 Claw & Ball Feet, George III, 4 In.	625.00
Chamber, Silver, Saucer Base, Beaded Edge, Snuffer, Matthew Boulton, England, 4 x 5 In.	108.00
Cloisonne, Crane Shape, Standing, Pine Sprays In Beak, 20 In., Pair	717.00
Cloisonne, Flower Panels, Lobed, Plum Ground, Gilt Brass Mounts, Japan, 1800s, 8 ¾ In.	316.00
Cloisonne, Masks, Lotus Scrolls, Prick, Mark, Chinese, 17 In., Pair	18960.00
Copper, Chamber, Hammered, Gustav Stickley, 9 x 7 ¼ In., Pair	620.00
Copper, Favrile Glass, Leaf Standard, Ruffle Rim, Round Foot, Arts & Crafts, 22 In., Pair	732.00
Copper, Figural, Dragon, Clouds, Jade Base, Mark, Chinese, 13 ¼ In., Pair	413.00

Candelabrum, 7-Light, Gilt Brass, Renaissance Revival Style, Scrolled Leafy Arms, 31 ½ In.
$244.00

Neal Auction Co.

Candelabrum, 7-Light, Silver, Central Sconce, Acanthus Arms, Domed Foot, Germany, c.1910, 24 ¼ In., Pair
$7963.00

Skinner, Inc.

Candlestick, Brass, Owl, Holding Flower Stem With Candle Cup, 6 ¾ In., Pair
$490.00

Skinner, Inc.

Candlestick, Bronze, Rococo, Green Glazed Porcelain, Continental, 1700s, 10 In., Pair
$1121.00

Brunk Auctions

Candlestick, Chamber, Brass, Adjustable, Toile Shade, Marked, France, 1800s, 15 ¾ In., Pair
$353.00

Cowan's Auctions

Candlestick, Plaster, George III, Figural, Classical Woman, Ebonized, Bronze Mounts, 1812, 9 In., Pair
$1553.00

Neal Auction Co.

Candlestick, Silver Plate, Richard Meier, Swid Powell, 1983, 9 x 3 ¾ In., Pair
$1875.00

Los Angeles Modern Auctions

TIP

Wave and call good-bye to "Grandma and the kids" when leaving in a cab for the airport. Make it sound as if the house is occupied.

Copper, G. Stickley, Hammered, Pyramid Shape, Square Base, Stamped, 20 x 7 In., Pair	65100.00
Copper, Hammered, Heart Shaped Handles, 9 x 5 In.	217.00
Crystal, Faceted Dangling Crystal Icicles, Swirl Design, Round Footed Base, 12 x 6 In., Pair	240.00
Earthenware, Figural, Cat, Billy Ray Hussey, 12 ¼ In., Pair	1610.00
Ecclesiastical, Gilt, Mirror, Swags, Banded Orb, Tripod Base, Italy, 1800s, 35 ½ In., Pair	889.00
Flint Enamel, Blue, Green Accents, Bennington, Vermont, 7 In.	705.00
Gesso, Figural, Angle, Kneeling, Holding Taper, Carved, Paint, Italy, 1800s, 15 ¼ In., Pair	472.00
Gilt Brass, Charles X, Spiral Ribbed, c.1835, 10 ¾ x 5 ¼ In.	799.00
Gilt Brass, Columnar, Scrolling Leaves, Tripod Stand, Dragon Shape Legs, c.1900, 29 In., Pair	472.00
Gilt Brass, Figural, Flower Shape Cup, Maiden Seated On Stem, Leaf Base, 1800s, 7 In., Pair.	1007.00
Gilt Bronze, Baluster Stem, Round Foot, Enamel, Leaves, France, 1800s, 9 In., Pair	1067.00
Gilt Bronze, Belle Epoque, Louis XV Style, c.1880, 10 In., Pair	615.00
Gilt Bronze, Empire Style, Patinated, Roman Centurion, Spear, Palm Tree Pole, 18 x 5 In., Pair	2340.00
Gilt Bronze, Empire, Black Dolphin Mounts, Tripod Feet, c.1905, 8 In., Pair	944.00
Gilt Bronze, Lion Supporting Castle Turret, Round Plinth, Farnce, 8 ½ In., Pair	1020.00
Gilt Bronze, Louis Philippe, Columnar, Round Foot, c.1850, 9 ½ In., Pair	281.00
Gilt Bronze, Rock Crystal, Fluted Leaf & Berry Cup, Round Base, c.1900, 7 ½ In., Pair	2214.00
Gilt Metal, Rococo Style, Figural, 10 In., Pair	47.00
Gilt Metal, Stamen Shape Cup, Petal Drip Tray, Winged Lion, Dragon, Scroll, 6 In., Pair	296.00
Gilt, Carved, Turned Column Shape, Fluted Base, Stepped Plinth, Italy, 27 In., Pair	305.00
Gilt, Trumpet, Leaf Carved Standard, Tripod Base, Paw Feet, Italy, c.1690, 37 In., Pair	533.00
Girandole, Cast Brass, Maiden, Tree, Glass Prisms, Marble Base, 18 In., Pair	123.00
Glass, Bell Shape Shade, Prisms, Brass Mounts, 1800s, 22 ½ In., Pair	1062.00
Glass, Blue, Clear & Gold Cups, Multicolor Rod Stem, Cenedese & Albarelli, Murano, 3 ½ x 8 ¾ In.	420.00
Glass, Deep Amber, Tapered, Pinched Socket, Saucer Base, 3 ⅝ In.	4760.00
Glass, Oil Spot, Pink & Purple Highlights, Candlecup, Stepped Round Foot, Austria, 16 In.	118.00
Glass, Red & White Air Twist Candy Stripes, Wafer, Red Rim, Flat Foot, 12 In.	1287.00
Glass, Tab Handle, Scalloped Rim, Heisey, 4 x 6 In.	19.00
Hurricane, Cranberry Glass, Enameled, Parcel Gilt, Pressed, Cut Glass Spears, 24 x 6 In., Pair	1722.00
Iron, Lemon Tree Form, Painted, Terra-Cotta Pot, c.1950, 18 In., Pair	1476.00
Iron, Rush Light, Forged, Riveted, Curved Tripod Stand, 21 ½ x 7 In.	176.00
Mahogany, Urn Shape Pricket, Graduated Rings, Spiral Stem, Wreath, Tripod Feet, 39 In.	858.00
Majolica, Gilt Metal, Monkey, Speak No Evil, Hear No Evil, Leaf Shape Stem, 9 In., Pair	1185.00
Maple, Turned, Treen, Yellow Stripes, c.1830, 10 In.	529.00
Marble, Column Shape, Applied Brass Putto, 8 In., Pair	307.00
Metal, Art Deco, Trumpet Shaped Tops, Fluted Column, Round Base, 63 ¾ x 12 In., Pair	861.00
Metal, Patinated, Figural, Vocalist Holding SongBook, Painter Holding Palette, 12 In., Pair	770.00
Nickel Over Bronze, Art Deco, Flowers, Figures, France, c.1930, 65 x 21 In., Pair	984.00
Pewter, Baluster, Engraved Flowers, Flagg & Homan, c.1840, 10 In., Pair	2585.00
Pewter, Baluster, Homan, Cincinnati, c.1850, 7 In., Pair	470.00
Pewter, Figural, Woman, Leaning Forward, Extending Sconce Above Head, 10 In., Pair	1007.00
Pewter, Pricket, Triangular, Flowers, Scroll Feet, Drip Pan, 1700s, 35 ½ In., Pair	444.00
Pewter, Turned Stem, 3 Scroll, Flower Carved Feet, c.1800, 17 ½ In., Pair	415.00
Plaster, Column Shape, Paint, 16 ½ In., Pair	12.00
Plaster, George III, Figural, Classical Woman, Ebonized, Bronze Mounts, 1812, 9 In., Pair .... *illus*	1553.00
Porcelain, Blue & White, Ceres, Wheat, Cybele, Lion, Cornucopia, 1700s, 13 In., Pair	20145.00
Porcelain, Cherubs, Playing Musical Instruments, 13 ½ In., Pair	180.00
Porcelain, Flowering Tree Shape, Perched Birds, Scrolling Base, Continental, 9 In., Pair	688.00
Porcelain, Gilt, Scalloped Rim, Stepped, Robed Man Stem, Pedestal Base, 1800s, 13 In., Pair	711.00
Porcelain, Willow Design, Blue & White, Canton, c.1835, 8 In., Pair	461.00
Porcelain, Woman, Nude, Masked, Standing, Cape, Ivory, Cobalt Blue, 1920, 12 ⅜ In.	3105.00
Pottery, Boy, Feather Crown, Cornucopia, Lion, Staffordshire, c.1810, 13 ½ In.	850.00
Pottery, Tall, Wide Base, Orange, Ben Owen, 17 In., Pair	978.00
Pressed Glass, Dolphin, Opaque White, 6-Petal Socket, Square Base, 10 x 4 In., Pair	259.00
Pressed Glass, Emerald Green, Hexagonal, Knop Extension, Flared Base, 7 x 4 In., Pair	1610.00
Pressed Glass, Petal & Loop, Electric Blue, 6-Petal Socket, Round Loop Base, 6 ¾ x 4 ¼ In.	460.00
Pricket, Gilt Brass, Gothic Revival, Cathedral Shape, Tripod Feet, England, 1800s, 25 In., Pair	489.00
Pricket, Lotus Shaped Cup, Tripod Base, Kylin Scrolls, Bronze, 20 ¼ In.	2370.00
Silver Plate, Baluster, Flower Heads, 3 Dolphin Supports, Tripartite Base, 12 In., Pair	100.00
Silver Plate, Baluster, Leaf & Grotesque Mask Design, Square Base, Scroll Toes, 14 In., Pair	403.00
Silver Plate, Baroque Style, Tapered, Masks, Scrolling Leaves, Paw Feet, U.S.A, c.1800, 21 In.	250.00
Silver Plate, Column, Ionic Capital, Square Foot, Leaves, Urns, Sheffield, 1800s, 11 In., Pair.	267.00
Silver Plate, Corinthian Column, James Dixon, Sheffield, 9 In., Pair	180.00
Silver Plate, Crane, Mother-Of-Pearl, Jade, Turquoise, Flowering Vines, 1800s, 20 In., Pair	6738.00
Silver Plate, Empire, Column Shape, Reeded Fish Scale & Leaf Bands, Tripod Hoof Feet, 8 In., Pair	1170.00
Silver Plate, Knopped Standard, Domed Base, Lion's & Ram's Masks, Putti, 7 In., Pair	184.00
Silver Plate, Lyre Shape, Fluted Oval Base, Reeded Border, c.1800, 13 ¼ In., Pair	1195.00

C

C

Silver Plate, Monkeys Perched In Tree, Round Foot, 14 In., Pair	478.00
Silver Plate, Pinecone Shape Cup, Quatrefoil Stem, Flared Foot, Berries, 1900s, 10 In., Pair	385.00
Silver Plate, Richard Meier, Swid Powell, 1983, 9 x 3 ¾ In., Pair *illus*	1875.00
Silver Plate, Sconce, Shell Back Plate, Center Cherub, 3 Scrolled Arms, c.1940, 16 x 13 In., Pair	1230.00
Silver Plate, Square Column Shape, Embossed Bamboo, c.1925, 7 ½ x 4 In.	430.00
Silver Plate, Thistle Sconce, Flared Rim, Knopped Stem, Paw & Ball Feet, c.1850, 9 ¼ In., Pair	858.00
Silver, Baluster Column, Spiral Knop, Stepped Base, Sheffield, c.1810, 11 ¼ In., Pair	295.00
Silver, Baluster Standard, Bell Shape Nozzle, Engraved Flowers, c.1935, 8 ½ x 3 ½ In., Pair	553.00
Silver, Baluster, Flowers, Stepped Circular Foot, Austria, c.1852, 10 ¼ In., Pair	478.00
Silver, Baluster, Scrolling Leaves, Circular Foot, 3 Acanthus Feet, Russia, c.1908, 9 In., Pair	508.00
Silver, Baluster, Square Base, Flower Banding, Beast Mask Feet, Portugal, c.1836, 9 ¾ In., Pair	267.00
Silver, Baluster, Urn Shape Nozzle, Circular Foot, Reeded Banding, Czech, c.1929, 12 In., Pair	568.00
Silver, Bell Shape, Applied Leaves, Scrolls, Cushion Cut Amethysts, Edward Oakes, 4 ¾ In., Pair. *illus*	11850.00
Silver, Bulbous Cup, Square, Tapering Stem, Etched Flowers, Stepped Round Foot, 12 In., Pair	279.00
Silver, Chantilly-Duchess, Gorham, 4 ¾ In., Pair	106.00
Silver, Column, Corinthian, Detachable Bobeche, Beaded Edge, Stepped Base, 10 x 4 In., Pair	676.00
Silver, Column, Flat Leaf Capital, Square Base, Urns, Branches, Orb Mark, Sheffield, 1886, 7 In., Pair	652.00
Silver, Columnar, Shaped Trefoil Base, Acanthus Design, Monogram, Germany, 11 In., Pair	717.00
Silver, Columnar, Square Base, Grape Design, 1800s, 12 ¾ In., Pair	805.00
Silver, Cone Shape Base, Gorham, 3 ½ In., Pair	72.00
Silver, Conical Stem, Reeded Collar & Rim, Spreading Reeded Foot, Czechoslovakia, c.1921, 12 In.	118.00
Silver, Conical, Clouds, Dragon, Pearl Of Wisdom, Square Stepped Foot, Chinese, 9 In., Pair	8365.00
Silver, Embossed, Scrolling Leaves, Round Foot, Beaded Trim, 1900s, 15 In., Pair	881.00
Silver, Flower Garland, Turned Standard, Denmark, c.1790, 7 ½ In., Pair	1380.00
Silver, George III, Gadrooned Sconce, Tapered Stem, Bat's Wing, Fluted Nozzle, 1766, 10 ½ In., Pair	5629.00
Silver, Heritage, Weighted, Reed & Barton, 12 In., Pair	240.00
Silver, Inverted Bell Shape Cup, Round Tapering Stem, Round Foot, England, 11 In., 4 Piece	2318.00
Silver, Lapis Lazuli, Rope Twist Column, Stepped Square Top, Base, Marked, 9 ¼ In., Pair	920.00
Silver, Neoclassical Style, Urn Nozzles, Fluted Columns, Stepped Base, 1903-06, 9 In., Pair	600.00
Silver, Orchid Pattern, Spread Foot, International, 3 ½ In., Pair	531.00
Silver, Reeded Column & Base, 1792, Ireland, 11 ¼ In., Pair	1770.00
Silver, Reeded Nozzle, Trumpet Base, Paw Feet, Acanthus Banding, Portugal, c.1814, 8 ¾ In., 4 Piece	1838.00
Silver, Reeded Shaft, Durgin, Gorham, 9 ½ In., Pair	531.00
Silver, Renaissance Revival, Embossed, Heraldic Crest, Dutch, c.1851, 8 ½ In., Pair *illus*	13035.00
Silver, Rococo, Leaves, Flowers, Relich & Co., 10 ½ In.	978.00
Silver, Square Stepped Base, Baluster Shape, Bird Feet, Austria, 23 In., Pair	896.00
Silver, Squared Bobeche, Tulip Shape Candle Cup, Howard & Co., c.1890, 11 In., Pair	1300.00
Silver, Talisman Rose, Frank Whiting, 8 In., Pair	127.00 to 207.00
Silver, Tapered, Chased Flowers, Jennings Silver Co., c.1925, 16 In., Pair	546.00
Silver, Tapered, Incised, Chased Roses, Domed Base, Footed, Mexico, c.1935, 10 ½ In., Pair	799.00
Silver, Tapered, Monogram, Gorham, 14 x 5 In., Pair	299.00
Silver, Tapered, Round Base, Cartier, 10 In., Pair	374.00
Silver, Weighted, S. Kirk & Sons, 3 ¼ In., Pair	175.00
Silver, Winged Figures, Flower Swags, Pierced & Chased, Germany, 7 In., Pair	384.00
Silvered Metal, Art Nouveau Style, Flower Shape, Knop Stem, Arched Feet, 1900s, 10 In., Pair	438.00
Silvered Metal, Figural, Vagabond, Haggard, Supported By Cane, Crutch, 11 In., Pair	1304.00
Spelter, Figural, Musician, Playing Fireplace Tools, Round Base, 12 In., Pair	711.00
Wood, Baluster, Turned, Multicolor, Italy, 26 In., Pair	215.00
Wood, Bulbous, Polychrome, Round Ebonized Base, 50 ½ In.	246.00
Wood, Rococo, Gesso, Carved, Pricket, Italy, 40 x 10 In., Pair	896.00
Wrought Iron, Gothic, Spiral Standard, Domed Openwork Base, Parcel Gilt, 27 ½ x 9 ½ In.	682.00
Wrought Iron, Spiral, Adjustable, Rattail Handle, Scrolled Legs, 11 In.	325.00
Wrought Iron, Spiral, Turned Wood Base, 6 ¾ In., Pair	452.00
Wrought Iron, Wide Drip Plate, Tripod Base, Stamped Samuel Yellin, 21 ¼ x 14 ½ In.	5890.00

CANDLEWICK *items may be listed in the Imperial Glass and Pressed Glass categories.*

CANDY CONTAINERS have been popular since the late Victorian era. Collectors have long favored the glass containers, but now all types, including tin and papier-mache, are collected. Probably the earliest glass container sold commercially was the Liberty Bell made in 1876 for sale at the Centennial Exposition. Thousands of designs were made until the cost became too high in the 1960s. By the late 1970s, reproductions were being made and sold without the candy. Containers listed here are glass unless otherwise described. A Belsnickle is a nineteenth-century figure of Father Christmas. Some candy containers may be listed in Toy or in other categories.

Airplane, Passenger, Original Closure & Paint	350.00

Candlestick, Silver, Arts & Crafts, Bell Shape, Applied Leaves, Scrolls, Bezel Set Cushion Cut Amethysts, Edward Oakes, 4 ¾ In., Pair
$11850.00

Skinner, Inc.

Cover The Earth From Cleveland

The Sherwin-Williams famous logo with the slogan "Cover the Earth" shows a globe covered with dripping paint. But if you look carefully, you will see the paint is not pouring on the North Pole; it is pouring on Cleveland, Ohio, the city where the paint company began 1866.

Candlestick, Silver, Renaissance Revival, Embossed, Heraldic Crest, Dutch, c.1851, 8 ½ In., Pair
$13035.00

Skinner, Inc.

Candy Container, Black Cat, Pumpkin Body, Black Flocking, Paper Face, 8 In. $460.00

Bertoia Auctions

Candy Container, Mouse, Silvertone, Cloth Bag Opens From Bottom, Dresden, Germany, 2 ¼ In. $431.00

Bertoia Auctions

Candy Container, Parrot Head, Silvertone, Gold Trim, Silk Bag, Dresden, Germany, 2 In. $690.00

Bertoia Auctions

Airplane, Glass, Rear Door, Propeller, Painted	90.00
Airplane, Liberty Motor, Tin, Glass, West Glass Co., c.1920, 1 ¼ x 4 ⅛ In.	2464.00
Airplane, P-38 Lightning, Flat Nose, Propeller, Wire Clip, 7 ⅛-In. Wingspan	140.00
Airplane, Spirit Of Goodwill, Original Closure, 4 ¹³⁄₁₆ In.	25.00 to 75.00
Airplane, Spirit Of St. Louis, Glass, Tin, 6 ³⁄₁₆-In. Wingspan	250.00
Airplane, U.S. Army, Red, Cardboard Wing	35.00
Amos 'n' Andy, Open Air Taxi, Victory Glass Co., c.1928, 2 ½ x 4 ½ In.	112.00
Barney Google & Ball, On Pedestal, Original Closure, 3 ¾ In.	180.00
Baseball Player, On Base, Glass, Painted, 5 In.	700.00
Bear On Circus Tub, Original Closure, 4 ¼ In.	300.00
Bellhop, Composition Head, Felt Cap & Outfit, Brass Buttons, Germany, 1930, 12 In.	315.00
Black Cat, Pumpkin Body, Black Flocking, Paper Face, 8 In. *illus*	460.00
Boat, Submarine, Original Closure, Periscope & Flag	250.00
Cannon, Rapid Gun Fire, Glass, Tin, Embossed, 7 ¾ In.	210.00
Car, Limousine, Trunk Spare Tire, Glass, Red Paint, 4 ¹³⁄₁₆ In.	55.00
Car, Sedan, 6 Vents, Painted Wheels, Glass, 2 ¼ x 4 ¼ x 1 ⅝ In.	30.00
Car, West Bros., Limousine, 2 ½ x 4 x 1 ⅞ In.	75.00
Carpet Sweeper, Baby Sweeper, Glass, Wire Handle, 2 ¾ x 2 ⅛ In. Base	300.00
Circus Animals, Clowns, Tin, Blue Ground, Lid, c.1925, 2 ¾ x 2 ½ In.	65.00
Clock, Paper Dial, Crooked Creek, Pa.	600.00
Dog, Papier-Mache, White Fur, Bushy Tail, Shaved Muzzle, Glass Eyes, France, c.1890, 7 In.	431.00
Doll, Baseball Player, Figural, At Bat, 1890s	823.00
Don't Park Here No. 2, Sign, Blue Paint, 4 ½ In.	250.00
Easter Bunny, Yellow Wheels, Green With Pink, Plastic, 6 ½ In.	25.00
Easter Egg, Tin, Chein, 1930s, 5 In.	60.00
Fire Engine, Ladder Truck, Painted Red Fireman, Glass, 2 ¼ x 5 x 1 ½ In.	100.00
Fire Engine, Large Boiler, Original Closure, Green Glass	75.00
Fire Engine, No. 11, Glass, 2 ⅛ x 4 ¾ x 1 ⅜ In.	15.00
Fire Engine, Original Closure, Stough, Tin Wheels, Glass, 1914, 3 ¼ x 5 x 2 In.	80.00
Flossie Fisher's Bed, Glass, Tin Bed Frame, George Borgfeldt Co., c.1916, 3 ¾ In.	3248.00
Grand Piano, Carnival Glass	850.00
Gun, Waisted Grip, Original Closure	15.00
Halloween, Devil, Pitchfork, Cardboard, Red & Black, Head Turns, 8 ¼ In.	240.00
Halloween, Jack-O'-Lantern, Glass Bead Eyes, Germany, 1920s, 4 x 3 ½ In.	150.00
Halloween, Jack-O'-Lantern, Pop Eyed, Tin Ring, Bail Handle	150.00
Harmonica, Sweettone	35.00
Jackie Coogan, Original Closure, Milk Glass, 5 In.	35.00
Jackie Coogan, Original Closure, Rose Color, 5 In.	35.00
Jeep, Willys-Overland, Original Closure	25.00
Jester, Papier-Mache, Pointed Hat, Silk Outfit, Metallic Paper Trim, Bells, c.1850, 4 In.	144.00
Kaleidoscope, Revolving Glass Tube, Tin, West Bros. Co., Journey G. Stough, c.1913, 7 In.	17550.00
Kewpie, By Barrel, Geo. Bergfeldt, 3 In.	50.00
Man In Top Hat, Cardboard, On A Spring, Sways, Germany, 1960, 9 In.	70.00
Man On Motorcycle, Sidecar, Victory Glass.	190.00
Merry Christmas From Santa, Old Lady, Shoe, Children, Cat, Fiddle, Handle, Tin, 1920s, 4 ½ In.	210.00
Mouse, Silvertone, Cloth Bag Opens From Bottom, Dresden, Germany, 2 ¼ In. *illus*	431.00
Owl, Original Closure, White Paint, Gold Color Screw Cap, 4 ⅜ In.	100.00
Pail, Tin Lithograph, Red Riding Hood & Wolf, c.1915, 4 Oz.	100.00
Parrot Head, Silvertone, Gold Trim, Silk Bag, Dresden, Germany, 2 In. *illus*	690.00
PEZ, Air Spirit, Eerie Spectres Series, Red, 1970s, 4 ¼ In.	127.00
PEZ, Casper The Friendly Ghost, Die Cut Stem, Austria, 1960s, 4 ¼ In.	86.00
PEZ, Diabolic, Eerie Spectres Series, Black Stem, 1970s, 4 ¼ In.	115.00
PEZ, Easter Bunny, Lavender, Ivory Head Top, A Style, Austria, 1950s, 4 ½ In.	115.00
PEZ, Frankenstein, Austria, 1960s, 4 ¼ In.	153.00
PEZ, Lions Club, Lion Head, Generic Stem, Convention, Nice, France, 1962, 4 In. *illus*	894.00
PEZ, Psychedelic Eye In Hand, Luv Pez, Late 1960s, 4 ¼ In. *illus*	380.00
PEZ, Santa Claus, Loop Ornament, No Feet, 1970s	25.00
PEZ, Scarewolf, Eerie Spectres Series, Purple Stem, 1970s, 4 ¼ In.	115.00
PEZ, Space Gun, Red Plastic, Permit	173.00
PEZ, Spaceman, Light Blue, 1950s, 4 ¼ In. *illus*	106.00
PEZ, Vamp, Eerie Spectres Series, Blue Stem, 1970s, 4 ¼ In.	153.00
PEZ, Zombie, Eerie Spectres Series, Orange Stem, 1970s, 4 ¼ In.	115.00
Pig, Pink, Pressed Paper, Glass Eyes & Nose, Pink, Germany, c.1890, 2 ¾ In.	150.00
Policeman, Pumpkin Head, Glass, c.1920, 4 ¾ x 2 ¼ In.	1512.00
Powder Horn, Hanger, Open At Large End, Ribbed, Prisms, Bands	20.00
Rabbit Pushing Chick In Shell Cart, Blue Tint, 3 ⅞ x 4 x 1 ⅝ In.	175.00

Rabbit With Wheelbarrow, Original Closure, Scroll Design On Base, 4 ¼ In.	100.00
Racer, Strough's, Original Cork Closure, Glass, 3 ¾ In.	100.00
Rocking Horse, Clown, Rider, Original Closure, 4 ¾ In.	125.00
Rolling Pin, Wood Handles, Metal Caps, Glass Center, 7 In.	70.00
Rooster, Original Closure & Paint	150.00
Santa Claus, Banded Coat	45.00
Santa Claus, Composition, Holly Branch, Fur Beard, Hair, Felt Clothes, 1920s, 15 In.	2242.00
Santa Claus, Double Cuff, Hands Together, Original Closure, 4 ⅜ In.	75.00
Santa Claus, Leaving Chimney, 5 In.	75.00
Santa Claus, Standing, Rabbit Fur Coat, Holding Tree, 10 In.	600.00
Soldier By Tent, World War I Doughboy Uniform, Original Closure, 1920s, 3 ¼ x 3 ⅜ In.	1680.00
Suitcase, Park Scene Decal, Milk Glass	150.00
Swan Boat, Rabbit & Chick Riding Inside, Victory Glass Co., Early 1900s, 2 ⅝ x 4 ¼ In.	1120.00
Telephone, Wood Transmitter No. 3, Original Closure, T.H. Stough, 4 ⅝ In.	75.00
Top, Glass Spinning Top, Winder, 4 ⅝ In.	55.00
Village, Church With Square Steeple, Tin Shell, Die Cut, 3 ½ In.	40.00
Village, Confectionery, Tin Shell, Die Cut, 2 ⅞ In.	20.00
Village, Drug Store, Tin Shell, Die Cut, 2 ⅞ In.	20.00
Village, Princess Theatre, Tin Shell, Die Cut, 2 ⅞ In.	20.00
Village, Schoolhouse, Flag, Tin Shell, 2 ¾ In.	20.00
Wheelbarrow, Glass, 6 In.	15.00
Windmill, Candy Guaranteed, Open Tower Top, Yellow Blades, Pewter Top	525.00

CANES and walking sticks were used by every well-dressed man in the nineteenth century, but by World War I the style had changed. Today canes are used by few but the infirm. Collectors prize old canes made with special features, like hidden swords, whiskey flasks, or risqué pictures seen through peepholes. Examples with solid gold heads or made from exotic materials are among the higher-priced canes. See also Scrimshaw.

Aqua, Square, Right Angle Handle, Twisted Bend, Tip, 32 In.	30.00
Automaton, Horse Head, Amber Glass Eye, Malacca Shift, 36 In.	920.00
Bakelite, Orange, Free-Form Handle, Turquoise Stone, Gold Metal Collar, 36 In.	1315.00
Bentwood, Rolled Over Handle, Carved Snake's Head, Shenandoah Valley, c.1875, 32 In.	259.00
Bird Grip, Wood Carved, Painted, Schtockschnitzler Simmons, Pa., c.1900, 35 In.	1185.00
Brass, Copper, Sword, Mushroom Knob Handle, Chinese Decoration, c.1920, 33 ¼ In.	590.00
Bulldog, Ivory, Amber Glass Eyes, Chased Gold Metal Collar, Hardwood Shaft, 36 In.	1315.00
Carved, Long Billed Bird's Head Handle, Rhinestone Eyes, Snake, Face Shaft, Paint, c.1920, 37 In.	881.00
Carved, Snake Handle, Mexico, 32 In.	225.00
Compass, Rose Gold Handle, Paneled, Snakewood Shaft, c.1862, 35 ¾ In.	6612.00
Copper Quartz Ore Knob Head, Cactus Shaft, Silver Band, Bisbee, Ariz., U.S.A.	1500.00
Dog's Head Grip, American Eagle, Stag, Horse Design, Pa., c.1900, 34 ¾ In.	533.00
Dog's Head Handle, Collar, Brampton Stoneware, Light Brown Glaze, Derbyshire, c.1840, 3 ¼ In.	701.00
Fish Vertebrae, Silver Collar, Engraved, 36 In.	444.00
Folk Art, Man, Flat Hat, Looking Up, Crooked Shaft, Hardwood, c.1890, 35 In.	383.00
Folk Art, Soldier, Musket, 1879, 18 ½ In.	420.00
French Bulldog, Smoky Quartz, Blue Sapphire Eyes, Silver Collar, c.1891, 38 In.	1972.00
Frog, Seated, On Sphere, Silver Collar, Wood Shaft, Brass Ferrule, 38 In.	2868.00
Glass, Aqua, Crooked, Spiral Reeding, 35 In.	35.00
Grapevine, Ivory, Clusters, Leaves, Ebonized Hardwood Shaft, 36 In.	1673.00
Gun Curio, Eagle Claw Holding Ball, Remington Gun, Gutta Percha, c.1858, 36 In.	12650.00
Hand Clenching Baton, Mahogany, Ivory Ferrule, c.1875, 35 ½ In.	206.00
Hardwood Shaft, Copper Baseball Knob, c.1900, 35 In.	575.00
Horn Handle, Tiger Maple, 8-Sided Shaft, Carved CT, Horn End Tip, c.1870, 38 In.	161.00
Horse & Dog Head Grip, Vines & Strawberries On Shaft, Brass Ferrule, 34 In.	113.00
Ivory Figure, Carved Stag, Wood, 36 ½ In.	234.00
Ivory Handle, Dog Head, Glass Eyes, Gold Plated Brass Collar, Monogram, 1800s	1195.00
Ivory Handle, Malacca Shaft, Scalloped Silver Collar, c.1697, 41 In.	2300.00
Ivory Handle, Stepped Partridgewood, Art Deco Style, 1920s, 33 ⅔ In.	402.00
Ivory Handle, Wild Boar, Sulphite Eyes, Rosewood Shaft, c.1895, 35 In.	2185.00
Ivory, Carved Hand, Inset Ring Stones, Cudgel, Cartouche, Silver Collar, Brass Ferrule, 1800s	615.00
Ivory, Carved Hound Handle, Gold Band, Inscribed, A.G. Walton, 34 In.	593.00
Ivory, Flower Ball Handle, Snakewood Shaft, c.1885, 35 ⅓ In.	501.00
Malacca, Python Snakeskin, Brass Ferrule, c.1910, 34 In.	805.00
Maple, Bird Handle, Glass Eyes, Snake Carved Shaft, Green Paint, c.1900, 36 ½ In. ....*illus*	88.00
Maple, Crook Handle, Stylized Faces, Leaves, Snakes, Lizards, 1924, 35 ½ In.	118.00
Meissen Handle, Songbirds, Branches, Leaves, Mahogany Shaft, Black Horn Ferrule, 33 In.	501.00
Musical, Flute, Ivory Knob, Metal Collar, Ebonized Hardwood, 35 In.	4481.00

C

Candy Container, PEZ, Lions Club, Lion Head, Generic Stem, Convention, Nice, France, 1962, 4 In.
$894.00

Hake's Americana & Collectibles

Candy Container, PEZ, Psychedelic Eye In Hand, Luv Pez, Late 1960s, 4 ¼ In.
$380.00

Hake's Americana & Collectibles

Candy Container, PEZ, Spaceman, Light Blue, 1950s, 4 ¼ In.
$106.00

Serious Toyz

C

Cane, Maple, Bird Handle, Glass Eyes, Snake Carved Shaft, Green Paint, c.1900, 36 ½ In.
$88.00

Garth's Auctions, Inc.

Cane, Wood, Foot Handle, Snake On Shaft, Black Paint, c.1900, 32 ¾ In.
$118.00

Garth's Auctions, Inc.

Cane, Wood, Stout, Snake, Painted, c.1900, 36 In.
$294.00

Garth's Auctions, Inc.

Painted Grip, Shaft Carved Animals, Pa., c.1900, 37 ¾ In.	326.00
Perfume Vial, Double, Green Glass, Hinged Caps, Silvered Metal Collar, 35 In.	508.00
Pink Shagreen Handle, Birch Shaft, Brass Collar, c.1915, 36 ½ In.	575.00
Presentation, Measuring Tool For Horses In Hands, To Zack Miller, 101 Ranch, 1925, 39 In.	1320.00
Puzzle, Bulbous Knob, Grooved Collar, Pieced Shaft, Glass Beads, 33 In.	177.00
Silver Cylinder Head, Contains Shaving Brush & Razor	950.00
Swagger Stick, Art Deco, Rosewood, Sterling Silver Cap, Monogram, 28 In.	110.00
Tortoiseshell, Mahogany, Wood Dome, Liquid Receptacle, Brass Cup, c.1890, 36 In.	708.00
Walking Stick, Antler Handle, Steel Parasol Shaft, Flowers, Bird, 36 In.	495.00
Walking Stick, Carved Head, Large Nose & Ears, Ceramic Eyes, Folk Art, 82 ½ In.	403.00
Walking Stick, Carved, Groundhog Pommel, 36 In.	181.00
Walking Stick, Ebony, Gold Filled Handle, Victorian, 19th Century, 36 In.	295.00
Walking Stick, Ebony, Gold Handle, Mark K & H, 36 ½ In.	374.00
Walking Stick, Elm, Ivory Handle, Angry Birds, Fruit Flowers, Gilt Collar, Bone Tip, c.1880, 35 In.	338.00
Walking Stick, Folk Art, Double Faced Finial, Diamonds, Twisting, c.1875, 37 In.	715.00
Walking Stick, Ivory & Silver Handle, c.1900, 36 In.	327.00
Walking Stick, Ivory, Cluster Of Human Skulls, Mahogany, Brass, 37 In.	215.00
Walking Stick, Ivory, Eagle's Head, Mouse In Beak, Mahogany Shaft, Brass Mount, 36 In.	400.00
Walking Stick, Ivory, Lion's Head, Mahogany Shaft, Brass Collar & Ferrule, 35 In.	399.00
Walking Stick, Ivory, Owl's Head, Rope Twist Mahogany Shaft, Brass Collar, 37 In.	399.00
Walking Stick, Ivory, Pharaoh's Horses, 3 Horse's Heads, Mahogany, Brass Mount, 35 In.	400.00
Walking Stick, Ivory, Silver Overlay, Senator Wolcott, Scrolled Band, Textured Wood, c.1892, 35 In.	518.00
Walking Stick, Maple, Ebony Handle, Gripping Hand Shape, Whalebone, 1800s, 36 In.	489.00
Walking Stick, Rosewood, Scrimshaw Ivory, Starfish, Spiral Twist Shaft, Engraved FJT, c.1855, 38 In.	6613.00
Walking Stick, Silver Horse Head, Wood Shaft, Brass Tip, Italy, 37 ¾ x 4 ½ In.	345.00
Walking Stick, Stag Antler, Carved Dog's Head Profile, Silver Mounted, c.1890, 4 ¼ In.	127.00
Wood, Carved, Frog, Snake, Twisted Shaft, Knob End, 32 In.	1610.00
Wood, Foot Handle, Snake On Shaft, Black Paint, c.1900, 32 ¾ In. *illus*	118.00
Wood, Horse Leg Grip, Carved, Painted, Pa., c.1900, 35 In.	178.00
Wood, Jockey Head, Carved, Painted, 36 In.	129.00
Wood, Stout, Snake, Painted, c.1900, 36 In. *illus*	294.00

CANTON CHINA is blue-and-white ware made near the city of Canton, in China, from about 1795 to the early 1900s. It is hand decorated with a landscape, building, bridge, and trees. There is never a person on the bridge. The "rain and cloud" border was used. It is similar to Nanking ware, which is listed in this book in its own category.

Basket, Underplate, Reticulated, Round, Shallow Handles, Flared Rim, 4 ¾ x 9 ¾ In.	575.00
Bowl, Lotus Blossom, 18th Century, 4 x 12 In.	265.00
Bowl, Pagoda, Lattice Inside Rim, 3 ¼ x 6 ½ In.	150.00
Bowl, Petal Shape, 1800s, 11 In.	403.00
Bowl, Salad, Notched Corner, c.1835, 5 x 9 ½ In., Pair	738.00
Bowl, Scalloped, 11 In.	210.00
Bowl, Vegetable, Cover, Village Scene, Flowers, Round, 1800s, 9 In.	92.00
Canister, Square, 19th Century, 6 x 6 In.	717.00
Chestnut Basket, Pierced Sides, Blue Out-Turned Rim, 3 ½ x 8 ¾ In.	115.00
Cider Jug, Foo Dog Finial, 1800s, 6 ½ In.	431.00
Cider Jug, Pagodas, Mountains, Loop Handle, Wide Spout, 1800s, 6 ½ In.	920.00
Dish, Octagonal, Deep, Late 1800s, 11 x 14 In.	237.00
Dish, Square, Shaped Rim, Riverscape, Pagodas, Boat, 1900s, 2 x 9 In.	89.00
Plate, Strainer, Canton Rose, Butterflies, Flowers, Round, c.1815, 2 ¾ x 18 ½ In.	1315.00
Platter, c.1850, 10 ½ x 13 ¾ In.	230.00
Platter, Octagonal, Island & Bridge, Sloped Corners, 1800s, 18 ⅜ x 15 In.	384.00
Platter, Slanted Corners, Rectangular, 11 x 13 ½ In.	345.00
Platter, Well & Tree, 1800s, 14 In.	374.00
Platter, Well & Tree, c.1810, 16 ¾ In.	269.00
Tureen, Sauce, Undertray, 1800s, 5 x 8 In.	345.00
Tureen, Soup, Cover, Riverscape, 2 Handles, Finial, c.1800, 12 In.	478.00

CAPO-DI-MONTE porcelain was first made in Naples, Italy, from 1743 to 1759. The factory moved near Madrid, Spain, reopened in 1771, and worked to 1821. Since that time, the Doccia factory of Italy acquired the molds and is using the crown and *N* mark. Societa Ceramica Richard is a modern-day firm often referred to as Ginori or Capo-di-Monte. This company also uses the crown and *N* mark.

Box, Cherubs, Flowers, Embossed, Marked, 2 x 3 In.	86.00
Box, Coffer Shape, Medieval Procession, Knights At Battle, Scroll Feet, 6 x 10 In.	554.00

Box, Ormolu Frame, Paw Feet, Figures, Leaves, Gold Ribbons, Green, 12 x 9 In.	546.00	
Bust, Young Boy, White Bisque, Cobalt Blue Porcelain Base, Marked Puci, 8 In.	40.00	
Centerpiece, Putti, Pulling Cart, 5 x 5 x 9 In.	221.00	
Figurine, Basket Of Flowers, Pink, Blue, Yellow Roses, Leaves, Marked, Italy, 13 x 17 In.	58.00	
Figurine, Horse, 12 x 11 In.	118.00	
Figurine, Horse, White, Wood Base, 9 x 12 In.	148.00	
Figurine, Sleigh, Swan, Flowers, Multicolor, 10 ½ x 15 In.	575.00	
Flagon, Hinge Lid, Figures, Carrying Flowers, Rope Twist Handle, Multicolor, Italy, c.1890, 18 In.	1880.00	
Garniture, Round, Segmented, Classical Maidens, 9 In.	527.00	
Jewelry Box, Architectural & Figure Panels, Brass Mounts, Italy, 1800s, 13 ½ x 18 In.	780.00	
Lamp, Swirled Black, Green, Tiered Metal Base, Dolphin Feet, Black Shaded, 32 x 10 In., Pair	138.00	
Lamp, Winged Women, Seated, Pierced Metal Base, Painted Fringe Shade, 15 x 27 In., Pair....	259.00	
Ring Box, White Bisque, Peach Flower, Burgundy Stamen, Green Leaves, 2 ⅛ x 1 ¾ In.	45.00	
Stein, Putti Finial, Winged Mermaid Handle, Gilt Accents, Figures, Trees, 10 In.	403.00	
Urn, Classical Figures In Cartouches, Ram's Head Handles, Pedestal Base, 12In., Pair	590.00	
Urn, Cover, Baluster, Mythological Figure Handles, Footed, 14 In.	310.00	
Urn, Cover, Handles, Family Scene, Cherub Knob, 20 x 14 In.	236.00	
Urn, Goat Mask Handles, 11 In., Pair	183.00	
Urn, Mermaid Handles, Footed, 20 ½ In.	590.00	
Vase, Cover, Stand, Scroll Snake Handles, Gilded Trim, Courtyard Scenes, Flowers, c.1890, 37 In.	490.00	
Vase, Frolicking Cherubs, Gilt Detail, 5 ¾ In.	*illus*	72.00
Vase, Lid, Crown On Cushion, Ram Mask, Figures In Relief, 12 ½ In.	*illus*	274.00
Vase, Mantel, Urn Shape, Gilt Enamel, Women Bearing Offerings, Square Base, 11 In., Pair ...	711.00	
Wedding Cup, Pedestal Base, Trophy Shape, 2 Handles, Figures, Gilt, 6 x 7 In.	92.00	
Wine Dispenser, Cover, 17 x 9 In.	236.00	

CAPTAIN MARVEL was introduced in February 1940 in Whiz comic books. An orphan named Billy Batson met the wizard, Shazam, and whenever he said the magic word he was transformed into a superhero. A movie serial was released in 1940. The comic was discontinued in 1954. A second Captain Marvel appeared in 1966, a third in 1967. Only the original was transformed by shouting "Shazam."

Figure, Captain Marvel Jr., Base, Plastic, Painted, Box, Kerr Co., 6 ¼ In.	*illus*	569.00
Ring, Compass, Rocket Raider, c.1946		460.00
Wristwatch, Flying Marvel Jr., Luminous, Vinyl-Covered Leather, Fawcett, 1948	*illus*	746.00

CAPTAIN MIDNIGHT began as a network radio show in September 1940. The first comic book appeared in July 1941. Captain Midnight was really the aviator Captain Albright, who was to defeat the Nazis. A movie serial was made in 1942 and a comic strip was published for a short time. The comic book version of Captain Midnight ended his career in 1948. Radio premiums are the prized collector memorabilia today.

Badge, Flight Commander, Mailer, Secret Squadron Commission, 1 ½ In.	173.00
Dog Whistle, 3-Way Mystery, Slides Open, Metal, Mailer, 1940, 5 In.	251.00
Jet Plane Decoder, Silver Dart, Silver Plastic, Red Nose Piece, 1957, 2 ½ In.	95.00
Patch, Insignia, Wings On Sides, Fabric, Mailer, 3 ¼ In.	253.00
Ring, Marine Corps Insignia, Goldtone Metal, Mailer, Story Folder, 1942	438.00
Ring, Mystic Sun God, Beveled Red Stone, Aztec Designs, Brass, Ovaltine Premium, 1946	810.00
Ring, Mystic-Eye, Eagle, Star, Chevrons, Brass, Adjustable, Mailer	285.00
Ring, Secret Compartment, Brass, Shield, Star, Wings On Sides, 1942	115.00
Ring, Whirlwind Whistling, Brass, Wing Design, Ovaltine Premium, Mailer, 1941	506.00

CARAMEL SLAG, see *Imperial Glass* category.

CARDS listed here include advertising cards (often called trade cards), baseball cards, playing cards, and others. Color photographs were rare in the nineteenth century, so companies gave away colorful cards with pictures of children, flowers, products, or related scenes that promoted the company name. These were often collected and stored in albums. Baseball cards also date from the nineteenth century, when they were used by tobacco companies as giveaways. Gum cards were started in 1933, but it was not until after World War II that the bubble gum cards favored today were produced. Today over 1,000 cards are issued each year by the gum companies. Related items may be found in the Christmas, Halloween, Movie, Paper, and Postcard categories.

Advertising, Humpty Dumpty Mechanical Bank, Shepard Hardware Co., 5 ½ x 3 ½ In.	*illus*	440.00
Baseball, Addie Joss, American Caramel, 1909-11		1058.00
Baseball, Addie Joss, T-205, Gold Border		944.00
Baseball, Al Mays, Kalamazoo Bats, 1887		8813.00

Capo-Di-Monte, Vase, Frolicking Cherubs, Gilt Detail, 5 ¾ In. $72.00

DuMouchelles Art Gallery

Capo-Di-Monte, Vase, Lid, Crown On Cushion, Ram Mask, Figures In Relief, 12 ½ In. $274.00

Leslie Hindman Auctioneers

TIP

If you are searching flea markets and yard sales, don't offer too little for a treasure. Being too cheap will mean that you may not hear about the other similar items that are not yet set out for sale. Offer a low but fair price, usually 20 percent off the market price.

Captain Marvel, Figure, Captain Marvel Jr., Base, Plastic, Painted, Box, Kerr Co., 6 ¼ In.
$569.00

Hake's Americana & Collectibles

Captain Marvel, Wristwatch, Flying Marvel Jr., Luminous, Vinyl-Covered Leather, Fawcett, 1948
$746.00

Hake's Americana & Collectibles

TIP

Replace broken or scratched watch crystals immediately. The crack may let moisture get to the works, and soon your watch will not tell time accurately.

Baseball, Babe Ruth, American Caramel, 1922	2350.00
Baseball, Babe Ruth, W-514, No. 2	767.00
Baseball, Clark Griffith, Cracker Jack, 1915	2644.00
Baseball, Cy Young, Portrait, Sovereign, 1909-11	1410.00
Baseball, Cy Young, T-205, Gold Border	519.00
Baseball, Jackie Robinson, Portrait, Bond Bread, 1947	1528.00
Baseball, Joe DiMaggio, Zeenut, Tab, 1935	14100.00
Baseball, Louis Lowdermilk, Red Cross Tobacco, Brown Background, 1912	21150.00
Baseball, Mickey Mantle Rookie, At Bat, Bowman, 1951	4700.00
Baseball, Mickey Mantle, Topps, No. 150 ....*illus*	305.00
Baseball, Mickey Mantle, Topps, No. 311, 1952	22325.00
Baseball, Mordecai Brown, T-205, Gold Border	425.00
Baseball, Sandy Koufax, Brooklyn Dodgers, Rookie, Topps, 1955	2350.00
Baseball, Topps Complete Set, 1967, 609 Cards	5015.00
Baseball, Tris Speaker, T-205, Gold Border	378.00
Baseball, Ty Cobb, T-206, Red Background, Polar Bear Back	566.00
Baseball, Walter Johnson, W-514, No. 94	295.00
Baseball, Willie Mays, Topps, 1952	2233.00
Basketball, Michael Jordan, Rookie, Signed, Chicago Bulls, Star, 1984-85	2644.00
Boxing, Jack Johnson, Turkey Red, 1911	940.00
Cigarette, Player's, Album Of Stars, 2nd Series, John Player & Sons, 1930s, 5 x 7 ¼ In.	36.00
Football, Knute Rockne, National Chicle, 1935	1058.00
Greeting, Valentine, Civil War, Soldier, Family, Embossed, Hand Colored, c.1861, 4 x 7 In.	707.00
Greeting, Valentine, Cruise Ship, Fold-Out, Blue, 12 In.	86.00
Greeting, Valentine, Die Cut, Embossed, Girl, Boy Inflating Heart, Germany, 4 ¾ In.	15.00
Greeting, Valentine, Lithograph, Embossed, Parchment, Glitter, Lace, Whitney, c.1899, 8 x 14 In.	83.00
Greeting, Valentine, Little Black Girl Maid, 1939, 3 ½ x 5 ½ In.	10.00
Greeting, Valentine, Omnibus, Dimensional, Lithograph, Embossed, Honeycomb Roof, 11 x 9 In.	531.00
Greeting, Valentine, Pinprick, Laid Paper, Hearts, Birds, Flowers, c.1830, 11 ½ x 10 ¼ In.	264.00
Greeting, Valentine, Sailboat, Children, Fold-Out, 12 In.	194.00
Greeting, Valentine, Ship, Couple, Child, Crepe Paper, Fold-Out 11 In.	86.00
Greeting, Valentine, Steamship, Dimensional, Lithograph, Embossed, Honeycomb, 12 x 12 In., Pair	205.00
Greeting, Valentine, Web, Rose, Leaves, Hand Colored, c.1850, 4 ½ x 7 ¼ In.	177.00
Trading, Bound For Mercury, Jets, Rockets, Spacemen Bowman, 1951, 6 ⅛ x 7 In.	1880.00

CARDER, *see Aurene and Steuben categories.*

CARLSBAD is a mark found on china made by several factories in Germany, Austria, and Bavaria. Many pieces were exported to the United States. Most of the pieces available today were made after 1891.

Vase, Flowers, Water Lilies, White Ground, 6 In.	12.00

CARLTON WARE was made at the Carlton Works of Stoke-on-Trent, England, beginning about 1890. The firm traded as Wiltshaw & Robinson until 1957. It was renamed Carlton Ware Ltd. in 1958. The company went bankrupt in 1995, but the name is still in use.

Biscuit Jar, Arvista, Flow Blue, Silver Plate Lid, Bail Handle, 6 ½ In.	75.00
Biscuit Jar, Burmese, Cobalt Blue Trim, Wild Flowers, Silver Plate Lid, Handle, 8 In.	100.00
Biscuit Jar, Classical Scene Relief, Green, White, Silver Plate Lid, Bail Handle, 6 ¾ In.	60.00
Biscuit Jar, Dutch Mill, Sailboat Scene, Flow Blue, Embossed Silver Plate Lid, Bail, 8 In.	60.00
Biscuit Jar, Floral & Leaf, Cream, Silver Plate Lid & Bail, 6 ½ In.	70.00
Pitcher, Abstract, Marked, Black Slip, 7 In. ....*illus*	518.00
Vase, Birds Of Paradise, Art Deco Orange, Burgundy Ground, Flared Rim, Footed, 10 x 5 In.	483.00
Vase, Delphinium, White, Pink Ground, c.1934, 5 In.	295.00
Vase, Flower Branches, Globular, c.1930	190.00
Vase, Garden, Daisies, Globular, c.1930, 5 ½ In.	300.00
Vase, Vert Royale, Leaves, Flowers, Butterflies, Spider, Trumpet Shape, Round Foot, 5 ¾ In.	196.00

CARNIVAL GLASS was an inexpensive, iridescent pressed glass made from about 1907 to about 1925. More than 1,000 different patterns are known. Carnival glass is currently being reproduced. Additional pieces may be found in the Northwood category.

Acanthus, Plate, Smoke Iridescent, 11 In.	175.00
Acorn Burrs, Pitcher, Water, Green	300.00
Acorn Burrs, Punch Set, Frost White, 8 Piece	3000.00

C

Acorn Burrs, Punch Set, Ice Blue, 8 Piece	13000.00
Acorn Burrs, Punch Set, Purple, 10 Piece	1050.00
Acorn Burrs, Spooner, Purple	35.00
Acorn, Bowl, Red & Silver Iridescent, Ruffled Edge, Fenton, 7 ½ In.	472.00
April Showers, Vase, Amethyst, 11 ½ In.	30.00
April Showers, Vase, Green, 11 ½ In.	30.00
Australian Kingfisher, Bowl, Master, Marigold, Ruffled Edge	95.00
Autumn Acorn, Plate, Blue, Fenton, c.1910, 9 In.	916.00
Basketweave, Basket, Marigold, 2 Sides Up	20.00
Basketweave, Basket, Ruffled Edge, Open Edge, Red	80.00
Basketweave, Bowl, Blue, Jack-In-The-Pulpit Shape, Fenton, 5 ¾ In.	60.00
Beaded Bull's-Eye, Vase, Purple, Flared, 11 In.	120.00
Beaded Cable, Rose Bowl, Aqua Opalescent	115.00 to 185.00
Beaded Cable, Rose Bowl, White	110.00
Beaded Shell, Spooner, Marigold	20.00
Bells & Beads, Bowl, Peach Opal, Crimped Edge, 7 In.	40.00
Birds & Cherries, Bonbon, Green, Card Tray Shape, Handles	135.00
Blackberry Spray, Bowl, Red, Jack-In-The-Pulpit, 6 ½ In.	200.00
Blackberry Spray, Hat, Ruffled Edge, Aqua Opalescent	220.00
Blackberry Spray, Hat, Ruffled Edge, Red	140.00
Blackberry, Basket, Green, Ruffled Edge, Open Edge	100.00
Blackberry, Vase, Open Edge, Blue, 7 ½ In.	375.00
Blackberry, Vase, Open Edge, Marigold, 9 ¼ In.	275.00
Brocaded Acorns, Vase, Fan Shape, Lavender, 8 ½ In.	500.00
Brocaded Palms, Dish, Mayonnaise, Pink	135.00
Broken Arches, Punch Set, Marigold, 14 Piece	200.00
Broken Arches, Punch Set, Purple, 10 Piece	1050.00
Butterfly & Fern, Water Set, Marigold, 7 Piece	210.00
Butterfly & Tulip, Bowl, Purple, Ruffled Edge, Footed, Square	850.00
Butterfly & Tulip, Bowl, Purple, Square, Footed	2400.00
Cannon Ball, Pitcher, Ice Green	45.00
Captive Rose, Plate, Blue, 9 In.	195.00
Captive Rose, Plate, Green, 9 In.	115.00 to 400.00
Captive Rose, Plate, Marigold, 9 In.	200.00
Circle Scroll, Spooner, Purple	75.00
Cobblestone, Bowl, Purple, Ruffled Edge	275.00
Cobblestone, Bowl, Ruffled Edge, Purple	145.00
Coin Spot, Compote, Ruffled Edge, Celeste Blue	300.00
Colonial, Candlestick, Celeste, 8 ½ In., Pair	120.00
Colonial, Candlestick, Russet, 8 ½ In., Pair	45.00
Columbia, Compote, Marigold, Ruffled Edge, Imperial	55.00
Columbia, Compote, Purple, Ruffled Edge	220.00
Concord, Bowl, Amethyst, 3-In-1 Edge	175.00
Constellation, Compote, White, Ruffled Edge	45.00
Corn, Bottle, Green	100.00
Cosmos & Cane, Compote, Cuspidor Shape, Marigold	500.00
Cosmos & Cane, Compote, Cuspidor Shape, Purple	3800.00
Cosmos & Cane, Compote, Honey Amber, Ruffled	230.00
Country Kitchen, Bowl, Square, White, Millersburg, 7 In.	105.00
Curved Star, Vase, Blue, 9 In.	130.00
Dahlia, Table Set, Amethyst, 4 Piece	350.00
Daisy & Drape, Vase, Aqua Opalescent	300.00
Daisy & Drape, Vase, Marigold, Footed, Flared, Scalloped Rim	275.00
Decorama, Tumbler, Marigold, Footed, Square	65.00
Diamond & Column, Vase, Amethyst, 14 In.	8.00
Diamond & Column, Vase, Marigold, 5 In.	23.00
Diamond & Sunburst, Wine Set, Purple, 6 Piece	300.00
Diamond Cut Shields, Pitcher, Water, Marigold	20.00
Diamond Lace, Water Set, Purple, 5 Piece	195.00
Diamond Point, Vase, Ice Blue, 11 In.	225.00
Diamond Point, Vase, Purple, 10 ½ In.	70.00
Diamond Point, Vase, Purple, Squat, 7 In.	55.00
Diamond Point Columns, Vase, Marigold, 5 ½ In. ....illus	$15.00
Diamond Ring, Rose Bowl, Marigold	10.00
Diving Dolphins, Rose Bowl, Marigold	125.00
Dogwood Sprays, Bowl, Peach Opalescent, Ruffled Edge, Footed, Dome	20.00

Card, Advertising, Humpty Dumpty Mechanical Bank, Shepard Hardware Co., 5 ½ x 3 ½ In.
$440.00

Wm Morford Antiques

Card, Baseball, Mickey Mantle, Topps, No. 150
$305.00

Philip Weiss Auctions

Carlton Ware, Pitcher, Abstract, Marked, Black Slip, 7 In.
$518.00

Humler & Nolan

Carnival Glass, Diamond Point Columns, Vase, Marigold, 5 ½ In.
$15.00

Carnival Glass, Good Luck, Bowl, Green, Piecrust Edge, Basketweave Back
$170.00

Carnival Glass, Grapevine Lattice, Tumbler, Marigold
$15.00

Carnival Glass, Hobstar, Sugar, Cover, Green, Marked IG
$15.00

Carnival Glass, Holly, Bowl, Red, Ruffled Edge
$275.00

Carnival Glass, Imperial Grape, Bowl, Purple, Ruffled Edge
$80.00

Dragon & Lotus, Bowl, Marigold, 9 In.	35.00
Dragon & Lotus, Bowl, Ruffled Edge, Amethyst	50.00
Dragon & Lotus, Bowl, Ruffled Edge, Aqua Opalescent	600.00
Dragon & Lotus, Bowl, Ruffled Edge, Cherry Red	1050.00
Drapery, Candy Dish, Blue	125.00
Drapery, Candy Dish, Green	225.00
Drapery, Candy Dish, Marigold	60.00
Drapery, Candy Dish, Purple	85.00
Drapery, Rose Bowl, Aqua	155.00
Drapery, Vase, Lime Green, 8 In.	155.00
Estate, Sugar & Creamer, Peach Opalescent	60.00
Fan, Gravy Boat, Peach Opalescent	15.00
Fantail, Bowl, Blue, Footed, Ruffled Edge	2000.00
Fantail, Chop Plate, Footed, Marigold	2100.00
Farmyard, Bowl, Purple, Ruffled Edge, 8 In.	9000.00
Farmyard, Bowl, Ruffled Edge, Purple Iridescent, 6 Ruffles	3750.00
Feathered Serpent, Bowl, Amethyst, Ruffled Edge, 10 In.	80.00
Field Flower, Tumbler, Marigold	20.00
Fine Cut & Roses, Rose Bowl, Footed, Ice Blue	150.00
Fisherman's Mug, Amethyst, Silver Iridescence, 4 In.	40.00
Fishscale & Beads, Plate, White, 6 In.	10.00
Floral & Grape, Water Set, Blue, 7 Piece	125.00
Florentine, Candlestick, Celeste Blue, 10 ½ In., Pair	85.00
Florentine, Candlestick, Ice Green, 8 ½ In., Pair	85.00
Florentine, Candlestick, Lavender, 8 ½ In., Pair	210.00
Four Flowers, Plate, Peach Opal, 6 In.	45.00
Four Pillars, Vase, Green, Ruffled Edge, 11 In.	125.00
Four Seventy Four, Punch Set, Emerald Green, 7 Piece	3700.00
Fruits & Flowers, Bonbon, Blue	65.00
Fruits & Flowers, Bonbon, Blue, Stippled	135.00
Fruits & Flowers, Bonbon, Green, Stippled	200.00
Fruits & Flowers, Bonbon, Ice Green	375.00
Fruits & Flowers, Bonbon, Sapphire	700.00
Fruits & Flowers, Bonbon, White	150.00
Fruits & Flowers, Plate, Purple, 7 In.	205.00
Garden Path, Chop Plate, Purple	900.00
Garland, Rose Bowl, Marigold	10.00
Good Luck, Bowl, Green, Piecrust Edge, Basketweave Back *illus*	$170.00
Good Luck, Bowl, Marigold, Ribbed Back	215.00
Good Luck, Bowl, Marigold, Ruffled Edge	115.00
Good Luck, Bowl, Purple, Ribbed Back, Ruffled Edge	195.00
Good Luck, Bowl, Purple, Ruffled Edge	150.00
Good Luck, Plate, Purple	210.00
Grape & Cable, Banana Boat, Marigold, Stippled, Banded	195.00
Grape & Cable, Bonbon, Purple, Handles, 6 In.	63.00
Grape & Cable, Bowl, Fruit, 3-Footed, Amethyst, 10 ½ In.	200.00
Grape & Cable, Bowl, Ribbed, Aqua Opalescent	2200.00
Grape & Cable, Bowl, Ribbed, Ice Blue	650.00
Grape & Cable, Candlestick, Green	105.00
Grape & Cable, Dish, Sweetmeat, Stemmed, Amethyst, Cover, c.1910, 9 In.	225.00
Grape & Cable, Hatpin Holder, Amethyst, 6 ½ In.	150.00
Grape & Cable, Hatpin Holder, Green, Footed	180.00
Grape & Cable, Humidor, Reninger Blue, Stippled	130.00
Grape & Cable, Pin Dish, Green	185.00
Grape & Cable, Plate, Green, Footed, 9 In.	45.00
Grape & Cable, Plate, Purple, 9 In.	75.00
Grape & Cable, Powder Jar, Lavender	240.00
Grape & Cable, Punch Set, Purple Iridescent, 10 ½ x 11 In.	450.00
Grape & Cable, Punch Set, Stippled, Blue, Small, 8 Piece	2000.00
Grape & Cable, Shot Glass, Purple	210.00
Grape & Cable, Table Set, Green, 4 Piece	165.00
Grape & Cable, Tumbler, Amethyst, 7 Piece	200.00
Grape & Gothic Arches, Water Set, Blue, 7 Piece	230.00
Grape Arbor, Tumbler, Ice Blue	28.00
Grape Delight, Nut Dish, Purple	25.00
Grape Delight, Rose Bowl, White, Ruffled Top, Footed	10.00

Carnival Glass, Inverted Thistle, Spooner, Amethyst
$100.00

Seeck Auctions

Carnival Glass, Lily Of The Valley, Tumbler, Blue
$75.00

Seeck Auctions

Carnival Glass, Orange Tree, Butter, Cover, Blue
$180.00

Seeck Auctions

> **TIP**
>
> *If you are moving, be sure to get special insurance coverage for damage to your antiques. You may want valuable pieces covered by your insurance, not by the mover's policy.*

Carnival Glass, Peacock, Bowl, Green, Ruffled Edge, Millersburg $160.00

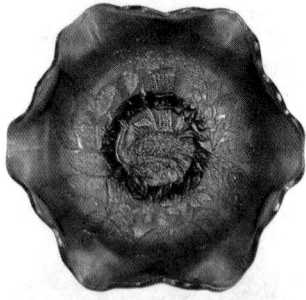

Seeck Auctions

Carnival Glass, Peacocks, Bowl, Purple, Piecrust Edge, Ribbed Back $95.00

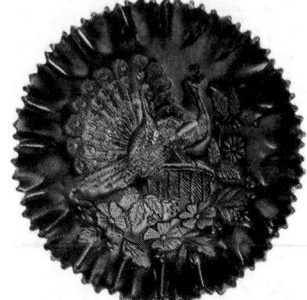

Seeck Auctions

Grapevine Lattice, Tumbler, Marigold	*illus*	$15.00
Grapevine Lattice, Tumbler, White		65.00
Greek Key, Tumbler, Purple		60.00
Hanging Cherries, Spooner, Green		55.00
Hattie, Bowl, Ruffled Edge, Blue, Iridescent		2300.00
Heart & Vine, Bowl, Blue, Ruffled Edge		50.00
Heart & Vine, Plate, Blue, 9 In.		165.00
Hearts & Flowers, Compote, Ruffled Edge, Blue		275.00
Hearts & Flowers, Compote, Ruffled Edge, Ice Green		250.00
Hearts & Flowers, Compote, Ruffled Edge, Marigold		50.00
Hearts & Flowers, Compote, Smoke, Ruffled Edge		2600.00
Hearts & Flowers, Compote, White, Ruffled Edge		65.00
Heavy Grape, Plate, Purple, 8 In.		95.00 to 105.00
Hobnail pattern is listed in this book as its own category.		
Hobstar & Cut Triangles, Bowl, Rose, Marigold		10.00
Hobstar, Sugar, Cover, Green, Marked IG	*illus*	$15.00
Holly, Bowl, Amber, Ruffled Edge		20.00
Holly, Bowl, Red, Ruffled Edge	*illus*	$275.00
Holly, Bowl, Teal Green, Ruffled Edge		255.00
Holly, Plate, Amethyst, 9 In.		245.00 to 300.00
Holly, Plate, Blue		145.00
Holly, Plate, Blue, 9 In.		125.00
Holly, Plate, Marigold, 9 In.		135.00
Homestead, Chop Plate, Amber		800.00
Homestead, Chop Plate, Emerald Green		3400.00
Homestead, Chop Plate, Purple		2000.00 to 3300.00
Homestead, Chop Plate, White		375.00
Honeycomb & Beads, Bowl, Tricorned Crimped Edge, Purple		35.00
Imperial Grape, Bowl, Purple, 10 ½ In.		40.00
Imperial Grape, Bowl, Purple, Ruffled Edge	*illus*	$80.00
Imperial Grape, Carafe, Emerald Green, Bulbous		1900.00
Imperial Grape, Carafe, Water, Emerald Green Iridescent		2300.00
Imperial Grape, Carafe, Water, Smoke		1550.00
Imperial Grape, Decanter, Wine, Purple		125.00
Imperial Grape, Tumbler, Purple		45.00
Imperial Grape, Water Set, Purple, 7 Piece		375.00
Imperial Grape, Wine Set, Marigold, 7 Piece		95.00
Imperial Grape, Wine Set, Purple, 7 Piece		225.00
Imperial Grape, Wine Set, Smoke, 5 Piece		150.00
Imperial Tiger Lily, Tumbler, Pink, 1970s, 4 ¼ In.		40.00
Inverted Thistle, Spooner, Amethyst	*illus*	100.00
Iris, Goblet, Buttermilk, Green		15.00
Lacy Dewdrop, Butter, Cover, Pearlized, Milk Glass		65.00
Lattice & Grape, Water Set, Tankard, Marigold, 7 Piece		60.00
Leaf & Beads, Nut Dish, Green, Rayed Interior		30.00
Leaf & Beads, Rose Bowl, Aqua Opalescent		205.00
Leaf & Beads, Rose Bowl, Blue		65.00
Leaf & Beads, Rose Bowl, Marigold		40.00
Leaf & Beads, Rose Bowl, Purple, 3-Footed, 5 ½ In.		75.00
Leaf & Beads, Rose Bowl, White		120.00
Leaf Chain, Plate, Marigold, 9 In.		170.00
Leaf Chain, Plate, White, 9 In.		45.00
Leaf Rays, Nappy, Purple		170.00
Leaf Swirl, Compote, Aqua, Ruffled Edge		85.00
Lily Of The Valley, Tumbler, Blue	*illus*	75.00
Loganberry, Vase, Marigold, Bulbous, Flared Rim		150.00
Lotus & Grape, Bowl, Blue, 3-In-1 Edge		80.00
Luster Rose, Pitcher, Water, Purple		900.00
Luster Rose, Spooner, Marigold		10.00
Luster Rose, Spooner, Purple		40.00
Luster Rose, Tumbler, Purple		105.00
Many Fruits, Punch Bowl, Dark Purple, 13 In.		175.00
Memphis, Punch Bowl, Ice Blue, Cups, 8 Piece		4500.00
Memphis, Punch Bowl, Purple, Cups, 8 Piece		350.00
Memphis, Punch Bowl, White, Cups, 8 Piece		1000.00
Memphis, Punch Set, Green, 8 Piece		2000.00

Mikado, Compote, Marigold, Round	70.00
Mikado, Compote, Ruffled Edge, Green	500.00
Milady, Pitcher, Water, Tankard, Marigold	500.00
Milady, Water Set, Tankard, Blue, 5 Piece	650.00
Moonprint, Butter, Marigold	10.00
Morning Glory, Vase, Funeral, Marigold, 14 In.	250.00
Morning Glory, Vase, Marigold, 5 In.	15.00
Morning Glory, Vase, Purple, Flared Mouth, 12 ½ In.	600.00
Octagon, Wine Set, Marigold, 8 Piece	65.00
Open Rose, Bowl, Amber	25.00
Orange Tree & Scroll, Water Set, Pitcher, Marigold, 7 Piece	400.00
Orange Tree, Butter, Cover, Blue .... *illus*	180.00
Orange Tree, Loving Cup, Green	230.00 to 900.00
Orange Tree, Loving Cup, Marigold	105.00
Orange Tree, Mug, Blue	70.00
Orange Tree, Mug, Purple	105.00
Orange Tree, Plate, Blue, 9 In.	120.00 to 450.00
Orange Tree, Powder Jar, Blue	125.00
Oriental Poppy, Tumbler, Ice Green	75.00
Pansy, Bowl, Amethyst, 9 In.	45.00
Pansy, Tray, Dresser, Purple, Iridescent	350.00
Parlor Panels, Vase, Purple, 11 In.	200.00
Peach, Tumbler, Blue	38.00
Peacock & Dahlia, Bowl, Vaseline, Ruffled Edge, 7 In.	190.00
Peacock & Grape, Bowl, Green, Footed	25.00
Peacock At The Fountain, Berry Bowl, Master, Ice Blue	275.00
Peacock At The Fountain, Berry Bowl, Purple	30.00
Peacock At The Fountain, Punch Set, Lime Green, 6 Piece	4600.00
Peacock At The Fountain, Table Set, Purple, 4 Piece	235.00
Peacock At Urn, Bowl, Master, Purple	180.00
Peacock Tail & Daisy, Bowl, Ruffled Edge, Marigold	1000.00
Peacock Tail, Dish, Hat Shape, Green, 6 ¼ In.	60.00
Peacock, Bowl, Green, Ruffled Edge, Millersburg .... *illus*	160.00
Peacock, Water Set, Amethyst, 5 Piece	300.00
Peacocks, Bowl, Marigold, Ribbed	225.00
Peacocks, Bowl, Purple, Piecrust Edge, Ribbed Back .... *illus*	95.00
Peacocks, Plate, Blue, Ribbed Back, 9 In.	525.00
Peacocks, Plate, Marigold, Ribbed Back, 9 In.	200.00
Persian Medallion, Bonbon, Red, Ruffled Edge	135.00
Persian Medallion, Bowl, Green, Ruffled Edge, 8 ½ In.	50.00
Persian Medallion, Plate, Marigold, 6 In.	10.00
Peter Rabbit, Plate, Green, 9 In.	2900.00
Pillow & Sunburst, Plate, Marigold, 9 In.	195.00
Pine Cone, Sauce Bowl, Blue	130.00
Pine Cone, Saucer, Blue, 6 In.	137.00
Pineapple, Sugar & Creamer, Marigold, Ruffled Edge	30.00
Plain Jane, Sugar & Creamer, Aqua Teal	30.00
Poinsettia & Lattice, Bowl, Blue, Footed, Ruffled Edge, Ribbed	475.00
Poinsettia & Lattice, Bowl, Horehound, Footed, Ruffled Edge, Ribbed	575.00
Poinsettia, Pitcher, Milk, Marigold	25.00 to 190.00
Poinsettia, Pitcher, Milk, Smoke	65.00 to 190.00
Poppy Show, Bowl, Ruffled Edge, Aqua Opalescent	9000.00
Poppy Show, Bowl, Ruffled Edge, Green Opalescent	1300.00
Poppy Show, Bowl, Ruffled Edge, Marigold	250.00
Poppy Show, Plate, Blue, 9 In.	425.00 to 1400.00
Poppy Show, Plate, Marigold, 9 In.	425.00 to 800.00
Poppy Show, Plate, Purple, 9 In.	1000.00 to 4100.00
Poppy Show, Vase, Marigold	275.00
Poppy Show, Vase, Plum Opalescent	145.00
Poppy, Compote, Marigold	1112.00
Poppy, Dish, Pickle, Blue	85.00
Poppy, Dish, Pickle, Ice Blue Opal	650.00
Poppy, Dish, Pickle, Purple	125.00
Pulled Loop, Vase, Aqua, Marigold Overlay, Flared, 10 ½ In.	120.00
Pulled Loop, Vase, Purple, Squat, 5 In.	301.00

Carnival Glass, Puzzle, Bonbon, Peach Opal
$25.00

Seeck Auctions

Carnival Glass, Rising Sun, Butter, Cover, Marigold
$55.00

Seeck Auctions

Carnival Glass, Rose Garden, Butter, Cover, Marigold
$210.00

Seeck Auctions

TIP

Save all labels and written information found on antiques to help determine past history of the object. Do not remove labels. To copy a bottle label you can try rolling the bottle on a scanner bed at the scan speed. It is easier than it sounds. Put a wide rubber band on the bottle if it has embossed lettering. It helps make a smoother roll.

C

Carnival Glass, Springtime, Creamer, Green
$70.00

Seeck Auctions

Carnival Glass, Victorian, Bowl, Ruffled, Purple
$170.00

Seeck Auctions

Carnival Glass, Wreath Of Roses, Rose Bowl, Marigold
$15.00

Seeck Auctions

TIP

In snowy weather, make tracks both in and out of your door. One set of tracks leaving the house is an invitation to an intruder. Or perhaps you could walk out of the house backward.

Puzzle, Bonbon, Peach Opal	*illus*	25.00
Question Marks, Bonbon, Peach Opalescent		10.00
Question Marks, Bonbon, Purple		20.00
Rays, Plate, Stippled, Marigold, 6 In.		20.00
Ribbon Tie, Bowl, 3-In-1 Edge, Blue		650.00
Ripple, Vase, Marigold, 5 ½ In.		30.00
Ripple, Vase, Marigold, Squat, 7 ½ In.		15.00
Rising Sun, Butter, Cover, Marigold	*illus*	55.00
Rose Garden, Butter, Cover, Marigold	*illus*	$210.00
Rose Show, Bowl, Ruffled Edge, Aqua, Opalescent		900.00
Rose Show, Bowl, Ruffled Edge, Horehound		1200.00
Rose Show, Bowl, Ruffled Edge, Ice Blue		525.00
Rose Show, Bowl, Ruffled Edge, Lime Green Opalescent		1700.00
Rose Show, Bowl, Ruffled Edge, Sapphire		2500.00
Rose Show, Plate, Blue, 9 In.		422.00
Rose Show, Plate, Ice Blue, 9 In.		675.00
Rose Show, Plate, Ice Green, 9 In.		375.00
Rose Show, Plate, Lime Green, Scalloped Edge, 9 In.		2000.00
Rose Show, Plate, Marigold, 9 In.		400.00
Rose Show, Plate, White, 9 In.		220.00
Rustic, Vase, Amethyst, 15 In.		70.00
Rustic, Vase, Funeral, Blue, 19 In.		375.00
Rustic, Vase, Funeral, Plunger Base, Green		2300.00
Rustic, Vase, Green, 15 In.		65.00
Scales, Plate, Amethyst, 6 In.		15.00
Scotch Thistle, Compote, Green, Crimped & Ruffled Edge		45.00
Seacoast, Pin Tray, Green, Millersburg		300.00
Shell & Sand, Plate, Purple, 9 In.		2400.00
Shell & Sand, Plate, Purple, Serrated Edge, 9 In.		2300.00
Shell & Sand, Plate, Smoke, Serrated Edge, 9 In.		750.00
Singing Birds, Mug, Blue		30.00
Singing Birds, Mug, Purple	25.00 to 50.00	
Singing Birds, Tumbler, Green	*illus*	30.00
Singing Birds, Tumbler, Purple	20.00 to 30.00	
Singing Birds, Water Set, Green, 7 Piece		255.00
Single Flower, Bowl, Peach Opalescent, Crimped Edge, Tricornered		40.00
Ski Star, Bowl, Tricornered, Crimped Edge, Dome, Footed, Peach		55.00
Ski Star, Plate, Dome Footed, Handgrip, Peach		45.00
Smooth Rays, Bowl, Peach Opal, Ruffled Edge		45.00
Smooth Rays, Compote, Ruffled Edge, Blue Opalescent		120.00
Spirilex, Vase, Blue, 11 In.		45.00
Spirilex, Vase, Peach Opalescent, 10 ½ In.		40.00
Springtime, Creamer, Green	*illus*	$70.00
Springtime, Spooner, Green, Ruffled Edge		210.00
Springtime, Spooner, Marigold		75.00
Stag & Holly, Bowl, Blue, Large		160.00
Stag & Holly, Plate, Marigold, Footed, 9 In.		155.00
Starfish, Bonbon, Purple		60.00
Starfish, Compote, Peach Opalescent		40.00
Starfish, Compote, Peach Opalescent, Ruffled Edge		15.00
Stippled Three Fruits, Plate, Ribbed Back, Aqua Opalescent		1300.00
Stippled Three Fruits, Plate, Ribbed Back, Purple		225.00
Stork & Rushes, Butter, Marigold		15.00
Sunflower, Pin Tray, Green, Loop Handle, Millersburg		300.00
Sunset, Bowl, Scalloped Rim, Indiana Glass, c.1960, 4 x 8 In.		50.00
Target, Vase, Purple, 9 ½ In.	26.00 to 28.00	
Ten Mums, Bowl, Blue, Ruffled Edge, Large		110.00
Thistle & Thorn, Bowl, Ruffled Edge, Marigold		30.00
Thistle, Banana Boat, Blue		190.00
Thistle, Plate, Marigold, c.1911, 9 In.		1650.00
Three Fruits, Plate, Amethyst, 9 In.		80.00
Three Fruits, Plate, Green, 9 ¼ In.		75.00
Tiger Lily, Tumbler, Pink, c.1965, 4 ¼ x 2 ¾ In.		40.00
Tornado, Vase, Green, Footed, Ruffled Edge		550.00
Tree Of Life, Salt & Pepper, Smoke		290.00

Tree Trunk, Vase, Funeral, Blue, Plunger Base, 18 In.	2200.00
Tree Trunk, Vase, Green, 10 In.	20.00
Tree Trunk, Vase, Marigold, 11 In.	20.00
Tree Trunk, Vase, Plunger Base, Blue, 20 In.	2600.00
Tree Trunk, Vase, Plunger Base, Purple, 18 In.	2400.00
Tree Trunk, Vase, Reninger Blue, Pinched Waist, 11 In.	205.00
Trumpet Twist, Candlestick, Celeste Blue, 6 ½ In., Pair	300.00
Two Flowers, Bowl, Blue, Ruffled, Footed	85.00
Two Flowers, Rose Bowl, Marigold, Footed	20.00
Victorian, Bowl, Ruffled, Purple ....illus	$170.00
Vintage, Bowl, Amethyst, 3-Footed, 6 In.	50.00 to 60.00
Vintage, Bowl, Amethyst, 7 In.	30.00
Water Lily, Sauce, Aqua, Ruffled Edge, Footed	55.00
Western Daisy, Bowl, Peach Opal, 9 In.	90.00
Wide Panel, Epergne, Green	600.00
Wide Panel, Vase, Smoke, 9 In.	425.00
Wild Rose, Syrup, Marigold	230.00
Wild Strawberry, Plate, Purple, Handgrip, 7 In.	145.00
Windmill, Tray, Dresser, Purple	175.00
Wishbone & Spades, Plate, Peach Opalescent, 6 In.	55.00
Wishbone & Spades, Sauce Bowl, Purple	95.00
Wishbone, Bowl, Blue Opalescent, 10 In.	550.00
Wishbone, Bowl, Green, 10 In.	105.00
Wishbone, Plate, Marigold, Ruffled Edge, Footed, 9 In. ....illus	55.00
Wishbone, Plate, Purple, Footed, 9 In.	175.00
Wreath Of Roses, Bonbon, Amethyst	80.00
Wreath Of Roses, Bonbon, Green	40.00 to 50.00
Wreath Of Roses, Punch Bowl, Marigold	245.00
Wreath Of Roses, Rose Bowl, Marigold ....illus	$15.00
Wreathed Cherry, Tumbler, Marigold	10.00
Wreathed Cherry, Water Set, Amethyst, 8 ¾-In. Pitcher, 4-In. Tumbler, 7 Piece	472.00
Zipper Loop, Lamp, Kerosene, Marigold, 8 In.	165.00 to 275.00
Zipper Stitch, Bottle, Wine, Marigold	35.00

CAROUSEL or merry-go-round figures were first carved in the United States in 1867 by Gustav Dentzel. Collectors discovered the charm of the hand-carved figures in the 1970s, and they were soon classed as folk art. Most desirable are the figures other than horses, such as pigs, camels, lions, or dogs. A jumper is a figure that was made to move up and down on a pole; a stander was placed in a stationary position.

Bear, Carved & Painted, Brown, White Saddle, Blue Ribbon Around Neck, 19 x 35 In.	400.00
Camel, Carved & Painted, Original Jewels & Fittings, Glass Eye, 58 x 52 In.	15000.00
Cat, Running, Wood, Cream, Blue Ribbon, Saddle, Twist Tail, Pole, c.1950, 53 x 47 In.	1175.00
Chariot, Elephant, Clown On Top Head, Red & Blue Howdah, Heyn, 78 x 65 In.	17500.00
Chariot, St. George & The Dragon, Carved, Painted, Allan Herschell, N.Y., 48 x 66 In. ....illus	5250.00
Dog, St. Bernard, Standing, Carved, Painted, Matheiu, Devos, c.1910, 31 x 35 In. ....illus	4375.00
Donkey, Fairground, Carved & Painted, White, Brown Saddle, Bayol, 25 x 36 In.	2375.00
Giraffe, Beige With Brown Spots, Carved & Painted, Spillman, 72 x 59 In.	8750.00
Goat, White, Marble Eyes, Orange Saddle, Dare, 58 x 6 In.	6870.00
Gorilla, Carved & Painted, Beige Fur, Orange Saddle, Mexico, 25 x 36 In.	750.00
Horse, 2-Seater, Horsehair Tail, Beige, Bristol, 45 x 30 In.	1750.00
Horse, Black, Leather Ears, Glass Eyes, Stirrups & Horsehair Tail, Herschell, 41 x 49 In.	875.00
Horse, Brown, White Saddle, Herschell, 41 x 50 In.	2000.00
Horse, Carved & Painted, White, Brown Saddle, Savage, 33 x 57 In.	1500.00
Horse, Jumper, Carved, Painted, Philadelphia Toboggan Co., Leo Zoeller, c.1910, 59 x 60 In. ....illus	2500.00
Horse, Jumper, Carved, Painted, Spillman, c.1925, 48 x 57 In.	2607.00
Horse, Jumper, Horsehair Tail, Carved Pistol & Stirrups, Goldstein, 84 x 50 In.	5625.00
Horse, Jumper, Long Stride, Painted, Carved Mane, Tail, Iron Mount, 51 x 82 In.	1770.00
Horse, Left Front Leg Raised, White, Multicolor Saddle, Blanket, Bridle, Jeweled, 60 x 60 In.	240.00
Horse, Prancer, Cast Fiberglass, Multicolor, Twisted Brass Pole, Stand, 71 x 59 In.	403.00
Horse, Prancer, Wood, Carved, Openwork Mane, Glass Eyes, Painted, 60 x 58 In.	5310.00
Horse, Rearing, Painted, White, Black Saddle, Wood, Leather, Gustav Bayol	4025.00
Horse, Runner, Carved, Paint, c.1900, 20 x 40 In.	243.00
Horse, Runner, Platform, Carved, Painted, Anderson Of Bristol, c.1900, 40 x 65 In. ....illus	1500.00
Horse, Runner, White, Carved & Painted, Brown Saddle, Parker, 82 x 32 In.	1875.00
Horse, Stander, Carved, Painted, E. Joy Morris, Philadelphia, c.1900, 51 x 52 In. ....illus	4000.00
Horse, Stander, White, Bridle & Horsehair Tail, Gold Saddle, 63 x 56 In.	938.00

C

Carousel Ladies
All horses on a carousel are mares.

Carousel, Chariot, St. George & The Dragon, Carved, Painted, Allan Herschell, N.Y., 48 x 66 In.
$5250.00

Bonhams & Butterfields

Carousel, Dog, St. Bernard, Standing, Carved, Painted, Matheiu, Devos, c.1910, 31 x 35 In.
$4375.00

Bonhams & Butterfields

Carousel, Horse, Jumper, Carved, Painted, Philadelphia Toboggan Co., Leo Zoeller, c.1910, 59 x 60 In.
$2500.00

Bonhams & Butterfields

CAROUSEL

Carousel, Horse, Runner, Platform, Carved, Painted, Anderson Of Bristol, c.1900, 40 x 65 In.
$1500.00

Bonhams & Butterfields

Carousel, Horse, Stander, Carved, Painted, E. Joy Morris, Philadelphia, c.1900, 51 x 52 In.
$4000.00

Bonhams & Butterfields

Carousel, Ostrich, Runner, Carved, Painted, Herschell-Spillman, N.Y., c.1910, 64 x 36 In.
$5250.00

Bonhams & Butterfields

Horse, White, Horse Shoes & Bridle Rings, Parker, 35 x 60 In.	3125.00
Kangaroo, Carved & Painted, Red Saddle On Back, Matheiu, 38 x 32 In.	5625.00
Ostrich, Runner, Carved, Painted, Herschell-Spillman, N.Y., c.1910, 64 x 36 In. ....*illus*	5250.00
Peacock, Carved & Painted, Blue Feathers, Gold & Red Plum, Original Saddle, 32 In.	5625.00
Rabbit, Carved & Painted, White, Brown Saddle, Bayol, 45 x 50 In.	4750.00
Snail, Carved, Painted, England, c.1950, 29 x 24 In. ....*illus*	1250.00
Stag, Prancer, Brown, Black Saddle, Dentzel, 79 x 49 In.	17500.00
Tiger, Stander, Carved & Painted, Angel On Shoulder, Dentzel, 50 x 72 In.	45000.00

CARRIAGE means several things, so this category lists baby carriages, buggies for adults, horse-drawn sleighs, and even strollers. Doll-sized carriages are listed in the Toy category.

Child's, Wooden Bed, Fringed Canopy, Spring Frame, Spoke Wheels, 1880s, 25 ½ x 30 In. ..*illus*	294.00
Conestoga Wagon, Painted, Tool Box, Signed, 1790-Marietta-Lancaster Co., 17 x 9 Ft. .*illus*	24780.00
Pram, Wicker, Iron Hardware, Lace Parasol, Rubber Wheels, Victorian, 65 x 43 x 26 In.	173.00
Sleigh, Brocade Upholstery, Curved Metal Runners, Painted, Push Handle, c.1890, 36 x 50 In.	383.00
Sleigh, Open, Wood, Red, Yellow Pin Stripe, Metal Clad Runners, Seat Cover, Child's, 22 x 37 In.	295.00

CASH REGISTERS were invented in 1884 because an eye on the cash was a necessity in stores of the nineteenth century, too. John and James Ritty invented a large model that resembled a clock and kept a record of the dollars and cents exchanged in the store. John Patterson improved the cash register with a paper roll to record the money. By the early 1900s, elaborate brass registers were made. More modern types were made after 1920.

National, Empire Style, Brass, Marble Shelf, Side Crank, 21 x 18 ½ In.	201.00
National, Marquee, Receipt Dispenser, Brass, 21 ½ In.	720.00
National, Model 5, Amount Purchased Embossed, Key	1017.00
National, Model 50, ¼ Brass, Ceramic, Oak, 21 x 11 In.	589.00
National, Model 57, Brass, 1900, 16 ½ x 17 ½ In.	489.00
National, Model 57, Brass, Wooden Shelf, Hinged Front, 5 Cents To 9 Dollars, 17 x 18 In.	489.00
National, Model 130, Nickel	935.00
National, Model 310, Bronze	1210.00
National, Model 312, Bronze	770.00
National, Model 313, Bronze, 21 x 10 x 16 In. ....*illus*	1180.00
National, Model 313, Bronze, Candy Store ....*illus*	396.00
National, Model 313, Bronze, Marble, Candy Store, 17 x 16 In.	201.00
National, Model 324, Money Must Be Registered Before Goods Are Wrapped	1100.00
National, Model 336, Bronze, 17 x 17 x 16 In.	360.00 to 367.00
National, Model Ra-132, Chrome, Marble Shelf, Candy, 1932, 18 ½ x 10 ½ In.	288.00

CASTOR JARS for pickles are glass jars about six inches in height, held in special metal holders. They became a popular dinner table accessory about 1890. Each jar had a top that was usually silver or silver plate. The frame, also of a silver metal, had a handle that arched above the jar and a hook that held a pair of tongs. By 1900, the pickle castor was out of fashion. Many examples found today have reproduced glass jars in old holders. Additional pickle castors may be found in the various Glass categories.

Pickle, Amber, Faceted, Cylindrical, Silver Plate Caddy, 4-Footed, Finial, 13 In.	230.00
Pickle, Blue Thumbprint Jar, Green Cucumbers, Silver Plate Cover, 1800s, 10 In.	207.00
Pickle, Brass, Bulbous, Splayed Foot, Cork Plug, c.1770, 4 In.	90.00
Pickle, Cover, Vertical Rib, Clear, Yellow Panes, Flowers, Silver Plated Lid, 6 In.	200.00
Pickle, Cranberry Glass, Optic Ribbed, Enameled Flowers, Silver Plated Holder, 10 In.	350.00
Pickle, Cranberry, Coin Spot, Cascading Flowers, 4-Footed Caddy, 10 In.	288.00
Pickle, Daisy & Button, Amber	569.00
Pickle, Diamond Quilted, Amber To Pink, Metal, Flower Embossed Caddy, Victorian Glass, 10 In.	115.00
Pickle, Paneled Sprig, Enameled Flowers, Single Arm, Wm Rogers Caddy, Northwood, 11 In. ...*illus*	115.00
Pickle, Pattern Glass, Vertical Zipper Highlights, Silver Plated Frame, 11 ½ In.	50.00
Pickle, Peachblow Insert, Flowers, Reed & Barton Silver Plated Frame, Hobbs, Brockunier, 9 ¾ In.	3500.00
Pickle, Pink Opalescent, Diamond Quilted, Middletown Silver Plated Frame, 10 In.	450.00
Pickle, Pink Satin Glass, Mother-Of-Pearl, Coin Spot, Enamel Flowers, Silver Plated Frame, 10 ½ In.	2400.00
Pickle, Prussian Blue, Coin Spot, Enameled Flowers, 4-Footed, Pierced Metal Holder, 13 In.	374.00
Pickle, Silver, Baluster Shape, England, 4 In., Pair	171.00
Pickle, Silver, Dome Lid, Pierced, Diamond, Leaves, Crescents, Bowl Shape Bottom, c.1770, 5 ½ In.	459.00
Pickle, Silver, Molded Band, Pierced Cap, Engraved, Wakely & Wheeler, England, c.1917, 8 x 3 ¾ In.	461.00
Pickle, Silver, Repousse Wreath & Flowers, Putti, Shaped Foot, Bulbous Center, Germany, 9 In.	196.00
Pickle, Translucent Cranberry, Enameled Flowers, Cylindrical, Reed & Barton Caddy, 10 In. ...	201.00
Pickle, Vaseline, Opalescent Drape, Silver Plate, 10 ¾ In.	700.00

Pickle, Windows, Opalescent, Cranberry, Metal Caddy, Hobbs Brockunier, 11 In.	201.00
Pickle, Yellow Satin, Diamond Quilted, Insert, Gilt, Rockford Silver Plated Frame, 12 In.	800.00

CASTOR SETS holding just salt and pepper castors were used in the seventeenth century. The sugar castor, mustard pot, spice dredger (shaker), bottles for vinegar and oil, and other spice holders became popular by the eighteenth century. These sets were usually made of sterling silver. The American Victorian castor set, the type most collected today, was made of silver plated Britannia metal. Colored glass bottles were introduced after the Civil War. The sets were out of fashion by World War I. Be careful when buying sets with colored bottles; many are reproductions. Other castor sets may be listed in various porcelain and glass categories in this book.

2 Bottles, Stand, Brass, Crystal, Stoppers, New Orleans, France, 9 ½ x 8 ¾ In.	180.00
5 Bottles, 2 Stoppers, 3 Lids, Silver Plate, Embossed, Tripod Base, Victorian, 14 ¾ In.	108.00
5 Bottles, Silver, Shell Feet, Ring Handle, England, 1764, 10 ¾ x 7 ½ In. ....*illus*	5904.00

CATALOGS *are listed in the Paper category.*

CAUGHLEY porcelain was made in England from 1772 to 1814. Caughley porcelains are very similar in appearance to those made at the Worcester factory. See the Salopian category for related items.

Bowl, Rock & Willow, Blue, Chinese Riverscape, Rim Lines, Diaper Border, c.1774, 7 ½ In.	1102.00
Punch Bowl, Pinecone, Printed, Center Spray, Fruit & Flower Frame, Swag Border, c.1778, 10 In.	1702.00

CAULDON Limited worked in Staffordshire, Great Britain, and went through many name changes. John Ridgway made porcelain at Cauldon Place, Hanley, until 1855. The firm of John Ridgway, Bates and Co. of Cauldon Place worked from 1856 to 1859. It became Bates, Brown-Westhead, Moore and Co. from 1859 to 1862. Brown-Westhead, Moore and Co. worked from 1862 to 1904. About 1890, this firm started using the words *Cauldon* or *Cauldon Ware* as part of the mark. Cauldon Ltd. worked from 1905 to 1920, Cauldon Potteries from 1920 to 1962. Related items may be found in the Indian Tree category.

Tub, Roman Scene, Molded Staved Barrel, Blue, 1800s, 4 ½ x 8 ½ In.	173.00

CELADON is the name of a velvet-textured green-gray glaze used by Chinese, Japanese, Korean, and other factories. The name refers both to the glaze and to pieces covered with the glaze. It is still being made. Only celadon-colored ceramics are listed here.

Bowl, Bushes, Trees, Chinese, 3 x 21 In.	590.00
Bowl, Conical Shape, Sea Green Glaze, Carved Lotus Petals, 6 ½ In.	119.00
Bowl, Flared, Carved Interior, Gilt Metal Rim Mounts, Footed Base, Chinese, 5 x 11 In.	345.00
Bowl, Flattened Rim, Flower Banding, Thailand, 1400s, 9 ⅛ In.	338.00
Bowl, Incised Clouds, Overlapping Petal Design, Pale Green, Blue, 1800s, 5 ⅞ In.	276.00
Bowl, Incised Flowers, 1 ¾ In.	115.00
Bowl, Incised Leaves, Carved Wood Cover, Stand, Jade Figural Finial, Chinese, 12 ½ In.	14938.00
Bowl, Lotus Petal Design, Glazed, Thailand, c.1500, 3 x 11 ½ In.	480.00
Bowl, Low, Slight Curled Lip, Crackle Glaze, 5 In. Diam.	1342.00
Bowl, Round Foot, San Duo, 3 Fruits, Gilt, Chinese, 1700s, 8 ½ In.	2726.00
Bowl, Sage Glaze, Clouds, 18th Century, 5 x 9 ½ In.	2700.00
Box, Cover, Carved Orchids, Chrysanthemum, Rocks, Shou Character, c.1905, 3 x 2 ¾ In.	922.00
Censer, Cover, Taotie Mask, Tripod Feet, Wood Base, Ring Handles, Apple Green, 3 In.	1673.00
Censer, Squat, Crackle, Lotus Blossom, 3 Animal Shape Feet, Hardwood Stand, 3 x 6 In.	992.00
Censer, Tripod, Incised Exterior, Flowers, Chinese, 12 In.	598.00
Charger, Central Flowers, c.1630, 14 ¾ In.	1400.00
Dish, Pedestal Base, Pinched, 7 In.	119.00
Dish, Shallow, Carved Flower Design, 6 In. Diam.	366.00
Ewer, Bamboo Shoot Shape, Red Marks, Chinese, 1800s, 7 ½ In.	178.00
Figurine, 2 Foo Dogs, 4 In.	359.00
Figurine, Guanyin, Seated, Double Lotus Throne, Holding Ruyi Scepter, 13 In.	717.00
Flask, Flattened Circular Shape, Dragon Moon, Elephant Head Handles, Ring, 7 ¼ In.	9560.00
Flask, Moon, Flowers, Leaves, Carved, Chinese, 10 ½ In.	12000.00
Garden Seat, Barrel Shape, Flower Bosses, Pierced Flowers Design, Scrolling Leaves, 19 In.	1845.00
Jar, Flowers, Incised, Stick Neck, 1900s, 9 In.	550.00
Jar, Lid, Sea Green Glaze, Oval, Ribbed, Chinese, 1800s, 7 ¾ In.	770.00
Jar, Storage, Bulbous Body, Clouds, Scrolling Leaves, Wood Stand, 1900s, 20 In.	246.00
Jar, Storage, Globular Shape, Ridged Round Lip, 2 Strap Handles, Crackled Glaze, 6 x 7 In.	123.00
Jar, Storage, Globular, Inverted Foot, 4 Lug Rings, Glazed, 5 In.	338.00
Mug, Crackled Sea Green Glaze, Chinese, 14 In.	1541.00

Carousel, Snail, Carved, Painted, England, c.1950, 29 x 24 In. $1250.00

Bonhams & Butterfields

Carriage, Child's, Wooden Bed, Fringed Canopy, Spring Frame, Spoke Wheels, 1880s, 25 ½ x 30 In. $294.00

Cowan's Auctions

Carriage, Conestoga Wagon, Painted, Tool Box, Signed, 1790-Marietta-Lancaster Co., 17 x 9 Ft. $24780.00

Conestoga Auction Co., Inc.

Don't Take Your Car to a Flea Market

Take your van, truck, or station wagon when you go to a farm auction, flea market or out-of-town show. You never know when you'll find the dining room table of your dreams.

Cash Register, National, Model 313, Bronze, 21 x 10 x 16 In.
$1180.00

DuMouchelles Art Gallery

Cash Register, National, Model 313, Bronze, Candy Store
$396.00

Showtime Auction Services

Castor, Pickle, Paneled Sprig, Enameled Flowers, Single Arm, Wm Rogers Caddy, Northwood, 11 In.
$115.00

Early Auction Co.

Planter, Floriform, Finger Mold Relief, Incised Lines, Asia, 1800s, 5 ½ x 11 ¼ In.	104.00
Platter, Raised Rim, Incised Lines, Round, Chinese, c.1640, 13 ¾ In.	1230.00
Teapot, Carved, Shou Character, Round Swirl Handle, Round Base, Zhen Wu Mark, 6 In.	4183.00
Vase, Baluster, Faux Ring Handles, Molded Design, Glazed, 7 In.	372.00
Vase, Birds On Nest, Flowering Branches, 14 x 7 In.	720.00
Vase, Bottle Shape, Green Glaze, Rings On Neck, Flared Lip, c.1800, 9 x 6 In.	173.00
Vase, Carved Design, Ju-I Lappets, Cranes, Bamboo, Korea, 11 In.	533.00
Vase, Cover, Carved, Bird, Pine Tree, Deer, Branches, Wood Base, Flower Shape, 6 ¼ In.	1315.00
Vase, Cover, Dragon & Phoenix Design, Carved Handles At Neck, Chinese, 4 In.	448.00
Vase, Cover, Flattened Shield Shape, Medallion, Taotie Mask, Dragon Shape Handles, 3 In.	329.00
Vase, Crackle Glaze, Curved, Handles, Swollen, 18th Century, 11 ½ In.	100.00
Vase, Cylindrical Neck, Flared Rim, Green Glaze, Meiping Shape, Chinese, 8 ¾ In.	5629.00
Vase, Double Gourd, Relief Molded, Vines, Flowers, Handles, Incised Mark, Chinese, 12 In. *illus*	8540.00
Vase, Elongated Oval, Narrow Neck, Rolled Rim, Dragons, Sea, c.1900, 9 ½ In.	490.00
Vase, Gourd Shape Base, Narrow Neck, Chinese, 8 In.	1200.00
Vase, Gray Crackle Glaze, Hu Shape, Chinese, 8 ½ In.	1422.00
Vase, Incised Bats, Peonies, Longevity Character, Sheep's Head Handles, c.1920, 14 ¼ In.	2032.00
Vase, Incised Flowers, Flared Neck, Late 1800s, 20 In.	948.00
Vase, Longquan, Baluster Shape, Flared Neck, Flowers, Late 1800s, 11 In.	329.00
Vase, Rectangular, Round Mouth & Foot, Blue Green Crackle Glaze, c.1890, 10 In.	28000.00
Vase, Ruffled Rim, Chinese, 7 ¾ In.	236.00
Vase, Square, Lung Chuan Ware, Chinese, 16th Century, 10 In. *illus*	1225.00
Vase, Wheel-Turned Design, Narrow Mouth, Lung Chuan, Chinese, c.1200, 5 ¼ In. *illus*	356.00

CELLULOID is a trademark for a plastic developed in 1868 by John W. Hyatt. Celluloid Manufacturing Company, the Celluloid Novelty Company, Celluloid Fancy Goods Company, and American Xylonite Company all used celluloid to make jewelry, games, sewing equipment, false teeth, and piano keys. The name *celluloid* was often used to identify any similar plastic. Celluloid toys are listed under Toy.

Box, 4 Children's Faces, Flowers, Cloth Interior, c.1890, 5 ¼ x 5 ¼ In.	115.00
Button, Yellow Kid, No. 33, Throwing Dice, Tin Rim, Easel Back, 1 ⅜ In.	443.00
Button, Yellow Kid, No. 79, Holding Pistols, Tin Back, 1 ¼ In.	183.00
Button, Yellow Kid, No. 101, Russia, Holding Flag, Tin Back, 1 ¼ In.	1112.00
Button, Yellow Kid, No. 128, France, Holding Flag, Tin Back, 1 ¼ In.	263.00
Button, Yellow Kid, No. 141, Japan, Holding Flag, Tin Back, 1 ¼ In.	275.00
Hair Comb, Egyptian, Scarab, Symbols, Art Deco, 6 x 4 In.	17.95
Hair Comb, Marbled, Fan Shape, c.1875, 6 ½ In.	110.00
Jewelry Box, Victorian Style, Lovers, Molded Relief, Mirror, French Ivory, c.1960, 4 ¾ x 3 ¾ In.	40.00
Place Card Holder, Whimsical Silhouettes, Courting Couples, 8 Piece	125.00
Shaving Mirror, Dish, French Ivory, Folds, 2 ½ x 6 ¾ In.	60.00
Toothbrush Holder, Raised Portrait Of Queen Victoria, Rectangular, 4 ½ In.	65.00

CELS *are listed in this book in the Animation Art category.*

CERAMIC ART COMPANY of Trenton, New Jersey, was established in 1889 by J. Coxon and W. Lenox and was an early producer of American belleek porcelain. It became Lenox, Inc. in 1906. Do not confuse this ware with the pottery made by the Ceramic Arts Studio of Madison, Wisconsin.

Basket, Sterling Foot & Handle, c.1900, 5 ¾ In.	158.00
Jug, Berries, Leaves, Brown Ground, Pallet Mark, c.1900, 5 ½ In.	144.00
Jug, Globular, Brown, Berries, Leaves, 5 ½ In.	265.00
Pitcher, Grapes, Leaves, c.1910, 11 ¾ In.	230.00
Stein, Blue, Boys Playing Rugby, 7 In.	1250.00
Tankard, Monks, Holding Barrel, Brown, 14 ¼ In.	395.00
Vase, Cylindrical, Windmill Winter Scene, Cottages, Hand Painted, Marked, 10 x 6 In.	196.00
Vase, Lorelei, Leaning Over Ledge, Waterfall, Oval, Signed, Grace Reid, Belleek, 8 In. *illus*	1126.00
Vase, Squat Gourd Shape, Stick Neck, Strap Handles, Scalloped Mouth, Flowers, 7 In.	1000.00

CERAMIC ARTS STUDIO was founded about 1940 in Madison, Wisconsin, by Lawrence Rabbett and Ruben Sand. Their most popular products were expensive molded figurines. The pottery closed in 1955. Do not confuse these products with those of the Ceramic Art Co. of Trenton, New Jersey.

Figurine, Angel With Arms Up	112.00
Figurine, Colonial Couple, Green, Brown, Orange, Dark Green & Pink Trim, 1940s	129.00
Figurine, Fighting Leopards	245.00

Figurine, Jackson & Southern Belle, c.1940s	229.00
Figurine, Peter Pan & Wendy, c.1940s, 5 ¼ In.	229.00
Salt & Pepper, Mother Skunk & Baby, 1940s	112.00

CHALKWARE is really plaster of Paris decorated with watercolors. One type was molded from Staffordshire and other porcelain models and painted and sold as inexpensive decorations in the nineteenth century. This type is very valuable today. Figures of plaster, made from about 1910 to 1940 for use as prizes at carnivals, are also known as chalkware. Kewpie dolls made of chalkware will be found in their own category.

Bust, Abraham Lincoln, Draped Shoulders, Pedestal, Signed, D. Morgan, 1865, 18 In. ......*illus*	663.00
Bust, Oliver Hazard Perry, Military Uniform, Painted, c. 1855, 10 In. ....*illus*	1880.00
Bank, Bird, Standing, Blue, Orange, Red & Black Paint, 1800s, 11 In., Pair	920.00
Bank, Dog, Hound, Seated, Bucket In Mouth, c.1900, 10 ½ In.	301.00
Bank, Penny, Dove, On Cherry Branch, Painted, c.1890, 11 In.	121.00
Figurine, Cat, Seated, White, Green Collar, c.1900, 6 In.	558.00
Figurine, Dog, Poodle, Standing, Painted, 19th Century, 7 ½ In., Pair	100.00
Figurine, Dog, Pug, Japanese Folk Art, Multicolor, Marked, 9 x 10 ½ In.	11.00
Figurine, Dog, Pug, Painted, Marked Cnr Cpyrt. 1979, Japan, 10 ½ In. x 9 In.	11.00
Figurine, Dog, Pug, Seated, Painted, c.1900, 6 In., Pair	200.00
Figurine, Dog, Spaniel, Yellow, Black, c.1870, 8 ¾ In.	1067.00
Figurine, Dog, White, Black Ears & Spots, Rectangular Stepped Base, 1800s, 8 x 5 In.	230.00
Figurine, Dove, Base, Painted Beak & Eyes, 10 ½ In.	79.00
Figurine, Dove, Perched On Cherry Branch, Painted, 1800s, 10 ½ In., Pair	450.00
Figurine, Dove, Perched On Fruiting Branch, c.1890, 11 In., Pair ....*illus*	889.00
Figurine, Dove, White, Brown, 1800s, 11 In., Pair	456.00
Figurine, Lion, Lying Down, Painted, 1800s, 10 x 10 ½ In., Pair	750.00
Figurine, Sailor, Painted, Incised Base, John Whiting, 1857, 14 ½ In.	200.00
Figurine, Sheep, White, Green Stand, 23 x 17 In.	575.00
Figurine, Squirrel, c.1850, 6 ½ In. ....*illus*	180.00
Figurine, Squirrel, Eating Nut, Painted Gray, Black, c.1875, 6 In.	35.00
Figurine, Stag, Lying Down, Base, 19th Century, 4 ¾ In., Pair	10073.00
Figurine, Stag, Lying Down, Painted, 1800s, 10 x 8 ½ In., Pair	1500.00
Figurine, Starlet, Provocative Pose, Blond Curls, 1920s, Art Deco Glass Stand, 14 In.	171.00
Fruit Basket, Footed Base, Multicolor, 1800s, 11 In.	1007.00
Fruit Compote, Grapes, Apples, Banana, Orange, Pear, 8 ½ In.	711.00
Lamp, Tennis Girl, Sitting On Ball, 1920s, 11 In.	85.00
Statue, Indian Brave, Arms Crossed, Plaster Of Paris, Bronze Painted, Signed, 1908, Life Size	3400.00
Tree, Mixed Fruit, Leaves, Medallion, Multicolor, Pedestal Base, 14 x 10 In. ....*illus*	1062.00

CHARLIE CHAPLIN, the famous comedian, actor, and filmmaker, lived from 1889 to 1977. He made his first movie in 1913. He did the movie *The Tramp* in 1915. The character of the Tramp has remained famous, and in the 1980s appeared in a series of television commercials for computers. Dolls, candy containers, and all sorts of memorabilia with the image of Charlie's Tramp are collected. Pieces are being made even today.

Automaton, Little Tramp, Papier-Mache, Wood, Eyes Roll, Cane Twirls, 1920s, 28 In.	4560.00
Candy Container, Glass, Figural Charlie Beside Container, L.E. Smith Co., c.1920, 4 In.	314.00
Candy Container, Leaning On Barrel, Cane, Hat, Glass, Painted, Borgfeldt	280.00
Dish, Porcelain, Green Glaze, 3 Sections, Figural Handle, c.1915, 5 ½ In.	143.00
Doll, Composition, Muslin, Side-Glancing Eyes, Painted Features, 13 In.	570.00
Doll, Kewpie Style, Bisque, Black Fleecy Wig, Flannel Suit, Germany, c.1915, 5 In.	371.00
Doll, Little Tramp, Composition Shoulder Head, Amberg & Sons, 32 In.	1368.00
Toy, Blue Jacket, Black Pants & Hat, Tin Lithograph, Cast Iron Shoes, B&R, Box, 8 ½ In. ....*illus*	1955.00
Toy, Figure, Walking, Tin, Flocked Hair, Goes In Circles, Cane Twirls, Schuco, 6 In.	460.00 to 684.00
Toy, Squeeze, Steel Band, Tin Lithograph, 7 ½ In. ....*illus*	288.00

CHARLIE MCCARTHY was the ventriloquist's dummy used by Edgar Bergen from the 1930s. He was famous for his work in radio, movies, and television. The act was retired in the 1970s.

Doll, Composition Head, Hands & Feet, Hinged Jaw, Cloth Body, Effanbee, 20 In.	1254.00
Doll, Composition, Painted Features, White Flannel Suit, Effanbee, c.1935, 16 In.	314.00
Dummy, Composition, Muslin, Jointed Jaw, Pull Mechanism, Effanbee, 19 ½ In. ....*illus*	316.00
Sign, Die Cut, 1940s, 14 ½ x 8 ½ In.	140.00
Toy, Benzine Buggy, Tin Lithograph, Windup, Marx, 8 In.	271.00
Toy, Car, Charlie McCarthy Driver, Head Turns, Tin Lithograph, Marx, 7 In.	158.00
Toy, Mortimer Snerd, Crazy Car, Tin Litho, Windup, 7 ¼ In.	345.00

Castor Set, 5 Bottles, Silver, Shell Feet, Ring Handle, England, 1764, 10 ¾ x 7 ½ In.
$5904.00

New Orleans Auction Galleries, Inc.

Celadon, Vase, Double Gourd, Relief Molded, Vines, Flowers, Handles, Incised Mark, Chinese, 12 In.
$8540.00

Neal Auction Co.

Celadon, Vase, Square, Lung Chuan Ware, Chinese, 16th Century, 10 In.
$1225.00

Skinner, Inc.

Celadon, Vase, Wheel-Turned Design, Narrow Mouth, Lung Chuan, Chinese, c.1200, 5 ¼ In.
$356.00

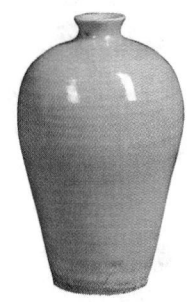

Skinner, Inc.

Ceramic Art Co., Vase, Lorelei, Leaning Over Ledge, Waterfall, Oval, Signed, Grace Reid, Belleek, 8 In.
$1126.00

Skinner, Inc.

Chalkware, Bust, Abraham Lincoln, Draped Shoulders, Pedestal, Signed, D. Morgan, 1865, 18 In.
$663.00

Garth's Auctions, Inc.

Chalkware, Bust, Oliver Hazard Perry, Military Uniform, Painted, c.1855, 10 In.
$1880.00

Garth's Auctions, Inc.

Toy, Mortimer Snerd, Crazy Car, Tin Lithograph, Windup, Marx, 8 In.	153.00
Toy, Walker, Mouth Motions, Tin Lithograph, Windup, Marx, 8 ¼ In. ....*illus*	230.00

CHELSEA porcelain was made in the Chelsea area of London from about 1745 to 1769. Some pieces made from 1770 to 1784 are called Chelsea Derby and may include the letter *D* for *Derby* in the mark. Ceramic designs were borrowed from the Meissen models of the day. Pieces were made of soft paste. The gold anchor was used as the mark, but it has been copied by many other factories. Recent copies of Chelsea have been made from the original molds. Do not confuse Chelsea porcelain with Chelsea Grape, a white pottery with luster grape decoration. Chelsea Keramic is listed in the Dedham category.

Dish, Leaf Mold, Green Rim, Purple Veins, Berries, Oval, Lobed, c.1770, 11 In.	500.00
Figurine, Flower Girl, Multicolor, 6 ¾ x 3 ½ In.	57.00
Plate, Exotic Bird, Standing Rock, Leafy Branches, 1760-65, 9 In.	1298.00
Plate, Round, Wavy Rim, Fruit, Leaves, Insects, Gilt Accents, 1763-65, 9 In.	3068.00
Platter, Botanical, Oval, Shaped Rim, Mark, c.1755, 12 ½ x 10 In.	489.00
Sauceboat, Footed, Loop Handle, Pour Spout, Stylized Leaf Design, Insects, Marked, 1700s, 7 In.	150.00
Sauceboat, Leaf Shape, Strawberry Vine, Berries, Blossoms, Branch Handle, c.1755, 7 In.	1652.00

CHELSEA GRAPE pattern was made before 1840. A small bunch of grapes in a raised design, colored with purple or blue luster, is on the border of the white plate. Most of the pieces are unmarked. The pattern is sometimes called Aynsley or Grandmother. Chelsea Sprig is similar but has a sprig of flowers instead of the bunch of grapes. Chelsea Thistle has a raised thistle pattern. Do not confuse these Chelsea patterns with Chelsea Keramic Art Works, which can be found in the Dedham category, or with Chelsea porcelain, the preceding category.

Cake Plate, Lugged, Blue Grape Swags, c.1830, 9 x 10 In.	78.00
Coffeepot, Panels, Footed, Scroll Handle, Purple, Grape Clusters, Finial, 9 ½ In.	110.00
Cup & Saucer, Purple Grapes	38.00
Cup & Saucer, Purple Grapes, Butterflies, Cherries	22.00
Jug, Flowers, Purple Sprig, Shouldered, Personalized, 1828, 7 In.	475.00
Plate, Luncheon, Blue Grape Swags, Raised, 7 In.	68.00

CHINESE EXPORT porcelain comprises all the many kinds of porcelain made in China for export to America and Europe in the eighteenth, nineteenth, and twentieth centuries. Other pieces may be listed in this book under Canton, Celadon, Nanking, Rose Canton, Rose Mandarin, and Rose Medallion.

Basin, Famille Rose, Figures, Flowers, Fold-Out Rim, 12 In. Diam.	657.00
Basin, Famille Rose, Flowering Plants, Fish, Aquatic Plants, 1800s, 14 ½ In.	551.00
Boat, Model, Famille Rose, Dragon Head, Pavilion Back, Figures, Stand, c.1875, 9 x 9 In.	799.00
Bottle, Armorial, Crests, Wolf, Standing On Shield, Wreath, 9 In.	1438.00
Bough Pot, Famille Rose, Interior Scenes, Squared Body, Leaf Handles, Gilt, 1800s, 9 ¼ In., Pair	4248.00
Bowl Set, Famille Rose, Figural Design, Flower Panel, Gilt Vine, 8 In., 2 Piece	239.00
Bowl, 4 Roundels, Figures, Round Foot, Wide Rim, 9 In. Diam.	508.00
Bowl, Black, Oil Spot, Footed, Chinese, 2 x 4 In.	270.00
Bowl, Blue & White, Flowers, Scrolling Leaves, 6 ½ In.	2390.00
Bowl, Blue & White, Magpies, Bridges, c.1620, 3 x 6 In.	1912.00
Bowl, Blue & White, Three Friends, Pine, Prunus, Bamboo, c.1900, 5 ¼ In., Pair	2726.00
Bowl, Carved Stand, 7 Worthies, Crane, Porpoise, Gilt Border, 1900s, 4 x 14 In.	502.00
Bowl, Cover, Black & Green, Gilt, Flowers, Leaves, Foo Dog Finial, Wire Bail Handle, 6 ½ In.	329.00
Bowl, Cover, Famille Rose, Allover Lotus Flower, Round Gilt Finial, Mark, 4 x 4 In.	1920.00
Bowl, Cover, Famille Rose, Figures, Fence, Garden, Pine, 5 Bracket Feet, 6 x 11 In.	760.00
Bowl, Cover, Round, Handles, Spherical Knop, Landscape Scenes, c.1800, 6 In.	492.00
Bowl, Famille Rose, 4 Roundels, Flowers, Pink, Marked, 6 In., Pair	1220.00
Bowl, Famille Rose, 8 Buddhist Treasures, Lotus Scrolls, Pink Ground, Mark, 3 x 6 In.	1007.00
Bowl, Famille Rose, 8 Immortals, Animals, Conical Shape, 10 ½ In.	186.00
Bowl, Famille Rose, Basket Shape, Underplate, Gold Handles, 1800s, 5 x 11 ½ In.	600.00
Bowl, Famille Rose, Bat, Peach, Calligraphy, 10 In.	388.00
Bowl, Famille Rose, Bell Shape, Fruits, Flowers, Butterflies, 4 In. Diam., Pair	10455.00
Bowl, Famille Rose, Birds, Flowers, Round Foot, Scalloped Rim, 10 In. Diam.	329.00
Bowl, Famille Rose, Blue & White, Mallow Blossoms, Leaves, Sweet Pea Vines, c.1900, 6 In., Pair	2706.00
Bowl, Famille Rose, Conical, Flared Sides, Footed, Shaped Lip Rim, Birds, Flowers, 7 ¾ In. Diam.	553.00
Bowl, Famille Rose, Figures, Scholar At His Desk, 8 In.	236.00
Bowl, Famille Rose, Flowers, Leaves, Buddhistic Chimes, Gilding, Round Panels, 6 In.	430.00
Bowl, Famille Rose, Flowers, Pink Ground, 3 x 5 ¾ In., Pair	8400.00

Bowl, Famille Rose, Flowers, Red, Green, Yellow Ground, c.1800, 3 x 6 In.	450.00
Bowl, Famille Rose, Flowers, Round Foot, 8 In. Diam.	390.00
Bowl, Famille Rose, Interior Flowers, Exterior Garden Scene, c.1910, 15 x 6 ½ In.	2370.00
Bowl, Famille Rose, Lotus, Molded Petals, Scalloped Rim, Marked, 1800s, 3 x 9 ¼ In. ....*illus*	1298.00
Bowl, Famille Rose, Painted, Immortal, Deer, Children, Peach Branch, 4 In., Pair	359.00
Bowl, Famille Rose, Painted, Insects, Flowers, 5 ½ In.	1554.00
Bowl, Famille Rose, Peony Interior, Garden Scenes Exterior, Round, 1700s, 8 In.	246.00
Bowl, Famille Rose, Pink Ground, Birds, Flowers, Insects, Marked, 5 In. Diam., Pair	1315.00
Bowl, Famille Rose, Pink Ground, Scrolling Leaves, Flowers, Round Foot, 4 In.	496.00
Bowl, Famille Rose, Ribbed, Round Base, Peach & Branches, 8 ½ In.	191.00
Bowl, Famille Rose, Round Reserves, Landscapes, Scrolling Leaves, 5 ¾ In.	5139.00
Bowl, Famille Rose, Scalloped, Butterflies, Flowers, White Ground, 2 ¾ x 6 In.	214.00
Bowl, Famille Verte, 4 Season Flowers, Iron Red Bat Interior, Mark, 1800s, 2 x 5 ½ In.	948.00
Bowl, Famille Verte, Flowers, Bamboo Leaf Band, Fruits, Painted, Square, 1800s, 2 ½ x 5 ¾ In.	237.00
Bowl, Famille Verte, Flowers, Insects, Gilt Rim, Round Foot, 7 In. Diam.	420.00
Bowl, Famille Verte, Insects, Flowers, Gilt Rims, Mark, Wood Stand, c.1945, 3 x 8 In., Pair	1659.00
Bowl, Fox Hunt Scene, Birds, Flowers, Scroll, Gilt Accents, Round Wood Base, 1700s, 15 In.	1840.00
Bowl, Glazed, Flowers, Birds, Leaf Design Band On Rim, 10 In.	338.00
Bowl, Pinstriped Foot, Flared Rim, Blue & White, Grape Vines, 6 Character Mark	374.00
Bowl, Rice, Cover, Flowers, Gilt Knob & Brackets, Bracket Foot, Signed, 5 x 9 In.	115.00
Bowl, Rice, Famille Rose, Inverted Bell, Entwined Willow, Plum Trees, Magpies, c.1930, 4 ⅜ In.	7687.00
Bowl, Rice, Famille Rose, Lotus Flowers, Scrolling Leaves, Bats, c.1930, 4 ⅝ In.	369.00
Bowl, Round Foot, Brown Matte Glaze, Blue Interior Glaze, 6 In. Diam.	1320.00
Bowl, Shallow, Multicolor, Flowers, Leaves, Blue Mark, 9 ¼ In.	329.00
Bowl, Steep Side, Yellow Ground, Green, Dragons, Phoenix Birds, Clouds, Marked, c.1930, 5 In.	246.00
Bowl, Twin Fish, Vertical Ribs Dividing Bowl, 6 Sections, 7 In.	338.00
Bowl, White, Iron Red & Black, Cockerel, Gilt Highlights, Marked, 7 ½ In.	269.00
Bowl, Yellow Ground, Red Dragons, Marked, 8 In. Diam., Pair	1080.00
Brush Washer, Famille Rose, Plum Shape, Fruit Plant, 7 In.	854.00
Brushpot, Blue & White, Figures In Landscape, 6 In.	488.00
Brushpot, Cylindrical, 2 Vendors, Seated Amidst Their Things, Blue & White, c.1895, 5 x 3 In.	354.00
Brushpot, Famille Rose, 2 Woodsmen, Crop, Inscriptions, Cylindrical, 5 x 4 In.	184.00
Brushpot, Famille Rose, Blue Ground, Peasants, Water Buffalo, 1800s, 5 ¾ In.	830.00
Cachepot, Armorial, Round, Lion Head Handles, Rings, Brass Base, 1800s, 10 x 12 ½ In., Pair	1845.00
Cachepot, Famille Rose, Flowers, Birds, Butterfly Reserves, Footed, 1900s, 12 x 14 In.	61.00
Censer, Famille Rose, Openwork, Lion Finial, Elephant Head Legs, Ring Handles, 1800s, 6 x 7 In.	225.00
Censer, Famille Rose, Yellow Ground, Applied Lion Handles, Shaped Panels, Tripod, 9 x 6 In.	4183.00
Chamber Pot, Famille Rose, Figures, Landscapes, Oblong, Handle, c.1780, 9 ¾ In.	738.00
Charger, Armorial, Landscape Border, Crest Motto, Pax In Bello, 1800s, 12 In.	375.00
Charger, Armorial, Neoclassical, Pink, Sepia, Gold, Shield, Bird, c.1800, 19 In.	207.00
Charger, Bird Of Paradise, Blue & White, Signed, 13 In.	575.00
Charger, Blue & White, Peony & Rockwork, Leaf Design Rim, c.1700, 15 In.	800.00
Charger, Blue & White, Rain Cloud, Bamboo & Chrysanthemum Spray, c.1851-74, 14 In.	470.00
Charger, Center Eagle, Spread Wings, Arrows, Laurel Branches, Iron Red Design, 18 In.	366.00
Charger, Dragon, Phoenix, Flowers, Marked, 1800s, 16 In., Pair	4392.00
Charger, Famille Rose, Bats, Peaches, Leaves, Wood Stand, c.1925, 12 In.	7190.00
Charger, Famille Rose, Domestic Scenes, Flowers, Fruit, Gilt, 18 In.	236.00
Charger, Famille Rose, Dragons, Clouds, Flaming Pearl, Chinese, 1900, 14 In.	4920.00
Charger, Famille Rose, Dragons, Flaming Pearl Of Wisdom, Multicolor, 1800s, 14 ½ In.	1076.00
Charger, Famille Rose, Flower Filled Urn, Greek Key Border, Bamboo Sprays, 1800s, 14 In.	767.00
Charger, Famille Rose, Flowering Peonies, Asters, c.1905, 14 ⅜ In.	430.00
Charger, Famille Rose, Flowers, Gilt Ground, c.1900, 16 In. Diam.	1912.00
Charger, Famille Rose, Foo Dogs, Peony Sprigs, Brown, 1700s, 15 In.	2200.00
Charger, Famille Rose, Magpies, Peony Bush, Flower Spray Rim, 1700s, 16 ¾ In.	1476.00
Charger, Famille Rose, Painted, 5 Iron Red Dragons, Pearl Of Wisdom, 14 ¼ In.	1135.00
Charger, Fruit Sprays, Blue & White, 12 In.	345.00
Charger, Stand, Famille Rose, Flowers, Multicolor, 13 In. Diam.	250.00
Chestnut Basket, Famille Rose, Mandarin, Flared Rim, c.1840, 4 x 9 In.	288.00
Cider Jug, Cover, Foo Dog Finial, Flower Sprigs, Butterflies, Dragon Border, 11 ½ In.	1500.00
Coffeepot, Dome Lid, Lighthouse Shape, Blue, Gilt, Entwined Handle, c.1800, 10 In.	173.00
Cup, Famille Rose, Lotus Blossom Shape, Marked, 1800s, 6 In., Pair	1838.00
Cup, Famille Rose, Maidens, Having Tea, 2 ⅝ In.	85.00
Cup, Stem, Flower Sprays, Everted Rim, Flared Foot, Blue & White, 1800s, 4 x 3 In.	1783.00
Cup, Tea, Saucer, Armorial, Heraldic Design, Handleless, 6 In.	338.00
Cup, Wine, Inverted Bell Shape, 2 Dragons, Flaming Pearl, Flames, Waves, c.1800s, 2 ¼ In.	1968.00

Chalkware, Figurine, Dove, Perched On Fruiting Branch, c.1890, 11 In., Pair
$889.00

Skinner, Inc.

Chalkware, Figurine, Squirrel, c.1850, 6 ½ In.
$180.00

DuMouchelles Art Gallery

Chalkware, Tree, Mixed Fruit, Leaves, Medallion, Multicolor, Pedestal Base, 14 x 10 In.
$1062.00

Conestoga Auction Co., Inc.

TIP
Bring a price guide book to an auction. It isn't possible to remember everything, but it is possible to look most items up. We think Kovels' Antiques & Collectibles Price Guide is the best.

Charlie Chaplin, Toy, Blue Jacket, Black Pants & Hat, Tin Lithograph, Cast Iron Shoes, B&R, Box, 8 ½ In. **$1955.00**

Bertoia Auctions

Charlie Chaplin, Toy, Squeeze, Steel Band, Tin Lithograph, 7 ½ In. **$288.00**

Bertoia Auctions

Charlie McCarthy, Dummy, Composition, Muslin, Jointed Jaw, Pull Mechanism, Effanbee, 19 ½ In. **$316.00**

Bertoia Auctions

Dish, European Scene In Center, Scrolling Gilt, 9 In. Diam.	620.00
Dish, Famille Rose, Bat Design, Marked, 7 In. Diam.	359.00
Dish, Famille Rose, Flowers, 8 Buddhist Emblems On Band, Flowers, 9 ⅝ In. Diam.	4481.00
Dish, Famille Rose, Nubian Head Profile, Flowers, 1700s, 9 In.	246.00
Dish, Famille Rose, Saucer Shape, Flowers, c.1925, 8 In.	492.00
Dish, Famille Rose, Shaped Rim, Medallion, Carp, 2 Dragons, Leaf Border, 1900s, 17 In.	615.00
Dish, Famille Rose, White Ground, Flower Head Design, Marked, 7 ½ In. Diam.	418.00
Dish, Famille Rose, White Ground, Leafy Branch, Flowers, Peaches, Bats, Saucer, 1900s, 8 In., Pair	1107.00
Dish, Sweetmeat, Cover, Cobalt Blue & White, Flowers, Compartments, 1800s, 8 In.	179.00
Ewer, White Glaze, Baluster, Square Handle, Loop Handles, Spout, 8 In.	359.00
Figurine, Famille Rose, Buddha, Stand, 7 ½ In.	201.00
Figurine, Crane, Standing, Rockwork Base, Turquoise, Yellow Beak & Feet, 1900s, 16 ¾ In.	430.00
Figurine, Famille Rose, Immortal & Boy, Flower Robe, 18 In.	508.00
Figurine, Famille Rose, Phoenix Bird, Perched On Rockwork, Multicolor, 1800s, 16 In.	615.00
Figurine, Famille Rose, Woman, Standing, Holding Ruyi Scepter, Feather Fan, 1800s, 17 In., Pair	1599.00
Figurine, Famille Verte, Boy, Seated, Yellow Robe, Flowers, 11 In.	1968.00
Figurine, Famille Verte, Official, Standing, Robed, Fitted Cap, Holding Lotus Leaf, 1700s, 10 ½ In.	522.00
Figurine, Fisherman, Beard, Robe, Trousers, Holding Huge Carp, Bamboo Hat, Crab, 30 In.	1599.00
Figurine, General, Riding Dragon, Horned, Lucite Stand, 15 x 16 In.	584.00
Figurine, Guanyin, Mercy Goddess, Seated, Long Robes, Marked, 13 In. ......*illus*	538.00
Figurine, Lion, Guardian, Male, Female, Ball, Cub, Multicolor, Stand, 1900s, 4 x 3 ½ In.	1098.00
Figurine, Mythical 3-Legged Frog, Green & Lavender Glaze, 1800s, 8 In.	267.00
Figurine, Throne, Cap, Long Robe, Blue & White, Dragons, Serpent Arms, 1900s, 25 x 16 In.	354.00
Flask, Famille Rose, Double Moon, Flowers, Riverscape, Red, Blue, Seal Mark, 7 ½ In., Pair	777.00
Flask, Famille Rose, Moon Shape, Flat Round Body, Splayed Foot, Dragon Handles, c.1925, 9 ¾ In.	2952.00
Ginger Jar, Blue, White, Urn Shape, Carved Lid & Stand, Pagoda, Flowers, 1800s, 7 In., Pair	4113.00
Ginger Jar, Dome Lid, Blue & White, Blossoms, 11 In.	430.00
Ginger Jar, Famille Rose, Flowers, Wood Base, 12 In., Pair	799.00
Ginger Jar, Famille Verte, Globular, Landscapes, People, Birds, Insects, Flowers, c.1855, 28 ½ In.	1107.00
Ginger Jar, Famille Verte, Scholar, White Ground, c.1980, 8 ¾ In.	504.00
Ginger Jar, Lid, Famille Verte, Bulbous, Figures, Pierced Hardwood Cover, 8 In.	10980.00
Hat Stand, Famille Rose, Birds, Flowers, Cylindrical, White Ground, c.1900, 11 x 5 In., Pair	1135.00
Incense Burner, Famille Rose, Elongated, Elephant Feet, Strap Handles, Pierced Top, c.1925, 9 ½ In.	553.00
Incense Burner, Famille Rose, Inverted Bowl Base, Bulbous Stem, Globe Top, 11 x 5 In.	600.00
Jar, Cover, Bulbous, Figures, Festive Procession, Cone Finial, 9 In.	549.00
Jar, Cover, Famille Jaune, Dragons, Lotus, Yellow Ground, 1800s, 17 In., Pair	2032.00
Jar, Cover, Famille Rose, Baluster, Birds Perched On Rocks, Multicolor, 16 In.	167.00
Jar, Cover, Famille Rose, Baluster, Peach Branches, Late 1800s, 17 In.	1100.00
Jar, Cover, Famille Rose, Bird, Flowers, Iron Red Ground, Gilt Metal Stand, 15 ½ In.	1170.00
Jar, Cover, Famille Rose, Cafe-Au-Lait Ground, Bird, Flowers, Cone Finial, 10 In., Pair	837.00
Jar, Cover, Famille Rose, Children Playing, White Ground, Round, c.1890, 9 ¼ In.	267.00
Jar, Cover, Famille Rose, Exterior Scenes, Foo Dog Finial, 18 In., Pair	502.00
Jar, Cover, Famille Rose, Peonies, Butterflies, Bulbous, Lotus Mouth Rim, c.1910, 9 In.	770.00
Jar, Cover, Famille Rose, Round, Bulbous, Flowers, Dragons, 12 In.	125.00
Jar, Cover, Famille Rose, Yellow Ground, Baluster, Domed, Bird & Flowers Panels, 21 In., Pair	366.00
Jar, Cover, Famille Verte, Baluster, Horses, c.1700, 6 In.	300.00
Jar, Cover, Famille Verte, Flowers, Bird, Bulbous, 1800s, 8 In.	203.00
Jar, Cover, Famille Verte, Urn Shape, Figures, Flowers, Wood Stand, 7 In.	780.00
Jar, Cover, Flambe Glaze, Oval, Splashes Of Purple & Crimson, 12 In.	148.00
Jar, Cover, Hexagonal, Blue & White, Landscape, Signed, 11 In., Pair	708.00
Jar, Cover, Porcelain, Knop Finial, Ribbed Bowl, Stem Foot, Geometrics, Blue, 11 In.	2510.00
Jar, Dome Lid, Famille Verte, Globular Finial, Figural Design, 8 In.	744.00
Jar, Famille Rose, Guests, Visiting Scholar, Chinese, 1800s, 14 In.	948.00
Jar, Famille Rose, Shouldered, Woman In Garden, Birds, Lid, 1800s	875.00
Jar, Famille Verte, Baluster, Warriors On Horseback, Masks, Foo Dog Finial, 25 In.	896.00
Jar, Famille Verte, Foo Dogs, Peony Scroll, Oval, Multicolor, c.1910, 4 In.	326.00
Jar, Famille Verte, Horseback Riders, Bulbous, 2 Boys Playing On Cover, 1800s, 11 ½ In.	948.00
Jar, Famille Verte, People, Landscape, Flower Border, 31 In.	326.00
Jar, Famille Verte, Warriors, Hundred Antiques, Flowers, Signed, 1800s, 12 ¼ In.	326.00
Jar, Oval, Cartouches, Birds, Flowers, Leafy Scrolls, Marked, 1800s, 10 In.	214.00
Jar, Temple, Cover, Bearded Figure, Family, Trees, Foo Dog Finial, Blue & White, 23 In., Pair	2070.00
Jardiniere, Famille Rose, Court Scenes, Flowers, Wood Stand, c.1900, 11 x 13 In.	299.00
Jardiniere, Famille Rose, Insects, Flowers, Gilt Design Orange Panels, c.1900, 7 ¾ In.	563.00
Jardiniere, Famille Rose, Plants, Animals, c.1790, 9 x 13 ½ In.	1495.00
Jardiniere, Flared Rim, Flowering Plants, Lappet Borders, 13 x 14 In.	244.00

Jug, Milk, Blue & White Figures, Flowers, Silver Mountings, c.1900, 6 ½ In.	1265.00
Mug, Ale, Famille Rose, Cylindrical, Strap Handle, Women, Children, Birds, 1800s, 5 ¾ In.	110.00
Mug, Armorial, Coat Of Arms, Berries & Vines, Gilt, c.1740, 6 In.	5463.00
Mug, Barrel Shape, Flower Sprays, Gilt Cartouches, Double Strap Handles, 5 In., Pair	244.00
Mug, Cider, Hand Painted, Flowers, Vase, Stool, Loop Handle, White Ground, 6 In.	207.00
Mug, Figural Scenes, 4 Landscapes, Cartouches, Handle, 5 In. .....*illus*	240.00
Pitcher, Cover, Flowers, Elongated Oval, Loop Handle, 8 ½ In.	863.00
Planter, Famille Rose, Openwork, Prosperity Symbols, Flowers, 1800s, 2 x 9 x 5 In.	600.00
Planter, Famille Rose, Woman, Children, Octagonal, Marked, c.1900, 2 x 8 x 6 In.	325.00
Plaque, Famille Rose, Mountains, Water Scene, Rectangular, 31 x 14 In.	267.00
Plaque, Famille Rose, Painted, Lotus Flowers, Signed, 21 x 13 In.	837.00
Plaque, Famille Rose, Painted, Riverscape, Frame, Signed, 1928, 21 x 13 In.	1076.00
Plaque, Famille Rose, Scholar, Teaching 5 Boys, Round, c.1890, 15 ½ In.	2032.00
Plaque, Famille Verte, Children At Play, Rosewood Frame, 18 x 13 In.	2520.00
Plaque, Famille Verte, Cockerel, Reticulated Wood Frame, 10 x 14 In.	837.00
Plaque, Famille Verte, Mountain, Water Scene, Inscribed, 14 x 10 In.	504.00
Plaque, Famille Verte, Pagoda, Mountains, Inscribed, Frame, 6 x 3 In.	239.00
Plate, 5 Bats, Peaches Roundels, Yellow Ground, Marked, 1800s, 9 ½ In.	593.00
Plate, Armorial, 2-Headed Falcon, Crowned Shield, Flower Border, Gilt Rim, 10 In., Pair	270.00
Plate, Armorial, Coat Of Arms, Family Crest, Gilt Flower Border, 18th Century, 8 ¾ In. ...*illus*	590.00
Plate, Armorial, Crown, Medallion, Bird, Dogs, 1700s, 9 In.	236.00
Plate, Armorial, Hexagonal, Jephson Impaling Chase, Coat Of Arms, Flowers, c.1730	4888.00
Plate, Armorial, Octagonal, Coat Of Arms, Honeycomb Border, Flowers, c.1750, 8 In.	4600.00
Plate, Blue Dragons, Clouds, Roundel, White Ground, Marked, 7 ½ In.	711.00
Plate, Blue Glaze, Flower Scrolling, Birds, Aquatic Plants, 8 ½ In.	551.00
Plate, Famille Rose, Central Panel, Chickens, Leaf Border, 9 In., Pair	549.00
Plate, Famille Rose, Flower Sprays, Gilt, 7 In. Diam., Pair	59.00
Plate, Famille Rose, Peach, Flowers, 1800s, Set Of 6	359.00
Plate, Famille Rose, Peonies, Green Lattice, Gold, Sacred Deer, Woodland, 10 In.	265.00
Plate, Famille Rose, Rosebuds, Fleur-De-Lis Border, Diaperwork, Scrolling Corbels, White, Pink, 9 In.	460.00
Plate, Famille Rose, Tobacco Leaf, Flowers, Leaves, Blue Underglaze, 1800s, 9 ¼ In., Pair	861.00
Plate, Famille Rose, Warrior, Riding Goat, Holding Flag, Pale Blue Ground, 1900s, 8 In. Diam.	4600.00
Plate, Famille Verte, Butterfly, Flowers, Green, White, Gilt, c.1900, 10 In.	173.00
Plate, Famille Verte, Woman, Fixing Hair, Garden, Brocade Ground, 1800s, 14 ¾ In.	1041.00
Plate, Flowers, Shrubbery, Pavilion, Pine Trees, c.1850, 9 In., Pair	345.00
Plate, Marie Antoinette, King Louis XVI, Roundel, Lidded Urn, Weeping Willow, 10 In.	496.00
Plate, Octagonal, Cowherd, Water Buffalo, Willow Trees, Flowers, Leaves, 1700s, 8 ¾ In., Pair	399.00
Plate, Sampan, Rough Seas, Figures, Birds, Scrolling Flower Border, c.1800, 9 In., Pair	1725.00
Plate, Soup, Dragon In Blue, Surrounded By Red Over Glaze, White Blossoms, 9 In.	53.00
Plate, South African Scenes, Grisaille, Chinese, c.1735, 9 In.	5750.00
Plate, Tobacco Leaf Design, Sprigs, Flowers, Enameled, 1700s, 10 In.	325.00
Plate, White Ground, Birds, Blossoming Tree, Flowers, Mid 1700s, 9 In. Diam.	213.00
Platter, Armorial, Coat Of Arms, Snug, Flowers, Gilt, Double Dart Border, 10 In.	1265.00
Platter, Armorial, Motto, Blue & Gilt Border, c.1785, 14 ¾ In. .....*illus*	460.00
Platter, Armorial, White, Mulberry Designs, Flowers, Scalloped Rim, Oval, 1700s, 11 In.	420.00
Platter, Blue & White, Lake Scene, Rectangular, 1700s, 11 ¾ x 14 ½ In.	553.00
Platter, Famille Rose, Figures, Landscape, Oval, 1900s, 18 ½ x 14 ¾ In.	259.00
Platter, Famille Rose, Lobed, Bird, Flower, Figure Cartouches, 1800s, 3 x 15 In.	179.00
Platter, Famille Rose, Oval, Scalloped Edge, Flower Sprays, Gilt, 13 In.	59.00
Platter, Famille Rose, Shaped Rim, Fort St. George, Crest, Harbor Views, c.1745, 14 In.	2124.00
Platter, Famille Verte, Figures, Village, Flowers, Birds, Diaperwork, 15 x 12 In., Pair	2300.00
Platter, Flower Basket, Urn, Blossoms, Bees, Gilt Lobed Edge, 1800s, 12 x 15 In.	345.00
Platter, Garden At Well, Flower Ring Urns, Notched Rim, 1700s, 16 x 13 In. .....*illus*	1200.00
Platter, Octagonal, Blue & White, Shaped, Flowers, Leaves, c.1860, 17 In.	999.00
Platter, Oval, Fishing Scene, Cobalt Blue Border, Birds, 1800s, 15 In.	1410.00
Platter, Oval, White & Cobalt Blue, Village, 1800s, 10 x 14 In.	259.00
Platter, Printed, Chinese River Scene, Islands, Connecting Bridges, Birds, Octagonal, c.1768, 13 In.	7207.00
Platter, Rectangular, Canted Corners, Emblem, 2 Trumpeting Angels, Blue, White, 13 In.	610.00
Punch Bowl, Aerostick Stage Balloon, Late 1800s, 10 ½ In.	4375.00
Punch Bowl, Cabbage Leaf Medallion, c.1890, 15 ½ In.	1200.00
Punch Bowl, Famille Rose, Bird, Flower, Figure Cartouches, Butterfly Gilt, 1800s, 5 x 11 In.	359.00
Punch Bowl, Famille Rose, Bird, Flower, Figure Cartouches, Stand, 1800s, 6 x 14 ¾ In.	535.00
Punch Bowl, Famille Rose, Enameled Figures, Landscape, Multicolor, 1900s, 17 x 7 ½ In.	1150.00
Punch Bowl, Famille Rose, Fish, Dragon Medallions, 19th Century, 10 In.	100.00
Punch Bowl, Famille Rose, Fox Hunt, Rondel, Flower Garlands, Swags, c.1755, 5 x 11 In.	1840.00
Punch Bowl, Figures, Flower Panels, Gilt, Paint, c.1900, 6 ¼ x 14 ¾ In.	548.00

Charlie McCarthy, Toy, Walker, Mouth Motions, Tin Lithograph, Windup, Marx, 8 ¼ In.
$230.00

Bertoia Auctions

Chinese Export, Bowl, Famille Rose, Lotus, Molded Petals, Scalloped Rim, Marked, 1800s, 3 x 9 ¼ In.
$1298.00

Brunk Auctions

Chinese Export, Figurine, Guanyin, Mercy Goddess, Seated, Long Robes, Marked, 13 In.
$538.00

Sloans & Kenyon

Chinese Export, Mug, Figural Scenes, 4 Landscapes, Cartouches, Handle, 5 In. $240.00

Cowan's Auctions

Chinese Export, Plate, Armorial, Coat Of Arms, Family Crest, Gilt Flower Border, 18th Century, 8 ¾ In. $590.00

Brunk Auctions

Chinese Export, Platter, Armorial, Motto, Blue & Gilt Border, c.1785, 14 ¾ In. $460.00

James D. Julia Inc.

Chinese Export, Platter, Garden At Well, Flower Ring Urns, Notched Rim, 1700s, 16 x 13 In. $1200.00

DuMouchelles Art Gallery

Punch Bowl, Flowers, Gilt Lattice, Rope Like Scroll Design On Rim, 1700s, 15 In.	1725.00
Sauce Bowl, Famille Verte, Cane, Pine Trees, Bats, c.1940, 3 In., Pair	184.00
Sauce, Famille Verte, Recessed Feet, Pine Tree, Crane, Bats, 3 In., Pair	492.00
Sauce, Flowering & Fruiting Plants, Yellow Ground, Late 1800s, 4 In., Pair	1353.00
Sauceboat, Famille Rose, Wavy Rim, European Subject, Dancing Figures, c.1775, 10 In.	649.00
Saucer, Famille Rose, Iron Red, Bats, Flowers, Character, Seal Mark, c.1945, 6 In.	307.00
Scepter, Ruyi, Inkstone, Dragons, Bats, Gilt, Carved Handle, Chinese, 13 In.	490.00
Scroll, 2 Levels Of Paradise, Mortals, Dieties, Demons, Ink, Paint, Frame, 74 x 44 ½ In.	5904.00
Soup, Dish, Armorial, Octagonal, Enamel & Gilt Crest, Dotted Green Rim Border, 1700s, 10 In.	296.00
Spoon Rest, Famille Rose, Scalloped, Flowers, Diamond Ground, Iron Red, Gilt, 3 ⅔ x 4 ⅔ In.	123.00
Teapot Stand, Armorial, Frederick Coat Of Arms, Shield, Gilt, Red, c.1740, 6 In.	748.00
Teapot, Armorial, Cylindrical, Twisted Handle, Straight Spout, c.1785-1820, 10 In.	239.00
Teapot, Bamboo, Melon Shape, Swirled Stem Shape Lid, Carved, 3 ½ In.	329.00
Teapot, Bulbous, Ball Finial, Loop Handle, Flowers, Chain From Handle To Spout, 5 In.	732.00
Teapot, Cadogan, Famille Verte, 2 Dragons, Pearl Of Wisdom, 6 In. *illus*	836.00
Teapot, Domed Lid, Armorial, Bulbous, Loop Handle, Crest, Lion, Shield, Helmet, Flowers, 1800s, 7 In.	944.00
Teapot, Famille Rose, Rose Color Ground, Flower Design, Cover, Finial, Loop Handle, 6 In.	1195.00
Teapot, Famille Rose, Scholar, Attendants, 1928, 7 x 5 In.	184.00
Teapot, Family Verte, Enameled Flowers & Butterfly, Serpentine Handle & Spout, 7 In.	770.00
Teapot, Globular, Blue, Green, Iron Red, Flowers, Leaves, Wire Handle, Marked, 4 In.	389.00
Teapot, Gold, Black Flowers, White Ground, Grisaille, c.1735, 5 ½ In.	575.00
Teapot, Oval, Gilded Finial, Straight Spout, Figural Scenes, 1700s, 6 In.	350.00
Teapot, Round, Bats, Inlaid Slip Design, Arched Handle, 5 In.	180.00
Teapot, Scenic Views, Grisaille, 5 ¼ In.	184.00
Tureen, Cover, Famille Rose, Flowers, Butterflies, Boar's Head Handles, Gilt, 8 ½ x 13 ½ In.	878.00
Tureen, Cover, Shaped Oval, Triangular Bands, Gilt Strap Handles, Berry Knop, c.1800, 6 x 13 In.	345.00
Tureen, Duck Shape, Brown, Blue, Pink, Chinese, 13 x 12 In., Pair	978.00
Tureen, Famille Rose, Warriors, Calligraphy, Metal Handles, Lid, 1800s, 7 x 11 In.	550.00
Tureen, Sauce, Underplate, Blue & Gilt, Dragon, Butterfly, Monogram, 1700s, 6 x 7 In.	978.00
Tureen, Soup, Cover, Armorial, Fruit Finial, Crests, Entwinded Handles, Flared Foot, 11 x 13 In.	1178.00
Tureen, Soup, Stand, Cartouches, Figures In Courtyard, Diapering, c.1795, 12 ½ In.	490.00
Tureen, Undertray, Cover, Famille Rose, Gilt, Stem Knop, Lotus Pod Handles, c.1800, 9 x 11 ½ In. *illus*	1348.00
Umbrella Stand, Blue Glazed, Molded Dragon Design, 27 In., Pair	418.00
Umbrella Stand, Famille Rose, Birds, Flowering Tree, 17 ½ In.	209.00
Umbrella Stand, Famille Rose, Dragons, Flowers, Gilt, Pendant Handles, 22 In.	1107.00
Umbrella Stand, Famille Rose, Flower Arrangements, Vases, c.1955, 18 In.	230.00
Urn, Cover, Bird Shape Handles, Foo Dog Finial, Mask Head Feet, Round Base, 21 x 9 In.	288.00
Urn, Cover, Famille Verte, Birds, Flowering Trees, Carved Teak Stands, 18 In., Pair	3450.00
Vase, Altar, Famille Jaune, Flowers, Symbols, Flared Neck, 1900s, 15 In., Pair	861.00
Vase, Archer's, Bulbous, Flared Neck, 2 Hollow Handles, Bamboo, Oxblood Glaze, 18 In.	861.00
Vase, Blue & White, Hawthorne Pattern, Wood Base, 13 In., Pair	861.00
Vase, Blue & White, Village, Landscape, Birds, 23 ½ x 10 In.	420.00
Vase, Blue On Celadon, Mountain Village, Foo Dog Handles, 23 x 8 In.	173.00
Vase, Blue, Flowers, Goldfish, Longevity Symbols, Dragon Handles, 17 x 8 In.	288.00
Vase, Bottle Shape, Art Nouveau, Blue Ground, Banding, Flowers, Leaves, 10 In.	89.00
Vase, Bottle Shape, Blue & White, Dragons, Flowers, Leaves, Stick Neck, 1800s, 9 In., Pair	167.00
Vase, Bottle Shape, Famille Rose, Pomegranate Trees, Birds, c.1900, 16 ⅛ In.	415.00
Vase, Bottle Shape, Tapering Cylindrical Body, Cloud Design, White Glaze, 4 In.	589.00
Vase, Bottle, Blue & White, Flower, Scroll Bands, c.1890, 15 ¼ In.	13145.00
Vase, Bottle, Flared Lip, White Ground, Flowers, Wavy Lines, 9 ¼ In.	184.00
Vase, Bottle, Pear Shape, Long Neck, 5 Dragons, Clouds, Raspberry Red Glaze, c.1930, 12 In.	984.00
Vase, Bottle, Pear Shape, Tapering Neck, Animals Of Zodiac, Blue & White, 1800s, 10 In.	615.00
Vase, Bottle, Sang-De-Boeuf, Globular, Cylindrical Neck, Marked, 1800s, 13 In., Pair	1076.00
Vase, Bulbous, Elongated Neck, Mirror Black, Gilt, Dragons, Plantain Leaves, c.1810, 5 ¼ In.	861.00
Vase, Bulbous, Tapered Neck, Round Foot, Marine Scenes, Flower Heads, Blue & White, 1800s, 7 In.	345.00
Vase, Cover, Famille Rose, Boys, Landscape, c.1890, 8 ½ x 5 ¾ In.	1434.00
Vase, Cover, Famille Rose, Lobed Rim, Foo Dog Handles, Cartouches, 16 In., Pair	527.00
Vase, Cover, Famille Rose, Turned Finial, Flowers, Scrolling Leaves, 18 In., Pair	341.00
Vase, Cover, Famille Rose, Urn Shape, Flowers, Green, Finial, Marked, 20 In., Pair	359.00
Vase, Cover, Hawthorne Design, Blue & White, Flowers, 7 In., Pair	1159.00
Vase, Double Gourd, Famille Rose, Children Playing, 12 ½ In.	551.00
Vase, Double Gourd, Flowers, Orange Glaze, Gilt, Swirling, Waves & Clouds, 1800s, 8 ½ In.	3185.00
Vase, Double Gourd, Fretwork, Lappet Borders, Stylized Flowers, Marked, 11 In., Pair	4920.00
Vase, Dragons, Clouds, Flowers, Butterflies, Famille Rose, Red Dragon Handles, 1800s, 22 In.	1541.00
Vase, Elongated Melon Shape, Purple Glaze, Butterflies, Flowers, Late 1800s, 16 In.	1300.00
Vase, Famille Jaune, Bulbous, Dragon, Ho Ho Bird, Yellow, Scroll Handles, 1800s, 18 x 14 In.	6040.00

Vase, Famille Jaune, Globular, Baluster, Shaped Handles, Pierced, Rotating Neck, 7 ½ In.	1107.00
Vase, Famille Noir, Bottle Shape, Black Ground, Flowering Tree, 12 In.	310.00
Vase, Famille Noir, Bulbous, Plum Branches, Black Green Ground, Dome Wood Cover, 14 In.	593.00
Vase, Famille Noir, Foo Dog, Riding Waves Panels, Black Ground, Marked, 14 In.	429.00
Vase, Famille Rose, 100 Butterfly, Trumpet Neck, Gilt Trim, c.1900, 15 ½ In.	6274.00
Vase, Famille Rose, 6-Sided, Flower Panels, Yellow Ground, Bronze Stand, c.1905, 13 In.	214.00
Vase, Famille Rose, Applied Water Dragons, Cicadas, White Ground, 1700s, 6 ½ In.	960.00
Vase, Famille Rose, Birds, Flowers, Landscapes, Blue Ground, c.1890, 27 ½ In.	2629.00
Vase, Famille Rose, Bottle Shape, Crested Love Birds, Flowering Branches, 6 In., Pair	922.00
Vase, Famille Rose, Bottle Shape, Flowers, Yellow Ground, 13 In.	239.00
Vase, Famille Rose, Bottle Shape, Scrolling Flowers, Village Scene, Mountains, 23 In.	248.00
Vase, Famille Rose, Bulbous Pear Shape, S-Handles, Round Foot, Birds, Flowers, c.1900, 15 In.	356.00
Vase, Famille Rose, Bulbous, Hundred Bats, Flared Neck, Gilt, Chinese, 14 ½ In.	6458.00
Vase, Famille Rose, Bulbous, Landscape, Footed, Tapered Neck, Flared Rim, 11 x 6 In., Pair	575.00
Vase, Famille Rose, Bulbous, Lotus Blossoms, Scrolls, Landscape Panels, Gilt, Magenta, 7 ¾ In.	1659.00
Vase, Famille Rose, Bulbous, Narrow Neck, Flare Rim, Pagoda, Trees, Flowers, 8 In.	598.00
Vase, Famille Rose, Bulbous, Stick Neck, Figures, Tree, White Ground, Marked, 8 In.	478.00
Vase, Famille Rose, Cylindrical, Narrow Neck, Horse, Pine Tree, Flared Rim, 11 In., Pair	478.00
Vase, Famille Rose, Double Gourd, Blue Ground, Flower Enamel, Landscape, 10 In., Pair	3600.00
Vase, Famille Rose, Dragon Handles, Bats, Clouds, 22 x 15 In.	5400.00
Vase, Famille Rose, Dragon Handles, Rings, Flowers, Leaves, 1900s, 15 In.	738.00
Vase, Famille Rose, Dragons, Phoenix, Clouds, Lavender Ground, Rosewood Base, 15 In.	4248.00
Vase, Famille Rose, Elephant Shape, Baluster Vase On Back, Orange, Turquoise, 11 In.	239.00
Vase, Famille Rose, Flared Rim, Woman, Palace, Flowers, Pink, Yellow, 13 ½ In.	674.00
Vase, Famille Rose, Flowering Branches, Rocks, Handles, 9 ½ In., Pair	575.00
Vase, Famille Rose, Flowering Prunus Tree, Pine, 15 In.	837.00
Vase, Famille Rose, Flowers, Bats, Turquoise Ground, 3 Strap Handles, 5 In.	1800.00
Vase, Famille Rose, Flowers, Birds, Yellow Ground, Branch Handles, 11 In., Pair	439.00
Vase, Famille Rose, Flowers, Scrolling, Geometric Neck Design, 7 x 4 In.	720.00
Vase, Famille Rose, Foo Dog Handles, Dragons, Flowers, Gilt, 1900s, 37 In., Pair	2214.00
Vase, Famille Rose, Genie Bottle Shape, Flowers, Tree, Pagoda, Lake, Mountains, 11 In.	240.00
Vase, Famille Rose, Globular, Stick Neck, Bats, Clouds, White, Red, Yellow, Marked, 15 In.	598.00
Vase, Famille Rose, Immortals, Round Foot, Flare Rim, 1900s, 16 In.	368.00
Vase, Famille Rose, Landscape, Warriors, 18 In.	4780.00
Vase, Famille Rose, Lid, Baluster, Scrolling Leaves, Bats, Turquoise Ground, 9 In.	305.00
Vase, Famille Rose, Long Neck, Flowering Trees, Birds, Footed, 13 In.	748.00
Vase, Famille Rose, Lozenge Shape, Riverscape, Iron Red Mark, 4 ½ In.	239.00
Vase, Famille Rose, Maple Tree, Branches, Cranes, Flowers, Deer, Marked, c.1890, 14 In. ....*illus*	1722.00
Vase, Famille Rose, Painted, Birds, Flowering Branches, 16 ½ In.	1135.00
Vase, Famille Rose, Painted, Scholars Playing, Pavilion, Oval, 19 In.	1076.00
Vase, Famille Rose, Painted, Warrior, Court Scene, 23 In.	1195.00
Vase, Famille Rose, Pear Shape, Elephant Head Handles, Turquoise Ground, 19 In.	1838.00
Vase, Famille Rose, Pear Shape, Woman Dressing, Screen, Signed, 12 ¼ In.	276.00
Vase, Famille Rose, Square, 4 Panels, Flowers, Peach, Diaper Pattern, 16 In.	199.00
Vase, Famille Rose, Square, Bats Among Clouds, Medallions, Pierced, 11 In.	310.00
Vase, Famille Rose, Squat, Shouldered, Figures, Buffalo, Tree, Rocks, 6 In.	269.00
Vase, Famille Rose, Symbols, Flowers, Landscapes, Handles, Chinese, 12 ¼ In.	3540.00
Vase, Famille Rose, Tapered Neck, Figures, Gardens, Pink, Foo Dog Handles, 11 In., Pair	295.00
Vase, Famille Rose, Tubular, Flare Neck, Lion Head Ring Handles, Stand, 1800s, 13 In., Pair	584.00
Vase, Famille Rose, Tulip Shape, Phoenix & Flowers, 25 In.	553.00
Vase, Famille Rose, Urn Shape, Gilt Mounts, Peonies, Leaves, Scroll Handles, 21 In., Pair	4920.00
Vase, Famille Rose, White Ground, Figures, Flared Rim, Handles, 1800s, 17 In.	299.00
Vase, Famille Rose, Women Picking Flowers, Round Foot, Signed, c.1930, 14 ½ In.	1103.00
Vase, Famille Verte, Bottle, Flowers Leaves, Chinese, 1800s, 11 ½ In.	1185.00
Vase, Famille Verte, Cartouches, Flower Scenes, Turquoise Stipple, 12 In.	149.00
Vase, Famille Verte, Cylindrical, Acrobats, Officials, Garden, 1800s, 7 ½ In.	430.00
Vase, Famille Verte, Figures Outside Walled City, Elephant Head Handles, 18 In.	3968.00
Vase, Famille Verte, Globular, Bottle Neck, Hundred Boys, Young Boys At Play, 14 In.	478.00
Vase, Famille Verte, Immortal Panels, Butterfly & Flower Ground, 21 ½ In.	593.00
Vase, Famille Verte, Leopards, Flowers, Butterflies, Rocks, 14 x 10 In.	1600.00
Vase, Famille Verte, Military, Landscape Cartouches, Purple Ground, Chinese, 1800s, 10 In., Pair	444.00
Vase, Famille Verte, Painted Warriors, On Horseback, Dragon Handles, 16 In.	8365.00
Vase, Famille Verte, Pear Shape, Bird Perched On Pine Tree, Fox, 10 In.	1076.00
Vase, Famille Verte, Peonies, Branches, Rocks, Chinese, c.1885, 10 In.	429.00
Vase, Famille Verte, Pheasant, Trees, Peonies, Birds, 19th Century, 18 In.	500.00
Vase, Famille Verte, Rolled Rim, Landscape, Figures, Trees, c.1700, 19 ½ In.	500.00

Chinese Export, Teapot, Cadogan, Famille Verte, 2 Dragons, Pearl Of Wisdom, 6 In.
$836.00

Sloans & Kenyon

Chinese Export, Tureen, Undertray, Cover, Famille Rose, Gilt, Stem Knop, Lotus Pod Handles, c.1800, 9 x 11 ½ In.
$1348.00

Skinner, Inc.

Chinese Export, Vase, Famille Rose, Maple Tree, Branches, Cranes, Flowers, Deer, Marked, c.1890, 14 In.
$1722.00

New Orleans Auction Galleries, Inc.

Christmas, Belsnickle, Santa Claus, Blue Robe, Feather Tree Sprig, Snow Flaked Base, 10 ½ In.
$805.00

Bertoia Auctions

Christmas, Button, Page's Toy Ship Quincy, Santa Claus, Sack, Toys, Cammall Badge Co., 1920s, 1 ¼ In. $75.00

Hake's Americana & Collectibles

Christmas, Card, Die Cut, Santa Claus, White Robe, Children Holding Hands, Germany, 10 ½ In. $748.00

Bertoia Auctions

Christmas, Lantern, Santa Claus Head, Hood, Mica, Composition, Painted, Paper Eyes, Teeth, 5 ½ In. $345.00

Bertoia Auctions

Christmas, Sign, Santa Claus, Unika Brand St. Nick Boots, Die Cut, Easel Back, 11 ¾ x 5 ⅝ In. $578.00

Wm Morford Antiques

Vase, Famille Verte, Square, Children Playing, Flowers, Tapered, Narrow Neck, 11 In.	777.00
Vase, Famille Verte, Tapered Square, Warriors, Butterflies & Leaf Neck, 1800s, 24 In., Pair	2370.00
Vase, Genie Bottle Shape, Blue & White, Flowers, Round Foot, Chien Lung, 4 In.	500.00
Vase, Gourd Shape, Blue & White, Many Flowers Design, Peonies, 1900s, 10 ½ In.	461.00
Vase, Gourd Shape, Blue Glaze, Purple Splash, Footed Base, 7 In.	676.00
Vase, Green Ground, Courtyard Scenes, 15 x 6 In.	1020.00
Vase, Grisaille, Yellow Ground, Flowers, Fruit, Scroll Handles, 11 ½ In.	1195.00
Vase, Hexagonal, Multicolor, Dragons, Flowers, Leaves, Marked, 8 ¼ In.	508.00
Vase, Iron Red, Blue & White, 5 Horned Dragons, Clouds, c.1930, 3 ¼ In.	276.00
Vase, Square, Long Neck, Tubular Handles, Blue & White, Leaf Scrolls, 1800s, 13 In.	1135.00
Vase, Squat, Turquoise, Crackled Glaze, Rust Rim, 6 In.	305.00
Vase, Tulipiere, Flat Octagonal, 5 Flower Holders, Ring Handles, Dragons, Lotus, 18 In.	153.00
Washbasin, Blue & White, Riverscape, Stand, Mahogany, 1800s, 16 x 27 In.	2252.00

CHINTZ is the name of a group of china patterns featuring an overall design of flowers and leaves. The design became popular with English makers about 1928. A few pieces are still being made. The best known are designs by Royal Winton, James Kent Ltd., Crown Ducal, and Shelley. Crown Ducal and Shelley are listed in their own sections.

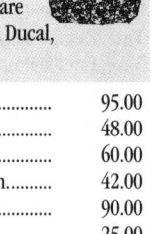

Angela, Cup & Saucer, Royal Albert, 1970s	95.00
Apple Blossom, Plate, James Kent, 9 In.	48.00
Balmoral, Plate, Pink, Yellow Flowers, Black Ground, Royal Winton, 1950s, 7 In.	60.00
Beeston, Sugar, Pink, Yellow Roses, Black Ground, Royal Winton, c.1940, 2 ¼ x 3 ½ In.	42.00
Biarritz, Plate, Yellow, Green, Blue, Royal Staffordshire, 1938, 7 ¾ x 9 In.	90.00
Blue Anemone, Plate, Luncheon, Royal Winton, 8 In.	25.00
Calico, Plate, Blue & White, Burleigh, England, 10 ½ In.	45.00
DuBarry, Plate, James Kent, 8 In.	155.00
Heather, Relish, Lord Nelson, 12 ¾ x 6 ⅞ In.	29.00
Hydrangea, Cup & Saucer, Royal Albert	128.00
Lady Gay, Sugar, Open, Royal Albert, 2 x 3 In.	19.00
Marion, Sugar Shaker, Royal Winton, 6 In.	162.00
Mayfair, Teapot, Stacking, Royal Winton, 5 ½ In.	795.00
Nocturne, Cup & Saucer, Royal Albert, 3 x 5 In.	30.00
Old Cottage, Dish, Roses, Asters, Oval, Molded Handles, Royal Winton, 7 x 11 In.	75.00
Pekin, Cup & Saucer, Black Ground, Demitasse, Royal Winton, 2 ¼ x 4 ¾ In.	62.00
Queen Anne, Cup & Saucer, Royal Winton, c.1935	50.00
Queen Anne, Relish, 3 Sections, Shaped, Royal Winton, 9 ½ In.	57.00
Rosalynde, Cup & Saucer, James Kent	65.00
Rose Du Barry, Ring Box, Round, Squat, 24K Gold Legs, Royal Winton, 1940s, 1 ½ x 1 ¾ In.	55.00
Stratford, Platter, Tulips, Lilacs, Round, Royal Winton, 1953, 12 ½ In.	325.00
Summertime, Cheese Dish, Royal Winton, 1951, 6 x 2 ½ In.	300.00
Sunshine, Relish, Royal Winton, c.1955, 6 x 4 In.	95.00
Sweet Pea, Plate, Pink, Blue, Yellow, Square, Royal Winton, c.1940, 6 In.	42.00
Sweet Pea, Platter, Royal Winton, c.1940, 9 ½ x 12 ½ In.	175.00
Trellis Rose, Teapot, Gold, Pink Flowers, James Kent, 1940s, 2 Pt.	55.00

CHOCOLATE GLASS, sometimes mistakenly called caramel slag, was made by the Indiana Tumbler and Goblet Company of Greentown, Indiana, from 1900 to 1903. It was also made at other National Glass Company factories. Fenton Art Glass Co. made chocolate glass from about 1907 to 1915. More recent pieces have been made by Imperial and others.

Cactus, Berry Set, 6 Piece	100.00
Cat On Hamper Cover, Dish, 5 ½ In.	891.00
Cactus, Butter, Cover, 9 ½ In.	604.00
Cord Drapery, Syrup, 7 In.	100.00
Wild Rose & Bowknot, Water Set, Pitcher & 5 Tumblers, 8 In.	518.00
Wild Rose & Festoon, Lamp, Oil, 10 In.	463.00

CHRISTMAS collectibles include not only Christmas trees and ornaments listed below, but also Santa Claus figures, special dishes, and even games and wrapping paper. A Belsnickle is a nineteenth-century figure of Father Christmas. A kugel is an early, heavy ornament made of thick blown glass, lined with zinc or lead, and often covered with colored wax. Christmas cards are listed in this section under Greeting Card. Christmas collectibles may also be listed in the Candy Container category. Christmas trees are listed in the section that follows.

Banner, Join Our Christmas Club Now, Wise Men, Camels, Linen, New York, 58 x 33 ½ In.	59.00
Belsnickle, Gold Robe, Holding Tree, 17 ½ In.	1320.00
Belsnickle, Red Robe, Hood, Holding Fir Tree, 11 In.	1020.00

Christmas, Tin, Biscuit, Santa Claus, Sack Of Toys, Elves, Letters, Huntley & Palmer, c.1935, 3 ¾ x 8 In.
$115.00

Bertoia Auctions

Christmas, Toy, Santa Claus, Holding Walking Stick, Composition, Cloth, Marked, Japan, 9 In.
$58.00

Bertoia Auctions

Christmas, Toy, Santa Claus, In Airplane, Blown Glass, Composition, Tinsel, Germany, 7 ½ In.
$489.00

Bertoia Auctions

Christmas Tree, Lamp, Glass, Queen Victoria, Aqua, Roped Corners, Quilted Panels, c.1885, 3 ½ In.
$202.00

American Glass Gallery

Christmas Tree, Ornament, Ali Baba, Extended Legs, Glass, Germany, 4 ½ In.
$920.00

Bertoia Auctions

Christmas Tree, Ornament, Dancing Girl, Bisque Head, Cotton, Crepe Paper, Heubach, Germany, 5 In.
$345.00

Bertoia Auctions

Christmas Tree, Ornament, Elf, Carrying Carrot, Pressed Cotton, Dresden, Germany, 2 ¼ In.
$690.00

Bertoia Auctions

Christmas Tree, Ornament, Foxy Grandpa, Glass, Clip, Germany, 4 ½ In.
$259.00

Bertoia Auctions

Christmas Tree, Ornament, Indian Head, Headdress, Blown Glass, Germany, 3 ½ In.
$690.00

Bertoia Auctions

Christmas Tree, Ornament, Moon Face, Embossed, Silvertone, Dresden, 2-Sided, Germany, 3 In.
$863.00

Bertoia Auctions

Christmas Tree, Ornament, Sailboat, Scrap Child, Wire Wrapped, Sebnitz, Germany, 3 ½ In.
$173.00

Bertoia Auctions

Christmas Tree, Ornament, Skeezix, Blown Glass, 4 In.
$230.00

Bertoia Auctions

Christmas Tree, Ornament, Victorian Woman, Bust, Glass, Clip, 4 ¼ In. $748.00

Bertoia Auctions

Christmas Tree, Ornament, Yellow Kid, Extended Legs, Glass, 4 In. $2588.00

Bertoia Auctions

Christmas Tree, Topper, Glass, Third Reich, Eagle, Swastika, 13 In. $207.00

The Stein Auction Co

Belsnickle, Santa Claus, Blue Robe, Feather Tree Sprig, Snow Flaked Base, 10 ½ In. ......*illus*	805.00
Belsnickle, Yellow Robe, Holding Tree, 10 ½ In..	540.00
Book, Jingle Bell, Actual Bells On Front, McLoughlin Brothers, 1955, 11 x 8 ½ In......................	30.00
Book, Night Before Christmas, Santa Claus, Reindeer, Sam'l Gabriel Sons, 1920s, 9 x 6 In.	50.00
Book, Santa's Circus, Pop-Up, White Plains Greeting Card Corp., 1952, 11 x 9 In.	35.00
Booklet, Rudolph Red Nosed Reindeer, 1st Edition, 38 Pages, 1939, 10 x 78 In.	475.00
Button, Page's Toy Shop Quincy, Santa Claus, Sack, Toys, Cammall Badge Co., 1920s, 1 ¼ In. *illus*	75.00
Candleholder, 2-Light, Santa Claus, Seated, Smoking Pipe, Composition, Germany, 6 x 8 In.	575.00
Candy containers are listed in the Candy Container category.	
Card, Die Cut, Holly, Campbell Art Co., Elizabeth, New Jersey, 1910, 6 x 3 ½ In.	18.00
Card, Die Cut, Santa Claus, White Robe, Children Holding Hands, Germany, 10 ½ In. ....*illus*	748.00
Catalog, Western Auto, 1975, 30 Page, 8 x 10 In.	28.00
Coloring Book, Santa Claus, Children, Toys, Reuben H. Lilja & Co., 23 Pages, 1940s, 14 x 10 In.	35.00
Display, Santa Claus, In Sleigh, Reindeer, Cast Iron, c.1900, 7 x 15 In........................	551.00
Doll, Santa Claus, Cloth, Velvet Outfit, Gold Brocade, 19 In.	175.00
Figure, Grandfather Frost, Children, Sack, Toys, Snow Man, Base Rocks, Russia, 17 x 10 In. ..	546.00
Figure, Polar Bear, Pulling Sleigh, St. Nick, Wood, Base, Painted, Russia, 27 x 7 In.................	1150.00
Figure, Santa Claus, Skiing, Metal, 3 In...	17.00
Figure, Santa Claus, Walking, Basket On Back, Sprig Tree, Lights, Germany, 11 In.	1380.00
Gift Wrap, Zippo Lighters, 1960s, 20 x 30 In.	21.00
Greeting Card, Hummingbirds, Butterfly, Christmas Hymn, Louis Prang, 1883, 7 x 6 In.	25.00
Lantern, Santa Claus Head, Hood, Mica, Composition, Painted, Paper Eyes, Teeth, 5 ½ In. ....*illus*	345.00
Lunch Box, Hinged Handle, Tin, Image Of Santa Claus Reading Rhymes, 1925, 4 ¾ x 3 In....	225.00
Mask, Parade, Santa, Cardboard, Germany, 13 ½ In..	240.00
Nativity Scene, Mother-Of-Pearl, Relief Carved, Pierced, Oval, c.1925, 6 x 8 In....................	492.00
Nodder, Man In Gray Robe, Blue Scarf, Bag, For Good Children, Papier-Mache, c.1910, 15 In.	7200.00
Pin, Santa Claus, Celluloid, Multicolor, Batterman Co., Brooklyn, Bastian Brothers, 1 ¼ In. ...	58.00
Pin, Santa Claus, Give Something Electrical, Multicolor, Celluloid, Bastian Brothers, 1 ¼ In. .	45.00
Pin, Santa Claus, Holly Wreath, Meet Me At Bowman's, Celluloid, 2-Sided, ¾ In.	52.00
Pin, Santa Claus, In Biplane, From Santa Claus Headquarters At Loeser's, c.1913, 1 ¼ In.	144.00
Pin, Santa Claus, In Biplane, Moon, Stars, Meet Me At Happyland, Lord & Gage, 1 ¼ In.	173.00
Pin, Santa Claus, Meet Me At Namm's, New York City, Celluloid, Back Paper, 1 ¼ In.............	56.00
Pin, Santa Claus, Your Old Friend Santa Is At Bailey's, c.1907, 1 ¼ In.	318.00
Pin, Santa's Good Conduct Pin, Image Of Santa Claus, Sack Of Toys, Celluloid, ⅞ In.	19.00
Plates that are limited edition are listed in the Collector Plate category or in the correct factory listing.	
Postcard, Holly, Berries, c.1900..	6.00
Postcard, Merry Christmas, Girl In Hat & Coat, Holding Pine Branches, c.1910....................	20.00
Postcard, Merry Christmas, Happy New Year, Children, Sleigh, Holly Leaves & Berries, 1911 ..	14.00
Postcard, Santa Claus, Sleigh, Blue Robe & Cap, Gold Stars, 1930	8.00
Postcard, Winter Scene, Hold-To-Light, 1906	135.00
Santa Claus, Sled, Reindeer, Tin, Celluloid, Japan, 8 In...	68.00
Sign, Santa Claus, Unika Brand St. Nick Boots, Die Cut, Easel Back, 11 ¾ x 5 ⅝ In. ....*illus*	578.00
Stocking, Baby's First, Red Quilted Plastic, Santa's Face On Front, 1930s, 11 x 5 In..............	35.00
Tin, Biscuit, Santa Claus, Sack Of Toys, Elves, Letters, Huntley & Palmer, c.1935, 3 ¾ x 8 In. *illus*	115.00
Tin, Father Christmas, Holding Lantern, Octagonal, 1950s, 5 x 3 In...........................	95.00
Toy, Handcar, Santa Claus, Christmas Tree, Mickey Mouse In Sack, Lionel, Box, 9 In.	1840.00
Toy, Santa Claus, Holding Walking Stick, Composition, Cloth, Marked, Japan, 9 In. ....*illus*	58.00
Toy, Santa Claus, In Airplane, Blown Glass, Composition, Tinsel, Germany, 7 ½ In. ....*illus*	489.00
Toy, Santa Claus, In Wood Wagon, Horse, Trees, 27 In.	805.00
Toy, Santa Claus, Riding Nodding Donkey, Composition, Feather Tree, Wheels, 11 In.............	690.00
Toy, Santee Claus Sleigh, Drawn By 2 Reindeer, Tin Lithograph, Strauss, 11 In........................	748.00

CHRISTMAS TREES made of feathers and Christmas tree decorations of all types are popular with collectors. The first decorated Christmas tree in America is claimed by many states, including Pennsylvania (1747), Massachusetts (1832), Illinois (1833), Ohio (1838), and Iowa (1845). The first glass ornaments were imported from Germany about 1860. Dresden ornaments were made about 135 years ago of paper and tinsel. Manufacturers in the United States were making ornaments in the early 1870s. Electric lights were first used on a Christmas tree in 1882. Character light bulbs became popular in the 1920s, bubble lights in the 1940s, twinkle bulbs in the 1950s, plastic bulbs by 1955. In this book a Christmas light is a holder for a candle used on the tree. Other forms of lighting include light bulbs. Other Christmas collectibles are listed in the preceding section.

Aluminum, 31 Branches, Stand, Box, 1950s, 4 Ft., 2 Piece	165.00
Aluminum, 94 Branches, Tripod Stand, Box, 6 Ft..	213.00
Aluminum, Pompom, Tripod Stand, 2 Ft.	39.00
Aluminum, Wood Poles, Tripod Stand, Silver Tree Co., Box, c.1960, 6 Ft................................	289.00

Bottle Brush, Composition Candles, Mercury Glass Ornaments, 3 ½ In.	42.00
Bottle Brush, Wood Base, 12 In.	25.00
Feather, 2-Tone Branches, Berries, Germany, c.1920, 25 In.	191.00
Feather, 14 Rows Of Branches, Germany, 89 In.	1875.00
Feather, Berries, Candle Topper, Plaster Pot, Germany, 6 In.	55.00
Feather, Glass Ornaments, Germany, 65 In.	880.00
Feather, Goose, Green, Red Berries, Paper Wrapped, c.1900, 24 In.	119.00
Feather, Sears & Roebuck, Box, c.1916, 33 In.	371.00
Fence, Cedar, 14 Ft. x 4 In.	150.00
Fence, Picket, White, Flex, Box	45.00
Fence, Twig, 5 Sections.	60.00
Fence, Wood, False Gate, 19th Century, 68 In., 4 Piece	125.00
Fence, Wood, Feather, Berries, Arch, c.1900, 10 x 10 x 3 In.	62.00
Garland, Gold Feather Tinsel, Glass Bell Feather Ornaments, Cotton Core, 8 Ft.	92.00
Garland, Mercury Glass, Blue Beads, 68 In.	10.00
Garland, Tinsel, Silver, Briton, Fireproof, Box, 12 Ft.	20.00
Lamp, Glass, Queen Victoria, Aqua, Roped Corners, Quilted Panels, c.1885, 3 ½ In. *illus*	202.00
Light, Santa Claus, Helmut, 2 ¾ In.	15.00
Ornament, Ali Baba, Extended Legs, Glass, Germany, 4 ½ In. *illus*	920.00
Ornament, Berry, Gold, Glass, c.1920, 1 ⅝ In. Diam.	15.00
Ornament, Church, Steeple, West Germany, 1950s, 1 ⅜ x 1 ¼ In.	10.00
Ornament, Dancing Girl, Bisque Head, Cotton, Crepe Paper, Heubach, Germany, 5 In. *illus*	345.00
Ornament, Elf, Carrying Carrot, Pressed Cotton, Dresden, Germany, 2 ¼ In. *illus*	690.00
Ornament, Figure Wearing Crown, Chenille Arms & Legs, 6 ½ In.	600.00
Ornament, Foxy Grandpa, Glass, Clip, Germany, 4 ½ In. *illus*	259.00
Ornament, Geisha Girl, Glass, Italy, 1960s, 5 In.	35.00
Ornament, Glass, Beetle, Wire Wrapped, 5 ¼ In.	480.00
Ornament, Glass, Candle Within A Ring, Multicolor, Occupied Japan, 2 ½ In., 12 Piece	75.00
Ornament, Glass, Eddie Cantor, Chenille Arms & Legs, 5 ½ In.	510.00
Ornament, Glass, Green, Mica Stripes, Shiny Brite, 1950s, 3 ½ In.	10.00
Ornament, Glass, Keystone Kop, 4 ½ In.	168.00
Ornament, Glass, Puss N Boots, Chenille Legs, 4 ¾ In.	900.00
Ornament, Gnome, On Pinecone, Frog, Flowers, Dresden, Germany, 3 In.	960.00
Ornament, Indian Head, Headdress, Blown Glass, Germany, 3 ½ In. *illus*	690.00
Ornament, Moon Face, Embossed, Silvertone, Dresden, 2-Sided, Germany, 3 In. *illus*	863.00
Ornament, Ocean Freighter, Dresden, Germany, 6 In.	960.00
Ornament, Sailboat, Scrap Child, Wire Wrapped, Sebnitz, Germany, 3 ½ In. *illus*	173.00
Ornament, Santa Claus, Composition, Wooden Arms & Legs, 8 In.	120.00
Ornament, Skeezix, Blown Glass, 4 In. *illus*	230.00
Ornament, Swiss Chalet, Dresden, Germany, 2 ½ x 2 ¾ In.	720.00
Ornament, Victorian Woman, Bust, Glass, Clip, 4 ¼ In. *illus*	748.00
Ornament, Yellow Kid, Extended Legs, Glass, 4 In. *illus*	2588.00
Stand, Aluminum, Folding, Quik & Ezy, 1950s, 16 x 6 x 6 In.	32.00
Stand, Cast Iron, 1920s, 9 x 4 In.	75.00
Stand, Cast Iron, Embossed, Santa Claus, Green, Red, 5 x 11 In.	231.00
Stand, Cast Iron, Green, Gold Paint, Shapes, c.1890, 12 x 12 In.	71.00
Stand, Cast Iron, Heart Shape Screws, Pointed Feet, 1920s, 7 x 7X 3 In.	49.00
Stand, Cast Iron, Merk, Patent 1891, 11 x 12 In.	148.00
Stand, Cast Iron, Raised Letters, North Bros Mfg., c.1900	100.00
Stand, Chrome, Handy Things Mfg., 1950, 26 In.	80.00
Stand, Chrome, Pot, Box, c.1958, 26 x 26 x 10 In.	84.00
Stand, Metal, Winter Scene, Lithographed, c.1945, 7 x 20 In. Diam.	64.00
Stand, Steel, Enamel, White, Precision Products, Box, 1960s, 17 In. Diam.	36.00
Topper, Candle, Circular Clear Lights, Silver Tinsel, Box, 1970s	20.00
Topper, Floral Bouquet, Urn, Handles, Embossed, 2-Sided, Dresden, 7 x 9 In.	767.00
Topper, Glass, Germany, Beads, Spheres, Lauscha, c.1925, 12 In.	245.00
Topper, Glass, Third Reich, Eagle, Swastika, 13 In. *illus*	207.00
Topper, Glass, Triple Indent, Tree, Painted, 1950s, 2 x 10 In.	20.00
Topper, Plastic, Metallic Finish, Steeple, Bells, c.1960, 13 ½ In.	16.00
Topper, Star, Tinsel, Angel Scrap, Czechoslovakia, c.1915, 8 In. Diam.	35.00
Topper, Victorian Lady, Porcelain, 8 In.	75.00

CHROME items in the Art Deco style became popular in the 1930s. Collectors are most interested in high-style pieces made by the Connecticut firms of Chase Brass & Copper Co. and Manning-Bowman & Co.

Ashtray, Dog, Crossbar, 5 x 5 In.	22.00
Ashtray, Elephants, Hamilton Products, 1930s, 4 x 2 In.	13.00

Cigar Store Figure, Indian, Brooks, Painted, 1880s, 69 In. $49500.00

Showtime Auction Services

Cigar Store Figure, Indian, Headdress, Carved, Painted, Mr. Wolf's Yankee Notions, c.1890, 84 In. $21240.00

Conestoga Auction Co., Inc.

Cigar Store Figure, Indian, Headdress, Carved, Painted, Right Hand Shields Eyes, Wheels, 83 ½ In. $80240.00

Conestoga Auction Co., Inc.

Cigar Store Figure, Indian, Princess, Headdress, Platform, 340, S.A. Robb, 195 Canal St., c.1851, 72 In. $43660.00

Conestoga Auction Co., Inc.

Bottle Opener, Dolphin Shape, 1960s, 6 ½ In.	30.00
Cigarette Case, Gold Wash Interior, Striped Texture, c.1950, 4 x 3 In.	55.00
Cigarette Lighter, Ships Wheel, U.S.A., 5 In.	85.00
Cocktail Shaker, Hand, Red Finger Nails, American Distilling Co., 1950s, 9 In.	40.00
Cocktail Shaker, Walnut Catalin Handle, Farber, 12 ¾ In.	65.00
Coffee Urn, Ball Shape, Art Deco, Bakelite, Manning Bowman, 1930s, 15 In.	175.00
Figurine, Horse, Saddle, 1960s, 4 ¼ In.	32.00
Percolator, Wood Handle, Manning Bowman, 11 ½ In.	75.00
Sugar & Creamer, Footed, Urn Shape, Manning Bowman	55.00
Tray, Glass, Lace & Cross-Stitch Insert, Farberware, 11 In.	25.00
Tray, Tiered, Folding, 3 Sections, Chase, 15 x 11 x 8 In.	150.00
Waffle Iron, Double, Wood Handle, Manning Bowman, 14 x 8 In.	85.00
Whiskey, Footed, Chase, Engraved	85.00

CIGAR STORE FIGURES of carved wood or cast iron were used as advertisements in front of the Victorian cigar store. The carved figures are now collected as folk art. They range in size from counter type, about three feet, to over eight feet high.

George Washington Head, Leaves, Flowers, Scrolled Tobacco Leaf Base, c.1790, 21 In.	900.00
Indian Chief, Carved, Painted, New England, c.1930, 71 x 18 In.	4830.00
Indian, Brooks, Painted, 1880s, 69 In. ....*illus*	49500.00
Indian, Hand Shielding Eyes, Holding Carved Cigars, 69 x 21 In.	431.00
Indian, Headdress, Carved, Painted, Mr. Wolf's Yankee Notions, c.1890, 84 In. ....*illus*	21240.00
Indian, Headdress, Carved, Painted, Right Hand Shields Eyes, Wheels, 83 ½ In. ......*illus*	80240.00
Indian, Princess, Headdress, Platform, 340, S.A. Robb, 195 Canal St., c.1851, 72 In. ....*illus*	43660.00
Indian, Raised Foot, Hand Raised To Forehead, Austin Productions, c.1963, 39 In.	323.00
Indian, Standing, Scouting Pose, Leg Raised, Cement, Wire Frame, c.1890s, 42 In.	2147.00
Man, Pine, Black, Rotund, Blue Coat, Hand Outstretched, Carved, Paint, 28 In.	3792.00
Smoking Butler, Ash Tray Stand, Multicolor, Wood, 39 In.	207.00

CINNABAR is a vermilion or red lacquer. Pieces are made with tens to hundreds of thicknesses of the lacquer that is later carved. Most cinnabar was made in the Orient.

Bottle, Snuff, Baluster, Twin Fish, 19th Century, 3 In.	300.00
Bottle, Snuff, Carved Figures, Landscape, Plum Blossom Stopper, Chinese, 1800s, 3 ¼ In.	296.00
Bottle, Snuff, Carved Immortals, Landscape, Scrolls, Oval, Brass Stopper, Chinese, c.1800, 3 In.	356.00
Bottle, Snuff, Firefly Shape, Head As Stopper, 19th Century, 3 In.	275.00
Bottle, Snuff, Pear Shape, Monkey, Flowers, 19th Century, 3 In.	175.00
Bowl, Carved, Dragon, Chasing Flaming Pearl, Chinese, 8 In.	269.00
Bowl, Enamel, Dragons, In Clouds, Bronze Lip, Copper Foot, Enamel Interior, 2 x 6 In.	874.00
Bowl, Jasper, Quanyin, Clouds, Chinese, 15 In.	600.00
Box, 2 Women, Willow Tree, Rocks, Round, Chinese, 3 ¼ x 2 In.	207.00
Box, 8 Buddhist Treasures, Lotus Scrolls, Round, Chinese, 4 In.	245.00
Box, Dragon, Chasing Flaming Pearl Of Wisdom, Round, Chinese, 3 ½ x 8 In.	956.00
Box, Dragons, Clouds, Incised Diaper Ground, Carved, Chinese, 15 ¼ In.	540.00
Box, Landscape, Scrolls, Flowers Carved, Layered, Round, Chinese, 3 x 7 In.	403.00
Box, Lid, 9 Flying Bats, Clouds, Peaches, Chinese, c.1905, 18 ½ In.	660.00
Box, Lid, Butterfly, Carved, Figures, Landscape, Chinese, 2 x 6 x 4 In.	1016.00
Box, Lid, Carved Central Flower, Scrolls, Yunnan Ware, Chinese, c.1590, 8 In.	65175.00
Box, Lid, Carved, Dragon, Scrolling, Rectangular, Marked, 5 ½ In.	478.00
Box, Lid, Carved, Rocky Landscape, Hunting Scenes, Geometric, 1800s, 2 ¾ x 6 ¾ In.	1422.00
Box, Lid, Carved, Scenic Landscape, Scrolls, Flowers, 7 In. Diam.	403.00
Box, Lid, Circular, Carved, Lotus Flowers, Branches, Marked, 6 ½ In.	2629.00
Box, Lid, Immortals, Landscape, Dragons, Phoenix, Scrolls, Carved, Chinese, 5 x 9 In.	504.00
Box, Lid, Landscapes, Vines, Carved, Round, Chinese, 5 ¼ x 10 In.	3776.00
Box, Lid, Peng, Samurai, Landscape, Greek Key Border, Children, 1800s, 6 x 12 ½ In. .....*illus*	5310.00
Box, Lid, Rectangular, Center Panel, 3 Scholars, Leaf Design, 6 In.	341.00
Box, Lion, Shishi, Carved, Black Interior, Chinese, c.1820, 13 x 9 In.	173.00
Box, Mythical Beasts, Black Interior, Carved, Round, 2 ½ x 7 In.	2415.00
Box, Wedding, Compressed Dome Cover, Black Lacquer Interior, 9 x 5 In.	817.00
Box, Wedding, Figures In Landscape, Panels, Leaves, Round, Lacquer Interior, 8 x 14 In.	9988.00
Plate, Figures, Landscape, Flower Carved, Wavy Brass Edge Rim, Mark, Chinese, c.1890, 9 In.	551.00
Platter, Carved Dragons, Flowers, Qianlong Mark, 15 In.	598.00
Screen, Calligraphy, Imperial Dragons, Lacquerwood Stand, 8 ¾ x 9 ¼ In.	307.00
Screen, Panel, Figures In Landscape, Gallery Top On Rectangular Base, 24 ½ In. ....*illus*	3172.00
Table, Alter, Carved Leaves, Flower Medallions, 4 Scrolling Supports, 13 ¾ In.	434.00
Teapot, Cover, Carved, Geometric, Flowers, Yixing Pottery, Chinese, 4 ¾ In. .....*illus*	558.00

Tray, Boys, Playing In Garden, 2 Women, Flowers, Trees, Crane, 15 x 10 In.	2074.00
Tray, Crane, Carved Pine & Prune Trees, Brocade Ground, Marked, 13 ½ In.	359.00
Tray, Iris, Carved, Brocade Ground, Key Fret Border, Wood Stand, Chinese, 14 x 11 ¼ In.	3308.00
Tray, Woman, Girl, Garden, Holding Flowering Branches, Pagodas, Trees, 10 In.	341.00
Umbrella Stand, Clouds, Dragon Carved, Wood Stand, c.1890, 23 ¼ In.	2596.00
Vase, Bottle Shape, Lotus Plants, Cartouches, Figural Scenes, Fret Borders, 19 In., Pair	2928.00
Vase, Bottle Shape, Saucer Foot, Garlic Mouth, Black On Red, Birds, Flowers, Scrolls, 1800s, 13 ½ In.	459.00
Vase, Cover, Figures, Landscape, Pine Trees, Mountains, Bronze Base, 12 In., Pair	558.00
Vase, Cover, Leaf Finial, Figures In Garden, 12 ½ In.	1860.00
Vase, Double Gourd, Flowers, Vinery, Peacock, Chinese, c.1855, 18 In.	575.00
Vase, Immortals, Trees, Rocks, Mountains, Flower Bands, Chinese, 9 In. ....*illus*	153.00
Vase, Jade, Peach, Leaves, Flowers, Brocade Ground, Narrow Neck, Flared Lip, 15 In.	418.00
Vase, Landscape, Tiger, 8 ⅛ In.	403.00
Vase, Square Sides, Man, Village Scenes, Flowers, Chinese, 12 ½ In., Pair	23600.00
Vase, Village, Figures Carved, Chinese, 10 ½ In.	127.00
Vase, Village, Figures, Flowers, Leaves, Carved, 11 In.	127.00

CIVIL WAR mementos are important collectors' items. Most of the pieces are military items used from 1861 to 1865. Be sure to avoid any explosive munitions.

Album, Photograph, Camp, Capt. Langdon's Quarters, 15 ½ x 17 In.	176.00
Broadside, Recruiting 66th New York Volunteer Infantry, Frame, 23 ¼ x 37 ¾ In.	4700.00
Cap, Forage, Confederate, North Carolina, Blue, Leather Visor, c.1860	14380.00
Cap, Shako, Leather, Plume, Brass Plate, Chin Strap, 7th N.Y. Militia, Model 1860	489.00
Cup, Pewter, Inscribed William M. Dufour Camp Belger, 1862, 2 ⅜ In.	2252.00
Cutlass, Model 1860, Naval, Leather Grip, Brass Guard, Scabbard, U.S.N. Dr 1863, 32 In. .....*illus*	374.00
Drum, U.S. Infantry, American Eagle, Shield, Replaced Rope, Paper Label, 16 ¾ x 15 In. .....*illus*	4025.00
Epaulets, Confederate Officer, Woven Gilt, Metal Fringe, Cardboard Box, c.1860	295.00
Hat, Kepi, Blue, Brass Wreath, 29 Emblem, Marked	149.00
Musket, Percussion, 58 Caliber, Walnut Stock, Bayonet Mounted, Muzzle Loading, c.1864	1185.00
Pipe, Briar, Carved, Cross, Shield, Co. B, 14 Reg., N.C.T. Sturgeon, Salmon, Vine, c.1861, 4 x 3 In.	1880.00
Surgeon's Medical Kit, Mahogany Case, Brass Nameplate, Tools, A.L. Hernstein, 6 x 16 In.	2233.00
Sword, Confederate, Staff Officer's, Pelican Insignia, Wire Wrapped Grip, Marked	9560.00
Sword, Scabbard, Cavalry, Confederate, Leather Wrapped Handle, Brass Pommel, 34 In.	2233.00
Sword, Scabbard, N.C.O., Emerson & Silver, Trenton, N.J., c.1863, 35 In.	633.00
Sword, Single Edge Blade, Eagle, Shield, Flags, Scrolled Flowers, Leaves, Iron Scabbard, c.1850, 40 In.	1164.00
Uniform Accessories, Chapeau Bras, Sash, Epaulettes, Tin Box, 1860s	1880.00
Uniform, USMA 1860 Cadet, Tail Coat, Handkerchiefs, Socks, Gloves, 12 Piece	2325.00

CKAW, *see Dedham category.*

CLARICE CLIFF was a designer who worked in several English factories, including A.J. Wilkinson Ltd., Wilkinson's Royal Staffordshire Pottery, Newport Pottery, and Foley Pottery after the 1920s. She is best known for her brightly colored Art Deco designs, including the Bizarre line. She died in 1972. Reproductions have been made by Wedgwood.

Autumn, Fantasque, Lotus Jug, Trees, Bushes, Cottage, 2 Handles, Marked, 1929-34, 11 ¾ In.	3851.00
Bizarre, Vase, Fir Trees, Beach, Cottage, Pen Outline, Flared Foot, Marked, c.1933, 19 In. .....*illus*	1778.00
Bizarre, Vase, Trees & Alpine House, Cone Shape, Ridged, Wilkinson, c.1930, 18 In.	356.00
Chintz, Fantasque, Planter, Oval, Water Lily Buds, Leaves, Marked, c.1930, 6 ⅞ In.	652.00
Cruiseware, Plate, Dessert, Amoebic Shape, Small Whale Swimming At Top, 1936, 10 In.	235.00
Cruiseware, Plate, Dinner, Stylish Figures, Whale, Amoebic Shape, 1936, 19 ¾ In.	237.00
Fantasque, Pitcher, Lotus Blossoms, Marked, 7 ⅞ In. ....*illus*	345.00
Fantasque, Pitcher, Petunia, Blue, Orange, Yellow, Brown & Yellow Bands, 9 In.	237.00
Gardenia, Fantasque, Lotus Jug, Art Deco Flower & Leaves, Handle, Marked, c.1931, 11 ¾ In.	1422.00
Gayday, Bizarre, Vase, Asters, Flower Sprays, Leaves, Marked, c.1930, 11 ⅞ In.	770.00
Lotus Blossom, Bowl, Leaves In Water, Newport Pottery Back Stamp, 1900s, 4 ⅛ x 8 ⅝ In. ...*illus*	61.00
Lucerne, Bizarre, Jug, Art Deco Castle, Mountain Landscape, Marked, c.1930, 11 ½ In.	7110.00
My Garden, Sugar Sifter, Flowers, Streaked Mushroom Ground, Cone Shape, 5 ½ In.	119.00
Rhodanthe, Cruet Set, Cone Shape, 3 Piece	369.00
Rhodanthe, Jam Pot, Cover, Bonjour Shape	277.00
Rhodanthe, Sugar Shaker, Cone Shape	308.00
Rhodanthe, Sugar Sifter, Conical, Bizarre Wilkinson Mark, c.1940, 5 ½ In.	403.00
Rhodanthe, Teapot, Bonjour Shape	369.00
Tonquin, Plate, Dinner, Brown, 10 In.	42.00
Tonquin, Plate, Dinner, Multicolor, 10 In.	94.00
Tonquin, Platter, Blue, Oval, 11 ⅝ In.	127.00

Cinnabar, Box, Lid, Peng, Samurai, Landscape, Greek Key Border, Children, 1800s, 6 x 12 ½ In.
$5310.00

James D. Julia Inc.

Cinnabar, Screen, Panel, Figures In Landscape, Gallery Top On Rectangular Base, 24 ½ In.
$3172.00

Leslie Hindman Auctioneers

Cinnabar, Teapot, Cover, Carved, Geometric, Flowers, Yixing Pottery, Chinese, 4 ¾ In.
$558.00

Leslie Hindman Auctioneers

Cinnabar, Vase, Immortals, Trees, Rocks, Mountains, Flower Bands, Chinese, 9 In.
$153.00

Skinner, Inc.

Civil War, Cutlass, Model 1860, Naval, Leather Grip, Brass Guard, Scabbard, U.S.N. Dr 1863, 32 In. **$374.00**

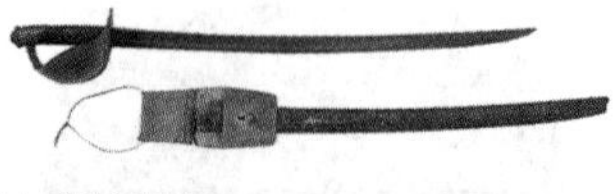

Leland Little Auction

Civil War, Drum, U.S. Infantry, American Eagle, Shield, Replaced Rope, Paper Label, 16 ¾ x 15 In. **$4025.00**

James D. Julia Inc.

Clarice Cliff, Bizarre, Vase, Fir Trees, Beach, Cottage, Pen Outline, Flared Foot, Marked, c.1933, 19 In. **$1778.00**

Skinner, Inc.

Clarice Cliff, Fantasque, Pitcher, Lotus Blossoms, Marked, 7 ⅞ In. **$345.00**

Humler & Nolan

Tonquin, Platter, Multicolor, Oval, 13 ⅞ In.	254.00
Vase, Landscape, Vines, Flowers, Oval Shape, Marked, 8 In.	230.00

CLEWELL was made in limited quantities by Charles Walter Clewell of Canton, Ohio, from 1902 to 1955. Pottery was covered with a thin coating of bronze, then treated to make the bronze turn different colors. Pieces covered with copper, brass, or silver were also made. Mr. Clewell's secret formula for blue patinated bronze was burned when he died in 1965.

Vase, Copper Clad, Crusty Patina, Marked, 6 In. ....*illus*	403.00
Vase, Copper Clad, Verdigris Patina, Marked, 8 ½ x 4 ½ In.	279.00

CLIFTON POTTERY was founded by William Long in Newark, New Jersey, in 1905. He worked there until 1909 making lines that included Crystal Patina and Clifton Indian Ware. Clifton Pottery made art pottery until 1911 and then concentrated on wall and floor tile. By 1914, the name had been changed to Clifton Porcelain and Tile Company. Another firm, Chesapeake Pottery, sold majolica marked *Clifton Ware*.

Humidor, Lid, American Indian, Stylized Bird, Pink, Brown, 6 ¾ In.	138.00
Vase, Green, Brown Flambe Glaze, Marked, 1906, 7 ¾ x 6 In.	155.00

CLOCKS of all types have always been popular with collectors. The eighteenth-century tall case, or grandfather's, clock was designed to house a works with a long pendulum. The name on the clock is usually the maker but sometimes it is a merchant or craftsman. In 1816, Eli Terry patented a new, smaller works for a clock, and the case became smaller. The clock could be kept on a shelf instead of on the floor. By 1840, coiled springs were used and even smaller clocks were made. Battery-powered electric clocks were made in the 1870s. A garniture set can include a clock and other objects displayed on a mantel.

4 Cherubs, 3 Holding Clock, Bronze, Marble Base, Bronze Band, France, 21 In.	6215.00
Advertising, A.R. Penny Druggist & Jeweler, Walnut, Calendar, 8-Day, Sidney, c.1885, 69 In. .... *illus*	29900.00
Advertising, Camel Belting, Figural, Dial On Hump, This Time Use Camel Belting, Metal, 6 In.	170.00
Advertising, Cheer Up, Bottle, Round, Red, White, Blue, Light-Up, Electric, 1940-50s, 15 In. ...	480.00
Advertising, Country Club Beer, Famous Since Days Of Pony Express, Wood, Frame, 1950s, 20 x 18 In.	150.00
Advertising, Dr Pepper, Deco Style, Good For Life, 5 Cents, 22 x 17 In.	3025.00
Advertising, Drink Frostie Root Beer, Family Favorite, Tin, Plastic Insert, 19 x 15 In.	130.00
Advertising, Dunlop Tires, Founder Of Pneumatic Tire Industry, Light-Up, Plastic, Round, 16 In.	226.00
Advertising, Ever-Ready Safety Razor, Man Shaving, Radio Blade, 1 Dollar, Round, 22 In.	1560.00
Advertising, Expert Hair Cutting, Woman Profile, Square Round Face, 20 x 20 In.	356.00
Advertising, Ford, Built For The Years Ahead, White, Yellow, Light-Up, Round, 1950s, 15 ½ In.	480.00
Advertising, Gem Damaskeene Razor, Man, Shaving Baby On Lap, 1 Dollar, Wood, 27 ½ In.	5400.00
Advertising, Genesee Beer, Rotary Clock Co., 1950s, 12 x 8 In.	66.00
Advertising, Hudson Coal, Round, 15 In.	141.00
Advertising, Iron City Beer, Barrel On Cradle, Wood, Paper Dial, Roman Numerals, 6 x 8 In..	226.00
Advertising, J. & P. Coats, Spool Cotton, Best Six Cord, Regulator, Oak, Glass, 37 In.	311.00
Advertising, Keen Kutter, Oak, Gallery, Pendulum, Key, 25 x 16 In.	424.00
Advertising, Liberty Flour, Hexagon, Neon, Red, White, Blue, 22 x 24 In.	9350.00
Advertising, Old Coon Cigars, Regulator, Oak, Carved Basket Weave, Glass Front, 20 In.	452.00
Advertising, Old Mr. Boston Fine Liquors, Figural, Bottle, Copper Color, Gilbert, 21 In.	113.00
Advertising, Original Eagle Clothiers, Building Shape, Cast Iron, 9 ½ x 12 ½ In.	28.00
Advertising, Pittsburgh Paints, Round, 12 In.	57.00
Advertising, Prescription Specialists, Neon, Electric, Round, 22 In.	452.00
Advertising, Purina Chows, Sanitation Products, Light-Up, Red, White, Blue, 1940-50s, 16 ¼ In.	360.00
Advertising, Rexall Drugs, R.N. Stripling Drug Store, Regulator, Oak, Pressed, 36 In.	623.00
Advertising, Ruppert Beer, Neon, 3 Colors, Motion, Bubble Face, 13 In.	8800.00
Advertising, Sinclair Gasoline, Round, Red, White, Black, Light-Up, 1956, 15 ½ In.	450.00
Advertising, Sunshine Premium Beer, Electric, Reverse Painted Glass, Metal, 9 x 11 In.	452.00
Advertising, U.S.G. Harness Oil, Lower Door, Pressed Tin, 15-Day, Seth Thomas, 29 ½ In. ......*illus*	2083.00
Advertising, Webb C. Ball Co., Cleveland School, Short Drop, Seth Thomas, 24 x 16 In.	297.00
Advertising, Western Mutual Ins. Co., Wagon Train, Metal, Glass, Lights, 1907, 15 In.	181.00
Advertising, Woody's Cafe, Woody Woodpecker, Plastic, Inset Date Dial, Animated, Alarm	90.00
Animated, Cupid, Grinding Wheel, Stool, Table, Bronze, Bell Strike, c.1840, 18 x 12 x 5 In.	11500.00
Ansonia, Bouncing Doll, Nickel Plated, Scrolls, Porcelain Doll On Spring Is Pendulum, 14 In.	537.00
Ansonia, Brass, Regulator, Prism, Round Face, Roman Numerals, Square Base, 11 x 7 In.	184.00
Ansonia, Knight, Seated, Spelter, Urn Finial, Cast Metal Base, 14 ¾ x 17 ¾ In.	489.00
Ansonia, Plato, Metal, Glass Cylinder, Flowers, 30-Hour, Tab Wind, 1903, 6 In.	254.00
Ansonia, Reflector, Walnut, Gilt, Beveled Mirrors, Pendulum, 8-Day Time & Strike, c.1885, 34 In. *illus*	1265.00
Ansonia, Shelf, Cast Metal, Column Supports, Porcelain Face, 11 ½ x 11 In.	144.00

Ansonia, Shelf, Delft, Blue & White, Time & Strike, Brass Movement, c.1910, 11 x 7 ½ In. ......*illus*	374.00
Ansonia, Shelf, Eastlake, Spring Driven, Nickel-Plated Pendulum, Bell, Hexagonal Case, 18 x 12 In.	118.00
Ansonia, Shelf, Figural, Hermes, Seated, Metal Rococo Case, Porcelain Dial	452.00
Ansonia, Shelf, Figural, Siren, Woman, Playing Flute, Metal Rococo Case, Porcelain Dial	452.00
Ansonia, Shelf, French Style, Brass, Giltwood, 13 x 7 In.	1200.00
Ansonia, Shelf, Iron, Arch, 4 Columns, Stepped Base, Time & Strike, Porcelain Dial, 13 In.	136.00
Ansonia, Shelf, Music & Poetry, 2 Statues, Time & Strike, Enamel Dial, c.1894, 21 In.	999.00
Ansonia, Shelf, Oak, Bronze, Sphinx Supports, North Wind Face Pendulum, Pan, 21 x 13 In.	575.00
Ansonia, Shelf, Parisian, Walnut, Columbia Head Top, Cameo Bust Pendulum, Arch, 25 In.	216.00
Ansonia, Shelf, Poetry, Girl Holding Book, Bronzed, Black Iron, Double Porcelain Dial, 21 In.	735.00
Ansonia, Shelf, Pompeii, Black Enamel, Cast Iron, Silver, 16 x 6 x 11 In.	995.00
Ansonia, Shelf, Porcelain, Flowers, Magenta, Gold Trim, Shaped, 11 x 10 In.	123.00
Ansonia, Shelf, Regulator, Crystal, Brass, 9 x 6 In.	210.00
Ansonia, Shelf, Rosalind, Iron, Black Enamel, Gilt, Woman, Angels, Brass 8-Day, 12 x 15 In. ...*illus*	295.00
Ansonia, Shelf, Rosalind, Mermaids On Ends, Black Iron, 8-Day, Black Dial, 12 In.	226.00
Ansonia, Shelf, Summer & Winter, 2 Statues, Urn Over Dial, c.1900, 22 x 23 In.	3456.00
Ansonia, Swinging Ball, Huntress, White Metal Statue, Tin Can Movement, Paper Dial, 23 In.	1130.00
Ansonia, Wall, Rosewood, Calendar, Round, Short Drop, Pinwheel, Rope Twist, c.1865, 25 x 16 In.	604.00
Art Deco, Cobalt Blue Enamel, Silver Hexagonal Plaques, Alarm, Oval, Bun Feet, 3 In.	826.00
Art Deco, Sheet Metal Rim, Glass Dial, Cream Paint, Lit Interior, c.1910, 40 x 8 ½ In.	1121.00
Atmos, Chrome, Beveled Glass, Open Moon Hands, Jean Leon Reutter, 9 x 7 x 5 In.	5750.00
Atmos, Chrome, Glass, Enameled Dial, Open Moon Hands, J.L. Reutter, 9 In.	6490.00
Austria, Shelf, Classical Scenes, Diana Finial, Flared Foot, Gilt, Enamel, Copper, c.1875, 8 ½ In.	1185.00
Automaton, Birdcage, Feathered Bird, Ball Shape Clock, Hoop Stand, 8 ½ In.	380.00
Banjo, A. Willard, Gilt, Beading, Glass Tablets, Country Home, Flame Finial, 8-Day, 34 In.	791.00
Banjo, Curtis & Dunning, Eglomise, War Of 1812 Scenes, Eagle Finial, Thermometer, c.1820, 40 In.	3300.00
Banjo, Federal, Mahogany, Eglomise, 8-Day, Eagle Finial, Painted Tablets, Gilt, 33 x 10 In.	3884.00
Banjo, Federal, Mahogany, Parcel Gilt, Eglomise Panels, Painted Metal Dial, Eagle Finial, 34 In.	456.00
Banjo, Federal, Mahogany, Woman, Winged Chariot Panel, Mass., c.1815, 33 In.	790.00
Banjo, Gilbert, Federal Style, Burl Wood, Painted, Flowers, Eagle Finial, 31 In.	300.00
Banjo, Gitow & Cuttle, Jeweled, Gilt, 8-Day, 41 x 13 In.	118.00
Banjo, H. Tifft, Walnut, Brass Finial, Scroll Sides, Weight Driven, 32 ½ In.	480.00
Banjo, Howard & Davis, No. 2, Rosewood, Weight Driven, 43 ½ In.	3955.00
Banjo, Howard, E. & Co., No. 5, Rosewood, Red, Gold & Black Paint, 29 In.	1475.00
Banjo, Ingraham Company, Nile Model, 8-Day, Spring, c.1915, 40 In.	646.00
Banjo, Ingraham, c.1880, 38 x 10 In.	354.00
Banjo, Mahogany, Brass Eagle Finial, Eglomise Panel, Shield, c.1847, 35 In.	1003.00
Banjo, Mahogany, Carved, Father Time, Cone Finial, c.1825, 57 In.	7703.00
Banjo, Mahogany, Carved, Lyre Front, Repainted Dial, Boston, c.1830, 40 ½ In. ....*illus*	1593.00
Banjo, Mahogany, Half Round Frame, Iron Dial, Roman Numerals, c.1824, 33 In.	3851.00
Banjo, New Haven, Whitney, Glass Tablet, Sailboat, Eagle Top, Time & Strike, 31 In.	79.00
Banjo, New Haven, Wilson, Mahogany, 30-Day, Oval Glass Scenic Panel, House, 40 In.	472.00
Banjo, Simon Willard, Mahogany, Brass, Eglomise, Vase, Eagle, Dolphin, Door, c.1815, 30 x 10 In.	984.00
Banjo, Walter H. Durfee, Eagle Finial, Painted Scene, 1800s, 41 x 10 ½ In.	1920.00
Banjo, Waltham, Mahogany, Eglomise, Eagle Finial, Painted Dial, c.1930, 41 x 10 In.	805.00
Banjo, Waltham, Reverse Painted, G. Washington, Mount Vernon, 8-Day, c.1920, 40 x 10 In.	1080.00
Banjo, Waterbury, Federal Style, War Of 1812 Reverse Painted Panel, Key, c.1920, 43 In.	575.00
Barometer, Wuersch, Mahogany, 34 In.	150.00
Beaupre, Pillar, Ebonized Case, Ormolu Mounts, Columns, France, 1800s, 15 ½ x 5 In.	295.00
Becker, G., Wall, Regulator, Porcelain Dial, 2 Brass Weights, Late 19th Century, 41 x 19 In.	523.00
Biedermeier, Wall Mahogany, Carved Crest, Triple Weight, Porcelain Face, 44 x 12 ½ In.	1955.00
Bigelow & Kennard, Bracket, Mahogany, Arched, Triple Fusee, Pineapple Finials, 18 x 16 In.	2655.00
Bigelow, Kennard & Co., Carriage, Mixed Metal, Brass, Flowers, Bug Relief Panels, 5 ½ x 5 In.	1989.00
Birdcage, Windup, Bird Rotates, Painted Ceramic Base, Japan, 11 In.	124.00
Birge & Fuller, Double Steeple, Wagon Spring, Zinc Dial, 30-Hour, c.1845, 24 ½ In. ......*illus*	1593.00
Bisque, Chariot, Drawn By Lions, Cast Bronze Face, Frieze, c.1890, 15 x 16 In.	1093.00
Black Forest, Cuckoo, Carved Crest, Bird, Maple Leaves, Grapes, Weights, Germany, 26 In.	207.00
Black Forest, Cuckoo, Hanging Pheasant, Rabbit, Oak Leaves, Eagle Top, 3-Weight, 36 In.	3245.00
Black Forest, Cuckoo, Walnut, Deer Head, Glass Eyes, Pheasant, Rabbit, Birds, Horn, 48 In.	791.00
Black Forest, Cuckoo, Walnut, Eagle, Acorns, 8-Day, Spring Movement, c.1870, 38 In. ..*illus*	1896.00
Black Forest, Cuckoo, Walnut, Stag's Head Crest, Leaves, 2 Standing Stags, 21 x 16 In.	246.00
Black Forest, Picture Frame, Pressed Brass, Dogs, Scrolls, Porcelain Dial, 2-Weight, 11 x 10 In.	158.00
Black Forest, Stag, Putti Holding Pitchfork, Shovel, Basket Of Fish, Oars, c.1837, 34 x 26 In.	3565.00
Black, Starr & Frost, Desk, Sterling Silver, Blue Enamel, Shaped Frame, Swiss, 5 x 3 In.	415.00
Booth, R., Woman's Head, Walnut, Arched, Teardrops, Scrolls, Gong & Beat Scale	136.00
Bracket, Ebonized, Gilt Metal, Stepped Cornice, Painted Dial, Button Feet, 14 In.	488.00

Clarice Cliff, Lotus Blossom, Bowl, Leaves In Water, Newport Pottery Back Stamp, 1900s, 4 ⅛ x 8 ⅝ In.
$61.00

Skinner, Inc.

Clewell, Vase, Copper Clad, Crusty Patina, Marked, 6 In.
$403.00

Humler & Nolan

Clock, Advertising, A.R. Penny Druggist & Jeweler, Walnut, Calendar, 8-Day, Sidney, c.1885, 69 In.
$29900.00

James D. Julia Inc.

Clock, Advertising, U.S.G. Harness Oil, Lower Door, Pressed Tin, 15-Day, Seth Thomas, 29 ½ In. **$2083.00**

Skinner, Inc.

Clock, Ansonia, Reflector, Walnut, Gilt, Beveled Mirrors, Pendulum, 8-Day Time & Strike, c.1885, 34 In. **$1265.00**

James D. Julia Inc.

Clock, Ansonia, Shelf, Delft, Blue & White, Time & Strike, Brass Movement, c.1910, 11 x 7 ½ In. **$374.00**

Leland Little Auction

Bracket, Ebonized, Ormolu, Gilt, Handle, Leaf Feet, Turkish Numerals, Musical, c.1765, 19 In.	14220.00
Bracket, Louis XV Style, Ormolu, Maroon Glaze, Enamel Dial, 1800s, 22 In.	1062.00
Bracket, Mahogany, Gilt Brass, Chimes, 8 Bells, 4 Gongs, Urn Finials, Carved Feet, 28 x 17 In.	6150.00
Bracket, Mahogany, Reeded Carved Top, Brass Inlay, Iron Dial, Lattice, Ball Feet, c.1820, 20 In.	2370.00
Bracket, Regency, Mahogany, Lyre, Crest, Rectangular, Filigree Ormolu, c.1830, 23 x 15 ¾ In.	575.00
Bracket, Rococo Style, Ormolu Mounted, Painted, Gilt Brass Leaves, 1900s, 12 In.	472.00
Brass, Enameled Round Dial, Beveled Glass, Footed, Top Handle, France, c.1915, 4 x 3 ¼ In.	215.00
Brass, Urn Shape, Serpent Pointer, Roman Numerals, Marble Base, 8 ¾ In.	2260.00
Brewster & Ingraham, Mahogany, Gallery, Hinged Bezel, Zinc Dial, c.1850, 11 In. Diam.	1304.00
Brown, J.C., Acorn, Mahogany, Zinc Dial, Reverse Painted, 8-Day, Spring, c.1845, 28 In. *illus*	17775.00
Brown, J.C., Shelf, Gothic, Rosewood, Ripple Front, Zinc Dial, 8-Day, Gong, c.1845, 20 In. *illus*	1422.00
Brown, J.C., Shelf, Mother-Of-Pearl, Zinc Dial, Roman Numerals, Hand Painted Flowers, 18 In.	948.00
Cachard, Gaspard, Louis XVI, White Marble, Fluted Columnar Case, Winged Putto, c.1780, 17 In.	588.00
Carriage, Badische, Gilt & White Metal, Roman Numerals, 6 x 5 In.	90.00
Carriage, Brass Case, Beveled Glass, Applied Floral Moldings, Handle, France, c.1900, 7 ¼ In.	489.00
Carriage, Brass, Beveled Glass, Hour Repeating, 8-Day, Time & Strike, France, 8 ½ In. *illus*	2573.00
Carriage, Brass, Gilt Twisted Rope Trim, Cased, Shaped Handle, Porcelain Dial, 1800s, 5 x 6 ½ In.	299.00
Carriage, Brass, Nickel Plate, Enamel Dial, Pilasters, Moon Dial, Alarm, Date, c.1885, 5 ¾ x 4 In.	6457.00
Carriage, Bronze, Beveled Glass Panels, Presentation, Inscription, France, c.1890, 4 ¾ In. *illus*	444.00
Carriage, Enameled Dial, Brass Scrollwork, Scroll Handle, Bun Feet, Leather Case, France, 7 In.	296.00
Carriage, Ferris Wheel Top, Reticulated Gallery, Silvered Metal, Hamburg, c.1910, 11 In.	1180.00
Carrier, A., Figural, Cherubs, Holding Orb, Patinated Metal, Onyx & Bronze, c.1910, 29 In.	1896.00
Cartel, Gilt Metal, Scrolling, Urn Finial, White Dial, France, 30 In.	1180.00
Cartel, Louis XV, Gilt Bronze, Scrolling Leaf Cast Case, Round Enamel Dial, 22 In.	406.00
Cartier, Pendulette, Agate, Gold Dial, Engine-Turned, Enamel, Diamond Hands, 1925, 3 In.	18960.00
Cartier, Travel, Square Case, Swiss Albertus Works, 14K Gold, Box, c.1975, 2 ¼ x 2 ½ In.	4674.00
Cartier, Travel, Square Dial, Brass & Steel Case, Quartz Movement, Swiss, 1900s, 2 ½ In.	480.00
Chinese, Shelf, Cloisonne, Brass, Glass, Pendulum With Woman's Face, Bowl Feet, 20 x 9 In.	1722.00
Chinese, Skeleton, Wheel, Enameled Face, Brass, Marble Base, 19 x 12 In.	150.00
Dasson, H., Shelf, Gilt Bronze, Scrolls, Flowers, Cherub, Playing Pipes, France, c.1880, 22 In.	5036.00
Deluxe Clock Co., Figural, Camel, Recumbent, Carved, Dial Case In Hump, Art Clock, 9 In.	102.00
Desk, Art Deco, Easel Back, Round, 8-Day, White Face, France, c.1925, 5 ½ x 5 ½ In.	276.00
Desk, Arts & Crafts, Copper, Mixed Metal, Enamel Chapters, 6 ¾ In.	117.00
Desk, Silver Plate, Roman Numerals, Monogram, 6 In.	92.00
Desprez, Charles, Shelf, Gothic Style, Carved, Bristol, c.1850, 19 x 14 In.	780.00
Dresser, Man In The Moon, Oak, Round, Moon Face, Child Poking, Metal Dial, 13 In.	113.00
Dresser, Pewter, Molded Swag, Rosettes & Tassels, Enameled Dial, Lenzkirch Movement, 6 In.	791.00
Dupont, Charles, Shelf, Porcelain, Cherubs, Flowers, France, 1800, 27 x 14 In.	475.00
Edin Watch Co., Wall, Bronze, Guilloche, Gilt, Beaded, Round, Lotus Hanger, 12 x 3 ½ In.	2271.00
Elgin, Bracket, Wood, Brass Face, Chime, Handle, 14 x 10 In.	210.00
Eli Terry, Shelf Empire Style, Mahogany, Ebonized, Rolled Glass Door, c.1825, 35 x 18 In.	150.00
Eli Terry, Shelf, Mahogany, Carved, Reverse Painted, 8-Day, Countwheel Strike, c.1825, 36 In. *illus*	1778.00
English, Shelf, Flower Swags, Courting Couple, Tin Lithograph, Arched, Windup, 12 x 11 In.	297.00
English, Shelf, Oak Base, Scrolled, Key, Pendulum, c.1890, 12 x 28 x 6 In.	2596.00
English, Tavern, Mahogany, Arched, Sliding Hood, 19th Century, 58 x 22 In.	1026.00
Figural, Andreas Hofer, Austrian Patriot, Gilt Bronze, Porcelain Dial, c.1810, 8 x 5 In.	230.00
Figural, Blue Spode Plate, On Easel, Cutout Metal Frame, Griffin Head & Feet, 11 In.	226.00
Figural, Courting Couple, Rococo Revival Case, Porcelain, Applied Flowers, c.1835, 16 x 9 In. *illus*	1168.00
Figural, Cupid, Bronze, Porcelain Face, Splayed Feet, 14 ½ x 6 In.	237.00
Figural, Cupid, Woman Holding Flowers, Fluted Column, Top Shape Feet, Gilt, 1900s, 11 x 8 In.	500.00
Figural, Father Time, Scythe, Baby New Year, Cattails, Rooster, Silver, Porcelain Dial, 13 In.	209.00
Figural, Lighthouse, Rotating, Barometer, 2 Thermometers, Brass, Nickel Plate, 1800s, 17 In.	4560.00
Figural, Owl, Blinking Eye, Wood, Carved, 9 In.	57.00
Figural, Palette, Brass Easel, Medieval Man & Woman, 10 ¾ x 10 In. *illus*	735.00
Figural, Putto, Holding Goblet, Bronze, Bell Strike Movement, Marked, 16 x 18 x 7 In.	201.00
Figural, Topsey, Blinking Eye, Cast Iron, Paper On Zinc, 30-Hour, c.1870, 16 ½ In. *illus*	1659.00
Figural, Will Rogers, White Metal, Copper-Flashed Finish, 13 x 13 In.	224.00
Figural, Winged Female, Bronze, Holding Book, Red Marble Base, 34 In.	1243.00
French, Porcelain Face, Set In Oil Painting, Punch & Judy Figures, Chime, 27 x 32 In. *illus*	2688.00
French, Repeater, Wood Case, Square, Applied Round Frame, Brass Handle, c.1800, 9 x 6 In.	720.00
French, Shelf, Bronze, Silver, Cherubs, Birds, Flower, Leaf, Berries, c.1900, 20 ½ In.	1659.00
French, Shelf, Bronze, Urn Finial, Inset Porcelain Dial, Scrolls, Flowers, c.1885, 13 x 9 In.	369.00
French, Shelf, Champleve, Gilt Bronze, Winged Figural Supports, Time & Strike, 19 In. *illus*	4464.00
French, Shelf, Empire, Bronze, Porcelain Dial, Griffin Relief Base, c.1820, 22 x 12 In.	1708.00
French, Shelf, Empire, Ebonized, Gilt, Portico, Pillars, Garland, 1800s, 20 x 10 In.	840.00
French, Shelf, Marble Inlay, Gilt Designs, Black, 11 ½ x 12 In.	115.00

C

French, Shelf, Perpetual Calendar, Barometer, Slate, Green Malachite, 8-Day, c.1875, 20 x 21 In.	1840.00
French, Shelf, Porcelain, Enamel, Cherub, Book, Painter's Palette, Flowers, 1800s, 18 ½ In....	2252.00
French, Silk Thread Movement, Black Man, Cane, Basket On Back, Cotton Bundle Face, 14 In.	7670.00
French, Silk Thread Movement, Picture, Gilt Frame, Enamel Ring, Pendulum Panel, 18 x 14 In.	590.00
French, Silk Thread Movement, Woman, Dog, Chariot, Tapers To Swan, Gilt, Ebony, Footed, 11 In.	3835.00
French, Wall, Brass, Enamel, Round Dial, Pressed Brass Case & Pendulum, 1900s, 52 In.	200.00
Gaston Jolly, Bracket, Musical, 3-Key Wind, Silent Chime, Brass Trim, Paw Feet, Paris, 26 In. ..illus	11400.00
German, African Man, Figural, Black Enamel, Hoop Earrings, Holding Face Of Clock, 12 In..	259.00
German, Dickory, Dickory, Dock, Wood, Shaped, Mouse, Bell Strike, 1910, 24 ½ In..................	254.00
German, Shelf, Cherubs, Flowers, Horns, Urn Finial, Porcelain, Enamel, Gilt, c.1890, 17 x 18 In.	1067.00
German, Shelf, Ebonized Wood, Onyx, Automaton, Gilt, Finial, c.1800, 17 x 10 In..................	450.00
German, Shelf, Engraved Gilt, Copper Face, Pendulum, Bells, Hipped Pediment, 1700s, 16 x 11 In.	2151.00
German, Shelf, Mahogany, Marquetry, c.1905, 17 ½ In..	84.00
German, Swinging Ball, Angel, Metal, Copper-Colored Ball, Metal Roman Numerals, 24 In....	509.00
German, Wall, Face, Chubby, Oak, c.1900, 19 x 16 In...	472.00
German, Wall, Walnut, Glass, 8-Day Spring Wound, 8 Tone Bars, Westminster, 1900s, 37 In...	219.00
Gilbert, Berkshire, Calendar, Oak, Colonettes, Reverse Painted, Pendulum, 8-Day, c.1890, 40 In.	1495.00
Gilbert, Calendar, Rosewood, Short Drop, Reverse Painted, 8-Day, Spring, 1850-1900, 22 ½ In.	460.00
Gilbert, Lenox Model, Wall, Oak, Calendar, Scale Design, Eglomise Door, c.1885, 35 x 15 In...	1035.00
Gilbert, Regulator, No. 10, Walnut, Fluted Decoration, Indented Panels, Paper Dial, 52 In......	735.00
Gilbert, Regulator, No. 21, Scroll Pediment, Flame Finial, Single Weight, 53 x 18 In.	540.00
Gilbert, Shelf, Cassius, Bell Top, Gilt-Metal Trim, 17 x 11 ¾ In.	378.00
Gilbert, Shelf, Orleans, Glass Case, Patinated Spelter Trim, Enamel Dial, 8-Day, c.1910, 11 In.	830.00
Gilbert, The Reliable, Lighter Time, Red Enamel, Oak Box, Light & Switch, 7 In......................	311.00
Globe, Time, Calendar, Metal, Wood, 24-Hour Dial, Silk String Movement, France, 1776, 22 In.	3390.00
Gothic Revival, Mahogany, Turned Drop Finial, Pendulum, White Face, Germany, 29 x 13 In.	720.00
Gothic Style, Oak, Barometer, c.1880, 24 x 10 In.	384.00
Guilmet, Wishing Well, Pendulum, Chain, Pulley, Bronze, Gilt, Cobalt Blue Tiles, 17 In.........	5015.00
Gustav Becker, Anniversary, Brass, Glass Dome, Porcelain Dial, Disc Pendulum, c.1855........	170.00
Gustav Becker, Regulator, 2-Weight, Domed Case, Enamel Dial, 43 x 15 x 6 ¼ In..................	513.00
Gustav Becker, Vienna Regulator, Walnut, Arched, Leaves, 3-Weight, Embossed Dial, 50 In. ..	1978.00
Gustav Becker, Wall, Oak, Spring Wound, Beveled Glass Door, Germany, c.1913, 32 In..........	288.00
Gustav Becker, Wall, Walnut, Turned Columns, Black Horse Top, Porcelain Dial, 42 In..........	339.00
Herman Miller, Chrome Plated Steel, Bronze, Aluminum, G. Rohde, 1930s, 11 x 6 In. ..illus	7150.00
Hirst, Shelf, Gothic Revival, Rosewood Case, Brass Inlay, Enameled Face, c.1850, 19 ½ In.	1062.00
Hour Lavigne, Shelf, White Marble Case, Gilt Brass, Signed, France, 1900s, 8 ¾ In.	443.00
Howard Miller, Brass Plated Metal Balls, Maple, Enamel Steel, G. Nelson, 3 x 13 ¾ In...........	372.00
Howard Miller, Kite, G. Nelson, c.1952, 16 ½ x 22 In. ....illus	1875.00
Howard Miller, Motion Notion, George Nelson, 6 x 5 ¼ In. ....illus	7500.00
Howard, E., No. 9, Figure 8, Walnut, Reverse Painted Throat, Open Moon Hands, 37 In.	4720.00
Howard, E., No. 70, Regulator, Oak, Reverse Painted, Black, Red, Glass Door, 30 x 15 In.	1566.00
Imhof, Bronze, Ball-Shaped Dial, Roman Numerals, 8-Day, Tempus Fugit, Swiss, 7 In............	396.00
Ingersoll, Who's Afraid Of The Big Bad Wolf, Red Metal, Alarm	226.00
Ingraham, Bugs Bunny Eating Carrot, Warner Brothers, Alarm, Square, Footed	79.00
Ingraham, Calendar, Oak Case, Molded Cornice, Roman Numerals, c.1870, 39 x 18 In.	180.00
Ingraham, Dresser, Lava Glass, Glossy & Textured, Tombstone Shape, 8 ½ x 6 ½ In..............	79.00
Ingraham, E., Shelf, Grecian Mosaic, Carved Concentric Circles, Hinged Door, 14 x 10 In.	378.00
Ingraham, E., Shelf, Wood, Faux Marble, Gilt Face, Scroll Feet, Shaped, 11 x 10 In.	70.00
Ingraham, E., Steeple, Glass Tablet, Etched Wreath & Flower, 18 ¾ x 10 ¼ x 4 In...................	270.00
Ingraham, Kitchen, Gingerbread, Oak, Calendar, 8-Day, Time & Strike	136.00
Ingraham, Shelf, Doric, Mosaic Candy Stripe Inlay, Time & Strike, 16 x 8 In.	324.00
Ingraham, Shelf, Gingerbread, Wood, Carved Flowers, Gilt Accents, Glass Front, 24 x 14 In. ..	58.00
Ingraham, Shelf, Neoclassical Style, Ebonized Wood, 6 Faux Onyx Columns, 11 x 20 In........	154.00
Ingraham, Shelf, Walnut, Gothic, Steeple, Round Face, Stenciled Door, Pillars, c.1835, 20 ¼ x 12 In...	1150.00
Ithaca Calendar Clock Co., Chronometer, Glass Door, Gilt Lettering, Carved Crest, c.1885, 33 x 16 In..	978.00
Ithaca Calendar Clock Co., Iron, Calendar, Pendulum, H.B. Horton's Patents, 1850-75, 19 In.	2070.00
Ithaca Calendar Clock Co., No. 1, Walnut, 8-Day, Time Only, Pendulum, 1875-1900, 74 In.	21850.00
Ithaca Calendar Clock Co., Regulator, Walnut, Zinc Dials, Rolling Date, 8-Day, 1883, 72 In. ..illus	24885.00
Ithaca Calendar Clock Co., Shelf, Library, Double Dial, Walnut, Semi-Steeple, Time, Strike, 25 In.	537.00
Ithaca Calendar Clock Co., Shelf, Walnut, Broken Pediment, Turned Spire, 25 x 12 In.........	384.00
Ithaca Calendar Clock Co., Wall, Iron Case, Figure 8, Flowers, Welch, c.1865, 21 x 9 In.	2070.00
Ithaca Calendar Clock Co., Wall, Walnut, Black Dials, Pediment, Kildare, c.1885, 32 x 13 In.	5175.00
Japy Freres, Figural, Birds, Putti, Bronze, Porcelain Face, Signed, 1800s, 14 ½ x 11 ¾ In.......	452.00
Japy Freres, Figural, Boy, Fishing, Oar, Net, Flowers, Gilt Metal, Marked G.K. & Co., 12 ¾ x 12 ½ In.	518.00
Japy Freres, Hot Air Balloon, Woven Basket, Fenced Platform Base, Bronze, Gold Dore, 27 In.	9440.00

Clock, Ansonia, Shelf, Rosalind, Iron, Black Enamel, Gilt, Woman, Angels, Brass 8-day, 12 x 15 In.
$295.00

Fontaine's Auction Gallery

Clock, Banjo, Mahogany, Carved, Lyre Front, Repainted Dial, Boston, c.1830, 40 ½ In.
$1593.00

Skinner, Inc.

Clock, Birge & Fuller, Double Steeple, Wagon Spring, Zinc Dial, 30-Hour, c.1845, 24 ½ In.
$1593.00

Skinner, Inc.

CLOCK

Clock, Black Forest, Cuckoo, Walnut, Eagle, Acorns, 8-Day, Spring Movement, c.1870, 38 In.
$1896.00

Skinner, Inc.

Clock, Brown, J.C., Acorn, Mahogany, Zinc Dial, Reverse Painted, 8-Day, Spring, c.1845, 28 In.
$17775.00

Skinner, Inc.

Clock, Brown, J.C., Shelf, Gothic, Rosewood, Ripple Front, Zinc Dial, 8-Day, Gong, c.1845, 20 In.
$1422.00

Skinner, Inc.

Clock, Carriage, Brass, Beveled Glass, Hour Repeating, 8-Day, Time & Strike, France, 8 ½ In.
$2573.00

Skinner, Inc.

Clock, Carriage, Bronze, Beveled Glass Panels, Presentation, Inscription, France, c.1890, 4 ¾ In.
$444.00

Skinner, Inc.

Clock, Eli Terry, Shelf, Mahogany, Carved, Reverse Painted, 8-Day, Countwheel Strike, c.1825, 36 In.
$1778.00

Skinner, Inc.

Clock, Figural, Courting Couple, Rococo Revival Case, Porcelain, Applied Flowers, c.1835, 16 x 9 In.
$1168.00

New Orleans Auction Galleries, Inc.

Clock, Figural, Palette, Brass Easel, Medieval Man & Woman, 10 ¾ x 10 In.
$735.00

Skinner, Inc.

Clock, Figural, Topsey, Blinking Eye, Cast Iron, Paper On Zinc, 30-Hour, c.1870, 16 ½ In.
$1659.00

Skinner, Inc.

Clock, French, Porcelain Face, Set In Oil Painting, Punch & Judy Figures, Chime, 27 x 32 In.
$2688.00

Theriault's

Clock, French, Shelf, Champleve, Gilt Bronze, Winged Figural Supports, Time & Strike, 19 In.
$4464.00

Leslie Hindman Auctioneers

Japy Freres, Hunter, Gun, Bird, Rabbit, Bronze, Marble, Porcelain Dial, 4-Toed Feet, 21 In. ...	537.00
Japy Freres, Shelf, Cherubs, Finial, Chains, Mask, Bronze, Dore, Marble Base, 16 x 10 In.	655.00
Japy Freres, Shelf, Marble, France, 16 x 9 In.	325.00
Japy Freres, Shelf, Renaissance Revival, Bronze, Urns, Acanthus, France, 1800s, 24 x 15 In...	960.00
Jennings Bros., Art Nouveau Spelter, Green, Sinuous, Open Handles, Alarm, 5 x 4 In.	81.00
Jerome & Co., Horolovar, Swinging Ball, Wood, Roman Numerals, Brass Feet, 10 In..............	102.00
Jerome & Co., Steeple, Painted Glass, Gothic Window, 15 x 8 In.	130.00
Jerome & Darrow, Shelf, Carved, Pillars, Painted, Flowers, Gilt, Bristol, 27 ¾ x 15 In...........	480.00
Jerome Chauncey, Mahogany, Ogee Case, Reverse Painting, c.1850, 26 x 15 ½ In.	177.00
Jerome Chauncey, School, Keyhole Drop, Faux Rosewood, Black & Bronze, c.1850, 16 In.	2370.00
Jerome Chauncey, School, Rosewood, 8-Sided, Short Drop, Tablet, 3 Girls, Goat, 23 In.........	113.00
Jugendstil, Copper, Brass, Art Glass, Rooster, Owl, Gilt Snake Hands, Austria, c.1900, 13 ¾ In. *illus*	1164.00
Junghans, Elephant, Brass, Swinging Pendulum, Windup, Germany, 1900s, 7 ½ x 11 In. .....*illus*	649.00
Junghans, Mystery, Elephant, Spelter, Gray, Trunk Dial, Swing Movement, 11 x 10 In.	270.00
Junghans, Swinging Arm, Diana Statue, Metal, Porcelain Dial, 8-Day, 14 In...........................	158.00
Junghans, Swinging Ball, Elephant, Bronze, 3-Day, Porcelain Dial, c.1900, 10 ¾ In.	209.00
Junghans, Swinging Ball, Kangaroo, Bronze, 3-Day, Porcelain Dial, c.1900, 10 ¾ In.	254.00
Kaiser, Birdcage, Brass, Alarm, 8 In.	90.00
Kienzle, Regulator, Black Forest, Key, Pendulum, 36 x 14 ½ In.	207.00
Kit Kat Klock, Blinking Eye, White Plastic, Black Bowtie, Eyes & Hands Light-Up, Tail Wags, Box	68.00
Kleinhemmel, Regulator, Vienna, 3-Weight, Carved Fan, Beads, Finials, 54 x 18 In...............	756.00
Kroeber, F., Wall, Walnut, Burl, Turned Columns, Zinc Dial, Strawberry Finial, c.1880, 37 In.	1778.00
Kroeber, Figural, Cupid, Winged, Holding Up Dial, Metal, Gold, Dolphin Head Base, 24 In.....	452.00
LeCoultre, Atmos, Glass, Brass Case, 9 In. ....*illus*	840.00
LeCoultre, Atmos, Perpetual Motion, Glass, Gilt Hands, Pendulum & Case, 9 x 8 ½ In. .....*illus*	531.00
LeCoultre, Shelf, Atmospheric, Brass Case, White Dial, c.1950, 9 x 8 In................. 720.00 to 1200.00	
Lenzkirch, Shelf, Domed Shape, Black & Burl, Time & Strike, 6 ¼ x 10 In.	194.00
L'Epee, Silver, Swing Handle, Enamel Face, Textured Surround, Black Lacquer, France, 2 In. .	830.00
L'Epine, Brass, Figural, Cherub On Chimera, Under Dome, Key, 5 ¾ x 4 In............................	288.00
Leroy, Balloon, Fruitwood, Brass Dial, Movement, Pendulum, Key, Paris, c.1840, 13 x 7 In.	230.00
Lespargot, Henry, Morbier, Porcelain Dial, Time & Strike, Metal, Steel Box, Repousse, 9 x 36 In.	478.00
Liberty & Co., Shelf, Pewter, Hammered, Tree Design, Enamel Face, David Veasey, 5 x 9 In.....	7200.00
Louis Philippe, Shelf, Marble, Gilt, Horse, Porcelain Face, Gallic Rooster, c.1850, 22 x 14 In.	1722.00
Louis XVI Style, Gilt Bronze, Fruit, Flaming Urn Finial, Fluted Columns, 1800s, 24 In.	3540.00
Lux, Animated, Happy Days, Beer Barrel, 2 Men, Lift Mugs, Windup, Metal, 1933, 3 ¾ x 3 ¾ In. ...*illus*	253.00
Lux, Black Cat, Red Bowtie, Pendulette Tail, 7 x 4 ½ x 1 In..	65.00
Lux, Cottage, White, Green Peaked Roof, Yellow Arched Door & Window, 6 x 4 ¼ In................	22.00
Lux, Country Scene, River, Cottages, Trees, Enamel, Cut Corners, Pendulum, 3 ½ x 3 In.	54.00
Lux, Cuckoo, Hunting Scene, Black Forest Style, Deer, Antlers, Guns, 8-Day, 17 x 10 In...........	38.00
Lux, Pendulette, Christmas Wreath, Metal Frame, Pink, Green, Pendulum, 6 In.......................	848.00
Lux, Pussy In The Well, 4 Women Looking Into Well, Pendulum, 6 ½ x 4 ¼ In.........................	151.00
Lux, Schmoo, Pink Plastic, Blue Pendulum, 6 x 4 In...	22.00
Macomb Calendar Clock Co., Walnut, Molded Plinth, Moon Phase, Pendulum, 1875-1900, 31 In.	1725.00
Mangiarotti, Angelo, Shelf, Molded Plastic, Black, Gilt Dial, Swiss, 1960s, 9 ½ In..................	300.00
Marit & Cie, Figural, War & Peace, Dore Bronze, White Marble, Porcelain Dial, 12 x 10 In.....	1610.00
Marit & Cie, Shelf, Figural, Woman Holding Scythe, Bronze, 19th Century, 13 x 15 In............	295.00
Marti, Shelf, Porcelain, Painted, Man & Woman In Park, Flowers, Scrolls, 1889, 10 In............	396.00
Mathey-Tissot, Travel, Art Deco, Swiss Movement, Side Buttons, Spring Loaded Doors, 2 x 1 ¼ In.	239.00
Mercedes, Art Nouveau Style, Gilt Metal, Pedestal Base, Continental, 16 In.	118.00
Milk Glass, Spring Driven, Plated Brass Case, Dolphin Relief, Davis Pat May 1877, 7 x 4 ¼ In.	224.00
Mitchell, Shelf, Bronze Dore, Brass Dial, Sunburst, Griffins, Paw Feet, 1800s, 17 In................	538.00
Musical, Wagner & Schubert, Metal, Embossed Instruments & Portraits, 8 In..........................	113.00
Mystery, Jefferson, Golden Minute, Gold Metal, Glass, Electric, 7 x 6 x 5 In.	54.00
Mystery, Statue, Black Marble, Gold Ormolu, Glass Bezel Pendulum, France, c.1880, 24 In.	6215.00
Mystery, Swinger, Upside Down Skeleton, Marble Base, Brass Feet, 25 In................................	920.00
Mystery, Woman Holding Wreath, Primavera Par Beuchon, White Metal, c.1880, 28 In.	1725.00
Napoleon III, Bronze, Enamel Face Atop Saddle Of Marching Horse, Urn, Late 1800s, 10 x 6 In.	615.00
New England Clock Co., Shelf, Mahogany, Gothic Steeple, 22 In...	59.00
New Haven, Fan, Copper, Rose Finish, Silver Leaves, Bird, Porcelain Numerals, 8 x 13 In.	136.00
New Haven, Shelf, Majolica, Putti, Scrolled Brass Frame, Low, Art Tile, c.1915, 12 x 10 In.	8060.00
New Haven, Shelf, Victorian, Birch Calendar, Black Dials, Arched Crest, Finials, c.1885, 32 x 17 In.	518.00
New Haven, Wall, Dickory Dock, Sliding White Mouse, Vertical Numbers, c.1910, 43 x 10 In..	1840.00
New Haven, Wall, Saturn, Oak, Spring Powered, Gold Painted Beat Plate, 35 x 15 In.	486.00
One Hand Clock Co., Metal, Round, Footed, Paper Dial, Warren, Pa., 9 In.............................	79.00
Oswald, Owl, Carved, Black Forest Style, Blinking Eye, Label, Germany, c.1930, 8 x 3 ½ In. ......*illus*	288.00

Clock, Gaston Jolly, Bracket, Musical, 3-Key Wind, Silent Chime, Brass Trim, Paw Feet, Paris, 26 In.
$11400.00

DuMouchelles Art Gallery

Clock, Herman Miller, Chrome Plated Steel, Bronze Support, Finish, Aluminum, G. Rohde, 1930s, 11 ½ x 6 ½ In.
$7150.00

Treadway Toomey Galleries

Clock, Howard Miller, Kite, G. Nelson, c.1952, 16 ½ x 22 In.
$1875.00

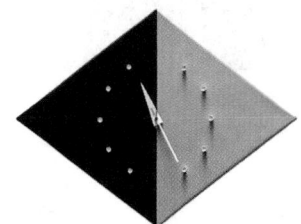

Los Angeles Modern Auctions

Clock, Howard Miller, Motion Notion, George Nelson, 6 x 5 ¼ In.
$7500.00

Los Angeles Modern Auctions

Clock, Ithaca Calendar Clock Co., Regulator, Walnut, Zinc Dials, Rolling Date, 8-Day, 1883, 72 In. $24885.00

Skinner, Inc.

Clock, Jugendstil, Copper, Brass, Art Glass, Rooster, Owl, Gilt Snake Hands, Austria, c.1900, 13 ¾ In. $1164.00

Skinner, Inc.

Clock, Junghans, Elephant, Brass, Swinging Pendulum, Windup, Germany, 1900s, 7 ½ x 11 In. $649.00

Brunk Auctions

Oswald, Owl, Carved, Blinking Eye, Germany, Prewar, 7 In.	403.00
Pendulette, Porcelain, Painted, Niagara Falls, 30-Hour, Germany, 4 x 3 In.	90.00
Pendulette, Wag The Wall, Painted Flowers, Graniteware, 30-Hour, Box, Germany, 2 ⅜ x 4 ½ In.	142.00
Perigord, Morbier, Brass, White Dial, Scrolling, France, 52 x 16 In.	207.00
Picard, H., Shelf, Napoleon III, Gilt Bronze, Marble, Shaped Case, Bellflowers, c.1850, 9 x 18 In.	738.00
Portico, French Empire Style, Gilt, Ebonized, Bell Strike, Flower Bezel, 4 Columns, 1800s, 18 In.	329.00
Portico, Marble Case, Fire Gilt Ormolu, 4 Columns, Enamel Dial, Brass, Swans, Flowers, 18 In.	1185.00
Portico, Wood, Gilt Metal, Round Dial, Leaves, 4 Spiral Supports, Vines, France, 21 x 10 In.	354.00
Potted Plant, Red Rose, Dial In Center Of Rose, Glass Dome, Carved Wood Stand, 8 In.	158.00
Pyramid, Sterling Silver, Purple Enamel, Ribbed Rays, Key Wind, Germany	1243.00
Raingo Freres, Shelf, Classical Figure, Bronze, Marble, Gold Trim, France, c.1870, 18 x 9 ½ In.	780.00
Regulator, Calendar, Oak, c.1900, 27 x 16 In.	254.00
Regulator, Jeweler's, Pinwheel Movement, Multi-Prong Pendulum, 75 x 16 In.	1053.00
Regulator, Vienna, Carved Wood Case, Columns, Base Finial, Porcelain Face, 40 x 18 In.	259.00
Regulator, Vienna, Grand Muller, Walnut, Front, Carved Crest & Columns, 58 x 22 In.	1035.00
Regulator, Wall, 3-Weight, 8-Day, Glass Door & Sides, Pendulum, c.1870, 49 x 18 x 8 In.	590.00
Renaissance Revival, Rosewood, Marble Face, Gold Incised, Finials, c.1870, 63 x 18 In. *illus*	4600.00
Rimbault, Stephen, Desk, George III, Ebonized, Musical, Brass Mounts, 8-Day, c.1765, 21 x 13 In. *illus*	17080.00
Sessions, Shelf, Black, Sarcophagus Shape, 6 Columns, Lion's Head Handles	102.00
Sessions, Shelf, Jupiter, Mission Oak, Metal Numbers, Pendulum, 16 ¾ x 8 In.	97.00
Sessions, Shelf, Temple Design, Painted Faux Marble, 6 Columns, Footed, 12 x 18 In.	213.00
Seth Thomas, Art Nouveau, Regulator, Crystal, Beveled Glass, c.1890, 14 x 8 ½ In.	431.00
Seth Thomas, Beulah, White Adamantine, Ormolu, 8-Day, Time & Strike, c.1905, 10 x 13 In.	173.00
Seth Thomas, Boston Kitchen, Oak, Gingerbread, Time & Strike, Painted Dial, Pat. 1870, 22 In.	141.00
Seth Thomas, Burglar, Fire Detective, Mahogany, Strike-A-Light Top, c.1860, 11 In.	633.00
Seth Thomas, Calendar, No. 4, Office, Rosewood, 2 Dials, 8-Day, 1868-1874, 27 x 15 In.	351.00
Seth Thomas, Calendar, No. 5, Mahogany, 2 Dials, Label, 20 x 12 ¾ In.	633.00
Seth Thomas, Calendar, No. 6, Office, 2 Dials, Rosewood Case, 32 x 15 In.	783.00
Seth Thomas, Calendar, No. 10, Office, Walnut, 8-Day, Silvered Pendulum, 1900-25, 48 In.	12650.00
Seth Thomas, Calendar, No. 10, Walnut, Burl Trim, Gallery Top, 8-Day, 36 x 22 In.	2950.00
Seth Thomas, Calendar, Parlor, Walnut, Acorn Finials, Hinged Door, c.1885, 37 x 23 In.	4485.00
Seth Thomas, Calendar, Parlor, Walnut, Reeded Columns, Carved Crest, c.1885, 27 ¼ x 14 ¾ In.	518.00
Seth Thomas, Calendar, Southern, Walnut Case, Arched Glass Door, 1879, 32 x 16 In.	1380.00
Seth Thomas, Mahogany Pillar & Scroll, Bonnet Top, Brass Finials, Early 1800s, 32 x 18 In.	748.00
Seth Thomas, Mahogany Pillar & Scroll, Reverse Painted Glass, Brass Finials, Conn., 32 In.	999.00
Seth Thomas, Mahogany Pillar & Scroll, Scrolled Crest, Reverse Painted, Lake	1475.00
Seth Thomas, Parlor, No. 3, Walnut, 2 Dials, Day, Date, Pendulum, 27 In.	452.00
Seth Thomas, Pillar & Scroll, Painted Tablet, House, Trees, 3 Finials, 24 x 12 In.	205.00
Seth Thomas, Pillar & Scroll, Wood Dial, Panel, Pendulum, Brass Finials, c.1815, 30 x 17 In. *illus*	2478.00
Seth Thomas, Regulator, Brass Case, Glass Sides, Crystal Column, 8-Day Time, c.1900, 9 In.	259.00
Seth Thomas, Shelf, Adamantine, 2 Movements, Sonora Chime, 4 Bells, 14 x 11 In.	270.00
Seth Thomas, Shelf, Arch Top, Burl Veneer, Time & Strike, 15 x 10 ½ In.	189.00
Seth Thomas, Shelf, Brass, Beveled Glass Case, 9 ¾ In.	354.00
Seth Thomas, Shelf, Fashion, No. 3, Walnut, Arched Glass Door, 2 Painted Dials, 8-Day, 32 In.	1180.00
Seth Thomas, Shelf, Federal, Mahogany, Pillar & Scroll, Swan's Neck Crest, c.1805, 32 x 18 In.	805.00
Seth Thomas, Shelf, Figural, Guardian Angel, Spelter, Scrolled Base, Porcelain Dial, 16 In.	226.00
Seth Thomas, Shelf, K.C.B. No. 2, Black, Red Adamantine Highlights, Gilt Metal, 11 x 18 In.	243.00
Seth Thomas, Shelf, Mahogany, Arched, Sonora Chime, Metal Dial, 15 In.	237.00
Seth Thomas, Shelf, Mahogany, Eglomise Picture, Baltimore Cemetery, c.1850, 26 x 15 In.	127.00
Seth Thomas, Shelf, Mahogany, Gothic Case, Westminster Chimes, Brass Dial, c.1900, 15 In.	448.00
Seth Thomas, Shelf, Mahogany, Molded, 4 Columns, Zinc Dial, Fruit, Flowers, c.1850, 19 In.	1041.00
Seth Thomas, Shelf, Mahogany, Round Face, Perpetual Calendar, 20 x 13 In.	633.00
Seth Thomas, Shelf, Mahogany, Round Top, Westminster Chimes, Early 1900s, 14 In.	546.00
Seth Thomas, Shelf, Red Adamantine, Rectangular, Arched Top, Celluloid Dial, 10 In.	68.00
Seth Thomas, Shelf, Rosewood, Sonora Chimes, c.1900, 14 x 15 In.	660.00
Seth Thomas, Shelf, Sonora Chime, Westminster Chime, Pendulum & Key, 1915-20, 14 In.	518.00
Seth Thomas, Shelf, Tyne, Adamantine, Arched, 2 Columns, Ormolu, 11 x 13 In.	194.00
Seth Thomas, Wall, King Bee, Oak, Gingerbread, Time, Strike, Alarm, 30-Hour, 30 x 14 In.	194.00
Seth Thomas, Wall, Oak, Round, 18 In. Diam.	266.00
Seth Thomas, Wall, Queen Bee, Oak, Gingerbread, Time, Strike, Alarm, 29 x 14 In.	297.00
Shelf, Abner Jones, Tablet, Mirror, 8-Day Time & Strike, Rectangular, Black, Gold, 1830s, 29 In.	1836.00
Shelf, Acorn, Building, Rectangular Stepped Base, c.1847, 24 In.	2573.00
Shelf, Balthazar, Mahogany, Cast Finials, Handle, Cherub Design, France, c.1850, 18 x 11 In.	690.00
Shelf, Brewster & Ingraham, Beehive, Gothic Style, Mahogany, 1800s, 19 x 11 In.	210.00
Shelf, Bronze, Champleve, Round, 2-Train Time & Strike Movement, 1900s, 21 x 10 ½ In.	2270.00

Shelf, Bronze, Enamel, Torcheres, Dolphins, Putto, Urn Finial, Leaves & Flowers, 14 ¼ In......	2950.00
Shelf, Circus Tent, Iron Front, Pagoda Top, Gilt Tassels, Brass Bezel Pendulum, c.1870, 21 In.	2015.00
Shelf, Cloisonne Enamel, Urn Finial, Columns, Gilt, Turquoise Ground, 18 ½ In.....................	1150.00
Shelf, Cloisonne, Blue, Stylized Feathers, 10 Open Columns, Panels, Nude Maidens, 9 x 9 In..	151.00
Shelf, Cloisonne, Brass, Flowers, 6 Column Supports, Urn Finial, Beveled Glass, 17 x 10 In. ...	863.00
Shelf, Cottage, Snakeskin Veneer, Faux Graining, Zinc Dial, Painted Glass, c.1855, 11 In.......	1041.00
Shelf, Egyptian Revival, Gilt Bronze, Marble, Onyx, Winged Sphinx, Griffons, 1800s, 17 x 20 In.	1845.00
Shelf, Empire Style, Applied Gilt Classical Figures, Stars, Faux Rouge Marble, 13 ¾ In...........	625.00
Shelf, Empire Style, Mahogany, Gilt Urn Finial, Figural Scrolls, Bun Feet, 1800s, 14 In.	269.00
Shelf, Empire, Love Crowning Psyche, Ormolu, Wood Base, France, 1800s, 15 In...................	1778.00
Shelf, Empire, Ormolu Lions, Swans, Arab Girl, Playing Mandolin, Hexagonal, 17 x 13 In......	2340.00
Shelf, Empire, Patina, Gilt Bronze Mounts, Enamel Dial, Sphinx Bust Top, Paw Feet, 17 x 9 In.	3510.00
Shelf, Empire, Patina, Gilt Bronze, Seated Classical Woman, Lute, Enamel Dial, 18 x 9 In......	2457.00
Shelf, Federal, Mahogany, Carved, Pillar & Scroll, Brass Urn & Spire Finials, 1800s, 32 In.	450.00
Shelf, Figural, Teddy Roosevelt On Horse, Iron, Gold Paint, Paper Dial, 10 ¾ In.	192.00
Shelf, Gilt Bronze, Tablet Frieze, Fluted Corinthian Columns, Swan Pendulum, 20 x 10 In.....	1076.00
Shelf, Ingraham, E., Wood, Gingerbread, 22 ¼ In.	210.00
Shelf, Lantern Style, Brass Barrel, Sevres Style Painted Panels, Classical Figures, 1800s, 17 In.	2596.00
Shelf, Louis XVI Style, Republic, Porcelain, Mounted Gilt Bronze, Brass, c.1900, 12 x 13 In. ...	1722.00
Shelf, Mahogany, Brass Accents, Porcelain Face, Flowers, Finials, Ball Feet, Key Wind, 1855, 12 x 6 In.	259.00
Shelf, Mahogany, Carved Gilded Fruit Basket, Gilded Columns, Flowers, c.1838-43, 27 In.......	948.00
Shelf, Mahogany, Carved, Mirror, Gilt, 8-Day, Brass, Pendulum, Iron Weights, c.1830, 31 In. ..*illus*	889.00
Shelf, Mahogany, Concave Dial, Footed, Eagle Finial, Flowers, 2 Women, Tree, c.1820, 36 In..	2133.00
Shelf, Mahogany, Gothic, Flowers, Spires, Ball Finials, Door, Peak, Zinc Dial, c.1840, 21 In. ..	5925.00
Shelf, Mahogany, Scroll, Stencil Design, Flowers, Eagle, Pillars, Paw Feet, 1800s, 33 x 17 ½ In.	236.00
Shelf, Mahogany, Scrolled Splat, Stenciled Columns, Wooden Dial, c.1835-40, 26 In.	2252.00
Shelf, Mahogany, Veneer, Pillar & Scroll, c.1827-29, 30 In..	796.00
Shelf, Majolica, Round, Rectangular Plinth, Oak Leaves, Lion Masks, Acorns, 1800s, 12 x 11 In..	551.00
Shelf, Marble, Gilt Bronze, Face, Sunburst, Pendulum, Time & Strike, Key, c.1890, 21 In. ....*illus*	5900.00
Shelf, Napoleon III Style, Brass, Enamel Dial, Key Wind, Scroll Legs, Boy Finial, c.1890, 15 In.	1003.00
Shelf, Napoleon III, Gilt Bronze, Gothic Cathedral Shape, Porcelain Dial, Gong, 1800s, 14 x 10 In.	427.00
Shelf, Napoleon III, Mahogany, Gilt Bronze, Columns, Lyre & Swan Pendulum, 1800s, 16 x 8 In.	615.00
Shelf, Napoleon III, Walnut, Brass Inlay, Chateau, Turret Finials, Gong, 1800s, 18 x 11 In......	677.00
Shelf, Petite Sonnerie, Black Marble, Stepped, Beveled Glass & Brass Door, France, 15 x 11 In.	203.00
Shelf, Regulator, Brass, Openwork Gallery, Finial, Columns, Key Wind, France, 14 x 7 In........	316.00
Shelf, Roman Figure, Gilt Bronze, Time & Strike, Pendulum, Silk Suspension, c.1790, 18 In. ...*illus*	4012.00
Shelf, Rosewood, Turned Finials, Columns, Roman Numerals, Moon Hands, c.1880, 11 In.....	2015.00
Shelf, Silver, Tortoiseshell Case, Inlaid Sterling Flowers, 4 ½ In.	345.00
Shelf, Spelter, Bronze, Bejeweled Woman, Holding Censor, Atop Elephant, 1800s, 21 x 15 In...	1353.00
Shelf, Trumpeter, Walnut, 4-Horn, Gothic Crest, Fluted Pillars, Hunting Song, c.1860, 35 In. .	3555.00
Ship's Bell, Ship's Wheel, Brass, Bronze, Wood, Presentation, Chelsea, 12 x 11 In....................	351.00
Skeleton, Brass, Glass Dome, c.1850, 17 x 11 In.	590.00
Skeleton, Full Strike, Cable-Driven Fusee, 2-Train, Wood Base, c.1860, 19 x 12 x 7 In............	2360.00
Spencer & Hotchkiss, Shelf, Mahogany, 8-Day, Reverse Painted, Pendulum, c.1835, 26 In. ..*illus*	4148.00
Stennis, E.O., Aurora, Girandole, Glass, Gilt, Eagle, Stamped, Case Made In Prison, 45 In.......	4068.00
Stick, Wood, Brass Numerals, Weight Driven, Drawer, Key, Dokei, Japan, 15 x 3 In.	1130.00
Stickley, L. & J.G., Shelf, Copper Face, Rectangular, 22 x 16 In.	5580.00
Swedish, Wall, Baroque Style, Carved Wood, Gilt Gesso Body, Brass Movement, 23 x 13 In......	118.00
Tall Case, A. Willard, Federal, Mahogany, Moon Phase, Brass Fluting, Ogee Feet, Finials, 89 In.	17250.00
Tall Case, Aaron Willard Mahogany, Pierced Fret, Iron Dial, Moon's Age, 8-Day, c.1790, 94 In.	21330.00
Tall Case, Aaron Willard, Mahogany, Curved Bonnet, Carved, Brass Ball, Spire Finials, 99 In.	12000.00
Tall Case, Art Deco, Mahogany, Moon Phase Dial, c.1930, 81 x 23 In..	720.00
Tall Case, Asahel Cheney, Cherry, Brass Dial, 8-Day, Movement, Putney, Vt., c.1800, 90 In. ....*illus*	11850.00
Tall Case, Bawo & Dotter, Mahogany, Brass Dial, 8-Day, German Movement, N.Y., c.1900, 95 In.	3911.00
Tall Case, Caleb Davis, Cherry, Inlay, Painted Moon Phase Dial, 8-Day, Brass Works, 97 In. ...	37375.00
Tall Case, Cherry, Broken Scroll Pediment, Bull's Eye Terminals, 8-Day, c.1820, 95 x 18 In. ...	1800.00
Tall Case, Cherry, Scalloped Door, 30-Hour, Chain, Single Weight, 1810-15, 100 In. ....*illus*	1293.00
Tall Case, Chippendale, Steeple Finials, Reeded Plinths, Fretwork, Painted............................	4600.00
Tall Case, Chippendale, Walnut, Scrolled Cornice, Carved, Arched, 1768, 99 x 20 In.	29000.00
Tall Case, Dutch Burl Walnut, Bombe, Carved, Brass Dial, Day, Month, Moon Phase, c.1770, 118 In.	7963.00
Tall Case, Elliott, Mahogany, Hinged Doors, Glass Inserts, Arched Bonnet, London, 88 x 20 In.	2128.00
Tall Case, Federal Style, Mahogany, Shaped Crest, Westminster Chimes, Germany, 1900s, 90 In.	518.00
Tall Case, Federal, Butternut, Painted Iron Dial, 8-Day Time & Strike, Iron Weights, c.1810, 88 In.	2370.00
Tall Case, Federal, Mahogany, Broken Arch Pediment, Moon Phase Dial, c.1810, 100 x 19 In.	4428.00
Tall Case, Federal, Mahogany, Tombstone Dial, Ship, Openwork Arch, Columns, c.1807, 88 In.	24885.00

Clock, LeCoultre, Atmos, Glass, Brass Case, 9 In.
$840.00

DuMouchelles Art Gallery

Clock, LeCoultre, Atmos, Perpetual Motion, Glass, Gilt Hands, Pendulum & Case, 9 x 8 ½ In.
$531.00

Fontaine's Auction Gallery

Clock, Lux, Animated, Happy Days, Beer Barrel, 2 Men, Lift Mugs, Windup, Metal, 1933, 3 ¾ x 3 ¾ In.
$253.00

Hake's Americana & Collectibles

Clock, Oswald, Owl, Carved, Black Forest Style, Blinking Eye, Label, Germany, c.1930, 8 x 3 ½ In.
$288.00

James D. Julia Inc.

Clock, Renaissance Revival, Rosewood, Marble Face, Gold Incised, Finials, c.1870, 63 x 18 In. $4600.00

Bob Courtney Auctions

Clock, Rimbault, Stephen, Desk, George III, Ebonized, Musical, Brass Mounts, 8-Day, c.1765, 21 x 13 In. $17080.00

Neal Auction Co.

Clock, Seth Thomas, Pillar & Scroll, Wood Dial, Panel, Pendulum, Brass Finials, c.1815, 30 x 17 In. $2478.00

James D. Julia Inc.

Clock, Shelf, Mahogany, Carved, Mirror, Gilt, 8-Day, Brass, Pendulum, Iron Weights, c.1830, 31 In. $889.00

Skinner, Inc.

Clock, Shelf, Marble, Gilt Bronze, Face, Sunburst, Pendulum, Time & Strike, Key, c.1890, 21 ½ In. $5900.00

Brunk Auctions

Clock, Shelf, Roman Figure, Gilt Bronze, Time & Strike, Pendulum, Silk Suspension, c.1790, 18 In. $4012.00

Brunk Auctions

Clock, Spencer & Hotchkiss, Shelf, Mahogany, 8-Day, Reverse Painted, Weights, Pendulum, c.1835, 26 In. $4148.00

Skinner, Inc.

Clock, Tall Case, Asahel Cheney, Cherry, Brass Dial, 8-Day, Movement, Putney, Vt., c.1800, 90 In. $11850.00

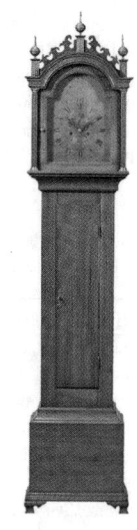

Skinner, Inc.

Clock, Tall Case, Cherry, Scalloped Door, 30-Hour, Chain, Single Weight, 1810-15, 100 In. $1293.00

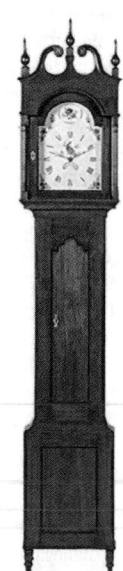

Cowan's Auctions

Tall Case, Federal, Maple, Birch Inlay, Iron Tombstone Dial, Moon Phase, Carved, c.1810, 91 In.		5629.00
Tall Case, French Provincial, Glazed Doors, Bracket Base, Enameled Face, 92 x 20 In.............		373.75
Tall Case, George II, Chinoiserie, Brass Dial & Finials, Silvered Ring, England, Signed, 88 In.		3450.00
Tall Case, George III, Mahogany, Brass Dial, Urn Finial, Pierced, Openwork Top, c.1790, 99 In.		1763.00
Tall Case, George III, Mahogany, Enamel Dial, Swan's Neck Pediment, 86 x 18 In...................		1100.00
Tall Case, George III, Oak, Inlaid, Swan's Neck Top, Brass Rosettes, Time & Strike, 83 In........		800.00
Tall Case, Gilbert, Regulator, No. 12, Oak, 8-Day, Open Moon Hands, 102 x 30 In.		4720.00
Tall Case, Gilt Bronze, Mahogany Parquetry, Putti, Swags, Enamel Dial, c.1920, 87 x 21In.....		14760.00
Tall Case, Gothic, Walnut, Carved, Steeple Accent Top, Weights, Pendulum, Bells, 110 x 23 In.		4600.00
Tall Case, Hanson Clock Co., Gothic Style, Walnut, Chiming, Moon Dial, c.1900, 82 x 25 In. ...		354.00
Tall Case, Hepplewhite, Cherry, Cove Molding, Scroll Top, Columns, Broken Arch, c.1820, 88 In.		529.00
Tall Case, Hepplewhite, Pine, Ship Painted Dial, Finials, Pewter Hands, 88 x 19 In.		1955.00
Tall Case, Hepplewhite, Walnut, Poplar, Broken Arch Pediment, Inlay, Bracket Feet, c.1810, 97 In.		1998.00
Tall Case, Howard Miller, Oak Case, 3 Chimes, Glass Side Shelves, 82 x 36 In.		1265.00
Tall Case, Isaac Rogers, Cherry, Ornate Brass Calendar Dial, London, 94 x 18 In.		1243.00
Tall Case, J. Wanamaker, Oak, Broken Arch, Pierced Gilt Brass Dial, 5 Tubes, 103 In.		8260.00
Tall Case, Jan Breukelaar, Burl Walnut, Metal Dial, 8-Day, Moon, Amsterdam, 1700s, 8 Ft. ..*illus*		3105.00
Tall Case, Jean Paturel A Rive De Gier, Walnut, Gilt Brass Face, France, 1800s, 100 x 24 In.....		2151.00
Tall Case, John Ashton Jr., Regency Style, Chinoiserie, Painted Dial, Gilt, Leek, c.1890, 77 x 22 In. *illus*		671.00
Tall Case, John Esterle, Mahogany, 8-Day, Brass Movement, 2-Weight, Pa., 102 In. ....*illus*		3304.00
Tall Case, John Ivison, George III, Mahogany, Time & Strike, Brass Engraved Dial, Signed, c.1810		2510.00
Tall Case, Mahogany, Arched Hood, Scroll Pediment, Spiral Pilasters, Shaped Door, 1800s, 94 In.		2714.00
Tall Case, Mahogany, Banded Waist Door, Brass Face, Shaped Bracket Feet, England, 77 x 16 In.		1955.00
Tall Case, Mahogany, Carved Scrolls, Beveled Glass, Moon Phase Dial, 8-Day, 99 In.		3795.00
Tall Case, Mahogany, Chimes, Painted Face, Lunar Calendar Dial, Tall Ship, 1800s, 96 x 98 In.		1673.00
Tall Case, Mahogany, Inlay, Swan's Neck, Painted Scenes, Signed Eccles, London, c.1820, 96 In.		830.00
Tall Case, Mahogany, Metal Dial, Moon, Swan's Neck Pediment, Time & Bell Strike, 1800s, 98 x 26 In.		1380.00
Tall Case, Mahogany, Swan's Neck Pediment, Painted Face, Roman Numerals, 87 In..............		1830.00
Tall Case, Marquetry Inlay, Pagoda Top, Barley Twist Stiles, Barometer, Scroll Feet, 1800s, 101 In.*illus*		4444.00
Tall Case, Marquetry, Domed Bonnet, Carved, Brass, Mother-Of-Pearl Inlay, c.1740, 101 x 21 In.		5975.00
Tall Case, Oak, Broken Arch Top, Arched Door, Painted Iron Dial, 4 Seasons, England, 90 In.		920.00
Tall Case, Oak, Carved, Arched Crest Bonnet, Silvered & Brass Moon Phase, c.1900, 90 In.		2500.00
Tall Case, Oak, John Ewer & Sir Oswald Temple, Carved King, Orb, Putti, 1653, 135 x 43 In. ..		76700.00
Tall Case, Oak, Pierced Fretwork, Engraved Dome, Brass Dial, England, c.1900, 77 x 17 In.		805.00
Tall Case, Oak, Scrolling Pediment, Brass Face, Glazed Door, Inlaid Columns, Bracket Feet, 81 In.		1298.00
Tall Case, Painted Iron Face, Broken Swan Pediment, England, 87 ½ In.		920.00
Tall Case, Pine, Grain Paint, Carved, Shaped Crest, c.1825-35, 83 In.		2726.00
Tall Case, Pine, Kettle Shape, Molded Cornice, Glazed Door, Diamond Pattern, c.1850, 90 x 23 In.		1230.00
Tall Case, Pine, Quarter Columns, 30-Hour Movement, New England, c.1825, 82 In. .....*illus*		999.00
Tall Case, Pine, Red Wash, Carved Scroll Crest, Hand Painted Dial, Ship & Figures, 84 In.......		826.00
Tall Case, Pine, Stained, Hourglass Shape, Time & Hour Strike, Sweden, 76 x 15 In.		492.00
Tall Case, Regency, Mahogany, Brass Inlay, Barometer, Thermometer, c.1810, 84 x 18 In. .....*illus*		3851.00
Tall Case, Renaissance Revival, Walnut, Green & Red Leaded Glass Door, Musical, 1800s, 92 In.		6463.00
Tall Case, Richardson, Flame Mahogany, Moon Phase, West Yorkshire, England, 94 In...........		961.00
Tall Case, Riley Whiting, Swan's Neck Crest, Spool Finials, Cove Cornice, c.1805, 86 ½ x 15 In.		805.00
Tall Case, Saml. Denton, Cottage, Oak, Brass Dial, 30-Hour, Engraved, Oxford, c.1785, 75 In.		770.00
Tall Case, Samuel Best, Cherry, Paneled Base, Dovetailed, Brass Movement, Ohio, 1806, 99 In. ..*illus*		4818.00
Tall Case, Samuel Breneiser, Federal, Cherry, Double Scroll Cresting, Carved, 97 In.		3250.00
Tall Case, Scandinavian, Carved, Painted, Pierced Gallery, Dial Window, Flower Border, 80 x 22 In.		1793.00
Tall Case, Seth Thomas, Burl Veneer, Fluted Columns, Metal Face, Triple Chime, 82 x 25 In....		863.00
Tall Case, Seth Thomas, Mahogany, Musical, Columns, Finials, c.1905, 102 In. x 25 In.		8050.00
Tall Case, Seth Thomas, Pine, Walnut Finish, Domed Bonnet, Silver Face, 82 x 21 In..............		540.00
Tall Case, Sheraton, Cherry, Broken Arch Pediment, Turned Columns, Shell Carved Door, 89 In.		1298.00
Tall Case, Silas Hoadley, Pine, Flat Top, Cutout Feet, Grain Painted, Conn., 84 In.		3495.00
Tall Case, Simon Willard, Mahogany, Iron Osborne Dial, 8-Day, Brass Time & Strike, c.1795, 97 In.		38513.00
Tall Case, Stanton Hackett, Arts & Crafts, Glass Door, Paper Label, 85 x 21 In.		1860.00
Tall Case, Symphonion, Walnut, 7 13-In. Musical Discs, c.1885, 88 ½ x 22 ½ In. ....*illus*		8125.00
Tall Case, T. Jeffrey, Mahogany, Pendulum, Cast Iron Weights, Brass Finials, Canterbury, 83 In. .*illus*		2370.00
Tall Case, Tho. Richardson, George III, Mahogany, Moon Dial, Eglomise Panel Bonnet, 90 x 22 In.		3690.00
Tall Case, Tiger Maple, Pagoda Top, Carved Heart, Moon Phase, Calendar, c.1795, 84 In.		5925.00
Tall Case, W. Smith, Mahogany, Chinese Scene Dial, Cantered Corners, c.1790, 89 x 25 In......		1912.00
Tall Case, Walnut, Shell & Leaf Hood, Long Door, Bombe Shape, Animal-Shape Feet, 92 In.		767.00
Tall Case, Waltham, Mahogany, Chime, Scroll Top, Brass Dial, Moon's Age, 8-Day, 1911, 95 In.		4148.00
Tall Case, Waterbury, Carved, Columns, Hood Door, Brass Dial, 8-Day, c.1915, 95 ½ In. .....*illus*		2489.00
Tall Case, Waterbury, Oak, Carved, Musical, 5-Tube, Oval Beveled Glass Door, 89 x 27 In........		904.00
Tall Case, William & Mary, Walnut, Seaweed, Marquetry, Gilt Finials, Glazed Door, 91 x 18 In.		9500.00

Clock, Tall Case, Jan Breukelaar, Burl Walnut, Painted Metal Dial, 8-Day, Moon Phase, Amsterdam, 1700s, 8 Ft. $3105.00

Cottone Auctions

Clock, Tall Case, John Ashton Jr., Regency Style, Chinoiserie, Painted Dial, Gilt, Leek, c.1890, 77 x 22 In. $671.00

Neal Auction Co.

Clock, Tall Case, John Esterle, Mahogany, 8-Day, Brass Movement, 2-Weight, Pa., 102 In. $3304.00

Clock, Tall Case, Pine, Quarter Columns, 30-Hour Movement, New England, c.1825, 82 In. $999.00

Clock, Tall Case, Samuel Best, Cherry, Paneled Base, Dovetailed, Brass Movement, Ohio, 1806, 99 In. $4818.00

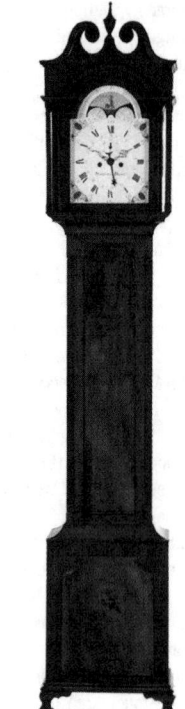

Conestoga Auction Co., Inc.

Garth's Auctions, Inc.

Garth's Auctions, Inc.

Clock, Tall Case, Marquetry Inlay, Pagoda Top, Barley Twist Stiles, Barometer, Scroll Feet, 1800s, 101 In. $4444.00

Clock, Tall Case, Regency, Mahogany, Brass Inlay, Barometer, Thermometer, c.1810, 84 x 18 In. $3851.00

Clock, Tall Case, Symphonion, Walnut, 7 13-In. Musical Discs, c.1885, 88 ½ x 22 ½ In. $8125.00

Skinner, Inc.

Skinner, Inc.

Bonhams & Butterfields

Tall Case, William IV, Mahogany, Swan's Neck Crest, Turned Columns, Cherub, c.1840, 95 In.	613.00
Tall Case, William Roach, Cherry, Peaked Cornice, Turned Columns, Cherubs, 1700s, 88 In.	826.00
Tall Case, Woolley, Flat Hood, Silvered, Gilt Metal Face, Crescent Shape, 1700s, 76 In.	1770.00
Terry & Andrews, Beehive, Painted Glass, 1897, 10 x 10 In.	130.00
Terry, Silas B., Cottage, Paper Veneer, Etched Tablet, Zinc Dial, 30-Hour, c.1855, 10 ½ In. ....*illus*	1225.00
Thwaites & Reed, Rosewood, Imperial Fan Clock, 8-Day, House Of Igor, Carl Faberge, 1984, 10 In.	738.00
Travel, Carriage Style, Turtle Top, Embossed, Alarm, c.1900, 5 ¼ x 2 ¾ In.	633.00
Vienna Regulator, Biedermeier Rosewood, Piecrust Bezel, Porcelain Dial, 1866, 40 In.	1356.00
Vincenti & Cie, Shelf, Spelter, Mantel, Figural, 2 Armored Soldiers, 1800s, 25 x 28 In.	499.00
Vulliamy, J., George III Style, Act Of Parliament, Gilt Crane, Rockwork, Bamboo, 47 x 23 In.	1755.00
Vulliamy, Shelf, Mahogany, Carved, Cathedral Style, 29 x 18 In.	3186.00
Wag-On-Wall, Wood, Brass Works, Weights, Pendulum, Germany, 1800s, 14 In.	176.00
Wall, Federal, Mahogany, Gilt, Tablet, Perry's Victory, Cone Finial, c.1820, 41 In.	1541.00
Wall, Floating Dial, Wood, Metal, Round, 1950s, 9 In.	275.00
Wall, Henry II Style, Walnut, Scrolls, Fruit & Berry Carved, 26 x 18 In.	244.00
Wall, Jellico, Amos, Oak, Carved, Painted Tin Dial, England, 1881, 24 x 14 In.	387.00
Wall, Mahogany, Carved, Lyre Front, Leafy Finial, Round Dial, c.1830, 41 In.	1778.00
Wall, Mahogany, Enamel Dial, Glass Case, Arched Cornice, Applied Leaves, 1900s, 45 x 14 In.	610.00
Wall, Regulator, Eastlake Style, Walnut Arched, Carved Basket Crest, Time & Strike, 36 In.	185.00
Walnut, Diamond Shape, Rays, Brass Sphere Finials, 37 In.	59.00
Warren Telechron, Shelf, Brass, Bakelite, Glass, Radiating Design, P. Frankl, 5 ¾ x 7 ¾ In.	1320.00
Waterbury, Calendar, Oak, Shaped Crest, Scrolls, 1889, 28 x 17 In.	359.00
Waterbury, Calendar, No. 43, Pressed Oak, 2 Dials Scrolls, 29 x 16 In.	513.00
Waterbury, Dresser, Abalone Shell, Paper Dial, 6 In.	68.00
Waterbury, Kitchen, Festus, Oak, Carved, Alarm, Time & Strike, Paper Dial	124.00
Waterbury, School, Rosewood, Calendar Dial, Octagonal, Short Pointed Drop, c.1885, 22 x 15 In.	777.00
Waterbury, Wall, Augusta, Oak, Calendar, Spiral Twist Columns, Acorn Finials, c.1885, 51 x 19 In.	2300.00
Waterbury, Wall, Prophet, Shaped Oak Case, Calendar, Feather & Scroll, 27 x 13 In.	184.00
Weill & Harburg, Carriage, Balance Wheel, Spring Driven, 8-Day, 1886, 10 x 8 x 7 In.	1180.00
Welch Spring & Co., Regulator, No. 5, Walnut, Calendar, Double Spring, Pendulum, c.1875, 38 In.	5175.00
Welch Spring & Co., Regulator, Walnut, Arched Crest, Urn Finials, Calendar, c.1850, 38 x 15 In.	5175.00
Welch, Auber, Arched, Molded Crest, Calendar, Columns, 2 Door, c.1865, 36 x 20 In.	1150.00
Welch, Briggs Rotary, Glass Dome, Stepped Base, Ormolu Feet, 8 In.	432.00
Welch, E.N., Wall, Walnut, Double Round, Paper Dial, Roman Numerals, 23 In.	170.00
Welch, Italian, No. 1, Rosewood, Arched, 2 Dials, Columns, 8-Day, Time, Calendar, 19 In.	432.00
Welch, Shelf, Gale, Calendar Dial, Walnut, Scrolling, Carved Crest, c.1885, 27 x 17 In.	575.00
Welch, Shelf, Patti Gerster, Rosewood, Spindled Gallery, Sandwich Glass Pendulum, 19 In.	1017.00
Westclox, Animated, Plastic, Calico Pony, Red, White Spots, Flower Pendulum, 7 In.	22.00
Westclox, Art Deco, Chrome, Painted Dials, Alarm, 1930-34, 3 ¼ In.	59.00
Westclox, Plastic, Globe & Stars, Convex, Metal Frame, Roman Numerals, Stem Wind, 3 In.	68.00
Western Union, Naval Observatory, Wood, Square, Spade Hands, Roman Numerals, 21 In.	194.00
Whitehall Hammond, Green Onyx, Square, Stepped, Bronze Horse, Electric, 9 x 16 In.	148.00
Wood, John, Pillar & Scroll, Inlaid, Painted Metal Dial, London, 35 In.	226.00
Wood, Robert, Bracket, Mahogany, Gilt, Silvered Dial, England, c.1800, 18 x 11 In.	5100.00
Wright, Russel, Wall, Plastic, Green, Raised White Letters, Electric	32.00

CLOISONNE enamel was developed during the tenth century. A glass enamel was applied between small ribbons of metal on a metal base. Most cloisonne is Chinese or Japanese. Pieces marked *China* are twentieth-century examples.

Basket, Hardstone Trees, Flowers, Multicolor, Round, Brass Handle, Chinese, 13 ½ In.	2509.00
Bottle, Double Gourd, Medallions, Birds, Landscape, Scroll & Flowers, Blue Lid, 11 ½ In.	89.00
Bowl, 4-Lobe Shape, Lotus Rim Band, Textured Ground, Chinese, c.1890, 5 ½ x 3 ½ In.	521.00
Bowl, Black Ground, Phoenix, Peonies, Chinese, Signed, 1700s, 3 ½ x 8 ½ In.	390.00
Bowl, Clouds, Longevity Symbols, Cobalt Blue Ground, Gilt Foot, 18th Century, 5 x 8 In.	1000.00
Bowl, Cover, Gilt Medallion, Dragon, Flaming Pearl, Lotus, Vines, Blossoms, 5 In., Pair	1984.00
Bowl, Cover, Octagonal, Flowers, Buddha, Lotus Blossoms, Dragon Toggle Handles, 11 x 11 In., Pair	3660.00
Bowl, Enamel, Blue Ground, Flowers, Footed, Temples, Fretwork Rim Border, 5 x 9 In.	489.00
Bowl, Flowers, Bamboo, Black Ground, Oval, Stand, Chinese, 1800s, 13 ½ x 7 ¼ In.	461.00
Bowl, Foo Dog Designs, Scalloped Rim, 3 x 6 ¾ In.	263.00
Bowl, Low, Round, 4 Winged Horses, Blue Waves, 3 In.	465.00
Bowl, Low, Sinuous White Dragon, Marked, 8 In.	366.00
Bowl, Narcissus, Curved Rim, Star Medallion, Flower Ground, Chinese, c.1935, 9 ½ In.	153.00
Bowl, Octagonal, Flowers, Turquoise Exterior, Green Interior, Chinese, 9 ¼ In.	196.00
Bowl, Scalloped Edges, Blue Ground, Red Dragon, Allover Flowers, Chinese, 22 In.	649.00
Bowl, Squat, Blue, White, Dragon, Pearl Of Wisdom, Carved Wood Stand, Gilt Rim, 12 In.	239.00

Clock, Tall Case, T. Jeffrey, Mahogany, Pendulum, Cast Iron Weights, Brass Finials, Canterbury, 83 In.
$2370.00

Skinner, Inc.

Clock, Tall Case, Waterbury, Carved, Columns, Hood Door, Brass Dial, 8-Day, c.1915, 95 ½ In.
$2489.00

Skinner, Inc.

CLOISONNE

Clock, Terry, Silas B., Cottage, Paper Veneer, Etched Tablet, Zinc Dial, 30-Hour, c.1855, 10 ½ In.
$1225.00

Skinner, Inc.

Cloisonne, Ewer, Lotus Blossoms, Buddhist Symbols, Monk's Cap, Dragon Handle, Tibetan, 1900s, 21 In.
$738.00

New Orleans Auction Galleries, Inc.

Cloisonne, Jardiniere, Applied Dog Head & Ring Handles, Chinese, 1800s, 10 ¾ In.
$649.00

Ivey-Selkirk Auctioneers

Cloisonne, Vase, Bands, Chinese Mythological Beast, Carved Handles, 25 ½ In.
$671.00

Leslie Hindman Auctioneers

Bowl, Squat, Round Foot, Black Ground, Forward Facing Dragon, 8 In.	147.00
Bowl, Squat, Scale Design, Lappet Border At Top, Round Foot, Gilt, 7 In.	149.00
Box, Bronze, Gilt, Lotus, Multicolor, 2 ¾ x 3 ½ In.	2700.00
Box, Butterfly, Flower Design, Foil, Oval, Japan, 1800s, 5 ¼ In.	259.00
Box, Cover, 5-Clawed Dragon, Lappet Border, Blue Ground, Marked, 2 ¼ x 4 In.	5612.00
Box, Cover, Blue Ground, Flowers, Vining, Chinese, 4 In.	657.00
Box, Cover, Circular, Turquoise Ground, Gilt, Dragon, Flowers, Marked, Chinese, 5 In.	1673.00
Box, Cover, Flowers, Cobalt Blue, Silver, P. Ovchinnikov, c.1915, 2 x 2 ¾ In.	489.00
Box, Cover, Round, Blue Ground, Dragon Chasing Flaming Pearl, Flowers, Marked, 4 ½ In.	896.00
Box, Cover, Round, Brass Foot Ring, Vining Fruit, Flowers, Blue, 2 x 3 In.	359.00
Box, Cover, Round, Flowers, Black Ground, Brass Foo Dog Finial, 6 ½ In. Diam.	59.00
Box, Cover, Seated Quail Shape, Yellow, Green, Blue, Gold, Enamel, 1900s, 6 ¾ In., Pair	399.00
Box, Cover, Tree Bark, Grapevine Design, Bird, Ball Finial, Japan, 5 x 4 In.	431.00
Box, Duck Shape, 4 x 4 ½ In.	472.00
Box, Flowers, Turquoise Ground, Chinese, 1800s, 3 x 2 In.	415.00
Box, Multicolor Flowers, Geometric, Chinese, c.1890, 1 ¼ x 2 ¼ In.	89.00
Box, Paste, Cover, Yellow Ground, Phoenix, Round, 2 ⅜ In.	236.00
Box, Peacock, On Brass, Removable Cover, 11 x 8 In.	109.00
Box, Peacock, Yellow Ground, Silver Rim, Lined Interior, Japan, c.1900, 5 x 2 In.	660.00
Box, Round, Calligraphy, Flowers, Turquoise, Round Foot, 4 ½ In. Diam.	1135.00
Buckle, 2 Parts, Shaped Edges, Dagger Shape Clasp, Chain, Marked, Russia, Late 1800s, 3 In.	200.00
Cachepot, Lobed Body, Gilt Rims, Butterflies, Flowers, Swastika, Blue Ground, 7 x 14 In.	649.00
Censer, 3 Legs, Foo Dog Finial, Lotus, Blue, Yellow Ground, Base, 1800s, 8 x 5 x 4 In.	200.00
Censer, Bowl, 3 Cylindrical Legs, 2 Square Handles, Turquois, Gilt, Flowers, 12 In.	250.00
Censer, Boy On 3-Legged Toad, Gilded, 19th Century, 8 In.	2100.00
Censer, Figural, Duck, Scrolls, Reticulated Lid, Chinese, c.1905, 6 ½ In., Pair	770.00
Censer, Lid, Duck Shape, Lotus Blossom, Open Mouth, 3 In.	137.00
Censer, Lid, Horse Shape, Reclining, Holes In Nostrils, 7 In.	1054.00
Censer, Mythical Bird Shape, Vase On Back, Birds, Lotus, Turquoise, Chinese, c.1904, 13 In., Pair	2205.00
Censer, Pierced Dome Cover, 2 Handles, Foo Dog Finial, Flower & Scroll Design, c.1900, 5 In.	472.00
Censer, Quatrefoil, Flowers, Scrolling Leaves, 2 Bar Handles, Chinese, 3 ½ In.	299.00
Censer, Turtle Shape, Chi Dragon, Clouds, Gilt Trim, Wood Base, 1800s, 3 x 4 x 2 In.	425.00
Charger, Multicolor Enamels, Round Flower Design, 12 In.	161.00
Crane, Red Cap, Standing, Rockwork Base, Plant Sprig In Mouth, Gilt Accents, 1900s, 17 In., Pair	1107.00
Cup, Silver, Cylindrical, Flared Foot, Loop Handle, Russia, c.1900, 3 ¼ In.	1300.00
Dish, 2 Ducks, Grass, Flowering Plants, Geometric Design Border, 12 In., Pair	366.00
Egg, Enamel, Silver, Circle & Teardrop Shapes, St. Petersburg, 1 ¼ x 1 In.	316.00
Egg, Romanov Eagle, Flowers, Silver Gilt Interior, Paul Ovchinnikov, Russia, 4 x 3 In.	2530.00
Ewer, Lotus Blossoms, Buddhist Symbols, Monk's Cap, Dragon Handle, Tibetan, 1900s, 21 In. ...*illus*	738.00
Figurine, Beast, Reclining, Geometric Design, Gilt Highlights, 11 ⅜ In., Pair	732.00
Figurine, Buddha, Seated, Hand In Lap, Lotus Position, Pale Blue Robe, Gilt, 14 In.	406.00
Figurine, Crane, Base, Multicolor, 1900s, 62 x 19 In., Pair	7768.00
Figurine, Duck, Gilt, Flowers, Lily Blossoms, Leaves, Scroll Design, 8 x 3 In., Pair	288.00
Figurine, Duck, Mandarin, Seated, Blue, Green, Wood Stand, Chinese, 3 ¼ x 4 ½ In.	413.00
Figurine, Horse Head, Turquoise, Multicolor, Gilt Accents, 12 x 8 In.	375.00
Figurine, Horse, Holding One Leg Up, Multicolor, Gilt Hooves, 1900s, 16 x 19 In., Pair	575.00
Figurine, Ivory, Woman With Instrument, 15 In.	1240.00
Figurine, Lamb, Standing, Multicolor, Scroll Design, Chinese, 16 ½ x 12 ½ In.	359.00
Figurine, Ox & Cart, Pulling Cart, Wood Base, Multicolor, Gilt Accents, 10 x 18 In.	1054.00
Figurine, Ram, Blue Ground, Flowers, Chinese, 18 ½ In.	478.00
Figurine, Rooster, On Rockwork Base, Gilt, 1900s, 38 In.	2952.00
Ginger Jar, Lid, Black Ground, Multicolor Enamel Flowers, 6 ¼ In.	178.00
Incense Burner, Mythical Winged Ram Shape, Reclining, Gilt Accents, 1900s, Pair	307.00
Incense Burner, Quail Shape, Lotus Scrolls, Turquoise Ground, Chinese, c.1900, 5 x 3 In., Pair	237.00
Jar, Cover, Globular Shape, Roosters & Flowers, c.1900, 13 ½ In.	184.00
Jar, Cover, Globular, Stylized Lotus Flowers, Foo Dog Finial, c.1900, 6 ¾ In.	207.00
Jar, Cover, Hundred Antiques Design, Red Ground, c.1900, 8 In.	356.00
Jar, Cover, Turquoise Ground, Dragons & Pearls, Bulbous, Pointed Finial, c.1890, 7 In.	521.00
Jar, Flowers, Black Ground, Lid, 3 ½ x 3 ½ In.	75.00
Jar, Hanging, Orb Shape, Pierced Cover, Hanging Cords, Chinese, c.1900, 4 ½ In.	81.00
Jardiniere, 4 Panels, Flowers, Diaper Design, Squat Bracket Feet, Lotus Blossoms, 9 In.	1736.00
Jardiniere, Applied Dog Head & Ring Handles, Chinese, 1800s, 10 ¾ In. ...*illus*	649.00
Jardiniere, Blue Ground, Hardstone Tree, White Prunus Blossoms, Chinese, 25 In., Pair	956.00
Jardiniere, Squat Shape, Rolled Lip, Flowers, Cranes, Round Wood Base, 15 In.	359.00
Kovsh, Enameled Silver, Stylized Flowers, Ivory, Olive Green, Marked, c.1908-26, 2 x 5 In.	4063.00
Mirror, Bird, Flower Cartouches, Chinese, 1800s, 9 x 8 ½ In.	474.00

Mirror, Etched Iris, Flowers, Stand, c.1900, 15 ½ x 8 In.	250.00
Pipe Case, Green & Blue Dragon, Black Ground, Clouds, Carved Ivory Skull Shape Ojime, 8 ⅝ In.	1159.00
Planter, Lobed, Enameled, Paneled, Lotus, Scrolling Vines, Chinese, 1900s, 3 ¾ x 8 ¾ In.	584.00
Plaque, Enamel, Calligraphy, Flower, Frame, Chinese, 1900s, 38 x 8 ¼ In., Pair	7768.00
Plaque, Figures, Mountains, Pavilion, Square, Inscribed, Wood Stand, Chinese, 1800s, 17 In.	10073.00
Plate, Buddha, Buddhism Symbols, Clouds, Marked, c.1790, 6 ¾ In.	2300.00
Pot, Archaic Designs, Bulbous, Tapered Base, Japan, 1800s, 5 x 6 In., Pair	369.00
Spoon, Serving, Silver Gilt Bowl, Stipple Ground, Bead Border, Russia, 1800s, 8 In., Pair	1440.00
Spoon, Silver, Gilt, Vasily Agafonov, Marked On Stem, c.1900, 4 ¼ In., 6 Piece	550.00
Tea Caddy, Cover, Dragons, 6 Shield Shape Reserves, Footed, c.1880, 6 ½ x 5 In.	345.00
Teapot, Flowers, Blue Ground, Birds, Butterflies, 19th Century, 3 x 6 In.	275.00
Tray, Yellow Dragons, Multicolor Ground, Shaped Rim, Chinese, 12 ¼ x 8 ½ In.	385.00
Trumpet, Tapering Shape, Scrolling Leaves, Gilt Banding & Mouthpiece, Asia, 16 In.	868.88
Urn, Bulbous, Rolled Rim, Flowers, Multicolor, Gilt Accents, Round Base, 13 In.	344.00
Urn, Lid, White Wisteria, Vine, Songbird, Mottled Olive Ground, Japan, c.1910, 9 ¼ In.	295.00
Urn, Yellow, Red Flowers, White Ground, Gilt Rim, 15 In., Pair	152.00
Vase, 3 Cow Figural Handles, 6 Legs, Chinese, 20 x 22 In.	805.00
Vase, Bands, Chinese Mythological Beast, Carved Handles, 25 ½ In. ....illus	671.00
Vase, Basket, Flowers, Double Gourd, Multicolor, Wood Base, 1900s, 15 ½ x 16 ½ In., Pair	300.00
Vase, Bird, Bamboo, Cherry Blossoms, Black Ground, Tapered, Japan, 3 ½ x 7 ½ In.	1870.00
Vase, Birds, Insects, Flowers, 6 Panels, Japan, 5 x 10 ½ In., Pair	1760.00
Vase, Blue Ground, Chrysanthemums, Cloud Band, Gilt Copper Rim, 6 In.	81.00
Vase, Blue Ground, Flower, Butterfly, Ovals, 5 In., Pair	148.00
Vase, Blue, Chrysanthemum, Impressed Insects, Japan, 5 ½ x 9 ½ In., Pair	4675.00
Vase, Bottle Shape, Birds, Flowers, Turquoise Ground, c.1800s ¾ In.	652.00
Vase, Buddhist Goddesses, Lotus, Phoenix, Turquoise, Chinese, 25 ½ In., Pair	660.00
Vase, Bulbous, Light Green, Deer Amongst Clouds, Wood Base, 5 In.	316.00
Vase, Bulbous, Round Spread Foot, 2 Ring Handles, Turquoise, Flowers, Gilt, 8 In., Pair	1554.00
Vase, Butterflies, Cartouches Of Flowers, Gold Stone Accents, c.1880, 10 In., Pair	184.00
Vase, Cartouches, Animals, Fish, Plants, Geometric Design, 12 In.	305.00
Vase, Cherry Blossoms, Birds, Green Ground, Tapered, Japan, 4 ½ x 9 ¾ In.	2200.00
Vase, Cobalt Blue Ground, Multicolor Flowers, Copper Wirework, 9 In.	178.00
Vase, Cover, Double Gourd, Birds, Flowers, Chinese, 11 ½ In., Pair	627.00
Vase, Dragon Roundels, Lotus Scrolls, White Ground, Chinese, c.1905, 14 In., Pair	3851.00
Vase, Dragons, Metallic, Blue Ground, Japan, 3 x 7 In., Pair	1210.00
Vase, Dragons, Phoenixes, Blue, Black Ground, Triangular Blade Panels, 12 In., Pair	245.00
Vase, Enamel, Prunus, Basket, Blue Ground, Japan, c.1900, 10 In.	203.00
Vase, Flowers, Birds, Blue Ground, Ando, Japan, 7 ½ x 12 In.	4070.00
Vase, Flowers, Birds, Butterflies, Square Baluster Shape, Hardwood Base, 12 In., Pair	316.00
Vase, Flowers, Birds, Dark Blue Ground, Green Interior, Japan, 4 ¾ In., Pair	230.00
Vase, Flowers, Branches, Black Ground, Lobed, Gilt Geometrics, Chinese, 8 ¾ In.	652.00
Vase, Flowers, Butterflies, Footed, Stretched Neck, Gilt, 1900s, 10 ¼ In., Pair	975.00
Vase, Gilt, Animal Shape Handles, Plantain Leaf Panels, Marked, Wood Stand, 7 In., Pair	1364.00
Vase, Gold Stone, Multicolor Designs, Japan, 1800s, 14 ½ In.	184.00
Vase, Goldfish, Seaweed, Pale Blue Ground, Silver Rim, 5 In., Pair	230.00
Vase, Hexagonal, Geometric Design, Flowers, Multicolor, Gilt Accents, Marked, 24 In., Pair	2232.00
Vase, Lobed, Baluster Shape, Scrolling Leaves, Dragon, Oval Base, 13 In., Pair	2108.00
Vase, Lotus, Scrolling Vines, Flowers, Blue, Gilded Dragon Handles, Rings, c.1750, 8 ¾ In. ....illus	22140.00
Vase, Moths, Multicolor, Black Ground, Bulbous, Pinched Neck, 6 In.	266.00
Vase, Narrow Neck, Gilt Rims, Scroll Flower Design, Green Ground, 3 In.	3466.00
Vase, Navy Blue Ground, Flying Moths, Japan, c.1925, 9 ½ In.	920.00
Vase, Peacock, Light Green Ground, Japan, 7 In., Pair	504.00
Vase, Pear Shape, Turquoise Ground, Flowers, c.1900-20, 8 In., Pair	325.00
Vase, Phoenix, Scrolled Flowers, Blue, Red, Gilt, Chinese, 20 In.	420.00
Vase, Prunus Tree, Doves, Flowers, Leaves, Silver & Copper Wirework, 47 In.	2645.00
Vase, Quatrefoil Shape, Scrolling Leaves, Gilt Copper Rim, Hardwood Stand, 14 In., Pair	620.00
Vase, Scenic, Birds, Bamboo, Chinese, 21 In.	325.00
Vase, Scrolling Leaves, Black Ground, Turquoise, Smokestack Shape, 9 In., Pair	244.00
Vase, Stepped Cover, Cylindrical, Jade Roundels, Round Foot, 15 ½ In.	1240.00
Vase, Tapered, Inlaid, Dragons, Clouds, 19th Century, 6 x 3 In.	275.00
Vase, Tapered, Temple, Mountains, Silver Wireworks, 1900s, 8 ½ In.	92.00
Vase, Totai, Treebark, Autumn Tones, Japan, 11 In.	144.00
Vase, Treebark, Squat, Narrow Neck, Flowers, Bird, Japan, 8 ½ In.	288.00
Vase, Turquoise Ground, Multicolor, Bulbous Base, Brass Foot, Narrow Neck, Flared Rim, 12 In.	161.00
Vase, Turquoise, Maroon, Fans, Flowers, Tall Narrow Neck, Chinese, 1800s, 14 ½ x 7 ½ In.	270.00
Vase, Urn Shape, Brass Applied Rim, Base, Asia, 1800s, 6 ½ x 3 ¼ In., Pair	230.00

Cloisonne, Vase, Lotus, Scrolling Vines, Flowers, Blue, Gilded Dragon Handles, Rings, c.1750, 8 ¾ In.
$22140.00

New Orleans Auction Galleries, Inc.

Clothing, Coat, Beaver & Raccoon, Coyote Fur Trim, c.1930, Woman's, Medium
$259.00

Allard Auctions

Clothing, Coat, Leopard Fur, A-Line, Knee-Length, 1960s
$956.00

Sloans & Kenyon

Clothing, Dress, Coat Style, Wool, Animal Print, Zip Front, 3 Gold Brooch Buttons, Valentino, Size 6-8
$738.00

New Orleans Auction Galleries, Inc.

Clothing, Hat, Driver, Yellow Cab Co.
$144.00

Victorian Casino Antique Auction

Clothing, Jacket, Lined, Pendleton, Portland, Oregon, Knockabout Brand, 31 In.
$55.00

Old Barn Auction

Vase, White Cranes, Butterflies, Green Flowers, Dark Ground, Baluster, Spread Foot, c.1900, 7 ⅜ In.	89.00
Vase, White Cranes, Pink Ground, Gold Rim, Japan, 3 ½ x 4 ¾ In.	440.00
Vessel, Drinking, Zun, Lotus, Peony, Flanges, Mark, Chinese, 1800s, 7 In.	2726.00
Water Pot, Barrel Shaped Coupe, Footed, Flowers, Gilt, Chinese, 5 ½ In.	2963.00
Wine Pot, Teapot Shape, Flowers, Luck Symbol, Ring Banded Handle, Aqua, Yellow, 1700s, 6 In.	1610.00
Wine, Ritual, Stand, Hundred Flowers, Gilt Edges, 1800s, 6 In.	459.00

CLOTHING of all types is listed in this category. Dresses, hats, shoes, underwear, and more are found here. Other textiles are to be found in the Coverlet, Movie, Quilt, Textile, and World War I and II categories.

Belt, 9 Concha, Sterling Buckle, Hand Tooled, Leather Strap, 42 In.	920.00
Belt, Belt Plate, Union Officer's, Gilt Brass, Eagle Plate, Robbins Co., c.1851, 38 ½ In.	588.00
Belt, Brown, Crocodile Skin, Gilt Metal Buckle, Cloth Bag, Judith Leiber, Saks 5th Avenue	236.00
Belt, Brown, Leather, Faux Ivory & Tiger's Eye Cabochons, Cloth Bag, Judith Leiber, 1980s	207.00
Belt, Leather, Ivory, Interlocking Gs, Gilt Metal Buckle, Gucci	207.00
Belt, Leather, Reversible, Tan, Bottle Green, Stamped, Hermes, 1 ¼ x 33 ¾ In.	307.00
Belt, Silver, 3 Cable Links, Turquoise Cabochons, Christian Dior, 27 In.	120.00
Boarding Cap, Revolutionary War Helmet, Leather, Captain S. Dunn, 13 ⅝ x 12 ¼ In.	19550.00
Boots, Cowboy, Tan Leather, Carved Designs, Woman's, Size 9.	22.00
Boots, High Heel, Lace-Up, Leather, Brown Uppers, Black Lowers, Woman's, c.1886	550.00
Boots, Leather, Trees, Ivory Mounts, England, c.1915, 23 x 10 ½ In.	124.00
Bra, Bullet, Cotton, Fagoted Bust, c.1965, Size 40B	38.00
Cap, Mink, Chocolate Brown, Black Silk Satin Lining, Label, Evans, Size 7	307.00
Cape, Hood, Wool Berber, Goat Hair, Red, Black, Atlas Mountains, Morocco, 1800s, Man's, 54 x 100 In.	1025.00
Cape, Velvet, Black, Feather Collar, Button Closure, 53 In.	201.00
Chaps, Angora, Tan, 1940s, 38 In.	1380.00
Chaps, Leather, Applied Longhorn Steers, Victor Ario Saddlery Co., c.1950, 38-In. Waist	288.00
Chasuble, White Silk Brocade, Gold Embroidery, Cross, 45 x 26 In.	240.00
Coat, American Indian Design, Red Suede, Shearling, Beaded, Fringe, Isaac Mizrahi, Knee-Length	657.00
Coat, Beaver & Raccoon, Coyote Fur Trim, c.1930, Woman's, Medium ....*illus*	259.00
Coat, Beaver, Calf-Length, Tuxedo Collar, Size 10-12, 48 In.	372.00
Coat, Chinchilla, Black, Full Collar, Long Sleeves, Alexandro, 47 In.	403.00
Coat, Driving, Wool, Leather, Charcoal Gray, Full-Length, Bernard Perris, Paris	359.00
Coat, Evening, Black Velvet, Swing Style, 4 Tiers, Black Ribbon Trim, Bill Blass, Size 4	120.00
Coat, Fur, Beaver, Raccoon, Coyote Trim, c.1950, Woman's Medium	259.00
Coat, Fur, Beckman Brothers, c.1950, Woman's Medium	288.00
Coat, Fur, Black, Long Lapel, Red Lining, Man's, 43 In.	288.00
Coat, Fur, Brown, Chevron Pattern, Leather Belt, Medium To Large, 48 In.	288.00
Coat, Leopard Fur, A-Line, Knee-Length, 1960s ....*illus*	956.00
Coat, Leopard, Large Cuffed Sleeves, Maroon Lining, N.L. Kaplan, 35 In.	345.00
Coat, Leopard, Wide Collar & Cuffs, Tan Satin Lining, Full-Length, Strouss Hirsberg, 36 In.	403.00
Coat, Mink, Black Satin Lining, Filigree Knot Pattern, Large, 41 In.	748.00
Coat, Mink, Black, Full-Length, Slit Pockets, Woman's, 50 In.	920.00
Coat, Mink, Brown, Collar, Satin Lining, Monogram, Full-Length, Medium To Large, 42 In.	460.00
Coat, Mink, Brown, Collarless, Medium, 29 In.	288.00
Coat, Mink, Brown, Slit Pockets, Marshall Field Label, Size 6 To 8, 48 In.	173.00
Coat, Mink, Full Collar, Long Sleeves, Label Ruth's Original St. Petersburg, Medium, 42 In.	633.00
Coat, Mink, Herringbone Pattern, Full-Length, Russia, Size 16, 51 In.	708.00
Coat, Mink, Purple Stripe, Peach Accents, Full-Length, Large, 48 In.	345.00
Coat, Platinum Mink, Sash, Pockets, J.P. Allen, Small-Medium, 39 ½ In.	173.00
Coat, Satin, Royal Blue, Embroidered, Flowers, Gold Thread, Chinese, c.1920, Size M	399.00
Coat, Trench, Midnight Blue, Cotton, Nylon, Silk Lining, Belt, Kaufmanfranco, Size 8	478.00
Coat, Wool, Navy, Swing, Stand-Up Collar, Cropped Sleeves, Balenciaga, c.1940, Size 10-12	922.00
Collar, Silk Embroidery, Dragons, Clouds, Vines, Metallic Thread, Chinese, 1800s, 12 x 29 In.	1003.00
Dress, Coat Style, Wool, Animal Print, Zip Front, 3 Gold Brooch Buttons, Valentino, Size 6-8 ...*illus*	738.00
Dress, Cocktail, Black, Bandage, Strapless, Draping Ribbons, Herve Eger Style	508.00
Dress, Mini, Psychedelic, Pink, Orange, Chartreuse, Green, Emilio Pucci, 1960s	635.00
Dress, Plaid Taffeta, Ruffled, Knee-Length, Bodice Ruffle Trim, Oscar De La Renta, Size 8	120.00
Dress, Prom, Off-The-Shoulder, Sweetheart Neckline, Black Velvet, 2 Layer Ruffle, 1980s	40.00
Dress, Silk, Red & White Polka Dot, Knee-Length, Pleats, Chanel Boutique, 1980s	359.00
Dress, Tunic Style, Front Half Zip, Belt, Silk, Emilio Pucci, 1960s	288.00
Dress, V Neck, Long Sleeves, Leaves, Flowers, Silk, 1960s	207.00
Gloves, Brown, Leather, Gold Clasp, Woman's, Hermes	236.00
Gloves, Buckskin Gauntlets, Upper Cuff With Stars, Flowers, Woman's, 11 x 5 In.	431.00
Gloves, Taupe, Suede, Woman's, Box, Hermes, c.1978	295.00
Gloves, White, Woman's, Box, c.1978	207.00

C

CLOTHING

Handkerchief, Brown Ground, Rose Spray, Burmel Original, 13 x 13 In.	7.00
Handkerchief, Linen, Appliqued Bows, Rolled Hems, 1920s, Pair	10.00
Handkerchief, Linen, Rolled Hem, Flower Appliques, Coral, 1920s	5.00
Handkerchief, Pink & Blue Flowers, Scalloped Edge, 12 x 12 In.	7.00
Handkerchief, Polka Dots, Carnations, Burmel Original, 12 x 12 In.	8.00
Hat, Ceremonial, Cloth, Silver Mounts, Birds, Flowers, Hanging Bells, Asia, 9 x 7 In.	118.00
Hat, Chapeau, Officer's, Red Ribbon, 1800-15	1150.00
Hat, Cocktail, Black Felt, Spray Of Feathers, Rhinestone Ornament, Adolpho, 7 In. Diam.	246.00
Hat, Driver, Yellow Cab Co. ....illus	144.00
Hat, Faux Pearl, Fuzzy Pink, Velvet, Band, Michael Terre, 1960s	48.00
Hat, Leopard Fur, Woman's, Adolfo II, Saks 5th Avenue	148.00
Hat, Pillbox, Velvet, Black, Grosgrain Strap, Adolfo II, 1960s	45.00
Hat, Pillbox, Wool Felt, Satin Trim, Black, Bow, c.1960	85.00
Hat, White Leather & Curly Tibetan Lamb Fur, GR Originals, 21 ¼ In.	185.00
Jacket, Cashmere, Charcoal Gray, Red Fox Fur Trim, Hood, Knee-Length, Burnello Cucinelli .	1135.00
Jacket, Evening, Plaid Taffeta, Wrap Style, Pleated Skirt, Gianfranco Ferre	120.00
Jacket, Fur & Leather, White Fox, Diamond Pattern, Belt, Satin Lining, Bricker, 32 In.	144.00
Jacket, Leather, Black, American Flag On Back, Argentina, Size 38	259.00
Jacket, Leopard, Tan Satin Lining, Small-Medium, 23 ½ In.	316.00
Jacket, Lined, Pendleton, Portland, Oregon, Knockabout Brand, 31 In. ....illus	55.00
Jacket, Mink, Beige, Lapel Collar, Novotny Of Ohio, 19 In.	259.00
Jacket, Mink, Brown, Wide Collar, Slit Pockets, Neiman Marcus Label, Size 6 To 8, 30 In.	863.00
Jacket, Mink, Tan Lining, 1950s, Medium, 31 In.	316.00
Jacket, Silk, Embroidered, Cream Ground, Flowers, c.1876, Child's	374.00
Kimono, Flower, Fruit, Turquoise Ground, Black Trim, Silk, Japan	207.00
Kimono, Paper, Black, Mounted In Shadowbox, 51 x 43 In.	117.00
Kimono, Wedding, Embroidered Silk, Purple Flowers, Japan, 1930s	500.00
Necktie, Dog Head Canes, Crook Canes, Tau Canes, Red Ground, Italian Silk, 57 In.	35.00
Necktie, Rayon, Dark Red, White Contrast, 1950s, 53 x 2 ⅞ In.	25.00
Nightgown, Lace Collar, Lace Front, 3 Pearl Buttons, Full Sleeves, 1880s, Bust 33 In.	145.00
Nightgown, Lace, Cotton, 3 Button Front, c.1800, Bust 38, 59 In.	145.00
Pants, Capri, Cotton, Blue, Black, Emilio Pucci, Size 10, 1960s	144.00
Robe, Blue, Silk, Embroidered Dragons, Clouds, Metallic Thread, Chinese, c.1900, 53 In.	2478.00
Robe, Court, Imperial, Gold Thread, Dragons, Flaming Pearls, Cranes, Chinese, c.1900	3220.00
Robe, Dragons, Symbols, Satin Stitching, Blue Silk, Chinese, 43 x 69 In.	2400.00
Robe, Dragons, Zodiac Figures, Silk Brocade, Metallic Thread, c.1900, 43 In.	2360.00
Robe, Embroidered, Dark Blue, Beige, Flowers, Roundels, Birds, Satin Stitch, Chinese	3107.00
Robe, Embroidered, Dragon, Peonies, Pavilion, Apricot Ground, Ocher, Chinese, 1800s, Woman's	1593.00
Robe, Embroidered, Dragons, Clouds, Cranes, Striped Blue Ground, Chinese, 1800s, Woman's	6125.00
Robe, Embroidered, Medallions, Symbols, Navy Ground, Chinese, 1800s, 43 x 54 In.	5760.00
Robe, Embroidered, Peonies, Lotus, Plum, Blue Ground, Chinese, 1800s, Woman's	4288.00
Robe, Embroidered, Peonies, Phoenixes, Frame, Chinese, c.1900, Woman's, 44 x 32 In.	148.00
Robe, Embroidered, Red & Blue Silk, Flower Design, Chinese, 55 In.	372.00
Robe, Flower Roundels, Peony, Wavy Ground, Chinese, c.1800, Woman's	9188.00
Robe, Imperial Court, Dark Blue Gauze, Embroidered, Phoenix, Sun, Flowers, Chinese	2070.00
Robe, Kesi, Winter, Dragons, Flowering Baskets, Bats, Objects, Blue, Lined Ground, Chinese	3555.00
Robe, Purple, Green Accents, Velvet, Gold Brocade, Asia, c.1905, 39 In.	354.00
Robe, Silk, Embroidered, 9 Dragons, Clouds, Bats, Buddhist Emblems, Chinese, 1700s, 54 ½ x 73 In.	4270.00
Robe, Silk, Embroidered, Blue, Turquoise, Silver Trim, Children At Play, Flowers, Chinese	1434.00
Robe, Silk, Embroidered, Butterflies, Blossoms, 4 Metal Buttons, Chinese, c.1900, 51 x 53 In. ...illus	1652.00
Robe, Silk, Embroidered, Figures, Flowers, Rocks, Chinese, 19th Century	425.00
Robe, Silk, Embroidered, Flowers, Chinese, 19th Century, 49 x 63 In.	1550.00
Robe, Silk, Needlework, Flowers & Butterflies, Chinese, 1800s, 44 In.	690.00
Robe, White Brocade, Flowers, Fruit, Chinese, 1800s, Woman's ....illus	398.00
Scarf, Blue Ground, Gold Rope Scrolling, Pink Flowers, Silk, Hermes	384.00
Scarf, Blue Ground, Peacocks, Flowers, Silk Twill, C. Latham, Hermes, France, 1971, 36 x 36 In.	425.00
Scarf, Blue Ground, Yellow, Pink, Blue Flowers, Christian Dior	89.00
Scarf, Brown Ground, Blue Scrolling, Geometric Design, Silk, Pucci	177.00
Scarf, Cowboy, Portrait, Dustin Farnum, Cotton, 1904, 23 x 23 In.	475.00
Scarf, Cream Ground, Pink & White Roses, Daisies, Silk, Chanel	236.00
Scarf, Geometric, Muslin, Signed, Emilio Pucci, 39 x 58 In.	155.00
Scarf, Green Ground, Blue Border, Hummingbirds, Silk, Box, Gucci	236.00
Scarf, Jacquard Silk, White, Black, Daimyo Princess Soleil Levant, Hermes, 1990, 36 x 35 In..	266.00
Scarf, Le Cle De Champs, Birds, Scrolls, Green, Hermes, 25 ½ In.	150.00
Scarf, Pink Peonies, Green Leaves, Silk, Hermes	236.00
Scarf, Samurai Design, Multicolor, Silk, Caty Latham, Hermes, France, 35 x 35 In.	259.00
Scarf, White Ground, Gold, Pink, Blue, Aqua Flowers, Silk, Box, Gucci	118.00

TIP
Don't hang valuable old clothing on wire hangers. This puts a strain on the shoulders. Store clothing flat or folded on a shelf.

C

Clothing, Robe, Silk, Embroidered, Butterflies, Blossoms, 4 Metal Buttons, Chinese, c.1900, 51 x 53 In.
$1652.00

Brunk Auctions

Clothing, Robe, White Brocade, Flowers, Fruit, Chinese, 1800s, Woman's
$398.00

Skinner, Inc.

Clothing, Shoes, High Button, Black, Khaki Canvas Spatterdash, Child's, 9 ¾ x 8 ½ In.
$30.00

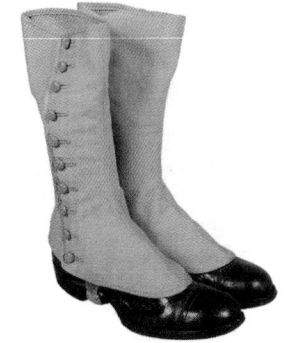

Conestoga Auction Co., Inc.

145

Clothing, Suit, Cocktail, Ribbed Silk Jacket, Skirt, White & Black Polka Dot, Print Trim, Valentino, Size 10
$153.00

New Orleans Auction Galleries, Inc.

Clothing, Suit, Top & Long Skirt, Black Velvet, Rhinestones, Oscar De La Renta, c.1985, Size 8-10
$276.00

New Orleans Auction Galleries, Inc.

Cluthra, Vase, Green, Flat Sides, Flask Shape, 10 In.
$575.00

Early Auction Co.

Scarf, White, Blue Border, Flower Vases, Multicolor, Silk, Gucci, c.1978	148.00
Scarf, White, Blue Border, Fruit Baskets, Butterflies, Silk, Box, Gucci	325.00
Scarf, White, Mauve Border, Multicolor Flowers, Silk, Box, Gucci	266.00
Scarf, White, Yellow Border, Floral Bouquets, Silk, Box, Gucci	177.00
Shawl, Boteh Pattern, Pieced Border, Paisley, Red, Harris, c.1860, 75 ½ x 68 In.	615.00
Shawl, Sea Green Ground, Tropical Fish, Lobster, Muslin, Hermes, 69 x 58 In.	269.00
Shawl, Turquoise, Amethyst Purple Border, Christian Dior, 53 x 53 In.	120.00
Shawl, White Ground, Multicolor, Figures, Birds, Children, Silk, Tassels, Chinese, 48 x 54 In..	489.00
Shawl, Wool, Paisley, Multicolor, Center Medallion, 1800s, 59 x 122 In.	227.00
Shawl, Wool, Paisley, Pink, Multicolor, Cream Medallion, c.1850, 65 x 132 In.	239.00
Shawl, Yellow, Cherry Blossoms, Leaves, Silk, Embroidered, Fringe, Chinese, c.1890, 69 x 69 In.	307.00
Shirt, Button-Up, Silk, Geometric Print, Emilio Pucci, 1960s	230.00
Shoes, High Button, Black, Khaki Canvas Spatterdash, Child's, 9 ¾ x 8 ½ In. ....*illus*	30.00
Shoes, Kidskin, Soles Inscribed & Dated, Caroline, Woman's, 1800	595.00
Shoes, Taupe, Leather, Lizard Skin, Cross Straps, Givenchy, 8 ½ In.	89.00
Skirt, Maxi, Silk, Multicolor, Emilio Pucci, Size 38	173.00
Skirt, Pencil, Belt Buckle, Khaki, Faux Pockets, Cotton, Casual Corner, 1970s, Size 5	22.00
Stole, Fox, Light Gray, Silk Chiffon Overlay, Fur Pelt Edges, 17 x 90 In.	2706.00
Stole, Fox, Silver Gray, 4 Pelts, Black Satin Lined, Shoulder Straps, Koslows, 12 x 100 In.	3690.00
Stole, Norwegian Blue Fox, Gray Satin Lining, Reynard, N.Y., 11 ½ In.	173.00
Suit, Cocktail, Ribbed Silk Jacket, Skirt, White & Black Polka Dot, Print Trim, Valentino, Size 10 *illus*	153.00
Suit, Top & Long Skirt, Black Velvet, Rhinestones, Oscar De La Renta, c.1985, Size 8-10 ....*illus*	276.00
Swim Trunks, Wool, Royal Blue, Dark Blue Anchors, Anchor Tag, 1930s, Men's	185.00
Swimsuit, Halter Style, White Cotton, Flared Skirt, Belted, Carolyn Schnuer, 1950s, 36 Bust	235.00
Top Hat, Black, Silk, Original Box, Knox, N.Y.	104.00
Tunic, Ceremonial, Black Skirt, Floral Top, Silver Dangles, Pakistan, c.1888, Woman's, 37 x 57 In.	854.00
Vest, Embroidered, Flowers, Butterflies, Cream, Gold Thread, Silk Tassels, Woman's, 39 In.	1054.00
Wrap, Alpaca, Camel Color, Giorgio Armani	269.00
Wrap, Black Crepe, Yellow Chiffon, Isabel Canovas, France, 64 x 64 In.	179.00
Wrap, Black Suede, Fringe Trim, Joseph Of London	359.00
Wrap, Black, Wool, Fox Trimmed, Henri Bendel	896.00
Wrap, Brown, Cashmere, Fox Trimmed, Adrienne Landau	1135.00
Wrap, Cobalt Blue Taffeta, Open Style, Ruffle Trim, Christian Dior	568.00
Wrap, Mink, Blond, Satin Lining, J.P. Allen, 77 In.	184.00
Wrap, Mink, Brown, Lines, Saks Fifth Avenue	201.00
Wrap, Navy Blue, Cashmere Blend, Wool, Christian Dior, Scotland	329.00
Wrap, Silk, Silver Tipped Ermine Trimmed, Brown, Golden Yellow	598.00

CLUTHRA glass is a two-layered glass with small bubbles and powdered glass trapped between the layers. The Steuben Glass Works of Corning, New York, first made it in 1920. Victor Durand of Kimball Glass Company in Vineland, New Jersey, made a similar glass from about 1925. Durand's pieces are listed in the Durand category. Related items are listed in the Steuben category.

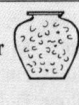

Shade, Green, Cylindrical Form, 2 ¼ In.	300.00
Vase, Green Mottled, Mounted As Lamp, 11 x 10 ½ In.	2006.00
Vase, Green, Flat Sides, Flask Shape, 10 In. ....*illus*	575.00
Vase, Pink, Signed, Steuben, 6 ¼ In.	700.00
Vase, Pink, White Opaque Handles, 10 ½ In.	750.00
Vase, Rose To Amber, Cluster Gold Ruby Flowers, Leaves, Flare Rim, 13 In.	2645.00

COALBROOKDALE was made by the Coalport porcelain factory of England during the Victorian period. Pieces are decorated with floral encrustations.

Cup & Saucer, Gilt Trim, Flower Cartouches, Cobalt Blue, Ground, c.1830, 6 x 3 ½ In.	165.00
Inkstand, Tray, 2 Pots, Duster, Candlestick, Flowers, Tray, c.1830, 14 ½ x 9 In.	5500.00
Sugar, Cover, Blue Leaves, Scallop Shell, Bird Finial, Signed John Rose, c.1825, 3 ¾ x 5 In.	450.00
Teapot, Blue, Pink, Green, Gilt, Scallops, Shells, Signed John Rose, c.1820, 6 x 6 In.	750.00

COALPORT ware has been made by the Coalport Porcelain Works of England from 1795 to the present time. Early pieces were unmarked. About 1810–25 the pieces were marked with the name *Coalport* in various forms. Later pieces also had the name *John Rose* in the mark. The crown mark has been used with variations since 1881. The date 1750 is printed in some marks, but it is not the date the factory started. Some pieces are listed in Indian Tree.

Bowl, Vegetable, Cover, Hunting Scene, Oval	810.00
Coffeepot, Demitasse, Harebell Turquoise, 7 ½ In.	554.00
Jardiniere, Mazarine Blue Panels, Children Playing, Fruit, Flowers, Leaf Scrolling, Gilt, 4 In., Pair	841.00

Plate Set, Athlone Blue, White, Blue Border, Gold Rim, 11 In., 10 Piece	420.00
Plate Set, Dinner, Flowers, Black & Gold Trim Border, 9 In., 8 Piece	173.00
Plate, Dinner, Countryware, 10 ¾ In.	76.00
Plate, Salad, Athlone, 8 In.	90.00
Tureen, Cover, Stand, Medallions, Exotic Animals, Gilt Handle, Insects, Cottage, Oval, c.1805, 8 In.	841.00
Urn, Landscape Cartouches, Cobalt Ground, Gilt Trim, Signed Peter Gosling, 8 ¼ In., Pair	489.00
Vase, Pinecone, Cylindrical, Blue Transfer, White Ground, c.1880, 8 x 8 ½ In.	115.00

COBALT BLUE glass was made using oxide of cobalt. The characteristic bright dark blue identifies it for the collector. Most cobalt glass found today was made after the Civil War. There was renewed interest in the dark blue glass in the late 1930s and dinnerware were made.

Decanter Set, Blown, Bottle Shape, Stopper, Footed Glasses, c.1800, 11 x 4 In., 5 Piece	180.00
Dish, Sweetmeat, Enamel Butterfly, Flowers, Embossed Silver Plate Lid, Bail, 5 In.	75.00
Pitcher, Silver Mica Highlights, Clear Handle, 5 In.	15.00
Rolling Pin, Glass, Gold Painted Ship, 1800s, 15 In.	144.00
Salt, Blown Glass, Ribbed, Footed, c.1810, 2 ½ In.	59.00
Vase, Cut To Clear, Floral Reserve, Square Foot, Germany, 14 x 8 In.	177.00
Vase, Rounded, Tapered, Galleried Rim, Chinese, 10 In.	184.00

COCA-COLA was first served in 1886 in Atlanta, Georgia. It was advertised through signs, newspaper ads, coupons, bottles, trays, calendars, and even lamps and clocks. Collectors want anything with the word *Coca-Cola*, including a few rare products, like gum wrappers and cigar bands. The famous trademark was patented in 1893, the *Coke* mark in 1945. Many modern items and reproductions are being made.

Ad, Coupon, Girl In Chair, Free 6-Pack To Costumers, Cardboard, 1940s, 6 ½ x 5 ½ In.	12.00
Ad, Welcome Home Soldier, Man In Easy Chair, Mom, Dog, December 1943, 10 ½ x 13 ½ In.	12.00
Aisle Marker, Grocery Store, Serve Coca-Cola At Home, Metal, Iron, 1950s, 12 x 29 ½ In.	150.00
Ashtray, Partners, Baseball, Round Shape, Red & White, Ceramic, 1950s, 7 ¼ In.	180.00
Ashtray, Standing Bottle Shape, Glass, 22 x 7 In.	250.00
Barrel Tag, There's Nothing Like A Coke!, Aluminum, Curved, Red, White, Yellow, 1956, 9 x 15 In.	90.00
Bingo Marker Card, Uncut Sheet, Take Time Out For The Pause That Refreshes, 1940s	12.00
Bookmark, 5 Cents, Heart Shape, Girl, Seated, Writing, Celluloid, 1899, 2 In.	660.00
Bookmark, Cardboard, Opera Star Lillian Nordica, 6 x 2 In.	853.00
Bookmark, Celluloid, Owl Shape, Frame, Under Glass, 1906, 3 In.	840.00
Bookmark, Heart Shape, Celluloid, Vintage Woman, c.1900, 2 ¼ In.	35.00
Bottle Carrier, Aluminum, Metal Signs, 1950s, 16 x 7 In.	42.00
Bottle Opener, Drink Coca-Cola In Bottles, Delicious & Refreshing, Bone, c.1920, 4 In.	115.00
Bottle Opener, Sword Shape, Purity Is Sealed In A Bottle, Drink Bottle Coca-Cola, c.1930, 3 In.	150.00
Bottle Redemption Card, Cardboard, Yellow, 6-Pack, Brail Handled Carriers, 1940s, 2 ¾ x 1 ½ In.	10.00
Bottle, 75th Anniversary, 1901-1976, 10 Oz.	5.00
Bottle, Birmingham Hutchinson, Aqua, Embossed, c.1900, 6 ¾ In.	1770.00
Bottle, Centennial Commemorative, Buffalo, New York, 1832-1982, 10 Oz.	15.00
Bottle, E.L. Husting Co., Milwaukee, Wis., Clear, Crown Top, 1920s	952.00
Bottle, Tuskegee, Ala., Hutchinson	3000.00
Bowl, Ice Cold Drink Coca-Cola Embossed, Green Glass, Vernonware, 1930s, 10 In.	518.00
Bowl, Pretzel, Metal & Aluminum, Round, 3 Bottle Shape Legs, 1930s, 4 ½ x 9 In.	150.00
Calendar, 1899, Hilda Clark, At Writing Desk, All Months Displayed, Cardboard, 13 x 7 ⅜ In. .. *illus*	25850.00
Calendar, 1908, Lady In Red, At Fountain, 7 x 14 In.	6900.00
Calendar, 1909, Lillian Nordica, 5 Cents, At Soda Fountains, Girl, Feather Fan, 7 x 3 ¾ In.	390.00
Calendar, 1919, Girl, With Knitting Bag, Pink Dress & Hat, Metal Strip, Full Pad, Frame, 37 x 18 In.	27140.00
Calendar, 1921, Autumn Girl, Sitting On Bench, Flowers, Full Pad, 38 ¼ x 18 ½ In. ....*illus*	1485.00
Calendar, 1929, Girl, With Long String Of Pearls, Seated, Holding Glass, Frame, 33 ½ x 20 ½ In.	120.00
Calendar, 1933, Village Blacksmith, Boy, Frederic Stanley, 12 x 24 ½ In.	201.00
Calendar, 1938, Girl At Shade, Holding Bottle, Paper Lithograph, 24 x 11 In.	908.00
Calendar, 1957, Going Skiing, Pause That Refreshes, Girl, Bottle, Ski Poles, 21 ¾ x 12 ¼ In. .	210.00
Cap, Baseball, Red, White Lettering, Stencil, Cotton, Size 6 ¾	55.00
Case Cart, Display Rack, Things Go Better With Coke, Red, White, Yellow, 1960s, 42 x 23 In.	150.00
Cigarette Case, Frosted Glass, Etched Circle, 50th Anniversary, 1886-1936, 1936, 5 ½ In.	300.00
Clock, Regulator, Pressed Oak, Glass, Gold Letters, Pendulum, 38 ½ In.	311.00
Clock, Sign, Fountain Service, Center Round Clock, Rectangular, White, Red, Gold, 1950s, 78 In.	450.00
Clock, Things Go Better With Coke, Drink Coca-Cola, Light-Up, Plastic, 17 x 17 In.	85.00
Cookie Jar, Polar Bear, Vending Machine, 11 x 9 x 6 In.	18.00
Cooler, Airline, Red, Attached Bottle Opener, Stainless Steel Interior, c.1950, 12 x 17 In.	429.00
Cooler, Drink Coca-Cola In Bottles, Metal, 19 x 18 In.	254.00
Cooler, Drink Coca-Cola, 12-Pack, Red & White, Metal Handle, Square, 1950s, 11 x 12 x 9 In.	270.00

Coca-Cola, Calendar, 1899, Hilda Clark, At Writing Desk, All Months Displayed, Cardboard, 13 x 7 ⅜ In. **$25850.00**

Wm Morford Antiques

Coca-Cola, Calendar, 1921, Autumn Girl, Sitting On Bench, Flowers, Full Pad, 38 ¼ x 18 ½ In. **$1485.00**

Wm Morford Antiques

Coca-Cola, Sign, Coca-Cola, Bottle, Tin, Round, 44 In. Diam. **$1121.00**

Showtime Auction Services

COCA-COLA

Coca-Cola, Sign, Edgar Bergen With Charlie McCarthy, CBS Sunday Evenings, 1949, 24 ¼ x 11 In.
$274.00

Serious Toyz

Coca-Cola, Sign, Talk About Refreshing, Girl With Umbrella, Bottle, Cardboard, Frame, c.1942, 21 x 32 In.
$660.00

Victorian Casino Antique Auction

Coca-Cola, Tray, 1909, Exhibition Girl, Holding Glass Of Coca-Cola, Oval, 13 x 10 ¾ In.
$1652.00

Showtime Auction Services

Snap! Crackle! Pop!
The phrase "Snap! Crackle! Pop!" without characters, first appeared on the Kellogg's Rice Krispies box in 1932.

Cooler, Model-W, 1950s, Acton Co., Box, 19 x 17 In.	186.00
Cooler, Pressed Steel, Portable, Embossed Side With Logo, Glascock Bros. Mfg., 30 x 17 In.	575.00
Dispenser Sign, Drink Coca-Cola Ice Cold, 2-Sided, Porcelain, Red & White, 1950s, 28 x 27 In.	720.00
Display, Autumn Leaves, Festoon, 5 Folds, Die Cut Cardboard, 1922, 84 In.	460.00
Display, Four Seasons, 5 Panels, Women, Die Cut Cardboard, Fabric Tape, 1922, 60 x 31 In.	16100.00
Display, Stop For A Pause, Go Refreshed, 1939	4950.00
Door Bar, Buvez Coca-Cola Glace, Red, Yellow, White, Porcelain, France, 1950s, 31 ½ In.	150.00
Door Push, Come In!, Have A Coca-Cola, Red, Yellow, Porcelain, Rounded Ends, 1941, 11 ¾ In.	360.00
Door Push, Ice Cold Coca-Cola In Bottles, Red & White, Porcelain, 2 ½ x 30 In.	275.00
Icebox, Countertop, Drink Coca-Cola, Wood, Stencil, Hinge, Square Handles, c.1910, 13 ½ x 25 ¾ In.	300.00
Ink Blotter, Bottle Image, Refreshing New Feeling, Over 60 Million A Day, c.1960, 7 ½ x 3 ½ In.	12.00
Jar, Chewing Gum, Lid, Coca-Cola, Square, Glass, Clear, Etched, 1913-19, 10 ½ In.	510.00
Jar, Lid, Pepsin Chewing Gum, Paper Label, Embossed, Rectangular, 11 x 9 In.	1610.00
Lampshade, Leaded Glass, Leaf Edge, Red, Green, 1920s, 16 In. Diam.	2950.00
Light, Bottle Shape, Milk Glass, Round Foot, Tin Bottle Cap, Red, White, 20 In.	13800.00
Menu Board, Drink Coca-Cola, Masonite, Wood, Red, White, Green, 1960s, 29 ½ x 17 ¼ In.	330.00
Menu, Soda, Cardboard, 1902, 4 x 6 In.	345.00
Mirror, Girl In Hat Holding Glass, At Fountains 10 Cents, Pocket, 1980s, 2 ¼ In.	10.00
Mirror, Girl Wearing Hat, Holding Coca-Cola Bottle, Pocket, 1916, 2 ¾ In.	106.00
Mobile, Cardboard, 2 12-Packs, Bottles, Good With Food, Serve Ice Cold, c.1954, 27 x 24 In.	230.00
Music Box, Ice Cold, Doll, Bottles, Square Base, Red & White, 1950s, 18 In.	270.00
Paper Doll, Christmas Greetings, Teen Girl, Prom, Cheerleading, Jeans, Beach, 11 ½ x 9 In.	15.00
Pennant, Cooperativa, Cuban Provinces, c.1930, 26 x 33 In.	190.00
Plate, 1905, Seated Girl, Seminude, Long Hair, Shaped Wood Frame, Vienna, 13 x 13 In.	270.00
Plate, Girl, Off-Shoulder Dress, Upswept Hair, Scrolling Leaf Border, Round, c.1905, 10 ¼ In.	1680.00
Plate, Vienna Art, Tin, Mounted In Shadowbox, Gesso Frame, Square, 1905, 16 In.	708.00
Playing Cards, Ice Skater, Play, Refresh, Have A Coke, 1956	85.00
Rack, Bag, For Home Refreshment, Sprite Boy, Red, White, 1940-50, 36 ½ x 15 In.	150.00
Rack, For 6-Packs, Black Metal Racks, Red Sign, 60 In.	303.00
Radio, Cooler, Drink Coca-Cola, Ice Cold, Have A Coke, Red & White, 1950s, 12 x 9 ¼ In.	360.00
Radio, Crystal, Red, White, Cooler Shape, 3 x 2 ¼ x 1 ½ In.	250.00
Radio, Drink Coca-Cola, Cooler Shape, c.1949	248.00
Sandwich Server, Refresh Yourself, Bottle & Glass, 1930s, 8 ¼ In. Diam.	360.00
Shade, Drink Coca-Cola, White Milk Glass, Green Border, Red, Ceiling, 1930s, 12 In.	390.00
Shade, Lamp, Coca-Cola, Leaded Glass, Leaves, Crown Top, White, Green, Brown, 1920s, 16 In. Diam.	10800.00
Sign, 2 Bottles, Mirror, 1930s, 3 x 7 In.	270.00
Sign, 6-Pack, Tin, Die Cut Embossed, 1956, 11 x 12 In.	633.00
Sign, 6-Pack, Yellow Version, Tin, Die Cut Embossed, 1958, 11 x 12 In.	1380.00
Sign, Bottle, Cutout, Tin, 1950s, 72 x 20 In.	780.00
Sign, Bottle, Tin & Wood, Silver Frame, 1947, 36 x 18 In.	360.00
Sign, Buvez, Self-Framed, Tin, 7 Cents, c.1951, 17 x 53 In.	141.00
Sign, Cap, Drink Coca-Cola, Red & White, Aluminum, 1940-50s, 16 In. Diam.	390.00
Sign, Cap, Drink Coca-Cola, Sign Of Good Taste, Round, Red, White, Yellow, 1950, 12 In. Diam.	330.00
Sign, Cap, Metal, Drink Coca-Cola, Round, Red & White, c.1950s, 12 In. Diam.	240.00
Sign, Cap, Porcelain, Red, White, Drink Coca-Cola In Bottles, 12 In.	240.00
Sign, Coca-Cola, Black, White, Yellow, Neon, Box, c.1970-80s, 11 x 23 In.	300.00
Sign, Coca-Cola, Bottle, Tin, Round, 44 In. Diam. *illus*	1121.00
Sign, Cooler, Arrow, Ice Cold, Red & White, Gold, Metal, 1930s, 16 x 32 In.	660.00
Sign, Curb, Drink Refresh, 2-Sided, Porcelain, Cast Iron Base, 30 In.	848.00
Sign, Diamond Shape, Cold Refreshment, Blue, Red, Cardboard, 1937, 21 x 21 In.	920.00
Sign, Drink Carioca-Cooler, Tropical Highball, 3-D, Cardboard, Billboard, 1940s, 7 x 9 In.	472.00
Sign, Drink Coca-Cola In Bottles, Lollipop Shape, Porcelain, Iron, Red & White, 1950s, 64 In.	450.00
Sign, Drink Coca-Cola In Bottles, Script, Truck Grill, Black, Silver, Metal, 17 x 7 In.	58.00
Sign, Drink Coca-Cola, 3 Bottles, Lined Up, Red, White, Green, Tin, Embossed, 1934, 54 x 16 In.	600.00
Sign, Drink Coca-Cola, Fountain Service, Yellow Ground, Porcelain, 1950s, 11 ¾ x 28 In.	450.00
Sign, Drink Coca-Cola, Ice Cold, Bottle, Flange, Round, Arrow, Red & White, Tin, 1956, 22 x 18 In.	420.00
Sign, Drink Coca-Cola, In 12 Oz. Cans, White, Red, Blue, Plexiglas, Light-Up, 1960s, 15 x 34 In.	270.00
Sign, Drink Coca-Cola, Red & Black, Light-Up, Plastic, Metal, 16 In. Diam.	230.00
Sign, Drink Coca-Cola, Red Ground, Tin, Green Frame, 1920s, 4 ½ x 9 In.	675.00
Sign, Drink Coca-Cola, Sign Of Good Taste, Light-Up, Round, Red & White, 1950s, 16 In. Diam.	360.00
Sign, Drink Coca-Cola, Take Enough Home, Round, Light-Up, Rotating, Red, Yellow, 1950s, 21 x 16 In.	960.00
Sign, Drink Coca-Cola, White Haired Boy, Bottle Cap Hat, Das Erfrischt, Germany, 1950s, 9 x 14 In.	200.00
Sign, Edgar Bergen With Charlie McCarthy, CBS Sunday Evenings, 1949, 24 ¼ x 11 In. *illus*	274.00
Sign, Electric, Round, Drink Coca-Cola, Pay When Served, Counter, Cast Metal, 13 x 14 In.	2990.00
Sign, Fishtail Logo, Tin, 1954, 20 x 42 In.	339.00
Sign, Fishtail, Be Really Refreshed, Tin, c.1959, 40 x 18 In.	207.00

Sign, Fountain Service, Drink Coca-Cola, Porcelain, Green, Red, Shield, 2-Sided, 1934, 14 x 27 In.	570.00
Sign, Girl, Behind Car Wheel, Hat, Scarf, Bottle, Gold Seal Stamp, 1911, 17 ½ x 14 ½ In.	120.00
Sign, Girl, Holding Glass Of Coke, Feather Hat, Paper, Frame, 1901, 15 x 20 In......................	14950.00
Sign, Girl, Holding Out Glass, Oval, Arrow Shape Corners, Green, Red, Tin, 1927, 20 ¼ x 14 ½ In.	1020.00
Sign, Girl, Marines Uniform, Standing, Holding Bottle, Stand-Up, Easel, 1940s, 63 In..............	660.00
Sign, Girl, Seated, Red Suit, Hat, Holding Bottle & Fur Stole, 1940, 50 x 30 In.	330.00
Sign, Girl, White Dress, Paper, Frame, 1912, 15 ½ x 23 In..	4025.00
Sign, Great Combination, Picture Of Hamburger, Bottle, Cardboard, Frame, 22 x 45 In...............	358.00
Sign, Hanging, Drink, Sign Of Good Taste, Tin, Plastic Frame & Lenses, Light-Up, 16 In..........	270.00
Sign, Hanging, Girl, Drink Carbonated Coca-Cola In Bottles, 5 Cents, Cardboard, 1902, 6 In. .	5250.00
Sign, Have A Drink Of Coca-Cola, Girl In Hammock, Matted, Frame, 1912, 10 ¾ x 20 In.........	5605.00
Sign, Ice Cold, Red & White, 2-Sided, Triangle, 1936, 22 ½ x 22 ½ In.	840.00
Sign, Ice Cold, Sign Of Good Taste, Bottle, Square Shape, Tin, 1960s, 27 ¾ x 19 ¾ In.	240.00
Sign, Jean Harlow, Die Cut, 1932, 15 x 42 In...	5750.00
Sign, Kay Display, Horseshoe, Bottle, Here's Refreshment, Wood & Metal, c.1934, 17 x 15 In. ..	690.00
Sign, Kay Display, Ye Who Enter Here On Refreshment Bent, Plywood, c.1940s, 39 x 11 In.	575.00
Sign, King Size, Coke, 6-Pack, Red, White, Green, Embossed, 1960, 36 x 31 In......................	900.00
Sign, Lantern, Take Cartons Home, Regular Size, Rotating, Light-Up, White, Red, Blue, 1960s, 24 ½ In.	210.00
Sign, Large Drinks, Crushed Ice, Soda Shop, Girl Holding Cup, Snowflake, Plexiglas, 13 x 29 ¾ In.	90.00
Sign, Now King Size With Squirt, Cardboard, Frame, 20 x 36 In.	170.00
Sign, On The Refreshing Side, Girl Seated, Cross-Legged, Boy, Holding Bottles, 1941, 50 x 30 In.	540.00
Sign, Pause Drink Coca-Cola, Bottle, Tin, Embossed, Red, Yellow, Frame, 1939, 54 x 18 In.....	840.00
Sign, Pause That Refreshes, Girl, Holding Bottle, Looking Over Shoulder, 1930s, 45 x 35 In....	390.00
Sign, Pause That Refreshes, Girl, Holding Bottle, Off-Shoulder Dress, 1947, 45 x 31 In..........	300.00
Sign, Pause!, 2 Girls, Clown, Holding Bottles, Vertical, 1950s, 27 x 16 In.	1440.00
Sign, Pause!, Ice Skater, Clown, Trainer, TV Camera, Cardboard, 16 x 27 In...........................	978.00
Sign, Picnic, 2 Women Silent Film Stars, Cardboard, 1923, 16 x 28 In....................................	6900.00
Sign, Pilaster, Serve Coke At Home, 6-Pack, White Ground, Red, Green, Tin, 1948, 41 x 16 In.	660.00
Sign, Pilaster, Take Home A Carton Of Quality Refreshment, 6-Pack, 1954, 40 ¾ x 16 In........	480.00
Sign, Play Refreshed, Girl, Fishing, Hat, Holding Bottle, Frame, 1950, 28 x 57 In.	900.00
Sign, Popcorn, Delicious With Ice Cold, Enjoy The Show, Light-Up, Square, 1950s, 15 ¾ x 15 In.	900.00
Sign, Refreshing, Houses, Strolling Couple, Masonite, Metal, 11 x 38 ½ In..............................	150.00
Sign, Refreshment!, Girl, Pink Dress, Bent Over, Picking Up Bottle From Tray, 1949, 50 x 30 In.	210.00
Sign, Refreshment, Bottle, 2-Sided, Gold Reeded Frame, 1951, 32 x 21 In.	330.00
Sign, Santa Claus, Bag Of Toys, Coke In Other Hand, Cardboard, 1953, 20 x 12 In..................	195.00
Sign, School Zone, Policeman, Thank You Resume Speed, 2-Sided, Round Logo Base, 1962, 65 In.	2700.00
Sign, School Zone, Thank You Resume Speed, Drive Refreshed, Bottle, Base, Metal, 1960s, 49 In.	570.00
Sign, Service Woman, Holding Up Bottle, Uniform, Life Size, Stand-Up, 1943, 64 x 26 In........	720.00
Sign, Sled, Curved Shape Ends, Elongated, Porcelain, Red, White, c.1960, 43 x 16 In.............	495.00
Sign, Sprite Boy, Please One Carton Of Coca-Cola To A Customer, Die Cut Cardboard, 21 x 16 In.	2875.00
Sign, Sprite Boy, Round, Tin, Yellow, Red, White, c.1940, 12 ¾ In. Diam......................	1140.00
Sign, Sprite Boy, Store Hour Discs, 10 ½ x 13 ½ In.	460.00
Sign, Straight-Sided Bottle, Embossed Tin, 36 x 12 In.	978.00
Sign, Take Home A Carton, Big King Size, 6-Pack, Red & White, Tin, 1958, 28 x 19 ¾ In.	540.00
Sign, Take Home A Carton, Drink Coca-Cola, 6-Pack, Bottle, Tin, Embossed, 1938, 54 x 18 In.	480.00
Sign, Talk About Refreshing, Girl With Umbrella, Bottle, Cardboard, Frame, c.1942, 21 x 32 In. *illus*	660.00
Sign, There's Nothing Like A Coke, Barrel, Aluminum, Red, White, Yellow, 1950s, 9 x 15 In.....	90.00
Sign, Tin, Fishtail, Enjoy That Refreshing New Feeling, Bottle, Ice Cold, c.1960, 18 x 54 In., Pair	403.00
Sign, Veneered Walnut Sides, Kay Display, Wood, 1930s, 30 x 12 In.......................................	3163.00
Stringholder, 6-Packs, Red, Yellow, Tin, Advertising Novelty Co., 13 ¼ x 15 ¾ In....................	920.00
Thermometer, Bottle Shape, Tin, 1950s, 16 ¾ x 5 ½ In...	110.00
Thermometer, Coke Bottle Shape, Metal, 16 x 5 In..	38.00
Thermometer, Masonite, Thirst Knows No Season, Bottle, Rectangular, Red, Green, 1940s, 17 In.	180.00
Thermometer, Sign Of Good Taste, White, Red, Cigar Shape, c.1948, 30 In............................	695.00
Thermometer, Things Go Better With Coke, Round, White, Green & Red, Pam, 1960s, 18 In. Diam.	540.00
Thermometer, Tin, Bottle, Embossed, Red & Gold, Rounded Ends, 1937, 16 In.	180.00
Thermometer, Tin, Drink Coca-Cola, Sign Of Good Taste, Oval, Red & White, 1950s, 30 In.....	180.00
Tip Tray, 1909, Exhibition Girl, With Glass Of Coke, Green, Oval, 16 ⅝ x 13 ⅝ In.	650.00
Tip Tray, 1921, Autumn Girl, Holding Glass Of Coke, Metal, 13 x 10 ½ In.	226.00
Toaster, Sandwich, Electric, Round, Aunt Sarah's, Paper Tag, Box, 1930s, 8 In........................	4200.00
Topper, Cash Register, Please Pay Cashier, Light-Up, 1940-50s, 6 ½ x 10 In.	300.00
Toy, Car, 1960 Ford, Tin Lithograph, Red, White, Refresh With Zest, Bottle, Box, Friction, Japan, 10 In.	236.00
Toy, Carrying Case, 6 Plastic Bottle, Cardboard, Marx, 1950s, 1 x 2 x 1 ¾ In., 3 Piece..............	95.00
Toy, Cooler, Glasscock, 1929	19800.00
Toy, Dispenser, Drink Coca-Cola, Red & White, Lever, Box, 1960s, 11 ½ In.	60.00
Toy, Fountain & Grill, Diner, Parking Lot, 1950s, 7 x 16 x 12 In..	240.00

Coffee Mill, Acme, Orange, Black Print, Sheet Iron Box, Lid, Cast Iron, Wall Mount, 12 x 4 ¼ In.
$94.00

Conestoga Auction Co., Inc.

Coffee Mill, Cast Iron, Open Hopper, Flange, Painted, Wooden Knob, 6 ½ In.
$53.00

Conestoga Auction Co., Inc.

Coffee Mill, Enterprise, No. 1, Gilt Stencil, Drawer, Cast Iron, Marked, 11 In.
$236.00

Brunk Auctions

Coffee Mill, Enterprise, No. 2, 2 Wheels, Red, Decal, Cast Iron, Drawer, Pat'd 1873, 12 ½ In.
$502.00

Conestoga Auction Co., Inc.

Coffee Mill, Enterprise, No. 5, 2 Wheels, Cast Iron, Drawer, Pat. 1873, 17 x 12 ⅝ In.
$590.00

Conestoga Auction Co., Inc.

Coffee Mill, Enterprise, No. 7, 2 Wheels, Painted, Decals, Eagle Finial, 17-In. Wheel
$440.00

Showtime Auction Services

Coffee Mill, Turkish Style, Tubular, Brass Folding Crank, c.1900, 8 ¾ In.
$24.00

Conestoga Auction Co., Inc.

Toy, Shopping Cart, Groceries, Lined, Red Wheels, 1950s, 20 x 13 ½ In.	180.00
Toy, Truck, Bottle, Rubber Tires, Metalcraft	850.00
Toy, Truck, Delivery, Wood & Metal, Wood Blocks With Logo, Red, Smith-Miller, 1940s, 13 In..	780.00
Toy, Truck, Delivery, Yellow, Holding Bottles, Smith-Miller, Box, c.1980, 13 In.	840.00
Toy, Truck, Delivery, Yellow, Red Product Cartons, Steel, New Era, 29 ½ In.	429.00
Toy, Truck, Ny-Lint Steel, Gmc, 18 Wheeler, Box	110.00
Toy, Truck, Panel Sides, Yellow, Marx, 1940, 20 ½ In.	250.00
Toy, Truck, Pressed Steel, Metalcraft, Open Side, Bottles, Decal, 11 In.	173.00
Toy, Truck, Red & Yellow, Rubber Wheels, Working Headlights, Metalcraft, 1933, 11 In.	236.00
Toy, Truck, Sprite Boy, Take Some Home Today, Yellow Trailer, Litho Wheels, Marx, c.1960, 20 In.	390.00
Tray, 1901, Hilda Clark, 5 Cents, Flowers, Leaf Border, Round, 9 ½ In.	1800.00
Tray, 1903, Hilda Clark, Holding Glass, Delicious, Refreshing, Round, 9 ¾ In.	1440.00 to 2750.00
Tray, 1903, Hilda Clark, Holding Glass, Drink Delicious Refreshing, Oval, 18 ½ x 15 ⅛ In.	540.00
Tray, 1905, Lillian Nordica, Tin Lithograph, Oval, 12 ¾ In.	1534.00
Tray, 1909, Exhibition Girl, Holding Glass Of Coca-Cola, Oval, 13 x 10 ¾ In. ....*illus*	1652.00
Tray, 1910, Coca-Cola Girl, Wide Brim Hat, Drink Delicious, 13 ¼ x 1 ½ In.	1200.00
Tray, 1916, Elaine Seated, Holding Glass, Hat, Roses, Rectangular, 19 x 8 ½ In.	150.00
Tray, 1925, Party Girl, Holding Glass, Fox Stole, Head Wrap, 13 ¼ x 10 ½ In.	150.00
Tray, 1927, Curb Service, Soda Jerk, Man, Holding Glasses, Red, Yellow, Black, 13 ¼ x 10 ½ In.	600.00
Tray, 1933, Frances Dee, Seated On Wall, Swimsuit, Holding Bottle, 13 ¼ x 10 ½ In.	120.00
Tray, 1934, Maureen O'Sullivan, Johnny Weissmuller, Back To Back, Holding Bottles, 10 x 13 In.	600.00
Tray, 1936, Hostess, Reclining In Chair, White Gown, Corsage, Holding Glass, 13 ¼ x 10 ½ In.	270.00
Tray, 1938, Girl At Shade, Yellow Dress, Floppy Hat, 13 x 10 ½ In.	122.00
Tray, 1939, Springboard Girl, Drink Coca-Cola, 13 ¼ x 10 ½ In.	130.00 to 139.00
Tray, 1941, Skater Girl, On Log, 13 ¼ x 10 ½ In.	164.00
Tray, 1942, 2 Girls At Green Car, 13 ¼ x 10 ½ In.	150.00 to 304.00
Tray, 1977, 75th Anniversary, Hilda Clark, Round, 12 ¼ In.	18.00
Tray, 1994, Smiles, Black Girl, Boy, Playing Checkers, 13 ¼ x 10 ½ In.	55.00
Tumbler, Holly Hobbie, Christmas Is Fun For Everyone, American Greetings, 1977, Pair	10.00
Vending Machine, Drink Coca-Cola In Bottles, Red, White, Key, 35 x 24 x 20 In.	450.00
Vending Machine, Ice Cold, 39 Bottles, 10 Cent, Red & White, 59 x 27 In.	863.00
Vending Machine, Vendo 44, Red, Metal Top, 16 ½ x 58 In.	2065.00

COFFEE MILLS are also called coffee grinders, although there is a difference in the way each grinds the coffee. Large floor-standing or counter-model coffee mills were used in the nineteenth-century country store. Small home mills were first made about 1894. They lost favor by the 1930s. The renewed interest in fresh-ground coffee has produced many modern electric mills and hand mills and grinders. Reproductions of the old styles are being made.

Acme, Orange, Black Print, Sheet Iron Box, Lid, Cast Iron, Wall Mount, 12 x 4 ¼ In. ......*illus*	94.00
Arcade, Imperial, No. 9022, Finger-Jointed Box, Drawer, Side Handle, Iron, 12 ¼ x 7 In.	83.00
Bronson-Walton, Dutch Scene, Cast Iron, Wood, 12 x 3 x 3 In.	264.00
Bronson-Walton, Patriotic Designs, Tin Lithograph, Wood, Cleveland, c.1910, 10 ½ In.	235.00
Bronson-Walton, Wall Mount, Dutch Girl, Cast Iron, Cleveland, Oh., 12 ¼ x 4 In.	94.00
Cast Iron, Open Hopper, Flange, Painted, Wooden Knob, 6 ½ In. ....*illus*	53.00
Challenge Fast, No. 1087, Wooden Box, Cast Iron, Drawer, Paper Label, 10 ½ x 5 ¾ In.	30.00
Charles Parker Co., Red, Blue, Gold, Flowers, Cast Iron, Wood Base, 1800s, 21 In.	460.00
Coles, 2 Wheels, Red Cast Iron, Eagle Finial, 27 ½ In.	504.00
Colonial, No. 1707, Daisies, Scrolls, Wood Box, Cast Iron, Crank Handle, 9 ¾ x 6 ¼ In.	153.00
Elgin National, 2 Wheels, No. 46, Cast Iron, Sheet Iron Hopper, 24 In.	590.00
Elgin National, No. 10, Cast Iron, Paint, Bird Finial., c.1900, 64 x 29 In.	999.00
Enterprise, 2 Wheels, Cast Iron, Red, Eagle Finial	540.00
Enterprise, 2 Wheels, Decals, Drawer, Paint, 1898, 17 In.	2040.00
Enterprise, 2 Wheels, Painted Yellow, Eagle Finial, 25-In. Wheels	770.00
Enterprise, 2 Wheels, Painted, Cast Iron, Wood Handle, Square Base, 1800s, 13 In.	345.00
Enterprise, 2 Wheels, Painted, Stenciled, Flowers, Wood Stepped Base, 13 In.	480.00
Enterprise, Eagle Finial, Decals, 34-In. Wheel	2475.00
Enterprise, No. 1, Gilt Stencil, Drawer, Cast Iron, Marked, 11 In. ....*illus*	236.00
Enterprise, No. 2, 2 Wheels, Cast Iron, Pat. Dec. 9, 1873, 8 ¾ In.	978.00
Enterprise, No. 2, 2 Wheels, Red, Decal, Cast Iron, Drawer, Pat'd 1873, 12 ½ In. ....*illus*	502.00
Enterprise, No. 2, Decals, Red Paint, 8 ¾ In., 12-In. Wheel	495.00
Enterprise, No. 5, 2 Wheels, Cast Iron, Drawer, Pat. 1873, 17 x 12 ⅝ In. ....*illus*	590.00
Enterprise, No. 6, 2 Wheels, Red, Gold, Eagle Finial, Drawer, Painted, c.1899, 5 In.	1320.00
Enterprise, No. 7, 2 Wheels, Painted, Decals, Eagle Finial, 17-In. Wheel ....*illus*	440.00
Enterprise, No. 7, Cast Iron, Red Paint, 17-In. Wheel, 22 ½ x 17 ¾ In.	288.00
Ever-Ready, No. 2, Lithograph, Tin, Iron, Hand Crank, Wood Board, 12 In.	113.00
J. Fisher, Wood, Square Shape, Drawer, Iron Bowl, Wood Grip Handle	59.00

Lane Bros., No. 14, Cast Iron, 20 x 10 x 14 In.	413.00
Peugeot Freres, Metal, Crank Handle, Wood Grip & Drawer, France, 15 x 9 In.	367.00
Turkish Style, Tubular, Brass Folding Crank, c.1900, 8 ¾ In. ....*illus*	24.00
Wilmot Castle, Cast Iron, Gold Lithograph, Glass Receiver, Patented 1891, 14 In. ....*illus*	236.00
Wood Veneer, Brass Receiver, Iron Mechanism, Mahogany Crank Knob, 10 x 5 In. ....*illus*	35.00
Zassenhaus, Kaffee, Ceramic, Dutch Children, Brass Tag, Gebr. Roittner, Salzburg, 15 ¾ In. ...*illus*	71.00

COIN SPOT is a glass pattern that was named by collectors for the spots resembling coins, which are part of the glass. Colored, clear, and opalescent glass was made with the spots. Many companies used the design in the 1870–90 period. It is so popular that reproductions are still being made.

Cruet, Cranberry, Opalescent, Clear Handle & Oval Faceted Stopper, 7 In., Pair	173.00

COIN-OPERATED MACHINES of all types are collected. The vending machine is an ancient invention dating back to 200 B.C., when holy water was dispensed in a coin-operated vase. Smokers in seventeenth-century England could buy tobacco from a coin-operated box. It was not until after the Civil War that the technology made modern coin-operated games and vending machines plentiful. Slot machines, arcade games, and dispensers are all collected.

Arcade, Basketball, Mike & Jake Basketball Star, 1 Cent, 2 Players, c.1947, 16 x 19 In. ....*illus*	421.00
Arcade, Bat-A-Ball, 5 Cent, Splatter Paint Wood, Glass Front Panel, 19 x 25 In.	805.00
Arcade, Cail-O-Scope Viewing, Diamonds, Nude Pictures, 1 Cent, Oak, 72 In.	2588.00
Arcade, Crane, Novelty Merchantman Mfg., Chicago, 41 x 21 x 19 In.	763.00
Arcade, Humpty Dumpty, Clown, 1 Cent, Flip Coin, Keys, Floor Model ....*illus*	3390.00
Arcade, Lift-O-Graph, Back Muscle, Monkey Climb, 10 Cent, International Mutoscope Reel Co., c.1938 ..*illus*	4025.00
Arcade, Pinball, Bally Hoo, 5 Cent	294.00
Arcade, Poison This Rat, Hitler, 1 Cent, Groetchen, 1940s, 17 x 24 In.	5175.00
Arcade, Strength Tester, Lung, Hygienic, Glass, Oak, Strong Man, Pedestal, 71 x 13 In.	1725.00
Bagatelle, Swastika, Joy Ball, Maple Board, Walnut Case, Turned Legs, 36 x 25 In.	472.00
Fortune Teller, Ask Swami, Brushed Stainless Steel, Lever, 8 x 8 In.	194.00
Fortune Teller, Oak Case, Best Novelty Co., Hartford, Conn., 16 ½ x 13 ½ x 5 In.	537.00
Gambling, Roulette Wheel, Wood Cabinet, Front Iron Lever, 5 Cent, c.1905, 11 x 11 In.	978.00
Gambling, Wheel, French Lodge, Tabletop, Riders On Horses, 48 x 28 In.	978.00
Gum, Adams, Chrome, 1 Cent, Stewart & McGuire DVC, 15 In.	403.00
Gum, Pulver, Kola-Pepsin, 1 Cent, 5 Cent Packages, Red & White, Wood, c.1900, 24 In.	5400.00
Gum, Pulver, One Cent Delivers A Tasty Chew, Yellow Kid, Porcelain, 20 x 8 In.	696.00
Gumball, Adams' Pepsin, Tutti Frutti, 1 Cent, Wood Cabinet, 29 x 12 In.	4888.00
Gumball, Dandy Vender, Ball-Gum, 1 Cent, 3-Reel, Push Knob, Counter	452.00
Gumball, E-Z Ball, 5 Cent, Cast Iron, Countertop, Green, Glass Globe, 23 x 9 In.	748.00
Gumball, Porcelain Base, Northwestern, Decal, 5 Cent	118.00
Music Box, Drums, Bells, Castanets, Rosewood, 8 Tunes, Swiss, c.1900, 23 x 11 In. ....*illus*	3360.00
Music, Boy, Whistling, Head Moves, 3 Songs, 2 Quarters, France, c.1895, 31 x 16 In.	20000.00
Mutoscope, Flip Card, Peep Show Movie, So French & So Nice, Oak, c.1933	1243.00
Skill, Ballgame, 1 Cent, Oak Cabinet, Early 1900s, 14 x 18 In.	690.00
Skill, Baseball, 1 Cent, Pinball Type Game, Red Wood Case, Aluminum, 10 x 17 In.	575.00
Skill, Baseball, 1 Cent, Wooden, Gumball, 22 x 21 In.	2070.00
Skill, Baseball, Wood Case, Aluminum Cast, Ball Game, B & M, 14 x 17 In.	4600.00
Skill, Gumball, 1 Cent, Play Ball, Wood Cabinet, Glass Front, Fill Bases, 14 x 14 In.	3565.00
Skill, Pace Peo Baseball, 1 Cent, Steel Case, Wood Base, 19 x 10 In.	1035.00
Slot, 1 Cent, Golden Falls, Wood Case, Cherries, 16 x 24 In.	1495.00
Slot, 3 Cherries, 10 Cent Slot, Cast Metal, Mounted On Base, 25 x 16 In.	826.00
Slot, Bally Showboat, 25 Cents, Metal, Light-Up, 1970s, 33 x 19 In.	403.00
Slot, Bally, 25 Cent, Electric, 3 Wheels, 41 x 25 In.	403.00
Slot, Caille, Big Six, 25 Cent, Upright, Single Wheel, Keys, c.1904 ....*illus*	18360.00
Slot, Dice, Yellow, Horsehead, 5 Dollar Jack Pot, 5 Cent, c.1900, 16 x 17 In.	16100.00
Slot, Jennings Sun Chief, 25 Cents, Light-Up, Keys	2475.00
Slot, Jennings, Golf Ball Payout, Walnut, 18 x 18 In.	8050.00
Slot, Jennings, Little Duke Jackpot, 1 Cent, 3 Discs, Side Gum, Keys, 1932	3051.00
Slot, Jennings, Sun Chief Blue Star Jackpot, 25 Cent, Light-Up, Keys, 1949	2760.00
Slot, Jennings, Sun Chief Jackpot, 25 Cent, Light-Up, Keys, 1949	2475.00
Slot, Jennings, Sun Chief, Thunder Hotel, Blue, Light-Up, 50 Cent, Keys	2376.00
Slot, Marvel, Gumball, 1 Cent, Green, 11 x 8 In.	177.00
Slot, Mills Extraordinary, Golf Ball Payout, 25 Cent, Wood, 1930s, 19 x 15 In.	5750.00
Slot, Mills, Ace Jackpot, 5 Cent, Keys, c.1948	960.00
Slot, Mills, Baseball, 5 Cent, Lithograph Play Field, 16 x 24 In.	5015.00
Slot, Mills, Bonus, 5 Cent, 1940s	2150.00

Coffee Mill, Wilmot Castle, Cast Iron, Gold Lithograph, Glass Receiver, Patented 1891, 14 In.
$236.00

Conestoga Auction Co., Inc.

Coffee Mill, Wood Veneer, Brass Receiver, Iron Mechanism, Mahogany Crank Knob, 10 x 5 In.
$35.00

Conestoga Auction Co., Inc.

Coffee Mill, Zassenhaus, Kaffee, Ceramic, Dutch Children, Brass Tag, Gebr. Roittner, Salzburg, 15 ¾ In.
$71.00

Conestoga Auction Co., Inc.

As always, the edited listings in *Kovels' Antiques & Collectibles Price Guide* aren't available on any website, but readers should visit Kovels.com for information on trends, tips, reproductions, marks, old prices, and more!

COIN-OPERATED MACHINE

Coin-Operated, Arcade, Basketball, Mike & Jake Basketball Star, 1 Cent, 2 Players, c.1947, 16 x 19 In.
$421.00

Coin-Operated, Arcade, Humpty Dumpty, Clown, 1 Cent, Flip Coin, Keys, Floor Model
$3390.00

Coin-Operated, Arcade, Lift-O-Graph, Back Muscle, Monkey Climb, 10 Cent, International Mutoscope Reel, c.1938
$4025.00

Coin-Operated, Music Box, Drums, Bells, Castanets, Rosewood, 8 Tunes, Swiss, c.1900, 23 x 11 In.
$3360.00

Coin-Operated, Slot, Caille, Big Six, 25 Cent, Upright, Single Wheel, Keys, c.1904
$18360.00

Coin-Operated, Slot, Mills, Q.T., V Or Triangle, 10 Cent, 3-Reel, Bell, Double Jackpot, Keys, c.1934
$1760.00

Coin-Operated, Slot, Mills, Silent Jackpot, 5 Cent, Keys, c.1931
$1695.00

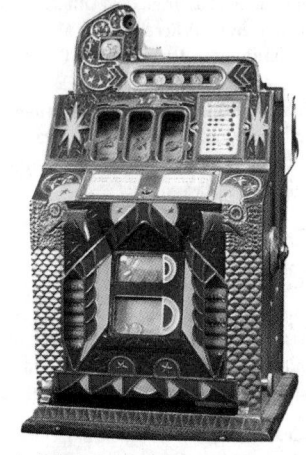

Coin-Operated, Slot, Puritan Baby Bell 3-Reel Jackpot, 1 Cent, Keys, Counter, c.1934
$1035.00

Coin-Operated, Slot, Watling, 25 Cent, Torch Front, Twin Jackpot, Keys
$1210.00

Slot, Mills, Bursting Cherry Jackpot, 5 Cent, Brown, 1939	1243.00
Slot, Mills, Castle Front, 10 Cent, 1930s, 16 x 16 In.	1150.00
Slot, Mills, Chevron Q.T., 1 Cent, 13 x 19 In.	1610.00
Slot, Mills, Cowboy, Standing, 25 Cent, Life Size	1920.00
Slot, Mills, Dewey, 5 Cent, Upright, Keys, c.1899	13500.00
Slot, Mills, Duplex, 25 Cent, Single Wheel, Upright, c.1899	126500.00
Slot, Mills, Golden Falls, Cherries, Flowers, 25 Cents, 26 In.	1680.00
Slot, Mills, Little Dewey, Upright, Single Wheel, 50 Cents, Keys, 48 In.	6600.00
Slot, Mills, Q.T., Sweetheart Double Jackpot, 1 Cent, 3 Reels, Bell, Side Vendor, Keys, 1941	2860.00
Slot, Mills, Q.T., V Or Triangle, 10 Cent, 3-Reel, Bell, Double Jackpot, Keys, c.1934 ....*illus*	1760.00
Slot, Mills, Silent Jackpot, 5 Cent, Keys, c.1931 ....*illus*	1695.00
Slot, Mills, Table Top, Pull Lever, 25 Cent, 1940s, 26 x 16 In.	978.00
Slot, Mills, Token Bell, 10 Cents, Chicago, c.1910, 26 x 15 x 15 In.	875.00
Slot, Puritan Baby Bell 3-Reel Jackpot, 1 Cent, Keys, Counter, c.1934 ....*illus*	1035.00
Slot, Rock-Ola, 5 Cent, Cast Iron, Paint, Wood Sides, Yellow, 25 x 15 In.	1380.00
Slot, Royal Bell Logo, Stand, Oak, 33 ½ x 18 In.	127.00
Slot, Stand, Art Nouveau, Oak, Door, Fitted Interior, Cast Metal Feet, 34 ¼ x 20 In.	230.00
Slot, Sun Chief, Indian's Head, 25 Cent, Light-Up, Floor, 60 In.	3163.00
Slot, Watling Baseball, Aluminum Casting, 5 Cent, 1930s, 15 x 24 In.	4313.00
Slot, Watling, 25 Cent, Torch Front, Twin Jackpot, Keys ....*illus*	1210.00
Slot, Watling, Rol-A-Top Twin Jackpot, 5 Cent, Keys, 1930s ....*illus*	2300.00
Slot, Watling, Rol-A-Top, 10 Cent, Steel Handle, Wood Sides, 1930s, 16 x 16 In.	3162.00
Spirometer, Strength Test, Lung, 1 Cent, c.1899	4500.00
Trade Stimulator, Ace, 1 Cent, Red, Blue, Yellow, 6 ¾ In.	270.00
Trade Stimulator, Bicycle, Oak Cabinet, 5 Cent, c.1910, 19 ½ x 6 In.	6490.00
Trade Stimulator, Fairest Wheel, c.1895, 25 x 18 In.	805.00
Trade Stimulator, Flip Ball, 1 Cent, Metal Case, Wood Top, Yellow, Red, 14 x 9 In.	460.00
Trade Stimulator, Kentucky Derby, Dice, Wood Cabinet, 10 ½ x 8 ½ In.	325.00
Trade Stimulator, Mills, Little Knocker, Cast Iron, Counter, c.1902 ....*illus*	64800.00
Trade Stimulator, Poison This Rat, Hitler Skill, U.S. War Bonds, 1 Cent, c.1940 ....*illus*	4425.00
Trade Stimulator, Poker, 1 Cent, Oak, Flower, Horseshoe, 1902, 11 x 10 In.	1840.00
Vending, Candy, Dog Patch Family, 10 Cent, Tin Lithograph, 23 In.	1093.00
Vending, Gum, Adam's, Metal, 6 Columns, 1 Cent, Keys	220.00
Vending, Gum, Chocolate, 1 Cent, L-Shape, Green, White, Red Paint, 10 x 9 In.	2185.00
Vending, Gum, Chocolate, Wooden, L-Shape, Champion, 32 x 10 In.	4600.00
Vending, Gum, Zeno Chewing, 1 Cent, Porcelain, Yellow, Black, c.1900, 17 In.	780.00
Vending, Gum, Zeno Chewing, 1 Cent, Wood Case, 16 ½ In.	374.00 to 960.00
Vending, Gum, Zeno, 1 Cent, Clockwork, Wooden, Tin, 17 x 10 In.	690.00
Vending, Hershey, U-Select-It, Coan Mfg. Co., 10 Cents	495.00
Vending, Hot Nuts, Red Glass, Silver King Mfg. Co., 1940s, 16 In.	245.00
Vending, Kandy King, 2 Column, Counter, Holli-Ware Mfg. Co., Keys	180.00
Vending, Match, Cast Iron, Relief Owl, Safety Matches, 1 Cent, 12 ½ In.	3277.00
Vending, Peanut, Smilin' Sam, Head Shape, Gum, 1 Cent, Red, 1940s, 14 In.	345.00
Vending, Peanut, Smilin' Sam, Head, Red, Yellow, Black Stand, Round Base, 43 In.	15600.00
Vending, Peanuts, Popcorn, Butter-Kist, Holcomb & Hoke Mfg. Co.	5700.00
Vending, Postage Stamp, 5 Cents, Get 2 2-Cent Stamps, Brass, c.1900, 23 ¾ x 11 ½ In.	3000.00
Vending, Postage Stamp, Porcelain, Metal, Shipman Mfg. Co., c.1938	141.00
Vending, Postage Stamp, Uncle Sam, 5 & 10 Cents, Porcelain, 8 x 20 In. ....*illus*	330.00
Vending, Prophylactics, Cellos, Red, White X, 25 Cent, 18 x 7 x 4 ¼ In.	243.00
Vending, Pulver Kola-Pepsin Gum, 1 Cent, Foxy Grandpa Inside, Keys, 1906 ....*illus*	1840.00

COLLECTOR PLATES are modern plates produced in limited editions. Some may be found listed under the factory name, such as Bing & Grondahl, Royal Copenhagen, Royal Doulton, and Wedgwood.

American Classics, Huckleberry Finn, 1983	26.00
Americans All, Artist Of The World Series, No. 498, Don Ruffin, 1984, 10 ¼ In.	19.00
Anheuser-Busch, Ganymeade, Budweiser Archives Series, No. 2359, Langeneckert, 1993, 8 In.	30.00
Arklow, Fox Chase Scene, Ireland, Green Border, Gilt, 4 ¼ In.	9.00
Bradford Exchange, Gold Collection, Sultry Yet Regal, Marilyn, 1995	25.00
Christian Bell Porcelain, Age Of Steam, Caboose, Engine, T. Xaras, 9 ½ In.	60.00
Collector's Gallery, San Francisco Tourist Scenes, c.1985, 10 In.	20.00
Danbury Mint, Broadway Limited, Great American Trains Collectible, Jim Deneen, 1991, 8 In.	28.00
Danbury Mint, Southwestern Limited, American Trains Series, Jim Deneen, 1991, 8 ¼ In.	28.00
D'Arceau Limoges, L'Opera, Sites Of Paris Series, France, 1982, 8 ½ In.	18.00
D'Arceau Limoges, Scarlet, Women Of The Century, No. 1, Box, 8 ½ In.	14.00
Davenport Pottery Co., Mr. Pickwick, Douglas Tootle, Wood Frame, 1886, 9 In.	50.00

Coin-Operated, Slot, Watling, Rol-A-Top Twin Jackpot, 5 Cent, Keys, 1930s $2300.00

Early Auction Co.

Coin-Operated, Trade Stimulator, Mills, Little Knocker, Cast Iron, Counter, c.1902 $64800.00

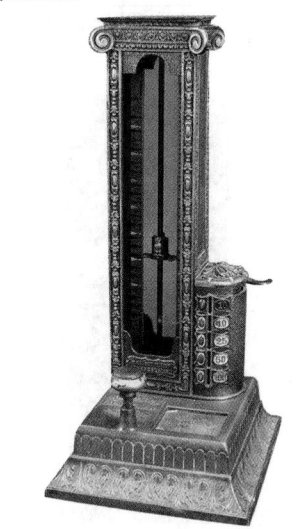

Victorian Casino Antique Auction

Coin-Operated, Trade Stimulator, Poison This Rat, Hitler Skill, U.S. War Bonds, 1 Cent, c.1940 $4425.00

Victorian Casino Antique Auction

Coin-Operated, Vending, Postage Stamp, Uncle Sam, 5 & 10 Cents, Porcelain, 8 x 20 In.
$330.00

Showtime Auction Services

Coin-Operated, Vending, Pulver Kola-Pepsin Gum, 1 Cent, Foxy Grandpa Inside, Keys, 1906
$1840.00

Victorian Casino Antique Auction

Comic Art, Cover, All-American Comics, No. 18, Green Lantern, Ink Marker, Moldoff, 1980s, 17 x 23 In.
$949.00

Hake's Americana & Collectibles

Franklin Mint, Kitchen Visitors, Gilt Rim, Carol Andres, c.1965, 8 ¼ In.	20.00
Goebel, Globetrotter, Hummel Annual, Germany, 1973, 7 ½ In.	25.00
Gorham, Flying High, Norman Rockwell, Four Seasons Series, 1949, 8 In.	17.00
Hamilton Collection, Peach Blossom, Precious Portraits, Bessie Gutmann, 1986, 8 ½ In.	18.00
Haviland Limoges, Lion, Bible Verse, Peaceable Kingdom, C.H. Field, c.1973, 9 ¾ In.	45.00
Helping Hands, Children, Food, Table, Patricia Buckley Moss, Certificate, c.1977, 8 In.	250.00
Holy Family, The First Holiday, Edna Hibel, 9 ¼ In.	35.00
Knowles, Alaska, Bears, Sleds, Totem Pole, White Porcelain, 8 In.	22.00
Knowles, Ashley, Gone With The Wind Series, Raymond Kursar, 1979	40.00
Knowles, Pondering On The Porch, Rockwell's Rediscovered Women, 8 ½ In.	12.00
Knowles, Scarlett's Green Dress, Gone With The Wind, Raymond Kursar, 1984	40.00
LMI, Why Me, Children's Hour Series Official Babysitter, No. 2391, Mike Hagel, 1981	30.00
Milestone Car Society, 1956 T Bird Convertible, Dream Machines, Phil Palma, Box, 1988, 8 ½ In.	15.00
Patience, Mare & Foal Nuzzling, Fred Stone, 9 ½ In.	75.00
Presidential, Washington To Kennedy, Portraits Border & Center, 1963, 10 In.	30.00
Reco, Little Miss Muffet, Mother Goose Series, Signed J. McClelland, 1981, 8 ½ In.	24.00
Spencer Gifts, 100 Anniversary Statue Of Liberty, White Ground, Japan, 1985, 9 In.	20.00
W.S. George, 500 Anniversary, Columbus Discovery, Box, Certificate, 1991, 8 ½ In.	25.00

COMIC ART, or cartoon art, is a relatively new field of collecting. Original art for comic strips, magazine covers, and even printed strips are collected. The first daily comic strip was printed in 1907. The paintings on celluloid used for movie cartoons are listed in this book under Animation Art.

Cartoon, New Yorker, Ink, Watercolor, Signed Charles Addams, 11 ¾ x 12 ¼ In.	8295.00
Comic Strip, Peanuts, 4 Panels, Signed Charles Schulz, Sept. 5, 1964, 7 ½ x 28 In.	11210.00
Cover, All-American Comics, No. 18, Green Lantern, Ink Marker, Moldoff, 1980s, 17 x 23 In. ....*illus*	949.00
Drawing, Blondie, Pen, Ink & Blue Pencil, Chic Young, Nov. 10, 1931, 5 ½ x 19 ½ In.	542.00
Drawing, Bringing Up Father, Pen, Ink, Blue Pencil, George McManus, 5 ½ x 21 ½ In.	260.00
Drawing, Our Boarding House, Pen, Ink, Blue Pencil, Gene Ahern, Jan. 3, 1937, 14 x 21 In.	136.00
Illustration Page, Abbie & Slats, R. Van Buren, March 3, 1933, 5 ½ x 22 In.	28.00
Illustration Page, Alley Oop, Jittery, W.T. Hamlin, August 27, 1948	475.00
Illustration Page, Family Circus, B. Keane, June 9, 1962	40.00
Illustration Page, Li'l Abner, Hamilton Fatback, Beauty & The Beast, Al Capp, Nov. 1, 1949, 7 x 22 In.	593.00
Illustration Page, Peanuts, Baseball Game, Patty, Charlie, C. Schulz, Aug. 5, 1952, 6 ¼ x 28 ½ In.	14690.00
Illustration Page, Peanuts, Charlie, Lucy, C. Schulz, July 19, 1960, 28 ½ x 6 ½ In.	15820.00
Illustration Page, Tarzan, Pursuit, 4 Panels, 1950, 6 ¼ x 21 ½ In.	260.00
Lithograph, Li'l Abner, Signed Al Capp, 31 x 35 In.	203.00
Sunday Page, Flash Gordon, Escape From Death Planet, Dan Barry, May 2, 1971	147.00
Sunday Page, Gasoline Alley, Hand Colored, Frank King, Aug. 18, 1946, 17 ½ x 22 In.	622.00
Sunday Page, Katzenjammer Kids, Dinglehoofer Topper, H. Knerr, July 28, 1935, 23 x 29 In.	1130.00
Sunday Page, Krazy Kat, Ignatz, Officer Pup, G. Herriman, Mar. 1, 1936, 16 ½ x 24 In.	16385.00
Sunday Page, Ming Foo, Brandon Walsh, Nov. 14, 1940, 13 ½ x 21 In.	706.00
Sunday Page, Peanuts, Snow Balls, Snoopy, Linus, Jan. 26, 1964, 17 x 23 ½ In.	30510.00
Sunday Page, Polly & Her Pals, Clifford Sterrett, May 17, 1930, 22 x 35 In.	2938.00
Sunday Page, Popeye, Rough House, Wimpy, Mary Ann, June 26, 1932, E. Segar, 17 x 21 ⅜ In.	11300.00
Sunday Page, Popeye, Wimpy, E. Segar, Oct.27, 1935, 22 x 23 In.	9322.00

COMMEMORATIVE items have been made to honor members of royalty and those of great national fame. World's Fairs and important historical events are also remembered with commemorative pieces. Related collectibles are listed in the Coronation and World's Fair categories.

Cup, Silver Jubilee, Queen's Wedding To Prince Philip, Blue, Crown, E.R., 1952-1977, 3 In.	25.00
Pin, Cuyahoga County Centennial, Bastian Brothers Back Paper, Celluloid, 1910, 1 ¼ In.	33.60
Program, Ice Skating, Great Lakes Exposition, 20 Pages, 1937, 9 x 12 In.	26.00

COMPACTS hold face powder. A woman did not powder her face in public until after World War I. By 1920, the beauty parlor, permanent waves, and cosmetics had become acceptable. A few companies sold cake face powder in a box with a mirror and a pad or puff. Soon the compact was designed by jewelers and made of gold, silver, and precious materials. Cosmetic companies began to sell powder in attractive compacts of less valuable metal or plastic. Collectors today search for Art Deco designs, commemorative compacts from World's Fairs or political events, and unusual examples. Many were made with companion lipsticks and other fittings.

Brass Filigree, Enamel Flowers, Stone Insets, France, 5 x 3 In.	149.00
Cartier, Diamond, Sapphire Clasp, 14K Gold Body, Mirror, Powder, 2 x 2 ¾ In.	2151.00
Cartier, Silver, Blue Enamel Band, 3 x 2 ½ In.	403.00

Cartier, Sterling, 14K Gold, Blue Stones, Ray Design, Mirror, Monogram, 1947, 2 ¼ x 2 ½ In.	900.00
Coty, Goldtone Weave, Mirror, Marked, 2 ½ In.	24.00
Enamel, Silver, Oval, Lid, Cavalier, Maiden, Sleeping Under Tree, Turquoise, c.1900, 3 In.	326.00
Flowers, Multicolor, Green Ground, Gold Trim, Mirror, Oval, England, 3 In.	30.00
Garrard Albemarle, Gold, Diamond & Enamel Clasp, England, 2 ½ x 2 In.	1495.00
Gold, 18K, Blue Enamel, Mirror, Art Deco, H. Dubret, 2 ⅜ x 1 ¾ In. ....*illus*	3555.00
Lalique, Glass, Birds, Sepia Patina, Fleurs D'Amour, Poudre Rachel, Roger Et Gallet, 3 In.	119.00
Leather, Green, Tooling, Brass, Mirror, Italy, 1960s, 3 In.	48.00
Silver Gilt, Peach Translucent Enamel, Blue Cabochon, Mirror, Russia, c.1915, 2 ¼ In.	5760.00
Silver, Lid, Engraved St. Mark Lion, Flowers, Blue Stone Latch, LVF Mark, c.1905, 3 x 3 In.	207.00
Sterling Silver, Engine Turned Rays, 14K Gold Latch, 3 Rubies, Engraved, Dec. 25, 1944	207.00
Sterling Silver, Engraved Flowers, 3 In.	118.00
Stratton, Enamel, Orange, Starburst, 3 In.	32.00
Stratton, RMS Queen Mary, Porcelain, Beveled Edges	250.00
Tiffany & Co., Gold, Ruby, Sterling Silver, 2 ½ x 2 ½ In.	403.00
Tropical Scene, Iridescent, Enamel, c.1925, 3 ½ x 2 In.	75.00

CONSOLIDATED LAMP AND GLASS COMPANY of Coraopolis, Pennsylvania, was founded in 1894. The company made lamps, tablewares, and art glass. Collectors are particularly interested in the wares made after 1925, including black satin glass, Cosmos (listed in its own category in this book), Martele (which resembled Lalique), Ruba Rombic (1928–32 Art Deco line), and colored glasswares. Some Consolidated pieces are very similar to those made by the Phoenix Glass Company. The colors are sometimes different. Consolidated made Martele glass in blue, crystal, green, pink, white, or custard glass with added fired-on color or a satin finish. The company closed for the final time in 1967.

Biscuit Jar, White Ribbed Panel Mold, Pink Flowers, Silver Plate Lid, Bail Handle, 8 In.	40.00
Bowl, Martele, Bird, Swallow, Green Wash, 1920s, 2 ½ x 9 ½ In.	132.00
Bowl, Martele, Fish, Green Wash, 1920s, 3 x 6 In.	147.00
Bowl, Martele, Five Fruits, Purple, 1920s, 2 ½ x 4 ½ In.	102.00
Bowl, Martele, Floral, Green Wash, 11 ½ In.	188.00
Bowl, Martele, Flower, Pink, 1920s, 6 ½ In.	109.00
Bowl, Martele, Flowers, Green Wash, 1920s, 4 x 10 In.	165.00
Butter, Cover, Crisscross, Camphor Tray, 7 In.	50.00
Butter, Cover, Crisscross, Cranberry, Cone Shape Finial, 8 In.	259.00
Charger, Martele, 5 Fruits, 1920s, 12 In.	222.00
Charger, Martele, Bird Of Paradise, Green Wash, 1920s, 12 In.	147.00
Charger, Martele, Bird Of Paradise, Orange Wash, 1920s, 12 In.	147.00
Compote, Fish, Amber Wash, 1920s, 6 ½ In.	147.00
Compote, Hummingbird, Amber Wash, 1920s, 6 ½ x 3 ½ In.	147.00
Compote, Hummingbird, Green Wash, 1920s, 3 ½ x 6 In.	147.00
Compote, Martele, Fish, Green Wash, 1920s, 3 ¼ In.	147.00
Condiment Set, Stand, Bulging, Yellow Cased, Loop Handle, c.1894-1900	144.00
Cruet, Crisscross, Bulbous, Frosted Cranberry, Faceted Stopper, 6 In.	475.00
Cruet, Crisscross, White Opalescent, 6 In.	350.00
Cruet, Pink Satin, Diamond Pattern, Squat, Camphor Handle, Ruffle Spout, Stopper, 7 In., Pair	173.00
Finger Bowl, Crisscross, Cranberry Translucent, 4 In.	75.00
Lamp, Cosmos, Opaline, Flowers, 9 In.	75.00
Pitcher, Water, Crisscross, Opalescent, Cranberry, Clear Handle, 9 In.	1600.00
Plate, Martele, Flowers, Green Wash, 1920s, 7 ½ In.	95.00
Plate, Martele, Olive Design, Orange Wash, 1920s, 8 ½ In.	72.00
Plate, Martele, Pheasant, Purple Wash, 1920s, 8 ½ In.	109.00
Plate, Pheasant, Green Wash, 1920s, 8 ½ In.	113.00
Saltshaker, Cranberry, Pear Shape, Metal Lid, 4 In.	345.00
Sugar & Creamer, White, Pink Flowers, Silver Plate Lid, Spout, Handles	70.00
Sugar, Crisscross, Translucent, Cranberry, Cover, 6 In.	300.00
Toothpick Holder, Crisscross, Cranberry, Bulbous, 2 In.	316.00
Tumbler, Crisscross, White Opalescent, 4 In.	144.00
Vase, Bittersweet, Purple Wash, 1920s, 9 ½ In.	188.00
Vase, Bittersweet, Yellow Wash, 1920s, 10 In.	169.00
Vase, Catalonian, Fan Shape, Amethyst, 1920s, 6 ½ In.	102.00
Vase, Hummingbird, Cream Ground, Flowers, Blue, Brown Detail, 5 ½ In.	30.00
Vase, Hummingbird, Green Wash, 1920s, 5 ¾ In.	185.00
Vase, Katydid, Purple Wash, 1920s, 7 ½ In.	280.00
Vase, Martele, Fan, Line 700, Blue Wash, 6 ½ In.	124.00

CONTEMPORARY GLASS, see *Glass-Contemporary.*

Compact, Gold, 18K, Blue Enamel, Mirror, Art Deco, H. Dubret, 2 ⅜ x 1 ¾ In. $3555.00

Skinner, Inc.

Cookie Jar, LaGardo Tackett, 2 Openings, Face Decorated Lids, Wrapped Handle, Schmid, 1958, 13 x 11 In. $406.00

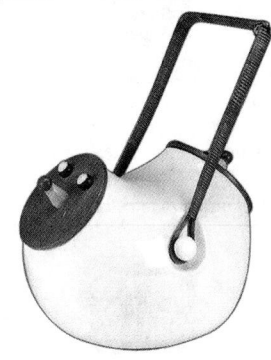

Los Angeles Modern Auctions

Copeland, Bust, Clytie, Pedestal, Impressed Mark, Parian, c.1886, 22 In. $2015.00

Skinner, Inc.

TIP

Remove pencil marks and other smudges with a Mr. Clean Magic Eraser or Scotch-Brite Easy Erasing Pad.

Copeland, Bust, The Bride, Veil, Pedestal, Inscribed, Crystal Palace Art Union, Parian, c.1875, 14 ¼ In.
$2726.00

Skinner, Inc.

Copeland, Figurine, Nude, Daphne, Leaning On Vine Wrapped Stump, Parian, England, c.1865, 21 ¾ In.
$504.00

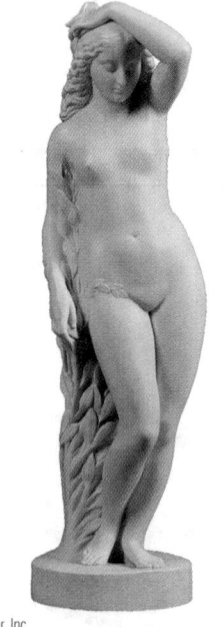

Skinner, Inc.

Copeland, Fruit Cooler, Lid, Strawberry Vines, Strawberry Finial, Twisted Handles, 1800s, 10 In., Pair
$2390.00

Neal Auction Co.

COOKBOOKS are collected for various reasons. Some are wanted for the recipes, some for investment, and some as examples of advertising. Cookbooks and recipe pamphlets are included in this category.

Arm & Hammer Baking Soda Cook Book, 1951, 6 x 4 ½ In., 18 Pages	10.00
Armour Ham Recipe Book, 60 Ways To Serve Armour's Star Hams, 26 Pages, 5 x 6 In.	10.00
Art Of Cooking & Serving, Sarah Field Splint, 1934, 254 Pages	18.00
Betty Crocker Cookbook & Linen, 1st Edition Hardcover, Spiral, 1965, 153 Pages	39.00
Betty Crocker, New Method Cake Recipes, 54 Party Cakes, 1946, 6 x 5 In.	8.00
Betty Crocker's Cookbook For Boys & Girls, Golden Books, 1978, 160 Pages	10.00
Betty Crocker's Cooky Carnival Cook Book, Copyright General Mills, 1957, 6 x 9 In.	12.00
Betty Crocker's Do-Ahead, 1st Edition, Color, General Mills, 1972, 160 Pages	40.00
Betty Crocker's Good & Easy, 1st Edition, Golden Press, 1971, 158 Pages	90.00
Betty Crocker's Microware Cookbook, Hardcover, Random House, 1981, 288 Pages	25.00
Betty Crocker's Picture Cook Book, 1st Edition, McGraw-Hill, 1950, Binder	54.00
Bride's Cookbook, San Francisco 1911, 1st Edition, Hardcover, 9 x 6 In.	43.00
Carnation Recipe Booklet, 100 Glorified Recipes, 1931, 5 x 7 In., 36 Pages	30.00
Christmas Goodies, Softcover, Random House, 8 x 10 In., 32 Pages	14.00
Cooking Magic, 500 Snacks, 250 Pies, Hardcover, 1956	100.00
Cooking The Scandinavian Way, Hardbound, c.1945, 260 Pages	9.95
Davis Cookbook, The Pure Food Kind, 1904	25.00
Del Monte Peaches Recipe Booklet, From California Packing Corp., 16 Pages, 1927, 5 x 6 In.	12.00
Dinah Shore Cook Book, By Dinah Shore, Dinah On Cover, c.1983, 500 Recipes	15.00
Fannie Farmer Junior Cook Book By Wilma Lord Perkins, Hardcover, 1944	24.00
Fun To Cook Book, Copyright 1974 Carnation Company, 48 Pages	25.00
Good Housekeeping Christmas Cookbook, Hearst Corp., 1967, 64 Pages	12.00
Jell-O Recipe Book, Through The Menu, Cherry Flavor On Cover, 1927, 4 x 5 In.	22.00
Jessie Marie Deboth's Cookbook, 1940, 6 x 8 In., 192 Pages	18.00
Joy Of Cooking, Hardback, Dust Jacket, 4300 Recipes, 1962, 849 Pages	65.00
Master Chefs Cookbook, Horn Of Plenty, 1964, 284 Pages	27.00
New Good Housekeeping, Hardcover, Dust Jacket, 1986, 10 x 9 In.	28.00
Perfect Hostess Cookbook, Mildred O. Knopf, 1972, 8 x 5 In., 499 Pages	32.00
Pet-Ritz Pie Shell Creations, Copyright 1979, Meredith Corp., 96 Pages	14.00
Philip Harben's Cookery Encyclopedic, 1955, 9 x 6 In., 480 Pages	47.00
Piggly Wiggly Supermarket Cookbook, 1920s, 220 Pages	15.00
Planning 1095 Meals A Year, Williams Bakery, c.1933, 24 Pages	6.95
Saturday Evening Post, All American Cookbook, 9 x 8 In., 96 Pages	15.00
Seagram's, Week End Bar & Barbecue, Softcover, 1960s, 34 Pages	10.00
Shredded Wheat, From The Field To The Table, 1911, 5 x 7 In., 84 Pages	25.00
Sixty-Five Delicious Dishes Made With Bread, The Fleischmann Co., 1919, 7 x 5 In., 32 Pages.	28.00
Star-Kist Tuna Recipe & Fact Book, Tuna Clipper On Cover, 1940s, 5 x 6 In.	15.00
The Cook Is In The Parlour, By Marguerite Gilbert McCarthy, 1947, 309 Pages	20.00
The New Connecticut Cookbook, 1st Edition, Woman's Club Of Westport, 1947, 338 Pages.	250.00
Trader Vic's Pacific Island Cook Book, Hardboard, Doubleday & Co., 1968, 6 x 9 In.	12.00
What Makes Jelly Jell?, General Foods, Softcover, 1951, 23 Pages	14.00
Williamsburg Art Of Cookery, By Helen Bullock, First Edition, 1938, 176 Pages	65.00
Wilton Cake Decorating Book, Celebrate, Wilton Enterprises, 1963, 160 Pages, 11 x 8 In.	12.00
Women's Evening Club, Brattleboro, Vermont, Spiral Bound, 1964, 100 Pages	15.00
Yes, Jell-O, Please, All Seven Flavors, Rose O'Neil, 1912, 6 x 4 In., 14 Pages	45.00

COOKIE JARS with brightly painted designs or amusing figural shapes became popular in the mid-1930s. Many companies made them and collectors search for cookie jars either by design or by maker's name. Listed here are examples by the less common makers. Major factories are listed under their own names in other categories of the book, such as Abingdon, Brush, Hull, McCoy, Metlox, Red Wing, and Shawnee. See also the Disneyana category.

Barn, Red Roof, Animals, Regal China, 12 x 14 In.	115.00
Clock Face, Sierra Vista, 10 ½ x 6 ½ In.	83.00
Cottage, Yellow, Blue Boar, Old Morris China Co., 8 In.	48.00
Dog, Toothache, American Bisque Co., 1950s, 14 In.	675.00
Flower Bouquet, Wood Lid, Hyalyn Pottery, c.1960	29.00
Fruit, Decal, Elephant Ear Handles, c.1940, 9 ½ In.	75.00
Goldilocks, Baby Bear, Regal, 13 In.	175.00
Jug Shape, Flowers, Cork Finial, Shawnee Pottery, 8 In.	170.00
Kool Aid Face, c.1934, 8 In.	113.00
LaGardo Tackett, 2 Openings, Face Decorated Lids, Wrapped Handle, Schmid, 1958, 13 x 11 In. *illus*	406.00
Leprechaun, Smiling, Pot Of Gold, U.S.A., 13 ¾ In.	95.00

Majic Bunny, Hat, American Bisque, 1950s, 12 ¼ In.	95.00
Mammy, Chrysanthemum Scarf, Gilt, c.1950, 11 In.	153.00
Merry-Go-Round, Elephant, Lion, Yellow, Red, American Bisque Co., 1950s, 10 In.	285.00
Owl, Holding Book, Tasseled Cap, Glasses, American Bisque Co., c.1958	160.00
Owl, On Stump, Winking, Mushrooms, Flowers, California Originals, 14 In.	50.00
Pig, In Wheelchair, Reading Book, 5 In.	55.00
Pig Head, Smiling, Rosy Cheeks, Top Hat, Polka Dot Tie, Japan, 7 ¼ In.	68.00
Rabbit, Holding Carrot, Green, Ribbed Lid, 1950s, 9 ¼ In.	47.00
Rooster, Crowing, White, Red, Purinton, 11 ½ In.	23.00

COORS ware was made by the Coors Porcelain Company of Golden, Colorado, a company founded with the help of the Coors Brewing Company. Its founder, John Herold, started the Herold China and Pottery Company in 1910. The company name was changed in 1920, when Herold left. Dishes were made from the turn of the century. Coors stopped making nonessential wares at the start of World War II. After the war, the pottery made ovenware, teapots, vases, and a general line of pottery, but no dinnerware—except for special orders. The company is still in business making industrial porcelain. For more prices, go to kovels.com.

COORS U.S.A.

Basket, Flower Frog, Pink, Ribbed, Handle, c.1935, 5 x 6 x 6 In.	38.00
Casserole, Rosebud Pattern, Lid, 8 ¾ x 4 ¾ In.	42.00
Creamer, Pink, Mello-Tone, 2 ½ x 5 In.	20.00
Pitcher, Octagonal, Square Knobbed Cover, Blossoms, Stems, Thermo, 7 ½ In.	105.00
Planter, Blue, Footed, 1930s, 9 x 3 In.	35.00
Planter, Rosebud, Turquoise, 1930s, 2 ½ x 3 ½ In.	26.00
Platter, Blue Trim, 20 x 8 In.	20.00
Vase, Shouldered, 2 Handles, Yellow, 1930s, 8 In.	95.00

COPELAND pieces listed here are those that have a mark including the word *Copeland* used between 1847 and 1976. Marks include *Copeland Spode* and *Copeland & Garrett*. See also Copeland Spode, Royal Worcester, and Spode.

Bust, Clytie, Pedestal, Impressed Mark, Parian, c.1886, 22 In. ....*illus*	2015.00
Bust, The Bride, Veil, Pedestal, Inscribed, Crystal Palace Art Union, Parian, c.1875, 14 ¼ In. ..... *illus*	2726.00
Bust, Woman, Spring, Parian, Impressed Mark, 12 x 7 x 5 ¼ In.	127.00
Figurine, Diana With Child, Seated, Panther, Oval Base, Inscribed, 1866, 19 In.	375.00
Figurine, Nude, Daphne, Leaning On Vine Wrapped Stump, Parian, England, c.1865, 21 ¾ In. ...*illus*	504.00
Figurine, Seminude, Nymph, Seated Among Tall Grass, Hand Mirror, Urn, Frog, 1800s, 9 In.	711.00
Fruit Cooler, Lid, Strawberry Vines, Strawberry Finial, Twisted Handles, 1800s, 10 In., Pair ...*illus*	2390.00
Garden Seat, Cobalt Blue Ground, Green Stylized Acanthus, Flared Rim, 20 In.	1725.00
Jug, Lotus, Cobalt Blue, Majolica, 8 ½ In.	384.00
Jug, Putti, Collecting Grapes, Drinking, Footed, Handle, c.1850, 8 In.	156.00
Plate, Blue Borders, Raised Flowers, 10 ½ In., 12 Piece	150.00
Shelf, Bracket, Ivy, Majolica, 7 ¼ x 9 In.	944.00

COPELAND SPODE appears on some pieces of nineteenth-century English porcelain. Josiah Spode established a pottery at Stoke-on-Trent, England, in 1770. In 1833, the firm was purchased by William Copeland and Thomas Garrett and the mark was changed. In 1847, Copeland became the sole owner and the mark changed again. W.T. Copeland & Sons continued until a 1976 merger when it became Royal Worcester Spode. The company was bought by the Portmeirion Group in 2009. Pieces are listed in this book under the name that appears in the mark. Copeland, Royal Worcester, and Spode have separate listings.

COPELAND
SPODE
ENGLAND

Cake Plate, Zoo Animals, Blue, Round Corners, Scalloped Rim, c.1890, 5 x 5 In.	125.00
Pitcher, Chicago, Historical Views, Jasperware, Frank E. Burley, 8 ½ In. ....*illus*	305.00
Plate, Dinner, Scalloped Rim, Rose Design, Ivory Ground, Gilt, 1900s, 11 In. Diam., 12 Piece.	89.00
Vase, Baluster, 1800s Women Visiting, Scroll Handles, Gilt, c.1900, 17 x 8 In.	1912.00

COPPER has been used to make utilitarian items, such as teakettles and cooking pans, since the days of the early American colonists. Copper became a popular metal with the Arts & Crafts makers of the early 1900s, and decorative pieces, like desk sets, were made. Other pieces of copper may be found in Arts & Crafts, Bradley & Hubbard, Kitchen, Roycroft, and other categories.

Aquarium, Hexagonal, Glass, Brass Finials, Ceramic Base, 1900s, 60 In.	960.00
Bed Warmer, Brass, Round, Hinged, Wood Handle, c.1885, 38 x 12 In.	61.00
Bed Warmer, Hot Water, Oval, Threaded Brass Cap, 5 ½ x 12 ½ In.	24.00
Bed Warmer, Round, Pierced, Shaped Handle, France, 32 ½ x 9 ½ In.	120.00
Boiler, Fish, Dovetailed, Bail Handles, 6 x 11 x 20 In.	354.00
Boiler, Incised Bands, Handles, 13 x 27 In.	120.00

Copeland Spode, Pitcher, Chicago, Historical Views, Jasperware, Frank E. Burley, 8 ½ In.
$305.00

Leslie Hindman Auctioneers

Copper, Bowl, Cover, Stone Arrowheads, Silver, Horn, Heinrichs, Shreve & Co., 7 ½ x 9 In.
$19840.00

Rago Arts & Auction Center

Copper, Chafing Dish, Lid, Hammered, Brass, Silver, Rabbits, Oak Base, Jos. Heinrichs, 12 x 19 In.
$2604.00

Rago Arts & Auction Center

Copper, Coal Scuttle, Lid, Hammered, Pearson, Inscribed JP, 1905, 14 ½ x 17 ½ In.
$5890.00

Rago Arts & Auction Center

C

Copper, Cuspidor, Figural, Turtle
$207.00

Showtime Auction Services

Copper, Kettle, Dome Lid, Gooseneck,
Dovetailed, Brass Handle, Acorn Finial,
1800s, 11 ⅔ In.
$53.00

Conestoga Auction Co., Inc.

Copper, Tankard, Arts & Crafts, Brass,
Footed, 22 In.
$450.00

Treadway Toomey Galleries

Bowl, Begging, Arabic Text Panels, Persia, 1800s, 12 In.	415.00
Bowl, Cover, Stone Arrowheads, Silver, Horn, Heinrichs, Shreve & Co., 7 ½ x 9 In. ....*illus*	19840.00
Bowl, Hammered, Novick, 7 ½ x 3 ½ In.	330.00
Bowl, Iron Handles, Continental, c.1925, 10 ½ In.	430.00
Box, Hammered, Aluminum Hardware, Arts & Crafts, 1920s, 6 ¼ x 2 ½ In.	600.00
Box, Hammered, Scroll Latch, Harry Dixon, 1 ¾ x 5 ¾ In.	992.00
Brazier, Brass Highlights, Pierced Cover, Brass Eagle Finial, Pedestal, 1800s, 36 x 22 In.	234.00
Bucket, Brass Mounts, Round, Tapered, Iron Swing Handle, 13 x 17 ½ In.	276.00
Bucket, Coal, Wrought Iron, G. Stickley, Marked, c.1905, 24 In.	12101.00
Bucket, Hand Hammered, Footed, Brass Loop Handle, Silver Scroll Design, 1900s, 18 x 13 In.	59.00
Cauldron, Hammered, Wrought Iron, Rolled Rim, Bail Handles, Turkey, 11 x 14 In.	276.00
Chafing Dish, Hammered, Oak Base, Lid, Marked, Charles Rohlfs, 15 x 13 ½ In.	496.00
Chafing Dish, Lid, Hammered, Brass, Silver, Rabbits, Oak Base, Jos. Heinrichs, 12 x 19 In. ....*illus*	2604.00
Clothes Boiler, Handles, c.1900, 14 x 28 x 12 In.	106.00
Coal Scuttle, Lid, Hammered, Pearson, Inscribed JP, 1905, 14 ½ x 17 ½ In. ......*illus*	5890.00
Coffee Service, Coffeepot, Sugar, Cover, Creamer, Tray, Geometric Design, 4 Piece	186.00
Coffeepot, Dome Lid, Gooseneck, Cone Shape, Wasted Body, Flared Foot, C-Handle, c.1850, 11 In.	170.00
Cup, Molded, Oval, Ruffled Rim, Applied Silver Flowering Branch, Gorham, 2 ½ In.	296.00
Cup, Presentation, Horn Handles, Silver Trim, J. Heinrichs, Marsellus & Pitt, 1903, 6 x 9 ½ In.	5580.00
Cuspidor, Figural, Turtle ......*illus*	207.00
Ewer, Asian, Embossed Brass, Mythical Animal Handle, Chain, Lid, 41 x 32 In.	336.00
Ewer, Lid, Tapered, Middle East, c.1910, 22 In.	59.00
Fountain, Hammered, Spigot, 2 Piece, Shaped Walnut Back, 1800s, 42 x 18 x 16 In.	366.00
Funnel, Lash's Bitters Co., c.1890, 7 ½ In.	83.00
Hand Warmer, Pierced Lid, Chrysanthemums, Leaves, Swing Handle, Japan, 5 ½ x 9 In.	176.00
Head, Elk, Patinated, Mounted, c.1895, 35 x 33 In.	4266.00
Humidor, Egyptian Head Form, Molded, Top Lifts, Copper Liner, 7 x 7 x 6 In.	369.00
Humidor, Hammered, Applied Lightning Bolts, Stone Finial, Arts & Crafts, Cylindrical, R.F., 5 x 7 In.	300.00
Kettle, Apple Butter, 2 Handles, Dovetailed, 19 In.	232.00
Kettle, Dome Lid, Gooseneck, Dovetailed, Brass Handle, Acorn Finial, 1800s, 11 ⅔ In. ....*illus*	53.00
Kettle, Gooseneck Spout, Iron Swing Handle, 1800s, 11 In.	385.00
Kettle, Round, Smokestack, Ring Handles, 13 ¼ x 17 In.	122.00
Kettle, Swing Handle, Iron Mounts, Stand, 1800s, 29 ½ In.	480.00
Kettle, Wrought Iron Tilter, Cupped Cap, Brass Knob, Hinged Spout Cover, Swing Handle, 9 x 10 In.	944.00
Lavabo, Embossed, Lidded Tank, Cartouche Panel, Lion Supports, Brass Spigots, c.1890, 17 x 12 In.	184.00
Lavabo, Lidded Tank, Repousse, Engraved, Brass, France, 1800s, 77 x 14 ½ In.	540.00
Molds are listed in the Kitchen category.	
Money Clip, Ceremonial Indian Dancer Head, Mexico, c.1945, 2 ½ In.	45.00
Pail, Apple Butter, Dovetail Base, Iron Bail, 1800s, 20 ½ x 26 In.	558.00
Pan, 2 Applied Handles, Rounded Corners, France, 6 x 20 x 16 In.	270.00
Pan, Brass Mounts, Handles, Round, 5 x 14 In.	399.00
Pan, Elongated, Rounded Corners, Shaped Handle, France, 4 ½ x 20 x 6 ½ In.	120.00
Pen Stand, Grape & Leaf Pattern, Reticulated Tray, 6 Bun Feet, Slag Glass, Riviere Studios....	68.00
Penholder, Hammered, Walrus Tusk Base, Albert Berry, 1 x 5 ½ In.	806.00
Plaque, Red Jacket, Seneca Chief, Embossed Wooded Scene, Frame, c.1950, 5 x 6 In.	2500.00
Plaque, Stylized Female Head, Hammered Ground, Beaded Ring, Art Deco Style, 12 In., Pair.	98.00
Plaque, Trees, Landscape, Oval, Signed, Hans Jauchen, March 10, 1930, 27 x 21 ½ In.	2480.00
Plate, Hammered, Free-Form Rim, Old Mission Kopperkraft, 6 In.	240.00
Pot, Cover, Spigot, 2 Handles, Bucket Shape, France, 15 ½ x 17 ½ x 18 In.	180.00
Pot, Cover, Wrought Iron Handle, France, c.1890, 18 ½ In.	413.00
Pot, Rice, 2 Handles, Cover, Barrel Shape, Hammered, 28 x 18 In.	295.00
Pot, Sauce, Lid, Dovetailed, Iron Handle, Tin Lining, c.1800, 8 x 14 x 22 In.	553.00
Sculpture, Buddha, Seated, Lotus Throne, Incised Base, Silvered, Chinese, 6 In.	889.00
Sculpture, Lion's Head, Green, c.1800, 12 x 13 In.	288.00
Shield, Wall Hanging, Figural Battle Scene, Polished, c.1920, 25 x 18 In.	403.00
Tankard, Arts & Crafts, Brass, Footed, 22 In. ......*illus*	450.00
Teakettle, Dovetail Construction, Swing Handle, Signed, Ward, Hartford, c.1850, 8 In.	1763.00
Teakettle, Gooseneck Spout, Bail Handle, Cover, Brass Finial, 1800s, 5 ¾ In.	316.00
Teakettle, High Wrought Iron Swing Handle, Dutch, 13 In.	69.00
Teakettle, Impressed L. Babb, Reading, Pa., c.1820, 12 ½ In.	237.00
Teakettle, Incised Pinwheel Lid, Pa., 1800s, Miniature, 6 In.	316.00
Teakettle, Lid, Gooseneck Spout, Handle, Schaum, 1800s, 9 In.	600.00
Teakettle, Signed R.M. Strattin & Co., 1800s, 11 In.	345.00
Teakettle, Stamped John Lay, York, Pa., 14 ¼ In.	1422.00
Teakettle, Swing Handle, Eagles Stamp, 1831, 14 In.	345.00
Teapot, Pewter Handle & Spout, Marked Rochester Stamping Works, N.Y., 8 ½ In.	145.00

COPPER

C

Copper, Cuspidor, Figural, Turtle
$207.00

Showtime Auction Services

Copper, Kettle, Dome Lid, Gooseneck, Dovetailed, Brass Handle, Acorn Finial, 1800s, 11 ⅔ In.
$53.00

Conestoga Auction Co., Inc.

Copper, Tankard, Arts & Crafts, Brass, Footed, 22 In.
$450.00

Treadway Toomey Galleries

Bowl, Begging, Arabic Text Panels, Persia, 1800s, 12 In.	415.00
Bowl, Cover, Stone Arrowheads, Silver, Horn, Heinrichs, Shreve & Co., 7 ½ x 9 In. ....*illus*	19840.00
Bowl, Hammered, Novick, 7 ½ x 3 ½ In.	330.00
Bowl, Iron Handles, Continental, c.1925, 10 ½ In.	430.00
Box, Hammered, Aluminum Hardware, Arts & Crafts, 1920s, 6 ¼ x 2 ½ In.	600.00
Box, Hammered, Scroll Latch, Harry Dixon, 1 ¾ x 5 ¾ In.	992.00
Brazier, Brass Highlights, Pierced Cover, Brass Eagle Finial, Pedestal, 1800s, 36 x 22 In.	234.00
Bucket, Brass Mounts, Round, Tapered, Iron Swing Handle, 13 x 17 ½ In.	276.00
Bucket, Coal, Wrought Iron, G. Stickley, Marked, c.1905, 24 In.	12101.00
Bucket, Hand Hammered, Footed, Brass Loop Handle, Silver Scroll Design, 1900s, 18 x 13 In.	59.00
Cauldron, Hammered, Wrought Iron, Rolled Rim, Bail Handles, Turkey, 11 x 14 In.	276.00
Chafing Dish, Hammered, Oak Base, Lid, Marked, Charles Rohlfs, 15 x 13 ½ In.	496.00
Chafing Dish, Lid, Hammered, Brass, Silver, Rabbits, Oak Base, Jos. Heinrichs, 12 x 19 In. ....*illus*	2604.00
Clothes Boiler, Handles, c.1900, 14 x 28 x 12 In.	106.00
Coal Scuttle, Lid, Hammered, Pearson, Inscribed JP, 1905, 14 ½ x 17 ½ In. ....*illus*	5890.00
Coffee Service, Coffeepot, Sugar, Cover, Creamer, Tray, Geometric Design, 4 Piece	186.00
Coffeepot, Dome Lid, Gooseneck, Cone Shape, Wasted Body, Flared Foot, C-Handle, c.1850, 11 In.	170.00
Cup, Molded, Oval, Ruffled Rim, Applied Silver Flowering Branch, Gorham, 2 ½ In.	296.00
Cup, Presentation, Horn Handles, Silver Trim, J. Heinrichs, Marsellus & Pitt, 1903, 6 x 9 ½ In.	5580.00
Cuspidor, Figural, Turtle ....*illus*	207.00
Ewer, Asian, Embossed Brass, Mythical Animal Handle, Chain, Lid, 41 x 32 In.	336.00
Ewer, Lid, Tapered, Middle East, c.1910, 22 In.	59.00
Fountain, Hammered, Spigot, 2 Piece, Shaped Walnut Back, 1800s, 42 x 18 x 16 In.	366.00
Funnel, Lash's Bitters Co., c.1890, 7 ½ In.	83.00
Hand Warmer, Pierced Lid, Chrysanthemums, Leaves, Swing Handle, Japan, 5 ½ x 9 In.	176.00
Head, Elk, Patinated, Mounted, c.1895, 35 x 33 In.	4266.00
Humidor, Egyptian Head Form, Molded, Top Lifts, Copper Liner, 7 x 7 x 6 In.	369.00
Humidor, Hammered, Applied Lightning Bolts, Stone Finial, Arts & Crafts, Cylindrical, R.F., 5 x 7 In.	300.00
Kettle, Apple Butter, 2 Handles, Dovetailed, 19 In.	232.00
Kettle, Dome Lid, Gooseneck, Dovetailed, Brass Handle, Acorn Finial, 1800s, 11 ⅔ In. ....*illus*	53.00
Kettle, Gooseneck Spout, Iron Swing Handle, 1800s, 11 In.	385.00
Kettle, Round, Smokestack, Ring Handles, 13 ¼ x 17 In.	122.00
Kettle, Swing Handle, Iron Mounts, Stand, 1800s, 29 ½ In.	480.00
Kettle, Wrought Iron Tilter, Cupped Cap, Brass Knob, Hinged Spout Cover, Swing Handle, 9 x 10 In.	944.00
Lavabo, Embossed, Lidded Tank, Cartouche Panel, Lion Supports, Brass Spigots, c.1890, 17 x 12 In.	184.00
Lavabo, Lidded Tank, Repousse, Engraved, Brass, France, 1800s, 77 x 14 ½ In.	540.00
Molds are listed in the Kitchen category.	
Money Clip, Ceremonial Indian Dancer Head, Mexico, c.1945, 2 ½ In.	45.00
Pail, Apple Butter, Dovetail Base, Iron Bail, 1800s, 20 ½ x 26 In.	558.00
Pan, 2 Applied Handles, Rounded Corners, France, 6 x 20 x 16 In.	270.00
Pan, Brass Mounts, Handles, Round, 5 x 14 In.	399.00
Pan, Elongated, Rounded Corners, Shaped Handle, France, 4 ½ x 20 x 6 ½ In.	120.00
Pen Stand, Grape & Leaf Pattern, Reticulated Tray, 6 Bun Feet, Slag Glass, Riviere Studios....	68.00
Penholder, Hammered, Walrus Tusk Base, Albert Berry, 1 x 5 ½ In.	806.00
Plaque, Red Jacket, Seneca Chief, Embossed Wooded Scene, Frame, c.1950, 5 x 6 In.	2500.00
Plaque, Stylized Female Head, Hammered Ground, Beaded Ring, Art Deco Style, 12 In., Pair.	98.00
Plaque, Trees, Landscape, Oval, Signed, Hans Jauchen, March 10, 1930, 27 x 21 ½ In.	2480.00
Plate, Hammered, Free-Form Rim, Old Mission Kopperkraft, 6 In.	240.00
Pot, Cover, Spigot, 2 Handles, Bucket Shape, France, 15 ½ x 17 ½ x 18 In.	180.00
Pot, Cover, Wrought Iron Handle, France, c.1890, 18 ½ In.	413.00
Pot, Rice, 2 Handles, Cover, Barrel Shape, Hammered, 28 x 18 In.	295.00
Pot, Sauce, Lid, Dovetailed, Iron Handle, Tin Lining, c.1800, 8 x 14 x 22 In.	553.00
Sculpture, Buddha, Seated, Lotus Throne, Incised Base, Silvered, Chinese, 6 In.	889.00
Sculpture, Lion's Head, Green, c.1800, 12 x 13 In.	288.00
Shield, Wall Hanging, Figural Battle Scene, Polished, c.1920, 25 x 18 In.	403.00
Tankard, Arts & Crafts, Brass, Footed, 22 In. ....*illus*	450.00
Teakettle, Dovetail Construction, Swing Handle, Signed, Ward, Hartford, c.1850, 8 In.	1763.00
Teakettle, Gooseneck Spout, Bail Handle, Cover, Brass Finial, 1800s, 5 ¾ In.	316.00
Teakettle, High Wrought Iron Swing Handle, Dutch, 13 In.	69.00
Teakettle, Impressed L. Babb, Reading, Pa., c.1820, 12 ½ In.	237.00
Teakettle, Incised Pinwheel Lid, Pa., 1800s, Miniature, 6 In.	316.00
Teakettle, Lid, Gooseneck Spout, Handle, Schaum, 1800s, 9 In.	600.00
Teakettle, Signed R.M. Strattin & Co., 1800s, 11 In.	345.00
Teakettle, Stamped John Lay, York, Pa., 14 ¼ In.	1422.00
Teakettle, Swing Handle, Eagles Stamp, 1831, 14 In.	345.00
Teapot, Pewter Handle & Spout, Marked Rochester Stamping Works, N.Y., 8 ½ In.	145.00

Majic Bunny, Hat, American Bisque, 1950s, 12 ¼ In.	95.00
Mammy, Chrysanthemum Scarf, Gilt, c.1950,11 In.	153.00
Merry-Go-Round, Elephant, Lion, Yellow, Red, American Bisque Co., 1950s, 10 In.	285.00
Owl, Holding Book, Tasseled Cap, Glasses, American Bisque Co., c.1958	160.00
Owl, On Stump, Winking, Mushrooms, Flowers, California Originals, 14 In.	50.00
Pig, In Wheelchair, Reading Book, 5 In.	55.00
Pig Head, Smiling, Rosy Cheeks, Top Hat, Polka Dot Tie, Japan, 7 ¼ In.	68.00
Rabbit, Holding Carrot, Green, Ribbed Lid, 1950s, 9 ¼ In.	47.00
Rooster, Crowing, White, Red, Purinton, 11 ½ In.	23.00

COORS ware was made by the Coors Porcelain Company of Golden, Colorado, a company founded with the help of the Coors Brewing Company. Its founder, John Herold, started the Herold China and Pottery Company in 1910. The company name was changed in 1920, when Herold left. Dishes were made from the turn of the century. Coors stopped making nonessential wares at the start of World War II. After the war, the pottery made ovenware, teapots, vases, and a general line of pottery, but no dinnerware—except for special orders. The company is still in business making industrial porcelain. For more prices, go to kovels.com.

COORS U.S.A.

Basket, Flower Frog, Pink, Ribbed, Handle, c.1935, 5 x 6 x 6 In.	38.00
Casserole, Rosebud Pattern, Lid, 8 ¾ x 4 ¾ In.	42.00
Creamer, Pink, Mello-Tone, 2 ½ x 5 In.	20.00
Pitcher, Octagonal, Square Knobbed Cover, Blossoms, Stems, Thermo, 7 ½ In.	105.00
Planter, Blue, Footed, 1930s, 9 x 3 In.	35.00
Planter, Rosebud, Turquoise, 1930s, 2 ½ x 3 ½ In.	26.00
Platter, Blue Trim, 20 x 8 In.	20.00
Vase, Shouldered, 2 Handles, Yellow, 1930s, 8 In.	95.00

COPELAND pieces listed here are those that have a mark including the word *Copeland* used between 1847 and 1976. Marks include *Copeland Spode* and *Copeland & Garrett.* See also Copeland Spode, Royal Worcester, and Spode.

Bust, Clytie, Pedestal, Impressed Mark, Parian, c.1886, 22 In. ....*illus*	2015.00
Bust, The Bride, Veil, Pedestal, Inscribed, Crystal Palace Art Union, Parian, c.1875, 14 ¼ In. ...... *illus*	2726.00
Bust, Woman, Spring, Parian, Impressed Mark, 12 x 7 x 5 ¼ In.	127.00
Figurine, Diana With Child, Seated, Panther, Oval Base, Inscribed, 1866, 19 In.	375.00
Figurine, Nude, Daphne, Leaning On Vine Wrapped Stump, Parian, England, c.1865, 21 ¾ In. ...*illus*	504.00
Figurine, Seminude, Nymph, Seated Among Tall Grass, Hand Mirror, Urn, Frog, 1800s, 9 In.	711.00
Fruit Cooler, Lid, Strawberry Vines, Strawberry Finial, Twisted Handles, 1800s, 10 In., Pair ...*illus*	2390.00
Garden Seat, Cobalt Blue Ground, Green Stylized Acanthus, Flared Rim, 20 In.	1725.00
Jug, Lotus, Cobalt Blue, Majolica, 8 ½ In.	384.00
Jug, Putti, Collecting Grapes, Drinking, Footed, Handle, c.1850, 8 In.	156.00
Plate, Blue Borders, Raised Flowers, 10 ½ In., 12 Piece	150.00
Shelf, Bracket, Ivy, Majolica, 7 ¼ x 9 In.	944.00

COPELAND SPODE appears on some pieces of nineteenth-century English porcelain. Josiah Spode established a pottery at Stoke-on-Trent, England, in 1770. In 1833, the firm was purchased by William Copeland and Thomas Garrett and the mark was changed. In 1847, Copeland became the sole owner and the mark changed again. W.T. Copeland & Sons continued until a 1976 merger when it became Royal Worcester Spode. The company was bought by the Portmeirion Group in 2009. Pieces are listed in this book under the name that appears in the mark. Copeland, Royal Worcester, and Spode have separate listings.

COPELAND SPODE ENGLAND

Cake Plate, Zoo Animals, Blue, Round Corners, Scalloped Rim, c.1890, 5 x 5 In.	125.00
Pitcher, Chicago, Historical Views, Jasperware, Frank E. Burley, 8 ½ In. ....*illus*	305.00
Plate, Dinner, Scalloped Rim, Rose Design, Ivory Ground, Gilt, 1900s, 11 In. Diam., 12 Piece.	89.00
Vase, Baluster, 1800s Women Visiting, Scroll Handles, Gilt, c.1900, 17 x 8 In.	1912.00

COPPER has been used to make utilitarian items, such as teakettles and cooking pans, since the days of the early American colonists. Copper became a popular metal with the Arts & Crafts makers of the early 1900s, and decorative pieces, like desk sets, were made. Other pieces of copper may be found in Arts & Crafts, Bradley & Hubbard, Kitchen, Roycroft, and other categories.

Aquarium, Hexagonal, Glass, Brass Finials, Ceramic Base, 1900s, 60 In.	960.00
Bed Warmer, Brass, Round, Hinged, Wood Handle, c.1885, 38 x 12 In.	61.00
Bed Warmer, Hot Water, Oval, Threaded Brass Cap, 5 ½ x 12 ½ In.	24.00
Bed Warmer, Round, Pierced, Shaped Handle, France, 32 ½ x 9 ½ In.	120.00
Boiler, Fish, Dovetailed, Bail Handles, 6 x 11 x 20 In.	354.00
Boiler, Incised Bands, Handles, 13 x 27 In.	120.00

Copeland Spode, Pitcher, Chicago, Historical Views, Jasperware, Frank E. Burley, 8 ½ In.
$305.00

Leslie Hindman Auctioneers

Copper, Bowl, Cover, Stone Arrowheads, Silver, Horn, Heinrichs, Shreve & Co., 7 ½ x 9 In.
$19840.00

Rago Arts & Auction Center

Copper, Chafing Dish, Lid, Hammered, Brass, Silver, Rabbits, Oak Base, Jos. Heinrichs, 12 x 19 In.
$2604.00

Rago Arts & Auction Center

Copper, Coal Scuttle, Lid, Hammered, Pearson, Inscribed JP, 1905, 14 ½ x 17 ½ In.
$5890.00

Rago Arts & Auction Center

Tray, Hammered, Lobed, Silver Hunting Scene In Low Relief, Gorham, 6 x 7 In.	444.00
Vase, Arts & Crafts, Hammered, Footed, Cylindrical, Ring Handles, c.1910, 6 ¼ x 8 ¼ In.	1080.00
Vase, Arts & Crafts, Hammered, Geometric Swirl Base, 4 x 5 ¾ In.	270.00
Vase, Bottle Shape, Birds, Lotus Pads, Japan, 7 In.	427.00
Vase, Hammered, Applied Design, 3 Handles, 9 x 12 In.	390.00
Vase, Hammered, Flared Mouth, Stickley Bros., 7 x 16 ½ In.	1020.00
Vase, Hammered, Horn Shape Handles, Stickley Bros., 11 x 9 ½ In.	1200.00
Vase, Wavy Shape, Impressed Designs, Hammered, Signed H. Wahlen, 6 x 17 In.	165.00

COPPER LUSTER *items are listed in the Luster category.*

CORALENE glass was made by firing many small colored beads on the outside of glassware. It was made in many patterns in the United States and Europe in the 1880s. Reproductions are made today. Coralene-decorated Japanese pottery is listed in the Japanese Coralene category.

Vase, Blossoms, White Ground, 9 ½ In.	210.00
Vase, Bulbous, Seaweed, 7 In.	56.00
Vase, Pink, Pinched Neck, 8 x 4 In.	182.00

CORDEY CHINA COMPANY was founded by Boleslaw Cybis in 1942 in Trenton, New Jersey. The firm produced gift shop items. In 1969 it was acquired by the Lightron Corp. and operated as the Schiller Cordey Co., manufacturers of lamps. About 1950 Boleslaw Cybis began making Cybis porcelains, which are listed in their own category in this book.

Bust, Gentleman, Curled White Hair, Tie, Marked, 6 ½ In.	57.00
Bust, Woman, Gilt Flower & Bow, Marked, 6 In.	46.00
Bust, Woman, Shawl, Pink Flower, Blond Hair, Marked, 6 In.	65.00
Bust, Woman, Tiara, Ruffled Collar, 6 ½ In.	48.00
Figurine, Woman, Flowers In Apron, Basket, Hat, Marked, c.1945, 16 In.	119.00
Figurine, Woman, Oriental, Multicolor, Red Shoe, Gilt, 11 ½ In.	142.00

CORKSCREWS have been needed since the first bottle was sealed with a cork, probably in the seventeenth century. Today collectors search for the early, unusual patented examples or the figural corkscrews of recent years.

African, Carved, Anri, 1920s, 5 ½ In.	495.00
Anchor, Embossed, Grapes, Leaves, Rope, Goblets, Germany, 5 x 4 In.	65.00
Antler Handle, Sterling End Cap, John Hasselbring, 19th Century, 10 ½ In.	325.00
Barrel Handle, Crosshatching, Steel, Ivory, 19th Century, 5 In.	795.00
Boar's Tusk, Upwards Curve, Chrome Cap, 4 ¼ In.	285.00
Bodeker Drug Co., Wood Handle, c.1898	35.00
Brass & Steel, Turned Bone, Boar Bristle Brush, 6 In.	280.00
Compression Spring, Wood, Steel, c.1920, 6 ½ In.	117.00
Double Lever, Buss & Sons, Iron, 7 In.	1293.00
Fawn Foot Handle, Steel Worm, 5 x 4 ¼ In.	34.00
Golf Bag, Cork Lining, Silver Plate Gold Club Screw, R. Blackinton & Co., c.1900, 4 In...........	359.00
Lady's Leg, Celluloid, Pink & White Stockings, 3 ⅝ In. ....*illus*	374.00
Metal, Gnarled Root Handle, Laurent Siret, Rochesfort Loire, 1900s, 6 ½ In.	35.00
Rack & Pinion King Screw, Bone Handle, Brush, England...........................	875.00
Rosewood Handle, Gripping Teeth, Brush	265.00
Spring Bell, Bennit Cap Style, Germany...	225.00
Wood Handle, Williamson Co., c.1898	35.00
Wood, France, c.1850, 7 In.	100.00
Yankee, No. 7, Nickel Plated Cast Iron, Hand Operated, Table Clamp, Gilchrist, c.1913 ...*illus*	334.00

CORONATION souvenirs have been made since the 1800s. Pottery, glass, tin, silver, and paper objects with a picture of the monarchs and date have been sold at many coronations. The pieces that mention King Edward VIII, the king who was never crowned, are not rare; collectors should be sure to check values before buying. Related pieces are found in the Commemorative category.

Beaker, Czar Nicholas II, Imperial 2-Headed Eagle, Enamel, 1896, 4 In...........................	850.00
Beaker, King Edward VII, Portrait, Enamel, Gold Band, 1902, 3 ⅞ In.	55.00
Box, Button, King Edward VII, Carriage, Bells, Scrolls, Pierced Silver, W. Comyns & Sons, 1902	695.00
Bracelet, Queen Elizabeth II, Coin Medallions, Links, Goldtone, 1953, 8 x ¾ In.......................	75.00
Compact, King George VII, Embossed Cameo King, Queen Portrait, Silver Plate, 1937, 1 ¾ In.	30.00
Compact, Queen Elizabeth II, Crown, Multicolor, Black Ground, Stratton Of England, 1953, 3 In.	65.00
Cookie Jar, King George VI, Sepia Portraits, Flags, Gilt Detail, 1937, 7 ½ In.	85.00

C

Corkscrew, Lady's Leg, Celluloid, Pink & White Stockings, 3 ⅝ In.
$374.00

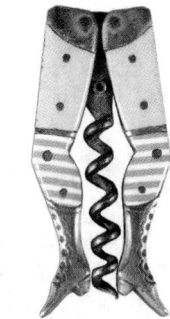

Showtime Auction Services

Corkscrew, Yankee, No. 7, Nickel Plated Cast Iron, Hand Operated, Table Clamp, Gilchrist, c.1913
$334.00

Auction Team Breker

Coverlet, Jacquard, Circle, Birds, Flowers, Cream, Black, Red, Fringe, 1852, 76 x 86 In.
$558.00

Garth's Auctions, Inc.

Coverlet, Jacquard, Red, White, Wool, Cotton, Absalom Klinger, Berks County, 1859, 92 x 88 In.
$71.00

Conestoga Auction Co., Inc.

Coverlet, Jacquard, Roses, Grapevines, Geometric, Wool, Cotton, Joseph Turnbaugh, Pa., 1851, 80 In.
$118.00

Conestoga Auction Co., Inc.

Coverlet, Jacquard, Wool & Cotton, Blue White, Birds Young, Buildings Border, c.1850, 73 x 83 In.
$176.00

Garth's Auctions, Inc.

Cowan, Bookends, Camel, Mottled Green & Brown Crackle Glaze, Marked, 8 ½ In.
$920.00

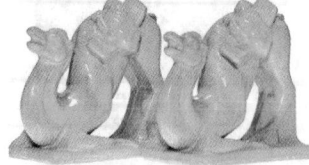

Humler & Nolan

Cup, King Edward VII, Base Queen Alexandra Lithophane Portrait, Gilt Rim, 1902, 2 ¾ In.	125.00
Dish, King Edward VII, Red Military Uniform, Scalloped Edge, Gilt, Royal Doulton, 1902, 6 In.	75.00
Fan, King Edward VII, Carlton Hotel, Crown, Flowers, Wood, Gilt, Signed H. Daudet, 1902, 11 In.	795.00
Jug, King George V, Figural, King & Queen Mary, Multicolor, Porcelain, 1911, 6 In., Pair	145.00
Jug, Queen Elizabeth II, Poole, 1953, 4 ½ In.	87.00
Jug, Queen Elizabeth, Poole, 1953	70.00
Jug, Queen Victoria, Blue Glazed, Full Portrait, Embossed, Wavy Rim, 1838, 7 ½ In.	550.00
Jug, Toby, King George VI, Bust, Military Attire, Royal Winton Grimwades Co., 1937, 2 ½ x 3 In.	98.00
Mug, King George VI, 2 Portraits, Flags, Crown, White Ground, 1937, 2 ¾ In.	100.00
Mug, King George VI, Horse, Grand National Race & Coronation, Royal Doulton, 1937, 5 ½ In.	185.00
Mug, Queen Elizabeth II, Black Transfer, Heraldic, Gold Trim, R. Guyatt, Wedgwood, 1953, 4 In.	65.00
Mug, Queen Victoria, Purple Transfer Portrait, Swansea, 1838, 2 ⅞ In.	975.00
Photographs In Nutshell, King George VI, Lacquered Case, 16 Photos, Box, 1937, 2 ½ x 1 ¾ In.	127.00
Pin, Crown, Queen Elizabeth II, Glass, Metal, Trifari, 1953	295.00
Pin, Lapel, King William IV, Shield Design, Enameled Stones, Multicolor, Round, 1830, 1 ¼ In.	195.00
Plaque, Queen Elizabeth II, Portrait, Porcelain, Round, 1953, 3 x 3 ¼ In.	75.00
Plate, King George V, Portraits, Countries Of Empire, Flow Blue, Royal Doulton, 1911, 10 ½ In.	135.00
Plate, King George VI, Pressed Glass, Beaded Dates, Etched, 1937, 9 ¾ In.	90.00
Plate, Queen Elizabeth II, Queen's Profile Portrait, Ivory Ground, Gilt Trim, Myott, 1953, 8 ¾ In.	65.00
Plate, Queen Elizabeth II, Sepia Portrait, Multicolor Surround, Scalloped Gilt Rim, 1953, 10 In.	23.00
Postcard, King George VI, Coronation Day Broadcast Photograph, Black & White, 1937	3.75
Program, King George VI, Maps, Portraits, Symbols, 1937, 11 ¼ x 8 ¼ In., 32 Pages	78.00
Program, Queen Elizabeth II, Canadian Market, Embossed Portraits, 40 Pages, 9 ¾ x 7 In.	68.00
Puzzle, Queen Elizabeth II, Carriage Procession, Wood, Box, 1953, 10 ¼ x 8 ¼ In.	75.00
Spoon, King Edward II, Geometric, Celtic Knot Bowl, Gold Wash, Sterling, 1902, 4 ¼ In.	40.00
Spoon, King George V, Sterling Ornate Designs, 1911, 4 ¼ In.	75.00
Tea Napkin Set, Queen Elizabeth II, London Scenes, Box, 1953, 6 Piece	55.00
Teaspoon Set, King George VI, Silver Plate, Oneida, 1936, 6 ⅛ In., 6 Piece	35.00
Throne, King Edward VII, Sterling Silver, London, 1936, 2 x 1 ¼ In.	475.00
Tin, Toffee, Queen Elizabeth II, Portraits, Hinged Lid, Blue, Geo. Horner & Co., Eng. 1953, 5 x 4 In.	45.00
Tumbler, King Edward VIII, Red, White, Blue Stripe, Wreath, Portrait, 1936, 4 ½ In.	38.00
Tumbler, King George VI, King & Queen, Portraits, Embossed, 1937, 4 ¼ In.	65.00

COSMOS is a pressed milk glass pattern with colored flowers made from 1894 to 1915 by the Consolidated Lamp and Glass Company. Tablewares and lamps were made in this pattern. A few pieces were also made of clear glass with painted decorations. Other glass patterns are listed under Consolidated Lamp and also in various glass categories. In later years, Cosmos was also made by the Westmoreland Glass Company.

Butter, Daisies, Cover, c.1900, 8 x 6 In.	175.00
Lamp, White, Flowers, Round Globe, Consolidated, 1900s, 15 In.	350.00
Lamp, White, Pink Trim, Pink, Yellow, Blue Flowers, 14 In.	595.00
Tile, Stippled Sapphire Blue, 8 x 4 In.	150.00

COVERLETS were made of linen or wool during the nineteenth century. Most of the coverlets date from 1800 to the 1880s. There was a revival of hand weaving in the 1920s and new coverlets, especially geometric patterns, were made. The earliest coverlets were made on narrow looms, so two woven strips were joined together and a seam can be found. The weave structures of coverlets can include summer and winter, double weave, overshot, and others. Jacquard coverlets have elaborate pictorial patterns that are made on a special loom or with the use of a special attachment. Quilts are listed in this book in their own category.

Jacquard, Black, Multicolor, Daniel Bordner, Millersburg, Pa., 1834, 82 x 76 In.	207.00
Jacquard, Blue, Red, Washington Corners, Capital Buildings, Flowers, 79 x 84 In.	474.00
Jacquard, Blue, Red, White, Lines, Designs, Henry Oberly, Womelsdorf, Pa., 97 x 79 In.	1094.00
Jacquard, Blue, White, Rose Sunburst, Bird, Bush Border, Wool, Cotton, 1842, 71 x 87 In.	206.00
Jacquard, Circle, Birds, Flowers, Cream, Black, Red, Fringe, 1852, 76 x 86 In. *illus*	558.00
Jacquard, Double Weave, Medallion, Eagles, Wool, Cotton, c.1845, 80 x 82 In.	121.00
Jacquard, Grapevine, Border, Sawtooth Medallion, Wool, Cotton, c.1850, 88 x 96 In.	844.00
Jacquard, Green, Brown, White, Pink, Wm. Ney, Myerstown, Pa., 82 x 62 In.	178.00
Jacquard, Green, Red, Black, White, Henry Keener 1847, Pa., 99 x 84 In.	504.00
Jacquard, Maroon, Green, Cream, Black, Eagle Corners, Diamond Border, Pa., 96 x 94 In.	770.00
Jacquard, Memorial Hall, Lettering, 1876, 77 x 87 In.	201.00
Jacquard, Purple, Green, Blue, Red, White, Arrow, Flowers, Fringe, Pa., 79 x 84 In.	119.00
Jacquard, Purple, White, Eagle Corners, Flower Border, Pa., 70 x 64 In.	89.00
Jacquard, Red, Black, Green, White, Bird, Tree Border, John Smith, 1835, 103 x 86 In.	444.00
Jacquard, Red, Black, Green, White, House, Palm Tree Border, Henry Keener, 1839, 100 x 80 In.	444.00

Jacquard, Red, Blue, Rose Center, Bird, Bush Border, Wool, Cotton, Adams, c.1859, 69 x 85 In.	382.00
Jacquard, Red, Blue, Snowflakes, Henry Oberly, Pa., 85 x 97 In.	533.00
Jacquard, Red, Green, Henry Brehem, Wolmelsdorf, 1837, 96 x 40 In.	425.00
Jacquard, Red, Green, Orange, Star, Eagle, Flowers, Wm. Ney, Myerstown, Pa., 86 x 84 In.	444.00
Jacquard, Red, Green, White, Black, Fringe, Henry Keener, 1838, 94 x 74 In.	474.00
Jacquard, Red, Green, White, Black, Star, Flowers, Fringe, Henry Oberly, 1839, 97 x 84 In.	652.00
Jacquard, Red, Purple, Black, Inscribed Henry Keener 1845, Pa., 96 x 88 In.	1659.00
Jacquard, Red, Purple, Green, Blue, White, Flowers, Star, Arrow, 84 x 80 In.	237.00
Jacquard, Red, White, Circles, Flowers, Henry Keener, Womelsdorf, 1844, 98 x 86 In.	652.00
Jacquard, Red, White, Green, Black, Peacock Border, Wreath Design, Pa., 96 x 84 In.	356.00
Jacquard, Red, White, Wool, Cotton, Absalom Klinger, Berks County, 1859, 92 x 88 In. *illus*	71.00
Jacquard, Roses, Grapevines, Geometric, Wool, Cotton, Joseph Turnbaugh, Pa., 1851, 80 In. *illus*	118.00
Jacquard, Snowflakes, Flowers, White, Brown, Black, Fringe, 84 x 96 In.	465.00
Jacquard, Triple Bird, Berry Border, Blue, Black, Brown, F. Gish, 1852, 92 x 82 In.	593.00
Jacquard, Wool & Cotton, Blue, White, Birds, Young, Buildings Border, c.1850, 73 x 83 In. *illus*	176.00
Overshot, Red, Blue, Geometric, Wool, Paper Label, Mohnton, 90 x 108 In.	147.00
Overshot, Red, White, Blue, Oberly, Pa., 86 x 76 In.	267.00
Wool, Embroidered, Black, Flowers, Fruit, Vines, Scrolling, Late 1700s, 88 x 78 In.	8295.00

COWAN POTTERY made art pottery and wares for florists. Guy Cowan made pottery in Rocky River, Ohio, a suburb of Cleveland, from 1913 to 1931. A stylized mark with the word *Cowan* was used on most pieces. A commercial, mass-produced line was marked *Lakeware*. Collectors today search for the Art Deco pieces by Guy Cowan, Viktor Schreckengost, Waylande Gregory, or Thelma Frazier Winter.

Bookends, Camel, Mottled Green & Brown Crackle Glaze, Marked, 8 ½ In. *illus*	920.00
Bookends, Elephant, Push-Pull, Primrose Yellow, Margaret Postgate, Impressed, 4 ¾ In.	560.00
Bookends, Pelican, Red Brown Glaze, Drexel Jacobson, 5 ¼ In. *illus*	1035.00
Bowl, Blue On Black, Banding, Tapered, Wide Rim, Drypoint Design, 3 ¾ In.	345.00
Bowl, Boat Shape, Oval Foot, Shaped Rim, Scrolled Up Handles, Oriental Red Glaze, 7 x 15 In.	58.00
Bowl, Flamingo, Oriental Red, Shaped, 15 In.	83.00
Bowl, Hand Thrown, Round Foot, Wide Rim, Blue, Gray, Lavender, Gold, 1927, 11 In. Diam.	920.00
Candleholder, Leaves, Loops, Arabian Night Glaze, Marked, 8 In., Pair *illus*	92.00
Charger, Thunderbird, Egyptian Blue Glaze, 15 In. Diam.	288.00
Compote, Seashore, Oval, Special Ivory, Interior Apple Blossom Pink, Mark, 6 ½ x 3 ¼ In.	18.00
Figurine, Bird, Wave, Mottled, Cream, Tan, 11 ½ In.	47.00
Figurine, Duet, 2 Women, Dancing, Ivory Glaze, Marked, 8 In.	288.00
Figurine, Giulia, Black, Semigloss Glaze, Marked, 10 In. *illus*	1150.00
Figurine, Heron, Wings Spread, Flower Frog Base, Ivory Glaze, 15 In.	345.00
Figurine, Woodland Nymph, Nude Woman, Seated On Stump, Long Hair, Ivory Glaze, 14 In.	2530.00
Flower Frog, Blue Luster, Marked, 1920s, 8 x 3 In.	110.00
Flower Frog, Debutante, Nude Woman, Arms Out, Leg Up, Flower Base, Ivory Glaze, 14 In.	633.00
Flower Frog, Flamingo, Oriental Red, 12 In.	83.00
Flower Frog, Grace, Woman, Leaning Backwards, Ivory Glaze, Marked, 6 ¼ In.	374.00
Flower Frog, Loveliness, Woman, Dancing Pose, Ivory Glaze, 12 In.	345.00
Flower Frog, Pavlova, Nude Woman With Long Scarf, Ivory Glaze, 6 In.	115.00
Flower Frog, Scarf Dancer, White, Impressed, 7 ⅛ In. *illus*	150.00
Flower Frog, Statuesque, Woman, Dancing Pose, Ivory Glaze, 13 In.	460.00
Jar, Strawberry, Turquoise Glaze, Marked, 5 ¾ In.	29.00
Lamp Base, Nude Woman, Square Stepped Base, Brown Matte Glaze, 12 In.	978.00
Pitcher, Striated Leaf Glaze, Orange, Yellow, Wide Spout, Loop Handle, 8 ⅞ In.	81.00
Plate, Sea, Light Green, Swirl Design, Thelma Frazier, Marked, 11 ½ In. Diam.	119.00
Plate, Spiraling Fish, Blue Glaze, 11 ½ In. *illus*	184.00
Plate, Sports, Art Deco Scene, Polo, Orange Brown Glaze, Viktor Schreckengost, 11 ⅛ In. *illus*	518.00
Vase, Abstract Flowers, Crackle Glaze, Die Stamped Lakeware, Signed, W. Atchley 31, 6 ½ In. *illus*	920.00
Vase, Arabian Night Blue, Tapered, Green Drips, Cylindrical, 2 Loop Handles, 9 In.	230.00
Vase, Azure Glaze, Impressed Mark, 9 In.	69.00
Vase, Azure Glaze, Tapered, Smokestack Rim, Half Moon Handles, Marked, 11 ⅜ In.	127.00
Vase, Bulbous, Shouldered, Lavender Luster Glaze, Purple, Blue Crystals, Dripped, 9 In.	230.00
Vase, Cashmere Glaze, Blue, Flared, Scalloped Rim, Waist Handles, Footed, 10 ¼ In.	95.00
Vase, Chinese Bird At Base, Round Foot, Flared Rim, Cobalt Blue, 11 In.	173.00
Vase, Cylindrical, Flared Rim, Round Foot, Oriental Red Glaze, Stripe Design	161.00
Vase, Cylindrical, Pinched Neck, Round Foot, Mottled Lavender, Green, Mauve, Drip Glaze, 7 In.	230.00
Vase, Delphinium Luster Glaze, Bulbous, Lavender & Blue, 10 In.	58.00
Vase, Elongated Oval, Narrow Rolled Rim, Magenta Luster Glaze	173.00
Vase, Elongated Oval, Narrow Rolled Rim, Marigold, 11 In.	161.00
Vase, Flower Band, Black On Green, Pear Shape, Flared Lip, 1931, 8 In.	575.00

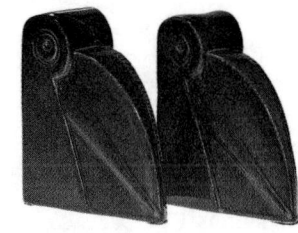

Cowan, Bookends, Pelican, Red Brown Glaze, Drexel Jacobson, 5 ¼ In. $1035.00

Humler & Nolan

Cowan, Candleholder, Leaves, Loops, Arabian Night Glaze, Marked, 8 In., Pair $92.00

Humler & Nolan

Cowan, Figurine, Giulia, Black, Semigloss Glaze, Marked, 10 In. $1150.00

Humler & Nolan

Cowan, Flower Frog, Scarf Dancer, White, Impressed, 7 ⅛ In. $150.00

Humler & Nolan

Cowan, Plate, Spiraling Fish, Blue Glaze,
11 ½ In.
$184.00

Humler & Nolan

Cowan, Plate, Sports, Art Deco Scene,
Polo, Orange Brown Glaze, Viktor
Schreckengost, 11 ⅛ In.
$518.00

Humler & Nolan

Cowan, Vase, Abstract Flowers, Crackle
Glaze, Die Stamped Lakeware, Signed,
W. Atchley 31, 6 ½ In.
$920.00

Humler & Nolan

Vase, Globular, Ribbed Design, Azurean Glaze, Turquoise Color, 10 In.	173.00
Vase, Gray & Mauve Glaze Over Brown, Red Clay, Incised, 6 ½ In. ....*illus*	633.00
Vase, Gypsy Moth, Delphinium Glaze, Swollen, 2 Moth Shape Handles, Narrow Rim, 13 ⅛ In.	431.00
Vase, Gypsy Moth, Marigold, Baluster, Pinched Neck, Sphinx Moth Handles, 13 In.	58.00
Vase, Lemon Tree, Mother-Of-Pearl Glaze, Square Shape, Pale Blue, Marked, 9 ¼ In.	115.00
Vase, Maple Leaf, Urn Shape, Round Foot, Rolled Rim, Green Matte Glaze, Turquoise Color	259.00
Vase, Marigold Glaze, Orange, Smokestack, Flare Rim, Lakewood Ware, 6 ⅜ In.	575.00
Vase, October Glaze, 4 Round Panels, Flowers, Birds, Bulbous, Narrow Neck, Handles, 12 In.	230.00
Vase, Oriental Red Glaze, Cylindrical Neck, Rectangular Handles, Round Foot, 10 ¾ In.	138.00
Vase, Ribbed, Thrown Design, Russet Brown Glaze, 11 ⅞ In. ....*illus*	81.00
Vase, Round Bulbous Shape, 2 Top Loop Handles, Blue Green Glaze, Azure	288.00
Vase, Round, Rolled Lip, Mottled Brown, Mauve, High Glaze, 1930, 8 In.	288.00
Vase, Squirrel, Urn Shape, Round Foot, Rolled Rim, Apple Green Glaze, 8 In.	345.00
Vase, Sunrise Glaze, Orange To Green, Marked, 16 ⅛ In. ....*illus*	230.00
Vase, Tapered, Cylindrical, Rolled Lip, Yellow, Clay, Glaze, 14 In.	633.00
Vase, Urn Shape, Sleeping Chinese Bird, Scroll, Round Foot, Jade Green, 11 In.	35.00
Vase, Yellow Luster Glaze, Orange Highlights, Signed, 7 In.	207.00

CRACKER JACK, the molasses-flavored popcorn mixture, was first made in 1896 in Chicago, Illinois. A prize was added to each box in 1912. Collectors search for the old boxes, toys, and advertising materials. Many of the toys are unmarked.

Ad, Magazine, Woman, Handing Out Cracker Jack For Halloween, 1954, 10 x 13 In.	9.25
Game, Board, Milton Bradley, Box, 1976	25.00
Pin, Woman, Celluloid, Give Away, Advertising Back Paper, Early 1900s, 1 ¼ In. ....*illus*	70.00
Toy, Bear, Stand-Up, Gray Veined, 1950s, 1 ¾ In.	10.00
Toy, Duck, Stand-Up, Plastic, Yellow, 1950s, 1 ⅞ In.	11.00
Toy, Magnifier, Round, Clear, Handle	5.00
Toy, Piano, Tin Lithograph, Folded, 1 ⅜ x 1 ¼ x ⁹⁄₁₆ In. ....*illus*	52.00
Toy, Pinball, Girl, Blue Dress, Jumping Rope	12.00
Toy, Pinball, Green Roadrunner	12.00
Toy, Pinball, Mother Goose, Flying On A Goose	10.00
Toy, Rake, Wood, Metal, 4 In.	25.00
Toy, Ring, Bust Of Woman, Yellow, White	14.00
Toy, Spinner, Orange, Plastic	16.00
Toy, Squirrel, Stand-Up, Pinkish Gray, Marbleized, 1940s, 1 ⅜ In.	8.00
Toy, Whistle, Red, White, Plastic, Embossed Jack	13.00
Toy, Yo-Yo, Red & Blue, Embossed Jack	16.00
Trolley, Tin Lithograph, Toonerville, Wheeled Base, Fontaine Fox, Penny Toy, 1 ¾ In.	230.00

CRACKLE GLASS was originally made by the Venetians, but most of the wares found today were made since the 1800s. The glass was heated, cooled, and refired so that many small lines appeared inside the glass. Most was made from about 1930 to 1980, although some is made today. The glass is found in many colors, but collectors today pay the highest prices for amberina, cranberry, or ruby red. Cobalt blue is also popular. More crackle glass may be listed in those categories in this book.

Apple, Gold, Clear Leaf, 4 In.	30.00
Basket, Blue, Applied Crystal Handle, Pilgrim, 4 ½ In.	30.00
Basket, Green Trim, Applied Handle, 7 In.	75.00
Bowl, Flower, Amber, Pilgrim, 6 ¼ In.	35.00
Bowl, Ruffled Rim, Pilgrim, 4 ½ In.	25.00
Bowl, Smoke, Crimped, Pilgrim, 6 ½ x 3 ½ In.	25.00
Creamer, Olive Green, Applied Handle, Molded Foot, Kanawha, 3 ⅜ In.	20.00
Creamer, Olive Green, Kanawha, 3 ⅜ In.	19.00
Cruet, Oil, Red, Pilgrim, 6 ¾ In.	30.00
Decanter, Blue, Stopper, 10 ¼ In.	45.00
Decanter, Wine, Fish, Green Eyes, Cork Stopper, 1960s, 16 In.	70.00
Light, Patio, Ruby Red, 4 x 4 ¾ In.	30.00
Pitcher, Amber, Left-Handed, Pilgrim, 3 ⅝ In.	20.00
Pitcher, Blue, Applied Blue Handle, 5 ⅝ In.	40.00
Pitcher, Blue, Kanawha, 6 In.	25.00
Pitcher, Blue, Molded Foot, Applied Blue Handle, Kanawha, 6 In.	25.00
Pitcher, Brown, 4 ½ In.	25.00
Pitcher, Cocktail, Amberina, Applied Handle, 7 ¼ In.	50.00
Pitcher, Heritage, Orange Amber, Applied Handle, 4 ⅜ In.	30.00
Pitcher, Olive Green, Applied Crystal Handle, Pilgrim, 3 ⅞ In.	15.00

Pitcher, Olive Green, Applied Crystal Handle, Pilgrim, 4 ⅝ In.	20.00
Pitcher, Orange & Yellow, Pilgrim, 3 ¼ In.	35.00
Pitcher, Red, Applied Handle, Pinched Waist, 3 ½ x 4 In.	35.00
Pitcher, Red, Gold Aurene, Rough Pontil, c.1930, 5 ½ In.	45.00
Pitcher, Root Beer Brown, Applied Handle, Pilgrim, 4 ⅝ In.	20.00
Pitcher, Ruby, Applied Yellow Handle, Pilgrim, 3 ½ In.	18.00
Pitcher, Tangerine, Applied Yellow Handle, Pilgrim, 3 ⅝ In.	18.00
Pitcher, Vintage Blue, Left-Handed, Pilgrim, 3 ½ In.	30.00
Pitcher, Window, Amber, Applied Crystal Handle, Pilgrim, 3 ¼ In.	15.00
Pitcher, Yellow, Applied Handle, Kanawha, 4 ³⁄₁₆ In.	20.00
Plate, Sherbet, Marigold, 6 In.	8.00
Tumbler, Liquor, Dark Amber, 3 ⅞ In.	20.00
Tumbler, Liquor, Green, Benedictine, 3 ⅞ In.	20.00
Tumbler, Liquor, Tangerine, 4 In.	22.00
Vase, Amberina, Kanawha, 4 ⅞ In.	20.00
Vase, Emerald Green, Pinched Sides, Pilgrim, 8 In.	50.00
Vase, Heart Shape, Rainbow, 5 x 2 In.	39.00
Vase, Ivy, Blue, Pinched Sides, Pilgrim, 3 ½ x 3 ⅝ In.	20.00
Vase, Rainbow, Heart, 5 In.	39.00
Vase, Top Hat, Green, Pinched, 4 ½ x 6 ¼ In.	30.00

CRANBERRY GLASS is an almost transparent yellow-red glass. It resembles the color of cranberry juice. The glass has been made in Europe and America since the Civil War. It is still being made, and reproductions can fool the unwary. Related glass items may be listed in other categories, such as Northwood, Rubina Verde, etc.

Basket, Clear Applied Twist Handle, Ruffled Edge, 9 x 8 ½ In.	40.00
Basket, Victorian, Opalescent Swirls, Ruffled Rim, Applied Clear Handle, 13 In.	59.00
Bell, Cranberry Cut To Clear, Zipper Cut Handle, 3 In.	45.00
Biscuit Barrel, Enameled Flowers, Silver Cover, Handle, c.1900, 10 x 5 In.	325.00
Bottle, Barber, Stars & Stripes, Cranberry Opalescent, 8 In.	1450.00
Bowl, Acid Etched Leaf Design, Cylindrical Body, 1800s, 9 In. Diam.	59.00
Bowl, Centerpiece, Cut To Clear, 9 x 9 In.	177.00
Bowl, Flashed Hobstar, Crosscut Diamond & Fan, Cranberry Cut To Clear, 3 x 6 In.	100.00
Bowl, Japanese Designs, Fans, Birds, Insects, Dragon Mounts, Gilt Bronze, France, c.1890, 13 ½ In.	1003.00
Bowl, Ribbed, Ruffled Rim, 3 Clear Applied Feet, 5 ¼ x 7 In.	201.00
Box, Enameled, Snowflake, Flowers, c.1900, 2 ½ x 4 ½ In.	210.00
Butter, Cover, Opalescent, Fern Pattern, Dome Shape, Ball Finial, 7 In.	173.00
Candy Dish, Cover, Etched, Bulbous, Jeanette, 1900s, 5 x 5 In.	65.00
Celery Vase, Thumbprint, Enamel Flowers, Aurora Silver Plate Frame, Handles, 8 In.	350.00
Compote, White Overlay, Cutback Flowers, 10 x 9 ¼ In.	200.00
Cruet, Star & Stripes, Opalescent, Faceted Stopper, 7 In. ....*illus*	230.00
Dish, Sweetmeat, Acid Cut Ground, Enamel Flowers, Silver Plate Lid, Bail Handle, 3 ¼ In.	175.00
Epergne, 3 Trumpet Vases, Brass Center Mount, Round Scalloped Base Bowl, 23 In.	219.00
Epergne, 5 Trumpet Vases, Ruffle Rims, Applied Rigaree, Metal Base, 20 In.	460.00
Epergne, Lily, 3 Hanging Baskets, Square Ruffled Base, Candy Cane Twist, 22 In.	1800.00
Jar, Condiment, Enameled Thumbprint, Silver Plate Frame, Spoon, 7 ¾ In.	184.00
Jar, Cover, White Crackle Overlay, Silver Plate Lid & Bail, 4 ½ In.	175.00
Jar, Silver Drum Shape Lid, 3 ½ x 3 In.	207.00
Jar, White Crackle Overlay, Silver Plate Lid, Bail Handle, 5 ½ In.	100.00
Lamp, Opalescent, Snowflake Pattern, 8 In.	600.00
Lamp, Optic Swirl, L.G. Wright, Miniature, 9 ½ In.	288.00
Lamp, Peg, Opalescent, Marble Base, Optic Diamond Oval Font, 22 In.	144.00
Lamp, Peg, Scalloped Font, In Brass Candlestick, Etched, France, 20 ½ x 6 ¼ In.	374.00
Letter Box, Courting Scene, Enamel, Gold Stencil Highlights, 3 ¼ x 7 In.	75.00
Perfume Bottle, Cut Glass, Lay Down, Cased, Cane Pattern, 7 ¼ In.	325.00
Perfume Bottle, Enamel Flowers, Metal Neck, Mechanical Plunger, 5 In.	140.00
Pitcher, Ribbed Lattice Patter, Opal, Cylindrical, Loop Handle, 5 In.	431.00
Pitcher, Rose Crackle Glaze, Crimped Rim, Applied Curved Handle, c.1890, 8 ¾ In.	161.00
Pitcher, Snowflake Pattern, Opalescent, Round Foot, Square Shape, Ruffle Rim, Clear Handle, 9 In.	1265.00
Salt Dip, Vaseline, Clear Applied Rigoree, Silver Plate Frame, 3 In.	950.00
Sugar Shaker, Melon Rib, Bulbous Bottom, Round Foot, Metal Lid, Ring Neck, 5 In., Pair	86.00
Sugar Shaker, Swirl, Red Interior Flashing, Ground Lip, Metal Top, 4 ⅝ In. ....*illus*	184.00
Sugar, Cover, Opalescent, Fern Pattern, Bulbous, Round Finial, 7 In.	173.00
Tankard, Clear Handle, Enameled Daisy Design, 12 In.	90.00
Vase, Applied White Flower, Leaf, Hat Shape, Wavy Rim, 4 ½ In.	59.00
Vase, Cut To Clear, Scenic, Stag, Game Bird, Forest, St. Louis, 13 ½ In.	350.00

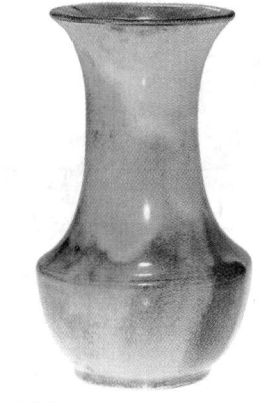

Cowan, Vase, Gray & Mauve Glaze Over Brown, Red Clay, Incised, 6 ½ In. **$633.00**

Humler & Nolan

Cowan, Vase, Ribbed, Thrown Design, Russet Brown Glaze, 11 ⅞ In. **$81.00**

Humler & Nolan

Cowan, Vase, Sunrise Glaze, Orange To Green, Marked, 16 ⅛ In. **$230.00**

Humler & Nolan

Cracker Jack, Pin, Woman, Celluloid, Give Away, Advertising Back Paper, Early 1900s, 1 ¼ In.
$70.00

Hake's Americana & Collectibles

Cracker Jack, Toy, Piano, Tin Lithograph, Folded, 1 ⅜ x 1 ¼ x ⁹⁄₁₆ In.
$52.00

Hake's Americana & Collectibles

Cranberry Glass, Cruet, Star & Stripes, Opalescent, Faceted Stopper, 7 In.
$230.00

Early Auction Co.

Cranberry Glass, Sugar Shaker, Swirl, Red Interior Flashing, Ground Lip, Metal Top, 4 ⅝ In.
$184.00

Glass Works Auctions

Vase, Etched, Flashed, Footed, Bulbous, Flared Rim, 12 ¾ x 7 In., Pair	300.00
Vase, Gilt, Enameled, Dog, Goat, Bulb Shape, Pointed Bottom, Pedestal Base, 15 In.	546.00
Vase, Painted, White Flowers, Gold Accents, Bulbous, Ruffled Rim, c.1940, 4 ½ x 3 ¼ In.	45.00
Vase, Trumpet Shape, Leaves, Mounted As Lamp, 11 In., Pair	366.00
Vase, Trumpet Shape, Silver Plate Rope & Reticulated Frame, Footed, 7 ½ In.	144.00
Vase, Tusk Shape, Thorn Body, 6 ¼ In., Pair	90.00
Water Pitcher, Coin Spot, Ribbed Handle, 6 Tumblers, 9 ½ In.	325.00

CREAMWARE, or queensware, was developed by Josiah Wedgwood about 1765. It is a cream-colored earthenware that has been copied by many factories. Similar wares may be listed under Pearlware and Wedgwood.

Basket, Fruit, Underdish, Oval, Brown & Green Leaves, 2 Handles, Pierced, c.1800, 10 In.	356.00
Basket, Stand, White, Blue Detail, Reticulated, 9 ¼ In.	177.00
Coffeepot, Black Transfer, Entwined Double Handle, Flower Terminals, c.1765, 11 x 9 In.	123.00
Figurine, Lion, Walking, Curly Main, Snarling, Head Turned, Rectangular Base, c.1780, 12 In.	8024.00
Figurine, Stag, Reclining, Leg Draped Over Side, Waisted Base, Berry Leaf Border, 13 In.	5664.00
Garniture Set, Urn Shape, Water Leaf Design, Footed Plinth, Magenta, Pointed Finial, c.1850, 9 In.	230.00
Jug, Ship, British Flag, Woman, Anchor, Grapevines, Loop Handle, Bulbous, 1800s, 9 In.	593.00
Jug, Thomas Jefferson, President Of The United States, Portrait, Vines, Poem, 7 In.	6000.00
Mold, 3 Tiers, Oval Shape, Scalloped Foot, Pierced Walls, Fish, Culinary, 1700s, 9 x 5 In.	306.00
Pepper Pot, Baluster, Scalloped Bands, Beaded Borders, Round Foot, Tortoiseshell Glaze, 5 In.	767.00
Pitcher, George Washington Greeting Indian, Liberty, Shield, Monument, 8 In.	7500.00
Pitcher, Peace, Plenty & Independence, Black Transfer, States, Ship, c.1810, 8 ½ In.	700.00
Pitcher, Washington In Glory, Peace & Independence, Eagle, Liberty Weeping, 8 In.	1950.00
Pitcher, Washington, Map, United States, Black Transfer, Floral Swag, Hope, c.1810, 11 ½ In.	2000.00
Plate, Allegorical Scene, Figure Seated, Open Book, 9 ¾ In.	150.00
Plate, Central Portrait Of Prince William Of Orange, Wave Edge, Flowers, 9 In. Diam.	360.00
Plate, Frederica Sophia Wilhelmina, Scalloped Edge, 10 In.	293.00
Plate, Our Lady Of Kevelaar, Holding Christ Child, Flower Border, Shaped Rim, c.1780, 10 In.	382.00
Plate, Portraits, Orange Tree, Scalloped Edge, c.1790, 10 In. Diam.	480.00
Plate, Portraits, William V & Wilhelmina, Orange Tree, Scalloped Edge, c.1790, 9 ¾ In. ...*illus*	390.00
Plate, Prince William V, Frederica, Facing Each Other, Orange Tree, Dutch Inscription, 9 ½ In. ...*illus*	294.00
Plate, Scalloped, Bust Portrait Of Prince William V, Scalloped, Dutch, 10 In.	270.00
Punch Bowl, 5 Historical Transfers, John Adams, Ship, Eagle, Poem, 5 x 11 In.	10000.00
Tea Bowl, William V & Wilhelmina, Round Foot, 1700s, 4 In., Pair	529.00
Teapot, Cover, Cylindrical, Ear Handle, Goddess, Chariot, Peacocks, Sun, Juno, 1770-82, 6 In.	2006.00
Teapot, Cover, Flower Sprays, Ribbed Spout, Double Twist Handle, Flower Finial, c.1780, 4 In.	150.00
Teapot, Cover, Square Shape, Canted Sides, Gardener, Flowers, Widow Knop, c.1775, 6 In.	1888.00
Teapot, Cover, Square Shape, Lion Knop, Blue & White, St. Anthony, Leaves, c.1785, 5 In.	1416.00

CROWN DERBY is the name given to porcelain made in Derby, England, from the 1770s to 1935. Andrew Planche and William Duesbury established Crown Derby as the first china-making factory in Derby. Pieces are marked with a crown and the letter *D* or the word *Derby*. The earliest pieces were made by the original Derby factory, while later pieces were made by the King Street Partnerships (1848–1935) or the Derby Crown Porcelain Co. (1876–90). Derby Crown Porcelain Co. became Royal Crown Derby Co. Ltd. in 1890. It is now part of Royal Doulton Tableware Ltd.

Egg Cup, Gilt Loops, Bands, White Ground, c.1810, 2 ¼ In.	185.00
Plate, Flowers, Cobalt Blue, Rust, White Ground, No. 2649, c.1920, 6 In.	60.00
Sugar, King's Pattern, Handles, 1810, 7 ¼ x 5 ½ In.	345.00

CROWN DUCAL is the name used on some pieces of porcelain made by A.G. Richardson and Co., Ltd., of Tunstall and Cobridge, England. The name has been used since 1916. Crown Ducal is a well-known maker of chintz pattern dishes.

Bowl, Vegetable, Cover, Bristol Blue, Round, 1931, 11 x 5 In.	145.00
Charger, Blue Peony, Flowers, Tube Lined, Charlotte Rhead, c.1935, 12 ½ In.	425.00
Compote, Pedestal, Delhi, Black, Red, Green, c.1925, 8 ½ x 4 In.	95.00
Creamer, Art Deco Designs, Black, Red, Green, Cream Ground, c.1925, 1 ½ x 3 ½ In.	12.00
Cup & Saucer, Gainsborough, Flowers, Cream Ground, 4 x 6 In.	13.00
Plate, Black, Primrose, White, Ivory Ground, 8 ⅝ In.	125.00
Plate, Bristol, Flowers, Birds, Pink Transfer, Scalloped Embossed Edge, Square, 10 x 8 ¾ In.	44.00
Plate, Chintz, Primrose, Black, White, Green, Yellow Ground, Octagonal, 8 ⅝ In.	125.00
Plate, Chintz, Rose Parade, Black Ground, 8 ½ In.	85.00
Plate, Gainsborough, Flower, 10 In.	11.00
Plate, Roses, Fruits, Cream Ground, Scalloped Rim, 11 In., Pair	40.00

Serving, Bowl, Blue Ivy, 9 x 1 ½ In.	50.00
Soup, Cream, Saucer, Tulips, Spring Flowers, Yellow Ground, 5 ¼ x 2 ¼ In.	75.00
Sugar Shaker, Bristol, Roses, Birds, Pink, Barrel Shape, 3 In.	29.00
Vase, Blush Exotic Bird, c.1920, 7 x 2 ⅓ In.	32.00
Vase, Chintz, Pink Roses, Gray Flowers, Black Ground, 1920s, 13 In.	275.00
Vase, Festival, Pink, Fuchsia, Pair	229.00
Vase, Festival, Pink, Purple Flowers, Pedestal Base, c.1926, 6 ½ In., Pair	229.00
Vase, Manchu, Green Dragon, Ribbed, Conical, Charlotte Rhead, c.1930, 5 In.	270.00
Vase, Muted Blues, Incised Bands, Charlotte Rhead, 4 ¾ In.	300.00

CROWN MILANO glass was made by the Mt. Washington Glass Works about 1890. It was a plain biscuit color with a satin finish decorated with flowers and often had large gold scrolls. Not all pieces are marked.

Biscuit Jar, Gilt Flowers, White, Yellow, Gold Plate Collar, Shaped Turtle Handle, 5 In.	518.00
Biscuit Jar, Rectangular, Cream With Scrolling Mums, Marked, 8 In.	200.00
Biscuit Jar, Yellow, Flowers, Embossed Crab, Silver Plate Lid, Melon Ribbed, 5 ½ In.	350.00
Card Holder, Shell Shape, Opalescent, Stemmed Pink Flowers, 6 In.	173.00
Castor Jar, Cream, Swirl Mold, Jeweled, Enamel, Gold Detail, Signed, 4 In.	125.00
Dish, Sweetmeat, Cover, Flower Bouquets, White Ground, Twist Handle, Globular, 4 In.	127.00
Dish, Sweetmeat, Opaque Glass, Rose Enamel Design, Embossed Gilt Silver Plate, Lid, 4 In.	135.00
Ewer, Swollen, Trifold Rim, Flower Garland, Medallions, Gaelic, Stamped, CM, 14 In.	1995.00
Lamp Base, Melon Ribbed Font, Dragon, Medallion, Pairpoint Silver Plate Foot, 15 In. ..*illus*	345.00
Pitcher, Water, Ribbed Body, Holly Leaves, Jeweled Berries, Rope Twist Handle, 7 In. ..*illus*	4025.00
Saltshaker, Shell Form, Enameled Flowers, 3 In.	100.00
Sugar & Creamer, Pink To White, Gold Enamel Flowers, Embossed Silver Plate Lid, Handle .	125.00
Syrup, Opal, Enameled Blossoms, Stippled Band, Embossed Flip Lid, Twist Handle, 7 In.	316.00
Toothpick Holder, Oak Leaves, Cylindrical, 2 ½ In.	375.00
Vase, Ball Shape, Narrow Cylindrical Neck, Pink Mums, Blue & Yellow Leaf Ground, 8 In.	374.00
Vase, Bulbous, Bottle Shape, Flaring Rim, Pink Mum, Green Stems, Blue Medallions, 8 In.	1610.00
Vase, Bulbous, Stick, Red & Gold Stippled Medallions, Scrolling Ground, 28 Jewels, 15 ½ In. ..*illus*	4025.00
Vase, Long Neck, Yellow Ground, Applied Gold, 10 ¾ In.	201.00
Vase, Narrow, Tapered, V-Shape Rim, White & Gilt, Flowers, Round Foot, 12 x 4 In.	115.00
Vase, White Opal, Enameled Flowers, 4 Gold Enameled Medallions, Signed, 6 ¼ In. ..*illus*	345.00

CRUETS of glass or porcelain were made to hold vinegar, oil, and other condiments. They were especially popular during Victorian times and have been made in a variety of styles since the eighteenth century. Additional cruets may be found in the Castor Set category and also in various glass categories.

Blown Mold, Sapphire Blue, Arched Panels, Flattened Rim, Tam-O'-Shanter Stopper, 6 In.	489.00
Blown Mold, Violet, Vertical Ribs, Flattened Rim, Tam-O'-Shanter Stopper, 6 ½ In.	546.00
Blue Opalescent, Swirl Pattern, Stopper, 6 In., Pair	173.00
Lacy Medallion, Purple, Gilt, Bell Shape Bottom, Loop Handle, Faceted Stopper, 8 In., Pair	403.00
Stopper, Bellaire, Circle Design, Findlay, c.1895, 5 ½ In.	23.00

CT GERMANY was first part of a mark used by a company in Altwasser, Germany (now part of Walbrzych, Poland), in 1845. The initials stand for C. Tielsch, a partner in the firm. The Hutschenreuther firm took over the company in 1918 and continued to use the *CT*.

C.T.

Bowl, Divided, Pink Flowers, White, Leaf Shape, Gilt Twig Handle	95.00
Bowl, Lily Of The Valley, Gilt, 10 ¾ In.	50.00
Bowl, Pink, White Flowers, Scalloped, Gilt, 11 x 10 In.	85.00
Cake Plate, Enameled Lilies, White, Gilt, c.1925, 10 ¼ x 9 ½ In.	85.00
Plate, Pink Flowers, White Ground, Gilt, Scalloped, Signed N.W. Poole, 8 ¼ In.	32.00
Plate, Pink Poppies, Scalloped Rim, 8 ½ In.	75.00
Plate, Pink Roses, Green Ground, Scalloped Rim, c.1905, 5 ⅛ In.	35.00
Plate, Reticulated, Flowers, Multicolor, 1920s, 9 In.	150.00

CUP PLATES are small glass or china plates that held the cup while a diner of the mid-nineteenth century drank coffee or tea from the saucer. The most famous cup plates were made of glass at the Boston and Sandwich factory located in Sandwich, Massachusetts. There have been many new glass cup plates made in recent years for sale to gift shops or collectors of limited editions. These are similar to the old plates but can be recognized as new.

Blue Green, Ship, Chancellor Livingston, 38 Scallops, 3 ½ In.	431.00
Blue, Eagle, Stars, Stippled, Blue, Alternation Bull's-Eye Scallops & Points, 3 ½ In.	747.00
Blue, Ship, 25 Flat Scallops Alternating With Points, 3 ¾ In.	403.00

Creamware, Plate, Portraits, William V & Wilhelmina, Orange Tree, Scalloped Edge, c.1790, 9 ¾ In.
$390.00

Cowan's Auctions

Creamware, Plate, Prince William V, Frederica, Facing Each Other, Orange Tree, Dutch Inscription, 9 ½ In.
$294.00

Cowan's Auctions

Crown Milano, Lamp Base, Melon Ribbed Font, Dragon, Medallion, Pairpoint Silver Plate Foot, 15 In.
$345.00

Early Auction Co.

TIP
Never leave the key under the doormat.

Crown Milano, Pitcher, Water, Ribbed Body, Holly Leaves, Jeweled Berries, Rope Twist Handle, 7 In.
$4025.00

Early Auction Co.

Crown Milano, Vase, Bulbous, Stick, Red & Gold Stippled Medallions, Scrolling Ground, 28 Jewels, 15 ½ In.
$4025.00

Early Auction Co.

Crown Milano, Vase, White Opal, Enameled Flowers, 4 Gold Enameled Medallions, Signed, 6 ¼ In.
$345.00

James D. Julia Inc.

TIP
Cruet tops for American glass pieces are almost always cut or pressed, not blown.

Clear, 6-Point Star, Bull's-Eyes With Rays, 15 Scallops With Shelf, New England, 4 In.		35.00
Clear, 12-Point Star, Stippled Ground, Peacock Eye & Single Point Rim, c.1840, 3 ¼ In.		127.00
Clear, Folded Rim, Kick Up Base, Pontil, 4 In.		184.00
Clear, George Washington, Star Border, Stippled Ground, Scalloped Edge, 3 ½ In.		9.00
Clear, Log Cabin With Flag, Flower Border, 66 Even Scallops, 3 ¼ In.		50.00
Clear, Log Cabin, Gabled Roof, Tree, Flag Pole, 1840 Election Symbols, 3 ¼ In.		104.00
Clear, Suspension Bridge, Bull's-Eye Border, 3 ¼ In.		46.00
Fiery Opalescent, Baskets, Rosettes, Leaves, Clear Rope Twist Rim, 3 ¾ In.		58.00
Fiery Opalescent, Scrolls, Rope Band, Stippled, 12-Sided, 81 Scallops, 4 In.		35.00
Fiery Opalescent, Ship, Benjamin Franklin, Sandwich, 3 ½ In.		259.00
Gray Blue, Opal & Black Inclusions, Peacock Eyes, Double Lines, 66 Scallops, 3 ¼ In.		81.00
Green, Ship, Chancellor Livingston, 38 Scallops, 3 ½ In.		431.00
Honey Amber, Log Cabin, 66 Even Scallops, 3 ¼ In.		633.00
Lacy, Sage Green, Amber Streaks, Boston & Sandwich, 3 ¼ In.		138.00
Lacy, Yellow Brown Tint, Scalloped Rim, 3 ¼ In.		288.00
Moonstone, Waffle Square Over Flowers & Leaves, 19 Scallops, Rope Twist Trim, 4 In.		374.00
Opaque White, Shields & Rosettes, 10-Sided, Rope Twist Rim, 3 ⅝ In.		58.00
Peacock Blue, Hearts, Squares In Swirls, 57 Even Scallops, 3 ½ In.		489.00
Peacock Blue, Waffle Square Over 8-Petal Flower, 55 Even Scallops, 3 ⅜ In.		184.00
Peacock Green, 8 Paneled Ovals, Scallop & Point Rim, Waffle Base, 4 In.		46.00
Sapphire Blue, Arches & Dots, Rayed Base, 57 Even Scallops, 3 In.		58.00
Ship, Green, Embossed Chancellor Livingston, Scalloped Rim, 3 ½ In.		46.00
Ship, Peacock Blue, Smoke Streaks, Scalloped Rim, 3 ½ In.		196.00
Sunburst, Peacock Blue, Scalloped Rim, Boston & Sandwich, 3 In.		374.00
Sunburst, Red Amber, Scalloped Rim, Boston & Sandwich, 3 ¼ In.		81.00
Yellow Green, 6-Point Star, Peacock Eyes, Alternating Large & Small Scallops, 3 ½ In.		173.00

CURRIER & IVES made the famous American lithographs marked with their name from 1857 to 1907. The mark used on the print included the street address in New York City, and it is possible to date the year of the original issue from this information. Earlier prints were made by N. Currier and use that name from 1835 to 1847. Many reprints of the Currier or Currier & Ives prints have been made. Some collectors buy the insurance calendars that were based on the old prints. The words *large, small,* or *medium folio* refer to size. The original print sizes were very small (up to about 7 x 9 in.), small (8.8 x 12.8 in.), medium (9 x 14 in. to 14 x 20 in.), large (larger than 14 x 20 in.). Other sizes are probably later copies. Other prints by Currier & Ives may be listed in the Card category under Advertising and in the Sheet Music category. Currier & Ives dinnerware patterns may be found in the Adams or Dinnerware categories.

Grand Racer Kingston, Lithograph, Frame, 1891, 20 x 27 In.	920.00
High Water In The Mississippi, Low Water In The Mississippi, Lithograph, 18 x 28 In., Pair	478.00
Life In The Wood, Returning To Camp, Lithograph, Frame, 1860, 19 x 28 In.	1093.00
Life In The Woods, Starting Out, Lithograph, Frame, 1860, 19 x 28 In.	1955.00
Papa's New Hat, Baby, Top Hat, Green, Red, Lithograph, Tramp Art Frame, 28 x 25 ½ In.	770.00
Small Hopes & Lady Mac, Lithograph, Frame, N.Y., 1878, 21 x 34 In.	690.00
Trotting Gelding Frank With J.O. Nay, His Running Mate, Lithograph, 1884, 19 x 30 In.	805.00

CUSTARD GLASS is a slightly yellow opaque glass. It was made in England in the 1880s and was first made in the United States in the 1890s. It has been reproduced. Additional pieces may be found in the Cambridge, Fenton, Heisey, and Northwood categories. Custard glass is called *Ivorina Verde* by Heisey and other companies.

Basket, Pink & Green Flower Spray, Applied Naturalistic Handle, 8 ¾ In.	*illus*	118.00
Candlestick, Dolphin, Opalescent, Stick With Petal Sockets, 1850s, 9 In.		235.00
Maize is its own category in this book.		
Swan, Bowl, Molded, Art Deco, Stylized Wings, 1930s, 3 x 5 ¼ In.		60.00
Vase, Blue Overlay Flowers, Amber Leaves & Feet, Foldover Rim, Oval, 9 ¾ In.		177.00
Water Set, Gild Flowers With Blue Scrolling, 7 Tumblers, 8 ½-In. Pitcher		250.00

CUT GLASS has been made since ancient times, but the large majority of the pieces now for sale date from the American Brilliant period of glass design, 1880 to 1905. These pieces have elaborate geometric designs with a deep miter cut. Modern cut glass with a similar appearance is being made in England, Ireland, Poland, and the Czech and Slovak republics. Chips and scratches are often difficult to notice but lower the value dramatically. A signature on the glass adds significantly to the value. Other cut glass pieces are listed under factory names, like Hawkes, Libbey, and Sinclaire.

Atomizer, Amethyst Cut To Clear, Engraved Leaf Design, Matte Finish, 5 In.	75.00
Banana Boat, Harvard Vesica, Crosscut Diamond & Fan, Green Cut To Clear, 5 x 10 In.	125.00

Banana Boat, Harvard, Cranberry Cut To Clear, 5 x 10 ½ In.	325.00
Banana Boat, Hobstars, 4 x 11 ½ In.	375.00
Berry Bowl, Hobstar, Cane, Strawberry Diamond & Fan, 5 In., 6 Piece	65.00
Bonbon, Star & Daisy, Engraved Scroll Flower Rim, Tiffany Silver, 7 ⅜ In.	385.00
Bottle, Water, Hobstar & Fan, 8 ¼ In.	23.00
Bowl, 13 Hobstars, Sawtooth Rim, 3 ½ x 8 In.	30.00
Bowl, Alhambra, Silver Rim, Meriden, Signed Wilcox, 4 ¼ x 8 ¾ In.	700.00
Bowl, Cane Center, Diamond Point Sides, Square, 9 In.	60.00
Bowl, Checkerboard, Hobstar, 3 x 9 In.	275.00
Bowl, Checkerboard, Hobstar, 3-Footed, Hawkes, 9 In.	485.00
Bowl, Checkerboard, Hobstar, 8 In.	485.00
Bowl, Cobalt Blue Layer Cut To Clear, Neoclassical Ormolu, Paw Feet, 9 x 7 In.	529.00
Bowl, Crossed Basketware, Lattice & Rosette, Hobstar Matte Glaze, 3 ¾ x 8 In.	200.00
Bowl, Emerald Green Cut To Clear, Flared, 12 Panes With Flowers, 4 x 15 In.	250.00
Bowl, Engraved Rooster, Rising Sun, 3 ¾ x 9 In.	750.00
Bowl, Genoa, Scalloped Edge, Sawtooth Rim, Clark, 4 x 9 In.	30.00
Bowl, Harvard, 7 In.	70.00
Bowl, Hobstar & Diamond, Emerald Green Cut To Clear, 4 x 8 ¾ In.	175.00
Bowl, Hobstar & Strawberry Diamond, Cane, Star & Fan Design, 3 ¾ x 8 In.	60.00
Bowl, Hobstar & Strawberry, Pedestal, Step Cut Stem, Hobstar Base, 5 x 8 In.	100.00
Bowl, Hobstar, Block & Strawberry Diamond, Triangular, Rounded Corners, c.1900, 5 x 9 In.	384.00
Bowl, Hobstar, Crosscut Diamond, Cranberry Cut To Clear, 3 ½ x 7 ¾ In.	225.00
Bowl, Hobstar, Crossed Basket Weave Lattice, Rosette, 3 ¾ x 8 In.	200.00
Bowl, Hobstar, File & Prism, Flat Bottom, 6-Sided, 3 ¾ x 10 In.	100.00
Bowl, Hobstar, Round, New York, c.1890, 8 In.	127.00
Bowl, Hobstar, Strawberry Diamond, Cane, Signed Clark, 3 x 8 ½ In.	150.00
Bowl, Hobstar, Strawberry Diamond, Cane, Star & Fan, 3 ¾ x 8 In.	60.00
Bowl, Hobstar, Strawberry Diamond, Prism & Fan, 4 x 11 ½ In.	75.00
Bowl, Hobstars With Cane Vesica Highlights, 8 In.	100.00
Bowl, Hobstars, Vesica, Banana Shape, 4 x 11 In.	40.00
Bowl, Low, Alternating Hobstar & Engraved Floral Vesica, 8 In.	125.00
Bowl, Low, Brunswick Pattern, 8 In.	50.00
Bowl, Marcella, Libbey, 9 In.	4275.00
Bowl, Napoleon's Hat, Carolyn Pattern, J. Hoare, 13 ¾ x 8 ¾ In.	1785.00
Bowl, Nordica, Clackmer, 9 In.	1475.00
Bowl, Orloff Pattern, Flared Edges, 9 x 3 ¾ In.	3250.00
Bowl, Pedestal, Triangle Design, Flowers, Oval, Signed, Ceki Finzi, 10 x 6 In.	110.00
Bowl, Poppy Pattern, Banana Shape, Fry, 11 ½ x 5 ½ In.	125.00
Bowl, Silver Rim, Snowflake, Ribbons, Hamilton & Diesinger, c.1897, 11 In.	600.00
Bowl, Star Cut Diamonds & Fan, Blue Cut To Clear, 4 x 8 ¾ In.	175.00
Bowl, Vegetable, Hobstar, Strawberry Diamond, Cane, Oval, 3 x 14 ½ In.	175.00
Bowl, Windsor, Dorflinger, 4 x 11 ½ In.	1900.00
Box, Cover, Beehive Shape, Russian Cut, Clear Buttons, 5 x 5 In.	250.00
Box, Hobstar, Silver Plate Ring, Hinged, Round, Hawkes, 6 ¼ In.	525.00
Butter, Dome Cover, Hobstar, Vesica, Nailhead Diamond & Fan, 5 ½ x 7 ½ In.	75.00
Cake Plate, Pedestal, Shoshone, US Glass, 4 x 9 In.	65.00
Candleholder, Facet Cut Knob Stem, 6-Sided, Pair	70.00
Candy Dish, Apple Green, Hexagonal Foot, Scalloped Rim, Cover, 1800s, 8 ⅝ In., Pair	147.00
Carafe, Hobstar & Cane, 8 ½ In.	175.00
Carafe, Hobstar Diamond, Dorflinger, 7 ¼ In.	125.00
Carafe, Hobstar, Prism, Strawberry Diamond & Fan, 8 In.	30.00
Carafe, Hobstar, Rays, Elongated Neck, 8 ½ In.	195.00
Carafe, Russian Pattern, Rayed Buttons, 7 ½ In.	165.00
Carafe, Water, Hobstar & File Design, 8 ½ In.	100.00
Celery Vase, 3 Rows Of Panels, Petal Shape Base & Rim, 1800s, 10 ½ x 5 ½ In., Pair	115.00
Centerpiece, Hobstar, Bowl, Rounded Body, 3 Splay Feet, Everted Rim, Foldover, 6 x 12 In.	266.00
Centerpiece, Intaglio, Pedestal, Rolled Rim, 5 ¾ x 13 ¼ In.	485.00
Chalice, Crosscut Diamond, Block, Star & Fan, Blue Cut To Clear, 11 ¼ In.	300.00
Chalice, Flashed Star, Crosscut Diamond, Notched Stem, Emerald Green Cut To Clear, 11 In.	300.00
Chalice, Hobstar Vesica With Wreath, Green Cut To Clear, 11 In.	100.00
Champagne Flute, Diamond & Fan Cut, 1850s, 5 ¾ In., 6 Piece	975.00
Cologne Bottle, Cranberry Cut To Clear, 7 In.	175.00
Cologne Bottle, Hobstar, Crosshatching, Squat, Stopper, 7 ½ In.	335.00
Cologne Bottle, Hobstar, Gargantuan, 8 ½ In.	435.00
Cologne Bottle, Hobstar, Strawberry Diamond, Vesica, 11 ¾ In.	225.00

C

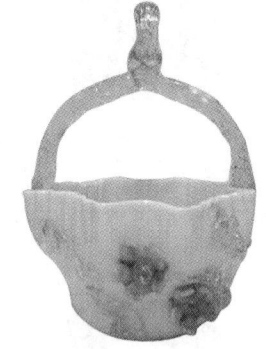

Custard Glass, Basket, Pink & Green Flower Spray, Applied Naturalistic Handle, 8 ¾ In.
$118.00

Ivey-Selkirk Auctioneers

Cybis, Boy & Girl Heads, White, Bisque, Wood Base, 7 In., Pair
$84.00

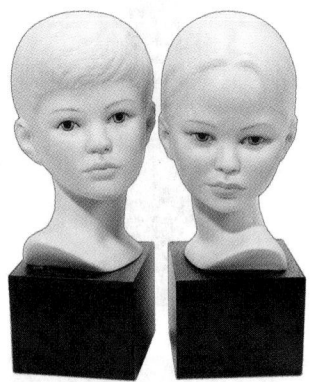

DuMouchelles Art Gallery

Czechoslovakia Glass, Lamp, Multicolor Flower Bouquet, Open Weave Light Base, 8 x 9 In.
$540.00

Cowan's Auctions

Daniel Boone, Pin, Bicentennial, 1734-1934, Birdsboro, Pa., Birthplace, Portrait, Ribbon, 2 In. $46.00

Hake's Americana & Collectibles

Daum, Lamp, Pine Trees, Helmet Shape Shade, 4 Iron Support Arms, Acid Cut, Cameo, 18 ½ In. $8625.00

James D. Julia Inc.

Compote, Emerald Cut To Clear, Green Bowl, Scalloped Rim, Clear Pedestal, 14 x 9 ½ In.	207.00
Compote, Emerald Green To Clear, Engraved Floral Wreath Border, 2 ¾ x 8 In.	10.00
Compote, Expanding Star, Scalloped Hobstar Foot, 12 In.	595.00
Compote, Hobstar, Strawberry Diamond, Engraved Flowers, Hobstar Base, Teardrop Stem, 8 In.	50.00
Compote, Hobstar, Strawberry Diamond, Teardrop Stem, Notched Foot, 8 ¼ x 7 ½ In.	125.00
Compote, Honeycomb, Downturned Rim Stem & Square, Star Cut Base, 7 ½ x 8 ½ In.	430.00
Compote, Jelly, Flute, Hobstar Foot, Scalloped Rim, 8 x 5 In.	120.00
Compote, Oval, Diamond Cut Border, Gadroon Band, Square Base, Ireland, 1800s, 7 In.	267.00
Compote, Oval, Pedestal, Hobstar, Vesica & Nailhead, Scalloped Base, 8 x 12 In.	1300.00
Compote, Pinwheel, Sawtooth Rim, Pedestal, 9 x 6 In.	148.00
Compote, Strawberry Diamond & Hobstar Design, Teardrop Stem, Notched Foot, 8 x 7 In.	125.00
Cruet, Pyramid Shape, Hobstar, 10 In.	145.00
Cruet, Strawberry Diamond, Prism & Fan Design, Double Gooseneck Handle, 7 In.	100.00
Cruet, Strawberry Diamond, Prism & Fan, Double Gooseneck Triple Notched Handle, 7 In.	100.00
Decanter Set, Cranberry Cut To Clear, 6-Point Star, Flashed Leaf, Stopper, Tray, 11 ¾ & 15 In., 2 Piece.	600.00
Decanter, Cranberry Cut To Clear, Handle, Triple Notched Handle, Hobstar Base, 8 In.	500.00
Decanter, Flute Motif, Red To Clear, 11 ¼ In.	245.00
Decanter, George III, Gilt Banding, Swags, Scalloped Honeycomb Stoppers, c.1815, 11 ½ In., Pair	492.00
Decanter, Globe Shape, Hobstars, Cut Rayed Bottom, Dorflinger, c.1900, 8 x 5 In.	175.00
Decanter, Harvard, Optic Bands, Scroll Handle, Silver Collar, Hinged Cover, Flowers, 11 In.	748.00
Decanter, Hobstar & Prism, Silver Spout & Stopper, Stag Horn Handle, Square, 9 In.	325.00
Decanter, Hobstar & Punty, Powder Blue Cut To Clear, Pyramid Shape, 17 In.	250.00
Decanter, Hobstar, Crosshatching, Neck Ring, Cut Handle, 10 In.	245.00
Decanter, Hobstar, Double Neck Ring, Triple Notched Handle, 12 ½ In.	865.00
Decanter, Hobstar, Faceted Neck Ring, 9 ¾ In.	275.00
Decanter, Hobstar, Fans & Checkerboard, Teardrop Stopper, 11 ½ In.	345.00
Decanter, Hobstar, Green To Clear, 16 ½ In.	225.00
Decanter, Hobstar, Honeycomb, Double Notched Handle, Stopper, 8 ¼ In.	960.00
Decanter, Hobstar, Notched Prism & Punties, 14 ½ In.	495.00
Decanter, Hobstar, Punties, Zipper Cutting, Flared Bottom, 14 ½ In.	495.00
Decanter, Hobstar, Stick Neck, Flat Rim, 11 ½ In., Pair	695.00
Decanter, Hobstar, Vesica & Crossed Bar, Scalloped, Mushroom Stopper, Snake Handle, 10 In.	200.00
Decanter, Lollipop Stopper, Etched Ship & Stars, 3 Coggle Bands, Flared Rim, c.1805, 9 In., Pair	1725.00
Decanter, Magnet & Grape, Fluted Neck, Star Cut Base, Engraved, Stopper, 13 ½ In.	259.00
Decanter, Panel Cut, Squat, Stopper, 7 ¾ In.	255.00
Decanter, Panel, Red To Clear, Flattened Stopper, 11 ¼ In.	265.00
Decanter, Panels, Pale Green Cut To Clear, Intaglio, Stopper, 11 In.	360.00
Decanter, Pyramid Shape, Cane, Strawberry Diamond, 17 In.	250.00
Decanter, Ships, Cobalt Blue Cut To Clear, Handle, Triple Notched Handle, 8 ¾ In.	300.00
Decanter, Thetis, Hobstar Squared Base, Stopper, 9 ¾ In.	795.00
Decanter, Trumpet Shaped Neck, Beaded Rim, Squat, Diamond Cuts, 1900s, 7 In.	119.00
Decanter, Tusk Design, Onion Shape, J. Hoare, 12 ½ In.	755.00
Decanter, Wheat, Stopper, 14 ½ In.	850.00
Decanter, Wine, Silver Flower Repousse Stopper, Monogram, Gorham, 10 In.	476.00
Dish, 5-Point Star, Hobstar Center, 6 1½ In.	25.00
Dish, Canoe Shape, Tangerine Cut To Clear, Crosscut Diamond & Fan, 8 In.	80 to 130.00
Dish, Folded, Cane Bars With Hobstar & Fan Border, 6 ¾ In.	100.00
Dish, Hobstar & Fan, Dark Amethyst Cut To Clear, Diamond Shape, 10 ¾ In.	175.00
Dish, Hobstar, Crosscut Diamond & Fan, Cranberry Cut To Clear, Oval, 8 ¼ In.	200.00
Dish, Hobstar, Nailhead Diamond & Fan, Pedestal, 3 x 6 In.	30.00
Dish, Mayonnaise, Flashed Hobstar, Meriden, 6 ¼ In.	205.00
Dish, Pedestal, Hobstar, Libbey, Scalloped Foot, 3 ½ x 6 In.	265.00
Dish, Stick, Geometric Cut Border, Step Cut Stem, Facet Cut Jewel Knob, 6 ½ x 8 In.	100.00
Epergne, Silver Plate, Trumpet Shape, Crosshatched, Triangular Base, Winged Horses, 1900s, 20 In.	306.00
Fernery, Hobstar & Fan, Silver Plate Insert, 3-Footed, 4 ½ x 7 ¾ In.	30.00
Finger Bowl, Strawberry Diamond & Fan, 5 x 2 ½ In.	99.00
Finger Bowl, Underplate, Russian, Cranberry Cut To Clear, Pair	700.00
Finger Bowl, Underplate, Russian, Green Turquoise Cut To Clear, Pair	700.00
Flagon, Stopper, White Overlay, Flowers, Gold Panels, Josephine Hutte, Poland, c.1850, 7 In., Pair	805.00
Goblet, Engraved, Landscape, Dog Chasing Stag, Panel Cut, Baluster Stem, Star Cut Foot, 7 In.	104.00
Goblet, Hobstar, Double Knobbed Teardrop Stem, 7 In.	135.00
Goblet, Shrimp Cocktail, Hobstar, Star & Fan, 6 ¾ In.	50.00
Humidor, Hobstar, Star, Split Strawberry Diamond, Barrel Shape, 6 ½ In.	175.00
Humidor, Marlboro, Dorflinger, Lid, 7 x 3 ½ In.	645.00
Humidor, Marlboro, Sterling Rim, Dorflinger, 9 ¼ In.	2875.00

C

Humidor, Notched Prisms, Hobstars, 9 x 6 In.	695.00
Ice Bucket, Pluto, Tab Handles, Signed J. Hoare, 5 ½ In.	150.00
Inkwell, Crosscut Diamond & Fan, Embossed Flowers, Silver Plate Flip Lid, 4 ½ In.	175.00
Inkwell, Ribbed, Sterling Top, 3 ½ x 3 ½ In.	825.00
Jam Jar, Intaglio, Sterling Top, Attached Underplate, 6 x 4 ¼ In.	195.00
Jar, Cover, Faceted Pagoda Lid, 6-Sided, Vial Shape, Elephant Busts, Handles, Rings, Chinese, 7 In.	3910.00
Jewelry Box, Hobstar Cut Lid, Sterling Collar, 3 ¾ x 7 ½ In.	450.00
Jug, Handle, Diamond, Strawberry Diamond & Fan, Dark Cranberry Cut To Clear, 10 In.	175.00
Knife Rest, Hobstar, 5 ½ In.	30.00
Knife Rest, Monarch, J. Hoare, 6 In.	325.00
Lamp, Electric, Crown, G.W. Huntley, 24 x 12 In.	2995.00
Loving Cup, Checkerboard, 2 Handles, 6 ¼ In.	380.00
Loving Cup, Hobnail Stars, Notched, Silver, Flared Top, 3 Loop Handles, Beaker Shape, c.1905, 6 ½ In.	295.00
Mug, Corset Shape, Cobalt Blue, Ray Highlights, 5 ¾ In.	50.00
Mug, Strawberry Diamond, Split Vesica & Fan, Blue Cut To Clear, Clear Handle, Corset Shape, 5 ¼ In.	160.00
Mustard, Sterling Collar, Orange Flame, Czechoslovakia, Finial, c.1925, 8 x 3 In.	85.00
Nappy, Tricornered, Handle, Hobstar & Looping Prism, 7 ½ In.	75.00
Pitcher, Champagne, Diamond, Strawberry & Hobstar, 10 ½ In.	230.00
Pitcher, Crosscut Diamond & Fan, Pattern Cut Handle, Dorflinger, 9 ½ In.	250.00
Pitcher, Diamond, Strawberry Diamond, Rosette, Fan, c.1910, 8 In.	89.00
Pitcher, Hobstar, Cylindrical, Flared Foot, Loop Handle, Wavy Rim, 1900s, 15 In.	2124.00
Pitcher, Hobstar, Triple Notched Handle, Footed, J. Hoare, 7 ¾ In.	495.00
Pitcher, Honeycomb Neck, Notched Handle, Hobstar Base, 8 ¾ In.	375.00
Pitcher, Queens, Hawkes, Hobstar Base, Triple Notched Handle, 8 ½ In.	1195.00
Plate, Chicago Variation, Scalloped Edge, 6 ½ In.	200.00
Plate, Greek Key, Meriden, 7 In.	1425.00
Plate, Hobstar, Checkerboard, 7 In.	175.00
Plate, Marquis, Scalloped Edge, J. Hoare, 7 In.	745.00
Powder Box, Hobstar, Cane, Strawberry Diamond & Zipper, Covered, 4 ½ In.	30.00
Powder Jar, Cover, Hobstar, Cane, Strawberry Diamond, Zipper, 4 ½ In.	30.00
Puff Box, Blown Out, J. Hoare, 4 x 4 In.	715.00
Punch Bowl, Cover, Diamond, Star, Strawberry Diamond & Fan, Green Cut To Clear, 11 ½ x 8 ½ In.	1200.00
Punch Bowl, Footed, Sawtooth Pedestal & Rim, 13 x 12 In.	268.00
Punch Bowl, Hobstar, Sawtooth Rim, Pedestal Stand, 14 x 15 In.	805.00
Punch Bowl, Hunt's Royal, 6 x 11 ½ In.	360.00
Punch Bowl, Mercedes, Signed, Clark, 14 ¼ In.	3995.00
Punch Bowl, Pinwheel Pattern, Sawtooth Rim, Scalloped, Footed, 14 In., 2 Piece.	150.00
Punch Bowl, Prima Donna, Pedestal Base, Crimped Edge, Clark, 13 ¾ x 14 In.	460.00
Punch Bowl, Stand, Hobstar & Fan, c.1910, 12 x 12 In.	150.00
Punch Bowl, Stand, Star & Diamond Panels, Ovalos, Spread Foot Base, 1900s, 8 ¾ x 10 ½ In.	148.00
Punch Bowl, Strawberry Diamond, Crosscut Diamond & Fan, Cobalt Blue Cut To Clear, 11 In., 2 Piece	700.00
Punch Bowl, Triumph, Anderson, 14 In.	1675.00
Punch Bowl, Triumph, Pedestal, Scalloped Rim, 14 In.	1675.00
Punch Cup, Hobstar Base, 3 In.	43.00
Ray, Leaf Shape, Hobstars, Crosshatching, 13 ¼ In.	1165.00
Relish, Folded, Hobstar & Fan, 6 ¾ In.	20.00
Relish, Folded, Hunt's Royal, 7 In.	75.00
Relish, Hobstar, Crosscut Diamond, Fan, 11 ½ In.	100.00
Relish, Hobstar, Strawberry Diamond & Fan, 7 ¼ In.	50.00
Relish, Hobstar, Vesica, Crosscut Diamond, Notched Fan Design, 7 ½ In.	20.00
Rose Bowl, Colonial, Dorflinger, 6 x 6 ½ In.	150.00
Rose Bowl, Dresden, Hobstar Base, Dorflinger, 6 ½ x 6 ½ In.	650.00
Rose Bowl, Russian Pattern, Football Shape, 9 ¾ In.	315.00
Serving Bowl, Orloff, Clark, Flared, 3 ¾ x 9 ½ In.	2585.00
Spooner, Drake, Corset Shape, Straus, 4 ¾ In.	40.00
Sugar & Creamer, Intaglio, Libbey	285.00
Sugar & Creamer, Prism & Starburst	40.00
Syrup, Prism Cut, Meriden, Silver Spout, Handle, 4 ½ In.	50.00
Tankard, Harvard, 11 ½ In.	125.00
Tankard, Russian, Star Cut Buttons, J. Hoare, Triple Notch Handle, 11 ½ In.	450.00
Tazza, Hobstar, Intertwined, Bronze Gilt Base, c.1900, 18 In.	413.00
Tazza, Intaglio & Geometric, Footed, 5 x 7 In.	115.00
Tazza, Scalloped Hobstar Foot, 10 In.	525.00
Tazza, Sinclair, Geometric, Intaglio Panels, Leaves, Grapes, 5 ¼ x 9 ½ In.	765.00
Tray, Hobstar Center, Floral Highlights, Prism & Fan Border, 13 ¼ In.	850.00

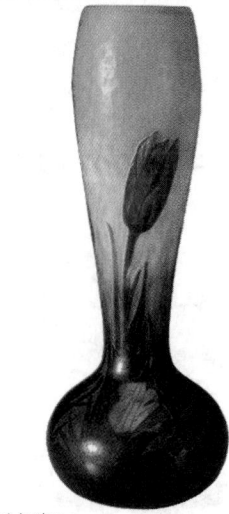

Daum, Vase, Crocus, Orange Blossoms, Acid-Cut Ground, Cameo, Marked, c.1910, 12 In.
$15340.00

Brunk Auctions

Daum, Vase, Harbor Scene, Sailboats, Square, Orange To Yellow, Cameo, Signed, 4 ½ In.
$1150.00

James D. Julia Inc.

Daum, Vase, Winter Scene, Orange, Brown Trees, Flat Sides, Cameo, Footed, Signed, 4 ¾ In.
$3163.00

Early Auction Co.

C

Davy Crockett, Bank, Dime Register,
Frontier, Tin Lithograph, 2 ⅝ x 2 ⅝ In.
$187.00

Wm Morford Antiques

Davy Crockett, Knife, Pocket, Davy
Portrait, 3 Folding Blades, Keychain
Loop, Imperial, c.1955, 3 ½ In.
$95.00

Hake's Americana & Collectibles

Garage Sale Know-How
Just heard of a new theory
about garage (tag) sales.
Gather together lots of stuff
especially inexpensive items.
Be sure there are some over
$10 items too. Put everything
out with a sign, "Every item
$1." A reader who did this
assures us that at the end of
the day he had more money
than he expected using the
normal method. Everything
sold—even items that could
have been worth less than $1.
It's a psychological thing.

Tray, Hobstar, Diamond & Fan, Cranberry Cut To Clear, Round, 8 ½ In.	200.00
Tray, Hobstar, Round, 12 In.	1840.00
Tray, Hobstar, Scalloped Edge, 15 ½ x 10 ¾ In.	850.00
Tray, Ice Cream, Duval Pattern, Straus, 15 x 10 In.	625.00
Tray, Ice Cream, Hobstar, Strawberry Diamond, Bull's-Eye & Fan, 15 x 10 ½ In.	350.00
Tray, Ice Cream, Hobstar, Zippered, 14 ½ x 10 In.	725.00
Tray, Roland Pattern, Pitkin & Brooks, 10 In.	695.00
Tray, Round, Catherine Wheel Pattern, 11 ¾ In.	900.00
Tray, Round, Gemini, 13 ½ In.	200.00
Tray, Round, Hobstar With Cross Design, Signed, 13 ¾ In.	4000.00
Trivet, Silver Overlay, Flowers, Butterfly, 10 In.	325.00
Tumbler, Creswick, Signed, Egginton, 3 ¾ In., 3 Piece	60.00
Tumbler, Hobstar, Strawberry Diamond & Fan, Flared, 3 ¾ In., 4 Piece	50.00
Tumbler, Hobstar, Strawberry Diamond & Fan, Flared, 4 In., 4 Piece	100.00
Tumbler, Hobstar, Strawberry Diamond, Nailhead Diamond, Vesica & Fan, Pair	50.00
Tumbler, Iced Tea, Hobstar, Sterling Mustache Protector, 5 ¼ In.	375.00
Tumbler, Russian Pattern, Star Cut Buttons, Cut Base, 4 In., Pair	90.00
Tumbler, Tall, Cranberry Cut To Clear, Strawberry Diamond, Crosscut Diamond, Star & Fan, 5 In.	50.00
Urn, Chestnut, Peaked Lid, Trapped Bubble, Lappet Rim, Crenellated Edge, Ireland, 1800s, 12 In., Pair	474.00
Vase, 2 Handles, Double Miter Hobnail, 10 ½ In.	1525.00
Vase, Amber Overlay, Oval, Panels Of Flowers, Star & Ribbed Borders, c.1900, 11 ¾ In.	415.00
Vase, American Eagle Holding Banner, 36 Stars, c.1865, 9 ½ In.	1200.00
Vase, Amethyst Cut To Clear, Scalloped Edge, 12 ½ x 7 In.	325.00
Vase, Bowling Pin Shape, Hobstars, Cane, 10 In.	435.00
Vase, Brazilian, Pinched Waist, Hawkes, 7 ½ In.	1325.00
Vase, Bronze, Empire, Serrated Rim, Spiral Lobed Body, 2 Handles, Busts, c.1800, 10 ½ x 5 ½ In.	1315.00
Vase, Butterfly & Daisy, Herringbone Stem, Facet Cut Knob, Scalloped Base, Tulip Shape, 14 In.	350.00
Vase, Butterfly & Daisy, Herringbone Stem, Tulip Shape, Scalloped Base, 12 In.	150.00
Vase, Center Flower Cut, Hobstar, Crosshatching, Pinched Neck, 10 In.	645.00
Vase, Cobalt Blue Cut To Clear, Cut Shell Shape, Pedestal Foot, 13 x 7 In.	148.00
Vase, Corset Shape, Hobstar, Crosscut Diamond, Nailhead Diamond & Fan, 9 ¾ In.	50.00
Vase, Cylinder Shape, Cranberry Cut To Clear, 16 In.	1000.00
Vase, Cylinder, Vesica & Diamond, Tangerine Cut To Clear, 12 In.	550.00
Vase, Daisy & Sunburst, Footed, Double Globe, 22 x 11 In.	413.00
Vase, Diamond & Fan, Olive Green Cut To Clear, 14 In.	25.00
Vase, Diamond & Hobstar, Paneled, Flared Foot, Fan Shape, Flattened Ruffle Rim, 13 x 14 In.	1416.00
Vase, Diamond & Medallion, Amethyst Cut To Clear, 12 In.	800.00
Vase, Diamond, Bar & Fan, Cobalt Blue Cut To Clear, 11 ½ In.	250.00
Vase, Diamond, Bar & Fan, Cranberry Cut To Clear, 11 ½ In.	550.00
Vase, Empire Style, Gilt Bronze, Athenienne Shape, 9 ½ x 3 ½ In.	554.00
Vase, Flaring, Cylindrical, Flowers, Theodore B. Starr, c.1915, 12 ¾ In.	239.00
Vase, Floral & Diamond Design, Emerald Green Cut To Clear, Pedestal, 8 In.	375.00
Vase, Floral Basket Medallion With Diamond, Powder Blue Cut To Clear, 12 In.	900.00
Vase, Flowers, Hoare Cut, Signed 14 x 4 ⅞ In.	129.00
Vase, Gothic Revival, Ruby, Panel Cut, Trefoils, Gilt Tracery, c.1865, 10 x 3 ¼ In., Pair	799.00
Vase, Hobstar & Prism, Hobstar Scalloped Base, Edge, Trumpet Shape, 11 ¾ In.	50.00
Vase, Hobstar, Crosscut Diamond & Fan, Trumpet Shape, 10 ¼ In.	25.00
Vase, Hobstar, Crosshatching, 4-Sided, 9 ¾ In.	425.00
Vase, Hobstar, Cut Panels, Tulip Shaped Body, c.1885, 14 x 5 In.	338.00
Vase, Hobstar, Cylindrical, 16 In.	895.00
Vase, Hobstar, Globular, Footed, 12 ¼ In.	395.00
Vase, Hobstar, Pin Shape, 10 In.	410.00
Vase, Hobstar, Strawberry Diamond, Crosscut Diamond, Vesica, Zipper & Fan, Chalice Shape, 13 ¾ In.	1000.00
Vase, Hobstar, Strawberry Diamond, Star & Fan, Hobstar Foot, Pedestal, Bulbous, 10 In.	175.00
Vase, Intaglio, Geometric, Hobstar Base, 14 ¼ In.	595.00
Vase, Iris, Rock Crystal Engraving, 16 In.	825.00
Vase, Nailhead Diamond, Zipper Swirl, Trumpet Shape, 12 In.	275.00
Vase, Notched Prismatic Panels, Flower Shaped, Round Shaped Foot, c.1900, 14 ½ In.	118.00
Vase, Othello, Clark, Step Cutting On Neck, Geometric Top, 16 ½ In.	1985.00
Vase, Pansy Pattern, Pedestal, 7 In.	235.00
Vase, Pinwheel & Fan, Chalice Shape, 12 In.	25.00
Vase, Rhine, Fan & Punty, Green Cut To Clear, 7 ½ In.	125.00
Vase, Rose Cut To Clear, Tapered, 10 x 4 In.	210.00
Vase, Rose, Chrysanthemum, 7 ½ In.	450.00
Vase, Scalloped Hobstar Foot, Flared Rim, 11 ½ In.	965.00
Vase, Sterling Collar, Flared, Pear Shape, Fluted Panels, Openwork, c.1900, 14 ½ In.	700.00
Vase, Strawberry Diamond, Cane & Fan, Amethyst Cut To Clear, Cylindrical, 11 ¾ In.	225.00

Vase, Sweet Pea, Comet Design, Signed, 6 ½ x 9 ½ In.	200.00
Vase, Trumpet, Dark Amethyst Cut To Clear, 14 In.	400.00
Vase, Trumpet, Flared, Scalloped Edge, Pedestal, 12 In.	148.00
Vase, Trumpet, Green Cut To Clear, 10 In.	250.00
Vase, Trumpet, Green Cut To Clear, 14 In.	350.00
Vase, Trumpet, Harvard, Dark Tangerine Cut To Clear, 14 In.	350.00
Vase, Trumpet, Royal Blue Cut To Clear, 14 In.	550.00
Vase, Tulip Shape, Butterfly & Daisy Design, Herringbone Cut Stem, 12 In.	160.00
Vase, Viola, Hobstar Base, Scalloped Edge, 17 ½ In.	1500.00
Vase, X-Ray Pattern, Cobalt Blue Cut To Clear, Tray, Round, 12 ½ In.	3750.00
Water Pipe, Cobalt Overlay, Cut To Clear Stars, Gilt, Long Neck, Middle East, c.1925, 11 In.	676.00
Wine, Cane & Flowers, Notched Teardrop Stem, 6 ½ In.	95.00
Wine, Cranberry Cut To Vaseline Cut To Clear, Acid Cut Field Scene, Tear Drop Stem, 5 In.	1600.00
Wine, Crosscut Diamonds, Faceted Stem, 5 ¼ In.	55.00
Wine, Fan, Facet Cut Hollow Stem, Rayed Base, Yellow Cut To Clear, 6 Piece	175.00
Wine, Green To Clear, Intaglio, 4 ¾ In.	115.00
Wine, Hobstar, Vesica & Fan, Blue Cut To Clear, 7 ½ In.	140.00
Wine, Parisian, Cranberry Cut To Clear, Dorflinger, 4 ⅝ In.	750.00
Wine, Parisian, Hobstar Base, Cranberry To Clear, 4 ½ In.	400.00
Wine, Red Cut To Clear, Faceted Teardrop Stem, 4 ¾ In.	295.00
Wine, Rhine, Amethyst Cut To Clear, Bell Shape, Hobstar Chain, Hollow Stem, 7 ½ In.	300.00
Wine, Rhine, Green Cut To Clear, Strawberry Diamond, Crosscut Diamond, 6 ½ In.	30.00
Wine, Strawberry Diamond, Crosscut Diamond & Fan, Green, 7 ½ In.	70.00

CYBIS porcelain is a twentieth-century product. Boleslaw Cybis came to the United States from Poland in 1939. He started making porcelains in Long Island, New York, in 1940. He moved to Trenton, New Jersey, in 1942 as one of the founders of Cordey China Co. and started his own company, Cybis Porcelains, about 1950. The firm is still working. See also Cordey.

CYBIS

Boy & Girl Heads, White, Bisque, Wood Base, 7 In., Pair .... *illus*	84.00
Carousel Goat, Persian Style Saddle, 12 x 12 In.	298.00
Carousel Horse, Bicentennial Flag, 13 x 12 In.	268.00
Carousel Horse, Blue 13 x 12 In.	298.00
Carousel Lion, Pastel Shield Saddle, 12 x 12 In.	208.00
Carousel Tiger, Indian Style Saddle, Black Base, 12 x 12 In.	238.00
Deer Mouse, In Clover, 3 ½ In.	195.00
Duckling, 4 In.	120.00
Eleanor Of Aquitaine, White Gown With Sky Blue Robe, 1971, 14 In.	850.00
Madonna & Child, Gilt, Wood Plinth, 13 ½ In.	173.00
Man, Seated, Folk Singer, Guitar, 12 In.	138.00
Owl, White, On Branch, 4 ½ In.	80.00
Peter Pan, Seated, On Tree Stump, Holding Flute, 7 ½ In.	58.00
Raccoon Eating Berries, 7 In.	65.00

CZECHOSLOVAKIA is a popular term with collectors. The name, first used as a mark after the country was formed in 1918, appears on glass and porcelain and other decorative items. Although Czechoslovakia split into Slovakia and the Czech Republic on January 1, 1993, the name continues to be used in some trademarks.

CZECHOSLOVAKIA GLASS

Bowl, Sawtooth Rim, 5 x 13 ½ In.	94.00
Compote, Cover, Cobalt Blue Cut To Clear, Paneled, Square Foot, 15 In.	207.00
Compote, Cover, Ruby Cut To Clear, Paneled, Square Foot, Clear Knop, 15 In.	118.00
Lamp, Multicolor Flower Bouquet, Open Weave Light Base, 8 x 9 In. .... *illus*	540.00
Perfume Bottle, Blue Cut Glass, Frosted Stopper, Nude Female, Dabber, 1920s, 9 x 6 In.	150.00
Perfume Bottle, Cut Glass, Dark Green, Oval, c.1920, 3 x 2 x 1 In.	75.00
Perfume Bottle, Frosted Fruit Design, Stopper, 10 ½ In.	25.00
Perfume Bottle, Pineapple Shape, White, Pink, Swirled, Stopper, c.1920, 3 ¼ In.	45.00
Vase, Clear To Mottled Red, Gold Wide Rim, 9 x 5 In.	115.00
Vase, Cobalt Blue, Yellow, Diamond Quilted Net, Beaker Shape, Trumpet Rim, 9 ¾ In.	748.00
Vase, Cranberry Overlay, Floral, Gold Stencil Highlights, Pedestal, 17 In.	150.00
Vase, Globular, Swimming Fish, Marked, 7 ¼ In.	89.00
Vase, Ruby Cut To Clear, Scenic Reserve, Scalloped Edge, 15 In.	177.00
Vase, Scenic, Flared Rim, Footed, 16 ½ In.	177.00

CZECHOSLOVAKIA POTTERY

Canister Set, Blue Iridescent, Flowers, 4 ½, 7 ½, 9 In., 13 Piece	80.00
Figurine, Peacock, Multicolor, c.1930, 18 In.	177.00
Serving Dish, Emerald Green, 3 Sections, Raised Ribs, 9 In.	35.00

Decoy, Canada Goose, Canvas, Carved & Painted Head, Marked JCP, North Carolina, c.1950, 24 In.
$413.00

Brunk Auctions

Decoy, Fish, Perch, Painted, Metal Fins, Tail, Faue, 6 ¾ In.
$288.00

Lang's Sporting Collectibles Inc.

Decoy, Turtle, Carved, Softwood Body, Sheet Iron Front Legs, Painted, c.1910, 10 ½ In.
$482.00

Garth's Auctions, Inc.

Dedham, Ibis, Plate, Blue & White Border, Scalloped Edge, Blue Stamp, 9 In.
$1185.00

Skinner, Inc.

Dedham, Scottie Dogs, Plate, Ink Stamp, 8 ½ In.
$1541.00

Skinner, Inc.

Delft, Puzzle Jug, Pierced Neck, Globular, Verse, 18th Century, 6 ¼ In.
$1200.00

Cowan's Auctions

Delft, Urn, Couple, Faces Below Snake Handles, c.1890
$196.00

Fox Auctions

Delft, Vase, Renaissance Revival, Seaside Scene, Blue & White, Signed, c.1915, 17 x 11 In.
$1353.00

New Orleans Auction Galleries, Inc.

DANIEL BOONE, a pre–Revolutionary War folk hero, was a surveyor, trapper, and frontiersman. A television series, which ran from 1964 to 1970, was based on his life and starred Fess Parker. All types of Daniel Boone memorabilia are collected.

Book, Little Golden Book, 1956	5.50
Candy Container, PEZ, Green, Austria	152.00
Figure, Bearskin Jacket, Coonskin Cap, Gun, Marx	80.00
Figure, Plastic, Rubber Head, Fake Coonskin Cap, Fess Parker, 1964, 5 In.	45.00
Knife, Folding, Schrade Walden Cut, 3 Blades, U.S.A.	90.00
Lunch Box, Daniel Swinging Musket, Indians, Aladdin Industries, 1955	250.00
Lunch Box, Fess Parker, Holding Gun, Fort, 1965	25.00
Lunch Box, Fighting Indians, Thermos, 1955	165.00
Lunch Box, Metal, Aladdin Industries, 1955	484.00
Medal, Club, Reading, Pa., 1967	9.99
Pin, Bicentennial, 1734-1934, Birdsboro, Pa., Birthplace, Portrait, Ribbon, 2 In. ....*illus*	46.00
Spoon, Silver, Tobacco Leaves, Daniel Boone, Gorham, c.1900, 5 In.	275.00

D'ARGENTAL is a mark used in France by the Compagnie des Cristalleries de St. Louis. The firm made multilayered, acid-cut cameo glass in the late nineteenth and twentieth centuries. D'Argental is the French name for the city of Munzthal, home of the glassworks. Later the company made enameled etched glass.

Bowl, Round, Cameo, Signed, 1 ¼ x 4 ¾ In.	345.00
Lamp, Cameo Glass, Red Poppies, Amber Ground, Domed Shade, 5 ¼ In.	2818.00
Perfume Lamp, Nasturtiums, Red Cut To Yellow Ground, Tapered, Metal Mount, 6 ½ In.	1304.00
Vase, Blossom, Leafy Branch Design, Burgundy To Amber, Tapered, Stepped Rim, 4 In.	374.00
Vase, Bougainvillea Flowers, Red, Amber Ground, Marked, c.1910, 8 ⅞ In.	826.00
Vase, Flower, Leaf Design, Burgundy To Amber, Stepped Rim, Cameo Signed, France, 3 ¾ In.	374.00
Vase, Frosted Blue, Ruby Cascading Branch, Swollen Bottom Stick, Signed, 11 In.	460.00

DAUM, a glassworks in Nancy, France, was started by Jean Daum in 1875. The company, now called *Cristalleries de Nancy*, is still working. The *Daum Nancy* mark has been used in many variations. The name of the city and the artist are usually both included. The term *martele* is used to describe applied decorations that are carved or etched in the cameo process.

Ashtray, Flowers, Lavender Ground, White Enamel, Gold Pinstripe, Flower Shape, Signed, 6 x 2 In.	978.00
Bowl, Mermaids Rim, Pate-De-Verre, Pale Purple, Etched, 8 In.	288.00
Bowl, Mottled Burgundy, Purple, Orange Foil, Cameo, Signed, 2 x 4 In.	215.00
Bowl, Mottled Yellow, Red Berries, Green Leaves, Oval, Quadrafold Rim, Cameo, Signed, 5 In.	460.00
Bowl, Purple, Foil Inclusions, Applied Nuggets & Insects, Square, Round Mouth, 4 x 5 In.	582.00
Bowl, Rose, Blue Design With Gilt Highlighted Stemmed Flowers, Signed, 4 In.	1100.00
Clock, Clear Egg Shape, Amber Butterfly, Frog & Lily Pad Base, Pate-De-Verre, Etched, 4 ¼ In.	259.00
Compote, Brown, Black Grapevines, Over Green, Black Foot, Cameo, Signed, c.1920, 11 x 11 ½ In.	4600.00
Compote, Cameo Footed, Quadrafold Coupe, Yellow & Blue, Cameo Foot, Signed, 6 In.	2750.00
Compote, Cobalt & Sky Blue, Gold Flakes, Pedestal Foot, Wide Wavy Rim, 5 ¼ x 11 ¼ In.	345.00
Creamer, Blue & Purple, 5 Violets On Green Stems, Cameo, Signed, 3 ½ In.	2100.00
Cruet, Winter Scene, Trees, Snow, Amber Ground, Loop Handle, Narrow Neck & Spout, Signed, 5 In.	2645.00
Dresser Box, Yellow & Blue Mottled With Blue Mottled Lid, Signed, 3 ½ x 5 ½ In.	100.00
Figurine, Alligator, Curved Tail, Head Upward Glancing, 16 ½ In.	219.00
Figurine, Confidences, Pate-De-Verre, Stainless Steel Base, 16 x 10 In.	434.00
Figurine, Coupe Riviera, Frosted, Lead Crystal, 1984, 4 x 15 ½ In.	575.00
Figurine, Deer, On Rocks, Engraved, 20 In.	127.00
Figurine, Dolphin, Clear Glass, Etched Signature, Chrome Base, 16 In.	186.00
Figurine, Dolphin, Tail Curling Upward, Engraved, 13 ½ x 7 In.	219.00
Figurine, Frog On Lily Pad, Pate-De-Verre, Signed, 2 ½ x 3 ¼ In.	230.00
Figurine, Frog, Yellow, Gold Eyes, Pate-De-Verre, Signed, 3 ¼ In.	184.00
Figurine, Polar Bear, Clear Crystal, 4 x 6 ½ In.	98.00
Figurine, Reflection Of The Nile, 2 Opposing Profiles, Cobalt Blue Glass, 12 In.	992.00
Lamp, Hanging, Leaves, Lavender Flowers, Yellow Ground, Bronze, Chains, Cameo, Signed, 19 In.	1725.00
Lamp, Pine Trees, Helmet Shade, 4 Iron Support Arms, Acid Cut, Cameo, 18 ½ In. ....*illus*	8625.00
Lamp, Table, Mottled Red, Foil, Cameo, Shaped Foot & Shade, Light-Up Base, c.1900, 20 x 10 In.	3963.00
Perfume Bottle, Mottled Yellow, Amber, Red Poppies, Ball Shape, Round Stopper, Cameo, 3 In.	575.00
Pitcher, Frosted White, 2 Women, Orange Umbrella, Rain, Pinch Sides, Handle, Signed, 3 In.	1035.00
Toothpick Holder, White Opaque, Black Enamel Kettle Scene, Tulip, Handles, 2 In.	1250.00
Tumbler, Mottled Red, Yellow, Sunflowers, Leafy Stems, Barrel Shape, Cameo, Signed, 3 ½ In.	1150.00
Vase, Art Deco, Red, White Cubist Inclusions, D'Avesn Loraine Series, 1920s, 9 ½ x 9 ½ In.	580.00
Vase, Ball Shape, Ice Blue Chipped Ice Ground, Pink Flowers, Signed, 3 In.	1800.00
Vase, Bulbous, Tapered, Yellow, Orange Orchids, Green Leaves, Frosted Ground, Cameo, 5 x 17 In.	4200.00

D

Vase, Carved Red Leaves & Flowers, Yellow, Cameo, Black Pedestal Base, Signed, c.1905, 16 In.	4600.00
Vase, Crocus, Orange Blossoms, Acid-Cut Ground, Cameo, Marked, c.1910, 12 In. ....*illus*	15340.00
Vase, Daffodil, Yellow Shaded To Green, Applied Yellow, Orange Flowers, 7 ½ In.	826.00
Vase, Enamel, Branches, Yellow Mottled Ground, Flower Shape, Round Foot, Cameo, Signed, 4 In.	2006.00
Vase, Enamel, Rain Scene, Trees, Pink & Green Mottled Ground, Square, Uneven Rim, Cameo, 4 In.	8338.00
Vase, Enamel, Red Flowers, Leaves, Pink & Green Frosted Ground, Broken Egg Shape, Signed, 3 In.	2760.00
Vase, Enamel, Violets, Green Leaves, Gold, White Mottled, Flared Rim, Cameo, Signed, 2 x 3 In.	2832.00
Vase, Enamel, Wheat, Frosted White To Purple, Brown, Green, Flattened Cylinder, Cameo, 9 In.	7670.00
Vase, Etched, Landscape, Enameled Mushrooms, c.1900, 6 x 4 ¼ In.	10158.00
Vase, Field & Tree Scene, French Cameo, Signed, 2 ¼ In.	1200.00
Vase, Flat Sides, Ruby, Gild Leafy Stemmed Iris, Cameo, Signed, 4 In.	375.00
Vase, Flowers, Leaves, Deep Red, Peach Mottled Ground, Pear Shape, Rolled Lip, Cameo, Signed, 9 In.	1610.00
Vase, Flowers, Stems, Shaded & Textured Rust Ground, Bulbous, Flared Rim, Cameo, 14 In.	4148.00
Vase, Flowers, Yellow & Orange, Elongated Tapered Neck, Round Foot, Cameo, 9 In.	3738.00
Vase, Footed Stick Form, Mottled Crimson & Opalescent, Thistles, Signed, 4 ½ In.	400.00
Vase, Footed, Cylindrical, Frosted Purple, Green With Amethyst Garden, Signed, 9 In.	700.00
Vase, Footed, Yellow With Crimson, Stemmed Flowers, Signed, 6 In.	1600.00
Vase, Globular Form, Pink With Art Deco Mountain Scene, Cameo, Signed, 5 In.	275.00
Vase, Gold Foil Inclusions, Dark Pink & Plum, Elongated Oval, Round Foot, 8 In.	575.00
Vase, Green Leaves, Blue Berries, Apricot Ground, Purple Saucer Foot, Narrow Body, Cameo, 9 In.	5463.00
Vase, Green Mottled Glass, Darker At Base, Matte Finish, 4 ¾ In.	414.00
Vase, Harbor Scene, Sailboats, Square, Orange To Yellow, Cameo, Signed, 4 ½ In. ....*illus*	1150.00
Vase, Ivy & Berry Design, 5-Color Cameo, Cut Square Shape, Signed, 4 ⅝ In.	900.00
Vase, Ivy, Gold Highlights, Cameo, Signed, 4 ¼ In.	95.00
Vase, Mottled Orange & Brown, Gold Foil Inclusions, Neck Handles, Incised, 1920s, 5 ½ In.	646.00
Vase, Mottled Orange With Green Leafy Stems, 11 Red Flowers, Signed, 6 ½ In.	1800.00
Vase, Mottled Yellow & Green, Long Stem Crimson Orchids, Cameo, Footed, Signed, 14 In.	2300.00
Vase, Mottled, Bulbous, Stick Form, Shades Of Red & Purple, Signed, 13 In.	150.00
Vase, Olives, Flared Rim, Footed, Wheel Cut, c.1931, 11 ¾ In.	3500.00
Vase, Opalescent Yellow, Textured, Mistletoe Branch, Leaves, Berries, Gold Rim, Genie Bottle, 9 ¼ In.	460.00
Vase, Orange Footed Stick, Mottled Yellow & White, Green Vines, Cameo, Signed, 17 In.	1200.00
Vase, Pink Flowers, Green Leaves, Marmalade Ground, Cameo, 2 ¼ x 3 ⅜ In.	1265.00
Vase, Pink, Green & White, Blue Flowers, Cameo, Signed, 3 ¼ In.	1300.00
Vase, Poppy Design, Leaves, Pink, Brown, Frosted, Orange Mottled Ground, Round Foot, 8 In.	6325.00
Vase, Poppy, Pink, Purple, Iridescent Frosted Round, Narrow Neck, Round Foot, Cameo, 7 In.	8338.00
Vase, Purple Crocus, Lilac & Frosted Ground, Hammered, Footed, Cameo, 4 ½ x 15 ½ In.	7150.00
Vase, Red, Red & White Striations, Spherical, Pierced Metal Mount, 10 In.	236.00
Vase, Roses, Violet, Green, Signed, 12 x 11 In.	1666.00
Vase, Silver Overlay Foot & Lip, Flowers, Stems, Pink, Green, Ball Shape, Stick Neck, Cameo, 8 In.	2415.00
Vase, Slender, Squared Rim, Round Foot, Raspberry Pink, Black, 25 In.	1610.00
Vase, Stick Form, Orange With Cinnamon Elongated Leafy Stemmed Flowers, Cameo, 31 In.	3600.00
Vase, Tall Trees, Brown, Green Ground, Cylindrical, Tricorner Rim, 5 ⅝ In.	2370.00
Vase, Trees, Meadow, Snow, Bulbous Bottom, Round Foot, Corseted, Slight Flare Rim, Cameo, 7 ¼ In.	3680.00
Vase, Tulips, Green Leaves, Orange Mottled Ground, Square Shape, Cameo, Signed, 4 In.	1380.00
Vase, Violets, Frosted Mottled Ground, Bulbous, Squat, Amber Foot, 4 x 5 ½ In.	2106.00
Vase, Winter Scene, Orange, Brown Trees, Flat Sides, Cameo, Footed, Signed, 4 ¾ In. .....*illus*	3163.00
Vase, Yellow With Lake Scene, Sailing Ships, Rectangular, Cameo, Signed, 4 ½ In.	750.00
Vase, Yellow, Pink Opaque Ground, Thistle, Cameo, 4 ¾ In.	650.00

DAVENPORT pottery and porcelain were made at the Davenport factory in Longport, Staffordshire, England, from 1793 to 1887. Earthenwares, creamwares, porcelains, ironstone, and other ceramics were made. Most of the pieces are marked with a form of the word *Davenport*.

DAVENPORT
LONGPORT
STAFFORDSHIRE

Coffeepot, Cypress, Elongated Handle & Spout, c.1850, 10 In.	125.00
Pitcher, Cover, Flowers, Leaves, Gaudy Ironstone, 9 ½ In.	68.00
Pitcher, Flowers, Leaves, Serpent Handle, Gaudy Ironstone, 9 ¼ In.	79.00
Plate, Flower Border, Lake Scene, Red, Transfer, c.1800, 10 In.	110.00

DAVY CROCKETT, the American frontiersman, was born in 1786 and died in 1836. The historical character gained new fame in 1954 when the Walt Disney television show ran a series of episodes featuring Fess Parker as Davy Crockett. Coonskin caps and buckskins became popular and hundreds of different Davy Crockett items were made.

Bank, Dime Register, Frontier, Tin Lithograph, 2 ⅝ x 2 ⅝ In. ....*illus*	187.00
Button, Image, Red Ground, Attached Ribbon With White Boot, c.1955, 1 ¼ In.	40.00
Canteen & Powder Horn, Plastic, Leather Pouch, Strap, Arrowhead, Box, 1955, 13 In.	558.00

Dental, Cabinet, Oak, Mirror, Large & Small Swivel, Pullout Drawers, Door, c.1910, 65 ½ In.
$2233.00

Garth's Auctions, Inc.

Dental, Tooth Key, Spring Latch, c.1850, 5 ½ In.
$176.00

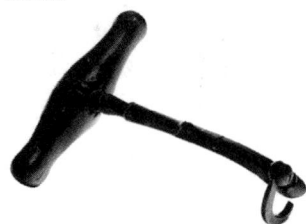

Garth's Auctions, Inc.

Denver, Jar, Cover, Speckled Matte Gray Glaze, Signed, 1913, 5 ½ x 7 In.
$434.00

Rago Arts & Auction Center

Depression Glass, Cameo, Goblet, Acid Etched, Green Stem, 8 In., 6 Piece
$173.00

Conestoga Auction Co., Inc.

Depression Glass, Cherry Blossom, Water Set, Pink, Pitcher, 6 Tumblers, 7 ¼ In. & 4 ¼ In.
$83.00

Specialists of the South, Inc.

Depression Glass, Floral, Salt & Pepper, Pink
$34.00

Tom Harris Auctions

Depression Glass, Homespun Lookalike, Lemonade Set, Cobalt Blue, Possibly By Hazel Atlas, 5 Piece
$70.00

Leighton Galleries, Inc

Cap, Coonskin, White	17.00
Cookie Jar, Full Figure, Holding Rifle, China, American Bisque, 1950s, 11 In.	158.00
Doll, Plastic, Sleep Eyes, Movable Arms & Legs, Ortune Toy, Box, c.1955, 7 In.	115.00
Figure, Bobbing Head, Molded Coonskin Cap, Composition, 1950s, 5 ½ In.	161.00
Hat, Indian Fighter, Coonskin, Official Tag, Weathermac Corp., Box, 13 In.	213.00
Knife, Pocket, Davy Portrait, 3 Folding Blades, Keychain Loop, Imperial, c.1955, 3 ½ In. ....*illus*	95.00
Pitcher & Mugs, Figural Coonskin Handle, Horton Ceramics, 1955, 7 Piece	115.00
Play Suit, Shirt, Pants, Cotton, Fringe, Coonskin Cap, Belt, Box, Size Medium	454.00
Sunglasses, Display, 6 Figural Glasses, Foster Grant, 1950s, 18 x 6 In.	258.00
Toy, Fix-It Stage Coach, Driver, 2 Horses, Plastic, Ideal, Box, 1950s, 6 x 15 In.	495.00
Toy, Paint The Story Of Davy Crockett, 5 Pictures, 5 Paint Jars, Easel, Box, 11 x 17 In.	115.00
Toy, Tool Kit, Hammer, Saw, Screwdriver, Metal Case, Box, 16 x 6 In., 11 Piece	415.00

DE VEZ was a signature used on cameo glass after 1910. E. S. Monot founded the glass company near Paris in 1851. The company changed names many times. Mt. Joye, another glass by this factory, is listed in its own category.

Bowl, Quadrafold, Lemon Yellow, Red Grapes, Signed, 4 ½ In.	500.00
Perfume Bottle, Footed Stick Form, Pink, Blue Pond Scene, 3 Geese, Signed, 7 ½ In.	225.00
Vase, Bulbous Stick Form, Yellow With Ruby Forest Scene, 3 Deer, Signed, 8 In.	850.00
Vase, Crimson Mountain Lake Scene, Footed, Conical, Bird Beak Rim, Signed, France, 6 In.	460.00
Vase, Cylindrical Form, Powder Blue, Lake Scene, Sailing Ship, Accented Leaves, Signed C, 10 In.	525.00
Vase, Cylindrical, Frosted Blue & Yellow, Amethyst Mountain Lake Scene, Signed, 8 In.	600.00
Vase, Frosted & Yellow, Lake Scene Of Mountains, Castle, Signed, 10 In.	600.00
Vase, Mottled Yellow, Crimson Stemmed Flowers, Signed, 4 In.	350.00
Vase, Poppies, Blooming, White Matte Ground, 5 ¼ In.	895.00
Vase, Yellow, Crimson Lake Scene, Shouldered, Narrow Neck, Signed, 5 In.	345.00

DECORATED TUMBLERS have been made by Anchor Hocking, Federal, Hazel Atlas, Libbey, and other companies since the 1930s, when the pyroglaze process of printing was introduced. The barware and other glasses feature drinking jokes, characters, or decorative geometric patterns. Swankyswigs are listed in their own category. Decorated tumblers may also be listed in Advertising, Coca-Cola, Pepsi-Cola, and many other categories.

All Dish Washer, Measurement Marks, Libbey, 1970s, 4 ½ In.	25.00
Bands Of Red Roses, Green Leaves, 10 Oz.	5.00
Beefeater Gin, Live A Little, Clear, Yellow, 5 ¾ In.	9.00
Clear, Dancing Colts, White, Gold, Libbey, 5 ¼ In.	7.50
Clear, Geese, In Flight, Trees, 5 In.	7.50
Clear, Multicolor Bands, Anchor Hocking, 6 In., 5 Piece	52.00
Clear, Ships, Ships Wheels, Red, Blue, c.1950, 4 ¾ In.	7.50
Flowers, Clear, Aqua, White, Hazel Atlas, 6 ½ In.	8.50
Frigidaire, Measurements, 4 ¾ In.	11.00
Hoe Down, Forest Green, Anchor Hocking, 5 ¼ In.	16.00
New Year's, Balloons, Clock At Midnight, Horns, Clear, Red, Green, 5 ¾ In.	8.00
Old Forester Bourbon, Clear, Gold, Anchor Hocking, 5 ½ In., 4 Piece	20.00
Partners All, Forest Green, Anchor Hocking, 5 ¼ In.	16.00
PRR 4902 Railroad, Train, Red, 1970s, 4 ½ In.	25.00
Roly Poly, PRR Railroad, Train, Red, 1970s, 2 ½ In.	25.00
Rooster, Metlox, c.1970, 5 ¼ In.	35.00
Treasure Island, One-Legged Pirate, Ship, Cabin, Gold Trim, Libbey, 5 In.	7.50
White Horse Scotch, Clear, Yellow, Diageo, 5 ½ In.	6.00

DECOYS are carved or turned wooden copies of birds, fish, or animals. The decoy was placed in the water or propped on the shore to lure flying birds to the pond for hunters. Some decoys are handmade; some are commercial products. Today there is a group of artists making modern decoys for display, not for use in a pond. Many sell for high prices.

Barrow's Goldeneye Hen, Signed, 13 ½ In.	189.00
Beaver, Ice Fishing, Wood, Carved, Painted, Moving Tail, Copper Foot Tabs, c.1910, 9 ½ In.	1528.00
Black Duck, Oscar Peterson, 1930s, 14 ½ In.	354.00
Bluebill, Feathered Marks, Carved, Old Wood, 13 x 6 In.	59.00
Brant Drake, Black Breast, Head, White Spotted Neck, Glass Eyes, Lead Weight Tether Ring, 17 In.	30.00
Brant, Preening, Glass Eyes, Painted Wood, 1900s, 16 In.	201.00
Canada Goose, Barrel Stave Shape, Slat Body, Painted, Elongated Tail, Arched Neck, c.1915, 30 In.	230.00
Canada Goose, Canvas, Carved & Painted Head, Marked JCP, North Carolina, c.1950, 24 In. ..*illus*	413.00
Canada Goose, Hollow Body, 2 Piece, c.1890, 10 x 23 In.	1126.00
Canada Goose, Metal Legs, Brown, Tan, 31 x 22 In.	201.00

Canada Goose, Wood & Canvas, Painted Head & Tail, 20th Century, 12 x 29 In.	490.00
Canvasback Drake, Wood, Hand Painted, Maryland, 7 ¼ x 14 In.	239.00
Catalog, Pike, Crackle Finish, Glass Eyes, Macatawa Bait Co., Box, 9 ½ In.	59.00
Common Goldeneye Hen, Working Decoy, Glass Eyes, Lead Weight, 17 In.	71.00
Coot, Wood, Painted, Back Bay Area, Virginia, c.1950, 10 ½ In.	295.00
Crow, Softwood, Applied Tail & Wings, Inset Glass Eyes, Pine Block Base, 1900s, 14 ½ In.	1175.00
Duck, Carved, Painted, Ken Harris, Woodville, N.Y., 6 x 17 In.	891.00
Duck, Glass Eyes, Carved, Painted, 3 Piece, Marked RA, 13 x 7 ¼ In.	118.00
Eider, Carved, Black & White Paint, Glass Eyes, Green Beak, c.1905, 20 ¼ In.	201.00
Fish, Butterfly Gar, Macatawa Bait Co., Crackle Finish, Glass Eyes, 14 In.	142.00
Fish, Ice Fishing, Wood, Weighted, Metal Fins, Glass Eyes, Carved Initials, 1900s, 9 In.	999.00
Fish, Muskie, Glass Eyes, Pointed Teeth, Signed Jim Strangland, 19 In.	94.00
Fish, Perch, Painted, Metal Fins, Tail, Faue, 6 ¾ In. ....*illus*	288.00
Fish, Rainbow Trout, Painted Tack Eyes, Oscar Peterson, 6 ¾ In.	2006.00
Fish, Stingray, Wooden, c.1900, 11 x 8 In.	185.00
Goose, 2 Parts, Hollow, Canada, c.1890, 10 x 24 In.	1126.00
Grouse, Metal, Peg Tripod Base, Painted, 8 x 7 In.	84.00
Hooded Merganser Drake, Wood, Title, Signed, 13 ¼ In.	59.00
Mallard Hen, Hollow Body, Flat Bottom, Dunville, Ontario, c.1950, 16 ½ In.	649.00
Merganser, Softwood, Painted, c.1900, 11 ½ In.	118.00
Pigeon, Blue, Red, Gray, Lead Feet, Red Glass Eyes, 12 In.	158.00
Pintail Drake, Hand Carved, Raised Feather, Glass Eyes, Signed, Dan Williams, 1985, 7 x 19 In.	144.00
Pintail Drake, Preening Shape, Carved Wings & Tail, Glass Eyes, 16 x 7 In.	316.00
Red-Breasted Merganser, Wood Carving, Signed, 17 ½ In.	59.00
Redhead Drake, Wood, Carved, Signed, 16 x 11 ½ In.	53.00
Scaup Drake, Black, White, Gray Beak, Glass Eyes, Lead Weight, Jimmy Bowden, 11 In.	212.00
Shorebird, Carved, Painted, Impressed Eye Socket, Frank Finney, 14 In.	472.00
Shorebird, Green Paint, Slender Neck, Elongated Beak, Glass Eyes, c.1915, 16 ½ In., Pair	1298.00
Shorebird, Sandpiper, Wood, Square Base, 5 x 10 In.	690.00
Shorebird, Softwood, Carved Beak, Base, c.1900, 11 In.	1293.00
Shorebird, Willet, Upright Wings, Mounted On Driftwood, Carved, Painted, Signed, David Rhodes	230.00
Shorebird, Yellowlegs, Carved Body, Split Tail, Painted, Glass Eyes, Mass., 1800s, 10 In.	4830.00
Swan, Tundra, Cedar, Glass Eyes, 22 In.	300.00
Swan, Wood, Carved, Painted, Signed, Roy White, North Carolina, 17 x 31 In.	295.00
Turtle, Carved, Softwood Body, Sheet Iron Front Legs, Painted, c.1910, 10 ½ In. ....*illus*	482.00
Widgeon, Tack Eyes, Dodge Co., Detroit, Mich., c.1890, 14 In.	5245.00
Wood Duck, Carved, Painted, Southern Mississippi River Valley, c.1925, 36 ¾ In.	153.00
Wood Duck, Painted, Branded C.E. Shannon, Southern Mississippi River Valley, c.1945, 15 In.	153.00

DEDHAM POTTERY was started in 1895. Chelsea Keramic Art Works was established in 1872 in Chelsea, Massachusetts, by members of the Robertson family. The factory closed in 1889 and was reorganized as the Chelsea Pottery U.S. in 1891. The firm used the marks *CKAW* and *CPUS*. It became the Dedham Pottery of Dedham, Massachusetts. The factory closed in 1943. It was famous for its crackleware dishes, which picture blue outlines of animals, flowers, and other natural motifs. Pottery by Chelsea Keramic Art Works and Dedham Pottery is listed here.

Bird In Potted Orange Tree, Plate, Blue & White, Blue Stamp, 8 ½ In.	296.00
Double Turtle, Plate, Blue & White, Blue Stamp, 8 ½ In.	593.00
Duck, Plate, Dinner, Blue & White, 10 In.	148.00
Duck, Plate, Dinner, Blue & White, Maud Davenport, 9 ⅞ In.	178.00
Flying Cock, Plate, Blue & White, Blue Stamp, 1896-1929, 8 ½ In.	385.00
Golden Gate, Plate, San Francisco, Poppy Border, Blue & White, H. Robertson, 10 In.	2370.00
Grape, Bowl, 6 In.	150.00
Grape, Bowl, Blue & White, 8 ⅞ In.	245.00
Ibis, Plate, Blue & White Border, Scalloped Edge, Blue Stamp, 9 In. ....*illus*	1185.00
Lobster, Plate, Blue & White, Blue Stamp, 8 ½ In.	533.00
Moth, Plate, Blue & White, Blue Stamp, 1929-43, 8 ¼ In.	337.00
Night & Morning, Pitcher, Owl, Rooster, Chelsea Keramic, c.1890, 5 In.	184.00
Pineapple, Plate, Dinner, Decorated Border, 9 ¾ In.	237.00
Polar Bear, Plate, Blue & White, Blue Stamp, 1931, 8 ½ In.	237.00
Pond Lily, Plate, Dinner, Blue & White, 10 ¼ In.	178.00
Rabbit, Bowl, Blue & White, Blue Stamp, 9 ¾ In.	148.00
Rabbit, Bowl, c.1910, 6 x 12 In.	823.00
Rabbit, Bowl, Cover, 4 ½ x 3 ¼ In.	184.00
Rabbit, Candlestick, Snuffer, Blue & White, Blue Stamp, 2 In., 3 Piece	237.00
Rabbit, Celery Dish, Blue & White, 6 ⅝ x 10 In.	207.00
Rabbit, Tile, Tea, Blue & White, Square, Round Border, 5 ½ In.	178.00

Depression Glass, Manhattan, Relish, 5 Sections, Ruby Red Inserts, 15 In. $29.00

Conestoga Auction Co., Inc.

Depression Glass, Mayfair, Bowl, Pink, 11 ¾ In. $18.00

Martin Auction Co.

Depression Glass, Mayfair, Candy Dish, Cover, Pink, 9 In. $10.00

Martin Auction Co.

Depression Glass, Royal Lace, Bowl, Pink, Footed, 10 ⅛ In. $23.00

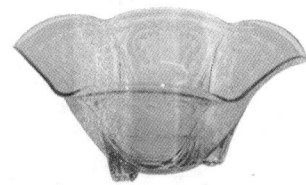

Tom Harris Auctions

Depression Glass, Royal Lace, Console, Blue, 3-footed, 10 x 4 ½ In. $48.00

Jeffrey S. Evans & Assoc.

Dick Tracy, Toy, B.O. Plenty, Holds Baby, Tin Lithograph, Windup, Box, Louis Marx, 8 ½ In. $325.00

Showtime Auction Services

Dick Tracy, Toy, Police Station, Lithographed Steel, Building, Patrol Car, Marx, 3 ½ x 8 ¾ In. $236.00

Conestoga Auction Co., Inc.

Scottie Dogs, Plate, Ink Stamp, 8 ½ In. ....*illus*	1541.00
Tapestry Lion, Plate, Blue & White Border, Blue Stamp, 8 ¼ In.	474.00
Turkey, Plate, Blue & White, Blue Stamp, 1896-1929, 8 ¼ In.	237.00
Vase, Brown Flambe Glaze, Lobed, Baluster Shape, Signed Hugh Robertson, 7 ½ x 4 In.	341.00
Vase, Green Mottled Design, Celadon Base, Incised Hugh Robertson, 10 In.	655.00
Vase, Green, Blue Flambe Glaze, Baluster Shape, Signed Hugh Robertson, 7 x 3 In.	465.00
Vase, Mottled Brown Glaze, Shouldered, Signed HRC, Hugh Robertson, 6 ¼ x 4 ½ In.	3472.00
Vase, Pillow, Insects, Leaves, Pale Blue, Robertson & Sons, Marked, 10 ¾ x 7 In., Pair	744.00
Vase, Sang-De-Boef Glaze, Textured, Hugh Robertson, Chelsea Keramic, 7 ½ x 3 ½ In.	4030.00

DEGENHART is the name used by collectors for the products of the Crystal Art Glass Company of Cambridge, Ohio. John and Elizabeth Degenhart started the glassworks in 1947. Quality paperweights and other glass objects were made. John died in 1964 and his wife took over management and production ideas. Over 145 colors of glass were made. In 1978, after the death of Mrs. Degenhart, the molds were sold. The *D* in a heart trademark was removed, so collectors can easily recognize the true Degenhart pieces.

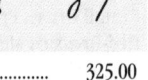

Figurine, Dog, Pooch, White, 3 ½ In.	15.00
Salt, Open, Bird, Berry In Mouth, Amber	15.00
Toothpick Holder, Tramp Shoe, Amber	18.00

DEGUE is a signature acid-etched on pieces of French glass made by the Cristalleries de Compiegne in the early 1900s. Cameo, mold blown, and smooth glass with contrasting colored rims are the types most often found.

Shade, Square, Tapered, Blue, Yellow, Pink, Signed, 5 x 3 x 2 In.	325.00
Vase, Footed, Urn, Mottled Purple, Blue Leaf, Stemmed Flowers, Signed, 20 In.	2000.00
Vase, Shouldered, Mottled Yellow, Crimson Flowers, Blue Stems, Signed, 9 ½ In.	2000.00

DELDARE, *see Buffalo Pottery Deldare.*

DELFT is a special type of tin-glazed pottery. Early delft was made in Holland and England during the seventeenth century. It was usually decorated with blue on a white surface, but some was polychrome, decorated with green, yellow, and other colors. Most delftware pieces were dishes needed for everyday living. Figures were made from about 1750 to 1800, and are rare. Although the soft tin-glazed pottery was well-known, it was not named delft until after 1840, when it was named for the city in Holland where much of it was made. Porcelain became more popular because it was more durable, and Holland gradually stopped making the old delft. In 1876 De Porceleyne Fles factory in Delft introduced a porcelain ware that was decorated with blue and white scenes of Holland that reminded many of old delft. It became popular with the Dutch and tourists. By 1990 all of the blue and white porcelain with Dutch scenes was made in Asia, although it was marked *Delft*. Only one Dutch company remains that makes the traditional old-style delft with blue on white or with colored decorations. Most of the pieces sold today were made after 1891, and the name *Holland* usually appears with the Delft factory marks. The word *Delft* appears alone on some inexpensive twentieth- and twenty-first-century pottery from Asia and Germany that is also listed here.

Apothecary Jar, Tobacco, Bulbous, Crowned Lions, Crest, Cream & Blue, 1700s, 12 In.	1610.00
Bowl, Bleeding, Enamel, Flowers, Holland, c.1790, 10 ¾ In.	368.00
Bowl, Chinoiserie Landscape, Floral Interior, England, c.1750, 3 ¾ x 9 ¼ In.	448.00
Bowl, Cover, Mask Heads, 4 Corner Spouts, Square Shape, Multicolor, c.1800, 10 In.	267.00
Bowl, Flared Rim, Flower Sprigs, Sprays, Birds, Blue, White, Round Foot, 1700s, 4 x 10 In.	863.00
Bowl, Flowers, Asian Figures, Landscape, Scalloped Rim, Fluted, Blue, Yellow, White, 1700s, 14 In.	652.00
Bowl, Octagonal, Flattened Rim, Chinoiserie Scenes, 11 In. Diam.	900.00
Bowl, Peacock Style, Late 1600s, 10 ⅜ In.	354.00
Bowl, Pointing Figure, Blue, White, Flower Border, c.1790, 2 x 12 In.	236.00
Bowl, White Ground, Blue Banding, Flowers, Leaves, Wide Rim, Round Foot, 9 In. Diam.	61.00
Candlestick, Crowned Griffin, Holding Heraldic Shield, Multicolor, c.1800, 15 In., Pair	896.00
Chair Model, Louis XV, Chaise, Blue & White Scenic Upholstery, Cabriole Legs, 8 ¾ x 5 ¼ In.	205.00
Charger, Asian Landscape, Scrolls, Diamond Border, Multicolor, 1700s, 13 ½ In.	770.00
Charger, Blue & White, Flower, Geometric Panels, Basket Center, 1700s, 13 ¾ In.	830.00
Charger, Blue & White, Flowers, Lattice Panels, Basket, 1700s, 14 In.	830.00
Charger, Blue & White, Scrolled Leaves, Center Bird, Flower Medallion, 1700s, 14 In.	415.00
Charger, Blue & Yellow Tulip, Flower Border, Holland, 12 ¼ In.	263.00
Charger, Flower, Leaves, Landscape, Multicolor, 1700s, 14 In.	652.00
Charger, Flowers, Urn, White, Blue, Yellow, Green, 14 In. Diam.	382.00
Charger, Painted, Chinese Style, c.1760, 14 In.	299.00
Charger, Sea Captain, Pipe, Looking At Ocean, Blue & White, Marked, c.1900, 15 ½ In.	374.00
Dish, Peacock Pattern, Cobalt Blue & White, Yellow Enamel Rim, 1700s, 12 ½ In. Diam.	444.00

Flower Brick, Checked Pattern, Flowers, 18th Century, 2 ½ x 6 In.	235.00
Flower Brick, Flower Pattern, 1700s, 6 ¼ In.	326.00
Jar, Cover, Blue, White, Bird, Flower, Rock Panels, Foo Dog Finial, Stand, 24 In., Pair	2457.00
Jar, Cover, Blue, White, Octagonal Shape, Peacock, Peony Reserves, Onion Knop, 15 x 8 ½ In., Pair	995.00
Jar, Cover, Blue, White, Woman, Cartouche, Flower Surround, 1700s, 15 ¾ In., Pair	1700.00
Jar, Cover, Lion Finial, Flower Design Panels, Blue & White, c.1890, 19 In.	764.00
Plaque, Scenic, Buildings, Blue & White, Frame, 1800s, 8 x 6 In.	118.00
Plaque, Shaped, Town Scene, Windmill, Waterway, Bridge, Blue & White, 1700s, 11 x 13 In.	295.00
Plaque, Winter Canal Scene, Windmill, Oval, Blue, Holland, 1800s, 23 x 19 In., Pair	2489.00
Plate, Bird & Flowers, Blue & White, 1700s, 9 In. Diam., 3 Piece	235.00
Plate, Flowers, Scrolled Leaves, Blue & White, 18th Century, 9 In.	235.00
Plate, Parrot On A Loop, Flowers, Leaves, Geometric Border, 9 In. Diam., Pair	295.00
Punch Bowl, Flower Sprays, Iron Red, Round Foot, 1700s, 10 In. Diam.	300.00
Puzzle Jug, Pierced Neck, Globular, Verse, 18th Century, 6 ¼ In. ....*illus*	1200.00
Tile, Owl, Cream, Blue Ground, Wood Frame, Marked, 6 ¼ In.	123.00
Tile, Sportsman Hunting Bird, Hunter With Dog, Castle, Holland, 1800s, 9 x 11 In., 2 Piece	413.00
Urn, Blue & White, Cover, Faience, c.1800, 15 ½ In.	177.00
Urn, Couple, Faces Below Snake Handles, c.1890 ....*illus*	196.00
Urn, Cover, Bean Jar Shape, Blue & White, 16 ½ In., Pair	300.00
Urn, Cover, Birds, Flowering Branches, Multicolor, c.1930, 14 ¾ In., Pair	388.00
Vase, Cover, Birds, Flowers, Leaves, Hexagonal, Fluted Sides, Foo Dog Finial, c.1800, 10 In.	415.00
Vase, Cover, Flower Panels, Octagonal Stand, Holland, c.1890, 15 ¾ In.	652.00
Vase, Flowers, Birds, Scrolls, Blue & White, Octangular Bottle Shape, c.1800, 11 ½ In., Pair	1541.00
Vase, Molded, Farming Hamlet, Sprigs, Scrolls, Blue & White, 1700s, 9 In., Pair	300.00
Vase, Octagonal, Flared Rim, Flowers, Scrolls, Late 1800s, 16 In., Pair	1100.00
Vase, Renaissance Revival, Seaside Scene, Blue & White, Signed, c.1915, 17 x 11 In. ......*illus*	1353.00
Vase, Wavy Border, Flowers, Leaves, Peacocks, Blue & White, Holland, c.1795, 11 In.	207.00

DENTAL cabinets, chairs, equipment, and other related items are listed here. Other objects may be found in the Medical category.

Cabinet, 2 Glass Doors, 10 Drawers, 6 Half Drawers, Metal Interior, Green, Mirror, 61 x 31 x 13 In.	288.00
Cabinet, Mahogany, 15 Drawers, 2 Doors, Glass Knobs, Milk Glass, Marble Base, 60 In.	763.00
Cabinet, Mahogany, Arched Shell Crest, 2 Marble Shelves, 2 Doors, 18 Drawers, 70 x 29 In.	4720.00
Cabinet, Mahogany, Revolving, Round, Marble Top, Drawers, Glazed Doors, c.1900, 40 In.	1220.00
Cabinet, Oak, 4 Hinged Arms, 3 Trays, 6 Over 7 Drawers, Paneled Sides	2950.00
Cabinet, Oak, 6 Drawers, Tambour Doors, Drop Lid, Harvard Dental Co., 75 x 30 In.	1175.00
Cabinet, Oak, Mirror, Large & Small Swivel, Pullout Drawers, Door, c.1910, 65 ½ In. ......*illus*	2233.00
Cabinet, Oak, Serpentine Center, Swing-Out Trays & Shelves, 21 Drawers, 59 x 26 In.	2360.00
Cabinet, Walnut, Metal Interior, W.D. Allison Co., 1950s, 59 x 27 ½ In.	985.00
Chair, Cast Iron, Folding, Reclining Back, Revolving Circular Seat, c.1920	345.00
Chest, Oak, Fitted Interior, Instruments, 25 Vials, 19 x 7 x 4 In.	308.00
Table, Dentist, Metal, Revolving, Milk Glass Top, 4 Glass Doors, Drawers, c.1910, 33 x 27 In.	3444.00
Tooth Key, Spring Latch, c.1850, 5 ½ In. ....*illus*	176.00
Tooth Mold Set, Plastic Drawer Case, Individual Teeth, 2 Tooth Keys, 6 ¼ In.	59.00

DENVER is part of the mark on an American art pottery. William Long of Steubenville, Ohio, founded the Lonhuda Pottery Company in 1892. In 1900 he moved to Denver, Colorado, and organized the Denver China and Pottery Company. This pottery, which used the mark *Denver,* worked until 1905, when Long moved to New Jersey and founded the Clifton Pottery. Long also worked for Weller Pottery, Roseville Pottery, and American Encaustic Tiling Company. Do not confuse this pottery with the Denver White Pottery, which worked from 1894 to 1955 in Denver.

DENVER
C T &.
P T Co

Jar, Cover, Speckled Matte Gray Glaze, Signed, 1913, 5 ½ x 7 In. ....*illus*	434.00
Vase, Raised Flowers, Green Matte Glaze, Scalloped Rim, Denaura, 1903, 6 x 5 ½ In.	1540.00

DEPRESSION GLASS is an inexpensive glass that was manufactured in large quantities during the 1920s and early 1930s. It was made in many colors and patterns by dozens of factories in the United States. Most patterns were also made in clear glass, which the factories called *crystal.* If no color is listed here, it is clear. The name *Depression glass* is a modern one and also refers to machine-made glass of the 1940s through 1970s. For more prices, go to kovels.com. Sets missing a few pieces can be completed through the help of one of the many matching services listed on our website.

Adam, Bowl, Cover, Pink, 9 In.	80.00
Adam, Bowl, Dessert, Green, 4 ¾ In.	22.00
Adam, Bowl, Pink, 8 In.	40.00
Adam, Butter, Cover, Pink	95.00

Dirk Van Erp, Lamp, Copper, Hammered, Rivets, Mica Shade, Windmill Stamp, c.1911, 20 x 18 In.
$23560.00

Rago Arts & Auction Center

Disneyana, Bottle, Milk, Mickey Mouse, 3 Little Pigs, Slogan, Sanitary Farm Dairies, 1930s, Qt.
$447.00

Hake's Americana & Collectibles

Disneyana, Doll, Pinocchio, Composition, Painted, Jointed Wood Arms, Legs, Felt Hat, Ideal, 1940s, 20 ½ In.
$374.00

Bertoia Auction

Disneyana, Inkwell, Mickey Mouse, Hinged Lid, Metal, Germany, c.1932, 2 ½ x 4 ½ In.
$1405.00

Hake's Americana & Collectibles

Disneyana, Jar, Condiment, Figural, Mickey Mouse, Lid, Black & White, Ceramic, Continental, 1930s, 6 In.
$173.00

Hake's Americana & Collectibles

Disneyana, Marionette, Prince From Snow White, Composition, Madame Alexander
$571.00

Hake's Americana & Collectibles

Adam, Grill Plate, Green, 9 In.	28.00
Adam, Plate, Dessert, Pink, 4 ¾ In.	25.00
Adam, Plate, Pink, Sherbet, 6 In.	10.00
Adam, Sugar, Cover, Pink	25.00
Adam, Tumbler, Pink, 4 ⅝ In.	30.00
Adam's Rib, Compote, Pink, Oval, 8 In.	18.00
Alice, Cup & Saucer, Jade-Ite, Fire-King	14.00
American Pioneer, Plate, Luncheon, Pink, 8 In.	12.00
American Sweetheart, Berry Bowl, Pink, 9 In.	45.00 to 65.00
American Sweetheart, Cup & Saucer, Monax	12.00
American Sweetheart, Cup & Saucer, Pink	19.00
American Sweetheart, Cup, Pink	15.00
American Sweetheart, Plate, Dinner, 9 ¾ In.	40.00
American Sweetheart, Plate, Dinner, Monax, 10 In.	25.00 to 26.00
American Sweetheart, Plate, Salad, Pink, 8 In.	15.00
American Sweetheart, Salver, Monax, 12 In.	25.00 to 28.00
American Sweetheart, Salver, Pink, 12 In.	22.00
American Sweetheart, Saucer, Monax	3.00
American Sweetheart, Sherbet, Pink, 4 ¼ In.	20.00
American Sweetheart, Sherbet, Pink, Footed, 4 ¼ In.	22.00
American Sweetheart, Soup, Cream, Monax, 4 ¾ In.	100.00
American Sweetheart, Soup, Flat, Pink, 9 ½ In.	57.00
American Sweetheart, Sugar, Pink	22.00
Apple Blossom pattern is listed here as Dogwood.	
Aramis, Tumbler, Cobalt Blue, Ribbed, 12 Oz., 5 In.	20.00
Aratura, Server, Yellow, Center Handle	50.00
Aunt Polly, Berry Bowl, Blue, 4 In.	12.00
Aunt Polly, Bowl, Fruit, Blue, 8 In.	40.00
Aunt Polly, Dish, Pickle, Blue, Handle, 7 ¼ In.	45.00
Aunt Polly, Dish, Pickle, Green, 2 Handles, Oval, 7 ¼ In.	20.00
Aurora, Bowl, Cereal, Cobalt Blue, 5 ½ In.	11.00
Aurora, Bowl, Cereal, Pink, 5 ⅜ In.	10.00
Aurora, Tumbler, Ritz Blue, 9 Oz., 4 ¾ In.	20.00
Autumn, Bowl, Seville Yellow, Oval, Footed, 5 ½ x 3 ¾ In.	30.00
Autumn, Console, Black, 2 Handles, Oval, Footed, 9 In.	45.00
Autumn, Console, Jade-Ite, 2 Handles, Oval, Footed, 9 In.	125.00
Avocado, Bowl, 2 Handles, Oval, 8 In.	11.00
Ballerina pattern is listed here as Cameo.	
Bamboo Optic, Console, Pink, Rolled Edge, 13 ½ In.	95.00
Bamboo Optic, Creamer, Green	10.00
Bamboo Optic, Plate, Luncheon, Pink, 8 In.	8.00
Bamboo Optic, Plate, Salad, Pink, Octagonal, 7 In.	6.00
Banded Rib pattern is listed here as Coronation.	
Beaded Block, Vase, Cobalt Blue, Footed, 5 ⅛ In.	25.00
Beaded Block, Vase, Opalescent, Ruffled	12.50
Block pattern is listed here as Block Optic.	
Block Optic, Bowl, Cereal, Green, 5 ½ In.	12.00
Block Optic, Goblet, Water, 9 Oz., 5 ¾ In.	15.00
Block Optic, Goblet, Water, Yellow, 7 ¼ In.	30.00
Block Optic, Pitcher, Bulbous, Green, 54 Oz., 7 ⅝ In.	65.00
Block Optic, Plate, Sandwich Server, 10 ¼ In.	12.00
Block Optic, Salt & Pepper, Green, 4 ¼ In.	45.00
Block Optic, Sherbet, Footed, 5 ½ Oz., 3 ½ In.	8.00
Block Optic, Sherbet, Footed, 6 Oz., 4 ¾ In.	10.00
Block Optic, Sugar Shaker, Footed, Pink	31.00
Block Panel, Berry Bowl, Pink, 4 ½ In.	12.00
Bouquet & Lattice pattern is listed here as Normandie.	
Bowknot, Cup, Green	10.00
Bubble, Creamer, Green	18.00
Bubble, Cup & Saucer, Blue	5.00
Bullseye pattern is listed here as Bubble.	
Buttons & Bows pattern is listed here as Holiday.	
Cabbage Rose pattern is listed here as Sharon.	
Cameo, Bowl, Cereal, Green, 5 ½ In.	40.00
Cameo, Bowl, Dessert, Platinum Trim, 4 ½ In.	7.00

D

Cameo, Bowl, Mayonnaise, Green, 5 In.	45.00
Cameo, Bowl, Vegetable, Green, Oval, 10 In.	30.00
Cameo, Cake Plate, Green, 3-Footed, 10 In.	40.00
Cameo, Candlestick, Green, Pair	95.00 to 110.00
Cameo, Console, Pink, 3-Footed, 11 In.	75.00
Cameo, Cookie Jar, Cover, Green	60.00
Cameo, Decanter, Green, Stopper, 10 In.	175.00
Cameo, Goblet, Acid Etched, Green Stem, 8 In., 6 Piece ......*illus*	173.00
Cameo, Pitcher, Juice, Green, 6 In.	77.00
Cameo, Plate, Salad, 7 In.	5.00
Cameo, Plate, Yellow, 9 ⅛ In.	15.00
Cameo, Relish, Green, 3 Sections, 3-Footed, 7 ½ In.	30.00
Cameo, Soup, Dish, Green, Rimmed, 9 In.	75.00
Cameo, Tumbler, Green, Booted, 5 In.	40.00
Cameo, Tumbler, Iced Tea, Green, Flat, 15 Oz., 5 ¼ In.	75.00
Candlewick pattern is listed in the Imperial Glass category.	
Cape Cod, Butter, Cover, Handle, 5 In.	28.00
Caprice pattern is included in the Cambridge Glass category.	
Cherry Blossom, Berry Bowl, Green, 8 ½ In.	50.00
Cherry Blossom, Bowl, Delphite, 2 Handles, 9 ½ In.	25.00
Cherry Blossom, Creamer, Green	22.00
Cherry Blossom, Creamer, Pink, 3 In.	16.00
Cherry Blossom, Cup & Saucer, Pink, 3 ½ In.	18.00
Cherry Blossom, Cup, Delphite	18.00
Cherry Blossom, Pitcher, Green, Scalloped Base, 6 ¾ In.	75.00
Cherry Blossom, Pitcher, Pink, Footed, 36 Oz., 8 In.	77.00
Cherry Blossom, Plate, Bread & Butter, Pink, 6 In.	12.00
Cherry Blossom, Plate, Dinner, Pink, 9 In.	28.00
Cherry Blossom, Platter, Green, 13 In.	75.00
Cherry Blossom, Sherbet, Green	20.00
Cherry Blossom, Sugar, Cover, Green, 3 ⅛ In.	16.00
Cherry Blossom, Tumbler, Delphite, Footed, 4 Oz., 3 ¾ In.	24.00
Cherry Blossom, Tumbler, Iced Tea, Pink, 5 In.	72.00
Cherry Blossom, Tumbler, Pink, Footed, 3 ⅝ In.	18.00
Cherry Blossom, Water Set, Pink, Pitcher, 6 Tumblers, 7 ¼ In. & 4 ¼ In. ......*illus*	83.00
Cherryberry, Sherbet, Green, Footed	10.00
Chevron, Pitcher, Milk, Blue, 4 ¼ In.	24.00
Chevron, Pitcher, Milk, Cobalt Blue, 4 In.	21.00
Chevron, Sugar & Creamer, Pink	30.00
Chinex Classic, Plate, Castle, 9 ¾ In.	25.00
Cloverleaf, Creamer, Black	12.50
Cloverleaf, Cup & Saucer, Black	7.50 to 15.00
Cloverleaf, Plate, Luncheon, Pink, 8 In.	10.00
Cloverleaf, Salt & Pepper, Green, Footed, 3 ¾ In.	60.00
Cloverleaf, Saucer, Black	3.00
Cloverleaf, Sherbet, Black, Footed, 3 In.	20.00
Cloverleaf, Sherbet, Green, Footed, 3 In.	10.00
Cloverleaf, Sugar & Creamer, Black, 3 ¾ In.	22.00
Colonial Block, Creamer, Pink	15.00
Colonial Block, Sugar, Cover, Pink	25.00
Colonial Block, Sugar, Cover, White	15.00
Colonial Fluted Rope, Cup & Saucer	12.00
Colonial Fluted, Bowl, Cereal, Green, 6 In.	18.00
Colonial Fluted, Cup & Saucer, Green	10.00
Colonial, Berry Bowl, Green, 4 ½ In.	20.00
Colonial, Berry Bowl, Green, 9 In.	32.00
Colonial, Butter, Cover, Green	60.00
Colonial, Creamer	16.00
Colonial, Cup	4.00
Colonial, Plate, Dinner, Pink, 10 In.	60.00
Colonial, Sherbet, Pink, 3 ⅞ In.	12.00
Colonial, Sugar, Cover, Green	45.00
Colonial, Whiskey, Pink, 1 ½ Oz., 2 ½ In.	18.00
Columbia, Bowl, Cereal, 5 In.	18.00
Columbia, Plate, Bread & Butter, 6 In.	3.00
Coronation, Berry Bowl, Ruby, 5 In.	9.00

The First TV Dinner
The TV dinner was introduced in 1953. Almost none of the original boxes and aluminum trays exist.

D

Disneyana, Pail, Minnie Mouse, Pluto Pulling Donald Duck, Wagon, Goofy, Tin Litho, Ohio Art, 1938, 7 ½ In.
$337.00

Disneyana, Pin, Donald Duck Beverages, Donald Holding Soda Bottle, Convention, Canada, 1950s, 2 In.
$220.00

Disneyana, Purse, Minnie Mouse, Mesh, Link Chain Handle, Cohn & Rosenberger, c.1934, 2 ⁹⁄₁₆ x 3 In.
$353.00

Disneyana, Stringholder, Snow White, Head, Plaster, Mouth Hole, Incised WDP, 6 ½ x 7 In. **$575.00**

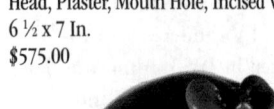

Hake's Americana & Collectibles

Disneyana, Toy, Ferdinand The Bull, Metal Bell, Wood, Pull Toy, N.N. Hill Brass Co., Copyright 1938, 9 In. **$1473.00**

Hake's Americana & Collectibles

Disneyana, Toy, Mickey Mouse, Slate Dancer, Tin Litho, Hand Crank, Steam, Germany, c.1930, 6 In. **$5750.00**

Bertoia Auction

Collectors Are Difficult to Please

Don't buy collectors something for their collection. Buy a book with information or something related to the collection, like a T-shirt picturing a bank for a bank collector.

Cube, Saucer, Pink, 5 ⅞ In.	14.00
Dancing Girl pattern is listed here as Cameo.	
Diamond pattern is listed here as Miss America.	
Diamond Line, Pitcher, Pink, 60 Oz.	48.00
Diamond Line, Tumbler, Pink, 9 Oz., 4 In.	12.00
Diana, Console, Flared, Scalloped, 12 In.	16.00
Diana, Cup & Saucer, Demitasse	12.00
Diana, Sherbet, Amber, Footed, Cone Shape	12.00
Dogwood, Berry Bowl, Pink, 8 ½ In.	50.00
Dogwood, Bowl, Cereal, Pink, 5 ¾ In.	25.00
Dogwood, Cup & Saucer, Pink	3.00
Dogwood, Grill Plate, Pink, Border Design, 10 ½ In.	25.00
Dogwood, Plate, Bread & Butter, Pink, 6 In.	5.00
Dogwood, Plate, Dinner, Pink, 9 ¼ In.	30.00
Dogwood, Plate, Luncheon, Pink, 8 In.	7.50
Dogwood, Sugar & Creamer, Pink, 2 ⅝ In.	25.00
Dogwood, Tumbler, 5 In.	65.00
Dogwood, Tumbler, Pink, 11 Oz.	5.00
Dogwood, Tumbler, Pink, Molded Band, 10 Oz., 4 ¾ In.	25.00
Doric & Pansy, Creamer, Children, Pink	40.00
Doric & Pansy, Plate, Children, Pink, 5 ¾ In.	11.00
Doric & Pansy, Sherbet, Pink, 6 In.	8.00
Doric, Berry Bowl, 4 ½ In.	12.00
Doric, Cup, Pink	12.00
Doric, Salt & Pepper, Pink	20.00
Doric, Tray, Square, Pink, 8 ¼ In.	40.00
Dutch Rose pattern is listed here as Rosemary.	
English Hobnail, Pitcher, Straight Sides, 64 Oz.	95.00
Fine Rib pattern is listed here as Homespun.	
Fire-King, Bowl, Chili, Yellow, 5 In.	7.00
Fire-King, Bowl, Shell, Jade-Ite, 6 ⅜ In.	17.00
Fire-King, Custard Cup, Blue Heaven, Scalloped Rim, 3 ¾ In.	5.00
Fire-King, Mixing Bowl, Swirl, Jade-Ite, 5 In.	250.00
Fire-King, Mug, Game Birds, Pheasant, 9 Oz.	9.00
Fire-King, Plate, Dinner, Fleurett, 9 ⅛ In.	6.00
Fire-King, Plate, Dinner, Honeysuckle, 9 ⅛ In.	9.00
Floral & Diamond Band, Berry Bowl, 8 In.	20.00
Floral & Diamond Band, Butter, Cover, Green	75.00
Floral, Bowl, Vegetable, Cover, 8 In.	55.00
Floral, Butter, Pink	110.00
Floral, Salt & Pepper, Pink ....*illus*	34.00
Floral, Sherbet, Green	30.00
Florentine No. 2, Berry Bowl, 4 ½ In.	6.25
Florentine No. 2, Bowl, Cereal, Green, 6 In.	48.00
Florentine No. 2, Coaster, 3 ⅜ In.	6.50
Florentine No. 2, Pitcher, Yellow, Footed, Cone, 28 Oz., 7 ½ In.	38.00
Florentine No. 2, Relish, Pink, 3 Sections, Oval, 10 In.	30.00
Florentine No. 2, Sherbet, 3 In.	4.00
Florentine No. 2, Soup, Dish	5.50
Florentine No. 2, Tumbler, Cocktail, 3 ¼ In.	5.50
Florentine No. 2, Tumbler, Cocktail, Yellow, 3 ¼ In.	15.00
Florentine No. 2, Tumbler, Green, Footed, 5 Oz., 3 ¼ In.	14.00
Florentine No. 2, Tumbler, Yellow, Footed, 4 ¹⁵⁄₁₆ In.	28.00
Flower & Leaf Band pattern is listed here as Indiana Custard.	
Forest Green, Pitcher, Ball, Textured, 84 Oz.	35.00
Fruits, Cup, Pink	12.00
Georgian, Berry Bowl, Green, 4 ½ In.	10.00
Georgian, Butter, Green	45.00
Georgian, Creamer, Green, Footed, 4 In.	18.00
Georgian, Sugar, Green, Footed, 4 In.	18.00
Hairpin pattern is listed here as Newport.	
Hex Optic pattern is listed here as Hexagon Optic.	
Hexagon Optic, Mixing Bowl, Green, Ruffled, 7 ½ In.	25.00
Hexagon Optic, Pitcher, Water, Iridescent Marigold, 64 Oz., 9 ½ In.	18.00
Hexagon Optic, Shaker, Pink	25.00

Hexagon Optic, Tumbler, Iridescent Marigold, 12 Oz., 5 In......	4.00
Hexagon Optic, Tumbler, Ultramarine, Flared Top, 11 Oz., 5 In.	24.00
Hocking Miscellany, Cookie Jar, Cover, Pink...	30.00
Hocking Miscellany, Vase, Pink, Basket Weave, Flared Rim, 6 x 5 In.	22.00
Holiday, Bowl, Vegetable, 9 ½ In...	32.00
Holiday, Candlestick, Pink, 3 In...	35.00
Holiday, Tumbler, Water, Pink, 10 Oz., 4 In...	20.00
Homespun Lookalike, Lemonade Set, Cobalt Blue, Possibly By Hazel Atlas, 5 Piece ......*illus*	70.00
Homespun, Berry Bowl Set, 7 Piece...	120.00
Homespun, Cup & Saucer, Pink...	30.00
Homespun, Platter, Pink, Oval...	20.00
Homespun, Tumbler, Banded, 5 ¼ In...	27.00
Honeycomb pattern is listed here as Hexagon Optic.	
Horizontal Ribbed pattern is listed here as Manhattan.	
Horseshoe pattern is listed here as No. 612.	
Indiana Custard, Berry Bowl, French Ivory, 5 ½ In...	15.00
Indiana Custard, Plate, Dinner, French Ivory, 9 ¾ In...	36.00
Indiana Custard, Sugar, French Ivory...	15.00
Iris & Herringbone pattern is listed here as Iris.	
Iris, Goblet, Water, 8 Oz., 5 ½ In...	27.00
Iris, Goblet, Wine, Iridescent, 4 In...	7.00 to 23.00
Iris, Pitcher, Water, 9 ½ In...	40.00
Iris, Plate, Bread & Butter, Iridescent, Jeannette Glass, 5 ½ In...	8.00
Iris, Sauce Bowl, Ruffled, 5 In...	14.00
Iris, Sherbet, 4 In...	28.00
Iris, Wine, 3 Oz., 4 ½ In...	22.00
Iris, Wine, 4 Oz., 5 ½ In...	27.00
Jadite, Measuring Cup, Green, Large Spout, Handle, 1950s, 7 In...	85.00
Jane-Ray, Bowl, Oatmeal, Jade-Ite, Fire-King, 5 ⅞...	25.00
Jane-Ray, Plate, Dinner, Ivory, Fire-King, 9 ⅛ In...	20.00
Jody, Serving Bowl, Yellow, 12 x 9 ½ In...	75.00
Jubilee, Tumbler, Water, Yellow, 10 In...	29.00
Lace Edge pattern is listed here as Old Colony.	
Laurel, Grill Plate, Ivory, 9 In...	20.00
Laurel, Plate, Salad, Jade Green, 7 ½ In...	17.00
Line 300 pattern is listed in the Paden City category as Peacock & Wild Rose.	
Lovebirds pattern is listed here as Georgian.	
Madrid, Cookie Jar, Amber, 7 ½ x 5 In...	60.00
Madrid, Cup, Green...	8.00
Madrid, Salt & Pepper, Amber ...	65.00
Madrid, Sugar, Amber ...	20.00
Majestic, Bowl, Mayonnaise, Emerald Green, c.1930s, 3 ¼ x 6 ½ In...	128.00
Manhattan, Candy Dish, Pink, 3-Footed, 6 ½ In...	16.00
Manhattan, Pitcher, Ball, Ribbed, Ruby, 24 Oz...	550.00
Manhattan, Relish, 5 Sections, Ruby Red Inserts, 15 In...*illus*	29.00
Manhattan, Sauce Bowl, 4 ½ In...	3.00
Martha Washington pattern is included in the Cambridge Glass category.	
Mayfair Open Rose, Bowl, Cereal, Pink, 5 ½ In...	20.00
Mayfair Open Rose, Bowl, Vegetable, Pink, Handle, 10 In...	28.00
Mayfair Open Rose, Pitcher, Juice, Pink, 8 In...	65.00
Mayfair Open Rose, Plate, Bread & Butter, Pink, 5 ¾ In...	13.00
Mayfair Open Rose, Saucer, Cup Ring...	45.00
Mayfair, Bowl, Pink, 11 ¾ In...*illus*	18.00
Mayfair, Candy Dish, Cover, Pink, 9 In...*illus*	10.00
Mayfair, Cookie Jar, Blue, 4 ½ In...	45.00
Mayfair, Plate, Dinner, Amber, 9 ⅜ In...	12.00
Mayfair, Sandwich Server, Green, Center Handle, 11 ½ In...	40.00
Mayfair, Sherbet, Pink, 3 ³⁄₁₆ In...	10.00
Mayfair, Tumbler, Amber, 4 In...	21.00
Miss America, Cake Plate, Pink, 10 ½ In...	25.00
Miss America, Compote, Martini Shape, Pink, 5 In...	35.00
Moderntone, Cup, Cobalt Blue ...	6.00 to 12.00
Moondrops pattern is listed in the New Martinsville category.	
Newport, Saltshaker, Cobalt Blue, 4 ¼ In...	25.00

Disneyana, Watch Fob, Mickey Mouse, Hunting, Pluto, Embossed Tin, Leather, 1930s, 1 ½ In.
$145.00

Hake's Americana & Collectibles

Disneyana, Wristwatch, Mickey Mouse, Silver Luster, Gold Electroplate, Leather, Ingersoll, Case, c.1940
$230.00

Hake's Americana & Collectibles

Doll, A.M., 240, Bisque Socket Head, Googly Eyes, Sculpted Topknot, c.1915, 10 In.
$448.00

Theriault's

D

Doll, Advertising, Miss Revlon, Vinyl Socket Head, Sleep Eyes, 5-Piece Body, c.1958, 10 In.
$224.00

Theriault's

Doll, Automaton, Juggling Clown, Papier-Mache, Paint, Cardboard Torso, Wood, Vichy, 30 In.
$29120.00

Theriault's

Doll, Automaton, Magician Clown, Surprises, Papier-Mache, Wood, Lambert, c.1890, 24 In.
$19040.00

Theriault's

No. 601 pattern is listed here as Avocado.	
No. 612, Bowl, Cereal, Yellow, 6 In.	25.00
No. 612, Cup & Saucer, Green	18.00
No. 612, Relish, Yellow, 3 Sections, Footed	25.00
No. 612, Tumbler, Green, Footed, 9 Oz., 4 ¾ In.	27.00
Normandie, Creamer, Pink, Footed	20.00
Normandie, Sugar, Pink, Footed, 2 Handles	20.00
Old Cafe, Olive Dish, Pink, 2 Handles, 6 In.	14.00
Old Colony, Plate, Lunch, Pink, 8 ¼ In.	20.00
Open Lace pattern is listed here as Old Colony.	
Open Rose pattern is listed here as Mayfair Open Rose.	
Oyster & Pearl, Bowl, 2 Handles, Red, 5 ½ In.	25.00
Oyster & Pearl, Bowl, Heart Shape, Pink, 5 In.	18.00
Oyster & Pearl, Candlestick, Pink, 4 ½ In.	20.00
Patrician, Butter, Cover, Spoke, Green, Round	140.00
Patrician, Grill Plate, Spoke, Yellow, 11 In.	10.00
Patrician, Sherbet, Spoke, Green, Footed	12.00
Patrician, Sugar & Creamer, Spoke, Green	25.00
Patrician, Tumbler, Spoke, Green, Footed, 5 ½ In.	80.00
Patrick, Cup & Saucer, Yellow	50.00
Peacock & Wild Rose pattern is listed in the Paden City category.	
Petal Swirl pattern is listed here as Swirl.	
Petalware, Cup, Pink	6.00
Petalware, Plate, Bread & Butter, Pink, 6 ½ In.	7.00
Petalware, Serving Bowl, Pink, 8 ¾ In.	49.00
Petalware, Sherbet, Footed, Pink, 4 ¼ In.	20.00
Pinwheel pattern is listed here as Sierra.	
Poinsettia pattern is listed here as Floral.	
Poppy No. 2 pattern is listed here as Florentine No. 2.	
Pretty Polly Party Dishes, see also the related pattern Doric & Pansy.	
Princess, Berry Bowl, Panels, Tab Handles, Green, 4 ½ In.	39.00
Princess, Bowl, Cereal, Green, 5 In.	29.00
Princess, Candy Jar, Green, 9 x 5 In.	45.00
Princess, Tumbler, Water, Green, Footed, 10 Oz., 5 ⅜ In.	30.00
Princess, Vase, Green, 8 In.	45.00
Provincial pattern is listed here as Bubble.	
Radiance pattern is listed in the New Martinsville category.	
Rainbow, Pitcher, Ball, Yellow, Ice Lip, Anchor Hocking, 1950s, 42 Oz.	29.00
Rope pattern is listed here as Colonial Fluted.	
Rosemary, Cup, Pink	11.00
Royal Lace, Bowl, Pink, Footed, 10 ⅛ In. .... *illus*	23.00
Royal Lace, Console, Blue, 3-footed, 10 x 4 ½ In. .... *illus*	48.00
Royal Lace, Cookie Jar, Cobalt Blue, 8 x 5 ½ In.	345.00
Royal Lace, Pitcher, Blue, Straight Sides, Ice Lip, 48 Oz.	185.00
Royal Lace, Pitcher, Straight Sides, Cobalt Blue, 48 Oz., 7 ½ In.	165.00
Royal Lace, Platter, Oval, Pink, Open Handle, 12 ¾ In.	30.00
Royal Lace, Platter, Pink, 13 In.	43.00
Royal Lace, Salt & Pepper, Green, 4 ⅛ In.	105.00
Royal Lace, Tumbler, Blue, 12 Oz.	120.00
Royal Lace, Tumbler, Juice, Cobalt Blue, 3 ⁷⁄₁₆ In.	40.00
Royal Ruby, Berry Bowl, 2 Handles, 4 ½ In.	8.00
Royal Ruby, Berry Bowl, 2 Handles, 8 In.	20.00
Royal Ruby, Bowl, 6 ½ In.	20.00
Sailboat pattern is listed here as Sportsman Series.	
Saxon pattern is listed here as Coronation.	
Sharon, Berry Bowl, Green, 5 In.	18.00
Sharon, Berry Bowl, Pink, 5 In.	10.00
Sharon, Berry Bowl, Yellow, 5 In.	8.00
Sharon, Bowl, Cereal, Pink, 6 In.	20.00
Sharon, Bowl, Fruit, Rose, 5 In.	15.00
Sharon, Bowl, Green, 10 ½ In.	52.00
Sharon, Bowl, Vegetable, Oval, Pink, 9 ½ In.	25.00
Sharon, Butter, Cover, Green	105.00
Sharon, Butter, Pink, 7 ¾ In.	50.00

Sharon, Creamer, Green	22.00
Sharon, Creamer, Pink, Footed	17.00
Sharon, Cup & Saucer, Green	30.00
Sharon, Cup & Saucer, Yellow	14.00
Sharon, Plate, Green, 7 ½ In.	34.00
Sharon, Platter, Oval, Pink, 12 In.	32.00
Sharon, Salt & Pepper, Green, 2 ⅜ In.	60.00
Sharon, Saltshaker, Amber	20.00
Sharon, Soup, Cream, Pink	30.00
Sierra, Creamer, Pink	20.00

Spiral Flutes pattern is listed in the Duncan & Miller category as Swirl.

Spoke pattern is listed here as Patrician.

Sportsman Series, Cocktail Shaker, Sailboats, 9 In.	65.00
Sportsman Series, Tumbler, Cobalt Blue, Windmills, 2 ⅜ In.	12.00
Sportsman Series, Tumbler, Sailboats, Cobalt Blue, 5 In., 5 Piece	50.00
Sunburst, Tray, Pickle, Oval, 8 ⅝ x 5 ¼ In.	9.00
Swirl, Serving Bowl, Ultramarine, Footed, 10 In.	28.00
Swirl, Soup, Dish, Ultramarine, 2 Handles, 5 In.	45.00
Tea Room, Salt & Pepper, 4 ⅛ In.	85.00
Thumbprint, Compote, Aqua, 1930s, 5 In.	18.00
Tulip, Pitcher, Water, Ice Lip, Celery Handle, 80 Oz.	70.00

White Ship pattern is listed here as Sportsman Series.

Wild Rose pattern is listed here as Dogwood.

Windmill pattern is listed here as Sportsman Series.

Windsor, Bowl, Pink, Footed, 7 ⅜ In.	45.00

DERBY has been marked on porcelain made in the city of Derby, England, since about 1748. The original Derby factory closed in 1848, but others opened there and continued to produce quality porcelain. The Crown Derby mark began appearing on Derby wares in the 1770s.

Bough Pot, D-Shape, Yellow & Gilt, Landscape, Villa Of Horace, Leaf & Berry Border, 10 In.	1062.00
Dish, Dessert, Pink, Roses, Buds, Peach Border, W. Billingsley, Gilt Rim, Heart Shape, c.1790, 10 In.	1201.00
Dish, Topographical Scene, Gilt Border, Mint Green, Oval, Marked, 1800s, 10 In., Pair	400.00
Figurine, 2 Cherubs, Sharing Book, White Biscuit, No. 45, 6 ¼ In.	173.00
Figurine, Boy, Standing, America, Feather Crown, Above Alligator, Gilded Base, 1800s, 9 In.	900.00
Figurine, Britannia, Standing, Helmet, Flowers, Shield, Reclining Lion, 1765-70, 15 In.	1180.00
Figurine, Cupid, Young & Old Woman, Gilded Rococo Base, Marked, 1800s, 8 In.	593.00
Figurine, Lion, Enamel, Gilded Trim Line, England, 1800s, 5 ⅜ In.	385.00
Figurine, Minerva, Standing, Plumed Helmet, Shield, Owl On Books, Gilt, 1765, 15 In.	1062.00
Figurine, Shakespeare, Bisque, Standing, Leaning On Stack Of Books, Pedestal, 1800s, 7 In.	237.00
Plate, Hand Painted, Fish, Landscape, Raised Gilt, Neoclassical Style, 10 In., Pair	153.00
Tray, No. 495, Notched Corners, Shaped Handles, Red, White, Blue Flowers, 20 x 16 ½ In.	351.00
Tureen, Cover, Japan Pattern, Gilt Lion Head Handle, 9 x 14 In., Pair	1814.00
Tureen, Sauce, Cover, Underplate, Parcel Gilt, Paint, Paw Feet, c.1800, 8 ½ x 5 In.	219.00
Vase, Jar Shape, Landscape, Lumley Castle, Wynyard Park, Gilt Neck, Foot Rim, 6 ½ In.	761.00

DICK TRACY, the comic strip, started in 1931. Tracy was also the hero of movies from 1937 to 1947 and again in 1990, and starred in a radio series in the 1940s and a television series in the 1950s. Memorabilia from all these activities are collected.

Crimestopper Club Kit, Wallet, ID Card, Secret Code Maker, 1961, Original Box	50.00
Flashlight, Secret Service, Metal Tube, Blue Enamel Paint, 1939, 3 In.	104.00
Pin, Air Detective, Airplane, Gold Metal, Bar Pinback, 2 ⅛ In.	75.00
Puppet, Hand, Cloth Body, Rubber Head, 1950s, 9 x 7 ½ In.	28.00
Toy, B.O. Plenty, Holds Baby, Tin Lithograph, Windup, Box, Louis Marx, 8 ½ In. ....*illus*	325.00
Toy, Crime Stoppers Lab No. 1, Book, Microscope, Fingerprint Kit, Box, 1950s, 13 In.	254.00
Toy, Junior Detective Kit, Type 1, c.1944, 8 x 12 In.	139.00
Toy, Pistol, Click, Pressed Steel, Decal, Marx, Box, 1930s, 8 ½ In.	253.00
Toy, Pistol, Siren, Pressed Steel, Glossy Red Paint, Decal, Tin Siren, Marx, 1934, 8 In.	115.00
Toy, Pistol, Sparkling Pop, Pressed Steel, Decals, Popping Noises, Sparks, Box, 1930s, 9 In.	247.00
Toy, Police Station, Lithographed Steel, Building, Patrol Car, Marx, 3 ½ x 8 ¾ In. ....*illus*	236.00
Toy, Squad Car With Siren, Flashing Light, Tin, Windup, Marx, Box, 1949, 11 In.	487.00
Wristwatch, Dick Tracy Holding Gun, Chrome Case, Leather Band, New Haven, Box, 1935	863.00
Wristwatch, Tan Leather Band, New Haven	45.00

DICKENS WARE *pieces are listed in the Royal Doulton and Weller categories.*

Doll, Bahr & Proschild, 204, Bisque Socket Head, Sleep Eyes, Human Hair, Composition, 14 In.
$374.00

Bertoia Auction

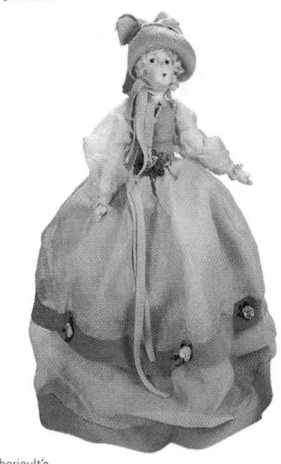

Doll, Cloth, Salon, Pressed & Painted Features, Elongated Sateen Body & Limbs, 1920s, 27 In.
$504.00

Theriault's

Doll, Clown, Musician, Composition Head, Glass Eyes, Painted Face, Trumpet, Clockwork, 24 In.
$1840.00

Bertoia Auction

D

183

Doll, Dewees Cochran, Grow-Up, Latex, Painted, Human Hair, Composition, Box, 1950s, 17 In. $1344.00

Theriault's

Doll, French, Boy Scout, Papier-Mache, Socket Head, 5-Piece Body, Mohair Wig, c.1910, 18 In. $616.00

Theriault's

Doll, German, Bisque Socket Head, Composition & Wood Body, Ball-Jointed, c.1900, 14 In. $448.00

Theriault's

DINNERWARE used in the United States from the 1930s through the 1950s is listed here. Most was made in potteries in southern Ohio, West Virginia, and California. A few patterns were made in Japan, England, and other countries. Dishes were sold in gift shops and department stores, or were given away as premiums. Many of these patterns are listed in this book in their own categories, such as Autumn Leaf, Azalea, Coors, Fiesta, Franciscan, Hall, Harker, Harlequin, Red Wing, Riviera, Russel Wright, Vernon Kilns, Watt, and Willow. For more prices, go to kovels.com. Sets missing a few pieces can be completed through the help of one of the many matching services listed on our website, www.kovels.com.

Ambassador, Bowl, Salad, Edwin Knowles, 7 ¼ In.	10.00
Ambassador, Plate, Bread & Butter, Edwin Knowles, 6 In.	8.00
Ambassador, Soup, Dish, Edwin Knowles, 7 ¾ In.	10.00
Apple Blossom, Bowl, Cereal, Homer Laughlin, 6 In.	22.00
Apple Blossom, Bowl, Fruit, Crooksville, 5 ⅜ In.	8.00
Apple Blossom, Bowl, Fruit, Homer Laughlin, 5 ¼ In.	8.00
Apple Blossom, Bowl, Salad, Homer Laughlin, 8 ⅛ In.	10.00
Apple Blossom, Bowl, Vegetable, Cover, Homer Laughlin	90.00
Apple Blossom, Cake Stand, Homer Laughlin	36.00
Apple Blossom, Creamer, Homer Laughlin, 10 Oz., 3 In.	24.00
Apple Blossom, Cup & Saucer, Homer Laughlin	24.00
Apple Blossom, Plate, Bread & Butter, Crooksville, 6 In.	7.00
Apple Blossom, Plate, Dinner, Homer Laughlin, 9 ⅞ In.	12.00
Apple Blossom, Platter, Johnson Brothers, 12 ¼ In.	21.00
Apple Blossom, Platter, Oval, Homer Laughlin, 13 ¼ In.	44.00
Apple Blossom, Platter, Oval, Homer Laughlin, 15 ⅝ In.	50.00
Apple Blossom, Soup, Dish, Crooksville, 8 In.	8.00
Apple Blossom, Sugar, Cover, Homer Laughlin, 2 ¾ In.	32.00
Apple Crunch, Cup & Saucer, Southern Potteries	18.00
Apple Jack, Bowl, Salad, Southern Potteries, 8 ¼ In.	12.00
Apple Jack, Bowl, Vegetable, Southern Potteries, 8 In.	44.00
Apple Jack, Sugar, Cover, Southern Potteries	36.00
Apple Trio, Cup, Blue Ridge	13.00
April, Cup & Saucer, Homer Laughlin	27.00
April, Plate, Bread & Butter, Homer Laughlin, 6 ¼ In.	8.00
April, Plate, Dessert, Homer Laughlin, 7 In.	13.00
April, Platter, Homer Laughlin, 15 ⅝ In.	90.00
Aristocrat, Bowl, Vegetable, Cover, Round, Homer Laughlin	100.00
Aristocrat, Bowl, Vegetable, Homer Laughlin, 9 ¼ In.	48.00
Aristocrat, Cup & Saucer, Homer Laughlin	26.00
Aristocrat, Gravy Boat, Underplate, Homer Laughlin	95.00
Aristocrat, Plate, Bread & Butter, Homer Laughlin, 6 ⅛ In.	7.00
Aristocrat, Platter, Oval, Homer Laughlin, 11 ½ In.	43.00
Aristocrat, Relish, 3 Sections, Homer Laughlin	40.00
Aristocrat, Sugar, Cover, Homer Laughlin	32.00
Becky, Coffeepot, Lid, Southern Potteries, 5 Cup, 6 ½ In.	140.00
Becky, Creamer, Southern Potteries, 8 Oz., 2 ¾ In.	24.00
Becky, Platter, Southern Potteries, 13 ¼ In.	56.00
Blossomtime, Platter, Oval, Edwin Knowles, 12 ½ In.	32.00
Blue Bells, Bowl, Fruit, Edwin Knowles, 5 ½ In.	8.00
Blue Bells, Plate, Bread & Butter, Edwin Knowles, 6 ¼ In.	4.00
Blue Bells, Plate, Dinner, Edwin Knowles, 10 ¼ In.	9.00
Blue Bells, Platter, Oval, Edwin Knowles, 12 ½ In.	38.00
Blue Bells, Sugar, Edwin Knowles, 3 ⅛ In.	12.00
Bramble, Creamer, Blue Ridge	12.00
Briar Rose, Bowl, Salad, Homer Laughlin, 7 ¾ In.	10.00
Briar Rose, Bowl, Vegetable, Rectangular, Homer Laughlin	119.00
Briar Rose, Cup & Saucer, Homer Laughlin	28.00
Briar Rose, Plate, Dinner, Homer Laughlin, 9 ⅝ In.	75.00
Briar Rose, Platter, Oval, Homer Laughlin, 11 ⅞ In.	50.00
Briar Rose, Soup, Dish, Homer Laughlin, 7 ¾ In.	22.00
Bryn Mawr, Bowl, Salad, Salem China, 7 ⅜ In.	8.00
Bryn Mawr, Bowl, Vegetable, Cover, Salem China	60.00
Bryn Mawr, Creamer, Salem China	15.00
Bryn Mawr, Gravy Boat, Footed, Salem China	56.00
Bryn Mawr, Plate, Bread & Butter, Salem China, 6 ½ In.	6.00
Bryn Mawr, Soup, Dish, Salem China, 8 ½ In.	9.00
Buttercup, Bowl, Vegetable, Round, Edwin Knowles, 8 In.	18.00

D

Buttercup, Creamer, Edwin Knowles, 8 Oz., 3 ¼ In.	18.00
Buttercup, Cup & Saucer, Edwin Knowles	10.00
Buttercup, Platter, Edwin Knowles, 15 ⅝ In.	38.00
Buttercup, Sugar, Cover, Edwin Knowles	18.00
Camellia, Berry Bowl, Johnson Bros.	12.00
Capri, Creamer, Homer Laughlin, 12 Oz., 3 ⅛ In.	14.00
Capri, Cup & Saucer, Homer Laughlin	8.00
Capri, Plate, Dinner, Homer Laughlin, 10 ¼ In.	9.00
Capri, Platter, Oval, Homer Laughlin, 15 ⅜ In.	36.00
Capri, Sugar, Homer Laughlin	10.00
Carlton, Bowl, Vegetable, Edwin Knowles, 9 ⅛ In.	28.00
Carlton, Creamer, Edwin Knowles, 10 Oz., 3 In.	16.00
Carlton, Cup & Saucer, Edwin Knowles	9.00
Carlton, Plate, Bread & Butter, Edwin Knowles, 6 ⅛ In.	4.00
Carlton, Platter, Edwin Knowles, 11 ¼ In.	28.00
Cashmere, Cup & Saucer, Homer Laughlin	18.00
Cashmere, Plate, Dinner, Homer Laughlin, 10 In.	20.00
Cashmere, Soup, Dish, Homer Laughlin, 8 ¼ In.	9.00
Chalet, Bowl, Fruit, Edwin Knowles, 5 ⅝ In.	6.00
Chalet, Plate, Bread & Butter, Edwin Knowles, 6 ¼ In.	4.00
Classic, Creamer, Edwin Knowles, 8 Oz., 3 ½ In.	22.00
Classic, Cup & Saucer, Edwin Knowles	20.00
Classic, Plate, Bread & Butter, Edwin Knowles, 6 ⅛ In.	8.00
Classic, Plate, Dinner, Edwin Knowles, 10 In.	8.00
Classic, Platter, Oval, Edwin Knowles, 13 In.	48.00
Classic, Relish, 3 Sections, Edwin Knowles	37.00
Classic, Sugar, Edwin Knowles, 3 ¼ In.	27.00
Coral Pine, Creamer, Edwin Knowles	16.00
Coral Pine, Saucer, Edwin Knowles	6.00
Damask Rose, Bowl, Fruit, Edwin Knowles, 5 ½ In.	8.00
Damask Rose, Bowl, Nut, Footed, Handle, Edwin Knowles	33.00
Damask Rose, Cup & Saucer, Edwin Knowles	8.00
Damask Rose, Relish, Edwin Knowles, 8 ¾ In.	16.00
Damask Rose, Salt & Pepper, Edwin Knowles	18.00
Damask Rose, Soup, Dish, Edwin Knowles, 7 ¾ In.	8.00
Dawn Rose, Bowl, Fruit, Edwin Knowles, 5 ⅜ In.	5.00
Dawn Rose, Bowl, Salad, Edwin Knowles, 8 In.	8.00
Dawn Rose, Bowl, Vegetable, Edwin Knowles, 8 In.	16.00
Dawn Rose, Creamer, Edwin Knowles	16.00
Dawn Rose, Cup & Saucer, Edwin Knowles	25.00
Dawn Rose, Plate, Dinner, Edwin Knowles, 10 ¼ In.	8.00
Dawn Rose, Platter, Oval, Edwin Knowles, 12 ⅝ In.	18.00
Debussy, Bowl, Fruit, Edwin Knowles, 5 ⅝ In.	8.00
Debussy, Bowl, Nut, Footed, Handle, Edwin Knowles	30.00
Debussy, Cup & Saucer, Edwin Knowles	8.00
Debussy, Relish, 3 Sections, Edwin Knowles	33.00
Desert Sand, Plate, Dinner, Johnson Brothers, 10 ½ In.	13.00
Desert Sand, Saucer, Johnson Brothers	2.00
Dubarry, Platter, Oval, Edwin Knowles, 11 ½ In.	30.00
Dunsmuir, Bowl, Oval, Viceroy, 11 x 8 In.	25.00
Ebonite, Cup & Saucer, Edwin Knowles	16.00
Eggshell Nautilus, Plate, Homer Laughlin, 10 ½ In.	8.00
Fantasy, Bowl, Vegetable, Edwin Knowles, 9 In.	32.00
Fantasy, Plate, Dinner, Edwin Knowles, 10 ¼ In.	9.00
Fantasy, Platter, Oval, Edwin Knowles, 12 ½ In.	28.00
Flamingo, Bowl, Fruit, Crooksville, 5 ¼ In.	8.00
Flamingo, Bowl, Vegetable, Oval, Crooksville, 9 ½ In.	16.00
Flamingo, Creamer, Crooksville	18.00
Flamingo, Cup & Saucer, Crooksville	8.00
Flamingo, Platter, Oval, Crooksville, 13 In.	18.00
Friendly Village, Cup & Saucer, Johnson Brothers	8.00
Friendly Village, Plate, Dinner, Johnson Bothers, 10 ½ In.	21.00
Game Birds, Mug, Johnson Brothers	25.00
Garland, Soup, Dish, Footed, Edwin Knowles	22.00
Golden Apple, Plate, Dinner, 10 In.	16.00
Greenbrier, Casserole, Dell Green, Paden City, Cover, 2 Qt.	55.00
Greenbrier, Chop Plate, Dell Green, Paden City, 12 ¾ In.	62.00

D

Doll, German, Bisque, Boy, Socket Head, Composition, Wood, Ball-jointed, Scottish Costume, c.1910, 18 In.
$3360.00

Theriault's

Doll, German, Bisque, Flapper, Bathing Beauty, Painted Face, Mohair Wig, c.1920, 6 ½ In.
$504.00

Theriault's

Doll, German, Fly-Lo Fairy, Bisque Head, Glass Eyes, Grace Putnam, Borgfeldt, c.1925, 10 In.
$1568.00

Theriault's

> **TIP**
> *Wash tea and coffee cups as soon as possible to avoid stains.*

Doll, Hertel & Schwab, 165, Bisque Socket Head, Googly Eyes, Mohair Wig, Jointed, 14 ½ In. $2875.00

Bertoia Auction

Doll, Jumeau, Bisque Socket Head, Paperweight Eyes, Human Hair, Composition, Bebe, 27 In. $5600.00

Theriault's

Doll, Jumeau, Toddler, Bisque, Socket Head, Paperweight Eyes, Composition, Wood, c.1882, 30 In. 24000.00

Theriault's

Greenbrier, Plate, Dinner, Dell Green, Paden City, 9 ¼ In.	13.00
Greenbrier, Plate, Salad, Dell Green, Paden City, 7 ¼ In.	12.00
Greenbrier, Soup, Dish, Dell Green, Paden City, 6 ⅛ In.	10.00
Greydawn, Blue, Cup & Saucer, Johnson Brothers	13.00
Greydawn, Blue, Plate, Dinner, Johnson Brothers, 9 ⅝ In.	14.00
Greydawn, Blue, Platter, Johnson Brothers, 12 ¼ In.	21.00
Greydawn, Green, Cup & Saucer, Johnson Brothers	14.00
Greydawn, Green, Gravy Boat, Johnson Brothers	25.00
Greydawn, Green, Plate, Dinner, Johnson Brothers, 10 In.	14.00
Harvest, Creamer, John B. Taylor	23.00
Heritage Hall, Bowl, Vegetable, Johnson Brothers, 8 ¼ In.	28.00
Heritage Hall, Plate, Dinner, Johnson Brothers, 9 ¾ In.	16.00
Little Bouquet, Bowl, Fruit, Crooksville, 5 ⅜ In.	8.00
Little Bouquet, Nut Dish, Handles, Footed, Crooksville	32.00
Little Bouquet, Plate, Bread & Butter, Crooksville, 6 In.	7.00
Little Bouquet, Saucer, Crooksville	9.00
Lupine, Plate, Teal Band, 1954, 10 ¼ In.	8.00
Malvern, Soup, Dish, Johnson Brothers, 8 In.	21.00
Mandarin Tricorne, Bowl, Fruit, Salem China, 5 ⅜ In.	26.00
Mandarin Tricorne, Bowl, Nut, Salem China, 3 ¾ In.	10.00
Mandarin Tricorne, Creamer, Salem China, 6 Oz., 2 ¼ In.	26.00
Mandarin Tricorne, Plate, Bread & Butter, Salem China, 6 ⅛ In.	8.00
Mandarin Tricorne, Relish, 3 Sections, Salem China	90.00
Maple Leaf, Bowl, Cereal, Salem China, 6 ⅛ In.	7.00
Maple Leaf, Bowl, Fruit, Salem China, 5 ¼ In.	7.00
Maple Leaf, Cup & Saucer, Salem China	9.00
Maple Leaf, Plate, Dinner, Salem China, 10 ⅛ In.	9.00
Maple Leaf, Soup, Dish, Salem China, 6 ⅝ In.	9.00
Margaret Rose, Platter, Johnson Brothers, 12 ¼ In.	35.00
Melody Lane, Gravy Boat, Salem China	32.00
Melody, Bowl, Cereal, Square, Johnson Brothers, 6 ⅛ In.	6.00
Minion, Bowl, Fruit, Green, Scalloped Edge, Paden City, 5 ½ In.	8.00
Noritake, Plate, Dinner, Imperial Blossom, 10 ½ In.	12.00
Noritake, Platter, Monteleone, Oval, c.1960, 13 In.	25.00
Old English, Plate, Dinner, Johnson Brothers, 10 ⅛ In.	21.00
Old Macdonald's Farm, Pitcher, Milk, Cow, Red Spout & Handle, Regal China, 8 In.	59.00
Old Mill, Charger, Johnson Brothers, 11 ⅜ In.	30.00
Old Mill, Mug, Johnson Brothers, 3 ⅜ In.	22.00
Parsley, Creamer, Salem China, 8 Oz., 2 ¾ In.	18.00
Parsley, Cup & Saucer, Square Handle, Salem China	9.00
Parsley, Plate, Dessert, Salem China, 7 ¼ In.	10.00
Parsley, Plate, Dinner, Salem China, 10 In.	10.00
Parsley, Platter, Oval, Salem China, 14 In.	38.00
Peach Bloom, Plate, Bread & Butter, Johnson Brothers, 6 ⅛ In.	18.00
Platter, Flowerpot, Round, Blue Ridge, 12 In.	40.00
Poinsettia, Creamer, Blue Ridge	16.00
Queen Rose, Bowl, Salad, Crooksville, 7 ¼ In.	8.00
Queen Rose, Platter, Oval, Crooksville, 13 ½ In.	45.00
Red Magnolia, Bowl, Wallace, 1950s, 6 ½ In.	18.00
Rosalee, Plate, Dinner, Paden City, 9 ⅞ In.	15.00
Rose Chintz, Plate, Dinner, Johnson Brothers, 9 ¾ In.	12.00
Rust Tulip, Bowl, Cereal, Salem China, 5 ⅞ In.	15.00
Rust Tulip, Bowl, Salad, Salem China, 7 ¼ In.	9.00
Rust Tulip, Creamer, Salem China, 8 Oz., 3 ¼ In.	24.00
Rust Tulip, Relish, 3 Sections, Salem China	38.00
Rust Tulip, Sugar, Cover, Salem China, 3 In.	34.00
Sandra, Bowl, Fruit, Salem China, 5 ½ In.	7.00
Sandra, Bowl, Salad, Salem China, 7 ¼ In.	10.00
Sandra, Gravy Boat, Salem China	50.00
Sandra, Sugar, Cover, Salem China, 3 ⅛ In.	18.00
Sheffield, Bowl, Fruit, Salem China, 5 ½ In.	8.00
Sheffield, Bowl, Vegetable, Cover, Salem China	60.00
Sheffield, Candleholder, Salem China	22.00
Sheffield, Sugar, Cover, Salem China	18.00
Sheraton, Plate, Salad, Square, Scalloped Edge, Johnson Brothers, 7 ¾ In.	15.00
Snowhite, Bowl, Oval, Johnson Brothers, 9 In.	33.00
Snowhite, Bowl, Round, Johnson Brothers, 8 ½ In.	32.00

D

Snowhite, Plate, Salad, Johnson Brothers, 8 In.	8.00
Southern Bell, Bowl, Fruit, Crooksville, 5 ⅜ In.	8.00
Southern Bell, Bowl, Salad, Crooksville, 7 ¼ In.	8.00
Southern Bell, Bowl, Vegetable, Crooksville, 9 ¾ In.	30.00
Southern Bell, Creamer, Crooksville	16.00
Southern Bell, Plate, Bread & Butter, Crooksville, 6 ¼ In.	5.00
Southern Bell, Platter, Oval, Crooksville, 11 ⅝ In.	22.00
Southern Bell, Soup, Dish, Crooksville, 8 In.	8.00
Southern Bell, Sugar, Cover, Crooksville	17.00
Spring Blossom, Bowl, Vegetable, Oval, Crooksville, 9 ¼ In.	26.00
Spring Blossom, Bowl, Vegetable, Round, Crooksville, 8 ¾ In.	36.00
Spring Blossom, Plate, Bread & Butter, Crooksville, 6 In.	5.00
Spring Blossom, Saucer, Crooksville	5.00
Spring Blossom, Sugar, Cover, Crooksville, 3 ⅛ In.	36.00
Summer Chintz, Plate, Bread & Butter, Johnson Brothers, 6 ¼ In.	6.00
Summer Chintz, Plate, Dinner, Johnson Brothers, 10 In.	21.00
Sweetie Pie, Bowl, Fruit, Blue Ridge	8.00
Trotter, Creamer, Crooksville	16.00
Trotter, Cup & Saucer, Crooksville	9.00
Woodhue, Creamer, Salem China	18.00
Woodhue, Cup & Saucer, Salem China	9.00
Woodhue, Platter, Oval, Salem China, 13 ¾ In.	18.00
Woodhue, Sugar, Salem China	17.00
Woodland, Plate, Dessert, Salem China, 7 ¼ In.	12.00
Woodland, Plate, Dinner, Salem China, 10 ¼ In.	15.00
Yorktown, Cup & Saucer, Salem China	21.00

DIONNE QUINTUPLETS were born in Canada on May 28, 1934. The publicity about their birth and their special status as wards of the Canadian government made them famous throughout the world. Visitors could watch the girls play; reporters interviewed the girls and the staff. Thousands of special dolls and souvenirs were made picturing the quints at different ages. Emilie died in 1954, Marie in 1970, Yvonne in 2001. Annette and Cecile still live in Canada.

Book, Family Secrets, Autobiography, 226 Pages	100.00
Calendar, 1947, Everybody Helps, String Hanger, 10 x 8 In.	24.00
Doll, Madame Alexander, Composition, 16 In.	365.00
Dolls, Composition, Carousel With Awning, Madame Alexander, 8 In., 5 Piece	969.00
Dolls, Composition, Madame Alexander, Suits, Bonnets, Name Tags, 1935, 5 Piece	845.00
Dolls, Composition, Nurse, Doctor, Basket, Madame Alexander, c.1935, 8 In.	2052.00
Dolls, Composition, Sleep Eyes, Madame Alexander, c.1935, 20 In., 5 Piece	3648.00
Dolls, Wooden Swing, Name Plate, Madame Alexander, c.1935, 8 In., 6 Piece	1083.00
Fan, Family Circle, Wood Handle, 1935	10.00
Handkerchief, Cotton, Hemmed Edge, Blue Ground, Red Dresses, 9 x 9 In.	65.00
Mirror, Pocket, Girls In Basket, 1936, 3 x 2 In.	7.00
Photograph, Baltimore Sun, Age 17, 1952, 8 x 10 In.	9.00
Photograph, Emilie Funeral, St. Agathe, Quebec, Canada, 1955, 9 x 7 In.	12.00
Pin, Girls, Home Museum, 2 ½ In.	20.00
Plate, Baby, Chrome Plated, Engraved, Heads, c.1935, 6 In.	25.00
Plate, Girls, High Chairs, 11 ¼ In.	17.00
Postcard, Dancing The Highland Fling, 1940s	18.00
Poster, Reunion, Nurses, Doctor, 1936, Color	150.00
Poster, Yvonne, 19 Months, Hat, Mittens, 1935, 29 ½ In.	18.00
Print, Girls In Class, Frame, 16 x 13 In.	22.00
Sign, Rexall Drugstore, Cod Liver Oil, Cardboard, c.1940, 24 x 29 In.	120.00
Spoon, Silver Plate, Figural Handle, Engraved, 6 In., 5 Piece	35.00

DIRK VAN ERP was born in 1860 and died in 1933. He opened his own studio in 1908 in Oakland, California. He moved his studio to San Francisco in 1909 and the studio remained under the direction of his son until 1977. Van Erp made hammered copper accessories, including vases, desk sets, bookends, candlesticks, jardinieres, and trays, but he is best known for his lamps. The hammered copper lamps often had shades with mica panels.

Centerpiece, Silver Plate, 3 Attached Candlesticks, Round, Copper, Hammered, 10 ½ x 14 In.	1240.00
Jardiniere, Copper, Hammered, Stamped, 13 x 17 In.	6820.00
Jardiniere, Copper, Hammered, Warty, Stamp, 9 ½ x 10 In.	5580.00
Lamp, Copper, Hammered, Gourd Shape, Marked, 21 x 17 In.	3224.00
Lamp, Copper, Hammered, Mica Shade, Leaf Design, 21 x 19 In.	7200.00

Doll, Jumeau, Fashion, Bisque Swivel Head, Blue Glass Eyes, Kid Body, Gusset-Jointed, c.1875, 17 In.
$7840.00

Theriault's

Doll, K * R, 101, Marie, Painted Face, Blond Mohair Wig, Braids, Incised, 19 ½ In.
$1495.00

Bertoia Auction

Doll, K * R, 109, Bisque Socket Head, Painted Eyes, Composition & Wood, Ball-Jointed, 15 In.
$9520.00

Theriault's

D

Doll, K * R, 115, Bisque Socket Head, Sleep Eyes, Wooden Body, Ball-Jointed, Toddler, 13 In.
$2576.00

Theriault's

Doll, Kathe Kruse, Boy, Cloth, Painted Face, Hair, Defined Hands, Disc-Jointed, c.1911, 16 In.
$5040.00

Theriault's

Doll, Kathe Kruse, Boy, Cloth, Painted Face, Molded Hair, Side Hip Joints, 17 In.
$3163.00

Bertoia Auction

Lamp, Copper, Hammered, Rivets, Mica Shade, Windmill Stamp, c.1911, 20 x 18 In. ....*illus*	23560.00
Lamp, Electric, Copper, Hammered, Riveted Base, Mica Shade, Marked, 19 x 18 In..................	10540.00
Pen Tray, Copper, Hammered, Jas Monogram, 12 x 4 In.....................	150.00
Vase, Copper, Hammered, Loop Handles, Mark, 7 ½ x 5 ½ In........................	1020.00
Vase, Copper, Hammered, Warty, Stamp, 4 x 4 ½ In........................	4030.00

DISNEYANA is a collectors' term. Walt Disney and his company introduced many comic characters to the world. Collectors search for examples of the work of the Disney Studios and the many commercial products modeled after his characters, including Mickey Mouse and Donald Duck, and recent films, like *Beauty and the Beast* and *The Little Mermaid*.

Ashtray, Mickey, Minnie, Pluto, Relief Figures Around Sides, China, 3 In.	230.00
Bank, Dime Register, Donald Duck, Money Bags, Tin, Gold Luster Trim, Cut Corners, 1939	153.00
Bank, Dime Register, Mickey, Minnie, Nephews, Tin Lithograph, Cut Corners, 1939, 3 In.........	285.00
Bank, Dime Register, Snow White, Metal, 2 ½ x 2 ½ In.	57.00
Bank, Elmer, Elephant, Playing Drum, Movable Trunk, Head Coin Slot, Japan, 1930s, 5 In.....	57.00
Bank, Three Little Pigs House Of Coins, Metal, Oilcloth, Chest Design, Zell, 1930s, 4 x 3 In.	508.00
Book, Donald Duck, Hardcover With Dust Jacket, 1936, 36 Pages, 10 ½ x 9 ½ In.	974.00
Book, The Clock Cleaner, Cloth, 1938..................	73.00
Bottle, Milk, Mickey Mouse, 3 Little Pigs, Slogan, Sanitary Farm Dairies, 1930s, Qt. ....*illus*	447.00
Bottle, Soakie Bubble Bath, Pinocchio, 1960, 9 ½ In..................	45.00
Bracelet, 10 Character Charms, Sterling Silver, 1940s, 7 In........................	120.00
Bracelet, Cuff, Mickey Mouse Pushing Minnie In Jalopy, Silvered Brass, c.1932	506.00
Candy Container, PEZ, Snow White, Turquoise Stem, Late 1960s, 4 ¼ In..................	115.00
Cel, see Animation Art category.	
Charm, Mickey Mouse Tipping Hat, Red & Black Enameled Metal, 1930s, ¾ In..................	86.00
Clock, Alarm, Mickey Mouse, Ivory Plastic, Luminous Hands, Ingersoll, Box, 1949, 5 In.........	230.00
Cookie Jar, Disney Cookie Bus, Yellow, Characters In Windows, D. Brecher....................	113.00
Cookie Jar, Donald Duck, Blue Sailor Jacket, American Bisque, 1950s, 12 ½ In. ... 250.00 to 329.00	
Doll, Donald Duck, Fabric, Oilcloth Head & Legs, Painted Features, 1930s, 13 In.	2875.00
Doll, Donald Duck, Indian Chief, Feathered Headdress, Bow, Felt, Stuffed, 1940s, 17 In.	924.00
Doll, Donald Duck, Velvet, Oil Cloth Eyes, Beak & Feet, Autographed, C. Nash, 1930s, 16 In.....	342.00
Doll, Dopey, Snow White, Composition Head, Clothed Body, Ideal, 11 ½ In....................	90.00
Doll, Jiminy Cricket, Wood, Felt, Swivel Head, Segmented Arms, Ideal, c.1940, 8 In.	456.00
Doll, Little Red Riding Hood, Cotton, Stuffed, Oilcloth Face, Painted, c.1934, 14 In.	408.00
Doll, Mickey Mouse, Felt, Stuffed, Oilcloth Eyes, Ear Tag, Steiff, 1930s, 7 In.	1414.00
Doll, Pinocchio, Composition, Painted, Jointed Wood Arms, Legs, Felt Hat, Ideal, 1940s, 20 ½ In. *illus*	374.00
Doll, Pinocchio, Composition, Wood, Jointed, Ideal, 8 In....................	57.00
Doll, Snow White, Composition, Ideal, 15 In.	73.00
Drum Set, Bass Drum, Floor Base, Cymbals, Wood Block, Characters, Child's	58.00
Fabric, Mickey Mouse & Beanstalk Scenes, 16 x 3 Ft.	45.00
Figurine Set, Snow White & Seven Dwarfs, Bisque, Painted, G. Borgfeldt, Box, 2 ¾ In............	283.00
Figurine, Ariel, No. 170, Resin Cast, Wood Stand, Giuseppe Armani, 12 ¼ In..................	230.00
Figurine, Dumbo, Porcelain, 1941, 5 ½ In....................	158.00
Figurine, Elmer, Tillie, Goebel, 1950s, 4 ¼ In....................	62.00
Figurine, Ferdinand The Bull, Ceramic, Brayton Laguna, c.1938, 4 x 8 x 7 In....................	230.00
Figurine, Mickey Mouse, Baseball Players, Bisque, 1930s, 3 ¼ In., 4 Piece....................	385.00
Figurine, Mickey Mouse, Open Mouth, Metal, 1930s, 2 ½ In....................	79.00
Figurine, Mickey Mouse, Oscar, Cast Metal, Standing, Round Pedestal Base, 9 In....................	920.00
Game, Three Little Pigs, Board, Accessories, Box, 1933....................	170.00
Inkwell, Mickey Mouse, Hinged Lid, Metal, Germany, c.1932, 2 ½ x 4 ½ In. ....*illus*	1405.00
Jar, Condiment, Figural, Mickey Mouse, Lid, Black & White, Ceramic, Continental, 1930s, 6 In. *illus*	173.00
Light Set, Silly Symphony, 8 Lights, Mazda Lamps, Noma	226.00
Light Set, Snow White, 12 Lights, Mazda, England, Box....................	328.00
Lunch Box, Sleeping Beauty, Metal, General Steel Wares, 1948....................	99.00
Marionette, Prince From Snow White, Composition, Madame Alexander ....*illus*	571.00
Mirror, Mickey Mouse In Relief, Silvered Brass, Round, 1932, 3 In....................	173.00
Napkin Ring, Mickey Mouse, Rope Twist, 2 x 3 x 5 In....................	184.00
Necklace, Minnie Mouse, 3 Charms, 2 Oval, 1 Heart Shape, Sterling Silver, 12 In.	213.00
Nodder, Donald Duck, Long Bill, Celluloid, Japan, 6 In....................	173.00
Nodder, Mickey Mouse, Instrument, Celluloid, Tin Base, Box, c.1930, 7 In....................	1380.00
Pail, Minnie Mouse, Pluto Pulling Donald Duck, Wagon, Goofy, Tin Litho, Ohio Art, 1938, 7 ½ In. ...*illus*	337.00
Painting, Bambi, Forest Secrets As Told To Thumper, Watercolor On Board, 1948, 24 In.........	6215.00
Painting, Snow White, Last Call For Dinner, Watercolor On Board, 1947, 20 x 24 In..............	6780.00
Pencil Holder, Mickey Mouse, Holding Pencil, Figural, Composition, 1930s, 4 ½ In....................	231.00
Phonograph, Donald Duck, Electric, Lionel, Walt Disney, c.1950	192.00
Pin, Donald Duck As Jockey, Riding Donkey, Die Cut Wood, 2 ½ In.	75.00

Pin, Donald Duck Beverages, Donald Holding Soda Bottle, Convention, Canada, 1950s, 2 In. .. *illus*	220.00
Pin, Pinocchio Comes To Town On Victor Records, Record Form, 1 ¼ In.	562.00
Plate, Mickey Mouse, Tambourine, Alphabet, 1930s, 7 ⅞ In.	295.00
Poster, Donald Duck Bread, Huey, Louie & Dewey, Normand Bros. Bakery, 22 x 17 In.	195.00
Purse, Mickey & Minnie Mouse, Mesh, Chain Handle, Cohn & Rosenberger, c.1934, 4 In.	173.00
Purse, Mickey Mouse, Minnie, Pluto, Metal, Chain, c.1934, 2 ¹⁄₁₆ x 2 ⅜ In.	390.00
Purse, Minnie Mouse, Mesh, Link Chain Handle, Cohn & Rosenberger, c.1934, 2 ⁹⁄₁₆ x 3 In. ....*illus*	353.00
Radio, Mickey Mouse, Sirocco & Wood, Carved, Mickey Playing Instrument, 1930s, 7 In.	531.00
Rug, Mickey & Minnie Mouse In Airplane, Donald Duck Parachutes, A. Smith, 1930s, 27 x 44 In.	362.00
Salt & Pepper, Donald Duck, Daisy, 20th Century	18.00
Schoolbag, Peter Pan, Canvas, Plastic Face Insert, Vinyl Strap, 1953, 13 In.	143.00
Shovel, Sand, Mickey & Minnie Digging, Tin Lithograph, Wood Handle, Ohio Art, 20 In.	648.00
Stringholder, Snow White, Head, Plaster, Mouth Hole, Incised WDP, 6 ½ x 7 In. ....*illus*	575.00
Tea Set, Mickey & Minnie Muse, Porcelain, White With Gold Trim, 1930, 21 Piece	500.00
Tea Set, Mickey, Minnie, Pluto, Wade Heath, Box Lid, 1930s, 12 x 19 In., 15 Piece	557.00
Toothbrush Holder, Dumbo, Ceramic, Colors, 3 Holders, c.1942, 3 ¾ In.	115.00
Toothbrush Holder, Mickey, Minnie, Figural, Porcelain, Maw, London, 1930s, 4 In., Pair	557.00
Toy, Bagatelle, Mickey Mouse, Spring Ejector, Wood Balls, Chad Valley, 1930s, 19 In.	949.00
Toy, Circus Train, Characters, Tin Litho, Windup, Lionel, 1930s, 3 6-In. Cars	934.00
Toy, Disneyland Parade Roadster, Tin Lithograph, Windup, Disney Characters, Marx, 11 In.	288.00
Toy, Disneyland Roller Coaster, Car, Characters, Windup, Tin Lithograph, Chein, 20 x 9 ½ In.	249.00
Toy, Donald Duck Delivery, Long Bill, Waves, Quacks, Pulls Cart, Fisher-Price, 1936, 11 In.	189.00
Toy, Donald Duck, Drummer, Tin Lithograph, Windup, Linemar, Box, 6 ¼ In.	431.00
Toy, Donald Duck, Open Car, Nodding Head, Clockwork, Tin Lithograph, Marx, Box, 5 ¼ In. ..	403.00
Toy, Donald Duck, Pluto Pulling Cart, Clockwork, Celluloid, Japan, 8 ½ In.	354.00
Toy, Donald Duck, Riding On Cart, Pull, Wood, Fisher-Price, No. 765, 8 x 6 ½ In.	45.00
Toy, Donald Duck, Tricycle, Cloth Pants, Celluloid, U.S. Flag, Japan, 1930s, 5 ¾ In.	354.00
Toy, Donald Duck, Walker, Composition, Clockwork, 11 ½ In.	403.00
Toy, Donald Duck, Zylophone, Wood, Metal, Pull, Fisher-Price, No. 185, 13 x 11 In.	136.00
Toy, Dopey, Sweeper, Musical, Whistle While You Work, Tin, Red Wood, 7 x 9 In.	285.00
Toy, Drum, Mickey, Minnie, Pluto, Instruments, Tin Litho, Ohio Art, 1930s, 3 ½ x 7 In.	173.00
Toy, Drum, Three Little Pigs, Big Bad Wolf, Tin Litho, Ohio Art, 1934, 9 In.	230.00
Toy, Ferdinand The Bull, Metal Bell, Wood, Pull Toy, N.N. Hill Brass Co., Copyright 1938, 9 In. ..*illus*	1473.00
Toy, Ferdinand The Bull, Tin Lithograph, Windup, Tail Spins, Rubber Horns, Marx, 1938, 6 In.	160.00
Toy, Goofy, Pushing Wheel Barrel, Key Wind, Tin Lithograph, Marx, 7 ½ In.	403.00
Toy, Jetliner, 4 Propellers, Disney Characters, Friction, Tin Lithograph, Japan, 7 ½ In.	431.00
Toy, Ludwig Von Drake, Tin Lithograph, Windup, Linemar, 5 ½ In.	147.00
Toy, Mickey & Minnie Mouse, Handcar, Tin, Round Railroad Track, Box, Lionel, 9 In.	1840.00
Toy, Mickey Mouse, Bus, Tin Litho, Fiberboard, Wood & Rubber Tires, 1950s, 8 x 19 In.	635.00
Toy, Mickey Mouse, Celluloid, 5 Fingers, Spring Tail, Windup, Germany, c.1930, 5 ½ In.	1770.00
Toy, Mickey Mouse, Circus Train, Tin Lithograph, 3 Lithograph Cars, 28 In.	690.00
Toy, Mickey Mouse, Cowboy, Riding Pluto, Celluloid, Rocker, Windup, Japan, Box, 8 In.	3738.00
Toy, Mickey Mouse, Crazy Car, Characters, Tin Lithograph, Windup, Marx, 6 In.	425.00
Toy, Mickey Mouse, Dipsy Car, Windup, Disc Wheels, Linemar, 5 ½ In.	316.00
Toy, Mickey Mouse, Ferris Wheel, 6 Gondolas, Tin Lithograph, Clockwork, Chein, 17 In.	382.00
Toy, Mickey Mouse, Ferris Wheel, Windup, Tin Lithograph, Chein, 16 ½ In.	294.00
Toy, Mickey Mouse, Ferris Wheel, Windup, Tin Lithograph, Face, Chein, 16 ½ In.	863.00
Toy, Mickey Mouse, Handcar, Tin Lithograph, Mickey & Donald, Wells-O-London, 8 In.	489.00
Toy, Mickey Mouse, Playing Xylophone, Tin Lithograph, Clockwork, Linemar, 6 In.	230.00
Toy, Mickey Mouse, Rambler, Legs Move, Celluloid, Box, Japan, 1934, 8 In.	1416.00
Toy, Mickey Mouse, Slate Dancer, Tin Litho, Hand Crank, Steam, Germany, c.1930, 6 In. ..*illus*	5750.00
Toy, Mickey Mouse, Tricycle, Lithograph, Celluloid, Bell, Clockwork, Linemar, 4 In.	431.00
Toy, Mickey Mouse, Walker, Tin Litho, Windup, Johann Distler, Germany, c.1930, 8 In.	5175.00
Toy, Mickey Mouse, Wood, Jointed, Lollipop Hands, Borgfeldt, 1931, 9 In.	854.00
Toy, Mickey Mouse, Wood, Rope Arms, Cord Tail, Rubber Ears, 1930, 6 In.	2657.00
Toy, Mickey, Traffic Cop, Blue Uniform, Traffic Booth, Morris Plastics, 1950s, 16 In.	173.00
Toy, Minnie Mouse, Knitting, Seated, Windup, Linemar, Box, 6 ½ In.	316.00
Toy, Minnie Mouse, Rocking Chair, Tin, Windup, Linemar, 1950s, 6 In.	506.00
Toy, Minnie Mouse, Seated In Rocker, Knitting, Ears Flap, Box, Windup, Linemar, 7 In.	266.00
Toy, Pail, Mickey Mouse, Tiny Tots, Tin Lithograph, Willow, 1950s, 5 ½ In.	158.00
Toy, Pinocchio, Riding Donkey, Rings Bell As It Rolls, Pull Cord, Fisher-Price, No. 494	147.00
Toy, Pinocchio, Tin Lithograph, Windup, Marked Linemar, 5 ½ In.	136.00
Toy, Pinocchio, Walker, Tin Lithograph, Long Nose, Buckets, Clockwork, Marx, 1939, 8 ¾ In..	259.00
Toy, Pinocchio, Walker, Windup, Tin Lithograph, Box, Linemar, 6 In.	271.00
Toy, Pluto, Bone, Mesh, Metal, Battery Operated, Japan, 3 In.	90.00
Toy, Pluto, Drum Major, Hat, Bell, Cane, Horn, Tin Lithograph, Windup, Box, Marx, 6 ½ In.	374.00

D

Doll, Kathe Kruse, Cloth, Pressed & Oil-Painted Features, Stitch & Disc-Jointed, c.1915, 17 In.
$2240.00

Theriault's

Doll, Kathe Kruse, Cloth, Pressed, Oil-Painted, Stitch & Disc-Jointed, c.1915, 17 In.
$3584.00

Theriault's

Doll, Kestner, 172, Gibson Girl, Bisque Shoulder Head, Glass Eyes, Mohair, Leather Body, 20 In.
$1035.00

Bertoia Auction

Doll, Kley & Hahn, 526, Bisque Socket Head, Painted, Composition, Wood, Ball-Jointed, c.1910, 17 In.
$4200.00

Theriault's

Doll, Lenci, Aligi, Felt Swivel Head, Pressed & Painted, Googly Eyes, c.1926, 17 In.
$4480.00

Theriault's

Doll, Lenci, Bombita, Felt Swivel Head, Pressed, Painted, Jointed, Felt Costume, 1925, 18 In.
$3360.00

Theriault's

Toy, Pluto, Party Pluto, Horn, Bells, Plastic, Windup, Marx, 1950s, Box, 10 In.	173.00
Toy, Rail Car, Donald Duck, Tin, Pluto, Long Bill, Doghouse, Round Track, Lionel, 10 In.	1725.00
Toy, Roll-Over Pluto, Watch Me Roll Over, Tin Lithograph, Marx, 1930s	125.00
Toy, Shaggy Dog, Squeak, Vinyl, Beige Fur, Disney Copyright, 1959, 5 In.	85.00
Toy, Smoking Butler, Mickey Mouse, Wood, Painted, 19 ½ In.	207.00
Toy, Telephone, Donald Duck, Candlestick, Wood, Metal, Die Cut Donald, c.1938, 7 In.	1251.00
Toy, Television, Record Player, Pressed Steel, Scrolled Images, Mouseketeers, 9 x 13 In.	144.00
Toy, Train Set, Metro Express, Windup, Walt Disney Characters, Tin Litho, Marx, 1949	950.00
Toy, Washer, Mickey Mouse & Minnie Washing Clothes, Tin Litho, Ohio Art, 1930s, 7 In.	490.00
Trinket Box, Mickey Mouse Figure On Top, Ceramic, White, Germany, 5 x 3 In.	230.00
Umbrella, Donald Duck, Yellow, Metal Frame, Wood Handle, 1930s, 18 In.	115.00
Watch Fob, Mickey Mouse, Hunting, Pluto, Embossed Tin, Leather, 1930s, 1 ½ In. ......*illus*	145.00
Watch Holder, Alice In Wonderland, Ceramic, Paper Label, 1960, 5 In.	11.00
Wristwatch, Donald Duck, Animated Hands, Metal Case, Link Band, Ingersoll, 1935	1574.00
Wristwatch, Mickey Mouse, Chromed Metal, Vinyl Band, Ingersoll, Box, 1947	288.00
Wristwatch, Mickey Mouse, Silver Luster, Gold Electroplate, Leather, Ingersoll, Case, c.1940 ... *illus*	230.00
Wristwatch, Three Little Pigs, Wolf, Chromed Metal, Link Band, Ingersoll, 1934, 5 In.	1149.00

DOCTOR, *see Dental and Medical categories.*

DOLL entries are listed by marks printed or incised on the doll, if possible. If there are no marks, the doll is listed by the name of the subject or country or maker. Notice that Barbie is listed under Mattel. G.I. Joe figures are listed in the Toy section. Eskimo dolls are listed in the Eskimo section and Indian dolls are listed in the Indian section. Doll clothes and accessories are listed at the end of this section. The twentieth-century clothes listed here are in mint condition.

A.M., 231, Fany, Bisque Socket Head, Blue Sleep Eyes, Pouty Lips, Jointed, Dress, Toddler, 13 In.	2850.00
A.M., 240, Bisque Socket Head, Googly Eyes, Sculpted Topknot, c.1915, 10 In. ....*illus*	448.00
A.M., 310, Just Me, Bisque Socket Head, Blue Googly Sleep Eyes, Composition, 10 In.	855.00
A.M., 323, Bisque Head, Impish Smile, Blue Googly Eyes, Composition, Toddler, 9 In.	627.00
A.M., 390, Bisque Head, Sleep Blue Eyes, Open Mouth, Teeth, Composition, Jointed, 26 In.	259.00
A.M., 390, Bisque, Brown Eyes, Pink Dress, Stamped Germany, 1800s, 17 In.	91.00
A.M., 390, Blue Eyes, Open Mouth, Teeth, Brown Human Hair, Composition, Jointed, 18 In.	127.00
A.M., Bisque Head, Blue Sleep Eyes, Open Mouth, Teeth, Chin Dimple, 26 In.	259.00
A.M., Bisque Head, Hands, Blond Wig, Open Mouth, Leather Jointed, Period Dress, 17 ½ x 18 In.	201.00
A.M., Boy, Bisque Head, Blue Googly Eyes, Impish Grin, Felt Costume, 7 In.	798.00
A.M., Nobbi Kid, Bisque Head, Blue Glass Googly Sleep Eyes, Papier-Mache Body, 7 In.	570.00
A.M., Porcelain, Sleep Eyes, Blond Curled Wig, Open Mouth, Composition, Jointed, 22 In.	144.00
Advertising, Borden's, Baby Beauregard, Hard Plastic Rattle, Bottle Fills, 1940s, 5 In.	150.00
Advertising, Buddy Lee, Ride 'Em, Lee Rider Cowboy Pants, Shirt, Jeans, Plastic, 1950s, 13 In.	285.00
Advertising, G.E. Radio, Band Leader, Composition, Wood, Jointed, Cameo, c.1930, 19 In.	1026.00
Advertising, Heinz Baby, Vinyl, Squeak, Removable Bib, Hungerford, 1950s, 9 In.	189.00
Advertising, Hobo Joe, California Restaurant Chain, 9 In.	150.00
Advertising, Jolly Green Giant, Vinyl, 9 In.	150.00
Advertising, Miss Revlon, Vinyl Socket Head, Sleep Eyes, 5-Piece Body, c.1958, 10 In. ....*illus*	224.00
Advertising, Nestle's, Hans, Vinyl, Red Beard, Molded Head, 1969, 12 ½ In.	65.00
Advertising, Reddy Kilowatt, Clear Red Lucite, Glow-In-Dark Head, 1950s, 5 ½ In.	195.00
Advertising, Sinclair Oil, Dino, Inflatable, 1960s, 48 In.	55.00
Al Jolson, Jazz Singer, Hard Rubber Head, Googly Eyes, Muslin Body, c.1927, 20 In.	627.00
Alexander dolls are listed in this category under Madame Alexander.	
Allied Grand, Jackie Robinson, Composition, Brooklyn Dodgers Uniform, 13 In.	1140.00
Alt, Beck & Gottschalk, 974, Bisque, Molded Hair, Bangs, Muslin Body, Stitch-Jointed, 18 In.	513.00
Alt, Beck & Gottschalk, Blue Scarf Lady, Bisque Shoulder Head, Muslin Body, Jointed, 21 In.	855.00
American Character, Annie Oakley, Plastic, Fringed Skirt, Vest, Holster, 1950s, 18 In.	342.00
American Character, Whimsies, Lena The Cleaner, Stuffed Vinyl, Jointed Legs, 1961, 19 In.	75.00
Armand Marseille dolls are listed in this category under A.M.	
Arranbee, Plastic, Painted Face, Clear Eyes, Blond, Walker, Cotton Dress, 21 In.	75.00
Automaton, 2 Bisque & Papier-Mache Dolls, Wood Music Box Base, Zinner & Sohne, 12 x 14 In.	1140.00
Automaton, Baby In Bathtub, Composite, Wicker, Sweet Heart, Manhattan Soap, 21 x 32 In.	354.00
Automaton, Bal Masque, Dancer, Seated, Bisque Head, Holding Mask, Lambert, Germany, 17 ½ In.	4129.00
Automaton, Bell Boy, Open Mouth, Blue Uniform, Tray, Clockwork, Germany, c.1920, 23 In.	575.00
Automaton, Birdcage, Rotating Bird, Softwood, Crank, 19th Century, 4 ¾ In.	147.00
Automaton, Chicago Band Box, Big Band Version, Restored, 34 x 46 In.	4400.00
Automaton, Erotic, Silver, Mother-Of-Pearl, Enameled Figures, Engaged In Pleasure, c.1890, 3 In.	9480.00
Automaton, Fisherman, Windmill, Pond, Papier-Mache, Glass Dome, Phalibois, c.1880, 25 In.	633.00
Automaton, Flower Seller, Black Woman, Flower Surprises, Silk, Gustave Vichy, c.1885, 25 In.	24200.00

Automaton, Girl With Lyre, Bisque, Paperweight Eyes, Strums, Head Turns, Velvet Base, 18 In.	2052.00
Automaton, Girl, Bisque Head, Green Dress, Table With Dolls, Simon & Halbig, 1800s, 24 In.	4715.00
Automaton, Goose Girl & Flock, Bisque, Painted, Papier-Mache, Platform, c.1890, 16 In.	86.00
Automaton, Juggling Clown, Papier-Mache, Paint, Cardboard Torso, Stool, Vichy, 30 In. ...*illus*	29120.00
Automaton, La Blanchisseuse Dans Le Jardin, Bisque, Woman Ironing, Phalibois, c.1870, 20 In.	374.00
Automaton, Little Drummer Girl, Silk Dress, Bonnet, Velvet & Wood Platform, 18 In.............	3420.00
Automaton, Little Girl, Mirror, Powder Puff, Velvet & Wood Base, Roullet & Decamps, 19 In..	7410.00
Automaton, Magician Clown, Surprises, Papier-Mache, Wood, Lambert, c.1890, 24 In. .....*illus*	19040.00
Automaton, Man, Black, Dapper, Spats, Gloves, Hat, Glass Eyes, Clockwork, Germany, 27 In..	3450.00
Automaton, Man, Black, Oversize Head, Clockwork, Windup, c.1925, 22 In.............................	805.00
Automaton, Man, Black, Papier-Mache Head, Hat, Jacket, Bowtie, Clockwork, Germany, 35 In.	575.00
Automaton, Man, Black, Seated, Dress Clothing, Eyes Move, Clockwork, 20 In........................	575.00
Automaton, Man, Black, Top Hat, Checkered Pants, Clockwork, 25 In.	1150.00
Automaton, Marquis Monkey Smoker, Silk Waistcoat, Key, Gustave Vichy, France, 1800s, 30 In.	7800.00
Automaton, Marquis Monkey, Playing Violin, Dog, Barrel, Divided Interior, 1800s, 16 In.	2880.00
Automaton, Marquis Smoker, Holding Hankie, Cigarette Holder, Lambert, c.1890, 23 In........	978.00
Automaton, Pig, Playing Harp, Leather Clothes, Giltwood, Key, 1800s, 13 ¼ In....................	2160.00
Automaton, Seated Lady With Party Mask, Velvet & Wood Box, France, c.1888, 16 In.............	3705.00
Automaton, Woman, 1700s Dress, Dressing Table, Hands & Head Move, Germany, c.1910, 14 ½ In.	978.00
Automaton, Woman, Playing Accordion, Papier-Mache Head, Glass Eyes, Windup, 1800s, 21 In.	2714.00
Averill, Bonnie Babe, Bisque Head, Painted Features, 2 Teeth, Cloth, Composition, 17 In.	342.00
Averill, Little Lulu, Cowgirl, Cloth, Dress, Gun, Holster, 15 In.	362.00
Averill, Nancy & Sluggo, Cloth, Painted Face, Stitch-Jointed, Felt Shoes, 1940s, 13 In., Pair	46.00
Averill, Tubby, Pressed Mask, Little Boy Attire, 1944, 14 In...	226.00
Bahr & Proschild, 204, Bisque Socket Head, Sleep Eyes, Human Hair, Composition, 14 In. ....*illus*	374.00
Barbie dolls are listed in this category under Mattel.	
Nancy Ann Storybook, Bebe, Muffie, Plastic, Sleep Eyes, Honey Hair, Pink & White Outfit, 8 In.	291.00
Bergmann dolls are also in this category under Simon & Halbig.	
Bergner, Bisque Head, 3 Faces, Crying, Laughing, Sleeping, Hood, Brass Knob At Crown, 12 In.	1083.00
Bisque Shoulder Head, Glass Paperweight Eyes, Mohair Wig, Cloth Body, 13 In.	1750.00
Bisque, Glass Eyes, 4 Teeth, Wood, Composition, Satin Clown Suit, Riding Rabbit, c.1902, 11 x 14 In...	1416.00
Bisque, Man, Shoulder Head, Mustache, Goatee, Molded Gray Helmet, Wood Block Body, 11 In.	1026.00
Black dolls are also included in the Black category.	
Bru Jne, Bisque Head, Amber Paperweight Eyes, Painted Features, Kid Body, Bonnet, 14 In.	8625.00
Bru Jne, Bisque Head, Blue Eyes, Blond Human Hair, Mona Lisa Smile, Green Dress, 14 In.	4956.00
Bru Jne, Bisque Shoulder Head, Paperweight Eyes, Kid, Gusset-Jointed, Wool Dress, 20 In.	10260.00
Bru Jne, Brevete, Bebe, Bisque Head, Brown Eyes, Lamb's Wool Wig, Kid Body, Silk Dress, 21 In.	21090.00
Bru Jne, Fashion, Bisque Swivel Shoulder Head, Gray Eyes, Kid Body, Silk Gown, 11 In...........	1938.00
Bruno Schmidt, 2048, Tommy Tucker, Bisque Head, Painted Hair, Teeth, Black Suit, Tie, 25 In.	912.00
Bucherer, Aviator, Papier-Mache Head, Metal Body, Jointed, Flannel Coat, 8 In......................	1254.00
Bucherer, Composition Head, Feet, Painted, Hands, Metal, Ball-Jointed, Cloche, 1920s, 8 In...	1062.00
Buffalo Bill, Papier-Mache Socket Head, Molded & Painted Features, c.1885, 14 In.	399.00
Captain Kangaroo, Vinyl, Cloth, Caricature Features, Blue Flannel Suit, Badge, 1960s, 20 In.	114.00
Catterfelder Puppenfabrik, 201, Baby, Domed Bisque Head, Dimples, Composition Body, 9 In.	171.00
Chinese Magician, Bisque Domed Head, Sculpted Face, Hair, Mustache, Beard, Kimono, Sash, 20 In.	460.00
Cloth, Boy, Muslin Face, Painted, Blue Glass Googly Eyes, Fleecy Hair, Overalls, 15 In.............	342.00
Cloth, Etta, Painted Eyes, Mary Pickford Curls, Organdy Ruffled Dress, c.1925, 19 In.	285.00
Cloth, Greta Garbo, Painted, Yarn Hair, Muslin Body, Felt Coat & Hat, 1930s, 15 In.................	1710.00
Cloth, Hawaiian Hula Girl, Grass Skirt, Black Wool Yarn Hair, 1940s, 11 ½ In.........................	45.00
Cloth, Salon, Pressed & Painted Features, Elongated Sateen Body & Limbs, 1920s, 27 In. ....*illus*	504.00
Cloth, Soldier, Painted Face, Wide Smile, Plush Velvet Royal Guard Costume, 1930s, 27 In.	171.00
Cloth, Tweedledee & Tweedledum, Felt, Painted, Plump Belly, Skinny Limbs, c.1940, 11 In., Pair	570.00
Clown, Musician, Composition Head, Glass Eyes, Painted Face, Trumpet, Clockwork, 24 In. ....*illus*	1840.00
Composition, Groucho Marx, Molded Black Hair, Painted Glasses, Muslin Body, c.1925, 16 In.	627.00
Composition, West Point Cadet, Painted Hair, Googly Eyes, Uniform, 1920s, 26 In.	513.00
Dean's Rag, Arthur Askey, Composition, Felt, Aviator Caricature, 1935, 12 In........................	855.00
Deluxe Reading, Suzy Smart, Plaid Skirt, Nylon Socks, Hairband, With Desk, 1960s, 25 In....	200.00
Denamur, Bebe, Bisque, Paperweight Eyes, Composition & Wood Jointed Body, 30 In..............	1368.00
Dewees Cochran, Grow-Up, Latex, Painted, Human Hair, Composition, Box, 1950s, 17 In. .....*illus*	1344.00
Doleac, Fashion, Bisque Swivel Head, Blue Glass Eyes, Kid, White Tiered Gown, 18 In.	3990.00
Dressel, Flapper, Bisque Head, Sleep Eyes, Brunette Human Hair, Edwardian Costume, 14 In.	1368.00
Dressel, Pouty Girl, Bisque Head, Painted Eyes, 12 In.	1074.00
Effanbee, Anne Of Green Gables, Composition, Brown Sleep Eyes, Auburn Braids, 14 In.........	627.00
Effanbee, Billy Bum, Vinyl, Jointed, 1979, 16 In.	65.00
Effanbee, Honey, Painted Face, Wig, 1950s, 14 In...	30.00
Effanbee, Little Lady, Yarn Hair, Blue Dress, Plaid Ruffles, 1945, 16 In................................	245.00

Doll, Lenci, Boy, Felt Swivel Head, Pressed, Painted, Stuffed Body, Tyrolean Costume, c.1926, 17 In. $1792.00

Theriault's

Doll, Lenci, Girl, Felt Swivel Head, Painted, Googly Eyes, Mohair, Jointed, c.1928, 13 In. $1232.00

Theriault's

Doll, Lenci, Girl, Felt, Pressed & Painted, Mohair Wig, Ciociara Costume, c.1940, 14 In. $784.00

Theriault's

Doll, Madame Alexander, Babs Skater, Plastic, Sleep Eyes, 5-Piece Body, Costume, c.1950, 14 In. **$1232.00**

Theriault's

Doll, Madame Alexander, Cissette, Gainsborough Lady, Plastic, Bendable Knees, 1957, 10 In. **$504.00**

Theriault's

Doll, Madame Alexander, Cissette, Going To A Matinee, Plastic, Bendable Knees, 1957, 10 In. **$560.00**

Theriault's

Effanbee, Mickey, Swivel Head, Brown Eyes, Mohair Wig, Cloth Body, 1945, 17 In.	190.00
Effanbee, Patsy Ann, Composition Socket Head, Molded Bob, Green Sleep Eyes, c.1935, 18 In.	456.00
Effanbee, Patsy Joan, Composition Socket Head, Molded Bob, Green Sleep Eyes, c.1935, 16 In.	399.00
Effanbee, Patsyette, Composition Socket Head, Auburn Hair, Painted Eyes, c.1935, 8 In.	285.00
Effanbee, Rosemary, Composition, Sleep Eyes, Open Mouth, 25 In.	136.00
Effanbee, Skippy, Composition, Painted Features, Sailor Suit, c.1931, 13 In.	342.00
Effanbee, Tintair, Hard Plastic, Socket Head, Blue Eyes, Platinum Blond, 1950s, 18 In.	336.00
Effanbee, W.C. Fields, Composition Shoulder Head, Molded Features, Top Hat, 1928, 18 In.	1140.00
Elmer Fudd, Vinyl, Hong Kong, 7 ½ In.	102.00
Fashion, Bisque Socket Head, Leather Body, Bisque Arms, Pierced Ears, Bonnet, 16 In.	4025.00
Fashion, Bisque Swivel Head, Glass Eyes, Closed Mouth, Blond Mohair Wig, Kid Body, c.1860, 15 In.	86.00
Fred Allen, Bobbin Head, Papier-Mache, Brown Hat, Blue Jacket, Red Tie, 1950s, 6 ½ In.	95.00
French, Bebe Moderne, Bisque Socket Head, Paperweight Eyes, Mohair, Wood, Composition, Box, 15 In.	1554.00
French, Bisque Shoulder Head, Molded Chignon, Hooped Skirt Holds Paper Fortunes, 8 In.	684.00
French, Boy Scout, Papier-Mache, Socket Head, 5-Piece Body, Mohair Wig, c.1910, 18 In. *illus*	616.00
French, Papier-Mache, Twill, Molded Curly Hair & Bow, Painted Features, c.1900, 30 In.	114.00
Freundlich, Baby Sandy, Composition, Molded Hair, 5-Piece Toddler Body, Box, 13 In.	513.00
Frozen Charlie, Porcelain, Molded Black Hair, Outstretched Arms, Germany, c.1880, 17 In.	285.00
Frozen Charlotte, Porcelain, Blue Eyes, Arms Out, Curled Fingers, Germany, 7 ½ In.	456.00
Frozen Charlotte, Porcelain, Molded Black Hair, Outstretched Arms, Germany, c.1880, 16 In.	456.00
Gaultier, Ebony Bisque Socket Head, Enamel Eyes, Black Fleecy Wig, Dress, Apron, c.1885, 13 In.	1254.00
Gaultier, Fashion, Bisque Head & Hands, Blue Eyes, Blond Human Hair, Kid Body, c.1872, 18 In.	2622.00
Gebruder Heubach dolls may also be listed in this category under Heubach.	
Gebruder Kuhnlenz, 165, Bisque, Open Mouth, Blue Eyes, White Dress, Germany, c.1890, 17 In.	59.00
German, Asian Child, Bisque Swivel Head, Glass Eyes, Peg-Jointed, Blue Slippers, c.1900, 6 ½ In.	1386.00
German, Asian Child, Bisque, Peg-Jointed, Black Mohair Pigtail, Silk Costume, c.1900, 5 In.	456.00
German, Bisque Socket Head, Composition & Wood Body, Ball-Jointed, c.1900, 14 In. *illus*	448.00
German, Bisque, Boy, Socket Head, Composition, Wood, Ball-Jointed, Scottish Costume, c.1910, 18 In. *illus*	3360.00
German, Bisque, Flapper, Bathing Beauty, Painted Face, Mohair Wig, c.1920, 6 ½ In. *illus*	504.00
German, Bisque, Young Man, Molded Brown Hair, Papier-Mache Limbs, Tyrolean Hat, 16 In.	1482.00
German, Fly-Lo Fairy, Bisque Head, Glass Eyes, Grace Putnam, Borgfeldt, c.1925, 10 In. *illus*	1568.00
German, Girl, Bisque Shoulder Head, Brown Glass Sleep Eyes, Open Mouth, Kid Body, 20 In.	46.00
German, Papier-Mache Shoulder Head, Molded Ringlets, Kid Body, Lace Dress, c.1860, 10 In.	228.00
German, Porcelain Shoulder Head, Black Molded Hair, Magenta Silk & Lace Dress, 1875, 17 In.	570.00
German, Topsyturvy, Bisque, 2 Faces, Black, White, Papier-Mache, Cloth, Skirt, 1880, 7 In.	456.00
German, Twins, Bisque, Blue Glass Eyes, Blond Hair, Loop-Jointed Arms & Legs, 5 In., Pair	228.00
German, Wooden Head, Painted Face, Cloth Body, c.1860, 22 ½ In.	1395.00
Gund, Clown, Celluloid Head, Cloth, 1940s, 19 In.	65.00
Gutsall, Boy, Muslin, Center-Seamed Face, Painted Features, Cotton Suit, 1893, 15 In.	228.00
Half Dolls are listed in the Pincushion Doll category.	
Handwerck, 109, Bisque, Blue Sleep Eyes, 4 Teeth, Ball-Jointed, Ruffled Bonnet, 28 In.	513.00
Handwerck, Bellhop, Bisque, Googly, Sculpted Hair, Ball-Jointed, Cap, Jacket, Pants, c.1917, 12 In.	115.00
Handwerck, Bisque Head, Sleep Eyes, Hair Lashes, Open Mouth, Jointed, Composition, 24 In.	196.00
Handwerck, Bisque Socket Head, Blue Sleep Eyes, 4 Porcelain Teeth, Blond Mohair, 30 In.	741.00
Handwerck, Brown Sleep Eyes, Pierced Ears, Open Mouth, 4 Teeth, Human Hair, 24 In.	288.00
Hertel & Schwab, 142, Bisque Head, Painted Eyes, Composition Bent-Limb Baby Body, 10 In.	114.00
Hertel & Schwab, 149, Bisque Head, Painted Features, Blond Mohair Wig, Jointed, 18 In.	7125.00
Hertel & Schwab, 165, Bisque Socket Head, Googly Eyes, Mohair Wig, Jointed, 14 ½ In. *illus*	2875.00
Heubach, 399, South Seas Baby, Brown Bisque Head, Painted Hair, Bangle Earrings, Beads, 12 In.	342.00
Heubach, 6970, Bisque Socket Head, Blue Sleep Eyes, Pouty, Composition & Wood, 11 In.	1824.00
Heubach, 7246, Boy, Bisque Socket Head, Brown Sleep Eyes, Pouty, Blue Suit, Cap, 15 In.	1140.00
Heubach, Bisque, 1-Piece, Googly Eyes, Molded White Bunny Suit, Egg, c.1912, 7 In.	456.00
Heubach, Bisque, Blue Intaglio Googly Eyes, Smile, Molded Bob, Kid Body, Dress, 11 In.	342.00
Heubach, Paperweight Eyes, Blond Human Hair, Bisque, Leather, c.1890, 21 In.	300.00
Heubach, Toddler, Bisque, Tilted Head, Sculptured Hair, Closed Mouth, c.1915, 8 ½ In.	173.00
Heubach, Whistling Jim, Bisque, Sculpted Hair, Googly Eyes, Muslin Body, Bellows, c.1915, 11 In.	175.00
Horsman, Ella Cinders, Composition Head, Arms & Legs, Painted, Muslin, c.1925, 18 In.	2508.00
Horsman, Nan, Composition Socket Head, Molded Bob, Sleep Eyes, Lashes, c.1939, 19 In.	228.00
Horsman, Poor Pitiful Pearl, Vinyl, Sleep Eyes, Straight Hair, 1963, 12 In.	40.00
Horsman, Tynie Baby, Bisque, Painted Hair, Sleep Eyes, Loop-Jointed, Germany, c.1924, 9 In.	150.00
Huret, Fashion, Bisque, Wood, Articulated, Painted, Dowel-Jointed, Satin Dress, c.1907, 18 In.	52.00
Ideal, Baby Mine, Plastic, Googly Eyes, Jointed, c.1952, 11 In.	55.00
Ideal, Betsy Wetsy, Vinyl, Sleep Eyes, Flannel Diaper, Bottle, Rattle, 1950s, 11 In.	118.00
Ideal, Betsy Wetsy, Vinyl, Socket Head, Sculpted Hair, Flannel Diaper, Rattle, 1950s, 11 In.	168.00
Ideal, Crissy, Growing Hair, Sleep Eyes, Box, 1973	85.00
Ideal, Deanna Durbin, Composition, Brown Sleep Eyes, Teeth, Striped Gown, c.1939, 21 In.	399.00
Ideal, Dorothy, Wizard Of Oz, Composition, Brown Sleep Eyes, Brunette Braids, 16 In.	3420.00

Ideal, Judy Garland As Little Nellie Kelly, Composition, Sleep Eyes, Wrist Tag, 1940, 20 In.	1482.00
Ideal, Miss, Blond, Blue Eyes, Blue Felt Skirt, Yellow Blouse, 10 In.	75.00
Ideal, Miss, Vinyl, Blue Eyes, Brunette, 5-Piece Body, Dress, Heels, Box, 1950s, 10 In.	224.00
Ideal, Patty Playpal, Plastic, Blue Dress, Shoes, Socks, 35 In.	113.00
Ideal, Scarecrow, Wizard Of Oz, Cloth, Felt, Jointed, Yarn Hair, 1939, 17 In.	1140.00
Ideal, Tammy, School Daze, Googly Eyes, Straight Leg, 12 In.	95.00
Ideal, Thumbelina, Moves Head, Blue Sleepy Eyes, Christening Outfit, 1970, 10 In.	550.00
Ideal, Toni, Plastic, Blue Sleep Eyes, Original Plaid Dress, Red Shoes, Tag, 1950s, 15 In.	114.00
Indian dolls are listed in the Indian category.	
J.D.K. dolls are also listed in this category under Kestner.	
Japanese, Samurai, Wood & Glass Case, 10 In.	325.00
Jumeau, Amber Eyes, Closed Mouth, Blond Mohair Wig, Wooden & Composition Body, Box, 14 In.	3163.00
Jumeau, Bisque Head, Blue Eyes, Human Hair Wig, Sausage Curls, Fully Jointed Body 16 In.	2300.00
Jumeau, Bisque Head, Blue Eyes, Long Painted Lashes, Pierced Ears, Honey Mohair Wig, 12 In.	3680.00
Jumeau, Bisque Head, Blue Paperweight Eyes, Honey Human Hair Wig, Chair, 1910, 19 In.	9200.00
Jumeau, Bisque Head, Open Mouth, Long Black Curly Hair, Red Dress, Jaunty Red Hat, 17 In.	2373.00
Jumeau, Bisque Socket Head, Blue Eyes, Composition & Wood, Jointed, Bebe, c.1877, 13 In.	9120.00
Jumeau, Bisque Socket Head, Open Mouth, Teeth, Blond Human Hair, Jointed, Bebe, 42 In.	7125.00
Jumeau, Bisque Socket Head, Paperweight Eyes, Human Hair, Composition, Bebe, 27 In. ...*illus*	5600.00
Jumeau, Bisque Socket Head, Spiral-Threaded Eyes, Jointed Body, Wool Sailor Suit, 14 In.	5700.00
Jumeau, Bisque, Glass Eyes, Human Hair Wig, Composition, 23 In.	1295.00
Jumeau, Bisque, Paperweight Eyes, Brunette Mohair, Checkered Dress, Beret, Bebe, 26 In.	5244.00
Jumeau, Bisque, Paperweight Eyes, Mohair Wig, Composition, Jointed, Bebe, c.1886, 9 ½ In.	173.00
Jumeau, Blue Eyes, Closed Mouth, Pierced Ears, Wood & Composition Body, Blond Mohair, 12 In.	4313.00
Jumeau, Blue Sleep Eyes, Open Mouth, Porcelain Teeth, Brown Human Hair, Chubby Body, 32 In.	708.00
Jumeau, Brown Eyes, Closed Mouth, Pierced Ears, Human Hair, Composition Body, c.1900, 18 In.	2300.00
Jumeau, Closed Mouth, Painted Features, Human Hair Wig, Ringlets, Bebe, 1910, 18 In.	2875.00
Jumeau, Fashion, Bisque Swivel Head, Blue Glass Eyes, Kid Body, Gusset-Jointed, c.1875, 17 In. ..*illus*	7840.00
Jumeau, Fashion, Bisque Swivel Head, Blue Glass Eyes, Leather Gusset Body, Ribbon Hat, 21 In.	3450.00
Jumeau, Fashion, Bisque Swivel Head, Brown Glass Eyes, Kid Body, Wedding Gown, 18 In.	3705.00
Jumeau, Porcelain Head, Glass Eyes, Pierced Ears, Jointed, Tete, Bebe, 27 In.	1912.00
Jumeau, Toddler, Bisque, Socket Head, Paperweight Eyes, Composition, Wood, c.1882, 30 In....*illus*	24000.00
Jumeau, Triste Bebe, Bisque Socket Head, Blue Eyes, Composition, Wood, c.1884, 25 In.	18810.00
Juro Novelty, Roller Derby Skater, Painted Face, Cloth Body, 16 In.	339.00
Juro, Pinky Lee, Vinyl, Caricature, Cloth Costume, Saddle Shoes, Booklet, 1950s, 24 In.	86.00
K * R, 101, Marie, Bisque Head, Blue Eyes, Heavy Lids, Brunette Mohair, Plaid Dress, 15 In.	1254.00
K * R, 101, Marie, Bisque Socket Head, Brunette Braids, Jointed, c.1910, 18 In.	2565.00
K * R, 101, Marie, Painted Face, Blond Mohair Wig, Braids, Incised, 19 ½ In. ....*illus*	1495.00
K * R, 101, Peter, Bisque Socket Head, Pouty Lips, Blond Mohair, Schoolboy Suit & Cap, 17 In.	1710.00
K * R, 107, Karl, Bisque Head, Painted Face, Petulant Lips, Composition, Sailor Suit, c.1910, 22 In.	403.00
K * R, 109, Bisque Socket Head, Painted Eyes, Composition & Wood, Ball-Jointed, 15 In. ... *illus*	9520.00
K * R, 114, Gretchen, Bisque, Painted Blue Eyes, Blond Wig, Pink Dress, c.1910, 25 In.	6555.00
K * R, 114, Hans, Bisque Socket Head, Blue Sleep Eyes, Pouty Mouth, Wool Coat, Pants, 18 In.	4275.00
K * R, 114, Hans, Bisque Socket Head, Brunette Wig, Jointed, c.1910, 18 In.	2850.00
K * R, 115, Bisque Domed Head, Pouty, Sleep Eyes, Sculpted Hair, Forelock, Composition, 12 In.	259.00
K * R, 115, Bisque Socket Head, Sleep Eyes, Wooden Body, Ball-Jointed, Toddler, 13 In. ...*illus*	2576.00
K * R, 115, Philip, Bisque Socket Domed Head, Molded Blond Curl, Pouty Face, 15 In.	2736.00
K * R, 117, Mein Liebling, Bisque Head, Sleep Eyes, Pouty, Mohair Bob, Jointed, 20 In.	4560.00
K * R, 126, Bisque Head, Blue Glass Sleep Eyes, 2 Teeth, Composition, Toddler, 17 In.	228.00
K * R, 131, Bisque Socket Head, Brown Googly Sleep Eyes, Brunette Mohair, Dress, 11 In.	3420.00
K * R, Bisque Socket Head, Blue Glass Flirty Eyes, Open Mouth, Composition Body, 16 In.	285.00
Kathe Kruse, Boy, Cloth, Painted Face, Hair, Stitch-Defined Hands, Disc-Jointed, c.1911, 16 In. ..*illus*	5040.00
Kathe Kruse, Boy, Cloth, Painted Face, Molded Hair, Side Hip Joints, 17 In. ....*illus*	3163.00
Kathe Kruse, Cloth, Painted, Pouty Face, Brown Eyes, Brown Human Hair, Blue Dress, 20 In.	684.00
Kathe Kruse, Cloth, Painted, Pouty Face, Brown Forelock Curl, Jointed, Folk Costume, 16 In.	2736.00
Kathe Kruse, Cloth, Painted, Pouty, Blond Human Hair Braids, Jointed, Romper Dress, 17 In.	2052.00
Kathe Kruse, Cloth, Pressed & Oil-Painted Features, Stitch & Disc-Jointed, c.1915, 17 In. .....*illus*	2240.00
Kathe Kruse, Cloth, Pressed, Oil-Painted, Stitch & Disc-Jointed, c.1915, 17 In. ....*illus*	3584.00
Kathe Kruse, Cloth, Swivel Head, Painted, Blond Human Hair, Stitch-Jointed, Pinafore, 20 In.	513.00
Kestner, 103, Boy, Bisque, Plump Face, Composition, Wood, Velvet Suit & Cap, 31 In.	1254.00
Kestner, 172, Gibson Girl, Bisque Shoulder Head, Glass Eyes, Leather, Mohair, 20 In. .....*illus*	1035.00
Kestner, 174, Bisque Head, Brown Sleep Eyes, 4 Teeth, Human Hair Wig, Striped Dress, 9 In. .	399.00
Kestner, 208, Baby Rose, Bisque, Blue Glass Sleep Eyes, Brunette Mohair Wig, Box, c.1915, 5 In.	285.00
Kestner, 211, Boy, Bisque Head, Open Mouth, 2 Teeth, Fleece Hair, Bent-Limb Body, 20 In.	456.00
Kestner, 243, Chinese Baby, Bisque, Brown Eyes, 2 Teeth, Silk Pajamas & Cap, c.1912, 13 In..	2280.00
Kestner, 243, Chinese Baby, Bisque, Open Mouth, Mohair Wig, Gump's Costume, c.1912, 16 In.	173.00

Doll, Madame Alexander, Cissy, Cole Porter Ice Capades, Plastic, 1964, 20 In.
$1456.00

Theriault's

Doll, Madame Alexander, Cissy, Lady In Red, Taffeta Gown, Tulle Stole, No. 2285, 1958, 20 In.
$1568.00

Theriault's

Doll, Madame Alexander, Elise, Plastic, Jointed, Opera Coat, Brocade Gown, Wrist Tag, 1963, 16 In.
$1456.00

Theriault's

Doll, Madame Alexander, Elise, Bride,
Hat & Veil, Box, c.1960, 20 In.
$259.00

Bertoia Auction

Doll, Madame Alexander, Eskimo,
Plastic, Bendable Knees, Brown Hair,
Alexander-Kins, 1966, 8 In.
$336.00

Theriault's

Doll, Madame Alexander, Fairy Queen,
Plastic, Mohair Wig, 5-Piece Body, Tulle
Gown, 1949, 14 In.
$1904.00

Theriault's

Kestner, Bisque Head, Brown Eyes, Painted Hair, Composition Body, 13 In.	196.00
Kestner, Bisque Head, Brown Glass Eyes, Blond, Pouty, Wood & Composition Body, Cape, 18 In.	1438.00
Kestner, Bisque Head, Mulatto, Brown Glass Eyes, Jointed, Silk Dress, Cap, Shoes, c.1885, 15 In.	1730.00
Kestner, Bisque Head, Sleep Eyes, Dimple Chin, Painted Hair, Composition Body, Baby, 13 In.	196.00
Kestner, Bisque Swivel Head, Blond Mohair, Peg-Jointed, Dress, Laced Boots, Mignonette, 6 In.	912.00
Kestner, Boy, Closed Mouth, Pouty, Blond, Ball-Jointed, Velvet Outfit, 16 In.	1208.00
Kestner, Composition Body, Porcelain Head, Open Mouth, Glass Eyes, Jointed, Toddler, 26 In.	508.00
Kestner, Gibson Girl, Bisque, Tilted Head, Haughty Look, Sleep Eyes, Pin-Jointed, c.1910, 20 In.	403.00
Kestner, Hilda, Bisque, Painted Hair, Forelock Curl, 2 Teeth, Composition Body, 15 In.	1482.00
Kestner, Hilda, Bisque, Sleep Eyes, Open Mouth, Wool Jacket, Cotton Dress, Shoes, c.1914, 15 In.	173.00
Kestner, Swivel Head, Painted, Blond Hair, Peg-Jointed, Painted Yellow Boots, Mignonette, 5 In.	570.00
Kewpie dolls are listed in the Kewpie category.	
Kley & Hahn, 526, Bisque Socket Head, Painted, Composition, Wood, Ball-Jointed, c.1910, 17 In. *illus*	4200.00
Klumpe, Matador, Felt, Flowers In Hair, Foil Label, 1950s, 8 In.	48.00
Knickerbocker, Little Lulu, Cloth, Pressed Mask Face, Painted, 17 In.	225.00 to 360.00
Lanternier, Cherie, Bisque Head, Open Mouth, Teeth, Composition, Jointed, Limoges, France, 17 In.	565.00
Laurel & Hardy, Felt, Pressed, Painted, Sons Of The Desert Costumes, c.1935, 13 In., Pair	342.00
Lenci Type, Raynal, Man Of The Court, Painted Features, Powdered Wig, Wood Cane, France, 19 In.	805.00
Lenci, Aligi, Felt Swivel Head, Pressed & Painted, Googly Eyes, c.1926, 17 In. *illus*	4480.00
Lenci, Anili, Felt, Painted, Brown Googly Eyes, Italian Costume, 1926, 16 In.	684.00
Lenci, Bambola, Felt, Painted Face, Swivel Head, Jointed, Blue Gown, 14 In.	625.00
Lenci, Bombita, Felt Swivel Head, Pressed, Painted, Jointed, Felt Costume, 1925, 18 In. *illus*	3360.00
Lenci, Boy, Felt Swivel Head, Pressed, Painted, Stuffed Body, Tyrolean Costume, c.1926, 17 In. *illus*	1792.00
Lenci, Character, Girl, Felt Swivel Head, Pouty Mouth, Jointed, Embroidered Costume, c.1935, 19 In.	115.00
Lenci, Clara Bow, Felt Swivel Head, Painted Googly Eyes, Felt Flapper Dress, 31 In.	6555.00
Lenci, Duck, Indian Outfit, Felt, Applique, Beak, Feet, Headdress, Quiver, Arrows, 1950s, 19 In.	1386.00
Lenci, Felt, Green Coat & Hat, Embroidered Flowers, 21 In.	380.00
Lenci, Felt, Painted Features, Googly, Eyes Face Left, Organdy Dress, Bonnet, 16 In.	1076.00
Lenci, Felt, Painted, Googly Eyes, Blond Mohair Ringlets, Green Dress, 19 In.	1254.00
Lenci, Felt, Painted, Googly Eyes, O-Shape Mouth, Petticoat, Apron, Pantalets, Broom, 9 In.	228.00
Lenci, Felt, Painted, Plump Scowling Face, Brunette Mohair, Jointed, Argyle Dress, 18 In.	627.00
Lenci, Girl, Felt Swivel Head, Blond Mohair Wig, Brown Eyes, c.1930, 21 In.	708.00
Lenci, Girl, Felt Swivel Head, Painted, Googly Eyes, Mohair, Jointed, c.1928, 13 In. *illus*	1232.00
Lenci, Girl, Felt, Pressed & Painted, Mohair Wig, Ciociara Costume, c.1940, 14 In. *illus*	784.00
Lenci, Girl, Googly Eyes, Blond Curly Hair, Red Shorts Set & Hat, 16 In.	848.00
Lenci, Girl, Sad Face, Closed Mouth, Red Felt Hat, Coat, White Dress, 19 In.	2300.00
Lenci, Italian Salon Lady, Swivel Head, Mohair Wig, Ungherese Costume, c.1930, 24 In.	81.00
Lenci, Lolita, Felt, Googly Eyes, Black Lace Dress, Mantilla & Fan, 1921, 28 In.	7125.00
Lenci, Mozart, Felt, Pressed, Painted, Googly Eyes, Jointed, c.1933, 11 In.	684.00
Lenci, Poupees Salon, Felt, Googly Eyes, Painted Features, Organdy Gown, 28 In.	6270.00
Lenci, Snake Charmer, Swivel Head, Felt, Painted, Turban, Flute, Snake, Basket, 23 In.	8550.00
Lenci, Woman, Googly Eyes, Wide Brim Hat, Blue Dress, Black Shoes, 25 In.	1003.00
Lillian Gish, Cloth, Padded Body, Painted Features, Ivory Satin Gown, Mary Green, 1940s, 11 In.	627.00
Madame Alexander, Alice In Wonderland, Composition, Wendy-Ann Body, c.1940, 13 In.	513.00
Madame Alexander, Angel, Plastic, Sleep Eyes, Curly Bangs, Taffeta Gown, Gold Wings, 8 In.	86.00
Madame Alexander, Babs Skater, Plastic, Sleep Eyes, 5-Piece Body, Costume, c.1950, 14 In. *illus*	1232.00
Madame Alexander, Baby Jane, Composition, Brown Sleep Eyes, Organdy Dress, 16 In.	627.00
Madame Alexander, Ballerina, Blue Eyes, Red Hair, Fashion Academy Award Tag, 18 In.	173.00
Madame Alexander, Beauty Queen Cisette, Plastic, Tosca Hair, Blue Bathing Suit, 1959, 10 In.	224.00
Madame Alexander, Beth, Little Women, Plastic, Sleep Eyes, 13 In.	57.00
Madame Alexander, Binnie Walker, Hard Plastic, Sateen Dress, Pinafore, Bonnet, Box, 1950s, 18 In.	35.00
Madame Alexander, Bride, Hard Plastic, Blue Sleep Eyes, Satin & Lace Dress, Bouquet, Veil, 20 In.	431.00
Madame Alexander, Bride, Plastic, Brunette, Tulle Gown, Pearl Necklace, 1959, 17 In.	280.00
Madame Alexander, Carmen, Composition, Sleep Eyes, Red Satin Dress, Black Lace, 21 In.	1368.00
Madame Alexander, Cissette, Ballerina, White Tutu, Flower, Ballet Slippers, 1950s, 10 In.	145.00
Madame Alexander, Cissette, Beauty Queen, Hard Plastic, Jointed, Swimsuit, Banner, c.1959, 10 In.	92.00
Madame Alexander, Cissette, Gainsborough Lady, Plastic, Bendable Knees, 1957, 10 In. *illus*	504.00
Madame Alexander, Cissette, Going To A Matinee, Plastic, Bendable Knees, 1957, 10 In. *illus*	560.00
Madame Alexander, Cissette, Plastic, Blond Hair, Blue Taffeta Dress, Bonnet, 1957, 10 In.	280.00
Madame Alexander, Cissy In Ice Capades, Plastic, Jester, Crown, 1960s, 20 In.	513.00
Madame Alexander, Cissy, Cole Porter Ice Capades, Plastic, 1964, 20 In. *illus*	1456.00
Madame Alexander, Cissy, Hard Plastic, Brown Hair, Sleep Eyes, Pink Striped Dress, c.1955, 20 In.	176.00
Madame Alexander, Cissy, Lady In Red, Taffeta Gown, Tulle Stole, No. 2285, 1958, 20 In. *illus*	1568.00
Madame Alexander, Cissy, Sleep Eyes, Navy Bolero Dress, 1955, 20 In.	525.00
Madame Alexander, Elise, Bride, Hat & Veil, Box, c.1960, 20 In. *illus*	259.00
Madame Alexander, Elise, Plastic, Jointed, Opera Coat, Brocade Gown, Wrist Tag, 1963, 16 In. *illus*	1456.00
Madame Alexander, Eskimo, Plastic, Bendable Knees, Brown Hair, Alexander-Kins, 1966, 8 In. *illus*	336.00

Madame Alexander, Fairy Queen, Plastic, Mohair Wig, 5-Piece Body, Tulle Gown, 1949, 14 In. ...*illus*		1904.00
Madame Alexander, Godey Lady, Plastic, 5-Piece Body, Taffeta Gown, Snood, 1950, 14 In....... *illus*		1120.00
Madame Alexander, Jane Withers, Composition, Sleep Eyes, Pink Cotton Dress, 1935, 13 In.		485.00
Madame Alexander, Jeanette MacDonald As Rose Marie, Cloth, Painted, 1936, 23 In.		1710.00
Madame Alexander, Little Betty, Red Hair, Green & Blue Scottish Outfit, 1938, 9 In.		160.00
Madame Alexander, Little Shaver, Cloth, Painted Eyes, Auburn Fleece Hair, c.1942, 7 In.		399.00
Madame Alexander, Little Women, Composition, Mohair, Cloth Tag, c.1933, 7 In., 4 Piece		741.00
Madame Alexander, Little Women, Hard Plastic, Original Costumes, Tags, c.1950, 5 Piece		1824.00
Madame Alexander, Margaret O'Brien, Composition, Bicolor Sleep Eyes, Braids, c.1946, 21 In.		1026.00
Madame Alexander, Margaret O'Brien, Composition, Sleep Eyes, Mohair Braids, c.1959, 14 In.		912.00
Madame Alexander, Mary Martin, Plastic, Sleep Eyes, Denim Shirt & Pants, 1950s, 17 In.		570.00
Madame Alexander, Mary Martin, Plastic, Sleep Eyes, South Pacific Costume, 1950, 14 In. ... *illus*		952.00
Madame Alexander, Mary Martin, Plastic, South Pacific Sailor Costume, 1950s, 15 In.		342.00
Madame Alexander, Mona Lisa, Brown Hair, Green Velvet Gown, Long Black Veil, 1900s, 8 In.		45.00
Madame Alexander, Plastic, Walker, Organdy Gown, Alexander-Kins, 1954, 8 In. ....*illus*		784.00
Madame Alexander, Princess Elizabeth, Composition, Mohair, Blue Silk Gown, 28 In.		342.00
Madame Alexander, Princess Elizabeth, Composition, Sleep Eyes, Human Hair, c.1935, 14 In.		12.00
Madame Alexander, Scarlett O'Hara, Composition, Green Satin Gown, Wrist Tag, 11 In.		570.00
Madame Alexander, Snow White, Composition, Sleep Eyes, Satin & Velvet Dress, c.1938, 18 In.		46.00
Madame Alexander, Snow White, Plastic, Sleep Eyes, 5-Piece Body, Wrist Tag, 1952, 18 In. ... *illus*		560.00
Madame Alexander, So-Lite Baby, Plastic, Vinyl, Cloth, Molded Hair, c.1961, 16 In.		57.00
Madame Alexander, Sonja Henie, Composition, Sleep Eyes, Teeth, Ski Costume, 1937, 21 In.		1083.00
Madame Alexander, Sonja Henie, Composition, Trousseau, Trunk, c.1938, 14 In.		2166.00
Madame Alexander, Sonja Henie, Vinyl Head, Hard Plastic Body, Skater, Curler Box, c.1951, 15 In..		32.00
Madame Alexander, Susie Q, Cloth, Painted, Googly Eyes, Blond Yarn Hair, c.1939, 16 In.		969.00
Madame Alexander, Sweet Tears Gift Set, Doll & Accessories On Box, 1965, 9 In.		140.00
Madame Alexander, Victoria, Composition, Ivory Satin Gown, Velvet Banner, 21 In.		5700.00
Madame Alexander, Victorian Bride, Plastic, Sleep Eyes, Ecru Satin Gown, Bustle, c.1951, 21 In.		1824.00
Madame Alexander, Wendy, First Sailor Dress, Plastic, Red Hair, Alexander-Kins, 1956, 8 In. . *illus*		448.00
Mark Twain, Papier-Mache, Painted, Mustache, Muslin & Felt Body, Germany, c.1890, 12 In.		314.00
Marotte, Arlette, Bisque Shoulder Head, Silk Jester Costume, Squeeker, Maple Handle, 12 In..		741.00
Martha Chase, George Washington, Stockinet, Pressed & Painted Features, Label, 25 In.		4560.00
Mattel, Baby Beans, Yawning, Blond, Cap, c.1970		28.00
Mattel, Baby Smile 'N Frown, Smiles When Hand Is Raised, Pouts When Lowered, 1965, 9 ½ In.		65.00
Mattel, Barbie, American Girl, Vinyl, Azure Eyes, Brunette, Suit, Box, 1965, 11 In.		280.00
Mattel, Barbie, Ash Blond Ponytail, Enchanted Evening Costume, Earrings, Stand, Box		904.00
Mattel, Barbie, Blond Bubble Cut, Bouncy Flouncy Costume, Sunglasses, Shoes, Box		226.00
Mattel, Barbie, Blond Bubble Cut, Pink Satin Outfit, Box, 11 In.		113.00
Mattel, Barbie, Blond Swirl Ponytail, Red Swimsuit, Box		226.00
Mattel, Barbie, Brunette Bob, Tricot Stripe, Turquoise Bottom, Box, 1965, 11 In.		201.00
Mattel, Barbie, Brunette Ponytail, Barbie-Q Costume, Accessories, Box, c.1960, 11 In.		912.00
Mattel, Barbie, Brunette Ponytail, Striped Swimsuit, Box, Montgomery Ward, 1972, 11 In.		283.00
Mattel, Barbie, Color Magic, Blond Hair, Multicolor Diamond Swimsuit		226.00
Mattel, Barbie, Copper Swirl Ponytail, Red Swimsuit, 11 In.		170.00
Mattel, Barbie, Fashion Queen, 3 Wigs, Box, 11 In.		254.00
Mattel, Barbie, No. 1, Blond Ponytail, Striped Swimsuit, 11 In.		1074.00
Mattel, Barbie, No. 1, Blond Ponytail, Striped Swimsuit, Earrings, Shoes, c.1958, 11 In.		3990.00
Mattel, Barbie, No. 3, Blond Ponytail, Striped Swimsuit, Earrings, Box		311.00
Mattel, Barbie, No. 4, Black Ponytail, American Airlines Outfit, Box, 11 In.		367.00
Mattel, Barbie, No. 5, Black Ponytail, Invitation To Tea Outfit, 11 In.		141.00
Mattel, Barbie, No. 5, Red Titian Ponytail, Plantation Belle Outfit		141.25
Mattel, Barbie, No. 5, Titian Bubble Cut, Nighty Negligee Outfit, Box, 11 In.		311.00
Mattel, Barbie, Twist 'N' Turn, 1966		13.00
Mattel, Barbie, Twist 'N' Turn, Blond Flip Hair, Pajama Pow Outfit, 11 In.		102.00
Mattel, Barbie, Twist 'N' Turn, Brunette Flip Hair, Party Wines Outfit, 11 In.		226.00
Mattel, Barbie, Walking Lively, Long Blond Hair, Pink Pants & Top, Yellow Purse, 1972		85.00
Mattel, Francie, Black, Red Hair, Original Swimsuit		537.00
Mattel, Francie, Black, Twist 'N' Turn, Painted Face, Long Lashes, Pierced Ears, 1967		450.00
Mattel, Francie, Blond Hair, Brown Eyes, Lashes, Bangs, Striped Suit, Box, 1967, 11 In.		280.00
Mattel, Francie, Brown Eyes & Hair, Tricot Suit, Pink & Green Squares, Box, 1965, 11 In.		448.00
Mattel, Francie, Brunette Hair, Bendable Legs, Box		311.00
Mattel, Francie, Twist 'N' Turn, Blond Hair, Orange Suit, Head Band, Shoes, Box, 1969, 11 In.		173.00
Mattel, Francie, Twist 'N' Turn, Brown Eyes & Hair, Tricot Suit, Pink Bottom, Box, 1967, 11 In.		280.00
Mattel, Francie, Twist 'N' Turn, Brown Eyes, Long Blond Hair, Neon Orange Suit, Box, 1969, 11 In.		1680.00
Mattel, Francie, Twist 'N' Turn, Brunette, Tricot Stripe, Pink Bottom, Belt, Tag, Stand, Box, 1967, 11 In.		1035.00
Mattel, Ken, Blond Flocked Hair, Blue Eyes, Red Swim Trunks, Red & White Jacket, 1962, 12 In.		224.00
Mattel, Ken, Brown Flocked Hair, Summer Shorts & Shirt, Vinyl Carrying Case, 1962		220.00

Doll, Madame Alexander, Godey Lady, Plastic, 5-Piece Body, Taffeta Gown, Snood, 1950, 14 In.
$1120.00

Theriault's

Doll, Madame Alexander, Mary Martin, Plastic, Sleep Eyes, South Pacific Costume, 1950, 14 In.
$952.00

Theriault's

Doll, Madame Alexander, Plastic, Walker, Organdy Gown, Alexander-Kins, 1954, 8 In.
$784.00

Theriault's

D

Doll, Madame Alexander, Snow White, Plastic, Sleep Eyes, 5-Piece Body, Wrist Tag, 1952, 18 In. $560.00

Theriault's

Doll, Madame Alexander, Wendy, First Sailor Dress, Plastic, Red Hair, Alexander-Kins, 1956, 8 In. $448.00

Theriault's

Doll, Mattel, Skipper, Blond Hair, Red Knit Suit, Sandals, Wrist Tag, Stand, Box, Booklet, 1964, 9 In. $112.00

Theriault's

Mattel, Ken, Mod Hair, Box	91.00
Mattel, Ken, Talking, Original Box & Clothes	34.00
Mattel, Midge, Blond Flip, Turquoise 2-Piece Swimsuit, Shoes, Box, Tag, Booklet, 11 In.	2760.00
Mattel, Midge, Blue Eyes, Freckles, Blond Hair, Turquoise Swimsuit, Box, 1965, 11 In.	224.00
Mattel, P.J., Long Blond Ponytail, Brown Eyes, Bendable Legs, Pink Swimsuit, 1969, 11 In.	280.00
Mattel, Shrinkin Violette, Talking, Eyelids Move, Attached Dress, Underpants, 1963, 17 In.	95.00
Mattel, Skipper, Blond Hair, Red Knit Suit, Sandals, Wrist Tag, Stand, Box, Booklet, 1964, 9 In. *illus*	112.00
Mattel, Skipper, Twist 'N' Turn, Blue Eyes, Blond Hair, Pink & Orange Suit, Box, 1967, 9 In.	168.00
Mego, Kristy McNichol, Blue Jeans, Red Jacket, White Shirt, 1978	90.00
Molly-'Es, Mamie Eisenhower, Plastic, Sleep Eyes, Musical Box Stand, c.1957, 16 In.	342.00
Mothereau, Bisque, Human Hair, Composition, Jointed, Cashmere Coat, Silk Bonnet, c.1880, 11 In.	259.00
Nancy Ann Storybook, Lavender & Lace, Plastic, Hair, 5-Piece Body, Organdy Gown, 1950s, 18 In.	784.00
Norah Wellings, Spanish Dancer, Felt, Googly Eyes, Black Yarn Wig, c.1935, 26 In.	513.00
Papago, Girl, Removable Head, Wide Arms, c.1990, 18 x 12 In.	748.00
Paper dolls are listed in their own category.	
Papier-Mache, Clown, Socket Head, Painted Cap, Face, Smile, Jointed, France, c.1900, 18 In.	115.00
Papier-Mache, Military Officer, Painted Eyes, Mustache, Jointed, Full Uniform, Sword, 13 In.	912.00
Papier-Mache, Pauline, Molded & Painted Features, Black Painted Hair, Leather Body, 18 In.	345.00
Papier-Mache, Woman, Shoulder Head, Closed Mouth, Kid Torso, Dress, Slippers, c.1840, 20 In.	288.00
Pincushion dolls are listed in their own category.	
Porcelain, Head, Tilted, Gray Sculpted Chignon, Muslin Body, White Dress, c.1860, 8 ½ In.	175.00
Porcelain, Woman, Shoulder Head, Black Molded Hair, Blue Snood, Muslin Body, Silk Gown, 14 In.	4332.00
Puppet, 3 Stooges, Composition Head, Painted, Cotton Felt Body, c.1935, 11 In., 3 Piece	1596.00
Puppet, Mr. Ed The Talking Horse, Pull String, Mattel, 1962	25.00
Queen Victoria, Poured Wax Shoulder Head, Blue Glass Eyes, Muslin, Black Silk Gown, 18 In.	1710.00
Rabery & Delphieu, Porcelain Head, Glass Eyes, Jointed Body, Hat, Long Dress, Marked, 24 In.	1793.00
Raggedy Andy, Painted Face, Eyelash, Shoebutton Eyes, Stitch-Jointed, Volland, 1920s, 16 In. *illus*	840.00
Raggedy Ann & Andy, Shoebutton Eyes, Wool Hair, Heart, Label, Georgene Novelties, 19 In., Pair	2016.00
Raggedy Ann & Andy, Silk-Screened Face, Wool Hair, Molly-'Es, c.1935, 18 In., Pair	2240.00
Raggedy Ann, Cloth, Wool Hair, Printed Face, Dress, Marked, Exposition Doll & Toy, 1935, 18 In.	4480.00
Raggedy Ann, Hand Painted Face, Shoebutton Eyes, Yarn Hair, Volland, c.1915, 17 In.	2352.00
Raggedy Ann, Painted Features, Wool Hair, Shoebutton Eyes, Heart, Volland, c.1922, 16 In.	1232.00
Ravca, Man, Stockinet, Stitch-Sculpted Head, Painted Face, Stitched Hair, c.1930, 15 In. *illus*	1120.00
Recknagel, Max, Bisque Head, Sculpted Hair, Painted Face, Smirk, Papier-Mache, Suit, 6 ½ In.	35.00
S & H dolls are also listed here as Simon & Halbig.	
S.F.B.J., 236, Bisque Head, Laughing Face, Tongue, Mohair, Composition, Wood, Toddler, 20 In.	684.00
S.F.B.J., 236, Bisque Head, Sleep Eyes, Open Mouth, 2 Teeth, Arms Extended, Bebe, 17 In.	474.00
S.F.B.J., 237, Boy, Bisque Head, Flocked Hair, Blue Eyes, Jointed, Sailor Suit, Red Anchor, 16 In.	2736.00
S.F.B.J., 252, Boy, Bisque Socket Head, Brown Sleep Eyes, Pouty Face, Toddler, 17 In.	5700.00
S.F.B.J., 301, Bisque, Sleep Eyes, Mohair Lashes & Wig, Jointed, Walks, Windup, 24 In.	627.00
S.F.B.J., Princess Elizabeth, Bisque Socket Head, Brown Human Hair, White Gown, 1938, 33 In.	3420.00
Sayco, Our Gang, Composition, Papier-Mache, Metal, Windup, Box, 1926, 26 In., 5 Piece	5244.00
Schmitt, Bisque Socket Head, Blue Eyes, Blond Mohair, Composition & Wood, 19 In.	10830.00
Schmitt, Bisque Socket Head, Spiral-Threaded Eyes, Composition & Wood Body, Bebe, 17 In.	9690.00
Schoenhut, Barney Google & Sparkplug, Wood, Painted Features, c.1922, 8-In. Barney	399.00
Schoenhut, Boy, Kermit, Teddy Roosevelt's Son, Camera, 8 In.	1298.00
Schoenhut, Boy, Wood, Brown Intaglio Eyes, Blond Hair, Spring-Jointed, White Sailor Suit, 21 In.	570.00
Schoenhut, Boy, Wood, Intaglio Eyes, Blond Mohair, Spring-Jointed, Boy's Suit & Cap, 16 In.	798.00
Schoenhut, Child, Pouty, Painted Face, Human Hair Wig, Pat. Jan 17, 18 ½ In. *illus*	748.00
Schoenhut, Man, Arab, Rifle, Sword, Turban, c.1900, 7 ½ In.	3540.00
Schoenhut, Man, Black African, Yellow Jug On Head, 7 ½ In.	1947.00
Schoenhut, Man, Great White Hunter, Rifle, Yellow Helmet, 7 ½ In.	1495.00
Schoenhut, Teddy Roosevelt, Safari Attire, Rifle, c.1900, 8 ½ In.	2360.00
Schoenhut, Toddler, Wood, Carved, Painted, Pouty Lips, Blond Bob, Spring-Jointed, 11 In.	171.00
Schoenhut, Woman, Wood Socket Head, Intaglio Eyes, Brown Mohair Coiled Braids, c.1911, 16 In.	6612.00
Shirley Temple dolls are included in the Shirley Temple category.	
Simon & Halbig, 890, Girl, Bisque, Blue Eyes, Blond Mohair Wig, Black Stockings, 5 In.	741.00
Simon & Halbig, 1039, Bisque Socket Head, Blue Flirty Eyes, Composition, Wood, Bebe, 22 In.	2736.00
Simon & Halbig, 1260, Bisque Head, Leather Body, Composition Arms, Human Wig, 15 In.	225.00
Simon & Halbig, 1329, Asian Child, Bisque, Jointed Composition Body, Silk Kimono, 15 In.	1824.00
Simon & Halbig, 1329, Asian Woman, Bisque Socket Head, Wood, Ball-Jointed, c.1900, 23 In. *illus*	3360.00
Simon & Halbig, 1388, Bisque Socket Head, Gray Glass Eyes, Smiling, Teeth, Ball-Jointed, 22 In.	9690.00
Simon & Halbig, Flapper, Bisque, Blue Glass Eyes, Open Mouth, Headband, 1915, 13 In.	1000.00
Simon & Halbig, Ondine, Cork Body, Jointed, Mechanical, Swims, c.1890, 16 In.	1695.00
Simon & Halbig, Porcelain Head, Sleep Eyes, Mohair Wig, Composition, Child, Jointed, 36 In. *illus*	299.00
Simon & Halbig, Porcelain Head, Sleep Eyes, Mohair Wig, Jointed Composition Body, 36 In.	399.00

DOORSTOP

Simon & Halbig, Sleep Eyes, Open Mouth, Composition Body, Jointed, 22 In. ....*illus*	106.00
Sonneberg, 137, Bisque, Big Blue Eyes, Pierced Ears, Composition, Wood, Jointed, Dress, 22 In.	1140.00
Steiff, Barney Google & Sparkplug, Felt, Pressed, Painted, Bead Eyes, 1925-27, 5-In. Barney ..	8265.00
Steiff, Captain, Sailor Cap, Glass Eyes, Beard, Felt, Movable Arms, 1900s, 15 In.	633.00
Steiff, Puck The Gnome, White Beard, Green Hat, Brown Boots, 7 In.	75.00
Steiner, Bisque Head, Blue Eyes, Blond Ringlets, Composition Body, Red Dress & Hat, 7 In.	3565.00
Steiner, Bisque Head, Blue Eyes, Closed Mouth, Mohair, Wood, Composition, Bonnet, Parasol, 32 In.	3163.00
Steiner, Bisque Head, Blue Wired Eyes, Chubby Cheeks, Blond Mohair, White Gown, 24 In.	5175.00
Steiner, Bisque Socket Head, Blue Eyes, Brunette Mohair, Jointed Composition, Bebe, 24 In.	6840.00
Steiner, Bisque Socket Head, Paperweight Eyes, Jointed Composition Body, Bebe, 24 In.	4560.00
Steiner, Gigoteur, Bisque, Lamb's Wool, Head Turns, Arms & Feet Move, Cries Mama, Bebe, 22 In.	3420.00
Steiner, Ma Poupee Et Son Trousseau, Bisque Socket Head, Clothes, Box, 16-In.	4845.00
Steiner, Series C, Bisque, Black Complexion, Closed Mouth, Fleecy Hair, Bebe, c.1884, 8 In.	173.00
Sterling Doll Co., Red Grange, Composition, Painted, Red Football Jersey, No. 77, 29 In.	456.00
Stockinet, Painted Googly Eyes & Ringlets, Stitch-Jointed Chubby Body, c.1920, 17 In.	57.00
Sustrac, Mignonette, Fashion, Bisque, Blue Glass Eyes, Blond Wig, 1877, 5 In.	2850.00
Terri Lee, Bonnie Lu, Plastic, Brown Skin, Black Curly Wig, Checkered Dress, 1950s, 16 In.	342.00
Terri Lee, Girl Scout, Hard Plastic, Auburn Hair, Green Outfit, Hat, 16 In.	159.00
Terri Lee, Plastic, Brown Eyes, Blond Curly Wig, Striped Pinafore, Shoes, 1950s, 16 In.	86.00
Valentine Co., Roxanne, Plastic, Sleep Eyes, Blond Hair, Pique Dress, Camera, 1950s, 18 In.	114.00
Ventriloquist Dummy, Bowtie, Straw Hat, Fake Cigarette Blowing Bubbles, 1940s	1350.00
Ventriloquist Dummy, Carved Wood, Clothes, Shoes, Hair, Hat, c.1875, 36 In.	4300.00
Ventriloquist Dummy, Man, Pine, Carved, Wool Suit, Painted, Spencer, 1937, 44 In. ....*illus*	264.00
Vogue, Ginnette, Vinyl, Sleep Eyes, 8 In.	280.00
Vogue, Jill, Blond Ponytail, Black Knit Top, Poodle Skirt, Heart Earrings, Sunglasses, 1958, 10 In.	195.00
Vogue, Jill, Plastic, Walker, Jointed, Sleep Eyes, 1958, 10 ½ In.	125.00
Volland, Belindy, Black, Muslin, Painted Face, Mother-Of-Pearl Eyes, Bandanna, c.1926, 15 In.	1792.00
Wax Head, Glass Eyes, Blond Hair, Wood Arms & Legs, 12 ½ In.	28.00
Woman, Wood, Carved, Painted Forehead Curls, Comb, Dowel-Jointed, Grodner Tal, c.1820, 21 In.	518.00
Wood, Carved Hair, Glass Eyes, Jointed, Floral Dress, Beaded Necklace, Italy, 16 In.	296.00
Wood, Carved, Paint Over Gesso, Inset Enamel Eyes, Velvet Robe, c.1800, 41 In. ....*illus*	1792.00
Wood, Carved, Painted Gesso, Glass Eyes, Dotted Eyebrows, Jointed, England, 1700s, 21 In. ....*illus*	2875.00
Wood, Painted Features, Tuck Comb, Dowel Jointed, Grodner Tal, c.1840, 9 In.	456.00

DOLL CLOTHES

Barbie, Barbie In Japan, Red & Gold Kimono, Belt, 3 Hair Ornaments	102.00
Barbie, Candy Striper Volunteer, No. 0889	170.00
Barbie, Easter Parade, No. 971	706.00
Barbie, Fun Flakes, Pink & White Knit, No. 3412	34.00
Barbie, Fur Cape, Mink, Silk-Like Lining, Hook & Eye, Label, Box, Sears Original	1150.00
Barbie, Gay Parisienne, Blue, 2 Fur Stoles, No. 1 Shoes, No. 964	622.00
Barbie, Glimmer Glamour, Hose, Belt, Shoes, Dress, Coat, No. 1547	509.00
Barbie, Poncho Put-On, Orange & Yellow Jumpsuit & Poncho, No. 3411	23.00
Barbie, Roman Holiday, Red, White & Blue, Striped Coat, No. 968	480.00
Barbie, Tennis Anyone, No. 941	57.00
Bebe Jumeau, Brown Velvet Jacket, Brown Taffeta Skirt, Lace Trim, Size 12	285.00
Bebe Jumeau, Shoes, Black Kidskin, Ankle Straps, Brown Silk Bows, c.1890, 4 In.	399.00
Bebe Jumeau, Shoes, Black Kidskin, Overcast Edge, Brown Silk Ribbon, c.1890, 4 In.	342.00
Bebe, Bonnet, Ivory Silk & Satin, Lace, Draped Form, c.1880	399.00
Bebe, Bonnet, Straw, Curled Bands, Crepe-De-Chine Loops, Satin Ruffles, Label, c.1890, 5 In.	12.00
Cap, Chinese, Black Silk, Jade, Coral Trim, Cotton Lining, Embroidered, Applique, c.1910, 5 In.	173.00
Dress, Burgundy Velvet, Hip Sash, Cord Trim, Gold Buttons, c.1900, For 20-In. Doll	285.00
Dress, Linen, Bronzed Green, Princess Style, Box Pleats, Plaid Trim, For 28-In. Doll	228.00
Dress, Rose Silk, Lace, High Waist, Bonnet, Silk Flowers, Ribbon, For 18-In. Doll	1145.00
Dress, Sheer Muslin, Fitted Jacket, Full Skirt, Faille Ribbons, France, c.1850, 12 In.	316.00
Dress, White Pique, Ribbed, Blue Braid Trim, Daisies, c.1888, For 35-In. Doll	342.00
Ken, The Yachtsman, No. 789, Box	198.00
Parasol, Faux Ivory, Dog Handle, Amber Glass Eyes, Silk Cover, Ruffled Edge, c.1890, 16 In.	316.00
Twiggy, Yellow Tunic, Knee-High Socks & Shoes, Purse, Box	254.00

DONALD DUCK *items are included in the Disneyana category.*

DOORSTOPS have been made in all types of designs. The vast majority of the doorstops sold today are cast iron and were made from about 1890 to 1930. Most of them are shaped like people, animals, flowers, or ships. Reproductions and newly designed examples are sold in gift shops.

Basket Of Flowers, Painted, Blue Ribbon Handle, Cast Iron, 1900s, 11 In.	123.00

Doll, Raggedy Andy, Painted Face, Eyelash, Shoebutton Eyes, Stitch-Jointed, Volland, 1920s, 16 In.
$840.00

Theriault's

Doll, Ravca, Man, Stockinet, Stitch-Sculpted Head, Painted Face, Stitched Hair, c.1930, 15 In.
$1120.00

Theriault's

Doll, Schoenhut, Child, Pouty, Painted Face, Human Hair Wig, Pat. Jan 17, 18 ½ In.
$748.00

Bertoia Auction

197

Doll, Simon & Halbig, 1329, Asian Woman, Bisque Socket Head, Wood, Ball-Jointed, c.1900, 23 In.
$3360.00

Theriault's

Doll, Simon & Halbig, Porcelain Head, Sleep Eyes, Mohair Wig, Composition, Child, Jointed, 36 In.
$299.00

Sloans & Kenyon

Doll, Simon & Halbig, Sleep Eyes, Open Mouth, Composition Body, Jointed, 22 In.
$106.00

Conestoga Auction Co., Inc.

Basket Of Fruit, Paint, Cast Iron, 12 ¾ In.	305.00
Basket, Mixed Flowers, Cast Iron, 10 ¾ In.	130.00
Basket, Woven, Blue Bow On Handle, Hurricane Style, Cast Iron, Painted, c.1910, 15 ¾ In.	59.00
Black Banjo Player, Sitting, Cast Iron, Spencer, 6 ½ x 6 In.	690.00
Black Boy, On Green Frog, Paint, Cast Iron, 6 ½ In.	1356.00
Carpenter Tools, Rectangular Panel, Red, Yellow, Blue Paint, Cast Iron, c.1900, 7 x 11 In.	237.00
Cat, Black, Curled Tail, Arched Back, Cast Iron, 10 In.	2110.00
Cat, Persian, Seated, Gray & White, Cast Iron, 7 x 9 ¼ In.	144.00
Cat, Reclining, Black & White Paint, Green Eyes, Cast Iron, c.1900, 6 x 10 In.	593.00
Cat, Seated, Bow, Cast Iron, England, 14 ¼ In.	431.00
Cat, Seated, Cast Iron, Creations Co., 8 ¼ In.	212.00
Cat, Seated, Head Turned, Cast Iron, Painted, Hubley, 9 x 6 ½ In.	181.00
Cat, Upright, Painted White, Green Eyes, Pink Ears, Hubley, 9 ¼ In.	71.00
Cats, Wearing Dresses, Multicolor, Cast Iron, c.1910, 6 In.	206.00
Charleston Dancers, Signed, Fish, Hubley, 8 ⅞ x 5 ⅜ In. ....*illus*	5463.00
Clown, Arms Outstretched, Red Outfit, White Ruffle, Iron, 1950s, 11 x 11 In.	125.00
Clown, Crossed Out, Crossed Legs & Arms, Books, Checkered Coat, 7 ⅜ x 5 ¾ In. ....*illus*	1725.00
Colonial Woman, Yellow, Paint, Cast Iron, 5 In.	170.00
Conestoga Wagon, Painted, Hollow Back, Cast Iron, c.1930, 11 ⅜ In.	83.00
Cottage, Ann Hathaway, Painted, 3-Piece Mold, Hubley, 6 ⅜ x 8 ⅜ In. ....*illus*	690.00
Cottage, Ann Hathaway, Tudor Style, 2 Chimneys, Trees, A.M. Greenblatt No. 14, 6 ¼ x 7 ⅜ In. *illus*	460.00
Cottage, Cape Cod, Thatched Roof, Picket Fence, Flowers, 5 x 7 ¼ In. ....*illus*	259.00
Cottage, Well, Brick Molding, Richardson, Mass., 5 x 8 In.	144.00
Covered Wagon, Oxen, Cast Aluminum, Headford Bros. & Hitchins, c.1895, 16 x 7 In.	375.00
Dancer, Flamenco, Holding Fan, Cast Iron, 9 ½ x 5 ¼ In.	144.00
Dog, Afghan Hound, White, Cast Iron, 10 x 15 In.	237.00
Dog, Boston Terrier, Cast Iron, 10 In.	124.00
Dog, Cockatoo, On Stump, Cast Iron, Albany Foundry Co., 12 In.	94.00
Dog, Cocker Spaniel, Painted Brown, Mottled, Cast Iron, 6 ¾ In.	35.00
Dog, Colonial Woman, Painted, Cast Iron, 10 ¾ x 5 ¾ In.	58.00
Dog, Double Scottie, Leaning, Cast Iron, Painted Black, 6 x 8 ½ In.	57.00
Dog, German Shepherd, Painted, Cast Iron, c.1900, 9 x 11 In.	210.00
Dog, German Shepherd, Standing, Ears Up, Brown & Black, 13 x 15 In.	226.00
Dog, Irish Setter, Pointing, Black, White, Cast Iron, 15 ½ In.	374.00
Dog, Japanese Spaniel, Black & White, Sitting Up, Marked, 9 In.	440.00
Dog, Russian Wolfhound, Cast Iron, c.1905, 9 ¾ x 15 In.	338.00
Dog, Scottie, Black Paint, Cast Iron, 9 ½ x 8 In.	147.00
Dog, Terrier, Black & White, Cast Iron, c.1931, 5 ½ In.	45.00
Dog, Terrier, Brown & White, Cast Iron, 9 In.	45.00
Dog, Terrier, Brown, White, Molded Fur, Cast Iron, 7 ½ In.	288.00
Dog, Terrier, Standing, Cast Iron, Brown, Black, 10 x 10 ½ In.	90.00
Dog, Terrier, Standing, Upswept Tail, Black & White, Cast Iron, Early 1900s, 23 In.	46.00
Dog, Wirehaired Fox Terrier, Cast Iron, Spencer, 7 ½ In.	35.00
Dolly, Girl Holding Baby Doll, Grace Drayton, Hubley, 9 ½ x 5 ½ In. ....*illus*	1265.00
Dutch Boy, Hands On Hip, Cast Iron, 9 In.	1062.00
Dutch Boy, Standing, Holding Basket Of Fruit, Top Hat, Cast Iron, 9 In.	207.00
Elephant, Palm Tree, Standing, Trunk Up In Tree, Cast Iron, 13 In.	148.00
Elephant, Raised Trunk, Cast Iron, Creation, Lancaster, Pennsylvania, 1930, 7 x 7 In.	195.00
Fireman, Holding Hose, Dalmatian, Fire Hydrant, Red Suit, Cast Iron, 7 ½ In.	122.00
Fisherman, Holding Oil Lamp, Yellow Raincoat, The Patrol, Cast Iron, 9 In.	57.00
Flower Basket, Bow On Top, Cast Iron, Painted	45.00
Flowers, 2-Sided, Grecian Urn Style Vase, Base, Embossed, Bradley & Hubbard, 10 x 5 In.	316.00
Flowers, Roses, Urn, Cream, Green, Peach, Marked, Hubley, 6 x 5 In.	45.00
Flowers, Woven Basket, Cast Iron, Marked, L.A.C.S., 10 x 8 In.	115.00
Fox Head, Black, Cast Iron, 6 In.	68.00
French Basket, Flowers, Bow Handle, Hubley No. 69, 10 x 6 In.	86.00
Giraffe, Cast Iron, Painted, 19th Century, 15 ¾ In.	15405.00
Girl Kicking Flower, Orange Plaid Skirt, 9 ¾ x 6 ¾ In. ....*illus*	1955.00
Gnome Elf, Standing, Cast Iron, Painted, 11 ½ In.	118.00
Golfer Caddy, Holding Bag Of Clubs, Cast Iron, Painted, 8 In.	317.00
Golfer, Putting, Hubley, 7 x 8 In.	230.00
Golfer, Swinging Pose, Maroon Jacket, Blue Knickers, Cast Iron, c.1900, 10 x 7 In.	368.00
Golfer, Woman, Wearing Dress, Hat, Holding Golf Club, Cast Iron, 8 ½ In.	178.00
Grapevine, Grapes, Leaves, Cast Iron, Albany Foundry, 7 x 6 In.	144.00
Griffin, Seated, Cast Iron, France, 9 ½ x 7 ½ In., Pair	183.00
Highland Lighthouse, Cape Cod, 2 Houses, c.1920s, 9 x 8 In.	876.00

Housekeeper, Weighted Quart Milk Bottle, Fabric Dress, 10 ½ In.		57.00
Jester, Seated, Long Nose, Pointed Hat, Multicolor, Cast Iron, Punch, 12 In.		444.00
Lighthouse, Tower, Guardhouse, Stairs, Rubber, 9 ¾ x 7 ⅜ In.		345.00
Lion, Cast Iron, c.1890, 7 x 9 In.		180.00
Lion, Standing, Looking Over Shoulder, Painted, Cast Iron, 7 x 9 In.		300.00
Little Red Riding Hood, Wolf, Cast Iron, Albany Foundry, N.Y., c.1900, 8 In.	*illus*	296.00
Major Domo, Standing, Dressed In Uniform, Judd Company, Cast Iron, 8 In.		119.00
Mammy, Cast Iron, Painted, c.1910, 12 In.		235.00
Mammy, Standing, Hands On Him, Red Dress, White Apron, Cast Iron, Hubley, 9 In.		89.00
Mammy, Weighted Quart Water Jar, Sack Dress, Lace Apron, Kerchief, 10 ½ In.		68.00
March Hare, Multicolor, Cast Iron, 8 In.		565.00
Merry Christmas, 3 Black & White Dogs, Red & Green Holly, Cast Iron, 8 In.	*illus*	142.00
Owl, Brown, On Grass, Cast Iron, 6 ¾ In.		362.00
Owl, Cast Iron, Bradley & Hubbard, 15 In.		1048.00
Owl, Perched, Pedestal, Cast Iron, Marked, Bradley & Hubbard, 16 x 5 In.		2147.00
Owl, White, Cast Iron, Bradley & Hubbard, 15 In.		1130.00
Owl, White, On Perch, White, Gray, Orange, Cast Iron, 9 In.		520.00
Parlor Maid, Holding Serving Tray, Fish, Hubley, Signed, 9 ¼ x 3 ½ In.	*illus*	1035.00
Pelican, Yellow, Green & White Paint, Iron, Marked, 14 ½ In.		4025.00
Penguin, Hollow, 2 Piece, Tuxedo, Top Hat, Hubley, 10 ½ In.		863.00
Penguin, Upward Glancing, Cast Iron, Painted, Signed, c.1930, 9 x 5 In.		1896.00
Pheasant, In Underbrush, Hubley, Signed, 7 x 8 In.		230.00
Pilgrim, Holding Gun, Standing, Bradley & Hubbard, c.1910, 10 In.		1243.00
Poppies, White Vase, Black Base, Hubley, 10 ⅝ x 7 ⅞ In.	*illus*	288.00
Punch & Judy, Painted, Red, White, Yellow, Cast Iron, c.1900, 11 In.		92.00
Punch, Seated, Dog, Paint, Cast Iron, England, 12 x 9 In.		676.00
Rabbit, Eating Cabbage, Multicolor, Paint, Cast Iron, 8 ½ In.		452.00
Rabbit, Sitting, Eating Carrot, Cast Iron, Creations Co., 1930, 9 In.		265.00
Ram, Cast Iron, Painted, 9 In.		523.00
Red Riding Hood, Shrubbery Embossed Base, 7 x 9 In.		1840.00
Red Riding Hood, Whimsical, Grace Drayton, Hubley, 9 ½ x 5 In.		1093.00
Rooster, Standing, Aroused Tail Feathers, Bradley & Hubbard, 9 ⅛ x 11 ⅛ In.	*illus*	5463.00
Roses, White Vase, Cast Iron, Hubley, 8 ¾ x 7 ⅞ In.		201.00
Sailing Ship, Paint, Cast Iron, 1930, 11 ½ x 11 In.		338.00
Skier, Woman, Holding Skis, Blue & Red, c.1930, 12 ⅜ x 5 In.	*illus*	1035.00
Soldier, Revolutionary, Cast Iron, Albany Fdry. Co., 9 In.		130.00
Squirrel, Eating Acorn, Sitting On Log, Bradley & Hubbard, 10 x 11 ½ In.		2588.00
Squirrel, Seated On Log, Cast Iron, c.1900, 12 x 10 In.		1896.00
Stagecoach, Fleur-De-Lis, Paint, Cast Iron, Creation Co., Copyright 1930, 7 x 8 ¾ In.		246.00
Sunbonnet Baby, Red Bonnet, White Lace, Bow, Blue Dress, Cast Iron, Painted, c.1900, 7 x 4 In.		123.00
Tulips, Paint, Cast Iron, Albany & National Foundry, 8 ½ x 7 In.		88.00
Tulips, Pot, Cast Iron, Multicolor Paint, c.1900, 9 x 7 In.		711.00
Tulips, Wicker Basket, 13 x 9 In.		920.00
Turkey, Cast Iron, Painted, Bradley & Hubbard, 12 ¾ In.		1652.00
Vase, Delphinium, Roses, Forget-Me-Nots, Blue Ribbon, Hubley, 9 In.		173.00
Whale, Cast Iron, Virginia Metalcrafters, 13 In.		153.00
Winged Putti, Holding Bow, Gilt Bronze, Leaf Pedestal, Demilune Base, Ring Handle Top, 17 ⅜ In.		207.00
Woman, Basket Of Flowers, Parasol, Base, Long Dress & Bonnet, 11 x 7 In.		711.00
Woman, Carrying Fruit On Her Head, 12 x 6 ½ In.	*illus*	1035.00
Woman, Southern Belle, Red Dress, Holding Flowered Hat, Cast Iron, 11 In.		46.00
Wrought Iron, Loop Handle, Twisted Shaft, Scrolled Supports, Stone Block, 28 In.		57.00

DOULTON pottery and porcelain were made by Doulton and Co. of Burslem, England, after 1882. The name *Royal Doulton* appeared on the company's wares after 1902. Other pottery by Doulton is listed under Royal Doulton.

Biscuit Jar, Cream Ground, Flowers, Barrel Shape, Silver Plate Lid, Bail, Signed, 6 ½ In.		80.00
Biscuit Jar, Red, Embossed Blue Leaves, Gold Detail, Bone Finial, Silver Plate Lid, Bail, 6 In.		110.00
Ewer, Flowers, Gilt, Dragon Handle, Cabochon Eyes, 14 In.		357.00
Figurine, Bather, Nude Maiden, On Globe, Lizard, 4 Frog Feet, Lambeth, c.1900, 12 ¾ In.		4709.00
Flask, Swollen, Loop Handle, Blue Smiling & Angry Face, Green Leaves, Lambeth, c.1905, 7 In.		2943.00
Ginger Jar, Cover, Ball Shape, Maidens Dancing In Garden, Red, Gold, Burslem, c.1900, 6 In.		99.00
Jardiniere, Medallions, Queen Victoria, Figures, Stems, Thistle, Rose, Lambeth, 1874, 8 ½ In.		1276.00
Jug, American Flags, Poem, America, Brown & Tan Glaze, Oval, Cylindrical Top, 7 ½ In.		275.00
Lamp, Kerosene, Flow Blue, 2 Handles, Poppy Design, Blue & White Shade, 21 In.		250.00
Pitcher, Stoneware, Salt Glazed, Raised Flowers, Golf Scene, Lambeth, c.1900, 8 ½ In.		1135.00
Pitcher, Water, Globular, Flower Shape Neck, Scroll Handle, Berry Swags, 3 Ball Feet, 1889, 15 In.		236.00

Doll, Ventriloquist Dummy, Man, Pine, Carved, Wool Suit, Painted, Spencer, 1937, 44 In.
$264.00

Garth's Auctions, Inc.

Doll, Wood, Carved, Paint Over Gesso, Inset Enamel Eyes, Velvet Robe, c.1800, 41 In.
$1792.00

Theriault's

Doll, Wood, Carved, Painted Gesso, Glass Eyes, Dotted Eyebrows, Jointed, England, 1700s, 21 In.
$2875.00

Bertoia Auction

Doorstop, Charleston Dancers, Signed, Fish, Hubley, 8 ⅞ x 5 ⅜ In.
$5463.00

Bertoia Auction

Doorstop, Clown, Crossed Out, Crossed Legs & Arms, Books, Checkered Coat, 7 ⅜ x 5 ¾ In.
$1725.00

Bertoia Auction

Doorstop, Cottage, Ann Hathaway, Painted, 3-Piece Mold, Hubley, 6 ⅜ x 8 ⅜ In.
$690.00

Bertoia Auction

Doorstop, Cottage, Ann Hathaway, Tudor Style, 2 Chimneys, Trees, A.M. Greenblatt No. 14, 6 ¼ x 7 ⅜ In.
$460.00

Bertoia Auction

Punch Bowl, Flowers, Footed, Marked Doulton Burslem England, 10 x 17 In. 71.00
Tyg, Kangaroos, Leaf Borders, Square Handles, Lambeth, Monogramed, c.1905, 6 ½ In. 9420.00
Urn, Commemorative, Inscribed, Deceased's Name, Age 33, Lambeth, c.1871, 18 ½ In. 896.00
Vase, 4 Round Holes, Long Creature Around Neck, Brown, Narrow Lip, Lambeth, c.1905, 6 In. 3139.00
Vase, Deer, Standing & At Rest, Bands, Hannah Barlow, Impressed Mark, 7 ⅝ In. .... *illus* 805.00
Vase, Gold, Blue, White Flowers, Red Glaze, Impressed Doulton Lambeth, c.1891, 9 ½ In. 115.00
Vase, Goose Girl, Maiden, Cascading Hair, Geese, Lambeth, c.1900, 20 In., Pair 17660.00
Vase, Jack & Jill, Little Bo Peep, Nursery Rhyme, Flowering Trees, Signed, 13 ¼ In., Pair 16680.00
Vase, Pear Shape, Footed, Grotesque Creature At Neck, Gray, Blue, Lambeth, 1903, 10 ½ In. ... 3532.00
Vase, Swirl Design, Cobalt Blue Ground, White Bead Rim, 10 In. 127.00
Vase, Tapered, Lizard Crawling On Neck, Spider, Leaves, Cream Flowers, Lambeth, c.1915, 11 In. 4121.00
Vase, Tapered, Relief Molded Stems, Leaves, Birds, Purple Flowers, Lambeth, 1916, 11 In., Pair 2551.00

DRESDEN china is any china made in the town of Dresden, Germany. The most famous factory in Dresden is the Meissen factory. Figurines of eighteenth-century ladies and gentlemen, animal groups, or cherubs and other mythological subjects were popular. One special type of figurine was made with skirts of porcelain-dipped lace. Do not make the mistake of thinking that all pieces marked *Dresden* are from the Meissen factory. The Meissen pieces usually have crossed swords marks, and are listed under Meissen. Some recent porcelain from Ireland, called *Irish Dresden,* is not included in this book.

Bowl, Centerpiece, Pierced, Applied Flowers, Handles, Footed, 4 x 9 In. 90.00
Bowl, Fruit, Bird, Flowers, Weaved Border, c.1870, 10 x 10 In. 47.00
Bowl, Pedestal, Scallop Rim, Reticulated, Flowers, Cherub, c.1900, 13 In. 633.00
Box, Flowers, Ribbon Handle, White Ground, Gilt Trim, 6 x 7 In. 60.00
Candelabrum, 5-Light, Applied Putti, Flowers, 16 In., Pair 240.00
Candelabrum, 5-Light, Scroll Arms, Flowers, Gilt Accents, Child, Footed Base, 18 In. 385.00
Candlestick, Flowers, Hand Painted, Gold Ground, Carl Thieme, Ovington Bros., 1890, 8 In.. 250.00
Compote, Cherub, Bird, Scalloped Bowl, Round Base, Flowers, Multicolor, 15 ½ x 9 In. 210.00
Compote, Figural, Multicolor, Gilt, Cherubs, Reticulated Bowl, 20th Century, 14 ½ x 10 ½ In. 173.00
Compote, Woman, Standing, Gilt, Grapes, Holding Basket Overhead, Flowers, Swags, c.1900, 18 In. 384.00
Figurine, Bird, Blue Flower Wreath Around Neck, Leaves, White, 1800s, 9 x 11 In. 86.00
Figurine, Dog, Pug, Seated, Ball Collar, White, Brown Spots, Marked, 11 In., Pair 791.00
Figurine, Tailor Riding Goat, Flower Pattern Coat, Hat, Boots, Early 1900s, 12 ½ In. 329.00
Figurine, Woman, Carrying 2 Baskets, White Ruffled, Netted Dress, Stamped, 1800s, 9 x 4 In. 153.00
Group, Allegorical, Classical Maidens, Cherub, 25 x 13 In. 708.00
Group, Aristocratic Family, Grandmother, Spring Bouquets, Rocky Base, 14 ¾ x 19 ¾ In. 2390.00
Group, Ballerina, 3 Dancers, Flowers, Marked, 7 x 8 In. 178.00
Group, Lavender Seller, Children, Rococo Base, Multicolor, Yardley's, 12 x 8 In. 58.00
Group, Men & Women, Playing Musical Instruments, Multicolor, 7 x 10 In. 113.00
Lamp, Figural, Man, Women, Talking, Period Clothing, Painted, c.1950, 10 x 11 In. 148.00
Pitcher, Hot Water, Cover, Enamel Victorian Dancers, Gilt Ground, c.1895, 9 In. 948.00
Plaque, 3 Fates, Giltwood Frame, Signed, 14 x 13 In. 1107.00
Plate, Flowers, Reticulated Border, Gold Accents, Hand Painted, Marked, 10 In. 127.00
Plateau, Oval, Raised On Scroll Feet, Ram's Heads, Busts Of Minerva, Gilt, 4 In. 178.00
Stein, Pewter Mounts, Ball Thumbpiece, Chinese Men, Palm Tree, Flowers, 1700s, 8 In. 15405.00
Tazza, Woman's Portrait, Blue Ground, Gilt Trim, c.1890, 8 In. 1230.00
Urn, 2 Handles, Men Around Woman In Chair, 14 ½ In. 354.00
Urn, Lid, Figures, Landscapes, Flower Panels, Gilt Rim, Handles, Mark, 1900s, 24 ½ In., Pair. 2478.00
Vase, 4 Panels, 2 Courting Couples, 2 Flowers, Yellow Ground, 12 ¼ In. 104.00
Vase, Cover, Couples' Scenes, Flowers, Cherubs, Crowns, Handles, Gilt, Stand, c.1900, 28 In., Pair 770.00
Vase, Cover, Figure, Flower Panels, Gilt, Marked, c.1890, 14 ½ In., Pair 889.00
Vase, Cover, Potpourri, Hunt Scene, Laurel Swags, Multicolor, Gilded Handles, c.1890, 20 In. ..... *illus* 490.00
Vase, Formally Dressed Figures, Gilt Ground, Tapered, c.1895, 9 In. 593.00

DUNCAN & MILLER is a term used by collectors when referring to glass made by the George A. Duncan and Sons Company or the Duncan and Miller Glass Company. These companies worked from 1893 to 1955, when the use of the name *Duncan* was discontinued and the firm became part of the United States Glass Company. Early patterns may be listed under Pressed Glass.

Canterbury, Goblet, 7 ¼ In. 34.00
Canterbury, Sherbet, 4 ¼ In. 8.00
Teardrop, Pitcher, Water, 64 Oz., 8 ½ In. 110.00
Teardrop, Tray, Lavender, c.1950, 13 x 10 In. 30.00
Teardrop, Wine, 5 In. 18.00
Willow, Champagne, 4 ⅝ In. 8.00

DURAND art glass was made from 1924 to 1931. The Vineland Flint Glass Works was established by Victor Durand and Victor Durand Jr. in 1897. In 1924 Martin Bach Jr. and other artisans from the Quezal glassworks joined them at the Vineland, New Jersey, plant to make Durand art glass. They called their gold iridescent glass Gold Luster.

Compote, Green Iridescent, White Interior, 5 ⅜ In.	950.00
Cookie Jar, Opalescent, Green Pulled Feather, Gold Tipped, Raspberry Finial, Signed, 12 In. .... *illus*	4600.00
Dresser Box, Cover, Iridescent Gold, Calcite, 8-Point Star, Squat, Round, 3 In.	161.00
Finger Bowl, Underplate, Ruby Glass, Optic Ribbed, Scalloped, 7 In.	374.00
Ginger Jar, Lid, Gold Orange, White Pulled Feather, Gold Trim, Applied Threading, 6 In. .... *illus*	575.00
Goblet, Optic Ribbed, Ruby Glass, Reeded Spanish Yellow Stem, Round Foot, 7 In.	230.00
Lamp Base, Blue Luster, Gold Threading, 10 In. .... *illus*	201.00
Lampshade, Iridescent Crackle, Elongated Trumpet Shape, Blue & White Over Gold, 8 In. ...*illus*	230.00
Vase, Blue Aurene, King Tut, Iridescent Swirls, Double Gourd Shape, 1975, 2 In.	230.00
Vase, Blue Aurene, Mandarin Yellow Leaves, Vines, Urn Shape, Round Foot, 1974, 3 In.	184.00
Vase, Blue Aurene, Tugged Leaves, Plum Ground, 1981, 5 ¼ In.	138.00
Vase, Blue Feathering, Gold Iridescent, Oyster White, Threading, 8 ¾ In.	518.00
Vase, Blue Iridescent, Bottle Form, Elongated Neck, 12 In.	1089.00
Vase, Blue Iridescent, Cylindrical, Rolled Rim, Slight Tapered, 5 In.	403.00
Vase, Blue Iridescent, Flared Rim, Footed, Signed, 9 ⅜ In.	1575.00
Vase, Blue Iridescent, Opalescent Pulled Webbing, Oval, Flared Rim, 10 ¼ In.	830.00
Vase, Blue Iridescent, Shouldered, Flared Mouth, 6 ½ In. .... *illus*	230.00
Vase, Blue Iridescent, Silvery Web Stringing Overlay, Tapered, Flared Rim, 7 x 3 In.	756.00
Vase, Blue Iridescent, White Swirl, 6 ½ In.	200.00
Vase, Blue Luster, Spider Webbing, Bulbous, Flared Rim, Signed, 8 In.	650.00
Vase, Blue, Pulled Feather, Flared Rim, Footed, 9 ¼ In.	450.00
Vase, Butterscotch Ground, Green Hearts, Vines, Signed, 7 ½ In.	700.00
Vase, Butterscotch Ground, Pulled Feather, Spider Webbing Overlay, 8 ½ In.	850.00
Vase, Butterscotch Ground, Spider Webbing Overlay, Pedestal, Signed, 14 ½ In.	650.00
Vase, Cobalt Blue, White Swirl Design, Flared Rim, 8 ¾ In.	1035.00
Vase, Gold & Olive Iridescent, Swirls, 10 ½ x 4 ¾ In. .... *illus*	1240.00
Vase, Gold Iridescent, Inverted Teardrop Shape, Flared Rim, Footed, 8 ½ In.	502.00
Vase, Gold Iridescent, Vertical Ribs, Oval, Flared Rim, c.1920, 8 ¼ In.	1136.00
Vase, Gold Luster, Green Vines, Cascading Tendrils, Amber, Green, Pedestal, Trumpet Shape, 12 In.	805.00
Vase, Gold, Blue Pulled Feather, Iridescent, Flared Cylinder, Silver Inscribed, c.1925, 10 ¾ In.	764.00
Vase, Green, White Pulled Feathers, Baluster Form, Flared Neck, Footed, 9 ½ x 6 ½ In.	380.00
Vase, Green, White, Pulled Feather, Engraved Flower Border, 10 In.	500.00
Vase, Iridescent Blue, Applied White, Yellow Streaks, Tapered, Cylinder, 10 ½ In.	920.00
Vase, Iridescent Blue, Silver, Swirls, King Tut, Pinched Neck, Rolled, 1987, 3 In.	288.00
Vase, King Tut, Bulbous, Flaring, Green Glass, Gold Coil Design, Signed, 6 ½ In.	800.00
Vase, King Tut, Gold Iridescent, Green, 6 ¾ In.	350.00
Vase, Orange Ground, Green Heart & Vine Design, Flaring Rim, Signed, 9 In.	748.00
Vase, Pink, White, Gold Moorish, Crackle, Ball Shape, Signed, 8 x 7 ½ In.	2100.00
Vase, Silver Blue Iridescent, Black Ground, Leaf & Vine Design, Signed, 6 ½ In. ....*illus*	1007.00
Vase, Temple, Cover, Urn Shape, Golden Threads, Green Leaves, Amber Rose Finial, 8 In.	345.00
Vase, Threaded Design, Gold Iridescent, Pulled Feather, Blue Tipped, Signed, 8 In.	805.00
Vase, Translucent Red, White Pulled Feather, 5 Crimped Side Handles, 9 In.	460.00
Vase, Translucent, Ruby & White Peacock Feather, Urn Shape, Round Foot, Flare Rim, 10 In.	805.00

DURANT KILNS was founded by Jean Durant Rice in 1910 in Bedford Village, New York. He hired Leon Volkmar to oversee production. The pottery made both tableware and artware. Rice died in 1919, leaving Leon Volkmar to run the business. After 1930 the name *Durant Kilns* was changed and only the *Volkmar* mark was used.

Vase, Kimball, Footed, Cylindrical, Orange Mottled, Signed, 8 ½ In.	350.00
Vase, Persian Green Crackle Glaze, Signed, 1913, 15 ¼ x 12 In. ....*illus*	1054.00

ELVIS PRESLEY, the well-known singer, lived from 1935 to 1977. He became famous by 1956. Elvis appeared on television, starred in twenty-seven movies, and performed in Las Vegas. Memorabilia from any of the Presley shows, his records, and even memorials made after his death are collected.

Doll, White Jump Suit, Hong Kong, Box, 1984, 12 In.	35.00
Figurine, Plastic, White Costume, AM Radio In Platform Base, Box, c.1977, 10 In.	11.00
Guitar, Plastic, Decals, 6 Strings, Fitted Cardboard Box, Emenee, 1956, 31 In.	863.00
Guitar, Styron Plastic, 4 Strings, Box, Selcol, England, 1957, 31 In.	288.00

E

Doorstop, Cottage, Cape Cod, Thatched Roof, Picket Fence, Flowers, 5 x 7 ¼ In.
$259.00

Bertoia Auction

Doorstop, Dolly, Girl Holding Baby Doll, Grace Drayton, Hubley, 9 ½ 5 ½ In.
$1265.00

Bertoia Auction

Doorstop, Girl Kicking Flower, Orange Plaid Skirt, 9 ¾ x 6 ¾ In.
$1955.00

Bertoia Auction

Doorstop, Little Red Riding Hood, Wolf, Cast Iron, Albany Foundry, N.Y., c.1900, 8 In.
$296.00

Skinner, Inc.

Doorstop, Merry Christmas, 3 Black & White Dogs, Red & Green Holly, Cast Iron, 8 In. $142.00

Conestoga Auction Co., Inc.

Doorstop, Parlor Maid, Holding Serving Tray, Fish, Hubley, Signed, 9 ¼ x 3 ½ In. $1035.00

Bertoia Auction

Doorstop, Poppies, White Vase, Black Base, Hubley, 10 ⅝ x 7 ⅞ In. $288.00

Bertoia Auction

Doorstop, Rooster, Standing, Aroused Tail Feathers, Bradley & Hubbard, 9 ⅛ x 11 ⅛ In. $5463.00

Bertoia Auction

Purse, Clutch, Blue Vinyl, Elvis Playing Guitar, Record Album, 1956, 5 x 10 In.	316.00
Skirt, Cotton, Wraparound Design, Music Theme, Song Titles, c.1956, 23 ½ In. ......*illus*	191.00
Wallet, Brown Vinyl, Elvis Playing Guitar, Folds, Snap Coin Pocket, 3 x 4 In.	211.00
Wallet, Rock & Roll, Vinyl, Comb, Emery Board, Photo Pages, Coin Holder, 1956, 3 ¼ x 4 ½ In.	311.00
Wristwatch, Guitar Second Hand, Leather Strap, Quartz, Box, Valdawn	40.00

ENAMELS listed here are made of glass particles and other materials heated and fused to metal. In the eighteenth and nineteenth centuries, workmen from Russia, France, England, and other countries made small boxes and table pieces of enamel on metal. One form of English enamel is called *Battersea* and is listed under that name. There was a revival of interest in enameling in the 1930s and a new style evolved. There is now renewed interest in the artistic enameled plaques, vases, ashtrays, and jewelry. Enamels made since the 1930s are usually on copper or steel, although silver was often used for jewelry. Graniteware is a separate category, and enameled metal kitchen pieces may be included in the Kitchen category.

Basket, Flowers, Multicolor, Rope Twist Handle, Silver Gilt, Moscow, c.1915, 5 In.	3840.00
Beaker, Flared Foot, Multicolor Scrolls, Rope Twist Rim, Silver Gilt, Cyrillic, 2 ¼ In.	2160.00
Bookends, Copper, Orange Tree Medallion, Cobalt Blue, Cauman, c.1925, 5 ½ x 6 In. ....*illus*	5036.00
Box, Blue, Gilt Bronze, Scrolls, Flowers, Wreath & Ribbon Design Lid, c.1900, 3 x 5 ½ In.	396.00
Box, Blue, Green Oval, Berries, Leaves, Silver, Chased, Mildred Watkins, c.1920, 1 ½ x 4 In.	6000.00
Box, Lid, Medallion, Leaves, Geometric, Bird Handles, Ball & Claw Feet, Silver Gilt, c.1950, 5 ¾ In.	840.00
Charger, Abstract Design, Purple, Copper, Signed J. Salinas, 1982, 19 In.	81.00
Cigarette Case, Flowers, Geometrics, Stippled Silver Gilt Ground, Moscow, 1883, 4 In.	1560.00
Cigarette Case, Flowers, Multicolor, Stippled Ground, Silver Gilt, c.1965, 4 ½ In.	570.00
Cigarette Case, Geometrics, Flowers, Green, Blue, Red, White, Silver Gilt, Rectangular, c.1915, 4 In.	9000.00
Cigarette Case, Multicolor Flowers, Blue Ground, Silver Gilt, Rectangular, Moscow, 1884, 3 ¾ In.	1920.00
Cup, Double, Screw Closure, Egg Shape, Silver Gilt, Stand, c.1980, 3 ½ In.	660.00
Dish, Blue Clown, Mask, Blue, White, Black, Green, Copper, Franz Bergmann, c.1955, 6 ½ In.	750.00
Dish, Blue, Green, Gold, Yellow, Copper, Mildred Ball, c.1955, 6 ¼ x 2 ½ In.	395.00
Dish, Copper Rim, Flower Sprays, Fruit, Butterflies, Yellow, Blue, Pink, Canton, 11 In.	310.00
Dish, Scalloped, Yellow Ground, Green, Dragon, Leafy Roundel, Vines, Chinese, 1800s, 5 In, Pair	12650.00
Egg, Scrolled Flowers, Beads, 2 Pieces, Silver, c.1970 ½ In.	450.00
Eggcup, Flower Rondels, Black & White, Scalloped Rim, Flared Base, Gold, c.1890, 5 ½ In.	2489.00
Ewer, Lotus, Scrolls, Bulbous Body, Long Neck, Dragon Handle, Chinese, 1800s, 8 ¾ In.	2818.00
Frame, Geometrics, Silver Base, Oval Opening, Strut Support, Russia, c.1888, 5 In.	3360.00
Frame, Royal Blue Ground, Silver Flower Swags, Ribbon Crest, St. Petersburg, c.1912, 2 ½ In.	3360.00
Jardiniere, Champleve, Quatrefoil Shape, Flowers, Greek Key Design, Shaped Feet, 11 In.	674.00
Kovsh, Flowers, Geometric, Silver Gilt, F. Ruckert, Russia, c.1905, 4 ¾ In.	7200.00
Kovsh, Red, Blue Flowers, Geometrics, Flared Foot, Flat Handle, Silver Gilt, 8 ¾ In.	2280.00
Mirror, Hand, Champleve, Gilt, Jade, Quatrefoil Shape, Silver Frame, Butterfly, c.1900, 7 x 3 In.	767.00
Paperweight, Multicolor, Gold, Margret Craver, 20th Century, 2 ⅞ x 2 ½ In. ....*illus*	6518.00
Pendant, Hammered Silver, Snake Link Chain, Blue Glass Rondels, Matsukata, 1970s, 2 ⅞ In. *illus*	1896.00
Plaque, Pond Life, Monogram, Frame, 20th Century, 11 x 11 In., Pair ....*illus*	4740.00
Plate, Abstract, Gold, Red, White, Copper, Edward Winter, c.1950, 4 ¾ In.	150.00
Plate, Abstract, Green, Black, Round, Copper, Oppi Untracht, c.1960s, 10 ½ In.	1200.00
Plate, Abstract, Pink, Peach, Blue, Gold, Green, Round, Copper, Bachrach, Mass., c.1955, 6 ⅞ In.	275.00
Plate, Abstract, Red & Aqua, Blue Ground, Round, Copper, Doris Hall, c.1950, 12 In.	120.00
Plate, Copper, Leaves, 1960s, 8 In.	69.00
Plate, Fish, Gold, Blue Ground, Copper, Marked, Hilary, c.1950, 4 ¾ In.	150.00
Plate, Flowers, Abstract, Orange, Blue Border, Round, Copper, Anne Marie Davidson, 1960s, 6 In.	175.00
Salt, Chair Shape, Pediment Back, Blue, Scroll Wires & Beads, Silver Bowl, Moscow, 1892, 4 ½ In.	1800.00
Snuffbox, Gilt, Flowers, Girl & Boy, Dog, Stream, Copper, Hinged Lid, France, 1 ¾ x 3 ⅛ In. ......*illus*	356.00
Spoon, Serving, Stipple Gilt Ground Bowl, Panel Handle, Khlebnikov, Russia, 1889, 7 ¾ In.	1140.00
Spoon, Silvered Gilt, Long Handle, Moscow, 1888, 7 ½ In.	480.00
Sugar & Creamer, Hinged Cover, Flowers, Gold, Raised Silver Beads, Gilt, Sbitnev, c.1910, 4 In.	9000.00
Teapot, Cat, Flower Design, Scrolled Handle, Feathered Cap Lid, Multicolor, c.1900, 9 In.	230.00
Teapot, Multicolor Spirals, Roundels, Green Glaze, Chinese, c.1890, 4 ¾ In.	267.00
Tray, Landscape, 8 Immortals, Gilt Metal Lip, Feet, 1700s, Canton, 12 x 8 In.	1380.00
Vase, Bird, Branch Filigree, Lobed, Silver Interior, White Jade Rim, Chinese, c.1905, 7 In.	2083.00
Vase, Courting Couple, Strolling, Dark Green Ground, Gilt Accents, Limoges, c.1900, 4 ⅛ In. ....*illus*	444.00
Vase, Red, Woman, 18th Century Dress, France, 2 ¼ In. ....*illus*	59.00
Vase, Woman Holding Basket, Landscape, Copper, Limoges, Signed, 1800s, 3 ½ In. ....*illus*	176.00
Vase, Woman, Red Gown, Garden, Flowers In Hair, Field, France, 4 In.	316.00
Vase, Zun, Flowers, Scrolls, Patterned Ground, Footed, Gilt, Multicolor, Chinese, 17 ½ In.	3981.00

ESKIMO

ERPHILA is a mark found on Czechoslovakian and other pottery and porcelain made after 1920. This mark was used on items imported by Ebeling & Reuss, Philadelphia, a giftware firm that was founded in 1866 and out of business sometime after 2002. The mark is a combination of the letters *E* and *R* (Ebeling & Reuss) and the first letters of the city, Phila(delphia). Many whimsical figural pitchers and creamers, figurines, platters, and other giftwares carry this mark.

Charger, Roses, Reticulated, Octagonal, Germany, 11 In.	65.00
Figurine, Cat, Tabby, Green Eyes, Germany, c.1933, 6 In.	79.00
Figurine, Dog, Spaniel, Sitting, Black, White, Germany, 4 In.	49.00
Teapot, Figural, Cat, Black, White, Red Collar, Marked, Germany, 8 In.	165.00
Teapot, Figural, Pig, Tail Handle, Paper Label, Germany, 7 ½ In.	200.00
Vase, Brown & Purple Matte Glaze, Flared Rim, Marked, Germany, 6 ¼ In.	39.00
Vase, Urn Shape, Ribbed Foot, Turquoise Interior, Czechoslovakia, c.1915, 10 In.	175.00

ES GERMANY porcelain was made at the factory of Erdmann Schlegelmilch from 1861 to 1937 in Suhl, Germany. The porcelain, marked *ES Germany* or *ES Suhl*, was sold decorated or undecorated. Other pieces were made at a factory in Saxony, Prussia, and are marked *ES Prussia*. Reinhold Schlegelmilch made the famous wares marked *RS Germany*.

Bowl, Bird, Hand Painted, Diamond Shapes, Mark, c.1902., 6 ¾ In.	225.00
Cup & Saucer, Roses, Gilt, Cup 2 ¼ x 3 ⅛ In., Saucer 5 ¼ In.	47.00
Plate, Etruscan, Goddess Of Fate, Portrait, 1900s, 11 ¾ In.	379.00
Potpourri Jar, Japanese Scenes, Red, Black Ground, 8-Sided, c.1890, 5 ¾ x 2 ¾ In.	285.00
Vase, Monk, Sipping From Mug Cartouche, Red Ground, Black Wavy Rim, c.1915, 12 In.	125.00
Vase, Sea Goddess, Holding Shell, Flowers, Turquoise, Gilt Beading, Shaped Handles, 5 x 3 In.	275.00

ESKIMO artifacts of all types are collected. Carvings of whale or walrus teeth are listed under Scrimshaw. Baskets are in the Basket category. All other types of Eskimo art are listed here. In Canada and some other areas, the term *Inuit* is used instead of Eskimo.

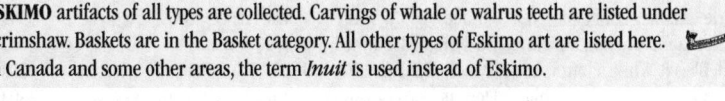

Basket, Cover, Baleen, Polar Bear & Hunter Finial, Omnik, Alaska, c.1968, 4 ½ x 4 ½ In.	1150.00
Basket, Cover, Coiled, Geometric Colored Design, 9 In., Pair	150.00
Basket, Cover, Cylindrical, Zigzag Band, Multicolor, Woven Sea Grass, c.1995, 11 x 9 In.	345.00
Basket, Cover, Hooper Bay, Colored Seagrass Design, c.1950, 5 x 4 ½ In.	77.00
Basket, Cover, Round, Diamond Design, Multicolor, Woven Sea Grass, c.1995, 11 x 10 In.	288.00
Basket, Cover, Soapstone Seal Finial, Woven Star Design, Jeannie Inuk-Puk, c.1958, 12 x 9 In.	403.00
Basket, Cover, Storage, Symbols, Woven Sea Grass, c.1992, 25 x 18 In.	1725.00
Basket, Cover, Stylized Figures, Blankets, Brown, Red, 8 x 6 ½ In.	196.00
Box, Ivory, Walrus, Carved, Oval, Seal Shape Knop, Painted, Bow Hunter, Bear, 3 In.	425.00
Container, Ivory, Wood Lid, Scrimshaw Figure, Animal, Geometrics, Bead, c.1885, 3 ½ x 2 In. *illus*	2695.00
Cribbage Board, Walrus Ivory, Nunivak Island, 16 ½ In.	764.00
Cribbage Board, Walrus Tusk, Scrimshaw Fish, Seals, Head, c.1950, 16 x 2 In.	1035.00
Cribbage Board, Walrus Tusk, Scrimshaw Seals, Walrus, Hunters, Boats, Bears, c.1940, 24 x 3 In.	1035.00
Cribbage Board, Walrus Tusk, War Scene, Carved, 16 In.	182.00
Cup, Basketry, Stepped Lid, Loop Handle, c.1930, 3 ½ x 4 ¼ In.	39.00
Doll, Traditional Dress, Wood Head & Body, Fur Collar & Cuffs, High-Top Moccasins, 16 In. *illus*	230.00
Figurine, Hunter & Seal, Soapstone, Green, Signed, Adamie Papyarluk, 1919, 9 In.	179.00
Figurine, Hunter, Goose, Black Soapstone, Signed Ey Ih Ii Abraham, 1900s, 8 In.	176.00
Figurine, Inuit, Seated, Hooded Parka, 8 x 5 ¼ In.	354.00
Figurine, Man, Standing, Carved Soapstone, 12 x 7 In. *illus*	605.00
Figurine, Otter, Wood Carving, Standing, 1800s, 1 x 6 In.	1035.00
Figurine, Walrus, Ivory Tusks, 4 ¾ x 8 In.	325.00
Figurine, Walrus, Reclining, Black, Johnny Tookalook, c.1987, 6 In.	359.00
Figurine, Woman, Reclining, Hands On Head, Serpentine, Kiawak Ashoona, 1933, 16 In.	1793.00
Kayak, Carved Wood Face, Sealskin Body, Carved Bone Harpoon, Model, 19 ½ In.	5650.00
Kayak, Figure Inside, Stone, Carved, Signed Chuck, 8 In.	68.00
Mask, Wood, Carved, Black Painted Hair, Red Lips, c.1900, 18 x 11 In.	2938.00
Mukluks, Greenland, Sealskin, 9 ½ In.	28.00
Mukluks, High Top, Cream Color, Ties, 1900-20	1000.00
Pipe, Walrus Ivory, Canoe, Seals, c.1900, 12 In.	2233.00
Snowshoes, Bear's Paw Style, Caned Surface, Wood Frame, c.1900, 30 x 23 In.	403.00
Stone Carving, Kneeling Figure, Spearing Fish, Through The Ice, 9 In.	288.00
Toy, Kayak, Carved Wood, Figure, Lined Clothing, Oars, Aleut, Late 1800s, 12 In.	748.00

Doorstop, Skier, Woman, Holding Skis, Blue & Red, c.1930, 12 ⅜ x 5 In.
$1035.00

Bertoia Auction

Doorstop, Woman, Carrying Fruit On Her Head, 12 x 6 ½ In.
$1035.00

Bertoia Auction

Doulton, Vase, Deer, Standing & At Rest, Bands, Hannah Barlow, Impressed Mark, 7 ⅝ In.
$805.00

Humler & Nolan

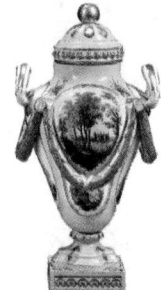

Dresden, Vase, Cover, Potpourri, Hunt Scene, Laurel Swags, Multicolor, Gilded Handles, c.1890, 20 In.
$490.00

Skinner, Inc.

E

Durand, Cookie Jar, Opalescent, Green Pulled Feather, Gold Tipped, Raspberry Finial, Signed, 12 In.
$4600.00

Early Auction Co.

F

Durand, Ginger Jar, Lid, Gold Orange, White Pulled Feather, Gold Trim, Applied Threading, 6 In.
$575.00

James D. Julia Inc.

Durand, Lamp Base, Blue Luster, Gold Threading, 10 In.
$201.00

Early Auction Co.

Durand, Lampshade, Iridescent Crackle, Elongated Trumpet Shape, Blue & White Over Gold, 8 In.
$230.00

Early Auction Co.

FABERGE was a firm of jewelers and goldsmiths founded in St. Petersburg, Russia, in 1842, by Gustav Faberge. Peter Carl Faberge, his son, was jeweler to the Russian Imperial Court from about 1870 to 1917. The rare Imperial Easter eggs, jewelry, and decorative items are very expensive today.

Bookmark, Russian Silver, Cabochon Sapphires, Signed, 5 ½ In.	8500.00
Box, Dome Lid, Silver, Scrolls, Flowers, Sprig Finial, Wavy Base, Mark, 6 x 5 In.	8400.00
Caviar Server, Egg Shape, Cobalt Blue, Clear, Gilt Pedestal, Late 1900s, 18 In.	1063.00
Cigarette Case, Pink Enamel, Chased Gold, Seed Pearls, H. Wigstrom, Russia, c.1910, 3 ¼ In.	12000.00
Compact, Silver Gilt, Blue Guilloche Enamel, Round, Domed, Mirror, St. Petersburg, 1 ¾ In.	2880.00
Compact, Silver Gilt, Guilloche Enamel, Round, Domed, Mirror, St. Petersburg, c.1910, 1 ¾ In.	2400.00
Frame, Jeweled Gold, Egg Shape, White Guilloche Face, Dark Blue Enamel Band, c.1910	57500.00
Locket, Blue Wavy Enamel, 2 Interior Photo Windows, 14K Gold Loop, St. Petersburg, c.1910, 1 In.	3120.00
Perfume Bottle, Peach, Enamel, Gold Band, Seed Pearls, Tubular, Mark Wigstrom, c.1900, 2 In.	7800.00
Salt & Pepper, Sterling, Rabbit Shape, Heads Facing, Amethyst Eyes, Marked, Box, c.1910	2530.00
Table Setting, Fork, Knife, Spoon, Napkin Ring, Silver, Purple & Green Enamel, Case, c.1900 ..*illus*	7963.00

FAIENCE refers to tin-glazed earthenware, especially the wares made in France, Germany, and Scandinavia. It is also correct to say that faience is the same as majolica or Delft, although usually the term refers only to the tin-glazed pottery of the three regions mentioned.

Box, Patch, White, Pink Flowers, Green Leaves, Shield Shape, Continental, 1700s, 4 ½ In.	150.00
Candlestick, Blue, Orange, White, 4 Scrolled Feet, 1800s, 10 In., Pair	180.00
Charger, Flowers, Leaves, Paint, Inscribed, 1800s, 14 In.	504.00
Charger, Wall, Pottery, Canal Landscape Design, Matte Glaze, 15 In. Diam.	830.00
Clock, Delft Design, Cabinet Shape, Devil's Face, Arched Cornice, Finials, Brass Face, Marked .	460.00
Figurine, Dog, Lying Down, Painted, France, 10 In.	180.00
Figurine, Foo Dog, Turquoise Glaze, Square Plinth, Chinese, 12 ½ In., Pair	144.00
Figurine, Pillows, 3 Graduated, Leaf Garlands, Yellow Tassels, Painted, France, 1800s, 12 x 18 In.	325.00
Figurine, Rome Warrior, Standing, Arms Crossed, Painted, 1800s, 17 In.	270.00
Jar, Lid, Blue & White, Flower, Insect Panels, Baluster, Dutch, 1700, 18 In., Pair	1020.00
Jug, Maroon Ground, Blue, White & Flowers, Scrolls, Pewter Mounts, 1733, 9 ¾ In.	230.00
Jug, Wine, Putti, Shell, Volutes, Birds' Nests, Medallions, Late 1800s, 10 x 7 In.	461.00
Pitcher, Baluster Shape, Flared Rim, Applied Handle, Blue, Ocher, Turquoise Glaze, 11 x 7 ½ In.	426.00
Pitcher, Yellow Roses, Gold Narrow Neck, High Spout, Marked 623, 16 x 7 In.	3720.00
Planter, Mother Nature, 2 Birds, Flowers, Avon, 10 ½ x 5 ¼ In.	213.00
Plate Set, Asparagus Relief, Basket Weave, France, c.1905, 13 In. Oval Platter, 10-In. Plate, 11 Piece	708.00
Plate, Enamel, Wildflower Stem, Entwined In Ribbon, Windmill, c.1900, 9 In.	267.00
Plate, Molded Edge, Flowers, White Ground, France, c.1760, 9 ¼ In.	115.00
Platter, Oval Shape, Landscape, Tree, Cavalry, Peasant Figures, 1800s, 29 In.	385.00
Saltcellar, Figural, Maid, Carrying Trays, Baroque Scrolls, c.1825, 6 ½ x 5 In., Pair	799.00
Tulipiere, Hunter, Dogs, French Village, Flowers, Serpentine, c.1925, 4 ½ x 8 In.	276.00
Vase, Dipped Brown Glaze, Elongated Oval, 2 Loop Handles, 26 In.	1150.00
Vase, Enamel, Flowers, Leaves, Fruit, Scroll Leaf Handles, c.1893, 76 In.	20145.00
Vase, Swan, Choisy-Le-Roi, Tall Green Leaves, Oval Base, 1867-89, 22 In.	4484.00
Vase, Tulipieres, Brown, Yellow, Blue Flowers, Waisted Round Feet, c.1775, 6 x 5 In., Pair	399.00
Vase, Turquoise Gloss, High Shouldered, Marked California Faience, 8 In.	69.00

FAIRINGS are small souvenir boxes and figurines that were sold at country fairs during the nineteenth century. Most were made in Germany. Reproductions of fairings are being made, especially of the famous *Twelve Months after Marriage* series.

Box, Cover, Baby In Basket, Gilt Smock, Toys, Polichinelle Figure, Staffordshire, 5 In. .....*illus*	280.00
Figurine, Baby On Dresser, Mirror, 4 In.	90.00
Figurine, Couple In Bed, Shall We Sleep First Or 1 Hour, 3 ⅜ In.	80.00
Figurine, Elephant, In Car, Trunk Up, Germany, c.1903, 5 x 4 In.	145.00
Figurine, Elephant, On Grass, Gray, c.1860, 3 x 3 In.	150.00
Figurine, Kittens In Vase, Blue Bows, 5 ¼ In.	48.00
Figurine, Man, 3 Legs, On Chimney, Lor 3 Legs, I'll Charge 2d, 9 x 2 x 9 In.	48.00
Figurine, Pig, Tennis Racket, Vase, 3 ¾ In.	110.00
Figurine, Woman In Bed, Baby, Nurse, c.1887, 9 x 9 ¼ In.	38.00
Figurine, Woman, Wicker Basket, Special Delivery, Precious Baggage, Germany, 3 x 4 In.	175.00
Trinket Box, Baby, In Basket, Holding Horn, Staffordshire, 6 x 6 In.	350.00
Trinket Box, Birds, Nest, 2 x 2 x 2 In.	75.00
Trinket Box, Boy Reading Book, Conta & Boehme, 2 x 2 ½ x 1 ½ In.	90.00
Trinket Box, Cradle Shape, Baby, Blanket	325.00
Trinket Box, Cutout Altar, Bible, Angel Kneeling, Purple, Gilt, 1860s, 5 x 2 ½ In.	139.00
Trinket Box, Dresser, Mirror, Watch, Germany, 1800s, 4 In.	76.00

Trinket Box, Elk Head, Gun, 2 x 3 x 1 In......................	99.00
Trinket Box, Flowers, Hand, Footed, 2 In. Diam.	75.00
Trinket Box, Grapes, Leaves, Relief, Parian, c.1960, 4 x 2 In.	60.00
Trinket Box, Hand, Holding Box, Gilt...........................	350.00
Trinket Box, Little Red Riding Hood, Staffordshire, 4 In..........	250.00
Trinket Box, One Man Band, Jesters Outfit, Drum, Horn, Symbols, Germany	52.00
Trinket Box, Table, Drape, Cup & Saucer On Top, Gilt, Conta & Boehme, 1 ⅞ x 1 ¾ In...........	45.00
Trinket Box, Woman, Rowing Boat, Blond, Conta & Boehme, 3 ½ x 4 In..........	85.00

FAIRYLAND LUSTER *pieces are included in the Wedgwood category.*

FAMILLE ROSE, *see Chinese Export category.*

FANS have been used for cooling since the days of the ancients. By the eighteenth century, the fan was an accessory for the lady of fashion and very elaborate and expensive fans were made. Sticks were made of ivory or wood, set with jewels or carved. The fans were made of painted silk or paper. Inexpensive paper fans printed with advertising were giveaways in the late nineteenth and early twentieth centuries. Electric fans were introduced in 1882.

Advertising, Borax, Little Cow Girl With Whip, Horse, 20 Mule Team, 14 x 7 ½ In.	495.00
Advertising, Drink Birchola, Lithograph, Woman, Cardboard, Wood Handle, 15 x 7 ⅝ In. .... *illus*	110.00
Bamboo Sticks, Boat Scene, Calligraphy, Paint, Ink, Chinese, 1944, 12 ¾ In.	1778.00
Celluloid, 16 Sticks, Painted Lithograph, Embossed, Applied Gold, 2-Sided, Victorian, 11 In...	86.00
Ebonized Wood Frame, Black Fabric, Embossed, Sequins, Silvered Stars, Brass Handle, 13 In.	104.00
Electric, Ceiling, Gyrating, Westinghouse, 1925..........	9900.00
Electric, Funeral Parlor, Candle Lights, Cast Iron, Label, Luminaire, Cincinnati, c.1910, 58 ½ In. *illus*	1003.00
Electric, Oscillating, Cast Iron, Brass Blades, Peerless, Counter .... *illus*	180.00
Ivory, 16 Ribs, Woven Silk Ribbon, Carved, Lily Of The Valley, 1800s, 9 ½ x 15 ½ In.	590.00
Ivory, Dragon Scene, Embroidery Silk, Reticulated Frame, Gilt Lacquer Box, c.1900, 10 ½ In.	600.00
Lace, Sequins, Black, 10 Sticks, Silver Dots, Ebonized Wood Frame, Handle, c.1885, 11 In......	69.00
Paper Lithograph, Painted, Applied Gold Detail, Mica Dots, 2-Sided, Victorian, 10 ½ In.	150.00
Paper, Painted, Ink, Colors, Figures, Garden, Reverse With Calligraphy, Inscribed, Signed, c.1925 *illus*	1225.00
Paper, Scholar, Boat, Willow, Calligraphy, Paint, Ink, Chinese, 12 ¼ In.	1348.00
Prunus, Calligraphy, Paint, Ink, Chinese, 1921, 12 ¼ In..........	4444.00
Prunus, Seals, Calligraphy, Bamboo Sticks, Paint, Ink, Signed, Chinese, 12 ½ In..........	8888.00
Satinwood, Schoolgirl, Watercolor, Birds, Flowers, Shells, c.1825, 14 ¾ In., Pair	705.00
Silk, Lotus Blossoms, Calligraphy, Ink, Paint, Chinese, 13 In.	2015.00
Theorem, Watercolor, On Velvet Cutout Flowers, Gilt, Turned Wood Handle, c.1890, 17 In......	2350.00
Tortoiseshell, Silk, Gilt, Continental, 15 In.	720.00
Wood, Carved, Hand Painted, Multicolor Ribs, Frame, Chinese, 15 ½ x 26 In. .... *illus*	1960.00
Wood, Ink On Paper, Blue, Liberty Bell, American Scenes Ovals, Hand, Frame, 1876, 11 x 20 In.	326.00
Wood, Lacquered, Sticks, Gilt, 2 Monks, Landscape, Paint, Glazed, Frame, c.1890, 20 x 10 In.	398.00

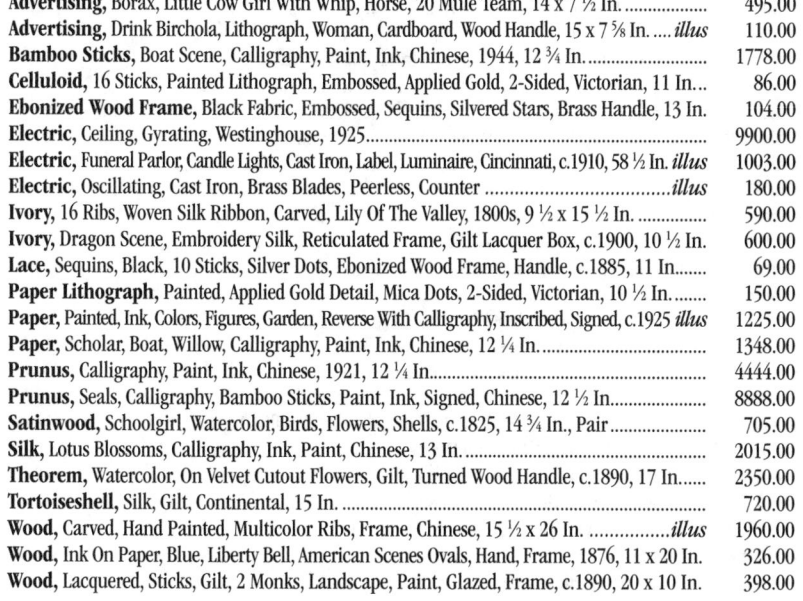

FAST FOOD COLLECTIBLES *may be included in several categories, such as Advertising, Coca-Cola, Decorated Tumbler, Toy, etc.*

FEDERZEICHNUNG, *see Loetz category.*

FENTON ART GLASS COMPANY was founded in 1905 in Martins Ferry, Ohio, by Frank L. Fenton and his brother, John W. Fenton. They painted decorations on glass blanks made by other manufacturers. In 1907 they opened a factory in Williamstown, West Virginia, and began making glass. The company is still in business, led by Fenton family members, but the company no longer makes art glass. Fenton is noted for early carnival glass produced between 1907 and 1920. Some of these pieces are listed in the Carnival Glass category. Many other types of glass were also made.

Apple Blossom, Bowl, Milk Glass, Fluted Edge, Pink To Red, 10 x 4 In..........	225.00
Aqua Crest, Basket, Handle, 5 In..........	62.00 to 102.00
Aqua Crest, Vase, Fan, 6 ⅝ In..........	30.00
Autumn Acorn, Bowl, Ruffled, Leaves, Iridescent Gold, Amber, 8 ½ In..........	65.00
Bell, Pink, Ruffled, 6 In..........	122.00
Blossoms & Berries, Bear, Mouse, Squirrel, Elephant, 4 Piece	100.00
Burmese, Basket, Fenced Garden, 11 In..........	175.00
Burmese, Candy Box..........	149.99
Burmese, Ewer..........	165.00
Burmese, Fairy Light, Wildflowers, 5 ½ In., 2 Piece..........	125.00
Burmese, Hat, Flowers, Bird Nest, Vine, 4 In.	99.00
Burmese, Hummingbird, Flowers, 4 ½ In..........	30.00

Durand, Vase, Blue Iridescent, Shouldered, Flared Mouth, 6 ½ In.
$230.00

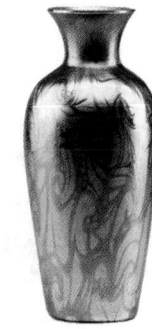

Early Auction Co.

Durand, Vase, Gold & Olive Iridescent, Swirls, 10 ½ x 4 ¾ In.
$1240.00

Rago Arts & Auction Center

Durand, Vase, Silver Blue Iridescent, Black Ground, Leaf & Vine Design, Signed, 6 ½ In.
$1007.00

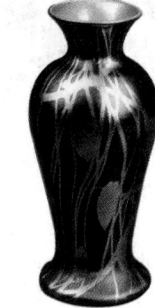

Skinner, Inc.

Durant Kilns, Vase, Persian Green Crackled Glaze, Signed, 1913, 15 ¼ x 12 In.
$1054.00

Rago Arts & Auction Center

Elvis Presley, Skirt, Cotton, Wraparound Design, Music Theme, Song Titles, c.1956, 23 ½ In.
$191.00

Hake's Americana & Collectibles

Enamel, Bookends, Copper, Orange Tree Medallion, Cobalt Blue, Cauman, c.1925, 5 ½ x 6 In.
$5036.00

Skinner, Inc.

Enamel, Paperweight, Multicolor, Gold, Margret Craver, 20th Century, 2 ⅞ x 2 ½ In.
$6518.00

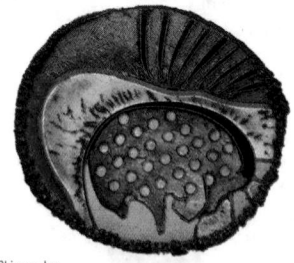

Skinner, Inc.

Enamel, Pendant, Hammered Silver, Snake Link Chain, Blue Glass Rondels, Matsukata, 1970s, 2 ⅞ In.
$1896.00

Skinner, Inc.

Burmese, Lamp, Hurricane, Flower	250.00
Burmese, Lamp, Rose Nectar, Lotus Mist, 27 ½ In.	700.00
Burmese, Perfume Bottle, Diamond Optic, Pink Roses	90.00
Burmese, Pitcher, Dragonfly, Blue, 7 ½ In.	150.00
Burmese, Vase, Blue, Blackberries, Blossoms	125.00
Burmese, Vase, Peacock, Flowers, Signed, 7 ¾ In.	225.00
Buttercup, Figurine, Frog	20.00
Butterfly & Berry, Lamp, Gone With The Wind, Lotus Mist	495.00
Cameo Opalescent, Cornucopia, c.1927, 5 ¼ In.	223.00
Candy Dish, Velva Rose, Dolphin Handles, Knopped Lid, Stretch Glass, 9 In.	55.00
Celeste Blue, Bowl, Cupped, Stretch Glass, 1920s, 8 In.	70.00
Celeste Blue, Candlestick, Blue & Ebony, 6 In.	385.00
Chameleon, Figurine, Elephant, Green	30.00
Charleton, Vase, Snow Crest, Ruby, 4 ½ In.	179.00
Coin Dot, Basket, Blue, 10 In.	55.00
Coin Dot, Basket, Cranberry, 7 In.	45.00
Coin Dot, Basket, Green Opalescent, 7 ¼ In.	370.00
Coin Dot, Vase, Cranberry, 11 In.	95.00
Coin Dot, Vase, French Opalescent, Ruffled Edge, c.1950, 10 In.	85.00
Coin Dot, Vase, Topaz, Flared Rim, c.1950, 6 In.	132.00
Coinspot, Vase, Cranberry, 5 In.	95.00
Cranberry Opalescent, Vase, Thousand Eye, 8 ½ In.	110.00
Crystal Crest, Vase, Fan, 7 In.	35.00
Daisy & Butterfly, Cat, Lotus Mist Green	55.00
Daisy & Button, Toothpick Holder, Hat Shape, Amber	25.00
Daisy & Fern, Lamp, Cranberry	450.00
Daisy & Fern, Lamp, Cranberry Opalescent, 3 Tiers	888.00
Diamond Optic, Vase, Cranberry, 8 ½ In.	75.00
Doll, Bridesmaid, Orange Ruby Slag, 1995	277.00
Emerald Crest, Compote, 3 ½ x 7 In.	44.00
Emerald Crest, Vase, 6 In.	38.00
Epergne, 4 Trumpet Vases, Ruffled Base Rim, 17 x 12 In.	288.00
Fairy Lamp, Green Iridescent, Embossed Fish, Signed, 4 ¾ In.	60.00
Favrene, Box, Black Base, Lid, Sand Carved, Chris Carpenter	200.00
Favrene, Vase, Butterfly Crest, 9 In.	275.00
Favrene, Vase, Flowers, Sandcarved, Blue, White Brass Mounts, Handles, 10 In.	150.00
Figurine, Bear, Orange With Black Hanging Hearts	770.00
Figurine, Cat, Blue Royale, Embossed, 3 ¾ x 2 ¾ In.	30.00
Figurine, Cat, Happy, Emerald Green, Milk Glass Ear	170.00
Figurine, Cat, Sitting, Hanging Hearts, Key Lime, Dave Fetty	550.00
Figurine, Cat, Sitting, Hanging Hearts, Orange Slice, Dave Fetty	425.00
Figurine, Cat, White Pearlized, 3 ¾ In.	38.00
Figurine, Cat, Winter Wonderland, 5 In.	45.00
Figurine, Donkey, White Satin	75.00
Figurine, Hippo, Blue Satin, White Flowers, 3 In.	55.00
Figurine, Lighthouse, Blue Satin, 9 In.	60.00
Figurine, Poinsettia, Fawn, Milk Glass, 3 ½ In.	40.00
Figurine, Satin, Hippo, Cameo Glass, Emerald Green, Carved, 3 In.	75.00
Figurine, Squirrel, Berries & Blossoms	35.00
Figurine, Whale, Vasa Murrhina, 5 In.	413.00
Forget-Me-Not, Tumbler, Enameled, Marigold	20.00
Forget-Me-Not, Water Pitcher, Tankard, Enameled, Marigold	120.00
Frame, Blue Satin, Blue Roses, Oval	50.00
Grape & Cable, Plate, Blue, c.1911, 9 In.	2136.00
Grape, Vase, 7 ½ In.	119.00
Hanging Hearts, Candlestick, Green, 11 ¾ In., Pair	3630.00
Heron Garden, Vase, 7 ½ In.	495.00
Hobnail, Basket, Blue Opal, 10 In.	155.00
Hobnail, Basket, Blue Opal, Footed, 8 In.	195.00
Hobnail, Basket, Blue Opalescent, 7 In.	55.00
Hobnail, Basket, Blue Opalescent, Clear Bamboo Handle, Ruffled Rim, Footed, 6 In.	30.00
Hobnail, Basket, Cranberry, 4 ½ In.	30.00
Hobnail, Basket, French Opal, 4 ½ In.	20.00 to 40.00
Hobnail, Basket, Milk Glass, Oval, 12 In.	65.00
Hobnail, Cat, Slipper, White, 3 x 5 In.	15.00
Hobnail, Console, Milk Glass, 8 ½ In.	15.00
Hobnail, Cornucopia, Opalescent, 6 In.	65.00
Hobnail, Creamer, Topaz Opal	60.00

F

Hobnail, Cruet, Topaz Opal	70.00
Hobnail, Decanter, Topaz Opalescent, Handle, 12 x 5 ½ In.	877.00
Hobnail, Fairy Lamp, Green	30.00
Hobnail, Jug, French Opal, 80 Oz.	195.00
Hobnail, Perfume Bottle, Stopper, Opalescent, 1940s, 5 ¾ x 4 In.	45.00
Hobnail, Rose Bowl, Amberina, 4 In.	22.00
Hobnail, Salt & Pepper, Milk Glass, 4 In.	30.00
Hobnail, Slipper, Blue, Opalescent.	23.00
Hobnail, Slipper, Topaz.	70.00
Hobnail, Vase, Blue Opalescent, Ruffled Edge, 1940s, 3 ¾ x 3 ⅝ In.	45.00
Hobnail, Vase, Blue, 6 In.	20.00
Hobnail, Vase, Fan, White Milk Glass, Ruffled Edge, 5 x 5 ¾ In.	35.00
Hobnail, Vase, Vaseline, 6 In.	35.00
Ivy, Ball, Cranberry, 9 In.	65.00
Ivy, Vase, Double Crimp, 6 In.	49.00
Lamp, Jupiter, Michael Dickinson	450.00
Lemon Server, Celeste Blue, Knobbed Handle, Stretch Glass, 1920s, 5 x 2 ⅜ In.	35.00
Lily Of The Valley, Candy Box, 7 In.	65.00
Moonstone, Candlestick, Jade Green, 8 In.	440.00
Mosaic, Vase, Narrow Baluster, Dark Iridescent, Red, Green, Applied Strands, c.1925, 10 ½ In.	325.00
Parrot Talk, Vase, 12 In.	195.00
Peach Crest, Basket, 10 In.	175.00
Peach Crest, Basket, Handle, 5 ½ In.	48.00
Peach Crest, Epergne, 1-Horn, Footed.	185.00
Peach Crest, Vase, 5 In.	10.00
Peach Crest, Vase, 8 ½ In.	20.00
Peach Crest, Vase, 9 In.	60.00
Peach Crest, Vase, Crimped, Flowers, 11 ½ In.	125.00
Peach Crest, Vase, White, Pink, Scalloped, Crimped Rim, Clear Ribbon, c.1945, 8 In.	46.00
Pilgrim, Vase, Cranberry, 6 ½ In.	35.00
Pitcher, Iridescent Blue, White Interior, 5 ¾ In.	75.00
Pitcher, Water, Apple, Iridescent Green, White Interior, 9 In.	125.00
Rosalene Remembrance, Vase, 11 ½ In.	850.00
Rosalene, Basket, White Flower, 8 ½ In.	90.00
Rosalene, Vase, Satin, Fenton Art Glass Collectors Or America 35th Anniversary	90.00
Rosalene, Vase, Vines, Footed, 6 In.	52.00
Rose Bowl, Pink, Velva, Scalloped, 3-Footed, Stretch Glass, 8 x 2 ⅝ In.	30.00
Rose Satin, Basket, Swirl, 11 In.	110.00
Royal Purple, Lamp, 20 In.	325.00
Salt & Pepper, Sea Mist Green, Vining Garden	35.00
Sign, Logo, Celeste Blue, 90th Anniversary, Oval, Stretch Glass, c.1995, 2 ¾ x 5 In.	48.00
Silver Crest, Bowl, 1950s, 7 x 3 In.	46.00
Silver Crest, Compote, White, Ruffled Rim, c.1950, 3 x 6 In.	22.00
Spiral Optic, Lamp, Oil, Cranberry Opalescent, 10 In.	395.00
Stretch Glass, Bowl, Florentine Green, Flared, Cupped, 1917-28, 6 ½ x 3 In.	35.00
Stretch Glass, Bowl, Green, Cupped, 9 x 2 In.	55.00
Topaz Opalescent, Cruet, Dot Optic, Crown Stopper, 1940s	120.00
Tumbler, Cobalt Blue Handle, Vaseline, Stretch Glass 4 ¾ In.	67.00
Vase, Crystal, Blue, Aqua, Blown, Delmer Stowasser, c.1975, 4 x 4 ½ In.	253.00
Vase, Fan, Green, Dolphin Handles, Stretch Glass, 5 ½ x 5 ½ In.	85.00
Vase, Iridescent Blue, Coralene Overlay, Signed, 6 ½ In.	50.00
Vase, Jack-In-The-Pulpit, Shading From Yellow To Deep Salmon, 10 In.	139.00
Vase, Raspberry, Black, White Pulled Design, Layered, Bulbous, Acid Etched Stamp, 10 ½ In.	207.00
Vase, Scenic, Cottage, White Satin Glass, Signed, 1993, 9 ¼ In.	75.00
Vase, Shouldered, Leaves, Red Ground, 9 x 5 In.	177.00
Vining Garden, Vase, Aurora, 4 ½ In.	29.00
Vintage, Bowl, Plum, Rippled Rim, 8 ¼ In.	113.00
Violets In The Snow, Compote, Round, Footed, 6 In.	35.00
Water Lily, Bowl, Marigold, 9 In.	89.00

FIESTA, the colorful dinnerware, was introduced in 1936 by the Homer Laughlin China Co., redesigned in 1969, and withdrawn in 1973. It was reissued again in 1986 in different colors and is still being made. New colors, including some that are similar to old colors, are introduced regularly. The simple design was characterized by a band of concentric circles beginning at the rim. Cups had full-circle handles until 1969, when partial-circle handles were made. Harlequin and Riviera were related wares. For more prices, go to kovels.com.

Chartreuse, Ashtray	56.00

Enamel, Plaque, Pond Life, Monogram, Frame, 20th Century, 11 x 11 In., Pair
$4740.00

Skinner, Inc.

Enamel, Snuffbox, Gilt, Flowers, Girl & Boy, Dog, Stream, Copper, Hinged Lid, France, 1 ¾ x 3 ⅛ In.
$356.00

Skinner, Inc.

Enamel, Vase, Courting Couple, Strolling, Dark Green Ground, Gilt Accents, Limoges, c.1900, 4 ⅛ In.
$444.00

Skinner, Inc.

Enamel, Vase, Red, Woman, 18th Century Dress, France, 2 ¼ In.
$59.00

DuMouchelles Art Gallery

Enamel, Vase, Woman Holding Basket, Landscape Background, Copper, Limoges, Signed, 1800s, 3 ½ In.
$176.00

Cowan's Auctions

Eskimo, Container, Ivory, Wood Lid, Scrimshaw Figure, Animal, Geometrics, Bead, c.1885, 3 ½ x 2 In.
$2695.00

Skinner, Inc.

Eskimo, Doll, Traditional Dress, Wood Head & Body, Fur Collar & Cuffs, High Top Moccasins, 16 In.
$230.00

James D. Julia Inc.

Eskimo, Figurine, Man, Standing, Carved Soapstone, 12 x 7 In.
$605.00

Old Barn Auctions

Chartreuse, Nappy, 8 ½ In.	30.00
Chartreuse, Plate, 9 In.	14.00
Chartreuse, Plate, Compartment, 10 ½ In.	55.00
Cobalt Blue, Bowl, Fruit, 11 ¾ In.	95.00
Cobalt Blue, Cake Server, Kitchen Kraft	88.00
Cobalt Blue, Candleholder, Bulb, Pair	40.00
Cobalt Blue, Candleholder, Tripod	60.00
Cobalt Blue, Casserole, 7 ¾ In.	275.00
Cobalt Blue, Compote, Fruit, 12 In.	95.00
Cobalt Blue, Compote, Sweets	60.00
Cobalt Blue, Cup & Saucer, After Dinner	89.00
Cobalt Blue, Jar, Cover, Kitchen Kraft, Small	65.00
Cobalt Blue, Marmalade	308.00
Cobalt Blue, Nappy, 8 ½ In.	46.00
Cobalt Blue, Pie Plate, Kitchen Kraft, 10 In.	30.00
Cobalt Blue, Pitcher, Disk, 7 In.	99.00 to 153.00
Cobalt Blue, Spoon, Kitchen Kraft	20.00
Cobalt Blue, Tray, Figure 8, 10 In.	99.00
Cobalt Blue, Vase, 8 In.	605.00
Forest Green, Ashtray	40.00
Forest Green, Cup & Saucer	33.00
Gray, Ashtray	28.00
Gray, Casserole, 7 ¾ In.	295.00
Gray, Chop Plate, 13 In.	75.00
Gray, Platter, 12 ½ In.	35.00
Gray, Saucer	11.00
Ivory, Candleholder, Bulb, Pair	15.00 to 20.00
Ivory, Compote, Fruit, 12 In.	50.00
Ivory, Compote, Sweets	40.00
Ivory, Mustard	113.00
Ivory, Pitcher, Disk	70.00
Ivory, Soup, Onion, Covered	357.00
Ivory, Tumblers, Juice, 3 ½ In., 4 Piece	25.00
Light Green, Ashtray	20.00
Light Green, Candleholder, Tripod	40.00
Light Green, Carafe, Footed, 8 ½ In.	81.00
Light Green, Compote, Fruit, 12 In.	60.00 to 80.00
Light Green, Compote, Sweets	65.00
Light Green, Cup & Saucer, After Dinner	59.00
Light Green, Fork, Kitchen Kraft	20.00 to 44.00
Light Green, Mixing Bowl, Kitchen Kraft, 8 In.	99.00
Light Green, Mixing Bowl, No. 2	120.00
Light Green, Pitcher, Water, Disk, 7 In.	60.00
Light Green, Salad Set, Fork & Spoon, Kitchen Kraft	244.00
Light Green, Spoon & Fork, Kitchen Kraft	85.00
Light Green, Sugar & Creamer, Stick Handle	35.00
Light Green, Vase, Bud, Footed, 6 ¼ In.	55.00
Medium Green, Ashtray	80.00
Medium Green, Bowl, Salad, Individual	77.00
Medium Green, Casserole, 7 ¾ In.	132.00
Medium Green, Cup & Saucer	52.00
Medium Green, Jar, Covered, Kitchen Kraft, Medium	110.00
Medium Green, Nappy, 8 ½ In.	93.00
Medium Green, Pitcher, Disk, 7 In.	700.00
Medium Green, Plate, 9 In.	35.00
Medium Green, Plate, Dinner, 10 In.	145.00
Medium Green, Platter, Oval, 12 ½ In.	195.00
Medium Green, Salt & Pepper, 2 ½ In.	150.00
Medium Green, Teapot, 6 Cup	770.00
Medium Green, Vase, 8 In.	595.00 to 629.00
Red, Ashtray	25.00 to 35.00
Red, Candleholder, Bulb, Pair	55.00
Red, Candleholder, Tripod, Pair	250.00
Red, Casserole, Individual, Kitchen Kraft	253.00
Red, Coffeepot, After Dinner	88.00
Red, Compote, Fruit, 12 In.	140.00
Red, Compote, Sweets	60.00 to 80.00

Red, Creamer, Individual	209.00
Red, Mixing Bowl, Cover Only, No. 4	990.00
Red, Mixing Bowl, Kitchen Kraft, 6 In.	99.00
Red, Mixing Bowl, No. 4	400.00
Red, Mixing Bowl, No. 5	285.00
Red, Pitcher, Disk, 7 In.	145.00
Red, Pitcher, Ice Lip, 6 ⅜ In.	165.00
Red, Relish, With Inserts, 1930s	499.00
Red, Salt & Pepper, Kitchen Kraft	93.00
Red, Soup, Onion, Cover	789.00
Red, Spoon, Kitchen Kraft	20.00
Red, Sugar & Creamer	25.00
Red, Syrup	385.00 to 450.00
Rose, Ashtray	45.00
Rose, Eggcup	53.00
Rose, Mug, Tom & Jerry, 3 In.	65.00
Rose, Nappy, 8 ½ In.	38.00
Rose, Pitcher, Disk, 7 In.	110.00
Rose, Sugar & Creamer	10.00
Rose, Teapot, 6 Cup	154.00
Rose, Vase, Bud, Footed, 1959, 6 In.	92.00
Turquoise, Bowl, Fruit, 11 ¾ In.	130.00
Turquoise, Bowl, Salad, Individual	71.00
Turquoise, Compote, Sweets	65.00
Turquoise, Mixing Bowl, No. 1	250.00
Turquoise, Mixing Bowl, No. 4	145.00
Turquoise, Nappy, 8 ½ In.	30.00
Turquoise, Pitcher, Disk, 7 In.	105.00
Yellow, Bowl, Onion, Cover	550.00
Yellow, Cake Lifter, Kitchen Kraft	80.00
Yellow, Candleholder, Bulb, Pair	35.00
Yellow, Casserole, French	165.00
Yellow, Casserole, Individual, Kitchen Kraft	110.00
Yellow, Compote, Fruit, 12 In.	85.00
Yellow, Cup	32.00
Yellow, Nappy, 8 ½ In.	88.00
Yellow, Pitcher, Juice, 6 In.	27.00 to 58.00
Yellow, Plate, 9 In.	7.50
Yellow, Plate, Dinner, 10 In.	15.00
Yellow, Soup, Onion, Covered	412.00
Yellow, Sugar & Creamer, Stick Handle	35.00
Yellow, Syrup	357.00
Yellow, Teapot, 6 Cup	88.00

FINCH, *see Kay Finch category.*

FINDLAY ONYX AND FLORADINE are two similar types of glass made by Dalzell, Gilmore and Leighton Co. of Findlay, Ohio, about 1889. Onyx is a patented yellowish white opaque glass with raised silver daisy decorations. A few rare pieces were made of rose, amber, orange, or purple glass. Floradine is made of cranberry-colored glass with an opalescent white raised floral pattern and a satin finish. The same molds were used for both types of glass.

Compote, Onyx, Hexagonal Bull's-Eye, c.1900, 7 In.	110.00
Muffineer, Onyx, Pierced Metal Top, c.1900, 3 x 5 In.	725.00
Pitcher, Onyx, Branched Tree Pattern, Clear, 1890s, 8 ½ x 7 ½ In.	125.00
Pitcher, Onyx, Raised Platinum Flowers, White Ground, c.1889	650.00
Pitcher, Onyx, Retort Pattern, Owl Face, Clear, 1890s, 9 ½ In.	95.00
Plate, Onyx, Dog, Ball Design Rim, 1887, 6 In.	139.00
Plate, Onyx, Priscilla Pattern, c.1895, 10 ½ In.	54.00
Spooner, Floradine, Oval, Frosted Red With White Inclusions, 4 ½ In.	650.00 to 1200.00
Spooner, Floradine, Oval, Opal Cream, Red Flowers, 4 In.	*illus* 2358.00
Spooner, Onyx, Priscilla Pattern, c.1895, 4 ½ x 3 In.	50.00
Sugar & Creamer, Floradine, Red, White Rosettes, 6-In. Sugar	*illus* 2473.00
Sugar Shaker, Onyx, Platinum Luster Design, c.1889, 5 ½ x 3 ½ In.	450.00
Sugar, Cover, Onyx, Silver Rosettes, 6 In.	*illus* 403.00
Syrup, Onyx, Opal Glass, Silver Flowers, 7 ½ In.	175.00

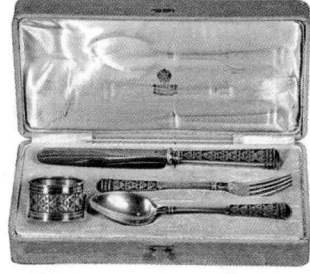
Faberge, Table Setting, Fork, Knife, Spoon, Napkin Ring, Silver, Purple & Green Enamel, Case, c.1900
$7963.00

Skinner, Inc.

Fairing, Box, Cover, Baby In Basket, Gilt Smock, Toys, Polichinelle Figure, Staffordshire, 5 In.
$280.00

Theriault's

Fan, Advertising, Drink Birchola, Lithograph, Woman, Cardboard, Wood Handle, 15 x 7 ⅝ In.
$110.00

Wm Morford Antiques

Fan, Electric, Funeral Parlor, Candle Lights, Cast Iron, Label, Luminaire, Cincinnati, c.1910, 58 ½ In. $1003.00

Brunk Auctions

Fan, Electric, Oscillating, Cast Iron, Brass Blades, Peerless, Counter $180.00

Victorian Casino Antique Auction

Fan, Paper, Painted, Ink, Colors, Figures, Garden, Reverse With Calligraphy, Inscribed, Signed, c.1925 $1225.00

Skinner, Inc.

FIREFIGHTING equipment of all types is wanted, from fire marks to uniforms to toy fire trucks. It is said that every little boy wanted to be a fireman or a train engineer 75 years ago and the collectors today reflect this interest.

Box, Fire Alarm, Red, House Shape, Metal, Wall Mount ....*illus*	243.00
Box, Fire Alarm, Street Corner, No. 589, 72 In.	961.00
Bucket, Erupting Volcano, Sea, D.S. Greenough, Painted, Handle, c.1812, 13 In.	10073.00
Bucket, Leather, Banner, Eagle, Salem, Black & Gold, Handle, Brass Rings, 1799, 12 x 9 In., Pair	7763.00
Bucket, Leather, Blue & Green Paint, Shield, Banner, Handle, L.W. Whitney, 1828, 12 x 9 In...	805.00
Bucket, Leather, Gilt, Brass Tacks, Shield, Motto, Black, Handle, France, 1800s, 13 x 11 In......	590.00
Bucket, Leather, Green Shield, Number 2, Red Ground, Paint, Handle, c.1830, 14 In.	770.00
Bucket, Leather, Iron, Strap, 1800s, 11 ½ x 10 In.	375.00
Bucket, Leather, Painted, Gold Gilt, Green Ground, J. Mason, W.F.S. No 1, 1848, 12 In.	518.00
Bucket, Leather, Shaking Hands, J.B. Kittridge, No. 2, F.F.C., c.1800, 13 In.	7833.00
Bucket, Leather, Stenciled, Dr. Robt M'Neill, Nos. 1 & 2, c.1800, 12 In., Pair	11000.00
Button, 9th Annual Convention, State Firemen's Assn., June, 1901, Fireman, 1 ¾ In................	69.00
Engine Bell, Brass, Cast Iron Cradle, Wood Base, 21 ½ x 10 ½ In.................................	880.00
Fire Mark, Continental, New York, Tin, Japanned, 3 x 7 In.	175.00
Fire Mark, Fire Pumper, Fire Department Insurance Co. Of Cincinnati, Cast Iron, 1841, 9 x 10 In.	220.00
Fire Mark, Protector, Firefighting Scene, Copper, Embossed, 1820s, 9 In...........................	1100.00
Grenade, Harden Star, Blue, Sealed, 8 In..	431.00
Grenade, Hayward's Hand, Clear, Smooth Base, Tooled Lip, 1875-95, 4 In.	345.00
Grenade, Hayward's Hand, Diamond Panel, Cobalt Blue, Tooled Mouth, c.1890, 6 ⅜ In........	460.00
Grenade, Minimax, Cobalt Blue, Twisted Double Spiral, Contents, England, 8 x 1 In.	175.00
Grenade, Rockfork Kalamazoo Automatic & Hand, Cobalt Blue, Swollen, 11 In.....................	556.00
Hat, Parade, Painted Shields, Northern Liberty Hose Co., 7, c.1825, 11 ¾ x 13 ½ In.	3792.00
Hat, Parade, T. Jefferson Portrait, Independent Hose Co., c.1824, 6 x 11 ½ In........................	6518.00
Helmet, Eagle Front Holder, Brass Shield, Fairmount Fire Co..	2875.00
Hydrant, Mueller, Cast Iron, 1960 ....*illus*	224.00
Model, Fire Pumper, Pump Pistons, Fly Wheel, Valves, Brass, Iron, 1920s, 21 x 32 In..............	8260.00
Parade Staff, Softwood, Fire Hose Form, Black, Gold, c.1875, 90 In.	823.00
Parade Torch, Turned Wood Handle, Copper Burner, 22 ½ In.	184.00
Respirator, Oxygen Tank, Mask, Inscribed Case, Inside Lid Instructions, 23 x 16 In. ......*illus*	148.00
Trumpet, Presentation, Nickel Plated Brass, Cairnes & Bros., New York	1380.00
Trumpet, Presentation, Silver Plate, Engraved, Flowers, Inscription, 1877, 18 ½ In. ......*illus*	1410.00
Trumpet, Presentation, Silver Plate, Incised Designs, Carrying Rings, 18 ½ In. ....*illus*	3163.00

FIREPLACES were used to cook food and to heat the American home in past centuries. Many types of tools and equipment were used. Andirons held the logs in place, firebacks reflected the heat into the room, and tongs were used to move either fuel or food. Many types of spits and roasting jacks were made and may be listed in the Kitchen category.

Andirons, Brass & Glass, Scroll Feet, Art Glass Balls, Pointed Finials, 1930s, 22 ½ In..............	384.00
Andirons, Brass Urn & Flame Finial, Angel Inserts, Round Jasperware, 12 x 7 In.	179.00
Andirons, Brass, Acorn Top, Arched Scroll Feet, c.1820, 17 x 17 In.	138.00
Andirons, Brass, Ball Feet, Pinecone Finial, 26 In.	132.00
Andirons, Brass, Ball Finials, Federal, c.1805, 18 ½ In..	385.00
Andirons, Brass, Bronze, Wrought Iron, Turned Standard, 26 x 14 In.	682.00
Andirons, Brass, Cannonball Top, Baluster Base, Scrolled Legs, Coin Feet, 1800s, 21 In.	227.00
Andirons, Brass, Colonial Revival, Urn Finials, Column Supports, Ball & Claw Feet, c.1910, 23 In.	300.00
Andirons, Brass, Dolphin, Fire Dogs, Bradley & Hubbard, c.1875	450.00
Andirons, Brass, Dutch Baroque Style, Flame Finial, Baluster Standard, Scrolled Feet, 30 In. ..*illus*	305.00
Andirons, Brass, Federal, Acorn Finial, Hexagonal Standard, Arched Legs, c.1800, 16 ¼ x 12 ¾ In.	430.00
Andirons, Brass, Federal, Hexagonal, Steeple Finial, Arched Legs, c.1810, 22 In.	711.00
Andirons, Brass, Federal, Iron, Faceted Tops, Ring Turnings, Spurred Legs, Early 1800s, 22 x 19 In.	431.00
Andirons, Brass, Federal, Knife Blade Finial, c.1790, 19 ½ In.	178.00
Andirons, Brass, Federal, Steeple Finial, New York, c.1810, 23 ½ In..	356.00
Andirons, Brass, Federal, Tapered Shaft, Urn Finial, Claw & Ball Feet, c.1790, 25 x 13 In........	956.00
Andirons, Brass, Federal, Urn Finial, Ring Turned Standard, Legs, Ball Feet, c.1820, 25 x 12 In.	546.00
Andirons, Brass, Federal, Urn Top, Engraved Leaves, Curved Legs, c.1810, 21 x 18 In.............	1610.00
Andirons, Brass, Gothic, Man's Head Top, Paneled Arch, Winged Griffin Supports, 25 ½ In. ...	248.00
Andirons, Brass, Iron, Donald Deskey, Sunset, 18 ½ x 8 ½ In...	403.00
Andirons, Brass, Iron, Elongated Acorn Top, Faceted Column Shaft, Spurred Legs, c.1800, 21 ¾ In.	1007.00
Andirons, Brass, Iron, Federal Style, Urn & Finial, 24 In.	70.00
Andirons, Brass, Iron, Knife Blade, Urn Finials, Arched Legs, Penny Feet, c.1800, 19 x 16 In.	230.00
Andirons, Brass, Iron, Knife Blade, Urn Finials, Brass Shield, Curved Legs, Penny Feet, 17 x 8 In.	948.00
Andirons, Brass, Iron, Ribbed Lemon Finials, Square Plinth, Slipper Feet, c.1800, 18 ¾ In.....	1007.00

F

Andirons, Brass, Iron, Steeple, Belted Ball, Faceted, Spurred Legs, Ball Feet, c.1815, 23 ¾ In. .	1007.00
Andirons, Brass, Iron, Steeple Top, Belted Spheres, Faceted Plinths, Slipper Feet, c.1800, 21 x 12 In.	1185.00
Andirons, Brass, Lemon Drop, 18 In.	240.00
Andirons, Brass, Louis XV Style, Lobed Column, Tripod Base, Paw Feet, Acorn Finial, 22 In.	100.00
Andirons, Brass, Spiral, Urn Shape Finial, 3-Footed, 21 In.	150.00
Andirons, Brass, Stylized Leaf Crest, Ribbed Arches, Beaded Legs, c.1890, 23 x 23 In.	1315.00
Andirons, Brass, Turned Finial, Double Ball Support, Scrolled Legs, Ball Feet, c.1890, 19 In.	275.00
Andirons, Bronze, Art Deco, Dragon Shape, Chinese, c.1920, 16 x 5 In.	795.00
Andirons, Bronze, Atlas Holding Urn, Flame Top, Griffin Finials, North Wind Face, 41 x 18 In.	4830.00
Andirons, Bronze, Ball Top, Strapwork, Tapered, Arched Legs, Arts & Crafts, 17 x 9 In.	148.00
Andirons, Bronze, Louis XVI Style, Flame Finials, Dogs, 1850s	424.00
Andirons, Bronze, Spiral Wrapped Dolphins, Fluted Column Standards, Urns, France, 1800s, 24 In.	2390.00
Andirons, Bronze, Winged Putto, Dolphin Feet, Central Urn, c.1900, 30 x 13 In.	1168.00
Andirons, Cast & Wrought Iron, Posset Cup Holder, Strapwork, 2 Scroll Feet, 33 In.	244.00
Andirons, Cast Iron, Acanthus Leaf, Scrolls, 23 In.	150.00
Andirons, Cast Iron, American Indians, Standing, Holding Hatchet, 1800s, 19 x 6 In.	1150.00
Andirons, Cast Iron, Arched Legs, Gooseneck, Out Turned Feet, c.1800, 18 ½ x 19 In.	403.00
Andirons, Cast Iron, Banded Ball Tops, Ring Turned Standards, c.1800s, 14 ¼ x 9 In.	610.00
Andirons, Cast Iron, Black Man, Waistcoat, Squatting, Hands On Knees, c.1900, 17 x 18 In.	459.00
Andirons, Cast Iron, Black, Men, Red Bandannas, Paint, 1800s, 19 x 12 In.	1035.00
Andirons, Cast Iron, Bulldog, Flop Ears, Black Paint, c.1905, 15 ½ x 24 In.	460.00
Andirons, Cast Iron, Cat, Figural, Inset Glass Eyes, c.1890, 18 x 10 ¼ In.	575.00
Andirons, Cast Iron, Cat, Figural, Sitting, Scrolled Logs, Glass Eyes, c.1875, 18 x 10 x 15 In. .	575.00
Andirons, Cast Iron, Dachshund, Seated, Stylized Body, c.1935, 18 x 15 ½ In.	930.00
Andirons, Cast Iron, George Washington, c.1890, 21 In.	546.00
Andirons, Cast Iron, Hessian Soldier, Black, 20 In.	81.00
Andirons, Cast Iron, Hessian Soldiers, Painted, Red Coats, Hats, Gold Eagle, 1800s, 17 ½ In. .	807.00
Andirons, Cast Iron, Liberty Head, Figural, Flared Scroll Feet, Billet Bars, 1800s	478.00
Andirons, Cast Iron, Male & Female Couple, Figural, c.1850, 16 ½ x 10 In. ....*illus*	1315.00
Andirons, Cast Iron, Owl, Figural, Amethyst Glass Marble Eyes, c.1900, 17 ½ In.	978.00
Andirons, Cast Iron, Renaissance Style, Scrolled Dragon Head, Twisted Pedestals, 27 In.	448.00
Andirons, Cast Iron, Scotsman, Long Pipe, Wearing Cap, Button Down Coat, 11 x 13 In.	288.00
Andirons, Cast Iron, Victorian, Owls, Perched, Glass Eyes, Marked, c.1900, 15 x 16 In.	431.00
Andirons, Copper, Disc, Stepped, Brass Ball Center, Machine Age, 9 x 17 ⅝ In.	1304.00
Andirons, Gilt Bronze, Louis XV Style, Upright Scrolled Acanthus Leaf, 30 In.	500.00
Andirons, Gilt Bronze, Napoleon III, Gilt Bronze, Orb, Stars, Wreath, Torches, Paw Feet, 11 x 12 In.	474.00
Andirons, Gilt Metal, Louis XVI Style, Columns, Leafy Swags, Paw Feet, 1800s, 14 x 7 x 19 In.	167.00
Andirons, Iron, Arts & Crafts, Cross Bar, Ball Finial, 35 ¾ x 15 In.	930.00
Andirons, Iron, Brass, Virginia Metalcrafters, Mid 1900s, 23 x 20 In.	316.00
Andirons, Iron, Forged, Balls, Rings, 18 x 14 In.	575.00
Andirons, Iron, Urn Top, Acorn Finial, Fluted Shaft, Claw & Ball Feet, c.1785, 28 x 24 ½ In. ..	5629.00
Andirons, Metal, Federal, Hexagonal Stem, Urn Finial, 24 x 12 In.	1112.00
Andirons, Silvered Bronze, Flower Column, Pineapple Finial, Swags, 1800s, 26 In.	1007.00
Andirons, Wrought Iron, Brass Tack Detail, Signed Bradley & Hubbard, 10 x 21 In.	660.00
Andirons, Wrought Iron, Crescent Finials, Attached Poker, Samuel Yellin, 26 x 10 In.	460.00
Andirons, Wrought Iron, Crescent Finials, Warming Brandy, Stores Poker, Scroll Feet, 26 x 10 In.	460.00
Andirons, Wrought Iron, North Wind Gods, 1800s, 29 In.	201.00
Andirons, Wrought Iron, Sunflower Design, Brass Collars, c.1910, 30 x 12 In.	748.00
Andirons, Wrought Iron, Sunflowers, Rings, Scrolled Lappets, England, c.1865, 27 ⅜ In. ...... *illus*	1960.00
Bellows, Box, Piston Type, Herringbone Marquetry, Walnut Knob & Nozzle, 1914, 23 In.	79.00
Bellows, Forge, Strap Iron Frame, Leather, Tack Bound Wood, Pump Lever, 31 x 40 In.	165.00
Bellows, Oak, Man's Face, Carved, Wrought Iron Snake Nozzle, 25 ½ In.	356.00
Bellows, Painted, Yellow, Red Flowers, Brass Nozzle, 1800s, 16 ½ In., Pair	206.00
Chenets, Andirons, Baroque Style, Bronze Dore, Mythological Creatures, 1900s, 15 In., Pair ..	508.00
Chenets, Andirons, Bronze, Garlands, Paw Feet, 1800s, 18 x 22 In.	2825.00
Chenets, Andirons, Gilt Bronze, Armorial Crest, C-Scroll Base, Gadrooned Knop Finials, 20 x 13 In.	265.00
Chenets, Andirons, Louis XV Style, Gilt Bronze, Cherubs, Holding Flames, Cloud, 1800s, 13 x 12 In. .	956.00
Chenets, Andirons, Louis XVI Style, Gilt Bronze, Pierced Scrolled Band, Torches, 11 x 14 In. ..	878.00
Chenets, Andirons, Louis XVI Style, Gilt Bronze, Pierced Scrolling Design, Fire Fender, 29 In., Pair	248.00
Chenets, Andirons, Napoleon III, Gilt Bronze, Griffins, Roman Breastplate, Scroll Base, 16 x 10 In.	717.99
Chenets, Andirons, Neoclassical, Gilt Bronze, Urns, Swags, Knobs, 16 In., Pair	688.00
Chenets, Andirons, Rococo Style, Gilt Bronze, Curving Leaves, Gilt Finish, 12 x 10 In.	259.00
Chenets, Andirons, Rococo, Bronze, Figural, Man, Woman Deity, On Throne, Waves, c.1850, 13 In.	575.00
Coal Bucket, Stickley Bros., Copper, Hammered, Handle, No. 117, 17 x 14 In.	2040.00
Coal Grate, Cast Iron, Brass, Demilune Top, Molded Urn, Open Work Skirt, 29 x 32 In.	1076.00
Coal Scuttle, Brass, Hammered, Peacock, Tree, Platypus Lid, Removable Liner, Victorian, 17 x 14 In. .	595.00
Coal Scuttle, Brass, Repousse, Trees, Peacocks, Trees, Turtles, Hammered, Footed, 18 x 15 In.	3472.00
Coal Scuttle, Brass, Wood Handle, 1900, 18 x 20 In.	37.00

Fan, Wood, Carved, Hand Painted, Multicolor Ribs, Frame, Chinese, 15 ½ x 26 In.
$1960.00

Skinner, Inc.

Findlay, Spooner, Floradine, Oval, Opal Cream, Red Flowers, 4 In.
$2358.00

Early Auction Co.

Findlay, Sugar & Creamer, Floradine, Red, White Rosettes, 6-In. Sugar
$2473.00

Early Auction Co.

Findlay, Sugar, Cover, Onyx, Silver Rosettes, 6 In.
$403.00

Early Auction Co.

The Queen's Bloomers
Queen Victoria's bloomers have gone up in price. A pair of her large cream-colored underpants embroidered with the letters *VR* sold in Scotland in 2011 for $14,950. The last pair we recorded sold in London in 2008 for $9,000.

Firefighting, Box, Fire Alarm, Red, House Shape, Metal, Wall Mount
$243.00

Victorian Casino Antique Auction

Firefighting, Hydrant, Mueller, Cast Iron, 1960
$224.00

Victorian Casino Antique Auction

Firefighting, Respirator, Oxygen Tank, Mask, Inscribed Case, Inside Lid Instructions, 23 x 16 In.
$148.00

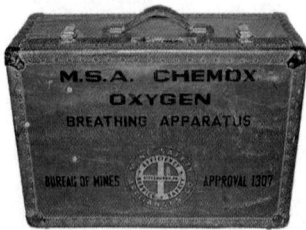

DuMouchelles Art Gallery

TIP

To clean very dirty brass or copper, boil it for two hours in a pan of water with a tablespoon of salt and a cup of white vinegar.

Coal Scuttle, Cover, Tole, Chinoiserie, Lion Mask Ring Handles, 16 ½ x 14 In. ....*illus*	1722.00
Coal Scuttle, Embossed, Gilt, Figures, Hinged Lid, Metal Insert, Japanned, 1800s, 14 x 23 ½ In. ..*illus*	1126.00
Coal Scuttle, Japanned Tin, Curved Reverse Painted Glass, Dog, Wharf, England, 18 ½ In.	1140.00
Coal Scuttle, Oak, Quartersawn, Liner, Carved, Oval Cartouche, Sunflower, c.1880, 21 x 13 In.	115.00
Coal Scuttle, Tin, Flower Painted, Cast Iron Figural Feet, Black, Gold, Victorian, 24 In..........	136.00
Fender & Seat, Wood, Molded, 1800s, 51 x 18 In..	403.00
Fender, Brass, Convex Rail, Ball Finials, Metal Screen Panel, 12 ½ x 49 ½ In........................	295.00
Fender, Brass, Leather, c.1900, 22 x 62 In..	885.00
Fender, Brass, Leather, Tufted, Nailhead Trim, Spindles, 26 x 62 In.	956.00
Fender, Brass, Openwork Lyres, Folding, c.1800, 21 x 14 In.	176.00
Fender, Brass, Serpentine, c.1820, 5 x 46 In.	460.00
Fender, Brass, Single Rail Over Pierced Frame, Cast Lion Masks, c.1900, 15 x 48 In...........	138.00
Fender, Brass, Wirework, Curved Brass Rail, Vertical Wires, Swags & Scrolls, 24 x 44 In.	1304.00
Fender, Bronze, Cast, Flower Garland, Greek Key Corners, Fluted Column, c.1880, 13 x 73 In.	374.00
Fender, Federal Brass, Wire, Caged, Scroll Design, Early 1800s, 12 x 36 ½ In.....................	148.00
Fender, Federal, Brass, Wirework, Serpentine, 4 Finials, 14 ½ x 60 ½ In...........................	322.00
Fender, Iron & Brass, Convex, Brass Rails, Pierced Grate, 37 ½ In...................................	177.00
Fender, Silvered Metal, Leather, Padded, Tufted Top, Slatted Gallery, c.1900, 23 x 55 In........	676.00
Fender, Wirework, Brass Rim, Finials, c.1810, 15 ½ x 60 In...	960.00
Fire Starter, G. Nelson, Bulbous, Footed, Top Removable Flint, Iron, Marked Howard Miller, 12 In.	480.00
Fireback, Cast Iron, Arched Lobed Crest, Lion, Waves, England, 1700s, 33 x 25 In.	948.00
Fireback, Iron, Arch, Rope Coils, Nesting Bird, Scrolls, Columns, Anchor, 1609, 29 x 35 In.	518.00
Footman, Brass, Openwork Skirt, Cabriole Legs, Side Handle, 11 x 18 In...........................	35.00
Footman, Brass, Pierced Top, Sides, Leaves, Handles, Cabriole Legs, 14 x 19 In.	359.00
Footman, Brass, Rectangular, Carrying Handles, Scrolled Legs, 11 x 21 In.	84.00
Footman, George III, Brass, Front Pulls, Side Handles, Faceted, Pad Feet, England, 11 ½ x 19 In.	315.00
Footman, Stool, Georgian Style, Brass, Red Interior, 10 x 21 In.	119.00
Fork, Wrought Iron, 3 Prongs, Twisted Grip, 49 In..	150.00
Grate, Brass & Steel, Pierced & Tiered, Urn Finials, Bulbous Legs, 31 x 23 x 16 In...................	984.00
Grate, Cast Iron, Victorian Style, 19 x 12 x 16 In.	174.00
Guard, Retour D'Egypte, Gilt, Patinated Bronze, Mask, Urns, Palmettes, Arabesques, 16 x 43 In.	2928.00
Hearth Crane, Standing, Iron, Trestle Type, Vertical Stile, Penny Feet, Top Rail, 26 x 49 In....	266.00
Kindling Box, Brass, Applied Wreath, Wood Handles, Sheet Iron Liner, c.1910, 16 x 17 In.	246.00
Log Holder, Wrought Iron, Curled Feet, 22 x 22 In..	390.00
Mantel is listed in the Architectural category.	
Screens are also listed in the Architectural and Furniture categories.	
Screen, 2-Panel, Victorian, Bamboo, Painted Plants, Birds, 43 x 42 In..........................	148.00
Screen, Black Mesh, Orange Diamond Spacers, 32 x 39 In...	89.00
Screen, Brass, Fan Shape Panels, Garland Support, Dolphin Head Handle, c.1905, 29 x 36 In.	676.00
Screen, Brass, Wire, Folding, Scroll Design, c.1800, 15 In..	356.00
Screen, Brass, Wire, Fox Hunt Scene, WJB Monogram, 33 x 42 In..................................	1440.00
Screen, Brass, Wirework, Folding, 2 Urn Finials, Swags & Scrolls, Early 1800s, 26 x 35 In.......	1185.00
Screen, Brass, Wirework, Folding, Rail Over Wire Mesh, Swags & Scrolls, 1800s, 24 x 36 In. ...	948.00
Screen, Cast Bronze, Stained Glass Center, Winged Lady Heads, Paw Feet, 32 x 39 In., c.1860.	3910.00
Screen, Cast Iron Spiral, Frame, Pedestal, Gold Leaf, Needlework, Flowers, Birds, Oval, c.1860, 40 In.	104.00
Screen, Fan Shape, Brass, 1900s, 27 x 36 In...	210.00
Screen, Fan Shape, Scalloped, Brass, 25 x 38 In.	112.00
Screen, Federal, Brass, Wire, Folding, c.1810, 24 x 33 In...	830.00
Screen, Gilt Metal, Flowers, Trophies, Wire Mesh, Trestle Base, 28 ½ x 26 ¾ In.	293.00
Screen, Gilt Metal, Shaped Mesh, Scrolling Leaves Frame & Feet, c.1900, 28 x 31 In.............	652.00
Screen, Glass Panel, Leaded, Stained, Multicolor Shapes, Brass Frame, c.1900, 37 x 24 In......	744.00
Screen, Iron, Scrolling Detail, Spider Web Corner Design, 38 x 45 In.	330.00
Screen, Leaded Glass Panels, Yellow Iris, Iron Frame, Bigelow & Kennard, 33 x 39 In.	8888.00
Screen, Louis XV Style, Gilt Bronze, Scrolled Flower Frame, Wirework Screen, 31 x 26 In........	489.00
Screen, Mesh, Crane Design, Wrought Iron Curled Feet, 42 x 9 ½ In.	1140.00
Screen, Mesh, Side Hook, Andiron Cutouts, 51 x 35 ½ In..	150.00
Screen, Pole, Needlework, Urn Finial, Shield Shape, Silk, Beads, Tripod Base, c.1810, 63 In....	900.00
Screen, Pole, Regency, Ebonized Wood, Chinoisserie, Landscape, Adjustable, 53 x 15 In.........	1888.00
Screen, Pole, Victorian, Ebonized Mahogany, Asian Scene, Scalloped, Gilt, 1800s, 54 x 16 In..	236.00
Screen, Rococo Revival, Giltwood, 2 Monkeys, Ivy, Tortoise & Hare, France, 1800s, 45 x 31 In. .*illus*	1304.00
Screen, Tole, Wading Bird, Rushes, Cast Iron Scrolled Base, England, 1800s, 45 x 25 In.	825.00
Tinder Box, Brass, 2 Lids, Flint, Firesteel, Cloth, Engraved, February 19, 1784, 1 ¾ x 3 In.	738.00
Tongs, Wrought Iron, Curved Tweezers Type, Copper, Iron Bird Cut Tips, 21 In....................	142.00
Tongs, Wrought Iron, Heart Shape Handle, 3 Scroll Plume, Leg Shape Arms, 16 In...............	115.00
Tongs, Wrought Iron, Hinged Arms, Spring Mounted Handles, Thumb Grip, 15 ½ In..............	266.00
Tool Set, Iron, Brass Caps, Twisted Shape, Curled Base Support, Arts & Crafts, 13 x 28 ½ In. ..	480.00

F

FISCHER porcelain was made in Herend, Hungary, by Moritz Fischer. The factory was founded in 1839 and is still in business. The wares are sometimes referred to as Herend porcelain.

Bowl, 2 Handles, Basketweave Design, Hand Painted, Birds, Berries, Flowers, 4 x 8 In.	81.00
Bowl, Openwork Rim, Blue Flowers, White Ground, Gilt, 9 ½ In.	170.00
Chocolate Pot, Lid, Chinese Bouquet, Rust, Basketweave, Wave Relief, Gilt, 6 ½ In.	161.00
Coffee & Tea Set, Coronation, Coffeepot, Teapot, Sugar & Creamer	230.00
Coffee Set, Printemps, Coffeepot, Sugar & Creamer, Flowers, 8 ½ In., 3 Piece	259.00
Figurine, Bird, Upward Wingspan, 13 ¼ In.	150.00
Figurine, Boy, Riding Goose, 8 x 10 In.	118.00
Figurine, Boy, With Boots, 7 ½ In. *illus*	96.00
Figurine, Dog, Brittany Spaniel, 10 x 12 In.	177.00
Figurine, Elephant, Raised Trunk, Blue, 4 In.	180.00
Figurine, Grasshopper, 3 In. *illus*	240.00
Figurine, Matador, Wrestling Bull, 7 x 11 ½ In.	265.00
Figurine, Penguin, Green, Herend, 4 In.	210.00
Figurine, Penguin, Red, Herend, 4 In.	360.00
Figurine, Rooster, 9 x 7 In.	148.00
Figurine, Stag, Braying, 12 x 12 In.	71.00
Flask, Moon Shape, Hungarian Soldier, Flowers, Gilded, Handles, Feet, c.1890, 13 In.	502.00
Ice Bucket, Rothschild Bird, Basketweave, Openwork, Naturalistic Handles, 6 x 11 In.	549.00
Serving Dish, Cover, Coronation, Flowers, Fruit Finial, 6 ½ x 10 ½ In.	161.00
Teapot, Rothschild Bird, 10 ½ In.	354.00
Tray, Centerpiece, Queen Victoria, Bird, 11 x 14 In.	308.00
Tray, Footed, Round, Scalloped Rim, Flowers, Gilt Accents, 3 x 10 In.	156.00
Tray, Queen Victoria, Coffeepot, Sugar & Creamer, Cup & Saucer, Herend	720.00
Tureen, Soup, Tray, 2 Handles, Oval, Bird Finial, Bird & Leaves Design, Herand	1250.00
Vase, Flowers, Gilt Detail, Scalloped Foot, Scalloped Edge, 10 ½ In.	71.00
Vase, Oval, Pedestal, Flowers, Pierced Sides, c.1935, 4 In.	388.00

FISHING reels of brass or nickel were made in the United States by 1810. Bamboo fly rods were sold by 1860, often marked with the maker's name. Lures made of metal, or metal and wood, were made in the nineteenth century. Plastic lures were made by the 1930s. All fishing material is collected today and even equipment of the past thirty years is of interest if in good condition with original box.

Bobber, Creek Chub, Wood, 7 In.	384.00
Bobber, Ideal Fishing Float Co., Multicolor Stripe, Richmond, Va., 1950s, 14 ¼ In. *illus*	891.00
Bobber, Muskie, Wood, Multicolor, 1970s, 18 x 3 In.	95.00
Bobber, Stamtdie Prods., Nibble-Nabber, Wood, Spring Loaded, 1940s, 8 ¾ In. *illus*	230.00
Book, Manual For Anglers, Frank Forrester, Peck & Snyder, 1877, 20 Pages, 4 ½ x 7 In.	212.00
Catalog, Heddon Dowagiac Bait Casting, 1922, 9 x 12 In., 16 Pages	1180.00
Catalog, Winchester Fishing Tackle, 32 Pages, 1924, 5 ½ x 8 ½ In.	132.00
Creel, Bill Mackowski, Brown Ash, Splint, Bird's-Eye, Maple Lid, Leather Straps	142.00
Creel, Ed Cumings, Lowboy Style, Broadhead Model, c.1935, 15 In.	142.00
Creel, Ed Cumings, Wooden Latch, Marked, c.1935, 6 x 12 In.	130.00
Creel, George Lawrence, Supreme Model, Leather Trim, Woven Willow, Strap, 15 x 10 In.	472.00
Creel, John Clark Saddlery Co., Split Willow, Leather Bound, Metal Snap Closure, c.1917, 17 In. *illus*	605.00
Creel, Leather, Pot Belly, Black Paint, Brass Loop Closure, England, 10 x 5 In.	2360.00
Creel, Willow, Leather Trim, Fishing Scene, Zippered Pouch, 1930s, 10 x 15 In. *illus*	345.00
Creel, Woven, Metal Over Leather, Handle, Fish-Shape Latch, c.1900, 14 x 10 In.	40.00
Fly Chest, Salmon, Drop Front, 11 Drawers, Brass Pulls, Leather Handle, 20 x 10 ½ In.	212.00
Fly, Carrie Stevens, Streamer, Size 6, Card	189.00
Fly, Morrissey, Salmon, Hand Tied, Frame, 1998, 7 x 9 In.	142.00
Fly, Popper, Red Wave, Glitter, Fuzzy Eyes, Signed Stan Gibbs, 6 In. *illus*	35.00
Gut Twister, Iron, Screw Foot, 3 Hooked-End Arms, 2 ¼ In.	106.00
Harpoon, Single Barb, Gold, Red Paint, Cape Cod, 1800s, 39 ½ In.	142.00
Hook, James M. Munn, 1890s, 2 ¼ In. *illus*	196.00
Hook, Payton Automatic, Guillotine Spring, 1890s, 4 ¼ In. *illus*	81.00
Line Dryer, Hardy Bros., Collapsible *illus*	115.00
Line Dryer, Vom Hofe, Folding, 10 Parts, Sack, Stamped 1995, 19 ½ x 19 1½ In.	177.00
Lure Box, Heddon, Baby Bass Bug, Copper Finish, Feathers, Intro Box	2360.00
Lure Box, Heddon, Dowagiac, Pine Tree, Blue Head, White Body, 1912	3068.00
Lure Box, Pflueger Neverfail, Minnow, Wood, 5 Hooks, 5 ⅞ x 2 ⅜ In.	384.00
Lure Box, Wood, Rainbow Finish, Painted Gills, Top Slide	767.00
Lure, Creek Chub, Bass Fly, Hummingbird, Floating, No. 300, 3 ⅛ In.	3186.00
Lure, Creek Chub, Bug Wiggler, Fly Rod ⅞ In.	200.00

Firefighting, Trumpet, Presentation, Silver Plate, Engraved, Flowers, Inscription, 1877, 18 ½ In.
$1410.00

Garth's Auctions, Inc.

Firefighting, Trumpet, Presentation, Silver Plate, Incised Designs, Carrying Rings, 18 ½ In.
$3163.00

Bertoia Auction

Fireplace, Andirons, Brass, Dutch Baroque Style, Flame Finial, Baluster Standard, Scrolled Feet, 30 In.
$305.00

Leslie Hindman Auctioneers

F

Fireplace, Andirons, Cast Iron, Male & Female Couple, Figural, c.1850, 16 ½ x 10 In. $1315.00

Neal Auction Co.

Fireplace, Andirons, Wrought Iron, Sunflowers, Rings, Scrolled Lappets, England, c.1865, 27 ⅜ In. $1960.00

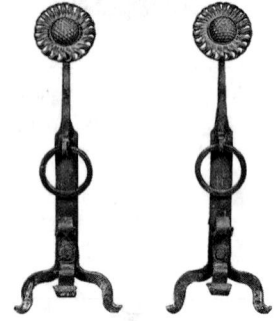

Skinner, Inc.

Fireplace, Coal Scuttle, Cover, Tole, Chinoiserie, Lion Mask Ring Handles, 16 ½ x 14 In. $1722.00

Neal Auction Co.

Fireplace, Coal Scuttle, Embossed, Gilt, Figures, Hinged Lid, Metal Insert, Japanned, 1800s, 14 x 23 ½ In. $1126.00

Skinner, Inc.

Lure, Creek Chub, Fly Rod, Feather Wings, Glitter, Red Eyes, 1920s, 1 ⅛ In.	189.00
Lure, Creek Chub, Fly Rod, Red & White, 1 ¼ In.	130.00
Lure, Creek Club, Bug Wiggler, Fly Rod, Shiny, 1 ¼ In.	266.00
Lure, Creek Club, Bug-A-Moth, Floater, No. 501, 1930s	974.00
Lure, Frog, Muskie, Wire-Covered Legs, Green, Yellow, Black Spots, Treble, c.1950, 7 In. *illus*	92.00
Lure, Haas Tackle Co., Liv-Minno, Painted Tail, Jointed Wood, Washer Eyes, Sapulpa, Okla., 3 In.	189.00
Lure, Heddon, Cade Cove, Mouse, Cork	18.00
Lure, Heddon, Dowagiac Underwater Expert, White, Aluminum, Brass Tail, 1903, 3 In.	3422.00
Lure, Heddon, Punkinseed, Perch Finish, Shiny	590.00
Lure, Heddon, Vamp, Fly Rod, Double Hook, 1920s	1770.00
Lure, Heddon, Vamp, Goldfish Scale Finish, Glass Eyes	502.00
Lure, Mansfield Tuttle's, Devil Bug Hair, Minnow, Spinner, Box, 2 ⅝ In. *illus*	58.00
Lure, Minnow, Balsa, Carved, Painted, 1950s, 4 ½ In. *illus*	35.00
Lure, Minnow, Creek Chub, Yellow Beetle, Metal Spinners, No. 3850	224.00
Lure, Mouse, Wood, Carved, Leather Tail, c.1940, 4 In. *illus*	138.00
Lure, Rat, Muskie, Wood Body, Leather Tail, Back, Weighted, c.1910, 6 ¾ In. *illus*	633.00
Lure, Shakespeare, Revolution, Worden Bucktail, Mickey Mouse Style Spinner	236.00
Lure, Spring Hook, Steel, Brass Rivets, c.1870, 7 ¼ In.	560.00
Lure, Winchester, Delavan Spoon, Nickel Finish, Model 9561, 1 x 1 ¾ In.	67.00
Lure, Winchester, Kidney Trolling Spoon, Nickel Finish, Model 9635, ¾ x 1 ⅛ In.	56.00
Maggot Box, Queen Anne Style, Walnut, Brass Hinges, Clasp, Straps, England, 1800s, 8 ½ x 4 In.	708.00
Minnow Bucket, Copper, Inner Lift-Out Bucket, Air Holes, Handles, 8 ¼ x 11 In.	472.00
Minnow Bucket, Copper, Oval Base, Galvanized Lift-Out Bucket, 8 ½ x 11 ½ In. *illus*	196.00
Minnow Bucket, Domed Cap, Springloaded Door, Perforated Lid, 16 In.	546.00
Minnow Bucket, Hourglass Shape, Blue Paint, Perforated Lid, Handles, 7 x 9 In.	443.00
Minnow Bucket, Lackawanna, Silver, Gold Scenic Stencil Over Green Paint, 20 Qt. *illus*	440.00
Minnow Bucket, Torpedo, Floating, Green Paint, Stenciled Finish, 26 In. *illus*	316.00
Minnow Trap, Camp, Glass, 3 Cones, Aluminum Lid, Checotah, Okla., 10 ½ In.	35.00
Minnow Trap, Orvis, Metal, Lid	25.00
Minnow Trap, Shakespeare, Model 771 ½, 9-Hole Perforated Swing Lid *illus*	58.00
Minnow Tube, Glass, Metal End Caps, Wire Frame, 5 ½ In. *illus*	173.00
Net, Barnes, Trout, Folding, Patent Nov. 9, 1909	236.00
Reel, Arthur Kovalovsky, Big Game, Gold Anodized Finish, c.1938, 6 ¼ In.	1770.00
Reel, Chapman & Son, Brass, Crank Handle, Pat. 1871, 1 ⅞ In. *illus*	196.00
Reel, Edward Vom Hofe, Salmon, Silver, Rubber, Right Hand Wind, 3 ½ In.	1062.00
Reel, Edward Vom Hofe, Trout, Peerless, Size 5, Pat Jan 23, 83, 2 In.	9735.00
Reel, Hendryx, Chrome Over Brass, Embossed, No. 300, 3 ½ In.	60.00
Reel, Herter's, Push Button, Spin Casting, No. 67	32.00
Reel, Herter's, Spinning, Salt Water, Stainless Steel, Box, No. 85	100.00
Reel, Mahogany, Brass, c.1890, 2 ¾ In.	280.00
Reel, Martin, Aluminum, Automatic, Mohawk, N.Y., 1939	50.00
Reel, Meek, Club Special, Casting, German Silver, 1 ¾ In.	4425.00
Reel, Pflueger Supreme, Model 1573, Level Wind, Free Spool, c.1920 *illus*	92.00
Reel, Philbrook & Paine, Fly, Salmon, 1880s, 3 ¾ In.	17700.00
Reel, Saracione, Monarch Lefty Kreh, 3 ½ In.	560.00
Reel, South Bend, Spinning, No. 720	10.00
Reel, Stan Bogdan, Salmon, Model O, Gold Tone, Right Hand Wind, 3 ¼ x 1 ¼ In.	2124.00
Rod, H.L. Leonard, Baby Catskill, Turned, Mortised, White Cedar Handle, 3 Sections, 5 Ft.	1416.00
Rod, Harisyo Ueda Co., Trolling, Bamboo, Tokyo, 6 ½ Ft.	150.00
Rod, Heddon Flyrod Wilder-Dilg, Fly, Intro Box, 1 ⅛ x ⅞ In.	708.00
Rod, Horton Mfg. Co., Expanding, Metal, 1905, 7 Ft.	100.00
Rod, Krider, German Silver Fittings, Signed, 14 Ft.	9735.00
Rod, Leonard, Travel, Tourister, 2 Butts, 2 Mids, 2 Tips, Mahogany Case, 10 Ft.	384.00
Rod, Leonard, Trout, Model 50, Twist Snake Guides, Bag, 8 Ft.	1416.00
Rod, Orvis, Trout, Madison Adirondack, Impregnated Shafts, Bag, 7 Ft. 6 In.	354.00
Rod, Orvis, Wes Jordon, Impregnated Shafts, Chrome Guides, 8 Ft.	767.00
Rod, Pezon & Michel, Trout, Super Parabolic Midget, 8 Ft.	649.00
Rod, Summers, Trout, Model 275, Bright Snake Guides, Bag, 7 Ft. 6 In.	2596.00
Rod, Thomas, Trout, Special, Straw-Colored Cane, Bag, 9 Ft.	236.00
Spear Head, Wrought Iron, 3 Center Tines, 11 ¼ x 7 ½ In. *illus*	316.00
Spear, Salmon, Cedar, Hand Carved, Northwest, 2 Sections, c.1890, 105 In.	295.00
Tackle Box, Fly Fishing, Walnut, Copper Fish Design, Rounded Rectangle, c.1900, 9 x 4 In.	288.00
Tackle Box, Mahogany, Lift-Out Drawer, Compartments, 3-Latch Lid, 10 x 20 x 8 In.	94.00
Tackle Box, Orvis, Mahogany, Brass Hardware, Fitted Interior, Joe Center, 1960s, 20 x 7 ½ In.	502.00
Tackle Box, Tournament Caster, Wood, Slots, Trays, Line Holders, c.1940, 20 x 12 In.	212.00
Tackle Box, Wood, Brass Hardware, 3 Lift-Out Trays, Victorian, 18 x 6 In.	118.00

Tackle Box, Wood, Drop Front, 2 Lift-Out Trays, 13 ¾ x 9 ¼ In. ....*illus*	104.00
Water Light, Otake Electric Plant Co., Brass, Wood, Glass, Japan, Stamped 1962	24.00

FLAGS *are included in the Textile category.*

FLASH GORDON appeared in the Sunday comics in 1934. The daily strip started in 1940. The hero was also in comic books from 1930 to 1970, in books from 1936, in movies from 1938, on the radio in the 1930s and 1940s, and on television from 1953 to 1954. All sorts of memorabilia are collected, but the ray guns and rocket ships are the most popular.

Book, In The Caverns Of Mongo, Hardcover, Dust Jacket, 1936, 7 ½ In., 220 Pages..................	230.00
Figure, Wood Composition, Pedestal Base, 1944, 4 ¾ In.	345.00
Pin, Movie Club, Follow The Adventures, Buster Crabbe, c.1938, 1 ¼ In.......................	1044.00
Rocket Fighter, Sparking, Schylling Collector Series, Box, 12 In.	45.00

FLORENCE CERAMICS were made in Pasadena, California, from World War II to 1977. Florence Ward created many colorful figurines, boxes, candleholders, and other items for the gift shop trade. Each piece was marked with an ink stamp that included the name *Florence Ceramics Co.* The company was sold in 1964 and although the name remained the same, the products were very different. Mugs, cups, and trays were made.

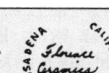

Dish, 3 Compartments, Applied Roses, Scalloped, Marked, 9 x 9 In.	40.00
Figurine, Abigail, Beige Dress, c.1950, 8 ½ In.	189.00
Figurine, Abigail, Rose Dress, c.1950, 8 ½ In.	199.00
Figurine, Betsy, Pale Green Dress, Gilt, Marked, 7 ½ In.	110.00
Figurine, Child Ballerina, Ruffled Tutu, Base, 1950s, 7 In.	140.00
Figurine, Chinese Girl, Gold Trim	112.00
Figurine, Choir Boy, c.1930s, 2 Piece	159.00
Figurine, Clarissa Girl, Maroon Dress, 7 ½ In.	329.00
Figurine, David, Green Suit, Holding Top Hat, Gilt, 7 ½ In.	95.00
Figurine, Deborah, Moss Green Dress, Holding Flowers, 9 ½ In.	450.00
Figurine, Delie, Maroon Dress & Muff, 1940, 7 ½ In.	252.00
Figurine, Dolores, Green Dress, Lace Trim, Shawl, Bonnet, Gloves, Umbrella, 8 In.	625.00
Figurine, Irene, Beige & Green Dress, 5 ½ In.	45.00
Figurine, Kay, Brown Hair, White Dress, Flowers, Marked, 7 In.	45.00
Figurine, Little Girl, Holding Bird, Seated, c.1950, 5 In.	95.00
Figurine, Louis XVI, 1940s, 10 ½ In.	332.00
Figurine, Matilda, Beige Dress With Red Trim, 8 ⅝ In.	239.00
Figurine, Matilda, Gray & Rose Dress, Gold Trim Bonnet, 1940s, 9 In.	165.00
Figurine, Melanie, Brown Hair, Blue Dress, Marked, 7 ½ In.	75.00
Figurine, Peter, Turquoise Tuxedo & Hat, 1930s, 9 ¼ In.	429.00
Figurine, Pheasants, White, 9 x 17 In.	150.00
Figurine, Pretty Little Pat, Turquoise Dress, 5 ⅞ In.	238.00
Figurine, Sarah, Gray Dress, Red Hat & Purse, Marked, 7 ½ In.	95.00
Figurine, Sue Ellen, Blue & Cream Dress, 6 In.	139.00
Figurine, Suzette, Green Dress, Pink Flowers, Blond, Holding Basket, 6 ¾ In.	52.00
Group, Story Hour, Mother Reading, Son & Daughter, 8 x 7 In.	1000.00
Head Vase, Violet, Hat, Ruffled Sleeves, Stamped, c.1950, 7 In.	145.00
Plaque, Woman, Blond, Umbrella, Hat, Stamped, 9 x 6 In.	75.00
Plaque, Woman, Brunette, Purse, Hat, Stamped, 9 x 6 In.	75.00

FLOW BLUE was made in England and other countries about 1830 to 1900. The dishes were printed with designs using a cobalt blue coloring. The color flowed from the design to the white body so that the finished piece has a smeared blue design. The dishes were usually made of ironstone china. More Flow Blue may be found under the name of the manufacturer.

Biscuit Jar, Marina, Fish, Seaweed, Brass Lid, Bail Handle, England, 7 ½ In.	10.00
Biscuit Jar, Poppies, Gold Highlights, Silver Plate Lid, Bail Handle, 7 In.	80.00
Bowl, Cover, Carnations, Rippled Rim, Melbourne, W.R. Grindley & Co., 12 In. ....*illus*	30.00
Bowl, Cover, Pelew, Octagonal, Footed, c.1850, 10 x 12 In.	207.00
Bowl, Cover, Transfer, Staffordshire, Marked Dunbarton, 5 ½ x 8 In.	69.00
Cake Plate, Daffodils, c.1900, 10 ½ In.	71.00
Creamer, Snowflake Pattern, 4 ⅛ In.	94.00
Creamer, Willow Pattern, Paneled, 5 ¾ In.	90.00
Cup & Saucer, Blue & White, Cashmere	36.00
Pitcher & Basin, Poppea Pattern, Flared & Shaped Rim, Grimwades, 12-In. Pitcher	277.00
Pitcher, Azalea, Leaves, White & Blue, Cylindrical, Rounded Bottom, Ruffle Rim, c.1920s, 7 x 5 In.	45.00
Pitcher, Oval, Nonpariel, Burgess & Leigh, c.1900, 7 ¾ x 9 ½ In.	81.00

Fireplace, Screen, Rococo Revival, Giltwood, 2 Monkeys, Ivy, Tortoise & Hare, France, 1800s, 45 x 31 In. $1304.00

Skinner, Inc.

Fischer, Figurine, Boy, With Boots, 7 ½ In. $96.00

DuMouchelles Art Gallery

Fischer, Figurine, Grasshopper, 3 In. $240.00

DuMouchelles Art Gallery

Fishing, Bobber, Ideal Fishing Float Co., Multicolor Stripe, Richmond, Va., 1950s, 14 ¼ In. $891.00

Lang's Sporting Collectibles Inc.

Fishing, Bobber, Stamtdie Prods., Nibble-Nabber, Wood, Spring Loaded, 1940s, 8 ¾ In.
$230.00

Lang's Sporting Collectibles Inc.

Fishing, Creel, John Clark Saddlery Co., Split Willow, Leather Bound, Metal Snap Closure, c.1917, 17 In.
$605.00

Lang's Sporting Collectibles Inc.

Fishing, Creel, Willow, Leather Trim, Fishing Scene, Zippered Pouch, 1930s, 10 x 15 In.
$345.00

Lang's Sporting Collectibles Inc.

Fishing, Fly, Popper, Red Wave, Glitter, Fuzzy Eyes, Signed Stan Gibbs, 6 In.
$35.00

Lang's Sporting Collectibles Inc.

Plate Set, Pelew, Staffordshire, 10 ¾ In., 6 Piece	184.00
Plate Set, Transfer, Staffordshire, Marked Brunswick, c.1900, 9 In., 6 Piece	69.00
Plate, Cashmere, 8 In.	95.00
Plate, Ships, Storm, Kent East Indiaman, 9 ¼ In.	181.00
Plate, Temple & Water Scene, Floral Border, Rippled Rim, Marked, 9 In.	12.00
Plate, Transferware, Diamond Shape, Closed Branch Handles, Marked Scinde, 9 In.	184.00
Plate, Transferware, Watteau, Doulton, Staffordshire, c.1900, 11 ¼ In.	58.00
Platter, Flowers, Ashworth Bros, c.1885, 19 In.	173.00
Platter, Kaolinware, 10 x 13 ½ In.	51.00
Platter, Nonpareil Castle Scene, Burgess & Leigh, c.1900, 15 ½ x 12 ¾ In.	173.00
Sardine Box, Undertray, Gilt, Flannel Daisy, Staffordshire, 7 x 7 ¾ In.	161.00
Tureen, Undertray, Cover, Gilt, Oval, Handles, Marked Luzerne, 10 ½ x 15 In.	81.00

FLYING PHOENIX, *see Phoenix Bird category.*

FOLK ART is also listed in many categories of this book under the actual name of the object. See categories such as Box, Cigar Store Figure, Paper, Weather Vane, Wooden, etc.

American Eagle, Spread Wings, Grasping Arrow, c.1930s, 13 x 23 In.	705.00
Ball, Potichomania, Aqua Green, Cutout Sepia Photographs, Colored Chalk, c.1900, 7 ½ In.	35.00
Bank, Freshwater Clam & Snail Shell, Recessed Sides, Coin Slot, Mirrors, 7 x 7 In.	295.00
Bird Tree, Wood, 7 Carved Birds, Multicolor, Daniel & Barbara Strawser, 1900s, 22 In.	264.00
Bird Tree, Wood, Carved, Painted Metal Leaves, Multicolor Blackbirds, c.1910, 39 In.	1600.00
Bird, Hardwood, Wrought Iron, Wings Open & Fold, Inner Compartment, 8 x 7 In.	123.00
Birdhouse, House, Wood & Tin, Hamilton County, Ohio, 1900s, 8 ½ In. ....*illus*	176.00
Black Man, Dancing, Metal Wire Attached, Carved, Painted, Stand, 20 In.	1150.00
Black Man, Holding Watermelon, Riding Alligator, Gray Dog, Pig, Marvin Bailey, 19 In.	230.00
Box, Pine, Paint, Chip Carved, Fans, Hearts, Eagle, Hills, Windmills, Tools, c.1900, 6 x 25 In.	617.00
Cage, Squirrel, Metal, Wood, Carved, Pierced, 1800s, 37 In.	46.00
Cage, Squirrel, Wood, Exercise Roller, Victorian, 21 x 32 In.	1200.00
Cane, Walking Stick, Snake Carved, Ball Pommel, Brass Tip, 46 ½ In.	403.00
Card Tray, Silent Butler, Black Man, Glass Eyes, Tray, Wood, Carved, 19 ½ In.	148.00
Carving, Sandstone Block, Mug, Pretzel, Recessed Compartment, c.1875, 4 x 7 In.	264.00
Case, Matchstick, Diamond Pattern, Stick Feet, 2 Hinged Doors, 6 x 8 In.	35.00
Clown, Painted, Carved, Walking Charlie, c.1925, 75 In. ....*illus*	518.00
Cow, Sheet Iron, Painted, c.1900, 32 x 48 In.	950.00
Cricket Cage, Molded Gourd, Chinese Characters, Ivory Lid, Birds, 1900s, 4 ½ In.	100.00
Cricket Cage, Molded Gourd, Ivory Dragon Lid, 19th Century, 4 ½ In.	100.00
Cricket Cage, Molded Gourd, Weave Pattern, Tortoiseshell Lid, c.1900, 5 ¾ In.	275.00
Cricket Cage, Molded Gourd, Wood Rim, Dragons, Clouds, Tortoiseshell Lid, 1800s, 6 ¾ In.	350.00
Deer Head, Buck, Hardwood, Black & White Paint, Carved, Wood Pedestal, c.1900, 40 In.	470.00
Eagle, Wood, Carved, Gilded, Feathers Down, 16 ¼ In.	1094.00
Eagle, Wood, Multicolor, Walnut Base, Bear, Ram, Tree, Painted, c.1900, 22 x 46 In.	3955.00
Flag Holder, Figural, Uncle Sam, Profile, Pedestal Base, 1950, 57 ½ In.	148.00
Frame, Tiger Maple Corners, Carved, Painted, Pennsylvania, 21 x 17 In.	1422.00
Horse, Prancing, Silhouette, Sheet Iron, Rectangular Base, c.1850, 24 In.	118.00
Horse, Running, Stand, Cast Iron, 19 In.	58.00
Horse, Wood, Horsehair Tail, Painted, 19th Century, 5 ½ x 7 In.	176.00
Lamp, Electric, Popsicle Stick, 10 Layer Base, 29 Circular Layers, Burlap Cover Shade, 32 ½ In.	224.00
Lion, Softwood, Cartoonish, Wild Teeth, Yellow, Colored Speckles, c.1900, 19 In.	764.00
Mailbox, Stainless Steel, Cylindrical, England, 28 ¾ x 15 In.	410.00
Man, Abraham Lincoln, Wood, Card Stock Ears, Painted Features & Shoes, c.1865, 21 In.	513.00
Man, Standing, Hands In Pocket, White Pine, Carved, Midwest, c.1920, 51 In.	600.00
Man, Standing, Wearing Hat, Bowtie, Elongated Nose, Face, Carved Wood, Late 1800s, 12 In.	1265.00
Man, Uniform, Hat Base, Carved, c.1875, 5 ½ In.	151.00
Mermaid, Brazilian Wood, Bottle Caps Scales, Lying On Side, Carved, ½ x 31 In.	337.00
Mermaid, Wood, Carved, Painted, Arms Behind Head, Seminude, 63 x 24 In.	565.00
Monk, Bearded, Torch, Skull, Signed, John Bastian, 1985, 9 ½ In.	51.00
Ostrich, Wood, Chain Saw Carved, Paint, Phil Wright, 60 x 47 In.	805.00
Owl, Carved, Wood Grain, Painted Feathers, Glass Eyes, Iron Beak, Stand, c.1930, 24 In. .... *illus*	1422.00
Parrot, Wood, Carved, Painted, 1800s, 19 ½ In.	118.00
Penguin, Wood, Carved & Painted, Standing, Square Base, 19 In.	1093.00
Picture, Pinprick Punch, Peafowl, Perched In Tree, Butterfly, c.1805, 9 x 8 In.	2013.00
Rattle, Carved, Painted Wood, Notched Slats, Forms Cube, Maple Handle, c.1890, 10 In.	337.00
Rooster, Wood, Carved, Painted, W. Schimmel, Penn., c.1875, 4 ½ In.	5451.00
Rooster, Wood, Red Leather Comb, Glass Eyes, Carved, Painted, c.1895, 17 x 12 In.	1304.00
Sailing Ship, Sheet Iron, 2-Masted Schooner, Directional, Paint, New England, c.1910, 38 x 39 In.	118.00

Seat, Tree Stump, Oak, Figure Of Woman, Carved, c.1905, 32 In.	182.00
Shelf, Hanging, Corner, Carved, Jesus Saves, Crosses, c.1950, 23 In.	121.00
Smoking Butler, Art Deco Style, Naked Woman, Painted Red, Black, 28 In.	266.00
Smoking Butler, Equestrian Man, Wearing Jodhpurs, Riding Boots, Cap, Painted, 29 ½ In.	235.00
Snake, Stripes, Black, White, c.1900, 11 ½ In.	118.00
Soldier, White Pine, Peaked Hat, Walking, Carved, New England, c.1790, 19 In.	2318.00
Spoon Rack, Shaped Pocket, Trellis, 3-Leaf Clovers, Painted, Roses, Schooner, 1908, 16 x 9 In.	690.00
Staff, Wood, Carved, Knob Finial, Tapering Shaft, 2 Snakes Encircling, Stand, c.1900, 62 In.	398.00
Toy, Noah's Ark, 41 Animals, Noah, Wife, Paint, c.1900, 9 ¾ x 18 ½ In.	2370.00
Trinket Box, Match Stickes, Recessed Lid, Raised Band & Knob, 5 x 8 ¾ In.	35.00
Uncle Sam, V For Victory Wreath, Carved Pine, 1940s, 17 ½ In.	118.00
Watch Hutch, Tombstone Shaped, Open Circle Center, Carved, 1760, 9 ¼ In.	705.00
Wedding Globe, Blown Glass, Cushion, Ormolu Leaves, Mirrors, France, c.1890, 16 In. *illus*	285.00
Whimsy, Mahogany, Scroll Cut, Basket, Tulips, Birds, Gold Paint, c.1875, 13 x 13 In. *illus*	2350.00
Whimsy, Rotating, Carved Wood, Thread, Inside Green Bottle, 3 Parts, Molded, 6 In.	59.00
Whimsy, Wood, Footed Church Steeple, 1 Piece Of Wood, Ball In Cage, Cross In Upper Ball, 6 ½ In.	142.00
Whirligig, Figure, Shaped Ears, Red Paint, Articulated Hands, Wood Block Base, c.1900, 22 ½ In.	805.00
Whirligig, Food Chain, Woman Chasing Chicken Chasing Grasshopper, Joe McFall, 1900s	512.00
Whirligig, Indian, Canoe, Pine, Painted, Stand, Round Base, c.1920, 14 x 12 In.	460.00
Whirligig, Johnny Bowline, Sailor Holding Oars, Painted Pine, Nantucket, c.1800s, 15 x 10 In.	1035.00
Whirligig, Man, Beard, Hat, Carved, Painted, Wood, c.1810, 22 In. *illus*	2070.00
Whirligig, Man, Mustache, Spinning Arm, Carved, Painted, 1985, 11 In.	57.00
Whirligig, People, In Line, Table, Carved, Painted, Andy Lunde, 1999	518.00
Whirligig, Softwood, Man In Top Hat, Painted, Signed Koosed, 1981, 13 In.	71.00
Whirligig, Soldier, Tack Eyes, Shako Style Hat, Ridged Paddles, Large Feet, Paint, c.1890, 21 In.	1687.00
Whirligig, Traffic Cop, Tin, Embossed, Safety First, Painted, 8 ¼ In.	259.00
Woman, Long Pleated Dress, Bare Feet, Curly Brown Hair, Square Base, Metal, Wood, Paint, 29 In.	375.00

FOOT WARMERS solved the problem of cold feet in past generations. Some warmers held charcoal, others held hot water. Pottery, tin, and soapstone were the favored materials to conduct the heat. The warmer was kept under the feet, then the legs and feet were tucked into a blanket, providing welcome warmth in a cold carriage or church.

Brass, Round, Screw Cap, Metal Handle, 19th Century, 9 ½ x 5 ¼ In.	220.00
Copper, Oval, Top Brass Ring, c.1900, 11 x 8 x 6 In.	55.00
Galvanized Metal, Ribbed, 9 x 12 In.	35.00
Hot Water, Soldered Sheet Copper, Wedge Shape, Fold Down Handles, 4 x 12 In.	30.00
Stoneware, Half Round, Denby, England, 11 x 5 x 5 In.	65.00
Stoneware, Jug Shape, Dorchester Pottery Works, Chain Pull, c.1880, 11 In.	200.00
Stoneware, Painted, Horse Heads, Denby, 4 ¾ x 2 ¾ In.	85.00
Stoneware, Triangular, End Knob, White, c.1880	33.00
Tin, Sycamore, Punched, Hearts, Turned Corner Posts, 1800s, 5 ¾ x 9 In.	176.00
Tin, Wood, Punched Hearts, Turning Wire Handle, Hinged Door, 1840s, 7 x 9 x 6 In.	275.00
Wood, Carved Top Edge, Cutout Hearts, Wood Know, Iron Handle, 10 x 6 x 7 In.	135.00
Wood, Metal, Horses, Bail Handle, Wood Grip	119.00
Wood, Punched Tin, Round, Bail Handle	250.00
Wood, Tin, Whale Oil Burner, Turnip Feet, Bail Handle, c.1850, 7 x 6 x 5 In.	300.00

FOOTBALL *collectibles may be found in the Card and the Sports categories.*

FOSTORIA glass was made in Fostoria, Ohio, from 1887 to 1891. The factory was moved to Moundsville, West Virginia, and most of the glass seen in shops today is a twentieth-century product. The company was sold in 1983; new items will be easily identifiable, according to the new owner, Lancaster Colony Corporation. Additional Fostoria items may be listed in the Milk Glass category.

American, Bowl, Fruit, 3-Footed, 11 ½ In.	50.00
American, Cake Plate, Pedestal, Pointed Skirt, 10 x 7 In.	145.00
American, Compote, 6 x 5 In.	5.00
American, Cruet, 6 ½ In.	30.00
American, Pitcher, Water, Crystal, 39 Oz.	85.00
American, Plate, Salad, 7 ¾ In.	12.00
American, Relish, 2 Sections, Handles	5.00
American, Relish, Cobalt Blue, 5 Sections, 14 In.	185.00
American, Soup, Cream, 2 Handles	40.00
American, Top Hat, 3 ¼ In.	24.00
American, Tray, Oblong, 10 ½ In.	142.00

Fishing, Hook, James M. Munn, 1890s, 2 ¼ In. $196.00

Lang's Sporting Collectibles Inc.

Fishing, Hook, Payton Automatic, Guillotine Spring, 1890s, 4 ¼ In. $81.00

Lang's Sporting Collectibles Inc.

Fishing, Line Dryer, Hardy Bros., Collapsible $115.00

Lang's Sporting Collectibles Inc.

Fishing, Lure, Frog, Muskie, Wire-Covered Legs, Green, Yellow, Black Spots, Treble, c.1950, 7 In. $92.00

Lang's Sporting Collectibles Inc.

Fishing, Lure, Mansfield Tuttle's, Devil Bug Hair, Minnow, Spinner, Box, 2 ⅝ In. $58.00

Lang's Sporting Collectibles Inc.

Fishing, Lure, Minnow, Balsa, Carved, Painted, 1950s, 4 ½ In.
$35.00

Lang's Sporting Collectibles Inc.

Fishing, Lure, Mouse, Wood, Carved, Leather Tail, c.1940, 4 In.
$138.00

Lang's Sporting Collectibles Inc.

Fishing, Lure, Rat, Muskie, Wood Body, Leather Tail, Back, Weighted, c.1910, 6 ¾ In.
$633.00

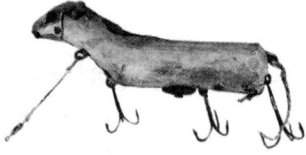

Lang's Sporting Collectibles Inc.

Fishing, Minnow Bucket, Copper, Oval Base, Galvanized Lift-Out Bucket, 8 ½ x 11 ½ In.
$196.00

Lang's Sporting Collectibles Inc.

Fishing, Minnow Bucket, Lackawanna, Silver, Gold Scenic Stencil Over Green Paint, 20 Qt.
$440.00

Lang's Sporting Collectibles Inc.

American, Tumbler, Flat, 5 Oz.	12.00
American, Whiskey, 2 ½ In., 2 Oz.	15.00
Autumn, Box, Handkerchief, Lid	1875.00
Baroque, Salt & Pepper, Chintz Etching, 2 ¾ In.	30.00
Baroque, Sherbet	7.00
Baroque, Sugar & Creamer	30.00
Baroque, Vase, Footed, 10 In.	45.00
Beacon, Sherbet, 5 ½ In.	50.00
Bedford, Toothpick Holder, 2 ¼ In.	50.00
Bookends, Rearing Horse, 7 ½ In.	65.00
Bracelet, Claret, 4 ½ In.	79.00
Cake Stand, Turned-Up Edge, 12 In Diam.	120.00
Capri, Cordial, Green, 2 ⅝ In.	56.00
Chintz Etch, Cake Plate, Center Handle, 6 x 12 In.	65.00
Chintz, Cup & Saucer	59.00
Chintz, Goblet, Water	28.00
Coin Glass, Bowl, Emerald Green, Patriot & Liberty Bell, Scalloped Rim, 8 x 5 x 3 In.	65.00
Coin, Bowl, Blue, Oval, 9 In.	102.00
Coin, Bowl, Oval, Emerald Green, 8 x 5 x 3 In.	65.00
Coin, Bowl, Scalloped, Ruby Red, 9 x 5 x 3 In.	55.00
Coin, Compote, Footed, 8 ½ In.	265.00
Coin, Pitcher, Olive Green	90.00
Coin, Salt & Pepper, Red	90.00
Coin, Sugar, Cover, Ruby Red, 6 ½ In.	45.00
Coin, Wedding Bowl, Green, Cover, 87 ½ In.	35.00
Colony, Bowl, Fruit, Turned-Up Ends, c.1952, 10 ½ In.	40.00
Colony, Bowl, Scalloped, Footed, 5 ½ In.	88.00
Colony, Compote, Cover, 6 ½ In.	48.00
Colony, Cracker Plate, 12 In.	29.00
Colony, Pitcher, Milk, Crystal, 16 Oz.	48.00
Colony, Plate, Center Handle, 11 In	24.00
Colony, Wine, 3 Oz.	12.00
Daisy, Bowl, Green, Rolled Edge, 11 In.	39.00
Dandelion, Toothpick Holder	55.00
Empire, Vase, Green, Clear Base, 9 ½ In.	125.00
Fairfax, Console, Topaz, Footed, 12 In.	35.00
Fairfax, Cup & Saucer, Pink Rose	10.00
Fairfax, Plate, Dinner, Blue, 9 ½ In.	30.00
Grapes & Leaves, Vase, Amber, Footed, 10 In.	165.00
Heart & Vine, Vase, Cream, Green, Iridescent Gold, Square Beaker Shape, Flared Foot, 12 In.	978.00
Heather, Salt & Pepper	61.00
Heather, Tray, Polished Bottom, 2 Handles, 10 In.	25.00
Heather, Vase, 2 Handles, 6 ¼ In.	55.00
Heirloom, Pitcher, Ruby, 9 In.	109.00
Heirloom, Vase, Green, Handles, 4 ½ In.	116.00
Holly, Goblet, 10 Oz.	22.00
Jamestown, Salt & Pepper, Shaker, Pink	44.00
Jamestown, Shaker, Pink	44.00
Jamestown, Wine, Amethyst, 4 Oz.	20.00
Jenny Lind, Tumbler, 4 Piece	125.00
June, Candlestick, Blue, Scroll, 5 In.	55.00
June, Cordial, Topaz, 1 Oz.	94.00
June, Goblet, Water, Rose Pink, 9 Oz.	75.00
June, Pitcher, Water, Azure Blue, 9 ¾ In.	875.00
June, Plate, Lunch, Rose Pink, 8 ¾ In.	29.00
June, Sugar & Creamer, Rose Pink, 3 ⅛ In.	60.00
June, Sugar, Azure Blue, Lid, 3 ⅜ In.	160.00
June, Wine, Topaz, 2 ½ Oz.	45.00
Lafayette, Relish, Divided, Oval, Underplate	48.00
Lido, Candy Box, Cover, 3 Sections	118.00
Lido, Ice Bucket, Steel Handle, 4 ½ x 6 In.	68.00
Mayflower, Cake Plate, Handles, 12 In.	30.00
Mayflower, Cruet, 3 Oz.	90.00
Mayflower, Goblet, 9 Oz.	20.00
Meadow Rose, Candlestick, 5 ¾ In.	39.00
Navarre, Bell, Blue, 6 ½ In.	120.00
Navarre, Bowl, Gold, Pedestal, 8 ¼ In.	95.00

Navarre, Candy Dish, Cover	118.00
Navarre, Plate, Salad, 7 ½ In.	20.00
Navarre, Sherbet, 4 ¼ In.	18.00
Navarre, Torte Plate, 14 In.	90.00
Oak Leaf Rose, Dish, Lemon	51.00
Oak Leaf Rose, Dish, Sweetmeat	47.00
Oak Leaf, Bonbon	40.00
Oak Leaf, Tray, Lunch, Rose	118.00
Romance, Dish, Mayonnaise, 6 ¾ In.	45.00
Romance, Sugar & Creamer	30.00
Sunray, Relish, 2 Sections, Handle, 4 x 6 ½ In.	15.00
Trojan, Bonbon, Topaz, 6 ¾ x 2 ¾ In.	40.00
Trojan, Bowl, Cream, Topaz, 6 In.	40.00
Trojan, Bowl, Dessert, Topaz, 4 ½ In.	35.00
Trojan, Celery Dish, Topaz, 11 ¾ In.	50.00
Trojan, Sauceboat, Topaz, 6 ¼ x 3 ⅝ In.	65.00
Versailles, Candlestick, Pink, 3 ½ In., Pair	75.00
Versailles, Compote, Pink, 6 ½ In.	100.00
Versailles, Ice Bucket, Green	150.00
Versailles, Sandwich Server, Center Handle, Topaz, 12 In.	95.00
Versailles, Soup, Dish, Flat, Green, 7 In.	100.00
Versailles, Tumbler, Green, Footed, 9 Oz.	35.00
Vesper, Pitcher, Amber, 1920s, 9 ¾ In.	350.00
Willowmere, Pitcher, Qt.	356.00
Willowmere, Salt & Pepper, Glass Lids	128.00
Windsor, Chalice, Royal Blue, Cover, 8 ½ In.	95.00

FOVAL, *see Fry category.*

FRAMES *are included in the Furniture category under Frame.*

FRANCISCAN is a trademark that appears on pottery. Gladding, McBean and Company started in 1875. The company grew and acquired other potteries. It made sewer pipes, floor tiles, dinnerware, and art pottery with a variety of trademarks. It began using the trade name *Franciscan* in 1934. In 1936, dinnerware and art pottery were sold under the name *Franciscan Ware.* The company made china and cream-colored, decorated earthenware. Desert Rose, Apple, El Patio, and Coronado were best-sellers. The company became Interpace Corporation and in 1979 was purchased by Josiah Wedgwood & Sons. The plant was closed in 1984, but a few of the patterns are still being made. For more prices, go to kovels.com.

Amapola, Baker, 14 ¾ In.	32.00
Amapola, Bowl, Vegetable, 9 ⅜ In.	35.00
Amapola, Creamer	10.00
Amapola, Plate, Bread & Butter, 6 ¾ In.	5.00
Amapola, Platter, 14 ⅛ In.	26.00
Antiqua, Bowl, Vegetable, Divided, 11 In.	25.00
Antiqua, Plate, Bread & Butter, 6 In.	3.00
Antique Green, Bread & Butter, 6 ¼ In.	12.00
Apple, Cup & Saucer	12.00
Apple, Cup & Saucer, Oversized	69.00
Apple, Mixing Bowl, 7 In.	95.00
Apple, Mixing Bowl, 8 In.	160.00
Apple, Plate, Dinner, 10 ⅝ In.	24.00
Apple, Platter, Oval, 14 In.	40.00
Apple, Relish, 10 ⅜ In.	20.00
Apple, Salt & Pepper, Cylindrical, 6 ¼ In.	75.00
Apple, Sugar, Lid	45.00
Apple, Tureen, Soup, Cover, Handles	489.00
Arcadia, Cup & Saucer	16.00
Autumn, Ashtray, 4 ¾ In.	4.50
Autumn, Bowl, Vegetable, Divided, 9 ¾ In.	16.00
Autumn, Butter, Cover	23.00
Autumn, Creamer, 3 ¼ In.	10.00
Autumn, Salt & Pepper	35.00
Beverly, Creamer	30.00
Beverly, Platter, Round, 14 In.	80.00
Beverly, Salt & Pepper	44.00

Fishing, Minnow Bucket, Torpedo, Floating, Green Paint, Stenciled Finish, 26 In.
$316.00

Lang's Sporting Collectibles Inc.

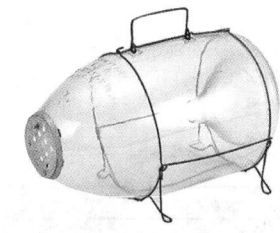

Fishing, Minnow Trap, Shakespeare, Model 771 ½, 9-Hole Perforated Swing Lid
$58.00

Lang's Sporting Collectibles Inc.

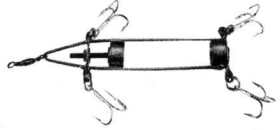

Fishing, Minnow Tube, Glass, Metal End Caps, Wire Frame, 5 ½ In.
$173.00

Lang's Sporting Collectibles Inc.

Fishing, Reel, Chapman & Son, Brass, Crank Handle, Pat. 1871, 1 ⅞ In.
$196.00

Lang's Sporting Collectibles Inc.

Fishing, Reel, Pflueger Supreme, Model 1573, Level Wind, Free Spool, c.1920
$92.00

Lang's Sporting Collectibles Inc.

Fishing, Spear Head, Wrought Iron, 3 Center Tines, 11 ¼ x 7 ½ In. $316.00

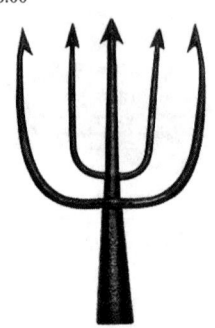

Lang's Sporting Collectibles Inc.

Fishing, Tackle Box, Wood, Drop Front, 2 Lift-Out Trays, 13 ¾ x 9 ¼ In. $104.00

Lang's Sporting Collectibles Inc.

Flow Blue, Bowl, Cover, Carnations, Rippled Rim, Melbourne, W.R. Grindley & Co., 12 In. $30.00

Conestoga Auction Co., Inc.

Folk Art, Birdhouse, House, Wood & Tin, Hamilton County, Ohio, 1900s, 8 ½ In. $176.00

Garth's Auctions, Inc.

Bird 'N Hand, Plate, Dinner, 10 ¼ In.	15.00
Blanc, Bowl, Vegetable, 10 ¾ In.	21.00
Blue Dawn, Plate, Dinner, 10 ¾ In.	15.00
Blue Dawn, Plate, Salad, 8 ¾ In.	10.00
Blueberry, Bowl, Fruit, 5 ¼ In.	8.00
Bountiful, Bowl, Cereal, 6 In.	15.00
Bountiful, Cup & Saucer	11.00
Bountiful, Plate, Dinner, 10 ⅝ In.	33.00
Cafe Royal, Bonbon, Heart Shape	49.00
Cameo, Plate, Bread & Butter, 6 ⅜ In.	8.00
Cantata, Plate, Dinner, 10 ⅜ In.	13.00
Cantata, Soup, Dish, 6 In.	10.00
Cantata, Teapot, Lid, 4 ⅞ In.	25.00
Carmel, Cup & Saucer	8.00
Carmel, Plate, Dinner, 10 ½ In.	15.00
Carmel, Plate, Salad, 8 ¼ In.	12.00
Chestnut Weave, Plate, Dinner, 10 ⅝ In.	13.00
Cloud Nine, Creamer	10.00
Cloud Nine, Cup & Saucer	8.00
Cloud Nine, Plate, Bread & Butter, 6 ⅛ In.	5.00
Cloud Nine, Plate, Dinner, 10 ¼ In.	12.00
Coronado Aqua, Plate, Bread & Butter, 6 ⅜ In.	5.00
Creole, Plate, Dinner, 10 ¾ In.	13.00
Daisy, Coffeepot, Lid	40.00
Daisy, Plate, Bread & Butter, 6 ½ In.	4.00
Daisy, Relish, 12 In.	15.00
Dessert Rose, Baker, Rectangular, 9 x 13 ¾ In.	229.00
Dessert Rose, Baker, Square, 9 ½ In.	89.00
Dessert Rose, Bonbon	99.00
Dessert Rose, Candy Box, Heart Shape	169.00
Dessert Rose, Piggy Bank	329.00
Dessert Rose, Teapot, 4 Cup	89.00
Dogwood, Plate, Dinner, 10 ⅝ In.	15.00
Dogwood, Sugar, Cover	35.00
Encanto, Plate, Dinner, 10 ½ In.	17.00
Encanto, Soup, Dish, 7 ⅜ In.	21.00
English Rock Rose, Plate, Dinner, 10 ¾ In.	16.00
Fan Tan, Creamer	12.00
Fan Tan, Cup & Saucer	7.00
Floral, Bowl, Vegetable, Divided, 10 ⅜ In.	25.00
Fruit, Plate, Bread & Butter, 6 ⅝ In.	4.00
Fruit, Plate, Salad, 8 ⅜ In.	15.00
Fruit, Plate, Serving Bowl, 9 ⅜ In.	42.00
Heritage, Coffeepot, Lid	40.00
Heritage, Creamer	10.00
Larkspur, Bowl, Vegetable, 7 ½ In.	20.00
Larkspur, Creamer	15.00
Larkspur, Plate, Bread & Butter, 6 ½ In.	4.00
Malibu, Plate, Bread & Butter	6.00
Maytime, Bowl, Fruit, 5 In.	15.00
Maytime, Plate, Dinner, 10 ⅛ In.	12.00
Maytime, Platter, 13 ¼ In.	18.00
Merry-Go-Round, Platter, 13 In.	21.00
Mesa, Chop Plate, 13 ¼ In.	85.00
Mesa, Soup, Dish, 7 ⅜ In.	30.00
Montecito, Platter, 13 ¼ In.	55.00
Porofino, Bowl, Pasta, Flowers, Food & Wine Center, 11 ¾ In.	55.00

FRANKART INC., New York, New York, mass-produced nude "dancing lady" lamps, ashtrays, and other decorative Art Deco items in the 1920s and 1930s. They were made of white lead composition and spray-painted. *Frankart Inc.* and the patent number and year were stamped on the base.

Bookends, Bears, Playing, c.1920, 4 ½ x 5 ¾ In.	250.00
Bookends, Nude Girl, Kneeling, 1920s, 5 x 3 x 3 In.	150.00
Clock, 2 Nude Women, Metal, Turquoise Paint, Arched Dial, 8 ½ In.	113.00
Lamp, Figure, Kneeling, Holding Flame Globe, Electrified, c.1920, 20 x 5 x 6 In., Pair	6000.00

FRANKOMA POTTERY was originally known as The Frank Potteries when John F. Frank opened shop in 1933. The factory is now working in Sapulpa, Oklahoma. Early wares were made from a light cream-colored clay from Ada, Oklahoma, but in 1956 the company switched to a red clay from Sapulpa. The firm made dinnerware, utilitarian and decorative kitchenwares, figurines, flowerpots, and limited edition and commemorative pieces. John Frank died in 1973 and his daughter, Joniece, inherited the business. Frankoma went bankrupt in 1990. The pottery operated under various owners for a few years and was bought by Joe Ragosta in 2008. It closed in 2010. The buildings, assets, name, and molds were sold at an auction in 2011.

Baker, Lazybones, Brown Satin, Whimsical Shape, 2 Qt.	30.00
Bean Pot, Plainsman, Woodland Moss, 1 ½ Qt.	45.00
Bookends, Charger Horse, Onyx Glaze, Ada Clay, 6 ¼ x 5 ¾ In.	130.00
Bookends, Dreamer Girl, Sorghum Glaze, c.1950, 5 ½ x 5 ½ In.	283.00
Bookends, Weeping Lady, Bronze Green Glaze, Marked, c.1938, 5 ½ x 5 ½ In.	226.00
Bowl, Desert Rose Glaze, Ball Shape, Ring Handles, Marked, 1940s, 5 ¾ x 5 ¼ In.	283.00
Bowl, Indian Bowl Maker, Coffee Glaze, Marked, 1973-93, 6 ½ x 5 ½ In.	198.00
Bowl, Vegetable, Divided, Wagon Wheel, Desert Gold, 13 ½ In.	35.00
Butter, Mayan Aztec, Marked, c.1960	40.00
Coffeepot, Lid, Blue, Green, 7 ¾ x 7 ¼ In.	30.00
Figurine, Flower Girl, Holding Pot, Green Glaze, Ada Clay, 5 ¾ x 2 ½ In.	162.00
Figurine, Greyhound, Running, Light Gray Glaze, 4 x 14 ½ In.	119.00
Figurine, Hunting Dog, Cream & Brown Glaze, 5 ½ x 7 ¾ In.	49.00
Figurine, Panther, Pacing, Pink Cream Glaze, Rectangular Base, 4 ¾ x 12 ½ In.	783.00
Figurine, Panther, Reclining, Onyx Glaze, 4 x 9 x 6 In.	22.00 to 46.00
Honey Pot, Plainsman, Prairie Green	15.00
Humidor, Cover, Scroll Band, Green Glaze, Globular, Tapered, Frank Potteries, 6 In.	1134.00
Planter, Ribbed Foot, Brown Trim, 8 x 5 x 4 In.	32.00
Plate, Bread & Butter, Blue, Green, 5 ¾ In.	5.00
Plate, Christmas, Laid In A Manger, 1969, 8 In.	33.00
Plate, Dessert, Blue, Green, 6 ¾ In.	6.00
Plate, Dinner, Blue, Green, 9 ¾ In.	7.00
Platter, Plainsman, Desert Gold, 11 ¼ In.	28.00
Trivet, Arrows To Atoms, c.1957, 6 In.	45.00
Trivet, Cantex, Roman, Laying Tiles, 6 In.	38.00
Trivet, Cherokee, Alphabet, Round, 6 In.	24.00
Trivet, Horseshoes, Brown, 6 ¼ In.	28.00
Trivet, Sooner State, Oklahoma, Prairie Green Glaze, Indian Shield, Round, 6 ½ In.	15.00
Vase, Dimpled, Peach, Marked, 5 x 5 In.	30.00
Vase, Fanned Top, Blue Gray Glaze, Marked, 7 x 8 In.	40.00
Vase, Hexagonal, Swirl, Marked, 3 x 5 In.	32.00
Vase, Prairie Green Glaze, Tapered, Bulbous Draped Base, Scalloped Rim, Ada Clay, 6 In.	81.00
Vase, Prairie Green, Oval, Concentric Rings, Pacing Leopard Mark, 4 x 3 ¼ In.	324.00
Vase, Squat, Verde Bronze Glaze, Marked, c.1933, 4 x 8 In.	3164.00
Warming Stand, Lazybones	35.00

FRATERNAL objects that are related to the many different fraternal organizations in the United States are listed in this category. The Elks, Masons, Odd Fellows, and others are included. Also included are service organizations, like the American Legion, Kiwanis, and Lions Club. Furniture is listed in the Furniture category. Shaving mugs decorated with fraternal crests are included in the Shaving Mug category.

Eagles, Flask, F.O.E., Eagle Shape, Beige, Weller, 5 ½ In.	76.00
Eagles, Tumbler, Lodge 1758, Waynesboro, Clear, Red, Libbey, 5 In.	6.00
Eastern Star, Pin, Josepha, Star, Enamel, Diamond, Scimitar, Crescent, Gavel, Gold, 2 In.	162.00
Eastern Star, Ring, Red Stone, Woman's, 10K Gold, Size 7 ¾ In.	85.00
Elks, Badge, West Virginia Reunion, Emblem, Enamel, 1912, 2 In.	50.00
Elks, Chair, Lodge, Leather & Carved Back, Elk Clock, Black Leather Seat, 33 x 25 In.	192.00
Elks, Vase, Presentation, Standing Elk, Trees, Albany Slip Glaze, Ohio, c.1907, 17 ½ In.	460.00
Improved Order Of Red Men, Diploma, Joseph Adams, Frame, c.1905, 21 x 27 In.	220.00
Knights Of Columbus, Badge, Cedar Point Picnic, 1946, 2 x 6 In.	20.00
Knights Of Columbus, Ring, Center Diamond, 14K Gold	446.00
Knights Of Pythias, Picture, Home, Springfield, Ohio, Oil, Canvas, J.E. Burks, c.1921, 36 x 55 In.	176.00
Knights Templar, Button, Convention, Welcome To Pittsburgh, W&H, 1898, 2 ⅛ In. ....*illus*	98.00
Lions Club, Sign, International, Pressed Composition, Embossed, Patina, 18 x 18 In. ....*illus*	132.00
Loyal Order Of Moose, Pitcher, 29th Annual Convention, Glass, 1917, 4 In.	25.00
Masonic, Apron, Winged Man, Woman, Vines, Symbols, Fringe, Silk, Painted, 17 x 18 In.	273.00
Masonic, Badge, Cross, Applied Emblems, Motto, St. George Commandery, 1922, 2 In.	81.00

Folk Art, Clown, Painted, Carved, Walking Charlie, c.1925, 75 In.
$518.00

James D. Julia Inc.

Folk Art, Owl, Carved, Wood Grain, Painted Feathers, Glass Eyes, Iron Beak, Stand, c.1930, 24 In.
$1422.00

Skinner, Inc.

Folk Art, Wedding Globe, Blown Glass, Cushion, Ormolu Leaves, Mirrors, France, c.1890, 16 In.
$285.00

Theriault's

Folk Art, Whimsy, Mahogany, Scroll Cut, Basket, Tulips, Birds, Gold Paint, c.1875, 13 x 13 In. $2350.00

Garth's Auctions, Inc.

Folk Art, Whirligig, Man, Beard, Hat, Carved, Painted, Wood, c.1810, 22 In. $2070.00

Cottone Auctions

Fraternal, Knights Templar, Button, Convention, Welcome To Pittsburgh, W&H, 1898, 2 ⅛ In. $98.00

Hake's Americana & Collectibles

Masonic, Button, Freemason, Metal, 1800s	12.00
Masonic, Flask, Green, Blown, Eagle On Reverse, 7 ¼ In.	711.00
Masonic, Jug, Cream Glaze, Inscribed In Gold, Handle, Symbols, England, 1809, 8 In.	1652.00
Masonic, Lapel Pin, Blue Enamel, Melee, 14K White Gold, Screwback	118.00
Masonic, Lodge Columns, Carved, Globe Topped Capital, Symbols, c.1900, 115 In., Pair	358.00
Masonic, Pin, Pentacle, Enameled, Inset Diamond, Gavel, Chain, c.1920, ¾ In.	43.00
Masonic, Ring, 10K Gold, Enamel Symbols, Star, Sword, Fez, Size 9	184.00
Masonic, Ring, Black Tablet, Inset Symbols, Sword, Crescent, Star, Gold, Chevron Mount	97.00
Masonic, Stick, Lumber Measuring, Emblems, Marked C.E. Dow, 43 ½ In.	184.00
Masonic, Tie Bar, Gold Tone, Emblem, Anson, c.1950, 1 ½ In.	15.00
Masonic, Uniform, Encampment, Wool Coat, Sleeve Patches, Pants, Badges, c.1930	238.00
Modern Woodmen Of The World, Plate, Green, Buffalo Pottery, c.1911, 7 ½ In.	78.00
Odd Fellows, Apron & Collar, Fringe, Embroidered Symbols, Orion Lodge 408, Reamstown, Penn.	178.00
Odd Fellows, Ax, Carved, Wood, Heart In Hand On Blade, c.1910, 30 In.	294.00
Odd Fellows, Banner, Parade, Cocalico Lodge 498, Adamstown, Penn.	356.00
Odd Fellows, Carving, Heart In Hand, Pine, Base, c.1875, 6 ¼ In.	529.00
Odd Fellows, Display Case, Oak, Inscribed Stony Fork Lodge No. 564, Penn., 36 ¾ x 24 In.	122.00
Odd Fellows, Minutes Ledger, I.O.O.F. Encampment No. 49, Greenfield, Indiana, 1856-92, 14 x 9 In.	144.00
Odd Fellows, Parade Staff, Heart-In-Hand, Carved, Gold Paint, 1800s, 70 In.	1215.00
Odd Fellows, Plaque, Ten Commandments, Hebrew, Wood, c.1890, 21 ¾ x 15 ¾ In. ....*illus*	783.00
Odd Fellows, Ritual Accoutrement, Model Of Ark Of The Covenant, Wood, 13 x 54 In.	130.00
Odd Fellows, Wood Ax, All-Seeing Eye, Scales, Heart-In-Hand Symbol, c.1900, 36 In.	518.00
Shriners, Champagne, Clear, Carnival Glass, Louisville, Ky., 1909	65.00
Shriners, Champagne, Clear, Carnival Glass, New Orleans, 1910	25.00
Shriners, Champagne, Clear, Carnival Glass, Rochester, N.Y., 1911	85.00

FRY GLASS was made by the H.C. Fry Glass Company of Rochester, Pennsylvania. The company, founded in 1901, first made cut glass and other types of fine glasswares. In 1922 it patented a heat-resistant glass called Pearl Ovenglass. For two years, 1926–1927, the company made Fry Foval, an opal ware decorated with colored trim. Reproductions of this glass have been made. Depression glass patterns made by Fry may be listed in the Depression Glass category. Some pieces of cut glass may also be included in the Cut Glass category.

FRY GLASS

Bean Pot, Opalescent, Qt.	128.00
Bowl, Ferner, Cut Flowers, Vines, Footed, Marked, 7 ¾ x 4 ½ In.	65.00
Bowl, Fruit, Royal Blue, Footed, Swirl Connector, 6 In.	300.00
Bowl, Sunbeam Pattern, Stars, Amorphic Shape, Lobed, 14 x 7 ½ In.	895.00
Candlestick, Turquoise, 12 ¾ In.	20.00
Casserole, Cover, Metal Frame & Handles, 1920s, 8 x 5 In.	75.00
Pitcher, Gray, Clear, Star Cut Base, c.1925, 11 In.	75.00
Pitcher, Swags, Etched, Clear, 7 ½ In.	26.00
Platter, Meat, Pearl Opalescent, 1920s, 12 ½ x 17 In.	65.00
Reamer, Pink, Paneled, Flat Open Handle, 6 x 2 In.	85.00
Tumbler, Clear, Black Petal Foot, c.1920, 3 x 2 ¼ In.	8.00
Vase, Albert Pattern, Clear, 10 In.	55.00
Vase, Diamond Optic, Green Threading, 9 ¼ x 6 In.	350.00
Vase, Green Transparent Base, 8 x 12 In.	425.00
Vase, Ribbed & Scalloped Rim, Green Threading, Bubbles, 6 x 7 ½ In.	375.00

FRY FOVAL

Bowl, Fruit, Ribbed Pearl Opalescent, Opaque Jade Foot, 12 x 7 ½ In.	325.00
Compote, Opalescent Milk Glass, Hand Blown, Green Stem & Foot, c.1925, 7 x 5 ½ In.	185.00
Vase, Pearl Blue, Shouldered, Flared Flat Rim, 5 ¼ In.	240.00

FULPER POTTERY COMPANY was incorporated in 1899 in Flemington, New Jersey. It made art pottery from 1909 to 1929. The firm had been making bottles, jugs, and housewares from 1805. Doll heads were made about 1928. The firm became Stangl Pottery in 1929. Stangl Pottery is listed in its own category in this book.

Basket, Green To Rose, Flambe Glaze, Handle, 6 x 9 In.	175.00
Bowl, Arts & Crafts, Green, Black, Marked, 8 x 2 In.	67.00
Bowl, Bulbous Ribbed Side, Mottled Blue Glaze, Green & Ivory Highlights, Shaped Rim, 4 x 14 In.	115.00
Bowl, Lotus, Blue Crystalline Glaze, Footed, Paper Label, 6 ½ x 11 ¼ In.	124.00
Bowl, Scalloped Rim, Vertical Ribbing Blue, Green Rim, Overglaze, Stamp, 9 ¼ In.	24.00
Candleholder, Green, Blue, Angled Handle, Arts & Crafts, 2 ¼ In., Pair	58.00
Candleholder, Multicolor, 4 ¾ x 1 ¼ In., Pair	34.00
Candlestick, Green Mottled Glaze, Flared Foot, Rim, Marked, c.1979, 9 ¾ In., Pair	380.00

F

Candlestick, Leopard Skin Glaze, Green, Crystals, Spread Foot, Cylindrical, 9 ¾ In., Pair.......	83.00
Candlestick, Yellow Glaze, Blue Gloss Overglaze, Marked, 8 ¾ In., Pair..................................	161.00
Compote, Blue & Tan Glaze, Figural Supports, Signed, 10 ½ x 7 ½ In....................................	540.00
Crock, Shaped Collar, Hog Ear Handles, Bird, Cobalt Blue, 11 ¾ In.	181.00
Doll's Head, Bisque, Blue Tin Sleep Eyes, Painted Features, Toddler Body, Sailor Suit, c.1917, 18 In.	855.00
Ewer, Squat, Loop Handle, Gloopy Green To Black Matte Glaze, 5 In..	259.00
Figurine, Female Nude, Turquoise Crystalline Glaze, Ebony Pedestal, 32 ½ x 8 In.	992.00
Humidor, Cover, Oatmeal Glaze, Bulbous, Round Foot, 4 In.	173.00
Jug, Green, Red Flambe Glaze, Stamped, 10 ¼ x 5 ¼ In.	310.00
Pitcher, Green, Over Purple, Marked, 4 In.	45.00
Pitcher, Mottled Green Glaze, 1920s, 4 In..	152.00
Teapot, Green Matte Glaze, Flared, Marked, 6 ½ x 10 ½ In.	106.00
Urn, 2 Handles, Hammered, Black Glaze, Marked, 12 x 11 In.	930.00
Urn, Chinese Blue Flambe, High Scrolled Handles, 15 x 7 ½ In.	744.00
Urn, Copper Dust Crystalline & Mirror Black Glaze, High Scrolled Handles, 15 x 7 ½ In..........	1612.00
Urn, Green & Amber Glaze, Beige Handles, 11 x 8 In.	1054.00
Urn, Hammered, Leopard Skin Crystalline Glaze, 2 Handles, Marked, 12 x 9 In. ....*illus*	930.00
Vase, Amber Glaze, Handles, 7 x 7 In..	215.00
Vase, Baluster, Frothy Blue & Green Glaze, Incised, 13 ¾ x 6 In.	992.00
Vase, Baluster, Green, Blue Glaze, 17 x 9 ½ In.	372.00
Vase, Baluster, Light Green, Crystals, Marked, 12 In.	127.00
Vase, Baluster, Mirror Black To Tan Glaze, 16 ½ x 9 In.	1984.00
Vase, Blue Glaze, 3 Shoulder Handles, 6 ¾ In.	101.00
Vase, Blue, Brown, Green Flambe Glaze, 3 Handles, Marked, 5 x 6 ½ In.	240.00
Vase, Bottle Shape, Cream Over Blue Matte Glaze, White Drips, 2 Handles, 11 In.	690.00
Vase, Bottle Shape, Dragon Around Neck, Cat's-Eye Flambe Glaze, 8 In.	1725.00
Vase, Bottleneck, Deep Green Drip Glaze, 8 In.	2645.00
Vase, Bud, 6-Sided, Blue Over Brown Glaze, Spread Foot, Striping Design, 6 ¾ In...................	219.00
Vase, Bud, Square, Shaped Square Foot, Cream, Pink, Striping, Famille Rose, Marked, 8 ½ In.	115.00
Vase, Bulbous, 2 Handles, Footed, Blue, 12 ¼ In.	649.00
Vase, Bulbous, Blue Flambe Drip, Tan Matte Glaze, 5 x 8 ½ In.	330.00
Vase, Bulbous, Flambe Glaze, Multicolor, Marked, 8 x 7 ½ In.	330.00
Vase, Bulbous, Flared, Mottled Blue, Green Glaze, Marked, 15 ½ In.	213.00
Vase, Bulbous, Gloppy Green Matte Glaze, 5 ¼ In.	288.00
Vase, Bulbous, Gray Over Tan, Cream Flambe Glaze, 2 Handles, 7 ¾ In..................................	219.00
Vase, Bulbous, Long Neck, Blue, Charcoal Matte Glaze, Impressed Marked, 5 ½ x 7 ¾ In.	480.00
Vase, Bulbous, Squat, Blue Crystalline Glaze Over Ivory, Round Foot, 3 Handles, 6 x 8 In........	115.00
Vase, Bulbous, Turquoise & Green Glaze, 3 Handles, Round Foot, 6 ½ In.	46.00
Vase, Bulbous, Yellow, Brown Flambe, Marked, 6 x 9 ½ In.	385.00
Vase, Buttress Shape, Blue Snowflake Crystals, Green Accents, Marked, 8 ⅜ In.	489.00
Vase, Cylindrical, Cucumber Green Glaze, Marked, 8 In.	259.00
Vase, Cylindrical, Flemington Green, Marked Remington, 10 ½ In.	167.00
Vase, Cylindrical, Green, Leopard Skin Crystalline Glaze, 15 ¾ x 5 ½ In...............................	1736.00
Vase, Cylindrical, Shouldered, Rolled Lip, Blue Flambe Glaze Over Cream, Marked, 16 In.	460.00
Vase, Elongated Oval, Chinese Blue Flame Glaze, Dripped, Amber & White, 10 In.	489.00
Vase, Elongated Oval, Round Foot, Ring Handles, Blue Crystals, Coffee Color Ground, 13 In...	288.00
Vase, Flared Base, Blue, Over White Crystalline Glaze, Marked, c.1920, 6 ½ In.	81.00
Vase, Flared Neck, Chinese Blue Flambe Glaze, Incised Mark, 15 ¼ x 7 In..............................	620.00
Vase, Flared, Copper Dust Crystalline Glaze, 11 ¼ x 8 ¼ In.	11160.00
Vase, Flared, Stepped & Fluted Rim, Leaves On Branch, Blue Glaze, Footed, Art Deco, 12 In. ...	216.00
Vase, Globular, Leopard Skin Crystalline Glaze, 2 Handles, Shaped Neck, Green, 3 ¾ In.	316.00
Vase, Globular, Mirrored Green, 2 Handles, Dripped Over Mottled Black, Rust, 8 In................	805.00
Vase, Gloppy Volcanic Glaze, Black & Green, Pear Shape, Marked, 12 ⅜ In.	4715.00
Vase, Grecian Style, 2 Handles, Flared Lip, Cobalt Blue Gloss, Crystalline Matte, 11 In.	345.00
Vase, Green, Blue Glaze, 2 Handles, Stamped, 4 ¾ x 5 ¾ In.	259.00
Vase, Ivory Crystalline Glaze, 12 ½ x 6 In.	496.00
Vase, Melon Shape, Green Matte Glaze, Marked, c.1900, 14 x 11 In.	316.00
Vase, Mirror Black Glaze, 2 Handles, Marked, 8 ½ x 9 In...	900.00
Vase, Mottled Blue Black Drip Over Wisteria Glaze, Handles, Marked, 10 ⅞ In. ....*illus*	748.00
Vase, Mottled Green Crystalline Glaze, Marked, 7 x 7 ½ In.	468.00
Vase, Multicolor Green Crystalline Glaze, Impressed Mark, 7 x 7 ½ In.	510.00
Vase, Narrow Neck, Brown & Green, Drip Glaze, Signed, Paper Label, 8 x 11 ½ In...................	660.00
Vase, Pear Shape, Elephant Head Handles, Caramel Over Brown Flambe Glaze, 5 In.	374.00
Vase, Pear Shape, Gloppy Oatmeal, 2 Handles, Flared Rim, Rust, Black, 12 In.	460.00
Vase, Rose & Tan, Vertical Striations, Handles, Marked, 7 ⅞ In. ....*illus*	460.00
Vase, Rose, Brown Matte Glaze, Marked, 12 In.	168.00

Fraternal, Lions Club, Sign, International, Pressed Composition, Embossed, Patina, 18 x 18 In.
$132.00

Wm Morford Antiques

Fraternal, Odd Fellows, Plaque, Ten Commandments, Hebrew, Wood, c.1890, 21 ¾ x 15 ¾ In.
$783.00

Garth's Auctions, Inc.

Fulper, Urn, Hammered, Leopard Skin Crystalline Glaze, 2 Handles, Marked, 12 x 9 In.
$930.00

Rago Arts & Auction Center

Fulper, Vase, Mottled Blue Black Drip Over Wisteria Glaze, Handles, Marked, 10 ⅞ In.
$748.00

Humler & Nolan

Fulper, Vase, Rose & Tan, Vertical Striations, Handles, Marked, 7 ⅞ In. $460.00

Humler & Nolan

Furniture, Armoire, Empire Style, Satinwood, Ormolu Mounts, 2 Doors, Lower Panel, 93 x 51 In. $922.00

New Orleans Auction Galleries, Inc.

Furniture, Armoire, French Provincial, Fruitwood, Carved, Shelves & Drawers, c.1900, 93 ½ In. $4148.00

Skinner, Inc.

Vase, Shoulder Handles, Green Matte Glaze, Impressed Mark, 6 x 10 ¼ In.	275.00
Vase, Shoulder Handles, Green Multitone Matte Glaze, Impressed Mark, 6 x 10 ¼ In.	300.00
Vase, Shouldered, Speckled Brown Matte Glaze, 11 ½ In.	84.00
Vase, Small Handles, Light Green Crystalline Glaze, Marked, 12 In.	157.00
Vase, Squat, Green, High Shoulder, 6 In.	489.00
Vase, Tan, Cream, Crystalline Glaze, Marked, 7 x 11 ¾ In.	330.00
Vase, Tapered Cylinder, Colonial Revival, Splotchy Green & Black, Brown, Ribbed, 10 In.	690.00
Vase, Tapered Cylinder, Pinched Neck, Gloppy Cream, Tan & Blue Flambe Glaze, 9 ¾ In.	345.00
Vase, Tapered, Copper Dust Crystalline & Mirror Black Flambe, Marked, 13 x 7 ½ In.	1488.00
Vase, Tapered, Round Foot, Leopard Skin Crystalline, Green, Swollen Shoulder, Narrow Neck, 12 In.	138.00
Vase, Urn Shape, Mirrored Black, Gray Glaze, 2 Loop Handles At Rim, Crystals, 6 ⅝ In.	173.00
Wall Pocket, Corner, Molded Fruit, Green Matte Glaze, 10 In.	73.00 to 95.00
Wall Pocket, Geometric Design, Crystalline Blue, Marked, 7 ½ In.	123.00
Water Cooler, Keg, Cobalt Blue Bird, Horizontal Rings, Bung Hole, Flemington, N.J., 13 ¼ In.	201.00

FURNITURE of all types is listed in this category. Examples dating from the seventeenth century to the 1970s are included. Prices for furniture vary in different parts of the country. Oak furniture is most expensive in the West; large pieces over eight feet high are sold for the most money in the South, where high ceilings are found in the old homes. Condition is very important when determining prices. These are NOT average prices but rather reports of unique sales. If the description includes the word *style,* the piece resembles the old furniture style but was made at a later time. It is not a period piece. Garden furniture is listed in the Garden Furnishings category. Related items may be found in the Architectural, Brass, and Store categories.

Altar, Anglo-Indian, Teak, Scalloped Pierced Apron, Drawer, Fluted Legs, 40 x 27 In.	480.00
Armchairs are listed under Chair in this category.	
Armoire, 2 Doors, Carved Panels, Flowers, Swag, Fitted Interior, 83 x 57 In.	748.00
Armoire, Art Deco, Macassar Ebony, Oak, Banded, Angled, Door, c.1920, 74 x 46 In.	1995.00
Armoire, Bamboo, Wire Mesh Caged Door, Shelves, Bamboo Shoot Trim, 85 x 40 In.	390.00
Armoire, Baroque, Walnut, Arched Cornice, Arched Doors, Scrolling, 19 x 17 In.	1664.00
Armoire, Burl Walnut, Carved Double Panel Doors, Venice, Italy, 84 x 74 In.	427.00
Armoire, Carved Crest, Column Sides, 2 Mirror Doors, Fitted Interior, 95 x 57 In.	1150.00
Armoire, Cherry, Arched Cornice, Carved Bird, 2 Paneled Doors, France, 92 x 53 In.	1364.00
Armoire, Cypress, 2 Doors, Raised Beveled Panels, 2 Drawers, c.1900, 87 x 49 In.	308.00
Armoire, Edwardian, Mahogany, Dentil Molding, 2 Paneled Doors, Drawer, 77 x 51 In.	400.00
Armoire, Empire Style, Satinwood, Ormolu Mounts, 2 Doors, Lower Panel, 93 x 51 In. ..*illus*	922.00
Armoire, French Provincial, Fruitwood, Carved, Shelves & Drawers, c.1900, 93 ½ In. ..*illus*	4148.00
Armoire, French Provincial, Mahogany, Stepped Cornice, 2 Glass Doors, 83 x 57 In.	688.00
Armoire, French Provincial, Oak, 2 Doors, Beveled Panels, Block Feet, 1700s, 89 x 56 In.	720.00
Armoire, French Provincial, Oak, 2 Doors, Shaped Panels, Bun Feet, 82 x 63 In.	800.00
Armoire, French Provincial, Oak, Carved Crest, Paneled Doors, Shelves, c.1900, 82 x 16 In.	1004.00
Armoire, French Provincial, Oak, Molded Cornice, 2 Doors, Block Feet, c.1850, 81 x 56 In.	1168.00
Armoire, French Provincial, Oak, Molded Cornice, 2 Paneled Doors, Flat Ball Feet, 84 x 60 In.	992.00
Armoire, French Provincial, Pine, Carved, Arched, Scrolled Crest, Paneled Doors, c.1820, 92 x 52 In.	2151.00
Armoire, Fruitwood, 2 Shaped Paneled Doors, 2 Drawers, 71 x 55 In.	119.00
Armoire, Fruitwood, Shaped Panel Doors, Fitted Interior, 1700s, 80 x 51 In.	1793.00
Armoire, Henry II Style, Beaded Crest, 2 Beveled Mirrors, Columns, 89 x 53 x 22 In.	366.00
Armoire, Henry II Style, Walnut, Arched Mirror Door, Urn Finials, Low Drawer, 98 x 46 In.	397.00
Armoire, Henry II Style, Walnut, Carved, Flat Dentil Top, 2 Glass Doors, Low Drawer, 84 x 52 In.	549.00
Armoire, Henry II, Rosewood, Arched Crest, Finials, Mirror Door, Drawer, 1800s, 99 x 46 In.	1159.00
Armoire, Louis Philippe, Rosewood, Beveled Mirror Door, Low Drawer, 103 x 49 In.	976.00
Armoire, Louis XIII, Pin & Barrel Hinges, Hewn Paneled Back, Painted, c.1775, 59 In.	21375.00
Armoire, Louis XIII, Shelves, Painted, Panel Doors, 63 In.	16312.00
Armoire, Louis XIV, Oak, 2 Doors, Carved, Figures, Block Feet, 1700s, 91 x 65 In.	900.00
Armoire, Louis XV Style, Oak, Carved, 2 Shaped Mirror Doors, c.1790, 91 x 55 In.	1708.00
Armoire, Louis XV Style, Walnut, 2 Doors, Shaped Crest, Paneled, 1700s, 112 x 64 In.	3660.00
Armoire, Louis XV Style, Walnut, Mirrored Doors, Flowers, Leaves, France, 1700s, 98 x 57 In.	1140.00
Armoire, Louis XV, 2 Panel Doors, Carved, 1700s, 94 x 62 In.	2074.00
Armoire, Louis XV, Fruitwood, 2 Panel Doors, Carved, Shaped Apron, 1700s, 88 x 57 In.	1315.00
Armoire, Louis XV, Oak, 2 Doors, Shaped Apron, Carved, 84 x 44 In.	793.00
Armoire, Louis XV, Oak, Drawer, Mirror Door, Peaked Crest, Carved, 98 x 41 In.	732.00
Armoire, Louis XV, Rosewood, 3 Mirrors, Bronze Gilt Mounts, 1800s, 96 x 63 In.	2745.00
Armoire, Louis XV, Walnut, 2 Mirror Doors, Scrolled Openwork Crest, 1800s, 106 x 55 In.	427.00
Armoire, Louis XV, Walnut, 2 Mirror Doors, Shaped, Carved, 98 x 54 In.	488.00
Armoire, Louis XV, Walnut, 3 Doors, Arched Mirror, Mother-Of-Pearl Inlay, 94 x 66 In.	360.00
Armoire, Louis XV, Walnut, 3 Mirror Doors, Carved, Leaves, 101 x 87 In.	480.00
Armoire, Louis XV, Walnut, 3 Mirror Doors, Shaped, Carved Crest, 99 x 66 In.	580.00

FURNITURE

Armoire, Louis XV, Walnut, Mirror Door, Carved Arched Crest, 96 x 41 In.	549.00
Armoire, Louis XVI Style, Walnut, 2 Mirror Doors, Arched, Carved Crest, 97 x 55 In.	427.00
Armoire, Louis XVI Style, Walnut, Carved, Arched Cornice, Paneled Doors, 100 x 76 In.	2390.00
Armoire, Louis XVI, Oak, 2 Doors, Carved Flower Baskets, 91 x 60 In.	366.00
Armoire, Mahogany, 2 Beveled Paneled Doors, 2 Drawers, American, 1800s, 91 x 62 In.	300.00
Armoire, Mahogany, 2-Panel Doors, Reeded, Stepped Cornice, Italy, 78 x 54 In.	625.00
Armoire, Mahogany, Brass & Leather Insets, 2 Doors, 3 Drawers, Grosfeld House, 62 x 36 In. .	620.00
Armoire, Mahogany, Flared & Molded Cornice, Ogee Case & Door, Drawer, c.1850, 101 x 58 In.	4674.00
Armoire, Mahogany, Flared Cornice, Paneled Doors, 2 Low Drawers, c.1820, 97 x 69 In.	2390.00
Armoire, Mahogany, Flared Cornice, Paneled Doors, Columns, Drum Feet, c.1840, 82 x 63 In. .	7170.00
Armoire, Mahogany, Molded Cornice, 2 Carved Panel Doors, Shaped Skirt, France, 83 x 53 In.	1830.00
Armoire, Mahogany, Molded Cornice, 2 Paneled Doors, Scalloped Skirt, c.1800, 85 x 58 In.	5378.00
Armoire, Mahogany, Ogee Cornice, 2 Paneled Doors, Ripple Moldings, c.1830, 89 x 66 In.	1434.00
Armoire, Mahogany, Panel Door, Gilt Columns, Leaf Feet, Carved, New York, c.1850, 79 x 39 In.	1912.00
Armoire, Mahogany, Paneled Doors, Ogee Molding, New Orleans, c.1835, 94 x 71 In.	3705.00
Armoire, Mahogany, Reeded Cornice, Doors, Leaf Carved Paw Feet, 1820, 84 x 60 In.	1107.00
Armoire, Mirror Door, 2 Carved Doors, Low Drawer, France, c.1890, 97 x 89 In.	793.00
Armoire, Mixed Wood, Marquetry, Stepped Cornice, 2 Doors, Drawers, 68 x 41 In.	580.00
Armoire, Neoclassical, Reeded Posts, Dentil Cornice, Painted, c.1800, 75 In.	28125.00
Armoire, Normandy Style, Oak, 2 Doors, 2 Lower Drawers, Scroll, 1700s, 93 x 70 In.	1920.00
Armoire, Oak, 3 Mirrors, 3 Doors, Shaped Cornice, Carved, 87 x 55 In.	518.00
Armoire, Ogee Molded Cornice, Paneled Doors, Shelves, Bracket Feet, 95 x 70 In.	1912.00
Armoire, Pine, Domed, Ebonized Accents, Paneled Doors, Drawers, Denmark, 89 x 81 In.	2337.00
Armoire, Pine, Faux Bamboo, Arched, 2 Panel Doors, 2 Drawers, c.1890, 96 x 60 In.	837.00
Armoire, Pine, Paint, Rectangular Top, 2 Paneled Doors, Flowers, Ball Feet, 75 x 50 In.	310.00
Armoire, Purpleheart, Mahogany, Molded Cornice, Doors, West Indies, c.1810, 67 x 48 In.	4183.00
Armoire, Renaissance Revival, 4 Doors, Triangle Arch, Leaves, Mirror, c.1865, 124 x 104 In. ...	5904.00
Armoire, Renaissance Revival, Mixed Wood, 2 Panel Doors, Twist Columns, 1700s, 94 x 73 In.	956.00
Armoire, Renaissance Revival, Walnut, Arched Cornice, Mirrored Doors, c.1850, 104 x 74 In. ..	1076.00
Armoire, Renaissance Style, Walnut, Gallery Top, Glazed Doors, Columns, 86 x 65 In.	1500.00
Armoire, Rococo Revival, Mahogany, Bonnet Top, Mirror Door, Drawers, 1850s, 111 x 56 In. ..	5900.00
Armoire, Rococo, Mixed Wood, 2 Carved Doors, c.1860, 101 x 64 In.	575.00
Armoire, Rosewood, Flower-Carved Crest, Finials, 2 Mirror Doors, Drawer, c.1850, 121 x 67 In.	10158.00
Armoire, Rosewood, Molded Cornice, Mirror Door, Drawers, Flower Roundels, c.1835, 97 x 103 In.	3444.00
Armoire, Scrolled Shaped Crest, Panel Doors, Divided Interior, Scroll Feet, 87 x 55 In.	984.00
Armoire, Victorian, Bamboo, Door, Lower Drawer, Caged Gallery Crest, 77 x 38 In.	219.00
Armoire, Victorian, Ebonized, Side By Side, Center Storage, Carved Shells, c.1880, 89 x 73 In.	978.00
Armoire, Victorian, Walnut, Carved, Marquetry, Glass Insets, Mirror Door, 4 Drawers, 91 x 53 In.	366.00
Armoire, Walnut, 2 Doors, Raised Panels, Relief Carved, 4 Shelves, Lock, 1700s, 115 x 78 In. ... *illus*	1955.00
Armoire, Walnut, Carved Cornice, 2 Shaped Doors, Shell Carved, France, 1700s, 115 x 78 In. .	1950.00
Armoire, Walnut, Carved Crest Over Mirrored Door, Cabinet Door, 3 Drawers, France, 90 x 59 In.	690.00
Armoire, Walnut, Carved Crest, Shaped Top, Door, Bottom Drawer, Gray Paint, 1900s, 95 x 50 In.	2700.00
Armoire, Walnut, Cypress, Flared Cornice, 2 Paneled Doors, Bracket Feet, c.1850, 108 x 78 In.	4183.00
Armoire, Walnut, Molded Ogee Cornice, 2 Arched Paneled Doors, Bracket Feet, 90 x 66 In.	1220.00
Armoire, Walnut, Scroll Carved, Door, Low Drawer, 88 x 47 In., 1800s	732.00
Armoire, Widdicomb, French Provincial Style, Walnut, Bonnet, Paneled Doors, 79 x 44 In.	359.00
Backbar, Walnut, Marble Top, Carved Crest, Columns, 2 Drawers, 2 Doors, Shelf, 96 x 50 In. .	1265.00
Banquette, Louis XV Style, Carved, Floral Needlepoint Top, 6 Cabriole Legs, 20 x 34 In.	413.00
Banquette, Louis XV Style, Walnut, Tufted Upholstery, Carved Rails, Scroll Feet, 15 x 68 In.	468.00
Bar Cart, Metal Basket Weave, 2 Tiers, Pierced Gallery, X-Stretcher, Wheels, c.1956, 27 x 34 In.	2250.00
Bar, Bamboo, Shaped Wood Top, Foot Rest, Fitted Back, 46 In.	354.00
Bar, Ebonized, Marble Top, Chinoiserie Panel, Figures, Pagoda Shape, c.1940, 44 x 84 In.	923.00
Bar, Teak, Laminate, 2 Sliding Doors, 3 Shelves, Casters, Verstergaard Jensen, 29 x 35 In.	533.00
Bed Steps, Mahogany, Tooled Leather Treads, Turned Rails, Legs, 29 x 17 In.	1016.00
Bed Steps, Poplar, Black Paint, 1800s, 18 x 14 In.	411.00
Bed Steps, Regency, Mahogany, 2 Hinged Steps, Chamber Pot, c.1850, 27 x 18 In. .... *illus*	1098.00
Bed Steps, William IV, Mahogany, 3 Steps, Red Leather Insert, Chamber Pot, 28 x 20 In.	800.00
Bed Steps, William IV, Mahogany, Hinged Treads, Pullout Drawer, Turned Feet, 24 x 19 In., Pair	1434.00
Bed Steps, Yellow Pine, 3 Supports, 62 x 41 In.	176.00
Bed, Art Deco, Brass, Ornate Headboard & Footboard Panels, c.1930, 43 ½ x 56 In.	738.00
Bed, Brass, Hammered Medallions On Head & Foot, Twisted Spindles, 1890s, 56 x 54 In.	3500.00
Bed, Brass, Iron Rails, c.1890, 62 ½ x 53 In.	115.00
Bed, Campaign, Mahogany, Cane, Hinged Body, Robinson & Sons, 1890s, 13 x 77 In.	995.00
Bed, Campaign, Poplar, Pine, Turned Posts, Folding, Rope Rails, Brown Red Paint, 54 x 77 In.	118.00
Bed, Campaign, Wrought Iron, Folding, Canvas, Curule Legs, Stretcher, c.1810, 28 x 76 In.	427.00
Bed, Canopy, Cherry, Shaped Headboard, Pencil Posts, Steps, Cassidy, 62 x 87 In.	424.00

Furniture, Armoire, Walnut, 2 Doors, Raised Panels, Relief Carved, 4 Shelves, Lock, 1700s, 115 x 78 In. $1955.00

Leland Little Auction

Furniture, Bed Steps, Regency, Mahogany, 2 Hinged Steps, Treads, Ironstone Chamber Pot, c.1850, 27 x 18 In. $1098.00

Neal Auction Co.

Furniture, Bed, Canopy, Rococo, Mahogany, Carved, Clustered Posts, Pleated Fabric, c.1835, 114 x 84 In. $5290.00

Leland Little Auction

As always, the edited listings in *Kovels' Antiques & Collectibles Price Guide* aren't available on any website, but readers should visit Kovels.com for information on trends, tips, reproductions, marks, old prices, and more!

Furniture, Bed, Four-Poster, Cannonball, Red Stain, Ohio, 32 x 47 In., Child's $206.00

Cowan's Auctions

Furniture, Bed, Half-Tester, Canopy, Rosewood, Arched Crest, Medallion, New Orleans, c.1870, 120 x 82 In. $6274.00

Neal Auction Co.

Furniture, Bed, Napoleon III, Ebonized, Porcelain Mounts, Bird, Branches, Pastoral Scenes, France, 1800s, Pair $7350.00

Skinner, Inc.

Furniture, Bed, Sleigh, Neoclassical, Mahogany, Scrolled Head & Footboard, Plinth Feet, c.1830, 78 x 43 In. $2749.00

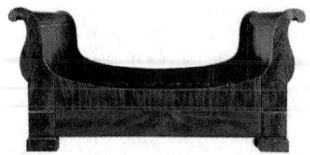

Neal Auction Co.

Bed, Canopy, Federal, Maple, Cherry, Reeded Posts, Arched, c.1810, 63 x 53 In.	206.00
Bed, Canopy, Mahogany, Column Supports, Shaped Frame, Molded Top, c.1850, 113 x 90 In.	10762.00
Bed, Canopy, Neoclassical, Mahogany, Paneled Headboard, Baluster Posts, c.1780, 62 x 81 In.	1600.00
Bed, Canopy, Neoclassical, Rococo Revival, Mahogany, Cluster Column Posts, 124 x 59 In.	11377.00
Bed, Canopy, Neoclassical, Tiger Maple, Turned Posts, Shaped Headboard, c.1850, 63 x 80 In.	1400.00
Bed, Canopy, Red, Yellow Striped Graining, 1900s, 81 x 52 x 76 In.	235.00
Bed, Canopy, Rococo Revival, Mahogany, Paneled Headboard, 109 x 54 In.	3936.00
Bed, Canopy, Rococo, Mahogany, Carved, Clustered Posts, Pleated Fabric, c.1835, 114 x 84 In. . . . *illus*	5290.00
Bed, Canopy, Tiger Maple, Birch, Scroll-Carved Headboard, c.1840, 72 x 81 In.	2760.00
Bed, Carved Columns, Flowers, Headboard 64 x 41 In., Footboard 41 ½ In., Pair	920.00
Bed, Chippendale, Mahogany, Tapered, Reeded, Carved, c.1790, 90 x 57 In.	7190.00
Bed, Curly Maple, Turned Spindles, Legs, Hinged Side, Ohio, c.1810, 32 x 39 In., Child's	499.00
Bed, Directoire Style, Walnut, Headboard, Triangular Crest, Bulb Finials, 44 x 37 In., Pair	338.00
Bed, Four-Poster, Brass, Steel, Tassel-Shape Feet, Italy, c.1970, 81 x 84 In.	492.00
Bed, Four-Poster, Cannonball, Red Stain, Ohio, 32 x 47 In., Child's . . . *illus*	206.00
Bed, Four-Poster, Cherry, Spiral Leaf Posts, Fruit Basket Carved Headboard, c.1825	2988.00
Bed, Four-Poster, Federal Style, Mahogany, Satinwood Stringing, Arched, 84 x 86 In.	299.00
Bed, Four-Poster, Federal, Maple, c.1820, 82 x 78 In.	1010.00
Bed, Four-Poster, George III Style, Mahogany, Carved, Greek Key Frieze, Arched, 97 x 73 In.	2091.00
Bed, Four-Poster, Neoclassical, Carved, Turned, Shaped Headboard, West Indies, 96 x 75 In.	7768.00
Bed, Four-Poster, Rope-Twist Columns, Gilt Tassels, Leaves, 84 x 54 In.	575.00
Bed, Four-Poster, Sheraton, Mahogany, Carved Posts, Upholstered, c.1820, 99 x 85 In.	1840.00
Bed, Four-Poster, Tester, Mahogany, Carved, Reeded, Phila., c.1825, 104 x 57 In.	4600.00
Bed, Half-Tester, Canopy, Rosewood, Arched Crest, Medallion, New Orleans, c.1870, 120 x 82 In. . . *illus*	6274.00
Bed, Half-Tester, Gothic Revival, Mahogany, Tapered Posts, Arched Panels, c.1840, 88 x 75 x In.	2440.00
Bed, Half-Tester, Rococo Revival, Mahogany, Pierced Carved Crest, 69 x 87 In.	11992.00
Bed, Iron, Brass, France, 72 x 38 In., Pair	458.00
Bed, Jenny Lind, Walnut, Carved, Lion's Heads, Flowers, Shells, Spindles, c.1880, 67 In.	575.00
Bed, Leather, Enameled Steel, Pace, Italy, 1980s, 36 x 84 In.	25.00
Bed, Louis XV Style, Oak, Gilt, Carved Headboard, Footboard, 74 x 53 In.	366.00
Bed, Louis XV Style, Oak, Headboard, Footboard, Carved Flower Basket, 73 x 54 In.	244.00
Bed, Louis XV Style, Rosewood, Shaped Head & Footboard, Flower-Carved Crest, 1800s, 77 x 54 In.	671.00
Bed, Louis XV Style, Walnut Veneer, Carved, Gilt, Flowers, Shell, Feathers, 66 x 81 In.	1534.00
Bed, Louis XV Style, Walnut, Headboard, Footboard, Scroll Crest, 1800s, 77 x 56 In.	244.00
Bed, Louis XV Style, Walnut, Headboard, Footboard, Shaped, Carved, 75 x 55 In.	244.00
Bed, Louis XV, Rosewood, Headboard, Footboard, Bronze Ormolu Mounts, 1800s, 73 x 59 In. . .	610.00
Bed, Louis XVI Style, Fluted Columns, Upholstered, Carved, Paint, France, c.1940, 79 x 64 In.	738.00
Bed, Louis XVI Style, Walnut, Applied Festoon Carvings, Finials, c.1890, 55 ½ x 56 In.	184.00
Bed, Low Posts, White Oak, Yellow Pine, 26 Rope Holes, Southern, c.1800, 34 x 77 In.	374.00
Bed, Mahogany, Columns, Flowers, Carved, 64 x 41 In., Pair	2875.00
Bed, Maple, Birch, Folding, Turned Posts, Red Paint, 1800s, 34 x 54 In.	118.00
Bed, Maple, Pine, Peaked Headboard, Turned Posts, Blue Paint, 1800s, 33 x 48 In.	332.00
Bed, Mixed Wood, Turned Posts, Peaked & Scrolled Headboard, Rope, c.1810, 52 x 51 In.	705.00
Bed, Napoleon III, Ebonized, Porcelain Mounts, Bird, Scenes, France, 1800s, Pair . . . . *illus*	7350.00
Bed, Neoclassical, Mahogany, Turned Posts, Pediment Head & Footboard, c.1820, 50 x 39 In. .	425.00
Bed, Opium, ¾ Surround Canopy, Geometric Carving, Flowers, Cabriole Legs, 1800s	236.00
Bed, Opium, Mahogany, Carved Column Canopy, Anglo-Colonial, c.1900, 71 x 48 In.	676.00
Bed, Parquetry, Shaped Headboard, Straight Footboard, 75 x 54 In.	92.00
Bed, Rosewood, Head & Footboard, Carved Crest, Finials, 1800s, 77 x 54 In.	488.00
Bed, Sleigh, Neoclassical, Mahogany, Scrolled Head & Footboard, Plinth Feet, c.1830, 78 x 43 In. *illus*	2749.00
Bed, Walnut, Arched Head & Footboards, Turned Legs, Rope, 1800s, 53 x 76 In.	115.00
Bed, Walnut, Carved, Paneled, Head & Footboard, Cabriole Legs, Venice, Italy, 77 x 67 In.	122.00
Bed, Walnut, Headboard, Footboard, Austria, 60 x 40 In., Pair	230.00
Bed, Walnut, Shaped Crest, 4 Finials, Flower, Basket Carved, 1800s, 73 x 52 In.	124.00
Bed, Walnut, Stepped Crest, Carved Footboard, 76 x 59 In.	671.00
Bed, Walnut, Urn Finials, Carved Headboard, Footboard, 77 x 58 In.	183.00
Bed, Wegner, Teak, Attached Extended Side Table & Lamp, 1966, 80 x 55 In.	770.00
Bed, Wood, Carved, Painted, Upholstered Headboard, Gilt Trim, c.1940, 44 x 79 In.	400.00
Bedroom Set, Art Nouveau, Maple, Mother-Of-Pearl Inlay, Galle, Bed, Armoire, c.1900 . . . . *illus*	1968.00
Bedroom Set, Blue Laminate Bed, Brass Accents, 2 Stands, Bed, 85 x 73 In.	266.00
Bedroom Set, Eastlake, Burl Walnut, Carved, Incised, Bed, Armoire, Dresser, c.1870	5175.00
Bedroom Set, Eastlake, Walnut, Burl Carved Panels, High-Back Bed, Chest, 3 Piece	1230.00
Bedroom Set, French Art Deco, Mahogany, Burl, Panels, 70-In. Armoire, 4 Piece	677.00
Bedroom Set, Kimbel & Cabus, Gothic Style, Walnut, Minton Tile, Carved, c.1890, 3 Piece	2689.00
Bedroom Set, R.J. Horner, Mahogany, Serpentine Fronts, Vanity, Dresser, Chest, Bed	6490.00
Bedroom Set, Renaissance Revival, Walnut, Marble, Dresser, Washstand, Bed, c.1890	1180.00
Bench, Arched Apron, Spindle Sides, Paper Label, Michigan Chair Co., 22 x 16 In.	120.00

Bench, Arts & Crafts, Carved, Openwork, Pierced Flower Stretcher, Shaped Sides, 27 x 31 In...	259.00
Bench, Arts & Crafts, Vertical Slatted Back, Sides, Cushion, 70 x 24 In.	1020.00
Bench, Arts & Crafts, Wood, Slatted Back, Notched Top Rail, Cushion, Label, Harden, 48 x 24 In.	270.00
Bench, Baroque, Plank Seat & Back, Shaped Legs, Stretchers, Spain, 17th Century, 33 x 59 In.	1304.00
Bench, Baroque, Walnut, Carved, 52 x 39 In.	702.00
Bench, Biedermeier, Walnut, Scroll Back, Carved, Upholstered, Tapered Legs, c.1850, 39 x 20 In.	2952.00
Bench, Blanket, Chippendale, Walnut, Lift Top, Shell Carved, 3 Drawers, Pa., 30 x 51 In.	474.00
Bench, Bootjack, Green Paint, 78 In.	81.00
Bench, Brass, Upholstered, Pace, 50 x 17 ½ In.	1560.00
Bench, Bucket, Drawers, Doors, Arched Cutout Feet, 54 x 42 x 15 In.	254.00
Bench, Bucket, Mortised, 3 Shelves, Shaped Ends, Pa., 1800s, 34 x 37 In.	529.00
Bench, Bucket, Pine, Painted, Square Backsplash, Shaped Sides, Lower Shelf, 34 x 66 In.	711.00
Bench, Bucket, Pine, Poplar, Curly Maple, 4 Shelves, 2 Doors, Pa., 1800s, 51 x 41 In.	1528.00
Bench, Bucket, Pine, Poplar, Drawers, Shelves, Scalloped Sides, c.1850, 58 x 43 In.	1093.00
Bench, Bucket, Pine, Shaped End Boards, 3 Shelves, Pa., 1800s, 47 x 42 In.	400.00
Bench, Bucket, Poplar, Open Shelves, Green Paint, Ohio, 1800s, 49 x 32 In.	705.00
Bench, Bucket, Red Paint	115.00
Bench, Bucket, Softwood, 2 Shelves, 2 Doors, Pa., 1800s, 50 x 45 In. ....*illus*	1180.00
Bench, Bucket, Wood, 3 Tiers, Gray, Salmon Paint, 1800s, 45 x 19 In.	374.00
Bench, Cast Iron, Black, Slatted Seat, Curved Ends, Bar Handles, Curled Legs, 26 x 66 In.	185.00
Bench, Cedar, Plank Top, 4 Block Legs, 13 x 73 In.	188.00
Bench, Contemporary, Leather, Rolled Arms, Button-Tufted Cushion, 29 x 59 In.	269.00
Bench, Corner, Pine, Shaped Crest, Spindle Back, Plank Seat & Supports, 36 In.	580.00
Bench, Curule, Beech, Frame, Cane, 19 x 26 In., Pair	708.00
Bench, Curule, William IV, Mahogany, Carved, Tufted Leather, Curved Legs, c.1830	4935.00
Bench, Deacon's, Pine, Fruit, Flower Stencil, 3 Part Back, Spindles, Paint, c.1840, 33 x 70 In.	334.00
Bench, Deacon's, Yellow Paint, Grape & Leaf Design, Plank Seat, 78 x 23 In.	2300.00
Bench, Edwardian, Metal, Upholstered, Heraldic Shields, Scrolling Panels, 17 x 60 In.	2337.00
Bench, Fer Forge, Iron, Raised Scrolls, Downswept Legs, c.1910, 28 x 31 In.	923.00
Bench, G. Nelson, Slats, Maple, Platform Design, c.1960, 14 ½ x 60 In.	499.00
Bench, G. Stickley, 2 Horizontal Back Slats, Low Stretcher, 43 x 13 In., Child's	3240.00
Bench, George III, Mahogany, Padded Top, Carved, Cabriole Legs, Ball & Claw Feet, 17 x 34 In.	325.00
Bench, Gothic Revival, Oak, Carved, High Back, Peaked Crest, Hinged Seat, Shields, 60 x 60 In.	460.00
Bench, Gothic Revival, Walnut, Triple Arch Back, Carved, Upholstered, c.1860, 59 x 74 In.	1495.00
Bench, Gothic Style, Oak, Ash, Carved Designs, Upholstered, Belgium, c.1895, 33 x 48 In.	708.00
Bench, Gray Paint, Rolling Back Rail, Panel Back, High Slatted Armrests, 1800s, 37 x 88 In. .	502.00
Bench, H. Bertoia, Oak, Enameled Iron, Slats, Paper Label, Knoll, 1950s, 15 x 66 In.	558.00
Bench, H. Bertoia, Redwood, Enameled Steel, Slats, 1950s, 15 ½ x 82 In.	589.00
Bench, H. Bertoia, Slatted Ash Top, Black Iron Legs, Knoll, 72 x 15 In.	1140.00
Bench, H. Bertoia, Wood, Slats, Metal, Knoll, c.1952, 15 x 82 In. ....*illus*	2250.00
Bench, Hall, Gothic Revival, Oak, Hooded, Arched Gallery, Pierced, Crest, c.1895, 105 x 68 In.	6457.00
Bench, Hall, Gothic Revival, Walnut, 3-Panel Back, Upholstered, Arms, c.1860, 58 x 33 In. ......*illus*	1495.00
Bench, Hall, Mahogany, Ebonized, Carved, Shell Crest Rail, H-Stretcher, 44 x 55 In.	300.00
Bench, Hall, R.J. Horner, Pierced Crest, Medallion, Putti, Lift Top Bench, Mirror, 90 In.	5310.00
Bench, Hall, Wood, Lift Plank Seat, 3 Parts, Leaf Design, 124 In.	1220.00
Bench, Hardwood, Carved, Coiled Dragon, Clouds, Hinged Seat, Japan, 1800s, 50 x 63 In.	500.00
Bench, Hardwood, Slatted Seat & Back, Scroll Arms, Tapered Legs, American, 51 In.	244.00
Bench, Hardwood, Spruce, Bootjack Ends, V-Shape Block Feet, 96 x 15 In.	230.00
Bench, Hide Strapwork Seat, Shaped Panel Ends, Longhorn Legs, 1900s, 21 x 49 In., Pair	2337.00
Bench, Johannes Hansen, Teak, Denmark, c.1960, 76 In.	2990.00
Bench, John Beringer, Brushed Aluminum, Vinyl, J.G. Furniture, 1970s, 18 x 110 In.	3224.00
Bench, Kilim Upholstery, Turned Legs, Turkey, 18 x 60 In.	2875.00
Bench, L. Hitchcock, Wood, Paint, Spindle Back, Arms, 34 x 17 In.	281.00
Bench, Louis XV Style, Beech, Upholstered, Double Seat, France, 1900s, 19 x 40 In.	531.00
Bench, Louis XVI Style, Carved Frieze, Padded Seat, Fluted Legs, Shaped Feet, 19 x 47 In.	246.00
Bench, Louis XVI Style, Mahogany, Upholstered, Egg & Dart Carved, Oval, 17 x 47 In.	214.00
Bench, M. Nakashima, Conoid, Walnut, Hickory, Shaped Seat, 24 Spindles, 87 In.	7703.00
Bench, Mahogany, Hinged Seat, Needlepoint Top, Ogee Base Molding, 17 x 44 In.	538.00
Bench, Mahogany, Plank Seat, Applied Bolster Ends, Molded Rails, 20 x 50 ½ In.	3393.00
Bench, Mahogany, Swan's Neck Arms, Upholstered, Winged Hairy Paw Feet, 29 x 55 In.	837.00
Bench, Mahogany, Upholstered Seat, Stretcher, 6 Carved Cabriole Legs, Claw Feet, 46 x 20 In.	374.00
Bench, Mahogany, Upholstered, Shaped Base, Bracket Feet, 16 x 36 In.	299.00
Bench, Mies Van Der Rohe, Barcelona, Black Leather, Chrome, c.1960, 18 x 36 In.	720.00
Bench, Mixed Wood, Curved Lattice Arms, Spindled Apron, Morocco, 1800s, 6 x 38 x In.	510.00
Bench, Neoclassical, Mahogany, Padded Seat, Gilt Ram's Heads Arms & Feet, 33 In.	512.00
Bench, Oak, Cherub Carved Panels, Paw Feet, 1800s, 39 x 45 In.	1215.00
Bench, Oak, Paneled Back, Base, Warriors, Lift Seat, Arms, England, c.1895, 41 x 53 In. .... *illus*	399.00

Furniture, Bedroom Set, Art Nouveau, Maple, Mother-Of-Pearl Inlay, Galle, Bed, Armoire, c.1900
$1968.00

New Orleans Auction Galleries, Inc.

Furniture, Bench, Bucket, Softwood, 2 Shelves, 2 Doors, Pa., 1800s, 50 x 45 In.
$1180.00

Conestoga Auction Co., Inc.

Furniture, Bench, H. Bertoia, Wood, Slats, Metal, Knoll, c.1952, 15 x 82 In.
$2250.00

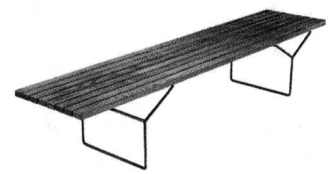

Los Angeles Modern Auctions

Furniture, Bench, Hall, Gothic Revival, Walnut, 3-Panel Back, Upholstered, Arms, c.1860, 58 x 33 In.
$1495.00

Leland Little Auction

Furniture, Bench, Oak, Paneled Back, Base, Warriors, Lift Seat, Arms, England, c.1895, 41 x 53 In.
$399.00

New Orleans Auction Galleries, Inc.

Furniture, Bench, Sam Maloof, Walnut, Woven Seat, Signed, May 1969, 16 x 29 ½ x 15 In.
$3438.00

Los Angeles Modern Auctions

Furniture, Bench, Venetian Rococo, Gilt, Carved, Needlepoint, Cabriole Legs, Hoof Feet, c.1790, 19 x 40 In.
$2390.00

Neal Auction Co.

Furniture, Bench, Wagon Seat, Bamboo Seat, Green Paint, Arms, 1800s, 29 ½ x 13 ½ In.
$708.00

Conestoga Auction Co., Inc.

Bench, P. Evans, Directional, Cityscape, Brass, Ultrasuede, 1970s, 16 x 26 In., Pair	2976.00
Bench, P. Evans, Directional, Cityscape, Olive Burl, Velvet, 18 x 26 In., Pair	2852.00
Bench, Pace Style, Steel Base, Tan Cushion, 1970s, 23 x 19 ½ In., Pair	900.00
Bench, Pew, Gothic Revival, Quartersawn Oak, Swivel Backrest, 40 ½ x 90 In.	805.00
Bench, Pew, Oak, Cross Carved Outside Armrest, 32 x 63 In.	210.00
Bench, Pew, Straight Top Rail, Canted Top Corners, England, c.1905, 34 x 86 In.	177.00
Bench, Phillip Lloyd Powell, Black Walnut, 1960s, 15 x 63 In.	1488.00
Bench, Phillip Lloyd Powell, Walnut, Sculpted, Shaped, 4 Circular Legs, 14 x 106 In.	8125.00
Bench, Piano, Mahogany, Carved, Adjustable, Glass Ball Toes, 20 x 15 In.	92.00
Bench, Pine, 3 Sections, Lift Seat, 1800s, 44 x 61 In.	173.00
Bench, Pine, Carved Top Rail, Vertical Back & Side Slats, Hinged Seat, 1800s, 77 In.	826.00
Bench, Pine, Cutout Ends, Single Board Top, Gray Over Red Paint, 1800s, 19 x 36 In.	353.00
Bench, Pine, Green Paint, 2 Demilune Cutout Supports, 1800s, 18 x 70 In.	1067.00
Bench, Pine, Locking Lift Seat, 1800s, 35 x 95 In.	374.00
Bench, Pine, Mortised, 1800s, 18 x 84 In.	141.00
Bench, Pine, Mortised, Blue Paint, Plank Legs, Arch Feet, 1800s, 21 x 48 In.	764.00
Bench, Pine, Painted, Rounded Ends, Arched Legs, Square Apron, 1900s, 20 x 71 In.	89.00
Bench, Pine, Plank Top, Painted, Splayed Plank Legs, American, 1800s, 18 x 79 In.	538.00
Bench, Pine, Poplar, Plank Seat, 3 Drawers, Lollipop Arms, Gray Paint, c.1790, 41 x 73 In.	3450.00
Bench, Plank, Rectangular Top, 4 Thick Angled Octagonal Legs, 25 x 62 In.	826.00
Bench, Quaker, Straight Crest Rail, Backrest, Shaped Ends, 1800s, 147 In.	550.00
Bench, Red Paint, Distressed Top, 2 Square Board Legs, Arch, 71 x 18 In.	173.00
Bench, Red Paint, Fruit & Flower Stencils, Scalloped Crest Rail, Spindles, 34 x 73 In.	185.00
Bench, Regency Style, Mahogany, Gilt Bronze Rosettes, Upholstered, 16 x 34 In.	1076.00
Bench, Regency Style, Mahogany, Upholstered, Outswept Arms, 42 In.	594.00
Bench, Regency Style, Wood, X-Shape Sides, Cane Seat, c.1960, 18 x 26 In.	923.00
Bench, Renaissance Revival, Oak, Blocked Panel Back, Owl Crest, Finials, Scroll Arms, 46 x 60 In.	3690.00
Bench, Renaissance Revival, Oak, Lift Seat, Paneled Back, Peaked Crest, 1800s, 61 x 60 In.	549.00
Bench, Robsjohn-Gibbings, Mahogany, Tufted Cushion, X-Leg, 33 ¾ x 13 ½ In.	1560.00
Bench, Rocker, Mammy's, Wood, Spindle Back, Arms, Flower Painted Back, 31 x 37 In.	420.00
Bench, Rococo Style, Gilt, High Shaped Arm Crest, Carved, Upholstered, c.1895, 35 x 46 In.	1007.00
Bench, Rose Valley, Oak, Brand, Rectangular, Shaped Apron, c.1910, 78 x 16 In., Pair	5000.00
Bench, Rosewood, Shaped Back, Arms, Block Legs, Shaped Apron, 1800s, 48 x 35 In.	2370.00
Bench, Roycroft, Ali Baba, Orb & Cross Mark, 19 ½ x 42 x 11 In.	7440.00
Bench, Sam Maloof, Walnut, Woven Seat, Signed, May 1969, 16 x 29 ½ x 15 In. .... *illus*	3438.00
Bench, Schoolhouse, Pine, Canted Backboard, Plank Seat, c.1845, 27 x 49 In.	1404.00
Bench, Shaker, Pine, Brown Paint, Plank Top, Arched Cutout Feet, 1800s, 6 ½ x 31 In.	206.00
Bench, Shaker, Pine, Iron Scrape, Bootjack Cutout Legs, 10 x 36 In.	351.00
Bench, Shoeshine, Inlaid Shoe, Heart, Diamond, Star, Hinged, Fitted Interior, 17 x 20 In.	48.00
Bench, Softwood, Red Paint, Mortised Leg, Shaped Cutout Legs, 1800s, 19 x 72 In.	354.00
Bench, Square, Upholstered, Wood Block Legs, W. Haines, c.1948, 15 x 20 In., Pair	281.00
Bench, Sycamore, Ebony Stringing, Curved, France, c.1937, 16 x 38 In.	1195.00
Bench, Teak Root, Carved, Shaped Back & Arms, 3 Legs, 32 x 68 x 34 In.	180.00
Bench, Telephone, Louis XV Style, Walnut, Upholstered Seat, Stand, Drawer, Arms, 34 x 37 In.	180.00
Bench, Tiger Maple, Single Board, Mortise & Tenon, Early 1800s, 78 x 21 In.	518.00
Bench, Venetian Rococo, Gilt, Carved, Needlepoint, Cabriole Legs, Hoof Feet, c.1790, 19 x 40 In. *illus*	2390.00
Bench, Victorian, Cast Iron, 4 Seasons Scenes, Green Paint, 35 x 70 In., Pair	1380.00
Bench, Wagon Seat, Bamboo Seat, Green Paint, Arms, 1800s, 29 ½ x 13 ½ In. *illus*	708.00
Bench, Wagon Seat, Natural Rush Seating, 19th Century, 35 x 32 In.	950.00
Bench, Wagon Seat, Oak, Turned Frame, Rush Seat, 1800s, 35 In., Pair	266.00
Bench, Wagon Seat, Slat Back, Double Wicker Seat, Stretchers, Arms, 28 x 35 In.	259.00
Bench, Walnut, Carved Sunflower Panels, Hinged Seat, Open Arms, Ohio, 1887, 39 x 48 In.	4370.00
Bench, William & Mary, Walnut, Embroidered Barley Twist Legs, 1600s, 16 x 29 In.	1195.00
Bench, Window, Louis XV Style, Upholstered, Pierced, Carved, Scroll, 20 x 48 In.	671.00
Bench, Window, Mahogany, Lyre Splat, Outstretched Legs, Paw Feet, c.1900, 34 x 48 In.	1168.00
Bench, Window, Oak, Square, Leather Seat, Brass Tacks, Arms, Baluster Legs, 29 x 25 In.	1830.00
Bench, Window, Walnut, Carved Leaves, Rolled Arms, Beaded Apron, Twist Legs, 32 x 66 In.	300.00
Bench, Window, Wrought Iron, Patina, Leather Upholstery, Robert Jones, 28 ¼ x 31 In. ... *illus*	600.00
Bench, Window, Yew, Rectangular, Carved, Shell, Leaf, Cabriole Legs, Italy, 17 x 28 In.	305.00
Bench, Windsor, Grain Painted, Stenciled, Straight Crest Rail, Scroll Arms, c.1830, 79 In.	950.00
Bench, Windsor, Mixed Wood, ½ Spindle Back, Grain Painted, Fruit Stencil, 35 x 72 In.	1175.00
Bench, Windsor, Mixed Wood, Spindle Arms, Back, Splayed Legs, Stretcher, 36 x 74 In.	1888.00
Bench, Wood, 4-Section Back, Fruit, Leaf Stencils, Open Arms, 8-Leg Base, c.1850, 35 x 78 In.	575.00
Bench, Wood, Chenille, Cabriole Legs, Italy, 1960s, 19 ½ x 19 ½ In.	930.00
Bench, Wood, Gilt, Carved, Upholstered Seat, c.1940, 18 x 21 In.	492.00
Bench, Wood, Painted, Bootjack Splats, Plank Seat, Scroll Arms, Turned Legs, 36 x 74 In.	397.00
Bench, Yellow Pine, Green Paint, Plank Top, Mortised Apron, Tapered Legs, 21 x 71 In.	538.00

Book Press, Georgian, Mahogany, Beech, Dovetailed Drawer, 1800s, 58 x 25 In. ....*illus*	1416.00
Book Press, Oak, Screw Drive, Removable Plates, Drawer, England, c.1750, 68 x 28 In. ..*illus*	1599.00
Bookcase, 2 Glass Doors, Fixed Interior Shelves, Red Decal, 56 x 58 In.	8680.00
Bookcase, 6 Shelves, Adjustable, Sweden, 28 x 77 In.	600.00
Bookcase, Art Deco, Rosewood, Stepped Top, Glass Door, c.1930, 51 x 24 In.	738.00
Bookcase, Arts & Crafts, 2 Glass Doors, 77 x 54 In.	1984.00
Bookcase, Arts & Crafts, 2 Leaded Glass Doors, Cutout Side Supports, 40 x 56 In.	1560.00
Bookcase, Arts & Crafts, Gallery Top, Cutout Hearts, 3 Shelves, 43 x 13 In.............................	900.00
Bookcase, Arts & Crafts, Oak, Glazed Doors, Flared Side Brackets, 56 x 46 In.	413.00
Bookcase, Barrister, Globe-Wernicke, Oak, 6 Sections, Lift Glass Panel, Ohio, c.1915, 89 x 34 In.	978.00
Bookcase, Barrister, Oak, 5 Shelves, 5 Lift Glass Doors, Fred Macey Co., Mich., c.1910, 75 x 34 In.	690.00
Bookcase, Barrister, Oak, Glass, 3 Shelves, Brass Pulls, Lundstrom, c.1905, 46 x 33 In.	138.00
Bookcase, Broken-Arch Pediment, Glazed Doors, Slant Front, 4 Drawers, 90 x 39 In...............	4183.00
Bookcase, Burl, Lacquer, Ormolu Mounts, 4 Doors, Top Shape Feet, 75 x 43 In........................	610.00
Bookcase, Chippendale Style, Mahogany, 2 Glass Doors, Epstein, c.1865, 75 x 45 In...............	518.00
Bookcase, Chippendale, Mahogany, Glass Doors, Drawers, Charleston, c.1775, 83 x 46 In. ...	50400.00
Bookcase, Crest, Glazed Cupboard Doors, Drop Front, Writing Surface, 1800s, 92 x 42 In.......	590.00
Bookcase, Dutch Marquetry, Doors, Drop Front, 2 Drawers, Bombe Base, 1900s, 84 x 50 In.	1298.00
Bookcase, Early American Style, Pine, 4 Glass Panel Doors, 1900s, 81 x 50 In.	570.00
Bookcase, Empire, Mahogany, Fold-Out Surface, Glass Doors, 1800s, 88 x 42 In.	657.00
Bookcase, Empire, Mahogany, Marble Top, Bronze Mounts, 2 Doors, 50 x 54 In.	1353.00
Bookcase, Empire, Oak, 3 Open Shelves, Columns, Drawers, 2 Doors, France, c.1850, 91 x 52 In.	4182.00
Bookcase, English Oak, Dentil Molding, Glass Doors, Stand, Stretchers, 51 x 61 In.	2596.00
Bookcase, Federal, Mahogany, Birch Inlay, Fold-Out Surface, 3 Doors, Drawers, c.1800, 57 x 38 In.	2607.00
Bookcase, Federal, Mahogany, Glass Doors, Folding Desk Top, 4 Drawers, Mass., c.1810, 62 x 41 In.	1700.00
Bookcase, French Provincial, Oak, Carved, 4 Shelves, 55 x 56 In...	366.00
Bookcase, G. Stickley, 2 Glass Doors, 2 Fixed Interior Shelves, Red Decal, 45 x 39 In.	8680.00
Bookcase, G. Stickley, 2 Glass Doors, Copper Hardware, 36 x 56 In..	11400.00
Bookcase, G. Stickley, Gallery Top, 2 12-Pane Doors, Through Tenons, 56 x 60 In.	1778.00
Bookcase, G. Stickley, Tree Of Life, Incised, 4 Shelves, Leather Facing, Tacks, 43 In.	1680.00
Bookcase, George III Style, Mahogany, Carved, Glass Doors, 3 Shelves, 100 x 48 In. ....*illus*	3286.00
Bookcase, George III Style, Mahogany, Glass Door, 3 Drawers, 1900s, 75 x 48 In.	805.00
Bookcase, George III Style, Mahogany, Swan's Neck Pediment, Glass Door, 100 x 48 In.	2868.00
Bookcase, George III, Mahogany, Glass Doors, Drawers, Writing Surface, c.1790, 82 x 42 In. .	1896.00
Bookcase, George III, Mahogany, Glass Upper Doors, Drawer, Lower Panel Doors, 95 x 47 In.	2106.00
Bookcase, George III, Mahogany, Molded Cornice, 2 Doors, 4 Drawers, Bracket Feet, 92 x 50 In.	2214.00
Bookcase, Georgian Style, Mahogany, Dentiled Cornice, 3 Glazed & 3 Panel Doors, 79 x 59 In.	868.00
Bookcase, Georgian Style, Mahogany, Swan's Neck Pediment, Glass Door, 1800s, 75 x 31 In. .	418.00
Bookcase, Georgian, Mahogany, Glass Doors, Drop Front, Side Doors, 4 Drawers, 85 x 76 In..	690.00
Bookcase, Globe-Wernicke, Tiger Oak, Leaded Glass Upper Shelf, 2 Open Shelves, 45 x 34 In.	633.00
Bookcase, Gothic Revival, Mahogany, 4 Glazed Doors, Tracery, Arches, 1800s, 76 x 65 In.	1434.00
Bookcase, Gothic Revival, Mahogany, Projecting Cyma Cornice, Arched Panel, 95 x 72 In.	3444.00
Bookcase, Gothic Revival, Mahogany, Shaped Pediment, Arch Doors, Scroll Feet, 1800s, 102 x 53 In.	3346.00
Bookcase, Gothic Revival, Oak, Carved, Ghoulish Plaque Scenes, 92 x 90 In..........................	1586.00
Bookcase, Gothic Revival, Walnut, Gilt, Doors, Drop Front, Drawers, c.1820, 100 x 45 In........	16605.00
Bookcase, Henry II Style, Oak, 2 Glass Doors, Spindle Columns, Leaves, 92 x 56 In.	1080.00
Bookcase, Henry II Style, Oak, Carved, 2 Arched Glass Doors, 2 Drawers, 2 Low Doors, 96 x 57 In.	1464.00
Bookcase, Henry II Style, Oak, Carved, 2 Glass Doors, Twist Columns, 1800s, 108 x 65 In.......	600.00
Bookcase, Henry II Style, Walnut, Arched Glass Doors, Drawers, Carved Doors, Crest, 109 x 61 In.	1342.00
Bookcase, L. & J.G. Stickley, Oak, Double Doors, 16 Panes, Decal, 55 x 39 ½ In. ....*illus*	5270.00
Bookcase, Limbert, Chestnut, Leaded Glass Door, 54 x 24 In.	2604.00
Bookcase, Limbert, Door, Divided Pane, Copper Pull, 30 x 15 In..	2160.00
Bookcase, Louis XIII Style, Carved, Oak, 3 Glass Doors, Spindle Columns, 81 x 84 In.............	1560.00
Bookcase, Louis XV Style, Walnut, Open Top Shelf, 3 Glass Doors, 72 x 75 In.	366.00
Bookcase, Louis XVI, Walnut, Carved Crest, 2 Shaped Glass Doors, 87 x 55 In.	793.00
Bookcase, Mahogany, 2 Glass Doors, Drop Front, 4 Drawers, Maddox, 82 x 35 In.	374.00
Bookcase, Mahogany, 2 Glass Doors, Shelves, 2 Lower Drawers, 62 x 48 In...........................	188.00
Bookcase, Mahogany, 2 Triple Arch Doors, Turned Feet, 50 x 49 In.	230.00
Bookcase, Mahogany, Bronze, Block Frieze, 2 Glass Doors, Columns, Plinth, c.1890, 60 x 56 In.	599.00
Bookcase, Mahogany, Carved Trim, Glass Doors, Adjustable Doors, 71 x 43 In.........................	403.00
Bookcase, Mahogany, Carved, Glass Doors, Shelves, Grand Rapids, c.1910, 50 x 40 In.	546.00
Bookcase, Mahogany, Finial Crest, 3 Beveled Glass Doors, Carved Leaves, 81 x 63 In...............	345.00
Bookcase, Mahogany, Flared Cornice, 2 Glass Doors, Melon Feet, c.1835, 97 x 54 In.	13742.00
Bookcase, Mahogany, Gadrooned Edge, 3 Glass Doors, Spiral Pillars, c.1890, 67 x 74 In.........	1610.00
Bookcase, Mahogany, Glass Doors, Diamond Molding, Drawer, Panel Doors, 1830, 105 x 66 In.	4270.00
Bookcase, Mahogany, Inlay, 4 Bubble Glass Doors, 7 Drawers, Slide-Out Desk, 86 x 65 In.	805.00
Bookcase, Mahogany, Molded Cornice, 2 Glazed Doors, Columns, Drawers, 1800s, 103 x 54 In.	7995.00

Furniture, Bench, Window, Wrought Iron, Patina, Leather Upholstery, Robert Jones, 28 ¼ x 31 In.
$600.00

F

Furniture, Book Press, Georgian, Mahogany, Beech, Dovetailed Drawer, 1800s, 58 x 25 In.
$1416.00

Furniture, Book Press, Oak, Screw Drive, Removable Plates, Drawer, Eng., c.1750, 68 x 28 In.
$1599.00

Furniture, Bookcase, George III Style, Mahogany, Carved, Glass Doors, 3 Shelves, 100 x 48 In.
$3286.00

Neal Auction Co.

TIP

Install locks on all garage doors and windows.

Furniture, Bookcase, L. & J.G. Stickley, Oak, Double Doors, 16 Panes, Decal, 55 x 39 ½ In.
$5270.00

Rago Arts & Auction Center

Furniture, Buffet, McCobb, 4 Drawers, 4 Pullout Shelves, Lane, c.1961, 32 x 75 In.
$2500.00

Los Angeles Modern Auctions

Bookcase, Mahogany, Molded Cornice, 4 Astragal Glass Doors, 4 Low Doors, 95 x 79 In.	3936.00
Bookcase, Mahogany, Molded Cornice, Glass Doors, Frieze Drawer, 88 x 49 In.	1180.00
Bookcase, Mahogany, Parcel Gilt, Stepped Cornice, Glass Doors, Columns, 66 x 46 In.	1586.00
Bookcase, Mahogany, Stepped Cornice, 2 Glass Doors, 2 Drawers, 1700s, 86 x 45 In.	3904.00
Bookcase, Mahogany, Stepped Cornice, 4 Glass Doors, 4 Cabinet Doors, 84 x 97 In.	875.00
Bookcase, Mahogany, Stepped Cornice, Shelves, 3 Arches, 3 Cabinet Doors, 86 x 86 In.	563.00
Bookcase, Neoclassical Style, Mahogany, Gilt, Pilasters, 4 Shelves, 1900s, 86 x 92 In.	896.00
Bookcase, Oak, Carved Cornice, Arched Doors, Garlands, Lion's Mask, 1800s, 108 x 66 In.	7170.00
Bookcase, Oak, Glass Panel Door, 3 Interior Shelves, c.1890, 61 x 34 In.	748.00
Bookcase, Parzinger, Lacquered Wood, Doors, Brass, 1950s, 88 x 38 x 16 In.	4650.00
Bookcase, Pine, Mixed Wood, Cornice, Glass Doors, Paneled Doors, 100 x 64 In.	717.00
Bookcase, Plum Pudding Mahogany, Lancet Glass Doors, 4 Drawers, c.1790, 87 x 42 In.	6100.00
Bookcase, Plum Pudding, William IV, 3 Shelves, Lower Drawers, Doors, 1800s, 90 x 55 In.	889.00
Bookcase, Quartersawn Oak, 3 Doors, Bowed Glass, Flint, N.Y., c.1890, 55 x 78 In.	1840.00
Bookcase, Regency Style, Mahogany, 3 Upper Shelves, 2-Door Cabinet, 60 x 36 In.	375.00
Bookcase, Regency, Mahogany, Brass Mounts, 4 Doors, Drawer, 69 x 26 In., Pair	8775.00
Bookcase, Regency, Mahogany, Ebonized, 4 Shelves, Reeded, Drawer Base, 47 x 36 In.	1287.00
Bookcase, Regency, Mahogany, Paneled Doors, Shaped Crest, Shelves, 43 x 36 In.	826.00
Bookcase, Renaissance Revival, Walnut, Gilt, Doors, Columns, Spindle Gallery, c.1835, 104 x 73 In.	3690.00
Bookcase, Revolving, Arts & Crafts, Oak, 3 Tiers, Spindle Sides, 49 x 22 In.	458.00
Bookcase, Revolving, Danish Modern, Rosewood, Vertical Slats, 1960s, 49 x 20 In.	930.00
Bookcase, Revolving, Mahogany, 3 Square Tiers, Open Sides, England, c.1910, 32 x 19 In.	316.00
Bookcase, Revolving, Mahogany, Flat, Turned Supports, Reeded Downswept Legs, 28 x 14 In.	92.00
Bookcase, Revolving, Square Top, Roped Edges, Carved Supports, X-Shape Base, 44 x 21 In.	551.00
Bookcase, Rococo Style, Swan's Neck Crest, Flower Painted Doors, Drop Front, 84 x 33 In.	1755.00
Bookcase, Roycroft, 5 Graduated Shelves, Slab Sides, Marked, 22 x 18 In.	14400.00
Bookcase, Roycroft, Mahogany, Leaded Glass Door, Marked, 55 x 40 In.	12400.00
Bookcase, Southern, Walnut, Stepped, Flared Cornice, Glass Doors, Paneled Doors, c.1850	2629.00
Bookcase, Step Back, Glass Top Doors, 2 Panel Doors, Applied Detail, 1880s, 91 x 50 In.	690.00
Bookcase, Stickley Bros., 2 Glass Doors, Gallery Top, Brass Ring Pulls, 48 In.	930.00
Bookcase, Victorian, Oak, 3 Glass Doors, Beaded, Carved, c.1900, 54 x 13 In.	210.00
Bookcase, Walnut, 2 Glass Doors, Brass Mounts, Carved Molding, 66 x 48 In.	1860.00
Bookcase, Walnut, 3 Glass & Paneled Doors, Glass Shelves, France, 87 x 73 In.	488.00
Bookcase, Walnut, Panel & Glass Doors, Geometric Molding, 1800s, 88 x 55 In.	793.00
Bookcase, Wicker, White Paint, 49 x 26 ½ In.	173.00
Bookcase, Wood, Banded Top, Inlaid Drawers, Open Shelves, Columns, c.1920, 39 x 43 In.	1476.00
Bookrack, Georgian Style, Turned Cross Stretcher, England, c.1900, 33 x 37 In., Pair	900.00
Bookstand, Revolving, Mahogany, 2 Tiers, c.1905, 35 x 19 In.	236.00
Bracket, Wall, Italian Baroque, Giltwood, Tiered Leaves, 12 x 14 In., Pair	2340.00
Bracket, Wall, Wood, Pierced, 17 ½ x 14 In., Pair	122.00
Breakfront, Chippendale Style, Arched Pediment, Fretwork Mullions, 1900s, 90 x 72 In.	6095.00
Breakfront, George III, Mahogany, 4 Glass Doors, Shelves, Lower Doors, c.1770, 105 x 108 In.	6683.00
Breakfront, Georgian Style, Mahogany, Glass Doors, Panel Doors, Drawers, c.1920, 92 x 83 In.	2390.00
Breakfront, Georgian, Mahogany, Drop Front, Glass, Pullout Desk, Inlay, 85 x 76 In.	690.00
Breakfront, Louis XVI Style, Parquetry, Glass Door, Recessed Panels, 65 x 64 In.	239.00
Breakfront, Mahogany, Glass Doors, Lower Doors, Council Craftsman, 93 x 78 In.	2856.00
Breakfront, Mixed Wood, Peaked Pediment, Glass Doors, Panel Doors, c.1850, 105 x 102 In.	5520.00
Breakfront, Regency Style, Mahogany, Serpentine, 4 Glass Doors, 3 Drawers, 75 x 59 In.	554.00
Breakfront, Yew, Mahogany, Broken Pediment, Glass Doors, Low Doors, 108 x 113 In.	3286.00
Buffet, Beveled Glass Doors, Open Shelf, 2 Frieze Drawers, Panel Doors, 1800s, 101 x 57 In.	708.00
Buffet, Black Forest, Purple Glass Doors, Carved Lower Drawers, Germany, 89 x 91 In.	2875.00
Buffet, Brown Marble Top, Drawers, Doors, Corner Doors, Hickory Chair Co., 40 x 76 In.	978.00
Buffet, Chippendale, Mahogany, 4 Doors, Brick Design, Brass Fish Handles, Chinese, 30 x 80 In.	330.00
Buffet, Empire, Oak, Mirror Back, Rectangular Top, Door, 2 Drawers, c.1910, 54 x 46 In.	127.00
Buffet, French Provincial, Fruitwood, Shaped & Molded Top, 6 Drawers, 1800s, 43 x 73 In.	1195.00
Buffet, Gothic Style, Oak, Leaf Crown, Carved Panel Doors, Column Pilasters, 98 x 58 In.	708.00
Buffet, Henry II Style, Oak, 6 Doors, 3 Drawers, Carved Supports & Panels, 93 x 59 In.	793.00
Buffet, Henry II Style, Oak, Spindle Column, 2 Glass Doors, Deer Head Mount, 109 x 53 In.	1140.00
Buffet, Henry II Style, Peaked Crest, Glass Doors, Drawers, Carved Doors, 1800s, 112 x 60 In.	732.00
Buffet, Henry II Style, Walnut, Carved, Upper Glass Doors, 2 Drawers, Doors, 1800s, 102 x 53 In.	1037.00
Buffet, Henry II Style, Walnut, Glass & Carved Doors, 2 Drawers, Open Middle, Ornate, 90 x 60 In.	732.00
Buffet, Henry II Style, Walnut, Open Shelves, Drawers, Carved Doors, Glass Doors, 1800s, 85 x 45 In.	732.00
Buffet, Henry II, Walnut, Crest, Finials, 2 Drawers, 5 Doors, Ornate Figural Carvings, 100 x 61 In.	458.00
Buffet, Henry II, Walnut, Openwork, Stepped Crest, Carved Doors, 2 Drawers, 103 x 59 In.	488.00
Buffet, Henry II, Walnut, Stepped Crest, 4 Drawers, 5 Doors, Ornate Carved Panels, 100 x 64 In.	1098.00
Buffet, Henry II, Walnut, Upper & Lower Carved Doors, Drawers, 88 x 56 In.	671.00
Buffet, Louis XV Style, Fruitwood, 4 Doors, Drawers, 1800s, 39 x 92 In.	388.00

Buffet, Louis XV Style, Molded Edge, 3 Drawers, 2 Arched Panel Doors, c.1820, 42 x 69 In.	2706.00
Buffet, Louis XV Style, Oak, Chestnut, Molded Crest, 2 Glass Doors, 2 Doors, c.1800, 89 x 54 In.	2460.00
Buffet, Louis XV Style, Oak, Shaped Cornice, 4 Drawers, 6 Doors, Carved Leaves, 80 x 76 In.	600.00
Buffet, Louis XV Style, Walnut, 2 Drawers, 2 Doors, Shaped Panels, 1700s, 38 x 55 In.	5166.00
Buffet, Louis XV, Oak, 2 Side Doors, Open Shelves, Lower Drawers, Doors, 86 x 59 In.	2196.00
Buffet, Louis XVI Style, Walnut, Carved, Marble Top, Mirror, 3 Drawers, 6 Doors, 92 x 64 In.	519.00
Buffet, Louis XVI, Walnut, Beveled Marble Top, 4 Drawers, 2 Doors, Center Shelf, 43 x 76 In.	2440.00
Buffet, Mahogany, Bleached, 3 Drawers, 4 Doors, Round Knobs, c.1950, 35 x 72 In.	875.00
Buffet, Mahogany, Oak, Open Side Shelves, Marble Shelf, Carved, c.1860	1159.00
Buffet, McCobb, 4 Drawers, 4 Pullout Shelves, Lane, c.1961, 32 x 75 In. ....*illus*	2500.00
Buffet, Mixed Wood, Carved Parquetry Doors, Panels, South America, 39 x 86 In.	227.00
Buffet, Neoclassical Style, Mahogany, Geometric Design, 2 Doors, Pilasters, 45 x 94 In.	938.00
Buffet, Neoclassical Style, Mixed Wood, Demilune, Flower Basket, Curved Doors, 37 x 54 In.	329.00
Buffet, Oak, Arched Volute Crest, Glass Doors, Carved Panel Doors, 95 x 56 In.	1793.00
Buffet, Renaissance Revival, Oak, Carved, Doors, Drawers, Iron Hardware, 1800s, 72 x 82 In.	671.00
Buffet, Walnut, 3 Glass Horizontal Doors, Bun Feet, France, 39 x 75 In.	397.00
Buffet, Walnut, Concave Top, Open Galleries, 4 Doors, Winged Griffins, 1800s, 108 x 71 In.	4720.00
Bureau, Bowfront, Mahogany, Banded Top, 4 Drawers, Bracket Feet, 32 x 30 In.	2844.00
Bureau, Burl, Ebonized, Inlay, Angular Oxbow Front, 4 Drawers, Bun Feet, 29 x 36 In.	2489.00
Bureau, Cherry, Drop Front, Writing Surface, Door, 4 Drawers, 1800s, 44 x 38 In.	384.00
Bureau, Chippendale, Mahogany, Block Front, Beaded, Tombstone Door, c.1770, 29 x 31 In.	14220.00
Bureau, Chippendale, Mahogany, Molded Top, 5 Drawers, Brass Bail Handles, 41 x 46 In.	207.00
Bureau, Chippendale, Mahogany, Serpentine, 4 Beaded Drawers, c.1760, 32 x 33 In.	2370.00
Bureau, Federal, Mahogany, Inlaid Diamond Banding, Beaded Drawers, c.1810, 37 x 39 In.	889.00
Bureau, French Provincial, Fruitwood, Banded Top, 2 Drawers, Bulb Feet, c.1850, 30 x 57 In.	738.00
Bureau, George III, Mahogany, Walnut, Slant Front, 6 Drawers, c.1780, 40 x 36 In.	1845.00
Bureau, George III, Mahogany, Writing Slide, 4 Drawers, Brass Bail Pulls, 32 x 35 In.	1652.00
Bureau, Hepplewhite, Cherry, 4 Drawers, French Feet, 40 In.	374.00
Bureau, Louis XV Style, Mahogany, Shaped Top, Leather, Ormolu Bands, c.1900, 32 x 65 In.	1722.00
Bureau, Louis XV Style, Oak, Slant Front, Shaped Back, Carved Leaves, Hoof Feet, 1800s, 39 x 37 In.	1230.00
Bureau, Louis XV Style, Walnut, Cupboard, Rectangular Top, Cabriole Legs, c.1900, 38 x 27 In.	338.00
Bureau, Louis XVI Style, Walnut, Mahogany, Marquetry, Gilt Mounts, 30 x 46 In.	938.00
Bureau, Mahogany, Brass Crossbands, Mirror, Drawers, c.1825, 65 x 39 In.	2337.00
Bureau, Neoclassical, Mahogany, Mirror, Drawers, 2 Half Round Drawers, c.1830, 55 x 35 In. ...*illus*	1220.00
Bureau, Oak, Bombe, Panel Doors, Drawers, Claw Feet, Flower Carvings, Dutch, 1800s, 38 x 26 In.	1422.00
Bureau, Pine, Grain Painted, 6 Drawers, Molded Bracket Base, 1866, 40 x 38 In.	652.00
Bureau, Serpentine, Graduated Drawers, Writing Surface, Bracket Feet, 1700s, 32 x 42 In.	8295.00
Bureau, Walnut, Cylinder, Carved, Shell Crest, Bird Returns, Allen & Bro., c.1870, 57 x 31 In.	5378.00
Cabinet, 2 Drawers, Leaf-Carved Skirt, Geometric Slat-Work Shelf, Chinese, 34 x 30 In.	325.00
Cabinet, 3 Pierced Panels, 2 Lattice-Carved Doors, Oval Pulls, Chinese, c.1890, 27 x 18 In.	984.00
Cabinet, A. Citterio, Maxalto, Wenge Wood, Enameled Steel, B & B Italia, 24 x 102 In.	2480.00
Cabinet, Adirondack, Twig, Bark, Mirror Top, Shelf, Mouse, Birds, 78 x 18 In.	460.00
Cabinet, Art Deco, Mahogany, Book-Painted Door, France, c.1920, 70 x 41 In.	465.00
Cabinet, Art Deco, Oak, 2 Doors, Fitted Interior, J. Klein, France, c.1939, 54 x 51 In.	1984.00
Cabinet, Art Deco, Rosewood, Brass & Bronze Trim, Glass Door, France, c.1930, 39 x 40 In.	1230.00
Cabinet, Arts & Crafts, Oak, Mirror Backsplash, Doors, Drawers, c.1930, 58 x 44 In.	1495.00
Cabinet, Baker's, Pine, 2 Plank Doors, Fitted Interior, Painted, c.1900, 84 x 44 In.	345.00
Cabinet, Bar, Black Lacquer, Soapstone, Figures, Drop Front, Doors, Chinese, c.1935, 41 x 38 In.	244.00
Cabinet, Bar, Rosewood, Rectangular, Drop Front, Shelves, Doors, c.1961, 44 x 45 In.	1500.00
Cabinet, Bar, Wood Inlays, Drop Front, Open Shelves, Italy, c.1955, 54 x 31 In.	488.00
Cabinet, Baroque, Walnut, Drawer, Door, Radiating Design, Continental, 39 x 28 In.	625.00
Cabinet, Baroque, Walnut, Gilt Metal, 9 Drawers, Inlaid Figures, Cabriole Legs, 1725, 63 x 42 In.	1638.00
Cabinet, Biedermeier, Bird's-Eye Maple, Walnut, Carved, Glass Doors, Drawers, c.1800s, 87 x 40 In.	1195.00
Cabinet, Biedermeier, Glass Door, Ebonized Spokes, Shelves, c.1810, 68 x 36 In. ....*illus*	1778.00
Cabinet, Biedermeier, Maple, 2 Glass Doors, Shelves, Shaped Crest, 67 x 54 In.	281.00
Cabinet, Biedermeier, Parquetry, Drop Front, Doors, Drawers, Hourglass Shape, 61 x 29 In.	3450.00
Cabinet, Black Lacquer, Fretted Doors, Fitted Interior, Gilt, Chinese, c.1850, 31 x 24 In.	676.00
Cabinet, Black Lacquer, Ivory Insets, Figures Scenes, 2 Doors, Chinese, 41 x 29 In.	2574.00
Cabinet, Black Lacquer, Orange Characters, Urns, Doors, Drawers, Chinese, 1800s, 49 x 43 In.	345.00
Cabinet, Black Lacquer, Soapstone Inlays, Carved, Gilt, 2 Doors, Chinese, c.1900, 30 x 23 In.	415.00
Cabinet, Blackwood, 9 Niches, Carved Openwork, Paw Feet, Chinese, 1800s, 61 x 41 In.	10413.00
Cabinet, Brass, Glass Doors, 12 Compartments, 17 x 16 In.	375.00
Cabinet, Burl Veneer, Marquetry, Bombe Marble Top, 2 Doors, 63 x 60 In.	2300.00
Cabinet, Cherry, Hinged Top, Paneled Door, Drawers, c.1860, 26 x 18 In.	2070.00
Cabinet, China, Arts & Crafts, Glass Door, 3 Interior Shelves, Mirrored Top, 61 x 50 In.	230.00
Cabinet, China, Bombe, Serpentine Crest, 2 Glass Doors, 3 Drawers, 1800s, 92 x 80 In.	956.00
Cabinet, China, Carved Doors, Crest, Apron, Interior Shelves, 1970, 36 x 72 In.	850.00

Furniture, Bureau, Neoclassical, Mahogany, Mirror, Drawers, 2 Half Round Drawers, c.1830, 55 x 35 In. $1220.00

Neal Auction Co.

Furniture, Cabinet, Biedermeier, Glass Door, Ebonized Spokes, Shelves, c.1810, 68 x 36 In. $1778.00

Skinner, Inc.

Furniture, Cabinet, G. Stickley, Safe-Craft, Mahogany, 2 Glass Doors, 2 Doors, Red Decal, 63 x 35 In. $2604.00

Rago Arts & Auction Center

Furniture, Cabinet, George III Style, Mahogany, Gallery, Beveled Glass, Mirror, c.1965, 82 x 41 In.
$1722.00

New Orleans Auction Galleries, Inc.

Furniture, Cabinet, Hvidt & Nielsen, Teak, 2 Sections, Tambour Door, Denmark, c.1960, 66 x 53 In.
$2315.00

Los Angeles Modern Auctions

Furniture, Cabinet, James Mont, Lacquered & Gilded Wood, 2 Doors, Gilded Metal, 1960s, 32 x 54 In.
$5270.00

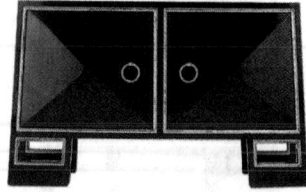

Rago Arts & Auction Center

Cabinet, China, Chippendale Style, Carved, Glass Doors & Shelves, Paw Feet, 81 x 49 In.	748.00
Cabinet, China, Queen Anne, Mahogany, Double Glass Doors, 5 Panes, Legs, 1920s, 42 x 49 In.	745.00
Cabinet, China, Rococo Style, Arch Cornice, Glass Doors, Canted Stiles, 1967, 85 x 66 In.	230.00
Cabinet, China, Rosewood, Carved, 2 Doors, Open Shelves, Pierced Galleries, 21 x 17 In.	711.00
Cabinet, China, William IV, Mahogany, Bowfront, Scrolling Crest, Drawers, 96 x 48 In.	4780.00
Cabinet, China, Wood, Open Shelves, 2 Drawers, 2 Doors, Red Paint, c.1820, 27 x 17 In., Child's	920.00
Cabinet, Chinoiserie, Double Doors, Drawer, Gallery, 17 x 31 In., Pair	702.00
Cabinet, Chinoiserie, Fruitwood, Carved, Doors, Drawers, Brass, Red, Gilt, 33 x 72 In.	305.00
Cabinet, Chinoiserie, Lacquer, Gold & Black, Shell Crest, 2 Doors, Drawers, 18 x 12 In.	2460.00
Cabinet, Chippendale Style, Gilt, Double Bonnet Top, Glass Doors, Chinese, 77 x 53 In.	3540.00
Cabinet, Chrome Steel, Laminated Wood, Block Design, 1970s, 30 x 80 In.	2356.00
Cabinet, Cinnabar, Figures, Landscape, Carved, 2 Doors, 3 Drawers, Chinese, 1900s, 19 x 16 In.	7170.00
Cabinet, Classical Revival, Arched, Column Pilasters, Adjustable Shelves, 91 x 35 In., Pair	4780.00
Cabinet, Cocobolo Wood, Parquetry, Carved, Inlaid, Signed, Mexico, 1965, 30 x 72 x 24 In.	1612.00
Cabinet, Contemporary, Mahogany, Molded Cornice, Glass Doors, 86 x 42 In., Pair	1195.00
Cabinet, Corner, Baroque, Walnut, Arched Paned Door, Lower Paneled Door, 84 x 33 In.	219.00
Cabinet, Corner, Biedermeier, Maple, Bombe, Bonnet, Glass Door, 74 x 34 In.	956.00
Cabinet, Corner, French Provincial, Walnut, Bowed Top, 2 Arch Paneled Doors, c.1790, 39 x 39 In.	984.00
Cabinet, Corner, George III, Mahogany, Carved, Brass, Paneled Doors, c.1790, 89 x 50 In.	2390.00
Cabinet, Corner, Georgian, Mahogany, Bowfront, Oak Interior, 4 Doors, 87 x 29 In.	805.00
Cabinet, Corner, Hanging, Chinoiserie, Bowfront, Shaped Back, Gilt, 1800s, 46 x 24 In.	1107.00
Cabinet, Corner, Hanging, French Provincial, Fruitwood, Bowfront, Panel Door, c.1810, 46 In.	1955.00
Cabinet, Corner, Hepplewhite Style, Mahogany, Broken Bonnet, Shelves, 78 x 32 In.	598.00
Cabinet, Corner, Mahogany, 2 Glass Doors, 2 Low Panel Doors, 76 ½ x 40 ½ In.	345.00
Cabinet, Corner, Mahogany, Glass Doors, Lower Paneled Doors, 1800s, 75 x 42 In.	177.00
Cabinet, Corner, Mahogany, Line Inlay, Glass Door, Diamond Mullion, 1700s, 27 x 15 In.	115.00
Cabinet, Corner, Poplar, Cherry Stain, Glass Doors, Arches, Lower Doors, c.1815, 87 x 56 In.	1476.00
Cabinet, Corner, Stripped Wood, Shaped Shelves, Glass Door, 69 x 28 In.	1409.00
Cabinet, Display, Bowed Glass Center, Flanked By Glass Doors, Stepped Base, 72 x 38 In.	316.00
Cabinet, Display, Carved, Flowers, Scrolls, Mirrored Interior, c.1900, 34 x 21 In.	398.00
Cabinet, Display, Demilune, Mirror Back, Glass Shelves, Velvet Lining, 25 x 14 In.	288.00
Cabinet, Display, Flat Top, 2 Beveled Glass Doors, Inlay, Gilt Metal, 89 x 58 In.	649.00
Cabinet, Display, French Provincial, Oak, Glass Door & Shelves, 34 x 30 In.	270.00
Cabinet, Display, Gilt, Serpentine Pediment, Flower Crest, Glass Door, 77 x 39 In.	919.00
Cabinet, Display, Glass Case, Stepped Cornice, Ring-Turned Legs, 66 x 28 In.	1416.00
Cabinet, Display, Kimbel & Cabus, Ebonized Cherry, Gilt, Porcelain Plaques, 79 x 48 In.	7440.00
Cabinet, Display, Lacquer, Cinnabar, Japanned, Doors, Drawers, 20 x 24 In.	563.00
Cabinet, Display, Mahogany, Leaf Crest, Beveled Mirror, Open Shelves, 2 Doors, 69 In.	384.00
Cabinet, Display, Mahogany, Peaked Top, 3 Glass Doors, Brass Knobs, 1800s, 20 x 13 In.	830.00
Cabinet, Display, Mahogany, Slanted Glass Top, 2 Glass Doors, Brass Gallery, 43 x 35 In.	500.00
Cabinet, Display, Mirrored, Lower Drawers, Painted Flower Bouquets, 1900s, 39 x 76 In.	767.00
Cabinet, Display, Oak, Backsplash, Glass Door, Convex Panels, Cabriole Legs, 1800s, 74 x 45 In.	295.00
Cabinet, Display, Oak, Carved, Glass Door, Interior Shelves, England, 1900s, 45 x 23 In.	230.00
Cabinet, Display, Ormolu, Masks, Marble Stiles, Glass Doors, 48 In.	863.00
Cabinet, Display, Red Lacquer, 4 Open Shelves, 2 Drawers, Chinese, 72 x 16 In.	207.00
Cabinet, Display, Shelves, Sliding Glass Panel Doors, 3 Drawers, c.1900, 54 x 49 In.	978.00
Cabinet, Display, Sheraton Style, Mahogany, Arch & Acorn Frieze, 2 Panel Doors, 1900s	767.00
Cabinet, Display, Triple Bow Crest, 3 Interior Shelves, c.1980, 78 x 49 In.	1265.00
Cabinet, Door, Shell, Flower Carvings, Scroll Feet, France, 1800s, 85 x 29 In.	385.00
Cabinet, Dutch Marquetry, Flowers, Doors, Drawers, 5 Legs, c.1890, 64 x 45 In.	10073.00
Cabinet, Ebonized, Marble Top, 4 Drawers, Open Compartment, c.1880, 36 x 17 In.	288.00
Cabinet, Empire Style, Chinoiserie, Ormolu Mounts, Marble Top, Shaped Skirt, 43 x 33 In.	250.00
Cabinet, Empire Style, Faux Marble Top, Pale Green Paint, Diamond Panel Doors, 37 x 70 In.	512.00
Cabinet, Empire Style, Mahogany, Marble Top, Doors, Ormolu Accents, 37 x 41 In.	1476.00
Cabinet, Empire Style, Rosewood, Brass Grill, Half Spirals, Paw Feet, 35 x 33 In., Pair	3540.00
Cabinet, Empire, Mahogany, Glass Door, Open Interior, Bronze Mounts, Paw Feet, 1800s, 55 x 43 In.	295.00
Cabinet, Filing, Amberg, Imperial, Oak, 15 Stacked Drawers, Oval Plaques, 76 x 16 In.	1298.00
Cabinet, Filing, Oak, 4 Drawers, Marked Property U.S. Air Force, 52 ½ x 16 ½ In.	161.00
Cabinet, Filing, P. Evans, Directional, Cityscape, Chromed Steel, 1970s, 61 x 20 In.	4340.00
Cabinet, Florence Knoll, Birch, Woven Cloth, Leather, Enameled Steel, 1940s, 31 x 72 In.	2852.00
Cabinet, Florence Knoll, Carrara Marble, Rosewood, Chrome, 10 Drawers, 26 x 75 In.	3720.00
Cabinet, Frank Lloyd Wright, Wood, Stacking, 2 Parts, Taliesin Design, Heritage, 35 x 44 In.	5400.00
Cabinet, French Empire Style, Mahogany, Gilt Metal Mounts, Ebonized, 41 x 38 In.	387.00
Cabinet, French Provincial, Maple, Flared Cornice, Doors, 86 x 47 In.	1434.00
Cabinet, French Provincial, Oak, 4 Drawers, Door, 32 x 32 In.	244.00
Cabinet, French Provincial, Oak, Door, Drawer, Intertwined Apron, 1700s, 37 x 29 In.	628.00
Cabinet, French Provincial, Oak, Molded Edge, 2 Doors, Scalloped Apron, c.1800, 34 x 68 In.	2952.00

Cabinet, French Provincial, Painted, Yellow Ground, Flowers, 32 x 36 In.		1063.00
Cabinet, French Provincial, Parcel Gilt, 2 Sunburst Carved Doors, Continental, 28 x 47 In.		384.00
Cabinet, French Provincial, Step Back, Rolling Crest, Doors, Iron Hardware, 73 x 36 In.		502.00
Cabinet, Fruitwood, Board Cornice, 4 Doors, 4 Linenfold Panels, Block Feet, c.1900, 73 x 45 In.		1045.00
Cabinet, G. Nakashima, Black Walnut, 3 Doors, c.1962, 32 x 76 In.		8060.00
Cabinet, G. Nakashima, Double Sliding Door, Walnut, Pandanus Cloth, 32 x 72 x 19 In.		13640.00
Cabinet, G. Nakashima, Kornblut, Walnut, 2 Doors, Burled Maple Handle, 1985, 18 x 22 In.		14400.00
Cabinet, G. Nakashima, Stereo, Walnut, 3 Grill Doors, Pandanus Cloth, 32 x 52 x 18 In.		6500.00
Cabinet, G. Nelson, Black Steel, 3 Walnut Drawers, Laminate Top, Herman Miller, 34 x 30 In.		840.00
Cabinet, G. Nelson, Primavera Wood, Black Surround, 5 Drawers, Herman Miller, 56 x 30 In.		660.00
Cabinet, G. Nelson, Walnut, Lacquer, Block Feet, Herman Miller, 22 ½ x 34 In.		744.00
Cabinet, G. Stickley, Safe-Craft, Mahogany, 2 Glass Doors, 2 Doors, Red Decal, 63 x 35 In.	*illus*	2604.00
Cabinet, George III Style, Mahogany, Gallery, Beveled Glass, Mirror, c.1965, 82 x 41 In.	*illus*	1722.00
Cabinet, George James Sowden, Wood, Silkscreen, Lacquered, Glass, c.1982, 63 x 24 In.		2480.00
Cabinet, Georges Guerin, Louis XVI Style, Mahogany, Marble Top, 16 x 51 In.		1599.00
Cabinet, Georgian Style, Painted, Glass Doors, Paneled Doors, 70 x 49 In.		1250.00
Cabinet, Georgian Style, Pine, Glass Pane Doors, 96 x 84 In.		688.00
Cabinet, Gilt Bronze, Ebonized, Tortoiseshell, Mirror, c.1880, 113 x 89 In.		19120.00
Cabinet, Gilt Incised, Sunflowers, Spindle Gallery, Grecian Urn, Brass Hinges, c.1876, 28 x 33 In.		4674.00
Cabinet, Gio Ponti, Walnut, 12 Drawers, Singer & Sons, 1950s, 40 x 66 In.		16120.00
Cabinet, Gun, Cherry, Arched Glass Doors, 3 Drawers, Henkel Harris, 1900s, 82 x 49 In.		2588.00
Cabinet, Gunni Omann, Teak, 4 Doors, Paper Label, Omann Jun, Denmark, 1950s, 50 x 71 In.		1860.00
Cabinet, Hanging, Chippendale, Mahogany, 2 Doors, Fish Scale Pagoda, Griffins, 1700s		7480.00
Cabinet, Hanging, Cincinnati Art, Walnut, Flower Carved Doors, A. Jordan, c.1910, 43 x 27 In.		7440.00
Cabinet, Hanging, Corner, Georgian, Oak, Panel Door, Fitted Interior, England, 1800, 41 x 34 In.		300.00
Cabinet, Hanging, Display, Hardwood, Rectangular, Plinth, Carved, Chinese, 24 x 18 In.		244.00
Cabinet, Hanging, Display, Pine, Door, 9 Glass Panels, Shelves, c.1850, 25 x 19 In.		633.00
Cabinet, Hanging, G. Nakashima, Black Walnut, Pandanus Cloth, 1973, 19 x 104 In.		44640.00
Cabinet, Hanging, George III Style, Mahogany, Swan's Neck Pediment, 1800s, 59 x 29 In., Pair		4674.00
Cabinet, Hanging, Mahogany, 2 Shelves, Scroll Supports, Door, 1800s, 22 x 16 In.		153.00
Cabinet, Hanging, P. Evans, Directional, Bronze, Wood, Slate, 1970s, 24 x 74 In.		13640.00
Cabinet, Hanging, Pine, Door, 1800s, 16 x 9 In.		92.00
Cabinet, Hanging, Post Office, Cubbyholes, Panel Door, Painted, c.1870, 31 x 37 In.		690.00
Cabinet, Hanging, Walnut, Door, Multicolor Border Designs, Carved Crest, c.1890, 24 x 14 In.		152.00
Cabinet, Hanging, Yellow Paint, Black Metal Hinges, 1800s, 19 x 13 In.		104.00
Cabinet, Hardwood, Applied Dragon Scrolls, Carved, Block Legs, Chinese, 34 x 63 In.		7605.00
Cabinet, Hardwood, Brass, Chinese, 1900s, 20 x 14 In., Pair		295.00
Cabinet, Henry II, Walnut, Bird's-Eye Maple Interior, Reeded Pillars, Shelf, 84 x 45 In.		840.00
Cabinet, Hvidt & Nielsen, Teak, 2 Over 2 Sliding Doors, 37 x 35 In.		1067.00
Cabinet, Hvidt & Nielsen, Teak, 2 Sections, Tambour Door, Denmark, c.1960, 66 x 53 In.	*illus*	2315.00
Cabinet, James Mont, Lacquered & Gilded Wood, 2 Doors, Gilded Metal, 1960s, 32 x 54 In.	*illus*	5270.00
Cabinet, Japanned, 2 Parts, 2 Glass Doors, Shelves, Birds, Scalloped Skirt, 72 x 41 In.		649.00
Cabinet, Jens Quistgaard, Teak, Tambour, Decal, Lovig, Denmark, 1960s, 32 x 79 In.		1240.00
Cabinet, John Keal, Bleached Mahogany, Glass Sliding Doors, Brown & Saltman, 40 x 58 In.		480.00
Cabinet, Kofod-Larsen, Rosewood, 2 Doors, 4 Drawers, Faarup, Denmark, 1960s, 31 x 80 In.		3596.00
Cabinet, Lacquer, Copper & Mother-Of-Pearl Inlay, Panel Doors, 2 Drawers, Chinese, 18 In.		122.00
Cabinet, Lacquer, Gilt, Landscape, 2 Panel Doors, Block Legs, 36 x 27 In.		488.00
Cabinet, Lacquer, Hardstone, Gilt, Drawers, Doors, Cloisonne Hardware, 36 x 24 In.		275.00
Cabinet, Library, Neoclassical, Cream, Gold, Arch, Glass Doors, Metal, 114 x 41 In., Pair		2963.00
Cabinet, Library, Walnut, 2 Doors, Shelves, 77 x 47 In.		351.00
Cabinet, Liquor, Art Deco, Mahogany, Satinwood, Chrome, Starburst, c.1930, 55 x 47 In.		1353.00
Cabinet, Liquor, Federal, Mahogany, 2 Drawers, 2 Doors, Paw Feet, c.1815, 45 x 30 In.		472.00
Cabinet, Liquor, George III Style, Mahogany, Manor Dollhouse Shape, 71 x 34 In.		2688.00
Cabinet, Loewy, Wood, Laminate, 4 Red & Orange Drawers, Door, Label, France		1560.00
Cabinet, Louis XV Style, Chinoiserie, Lacquer, Domed Cornice, Landscape, 69 x 48 In.		2952.00
Cabinet, Louis XVI Style, Burl Walnut Veneer, Bowed Glass, Tiffany Co., Paris, c.1900, 82 x 59 In.	*illus*	1680.00
Cabinet, Louis XVI Style, Mahogany, Gallery, Open Shelf, 2 Doors, c.1920, 29 x 19 In., Pair		690.00
Cabinet, Louis XVI, Rosewood Inlay, Beveled Marble Top, Drop Front, Drawer, 41 x 39 In.		300.00
Cabinet, M. Baughman, Olive Burl, Chrome Platform, 3 Doors, T. Coggin, 66 x 34 In.		1560.00
Cabinet, Mahogany, Ebonized, Fretwork Gallery, Mirrors, Spindles, Birds, c.1885, 60 x 60 In.		3444.00
Cabinet, Marquetry, Wood Veneer, Serpentine Front, Fitted Interior, 17 x 13 In.		1121.00
Cabinet, McCobb, Brass, Teak, 2 Bifold Doors, Fitted Interior, Tag, Calvin, 71 x 34 In.		4800.00
Cabinet, Meeks, Neoclassical, Mahogany, Marble Top, Cylindrical Pedestal, 30 x 15 In.		1076.00
Cabinet, Metal, Wood, 12 Drawers, 4 Cabinet Doors, c.1910		1107.00
Cabinet, Mixed Wood, Carved, Minerva Head Crest, Medallion Door, Drawer, c.1880, 30 x 21 In.		823.00
Cabinet, Mixed Wood, Portrait Frieze, 2 Doors, Flower, Leaf Inlay, Dutch, 86 x 68 In.		2952.00
Cabinet, Music, Amber Glass Door, 47 x 19 ½ In.		8060.00

Furniture, Cabinet, Louis XVI Style, Burl Walnut Veneer, Bowed Glass, Bronze, Tiffany Co., Paris, c.1900, 82 x 59 In. $1680.00

Cowan's Auctions

Furniture, Cabinet, Neoclassical, Mahogany, Carved Frieze, Door, Pedestal, Continental, 1800s, 56 x 21 In. $3585.00

Neal Auction Co.

Furniture, Cabinet, Neoclassical, Mahogany, Drawer, Door, Egyptian Columns, c.1825, 44 x 25 x 28 In. $7170.00

Neal Auction Co.

Furniture, Cabinet, P. Evans, Enameled Steel, Slate, Bronze, 1969, 31 ½ x 72 In. $24800.00

Rago Arts & Auction Center

Furniture, Cabinet, Regency, Rosewood, Gilt Metal Grid Door, Leafy Brass Inlay, Scrolling Feet, 25 x 23 In. $6490.00

Ivey-Selkirk Auctioneers

Furniture, Cabinet, Renaissance Revival, Rosewood, Cherry, Plaques, Inlay, Bronze, c.1865, 52 x 72 In. $14340.00

Neal Auction Co.

Furniture, Cabinet, Telephone, Art Deco, Gilt Bronze, Iron, Gothic, Door, 1920s, 52 ½ x 18 ¾ In. $1416.00

Brunk Auctions

Cabinet, Music, Empire Revival, Mahogany, Panel Door, Bowfront Drawer, c.1900, 42 x 21 In.	288.00
Cabinet, Music, Sheraton, Mahogany, Paneled Doors, Drawer, Phila., c.1810, 27 x 21 In.........	1185.00
Cabinet, Music, Victorian, Cherry, Mirror Gallery, Swag, Bead Panel Doors, 6 Drawers, 42 x 28 In.	565.00
Cabinet, Napoleon III, Brass, Mixed Wood, Glass Door, Shelves, Flower Mounts, 1800s, 27 x 20 In.	474.00
Cabinet, Neoclassical, Mahogany, Carved Frieze, Door, Pedestal, Continental, 1800s, 56 x 21 In. ...*illus*	3585.00
Cabinet, Neoclassical, Mahogany, Drawer, Door, Egyptian Columns, c.1825, 44 x 25 x 28 In. ...*illus*	7170.00
Cabinet, Neoclassical, Mahogany, Satinwood, 36 x 19 In.	500.00
Cabinet, Neoclassical, Marquetry, D-Shape, Door, 1800s, 35 x 29 In., Pair	3750.00
Cabinet, Neoclassical, Satinwood, Flower Roundel Inlays, 2 Doors, 3 Drawers, 38 x 64 In.......	1280.00
Cabinet, Oak, 2 Doors, Fitted Interior, Side Pedestals, c.1940, 38 x 43 In.	800.00
Cabinet, Oak, 2 Glass Doors, Openwork, 2 Flour Bins, Marked, c.1900-10..........................	460.00
Cabinet, Oak, 2 Panel Doors, Crown Molding, 2 Drawer Base, England, 1700s, 72 x 55 In.	690.00
Cabinet, Oak, Brass Hinges, Hanging, c.1895, 27 x 28 x 9 In.	259.00
Cabinet, Oak, Dentil Cornice, Paneled Doors, Flowers, Beading, 10 Drawers, Bun Feet, 70 x 51 In.	1422.00
Cabinet, Oak, Fruitwood, Molded Cornice, 12 Panel Doors, Shelves, Plinth, 78 x 95 In...........	1230.00
Cabinet, Oak, Pine, Shaped Top, Rounded Corners, Door, Columns, 1800s, 41 x 51 In............	500.00
Cabinet, Oak, Rectangular, Molded Edge, Drawer, 2 Doors, Plinth Base, 36 x 35 In.................	711.00
Cabinet, Oak, Shaped Top, 2 Frieze Drawers, 2 Doors, 1800s, 38 x 66 In.	1035.00
Cabinet, P. Evans, Directional, Bronze, Composite, Slate, Laminate, c.1977, 31 x 48 In.	8060.00
Cabinet, P. Evans, Directional, Cityscape, Flip Top Bar, Chromed Steel, Brass, 1970s, 35 x 36 In.	6200.00
Cabinet, P. Evans, Directional, Faceted, Chrome Plate, Maple Burl, Fiberglass, 1970s, 33 x 104 In.	27280.00
Cabinet, P. Evans, Directional, Model PE-39, Steel, Bronze, c.1969, 36 x 24 In......................	6820.00
Cabinet, P. Evans, Enameled Steel, Slate, Bronze, 1969, 31 ½ x 72 In. ....*illus*	24800.00
Cabinet, Painted, Flowers, Gilt Accents, 2 Glass Doors, 2 Drawer Bombe Base, 85 x 44 In.	690.00
Cabinet, Parquetry, Ribbon, Swags, Marble Top, Demilune, Ormolu Mounts, 36 x 40 In.	595.00
Cabinet, Parzinger, Lacquered Wood, Marble, Brass, 1950s, 35 x 103 In...............................	11780.00
Cabinet, Parzinger, Mixed Wood, Lighted Top Section, Glass Doors, Drawers, 87 x 60 In.	1000.00
Cabinet, Pine, 2 Doors, Shaped Painted Backsplash, Iron Hardware, Monterey, c.1935, 36 x 57 In.	3250.00
Cabinet, Pine, Molded Cornice, 2 Paneled Doors, Drawer, Bun Feet, 1900s, 80 x 48 x 26 In.....	1045.00
Cabinet, Pine, Rectangular Ebonized Top, 2 Doors, Arched Panel, Base, 1800s, 39 x 47 In......	461.00
Cabinet, Pine, Upper & Lower Double Doors, Block Feet, 73 x 38 In.	546.00
Cabinet, Post Office, Oak, 2 4-Panel Doors, Fitted Interior, 1870s, 83 x 42 In.....................	432.00
Cabinet, R.J. Horner, Curved Glass Front, Bonnet Top, Griffins, Paw Feet, 75 x 45 In...............	5605.00
Cabinet, Record, Herzog, Bow Door, Interior Shelf, Bun Feet..	690.00
Cabinet, Record, Oak, 5 Drawers, Cylinder, Pegs..	316.00
Cabinet, Rectangular, 4 Frieze Drawers, 3 Center Drawers, Doors, Chinese, 37 x 62 In.	177.00
Cabinet, Regency Style, Rosewood, 2 Glass Doors, 2 Brass Grill Doors, England, c.1905, 55 x 49 In.	345.00
Cabinet, Regency, Rosewood, Gilt Metal Grid Door, Leafy Brass Inlay, Scrolling Feet, 25 x 23 In. .*illus*	6490.00
Cabinet, Regency, Walnut, Greek Key, Grill Door, Paneled Uprights, c.1805, 36 x 35 In., Pair..	3444.00
Cabinet, Renaissance Revival, Oak, 2 Doors, Carved, Side Handles, Ball Feet, 37 x 53 In.	660.00
Cabinet, Renaissance Revival, Rosewood, Cherry, Plaques, Inlay, Bronze, c.1865, 52 x 72 In. ..*illus*	14340.00
Cabinet, Robsjohn-Gibbings, Bleached Mahogany, Brass, Widdicomb, 1950s, 35 x 72 In.	1488.00
Cabinet, Robsjohn-Gibbings, Mahogany, Brass, 2 Doors, Widdicomb, 1940s, 31 x 34 In.	372.00
Cabinet, Rococo Revival, Rosewood, Open Shelves, Mirrors, Carved Crest, c.1865, 67 x 47 In.	1968.00
Cabinet, Rosewood, 5 Compartments, 2 Doors, Carved Lotus Scrolls, Chinese, 1800s, 51 x 20 In.	7968.00
Cabinet, Rosewood, Burl, Panel Doors, 5 Drawers, Chinese, 1900s, 28 x 19 In.........................	354.00
Cabinet, Rosewood, Carved, Chinese, 1900s, 37 ½ x 24 In.	120.00
Cabinet, Rosewood, Mother-Of-Pearl Inlay, 2 Glass Doors, Cherry Blossoms, 78 x 42 In.	450.00
Cabinet, Rosewood, Rectangular, Turret Corners, Flower Garland, Leaves, c.1865, 43 x 34 In.	2415.00
Cabinet, Rosewood, Shelves, Turned Spindles, Fretwork Gallery, Mirror Doors, c.1850, 60 x 36 In.	1599.00
Cabinet, Scholar's, 4 Doors, Lower Drawers, Block Feet, Chinese, c.1900, 67 x 44 In.	188.00
Cabinet, Sewing, Chinoiserie, Lacquer, Shaped Top, 2 Supports, Stretcher, 28 x 25 In...........	488.00
Cabinet, Sheraton Style, Nymph Painted Door, 2 Glass Side Doors, England, 1800, 48 x 48 In.	3660.00
Cabinet, Sheraton, Mahogany, Cushion Frieze Drawer Over 3 Drawers, 34 x 21 In...................	123.00
Cabinet, Smoking, Arts & Crafts, Oak, Brass Round Plate, Door, 12 ½ x 12 ½ In......................	270.00
Cabinet, Smoking, G. Stickley, Drawer, Door, Shaped Base, Paper Label, 28 ¾ x 20 In.	2728.00
Cabinet, Spanish Baroque, Pine, 2 Baluster Doors, 2 Drawers, Trestle Base, 66 x 38 In...........	770.00
Cabinet, Specimen, Chippendale Style, Walnut, 4 Drawers, Bracket Feet, c.1815, 9 ½ x 17 In.	460.00
Cabinet, Spice, 8 Drawers, c.1900, 17 ½ In...	180.00
Cabinet, Spice, Cherry, Step Back, 8 Drawers, Wood Knobs, 1800s, 11 x 18 In.	490.00
Cabinet, Spice, Pine, 27 Drawers, Shaped Bracket Base, Molded Cornice...............................	920.00
Cabinet, Spice, Tin, Scroll Crest, 8 Drawers, White & Salmon Paint, Victorian, 14 x 9 In.	89.00
Cabinet, Stereo, Multisonic, Splayed Legs, Grundig-Majestic, 32 x 58 In.	236.00
Cabinet, Tambour Slide Front, 7 Interior Drawers, Mohler Rabique, 30 x 20 In.	230.00
Cabinet, Teak, Chromed Steel, White Oak, Tambour Doors, Denmark, 1960s, 31 x 78 x 19 In.	2480.00

F

Cabinet, Telephone, Art Deco, Gilt Bronze, Iron, Gothic, Door, 1920s, 52 ½ x 18 ¾ In. ....*illus*		1416.00
Cabinet, Tiger Maple, 6 Pigeonholes, c.1850, 23 ½ x 19 ¾ In..		304.00
Cabinet, Victorian, Carved Crest, 4 Doors, Shelves, 2 Drawers, Marble Top Base, 98 x 62 In.....		460.00
Cabinet, Victorian, Mahogany, Brass Wreath Mounts, 2 Doors, Cabriole Legs, 35 x 38 In.........		156.00
Cabinet, Victorian, Mahogany, Rail Gallery, Drawer, Triple Panel Door, Side Pilasters, 39 x 28 In.		250.00
Cabinet, Victorian, Rosewood, Shaped Top, 3 Doors, Carved Stiles, 37 x 56 In.		575.00
Cabinet, Victorian, Walnut, Carved, Drawer, Door, Oval Woman Medallion, c.1860, 44 x 34 In.		948.00
Cabinet, Victorian, Walnut, Flower Carved Doors, Shelves, Ball & Stick, 34 x 20 In.................		357.00
Cabinet, Victorian, Walnut, Shaped Crest, Door, 3 Drawers, c.1890, 71 x 31 In.		230.00
Cabinet, Walnut, 2 Doors, Drop Sides, Black Laminate Top, Glenn Of California, 33 x 32 In...		180.00
Cabinet, Walnut, Carrara Marble Top, Inlaid Frieze, Domed Mirror Plate, 35 x 61 In.		430.00
Cabinet, Walnut, Cherry, Triple Panel Door, Shelves, Dovetailed Drawer, N.C., 1800s, 39 x 27 In. *illus*		1440.00
Cabinet, Walnut, Door, Drawer, Carved Scrolls & Profiles, Brittany, 70 x 32 In.		458.00
Cabinet, Walnut, Door, Interior Shelves, Drawer, Painted, Lammert, 1930s, 61 x 36 In...........		288.00
Cabinet, Walnut, Molded Top, 2 Drawers, 2 Doors, Masks, Leaf Garland, Italy, 1600s, 34 x 35 In.		1188.00
Cabinet, Walnut, Scalloped Glass Doors, Drawer, Shaped Base, Cabriole Legs, 1800s, 28 x 18 In.		837.00
Cabinet, Watering, Zinc, 2 Doors, 3 Shelves, Quatrefoil Cutouts Over All, 30 x 51 x 31 In.		984.00
Cabinet, William & Mary, Walnut, Drawers, Door, Trumpet Legs, 1700s, 64 x 45 In.................		4270.00
Cabinet, William IV, Rosewood, Marble Top, Drawer, Grillwork Doors, 37 x 42 In.		354.00
Cabinet, Wood, Veneers, 4 Flat Doors, Bakelite Pulls, c.1930, 59 x 47 In...............................		615.00
Cabinet, Wormley, Lacquered Rosewood, Printing Block Panels, Dunbar, 1950s, 30 x 65 ½ In.		1364.00
Cabinet, Wormley, Mahogany, 5 Drawers, Dunbar, c.1950, 30 x 30 In., Pair...........................		1410.00
Cabinet, Wormley, Mahogany, Enameled Brass, Aluminum, Dunbar, 1960s, 15 x 32 In...........		372.00
Cabinet-On-Chest, Georgian, Oak, Molded Cornice, Arch-Paneled Grill Doors, 1700s, 76 x 56 In.		708.00
Cabinet-On-Stand, Chinoiserie, Red Lacquer, Flowers, Mountains, 2 Doors, 40 x 33 In.........		236.00
Cabinet-On-Stand, Lacquer, Gilt, Figures, 2 Upper Doors, Drawers, Chinese, 1800s, 60 x 39 In.		915.00
Cabinet-On-Stand, Teak, 2 Doors, Sliding Trays, Shelves, Denmark, c.1955, 57 x 47 In. .... *illus*		1076.00
Candlestand, Birch, Painted, Oval Tilt Top, Urn Standard, Spider Leg Base, c.1810, 28 In.		1150.00
Candlestand, Birch, Square Top, Painted, Splayed Tripod Feet, c.1800, 27 x 14 In...................		460.00
Candlestand, Cherry, Red Paint, Urn Standard, Tripod, New England, 1900s, 28 x 18 In.		504.00
Candlestand, Cherry, Shaped Top, Serpentine Edge, Turned Stem, Tripod, c.1800, 27 x 18 In.		1947.00
Candlestand, Cherry, Square Tray Top, Cabriole Legs, Pad Feet, 1700s, 29 x 20 In..................		889.00
Candlestand, Cherry, Yellow Pine, Drawer, Tripod, Piedmont, c.1850, 28 In. ....*illus*		316.00
Candlestand, Chippendale, Cherry, Octagonal, Turned Pedestal, Cabriole Legs, 27 x 15 In.....		234.00
Candlestand, Chippendale, Mahogany, Tilt Dish Top, Birdcage Support, 1700s, 30 x 19 In......		400.00
Candlestand, Chippendale, Walnut, Round Tilt Top, Birdcage Support, Pad Feet, c.1795, 29 x 19 In.		1067.00
Candlestand, Chippendale, Walnut, Round Tilt Top, Rotating Support, 1700s, 28 x 22 ½ In. .		300.00
Candlestand, Chippendale, Wood, Tripod Base, c.1805, 27 x 19 In.		1680.00
Candlestand, Federal, Birch, Cherry, Single-Board Top, Tripod, Snake Feet, c.1800, 26 x 17 In.		235.00
Candlestand, Federal, Birch, Oval Tilt Top, Urn Post, Shaped Legs, Tripod, c.1805, 28 x 15 In.		533.00
Candlestand, Federal, Cherry, Drawer, Square, Rounded Corners, Vase Support, 1800s, 28 x 19 In.		1067.00
Candlestand, Federal, Cherry, Inlay, Cut-Corner Top, Urn Post, Curved Legs, c.1815, 26 x 16 In.		3450.00
Candlestand, Federal, Cherry, Octagonal Top, Splayed Spider Legs, 28 x 17 In........................		345.00
Candlestand, Federal, Mahogany, Inlay, Shaped Tilt Top, Baluster, Reeded Legs, c.1800, 30 x 25 In.		1353.00
Candlestand, Federal, Mahogany, Octagonal Tilt Top, 3 Arched Legs, c.1800, 29 x 17 In.........		546.00
Candlestand, Federal, Mahogany, Octagonal Top, Pear Stem, Tripod Cabriole Legs, 25 x 16 In.		293.00
Candlestand, Federal, Mahogany, Oval Tilt Top, Birdcage Support, Urn Pedestal, c.1800, 42 In.		690.00
Candlestand, Federal, Mahogany, Tilt Top, Molded Edge, Turned Support, c.1780, 28 x 21 In.		415.00
Candlestand, Federal, Mahogany, Tilt Top, Vase & Ring Turned Post, Tripod, Pad Feet, 1800s, 28 In.		1041.00
Candlestand, Federal, Mahogany, Tripod Feet, 1800s, 28 ½ x 16 In.......................................		140.00
Candlestand, Federal, Maple, Octagonal Top, Turned Pedestal, Tripod Base, c.1810, 28 x 20 In.		194.00
Candlestand, Federal, Tiger Maple, Square Top, Lyre Leg Base, New England, 28 x 17 In........		978.00
Candlestand, George III, Mahogany, Dish Top, Vase Stem, Spider Legs, Pad Feet, 1700s, 27 In.		915.00
Candlestand, Georgian, Mahogany, Round Dish Top, Baluster Turned Stem, 13 In.................		427.00
Candlestand, Grain Painted, Square Top, Scroll Cut Corner, Carved Legs, Pad Feet, 1800s, 26 In.		711.00
Candlestand, Iron, Open Work Top, Square Shaft, 3 Curved Legs, Round, 27 In......................		165.00
Candlestand, Iron, Tripod Base, c.1800, 45 In..		365.00
Candlestand, Mahogany, Dish Top, Weighted Base, Adjustable Column Post, 8 ½ In..............		294.00
Candlestand, Mahogany, Shaped Tilt Top, Carved Pineapple Shaft, Scroll Feet, c.1800, 29 x 26 In.		1315.00
Candlestand, Maple, Oval Top, Reeded Standard, Tripod Base, New England, c.1815, 27 ½ x 17 In.		356.00
Candlestand, Maple, Round Top, Turned Pedestal, Tripod Base, Slipper Feet, 27 In................		443.00
Candlestand, Mixed Wood, Round Top, Sausage Turned Column, 27 x 16 In..........................		104.00
Candlestand, Neoclassical, Mahogany, Carved, Leaves, Reeded Legs, N.Y., c.1825, 22 x 19 In. ..*illus*		956.00
Candlestand, Oval Top, Baluster, Reeded Tripod Splayed Legs, American, 1800s, 30 x 24 In. ..		295.00
Candlestand, Painted, Shaped Square Top, Vase Turned Pedestal, Tripod, 1700s, 26 x 15 In...		115.00
Candlestand, Pine, Square, Shaped Gallery, Candleholders, Footstool Base, 1800s, 30 x 15 In.		148.00
Candlestand, Queen Anne, Cherry, 2-Board Serpentine Top, Ring & Urn Shaft, 1700s, 28 x 16 In.		288.00

Furniture, Cabinet, Walnut, Cherry, Triple Panel Door, Shelves, Dovetailed Drawer, N.C., 1800s, 39 x 27 In. $1440.00

Brunk Auctions

Furniture, Cabinet-On-Stand, Teak, 2 Doors, Sliding Trays, Shelves, Denmark, c.1955, 57 x 47 In. $1076.00

Neal Auction Co.

Furniture, Candlestand, Cherry, Yellow Pine, Drawer, Tripod, Piedmont, c.1850, 28 In. $316.00

Leland Little Auction

Furniture, Candlestand, Neoclassical, Mahogany, Carved, Leaves, Reeded Legs, N.Y., c.1825, 22 x 19 In.
$956.00

Neal Auction Co.

Furniture, Canterbury, Hepplewhite Style, Drawer, Banding, Line & Barberpole Inlays, c.1890, 19 x 17 In.
$413.00

Brunk Auctions

Furniture, Canterbury, Walnut, Carved, Pierced Sides, Drawer, Casters, England, c.1850, 23 x 24 In.
$837.00

Neal Auction Co.

TIP

To deodorize a drawer, try this. Put uncooked coffee grounds in the leg of an old pair of panty hose. Tie it shut. Then put the bundle in the drawer for a few days.

Candlestand, Queen Anne, Cherry, Shaped Top, Diamond Inlay, Snake Feet, 1700s, 27 x 19 In. — 4600.00
Candlestand, Queen Anne, Cherry, Tripod Legs, c.1780, 26 x 17 ½ In. — 296.00
Candlestand, Queen Anne, Cuban Mahogany, Round Top, Turned Pedestal, 3 Legs, 1800s, 27 In. — 316.00
Candlestand, Queen Anne, Walnut, Round Dish Top, Birdcage Pedestal, c.1760, 29 x 24 In. .. — 5000.00
Candlestand, Queen Anne, Walnut, Round Top, Tripod Base, Pa., c.1765, 27 x 22 In. — 889.00
Candlestand, Queen Anne, Wood, Drawer, Turned Stem, Tripod, New England, c.1780, 26 x 16 In. — 3750.00
Candlestand, Tiger Maple, Rectangular, Rounded Corners, Baluster, Tripod, 1847, 29 x 24 In. — 540.00
Candlestand, Tiger Maple, Round Top, Baluster Support, Curved Feet, 1800s, 27 x 16 In........ — 237.00
Candlestand, Tiger Maple, Round Tray Top, Tripod Base, c.1890, 29 x 21 In. — 304.00
Candlestand, Tilt Top, Leaf Carved, Paw Feet, c.1825, 30 x 27 In............... — 956.00
Candlestand, Tilt Top, Walnut, Round, 22 x 16 In. .... — 57.00
Candlestand, Walnut, Inlay, 2 Tiers, 10-Sided Top, Bulbous Standard, England, c.1690, 29 x 15 In. — 215.00
Candlestand, Walnut, Octagonal Top, Arched Tripod Base, N.C., c.1850, 27 In...................... — 374.00
Candlestand, Walnut, Octagonal Top, Turned Stem, Tripod Base, N.C., c.1850, 26 x 15 In. ...... — 863.00
Candlestand, Walnut, Tilt Top, Molded Edge, Birdcage Support, Tripod, Pa., c.1780, 29 x 39 In. — 2185.00
Candlestand, Wood, Round Dish Top, Tapered Pedestal Support, 1800s, 29 In........................ — 443.00
Candlestand, Wrought Iron, 3 Scrolled Legs, Center Shaft, Spring, Rush Stirrup, 18 In........... — 502.00
Candlestand, Wrought Iron, Adjustable, 2 Cups, Penny Feet, 60 In. .... — 474.00
Candlestand, Wrought Iron, Shaft, Slide, 3 Arched Legs, c.1800, 53 x 13 In. .... — 403.00
Canterbury, Art Deco, Mahogany, Burl Walnut, Slatted Brass Rack, Door, c.1920, 39 x 18 In.. — 461.00
Canterbury, Federal, Mahogany, 4 Compartments, Drawer, Casters, 16 x 19 In..................... — 316.00
Canterbury, Hepplewhite Style, Drawer, Banding, Line & Barberpole Inlays, c.1890, 19 x 17 In. *illus* — 413.00
Canterbury, Mahogany, Openwork Lyre Sides, Drawer, Flower Carved, c.1860, 21 x 26 In....... — 474.00
Canterbury, Mahogany, Turned Stiles, Drawer, Curved Top, Handle, Casters, 19 x 19 In......... — 259.00
Canterbury, Regency Style, Mahogany, Drawer, Caster, 1800s, 21 x 21 In. .... — 413.00
Canterbury, Regency Style, Mahogany, Lyre Shape, 25 x 18 In. .... — 188.00
Canterbury, Regency Style, Mahogany, Turned Spindles, 4 Partitions, Shelf, 20 x 15 In......... — 308.00
Canterbury, Regency, Mahogany, Curved Top, Drawer, Dividers, Casters, 1800s, 21 x 18 In...... — 504.00
Canterbury, Regency, Mahogany, Drawer, 4 Sections, Slats, Handle, 1800s, 20 x 20 In. .... — 499.00
Canterbury, Regency, Rosewood, 2 Shelves, X-Shape Dividers, Drawer, 48 x 19 In. .... — 3627.00
Canterbury, Rosewood, Drawer, Straight Uprights, Round Reeded Legs, c.1900...................... — 474.00
Canterbury, Sheraton, Mahogany, Turned Post, Ball Finials, Pierced Dividers, Drawer, 19 x 17 In. — 413.00
Canterbury, Turned Post, Ball Finials, Pierced Dividers, Drawer, Turned Feet, 18 x 18 In........ — 443.00
Canterbury, Victorian, Burl, Rectangular, Marquetry, Flowers, Gilt, Openwork, 35 x 20 In. .... — 830.00
Canterbury, Walnut, Carved, Pierced Sides, Drawer, Casters, England, c.1850, 23 x 24 In. . *illus* — 837.00
Canterbury, Walnut, Oval, Finials, Slotted Compartments, Drawer, Casters, 39 x 29 In. .... — 984.00
Canterbury, William IV, Rosewood, Drawer, Scroll Uprights, Spindles, c.1850, 19 x 22 In. ...... — 1778.00
Card Catalog, Library, Oak, 15 Drawers, Legs, Gaylord, 33 x 46 ½ In. .... — 490.00
Card Stand, Black Forest, Bear, Holding Tray, Oval Base, 21 ½ In. .... *illus* — 837.00
Cart, Brass, Steel, 2 Tiers, Black Glass Shelves, Paw Feet, France, c.1940, 28 x 33 In. .... — 1168.00
Cart, Chrome Handle, Tray, Low Shelf, c.1960, 30 x 30 In. .... — 431.00
Cart, Danish Style, Teak, Blond Wood, Casters, 25 x 32 In............................. — 118.00
Cart, Ebonized Faux Bamboo, Brass, Glass Shelves, 3 Tiers, c.1960, 34 x 31 In. .... — 923.00
Cart, Glass, Brass, Gallery, Shelf, Tube Supports, Handle, Spoked Wheels, 33 x 37 In................ — 72.00
Cart, Kittinger, Mahogany, 2 Tiers, Gallery Back, 2 Slides, 2 Drawers, 35 ½ x 36 In. .... — 374.00
Cart, Painted, Slats, 2 Back Wheels, 2 Smaller Front Wheels, 20 x 64 x 23 In. .... — 270.00
Cart, Tea, Mahogany, Removable Glass Tray, 2 Open Shelves, 31 x 32 In. .... — 61.00
Cart, Tea, Renaissance Revival, Oak, 2 Gallery Shelves, Carved Legs, Wheels, 29 x 27 In.......... — 397.00
Cart, Wine, Round Wood Top, Divided Bottle Holders, Raised Wheels, 36 ½ x 47 In................. — 1968.00
Cellarette, Arts & Crafts, Redwood, Door, Strap Hardware, 17 ½ x 17 ½ In. .... — 270.00
Cellarette, Carved Hardwood, Elephant Shape, Hinged Door, Ivory Tusks, 1800s, 29 x 41 In.... — 6518.00
Cellarette, Drop Front, Carved, Jamestown, 36 x 23 In. .... — 600.00
Cellarette, Federal, Walnut, Eagle Inlay, Lift Top, Stand, X-Stretcher, c.1800, 36 x 19 In.......... — 2032.00
Cellarette, Federal, Walnut, Hinged Top, Stand, Inscribed, Orton, 38 x 18 In. .... *illus* — 35400.00
Cellarette, George III, Mahogany, Brass Bound, Octagonal, Hinged Top, Bail Handles, 23 x 24 In. — 1375.00
Cellarette, George III, Mahogany, Fitted Metal Interior, Brass Handles, c.1790, 25 x 17 In. ...... — 1049.00
Cellarette, George III, Mahogany, Hexagonal, Hinged Cover, Brass, Reeded Legs, 27 x 18 In... — 750.00
Cellarette, George III, Mahogany, Inlay, Hexagonal, Hinged Top, Spigot, 1700s, 27 In............ — 956.00
Cellarette, George III, Mahogany, Rectangular, Hinged Top, Lion Mask Ring Handles, 20 x 27 In. — 915.00
Cellarette, George III, Satinwood, Inlaid Mahogany, Octagonal, Hinged Lid, Stand, c.1790, 30 In. — 646.00
Cellarette, Hepplewhite, Mahogany, Eagle, Snake Inlays, Drawer, Tapered Legs, 42 x 21 In. ... — 748.00
Cellarette, Mahogany, Brass, Octagonal, Lion's Head Handles, X-Stretcher, 23 x 27 In. .... — 1380.00
Cellarette, Mahogany, Star Design Top, Base Drawer, Raised Tapered Legs, 37 x 21 In. .... — 1035.00
Cellarette, Mahogany, String Inlay, Hinged Top, Sham Drawer, Stand, Square Legs, 28 x 17 In. — 770.00
Cellarette, Regency, Mahogany, Tin Liner, Paw Feet, c.1820, 34 x 24 ½ In. .... — 978.00
Cellarette, Rosewood, Sarcophagus Shape, Inlaid Highlights, Gilt, Fitted, 9 ½ x 13 In. .... — 826.00
Cellarette, William IV, Mahogany, Sarcophagus Shape, Domed Lid, 1800s, 23 x 40 In............ — 896.00

Cellarette, Wood, Square Top, Open Shelf, Door, Lock, Jamestown, 22 x 22 In.	2760.00
Chair & Ottoman, Eames, Rosewood, Leather Upholstery, Herman Miller, 32 In.	1725.00
Chair & Ottoman, Milo Baughman, Black Leather, Wood Arms & Legs, 1960s, 36 In.	613.00
Chair Set, Aesthetic Revival, Gilt, Faux Bamboo Back & Legs, 36 In., 12	677.00
Chair Set, Afra & Tobia Scarpa, Artona, Rosewood, Birch, Leather, Brass, 1975, 31 In., 8	24800.00
Chair Set, Art Deco, Walnut, Carved Flower Back, Cushion Seat, France, 18 x 36 In., 6	1140.00
Chair Set, Arts & Crafts, Vertical Splats, Square Legs, Leather, Stretcher, 44 In., 8	976.00
Chair Set, Brass, Tufted Velvet, Low Arms, Mastercraft, c.1970, 44 x 22 In., 8	3100.00
Chair Set, Chippendale, Carved Crest, Pierced Splat, Slip Seat, Cabriole Legs, c.1875, 40 x 24 In., 4.	1150.00
Chair Set, Chippendale, Cherry, Ladder Back, Marked, c.1795, 37 x 19 In., 4	1185.00
Chair Set, Chippendale, Cherry, Upholstered Slip Seats, Beaded Legs, c.1795, 39 In., 4	3851.00
Chair Set, Chippendale, Mahogany, Yoke Crest Rail, Openwork Splat, Armchair, 39 In., 7	777.00
Chair Set, Chrome, Bronze, Swan Arm Ends, Padded Seat, c.1960, 32 x 26 In., 4	923.00
Chair Set, Classical Revival, Mahogany, Arched Carved Crest Rail, Upholstered, 32 In., 6	676.00
Chair Set, Curly Maple, Saber Legs, Cane Seat, c.1850, 33 In., 6	1293.00
Chair Set, Eero Saarinen, Laminated Walnut, Wool, 1950s, 32 x 22 In., 8	2976.00
Chair Set, Empire, Carved Crest Rail, Shaped Splat, Medial Rail, Fluted Legs, c.1830, 33 In., 6	269.00
Chair Set, George III Style, Mahogany, Carved, Arched Crest Rail, 2 Armchairs, 8	671.00
Chair Set, George III Style, Mahogany, Carved, Shaped Crest Rail, 2 Armchairs, 12	5676.00
Chair Set, George III Style, Mahogany, Flared Openwork Splats, Upholstered, 8	3438.00
Chair Set, George III, Mahogany, Carved Crest, Pierced Splat, Upholstered, c.1785, 37 In., 6 ..	1422.00
Chair Set, Georgian Style, Mahogany, Shaped Splat, Slip Seat, 4	813.00
Chair Set, Georgian Style, Mahogany, Upholstered Seat, 4	813.00
Chair Set, Georgian, Mahogany, Inlaid, Pierced Crest, Slip Seat, c.1800, 36 x 22 In., 4	920.00
Chair Set, Georgian, Oak, Stylized Fan & Lyre Splat, Padded Seat, c.1910, 37 In., 8	1230.00
Chair Set, Gilt Metal, Faux Bamboo, Lattice Design, Splay Feet, c.1900, 34 In., 4	1230.00
Chair Set, Henry II Style, Walnut, Pierced Rail, Upholstered Seat & Back, 34 x 18 In., 8	153.00
Chair Set, Hepplewhite Style, Mahogany, Carved, Arched Crest, Vase Shape Splat, 8	1554.00
Chair Set, Iron, Black, Tapered Backrest, Round Seat, Brass Finials, 39 x 14 In., 4	207.00
Chair Set, L. & J.G. Stickley, Oilcloth, Tacks, Onondaga Shops, 35 ½ x 19 In., 6	4030.00
Chair Set, L. & J.G. Stickley, Spindle Back, Tacked Leather, 41 ½ x 17 ½ In., 6	3720.00
Chair Set, Ligne Roset, Brown Leather, Steel Frame, 32 In., 6	531.00
Chair Set, Louis XV Style, Fruitwood, Carved, Shaped, Flower Crest, Peg Feet, c.1900, 36 In., 4	461.00
Chair Set, Louis XV Style, Fruitwood, Shaped Cane Back, Shield Crest, c.1910, 37 In., 4	799.00
Chair Set, Louis XV Style, Gilt, Padded Back, Seat, Floral Crest, Cabriole Legs, 38 In., 8	1045.00
Chair Set, Louis XVI Style, Fruitwood, Leaf Carved Domed Crest, Upholstered, 40 In., 8	1135.00
Chair Set, Mahogany, Ebonized Crest, Brass Rings, 2 Panel Splat, Saber Legs, c.1825, 35 In., 8	2460.00
Chair Set, Mahogany, Gondola, Concave Rail, Curved Stiles, Bowed Seat, c.1890, 31 In., 4	584.00
Chair Set, Marco, Upholstered Back, Seat, Chrome, Brueton, 29 ½ In., 8	1000.00
Chair Set, Mies Van Der Rohe, Brno, Stainless Steel, Leatherette, Knoll, 1980s, 32 In., 6	2728.00
Chair Set, Mixed Wood, Ladder Back, 3 Slat Back, Egg & Cove Finials, Splint Seat, 37 In., 4 ...	81.00
Chair Set, Nanna Ditzel, Fanback, Wood, Cutouts, Tubular Base, Trinidad, 32 In., 12	3911.00
Chair Set, Neoclassical Style, Walnut, Upholstered Back, Seat, Arms, 4	531.00
Chair Set, Neoclassical, Mahogany, Reeded Top Rail, Scroll Splat, Slip Seat, 33 In., 4	1599.00
Chair Set, Neoclassical, Mahogany, Shaped Crest Rail, Diamond, Sunburst, Inlaid Slats, 8	2151.00
Chair Set, Neoclassical, Mahogany, Shell Carved Crest Rail, Reeded Leaf Slat, c.1810, 7	1195.00
Chair Set, Oak, Ladder Back, Rush Seat, France, 46 x 18 In., 6	244.00
Chair Set, Office, Modern, Chrome, Italian Leather, Button Tufted, Swivel, 32 x 23 In., 4	359.00
Chair Set, Queen Anne, Vase Shape Splat, Serpentine Stretcher, Cabriole Legs, 6	2820.00
Chair Set, Regency, Mahogany, Paneled Back, Spiral Ribbed Splat, 32 In., 6	1230.00
Chair Set, Steer Horn, Cow Hide, Entwined Horns, Outswept Legs, c.1890, 39 In., 4	1175.00
Chair Set, Suede, Square Back, Scrolled Stiles, Chrome Nailheads, Round Legs, 40 x 27 In., 6	717.00
Chair Set, Thomas Moser, Cherry, Arched Cage Back, Continuous Arm, 8	2825.00
Chair Set, Upholstered, Metal, Lucite, Open Arms, Charles H. Jones, 1970s, 36 x 22 In., 6	9500.00
Chair Set, Victorian, Mahogany, Balloon Back, Velvet Seat Upholstery, 36 x 19 In., 4	299.00
Chair Set, Wegner, Teak, Black Leather Backrest & Seat, c.1950, 31 In., 6	4444.00
Chair Set, Wegner, Teak, Cow Horn-Shaped Backrest, Leather Seat, c.1958, 29 In., 8	44438.00
Chair Set, Windsor, Elm, Mixed Wood, Pierced Wheel Splat, Round Legs, 1800s, 35 In., 8	1476.00
Chair Set, Windsor, Hoop Back, 8 Spindles, Black Paint, 1800s, 42 x 20 In., 6	863.00
Chair, 1600s Style, Carved Armorial Back, Leather, Open Arms, Paw Feet, 73 In., Pair	22420.00
Chair, Aalto, Lounge, Cantilever, Laminate Bent Birch, Finland, 1960s, 30 x 24 In., Pair	1534.00
Chair, Aalto, Lounge, Taupe, Birch Curvilinear Frame, Dated 1936, 29 x 29 In.	1125.00
Chair, Adirondack, Cedar, Single Plank Back, Broad Arms, 39 x 37 In., Pair	1612.00
Chair, Aesthetic Revival, Curved Tablet Back, Incised Greek Key, Lattice Splat, 32 In.	111.00
Chair, Aesthetic Revival, Mahogany, Mixed Metal Inlay, Upholstered, 34 x 21 In., Pair	992.00
Chair, Aesthetic Revival, Multicolor, Oval Padded Back, Turned Uprights, c.1870	610.00
Chair, Aesthetic Revival, Slab Seat, Back, Carved Arms, 23 x 18 In.	210.00

Furniture, Card Stand, Black Forest, Bear, Holding Tray, Oval Base, 21 ½ In.
$837.00

Neal Auction Co.

Furniture, Cellarette, Federal, Walnut, Hinged Top, Stand, Inscribed, Orton, 38 x 18 In.
$35400.00

Brunk Auctions

Furniture, Chair, Art Deco, Arched Fluted Back, Needlepoint Seat, Tapered Legs, France, 35 In.
$354.00

Ivey-Selkirk Auctioneers

Furniture, Chair, Art Deco, Skyscraper,
Overstuffed Seat & Back, Red Paint,
1900s, 36 In., Pair
$478.00

Sloans & Kenyon

Furniture, Chair, Banister Back, Mixed
Wood, Shaped Crest, Turned Stiles, Legs,
Stretchers, 1700s, 42 In.
$235.00

Garth's Auctions, Inc.

Furniture, Chair, Bergere, Ebony, Cane
Back, Prince Of Wales Feather Medallion,
Closed Arms, 1800s
$2510.00

Neal Auction Co.

Furniture, Chair, Black Forest, Standing
Bear, Carved, Tree Trunk Front Legs,
c.1870, 29 x 16 In.
$1541.00

Skinner, Inc.

Chair, Alexander Begge Casalino, Fiberglass, Molded, Yellow, 23 ½ x 16 ½ In., Child's, Pair	350.00
Chair, Aluminum, Cone Shape, Metal Rod Legs, 29 x 22 In.	1521.00
Chair, Anglo-Colonial, Ebony, Carved, Acanthus, Cane Back, Seat, Scroll Arms, c.1835	8664.00
Chair, Arne Jacobsen, Egg, Wing, Leather, Metal Swivel Base, Fritz Hansen, c.1960, 42 x 35 In.	5000.00
Chair, Arne Norell, Lounge, Safari, Rosewood, Brass, Leather, Sweden, 1960s, 28 x 27 In., Pair	1488.00
Chair, Art Deco, Arched Fluted Back, Needlepoint Seat, Tapered Legs, France, 35 In. ....*illus*	354.00
Chair, Art Deco, Birch, Arms, Metal Tag, Mueller Furniture, 23 x 30 In.	1080.00
Chair, Art Deco, Leather Upholstery, Arms, Banded Legs, 34 x 24 In., Pair	1230.00
Chair, Art Deco, Leather, Brass Studs, Velvet Pillow, c.1910, 32 x 33 In.	354.00
Chair, Art Deco, Mahogany, Upholstered, Open Arms, France, 39 x 24 In.	1850.00
Chair, Art Deco, Oval Back, Tassel Carved, Upholstered, France, c.1930, 37 x 17 In., Pair	1968.00
Chair, Art Deco, Skyscraper, Overstuffed Seat & Back, Red Paint, 1900s, 36 In., Pair ....*illus*	478.00
Chair, Art Nouveau, Mahogany, Pierced Back, Scroll Arms, Upholstered, c.1900, 46 x 23 In. ...	489.00
Chair, Art Nouveau, Wood, Bird Arm Supports, Ornate Carved Back, Cushion, c.1900, 52 x 40 In.	546.00
Chair, Arts & Crafts, Leather Back, Seat, Nailheads, Open Arms, c.1915, 42 x 24 In., Pair	984.00
Chair, Arts & Crafts, Oak, Ladder Back, Faux Leather, Slip Seat, 1900s, 37 x 17 In.	2868.00
Chair, Austin Model, Easy, Leather, Hancock & Moore Furniture Co., 1994, Pair	1093.00
Chair, Axel Bender Madsen & Ejnar Larsen, Leather, Teak, Arms, c.1955, 32 x 28 In., Pair	2232.00
Chair, Bachelor's, Square Seat & Back, W-Shape Metal Base, Arms, c.1962, 29 x 21 In., Pair...	1125.00
Chair, Banister Back, Black Paint, Shaped Crest, Vase & Ring Turned Stiles, Late 1700s, 44 In.	593.00
Chair, Banister Back, Black Paint, Wicker Seat, Curved Arms, 1700s, 50 In.	9480.00
Chair, Banister Back, Carved, Black Paint, Prince Of Wales Crest, Rush Seat, c.1710, 47 In.....	9480.00
Chair, Banister Back, Crest, Wicker Seat, Scrolled Handholds, Painted, Arms, 1700s, 46 In......	1304.00
Chair, Banister Back, Leaf Pierced, Shaped Top, Turned Stiles, Urn Finials, Rush Seat, 1700s, 46 In.	708.00
Chair, Banister Back, Mixed Wood, Shaped Crest, Turned Stiles, Legs, Stretchers, 1700s, 42 In. ....*illus*	235.00
Chair, Banister Back, Rush Seat, Painted, Arms, Turned Finials	200.00
Chair, Banister Back, Shaped Top Rail, Pad Seat, 49 In.	115.00
Chair, Barcelona, Mies Van Der Rohe, Leather, Knoll, c.1953, 30 x 30 In., Pair	3220.00
Chair, Baronial, Walnut, Embossed Leather, Warrior, Shield, Arms, 52 In.........................	861.00
Chair, Baroque, Leather, Walnut, Plank Arms, Square Legs, Entwined Stretchers, 19 ½ In., Pair	490.00
Chair, Baroque, Putti, Leaves, Figural Arm Supports, Carved, Upholstered, Venice, 1800s, 48 In.	1320.00
Chair, Baroque, Walnut, Carved Back, Heart Cutout, Bobbin Turned Legs, 34 In., Pair	205.00
Chair, Baroque, Walnut, Carved, Winged Lion Shape, Cherub Crest, 1800s, 50 x 34 In............	295.00
Chair, Baroque, Walnut, Cherub Crest, Open Back, Leather Seat, Carved, 39 x 21 In...............	497.00
Chair, Baroque, Walnut, Gilt, Leather Back & Seat, Nails, Arms, Italy, c.1650, 47 x 26 In.	480.00
Chair, Barrel, Cane Back & Sides, Downswept Arms, Upholstered, 1800s, 30 x 24 In...............	1107.00
Chair, Barrel, Ornate Carvings, Flower Upholstery, Deutch Brothers, 37 x 37 In.	230.00
Chair, Beech, Openwork, Square Back, Upholstered, H-Stretcher, Italy, 1800s, Pair	156.00
Chair, Bembe & Kimbel, Oak, Carved, Padded, Arms, c.1857, 40 x 24 In...........................	17925.00
Chair, Bentwood, Ball Design Back, Woven Compass Seat, Painted, c.1810, 33 In., Pair..........	53.00
Chair, Bergere, Biedermeier, Fruitwood, Upholstered, Closed Arms, Cabriole Legs, 34 x 23 In., Pair	878.00
Chair, Bergere, Domed Back, Leaf Crest, Cabriole Legs, Peg Toes, 36 In., Pair	2337.00
Chair, Bergere, Ebony, Cane Back, Prince Of Wales Feather Medallion, Closed Arms, 1800s...*illus*	2510.00
Chair, Bergere, Empire, Mahogany, Upholstered, Closed Arms, 37 x 35 In.	2574.00
Chair, Bergere, Fruitwood, Padded Back, Cabriole Legs, Closed Arms, c.1920, 34 In., Pair	676.00
Chair, Bergere, Gilt, Carved Crest, Gilt, Silk Upholstery, Closed Arms, France, 37 x 25 In., Pair	460.00
Chair, Bergere, Gilt, Dome Back, Rope Carved, Flower Crest, Closed Arms, c.1875, 40 ½ In......	1722.00
Chair, Bergere, Louis XVI Style, Dome Back, Rosettes, Closed Arms, Peg Feet, c.1890, 33 In., Pair	738.00
Chair, Bergere, Louis XVI Style, Gilt, Scrolling Crest, Closed Arms, c.1900, 32 In., Pair	738.00
Chair, Bergere, Louis XVI Style, Parcel Gilt, Medallion Back, Upholstered, Closed Arms, c.1910, 34 In.	553.00
Chair, Bergere, Louis XVI Style, Silk Upholstery, Closed Arms, c.1960, 35 x 27 In., Pair	492.00
Chair, Bergere, Louis XVI, Loose Seat Cushion, Upholstered, Closed Arms, 1900s, 39 In., Pair .	1016.00
Chair, Bergere, Louis XVI, Molded Crest Rail & Stiles, Fluted Legs, Closed Arms, 1700s............	866.00
Chair, Bergere, Mahogany, Rectangular Back, Reeded, Carved Closed Arms, c.1800, Pair	5378.00
Chair, Bergere, Mahogany, Square Back, Upholstered, Gilt Paint, Closed Arms, Pair................	750.00
Chair, Bergere, Rectangular Padded Back, Curved Crest, Closed Arms, Saber Legs, c.1850, 48 In.	984.00
Chair, Bergere, Restauration, Mahogany, Padded, Rolled Crest, Closed Arms, c.1840, 37 In.....	799.00
Chair, Bergere, Upholstered, Carved Legs, Closed Arms, c.1940, 31 x 30 In.	1476.00
Chair, Biedermeier, Black Lacquer, Openwork Back, Pad Seat, Cabriole Legs, 36 x 18 In., Pair	760.00
Chair, Biedermeier, Burl Maple, Klismos, Fabric Seat, 32 x 24 ½ In., Pair	1860.00
Chair, Biedermeier, Mahogany, Burl Veneer, Fan Shape Back, 35 x 17 In..............................	121.00
Chair, Biedermeier, Pierced Vase Shape Splat, Round Seat, Swivel, Tripod Legs, 20 In.............	551.00
Chair, Biedermeier, Satin Birch, Shaped Crest, Pierced Splat, Rosette, Pad Seat, 33 x 19 In., Pair	690.00
Chair, Birch, Peacock Design, Cane Back, Arms, 1930, 32 In., Pair	795.00
Chair, Bird, Wool, Chromed Steel, Preben Fabricius & Jorgen Kastholm, Germany, 1960s, 44 x 30 In.	434.00
Chair, Bishop's, Gothic Style, High Back, Plank Seat, Arch, Quatrefoil, Pierced, Arms, c.1890, 78 In.	353.00
Chair, Black Forest, Standing Bear, Carved, Tree Trunk Front Legs, c.1870, 29 x 16 In. ...*illus*	1541.00

Chair, Boudoir, Painted, Upholstered, 1900s, 39 x 24 ½ In., Pair	310.00
Chair, Campaign, Regency, Mahogany, Cane Back, Seat, Arms, England, 1800s, 37 x 26 In.	1416.00
Chair, Campaign, Slatted Back, Folding Arms, Cane Seat, Burke Co., Ireland, c.1850, 31 In., Pair	2952.00
Chair, Campaign, Wrought Iron, Brass Finials, Leather Back, France, c.1920, 32 x 23 In., Pair	1599.00
Chair, Cane Back, Seat, Gold Painted, Cornucopia Arm Supports, M. Castaing, 1900s, 35 x 21 In.	5900.00
Chair, Cane Back, Seat, Slatted Arms, David Wolcott Kendall, 35 x 29 In., Pair	1364.00
Chair, Carved Crest, Paw Feet, Flower Upholstery, Downswept Arms, 39 x 25 In., Pair	305.00
Chair, Carved Crest, Rope Twist Trim, Upholstered, 41 x 24 In., Pair	345.00
Chair, Carved Lotus Yoke Back, Curved Open Arms, Chinese, 1800s, 42 In., Pair	1778.00
Chair, Carved Panels, Upholstered Seat, Open Arms, Ball & Claw Feet, Chinese	502.00
Chair, Carved Stretcher, Apron, Leather Seat, Elidio Gonzales, c.1970, 16 x 39 In.	270.00
Chair, Carved, Pierced Back, Medallion, Chinese, 35 x 23 In., Pair	920.00
Chair, Carved, Scroll Arms, Upholstered, Sweden, c.1890, 45 x 26 In.	690.00
Chair, Carved, Serpentine Crest Rail, Open Arms, 38 x 26 In., Pair	300.00
Chair, Charles II, Wing Mermaid Rail, Carved, Pierced, Oval Cane Back, Seat, 46 x 23 ½ In.	374.00
Chair, Chinese Chippendale, Faux Bamboo, Cushion, Open Arms, c.1960, 37 x 23 In., Pair	492.00
Chair, Chippendale Style, Mahogany, Carved, Square Back, Paw Feet, 1900s, 40 In.	415.00
Chair, Chippendale Style, Mahogany, Openwork Splat, 1800s, 38 x 22 In.	508.00
Chair, Chippendale Style, Mahogany, Pierced Splat, Needlework, Cabriole Legs, c.1900, 41 In.	307.00
Chair, Chippendale Style, Mahogany, Pierced Splat, Rococo Designs, Arms, Claw Feet, 39 In.	118.00
Chair, Chippendale Style, Mahogany, Pierced Splat, Square Legs, England, 1800s, 38 x 22 In., Pair	360.00
Chair, Chippendale Style, Mahogany, Serpentine Crest Rail, Pierced Splat, Arms, c.1910	175.00
Chair, Chippendale Style, Mahogany, Yoke Back Crest Rail, Openwork Splats, 40 x 24 In., Pair	191.00
Chair, Chippendale Style, Serpentine Crest, Ears, Openwork Splat, 1800s, 37 x 28 In.	508.00
Chair, Chippendale, Cherry, Slip Seat, Pierced Vase Splat, Shaped Crest, Square Legs, c.1790, 38 In.	705.00
Chair, Chippendale, Mahogany, 4 Ribbon Splats, Flower Carved, Phila., c.1780, Pair	1458.00
Chair, Chippendale, Mahogany, Carved, New York, c.1760-80, 39 ½ In.	3555.00
Chair, Chippendale, Mahogany, Carved, Pierced, Shaped Crest, Slip Seat, c.1790, 38 x 22 In.	431.00
Chair, Chippendale, Mahogany, Crest With Carved Ends, Cabriole Legs, 1790s, 38 In.	885.00
Chair, Chippendale, Mahogany, Molded Crest Rail, Shells, Leaves, Cabriole Legs, c.1900, Pair	325.00
Chair, Chippendale, Mahogany, Open Arms, England, 1700s, 37 x 22 In.	177.00
Chair, Chippendale, Mahogany, Pierced Splat, Bead Molded Legs, 1700s, 38 x 22 In.	748.00
Chair, Chippendale, Mahogany, Pierced Splat, Leaves, Leaf Carved Arms, c.1765, 39 In.	5412.00
Chair, Chippendale, Mahogany, Pierced Splat, Open Arms, Slip Seat, Phila., c.1760, 36 x 27 In.	1495.00
Chair, Chippendale, Mahogany, Pierced Splat, Scroll Crest, 1700s, 38 x 23 In.	1265.00
Chair, Chippendale, Mahogany, Pierced Splat, Scrolled Ears, Slip Seat, 1700s, 38 In. ......*illus*	431.00
Chair, Chippendale, Mahogany, Pierced Splat, Serpentine Crest Rail, Padded Seat, 1700s, Pair	500.00
Chair, Chippendale, Mahogany, Scroll Ears, Pierced Splat, Square Legs, c.1840, 38 In.	173.00
Chair, Chippendale, Mahogany, Shaped Crest, Pierced Eye Splat, Square Legs, c.1790, 18 In., Pair	770.00
Chair, Chippendale, Mahogany, Yoke Crest, Pierced Splat, Scroll Arms, 1700s, 42 x 24 In., Pair	2032.00
Chair, Chippendale, Mahogany, Yoke Crest, Ribbon Splat, H-Stretcher, 39 x 22 In., Pair	1135.00
Chair, Chippendale, Maple, Pierced Splat, Rush Seat, Turned Legs, New England, 40 x 19 In.	322.00
Chair, Chippendale, Shell & Leaf Carved, Triangular Brackets, c.1765, 39 In.	3444.00
Chair, Chippendale, Townsend School, Mahogany, Spiral Scrolls, 1700s, 39 In. ....*illus*	1645.00
Chair, Chippendale, Walnut, Carved, Open Arms, Delaware Valley, c.1770	2252.00
Chair, Chippendale, Walnut, Pierced Splat, Carved Terminals, Cabriole Legs, 1700s, 39 In.	563.00
Chair, Chippendale, Walnut, Serpentine Crest Rail, Pierced Splat, Marlboro Legs, 38 In. ...... *illus*	106.00
Chair, Chippendale, Walnut, Serpentine Crest, Pierced Splat, Cabriole Legs, c.1750, 38 In., Pair	3437.00
Chair, Chippendale, Walnut, Shaped Crest, Scalloped Shell & Ears, Slip Seat, 40 x 20 In.	4313.00
Chair, Chippendale, Walnut, Shell Carved Crest, Slip Seat, Mass., c.1770, 36 In.	500.00
Chair, Chippendale, Wood, Open Fan Slat Back, Rush Seat, New England, 1700s, 18 x 37 In.	173.00
Chair, Chippendale, Yellow Pine, Shaped Splat, 39 x 20 In.	187.00
Chair, Club, Arched, Rolled Back & Arms, Upholstered, Turned Legs, c.1910, 32 x 31 In., Pair	738.00
Chair, Club, Art Deco, Arched Back, Arms, Reeded Columns, Upholstered, c.1930, 36 x 24 In., Pair	1230.00
Chair, Club, Art Deco, Beech, Leather, Brass, Golden Brown, 1930s, 31 x 26 In., Pair	2976.00
Chair, Club, Art Deco, Burl, Leather Upholstery, 23 x 31 In., Pair	1353.00
Chair, Club, Art Deco, Chromed Steel, Tiger Maple, Mohair, 1930s, 34 x 26 In., Pair	1736.00
Chair, Club, Art Deco, Leather, Mustache Back, 22 x 36 In., Pair	2480.00
Chair, Club, Art Deco, Leather, Nailheads, 28 x 24 In., Pair	984.00
Chair, Club, Art Deco, Macassar Curved Arms, Upholstered, 29 x 27 In., Pair	1722.00
Chair, Club, Art Deco, Shaped Back, Straight Arms, Stepped Legs, France, c.1930, 33 x 25 In., Pair	923.00
Chair, Club, Art Deco, Wood Scrolled Arms, Upholstered, Platform Base, 33 x 28 In., Pair	5400.00
Chair, Club, Black Leather, Polished Aluminum, Signed Leolux, 32 x 34 In., Pair	2232.00
Chair, Club, Ebonized, Padded Seat & Back, Downswept Arms, 31 In., Pair	307.00
Chair, Club, Leather, Brown, Tufted, 29 x 36 In., Pair	900.00
Chair, Club, Leather, Brown, Tufted, Brass Tacks, 1900s, 30 x 26 In., Pair	2400.00
Chair, Club, Mahogany Trim, Upholstered, France, c.1940, 33 x 34 In., Pair	248.00

Furniture, Chair, Chippendale, Mahogany, Pierced Splat, Scrolled Ears, Slip Seat, 1700s, 38 In.
$431.00

Leland Little Auction

Furniture, Chair, Chippendale, Townsend School, Mahogany, Spiral Scrolls, 1700s, 39 In.
$1645.00

Cowan's Auctions

Furniture, Chair, Chippendale, Walnut, Serpentine Crest Rail, Pierced Splat, Marlboro Legs, 38 In.
$106.00

Conestoga Auction Co., Inc.

Furniture, Chair, Club, Robsjohn-Gibbings, Mahogany, Upholstered, 1950s, 30 x 30 x 33 In.
$3348.00

Rago Arts & Auction Center

Furniture, Chair, D. Knorr, Steel, Knoll, 1949, 28 x 22 In.
$2500.00

Los Angeles Modern Auctions

Furniture, Chair, Desk, Renaissance Revival, Walnut, Ebonized, Swivel, Arms, c.1865, 40 x 24 In.
$3936.00

New Orleans Auction Galleries, Inc.

Furniture, Chair, Eames, Lounge, Rosewood, Black Leather, Herman Miller, c.1956, 33 In.
$1750.00

Los Angeles Modern Auctions

Furniture, Chair, Eames, Plywood, Molded, c.1945, 14 ½ x 14 ½ In., Child's
$8750.00

Los Angeles Modern Auctions

Chair, Club, Modernist, Fiberglass, Crucible Furniture Co., 1970s, 27 x 30 In., Pair	2500.00
Chair, Club, Paquebot, Ultrasuede, Ebonized Mahogany Feet, France, c.1930, 30 x 32 In., Pair	3596.00
Chair, Club, Robsjohn-Gibbings, Mahogany, Upholstered, 1950s, 30 x 30 x 33 In. ....*illus*	3348.00
Chair, Club, Roger Sprunger, Wool, Chromed Steel, Dunbar, 1980s, 29 x 31 In.	434.00
Chair, Club, Straight Back & Arms, Upholstered, c.1950, 40 x 28 In.	1975.00
Chair, Club, Tan Faux Leather, 1950s, 32 x 34 In., Pair	279.00
Chair, Club, Wool, Ebonized Wood, 1980s, 30 x 33 In., Pair	124.00
Chair, Cockpen, Mahogany, Openwork, Upholstered Seat, c.1890, 37 In., Pair	3851.00
Chair, Corner, Black Paint, Shaped Back, Scroll Arms, Turned Stiles, 1700s, 30 In.	563.00
Chair, Corner, Chippendale Style, Horseshoe Arms, Pierced Twin Splats, Pad Seat, c.1820	207.00
Chair, Corner, Chippendale Style, Mahogany, Strapwork Splats, Straight Legs, c.1900, 32 In.	441.00
Chair, Corner, Chippendale, Mixed Wood, Black Over Red Paint, Rush Seat, 30 In.	646.00
Chair, Corner, Ebonized, Gilt, Bird, On Wreath, Pierced Panels, c.1885, 27 In.	461.00
Chair, Corner, Faux Bamboo, Gilt, Rail Back, 3 Posts, Cane Seat, c.1890, 30 x 17 In.	295.00
Chair, Corner, Georgian, Elm, Divided Splat, Curved Arms, England, 1700s, 29 x 29 In.	460.00
Chair, Corner, Georgian, Mahogany, Scroll Arms, Open Side Splats, Slip Seats, c.1775, 33 In. .	1722.00
Chair, Corner, Georgian, Mahogany, Scroll Arms, Pierced Splats, Marlboro Legs, c.1775, 31 In.	940.00
Chair, Corner, Louis XV Style, Fruitwood, Downswept Arms, Peg Feet, 1800s, 33 In.	1599.00
Chair, Corner, Mahogany, Arched Crest Rail, Turned Uprights, c.1900, 32 In.	836.00
Chair, Corner, Mahogany, Carved Splats, Scroll Arms, Rush Seat, Ball & Claw Feet, 33 In.	107.00
Chair, Corner, Mahogany, Double Pierced Splat Back, Velvet Upholstery, England, 1700s	230.00
Chair, Corner, Mahogany, Northwind Carved Back, Needlepoint Seat, Paw Feet, 31 x 30 In.	403.00
Chair, Corner, Mahogany, Turned Supports, Shaped Splats, Molded Edges, c.1800, 31 In.	799.00
Chair, Corner, Maple, Ash, Shaped Back, Arched Slats, Vase & Ring Turned Stiles, 1700s, 31 In.	237.00
Chair, Corner, Maple, Rush Seat, Raised Back, Shaped Double Splat, Arms, 1700s	345.00
Chair, Corner, Maple, Scrolled Handholds, Shaped Splats, New Eng., 1700s, 30 In.	652.00
Chair, Corner, Queen Anne, Mahogany, Pierced Splats, Upholstered, 1700s, 33 x 24 In.	472.00
Chair, Corner, Queen Anne, Walnut, Carved, Shaped Splat, X-Stretcher, c.1750, 31 In.	1541.00
Chair, Corner, Walnut, Yellow Pine, Solid Splat, X-Stretcher, Upholstered, N.C., c.1800, 30 x 31 In.	575.00
Chair, Corner, Wood, Mother-Of-Pearl Inlay, Chinese, 29 x 29 In., Pair	115.00
Chair, D. Knorr, Steel, Knoll, 1949, 28 x 22 In. ....*illus*	2500.00
Chair, Dagobert, Oak, Carved Base, Barrel Seat, Lion's Heads, Leather, 40 x 25 In.	330.00
Chair, Dan Johnson, Lounge, Gazelle, Bronze, Woven Cane, 1950s, 27 x 23 In.	7440.00
Chair, David Reuland, Chrome, Yellow Zigzag Wire Seat, Back, Thonet, 18 x 31 In., Pair	138.00
Chair, Deck, Hardwood, Folding, Queen Mary Plaque, 37 x 58 In.	354.00
Chair, Deck, Maple, Cane, Shaped Crest Rail, Stenciled SS Etruria, 1905	641.00
Chair, Desk, American Oak, Bentwood, Swivel Base, Casters, c.1900, 41 ½ x 22 In.	92.00
Chair, Desk, Renaissance Revival, Walnut, Ebonized, Swivel, Arms, c.1865, 40 x 24 In. ...*illus*	3936.00
Chair, Desk, Swivel, Walnut, Tilt & Height Control, White Palm Tree Covering, 1920s, 27 In. ..	1275.00
Chair, Desk, Wood, Leather, Carved, Adjustable, Swivel, 46 x 30 In.	275.00
Chair, Diapered, Reticulated, Jeweled Design, Painted, Needlepoint Seat, c.1875	976.00
Chair, Don Shoemaker, Rosewood, Leather, Open Arms, Mexico, 1970s, 31 x 22 In.	465.00
Chair, Dragon, Red Lacquer, Arms, Chinese, Pair	269.00
Chair, Eames, Aluminum, Tan Leather Sling Seat, 5 Point Base, Casters, 21 x 36 In.	900.00
Chair, Eames, Ash Laminate, Rubber, Steel, Herman Miller, 1940s, 29 x 19 ½ In.	310.00
Chair, Eames, LCM, Plywood Frame, Leather, Herman Miller, c.1950, 22 x 24 In.	300.00
Chair, Eames, Lounge, LCW, Rosewood, Tag, Herman Miller, 1945-48, 27 x 22 In.	3348.00
Chair, Eames, Lounge, Ottoman, Black Leather	2115.00
Chair, Eames, Lounge, Ottoman, Leather, Plywood, Walnut Veneer, Herman Miller, 32 & 17 In.	950.00
Chair, Eames, Lounge, Rosewood, Black Leather, Herman Miller, c.1956, 33 In. ....*illus*	1750.00
Chair, Eames, Plastic Shell, Upholstered, Cast Aluminum Base, Herman Miller, 32 In., Pair ...	236.00
Chair, Eames, Plywood, Molded, c.1945, 14 ½ x 14 ½ In., Child's ....*illus*	8750.00
Chair, Eames, Plywood, Molded, Herman Miller, c.1945, 27 x 22 In. ....*illus*	2250.00
Chair, Eames, Rosewood Laminate Shell, Black Leather, Aluminum Foot, 33 In.	2963.00
Chair, Eames, Steel, Birch, Rope Edge, Red Fiberglass Shell, 1950s, 26 In.	6250.00
Chair, Ebonized Wood, Gold Stencils, Arched Crest, Cane Seat, Turned Legs, 32 In., Pair	111.00
Chair, Ebonized Wood, High Back, Downswept Sides, Upholstered, c.1940, 51 x 24 In., Pair....	1353.00
Chair, Ebonized Wood, Silk Upholstery, Spoon Back, 1960s, 35 x 22 In., Pair	1240.00
Chair, Edwardian, Brass, Shaped Crest, Spindle Back, Bulbous Legs, Peg Feet, c.1900, 42 In., Pair	738.00
Chair, Eero Aarnio, Pastil, Lounge, White Fiberglass, Green Wool, Finland, 1960s, 20 x 36 In.	1178.00
Chair, Eero Saarinen, Ottoman, Knoll, c.1948, 35-In. Chair, 16-In. Ottoman ....*illus*	1250.00
Chair, Eero Saarinen, Tulip, White Molded Pedestal, Upholstered, Knoll, 25 x 32 In.	210.00
Chair, Egyptian Revival Style, Bronze, Iron, Lioness, Sphinx, P.E. Gurin, c.1930, 39 x 18 In. ...	345.00
Chair, Egyptian Style, Walnut, Carved Stiles, Scroll Top, Sphinx Arm Supports, c.1885, 37 In.	1353.00
Chair, Elizabethan Style, Oak, Carved, Knight, Dragons, Lion Arms, Turned Legs, 47 In.	338.00
Chair, Elm, Horseshoe Back, Carved, Pierced, Deer Arm Supports, Chinese, 35 x 25 In.	230.00
Chair, Elm, Mahogany, Crest, Pierced Splat, Padded Seat, Dutch, c.1800, 37 In., Pair	307.00

Chair, Elm, Sloped, Diamond, Cutout Back, Arms, c.1790, 36 In., Pair	615.00
Chair, Empire Style, Beech, Parcel Gilt, Figural Open Arms, Upholstered, 36 In., Pair	1298.00
Chair, Empire Style, Gilt Mounted, Upswept Arms, Scroll Supports, Block Feet, c.1900, 37 In., Pair	2706.00
Chair, Empire Style, Mahogany, Leather, Female Busts, Padded Arms, Paw Feet, c.1900, 38 In., Pair	1168.00
Chair, Empire Style, Scrolled Arm Supports, Cabriole Legs, 17 In., Pair	504.00
Chair, Empire, Mahogany, Eagle Stretcher, Saber Legs, 33 x 18 In.	920.00
Chair, Empire, Walnut, Rectangular Back, Downswept Arms, Shepherd's Crook, 1800s, 36 In., Pair	490.00
Chair, Esherick, Cherry, Walnut, Carved, Saddle Leather, c.1960, 33 x 20 In.	33480.00
Chair, Esherick, Hammer Handle, Hickory, Hide, 1950s, 31 x 21 In.	19840.00
Chair, Fauteuil, Beech, Open Upholstered Arms, c.1770, Pair	2375.00
Chair, Fauteuil, Beech, Padded Oval Back, Flower Crest, Upholstered Arms, c.1920, 38 In., Pair	799.00
Chair, Fauteuil, Cream Paint, Molded, Carved Backs, Open Upholstered Arms, Pair	478.00
Chair, Fauteuil, Directoire, Beech, Carved, Scroll Back, Padded Arms, Seat, c.1810, 35 In.	307.00
Chair, Fauteuil, Elm, High Back, Carved Legs & Feet, Open Upholstered Arms, c.1900, 49 x 27 In.	461.00
Chair, Fauteuil, Empire Style, Mahogany, Gilt Swan, Open Upholstered Arms, c.1800s, 35 In., Pair	861.00
Chair, Fauteuil, Empire Style, Painted, Crest, Urn Splat, Rounded Arms, Peg Feet, 35 In., Pair	369.00
Chair, Fauteuil, Empire, Mahogany, Scroll Back, Maiden's Head Uprights, Arms, 36 In., Pair..	3075.00
Chair, Fauteuil, Gilt, Carved Crest, Padded Seat, Arms, c.1850, 42 In., Pair	5904.00
Chair, Fauteuil, Gilt, Carved, Columns, Brocade, Open Upholstered Arms, c.1900, 41 x 26 In., Pair	2440.00
Chair, Fauteuil, Gilt, Finials, Fluted Legs, Open Upholstered Arms, c.1795, 40 In. ....illus	1230.00
Chair, Fauteuil, Louis XIV Style, Gilt, Padded Back, Seat, Open Upholstered Arms, c.1875, 45 In.	738.00
Chair, Fauteuil, Louis XV Style, Cane Back, Open Upholstered Arms, 41 x 23 In., Pair	234.00
Chair, Fauteuil, Louis XV Style, Fruitwood, Carved, Open Upholstered Arms, 1800s, 37 x 25 In.	418.00
Chair, Fauteuil, Louis XV Style, Fruitwood, Open Upholstered Arms, Peg Feet, 1900s, 39 In.	492.00
Chair, Fauteuil, Louis XV Style, Fruitwood, Padded Back, Upholstered Arms, c.1950, 35 In., Pair..	246.00
Chair, Fauteuil, Louis XV Style, Gilt, Carved Crest, Padded, Open Upholstered Arms, c.1885, 42 In. .illus	984.00
Chair, Fauteuil, Louis XV Style, Gilt, Carved, Open Upholstered, Arms, 33 x 23 In., Pair	183.00
Chair, Fauteuil, Louis XV Style, Mahogany, Open Upholstered Arms, France, 1890s, 37 x 28 In.	354.00
Chair, Fauteuil, Louis XV Style, Shell Carved Crest, Needlework Upholstery, Padded Back, 40 In.	384.00
Chair, Fauteuil, Louis XV Style, Walnut, Carved Crest, Open Upholstered Arms, c.1805, 35 In., Pair	215.00
Chair, Fauteuil, Louis XV Style, Walnut, Carved, Shaped Back, Scroll Arms, Pair	1464.00
Chair, Fauteuil, Louis XV, Fruitwood, Carved, Open Upholstered Arms, France, c.1780, 15 In., Pair	2252.00
Chair, Fauteuil, Louis XV, Painted, Cane Back, Open Upholstered Arms, c.1750, Pair	1875.00
Chair, Fauteuil, Louis XV, Walnut, Flat Back, Arched Crest Rail, Open Upholstered Arms, c.1750	960.00
Chair, Fauteuil, Louis XVI Style, Beech, Carved, Fluted Legs, Open Upholstered Arms, c.1890, 38 In.	1353.00
Chair, Fauteuil, Louis XVI Style, Beech, Gilt, Ebonized, Open Upholstered Arms, c.1800, 38 In., Pair	2124.00
Chair, Fauteuil, Louis XVI Style, Carved Flowers, Fluted Legs, Open Upholstered Arms, 19 In., Pair	415.00
Chair, Fauteuil, Louis XVI Style, Finials, Fluted, Open Upholstered Arms, 1900s, 38 In., Pair...	1722.00
Chair, Fauteuil, Louis XVI Style, Gilt, Carved Floral Crest, Padded Back, Arms, Seat, 39 In.	649.00
Chair, Fauteuil, Louis XVI Style, Painted, Silk, Open Upholstered Arms	352.00
Chair, Fauteuil, Louis XVI, Gilt, Oval Back, Carved Crest, Open Upholstered Arms, 33 In., Child's	1845.00
Chair, Fauteuil, Mahogany, Dome Back, Scrolling Arms, Saber Legs, Scroll Toes, c.1850, 36 In., Pair	1230.00
Chair, Fauteuil, Mahogany, Tapered Back, Crest, Open Upholstered Arms, c.1900, 36 ½ In., Pair .	399.00
Chair, Fauteuil, Oak, Padded Seat & Back, Shell, Flower Crest, Open Upholstered Arms, 1800s, 42 In.	1168.00
Chair, Fauteuil, Oval Back, Painted, Open Upholstered Arms, c.1780, 17 In., Pair	711.00
Chair, Fauteuil, Regency Style, Fruitwood, Open Upholstered Arms, Curved Legs, 1900s, 45 In., Pair	676.00
Chair, Fauteuil, Regency, Fruitwood, Carved Crest, Open Upholstered Arms, 43 In., Pair	2337.00
Chair, Fauteuil, Walnut, Leather, Carved Crest, Open Upholstered Arms, France, c.1895, 49 x 26 In.	244.00
Chair, Fauteuil, Wood, Molded, Open Upholstered Arms, Cabriole Legs, 34 x 27 In., Pair	403.00
Chair, Faux Leather, Brass Nail Trim, Dog Mask Carvings, 1800s, 38 x 30 In.	805.00
Chair, Federal Style, High Back, Arched Crest, Upholstered, Shaped Arms, c.1905, 49 x 26 In. .	420.00
Chair, Federal, Bentwood, Slats, Hoof Feet, DMM Monogram, S. Gragg, c.1825, 34 In. ....illus	7080.00
Chair, Federal, Iron, Flower Crest, Openwork Seat, Arms, Robert Wood, Phila., c.1850 ....illus	3050.00
Chair, Federal, Mahogany, Barrel Back, Upholstered, Arms, 33 x 23 In.	460.00
Chair, Federal, Mahogany, Burl, Carved, Tablet Crest Rail, Lyre Splat, Scroll Arms, c.1820, Pair	4481.00
Chair, Federal, Mahogany, Carved, Joseph Barry, c.1815, Pair	1708.00
Chair, Federal, Mahogany, Carved, Serpentine Crest, Scroll Arms, c.1795, 45 In.	5629.00
Chair, Federal, Mahogany, Inlay, Scrolled Tablet Crest Rail, Shaped Arms, c.1820, Pair	1200.00
Chair, Federal, Mahogany, Paneled Crest Rail, Rosette Carved Slat, Scroll Arms, c.1820, Pair..	610.00
Chair, Federal, Mahogany, Satinwood, Upholstered, Arms, Reeded Legs, 1810, 46 x 26 In.	5463.00
Chair, Federal, Mahogany, Shieldback, Heart Shape, Upholstered Seat, Pair	1800.00
Chair, Federal, Mahogany, Square Back, Stepped Crest Rail, Urn Slat, Philadelphia, c.1800	2000.00
Chair, Federal, Rosewood, Gilt Bronze, Carved, Tablet Carved, Scrolling Arms, c.1815	4780.00
Chair, Federal, Square Back, Mahogany, Reeded Slats, Upholstered Seat, Pair	1600.00
Chair, Federal, Walnut, Upholstered, Open Arms, c.1940, 38 x 24 In., Pair	1968.00
Chair, Finn Juhl, Diplomat, Teak, Wool, France & Sons, 1960s, 37 x 27 In., Pair	1240.00

Furniture, Chair, Eames, Plywood, Molded, Herman Miller, c.1945, 27 x 22 In.
$2250.00

Los Angeles Modern Auctions

Furniture, Chair, Eero Saarinen, Ottoman, Knoll, c.1948, 35-In. Chair, 16-In. Ottoman
$1250.00

Los Angeles Modern Auctions

Furniture, Chair, Fauteuil, Gilt, Finials, Fluted Legs, Open Upholstered Arms, c.1795, 40 In.
$1230.00

New Orleans Auction Galleries, Inc.

Furniture, Chair, Fauteuil, Louis XV Style, Gilt, Carved Crest, Padded, Open Upholstered Arms, c.1885, 42 In.
$984.00

New Orleans Auction Galleries, Inc.

Furniture, Chair, Federal, Bentwood, Slats, Hoof Feet, DMM Monogram, S. Gragg, c.1825, 34 In.
$7080.00

Brunk Auctions

Furniture, Chair, Federal, Iron, Flower Crest, Openwork Seat, Arms, Robert Wood, Phila., c.1850
$3050.00

Neal Auction Co.

Furniture, Chair, Frank Lloyd Wright, Padded, Metal Office Furniture Co., c.1936, 35 x 18 In.
$25000.00

Los Angeles Modern Auctions

Furniture, Chair, G. Nakashima, Lounge, Black Walnut, Spindle Back, Plank Seat, Marked, 1954, 31 In.
$3063.00

Skinner, Inc.

Chair, Flared Tablet Back, Painted, 5 Spindles, Shaped Seat, Bamboo Turned Legs, c.1810, 35 In.	230.00
Chair, Florence Knoll, Chromed Metal Frame, Upholstered, 28 x 32 In.	593.00
Chair, Flower, Leaf Painted Crest, Pinstripes, Brown Ground, 1800s, 30 In., Child's	474.00
Chair, Folding, Gilt Metal, Brass Mounts, Finials, Leather, Scroll Legs, 28 x 28 In., Pair	1404.00
Chair, Folding, Maple, Cane Panel, Reclined Back, Arched Crest Rail, Open Arms, 31 In.	215.00
Chair, Frank Lloyd Wright, Padded, Metal Office Furniture Co., c.1936, 35 x 18 In. ....*illus*	25000.00
Chair, Frankl, Lounge, D, Lacquered Wood, Upholstered, 1930s, 27 x 25 In., Pair	4000.00
Chair, Frankl, Speed, Mohair, Walnut, Frankl Studios, 1930s, 27 x 37 In.	2728.00
Chair, Fruitwood, Shaped Back, Serpentine Seat Rail, Cabriole Legs, 1800s, 38 x 23 In.	168.00
Chair, Fruitwood, Shaped Padded Back, Leaf Carved Arms, Shell, Flower Apron, c.1920, 30 x 57 In.	338.00
Chair, G. Magnusson, Fiberglass, Shaped Seat & Back, Black Metal Rod Base, 28 In.	385.00
Chair, G. Mulhauser, Lounge, Walnut, Laminate, Upholstered, Plycraft, 1950s, 32 x 29 In., Pair	620.00
Chair, G. Nakashima, Lounge, American Black Walnut, 1 Arm, 1960s, 33 x 31 x 28 In.	8680.00
Chair, G. Nakashima, Lounge, Black Walnut, Hickory, Spindle Back, 1 Arm, 1960s, 33 x 31 In.	8680.00
Chair, G. Nakashima, Lounge, Black Walnut, Spindle Back, Plank Seat, Marked, 1954, 31 In. ..... *illus*	3063.00
Chair, G. Nakashima, Stool, Walnut, Grass Seat, Spindle Back, Tapered Legs, 27 x 13 In.	1000.00
Chair, G. Nakashima, Walnut, Bowed Back, Woven Grass Seat, c.1970, 27 x 23 In.	7480.00
Chair, G. Nelson, Catenary, Chrome Plated Steel, Black Leather, Herman Miller, 28 In., Pair...	2573.00
Chair, G. Nelson, Coconut, Herman Miller, 1955, 32 x 40 In. ....*illus*	3438.00
Chair, G. Piretti, Plona, Molded Plastic Seat, Aluminum Frame, Folding, Castelli, 27 x 29 In., Pair	600.00
Chair, G. Stickley, 2 Slat Back, Rabbit Ear, Red Decal, 38 x 18 ¾ In.	2728.00
Chair, G. Stickley, 5 Vertical Side Slats, Cushion, Arms, 32 x 36 In.	5060.00
Chair, G. Stickley, Ladder Back, 4 Slats, Arms, Leather Upholstery, 40 In.	1380.00
Chair, G. Stickley, Ladder Back, Leather Seat, Arms, Red Decal, 26 x 23 In.	540.00
Chair, G. Stickley, Leather Tacks, Arms, Red Decal, 37 x 26 In.	3596.00
Chair, G. Stickley, Morris, Bow Arms, Loose Leather Cushions, 38 x 28 In.	17360.00
Chair, G. Stickley, Morris, Bow Arms, Spring Seat, Leather Cushions, Red Decal, 41 x 30 In.....	5270.00
Chair, G. Stickley, Morris, Chestnut, Bow Arms, Flaring Legs, c.1901, 39 In.	7440.00
Chair, G. Stickley, Oak, Ladder Back, 4 Slats, Arms, Green Leather, 40 In.	1380.00
Chair, G. Stickley, Vertical Side Slats, Horizontal Back Slats, Flat Arms, Cushion, 32 x 38 In.....	4800.00
Chair, G. Stickley, Wood, Slatted V Back, Leather Seat, Arms, 26 x 21 In.	720.00
Chair, Gainsborough, Mahogany, Leather, Tacks, Arched Back, Open Arms, 40 x 31 In.	1035.00
Chair, Gainsborough, Mahogany, Padded Seat & Back, Outscrolled Arms, c.1890, 40 In.	1045.00
Chair, Gehry, Maple, Cross-Checked Slats, Open Arms, Knoll, 34 x 29 In.	1364.00
Chair, George III Style, Mahogany, Flower Carved Rail, Splat, c.1985, 37 In., Pair	738.00
Chair, George III Style, Mahogany, Oval Back, Prince Of Wales Plume Splat, Upholstered, c.1890, 14 In.	830.00
Chair, George III Style, Mahogany, Pierced Splat, Shaped Crest Rail, H-Stretcher, Arms, 40 In.	246.00
Chair, George III Style, Mahogany, Upholstered Seat, Shaped Pierced Splat, Arms, Pair	750.00
Chair, George III Style, Rectangular Back, Arched Crest, Downswept Arms, c.1950, 39 In., Pair	518.00
Chair, George III, Mahogany, Leaf Carved Serpentine Crest, Pierced Splat, Curved Arms	1416.00
Chair, George M. Niedecken, Wide Slat Back, Angled, 1909, 23 x 33 In., Pair	2040.00
Chair, Georgian Style, Carved, Gilt Leaf Highlights, Open Arms, Baker, 40 x 26 In., Pair	885.00
Chair, Georgian Style, Mahogany, Scroll Back, Shell Carved Knees, Upholstered, England, c.1910	127.00
Chair, Georgian Style, Mahogany, Shaped Back, Curved Arms, Acanthus Knee, 35 In.	563.00
Chair, Georgian, Mahogany, Flared Arms, Greek Key Carving, Pierced Stretchers, 1700s	1342.00
Chair, Gilt, Ball Finials, Turned Splats, Spindle Apron, Shaped Feet, 1900s, 33 In., Pair	615.00
Chair, Gilt, Carved, Painted, Silk Upholstery, Open Arms, c.1930, 33 x 24 In., Pair	677.00
Chair, Gilt, Carved, Pierced Back, Shell Crest, 1800s, 35 x 17 In.	214.00
Chair, Gilt, Pierced Crest, Seat Rail, Scroll Arms, Upholstered, c.1985, 48 x 30 In., Pair	837.00
Chair, Gio Ponti, Lounge, Leather, Mohair, Walnut, Italy, 1952, 31 ½ x 28 ½ In. ....*illus*	4340.00
Chair, Gio Ponti, Lounge, Pieghevole, Walnut, Linen, Brass, Reguitti, 1958, 28 x 19 In., Pair..	2480.00
Chair, Gio Ponti, Walnut, Slat Back, Cane Seat, Open Arms, Singer & Sons, 1950s, 33 x 22 In.	930.00
Chair, Giulia Veronesi, Lounge, Perla, Walnut, Wool, ISA, c.1952, 31 x 34 In.	7440.00
Chair, Golden Oak, Lyre, Heraldic Carved Crest, Curved Seat, Turned Legs, Arms, 36 x 24 In. ...	69.00
Chair, Gondola, Rosewood, Dome, Tufted, Pad Back, Downswept Arms, c.1875, 32 In.	492.00
Chair, Gothic Revival, Carved, Crocket Finials, Paneled Stiles, Arched Backrest, c.1845	425.00
Chair, Gothic Revival, Mahogany, Lotus Leaf Crest, Columns, Arches, c.1835, 35 In., Pair	2337.00
Chair, Gothic Revival, Oak, Arch Back, Quatrefoil Roundel, Twist Stiles, Turned Arms, c.1850, 52 In.	5166.00
Chair, Gothic Revival, Oak, Towering Back, Arches, Scroll Arms, Pierced Apron, c.1855, 84 In.	3936.00
Chair, Gothic Revival, Rosewood, Leaf Carved Plume, Turned Posts, Spire Finials, c.1855, 55 In.	861.00
Chair, Gothic Revival, Spindle Back, Openwork Crest, Velvet Seat, Turned Legs, 38 In.	142.00
Chair, Gothic Revival, Walnut, Acorn Finials, 2 Arch Back, Quatrefoil Crest, Arms, c.1855, 48 In.	3444.00
Chair, Gothic Revival, Walnut, Carved, Fleur-De-Lis Embossed Leather, Arms, 1800s, 64 x 26 In.	840.00
Chair, Gothic Revival, Walnut, Carved, Pierced Splat, Scroll Arms, Needlepoint Seat, c.1876 ...	1195.00
Chair, Gothic Revival, Walnut, Twist Columns, Elongated Oval Back, Flowers, 1800s, 50 x 20 In.	288.00
Chair, Grain Painted, Bannister Back, Shaped Crest, Vase & Ring Turnings, 1800s, 44 In.	770.00
Chair, H. Bertoia, Diamond, Chrome Wire Frame, Seat Cushion, Knoll, 30 ½ In., Pair	225.00

Chair, H. Bertoia, Diamond, Orange Cover, Metal Supports, Knoll, c.1960, 17 x 45 In., Pair	1150.00
Chair, H. Bertoia, Diamond, Wool Upholstery, Wire Mesh Frame, 1970s, 28 x 44 x 32 In..........	354.00
Chair, H. Bertoia, Wire, Cushion, c.1952, 23 ¾ x 15 ¾ In., Child's............................	115.00
Chair, Hall, Carved Crest, Crown, 2 Headed Eagle, Upholstered, Ball & Claw Feet, 1800s, 53 In.	460.00
Chair, Hall, Gothic Revival, Walnut, Tracery Back, Crocket Crest, Barley Twist Legs, c.1850.....	676.00
Chair, Hall, Mahogany, Concave Back, Trestle Legs, c.1800	235.00
Chair, Hall, Renaissance Revival, Pierce Carved, Grotesque Mask, Plank Seat, 38 In................	427.00
Chair, Hall, Renaissance Revival, Plank Back, Grotesque Mask, Trapezoid Seat, 46 In., Pair ...	976.00
Chair, Hall, Rococo Revival, Rosewood, Open Carved Back, Scrolls, Lift Seat, c.1850, 50 In., Pair	2214.00
Chair, Hall, Victorian, Mahogany, Shaped Pierced Back, Finial, England, 43 x 17 In., Pair......	354.00
Chair, Hall, Walnut, Backrest Owl Carvings, Plank Seat, Trestle Base, c.1910, 19 In.	593.00
Chair, Hall, Walnut, Carved, Cherubs, Scrolls, Lion's Mask, c.1855, 49 In...............	460.00
Chair, Hans Olsen, Teak, Leather Arms, Suede Sling Seat, V. Mobelindustri, Sweden, 26 x 30 In., Pair .	1200.00
Chair, Henry II Style, Walnut, Cane Seat, Turned Spindle Back, Carved Arms, 40 x 25 In.........	92.00
Chair, Henry II Style, Walnut, Openwork Crest, Cane Seat, Spiral Carved Legs, 43 x 18 In., Pair	366.00
Chair, Henry IV Style, Ebonized, Needlework, Flower Carved Arms, Turned Legs, 1800s, 54 In.	984.00
Chair, Hepplewhite Style, Pierced Shieldback, Carved Arms, Upholstered Seat, 37 In........	144.00
Chair, Hepplewhite, Mahogany, Arched Back Rail, Carved Splat, Urn, c.1815, 21 In........	276.00
Chair, Hepplewhite, Mahogany, Pierced Splat, Slip Seat, c.1800, 38 x 21 In., Pair............	518.00
Chair, Hepplewhite, Mahogany, Shield Back, Lyre Splat, c.1800, 37 x 19 In., Pair	118.00
Chair, Hepplewhite, Mahogany, String Inlay, Arched, Pierced Splat, Baluster Arms, c.1815, 28 In.	492.00
Chair, Hepplewhite, Mahogany, String Inlay, Square Back, Pierced, Drapery Swag, c.1800, 35 In.	922.00
Chair, Hickory, Arms, Paper Label, Hoosier Hickory Mfg. Co., 48 x 30 In. ....*illus*	1364.00
Chair, Hitchcock Type, Eagle Slats, Rush Seat, New England, c.1830, 33 In., Pair ....*illus*	235.00
Chair, Horseshoe Carved Back, Shaped Splat, Spindles, Juma, Chinese, c.1850, 38 In.	3198.00
Chair, I. Kenmochi, Lounge, Cane, Yamakawa Rattan, Japan, 1960s, 33 In., Pair ....*illus*	992.00
Chair, Iron, Flower Splat, Green Paint, Upholstered, 38 x 25 In., Pair....................	615.00
Chair, J. Hoffmann, Bentwood, Cane Seat, Stendig Label, Thonet & Sons, 32 x 20 In.	89.00
Chair, J. Hoffmann, Bentwood, Openwork Back, Arms, Curved Rail, Pad Seat, 20 x 30 In., Pair	2640.00
Chair, J.M. Young, Morris, Beige Leather Cushions, 37 x 32 In.	1984.00
Chair, J.M. Young, Morris, Slatted Sides, Foam Cushions, 38 x 30 ½ In............	2356.00
Chair, Jack Lenor Larsen, Arched Back, Upholstered Seat, Back, Signed, 33 x 22 In............	325.00
Chair, Jacobean Style, Curule, Shaped Back, Rosettes, Turned Stretcher, Arms, c.1885, 35 x 23 In.	148.00
Chair, Jacobean Style, Walnut, Carved, High Back, Open Crest Rail, Upholstered, 53 x 21 In. ..	209.00
Chair, Jacobean, Walnut, Carved, Openwork Back, Scrollwork, Cane, c.1685, 61 ¾ In. ....*illus*	16590.00
Chair, Jean Royere, Trefle, Bleached Mahogany, Woven Silk, France, 1920s, 32 x 19 In...........	4650.00
Chair, Jindrich Halabala, Lounge, Bentwood, Upholstered, Czechoslovakia, 1930s, 28 x 29 In., Pair	3240.00
Chair, Kem Weber, Lounge, Chrome, Leather, Maple, Lloyd Mfg., 1934, 33 x 29 In., Pair.........	13640.00
Chair, Kofod Larsen, Molded Wood, Iron Frame, Upholstered Seat, 1950s, 29 x 22 In..........	950.00
Chair, Kofod Larsen, Vinyl Upholstery, Brass Rod Arms, c.1950, 28 x 22 In..................	975.00
Chair, Ladder Back, 3 Arched Slats, Rush Seat, Black Paint, Bergen County, N.J., 1700s, 38 In.	115.00
Chair, Ladder Back, 3 Arched Slats, Woven Hide Seat, Delaware Valley, 1800s, 37 In............	110.00
Chair, Ladder Back, 3 Slats, Velvet Cushion, 1800s, 44 x 20 In., Pair....................	62.00
Chair, Ladder Back, 4 Arched Back Slats, Rush Seat, Stile Finials, c.1810, 42 x 22 In.	374.00
Chair, Ladder Back, 4 Arched Splats, Lemon Finials, Splint Seat, 44 x 23 In....................	351.00
Chair, Ladder Back, 5 Slats, Turned Finials, Rush Seat, Box Stretchers, Stained, Pa., 48 x 24 In.	2340.00
Chair, Ladder Back, Oak, Carved, Rush Seat, Spindle Stretcher, Squat Legs, 1800s, 49 x 18 In.	150.00
Chair, Ladder Back, Oak, Rush Seat, Turned Finials, Arms, 1700s, 44 x 22 In.	550.00
Chair, Ladder Back, Rush Seat, Cabriole Legs, 41 x 22 In., Pair..............	488.00
Chair, Ladder Back, Wood, Black Paint, Yellow Stripes, Rush Seat, c.1790, 49 In.	294.00
Chair, Ladder Back, Woven Seat, Turned Legs, Stretcher, Shaped Arms, 1700s	415.00
Chair, Laminated Birch, Puzzle Design, Red Stain, Rounded Back, Block Legs, 33 In., Pair.....	984.00
Chair, Laminated Wood, Steel, Shaped Back, Triangular Plank Seat, Tripod Base, 39 In., Pair	984.00
Chair, Le Corbusier, Lounge, Black Leather, Chrome, Swivel, 25 x 25 In.	2021.00
Chair, Leather, Nailhead Trim, Carved Crest, Stanford Furniture, 43 x 27 In., Pair.................	1098.00
Chair, Leather, Nailheads, Shaped Back, Carved Arms, Legs, Stanford Furniture, 41 x 39 In....	305.00
Chair, Limbert, Drop-In Spring Seat, Arms, Branded Mark, 32 x 32 x 33 In.	1860.00
Chair, Limbert, Morris, Corbels, Long Flat Arms, Arched Skirt, Cushions, 36 x 32 In.	1178.00
Chair, Limbert, Oak, Pierced Inverted Heart Back, Branded Mark, 38 In. ....*illus*	940.00
Chair, Limbert, Saddle Seat, Ladder Back, Mark, 42 x 19 In...................	310.00
Chair, Limbert, Vertical Slat Back, Sides, Leather Seat, Arms, 28 x 23 In...................	510.00
Chair, Lolling, Federal, Mahogany, High Back, Block Legs, Stretcher, Scroll Arms, c.1795, 43 In.	9480.00
Chair, Lolling, Federal, Mahogany, Mixed Wood, Arms, Upholstered, New Eng., c.1800s, 43 x 26 In.	1440.00
Chair, Lolling, Mahogany, Arched, Turned Reeded Arms, Legs, c.1950, 44 x 27 In., Pair..........	861.00
Chair, Lolling, Queen Anne Style, Mahogany, Ball & Claw Front Feet, Arms, 1900s, 41 x 29 In.	127.00
Chair, Louis XIII Style, Walnut, Upholstered, Open Arms, 45 x 24 In., Pair..............	580.00
Chair, Louis XIV Style, Oak, Shell Crest, High Back, Upholstered Splat, Seat, 47 x 23 In.	179.00

Furniture, Chair, G. Nelson, Coconut, Herman Miller, 1955, 32 x 40 In.
$3438.00

Los Angeles Modern Auctions

Furniture, Chair, Gio Ponti, Lounge, Leather, Mohair, Walnut, Italy, 1952, 31 ½ x 28 ½ In.
$4340.00

Rago Arts & Auction Center

Furniture, Chair, Hickory, Arms, Paper Label, Hoosier Hickory Mfg. Co., 48 x 30 In.
$1364.00

Rago Arts & Auction Center

Furniture, Chair, Hitchcock Type, Eagle Slats, Rush Seat, New England, c.1830, 33 In., Pair
$235.00

Garth's Auctions, Inc.

Furniture, Chair, I. Kenmochi, Lounge, Cane, Yamakawa Rattan, Japan, 1960s, 33 In., Pair
$992.00

Rago Arts & Auction Center

Furniture, Chair, Jacobean, Walnut, Carved, Openwork Back, Scrollwork, Cane, c.1685, 61 ¾ In.
$16590.00

Skinner, Inc.

Furniture, Chair, Limbert, Oak, Pierced Inverted Heart Back, Branded Mark, 38 In.
$940.00

Cowan's Auctions

TIP
To remove white marks from tabletops, rub with olive oil, then a rag dipped in alcohol.

Chair, Louis XIV Style, Walnut, High Back, Acanthus Carved, Gilt, Padded Arms, 58 In.	150.00
Chair, Louis XIV Style, Walnut, Upholstered, Carved Armrests, 74 x 26 In.	427.00
Chair, Louis XV Style, Brass, Faux Tortoiseshell, Cast Brass, Upholstered, Swivel, c.1985, 44 x 25 In.	767.00
Chair, Louis XV Style, Fruitwood, Shaped, Padded Back, Scroll Crest, 37 In., Pair	492.00
Chair, Louis XV Style, Gilt, Balloon Back, Leaf Crest, Cabriole Legs, 1800s, 34 In.	584.00
Chair, Louis XV Style, Gilt, Round Back, Shield Crest, Cabriole Legs, 1800s, 37 In.	369.00
Chair, Louis XV Style, Walnut, Upholstered, Carved Crest, 38 x 21 In., Pair	153.00
Chair, Louis XV Style, Walnut, Upholstered, Carved Crest, Arms, 40 x 27 In., Pair	366.00
Chair, Louis XV Style, Walnut, Upholstered, Curved Back, Carved Arms, 26 x 25 In.	305.00
Chair, Louis XV, Walnut, Carved, Upholstered, Open Arms, 40 x 27 In., Pair	854.00
Chair, Louis XVI Style, Dome Crest, Pierced Lyre Splat, Fluted Legs, c.1850, 37 In.	492.00
Chair, Louis XVI Style, High Back, Upholstered, Fluted Legs, Jansen, c.1940, 35 x 18 In., Pair	1230.00
Chair, Louis XVI Style, Open Back, White Paint, Upholstered, Child's, Pair	406.00
Chair, Louis XVI Style, Parcel Gilt, Paint, Upholstered, Arms, Fluted Legs, 36 In.	976.00
Chair, Louis XVI Style, Shaped Back, Upholstered, c.1940, 33 x 20 In.	246.00
Chair, Louis XVI Style, Wood, Carved, Upholstered, Arm Pads, 34 ¾ In.	322.00
Chair, Louis XVI, Scrolled Back, Bowed Seat, Silk, Arm Supports, 1700s, 36 x 24 In.	478.00
Chair, Lounge, Bentwood, Leatherette, Paper Label, Thonet, 31 ½ x 26 ½ In.	465.00
Chair, Lounge, Leather, Brass, Enameled Steel, Open Arms, Italy, 1960s, 29 x 25 ½ In., Pair	806.00
Chair, Lounge, Mahogany, Enameled Metal, Open Arms, 1980s, 28 ½ x 26 In.	248.00
Chair, Lounge, Oak, Wool, Guillerme & Chambron, France, 1960s, 32 x 29 In., Pair	496.00
Chair, Lounge, Ottoman, Black Leather, Swivel Base, Casters, 1900s, 40 x 31 In.	2115.00
Chair, Lounge, Ottoman, Twig Frame, Woven Splint Seat & Back, Arms, 26 x 39 In.	1680.00
Chair, Lounge, Teak, Vertical Slat Back, Cushion, Arms, DUX, Denmark, 30 x 23 In., Pair	868.00
Chair, Lounge, White, Adjustable, 1985, 38 x 65 In.	119.00
Chair, M. Newson, Embryo, Neoprene, Stainless Steel, Aluminum, Austria, 1990s, 31 x 32 In. ... *illus*	2108.00
Chair, Mahogany, Adjustable, Arched, Padded Back, Seat, Arms, Book Rest, c.1820	3107.00
Chair, Mahogany, Balloon Back, Turned Spindles, Horseshoe Arms, Claw Feet, c.1900	150.00
Chair, Mahogany, Beaded, Flower Carved Rail, Leather Seat, c.1775, 38 In., Pair	399.00
Chair, Mahogany, Carved, Arched Back, Upholstered Seat, c.1810, Pair *illus*	5856.00
Chair, Mahogany, Carved, Concave Crest, Open Arms, Upholstered, Boston, c.1820, 38 x 21 In., Pair	2640.00
Chair, Mahogany, Carved, Shaped Crest Rail, Scroll Arms, c.1800s	717.00
Chair, Mahogany, Carved, Vase Shape Splat, Upholstered, 1700s, 38 In. *illus*	1342.00
Chair, Mahogany, Concave Figured Top Rail, Vase Splat, Scroll Arms, Saber Legs, c.1835, 35 In.	461.00
Chair, Mahogany, Curved Crest Rail, Pieced Splat, Padded Seat, 1700s	1625.00
Chair, Mahogany, Curved Seat, Leaves, Dragons, Lion's Heads, Curved Legs, Arms, Pair	450.00
Chair, Mahogany, Domed Leaf Carved Crest, Pierced, c.1785, 38 In., Pair	1599.00
Chair, Mahogany, Double Dome Crest, Interlaced Splat, H-Stretcher, c.1785, 38 In., Pair	1599.00
Chair, Mahogany, Ebonized, Carved Bat, Open Arms, Cushion, Chinese, c.1820, 40 x 24 In., Pair	1220.00
Chair, Mahogany, Flower Carved Crest, Pierced Splat, Pad Seat, c.1875, 38 In., Pair	1353.00
Chair, Mahogany, Gondola Shape, Flower Crest, Shaped Splat, Cabriole Legs, c.1850, 35 In., Pair	153.00
Chair, Mahogany, Leaf, Shell Carved, Upholstered, Open Arms, c.1890, 39 x 28 In.	1150.00
Chair, Mahogany, Leather, Lion End Caps, Arms, c.1890, 38 In., Pair	2370.00
Chair, Mahogany, Leather, Spindle Gallery, Fluted Stiles, Arms, c.1890, 38 ½ In., Pair	2489.00
Chair, Mahogany, Leather, Straight Back, Arms, Leaf, Husk Carvings, 1800s, 27 ½ In., Pair	5036.00
Chair, Mahogany, Openwork Arm Supports, Apron, Upholstered, France, 42 x 36 In., Pair	633.00
Chair, Mahogany, Scrolled Crest Rail, Stiles, Bronze Mounted, Cabriole Legs, c.1820	1434.00
Chair, Mahogany, Serpentine Crest Rail, Shaped Arms, Upholstered, c.1785, 40 ½ In. ...*illus*	575.00
Chair, Mahogany, Shaped Back, Scroll Arms, Flower Terminals, S-Scroll Legs, c.1830, 37 In.	1076.00
Chair, Mahogany, Tan Leather, Brass Tacks, Carved Arms, Legs, c.1910, 44 x 26 In.	345.00
Chair, Mahogany, Tub, Steel Studs, Leather, Shaped Skirt, Arms, 1800s	1528.00
Chair, Mahogany, Upholstered, Arched Back, Round Seat, Padded Arms, 30 x 24 In.	478.00
Chair, Mahogany, Upholstered, Tufted, Open Arms, c.1910, 37 x 26 In., Pair	944.00
Chair, Mahogany, Yew, Shaped Crest, Splats, Arms, Box Stretcher, England, c.1800, 48 In.	1970.00
Chair, Maple, Ash, Arched Slats, Turned Stiles, Splint Seat, Scroll Arms, 1700s, 45 In.	237.00
Chair, Maple, Ash, Bannister Back, Carved Crest, Spindles, Spanish Feet, 1700s, 43 In., Pair	1778.00
Chair, Maple, Ash, Paint, Bannister Back, Prince Of Whales Crest, 1700s, 47 In.	3081.00
Chair, Maple, Pine, Carved, Cane Back Seat, Black Paint, New England, c.1710, 49 ¼ In.	368.00
Chair, Maple, Scroll Crest, Winged Lion Sphinxes, Shaped Seat Rail, Arms, N.Y., 1800s	1342.00
Chair, Marcel Breuer, Lounge, Birch, Mohair Upholstery, England, 1980s, 33 x 24 In.	992.00
Chair, Marcel Breuer, Wassily, Black Leather, Steel Tube Frame, Knoll, Italy, 31 x 29 In.	960.00
Chair, Marcel Breuer, Wassily, Tubular Steel, Leather, Knoll, c.1925, 29 x 31 In., Pair	976.00
Chair, Marco Zanuso, Multicolor Upholstery, Arms, Artflex, France, 31 x 32 In.	1140.00
Chair, Marquetry, Shaped Back, Upholstered, Cabriole Legs, Dutch, 1700s, 43 x 20 In.	253.00
Chair, Max Gottschalk, Lounge, Saddle Leather, Chromed Tubular Steel, 29 x 26 In.	1054.00
Chair, McCobb, Black Leather, Widdicomb, c.1962, 36 x 28 In. ...*illus*	2500.00
Chair, Meeks, Rococo Revival, Stanton Hall, Rosewood, Concave Back, Pierced Flowers, c.1865, 41 In.	2091.00

Chair, Mies Van Der Rohe, Leather, Steel Base & Arms, Square Back, 1929, 34 x 28 In.	4063.00
Chair, Mies Van Der Rohe, Mr. Arm, Tubular Steel Frame, Leather, Knoll, 1927, 32 x 21 In.	1350.00
Chair, Mies Van Der Rohe, Mr. Lounge, Tubular Stainless Steel, Tufted Leather, Knoll, 33 x 24 In.	2242.00
Chair, Milo Baughman, Chromed Steel, Chenille, Oak, Thayer Coggin, 32 x 21 In., Pair	372.00
Chair, Milo Baughman, Lounge, Metal, Ultrasuede Cushions, Thayer Coggin, 29 x 30 In.	1200.00
Chair, Milo Baughman, Lounge, Upholstered, Chrome Steel, Thayer Coggin, 27 x 28 In.	527.00
Chair, Milo Baughman, Upholstered, Curved Back, Swivel, 1980, 28 x 34 In., Pair	5400.00
Chair, Milo Baughman, Upholstered, Cushion, Thayer Coggin, c.1990, 40 x 18 In., Pair	1200.00
Chair, Ming Style, Wood, Yoke Crest Rail, Curved Arms, Box Stretcher, 45 x 23 In., Pair	12870.00
Chair, Morris, Oak, Adjustable, Leather Cushions, c.1900, 25 x 18 In., Child's	385.00
Chair, Morris, Oak, Twisted Side Spindles, Lion's Heads, Padded, Paw Feet, 34 In.	615.00
Chair, Napoleon III, Ebonized, Shaped Padded Back, Seat, Ormolu Leaf Crest, c.1870, 39 In., Pair	738.00
Chair, Neoclassical, Gilt, Turned, Fluted Legs, Upholstered, c.1810, 44 x 26 In., Pair	6547.00
Chair, Neogrecque, Mahogany, Rounded Back, Shaped Arms, Lion's Heads, Paw Feet, 1800s	976.00
Chair, Nickel, Tubular, Suede Upholstery, Emile Guillot, c.1928, 33 x 27 In.	896.00
Chair, Norman Cherner, Bernardo, Plywood, Molded, Vinyl Upholstery, 30 x 17 ½ In.	1035.00
Chair, Nutting, Chippendale Style, Mahogany, Scrolled Leaf Crest, Arms, c.1905, 39 In.	1265.00
Chair, O. Niemeyer, Lounge, Ottoman, Mohair, Brushed Steel, Plastic, 1960s, 28 x 30 In.	8680.00
Chair, Oak, Carved Solid Back Panel, Ram's Head Handrests, Box Stretcher, 50 x 30 In., Pair.	1416.00
Chair, Oak, Carved Spiral Stiles, Bird, Dragon, Upholstered, Turned Legs, c.1900, 53 x 26 In. .	326.00
Chair, Oak, Pierced, Carved Back & Legs, Scroll Arms, Upholstered, c.1890, 49 x 25 In.	230.00
Chair, Oak, Shaped Crest, Baluster Splat, Outscrolled Arms, Box Stretcher, c.1800, 40 In.	461.00
Chair, Oak, Shaped Pierced Back, Leaf Carved, Splayed Legs, England, 38 In.	62.00
Chair, Oak, Shaped Pierced Crest, Gallery Spindle Back, Outscrolled Arms, c.1835, 33 In.	461.00
Chair, Ottoman, Leather, Brown, Casters, Whittemore-Sherrill, 38 x 32 In.	1098.00
Chair, Ottoman, Peter Maly, High Back, Fabric & Faux Suede, Open Arms, 40 x 30 In.	236.00
Chair, Ottoman, Sheet Metal, Paint, Curved, Trudo Mfg. Co., Mass., 39 x 21 In.	1872.00
Chair, Ottoman, Sling, Iron & Brass, Upholstered, Leather Arms, 32 x 24 In.	1599.00
Chair, Ottoman, Wood Carved, Upholstered, Arms, 1800s, 44 x 29 In.	854.00
Chair, Oval Pierced Splat, Serpentine Arms, Shield Shape Seat, Spade Feet, 1800s, Pair	3050.00
Chair, P. Evans, Lounge, Ottoman, Cityscape, Chromed Steel, Vinyl, Directional, 1970s	4960.00
Chair, P. Evans, Sculpted Bronze, Composite, Leatherette, Directional, 1970s, 32 In., Pair	14880.00
Chair, P. Friedeberg, Hand & 3 Feet, Mahogany, Signed, Mexico, 24 In. ....*illus*	8625.00
Chair, P. Friedeberg, Hand, Mahogany, Carved, Pedestal Base, Signed, 20 x 22 x 34 In.	7200.00
Chair, Padded Back, Seat, Armorial Crest, Open Arms, Scrolling Finials, Stretcher, 47 In., Pair	767.00
Chair, Paint, Yoked Crest, Turned Front Legs, Spanish Feet, c.1765, 41 In. ....*illus*	1838.00
Chair, Paul Laszlo, Cage Back, Round Legs, Plush Seat, Paddle Arms, c.1952, 32 x 35 In., Pair	7500.00
Chair, Peter Hvidt, Teal, Curved Back, Finger Joints, Leather Seat, 27 ⅝ In.	337.00
Chair, Piano, Rococo Revival, Rusalie, Rosewood, Upholstered, Swivel, c.1850, 32 In. ....*illus*	7995.00
Chair, Piano, Victorian, Carved & Pressed Spindle Back, Swivel, Claw & Glass Ball Feet, 38 x 16 In.	330.00
Chair, Pierced Crest, Leaf Carved Holds, Upholstered, Stretcher, Italy, 54 x 26 In.	460.00
Chair, Pine, Curved Yoke Band, Arms, Openwork Splat, Chinese, 37 x 25 In., Pair	922.00
Chair, Planter's, Mahogany, Scroll Crest, Cane Seat, Arms With Boot Rests, 34 In.	777.00
Chair, Plastic, Arched Back, Shaped Arms, Barrel Seat, Metal Legs, c.1950, 31 x 25 In.	3438.00
Chair, Pony Shape, Upholstered, Round Ears, Legs, Round Metal Feet, 1973, 35 x 45 In.	4063.00
Chair, Poplar, Plank Seat, Flowers, Grandmother, Grandfather, Paint, 1800s, 33 x 18 In., Pair	118.00
Chair, Potty, French Provincial, Walnut, Carved, Cane Back, Hinged Seat	2271.00
Chair, Potty, Pine, Red Paint, Slide Lid, Chamber Pot, c.1850, 44 In.	468.00
Chair, Poul Kjaerholm, Sling Seat, Brown Leather, Steel Frame, 1965, 28 x 25 In., Pair	2133.00
Chair, Poul Volther, Footstool, Brushed Steel, Leather, Corona, Denmark, 1961, 29 x 34 In. ......*illus*	2450.00
Chair, Prairie School, Barrel Back, Vertical Slats, Open Arms, Low Stretcher, 30 x 29 In., Pair	434.00
Chair, Prayer, French Provincial, Ladder Back, Wide Top Rung, Woven Seat, 33 x 16 In.	92.00
Chair, Queen Anne Style, Domed Pierced Crest, Baluster Splat, 46 In., Pair	1599.00
Chair, Queen Anne Style, Mahogany, Shell Carved Crest, Pad Seat, c.1890, 42 x 20 In.	1380.00
Chair, Queen Anne Style, Mahogany, Shell Carved Crest, Upholstered, c.1890, 41 In. ......*illus*	230.00
Chair, Queen Anne Style, Vase Shape Splat, Carved Arms, Turned Legs, c.1900, 42 ½ In. .....*illus*	118.00
Chair, Queen Anne Style, Walnut, Padded Rectangular Back, Outscrolled Arms, 1800s, 41 In.	307.00
Chair, Queen Anne Style, Walnut, Shell Carved Crest, Knees, Philadelphia, 41 ½ In.	173.00
Chair, Queen Anne, Black Paint, Yoked Crest Rail, Vase Shape Splat, 1700s, 40 In.	4444.00
Chair, Queen Anne, Burl Walnut, Fiddle Splat, Upholstered, Slip Seat, 39 x 21 In., Pair	896.00
Chair, Queen Anne, Ladder Back, 5 Slats, Delaware Valley, 1700s	1659.00
Chair, Queen Anne, Mahogany, Rolling Top Rail, Arms, Cabriole Legs, Pad Feet, 34 In.	354.00
Chair, Queen Anne, Mahogany, Serpentine Crest Rail, Urn Shape Splat, c.1770	500.00
Chair, Queen Anne, Mahogany, Vase Shape Splat, Balloon Seat, Cabriole Legs, 1700s	5463.00
Chair, Queen Anne, Mahogany, Yoke Crest, Vase Shape Splat, Balloon Seat, c.1790, 37 In.	173.00
Chair, Queen Anne, Maple, Carved, Turned, Arms, Massachusetts, c.1730-40, 42 In.	3318.00
Chair, Queen Anne, Mixed Wood, Baluster Splat, Woven Seat, Hudson Valley, c.1770, 38 ½ In. *illus*	441.00

Furniture, Chair, M. Newson, Embryo, Neoprene, Stainless Steel, Aluminum, Austria, 1990s, 31 x 32 In.
$2108.00

Furniture, Chair, Mahogany, Carved, Arched Back, Upholstered Seat, c.1810, Pair
$5856.00

Furniture, Chair, Mahogany, Carved, Vase Shape Splat, Upholstered, 1700s, 38 In.
$1342.00

Furniture, Chair, Mahogany, Serpentine Crest Rail, Shaped Arms, Upholstered, c.1785, 40 ½ In.
$575.00

Furniture, Chair, McCobb, Black
Leather, Widdicomb, c.1962, 36 x 28 In.
$2500.00

Los Angeles Modern Auctions

Furniture, Chair, P. Friedeberg, Hand &
3 Feet, Mahogany, Signed, Mexico, 24 In.
$8625.00

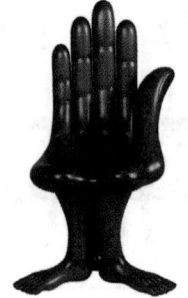

Cottone Auctions

Furniture, Chair, Paint, Yoked Crest,
Turned Front Legs, Spanish Feet, c.1765,
41 In.
$1838.00

Skinner, Inc.

Furniture, Chair, Piano, Rococo Revival,
Rusalie, Rosewood, Upholstered, Swivel,
c.1850, 32 In.
$7995.00

New Orleans Auction Galleries, Inc.

Chair, Queen Anne, Mixed Wood, Shaped Splat, Rush Seat, Open Arms, 1700s, 43 x 26 In.......	300.00
Chair, Queen Anne, Spoon Shape Back, Japanned, Bird, Shell, Pad Seat, 43 x 20 In., Pair	1872.00
Chair, Queen Anne, Tiger Maple, Vase Shape Splat, Molded Crest, Trapezoid Seat, c.1740, 38 In.	711.00
Chair, Queen Anne, Tiger Maple, Vase Shape Splat, Rush Seat, Turned Legs, 1700s	173.00
Chair, Queen Anne, Tiger Maple, Vase Shape Splat, Slip Seat, 1700s, 40 In...............................	2185.00
Chair, Queen Anne, Walnut, Raised Crest, Vase Shape Splat, Cabriole Legs, 1700s, 42 In..........	4025.00
Chair, Queen Anne, Walnut, Seaweed Carved Crest, Open Arms, Stretcher, c.1730, 41 x 25 In..	633.00
Chair, Queen Anne, Walnut, Serpentine Beaded Crest, Raking Stiles, 1700s, 39 In., Pair..........	2844.00
Chair, Queen Anne, Walnut, Shaped & Rolled Crest, Slip Seat, Cabriole Legs, 40 In....................	690.00
Chair, Queen Anne, Walnut, Shaped Back Splat, Slip Seat, 40 x 22 In...................................	780.00
Chair, Queen Anne, Walnut, Shell Carved Splat, Legs, Slip Seat, c.1750	11258.00
Chair, Queen Anne, Walnut, Vase Shape Splat, Cabriole Legs, Pa., c.1750	3081.00
Chair, Queen Anne, Yoke Shaped Crest, Flat Stiles, Carved Legs, Phila., c.1765, 40 ¾ x 20 ½ In.	4313.00
Chair, Regency Style, Black Lacquer, Parcel Gilt, Cane Back, Curule Front Legs, 35 x 25 In., Pair	1170.00
Chair, Regency Style, Cane Back & Seat, Arms, Lion Cabriole Legs, Paw Feet, 37 x 25 In., Pair	4972.00
Chair, Regency Style, Captain's, Mahogany, Barrel Back, 31 In., Pair..................................	523.00
Chair, Regency Style, Ebonized, X-Frame, Rattan Seat & Back, Reeded Arms, 32 x 22 In.	150.00
Chair, Regency Style, Mahogany, Cane, Arched Back, Turned Legs, Pair	1793.00
Chair, Regency Style, Spinning, Banjo Backrest, Octagonal Seat, H-Stretcher, 17 x 40 In.........	148.00
Chair, Regency Style, Walnut, Needlework, Open Arms, c.1900, 47 In., Pair...........................	2629.00
Chair, Regency, Barrel Back, Leather, Brass Tacks, Reeded Legs, Casters, Arms, c.1810, 32 In. .... *illus*	1410.00
Chair, Regency, Carved, Leather, Sliding Foot Rest, Padded Arms, c.1830, 44 In....................	1840.00
Chair, Regency, Mahogany, Adjustable, 4 Step Ladder, Scroll Arms, 36 x 22 In.	920.00
Chair, Regency, Mahogany, Cane Seat, Scroll Arms, 4 Leather Steps, 29 x 22 In......................	4680.00
Chair, Regency, Mahogany, Carved, Bowed Crest Rail, Tufted Back, Arms, Upholstered	1793.00
Chair, Regency, Mahogany, Tiered Rail, Applied Blind Cartouche, Plank Seat, 35 x 17 In., Pair	1287.00
Chair, Regency, Parcel Gilt, Decorated Crest Rail, Classical Figure, Cane, c.1815, Pair.............	1875.00
Chair, Regency, Rosewood, Beech, Brass Inlay, Lyre Back, Saber Legs, c.1825, 33 In., Pair.......	553.00
Chair, Regency, Rosewood, Brass Inlaid Splat, Curved Rail, Cane Seat, 32 x 18 In..................	293.00
Chair, Renaissance Revival, Burl Walnut, Carved, Applied Rosettes, Lion's Heads, c.1871	2074.00
Chair, Renaissance Revival, Burl Walnut, Incised, Handle Top, Upholstered, c.1870, 35 x 18 In.	69.00
Chair, Renaissance Revival, Inlay, Shield Shape Back, Upholstered Arms, c.1870	125.00
Chair, Renaissance Revival, Oak, Elm, Arched Back, Lion's Heads, Scroll Arms, 1800s.............	4183.00
Chair, Renaissance Revival, Oak, Rush Seat, Carved Back, Legs, Arms, 1800s, 45 x 21 In., Pair.	275.00
Chair, Renaissance Revival, Shaped Splat, Arched Crest Rail, Padded Seat, c.1875, Pair	200.00
Chair, Renaissance Revival, Walnut, Gilt, Carved Crest, Drop Crest Seat Rail, Hoof Feet, c.1869, 44 In.	8610.00
Chair, Renaissance Revival, Walnut, Leather, Storage Seat, Carved Crest, c.1870, 43 x 25 In., Pair	920.00
Chair, Renaissance Revival, Walnut, Trophy Crest, Griffins, Carved Stiles, c.1875	1195.00
Chair, Risom, Maple, Plastic, Knoll, 1950s, 31 x 20 ½ In., Pair...	310.00
Chair, Robsjohn-Gibbings, Lounge, Lacquered Mahogany, Leather, 1950s, 34 In....................	1116.00
Chair, Robsjohn-Gibbings, Lounge, Leather, Lacquered, Widdicomb, 1950s, 30 x 30 In.	3596.00
Chair, Robsjohn-Gibbings, Lounge, Mahogany, Linen, Widdicomb, 1950s, 31 x 27 In..............	4030.00
Chair, Robsjohn-Gibbings, Lounge, Mahogany, Upholstered, Widdicomb, 1950s, 31 x 24 In....	2728.00
Chair, Robsjohn-Gibbings, Mahogany, Webbing, Brass, Widdicomb, 1950s, 36 x 22 In., Pair...	4650.00
Chair, Rococo Revival, Rosewood, Arched Crest, Pierced Stiles, Serpentine Seat Rail, c.1850, Pair	3660.00
Chair, Rococo Revival, Rosewood, Carved, New York, c.1860, 40 x 18 In...............................	1067.00
Chair, Rococo Revival, Rosewood, Carved, Pierced Crest, Upholstered, c.1855, 30 x 26 In., Pair	2988.00
Chair, Rococo Revival, Rosewood, Flower Carved, Upholstered, Cabriole Legs, c.1900, 46 In.....	2460.00
Chair, Rococo Revival, Rosewood, Laminated, Carved Splat, c.1860, 46 In., Pair....................	538.00
Chair, Rococo Revival, Rosewood, Laminated, Concave Back, Pinched Waist, c.1850, 43 In. ...	4674.00
Chair, Rococo Revival, Rosewood, Openwork Crest, Cabriole Legs, c.1890, 45 x 21 In.............	1076.00
Chair, Rococo Revival, Rosewood, Oval Back, Leafy Crest, Scroll Arms & Legs, Velvet, 45 In.....	74.00
Chair, Rococo Revival, Rosewood, Pierced Shaped Back, Grapes & Vines, c.1865, 42 In.	3198.00
Chair, Rococo Revival, Walnut, Carved Crest, Arms, Upholstered, England, c.1860, 40 x 30 In.	288.00
Chair, Rococo Revival, Walnut, Carved, Scrolled, Upholstered, c.1850, 41 x 18 In..................	295.00
Chair, Rococo Revival, Walnut, Carved, Upholstered, 48 ½ x 29 ½ In.	863.00
Chair, Rococo Revival, Walnut, Open Carved Leaves, Serpentine Front Rail, 42 In.	184.00
Chair, Rococo Revival, Walnut, Shieldback, Upholstered, Padded Arms, 1800s, Child's .....*illus*	717.00
Chair, Rococo Style, Sleepy Hollow, Walnut, Carved, Tufted, Late 1800s................................	81.00
Chair, Rohde, Lounge, Chrome Plated Steel, Vinyl Upholstery, Troy Sunshade, 28 x 34 In.	1800.00
Chair, Rosewood, Arched Crest, Finials, Bamboo Turned Stiles, Arms, c.1850, 56 In.	3936.00
Chair, Rosewood, Bowed Crest, Square Back, Scroll Arms, Cabriole Legs, c.1830	2806.00
Chair, Rosewood, Carved Back, Coin Design, Chinese, 1800s	593.00
Chair, Rosewood, Curved Splat, Chinese, 1800s, 28 x 18 In...	3430.00
Chair, Rosewood, Inlay, Curved Splat, Carved Lotus Inset, Arms, Chinese, 1800s, 37 x 23 In....	3185.00
Chair, Rosewood, Mahogany, Pierced Splat, Open Arms, Chinese, 38 x 23 In.........................	531.00
Chair, Rosewood, Marble Inset Back, Carved Crest, Splat, Arms, Chinese, 39 In., Pair	1793.00

Chair, Rosewood, Phoenixes, Open Scroll Back & Arms, Square Legs, Stretcher, 1800s, 21 In., Pair	674.00
Chair, Rosewood, Scalloped Apron, Reticulated Back & Arms, Straight Legs, Chinese.............	1434.00
Chair, Rosewood, Scrolled Uprights, Scroll Arms, Carved Curule Legs, Casters, c.1830	2032.00
Chair, Roycroft, 2 Horizontal Slats, Red Leather Cushion, Marshal P. Wilder, 17 x 35 In.	1560.00
Chair, Roycroft, Mahogany, Leather, Back Slats, Brass Tacks, Arms, 43 ¾ x 21 In., Pair	4960.00
Chair, Roycroft, Meditation, Wide Horizontal Back Slat, Leather, 34 x 24 In................	3720.00
Chair, Roycroft, Tall Back, Pinched Slats, Black Cushion, Mark, 37 x 17 In.	372.00
Chair, Rubber Strap, Gray Tubular Frame, 33 x 20 In., Pair	30.00
Chair, Sam Maloof, Walnut, Spindle Back, Curved Legs, Arms, 1965, 39 In.	4063.00
Chair, Satinwood, Square Back, Padded Arms, Seat, Upholstered, Casters, 1800s	492.00
Chair, Savanarola, Oak, Rectangular Back, Medallion, Shaped Arms, X-Base, c.1805, 35 In....	184.00
Chair, Savonarola, Carved Back, Apron, Paw Feet, 39 x 25 In..........................	184.00
Chair, Savonarola, Carved, Scrolling Leaves, Bust Finials, Concave Seat, 42 x 25 In., Pair....	2124.00
Chair, Savonarola, Northwind, Carved Griffin, Turned Stretchers, 41 x 24 In.	403.00
Chair, School, Oak, Cast Iron, Salesman's Sample, A.H. Andrews & Co., c.1878, 15 x 24 In......	805.00
Chair, Scroll Carved Stretcher, Legs, Velvet Upholstery, 46 ½ In........................	138.00
Chair, Scrolled Crest, Baluster Splat, Cabriole Legs, Pad Feet, c.1800, 39 In.	184.00
Chair, Sedan, Rattan Dome, Lacquer Sides, Panel Doors, Pagoda Shape, Chinese, c.1870, 79 x 39 In.	7768.00
Chair, Sergio Rodrigues, Rosewood, Beige Leather, Open Arms, Brazil, 30 x 24 In.	248.00
Chair, Serpentine Top Rail, Pierced Splat, Scroll Arms, Carved Supports, 1700s, 38 x 27 In.....	1170.00
Chair, Shaker, Maple, Red Brown Stain, 3 Shaped Slats, Splint Seat, c.1835, 41 In., Pair	585.00
Chair, Shaker, Maple, Red Paint, Pinned Top Slat, Tilter, c.1840, 40 In.	245.00
Chair, Shaker, Woven Tape Seat & Back, Ball Arm Rests, 17 ½ In., Child's.............	230.00
Chair, Sheraton, Rosewood, Cane Seat & Back, Painted Flowers, 1800s, 27 x 15 In., Child's	60.00
Chair, Sheraton, Tiger Maple, Curved Crest, Acanthus Leaves Slat, Turned Legs, c.1825, 32 In., Pair	177.00
Chair, Shield Back, Vertical Splats, Square Legs, Spade Feet, 37 In......................	59.00
Chair, Sigurd Ressel, Falcon, Sling Seat, Padded, Metal Pedestal Base, 40 x 29 In..................	216.00
Chair, Slat Back, Grain Painted, Rush Seat, Stretcher, Arms, New England, c.1850, 41 In........	711.00
Chair, Sling Seat, Black Leather, Steel T-Shaped Support, Littell, c.1952, 32 In., Pair	830.00
Chair, Sling, Steel, Polished, Scrolled Back, Riveted Seat, Stretcher, Pair	671.00
Chair, Slipper, Louis XV Style, Tufted Back, Cushion Seat, Cabriole Legs, 38 In.	207.00
Chair, Slipper, Rococo Revival, Faux Rosewood, Carved Back, Spiral Posts, c.1850, 46 x 19 In.	184.00
Chair, Slipper, Rococo, Walnut, Carved Oval Back, Scroll Arms, Needlepoint, 1800s	598.00
Chair, Slipper, Rolled Back, Upholstered, Turned Legs, France, c.1890, 32 x 23 In.	338.00
Chair, Slipper, Square Seat & Back, Tufted Upholstery, Wood Feet, c.1948, 31 x 28 In...........	2125.00
Chair, Slipper, Victorian, Mahogany, Tufted Leather, Serpentine, Cabriole Legs, 34 x 22 In.......	761.00
Chair, Smokey Tunis, Poplar, Carved, Stained, Signed, c.1969, 44 x 16 In.	620.00
Chair, Spindle Back, Black Paint, Splint Seat, Double Stretcher, Arms, 44 x 23 In..............	805.00
Chair, Spindle Back, Leather Upholstery, Turned Legs, 42 x 22 In.	677.00
Chair, Square Back, Tufted Upholstery, Square Arms, Tapered Wood Feet, c.1959, 28 In..........	625.00
Chair, Steer Horn Backs, Rounded Padded Seat, c.1900, Pair	1434.00
Chair, Steer Horn, Tooled Saddle Leather, Chromed Steel Stretchers, 1800s, 51 In. ....illus	4980.00
Chair, Stendig, Ebonized, Spindles, Upholstered Seat, Round Legs, Label, 37 In., Pair.............	207.00
Chair, Stickley Bros., Morris, Vertical Arm Slats, Leather Cushions, 41 x 30 ½ In.................	527.00
Chair, Stickley, 4 Horizontal Slats, Pebble Cushion, Arms, 39 In........................	889.00
Chair, Stool, P. Volther, Corona, Oval Segments, Leather, Brushed Steel, 36 In.	4740.00
Chair, Stretcher, Chinese, Hardwood, Horseshoe Back, Pierced Splat, Dish Seat, Pair	1220.00
Chair, Sweetheart, Heart Shape, Pierced Back Splat, Upholstered, Cabriole Legs, 32 x 36 In....	300.00
Chair, Swivel, Blond Wood Base, Tweed Upholstery, 1960s, 30 x 26 In......................	295.00
Chair, Tall Scrolled Back, Carved Supports, Padded Arms, Reeded Legs, c.1800	2562.00
Chair, Teak, Carved Back, Pierced Leaves, Round Seat, Animal Shape Feet, 1800s, 38 x 19 In.	207.00
Chair, Teak, Mixed Wood, Carved, Scrolled, Pierced, Chinese, c.1900, 37 x 22 In., Pair	805.00
Chair, Thonet, Beech, Dark Stain, Ink Stamp, Paper Label, Austria, c.1905, 39 In. ....illus	1178.00
Chair, Thonet, Lounge, Laminated Wood, Vinyl, 1950s, 32 x 22 In........................	496.00
Chair, Throne, Renaissance Revival, Oak, Inset Garden Of Eden Scene, 1800s, 57 x 28 In.......	896.00
Chair, Throne, Rosewood, Carved, Mother-Of-Pearl, Marble Insets, Chinese, c.1920, 40 x 27 In., Pair	6900.00
Chair, Tiger Oak, Lyre Crest, Turned Back, Side Slats, Arms, Swivel, c.1900, 46 x 25 In.	153.00
Chair, Tommi Parzinger, Lounge, Mahogany Open Arms, Upholstered, 1950s, 32 x 25 In........	14880.00
Chair, Tufted Leather, Open Arms, Swivel Base, 44 x 26 In.	369.00
Chair, Upholstered Square Seat & Back, Spindle Arm Rails, Scroll Feet, 41 In................	91.00
Chair, V. Kagan, Lounge, Barrel, Walnut, Fabric, 1970s, 31 x 33 In.	2480.00
Chair, V. Kagan, Lounge, Wing, Ottoman, Walnut, Wool, 1950s, 40 x 31 In..............	11780.00
Chair, V. Panton, Cone, Chromed Steel, Leather Cushion, Plastic, Plus-Linje, 1950s, 30 x 25 In.	496.00
Chair, V. Panton, Lounge, Tufted Fabric, Aluminum, Fritz Hansen, 1990s, 43 x 23 ½ In..........	620.00
Chair, V. Panton, Peacock, Wire Collection, Plus-Linje, Denmark, 1950s, 16 x 38 In. ......illus	4375.00
Chair, Vesey, Napoleonic Campaign, Adjustable, Chrome, Leather, c.1958, 40 In., Pair.............	16120.00
Chair, Victorian, Oak, Flower & Figure Carved Base, Back, Round Seat, 59 In........................	374.00

Furniture, Chair, Poul Volther, Footstool, Brushed Steel, Leather, Corona, Denmark, 1961, 29 x 34 In. $2450.00

Skinner, Inc.

Furniture, Chair, Queen Anne Style, Mahogany, Shell Carved Crest, Upholstered, c.1890, 41 In. $230.00

Leland Little Auction

Furniture, Chair, Queen Anne Style, Vase Shape Splat, Carved Arms, Turned Legs, c.1900, 42 ½ In. $118.00

Garth's Auctions, Inc.

Furniture, Chair, Queen Anne, Mixed Wood, Baluster Splat, Woven Seat, Hudson Valley, c.1770, 38 ½ In. $441.00

Garth's Auctions, Inc.

Furniture, Chair, Regency, Barrel Back, Leather, Brass Tacks, Reeded Legs, Casters, Arms, c.1810, 32 In. **$1410.00**

Cowan's Auctions

Furniture, Chair, Rococo Revival, Walnut, Shieldback, Upholstered, Padded Arms, 1800s, Child's **$717.00**

Neal Auction Co.

Furniture, Chair, Steer Horn, Tooled Saddle Leather, Chromed Steel Stretchers, 1800s, 51 In. **$4980.00**

Neal Auction Co.

Chair, Victorian, Rosewood, Carved Crest, Floral Skirt, Leaf Carved Legs, 35 In., Pair	295.00
Chair, Victorian, Upholstered, Paw Grips, Reeded Arms, Ring Turned Legs, 46 In., Pair	444.00
Chair, Victorian, Walnut, Hinge Lift Plank Seat, Carved Back, 46 x 20 In.	259.00
Chair, W. Platner, Lounge, Walnut, Leather, Brass, L. Leopold, 1970s, 29 x 37 In. ....*illus*	1364.00
Chair, Walnut, Burl, Pierced & Carved Back, Urn, Turned Legs, c.1885, 34 In., Pair	1845.00
Chair, Walnut, Carved, Inlaid Crest, Scrolled Crest Rail, Paneled Back, 1700s, 39 In., Pair	155.00
Chair, Walnut, Carved, Turned Uprights, Gilt, Scrolled Back, Seat, Arms, Hoof Feet, c.1890	358.00
Chair, Walnut, Leaf Carved Crest, Tufted Upholstery, Oval Back, Seat, Open Arms, 39 x 24 In.	61.00
Chair, Walnut, Open Back & Arms, Barrel Seat, Arched Base, Digbert, 33 ½ x 23 In., Pair	336.00
Chair, Walnut, Scroll Carved Open Arms, Upholstered, 40 x 30 In.	144.00
Chair, Walnut, Shaped, Reclining Putti, Arms, Outswept Dolphin Legs, X-Stretcher, Italy, 1800s	3904.00
Chair, Walnut, Shell Carved Crest, Arms, Scrolled Ears, Slip Seat, Phila., c.1770, 40 x 30 In.	20700.00
Chair, Walnut, Square Seat & Back, Barley Twist, Ring-Turned Feet, Arms, 1700s, 43 In., Pair	2015.00
Chair, Walnut, Upholstered Seat & Back, Tapestry, Scroll Legs, Stretcher, Belgium, 44 In., Pair	3185.00
Chair, Walnut, Upholstered, Kodawood, c.1950, 32 x 19 In., Pair	150.00
Chair, Walnut, Vertical Back Slat, Turned Supports, Stretcher, 38 x 22 In., Pair	92.00
Chair, Wedding, Carved, Names, Hearts, Painted, Cane Seat, 1845, 1850, 36 & 38 In., Pair	374.00
Chair, Wegner Style, Papa Bear, Maple, Canted Tufted Back, Trapezoid Seat, c.1950, Pair	1107.00
Chair, Wegner, Cord Seat & Back, Flat Oak Arms, c.1950, 28 x 27 In., Pair	3911.00
Chair, Wegner, Easy High Back, White Oak, Upholstered, 37 x 29 In.	306.00
Chair, Wegner, Fried Egg, Teak, Wool Upholstery, V. Birksholm, c.1956, 39 x 28 In.	45000.00
Chair, Wegner, Metal, Triangle Wood Back, Black Seat, Swivel, Signed, 1955, 29 x 29 In.	26000.00
Chair, Wegner, Oak, Black Plastic, Carl Hansen, 1950s, 30 x 20 In.	465.00
Chair, Wegner, Papa Bear, Ottoman, Teak, Leather, Brass Tacks, A.P. Stolen, 1950s, 39 In. .... *illus*	6820.00
Chair, Wegner, Peacock, Johannes Hansen, Denmark, c.1947, 42 In. ....*illus*	2500.00
Chair, Wegner, Teak, Leather Seat, Steel Base, Swivel, J. Hansen, c.1960, 29 x 30 In.	14400.00
Chair, Wegner, Valet, Hinged Saddle Seat, Tripod Base, 1953, 37 x 19 In.	5915.00
Chair, Wegner, Valet, Shaped Seat & Back, Johannes Hansen, c.1953, 37 ½ In. ....*illus*	10000.00
Chair, Wegner, Valet, Teak, Shaped Back, 3 Legs, Denmark, c.1953, 38 x 19 In.	7768.00
Chair, Wegner, Wishbone, Beech, Woven Seat, Denmark, 29 x 22 In.	148.00
Chair, William & Mary Style, Walnut, Flower Carvings, Needlepoint, Arms, c.1905, 18 x 21 In.	889.00
Chair, William & Mary, Banister Back, Woven Seat, New Hampshire, c.1750, 44 ½ In.	7000.00
Chair, William & Mary, Blue Paint, Carved Yoked Crest Rail, Rush Seat, 1700s, Pair	450.00
Chair, William & Mary, Oak, Turned Legs, X-Shape Stretcher, Arms, 1750, 45 x 27 In.	657.00
Chair, William & Mary, Yoke Crest, Urn Splat, Rush Seat, Scrolling Arms, c.1800	325.00
Chair, William IV, Mahogany, Carved, Bead Molded, Lion's Head, Arms, Ireland, c.1810 .*illus*	956.00
Chair, Windsor, Arrow Back, Drum, Cannon, Flags, Crossed Slats, c.1815, 35 In., Pair ....*illus*	705.00
Chair, Windsor, Bamboo Turnings, Spindle Back, Arms, 1800s, 34 x 16 In.	374.00
Chair, Windsor, Bent Rod Back, Red, Black Stripes, Painted Vines, New England, Pair	3081.00
Chair, Windsor, Birdcage, 7 Spindles, Flared Back, Ring-Turned Finials, Painted, 36 In.	288.00
Chair, Windsor, Bow Back, 8 Spindles, Shaped Seat, Bamboo Turned Legs, c.1800, 37 In.	374.00
Chair, Windsor, Bow Back, Bamboo Turned Legs, Paint, 38 ½ In., Pair ....*illus*	2585.00
Chair, Windsor, Bow Back, Bamboo Turned Spindles, Curved Stretcher, c.1800, 39 x 18 In.	711.00
Chair, Windsor, Bow Back, Braced, Swelled Spindles, Vase & Ring Turnings, N.Y., c.1790, 37 In. *illus*	429.00
Chair, Windsor, Bow Back, Mixed Wood, Bamboo Turned Legs, c.1800, 35 ½ In.	499.00
Chair, Windsor, Bow Back, Mixed Wood, c.1810, 33 ½ In. ....*illus*	705.00
Chair, Windsor, Bow Back, Saddle Seat, Turned Supports & Legs, Arms, 1700s, 36 In.	173.00
Chair, Windsor, Bow Back, Splayed Legs, Black Finish, c.1810, Pair	356.00
Chair, Windsor, Brace Back, Bow Back, Blue Paint, c.1790-95, 37 x 17 In.	551.00
Chair, Windsor, Brace Back, Bow Back, Pipe Stem Turnings, Arms, 1700s, 38 x 17 In.	690.00
Chair, Windsor, Brace Back, Bow Back, Vase & Ring Turnings, c.1795, 37 x 17 In.	429.00
Chair, Windsor, Brace Back, Red Paint, Continuous Arm, c.1780-90, 35 In.	948.00
Chair, Windsor, Comb Back, 5 Spindle Crest, Arched Back, Arm Rests, Dish Seat, 46 x 22 In.	1638.00
Chair, Windsor, Comb Back, 7 Spindles, Mixed Wood, Arms, 46 In. ....*illus*	940.00
Chair, Windsor, Comb Back, Eared, Bamboo Turned Legs & Arms, c.1800, 37 In.	2350.00
Chair, Windsor, Comb Back, Painted, Serpentine Crest, Vase Shape Supports, 1700s	1300.00
Chair, Windsor, Comb Back, Poplar, Arms, Plank Seat, New England, 43 x 25 In.	720.00
Chair, Windsor, Fanback, Black Paint, Curved Crest Rail, Carved Seat, c.1790	1185.00
Chair, Windsor, Fanback, Green Paint, Arched Crest, Scroll Ears, H-Stretcher, c.1790, 37 In.	748.00
Chair, Windsor, Fanback, Green Paint, c.1785.	1304.00
Chair, Windsor, Fanback, Saddle Seat, Paint, Vase & Ring Turned Legs, 1700s, 40 In., Pair	2083.00
Chair, Windsor, Fanback, Scroll Crest, Knuckle Handholds, Saddle Seat, Arms, c.1795, 41 x 16 In.	2370.00
Chair, Windsor, Federal, Bamboo Turned Spindles, Tablet Crest Rail, Stiles, Arms, 35 In.	430.00
Chair, Windsor, Hickory, Pine, 7 Spindles, Arched, Dish Seat, Splayed Legs, 37 x 15 In.	88.00
Chair, Windsor, Hickory, Pine, 7 Spindles, Stepped Top Rail, Dish Seat, 36 x 16 In., Pair	293.00
Chair, Windsor, Hoop Back, Arms, Blue Paint, Pa., c.1795.	652.00
Chair, Windsor, Hoop Back, Saddle Seat, Black Paint, T.C. Haywood, 38 x 28 ½ In.	1521.00

Chair, Windsor, Low Back, Ring Turned, c.1765, 30 In. ....*illus*	948.00
Chair, Windsor, Mixed Wood, Continuous Arm, Splayed Base, H-Stretcher, c.1950, 39 In., Pair	382.00
Chair, Windsor, Mustard Paint, Arms, 22 x 13 In., Child's	316.00
Chair, Windsor, Pine, Green Paint Over Red, Bamboo Turned, Stretcher, Arms, c.1850, 34 In..	294.00
Chair, Windsor, Queen Anne, Yew, Arms, c.1850	1337.00
Chair, Windsor, Sack Back, Black Paint, Splayed Legs, New York, c.1790	1896.00
Chair, Windsor, Sack Back, Cutout Arms, 1700s, 36 x 23 In.	460.00
Chair, Windsor, Sack Back, Green Paint, Baluster Turned Handhold, Philadelphia, 1700s.......	325.00
Chair, Windsor, Sack Back, Green, Blue Paint, Arms, c.1810	2015.00
Chair, Windsor, Sack Back, Painted, c.1800, 36 In.	2070.00
Chair, Windsor, Sack Back, Red Over Green Paint, Curved Arm Supports, R.I., c.1790	7703.00
Chair, Windsor, Sack Back, Saddle Seat, H-Stretcher, Turned Legs, Pa., c.1790........................	948.00
Chair, Windsor, Sack Back, Tiger Maple, Bowed, Swelled Stretcher, Arms, c.1790, 36 In.	1541.00
Chair, Windsor, Sack Back, Walnut, Ash, Knuckle Handholds, Saddle Seat, Arms, c.1795, 38 In.	593.00
Chair, Windsor, Sack Back, Wood, Double Baluster, Knuckle Arms, c.1880, 37 In.....................	881.00
Chair, Windsor, Sack Back, Yellow Pinstriping, Pa., c.1790	889.00
Chair, Windsor, Scrolled Ears, Black Paint, Philadelphia, c.1750, 45 x 25 In........................	8400.00
Chair, Windsor, Tall Back & Sides, Bamboo Turned Legs, c.1810, 49 In. ....*illus*	764.00
Chair, Windsor, William IV, Mixed Wood, Ship Wheel Splat, Open Arms, c.1820, 35 In.	276.00
Chair, Windsor, Wood, Baluster Turned Legs, c.1775, 35 In.........................	411.00
Chair, Windsor, Wood, Blue Paint, Arms, England, c.1890, 32 x 18 In., Child's	480.00
Chair, Windsor, Wood, Half Spindle, Rabbit Ear Posts, Painted, c.1830, 34 In.	206.00
Chair, Windsor, Wood, Plank Seat, Red Paint, c.1810, 34 x 20 In.	354.00
Chair, Windsor, Wood, Square, Arched Crest, Bamboo Turned Spindles, c.1805, 36 In.............	1145.00
Chair, Windsor, Writing, Federal, Balloon Writing Surface, Drawers, 37 In.....................	3802.00
Chair, Wing, Arched Crest Rail, Scroll Arms, Upholstered, 1900s, 46 x 33 In.....	598.00
Chair, Wing, Black Leather, Loose Cushions, Nail Trim, 1900s, 41 x 32 In.	738.00
Chair, Wing, Butterfly, Upholstered, Paw Feet, 45 x 37 In., Pair	633.00
Chair, Wing, Carved, Upholstered, Scroll Arms, Legs, England, 1940s, 39 x 33 In.....................	1200.00
Chair, Wing, Chippendale Style, Mahogany, Leather, Scrolling Arms, Brass Nailheads, 48 x 31 In., Pair	2988.00
Chair, Wing, Chippendale, Mahogany, Upholstered, 1700s, 50 x 36 ½ In.	62.00
Chair, Wing, Chippendale, Upholstered, 1700s, 20 x 46 In.	1840.00
Chair, Wing, Federal, Mahogany, Carved, Serpentine Crest, Upholstered, c.1800, 43 x 34 In. ....*illus*	2278.00
Chair, Wing, George III Style, Mahogany, Domed Padded Back, Scroll Arms, c.1885, 49 In......	1599.00
Chair, Wing, George III Style, Mahogany, Upholstered Back, Square Legs, c.1900, 43 In.	1265.00
Chair, Wing, George III Style, Mahogany, Upholstered, Arms, Ireland, c.1925, 49 In...............	1230.00
Chair, Wing, Guglielmo Ulrich, Lounge, Ebonized Wood, Velvet, 1940s, 39 x 30 In., Pair	9920.00
Chair, Wing, Leather, Cabriole Legs, Hickory Chair Co., c.1980, 44 x 31 In.	369.00
Chair, Wing, Leather, Tufted, Green, Brown, England, c.1905, 50 x 33 In.	2832.00
Chair, Wing, Long-Haired Lamb, Sycamore, France, 1930s, 41 x 33 ½ In. ....*illus*	6200.00
Chair, Wing, Louis XVI Style, Flower Carved Arms, Legs, Upholstered, 40 x 29 In.	270.00
Chair, Wing, Louis XVI Style, Upholstered, Curved Crest, Fluted Legs, Arms, 45 In.	465.00
Chair, Wing, Mahogany, Carved Scroll, Rosettes, Upholstered, Hoof Feet, 1700s, 49 In.	2875.00
Chair, Wing, Mahogany, Scroll Arms, Carved Knees, Hickory, 45 In..	238.00
Chair, Wing, Queen Anne Style, Leather, Tufted, c.1970, 37 x 28 In.	246.00
Chair, Wing, Queen Anne Style, Mahogany, Stretchers, Upholstered, c.1900, 47 x 35 In., Pair .	480.00
Chair, Wing, Queen Anne Style, Mahogany, Upholstered, Outscrolled Arms, c.1910, 37 In.	430.00
Chair, Wing, Queen Anne Style, Mahogany, Upholstered, Pad Feet, 1800s, 42 In.	430.00
Chair, Wing, Queen Anne, Mahogany, Arched Crest, Rolled Arms, Cabriole Legs, 1800s, 46 In.	633.00
Chair, Wing, Queen Anne, Walnut, Upholstered, Scroll Arms, Cabriole Legs, Pad Feet, 1700s...	1952.00
Chair, Wing, Sheraton, Mahogany, Upholstered, Turned Front Legs, c.1815	577.00
Chair, Wing, Sheraton, Mahogany, Upholstered, Turned Legs, Cup Casters, Arms, 47 x 31 In...	3450.00
Chair, Wing, Upholstered, Ball & Claw Feet, c.1890, 17 x 45 In.....................	81.00
Chair, Wing, Walnut, Upholstered, Angular Armrest, Dunbar, 31 x 29 In., Pair........................	1470.00
Chair, Wing, Walnut, Upholstered, Cabriole Legs, Trifid Feet, England, 1700s	3450.00
Chair, Wing, Welted Seat Cushion, Trapunto Appliques, 28 x 42 In.	575.00
Chair, Wood, Banister Back, Double Arch Crest, Turned Legs & Stretchers, Arms, 1700s, 46 In.	1175.00
Chair, Wood, Black Paint, Banister Back, Shaped Crest, Turned Arms, Stretcher, 1700s, 45 In.	558.00
Chair, Wood, Carved, Eagles, Openwork Back, Padded Seat, 1825, 38 x 16 In...........................	850.00
Chair, Wood, Carved, Tilt Headrest, Footrest, 2-Tiered Armrest, Chinese, 1900s, 34 x 45 In.	780.00
Chair, Wood, Carved, Upholstered, Paw Armrests, Scrolled Stretcher, 45 In.	207.00
Chair, Wood, Horseshoe Back, Arms, Spindles, Chinese, 1900s, 36 x 26 In., Pair	461.00
Chair, Wood, Inlays, Horseshoe Back, Cushion Seat, Syria, 32 x 26 In., Pair	1680.00
Chair, Wood, Leather, Mechanical, Reclining Back, Footrest, Paris, c.1900, 49 x 24 In............	677.00
Chair, Wood, Rectangular, Pierced Splat, Round Stone Medallions, Squared Legs, Arms, 29 In., Pair	427.00
Chair, Wood, Tablet Top, Green, Multicolor Fruit, Flowers, James Huey, 32 In., Pair	470.00

Furniture, Chair, Thonet, Beech, Dark Stain, Ink Stamp, Paper Label, Austria, c.1905, 39 In.
$1178.00

Rago Arts & Auction Center

Furniture, Chair, V. Panton, Peacock, Wire Collection, Plus-Linje, Denmark, 1950s, 16 x 38 In.
$4375.00

Los Angeles Modern Auctions

Furniture, Chair, W. Platner, Lounge, Walnut, Leather, Brass, L. Leopold, 1970s, 29 x 37 In.
$1364.00

Rago Arts & Auction Center

Furniture, Chair, Wegner, Papa Bear, Ottoman, Teak, Leather, Brass Tacks, A.P. Stolen, 1950s, 39 In.
$6820.00

Rago Arts & Auction Center

Furniture, Chair, Wegner, Peacock, Johannes Hansen, Denmark, c.1947, 42 In.
$2500.00

Los Angeles Modern Auctions

Furniture, Chair, Wegner, Valet, Shaped Seat & Back, Johannes Hansen, c.1953, 37 ½ In.
$10000.00

Los Angeles Modern Auctions

Furniture, Chair, William IV, Mahogany, Carved, Bead Molded, Lion's Head, Arms, Ireland, c.1810
$956.00

Neal Auction Co.

Furniture, Chair, Windsor, Arrow Back, Drum, Cannon, Flags, Crossed Slats, c.1815, 35 In., Pair
$705.00

Garth's Auctions, Inc.

Chair, Wood, Tufted Leather, Open Scroll Arms, Curule Base, France, c.1890, 38 x 26 In.	3690.00
Chair, Wormley, Mahogany, Leather, A-Frame, Dunbar, c.1950, 27 x 25 In., Pair	1793.00
Chair, Wrought Iron, Leather Seat & Back, c.1950, Pair	633.00
Chair, Wrought Iron, Radiating Scrolls & Lines, Arms, White Paint, c.1940, 45 In., Pair	1968.00
Chair, Rocker, is listed under Rocker in this category.	
Chair-Table, Pine, 3-Board Top, 1800s, 30 x 40 x 58 In.	235.00
Chair-Table, Pine, Birch, Turned Posts, Pinned Arms, Octagon Top, 27 x 46 In.	558.00
Chair-Table, Pine, Red Stain, 2-Board Top, Trestle Base, 27 x 55 In.	660.00
Chair-Table, Pine, Tilt Overhang, Cutout End, Paint, c.1800, 29 x 66 In.	4503.00
Chair-Table, R.E. Cahoon Jr., Painted, Bird, Flowers, Planks, Shelf, 30 x 54 In.	2875.00
Chair-Table, Shoefoot Base, 38 In. Diam.	1265.00
Chair-Table, Wood, Pine, Pinned Stretcher, Arms, 1800s, 27 x 43 In.	588.00
Chair-Table, Wood, Round Pine Top, Scrolled Arm Supports, Drawer, 1800s, 29 x 57 In.	472.00
Chaise Longue, Copper, Upholstered, Riveted Trim, Arms, c.1980, 27 x 67 In.	1968.00
Chaise Longue, Ebonized Wood, Spindle Arm Support, Arched Back, 1800s, 70 In.	81.00
Chaise Longue, French Provincial, Oak, Outscrolled Armrest, 1800s, 32 x 21 In.	738.00
Chaise Longue, H. Probber, Velvet, Mahogany, 1 High Arm, 1950s, 29 x 61 In.	2976.00
Chaise Longue, J. Bernett, Landscape, Aluminum, Leather, B & B Italia, 24 x 60 x 33 In.	3600.00
Chaise Longue, Le Corbusier, Chrome, Pony Skin Upholstery, Cassina, 64 x 17 In.	1652.00
Chaise Longue, Le Corbusier, Jeanneret & Perriand, Chromed Steel, Leather, 63 In.	711.00
Chaise Longue, Louis XV Style, Painted Frame, Floral Fabric, Tassels, 32 x 64 In.	554.00
Chaise Longue, Oak, Upholstered, Rounded End, Stepped Block Feet, c.1885, 80 In.	531.00
Chaise Longue, Orange Ultrasuede, Polished Aluminum, Leolux, 1990s, 32 x 63 In.	279.00
Chaise Longue, Padded Back, Seat, Round Legs, Multicolor, Gilt Accents, 39 x 36 In.	738.00
Chaise Longue, Robsjohn-Gibbings, Mahogany, Brass, Wool, 1950s, 33 x 62 In.	12400.00
Chaise Longue, Van Keppel & Green, Upholstered, Adjustable, Metal Base, c.1956, 23 x 72 In.	3750.00
Chaise Longue, Victorian, Shaped Rails, Tufted, 33 x 39 In., Child's	184.00
Chaise Longue, Wrought Iron, Grass Wrapped, 31 x 68 In.	236.00
Chest, 4 Graduated Drawers, Bracket Feet, N.C., c.1810, 52 x 39 In.	805.00
Chest, 7 Drawers, Carved Base, Cabriole Legs, Pa., c.1790, 63 x 43 In.	2185.00
Chest, Alexander Roux, Rosewood, White Marble Top, 3 Drawers, Pilasters, c.1850, 45 x 21 In.	2270.00
Chest, Arched Drawers Over 6 Drawers, Side Panels, Bracket Feet, c.1750, 68 x 38 In.	4740.00
Chest, Bachelor's, Cherry, Maple Banding, 7 Drawers, c.1815-40	1265.00
Chest, Bachelor's, Chippendale, Mahogany, Serpentine, 4 Drawers, 1700s, 34 x 39 In.	3055.00
Chest, Bachelor's, George III, Mahogany, Crossbanded Top, 3 Graduated Drawers, 34 x 34 In.	984.00
Chest, Bachelor's, Georgian Style, Burl, Dressing Slide, 4 Drawers, Bracket Feet, 29 x 24 In.	1315.00
Chest, Bachelor's, Mahogany, Bowfront, Banded Inlay, 4 Drawers, Turned Feet, 1800s, 37 x 38 In.	805.00
Chest, Bachelor's, Mahogany, Gallery, Tapered Columns, Crossbanded, c.1840, 52 x 43 In.	717.00
Chest, Baroque, Oak, Iron Mounts, Pierced Scrolls, Flowers, Well Interior, 1600s, 25 x 46 In.	1185.00
Chest, Baroque, Walnut, Carved, Drawer, Panel Door, Paw Feet, Italy, 1600s, 31 x 26 In.	944.00
Chest, Biedermeier, 8 Drawers, Spindle Column, Paw Feet, 1800s, 69 x 46 In.	540.00
Chest, Biedermeier, Frieze Drawers, Column Pilasters, Block Feet, 30 x 37 In.	649.00
Chest, Biedermeier, Fruitwood, Marble Top, 4 Drawers, Bun Feet, c.1830, 34 x 37 In.	1375.00
Chest, Birch, Mahogany Veneer, Shaped Backsplash, 7 Drawers, Pineapple Posts, c.1825, 49 x 41 In.	385.00
Chest, Bird's-Eye Maple, 4 Drawers, Inlaid Diamond Escutcheons, 1800s, 22 x 14 In.	1610.00
Chest, Bird's-Eye Maple, Arched Backsplash, 6 Drawers, 46 In.	646.00
Chest, Bird's-Eye Maple, Shaped Backsplash, Scroll Stiles, 6 Drawers, c.1835, 47 x 43 In.	610.00
Chest, Blanket, Bayberry Blue Paint, Dovetailed, Bracket Feet, 21 x 38 x 17 In.	2925.00
Chest, Blanket, Blue Paint, Hinged Top, Drawer, New England, c.1810, 31 x 42 In.	4500.00
Chest, Blanket, Blue Stain, Drawers, Ball Feet, 1800s, 26 x 49 In.	300.00
Chest, Blanket, Blue Gray Paint, 6-Board, Bootjack Ends, Brass, 1700s, 25 x 48 In.	345.00
Chest, Blanket, Brown Stain, Lift Top, Scrolled Bootjack Ends, 1700s, 24 ½ x 19 In.	358.00
Chest, Blanket, Burl Veneer, Coffered Lid, Brass Hinges, Escutcheon, Brass Feet, 13 x 14 In.	489.00
Chest, Blanket, Camphorwood, Brass Drop Handles, Chinese, 18 x 38 In.	1287.00
Chest, Blanket, Camphorwood, Carved, c.1910, 18 ½ x 34 ½ In.	119.00
Chest, Blanket, Camphorwood, Lift Top, Carved Figures, Chinese, 1900s, 18 x 38 In.	92.00
Chest, Blanket, Camphorwood, Lift Top, Carved Figures, Chinese, Mid 1900s, 23 x 41 In.	316.00
Chest, Blanket, Cedar, Dovetailed, Brass Bands, Handles & Corner Brackets, 19 x 39 In.	123.00
Chest, Blanket, Cedar, Wood, Inlaid, Lift Top, Waterfall, Shaped Apron, 1900s, 21 x 45 In.	161.00
Chest, Blanket, Cherry, Drawer, Red Paint, Turned Feet, c.1850, 29 x 48 In.	176.00
Chest, Blanket, Cherry, Pine, Poplar, Iron Handles, Runner Base, 12 x 18 In.	590.00
Chest, Blanket, Cherry, Walnut, Paint, 2 Drawers, Turned Feet, 27 x 43 In.	1410.00
Chest, Blanket, Chip Carved, Paneled, Arches, Wrought Iron, 57 x 27 In.	178.00
Chest, Blanket, Chippendale, Pine, Hinged Top, 2 False Drawers, Base Drawer, 33 x 37 In.	293.00
Chest, Blanket, Chippendale, Pine, Hinged, 2 False Drawers, 2 Drawers, 36 x 38 In.	468.00
Chest, Blanket, Chippendale, Walnut, Bracket Feet, 30 ½ x 47 In.	1185.00

Chest, Blanket, Chippendale, Walnut, Dovetailed, Hinged, Till, Drawers, c.1800s, 25 x 44 In. ...	470.00
Chest, Blanket, Chippendale, Walnut, Drawers, Strap Hinges, Tulip Finials, c.1800, 28 x 50 In.	823.00
Chest, Blanket, Chippendale, Walnut, Interior Till, Bracket Feet, c.1790, 25 ½ x 48 In............	840.00
Chest, Blanket, Chippendale, Walnut, Poplar, Drawers, Secret Compartment, 29 x 52 In........	823.00
Chest, Blanket, Chippendale, Walnut, Shaped Apron, Pa., c.1800, Child's, 19 x 24 In.	889.00
Chest, Blanket, Dutch Baroque Style, Oak, Fan, Beads, Leaves, Trestle Feet, c.1910, 26 x 54 In.	711.00
Chest, Blanket, Empire, Walnut, Black Lacquer, Veneered Frieze, 27 x 40 In.	239.00
Chest, Blanket, Faux Mahogany Grain, Cutout Ends, 6-Board, c.1790, 24 x 39 In.	276.00
Chest, Blanket, Federal, Cherry, Hinged Lid, Drawer, Turned Legs, 30 x 33 In...................	1107.00
Chest, Blanket, Gothic Style, Oak, Spindled Columns, Needlepoint Panels, 27 x 26 In........	480.00
Chest, Blanket, Grain Painted, Lift Top, Interior Till, c.1800, 17 x 38 In.	230.00
Chest, Blanket, Grain Painted, Pine, Hinged, Pa., c.1850, 22 x 36 In................................	318.00
Chest, Blanket, Grain Painted, Red & Yellow Sponge, Hinged, Turned Feet, 1800s, 48 x 23 In.	276.00
Chest, Blanket, Grain Painted, Red, Orange Flame, Lid, Pa., 24 x 43 In..........................	889.00
Chest, Blanket, Green Paint, Bracket Feet, Pa., 1800s, 25 ½ x 46 In.	593.00
Chest, Blanket, Mixed Wood, 2 Drawers, Pa., 1700s, 50 x 23 In..	144.00
Chest, Blanket, Oak, Carved, Flowers, Stars, Hinged Top, Iron Hardware, Square Legs, 34 x 54 In.	944.00
Chest, Blanket, Oak, Hinged Top, Paneled, 2 Drawers, Casters, 1800s, 34 x 43 In.............	236.00
Chest, Blanket, Oak, Lift Top, Footed, 3 Recessed Front Panels, 1700s, 24 x 46 In.	690.00
Chest, Blanket, Old English Style, Oak, Carved, Gothic Arches, Lift Top, 19 x 41 In...........	288.00
Chest, Blanket, Paint, Dovetailed, Bracket Feet, 1800s, 23 x 44 x 19 ¾ In. ....*illus*	558.00
Chest, Blanket, Paint, Iron Handles, Brass Name Plate, Late 1700s, 41 x 21 In.	489.00
Chest, Blanket, Painted, 2 Drawers, Hinged Top, Feathered Design, Brass, 38 x 38 In........	748.00
Chest, Blanket, Painted, Tree Of Life, Zigzags, Splotches, Hinged Lid, c.1800, 16 x 31 In.	1668.00
Chest, Blanket, Pine, 6-Board, Dovetailed, Bracket Base, 1700s, 21 x 41 In.	431.00
Chest, Blanket, Pine, Blue Paint, 6-Board, Lift Top, Well With Till, 1700s, 12 x 29 In........	237.00
Chest, Blanket, Pine, Blue Paint, Molded Top, Bootjack, Bracket Feet, 1800s, 21 x 42 In....	345.00
Chest, Blanket, Pine, Blue Paint, Red Designs, c.1820, 25 x 53 In.	207.00
Chest, Blanket, Pine, Cast-Iron Hinges, Handles, Lock, Clasp, Korea, c.1850, 21 x 34 In.....	584.00
Chest, Blanket, Pine, Dovetailed, Till, Lid, Turned Feet, 18 x 33 In..................................	441.00
Chest, Blanket, Pine, Dovetailed, Turned Feet, American, c.1830, 13 x 24 In., Child's.............	316.00
Chest, Blanket, Pine, Flame Grain Painted, Moldings, Till, Hinged, 1800s, 23 x 37 In.	235.00
Chest, Blanket, Pine, Grain Paint, Applied Molding, Till, Bootjack Ends, 25 x 43 In.	764.00
Chest, Blanket, Pine, Grain Painted, 2 Drawers, Strap Hinges, 1800s, 30 x 39 In.	360.00
Chest, Blanket, Pine, Grain Painted, Bracket Feet, c.1850	411.00
Chest, Blanket, Pine, Grain Painted, Lid, 2 Drawers, Scalloped Skirt, c.1810, 42 x 42 In.	6518.00
Chest, Blanket, Pine, Grapes, Flowers, Painted, Paneled, Lift Top, 1800s, 33 ½ x 66 In............	403.00
Chest, Blanket, Pine, Hinged, Notched Trestles, 24 x 43 In...	293.00
Chest, Blanket, Pine, Lift Top, 2 Drawers, Molded, Scrolled Apron, Late 1700s, 36 x 40 In.......	345.00
Chest, Blanket, Pine, Lift Top, Drawer, Bracket Feet, Shaped Skirt, c.1820, 36 x 44 In.......	345.00
Chest, Blanket, Pine, Oak, Hinged Top, Open Interior, New England, c.1800, 23 x 40 In.	420.00
Chest, Blanket, Pine, Orange, Yellow Paint, Cutout Feet, c.1835, 15 x 21 x 12 In..............	1880.00
Chest, Blanket, Pine, Paint, 6-Board, Bootjack Ends, c.1830, 24 x 45 In.	1205.00
Chest, Blanket, Pine, Painted, Flip Top, Bracket Feet, 1800s, 19 x 35 In.	267.00
Chest, Blanket, Pine, Poplar, Paint, Bracket Feet, 24 x 49 In...	353.00
Chest, Blanket, Pine, Poplar, Scratch Beaded Drawers, Bracket Feet, Pa., 1800s, 25 x 49 In. ......*illus*	705.00
Chest, Blanket, Pine, Red Paint, Molded Edge, Pin Hinges, Drawer, Arched Apron, c.1800, 41 x 41 In.	805.00
Chest, Blanket, Pine, Red, Brown Vinegar Paint, c.1825, 23 x 41 In.	460.00
Chest, Blanket, Pine, Scalloped Apron, Southern, c.1803, 14 x 27 In................................	356.00
Chest, Blanket, Pine, Yellow, Ocher Paint, Pa., c.1820, 24 x 49 In.	889.00
Chest, Blanket, Poplar, Brown Flame Graining, Dovetailed, Till, Drawer, c.1850, 24 x 50 In.	294.00
Chest, Blanket, Poplar, Brown Paint, Drawer, Cutout Ends, Valanced Skirt, 1700s, 25 x 27 In.	13035.00
Chest, Blanket, Poplar, Cream, Blue Paint, Dovetailed, Turned Feet, c.1875, 25 x 24 In...........	646.00
Chest, Blanket, Poplar, Dovetailed, Bracket Feet, c.1850, 15 x 27 In................................	411.00
Chest, Blanket, Poplar, Oak Graining, 2 Drawers, Till, Turned Feet, Henry Lapp, 28 x 50 In. ...	588.00
Chest, Blanket, Poplar, Painted, 1-Board Top, Dovetailed, Till, Hinged, c.1850, 26 x 38 In.	588.00
Chest, Blanket, Poplar, Painted, 6-Board, Till, Lid, Hinged, Molding, 21 x 40 In......................	843.00
Chest, Blanket, Poplar, Painted, Dovetailed, Molded Edge, Bracket Feet, 1800s, 36 x 17 In.......	499.00
Chest, Blanket, Poplar, Panels, Bracket Feet, Till, 2 Drawers, Painted, c.1850, 24 x 38 In. *illus*	1175.00
Chest, Blanket, Poplar, Red Flame Graining, Hinged, Till, Turned Feet, c.1850, 23 x 44 In.......	235.00
Chest, Blanket, Poplar, Red Paint, Till, Hinged, Dovetailed Bracket Feet, c.1800, 24 x 46 In.....	176.00
Chest, Blanket, Poplar, Red, Black & Yellow Compass Stars, Drawers, 28 x 42 In.	940.00
Chest, Blanket, Poplar, Yellow Ocher Sponge Paint, Pa., 13 ½ In....................................	356.00
Chest, Blanket, Pumpkin Pine, 3 Drawers, Bail Handles, Block Feet, 1800s............................	254.00
Chest, Blanket, Putty Paint, Stamped Designs, Oak Leaves, c.1810, 22 x 43 In. ....*illus*	4740.00
Chest, Blanket, Red & Black Paint, Shaped Feet, c.1800, 23 x 38 In.	663.00

Furniture, Chair, Windsor, Bow Back, Bamboo Turned Legs, Paint, 38 ½ In., Pair
$2585.00

Garth's Auctions, Inc.

Furniture, Chair, Windsor, Bow Back, Braced, Swelled Spindles, Vase & Ring Turnings, N.Y., c.1790, 37 In.
$429.00

Skinner, Inc.

Furniture, Chair, Windsor, Bow Back, Mixed Wood, c.1810, 33 ½ In.
$705.00

Garth's Auctions, Inc.

As always, the edited listings in *Kovels' Antiques & Collectibles Price Guide* aren't available on any website, but readers should visit Kovels.com for information on trends, tips, reproductions, marks, old prices, and more!

Furniture, Chair, Windsor, Comb Back, 7 Spindles, Mixed Wood, Arms, 46 In.
$940.00

Cowan's Auctions

Furniture, Chair, Windsor, Low Back, Ring Turned, c.1765, 30 In.
$948.00

Skinner, Inc.

Furniture, Chair, Windsor, Tall Back & Sides, Bamboo Turned Legs, c.1810, 49 In.
$764.00

Garth's Auctions, Inc.

Furniture, Chair, Wing, Federal, Mahogany, Carved, Serpentine Crest, Upholstered, c.1800, 43 x 34 In.
$2278.00

Neal Auction Co.

Chest, Blanket, Red Paint, Inscribed L.K. Boston 1809, 23 x 36 In.	288.00
Chest, Blanket, Red Paint, Lift Top, Molded Base, 1800s, 48 x 19 In.	144.00
Chest, Blanket, Red Paint, Lift Top, Molded, Till, Cutout Ends, c.1805, 26 x 39 In.	948.00
Chest, Blanket, Renaissance Revival, Oak, Lift Top, Paneled, Rosettes, Block Feet, c.1890	329.00
Chest, Blanket, Rosewood, Grain Painted, Molded Lid, Turned Feet, c.1825, 29 x 51 In.	225.00
Chest, Blanket, Shaker, Pine, Orange Stain, Dovetailed, Lock, Key, Till, c.1840, 14 x 24 In.	585.00
Chest, Blanket, Shaker, Pine, Red Paint, Overhang, Arched Base, c.1825, 35 x 42 In.	4095.00
Chest, Blanket, Sheraton, Cherry, Dovetailed, Beaded Edge, Turned Feet, 28 x 50 In.	424.00
Chest, Blanket, Sponge Paint, Dovetailed, Hinge & Lock, Turned Feet, 26 x 49 In.	311.00
Chest, Blanket, Tiger Maple, 6-Board, Molded Top, Strap Hinges, c.1800, 25 x 47 In.	748.00
Chest, Blanket, Walnut, Carved Panels, Lift Top, Cookie Corners, Drawer, Footed, 20 x 24 In.	767.00
Chest, Blanket, Walnut, Cedar, Lift Top, Hand Painted, Flowers, c.1920s, 29 x 45 In.	230.00
Chest, Blanket, Walnut, Dovetailed, Hinged, Turned Spool Feet, c.1805, 22 x 37 In.	345.00
Chest, Blanket, Walnut, Open Interior, 1700s, 27 x 47 In.	708.00
Chest, Blanket, Walnut, Strap Hinges, 2 Drawers, Bracket Feet, 1800s, 29 x 50 In.	708.00
Chest, Blanket, William & Mary, Oak, Carved, Leaf Design, Bracket Feet, 1600s, 27 x 45 In.	593.00
Chest, Blanket, Wood, Burnt Sienna & Mustard Paint, 6-Board, Turned Feet, c.1830, 24 x 36 In.	237.00
Chest, Blanket, Wood, Lift Top, Drawer, Red Paint, 40 x 32 In.	863.00
Chest, Blanket, Wood, Molded Lid, Interior Till, Drawers, 32 x 51 In.	165.00
Chest, Blanket, Wood, Painted, Hinged Top, 2 Drawers, 1800s, 40 x 43 In.	118.00
Chest, Blanket, Wood, Painted, Molded Lid, Dovetailed, Till, Bracket Feet, c.1810, 23 x 50 In.	236.00
Chest, Blanket, Wood, Painted, Molded Lid, Till, Hinges, Dovetailed, Pa., 1800s, 26 x 50 In. ... *illus*	2147.00
Chest, Blanket, Wood, Red, Mother-Of-Pearl Inlays, Lift Top, Iron Handles, Bali, c.1915, 14 x 23 In.	183.00
Chest, Blanket, Yellow Pine, Hinged, Painted Flowers, Symbols, N.C., c.1845, 28 x 48 In.	6900.00
Chest, Blanket, Yellow Pine, Paint, Turned Feet, Molded Edge, Fitted Interior, c.1850, 26 x 49 In.	690.00
Chest, Blue Paint, 7 Small Drawers, Cutout Feet, 1800s, 21 x 14 In.	1998.00
Chest, Borge Mogensen, Teak, 7 Drawers, Straight Tapered Legs, 57 x 39 In.	948.00
Chest, Burl Walnut, 5 Drawers, Molded Top, England	2749.00
Chest, Burl Walnut, Tunbridge Inlay, Spire Gallery, Watch Holder, Drawers, c.1875, 20 x 18 In.	770.00
Chest, Burl, 5 Drawers, Inverted V Shape, Tapered Legs, 36 x 45 In.	984.00
Chest, Burl, Shaped Top, 4 Serpentine Drawers, 1800s, 33 x 28 In.	1840.00
Chest, Butler's, Chippendale, Walnut, 5 Drawers, Bracket Feet, Pa., c.1770, 32 x 32 In.	474.00
Chest, Butler's, Mahogany, Drop Front, 3 Lower Drawers, c.1750, 40 ½ x 41 ½ In.	282.00
Chest, Butler's, Mahogany, Line Inlay, Drop Front, Fitted Interior, Drawers, c.1800, 45 x 49 In.	1230.00
Chest, Butler's, Tiger Maple, Oval Inlays, Drop Drawer, 3 Drawers, Columns, c.1840, 41 x 43 In.	1840.00
Chest, Campaign, 4 Drawers, Metal Mounts, Hekman, 14 ½ x 18 In.	144.00
Chest, Campaign, Brass Bound, 6 Drawers, 57 x 21 In.	688.00
Chest, Campaign, Brass Bound, Cock-Beaded, Hinged Lid, Desk, Drawers, 1800s, 47 x 39 In.	1725.00
Chest, Campaign, Camphorwood, 2 Stacking Sections, 5 Drawers, 1800s, 43 x 39 In.	1896.00
Chest, Campaign, Camphorwood, Brass, Drawers, Fitted, Stencils, England, c.1890, 38 x 34 In.	3437.00
Chest, Campaign, Fruitwood, Brass, 5 Drawers, England, 40 x 35 In.	1750.00
Chest, Campaign, Mahogany, 2 Parts, England, 1800s, 36 x 30 In.	2230.00
Chest, Campaign, Mahogany, 5 Drawers, England, 42 x 35 In.	1050.00
Chest, Campaign, Mahogany, 5 Drawers, Handles, Bracket Feet, England, 1800s, 40 x 35 In.	1875.00
Chest, Campaign, Mahogany, Molded Edges, Hinged Drawer, Writing Surface, 1800s, 49 x 45 In.	1840.00
Chest, Campaign, Regency, Mahogany, Brass Bound, Drawers, Shaped Feet, 1800s, 48 x 30 In.	5000.00
Chest, Campaign, Victorian, Teak, Brass Mounts, 3 Drawers Over 2 Drawers, 40 x 39 In.	1521.00
Chest, Campaign, Walnut, Hinged, Brass Fittings, 2 Drawers, Continental, c.1875, 27 x 48 In.	610.00
Chest, Cherry, 3 Drawers, Fluted Stiles, Tapered Legs, Kindel, 1900s, 33 x 40 In.	431.00
Chest, Cherry, 4 Drawers, Shaped Skirt, Splayed Legs, 43 x 36 In.	793.00
Chest, Cherry, 4 Drawers, Tulip Inlay, Ring-Turned Columns, Ball Feet, c.1835, 47 x 40 In.	652.00
Chest, Cherry, 6 Graduated Drawers, Brass Handles, Bracket Feet, c.1790, 59 x 42 In.	1093.00
Chest, Cherry, Chippendale, 4 Drawers, Brass Handles, Bracket Feet, 41 x 44 In.	345.00
Chest, Cherry, Cock-Beaded, Lift Top, 2 False Drawers, 2 Drawers, Bracket Feet, 44 x 42 In.	600.00
Chest, Cherry, Mahogany, Shaped Backsplash, Columns, 5 Drawers, c.1835, 72 x 46 In.	805.00
Chest, Cherry, Pine, 5 Drawers, Bracket Feet, Carved Drop, 1790s, 53 x 38 In.	1025.00
Chest, Cherry, Rectangular Top, Drawers, Glass Knobs, c.1825, 47 x 42 In.	200.00
Chest, Cherry, Tiger Maple Insets, 2 Drawers Over 3 Drawers, c.1850, 56 x 44 In.	3540.00
Chest, Cherry, Yellow Pine, 2 Drawers, Ring Turned Feet, American, 1800s, 14 x 19 In.	837.00
Chest, Chippendale Style, 4 Drawers, Bracket Feet, American, 1800s, 41 x 42 In.	345.00
Chest, Chippendale Style, Mahogany, Block Front, Ogee Bracket Feet, 30 x 31 x 19 In.	978.00
Chest, Chippendale Style, Mahogany, Bowfront, String Inlay, 4 Drawers, 1800s, 33 x 36 In.	575.00
Chest, Chippendale Style, Mahogany, Carved Cartouche, Broken-Arch Cornice, 1900s, 40 In.	1500.00
Chest, Chippendale Style, Mahogany, Writing Slide, 5 Drawers, Bracket Feet, 31 x 36 In.	649.00
Chest, Chippendale, 4 Drawers, Beaded Edge, String Inlay, Bracket Base, 36 x 38 In.	920.00
Chest, Chippendale, 4 Drawers, Beaded, Ogee Bracket Feet, Conn., 34 x 42 In.	7020.00

Chest, Chippendale, 4 Drawers, Dovetailed, Bracket Feet, 37 x 38 In.	558.00
Chest, Chippendale, Cherry, 4 Cock-Beaded Drawers, Bracket Feet, c.1780, 38 x 40 In.	1035.00
Chest, Chippendale, Cherry, 4 Drawers, Bracket Feet, New England, 41 x 44 In.	345.00
Chest, Chippendale, Cherry, Line Inlay, 9 Drawers, Fluted Columns, Pa., c.1790, 63 x 40 In.	1126.00
Chest, Chippendale, Cherry, Mixed Wood, 4 Drawers, Dovetailed, Columns, c.1790, 37 x 39 In.	1380.00
Chest, Chippendale, Cherry, Molded Edge, 4 Graduated Drawers, Columns, c.1850, 36 x 38 In.	345.00
Chest, Chippendale, Cherry, Molded Top, 4 Drawers, Bracket Feet, 1700s, 32 x 35 In.	5750.00
Chest, Chippendale, Cherry, Overhanging Serpentine Top, 4 Drawers, 1700s, 33 x 39 In.	1541.00
Chest, Chippendale, Cherry, Pine, 4 Graduated Drawers, Bracket Feet, c.1760, 38 x 40 In.	1058.00
Chest, Chippendale, Cherry, Pine, 4 Graduated Drawers, Columns, c.1790, 39 x 41 In.	353.00
Chest, Chippendale, Mahogany, 4 Drawers, Bracket Feet, England, 1700s, 33 x 34 In.	944.00
Chest, Chippendale, Mahogany, 4 Drawers, Pa., c.1770, 33 ½ x 37 In.	770.00
Chest, Chippendale, Mahogany, 4 Drawers, Serpentine, Bracket Feet, 36 x 40 In.	2875.00
Chest, Chippendale, Mahogany, 4 Serpentine Drawers, Brass Bail Pulls, Mass., c.1800, 32 x 41 In.	3840.00
Chest, Chippendale, Mahogany, Block Front, 4 Drawers, Bracket Feet, c.1780, 30 x 38 In.	2875.00
Chest, Chippendale, Mahogany, Bowfront, 4 Drawers, Fan Spandrels, Apron, c.1800, 35 x 44 In.	3163.00
Chest, Chippendale, Mahogany, Drawers, Bracket Base, c.1790, 33 x 38 In.	500.00
Chest, Chippendale, Mahogany, Inlay, 7 Drawers, England, 1800s, 42 x 43 In.	590.00
Chest, Chippendale, Mahogany, Serpentine, Scratch Beaded Drawers, Ogee Bracket Feet, 31 x 35 In.	7110.00
Chest, Chippendale, Maple, 6 Molded Graduated Drawers, Bat's Wing Brasses, 50 x 37 In.	4972.00
Chest, Chippendale, Maple, 7 Drawers, New England, c.1765, 55 x 36 In.	4740.00
Chest, Chippendale, Maple, Chestnut, 7 Graduated Drawers, Bracket Feet, 1780s, 60 x 38 In.	999.00
Chest, Chippendale, Maple, Flared Crown, 6 Drawers, Bracket Feet, 59 x 43 In.	488.00
Chest, Chippendale, Maple, Molded Cornice, 5 Drawers, Bracket Feet, c.1780, 43 x 37 In.	1093.00
Chest, Chippendale, Mixed Wood, 8 Drawers, Fluted Columns, c.1820, 71 x 50 In.	4140.00
Chest, Chippendale, Paint, 6 Thumb-Molded Drawers, Bracket Feet, Late 1700s, 53 x 36 In.	5333.00
Chest, Chippendale, Walnut, 2 Drawers, Molded Edge, Ogee Bracket Feet, 1700s, 35 x 40 In.	2196.00
Chest, Chippendale, Walnut, 4 Drawers, Butler's Slide, 1700s, 34 x 39 In.	1545.00
Chest, Chippendale, Walnut, 4 Drawers, Delaware, c.1780, 34 ½ x 37 ½ In.	43113.00
Chest, Chippendale, Walnut, 4 Drawers, Fluted Columns, Ogee Feet, 1700s, 39 x 30 In.	2070.00
Chest, Chippendale, Walnut, 5 Drawers, Batwing Brasses, Bracket Feet, Late 1700s, 47 x 38 In.	359.00
Chest, Chippendale, Walnut, 6 Long Drawers, Bracket Base, c.1790, 47 x 39 In.	600.00
Chest, Chippendale, Walnut, 8 Drawers, Bracket Feet, c.1810, 62 x 40 In.	944.00
Chest, Chippendale, Walnut, 8 Drawers, Bracket Feet, Pa., c.1790, 46 x 41 In.	1080.00
Chest, Chippendale, Walnut, 8 Drawers, Columns, Ogee Bracket Feet, Pa., c.1770	1659.00
Chest, Chippendale, Walnut, 9 Drawers, Fluted Pilasters, Bracket Feet, Pa., 54 x 40 In.	1404.00
Chest, Chippendale, Walnut, 9 Graduated Drawers, Bracket Feet, Pa., c.1770, 34 x 39 In.	2490.00
Chest, Chippendale, Walnut, Pa., c.1770, 78 ½ x 41 In.	2133.00
Chest, Chippendale, Walnut, Poplar Ogee Feet, Fluted Columns, 1700s, 41 x 21 In.	1880.00
Chest, Curly Maple, Stepped Cornice, Central Fan, 4 Drawers, Connecticut, c.1775, 51 x 41 In. *illus*	900.00
Chest, Directoire, 6 Drawers, Brass Pulls, Fluted Stiles, Square Legs, France, c.1800, 50 x 36 In.	1422.00
Chest, Dower, Baroque, Hinged Top, Scrolling Leaves, Carved Front Panel, 24 x 64 In. 826.00 to	1770.00
Chest, Dower, Goan Teak, Iron Hinges, Lid, c.1820, 18 x 48 In.	580.00
Chest, Dower, Grain Painted, Yellow, Black, Heart, Pinwheels, Drawers, Lift Top, 30 x 50 In.	7500.00
Chest, Dower, Mixed Wood, Painted, Tulips, Hinged, 3 Drawers, Pa., 1700s, 27 x 51 In.	41400.00
Chest, Dower, Painted, Arched Panels, Inscribed Gorge Weit, Pa., 1794, 25 x 48 In.	1304.00
Chest, Dower, Painted, Hinged Lid, Compass Stars, Elizabeth Kriss, 1798, 27 x 50 In.	12000.00
Chest, Dower, Painted, Salmon Paint, Ocher Ground, Diamond Pattern, Pa., c.1800, 29 x 51 In.	4740.00
Chest, Dower, Pine, Grain Painted, Lift Top, 2 Drawers, Pa., c.1805, 27 ½ x 48 In.	296.00
Chest, Dower, Pine, Green, Yellow Sponge, Recessed Arches Pa., c.1775, 20 x 49 In.	770.00
Chest, Dower, Renaissance Revival, Gilt, Ornate Griffin Corners, Carved, Italy, c.1700, 34 x 68 In.	3480.00
Chest, Dower, Roycroft, Lift Top, Copper Straps, Hinges, 39 x 21 In.	21600.00
Chest, Dower, Yellow Paint, Cloisonne, Lid, Fitted Interior, Silk Lining, Chinese, 20 x 9 ¾ In.	6600.00
Chest, Drawers, Grain Painted, c.1830, 44 x 39 In.	715.00
Chest, Dutch Baroque, Oak, Carved Husk Pendant, Doors, 3 Bombe Drawers, 1700s, 104 x 71 In.	593.00
Chest, Elidio Gonzales, Wood, 2 Doors, Carved Flowers, c.1970, 28 x 28 In.	900.00
Chest, Empire, Mahogany, 3 Drawers Over 4 Drawers, Stiles, 45 x 43 In.	460.00
Chest, Empire, Mahogany, 4 Drawers, Bun Feet, c.1840, 39 x 43 In.	89.00
Chest, Empire, Mahogany, 4 Drawers, Turned Columns, Cock-Beaded, c.1840, 42 x 22 ¼ In.	431.00
Chest, Empire, Mahogany, 5 Drawers, Columns, Paw Feet, 1800s, 42 x 45 In.	237.00
Chest, Empire, Mahogany, 5 Drawers, Reeded Columns, c.1850, 40 x 45 ½ In.	230.00
Chest, Empire, Mahogany, 7 Graduated Drawers, 1800s, 59 x 39 In.	633.00
Chest, Empire, Mahogany, Marble Top, Turned Columns, Mirror, c.1850, 80 x 43 In.	690.00
Chest, Empire, Mahogany, Serpentine Top, 4 Drawers, Turned Feet, c.1850, 40 x 43 x 19 In.	155.00
Chest, Empire, Mahogany, Tilt Mirror, Columns, Acorn Finial, 3 Drawers, 1800s, 86 x 47 In.	269.00
Chest, Empire, Maple, Projecting Frieze Drawer, Wood Pulls, Bun Feet, 1800s, 41 x 45 In.	239.00

Furniture, Chair, Wing, Long-Haired Lamb, Sycamore, France, 1930s, 41 x 33 ½ In.
$6200.00

Rago Arts & Auction Center

Furniture, Chest, Blanket, Paint, Dovetailed, Bracket Feet, 1800s, 23 x 44 x 19 ¾ In.
$558.00

Garth's Auctions, Inc.

Furniture, Chest, Blanket, Pine, Poplar, Scratch Beaded Drawers, Bracket Feet, Pa., 1800s, 25 x 49 In.
$705.00

Cowan's Auctions

Furniture, Chest, Blanket, Poplar, Panels, Bracket Feet, Till, 2 Drawers, Painted, c.1850, 24 x 38 In.
$1175.00

Garth's Auctions, Inc.

Furniture, Chest, Blanket, Putty Paint, Stamped Designs, Oak Leaves, c.1810, 22 x 43 In. $4740.00

Skinner, Inc.

Furniture, Chest, Blanket, Wood, Painted, Molded Lid, Till, Hinges, Dovetailed, Pa., 1800s, 26 x 50 In. $2147.00

Conestoga Auction Co., Inc.

Furniture, Chest, Curly Maple, Stepped Cornice, Central Fan, 4 Drawers, Connecticut, c.1775, 51 x 41 In. $900.00

Cowan's Auctions

Furniture, Chest, Empire, Poplar, Faux Mahogany Paint, 4 Drawers, Applied Turnings, c.1850, 39 x 40 In. $764.00

Garth's Auctions, Inc.

Chest, Empire, Pine, Red & Black Flame Graining, Turned Feet, Columns, 1800s, 41 x 43 In.. 235.00
Chest, Empire, Poplar, Faux Mahogany Paint, 4 Drawers, Applied Turnings, c.1850, 39 x 40 In. *illus* 764.00
Chest, Empire, Poplar, Flame Graining, Dovetailed, 4 Drawers, Step Back, c.1835, 56 x 47 In. ... *illus* 411.00
Chest, Empire, White Pine, Red Paint, 2 Upper, 5 Lower Drawers, Apron, c.1840, 21 x 12 In., Child's 748.00
Chest, Federal, Applewood, Rectangular Top, 4 Cock-Beaded Drawers, c.1815, Child's 1400.00
Chest, Federal, Birch, 4 Graduated Drawers, Shaped Apron, French Feet, c.1805, 39 x 41 In.... 403.00
Chest, Federal, Bird's-Eye-Maple, 3 Drawers, Rossette Brass Pulls, Bracket Feet, 12 x 13 In. 644.00
Chest, Federal, Cherry, 4 Drawers, French Feet, c.1820, 36 x 40 In. 1770.00
Chest, Federal, Cherry, 4 Drawers, Molded Top, Shaped Skirt, Block Feet, c.1810, 38 x 41 In.... 474.00
Chest, Federal, Cherry, Birch, Bowfront, 4 Drawers, Cock-Beaded, French Feet, c.1800, 34 x 40 In. 978.00
Chest, Federal, Cherry, Birch, Inlay, 4 Drawers, Shaped Apron, French Feet, c.1805, 38 x 43 In. 1725.00
Chest, Federal, Cherry, Bombe, Inlaid Stringing, 4 Drawers, French Feet, c.1800, 35 x 41 In. .. 17775.00
Chest, Federal, Cherry, Carved & Inlaid, 4 Drawers, Brass Bail Pulls, c.1795, 36 x 37 In.......... 3555.00
Chest, Federal, Cherry, Cove-Molded Cornice, Diamond Banding, c.1800, 64 x 44 In. 1900.00
Chest, Federal, Cherry, Inlaid, Cock-Beaded, Oval Corners, Drawers, Early 1800s, 43 x 43 In. . 1067.00
Chest, Federal, Cherry, Inlay, 4 Graduated Drawers, French Feet, c.1800, 34 x 40 In............... 1342.00
Chest, Federal, Cherry, Mahogany, Swell Front, 4 Cock-Beaded Drawers, c.1810, 37 x 40 In. ... 1185.00
Chest, Federal, Cherry, Serpentine, Cock-Beaded Drawers, Reeded Pilasters, c.1815, 40 x 40 In. 1000.00
Chest, Federal, Cherry, Tiger Maple, 2 Cock-Beaded Drawers, Eagle, Shield, c.1800, 46 x 46 In. 2015.00
Chest, Federal, Mahogany, 4 Drawers, Cornucopia Brasses, Bracket Feet, Late 1700s, 34 x 33 In. 1195.00
Chest, Federal, Mahogany, 4 Drawers, Flared Bracket Feet, c.1820, 36 x 41 In........................... 276.00
Chest, Federal, Mahogany, 4 Drawers, Molded Cornice, Brass Handles, c.1790, 34 x 44 In. 2032.00
Chest, Federal, Mahogany, 4 Drawers, Reeded Stiles, Scalloped Skirt, 40 x 43 x 21 In. ....*illus* 837.00
Chest, Federal, Mahogany, 5 Drawers, 5 Lower Doors, Shaped Skirt, c.1810, 41 x 43 In. 516.00
Chest, Federal, Mahogany, 5 Drawers, Paper Label, John F. Dolan, c.1800, 41 x 43 In............... 1300.00
Chest, Federal, Mahogany, Bird's-Eye Maple, Reeded Columns, Apron, c.1820, 40 x 43 In........ 2390.00
Chest, Federal, Mahogany, Bowfront, 2 Parts, Tilt Mirror, Pilasters, Shaped Apron, 1800s, 79 x 47 In. 3585.00
Chest, Federal, Mahogany, Bowfront, 4 Drawers, Fluted Stiles, Shaped Apron, 1800s, 39 x 41 In. 717.00
Chest, Federal, Mahogany, Bowfront, 4 Drawers, Reeded Stiles, c.1820, 46 x 45 In. 1554.00
Chest, Federal, Mahogany, Bowfront, Crossbanded Drawers, c.1800, 39 x 42 In. 1314.00
Chest, Federal, Mahogany, Bowfront, Plank Top, Reeded Edge, 4 Drawers, 1800s, 33 x 36 In... 1434.00
Chest, Federal, Mahogany, Bowfront, Turret Corners, 4 Drawers, Rope Columns, 42 x 42 In. .. 1265.00
Chest, Federal, Mahogany, Inlaid Birch, 4 Drawers, New England, c.1815, 40 x 42 In. ....*illus* 5175.00
Chest, Federal, Mahogany, Inlaid, 4 Drawers, Checkerboard Banding, 1800s, 20 x 17 In. 1265.00
Chest, Federal, Mahogany, Inlay, 4 Drawers, French Feet, Southern, c.1790, 36 x 44 In........... 2032.00
Chest, Federal, Mahogany, Molded Top, 4 Drawers, Shaped Apron, c.1800, 40 x 42 In. 1434.00
Chest, Federal, Mahogany, Parquetry, Bowfront, 5 Drawers, 36 x 42 In............................... 1255.00
Chest, Federal, Mahogany, String Inlay, 5 Drawers, Shaped Apron, French Feet, c.1800, 45 x 46 In. 1342.00
Chest, Federal, Mahogany, Walnut, 7 Graduated Drawers, Oval Brasses, c.1845, 68 x 43 In. 1725.00
Chest, Federal, Mixed Wood, 4 Drawers, Brass Pulls, c.1890, 32 x 37 In............................... 840.00
Chest, Federal, Mixed Wood, Serpentine Front, 5 Drawers, Scalloped Apron, 1700s, 40 x 51 In. 2390.00
Chest, Federal, Serpentine, Inlays, 4 Graduated Drawers, Drop Skirt, c.1790, 37 x 41 In.......... 4140.00
Chest, Federal, Tiger Maple, Cherry Inlay, 6 Cock-Beaded Drawers, Bracket Feet, 1816, 45 x 43 In. 658.00
Chest, Federal, Tiger Maple, Rosewood, Bowfront, 4 Drawers, Columns, 1800s, 48 x 45 In. ....*illus* 2271.00
Chest, Federal, Walnut, 4 Drawers, Bracket Feet, 39 ½ x 33 ½ In............................... 184.00
Chest, Federal, Walnut, 5 Drawers, Brass Handles, Scalloped Apron, c.1805, 38 x 36 In. 1150.00
Chest, Federal, Walnut, Barber Pole Inlay, 4 Drawers, Bracket Feet, Pa., c.1805, 42 x 40 In. 711.00
Chest, Federal, Walnut, Parquetry, 5 Drawers, Cock-Beaded, Serpentine Apron, 1800s, 40 x 41 In. 837.00
Chest, Federal, Walnut, Poplar, 4 Drawers, French Feet, Pa., c.1800, 38 x 42 In. 1800.00
Chest, French Empire, Mahogany, Marble Top, Drawers, Columns, c.1810, 36 x 51 In. 1968.00
Chest, G. McCabe, Orange Crate Modern, 6 Drawers, c.1968, 29 x 60 In. 344.00
Chest, G. Nakashima, Black Walnut, Overhang, 1973, 50 x 40 x 21 In................................... 9920.00
Chest, G. Nelson, Hardwood, 2 Banks Of Drawers, Steel Legs, Herman Miller, 33 x 67 In......... 3200.00
Chest, G. Nelson, Rosewood, Porcelain Pulls, Herman Miller, 41 x 40 In. 2596.00
Chest, G. Stickley, Harvey Ellis, Mirror, 4 Drawers, Red Decal, 66 x 48 In............................. 5270.00
Chest, G. Stickley, Oak, 4 Drawers, Hidden Safe, Signed, c.1900, 30 x 19 In.......................... 3335.00
Chest, George II Style, Mahogany, 4 Cock-Beaded Drawers, c.1890, 32 x 35 In........................ 444.00
Chest, George II Style, Mahogany, 6 Drawers, Bracket Feet, 1800s, 16 x 16 In. 427.00
Chest, George II, Figured Mahogany, Bowfront, 5 Drawers, c.1800, 40 x 34 x 21 In. ....*illus* 1793.00
Chest, George II, Figured Oyster Veneer, 5 Drawers, Bracket Feet, c.1700s, 41 x 44 In.............. 2242.00
Chest, George II, Herringbone Inlay, Walnut, Canted Corners, Stiles, c.1725, 56 x 43 In. 1593.00
Chest, George II, Mahogany, 5 Drawers, Serpentine Skirt, Bracket Feet, England, 1700s, 41 x 41 In. 674.00
Chest, George II, Mahogany, Molded Top, 4 Drawers, Bracket Feet, 1700s, 27 x 27 In............... 1076.00
Chest, George II, Mahogany, Thumb-Molded Edge, Pullout Surface, Drawers, c.1755, 30 x 30 In. 533.00
Chest, George II, Mahogany, Thumb-Molded Edge, Spurred Bracket Feet, c.1770, 39 x 41 In. . 470.00
Chest, George III Style, Mahogany, 4 Drawers, Swell Front, Dressing Slide, 34 x 37 In.............. 805.00

Chest, George III Style, Mahogany, Bowfront, 5 Drawers, Bracket Feet, 38 x 46 In.		819.00
Chest, George III Style, Mahogany, Bowfront, Crossbanded Top, 4 Drawers, Bracket Feet, 34 x 36 In.		468.00
Chest, George III Style, Mahogany, Inlay, 5 Drawers, 1800s, 36 x 45 In.		500.00
Chest, George III Style, Mahogany, Inlay, Bowfront, Drawers, Base, French Feet, 35 x 40 In.		923.00
Chest, George III Style, Satinwood, Bowed, 5 Drawers, Shaped Feet, 41 x 41 In.		469.00
Chest, George III, Fruitwood, 2-Board Top, 4 Drawers, Bracket Feet, c.1755, 34 x 27 In.		805.00
Chest, George III, Mahogany, 4 Beaded Drawers, Drop Handles, 30 x 27 In.		2106.00
Chest, George III, Mahogany, 5 Drawers, Shaped Apron, French Feet, c.1800, 42 x 38 In.		837.00
Chest, George III, Mahogany, Bowfront, 3 Drawers, Block Feet, c.1800, 35 x 39 In.		1058.00
Chest, George III, Mahogany, Bowfront, 4 Drawers, Shaped Apron, French Feet, 1700s, 34 In.		1830.00
Chest, George III, Mahogany, Inlay, Bowfront, 4 Drawers, Brass Lion Drop Handles, 36 x 42 In.		1521.00
Chest, George III, Mahogany, Molded Edge, 5 Drawers, Bracket Feet, c.1785, 37 x 38 In.		1722.00
Chest, George III, Mahogany, Oak, 6 Drawers, Shaped Bracket Feet, 1700s, 47 x 41 In.		470.00
Chest, George III, Mahogany, Pine, 5 Drawers, Bracket Feet, c.1800, 37 x 40 In.		1003.00
Chest, George III, Mahogany, Pine, 20 Drawers, Brass Pulls, c.1810, 49 x 51 In.		2400.00
Chest, George III, Mahogany, Serpentine, 5 Drawers, Bracket Feet, c.1780, 35 x 36 In.		2318.00
Chest, George III, Mahogany, Serpentine, Crossbanded Top, 4 Beaded Drawers, 32 x 40 In.		1989.00
Chest, George III, Mahogany, Serpentine, 4 Drawers, Bracket Feet, 33 x 41 In.		1750.00
Chest, George III, Satinwood, Feather Inlaid Oak, 6 Drawers, Reeded Columns, 1700s, 32 x 54 In.		1998.00
Chest, George III, Walnut, 6 Drawers, Chevron Banding, Bracket Feet, c.1780, 40 x 40 In.		2214.00
Chest, George III, Walnut, Crossbanded, 5 Drawers, Batwing Escutcheons, Bracket Feet, 38 x 39 In.		1111.00
Chest, Gilt Rosettes, Scrolled Backsplash, Drawers, Columns, Mass., c.1820, 53 x 45 In.		2032.00
Chest, Gustavian, Blue Paint, Faux Marble Top, Serpentine Edges, Sweeden, c.1800, 31 In.		4740.00
Chest, Half Drawers Over 4 Drawers, Shaped Supports, Curved Legs, 48 x 43 In.		200.00
Chest, Henredon, Lingerie, Chinese, Chippendale Style, Mahogany, 7 Drawers, 60 x 23 In.		489.00
Chest, Henredon, Mahogany, 4 Drawers, Shaped Ball Feet, 47 x 51 x 23 In.		570.00
Chest, Hepplewhite Style, Mahogany, 4 Drawers, Slide, 33 x 19 In.		633.00
Chest, Hepplewhite Style, Mahogany, Inlay, 5 Drawers, England., 1800s, 36 x 36 In.		590.00
Chest, Hepplewhite, Birch, Pine, Drawers, Cock-Beaded, Bracket Feet, c.1810, 37 x 43 In.		734.00
Chest, Hepplewhite, Birch, Scrolled Apron, 4 Drawers, French Feet, c.1800, 36 x 40 In.		764.00
Chest, Hepplewhite, Cherry, 4 Drawers, c.1810, 41 x 38 ½ In.		770.00
Chest, Hepplewhite, Cherry, Kite Escutcheons, Shaped Skirt, c.1800, 42 x 40 In.		823.00
Chest, Hepplewhite, Cherry, Line Inlay, Drawers, French Feet, c.1790, 34 x 41 In.		1058.00
Chest, Hepplewhite, Mahogany, 4 Drawers, Bracket Feet, c.1820, 9 ½ x 9 ¾ In.		1422.00
Chest, Hepplewhite, Mahogany, Bowfront, Reeded, Bracket Feet, c.1800, 37 x 39 In.		1293.00
Chest, Hepplewhite, Mahogany, Fan Corners, Dovetailed, 2 Over 3 Drawers, 36 x 37 In.		1921.00
Chest, Hepplewhite, Mahogany, Inlay, Bowfront, 4 Drawers, New England, c.1800		977.00
Chest, Hepplewhite, String Inlay, 4 Drawers, French Feet, New England, c.1785, 37 x 40 In.		1093.00
Chest, Hepplewhite, Tiger Maple, Mahogany, Bowfront, Flared Feet, c.1810, 36 x 40 In.		4888.00
Chest, Hepplewhite, Walnut, 8 String Inlaid Drawers, French Feet, c.1800, 64 x 45 In.		1840.00
Chest, Hepplewhite, Walnut, Barber Pole Inlay, 9 Graduated Drawers, c.1820, 64 x 41 In.		1541.00
Chest, Hepplewhite, Walnut, Poplar, 5 Drawers, Inlay, Cutout Feet, 39 x 39 In.		1645.00
Chest, Hepplewhite, Walnut, Poplar, Bonnet, Shaped Skirt, Cutout Feet, c.1810, 48 x 48 In.		999.00
Chest, Hepplewhite, Walnut, Poplar, Pine, Bowfront, 4 Drawers, Inlaid Fan, 42 x 40 In.		2115.00
Chest, Hepplewhite, Walnut, Poplar, String Inlay, Ivory Shields, 4 Drawers, c.1810, 38 x 21 In.		764.00
Chest, Hepplewhite, Walnut, Yellow Pine, String Fan Inlay, c.1820, 42 x 41 In.		1410.00
Chest, Hinged Top, Fitted Interior, Red Lacquer, Brass Hardware, Korea, 12 x 14 In.		288.00
Chest, Hvidt & Nielsen, Teak, 6 Graduated Drawers, c.1960, 37 x 35 In.		1185.00
Chest, Italian Baroque, Walnut, Fruitwood, 3 Long Drawers, Turned Feet, 37 x 52 In.		2808.00
Chest, Italian Style, Peach Paint, Birds, Butterfly & Leaves, 2 Drawers, 1900s, 29 x 31 In.		375.00
Chest, Josef Frank, Wood, 14 Drawers, Svenskt Tenn, Sweden, 55 x 28 In.		4025.00
Chest, Kiri Wood, 2 Sliding Doors, 8 Drawers, Black Iron Handles, Japan, 57 x 36 In.		748.00
Chest, Kiri Wood, Sliding Doors, 3 Drawers Over 5 Drawers, Iron Handles, c.1905, 57 x 36 In.		518.00
Chest, Kittinger, Chippendale Style, Mahogany, 5 Drawers, Canted Corners, 34 x 42 In.		460.00
Chest, Kittinger, Mahogany, Bowfront, 5 Drawers, Block Feet, 36 x 38 In.		2133.00
Chest, Kittinger, William & Mary, Mirror, Drawers, 1960s, 45 x 39 In.		750.00
Chest, Lingerie, Black Lacquer, Gilt Flowers, Scenes, 5 Drawers, Chinese, c.1910, 45 x 13 In.		150.00
Chest, Lingerie, Louis XVI Style, Gilt, Marble Top, Rounded Corners, 5 Drawers, 41 x 16 In.		610.00
Chest, Lingerie, Marquetry, Parquetry, Ormolu, Marble Top, 5 Drawers, 32 x 16 In.		250.00
Chest, Lingerie, Wood, Marble Top, Bronze Gallery, 5 Banded Drawers, c.1910, 39 x 19 In.		492.00
Chest, Louis Philippe Style, Walnut, Marble Top, 4 Drawers, 39 x 49 In.		732.00
Chest, Louis Philippe, Cuban Mahogany, Marble Top, 4 Drawers, France, 1840, 37 x 52 In.		4200.00
Chest, Louis Philippe, Walnut, Marble Top, 4 Drawers, Bracket Feet, 1800s, 38 x 46 In.		450.00
Chest, Louis XV, Bombe, Walnut, Beveled Marble Top, 3 Drawers, 1800s, 35 x 47 In.		540.00
Chest, Louis XV, Mahogany, Carved, Serpentine, 4 Lined Drawers, Cabriole Legs, 40 x 22 In.		427.00
Chest, Louis XV, Walnut, Rose Marble Top, 4 Drawers, Carved Apron, 1800s, 40 x 54 In.		1098.00

Furniture, Chest, Empire, Poplar, Flame Graining, Dovetailed, 4 Drawers, Step Back, c.1835, 56 x 47 In.
$411.00

Garth's Auctions, Inc.

Furniture, Chest, Federal, Mahogany, 4 Drawers, Reeded Stiles, Scalloped Skirt, 40 x 43 x 21 In.
$837.00

Neal Auction Co.

Furniture, Chest, Federal, Mahogany, Inlaid Birch, 4 Drawers, New England, c.1815, 40 x 42 In.
$5175.00

James D. Julia Inc.

Furniture, Chest, Federal, Tiger Maple, Rosewood, Bowfront, 4 Drawers, Columns, 1800s, 48 x 45 In.
$2271.00

Neal Auction Co.

Furniture, Chest, George II, Figured Mahogany, Bowfront, 5 Drawers, c.1800, 40 x 34 x 21 In.
$1793.00

Neal Auction Co.

Furniture, Chest, Mahogany, 22 Drawers, Double Wellington Locks, England, c.1900, 45 x 41 In.
$1554.00

Neal Auction Co.

Furniture, Chest, Mahogany, Carved, 4 Drawers, Turned Columns, Glass Pulls, 1800s, 13 x 12 x 9 In.
$1195.00

Neal Auction Co.

Furniture, Chest, Mule, Pine, Painted, Tapered Feet, Brass Hardware, c.1825, 35 ½ x 39 ¾ In.
$10281.00

Garth's Auctions, Inc.

Chest, Mahogany, 3 Drawers, Bat Escutcheons, Bail Pulls, Ogee Feet, 1800s, 35 x 47 In.	956.00
Chest, Mahogany, 4 Drawers, Brass Handles, Block Feet, American, 25 x 40 In.	240.00
Chest, Mahogany, 4 Drawers, England., c.1800, 32 x 37 In.	1298.00
Chest, Mahogany, 4 Graduated Drawers, Twisted Rope Edge, Bracket Feet, England, 41 x 49 In.	780.00
Chest, Mahogany, 5 Drawers, Ivory Key Holes, Shaped Skirt, Block Feet, c.1850, 40 x 43 In.	570.00
Chest, Mahogany, 6 Drawers, Scotland, 1800s, 47 x 48 In.	316.00
Chest, Mahogany, 6 Graduated Drawers, Scotland, c.1825, 51 x 50 In.	518.00
Chest, Mahogany, 8 Drawers, Reeded Columns, Scotland, 1850s, 43 x 51 In.	259.00
Chest, Mahogany, 22 Drawers, Double Wellington Locks, England, c.1900, 45 x 41 In. ...*illus*	1554.00
Chest, Mahogany, Bowfront, 2 Short Over Cock-Beaded Drawers, Bracket Feet, 40 x 39 In.	708.00
Chest, Mahogany, Bowfront, 5 Drawers, Carved Knobs, Columns, Scotland, c.1860, 41 x 51 In.	610.00
Chest, Mahogany, Bowfront, 6 Drawers, Reeded, Oval Brass Handles, American, 34 x 42 In.	390.00
Chest, Mahogany, Carved, 4 Drawers, Turned Columns, Glass Pulls, 1800s, 13 x 12 x 9 In. ...*illus*	1195.00
Chest, Mahogany, Fold Front, Iron Hinges, Handles, Carved Stand, Chinese, c.1875, 26 x 31 In.	122.00
Chest, Mahogany, Molded Top, 4 Drawers, Turned Feet, c.1800, 42 x 44 In.	976.00
Chest, Mahogany, Projecting Drawer Over 5 Drawers, Painted, Garland, 1800s, 60 x 41 In.	3965.00
Chest, Mahogany, Rectangular Top, 6 Drawers, Splayed Legs, 52 x 43 In.	488.00
Chest, Mahogany, Rectangular Top, Round Edge, 5 Drawers, Columns, Ball Feet, 44 x 45 In.	1315.00
Chest, Mahogany, Rectangular, 3 Drawers, Turned Legs, 1800s, 39 x 40 In.	413.00
Chest, Mahogany, Rectangular, 4 Graduated Drawers, Bracket Feet, 42 x 43 In.	366.00
Chest, Mahogany, String Inlay, Drop Front, Fitted Interior, 3 Drawers, c.1850, 46 x 49 In.	615.00
Chest, Mahogany, Tiger Maple, Drop Front, 4 Drawers, Bracket Feet, 1800s, 44 x 43 In.	518.00
Chest, Maple, Chestnut, Dovetailed, 6 Drawers, Molded Cornice, Bracket Feet, c.1790, 51 x 38 In.	588.00
Chest, Marble Top, String Inlays, Drop Drawer, 3 Low Drawers, Cabriole Legs, 46 x 21 In.	345.00
Chest, Marquetry, 3 Drawers, Bracket Feet, Italy, c.1820, 34 x 45 In.	4148.00
Chest, McCobb, Mahogany, 7 Drawers, Drop Front Drawer, Calvin, 36 x 53 In.	1020.00
Chest, McCobb, Mr. & Mrs. Chest, Maple, Brass, Winchendon, 1950s, 33 x 72 In.	2232.00
Chest, McCobb, Walnut, 6 Drawers, Directional, 1960s, 47 x 40 In.	1195.00
Chest, Mixed Wood, Bowfront, Banded Top, 4 Beaded Drawers, England, c.1790, 38 x 40 In.	978.00
Chest, Mule, Basswood, Blue Paint, 5 Drawers, New England, 1700s, 46 x 43 In.	652.00
Chest, Mule, Chippendale, Maple & Pine, Bracket Feet, c.1790, 49 x 39 In.	1293.00
Chest, Mule, Faux Grain Paint, 3 Drawers, Cutout Feet, c.1800, 46 x 40 x 19 In.	1998.00
Chest, Mule, Federal, Pine, Red Paint, Flip Top, Drawers, Bail Handles, 47 x 38 In.	359.00
Chest, Mule, Fluted Columns, 6 Drawers, Bracket Feet, c.1750-55, 33 x 66 In.	1778.00
Chest, Mule, Hinged Top, 2 Drawers, New York, 1700s, 38 x 41 In.	230.00
Chest, Mule, Mahogany, Hinged Top, Ogee Bracket Feet, c.1770, 43 x 71 In.	1912.00
Chest, Mule, Mixed Wood, 2 Drawers, 2 Faux Drawers, Applied Molded Edges, c.1820, 44 x 45 In.	805.00
Chest, Mule, Oak, Hinged Top, Molded Edge, Panels, 2 Drawers, England, c.1820, 36 x 55 In.	3444.00
Chest, Mule, Oak, Hinged Top, Paneled Sides, 3 Drawers, Block Feet, c.1770, 41 x 59 In.	717.00
Chest, Mule, Oak, Hinged, Molded Edge, 3 Inset Panels Over 2 Drawers, Ogee Feet, 1870s	3440.00
Chest, Mule, Oak, Lift Top, 4 Drawers, England, 1700s, 50 x 57 ½ In.	374.00
Chest, Mule, Painted, 5 Drawers, Shaped Feet, New England, c.1790, 44 x 36 In.	326.00
Chest, Mule, Pine, 2 Drawers, Lift Top, Vinegar Grain, New England, c.1810, 42 x 42 In.	6518.00
Chest, Mule, Pine, Half Moon Ends, c.1850, 11 x 10 x 5 In.	5875.00
Chest, Mule, Pine, Hinged Lid, Dovetailed Drawers, Cutout Feet, 1800s, 45 x 40 In.	705.00
Chest, Mule, Pine, Painted, Lift Top, Drop Front, Shelf, Drawers, Cutout Feet, c.1810, 42 x 44 In.	529.00
Chest, Mule, Pine, Painted, Strap Hinges, Drawers, Applied Molding, c.1810, 30 x 23 In.	690.00
Chest, Mule, Pine, Painted, Tapered Feet, Brass Hardware, c.1825, 35 ½ x 39 ¾ In. ...*illus*	10281.00
Chest, Mule, Pine, Red Finish, 2 Drawers, Snipe Hinges, Bootjack Ends, c.1760, 40 x 34 In.	999.00
Chest, Mule, Pine, Red Paint, Scrolled Apron, Lift Top, Cutout Feet, c.1800, 38 x 40 In.	482.00
Chest, Mule, Poplar, Pine, 2 Drawers, Faux Inlay, New England, c.1810, 39 x 43 In.	529.00
Chest, Mule, Queen Anne, Pine, Paint, Shaped Skirt, Cutout Feet, c.1765, 48 x 40 In.	3643.00
Chest, Multicolor, Scenes, Women, Children, 2 Drawers, Doors, Tibet, 36 x 58 In.	575.00
Chest, Neoclassical, Poplar, Flame Mahogany Veneer, Drawers, Shaped Crest, 49 x 42 In.	264.00
Chest, Oak, 3 Graduated Drawers, Brass Handles, Block Feet, American, c.1900, 25 x 20 In.	173.00
Chest, Oak, 8 Drawers, Carved Flowers & Leaves, Cast Pulls, Side Lock, 57 x 40 In.	922.00
Chest, Oak, Carved, Paneled, 4 Drawers, Applied Moldings, Bun Feet, England, c.1700, 36 x 38 In.	1440.00
Chest, Ocher, Red Paint, Lift Top, Side Handles, 2 Drawers, Iron Mounts, c.1820, 30 x 51 In.	720.00
Chest, Oyster Veneer, 4 Graduated Drawers, England, c.1790, 36 x 38 In.	2300.00
Chest, Painted, Flag, George Washington, Red, White, Blue Pilasters, 1900s, 14 x 22 In.	800.00
Chest, Pine, 6 Graduated Drawers, Brass Handles, Bracket Base, c.1780, 54 x 39 In.	805.00
Chest, Pine, Black Paint, 6 Drawers, Teardrop Pulls, Turnip Feet, c.1710, 43 x 38 In.	10073.00
Chest, Pine, Faux Mahogany, Painted, 3 Drawers, Bracket Feet, 36 x 36 In.	186.00
Chest, Pine, Molded Cornice, 4 Drawers, Turned Legs, Dutch, c.1700, 26 x 21 In.	1265.00
Chest, Pine, Painted, Applied Moldings, 3 Lower Drawers, Bracket Feet, 1700s, 29 x 23 x 50 In.	1840.00
Chest, Pine, Painted, Turned Wood Pulls, Brass Escutcheons, Early 1700s, 37 x 43 In.	2607.00

Chest, Pine, Red & Black Smoke Designs, New England, c.1810, 17 ½ x 45 ½ In.	889.00
Chest, Poplar, 9 Drawers, Pa., 1800s, 29 x 53 In.	400.00
Chest, Poplar, Carved Pinwheels, Painted, 4 Drawers, Matchstick Corners, c.1805, 52 x 42 In.	13035.00
Chest, Poplar, Scrolled Cornice, Stepped Top, 8 Drawers, Bracket Feet, c.1850, 49 x 39 In.	911.00
Chest, Queen Anne Style, Oak, 8 Drawers, Carvings, Cabriole Legs, England, c.1900, 66 x 51 In.	960.00
Chest, Queen Anne, Cherry, Pine, Shell Carving, 1700s, 73 ½ In. ....*illus*	2350.00
Chest, Queen Anne, Walnut, 5 Short Over 4 Long Drawers, Bracket Feet, c.1760, 60 x 37 In.	2015.00
Chest, Queen Anne, Walnut, Arched Drawers, Paneled Sides, c.1770, 66 x 40 In.	13000.00
Chest, Queen Anne, Walnut, Carved Swan's Neck Crest, Shells, 11 Drawers, Mass., 77 x 38 In.	3042.00
Chest, Queen Anne, Walnut, Fan Carved, Molded Cornice, Drawers, c.1750, 71 x 38 In.	9500.00
Chest, Queen Anne, Walnut, Fan Carved, Scroll Top, Brass Bail Handles, c.1770, 84 x 39 In. .	14220.00
Chest, Queen Anne, Walnut, Herringbone Inlay, Thumb-Molded Edge, 5 Drawers, 37 ¾ In. ......*illus*	5629.00
Chest, Red Lacquer, 2 Doors, Metal Accents, Chinese, 68 x 43 In.	275.00
Chest, Red, Carved, Parcel Gilt, 5 Drawers, Hidden Pulls, Block Legs, Chinese, 28 x 40 In.	575.00
Chest, Regency, Mahogany, Bowfront, 5 Drawers, Shaped Apron, French Feet, 1800s, 42 x 39 In.	1952.00
Chest, Regency, Mahogany, Bowfront, Crossbanded, 5 Drawers, Bracket Feet, 1800s, 40 x 41 In.	652.00
Chest, Regency, Mahogany, Bowfront, Inlaid Top, 5 Drawers, Bracket Feet, 39 x 42 In.	429.00
Chest, Regency, Mahogany, Bowfront, Reeded Edge, 5 Drawers, 1800s, 42 x 42 In.	717.00
Chest, Renaissance Revival, Walnut, Burl, Stringing, Serpentine, 4 Drawers, 34 x 30 In.	4444.00
Chest, Rococo, Mahogany, Marble Top, Arched Mirror, Scroll Crest, 2 Drawers, 1800s, 85 x 48 In.	1434.00
Chest, Rosewood, Carved Figures, Dog Feet, Pine Handles, Chinese, c.1900, 24 x 40 In.	858.00
Chest, Shaker, Pine, Blue Paint, Double Case, 6 Drawers, Middle Foot, c.1845, 40 x 19 In.	13456.00
Chest, Shaker, Pine, Butternut, Beech, 7 Drawers, Walnut Pulls, c.1840	3510.00
Chest, Sheraton Style, Mahogany, Bowfront, Cock-Beaded Drawers, Columns, 45 x 40 In.	885.00
Chest, Sheraton Style, Mahogany, Bowfront, Turreted Corners, Drawers, 39 x 41 In.	1045.00
Chest, Sheraton Style, Mahogany, Turned Pilasters, Shaped Backsplash, 4 Drawers, 43 x 44 In.	345.00
Chest, Sheraton Style, Mahogany, Turret Corners, 4 Drawers, Crossbanded, 40 x 43 In.	518.00
Chest, Sheraton, Cherry, 4 Drawers, Baluster Feet, c.1825, 45 x 43 In.	492.00
Chest, Sheraton, Cherry, Bowfront, 4 Drawers, Maple Veneer Drawer Fronts, c.1820, 40 x 40 In.	1610.00
Chest, Sheraton, Cherry, Poplar, 4 Drawers, Reeded Stiles, Turned Feet, c.1830, 48 ½ x 42 In..	646.00
Chest, Sheraton, Cherry, Reeded Top, 4 Drawers, Cock-Beaded, Turned Feet, 1800s, 44 x 39 In.	764.00
Chest, Sheraton, Cherry, Walnut, 6 Cock-Beaded Drawers, Turned Feet, 1800s, 48 x 41 In.	705.00
Chest, Sheraton, Curly Maple, Cherry, 4 Graduated, c.1830, 49 x 41 In.	441.00
Chest, Sheraton, Mahogany, Bowfront, 4 Drawers, New England, c.1815, 42 x 43 In.	531.00
Chest, Sheraton, Mahogany, Bowfront, Porringer Corners, 4 Drawers, c.1810, 40 x 42 In.	1495.00
Chest, Sheraton, Mahogany, Line Inlay, Serpentine, 4 Drawers, Bracket Feet, 37 x 44 In.	295.00
Chest, Sheraton, Pine, Poplar, 4 Graduated Drawers, Turned Feet, 1800s, 44 x 21 In.	489.00
Chest, Sheraton, Walnut, Cock-Beaded, Diamond Edge, Turned Feet, c.1835, 44 x 42 In.	999.00
Chest, Specimen, Mahogany, Drawer, Cupboard Door, 6 Interior Drawers, 1800s, 16 x 10 In..	89.00
Chest, Specimen, Mahogany, Flip Top, 24 Drawers, Late 1800s, 16 x 19 In.	365.00
Chest, Specimen, Mahogany, Molded Edge, 8 Drawers, Base, 1870s, 25 x 19 In.	657.00
Chest, Spice, Pine, 10 Marked Drawers, Bracket Feet, c.1920, 17 ¾ x 9 ½ In.	122.00
Chest, Spice, Red Grain Painted, 17 Drawers, Pa., c.1850, 17 x 18 In.	4740.00
Chest, Spice, Vine, Berry Inlay, Door, 11 Interior Drawers, Bun Feet, c.1740	30810.00
Chest, Sugar, Cherry, Hinged Lid, Stand, Scratch Beaded Drawer, 33 x 23 In.	2468.00
Chest, Sugar, Cherry, Lift Top, Paneled, Drawer, Turned Legs, c.1825, 41 x 41 x 18 In.	1130.00
Chest, Sugar, Federal, Walnut, Hinged Lid, Open Interior, Divider, Drawer, Tenn., 1800s, 36 x 34 In.	2006.00
Chest, Sugar, Walnut, 2-Board Top, Beaded Drawer, Turned Legs, Ball Feet, 1825, 34 x 35 In..	1116.00
Chest, Sugar, Walnut, Poplar, Hinged Top, Fitted Interior, 2 Drawers, N.C., c.1825	8625.00
Chest, Tabletop, Red, 6 Drawers, Dovetailed, 1800s, 15 x 48 In.	1150.00
Chest, Tansu, 3 Drawers, Door, Stacked, Sendai, Japan, 41 ½ x 43 In.	230.00
Chest, Tansu, Red Stain, 8 Drawers, Iron Hardware, Japan, 35 x 46 In.	633.00
Chest, Tansu, Wood, 3 Kimono Drawers, 4 Smaller Side Drawers, Japan, 25 x 46 In.	185.00
Chest, Teak, 5 Carved Drawers, Chinese, 20th Century, 41 x 36 x 18 In.	288.00
Chest, Tiger Maple, 4 Drawers, Split Columns, Carved Feet, N.C., 1800s, 25 x 19 In.	4140.00
Chest, Tiger Maple, Mixed Wood, 6 Drawers, New England, c.1810, 49 x 44 In.	1140.00
Chest, Walnut, 3 Arched Drawers, Over 5 Graduated Drawers, Pa., c.1750, 54 x 39 In.	3555.00
Chest, Walnut, 4 Drawers, Brown Paint, Southern, Signed Gabriel, 1875, 44 x 41 In.	649.00
Chest, Walnut, 4 Drawers, Shaped Backsplash, c.1860-75, 43 x 40 In.	230.00
Chest, Walnut, 4 Graduated Beaded Drawers, Scrolled Skirt, N.C., c.1830, 41 x 41 In.	1955.00
Chest, Walnut, 4 Graduated Drawers, Wood Knobs, Turned Feet, c.1820, 49 x 41 In.	518.00
Chest, Walnut, 6 Graduated Drawers, Locking Bar, c.1880, 58 x 38 In.	690.00
Chest, Walnut, Curly Maple, Poplar, Broken-Arch Backsplash, Glove Drawers, 42 x 30 In.	881.00
Chest, Walnut, Drawers, Notched Corners, Shaped Apron, Shell, Cabriole Legs, 1800s, 43 x 46 In.	950.00
Chest, Walnut, Fruitwood, 4 Drawers, Chamfered, Brass Bail Handles, 1700s, 38 x 53 In.	2629.00
Chest, Walnut, Marquetry Top, 3 Drawers, Shaped Apron, Italy, 1700s, 33 x 41 In.	3227.00

F

Furniture, Chest, Queen Anne, Cherry, Pine, Shell Carving, 1700s, 73 ½ In. $2350.00

Cowan's Auctions

Furniture, Chest, Queen Anne, Walnut, Herringbone Inlay, Thumbmolded Edge, 5 Drawers, 37 ¾ In. $5629.00

Skinner, Inc.

Furniture, Chest, William & Mary, Maple, Molded Edge, 5 Drawers, Bun Feet, 36 x 36 ¾ In. $1888.00

Northeast Auctions

Furniture, Chest-On-Chest, George III, Walnut, Molded Cornice, 8 Drawers, Bracket Feet, 70 x 44 ½ In. **$2440.00**

Leslie Hindman Auctioneers

Furniture, Commode, Bombe, Serpentine Marble, Door, Painted Scene, Ormolu Mounts, France, 44 x 39 In. **$4148.00**

Skinner, Inc.

Furniture, Commode, Faux Marble Top, 4 Drawers, Painted, Trees, Cabriole Legs, Italy, c.1790, 33 x 41 In. **$2988.00**

Neal Auction Co.

Furniture, Commode, Louis XV Style, Burl Mahogany, Marble Top, Cabriole Legs, c.1910, 36 x 48 In. **$799.00**

New Orleans Auction Galleries, Inc.

Chest, Walnut, Mirror, 6 Drawers, Gallery, c.1875, 23 ½ x 75 ½ In.	374.00
Chest, Walnut, Mixed Wood, Shaped Backsplash, 4 Drawers, Southern, 48 x 43 In.	708.00
Chest, Walnut, Pierced Gallery, Flowers, 7 Drawers, Reeded Pilasters, Base, c.1890, 61 x 38 In.	2151.00
Chest, Walnut, Rectangular Gallery Top, 6 Drawers, c.1885, 60 x 37 In.	748.00
Chest, White Pine, Shaped Backsplash, 4 Drawers, Base Inlaid Heart, 13 x 12 In.	350.00
Chest, William & Mary Style, Yew, Ebony Inlay, 5 Drawers, Southampton, c.1990, 33 x 33 In.	4743.00
Chest, William & Mary, Mahogany, Maple, 2 Sections, Drawers, Turned Legs, 68 x 40 In.	1998.00
Chest, William & Mary, Maple, Molded Edge, 5 Drawers, Bun Feet, 36 x 36 ¾ In. ....*illus*	1888.00
Chest, William & Mary, Oak, 4 Drawers, Raised Panels, 38 x 44 In.	1000.00
Chest, William & Mary, Oyster Veneer, 5 Drawers, Bun Feet, 1700s, 37 x 38 In.	4444.00
Chest, William & Mary, Yew, Elm, 3 Molded Drawers, Raised Design, c.1690, 34 x 38 In.	1955.00
Chest, Wood, Carved, Raised Legs, England, 27 x 38 In.	369.00
Chest, Wood, Painted Panels, 2 Doors, 3 Drawers, Carved, Chinese, 63 x 65 In.	861.00
Chest, Wood, Shaped Gallery, 5 Serpentine Block Drawers, Cabriole Legs, 54 x 30 In.	185.00
Chest, Yellow, Green, Paint, Gilt, Roses, Bombe Shaped Top, 1800s, 32 x 50 In.	2950.00
Chest, Yew, Molded Top, 11 Graduated Drawers, Oval Brasses, Bracket Feet, 61 x 26 In.	1554.00
Chest-On-Chest, Chippendale, Cherry, 10 Drawers, Shell Carving, Conn., c.1775, 80 x 51 In.	2596.00
Chest-On-Chest, Chippendale, Cherry, 10 Drawers, Shell, New England, 1700s, 87 x 39 In.	5310.00
Chest-On-Chest, Chippendale, Cherry, Dentil Molded Cornice, Beaded Drawers, Fan, 1700s, 76 In.	6518.00
Chest-On-Chest, Chippendale, Mixed Wood, 10 Drawers, Carved, England, c.1790, 81 x 47 In.	2875.00
Chest-On-Chest, Chippendale, Walnut, 7 Drawers Over 5 Drawers, Columns, 1795, 80 x 43 In.	5214.00
Chest-On-Chest, Chippendale, Walnut, Bonnet Top, Flame Finials, Drawers, c.1770, 91 x 69 In.	7000.00
Chest-On-Chest, Empire, Mahogany, 7 Graduated Drawers, Germany, 1800s, 59 x 39 In.	575.00
Chest-On-Chest, Federal Style, Cherry, Drawers, Chamfered, c.1910, 67 x 49 In.	837.00
Chest-On-Chest, Federal, Mahogany, Inlay, Dentil Molded Cornice, c.1790, 69 x 42 In.	1016.00
Chest-On-Chest, George II, Walnut, Boxwood Inlay, 5 Drawers, Cabriole Legs, 71 x 44 In.	575.00
Chest-On-Chest, George III Style, Mahogany, Dentillated Cornice, 3 Drawers, 74 x 44 In.	2214.00
Chest-On-Chest, George III, Walnut, Molded Cornice, 8 Drawers, Bracket Feet, 70 x 44 ½ In. ....*illus*	2440.00
Chest-On-Chest, Mahogany, 5 Drawers Over 3 Drawers, c.1800, 67 x 42 In.	1722.00
Chest-On-Chest, Mahogany, 8 Drawers, Reeded Stiles, c.1800, 68 x 42 In.	1076.00
Chest-On-Chest, Mahogany, Molded Cornice, 8 Drawers, c.1785, 74 x 44 In.	2706.00
Chest-On-Chest, Mahogany, Molded Cornice, Dressing Slide, Bracket Feet, c.1790, 72 x 41 In.	2390.00
Chest-On-Chest, Queen Anne Style, Mahogany, Mixed Wood, 8 Drawers, c.1905, 28 ½ x 24 In.	1140.00
Chest-On-Chest, Queen Anne, Maple, Mixed Wood, 8 Drawers, Fan, New Eng., 70 x 38 In.	2040.00
Chest-On-Chest, Queen Anne, Maple, Molded Cornice, 5 Drawers, Cabriole Legs, 1740, 71 In.	1175.00
Chest-On-Chest, Queen Anne, Tiger Maple, 9 Graduated Drawers, New Eng., 1700s, 73 x 41 In.	2124.00
Chest-On-Chest, Walnut, 8 Drawers, Scrolled Bracket Base, England, 1700s, 68 x 39 In.	863.00
Chest-On-Frame, Black Lacquer, Gilded Scenes, Bronze Handles, Chinese, 18 x 36 In.	244.00
Chest-On-Frame, George II Style, Yew, 5 Drawers, 1800s, 56 x 40 In.	1625.00
Chest-On-Frame, George III Style, Chinoiserie, Drawers, Handles, Gilt, 37 x 41 In.	2562.00
Chest-On-Frame, Gilt, Lift Top, Rounded Corners, Carved Apron, Cabriole Legs, 32 x 26 In.	1037.00
Chest-On-Frame, Jacobean Style, Walnut, Burl, 3 Drawers, Trestle, 38 x 38 In.	246.00
Chest-On-Frame, Maple, Thumb-Molded Drawers, Carved Fan, 1700s, 59 x 39 In.	1304.00
Chest-On-Frame, Sheraton, Pine, Painted, Hinged Lid, Turned Legs, 1800s, 38 x 34 In.	345.00
Chest-On-Frame, Storage, Red Lacquer, Gilt Lotus, Horse Hoof Feet, Chinese, 33 x 22 In.	123.00
Chest-On-Frame, Walnut, Burl, 5 Drawers, Scalloped Skirt, 56 x 35 In.	1673.00
Chest-On-Frame, William & Mary, Walnut, Oyster Veneer, 5 Drawers, 45 x 38 In.	1188.00
Chiffonier, Louis XVI, Walnut, 4 Drawers, Drop Ring Handles, 42 x 30 In.	995.00
Chiffonier, Mahogany, Rolling Back Board, Leaf Crest, 4 Drawers, England, 1800s, 65 x 72 In.	826.00
Chiffonier, Regency, Mahogany, Brass Gallery, Drawer, Doors, Scroll Supports, 1815, 49 x 35 In.	1793.00
Chiffonier, William IV, Mahogany, Grecian Pediment, Wreath, Paneled Doors, c.1835, 48 x 37 In.	1098.00
Chifforobe, Maple, 6 Drawers, Wardrobe, Slide-Out Hanger, 1900s, 59 x 43 In.	92.00
Chifforobe, Oak, Drawers, Paneled Door, Larkin Soap Co., c.1900, 40 x 19 In.	316.00
Clothespress, Red Lacquer, Gilt Butterflies & Flowers, 2 Doors, Chinese, 1800s, 70 x 44 In.	1778.00
Coat Hook, Bronze, Dragons, Wall Mount, c.1880, 7 ½ x 14 ½ In.	144.00
Coat Rack, Aluminum, Leather, Walnut, Brass, Painted, Italy, 1960s, 94 In.	17360.00
Coat Rack, G. Stickley, Double, 6 Hooks, 72 x 14 x 22 In.	2108.00
Coat Rack, Georgian Style, Mahogany, Turned Finial, 3 Tiers, Support, Tripod Feet, 73 In.	1315.00
Coat Rack, Mahogany, 2 Tiers, Urn Finial, Reeded, Circular Base, 82 x 25 In.	510.00
Coat Rack, Roycroft, Shoe Feet, Marked, 73 In.	3596.00
Coat Rack, Shaker, Tiger Maple, Ring Turnings, 1830s, 84 In.	162.00
Coat Rack, Wrought Iron, Painted Top Balls, Tripod, France, c.1950, 18 ½ x 69 In.	480.00
Coffer, Baroque, Walnut, Paneled, Carved, Italy, c.1700, 10 x 21 In.	944.00
Coffer, George II, Oak, 4-Panel Inset Hinged Top, Side Till, c.1750, 21 x 50 In.	353.00
Coffer, Jacobean, Oak, Carved, England, c.1790, 19 x 38 ¼ In.	504.00
Coffer, Jacobean, Oak, Diamond Panels, Interior Till, England, 1700s, 26 x 48 In.	2415.00

Coffer, Maple, Carved Panels, St. George, Slaying Dragon, Lift Top, Paw Feet, c.1700, 27 x 63 In.	1438.00
Coffer, Oak, Carved Stylized Leaves, Rectangular Plank Top, Drawers, Block Feet, 1700s, 29 x 49 In.	461.00
Coffer, Oak, Chip-Carved Edge, Flower Design, Rectangular Hinged Top, Molded Legs, 31 x 43 In.	415.00
Coffer, Oak, Raised Panel Front, Pegged, Lift Top, Wooden Strap Hinges, 1600s, 34 x 50 In.	460.00
Coffer, Rosewood, Oak, Carved Octagon, Marquetry, Flowers, Vases, Bun Feet, c.1830, 27 x 51 In.	1195.00
Coffer, Walnut, Mahogany, Arched Inset Panels, Hinged, Italy, 45 x 23 In.	1168.00
Commode, 3 Drawers, Ebonized Pilasters, Gilt Mask Capitals, c.1810, 36 x 49 In.	2655.00
Commode, Art Deco, Burl, Banded, 4 Drawers, c.1910, 33 x 39 In.	900.00
Commode, Art Deco, Mirror, Stepped Top, 3 Drawers, Tapered Legs, 32 x 32 In., Pair	3198.00
Commode, Art Deco, Rosewood, Brass Mounts, 2 Drawers, c.1925, 36 x 32 In.	470.00
Commode, Baroque, Oak, Bombe, Shaped Top, 3 Drawers, Ball Feet, 1800s, 30 x 40 In.	588.00
Commode, Baroque, Pine, Scalloped Edges, 4 Drawers, Ogee Bracket Feet, 1700s, 33 x 36 In.	230.00
Commode, Baroque, Walnut, Carved, Banded Border, Plank Top, 3 Drawers, Italy, 39 x 54 In.	3760.00
Commode, Baroque, Walnut, Marquetry, Drawers, Leafy Scrolls, Bracket Feet, 32 x 45 In.	3520.00
Commode, Baroque, Walnut, Parquetry, 2 Drawers, Cabriole Legs, 1700s, 32 x 52 In.	770.00
Commode, Baroque, Walnut, Short Drawers, Burnished Scrolling, Bun Feet, 37 x 25 In.	1875.00
Commode, Biedermeier, Fruitwood, Rounded Rectangular Top, 3 Drawers, c.1850, 33 x 49 In.	1476.00
Commode, Bombe, Banded Inlay, 4 Drawers, Scalloped Skirt, Flare Feet, c.1800, 32 x 47 In.	6274.00
Commode, Bombe, Marble Top, Parquetry, 3 Drawers, France, c.1890, 36 x 51 In.	1150.00
Commode, Bombe, Ormolu, Marble Top, Hand Painted, 2 Doors, 36 x 40 In.	2963.00
Commode, Bombe, Serpentine Marble, Door, Painted Scene, Ormolu Mounts, France, 44 x 39 In. *illus*	4148.00
Commode, Bronze, Gilt, Parquetry, Bombe, Marble Top, 4 Drawers, Busts, 35 x 47 In.	861.00
Commode, Burl Veneer, Marble Top, String Inlay, Demilune, 2 Drawers, France, 31 x 31 In.	546.00
Commode, Burl Walnut, Serpentine Top, 3 Drawers, Ormolu, Bracket Feet, 1700s, 32 x 46 In.	1150.00
Commode, Burl, Bombe, Black Marble Top, 4 Drawers, Ormolu Head Mounts, 34 x 50 In.	201.00
Commode, Campaign, Mahogany, Brass Mounts, Green Marble, 3 Drawers, 31 x 19 In., Pair.	738.00
Commode, Charles X, Mahogany, Drop Front, Marble Top, 5 Drawers, 1800s, 40 x 45 In.	900.00
Commode, Demilune, Banded Inlay, 2 Doors, Spade Feet, 34 ½ x 33 In.	403.00
Commode, Directoire, Bombe, Marble Top, Parquetry, Ormolu, Apron, c.1810, 33 x 31 In.	388.00
Commode, Dutch Style, Marquetry, Drawer, Fluted Legs, 24 x 20 In.	956.00
Commode, Ebonized, Yew, 3 Drawers, Pilasters, Paw Feet, 1800s, 30 x 33 In.	861.00
Commode, Edwardian, Oak, 5 Drawers, Pedestal, Base, c.1900, 34 x 21 In., Pair	717.00
Commode, Empire Style, Mahogany, Marble Top, Columns, Turreted Feet, 1800s, 29 x 32 In.	1845.00
Commode, Empire, Mahogany, Marble Top, Bronze Mounts, 3 Drawers, 1800s, 36 x 51 In.	1673.00
Commode, Faux Marble Top, 4 Drawers, Painted, Trees, Cabriole Legs, Italy, c.1790, 33 x 41 In. *illus*	2988.00
Commode, French Empire Style, Marble Top, 4 Drawers, Columns, 30 x 28 In., Pair	1464.00
Commode, French Provincial, Walnut, Carved, Marble, Cabriole Legs, 1800s, 39 x 46 In.	3286.00
Commode, French Provincial, Walnut, Carved, Serpentine, Drawers, 38 x 51 In.	3884.00
Commode, French Provincial, White Cherry, Carved Detail, 3 Drawers, c.1810, 33 x 48 In.	1840.00
Commode, Fruitwood, Marble Top, Ormolu, Demilune, 2 Drawers, 2 Doors, c.1790, 34 x 44 In.	748.00
Commode, Georgian, Mahogany, Banded Gallery Top, 3 Drawers, Doors, 1700s, 34 x 32 In.	1434.00
Commode, Georgian, Mahogany, Scalloped Edge, Tray Top, 2 Doors, Drawer, 28 x 23 In.	470.00
Commode, Georgian, Mahogany, Shaped Tray Top, 2 Doors, Drawer, Square Legs, 31 x 21 In.	1195.00
Commode, Georgian, Mahogany, Shaped Tray Top, Tambour Door, 2 Drawers, 30 x 19 In.	1315.00
Commode, Gilt, White Paint, 3 Drawers, Shaped Skirt, Scroll, Flowers, Leaves, 37 x 54 In.	420.00
Commode, Italian Neoclassical, Walnut Inlay, Book Matched Veneer, Drawers, 38 x 47 In.	2074.00
Commode, Italianate, Painted, Flowers, Shaped Front, Drawers, 32 x 35 In.	1058.00
Commode, Kingwood, Bombe, Marble Top, 3 Drawers, c.1900, 32 x 17 In., Pair	1722.00
Commode, Kingwood, Bombe, Marquetry, Marble Top, Drawers, Dutch, 33 x 29 In.	717.00
Commode, Kingwood, Mahogany, Bowfront, Marble Top, Drawers, Doors, Italy, c.1820, 36 x 20 In.	2091.00
Commode, Kingwood, Marble Top, 11 Drawers, 4 Leather Drawers, France, c.1900, 38 x 40 In.	1230.00
Commode, Louis Philippe, Mahogany, Marble Top, Frieze Drawer, Block Feet, c.1835, 38 x 50 In.	1845.00
Commode, Louis Philippe, Shaped Marble Top, Blind Drawer, 4 Drawers, c.1850, 38 x 50 In.	984.00
Commode, Louis Philippe, Walnut, Marble Top, 3 Drawers, Bracket Feet, 37 x 49 In.	1080.00
Commode, Louis Philippe, Wood, Marble Top, 4 Drawers, France, c.1850, 36 x 51 In.	984.00
Commode, Louis XIV Style, Banded Marquetry, Marble Top, 3 Drawers, France, 30 x 23 In.	633.00
Commode, Louis XV Style, Bombe, 3 Serpentine Drawers, Scroll, Italy, 1900s, 31 x 41 In.	316.00
Commode, Louis XV Style, Bombe, Green, Painted, Flowers, 3 Drawers, 32 x 47 In.	584.00
Commode, Louis XV Style, Bombe, Parquetry, Marble Top, Drawers, 51 x 20 In.	1064.00
Commode, Louis XV Style, Burl Mahogany, Marble Top, Cabriole Legs, c.1910, 36 x 48 In. *illus*	799.00
Commode, Louis XV Style, Inlay, 2 Drawers, Red & Gilt Scroll, Ormolu, 33 x 51 In.	390.00
Commode, Louis XV Style, Kingwood, Marble Top, Ormolu Band, 2 Drawers, 1800s, 29 x 21 In.	615.00
Commode, Louis XV Style, Mahogany, Faux Book Front, Drawer, Egypt, 1900s, 29 x 16 In. *illus*	472.00
Commode, Louis XV Style, Mahogany, Marble Top, 3 Drawers, Splayed Legs, c.1950, 33 x 43 In.	922.00
Commode, Louis XV Style, Marble Top, 2 Drawers, Marquetry, Gilt, 1900s, 34 x 50 In.	777.00
Commode, Louis XV Style, Marquetry Veneers, 2 Drawers, Bronze Mounts, France, 32 x 17 In.	767.00

Furniture, Commode, Louis XV Style, Mahogany, Faux Book Front, Drawer, Egypt, 1900s, 29 x 16 In. $472.00

Brunk Auctions

Furniture, Commode, Louis XVI, Kingwood, Inlay, Marble Top, Drawers, Bronze Mounts, c.1790, 50 x 25 In. $1830.00

Neal Auction Co.

Furniture, Commode, Louis XVI, Mahogany, Carved, Marble Top, 4 Drawers, Fluted Stiles, 1800s, 39 x 51 In. $2460.00

Neal Auction Co.

Furniture, Credenza, Renaissance Revival, Walnut, Bird's-Eye Maple, Mirror, c.1880, 98 x 47 In. $5750.00

Bob Courtney Auctions

Furniture, Cupboard, Cherry, Poplar, Glass Doors, Drawers, Panel Doors, Ohio, c.1850, 84 x 50 In. $2233.00

Garth's Auctions, Inc.

Furniture, Cupboard, Corner, 8-Pane Door, Paneled Door, 3 Butterfly Shape Shelves, Pa., 85 In. $1534.00

Conestoga Auction Co., Inc.

Furniture, Cupboard, Corner, Blue Paint, 2 8-Pane Doors, 2 Lower Doors, 85 x 53 In. $6490.00

Ivey-Selkirk Auctioneers

Commode, Louis XV Style, Marquetry, Marble Top, Drawers, France, 1900s, 16 x 11 In., Pair .	472.00
Commode, Louis XV Style, Tulipwood, Fruitwood Inlay, Bombe, c.1900, 37 x 48 In................	823.00
Commode, Louis XV Style, Walnut, Bowed, 3 Drawers, c.1790, 38 x 47 In................	2952.00
Commode, Louis XV, Cherry, Gilt Metal, Bombe, Drawers, Scroll Feet, 33 x 38 In................	5938.00
Commode, Louis XV, Inlaid, Marble Top, 3 Drawers, Cabriole Legs, 36 x 50 x 22 In.	450.00
Commode, Louis XV, Mahogany, Molded Edge, 3 Drawers, Cabriole Feet, 1700s, 25 x 19 In.....	2460.00
Commode, Louis XV, Rosewood, Kingwood, Marble Top, Bombe, Signed, Lapie, 34 x 49 In......	6150.00
Commode, Louis XV, Walnut, Bronze Mounts, 5 Drawers, Paneled Sides, 36 x 49 In.	2925.00
Commode, Louis XV, Walnut, Molded Top, Drawers, Cabriole Legs, Pad Feet, 1700s, 20 x 25 In.	2875.00
Commode, Louis XVI Style, Kingwood, Marquetry, Marble Top, 5 Drawers, 1890, 33 x 15 In., Pair	1195.00
Commode, Louis XVI Style, Mahogany, Marble Top, Fluted Columns, 5 Drawers, 36 x 53 In. ..	2813.00
Commode, Louis XVI Style, Oval Marble Top, Drawer, Door, Shelf, Fluted Legs, 1800s, 30 In...	470.00
Commode, Louis XVI, Kingwood, Inlay, Marble Top, Drawers, Bronze Mounts, c.1790, 50 x 25 In. *illus*	1830.00
Commode, Louis XVI, Mahogany, Carved, Marble Top, 4 Drawers, Fluted Stiles, 1800s, 39 x 51 In. *illus*	2460.00
Commode, Louis XVI, Mahogany, Marble Top, Ormolu, Drawers, c.1795, 33 x 49 In................	1599.00
Commode, Louis XV-XVI, Burl Veneer, Bombe, Marble, Kidney Shape, 36 x 23 In................	817.00
Commode, Mahogany, D-Shape Top, 2 Drawers, Tambour Doors, Gilt Mounts, Dutch, 33 x 22 In.	350.00
Commode, Mahogany, Lift Top, Drawer, 2 Doors, 26 x 18 In.	115.00
Commode, Mahogany, Marble Top, 4 Drawers, c.1890, 36 x 51 In.	1912.00
Commode, Mahogany, Marble Top, Bombe, Drawers, Sunburst Pattern, c.1885, 34 x 47 In.	2091.00
Commode, Mahogany, Marble Top, Crossbanded, Shelf Interior, Base Molding, c.1830, 30 x 21 In.	598.00
Commode, Mahogany, Parquetry, Brass, Marble Top, Drawers, Wedgwood Inset, c.1905, 29 x 24 In.	239.00
Commode, Mahogany, Shaped Tray Top, Tambour Door, Drawer, 50 x 35 In.	956.00
Commode, Mahogany, Step, Carpeted Top, Enamel Pot, Pullout Panel, 1800s, 18 x 18 In......	118.00
Commode, Marble Top, Bowfront, 3 Drawers, Ormolu Mounted, Splayed Legs, 1900s, 33 x 45 In.	295.00
Commode, Marble Top, Inlays, 6 Drawers, Italy, c.1820, 34 x 45 In., Pair	2440.00
Commode, Marbleized Surface, Green Painted Vines, Cabriole Legs, 32 x 42 In.	2950.00
Commode, Mixed Wood, Drawers, Crossbanded Inlay, Tapered Legs, 1790s, 15 x 20 In...........	705.00
Commode, Mixed Wood, Marble Top, Geometric Inlays, Shaped Case, 3 Drawers, 36 x 50 In..	5557.00
Commode, Napoleon III Style, Burl, Broken Pediment, Doors, Plaques, 1900s, 72 x 67 In.	1998.00
Commode, Painted, Shaped Top, Flowers, 2 Drawers, Cabriole Legs, Italy, c.1800, 29 x 28 In., Pair	984.00
Commode, Parchment, Banded Top, 9 Drawers, Allover Inlaid Instrument, 34 x 48 In...........	984.00
Commode, Parchment, Macassar, 3 Drawers, Tapered Legs, 34 x 47 In.	738.00
Commode, Parquetry, 4 Drawers, France, c.1890, 39 x 23 ½ In........................	369.00
Commode, Parquetry, Carved Backsplash, Drawer, France, 39 x 51 In.	518.00
Commode, Parquetry, Serpentine, Leaves, Cock-Beaded, Splayed Legs, Italy, 1800s, 36 x 57 In.	4250.00
Commode, Pine, Paint, Pa., 1800s, 33 x 23 In.	460.00
Commode, Provincial, Louis XV, Cherry, 2 Drawers, Incised, Cabriole Legs, 32 x 50 In.	1625.00
Commode, Provincial, Louis XV, Walnut, Cherry, Molded Top, Drawers, 32 x 49 In.............	1375.00
Commode, Regency Style, Burl Walnut, Serpentine Front, Bombe, Brass, 1800s, 30 x 33 In......	657.00
Commode, Renaissance Revival, Walnut, Shaped Marble Top, Drawer, Paneled Door, 30 x 19 In.	365.00
Commode, Rococo Style, Bombe, Serpentine Top, Painted, Cabriole Legs, 35 x 49 In.	1353.00
Commode, Rococo Style, Diamond Parquetry, Bombe Shape, 2 Drawers, 28 ½ x 36 In.	1170.00
Commode, Rosewood, Turreted Ends, 4 Drawers, Barrel Shaped, c.1850, 36 x 43 In.	2706.00
Commode, Serpentine Top, 3 Drawers, Brass Pulls, Shell, Scroll Feet, 37 x 49 In.	2963.00
Commode, Victorian, Walnut, White Marble Top, c.1870, 30 x 31 In.	144.00
Commode, Walnut, Banded, Serpentine, Strapwork Veneer, 3 Drawers, Germany, 34 x 38 In. .	813.00
Commode, Walnut, Bombe, Banded, 6 Drawers, Shaped Top, Cabriole Legs, 30 x 36 In..........	345.00
Commode, Walnut, Drawer, Door, Figural Stiles, Paw Feet, Carved, Italy, c.1800, 25 x 28 In. ..	2135.00
Commode, Walnut, Marble Top, Demilune, Drawers, Apron, Cabriole Legs, 35 x 40 In.	1135.00
Commode, Walnut, Marquetry, 2 Drawers, Leaves, Italy, 1700s, 33 x 35 In........................	823.00
Commode, Walnut, Open Sides, Mirror Back, Marble Top, Drawer, Doors, c.1900, 59 x 51 In..	720.00
Commode, Walnut, Round Crossbanded Top, 3 Drawers, c.1770-80, 30 In.	1080.00
Commode, Walnut, White Marble Top, Secretary Drawer, 4 Lower Drawers, c.1890, 36 x 47 In.	1554.00
Commode, Wood, Bombe, Marble Top, 2 Bronze Mount Drawers, Fluted Legs, 35 x 60 In........	2952.00
Commode, Wood, Horizontal Grain, 4 Shelves, c.1950, 34 x 41 In.	615.00
Commode, Wood, Shaped Marble Top, 4 Bronze Trim Drawers, Columns, France, c.1920, 32 x 41 In.	1046.00
Commode, Yellow, Painted Flowers, 4 Drawers, Venice, Italy, 37 x 45 In.	366.00
Counter, Pastry, Marble, Butcher Insets, 2 Drawers, Grain Painted Panels, 1800s, 33 x 77 In..	1320.00
Cradle, Acadian, Cypress, Carved, Uprights, Spindle Sides, Mesh Bottom, Rockers, 33 x 40 In.	615.00
Cradle, Arts & Crafts, Wood, Slats, A Frame Sides, 50 x 24 In.	390.00
Cradle, Bentwood, 21 Slats, Boat Shape, Floor Stand, Iron Wheels, c.1850, 30 x 49 In.	316.00
Cradle, Bentwood, Canoe Shape, Geometric Design, Iron Wheels, 1800s, 24 x 45 In.............	300.00
Cradle, Bentwood, Canoe-Shaped, Geometric, Suspended, 1890s, 24 x 45 In................	300.00
Cradle, Carved, Painted, Christmas Tree, Animals, Flowers, Bird, 1900s, 12 x 22 In..................	1400.00
Cradle, Cherry, Dovetail, Cutout Designs, 20 x 40 In...	132.00

F

Cradle, Cherry, Heart Cutouts, Pa., c.1810, 22 ½ x 40 ½ In.	119.00
Cradle, Pine, Painted, Rocking, Turned Posts, Pa., 1800s	61.00
Cradle, Pine, Rectangular Case, Arched, 2 Rockers, 36 In.	310.00
Cradle, Walnut, Cutout Headboard & Footboard, Cheese Cutter Rockers, c.1800, 23 x 30 x 43 In.	136.00
Cradle, Walnut, Shaped Ends, Cast Iron Rocking Mechanism, Foot Pedal, 40 x 39 In.	119.00
Cradle, Windsor, Rails, Pa., c.1800	3792.00
Credenza, Arne Vodder, Danish Modern, Teak, Sliding Doors, Shelves, Drawers, c.1958, 30 x 72 In.	1722.00
Credenza, Burl, 4 Drawers, 4 Doors, Splayed Legs, Italy, c.1950	4800.00
Credenza, Danish Modern, Oak, Sliding Doors, 44 x 71 In.	380.00
Credenza, Faux Marble Top, Painted, Flowers, 2 Doors, Columns, Italy, 1800s, 44 x 53 In.	2390.00
Credenza, G. Nakashima, Cherry, Burlap Lined Doors, c.1970, 32 x 84 In.	11353.00
Credenza, Marble Top, Applied Metal Maidens, 2 Doors, Boule Inlay, Red Lacquer, 44 x 54 In.	316.00
Credenza, Rectangular, 4 Drawers, Sliding Doors, Tapered Feet, Denmark, c.1960, 31 x 95 In.	1063.00
Credenza, Regency Style, Mahogany, Figured Cabinet Doors, Open Shelves, c.1900, 31 x 83 In..	307.00
Credenza, Regency, Bird's-Eye Maple, Mirrored, Marble Top, Brass Columns, England, 50 x 82 In.	2300.00
Credenza, Renaissance Revival, Walnut, Bird's-Eye Maple, Mirror, c.1880, 98 x 47 In. ...*illus*	5750.00
Credenza, Teak, 2 Tambour Doors, Fitted Interior, Henrik Worts, c.1960, 36 x 63 In.	823.00
Credenza, Victorian, Walnut, Maple, Gilt Metal, D-Shape Top, Convex Doors, c.1870, 43 x 68 In.	3750.00
Credenza, Walnut, Relief Molded Plaques, Putti, Maidens, Allen Bros., 43 x 53 In.	3835.00
Crib, Mahogany, Sleigh Bed, Curved Crest Rail, Spindles, Casters, 1800s, 22 x 42 In.	575.00
Crib, Maple, Spindled, Finials, Casters, c.1850, 28 x 18 ½ x 38 ½ In.	56.00
Cupboard, 2 Sections, Oak, Pewter, Frieze Pediment, 3 Open Shelves, 5 Drawers, Hooks, 84 x 61 In.	2015.00
Cupboard, 3 Drawers, 2 Doors, Grain Paint, c.1840, 48 ½ x 41 ¾ In.	304.00
Cupboard, 4-Panel Door, Shaped Apron, Block Feet, American, 1800s, 49 x 40 In.	413.00
Cupboard, Baroque, Walnut, Shelves, Pilasters, Drawers, Squat Legs, Bun Feet, 1700s, 90 x 36 In.	1067.00
Cupboard, Base, Pine, 3 Drawers, 2 Doors, Red, Jacob Blatt Attr., Pa., c.1845, 35 x 44 In.	3318.00
Cupboard, Blue Paint, Open Top Shelf, Serpentine Sides, Lower Plank Door, 60 x 42 In.	456.00
Cupboard, Bonnetiere, Louis XIII Style, Walnut, Door, Carved Design, Block Feet, 79 x 37 In.	900.00
Cupboard, Bonnetiere, Louis XV Style, Oak, Shaped Panel Door, 71 x 31 In.	580.00
Cupboard, Bonnetiere, Louis XV, Walnut, Stepped Cornice, Panel Door, Apron, 1700s, 81 x 45 In.	657.00
Cupboard, Bonnetiere, Walnut, Elm, Paneled, Carved Rosette, Molded Frame, 1700s, 73 x 31 In.	1159.00
Cupboard, Book Press, Mixed Wood, 2 Glass Doors, 2 Paneled Doors, Virginia, c.1825, 85 x 41 In.	4012.00
Cupboard, Cherry, Green, White, Raised Panel Doors, Shelf, Shaped Skirt, c.1835, 85 x 40 In.	646.00
Cupboard, Cherry, Pine, Step Back, 4 Doors, 2 Sections, Block Feet, c.1850, 64 x 40 In.	4406.00
Cupboard, Cherry, Poplar, Glass Doors, Drawers, Panel Doors, Ohio, c.1850, 84 x 50 In. *illus*	2233.00
Cupboard, Chestnut, Upper Panel Doors, Open Shelf, 3 Low Doors, Drawer, Pa., c.1870, 63 x 42 In.	207.00
Cupboard, Chimney, Pine, Paneled Door, 5 Shelves, c.1830, 54 x 20 In.	823.00
Cupboard, Chimney, Pine, Raised Panel Doors, 1800s, 79 x 28 In.	940.00
Cupboard, Chimney, Red, Yellow, Blue, 90 x 28 In.	7703.00
Cupboard, Chimney, Walnut, Poplar, Cornice, Paneled Doors, Iron, Brass Latches, 85 x 17 In.	1410.00
Cupboard, Chinoiserie, Pine, Painted, 2 Doors, Gilt Relief Carvings, 1800s, 20 x 28 In.	89.00
Cupboard, Chippendale Style, Maple, Step Back, Glass Panel Doors, Pie Shelf, c.1955, 86 x 63 In.	5993.00
Cupboard, Contemporary, Neoclassical Style, Black Lacquered Cabinet, Ormolu, Gilt, 64 x 52 In.	3227.00
Cupboard, Corner, 2 Glass Doors Over 2 Paneled Doors, String Inlay, Pa., 81 x 47 In.	345.00
Cupboard, Corner, 2 Glass Paned Doors, 2 Low Panel Doors, Arched Apron, c.1820, 91 x 51 In.	2645.00
Cupboard, Corner, 2 Sections, Arched Doors, Shelves, 2 Lower Doors, 1700s, 89 x 42 In.	1410.00
Cupboard, Corner, 4 Raised Panel Doors, Green Paint, c.1800, 90 x 47 In.	985.00
Cupboard, Corner, 8-Pane Door, Paneled Door, 3 Butterfly Shape Shelves, Pa., 85 In. ..*illus*	1534.00
Cupboard, Corner, Blue Paint, 2 8-Pane Doors, 2 Lower Doors, 85 x 53 In. ...*illus*	6490.00
Cupboard, Corner, Cherry, 2 Glass Doors, Shelves, Scalloped Skirt, c.1830, 86 x 54	770.00
Cupboard, Corner, Cherry, 12-Pane Upper Door, 2-Door Panel Base, Bracket Feet, 86 In.	2185.00
Cupboard, Corner, Cherry, 12 Panes, Paneled Doors, Molded Cornice, c.1835, 90 x 43 In. ..*illus*	3290.00
Cupboard, Corner, Cherry, Poplar, 2 Paneled Glass Doors, Cutout Feet, c.1835, 88 x 22 In.	823.00
Cupboard, Corner, Chippendale, Chinoiserie, Hanging, Painted Door, c.1800, 43 x 32 In.	1003.00
Cupboard, Corner, Chippendale, Mixed Wood, 4 Paneled Doors, 81 x 47 In.	472.00
Cupboard, Corner, Chippendale, Pine, 2 Glass Doors, Drawer, Southern, 1700s, 80 x 46 In.	295.00
Cupboard, Corner, Chippendale, Stepped Cornice, Panel Doors, c.1790, 76 x 36 In.	3738.00
Cupboard, Corner, Chippendale, Walnut, Glass Doors, Paneled Doors, c.1790, 78 x 40 In.	6600.00
Cupboard, Corner, Federal, 12-Pane Door, Lower Door, 2 Sections, 83 x 48 In. ...*illus*	767.00
Cupboard, Corner, Federal, Cherry, 4 Paneled Doors, Carved Apron, 1800s, 90 x 48 In.	7080.00
Cupboard, Corner, Federal, Cherry, 9-Pane Door, Drawers, 2 Sections, Pa., 86 x 51 In. ...*illus*	1121.00
Cupboard, Corner, Federal, Cherry, Glass Door, Lower Paneled Door, c.1820, 84 x 41 In.	3318.00
Cupboard, Corner, Federal, Cherry, Glazed Door, Shelves, c.1800, 85 x 43 In.	2700.00
Cupboard, Corner, Federal, Mahogany, Swan Pediment, Arched Glass Door, Drawer, 95 x 40 In.	5557.00
Cupboard, Corner, Federal, Walnut, Broken Arch, Star, Fan, Inlay, Tennessee, 92 x 50 In. ...*illus*	42480.00
Cupboard, Corner, French Provincial, Mullioned Door, Open Shelf, c.1890, 85 x 33 In.	185.00

Furniture, Cupboard, Corner, Cherry,
12 Panes, Paneled Doors, Molded
Cornice, c.1835, 90 x 43 In.
$3290.00

Garth's Auctions, Inc.

Furniture, Cupboard, Corner, Federal,
12-Pane Door, Lower Door, 2 Sections,
83 x 48 In.
$767.00

Conestoga Auction Co., Inc.

Furniture, Cupboard, Corner, Federal,
Cherry, 9-Pane Door, Drawers, 2 Sections,
Pa., 86 x 51 In.
$1121.00

Conestoga Auction Co., Inc.

FURNITURE

Furniture, Cupboard, Corner, Federal, Walnut, Broken Arch, Star, Fan, Inlay, Tennessee, 92 x 50 In.
$42480.00

Brunk Auctions

Furniture, Cupboard, Corner, Mahogany, Painted Interior, Shelves, c.1900, 81 x 42 ½ In.
$1778.00

Skinner, Inc.

Furniture, Cupboard, Corner, Poplar, 9-Pane Door, 1 Drawer & 2 False, Glass Pulls, c.1850, 83 x 44 In.
$7638.00

Garth's Auctions, Inc.

Cupboard, Corner, French Provincial, Pine, Serpentine Crest, Doors, Pillars, c.1790, 85 x 33 In.	575.00
Cupboard, Corner, George III, Mahogany, c.1750, 52 x 31 In.	830.00
Cupboard, Corner, Glass Door Over 2 Panel Doors, Paint Decorated, c.1835, 82 x 44 In.	8505.00
Cupboard, Corner, Glass Door, Drawer, Lower Paneled Door, Scalloped, 1800s, 79 x 32 In.	4266.00
Cupboard, Corner, Green Paint, Upper Glass Door, Lower Door, Carved, 1800s, 85 x 51 In.	1208.00
Cupboard, Corner, Hanging, Molded Frieze, Paneled Cupboard Door, Blue Interior, 30 x 24 In.	384.00
Cupboard, Corner, Hanging, Oak, Dentil Molded Cornice, Paneled Door, 1800s, 45 x 36 In.	472.00
Cupboard, Corner, Hanging, Pine, Gray Green Paint, Door, Molding, 48 x 16 In.	294.00
Cupboard, Corner, Hanging, Walnut, Paneled Door Front, England, 1700s, 37 x 17 In.	173.00
Cupboard, Corner, Mahogany, 2 Doors, Cabriole Legs, Hairy Paw Feet, c.1800, 60 ½ x 26 In.	550.00
Cupboard, Corner, Mahogany, Broken-Arch Pediment, 2 Glass Doors, 83 x 44 In.	345.00
Cupboard, Corner, Mahogany, Painted Interior, Shelves, c.1900, 81 x 42 ½ In. *illus*	1778.00
Cupboard, Corner, Mahogany, Pineapple Finials, Glass Mullioned Door, Drawers, c.1850, 95 x 46 In.	1075.00
Cupboard, Corner, Molded Cornice, Scalloped, 2 Glass Doors, Daniel Pabst, c.1875, 92 x 63 In.	1900.00
Cupboard, Corner, Neoclassical, Maple, Door, Maiden, Scroll, 1800s, 39 x 36 In.	1107.00
Cupboard, Corner, Oak, Paneled Door, England, 1800s, 38 x 31 In.	413.00
Cupboard, Corner, Overhanging Cornice, Inlaid Frieze Panel, Panel Door, 1800s, 46 x 35 In.	708.00
Cupboard, Corner, Panel Doors, Gray Paint, 1800s, 76 x 40 In.	712.00
Cupboard, Corner, Pine, 2 Sections, Upper Glass Door, Lower Door, Bracket Feet, 1800s, 83 x 36 In.	516.00
Cupboard, Corner, Pine, 2 Shelves, Lower Paneled Door, Early 1800s, 72 In.	575.00
Cupboard, Corner, Pine, 6-Panel Glazed Door, 2 Shelves, c.1830, 83 x 25 In.	1035.00
Cupboard, Corner, Pine, Barrel Back, 3 Shaped Shelves, Raised Panel Doors, Painted, 79 x 42 In.	2585.00
Cupboard, Corner, Pine, Cherry, Upper Paned Doors, Lower Panel Doors, Pa., 1800s, 7 x 45 In.	835.00
Cupboard, Corner, Pine, Glass Door Over Paneled Door, Red, Black Stipple, Pa., c.1835, 82 x 44 In.	8505.00
Cupboard, Corner, Pine, Green Paint, Lower Door, Upper Open Shelves, 1800s, 73 x 43 In.	356.00
Cupboard, Corner, Pine, Molded Cornice, 12-Pane Door, Recessed Panels, 1800s, 78 x 44 In.	500.00
Cupboard, Corner, Pine, Molded, Open Shelves, Panel Door, 37 x 21 In.	690.00
Cupboard, Corner, Pine, Paint, Upper & Lower Panel Door, 1800s, 76 x 38 In.	652.00
Cupboard, Corner, Pine, Paneled Doors, Flat Bracket Base, Early 1800s, 82 x 25 In.	978.00
Cupboard, Corner, Pine, Reeded Cornice, Arched Frieze, Shelves, Door, c.1800, 7 Ft. 9 In.	920.00
Cupboard, Corner, Poplar, 9-Pane Door, 1 Drawer & 2 False, Glass Pulls, c.1850, 83 x 44 In. *illus*	7638.00
Cupboard, Corner, Poplar, 12-Pane Glass Door, 2 Lower Paneled Doors, Apron, c.1850, 74 x 43 In.	1880.00
Cupboard, Corner, Poplar, 2 Scalloped Paned Doors, 3 Drawers, Columns, 1800s, 85 x 44 In.	2075.00
Cupboard, Corner, Poplar, Stained, Glass Door, Reeded Panel Doors, 101 x 44 In.	972.00
Cupboard, Corner, Red Paint, Glass Panel Door, 2 Lower Doors, Pa., 1800s, 82 x 45 In.	1067.00
Cupboard, Corner, Shaker, Brown Paint, 4 Shelves, Door, c.1800, 86 x 50 In.	173.00
Cupboard, Corner, Shaped Shelves, Lower Door, Blue Paint, England, 1780s, 43 x 22 In.	1145.00
Cupboard, Corner, Softwood, Blind Door, Molded Cornice, Arched Top, Paneled Doors, 82 x 66 In.	354.00
Cupboard, Corner, Softwood, Grain Painted, Dovetailed Drawers, Pa., 93 x 55 In. *illus*	5085.00
Cupboard, Corner, Victorian, Painted Flowers, 3 Shelves, 2 Doors, Scalloped, 1800s, 30 x 11 In.	227.00
Cupboard, Corner, Walnut, 2 Sections, Glass Upper Doors, Drawer, Low Doors, 53 x 82 In.	593.00
Cupboard, Corner, Walnut, 4 Paneled Doors, Shaped Skirt, Block Feet, 1800s, 80 x 44 In.	2040.00
Cupboard, Corner, Walnut, Arched Panel Doors Over 2 Doors, Bracket Feet, Pa., 82 ¼ In. *illus*	1645.00
Cupboard, Corner, Walnut, Inlay, Finials, Arched Glass Doors, Panel Doors, c.1800, 105 x 56 In.	18600.00
Cupboard, Corner, Walnut, Molded Cornice, 2 Glass Doors, Drawer, 2 Lower Doors, 1800s, 84 x 43 In.	1080.00
Cupboard, Corner, Walnut, Molded Cornice, 2 Glass Doors, Shaped Skirt, c.1820, 84 x 50 In.	940.00
Cupboard, Corner, Walnut, Poplar, Inlaid, 4-Panel Doors, Vines, 74 x 39 In.	999.00
Cupboard, Corner, Walnut, Yellow Pine, 2 Glass Doors, 2 Lower Doors, 1800s, 80 x 56 In.	1778.00
Cupboard, Corner, White Paint, 2 Upper & Lower Paneled Doors, Drawer, 1800s, 85 x 35 In.	1495.00
Cupboard, Corner, Yellow Pine, Paneled Doors, Molded Cornice & Base, c.1795, 38 x 21 In. *illus*	1003.00
Cupboard, Court, Flat Top, 3 Paneled Doors, Leaf Carved, 1700s, 67 x 63 In.	325.00
Cupboard, Court, Paneled Doors, Interior Shelves, Scroll Supports, 1790s, 70 x 68 In.	4375.00
Cupboard, Court, Walnut, Marble Top, 2 Sections, Glass Front, Carved Crest, France, 97 x 55 In.	1265.00
Cupboard, Curly Maple, Doors, Drawers, Pie Shelf, Bracket Feet, 41 x 30 In.	367.00
Cupboard, Dutch, Pine, Glass Doors, Open Shelf, 2 Drawers, 2 Paneled Doors, c.1910, 85 x 49 In.	772.00
Cupboard, Dutch, Poplar, Upper Glass Doors, Shelf, 2 Drawers, Doors, Pa., 1800s, 87 x 54 In.	2750.00
Cupboard, Faux Mahogany, Step Back, 2 Sections, Paneled Doors, Drawers, c.1850, 86 x 50 In.	4700.00
Cupboard, Federal, Softwood, Molded Cornice, 6-Pane Upper Doors, 87 x 56 In.	3068.00
Cupboard, Federal, Walnut, Step Back, Glass Doors, Drawers, Panel Doors, c.1815, 86 x 64 In.	5500.00
Cupboard, French Provincial, Oak, Frieze Carved, 2 Arched Glass Doors, c.1890, 85 x 50 In.	1150.00
Cupboard, French Provincial, Oak, Molded Top, 4 Shelves, 2 Drawers, 2 Paneled Doors, 84 In.	1610.00
Cupboard, French Provincial, Walnut, Arched Cornice, Upper, Paneled Doors, 1700s, 95 x 38 In.	3107.00
Cupboard, French Provincial, White Paint, Step Back, 2 Arched Glass Doors, 90 x 51 In.	472.00
Cupboard, George III, Mahogany, Glass Upper Doors, Drawer, 2 Paneled Doors, c.1770, 86 x 39 In.	948.00
Cupboard, Hanging, Chippendale, Oak, Glass Door, Pilasters, England, c.1800, 37 x 31 In.	720.00
Cupboard, Hanging, Chippendale, Tiger Maple, Arched Glass Door, Drawer, Pa., c.1765, 32 x 28 In.	4000.00

Cupboard, Hanging, Corner, Chestnut, Ogee, Cornice, Door, Shelves, 52 x 36 In.	245.00
Cupboard, Hanging, Curly Maple, Walnut, Poplar, Dovetailed Drawer, Panel, 1800s, 28 x 12 In.	392.00
Cupboard, Hanging, Ecclesiastical, Oak, Dentillated Cornice, Paneled Door, England, 30 x 25 In.	215.00
Cupboard, Hanging, Georgian, Oak, Arched Panel, c.1750, 42 ½ x 28 In.	652.00
Cupboard, Hanging, Grain Painted, 2 Paneled Doors, Fitted Interior, 22 x 19 In.	356.00
Cupboard, Hanging, Mixed Wood, Blind Doors, Shelf, Red Over Blue Paint, c.1810, 21 x 36 In.	499.00
Cupboard, Hanging, Mixed Wood, Glass Door, Beveled Mullions, 26 x 23 In.	150.00
Cupboard, Hanging, Pierced Crest, Glass Door, Raised Panel, Brown, Blue, Paint, 34 x 19 In.	441.00
Cupboard, Hanging, Pine, Chestnut, Paneled Door, Painted, 21 x 16 In.	705.00
Cupboard, Hanging, Pine, Door, Blue Gray Paint, c.1870, 30 x 26 In.	795.00
Cupboard, Hanging, Pine, Door, Open Shelf, 1800s, 36 x 25 In.	182.00
Cupboard, Hanging, Pine, Picture Frame Molding, Double Doors, Brown Paint, 20 x 12 In.	181.00
Cupboard, Hanging, Red Paint, Drawers, Pigeonholes, 36 x 37 In.	705.00
Cupboard, Hanging, Walnut, Red Paint, Dovetailed Case, Applied Molding, Door, 24 x 20 In.	1175.00
Cupboard, Hanging, Wood, Painted, Stepped Crest, Paneled Door, Drawer, Pa., c.1900, 39 x 17 In.	89.00
Cupboard, Hepplewhite, Mixed Wood, Glass Doors, Shelf, 4 Drawers, c.1800, 77 x 40 In.	830.00
Cupboard, Jackson Press, Glass Doors, Drawers Over Doors, 1800s, 77 x 44 In.	767.00
Cupboard, Jelly, Blue Paint, Yellow Stencil, 2 Doors, 2 Drawers, Pa., 42 x 42 In.	1094.00
Cupboard, Jelly, Mixed Wood, Drawer, Slides, 2 Fluted Panel Doors, 45 x 47 In.	2185.00
Cupboard, Jelly, Oak, Grained, 2 Frieze Drawers, 2 Paneled Doors, 46 x 37 In.	234.00
Cupboard, Jelly, Pine, 1 Door, 3 Shelves, Bracket Base, American, 64 x 27 In.	403.00
Cupboard, Jelly, Pine, Carved Backsplash, 2 Drawers, 2 Doors, Stippled, Pa., c.1850, 62 x 42 In.	563.00
Cupboard, Jelly, Pine, Faux Bird's-Eye Maple, Drawer Over 2 Paneled Doors, 43 x 43 In.	308.00
Cupboard, Jelly, Pumpkin Pine, Plank Top, 2 Paneled Doors, Mushroom Knobs, 5 Shelves	345.00
Cupboard, Jelly, Shaped Oak Gallery, Drawers, Paneled Doors, 46 x 41 In.	478.00
Cupboard, Jelly, Softwood, Backsplash, Drawer, 2 Paneled Doors, Cutout Feet, c.1850, 48 x 43 In.	590.00
Cupboard, Jelly, Softwood, Drawer, Paneled Doors, Shelves, Backsplash, c.1850, 48 x 43 In. *illus*	590.00
Cupboard, Jelly, Softwood, Grain Painted, Backsplash, Drawers, Paneled Doors, 53 x 43 In.	384.00
Cupboard, Jelly, Walnut, Green Paint, Dovetailed Drawers, Doors, Shelves, 48 x 42 In. ...*illus*	767.00
Cupboard, Kitchen, Pine, Green Paint, Reeded Square Cornice, 2-Panel Doors, 1800s, 62 x 49 In.	273.00
Cupboard, Kitchen, Pine, White Paint, Shaped Crest, 2-Panel Doors, 2 Drawers, 1800s, 75 x 42 In.	207.00
Cupboard, Louis XV Style, Oak, Upper Shelf, Drawer, 2 Paneled Doors, 50 x 31 x 15 In.	510.00
Cupboard, Louis XV, Oak, Glass & Panel Door, Carved, 73 x 29 In.	793.00
Cupboard, Louis XV, Walnut, Drawer, Door, Paneled, 30 x 26	488.00
Cupboard, Louis XV, Walnut, Marble Top, Burled Insets, Drawer, Door, Carved, 36 x 25 In.	366.00
Cupboard, Mahogany, Inlay, Molded Cornice, Mullioned Glass Doors, Shelves, 91 x 74 In.	2489.00
Cupboard, Mahogany, Step Back, 2 Paneled Doors, 8 Low Drawers, 60 x 28 ½ In.	450.00
Cupboard, Mahogany, Upper, Lower Doors, Gadrooned Oval, 1800s, 84 x 49 In.	1920.00
Cupboard, Maple, Yellow Paint, 2 Sections, Doors, 2 Drawers, Block Feet, c.1830, 81 x 49 In.	2252.00
Cupboard, Milk, Softwood, Plank Top, Double Paneled Door, Yellow, 43 x 38 In.	260.00
Cupboard, Milk, Softwood, Yellow Paint, Plank Top, Paneled Door, Cutout Feet, c.1850, 43 x 38 In.	2596.00
Cupboard, Mixed Wood, Double Panel Door, Green, 19th Century, 67 x 45 x 14 In.	1410.00
Cupboard, Oak, 2 Sections, Frieze Pediment, 2 Shelves, 2 Drawers, Apron, 1800s, 66 x 48 In.	1541.00
Cupboard, Oak, 2 Sections, Lower Paneled Doors, Arched Crest, 2 Glass Doors, c.1900, 79 x 54 In.	805.00
Cupboard, Oak, Carved Pediment, 2 Glass Doors, 2 Drawers, 2 Paneled Doors, 71 ½ x 38 In.	288.00
Cupboard, Oak, Carved, Inlay, Landscape Painted Doors, Drop Front, Drawer, 56 x 36 In.	460.00
Cupboard, Oak, Carved, Step Back, Frieze, Drawer, Paneled Door, Columns, c.1890	748.00
Cupboard, Oak, Dentil Molded Cornice, 2 Open Shelves, 3 Drawers, 2 Doors, 76 x 65 In.	2370.00
Cupboard, Pine, Blue Paint, 2 Paneled Doors, Pa., 1800s, 55 x 42 In.	830.00
Cupboard, Pine, Blue Paint, Glass Doors, Drawer, Panel Doors, England, c.1850, 75 x 41 In.	1220.00
Cupboard, Pine, Blue Paint, Hinged Door, Bracket Feet, 1800s, 54 x 31 In.	207.00
Cupboard, Pine, Blue Paint, Open Top Shelves, 2 Drawers, 2 Lower Doors, Pa., c.1790, 78 x 56 In.	3318.00
Cupboard, Pine, Blue Wash Over White Paint, Board & Batten Door, Peaked Crest, 69 x 35 In.	646.00
Cupboard, Pine, Door, Iron Hinges, White Paint, Bootjack Cutout Base, 2 Shelves, c.1810, 74 x 36 In.	177.00
Cupboard, Pine, Drawer, Door, Fluted Side Uprights, Block Feet, 29 x 20 In., Pair	276.00
Cupboard, Pine, Elm, 4 Doors, Scrolled Ends Top, Tabletop, Chinese, 1900s, 24 x 29 In.	59.00
Cupboard, Pine, Flared Cornice, Plate Racks, 3 Drawers, 2 Doors, 1700s, 79 x 58 In.	1464.00
Cupboard, Pine, Flat Top, Stenciled Panel Doors, Drawers, Painted, 94 x 48 In.	1298.00
Cupboard, Pine, Gray Paint, Drop Front, Upper Shelf, Slots, Pigeonholes, 1800s, 47 x 36 In.	499.00
Cupboard, Pine, Green Paint, Scalloped Base, c.1820, 65 x 48 In.	1074.00
Cupboard, Pine, Lacquered, 2 Doors, Shaped Skirt, Block Feet, Chinese, 72 x 36 In.	243.00
Cupboard, Pine, Painted, 2 Doors, 6 Lower Drawers, Stepped Cornice, 1700s, 75 x 49 In.	889.00
Cupboard, Pine, Painted, 2 Sections, Shelf, Cabinet Doors, 2 Drawers, 78 x 47 In.	313.00
Cupboard, Pine, Painted, Pierced Gallery, Shelves, Drawer, Doors, c.1900, 38 x 20 In.	264.00
Cupboard, Pine, Painted, Red, Blue, Step Back, 6-Pane Doors, 3 Drawers, 2 Doors, 85 In.	6900.00
Cupboard, Pine, Plank Door, Green Paint, Tobacco Leaf Design, Bootjack Ends, 1800s	920.00

Furniture, Cupboard, Corner, Softwood, Grain Painted, Dovetailed Drawers, Pa., 93 x 55 In.
$5085.00

Conestoga Auction Co., Inc.

Furniture, Cupboard, Corner, Walnut, Arched Panel Doors Over 2 Doors, Bracket Feet, Pa., 82 ¼ In.
$1645.00

Cowan's Auctions

Furniture, Cupboard, Corner, Yellow Pine, Paneled Doors, Molded Cornice & Base, c.1795, 38 x 21 In.
$1003.00

Brunk Auctions

FURNITURE

Furniture, Cupboard, Jelly, Softwood, Drawer, Paneled Doors, Shelves, Backsplash, c.1850, 48 x 43 In.
$590.00

Conestoga Auction Co., Inc.

Furniture, Cupboard, Jelly, Walnut, Green Paint, Dovetailed Drawers, Doors, Shelves, 48 x 42 In.
$767.00

Brunk Auctions

Furniture, Cupboard, Pine, Step Back, Glass Doors, Drawers, 2 Paneled Doors, Ohio, 1800s, 92 In.
$2585.00

Cowan's Auctions

264

Cupboard, Pine, Poplar, Painted, Canted Top, Open Shelves, Cutout Feet, 81 x 52 In.	1528.00
Cupboard, Pine, Poplar, Yellow, Painted, 2 Sections, Doors, Drawers, 85 x 53 In.	1410.00
Cupboard, Pine, Red Paint, Breadboard Doors, Overhanging Top, Ohio, 1800s, 40 x 36 In.	499.00
Cupboard, Pine, Red Paint, Molded Cornice, Shelves, Drawer, 4 Doors, Late 1700s, 88 x 76 In.	11850.00
Cupboard, Pine, Red Paint, Step Back, 3 Shelves, Door, Iron Hinges, Trestle Feet, 1700s, 67 x 36 In.	3555.00
Cupboard, Pine, Salmon Grain Paint, Raised Panel Doors, c.1820, 68 x 46 In.	4503.00
Cupboard, Pine, Step Back, Canted Upper Shelves, 26 x 18 In.	2370.00
Cupboard, Pine, Step Back, Glass Doors, Drawers, 2 Paneled Doors, Ohio, 1800s, 92 In. *illus*	2585.00
Cupboard, Pine, Step Back, Molded Crown, Shelves, Recessed Panel Doors, 67 x 53 In.	299.00
Cupboard, Pine, Step Back, Open Shelves, 2 Doors, 37 x 22 In.	633.00
Cupboard, Pine, Yellow Paint, 2 Doors, 2 Circle Design, Stepped Crest, 1800s, 80 x 50 In.	334.00
Cupboard, Plum Pudding Mahogany, 16 Drop Front Doors, France, c.1870, 74 x 47 In.	1845.00
Cupboard, Poplar, Brown Paint, 2 Paneled Doors, Shelves, Shoe Feet, c.1850, 74 x 42 In.	230.00
Cupboard, Poplar, Cutout Feet, Paneled Doors, 3 Drawers, Pie Shelf, c.1810, 95 x 60 In.	2233.00
Cupboard, Poplar, Green Over Brown Paint, Step Back, Open Shelves, Doors, 75 x 42 In.	2233.00
Cupboard, Poplar, Shaped Gallery, 2 Bowed Drawers, 2 Doors, Turned Feet, c.1850, 51 x 43 In.	558.00
Cupboard, Poplar, Shaped Sides, Crest, Open Shelves, 3 Drawers, 2 Doors, 50 x 83 In.	237.00
Cupboard, Poplar, Step Back, Yellow Paint, Board & Batten Doors, Pie Shelf, 85 x 50 In.	1528.00
Cupboard, Regency Style, Mahogany, Dentil Molded Cornice, Geometric Door, 61 x 23 In.	266.00
Cupboard, Shaker, Pine, 4 Paneled Doors, Bracket Feet, 1800s, 67 x 35 In.	1058.00
Cupboard, Shaker, Pine, Yellow Paint, 2 Doors, 7 Drawers, c.1835, 72 x 33 In.	28910.00
Cupboard, Softwood, Grain Painted, Molded Cornice, Plank Door, Shelves, 35 x 24 In.	384.00
Cupboard, Softwood, Plank Top, Pie Board Ends, Drawer, Paneled Doors, c.1850, 45 x 43 In.	590.00
Cupboard, Softwood, Step Back, Molded Cornice, Glass Doors, Drawers, Cutout Feet, 80 x 52 In.	805.00
Cupboard, Tabletop, Grain Painted, Triangular Pediment, 2 Doors, 1800s, 28 x 17 In.	563.00
Cupboard, Victorian, Oak, 3 Upper Shelves, Iron Hooks, 3 Drawers, Base Shelf, 83 x 69 In.	2808.00
Cupboard, Victorian, Panel Door, 4 Painted Flower Sprays, 1800s, 55 x 23 In.	230.00
Cupboard, Walnut, Arched Panel Doors, Pie Shelf, 3 Drawers, 2 Doors, c.1780, 89 x 56 In.	10665.00
Cupboard, Walnut, Door, Carved Round Flower, Bracket Feet, 29 x 29 In.	480.00
Cupboard, Walnut, Molded Cornice, 2 Doors, Recessed Panels, Shelves, c.1835, 20 x 17 In.	800.00
Cupboard, Walnut, Paneled Door, Applied Molding, Bun Feet, c.1890, 72 x 33 In.	127.00
Cupboard, Walnut, Raised Panel Doors, Heart, Rattail Hinges, Pa., c.1890, 47 x 35 In.	2252.00
Cupboard, Walnut, Step Back, 2 Sections, Angled Cornice, Panel Doors, Shelves, 81 x 17 In.	2760.00
Cupboard, Walnut, Step Back, 6-Pane Doors, 3-Panel Lower Section, 80 x 64 In.	1928.00
Cupboard, Walnut, Step Back, 2 Arch Panel Doors, Drawers, Apron, 1800s, 88 x 55 In.	1003.00
Cupboard, Walnut, Step Back, Paneled Glass Doors, 2 Drawers, Cutout Feet, c.1850, 83 x 56 In.	2115.00
Cupboard, White Paint, Open Shelves, Flower Carved, Finials, 2 Doors, 2 Drawers, 81 x 52 In.	549.00
Cupboard, William III, Oak, Court Style, Paneled Cupboard Doors, 64 x 61 In.	1375.00
Cupboard, Wood, Black, Red Paint, Stenciled, Step Back, Glazed Doors, Drawers, c.1895, 86 x 59 In.	7050.00
Cupboard, Wood, Blue Paint, Step Back, 17 Drawers, Knobs, New England, c.1850, 68 x 33 In. *illus*	7762.00
Cupboard, Wood, Blue Paint, Step Back, Open Shelves, Door, Bootjack Feet, 1800s, 73 x 44 In.	770.00
Cupboard, Wood, Carved Crest, Painted Flower Panels, Blue, Gold, Austria, 1850s, 73 x 43 In.	2450.00
Cupboard, Wood, Grain Painted, Open Hooded Top, Shelves, Demilune Cutouts, c.1890, 81 x 39 In.	2070.00
Cupboard, Wood, Painted, Step Back, 2 Glazed Doors, 2 Drawers, Stepped Base, c.1840, 48 x 26 In.	206.00
Cupboard, Wood, Paneled Doors, Board Top, White Paint, 1800s, 85 x 51 In.	1180.00
Cupboard, Wood, Pediment, Painted, Stag Hunt, Windmill, 2 Paneled Doors, 1800s, 79 x 53 In.	3851.00
Cupboard, Yellow Pine, Gallery, Crock Shelf, Paneled Doors, 54 x 51 In.	690.00
Cupboard, Yellow Pine, Peaked Cornice, Half Moon Cutouts, Slab Doors, 1800s, 84 x 37 In.	978.00
Cupboard, Yellow Pine, Scalloped Top, Open Shelves, 2 Doors, North Carolina, c.1805, 80 x 48 In.	1265.00
Daybed, Adjustable, Leather, Enameled Metal, Swiss, 33 x 79 In.	620.00
Daybed, Arts & Crafts, Slanted Headrest Supports, Leather, Paper Label, J.M. Young, 29 x 78 In.	1140.00
Daybed, Charles X, Mahogany, Sleigh Shape, Bracket Feet, 57 x 26 In.	510.00
Daybed, Empire, Oak, Sleigh Shape, Rounded Side Rails, France, c.1860, 41 x 65 In.	923.00
Daybed, Fruitwood, Flower Carvings, Upholstered, Cabriole Feet, 34 x 79 In.	415.00
Daybed, G. Jensen, Oak, Cushion, Headboard Curve, 1967, 78 x 36 x 20 In.	1020.00
Daybed, G. Stickley, Vertical Slatted Ends, Leather Seat, Red Decal, 84 x 36 In.	1920.00
Daybed, George III Style, Mahogany, Bench Design, Chair Back Ends, 35 x 97 In.	431.00
Daybed, L. & J.G. Stickley, Slatted, Leather Spring Seat, Pillow, 28 x 80 In.	2232.00
Daybed, Louis Philippe, Mahogany, Carved, Scrolled Head & Footboard, Paneled, 43 x 75 In.	1434.00
Daybed, Louis XV Style, Needlepoint Upholstery, Signed Jansen, c.1900, 31 x 86 In.	800.00
Daybed, Low Square Back, 1 Arm, Wood Tapered Feet, W. Haines, c.1948, 27 x 73 In.	1125.00
Daybed, Meeks, Rosewood, Faceted Baluster Corner Posts, c.1835, 29 x 80 In. *illus*	799.00
Daybed, Meridienne, Rosewood, Continuous Arm, Pierced, Scrolls, Tuthill King, 38 x 40 In.	9440.00
Daybed, Mies Van Der Rohe, Tufted Leather, Bolster Support, Wood, Steel Frame, Knoll, 78 x 15 In.	3000.00
Daybed, Parzinger, Lacquered Wood, Silk, 1940s, 29 x 62 In.	7440.00
Daybed, Richard Stein, Birch, Upholstered, Knoll, 1950s, 25 x 76 In.	682.00

Daybed, Tiger Maple, Scroll Arms, Turned Legs, Beehive Finials, 1850s, 9 ½ In., Pair	585.00
Daybed, Wegner, Brown Leather Platform, 4 Cylindrical Steel Legs, 16 x 75 In..........................	3851.00
Daybed, Wegner, Teak, Cane Back, White Upholstered Seat, c.1956, 27 x 78 In.......................	1593.00
Daybed, Wool, Burl, Chrome Plated Steel, 1930s, 34 x 76 In..	682.00
Desk, 2 Upper Hutch Doors, Stepped Cornice, Drawer, Turned Legs, 61 x 37 In.	367.00
Desk, 3 Drawers, Raised Center, Cylindrical Supports, Baughman, 1953, 30 x 57 In..................	1250.00
Desk, Accountant's, Provincial, Pine, Turned Legs, Stretcher, 60 x 64 In.................................	469.00
Desk, Anglo-Indian, Rosewood, Carved, Shelf, Writing Surface, Trestle Base, c.1860, 48 x 38 In. *illus*	1353.00
Desk, Arched Cornice, Glass Doors, Drop Front, Shaped Skirt, Cabriole Legs, Italy, 90 x 43 In.	1195.00
Desk, Architect's, Chippendale, Mahogany, Hinged Top, 3 Drawers, Pierced Brackets, 31 x 46 In.	1652.00
Desk, Architect's, Wood, Leather Slant Front, 3 Doors, 3 Drawers, France, c.1940, 54 x 55 In...	1230.00
Desk, Art Deco, Mahogany, Central Drawer, 6 Side Drawers, c.1940, 30 x 48 In.......................	2091.00
Desk, Art Deco, Walnut, Rectangular, Leather Inset Top, Paneled Door, 29 x 56 In.	488.00
Desk, Arts & Crafts, Slant Front, Oak, Brass Rail Gallery, Fitted Interior, 3 Drawers, Door, 43 x 33 In.	345.00
Desk, Arts & Crafts, Slant Front, Oak, Slatted Sides, Square Legs, H-Stretcher, 43 x 40 In.........	549.00
Desk, Austro-German, Inset Leather, Mounted On Crossed Antler Base, Drawers, 30 x 48 In. ....*illus*	6518.00
Desk, Baronial Style, Drop Front, Walnut, Plaques, Pillars, c.1900, 45 x 32 In. ....*illus*	861.00
Desk, Bombe, Louis XV Style, Fitted Interior, Parquetry, Bronze Mounts, 1900s, 36 x 36 In. *illus*	295.00
Desk, Borsani, Adjustable Return, Chrome, Wood, Painted Glass, Techno, 1950s, 29 x 99 In. ..	4650.00
Desk, Brass, Iron Trim, Demilune, Glass, Leather Top, 6 Drawers, c.1960, 30 x 70 In.	2223.00
Desk, Bronze, Marquetry, Ebonized, Foldover Writing Flap, Brass Inkwells, 36 x 30 In............	1434.00
Desk, Burl Walnut, Brass Banded, Silver Presentation Shield, Leather Surface, Inkwells, 20 x 10 In.	305.00
Desk, Burl Walnut, Twin Pedestal, 9 Drawers, Egg & Dart Molding, c.1890, 32 x 74 In............	1220.00
Desk, Burl, Marquetry, Slant Front, Fruitwood Veneer Bouquets, Cabriole Legs, 37 x 33 In......	563.00
Desk, Butler's, Campaign, Mahogany, Brass Mounts, 4 Drawers, 36 In....................................	1230.00
Desk, Butler's, Cherry, Paneled Drawer, 2 Doors, Scroll Columns, 43 x 45 In..........................	492.00
Desk, Butler's, Drop Front, Mahogany, Gallery Top, 2 Paneled Doors, Columns, 1800s, 54 x 46 In.	1673.00
Desk, Butler's, Empire, Drop Drawer, 3 Base Drawers, Glass Pulls, 50 x 53 ¾ In.	374.00
Desk, Butler's, Empire, Drop Front, Mahogany, Fitted Interior, 3 Drawers, 1800s, 47 x 47 In. ..	341.00
Desk, Butler's, Federal, Mahogany, Fitted Drawer, Beaded Drawers, Lion's Head Handles, 45 x 48 In.	995.00
Desk, Butler's, Federal, Mahogany, Inlaid, Drawer, Fitted Interior, 3 Lower Drawers, 41 x 10 ½ In.	460.00
Desk, Butler's, Sheraton, Maple, Drop Front, 3 Drawers, Inlaid Corner Fans, 1800s, 46 x 41 In. *illus*	2565.00
Desk, Butler's, Sheraton, Mixed Wood, Drop Front, Doors, Drawers, c.1830, 41 x 72 In.	748.00
Desk, Cabinet, Moore, Walnut, Paneled Door, Pullout Surface, Fitted Interior	11018.00
Desk, California Spanish Revival, Slant Front, Flower Design, Spool Legs, 30 x 26 In...............	1920.00
Desk, Campaign, Anglo-Indian, Teak, Wood, Brass, Kneehole, 1800s, 30 x 35 In.	316.00
Desk, Campaign, Drop Front, Hardwood, 2 Sections, 3 Drawers, Bracket Feet, 1800s, 43 x 40 In.	1076.00
Desk, Campaign, Mahogany, Double Pedestal, Leather Top, Drawers, 1800s, 31 x 55 In...........	956.00
Desk, Campaign, Mahogany, Leather Top, 5 Drawers, England, 1800s, 30 x 42 In.	1180.00
Desk, Campaign, Mahogany, Leather Top, 9 Drawers, Pedestal Supports, 1800s, 31 x 54 In.....	1315.00
Desk, Campaign, Maple, Double Pedestal, Gilt, Leather, Brass Shelves, 1800s, 50 x 52 In.........	1434.00
Desk, Campaign, Pedestal, Mahogany, Brass Bound, 9 Drawers, England, 39 x 53 In..............	1875.00
Desk, Campaign, Wood, Leather Top, Folding, Saw Horse Base, c.1960, 29 x 55 ½ In.	22460.00
Desk, Chair, Wood, Pierced Leaves, Birds, Cupboard Doors, Drawers, Slots, Flowers, Asia, 56 x 43 In.	649.00
Desk, Chalet, G. Stickley, No. 505, Pierced Top, Beveled Front, Shoefoot Base, 24 x 17 In.	240.00
Desk, Chinese Chippendale, Slant Front, Mahogany, 4 Drawer, 1700s, 100 x 48 In.	20400.00
Desk, Chinoiserie Style, Painted, 5 Drawers, Curved Legs, Rectangular, Round Corners, 29 x 50 In.	406.00
Desk, Chippendale Style, Mahogany, 5 Drawers, Cabriole Legs, 28 ½ x 41 ½ In.	245.00
Desk, Chippendale Style, Mahogany, 5 Drawers, Kneehole Center, 1900s, 30 x 42 In.	4500.00
Desk, Chippendale Style, Maple, Slant Front, 4 Drawers, Fluted Columns, Ogee Feet, 42 x 38 In.	489.00
Desk, Chippendale Style, Walnut, Ball & Claw, 5 Drawers, Reeded Edge, 1800s, 32 x 66 x 34 In.	540.00
Desk, Chippendale, Drop Front, Mahogany, Fitted Interior, 4 Drawers, c.1755, 43 x 36 In........	690.00
Desk, Chippendale, Drop Front, Scrolled Top, 2 Doors, 4 Drawers, N.Y., 1700s, 95 x 51 In........	2950.00
Desk, Chippendale, Drop Front, Tiger Maple, 4 Drawers, Ogee Feet, Rhode Island, 43 x 36 In.	8050.00
Desk, Chippendale, Drop Front, Tiger Maple, Fitted Interior, 4 Drawers, Bracket Feet, 41 x 38 In.	4012.00
Desk, Chippendale, Drop Front, Walnut, Fitted Interior, 4 Drawers, c.1890, 44 x 41 In.	1440.00
Desk, Chippendale, Drop Front, Walnut, Panels Doors, Drawers, 1900s, 87 x 45 In................	1920.00
Desk, Chippendale, Slant Front, 4 Drawers, Beaded, Slides, 1700s, 22 x 42 In.	1725.00
Desk, Chippendale, Slant Front, Birch, Carved Shell, Cubbyholes, Drawers, Feet, 1700s, 43 x 40 In.	690.00
Desk, Chippendale, Slant Front, Birch, Shell Drop Pediment, Drawers, Feet, c.1765, 44 x 42 In. ..*illus*	1845.00
Desk, Chippendale, Slant Front, Cherry, Dovetail, Brass Pulls, Ogee Feet, 42 x 36 x 20 In.	1356.00
Desk, Chippendale, Slant Front, Cherry, Fitted Interior, 4 Drawers, New England, c.1780, 41 x 37 In.	563.00
Desk, Chippendale, Slant Front, Cherry, Tiger Maple, Fitted Interior, 4 Drawers, c.1800, 40 x 36 In.	351.00
Desk, Chippendale, Slant Front, Curly Maple, Pine, Graduated Drawers, 43 x 37 In.	1645.00
Desk, Chippendale, Slant Front, Mahogany, 4 Drawers, Ball & Claw Feet, Mass., 44 x 42 In.....	1638.00

F

Furniture, Cupboard, Wood, Blue Paint, Step Back, 17 Drawers, Knobs, New England, c.1850, 68 x 33 In. $7762.00

James D. Julia Inc.

Furniture, Daybed, Meeks, Rosewood, Faceted Baluster Corner Posts, c.1835, 29 x 80 In. $799.00

New Orleans Auction Galleries, Inc.

Furniture, Desk, Anglo-Indian, Rosewood, Carved, Shelf, Writing Surface, Trestle Base, c.1860, 48 x 38 In. $1353.00

Neal Auction Co.

> **TIP**
> To clean furniture, dip your dusting cloth in ½ cup of vinegar mixed with a teaspoon of olive oil.

Furniture, Desk, Austro-German, Inset Leather, Mounted On Crossed Antler Base, Drawers, 30 x 48 In.
$6518.00

Skinner, Inc.

F

Furniture, Desk, Baronial Style, Drop Front, Walnut, Plaques, Pillars, c.1900, 45 x 32 In.
$861.00

New Orleans Auction Galleries, Inc.

Furniture, Desk, Bombe, Louis XV Style, Fitted Interior, Parquetry, Bronze Mounts, 1900s, 36 x 36 In.
$295.00

Brunk Auctions

Furniture, Desk, Butler's, Sheraton, Maple, Drop Front, 3 Drawers, Inlaid Corner Fans, 1800s, 46 x 41 In.
$2565.00

Garth's Auctions, Inc.

Desk, Chippendale, Slant Front, Mahogany, Eagle Inlay, c.1910, 42 x 42 In.	527.00
Desk, Chippendale, Slant Front, Mahogany, Oxbow, Hinged Lid, Pigeonholes, c.1780, 44 x 42 In.	1645.00
Desk, Chippendale, Slant Front, Mahogany, Pigeonholes, Short Drawers, c.1780, 42 x 40 x 22 In.	1840.00
Desk, Chippendale, Slant Front, Mahogany, Reverse Serpentine, Sun Bleached, c.1795, 43 x 42 In.	4740.00
Desk, Chippendale, Slant Front, Mahogany, Shaped Drawers, Secret Compartment, 1700s, 41 In.	20145.00
Desk, Chippendale, Slant Front, Maple, Rectangular, 4 Drawers, Ogee Bracket Feet, 41 x 37 In.	1098.00
Desk, Chippendale, Slant Front, Mixed Wood, 4 Drawers, Carved, c.1780, 43 x 40 In.	1840.00
Desk, Chippendale, Slant Front, Tiger Maple, 4 Drawers, Agee Feet, c.1780, 45 x 33 In.	3555.00
Desk, Chippendale, Slant Front, Walnut, Fitted Interior, 4 Drawers, Pa., c.1770	1422.00
Desk, Chippendale, Slant Front, Walnut, Fitted Interior, Bracket Feet, 1800s, 42 x 44 In.	850.00
Desk, Chippendale, Slant Front, Walnut, Fluted Columns, Bracket Feet, c.1775, 43 x 45 In.	1582.00
Desk, Cutler, Roll Top, C Roll, Oak, 7 Drawers, Interior Slots, Kick Panel, 45 x 60 In.	173.00
Desk, Danish Teak, Floating Top, 6 Drawers, c.1950, 29 x 60 In.	359.00
Desk, Davenport, Cherry Stick & Ball, Lift Top, Fitted Interior, Doors, Carved, 28 x 47 In.	294.00
Desk, Davenport, Regency, Mahogany, Leather Top, Opens To Desk, c.1820, 35 x 25 In.	1135.00
Desk, Davenport, Regency, Mahogany, Swivel Lift Top, Leather, 4 False Drawers, c.1810, 34 x 15 In. *illus*	956.00
Desk, Davenport, Slant Front, Mahogany, 8 Side Drawers, 33 ½ x 21 ¾ In.	288.00
Desk, Davenport, Walnut, Serpentine Lift Top, Leaf Scrolled Supports, 4 Drawers, 33 x 22 In.	1195.00
Desk, Drop Front, 4 Drawers, Raised Bracket Feet, 37 x 24 In.	185.00
Desk, Drop Front, Burl, Rosette Carved Door, 2 Drawers, Cabriole Legs, 61 x 36 In.	519.00
Desk, Drop Front, Inlays, Ormolu Mounts, Fitted Interior, Drawer, Bombay Shape, 33 x 30 In.	460.00
Desk, Drop Front, Lady's, Walnut, Gallery, Leather Writing Surface, Continental, 37 x 33 In. *illus*	837.00
Desk, Drop Front, Mahogany, 2 Drawers, Tapered Square Legs, Spade Feet, Inlay, 1800s, 40 x 36 In.	236.00
Desk, Drop Front, Mahogany, 3 Drawers, Bracket Feet, England, c.1800, 43 x 38 In.	177.00
Desk, Drop Front, Mahogany, Fitted, 3 Drawers, England, c.1790, 43 x 42 In.	560.00
Desk, Drop Front, Mahogany, Roll Top, Cutout Gallery, 1800s, 47 x 29 In.	359.00
Desk, Drop Front, Maple, Slide Supports, 4 Drawers, Fitted Interior, 1800s, 38 x 38 In.	173.00
Desk, Drop Front, Oak, Slide Supports, Drawer, Fitted Interior, England, c.1785, 31 x 21 In.	460.00
Desk, Drop Front, Queen Anne, Cherry, Book Rest, Fitted Interior, Drawers, c.1725, 39 x 32 In.	836.00
Desk, Drop Front, Reticulated Gallery, Drawer, Ormolu Mounts, Bombe, France, 35 x 27 In.	805.00
Desk, Drop Front, Walnut Veneer, Marquetry, Ormolu, Continental, c.1900, 61 x 29 In.	978.00
Desk, Drop Front, Walnut, 2 Parts, Cabinet, Drawer, Turned Legs, Victorian, 59 x 36 In.	127.00
Desk, Drop Front, Walnut, Fitted Interior, 3 Drawers, Beaded Borders, Carved Flowers, 39 x 33 In.	702.00
Desk, Drop Front, Walnut, Inlaid, Figures, Vines, 3 Shaped Drawers, Dutch, c.1800, 40 x 41 In.	690.00
Desk, Drop Front, Walnut, Inset Leather, 2 Drawers, Cabriole Legs, England, 41 x 35 In.	1195.00
Desk, Drop Front, William IV, Rosewood, Pedestal, 6 Drawers, Doors, 1850s, 59 x 54 In.	1016.00
Desk, Drop Front, Wood, Telescoping Fitted Interior, 7 Drawers, Carved, Chinese, c.1820, 40 x 35 In.	889.00
Desk, Drop Leaf, Wellington, Regency Style, Mahogany, Fitted Interior, Drawers, 51 x 30 In.	956.00
Desk, Elm, Painted Flower Band, Side Drawers, Pullout Slide, c.1850, 32 x 37 In.	738.00
Desk, Empire Style, Mahogany, Leather Top, 3 Drawers, Square Legs, 30 x 51 In.	1500.00
Desk, Empire, Mahogany, Flip Top, Backsplash, Frieze Drawers, Fitted Interior, 43 x 32 In.	299.00
Desk, Federal, Bird's-Eye Maple, Cherry, 2 Doors, Slant Drop Drawer, 3 Drawers, 53 x 40 In.	1170.00
Desk, Federal, Cherry, Molded Top, Fitted Interior, Cock-Beaded Drawers, c.1810, 43 x 39 In.	950.00
Desk, Federal, Drop Front, Cherry, Molded Cornice, Drawers, Bracket Base, 69 x 44 In.	2500.00
Desk, Federal, Slant Front, Cherry, 4 Drawers, Brass Handles, Bracket Feet, 42 x 40 In.	1287.00
Desk, Federal, Slant Front, Cherry, Fitted Interior, Pa., c.1805, 42 x 40 ½ In.	1659.00
Desk, Federal, Slant Front, Maple, Mahogany, Upper Doors, Drawers, c.1810, 55 x 39 In.	500.00
Desk, Federal, Slant Front, Tiger Maple, Drawers, Vermont, c.1820, 43 x 41 In. *illus*	6518.00
Desk, Federal, Slant Front, Walnut, Fitted Interior, Dovetailed Drawers, c.1810, 44 x 41 In. *illus*	1770.00
Desk, Frank Lloyd Wright, Rectangular, Side Drawers, Recessed Handles, Heritage, 52 x 20 In.	1800.00
Desk, Frank Lloyd Wright, Walnut, Carved Repeat Design, 2 Banks Of Drawers, Henredon, 52 In.	540.00
Desk, French Provincial, Cherry, Central Frieze, 2 Drawers, Scalloped Apron, c.1875, 31 x 77 In.	2214.00
Desk, Fruitwood, Drawer, Carved Skirt, Shaped Legs, Paw Feet, 30 x 49 In.	230.00
Desk, Fruitwood, Leather Flat Lid, Drawer, Turned Legs, England, c.1840, 30 x 32 In.	546.00
Desk, G. Nelson, Wood, Metal Frame, Tambour, Herman Miller, 29 x 54 In.	3500.00
Desk, G. Stickley, Chalet, Quartersawn Oak, Trestle Feet, 46 x 24 In.	2070.00
Desk, G. Stickley, Drop Front, Chamfered, 52 x 26 x 11 In.	2480.00
Desk, G. Stickley, Drop Front, Open Low Shelf, Branded Mark, H. Ellis, 44 x 11 ¼ In.	3224.00
Desk, G. Stickley, Drop Front, Walnut, Fitted Interior, Drawer, Medial Shelf, 43 ½ x 30 In.	744.00
Desk, George III Style, Drop Front, Mahogany, Marquetry, Urns & Leaves, 34 In.	277.00
Desk, George III Style, Mahogany, 8 Upper Drawers, Door, Lower Drawer, High Legs, 41 x 34 In.	500.00
Desk, George III Style, Mahogany, Inset Leather, 2 Pedestals, Bowed Center, 1800s, 31 x 60 In.	676.00
Desk, George III Style, Mahogany, Writing Surface, Cabriole Legs, 30 x 60 In.	1986.00
Desk, George III, Mahogany, Keyhole, Convex Drawers, Hinged Surface, 1700s, 30 x 47 In.	8225.00
Desk, George III, Mahogany, Keyhole, Twin Pedestals, Paneled Cabinet, 31 x 33 In. *illus*	1098.00

Desk, Georgian Style, Slant Front, Mahogany, Cubbyholes, Drawers, Prospect Door, 42 x 40 In. — 359.00

Desk, Gilt Leather Top, Parquetry, 3 Drawers, Cabriole Legs, 32 x 48 In. 688.00

Desk, Gothic Style, Ebonized, Gilt Incised, Lift Top, Gallery, Drawer, Brass Straps, c.1885, 37 x 23 In. — 1353.00

Desk, Hepplewhite Style, Lady's, Brass Gallery, Satinwood, Top Drawers, Inlay, 38 x 42 In. 837.00

Desk, Hepplewhite Style, Mahogany, Leather, Brass Tacks, Tapered Legs, Swivel, c.1910, 33 x 24 In. — 1062.00

Desk, Hepplewhite, Mahogany, Crossbanded, 2 Doors, 2 Drawers, c.1790, 46 x 35 In. 2390.00

Desk, Hollywood Style, Smoked Glass, Gilt, Wood Trim, Brass Pulls, 1940s, 30 x 55 In. ...*illus* 770.00

Desk, Home Office, G. Nelson, Walnut, Leather, Steel, Aluminum, Herman Miller, c.1946, 41 x 54 In. — 6200.00

Desk, Irish Chippendale, Walnut, Leather Lined Interior, Drawers, Cabriole Legs, 1800s, 40 x 23 In. — 1416.00

Desk, Jens Mellerup, Black Walnut, 3 Drawers, Sawbuck Base, 30 x 56 In. 593.00

Desk, Keyhole, Mahogany, Writing Slide, 7 Drawers, Pedestals, Cupboard Doors, 31 x 31 In. 368.00

Desk, Kimbel & Cabus, Drop Front, Ebonized Cherry, Printed Paper Inlay, 36 x 24 In. 1178.00

Desk, Kimbel & Cabus, Drop Front, Oak, Nickel Plated Brass, 56 x 36 x 20 In. 4030.00

Desk, Kimble & Cabus, Drop Front, Walnut, Minton Transfer Decorated Tiles, 60 x 46 In. 5270.00

Desk, Kneehole, Chinoiserie, Figures, Boats, Landscape, Drawers, Door, Chinese, c.1900, 36 x 48 In. — 456.00

Desk, Kneehole, Feather Banded Walnut, Drawers, Recessed Cupboard, c.1740, 30 x 31 In...... 5313.00

Desk, Kneehole, Mahogany, Writing Slide, 6 Drawers, Door, c.1775, 33 x 35 In. 1126.00

Desk, Knoll, Walnut Top, 4 Drawers, Polished Steel Frame, 76 x 29 In. 360.00

Desk, Larkin, Oak, c.1900, 62 x 30 x 12 In. 259.00

Desk, Leather Shaped Top, Drawer, Cluster Columnar Legs, X-Stretcher, 30 x 60 In. 540.00

Desk, Leather, Kneehole Center, 5 Drawers, Door, Carved, Cutler Furniture Co., c.1890, 30 x 72 In. . 748.00

Desk, Library, Arts & Crafts, Oak, Drawer, Open Shelf Bookcase Sides, c.1915, 29 x 48 In. 431.00

Desk, Lift Top, Lower Shelf, Texture Carving, Appliques, c.1900, 32 x 20 In. 118.00

Desk, Lift Top, Pine, Tapered Legs, Blue Paint, Georgia, 1800s, 30 x 26 In. 518.00

Desk, Limbert, Drop Front, 34 x 17 In. 1440.00

Desk, Louis XIV Style, Ormolu, 6 Drawers, Scrolled Rosettes, Lion's Head, 1900s, 71 x 34 In..... 777.00

Desk, Louis XV Style, Elm, Fruitwood, Canted Corners, Drawers, c.1900, 30 x 69 In.................. 615.00

Desk, Louis XV Style, Lady's, Kingwood, Walnut, Ormolu Trim, Marble Top, c.1900, 38 x 29 In. 1495.00

Desk, Louis XV Style, Lady's, Ormolu, Leather, 3 Frieze Drawers, Cabriole Legs, 1900s, 31 x 70 In.. 295.00

Desk, Louis XV Style, Marquetry, Slant Front, Openwork Brass Gallery, Drawers, 37 x 31 In...... 667.00

Desk, Louis XV Style, Oak, 4 Drawers, Paneled Door, Carved, 30 x 57 x 26 In. 360.00

Desk, Louis XV Style, Oak, Parquet Top, 5 Drawers, Cabriole Legs, 60 x 31 In........................... 330.00

Desk, Louis XV, Beech, Cross Grain Panel Top, 3 Drawers, 31 x 63 In. 244.00

Desk, Louis XV, Walnut, Parquet Top, Shaped Apron, Drawer, Cabriole Legs, 31 x 31 In. 240.00

Desk, Louis XVI Style, Burl, Mahogany, Brass Bound, Ormolu Millwork Banding, 29 x 60 In... 922.00

Desk, Louis XVI Style, Leather Top, 3 Drawers, Bronze Mounts, Sabots, c.1940, 30 x 47 In. 1968.00

Desk, Louis XVI Style, Mahogany, Brass Mounts, Leather Insets, 4 Drawers, Tapered Legs, 30 x 51 In. 1404.00

Desk, Louis XVI Style, Mahogany, Square Legs, Ring-Turned Feet, c.1895, 30 x 45 In. 1722.00

Desk, Louis XVI Style, Parcel Gilt, Ormolu, Leather, 9 Drawers, Fluted Legs, 30 x 55 In. 2940.00

Desk, Louis XVI, Drop Front, Burl, Parcel Gilt, Lift Top, Fitted, 4 Drawers, France, c.1720, 36 x 40 In. . 9440.00

Desk, Louis XVI, Mahogany, Brass Mounts, Leather, Drawers, Kneehole Shape, Slides, 29 x 63 In. 2223.00

Desk, Mahogany, Leather Inset, 3 Drawers, Banded, Inlays, Tapered Legs, c.1900, 31 x 48 In. . 1230.00

Desk, Mahogany, Leather Inset, 5 Drawers, Lid Top, Fitted Interior, 45 x 24 In........................ 250.00

Desk, Mahogany, Marble Top, Gallery, Shelf, Convex Cupboard Doors, 1800s, 53 x 54 In. 354.00

Desk, Mahogany, Spindle Gallery, Leather Surface, Round Legs, c.1900, 44 x 51 In. 1599.00

Desk, Mahogany, Trestle Base, Carved, Leopold Eidlitz, c.1880, 31 x 27 In............................... 1488.00

Desk, Mahogany, Wreath Glass Doors, 3 Low Drawers, Columns, c.1820, 88 x 23 In................ 3107.00

Desk, Marquetry, Flower Medallion, Swags, Drawer, Ormolu, Cabriole Legs, 29 x 40 In............ 431.00

Desk, Mechanical, Edwardian, Mahogany, Flip Top, Stretcher Shelf, Gallery, c.1910, 31 x 26 In. 861.00

Desk, Oak, 5 Drawers, Spindle Gallery, Carved Legs, Ball Feet, 1800s, 32 x 51 In...................... 420.00

Desk, Oak, Kidney Shape, 3 Drawers, Side Bowfront Doors, England, c.1910, 30 x 56 In. 2952.00

Desk, Oak, Lift Top, Marble Sink Inside, 5 Drawer, Door, 30 x 40 In. 207.00

Desk, Oak, Plank Top, 2 Square Drawers, Block Legs, Rustic Style, France, 1700s, 66 x 31 In.. 600.00

Desk, Painted, Beadboard Cottage, 2 Upper Doors, Writing Surface, c.1900, 58 x 40 In. 518.00

Desk, Parquetry Border, Gilt Leather Inset, 3 Frieze Drawers, Mounts, France, c.1890, 29 x 56 In. 4880.00

Desk, Parsons Style, Faux Shagreen Finish, Shaped Apron, Square Legs, 29 x 72 In. 1000.00

Desk, Partners, Federal, Mahogany, String Inlay, 7 Drawers, Square Legs, c.1800, 29 x 51 In. . 7703.00

Desk, Partners, George III Style, Mahogany, 2 Pedestals, 3 Drawers, Leather Top, 1800s, 62 In. 7050.00

Desk, Partners, Mahogany, Leather Top, 5 Drawers, 1830s, 31 x 60 In. 10000.00

Desk, Partners, Oak, Carved Columns, 5 Drawers, Art Nouveau Design, Bun Feet, 31 x 63 In.. 805.00

Desk, Partners, Pedestal, Campaign Style, Satinwood, Drawers, Leather, Brass, Baker, 30 x 72 In. 2952.00

Desk, Partners, Rosewood, Marble Inset Top, 8 Drawers, Footrest, Chinese, c.1800, 35 x 76 In. 10800.00

Desk, Pay, Oak, Brass Gallery, Drawers, Open Storage, Continental, 1800s, 46 x 37 In. 708.00

Desk, Pedestal, George III Style, Mahogany, 9 Drawers, Carved Trim, 30 x 48 In...................... 313.00

Desk, Pedestal, Walnut, Leather Inset, 9 Drawers, 2 Doors, Leaves, Masks, 1800s, 34 x 72 In. .. 652.00

Desk, Pine, Painted, Drawer, Shelves, Cutout Stars, Square Legs, Pa., 1800s, 28 x 36 In. 207.00

Furniture, Desk, Chippendale, Slant Front, Birch, Shell Drop Pediment, Drawers, Feet, c.1765, 44 x 42 In. $1845.00

New Orleans Auction Galleries, Inc.

Furniture, Desk, Davenport, Regency, Mahogany, Swivel Lift Top, Leather, 4 False Drawers, c.1810, 34 x 15 In. $956.00

Neal Auction Co.

Furniture, Desk, Drop Front, Lady's, Walnut, Gallery, Leather Writing Surface, Continental, 37 x 33 In. $837.00

Neal Auction Co.

Furniture, Desk, Federal, Slant Front, Tiger Maple, Drawers, Vermont, c.1820, 43 x 41 In. $6518.00

Skinner, Inc.

Furniture, Desk, Federal, Slant Front, Walnut, Fitted Interior, Dovetailed Drawers, c.1810, 44 x 41 In.
$1770.00

Brunk Auctions

Furniture, Desk, George III, Mahogany, Keyhole, Twin Pedestals, Paneled Cabinet, 31 x 33 In.
$1098.00

Leslie Hindman Auctioneers

Furniture, Desk, Hollywood Style, Smoked Glass, Gilt, Wood Trim, Brass Pulls, 1940s, 30 x 55 In.
$770.00

Skinner, Inc.

Furniture, Desk, Rohde, Leatherette, Brass, Double Pedestal, 6 Drawers, Herman Miller, 1940s, 29 x 56 In.
$4030.00

Rago Arts & Auction Center

Desk, Pine, Painted, Lift Top, Shaped Gallery, Beaded, Drawer, Square Legs, c.1805, 40 x 25 In.	563.00
Desk, Plantation, Carved Shell, Leaf, Scroll Crest, Cubbyholes, Column Supports, 68 x 51 In..	575.00
Desk, Plantation, Drop Front, 2 Sections, Arched Crest, Drawer, 1800s, 59 x 29 In......................	403.00
Desk, Plantation, Federal, Panel Doors, Fitted Interior, Drawer, c.1890, 61 x 30 In.................	180.00
Desk, Portable, Sandalwood, Carved, Sloped Front, Engraved, Colonial India, 12 x 9 In.........	922.00
Desk, Postmaster's, Oak, Sorting Rack, Turned Legs, Drawer, 32 Cubbies, c.1900, 38 In.........	546.00
Desk, Provincial, Slant Front, 4 Drawers, Writing Surface, Medial Door, Bracket Feet, 40 x 27 In.	178.00
Desk, Queen Anne Style, Burl Walnut, Tooled Leather Top, Drawers, Scalloped Apron, 30 x 57 In.	538.00
Desk, Queen Anne Style, Slant Front, Walnut, Faux Book, Mirror Top, Drawer, c.1905, 54 x 26 In.	4043.00
Desk, Queen Anne, Mahogany, Hinged Lid, Interior Compartment, c.1750, 42 x 29 In............	8800.00
Desk, Red, Hinged Lid, Crowned Woman, Holding Cross, Chalice, Chariot, c.1850, 11 x 35 In.	326.00
Desk, Regency Style, Drawers, Trestle Base, Brass Gallery, Kittinger, 1900s, 31 x 47 In.	2242.00
Desk, Regency Style, Figured Mahogany, Stepped, Drawers, Inset Gilt Tooled Leather, 35 x 39 In.	1076.00
Desk, Regency Style, Mahogany, Shaped Top, Wire Mesh Doors, 2 Frieze Drawers, 37 x 47 In..	1125.00
Desk, Renaissance Revival, Carved, Slant Front, Crowned Crest, Grotesques, X-Stretcher, 51 x 34 In.	1164.00
Desk, Renaissance Revival, Drop Front, Walnut, 2 Doors, Pigeonholes, c.1875, 62 x 42 In.......	2588.00
Desk, Renaissance Revival, Oak, Carved, Leaves & Flowers, 1880s, 31 x 53 x 26 In.	780.00
Desk, Robsjohn-Gibbings, Bleached Mahogany, Leg, 4 Drawers, 1950s, 30 x 46 In.	682.00
Desk, Rococo, Drop Front, Rosewood, Bead Molded Surround, Fitted Interior, 59 x 26 In.	369.00
Desk, Rohde, Leatherette, Brass, Double Pedestal, 6 Drawers, Herman Miller, 1940s, 29 x 56 In. .*illus*	4030.00
Desk, Rohlfs, Slant Front, Shaped Carvings, Finials, c.1899, 56 ½ x 25 In...............................	40300.00
Desk, Roll Top, French Provincial, Fruitwood, Inlaid, Tambour, Shaped Top, Drawers, 39 x 48 In.	554.00
Desk, Roll Top, Fruitwood, Inlays, Fitted Interior, 4 Drawers, France, 1800s, 38 x 36 In.	1062.00
Desk, Roll Top, Hepplewhite, Mahogany, 4 Drawers, Pullout Leather Surface, 40 In.................	861.00
Desk, Roll Top, Louis XVI Style, Hinged, Putti With Garlands, 1900s, 33 x 27 In.	858.00
Desk, Roll Top, Mahogany, Satinwood, Leather, Fitted Interior, Reeded Legs, c.1890, 40 x 43 In.	2270.00
Desk, Roll Top, Marquetry, Brass Gallery, Fitted Interior, 4 Drawers, 42 x 35 In.	633.00
Desk, Roll Top, Pullout Writing Surface, 2 Frieze Drawers, Cupboard Doors, 48 x 44 In.	590.00
Desk, Roll Top, S Roll, Oak, Double Pedestal, Sliding Tambour Top, Drawers, 46 x 48 In........	460.00
Desk, Roll Top, S Roll, Victorian, Cherry, 21 Cubbyholes, Writing Surface, Hinged Panels, 51 x 54 In..	748.00
Desk, Roll Top, Sliding Tambour Cover, Fitted Interior, c.1890, 53 x 30 In...........................	127.00
Desk, Roll Top, Walnut, Burl, Glass Top, Rotating Carousels, 6 Tier, Leather Top, c.1875, 48 x 54 In.	10925.00
Desk, Roll Top, Wormley, 3 Sections, I-Stretcher, Block Legs, 1967, 35 x 76 In.	3750.00
Desk, Satinwood, Painted Swags, Medallions, Gallery, Fitted Drawer, Shelf, 40 x 22 In............	1315.00
Desk, School, Shaker, Slant Front, Cherry, Pine, Raised Edging, Back Shelf, Brass, 29 x 19 In.	205.00
Desk, Schoolmaster's, Cherry, Poplar, Turned Legs, Lift Top, Fitted Interior, Gallery, 37 x 31 In.	118.00
Desk, Schoolmaster's, Slant Front, Country Sheraton, Softwood, Grain Painted, 36 x 38 In. ...	561.00
Desk, Schoolmaster's, Slant Front, Red Wash, Breadboard Ends, 19th Century, 33 x 31 In.......	65.00
Desk, Schoolmaster's, Slant Front, Walnut, Drawer, Shaped Gallery, Square Legs, c.1820	533.00
Desk, Severin Hansen, Teak, Brass, Signed, Haslev, Denmark, 1960s, 29 x 56 In.	1612.00
Desk, Shaker, Sister's, Pine, Slant Hinged Lid, Walnut Finish, Compartments, 33 x 20 In.	2574.00
Desk, Sheraton, Lady's, Curly Maple, Paneled Doors, Folding Writing Surface, c.1830, 47 x 31 In. .*illus*	6756.00
Desk, Sheraton, Mahogany, Bird's-Eye Maple, Blind Door, 3 Drawers, 53 x 40 In.	2013.00
Desk, Slant Front, 3 Drawers, Brass Handles, Pigeonholes, 39 x 37 ½ In.	443.00
Desk, Slant Front, 4 Drawers, 8 Pigeonholes, Bracket Feet, c.1800, 44 x 42 In........................	717.00
Desk, Slant Front, Birch, Pine, 4 Drawers, Hinged Lid, Bracket Feet, c.1795, 43 x 38 In.	1058.00
Desk, Slant Front, Carved Merchants Crest, Glass Doors, Cream, Red Paint, Italy, 1800s, 91 x 36 In.	2280.00
Desk, Slant Front, Cherry, S-Curve Legs, Bookshelf Stretcher, c.1900, 43 x 28 In......................	288.00
Desk, Slant Front, Chippendale, Cherry, 5 Drawers, Southern, c.1790, 46 x 40 In.	326.00
Desk, Slant Front, Edwardian, Graduated Drawers, Scroll Inlay, Bracket Feet, c.1900, 39 x 25 In.	770.00
Desk, Slant Front, Empire Revival, Walnut, 4 Drawers, Columns, Paw Carved Feet, 42 x 36 In.	575.00
Desk, Slant Front, Federal Style, Mahogany, 4 Drawers, Hidden Panel, Bracket Feet, 43 x 37 In..	627.00
Desk, Slant Front, Fitted Interior, 4 Drawers, c.1820, 41 x 36 In.	374.00
Desk, Slant Front, Gothic Revival, Ebonized, Gilt, Upper Cupboard, Shed Roof, c.1885, 38 x 22 In.	2952.00
Desk, Slant Front, Hepplewhite, Cherry, 4 Drawers, Cock-Beaded, Bracket Feet, c.1819, 43 x 41 In.	499.00
Desk, Slant Front, Hepplewhite, Cherry, Banded Inlay, Drawers, Fitted Interior, 41 x 43 In.	499.00
Desk, Slant Front, Hepplewhite, Grain Painted, Drawer, Compartment Storage, 30 x 33 In.	329.00
Desk, Slant Front, Hepplewhite, Walnut, Banding, 4 Drawers, French Feet, c.1800, 44 x 38 In.	1880.00
Desk, Slant Front, Japanned, Oblong Top, 4 Drawers, Bracket Feet, Figures, Buildings, 39 x 38 In.	1298.00
Desk, Slant Front, Ledger, Empire, Mahogany, 5 Drawers, Turned Feet, c.1840, 50 x 44 In.......	374.00
Desk, Slant Front, Mahogany, 4 Drawers, 42 x 38 In..	360.00
Desk, Slant Front, Mahogany, Inlay, 5 Drawers, Block Feet, Brass Handles, 22 x 22 In., Child's	625.00
Desk, Slant Front, Mahogany, Valance Compartments, Drawers, Bracket Feet, 41 x 36 In.........	385.00
Desk, Slant Front, Maple, 4 Drawers, Bracket Feet, Brass Handles, American, 38 x 36 In..........	375.00
Desk, Slant Front, Maple, Mahogany, Serpentine, 4 Drawers, Talon Feet, 1800s, 44 x 41 In.	2070.00

Desk, Slant Front, Master's, Pine, Rectangular, Dovetailed, 6 Drawers, Ball Feet, c.1890, 50 x 33 In.	1610.00
Desk, Slant Front, Ormolu, Bombe Shape, Reticulated Gallery, Cabriole Legs, France, 35 x 27 In.	805.00
Desk, Slant Front, Oxbow, Ogee Feet, c.1775, 42 x 42 x 23 In.	7475.00
Desk, Slant Front, Pine, 3 Drawers, Iron Handles, c.1800, 33 x 37 In.	316.00
Desk, Slant Front, Pine, Fitted Interior, 3 Drawers, Ocher Sponge, Swirl Paint, 42 x 36 In.	7110.00
Desk, Slant Front, Pine, Gray Paint, 4 Drawers, Shaped Skirt, c.1800, 39 x 40 In.	1185.00
Desk, Slant Front, Pine, Raised Pencil Lip, Till, Shelf, Bracket Feet, Painted, 13 x 17 In.	823.00
Desk, Slant Front, Queen Anne, Maple, Cherry, Blocked, Drawers, Pad Feet, 1700s, 45 x 38 In.	5036.00
Desk, Slant Front, Queen Anne, Pine, Dovetailed Drawers, Sliding Cover, 1700s, 35 x 21 In. .....*illus*	4230.00
Desk, Slant Front, Queen Anne, Tiger Maple, 4 Drawers, Brass, Bracket Feet, 1700s, 42 x 36 In.	2185.00
Desk, Slant Front, Queen Anne, Tiger Maple, 6 Drawers, 6 Compartments, c.1750, 40 x 36 In.	4029.00
Desk, Slant Front, Tiger Maple, 4 Drawers, Ogee Bracket Feet, c.1780, 45 x 33 In.	3555.00
Desk, Slant Front, Walnut, 2 Parts, Arched Gallery, Doors, Bird, Drawers, c.1870-90, 62 x 42 In.	3444.00
Desk, Slant Front, Walnut, 3 Parts, Carved Vinery, Hinged Lid, Drawers, c.1885, 66 x 30 In.	316.00
Desk, Slant Front, Walnut, Parquetry, Fitted Interior, c.1800, 43 x 49 In.	1000.00
Desk, Slant Front, William & Mary, Walnut, 4 Drawers, Inlay, Bun Feet, c.1690, 39 x 38 In.	9480.00
Desk, Spinet, Rosewood, Hinged Folding Top, Fitted Interior, Baluster Legs, c.1850, 32 x 47 In.	75.00
Desk, Stand, Black Forest, Owl, Glass Eyes, 10 ½ In.	518.00
Desk, Stickley Bros., 2 Tier Drawers, Slated Base, Low Stretcher, 36 x 23 In.	450.00
Desk, Stickley, Arts & Crafts, Oak, 3 Drawers, Lower Shelf, Block Legs, 29 x 60 In.	790.00
Desk, Table Top, Black Lacquer, Gilt Chinoiserie Scene, Fitted Interior, Drawer, 10 x 17 In.	176.00
Desk, Table Top, Shaker, Cherry, Pull Down Writing Surface, c.1890, 24 x 31 In.	936.00
Desk, Table, Inset Leather Top, 2 Bronze Trim Drawers, Tapered Legs, France, c.1920, 30 x 39 In.	861.00
Desk, Table, Louis XV Style, Kingwood, Ormolu, 3 Drawers, France, 32 x 55 In.	2430.00
Desk, Table, Wood, Leather Inset Top, 5 Bronze Trim Drawers, Pilasters, France, c.1930, 30 x 51 In.	3198.00
Desk, Tambour Doors, Cherry, Drawers, Pigeonholes, c.1800, 46 x 39 x 21 In.	2070.00
Desk, Tambour, Federal Style, Mahogany, Inlay, Fitted Top, Fold-Out Writing Surface, 44 x 36 In.	184.00
Desk, Tambour, Federal, Mahogany, Fitted Interior, 2 Drawers, 42 x 36 In.	590.00
Desk, Tambour, Federal, Mixed Wood, Fitted Interior, 3 Drawers, c.1800, 46 x 39 In.	2070.00
Desk, Teak, Chrome Steel, 5 Drawers, Peter Hvidt, France & Sons, 1960s, 29 ½ x 71 In.	589.00
Desk, Teak, Curved Top, A-Shape Legs, 6 Drawers, Povl Dinesen, Stamped, c.1960, 30 x 59 In.	1063.00
Desk, Teak, Tray Top, 6 Drawers, Kneehole, Lovig, c.1970, 29 x 61 In.	499.00
Desk, Travel, Mahogany, Silver, Tambour Top, Fitted Interior, Drawer, 1800s, 28 x 45 In.	472.00
Desk, Walnut, 2 Drawers, Spiral Carved Stretcher & Legs, 1800s, 30 x 43 In.	671.00
Desk, Walnut, 10 Drawers, Twisted Legs, Stretcher, Carved, 40 x 52 In.	488.00
Desk, Walnut, Carved Geometrics, Trestle, Cutouts, A. Jordan, Cincinnati Art, c.1910, 30 x 38 In.	2356.00
Desk, Walnut, Kneehole, Reeded Edge Top, Paneled Door Pedestals, Drawers, 1800s, 31 x 49 In.	239.00
Desk, Walnut, String Inlay, Sliding Writing Surface, Drawers, Hoof Feet, Italy, c.1765, 29 x 51 In.	1348.00
Desk, William IV, Mahogany, Beveled Edge, 2 Drawers, Lobed Legs, Casters, c.1850, 29 x 47 In.	780.00
Desk, Wood, Double Pedestal Base, 2 Drawers, Dragon Carved, Chinese, 1900s, 31 x 84 In.	885.00
Desk, Wood, Faux Malichite Top, Partly Clad Women Legs, Carved, Phyllis Morris, 30 x 60 In.	2500.00
Desk, Wood, Straight Metal Legs, Stretcher, 4 Drawers, Fold-Out Hinged Gallery, 34 x 64 In.	863.00
Desk, Wooton Type, Budget, Roll Top, Drop Desk Door, Signed, Zue Jackson	7345.00
Desk, Wooton, Drop Front, Burl Walnut, Fitted Interior, Leather Surface, c.1874, 76 x 46 In. .....*illus*	8963.00
Desk, Wooton, Drop Front, Walnut, 2 Doors, Pigeonhole Shelves, c.1875, 62 x 42 In.	1150.00
Desk, Wooton, Renaissance Revival, Drop Front, Walnut, Maple, Fitted Interior, 1874, 64 x 42 In. .*illus*	4406.00
Desk-Bookcase, Drop Front, Mahogany, Glass Doors, 3 Drawers, Eng., c.1810, 92 x 42 In.	1725.00
Desk-Bookcase, Queen Anne, Oyster Veneer, Paneled Doors, Interior Shelves, c.1800, 80 x 46 In.	1770.00
Dinette Set, Flame Back Chairs, Faux Leather, White Laminate Table, c.1960, 44 & 54 In., 7 Piece	180.00
Dining Set, Biedermeier, Satinwood, Fruitwood, Table, 6 Chairs, Lyre Splat, 31 x 50 In., 7 Piece	750.00
Dining Set, Heywood-Wakefield, Birch, Butterfly Drop Leaf, Gardner, 29 x 52 In., 5 Piece	200.00
Dining Set, James Mont, Multicolor Wood, Upholstered Chair Seat, 2 Armchairs, 1940s, 9 Piece	2232.00
Dining Set, John Risley, Figures, Enameled Steel, Glass, Round Table, 2 Armchairs, 1960s, 5 Piece	4340.00
Dining Set, Nakashima, Black Walnut, Square Table, Captain's Chairs, 29 x 35 In., 3 Piece	3720.00
Dresser, Arts & Crafts, Mahogany, Mother-Of-Pearl Inlays, Mirror, 47 x 21 In.	450.00
Dresser, Burl Walnut, 4 Drawers, Carved Shaped Mirror, Venice, 37 x 54 In.	793.00
Dresser, Burl, Gallery Top, 5 Drawers, 2 Doors, Wood Knobs, c.1820, 45 x 72 In.	2340.00
Dresser, Campaign, Mahogany, Brass Mounts, 5 Graduated Drawers, 47 x 21 In.	554.00
Dresser, Chippendale Style, Flame Birch, Bracket Base, 4 Drawers, Drop Ball Pulls, 34 x 38 In.	460.00
Dresser, Corner, Oak, Stepped Cornice, Plate Shelves, Paneled, Drawers, Wales, c.1850, 78 x 95 In.	2988.00
Dresser, Danish Modern, Teak, 8 Drawers, 30 x 58 In.	748.00
Dresser, Dog Kennel, Cream Paint, 2 Open Shelves, Central Cove, Doors, 1900s, 84 x 62 In.	944.00
Dresser, Empire, Mahogany Veneer, 4 Drawers, Columnar Stiles, 48 x 44 In.	460.00
Dresser, Empire, Mahogany, Flame Grain, Overhung Drawer, Columns, 4 Low Drawers, 48 x 44 In.	460.00
Dresser, Federal, Mahogany, Poplar, 6 Drawers, Bracket Feet, Label E.G. Clark, c.1820, 39 x 44 In.	738.00
Dresser, Frankl, Cream Lacquer, 7 Drawers, Brass X Pulls, Johnson Furniture Co., 40 x 45 In.	870.00

Furniture, Desk, Sheraton, Lady's, Curly Maple, Paneled Doors, Folding Writing Surface, c.1830, 47 x 31 In.
$6756.00

Garth's Auctions, Inc.

Furniture, Desk, Slant Front, Queen Anne, Pine, Dovetailed Drawers, Sliding Cover, 1700s, 35 x 21 In.
$4230.00

Garth's Auctions, Inc.

Furniture, Desk, Wooton, Drop Front, Burl Walnut, Fitted Interior, Leather Surface, c.1874, 76 x 46 In.
$8963.00

Neal Auction Co.

Furniture, Desk, Wooton, Renaissance Revival, Drop Front, Walnut, Maple, Fitted Interior, 1874, 64 x 42 In. $4406.00

Cowan's Auctions

Furniture, Dresser, G. Nakashima, Black Walnut, 8 Drawers, Double Overhang, 1960, 32 x 76 In. $10540.00

Rago Arts & Auction Center

Furniture, Dresser, G. Nakashima, Walnut, 4 Drawers, Brass, Widdicomb, 1958, 32 x 36 ¾ In. $4650.00

Rago Arts & Auction Center

Furniture, Dresser, Tiger & Curly Maple, 2 Hidden Drawers, Diamond, Flower Carving, Label, 57 x 48 In. $1208.00

Cottone Auctions

Dresser, Frankl, Cream Lacquer, 10 Drawers, Brass X Pulls, Johnson Furniture Co., 73 x 32 In.	1320.00
Dresser, Frankl, Mahogany, Brass, Johnson Furniture, 1940s, 45 x 40 In.	527.00
Dresser, G. Nakashima, Black Walnut, 3 Drawers, 30 x 36 In.	5580.00
Dresser, G. Nakashima, Black Walnut, 3 Drawers, 32 x 36 In.	4650.00
Dresser, G. Nakashima, Black Walnut, 8 Drawers, Double Overhang, 1960, 32 x 76 In. *..illus*	10540.00
Dresser, G. Nakashima, Walnut, 4 Drawers, Brass, Widdicomb, 1958, 32 x 36 ¾ In. *.......illus*	4650.00
Dresser, G. Nelson, Thin-Edge, Rosewood, Porcelain, Aluminum, Herman Miller, 1950s, 31 x 34 In.	1364.00
Dresser, G. Stickley, 9 Drawer, V Pulls, Red Decal, 50 ½ x 36 x 20 In.	9300.00
Dresser, G. Stickley, Mirror, Adjustable, 4 Drawers, Red Decal, c.1902, 63 x 48 In.	8060.00
Dresser, George II, Oak, Low, Planked Top, Cock-Beaded, 3 Drawers, Shaped Apron, 31 x 75 In.	1700.00
Dresser, Jean-Michel Frank Style, Parchment On Wood, Brass, 4 Drawers, 29 x 41 x 21 In.	2480.00
Dresser, Kipp Stewart, Walnut, 8 Drawers, Enameled Panel, John Stuart, 51 x 20 In.	620.00
Dresser, Louis XV Style, Painted, Pink & White Marble Top, Segmented Mirror, Italy	944.00
Dresser, Louis XV Style, Walnut, Marble Top, Adjustable Mirror, Carved & Shaped, 84 x 49 In.	450.00
Dresser, Louis XVI Style, Oak, Trifold Mirror, 2 Tier Marble Top, Drawers, Doors, 81 x 42 In. ..	431.00
Dresser, Mahogany, Metal Label Hickory Chair, 1900s, 36 x 63 In.	327.00
Dresser, Mahogany, Mirror, 2 Drawers, Over 4 Drawers, Tapered Pilasters, c.1820, 69 x 38 In.	1952.00
Dresser, Marquetry, Roses, 4 Drawers, Central Flip Top, Turned Legs, 1815, 32 x 37 In.	119.00
Dresser, McCobb, Maple, Double, Brass, 8 Drawers, Winchendon, 1950s, 32 x 60 In.	1240.00
Dresser, Mirror, Faux Bamboo, 5 Drawers, Partial Gallery, Turned Feet, 75 x 30 In.	2015.00
Dresser, Modern, Walnut, 8 Drawers, American Of Martinsville, 32 x 58 In.	2100.00
Dresser, Oak, 2 Open Display Shelves, Metal Hooks, Stepped Base, 5 Drawers, England, 77 x 71 In.	1416.00
Dresser, Oak, 2 Parts, Central Cupboard, Shelves, Drawers, Gadroon Apron, c.1760, 80 x 68 In.	1000.00
Dresser, Oak, Molded Top, Apron With 3 Drawers, Square Legs, c.1760, 34 x 83 In.	2271.00
Dresser, Oak, Tilt Mirror, 2 Drawers, Curvy Front, c.1910, 71 x 42 In.	495.00
Dresser, Oak, Tilt Mirror, Serpentine Front, Cabinet Door, 5 Drawers, c.1900, 70 x 36 In.	403.00
Dresser, Parchment Covered, Bowfront Top, 6 Drawers, Gilt, Lucite Pulls, 1920s, 36 x 71 In.	3063.00
Dresser, Parzinger, 8 Drawers, Lacquered Wood, Brass, 1960s, 32 x 60 x 18 In.	1860.00
Dresser, Parzinger, Undulating, 6 Drawer, Mahogany, Chrome Plated, 1960s, 31 x 84 x 20 In.	9920.00
Dresser, Queen Anne, Burl, Inlays, Carved Knees, Ireland, c.1800, 34 x 57 In.	1416.00
Dresser, Regency, Mahogany, 4 Drawers, Shaped Backsplash, Twist Columns, c.1830, 46 x 43 In.	460.00
Dresser, Rococo Revival, Flame Veneer, Marble Top, Carved, Shaped Mirror, 4 Drawers, 34 x 44 In.	230.00
Dresser, Satinwood, Tilt Mirror, Upright Supports, 3 Drawers, England, c.1900, 62 x 36 In.	288.00
Dresser, Sheraton, Cherry, 4 Graduated Drawers, 2-Board Top, Brass Escutcheons, 40 x 43 In.	460.00
Dresser, Tiger & Curly Maple, Hidden Drawers, Diamond, Flower Carving, Label, 57 x 48 In. *.illus*	1208.00
Dresser, Victorian, Ash, 4 Drawers, Tilt Mirror, Shaped Carved Crest, 1895, 83 x 42 In.	184.00
Dresser, Victorian, Carved Gallery, Mirror, 2 Glove Boxes, Marble Shelf, 4 Drawers, 80 x 42 In.	201.00
Dresser, Victorian, Walnut, Marble Top, Carved Crest, Mirror, 6 Drawers, 75 x 47 In.	633.00
Dresser, Victorian, Walnut, Marble Top, Mirror, Carved, Candle Shelves, 3 Drawers, 93 x 48 In.	288.00
Dresser, Walnut, Arched Spindled Mirror, Flanked By 2 Marble Top Chests, 1870s, 71 x 63 In.	418.00
Dresser, Welsh, Corner, Oak, Shelves, Paneled Drawers, Stretcher Shelf, c.1790, 77 x 95 In. .....*illus*	2988.00
Dresser, Welsh, Elm, Scalloped Crest, Plate Shelves, Arched Side Doors, Drawers, 1700s, 84 x 89 In.	3585.00
Dresser, Welsh, Oak, Upper Shelves & Doors, Lower Drawers, Dovetailed, Inlay, c.1890, 78 x 54 In. *illus*	1534.00
Dresser, Wood, Parchment Panels, Greek Key Ebonized Frame, 2 Drawers, c.1950, 51 x 42 In.	1800.00
Dresser, Wormley, Mahogany, 4 Fluted Drawers, Dunbar, 1940s, 31 x 50 In.	2728.00
Dry Sink, 2 Doors, Red Paint, c.1850, 31 x 38 In.	729.00
Dry Sink, Arched Backsplash, Drawer Over Doors, Blue Paint, 35 x 41 In.	1175.00
Dry Sink, Cupboard, Doors, Drawer, Mustard Yellow Over Cream Paint, 71 x 43 In.	1880.00
Dry Sink, Federal, Mahogany, Brass Rosettes, Gallery, Inset Bowl, 7 Drawers, c.1810, 37 x 18 In..	598.00
Dry Sink, Mahogany, Hinged, Zinc Interior, Drawer, Panel Doors, Columns, 1800s, 32 x 30 In.	717.00
Dry Sink, Oak, Door, Tray Top, 1800s, 38 x 19 In.	230.00
Dry Sink, Painted Pine, Rectangular Top, 2 Panel Doors, Cutout Feet, 49 x 42 In.	1058.00
Dry Sink, Painted, Poplar, Hinged Top, Applied Moldings, Drawers, Doors, 37 x 42 In.	460.00
Dry Sink, Pine, 2 Parts, Work Station, 2 Drawers, 2 Upper & 2 Lower Doors, 1800s, 89 x 42 In.	460.00
Dry Sink, Pine, Carved Backsplash, 4 Drawers, 2 Doors, 38 x 60 In.	330.00
Dry Sink, Pine, Green Paint, 2 Hinged Doors, Planks, 1800s, 33 x 43 In.	148.00
Dry Sink, Pine, Nailed Apron, Scrolled, Zinc Lining, Tapered Legs, Painted, 1800s, 33 x 24 In.	1528.00
Dry Sink, Pine, Painted, Rounded Back, Drawer, 2 Cabinet Doors, Block Feet, 1880s, 34 x 42 In. .	267.00
Dry Sink, Pine, Poplar, Backsplash, Drawer, Applied Panel, Doors, Painted, 36 x 47 In.	1175.00
Dry Sink, Pine, Red, Blue Paint, Pa., 1800s, 30 x 45 In.	911.00
Dry Sink, Pine, Slab Arched Sides, 1800s, 34 x 50 In.	652.00
Dry Sink, Poplar, 2 Paneled Upper Doors & Drawers, 2 Lower Doors, 72 x 36 In.	358.00
Dry Sink, Poplar, Chestnut, Drawers, Raised Panel Door, Hood, Green, Cream, 47 x 50 In.	1293.00
Dry Sink, Poplar, Green Paint, Zinc Lining, 1800s, 38 x 62 In.	1528.00
Dry Sink, Poplar, Paneled Doors, Cutout Base, Green Gray Paint, c.1850, 30 x 49 In.	1058.00
Dry Sink, Poplar, Yellow Stain, Drawer, 2 Doors, 38 x 49 In.	1896.00

Dry Sink, Softwood, Unpainted, Shaped Backsplash, Raised Panel Doors, Cutout Feet, 41 x 44 In.	384.00
Dumbwaiter, 3 Graduated Dish Tiers, Tripod Base, 1800s, 48 In.	356.00
Dumbwaiter, Brass, Glass, 3 Round Tiers, Putti Finial, Reeded Columnar Supports, Leaf Base, 54 In.	443.00
Dumbwaiter, George III Style, Mahogany, 3 Graduated Tiers, 3 Splayed Legs, 44 x 26 In.	185.00
Dumbwaiter, George III Style, Mahogany, 3 Tiers, Baluster Supports, Tripod Base, 43 x 23 In. ...*illus*	777.00
Dumbwaiter, Georgian Style, 3 Tiers, Pierced Brass Gallery, Pedestal, Tripod Base, 50 x 30 In.	657.00
Dumbwaiter, Louis XVI, Kingwood, 2 Tiers, Folding Hinged Compartments, Ormolu, 27 In. *illus*	896.00
Dumbwaiter, Mahogany, 3 Tiers, Rosettes, Ball Beaded Feet, c.1850, 43 x 42 In.	690.00
Dumbwaiter, Mahogany, 3 Tiers, Stepped Plinth, Disc Feet, c.1830, 30 x 36 In.	1708.00
Easel, Aesthetic, Faux Bamboo, Gold Leaf, Geometric Structure, c.1880, 76 x 36 In.	1150.00
Easel, Black Forest Style, Carved Boughs, Branches, Leaves, c.1890, 72 x 35 In.	652.00
Easel, Gilt Incised, Crest, Ram's Horns, Altar Table, Birds, Elephant Trunk Feet, c.1865, 80 In.	2337.00
Easel, Gilt Wood, Carved, Hinged Leg, Curved Front Legs, 79 x 18 In.	1098.00
Easel, Louis XIV Style, Carved Wood, Gilt, Scrolling Leaves, 1800s, 98 x 38 In.	2700.00
Easel, Renaissance Revival, Carved, Ebonized, Gilt Incised, Strapwork Stretcher, c.1870, 83 x 34 In.	1464.00
Entertainment Center, Doors, Open Glass Shelf Units, 1970s, 75 ½ x 73 In.	59.00
Etagere, Biedermeier, Gilt, Round Top, 3 Tiers, 3 Serpent Shape Supports, Tripod Base, 57 In.	4444.00
Etagere, Bleached Walnut, Leaf Carved Broken-Arch Pediment, 3 Tiers, Top-Shaped Feet, 38 x 41 In.	275.00
Etagere, Bronze, Leather, 4 Tiers, Gilt Embossed, c.1940, 36 x 16 In.	800.00
Etagere, Cherry, 4 Tiers, Mirror Back, Scrolling Leaves, c.1900, 61 x 31 In.	219.00
Etagere, Faux Bamboo, Gold Paint, 5 Tiers, X-Frame Sides, 82 x 18 In., Pair	1125.00
Etagere, George IV, Mahogany, Balustered Gallery, 2 Shelves, Drawers, 48 x 26 In.	2500.00
Etagere, Gothic Revival, Rosewood, 3 Towering Arch Crests, Crockets, Spires, c.1855, 112 x 55 In.	14145.00
Etagere, Hanging, Mahogany, Fretwork, Pierced Gallery Shelves, Columns, Mirror, c.1910, 50 x 35 In.	956.00
Etagere, Hardwood, 3 Tiers, Metal Trim, India, 1700s, 78 ½ x 36 In.	1968.00
Etagere, Mahogany, 3 Tiers, Shaped Shelves, Medial Drawer, Turned Finials, 52 x 18 In.	1035.00
Etagere, Mahogany, 4 Tiers, 71 x 25 In., Pair	2000.00
Etagere, Mahogany, 4 Tiers, Drawers, Turned Supports, Casters, c.1850, 53 x 24 ½ In. ...*illus*	896.00
Etagere, Mahogany, Shell, Grape Crest, Mirror, 6 Shelves, Ornately Carved, 80 x 49 In.	805.00
Etagere, Moorish, Mahogany, Mirror, Open Shelves, Carved Door, 60 x 33 In.	1178.00
Etagere, Neoclassical Style, Patinated Metal, 3 Tiers, Crisscross Open Back, 36 x 26 In.	2500.00
Etagere, Regency Style, Mahogany, 3 Shelves, Drawer, Bamboo Turned Supports, Legs, 60 x 20 In.	240.00
Etagere, Regency, Mahogany, 4 Tiers, Drawer, Turned Spindles, Casters, 61 x 18 x 18 In.	1652.00
Etagere, Regency, Mahogany, 4 Tiers, Turned Feet, Brass Casters, 53 x 15 In.	1534.00
Etagere, Renaissance Revival, Rosewood, Arched Crest, Pierced Fretwork, Shelves, 1800s, 73 x 33 In.	1353.00
Etagere, Renaissance Revival, Rosewood, Crest, Spindles, Mirror, Marble Top, c.1860, 91 x 37 In.	2562.00
Etagere, Rococo, Rosewood, Corner, Carved, 3 Graduated Tiers, 2 Shelves, 76 x 30 In.	299.00
Etagere, Rococo, Rosewood, Dome Top, Mirrored Back, Serpentine Base, 1860s, 103 x 53 In.	4481.00
Etagere, Rococo, Rosewood, Reticulated Gallery, 3 Shelves, Drawer, N.Y., c.1850, 41 x 21 In.	1195.00
Etagere, Rococo, Walnut, Marble, Carved, Pierced, 6 Shelves, Mirror, 93 In.	1169.00
Etagere, Rosewood, 3 Tiers, Low Drawer, Barley Twist Columns, 1850s, 45 x 19 In.	777.00
Etagere, Rosewood, Mirror, Marble Top, Carved Frame, Shelves, c.1875, 99 x 53 In.	4920.00
Etagere, Walnut, Pierced, Carved, Mirror, Corner, Marble Shelf, Drawer, c.1885, 102 In. ...*illus*	1150.00
Etagere, Wood, Open Shelves, Carved Apron, Chinese, 31 x 21 In., Pair ...*illus*	335.00
Etegere, Rosewood, Pierced Scrolling Side Supports, 2 Mirror Back Open Shelves, 1800s, 60 x 26 In.	325.00
Folio Stand, Regency Style, Mahogany, Carved, Adjustable Slat Supports, Stretchers, 40 x 26 In.	615.00
Footstool, Chippendale Style, Mahogany, Needlepoint, c.1890, 17 x 18 In.	264.00
Footstool, Chippendale, Mahogany, Block Legs & Stretcher, Upholstered, c.1795, 22 x 17 In.	711.00
Footstool, Chippendale, Mahogany, Faux Leather Top, Brass Nailhead Trim, Claw Feet, 9 x 17 In.	538.00
Footstool, Empire Revival, Mahogany, Ogee Bracket Feet, Upholstered Top, c.1880, 7 x 15 In.	399.00
Footstool, Federal, Mahogany, Reeded Flared Ends, Turned Feet, Upholstered, c.1800, Pair ...*illus*	836.00
Footstool, Fiddle Shape Top, Chamfered Legs, Grain Painted, c.1910, 12 ½ x 14 ½ In. ...*illus*	235.00
Footstool, Gilt, Padded Rectangular Top, Upholstered, Bun Feet, c.1875, 4 x 13 In., Pair	430.00
Footstool, Gilt, Padded Top, Cabriole Legs, Scrolled Toes, c.1875, 8 x 9 In.	430.00
Footstool, Inlaid Star, Rectangular, Turned Legs, 8 x 14 In.	91.00
Footstool, L. & J. G. Stickley, Upholstered, Paper Label, 13 ¼ x 19 ¼ In.	558.00
Footstool, Louis XV, Gilt, Flower Carved Frame, Cabriole Legs, Scroll Feet, c.1900, 6 x 13 In.	246.00
Footstool, Mahogany, Rectangular Cyma Frame, X-Supports, Cushion Top, c.1835, 16 x 23 In., Pair	115.00
Footstool, Needlework Panel, Equestrian Scene, Maitland-Smith, c.1990, 17 x 18 In.	649.00
Footstool, Painted Wood, Flowers, Shaped Skirt & Sides, Block Feet, 1800s, 6 x 11 In.	237.00
Footstool, Pine, 5-Board, Painted, Bittersweet, Stencil, Fruits, Leaves, c.1830, 6 ½ x 18 In.	470.00
Footstool, Pine, Black, Tacks, 19th Century, 9 ¼ x 15 In.	147.00
Footstool, Pine, Grain Painted, Stenciled Bird, Branch, 1800s, 6 x 7 x 13 In.	151.00
Footstool, Plank, Painted, Demilune Cutout Legs, 7 ¾ x 14 ¼ In.	181.00
Footstool, Provincial Louis XV Style, Fruitwood, Needlework Seat, c.1890, 10 x 24 In.	413.00
Footstool, Regency, Rosewood, Serpentine, Gilt, Stretchers, Miles & Edwards, c.1825	1135.00

Furniture, Dresser, Welsh, Corner, Oak, Shelves, Paneled, Drawers, Stretcher Shelf, c.1790, 77 x 95 In.
$2988.00

Neal Auction Co.

Furniture, Dresser, Welsh, Oak, Upper Shelves & Doors, Lower Drawers, Dovetailed, Inlay, c.1890, 78 x 54 In.
$1534.00

Brunk Auctions

Furniture, Dumbwaiter, George III Style, Mahogany, 3 Tiers, Baluster Supports, Tripod Base, 43 x 23 In.
$777.00

Neal Auction Co.

Furniture, Dumbwaiter, Louis XVI, Kingwood, 2 Tiers, Folding Hinged Compartments, Ormolu, 27 In. $896.00

Neal Auction Co.

Furniture, Etagere, Mahogany, 4 Tiers, Drawers, Turned Supports, Casters, c.1850, 53 x 24 ½ In. $896.00

Neal Auction Co.

Furniture, Etagere, Walnut, Pierced, Carved, Mirror, Corner, Marble Shelf, Drawer, c.1885, 102 In. $1150.00

James D. Julia Inc.

Footstool, Rhinoceros, Leather, Abercrombie, 16 ½ x 31 In.	561.00
Footstool, Rococo, Mahogany, Serpentine Seat, Flowers, Cabriole Legs, c.1850, 15 x 18 In.	299.00
Footstool, Rococo, Rosewood, Needlepoint Top, Carved Frame, Cabriole Legs, 17 x 25 In.	598.00
Footstool, Softwood, Mortised, Shaped Skirt, Demilune Cutout Legs, 6 x 16 In.	102.00
Footstool, Walnut, Tapestry, Cabriole Legs, Acanthus Knees, Hoof Feet, France, 18 ½ In. .. *illus*	429.00
Footstool, Wood, Bootjack Ends, Black, White, Paint, 19th Century, 5 x 8 In.	176.00
Frame, Baroque, Giltwood, Carved, Leaf, Fruit Twisted Ribbon, c.1790, 65 ½ x 54 ½ x 7 ½ In. ..... *illus*	3540.00
Frame, Black Forest, Lindenwood, Leaf Carved, Arched, Gilt Liner, c.1880, 39 x 25 In.	338.00
Frame, Carved, Spanish Style, Whitewash, c.1930, 27 x 22 In.	523.00
Frame, Gesso Gilt, Scrollwork, Leaves, Round Opening, James Hanna, 51 x 44 In.	235.00
Frame, Grain Painted, 1800s, 26 x 22 ½ In.	563.00
Frame, Mirror, Oval, Figural Putti Surround, Fruit, Masks, Faience, Ginori, Italy, 31 x 19 In. .	432.00
Frame, Neoclassical, Gilt, 3 Finials Crest, Columns, Winged Cherub, 1800s, 21 In., Pair	948.00
Frame, Pine, Carved Zigzag Design, Cutout Corner Leaves, 24 x 19 In.	298.00
Frame, Third Republic, Gilt, Cove Molded, Carved Oak Leaves, c.1875, 23 x 20 In.	553.00
Glider, Hickory, 2 Seat, Basket Weave Back, Branded Mark, 31 x 50 x 32 In.	2976.00
Gun Stand, Mahogany, Brass, Hinged Lid, Eagle, Square Legs, Stretchers, 18 x 33 In.	711.00
Hall Rack, Mirror, Cast Iron, Hunter, Dog, Top Lettering, Gold Paint, c.1900, 77 In.	633.00
Hall Stand, Art Deco, Oak, Rounded Top, 4 Hooks, Mirror, Lower Door, c.1920, 70 x 27 In.	156.00
Hall Stand, Art Nouveau, Walnut, Mirror, Iron Hooks, Drawer, Carved, 79 x 44 In.	488.00
Hall Stand, Cast Iron, Adjustable Mirror, White Paint, 79 In.	460.00
Hall Stand, Cast Iron, Mirror, Leafy Branching Arms, Umbrella Rest, Victorian, 75 x 26 In. ...	610.00
Hall Stand, Cast Iron, Oval Mirror Plate, Scrolling Hooks, Leaf Design, Victorian, 70 In.	244.00
Hall Stand, Gothic Revival, Mahogany, Mirror Plate, Trefoil, Spiral Shape, 75 x 30 In.	1107.00
Hall Stand, Henry II Style, Burl Walnut, Mirror, Arched, Ormolu Hooks, 84 x 39 In.	153.00
Hall Stand, Herter Bros., Mirror, Marquetry, Ebonized, Gilt Incised, 102 x 46 In.	2460.00
Hall Stand, Mahogany, Umbrella Stand, Lift Top Glove Box, Mirror, Hooks, 1900s, 74 x 26 In.	161.00
Hall Stand, Marble, Carved Top, Mirror, Turned Columns, Lower Shaped Shelf, 78 x 38 In.	374.00
Hall Stand, Mirror, Carved, Tree Trunk, Stag's Head, Ink Wells, Marble Top, c.1850, 108 x 53 In. *illus*	7800.00
Hall Stand, Mirror, Carved, Turned Columns, Marble Top, Low Shaped Shelf, 77 ½ x 38 In.	374.00
Hall Stand, Napoleon III Style, Walnut, Oval Mirror, Brass Hooks, Drawer, 92 x 49 In.	900.00
Hall Stand, Oak, Armchair Base, Lift Seat, High Back, Mirror, 4 Garment Hooks, c.1895, 81 x 30 In.	575.00
Hall Stand, Oak, Stepped Cornice, Fretwork Panels, Oval Mirrors, Demilune, 1800s, 90 x 40 In.	1076.00
Hall Stand, Walnut, Mirror, Turned Hooks, Marble, Drawer, Umbrella Holder, c.1870, 90 In. *illus*	805.00
Hall Stand, Tiger Oak, Carved Crest, Arched Mirror, Hooks, Storage Seat, Victorian, 82 x 30 In.	374.00
Hall Stand, Walnut, Beveled Mirror, Marble Surface, Hooks, Umbrella Stand, 1800s, 90 x 73 In.	4720.00
Hall Stand, Walnut, Leaf Carved Crest, Drawer, Marble Top, Mirror, Umbrella Hook, 89 x 38 In.	444.00
Hall Stand, Walnut, Marble Top, Drawer, Oval Mirror, Hooks, c.1890, 79 x 33 In.	179.00
Hall Stand, Walnut, Mirror, 6 Hooks, Umbrella Rack, Marble Top, Victorian, c.1875, 101 x 44 In.	1495.00
Hall Tree, Bamboo, Arched Top, Openwork Design, 89 x 36 In.	281.00
Hall Tree, Black Forest, 4 Cubs, Mother Bear, Lindenwood, Glass Eyes, 5 Arms, c.1910, 93 x 28 In.	2185.00
Hall Tree, Gothic Style, Carved, Pierced Wood, Hooks, Umbrella Bar, 87 x 38 In.	427.00
Hall Tree, Mahogany, Garment Pegs, Projecting Cove, Lunar Crest, c.1835, 79 x 35 In.	307.00
Hall Tree, Moroccan, Inlaid Bone, Serpentine Shaped Bonnet, Base, c.1820, 82 x 47 In.	896.00
Hall Tree, Oak, Hooks, Umbrella Stand, Shaped, Carved, France, 82 x 26 In.	397.00
Hall Tree, Oak, Oval Plate, Ornate Carved, Inlays, Brittany, 82 x 46 In.	397.00
Hall Tree, Parquetry, Walnut, Mother-Of-Pearl, Menard Illinois State Prison, 81 x 36 In.	940.00
Hall Tree, Renaissance Revival, Cast Iron Shell Shape Tray, c.1890, 87 x 33 In.	351.00
Hall Tree, Renaissance Revival, Walnut, Carved, Scroll Pediment, Block Feet, c.1875, 105 x 59 In.	720.00
Hall Tree, Wood, Carved, Hinged Top, Umbrella Sections, Copper Inserts, 79 x 36 In.	184.00
Hat Rack, Bronze & Marble Fittings, Carved, Figures, Scrolls, 69 x 19 In.	183.00
Hat Rack, Deer Antlers, Wood Base, Carved, Log, Leaves, Acorns, Pegs, c.1910, 35 In.	767.00
Hat Rack, Oak, Carved, Brass Hooks, c.1880, 86 x 10 x 16 In.	1600.00
Hat Rack, Renaissance Revival, Carved Wood, Wall Mount, 17 x 53 In.	122.00
Hat Rack, Walnut, 4 Carved Arms, Turned Standard, 72 x 25 In.	183.00
Headboard, G. Nakashima, Plank, Black Walnut, c.1960, 36 x 92 In.	5890.00
Headboard, G. Nakashima, Storage Area, Black Walnut, 1962, 35 x 58 In.	4030.00
Headboard, P. Evans, Directional, Cityscape, Illuminated, Storage, 1970s, 85 x 86 In.	5580.00
Highboy, 2 Panel Doors, Columns, Drawer, Swiss Paint Design, Shaped Feet, 30 x 26 In.	1121.00
Highboy, Cherry, Full Bonnet, 9 Drawers, Shell Carved, Harden, Queen, 39 x 84 In.	960.00
Highboy, Chippendale Style, Mahogany, Bonnet Top, 2 Parts, Drop Bail Pulls, 1900s	460.00
Highboy, George I, Walnut, Inlay, 5 Drawers, Cabriole Legs, 1700s, 51 x 38 In.	4270.00
Highboy, Metal, 5 Drawers, Shaped Gallery, Simmons, 1920s, 36 x 40 In.	1600.00
Highboy, Oak, 5 Drawers, Arched Skirt, Ball Feet, Brass Hardware, Early 1700s, 41 x 40 In. ...	460.00
Highboy, Queen Anne Style, 3 Parts, Bonnet Top, Drawers, Carvings, Henkel Harris, 89 x 41 In.	2070.00
Highboy, Queen Anne, Cherry, 2 Parts, Scroll Apron, Cabriole Legs, 1700s, 71 x 39 In.	1725.00

Highboy, Queen Anne, Cherry, Broken Pediment, Flame Finial, Shell, Shaped Skirt, c.1760, 91 In..		1438.00
Highboy, Queen Anne, Cherry, Carved Shell Design, Shaped Apron, Brass, 1760-80, 76 x 37 In.		5640.00
Highboy, Queen Anne, Cherry, Maple, Cornice, 5 Drawers, Carved Shell, 64 x 39 In.		1888.00
Highboy, Queen Anne, Mahogany, Bonnet Top, Fan Carved, Apron Drops, 1700s, 86 x 41 In. ..		3450.00
Highboy, Queen Anne, Maple, 6 Drawers, Carved Fan, Cabriole Legs, New Eng., c.1765, 66 x 38 In.		4266.00
Highboy, Queen Anne, Maple, 6 Drawers, Scrolled Apron, Cabriole Legs, 1700s, 77 x 40 In.		6900.00
Highboy, William & Mary, Walnut, 2 Parts, 8 Drawers, 6 Turned Legs, c.1705, 63 x 36 In.		1840.00
Highboy, William & Mary, Walnut, 8 Drawers, Turned Legs, Brass Handles, 1700s, 61 x 39 In. ....*illus*		1434.00
Highboy, Wood, Brass Pulls, 3 Drawers, James Mont, 1940s, 30 x 31 In.		4800.00
Highchair, 5 Spindles, Bentwood Backrest, Saddle Seat, 38 x 15 In.		29.00
Highchair, Arts & Crafts, Oak, Slatted Back, Saddle Seat, W.F. Whitney Co., Mass., 17 x 19 In..		300.00
Highchair, Birch, Mixed Wood, Red Paint, Footrest, 1800s, 38 x 18 In. ....*illus*		354.00
Highchair, Faux Bamboo, Woven Seat, Yellow Paint, 1800s, 35 x 12 In.		177.00
Highchair, Louis XVI Style, Beech, Cream Paint, Cane Seat & Back, Reeded Legs		649.00
Highchair, Oak, Turned Spindle Back, Pressed Back, Finials, c.1900, 38 ½ x 16 In.		58.00
Highchair, Windsor, Hide Seat, Green Paint, c.1810, 36 x 19 In.		708.00
Highchair, Wooden, Ladder Back, Double Box Stretcher, Round Legs, Woven Seat		207.00
Humidor, Engraved Figures, Landscape, Black Enamel, Gilt, Pewter Lining, Lid, 1800s, 14 x 8 In.		127.00
Humidor, Stand, Ebonized, Carved Swags, Beading, Turned Legs, 1900s, 26 x 19 In.		178.00
Humidor, Walnut, Folding Doors, Fitted Interior, Carved Trestle Legs, 1930s, 24 x 16 In.		90.00
Huntboard, Federal Style, Mahogany, Drawer, 2 Doors, 6 Square Legs, 41 x 70 In.		533.00
Huntboard, Mahogany, Backsplash, 2 Drawers, Spiral Legs, Stretcher Shelf, c.1820, 52 x 59 In.		13145.00
Huntboard, Oak, 2 Frieze Drawers, Fluted, Carved Legs, Paw Feet, c.1890, 36 x 82 In.		1076.00
Huntboard, Pine, 2 Drawers, Nail Construction, c.1850, 48 x 48 x 23 In.		2760.00
Huntboard, Pine, Blue & Gray Paint, 3 Drawers, Brass Handles, Square Legs, 1800s, 35 x 74 In.		2128.00
Huntboard, Southern, Walnut, Yellow Pine, 2 Doors, Drawer, 1800s, 40 x 57 In.		1121.00
Huntboard, Yellow Pine, 3 Drawers, 4 Doors, Columns, Bow Backsplash, c.1825, 51 x 62 In..		1840.00
Huntboard, Yellow Pine, Cut Nail Construction, 19th Century, 31 x 57 x 22 In.		2990.00
Huntboard, Yellow Pine, Drawer, Tall, Tapered Legs, 1800s, 41 x 50 In.		1020.00
Hutch, Oak, Arched Cornice, Panel Doors, Serpentine Base, 3 Drawers, France, 1700s, 97 x 53 In.		1534.00
Hutch, Pine, 2 Open Shelves, 2 Doors, 1800s, 67 x 40 ½ In.		288.00
Hutch, Pine, Plate Rack, Rolling Frieze, 7 Drawers, Door Bottom Center, Bun Feet, 83 x 60 In.		1062.00
Hutch, Pine, Scalloped Sides, 5 Open Shelves, Shaped Apron, Red Wash, c.1790, 75 x 48 In....		690.00
Ice Cart, Elm, Rectangular, Iron Mounts, Chinese, 65 In.		397.00
Jardiniere, Mahogany, Oval Bowl, 4 Ram Mask Supports, X-Stretcher, Birds, Hoof Feet, 31 In.		4216.00
Jardiniere, Regency Style, Mahogany, Slatted Tapered Body, Splayed Feet, 36 x 15 In.		98.00
Jardiniere, Regency, Mahogany, Brass Swing Handle, Reeded Body, Pedestal, 20 ½ x 14 ½ In.		644.00
Kas, Grain Painted, Molded Cornice, 2 Doors, Shelves, Hudson Valley, c.1830, 76 x 60 In.		2100.00
Kneeler, Prie-Dieu, Carved Frame, Upholstered, Blue, Flowers, France, 1800s, 36 x 20 In.		214.00
Kneeler, Prie-Dieu, Napoleon III, Oak, Upholstered Rests, Scrolls, Flowers Cross, Carved, c.1875, 36 In.		338.00
Kneeler, Prie-Dieu, Wood, Carved Scrolls, Cross, Dark Finish, Upholstered, France, 37 x 18 In.		214.00
Lap Desk, Anglo-Indian, Ivory, Quillwork, Ebonized, Inlaid Lid, Center Compartment, 9 x 16 In.		2196.00
Lap Desk, Campaign Style, Rosewood, Hinged, Lid, Brass Edges, Fitted Interior, c.1875, 5 x 16 In.		184.00
Lap Desk, Camphorwood, Brass Mounts, Chinese, 1800s, 19 ½ x 17 In.		237.00
Lap Desk, Drop Front, Mahogany Drawer, Fitted Interior, Legs, Brass, c.1875, 24 x 15 ¾ In.		522.00
Lap Desk, Ebony, Bone Inlay, Folding, Fitted Interior, India, 1800s, 17 In.		150.00
Lap Desk, Faux Red Grain, Hinged, Brass Key Escutcheon, 5 x 15 x 10 In.		79.00
Lap Desk, George II, Hinged Flap, Walnut, Reverse Painted, 18 x 11 In.		531.00
Lap Desk, Lid, Parquetry, Geometric Design, Compartments, 1800s, 4 x 11 In.		295.00
Lap Desk, Mahogany, Brass Banding, Williams Gaimes, c.1810, 6 x 18 In.		615.00
Lap Desk, Mahogany, Brass Inlay, Scrollwork, Hinged Top, Writing Surface, Handles, 6 x 16 In.		306.00
Lap Desk, Mahogany, Brass Mounted, Side Drawer, Swing Handle, Writing Surface, 7 x 13 In.		306.00
Lap Desk, Mahogany, Hinged Top, Fitted Interior, Brass Fittings, England, c.1820, 6 x 19 ¾ In.		145.00
Lap Desk, Mahogany, Rectangular, Fitted Interior, Brass Handles, Label, England, 1820, 14 x 9 In.		356.00
Lap Desk, Rosewood Veneer, Holly, Mother-Of-Pearl Inlay, Velvet Lining, 16 x 11 In.		83.00
Lap Desk, Rosewood, Brass, Fitted Interior, Purple Velvet, Writing Surface, Bottles, c.1880, 11 In.		504.00
Lap Desk, Stand, Mahogany, Brass Bound, Leather Writing Surface, Beaded Legs, 1800s, 34 x 18 In.		711.00
Lap Desk, Victorian, Mahogany, Sloped Lid, Writing Slide, Drawer, Ball Feet, 16 x 11 In.		123.00
Lap Desk, Victorian, Rosewood, Geometric Inlay, Lid, Writing Surface, 1800s, 5 x 10 In.		184.00
Lap Desk, Victorian, Walnut, Brass Shield, Sloped Writing Surface, c.1865, 5 ½ x 10 In.		184.00
Lap Desk, Walnut, Line Inlays, Brass Plate, Fitted Interior, Leather, c.1850, 6 x 12 In.		276.00
Lap Desk, Walnut, Slanted Leather Surface, Fitted Interior, Legs, Brass, c.1875, 26 x 19 In. ...		492.00
Lap Desk, William IV, Rosewood, Brass Inlaid, Handles, Felt Lined Surface, 7 x 20 In.		430.00
Lectern, Gothic Revival, Cherry, Carved Arch, Turned Columns, 1900s, 36 x 33 In.		374.00
Lectern, Mahogany, Putti Supports, Music Instruments, Heads, Tripod Base, c.1905, 60 In.		1422.00
Lectern, Pine, Lift Top, Slanted, Fitted Interior, 2 Lower Drawers, 40 x 36 In.		173.00

F

Furniture, Etagere, Wood, Open Shelves, Carved Apron, Chinese, 31 x 21 In., Pair
$335.00

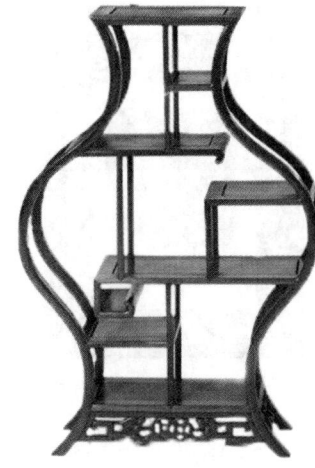

Leslie Hindman Auctioneers

Furniture, Footstool, Federal, Mahogany, Reeded Flared Ends, Turned Feet, Upholstered, c.1800, Pair
$836.00

Neal Auction Co.

Furniture, Footstool, Fiddle Shape Top, Chamfered Legs, Grain Painted, c.1910, 12 ½ x 14 ½ In.
$235.00

Garth's Auctions, Inc.

Furniture, Footstool, Walnut, Tapestry, Cabriole Legs, Acanthus Knees, Hoof Feet, France, 18 ½ In.
$429.00

Skinner, Inc.

Furniture, Frame, Baroque, Giltwood, Carved, Leaf, Fruit Twisted Ribbon, c.1790, 65 ½ x 54 ½ x 7 ½ In. **$3540.00**

Brunk Auctions

Furniture, Hall Stand, Mirror, Carved, Tree Trunk, Stag's Head, Ink Wells, Marble Top, c.1850, 108 x 53 In. **$7800.00**

Cowan's Auctions

Furniture, Hall Stand, Walnut, Mirror, Turned Hooks, Marble, Drawer, Umbrella Holder, c.1870, 90 In. **$805.00**

Leland Little Auction

Lectern, Oak, Pedestal Shape, Gilt Cross, Arch, c.1910, 35 x 18 In., Pair	950.00
Lectern, Rococo Style, Gilt, Eagle Carved, Scroll Supports, Shaped Feet, 6 ¾ x 21 In.	995.00
Library Ladder, Esherick, Cherry, 3 Steps, Twisted Post, Certificate, 1970, 25 x 51 In.	45000.00
Library Ladder, Esherick, Oak, Cherry, Carved, c.1965, 35 x 17 x 25 In. *illus*	53320.00
Library Ladder, Mahogany, Folding, 4 Rungs, Brass Treads, 54 In.	676.00
Library Ladder, Pine, Cast Iron Track Support, 95 ½ In.	478.00
Library Ladder, Walnut, 4 Steps, Stretcher Base, 80 x 22 In.	690.00
Library Ladder, William IV Style, Oak, 5 Rungs, Hand Rail, Box Stretcher, c.1950, 87 x 41 In.	799.00
Library Steps & Chair, Anglo-Indian, Teak, Folding, 1800s	230.00
Library Steps, Mahogany, Concave & Convex Compartments, Turned Feet, Leather, 25 x 19 In.	805.00
Library Steps, Mahogany, Drawer, Cupboard, Tooled Leather, Turned Legs, Eng., 1800s, 24 x 27 In.	805.00
Library Steps, Mahogany, Through Tenon Construction, Brass, Rubber Mounted, c.1890, 77 x 34 In.	7670.00
Library Steps, Oak, 4 Risers, c.1900, 77 x 24 In.	826.00
Library Steps, Oak, Folding, 4 Steps, 35 In.	313.00
Library Steps, Oak, Treads, Bannister, Block Support, 4 Steps, England, c.1890, 66 x 20 In.	1107.00
Library Steps, Regency Style, Leather, Pine, Fruitwood, 1900s, 102 x 12 In.	2124.00
Library Steps, Regency, Bamboo Turned Posts, Leather Wedge Treads, 79 x 19 In.	995.00
Library Steps, Regency, Mahogany, Tooled Leather, Columns, Metal Work Doors, 27 x 19 In.	354.00
Linen Press, Camphor, Carved, 2 Parts, Paneled Doors, Flowers, Fans, Drawers, 1800s, 85 x 53 In.	2013.00
Linen Press, Carved, Paneled Doors, 3 Drawers, Gilt Bronze, Continental, c.1770, 101 x 63 In. *illus*	1793.00
Linen Press, Cherry, 2 Parts, Hinged Doors, Stepped Cornice, 3 Lower Drawers, c.1795, 76 x 48 In.	4444.00
Linen Press, Chippendale, Cherry, 2 Panel Doors, 2 Large Drawers, Pa., c.1800, 75 x 44 In.	1580.00
Linen Press, Federal, Cherry, Paneled Doors, Reeded, Beaded, Reeded Feet, c.1800, 78 x 38 In.	2415.00
Linen Press, Federal, Mixed Wood, 2 Panel Doors, Over 4 Drawers, New York, c.1800, 84 x 51 In.	2645.00
Linen Press, Federal, Mixed Wood, 2 Panel Doors, Over Drawer, 2 Doors, Carved, 78 x 39 In.	2415.00
Linen Press, Federal, Mixed Wood, Curved Top, Inlaid, Carved, 2 Doors, N.Y., c.1810, 96 x 55 In.	4600.00
Linen Press, George III, Mahogany, Dovetailed Drawers, Ivory Escutcheons, c.1800, 84 x 51 In. *illus*	2124.00
Linen Press, Georgian Style, Mahogany, 2 Cupboard Doors, 4 Drawers, 67 x 49 In.	2125.00
Linen Press, Hepplewhite, Fruitwood, 2 Section, Lattice Frieze, Doors, Shelves, Drawers, 76 x 46 In.	2950.00
Linen Press, Hepplewhite, Mahogany, Paneled Doors, Interior Shelves, Drawers, c.1810, 76 x 50 In.	2714.00
Linen Press, Mahogany, 2 Paneled Doors, 4 Drawers, Bracket Feet, c.1880, 56 x 49 In.	960.00
Linen Press, Mahogany, Banded Doors, Fitted Interior, Bracket Feet, 44 x 22 In.	915.00
Linen Press, Mahogany, Frieze, Doors, Spurred Bracket Feet, Drawers, c.1800, 84 x 50 In.	2645.00
Linen Press, Mahogany, Interior Shelves, Lower Drawers, c.1850, 84 x 48 In. *illus*	1722.00
Linen Press, Mahogany, Pine, Double Pediment, Paneled Doors, Drawers, N.C., c.1820, 91 x 47 In.	5520.00
Linen Press, Mahogany, Serpentine Front, 2 Doors, 6 Drawers, Block Feet, 81 x 38 In.	510.00
Linen Press, Mahogany, Stepped Cornice, 2 Doors, 4 Drawers, c.1780, 77 x 50 In.	3050.00
Linen Press, Molded Cornice, Cupboard Doors, 2 Over 3 Drawers, 1800s, 80 x 50 In.	1652.00
Linen Press, Poplar, Raised Panel Doors, Drawer, Red Paint, c.1870, 42 x 18 In.	1763.00
Linen Press, Regency, Mahogany, 2 Paneled Door, 8 Drawers, Ball Feet, c.1820, 44 x 87 In.	2510.00
Linen Press, Satinwood, Ormolu Mounts, 2 Doors, Fitted Interior, 4 Drawers, France, 65 x 32 In.	748.00
Linen Press, Sheraton, Cherry, 2 Doors, Drawer, c.1820, 25 x 21 In.	3318.00
Linen Press, Sheraton, Mahogany, Doors, Sliding Trays Top, 3 Drawer Base, 68 x 48 In.	920.00
Linen Press, Walnut, 2 Parts, Panel Doors, Drawers, Bracket Feet, c.1755, 85 x 62 In.	10350.00
Love Seat, Art Deco, Mahogany, Silk Velvet, 1930s, 30 x 49 In.	1178.00
Love Seat, Charles Hollis Jones, Acrylic Base, Cotton, 1960s, 23 x 52 In.	3100.00
Love Seat, Louis XVI Style, Oval Padded Back, Carved Crest, Leaf Frame, Reeded Legs, 37 x 49 In.	295.00
Love Seat, Mahogany, Carved Crest, Cherubs, Scrolling, Tufted Back, Paw Feet, 38 x 46 In.	173.00
Love Seat, Meeks, Rosewood, Serpentine Crest, Pierced, Grapevines, c.1880, 48 x 65 In.	3245.00
Love Seat, Sheraton Style, Mahogany, Arched Back, Upholstered, c.1950, 33 x 53 In., Pair	523.00
Lowboy, Chippendale Style, Mahogany, 4 Drawers, Central Shell, Carved, Shaped, 1900s, 30 x 35 In.	5 75.00
Lowboy, Chippendale Style, Mahogany, 4 Drawers, Shell Design, Cabriole Legs, 1900s, 30 x 36 In.	207.00
Lowboy, Chippendale Style, Walnut, 4 Drawers, Shell & Tassel Knees, Brass, c.1900, 28 x 30 In.	489.00
Lowboy, Chippendale, Walnut, 3 Drawers, Shell Carved Knees, Ball & Claw Feet, 29 In.	1438.00
Lowboy, Mahogany, 3 Drawers, Shell Carved Center, Councill Craftsman, 1990s, 32 x 33 In.	506.00
Lowboy, Mahogany, Bowfront, 3 Drawers, Square Legs, Spade Feet, England, 1800s, 30 x 32 In.	177.00
Lowboy, Oak, Rectangular, 3 Drawers, Cabriole Legs, England, c.1820, 30 x 43 In.	430.00
Lowboy, Queen Anne Style, Mahogany, 3 Drawers, Batwing Brasses, 1900s, 27 x 30 In. *illus*	209.00
Lowboy, Queen Anne Style, Mahogany, Rectangular, 4 Drawers, Shell, Cabriole Legs, 31 x 33 In.	366.00
Lowboy, Queen Anne Style, Walnut, 2 Drawers, Cabriole Legs, c.1975, 30 x 29 In.	150.00
Lowboy, Queen Anne Style, Walnut, 3 Drawers, Carved Apron, Cabriole Legs, 29 x 34 In.	3320.00
Lowboy, Queen Anne, Mahogany, Fan Carved Drawer, Cabriole Legs, 1700s, 31 x 32 In.	1840.00
Lowboy, Walnut, Inlaid, 3 Drawers, Cabriole Legs, Pad Feet, 1800s, 28 x 29 In.	400.00
Mirror, 4 Color Prints In Panels, Carved Frame & Moldings, Victorian, 62 x 34 x 2 In.	230.00
Mirror, Adam Style, Giltwood, Basket Of Flowers, Ebonized, Faux Marble, c.1930, 54 x 23 In., Pair	546.00

Mirror, Adam Style, Giltwood, Oval, Scrolling Leaves, Shaped Crest, 47 x 22 In.	413.00
Mirror, Adam Style, Giltwood, Urn, Flower, Sheaf Crest, Carved, 1900, 55 x 25 In., Pair	1062.00
Mirror, Antler Veneer, Framed By Horns & Segments, 1900s, 51 x 41 In.	296.00
Mirror, Arched, Birds, Clouds, Flowers, Gray Paint, Giltwood, Venice, Italy, 1700s, 31 x 32 In.	474.00
Mirror, Art Deco, Bronze, Painted Scroll Frame, France, c.1940, 36 x 26 In.	584.00
Mirror, Art Deco, Parcel Gilt, Rectangular, Beveled, Ring, Swags Of Drapery, 1900s, 75 x 44 In.	1225.00
Mirror, Art Deco, Silver Plate, Diana Huntress, 2 Stags, Rectangular, France, 29 x 15 In.	1230.00
Mirror, Art Nouveau Style, Walnut, Pierced Frame, Giltwood, Carved Lilies, Leaves, 54 x 37 In., Pair	1638.00
Mirror, Art Nouveau Style, Wood, Carved, Parcel Gilt Lily Overlay, 48 x 36 In.	805.00
Mirror, Art Nouveau, Giltwood, Shaped, Wreath, Scrolls, Carved, c.1900, 78 x 47 In.	1180.00
Mirror, Arts & Crafts, Copper, Repousse Flower Frame, Rectangular, England, 15 x 19 In.	1440.00
Mirror, Arts & Crafts, Wood Surround, Rectangular, Iron Hooks, 32 x 22 In.	480.00
Mirror, Arts & Crafts, Wood, Notched Frame, Iron Hooks, 32 x 26 In.	540.00
Mirror, Ballroom, Empire, Oak, Gesso, Carved, Gold Leaf, Eagle, Egg & Dart, 99 x 60 In.	3346.00
Mirror, Baroque, Carved Wood, C-Scroll Frame, 1600s, 14 1/4 x 12 In.	858.00
Mirror, Baroque, Composition, Ornate Carvings, 2 Sconces, 3 Arms Each, Italy, 1800s, 101 x 70 In.	3068.00
Mirror, Baroque, Giltwood, Carved Leaves, High Relief Crest, Italy, 1600s, 24 x 21 In.	674.00
Mirror, Baroque, Sterling Repousse, Shells, Scrolling, Diamonds, Easel Back, 35 x 25 In.	1912.00
Mirror, Baroque, Winged Putti, Continental, 19th Century, 39 x 31 In.	588.00
Mirror, Beaux Arts, Giltwood, Pierced Flowers, Beaded Molding, Beveled, c.1885, 71 x 59 In.	1912.00
Mirror, Beveled, Cast Metal, Cherub Frame, Footed, c.1905, 11 In.	40.00
Mirror, Bilbao, Giltwood, Sienna Marble, Carved, Urn & Flower Spray Crest, 1700s, 39 x 18 In.	2629.00
Mirror, Carved Frame, Square, Scrolling Waves, c.1850, 16 x 14 In.	403.00
Mirror, Cheval, Louis XV Style, Carved Leaf Crest, Beveled Mirror, Wishbone Stand, 72 In.	708.00
Mirror, Cheval, Mahogany Frame, Scrolled Uprights, Trestle Base, c.1855, 80 x 30 In.	575.00
Mirror, Cheval, Mahogany, Carved, Sunburst Crest, Columns, Candlearms, c.1810, 76 x 39 In. *illus*	2988.00
Mirror, Cheval, Mahogany, Inlay, Oval, Lyre Shape Support, 4-Leg Base, c.1900, 69 In.	345.00
Mirror, Cheval, Mahogany, Serpentine, Shell Carved Crest, Curved Legs, 72 In.	826.00
Mirror, Cheval, Napoleon III, Mahogany, Scrolling Supports, 2 Candlearms, 70 In.	677.00
Mirror, Cheval, Neoclassical, Walnut, Gilded, Palmetto Crest, Urn Finials, c.1765, 85 x 45 In.	2952.00
Mirror, Cheval, Regency, Mahogany, Ring-Turned Frame, Brass Knobs, c.1810, 53 x 24 In. *illus*	1195.00
Mirror, Cheval, Turned Supports, Axe Head Finials, Drawer, Turned Stretcher, 1800s, 81 x 46 In.	345.00
Mirror, Cheval, Victorian, Fruitwood, Domed, Turned Support, Downswept Legs, c.1870, 11 In.	232.00
Mirror, Chinoiserie, Faux Giltwood, Pagoda Crest, Flower Urns, Divided Panes, c.1930, 78 x 61 In.	345.00
Mirror, Chinoiserie, Giltwood, Pagoda Crest, Flower Carved Frame, Phoenix Side Mounts, 53 In.	978.00
Mirror, Chippendale Style, Burl, Giltwood, Plume Crest, Scroll Corners, Leaf Stiles, 53 x 27 In.	2844.00
Mirror, Chippendale Style, Mahogany, Gilt, Carved Crest, Flowers, Leaves, c.1940s, 45 x 26 In.	368.00
Mirror, Chippendale Style, Mahogany, Giltwood, Carved, Serpentine Crest, 41 x 23 In.	149.00
Mirror, Chippendale Style, Mahogany, Shaped Edges, Giltwood, Phoenix, 46 x 21 In.	215.00
Mirror, Chippendale Style, Pine, Gesso, Shaped, Wing Crest, Carved, 1900s, 62 x 32 In.	1062.00
Mirror, Chippendale Style, Tiger Maple, Full Fretwork, 22 x 13 In.	148.00
Mirror, Chippendale Style, Tiger Maple, Scrolling Fretwork Frame, Rectangular, 39 x 21 In.	590.00
Mirror, Chippendale, Giltwood, Carved Flowers, Shells, Stippled, Shaped, Eng., 1700s, 59 x 29 In.	1180.00
Mirror, Chippendale, Giltwood, Pagoda Crest, Seated Monkey, Arches, c.1850, 64 x 27 In.	940.00
Mirror, Chippendale, Mahogany Veneer, Pine, Pierced, Giltwood, Phoenix, c.1800, 43 1/2 In. *illus*	294.00
Mirror, Chippendale, Mahogany Veneer, Scrolled Frame, Ogee Molded Liner, Late 1700s, 40 x 24 In.	735.00
Mirror, Chippendale, Mahogany, Carved, Phoenix Crest, Scrolling, c.1790, 32 x 18 In., Pair	345.00
Mirror, Chippendale, Mahogany, Carved, Scrolling, Giltwood, Wrought Iron Hanger, 37 x 19 In.	575.00
Mirror, Chippendale, Mahogany, Cutout Carved, c.1780, 51 3/4 x 25 In.	356.00
Mirror, Chippendale, Mahogany, Fretwork, Molded Crested Frame, c.1820, 40 x 20 In.	1150.00
Mirror, Chippendale, Mahogany, Giltwood, Feather Crest, Inset Shell, American, 1700s, 19 x 35 In.	374.00
Mirror, Chippendale, Mahogany, Giltwood, Phoenix Crest, Scrolling, 1700s, 36 In.	1725.00
Mirror, Chippendale, Mahogany, Giltwood, Shell Crest, Scrolled Ears, 1700s, 34 In.	2300.00
Mirror, Chippendale, Mahogany, Holly Line Inlay, Applied Pediment, Drop, Ears, 23 1/2 x 13 In.	153.00
Mirror, Chippendale, Mahogany, Parcel Gilt, Eagle Crest, Shaped, Carved Frame, c.1790, 31 x 18 In.	472.00
Mirror, Chippendale, Mahogany, Parcel Gilt, Frame, Pierced Medallion, 30 x 18 1/2 In.	117.00
Mirror, Chippendale, Mahogany, Parcel Gilt, Scrolled Pediment, England, c.1800, 55 x 28 In.	472.00
Mirror, Chippendale, Mahogany, Pine, Scrolled Frame, Pierced Gilded Shell Crest, c.1790, 26 In.	118.00
Mirror, Chippendale, Mahogany, Rectangular, Pierced Crest & Apron, Leaves, c.1790, 43 x 25 In.	863.00
Mirror, Chippendale, Mahogany, Scroll Top, Giltwood, Spread Wing Eagle, 1700s, 32 x 16 In.	150.00
Mirror, Chippendale, Mahogany, Scrolled Frame, Molded, 1700s, 33 x 19 In.	207.00
Mirror, Chippendale, Mahogany, Scrolled Pediment, Ears, Base, c.1800, 30 x 17 In.	600.00
Mirror, Chippendale, Mahogany, Shaped Frame, c.1800, 19 x 12 In., Pair	413.00
Mirror, Chippendale, Mahogany, Shaped, Arched Crest, Frame Surround, c.1790, 19 x 15 In.	540.00
Mirror, Chippendale, Parcel Gilt, Mahogany, Pierced Crest, Raised Shell, c.1780, 35 x 19 In.	403.00

Furniture, Highboy, William & Mary, Walnut, 8 Drawers, Turned Legs, Brass Handles, 1700s, 61 x 39 In.
$1434.00

Sloans & Kenyon

Furniture, Highchair, Birch, Mixed Wood, Red Paint, Footrest, 1800s, 38 x 18 In.
$354.00

Brunk Auctions

Furniture, Library Ladder, Esherick, Oak, Cherry, Carved, c.1965, 35 x 17 x 25 In.
$53320.00

Rago Arts & Auction Center

Furniture, Linen Press, Carved, Paneled Doors, 3 Drawers, Gilt Bronze, Continental, c.1770, 101 x 63 In. **$1793.00**

Neal Auction Co.

Furniture, Linen Press, George III, Mahogany, Dovetailed Drawers, Ivory Escutcheons, c.1800, 84 x 51 In. **$2124.00**

Brunk Auctions

Furniture, Linen Press, Mahogany, Interior Shelves, Lower Drawers, c.1850, 84 x 48 In. **$1722.00**

New Orleans Auction Galleries, Inc.

Mirror, Chippendale, Tiger Maple, Shaped Crest, Ears, c.1890, 19 x 31 In., Pair	660.00
Mirror, Contemporary, Giltwood, Dentil Molded Frame, Beveled, 1900s, 60 x 38 In.	388.00
Mirror, Convex Girandole, Wood, Giltwood, Eagle, Leaf Crest, Applied Spheres, Chain, 56 x 33 In.	3318.00
Mirror, Convex, Giltwood, 12 Spheres, Reeded Ebonized Liner, Round, c.1925, 15 In.	185.00
Mirror, Convex, Giltwood, Basket, Fruit, Cornucopia Frame, Carved, Round, 1800s, 40 x 30 In.	1888.00
Mirror, Convex, Regency, Giltwood, Reeded Cavetto Frame, Round, 46 In.	7020.00
Mirror, Copper, Wood, Diamond Shape, Rope Hanger, Dutch, c.1905, 12 x 18 In.	720.00
Mirror, Courting, Pine, Coffin Crest, Flowers, Continental, 18th Century, 16 x 11 In.	529.00
Mirror, Directoire, Giltwood, Shell Centered Rest, Acanthus Leaves, France, c.1820, 65 x 40 In.	1434.00
Mirror, Dressing, Bronze, Oval, Flowers, Cabochon Crest, Cherubs, Paw Feet, 1800s, 27 x 16 In.	8664.00
Mirror, Dressing, Empire, Mahogany, Swivel, Turned Posts, Roll Front Drawers, 26 x 23 In.	81.00
Mirror, Dressing, Koloman Moser, Beech, Marble, Brass, 2 Drawers, 2 Doors, 82 x 59 In. *illus*	5580.00
Mirror, Dressing, Mahogany, Shaped Supports, Base Drawers, c.1850, 38 x 25 In.	461.00
Mirror, Dressing, Sheraton, Mahogany, Line Inlay, Bowfront, Drawers, Ball Feet, 19 x 17 In.	71.00
Mirror, Dutch Baroque, Giltwood, Carved, Stippled, 6 Candle Shelves, c.1895, 22 x 62 In., Pair	1770.00
Mirror, Dutch Baroque, Lacquer, Giltwood, Wave & Rope Twist Bands, 50 ½ x 43 ½ In.	8190.00
Mirror, Eagle, Wreath, Putti, Openwork Crest, Pierced Leaf Surround, c.1700, 36 x 20 In.	1476.00
Mirror, Edwardian, Burl Walnut, 3 Parts, Scalloped Crest, Shaped Plate, c.1900, 27 x 30 In.	123.00
Mirror, Edwardian, Sterling, Beveled, Engraved Frame, Shield, Arched Top, c.1911, 18 x 12 In.	615.00
Mirror, Empire Revival, Mahogany, Ogee Molded Frame, c.1910, 44 x 50 In.	138.00
Mirror, Empire Style, Giltwood, Leaf Molded Crest, Flower Basket Spray, Pillars, 53 x 40 In.	738.00
Mirror, Empire Style, Mahogany, Rectangular, Pyramid Pediment, Ormolu, c.1900, 67 x 42 In.	799.00
Mirror, Empire, Mahogany Veneer, c.1830, 36 x 25 ½ In.	150.00
Mirror, Empire, Mahogany, Giltwood, 2 Ball Topped Columns On Pedestals, 1800s, 64 x 31 In.	830.00
Mirror, Empire, Mahogany, Giltwood, Applied Cornucopia, Wheat, France, 1800s, 47 x 22 In.	300.00
Mirror, Empire, Mahogany, Split Posts, c.1820, 23 x 21 In. *illus*	330.00
Mirror, Etched Flower Sprays, Banded Roping, Glass Rosettes, Venice, Italy, 51 x 32 In.	738.00
Mirror, Etched Venetian Glass, 8-Sided, Segmented Frame, Rosette Mounts, 49 x 28 In. *illus*	1107.00
Mirror, Fan Shape, Easel Back, Beveled, Spelter, Tassels, c.1890, 9 x 17 In.	201.00
Mirror, Faux Bamboo, France, 19th Century, 21 x 18 In.	249.00
Mirror, Federal Style, Carved Marble, Broken-Arch Pediment, Eagle Medallions, c.1900, 60 x 35 In.	1107.00
Mirror, Federal Style, Mahogany Inlaid, Giltwood, Urn Finial, Flower Stems, 1932, 56 x 24 In.	1067.00
Mirror, Federal, Ball Pendants Over Cornice, Ship, Carved Columns, c.1830, 41 x 22 In.	360.00
Mirror, Federal, Chinoiserie Design, Black, 1800s, 20 x 20 ½ In.	259.00
Mirror, Federal, Convex, Carved Eagle, c.1780, 34 ¾ In. *illus*	470.00
Mirror, Federal, Convex, Eagle Mount, 12 Applied Spheres, Flower Scroll Base, 1800s, 43 x 27 In.	1265.00
Mirror, Federal, Convex, Round, 18 Spherules, Eagle Crest, Pendant Apron, c.1805, 41 x 25 In.	345.00
Mirror, Federal, Giltwood, Applied Hunt Panel, Columns, Carved, 1800s, 59 x 32 In.	1304.00
Mirror, Federal, Giltwood, Convex, Round, Leaf Tip, Eagle Perched On Base, c.1800, 41 x 27 In.	2013.00
Mirror, Federal, Giltwood, Embossed Leaf Frame, Battle Of Lexington, 38 x 19 In.	212.00
Mirror, Federal, Giltwood, Gesso Frame, Lighthouse Reverse Painted Panel, c.1800, 45 x 23 In.	489.00
Mirror, Federal, Giltwood, Gesso, Acorn In Relief, New England, c.1825, 29 x 20 ¾ In. *illus*	1659.00
Mirror, Federal, Giltwood, Gesso, Reverse Painted, War Of 1812, Beading, c.1815, 40 x 22 In.	948.00
Mirror, Federal, Giltwood, Reverse Painted, Urns, Reeded Columns, c.1810, 38 x 32 In.	1003.00
Mirror, Federal, Gold Finish, Oval Crest, Flanking Urns, Flower Shape Sconce, 1900s, 41 x 15 In.	144.00
Mirror, Federal, Mahogany Veneer, Carved Acorn Drops On Cornice, Half Columns, 1800s, 36 In.	830.00
Mirror, Federal, Mahogany, Cheval, Rectangular, Crest, Trestle Base, Candlearms, 38 x 75 In.	2185.00
Mirror, Federal, Mahogany, Half Columns, Powder Stencil, 30 ¾ x 16 In. *illus*	130.00
Mirror, Federal, Mahogany, Home, Pond Scene, Column, P. Wayne, c.1820, 26 ¾ x 13 In.	119.00
Mirror, Federal, Pine, Applied Half Turnings, Architectural Crest, Giltwood, 32 x 20 In.	382.00
Mirror, Federal, Reverse Painted Panel, Landscape, Black, Gold Frame, 1800s, 12 x 25 In.	69.00
Mirror, Flame Mahogany Veneer, Ogee Form, Gold Liner & Edge, 33 In.	111.00
Mirror, Flower & Shell Crest, Carved, Gilded, Rectangular, Continental, c.1890, 62 In.	478.00
Mirror, Fornasetti, Label, Italy, c.1960, 18 ½ In. Diam. *illus*	1750.00
Mirror, Fruitwood, Silver Clad, Rectangular, Flowers, Carved Borders, 1800s, 13 x 11 In.	858.00
Mirror, Full-Length, Black, Giltwood Garland Surround, 64 x 28 In.	214.00
Mirror, G. Nakashima, Walnut, Extended Frame, Widdicomb, 1950s, 37 x 46 In.	1736.00
Mirror, G. Stickley, Divided Pane, 4 Hooks, 27 ¾ x 42 ½ In.	3720.00
Mirror, George II Style, Giltwood, Shaped Plate, Swan Neck Pediment, Shell Crest, 40 x 19 In.	1230.00
Mirror, George II Style, Giltwood, Swan Neck Pediment, Carved Frame, 63 x 38 In.	2000.00
Mirror, George II Style, Mahogany, Parcel Gilt, Leaves, Shells, Shaped Frame, 40 x 23 In.	527.00
Mirror, George II, Walnut, Parcel Gilt, Rectangular, Molded Corners, c.1750, 36 x 24 In.	613.00
Mirror, George II, Walnut, Swan Neck Crest, Applied Leaves, Flowers, c.1750, 52 x 27 In.	3159.00
Mirror, George III Style, Gesso, Cherubs, Eagles, Flower, Scrolls, Rectangular, 36 x 17 In.	369.00
Mirror, George III Style, Giltwood, Leaves, Openwork Crest, Bouquet & Urn, 1800s, 45 x 21 In.	448.00
Mirror, Georgian Style, Giltwood, Broken Pediment, Crackle Finish, Shaped, 1970s, 54 x 28 In.	1650.00

Mirror, Gilt Gesso, Oval, Carved, Shaped Pediment, Scroll, Flowers, Late 1800s, 46 x 29 In.....	230.00
Mirror, Gilt Gesso, Oval, Deep Dish, Fruit, Nuts, Leaves, 1800s, 32 x 28 In..............................	230.00
Mirror, Gilt Metal, Sunburst, Round Beveled, Interlacing Rays, c.1950, 52 In. Diam................	676.00
Mirror, Giltwood, Arched, Openwork Crest, 1800s, 69 x 29 In..	288.00
Mirror, Giltwood, Arched, Pierced Crest, Carved, c.1800, 37 x 20 ½ In................................	386.00
Mirror, Giltwood, Banded Frame, Central Plate, c.1870, 38 x 31 In.	1599.00
Mirror, Giltwood, Bronze, Enamel, Oval, Putti, Easel, Alphonse Giroux, c.1875, 12 x 10 In.	2300.00
Mirror, Giltwood, Bull's-Eye, Openwork Flowers, Scrolled Leaves, Eagle, c.1905, 50 x 37 In. ...	474.00
Mirror, Giltwood, Cartouche Shape, Pierced Rocaille Crest, 2 Phoenixes, 1760, 47 x 53 In......	7080.00
Mirror, Giltwood, Carved Flowers, Swags, c.1925, 30 x 40 In.	127.00
Mirror, Giltwood, Carved, Domed Crest, Leaves, Blossoms, 2-Handled Urn, 1800s, 29 x 19 In.	657.00
Mirror, Giltwood, Carved, Medusa Mask Crest Rail, 2 Elongated Palmettes, 1800s, 79 x 61 In.	1045.00
Mirror, Giltwood, Carved, Peaked Crest, France, 1800s, 46 ½ x 22 In.....................................	1220.00
Mirror, Giltwood, Convex, Gilt, Fruit Basket Crest, Acanthus Base, 1800s, 38 In., Pair.............	6325.00
Mirror, Giltwood, Crest, Putti, Garlands, Beading, Egg & Dart Molding, France, 1800s, 60 x 33 In.	1348.00
Mirror, Giltwood, Domed, Pierced, Scrolling Leaf Crest, Dentil, Pendants, c.1890, 70 x 35 In..	1968.00
Mirror, Giltwood, Faux Bamboo, Beveled, Carved, France, 48 x 40 In.	553.00
Mirror, Giltwood, Faux Bamboo, Flower Wreath Crest, Tassel Roping, 1800s, 64 x 37 In.	830.00
Mirror, Giltwood, Gesso, Carved Flowers, France, c.1880, 54 x 31 In.	923.00
Mirror, Giltwood, Gesso, Incised, Carved, Cartouche Shape, Italy, 1800s, 28 ½ x 18 ½ In.	400.00
Mirror, Giltwood, Gesso, Rectangular, Grape Leaves, Spiral Columns, 1800s, 35 x 23 In.........	1076.00
Mirror, Giltwood, Louis XVI, Double Pane Edge, Bead & Flower Carved, Pierced, 1800s, 79 x 51 In.	3355.00
Mirror, Giltwood, Masque Centered Leafy Fan, Mermaids, Italy, c.1910, 53 x 34 In.	615.00
Mirror, Giltwood, Matte Gilt, Rectangular, c.1820, 46 ½ x 28 In..	1016.00
Mirror, Giltwood, Neoclassical Style, Rectangular, Dentil Frame, 1800s, 44 x 38 In.	553.00
Mirror, Giltwood, Open Flower Carved Frame, c.1950, 32 x 27 In..	185.00
Mirror, Giltwood, Openwork Scroll Frame, Italy, c.1910, 19 x 14 In., Pair...............................	1476.00
Mirror, Giltwood, Openwork, Flower Basket, Fruit, Carved, c.1910, 47 In.	259.00
Mirror, Giltwood, Oval, Carved, Eagle Finial, Leaf Openwork, c.1760, 40 In............................	1000.00
Mirror, Giltwood, Oval, Pebble Design, Fruit, Acorns, 1800s, 32 x 28 In.................................	717.00
Mirror, Giltwood, Pierced, Carved Crest, France, 1800s, 93 ½ x 57 In...................................	2745.00
Mirror, Giltwood, Rectangular, Beveled Panel, Leaves, c.1950, 84 x 72 In.	2006.00
Mirror, Giltwood, Rectangular, c.1890, 30 x 22 In.	288.00
Mirror, Giltwood, Rectangular, Flower Crest, Molded Dentil Frame, c.1950, 69 x 40 In...........	2214.00
Mirror, Giltwood, Rectangular, Opposing Bird Head Crest, Plume, Leaves, Shell, 1718, 22 x 15 In.	288.00
Mirror, Giltwood, Reverse Painted, Beaded Molding, Flower, Leaf, Carved, c.1850, 39 x 27 In.	478.00
Mirror, Giltwood, Ribbon & Wreath Crest, Flower Carved Frame, c.1910, 55 x 40 In.	492.00
Mirror, Giltwood, Rococo, Ebonized Slip, Flower Accents, c.1875, 31 x 27 In.	369.00
Mirror, Giltwood, Round, Raised Fruit & Laurel Border, Paint, Italy, c.1800, 20 In...................	770.00
Mirror, Giltwood, Scroll, Flower Carved Crest, Frame, Italy, 1800s, 80 x 50 In........................	1586.00
Mirror, Giltwood, Scrolled Leaves, Flower Trim, Continental, 1700s, 52 x 18 In.......................	1541.00
Mirror, Giltwood, Shell & Leaf Crest, Molded Scroll Frame, Rectangular, c.1885, 66 x 42 In. ..	984.00
Mirror, Giltwood, Shell Crest, Acanthus, Swags, c.1910, 32 x 42 In.	478.00
Mirror, Giltwood, Split Baluster Frame, Fleur-De-Lis Corners, Gilt, c.1800, 47 x 31 In.	1673.00
Mirror, Gold, Red, Green Lacquer, Ornate Dragons, Figures, Carved, Chinese, c.1900, 28 x 16 ½ In.	115.00
Mirror, Gothic Revival, Walnut, Carved, Crest, Flower Finial, Ripple Molding, c.1865, 39 x 21 In.	239.00
Mirror, Hanging, Giltwood, Oval, Leaves, Ribbon Banding, 1900s, 36 x 31 In.	389.00
Mirror, Italian Rococo, Giltwood, Shaped Shell, Flowers, Scroll Frame, Crest, 50 x 24 In.	995.00
Mirror, Ivory, Oval, Swelled Scalloped Crest, Leaves, Griffins, Serpents, France, c.1800, 34 In., Pair	3851.00
Mirror, Karl Springer, Mirrored Glass, Satinwood, Chromed Steel, Octagonal, 1980s, 30 In. ...	1054.00
Mirror, Laurel & Berry Wreath Crest, Rose, Leaf Frame, c.1940, 37 x 42 In.	215.00
Mirror, Louis Philippe, Damascene Gilt, Matte Frame, Greek Key Edge, c.1820, 43 x 32 In......	1554.00
Mirror, Louis Philippe, Giltwood, France, c.1880, 62 x 53 In.	984.00
Mirror, Louis Philippe, Silver Gilt, Incised Greek Key, c.1840, 47 x 32 In.	1353.00
Mirror, Louis XV Style, Giltwood, Arched, Leaf Crest, Shield, Beaded Rabbet, 1800s, 77 x 48 In.	2749.00
Mirror, Louis XV Style, Giltwood, Carved, Molded Frame, c.1890, 26 x 22 In.	295.00
Mirror, Louis XV Style, Giltwood, Carved, Scrolls, Grapevines, Putti, Bird, c.1900, 54 x 42 In. .	2390.00
Mirror, Louis XV Style, Giltwood, Serpentine Crest, Gilt Basket, Garlands, c.1815, 63 x 31 In. .	584.00
Mirror, Louis XV, Giltwood, Pierced Crest, Rectangular, 1800s, 60 x 43 In.	1342.00
Mirror, Louis XVI Style, Bronze, Wreath Cartouche, c.1890, 5 x 3 In.	195.00
Mirror, Louis XVI Style, Giltwood, Arched, Crest, Scrolls, Paneled Ground, c.1890, 72 x 39 In., Pair	5658.00
Mirror, Louis XVI Style, Giltwood, Female Mask, Flowers, Urn, Beaded, Oval, c.1900, 58 x 38 In.	2091.00
Mirror, Louis XVI Style, Giltwood, Openwork Frame, Flower Crest, Carved, 68 x 33 In., Pair ...	8302.00
Mirror, Louis XVI, Giltwood, Rectangular, Hearts, Ribbon, Crest, Pineapple Carved, 61 x 37 In.	2133.00
Mirror, Louis XVI, Pine, Urn, Garland Panel, Putty Paint, France, c.1790, 115 x 44 In.............	1888.00
Mirror, Louis XVI, Provincial Style, Giltwood, Leaf Crest, Bellflowers, 1900s, 39 x 23 In.	837.00

Furniture, Lowboy, Queen Anne Style, Mahogany, 3 Drawers, Batwing Brasses, 1900s, 27 x 30 In.
$209.00

Sloans & Kenyon

Furniture, Mirror, Cheval, Mahogany, Carved, Sunburst Crest, Columns, Brass Candlearms, c.1810, 76 x 39 In.
$2988.00

Neal Auction Co.

Furniture, Mirror, Cheval, Regency, Mahogany, Ring-Turned Frame, Brass Knobs, c.1810, 53 x 24 In.
$1195.00

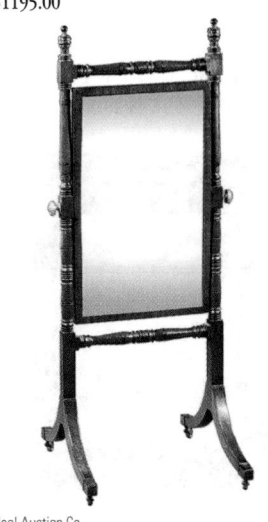

Neal Auction Co.

Furniture, Mirror, Chippendale, Mahogany Veneer, Pine, Pierced, Giltwood, Phoenix, c.1800, 43 ½ In. $294.00

Garth's Auctions, Inc.

Furniture, Mirror, Dressing, Koloman Moser, Beech, Marble, Brass, 2 Drawers, 2 Doors, 82 x 59 In. $5580.00

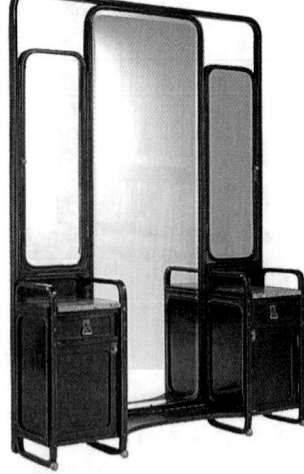

Rago Arts & Auction Center

Furniture, Mirror, Empire, Mahogany, Split Posts, c.1820, 23 x 21 In. $330.00

Cowan's Auctions

Mirror, Mahogany Veneer, Scrolled Crest & Base, c.1790, 33 In.	147.00
Mirror, Mahogany Veneer, String Inlay, Giltwood, Garlands & Phoenix Crest, c.1790, 29 In.	294.00
Mirror, Mahogany, Bellflower, Drape Carved Crest, c.1950, 30 x 46 In.	102.00
Mirror, Mahogany, Carved, Fans, Abstract Devices, Late 1700s, 28 x 11 In.	368.00
Mirror, Mahogany, Carved, Shaped, 1900s, 47 x 46 In.	115.00
Mirror, Mahogany, Chippendale Style, c.1785, 37 ½ x 23 In.	430.00
Mirror, Mahogany, Horseshoe Shape, Brass Hooks, c.1890, 30 x 25 ½ In.	300.00
Mirror, Mahogany, Parcel Gilt, Mountain Scene Panel, Carved Animals, Italy, 58 x 26 In.	1112.00
Mirror, Mahogany, Stepped Top, Silvered, Birds, Urns, Flowers, c.1700, 35 x 17 In.	1180.00
Mirror, Maple, Sculptural, Carved Profile Frame, Michael Joerling, 35 x 34 In.	690.00
Mirror, Metal, Bronzed, Porcelain, Medallions, Flowers, Openwork Frame, France, c.1890, 20 ¾ In.	613.00
Mirror, Metal, Elongated Octagon, Draped Beading, Applied Beads On Frame, 1993, 76 x 54 In.	3125.00
Mirror, Milk Glass, Canted Rectangle, Flower Crest, Shield Cornice, Banding, c.1900, 56 x 35 In.	1845.00
Mirror, Multicolor, Giltwood, Pierced Crest, Shells, 1900s, 33 x 26 In, Pair	777.00
Mirror, Napoleon III, Giltwood, Caryatids, Putti, Scrolled Leaves, c.1865, 99 x 55 In.	11353.00
Mirror, Napoleon III, Giltwood, Domed Crest, Molded Egg & Dart Frame, c.1865, 47 x 36 In.	615.00
Mirror, Napoleon III, Giltwood, Incised Leaves & Flowers, c.1865, 63 x 37 In.	1045.00
Mirror, Napoleon III, Giltwood, Lattice Incised Frame, c.1890, 41 x 37 In.	246.00
Mirror, Napoleon III, Giltwood, Leaves & Flowers, c.1865, 63 x 37 In.	1845.00
Mirror, Napoleon III, Giltwood, Oval, Bowknot Crest, c.1865, 42 x 32 In.	461.00
Mirror, Napoleon III, Giltwood, Rectangular, Canted Corners, Egg & Dart Frame, c.1865, 60 x 42 In.	922.00
Mirror, Neoclassical Style, Giltwood, Carved Ribbon Crest & Swags, Leaves, 41 x 24 In.	329.00
Mirror, Neoclassical Style, Walnut, Molded Cornice, Column Stiles, Austria, 1800s, 61 x 42 In.	127.00
Mirror, Neoclassical, Ebonized, Giltwood, Split Balusters, Inscribed, c.1825, 43 x 20 In.	600.00
Mirror, Neoclassical, Gilt Gesso, Carved, Girandole, Eagle, c.1825, 37 x 20 In. ....*illus*	3081.00
Mirror, Neoclassical, Giltwood, Carved, Blocked Cornice, Acorn Pendants, Rosettes, 38 x 23 In. ..*illus*	418.00
Mirror, Neoclassical, Giltwood, Flat Crest Rail, Rose & Leaf, Twisted Rope, c.1825, 28 x 15 In.	275.00
Mirror, Neoclassical, Giltwood, Gesso, Turned Half Columns, Acanthus Leaf, c.1850, 38 x 20 In.	194.00
Mirror, Neoclassical, Giltwood, Pink Marble, Scrolling Leaf Crest, Finials, Spain, c.1800, 45 x 19 In.	4740.00
Mirror, Neoclassical, Giltwood, Reverse Painted Panel, Stepped Cornice, c.1810, 21 x 12 In.	100.00
Mirror, Neoclassical, Giltwood, Ribbon Wreath Crest, Warriors, Paw Feet, 1800s, 66 x 29 In.	1968.00
Mirror, Neoclassical, Giltwood, Scrolling Leaf Corners, Raised Panel, c.1830, 42 x 23 In.	400.00
Mirror, Neoclassical, Giltwood, Stepped Cornice, Spherules, Double Column Frame, c.1810, 37 In.	250.00
Mirror, Neoclassical, Marble, Parcel Gilt, Italy, 1900s, 59 x 39 ½ In.	236.00
Mirror, Neoclassical, Pine, Artichoke Finial, Leaf Drop, Pear Shape, Carved, Italy, 1800s, 40 x 42 In.	1652.00
Mirror, Neoclassical, Urn Crest, Garlands, Mirrored Frame, Pendant, 1800s, 63 x 29 In.	2100.00
Mirror, Oak, Rectangular, Ogee Molded Frame, c.1910, 30 x 46 In.	259.00
Mirror, Octagonal, Segmented Surround, Rosettes, Etched Flowers, 44 x 31 In.	419.00
Mirror, Oscar Bach, Bronze, Arched Grape Leaf Crest & Low Corners, 19 x 35 In.	420.00
Mirror, Oval, Gilded Gesso Frame, Urn Of Flowers, Late 1700s, 42 x 22 In.	461.00
Mirror, Painted, Arch, Wavy Frame, Scrolling Edge & Ears, Orange & Gold Wash, 1800s, 11 x 8 In.	144.00
Mirror, Parcel Gilt Music Trophy, Urn Crest, Beaded, Dentil Frame, Black Paint, Sweden, 57 x 25 In.	1287.00
Mirror, Parcel Gilt, Flowers, Swags, Cabochon Crest, Faux Marble Frame, Italy, c.1790, 50 x 35 In.	1845.00
Mirror, Pier, Aluminum, Bronze, France, 1970s, 64 x 27 In.	434.00
Mirror, Pier, Empire Style, Walnut, Cornice, Domed Panel, Figure, Drum, Flag, 1800s, 78 x 35 In.	2460.00
Mirror, Pier, Empire, Giltwood, Ebonized, Sphinx, 2 Obelisks, Fluted Columns, 1800s, 64 In., Pair	2573.00
Mirror, Pier, Federal, Giltwood, Dragon Tablet, Carved, Ebonized, Reeded Pilasters, 37 x 23 In.	1287.00
Mirror, Pier, Federal, Mahogany, Blocked Crest, Reeded Stiles, Reverse Painted, 40 x 21 In.	359.00
Mirror, Pier, Figures & Landscape Panel, Flowers, Red, c.1921, 66 x 45 In.	861.00
Mirror, Pier, French Provincial, Walnut, Carved, Landscape Vignette, 60 x 17 In.	199.00
Mirror, Pier, Giltwood, Ebonized, Reeded Pilasters, Gold Leaf Corners, c.1835, 54 x 30 In.	1722.00
Mirror, Pier, Giltwood, Gouache Figures, Garland Panels, Beaded Frame, Sweden, 50 x 22 In.	595.00
Mirror, Pier, Giltwood, Mica Classical Frieze, Scroll Pilasters, Reeded Columns, c.1810, 54 x 35 In.	3585.00
Mirror, Pier, Giltwood, Molded Cornice, Frieze Carved Urn, Fluted Supports, c.1920, 81 x 52 In.	4182.00
Mirror, Pier, Giltwood, Molded Cornice, Round Pendants, Split Column, 1800s, 32 x 19 In.	837.00
Mirror Pier, Giltwood, Molded Frame, Cylindrical Columns, c.1800, 46 In.	956.00
Mirror, Pier, Giltwood, Paint, Gallery Crest, Birds, Cherry Branches, 2 Drawers, 1800s, 92 x 33 In.	1093.00
Mirror, Pier, Giltwood, Stepped Crest, Flowers, Fluted Pilasters, Onyx Top Shelf, c.1885, 113 x 32 In.	2214.00
Mirror, Pier, Louis XVI Style, Giltwood, Rectangular, Ribbon Carved Frame, 1800s, 74 x 47 In.	2271.00
Mirror, Pier, Louis XVI Style, Multicolor, Molded Frame, Pastoral Landscape, c.1910, 50 x 27 In.	676.00
Mirror, Pier, Mahogany, Molded Cornice, Pineapple & Spiral Columns, 1800s, 40 x 21 In.	369.00
Mirror, Pier, Napoleon III Style, Giltwood, Figural Painting, c.1910, 49 x 28 In.	180.00
Mirror, Pier, Neoclassical, Giltwood, Molded Frame, Anthemion Mounts, c.1810, 48 x 24 In.	1315.00
Mirror, Pier, Oil On Canvas Napoleonic Scene, Lower Pane, Ribboned Frame, c.1875, 60 x 29 In.	1845.00
Mirror, Pier, Parcel Gilt, Landscape, Figures Panel, Beaded Frame, c.1875, 46 x 30 ½ In.	584.00
Mirror, Pier, Pine, Fluted Columns, Scrollwork, Classical Bust, Silvered, c.1890, 83 x 57 In.	235.00

Mirror, Pier, Queen Anne, Walnut, Parcel Gilt, Divided Pane, Shaped Frame, 44 x 18 In.	468.00
Mirror, Pier, Regency, Parcel Gilt, Reeded Pilasters, Tablet, Flower, Leaf Carved, 53 x 29 In.	5557.00
Mirror, Pier, Rococo Style, Giltwood, Chinoiserie Landscape, Continental, 1800s, 72 x 44 In. ... *illus*	1195.00
Mirror, Pier, Victorian Style, Giltwood, Shield & Scroll Crest, Arched Top, 63 x 30 In.	488.00
Mirror, Pier, Walnut, Shelf, Pilaster, Chalet Roof Crest, Pendant Finials, c.1885, 91 x 24 In. ...	345.00
Mirror, Pine, Carved, c.1710, 10 ½ x 6 ¼ In. ......*illus*	3819.00
Mirror, Pine, Waxed, Molded Leaf Carving, Oval, Beveled Glass, 37 In.	369.00
Mirror, Pine, Yellow Oval Frame, David Good, Ohio, c.1850	823.00
Mirror, Plume Crest, 2 Phoenixes, Openwork Carved Frame, c.1910, 72 In.	575.00
Mirror, Queen Anne, Burl Veneer, Broken Pediment, Scrolling, 1700, 31 x 15 In.	119.00
Mirror, Queen Anne, Giltwood, Leaf & Tassel Design, England, c.1710, 17 ¾ x 62 In.	5036.00
Mirror, Queen Anne, Mahogany, Rectangular, Scrolled Crest, Round Shell, c.1755, 43 x 18 In.	690.00
Mirror, Queen Anne, Pine, Scrolled Crest, Painted, Red, White Flowers, Leaves, 1700s, 16 x 9 In..	7110.00
Mirror, Queen Anne, Pine, Shaped Crest, Mortise & Tenon, Rectangular, 1700s, 16 x 10 In.	237.00
Mirror, Queen Anne, Walnut, Gilt Gesso, Scrolled & Pierced Crest, 1700s, 31 In.	210.00
Mirror, Queen Anne, Walnut, Shaped Crest, Beveled Glass, Rectangular, c.1750, 35 x 15 In. ...	1778.00
Mirror, Rectangular, Scrolled Oval Medallion Crest, Giltwood, Venice, c.1905, 112 x 72 In.	3585.00
Mirror, Regency Style, Giltwood, Concave, Carved Leaves & Berries, Reeded, Ebonized, c.1885, 31 In.	738.00
Mirror, Regency Style, Giltwood, Convex, Eagle Crest, Ebonized, c.1890, 36 x 22 In.	1230.00
Mirror, Regency, Carved, Giltwood, Oval, 1846, 40 In.	623.00
Mirror, Regency, Giltwood, Bull's-Eye, Spherules, Ebonized Reeded Rabbet, c.1810, 17 In.	598.00
Mirror, Regency, Giltwood, Convex, Black Trim, Eagle Crest, England, c.1810, 40 x 25 In., Pair	5333.00
Mirror, Regency, Giltwood, Convex, Eagle, Applied Scrolls, Ebonized, c.1810, 41 x 23 In.	5412.00
Mirror, Regency, Giltwood, Half Columns, Wheat & Grapevine Ornaments, c.1850, 47 x 22 In.	230.00
Mirror, Regency, Giltwood, Leaves, Serpentine Top, Pendant Crest, Sweden, c.1750, 60 x 25 In.	1960.00
Mirror, Regency, Giltwood, Pierced Shell, Scrolling, Diaper Ground, 1700s, 30 x 22 In.	750.00
Mirror, Reverse Painted Glass, Aluminum Scrolled Crest, M. Aubert, 1960s, 44 x 22 In.	527.00
Mirror, Reverse Painted, Woman On Stage, Applied Turnings, Rosettes, c.1835, 25 x 13 In. ...... *illus*	441.00
Mirror, Reverse Painted, Wood, Painted Black, Gold, Split Spindle, c.1830, 22 x 12 In.	482.00
Mirror, Rococo Revival, Giltwood, Oval, Leaf Crest, Bellflowers, Shell, c.1865, 100 x 42 In.	5412.00
Mirror, Rococo Revival, Wood, Gold Paint, Pierced, Scrolled Crest, c.1860, 64 x 33 In., Pair ...	1840.00
Mirror, Rococo Style, Flower Painted, Shaped Frame, Pane, Italy, 29 x 17 In.	384.00
Mirror, Rococo Style, Giltwood, Carved, Flower Swags, Shells, Rectangular, 1900s, 50 x 38 In.	132.00
Mirror, Rococo Style, Giltwood, Openwork Leaf Pediment, Fruited Branches, c.1900, 42 x 21 In.	646.00
Mirror, Rococo Style, Giltwood, Pierced Frame, Beveled Glass, 1800s, 51 x 29 In.	118.00
Mirror, Rococo Style, Giltwood, Scrolling Leaves Crest, Domed Plate, 1900s, 51 x 30 In.	861.00
Mirror, Rococo, Ebonized, Giltwood, Arched Top, Grapevine Crest, Strapwork, c.1850, 45 x 25 In.	1098.00
Mirror, Rococo, Giltwood, Acanthus Carved Crest, Flower Swags, 1800s, 43 x 21 In., Pair	1195.00
Mirror, Rococo, Giltwood, Flared Scroll Frame, Smoky Divided Panes, c.1950, 47 x 44 In.	259.00
Mirror, Rococo, Giltwood, Oval, Pierced, Carved Crest, Scrolls, Leaves, c.1850, 95 x 43 In.	1315.00
Mirror, Rococo, Walnut, Giltwood, Flower Basket, Vine, Beveled, Arched, c.1790, 36 x 15 In.	474.00
Mirror, Rosewood, Burl Walnut Trim, Line & Gazelle Design, c.1920, 34 x 65 In.	123.00
Mirror, Rosewood, Carved, Shou Characters, Bats, Painted Glass Panel, 1800s, 63 x 23 In.	119.00
Mirror, Rosewood, Lotus Design, Carved, Pierced, Chinese, c.1900, 21 x 22 In.	237.00
Mirror, Shaker, Tiger Maple, Cherry, Brass Ring Hanger, Silvered Glass, c.1835, 7 x 5 In.	1638.00
Mirror, Shaped, Scalloped, Silver Sconce, Portugal, 16 x 7 In., Pair	7898.00
Mirror, Shaving, Brass, Oval Tray, Ornate Wishbone Frame, c.1900, 64 In.	240.00
Mirror, Shaving, Federal, Bowfront, 3 Drawers, Turned Supports, c.1800s, 26 x 25 In.	118.00
Mirror, Shaving, Federal, Mahogany, Inlay, Stepped Base, Oval, Drawers, c.1810, 24 x 19 In...	151.00
Mirror, Shaving, G. Stickley, Swivel, Branded, 21 ½ x 26 In. .....*illus*	1488.00
Mirror, Shaving, Georgian, Mahogany, Urn Finials, 3 Drawers, Bracket Feet, 1700s, 24 x 16 In.	296.00
Mirror, Shaving, Mahogany Veneer, Pine, Inlaid Bowfront Case, Drawer, 19 x 16 In.	88.00
Mirror, Shaving, Mahogany, Compartment, Spiral Supports, Shell Feet, England, c.1879, 32 x 31 In.	356.00
Mirror, Shaving, Mahogany, Round, Pivoting Plate, Scroll Arms, c.1830, 19 In.	350.00
Mirror, Shaving, Mahogany, Serpentine Front, Oval Pane, 3 Drawers, England, c.1800, 24 In.	184.00
Mirror, Shaving, Sheraton, Mahogany, Pa., c.1820, 20 x 18 ¾ In.	89.00
Mirror, Sheraton, Gilt Shell Crest Panel, Twisted Column, c.1820, 30 x 20 In.	127.00
Mirror, Sheraton, Giltwood, Classical Frieze, Reeded Pilasters, c.1790, 43 x 25 In.	184.00
Mirror, Sheraton, Giltwood, Reverse Painted Landscape, Carved, 35 ½ x 17 ½ In.	207.00
Mirror, Sheraton, Giltwood, Reverse Painted, Columns, Harbor Scene, c.1835, 36 x 22 In.	173.00
Mirror, Sheraton, Tabernacle, Giltwood, House, Lake, Early 1800s, 30 x 20 In.	115.00
Mirror, Sheraton, Tabernacle, Reverse Painted, Turned Columns, 1800s, 38 x 19 In.	115.00
Mirror, Silver, Cartouche Shape, Chased, Embossed, Madonna, Figures, Italy, c.1750, 18 x 14 In.	1304.00
Mirror, Silver, Oval, Leaves, Chinese Temple Finial, Pierced, Fret, 2 Phoenixes, 1900s, 57 x 34 In.	2460.00
Mirror, Smoke Design, Gray On Beige, Square, c.1840, 15 ½ x 13 ¼ In.	403.00
Mirror, Stencil Design, Hitchcock, 1830, 22 x 20 In.	840.00

Furniture, Mirror, Etched Venetian Glass, 8-Sided, Segmented Frame, Rosette Mounts, 49 x 28 In.
$1107.00

Neal Auction Co.

Furniture, Mirror, Federal, Convex, Carved Eagle, c.1780, 34 ¾ In.
$470.00

Cowan's Auctions

Furniture, Mirror, Federal, Giltwood, Gesso, Acorn In Relief, New England, c.1825, 29 x 20 ¾ In.
$1659.00

Skinner, Inc.

Furniture, Mirror, Federal, Mahogany, Half Columns, Powder Stencil, 30 ¾ x 16 In.
$130.00

Conestoga Auction Co., Inc.

Furniture, Mirror, Fornasetti, Label, Italy, c.1960, 18 ½ In. Diam.
$1750.00

Los Angeles Modern Auctions

Furniture, Mirror, Neoclassical, Gilt Gesso, Carved, Girandole, Eagle, c.1825, 37 x 20 In.
$3081.00

Skinner, Inc.

Mirror, Toilet, Mahogany, Urn Finials, 3 Drawers, Cock-Beaded, Bracket Feet, 1700s, 25 x 17 In.		329.00
Mirror, Toilet, Walnut, Drawers, Bracket Feet, c.1740, 28 x 18 In.		299.00
Mirror, Transitional Style, Gilt Gesso, 1800s, 55 x 28 In., Pair		150.00
Mirror, Vanity, Art Nouveau, Gilt Metal, Carved Leaves, Figures, 11 ½ x 14 In.		325.00
Mirror, Venetian Glass, Elongated Octagon, Leaf Design Frame, 47 x 29 In.		930.00
Mirror, Venetian Glass, Plumed Crest, Engraved, Inset Blue Glass, 1800s, 49 x 25 In.	*illus*	823.00
Mirror, Venetian Style, Carved, Multicolor, Scrolled, Pierced Acanthus Crest, 42 x 21 In.		837.00
Mirror, Venetian Style, Heart Shape, Flowers, Beveled, 25 x 22 In., Pair		478.00
Mirror, Venetian Style, Rossin, Oval, Scalloped Edge, 1900s, 37 x 25 In., Pair		4428.00
Mirror, Victorian, Giltwood, Gesso, Oval, Leaf & Flower Crest, Carved, 53 x 35 ½ In.		115.00
Mirror, Victorian, Giltwood, Open Crest, Carved, 70 x 36 In.		374.00
Mirror, Victorian, Iron, Wreath Border, Crown Crest, c.1890, 17 In.		236.00
Mirror, Victorian, Walnut, Hat Rack, 6 Garment Pegs, Shelf, Shaped Design, 42 x 26 In.		207.00
Mirror, Walnut, American Federal Shield Shape Frame, Giltwood, Gesso, c.1890, 16 x 13 In.	*illus*	705.00
Mirror, Walnut, Branchwork Frame, Oak Leaves, Flowers, c.1900, 29 x 20 In.		369.00
Mirror, Walnut, Carved Panel, Beveled, Twist Column, c.1890, 94 x 36 In.		338.00
Mirror, Walnut, Flat Crest, Opposing Gothic Arches, Square Quatrefoils, c.1835, 46 In.		584.00
Mirror, Walnut, Openwork Leaf Scrolls, 2 Rampant Lions, Medallion, c.1900, 54 x 35 In.		529.00
Mirror, Walnut, Prince Of Wales Feather Finial, Candlearms, c.1835, 42 x 22 In.		553.00
Mirror, Walnut, Wall, Arched Crest, Horns, Flower Design, Cutout Hearts, 24 In.		273.00
Mirror, Wendell Castle, Walnut, Shaped, Drip Design, Marked, 26 x 16 In.	*illus*	13035.00
Mirror, William & Mary Style, Chinoiserie, Black Ground, Shaped Divided Plate, 47 x 18 In.		576.00
Mirror, William IV, Mahogany, Arched Plate, Molded Frame, Hinged Storage, c.1835, 29 x 27 In.		153.00
Mirror, Wood Frame, Ebonized Flowers, Urns, Ivory Inlaid, Germany, 1876, 12 x 9 In.		633.00
Mirror, Wood, Carved Eagle Surround Frame & Crest, Continental, 26 x 33 In.		776.00
Mirror, Wood, Carved, 2 Eagles, Leaves, Fruit, Upper, Lower Shelves, Beveled, 1900s, 54 x 29 In.		288.00
Ottoman, Cowhide Upholstery, Round, c.1985, 17 x 40 In.		923.00
Ottoman, Empire, Mahogany, Upholstered, Rectangular, Scroll Feet, c.1830, 37 x 18 In.		919.00
Ottoman, Frank Lloyd Wright, Hexagonal, Upholstered, Heritage, 30 x 27 In.		2160.00
Ottoman, Karl Springer, Wool Upholstery, Brass Casters, 17 ½ x 25 In., Pair		341.00
Ottoman, Mahogany, Square Shape, Upholstered Slip Seat, Bracket Feet, c.1820, 16 x 18 In., Pair		366.00
Ottoman, Thayer-Coggin, Square Seat, Tapered Wood Legs, c.1955, 15 x 21 In., Pair		688.00
Overmantel Mirror, see Architectural category.		
Pedestal, Alabaster Top, Column, Gilt Bronze Cupid Supports & Ornate Base, c.1900, 27 x 20 In.		1230.00
Pedestal, Baptismal, Gothic Revival, Oak, Octagonal, Bowl, Base, c.1885, 39 x 19 In.		1353.00
Pedestal, Belle Epoque, Red Lacquer, Round, Winged Dragon Masks, c.1900, 41 In., Pair		1586.00
Pedestal, Black Marble, Round, 37 x 16 In.		390.00
Pedestal, Bronze & Gilt Accents, Carved, Center Urn, Columnar Supports, c.1885, 46 x 24 In.		6038.00
Pedestal, Bronze, Marble Top, Reeded Legs, Paw Feet, Leaf Standard, Italy, 40 x 14 In., Pair		4575.00
Pedestal, Bronze, Square Top, Tapered, Scroll Feet, Rosettes, Leaves, 33 In.		478.00
Pedestal, Carved, Oak, Egyptian Woman, Flowers, Marble Top, Base, 1800s, 19 In., Pair		240.00
Pedestal, Carved, Wood, Griffin, Round Top, Late 1800s, 19 ½ In.		356.00
Pedestal, Cherry, Lion Mask Handles, Turned Column, Leaves, Cattails, c.1875, 42 In.		3050.00
Pedestal, Cherry, Revolving Top, Incised Tapered Stem, Turned Base, Ball Feet, c.1870, 39 In.		2135.00
Pedestal, Corner, Black Marble Top, Ormolu Capital, Spiral Black Marble Column, 37 x 25 In.		219.00
Pedestal, Ebonized, Granite Top, Egret Shape Stand, Platform, Shaped Feet, c.1885, 36 x 16 In.		3690.00
Pedestal, Faux Burl Veneer, Faux Black Marble, Octagonal, 1900s, 47 x 12 In., Pair		239.00
Pedestal, George III, Mahogany, Rectangular, Applied Moldings, 48 x 13 In.		702.00
Pedestal, Gilt, Carved, Marble Top, Apron Garland, Round, Painted, c.1940, 32 x 11 In.		523.00
Pedestal, Gilt, Glass Jewels, Fabric Top, Strapwork Corners, Fluted Legs, 39 x 16 In.		4780.00
Pedestal, Gilt, Round, Dentil Carved Frieze, Iron Supports, Scroll Feet, 44 x 14 In.		1722.00
Pedestal, Gilt, Square Top, Fleur-De-Lis Design, Tapered, Support, 42 In.		2006.00
Pedestal, Green Marble, Spiral Turned, Square Swivel Top, Octagonal Base, 1800s, 31 x 14 In.		671.00
Pedestal, Hardwood, Round Marble Top, Pierced Carved Frieze, Stretcher, Cabriole Legs, 36 In.		186.00
Pedestal, Italian Style, Green Marble, Round Top, 1900s, 44 In.		478.00
Pedestal, Italian Style, Marble, Gilt Detail, 1900s, 45 In.		568.00
Pedestal, Kimbel & Cabus, Ebonized Cherry, Gilded, 38 x 15 x 15 In.		2976.00
Pedestal, Limbert, Shoe Feet, Branded Mark, 36 x 16 ½ x 16 ½ In.		3720.00
Pedestal, Louis Philippe, Green Marble, Tapered Body, Busts, Stepped Base, 43 x 14 In.		837.00
Pedestal, Louis XVI Style, 4 Curled Ram's-Head Supports, Gilt, Triangular Base, 58 In., Pair		1063.00
Pedestal, Louis XVI Style, Gilt Bronze, Porcelain, Tripod Brass Stand, 32 x 12 In., Pair		3936.00
Pedestal, Louis XVI Style, Marble, Gilt Bronze, Tapered, Stepped Base, c.1890, 45 x 13 In.		5378.00
Pedestal, Mahogany, Round Top, Maiden's-Head Standard, Round Base, Italy, c.1890, 36 x 13 In.		492.00
Pedestal, Marble, Carved, Fluted, Bellflowers, Ribbons, Garlands, Italy, 1800s, 44 x 17 In., Pair		4780.00
Pedestal, Marble, Gilt Bronze, Round Top, Cylindrical Column, Round Base, 46 x 14 In.		594.00
Pedestal, Marble, Gilt, Square Top, Serpentine Edge, Cabriole Legs, X-Stretcher, 47 In., Pair		948.00

Pedestal, Marble, Square Top, Ringed Capitals, Square Stepped Base, 1900s, 51 x 10 In., Pair	956.00
Pedestal, Napoleon III Style, Marble, Gilt Bronze, Alternating Masks, France, 47 In.	4481.00
Pedestal, Neoclassical, Faux Marble, Ebonized, Square Top, Gilt Banded, Back Opens, 32 In., Pair	492.00
Pedestal, Neoclassical, Marble Top, Round Column, 25 x 20 In.	984.00
Pedestal, Neoclassical, Marble, Round Top, Cylindrical Base, 25 x 20 In.	492.00
Pedestal, Neoclassical, Walnut, Carved, Square Top, Column Support, Square Base, 42 In.	156.00
Pedestal, Oak, Gadrooned Top, Carved & Twisted Stem, Griffin, Brass Mounts, 37 x 19 In.	183.00
Pedestal, Oak, Quartersawn, Cat Face, Rings, Carved Scrolling, Leaves, 44 x 15 ½ In.	374.00
Pedestal, Oak, Spiral Support, France, 1800s, 47 x 16 In.	366.00
Pedestal, Oak, Square Top, Turned, Square Paneled Support, Stepped Base, 39 x 11 In.	207.00
Pedestal, Ormolu, Marble Top, Spiral Turned Support, Round Foot, 37 x 25 In.	460.00
Pedestal, Pine, Carved, Bird, Downturned Head, Long Neck, Turned Base, 40 x 11 ½ In.	532.00
Pedestal, Renaissance Revival, Oak, V Shape, Carved Face, Leaves, Square Base, 1800s, 49 x 13 In.	420.00
Pedestal, Renaissance Revival, Rosewood, Hexagonal Top, Gilt Banding, Hoof Feet, c.1890, 38 In.	3355.00
Pedestal, Renaissance Revival, Walnut, Ebonized, Carved, Gilded, Square, Swags, c.1850, 39 x 14 In.	2074.00
Pedestal, Rosewood, Carved, Round Stretcher, Chinese, 34 x 12 In., Pair	384.00
Pedestal, Rosewood, Gilt, Round Top, Tapered Support, Base Molding, Bracket Feet, 44 In.	7469.00
Pedestal, Rustic, Driftwood, Rounded Top, Twisted Base, 3 Splayed Supports, 29 x 15 In.	246.00
Pedestal, Stand, Wood, Painted, Chinese Man, Kneeling, Tray On Head, 1800s, 31 In., Pair	5925.00
Pedestal, Walnut, Bronze, Dish Top, Stretcher With Finial, Paw Feet, Disc Base, c.1890, 38 In.	1342.00
Pedestal, Winged Phoenix, Marble Top, Shield Front, Draped Chain, Tripod Base, c.1890, 44 x 19 In.	1150.00
Pedestal, Wood, Black Figure, Holding Round Top, Rocaille Base, Paw Feet, 1800s, 35 In., Pair	5490.00
Pedestal, Wood, Ebonized, Gilt, Square, Canted Corners, Festoons, Scrolling Pilasters, 21 x 23 In.	649.00
Pedestal, Wood, Marquetry, Garlands, 46 x 15 In., Pair	403.00
Pedestal, Wood, Shaped Shelf, Scrolled, Tasseled, Black Figures, c.1900, 36 ¾ In., Pair	1434.00
Pew, Oak, Carved, Scrolled Armrest, Arch Panel Support, c.1910, 50 x 38 In.	120.00
Pie Safe, Green Paint, Scalloped Base, Flowers, Hourglass Vents, Carved Feet, c.1840, 34 x 16 In.	288.00
Pie Safe, Mixed Wood, 2 Doors, Tin Punched Panels, Painted Urns, Drawers, c.1840, 59 x 54 In.	27140.00
Pie Safe, Mixed Wood, Punched Tin Panels, Arch, Star Designs, 2 Drawers, c.1850, 45 x 53 In.	1495.00
Pie Safe, Painted, Ebonized, Paneled Doors, Tall Bracket Feet, c.1890, 56 x 57 In.	956.00
Pie Safe, Pine, 2 Drawers, 2 Doors, Punched Tin Panels, 59 x 45 In.	275.00
Pie Safe, Pine, Cutout Gallery, 2 Doors, Drawers, Painted, Punched, Tapered Legs, 66 x 63 In.	4600.00
Pie Safe, Pine, Hanging, Punched Tin Panels, c.1900, 19 x 21 In.	2950.00
Pie Safe, Poplar, Drawer, Butterfly Punched Tin Panels, Gray Paint, c.1850, 58 x 39 In.	1410.00
Pie Safe, Poplar, Pine, 12 Star Tines, Drawer, High Legs, Gray Paint, 66 x 41 In.	1410.00
Pie Safe, Poplar, Punched Fylfot Tins, 54 x 38 ¼ In.	948.00
Pie Safe, Poplar, Yellow Pine, 6 Inset Punched Tin Panels, 79 x 45 In.	2640.00
Pie Safe, Softwood, Grain Painted, Punched Tin Panels, Gallery Back, 1800s, 58 x 42 In. ..... illus	735.00
Pie Safe, Softwood, Molded Cornice, Upper Doors, Punched Tin Panels, Drawers, 74 x 44 In.	1298.00
Pie Safe, Softwood, Yellow Pine, Poplar, Gallery, Punched, Fylfot, Fan Designs, 53 x 49 In.	1150.00
Pie Safe, Tin, Punched Pinwheel Design, 1800s, 38 ½ x 40 In.	830.00
Pie Safe, Walnut, Poplar, Drawer, Doors, Painted, Star-Punched Tin Panels, 52 x 39 In.	1410.00
Pie Safe, White Pine, Tin, 2 Drawers, Over 2 Pierced Doors, Virginia, c.1850, 49 x 54 In.	1265.00
Pie Safe, Yellow Pine, 2 Doors, Punched Tin Panels, Side Panels, Painted, 1800s, 54 x 46 In. illus	4248.00
Pie Safe, Yellow Pine, Scalloped Gallery, 2 Framed Tin Doors, 2 Drawers, c.1835, 58 x 54 In.	2588.00
Pipe Rack, Oak, Cutout Crest, 2 Rack Rows, Slide-Out Shelf, Drawer, England, 28 x 14 In.	460.00
Planter, Biedermeier, Corner, Bronze Arch Frieze, Gadroon Molding, Walnut Base, 29 x 18 In., Pair	191.00
Planter, Hardwood, Brass Bound Handles, Stand, 26 In.	469.00
Planter, Wicker, Ball Feet, 34 x 32 In.	92.00
Rack, Baking, Brass, Iron, Marble Top, 3 Tiers, 90 x 90 In.	750.00
Rack, Baking, French Provincial, Oak, Arched Plank Top, Finials, Drawer, Spindles, 37 x 33 In.	777.00
Rack, Baking, French Provincial, Walnut, Urn Finials, Shaped Crest, Spindled Door, 34 x 38 In.	956.00
Rack, Baking, Louis XV Style, Shaped Crest, Garlands, Wheat Sheaf, Stiles, Squat Legs, 29 x 31 In.	276.00
Rack, Baking, Oak, Cage Spindle, Door, Flowers, Wheat, Row Of Finials, France, 41 x 39 In.	540.00
Rack, Baking, Walnut, Shaped Crest, Turned Spindles, Door, Slatted, Scroll Feet, c.1800, 42 x 31 In.	3173.00
Rack, Blanket, George III Style, Mahogany, Line Strung Uprights, c.1950, 34 x 26 In.	338.00
Rack, Drying, Pine, Mortised Construction, 1800s, 46 ½ x 40 In.	88.00
Rack, Drying, Shaker, Collapsible, 4 Split Legs, Hinged Joints, Metal Braces, 1800s, 48 x 65 In.	52.00
Rack, Kindling, Pressed Brass, Lion Mask, Flanked By Lions, 6 Paw Feet, 30 In.	232.00
Rack, Magazine, Barrel Shape, Wood, Brass Frame, 19th Century, 18 x 14 In.	71.00
Rack, Magazine, Brass, Swan Shape, Jansen, c.1955, 14 ½ x 23 In.	523.00
Rack, Magazine, Oak, Brass, Stand, Tripod Legs, Stretcher, Rotates, Hall Birmingham, 33 In.	156.00
Rack, Plate, French Provincial, Molded Cornice, Glass Doors, Open Shelves, 49 x 60 In.	127.00
Rack, Plate, Hanging, Red Grain Paint, Shaped Sides, Gallery, 13 Pegs, 1800s, 11 x 71 In.	823.00
Rack, Plate, Pine, Hanging, Dovetailed, Blue Over Blue Paint, c.1830, 45 x 37 In.	764.00
Rack, Quilt, French Provincial, Pine, Distressed, Open Wood Bar, 1800s, 32 x 94 In.	299.00

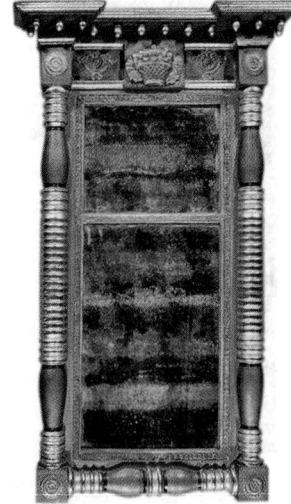

Furniture, Mirror, Neoclassical, Giltwood, Carved, Blocked Cornice, Acorn Pendants, Rosettes, 38 x 23 In.
$418.00

Neal Auction Co.

Furniture, Mirror, Pier, Rococo Style, Giltwood, Chinoiserie Landscape, Continental, 1800s, 72 x 44 In.
$1195.00

Neal Auction Co.

Furniture, Mirror, Pine, Carved, c.1710, 10 ½ x 6 ¼ In.
$3819.00

Garth's Auctions, Inc.

Furniture, Mirror, Reverse Painted, Woman On Stage, Applied Turnings, Rosettes, c.1835, 25 x 13 In. $441.00

Garth's Auctions, Inc.

Furniture, Mirror, Shaving, G. Stickley, Swivel, Branded, 21 ½ x 26 In. $1488.00

Rago Arts & Auction Center

Furniture, Mirror, Venetian Glass, Plumed Crest, Engraved, Inset Blue Glass, 1800s, 49 x 25 In. $823.00

Cowan's Auctions

Rack, Quilt, Pine, Blue, Green Paint, Pa., c.1800, 36 ¾ x 37 In.	474.00
Rack, Towel, Edwardian, Fruitwood, Faux Bamboo, Arched Sides, 4 Rails, 33 x 24 In.	111.00
Rack, Towel, Mahogany, Line Inlay, 4 Bar Rails, England, 34 x 27 In.	148.00
Rack, Wine, Metal, Scroll Design, Doors, Paint, 38 x 14 In.	92.00
Rack, Wine, Rustic, Pine, Rectangular, Rounded, Upright, 11 Banks Of 3 Holes, 50 x 13 x 7 In.	861.00
Rack, Wrought Iron, Brass, Round Shelf, Downswept Legs, Adjustable, Paris, c.1920, 64 x 20 In.	615.00
Recamier, Carved Backrest, Reeded Seat Rail, Downswept Legs, Upholstered, 1800s, 34 x 86 In.	2133.00
Recamier, Carved Scrolling Top Rail, Shaped Seat, Cabriole Legs, Scroll Feet, 33 x 42 In.	2360.00
Recamier, Louis Philippe, Rosewood, Carved Back, Pierced, Upholstered, c.1850 ....*illus*	956.00
Recamier, Mahogany, Carved, Turned Feet, 31 x 63 In. ....*illus*	2300.00
Recamier, Mahogany, Tall Curved Arms, Bolster, Rosettes, Paw Legs, c.1835, 33 x 22 In.	3444.00
Recamier, Regency, Beech, Upholstered, Scrolling Side, c.1815, 31 x 25 In.	478.00
Recamier, Regency, Rosewood, Cane Back, Faux Wood Paint, Scrolling Leaves, 38 x 70 In.	4481.00
Recamier, Rosewood, Serpentine Back, Molded Panel Arm Supports, c.1835, 36 x 82 In.	3444.00
Recamier, Walnut, Gilt, Padded Arm, Bolsters, Scroll Footboard, Block Feet, c.1835, 40 x 29 In.	4182.00
Rocker, Arts & Crafts, Slat Back, Leather Seat, Arms, 27 x 26 In.	210.00
Rocker, Campeche, Cherry, Carved, Scalloped Crest, Leather Sling Back, Arms, c.1810 ...*illus*	2510.00
Rocker, Cherry, Half Round Crest, Nailhead Trim, Serpentine Arms, c.1800, 42 In.	11950.00
Rocker, Cream Paint, Red Dot Design, Harbor Scenes, Arms, 1800s, 41 x 26 In.	230.00
Rocker, Danish Modern, Mahogany, Tufted Black Leather, 1900s, 28 x 27 In.	660.00
Rocker, Danish Modern, Teak, Cushion Seat, Back, Edvard Larsen, 26 x 26 In.	414.00
Rocker, Eames, Molded Fiberglass, Steel Rods, Herman Miller, 27 x 25 In.	1755.00
Rocker, Eames, Zenith, Parchment Fiberglass, Herman Miller, c.1952, 27 In. ....*illus*	2813.00
Rocker, Eames, Zenith, Rope Edge, Molded Fiberglass, Steel, Birch, Herman Miller, 27 x 25 In.	930.00
Rocker, Franco Albini, Rattan, Bamboo, 23 x 36 In.	180.00
Rocker, G. Henkel, Mahogany, Laminated, Arched Pierced Back, Swirling Leaves, 41 In.	826.00
Rocker, G. Stickley, No. 2603, 4 Slat Back, Rope Seat, Cut Corner Arms, 27 x 30 In.	660.00
Rocker, G. Stickley, Slatted Sides, Back, Foam Cushions, Branded, 39 x 29 In.	1984.00
Rocker, L. & J.G. Stickley, 5 Slat Back, Arched Seat Rail, Cushion, Arms, 28 x 28 In.	270.00
Rocker, L. & J.G. Stickley, Bent Arm, Drop-In Spring Seat, Partial Decal, 42 x 30 ½ In. ...*illus*	3348.00
Rocker, L. & J.G. Stickley, No. 425, 5 Vertical Back Slats, Cushion, 20 x 27 In.	330.00
Rocker, L. & J.G. Stickley, No. 499, Vertical Slat Sides, Leather Cushions, Drop Arms, 31 x 38 In.	3600.00
Rocker, Ladder Back, Scroll Arms, Splint Seat, Red Paint, 1800s, 40 In.	118.00
Rocker, Limbert, Arts & Crafts, Oak, Slat Back, Green Drop-In Upholstered Seat	236.00
Rocker, Lincoln, Rococo Revival, Mahogany, Carved Shaped Back, Open Arms, 44 In.	246.00
Rocker, Lincoln, Tiger Maple, Cane Seat & Back, Scroll Arms, 1800s, 43 x 22 In.	1610.00
Rocker, Lollipop, Curved Spindle Back, Leather Seat, Twist Stretcher, 1800s, 32 x 21 In.	508.00
Rocker, Mahogany, Scroll & Masks Carved Back, Uprights, Apron, Shaped Seat, c.1900	489.00
Rocker, Mahogany, Spiral Reeded Frame, Padded Back, Seats, Arm	431.00
Rocker, Maple, Ladder Back, 5 Curved Slats, Dipped Arm Rests, Rush Seat, 43 x 25 In.	146.00
Rocker, Oak, Pressed Back, c.1890, 47 x 23 x 30 In.	127.00
Rocker, Oak, S-Curve Panel Seat, Turned Spindles, Shaped Arms, c.1900	184.00
Rocker, Oak, Shaped Back, Curved Spindle Arms, c.1890	150.00
Rocker, Pine, Woven Seat, Finial, Green Paint, 1800s, 19 In., Child's	326.00
Rocker, Platform, Eastlake, Turned Frame, Fabric Sling Seat & Back, 39 ¾ In.	37.00
Rocker, Platform, Oak, Velvet Upholstery, Carved, Victorian, 39 x 27 In.	94.00
Rocker, Shaker, Ladder Back, Woven Cloth Seat, Red Finish, 1800s, 40 In.	165.00
Rocker, Shaker, Maple, 3 Slats, Tape Seat, Mt. Lebanon, N.Y., 28 ½ In., Child's ....*illus*	1170.00
Rocker, Shaker, Maple, Black Paint, Shawl Bar, 4 Shaped Slats, Wool Tape Seat, 41 In.	1404.00
Rocker, Shaker, Maple, No. 3, 1800s, 34 In.	206.00
Rocker, Shaker, Maple, Red Stain, Acorn Finials, 4 Slats, Mushroom Cap Arms, c.1880, 41 In.	936.00
Rocker, Shaker, Maple, Shawl Bar, 4 Slats, Curved Arms, Red, Black Tape Seat, c.1880, 40 In.	293.00
Rocker, Shaker, No. 6, Web Seat & Back, Acorn Finials, Arms, Mt. Lebanon, c.1865, 40 ¾ In. .*illus*	316.00
Rocker, Soren-Georg Jensen, Teak, Black Leather, Tonder Monelfabrik, Norway, 23 x 30 In.	1560.00
Rocker, Stickley Bros., Mixed Slat Back, Open Arms, Black Cushion, 42 x 25 ½ In.	558.00
Rocker, Stickley, Oak, Domed Crest, Leather Slip Seat, c.1910, 34 x 29 In.	657.00
Rocker, Twig, Bentwood Back & Arms, Plank Seat, Tennessee, 1800s, 38 ½ In. ....*illus*	598.00
Rocker, Twig, Green Paint, Gold Highlights, Weaved Scrolled Back, Va., c.1900, 44 x 29 In.	920.00
Rocker, V. Kagan, Sculpted Walnut, Wool, 1970s, 37 x 32 In.	14880.00
Rocker, Walnut, Upholstered, c.1890, 40 x 23 In.	58.00
Rocker, Windsor, Comb Back, Serpentine Crest, Spindles, Birdcage, Arms, H-Stretcher, 41 In.	144.00
Rocker, Windsor, Firehouse, 8 Spindle Back, Black Paint, White Stripes, 16 ¾ x 14 In., Child's *illus*	35.00
Rocker, Windsor, Mahogany, Bamboo Turned, S-Scroll Arms, Yellow, Black, Brown, 1800s, 42 In.	121.00
Rocker, Windsor, Mixed Wood, High Half-Arrow Back, Black Over Red Paint, 42 In.	147.00
Rocker, Windsor, Painted, Roses On Crest, Pinstripes, Pa., Child's, c.1830, 19 ½ In. ....*illus*	119.00
Schrank, Walnut, 2 Panel Doors, 4 Drawers, Ogee Feet, Pa., c.1775, 84 x 60 In.	30810.00

Schrank, Walnut, 2 Panel Doors, 5 Drawers, Brass, Pa., c.1750, 80 x 84 In.	854.00

Screens are also listed in the Architectural and Fireplace categories.

Screen, 2-Panel, Carved & Pierced Cherubs, Shields, Fabric Inset Panels, 72 x 23 In.	288.00
Screen, 2-Panel, Landscape Painted, Molding, France, c.1900, 93 x 31 In.	173.00
Screen, 2-Panel, Women, Landscapes, Silk, Carved Frame, 64 x 37 In.	395.00
Screen, 3-Panel, Arched Pediment, Spindles, Painted Flowers, Victorian, 69 x 71 In. ......*illus*	177.00
Screen, 3-Panel, Crane In Pond, Bamboo, Gilt, Japan, 1800s, 61 x 23 In.	1364.00
Screen, 3-Panel, Folding, Arched, Stylized Leaf Needlepoint, Multicolor, 79 x 60 In.	427.00
Screen, 3-Panel, Gilt, Ruffled Mirror Top, Gold Brocade, Carved Feet, 68 x 76 In.	3050.00
Screen, 3-Panel, Italian Garden, Birds, Wood Frames, Painted, 72 x 65 In.	1185.00
Screen, 3-Panel, Kesi, Figures, Heavenly Landscape, Gilt Frame, Chinese, 1800s, 32 x 23 In. ..	296.00
Screen, 3-Panel, Leather, Wavy Top, Flowers, Painted, 69 x 51 In.	184.00
Screen, 3-Panel, Louis XVI Style, Tromp L'Oeil Niche, Flower Filled Urn, Faux Marble, 84 x 72 In.	461.00
Screen, 3-Panel, Mashrabiya Ottoman, 70 x 69 In.	633.00
Screen, 3-Panel, Neoclassical, Oil On Canvas, 3 Graces, Putti, Gilt Frame, c.1800, 71 x 67 In. .....*illus*	4740.00
Screen, 3-Panel, Parrots, Oil On Wood, Signed, Marie Atkinson Hull, c.1925, 69 x 60 In. ..... *illus*	14640.00
Screen, 3-Panel, Ships, Oil On Canvas, Germany, c.1820, 60 x 38 In.	575.00
Screen, 3-Panel, Village Scene, Oil On Canvas, Wood, Faux Leather, England, c.1910, 73 x 66 In.	489.00
Screen, 4-Panel, Birds, Flowers, Blue Ground, Chinese, c.1910, 69 x 64 In.	489.00
Screen, 4-Panel, Birds, Watery Landscape, Gilt Ground, Japan, 36 x 19 In.	854.00
Screen, 4-Panel, Black, Gold Lacquer, Women, Palace, Ivory, Mother-Of-Pearl, Chinese, c.1900, 72 In..	980.00
Screen, 4-Panel, Black Lacquer, Soapstone, Mother-Of-Pearl Inlay, 72 x 72 In.	239.00
Screen, 4-Panel, Carved Wood & Bone, Flowering Plants, Japan, 48 x 56 In.	1178.00
Screen, 4-Panel, Coromandel, Asian Figures, Landscape, c.1940, 72 x 76 In.	923.00
Screen, 4-Panel, Coromandel, Tea Production Scene, Figures, Fields, 73 x 64 In.	3904.00
Screen, 4-Panel, Dressing, Gilt, Silk, Shaped Surround, France, 72 x 96 In.	369.00
Screen, 4-Panel, Empire Style, Mahogany, Gilt Mounts, Pleated Silk, Diamond Design, 52 x 20 In.	527.00
Screen, 4-Panel, Folding, Silk Embroidered, c.1890, 69 x 64 In.	179.00
Screen, 4-Panel, Gilt On Paper, Celebration Scene, Dancing, Signed, Japan, 1800s, 32 x 68 In.	551.00
Screen, 4-Panel, Green, Yellow Needlework Flowers, Red Silk, 1800s, 77 x 69 In.	830.00
Screen, 4-Panel, Hardstone, Figures, Courtyard, Black Ground, 72 x 72 In.	150.00
Screen, 4-Panel, Hardstones, Flowers, Vases, Gold Ground, Black Lacquer Frame, Chinese, 71 x 72 In..	1035.00
Screen, 4-Panel, Leather, Figures, Chinoiserie Painted, c.1905, 72 x 76 In.	413.00
Screen, 4-Panel, Louis XVI Style, Paint, Gilt, Courtiers, Flowers, Ball Feet, France, 56 x 68 In.	1715.00
Screen, 4-Panel, Mahogany, Carved, Pierced, Silk Panels, Birds, Trees, Chinese, 78 x 108 In....	4720.00
Screen, 4-Panel, Mahogany, Oval Inset Glass, Carved Flowers & Scroll, France, 78 x 80 In.	600.00
Screen, 4-Panel, Metal, Incised Design, Gray, c.1960, 67 x 48 In.	430.00
Screen, 4-Panel, Mother-Of-Pearl Inlays, Birds, Branches, Chinese, 72 x 96 In.	173.00
Screen, 4-Panel, Paper, Figures Playing Go, Gilt, Landscape, Japan, 31 x 17 In.	2684.00
Screen, 4-Panel, Red & White Dahlias, Leaves, Japan, Signed, 70 x 28 In.	259.00
Screen, 4-Panel, Rosewood Frame, Carved Diety Scenes, Chinese, 72 x 72 In.	1722.00
Screen, 4-Panel, Rosewood, Carved, Figures, Landscape, 72 x 72 In.	735.00
Screen, 4-Panel, Silk, Embroidered, Flowers, Butterflies, Gilt Frame, 1800s, 63 x 43 In.	750.00
Screen, 4-Panel, Table, Traders, Immortals Plaques, Carved Bone, Wood, c.1890, 9 ½ x 9 In..	553.00
Screen, 4-Panel, Victorian Style, Walnut, Carved, 1920s, 77 x 84 In.	932.00
Screen, 4-Panel, Wood, Shaped, Carved, Grape & Vine Painted, 67 x 46 In.	61.00
Screen, 4-Panel, Wood, Sheesham, Carved, East Indian, 1900s, 73 x 61 In.	253.00
Screen, 5-Panel, Birds, Trees, Orange, Black, Green, Silk, 58 x 52 In.	415.00
Screen, 5-Panel, Floral Tapestry, Brass Nailhead Trim, Folding, 1900s, 72 x 112 In.	538.00
Screen, 6-Panel, Black Lacquer, Peacocks, Birds Of Paradise, Trees, 72 x 96 In.	259.00
Screen, 6-Panel, Black Lacquered Wood, Inlays, Women, Boys, Landscapes, 45 x 59 In.	2360.00
Screen, 6-Panel, Blossoming Trees, Flowers, Painted, Chinese, c.1900, 21 x 54 In.	127.00
Screen, 6-Panel, Chinoiserie, Silk Mounted To Board, Ink, Gilt, Plants, Fruit, Flowers, 98 x 130 In.	1968.00
Screen, 6-Panel, Coromandel, Black Lacquer, Pavilion Figure Scenes, Chinese, 73 x 96 In.	236.00
Screen, 6-Panel, Coromandel, Landscape, Figure, Pavilions, 70 x 84 In.	1434.00
Screen, 6-Panel, Coromandel, Shore, Birds, Trees, Black Lacquer, Gilt, 72 x 86 In.	288.00
Screen, 6-Panel, Coromandel, Village Scene, Animals, Figures, Carved, Painted, 72 x 16 In....	288.00
Screen, 6-Panel, Courtyard, Waves, Hundred Antiques, Black Ground, Chinese, 1800s, 108 x 20 In.	2640.00
Screen, 6-Panel, Ebonized, Painted Asian Mountain Landscapes, Folding, 48 x 60 In.	184.00
Screen, 6-Panel, Flower Scenes, Ducks, Deer, 73 In.	372.00
Screen, 6-Panel, Flowers, Birds, Silver Foil Ground, Japan, 1900s, 83 ½ x 110 In.	920.00
Screen, 6-Panel, Ink On Silk, Scenes Of Children Playing, Korea, 1700s, 78 x 132 In.	5925.00
Screen, 6-Panel, Ivory, Mother-Of-Pearl Inlay, Birds, Monks, Animals, 1800s, 39 x 48 In.	1800.00
Screen, 6-Panel, Leaf, Flower Painted, Leather, Arched Top, c.1890, 81 x 60 In.	2714.00
Screen, 6-Panel, Village Scenes, Ink & Color On Paper, Korea, 1900s, 67 x 102 In.	1175.00
Screen, 8-Panel, Birds, Flowers, Branches, Coromandel, Incised Lacquer, Folding, 49 x 80 In.	210.00

Furniture, Mirror, Walnut, American Federal Shield Shape Frame, Giltwood, Gesso, c.1890, 16 x 13 In.
$705.00

Garth's Auctions, Inc.

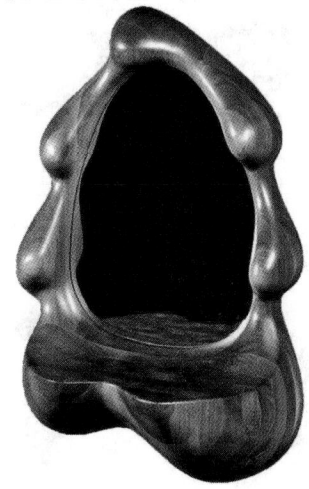

Furniture, Mirror, Wendell Castle, Walnut, Shaped, Drip Design, Marked, 26 x 16 In.
$13035.00

Skinner, Inc.

Furniture, Pie Safe, Softwood, Grain Painted, Punched Tin Panels, Gallery Back, 1800s, 58 x 42 In.
$735.00

Conestoga Auction Co., Inc.

Furniture, Pie Safe, Yellow Pine,
2 Doors, Punched Tin Panels, Side
Panels, Painted, 1800s, 54 x 46 In.
$4248.00

Brunk Auctions

Furniture, Recamier, Louis Philippe,
Rosewood, Carved Back, Pierced,
Upholstered, c.1850
$956.00

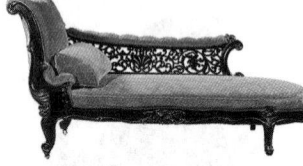

Neal Auction Co.

Furniture, Recamier, Mahogany, Carved,
Turned Feet, 31 x 63 In.
$2300.00

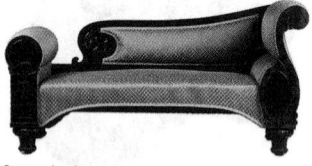

Cottone Auctions

Furniture, Rocker, Campeche, Cherry,
Carved, Scalloped Crest, Leather Sling
Back, Arms, c.1810
$2510.00

Neal Auction Co.

Screen, 8-Panel, Floor, Lacquer, Asian Figures, Black Ground, Gilt, 95 x 114 In.	1220.00
Screen, 8-Panel, Folding, Paper, Ink, Scholars, Hermits, Landscapes, Inscribed, Korea, 28 x 112 In.	4148.00
Screen, 8-Panel, Jade, Soapstone, Ivory Inlays, Figures, Landscape, Chinese, 1800s, 83 x 104 In.	22050.00
Screen, 8-Panel, Leaves, Flowers, Wood, Paint, 71 x 80 In.	156.00
Screen, 12-Panel, Parcel Gilt, Lacquer, Cranes, Taking Flight, Pines, Chinese, 1900s, 90 x 192 In.	590.00
Screen, 3-Panel, Center Mirror, Scrolled Flower Sides, Embroidery, England, 1700s, 47 x 54 In.	1304.00
Screen, 3-Panel, Stained Glass, Arched Top, Peacock, Multicolor, 34 x 32 In.	240.00
Screen, Aalto, Birch, Finmar, Finland, 1930s, 59 x 79 In.	3224.00
Screen, Alabaster, Lattice, Foliage, Rectangular, Interior Arch, Carved, c.1900, 15 x 10 In.	1920.00
Screen, Embroidery, Birds, Flowers, Rosewood Stand, Foo Dog Feet, Chinese, c.1800, 73 x 46 In.	17925.00
Screen, Louis XVI Style, Gilt, Carved, Tapestry Inset, Girl, Flowers, Trestle Base, 39 x 23 In.	538.00
Screen, Mahogany, 2 Sliding Panels, Lift Panel, Fabric, Animal Brass Caps, 68 x 56 In.	59.00
Screen, Mosaic Glass, Iron Frame, Roses, Leaves, , Bigelow & Kennard, c.1900, 32 x 39 ½ In. *illus*	10665.00
Screen, Needlework, Turned & Molded Frame, Simulated Bamboo, Scrolled Toes, 1800s, 44 x 31 In.	307.00
Screen, Rococo, Rosewood, Carved, Pierced Frame, Scrolling, Gilt, Velvet, 58 x 19 In.	299.00
Screen, Rococo, Rosewood, Pierced Scroll Crest, Birds, Arched Trestle Legs, Scroll Toes, c.1850	1098.00
Screen, Table Trestle Stand, Brackets, Wood, Abalone Inlay, Silk Robe Piece, Chinese, 30 ½ x 20 In.	1200.00
Screen, Table, Dreamstone Marble Inset, Imaginary Landscape, Chinese, 21 x 16 In.	3585.00
Screen, Table, Dreamstone, Rosewood, Fretwork, Mountains, Clouds, Gray, Russet, White, 21 In.	1599.00
Screen, Table, Duan Stone, Carved, Mountain Landscape, Pavilions, Waterfall, Chinese, 30 x 21 In.	2390.00
Screen, Table, Famille Rose, Goddess Of Mercy, Attendant, Rosewood Frame & Stand, 22 In.	360.00
Screen, Table, Glass, Sterling Overlay, Wirework Curlicues, Black, Starr & Frost, c.1920, 9 x 10 In.	356.00
Screen, Table, Hardstone Plague, Rosewood Openwork Carved Frame, Chinese, 1900s, 27 In.	2250.00
Screen, Table, Inset Porcelain Tile, Figures Boating, Openwork Frame, c.1900, 14 x 10 In.	369.00
Screen, Table, Jade & Mother-Of-Pearl Inlay, Buddha, Rosewood Frame, c.1900, 20 x 13 In. .. *illus*	1560.00
Screen, Table, Jade Goddess Panel, Pierced, Carved, Ebonized Frame, 16 ½ x 10 In.	334.00
Screen, Table, Jadeite, Unicorn, Deer, Crane, Flowers, Rosewood, Stand, Chinese, c.1920, 5 x 4 In.	6572.00
Screen, Table, Rosewood, Carved Soapstone, Figures, Mountains, Chinese, 1800s, 15 x 10 In. ....*illus*	3981.00
Screen, Table, Rosewood, Ivory Landscape Panel, Fretwork Border, Stand, Chinese, 1900s, 19 In.	1107.00
Screen, Table, Rosewood, White Jade, Figure, 10 Arms, 10 ½ x 18 ½ In.	497.00
Screen, Table, White Jade, Plaque, 2 Dragons, Clouds, Pearl, Carved Stand, Branches, 9 x 12 In.	799.00
Screen, Table, White Jade, Rectangular, Sages, Scroll, Garden, Fretwork Frame, c.1905, 13 x 14 In.	1168.00
Screen, Table, Wood, Buddha, Clouds, Pagoda, Scrolling Leaves, Pierced, 1800s, 34 x 22 In. ..	2318.00
Seat, Rococo Revival, Flower Carved, Scroll Arms, Upholstered, Cabriole Legs, 22 x 33 In.	563.00
Secretary, 2 Glass Doors, 3 Drawer Top, 3 Lower Drawers, Turned Legs, c.1820, 76 x 42 In.	805.00
Secretary, 2 Sections, 2 Paneled Glass Doors, 6 Drawers, Carved, Turned Legs, 1800s, 76 x 42 In.	805.00
Secretary, Biedermeier, Burl, Drawer, Pulls, Fitted Interior, 2 Lower Doors, Dutch, c.1810, 57 x 40 In.	1265.00
Secretary, Biedermeier, Drop Front, 3 Long Drawers, Frieze Drawer, c.1830, 65 x 41 In. *illus*	1180.00
Secretary, Biedermeier, Oak, Roll Top, Bowed Cupboard Doors, Griffin, c.1850, 82 x 47 In.	2706.00
Secretary, Butler's, Mahogany, Drop Front, Pigeonholes, 5 Drawers, Inlaid, c.1810, 42 x 42 In.	1610.00
Secretary, Chippendale Style, Birch, Slant Front, 2 Sections, Bonnet Top, 4 Drawers, 1800s, 87 In.	1265.00
Secretary, Chippendale Style, Oak, Slant Front, 4 Drawers, Leather Top, Bail Handles, 41 x 36 In.	329.00
Secretary, Chippendale, Cherry, 2 Panel Doors, Slant Front, 4 Drawers, Conn., c.1820, 77 x 37 In.	1778.00
Secretary, Chippendale, Drop Front, Cherry, 3 Shelves, Thumb-Molded Drawers, c.1790, 80 In. *illus*	8295.00
Secretary, Chippendale, Drop Front, Cherry, Bonnet Top, Inlays, 2 Doors, 4 Drawers, c.1770, 88 x 40 In.	8295.00
Secretary, Drop Front, 2 Glass Paned Doors, Divided Interior, 4 Drawers, N.C., c.1810, 95 x 46 In.	5520.00
Secretary, Drop Front, Cherry, Bonnet Top, Carved, 2 Panel Doors, 3 Drawers, c.1770, 88 x 40 In.	8295.00
Secretary, Drop Front, Country French, Lower Drawers, 1800s, 59 x 42 In.	345.00
Secretary, Drop Front, Drawer, 2 Doors, Asian Style, 1900s, 55 x 39 In.	138.00
Secretary, Drop Front, Empire Style, Ribbon Mahogany Veneer, 55 x 38 In.	472.00
Secretary, Drop Front, Empire, Bronze, Mahogany, Marble, Fitted, c.1810, 58 x 41 In.	956.00
Secretary, Drop Front, Empire, Mahogany, Ormolu Accents, Granite Top, Doors, 1800s, 56 x 36 In.	881.00
Secretary, Drop Front, Kingwood Parquetry, Gilt, Gallery, Drawer, Leather Inset, c.1910, 55 x 22 In.	1230.00
Secretary, Drop Front, Louis XV Style, Kingwood, Marble Top, Shaped, Flower Inlay, 1800s, 53 In.	1230.00
Secretary, Drop Front, Louis XVI, Walnut, Marble Top, Inlaid Star, Tambour Door, 50 x 23 In.	944.00
Secretary, Drop Front, Mahogany, 7 Drawers, Brass Bail Handles, c.1850, 57 x 46 In.	179.00
Secretary, Drop Front, Mahogany, Paneled Cabinet Doors, Octagonal Pilaster, 55 x 44 In.	3444.00
Secretary, Drop Front, Marble Top, Inlaid Flower Drawer, 3 Lower Drawers, France, 57 x 29 In.	1725.00
Secretary, Drop Front, Marquetry, Bronze Mounts, Marble Top, 4 Drawers, 1900s, 48 x 25 In.	418.00
Secretary, Drop Front, Panes, Arched & Fitted Interior, 2 Drawers, c.1840, 53 x 35 In.	984.00
Secretary, Drop Front, Walnut, Arched Crest, Mirrored Doors, Drawers, c.1800, 94 x 42 In. ......*illus*	12810.00
Secretary, Eastlake, Roll Top, Oak, Molded Crest, Glazed Doors, Drawers, 93 x 47 In.	837.00
Secretary, Edwardian, Mahogany, 6 Drawers, Ebonized Pulls, Mother-Of-Pearl Inlay, 51 x 48 In.	593.00
Secretary, Edwardian, Mahogany, Inlay, Glazed Doors, Shelves, Drawers, 92 In. ....*illus*	1554.00
Secretary, Empire, Mahogany, 2 Sections, Molded Cornice, Ball Feet, c.1835, 68 x 42 In.	575.00
Secretary, Empire, Mahogany, Bird's-Eye Maple, Pilasters, Gothic Arch Door, 104 x 47 In.	657.00

F

Secretary, Empire, Mahogany, Molded Crest, Glazed Doors, Felt Surface, 81 x 45 In................	329.00
Secretary, Empire, Pine, 2 Sections, Hinged Top, Tombstone Doors, 1800s, 19 x 15 In.	490.00
Secretary, Federal, Cherry, Satinwood, Inlaid, 2 Sections, 3 Drawers, Crossbanded, 50 x 40 In. ..	2300.00
Secretary, Federal, Drop Front, Mahogany, c.1900, 72 x 73 In.	4000.00
Secretary, Federal, Mahogany, 2 Sections, Shaped Cornice, 2 Doors, 4 Drawers, 70 x 40 In.....	4600.00
Secretary, Federal, Mahogany, Foldover Desk, Gothic Arch Glass Doors, c.1820, 75 x 34 In.....	1195.00
Secretary, Federal, Slant Front, Cherry, Vine Inlay, Graduated Drawers, c.1800, 95 In. ...*illus*	22705.00
Secretary, Federal, Slant Front, Mahogany, Inlays, Glass Doors, 3 Drawers, c.1800s, 97 x 44 In.	3466.00
Secretary, Fold-Out Front, Pine, 2 Sections, Doors, Drawers, Stencil, c.1825, 77 In. ....*illus*	9988.00
Secretary, George I, Drop Front, Walnut, Glass Door, Drawers, c.1720, 82 x 29 In.	11800.00
Secretary, George II Style, Japanned, Scrolled Crest, Etched Glass Doors, Bird, 87 x 35 In.......	7080.00
Secretary, George II, Drop Front, Walnut, Mirrored Cupboard Door, 67 x 26 In.	3750.00
Secretary, George III, Drop Front, Mahogany, Glass Doors, 4 Drawers, c.1800, 87 x 39 In.......	1152.00
Secretary, George III, Drop Front, Mahogany, Glass Panel Doors, 78 x 31 In...........................	938.00
Secretary, George III, Drop Front, Walnut, Inlaid Frieze, Arched Doors, Drawers, 86 x 41 In. .	3444.00
Secretary, George III, Mahogany, 2 Sections, 2 Doors, Pigeonholes, 1700s, 89 x 46 In............	1116.00
Secretary, Georgian, Slant Front, Walnut, 2 Panel Upper Doors, 6 Drawers, c.1790, 83 ½ In..	3738.00
Secretary, Hepplewhite, Mahogany, 2 Sections, Tambour Doors, Fold-Out, c.1800, 49 In.	3738.00
Secretary, Hepplewhite, Mahogany, Tambour Doors, 2 Drawers, c.1800, 43 x 33 In.................	356.00
Secretary, Louis Philippe, Drop Front, Walnut, Marble, Carved Door, 3 Drawers, 59 x 37 In. ..	1287.00
Secretary, Louis XV Style, Drop Front, Oak, 2 Drawers, Interior Compartments, 40 x 35 ½ In.	360.00
Secretary, Mahogany, Drop Front, Swan Pediment, 2 Doors, 4 Drawers, 1700s, 96 x 46 In......	2160.00
Secretary, Mahogany, Molded Cornice, Upper Glass Doors, 4 Lower Drawers, 1800s, 92 x 50 In.	1265.00
Secretary, Mahogany, Swan Neck Pediment, Urn, Fretwork, Doors, 2 Sections, 1700s, 99 x 47 In.	4000.00
Secretary, Mahogany, Upper Glass Doors, Foldover Writing Surface, 2 Panel Doors, 92 x 45 In.	738.00
Secretary, Meeks, Rosewood, Roll Top, Grillwork Doors, Trestle Stand, c.1865, 68 x 38 In. ...*illus*	2214.00
Secretary, Neoclassical Style, Walnut, Crossbanded, 2 Sections, Hinged Lid, 1800s, 71 In........	1175.00
Secretary, Neoclassical, Mahogany, Glazed Panel Doors, Drop Front, 104 x 54 In....................	4920.00
Secretary, Neoclassical, Rococo Revival, Slant Front, Mahogany, Arched Glass Doors, 88 x 41 In.	1168.00
Secretary, Queen Anne Style, Slant Front, Walnut, Mirrored Door, Drawers, 81 x 24 In.	2337.00
Secretary, Queen Anne, Cherry, Bonnet Top, Upper Doors, 3 Drawers, Conn., c.1760, 90 x 37 In.	7000.00
Secretary, Queen Anne, Slant Front, Mahogany, Mirrored Doors, Shelves, 1700s, 90 x 39 In. ...*illus*	4248.00
Secretary, Queen Anne, Slant Front, Swivel Mirror, Japanned, Serpentine Front, 39 x 18 In. ..	444.00
Secretary, Regency, Mahogany, 3 Glazed Doors, Arched, Lower Panel Doors, 78 x 72 In..........	1888.00
Secretary, Regency, Mahogany, Moorish Arch Panel Doors, Drawers, 80 x 43 In.	1968.00
Secretary, Renaissance Revival, Mahogany, 2 Sections, Stepped Cornice, Glazed Doors, 7 Ft...	750.00
Secretary, Rococo Style, Painted, Upper Glass Doors, 2 Drawers, Italy, 90 x 61 In.	500.00
Secretary, Serpentine Marble Top, Drop Front, 7 Drawers, Vines, Flowers, 1800s, 49 x 26 In...	1476.00
Secretary, Sheraton, Maple, Molded Cornice, Blind Door, 3 Drawers, Writing Surface, 52 x 40 In.	472.00
Secretary, Slant Front, 2 Sections, 2 Doors, Cut Corner, Bracket Feet, 86 x 41 In	1527.00
Secretary, Slant Front, Painted, Domed Crest, 2 Panel Doors, Leaves, Rosettes, c.1900, 88 x 34 In.	1230.00
Secretary, Slant Front, Walnut, Divided Glass Doors, 4 Drawer Base, 1900s, 85 x 23 In.	480.00
Secretary, Victorian, Roll Top, Carved Crest, 2 Glass Doors, 96 x 37 In...........................	2070.00
Secretary, Victorian, Slant Front, Oak, 3 Drawers, 3 Glass Doors, Molded Crest, 1800s, 93 x 51 In.	805.00
Secretary, Victorian, Walnut, Bonnet Top, Roll Top, Interior Drawers, 81 x 38 In. ....*illus*	848.00
Secretary, Wooton, Extra Grade, Bird's-Eye Maple & Ebony Incised, 76 x 44 In........................	22420.00
Secretary, Wooton, Standard Grade, 2 Hinges, Walnut, Renaissance Revival Gallery, 68 In.....	10620.00
Semainier, Aesthetic Revival, 7 Drawers, Maroon Birds, Branch Panels, 56 x 30 In.	1755.00
Semainier, Chinoiserie, Black Paint, Gold Detail, 7 Drawers, 60 x 28 In.	594.00
Semainier, French Provincial, 7 Drawers, Ebonized Molding, Base, c.1825, 59 ¾ x 22 ½ In. .....*illus*	1007.00
Semainier, Louis XVI Style, Mahogany, Marble Top, 7 Drawers, 61 x 36 In.	375.00
Semainier, Ormolu, Painted, Marble Top, 7 Drawers, Couple, Ruins, France, 1800s, 54 x 28 In.	1304.00
Server, 3 Tiers, Gallery, Turned Block Legs, Casters, England, 1800s, 41 x 29 In.	944.00
Server, Art Nouveau, Walnut, 2 Drawers, 2 Doors, Open Shelf, Gilt Mounts, 1900s, 42 x 47 In.	568.00
Server, Arts & Crafts, Oak, Carved, Chased Copper, Leaded Glass Doors, c.1880, 63 x 75 In. .....*illus*	2215.00
Server, Breakfast, Walnut, Black, Marble Top, Ormolu Mounts, Drawers, Doors, Carved, 37 x 49 In.	345.00
Server, Cabinet, Mahogany, Drawers, Recessed Panel Drawers, c.1840, 49 x 49 In....................	738.00
Server, Chinese, Hardwood, Banded Top, 3 Frieze Drawers, 35 x 50 In..............................	627.00
Server, Cy Mann, Chromed Steel, Glass, Marble, 1970s, 29 x 62 In....................................	2108.00
Server, Eastlake, Burl Walnut, Marble Top, Frieze Drawers, Paneled Doors, Shelves, 36 x 54 In.	448.00
Server, Edwardian, Mahogany, Marble Top, Backsplash, Faux Drawers, c.1890, 33 x 18 In.......	657.00
Server, Empire, Mahogany, Marble Top, Oval Mirror, Dolphin Shape Supports, c.1840, 69 x 44 In.	1725.00
Server, Federal, Mahogany, Bowfront, Inlay, Cutlery, Bottle Drawers, Doors, 47 ½ x 23 In. .*illus*	3660.00
Server, Federal, Mahogany, Satinwood, Turret Corners, 2 Drawers, Reeded Legs, Ivory, 35 x 32 In.	3450.00
Server, French Provincial, Walnut, Molded, Relief Carved Frieze & Doors, 1700s, 37 x 52 In...	3200.00

Furniture, Rocker, Eames, Zenith, Parchment Fiberglass, Herman Miller, c.1952, 27 In.
$2813.00

Los Angeles Modern Auctions

Furniture, Rocker, L. & J.G. Stickley, Bent Arm, Drop-In Spring Seat, Partial Decal, 42 x 30 ½ In.
$3348.00

Rago Arts & Auction Center

Furniture, Rocker, Shaker, Maple, 3 Slats, Tape Seat, Mt. Lebanon, N.Y., 28 ½ In., Child's
$1170.00

Willis Henry Auctions, Inc.

F

Furniture, Rocker, Shaker, No. 6, Web Seat & Back, Acorn Finials, Arms, Mt. Lebanon, c.1865, 40 ¾ In.
$316.00

James D. Julia Inc.

Furniture, Rocker, Twig, Bentwood Back & Arms, Plank Seat, Tennessee, 1800s, 38 ½ In.
$598.00

Neal Auction Co.

Furniture, Rocker, Windsor, Firehouse, 8 Spindle Back, Black Paint, White Stripes, 16 ¾ x 14 In., Child's
$35.00

Conestoga Auction Co., Inc.

Server, G. Stickley, 2 Drawers, Branded, 38 ½ x 42 In.	2232.00
Server, George III Style, Mahogany, 31 x 44 In.	281.00
Server, George III, Mahogany, Bowfront, 2 Drawer, Feather Banded Edge, c.1800, 31 x 47 In.	896.00
Server, Georgian Style, Mahogany, Shaped, Leaf Carved Top, Reeded Legs, c.1890, 36 x 62 In.	3884.00
Server, Henry II Style, Oak, 2 Drawers, Spindle Columns, 2 Shelves, Flip Top, 38 x 39 In.	510.00
Server, Henry II Style, Oak, Lift Top, 2 Drawers, Medial & Base Stretcher Shelf, 39 x 46 In.	915.00
Server, Henry II Style, Oak, Lift Top, Marble Inside, 2 Drawers, Base Shelf, Carved, 40 x 48 In.	610.00
Server, Henry II Style, Oak, Marble, Rail Gallery Top, 2 Drawers, Open Shelves, 68 x 54 In.	580.00
Server, Henry II Style, Walnut, Rail Crest, Open Shelves, 2 Drawers, 73 x 45 In.	519.00
Server, Henry II, Walnut, Marble Top, Openwork Crest, Side Shelves, 2 Drawers, Carved, 71 x 53 In.	549.00
Server, Henry II, Walnut, Marble, 3 Drawers, 2 Doors, Carvings, Base Shelf, 83 x 48 In.	854.00
Server, Irish Chippendale, Mirror, Broken-Arch Pediment, Carved, Shells, Leaves, Feet, 33 x 60 In.	826.00
Server, Iron, Serpentine, Hammered, 2 Doors, Rod Handles, 34 x 52 In.	366.00
Server, Louis XV Style, Oak, 2 Drawer, 2 Doors, Carved, Open Medial Shelf, 48 x 17 In.	396.00
Server, Louis XV Style, Walnut, Carved, Doors, Frieze Drawers, Bronze Pulls, c.1895, 42 x 63 In. *illus*	2360.00
Server, Louis XV, Mixed Wood, 2 Side Doors, Open Shelves, Leaf Carved, 1800s, 41 x 70 In.	1118.00
Server, Louis XV, Oak, Shaped Crest, High Shelf, 2 Drawers, 2 Doors, Carved, 67 x 44 In.	671.00
Server, Louis XV, Walnut, Carved Gallery, Open Shelves, 2 Doors, 38 x 58 In.	458.00
Server, Louis XV, Walnut, Marble Top, 2 Drawers, 2 Shelves, Paneled, Carved, 76 x 49 In.	671.00
Server, Louis XVI Style, Mahogany, Marble Top, Demilune, Gallery, Drawer, c.1900, 37 x 62 In.	1353.00
Server, Louis XVI Style, Marble Top, D-Shape, Cream Color, Panel Door, Columns, 40 x 51 In.	1016.00
Server, Mahogany, 2 Drawers, 2 Tiers, Turned, Carved Supports, Caribbean, 1800s, 49 x 29 In.	1534.00
Server, Mahogany, Drawer, Columns, Pullout Slides, 2 Shelves, France, 36 x 38 In.	984.00
Server, Mahogany, Inlays, Splash Rail, Drawer, Doors, France, c.1890, 35 x 42 In.	478.00
Server, Mahogany, Poplar, Scroll Backsplash, Columns, Drawers, Crossbanding, 1800s, 58 x 48 In.	588.00
Server, Maple, 4 Drawers, 2 Doors, Bun Feet, 1800s, 34 x 70 In.	1125.00
Server, Normandy Style, Oak, 2 Drawers, 2 Doors, Shaped Skirt, Carved Leaves, 39 x 47 In.	960.00
Server, Oak, Carved Trim, Panels, 3 Drawers, 3 Doors, c.1800, 40 x 54 In.	3450.00
Server, Oak, Quartersawn, Winged Lady Supports, Basket Crest, Glass Doors, c.1880, 48 x 48 In.	1093.00
Server, Oak, Shelves, Beveled Mirror, Drawers, Cupboard Doors, c.1910, 72 x 54 In.	708.00
Server, Poplar Grained, Drawer, 2 Paneled Doors, Shaped Apron, Spurred Feet, 48 x 45 In.	3000.00
Server, Queen Anne, Cherry, Overhanging Top, Drawers, Apron, Pad Feet, 1700s, 31 x 30 In.	5629.00
Server, Rectangular, Canted Corners, 4 Drawers, Ormolu, Bracket Feet, c.1850, 38 x 46 In. *illus*	1045.00
Server, Regency, Mahogany, 2 Tiers, Oval, Tripod Base, England, c.1810, 41 x 25 In.	354.00
Server, Renaissance Revival, Oak, 2 Doors, 2 Drawers, Shelf, Carved, 1800s, 45 x 59 In.	366.00
Server, Rosewood, 2 Drawers, 2 Doors, Raised Gallery Sides, Carved Blossoms, 31 x 38 In.	180.00
Server, Server, Edwardian, Satinwood, Brass Gallery, Drawers, c.1790, 62 x 41 In.	708.00
Server, Shaped Marble Top, Frieze Drawers, Open Shelf, Doors, Carved Flowers, 39 x 46 In.	236.00
Server, Sheraton, Pine, Turned Feet, Posts, Shelf, Drawers, Scrolled Crest, 1800s, 41 x 36 In.	764.00
Server, Stickley Bros., 2 Drawers, Medial Shelf, 48 x 20 In.	1920.00
Server, Stickley Bros., Oak, Drawer, 2 Low Shelves, 38 x 38 In.	1054.00
Server, Teak, Rectangular, 3 Sliding Doors, Metal Handles, 60 x 15 In.	80.00
Server, Victorian Style, Mahogany, 2-Tier Glass Shelves, Lower Railing Gallery, 38 x 40 In.	188.00
Server, Victorian, Walnut, 3 Drawers, 2 Panel Doors, Carved Design, Shaped Skirt, 38 x 60 In.	201.00
Server, Walnut, Veneer, 2 Faceted Drawers Over Long Drawer, Panel Doors, c.1835, 58 x 51 In.	353.00
Server, William IV, Mahogany, 2 Open Shelves, Turned Supports, c.1850, 43 x 48 In.	1230.00
Server, Wood, Mirror, Parquetry, Marble Top, Ormolu Mounts, 61 x 49 In.	1098.00
Settee, 3 Seat, Arrow Back, Pa., c.1835, 35 x 71 ½ In.	1422.00
Settee, 3 Seat, Fruit Design, Green Ground, Paint, Pa., c.1835, 35 x 79 In.	1154.00
Settee, Adams, Triple Back, Cane Seat, Lattice Back, Upholstered, Painted, 62 x 32 In.	2588.00
Settee, Art Deco, Arch Back, Continuous Arm, Rope Carved Apron, 5 Legs, c.1930, 36 x 48 In.	4182.00
Settee, Art Deco, Wood, Woven Back, Seat, Looped Open Arms, c.1960, 30 x 42 In.	800.00
Settee, Arts & Crafts, Oak, Stickley Style, 12 Slat Back, Arms, 79 x 21 In.	403.00
Settee, Bamboo, Rattan, 3 Sections, Tropical Palm & Floral Upholstery, 29 x 75 In.	89.00
Settee, Burl Walnut, Double Chair Back, Needlepoint, Leaf Carved, c.1905, 28 x 32 In., Pair	1067.00
Settee, Burl, Ebonized, Triple Back, Upholstered, Urn Finials, Frame, 1800s, 70 In.	1240.00
Settee, Carved Bird Crest, Shaped Arm Rest, Apron, Upholstered, Deutch Brothers, 36 x 56 In.	345.00
Settee, Charles Pfister, Wool, Enameled Metal, Knoll, 1970s, 26 x 60 In., Pair	682.00
Settee, Chinese Style, Mahogany, Carved, Pierced Geometric Design Back, Arms, 30 x 74 In.	281.00
Settee, Chippendale Style, Mahogany, Camelback, Scroll Arms, Tapered Legs, 1900s, 29 x 48 In.	492.00
Settee, Chippendale, Mahogany, Arched Camelback, Arms, Gothic Panels, c.1765, 41 x 74 In.	5658.00
Settee, Directoire, Carved Sloped Back, Painted Needlepoint, Tapered Reeded Legs, c.1820, 36 x 90 In.	4305.00
Settee, Double Fan Shape, Channel Padded Back, Outswept Arms, 1800s, 31 x 61 In.	325.00
Settee, Duncan Phyfe Style, Harp Shape, Scrolling Feet, Upholstered, 32 x 79 In.	295.00
Settee, Elm, Openwork Back, Arms, Turned In Legs, Silk Seat Cushion, Chinese, 37 x 55 In.	313.00
Settee, Empire Style, Flame Mahogany, Upholstered, Curved Arms, Shaped Back, 37 x 72 In.	406.00

Settee, Figured Crest Rail, Flower Carving, Rolled Arms, Carved Legs, Paw Feet, c.1815, 35 x 78 In. ... 885.00
Settee, Flowers, 3 Panel Bootjack Back, Plank Seat, Shaped Crest Rail, Scroll Arms, 18 x 75 In. ... 295.00
Settee, G. Stickley, Slatted Back, Loose Cushions, Arms, 38 x 71 ½ In. ... 2232.00
Settee, G. Stickley, Willow Woven, Level Back & Sides, Striped Cushions, 33 x 88 In. ... 4340.00
Settee, George III Style, Mahogany, Domed Back, Padded, Cabriole Legs, 19th Century, 43 x 50 In. ... 735.00
Settee, George III, Mahogany, Sheraton Style, Reeded Crest Rail, Arms, Upholstered, 35 x 59 In. ... 1107.00
Settee, George III, Pine, Paneled Back, Scroll Arms, Plank Seat, 3 Drawers, 1800s, 40 x 71 In. ... 2390.00
Settee, Georgian Style, 3 Flower Carved Backs, Lion's Head Arms, Leather Seat, c.1910, 71 In. ... 546.00
Settee, Gilt, 3-Panel Serpentine Back, Carved Putti, c.1890, 20 x 63 In. ... 2726.00
Settee, Gilt, Flower Crest, Domed, Padded, Closed Arms, Carved Apron, c.1875, 39 x 40 In. ... 676.00
Settee, Half-Spindle Back, Plank Seat, Scroll Arms, Turned Legs, Fruit Stencil, 34 x 79 In. ... 287.00
Settee, Hardwood, Bamboo Turnings, Paint, Splint Seat, 28 x 37 In. ... 235.00
Settee, Italian, Rococo, Breakfast At Tiffany's Style, 1880s, 44 x 65 x 25 In. ... 3095.00
Settee, Leather, Rounded Back & Arms, Turned Spherical Feet, England, 56 In. ... 2074.00
Settee, Louis XIII, Walnut, Carved Crest, 8 Legs, Arms, Upholstered, 1800s, 48 x 65 In. ... 244.00
Settee, Louis XV Style, Button Tufted Velvet, Fruitwood, Cream, Gilt, c.1890, 31 x 45 In. ... 448.00
Settee, Louis XV Style, Fruitwood, Cane Back, Serpentine Crest, Seat Rails, c.1890, 37 x 48 In. ... 203.00
Settee, Louis XV Style, Fruitwood, Scroll Leaf Crest, X-Stretchers, c.1900s, 43 x 69 In. ... 1599.00
Settee, Louis XV Style, Gilt, Pierced Leaf Crest, Upholstered, Cabriole Legs, 50 In. ... 1159.00
Settee, Louis XV Style, Oak, Carved, Painted, Upholstered, 1900s, 34 x 33 In. ... 236.00
Settee, Louis XV, Walnut, Carved Crest, Upholstered, Arms, 6 Legs ... 549.00
Settee, Louis XV, Walnut, Leather, Double Seat & Back, Yellow, Carved Legs, 38 x 59 In. ... 397.00
Settee, Louis XV, Walnut, Molded & Carved Frame, Cabriole Legs, 1700s, 38 x 91 In. ... 1076.00
Settee, Louis XVI Style, Carved Leaves, Padded Back, Seat, Armrest, 1800s, 34 x 41 In. ... 384.00
Settee, Louis XVI Style, Gilt, Needlepoint Upholstery, Oval Back, Open Arms, c.1810, 38 x 51 In. ... 299.00
Settee, Louis XVI Style, Gilt, Oval Back, Gadrooned Crest Rail, c.1910, 33 x 52 In. ... 448.00
Settee, Louis XVI Style, Pine, Carved Frame, Upholstered, 73 In. ... 671.00
Settee, Louis XVI Style, Scrolling, Carved Crest, Scroll Arms, Gold Finish, 39 x 47 In. ... 259.00
Settee, Louis XVI, Cane Back, Double Cane Arms, Olive Paint, Seafoam Fabric, 68 x 29 In. ... 3075.00
Settee, Louis XVI, Mahogany, Dome Back, Arms, Ormolu, Upholstered, c.1775, 38 x 68 In. ... 1845.00
Settee, Mahogany, Leaf Crest, Scroll Arms, Serpentine Front Rail, Upholstered, 1800s, 38 x 86 In. ... 1298.00
Settee, Mahogany, Lyre Shape, Rolling Top Rail, Carved Crest, Serpentine Rail, 1800s, 37 x 82 In. ... 236.00
Settee, Mahogany, Reeded Frame, Scroll Arms, Upholstered, 40 x 72 In. ... 1521.00
Settee, Mixed Wood, Bamboo Turned Legs, 1-Board Seat, Scroll Arms, Spindles, c.1800, 35 In. ... 617.00
Settee, Neoclassical, Fruitwood, Inlaid, Shaped Back, Stylized Leaf Splats, c.1810, 36 x 61 In. ... 837.00
Settee, Neoclassical, Mahogany, Dome Top, Ormolu, Bolster, Cornucopia, c.1835, 42 x 27 In. ... 1722.00
Settee, Oak, Kidney Shape, Panel Back, C-Scoll Arms, Serpentine Doors, 1800s, 35 x 37 In. ... 633.00
Settee, Oak, Slatted Back, Sculpted Arms, Green Cushions, Dux, Denmark, 49 x 28 In. ... 300.00
Settee, Pesce, Rounded Foam, Upholstered, C&B, Italy, 62 x 36 x 26 In. ... 660.00
Settee, Pierced Triple Back, Bird, Ribbon, Oak Leaf, Dolphin Arms, Mask, Paw Feet, 40 x 74 In. ... 1736.00
Settee, Queen Anne Style, Upholstered, Button Tufted, Scrolled Open Arms, 37 In. ... 203.00
Settee, Queen Anne, Mahogany, Double Back, Shaped Splats, Upholstered, England, 40 x 42 In. ... 472.00
Settee, Regency, Gilt Stenciled, Black Ground, Basket Weave Seat & Back, 81 In. ... 1298.00
Settee, Rococo Revival, Carved Serpentine Crest Rail, Scroll Arms, Upholstered, 36 x 33 In. ... 155.00
Settee, Rococo, Red Paint, Wing Back, Scroll Arms, Serpentine Seat, 1800s, 44 x 65 In. ... 3998.00
Settee, Russell Woodard, Sculptura, Black Wire Mesh, 1950s, 53 x 27 In. ... 660.00
Settee, Scrolled Triple Back, Pierced Vase Shape Splat, Outswept Arms, Claw Feet, 36 x 46 In. ... 1045.00
Settee, Shaped Seat & Back, Carved Ribbon Crest, Open Arms, Upholstered, c.1790, 33 x 41 In. ... 461.00
Settee, Sheraton Style, Mahogany, Carved Fruit, Reeded Open Arms, Legs, 1890s, 35 x 64 In. ... 1845.00
Settee, Sheraton, Mahogany, Rectangular Back, Down Curved Arms, Reeded Supports, 36 x 76 In. ... 590.00
Settee, Sheraton, Mahogany, Upholstered Square Back, Reeded Arms & Legs, 1800s, 34 x 50 In. ... 777.00
Settee, Stickley Bros., Mother-Of-Pearl & Copper Inlay, 39 x 82 x 32 In. ... 4650.00
Settee, Teak, Arched Crest, Upholstered, Leaf Carved Arms, Swans, Flowers, c.1850, 37 x 76 In. ... 2875.00
Settee, Teak, Cane, Upholstd Cushions, Peter Hvidt, France & Sons, 1960s, 33 x 87 In. ... 868.00
Settee, Teak, Mohair, Risom, 1960s, 35 x 57 In. ... 558.00
Settee, Tiger Maple, Straight Crest, Scroll Arms, Cushion, Converts To Bed, 1840s, 81 In. ... 3795.00
Settee, Victorian, Burl Veneer, Carved, Shaped Seat & Back, Curved Arms, 44 x 68 In. ... 173.00
Settee, Victorian, Mahogany, Carved Frame, Tufted Oval Back, Cabriole Legs, 1800s, 36 x 55 In. ... 259.00
Settee, Victorian, Walnut, Carved Grapes, Scalloped Back Rail, Skirt, Upholstered, c.1880, 35 x 51 In. ... 288.00
Settee, Victorian, Walnut, Fruit Carved Crest, Tufted Upholstery, 60 x 29 In. ... 192.00
Settee, Walnut, Carved Flowers Splat, Outswept Arms, Square Legs, 36 x 39 In. ... 316.00
Settee, Walnut, Flower Carved Frame, Downswept Arms, Upholstered, c.1790, Italy, 38 x 70 In. ... 2706.00
Settee, Walnut, Flower Carving, Open Scroll Arms, Upholstered, Continental, 50 In. ... 649.00
Settee, Walnut, Louis XV Style, Padded Back, Downswept Arms, Upholstered, c.1850, 41 x 54 In. ... 1845.00
Settee, Walnut, Shaped Dome Back, Cabriole Legs, Scroll Feet, Velvet, 1700s, 43 x 65 In. ... 896.00
Settee, William & Mary Style, Double Arched Back, Columns, Arms, Scroll, 1900s, 52 x 30 In. ... 213.00

Furniture, Rocker, Windsor, Painted, Roses On Crest, Pinstripes, Pa., Child's, c.1830, 19 ½ In.
$119.00

Furniture, Screen, 3-Panel, Arched Pediment, Spindles, Painted Flowers, Victorian, 69 x 71 In.
$177.00

Furniture, Screen, 3-Panel, Neoclassical, Oil On Canvas, 3 Graces, Putti, Gilt Frame, c.1800, 71 x 67 In.
$4740.00

> **TIP**
> *To get candle wax off your antique table, use a hair dryer set on low heat. Melt the wax, then wipe it off.*

Furniture, Screen, 3-Panel, Parrots, Oil On Wood, Signed, Marie Atkinson Hull, c.1925, 69 x 60 In.
$14640.00

Neal Auction Co.

Furniture, Screen, Mosaic Glass, Iron Frame, Roses, Leaves, Bigelow & Kennard, c.1900, 32 x 39 ½ In.
$10665.00

Skinner, Inc.

Furniture, Screen, Table, Jade & Mother-Of-Pearl Inlay, Buddha, Rosewood Frame, c.1900, 20 x 13 In.
$1560.00

DuMouchelles Art Gallery

Settee, Windsor, Arrow Back, Tablet Top, Scroll Arms, Stenciled, c.1835, 78 In. ....*illus*	3408.00
Settee, Windsor, Mixed Wood, Shaped Crest, Bamboo Turned Legs, Black Paint, 38 In............	2820.00
Settee, Wing, Scalloped Wood Trim, Upholstered, 1900s, 31 x 46 In..	188.00
Settee, Womb, Eero Saarinen, Metal Legs, Curved Back, Flat Arms, Knoll, 1947, 35 x 62 In.....	3375.00
Settee, Wood, Shaped Arched Back, Carved, Painted, Upholstered, France, c.1940, 37 x 56 In.	984.00
Settle Bench, Pine, Panel Back, Shaped Sides, 64 x 48 In.	392.00
Settle, Arts & Crafts, Vertical Slat Sides, Backs, 3 Seat Cushions, 84 x 30 In............................	570.00
Settle, G. Stickley, Loose Seat Cushion, 27 x 78 In...	7440.00
Settle, Grain Painted, Striping, Stencil Detail, 1800s, 33 x 72 In..	118.00
Settle, Harden, Drop Arm, Vertical Slats, Black Leather Cushion, 36 x 61 In.	682.00
Settle, L. & J.G. Stickley, Knock Down, Drop In Spring Seat, Decal, 34 x 78 x 36 In. ....*illus*	6820.00
Settle, Oak, Carved, Paneled Back, Plank Seat, Shaped Arms, England, 1800s, 46 x 49 In.	480.00
Settle, Painted Brown, Yellow, White Striping, Fruit, Leaves, Scroll Arms, 37 x 75 In.	529.00
Settle, Pine, High Back, Curved Arms, Flared Base, Brown Paint, c.1810, 58 x 51 In.	2280.00
Shelf Unit, Softwood, Grain Painted, Mortised Shelves, Arched Cutout Feet, 57 x 42 In.	384.00
Shelf Unit, Wood, 6 Tiers, Collapsible, 74 x 72 In.	183.00
Shelf, Aalto, Wooden, 2 Tiers, Triangular Supports, c.1938, 25 x 36 In.	875.00
Shelf, Blackamoor Figure Support, Gilt, Carved, Painted, Italy, 1800s, 12 x 13 In., Pair..........	1304.00
Shelf, Corner, Hanging, 3 Graduated Tiers, Scalloped Edges, 32 In.	148.00
Shelf, Corner, Hanging, Mahogany, 3 Shelves, Cutout, Birds, Painted, c.1890, 15 x 9 In. .*illus*	999.00
Shelf, Corner, Hanging, Regency Style, Brass, Glass, 3 Tiers, 36 x 30 In., Pair	1250.00
Shelf, Corner, Hanging, Walnut, Cutout Top, Base, Graduated Shelves, c.1870, 30 x 18 In.......	230.00
Shelf, Corner, Hanging, Wood, Carved, 3 Tiers, c.1910, 26 x 17 In.	69.00
Shelf, Ebony, Carved, Inlaid, Pierced, Crysanthemums, Birds, Japan, 1800s, 17 x 18 x 17 In. ...	200.00
Shelf, George III, Mahogany, 3 Tiers, Serpentine Shelves, Openwork Gallery, England, 30 x 34 In.	474.00
Shelf, Georgian, Gilt, Carved As Doric Capitals, Garland Draping, 108 x 20 In........................	881.00
Shelf, Gilt, Blackamoor Bracket, Draped Gilt Embroidery, c.1800s, 14 In., Pair	2689.00
Shelf, Gothic Revival, Mahogany, Gallery, 2 Over 3 Medallion Doors, 33 x 30 In....................	425.00
Shelf, Hanging, Birch, Pine, Painted, Scalloped Cornice & Apron, Pinwheel, c.1800, 18 x 62 In.	885.00
Shelf, Hanging, Chippendale Style, 4 Shelves, Chinese Style Fretwork, Early 1900s, 36 x 29 In.	144.00
Shelf, Hanging, Ebonized, Chinese Style, Pagoda Crest, Pierced Fret Supports, 31 x 32 In.	553.00
Shelf, Hanging, Federal, Pierced Fretwork, 3 Shelves, 2 Drawers, Ivory Pulls, c.1800, 29 x 23 In.	329.00
Shelf, Hanging, Japanned, 3 Shelves, Ring-Turned Supports, Gold, Figures, Battle, 26 x 24 In.	796.00
Shelf, Hanging, Pine, 3 Open Tiers, 1800s, 21 x 49 In..	201.00
Shelf, Hanging, Pine, Gray Paint, 4 Tiers, Shaped Sides, New England, c.1815, 41 x 25 In.......	460.00
Shelf, Hanging, Pine, Projecting Cornice, 3 Shelves, Scalloped Supports, c.1900, 43 x 39 In. ..	492.00
Shelf, Hanging, Pine, Scalloped Sides, 32 ½ x 24 ¾ In...	652.00
Shelf, Hanging, Regency, Mahogany, 3 Reeded Shelves, Panel Back, 23 x 41 In........................	293.00
Shelf, Hanging, Regency, Painted, Parcel Gilt, Columnar Supports, 42 x 42 In.........................	625.00
Shelf, Hanging, Regency, Red Japanned, 3 Tiers, Flower Design, Shaped Crest, 28 In.	649.00
Shelf, Hanging, Walnut, Mustard Paint, 3 Shelves, Cutout Ends, Scrollwork, 30 x 32 In.	176.00
Shelf, Hanging, Wrought Iron, Wood, Shaped Grid Crest, Lyre, Gothic Arches, c.1890, 42 x 32 In.	474.00
Shelf, Mahogany, 4 Tiers, Whale Sides, Open Back, American, Early 1800s, 33 x 25 In.............	546.00
Shelf, Mahogany, Shaped, Pierced Masonic Symbols, Gold & Silver Paint, c.1890, 22 x 13 In..	2489.00
Shelf, Mahogany, Stepped Side Panels, 4 Open Shelves, England, 1800s, 21 x 21 In.	59.00
Shelf, Metal Frame, Glass Shelves, Belloggetti, Italy, 61 x 26 In., Pair..	610.00
Shelf, Neoclassical Style, Gilt, Acorn Pendants, Eagle, Pineapple Terminal, 1900s, 12 x 14 In., Pair	400.00
Shelf, Shaker, Cherry, Pine, 3 Shelves, Dovetailed Case, c.1840, 26 x 31 In.	702.00
Shelf, Softwood, Scroll Cut, Pierced, Green, c.1875, 13 In.	999.00
Shelf, Victorian Style, Rosewood, 4 Tiers, Lower Drawer, Turned Finials, Spindles, 62 x 19 In.	700.00
Shelf, Walnut, 3 Open Tiers, 1950s, 29 ½ x 48 In..	1054.00
Shelf, Walnut, Pierced Backboard, Leaves, Shaped Skirt, Bracket, 7 x 23 In.	128.00
Shelf, Walnut, Whale End, 4 Shaped Tiers, 1800s, 35 x 26 In..	1058.00
Shelf, Walnut, Whaleback, Shaped Sides, 2 Tiers, 2 Drawers, Whalebone Pulls, 1800s, 23 In...	1725.00
Shrank, Chippendale, Walnut, 2 Panel Doors, 5 Drawer Base, c.1775, 84 x 60 In.....................	30810.00
Sideboard, 5 Marquetry Doors, Marble Top, Shaped, 38 x 88 In.	805.00
Sideboard, Art Deco, Burl, Glass Top, 4 Rounded Doors, Fluting, 2 Carved Bases, c.1940, 38 x 85 In.	861.00
Sideboard, Art Deco, Burl, Satinwood Trim, 4 Doors, Shelf, Scroll Base, France, c.1930, 48 x 78 In.	1599.00
Sideboard, Art Deco, Macassar, Doors, Nickeled Bronze Insets Panels, c.1930, 38 x 70 In.	1046.00
Sideboard, Art Deco, Rosewood, 2 Curved Doors, 4 Drawers, France, 1930s, 40 x 63 In.	3800.00
Sideboard, Art Deco, Walnut, Fitted Bar Interior, Carved Panel, Italy, c.1935, 38 x 71 In.........	1116.00
Sideboard, Art Deco, Walnut, Painted Fruit, 2 Doors, 3 Drawers, Carved, France, c.1930, 41 x 70 In.	923.00
Sideboard, Art Deco, Wood, Red Marble Top, 2 Rounded Doors, Fitted Interior, c.1930, 34 x 49 In.	1230.00
Sideboard, Arts & Crafts, Oak, Beveled Mirrors, Shelf, Drawers, Doors, c.1890, 90 x 71 In. *illus*	1708.00
Sideboard, Arts & Crafts, Oak, Dish Rail, 4 Drawers, Doors, 44 x 54 In.	813.00
Sideboard, Ash, Oak, 2 Drawers, 2 Cabinet Door, 6 Legs, Stretchers, American, 1920s, 42 x 60 In.	104.00

F

Sideboard, Birch, Marble Top, 8 Drawers, 2 Files, Saddle Pulls, Knoll, 26 x 75 In. 2700.00
Sideboard, Black Lacquer, 3 Red Drawers, Bail Handles, Square Legs, Chinese, 1900s, 35 x 79 In.. 59.00
Sideboard, Butler's, Walnut, String Inlay, Drop Front, Drawers, 1800s, 54 x 61 In. 6900.00
Sideboard, Cherry, Maple, Cock-Beaded, Inlaid Drawers, Opalescent Pulls, c.1814, 40 x 41 In. 5629.00
Sideboard, Cherry, Walnut, Dentil Cornice, Vase Shape Supports, 3 Drawers, 1800s, 86 x 77 In. 4481.00
Sideboard, Chippendale Style, Brass Rail, 6 Drawers, Carved, Shaped Skirt, Stanley, 40 x 61 In. 460.00
Sideboard, Classical Revival, Quartersawn Oak, Hooded, Winged Lion Supports, c.1880, 89 x 67 In. 2530.00
Sideboard, Curly Maple, Butternut, Block Front, 12 Drawers, Center Desk, 47 x 56 In............. 1175.00
Sideboard, Edwardian, Mahogany, Crossbanding, Gallery, Drawers, Doors, 37 x 63 In........... 652.00
Sideboard, Edwardian, Mahogany, Scrolling Leaves, Bellflower, Drawer, 2 Doors, 37 x 72 In.. 1380.00
Sideboard, Elizabethan Revival, Oak, Cabinet Doors, 2 Drawers, Spiral Legs, 1900s, 44 x 54 In. 219.00
Sideboard, Empire Style, Mahogany, Arched Backsplash, Shell Carved Crest, 3 Doors, 59 x 56 In. 518.00
Sideboard, Empire Style, Mahogany, Marble Top, 4 Upper Drawers, 4 Doors, 41 x 91 x 23 In. 600.00
Sideboard, Empire, Mahogany, Shaped Backsplash, 4 Drawers, 2 Doors, Carved, c.1850, 57 x 46 In. 374.00
Sideboard, Federal Style, Mahogany, Bowfront, Broken-Arch Back, Drawers, c.1900, 55 x 75 In. 956.00
Sideboard, Federal Style, Mahogany, Frieze Drawer, Brass Pulls, C.R. Senner, 1900s, 34 x 54 In. 896.00
Sideboard, Federal, Mahogany Veneer, 5 Drawers, 2 Hinged Doors, Fan Inlay, c.1795, 43 x 65 In. 2370.00
Sideboard, Federal, Mahogany, 3 Drawers, 4 Cabinet Doors, Fluted Shafts, c.1820, 39 x 58 In. 1200.00
Sideboard, Federal, Mahogany, 3 Drawers, 4 Doors, 2 Drawers, Kentucky, c.1820, 44 x 73 In. 2242.00
Sideboard, Federal, Mahogany, Birch, Marble Top, Arched Door, Square Legs, 38 x 45 In. 1778.00
Sideboard, Federal, Mahogany, Drawer, Doors, Square Legs, Spade Feet, c.1800, 41 x 67 In.... 3286.00
Sideboard, Federal, Mahogany, Inlay, Bowed, 5 Drawers, Door, Tapered Legs, 12 x 18 ¾ In. .. 2106.00
Sideboard, Federal, Mahogany, Inlay, Kidney Shape, Drawers, Doors, c.1800, 41 x 80 In. 2800.00
Sideboard, Federal, Mahogany, Line Inlay, Shaped Front, Drawer, 4 Doors, c.1800, 40 x 71 In. 1045.00
Sideboard, Federal, Mahogany, Pine, Drawer, Tapered Legs, N.C., c.1820, 33 x 48 In. 2478.00
Sideboard, Federal, Mahogany, Veneer, Tambour Doors, Drawers, Cock-Beaded, c.1800, 42 x 63 In. 889.00
Sideboard, Federal, Tiger Maple, River Birch, 4 Drawers, 2 Doors, Southern, 46 x 71 In. 9440.00
Sideboard, Finn Juhl, Teak, Sliding Doors, Fitted Interior, Baker, 31 x 78 In. 2600.00
Sideboard, French Provincial, Painted, Rounded Cornice, Shelves, Cupboard Doors, 78 x 54 In. 1845.00
Sideboard, G. Stickley, 4 Drawers, 2 Doors, 8 Legs, Plate Rail, Decal, 70 x 25 In..................... 13200.00
Sideboard, G. Stickley, Gallery, 2 Doors, 7 Drawers, Paper Label, H. Ellis, 42 x 54 In............... 7440.00
Sideboard, G. Stickley, Plate Rail, Strap Hinges, Red Decal, Paper Label, 48 x 56 In. ....*illus* 5580.00
Sideboard, George III, Mahogany, Bowfront, 3 Drawers, Tapered Legs, 33 x 39 ½ In. 1112.00
Sideboard, George III, Mahogany, Bowfront, Inlaid Bowl, Spade Feet, c.1820, 35 x 72 In. ... *illus* 3444.00
Sideboard, George III, Mahogany, Carved, Inlay, 2 Drawers, 2 Doors, c.1795, 74 x 35 In. .... *illus* 4481.00
Sideboard, George III, Mahogany, D-Shape Top, Frieze Drawer, Convex Doors, Turned Legs, 38 x 61 In. 944.00
Sideboard, George III, Mahogany, Inlay, Double Pedestal, 2 Drawers, Late 1700s, 34 x 63 In. 2988.00
Sideboard, George III, Pine, Bowfront, 3 Drawers, 2 Cupboard Doors, Base, c.1790, 35 x 69 In. 2185.00
Sideboard, George III, Satinwood, Mahogany, Serpentine, Drawers, c.1770, 34 x 58 In........... 6250.00
Sideboard, Gilt, Inlay, Central Mirror, Side Mirrors, Shelves, c.1880, 73 x 67 In. 1593.00
Sideboard, Gothic Revival, Mahogany, Backsplash, Drawers, Column Legs, England, 60 x 79 In. 3105.00
Sideboard, Henry II, Walnut, 3 Drawers, Carved, Ring Handles, Block Feet, 1800s, 40 x 60 In. 570.00
Sideboard, Henry II, Walnut, Lower Shelf, 3 Drawers, Baluster Supports, 1800s, 45 x 137 In. 900.00
Sideboard, Hepplewhite Style, Mahogany, Banded, c.1890, 36 x 39 In.. 1416.00
Sideboard, Hepplewhite Style, Mahogany, Serpentine, Stringing, Cabinet Doors, 1800s, 29 x 64 In. 896.00
Sideboard, Hepplewhite Style, Mahogany, Urn, Flower, Inlay, Gallery, 4 Drawers, Doors, 78 x 32 In. 1840.00
Sideboard, Hepplewhite, Mahogany Inlay, Burl Veneer, Bowfront, Drawers, Doors, 43 x 75 In. 1888.00
Sideboard, Hepplewhite, Mahogany, Bowfront, Banded Edge, Drawer, 2 Doors, 1790, 36 x 48 In. 1076.00
Sideboard, Hepplewhite, Mahogany, Inlay, 6 Drawers, 2 Doors, New England, 38 x 65 In. 3402.00
Sideboard, Hepplewhite, Mahogany, Inlay, Serpentine Front, Ivory Stringing, c.1790, 40 x 36 In. 4182.00
Sideboard, Hepplewhite, Mahogany, Inlay, Serpentine, Frieze Drawer, Spade Feet, 37 x 73 In. 1534.00
Sideboard, Hepplewhite, Mahogany, Urn, Flower Inlay, 6 Drawers, 2 Doors, c.1800, 41 x 79 In. 4266.00
Sideboard, Hepplewhite, Mixed Wood, Inlay, Raised Tapered Legs, 5 Drawers, Karges, 36 x 72 In. 1035.00
Sideboard, Hepplewhite, Walnut, Tambour Door, Frieze Drawer, Spade Feet, c.1800, 38 x 56 In. 956.00
Sideboard, Italian Renaissance Revival, Carved, Figures, Caryatids, Frieze Drawers, 69 x 28 In. 1409.00
Sideboard, Jacobean Style, Oak, 3 Paneled Drawers, Stretcher, 31 x 63 In. 1375.00
Sideboard, Jules Leleu, Art Deco, Rosewood, Ebony, Brass, 2 Doors, France, c.1950, 34 x 64 In. 3800.00
Sideboard, Limbert, Arched Mirror Back, Copper Hardware, Doors, Drawers, 66 x 24 In........ 4200.00
Sideboard, Limbert, Plate Rail, Doors, Drawers, Branded Mark, 44 x 45 x 19 In. 1984.00
Sideboard, Louis XV Style, Walnut, 5 Drawers, Serpentine, Marble Top, 1800s, 44 x 102 In..... 1680.00
Sideboard, Louis XV Style, Walnut, Parquet, 4 Doors, 2 Drawers, Carved Panels, 40 x 91 In.... 488.00
Sideboard, Louis XV, Oak, Parquet Top, Rounded, 4 Doors, 2 Drawers, Carved, 44 x 87 In. 1037.00
Sideboard, Louis XV, Oak, Shaped Marble Top, 3 Drawers, Carved, 41 x 93 In. 1220.00
Sideboard, Louis XV, Walnut, 2 Drawers, 2 Doors, Carved, 1700s, 31 x 53 In. 732.00
Sideboard, Louis XV, Walnut, 3 Drawers, 2 Panel Doors, 1700s, 38 x 52 In. 1314.00
Sideboard, Louis XV, Walnut, Parquet Top, 2 Drawers, 3 Doors, Carved Burl Panels, 41 x 79 In. 580.00

Furniture, Screen, Table, Rosewood, Carved Soapstone, Figures, Mountains, Chinese, 1800s, 15 x 10 In. $3981.00

Furniture, Secretary, Biedermeier, Drop Front, 3 Long Drawers, Frieze Drawer, c.1830, 65 x 41 In. $1180.00

Furniture, Secretary, Chippendale, Drop Front, Cherry, 3 Shelves, Thumb-Molded Drawers, c.1790, 80 In. $8295.00

Furniture, Secretary, Drop Front, Walnut, Arched Crest, Mirrored Doors, Drawers, c.1800, 94 x 42 In. $12810.00

Neal Auction Co.

Furniture, Secretary, Edwardian, Mahogany, Inlay, Glazed Doors, Shelves, Drawers, 92 In. $1554.00

Neal Auction Co.

Furniture, Secretary, Federal, Slant Front, Cherry, Vine Inlay, Graduated Drawers, c.1800, 95 In. $22705.00

Neal Auction Co.

Sideboard, Louis XVI, Parquetry, Mirror, Marble, Ormolu, 3 Doors, 64 x 52 In.	1464.00
Sideboard, Mahogany, 4 Drawers, 2 Side Drawers, Doors, White Furniture Co., 36 x 64 In.	345.00
Sideboard, Mahogany, Bowfront, 3 Drawers, Door, 6 Square Legs, 1800, 36 x 60 In.	1007.00
Sideboard, Mahogany, Bowfront, Inlays, 5 Drawers, c.1820, 38 x 66 In.	1673.00
Sideboard, Mahogany, Bowfront, Inlays, Drawers, Pedestal Doors, Eng., 1800s, 38 x 88 In.	2390.00
Sideboard, Mahogany, Fluted Columns, Paw Feet, 3 Drawers, 4 Doors, c.1820-25, 44 x 62 In.	1528.00
Sideboard, Mahogany, Fremarc, 3 Drawers, 4 Cupboard Doors, Block Feet, 36 x 84 In.	250.00
Sideboard, Mahogany, Maidou, Rosewood, Rohde, 4 Doors, Herman Miller, 1940s, 72 x 33 In.	1440.00
Sideboard, Mahogany, Marble Top, Mirror, Acanthus Brackets, Doors, Paw Feet, c.1835, 56 x 75 In.	1476.00
Sideboard, Mahogany, Marble Top, Stenciled, Brass, Mirror, Cornucopia, c.1835, 66 x 72 In.	7072.00
Sideboard, Mahogany, Marble, Stenciled, Mirror, Drawers, Doors, Scrolls, c.1820, 61 x 77 In.	5975.00
Sideboard, Mahogany, Mirrored Back, Side Panels, Marble Drop Center, 60 x 74 In.	1195.00
Sideboard, Mahogany, Yew Band, Shell Inlay, Drawers, Tapered Legs, Hekman Copley, 37 x 68 In.	1071.00
Sideboard, Maple Veneer, Marble Top, Swell Front, 9 Drawers, Gilt Leaf, Shell Pulls, 85 x 36 In.	403.00
Sideboard, Mixed Wood, Silver Hardware, 2 Doors, 3 Drawers, T. Philbrick, 42 x 60 In.	10350.00
Sideboard, Oak, 2 Parts, Turned Columns, Cabinet Doors, Slide Out, Germany, c.1900, 78 x 51 In.	431.00
Sideboard, Oak, Carved Backsplash, Shaped Top, 4 Doors, 5 Drawers, 47 x 103 In.	518.00
Sideboard, Oak, Doors, Drawers, Paper Label, Lifetime, 42 ½ x 60 In. ....*illus*	1240.00
Sideboard, Painted, 3 Drawers, 2 Recessed Hinged Doors, Pilasters, Turned Feet, c.1835, 49 x 49 In.	2489.00
Sideboard, Porcelain, White, Monel Metal, Ransom Barton Co., c.1900, 36 x 73 In.	9500.00
Sideboard, Queen Anne Style, Mirror Top, Shelf Over 3 Drawers, 3 Doors, c.1910, 85 x 72 In.	288.00
Sideboard, Queen Anne Style, Oak, Mirror Panel Top, 2 Drawers, 2 Lower Doors, 69 x 54 In.	288.00
Sideboard, Rectangular, 3 Drawers, Lower Shelf, Square Legs, W. Haines, c.1950, 32 x 60 In.	688.00
Sideboard, Red Lacquered, 5 Drawers, Carved Openwork Apron, Block Legs, c.1920, 35 x 55 In.	237.00
Sideboard, Regency Style, Oak, Bowfront, 5 Drawers, Brass Bail Handles, 1900s, 37 x 66 In.	418.00
Sideboard, Regency, Mahogany, Inlay, Incurved Sides, Doors, Bowed Apron, c.1800, 37 x 61 In.	575.00
Sideboard, Renaissance Revival, Mahogany, Drawers, Doors, Backsplash, c.1850, 59 x 80 In.	1410.00
Sideboard, Renaissance Revival, Oak, 3 Doors, Lower Shelf, Pillars, Carved, 1800s, 42 x 89 In.	960.00
Sideboard, Renaissance Style, Oak, Parquet Top, Doors, Drawers, Iron Stretcher, 48 x 96 In.	336.00
Sideboard, Rococo Revival, Walnut, Game Birds, Open Shelves, Doors, Fox Heads, c.1865, 74 In.	6150.00
Sideboard, Saint Hubert, Walnut, Open Shelves, Low Doors, Carved, Rounded, 1800s, 98 x 76 In.	915.00
Sideboard, Satinwood Inlays, Shaped Top, 2 Doors, 2 Drawers, Councill Craftsman, 36 x 56 In.	1428.00
Sideboard, Sheraton Style, Mahogany, 2 Doors, Drawer, Reeded Legs, England, 35 x 66 In.	840.00
Sideboard, Sheraton, Mahogany, Tambour Door Top, Low Door, 6 Drawers, c.1810, 47 x 76 In.	3600.00
Sideboard, Sheraton, Maple, Shaped Backsplash, 3 Drawers, 4 Doors, N.C., c.1810, 51 x 63 In.	4830.00
Sideboard, Southern Federal, Shaped, Mixed Wood, Inlays, 4 Doors, Drawer, c.1800, 39 x 66 In.	21850.00
Sideboard, Steel, Enamel, Pediment Backsplash, Drawers Over Doors, Ed. Higgins, 34 x 60 In.	440.00
Sideboard, Teak, Tapered Top, Flared Legs, Spindle Stretcher, Italy, c.1950, 36 x 98 In.	1107.00
Sideboard, Tiger Oak, Mirror Backsplash, 2 Drawers, Open Shelves, Paw Feet, 46 x 48 In.	316.00
Sideboard, Victorian, Walnut, Mirror Back, Candle Shelves, Drawers, Panel Doors, 71 x 53 In.	212.00
Sideboard, Walnut, Burl, Black Marble Top, 4 Drawers, 2 Doors, Mirror, Carved, Italy, 39 x 75 In.	366.00
Sideboard, Walnut, Burl, High, Shaped Backsplash, Carved Scrolls, 3 Doors, Italy, 39 x 79 In.	519.00
Sideboard, Walnut, Louis XV, Walnut, Serpentine, Carved, 40 x 88 In.	976.00
Sideboard, Walnut, Marble Top, 4 Drawers, 2 Doors, Base Shelf, Carvings, Continental, 96 x 50 In.	460.00
Sideboard, William IV, Mahogany, Backsplash, Pedestal Drawers, Doors, c.1820, 52 x 89 In.	3050.00
Sideboard, William IV, Mahogany, Inlaid Bands, Door, 3 Drawers, Side Bases, c.1835, 42 x 82 In.	2706.00
Sideboard, Wood, Bleached, Bronze Trim, Parchment Panels, 4 Doors, France, c.1940, 40 x 96 In.	7380.00
Sideboard, Wood, Molded Marble Top, 4 Bronze Trim Drawers, 4 Doors, France, c.1910, 39 x 77 In.	2214.00
Sideboard, Wood, Sliding Doors, Slant Legs, Box Shape, c.1950s, 30 x 72 In.	813.00
Silver Chest, 5 Silverware Drawers, Brass Escutcheons, Bellflower Inlay, 1900s, 43 x 22 In.	598.00
Silver Chest, Campaign Style, Mahogany, Brass Plaque, Lined, Square Legs, 30 x 25 In.	861.00
Silver Chest, Marble Top, 2 Doors, 7 Interior Drawers, 30 x 36 In.	345.00
Sofa, 6 Seats, Modular Shape, Wool, Chrome, Enameled Steel, Artfort, Dutch, 1960s, 24 x 86 In.	1240.00
Sofa, Armchair, Poul Jeppesens, Rosewood, Wool, Denmark, Ole Wanscher, 30 x 69 In.	2728.00
Sofa, Belter, Henry Clay, Rosewood, Triple Arch Back, Continuous Arm, 78 In.	885.00
Sofa, Biedermeier, Burl, Shaped Back, Footed, Outswept Arms, Upholstered, 35 x 78 In.	2500.00
Sofa, Biedermeier, Satin Birch, Upholstered, Downswept Arms, Applied Carvings, 32 x 82 In.	1380.00
Sofa, Burl, Faux Leather, Brass, Uptown Furniture Manufacturing, 36 x 84 In.	434.00
Sofa, Camelback, Scroll Arms, Upholstered, Southwood Label, 84 In.	506.00
Sofa, Charles Pfister, Even Arm Shape, Black Legs, Upholstered, Knoll, 60 x 24 In.	180.00
Sofa, Chesterfield, Leather, Button Tufted, Loose Seat Cushion, Rolled Arms, 24 x 78 In., Pair	1016.00
Sofa, Chesterfield, Leather, Tan, Tufted, Ball Feet, 62 In., Pair	938.00
Sofa, Chesterfield, Leather, Tufted, Rounded Arms, c.1910, 29 x 75 In., Pair	4248.00
Sofa, Chippendale Style, Chinoiserie, Camelback, Lacquered, 35 x 75 In.	234.00
Sofa, Chippendale Style, Mahogany, Camelback, Arched Rail, Rolled Arms, Claw Feet, c.1935, 88 In.	403.00
Sofa, Chippendale Style, Mahogany, Carved Frame, Upholstered, Down Cushion, 1900s, 35 x 85 In.	2242.00

Sofa, Chippendale Style, Mahogany, Upholstered, Camelback, Straight Legs, 75 In.	213.00
Sofa, Chippendale, Camelback, Rolled Arms, Upholstered, 1900s, 84 x 38 In.	472.00
Sofa, Chippendale, Mahogany, Upholstered, Shaped Back, Rolled Arms, England, 39 x 80 In..	558.00
Sofa, Chrome Steel, Boucle, Cassina, Italy, 1990s, 32 x 87 In.	434.00
Sofa, Classical Revival, Mahogany, Leather, Box Form, Carved Acanthus, 33 x 80 In.	738.00
Sofa, Duncan Phyfe, Carved Swag & Tassel Frame, Cornucopia, Fluted Legs, 36 x 78 In.	10350.00
Sofa, Eastlake, Mahogany, Upholstered, Seat, Spindle Top Crest Rail, c.1890, 39 x 67 In.........	155.00
Sofa, Empire, Carved, Shaped Back, Double Scroll Arms, Carved Feet, Upholstered, 36 x 80 In.	173.00
Sofa, Empire, Mahogany, Carved Crest, Serpentine Seat Rail, Scroll Legs, c.1840, 38 x 89 In...	1035.00
Sofa, Empire, Mahogany, Leaf Carved Back, Reeded, Carved Arms, Upholstered, 34 x 84 In.....	296.00
Sofa, Federal Style, Mahogany, Cornucopia Crest Rail, Eagle's Head, 19th Century, 82 x 35 In.	1550.00
Sofa, Federal Style, Mahogany, Eagle Crest, Carved, Flared Arms, Legs, Upholstered, 82 In.	735.00
Sofa, Federal Style, Mahogany, Tablet Shape Crest, Reeded Arms, Scroll Legs, 1900s, 32 x 84 In.	538.00
Sofa, Federal, Mahogany Arm Supports & Legs, Flat Back, Upholstery, c.1810, 39 x 78 In........	5400.00
Sofa, Federal, Mahogany, Reeded Crest, Arms, Melon Supports, Brass Casters, c.1810, 81 In.. *illus*	4183.00
Sofa, Flemish Style, Straight Back, Carved Skirt, Tapestry Upholstery, c.1910, 38 x 58 In.........	115.00
Sofa, Florence Knoll, Tuxedo Style, 6 Tufted Cushions, Chromed Metal Legs, 29 x 90 In.	2133.00
Sofa, Frits Henningsen, Wool, Mahogany, Denmark, 1940s, 32 x 51 In.	5270.00
Sofa, George III Style, Arched & Padded, Camelback, Out Curved Arms, 1900s, 35 x 78 In.......	1968.00
Sofa, George III Style, Mahogany, Camelback, Outscrolled Arms, Serpentine Seat, 38 x 80 In.	799.00
Sofa, George III Style, Mahogany, Domed Back, Reeded Uprights & Arms, c.1900, 36 x 80 In..	861.00
Sofa, George III, Mahogany, Beaded Crest, Central Shell, Carved, Upholstered, c.1790, 37 x 84 In.	1793.00
Sofa, George III, Mahogany, Upholstered, Serpentine Back, Downswept Arms, Carved, 32 x 77 In.	702.00
Sofa, George Nelson, Marshmallow, 34 Multicolor Cushions, Irving Hunter, 1980s, 31 x 103 In.	7500.00
Sofa, Georgian Style, Mahogany, Carved, Molded High Back, Button Tufted Back, c.1910, 40 x 55 In.	717.00
Sofa, Giovanni Offredi, Wave, Leather, Chromed Steel, Plastic, Saportit, 1980s, 29 x 97 In.	1860.00
Sofa, Grecian, Ebonized, Gilt, Scrolled Back, Arm, Outswept Legs, Upholstered, 1800s, 33 x 80 In.	3567.00
Sofa, Hepplewhite, Camelback, Rolled Arms, Upholstered, 1900s, 30 x 47 In............................	480.00
Sofa, High Wing, Leather, Tan, Tufted, Rolled Arms, France, c.1905, 36 x 70 In.	2242.00
Sofa, Kem Weber, Chrome, Leather, Lloyd Manufacturing, c.1935, 33 x 63 x 36 In. ....*illus*	938.00
Sofa, Kimble & Cabus, Walnut, Cotton, Ball Feet, 31 x 68 x 26 In....................................	5270.00
Sofa, Leather, Black Trim, Loose Cushion Seats, Black Tapered Legs, France, 32 x 64 In.........	1722.00
Sofa, Louis XV Style, Gilt, Carved, Upholstered, France, c.1900, 41 x 64 In............................	2745.00
Sofa, Louis XV Style, Gilt, Upholstered, Shaped Frame, Flower Carved, c.1890, 32 x 61 In........	671.00
Sofa, Louis XV, Walnut, Upholstered, Shaped, Carved Frame, Outswept Arms, France, 39 x 82 In.	9150.00
Sofa, Louis XVI Style, Mahogany, Padded Back, 3-Cushion Seat, Rolled Arms, Carved, 32 x 20 In.	676.00
Sofa, Louis XVI Style, Walnut, Bowed Seat, Rope Twist Legs, Top Shape Feet, Pad Arms, 40 x 54 In.	239.00
Sofa, Louis XVI Style, Walnut, Flower Carved Crest, Laurel Carved Arms, Ball Feet, 41 x 74 In.	1912.00
Sofa, Louis XVI, Scroll Arms, Neoclassical Design Upholstery, Aubusson, c.1800, 38 x 73 In. ....*illus*	2135.00
Sofa, Mahogany, Arched Back, Eagle, Scroll Arms, Paw Feet, Acanthus Brackets, 39 x 91 In.	3321.00
Sofa, Mahogany, Back Scrolled Crest, Rolled Arms, Gadrooned Rail, c.1830, 36 x 86 In...........	500.00
Sofa, Mahogany, Brass, Molded Crest Rail, Scroll Arms, Reeded Seat Rail, c.1815, 35 x 77 In..	2337.00
Sofa, Mahogany, Carved, Cornucopia, Eagle, Sheffield, Outscrolled Arms, c.1825, 88 In.	1000.00
Sofa, Mahogany, Carved, Molded Back & Feet, Outswept Arms, Upholstered, 91 In.	688.00
Sofa, Mahogany, Cupid's Bow Crest, Flowers, Baluster Arm Supports, Reeded Legs, c.1900, 39 x 72 In.	1554.00
Sofa, Mahogany, Gilt, Scrolled Crest, Beaded Seat Rail, Half Round Feet, c.1800, 35 x 84 In....	2135.00
Sofa, Mahogany, Green Paint, Upholstered, Flared Arms, c.1905, 33 x 38 In.	1035.00
Sofa, Mahogany, Marquetry, Scrolled Leaves, Swan & Lyre Crest, Upholstered, 1800s, 45 x 81 In.	1464.00
Sofa, Mahogany, Molded Crest Rail, Arms, Upholstered, c.1820, 37 x 83 In.	1195.00
Sofa, Mahogany, Molded Crest Rail, Terminals, Outscrolled Arms, c.1825, 75 In.......................	300.00
Sofa, Mahogany, Palmette Terminals, Scroll Arms, Rosettes, Outswept Legs, 1815, 35 x 84 In.	3286.00
Sofa, Mahogany, Rolled Crest, Flat Carved Arms, Upholstered, Baltimore, c.1825, 32 x 74 In...	920.00
Sofa, Mahogany, Scroll Crest Rail, Leaf Roundels, Scroll Arms, Paw Feet, c.1850, 37 x 83 In...	2091.00
Sofa, Mahogany, Scrolled Back, Rounded Shell Carved Arms, Upholstered, Pa., c.1820, 32 x 79 In.	1952.00
Sofa, Mahogany, Serpentine Back, Paneled Arm Supports, Scroll Feet, c.1835, 36 x 82 In........	2952.00
Sofa, Mahogany, Turned Crest Rail, Carved Scroll Ends, Upholstered, c.1825, 37 x 96 In.........	600.00
Sofa, Marshmallow, Leather, Brush & Enamel Steel, White Disc Seat & Back, 1990s, 32 x 52 In.	1240.00
Sofa, Modular, H. Probber, Silk Velvet, Brushed Metal, 1970s, 25 x 99 In.	7440.00
Sofa, Neoclassical, Mahogany, Circular Arms, Lyre Clock Facades, c.1830, 35 x 84 In. ....*illus*	3851.00
Sofa, Neoclassical, Mahogany, Molded Top Rail, Shell Carved Arms, Ball Feet, c.1825, 36 x 87 In.	5166.00
Sofa, Neoclassical, Mahogany, Reeded Top Rail, Scroll Arms, Saber Legs, c.1825, 35 x 90 In. ..	3198.00
Sofa, Piedmontese Style, Walnut, Arched Back, Scroll Arms, Cabriole Legs, Italy, 40 x 111 In..	2151.00
Sofa, Pine, Dovetailed, Canted Base, Red & Cream Cushions, 1800s, 31 x 56 In......................	734.00
Sofa, Pine, Oak, Serpentine Crest, Arms, Red Brown Paint, 1800s, 13 x 26 In...........................	1087.00
Sofa, Provincial, Louis XV, Walnut, Padded Backrest, Loose Cushion, 66 In..............................	1280.00
Sofa, Rataplan, Roberto Tapinassi, Reclining Arm, Leather, Chrome, Rubber, 1980s, 30 x 73 In.	1860.00

Furniture, Secretary, Fold-Out Front, Pine, 2 Sections, Doors, Drawers, Stencil, c.1825, 77 In.
$9988.00

Garth's Auctions, Inc.

Furniture, Secretary, Meeks, Rosewood, Roll Top, Grillwork Doors, Trestle Stand, c.1865, 68 x 38 In.
$2214.00

New Orleans Auction Galleries, Inc.

Furniture, Secretary, Queen Anne, Slant Front, Mahogany, Mirrored Doors, Shelves, 1700s, 90 x 39 In.
$4248.00

Brunk Auctions

Furniture, Secretary, Victorian, Walnut, Bonnet Top, Roll Top, Interior Drawers, 81 x 38 In.
$848.00

Conestoga Auction Co., Inc

Furniture, Semainier, French Provincial, 7 Drawers, Ebonised Molding, Base, c.1825, 59 ¾ x 22 ½ In.
$1007.00

Skinner, Inc.

Furniture, Server, Arts & Crafts, Oak, Carved, Chased Copper, Leaded Glass Doors, c.1880, 63 x 75 In.
$2215.00

Neal Auction Co.

Sofa, Recamier, Empire Style, Velvet Upholstery, Scrolled Feet, c.1910, 34 x 57 In.	492.00
Sofa, Regency, Mahogany, Rounded Corners, Scroll Arms, Shell Seat Rail, 1835, 85 In.	1075.00
Sofa, Renaissance Revival, Rosewood, Gilt, Open Arms, Winged Masks, Saber Legs, 37 x 79 In.	11992.00
Sofa, Risom, Walnut Frame, Curved Sides, Upholstered, 78 x 30 In.	2280.00
Sofa, Robsjohn-Gibbings, Mahogany, Wool, 3 Seats, Widdicomb, 1940s, 31 x 74 In.	1240.00
Sofa, Rococo Revival, Rosewood, Upholstered, Triple Back, Pierced Crests, c.1875, 49 x 80 In.	1725.00
Sofa, Rococo, Rosewood, Serpentine Back, Fruit & Flower Crest, Cabriole Legs, 1800s, 40 x 67 In.	1434.00
Sofa, Rosewood Veneer, Upholstered, Italy, c.1940, 32 x 90 ½ In.	248.00
Sofa, Rosewood, Arched Back, Pierced Crest, Scrolling Vine Frieze, Acorn Finials, c.1835, 45 x 82 In.	6765.00
Sofa, Rosewood, Gilt Incised, 3 Part Back, 2 Chair Backs, Plaque, Trumpet Legs, c.1865, 38 x 74 In.	1845.00
Sofa, Sectional, D. Chadwick, Upholstered, Plastic Black Base, Herman Miller, 1970s, 150 In., 6 Piece	1680.00
Sofa, Serpentine Arch Rail, Carved Crest, Tufted Upholstery, c.1850, 39 x 83 In.	288.00
Sofa, Serpentine Molded Back, Carved Crest, Tufted Upholstery, c.1890, 39 x 73 In.	575.00
Sofa, Sheraton Style, Mahogany, Upholstered Back, Sides, Loose Cushion, 1900s, 36 x 80 In.	448.00
Sofa, Sheraton, Mahogany, Carved, Arched Crest, Reeded Arm Supports, c.1825, 35 x 77 In.	805.00
Sofa, Sheraton, Mixed Wood, Shaped Back, Reeded Arms, 6 Legs, New Eng., 1800s, 38 x 69 In.	1093.00
Sofa, Sling, George Nelson, Leather, Chromed Steel, Herman Miller, 1960s, 30 x 88 In.	1984.00
Sofa, Stanton Hall, Rosewood, Carved Crest, Apron, Serpentine Arms, Tufted, c.1850, 48 x 64 In.	2988.00
Sofa, V. Kagan, Microfiber, Walnut, Dreyfuss, 30 x 109 In.	2108.00
Sofa, V. Kagan, Sculpted Walnut, Jack Lenor Larsen Velvet, 1970s, 31 x 82 In.	3720.00
Sofa, V. Kagan, Swan Back, Ultra Suede, Enameled Steel, 1960s, 32 x 115 In.	11160.00
Sofa, Victorian, Burl Walnut, Upholstered, Arched Arms, 30 x 76 In.	239.00
Sofa, Victorian, Carved 3-Section Back, Padded Arms, Shaped Skirt, Upholstered, 42 x 71 In.	288.00
Sofa, Victorian, Walnut, Carved Crest, Button Tufted Velour Upholstery, 39 x 62 In.	107.00
Sofa, Victorian, Walnut, Carved Flowers, Upholstered, c.1900, 146 x 46 In.	288.00
Sofa, W. Platner, Walnut, Stainless Steel, Leather, 3 Seats, Lehigh Leopold, 1970s, 28 x 93 In.	9920.00
Sofa, White Haitian Cotton, 1970s, 26 x 104 In.	30.00
Sofa, William IV, Mahogany, 2 Eagles On Crest, Scroll Arms, Upholstered, c.1840, 45 x 87 In.	956.00
Sofa, Wood Ends, White Leather, c.1970, 27 x 82 In.	430.00
Sofa, Wood, Upholstered, Carved, Painted Frame, c.1940, 37 x 79 In.	861.00
Sofa, Wormley, 3 Seats, Walnut, Wide Wale Corduroy, 1950s, 28 x 89 In.	9300.00
Sofa, Wormley, Curved Shape, Tufted Upholstery, Dunbar, 98 x 29 In.	1680.00
Sofa, Wormley, Even Arms & Back, Angled Arms, Ash, Cushions, Dunbar, 79 x 28 x 28 In.	3000.00
Sofa, Wormley, Sculpted Mahogany, Cotton Velveteen, Dunbar, 1950s, 29 x 90 In.	5270.00
Sofa, Wormley, Sectional, Upholstered, Mahogany, Leather, Dunbar, 1950s, 29 x 54 In.	527.00
Stand, 1st Empire Style, Mahogany, Gilt Brass, Vertical Mirror, Baluster Vase, 120 x 21 In., Pair	4182.00
Stand, 3 Tiers, Gilt Metal, Allover Scrolling, Mask Finials, Paw Feet, 29 x 11 In.	134.00
Stand, Art Deco, Burl, Rosewood, Brass, Chrome Steel, 24 x 28 In., Pair	372.00
Stand, Art Deco, Nickel, Over Bronze, c.1920, 23 ½ x 22 In., Pair	923.00
Stand, Arts & Crafts, Mahogany, Mother-Of-Pearl Inlays, Marble Top, Drawer, 15 x 14 In., Pair	660.00
Stand, Arts & Crafts, Rectangular Top, Drawer, Medial Shelf, 16 x 14 In.	240.00
Stand, Baker, Marble Top, Brass Capped Columns, Platform Base, 34 x 22 In.	119.00
Stand, Birch, Mortised & Pinned, Red Paint Trace, Turned Legs, 23 x 17 In.	542.00
Stand, Bird's-Eye Maple, Studio, c.1985, 30 x 24 In., Pair	155.00
Stand, Blackamoor, Boy, Ebonized, Gilt, Painted, Continental, c.1900, 66 In. ....*illus*	1778.00
Stand, Book, Mahogany, Tilt Top, Tripod Pedestal Base, c.1985, 43 In.	150.00
Stand, Book, Regency, Satinwood Crossbanded, Inlays, Drawer, Tripod Base, c.1805, 30 x 20 In.	1659.00
Stand, Boot & Whip, Mahogany, Ball Finials, England	384.00
Stand, Brass, Faience Tile, Pierced Leaf Frame, Scarab Beetle, Flared Legs, 1800s, 34 In.	2214.00
Stand, Brass, Walnut, Turned, Carved Standard, Tripod Legs, 29 x 15 In.	153.00
Stand, Butler's, Mahogany, Tray, Cutout Handles, England, 1800s, 27 x 20 In.	219.00
Stand, Campaign Style, Mahogany, Brass Mounts, 2 Drawers, Tapered Legs, 28 x 15 In., Pair.	738.00
Stand, Camphorwood, Brass Inlaid, Writing Box, Velvet Surface, Chinese, 1800s, 21 x 21 In.	474.00
Stand, Card, Renaissance Revival, Mahogany, Medallion, Putti, Fluted Column, c.1865, 32 In.	610.00
Stand, Cherry, Chestnut, Shaped Top, Drawer, Turned Legs, c.1850, 30 x 19 In.	999.00
Stand, Cherry, Gilt, Round Top, Chain Design Swags, Low Shelf, 3 Supports, c.1875, 36 x 17 In.	799.00
Stand, Cherry, Poplar, Beaded Skirt, Tapered Legs, Black, Red Paint, 31 x 22 In.	646.00
Stand, Cherry, Poplar, Single Board, Drawers, Vase Shape Standard, Curved Feet, c.1850, 29 x 23 In.	151.00
Stand, Cloisonne, Dragon, Phoenix, Shaped Skirt, Open Base, Chinese, 16 ½ x 14 ½ In.	1416.00
Stand, Crock, Softwood, Bowfront Shelves, Red & Green Paint, c.1900, 22 x 35 In.	206.00
Stand, Dictionary, Oak, Iron Frame, Pat. Dec. 10 1895, 39 x 19 In.	248.00
Stand, Drawer, Splayed Legs, Paint, Ohio, c.1850, 30 x 21 In.	823.00
Stand, Dressing Mirror, Mahogany, Rooftop Frame, Cupola, Lift Top, 1800s, 26 x 16 In.	356.00
Stand, Dressing, Federal, Mahogany, Pivoting Mirror, Drawers, 6 Turned Legs, c.1815, 26 x 26 In.	300.00
Stand, Drink, L. & J.G. Stickley, Round, Leather Top, Wide Apron, Splayed Legs, 18 x 29 In.	3600.00

Stand, Drop Leaf, Pine, Turned Legs, Drawer, Red & Brown Graining, Maine, 1800s, 29 x 16 In.	235.00
Stand, Easel, Eastlake, Gilt, Ebonized, Folding, Lyre Base, Inlays, Carvings, c.1875, 78 x 28 In.	3000.00
Stand, Ebonized, 2 Drawers, Ivory Pulls, Medial Shelf, Chinese, 38 ½ x 22 In.	118.00
Stand, Empire, Mahogany, 2 Drawers, Turned Standard, 30 x 19 In.	238.00
Stand, Federal, Bird's-Eye Maple, Drawer, Tapered Legs, Banded Cuff, c.1800, 29 x 16 In.	1495.00
Stand, Federal, Cherry, Drawer, Drop Leaves, Turned Post, Scroll Tripod Base, 28 x 17 In.	259.00
Stand, Federal, Cherry, Square, Drawer, Cock-Beaded Edge, Inlay, Square Legs, c.1810, 29 x 18 In.	1150.00
Stand, Federal, Mahogany, Drawer, Inlaid Urn, String Inlay, Square Legs, c.1810, 27 x 17 In.	633.00
Stand, Federal, Maple, Mahogany, Drawer, Shelf, Curved Gallery, Vase & Ring, Legs, 30 x 20 In.	3081.00
Stand, Federal, Painted, Leaves, Smoke Design, Drawer, Square Tapered Legs, 1800s, 29 x 20 In.	1778.00
Stand, Fern, Chinese, Hardwood, Round Inset Marble Top, Pierced Skirt, Stretcher, 36 x 14 In.	308.00
Stand, Fern, Pierce Carved, Marble Insert, Frieze, Cabriole Legs, Oriental, c.1875, 35 x 19 In. *illus*	460.00
Stand, Fern, Walnut, Round, Molded, Tri Legs, Triangular Shelf Stretcher, c.1885, 44 In., Pair	3198.00
Stand, Folio, Walnut, 2 Tiers, 2 Hinged Compartments, Pierced Crest, Flowers, c.1895, 50 x 23 In.	863.00
Stand, Frankl, Lacquer, Drop Front, 2 Drawers, X Pulls, Johnson Furniture Co., 24 x 25 In., Pair	1320.00
Stand, Frankl, Teak, Birch, Leather, Brass, Johnson Furniture Co., 1940s, 21 x 24 In., Pair	6200.00
Stand, G. Nakashima, Black Walnut, Drawer, c.1960, 21 x 22 x 21 In., Pair	9300.00
Stand, G. Stickley, Oak, Peg Construction, X-Shaped Stretcher, 26 x 20 In.	518.00
Stand, G. Stickley, Tree Of Life, Mahogany, 4 Leather Shelves, Cutout Base, 43 x 13 In.	2480.00
Stand, George III, Mahogany, Brass, Square Tapered Legs, England, 17 ¾ x 11 ½ In.	504.00
Stand, George III, Mahogany, Conch Shell Inlay, Brass Handles, Block Legs, c.1820, 30 x 21 In.	863.00
Stand, George III, Mahogany, Inlaid, Banded Edge, Drawer, Brass Knob, 1800s, 28 x 15 In.	345.00
Stand, George III, Satinwood, Inlaid Mahogany, Tambour Door, Drawer, Gallery, 31 x 14 In. *illus*	889.00
Stand, Georgian, Walnut, Ring-Turned Disc, Spindles, Drawers, Arched Legs, Pad Feet, 1700s, 31 In.	369.00
Stand, Hall, Onyx, Bronze, Square, Openwork Apron, Shelf, Spiral Legs.c.1895, 33 In.	593.00
Stand, Hall, Renaissance Revival, Ebonized, Griffin Carved, Drip Pans, c.1880, 103 x 48 In.	488.00
Stand, Hall, Victorian, Walnut, Marble Top, Pierce Carved, Drawers, Mirror, c.1865, 84 x 32 In.	230.00
Stand, Hardwood, Inset, Marble Top, Flower & Scroll Carved, 36 In.	180.00
Stand, Hepplewhite, Mahogany, Line & Cuff Inlay, Drawer, Tapered Legs, 28 x 18 In.	518.00
Stand, Hepplewhite, Walnut, Pine Top, Drawer, Tapered Legs, Pa., c.1890, 28 ½ x 24 In. *illus*	472.00
Stand, Incense, Rosewood, Marble Top, Mother-Of-Pearl, Carved Scrolls, Chinese, 1800s, 45 ½ In.	980.00
Stand, James Mont, Wood, Brass Pulls, 3 Drawers, 23 x 18 In., Pair	4800.00
Stand, Jardiniere, Bronze, Round Bowl, 3 Supports, Rabbit Figure, Claw Feet, 42 x 13 In.	259.00
Stand, Kettle, Cherry, Drawer, Wood Knob, Tapered Legs, England, 1700s, 28 x 12 In.	575.00
Stand, Kettle, George III, Satinwood, Marquetry, Penwork, Scalloped Gallery, 27 x 11 In.	1375.00
Stand, Kettle, Hepplewhite, Mahogany, Mixed Wood, Inlay, Scalloped, Candle Slide, 21 x 12 In.	480.00
Stand, Kittinger, Lacquered Wood, Drawer, 2 Open Shelves, 1950s, 29 x 16 ½ In., Pair	186.00
Stand, Lacquer, Gilt, Ornate Carving, Painted, Japan, 1800s, 9 ¾ x 8 ½ In., Pair	474.00
Stand, Louis XV Style, 2 Tiers, Painted, Flowers, Brass Gallery, c.1900, 28 x 16 In.	236.00
Stand, Louis XVI Style, Mahogany, Round Marble Top, Flowers, Cabriole Legs, 45 In., Pair	625.00
Stand, Magazine, Arts & Crafts, Wood, Dark Finish, Cutout Design, Folding, 16 x 33 In.	60.00
Stand, Magazine, Bamboo, Rattan, Woven & Patterned Sides, Central Handle, 20 In.	415.00
Stand, Magazine, G. Stickley, Branded Mark, 30 x 27 x 12 In.	232.00
Stand, Magazine, G. Stickley, No. 514, Leather Facing, 3 Shelves, Panel Sides, 15 x 15 In.	3600.00
Stand, Magazine, G. Stickley, No. 548, 4 Shelves, Red Decal, 44 x 15 x 15 In.	4340.00
Stand, Magazine, Harvey Ellis, 3 Open Shelves, G. Stickley, 42 x 21 In.	1488.00
Stand, Magazine, Roycroft, Shaped Top, Open Shelves, 38 x 18 In.	5890.00
Stand, Magazine, Stickley Bros., No. 4602, Oak, 5 Shelves, Slatted Sides, 16 x 47 In.	1020.00
Stand, Magazine, Victorian, Walnut, Pierced Scrolled Sides & Skirt, 26 x 19 x 20 In.	170.00
Stand, Magazine, Wormley, Walnut, Green Metal Label, 1940s, 24 x 28 x 16 In.	1984.00
Stand, Mahogany, 2 Drawers, Brass Pulls, Turned Legs, 31 x 16 In.	316.00
Stand, Mahogany, Green Tooled Leather Top, 2 Tiers, Square Legs, 1800s, 33 x 14 In.	148.00
Stand, Mahogany, Kidney Shape, Brass Gallery, 3 Drawers, Shelf, 1800s, 36 x 23 In.	264.00
Stand, Marble Top, Drawer, Door, Ring Handles, Ball Feet, France, 1900s, 29 x 17 In.	89.00
Stand, Marble Top, Round, Elephant Shape Support, Tusks, Shaped Stretcher, 30 x 20 In.	1541.00
Stand, Music Box, Burl, Banded Veneer, Shaped Top, Drawer, Cabriole Legs, 31 x 41 In.	690.00
Stand, Music, Ebony, Carved Gallery, 3 Open Shelves, Drawer, Carved, 47 x 19 In.	150.00
Stand, Music, Neoclassical, Mahogany, Carved, 6 Compartments, American, c.1825, 35 x 23 In.	633.00
Stand, Music, Regency Style, Mahogany, Scroll Inlay, Brass, Lyre Support, c.1895, 45 In.	563.00
Stand, Music, Walnut, Studio, 1980s, 41 ½ x 23 In.	248.00
Stand, Music, Wendell Castle, Walnut, Sculpted, 1977, 44 x 24 x 20 In.	33480.00
Stand, Music, William IV, Mahogany, Candlesticks, Ribbed Standard, c.1835, 55 ½ In. *...illus*	553.00
Stand, Music, William Keyser, Rosewood, Ash, c.1986, 55 x 24 In.	4340.00
Stand, Music, Wrought Iron, Adjustable, Scrollwork, France, 67 x 19 x 20 In.	180.00
Stand, Napoleon III, Ebonized Wood, Oval, Dog Head Handles, Stretcher, 1800s, 29 x 18 In.	418.00

Furniture, Server, Federal, Mahogany, Bowfront, Inlay, Cutlery, Bottle Drawers, Doors, 47 ½ x 23 In.
$3660.00

Neal Auction Co.

Furniture, Server, Louis XV Style, Walnut, Carved, Doors, Frieze Drawers, Bronze Pulls, c.1895, 42 x 63 In.
$2360.00

Brunk Auctions

Furniture, Server, Rectangular, Canted Corners, 4 Drawers, Ormolu, Bracket Feet, c.1850, 38 x 46 In.
$1045.00

New Orleans Auction Galleries, Inc.

Furniture, Settee, Windsor, Arrow Back, Tablet Top, Scroll Arms, Stenciled, c.1835, 78 In.
$3408.00

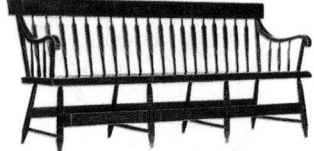

Garth's Auctions, Inc.

Furniture, Settle, L. & J.G. Stickley, Knock Down, Drop-In Spring Seat, Decal, 34 x 78 x 36 In. $6820.00

Rago Arts & Auction Center

Furniture, Shelf, Corner, Hanging, Mahogany, 3 Shelves, Cutout, Birds, Painted, c.1890, 15 x 9 In. $999.00

Garth's Auctions, Inc.

Furniture, Sideboard, Arts & Crafts, Oak, Beveled Mirrors, Shelf, Drawers, Doors, c.1890, 90 x 71 In. $1708.00

Neal Auction Co.

TIP

When moving a chest of drawers or a cabinet with doors a long distance, tape the drawers and doors shut with masking tape or tie them shut with rope.

Stand, Neoclassical, Composition, Canted Corners, Lion's Paw Base, 16 x 19 In., Pair	448.00
Stand, Overhanging Cut Corner Top, Wide Splayed Legs, 28 x 16 In.	316.00
Stand, Painted, Round Top, Morning Glory Design, Baluster, Continental, 1800s, 26 In.	118.00
Stand, Parquetry, Cabriole Legs, Italy, 18 ½ x 23 ¾ In., Pair	390.00
Stand, Parquetry, White Marble Top, 2 Drawers, Ormolu Mounts, 28 x 15 In., Pair	374.00
Stand, Parzinger, Lacquered Wood, 2 Drawers, Nickel Plated Brass, 1960s, 21 x 24 In. ...*illus*	3100.00
Stand, Peter Hvidt, Teak, Wall Mount, Soborg, 8 ½ x 19 In.	595.00
Stand, Pine, Poplar, Deep Apron, Splay Leg, Bulb & Spike Feet, 28 x 20 In.	518.00
Stand, Pine, Vernacular Painted, Drawer, 1800s, 29 x 17 In.	196.00
Stand, Plant, 5 Tiers, Green Paint, 1800s, 56 x 51 In.	259.00
Stand, Plant, 9 Arms, Saucer Ends, Tripod Base, Cast Iron, c.1890, 28 In.	88.00
Stand, Plant, Arts & Crafts, Maple, Inset Leather Panel, Zinc Tray, 29 x 27 In.	186.00
Stand, Plant, Brass Bands, Gilt Open Bar Top, Red Paint, Flared Base, 33 ½ x 15 ½ In.	153.00
Stand, Plant, Brass, Green Onyx Top, Ormolu Mounts, Curved, Pierced, France, c.1900, 31 In.	200.00
Stand, Plant, Brass, Round, Reticulated, Scroll Supports, Dolphin Heads, c.1910, 24 x 12 In., Pair.	215.00
Stand, Plant, Cast Iron, 4-Tier Openwork, 47 x 38 In.	431.00
Stand, Plant, Gothic Rival, Mahogany, Round Top, Cluster Column, Acorn Pendants, c.1850, 35 In.	2560.00
Stand, Plant, Iron, Basket, Scrolled Edges & Legs, S-Design Base, 63 In.	153.00
Stand, Plant, Limbert, Oak, Arched Apron, Shelf, 10 x 10 In.	720.00
Stand, Plant, Mahogany, Hexagonal Top, Pierced Frieze, c.1890, Chinese, 29 In., Pair	5750.00
Stand, Plant, Mahogany, Round Dish Top, Baluster Support, Ball & Claw Feet, 42 x 12 In.	234.00
Stand, Plant, Marble Top, Beaded Edge, Carved Vines, Foo Dog Masks, Claw Feet, c.1890, 32 In.	345.00
Stand, Plant, Rosewood, Marble, Square Legs, Claw Feet, Carved, Chinese, 1800s, 32 x 18 In.	1107.00
Stand, Plant, Round Top, Beaded Edge, Plaque, Dragon, Carved, Flower Stretcher, 1800s, 18 In.	5750.00
Stand, Plant, Walnut, Burled, Round Marble Top, Tripod Base, c.1880, 35 x 22 In.	230.00
Stand, Plant, Wood, Carved, Square Top, Dragon, Clouds, Pedestal, Claw Feet, c.1920, 54 In. .	799.00
Stand, Poplar, Butternut, 2 Draws, Decorated, Turned Legs, c.1875, 31 x 18 In.	676.00
Stand, Portfolio, Ebonized, Incised, Painted, Folding Legs, Trestle Base, c.1890, 41 In.	732.00
Stand, Portfolio, Rosewood, Carved, Fretwork Panel, Brass Fittings, Casters, 1800s ....*illus*	2318.00
Stand, Portfolio, Walnut, Adjustable Leaves, Flower Crest, Stretcher Shelf, c.1890, 46 In.	1195.00
Stand, Red Paint, Drop Leaf, 2 Drawers, Turned Legs, Mid 1800s, 24 ½ In.	138.00
Stand, Renaissance Revival, Walnut, Marble Inset Top, Tripod, c.1870, 31 ½ x 16 In.	546.00
Stand, Rococo Revival, Walnut, Carved, Marble Top, Drawer, Door, c.1860, 32 x 19 In.	738.00
Stand, Rosewood Scroll Carved Apron, Curved Legs, Chinese, 1800s, 17 x 12 ½ In.	474.00
Stand, Rosewood, 2 Open Shelves, Chinese, 30 x 16 In.	260.00
Stand, Rosewood, Carved, Mother-Of-Pearl Inlay, Chinese, 2 Tiers, 30 ½ x 16 In.	431.00
Stand, Rosewood, Carved, Scroll Design, 2 Tiers, Block Legs, Chinese, 1800s, 36 x 13 In.	2083.00
Stand, Rosewood, Dragon Roundel, Openwork Lotus, Scrolls, Chinese, 1800s, 4 ½ In.	3185.00
Stand, Rosewood, Hexagonal Marble Top, Carved Flowers, Lion Masks, 6 Legs, 1800s, 31 ¾ In.	1422.00
Stand, Rosewood, Marble Inlay, 5-Sided Top, Carved Apron, Paw Feet, Chinese, 1800s, 18 In. .	593.00
Stand, Rosewood, Marble Top, Carved Openwork Apron, Paw Feet, Chinese, 1800s, 18 In.	796.00
Stand, Rosewood, Marble, Pierced Apron, Flowers, Phoenixes, Shelf, Cabriole Legs, 1800s, 17 ½ In.	1470.00
Stand, Rosewood, Shelf, Stylized Dragon, Beaded Skirt, Chinese, 16 x 12 In.	179.00
Stand, Satinwood, Zinc-Plated Steel, Enameled Wood, 1940s, 49 x 37 In., Pair	341.00
Stand, Sewing, Wicker, Lift Lid, Low Shelf, Brown, Label JM Virgin & Son, Maine, 15 ½ x 12 ½ In.	138.00
Stand, Shaker, Tiger Maple, Red Finish, Round Top, Spider Leg Base, 27 x 17 In.	2926.00
Stand, Shaker, Weaver's, Maple, Green, Black Paint, Round Top, T Base, 25 x 16 In.	1463.00
Stand, Shaving, Edwardian, Mahogany, 3 Drawers, Mirror, Glass, Shelf, 68 In.	345.00
Stand, Shaving, Mahogany Inlay, Mirror, Shield Shape, Adjustable Brass Standard, 60 x 16 In.	299.00
Stand, Shaving, Mahogany, Poplar, 2 Mirrors, 3 Drawers, French Feet, 1800s, 25 x 40 In.	92.00
Stand, Shaving, Renaissance Revival, Walnut, Carved, Mirror, Marble Top, Drawer, c.1890, 69 In. .*illus*	366.00
Stand, Shaving, Renaissance Revival, Walnut, Mirror, Marble Top, Arched Legs, c.1890, 70 x 24 In.	366.00
Stand, Shaving, Victorian, Mahogany, Carved, Adjustable Mirror, Drawer, c.1880, 70 x 21 In. ... *illus*	518.00
Stand, Sheraton Style, Mahogany, Rope Turned Legs, Drawers, c.1910, 17 x 19 In.	235.00
Stand, Sheraton, 2 Drawers, Cookie Cutter Corners, c.1820, 27 ½ In.	489.00
Stand, Sheraton, Cherry, Poplar, Drawer, Turned Legs, c.1835, 30 x 18 In.	705.00
Stand, Sheraton, Cuban Mahogany, 2 Maple Drawers, Drop Leaf, Brass, 1800s, 29 x 18 In.	489.00
Stand, Sheraton, Curly Maple, 2 Drawers, 29 x 17 ½ In. ....*illus*	633.00
Stand, Sheraton, Curly Maple, Poplar, Bowed Drawer, Turned Legs, 28 x 20 In.	705.00
Stand, Sheraton, Mahogany, Bird's-Eye Maple Drawer Front, Turned Legs, 28 x 16 In.	1955.00
Stand, Sheraton, Mahogany, Drawers, Turned Tapered Legs, c.1890, 30 x 21 In.	307.00
Stand, Sheraton, Mixed Hardwood, Birch Overhanging Top, Drawer, 1800s, 29 x 21 In.	345.00
Stand, Sheraton, Pine, Poplar, False Drawer, Red & Black Graining, Brown Top, 22 x 24 In.	382.00
Stand, Sheraton, Tiger Maple, 2-Board Top, Drawer, Tapered Legs, Spool Cuffs, c.1850, 27 x 28 In.	1150.00
Stand, Sheraton, Walnut, 2 Drawers, 2-Board Top, Turned Legs, 1800s, 29 x 22 In.	206.00
Stand, Silver Inlay, Goddess Riding Phoenix, Flowers, Chinese, c.1890, 21 x 11 In.	148.00

F

Stand, Smoking, Art Deco, Iron, Round, Compartment, Column, Flared Base, c.1930, 27 x 13 In.		123.00
Stand, Smoking, Brass, Shaped Handles, Marble Ashtray, Ship Medallion, Oscar Bach, 41 In.		480.00
Stand, Smoking, Wood, Adam & Eve, Serpent, Match Holder, Square Pedestal, Virginia, 35 In., Pair		489.00
Stand, Teak, Carved, Birds, Flowers, Marble Top, 32 x 15 In.		260.00
Stand, Teakettle, George III, Mahogany, Shaped Gallery, Pullout Candleholders, 12 x 27 In.		920.00
Stand, Tray, Papier-Mache, Victorian, Chinoiserie, Flowers, Black Ground, 20 ½ x 24 ½ In.		478.00
Stand, Tray, Papier-Mache, Victorian, Oval, Gilt Bead, Flower & Ring Band, 19 x 29 In.		936.00
Stand, Twig, Split Oak Basketry Top, Painted, 17 x 14 ½ In.		178.00
Stand, Victorian, Walnut, Brown Marble, Burled Panels, Incised Carvings, 31 x 25 In.		228.00
Stand, Victorian, Walnut, Marble, Turtle Top, 27 x 32 x 20 In.		158.00
Stand, Walnut, 3 Drawers, Board Top, Fiddleback Drawer Fronts, 1800s, 30 x 26 In.		235.00
Stand, Walnut, Carved Apron, Reeded Legs, France, 1800s, 13 ½ x 10 ½ In.		142.00
Stand, Walnut, Mahogany, Inlaid Star, Drawers, c.1850, 30 x 21 In.		430.00
Stand, Walnut, Red Wash, Drawer, Cabriole Legs, 28 x 20 In.		470.00
Stand, Walnut, Ripple Molded Drawer, c.1850, 30 x 21 In.		118.00
Stand, Walnut, Square Tile Top, Incised Support, 4 Arched Legs, c.1880, 30 x 15 In.		359.00
Stand, Walnut, White Marble Top, 4 Curved Legs, Upright Finial, c.1880, 30 x 16 In.		127.00
Stand, William & Mary, Wood, Green Paint, 2 Cutout Supports, 34 x 28 ½ In.		257.00
Stand, Wood, Gilt, Acrobat, Legs Overhead, Head Between Thighs, Glass Tops, 46 In., Pair		14220.00
Stand, Wood, Red Marble Top, Carved Apron, Legs, 36 ½ x 11 In., Pair		690.00
Stand, Wood, Reticulated Apron, Chinese, 17 x 14 In., Pair		269.00
Stand, Wood, Round, Pierced Roundel, Dragon, Clouds, C-Scroll Band, Squat Feet, 3 ½ In.		4392.00
Stand, Wood, Young Man, Holding 2 Trays, Standing On Cushion, Paw Feet Base, c.1900, 60 In.		948.00
Steps, Shaker, Sister's, Pine, Red Paint, 2 Steps, c.1850, 16 x 20 In.		1463.00
Stool Set, Iron, Openwork Molded Seat, Tripod Base, Gold Paint, 4 Piece		544.00
Stool Set, Lucite, Chrome, Faux Cheetah Upholstery, c.1970, 27 x 13 ½ In., 4 Piece		984.00
Stool, A. & P. Castiglioni, Mezzadro, Chrome, Beech, Enamel, Zanotta, 1957, 21 In. ....*illus*		2500.00
Stool, Arts & Crafts, Oak, Leather Seat, 17 x 21 x 13 In.		236.00
Stool, Bamboo, Interlaced Rods, Needlepoint, Upholstered Square Seat, 17 x 15 In.		326.00
Stool, Bar, Brass Frame, Upholstered Seat, France, c.1930, 34 x 16 ½ In.		308.00
Stool, Bar, Metal, White Paint, Openwork, Backrest, Yellow Vinyl Seat, 47 x 20 In.		177.00
Stool, Baroque, Oak, Dark Finish, Turned Legs, Base Stretcher, England, c.1800, 19 x 16 In.		480.00
Stool, Bat Shape, 3 Legs, Chinese, 1800s, 21 ½ x 17 In.		1395.00
Stool, Brown Leather Seat, J.M. Young, 17 x 23 In.		161.00
Stool, Burl Walnut, Inlay, Crescent Shape, Festoon, Club Shape Legs, 14 x 17 In.		118.00
Stool, Burl, Natural Trunk, Figural Carving, 24 In.		413.00
Stool, Curly Maple, Bootjack Ends, Shaped Apron, 1800s, 9 x 16 In.		230.00
Stool, Don Shoemaker, Rosewood, Leather, Folding, Mexico, 1960s, 18 ½ x 20 In.		186.00
Stool, Drafting, Wood, Metal, Toledo Metal Furniture Co., c.1925, 24 x 15 ¼ In.		675.00
Stool, Elm, Rectangular, Square Legs, Stretcher, Chinese, 19 In.		209.00
Stool, Empire, Fruitwood, Reeded, Upholstered, Base, c.1810, 18 x 22 In.		976.00
Stool, Empire, Mahogany, Curule, Ram's Head Ends, Arched Legs, Hoof Feet, 28 In.		945.00
Stool, Enameled Cast Iron, Aluminum, Faux Leather, Adjustable, 1930s, 21 x 18 In.		248.00
Stool, Erik Buck, Bar, Teak, Black Leather, Denmark, 33 In.		531.00
Stool, Erik Buck, Teak, Rosewood, Vinyl Seat, O. Maskinsnedkeri, 1969, 16 x 30 In., Pair		1440.00
Stool, Federal, Mahogany, Lift Top, Embroidered Seat, Eagle, Flag, 13 x 15 In., Pair		1076.00
Stool, G. Nakashima, Greenrock, Black Walnut, Vinyl, 14 ½ x 21 x 21 In.		3720.00
Stool, G. Nakashima, Walnut, Grass Seat, c.1970, 12 ½ x 18 In., Pair		2760.00
Stool, G. Stickley, Leather Seat, Red Decal, 15 ½ x 20 ½ In.		2490.00
Stool, G. Stickley, No. 301, Wood, Leather Seat, 21 x 17 In.		1080.00
Stool, George III, Mahogany, Padded Seat, Drop-In, Chamfered Legs, Pair		4063.00
Stool, George III, Mahogany, Padded Seat, Square Legs, c.1800, 17 x 18 In.		184.00
Stool, Georgian Style, Mahogany, Oval, Cabriole Legs, Ball & Claw Feet, 19 x 23 In.		215.00
Stool, Georgian, Mahogany, Overupholstered Top, Cabriole Legs, Pad Feet, 18 x 19 In.		385.00
Stool, Gout, G. Stickley, Branded Signature, 4 ½ x 12 In.		527.00
Stool, H. Werner, Walnut, Shaped, Single Piece, Signed, 1997, 21 x 53 In.		2232.00
Stool, Iron Frame, Open Splat Back, Upholstered Seat, 40 x 20 In., Pair		61.00
Stool, Ivory, Leather, Wood, Curved, Flared, 21 x 21 In.		1072.00
Stool, Kilim, Padded Square Top, Square Legs, Box Stretcher, Upholstered, 19 x 18 In.		184.00
Stool, L. & J.G. Stickley, No. 131, Monk, Leather, Tapered Legs, Onondaga Shop, 16 x 12 In.		390.00
Stool, Leather Upholstery, Woman's Boot Shape Legs		594.00
Stool, Louis XV Style, Cream Paint, Scrolled Seat Rail, Cabriole Legs, 14 x 27 In., Pair		1076.00
Stool, Louis XV Style, Fruitwood, Padded Top, Cabriole Legs, 18 x 28 In.		338.00
Stool, Louis XV Style, Fruitwood, Shield Carving, Square, Tapestry, Cabriole Legs, c.1800, 16 x 19 In.		430.00
Stool, Louis XV, Gilt, Upholstered Top, Floral Carved Skirt, Cabriole Legs, 1700s		375.00
Stool, Mahogany, Carved, Needlepoint Seat, Curule Supports, 14 x 18 In., Pair		369.00

Furniture, Sideboard, G. Stickley, Plate Rail, Strap Hinges, Red Decal, Paper Label, 48 x 56 In.
$5580.00

Rago Arts & Auction Center

Furniture, Sideboard, George III, Mahogany, Bowfront, Inlaid Bowl, Spade Feet, c.1820, 35 x 72 In.
$3444.00

New Orleans Auction Galleries, Inc.

Furniture, Sideboard, George III, Mahogany, Carved, Inlay, 2 Drawers, 2 Doors, c.1795, 74 x 35 In.
$4481.00

Neal Auction Co.

Furniture, Sideboard, Oak, Doors, Drawers, Paper Label, Lifetime, 42 ½ x 60 In.
$1240.00

Rago Arts & Auction Center

F

Furniture, Sofa, Federal, Mahogany, Reeded Crest, Arms, Melon Supports, Brass Casters, c.1810, 81 In. $4183.00

Neal Auction Co.

Furniture, Sofa, Kem Weber, Chrome, Leather, Lloyd Manufacturing, c.1935, 33 x 63 x 36 In. $938.00

Los Angeles Modern Auctions

Furniture, Sofa, Louis XVI, Scroll Arms, Neoclassical Design Upholstery, Aubusson, c.1800, 38 x 73 In. $2135.00

Neal Auction Co.

Furniture, Sofa, Neoclassical, Mahogany, Circular Arms, Lyre Clock Facades, c.1830, 35 x 84 In. $3851.00

Skinner, Inc.

TIP

If a chair rung is loose, try putting a sliver of wood or a small wad of steel wool into the hole, then put glue in the hole and on the rung and push the rung into the hole.

Stool,	Mahogany, Curule, Upholstered, Arched Legs, Straight Ball Stretcher, 16 In., Pair	1298.00
Stool,	Mahogany, Flame, Flower Needlepoint, Crotch Cut Veneers, Bracket Feet, c.1835	461.00
Stool,	Mahogany, Round Leather Seat, 3-Part Base, Scroll Feet, Adjustable, 20 In.	110.00
Stool,	Mahogany, Spool Turned, Beadwork Upholstery, Finials & Drops, 1800s, 16 In., Pair	770.00
Stool,	Maple, Butcher Block, Round, 3 Removable Legs, c.1905, 28 x 36 In.	300.00
Stool,	Neoclassical, Gilt, X-Shape, Fan Carved Frieze, Serpent Shape Legs, 1800s, 18 x 33 In., Pair	5925.00
Stool,	Neoclassical, Mahogany, Red Leather, Molded, Bracket Feet, c.1850, 15 x 20 In., Pair	598.00
Stool,	Oblong, Flower Upholstery, 4 Turned Maple Legs, c.1860, 8 x 9 In.	245.00
Stool,	P. Urquiola, Re-Trouve Pout, Steel, Mesh, Black, Emu, Italy, 18 x 17 In., Pair	780.00
Stool,	Painted, Bowed Seat, Rectangular, Reeded Apron, 4 Legs, 18 In., Pair	276.00
Stool,	Philippe Starck, Bubu, Red, XO, c.1986, 17 x 13 In.	85.00
Stool,	Piano, Empire, Mahogany, Octagonal, Adjustable, Upholstered, Scroll Foot, 21 x 14 In.	104.00
Stool,	Piano, Mahogany, Carved, Upholstered, Adjustable, c.1885, 20 x 23 In.	345.00
Stool,	Piano, Regency, Mahogany, Leather Seat, Baluster, Carved Feet, 20 ½ In. ....*illus*	366.00
Stool,	Piano, Square Seat, Adjustable, Carved Legs, Block & Ball Feet, c.1920, 21 x 17 In.	1599.00
Stool,	Piano, Victorian, Rosewood, Embroidered Seat, Baluster, c.1870, 21 x 14 In.	61.00
Stool,	Pine, Green Paint, Splayed Legs, 7 ¾ x 10 In.	30.00
Stool,	Pine, Painted, Turned Leg, c.1700, 17 In.	332.00
Stool,	Pine, Pinstripe, Painted, Flowers, 1800s	91.00
Stool,	Pine, Scroll Cut Skirt, Ends, Multicolor, 1800s, 9 ¾ x 8 In.	157.00
Stool,	Porcelain Top, Round, Flowers, Bamboo Twisted Legs, Chinese, c.1830, 18 In.	1150.00
Stool,	Queen Anne, Oak, Rectangular Slip Seat, Cabriole Legs, Pad Feet, 1700s, 19 x 22 In.	299.00
Stool,	Regency Style, Carved, Parcel Gilt, Ebonized, Upholstered, 15 In., Pair ....*illus*	1896.00
Stool,	Regency, Rosewood, Scrolled Volute Feet, c.1820, 6 x 14 In., Pair	1195.00
Stool,	Robsjohn-Gibbings, Diphros, Walnut, Leather, Sardis Of Athens, 1950s, 16 x 22 In.	4650.00
Stool,	Rococo, Rosewood, Needlepoint Top, c.1850, 8 x 13 In.	246.00
Stool,	Shaker, Walnut, Arch Design, Shaped Back Legs, 25 x 17 In.	2223.00
Stool,	Sori Yanagi, Butterfly, Rosewood Laminate, Curvilinear, 1956, 15 x 17 In., Pair	3555.00
Stool,	Sori Yanagi, Butterfly, Rosewood, Metal Rod, Tendo, 1956, 15 ¾ x 16 ½ In. ....*illus*	5938.00
Stool,	Step, Painted, Mortised Plank Legs, Skirt, Scrubbed Top, 8 ¼ x 14 In.	71.00
Stool,	Tractor Seat, Cast Iron, Raised Text, Cylindrical Support, Footrest, c.1900, 31 In.	850.00
Stool,	Victorian, Leather Seat, Brown, Black, Bronze, Boot Legs, 23 x 15 In.	1476.00
Stool,	Walnut, Carved, Winged Griffin, Curling Tail, Backrest, c.1860, 26 x 15 In.	805.00
Stool,	Walnut, Glass Mounted, Square Top, Block Legs, Double Knuckle Paw Feet, 13 x 22 In.	2952.00
Stool,	Walnut, Rectangular, Upholstered Seat, Turned Legs, Box Stretcher, 20 In.	504.00
Stool,	Windsor, Oak, Turned Legs, Painted, 1900s, 25 x 21 In.	326.00
Stool,	Wood, Baseball Mitt Seat, Leather, Baseball Bat Legs, Swivel, c.1965, 46 In., Pair ..*illus*	1126.00
Stool,	Wood, Carved, Kenya, Africa, 9 x 11 In.	48.00
Storage Unit,	Fritz Haller, Metal, Brown Lacquer, Chrome Steel, Herman Miller, 60 x 57 In.	1920.00
Storage Unit,	Wood, Stacked Cubes, Askew, White Lacquer, 1960s, 26 x 73 In.	420.00
Table,	Aalto, Birch, Molded Plywood, Aalto Design, Sweden, 23 x 19 In., Pair	900.00
Table,	Acrylic, Chrome Steel, Glass Top, 1970s, 28 x 72 In.	1240.00
Table,	Adam Style, Satinwood, Parquetry, Parcel Paint, Demilune, Carved, 33 x 57 In.	750.00
Table,	Aesthetic Revival, Brass, Pierced, Inset Longwy Tiles, Outswept Legs, c.1885, 31 x 13 In. .. *illus*	1845.00
Table,	Aesthetic Revival, Brass, Relief Bird, Leaves, Flowers, Stretcher Shelf, 25 x 19 In.	2689.00
Table,	Aesthetic Revival, Brass, Wrought Iron, Pierced, Moorish Openwork, Leaves, 17 x 42 In.	413.00
Table,	Aesthetic Revival, Oak, Overhung Top, 2 Doors, 28 x 52 In.	259.00
Table,	Alabaster Top, Wrought Iron Base, Bronze Rondels, c.1940, 29 x 32 In.	738.00
Table,	Alexander Roux, Rosewood, 2 Drop Leaves, Center Post, 30 x 36 In.	1180.00
Table,	Alexander Roux, Rosewood, Drawers, Turned Legs, Label, c.1880, 26 x 53 In.	1500.00
Table,	Altar, Carved Apron, Raised, 4 Square Legs, Chinese, 21 x 69 In.	305.00
Table,	Altar, Elm, Brown Lacquer, Carved Apron, c.1850, 34 x 72 In.	1076.00
Table,	Altar, Elm, Openwork Side Supports, Carved, Block Feet, Chinese, 36 x 100 In.	500.00
Table,	Altar, Elm, Pierced Apron, Ladder Supports, Chinese, 42 x 82 In.	688.00
Table,	Altar, Frieze Fitted, 2 Sliding Doors, Front Stretcher, Chinese, 1800s, 32 x 53 In.	799.00
Table,	Altar, Hardwood, Carved Apron, Geometric Design, Cartouche, Stretchers, 39 x 82 In. ..	992.00
Table,	Altar, Hardwood, Shaped Brackets, Apron, Chinese, 28 x 29 In.	1188.00
Table,	Altar, Mahogany, Tray Top, Lower Shelf, Pierced Apron, 29 x 72 In.	250.00
Table,	Altar, Mixed Wood, 3 Drawers, Overhung Top, Chinese, 1900s, 26 x 55 In.	295.00
Table,	Altar, Plank Top, Reticulated Apron, Carved Feet, Chinese, 1900s, 32 x 97 In.	5079.00
Table,	Altar, Red Lacquer, Swirl Cutout Apron, Slant Ends On Top, 1900s, 36 x 47 In.	356.00
Table,	Altar, Rosewood, Carved Apron, Pi Disks, Garland, Chinese, 1800s, 49 x 36 In.	1348.00
Table,	Altar, Square Legs, Brackets, Chinese, 1800s, 34 x 71 In.	531.00
Table,	Altar, Walnut, Raised Ends, Carved Brackets, Pierced Flowers, 40 x 112 In.	8540.00
Table,	Anglo-Indian, Rosewood, Round, Gadrooned, Carved, Lotus Support, 30 x 24 In.	1434.00
Table,	Art Deco, Burl, Nickel-Plated Brass, Curved Slat Base, 1930s, 24 x 24 In.	434.00

Table, Art Deco, Ebonized, Reverse Painted Glass Top, Round, c.1940, 25 x 23 In., Pair		738.00
Table, Art Deco, Maple, Cutting Block Top, Stepped, Drawer, 34 x 48 In.		2600.00
Table, Art Deco, Tiger Maple, Parchment Cover, 3 Drawers, c.1930, 27 x 19 In., Pair		1599.00
Table, Art Deco, Walnut, Round Top, 4 Curved Supports, 1900s, 30 x 35 ½ In., Pair		1353.00
Table, Art Deco, Wrought Iron, Scrolls, c.1940, 32 ½ x 53 In.		738.00
Table, Art Nouveau, Hardwood, Bamboo, Shaped Top, Lily Pad Edges, Trestle, 30 x 30 In.		770.00
Table, Art Nouveau, Walnut, Marble Top, Door, Drawer, 47 x 15 In.		61.00
Table, Arts & Crafts, Oak Top, Octagonal, Wicker Supports, 24 x 20 ½ In.		1116.00
Table, Arts & Crafts, Round, Crosscut Stretcher, Label, Charles Greenman, 29 x 29 In.		960.00
Table, Arts & Crafts, Wood, Dark Stain, Round, Cross Stretcher, 30 x 27 In.		460.00
Table, Baker's, Iron, Marble, Fleur-De-Lis Apron, Brass Mounts, Casters, 1800s, 31 x 39 In. *illus*		2074.00
Table, Baker's, Mahogany, Shell Inlay, Oval, Tapered Legs, 28 x 18 In.		95.00
Table, Baker's, Rose Marble Top, Iron Base, S Mounts, 30 x 48 x 29 In.		3600.00
Table, Baker's, Wood, Cast Iron, Bronze Mounts, Scrolled Legs, 30 x 49 In.		800.00
Table, Bamboo, Armorial Crest, Floral Crossbanded, Folding Shelves, Painted, 29 x 21 In.		354.00
Table, Baroque, Oak, Demilune, Pinned Joints, England, 29 ½ x 36 In.		649.00
Table, Baroque, Pine, Overhung Top, Stretcher Base, Drawer, Continental, 1700s, 32 x 49 In..		540.00
Table, Baroque, Walnut, Round, Brass Nailhead Trim, Tripart Base, Paw Feet, Italy, 30 x 44 In.		2748.00
Table, Baroque, Walnut, Urn Shape Trestle Supports, Scrolling Base, Stretcher, 31 x 64 In.		2250.00
Table, Basque Style, Bronze Faux Bamboo Frame, Marble Top & Shelf, c.1950, 26 x 25 In.		1350.00
Table, Biedermeier, Birch, Oval, Fluted Frieze, Scalloped, Column Support, 1800s, 29 x 35 In.		1164.00
Table, Biedermeier, Maple, Ebonized, Drawer, Column Support, 1800s, 30 ½ x 29 In. *illus*		984.00
Table, Biedermeier, Oak, Oval, Gallery, Rectangular Base, c.1890, 25 x 20 In.		215.00
Table, Black Lacquer, Inset Lacquer Panel, Flowers, 17 x 56 In.		2691.00
Table, Black Lacquer, Painted Scenes, Multicolor, Carved, Chinese, 1900s, 33 x 55 In.		2200.00
Table, Bouillotte, Kingwood, Marquetry, Marble Top, Candle Slides, Drawer, 1800s, 30 x 24 In.		2032.00
Table, Brass Inlay, Rectangular, D-Shape Leaves, 4 Drawers, 28 x 37 In.		2015.00
Table, Brass, Mirror Top, 2 Tiers, France, 25 x 20 In.		563.00
Table, Brass, Wood, Glass Top, Gilt Glass Shelf, Scrolled Legs, c.1950, 17 x 24 In., Pair		1107.00
Table, Britton Style, Oak, Draw Leaf, Trestle Base, Shaped Apron, 29 x 66 In.		540.00
Table, Bronze, Ebonized Top, X-Shape Base, Folding, c.1950, 29 x 76 In.		1107.00
Table, Bronze, Marble Top, Urn Finial, Curved Legs & Stretcher, 31 x 36 In.		920.00
Table, Bronze, Onyx, Pedestal, Shelf, Griffin Head Feet, c.1890, 32 x 18 In.		518.00
Table, Bronze, Rose Marble Top, Caryatid Supports, 2 Openwork Bases, 37 x 57 In.		1093.00
Table, Bronze, Round Rose Breccia Marble Top, 3 Elephant Supports, 38 x 32 In.		575.00
Table, Bureau, Louis XV, 2 Drawers, Scalloped Apron, 31 x 70 In.		1063.00
Table, Butler's, Dutch Colonial, Walnut, Oval, Panel Sides, Door, 31 x 29 In.		92.00
Table, Cafe, Neoclassical, Gilt Bronze, Onyx Top, Enameled Legs, c.1890, 29 x 25 In. *illus*		7320.00
Table, Campaign, Pine, 8-Sided, Crossed Legs, c.1775, 38 In.		3375.00
Table, Cane Sides, Shelf, 24 x 36 In.		210.00
Table, Card, Art Nouveau, Mahogany, Shaped Top, Pierced Apron, 29 x 35 In.		6844.00
Table, Card, Axel Bender Madsen, Teak, Leather, Willy Beck, Denmark, 1960s, 28 x 20 In.		1984.00
Table, Card, Chippendale, Mahogany, Hinged Top, Apron Drawer, 1700s, 28 x 35 In.		6900.00
Table, Card, Chippendale, Mahogany, Veneer, Foldover Top, Drawer, c.1770, 28 ½ x 36 In. ... *illus*		6518.00
Table, Card, Chippendale, Shaped Apron, Square Legs, Folding, 1800s, 29 x 36 In.		300.00
Table, Card, Empire Style, Rotates, Pedestal Base, Folding, Scroll Feet, c.1910, 30 x 40 In.		219.00
Table, Card, Empire, Mahogany, Flip Top, c.1830, 30 x 34 In.		89.00
Table, Card, Empire, Mahogany, Folding Top, Piecrust Edge, Lyre Pedestal, c.1810, 28 x 34 In.		179.00
Table, Card, Federal Style, Mahogany, Demilune, Foldover Top, Barber Pole, c.1890, 31 x 36 In.		646.00
Table, Card, Federal, Birch, Hinged Top, Swelled Front, c.1805, 28 x 36 In.		230.00
Table, Card, Federal, Cherry Inlay, Demilune, Folding Top, Beaded Apron, c.1800, 28 x 34 In.		770.00
Table, Card, Federal, Flame Birch, Inlaid Mahogany, Reeded Legs, c.1810, 30 x 36 In., Pair		28440.00
Table, Card, Federal, Mahogany, 5 Reeded Legs, Birch Gate, New York, c.1810, 31 x 36 In.		1800.00
Table, Card, Federal, Mahogany, Bowed Hinged Top, Turret Corners, Lunette Inlay, 30 x 36 In.		1093.00
Table, Card, Federal, Mahogany, Flip Top, Frieze Drawer, Glass Pulls, 1800s, 29 x 35 In.		299.00
Table, Card, Federal, Mahogany, Folding Top, Cock-Beaded, Square Legs, c.1800, 30 x 36 In.		652.00
Table, Card, Federal, Mahogany, Folding Top, Oval Corners, String Inlay, c.1795, 29 x 36 In.		1185.00
Table, Card, Federal, Mahogany, Inlay, Folding Top, Square Tapered Legs, 1800s, 30 x 17 In.		2370.00
Table, Card, Federal, Mahogany, Inlay, Reeded Legs, Serpentine Front, 31 x 36 In.		572.00
Table, Card, Federal, Mahogany, Inlay, Serpentine Foldover Top, Reeded Legs, c.1800, 29 x 37 In.		7170.00
Table, Card, Federal, Mahogany, Line Inlay, Demilune, 1800s, 29 ½ x 36 In.		267.00
Table, Card, Federal, Mahogany, Maple, Inlay, Reeded Legs, Shaped Top, c.1815, 30 x 36 In., Pair		15405.00
Table, Card, Federal, Mahogany, String Inlaid Edge, Hinged Top, Square Legs, c.1795, 29 x 35 In.		533.00
Table, Card, Federal, Maple, Demilune, Foldover Top, Plain Frieze, 30 x 34 In.		2691.00
Table, Card, Federal, Mixed Wood, Inlay, Foldover, Charleston, 29 x 18 In.		30680.00
Table, Card, Federal, Satinwood, Flame Birch, Inlay, Serpentine Fold-Out Top, c.1810, 30 x 37 In.		1058.00

Furniture, Stand, Blackamoor, Boy, Ebonized, Gilt, Painted, Continental, c.1900, 66 In.
$1778.00

Skinner, Inc.

Furniture, Stand, Fern, Pierce Carved, Marble Insert, Frieze, Cabriole Legs, Oriental, c.1875, 35 x 19 In.
$460.00

James D. Julia Inc.

Furniture, Stand, George III, Satinwood, Inlaid Mahogany, Tambour Door, Drawer, Gallery, 31 x 14 In.
$889.00

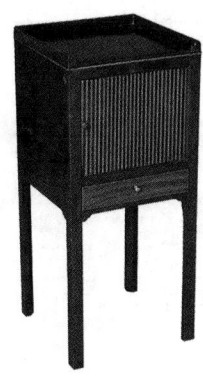

Skinner, Inc.

Furniture, Stand, Hepplewhite, Walnut, Pine Top, Drawer, Tapered Legs, Pa., c.1890, 28 ½ x 24 In.
$472.00

Conestoga Auction Co., Inc.

Furniture, Stand, Music, William IV, Mahogany, Candlesticks, Ribbed Standard, c.1835, 55 ½ In.
$553.00

New Orleans Auction Galleries, Inc.

Furniture, Stand, Parzinger, Lacquered Wood, 2 Drawers, Nickel Plated Brass, 1960s, 21 x 24 In.
$3100.00

Rago Arts & Auction Center

Table, Card, Federal, Satinwood, Leaf, Bellflower, Demilune, Fold-Out Top, c.1790, 30 x 36 In.	5405.00
Table, Card, Federal, Serpentine Foldover Top, Shell Inlay, Square Legs, c.1790, 29 x 36 In.....	1342.00
Table, Card, Federal, Wood, Inlay, Demilune, Swing Leg, Charak, Boston, c.1932, 31 x 36 In...	460.00
Table, Card, George III Style, Mahogany, Carved Cabriole Legs, Paw Feet, 28 x 33 In.	1304.00
Table, Card, George III, Mahogany, Carved, Hinged Top, Pierced Apron, Square Legs, 29 x 34 In.	1888.00
Table, Card, George III, Satinwood, Demilune, Fan Inlay, Spade Feet, 30 x 36 In.................	1265.00
Table, Card, Georgian, Mahogany, Shell Inlay, Gateleg, Octagonal Hinged Top, c.1790, 29 x 31 In.	368.00
Table, Card, Hepplewhite Style, Mahogany Inlay, Shaped Drop Leaf, c.1910, 30 ½ x 36 In., Pair	2250.00
Table, Card, Hepplewhite, Birch, Square Tapered Legs, Mortised Apron, Hinged Top, 27 x 31 In.	646.00
Table, Card, Hepplewhite, Mahogany, Demilune, Banded Inlay, Tapered Legs, c.1790, 30 x 36 In.	460.00
Table, Card, Hepplewhite, Mahogany, Flower Inlay, Foldover, New England, c.1800, 29 x 36 In.	593.00
Table, Card, Hepplewhite, Mahogany, Foldover, New England, c.1800, 30 x 35 In.	2015.00
Table, Card, Hepplewhite, Mahogany, Hinged Leaf, Banded Inlay, 1700s, 29 x 36 In................	1380.00
Table, Card, Hepplewhite, Mahogany, Inlaid, Foldover, Drawer, Pa., c.1800, 29 x 36 In.	444.00
Table, Card, Hepplewhite, Mahogany, Inlaid, Serpentine Front, Cock-Beaded, c.1780, 30 x 35 In.	1495.00
Table, Card, Hepplewhite, Mahogany, Inlay, Demilune, Hinged Leaf, c.1800, 29 x 36 In..........	1610.00
Table, Card, Hepplewhite, Mahogany, Pine, Inlay, Stringing, D-Shape Apron, c.1800, 28 x 36 In.	264.00
Table, Card, Mahogany, Bird's-Eye Maple Panels, c.1800, 28 x 36 In................................	4503.00
Table, Card, Mahogany, Carved Shell Frieze, Shaped Base, Carved Feet, 1800s, 30 x 34 In.	237.00
Table, Card, Mahogany, Carved, Fold Top, Gilt Stencil, Paw Feet, Swivel, 30 x 36 In..................	1989.00
Table, Card, Mahogany, Crossbanded, Swivel Top, Trestle, Stretcher, c.1820, 31 x 36 In.	2390.00
Table, Card, Mahogany, D-Shape, Hinged Top, Stencil, Swelled Stem, Swivel, c.1840, 30 x 36 In.	590.00
Table, Card, Mahogany, Pedestal Base, Lyre Legs, Paw Feet, Casters, N.Y., 28 x 35 In.	1093.00
Table, Card, Mahogany, Swivel Top, Spiral Reeded Standard, Saber Legs, c.1815, 29 x 36 In. ..	1098.00
Table, Card, Neoclassical, Mahogany, Lyre Base, Shaped Apron, Rectangular Top, 30 x 36 In..	708.00
Table, Card, Neoclassical, Mahogany, Ogee Molded Apron, Paw Feet, c.1820, 30 x 36 In.	450.00
Table, Card, Neoclassical, Mahogany, Swelled Front, Hanging Pendants, c.1820, 28 x 36 In....	175.00
Table, Card, Queen Anne, Mahogany, Scalloped, Skirt, Painted, Cabriole Legs, c.1905, 30 x 34 In.	177.00
Table, Card, Queen Anne, Walnut, Tooled Leather, Rectangular, Hinged Top, Pad Feet, 29 x 33 In.	1534.00
Table, Card, Regency, Mahogany, Inlay, Felt Interior, Bulbous Stem, Swivel, c.1810, 29 x 36 In., Pair	3220.00
Table, Card, Sheraton, Mahogany, Foldover Top, Philadelphia, 29 x 35 ½ In.	267.00
Table, Card, Sheraton, Mahogany, Hinged, Reeded Edge, Drawer, Turned Legs, c.1825, 30 x 17 In.	411.00
Table, Card, Tilt Top, Painted Flowers, Splayed Legs, Brass End Caps, 28 x 27 In.	238.00
Table, Card, Tulipwood, Bronze, Inlay, Felt Interior, Demilune, France, 1800s, 30 x 35 In........	1541.00
Table, Cast Iron, Central Scroll & Quiver Design, X Frame, 34 x 48 In.	615.00
Table, Cast Iron, Diamond & Scroll Pattern, Arches, Fluted Columns, c.1870, 34 x 53 In., Pair	1230.00
Table, Cast Iron, Marble, Square Top, Column, Curved Shaped Feet, 30 x 35 In.......................	94.00
Table, Cast Iron, Riveted, 4 Apron Drawers, Column Legs, 17 x 52 In................................	1554.00
Table, Cast Iron, Round Top, Cabriole Legs, Stretcher Shelf, c.1880, 30 x 24 In.	717.00
Table, Cast Stone, Faux Bois, Tripod Base, c.1940, 31 x 45 In...................................	923.00
Table, Cedric Hartman, Granite, Brass, Round Top, 3 Tubular Legs, 1970s, 23 x 17 In., Pair ...	6820.00
Table, Center, Aesthetic Revival, Mahogany, Inlay, Octagonal, Spider Supports, c.1885, 29 x 39 In.	8365.00
Table, Center, Arts & Crafts, Oak, Round, 6 Supports, Concave Hexagonal Shelf, 30 x 33 In. ...	366.00
Table, Center, Bronze, Round Beveled Glass Top, 4 Winged Women, Scroll Feet, 30 x 42 In......	1896.00
Table, Center, Charles X, Mahogany, Ebonized, Marble, Dish Top, Hexagonal, 30 x 39 In........	3125.00
Table, Center, Chippendale Style, Mahogany, Round Top, Gadrooned Border, X-Stretcher, 36 In.	519.00
Table, Center, Elm, Square Top, Corner Arches On Apron, Block Legs, 1800s, 34 x 40 In.	273.00
Table, Center, Empire Style, Gilt, Round Marble Top, 3 Crocodile Supports, 30 In....................	1220.00
Table, Center, Empire, Gilt, Marble Top, Rectangular, Grapevines, Pinecone, 31 x 47 In.	2370.00
Table, Center, Empire, Mahogany, Round Top, Squared Support, Paw Feet, c.1830, 29 x 38 In.	100.00
Table, Center, Empire, Marble Top, 12-Sided, 3 Scroll Legs, Cyma Apron, c.1835, 31 x 35 In....	2950.00
Table, Center, Federal, Mahogany, Drop Leaf, Butterfly Supports, Columns, c.1820, 28 x 35 x 22 In.	5060.00
Table, Center, Gothic Revival, Rosewood, 6-Sided Marble Top, c.1845, 40 x 36 In. ....*illus*	47800.00
Table, Center, Habersham Style, Marble Top, Shaped Apron, 4 Column Legs, 28 x 34 In.	180.00
Table, Center, Jacobean, Walnut, Molded Edge, Drawer, Turned Legs, H-Stretcher, 27 x 35 In..	649.00
Table, Center, Louis XIII Style, Oak, Round, Beaded Edge, Twist Column, 2 Lions, 30 x 28 In..	390.00
Table, Center, Louis XV Style, Mahogany, Sprig Inlay, Gilt, Banded Top, Cabriole Legs, 30 x 29 In.	300.00
Table, Center, Louis XV Style, Oak, Walnut, Square, Carved Frieze, Cabriole Legs, 1800s, 30 x 34 In.	1476.00
Table, Center, Louis XV Style, Rosewood, 2 Drawers, Cabriole Legs, 28 ½ x 51 x 33 In.	1140.00
Table, Center, Louis XV, Shaped Top, Carved Frieze, Stretchers, Cabriole Legs, 29 x 44 In........	649.00
Table, Center, Louis XVI Style, Pickled Oak, Carved, Scalloped Apron, Bun Feet, 30 x 50 In......	1476.00
Table, Center, Louis XVI, Gilt, Marble Top, Fluted Frieze, Swag, 6 Ft. 7 In.................	3438.00
Table, Center, Mahogany, Beaded Skirt, Curved, Splayed Base, c.1830, 28 x 34 In.	403.00
Table, Center, Mahogany, Gilt Bronze Mounted, Pedestal, France, c.1825, 27 x 28 In.	2460.00
Table, Center, Mahogany, Plank Round Top, Dentil Carved Frieze, 6 Supports, 1800s, 31 x 49 In.	3198.00
Table, Center, Mahogany, Round Tilt Top, Bulbous Stem, Stepped Base, c.1825, 29 In..............	2091.00

Table, Center, Mahogany, Round Tilt Top, Piecrust Gallery Edge, 3-Footed, 29 x 30 In.	330.00
Table, Center, Mahogany, Round, Turned Bulbous Support, Platform Base, c.1850, 29 x 35 In.	230.00
Table, Center, Metal, Faux Bamboo Painted, Marble Slab Top, 1900s, 37 x 78 In.	180.00
Table, Center, Napoleon III, Ebonized, Flower Basket, Shaped Frieze, 1800s, 30 x 31 In.	1107.00
Table, Center, Neoclassical, Black Paint, Fruit, Vine, Round Top, c.1835, 29 x 36 In.	750.00
Table, Center, Neoclassical, Iron, Gilt, Glass Top, Scrolls, Tapered Legs, 30 x 54 In.	492.00
Table, Center, Neoclassical, Mahogany, Shaped Corners, Acanthus Pedestal, 30 x 50 In.	154.00
Table, Center, Neoclassical, Mahogany, Veneer, Tilt Top, Corner Columns, c.1835, 38 x 39 In.	1830.00
Table, Center, Neoclassical, Pietra Dura, Gilt, Round Top, Compass Stars, Urn Base, 1900s, 35 In.	7320.00
Table, Center, Neogrecque, Rosewood, Inlay, Parcel Gilt, Center Column, c.1865, 31 x 35 In. ..*illus*	4674.00
Table, Center, Oak, Round, Molded Top, Box Stretcher, Turned Legs, 29 x 23 In.	236.00
Table, Center, Oval Top, Inlay, Ebonized Legs, Gilt, Medallions, c.1880, 31 x 49 In.	2875.00
Table, Center, Red Lacquer, Carved, 3 Drawers, Openwork Brackets, Chinese, 36 x 38 In.	711.00
Table, Center, Regency Style, Mahogany, Inlay, Round, 31 x 56 In.	469.00
Table, Center, Renaissance Revival, Walnut, Marble, Carved, Turned Standard, c.1865, 31 x 35 In.	1265.00
Table, Center, Renaissance Revival, Walnut, Rectangular, Baluster, Paw Feet, 1800s, 29 x 32 In.	144.00
Table, Center, Rococo Revival, Rectangular, Frieze, Carved, Putti, Snail Feet, c.1865, 29 x 32 In.	288.00
Table, Center, Rococo Revival, Walnut, Marble, Figural Supports, James G. Blake, c.1850, 57 x 43 In. *illus*	16730.00
Table, Center, Rococo Revival, Walnut, Serpentine Marble Top, Stretcher, 1800s, 29 x 52 In.	418.00
Table, Center, Rosewood, Chestnut, Round Slate Top, Painted, Flowers, Pedestal, c.1830, 34 In.	3738.00
Table, Center, Round Top, Frieze Drawer, Ebonized, Tripod Pedestal, c.1810, 30 x 19 In.	767.00
Table, Center, Victorian, Mahogany, Inlaid Top, Octagonal, Pedestal, 28 x 34 In.	531.00
Table, Center, Victorian, Marble Top, Cast Iron, Round, Fluted, Ribbed Stem, 27 x 24 In.	184.00
Table, Center, Victorian, Oak, 2 Tiers, Shaped Lower Shelf, 24 x 32 In.	259.00
Table, Center, Victorian, Walnut, Geometric Inlay, Octagonal Top, Tripod Base, 29 x 30 In.	344.00
Table, Center, Victorian, Walnut, Incised Carving, 30 ½ x 30 In.	120.00
Table, Center, Victorian, Walnut, Marble Top, Urn Finial, Scroll Legs, c.1865, 29 x 30 In.	460.00
Table, Center, Victorian, Walnut, Round Top, Bulbous Standard, 3 Splay Legs, Scroll Toes, 54 In.	369.00
Table, Center, William IV, Mahogany, Round Tilt Top, Cylindrical Stem, 1800s, 48 In.	1168.00
Table, Charles II, Oak, Gateleg, D-Shape Leaves, Frieze Drawers, Brass Pull, Block Legs, 29 x 22 In.	585.00
Table, Cherry, 2-Board Top, Drawer, North Carolina, 29 x 23 In.	1200.00
Table, Cherry, Figured Maple Legs, Drawer, Flame Grain, 1800s, 30 x 20 In.	413.00
Table, Chinoiserie, Ebonized, Dish Top, Gilt, Tripod, Pad Feet, c.1875, 30 x 16 In.	246.00
Table, Chippendale Style, Mahogany, Bamboo, Removable Silver Plated Tray, 21 x 19 In.	1455.00
Table, Chippendale Style, Mahogany, Round, Beaded Edge, Paw Feet, 29 x 36 In.	240.00
Table, Chippendale Style, Round Top, Birdcage, Baluster Pedestal, Tripod, 31 x 32 In.	4900.00
Table, Chippendale Style, X-Stretcher, Metal Tag, Council, 18 x 38 In.	60.00
Table, Chippendale, Battened Top, Octangular, North Carolina, c.1775, 28 x 33 In.	920.00
Table, Chippendale, Mahogany, Blind Fretwork Apron, Chamfered Legs, 28 x 35 In.	837.00
Table, Chippendale, Mahogany, Tilt Top, Round, Column Pedestal, Tripod, 1800s, 27 x 36 In.	657.00
Table, Chippendale, Oval Maple Top, Overhung, Box Stretcher, 26 x 33 In.	527.00
Table, Chippendale, Slab, Marble Top, Drawer, Reeded Legs, 1900s, 34 x 56 In.	385.00
Table, Coaching, Edwardian, Mahogany, Bisected Top, Folding, Railed Supports, c.1900, 27 x 30 In.	461.00
Table, Coffee Mill Base, Pine Top, The Chas Parker Company, American, 1880s, 22 x 48 In.	460.00
Table, Coffee, Arts & Crafts Style, Wood, Drawer, Twist Legs, 42 x 26 In.	1080.00
Table, Coffee, Black Paint, Glass Inset, Gilt Flowering Tree, Silver Leaf, Hoof Feet, 18 x 54 In.	676.00
Table, Coffee, Black Wood, Tubular Steel Frame, Wolfgang Hoffman, Howell, 34 x 20 In.	540.00
Table, Coffee, Brass, Glass Top, Downswept Legs, X-Stretcher, c.1960, 17 x 29 In.	492.00
Table, Coffee, Brass, Glass, Enameled Metal, Oval, Mathieu Mategor, 1960s, 16 x 42 In.	682.00
Table, Coffee, Bronze Abstract Base, Glass Top, Engraved Silas Seandel, 15 x 35 In.	496.00
Table, Coffee, Bronze, Gilt Reverse Painted Glass Top, X-Stretcher, c.1940, 16 x 53 In.	1107.00
Table, Coffee, Bronze, Glass Top, c.1960, 17 x 73 In.	369.00
Table, Coffee, Bronze, Marble, Festoon Frieze, 4 S-Curve Legs, 21 x 33 ½ In.	219.00
Table, Coffee, Bronze, Michelangelo's Creation Of Adam, 2 Pedestal Bases, 18 x 65 In.	1610.00
Table, Coffee, Bronze, Mirrored Top, Column Legs, Shaped Stretcher, c.1940, 17 x 30 In.	861.00
Table, Coffee, Bronze, Patinated, Etched, Enamel, Oval Top, Asian Scene, Laverne, 18 x 66 In.	2600.00
Table, Coffee, Bronze, Shaped Marble Top, Pierced Apron, Splayed Legs, 18 x 47 In.	183.00
Table, Coffee, Burl Walnut, Brass Checkerboard, Black Platform Base, c.1970, 12 x 51 In.	1046.00
Table, Coffee, Burl, Square, Milo Baughman, 1960s, 40 x 40 In.	5800.00
Table, Coffee, Carved Glass Top, Brass, Ebonized, Free-Form, 3 Legs, 1940s, 15 x 40 In.	124.00
Table, Coffee, Ceramic Tile Top, Wrought Iron Base, Shaped Stretcher, France, c.1960, 17 x 40 In.	1353.00
Table, Coffee, Charles Hollis, Glass Top, 2 Bronze Metal Bases, 48 x 20 In.	1560.00
Table, Coffee, Chevron Veneer Top, 2 Pedestal Legs, c.1930, 20 x 20 In., Pair	492.00
Table, Coffee, Chrome Steel, Brass, Glass, 1980s, 16 ½ x 36 In.	186.00
Table, Coffee, Copper, Chrome, Brass Tacks, 14 ½ x 30 ½ In.	461.00
Table, Coffee, Cross Grain Starburst Veneer, 2 Drawers, Stretcher Shelf, Brass, Mounts, 20 x 42 In.	610.00

Furniture, Stand, Portfolio, Rosewood, Carved, Fretwork Panel, Brass Fittings, Casters, 1800s
$2318.00

Neal Auction Co.

Furniture, Stand, Shaving, Renaissance Revival, Walnut, Carved, Mirror, Marble Top, Drawer, c.1890, 69 In.
$366.00

Neal Auction Co.

Furniture, Stand, Shaving, Victorian, Mahogany, Carved, Adjustable Mirror, Drawer, c.1880, 70 x 21 In.
$518.00

Cottone Auctions

Furniture, Stand, Sheraton, Curly
Maple, 2 Drawers, 29 x 17 ½ In.
$633.00

Cottone Auctions

Furniture, Stool, A. & P. Castiglioni,
Mezzadro, Chrome, Beech, Enamel,
Zanotta, 1957, 21 In.
$2500.00

Los Angeles Modern Auctions

Furniture, Stool, Piano, Regency,
Mahogany, Leather Seat, Baluster, Carved
Feet, 20 ½ In.
$366.00

Leslie Hindman Auctioneers

Furniture, Stool, Regency Style, Carved,
Parcel Gilt, Ebonized, Upholstered,
15 In., Pair
$1896.00

Skinner, Inc.

Table, Coffee, Danish Modern, Teak Top, V-Shape Legs, 68 x 18 In.		300.00
Table, Coffee, Danish Modern, Teak, Beveled Edges, Cube Base, 19 ½ x 31 In.		518.00
Table, Coffee, Driftwood, Stacked, 10 x 38 In.		523.00
Table, Coffee, Eastlake, Walnut, White Marble Top, Trestle Base, c.1875, 17 ¾ x 32 In.		127.00
Table, Coffee, Eero Saarinen, Tulip, Walnut, Round Top, White Metal Spread Base, 15 x 42 In.		593.00
Table, Coffee, Embossed, Lacquered Leather, Baker Furniture, 17 x 30 In.		403.00
Table, Coffee, Esherick, Cherry, Biomorphic, Top, Label, 1960, 60 x 40 In.		30000.00
Table, Coffee, Figured Wood Veneer, Brass Banding, Baker Furniture Label, 60 x 16 In.		368.00
Table, Coffee, Flower Lacquered Top, Red, Lacque De Fram Label, France, c.1960, 16 ½ x 39 In.		554.00
Table, Coffee, Frankl, Enameled Cork, Mahogany, Johnson Co., 1940s, 14 x 71 In.		4650.00
Table, Coffee, G. Nakashima, English Oak Burl, Oak Base, 1965, 12 x 54 In.		21080.00
Table, Coffee, G. Nakashima, English Walnut, Plank, c.1966, 13 x 62 In.		7440.00
Table, Coffee, G. Nakashima, Walnut, Slab, Marked, c.1970, 67 x 36 In.		16120.00
Table, Coffee, Geometric Copper Top, Wrought Iron Base, c.1950, 17 ½ x 39 In.		615.00
Table, Coffee, Glass Top, Bronze Horse Supports, Brass Stretcher, Base, France, c.1960, 16 x 55 In.		2214.00
Table, Coffee, Glass Top, Chrome, Brass Frame, 1960s, 36 x 16 In.		210.00
Table, Coffee, Glass Top, Chromed Steel Legs, Pace, 1970s, 18 ¾ x 42 In.		558.00
Table, Coffee, Glass Top, Mixed Metals, Green, White Paint, Italy, 1900s, 18 x 41 In.		300.00
Table, Coffee, Glass Top, Oval, X-Stretcher, Hoof Feet, 1970, 17 x 55 In., Pair		523.00
Table, Coffee, Glass, Wood, Round, Free-Form Base, 1960s, 15 x 49 In.		186.00
Table, Coffee, Gordon & Jane Martz, Walnut, Inset Black Tiles, Round, 36 x 20 In.		180.00
Table, Coffee, Heckman, Mahogany, Drawer, Tray Top, X-Stretcher, Beveled Edge, 1900s, 26 x 28 In.		240.00
Table, Coffee, J. Adnet, Enamel, Wrought Iron, Bronze, Glass, France, 1950s, 20 x 30 In.		930.00
Table, Coffee, Karl Springer, Fossil Stone, Brass Inlay, Square, 40 x 15 In.		360.00
Table, Coffee, Karl Springer, Lacquered Parchment, Brass, 1970s, 18 x 42 In.		589.00
Table, Coffee, Knoll, Square, Marble Top, Square Metal Legs, 1954, 17 x 36 In.		938.00
Table, Coffee, Leather Book Shape, 3 Drawers, Raised Ball Feet, 17 x 35 In.		584.00
Table, Coffee, Louis XV Style, Shaped Onyx Top, Bronze Curved Stretcher, 18 x 46 In.		519.00
Table, Coffee, Louis XV, Walnut, Inlaid Marble Top, Carved Apron, 1800s, 30 x 80 In.		1200.00
Table, Coffee, Louis XV, Walnut, Tray Top, Shaped Apron, Flowers, Cabriole Legs, 20 x 36 In.		150.00
Table, Coffee, Louis XVI Style, Gilt Metal, Smoked Mirror Glass, Acorn Finials, 34 x 19 In.		461.00
Table, Coffee, Lucite, Curved, American Studio, 1970s, 18 x 60 In.		744.00
Table, Coffee, Lucite, Polished Aluminum Base, Overhung Glass Top, 1980s, 16 x 60 In.		496.00
Table, Coffee, M. Baughman, Burl, Square Top, Round Metal Base, T. Coggin, 40 x 40 x 15 In.		510.00
Table, Coffee, Mahogany, Carved Rim, Apron, Legs, 1900s, 20 x 39 In.		115.00
Table, Coffee, Mahogany, Glass Top, Kidney Shape, Fretwork Surround, 19 x 36 In.		120.00
Table, Coffee, Mahogany, Glass, Flowers, Diaper Border, Claw Feet, c.1900, 16 x 35 In.		148.00
Table, Coffee, Mahogany, Vitrine, Lift Top, Ferguson Furniture Co., 1900s, 19 x 38 In.		600.00
Table, Coffee, Maple Frame, Mosaic Inlay Top, Rectangular, Ebonized Base, c.1960, 22 x 39 In.		1280.00
Table, Coffee, Marble, Inlaid Squares, Rectangular, X-Stretcher, Spheres, 1900s, 16 x 44 In.		4444.00
Table, Coffee, Max Kuehne, Silver Leaf, Multicolor, Gesso Wood, 1930s, 16 x 64 In.		10540.00
Table, Coffee, McCobb, Brass Supports, White Glass Top, Rectangular, Directional, 48 x 18 In.		1440.00
Table, Coffee, Melt Coated Welded Steel Base, Abstract Design, Glass Top, c.1960, 15 x 65 In.		4063.00
Table, Coffee, Metal, Inset Glass, Circle Designs, Rectangular, 18 x 55 In.		492.00
Table, Coffee, Mies Van Der Rohe, Barcelona, Stainless Steel, Glass, Knoll, 1960s, 17 x 48 In.		806.00
Table, Coffee, Milo Baughman, Clear Acrylic, Lacquered Wood, Steel Legs, T. Coggin, 36 x 16 In.		3240.00
Table, Coffee, Oriental Design, Leather Panel, Green Paint, Gilt, Processional, 47 x 25 In.		354.00
Table, Coffee, Osvaldo Borsani, Glass, Mahogany, Brass, 1950s, 60 x 28 In.		2356.00
Table, Coffee, Oval, Marble Top, Fluted Tapered Legs, Carved, Gold Paint, 1900s, 19 x 54 In.		240.00
Table, Coffee, P. Evans, Directional, Cityscape, Cantilevered, 1970s, 60 x 48 In.		5890.00
Table, Coffee, Painted, White Wash, Flowers, Variegated Marble Top, Oval, 15 x 28 In.		173.00
Table, Coffee, Parzinger, Brass, Bleached Mahogany, 17 x 44 In.		930.00
Table, Coffee, Paul Lazlo, White Oak, Brown Saltman, 12 x 60 In.		527.00
Table, Coffee, Philip & Kelvin Laverne, Bronze, Patinated, 2 Etched Nudes, 1960s, 18 x 65 In.		3555.00
Table, Coffee, Philip & Kelvin Laverne, Chan, Bronze, Enameled, Kidney Shape, 1965, 17 x 64 In.		10158.00
Table, Coffee, Philip & Kelvin Laverne, Chan, Bronze, Pewter, Etched, Multicolor, 17 ½ x 45 In. *..illus*		4340.00
Table, Coffee, Philip & Kelvin Laverne, Patina, Polychrome Bronze, Pewter, 1960s, 16 x 60 x 31 In.		5890.00
Table, Coffee, Pietra Dura Marble Top, Vines, Birds, 4 Legs, 15 ¾ x 36 In.		374.00
Table, Coffee, Pine, Scalloped Apron, Green Paint, 24 x 53 In.		230.00
Table, Coffee, Poul Kjaerholm, PK 61, Chrome, Slate, E. Kold Christensen, 1950s, 13 x 32 In.		2728.00
Table, Coffee, Queen Anne Style, Mahogany, Gateleg, Spindles, Baker Furniture, 18 x 38 In.		529.00
Table, Coffee, Ramsey, Gilded Wrought Iron, Glass, 1940s, 12 x 39 x 20 In.		1612.00
Table, Coffee, Removable Tray, Round Top, Bamboo Design Legs, Splay Feet, c.1948, 19 x 25 In.		938.00
Table, Coffee, Resin Topped Marble, Chrome Steel, Lacquered Wood, 1970s, 16 x 48 In.		744.00
Table, Coffee, Ron Seff, Chromed Steel, Brass, Glass, 1970s, 19 x 55 In.		2480.00
Table, Coffee, Rosewood, Rectangular, Carved Apron, Block Legs, c.1900, 30 x 16 In.		1076.00

Table, Coffee, Rosewood, Rectangular, Shaped Skirt, Cabriole Legs, Low, 47 x 24 In............	896.00
Table, Coffee, Round Glass Top, 7 Painted Metal Legs, Star Stretcher, 1953, 16 x 43 In.	4375.00
Table, Coffee, Round, Marble Top, Mahogany, Legs, Metal Tag, Dunbar, 1957, 48 In.	1020.00
Table, Coffee, Shaped, Engraved Asian Landscape Top, White, Heritage, 15 x 46 In.	305.00
Table, Coffee, Spanish Style, Oak, Curled Iron Stretcher, 18 x 35 In.	122.00
Table, Coffee, Square Top, Inlaid Design, Asian Style, Scrolled Legs, 1900s, 39 x 39 In.	299.00
Table, Coffee, Steel, Brass, Distressed, Mirror Top, Tapered Legs, Shaped Stretcher, c.1960, 16 x 40 In.	430.00
Table, Coffee, Stepped Lacquered Mahogany Base, Round Glass Top, 1940s, 18 ½ x 30 In.	434.00
Table, Coffee, Tray On Stand, Low, Round, 4 Turned Legs, Persia, 18 x 47 In..........................	201.00
Table, Coffee, Triangular Glass Top, Mesh Metal Base, Curved Design, Shelf, c.1956, 20 x 34 In.	6250.00
Table, Coffee, V. Kagan, Snail, Laminated Walnut, Glass, 1960s, 15 x 42 x 37 In.	1488.00
Table, Coffee, V. Kagan, Tri-Symmetric, Walnut, Glass, Emilio Pucci, 1990s, 15 x 60 In.	3472.00
Table, Coffee, W. Rizzo, Bar, Brushed Chromed Steel, Revolving, Laminated, 1970s, 13 x 45 In. *illus*	3720.00
Table, Coffee, Walnut, 6 Legs, 1950s, 16 ½ x 72 In.	558.00
Table, Coffee, Walnut, Claw Foot, 34 x 19 ½ In...	173.00
Table, Coffee, Walnut, Laminate, John Keal, Brown-Saltman, 1960s, 15 x 96 In.	372.00
Table, Coffee, Walnut, Marble, Round, Bertha Schafer, Italy, 1950s, 15 x 40 In.	2400.00
Table, Coffee, Walnut, Round Chopping Block, 19 ¼ x 34 In.	285.00
Table, Coffee, Walnut, Sculpted, Wavy Square, Circular Legs, 18 x 28 In.................................	2500.00
Table, Coffee, Wegner, Teak, Laminate, Oak, Round, Reversible Top, c.1960, 37 In.	1007.00
Table, Coffee, Wood, Paint, Inset Marble Top, Hoof Feet, c.1960, 14 x 30 In.	492.00
Table, Coffee, Wood, Sculpted Shape, Signed Devon Dennett, 1947, 15 x 39 ½ In.	155.00
Table, Coffee, Wood, World Map Top, Brass Trim, France, c.1970, 21 x 31 In...........................	492.00
Table, Coffee, Wormley, Mahogany, Round, Curved, Continuous Legs, Drexel, c.1960, 19 x 37 In.	795.00
Table, Coffee, Wormley, White Oak, Laminate, Dunbar, c.1950, 16 x 86 In.	478.00
Table, Coffee, Woven Fiber, Brass Plated Metal, Travertine Top, France, 1970s, 13 x 38 In........	1240.00
Table, Coffee, Wrought Iron, Glass, Hammered, Knotted X-Shape Stretcher, c.1950, 16 x 44 In.	1968.00
Table, Conference, Renaissance Revival, Oak, Griffins, Trestle Base, c.1900, 95 x 42 In. ...*illus*	978.00
Table, Conservatory, Cast Iron, Onyx, Round, Pierced Frieze, Ring Stretchers, c.1865, 30 x 19 In.	553.00
Table, Console, Amboyna, Silver Foil Glass Top, J. Asnet, c.1940, 33 ½ x 84 ½ In.	5875.00
Table, Console, Antico Verde, Bronze Leaf, Bead Mounts, 4 Pedestal Legs, c.1890, 113 x 30 In.	2133.00
Table, Console, Art Deco, Wrought Iron Line & Scroll Design, Marble Top, 35 x 44 In., Pair	430.00
Table, Console, Asian Style, 3 Drawers, Shaped Metal Stretcher, Bamboo Trim, 39 x 74 In.......	360.00
Table, Console, Belle Epoque, Beech, Gilt, Marble Top, Carved Leaves, c.1900, 40 x 47 In.	359.00
Table, Console, Biedermeier, Ebonized, Parcel Gilt, Marble Top, D-Shape, Stretcher, 32 x 39 In., Pair.	4688.00
Table, Console, Biedermeier, Olive Wood, Shaped Apron, Drawer, Cabriole Legs, 29 x 46 In.....	750.00
Table, Console, Cantilever, Walnut, Walnut Veneer, Rectangular Top, Diagonal Support, 34 x 76 In.	1600.00
Table, Console, Carved Eagle Base, Spread Wing, Inlay, Distressed Gold, 1900s, 31 x 34 In., Pair	1035.00
Table, Console, Cherry, Demilune, String Inlay, Bellflower, Tapered Legs, c.1800-10, 29 x 40 In.	1763.00
Table, Console, Ebonized Wood, Enamel Steel, 1990s, 29 x 51 In.	372.00
Table, Console, Federal, Cherry, Demilune, 3 Square Tapered Legs, Straight Skirt, 1800s, 29 x 37 In.	337.00
Table, Console, Federal, Mahogany, D-Shape, Hinged Top, Reeded, Fluted Legs, 1800s, 30 x 36 In...	418.00
Table, Console, George III Style, Mahogany, Demilune, Hinged, Flip Top, Pad Feet, 29 x 30 In.	568.00
Table, Console, Gilt, Carved, Shell, Shaped Openwork Apron, Cabriole Legs, 36 x 47 In.	313.00
Table, Console, Gilt, Faux Marble, Pierced Leaf Frieze, Shell Stretcher, c.1900, 32 x 26 In........	1107.00
Table, Console, Gilt, Marble Top, Carved Apron, Garland, Leaf Carved Legs, c.1890, 33 x 54 In.	1912.00
Table, Console, Gilt, Marble Top, Scrolling Leaf Base, Cabriole Legs, Scroll Feet, c.1900, 32 x 35 In.	413.00
Table, Console, Gilt, Marble Top, Shaped, Shell Carved, Pierced Stretcher, c.1820, 35 x 33 In..	1722.00
Table, Console, Gilt, Serpentine Top, 2 Blackamoor Figures Supports, Italy, 1800s, 40 x 64 In.	3555.00
Table, Console, Gothic Revival, Walnut, Carved, Marble Top, Serpentine Stretcher, 32 x 50 In.	3068.00
Table, Console, Hepplewhite Style, Cherry, Demilune, Inlay, Tapered Legs, 1900s, 30 x 40 In., Pair...	646.00
Table, Console, Hepplewhite, Cherry, Demilune, Inlay, c.1800, 28 x 45 In...............................	1058.00
Table, Console, Louis V, Beech, Gilded, Pierced Apron, Cabriole Legs, c.1910, 33 x 72 In.	270.00
Table, Console, Louis XV Style, Shaped Marble Top, Carved Apron, Cabriole Legs, 35 x 63 In...	744.00
Table, Console, Louis XV, Gilded, Scrolled Mirror & Apron, Cabriole Legs, 1800s, 59 x 44 In.	1320.00
Table, Console, Louis XV, Walnut, Marble Top, Molded Edge, Leaves, c.1750, 38 x 101 In.	3000.00
Table, Console, Mahogany, 2 Drawers, Ring Handles, Lower Shelf, Baker Furniture, 29 x 46 In.	563.00
Table, Console, Mahogany, 3 Drawers, Crossed Saber Gallery, Brass Trellis Back, 63 x 42 In....	1000.00
Table, Console, Mahogany, Carved, Triangular, 3 Cabriole Legs, Carved Apron, 24 x 27 In.......	63.00
Table, Console, Mahogany, Gilt Bronze Mounts, Marble Top, Frieze Drawer, Fluted Legs, 30 x 21 In.	837.00
Table, Console, Mahogany, Marble Top, Frieze Drawer, Animal Shape Legs, 1800s, 28 x 58 In.	948.00
Table, Console, Mahogany, Marble, Mirrored Back, Stone Columns, Paw Feet, c.1810-15, 36 x 44 In..	1645.00
Table, Console, Marble, Wrought Iron, Scrollwork, Leaves, Stamped, c.1925, 36 x 65 In.	30000.00
Table, Console, Marquetry, Demilune Top, Flowers, Door, 31 x 35 In.	372.00
Table, Console, Mixed Wood, Marble, Faceted Tapered Stem, Scrolled Feet, c.1830, 29 x 35 In., Pair	1495.00

F

Furniture, Stool, Sori Yanagi, Butterfly, Rosewood, Metal Rod, Tendo, 1956, 15 ¾ x 16 ½ In.
$5938.00

Los Angeles Modern Auctions

Furniture, Stool, Wood, Baseball Mitt Seat, Leather, Baseball Bat Legs, Swivel, c.1965, 46 In., Pair
$1126.00

Skinner, Inc.

Furniture, Table, Aesthetic Revival, Brass, Pierced, Inset Longwy Tiles, Outswept Legs, c.1885, 31 x 13 In.
$1845.00

Neal Auction Co.

As always, the edited listings in *Kovels' Antiques & Collectibles Price Guide* aren't available on any website, but readers should visit Kovels.com for information on trends, tips, reproductions, marks, old prices, and more!

Furniture, Table, Baker's, Iron, Marble, Fleur-De-Lis Apron, Brass Mounts, Casters, 1800s, 31 x 39 In.
$2074.00

Neal Auction Co.

Furniture, Table, Biedermeier, Maple, Ebonized, Drawer, Column Support, 1800s, 30 ½ x 29 In.
$984.00

Neal Auction Co.

Furniture, Table, Cafe, Neoclassical, Gilt Bronze, Onyx Top, Enameled Legs, c.1890, 29 x 25 In.
$7320.00

Neal Auction Co.

Furniture, Table, Card, Chippendale, Mahogany, Veneer, Foldover Top, Drawer, c.1770, 28 ½ x 36 In.
$6518.00

Skinner, Inc.

Table, Console, Oak, 3 Drawer, Painted, Sarried, Ltd., 32 x 54 In.	244.00
Table, Console, Orange Paint, Drawers, Cupboard Doors, Chinese, 1800s, 28 x 52 In.	767.00
Table, Console, P. Evans, Directional, Cityscape, Chrome Plated Steel, Rass, 1970s, 34 x 66 In.	2232.00
Table, Console, P. Evans, Directional, Patchwork, Fiberglass, Bronze, Hanging, 1970s, 97 x 14 In.	4340.00
Table, Console, Philip & Kelvin Laverne, Bronze, Patinated, Multicolor, c.1962, 33 x 96 In.	57040.00
Table, Console, Pierre Giraudon, Fractured Resin, France, 1970s, 39 x 59 In.	11160.00
Table, Console, Pine, Cherry, Demilune Overhanging Top, Tapered Legs, 29 x 36 In.	356.00
Table, Console, Pine, Sycamore, 3 Drawers, Square Block Legs, 30 x 76 In.	438.00
Table, Console, Pine, Tapered Post Legs, 1900s, 30 ¼ x 20 In.	104.00
Table, Console, Queen Anne, Mahogany, Marble Top, Cabriole Legs, Pad Feet, England, 30 x 60 In.	4888.00
Table, Console, Regency Style, Mahogany, Gilt, Marble Top, Rocaille Carved Drawer, 35 x 41 In., Pair	2390.00
Table, Console, Regency, Mahogany, Burl, Demilune, Pierced Gallery, Base, 38 x 34 In.	1845.00
Table, Console, Renaissance Revival, Oak, Carved, Lion's Head, Lower Shelf, Ball Feet, 35 x 42 In.	480.00
Table, Console, Rococo Style, Cast Iron, Marble, Serpentine Top, c.1842, 33 x 61 In.	8066.00
Table, Console, Rococo Style, Fruitwood, Marble Top, Serpentine, Flowers, 1900s, 31 x 54 In.	191.00
Table, Console, Rococo Style, Gilt, Carved, Serpentine Marble Top, Garland, Shells	3705.00
Table, Console, Rococo Style, Wood, Carved, Shell Stretcher, Finial, Faux Marble Top, 35 x 56 In.	416.00
Table, Console, Rococo, Mahogany, Serpentine Top, Drawer, Cabriole Legs, c.1865, 30 x 29 In., Pair	1845.00
Table, Console, Rosewood, Bronze, Marble Top, Columns, Curved Base, Eagle Feet, c.1800, 68 In.	12548.00
Table, Console, Shagreen, Glass, 1980s, 31 x 29 In.	806.00
Table, Console, Victorian, Mahogany, Drawer, 2 Columns, Scroll Legs, 1880s, 30 x 48 In.	184.00
Table, Console, Walnut Veneer, Molded Top, 2 Drawers, Brasses, Brass Bound Feet, 29 x 63 In.	58.00
Table, Console, Walnut, 2 Drawers, Turned Legs, Continental, Early 1800s, 30 x 63 In.	863.00
Table, Console, Walnut, Carved, Bowfront, Scrolled Apron, 2 Griffin Supports, c.1850, 28 x 79 In.	2988.00
Table, Console, Walnut, Carved, Serpentine Top, Shaped Skirt, Cabriole Legs, Italy, 31 x 48 In.	793.00
Table, Console, Walnut, Demilune, Flowers, Vines, Game Board, 1800s, 29 x 36 In.	598.00
Table, Console, Walnut, Demilune, Wavy Piecrust Surround, Leaf Carved, 31 x 36 In.	413.00
Table, Console, White Marble Top, Walnut, Single Drawer, Long Cabriole Legs, 31 x 29 In.	118.00
Table, Console, Wood, Arch & Tassel Design, Cream, Gold Paint, 1900s, 32 x 42 In.	277.00
Table, Console, Wood, Demilune, Marble Top, Bronze Galley, Shelf, 36 x 34 In., Pair	3729.00
Table, Console, Wood, Faux Marble Top, Carved Apron, Cabriole Legs, Paint, c.1870, 36 x 48 In.	185.00
Table, Console, Wrought Iron, Glass Top, Scrolled Front, Sides, 36 x 68 In.	239.00
Table, Contemporary, Fruitwood, Nubian Figures, Glass Top, 21 x 55 In.	478.00
Table, Corner, Fan Shape Marble Top, Openwork Apron, Gourd, Vines, Chinese, 1800s, 32 x 18 In.	1041.00
Table, Corner, Federal, Bowfront, Mahogany, Door, Drawer, Hinged Top, c.1800, 32 x 29 In. *illus*	3555.00
Table, Corner, Oak, Wedge Shape Top, Pedestal Base, c.1910, 30 x 39 In.	179.00
Table, Country French Style, Oak, 2 Drawers, Low Stretcher, 30 x 54 In.	183.00
Table, Country French Style, Walnut, Carved Molded Skirt, Brass, 2 Leaves, c.1950, 30 x 77 In.	978.00
Table, Cricket, Pine, Painted, Cream Painted Tripod Base, Turned Legs, Peg Feet, 29 x 30 In.	620.00
Table, Cypress, Paneled Frieze, Scalloped Apron, 8 Cabriole Legs, 32 x 144 In.	1722.00
Table, D. Cooper, Butterfly, c.1942, 14 x 22 In. *illus*	1250.00
Table, Danish Modern, Teak, Floating Lower Shelf, Metal Tag, France & Sons, 17 x 59 In.	575.00
Table, Demilune, Federal, Mixed Wood, Line Inlays, c.1805, 28 ½ x 48 ½ In., Pair	708.00
Table, Demilune, Lacquer Top, Closed Apron, Cabriole Legs, Chinese, 1900s, 32 x 25 In., Pair	1020.00
Table, Demilune, Louis XVI Style, Mahogany, Shaped Marble Top, Metal Mounts, 32 x 40 In.	305.00
Table, Demilune, Louis XVI, Walnut, Frieze Drawer, Reeded Legs, c.1950, 34 x 40 In.	489.00
Table, Demilune, Mixed Wood, Marble Top, Flower String Inlay, 2 Drawers, 30 x 26 In., Pair	1150.00
Table, Dessert, Louis XVI Style, Marble Inset, Gallery Top, 3 Tiers, Cabriole Legs, 35 x 16 In.	671.00
Table, Dining, Aalto, Birch, Laminate, Sweden, 1950s, 28 ½ x 72 In.	1612.00
Table, Dining, Art Deco, Oak, Rectangular Top, Curved Ends, C-Shape Supports, 1900s, 31 x 30 In.	58.00
Table, Dining, Art Deco, Rosewood, Block Base, 100 In.	1755.00
Table, Dining, Arts & Crafts, Oak, Round, Planked Top, Square Legs, Peg Feet, c.1910, 30 x 48 In.	2151.00
Table, Dining, Ash, Square Top, Molded Border, Turned & Reeded Legs, c.1900, 28 x 41 In.	92.00
Table, Dining, Baroque, Mahogany, 2 Pedestal, Rectangular, Plank Stretcher, 31 x 96 In.	531.00
Table, Dining, Biedermeier, Swags, Apron, Ebonized Feet, 2 Leaves, 1830, 31 x 50 In.	615.00
Table, Dining, Ceramic Tesserae, Brass, Enameled Wood, Italy, 1950s, 30 x 54 In.	1488.00
Table, Dining, Cherry, Molded Edge, Faceted Legs, Leaf, 1800s, 17 x 11 In.	300.00
Table, Dining, Chippendale Style, Mahogany, 3 Pedestal, Band Inlay, 31 x 144 In.	4481.00
Table, Dining, Chippendale, Mahogany, Drawer, Batwing Brass, England, 1700s, 28 x 30 In.	480.00
Table, Dining, Chippendale, Mahogany, Oak, 4 Swing Legs, Leaves, 1700s, 67 x 52 In.	1020.00
Table, Dining, Drop Leaf, Cherry, Demilune Ends, Square Tapered Legs, Thomas Moser, 138 In.	735.00
Table, Dining, Drop Leaf, Chippendale, Mahogany, Scrolled Apron, 1700s, 27 x 48 In.	3163.00
Table, Dining, Drop Leaf, Chippendale, Walnut, Rectangular, Cabriole Legs, c.1770, 28 x 49 In.	3200.00
Table, Dining, Drop Leaf, Chippendale, Walnut, Rectangular, Scalloped Apron, 1700s, 27 x 48 In.	598.00
Table, Dining, Drop Leaf, Federal, Fly Legs, c.1900, 29 x 116 In.	1353.00

Table, Dining, Drop Leaf, Federal, Mahogany, 2 Parts, D-Shape Ends, Inlay, c.1800, 30 x 42 In.			2530.00
Table, Dining, Drop Leaf, Federal, Walnut, Rounded Ends, Square Legs, 1900s, 29 x 54 In.			179.00
Table, Dining, Drop Leaf, Federal, Walnut, String Inlays, Tapered Legs, c.1790, 29 x 58 In.			657.00
Table, Dining, Drop Leaf, Mahogany, Demilune Ends, Square Legs, c.1785, 28 x 108 In.			1195.00
Table, Dining, Drop Leaf, Mahogany, Inlay, Drawer, Brass Casters, Baker Furniture, 29 x 26 In.			748.00
Table, Dining, Drop Leaf, Maple, Gatelegs, Denmark, 30 x 60 In.			118.00
Table, Dining, Drop Leaf, Maple, Tapered Square Legs, 1800s, 28 x 38 In.			354.00
Table, Dining, Drop Leaf, Queen Anne, Cherry, Molded Edge, Cabriole Legs, 1700s, 27 x 36 In.			1610.00
Table, Dining, Drop Leaf, Queen Anne, Mahogany, Rounded, Tapered Legs, Pad Feet, 29 x 49 In.			944.00
Table, Dining, Drop Leaf, Queen Anne, Tiger Maple, Gateleg, Frieze Drawer, 28 x 51 In.			1434.00
Table, Dining, Drop Leaf, Queen Anne, Tiger Maple, Scalloped Skirt, Pad Feet, England, 28 x 48 In.			4313.00
Table, Dining, Drop Leaf, Queen Anne, Walnut, Oval, Cutout Skirt, Cabriole Legs, 28 x 44 In.			978.00
Table, Dining, Drop Leaf, Shaker, Cherry, Boxed Sliding Leaf Supports, 68 x 15 In.			44480.00
Table, Dining, Drop Leaf, Sheraton, Curly Maple, Rectangular, Turned Legs, c.1840, 30 x 42 In.			978.00
Table, Dining, Drop Leaf, Sheraton, Tiger Maple, Rectangular, Cup Casters, 29 x 48 In.			1380.00
Table, Dining, Drop Leaf, Sheraton, Tiger Maple, Turned Legs, c.1840, 30 x 48 In.			575.00
Table, Dining, Drop Leaf, Tapered Square Legs, 1800s, 29 x 16 In.			325.00
Table, Dining, Drop Leaf, Wood, Oval, Gateleg, 8 Bobbin Turned Legs, 1800s, 28 x 32 In.			177.00
Table, Dining, Duncan Phyfe Style, 2 Baluster Pedestals, Oval Top, Fluted Legs, 1800s, 29 x 76 In.			299.00
Table, Dining, Eero Saarinen, Tulip, Marble, Iron, Painted Wood, Knoll, 1960s, 29 x 78 In.			3100.00
Table, Dining, Eero Saarinen, White Enamel, Pedestal Base, Round Top, Spread Foot, 1956, 29 In.			450.00
Table, Dining, Enameled Iron Tube Legs, Square Glass Top, Tobias & Afra Scarpa, 1980s, 29 x 64 In.			124.00
Table, Dining, Farm, Pine, Rectangular, Turned Legs, 30 x 84 In.			633.00
Table, Dining, Federal Style, Mahogany, 3 Parts, Oval, Square Apron, Block Legs, 30 x 46 In.			2066.00
Table, Dining, Federal Style, Mahogany, 3 Pedestal, Urn Support, Saber Legs, 1900s, 30 x 88 In.			1440.00
Table, Dining, Federal Style, Mahogany, Round, Extension, Leaf Box, 5 Curved Legs, 50 In. Diam.			4500.00
Table, Dining, Florence Knoll, Rosewood, Chrome Plated Steel Pedestal, 1960s, 28 x 78 In. ......*illus*			1736.00
Table, Dining, Frankl, Black Oval, Fluted Pedestal, Brass Legs, Leaves, Johnson Furniture, 100 x 29 In.			960.00
Table, Dining, French Provincial Style, Round, Mahogany, Baluster Pedestal, 1900s, 52 x 52 In.			657.00
Table, Dining, French Provincial, Walnut, Parquetry, Scalloped, 2 Leaves, Apron, 1900s, 31 x 59 In.			717.00
Table, Dining, G. Nakashima, Black Walnut, Turned Legs, 29 x 84 In.			4960.00
Table, Dining, G. Nakashima, Boat Shape, Walnut, Rosewood, 1965, 29 x 60 x 40 In.			5270.00
Table, Dining, G. Nakashima, Frenchman's Cove, Black Walnut, Rosewood, 1965, 29 x 80 In.			9920.00
Table, Dining, G. Nakashima, Walnut, 3 Butterfly Joints, Tapered Legs, c.1952, 72 In.			3555.00
Table, Dining, George III Style, Mahogany, Crossbanded Top, Pedestal, Tripod Base, 30 x 75 In.			1121.00
Table, Dining, George III Style, Mahogany, Inlaid Rosewood, Pedestal, Rounded Corners, 96 x 52 In.			3540.00
Table, Dining, George III Style, Mahogany, Leaf, Carved Apron, Cabriole Legs, 30 x 42 In.			375.00
Table, Dining, George III Style, Mahogany, Oval, Gadrooned Edges, 31 x 120 In.			1168.00
Table, Dining, George III Style, Mahogany, Rectangular, 2 Pedestals, Base, 32 x 45 In.			1722.00
Table, Dining, George III Style, Mahogany, Rectangular Top, 3 Pedestals, Splayed Legs, 30 x 45 In.			2706.00
Table, Dining, Georgian Style, Mahogany, 3 Pedestal, Reeded Edge, Legs, Brass Feet, 29 x 108 In.			1912.00
Table, Dining, Georgian Style, Satinwood, Mahogany, 2 Leaves, 91 x 47 In.			375.00
Table, Dining, Glass Top, 4 Cylindrical Chrome Supports, Arched Legs, Brueton, 60 x 60 In.			500.00
Table, Dining, Glass Top, Acanthus Supports, Scrolls, Medallions, Carved, Gilt Paint, 30 ½ x 96 In.			732.00
Table, Dining, Harvest, Yellow Pine, Plank Top, Tapered Legs, c.1850, 30 x 107 In.			1495.00
Table, Dining, Hepplewhite, Mahogany, 3 Parts, c.1810, 31 x 86 In.			420.00
Table, Dining, Inlaid Detail, Dutch Style, 19th Century, 65 x 28 In.			531.00
Table, Dining, Knoll, Round Wood Top, Black Star Shape Legs, 1948, 28 x 48 In.			1875.00
Table, Dining, L. & J.G. Stickley, 5 Post Pedestal, 2 Leaves, Decal, 30 x 48 In.			2728.00
Table, Dining, Laminate, Chrome Steel, 1950s, 29 x 60 In.			496.00
Table, Dining, Lewis Butler, Mahogany, Walnut, Knoll, 29 ¾ x 59 In.			1736.00
Table, Dining, Limbert, Round Top, Cross Stretcher, Extension Branded, 30 x 48 In.			620.00
Table, Dining, Limbert, Round Top, Pedestal Base, 2 Leaves, 45 x 29 In.			1200.00
Table, Dining, Linet Roset, Rectangular Top, Square Legs, Undertable Leaf, 30 x 72 In.			325.00
Table, Dining, Louis XVI Style, Ebonized, Bronze, Fluted Legs, 3 Leaves, c.1940, 30 x 43 In.			1599.00
Table, Dining, M. Baughman, Burl, Square, 2 Leaves, T. Coggin, 39 x 39 In.			960.00
Table, Dining, Mahogany, 2 Column Stems, 8 Leaves, Boston, c.1830, 30 ½ x 53 ½ In.			3198.00
Table, Dining, Mahogany, 4 Leaves, Tapered Round Legs, Ormolu Capitals, c.1920, 29 x 40 In.			5166.00
Table, Dining, Mahogany, Bird's-Eye Maple, Banded, 3 Pedestal, Saber Legs, 28 x 97 In.			3585.00
Table, Dining, Mahogany, Columnar Pedestal Supports, Base, Paw Feet, 8 Leaves, 30 x 60 In.			1763.00
Table, Dining, Mahogany, Ebonized, Round, Tripart Base, Paw Feet, 29 x 57 In.			598.00
Table, Dining, Mahogany, Extension, U-Shape Supports, Barbara Barry, 30 x 86 In.			3000.00
Table, Dining, Mahogany, Pineapple Pillar & Claw Pedestal, Victorian, 29 x 54 In.			483.00
Table, Dining, Mahogany, Round, 4 Supports, Splayed Paw Feet, 4 Leaves, c.1910, 29 x 62 In.			938.00
Table, Dining, Mahogany, Round, Bulbous Turned Pedestal, Saber Legs, Leaves, 30 x 99 ½ In.			4880.00
Table, Dining, Mahogany, Round, Caryatid Carved Supports, 8 Leaves, c.1870, 30 x 60 In.			2530.00

Furniture, Table, Center, Gothic Revival, Rosewood, 6-Sided Marble Top, c.1845, 40 x 36 In.
$47800.00

Neal Auction Co.

Furniture, Table, Center, Neogrecque, Rosewood, Inlay, Parcel Gilt, Center Column, c.1865, 31 x 35 In.
$4674.00

New Orleans Auction Galleries, Inc.

Furniture, Table, Center, Rococo Revival, Walnut, Marble, Figural Supports, James G. Blake, c.1850, 57 x 43 In.
$16730.00

Neal Auction Co.

Furniture, Table, Coffee, Philip & Kelvin Laverne, Chan, Bronze, Pewter, Etched, Multicolor, 17 ½ x 45 In.
$4340.00

Rago Arts & Auction Center

Furniture, Table, Coffee, W. Rizzo, Bar, Brushed Chromed Steel, Revolving, Laminated, 1970s, 13 x 45 In. $3720.00

Rago Arts & Auction Center

Furniture, Table, Conference, Renaissance Revival, Oak, Griffins, Trestle Base, c.1900, 95 x 42 In. $978.00

James D. Julia Inc.

Furniture, Table, Corner, Federal, Bowfront, Mahogany, Door, Drawer, Hinged Top, c.1800, 32 x 29 In. $3555.00

Skinner, Inc.

Furniture, Table, D. Cooper, Butterfly, c.1942, 14 x 22 In. $1250.00

Los Angeles Modern Auctions

TIP

Baking soda and vinegar or lemon juice can be used to remove rust.

Table, Dining, Mahogany, Round, Scroll Centered X-Stretcher, Cabriole Legs, 1800s, 29 x 57 In.	615.00
Table, Dining, Mahogany, Satinwood, Burl, Round, Saber Legs, c.1950, 29 x 84 In.	3286.00
Table, Dining, Mahogany, Sunburst Inlay, 4 Columns, Birdcage, Saber Legs, 1900s, 29 x 68 In..	777.00
Table, Dining, Maple, Poplar, Tapered Legs, Leaf, Red, Blue, Painted, 1800s, 31 x 43 In.	499.00
Table, Dining, Neoclassical, Rosewood, Rotating Oval, 5 Leaves, Scrolled Legs, c.1830, 56 x 43 In. *illus*	2689.00
Table, Dining, Neoclassical, Square Top, Urn Shape Base, Zinc Veneer, 32 x 36 In.	1180.00
Table, Dining, Oak, Round, Cylindrical Pedestal Base, Quadruped Cabriole Legs, 29 x 54 In....	180.00
Table, Dining, Olive Wood, Burl, 2 Leaves, Rectangular, Square Block Legs, 28 x 66 In.	531.00
Table, Dining, Oval, Pedestal Base, Extension Supports, 5 Leaves, c.1840, 90 x 48 In.	1076.00
Table, Dining, P. Evans, Directional, Cityscape, Brass, 1970s, 30 x 72 In.	4340.00
Table, Dining, P. Evans, Directional, Cityscape, Chromed Steel, Glass, 1970s, 30 x 72 In.	3720.00
Table, Dining, Queen Anne Style, Curly Maple, Hardwood, Breadboard Top, c.1970, 20 x 102 In.	705.00
Table, Dining, Queen Anne Style, Walnut, Double Pedestals, Racetrack Top, 1900s, 29 x 115 In.	359.00
Table, Dining, Queen Anne, Mahogany, Birdcage Design, Dish Top, Urn Post, 1700s, 30 x 34 In.	3738.00
Table, Dining, Regency Style, 2 Pedestal, Reeded Saber Legs, England, 1800s, 29 x 62 In.	660.00
Table, Dining, Regency Style, Mahogany, 2 Pedestal, Scrollwork & Leaves, Squat Ball Feet, 29 In.	3660.00
Table, Dining, Regency Style, Mahogany, Double Baluster Pedestal, Reeded Edge, 1900s, 30 x 80 In.	269.00
Table, Dining, Regency Style, Mahogany, Round Top, Pedestal Base, Splay Legs, 1900s, 60 In.	1840.00
Table, Dining, Regency Style, Mahogany, Round, Banded Top, 4 Turned Supports, 62 In. Diam.	2032.00
Table, Dining, Regency Style, Mahogany, Round, Birdcage, Scrolled Capitals, 1900s, 66 x 66 In.	508.00
Table, Dining, Regency, Mahogany, 2 Pedestal, Ring Turned, Reeded Legs, c.1800, 28 x 106 In..	2689.00
Table, Dining, Renaissance Style, Oak, Carved, Turned Legs, Box Stretchers, 33 x 60 In.	2689.00
Table, Dining, Robsjohn-Gibbings, Mahogany, Laminate, Brass, 1950s, 30 x 68 In.	1860.00
Table, Dining, Round, Flared Legs, Base Stretcher, 4 Leaves, Grand Rapids, 30 x 50 In.	1984.00
Table, Dining, Shaker, Walnut, Pegged Top, Trestle Base, Center Stretcher, c.1840, 25 x 72 In.	1170.00
Table, Dining, Shaped Apron, Cabriole Legs, Carved, Paint, 2 Leaves, France, c.1960, 30 x 65 In..	1168.00
Table, Dining, Sheraton, Gateleg, 6 Turned & Fluted Legs, Brass Casters, 28 x 60 In.	575.00
Table, Dining, Steel, Bookjack Ends, Rectangular, Ed Higgins, c.1950, 30 x 72 In.	1755.00
Table, Dining, Stickley Bros., Round, 5 Legs, 4 Leaves, 40 x 29 In.	780.00
Table, Dining, Teak, Oval, Board, 4 Set Double Cylindrical Metal Legs, T-Shape Stretcher, 30 x 65 In.	102.00
Table, Dining, Tiger Maple, Ebonized Frieze, Turned Legs, H-Stretcher, 30 x 90 In.	793.00
Table, Dining, Victorian, Drop Leaves, Oval Top, 5 Legs, c.1900, 29 x 45 In.	115.00
Table, Dining, Victorian, Walnut, Round, Center Leg, 6 Leaves, c.1880, 44 x 30 In.	4950.00
Table, Dining, Walnut, Oval, Cylindrical Legs, 2 Leaves, Design Research, 1960, 48 x 72 In.	1304.00
Table, Dining, Walnut, Shaped Top, Scalloped Edge, Scrolled Apron, France, 1800s, 27 x 51 In.	764.00
Table, Dining, William & Mary Style, Mahogany, Turned Legs, Oval Top, 1900s, 48 x 52 In.	59.00
Table, Dining, Wood, 7 Tapered Legs, Curvy Heart & Kidney Shape, c.1950, 30 x 46 In.	3750.00
Table, Dining, Wood, Downswept Legs, Splayed Bronze Cap Feet, Italy, c.1955, 29 x 46 In.	984.00
Table, Dining, Wormley, Walnut, Dunbar, 1950s, 28 ½ x 88 In.	868.00
Table, Dining, Wormley, Walnut, Square Top, Block Legs, Dunbar, 24 x 40 In.	144.00
Table, Dining, Wrought Iron, Glass Top, Scrolled Sides, Brass Mounts, 30 x 72 In.	418.00
Table, Directoire, Mahogany, Leather Inset Top, Drawers, c.1800, 31 x 45 In.	2813.00
Table, Display, Gilt, Glass Inset Top & Sides, 2 Doors, Carved Legs, 23 x 25 In.	460.00
Table, Drafting, George III, Mahogany, Metamorphic Top, 3 Drawers, c.1780, 31 x 43 In.	3286.00
Table, Drafting, Georgian, Mahogany, Rectangular, Pedestal Base, Tripod Feet, 31 x 30 In.	326.00
Table, Drafting, Queen Anne, Mahogany, Tilt Top, Drawers, Tripod Base, c.1750, 30 x 22 In.	2629.00
Table, Drafting, Regency Style, Medial Shelf, Turned Stretcher, Trestle Legs, 29 x 38 In.	625.00
Table, Draw Leaf, Oak, Trestle Base, England, c.1900, 30 x 30 In.	115.00
Table, Draw Leaf, Overhanging Top, Carved Apron, France, 32 x 44 In.	518.00
Table, Dressing, 4 Drawers, Scrolled Apron, Cabriole Legs, Paw Feet, 1700s, 29 x 34 In.	1126.00
Table, Dressing, Beau Brummel, Hepplewhite, Inlaid Mahogany, Lid, 2 Drawers, 1800s, 32 x 18 In.	920.00
Table, Dressing, Beau Brummel, Mahogany, Lid, Fold-Out Mirror, c.1800, 32 x 28 In.	863.00
Table, Dressing, Beau Brummel, Mahogany, Lid, Mirror, Drawers, Washbowl, c.1800, 35 x 24 In.	1076.00
Table, Dressing, Beau Brummel, Mahogany, Inlay, Lid, Mirror, Bowl, Bidet, c.1800, 35 x 24 In. *illus*	1076.00
Table, Dressing, Beau Brummel, Satinwood, Band Mahogany, c.1805, 35 x 23 In.	416.00
Table, Dressing, Carmen Spera, Painted Glass, Memphis, c.1980, 51 x 60 ½ In. ....*illus*	613.00
Table, Dressing, Charles X, Mahogany, Gilt Bronze Mounts, Marble Top, Round Mirror, 59 x 32 In.	2925.00
Table, Dressing, Chippendale, Mahogany, Cabriole Legs, Claw Feet, Scrolled Apron, 30 x 20 In.	1175.00
Table, Dressing, Chippendale, Mixed Wood, 4 Drawers, Philadelphia, c.1780, 30 x 35 In.	10200.00
Table, Dressing, Chippendale, Walnut, 3 Drawers, Fan Carved, Delaware Valley, 29 x 33 In.	2607.00
Table, Dressing, Crossbanded, Hinged Rectangular, Sham Drawer, c.1800, 33 x 27 In.	398.00
Table, Dressing, Empire Style, Mahogany, Oval Mirror, Scroll Yoke Supports, Drawer, 64 x 31 In.	598.00
Table, Dressing, Federal, Walnut, Inlay, Serpentine Front, Brass Pulls, c.1800, 29 x 29 x 22 In.	9200.00
Table, Dressing, French Directoire Style, Fruitwood, Banded Inlay, 2 Drawers, 1900s	575.00
Table, Dressing, French Provincial, Fruitwood, Lift Top, Mirror, Cabriole Legs, 29 x 33 In.	956.00
Table, Dressing, Gentleman's, Regency, Mahogany, Hinged Top, Pullout Slide, c.1815, 30 x 21 In.	480.00

Table, Dressing, George I, Walnut, Inlay, Molded Top, Drawers, Pad Feet, 28 x 29 In.	2151.00
Table, Dressing, George II, Mahogany, 3 Drawers, Arched Scrolling Apron, 31 x 31 In.	1875.00
Table, Dressing, Georgian Style, Mahogany, Serpentine Top, Drawer, Square Legs, 29 x 36 In.	148.00
Table, Dressing, Georgian, Mahogany, Shaped Corners, 3 Frieze Drawers, 1700s, 27 x 28 In.	889.00
Table, Dressing, Kittinger, Mahogany, 3 Drawers, Tray Top, Cabriole Legs, 30 x 30 In.	533.00
Table, Dressing, Lacquer, Gilt Design, Hinged Top, Mirror, Drawer, c.1900, 32 x 14 In.	546.00
Table, Dressing, Lacquer, Metal, Japanese Style, Peacock, 2 Doors, 3 Drawers, c.1900, 15 x 14 In.	237.00
Table, Dressing, Louis XV Style, Fruitwood, Hinged Center, Scalloped Apron, 1800s, 29 x 24 In.	300.00
Table, Dressing, Louis XV Style, Parquetry, Shaped Top, 7 Drawers, 30 x 47 In.	1250.00
Table, Dressing, Mahogany, 3 Drawers, Tapered Square Legs, England, 1800s, 30 x 31 In.	234.00
Table, Dressing, Mahogany, Ebonized, Breakfront Top, 3 Drawers, Square Legs, 1800s, 30 x 36 In.	889.00
Table, Dressing, Mahogany, Fitted, Split Top, 13 Piece Dresser Set, Berkey & Gay, 31 x 23 In.	518.00
Table, Dressing, Mahogany, Hinged Top, 2 Drawers, Square Legs, Stretcher, 1800s, 29 x 16 In.	266.00
Table, Dressing, Mahogany, Mirror, Column Supports, Marble Top, Trestle, c.1840, 82 x 42 In.	2151.00
Table, Dressing, Mahogany, Mirror, Marble Top, Recessed Drawers, 1800s, 65 x 36 In. ....illus	529.00
Table, Dressing, Mahogany, Mirror, Scroll Supports, 4 Drawers, Reeded Legs, N.Y., 44 x 38 In.	3042.00
Table, Dressing, Mahogany, Mirror, Spiral Supports, 6 Drawers, Shelf, c.1825, 66 x 38 In.	1076.00
Table, Dressing, Mahogany, Mirror, Turned Supports, Drawers, Trestle Base, c.1830, 58 x 37 In. . illus	1195.00
Table, Dressing, Mahogany, Scrolled Backsplash, 3 Drawers, Vase Shape Legs, 41 x 33 In.	708.00
Table, Dressing, Mirror, Queen Anne, Burl, Pierced Crest, 6 Drawers, Bun Feet, 30 In.	732.00
Table, Dressing, Neoclassical, Mahogany, Marble, Mirror, Lyre Supports, c.1810, 82 x 38 x 27 In. illus	2629.00
Table, Dressing, Oak, Tilt Mirror, 2 Drawers, Frieze Drawer, Column Legs, c.1900, 54 x 36 In..	219.00
Table, Dressing, Pine, Drawer, Backsplash, Fruit Decoration, c.1820, 34 x 32 In.	264.00
Table, Dressing, Pine, Marble Top, Backsplash, 2 Drawers, England, 1800s, 42 x 51 In.	2032.00
Table, Dressing, Pine, Mustard Yellow Paint, Shaped Top, Drawer, Shells, Grapes, c.1820, 27 x 35 In.	4444.00
Table, Dressing, Queen Anne, 3 Drawers, Japanned, England, 1700s, 28 x 30 In.	1180.00
Table, Dressing, Queen Anne, Cherry, 4 Drawers, Carved Flowers, Shaped Skirt, c.1750, 31 x 30 In.	5333.00
Table, Dressing, Queen Anne, Cherry, Molded Top, Frieze Drawer, Cabriole Legs, 1700s, 25 x 31 In.	984.00
Table, Dressing, Queen Anne, Mahogany, Drawer, Cabriole Legs, Pad Feet, 26 x 31 In.	425.00
Table, Dressing, Queen Anne, Mahogany, Drawer, England, 1700s, 29 x 32 In.	767.00
Table, Dressing, Queen Anne, Mahogany, Rectangular, 2 Drawers, Pad Feet, c.1740, 28 x 35 In.	7050.00
Table, Dressing, Queen Anne, Oak, Drawer, Cabriole Legs, England, c.1800, 28 x 29 In.	240.00
Table, Dressing, Queen Anne, Oak, Drawer, Pad Feet, England, 1700s, 29 x 30 In.	600.00
Table, Dressing, Queen Anne, Walnut, String Inlaid Drawers, Stocking Feet, 1700s, 28 x 31 In.	1000.00
Table, Dressing, Rosewood, Hinged Top, Triple Mirror, Marble, Spiral Supports, 1800s, 34 x 23 In.	472.00
Table, Dressing, Sheraton, Backsplash Drawers, Low Shelf, Tiger Striped Paint, c.1820, 43 x 34 In.	3555.00
Table, Dressing, Sheraton, Pine, Backsplash, Ears, 3 Drawers, Turned Legs, c.1840, 37 x 29 In.	460.00
Table, Dressing, Sheraton, Pine, Drawers, Scroll Crest, Gilt Stencil, Turned Legs, c.1835, 40 x 35 In.	294.00
Table, Dressing, Sheraton, Stencil, Painted, Scrolled Backsplash, Drawer, c.1810, 34 x 29 In. ... illus	920.00
Table, Dressing, Sheraton, Tiger Maple, 4 Drawers, Mirror, N.Y., 58 x 43 In.	1955.00
Table, Dressing, Stool, Demilune Top, Carved Frieze Drawer, Paint, Gilt, 1900s, 34 x 47 In.	598.00
Table, Dressing, Victorian, Walnut, Marble Top, Columns, Tilt Mirror, Austria, 1800s, 62 x 23 In.	345.00
Table, Dressing, Walnut, Checkerboard Inlay, 3 Drawers, Cabriole Legs, c.1750, 29 x 33 In.	1434.00
Table, Drop Leaf, Chippendale, Gateleg Support, c.1780, 28 x 43 In.	489.00
Table, Drop Leaf, Chippendale, Mahogany, Double Gateleg, England, 1700s, 15 x 30 In.	420.00
Table, Drop Leaf, Chippendale, Mahogany, Paduck, Gateleg, Chamfered Legs, c.1790, 28 x 42 ½ In. illus	489.00
Table, Drop Leaf, Chippendale, Mahogany, Shaped Skirt, Cabriole Legs, 1700s, 28 x 48 In.	1320.00
Table, Drop Leaf, Chippendale, Walnut, Cross Stretcher, Square Legs, Marlboro Feet, 29 x 35 In. .	1058.00
Table, Drop Leaf, Chippendale, Walnut, Frieze Drawers, X-Stretcher, 29 x 24 In.	1374.00
Table, Drop Leaf, Federal, Carved, Column Supports, Splayed Legs, N.Y., c.1820, 29 x 36 In.	5290.00
Table, Drop Leaf, Federal, Cherry, Shaped Leaves, Reeded Legs, Casters, c.1810, 37 x 44 In.	411.00
Table, Drop Leaf, Federal, Mahogany, Acanthus Leaf, Carved, 1800s, 28 x 40 In.	230.00
Table, Drop Leaf, Federal, Mahogany, Carved Leaf Legs, Mid Atlantic, 1800s, 28 x 40 In.	230.00
Table, Drop Leaf, Fruitwood, Rounded Rectangular Top, Leaves, Round Legs, 1800s, 31 x 40 In.	861.00
Table, Drop Leaf, G. Nelson, Walnut, Gateleg, Herman Miller, c.1950, 40 x 65 In.	480.00
Table, Drop Leaf, George III, Mahogany, Curved Leaves, Gateleg, c.1790, 28 x 35 In.	568.00
Table, Drop Leaf, George III, Mahogany, Oak, String Inlay, Rounded Corners, Drawer, 28 x 44 In.	353.00
Table, Drop Leaf, Harvest, Cherry, Rectangular, Round Legs, Pad Feet, 1900s, 21 x 66 In.	474.00
Table, Drop Leaf, Harvest, Pine, Birch Legs, 1800s, 28 x 90 In.	2880.00
Table, Drop Leaf, Hepplewhite Style, Cherry, Frieze Drawer, 1900s, 29 x 44 In.	239.00
Table, Drop Leaf, Hepplewhite, Cherry, New England, 1800s, 48 x 48 In.	115.00
Table, Drop Leaf, Hepplewhite, Cherry, Rectangular, Tapered Legs, c.1800, 29 x 44 In.	184.00
Table, Drop Leaf, Hepplewhite, Mahogany, Pine, Drawer, Reeded Legs, c.1820, 30 x 36 In.	230.00
Table, Drop Leaf, Hepplewhite, Mahogany, Single-Board Top, Drawer, c.1815, 29 x 40 In.	676.00
Table, Drop Leaf, Hepplewhite, Walnut, Rectangular, Barrel Jointed, 1800s, 28 x 42 In.	441.00

Furniture, Table, Dining, Florence Knoll, Rosewood, Chrome Plated Steel Pedestal, 1960s, 28 x 78 In. $1736.00

Furniture, Table, Dining, Neoclassical, Rosewood, Rotating Oval, 5 Leaves, Scrolled Legs, c.1830, 56 x 43 In. $2689.00

Furniture, Table, Dressing, Beau Brummel, Mahogany, Inlay, Lid, Mirror, Bowl, Bidet, c.1800, 35 x 24 In. $1076.00

Furniture, Table, Dressing, Carmen Spera, Painted Glass, Memphis, c.1980, 51 x 60 ½ In. $613.00

Furniture, Table, Dressing, Mahogany, Mirror, Marble Top, Recessed Drawers, 1800s, 65 x 36 In.
$529.00

Cowan's Auctions

Furniture, Table, Dressing, Mahogany, Mirror, Turned Supports, Drawers, Trestle Base, c.1830, 58 x 37 In.
$1195.00

Neal Auction Co.

Furniture, Table, Dressing, Neoclassical, Mahogany, Marble, Mirror, Lyre Supports, c.1810, 82 x 38 x 27 In.
$2629.00

Neal Auction Co.

Table, Drop Leaf, Jacobean Style, Oak, Gateleg, Dark Stain, England, 1800s, 31 x 30 In...........	240.00
Table, Drop Leaf, Jacobean Style, Oak, Rectangular, Flower Carved Legs, c.1920, 31 x 84 In....	2300.00
Table, Drop Leaf, Mahogany, Drawer, Vase Shape Pedestal, Paw Feet, 37 x 24 In.......................	799.00
Table, Drop Leaf, Mahogany, Drawers, Pedestal, Splayed Legs, England, c.1830, 29 x 36 In.....	518.00
Table, Drop Leaf, Mahogany, Oval, Lip Molded Edge, Drawer, 1700s, 49 x 47 In.......................	450.00
Table, Drop Leaf, Mahogany, Platform Base, Ball & Claw Feet, 30 x 41 In.	1150.00
Table, Drop Leaf, Mahogany, Rectangular Top, Shaped Frieze, Spade Feet, c.1810, 28 x 42 In.	799.00
Table, Drop Leaf, Mahogany, Stenciled Apron, Beribboned Lyre, Paw Feet, c.1800	1599.00
Table, Drop Leaf, Mahogany, Swing, Tapered Legs, c.1800, 29 x 42 In.	259.00
Table, Drop Leaf, Marquetry, Drawer, Cabriole Legs, Brass Mounts, c.1905, 20 ¾ x 9 In.	230.00
Table, Drop Leaf, Mixed Wood, Drawer, Carved, Shaped, c.1800, 28 x 36 In.	546.00
Table, Drop Leaf, Mixed Wood, Line Inlays, Butterfly Supports, Tapered Legs, Eng., 1800s, 28 x 38 In.	430.00
Table, Drop Leaf, Pine Top, Oak Base, Drawers, Turned Legs, 29 x 60 In...............................	708.00
Table, Drop Leaf, Queen Anne Style, Mahogany, Oval Top, Shaped Skirt, 1800s, 28 x 52 In......	299.00
Table, Drop Leaf, Queen Anne, Mahogany, England, 1700s, 28 x 45 In.	590.00
Table, Drop Leaf, Queen Anne, Mahogany, Mixed Wood, Gatelegs, England, 1700s, 28 x 40 In.	240.00
Table, Drop Leaf, Queen Anne, Mahogany, Shaped Skirt, Ball & Claw Feet, 1700s, 27 x 38 In. .	2760.00
Table, Drop Leaf, Queen Anne, Oak, Maple, Oval Top, 1700s, 27 x 27 In.	540.00
Table, Drop Leaf, Queen Anne, Walnut, Apron, Cabriole Legs, Pad Feet, American, 27 x 47 In. ...*illus*	558.00
Table, Drop Leaf, Queen Anne, Walnut, Arched Apron, Pa., c.1765, 28 x 45 In.........................	1500.00
Table, Drop Leaf, Queen Anne, Walnut, Gateleg, Serpentine Skirt, Cabriole Legs, 1700s, 27 x 20 In.	590.00
Table, Drop Leaf, Queen Anne, Walnut, Round, Swing Leg Supports, c.1750, 27 x 32 In..........	460.00
Table, Drop Leaf, Queen Anne, Walnut, Rounded, Turned Legs, 1740, 27 x 45 In.....................	558.00
Table, Drop Leaf, Queen Anne, Walnut, Swing Leg, Oval, Cabriole Legs, 28 x 42 In.	470.00
Table, Drop Leaf, Regency, Mahogany, Inlay, 2 Drawers, Trestle, Brass Caps, c.1815, 28 x 58 In. *illus*	610.00
Table, Drop Leaf, Rosewood, Inlay, Rectangular, 2 Frieze Drawers, Pedestal, 1800s, 28 x 59 In.	306.00
Table, Drop Leaf, Sheraton, Cherry, Frieze Drawer, Reeded Legs, Brass Feet, c.1810, 21 x 42 In. *illus*	1342.00
Table, Drop Leaf, Sheraton, Curly Maple, Poplar, Turned Legs, c.1850, 29 x 39 In.	940.00
Table, Drop Leaf, Sheraton, Mahogany, Frieze Drawers, Reeded Legs, 1700s, 30 x 45 In.	359.00
Table, Drop Leaf, Sheraton, Red Paint, Round Corners, Turned Legs, 1800s, 29 x 42 In.	516.00
Table, Drop Leaf, Sheraton, Rounded Leaves, Scrubbed Top, Turned Legs, c.1835, 36 x 35 ½ In. *illus*	206.00
Table, Drop Leaf, Sheraton, Walnut, Pa., c.1830, 28 x 42 ½ In...	89.00
Table, Drop Leaf, William & Mary, Gateleg, Ring & Block Turned Legs, 1700s, 28 x 40 In........	2400.00
Table, Drop Leaf, William & Mary, Gateleg, Turned Legs, c.1750, 28 x 36 In.	178.00
Table, Drop Leaf, William & Mary, Mahogany, Gateleg, Banded Edge, Scroll Feet, c.1700, 33 x 29 In.	1304.00
Table, Drop Leaf, William & Mary, Oak, Gateleg, Demilune, Drawer, Turned Legs, c.1790, 41 x 20 In.	374.00
Table, Drum, Federal, Mahogany, Round, Column Support, Saber Legs, c.1815, 30 x 32 In.....	4780.00
Table, Drum, Mahogany, Leather, Round, Downswept Legs, Baker, c.1950, 28 x 38 In.............	478.00
Table, Dutch Rococo, Mahogany, Gallery, Ogee Mounted Frieze, Cabriole Legs, 1700s, 30 x 38 In.	1434.00
Table, Eames, Conference, Walnut, Rubber, Steel Aluminum, Herman Miller, 1960s, 29 x 96 In.	527.00
Table, Eames, Surfboard, Laminate, Birch Top, Wire Work Frame, c.1951, 89 x 30 In..............	472.00
Table, Eastlake, Marble Top, Carved Frieze, X-Shape Pedestal, c.1800s, 29 x 28 In....................	179.00
Table, Eastlake, Pietra Dura, Flowers, Multicolor, Ebonized Tripod Base, Paint, 24 x 21 In......	374.00
Table, Eastlake, Walnut, Marble Top, Carved Splayed Legs, Victorian, 21 x 29 In.	147.00
Table, Ebonized, Brass Inlays, Leather Top, Shaped Apron, Cabriole Legs, 26 x 30 In.	1076.00
Table, Ebonized, Gilt, Bronze, Leaping Lion, Flowers, Shaped Apron, Fluted Legs, c.1865, 32 x 47 In.	5904.00
Table, Ebonized, Gilt, Demilune Ends, Trestle Base, Spindle Gallery, c.1885, 30 x 38 In.	1353.00
Table, Ebonized, Inlaid, Marble Top, Chevron Frieze, Pierced Skirt, Flowers, c.1875, 28 x 39 In.	1353.00
Table, Ebonized, Marquetry, Drop Conjoined Scrolls, Pierced Leaf Gallery, c.1885, 28 x 39 In.	4428.00
Table, Edwardian, Mahogany, Shell Shape Inlays, Oval Top, Gallery, Stretcher, c.1910, 48 x 23 In.	179.00
Table, Edwardian, Oak, Overhanging Top, Stretchers, 1800s, 28 x 28 In...............................	239.00
Table, Edwardian, Rosewood, Handkerchief Foldover, Inlays, Frieze Drawer, c.1900, 28 x 33 In.	598.00
Table, Eero Saarinen, Tulip, Laminate, Enameled Cast Iron, Round, Knoll, 1950s, 16 x 54 In.	620.00
Table, Elm, Square, Cabriole Legs, Box Stretcher, Black & Gold Lacquered, c.1800, 34 x 34 In.	4288.00
Table, Empire Revival, Walnut, Leather Top, Twist Support, 3 Scrolled Feet, 1900s, 28 x 29 In.	150.00
Table, Empire Style, Tole Tray Top, Swan Mounts, Stenciled Vine Design, Italy, c.1950, 23 x 25 In...	826.00
Table, Empire, Ebonized, Oval, Tray Top, Butler Handles, Painted, X-Form Base, 1800s, 18 x 19 In.	508.00
Table, Empire, Mahogany, Round Granite Top, Column Supports, 3 Parts, c.1800, 28 x 32 In.	861.00
Table, Empire, Mahogany, Shaped White Marble Top, c.1840, 30 ½ x 35 In.	310.00
Table, Encyclopedia, L. & J.G. Stickley, Square Top, 2 Divided Shelves, Slated Sides, 27 x 27 In.	7200.00
Table, Farm, 2-Board Top, Dovetailed Drawers, Turned & Splayed Legs, Pa., 29 x 60 In. ...*illus*	1955.00
Table, Farm, Cypress, Plank Top, Fitted Drawer, Square Legs, H-Stretcher, c.1850, 75 x 29 In. ...*illus*	861.00
Table, Farm, French Provincial, Oak, Rectangular, Conforming Frieze, c.1805, 31 x 57 In.	861.00
Table, Farm, French Provincial, Plank Top, Drawers, Hinged, Peg & Mortise, 1800s, 79 x 30 In. *illus*	837.00
Table, Farm, Oak, 2 Drawers, Green Apron, Legs, Quebec, 38 x 100 In.	1035.00
Table, Farm, Oak, Drawer, Turned Legs, France, 30 x 79 In...	244.00

F

Table, Farm, Pine, Green Paint, Rectangular, Drawer, 1800s, 29 x 61 In.	1422.00
Table, Faux Marble Top, Carved, Reeded Apron, Legs, White Paint, Italy, 1900s, 20 x 32 In.	354.00
Table, Faux Marble Top, Paint, Garland Carved Skirt, Arched Stretcher, 1900s, 22 x 21 In.	299.00
Table, Faux Marble Top, Yellow, Black Striped, Drawer, Bamboo Skirt, 1800s, 33 x 30 In.	5629.00
Table, Federal Style, Mahogany, Reticulated Gallery Top, Square Tapered Legs, 1800s, 34 x 35 In.	956.00
Table, Federal, Mahogany, 2 Drawers, Tapered Legs, c.1950, 32 x 30 In.	150.00
Table, Federal, Mahogany, Bowfront, Lift Top, Fitted Interior, Gallery, c.1810, 40 x 29 In. ..... *illus*	1912.00
Table, Federal, Mahogany, Double Pedestal, Sunburst, Ball & Claw Feet, 1800s, 29 x 76 In.	388.00
Table, Federal, Mahogany, Drawer, c.1820, 29 x 23 In.	590.00
Table, Federal, Mahogany, Inlaid, 2 Parts, Demilune Tops, Hinged, Swing Legs, c.1810, 30 x 44 In.	1659.00
Table, Federal, Mahogany, Mixed Wood, 2 Drawers, Turned Legs, c.1840, 29 x 25 In.	295.00
Table, Federal, Mahogany, Rounded Drop Leaves, Beaded, Vase Support, c.1820, 29 x 22 In.	356.00
Table, Federal, Mahogany, Stringing, Bowfront, Square Legs, c.1800, 33 x 35 In.	17775.00
Table, Federal, Mixed Wood, Tray Top, Drawer, Tennessee, 1800s, 31 x 28 In.	1180.00
Table, Federal, Pine, Overhung Top, Drawer, Red Paint, 1800s, 30 x 50 ½ In.	480.00
Table, Federal, Walnut, Drawer, Tapered Legs, Southern, 1800s, 31 x 27 In.	600.00
Table, Federal, Walnut, Mixed Wood, Line Inlays, Drawer, c.1840, 28 x 21 In.	531.00
Table, Federal, Walnut, Overhung Top, Drawer, Turned Legs, c.1840, 29 x 24 In.	1416.00
Table, Fer Forge, Metal, Marble Top, Apron, 6 Hammered Legs, France, c.1920, 34 x 104 In.	8302.00
Table, Figural, Black Enamel Metal Rods, John Risley, 1970s, 19 x 14 In.	2480.00
Table, Figural, Greyhound Dog Support, Round Onyx Top, Marble Base, 30 x 17 In.	1560.00
Table, Figural, Mermaid Support, Glass Tray In Hands, 20 ½ x 32 In.	460.00
Table, Figural, Tortoise Support, Smoky Glass Top, 17 x 32 In.	2040.00
Table, Finn Juhl, Walnut, Asymmetrical, Baker Furniture, 20th Century, 64 x 22 In.	480.00
Table, Finn Juhl, Walnut, Square Top, Open Medial Shelf, France & Sons, 28 x 22 In.	390.00
Table, Flip Top, Mahogany, Round, Carved Pedestal, c.1820, 29 x 51 In.	4481.00
Table, Fold Top, William & Mary, Walnut, Demilune, Slides, Drawers, c.1690, 26 x 28 In.	2460.00
Table, Folding, Wegner, Teak, Round Top, Swivel Leg, Fritz Hansen, 37 x 28 In.	600.00
Table, Frankl, Big Foot, Lacquered Cork, Mahogany, Johnson, c.1948, 15 x 72 In. ....*illus*	15000.00
Table, Frankl, Low, Cork, Mahogany, Johnson Furniture Co., c.1948, 14 x 48 In.	992.00
Table, Free-Form, Karl Springer, Brass, Granite, 1970s, 18 x 26 In.	5270.00
Table, French Boulle, Ebonized Wood, Drawer, Cabriole Legs, Bronze Mounts, c.1890, 28 x 32 In.	7768.00
Table, French Provincial, Fruitwood, 3 Drawers, Tapered Legs, 30 x 67 In.	1121.00
Table, French Provincial, Fruitwood, Farm, Scalloped Frieze, Cabriole Legs, c.1900, 29 x 71 In.	2460.00
Table, French Provincial, Fruitwood, Molded Edge, Shell, Scroll Toes, c.1900, 29 x 39 In.	276.00
Table, French Provincial, Fruitwood, Planked Top, Pullout Leaves, Drawer, c.1820, 31 x 33 In.	1845.00
Table, French Provincial, Fruitwood, Scalloped Apron, c.1800, 32 x 76 In.	1093.00
Table, French Provincial, Mahogany, Carved, Rectangular, Cabriole Legs, 1800s, 31 x 57 In.	2748.00
Table, French Provincial, Oak, Baluster Turned Legs, Low Stretcher, Drawer, 1800s, 29 x 76 In.	1195.00
Table, French Provincial, Oak, Frieze Panel, Round Legs, c.1820, 30 x 26 In.	799.00
Table, French Provincial, Walnut, Molded Top, Shaped Apron, Drawer, Cabriole Legs, 28 x 38 In.	1315.00
Table, G. Nakashima, Kevin, Free Edge Slab Top, Asymmetrical Base, 20 x 32 In.	26738.00
Table, G. Nakashima, Trestle, Walnut, Plank, Trestle Base, c.1955, 28 ½ x 84 In.	7480.00
Table, G. Nakashima, Walnut, Convex Top, c.1960, 25 x 20 In.	16415.00
Table, G. Nakashima, Walnut, Demilune, 3 Legs, Hickory Stretcher, Widdicomb, 1958, 30 x 21 In.	1080.00
Table, G. Nakashima, Walnut, Slab Top, Free-Form, 1971, 13 x 66 In.	8575.00
Table, G. Nelson, Ebonized Birch, Gateleg, Herman Miller, 30 x 18 ½ In.	702.00
Table, G. Stickley, Clip Corner, Medial Shelf, 29 x 24 In.	2356.00
Table, G. Stickley, Director's, Base Stretcher, Red Decal, 30 x 72 In.	21080.00
Table, G. Stickley, Mahogany, Spindle Sides, Stretcher Shelf, 36 x 24 In.	1140.00
Table, G. Stickley, Round, 5 Legs, 4 Leaves, Red Decal, 28 ¾ x 54 In.	3100.00
Table, G. Stickley, Spindled, Round, Paper Label, c.1905, 29 x 29 ½ In.	5890.00
Table, Game, Andre Arbus, Leather Top, 4 Drawers, Chrome Sabots, 31 x 39 In.	2460.00
Table, Game, Backgammon, Red Paint, American, 1900s, 31 x 40 x 21 In.	938.00
Table, Game, Black Lacquer, 3 Drawers, Ivory Pulls, Birdcage Support, Paw Feet, 32 x 24 In. .	267.00
Table, Game, Black Lacquer, Parcel Gilt, Fold Top, Chinoiserie, Drawer, 30 x 39 In.	995.00
Table, Game, Brass, Mother-Of-Pearl, Hinged Top, Shaped, Beaded Edge, Turned Stem, 29 x 27 In.	1830.00
Table, Game, Bullnose Top, Ogee Skirt, Pedestal Base, Columns, Scroll Feet, c.1835, 29 x 36 In.	3444.00
Table, Game, Burl, Marquetry, Scrolling Leaves, Hinged Top, Cabriole Legs, 1800s, 32 x 36 In.	1659.00
Table, Game, Chinese Chippendale, Hinged, Swing Leg, Applied Fretwork, Eng., 49 x 43 In.	748.00
Table, Game, Chippendale, Mahogany, Cabriole Legs, Ball & Claw Feet, c.1780, 30 x 35 In.	14220.00
Table, Game, Chippendale, Mahogany, Double Fold, Rear Gateleg, Hinged Top, 20 x 33 In.	777.00
Table, Game, Chippendale, Mahogany, Foldover Top, Scalloped Skirt, Cabriole Legs, 30 x 30 In.	717.00
Table, Game, Chippendale, Mahogany, Serpentine Lift Top, Reeded Block Legs, c.1790	273.00
Table, Game, Demilune, Foldover, Baize, Square, Tapered Legs, 30 x 43 In.	1135.00
Table, Game, Edwardian, Mahogany, Tooled Leather, Drawer, Stretcher Shelf, c.1900, 30 x 44 In.	366.00

Furniture, Table, Dressing, Sheraton, Stencil, Painted, Scrolled Backslpash, Drawer, c.1810, 34 x 29 In. **$920.00**

Leland Little Auction

Furniture, Table, Drop Leaf, Chippendale, Mahogany, Paduck, Gateleg, Chamfered Legs, c.1790, 28 x 42 ½ In. **$489.00**

Leland Little Auction

Furniture, Table, Drop Leaf, Queen Anne, Walnut, Apron, Cabriole Legs, Pad Feet, American, 27 x 47 In. **$558.00**

Cowan's Auctions

Furniture, Table, Drop Leaf, Regency, Mahogany, Inlay, 2 Drawers, Trestle, Brass Caps, c.1815, 28 x 58 In. **$610.00**

Leslie Hindman Auctioneers

Furniture, Table, Drop Leaf, Sheraton, Cherry, Frieze Drawer, Reeded Legs, Brass Feet, c.1810, 21 x 42 In. $1342.00

Neal Auction Co.

Furniture, Table, Drop Leaf, Sheraton, Rounded Leaves, Scrubbed Top, Turned Legs, c.1835, 36 x 35 ½ In. $206.00

Garth's Auctions, Inc.

Furniture, Table, Farm, 2-Board Top, Dovetailed Drawers, Turned & Splayed Legs, Pa., 29 x 60 In. $1955.00

Cottone Auctions

Furniture, Table, Farm, Cypress, Plank Top, Fitted Drawer, Square Legs, H-Stretcher, c.1850, 75 x 29 In. $861.00

New Orleans Auction Galleries, Inc.

Table, Game, Empire Style, Mahogany, Flip Top, Dished Surface, Brass Edge, c.1850, 29 x 44 In. *illus*	1168.00
Table, Game, Empire, Mahogany, Rectangular, Folding Top, Pedestal Base, 1800s, 31 x 34 In.	345.00
Table, Game, Federal, Line & Diamond Inlay, Foldover Top, Demilune, c.1810, 30 x 36 In.	400.00
Table, Game, Federal, Mahogany, D-Shape Top, Hinged, Square Legs, c.1815, 30 x 36 In.	1045.00
Table, Game, Federal, Mahogany, Foldover Top, Curly Maple Panel, Tapered Legs, c.1820, 28 x 36 In.	598.00
Table, Game, Federal, Mahogany, Foldover Top, Line Strung, Crossbanded, c.1800, 35 x 32 In.	922.00
Table, Game, Federal, Mahogany, Foldover Top, String Inlays, c.1920, 30 x 36 In.	403.00
Table, Game, Federal, Mahogany, String Inlay, Foldover Top, Square Legs, c.1800, 30 x 35 In.	1708.00
Table, Game, French Provincial, Oak, Checkerboard Hinged Top, 3 Faux Drawers, 31 x 30 In.	956.00
Table, Game, Fruitwood, Inlaid, Foldover Top, Swivel, Block Square Legs, c.1790, 30 x 33 In.	369.00
Table, Game, George II, Mahogany, Shaped Flip Top, Drawer, Cabriole Legs, c.1740, 28 x 35 In.	1830.00
Table, Game, George II, Walnut, Hinged Top, Frieze Drawer, Pad Feet, c.1740-50, 29 x 34 In.	1076.00
Table, Game, George III, Mahogany, Triple Top, Fitted Interior, Rectangular, c.1890, 30 x 35 In.	984.00
Table, Game, Georgian, Mahogany, Acanthus Leaf Knees, Ball & Claw Feet, 1740s, 29 x 34 In.	764.00
Table, Game, Georgian, Mahogany, Foldover Top, Carved Edge, Cabriole Legs, 1740s, 28 x 36 In.	3050.00
Table, Game, Georgian, Mahogany, Shaped Foldover Top, Drawer, 1700s, 29 x 34 In.	1315.00
Table, Game, Handkerchief Top, Mahogany, Wells, Blaize Surface, Tapered Legs, c.1900, 29 x 29 In.	1045.00
Table, Game, Handkerchief, Mahogany, Brass, Fitted, Ireland, c.1885, 29 x 22 In.	652.00
Table, Game, Hepplewhite, Flip Top, Gatelegs, Shaped Apron, 28 x 36 In.	550.00
Table, Game, Hepplewhite, Serpentine, Inlaid, Foldover, 1800s, 30 x 36 In.	1380.00
Table, Game, Loo, Walnut, Molded Edge, Bulbous Standard, Splayed Legs, c.1875, 21 x 42 In.	2091.00
Table, Game, Louis XV Style, Inlaid Birds, Leaves, Hinged Top, Cabriole Legs, 31 x 31 In.	443.00
Table, Game, Louis XVI Style, Mahogany, Brass, Convertible, Writing, Fluted Legs, c.1900, 29 x 49 In.	2015.00
Table, Game, Louis XVI, Rectangular Dish Top, Inlaid Gameboard, Square Legs, c.1805, 29 x 34 In.	1230.00
Table, Game, Mahogany, Demilune, Foldover, Green Lined Surface, c.1740, 28 x 36 In., Pair	8775.00
Table, Game, Mahogany, Demilune, Hinged, Interior Storage, Tapered Legs, c.1910, 29 x 33 In.	1045.00
Table, Game, Mahogany, Flip Top, Turned Pedestal, Platform Base, Paw Feet, 1800s, 29 x 36 In., Pair	3198.00
Table, Game, Mahogany, Fold Open, 4 Animal Shape Legs, Paw Feet, c.1835, 30 x 37 In., Pair	7072.00
Table, Game, Mahogany, Fold Open, Ribbon Edge, Carved, Stretcher, c.1950, 28 x 32 In.	1722.00
Table, Game, Mahogany, Fold-Out Hinged Top, Money Pockets, Carved Apron, 1800s, 28 x 30 In.	646.00
Table, Game, Mahogany, Foldover Swivel Top, Pillar Support, Paw Feet, c.1802, 30 x 36 In.	1016.00
Table, Game, Mahogany, Foldover Top, Drawer, Angles Corners, Cabriole Legs, c.1720, 28 ½ x 32 In.	468.00
Table, Game, Mahogany, Foldover Top, Drawer, England, 1700s, 28 x 26 In.	1020.00
Table, Game, Mahogany, Foldover Top, Tapered Supports, Trestle Base, 1800s, 30 x 36 In.	9261.00
Table, Game, Mahogany, Foldover, Flower Carved Frieze, Lyre Pedestal, Paw Feet, c.1825, 30 x 30 In.	338.00
Table, Game, Mahogany, Inlaid Chessboard, Interior Roulette Wheel, Saber Legs, 32 x 36 In.	896.00
Table, Game, Mahogany, Ogee Molded Apron, Baluster Support, 29 x 36 In.	125.00
Table, Game, Mahogany, Tiger Stripe Base, Flat Bun Feet, Swivel, Flip Top, 26 x 32 In.	244.00
Table, Game, Mahogany, Tilt Top, Shaped Rectangular Top, Scroll Feet, Victorian, 31 x 36 In.	458.00
Table, Game, Marquetry, Flip Top, Bronze Trim, Drawer, France, c.1920, 30 x 29 In.	369.00
Table, Game, Marquetry, Foldover Top, Bonze, Leather Inset, Flower Reserve, c.1910, 30 x 33 In.	984.00
Table, Game, Mother-Of-Pearl, Inlay, Wood, Hinged Top, Cabriole Legs, Syria, c.1890, 32 x 32 In.	4130.00
Table, Game, Napoleon III, Brass Inlay, Shaped Top, Flowering Urn, Fluted Legs, 31 x 36 In.	1464.00
Table, Game, Neoclassical, Mahogany, Foldover Top, Carved, Gilt Stencil, Paw Feet, c.1810, 36 x 19 In. *illus*	2749.00
Table, Game, Papier-Mache, Tilt Top, Painted, Gilt & Black, Flower Border, c.1820, 28 x 18 In.	275.00
Table, Game, Queen Anne Style, Hinged Top, Cabriole Legs, Tassel Knees, Pad Feet, 29 x 36 In.	354.00
Table, Game, Queen Anne, Mahogany, Gateleg, Hinged, Frieze Drawer, Square Stiles, 29 x 30 In.	429.00
Table, Game, Queen Anne, Walnut, Flip Top, Leather Inset, Tapered Legs, Pad Feet, 27 x 30 In. *illus*	4216.00
Table, Game, Regency, Mahogany, Hinged Top, 2 Counters, Ring-Turned Stem, c.1820, 31 x 37 In.	1342.00
Table, Game, Regency, Penwork, Checkerboard Top, Flower, Figure Border, Tripod Legs, 28 x 19 In.	3627.00
Table, Game, Regency, Rosewood, Foldover Top, Carved, Molded Edge, Casters, 29 x 36 In.	956.00
Table, Game, Renaissance Revival, Burl Panels, Inlaid Instruments, Pedestal Base, 36 In.	1475.00
Table, Game, Rococo, Rosewood, Carved Skirt, Scroll Legs, c.1840, 29 x 41 In.	488.00
Table, Game, Rosewood, Brass Checkerboard Inlay, Drawer, Trestle Base, 28 x 22 x 18 In.	920.00
Table, Game, Rosewood, Leaf Carved Standard, Scrolled Feet, c.1835, 29 x 35 In.	593.00
Table, Game, Rosewood, Marble & Black Wood Inlay, Chinese, c.1890, 30 ½ In. *illus*	3981.00
Table, Game, Satinwood, Foldover Top, Inlaid Flowers, Urn, Spade Feet, 1800s, 30 x 36 In., Pair	10158.00
Table, Game, Sheraton Style, Double Hinged Top, Green Leather, Round, 5 Legs, 31 x 42 In.	575.00
Table, Game, Sheraton, Mahogany, Flip Top, Swing Leg, Carved, New England, c.1805, 30 x 37 In.	1035.00
Table, Game, Snooker, Felt, Slate, Cues, Balls, Triangle, Pine Case, England, c.1890, 11 x 20 In.	385.00
Table, Game, Square, Reversible Top Lifts, Backgammon, Continental, 1920s, 29 x 32 In.	240.00
Table, Game, Square, Ring-Turned Legs, William Haines, Gold Stamp, c.1948, 30 x 36 In.	10000.00
Table, Game, Walnut, Ebonized, Inlaid Gameboard, Drawer, c.1865, 28 x 33 In. *illus*	984.00
Table, Game, Walnut, Square Marble Top, Molded Edge, Turned Vase Shape Stem, 1800s, 29 x 21 In.	1195.00
Table, George II, Bowed, D-Shaped Leaves, Cabriole Legs, Gateleg, 28 x 13 In.	1287.00

Table, George III Style, Mahogany, Serpentine Front, 4 Inlaid Drawers, Leaf Medallions, 36 x 74 In.		1872.00
Table, George III Style, Pedestal, Square Dish Top, Bulbous Standard, c.1800s, 35 x 9 In., Pair		615.00
Table, George III, Mahogany, Blind Fretwork, Carved Frieze, 34 x 62 In.		2988.00
Table, George III, Mahogany, Brass Mounts, Gray Baize Panel, 2 Drawers, Tapered, 30 x 47 In.		4387.00
Table, George III, Mahogany, Gallery Top, Pierced Handles, Tambour Door, Drawer, 30 ½ x 20 In.		1755.00
Table, George III, Mahogany, Piecrust Top, Turned Standard, 3 Splayed Legs, c.1800, 27 In.		246.00
Table, George III, Mahogany, Satinwood Inlays, Hinged Top, Well, Drawer, Shelf, 29 x 20 In.		1404.00
Table, George III, Mahogany, Tilt Top, Spiral Fluted Pedestal, Leaf Carved Tripod Legs, 28 x 31 In.		1053.00
Table, George III, Mixed Wood, Inlays, Drawer, Oval, X-Stretcher, 23 ½ x 21 In.		1404.00
Table, Georgian Style, Mahogany, Scalloped Apron, Medial Shelf, 26 x 21 In., Pair		688.00
Table, Georgian, Mahogany, Crossbanded, Drop Leaf, Drawers, Trestle Base, c.1795, 29 x 38 In.		717.00
Table, Gilt Aluminum Scrolled Flower Stem, Base, Round Glass Top, 1970s, 17 x 19 In., Pair		279.00
Table, Gilt Iron Frame, Marble Top, Round, Maitland Smith, 1980s, 21 x 23 In.		465.00
Table, Gilt Metal, Marble, Round Top, Tripod Branch Base, 20 ½ x 16 ½ In.		239.00
Table, Gilt, Eagle Masks, Pierced Scrolled, Cabriole Legs, Sino-Tibetan, 17 ½ x 81 In.		430.00
Table, Gilt, Mahogany, Round, Gadrooned Edge, Pedestal, Octagonal Standard, c.1900, 29 x 60 In.		1476.00
Table, Gilt, Marble Top, Rectangular, Carved Apron, Cabriole Legs, c.1985, 34 x 57 In.		6573.00
Table, Gilt, Pietra Dura, Inlaid Flowers, Shell, Birds, Beaded Wreath, Mask Capitals, 19 x 33 In.		2950.00
Table, Gilt, Rectangular Marble Top, Scrolled Frieze, Column Legs, c.1890, 29 x 41 In.		1599.00
Table, Gilt, Rectangular Marble Top, Wavy Carved Frieze, Leg Tops, c.1890, 33 x 46 In., Pair		1968.00
Table, Gilt, Round Marble Top, Shell & Fret Carved Apron, Saber Legs, X-Stretcher, 28 In., Pair		711.00
Table, Gilt, Shaped Marble Top, Ornate Flower & Leaf Carved, 1800s, 38 x 81 In.		2415.00
Table, Gilt, Shaped Marble Top, Pierced Shell Frieze, Scrolled Legs, Toes, c.1890, 35 x 38 In., Pair		4920.00
Table, Glass Mosaic, Wrought Iron, Serpent Design, Round, 30 x 36 In.		1989.00
Table, Glass Top, Chrome Plated Steel Legs, Brueton, 16 x 72 In.		682.00
Table, Glass Top, Iron, Curved X-Shape Base, c.1970, 29 x 55 In.		246.00
Table, Glass Top, Round, 3 Putto Base, Parcel Gilt Wings, Pants, 1900s, 24 x 30 In.		488.00
Table, Glass Top, Wrought Iron, Scrolled Legs, Gilt Stretcher, 2 Putti Panels, c.1920, 20 x 23 In.		460.00
Table, Glass, Bronze & Iron Tapered Legs, 2 Glass Tier Shelves, Italy, c.1960, 17 x 23 In., Pair		1476.00
Table, Gothic Revival, Mahogany, Rippled Skirt, Arched Legs, American, c.1840, 30 x 36 In.		299.00
Table, Gothic Revival, Rosewood, Sienna Marble, Carved, Support, American, c.1850, 30 x 26 In.		1554.00
Table, Gothic Style, Oak, Shaped, Carved Royal Figures, Swags, 2 Doors, France, c.1875, 40 x 69 In.		3965.00
Table, Green Lacquer, Rectangular, Shelf, Square Tapered Legs, W. Haines, c.1948, 24 x 20 In.		531.00
Table, Green Painted Openwork Skirt, Shaped Legs, Stretcher, Carved, 30 x 33 In.		201.00
Table, Habersham Style, Mahogany, Carved Apron, Leaves, Roses, 6 Legs, 33 x 71 In.		210.00
Table, Hardwood, Carved, Standing Camel Base, Octagonal Top, Egypt, 1900s, 27 x 28 In. *illus*		7703.00
Table, Hardwood, Inset Marble, Square Shelf, Carved Apron, Chinese, 30 x 24 In.		780.00
Table, Hardwood, Slab, Shaped Marble Top, Fluted Apron, Carved Flowers, 33 x 63 In.		1770.00
Table, Harvest, Sawbuck, 2-Board Top, Breadboard Ends, X-Shape Supports, 30 x 28 x 80 In.		561.00
Table, Henry II Style, Oak, Round, Carved Pedestal Base, Animal Heads, 28 x 45 x 40 In.		540.00
Table, Henry II, Oak, Pedestal, Round, Carved Base, 29 x 51 In.		397.00
Table, Henry II, Walnut, Rounded, Columns, Turned Leg Supports, 29 x 50 In.		183.00
Table, Hugh Acton, White Marble Top, Round, Polished Steel Base, 36 x 30 In.		450.00
Table, I. Barringer & T. Muller, Shaped Top, Frame Support, Kittinger, 24 x 15 In., Pair		390.00
Table, Indian, Wood, Ivory Inlay, Round, Gateleg, 31 x 46 In.		418.00
Table, Inset Leather Top, 2 Drawers, 2 Slides, Turned Legs, England, c.1860, 29 x 51 In.		738.00
Table, Iron, Fer Forge, Marble Top, Openwork Apron, Flared Pedestal, c.1930, 34 x 41 In.		1845.00
Table, Iron, Glass Top, Snakes, Nest, 20 ½ x 36 In.		1840.00
Table, Iron, Marble Top, Scrollwork Stretcher & Base, 22 x 41 x 25 In.		150.00
Table, J. Adnet, Mahogany, Stitched Leather, Top, Round, France, 1950s, 16 x 20 In.		682.00
Table, Jacobean Style, Oak, Round, Base Stretcher, Carved Apron, England, 1800s, 28 x 30 In.		420.00
Table, Jacobean Style, Walnut, Recessed Carved Patera Freize, Baluster Legs, 22 x 22 In.		123.00
Table, Janus, Wormley, Natzler Tiles, Mahogany, Brass, Label, Dunbar, 17 x 15 In., Pair		12400.00
Table, Jean Prouve, Grand Compass Base, Enameled Steel, France, 1950s, 27 x 66 ¾ In.		4960.00
Table, Joe Columbo, Card, Chromed Steel, Green Felt, Leather, Italy, 1960s, 28 x 39 In.		527.00
Table, John Dickinson, Enameled Plaster, 3-Footed, 1970s, 20 x 16 In. *illus*		11160.00
Table, John Keal, Bleached Mahogany, Brown Saltman, 1960s, 18 x 20 In., Pair		248.00
Table, John Mortenson, Rosewood, Round, Pedestal Base, 2 Leaves, Heltborg Mobler, 51 x 28 In.		720.00
Table, Kang, Walnut, Carved Dragons On Aprons & Feet, Chinese, c.1700 *illus*		1838.00
Table, Karl Springer, Fossil Stone, Rectangular, Block Legs, 60 x 30 In.		900.00
Table, Kem Weber, Black Wood Top, Chromed Steel Tube Frame, Lloyd, 29 x 32 In.		150.00
Table, Kimble & Cabus, Walnut Drawers, Octagonal, 8 Legs, 30 x 48 In.		744.00
Table, Kingwood, Breche D'Aleps Marble Top, Molded Edges, 2 Drawers, Cabriole Legs, 30 x 25 In.		1722.00
Table, Kitchen, Mahogany, Marble, Shelf, Drawer, Carvings, Iron Handles, Italy, 1975, 40 x 32 In.		458.00
Table, L. & J.G. Stickley, Book, Open Shelves, Slats, Partial Decal, 29 x 27 In. *illus*		7440.00
Table, Lacquer, Red, Green, Pheasant Cartouches, Rectangular, Chinese, c.1890, 14 x 41 In.		415.00

Furniture, Table, Farm, French Provincial, Plank Top, Drawers, Hinged, Peg & Mortise, 1800s, 79 x 30 In. $837.00

Neal Auction Co.

Furniture, Table, Federal, Mahogany, Bowfront, Lift Top, Fitted Interior, Gallery, c.1810, 40 x 29 In. $1912.00

Neal Auction Co.

Furniture, Table, Frankl, Big Foot, Lacquered Cork, Mahogany, Johnson, c.1948, 15 x 72 In. $15000.00

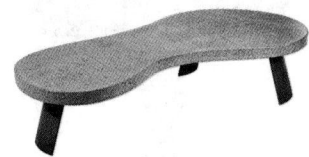

Los Angeles Modern Auctions

Furniture, Table, Game, Empire Style, Mahogany, Flip Top, Dished Surface, Brass Edge, c.1850, 29 x 44 In. $1168.00

New Orleans Auction Galleries, Inc.

Furniture, Table, Game, Neoclassical, Mahogany, Foldover Top, Carved, Gilt Stencil, Paw Feet, c.1810, 36 x 19 In. $2749.00

Neal Auction Co.

Furniture, Table, Game, Queen Anne, Walnut, Flip Top, Leather Inset, Tapered Legs, Pad Feet, 27 x 30 In. $4216.00

Leslie Hindman Auctioneers

Furniture, Table, Game, Rosewood, Marble & Black Wood Inlay, Chinese, c.1890, 30 ½ In. $3981.00

Skinner, Inc.

Cocktail or Coffee

When Prohibition ended in 1933, furniture makers started to sell low "cocktail tables" to be used in front of sofas to serve the newly legal mixed drinks. The public objected to the name, so it was renamed a "coffee table."

Table, Landscape Scene, Bird, Insects, Japanned, Ball & Claw Feet, c.1890, 28 x 37 In.		345.00
Table, Leather Cover, 2 Stacked Books Shape, 2 Side Drawers, 17 x 36 In.		173.00
Table, Leather Top, 3 Drawers, Carved, Santa Fe, 1980s, 29 x 60 In.		690.00
Table, Leather Top, Longhorn Stretcher, Oval, Brass Tacks, c.1900, 30 x 40 In.		415.00
Table, Library, Aesthetic Revival, Walnut, Leather, Splayed Legs, c.1885, 26 x 42 In.	*illus*	2091.00
Table, Library, Arts & Crafts, Fumed Oak, 2 Drawers, Copper Pulls, Stretcher, 31 x 48 In.		558.00
Table, Library, Classical Revival, Mahogany, Marble Top, Serpentine Legs, 30 x 60 In.		369.00
Table, Library, G. Stickley, Overhung, Drawer, Iron Pull, Low Stretcher, 48 x 30 In.		1440.00
Table, Library, Limbert, Turtle Top, Drawer, Branded Mark, 29 ½ x 48 In.	*illus*	2728.00
Table, Library, Lion Masks, Leaf Scrolls, Paw Feet, Carved, 30 x 49 In.		600.00
Table, Library, Mahogany, 6 Drawers, Drop Leaf, Leather Top, Reeded Legs, c.1890, 84 x 42 In.		1320.00
Table, Library, Mahogany, Leather Top, 3 Frieze Drawers, Turned Legs, 30 x 78 In.		3286.00
Table, Library, Mahogany, Marble Top, Trestle Base, Arched Stretcher, c.1835, 32 x 53 In.		4182.00
Table, Library, Mahogany, Oval Top, Drawer, Standards, Turned Stretcher, c.1835, 31 x 71 In.		861.00
Table, Library, Mahogany, Oval, Carved Seated Griffins, Shelf, Scroll Feet, c.1870s, 30 x 54 In.		1645.00
Table, Library, Napoleon III, Mahogany, Gilt Brass, Drawers, Columnar Supports, 28 x 54 In.		2390.00
Table, Library, Rectangular Leather Top, 6 Drawers, Turned Legs, Casters, 32 x 84 In.		944.00
Table, Library, Regency, Mahogany, Gilt Tooled Leather, Outswept Legs, 1800s, 31 x 60 In.		2600.00
Table, Library, Renaissance Revival, Walnut, Leather, Gilt, Phila 1876 Paris 1878, c.1876, 68 x 50 In.		5078.00
Table, Library, Rococo, Rosewood, Serpentine Marble Top, Scroll Trestle, c.1850, 31 x 46 In.		7170.00
Table, Library, Rosewood, Gilt Leaves, Lyre Pedestal, Paw Feet, Stretchers, c.1825, 30 x 48 In.		5166.00
Table, Library, Walnut, Inlaid Apron, 4 Carved Drawers, Plank Stretcher, c.1895, 30 x 84 In.		2070.00
Table, Library, William IV, Mahogany, Gilded, Trestle Base, Turned Stretcher, c.1850, 29 x 55 In.		1315.00
Table, Library, William IV, Oak, Writing Surface, Melon Feet, Drawers, c.1840, 30 x 66 In.		2032.00
Table, Limbert, No. 1162, 2 Drawers, Copper Hardware, 42 x 29 In.		210.00
Table, Louis Philippe, Mahogany, Marble, Drawer, Scrolled Supports, Paw Feet, 1850, 38 x 42 In.		1968.00
Table, Louis XIV Style, Gilt, Marble Top, Pierced Apron, Cabriole Legs, 1900s, 40 x 37 In.		360.00
Table, Louis XIV Style, Marble Top, Flowers, Scrolling Leaves, Square Legs, 1900s, 32 x 48 In.		1121.00
Table, Louis XV Style, Marquetry, Round, Inlaid Flowers, Vase Shape Column, 1900s, 30 x 27 In.		115.00
Table, Louis XV Style, Oak, Marble Top, Drawer, Door, Cabriole Legs, 34 x 17 In.		210.00
Table, Louis XV Style, Oak, Parquet Top, Carved Trestle Base, 29 x 94 x 43 In.		900.00
Table, Louis XV Style, Oak, Parquet Top, Draw Leaf, Scalloped Skirt, Cabriole Legs, 29 x 43 In.		390.00
Table, Louis XV Style, Paul Sormani, Ormolu, Oval Marble Top, ¾ Gallery, Drawer, 31 In., Pair		3245.00
Table, Louis XV Style, Walnut, Carved Cabriole Legs, Stretcher, 29 x 49 In.		122.00
Table, Louis XV Style, Walnut, Parquet Top, Carved & Shaped Apron, 31 x 96 In.		549.00
Table, Louis XV Style, White Marble Top, Gilt, Paint, c.1800, 29 In.		210.00
Table, Louis XV, Marquetry, Gilt Bronze, Oval, Banded Flower, Cabriole Legs, c.1910, 29 x 42 In.		717.00
Table, Louis XV, Parquetry, Marble Top, Drawer, Open Shelf, Door, 32 x 19 In.		214.00
Table, Louis XV, Rosewood, Marble Top, Bronze Ormolu, 2 Drawers, Medial Shelf, 1800s, 35 x 15 In.		427.00
Table, Louis XV, Walnut, Side Drawer, Shell Carved, Cabriole Legs, Hoof Feet, 33 x 40 In.		2988.00
Table, Louis XVI Style, Dressing Mirror, Serpentine Base, Drawer, Parquetry, Bronze, 30 x 27 In.		717.00
Table, Louis XVI Style, Ebonized, Marble Top, Bronze Trim, 2 Drawers, c.1940, 26 x 19 In., Pair		1845.00
Table, Louis XVI Style, Fruitwood, Marble Top, Brass, Heads, Splayed Legs, c.1950, 30 x 27 In., Pair		3690.00
Table, Louis XVI Style, Fruitwood, Marble Top, Round, 19 x 36 In.		313.00
Table, Louis XVI Style, Gilded, Marble Top, Scrolled Leaf Pierced Apron, Turned Legs, 31 x 47 In.		1793.00
Table, Louis XVI Style, Gilt Bronze, Marble Top, 2 Drawers, Cabriole Legs, Sabots, 30 x 24 In.		488.00
Table, Louis XVI Style, Gilt, Marble Top, Sunflowers, Bellflower, Urn Stretcher, c.1850, 34 x 67 In.		2460.00
Table, Louis XVI Style, Marquetry, Shaped Top, Ormolu Mounts, 1900s, 30 x 40 In.		296.00
Table, Louis XVI Style, Round Marble Top, Reeded Legs, France, c.1900, 16 x 17 In.		288.00
Table, Louis XVI, Gilt Bronze, Oval, 3 Mirrors, Leaf Gallery, Ebonized, Fluted Legs, 21 x 56 In.		17550.00
Table, Louis XVI, Mahogany, Leather Top, Gallery, Frieze Drawer, Tapered Legs, 31 x 33 In.		1404.00
Table, Louis XVI, Mahogany, Shaped Top, Gallery, Hinge, Lyre Shape Legs, Splay Feet, 30 x 33 In.		2252.00
Table, Louis XVI, Oak, 2 Drawer, Gilt Swags, Turned Legs, Finial On Stretcher, 30 x 39 In.		671.00
Table, Louis XVI, Walnut, Marble Top, Arched Crest, Drawer, Door, Stretcher Shelf, 49 x 17 In.		244.00
Table, Louis XVI, Walnut, Overhung 2-Board Top, Drawer, c.1790, 30 x 51 In.		649.00
Table, Louis XVI, Wood, Leather Top, Ormolu Mounts, 2 Drawers, c.1790, 30 x 59 In.		920.00
Table, Louis, XV Style, Cherry, Banded Top, Scallop Frieze, Drawer, Pullout Slide, c.1820, 31 x 62 In.		2706.00
Table, Low, Mother-Of-Pearl Inlay, Rectangular, Pierced Apron, Claw Feet, Chinese, 11 x 33 In.		2728.00
Table, Low, Neoclassical, Gilt Metal, Marble, Round Gallery Top, X-Stretcher, Finial, 17 x 28 In.		372.00
Table, Low, Red Lacquer, Lotus Flowers, Bamboo Leaves, Gold Trim, Japan, 1800s, 8 ¾ x 28 In.		237.00
Table, Low, Rococo Style, Mahogany, Shaped Rectangular Top, Pierced Frieze, Shelf, 18 x 35 In.		465.00
Table, M. Baughman, Chrome Base, Smoky Glass Top, Thayer-Coggin, 28 x 78 In.		1080.00
Table, M. Sheets, Travertine Top, Walnut Base, Round, c.1946, 17 x 38 In.	*illus*	3125.00
Table, Mahogany, 2 Carved Egret Sides, Fitted With Rectangular Top, 26 x 20 In.		132.00
Table, Mahogany, 2 Drawer, Carved Edge, Herter Style, 29 x 28 In.		6200.00
Table, Mahogany, 2 Pedestals, Cabriole Legs, Ball & Claw Feet, Henredon, 45 x 76 In.		590.00

Table, Mahogany, Book Support, Hinged, 3 Scrolled Legs, c.1875, 32 x 18 In............................	369.00
Table, Mahogany, Brass Inlays, Round, Molded Top, Pedestal Stem, Tripod Base, 28 x 34 In. ..	819.00
Table, Mahogany, Brass, 3 Leather Steps, Hinged Compartment, 27 x 16 In., Pair.....................	1673.00
Table, Mahogany, Brass, Scrolled Backsplash, 4 Drawers, Boston, c.1820, 37 x 40 In................	1912.00
Table, Mahogany, Brass, Tambour Doors, Drawer, R. Rutili, Johnson Furniture, 23 x 22 In., Pair	2450.00
Table, Mahogany, Carved, Marble Top, Blocked Trestle, c.1810, 46 x 22 In. ....*illus*	2390.00
Table, Mahogany, Fruitwood, Turtle Top, Sunburst Pattern, Ormolu Bands, c.1905, 28 x 27 In.	867.00
Table, Mahogany, Gilt, Round Marble Top, Lotus Standard, Paw Feet, c.1830, 29 x 34 In.........	9560.00
Table, Mahogany, Marble Top, Pierced Skirt, Masks, Garland, Hairy Paw Feet, Ireland, 30 x 53 In. ..	9859.00
Table, Mahogany, Marquetry, Marble Top, Round, Pedestal, 31 x 42 In...............................	305.00
Table, Mahogany, Octagonal Top, Flared Stem, Arched Scroll Legs, c.1800, 28 x 41 In.	2390.00
Table, Mahogany, Ormolu Mounts, Ebonized Drawer, Fluted Legs, Cross Stretcher, c.1910, 30 x 51 In.	518.00
Table, Mahogany, Ormolu, Brass Gallery, Leather Inset Slide, Drawer, Shelf, c.1875, 27 x 17 In., Pair	861.00
Table, Mahogany, Oval Marble Top, Center Urn Pedestal, Shaped Legs, Victorian, 29 x 30 In...	173.00
Table, Mahogany, Oval, Gadrooned Edge, Scroll Legs, Ball & Claw Feet, 1800s, 30 x 95 In.......	8365.00
Table, Mahogany, Parcel Gilt, Round, Faceted, Gadrooned, 3 Paw Feet, 1800s, 30 x 54 In........	2988.00
Table, Mahogany, Piecrust, Spiral Urn Pedestal, Carved Knees, Scrolling Feet, 28 x 32 In........	2875.00
Table, Mahogany, Rectangular, 2 Long Drawers, Straight Legs, 1700s, 27 x 20 In.....................	276.00
Table, Mahogany, Reeded Edge, Frieze Drawer, Vase-Shape Pedestal, 29 x 44 In.	399.00
Table, Mahogany, Round Ball & Stick Apron, Stretcher, Ball & Claw Feet, c.1900, 30 x 32 In...	403.00
Table, Mahogany, Round Marble Top, 3 Leaf Carved Paw Feet, New York, c.1825, 30 x 36 In....	2151.00
Table, Mahogany, Round Marble Top, Turned Pedestal, Triangular Base, c.1815, 30 x 36 In.......	8302.00
Table, Mahogany, Round Top, Pedestal, Accordion Mechanism, 29 x 50 In.	4888.00
Table, Mahogany, Round, Flame Veneer Top, Bulbous Stem, Brass Paw Feet, c.1820, 29 x 42 In.	1673.00
Table, Mahogany, Round, Inset Ormolu, Flower Edge, Tapered Support, c.1950, 28 x 20 In., Pair	1236.00
Table, Mahogany, Scalloped Leather Top, Drawer, 5 False Drawers, Pedestal Tripod Base, 28 In.	173.00
Table, Mahogany, Tilt Top, Round, Vase Shape Pedestal, Tripod Base, c.1800, 28 x 29 In.	246.00
Table, Mahogany, Tray Top, Door, Drawer, Tapered Legs, 1800s, 29 x 10 In.	489.00
Table, Mahogany, White Marble Top, Frieze Drawer, Panel Door, Flared Scrolls, c.1890, 38 x 36 In.	3585.00
Table, Mahogany, White Marble Top, Ogee Molded Frieze Drawer, Scrolled Stiles, c.1820, 39 x 42 In.	4475.00
Table, Mahogany, Yew Bands, Fan Inlays, Drawer, Tapered Legs, Hekman, c.1985, 30 x 54 In.	327.00
Table, Maple, Pine, Red Paint, Turned Splayed Legs, Butterfly Leaf Supports, Oval Top, 29 x 38 In.	1293.00
Table, Marble Top, Bronze Band, Medial Shelf, Downswept Legs, France, c.1940, 22 x 28 In....	615.00
Table, Marble Top, Bronze Mounts, Inlay, 4 Drawers, 28 ¾ x 13 ¾ In., Pair	1017.00
Table, Marble Top, Bronze Trim, 2 Bowfront Drawers, Fluted Pilasters, c.1940, 27 x 18 In.......	984.00
Table, Marble Top, Cast Iron, Scrolled Openwork, 32 x 62 ½ In., Pair....................................	2706.00
Table, Marble Top, Cast Iron, Scrolls, Fleur-De-Lis, Trestle Shape, c.1920, 30 x 36 In.	1168.00
Table, Marble Top, Ebonized Wood & Metal Base, c.1960, 15 ½ x 29 In., Pair	984.00
Table, Marble Top, Gallery, Kidney Shape, Oval Medial Shelves, Trestle Base, c.1890, 26 x 25 In.	356.00
Table, Marble Top, Gilt, Carved Base, Paw Feet, 1900s, 29 ½ x 32 ½ In...............................	575.00
Table, Marble Top, Pierced Apron, Bust Topped Cabriole Legs, 37 x 31 In.............................	546.00
Table, Marble Top, Round, Pedestal, 4 Carved Arched Legs, 30 x 32 In...................................	281.00
Table, Marble Top, Round, Pierced Skirt, Rosette Topped Legs, Painted, Italy, 30 x 30 In., Pair	538.00
Table, Marble Top, Wrought Iron, Round, Inset Flowers, Alphabet, Scrolled Legs, Gilt, 30 x 40 In.	799.00
Table, Marquetry, Gilt, Bronze Mounts, Flower Top, Drawer, 30 x 46 In.	861.00
Table, Marquetry, Leather Top, Shaped, Drawer, Ormolu Mounts, 33 x 44 In.	575.00
Table, Marquetry, Slender Curved Legs, Drawer, Oval, Edge Band, Gilt, 1900s, 17 x 28 In.	351.00
Table, McCobb, Birch, Drawer, Shelf, Black Iron Frame, 18 x 22 In., Pair..............................	1920.00
Table, Metal, Flip Top, Wrought Iron, Downswept Legs, c.1950, 29 x 31 In.	215.00
Table, Mies Van Der Rohe, Barcelona, Glass Top, X-Form Steel Frame, 1970s, 17 x 40 In.........	652.00
Table, Milo Baughman, Dining, Mixed Wood, Brush Steel Legs, Leaves, T. Coggin, 1970s, 29 x 84 In.	1178.00
Table, Mixed Wood Veneers, Flower Inlays, Ormolu Mounts, 3 Drawers, c.1910, 43 x 25 In.	633.00
Table, Mixed Wood, Inlaid Top, Round, Carved Flower Apron, Legs, Urn Finial Stretcher, 28 x 26 In.	259.00
Table, Mixed Wood, Painted, 3-Board Top, Turned Legs, Mid 1800s, 29 x 36 x 83 In................	374.00
Table, Mixed Wood, Red & Yellow Turkey, Wavy Ocher Apron, Paint, 1954, 29 x 32 In.	15600.00
Table, Mixed Wood, Shell Inlay, Tripod Base, c.1820, 29 x 24 ½ In.	935.00
Table, Mixing, Empire, Mahogany, Faux Marble Slate Top, Carved Legs, 28 x 39 x 21 In. *illus*	345.00
Table, Mixing, Federal, Mahogany, Shaped Gallery, Marble Top, Stretcher Shelf, 1800s, 35 In.	2510.00
Table, Mixing, Mahogany, Marble Top, Cupboard, Door, Pointed Arches, Egypt, c.1835, 37 x 41 In.	5166.00
Table, Mixing, Mahogany, Marble Top, Scroll Brackets, Mirrored Cupboard Door, 41 x 36 In. .	5658.00
Table, Mixing, Neoclassical, Mahogany, Frieze Drawer, Door, Bracket Feet, 1800s, 35 x 36 x 19 In. *illus*	3075.00
Table, Mixing, Paneled Frieze Drawer, Scrolled Ends, Door, Bracket Feet, 1800s, 36 x 36 In......	3075.00
Table, Modern, Oak, Dark Finish, Lazy Susan On Top, Turned Legs, Cross Stretcher, 30 x 66 In.	660.00
Table, Molded Apron, Intricate Carving, Gilt, Red Paint, Chinese, 25 x 20 In., Pair..................	188.00
Table, Monastery, Oak, Rectangular, Beam Stretcher, 28 x 98 x 35 In.	900.00

Furniture, Table, Game, Walnut, Ebonized, Inlaid Gameboard, Drawer, c.1865, 28 x 33 In.
$984.00

New Orleans Auction Galleries, Inc.

Furniture, Table, Hardwood, Carved, Standing Camel Base, Octagonal Top, Egypt, 1900s, 27 x 28 In.
$7703.00

Skinner, Inc.

Furniture, Table, John Dickinson, Enameled Plaster, 3-Footed, 1970s, 20 x 16 In.
$11160.00

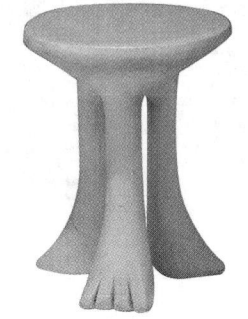

Rago Arts & Auction Center

Furniture, Table, Kang, Walnut, Carved Dragons On Aprons & Feet, Chinese, c.1700
$1838.00

Skinner, Inc.

Furniture, Table, L. & J.G. Stickley, Book, Open Shelves, Slats, Partial Decal, 29 x 27 In.
$7440.00

Rago Arts & Auction Center

Furniture, Table, Library, Aesthetic Revival, Walnut, Leather, Splayed Legs, c.1885, 26 x 42 In.
$2091.00

New Orleans Auction Galleries, Inc.

Furniture, Table, Library, Limbert, Turtle Top, Drawer, Branded Mark, 29 ½ x 48 In.
$2728.00

Rago Arts & Auction Center

Furniture, Table, M. Sheets, Travertine Top, Walnut Base, Round, c.1946, 17 x 38 In.
$3125.00

Los Angeles Modern Auctions

Table, Money, Red Lacquer, Carved, Drawers, Chinese, Early 1800s, 34 x 31 In. ....*illus*	1230.00
Table, Mother-Of-Pearl Inlay, Octagonal, Signed, 23 x 16 In., Pair..............................	359.00
Table, Multicolor, Marble Top, Frieze Drawer, Cabriole Legs, c.1700s, 27 x 41 In............	1476.00
Table, Nagato, Christian Liaigre, Raw Oak, Steel, Holly Hunt, 18 x 15 In.............................	3224.00
Table, Napoleon III, Ebonized, Serpentine Top, Chariot, Drawer, Cabriole Legs, c.1850, 30 x 48 In..	1830.00
Table, Neogothic, Oak, Column Supports, U-Shape Stretcher, 30 x 87 In...........................	671.00
Table, Nesting, Chinoisiere, Lacquer, Flowers, Paw Feet, Eng., c.1860, 27 x 17 In., 3 Piece......	246.00
Table, Nesting, Chippendale Revival, Mahogany, 1900s, 24 x 25 In., 3 Piece	120.00
Table, Nesting, Flower Top, Black, Paint, Gilt Cabriole Legs, 22 x 26 In., 3 Piece...............	214.00
Table, Nesting, George III Style, Mahogany, String Inlay, Largest 23 x 23 In., 4 Piece..............	461.00
Table, Nesting, Louis XV Style, Onyx Top, Pierced Gallery, Brass Legs, 18 x 21 In., 3 Piece........	488.00
Table, Nesting, Oak, Teak, Dunbar, 20 ½ x 24 ½ In., 3 Piece....................................	868.00
Table, Nesting, Polished Nickel, Floating Glass, France, 1960s, 15 x 19 x 13 In., 3 Piece	7800.00
Table, Nesting, Poul Kjaerholm, PK 71, Chrome, Acrylic, Fritz Hansen, 1970s, 12 x 11 In., 3 Piece	1984.00
Table, Nesting, Red Lacquer, Gilt Chinoiserie, Pierced Trestle Sides, Dragon Feet, 28 x 21 In., 4 Piece	1872.00
Table, Nesting, Rosewood, Rectangular Tops, Tapered Legs, Largest 18 x 22 In., 3 Piece	335.00
Table, Nesting, Scrolling Leaves, Leather Embossed Top, Tapered Columns, 24 x 20 In., 3 Piece	177.00
Table, Nesting, Wood, Eggshell Finish, 22 x 24 In. To 12 ¾ x 19 In., 3 Piece.....................	720.00
Table, Nickel Over Bronze, Round Marble Top, Cast Iron Base, France, c.1930, 28 x 20 In.......	430.00
Table, Oak Veneer, Rectangular, Austere Frieze, Drawer, Shoe Feet, Trestle Base, 31 x 72 In.....	711.00
Table, Oak, 4 Figural Supports, Railing Stretcher, Ornate Carvings, Brittany, 30 x 44 In.........	732.00
Table, Oak, Flared Carved Base, 1700s, 19 x 24 In.	288.00
Table, Oak, Gateleg, Oval Drop Leaves, End Drawer, Box Stretcher, England, 29 x 20 In.........	738.00
Table, Oak, Glass Tray Top, Carved, Leaf Handles, Flowers, Spiral Legs, Stretchers, 21 x 30 In.	207.00
Table, Oak, Iron Hardware Corners, Drawer, Inlaid Geometric, Splay Block Legs, 1800s, 25 x 34 In.	430.00
Table, Oak, Lion Pull, Carved Border & Legs, Stretcher Shelf, 30 x 42 In........................	316.00
Table, Oak, Marble Top, Flower Carved Panel Over Door, Shelf, c.1910, 64 x 24 In.	385.00
Table, Oak, Oval Top, Column Supports, Tapered Feet, England, 30 x 39 In......................	738.00
Table, Oak, Rectangular Top, Horn Covered Standard, Tripod Base, 1800s, 29 x 21 In. ...*illus*	1159.00
Table, Oak, Round, 4 Leaves, 1900s, 48 x 30 ½ In..	1380.00
Table, Oak, Round, Flower & Dart Carved, Cabriole Legs, Scrolled Stretcher, 32 x 31 In.	244.00
Table, Oak, Serpentine Square Top, 2 Tiers, Spiral Turned Cabriole Legs, 1800s, 29 x 26 In. ...	196.00
Table, Oak, Shaped Top, Drawer, Double Doors, Carved, Chinese, 38 ½ x 40 ½ In.	288.00
Table, Oak, Twisted Legs, c.1900, 29 x 19 x 19 In..	259.00
Table, Oak, Walnut, Square Top, Drawer, Splayed Legs, England, 1800s, 28 x 19 In................	288.00
Table, P. Evans, Cityscape, Octangular, Brass & Chrome Base, Glass Top, Directional, 24 x 25 In.	2760.00
Table, Papier-Mache, Bejeweled, Eagle Supports, Multicolor, France, c.1910, 29 x 33 In. ..... *illus*	2390.00
Table, Papier-Mache, Mother-Of-Pearl, Round, Scalloped Top, Gilt, Paint, Eng., 1800s, 28 x 22 In..	598.00
Table, Parquetry, Shaped Top, 6 Reeded Legs, Kiel Furniture, c.1925, 30 x 38 In................	138.00
Table, Parsons, Pigskin, Wood Base, c.1975, 29 ½ x 84 In.......................................	496.00
Table, Parsons, White, 36 ½ x 22 x 20 In., Pair	148.00
Table, Partners, Victorian, Mahogany, Gilt Leather, 3 Drawers, Square Legs, 31 x 72 In.	3555.00
Table, Parzinger, Burl, Inset Center, Round, 4 Angular Legs, Charak, 17 x 36 In................	948.00
Table, Parzinger, Mahogany, Brass, 2 Round Tiers, Square Base, 1950s, 61 x 22 In.	992.00
Table, Pastry, Marble, Wrought Metal, Rectangular, Scrolling Frieze & Legs, Stretcher, 31 x 48 In.	4960.00
Table, Pedestal, Burl, Round Top, Star Design, Inlay, Barley Twist Column, Tripod, 29 x 36 In.	438.00
Table, Pedestal, Hardwood, Marble Inset, Round, Pierced Frieze, Vine Design Legs, 32 x 16 In.	744.00
Table, Pedestal, Mahogany, Round Top, Reeded Column, Tripod Base, Paw Feet, 28 x 44 In.	240.00
Table, Pedestal, Neoclassical Style, Mahogany, Round, S-Scroll Supports, Tripod, Ball Feet, 32 In.	156.00
Table, Pedestal, Oak, Shaped Apron, Carved Support, France, 26 x 30 In........................	366.00
Table, Pedestal, Victorian, Mahogany, Carved, Paw Feet, 36 x 29 In............................	288.00
Table, Pedestal, Wood, Carved, Marble Top, Curved Legs, Chinese, 32 x 14 In....................	510.00
Table, Pembroke, Cherry, Poplar, Oak, c.1800, 25 x 22 In.	1200.00
Table, Pembroke, Chippendale, Mahogany, Drawer, Cross Stretcher, Phil., c.1780, 29 x 20 In..	948.00
Table, Pembroke, Chippendale, Walnut, Marlboro Legs, Stretcher, c.1790, 29 x 34 In.	1200.00
Table, Pembroke, Dining, Sheraton, Cherry, Mahogany, c.1810, 29 x 34 In......................	345.00
Table, Pembroke, Drawer, Skirt With Rosette Carved Corners, Paw Feet, 28 x 39 In..............	3352.00
Table, Pembroke, Drawers, Leaves, Swing Supports, Tapered Legs, c.1820, 29 x 38 In.	144.00
Table, Pembroke, Federal, Mahogany, Frieze Drawers, X-Stretcher, 1700s, 30 x 21 In..............	837.00
Table, Pembroke, Federal, Mahogany, Oval, String Inlay, Drawer, Tapered Legs, c.1800, 28 x 18 In.	1230.00
Table, Pembroke, Federal, Mahogany, String Inlay, Oval Corners, Square Legs, Cuffs, 29 x 20 In.	1126.00
Table, Pembroke, Federal, Mahogany, String Inlay, Square Legs, Conch Shell, c.1790, 28 x 21 In.	490.00
Table, Pembroke, Federal, Mahogany, Turned, Reeded Legs, Ball Feet, c.1810, 29 x 20 In.	326.00
Table, Pembroke, Federal, Maple, Notched Corners, Box Frame, New England, 28 x 18 In.......	1053.00
Table, Pembroke, Flame Mahogany, Drawer, c.1805, 29 x 32 In.	575.00
Table, Pembroke, George II, Mahogany, c.1790, 28 x 33 In..	356.00

F

Table, Pembroke, George III Style, Mahogany, Drawer, 38 x 49 In..	594.00
Table, Pembroke, George III, Mahogany, Banded, Drawer, Tapered Legs, 28 x 21 In.................	460.00
Table, Pembroke, George III, Mahogany, Beaded Drawer, 27 x 24 In..................................	1053.00
Table, Pembroke, George III, Mahogany, Drawer, Rounded, 1740s, 28 x 35 In.........................	1673.00
Table, Pembroke, George III, Mahogany, Inlaid, Curved Leaves, Drawer, c.1800, 28 x 17 In. ...	805.00
Table, Pembroke, Hepplewhite Style, Mahogany, Drawer, Square Legs, 28 x 19 In.	58.00
Table, Pembroke, Hepplewhite, Drawer, Beaded, England, c.1790, 29 x 30 In.	978.00
Table, Pembroke, Hepplewhite, Mahogany, Oval Top, c.1800, 28 x 40 In............................	900.00
Table, Pembroke, Mahogany, Drawer, Turned Legs, 1800s, 28 x 21 In.	708.00
Table, Pembroke, Mahogany, Flower Inlays, Drawer, Council Craftsman, 27 x 16 In., Pair......	714.00
Table, Pembroke, Mahogany, Pine Line Inlay, D-Shape Leaves, 29 x 20 In.	600.00
Table, Pembroke, Mahogany, Rectangular, Frieze Drawer, Square Leg, 1800s, 29 x 30 In........	354.00
Table, Pembroke, Queen Anne, Poplar, Pine, Pad Feet, 1700s, 30 x 33 In.................................	2520.00
Table, Pembroke, Satinwood, Banded Top, Painted, Bellflower, Square Legs, c.1800s, 30 x 33 In..	1912.00
Table, Pembroke, Sheraton, Mahogany, Drawer, Reeded Legs, c.1810, 30 x 34 In.	575.00
Table, Persian Designs, Door, Octagonal, Carved, Painted, Signed Louie Doud, 1909, 28 x 25 In.	154.00
Table, Pesce, Sansone, Polyurethane, Poured, Melted, Cast, 1980, 28 x 55 x 71 In. ....*illus*	37500.00
Table, Philip LaVerne, Bronze, Enamel, Etched Zodiac, Tubular Legs, c.1965, 15 ½ x 36 In....	1434.00
Table, Philip Lloyd Powell, Black Walnut, Pedestal, Triangular Top, 3-Footed, 1960s, 21 x 21 In.	1984.00
Table, Picnic Set, Slats, 4 Armchairs, Red, White Paint, Eng., 1900s, 27 x 34 In........................	540.00
Table, Pier, Art Deco, Mahogany, Fruitwood, Reeded Frieze, Brass Mounts, c.1910, 40 x 51 In.	600.00
Table, Pier, Baroque, Wood, Cream, Sienna Paint, Italy, 1900s, 33 x 44 In., Pair......................	3120.00
Table, Pier, Chippendale, Mahogany, Marble Top, Shell, Flower Carved Knees, 1760s, 31 x 39 In.	2596.00
Table, Pier, Classical Revival, Mahogany, Scroll Columns, Serpentine Shelf, 36 x 40 In.	461.00
Table, Pier, Empire Revival, Mahogany, 2 Scroll Supports, Mirror, c.1910, 35 x 48 In..............	518.00
Table, Pier, Empire, Mahogany, Shaped Platform, Columns, Mirror Back, Ogee Skirt, 35 x 40 In.	575.00
Table, Pier, George IV, Mahogany, Marble Top, Gilt Brackets, Mirrored Back, 36 x 69 In., Pair	8610.00
Table, Pier, Gilt, Marble, Gilt Bronze, Backsplash, Hoof Feet, France, 65 x 97 In.	38838.00
Table, Pier, Mahogany, Canted Corners, Ogee Frieze, Curved Yoke Shape Supports, c.1835, 37 x 42 In.	460.00
Table, Pier, Mahogany, Carved, Gilt Stencil, Marble Top, Frieze, Columns, c.1810, 37 x 44 In..	9859.00
Table, Pier, Mahogany, Gilt, Marble Top, Mirrored, Column Legs, Paw Feet, c.1825, 41 x 40 In.....	6573.00
Table, Pier, Mahogany, Gilt, Stencil, Ebonized, Marble Top, Columns, Mirror, c.1835, 41 x 38 In. ...*illus*	4674.00
Table, Pier, Mahogany, Marble Top, Frieze, Scroll Columns, Bowed Platform, 37 x 42 In.	1230.00
Table, Pier, Mahogany, Marble Top, Gilt Stencil Flowers, Column Supports, 1800s, 36 x 42 In.	2988.00
Table, Pier, Mahogany, Mirror Back, Turned Column Supports, 1800s, 15 ¼ In.......................	207.00
Table, Pier, Mahogany, Ogee Molded Apron, Column Supports, 35 x 47 In.	850.00
Table, Pier, Mahogany, Ogee Molded Frieze, Scrolled Front Supports, Mirror, c.1835, 40 x 48 In.	1003.00
Table, Pier, Mahogany, Satinwood Inlay, Lyre Shape Supports, Rounded Feet, 1800s, 33 x 45 In.	1076.00
Table, Pier, Mahogany, Veneer, Marble Top, Mirror, Swan Feet, c.1825, 39 x 32 In. ....*illus*	2370.00
Table, Pier, Marble Top, Ogee Frieze, Column Supports, Stretcher Shelf, 33 x 39 In..................	2629.00
Table, Pier, Marble Top, Shaped Apron, Mirror Back Base, c.1840, 29 x 31 In...........................	708.00
Table, Pier, Marble, Gilt, Cove Molded, Gadrooning, c.1825, 41 x 40 In..................................	800.00
Table, Pier, Parcel Gilt, Flower, Leaf, Carved, Cream Paint, 4 Shaped Mirrors Back, 1800s, 41 x 60 In..	1770.00
Table, Pier, Rococo, Mahogany, Marble Top, Mirror Back, Lyre Supports, c.1850, 38 x 40 In..	1315.00
Table, Pier, Rosewood, Marble Top, Columns, Stenciled, Mirror, Paw Feet, c.1905, 37 x 42 In.	7995.00
Table, Pier, Rosewood, Marble Top, Bronze Figures, Banding, Columns, Paw Feet, c.1900, 37 x 42 In.	7072.00
Table, Pier, Rosewood, Mother-Of-Pearl Inlays, Marble Top, Carved Skirt, Chinese, 34 x 41 In.	1416.00
Table, Pier, Walnut, Painted Flowers, Trestle Base, Gilt Top Edge, 1800s, 31 x 60 In..................	269.00
Table, Pine Top, Queen Anne, Pine, Poplar, Drawer, Turned Legs, 1700s, 29 x 58 In.................	259.00
Table, Pine Top, Walnut, Scrubbed Top, Turned Legs, Holmes County, 28 x 60 In.	1175.00
Table, Pine, Paint, Rectangular, Splayed Vase & Ring-Turned Legs, Pad Feet, c.1725, 25 x 23 In.	444.00
Table, Pine, Board Ends, 2 Frieze Drawers, Turned Legs, 32 x 88 In.	923.00
Table, Pine, Breadboard End Top, Bracketed Skirt, Ireland, 1800s, 59 x 61 In...........................	633.00
Table, Pine, Cherry, Overhung Top, Drawer, Base Stretcher, 37 x 22 In.	184.00
Table, Pine, Drawer, Overhung Top, Turned Legs, 1800s, 27 x 29 In..	110.00
Table, Pine, Painted, Lower Shelf, Square Supports, Arched, 1800s, 29 x 54 x 38 In.	415.00
Table, Pine, Paneled, Paint, 1800s, 34 x 70 In..	1072.00
Table, Pine, Poplar, Drawer, Paint Decorated, 1800s, 30 x 22 In.	480.00
Table, Pine, Sawbuck, Mustard & Brown Paint, Rectangular Single-Board Top, c.1800, 29 x 60 In. ..	1348.00
Table, Pine, Scrubbed Top, White Washed Base, Square Legs, c.1850, 30 x 35 In......................	288.00
Table, Pine, Stained, Drawer, Overhung Top, Splayed Legs, 1800s, 29 x 19 In.	282.00
Table, Pivoting, Checkerboard Top, Gilt Border, Tripod Cabriole Base, France, c.1890, 30 x 34 In.	1035.00
Table, Polished Aluminum, Free-Form Base, Round Glass Top, 26 x 19 In.	496.00
Table, Potter, Mortise & Tenon Base, Box Stretcher, c.1920, 33 x 60 In..................................	1107.00
Table, Pottier & Stymus, Renaissance Revival, Burl Walnut, Ebonized, Incised, Marble, 30 x 57 In..	2689.00
Table, Pottier & Stymus, Renaissance Revival, Marquetry, Ebonized, Bronze, Stretcher, 31 x 49 In.	4183.00

Furniture, Table, Mahogany, Carved, Marble Top, Blocked Trestle, c.1810, 46 x 22 In.
$2390.00

Neal Auction Co.

Furniture, Table, Mixing, Empire, Mahogany, Faux Marble Slate Top, Carved Legs, 28 x 39 x 21 In.
$345.00

Cottone Auctions

Furniture, Table, Mixing, Neoclassical, Mahogany, Frieze Drawer, Door, Bracket Feet, 1800s, 35 x 36 x 19 In.
$3075.00

Neal Auction Co.

Furniture, Table, Money, Red Lacquer, Carved, Drawers, Chinese, Early 1800s, 34 x 31 In.
$1230.00

New Orleans Auction Galleries, Inc.

F

Furniture, Table, Oak, Rectangular Top, Horn Covered Standard, Tripod Base, 1800s, 29 x 21 In.
$1159.00

Leslie Hindman Auctioneers

Furniture, Table, Papier-Mache, Bejeweled, Eagle Supports, Multicolor, France, c.1910, 29 x 33 In.
$2390.00

Neal Auction Co.

Furniture, Table, Pesce, Sansone, Polyurethane, Poured, Melted, Cast, 1980, 28 x 55 x 71 In.
$37500.00

Los Angeles Modern Auctions

Table, Provincial Directoire, Walnut, Demilune, Flip Top, 5 Legs, Casters, 29 x 50 In.	1169.00
Table, Provincial, Fruitwood, 2 Drawers, France, 1800s, 31 x 64 In.	1320.00
Table, Provincial, Louis XV, Parquetry, Cherry, Tric Trac, Leather Insert, 1700s, 29 x 29 In.	1125.00
Table, Provincial, Pine, Frieze Fitted, 2 End Drawers, c.1850, 30 x 72 In.	522.00
Table, Pub, Mahogany Top, Cast Iron Trestle Base, England, c.1890, 31 x 18 In.	230.00
Table, Pub, Victorian, Cast Iron, Round Wood Top, 3 Legs, Undertier, c.1900, 30 x 24 In.	207.00
Table, Queen Anne Style, Mahogany, Tripod, Tilt Top, Baluster, Splayed Legs, c.1850, 29 In.	430.00
Table, Queen Anne Style, Pine, Maple, Brass Handles, Pa., 29 ½ x 57 In.	1170.00
Table, Queen Anne Style, Scalloped Apron, Chinoiserie, Red Japanned, Cabriole Legs, 30 x 36 In.	2574.00
Table, Queen Anne Style, Tilt Top, Mahogany, 3 Legs, c.1875, 28 x 31 In.	672.00
Table, Queen Anne Style, Walnut, Round Top, Drawer, Cabriole Legs, Pad Feet, 1900s, 29 x 24 In.	259.00
Table, Queen Anne, Birch, Octagonal Top, Turned Legs, 1700s, 26 x 29 In.	2400.00
Table, Queen Anne, Mahogany, Tilt Top, Oval, Birdcage Stem, c.1760, 29 x 23 In.	1300.00
Table, Queen Anne, Maple, 4 Molded Drawers, Cabriole Legs, Pa., 29 x 33 In.	12870.00
Table, Queen Anne, Maple, New England, c.1770, 26 ½ x 33 In.	3318.00
Table, Queen Anne, Maple, Oval Top, Stretcher Base, 1700s, 25 x 29 In.	1180.00
Table, Queen Anne, Maple, Shaped Apron, New England, c.1700, 26 x 32 In.	1422.00
Table, Queen Anne, Walnut, 2-Board Top, Dovetailed, Turned Legs, c.1700, 39 x 34 In.	25300.00
Table, Queen Anne, Walnut, Crossbanded Top, Drawer, Tapered Legs, 28 x 31 In.	819.00
Table, R. Lauren, Alligator Tray Top, Brass Base, 30 ½ x 29 In.	868.00
Table, Rattan, Painted, Medial Shelf, Splayed Legs, 36 x 20 In.	288.00
Table, Refectory, Baroque, Oak, Plank Top, Spiral Twist Legs, H-Stretcher, 1900s, 30 x 87 In.	388.00
Table, Refectory, Jacobean, Walnut, Oak, c.1790, 31 x 96 In.	2370.00
Table, Refectory, Provincial, Fruitwood, Tapered Round Legs, H-Stretcher, 30 x 26 In.	2706.00
Table, Refectory, Renaissance Style, Walnut, 3 Carved Apron Drawers, Iron Stretcher, 32 x 77 In.	1195.00
Table, Refectory, Walnut, Chip Carved Apron, Trestle Base, c.1890, 32 x 114 In.	2133.00
Table, Refectory, Walnut, Palmetto Carved Edge, Shaped Supports, Spain, c.1910, 36 x 81 In.	2952.00
Table, Regency Style, Burl, Ebonized Inlays, Oval Top, Column Legs, Urn Finial, 29 x 48 In.	1024.00
Table, Regency Style, Ebonized, Drawer, Low Shelf, c.1950, 28 x 21 In.	123.00
Table, Regency Style, Mahogany, Pedestal, Round Top, Saber Legs, 44 x 31 In.	239.00
Table, Regency Style, Mahogany, Splayed Pedestal Base, 29 x 62 In.	625.00
Table, Regency Style, Mahogany, Tilt Top, Oval, Banded, Splayed Reeded Legs, 29 x 67 In.	1968.00
Table, Regency Style, Mahogany, Triple Pedestal, Saber Legs, Leaves, 29 x 95 In.	388.00
Table, Regency Style, Maple, Round Top, Crossbanded, Column, Quatrefoil Base, 30 x 30 In.	275.00
Table, Regency Style, Oblong, Baluster Double Pedestal, Saber Tripod Base, 1900s, 64 x 42 In.	269.00
Table, Regency Style, Rosewood, String Inlay, Scroll Brackets, Trestle Base, 28 x 49 In.	4270.00
Table, Regency Style, Walnut, Drop Leaf, Pedestal, 4 Saber Legs, 1900s, 28 x 35 In.	329.00
Table, Regency, Calamander Wood, Inlays, 3 Drawers, Arch Handle, Tapered Legs, Shelf, 44 x 22 In.	3830.00
Table, Regency, Mahogany, Inlay, 2 Demilune Leaves, 2 Drawers, Square Legs, 30 x 39 In.	948.00
Table, Regency, Mahogany, Pembroke, 2 Demilune Leaves, 2 Drawers, Square Legs, 1800s, 28 In.	385.00
Table, Regency, Mahogany, Rectangular, D-Shape Drop Leaves, Trestle Base, 29 x 36 In.	1416.00
Table, Regency, Mahogany, Rectangular, Round Corners, 4-Footed, c.1815, 29 x 54 In.	999.00
Table, Regency, Mahogany, Tilt Top, 8-Sided, Inlay, Pedestal, Tripod Feet, c.1880, 33 x 21 In.	300.00
Table, Regency, Mahogany, Tilt Top, Pedestal, Rectangular, Round Corners, 1800s, 27 x 22 In.	144.00
Table, Regency, Rosewood, Banded, Drop Leaves, Drawers, 29 x 61 In.	531.00
Table, Regency, Rosewood, Round Top, Gilt Tooled Leather, 3 Part Base, c.1825, 30 x 50 In.	6150.00
Table, Renaissance Revival Style, Walnut, Burl Walnut, Marble Inset, Round, c.1870, 30 x 23 In.	1035.00
Table, Renaissance Revival, Burl Inlay, Ebonized, Oval Top, Hoof Feet, c.1870, 30 x 22 In.	717.00
Table, Renaissance Revival, Mahogany, Flower, Rope Twist Carved, Column, c.1890, 11 Leaves	3680.00
Table, Renaissance Revival, Oak Parquet, Top Draw Leaf, 30 x 51 In.	397.00
Table, Renaissance Revival, Oak, Draw Leaf, Splayed, Carved Supports, Iron Stretcher, 30 x 67 In.	488.00
Table, Renaissance Revival, Rosewood, Ebonized, Gilt, Scene, Fluted Legs, Paw Feet, c.1865, 30 x 44 In.	3444.00
Table, Renaissance Revival, Rosewood, Gilt, Inlay, Finial, Scroll Feet, c.1865, 30 x 45 In.	3444.00
Table, Renaissance Revival, Rosewood, Gilt, Marble Top, Wolf's Head, c.1865, 29 x 38 In.	3444.00
Table, Renaissance Revival, Rosewood, Marble Top, Leaves, Octagonal Pedestal, c.1865, 30 x 39 In.	1722.00
Table, Renaissance Style, Elm, Frieze Drawers, Ring-Turned Legs, Box Stretcher, 33 x 65 In.	1220.00
Table, Renaissance Style, Oak, Coffee, Round, Carved, Urn Shape Legs, 19 x 35 x 35 In.	270.00
Table, Renaissance Style, Oak, Parquet Top, Scrolled Iron Stretcher, Trestle Base, 30 x 71 x 39 In.	660.00
Table, Renaissance Style, Walnut, Square Column Legs, Low Stretcher, 30 x 79 In.	610.00
Table, Rent, Mahogany, 4 Drawers, 4 Faux Drawers, 8-Sided Pedestal, c.1825, 29 x 41 ⅝ In. ..*illus*	2151.00
Table, Rent, Regency, Mahogany, Leather, Round, 4 Frieze Drawers, Splayed Legs, 1800s, 21 x 27 In.	2510.00
Table, Richard Schultz, White Aluminum Frame, Steel Top, Knoll, 1982, 28 x 16 In., Pair	600.00
Table, Robsjohn-Gibbings, Lacquered, Mahogany Drawer, Shelf, Widdicomb, 18 x 26 In., Pair	960.00
Table, Robsjohn-Gibbings, Maple, 3 Tiers, 2 Drawers, Rectangular, 24 x 28 In.	889.00
Table, Robsjohn-Gibbings, Walnut, Drawer, Shelf, Widdicomb, 27 x 23 In.	1195.00
Table, Robsjohn-Gibbings, Walnut, Round, Tapered Legs, Label, Widdecomb, 50 x 26 In.	600.00
Table, Rococo Revival, Rosewood, Marble Top, Gadroon Frame, Drawer, Door, c.1875, 30 x 19 In.	676.00

Table, Rococo Revival, Rosewood, Veneers, New York, c.1860, 28 ½ x 30 In.	3318.00
Table, Rococo Revival, Walnut, Marble Top, Oval, Carved Legs & Support, 30 x 24 In.	184.00
Table, Rococo Style, Gilt Wood, Serpentine Edge, Carved Legs, X-Stretcher, 33 x 80 In.	2510.00
Table, Rococo Style, Gilt, Marble Top, Ornate, Carved Apron & Stretcher, c.1975, 36 x 67 In.	750.00
Table, Rococo Style, Sienna Marble Top, Applied Gilt Mask, Scrolls, Carved, 1900s, 34 x 45 In.	978.00
Table, Rococo, Cast Iron, Marble Top, Lyre Supports, Scroll Stretcher, c.1850, 29 x 48 In.	598.00
Table, Rococo, Gilt, Pietra Dura Top, Marble, Flowers, Carved Tripod Base, 30 In.	2065.00
Table, Rococo, Mahogany, Tilt Top, Round, Carved Edge, Fluted Baluster, Tripod Legs, 27 x 26 In.	1778.00
Table, Rococo, Rosewood, Marble Top, Beaded Skirt, Scrolls, Stretcher Shelf, c.1850, 29 x 35 In.	366.00
Table, Rococo, Rosewood, Marble Top, Carved Flowers, Scrolls, Pendants, c.1850, 30 x 36 In.	776.00
Table, Rococo, Rosewood, Marble Top, Stretchers, Beaded, Fretwork, Finial, c.1850, 30 x 47 In.	3444.00
Table, Rococo, Rosewood, Serpentine Marble Top, Pierced Leaf Apron, Stretcher, c.1850, 30 x 46 In.	3660.00
Table, Rococo, Rosewood, White Marble Top, Carved Flowers, Masques, Scrolls, c.1850, 31 x 45 In.	4302.00
Table, Rococo, Walnut, Marble Top, Tortoise Shape, Flowers, C-Scroll, Basket Finial, c.1850, 29 x 52 In.	1230.00
Table, Roger Sprunger, Bronze Base, Round Glass Top, Dunbar, 1970s, 29 x 36 In.	1116.00
Table, Rosewood, 2 Tiers, Red Marble, Pierced, Foo Dog, Chinese, 1800s, 31 x 22 In. ......*illus*	2015.00
Table, Rosewood, Boxwood, Ormolu Gallery, Drawer, Medial Shelf, New York, 1900s, 28 x 30 In.	563.00
Table, Rosewood, Brass Inlays, 2 Drawers, Fitted Interior, Harp Stem, c.1820, 31 x 25 In.	885.00
Table, Rosewood, Marble Inset, Shaped Apron, Stretcher Shelf, Chinese, 1890, 31 x 20 In.	1968.00
Table, Rosewood, Openwork Apron, Scrolls, Rectangular, Chinese, 1800s, 23 x 24 In.	711.00
Table, Rosewood, Rectangular, Flower Carved Apron, Scrolled Toes, Chinese, 13 x 36 ½ In.	276.00
Table, Rosewood, Satinwood Band, 2 Leaves, Italy, c.1950, 30 x 109 In.	615.00
Table, Round Marble Top, Openwork Apron, Gourd & Vine Design, Dragon, Chinese, 1800s, 26 In.	735.00
Table, Round Onyx Top, Brass Gallery, Pedestal Base, Paint, c.1910, 30 ½ x 16 In.	472.00
Table, Round Top, Scalloped Frieze, Shaped Legs, Round Stretcher Base, Turquoise Finish, 35 In.	553.00
Table, Round, Gilt, Porcelain Round Top, Beaded Rim, Incurved Legs, Arched Stretcher, 27 x 20 In.	3125.00
Table, Round, Glass Top, Round, 3 Chrome Downswept Legs, c.1960, 27 x 27 In., Pair	923.00
Table, Round, Nickel Plated Brass Frame, Parchment, 2 Tiers, c.1935, 28 x 26 ½ In.	3411.00
Table, S. Kuramata, Steel, Broken Laminated Glass, Sally, Memphis, 1987, 30 x 21 In. ...*illus*	2813.00
Table, Sawbuck, Cherry, Oak, c.1920, 29 x 71 In.	560.00
Table, Sawbuck, Pine, 2-Board Top, Brown Paint, 29 x 42 In.	588.00
Table, Sawbuck, Pine, 3-Board Top, Trestle Base, 1700s, 29 x 71 In.	320.00
Table, Serving, Federal, Mahogany, 3 Drawers, Stretcher Shelf, Ball Feet, c.1830, 35 x 34 In. ....*illus*	1076.00
Table, Serving, George III Style, Mahogany, Carved, Serpentine Reeded Apron, 1900s, 35 x 84 In.	940.00
Table, Serving, Georgian, Mahogany, Bowfront, 2 Frieze Drawers, Spade Feet, c.1830, 33 x 61 In.	6573.00
Table, Serving, Gothic Revival, Walnut, Drawer, Fluted Legs, Shelf, Turnip Feet, 1800s, 29 x 36 In.	1434.00
Table, Serving, Hepplewhite, Mahogany, Bowfront, Drawer, Arched Apron, 29 x 37 In.	531.00
Table, Serving, Mahogany, Inset Marble Top, Fitted Interior, c.1850, 29 x 19 In.	984.00
Table, Serving, William IV, Mahogany, Shaped Backsplash, Stretcher Shelf, c.1840, 37 x 53 In.	1554.00
Table, Sewing, Biedermeier, Recessed Top, Frieze Drawer, Stretchers, 28 x 19 In.	295.00
Table, Sewing, Biedermeier, Walnut, Canted Top, Compartments, Hoof Feet, c.1835, 29 x 22 In.	399.00
Table, Sewing, Black Lacquer, Gilt, Figural Reserves, Leaf Borders, Baluster Supports, 29 x 26 In.	500.00
Table, Sewing, Cherry, 2 Scratch Beaded Drawers, Vase & Ring Legs, Scrolling, c.1830, 28 x 20 In.	830.00
Table, Sewing, Cherry, Mahogany, Drawer, Drop Leaf, c.1830, 29 x 20 In.	215.00
Table, Sewing, Chinoiserie, Hinged Top, Turned Trestle Supports, Stretcher, 1800s, 26 x 15 In.	366.00
Table, Sewing, Curly Maple, 2 Drawers, Tapered Turned Legs, 28 x 20 In.	413.00
Table, Sewing, Drop Leaf, Birch, 2 Drawers, New England, c.1830, 30 x 17 In.	91.00
Table, Sewing, Drop Leaf, Mahogany, Drawer, c.1835, 28 x 18 In.	210.00
Table, Sewing, Drop Leaf, Sheraton, Turned & Rope Spiral Legs, Drawers, Reeded Edge, 33 x 17 In.	382.00
Table, Sewing, Drop Leaf, Tiger Maple, 3 Drawers, Inkwell, Shoe Feet, c.1830, 30 x 18 In.	1265.00
Table, Sewing, Drop Leaf, Walnut, 2 Drawers, Spindle Shape Legs, 1800s, 29 x 18 In.	236.00
Table, Sewing, Empire, Mahogany, Drop Leaf, 3 Drawers, c.1850, 29 x 20 In.	546.00
Table, Sewing, Empire, Mahogany, Gilt Figures Band, Bowl, Drawer, Arched Base, 22 x 16 In.	439.00
Table, Sewing, Empire, Mahogany, Octagonal Lift Top, Lyre Shape Supports, c.1830, 31 x 21 In.	460.00
Table, Sewing, Federal Style, Mahogany, Square Top, 2 Drawer, Reeded Legs, 1936, 29 x 20 In.	711.00
Table, Sewing, Federal, Cherry, 2 Drawers, Turned Legs, Arrow Feet, 29 x 19 x 18 In.	509.00
Table, Sewing, Federal, Mahogany, 2 Drawers, Rounded Edge, Skirt, Square Legs, 29 x 19 In.	830.00
Table, Sewing, Federal, Mahogany, Birch, 2 Drawers, Spiral Turned Legs, c.1810, 29 x 18 In.	900.00
Table, Sewing, Federal, Mahogany, Carved, 2 Drawers, Writing Surface, c.1815, 30 x 19 In. .*illus*	2318.00
Table, Sewing, Federal, Mahogany, Drawer, Lion's Head Handles, Bag Slide, 29 x 22 In.	1955.00
Table, Sewing, Federal, Mahogany, Inlaid, Octagonal, Bag Drawer, Reeded Legs, c.1810-15, 29 x 19 In.	1778.00
Table, Sewing, Federal, Mahogany, Lift Top, Carved Paw Feet, 2 Drawers, c.1820, 24 x 16 In.	863.00
Table, Sewing, Federal, Mahogany, Lift Top, Slide Out Basket, Pedestal, Tripod, c.1825, 29 x 20 In.	633.00
Table, Sewing, Federal, Mahogany, Turret Corners, 2 Drawers, Splayed Legs, 31 x 22 In.	633.00
Table, Sewing, Federal, Reeded Top, 3 Drawers, Tapered Round Legs, c.1815, 29 x 26 In.	1554.00
Table, Sewing, Federal, Tiger Maple, Square Top, Drawer, Tapered Legs, 1800s, 27 In.	300.00
Table, Sewing, G. Stickley, Drop Leaf, 2 Drawers, Red Decal, 28 x 18 ¾ In.	1984.00

Furniture, Table, S. Kuramata, Steel, Broken Laminated Glass, Sally, Memphis, 1987, 30 x 21 In.
$2813.00

Los Angeles Modern Auctions

Furniture, Table, Serving, Federal, Mahogany, 3 Drawers, Stretcher Shelf, Ball Feet, c.1830, 35 x 34 In.
$1076.00

Neal Auction Co.

Furniture, Table, Sewing, Federal, Mahogany, Carved, 2 Drawers, Writing Surface, c.1815, 30 x 19 In.
$2318.00

Neal Auction Co.

TIP
Watch out for sideboards or sofas that have been altered to a smaller, more easily sold size.

Table, Sewing, G. Stickley, Drop Leaf, 3 Drawers, Iron Pulls, Red Decal, 18 x 16 In.	3000.00
Table, Sewing, George III, Rosewood, 2 Drawers, Rectangular, Conforming Apron, 28 x 16 In.	2596.00
Table, Sewing, Gothic Revival, Mahogany, Beaded, Drawer, Arched Legs, c.1830, 30 x 25 In.	2271.00
Table, Sewing, Hepplewhite, Birch, Pine, Breadboard Top, Hinged Leaf, 1800s, 42 x 27 In.	646.00
Table, Sewing, Hepplewhite, Mahogany, Reeded Legs, H-Stretcher, Apron, Bag, c.1800, 29 x 32 In.	147.00
Table, Sewing, Hepplewhite, Walnut, Drawer, Bellflower Inlay, Square Legs, 28 x 22 In.	1140.00
Table, Sewing, Iron, Patinated, Brass Top, Rivets, 6 Drawers, Stretchers, 30 x 74 In.	2988.00
Table, Sewing, Mahogany, 2 Convex Drawers, Turned Legs, 31 x 18 In.	120.00
Table, Sewing, Mahogany, 2 Drawers, Feather Carved, Spiral Turned Legs, c.1820, 28 x 23 In.	235.00
Table, Sewing, Mahogany, 3 Drawers, Pilasters, Carved Standard, Paw Feet, Base, c.1885, 30 x 19 In.	338.00
Table, Sewing, Mahogany, Adams Style, Inset Leather Surface, Leaf Band, Drawer, Slide, 28 x 20 In.	1845.00
Table, Sewing, Mahogany, Banded Top, Acanthus Pedestal, Hairy Paw Feet, c.1835, 30 x 24 In.	461.00
Table, Sewing, Mahogany, Canted Corners, 2 Drawers, Baluster Stem, Paw Feet, 1800s, 33 x 23 In.	896.00
Table, Sewing, Mahogany, Carved, Drawers, Acanthus Vase Shape Pedestal, Paw Feet, 30 x 21 In.	1195.00
Table, Sewing, Mahogany, Carved, Foldover Bowfront Top, Drawer, Urn Pedestal, 34 x 23 In.	2390.00
Table, Sewing, Mahogany, Drawer, Middle Shelf, Turned Legs, c.1820, 29 x 18 In.	863.00
Table, Sewing, Mahogany, Drop Leaf, Drawers, Easel, Writing Surface, c.1835, 30 x 20 In.	276.00
Table, Sewing, Mahogany, Drop Leaf, Inlay, 2 Drawers, c.1820, 30 x 17 In.	1098.00
Table, Sewing, Mahogany, Frieze Drawers, Acanthus Carved Legs, c.1810, 30 x 21 In.	461.00
Table, Sewing, Mahogany, Hinged Lid, Rosewood Drawers, Work Bag, Curved Base, 29 x 28 In.	738.00
Table, Sewing, Mahogany, Mixed Wood, Drop Leaf, 2 Drawers, c.1830, 28 x 18 In.	575.00
Table, Sewing, Mahogany, Tiger Maple, Drop Leaf, Drawers, Work Bag, c.1810, 29 x 18 In.	1315.00
Table, Sewing, Maple, Ogee Frieze Drawer, Turned Legs, Peg Feet, 1800s, 29 x 26 In.	1180.00
Table, Sewing, Neoclassical, Mahogany, Baize Lined, New York, Early 1800s, 32 x 23 x 23 In. *...illus*	3466.00
Table, Sewing, Neoclassical, Mahogany, Bolection Front Drawers, Column Base, c.1820, 29 x 22 In.	180.00
Table, Sewing, Neoclassical, Mahogany, Turned Corners, Drawers, Brass Plaque, c.1815, 31 x 22 In.	1700.00
Table, Sewing, Oak, Rectangular Top, Frieze Drawer, Tapered Square Legs, 1800s, 29 x 25 In.	590.00
Table, Sewing, Pine Top, Walnut, 2 Asymmetrical Drawers, Molded Apron, 1740, 28 x 51 In.	822.00
Table, Sewing, Pine, Rectangular, 2-Board Top, Dovetailed Drawer, Square Legs, 1800s, 27 x 46 In.	362.00
Table, Sewing, Pine, Red Paint, Scrubbed Top, Rectangular, Square Legs, 1800s, 25 x 34 In.	182.00
Table, Sewing, Pine, Scrubbed Single-Board Top, Drawer, Paint, c.1850, 30 x 43 In.	844.00
Table, Sewing, Pine, Scrubbed Top, Drawer, Tapered Legs, Gray Paint, 30 x 43 In.	705.00
Table, Sewing, Poplar, Drawer, Tapered Legs, Lambs Tongue Corners, 29 x 26 In.	863.00
Table, Sewing, Poplar, Mixed Wood, Drawer, Tapered Legs, Paint, c.1820, 30 x 27 In.	863.00
Table, Sewing, Queen Anne, Cherry, Pine, Drawer, Turned Legs, Duck Feet, 27 x 45 In.	940.00
Table, Sewing, Queen Anne, Pine, Drawer, Turned Legs, Scrubbed Top, 29 x 48 In.	1687.00
Table, Sewing, R. Solberg, Teak, Leather, Round, Hinged Top, Denmark, c.1965, 23 ½ x 17 In.	450.00
Table, Sewing, Regency, Chinoiserie Lacquer, Hinged, Gilt Scene, Mirror Interior, Pedestal, 31 x 25 In.	1521.00
Table, Sewing, Regency, Mahogany, Hinged Drop Leaves, Drawers, Ebony, c.1815, 27 x 18 In.	345.00
Table, Sewing, Regency, Mahogany, Hinged, Fitted Interior, Curved Supports, c.1820, 30 x 22 In.	625.00
Table, Sewing, Regency, Mixed Wood, Banded, Hinged, Tapered Legs, c.1825, 27 x 22 In.	553.00
Table, Sewing, Regency, Rosewood, Folding, Swivel Top, C-Scroll Support, Tripod Base, 31 x 21 In.	644.00
Table, Sewing, Regency, Rosewood, Marquetry, Trestle Supports, Stretcher, c.1820, 28 x 28 In.	9375.00
Table, Sewing, Regency, Rosewood, Rectangular, Brass Inlay, Trestle Base, c.1815, 27 x 18 In.	646.00
Table, Sewing, Regency, Rosewood, Rounded Corners, 2 Drawers, U-Shape Support, 30 x 17 In.	1342.00
Table, Sewing, Regency, Satinwood, Mahogany, Round, Silk Bag, X-Stretcher, 1800s, 30 x 19 In.	588.00
Table, Sewing, Renaissance Revival, Black Walnut, Mixed Wood, Drawer, c.1885, 24 x 20 In.	1035.00
Table, Sewing, Rococo Style, Lacca Povera, Painted, Garden, Shaped Apron, Hoof Feet, 28 x 26 In.	1625.00
Table, Sewing, Rococo, Banded Walnut, Shaped Top, Pieced Shell Carved Frieze, 29 x 39 In.	1875.00
Table, Sewing, Rococo, Rosewood, Carved, Drawer, Pullout Compartment, Stretchers, 33 x 21 In.	837.00
Table, Sewing, Rococo, Rosewood, Lift Top, Serpentine, Beaded Edge, Scroll Legs, c.1850, 30 x 20 In.	4182.00
Table, Sewing, Rococo, Walnut, 2 Drawers, Cabriole Legs, Hoof Feet, Continental, 27 x 38 In.	1125.00
Table, Sewing, Rosewood, Gilt, Slide, 2 Drawers, Reeded Basket, Scroll Supports, c.1825, 29 x 21 In.	7170.00
Table, Sewing, Sawbuck, Pine, Breadboard Ends, Red Paint, 3 Supports, c.1820, 29 x 34 In.	3819.00
Table, Sewing, Shaker, Birch, Pine, Upper, Lower Drawers, Extended Surface, c.1850, 38 x 32 In.	1755.00
Table, Sewing, Shaker, Butternut, Cherry, Dovetailed, Hancock, c.1840, 25 x 19 ½ In. *....illus*	4388.00
Table, Sewing, Sheraton, Cherry, Mahogany, 2 Drawers, Pa., c.1830, 29 x 18 In.	316.00
Table, Sewing, Sheraton, Mahogany, 2 Drawers, Cock-Beaded, Silk Bag, c.1890, 29 x 22 In.	4720.00
Table, Sewing, Sheraton, Mahogany, 2 Drawers, Reeded & Turned Legs, Ball Feet, 29 x 22 In.	1062.00
Table, Sewing, Sheraton, Mahogany, Burl, Rosette Corners, Reeded Legs, c.1820, 27 x 20 x 16 In.	1582.00
Table, Sewing, Sheraton, Mahogany, Drop Leaf, 2 Drawers, Reeded Legs, Wood Pulls, 28 x 20 In.	489.00
Table, Sewing, Sheraton, Mahogany, Hinged Lid, Demilune Wells, Drawers, c.1840, 29 x 26 In. *. illus*	354.00
Table, Sewing, Sheraton, Mahogany, 3 Drawers, Turned Legs, New Eng., c.1810, 30 x 21 In.	708.00
Table, Sewing, Sheraton, Mahogany, Reeded Edge, Cock-Beaded, c.1820, 29 x 18 x 16 In.	1150.00
Table, Sewing, Sheraton, Tiger Maple, Pine, 2 Drawers, Turned Legs, Ball Feet, c.1825-30, 28 x 25 In.	660.00
Table, Sewing, Smoke Design, Drawer, Rectangular, Square Legs, Brass Pulls, c.1805, 29 x 20 In.	652.00
Table, Sewing, Softwood, Federal, Drawer, Turned Legs, 28 x 18 x 17 In.	283.00

Table, Sewing, Square, 2 Drawers, Pedestal, 4-Part Paw Support, American, 1800s, 30 x 23 In.	354.00
Table, Sewing, Victorian, Rosewood, Leather Inset Slide, c.1840, 29 x 29 In.	2000.00
Table, Sewing, Walnut, 2 Shaped Drawers, Square Overhang Top, Square Legs, 1800s, 28 x 20 In.	148.00
Table, Sewing, Walnut, Scrubbed Top, Drawer, Turned Legs, Painted, 30 x 60 In.	499.00
Table, Sewing, Wicker, Pine, Plank Top, Arched Apron, Shelf, 1900s, 30 x 42 In.	250.00
Table, Sewing, Yellow Pine, Poplar, Scrubbed Top, Drawer, Tapered Legs, 28 x 41 In.	219.00
Table, Shaped Marble Top & Backsplash, Drawer, Carved Supports, Shelf, 36 x 21 In.	316.00
Table, Sheraton, Cherry, 3 Sections, Turned & Reeded Legs, Brass Casters, c.1810, 46 x 131 In. *.illus*	2651.00
Table, Sheraton, Cherry, Cutout Corners, Drawer, Turned Splayed Legs, c.1830, 27 x 17 In.	260.00
Table, Sheraton, Cherry, Drawer, Turned Legs, c.1830, 28 x 19 In.	280.00
Table, Sheraton, Cherry, Hinged Demilune Leaves, Turned Legs, c.1850, 28 x 21 In.	127.00
Table, Sheraton, Cherry, Overhanging Top, Drawer, Turned Legs, c.1825, 30 x 22 x 17 In.	369.00
Table, Sheraton, Mahogany, 3 Drawers, Turned Legs, Mass., 33 x 31 In.	1422.00
Table, Sheraton, Mahogany, Hinged Drop Leaves, Rectangular, Spiral Twist Legs, c.1830, 29 x 62 In.	472.00
Table, Sheraton, Mahogany, Tilt Top, Tripod Base, Scroll Reeded Legs, Column, c.1835, 29 x 30 In.	206.00
Table, Sheraton, Maple, Drawer, Turned Legs, c.1800, 29 x 20 In.	96.00
Table, Sheraton, Maple, Mixed Wood, Drawer, Turned Legs, 1800s, 28 x 21 In.	649.00
Table, Sheraton, Mixed Wood, 2 Drawers, Faux Front Turned Legs, New England, c.1820	1150.00
Table, Sheraton, Scroll Backsplash, Painted Berries, Leaves, Mustard, New Eng., c.1810, 34 x 29 In.	920.00
Table, Shrine, Pine, Carved Throne, 3 Drawers, Carved Apron, Square Legs, 44 x 33 In.	676.00
Table, Side, Art Deco Style, Rosewood, Round, Ivory Inset, 6 Double Supports, 20 x 32 In., Pair	1830.00
Table, Side, Arts & Crafts, Oak, Round, Square Legs, X-Stretcher, Shelf, 1900s, 30 x 26 In.	577.00
Table, Side, Arts & Crafts, Round, Lower Tier With Cross Stretchers, Square Legs, 27 In.	460.00
Table, Side, Bear Shape, Standing On Hind Legs, Holding Tray, Shaped Base, c.1900, 35 In.	2370.00
Table, Side, Blond Wood, Round, Square Feet, William Haines, c.1948, 26 x 24 In.	875.00
Table, Side, Bronze, Standing Female Figure, Square Top, 27 x 14 In.	625.00
Table, Side, Burl, Round, Pierced Gallery & Apron, Pedestal, Ball & Claw Feet, 21 x 29 In.	345.00
Table, Side, Cherry, 2-Board Top, Drawer, Cabriole Legs, 29 x 37 In.	4183.00
Table, Side, Cherry, Spindle Frieze, Circular Shelf, Twist Legs, Outswept Feet, c.1875, 30 x 23 In.	299.00
Table, Side, Chippendale, Mahogany, 2 Drawers, Molded Edge, 28 x 31 In.	708.00
Table, Side, Conant & Ball, Mahogany, 2 Tiers, Galleries, Turned Supports, 27 x 18 In.	98.00
Table, Side, Ebonized, Gilt, Marquetry, Flowers, Birds, Pedestal, Round, Paw Feet, c.1865, 30 In.	2952.00
Table, Side, Edwardian, Iron, Marble Top, Demilune, Flower Stretcher, Toes, c.1905, 30 x 31 In.	276.00
Table, Side, Edwardian, Mahogany, Gilt, Shield Stretchers, Iron Supports, 1900s, 30 x 19 In.	307.00
Table, Side, Elm, 3 Tiers, Openwork Weave, Shelf, 1900s, 31 x 18 In.	219.00
Table, Side, Empire Style, Mahogany, 2 Drawers, Pedestal, Leaves, Paw Feet, 30 x 23 In.	180.00
Table, Side, Empire Style, Mahogany, Marble Top, Drawer, Mirror Back, 1800s, 36 x 51 In.	984.00
Table, Side, Empire, Mahogany, Marble Top, Column Supports, Stretcher, c.1800, 36 x 41 In.	2337.00
Table, Side, Empire, Mahogany, Round Granite Top, Ormolu Column Supports, c.1800, 35 x 18 In.	615.00
Table, Side, Federal Style, Oak, Drop Leaf, Frieze Drawer, Spade Feet, 1800s, 29 x 13 In.	299.00
Table, Side, Federal, Mahogany, Drawer, Cock-Beaded Edge, Tapered Legs, 1800s, 29 x 21 In.	461.00
Table, Side, Federal, Painted, Scrub Top, Straight Apron, c.1805, 30 x 34 In.	652.00
Table, Side, French Provincial, Fruitwood, Arched Aprons, Cabriole Legs, c.1750, 30 x 35 In.	461.00
Table, Side, French Provincial, Fruitwood, Scalloped Frieze, Cabriole Legs, c.1795, 26 x 37 In.	1168.00
Table, Side, Georgian Style, Mahogany, Tray Top, Pierced Loop Gallery, 30 x 24 In.	708.00
Table, Side, Georgian, Walnut, Breakfront Top, Cabriole Legs, Pad Feet, England, 1700s, 29 x 34 In.	858.00
Table, Side, Gilt Metal, Glass, Round, X-Stretcher, Scroll, Leaf Feet, 20 In., Pair	461.00
Table, Side, Gilt Metal, Round Marble Top, 3 Dragonfly Female Supports, Flowers, 29 x 24 In.	708.00
Table, Side, Gothic Revival, Mahogany, Pierced Aprons, Turned Spindles, c.1885, 29 x 22 In.	2706.00
Table, Side, Gothic Revival, Mahogany, Round, Hexagonal Pedestal, Trefoil Feet, c.1835, 28 x 23 In.	2706.00
Table, Side, Hardwood, Carved, Reclining Camel Shape, Octagonal Top, 1900s, 16 x 28 In.	6518.00
Table, Side, Hardwood, Marble Inset Top, Pierced Frieze, Tapered Legs, Chinese, 36 In.	85.00
Table, Side, Hardwood, Mother-Of-Pearl Inlay, Inset Stone Top, Carved Apron, Shelf, 24 In.	744.00
Table, Side, Hepplewhite Style, Satinwood, Door, Banded Square Legs, 33 x 15 In.	207.00
Table, Side, Jacobean Style, Rectangular, Frieze Drawer, Ring-Turned Legs, Ball Feet, 20 x 18 In.	276.00
Table, Side, Louis XV Style, Fruitwood, Marquetry, Pierced Gallery, Drawer, c.1935, 29 x 18 In., Pair	1107.00
Table, Side, Louis XV Style, Mahogany, Rosewood, Marble Top, Drawer, c.1950, 28 x 18 In., Pair	553.00
Table, Side, Louis XV Style, Marble Top, Frieze Drawer, Door, Scrolls, Cabriole Legs, 35 x 15 In.	207.00
Table, Side, Louis XV Style, Shaped Marble Top, Bowed Ends, 2 Drawers, 1900s, 29 x 22 In.	235.00
Table, Side, Louis XV Style, Walnut, Round Inlaid Top, 2 Doors, Late 1800s, 29 x 12 In.	250.00
Table, Side, Louis XVI Style, 2 Tiers, Trefoil Top, Brass Gallery, France, 1900s, 31 x 18 In.	207.00
Table, Side, Louis XVI Style, Bronze, Gilt, Marble Top, Masques, Tapered Legs, Hoof Feet, 22 x 28 In.	488.00
Table, Side, Louis XVI Style, Gilt Metal, Round Gallery Tiers, Fluted Support, 29 In., Pair	549.00
Table, Side, Louis XVI Style, Gilt, Oval Marble Top, Gallery, Round Legs, 19 x 16 In.	352.00
Table, Side, Louis XVI Style, Marble Top, Drawer, Cabriole Legs, France, 1900s, 26 In.	490.00
Table, Side, Louis XVI Style, Square Marble Top, Acanthus Fluted Legs, Shelves, 33 In., Pair	1464.00
Table, Side, Mahogany, 6-Sided & Scalloped Top, Spindle Supports, 3-Footed, 1900s, 27 x 20 In.	525.00

Furniture, Table, Sewing, Neoclassical, Mahogany, Baize Lined, New York, Early 1800s, 32 x 23 x 23 In.
$3466.00

Neal Auction Co.

Furniture, Table, Sewing, Shaker, Butternut, Cherry, Dovetailed, Hancock, c.1840, 25 x 19 ½ In.
$4388.00

Willis Henry Auctions, Inc.

Furniture, Table, Sewing, Sheraton, Mahogany, Hinged Lid, Demilune Wells, Drawers, c.1840, 29 x 26 In.
$354.00

James D. Julia Inc.

Furniture, Table, Sheraton, Cherry, 3 Sections, Turned & Reeded Legs, Brass Casters, c.1810, 46 x 131 In. $2651.00

Garth's Auctions, Inc.

Furniture, Table, Side, Walnut, String & Star Inlay, Frieze Drawer, 29 x 21 x 18 In. $2151.00

Neal Auction Co.

Furniture, Table, Tavern, Pine, Oval, Baluster Turned Legs, Square Stretcher, 1700s, 25 ½ x 32 In. $558.00

Cowan's Auctions

Furniture, Table, Tea, G. Stickley, Partial GS & Co. Paper Label, c.1900, 22 x 22 In. $4650.00

Rago Arts & Auction Center

Table, Side, Mahogany, Brass, Drawer, Saber Legs, Crescent, Stretcher, Russia, 30 x 19 In.	2963.00
Table, Side, Mahogany, Carved, Tray Top, Pierced Apron, Cabriole Legs, 31 x 32 In.	219.00
Table, Side, Mahogany, Drawer, Urn Support, 4 Splayed Legs, 22 In. Diam.	63.00
Table, Side, Mahogany, Gadrooned Edge, Fluted Frieze, Spiral Legs, 1800s, 29 x 35 In.............	2032.00
Table, Side, Mahogany, Marble Top, Kidney Shape, Ormolu, Pierced Gallery, Drawer, 30 x 28 In.	461.00
Table, Side, Mahogany, Round, H-Stretcher, Circular Raised Platform, Hekman, 28 x 20 In....	180.00
Table, Side, Mahogany, Scalloped Gallery Top, X-Stretcher, Square Legs, England, 23 x 24 In.	281.00
Table, Side, Mahogany, Shaped Gallery & Apron, Column Supports, 2 Drawers, 34 x 14 In.	415.00
Table, Side, Mahogany, Square Top, Sword Design Brass Gallery, X-Supports, Drawer, 29 x 26 In.	344.00
Table, Side, Mahogany, Tilt Top, Scroll Border, Urn, Column Standard, Tripod, c.1805, 29 In..	369.00
Table, Side, Marble Top, Molded Edge, Paneled Frieze, Cabriole Legs, 27 x 30 In.	1230.00
Table, Side, Mixed Wood, Demilune, Parquetry, Frieze Drawer, Door, 1900s, 32 x 37 In., Pair..	1016.00
Table, Side, Mixed Wood, Tilt Top, Round, Turned Standard, Tripod Base, 28 x 42 In.	208.00
Table, Side, Moorish Style, Wood, Mother-Of-Pearl, Octagonal, Faux Arabic, 15 x 15 In.........	429.00
Table, Side, Moroccan Style, 8-Sided, 1900s, 16 ½ x 16 In..	375.00
Table, Side, Mother-Of-Pearl Inlay, Tilt Top, Octagonal, Arched Feet, Syria, 26 x 20 In., Pair...	418.00
Table, Side, Mother-Of-Pearl Inlay, Tray Top, Phoenixes, Gardens, Block Legs, 1800s, 18 x 24 In.	178.00
Table, Side, Neoclassical, Fruitwood, Drawer, Drop Leaf, Carved Lines, 27 x 36 In.	413.00
Table, Side, Neoclassical, Kingwood, Parquetry, Round Top, Drawer, Square Legs, c.1800, 23 x 28 In.	1230.00
Table, Side, Neoclassical, Walnut, Curule Supports, Bulbous Stretcher, Runners, 29 x 51 In. ..	738.00
Table, Side, Neoclassical, Walnut, Molded Edge, Fluted Apron, Drawer, 29 x 31 In.	325.00
Table, Side, Oak, Drawer, Carved Apron, Shelf, Tapered Legs, Pad Feet, 29 x 27 In.	296.00
Table, Side, Oak, Frieze Drawer, Feather Ankles, Cabriole Legs, Ireland, 1700s, 28 x 27 In.	1416.00
Table, Side, Oak, Inlaid, Deer, Palm Tree, Turned Column, Carved Base, c.1890, 29 x 26 In. ...	235.00
Table, Side, Oak, Plank Top, Square Legs, Box Stretcher, c.1800, 29 x 36 In.	676.00
Table, Side, Oval, ¾ Gallery, Drawer, Shelf Between Tapered Legs, Continental, 30 x 19 In.	183.00
Table, Side, Pine, Waxed & Stained, Plank Top, Drawer, Square Legs, 1800s, 31 x 48 In..........	353.00
Table, Side, Porcelain Insert, Gallery Top, Birds, Leaves, Scroll Base, Continental, 31 x 39 In..	900.00
Table, Side, Quartersawn Oak, Drawer, Brass Leaves, Reeded Legs, Stretcher, c.1900, 29 x 46 In.	115.00
Table, Side, Regency Style, Gilt, Granite Top, Urn, Fluted Legs, Shaped Feet, 37 x 36 In............	1845.00
Table, Side, Regency, Mahogany, 2 Drawers, Rounded Corners, Reeded Legs, 1900s, 30 x 21 In.	270.00
Table, Side, Regency, Mahogany, Hand Painted, Oval Tray Top, Shaped Apron, 27 x 28 In.	240.00
Table, Side, Regency, Rosewood, Dish Top, Leaves, 2 Shelves, Fluted Column, c.1820, 30 x 20 In.	944.00
Table, Side, Rosewood, Cloud Design Apron, Stretchers, Bun Feet, 1800s, 22 x 16 In.	215.00
Table, Side, Rosewood, Drawer, Scroll Grillwork, Turned Stretcher, Trestle Base, c.1835, 28 x 22 In.	615.00
Table, Side, Rosewood, Square Top, Relief Carved Apron, Reeded Legs, Square Stretchers, 30 x 16 In.	584.00
Table, Side, Round Marble Top, Carved Cherubs, Turned Stretcher, Tripod Legs, 18 x 22 In.....	288.00
Table, Side, Round Top, Inlaid Flower, Shaped Square Support & Base, Paw Feet, 34 In. Diam.	63.00
Table, Side, Round Top, Removable, 4 Legs, Wood Stretcher, Folding, Africa, 17 In.	156.00
Table, Side, Round, Glass Top, Metal Wavy Legs, DeRossi, c.1980, 19 In., Pair......................	2250.00
Table, Side, Round, Leather Top, Shaped Shelf, Block Legs, Charak Modern, c.1965, 28 x 28 In.	3438.00
Table, Side, Shaped Carved Skirt, Round, Carved Legs, X-Stretcher, 28 x 20 In.	207.00
Table, Side, Sheraton, Mahogany, Drawer, Round Corners, Turned Legs, c.1800s, 30 x 21 In...	127.00
Table, Side, Sheraton, Painted Design, 2 Drawers, Brass Rosette Pulls, 27 x 27 In.	403.00
Table, Side, Square, Shelf, Block Legs, c.1948, 25 x 22 In., Pair.................................	1875.00
Table, Side, Teak, Canvas Magazine Sling, Square Legs, c.1960, 18 x 18 In.	125.00
Table, Side, Teak, Curved Top, Slatted Lower Shelf, Round Legs, c.1960, 23 x 30 In., Pair........	469.00
Table, Side, Teak, Rounded Top, Square Legs, Denmark, c.1960 In.	113.00
Table, Side, Tole, 2 Tiers, Round, Scalloped Gallery, Drawer, 4 Legs, Maitland-Smith, 25 x 19 In.	563.00
Table, Side, Victorian, Mahogany, Marble Top, Drawer, Arched Feet, 29 x 32 In.	489.00
Table, Side, Victorian, Twist Legs, Carved & Twist Stretchers, Ball & Claw Feet, 25 x 43 In. ...	460.00
Table, Side, Walnut, String & Star Inlay, Frieze Drawer, 29 x 21 x 18 In. ....*illus*	2151.00
Table, Side, Wood, Indian Bone Inlay, Octagonal, Flower Design, 24 x 26 x 26 In.....................	480.00
Table, Snakewood, Carved Frieze, Scroll, Vines, Bats, Curved Legs, Chinese, 1800s, 14 x 46 In.	8850.00
Table, Sofa, Mahogany, Parcel Gilt, Marble Top, Molded Apron, Shaped Legs, 30 x 20 In.	2337.00
Table, Spanish Colonial, Carved, Drawer, Pinwheels, 1600s, 14 ½ x 20 In.	650.00
Table, Spanish Style, Spiral Turned Legs, Box Stretcher, 1800s, 28 x 19 ½ In.	375.00
Table, Spanish Style, Wrought Iron, Twisted, Painted Top, Scrolled Base, c.1925, 29 x 11 ½ In.	550.00
Table, Stanley J. Friedman, Clone, Eggcup Shape, Metallic Brown, Brueton, 20 x 21 In., Pair .	600.00
Table, Stickley Bros., Crossed Stretcher, 28 ½ x 35 ¾ In.	930.00
Table, Stickley Bros., No. 184, Blind Drawer, Slated Sides, 36 x 24 In.	720.00
Table, Stickley Bros., No. 2516, Round Top, Round Stretcher Shelf, 30 x 30 In........................	1320.00
Table, Stickley Bros., No. 2615, Copper Top, Arched Apron, 18 x 28 In.	2040.00
Table, Stickley Bros., No. 2812, Drawer, Copper Hardware, Slat Sides, Stretcher Shelf, 24 x 22 In.	1440.00
Table, Stickley Bros., No. 2882, Slat Sides, Low Stretcher, Signed Tag, 30 x 18 In.	720.00
Table, Stickley Bros., Reversible, Oval, Tray Top, 29 x 28 x 17 In.	2604.00
Table, Sunderland, Mahogany, Turned Trestle Base, Scroll Feet, Rectangular, 31 x 41 In........	502.00

Table, Syrian, White Metal, Octagonal, Repousse, Rosettes, Scrolling Leaves, 22 x 20 In., Pair	657.00
Table, Tabouret, G. Stickley, Overhung Top, Wide Apron, Paper Label, 20 ½ x 18 In.	1612.00
Table, Tabouret, Limbert, Octagon Top, Splayed Legs, Cutout Details, 15 x 18 ½ In.	390.00
Table, Tabouret, Rosewood, Marble, Pierced Apron, Medial Shelf, Masks, Chinese, 32 x 15 In.	767.00
Table, Tavern, Chippendale, Pine, Maple, Salmon Paint, Rosewood Graining, c.1775, 28 x 28 In.	235.00
Table, Tavern, Chippendale, Walnut, Cut Corner Top, Drawer, Tapered Legs, c.1780, 29 x 40 In.	546.00
Table, Tavern, Chippendale, Walnut, Oval Top, Block Legs, American, c.1780, 27 x 33 In.	489.00
Table, Tavern, Country English, Red Walnut, Drawer, Plank Top, Box Stretcher, c.1880, 30 x 41 In.	720.00
Table, Tavern, Farm, Red Paint, Scrub Top, 2 Drawers, Drop Leaf, Turned Legs, 1800s, 54 x 45 In.	345.00
Table, Tavern, Federal, Pine, Maple, Breadboard Top, Drawer, Square Legs, c.1800, 28 x 35 In.	2015.00
Table, Tavern, Federal, Tiger Maple, Board Top, Drawer, Square Legs, H-Stretcher, c.1890, 27 x 32 In.	748.00
Table, Tavern, Frieze Drawer, Tapered Club Legs, Pad Feet, 27 x 43 In.	2655.00
Table, Tavern, George III, Oak, Gateleg, Oval Top, D-Shape Drop Ends, Turned Legs, 29 x 45 In.	700.00
Table, Tavern, Hepplewhite, Pine, Square Tapered Legs, Breadboard Top, Paint, 37 x 23 In.	499.00
Table, Tavern, Jacobean Style, Vine Carved Apron, 2 Drawers, Turned Legs, Stretchers, 30 x 70 In.	613.00
Table, Tavern, Maple, Pine, Oval Top, Single Board, Turned Stretcher Base, 1700s, 26 x 32 In.	2703.00
Table, Tavern, Maple, Pine, Oval, Beaded Skirt, Stretchers, Vase, Ring-Turned Legs, 1700s, 24 x 34 In.	474.00
Table, Tavern, Moravian, Walnut, Lift Top, Splayed Turned Legs, 29 x 39 ½ In.	2015.00
Table, Tavern, Oak, Pine, Scrubbed Top, Breadboard Ends, Square Stretcher, 25 x 62 In.	1610.00
Table, Tavern, Oval Top, Rectangular Base, Tapered Turned Legs, 26 x 37 In.	590.00
Table, Tavern, Oval Top, Splayed Vase Turned Base, Square Stretcher, American, 25 x 28 In.	590.00
Table, Tavern, Pine, Green Paint, Drawer, Baluster Legs, Rectangular, 1700s, 23 x 26 In.	474.00
Table, Tavern, Pine, Green Paint, Rectangular, Plank Top, Square Apron & Legs, 1900s, 30 x 80 In.	504.00
Table, Tavern, Pine, Maple, Oak, Stretcher Base, Splayed Legs, Grain Painted, c.1800, 19 x 34 In.	575.00
Table, Tavern, Pine, Oval, Baluster Turned Legs, Square Stretcher, 1700s, 25 ½ x 32 In. ......illus	558.00
Table, Tavern, Pine, Overhung Top, Low Stretcher, 1800s, 28 x 47 In.	420.00
Table, Tavern, Queen Anne Style, Curly Maple, Oval Top, Splayed Legs, 27 x 31 In.	295.00
Table, Tavern, Queen Anne Style, Turned Legs, Box Stretcher, 1900s, 25 x 37 In.	529.00
Table, Tavern, Queen Anne, Birch, Pine, Drawer, Ring-Turned Legs, Button Feet, c.1755, 28 x 42 In.	1438.00
Table, Tavern, Queen Anne, Maple, Red Finish, Pine Breadboard Top, Stretcher, Drawer, 25 x 36 In.	881.00
Table, Tavern, Queen Anne, Maple, Shaped Top, Splayed Legs, c.1800, 27 x 30 In.	1100.00
Table, Tavern, Queen Anne, Pine, Hardwood, Turned Legs, Stretcher, 1700s, 32 x 27 In.	1567.00
Table, Tavern, Queen Anne, Pine, Maple, Turned Legs, Box Stretcher, Blue Paint, 26 x 28 In.	1058.00
Table, Tavern, Queen Anne, Walnut, Drawers, Ringed Cabriole Legs, 1700s, 29 x 47 In.	750.00
Table, Tavern, Scrub Top, Painted, Breadboard Ends, Scalloped Apron, c.1790, 27 x 36 In.	3000.00
Table, Tavern, William & Mary, Curly Maple, Drawer, Cleated Ends, 1700s, 27 x 46 In.	345.00
Table, Tavern, William & Mary, Drawer, Black & Gold Paint, Stretcher Base, 28 x 34 In.	1150.00
Table, Tea, Art Nouveau, Walnut, Marquetry, 2 Tiers, Stylized Flowers, Leaves, Gauthier, 30 x 29 In.	1673.00
Table, Tea, Baroque, Mahogany, Bombe, Tray Top, Drawer, Dutch, c.1800, 31 x 34 In.	354.00
Table, Tea, Cherry, Rectangular, Shaped Corners, Beaded Skirt, Splayed Legs, Late 1700s, 26 x 29 In.	1304.00
Table, Tea, Cherry, Round Scalloped Top, Rope Pedestal, Cabriole Feet, 1800s, 27 x 17 In.	152.00
Table, Tea, Chippendale Style, Mahogany, Piecrust Top, Baluster Support, Paw Feet, 31 x 31 In.	207.00
Table, Tea, Chippendale Style, Walnut, Tilt Top, Dish Top, Pedestal, Slipper Feet, 28 In.	413.00
Table, Tea, Chippendale, Mahogany, Chinese, Raised Pierced Galley, Carved, 29 x 34 In.	397.00
Table, Tea, Chippendale, Mahogany, Tilt Top, Snake Feet, Column, Fluting, c.1760, 28 x 30 In.	940.00
Table, Tea, Chippendale, Mahogany, Octagonal, Tripod Base, England, c.1800, 29 x 33 In.	420.00
Table, Tea, Chippendale, Walnut, Dish Top, Birdcage Standard, Tripod Legs, Pa., c.1770, 30 x 34 In.	2607.00
Table, Tea, Chippendale, Walnut, Round Top, Turned Post, Ball & Tripod Base, 29 In.	184.00
Table, Tea, Chippendale, Walnut, Shaped Skirt, Tapered Legs, Oval Corners, c.1775, 29 x 27 x 21 In.	2233.00
Table, Tea, Federal, Tiger Maple, Turned Support, Arched Legs, c.1810, 27 x 23 In.	500.00
Table, Tea, Federal, Walnut, Shaped Skirt, Turned Legs, 1800, 28 x 33 In.	2478.00
Table, Tea, Fruitwood, Round Top, Turned Pedestal Base, 3 Ball Feet, 26 In. Diam.	502.00
Table, Tea, G. Stickley, Partial GS & Co. Paper Label, c.1900, 22 x 22 In. ......illus	4650.00
Table, Tea, George II, Mahogany, Dish Top, Cabriole Legs, Slipper Feet, 28 x 28 In.	1250.00
Table, Tea, George II, Mahogany, Piecrust Top, Cabriole Legs, c.1760, 29 x 37 In.	593.00
Table, Tea, George II, Mahogany, Piecrust Top, Cabriole Tripod Legs, c.1760, 28 ½ x 29 In.	5925.00
Table, Tea, George II, Tray Top, Drawer, c.1760, 28 ¼ x 30 ½ In.	1033.00
Table, Tea, George III, Mahogany, Rectangular, Fold-Out Top, Side Drawer, c.1790, 28 x 28 In.	1528.00
Table, Tea, George III, Mahogany, Round Tilt Top, Turned Support, Tripod Feet, c.1790, 28 x 34 In.	353.00
Table, Tea, George III, Mahogany, Scalloped Rectangular Top, Carved Cabriole Legs, 27 x 27 In.	2015.00
Table, Tea, George III, Mahogany, Tilt Top, Spindled Birdcage, Arched Legs, Ball Feet, 28 x 30 In.	837.00
Table, Tea, Georgian Style, Mahogany, Scalloped Apron, 29 x 35 In.	500.00
Table, Tea, Georgian Style, Square Dish Top, Scalloped Apron, Bow Legs, 29 x 35 In.	500.00
Table, Tea, Mahogany, Dish Top, Turned Pedestal, 3 Arched Legs, Slipper Feet, 1700s, 28 x 22 In.	690.00
Table, Tea, Mahogany, Square Top, Tripod Base, Kittinger, Williamsburg, 25 x 28 In.	150.00
Table, Tea, Mahogany, Tray Top, Inlay, Brass Handles, Hexagonal Tops, 27 x 27 In., Pair	538.00
Table, Tea, Maple, Drop Leaf, Carved, Oval, Cabriole Legs, Pad Feet, 26 x 27 In.	2950.00

Furniture, Table, Teak, 6-Sided, 2 Tiers, Marble Top, Carved, Flowers, Chinese, 48 ¾ x 16 ⅜ In.
$1541.00

Skinner, Inc.

Furniture, Table, Tilt Top, Mahogany, Carved Top, Birdcage Mechanism, Snake Feet, c.1855, 27 ½ In.
$646.00

Cowan's Auctions

Furniture, Table, Tilt Top, Mixed Wood, Inlay, 5-Point Star, Order Of Eastern Star, c.1890, 29 x 21 In.
$264.00

Garth's Auctions, Inc.

Furniture, Table, Tilt Top, Mixed Wood, Inlay, Mariner's Compass, Ivory Hearts, c.1860, 29 x 20 In.
$1778.00

Skinner, Inc.

Furniture, Table, Tilt Top, Regency, Burl Walnut, Crossbanding, Inlay, Pedestal, Casters, 27 x 39 x 52 In.
$1652.00

Ivey-Selkirk Auctioneers

Furniture, Table, Tilt Top, Tea, Chippendale, Mahogany, Piecrust Edge, Carved Legs, Ball & Claw Feet, 1700s, 26 ⅝ x 29 ⅝ In.
$2749.00

Neal Auction Co.

Table, Tea, Maple, Yellow Pine, Oval, Block Turned Legs, Pad Feet, Brackets, c.1750, 27 x 35 In.	1541.00
Table, Tea, Oak, Lift Tray, Carved Side Panel Legs, Stretcher, 1920s, 20 x 26 In.	173.00
Table, Tea, Queen Anne Style, Cherry, Porringer Top, Pad Feet, Eldred Wheeler, 28 x 33 In.	690.00
Table, Tea, Queen Anne Style, Mahogany, Tray Top, Cabriole Legs, Spoon Feet, 1900s, 19 x 34 In.	215.00
Table, Tea, Queen Anne, Cherry, Round Top, Baluster Support, Curved Feet, c.1770, 28 x 35 In.	296.00
Table, Tea, Queen Anne, Cherry, Scalloped Top, Eldred Wheeler, Labeled, 29 x 21 In.	288.00
Table, Tea, Queen Anne, Mahogany, Dish Top, Candle Slides, Henkel-Harris, 27 x 30 In.	300.00
Table, Tea, Queen Anne, Mahogany, Round Dish Top, Tilt, Fluted Support, Slipper Feet, 29 In.	649.00
Table, Tea, Queen Anne, Mahogany, Tray Top, c.1760, 30 x 34 In.	1422.00
Table, Tea, Queen Anne, Mahogany, Urn Standard, c.1760, 27 x 28 In.	948.00
Table, Tea, Queen Anne, Maple, Oval Overhanging Top, Pad Feet, Cutout Apron, 27 x 26 In.	2370.00
Table, Tea, Queen Anne, Maple, Porringer Top, Splayed Legs, New England, 1700s, 25 x 36 In.	5428.00
Table, Tea, Rosewood, Floating Panel, Openwork Apron, Chinese, 1800s, 31 x 20 In.	984.00
Table, Tea, Star Design Parquetry, Round, Tripod Legs, 1800s, 29 x 27 In.	575.00
Table, Tea, Tiger Maple, 3-Board Tilt Top, Vase Turned Pedestal, Slipper Feet, 1700s, 27 x 36 In.	748.00
Table, Tea, Tilt Top, Queen Anne, Walnut, Serpentine Top, Baluster Pedestal, 1700s, 27 x 35 In.	478.00
Table, Tea, Tole Tray Top, Gilt Pierced Gallery, Painted Fruit, Flowers, Tripod Base, Claw Feet, 23 In.	359.00
Table, Teak, 6-Sided, 2 Tiers, Marble Top, Carved, Flowers, Chinese, 48 ¾ x 16 ⅜ In. *illus*	1541.00
Table, Teak, Dux, Sweden, 1960s, 20 ½ x 30 In., Pair	279.00
Table, Teak, Inset Round Marble Top, Pierced Apron, Carved Legs, 20 x 16 In.	122.00
Table, Teak, New World Collection, Baker Furniture, 30 x 34 In.	460.00
Table, Teak, Pierced Apron, Trestle Legs, Carved, Chinese, c.1950, 33 x 85 In.	518.00
Table, Teak, Pierced, Carved, Marble Top, 21 x 22 ½ In.	170.00
Table, Teak, Pierced, Carved, Mother-Of-Pearl Top, 39 x 14 In.	237.00
Table, Telephone, Oak, Square Top, Square Legs, Low Back Chair, American, c.1920, 30 x 16 In.	115.00
Table, Tiger Maple, Drawer, New England, 1800s, 27 x 19 In.	480.00
Table, Tiger Maple, White Pine, Overhung Top, Drawer, c.1850, 30 x 50 In.	460.00
Table, Tile Top, 6 Hispano-Moresque, 14 Black & Orange, California, 18 x 24 In.	112.00
Table, Tilt Top, Chippendale Style, Mahogany, Piecrust Top, Tripod Legs, 1900s, 29 x 31 In.	345.00
Table, Tilt Top, Chippendale, Cherry, Tripod Base, Virginia, c.1790, 29 x 36 In.	1280.00
Table, Tilt Top, Chippendale, Mahogany, Spiral Support, Tripod Base, England, 1700s, 28 x 27 In.	960.00
Table, Tilt Top, Chippendale, Mahogany, Spiral Turned Support, Tripod Base, 1700s, 28 x 32 In.	900.00
Table, Tilt Top, Chippendale, Round, Piecrust, c.1950, 27 ¾ x 28 In.	80.00
Table, Tilt Top, Chippendale, Walnut, Pa., c.1700, 29 x 34 ¾ In.	3000.00
Table, Tilt Top, Edwardian, Mahogany, Rosewood Marquetry Flowers, Shaped Top, Urn, 30 x 23 In.	489.00
Table, Tilt Top, George III Style, Mahogany, Round, Dish Edge, Carved, Tripod Legs, 30 In., Pair	120.00
Table, Tilt Top, George III, Mahogany, Birdcage Support, Fluted Pedestal, Tripod Base, 26 x 24 In.	1287.00
Table, Tilt Top, George III, Mahogany, Round, Baluster Pillar, Tripod Legs, Pad Feet, 1700s, 15 In.	356.00
Table, Tilt Top, Mahogany, Birdcage Support, Piecrust Top, Carved, Tripod Feet, 1900s, 31 x 28 In.	138.00
Table, Tilt Top, Mahogany, Carved Top, Birdcage Mechanism, Snake Feet, c.1855, 27 ½ In. *illus*	646.00
Table, Tilt Top, Mahogany, Inlay, Carved, Tripod Base, Continental, 29 x 24 In.	201.00
Table, Tilt Top, Mahogany, Octagonal Top, String Inlay, Pedestal, 1800s, 26 x 23 In.	288.00
Table, Tilt Top, Mahogany, Reeded Edge, Ring-Turned Standard, Tripod Base, c.1830, 29 x 28 In.	431.00
Table, Tilt Top, Mahogany, Round, Tapered Stem, Triangular Base, 3 Paw Feet, c.1805, 30 x 41 In.	1912.00
Table, Tilt Top, Mahogany, Turned Standard, Tripod Base, c.1850, 28 x 25 In.	1035.00
Table, Tilt Top, Mixed Wood, Inlay, 5-Point Star, Order Of Eastern Star, c.1890, 29 x 21 In. *illus*	264.00
Table, Tilt Top, Mixed Wood, Inlay, Mariner's Compass, Ivory Hearts, c.1860, 29 x 20 In. *illus*	1778.00
Table, Tilt Top, Papier-Mache, Oval, Scalloped, Painted Flowers, Platform Base, c.1880, 27 x 22 In.	345.00
Table, Tilt Top, Papier-Mache, Victorian, Mother-Of-Pearl Inlay, Flowers, 28 x 24 In.	460.00
Table, Tilt Top, Queen Anne, Mahogany, Column Standard, Arched Tripod Base, 1700s, 28 x 35 In.	460.00
Table, Tilt Top, Regency, Burl Walnut, Crossbanding, Inlay, Pedestal, Casters, 27 x 39 x 52 In. *illus*	1652.00
Table, Tilt Top, Regency, Calamander Wood, Column, Egg, Dart Ring, Stepped Base, 30 x 48 In.	17550.00
Table, Tilt Top, Regency, Rosewood, Octagonal, Fluted Column, 3 Curled Feet, 29 x 33 In.	984.00
Table, Tilt Top, Regency, Rosewood, Round, Lotus & Ribbed Base, 28 x 48 In.	3198.00
Table, Tilt Top, Regency, Rosewood, Round, Lotus Carved Support, Rope Collar, Paw Feet, 29 x 50 In.	2829.00
Table, Tilt Top, Round, Teak, Leaves, Vines, Scalloped Pierced Apron, Serpents, 1800s, 31 In.	413.00
Table, Tilt Top, Stickley Bros., Round, Cane Triangular Support, 30 x 29 In.	720.00
Table, Tilt Top, Tea, Chippendale, Mahogany, Birdcage, Ring-Turned Post, c.1795, 29 x 30 In.	1541.00
Table, Tilt Top, Tea, Chippendale, Mahogany, Piecrust Edge, c.1795, 26 ⅝ x 29 ⅝ In. *illus*	2749.00
Table, Tilt Top, Tea, Chippendale, Maple, Reeded, Bulbous Shaft, Ball & Claw Feet, 29 x 34 In.	499.00
Table, Tilt Top, Tea, Federal, Mahogany, American Eagle, Inlaid, 28 x 16 In.	10000.00
Table, Tilt Top, Tea, George III, Cherry, Ring, Turned Pedestal, Tripod, Pad Feet, 28 x 29 In.	389.00
Table, Tilt Top, Tea, Georgian Style, Pierced Shell Edge, Columnar Pedestal, Ball & Claw Feet	885.00
Table, Tilt Top, Tea, Mahogany, Baluster Turned Pedestal Support, Tripod Base, Slipper Feet, 29 In.	502.00
Table, Tilt Top, Tea, Mahogany, Dish Top, Birdcage Support, Tripod Base, Pad Feet, 1700s, 29 In.	2252.00
Table, Tilt Top, Tea, Mahogany, Piecrust, Carved, 3 Tapered Legs, c.1750, 28 x 29 In.	956.00

Table, Tilt Top, Tea, Mahogany, Rectangular, Carved Support, Tripod Legs, c.1790, 28 x 28 In.	2300.00
Table, Tilt Top, Tea, Mahogany, Round Dish Top, Vase Shape Turned Standard, Claw Feet, 28 x 25 In.	478.00
Table, Tilt Top, Tea, Queen Anne Style, Mahogany, Round, Pedestal, Tripod Base, 1800s, 28 x 33 In.	239.00
Table, Tilt Top, Tea, Queen Anne Style, Mahogany, Turned Pedestal, Tripod, Pad Feet, 28 x 30 In...	269.00
Table, Tilt Top, Tea, Queen Anne Style, Round, Turned Pedestal, Tripod Base, Pad Feet, 27 x 34 In.	269.00
Table, Tilt Top, Tea, Queen Anne Style, Walnut, Inlaid Satinwood Patera Top, 28 x 34 In.........	478.00
Table, Tilt Top, Tea, Queen Anne, Cherry, Round, Birdcage Support, Pedestal, 1700s, 29 x 30 In.	266.00
Table, Tilt Top, Tea, Walnut, Inlay, Deer, Flowers, Pedestal, Tripod Base, 1800s, 28 x 36 In.	900.00
Table, Traccia, Meret Oppenheim, Gilt Bronze, Gilt Wood, Ostrich Foot Base, Oval, 25 x 27 In.	1912.00
Table, Tray, Brass Top, Wood, Bail Handles, Cabriole Legs, c.1900, 20 ½ x 43 In.	403.00
Table, Tray, Chinoiserie Style, Ebonized, Scalloped, Flower Gilt, Cabriole Legs, c.1950, 17 x 34 In....	369.00
Table, Tray, Mahogany, Rectangular, Beaded Skirt, Drawer, Square Beaded Legs, c.1800, 30 x 32 In. .	4740.00
Table, Tray, Stand, George III, Mahogany, X-Stretcher, 23 x 29 In.	219.00
Table, Tray, Stand, Georgian, Mahogany, c.1800, 29 x 19 In.	354.00
Table, Tray, Stand, Papier-Mache, Gilt, Greek Key Border, Chinoiserie Landscape, 21 x 26 In. .	1750.00
Table, Tray, Wormley, Walnut, Tagged, Dunbar, 1940s, 26 x 24 x 20 In.	1365.00
Table, Tray, X-Shape Stand, Oak, Gallery Pierced Side Handles, England, c.1890, 37 x 28 In...	246.00
Table, Trestle, Carved Frieze, Lyre Shaped Legs, Scrolled Supports, 1900s, 33 x 60 In.	2868.00
Table, Trestle, Carved, Shaped Supports, X-Stretcher, Continental, 30 x 38 In.	1434.00
Table, Trestle, Cherry, 28 ½ x 59 ½ In.	710.00
Table, Trestle, G. Nakashima, Black Walnut, Rosewood, 1960s, 29 x 72 In.	5270.00
Table, Trestle, Henredon, Oak, 2 Carved Drawers, I-Stretcher, Baluster Legs, Square Feet, 30 x 74 In.	575.00
Table, Trestle, Pine, 119 x 40 In.	439.00
Table, Trestle, Pine, Mortised, Pinned, Faux Mahogany Graining, Scrubbed Top, 1800s, 33 x 84 In.	1116.00
Table, Trestle, Stickley Bros., Quartersawn Oak, Label, 29 x 48 In.	1984.00
Table, Turn Top, Mahogany, Leaf Carved Legs & Stretcher, 35 x 30 In.........................	158.00
Table, V. Kagan, Venetian Glass Tiles, Bronze, Walnut, Round Top, 1950s, 17 x 27 In.	8680.00
Table, V. Kagan, Venetian Glass Tiles, Bronze, Walnut, Round, 1950s, 15 x 24 In.	3596.00
Table, Victorian, Burl Walnut, Border & Medallion Inlays, Oval, England, 1860s, 16 x 37 In....	288.00
Table, Victorian, Faux Bamboo, Chinese Style, Drawers, 32 x 35 In............................	608.00
Table, Victorian, Mahogany, 2 Tiers, Barley Twist Supports, Gargoyle Feet, Claw Foot, 31 x 36 In.	269.00
Table, Victorian, Mahogany, Shaped Marble Top, Carved Legs, Stretcher Finial, 30 x 30 In......	215.00
Table, Victorian, Mahogany, Shaped, Marble Top, Acanthus Carved, Stretcher Finial, 29 x 30 In.	610.00
Table, Victorian, Marble Top, Cyma Curved Legs, Gallery Stretcher, c.1875, 29 x 32 In.	345.00
Table, Victorian, Marble Top, Shaped Pendants, Turned Shaft, c.1890, 31 x 23 In.	40.00
Table, Victorian, Marquetry, Ormolu, Turtle Top, Masks, Cabriole Legs, 1875, 29 x 51 In.	889.00
Table, Victorian, Rosewood, Barrel Cylinder, Y-Shape Support Gates, Pedestal, 29 x 37 In.	288.00
Table, Victorian, Walnut, Cyma Curved Legs, c.1875, 29 x 22 In................................	104.00
Table, Victorian, Walnut, Inset Marble Top, Incised Carving, Star Cut Legs, c.1880, 27 x 20 In.	201.00
Table, Victorian, Walnut, Marble Top, Carved, 1860s, 28 ½ x 20 ½ In.	978.00
Table, Victorian, Walnut, Marble Top, Oval, Shaped Frame, c.1875, 30 x 35 In.	480.00
Table, Victorian, Walnut, Oval Marble Top, Carved Apron & Splayed Legs, 1800s, 29 x 28 In. ..	374.00
Table, Victorian, Walnut, Oval Marble Top, Carved, 1860s, 30 x 25 ½ In........................	316.00
Table, Vittorio Introini, Chromed Steel, Glass, Saporiti, 1972, 28 x 36 In.........	4340.00
Table, W. Platner, Chrome Plated Steel, Round Glass Top, c.1965, 14 x 30 In.	1093.00
Table, W. Platner, Glass Top, Bronze Steel, Round, Knoll, 15 x 42 In.	1054.00
Table, Walnut, Burl, Black Marble Top, Carved Gallery, Door, Italy, 37 x 21 In., Pair	275.00
Table, Walnut, Cabriole Legs, Venice, Italy, 31 x 77 In.	366.00
Table, Walnut, Carved Apron, Pedestal Base, X-Stretcher, American, c.1885	207.00
Table, Walnut, Drawer, Whalebone Diamond Shape Escutcheon, c.1800, 28 x 36 In.	978.00
Table, Walnut, Line Inlays, Drawer, c.1815, 28 x 23 In.	600.00
Table, Walnut, Mahogany, 6-Sided, Oyster Veneers, Barley Twist Stem, c.1690, 25 x 15 In........	461.00
Table, Walnut, Marble Top, Greek Key Apron, Urn On Stretcher, c.1900, 40 x 62 In.	1353.00
Table, Walnut, Marble, Round, Shaped Apron, Pedestal, Carved, 31 x 47 In.	427.00
Table, Walnut, Oval Marble Top, Carved Apron & Feet, 37 x 29 In.	690.00
Table, Walnut, Oval Top, Drawer, Splayed Legs, Line Inlays, Gilt Traces, c.1820, 17 x 23 In......	25200.00
Table, Walnut, Pewter Inlay, Magazine, 3 Tier Open Shelves, Martinsville, 22 x 20 In.	400.00
Table, Walnut, Pine, Line Inlays, North Carolina, c.1820, 29 x 22 In.	2520.00
Table, Walnut, Plank Top, Low, Square, 6 Drawers, Iron Handles, Block Feet, 19 x 42 x 42 In.	360.00
Table, Walnut, Poplar, Drawer, Inlaid Top, c.1820, 29 x 19 In...........................	12000.00
Table, Walnut, Round Top, Sunburst Veneer, 3 Masque Carved Splayed Legs, c.1850, 29 x 41 In.	2952.00
Table, Walnut, Yellow Pine, Drawer, Southern, 1800s, 29 x 31 In.	413.00
Table, White Pine, Drawer, Square Legs, c.1850, 29 x 25 In....................................	546.00
Table, Whitewashed Mahogany, Glass Top, Tiers, Grosfeld House, 1940s, 17 x 17 In., Pair	682.00
Table, William & Mary, Ebonized, Banding Inlay, Barley Twist Legs, Bun Feet, c.1695, 28 x 47 In.	6150.00
Table, William & Mary, Gateleg, D-Shape Leaves, Drawer, Wood Pull, 28 x 15 In.	1404.00
Table, William & Mary, Oak, Baluster Legs, Stretchers, Half Ball Feet, c.1680, 27 x 31 In.	593.00

Furniture, Umbrella Stand, Fornasetti, Transfer, Musical Instrument, Label, Italy, c.1965, 25 x 16 In.
$1045.00

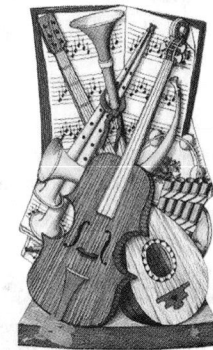

New Orleans Auction Galleries, Inc.

Furniture, Vanity, Art Deco, Mahogany, Ebony Bands, Beveled Glass, 2 Inlaid Supports, 64 x 48 ½ In.
$744.00

Leslie Hindman Auctioneers

F

Furniture, Vitrine, Louis XV Style, Parquetry, Glazed Case, Doors, Drawer, Bronze, 1800s, 46 x 30 In. $9261.00

Neal Auction Co.

Furniture, Vitrine, Louis XV Style, Vernis Martin Panels, Ormolu Mounts, Continental, 58 x 24 In. $450.00

Cowan's Auctions

> **TIP**
> If the drawer on your antique-looking furniture is held together with new screws, nails, or staples, it is not an antique.

Table, William & Mary, Walnut, Overhung Top, Gateleg, c.1740, 25 ¾ x 12 In.	3318.00
Table, William & Mary, Walnut, Yellow Pine, Drawer, Demilune Drop Leaf, c.1700, 27 x 43 In.	5040.00
Table, William IV, Mahogany, Tilt Top, Dentil Border, Splayed Legs, 28 ½ x 35 In.	625.00
Table, William IV, Rectangular Top, Rounded Corners, Turned, Reeded Legs, Extension, 28 x 42 In.	549.00
Table, William IV, Rosewood, Crossbanded, 2 Drawers, Trestle Support, c.1835, 30 x 58 In.	1659.00
Table, Wine, English Oak, Collapsible Round Top, Gateleg, 28 In.	295.00
Table, Wine, Georgian, Burl, Round Dish Top, Baluster Post, Ivory, Tripod Legs, Pad Feet, 23 x 17 In.	7110.00
Table, Wood, 2 Doors, Fitted Interior, Scrolled Feet, Carved, Painted, Gilt, Tibet, c.1905, 13 x 21 In.	489.00
Table, Wood, Drawer, Gilt Garland, Green Paint, Lower Shelf, 34 x 48 In.	185.00
Table, Wood, Geometric Veneer Top, Round, Shelf, Shaped Legs, c.1940, 23 x 29 In.	584.00
Table, Wood, Marble Inset, Ornate, Carved Stretcher & Legs, Chinese, c.1910, 18 x 18 In., Pair	978.00
Table, Wood, Marble Top, 3 Drawers, Flower Inlays, Metal Mounts, France, 34 x 32 In.	1725.00
Table, Wood, Marble Top, Banded, Inlay, 2 Drawers, Fluted Legs, c.1940, 26 x 18 In., Pair	738.00
Table, Wood, Marble Top, Openwork Frieze, Shaped Stretcher, Carved, Painted, c.1890, 30 x 40 In.	2214.00
Table, Wood, Metal, Adjustable, Mechanical Base, c.1920, 26 x 70 In.	1476.00
Table, Wood, Reverse Painted Mirror Top, Ornate Carved Pedestal, Paw Feet, 30 x 43 In.	259.00
Table, Wood, Round Glass Top, Carved Feather Plume Support, c.1950, 18 x 30 In.	308.00
Table, Wood, Round Top, Urn Shape Support, Pedestal Base, W. Haines, c.1948, 28 x 42 In.	156.00
Table, Wood, Round, Starburst Inlay Top, Spindle & Balls Rail Base, Ebonized, c.1955, 20 x 26 In.	820.00
Table, Wood, Shaped Leather Top, Inlay, Drawer, Ormolu Mounts, 33 x 44 In.	575.00
Table, Wood, Shaped Marble Top, Drawer, 2 Doors, Turned Legs, c.1940, 26 x 18 In., Pair	369.00
Table, Wood, Shaped Top, Swan Support, 3 Legs, Stain, c.1940, 23 x 25 In., Pair	523.00
Table, Wood, Wrought & Cast Iron Base, c.1930, 30 x 22 In.	338.00
Table, Wormley, Extension, Mahogany, Dunbar, c.1950, 14 In. Leaves, 30 x 42 In.	705.00
Table, Wormley, Mahogany, Leather Top, 4 Drawers, Dunbar, 1940s, 18 x 20 x 26 In., Pair	420.00
Table, Wormley, Round, Mahogany Base, Dunbar, 16 ¼ x 21 ¼ In.	1440.00
Table, Wormley, Walnut, Walnut Burl, Tiffany Glass Tiles, X-Stretcher, 1956, 20 x 24 In.	2108.00
Table, Writing, Arts & Crafts, Carved, Pierced Openwork, 35 x 36 In.	460.00
Table, Writing, Chippendale, Pine, Vernacular, Scratchbeaded Drawer, Legs, 30 x 24 In.	206.00
Table, Writing, George III Style, Mahogany, Drawers, 47 x 24 In.	406.00
Table, Writing, George III, Mahogany, 6 Upper Drawers, Leather Inset, c.1800, 37 x 51 In.	1088.00
Table, Writing, George III, Mahogany, Leather Inset, Drawers, c.1780, 30 x 57 In.	4063.00
Table, Writing, Georgian Style, Mahogany, 2 Drawers, 47 x 21 In.	438.00
Table, Writing, Georgian, Mahogany, Curved Shelf, Tapered Legs, Pad Feet, Eng., 1700s, 29 x 24 In.	5925.00
Table, Writing, Georgian, Style, Mahogany, 4 Drawers, 30 x 47 In.	438.00
Table, Writing, Hepplewhite Style, Rectangular, Leather Top, 2 Drawers, 29 x 39 In.	1062.00
Table, Writing, Louis XVI Style, Marble Top, Ormolu Base, Drawer, X-Stretcher, 31 x 52 In.	1652.00
Table, Writing, Mahogany, Bowfront, Leather, Drawers, Tapered Legs, Spade Feet, 1800s, 30 x 36 In.	118.00
Table, Writing, Mahogany, Leather, Inset, Drawer, Turned Legs, Casters, 29 x 34 In.	359.00
Table, Writing, Mahogany, Shaped Top, Line Inlay, 4 Drawers, Square Feet, Tapered, 32 x 37 In.	148.00
Table, Writing, Pine, Marble Top, 2 Drawers, Concave Stretcher, Shelf, c.1895, 31 x 50 In.	553.00
Table, Writing, Regency, Mahogany, Gallery Top, Geometric Inlay, c.1880, 29 x 33 In.	2489.00
Table, Writing, Regency, Rosewood, Drop Front, Fitted Interior, Drawer, 37 x 23 In.	861.00
Table, Writing, Satinwood, Scalloped Gallery, 4 Drawers, c.1900, 50 x 30 In.	738.00
Table, Wrought Iron, Demilune, Scrolled Base, 28 x 24 ½ In., Pair	923.00
Table, Wrought Iron, Marble Top, Grape Leaves, Vines, Cross Stretcher, Painted, 1900s, 32 x 48 In.	295.00
Table-Bench, Pine, Plank Top, Slab Arched Ends, Top Flips To Bench Seat, 31 x 58 In.	304.00
Tabouret, Arts & Crafts, Round, Cutout Base, Charles Greenman, 14 x 16 In.	270.00
Tabouret, Hardwood, Marble Top, Carved Scroll, 4 Legs, Curved Stretcher, Chinese, 1800s, 18 In.	201.00
Tabouret, Hardwood, Round, 5 Scroll Legs, Shelf, Pierced Apron, Chinese, 21 x 16 In.	115.00
Tabouret, Hardwood, Shaped Beaded Top, Marble, Pierced, Square Stretcher, 23 x 18 In.	369.00
Tabouret, Louis XVI, Painted, Parcel Gilt, Padded Seat, Round Fluted Legs, c.1790, 16 x 22 In.	1000.00
Tabouret, Mixed Metal, 8-Sided, Raised & Pierced Design, Middle Eastern, 31 x 22 In., Pair	5100.00
Tabouret, Rosewood, Marble Inset, Pierced Leaf Scrolls, Lion Masks, Paw Feet, Ball, 1800s, 18 ½ In.	796.00
Tabouret, Rosewood, Marble Top, Carved Skirt, Cabriole Legs, Ball & Claw Feet, 24 x 16 In.	418.00
Tabouret, Wood, Cut Corner, Arched Apron, Cross Stretcher Base, 16 x 18 In., Pair	1020.00
Tantalus, Oak, 3 Cut Glass Decanters, Faceted Stoppers, Silver Plate Handles, c.1895, 14 x 7 In.	984.00
Tea Cart, Duncan Phyfe, Drop Leaf, Removable Glass Tray, Low Shelf, 18 x 30 In.	106.00
Tea Cart, Gilt Metal, Glass Top, Roping & Tassels, Shelf, Wheels, 28 x 33 In.	326.00
Tea Cart, Lucite, Chrome Covered Wheels, c.1950, 33 x 19 In.	777.00
Tea Cart, Mahogany, 3 Tiers, Gallery, Brass Cup Casters, 34 x 32 In.	1434.00
Teapoy, Satinwood, Telescoping Top, Fitted Interior, 4 Compartments, c.1850, 30 x 18 In.	359.00
Teapoy, William IV, Rosewood, Sarcophagus Shape, 3 Drawers, Fitted Interior, 31 x 18 In.	837.00
Umbrella Stand, Arts & Crafts, Wood, Chamfered Posts, Zinc Drip Pan, 25 ½ x 27 ¼ In.	248.00
Umbrella Stand, Black Forest, Black Bear, Composite, Chain, 33 x 14 In.	115.00
Umbrella Stand, Brass, Enamel Metal, Italy, 1950s, 29 x 14 In.	403.00

Umbrella Stand, Bronze, Birds, Leaves, Flowering Branches, Chinese, c.1890, 24 In............	148.00
Umbrella Stand, Bronze, Tubular, Birds, Plants, Pine Tree, Key Fret Border, c.1900, 24 ½ In.	676.00
Umbrella Stand, Cast Iron, Center Arch, 2 Scrolled Columns, 1800s, 42 x 24 In.	764.00
Umbrella Stand, Fornasetti, Pompeii Scenes, Orange, Brown, Cylinder, Metal, c.1950, 23 In.	470.00
Umbrella Stand, Fornasetti, Transfer, Musical Instrument, Label, Italy, c.1965, 25 x 16 In. *illus*	1045.00
Umbrella Stand, G. Stickley, Arts & Crafts, Oak, Copper Drip Pan, 33 x 12 In.	920.00
Umbrella Stand, G. Stickley, No. 100, Slats, Flared, Iron Hoops, Red, Decal, 12 x 24 In..........	2160.00
Umbrella Stand, Oak, Slats, Brass, Lion's Mask Handles, Tapered Legs, Pad Feet, 30 x 12 In..	239.00
Umbrella Stand, Oak, Stick & Ball, Metal Drip Pan, 27 x 9 In...	173.00
Umbrella Stand, Pinwheel Design, Cast Iron, c.1920, 28 In.	210.00
Umbrella Stand, Walnut, Peaked Crest, Finial, Scrolls, Carved, France, 43 x 26 In.................	549.00
Umbrella Stand, Wood, Dog, Sitting Next To Tree Stump, 33 x 34 In...............................	17700.00
Vanity, Art Deco, Mahogany, Ebony Bands, Beveled Glass, 2 Inlaid Supports, 64 x 48 ½ In. ....*illus*	744.00
Vanity, Chippendale Style, Mahogany, 5 Drawers, Scrolling Leaves, Cabriole Legs, 32 x 43 In..	177.00
Vanity, Louis XV, Pine, 5 Drawers, Shaped Apron, Cabriole Legs, 1800s, 27 x 47 In.	590.00
Vanity, Queen Anne Style, Mahogany, 2 Pedestals, Trifold Mirror, 1920s, 65 x 46 In.	82.00
Vitrine, Art Deco, Rosewood, Glass Door, Brass Trim Doors, Platform Base, France, 58 x 32 In.	1230.00
Vitrine, Biedermeier, Mahogany, Arched Panel Glass Doors, 65 x 29 In.	531.00
Vitrine, Bronze, Glass, Mirror, Illuminated, Brass Tag, Mastercraft, 1980s, 84 x 32 In., Pair....	2480.00
Vitrine, Burl Walnut, Marquetry, Glazed Cabinet, Scenic Panel, Drawer, Galle, c.1900, 52 x 25 In.	16730.00
Vitrine, Chinese Style, Mahogany, Broken-Arch Crest, Door, Fretwork, 75 x 25 In.................	1416.00
Vitrine, Edwardian, Mahogany, Satinwood Inlay, Hinged Door, Paneled Base, 29 x 17 In.	400.00
Vitrine, Edwardian, Oak, Tea Tray Top, 30 x 31 In..	187.00
Vitrine, Fruitwood, Bowed, Ormolu Frieze, Glass Door, Landscape Painted Door, 68 x 30 In....	522.00
Vitrine, Kingwood, Bronze Mounts, Silk Interior, Flower Frieze, Lift Top, c.1910, 30 x 27 In....	1896.00
Vitrine, Louis XIII Style, Oak, Glass Door, Carved, Diamond Design, Ball Feet, 71 x 34 In........	450.00
Vitrine, Louis XV Style, Parquetry, Glazed Case, Doors, Drawer, Bronze, 1800s, 46 x 30 In. *illus*	9261.00
Vitrine, Louis XV Style, Satinwood, Oval Hinged Top, Frieze, Cabriole Legs, c.1900, 30 x 20 In.	307.00
Vitrine, Louis XV Style, Serpentine Glass Door, Bombe Door, Painted, c.1900, 68 x 30 In.	1150.00
Vitrine, Louis XV Style, Vernis Martin Panels, Ormolu Mounts, Continental, 58 x 24 In. ...*illus*	450.00
Vitrine, Louis XV Style, Vernis Martin Style Panels, Ormolu Door, Demilune, Spain, 65 x 27 In.	294.00
Vitrine, Louis XV Style, Walnut, Ormolu, Peaked Crest, Shaped Glass Door, Shelves, 67 x 25 In.	305.00
Vitrine, Louis XV, Mahogany, Gold Leaf, Lift Top, Inset Glass, X-Stretcher, Flower Urn, 29 x 26 In.	900.00
Vitrine, Louis XVI Style, Gilt, Garland Carved Door, Crest, 4 Shelves, France, c.1900, 70 x 28 In.	1342.00
Vitrine, Louis XVI Style, Gilt, Garland Carved Frieze, Jasperware Medallion, 64 x 26 In.	2706.00
Vitrine, Louis XVI Style, Mahogany, Marble Top, Pierced Gallery, Glazed Door, c.1905, 56 x 27 In.	676.00
Vitrine, Louis XVI Style, Mahogany, Ormolu, Concave Door, Hanging, c.1900, 36 x 24 In.	558.00
Vitrine, Mahogany, Demilune, Flower Inlays, Glazed Doors, Drawer, 66 x 25 In., Pair	1830.00
Vitrine, Mahogany, Glass Door, Painted Panels, Bronze Mounts, France, c.1900, 61 x 37 In....	660.00
Vitrine, Mahogany, Glass Door, Shelves, Carved, Mechanics Furniture Co., c.1910, 50 x 25 In.	480.00
Vitrine, Mahogany, Mother-Of-Pearl, Wood Inlay, Carved, Door, Shelves, c.1890, 47 x 44 In. *illus*	1912.00
Vitrine, Mahogany, Mother-Of-Pearl, Glass Door, Mirror Back, c.1900, 58 x 23 In....................	300.00
Vitrine, Mahogany, Round, Hinged Top, Flower Inlays, Low Shelf, Paw Feet, c.1890, 30 x 22 In.	488.00
Vitrine, Mahogany, Scrolled Ormolu Mounts, Mirror, Glass Doors, 72 x 40 In.	1150.00
Vitrine, Metal, 2 Glass Doors, Arched Top, c.1910, 69 x 27 In..	1353.00
Vitrine, Napoleon III Style, Ebonized, Brass, 2 Parts, Arched Top, Glazed Doors, 84 x 48 In.....	2375.00
Vitrine, Oak, Domed Cornice, Door, 2 Drawers, Shaped Stretcher, Bun Feet, 1800s, 67 x 34 In.	492.00
Vitrine, Ormolu, Hand Painted, Bombe Case, Putti, Doves, Garlands, Glass Door, France, 63 x 26 In.	3185.00
Vitrine, Parquetry, Ormolu Mounts, 3 Glass Shelves, Cabriole Legs, France, 56 x 26 In............	305.00
Vitrine, Provincial, Walnut, Molded Fruit Basket Cornice, Glazed Door, Drawers, 43 x 29 In...	2091.00
Vitrine, Regency, Glass, Bronze Pierced Gallery, Serpentine Sides, France, 1800s, 54 x 27 In...	1380.00
Vitrine, Renaissance Revival, Oak, Fruit, Animal Head, Carved, c.1880, 58 x 34 In.	451.00
Vitrine, Rococo, Rosewood, Pierced Scroll Crest, Fretwork, Glazed Door, Mirror, c.1850, 93 In.	7320.00
Vitrine, Rosewood, Ormolu, Glazed Doors, Mirror, Flat Top, Floral Frieze, 67 x 36 In..............	1298.00
Vitrine, Walnut, 6-Sided, Round Top, William Freeman, England, c.1890, 27 x 16 ½ In.	259.00
Vitrine, Wood, Curved Glass, Painted, Flower, Bronze, Cabriole Legs, France, c.1920, 55 x 26 In.	492.00
Vitrine, Wood, Marble Top, Beveled Glass Doors, Carved Lower Panel, c.1940, 77 x 24 In., Pair	1476.00
Wall Unit, G. Nelson, Walnut, 2 Upper Doors, Shelves, 7 Drawers, Henry Miller, 49 x 95 In.	1440.00
Wall Unit, Poul Cadovius, Royal System, Rosewood, Shelves, Doors, Drawers, 1950s, 88 x 127 In.	3224.00
Wardrobe, 2 Doors, 3 Drawers, Side Mirror Doors, Carved, England, c.1890, 83 x 76 In...........	403.00
Wardrobe, 2 Doors, Drawer, Carved, Cherubs, Lions, Gargoyles, Continental, 1800s, 84 x 52 In.	1265.00
Wardrobe, Art Nouveau, Oak, Carved Crest, Single Door, Acanthus Panels, Drawer, 70 In.......	123.00
Wardrobe, Arts & Crafts, Mahogany, 2 Paneled Doors, 6 Panes, Tin Mullions, 78 In................	98.00
Wardrobe, Arts & Crafts, Oak, Door, Carved Stylized Flowers, Inset Mirror, 73 In.	154.00
Wardrobe, Cherry, Raised Panel Door, Pintle Hinges, Drawer, Peg Racks, Ohio, 1800s, 75 x 42 In.	999.00
Wardrobe, Gentleman's, Mahogany, William IV, Carved, Applied Beading, Drawers, 77 x 94 In.	1708.00

Furniture, Vitrine, Mahogany, Mother-Of-Pearl Wood Inlay, Carved, Door, Shelves, c.1890, 47 x 44 In. **$1912.00**

Neal Auction Co.

Furniture, Wardrobe, Meeks, Mahogany, Stenciled, 2 Doors, Columns, Carved, Eagle, Paw Feet, 94 In. **$4888.00**

Cottone Auctions

You Can't "Feed" Wood

If you own antique wooden furniture, do not use the new polishes that contain silicone or linseed oil or those that claim to "feed the wood." Wood in furniture is dead. It can be oiled or greased or waxed to look darker and shiny, but the coating is a cosmetic, not a cure. Rub old wooden furniture with a true wax like beeswax or carnauba wax, let it dry, then buff to a lustrous finish.

Furniture, Washstand, Pine, Closed Plank Base, Half Shelf, 37 x 22 x 18 In. $180.00

DuMouchelles Art Gallery

Furniture, Wine Cooler, Regency, Mahogany, Sarcophagus Shape, Paw Feet, Tin Liner, c.1820, 17 x 34 In. $1673.00

Neal Auction Co.

TIP

Ordering a new mattress and bedsprings to use on your antique bed or in your old house? Check the size of the bedsprings, including the height. Then measure the width and height of your stairs. Often there are problems getting up the stairs. You may need to get two springs to use under a king or queen mattress. Sometimes even the mattress will be too big and too rigid to make it up the stairs.

Wardrobe, Mahogany, 2 Paneled Doors, Interior Shelves, Germany, c.1900, 76 x 46 In.	150.00
Wardrobe, Mahogany, Doors, Fitted Interior, Drawers, 1800s, 66 x 48 In.	444.00
Wardrobe, Mahogany, Molded Cornice, Paneled Doors, Ripple Molding, Bracket Feet, 87 x 60 In.	1195.00
Wardrobe, Meeks, Mahogany, Stenciled, 2 Doors, Columns, Carved, Eagle, Paw Feet, 94 In. *illus*	4888.00
Wardrobe, Mixed Wood, Paneled Door, Red Paint, North Carolina, c.1850, 74 x 46 In.	1150.00
Wardrobe, Neoclassical, Mahogany, Molded Cornice, Paneled Doors, Ionic Columns, 90 x 69 In.	5676.00
Wardrobe, Neoclassical, Mahogany, Molded Cornice, Paneled Doors, Paw Feet, c.1825, 90 x 62 In.	1900.00
Wardrobe, Oak, Panel Door, Fitted Interior, England, c.1950, 72 x 30 In.	160.00
Wardrobe, Oak, Quartersawn, Beveled Mirror, c.1890	2070.00
Wardrobe, Pine, Bird, Flower Panels, 2 Doors, Drawer, Painted, 1827, 72 x 45 In.	1080.00
Wardrobe, Pine, Painted, 2-Panel Doors, Stepped Cornice, Interior Shelves, 1800s, 76 x 47 In.	711.00
Wardrobe, Pine, Panel Door, Low Drawer, England, 1800s, 83 x 36 In.	178.00
Wardrobe, Pine, Paneled Doors, Bun Feet, Interior Shelves, Red Paint, c.1830, 70 x 46 In.	940.00
Wardrobe, Poplar, 2 Paneled Doors, Blue Paint, c.1800, 70 x 44 In.	1265.00
Wardrobe, Poplar, 2 Paneled Doors, Removable Cornice, Hooks, Shelf, 2 Parts, c.1850, 81 In.	470.00
Wardrobe, Scottish Regency, Mahogany, Peaked Crest, Central 4 Doors, 3 Drawers, 77 x 80 In.	2340.00
Wardrobe, Walnut, 2 Doors, Carved, Austria, 80 x 49 In.	196.00
Wardrobe, Walnut, 3 Doors, Beveled Mirror, Ball Feet, Germany, 1900s, 73 x 59 In.	104.00
Wardrobe, Walnut, Carved, Female, Lion, Knights, 2 Doors, c.1890, 86 x 59 In.	4370.00
Washstand, Bird's-Eye Maple, Bronze, Marble, Backsplash, 2 Drawers, 2 Doors, 1825, 41 x 30 In.	2749.00
Washstand, Corner, Federal, Cherry, Arched Back, Pierced Deck, Stretcher, c.1810, 39 x 25 In.	250.00
Washstand, Corner, Federal, Mahogany, Satinwood Inlay, Bowfront, Drawer, 2 Tiers, 43 x 23 In.	489.00
Washstand, Corner, Hepplewhite, 3 Tiers, Outswept Legs, England, Late 1700s, 33 x 18 In.	184.00
Washstand, Corner, Mahogany, String Inlay, Scalloped Backsplash, Drawer, c.1815, 44 x 25 In.	676.00
Washstand, Corner, Regency, Mahogany, Drawer, Pitcher, Basin, 2 Tiers, France, 1800s, 40 x 27 In.	236.00
Washstand, Corner, Regency, Mahogany, Inlays, Shelf, Drawer, Shell Apron, 1800s, 40 In.	948.00
Washstand, Corner, Regency, Mahogany, Lift Top, Inlay, Saber Legs, Stretcher, 1800s, 32 x 23 In.	269.00
Washstand, Corner, Sheraton, Cherry, 2 Tiers, New England, c.1815, 28 ¾ x 23 In.	563.00
Washstand, Drawer, Gold Stencil, Black Paint, Shelf, Towel Rails, Maine, c.1810, 31 x 36 In.	273.00
Washstand, Edwardian, Mahogany, Gallery Top, Paneled Door, Turned Legs, 32 x 17 In., Pair	1672.00
Washstand, Empire, Mahogany, Lift Top, Fitted Interior, Pewter Lavabo, Basin, 1800s, 37 x 46 In.	480.00
Washstand, Empire, Tiger Maple, Scrolled Backsplash, Shaped Sides, Shelf, c.1840, 36 x 20 In.	400.00
Washstand, Federal, Gallery Top, Drawer, Lower Shelf, Turned Legs, 1800s, 33 x 19 In.	295.00
Washstand, Federal, Mahogany, Drawers, Turned Legs, 39 x 34 In.	299.00
Washstand, Federal, Mahogany, Hinged Lid, Drawer, Door, Reeded Legs, 33 x 17 In.	144.00
Washstand, G. Stickley, Iron Faceted Pulls, Slat Back, c.1901, 44 x 40 In.	5270.00
Washstand, Gilt, Drawer, Mirror, 2 Pierced Tiers, Glass, Block Legs, Chinese, 71 x 18 In.	460.00
Washstand, Gilt, Gilt Crest, Mirror, Shelf, Drawer, Carved, Chinese, 71 x 18 In.	460.00
Washstand, Gilt, Painted, Panel, Pierced, Round Basin, Folding Legs, Chinese, 72 x 18 In.	316.00
Washstand, Hepplewhite, Corner, Mahogany, False Drawers, Base Shelf, 34 x 26 In.	206.00
Washstand, Hepplewhite, Tiger Maple, Backsplash, Shelf, Drawer, 33 x 18 In.	1380.00
Washstand, Hepplewhite, Walnut, Cherry, Poplar, Shaped Gallery, Drawer, 32 x 17 In.	147.00
Washstand, L. & J.G. Stickley, Slatted Backsplash, Child's, 34 x 30 x 15 In.	2852.00
Washstand, Louis XV Style, Walnut, 2 Doors, Marble Top, Mirror, Carved Crest, 91 x 46 In.	575.00
Washstand, Mahogany, Gallery, Fitted Top, Open Shelf, Drawer, Square Legs, 1800s, 41 In.	354.00
Washstand, Mahogany, Marble Top, Backsplash, Drawer, Doors, Columns, c.1820, 38 x 28 In.	777.00
Washstand, Mahogany, Shaped Backsplash, Turned Towel Rack, Legs, 47 x 34 In.	657.00
Washstand, Ocher Paint, Black Pinstripes, Shaped Backboard, Shelf, c.1835, 35 In.	150.00
Washstand, Pine, Closed Plank Base, Half Shelf, 37 x 22 x 18 In. *illus*	180.00
Washstand, Pine, Gallery Shelf, Drawer, Smoke Graining, Red, Square Legs, c.1835, 28 x 18 In.	323.00
Washstand, Pine, Shaped Backsplash, Turned Legs, Painted, New England, c.1825, 38 x 17 In.	178.00
Washstand, Pine, Shaped Gallery, Drawer, Turned Legs, Painted, Fruit, c.1820, 36 x 16 In.	118.00
Washstand, Regency, Mahogany, 3 Tiers, Brass Rods, Inserts, 1800s, 20 x 27 In.	976.00
Washstand, Sheraton, Basswood, Yellow Paint, c.1815, 32 x 16 In.	652.00
Washstand, Sheraton, Mahogany, Dovetailed Gallery, Faux Drawer, Turned Legs, 1800s, 37 x 29 In.	235.00
Washstand, Sheraton, Painted, Flowers, Shaped Gallery, Drawer, Shelf, 1800s, 37 x 22 In.	89.00
Washstand, Sheraton, Pine, Gilt Stencil, Flowers, Turned Legs, Scroll Crest, c.1835, 38 x 18 In.	323.00
Washstand, Sheraton, Pine, Scrolled Backsplash, Drawer, Low Shelf, Yellow Paint, 1800s, 37 x 17 In.	948.00
Washstand, Sheraton, Yellow Paint, Flared Backsplash, Fruit Design, Drawer, 1800s, 36 x 21 In.	316.00
Washstand, Ship's, Victorian, Mahogany, Slant Top, Spigot, Baluster Legs, 1800s, 40 x 25 In.	403.00
Washstand, Victorian, Walnut, Marble Top, Arched Backsplash, Drawer, c.1865, 41 x 32 In.	345.00
Whatnot Shelf, Corner, Distressed Paint, Doors, Shaped Top, 76 x 16 In.	92.00
Whatnot Shelf, Mahogany, 3 Shelves, Pierced, Carved, Drawer, 59 x 26 In.	122.00
Whatnot Shelf, Regency, Mahogany, 4 Shelves, Drawers, Eng., 1800s, 55 x 20 In.	708.00
Whatnot Shelf, Regency, Mahogany, Shelves, 2 Drawers, Ring-Turned Supports, 59 x 20 In.	1521.00
Whatnot Shelf, Steel, Pyramid, Tapered Shelves, 68 In.	325.00
Window Seat, Contemporary, Upholstered, H-Stretcher, 1900s, 20 x 60 In.	239.00

F

Window Seat, George II Style, Side Swept Scroll Arms, H-Stretcher, 1900s, 25 x 52 In.............	269.00
Window Seat, George III Style, Mahogany, Scroll Ends, Leather Seat, 27 x 62 In.......................	950.00
Window Seat, Louis XVI Style, Gilt, Shaped, Padded Outscrolled Arms, 1900s, 25 x 34 In.	246.00
Wine Cooler, George III, Mahogany, Banded Inlay, Octagonal, Splayed Legs, 29 x 20 In.	1298.00
Wine Cooler, Mahogany Inlay, Octagonal, Hinged Lid, 2 Brass Handles, Bracket Feet, 18 In...	652.00
Wine Cooler, Mahogany, Gilt, Flared Basket Shape, Swing Handle, Stand, c.1805, 21 x 14 In.	978.00
Wine Cooler, Regency Style, Mahogany, Lion Ring Handles, Eng., 1800s, 23 x 24 In.	590.00
Wine Cooler, Regency, Mahogany, Round, Brass Handles, Removable Metal Bucket, 19 x 22 In.	1053.00
Wine Cooler, Regency, Mahogany, Sarcophagus Shape, Paw Feet, Tin Liner, c.1820, 17 x 34 In. *illus*	1673.00
Wine Cooler, Rosewood, Brass Mounts, Stand, George Zee, Hong Kong, 35 x 18 In., Pair........	173.00

G. ARGY-ROUSSEAU is the impressed mark used on a variety of objects in the Art Deco style. Gabriel Argy-Rousseau, born in 1885, was a French glass artist. In 1921, he formed a partnership that made pate-de-verre and other glass. The partnership ended in 1931 and he opened his own studio. He worked until 1952 and died in 1953.

G-ARGY-
ROUSSEAU

Bowl, Anemones, Pate-De-Verre, c.1920, 3 x 4 ½ In..	4780.00
Bowl, Pate-De-Verre, c.1920, 2 ½ x 3 ¼ In...	2629.00
Bowl, Translucent Yellow, Molded Berries, Mottled Amber Leaves, 4 x 5 In.	2844.00
Pendant, Cameo, Brown Beetle, Blue Mottled, Yellow Ground, Pate-De-Verre, 1 ½ In. ....*illus*	288.00
Vase, Brown, Red Flower Heads, Panels, Pate-De-Verre, Signed, c.1910, 9 ⅛ In. ....*illus*	3690.00
Vase, Purple, Green Flowers, Pate-De-Verre, Signed, 5 x 10 ½ In.	9350.00

GALLE was a designer who made glass, pottery, furniture, and other Art Nouveau items. Emile Galle founded his factory in France in 1874. After Galle's death in 1904, the firm continued to make glass and furniture until 1931. The name *Galle* was used as a mark, but it was often hidden in the design of the object. Galle glass is listed here. Pottery is in the next section. His furniture is listed in the Furniture category.

Gallé

Atomizer, Purple Iris, Peach Ground, Brass Collar & Stem, Cloth Pump, 8 ½ In.	590.00
Bottle, Orange Flowers, Etched, Pale Orange Ground, Brass Fitting, Cameo, Signed, 11 In. .....*illus*	551.00
Bowl, Amber Aquatic Vegetation, Blue Shaded To White Ground, Angular Cut Rim, 4 x 4 In...	711.00
Bowl, Red Flowers, Yellow & White Ground, 2 ¼ x 6 ¼ In.	1007.00
Cordial, Enameled Cherry & Leaf Design, Smoke Color Glass, Gold Highlights, Pedestal Foot, 2 x 2 In.	173.00
Incense Burner, Amber, Crimson Flowers, Bronze Embossed Flowers, Cameo, Signed, 7 In. ... *illus*	1495.00
Lamp, Art Nouveau, Red, Light Green, Cameo, Signed, 26 In.	2185.00
Lamp, Leaves, Blue Cut To Green, Peach Ground, Cameo, Vase Shape, 29 In.	1715.00
Lamp, Maroon & Blue Flowers, Amber Ground, Cameo, Fabric Shade, 21 In............................	1185.00
Lamp, Red Berries, Green Leaves, Cameo, Signed, France, 10 x 26 In.	4313.00
Lamp, Red Flowers & Leaves, Cone Top, Flared Foot, Tapered Base, Cameo, Signed, 22 In........	19550.00
Perfume Bottle, Purple Flowers, Frosted Ground, Cameo, Floral Stopper, Silver Lid, Signed, 3 In.	1725.00
Perfume Bottle, Purple Flowers, Iridescent Ground, Bulbous, Stepped Silver Foot, Signed, 3 In.	1725.00
Perfume Bottle, Red Flowers, Yellow Ground, Bulbous Base, Elongated Neck, 6 ¾ In.............	296.00
Perfume Lamp, Red Wildflowers, Yellow Ground, Pillow Form, Gold Mount, 6 ¾ In.	1778.00
Tankard, Topaz, Rolled Leaf, Ridges, Swirl, Flower, Stems, Serpentine Handle, Angled Rim, 13 In.	2530.00
Vase, Acid Etched Lavender Leaves, Frosted Ground, Cameo, c.1900, 6 In.	2468.00
Vase, Amber, Purple, Trees, Over Mountain Lake, Cameo, Signed, c.1900, 5 In........................	430.00
Vase, Aquatic Plants, Tapered, Orange Over Frosted, Cameo, 2 Handles, 6 ¼ In.	2032.00
Vase, Aubergine Iris On Amber, Tapered, Cameo Signed, c.1900, 5 ¼ In.........................	546.00
Vase, Banjo Form, Frosted Yellow, Ruby Leaves & Berries, Signed, 5 ½ In.	550.00
Vase, Bleeding Hearts, Leaves, Red, Yellow, Urn Shape, Pedestal Foot, Cameo, Signed, 9 In......	4600.00
Vase, Blossoms, Red, Yellow Ground, Frosted, Cameo Signed, 5 ½ x 15 In.	3240.00
Vase, Blue Blossoms, Footed, Cameo, Signed, 6 ½ x 4 In.	992.00
Vase, Blue Daisies, Yellow, Pink, Frosted Ground, Cameo, Signed, 7 ½ x 10 ½ In.	7200.00
Vase, Blue Mountain, Purple Leafy Tree, Bulbous, Rolled Rim, Cameo, Signed, 5 In.	3163.00
Vase, Bottle Shape, Trailing Enamel Flowers, Gilt, Signed, c.1900, 15 ¼ In. ....*illus*	7768.00
Vase, Branch & Leaf Design, Teardrop Shape, Pink, Yellow & White, Berry, Signed, 4 ⅝ In.	1900.00
Vase, Brown & Green Stems, Leaves, Light Green, Cylindrical, Bulbous Base, 17 In.	1348.00
Vase, Brown Leaves, Berries, Branches, Chartreuse Ground, Swollen, Narrow Rim, 4 In.	489.00
Vase, Bud, Frothy White, Purple Overlay, Cut Leaves, c.1910, 3 In...	590.00
Vase, Bud, Tapered, Narrow, Round Foot, Peach, Light Green Etched Flowers, Leaves, Signed, 8 In.	561.00
Vase, Bud, Wisteria, Lavender Over Pink, Cameo, Tapered, Purple Foot, 16 In..........................	3346.00
Vase, Bulbous, Narrow Neck, Flared Lip, Etched Lavender Leaves, Frosted White, Cameo, 1900s, 9 In..	720.00
Vase, Burgundy, Pink Leaves & Berries, Yellow Ground, Bulbous, Cameo, Signed, 5 x 8 ½ In...	3300.00
Vase, Butterfly, Purple Lupine, Cut To Pale Green, Pillow Form, Loop Handles, 9 In.	1778.00
Vase, Chrysanthemums, Ocher, Yellow, Bulbous, Tapered, Cameo, 6 ½ In..............................	1136.00
Vase, Chrysanthemums, Orange, Frosted, Apricot, Baluster, Elongated Neck, Cameo, Signed, 11 In.	2070.00
Vase, Chrysanthemums, Translucent Green, Enameled, Long Neck, Bulbous Base, 23 In........	5079.00

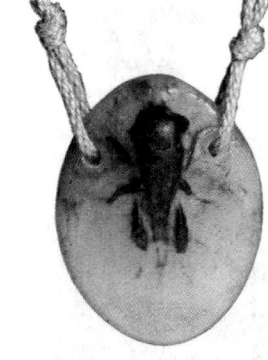

G.Argy-Rousseau, Pendant, Cameo, Brown Beetle, Blue Mottled, Yellow Ground, Pate-De-Verre, 1 ½ In. $288.00

Early Auction Co.

G.Argy-Rousseau, Vase, Brown, Red Flower Heads, Panels, Pate-De-Verre, Signed, c.1910, 9 ⅛ In. $3690.00

New Orleans Auction Galleries, Inc.

Galle, Bottle, Orange Flowers, Etched, Pale Orange Ground, Brass Fitting, Cameo, Signed, 11 In. $551.00

Skinner, Inc.

G

GALLE

Galle, Incense Burner, Amber, Crimson Flowers, Bronze Embossed Flowers, Cameo, Signed, 7 In.
$1495.00

Early Auction Co.

Galle, Vase, Bottle Shape, Trailing Enamel Flowers, Gilt, Signed, c.1900, 15 ¼ In.
$7768.00

Sloans & Kenyon

Galle, Vase, Fuchsia, Leaves, Flattened Oval, Flared Rim, Cameo, Signed, 4 x 4 ¾ In.
$3450.00

James D. Julia Inc.

Vase, Clematis, Vines, Blue, Purple, Yellow, Elongated Oval, Round Foot, Cameo, Signed, 10 In.	3163.00
Vase, Cylindrical, Citron, Plus On Royal Blue & Cobalt Stems, Footed Cameo, Signed, 15 In. ..	9000.00
Vase, Cylindrical, Yellow With Purple Cascading Wisteria Leafy Branch, Signed, 24 In............	1500.00
Vase, Daffodils, Yellow, Green Cut To Gold Cut To White, Tapered, c.1885, 10 ⅝ In.	3981.00
Vase, Dragonfly, Amber, Plants, Frosted, Blue, Cylindrical, Stepped Waist, Round Foot, Cameo, 12 In.	5520.00
Vase, Dragonfly, Amber, Pond, Frosted, Green, Banjo Shape, Rolled Lip, Cameo, Signed, 7 In..	3163.00
Vase, Dragonfly, Pond, Lilies, Flowers, Cameo, Signed, 6 ½ x 3 ¼ In.	748.00
Vase, Etude, Overlay Glass, c.1900, 4 In.	885.00
Vase, Fern, Frosted, Green, Stick Shape, Stepped Rolled Lip, Cameo, Signed, 12 In.	1840.00
Vase, Ferns, Crimson Over Green, Cameo, Elongated Neck, Bulbous Base, 17 ½ In................	3107.00
Vase, Fire Polished Red, Red Flowers, Bulbous, Tapered, Stand-Up Rim, 3 In.	1062.00
Vase, Flowering Vine, Lavender & Pink Over White, Bulbous, Spiral Fluting, 4 In.	1136.00
Vase, Flowers, Frosted, Purple, Stems, Hexagonal, Tapered Neck, Cameo, Signed, 8 ½ In.	575.00
Vase, Flowers, Leaves, Blue, Gray, Mottled Yellow Ground, Pear Shape, Cameo, Signed, 9 In....	3163.00
Vase, Flowers, Leaves, Blue, Purple, Yellow, Bulbous, Flared Rim, Multilayer, Cameo, Signed, 5 In.	1725.00
Vase, Fond De La Mer, Seaweed, Mottled, Foil Inclusions, 3 Shells, 10 In........................	21510.00
Vase, Fuchsia, Leaves, Flattened Oval, Flared Rim, Cameo, Signed, 4 x 4 ¾ In. ....*illus*	3450.00
Vase, Grapevine, Amber Over White To Crimson, Cameo, Elliptical Neck, 12 In......................	2629.00
Vase, Green Summer Landscape, Pink To Frost Ground, Cameo, Signed, 2 ½ x 8 In.	1920.00
Vase, Green, Brown, Landscape, Shouldered, Cameo, Signed, 18 ½ x 6 ¼ In.	1860.00
Vase, Hydrangea, Violet & Ocher Over White, Cameo, Bulbous, Flared Rim, 7 ½ In.	1434.00
Vase, Irises, Wheel Curved, Fire Polished, Cylindrical, Cameo, Signed, 12 ½ x 4 In.	1860.00
Vase, Lake Landscape, Green & Ocher Over White, Cameo, Pulled Rim, 7 ¼ In.	1434.00
Vase, Lake Scene, Green, Blue, Amber Ground, Cameo, Signed, c.1904, 4 ¼ In.	531.00
Vase, Landscape, Blue, Purple, Green To Yellow Ground, Monumental Shape, Cameo, 7 x 18 ½ In.	7200.00
Vase, Landscape, Blue, Purple, Green, Yellow, Frosted, Wavy Rim, Cameo, Signed, 7 x 18 In....	6600.00
Vase, Landscape, Brown Cut To Green, Blush Sky, Oval, c.1905, 7 ½ In.........................	1225.00
Vase, Lavender, Green Wisteria, Frosted, Pink Body, Flared, Cameo, Signed, 7 x 22 ½ In.	2200.00
Vase, Leafy Branch, Frosted, Yellow, Dark Purple, Stems, Double Gourd, Cameo, Signed, 5 In.	460.00
Vase, Leafy Flowers, Frosted, Purple, Stems, Bulbous Stick Shape, Cameo, Signed, 6 In..........	201.00
Vase, Leaves & Berries, Pink & Orange Over White, Cameo, Bottle Shape, 7 In.	1136.00
Vase, Leaves, White Shaded To Peach, Green, c.1900, 13 ¼ In.	1793.00
Vase, Magenta & Burgundy Flowers, Leaves, Yellow Ground, Cameo, 9 x 8 ½ In.	4800.00
Vase, Mountains, Blue, Brown, Leaves, Frosted & Yellow Ground, Elongated Oval, Cameo, Signed, 5 In.	2070.00
Vase, Mt. Fuji, Mottled Green Orange Ground, Signed E G Depose, 8 In.	2825.00
Vase, Orange, Green Flowers, Yellow Ground, Cameo, Signed, 4 ½ x 9 ½ In.	3080.00
Vase, Periwinkles, Magenta, Rose, Frosted & Yellow Ground, Cameo, 3 x 11 In.	1680.00
Vase, Plum Branches, Ocher & Violet Over Yellow, Cameo, Oval, 8 In........................	2988.00
Vase, Polar Bear, Ice Floes, Blue & White, Cameo, Signed, 14 ¼ In. ....*illus*	44840.00
Vase, Poppies, Pink & Green Over White, Cameo, Cylindrical, Footed, 6 ½ In.	1434.00
Vase, Purple Chrysanthemums, Orange, Pedestal Foot, Flared Lip, Cameo, Signed, 6 In.	1150.00
Vase, Purple Flowers, Yellow, Genie Bottle Shape, Rolled Rim, Cameo, Signed, 7 In................	1770.00
Vase, Purple Iris, Kidney Shape Bottom, Trumpet Stem, Cameo, 8 In.	885.00
Vase, Purple Wildflowers, Pink Ground, Tapered Pillow Shape, Shaped Rim, 5 In.	563.00
Vase, Red Blossoms, Yellow, Frosted Highlights, Flared, Cameo, Signed, 5 ½ x 15 In............	2970.00
Vase, Red Leaves & Berries, Frosted Ground, Thin Stem, Bulbous Base, Cameo, 13 ½ In............	1416.00
Vase, Red Roses, Branches, Frosted Ground, Yellow Rim, Tapered, Cameo, Signed, 4 x 17 ¼ In.	5700.00
Vase, Red, Burgundy Flowers, Leaves, Frosted Yellow, Footed, Cameo, 2 ½ x 8 In.	1760.00
Vase, Red, Burgundy Roses, Yellow, Frosted Ground, Squat, Shouldered, Cameo, 9 ½ x 7 In.	605.00
Vase, Red, Pink Magnolia Blossoms, Yellow, Frosted Ground, Oriental Signed, 6 x 17 In.	5500.00
Vase, Red, Purple Wild Roses, Yellow, Frosted Ground, Signed, 4 ¼ x 14 ½ In.	2860.00
Vase, Red, Roses, Yellow Ground, Cameo, Signed, 4 x 11 ¾ In.	3850.00
Vase, Roses, Red, Burgundy, Yellow Frosted Ground, Cameo, Signed, 9 ½ x 7 In.	6600.00
Vase, Spider Web, Leaves, Blue, Burgundy & Frost, Round, Square Foot, 3 ⅛ In.	2760.00
Vase, Stick, Pink With Grasshopper On Green & Blue Leaves, Signed, 5 In.	450.00
Vase, Stick, Pink With Purple & Green Stemmed Flower, Signed, 8 In...........................	650.00
Vase, Tapered, Round Foot, Ivory Ground, Acid Cut Leaves & Berries, Amber, Cameo, c.1900, 6 In.	1650.00
Vase, Thistles, Amber Ground, Lobed, Cameo, Engraved Galle Depose, c.1900, 9 ¾ In.............	2360.00
Vase, Urn Form, Citron With 2 Random Branches Of Blue Leaves, Footed, Cameo, Signed, 10 In.	900.00
Vase, Vines, Green, Textured & Fire Polished Clear Ground, Lobed, 8 ½ In.	1554.00
Vase, Water Lily, Yellow Ground, Violet, Crescent Shape, Cameo, Signed, c.1900, 5 ⅜ x 7 ½ In.	2032.00
Vase, Water Scene, Iris, Blue Shaded To White Ground, Tapered, Flared Rim, 16 In................	2695.00
Vase, Waterscape, Pond Lilies, Overlaid & Etched, Cameo, Signed, 4 ½ In. ....*illus*	593.00
Vase, Waterway, Trees, Leaves, Green, Cameo, Cylindrical, 9 ½ x 5 ¾ In.	920.00
Vase, Wildflowers, Dark Green Shaded To Blue & White, Bulbous, Squat, 4 In........................	830.00
Vase, Windswept Flowers, Purple, Green, White, Fire Polished, Frosted & Peach, 5 In..............	1955.00

G

Vase, Wisteria, Violet Over White, Cameo, Ball Shape, Pulled Elliptical Rim, 5 ¾ In.	1135.00
Wall Pocket, White Bonnet With Blue Ribbon, Yellow Floral Highlights, Signed, 11 In.	800.00

GALLE POTTERY was made by Emile Galle, the famous French designer, after 1874. The pieces were marked with the initials *E. G.* impressed, *Em. Galle Faiencerie de Nancy*, or a version of his signature. Galle is best known for his glass, listed above.

Candlestick, Rampant Lion, Imari Palette, Standing, Faience, Late 1800s, 17 In., Pair	2115.00
Figurine, Cat, Yellow, Blue & White, Circles & Hearts, Applied Eyes, Faience, c.1890, 13 In. ....*illus*	354.00
Plate, Raised Enamel, 2 Butterflies, Gilt, Square, Marked, E&G Depose, France, 8 In. .....*illus*	288.00

GAME collectors like all types of games. Of special interest are any board games or card games. Transogram and other company names are included in the description when known. Other games may be found listed under Card, Toy, or the name of the character or celebrity featured in the game.

Annie Oakley, Milton Bradley, Board, 1955, 9 ½ x 19 In.	31.00 to 55.00
Barney Google & Spark Plug, Milton Bradley, Board, Frame, 1923, 17 x 17 In.	475.00
Basketball, Tiddlywinks Type, Inset Playing Field, Net Backstops, McLoughlin, 20 x 11 In.	472.00
Bean Bag, Dart, Zorro, Vinyl, Box, c.1955	95.00
Board, Checkers & Backgammon, Black, Red, Gold, Gray, Pine, Folding, 16 x 15 In.	588.00
Board, Checkers & Backgammon, Paint, Square, Red, Brown, 16 In.	662.00
Board, Checkers & Backgammon, Pine, Painted, Early 1900s, 17 x 17 In.	148.00
Board, Checkers, Black & Gold Paint, Square, 1800s, 15 In.	518.00
Board, Checkers, Black & White, Gold Trim, Blue Border, c.1900, 14 x 14 ½ In. ....*illus*	1808.00
Board, Checkers, Mother-Of-Pearl, Wood Frame, 1900s, 19 x 19 In.	185.00
Board, Checkers, Painted, Yellow, Brick Red, Black Border, Yellow Scrolls, 13 x 13 In.	2925.00
Board, Checkers, Pine, Green, Black, Applied Trim, Signed, James H. Hale, c.1850, 10 x 9 ¾ In.	1528.00
Board, Checkers, Pine, Painted Blue, Red, Green Ground, Raised Edge Trim, 14 ¾ x 14 ½ In.	472.00
Board, Checkers, Pine, Red, Black Squares, Piece Trays, Gallery, Border, 27 x 18 ¾ In. ...*illus*	325.00
Board, Checkers, Red, Yellow, Black, Quebec, 30 x 19 In.	562.00
Board, Checkers, Wood, Multicolor Paint, Gilt Stenciled, Square, Vase, Grain, Leaves, 1800s, 20 x 20 In.	1541.00
Board, Checkers, Wooden, Hand Painted, Splatter Design Around Edges, 1880s, 15 x 19 In.	520.00
Board, Chess & Backgammon, Wood, Diamond Inlay, c.1900, 23 x 24 In.	201.00
Board, Parcheesi, Painted Multiple Colors, Wood, 1800s, 16 ½ x 16 ½ In. ....*illus*	4680.00
Board, Parcheesi, Painted, Red, Black, Green, Blue, Ivory, 18 x 18 In.	4388.00
Board, Parcheesi, Pine, Decoupage, Stag Corners, c.1890, 17 ¾ x 21 In.	3034.00
Board, Parcheesi, Pinwheels, Pipe Tongs, 19th Century, Quebec, 18 x 31 In.	5625.00
Board, Skittles, Green Felt, Folding	128.00
Branded, Chuck Connors, Western Themes, Milton Bradley, Board, 1966, 10 x 19 In.	155.00
Captain Kangaroo, Wood Figures, Milton Bradley, Board, 1956	40.00
Carnival, Ball Toss, Bust Of Hitler, Hit Nose & Jackass Ears Pop Up, Springloaded, 36 x 37 In.	2588.00
Checkerboard, Russet & Ivory Squares, Leafy Sprigs, New England, c.1890, 14 x 18 ½ In.	978.00
Chess Set, 32 Pieces, Wood, Turquoise, Carved, Indian Theme, D. Hyde, 1980s, 22 x 22 In.	1265.00
Chess Set, Aluminum Pieces, Plexiglass, Felt Board, Walnut Box, Austin Cox, Alcoa, 1966, 19 x 19 In.	960.00
Chess Set, Board, Bone, Inlays, Carved, Red, Green Enamel Pieces, 26 In.	288.00
Chess Set, Bone, 32 Carved Pieces, Hardwood Board, Storage Case, Bone Inlaid, 26 x 26 In.	184.00
Chess Set, Ivory Carved On Mystery Ball, Chinese, Case, 18 ½ x 9 ¼ In.	518.00
Chess Set, Ivory Figures Riding Horses, Camels & Elephants, Fitted Case, India, 6 In., 32 Pieces	1952.00
Chess Set, Ivory Folding Case, Chinese, 6 ½ In., 32 Piece	649.00
Chess Set, Ivory Pieces, White & Red, Lacquer Box, Chinese, 4 ½ In.	896.00
Chess Set, Ivory Pieces, Wood Folding Board, Ivory Plaques, Chinese, 3-In. King	1180.00
Chess Set, Leather Board, Carved Wood Pieces, 18 x 18 In.	150.00
Croquet, Wood, 6 Mallets, 6 Balls, Original Carrying Case, c.1920, 20 x 22 In.	210.00
Dexterity Puzzle, 2 Dice, Young Woman's Head, Tin, Glass, Germany, 1 ¾ In.	52.00
Dexterity Puzzle, Black Man, Top Hat, Try To Get White Teeth In Mouth, Tin, Glass, 2 ½ In.	139.00
Dexterity Puzzle, Cat, Felix, Reg. U.S. Pat. Off., Germany, 1920s, 2 ¼ In. ....*illus*	75.00
Dexterity Puzzle, Devil, Tin Rim, Mirror Back, Tin Lithograph, Patent, Germany, 2 ⅝ In. ....*illus*	612.00
Doctor, Doctor, Diagnosis Mr. Ilbent's Illness, Ideal, 1978	55.00
Dominoes, Punch & Judy Box, 1914	65.00
Errand Boy, McLoughlin, Board, Mat, Folding Frame, Box, c.1891, 19 ½ x 42 In.	118.00
Fast Mail, Railroad Theme, Spinner, Milton Bradley, Board, Inset, Frame, 22 x 22 In.	649.00
Fess Parker Wilderness Trail, American Tradition Co. & Transogram, Board, 1964	65.00
Fess Parker Wilderness Trail, American Tradition Co., Card, 1964	65.00
Frog Fishing, La Peche Aux Grenouiles, 24 Embossed Copper Frogs, 3 Poles, France, 18 x 9 In.	389.00
Gambling, Dice Cups, Leather, Bone Wood, c.1900, 3 Piece	146.00
Game Of Shopping, Board, Frame, c.1890, 20 x 20 In.	450.00
Go On Or Run For The Stake, McLoughlin Bros., Board, Frame, 18 x 18 In.	450.00

Galle, Vase, Polar Bear, Ice Floes, Blue & White, Cameo, Signed, 14 ¼ In.
$44840.00

Brunk Auctions

Galle, Vase, Waterscape, Pond Lilies, Overlaid & Etched, Cameo, Signed, 4 ½ In.
$593.00

Skinner, Inc.

G

Galle Pottery, Figurine, Cat, Yellow, Blue & White, Circles & Hearts, Applied Eyes, Faience, c.1890, 13 In.
$354.00

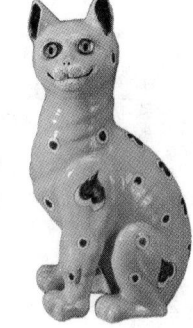

Brunk Auctions

Galle Pottery, Plate, Raised Enamel, 2 Butterflies, Gilt, Square, Marked, E&G Depose, France, 8 In.
$288.00

James D. Julia Inc.

Game, Board, Checkers, Black & White, Gold Trim, Blue Border, c.1900, 14 x 14 ½ In.
$1808.00

Garth's Auctions, Inc.

Game, Board, Checkers, Pine, Painted Red, Black Squares, Piece Trays, Gallery, Border, 27 x 18 ¾ In.
$325.00

Conestoga Auction Co., Inc.

Game, Board, Parcheesi, Painted Multiple Colors, Wood, 1800s, 16 ½ x 16 ½ In.
$4680.00

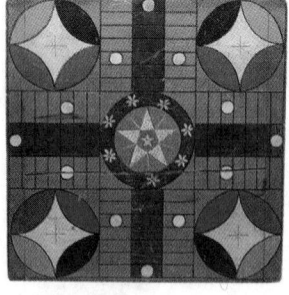

Norman C. Heckler & Company

Game, Dexterity Puzzle, Cat, Felix, Reg. U.S. Pat. Off., Germany, 1920s, 2 ¼ In.
$75.00

Hake's Americana & Collectibles

Golf, Spinning Wheel, Handheld, Landscape Scene, Celluloid, Nickel Plate Case, c.1950, 3 ¾ In..	201.00
Gumps At The Seashore, Spinner, 4 Wood Markers, Milton Bradley, Board, 1930s, 13 x 7 In.	115.00
Jigsaw Puzzle, Boy, Hunting, 22 Rifle, Whitman, 300 Piece, 1940s, 16 x 18 In.	50.00
Jigsaw Puzzle, Cheyenne, Clint Walker, Horse, Milton Bradley, 1959, 9 x 12 In.	50.00
Jigsaw Puzzle, Ring Around The Rosie, Milton Bradley, 30 Piece, 12 x 17 ½ In.,	35.00
Jigsaw Puzzle, United States Map, Laminated Cardboard, McLoughlin, 1890s, 13 ½ x 21 In. ...*illus*	224.00
Jigsaw Puzzle, Wild Bill Hickok & Jingles, 100 Piece, 1956	25.00
Jigsaw Puzzle, Wooster River Boat, Lithograph Paper, Wood Box, McLoughlin, 38 x 13 In.	885.00
Jigsaw Puzzle, Wyatt Earp, Full Body, Hugh O'Brien, 1950s, 17 x 21 In.	75.00
Jolly Marble, 5 Marbles, c.1892	429.00
Life's Mishaps, McLoughlin Brothers, Board, New York, 14 x 7 In.	165.00
Little Red Hen, Barnyard Friends, Board, Frame, 1950, 13 x 13 In.	140.00
Mahjong, Bone & Bamboo Tiles, Wooden Box, Brass Handles, 5 Drawers, 10 x 6 In.	316.00
Mahjong, Bone Over Bamboo Tiles, Wood Box, Brass Trim, Fitted Interior, 6 x 9 ½ In.	288.00
Mahjong, Carved Case, Drawers, Bamboo & Bone Tiles, c.1890, 9 ½ x 9 ½ In. ...*illus*	690.00
Mary Poppins Carousel, Parker Brothers, Board, 1964	25.00
Messenger Boy & Checkers, Milton Bradley, Board, Box, 17 x 9 ¾ In.	175.00
Monopoly, Parker Brothers, Board, Box, 1936, 6 ½ x 7 ½ In.	125.00
Moon Mullins Gets The Run-A-Round, Emmy Kicking Moon Out, Milton Bradley, Board, 1930s	115.00
Motor Race, Tin Litho Board, 6 Iron Cars, Spinner, Wolverine, 1925, 16 ½ x 16 ½ In. ...*illus*	278.00
Newlywed Game, Pressman Toy Corp., Board, 1960s	28.00
Old Maid Card Game, Whitman Publishing Company, 45 Cards, 1937	60.00
Ouija, Board, Parker Brothers, Box, c.1940	350.00
Our Gang Tipple Topple, Board, Lithographed Paper, Hinged Pegs, All-Fair, 1920s, 17 In.	456.00
Poker Set, Golf Theme, Rectangular Chip Holder, Card Slots, Raised Images, c.1950, 4 x 9 x 4 ½ In..	299.00
Psychic, Baseball, Parker Brothers, Board, Box, 1935	57.00
Punch & Judy, Baby, Litho Art, Board, Frame, c.1890, 16 x 16 In.	1250.00
Puzzle Cube, Aunt Louisa, Yankee Doodle, Wood, Lithograph, McLoughlin Bros., 10 x 13 In..	1416.00
Puzzle, Blocks, Wood, Chromolithograph, Jack & Beanstalk, McLoughlin Bros., Box, 10 x 11 In.	1200.00
Puzzle, Jig-O-Pin, Wood, Box, c.1932	173.00
Puzzle, Santa Claus, At Window, Girls In Bed, Scroll, Milton Bradley, Mat, Frame, 26 x 21 In..	118.00
Roulette Wheel, Table, Adjustable, Turned Pedestals, Stretcher, Claw Feet, L. Rude Mfg.	1475.00
Rummikub, Score Pad, Box, 1 ½ x 13 In.	61.00
Sherlock Holmes, Parker Brothers, Card, Instructions, Box, 1904	75.00
Skeezix Visits Nina, Spinner, 4 Markers, Milton Bradley, Board, 1930s, 14 x 7 ½ In.	115.00
Snake, Paper Litho On Wood, 34-Star American Flag, Fisher & Brother, Board, 18 x 23 In.	374.00
Sock Me Here Pony, Carnival Ball Toss, Leather Covered, c.1900, Life Size, Pair	10500.00
Table Billiards, Metropolitan, Flame Figured Mahogany, Brunswick, Blake, Callender, c.1938	295.00
Table, Arcade, Electric, Wood Frame, Figures, Steel Marbles, 13 x 23 In.	58.00
Table, Craps, Claw Feet Legs, Carrying Case, 128 x 54 In.	720.00
Table, Foos Ball, Mahogany, Glass Covered, Wood Players, Beads, South Cone Furn., 35 x 58 In.	915.00
Target, Ball Toss, Painted Metal, Peeping Tom, Partially Dressed Woman, France, 17 x 20 In.	719.00
Target, Seven Dwarfs, Snow White On Cover, Cardboard Dwarfs, American Toy Co., 1938	310.00
Touring, Parker Brothers, Card, Box, 1920s	12.00
Uncle Wiggly, Die Cut Markers, Cards, Milton Bradley, Board, 1949, 19 x 10 In.	95.00
Wa-Hoo, Wood, Painted, Board, USA, 1970s, 15 x 15 In.	22.00
Wheel, Big Six Gaming Wheel, Red Pole, Blue Dice Edges, H.C. Evans, c.1890, 60 In.	2607.00
Wheel, Crown & Anchor, Wood Stand, Cast Iron Base, Playing Card Decals, Evans, 50 x 32 In.	826.00
Wheel, Lodge, Hand Painted, Wooden Post, 3 Cast Iron Feet, 1 To 48, 67 x 40 In.	690.00
Wonderful World Of Oz, Folding Board, Instructions, Tokens, Spelling Cubes, Cup, 20 x 10 In.	323.00

GAME PLATES are plates of any make decorated with pictures of birds, animals, or fish. The game plates usually came in sets consisting of twelve dishes and a serving platter. These sets were most popular during the 1880s.

Fish Set, Various, Cobalt Blue Border, Gilt Rim, Signed A. Holland, Wedgwood, 9 In., 10 Piece	354.00
Game Bird, In Flight, Scalloped Rim, Limoges, 1890s, 8 In.	99.00
Mallard Duck, Pheasant, Decal, 22K Gold, c.1910, 8 ½ In.	32.00

GARDEN FURNISHINGS have been popular for centuries. The stone or metal statues, wire, iron, or rustic furniture, urns and fountains, sundials, and small figurines are included in this category. Many of the metal pieces have been made continuously for years.

Arbor, White Paint, Openwork, Pointed Arch, Iron, 100 x 51 In.	219.00
Armillary Sphere, Bronze, 2 Dolphins, Arrow, Stone Base, c.1885, 48 x 27 In.	3936.00
Barrel, Famille Verte, Birds, Flowers, Pierced Coins, Vinery, Tree, Chinese, c.1855, 18 In.	2300.00
Barrel, Rose Medallion, Hexagonal Shape, Chinese, 1800s, 19 x 12 In.	920.00
Bench, Arched Back, Legs, Grapevines, Pierced Seat, White, Cast Iron, 31 x 45 In.	2440.00

Bench, Arched, Pierced, Slab Seat, Flared Legs, Cast Stone, Colvin & Hastings, 42 x 78 x 16 In.	2280.00
Bench, Back Splats, Neoclassical Urns, Garland, Cast, Wrought Iron, X-Shape Base, c.1900....	1440.00
Bench, Camelback, Entwined Strapping Arcs, Slatted Seat, Penny Feet, Iron, 1700s, 63 x 21 In.	1840.00
Bench, Curved Seat, Cherub Supports, Concrete, 3 Sections, 16 x 50 In.	63.00
Bench, Geometric Designs, Plank Seat, Wrought Iron, 45 x 64 x 20 In.	1320.00
Bench, Gothic, Arched Back, Shield, Quatrefoil Uprights, Scroll Arms, Iron, c.1890, 38 x 48 In.	837.00
Bench, Grapevines, Black Paint, Cast Iron, 33 x 43 In..	207.00
Bench, Neoclassical Style, Pierced Lattice, Outscrolled Arms, Curule Legs, Iron, 22 x 33 In.....	184.00
Bench, Regency Style, Wood Saddle Seat, X-Round Base, Cast Iron, c.1950, 17 x 50 In., Pair..	1722.00
Bench, Roses, Slat Back, Shaped Arms, Oval Finials, Walnut, Inset Majolica Tiles, 44 x 48 In.	120.00
Bench, Scrollwork, X-Stretcher, Double Back, Arms, Cabriole Legs, Painted, Iron, 31 x 33 In..	180.00
Bench, Shaped Crest Rail, Slat Back, Seat, Outscrolled Arms, Stretcher, Teak, 1900s, 42 x 66 In.	3250.00
Bench, Victorian, James Bebe, Twig, Cast Iron, c.1870, 33 ½ x 50 x 20 In......................	4080.00
Bench, Victorian, Pierced Back, Wood Slat Seat, Cast Iron, White Paint, Coalbrookdale, 33 x 58 In.	1989.00
Bench, Victorian, Rounded, Pierced Lily-Of-The-Valley Back, White, Cast Iron, 33 ½ x 62 In.	1872.00
Bench, Victorian, White Paint, Open Work, Slat Plank Seat, Paw Feet, Iron, 35 x 56 In., Pair..	900.00
Bench, White Paint, Scroll Back & Arms, Cabriole Legs, Cast Iron, 34 x 41 In.	915.00
Bench, Wire, White, Ohio In Wirework, Shaped Back, Arms, Bromwell Co., c.1855, 37 In. ...... *illus*	529.00
Birdbath, Baroque Style, Round Bowl, Leaf Carved Pedestal, Marble, c.1800, 48 x 24 In.........	3776.00
Birdbath, Fluted Column, Gadrooned Bowl, Cement, 35 x 23 In...	357.00
Birdbath, Round Bowl, Figural Pedestal Base, 3 Winged Seahorses, Concrete, 39 x 35 In.	345.00
Birdbath, Round, Flared Molded Edge, Baluster Stem, Egg & Dart Base, Iron, 43 x 30 In.......	400.00
Birdbath, Round, Scalloped Rim, Cast Iron, 32 In...	201.00
Birdbath, Shallow Bowl, Tapered Column, Block Base, Marble, c.1910, 34 x 18 In.	1230.00
Birdbath, Shell Shape Dish, Putti Base, Perched Bird, Cast Lead, 31 x 15 In......................	1003.00
Birdhouse, Country House Shape, Wire, Painted Green, Yellow, Brown, 1800s, 25 x 26 In.......	663.00
Boot Scraper, Cast Iron, c.1810, 9 x 4 In.	105.00
Boot Scraper, Cast Iron, Stone Base, 1800s, 13 x 15 ½ In.	288.00
Boot Scraper, Dachshund, Standing Profile, 2 Round Feet, Bronze, 7 In..........................	474.00
Boot Scraper, Pointer, Full Figure, Cast Iron, 15 x 18 ½ In...	454.00
Chair Set, Oval Back, Host Chair, 4 Sides, Spring Steel, c.1925, 43 In., 37 ½ In., 5 Piece ...... *illus*	1035.00
Chair, Curved Back, Woven Seat, Twist Legs, Cross Stretcher, Wrought Iron, c.1920, 32 In.......	780.00
Chair, Fern Design, Pierced, Outswept, Bracketed Legs, Arms, Cast Iron, 33 x 24 In., Pair.....	2440.00
Chair, Rolled Back, Seat, Scrolling Arms, Downswept Legs, Usine Sauveur Arras, 31 In., Pair..	9120.00
Chair, Tete-A-Tete, Wrought Iron, Central Table, Russel Woodard, c.1950, 29 x 69 In...............	900.00
Cross, Figure Of Mary, Pierced, Flower, Cast Iron, 65 x 38 In.	676.00
Dining Set, Fern Design, Table, Glass Top, Metal, Painted, 6 Chairs, 29 x 68 In...................	2375.00
Figure, 2 Frolicking Maidens, Seminude, Holding Ribbon, Pedestal, Marble, 79 x 19 In.	8302.00
Figure, Bird, Rook, Perched, Black, Yellow, Green, Clay, 8 ½ In.	69.00
Figure, Bust, Woman, Egyptian Revival Style, Copper, Stone, White Wash, 1800s, 31 x 21 In. ..... *illus*	837.00
Figure, Ceres, Goddess Of Harvest, Holding Wheat Sheath, Concrete, 59 x 22 In...................	161.00
Figure, Children Depicting The Four Seasons, Plinth Base, Concrete, 25 In., 4 Piece	777.00
Figure, Closed Red Umbrella, C-Scroll Handle, Base, Cast Iron, Lead, 106 x 23 In...................	1112.00
Figure, Crane, Open Beak Water Spout, Standing, Patinated Bronze, 79 In., Pair..................	3346.00
Figure, Dog, Dalmatian, Seated, White & Black Paint, Cast Stone, 1900s, 30 x 13 In., Pair.....	575.00
Figure, Dog, Greyhound, Reclining, Plinth Base, Cement, 1900s, 16 x 27 In., Pair..............	1016.00
Figure, Dog, Poodle, Painted Brown, Rectangular Base, 27 ½ In., Pair............................	100.00
Figure, Dog, Reclining, Glass Eyes, Brown, Earthenware, c.1900, 21 ¼ x 6 In........................	575.00
Figure, Dog, Spaniel, Paw On Flower Basket, 26 In., Pair	200.00
Figure, Duck, Mound Of Leaves, 2 Parts, Red, Black, Green Paint, Iron, Cement, c.1900, 13 In.	326.00
Figure, Eagle, Arched Wings, Sideward Glancing, Round Base, Cement, 1981, 24 In., Pair......	657.00
Figure, Eagle, Spread Wing, Perched On Square Base, Lead, c.1900, 17 x 46 In., Pair..............	4025.00
Figure, Flower Filled Basket, Cement, 1900s, 12 In., Pair..	329.00
Figure, Gargoyles, Perched On Sphere, Pedestal Stand, Wings Up, Sandstone, 52 x 14 In., Pair	563.00
Figure, Goose, White Paint, Cast Iron, 26 In., Pair...	173.00
Figure, Heron, Metal, 18 In..	150.00
Figure, Hound, Resting, Cast Stone, 8 x 27 In., Pair	878.00
Figure, Labrador Pup, Sitting, Cast Cement, 24 In..	270.00
Figure, Lion, Reclining, Limestone, 14 x 4 x 8 In...	300.00
Figure, Lion, Seated, Paw On Shield, Cast Stone, 20 x 16 In., Pair	89.00
Figure, Lion, Standing, Open Mouth, Stand, Concrete, 30 x 42 In., Pair	313.00
Figure, Man, Wearing Toga, Cast Cement, 42 In...	389.00
Figure, Mythological Sirens, Entwined, Rocky Base, Patinated Metal, 1900s, 51 x 44 In.	5795.00
Figure, Pagoda, Cement, 15 x 15 In...	59.00
Figure, Peacock, Lead, 36 In., Pair..	1650.00
Figure, Putti, Holding Dolphin, Verdigris Patina, 29 In..	770.00
Figure, Rabbit, Seated, White Paint, Cast Iron, c.1910, 12 In. .... *illus*	385.00

Game, Dexterity Puzzle, Devil, Tin Rim, Mirror Back, Tin Lithograph, Patent, Germany, 2 ⅝ In.
$612.00

Hake's Americana & Collectibles

Game, Jigsaw Puzzle, United States Map, Laminated Cardboard, McLoughlin Bros., 1890s, 13 ½ x 21 In.
$224.00

Hake's Americana & Collectibles

Game, Mahjong, Carved Case, Drawers, Bamboo & Bone Tiles, c.1890, 9 ½ x 9 ½ In.
$690.00

James D. Julia Inc.

Game, Motor Race, Tin Litho Board, 6 Iron Cars, Spinner, Wolverine, 1925, 16 ½ x 16 ½ In.
$278.00

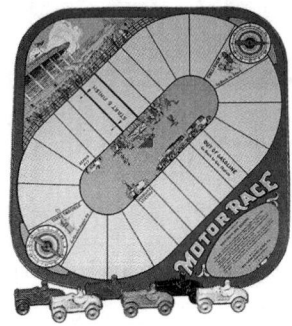

Serious Toyz

Garden, Bench, Wire, White, Ohio In Wirework, Shaped Back, Arms, Bromwell Co., c.1855, 37 In.
$529.00

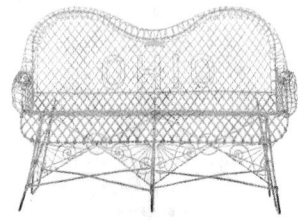

Garth's Auctions, Inc.

Garden, Chair Set, Oval Back, Host Chair, 4 Sides, Spring Steel, c.1925, 43 In., 37 ½ In., 5 Piece
$1035.00

Leland Little Auction

Garden, Figure, Bust, Woman, Egyptian Revival Style, Copper, Stone, White Wash, 1800s, 31 x 21 In.
$837.00

Neal Auction Co.

Broken Dishes

The French term for a mosaic made from broken dishes is *pique assiette*. The term is also used by English-speaking artists.

Figure, Seated Dogs, Paw On Flower Basket, Cast Stone, c.1905, 25 In., Pair	851.00
Figure, Whippet, Seated, Full Body, Glass Eyes, Tan Paint, Cast Iron, c.1890, 19 In.	1304.00
Figure, Woman, Classical Garment, Holding Flower Swag, Square Base, Cement, 49 In.	489.00
Figure, Woman, Nude, Seated On Stool, Holding Platter, Romania, c.1900, 37 x 24 In.	3690.00
Figure, Woman, Standing, Holding Object, Draped Robe, Cast Concrete, 51 In., Pair	403.00
Flowerpot, Coggled Band, Manganese Splash, Pottery, Penn., 12 x 13 In.	415.00
Fountain, 2 Dolphins, Ocean Wave, Pedestal Base, Mouth, Spout, Bronze, 46 In.	219.00
Fountain, 2 Putti, Seated On Satyr, Grape Clusters, Stone, c.1940, 41 x 38 x 14 In.	3444.00
Fountain, 3 Tiers, Round Graduated Bowls, 3 Swan Pedestal Base, Bronze, 39 x 22 In.	518.00
Fountain, Baroque Style, Bowl Over Support, Pan Figures, Bronze, 85 x 48 In.	3938.00
Fountain, Bird, Child, Seated, Arms Out, Bronze, J. Scudder, c.1915, 32 x 12 In.	52900.00
Fountain, Boy, Fishing, Sitting On Stump, Fish On Rod, Verdigris Finish, 59 ½ x 17 In.	1560.00
Fountain, Boy, Seated, Playing Flute, Cast Lead, 17 In.	549.00
Fountain, Bullfrog, Leaping, Dragonfly, Water Flow From Frog's Mouth, Bronze, 26 In.	259.00
Fountain, Cherub On Swan, Masks, On Bowl, Putti, Dolphin Supports, Bronze, 72 In.	5378.00
Fountain, Cherub Riding Dolphin, 2-Tiered Shell Basin, Urn, Square Base, Lead, 56 x 26 In.	1076.00
Fountain, Child, Holding Fish, Bronze, Roman Bronze Works, c.1920, 41 In.	10800.00
Fountain, Child, Holding Fish, White Metal, 1900s, 22 ½ x 11 ½ In.	434.00
Fountain, Children At Water Fountain, Bronze, 46 x 44 x 26 In.	3206.00
Fountain, Crocodile, Raised Head & Tail, Open Mouth, Bronze, 47 In.	863.00
Fountain, Dog, Seated, Chain Leash, Pot Metal, 36 In.	288.00
Fountain, Harem Girl, Standing, Tall Vase, Bull Elephant Head, Bronze, 72 In.	920.00
Fountain, Lion's Head, Mouth Spout, Wall Mount, Bronze, 16 ½ x 8 In.	259.00
Fountain, Neoclassical Masks, Flared, Wavy Rim, Fluted Pedestal, Lead, 44 x 34 In., Pair	1872.00
Fountain, Nude Bather, Women, Bird Heads, Dolphins, Marble, 3 Parts, 1800s, 84 x 52	6900.00
Fountain, Pan, 2 Flutes, Cast Lead, 36 x 10 In.	369.00
Fountain, Pedestal, 3 Lion's Head Support Column, Round Bowl, Bronze, 58 x 23 In.	575.00
Fountain, Raised Bowl, Putto Supports, Garlands, Pedestal Spouting Lion Mask, Bronze, 58 x 39 In.	978.00
Fountain, Round Bowl, Pedestal Base, Spout In Center, Concrete, 47 x 19 In.	104.00
Fountain, Round Gadrooned Basin, Putti, Pedestal, Square Column, Bronze, 68 x 30 In.	1150.00
Fountain, Shell Basin, 2 Children, Goose, Head Spout, Column Pedestal, Bronze, 85 x 45 In.	920.00
Fountain, Shell Basin, Dolphin Pedestal, Putti, Spouting Dolphin, Bronze, 78 x 37 In.	920.00
Fountain, Spouting Elephant Heads & Girl, Over 3 Elephant Pedestal Base, Bronze, 99 x 59 In.	1725.00
Fountain, Spouting Pacific Marlin, Rising Vertically, Round Marble Base, 42 In.	1150.00
Fountain, Statue, Naked Boy, Seated On Rock, Blowing Bugle, Cast Bronze, 44 In.	4428.00
Fountain, Swan, Spread Wings, Bronze, 44 x 50 x 47 In.	2612.00
Fountain, Urn, Leaf Handles, 3 Swans Support, Pedestal Base, Cast Iron, 1900s, 70 In.	1845.00
Fountain, Urn, On Pedestal, Fleur-De-Lis, Basin, Cast Cement, 73 x 50 In.	738.00
Fountain, Wall, Dolphins, Shell, Spouting Head, 2 Mermaids, Bronze, 70 x 40 In.	748.00
Fountain, Wall, Fountain, Lion's Head, Footed Dish, 2 Piece	236.00
Fountain, Water Lily Shape, Bronze, 19 x 37 In.	1150.00
Fountain, Winged Boy, Holding Fish, Bronze, Patina, c.1920, 28 In.	1722.00
Hitching Post, Black Head Finial, Cast Iron, 1800s, 52 ½ In.	1422.00
Hitching Post, Black Jockey, Cast Iron, Painted, 35 In.	295.00
Hitching Post, Black Jockey, Painted, Base, Cast Iron, 1910, 36 x 15 x 14 In.	265.00
Hitching Post, Horse Head, Cast Iron, L.T. Barnum Wire & Iron Works, 6 Ft.	935.00
Hitching Post, Horse Head, Fluted Post, Nose Ring, Cast Iron, 1800s, 44 ½ In. ....*illus*	2032.00
Hitching Post, Horse Head, Mouth Ring, Fluted Post, Cast Iron, 1800s, 45 x 6 In.	2032.00
Hitching Post, Horse Head, Nose Ring, White Paint, Cast Iron, 1800s, 13 In.	92.00
Hitching Post, Jockey, Green & White, Plinth Base, Cast Iron, 24 In.	176.00
Hitching Post, Jockey, Plinth Base, Cast Iron, 47 In. ....*illus*	1175.00
Hitching Post, Tree Trunk, Cast Iron, c.1880, 64 In.	452.00
Jardiniere, 3 Dragons, Waves, Clouds, Flames, Bulbous, Chinese, 8 ½ In.	540.00
Jardiniere, Blue & White, Dragons, Lucky Symbols, Chinese, Porcelain, 12 ½ x 11 In., Pair	418.00
Jardiniere, Blue, White, Peonies, Key Border, Porcelain, Wood Stand, Chinese, 1800s, 32 x 16 In.	799.00
Jardiniere, Cherubs, Latin Text, Octagon Shape, Pottery, 15 ½ x 16 ½ In.	288.00
Jardiniere, Cloisonne, Bulbous, Splayed Foot, Multicolor, Stand, Chinese, c.1925, 12 x 15 In.	1107.00
Jardiniere, Cobalt Insets, Gilt Metal Mounts, Stand, Porcelain, 1900s, 32 x 15 In.	2868.00
Jardiniere, Flowers, Scrolls, Cloisonne, Carved Wood Stand, Chinese, c.1910, 6 ½ x 11 In.	2070.00
Jardiniere, Openwork Rope Design, Round Side Handles, Iron, 20 In.	438.00
Jardiniere, U-Shape, Molded Sides, Putti, Swag Garland, Rolled Rim, Stone, 29 x 34 In., Pair	2100.00
Lamp, Pagoda Top, Sphere, Blooming Lotus, Elephants, Cloisonne, c.1855, 35 In.	920.00
Lawn Jockey, Black, Concrete, Multicolor Paint, 44 x 24 In.	201.00
Lawn Jockey, Black, Holding Lantern, Square Base, Cast Iron, 43 x 19 In.	690.00
Lawn Jockey, Black, Horse Tie, Blue Jacket, White Hat, Cast Iron, 39 In.	2200.00
Lawn Jockey, Painted, Aluminum Hat, Iron Plinth, 40 x 11 x 11 In.	540.00
Lawn Jockey, Painted, Holding Lantern, Molded Plinth, Iron, 1800s, 36 x 11 In.	460.00

G

Pedestal, Square Column Shape, Black, Relief Design, Cast Iron, 32 x 19 In.	219.00

Plant Stand, see Furniture, Stand, Plant

Planter, 8 Tiles, Pink Musical Designs, Leaves, Acorn Finials, Brass, Porcelain, 11 x 25 In.	325.00
Planter, Art Nouveau, Applied Children, Nude Woman On Sides, Bronze, 6 ½ x 11 In.	492.00
Planter, Arts & Crafts, Oval, 4 Post Legs, Embossed Squares, Copper, c.1910, 5 x 8 In.	460.00
Planter, Box, Peacock, Cast Concrete, Copper Finish, Calif., 12 x 12 x 49 In., Pair	345.00
Planter, Copper Liner, Underplate, Applied Dolphins, Leaves, Bronze, France, c.1900, 8 x 22 In.	805.00
Planter, Dragons Amidst Waves, Archaic Style, Blue Glaze, Oval, Flat Rim, 5 x 5 In.	118.00
Planter, Ebonized Wood, Bronze Openwork, Mother-Of-Pearl Inlay, Oval, 8 x 15 In.	1063.00
Planter, Figural, African Elephant, Basket Saddle Flowerpot, Bronze, 18 ½ In.	460.00
Planter, Figural, Swan, Aluminum, Painted, 1960s, 29 x 41 In.	1895.00
Planter, Floor, Burro Shape, Standing, Open Burden Basket, Bronze, 48 In.	489.00
Planter, Foo Dog Mask Head Handles, Calligraphy, Gilt Bronze, 6 In.	863.00
Planter, Masks, Flowers, Pedestal Shape, Iron, 44 x 22 In., Pair	288.00
Planter, Regency Style, Fluted, Wreaths, Footed, Cast Iron, c.1910, 115 x 28 In., Pair	492.00
Planter, Round, Footed, Vase Shape, S-Curve Bird Head Handles, Cast Iron, 37 x 35 In.	690.00
Planter, Round, Leaf Border, Reeded, Round Stand, Cast Stone, 25 In. Diam	177.00
Planter, Squat, Bulbous, Vines, Flowers, Pottery, Metal Rim, Enamel, Gilt, 8 In. Diam., Pair	119.00
Planter, Thistle Design, Cast Stone, 35 In., Pair	236.00
Planter, Woven Wire Basket, Scroll Sides, Leaf Shape Supports, Cast Iron, c.1855, 27 x 17 In.	1035.00
Rack, 3 Tiers, Semicircular, Painted, Wrought Iron, 28 x 39 In.	176.00
Seat, Barrel Shape, Blue & White, Latticework, Flowers & Birds, Staffordshire, c.1900, 18 x 14 In.	633.00
Seat, Blue & White, Flowers, Barrel Shape, Pierced Symbols, Chinese, 19 In.	215.00
Seat, Blue & White, Foo Dog, Lotus Scroll, Studded Borders, 18 x 11 ½ In., Pair	351.00
Seat, Blue, White, Birds, Landscape, Barrel Shape, Pierced, Chinese, 18 In.	338.00
Seat, Cash Symbols, Peonies, Leaves Barrel Shape, Pierced Design, White Glaze, 18 In., Pair	399.00
Seat, Celestial Dragon & Celestial Pearl, Black, Yellow, White, 18 In., Pair	338.00
Seat, Central Serpentine Cutout, Flowering Bamboo, Bracket Feet, Hexagonal, 1800s, 19 In.	613.00
Seat, Cranes, Clouds, Flowers, Foo Dog Mask Lugs, Blue, White, Chinese, 1800s, 16 In.	2252.00
Seat, Famille Jeune, Yellow Ground, Barrel Shape, Porcelain, Chinese, c.1890, 18 In., Pair	1778.00
Seat, Famille Rose, Family Scenes, Openwork Cash Coins, Blue Ground, Chinese, 1800s, 19 In.	613.00
Seat, Famille Rose, Figural Panels, Hexagonal Shape, Chinese, 19 In., Pair	1045.00
Seat, Famille Rose, Figures, Flower & Butterfly Bands, 18 In., Pair	920.00
Seat, Famille Rose, Pierced, Panels, Figures, Birds & Flowers, Chinese, c.1850, 18 In. .....illus	1434.00
Seat, Famille Rose, Yellow Ground, Pierced Top, Gilt Brass, Hexagonal, 19 x 13 In., Pair	4972.00
Seat, Faux Bois Design, Barrel Shape, Porcelain, c.1920, 17 ½ In.	690.00
Seat, Fitzhugh Pattern, Wavy Borders, Leafy Twigs, Rondels, Blue, White, Hexagonal, 1900s, 19 In.	2875.00
Seat, Leaves & Birds, Barrel Shape, Mother-Of-Pearl Inlay, Hardwood, 13 In., Pair	620.00
Seat, Majolica, Red, White, Tufted, Garlands, Fruit Swags, Leg Leaves, Marked, Wedgwood, 18 In.	536.00
Seat, Orange, Blue, Gilt, Imari Style, Drum Shape, 1900s, 19 In., Pair	2500.00
Seat, Peaches, Peonies, Lotus, Pierced Symbols, Octagonal Barrel, 18 In., Pair	9225.00
Seat, Porcelain, Blue & White, Flowers, Figures, Barrel Shape, Chinese, 19 In., Pair	389.00
Seat, Rose Medallion, Barrel Shape, Multicolor, Gilt Knobs, 1800s, 19 In.	2015.00
Seat, Rose Medallion, Figures In Garden, Flowers, 18 x 12 In.	7500.00
Seat, White Ground, Figures, Flowers, Dots, Hexagonal, Porcelain, Chinese, 18 In., Pair	207.00
Seat, Yellow, Gold Dragons, White Flowers, Hexagonal, Drum Shape, Chinese, 15 In.	2880.00
Settee, Back, Seat Cushion, Iron, Patinated, 56 In.	219.00
Settee, Branches, Leaves, Acorns, Intertwined Snake Legs, Green, Iron, c.1890, 32 x 49 In. ....illus	3200.00
Settee, Fern Pattern, Scrollwork Seat, Cast Iron, 33 x 54 In. ....illus	4880.00
Settee, Pierced, Scrolled Oak Leaves, Ivy, Lion's Heads, Paw Feet, Iron, 37 x 59 In., Pair	7170.00
Sundial, Brass, Father Time, Grow Old Along With Me, Best Is Yet To Be, Bird, 1900s, 12 In.	207.00
Sundial, Compass, Equatorial, Swag & Flower Design, Octagonal, Germany, 1700s, 2 ¼ In.	1035.00
Sundial, Compass, Equinoctial, Brass Plate, Bled Steel Needle, 1800s, 5 In.	178.00
Sundial, Compass, Wood, Beringer Style, 4 Dials, Brass Gnomons, 9 In.	429.00
Sundial, Let Not The Sun Go Down Upon Your Anger, Bronze, C.E. Going, 1700s, 12 In.	518.00
Sundial, Noon Signal, Marble Base, Arabic Numerals, Brass Cannon, c.1850, 13 In.	1593.00
Sundial, Round Plate, Inscribed, Roman Numerals, Sun Face, Scrolled Axis, 3 x 5 In.	178.00
Sundial, Sailboat, Arabic Chapter Ring, Weller Column, Stand, Cast Iron, 1900s, 35 x 12 In.	690.00
Tree Tub, Putti, Fern Handles, Lion Masques, Patinated Brass, 31 x 34 In.	2952.00
Trellis, Pierced Oval Shape, Scroll, Arrow Design Center, White Paint, Iron, 71 x 37 In.	31.00
Urn, Cover, Ram's Heads, Swags, Wood Base, Iron, 1800s, 12 ½ In.	71.00
Urn, Curved Pierced Handles, Stepped Base, Cast Iron, c.1900, 22 x 33 In., Pair	1416.00
Urn, Egg & Dart Rim, Body, Handles, Fluted Pedestal, Iron 20 x 15 In.	121.00
Urn, Egg & Dart Rim, Handles, Bacchanalian Frieze, Cast Iron, Townley, c.1880, 45 x 21 In.	3198.00
Urn, Figures, Tropical Garden, Cream Ground, Blue, Tapered, Rolled Rim, c.1922, 19 In.	3450.00
Urn, Gadrooned Rim, Fluted Body, Flared Base, Iron, 24 x 18 In., Pair	357.00

Garden, Figure, Rabbit, Seated, White Paint, Cast Iron, c.1910, 12 In.
$385.00

Skinner, Inc.

G

Garden, Hitching Post, Horse Head, Fluted Post, Nose Ring, Cast Iron, 1800s, 44 ½ In.
$2032.00

Neal Auction Co.

Garden, Hitching Post, Jockey, Plinth Base, Cast Iron, 47 In.
$1175.00

Cowan's Auctions

Garden, Seat, Famille Rose, Pierced, Panels, Figures, Birds & Flowers, Chinese, c.1850, 18 In.
$1434.00

Neal Auction Co.

Garden, Settee, Branches, Leaves, Acorns, Intertwined Snake Legs, Green, Iron, c.1890, 32 x 49 In.
$3200.00

Skinner, Inc.

Garden, Settee, Fern Pattern, Scrollwork Seat, Cast Iron, 33 x 54 In.
$4880.00

Neal Auction Co.

Garden, Urn, Leaves, Acanthine Lion's Head Handles, Iron, Kramer Bros., Oh., c.1850, 52 In.
$4183.00

Neal Auction Co.

Urn, Green Glaze, 1900s, 34 x 21 In.		527.00
Urn, Handles, Plinth Base, Cast Iron, Walbridge & Co., 27 In.		265.00
Urn, Handles, Rings, Patina, Cast Iron, 21 x 18 In.		2091.00
Urn, Leaves, Acanthine Lion's Head Handles, Iron, Kramer Bros., Oh., c.1850, 52 In.	*illus*	4183.00
Urn, Lid, Ram's Head, Fruit Swags, Ribbons, Pedestal Base, Cement, 84 x 27 In.		1438.00
Urn, Lobed, Kneeling Nude Support, Cast Stone, 53 x 26 In.		369.00
Urn, Multicolor Fruit, Cast Iron, 7 In.		28.00
Urn, Neoclassical, Pedestal Base, Iron, 26 ½ In., Pair		688.00
Urn, Reeded, Classical Figures, Putto, Lion Handles, Marble, Gilt Metal, Patinated, 15 x 8 In., Pair		760.00
Urn, Ribbed, Gadrooned Top, Putti, Ram's Heads, Pedestal, Cast Iron, 48 x 31 In., Pair		3198.00
Urn, Rosette Designs, Downswept Column, Zinc, c.1910, 34 x 23 In.		738.00
Urn, Shaped Openwork Handles, Stepped Square Stand, Iron, 36 x 47 In.		688.00
Urn, Shaped Sides, Square Foot Base, Leaf Design, Cast Stone, 19 x 16 In.		575.00
Urn, Squat, Melon Shape, Scrolled Arms, Round Pedestal, Cast Iron, 1900s, 20 x 23 In.		120.00
Urn, Vase Shape, Square Foot, Relief Design, Black, Cast Iron, 51 In., Pair		1093.00
Urn, Wide Mouth, Base, Cement, 21 In., Pair		92.00

GARDNER Porcelain Works was founded in Verbiki, outside Moscow, by the English-born Francis Gardner in 1766. The Gardner family retained ownership of the factory until 1891 and produced porcelain tablewares, figurines, and faience.   ГАРДНЕРЪ

Cup & Saucer, Gilt Scrolling, Rose Bouquets, White Ground, c.1890	325.00
Figurine, Mother Carrying Son, Father Carrying Daughter, Russia, c.1830, 12 In., Pair	8400.00
Jug, Cream, Baluster, Pastoral Scene, 5 ¼ In.	1350.00

GAUDY DUTCH pottery was made in England for the American market from about 1810 to 1820. It is a white earthenware with Imari-style decorations of red, blue, green, yellow, and black. Only sixteen patterns of Gaudy Dutch were made: Butterfly, Carnation, Dahlia, Double Rose, Dove, Grape, Leaf, Oyster, Primrose, Single Rose, Strawflower, Sunflower, Urn, War Bonnet, Zinnia, and No Name. Other similar wares are called Gaudy Ironstone and Gaudy Welsh.

Bowl, Single Rose, Footed, 5 ½ x 2 ¾ In.	325.00
Creamer, Oyster, 4-Footed, 4 ½ In.	110.00
Cup, Yellow Hearts, Handleless, 2 ½ In.	225.00
Plate, Butterflies, Vase With Flowers, 10 ½ In.	795.00
Tea Set, Oyster, Teapot, Sugar & Creamer, Cover	1541.00
Tea Set, Single Rose, Teapot, Sugar & Creamer, 6 ½ In.	770.00
Waste Bowl, Single Rose, 1800s, 3 x 6 ⅜ In.	207.00

GAUDY IRONSTONE is the collector's name for the ironstone wares with the bright patterns similar to Gaudy Dutch. It was made in England for the American market after 1850. There may be other examples found in the listing for Ironstone or under the name of the ceramic factory.

Cup & Saucer, Cobalt Blue, Red & Orange Flowers, Ribbed, Gilt	185.00
Plate, Aurora, 9 In.	85.00
Plate, Seeing Eye, Ceres Shape, c.1856, 5 In.	79.00
Plate, Seeing Eye, Paneled, 8 ½ In.	79.00
Platter, Flowers, Vase, Bird, Clouds, Russet, Gold, Dark Blue	690.00
Punch Bowl, Blow Blue, Green, Orange, Flowers, Footed	395.00
Relish, Leaf Shape, Flowers, 8 ¾ x 5 In.	98.00
Soup, Dish, Chrysanthemum, 7 ⅜ In.	55.00

GAUDY WELSH is an Imari-decorated earthenware with red, blue, green, and gold decorations. Most Gaudy Welsh was made in England for the American market. It was made from 1820 to about 1860.

Chamber Pot, Copper Luster Accents, Molded Handle, 2 x 3 In.	94.00
Plate, Dessert, Wagon Wheel, 6 In.	57.00
Urn, Bowl, Flowers, Blue & Red, Copper Luster, 11 ¼ In.	59.00

GEISHA GIRL porcelain was made for export in the late nineteenth century in Japan. It was an inexpensive porcelain often sold in dime stores or used as free premiums. Pieces are sometimes marked with the name of a store. Japanese ladies in kimonos are pictured on the dishes. There are over 125 recorded patterns. Borders of red, blue, green, gold, brown, or several of these colors were used. Modern reproductions are being made.

Bowl, Geisha, Flowers, Mountains, Scalloped Rim, 7 In.	45.00
Bowl, Nut, Oriental Scene, Scalloped Red Rim, 3-Footed, 2 x 8 In.	39.00

G

Cup & Saucer, 2 Geisha Near River, Green Trim	25.00
Cup & Saucer, 4 Portraits, Lithophane, 1930s	199.00
Cup & Saucer, Huts, Island, Geisha In Boat, c.1920	42.00
Cup, 3 Geisha On Porch, Cobalt Blue Trim, Bamboo Handle, 2 x 4 In.	18.00
Dresser Box, Geisha, Flowering Cherry Trees, Mountains, Gold Lattice, Lid, 3 In. Diam.	65.00
Sugar, Geisha On Bridge, Red Trim, Loop Finial, 4 x 5 In.	55.00

GENE AUTRY was born in 1907. He began his career as the "Singing Cowboy" in 1928. His first movie appearance was in 1934, his last in 1958. His likeness and that of the Wonder Horse, Champion, were used on toys, books, lunch boxes, and advertisements.

Doll, Plastic, Painted Hair, Checkered Shirt, Jeans, Boots, Holster, Terri Lee, 16 In.	2736.00
Doorstop, Horse, Inscribed Gene Autry's Champion, Brown, Cast Iron, 10 ½ In.	267.00
Guitar, Emenee Musical Toys, Box, 32 In.	113.00
Gun & Holster, Leslie-Henry Guns, Box	650.00
Gun, Revolver, Cap, Red Handle, Cast Iron, 8 ½ In.	113.00
Lunch Box, Melody Ranch, Cork Stopper, Red Top, Universal, 1954	149.00
Pin, Gene On Champ, Waving Hat, Blue Ground, Late 1940s, 1 ¾ In.	52.00
Songbook, Cowboy Songs, No. 2, 28 Songs, Gene & Champion On Cover	25.00

GIBSON GIRL black-and-blue decorated plates were made in the early 1900s. Twenty-four different 10 ½-inch plates were made by the Royal Doulton pottery at Lambeth, England. These pictured scenes from the book *A Widow and Her Friends* by Charles Dana Gibson. Another set of twelve 9-inch plates featuring pictures of the heads of Gibson Girls had all-blue decoration. Many other items also pictured the famous Gibson Girl.

Plate, A Message From The Outside World, 10 ½ In.	150.00
Plate, Mr. Waddles Arrives Late & Finds Her Card Filled, 10 ½ In.	125.00
Plate, She Becomes A Trained Nurse, 10 ½ In.	140.00
Plate, She Goes To The Fancy Dress Ball As Juliet, 10 ½ In.	155.00
Plate, Some Think She Remained In Retirement Too Long, c.1900, 10 ½ In.	265.00
Plate, They Go Fishing, 10 ½ In.	130.00

GILLINDER pressed glass was first made by William T. Gillinder of Philadelphia in 1863. The company had a working factory on the grounds at the Centennial and made small, marked pieces of glass for sale as souvenirs. They made a variety of decorative glass pieces and tablewares.   **GILLINDER**

Plate, Ulysses Grant Portrait, Peace, Green, Maple Leaf Border, c.1885	85.00

GIRL SCOUT collectors search for anything pertaining to the Girl Scouts, including uniforms, publications, and old cookie boxes. The Girl Scout movement started in 1912, two years after the Boy Scouts. It began under Juliette Gordon Low of Savannah, Georgia. The first Girl Scout cookies were sold in 1928.

Calendar, 1954, Black & Asian Scouts, 10 x 17 In.	20.00
Calendar, 1955	20.00
Catalog, Equipment, 1953, 8 x 8 In., 24 Pages	20.00

GLASS-ART. Art glass means any of the many forms of glassware made during the late nineteenth or early twentieth century. These wares were expensive when they were first made and production was limited. Art glass is not the typical commercial glass that was made in large quantities, and most of the art glass was produced by hand methods. Later twentieth-century glass is listed under Glass-Contemporary, Glass-Midcentury, or Glass-Venetian. Even more art glass may be found in categories such as Burmese, Cameo Glass, Tiffany, and other factory names.

Basket, Cranberry, Opalescent Satin, Silver Stand, Quilted Bowl, Enamel, Ruffled, Wilcox, 14 x 12 In.	460.00
Basket, Green Iridescent, Sterling Overlay Flowers, Handle, Flared Base, Rim, 19 x 11 In.	874.00
Basket, Pink, Green Spatter, Cased, Clear Applied Thorn Handle, Star Shape, 6 x 6 In.	50.00
Basket, Pink, Yellow Mottled, Cased, Clear Thorn Handle, 5 ½ In.	50.00
Basket, White With Cranberry Interior, Clear Applied Thorn Handle, 7 ½ x 6 ½ In.	50.00
Biscuit Jar, Amber, Coralene Flowers, Butterflies, Silver Plate Lid, Bail Handle, 7 In.	325.00
Biscuit Jar, Brown, Sailboat Scene, Silver Plate Lid, Bail Handle, Handley, 7 In.	50.00
Biscuit Jar, Brown, White Mottled Ground, Sailboat Scene, Silver Plate Lid, Handle, 7 In.	25.00
Biscuit Jar, Cased, Yellow, White Swirls, Enamel Birds, Flowers, Silver Plate Lid, Handle, 7 In.	125.00
Biscuit Jar, Frosted Satin, Enamel Iris, Silver Plate Lid, Bail Handle, 6 ½ In.	90.00
Biscuit Jar, Painted Scene, 4 Koi Fish, Silver Plate Lid, Bail Handle, Lott Nancy, 7 ¾ In.	90.00
Biscuit Jar, Pink, Amber, Geometric, Pink Enamel Flowers, Silver Plate Lid, Handle, 8 ½ In.	150.00

Glass-Art, Syrup, Polka Dot, Opaque Blue Overlay, Applied Handle, Metal Top, 5 ¾ In.
$546.00

Glass Works Auctions

Glass-Blown, Creamer, Cobalt Blue, 19 Vertical Ribs, Flared Rim, Solid Handle, Pontil, c.1820, 4 ⅝ In.
$585.00

Norman C. Heckler & Company

Glass-Blown, Milk Pan, Citron Yellow, Folded Rim, Burst Bubble, Zanesville, Oh., 10 ¼ In.
$2115.00

Garth's Auctions, Inc.

TIP

If garage windows are painted, burglars won't be able to tell if cars are home or not. Use translucent paint to get light in the closed garage, if it has an entrance to your house.

Glass-Blown, Pokal, Amber, Enameled, Cavalier, Hand Painted, 12 ½ In. $138.00

The Stein Auction Co.

Glass-Bohemian, Chalice, Green Translucent, Dwarfs Harvesting Grapes, Holbein, Lobmeyr, 10 In. $1333.00

Early Auction Co.

Glass-Bohemian, Vase, Red Cut To Clear, Etched Design, Beading, Gilded, 12 ¼ In. $296.00

Skinner, Inc.

Biscuit Jar, White Opaque, Pink Orchids, Silver Plate Lid, Bail Handle, 6 ½ In.	45.00
Bottle, Hourglass Shape, Applied Ribbons, Flowers, Stopper, Italy, 12 In.	145.00
Bottle, Oval, Narrow Rim, Iridescent Blue & White, Stopper, Signed, France, 12 x 6 In.	375.00
Bowl, Blue, White Cased, Ruffled Rim, 6 ¾ In.	60.00
Bowl, Centerpiece, Deep Purple & Blue Swirl, Gold, Wide Ruffle Rim, Wavy, B. Hawn, 7 In.	173.00
Bowl, Clambroth, Gold, Red, Clear Foot, Rippled Rim, Victorian, 9 In.	90.00
Bowl, Flared Corners, Pointed Edge, Orange, 6 x 2 In.	36.00
Bowl, Flaring Rim, Round Foot, Gold Iridescent, U.S.A., 6 In. Diam.	98.00
Bowl, Flowers, Leaves, Vines, Gold, Green, Pink, Silver Accents, Squat, Flared Center, 8 In.	920.00
Bowl, Opalescent, Blue Pulled Feather Design, Oval, Folded-In Rim, Signed, C. Lotton, 1972, 4 In.	288.00
Bowl, Red, Mottled Multicolor, Metallic Accents, Threaded & Ruffled Rim, 22 x 17 In.	138.00
Bowl, Reeded & Ruffled Rim, Mottled Blue & Yellow, Metallic Flecks, 20 x 18 In.	127.00
Bowl, Rose, Quilted, Yellow & Green, Squat, Ruffle Rim, 4-Footed, 6 In.	59.00
Bowl, Ruffled, Blue Cased, Silver Mica Highlights, White Exterior, 7 In.	10.00
Cake Stand, Scalloped Edge, Pedestal, Diamond Facets, 1940s, 10 x 7 In.	179.00
Charger, White Opalescence, Blue Tints, Spiral Design, Signed J. Landier, 13 ¾ In.	546.00
Cigar Holder, Cut Overlay, Pink To Opal, Oval & Crosshatch Cuttings, Serrated Rim, 3 ⅛ In.	127.00
Claret Jug, Metal Mounts, Art Nouveau, Green Glass, Square Leaf Handle & Finial, c.1905, 15 In.	313.00
Compote, Ferns, Lattice, Smoky Amber Glass, Square Base, Wide Flared Rim, France, 3 ¼ x 11 ¾ In.	58.00
Decanter, Amber Iridescent, Stopper, Ball Shape, Bottle Neck, Ruffled Rim, 12 x 4 In.	115.00
Decanter, Clear, Leaves Ormolu Mounts, Scroll Footed Base, St. Louis Crystal, France, 12 ½ x 6 ½ In.	1265.00
Decanter, Stopper, Bottle Shape, Flowers, Birds, Handle, Gilt Over Orange Enamel, 10 In.	385.00
Dish, Flared Ruffled Rim, Gold Iridescent, 6 In. Diam.	98.00
Dish, Sweetmeat, Amber, Thumbprint, Enamel Flowers, Insects, Silver Plate Lid, Bail Handle, 5 ½ In.	100.00
Dish, Sweetmeat, Brown, Green Mottled Border, Flowers, South Devon, Silver Plate, 3 ½ x 5 In.	60.00
Epergne, Cranberry Swirl, Ribbed, Vines Leaves, Gold Flecks, 3 Flutes, c.1900, 16 In.	550.00
Ewer, Dahlia Pattern, Amethyst, Upswept Spout, Pink Mottled, Handle, Pear Shape, 13 In.	2360.00
Figurine, Cockerels, Multicolor, 11 ¾ In., Pair	84.00
Jar, Cabinet, Yellow, Flared Rim, Tapered Neck, Chinese, 4 In.	270.00
Pitcher, Daffodil Pattern, Blue Opalescent, Ruffle Rim, Loop Handle, Baluster, 10 In.	1064.00
Pitcher, Water, Pink, Brown Mottled Highlights, Silver Mica, Clear Ribbed Handle, 8 In.	150.00
Pitcher, Water, Red, Yellow Flowers, Square Shape, Flare Spout, Loop Handle, Tumbler, 9 In.	86.00
Portrait, Clear, Sulphide, Gentleman In Profile, c.1830, 2 ¼ x 2 ⅛ In.	443.00
Rose Bowl, Yellow, Amber Flowers, Brown Branches, Scalloped Rim, Mother-Of-Pearl, 4 In.	86.00
Sugar Shaker, Light Blue, Pearlescent, Smokestack, Zigzag Design, 6 In.	460.00
Syrup, Polka Dot, Opaque Blue Overlay, Applied Handle, Metal Top, 5 ¾ In. *illus*	546.00
Tumbler, Opal Glass, Blue Pulled Feather Design, Iridescent, Rounded Bottom, 1972, 4 In.	173.00
Vase, Art Nouveau, Gilt Overlay, Swirling Lotus Stems, Purple Floating Flowers, c.1880, 11 In.	369.00
Vase, Art Nouveau, Green Iridescent, Flattened, Elongated Neck, Austria, 7 ¾ In.	207.00
Vase, Blue To White Overlay, Flowers, Long Neck, Crimped, 2 Twig Shape Handles, 8 ½ In.	30.00
Vase, Bottle Shape, Flared Mouth, 4 Twist Handles, Iridescent, Oil Spot, 9 In.	2684.00
Vase, Bottle Shape, Swollen Center, Blue, Dark Swirls, Applied Strands, Iridescent, Signed, 8 In.	259.00
Vase, Cameo, Round Foot, Swollen Shoulder, Frosted White, Burgundy Flowers, France, 7 In.	92.00
Vase, Clear, Gold Rim, Rose Color Flowers, Rectangular, Enameled, Signed, 12 x 9 In.	403.00
Vase, Cobalt Blue To Clear, Gilt Band Of Figures, Square Foot, 12 In., Pair	1830.00
Vase, Cylindrical, Waisted Neck, Ruffled Rim, Iridescent Dark Blue, White Striations, 7 In.	81.00
Vase, Dragonflies, Cattails, Royal Blue, Teal, Cylindrical, Slightly Swollen, Squared Rim, 7 ¾ In.	489.00
Vase, Elongated Pear Shape, Wood Base, Birds, 2 Seals, Etched, Chinese, 15 In.	156.00
Vase, Emerald Green, Yellow, Blue, Crisscross Threading, Tri-Throated, Human Heart Shape, 7 In.	345.00
Vase, Fan, Translucent Jade Green, Ribbed, Domed Alabaster Foot, 11 In.	237.00
Vase, Genie Bottle, Ruffle Rim, Iridescent Purple, Silver Strands, c.1900, 8 ½ In.	144.00
Vase, Gilt Enamel Fish, Lotus, Cranes, Continental, c.1890, 11 ¼ In., Pair	863.00
Vase, Goblet Shape, Gilt & Enamel, Ruby, Portrait Medallions, Flowers, Scalloped, 1800s, 13 In.	1763.00
Vase, Gold & Amber Iridescent, White Waves, Pontil, c.1900, 10 In.	399.00
Vase, Gold Iridescent, Baluster, Neoclassical Head, Gilt Laurel Wreath, Signed, Austria, c.1915, 8 ½ In.	215.00
Vase, Gold, Purple, Round Foot, Tapered, Flared Rim, c.1900, 5 x 3 In.	153.00
Vase, Gourd Shape, Pinched Rim, Black Glaze, Pink Swirl Drips, 5 In.	104.00
Vase, Green & Pink Iridescent, Rolled Rim, 10 ½ In.	8260.00
Vase, Green Iridescent, Acid Cut, Round Foot, Stick Shape, Chalice Shaped Top, Leaves, c.1900, 10 In.	1168.00
Vase, Green Iridescent, Blue Threading Design, Cylindrical, Swollen Foot, Slight Pinched Waist, 11 In.	115.00
Vase, Green Iridescent, Silver Drip Overlay, Oval Shape, Narrow Rim, Pontil, c.1900, 4 In.	399.00
Vase, Green Iridized, Silver Overlay, La Pierre Mfg., c.1910, 11 In.	369.00
Vase, Green Pulled Feathers, Silvery Blue, Shouldered, Flare Rim, Orient & Flume, 1978, 7 In.	230.00
Vase, Green, Gold, Purple, Pulled Feather Design, c.1900, 7 In.	492.00
Vase, Green, Sterling Silver Iris Overlay, 8 In., Pair	700.00
Vase, Green, Yellow, Lavender, Ebony, Swirling Feathers, Unfurling Flower Shape, 10 ¼ In.	173.00

Vase, Handkerchief Shape, Multicolor, Stephen Nelson, 22 ½ x 16 ½ In.	748.00
Vase, Harvest Moon, Trees, Wisteria, Tangled Branches, Dark Blue, Urn Top, Tapered Bottom, 10 ¾ In.	460.00
Vase, Iridescent Blue, Swirl Design, Threading, Water Sprinkler Shape, Curved Neck, 7 In.	150.00
Vase, Iridescent Ruby Red To Yellow, Ruffle Rim, Pedestal Foot, 9 In.	345.00
Vase, Iridescent White, Trumpet Shape, Metal Round Foot Base, 15 In.	41.00
Vase, Iridescent, Amethyst, Blue, Green, Swirl Design, Baluster, Ruffled Rim, Signed, 7 In.	207.00
Vase, Opal Glass, Red, Silver Hooked Feather Design, Elongated Oval, Flared Rim, 1974, 9 In.	633.00
Vase, Oval Shape, Narrow Rim, Iridescent Gold, Green, Orange & Yellow Lines, 6 ½ In.	69.00
Vase, Pale Green To Cranberry Peach, Crackle Glaze, Flared Base, Cylindrical, 12 In.	69.00
Vase, Peach & White Overlay, Fruit Spray, Crimped Ruffled Rim, Square Handles, 7 In., Pair	30.00
Vase, Pink Flowers, Blue Vines, Clear Ground, Tapered, Shouldered, Rolled Wide Rim, 8 In.	115.00
Vase, Purple & Blue Spatter, Aventurine Spots, Bulbous Base, 8-Petal Rim, 6 In.	115.00
Vase, Purple Iridescent, Green Feathery Plumes, White, Urn Shape, Round Foot, 12 ¾ In.	374.00
Vase, Purple, Gold, Green Iridescent, Ribbed, Half Twist Neck, Spread Foot, Swollen Mouth, 12 In.	259.00
Vase, Red To Clear, Narrow Neck, Flared Rim, Elongated Circle Design, Dot Pattern, 7 In.	29.00
Vase, Rose, Ball Shape, Pinched Neck, Ruffled Rim, Dark Pink Satin, Lines, 5 x 6 In.	173.00
Vase, Sapphire Blue Butterflies, Sparkly Wings, Pink Flowers, Green Leaves, 6 ½ In.	345.00
Vase, Square, Rounded, Stretched Swirl, Multicolor, Flowers, Blue Interior, Millefiori, 10 x 7 In.	138.00
Vase, Swollen Top, Narrow Base, Round Foot, Cameo, Yellow, Flowers, 12 In.	250.00
Vase, Trumpet Shape, Cobalt Blue Leaf Design, 12 In.	134.00
Vase, Tulip Shape Top, Narrow Neck, Sage Green Oval, Gilt Metal Leaves, Art Nouveau, 9 In.	593.00
Vase, White, Pink, Amber, Acorns, Leaves, Ruffled Rim, Smokestack, Stevens & Webb, 6 In.	59.00
Vase, White Iridescent, Green Lip Wrap, Squat, Ruffled Rim, Footed Acanthus Leaf Stand, 6 In.	86.00
Vase, Yellow, Pink Flower Heads, Blue Black Leaves, Scrolling Vines, Urn, Downward, 9 ¾ In.	3105.00

GLASS-BLOWN. Blown glass was formed by forcing air through a rod into molten glass. Early glass and some forms of art glass were hand blown. Other types of glass were molded or pressed.

Bird Waterer, Molded, Cone Shape, 8 Vertical Ribs, Cobalt Ball Finial, Rigaree Wafer, 5 ½ x 2 ½ In.	161.00
Bowl, Aqua, Flared Out, Tooled Rim, Pontil, 4 x 12 In.	439.00
Bowl, Cobalt Blue, Flint, Cup Shape, 16 Raised Radius Lines, 5 x 3 In.	177.00
Carafe, Pillar Mold, 8 Ribs, Opaque White, Applied Wide-Collar Neck Ring, 6 ¾ In.	150.00
Celery Vase, Pillar Mold, 8 Ribs, Applied Blue Ribs, Baluster Stem, Footed, 10 In.	1610.00
Celery Vase, Pillar Mold, Yellow, 8 Ribs, Scalloped, Knop Stem, Footed, 10 In.	345.00
Compote, 12 Vertical Ribs, Flared Rim, Baluster Stem, 4 ¾ In.	112.00
Compote, Cover, Pillar Mold, 8 Ribs, Baluster Stem, Footed, Pear-Shaped Finial, 10 In.	805.00
Compote, Dome Ribbed Cover, Pillar Mold, 8 Ribs, Baluster Stem, Footed, 16 In.	460.00
Compote, Round Bowl, Hollow Knopped Shaft, Biscuit, Disk Base, Early 1800s, 7 x 9 In.	207.00
Creamer, Blue Thread Wrap, Bulbous, Pulled Spout, Applied Handled, 4 In.	266.00
Creamer, Cobalt Blue Cased, Opal Inside, Low Shoulder, Opal Handle, c.1880, 5 In.	104.00
Creamer, Cobalt Blue, 19 Vertical Ribs, Flared Rim, Solid Handle, Pontil, c.1820, 4 ⅝ In. *..illus*	585.00
Creamer, Olive Green, White Splotches & Stringed Rim, Flared Neck, Pontil, 4 In.	439.00
Creamer, Purple Blue, Bulbous, Tapered, Flared Rim, Shaped Handle, 5 ⅜ In.	380.00
Cruet, Reeded, Clear, Applied Handle, Pad Foot, Pewter Cap, 7 ¼ In.	254.00
Decanter, 3-Mold, Aquamarine, Square, Diamond Diaper Pattern, Ribbed Panels, 1800s, 7 In.	1067.00
Decanter, 8 Flute, Canary Yellow, Double Ring Mouth, 11 In.	259.00
Decanter, 8 Flute, Sapphire Blue, Shouldered, Applied Bar Lip, c.1860, Qt., 10 In.	748.00
Decanter, 12 Panel, Deep Emerald Green, Shouldered, Applied Bar Lip, Qt., 10 In.	1265.00
Decanter, Cobalt Blue, Shell & Ribbing Molded, Ball Stopper, 9 In.	805.00
Decanter, Cordial Set, Orange, Black Stopper, Rim, Black Stem, Orange Bowl, 11 In., 6 Piece	81.00
Decanter, Marbrie Loop, Gray Tint, Opal Loopings, 3 Neck Rings, Flared Lip, 8 In.	127.00
Decanter, Prism Cut, Flowers, Swag, Diagonal Cut Stopper, c.1800s, 10 x 3 ¼ In., Pair	546.00
Decanter, Stylized Pig Shape, Clear, Sapphire Blue Ears & Tail, Rigaree, 7 x 9 In.	161.00
Decanter, Threaded, Blue Roundels, Footed, 10 x 4 In.	118.00
Drapery Rod Finials, Hobnail, Translucent Starch Blue, Pyriform Body, Applied Prunt, 4 ¾ x 3 In.	150.00
Epergne, Victorian, Apple Green Opaline, Ruffled Bowl, Basket Shape Holders, c.1890, 23 x 12 In.	538.00
Fly Trap, Clear, Applied Shell Style Feet, c.1870, 6 ¾ x 5 In.	92.00
Goblet, Cased White, Opal Inside, Gray Tinted Stem & Foot, c.1850, 5 ½ In.	978.00
Goblet, Turquoise, Twisted Stem, Amethyst Bowl, Bellflower Shape, 8 In., 6 Piece	69.00
Hat Stand, Victorian, Flared Bottom, c.1890, 12 In.	75.00
Hat, Yellow, Rolled Rim, 3 In.	140.00
Hourglass, Triple, Flint, Brass Frame, Engraved, Stamped, 10 ½ x 6 ½ In.	372.00
Jar, Golden Amber, Pear Shape, Flared Ring Lip, 7 ⅝ In.	280.00
Jar, Tinned Sheet Iron Lid, Short Neck, 10 In.	71.00
Jug, Clear, Fluted Bottom, Applied Curled Strap Handle, Pt.	546.00
Jug, Clear, Raised Gold Leaves & Vines, Faceted Ball Stopper, Victorian, 8 In.	49.00

Glass-Bohemian, Wedding Cup, Gilt Metal, Transparent Enamel Flowers, Fritz Heckert, 7 ¾ In.
$1610.00

Fox Auctions

G

Glass-Contemporary, Bowl, Opal Glass, Iridescent Drop Leaf, Cased, Rolled Rim, Charles Lotton, 2004, 5 ½ In.
$405.00

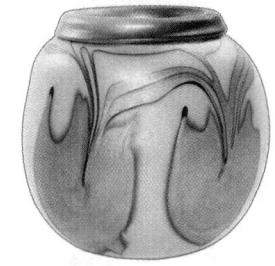

Early Auction Co.

Glass-Contemporary, Sculpture, Multicolor, John Littleton, 1988, 12 ¼ x 17 In.
$434.00

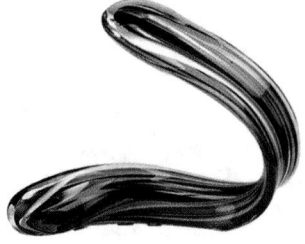

Rago Arts & Auction Center

TIP

For a pollution-free glass cleaner use a mixture of white vinegar and water.

Glass-Contemporary, Vase, Bud, Paperweight, St. Louis, Millefiori, 150th Anniversary, SL 1845-1995, 5 ⅜ In. $1035.00

James D. Julia Inc.

Glass-Contemporary, Vase, Cobalt Blue, Iridescent Blue Leaves, Pulled Feather, Orient & Flume, 1979, 7 ¼ In. $316.00

Humler & Nolan

Glass-Contemporary, Vase, Seashell, Iridescent, Leaf & Seaweed, White Oil Spot, Signed Muller, 9 In. $403.00

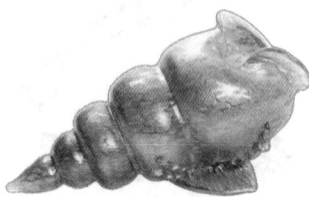

Early Auction Co.

TIP

Rust spots on bottles can be removed with steel wool or a knife blade.

Milk Pan, 8 Curves, Swirled Lines, Flint, Ground Pontil, 9 In.	94.00
Milk Pan, Citron Yellow, Folded Rim, Burst Bubble, Zanesville, Oh., 10 ¼ In. ....*illus*	2115.00
Milk Pan, Cobalt Blue, Rolled Rim, Broken Pontil, 3 ½ In.	384.00
Milk Pan, Pale Green, Folded Rim & Foot, c.1825, 8 ¼ In.	823.00
Molasses Jug, Bellflower, Vine, Applied Handle, Britannia Lid, 7 x 5 In.	150.00
Molasses Jug, Peace & Plenty, Opaque White, Oval, Wheat Wreath, Steam Ship, 5 ½ x 4 In.	207.00
Molasses Jug, Reverse Colonial, Sage Green, Tapered, Hexagonal, Hollow Handle, 7 x 5 In.	2645.00
Mug, Clear, Engraved Stylized Tulips, Pinched Edge, Strap Handle, 6 In.	259.00
Mug, Pillar Mold, 9 Ribs, Cobalt Blue, Pinched Waist, 5 ½ In.	489.00
Mug, Sunburst, Diamond Diaper, Ribs, Cylindrical, Rayed Base, 3 ⅜ In.	1840.00
Pitcher, Amber, Crimped, Pad Foot, Neck, Flared Rim, Pulled Spout, Loop Handle, 9 In.	5015.00
Pitcher, Green Aqua, Bulbous, Wide Flaring Neck, Applied Crimped Foot, 6 In.	351.00
Pitcher, Hunter Green Cased, Opal Inside, Bulbous, Squat, Opaque Black Handle, 7 In.	81.00
Pitcher, Jade Green Cased, Opal Inside, Pear Shaped, Opal Foot & Handle, 8 In.	92.00
Pitcher, Lily Pad, Aqua, Squat, Globular, Double Rib Handle, Crimped Foot, c.1840, 6 ½ In.	3450.00
Pitcher, Overshot, Clear, Tankard, Pinched Spout, Twisted Rope Handle, 9 ½ In.	127.00
Pitcher, Squat Sphere, Flared Neck, Threaded Rim, Shaped Hollow Handle, 8 In.	392.00
Pokal, Amber, Enameled, Cavalier, Hand Painted, 12 ½ In. ....*illus*	138.00
Salt, Amber, Goblet Form, Globular, Short Stem, c.1840, 3 ¼ x 2 In.	345.00
Salt, Colorless, Ribbed & Diamond Bands, Folded Rim, c.1830, 2 ¼ x 2 ¼ In.	150.00
Salt, Deep Amethyst, Slumped Low Shoulder, c.1820, 1 ¾ x 2 x 2 ½ In.	978.00
Salt, Master, Amethyst, Reeded, Footed, Flared, Folded Rim, 2 ¼ In.	142.00
Smoke Bell, Cut, Frosted, Applied Green Hanging Ring, 8-Petal Rim, Vine, Berries, 6 ¾ x 5 In.	104.00
Snow Globe, Compressed, Funnel Shape, Folded Rim, Foot, Pontil, 1840-70, 12 x 4 In.	69.00
Sugar, Baluster, Clown Hat Lid, Finial, c.1830, 7 ½ In.	470.00
Sugar, Dome Cover, Clear, Folded Rim, Chain Pattern Band, Round Foot, 1800s, 5 In.	563.00
Syrup, 10 Panels, Amethyst, Pinched Waist, Neck Ring, c.1850, Qt., 10 ½ In.	489.00
Syrup, Pillar Mold, 8 Ribs, Cone Shape, Concave Neck Ring, Britannia Nozzle, 8 In.	173.00
Syrup, Pillar Mold, Canary Yellow, 8 Ribs, Neck Ring, Cylindrical, Silver Nozzle, 11 In.	288.00
Syrup, Pillar Mold, Electric Blue, 8 Ribs, Cylindrical, Britannia Nozzle, 11 In.	403.00
Toddy Lifter, Clear, Flute & Honeycomb Design, Applied Ring, 13 In.	207.00
Tumbler, Ale, 12 Flutes, Engraved Hops & Barley, Footed, 5 ⅜ In.	58.00
Tumbler, Clear, Engraved Garland & Bows, 3 ¾ In.	81.00
Tumbler, Flip, Clear, Engraved Stylized Tulips, 7 ¾ In.	230.00
Vase, Hyacinth, Light Sienna, Cone Shape, Cupped Top, Pontil, c.1880, 8 x 3 In.	104.00
Vase, Marbrie Loop, Clear, Blue Loopings, Rigaree, Gemel Flask Shape, Clear Foot, 8 In.	184.00
Vase, Trumpet, Marbrie Loop, Opal, Rose Loopings, 8-Petal Rim, Dome Foot, 10 ⅜ In.	288.00
Vase, Trumpet, Opal, Red & Blue Swirled Threads, 8-Petal Rim, Dome Foot, 12 In.	374.00
Whimsy, Bellows, Clear, Applied Prunts, Rigaree, Threading, Handles, 8 In.	69.00
Whimsy, Hat, Curled Rim, Amber, Sheared, Pontil, 2 ½ In.	176.00
Whimsy, Pipe, Mottled, Multicolor, Opal Cased Interior, Applied Bowl, c.1850, 10 ½ In.	46.00
Wig Stand, Flared Rim Saucer, Reeded Stem, Flattened Ball Pad, 9 ½ In.	94.00
Witch's Ball, Aquamarine, Red, Blue Side Stripe, Rough Pontil, 1850-80, 3 In.	81.00
Witch's Ball, Cornflower Blue, 12 Opal Swirled Stripes, 1880-1920, 7 In.	104.00
Witch's Ball, Dark Steel Blue, Opal Spatter, c.1865, 3 ⅝ In.	69.00
Witch's Ball, Marbrie Loop, Clear, Red & Green Loopings, c.1880, 5 ¾ In.	288.00
Witch's Ball, Marbrie Loop, Opal, Rose Loopings, Baluster Stand, c.1880, 12 In.	460.00

GLASS-BOHEMIAN. Bohemian glass is an ornate overlay or flashed glass made during the Victorian era. It has been reproduced in Bohemia, which is now a part of the Czech Republic. Glass made from 1875 to 1900 is preferred by collectors.

Basket, Iridescent, Cased Amber, Clear Loop Handles, Wilhelm Kralik, 15 In.	58.00
Beaker, Ruby Stain, Engraved, American Views, Washington, Niagara, 4 ½ x 3 In.	2070.00
Biscuit Jar, Green, Lobed Shape, Silver Plate Mountings, Handle, 7 ½ x 6 ½ In.	345.00
Bowl, Cream, Green, Rose, Pink, Yellow Roses, 10 In.	40.00
Bowl, Pedestal, White Ground, Flowers, Cranberry Interior, Gold Band, 12 x 8 In.	81.00
Box, Trunk Shape, Amber, Ormolu Mounted, Hinged Lid, Flowers, Gilt Ribbon Design, 1800s.	177.00
Candelabrum, 5-Light, White To Green, Painted Flowers, Gilt, Drops, 21 x 22 In.	387.00
Candle Pricker, Black Hyalith, Gilt, Count Buquoy Glassworks, c.1835, 12 In.	345.00
Centerpiece, Amethyst Cut To Clear, 1900s, 8 x 11 In.	118.00
Centerpiece, Faceted Knobs, Trumpet Shape, Foldover Ruffle Rim, Scalloped Foot, 14 ½ In.	230.00
Chalice, Green Translucent, Dwarfs Harvesting Grapes, Holbein, Lobmeyr, 10 In. ....*illus*	1333.00
Compote, Art Nouveau, Orange Iridescent, Ruffled Rim, 3-Legged Stand, Austria, 9 x 10 In.	177.00
Compote, White Overlay, Flower Border, Ruffled Foldover Rim, Silver Base, 1800s, 9 In.	429.00
Cordial Set, Art Nouveau, 2 Green Stem, 2 Rose Stem, Stylized Flowers, Meyer's Neffe, 6 In., 4 Piece.	293.00

Decanter Set, Cranberry To Clear, Gold Designs, Decanter, Glasses, c.1910, 11 In., 5 In., 7 Piece	1610.00
Decanter Set, Victorian Style, 3 Bottles, Cranberry, Celadon, Blue To Clear, Stoppers, 16 x 10 In.	461.00
Decanter Set, Wine Goblet, Ruby Flash, Engraved, Stag, Castle, 14 In., 7 Piece	80.00
Decanter, Gilt Scroll, Cobalt Glass, Wrapped Around Slender Neck, Stopper, 1800s, 12 In.	489.00
Dish, Jar Flowers, Multicolor, Gilt Vermicelli Ground, c.1890, 6 In., Pair	215.00
Jar, Cover, Cranberry, Ribbed, Pear Shape, Flame Finial, Gilt Accents, 8 In.	173.00
Jewelry Box, Ruby Flash, Engraved Castle Scene Cover, Casket Shape, 3 x 4 In.	75.00
Perfume Bottle, Birth Of Venus, Green, Stopper, Signed Ingrid, 7 ¼ x 4 In.	1240.00
Perfume Bottle, Black Hyalith, Gilt Snake, Cane, Count Buquoy Glassworks, c.1835, 3 In.	115.00
Pokal, White Overlay, Cut To Clear, Scrolls, Facets, Flutes, Gold Enamel, Cover, 15 In.	1380.00
Punch Bowl, Notched Lid, Baluster, Engraved, Stags, Wooded Landscape, Red, 15 In.	1342.00
Urn, Cover, Amethyst Cut To Clear, Gilt Metal, 16 x 9 In.	148.00
Vase, Amber To Clear, Diamond Pattern, Blue Enamel Rays, Wide Rim, Round Foot, 8 In.	196.00
Vase, Art Nouveau, Blue, Inside Scrolled White Metal Frame, 15 ¾ x 5 In.	434.00
Vase, Cobalt Blue Cut To Clear, Lattice, Chrysanthemum, Bull's-Eye Stripes, 14 In.	123.00
Vase, Cobalt Blue, Gilded, Baluster, c.1905, 16 In.	649.00
Vase, Cranberry Cased, Overlay, Flared Rim, Gilt, 1900s, 8 ¼ x 6 In.	104.00
Vase, Cranberry Cut To Clear, Windows, Trees, Spots, Bell Shape, 12 In.	148.00
Vase, Cranberry Flashed, Gilt Handles, Trumpet Foot, Man & Maid, 1900s, 16 In., Pair	4594.00
Vase, Cranberry Overlay, Enamel Flower Design, Gold, Flared Rim, Round Foot, 12 In.	150.00
Vase, Cranberry Overlay, Gold Flower & Woman Cartouche Enamel, Bulbous, 6 In.	196.00
Vase, Cranberry To Clear, Pedestal Base, 12 x 5 In., Pair	236.00
Vase, Cranberry, Gold Overlay, Applied Enamel Flowers, 10 ¼ In.	125.00
Vase, Elk, Landscape, Blue, Etched, Footed, 9 ¼ In., Pair	130.00
Vase, Enameled, White, Green Coins, Interior, 6 x 3 ¾ In.	118.00
Vase, Gilded White To Green, Tulip Shape, Knopped Stem, Round Foot, Overlay, 14 In., Pair	889.00
Vase, Green, Gilded, Tapered Body, Round Foot, Enameled Design, Hearts, Stars, 14 ½ In.	237.00
Vase, Mottled Purple, Pink, Gold, Art Deco Design Around Neck, Baluster, Austria, 5 ½ In.	184.00
Vase, Panel & Diamond Design, Flower Band, Flaring Neck, Spread Foot, 10 In.	474.00
Vase, Purple Iridescent, White Threading Design, Cone Shape, Foldover Rim, Pallme-Koenig, 7 In.	144.00
Vase, Red Cut To Clear, Etched Design, Beading, Gilded, 12 ¼ In. ....*illus*	296.00
Vase, Ruffled Rim, Iridescent, Gilt Metal Holder, Kralik, Austria, c.1900, 14 ¾ x 11 In.	2895.00
Vase, Seafoam Green Shaded To Blue, Iridescent Swirls, Swollen, Rindskopf, c.1900, 10 In.	613.00
Vase, Smokestack, Dark Green, Pulled Feather, Pink, Iridescent, Rindskopf, c.1900, 12 In., Pair	259.00
Vase, Swirl Design, Burgundy, Yellow, Purple, Cylindrical, Tapered, Ruffled Rim, Rindskopf, 10 In.	518.00
Vase, Tango, Red, Black Rims, Cylindrical, Flared Rim, Round Foot, Kralik, 10 In., Pair	69.00
Vase, White Cased, Cut To Clear, Crosshatching, Baluster, 9 In., Pair	98.00
Vase, White To Ruby, Gold Enamel, Flower Design, 1800s, 8 ⅜ In., Pair	770.00
Wedding Cup, Gilt Metal, Transparent Enamel Flowers, Fritz Heckert, 7 ¾ In. ....*illus*	1610.00
Wine, Cobalt, Sunburst, Star, 4 ¾ In.	18.00
Wine, Garnet Overlay, Clear Paneled Stem, Garnet Foot, 6 In., 6 Piece	74.00
Wine, Rhine, Gold, Applied Floral Highlights, 8 In.	170.00

GLASS-CONTEMPORARY includes pieces by glass artists working after 1970. Many of these pieces are free-form, one-of-a-kind sculptures. Paperweights by contemporary artists are listed in the Paperweight category. Earlier studio glass may be found listed under Glass-Midcentury or Glass-Venetian.

Ashtray, Ruby Red, Leaf Shape, Anchor Hocking, 5 x 4 x 1 In.	12.00
Basket, Macchia Loop, Brown, Yellow, Orange, Signed Dale Chihuly, c.1983, 5 x 8 In.	3680.00
Basket, Seaform, Aqua, Maroon, White, Black Rim, Signed Dale Chihuly, c.1981, 6 x 13 In.	4140.00
Bowl, Cityscape, Blown, Red, Black, Paint, Signed Jay Musler, c.1987, 6 ½ x 14 In.	4641.00
Bowl, Cover, Smoky Gold, Bent Cut, Brass Handle, Fontana Arte, 1940s, 5 ½ x 8 ¼ In.	1116.00
Bowl, Cranberry Color, Black Vines, Green Leaves, Round, Bulbous, Signed C. Lotton, 1988, 8 In.	633.00
Bowl, Divination, Swirl Design, Double Walled, Footed, Signed Larry Newsom, 1997, 10 x 11 In.	575.00
Bowl, Embossed Flowers, Purple, Flared Rim, Inscribed Kent Ipsen, 1974, 8 ½ x 13 ½ In.	345.00
Bowl, Fused Glass Threads, Folded Ruffle Rim, Thermo Formed, Signed Z, 1988, 6 x 13 In.	10370.00
Bowl, Handkerchief, Green, Purple, Silver Ribbed Highlights, 1998, 7 ¼ x 11 In.	80.00
Bowl, Opal Glass, Iridescent Drop Leaf, Cased, Rolled Rim, Charles Lotton, 2004, 5 ½ In. ....*illus*	405.00
Bowl, Opal Iridescent, Green Band Of Threading, Rounded Rectangular, Quadrafold, Rim, 7 In.	86.00
Bowl, Purple, Blue Swirls, Pinched, Wavy Rim, Susan Glass, 1994, 23 x 17 In.	748.00
Bowl, Ribbed, Cranberry Stripes, Irregular Rim, Dale Chihuly, 8 x 16 In.	1560.00
Bowl, Yellow Interior, Gold, Orange, Flared, Labino, 5 ½ x 7 In.	240.00
Charger, Amethyst, Textured, Glen Lukens, 15 In.	110.00 to 120.00
Charger, Geometrics, Orange, Fused Enamel, Signed Maurice Heaton, 15 In.	165.00
Drinking Vessel, Blue, Yellow, Red Swirl, Kurt Walstab, 7 ¼ x 2 ½ In.	248.00

Glass-Venetian, Bottle, Applied Design, Cenedese, Fulvio Bianconi, Italy, c.1950, 13 ½ x 4 In.
$1984.00

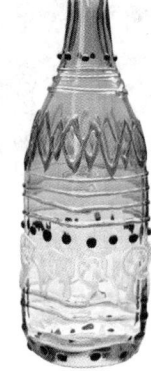

Rago Arts & Auction Center

Glass-Venetian, Figurine, Pulcini Bird, Copper Leg & Foot, Vistosi, Murano, 1960s, 7 ¼ x 8 In.
$4030.00

Rago Arts & Auction Center

Glass-Venetian, Hourglass, Clessidra, Red Orange, Venini, 1950s, 12 x 5 In.
$372.00

Rago Arts & Auction Center

Glass-Venetian, Sculpture, Pulcini, Chicks, Copper Legs, Vistosi, Alessandro Pianon, Italy, 1960s, 10 x 6 In.
$3472.00

Rago Arts & Auction Center

Glass-Venetian, Vase, Green, Design, Fuga, Italy, 1940s, 9 x 8 In. $1116.00

Rago Arts & Auction Center

Glass-Venetian, Vase, Pezzi-Pezze, Multicolor, Michele Burato, Signed, 2002, 14 ½ x 13 In. $744.00

Rago Arts & Auction Center

Glass-Venetian, Vase, Wrapped In Multicolor Strands, Simone Cenedese, 1997, 17 x 14 In. $1440.00

DuMouchelles Art Gallery

Glass-Venetian, Vase, Yellow, White, Brown, Etched 3-Line Mark, Venini, 1950s, 8 ¼ x 4 ½ In. $13640.00

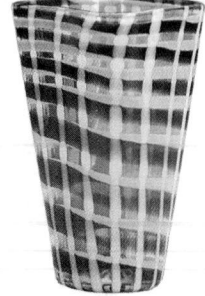

Rago Arts & Auction Center

Figure, Conch Shell Shape, Rose, Pink, Gwenn Knight, 9 x 11 In.	210.00
Figure, Owl, Maroon, Clear, Labino, 4 In.	108.00
Horn, Cobalt Blue, Paul Baker, c.1990, 14 x 9 ¼ In.	633.00
Jar, Cover, Mottled Turquoise, Black Leaves, Red Octopus, Ball Finial, Signed, D. Smallhouse, 10 In.	431.00
Perfume Bottle, Stopper, Faceted Amber, Cut To Clear, Signed Brian Maytum, 6 ¼ x 4 In.	74.00
Sculpture, After Glow, Clear, Tear Shape, Christopher Ries, 16 x 12 In.	2160.00
Sculpture, Bored Man, David Reekie, Lost Wax Cast, Black Enamel, c.1990, 6 In.	777.00
Sculpture, Magicscope Glass, Triangular, Stainless Steel, Feliciano Bejar, 1979, 10 x 2 In.	1736.00
Sculpture, Multicolor, John Littleton, 1988, 12 ¼ x 17 In. ....*illus*	434.00
Urn, Cranberry Color, Frosted, Tulips, Leaves, Clear Ball & Ebony Base, Corriea, 1996, 13 In.	230.00
Vase, 3 Hawthorn Trees, White Blooms, Golden Yellow, Blue, Baluster, Orient & Flume, 7 In.	350.00
Vase, 6 Tall Orange Flowers, Leaves, Cobalt Blue, Black, Cylindrical, Bulbous Top, C. Lotton, 13 In.	978.00
Vase, Amber Iridescent, Pulled Feather, Gourd Shape, Red Interior, Signed C. Lotton, 1973, 10 In.	690.00
Vase, Black Glass, Enamel Parrot, Silver Overlay, Cherry Blossoms, Rockwell, 12 ¼ In.	394.00
Vase, Blue & Silver Sand Dollars, Vines, Morning Glory, Oval, Signed C. Lotton, 1973, 8 In.	633.00
Vase, Blue Aurene, Red Flame Design, Baluster Shape, Flared Rim, Orient & Flume, 1979, 7 In.	173.00
Vase, Blue Iridescent, Gold Pulled Feather Design, Ball Shape, Signed C. Lotton, 1971, 3 In.	345.00
Vase, Blue Iridescent, Hooked Feather Design, Flared Rolled Rim, Signed C. Lotton, 1972, 8 In.	518.00
Vase, Blue, Tan Swirls, Blue Lip, Applied Blue Twist, c.1966, 4 ½ In.	219.00
Vase, Blue, White Flowers, Rolled Rim, Orient & Flume, 1981, 7 ¼ In.	288.00
Vase, Bud, Orange Red, Bulbous, Wide Neck, Brian Lonsway, c.1977, 3 In.	83.00
Vase, Bud, Paperweight, St. Louis, Millefiori, 150th Anniversary, SL 1845-1995, 5 ⅜ In. ..*illus*	1035.00
Vase, Celebration, Purple To White, Signed Cynthia England, 1998, 9 x 10 In.	149.00
Vase, Clear Globe, Metallic Coiled Tendrils, Double Ring Neck, Signed Benn, 1974, 4 In.	69.00
Vase, Cobalt Blue Iridescent, Cascading Lava, Free-Form, Signed C. Lotton, 1972, 6 In.	518.00
Vase, Cobalt Blue Iridescent, Pulled Feather Design, Bulbous, Signed C. Lotton, 1972, 5 In.	288.00
Vase, Cobalt Blue Iridescent, Vertical Coil Design, Elongated Oval, Narrow Neck, 1989, 9 In.	288.00
Vase, Cobalt Blue Star Flowers, Vine, Caramel, Violet, Bulbous, Narrow Rim, 1976, 4 In.	81.00
Vase, Cobalt Blue, Iridescent Blue Leaves, Pulled Feather, Orient & Flume, 1979, 7 ¼ In. ..... *illus*	316.00
Vase, Coral & Green Feathers, Yellow, Threading, Urn Shape, Orient & Flume, Signed, 8 In.	173.00
Vase, Cranberry, Deep Scalloped Edge, Twist From Base, 11 ½ In.	150.00
Vase, Curling Leaves, Purple, White, Blue, Green, Gourd Shape, Orient & Flume, 1984, 8 In.	288.00
Vase, Dance To Joy, Etched, Figural Handles, William Bernstein, 18 x 10 In.	805.00
Vase, Elongated Oval, Purple, Gold Iridescent, Signed J. Novaro, France, 12 x 8 In.	313.00
Vase, Flattened Rim, Oval Body, Internal Bubble Design, Multicolor Swirls, 1986, 6 In.	403.00
Vase, Gold & Blue, Iridescence, Signed R. Eichholt, 1997, 5 x 7 In.	119.00
Vase, Gold Leaves At Rim, Horizontal Fuchsia Design, Baluster Shape, Flared Rim, S. Alcaraz, 8 In.	69.00
Vase, Golden Base, Burgundy Leaves, Opal Tipped, Footed, Flared Rim, Swollen Shoulder, 1978, 8 ⅝ In.	230.00
Vase, Golden Honey Amber, Aerial Patterns, Iridescent Flakes, Cylindrical, 1979, 12 In.	518.00
Vase, Golden Yellow & Amber, Green Leaves, Pink, Feather Design, Signed, 1973, 7 ½ In.	115.00
Vase, Green Swirl Leaves, Sweet Pea, Wide Ruffled Rim, Narrow Stem, Round Foot, S. Alcaraz, 7 In.	115.00
Vase, Green, Red Dots, Ribbing, Orange Spread Foot, Oval, Swollen Top, Flare Rim, Transjo, 9 ⅜ In.	173.00
Vase, Iridescent Blue, Feather Design, Cylindrical, Pinched Neck, Flared Rim, 1981, 10 In.	288.00
Vase, Iridescent Blue, Purple, Swirl, Round Foot, Pear Shape, Narrow Rim, B. Cox, 1991, 8 In.	460.00
Vase, Iridescent Blue, Web Pattern, 2 Handles On Shoulder, Pinched Neck, Strini, 1998, 13 In.	230.00
Vase, Iridescent, Blue & White Wave Pattern, Gourd Shape, Narrow Rolled Rim, 1972, 8 In.	518.00
Vase, Iridescent, Green Waves, Tapered, Flower Shape Top, Rim Bent Inward, 13 In.	173.00
Vase, Jade Green, Mocha Bamboo Stalks, Leafy, Tapered, Heilman-Reisler, 1979, 9 In.	115.00
Vase, Lilac, Blue, Trumpet Shape, Ribbed, Ruffled Rim, Round Foot, Lundberg, 13 ½ In.	345.00
Vase, Morning Glories, Stems, Pink, Lavender, White, Cobalt Blue, Elongated Oval, C. Lotton, 10 In.	1035.00
Vase, Morning Glory, Opal, Blue, Green Leaves, Ball Shape, Narrow Flared Rim, 1973, 7 In.	748.00
Vase, Opal, Iridescent Blue Hooked Feather Design, Squat, Rolled Rim, C. Lotton, 1989, 6 In.	460.00
Vase, Opalescent, Gold, Pulled Feather, Stick Neck, Water Sprinkler, C. Lotton, 1977, 13 In.	690.00
Vase, Opalescent, Silver Blue Pulled Feather, Oval Shape, Signed, C. Lotton, 1972, 2 ½ In.	345.00
Vase, Orange Sherbet, Iridescent Green Leaves, Round Bottom, Tapered Neck, 1988, 5 In.	575.00
Vase, Orchid Body, Gold Iridescent Flag Pattern, Blue, Baluster, Footed, Flared Rim, 1980, 9 In.	288.00
Vase, Peach, Amethyst Wisteria, Elongated Oval, Flared Rim, Signed C. Lotton, 1974, 11 In.	575.00
Vase, Planets, Rocky Landscape, Orange Sun, Globe Shape, Narrow Rim, 1987, 5 In.	184.00
Vase, Pulled Feather, Blue Diagonal Swirls, Glossy, Pear Shape, Swollen Neck, 1974, 10 In.	1438.00
Vase, Pulled Netted Pattern, Pink, Caramel, Blue Iridescent, Baluster, 1976, 6 In.	207.00
Vase, Quiet Down There, Green, Blue, Cylindrical, Marked B. Young, 1981, 8 ½ x 5 In.	806.00
Vase, Red Blanket Cylinder, Red, Yellow, Inset White & Red Cards, Chihuly, 2000, 8 x 7 In.	5040.00
Vase, Red, Blue Iridescent Pulled Feather, Stick, Signed Charles Lotton, 1982, 9 In.	1150.00
Vase, Red, Pulled Silvery Gold Plumes, Bulbous, Pinched Neck, Flower Petal Rim, 1992, 5 In.	345.00
Vase, Sand Dollar Design, Opal Glass, Blue Vines, Amber Leaves, Free-Form Rim, 1973, 7 In.	920.00
Vase, Seashell, Iridescent, Leaf & Seaweed, White Oil Spot, Signed Muller, 9 In. ....*illus*	403.00

G

Vase, Silvery Blue Feather Design, Plum Color, Narrow Baluster, Flare Rim, Carlson, 1978, 8 In.	127.00
Vase, Spheres, Flared, Multicolor Luster, Paint, Signed, A. Corradetti, 1991, 18 x 15 In.............	179.00
Vase, Teaser, 2 Lobed, Murrines, Multicolor, Signed S.R. Powell, 1995, 22 x 30 In.	21600.00
Vase, Translucent Amber, Yellow Flowers, Green Hearts, Vines, Cylindrical, Swollen Top, 1974, 12 In.	978.00
Vase, Translucent Gold, Sphere, Signed Dominick Labino, 1979, 3 ½ x 4 ½ In.........................	248.00
Vase, Trumpet Shape, Footed, Leaves, James Lundberg, 15 x 6 In.	354.00
Vase, Trumpet Shape, Frosted, Red Hatching, Fritz Dreisbach, 9 ½ x 5 ½ In...........................	118.00
Vase, White, Green, Ball Standard, Steven Maslach, 1992, 11 In.	208.00
Vase, Yellow Flowers, Green Hearts & Vines, Bulbous, Slight Flared Rim, Signed C. Lotton, 1974, 8 In.	1333.00
Vase, Yellow Rim, Multicolor, Abstract, Earl O. James, 11 x 8 ½ In..........................	240.00
Vase, Yellow, Rust, Red Swirl Design, Signed Charles Lotton, c.1974, 9 ¼ x 5 ¾ In..................	826.00

GLASS-CUT, *see Cut Glass category.*

GLASS-DEPRESSION, *see Depression Glass category.*

GLASS-MIDCENTURY refers to art glass made from the 1940s to the early 1970s. Some glass factories, such as Baccarat or Orrefors, are listed under their own categories. Earlier glass may be listed in the Glass-Art and Glass-Contemporary categories. Italian glass may be found in Glass-Venetian.

Bottle, Ball Stopper, Slender Neck, Black & Gold Stripe Design, Morandiane, c.1946, 20 In.....	2375.00
Bowl, Green Plants, Flowers, Phoenix Overlay, White Ground, Silver Handle, c.1950, 7 In.......	180.00
Bowl, Red, Scalloped Rim, Medallions, Liberty Bell, Man's Head, c.1950, 9 x 5 In...................	35.00
Bowl, Speckled Blue & Orange, Monart Ware, Labeled, c.1950, 5 x 12 In...............................	492.00
Figurine, Stylized Bird, Elongated Neck, Blue, Magenta, Murano, 3 x 18 In...........................	27.00
Plaque, Stylized Chicken, Chicks, Faux Wire Ground, Higgins, 14 x 7 In., Pair......................	351.00
Sculpture, Elfo III, Face, Yellow, Green, Signed Max Ernst, Fucina Degli Angeli, 1966, 6 x 6 In.	2976.00
Thermos & Tray, Salmon Glass, Metal, H. Dreyfuss, American Thermos Co., 10 x 6 In............	2880.00
Tray, Purple, Blue & Green Elongated Rectangles, Fused, Higgins, 14 x 7 In.	49.00
Vase, Blue Aurene, Pouch Shaped, Gathered Neck, Glass Cord, Threaded Ruffle Rim, 8 In.	230.00
Vase, Emerald Green, Cylindrical, Applies Spiraling Trails, 12 x 7 In................................	154.00
Vase, Mezza Filligrana, Black, White, Swirled, Dino Martens, 1950s, 18 x 7 ½ In.	1364.00
Vase, Variegated Yellow, Iridescent Blue Heart & Vine, Urn Shape, Flared Flat Rim, 1973, 7 In.	575.00
Water Set, Yellow & Clear Cased, Orange Rim, c.1970, 9-In. Pitcher, 7 Piece......................	65.00

GLASS-PRESSED, *see Pressed Glass category.*

GLASS-VENETIAN. Venetian glass has been made near Venice, Italy, since the thirteenth century. Thin, colored glass with applied decoration is favored, although many other types have been made. Collectors have recently become interested in the Art Deco and fifties designs. Glass was made on the Venetian island of Murano from 1291. The output dwindled in the late seventeenth century but began to flourish again in the 1850s. Some of the old techniques of glassmaking were revived, and firms today make traditional designs and original modern glass. Since 1981, the name *Murano* may be used only on glass made on Murano Island. Other pieces of Italian glass may be found in the Glass-Contemporary and Glass-Midcentury categories of this book.

Angel, Praying, Gold Flake, Murano, 7 ¾ In..	75.00
Ashtray, Heart Shape, Silver, Rows Of Concentric Bubbles, Pink Trim, Murano, 1940s, 5 x 4 In.	50.00
Ashtray, Pink, White Ribbon, Gold Mica Highlights, Murano, 7 ½ In.	30.00
Bottle, Applied Design, Cenedese, Fulvio Bianconi, Italy, c.1950, 13 ½ x 4 In. ....*illus*	1984.00
Bowl, Centerpiece, Blown, Blue, White Stripes, Crimped Rim, 6 x 9 ½ In...........................	210.00
Bowl, Centerpiece, Murano, Red, White Swirls, Gold Flecks, Fratelli Toso, 22 x 18 In.	414.00
Bowl, Clear, Pink, White Ribbon, Folded, 7 ½ In.	40.00
Bowl, Mezza Filigrana, Applied Base, Gold Inclusions, Murano, 2 x 6 In.	148.00
Bowl, Oriente Hat Shape, Multicolor Collage, Dino Martens, Italy, 1960s, 5 x 11 In.............	2356.00
Bowl, Round, 4 Mouth Blown Fish, Iridescent Green, Blue Rim, Murano, 13 In. Diam.	173.00
Candlestick, Blown, Blue, Ruffled Edge, Gold Pedestal Beading, 5 x 5 In...........................	420.00
Centerpiece, Cobalt Blue To Clear, Footed, Flared Bowl, 1900s, 15 x 14 In.........................	236.00
Decanter, Wine Glass Set, Amber, Turkish Style, 7 Piece	84.00
Figurine, Birds, Pink, Gold Flecks, Applied Wings, Black Bead, Eyes, 5 & 7 In., 2 Piece	238.00
Figurine, Bride, Veil, c.1950, 12 ¾ x 3 ¼ In...	1240.00
Figurine, Man, White Opaque, Green Trousers, Hat, 17 In.	531.00
Figurine, Pheasant, Tail Raised, Red, Clear, Gold Inclusions & Comb, 9 x 21 In...................	154.00
Figurine, Pulcini Bird, Copper Leg & Foot, Vistosi, Murano, 1960s, 7 ¼ x 8 In. ....*illus*	4030.00
Hourglass, Clessidra, Red Orange, Venini, 1950s, 12 x 5 In. ....*illus*	372.00
Lamp, Pink Bubble, Fluted, Twist Top, Metal Base, 13 ½ x 21 In.......................	144.00

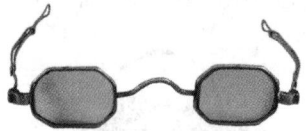

Glasses, Brass, Tinted, Pre-Civil War
$148.00

Showtime Auction Services

Gouda, Lamp Base, Oil, Stylized Flower, Fitted Brass Insert, Glazed, 14 ½ In.
$356.00

Skinner, Inc.

Graniteware, Bucket, Confetti, End-Of-Day, White Interior, Riveted Ears, Bail Handle, 3 ⅝ x 3 ¾ In.
$177.00

Conestoga Auction Co., Inc.

Graniteware, Coffeepot, Cobalt Blue & White Swirl, Lid, Black Knob, Weld Handle, 7 ¾ In.
$130.00

Conestoga Auction Co., Inc.

339

Graniteware, Cream Can, Green & White Swirl, Blue Rim, Wire, Wood Handle, Sheet Iron Lid, 8 x 4 In.
$83.00

Conestoga Auction Co., Inc.

Graniteware, Creamer, End-Of-Day, Multicolored Confetti, Riveted Loop Handle, Pinch Spout, 2 ½ x 2 In.
$212.00

Conestoga Auction Co., Inc.

Graniteware, Double Boiler, Blue & White Swirl, Lid, Hollow Handles, 8 x 6 ⅞ In.
$12.00

Conestoga Auction Co., Inc.

Graniteware, Milk Can, Red & White, Mottled, Wire Bail Handle, Lid, 8 ½ x 5 ¼ In.
$83.00

Conestoga Auction Co., Inc.

Martini Glass Set, Blown, Swan Stem, Gold Flecks, 5 ½ x 4 ¾ In., 12 Piece 575.00

Obelisk, Black, Inscribed Venini Murano, 9 ¾ In. 259.00

Sculpture, Bird, Green, Signed Luciano Caspari Salviati, 1960, 7 x 5 In. 217.00

Sculpture, Block Aquarium Shape, Glass, 3 Fish, Multicolor, Copper, Murano, c.1950, 4 x 5 In. 470.00

Sculpture, Pulcini, Chicks, Copper Legs, Vistosi, Alessandro Pianon, Italy, 1960s, 10 x 6 In. . *illus* 3472.00

Vase, Amber, Tortoiseshell Pattern, Multicolor Murrines, Tapered, Squat, 14 In. 74.00

Vase, Blue, Diagonal Red & Green Decoration, Bottle Form, Murano, 11 In. 563.00

Vase, Blue, White Latticinio, Trumpet Shape, 15 ¼ & 15 ¾ In., 2 Piece 325.00

Vase, Bottle Shape, Ribbed Design, Murano, 8 In. 75.00

Vase, Bubbles, Blown, Murano, 15 x 12 ½ In., Pair 708.00

Vase, Bulbous, Blue, Applied Fruit, c.1934, 9 In. 230.00

Vase, Bulbous, Pinched Neck, Blue, White, Fenico, c.1930, 11 ¾ x 7 In. 9920.00

Vase, Cobalt Blue Stripes, Gold Infused Clear Ground, Signed Seguso, 10 In. 413.00

Vase, Cobalt Blue, Looped Purple Inclusions, Handle, Dino Martens, c.1938, 8 ½ x 10 ½ In.... 495.00

Vase, Cranberry Cut To Clear, Leaves & Berries, Tapered, Bulbous Top, Footed, 8 In. 118.00

Vase, Fili Applicati, Green Translucent, Cone, Applied Red Canes, Venini, 11 ½ In. 450.00

Vase, Frosted, Blue & Red Designs, Cylindrical, Ermanno Nason Cenedese, Italy, 12 ¾ x 5 ½ In. 888.00

Vase, Gold Flecks, Applied Wavy Handles, Engraved Vetreria Murano, Mario Gambaro, 13 In.. 179.00

Vase, Green, Design, Fuga, Italy, 1940s, 9 x 8 In. .... *illus* 1116.00

Vase, Honey Amber, Ribbed With Stretched Columns, Rounded Bottom, Murano, 12 In. 345.00

Vase, Inciso, Amber, Clear Cased, Tapered Triangular Shape, Signed A. Barbini, c.1962, 14 In. 1210.00

Vase, Lattice Design, Flared, Archimede Seguso, Murano, 7 ½ x 8 ¼ In. 1054.00

Vase, Millefiori Flowers, Green, Orange, White, Blue, Clear, Double Handle, Murano, 3 x 3 In. 120.00

Vase, Millefiori, Murano, Italy, 7 ¼ In. 150.00

Vase, Multicolor Triangles, Ercole Barovier, Barovier Toso, Italy, 1960s, 12 x 8 In. 10540.00

Vase, Pezzi-Pezze, Multicolor, Michele Burato, Signed, 2002, 14 ½ x 13 In. .... *illus* 744.00

Vase, Red, Silver Leaf, Gondola, Footed, Flared Rim, c.1925, 10 In. 450.00

Vase, Ribbon, Pink, White, Flared Rim, 11 ½ In. 293.00

Vase, Round, Ruffle Rim, Green, Venini Fazzoletto, Etched Signature, 3 x 4 In. 125.00

Vase, Scozzese, White, Green, Black Check, Italy, Fulvio Bianconi, 1950s, 10 x 3 ½ In. 14880.00

Vase, Urn Shape, Green Handles, Foldover Petal Rim, Pink, Flowers, Leaves, Murano, 7 In. 144.00

Vase, White & Brown Pattern, Corset Shape, Flaring Foot & Rim, Signed, Murano, 7 In. 230.00

Vase, White Zanfirico, Gold Aventurine, Green Ribbon, Baluster, Footed, 9 x 4 In., Pair 155.00

Vase, Wrapped In Multicolor Strands, Simone Cenedese, 1997, 17 x 14 In. .... *illus* 1440.00

Vase, Yellow, White, Brown, Etched 3-Line Mark, Venini, 1950s, 8 ¼ x 4 ½ In. .... *illus* 13640.00

GLASSES for the eyes, or spectacles, were mentioned in a manuscript in 1289 and have been used ever since. The first eyeglasses with rigid side pieces were made in London in 1727. Bifocals were invented by Benjamin Franklin in 1785. Lorgnettes were popular in late Victorian times. Opera Glasses are listed in their own category.

Brass, Tinted, Pre-Civil War .... *illus* 148.00

Folding, 14K White Gold Frame & Neck Chain, Pince Nez Oxford, 4 x 2 In., 17-In. Chain 161.00

Lorgnette, Diamonds, 14K Gold, c.1840, 3 x 1 ½ In. 575.00

Lorgnette, Fluted Column, Leaf Finial, 14K Gold Case, St. Petersburg, c.1900, 5 ½ In. 1560.00

Lorgnette, Silver Marcasite, 6 In. 95.00

Lorgnette, Tortoiseshell, Shaped, Inlaid Gilt Monogram, Folding Lens, 5 ¾ In. 49.00

Magnifying, Mother-Of-Pearl Handle, 7 ½ In. 60.00

GLIDDEN POTTERY worked in Alfred, New York, from 1940 to 1957. The pottery made stoneware, dinnerware, and art objects.

Ashtray, Butterfly, Fern, Square 45.00

Pitcher, Boston Spice, Large, 9 In. 350.00

Plate, Bird, Square, Rounded Corners, 8 In. 150.00

Plate, Fish, Teal, Green, Square, 8 x 4 In., 4 Piece 240.00

Tray, Powder Blue, Detachable Handle, Marked, 12 x 9 In. 195.00

Vase, Squared, Blue Speckled Glaze, Marked, 7 ½ x 6 ¼ In. 40.00

GOEBEL is the mark used by W. Goebel Porzellanfabrik of Oeslau, Germany, now Rodental, Germany. The company was founded by Franz Detleff Goebel and his son, William Goebel, in 1871. It was known as F&W Goebel. Slates, slate pencils, and marbles were made. Soon the company began making porcelain tableware and figurines. Hummel figurines were first made by Goebel in 1935 and are now being made by another company. Goebel is still in business. Old pieces marked *Goebel Hummel* are listed under Hummel in this book.

Ashtray, Friar Tuck, c.1956, 3 ½ x 5 In. 65.00

Figurine, Accompanist, Girl, Playing Banjo, Canary, 7 ½ In. 95.00

Figurine, Christ Child, Halo, c.1950, 8 In. 95.00

Figurine, First Date, Boy, Bouquet Of Flowers, 9 In.	175.00
Figurine, Good News Boy, Red Hair, 4 ⅜ In.	69.00
Figurine, Rabbit, Yellow, Mark, West Germany, 4 In.	13.00
Toby Jug, Man, Orange Top Coat, Plume In Hat, Rosy Checks, c.1945, 3 ½ In.	44.00

GOLDSCHEIDER was founded by Friedrich Goldscheider in Vienna in 1885. The family left Vienna in 1938 and the factory was taken over by the Germans. Goldscheider started factories in England and in Trenton, New Jersey. The New Jersey factory started in 1940 as Goldscheider-U.S.A. In 1941 it became Goldscheider-Everlast Corporation. From 1947 to 1953 it was Goldcrest Ceramics Corporation. In 1950 the Vienna plant was returned to Mr. Goldscheider and the company continues in business. The Trenton, New Jersey, business, called Goldscheider of Vienna, imports all of the pieces.

Bust, Woman, Lowered Head, Gold Crown, Blue Dress, 7 x 6 ½ In.	47.00
Figurine, 2 Putti, Feeding Goat Grapes, Signed Petru, Austria, 9 x 9 In.	300.00
Figurine, Asian Woman & Deer Seated, Multicolor, Signed, 7 ¾ x 4 ¼ In.	360.00
Figurine, Ladyrose, With Bouquet Of Roses, Rose Colored Gown, Marked, 6 ¾ In.	50.00
Figurine, Parrot, On Stump, Green, Blue, Everlast Model, c.1942, 13 ½ In.	201.00
Figurine, Woman, Basket, Signed Goldscheider, 47 x 19 ½ In.	1265.00
Figurine, Woman, Child, Dancing, Green, Yellow, Signed Gruber, Impressed K, 13 In.	180.00

GOLF, see Sports category.

GONDER CERAMIC ARTS, INC., was opened by Lawton Gonder in 1941 in Zanesville, Ohio. Gonder made high-grade pottery decorated with flambe, drip, gold crackle, and Chinese crackle glazes. The factory closed in 1957. From 1946 to 1954, Gonder also operated the Elgee Pottery, which made ceramic lamp bases.

Basket, Pink Glaze, Ribbed, Footed, c.1950, 6 x 8 x 4 In.	25.00
Vase, Double Offset Handles, Lilac, Flared Rim, 9 In.	28.00
Vase, Shell Fan Shape, Lilac, 8 ¼ x 12 In.	46.00

GOOFUS GLASS was made from about 1900 to 1920 by many American factories. It was originally painted gold, red, green, bronze, pink, purple, or other bright colors. Many pieces are found today with flaking paint, and this lowers the value.

Bowl, Charter Oak Leaf & Acorn, Ruffled Edge, Gold, Red, 9 ½ x 3 In.	10.00
Compote, Scalloped Rim, Peaches, Leaves, 12 ¾ In.	17.00
Plate, La Belle Rose, Footed, Gold, Red Roses, 11 In.	15.00

GOSS china has been made since 1858. English potter William Henry Goss first made it at the Falcon Pottery in Stoke-on-Trent. The factory name was changed to Goss China Company in 1934 when it was taken over by Cauldon Potteries. Production ceased in 1940. Goss China resembles Irish Belleek in both body and glaze. The company also made popular souvenir china, usually marked with local crests and names.

Cup & Saucer, Crested, City Of Edinburgh, Straight-Sided, c.1900	71.00
Figurine, House, Window In Thrums, Unglazed, 2 ¼ In.	145.00
Loving Cup, Arms Of Goss, Relief, 2 Handles, 4 ½ In.	195.00
Mug, Crested, Great Malvern, Handleless, c.1875, 1 ½ x 1 ¾ In.	48.00
Pot, Crested, Arms At Abbotsford, Watch Weel, Globular, Scalloped & Gilt Rim, 1 ¾ In.	24.00
Pot, Crested, Swansea, Wales, 2 Handles, Marked, c.1900, 2 ½ In.	62.00
Urn, Pembrooke Dock, Gilt Rim, Footed, 2 Handles, 4 x 2 In.	64.00

GOUDA, Holland, has been a pottery center since the seventeenth century. Two firms, the Zenith pottery, established in the eighteenth century, and the Zuid-Hollandsche pottery, made the brightly colored art pottery marked *Gouda* from 1898 to about 1964. Other factories followed. Many pieces featured Art Nouveau or Art Deco designs. Pattern names in Dutch, listed here, seem strange to English-speaking collectors.

Ashtray, Marked Juliana, 6 ½ In.	40.00
Candlestick, Band Of Flowers, Matte Glaze, Anjer Pattern, c.1915, 14 In., Pair	711.00
Candlestick, Berna Pattern, Sea Creatures, c.1924, 19 In.	326.00
Charger, Clematis, Flowers, Wall, High Glaze, c.1920, 14 In.	296.00
Charger, Flowers & Leaves, Matte Glaze, c.1927, 14 In. Diam.	1778.00
Charger, Wall, Damascus Holland, Leafy Border, Blue, Cream, Yellow, Matte Glaze, c.1918, 12 In.	444.00
Flowerpot, Hanging, Massa Pattern, Matte Glaze, Holland, c.1915, 6 In.	184.00
Jardiniere, Ajour Pattern, Elongated Oval, 2 Handles, Stylized Design, c.1915, 17 In.	337.00
Jardiniere, Stylized Flowers & Leaves, High Glaze, c.1912, 8 In.	245.00

G

Grueby, Vase, 3 Daffodils, Yellow & Ivory, Ruth Erickson, Stamped, 1914, 11 x 9 In. $9920.00

Rago Arts & Auction Center

Grueby, Vase, Green Matte Glaze, Yellow Narcissus, Stamped, 11 ½ x 5 ½ In. $6820.00

Rago Arts & Auction Center

Grueby, Vase, Oatmeal Glaze, Marked, 11 In. $1416.00

Morphy Auctions

TIP
Think about the problems of owning a cat and a large collection of ceramics.

Gustavsberg, Bowl, Cherub, Flowers, Wilhelm Kage, Marked, 2 ¾ In. $115.00

Humler & Nolan

Gustavsberg, Box, Cover, Nude Females, Different Poses, Wilhelm Kage, Marked, 5 ¾ In. $403.00

Humler & Nolan

Gustavsberg, Charger, Woman Riding Dolphin, Band Of Stars Rim, Wilhelm Kage, Marked, 13 ½ In. $345.00

Humler & Nolan

TIP

Do not wipe gold or platinum decorated glasses while they are hot from the dishwasher. The metalic color will rub off.

Jug, Jacoba, Dagmar Pattern, Flowers, Round Foot, Loop Handle, c.1922, 10 In.	296.00
Lamp Base, Oil, Stylized Flower, Fitted Brass Insert, Glazed, 14 ½ In. ...*illus*	356.00
Lamp Base, Suled Pattern, Matte Glaze, Stylized Leaves, 15 In.	306.00
Plaque, Country Landscape, High Glaze, c.1905, 14 x 20 In.	3081.00
Plaque, High Glaze, Mother & Baby, Seated By Fireplace, c.1905, 16 x 23 In.	1422.00
Sign, Regina, Flower Border, Holland, c.1925, 4 x 7 In.	237.00
Tobacco Jar, Cover, Flowers, Band Of Leaves, c.1925, 7 In., Pair	326.00
Vase, Abstract, Square, Round Foot, Narrow Swollen Neck, Rolled Rim, c.1920, 17 In.	1778.00
Vase, Bejo Pattern, Bird, Flowers, Leaves, Bottle Shape, Matte Glaze, c.1921, 9 In.	1659.00
Vase, Corona Pattern, Slender Bottle Shape, Bottom Loop Handles, Matte Glaze, c.1915, 15 In., Pair	490.00
Vase, Cover, Flowers, Leaves, Glaze, Shouldered, Pinched Waist, Round Foot, c.1898, 11 In.	1896.00
Vase, Elongated Oval, Round Foot, Rolled Rim, White Ground, Leaves, c.1930, 11 In.	474.00
Vase, Flowers & Leaves, Basket Handles, High Glaze, c.1908, 9 In.	948.00
Vase, Flowers & Leaves, Gourd Shape, Pinched Sides, c.1898, 9 In.	326.00
Vase, Flowers & Leaves, Multicolor, 10 ½ In.	115.00
Vase, Flowers & Leaves, Semimatte, c.1925, 16 In.	770.00
Vase, Flowers, Globular, Upturned Loop Handles, c.1905, 4 In.	474.00
Vase, Flowers, High Glaze, 2 Loop Handles At Rim, Round Foot, Green, Yellow, 11 ⅞ In.	138.00
Vase, Horse Drawn Cart, Woodsman, High Glaze, Signed, c.1908, 12 In.	474.00
Vase, Luka Geometric Pattern, Elongated Oval, Round Foot, Rolled Rim, c.1928, 9 In.	889.00
Vase, Magpie, Flowers, Baluster, Narrow Neck, Rolled Lip, Matte Glaze, c.1920, 17 In.	3081.00
Vase, Pansy, Art Nouveau, Green, Yellow, Purple, Bell Shape, Flare Rim, Round Foot, 7 ⅜ In.	403.00
Vase, Portrait, Dutch Man, Flower & Leaf, 2 Square Handles, Narrow Neck, c.1910, 13 In.	267.00
Vase, Squat Bottle Shape, Flower Pattern, Brown, Orange, Green, Gold, Signed, c.1900, 4 In.	98.00
Vase, Srebo Pattern, Stylized Leaves, Flowers, Matte Glaze, Cylindrical, Trumpet Rim, c.1915, 10 In.	245.00
Vase, Stylized Flowers, Leaves, Bell Shape, Round Foot, Narrow Neck, Flare Rim, c.1898, 7 In.	385.00
Vase, Stylized Flowers, Leaves, Narrow Neck, Rolled Rim, High Glaze, c.1910, 22 In.	1541.00
Vase, Tulips, Green, Red, Yellow, Purple, High Glaze, Shaped Neck, 11 ⅝ In.	345.00
Vase, Urn Shape, Round Foot, Narrow Rim, Stylized Butterflies, Matte Glaze, c.1920, 12 In.	2370.00

GRANITEWARE is enameled tin or iron used to make to make kitchenware since the 1870s. Earlier graniteware was green or turquoise blue, with white spatters. The later ware was gray with white spatters. Reproductions are being made in all colors. There is a second definition of the word *graniteware*, meaning a blue speckled pottery. Only the metal graniteware is listed here.

Baking Dish, Cover, Blue, White Mottling, Pouring Spout, Handle, c.1910, 2 x ¾ In.	75.00
Baking Pan, Blue & White, Large Swirl, White Interior, Black Rim, Rim Handles, 11 x 9 In.	35.00
Berry Bucket, Blue & White, Wire Bail, Wood Grip, Riveted Handles, Cover, 5 x 4 In.	59.00
Berry Bucket, Gray, Bail Handle, Tin Cover, 7 x 4 ½ In.	60.00
Bowl, Green, White Interior, 4 ½ In.	35.00
Bucket, Confetti, End-Of-Day, White Interior, Riveted Ears, Bail Handle, 3 ⅝ x 3 ¾ In. ...*illus*	177.00
Bucket, Dinner, Light Blue & White, Large Swirl, Domed Pressed Lid, Oval, 3 Piece, 7 x 9 ½ In.	35.00
Cake Pan, Green, 9 x 7 In.	275.00
Canister Set, Red, White Checker, Swirl Interior, 1930s, 4 ½ x 4 ½ To 3 x 2 ¾ In., 5 Piece	175.00
Canister Set, Red, White Detail, France, c.1920, 5 ½ To 8 In., 5 Piece	198.00
Canister Set, Red, White Lacy Trim, Lettering, Cafe, Pates, Chocolat, France, 3 Piece	125.00
Canister, Robin's-Egg Blue, Cover, 5 ¼ x 8 In.	36.00
Canister, White, Gold Trim, Lettering, Rose Bands, Cover, Chicoree, 7 x 4 ¾ In.	65.00
Chamber Pot, Blue & White, Swirl, 8 In.	70.00
Chamber Pot, Blue Swirl, White, Rolled Black Rim, White Interior, Loop Handle, 4 ¾ x 10 In.	12.00
Coffee Carrier, Blue, White, Large Swirl, Seamed, Conical, Black Cover, Stirrup Handle, 8 x 5 In.	71.00
Coffee Flask, Gray Mottled, Stamped Threaded Neck, Cap, Seamed Top, Bottom, 6 x 4 In.	24.00
Coffeepot, Blue & White, Large Swirl, Black Rims, Knob, Handle, Molded Hinged Lid, 10 x 7 In.	35.00
Coffeepot, Blue & White, Large Swirl, White Interior, Pressed Molded Lid, Knob, 12 x 9 ½ In.	94.00
Coffeepot, Blue, Large Swirl, White Interior, Pinch Spout, Ears, Lid, Wire Bail, 11 x 8 ½ In.	35.00
Coffeepot, Cobalt Blue & White Swirl, Lid, Black Knob, Weld Handle, 7 ¾ In. ...*illus*	130.00
Coffeepot, Gray Mottled, Hinged Tinned Sheet Steel Rim, Black Wood Knob, 4 ¾ x 3 In.	83.00
Coffeepot, Green, White Mottled, Signed Elite Austria, 10 ½ x 5 ¾ In.	120.00
Coffeepot, Snow On The Mountain, Red & White, France, 1930s, 9 x 10 In.	80.00
Coffeepot, White, Trailing Flowers, Leaves, Gold Detail, Lid, France, c.1900, 9 ½ x 4 ¾ In.	125.00
Colander, Green, Black Rim, Handles, Marked Oto, 5 ¼ x 10 ¾ In.	24.00
Colander, Yellow, Black Rim & Handles, 4 ¼ x 8 ¼ In.	35.00
Cream Can, Green & White Swirl, Blue Rim, Wire & Wood Handle, Sheet Iron Lid, 8 x 4 In. *illus*	83.00
Creamer, End-Of-Day, Multicolored Confetti, Riveted Loop Handle, Pinch Spout, 2 ½ x 2 In. ...*illus*	212.00
Cup, Green, White Interior, Black Rim, 2 ¾ x 3 In., Pair	18.00
Double Boiler, Blue & White Swirl, Lid, Applied Hollow Handles, 5 x 10 ⅝ In.	12.00

Double Boiler, Blue & White Swirl, Lid, Hollow Handles, 8 x 6 ⅞ In. ....*illus*	12.00
Dust Pan, Robin's-Egg Blue Handle, White Pan, c.1910, 5 ½ x 3 ¼ In.	135.00
Funnel, Canning Jar, Blue & White, Large Swirl, Riveted Loop Handle, Cobalt Blue Rim, 2 x 5 In.	12.00
Funnel, Gray, 7 x 5 ½ In.	15.00
Ladle, Gray, 14 ½ x 4 ¾ In.	25.00
Laundry Set, White, Lavender Flowers, Wall Holder, 3 Cups, Soda, Sand, Seife, France, Pre 1920	400.00
Lunch Pail, Blue & White, Swirl, Bail Handle, Lid, 6 In.	70.00
Matchbox, White, Red Gingham, Allumettes, Stripes, 1930s, 6 ¼ x 4 ½ In. .... 85.00 to 150.00
Measuring Set, Long Handle, Blue, White Interior, 2 ½ To 4 In., 4 Piece...........................	125.00
Milk Can, Brown & White, Black Rim, Riveted Ears, Wire Bail, Strap Handle, 9 ¼ In...............	443.00
Milk Can, Dome Lid, Green & White Swirl, Black Rim, Rivets, Handle, Wire Bail, 12 x 6 In.....	266.00
Milk Can, Green & White, Large Swirl, Black Rim, White Interior, Welded Wire Ears, 9 x 5 In.	266.00
Milk Can, Red & White, Mottled, Wire Bail Handle, Lid, 8 ½ x 5 ¼ In. ....*illus*	83.00
Milk Pail, Blue, Blue & White Check Band, Lustacru Pattern, Laitiere, 10 In............................	185.00
Mold, Lobster, On Crown, Light Blue, Serrated Rim, Embossed, 2 ½ x 6 ½ In.	12.00
Muffin Pan, 8 Cup, Blue & White, Large Swirl, White Lining, Black Edge, 14 ¼ x 7 ¼ In.	35.00
Muffin Pan, Lavender, Large Swirl, Black Edging, 8 Cup, 14 ½ x 7 ¼ In.	12.00
Muffin Pan, Light Blue Swirl, Both Sides, 10 ¾ In..	35.00
Onion Keeper, White, Violets, Cutout Hearts, Germany, Pre 1940s..	215.00
Pail, Blue, White, Bail Handle, Wood Grip, 4 x 4 ¾ In...	115.00
Pan, Lavender, White, Large Swirl, Pressed Dome Lid, Riveted Tab, Wire Handles, 14 ½ x 8 In.	24.00
Pan, Lid, White, Turquoise Trim, 2 Qt.	26.00
Pan, Red, White Gingham Band, Red Handle, 1 ½ In.	22.00
Pitcher, Blue, Green, White Swirl, France..	95.00
Pitcher, Blue, White, France, 1930s..	165.00
Pitcher, Mint Green, Forest Green Trim, France, c.1910, 14 ¾ x 8 In.	225.00
Pitcher, Water, Blue Trim, White Ground, 11 ½ In.	23.00
Pitcher, White, Gray Mottled, 10 ½ x 8 In...	56.00
Pot, Hot Water, Cover, Painted Flower, Cattail, Caterpillar, France	115.00
Pot, White, Red Piping, Open Handles, 6 ¼ x 10 ¼ In.	26.00
Refrigerator Dish Set, White, Black Rim, 5 ¼ x 4 ¼ & 8 ¼ x 5 ¼ In., 3 Piece.........................	34.00
Salt Box, Guirland Roses, Blue & White Stripes, Sel, Wall Hanger, France..............................	110.00
Salt Box, White, Hanging Hook, France, c.1900..	45.00
Scoop Set, Graduated, Blue, White Interior, Welded Loop Handle, 5, 4 ¼, 3 ½ In., 3 Piece.......	130.00
Skillet, Wood Handle, Blue, Hanging Loop, France, Pre 1910	125.00
Skimmer, Perforated, Mottled Green & White, Blue Handle, 14 ⅛ In.	24.00
Soap Dish, Red & White Stripe Checks, Wall Hanger..	14.00
Soap Dish, White, Hanging, c.1930, 6 ⅛ x 4 ½ In.	38.00
Strainer, Gray, 3-Footed, 8 x 3 In.	18.00
Strainer, Gray, Loop Handles, Footed, 4 x 10 In.	19.00
Strainer, Gray, White Mottling, Long Handle, Kettle Hook, Pre 1910, 7 ½ In..........................	85.00
Teakettle, Blue & White, Wood Handle, 9 ½ x 10 ½ In...	35.00
Teapot, Green & White, Large Swirl, Welded Loop Handle, Gooseneck Spout, 8 ¾ x 5 In..........	142.00
Teapot, Painted, Cattails, Carnations, Flowers, Pink Shaded To White, Pewter, 6 x 9 In.	245.00
Teapot, Silver On Metal, Lid, 1900s, 1 Cup, 5 ½ In...	115.00
Trivet, French Country Recipe, Painted, White, Red, Blue, Bird, Holding Herbs, France	45.00
Washtub, Gray & White, Handles, 10 x 22 ¼ In..	95.00
Water Carrier, Blue & White Mottled, Flip Lid, 15 x 10 ½ In...	155.00

GREENTOWN glass was made by the Indiana Tumbler and Goblet Company of Greentown, Indiana, from 1894 to 1903. In 1899, the factory became part of National Glass Company. A variety of pressed glass was made. Additional pieces may be found in other categories, such as Chocolate Glass, Holly Amber, Milk Glass, and Pressed Glass.

Holly, Saltshaker, Beaded Detail, Metal Lie, 3 In...	316.00
Holly, Tumbler, White, Opalescent, 4 In.	9000.00

GRUEBY FAIENCE COMPANY of Boston, Massachusetts, was founded in 1894 by William H. Grueby. Grueby Pottery Company was incorporated in 1907. In 1909, Grueby Faience went bankrupt. Then William Grueby founded the Grueby Faience and Tile Company. Grueby Pottery closed about 1911. The tile company worked until 1920. Garden statuary, art pottery, and architectural tiles were made until 1920. The company developed a green matte glaze that was so popular it was copied by many other factories making a less expensive type of pottery. This eventually led to the financial problems of the pottery. Cuerda seca and cuenca are techniques explained in the Tile category. The company name was often used as the mark, and slight changes in the form help date a piece.

Bowl, Squat, Bulbous, Incised Vertical Lines, Green, 5 In. Diam...	489.00
Figure, Scarab, Green Matte Glaze, 1905, 1 ½ x 4 In. .... 276.00 to 306.00

Halloween, Costume, Lucille Ball, Gold Fabric Dress, Plastic Mask, Box, Child's, 1960s, Medium
$253.00

Hake's Americana & Collectibles

Halloween, Jack-O'-Lantern, Black Cat, Green Eyes, Paper Face, Candleholder, Handle, Germany, 4 In.
$633.00

Bertoia Auctions

Halloween, Jack-O'-Lantern, Devil Ears, Grin, Paper Face, Candleholder, Germany, 3 In.
$288.00

Bertoia Auctions

Halloween, Jack-O'-Lantern, Eyeglasses, Large, Nose, Hair, Painted, Candleholder, 4 ½ In.
$316.00

Bertoia Auctions

Halloween, Lantern, Foot, Figural, Composition, Painted, Insert, Debossed Ghosts On Toes, 7 ½ In.
$4025.00

Bertoia Auctions

Halloween, Noisemaker, Spinner, Witch, Die Cut Cardboard, Germany, 11 In.
$115.00

Bertoia Auctions

Hampshire, Pitcher, Green Matte Glaze, Leaf Spout & Handle, Impressed Mark, c.1890, 8 ½ In.
$415.00

Skinner, Inc.

Lamp, Green Matte, Melon Lobed, Bronze Mount, Leaded Glass Shade, E. Felton, 18 In.	10120.00
Tile, Grapes, Oak Frame, 9 x 9 In.	236.00
Tile, Landscape, Green, Brown, Wood Frame, 11 ¾ In.	202.00
Tile, Lioness, Cub, Green Matte Glaze, Russell Crook, 7 x 11 ½ In.	4960.00
Tile, Musician, Blue Matte Flowers, Yellow Brown Ground, Frame, 11 ¾ In.	213.00
Tile, Pines, Green, Blue, Paper Label, 6 In.	1860.00
Tile, Stag, Tree, Green, Blue, Cream, Signed, 4 In.	1725.00
Tile, Tall Ship, White Sails, Brown Bow, Blue Water, 6 In.	1054.00
Vase, 3 Daffodils, Yellow & Ivory, Ruth Erickson, Stamped, 1914, 11 x 9 In. *illus*	9920.00
Vase, 5 Buds, Stems, Broad Leaves, Green Matte Glaze, Oval, Flared Rim, c.1905, 7 ⅜ In.	2328.00
Vase, Blue Matte Glaze, Spherical, 3 ¾ x 4 In.	1984.00
Vase, Dark Green Glaze, Yellow Blossoms, Squat, 4 ½ x 5 ¼ In.	3100.00
Vase, Green Matte Glaze, 2 Rows Of Leaves, Cylindrical, W. Post, 11 ½ x 5 ¾ In.	1860.00
Vase, Green Matte Glaze, Carved, Leaves, Square, Squat, 2 ⅞ In.	633.00
Vase, Green Matte Glaze, Cylindrical, Impressed, 5 x 11 In.	900.00
Vase, Green Matte Glaze, Leaves, Buds, Flared Mouth, 8 ¾ x 4 ½ In.	2852.00
Vase, Green Matte Glaze, Leaves, Faience Stamp, 12 x 6 In.	4030.00
Vase, Green Matte Glaze, Leaves, Oval, 6 ¾ x 4 ½ In.	2852.00
Vase, Green Matte Glaze, Pinched Waist, Impressed Mark, 9 ¾ x 5 ½ In.	868.00
Vase, Green Matte Glaze, White Base Runs, Bulbous, Ridged, 10 ¼ x 3 ¾ In.	1860.00
Vase, Green Matte Glaze, Yellow Narcissus, Stamped, 11 ½ x 5 ½ In. *illus*	6820.00
Vase, Leathery Burnt Sienna Matte Glaze, Cylindrical, Swollen, Wide Mouth, c.1905, 8 In.	2252.00
Vase, Leaves, Mottled Green Matte Glaze, Carved, 5 x 7 ½ In.	2860.00
Vase, Oatmeal Glaze, Marked, 11 In. *illus*	1416.00
Vase, Pear Shape, Thick Green Glaze, Hand Tooled Leaf Design, 7 In.	460.00
Vase, Vertical Leaves, Suspended Green Matte Glaze, Tapered, 4 ½ x 7 ¾ In.	2640.00

GUN, *see Toy*

GUNDERSEN glass was made at the Gundersen Glass Works of New Bedford, Massachusetts, from 1939 to 1952 and by its successor, Gundersen/Pairpoint, from 1952 to 1957. Gundersen Peachblow is especially famous.

Fairy Lamp, Burmese, Base, 6 In.	225.00
Vase, Burmese, Bulbous Base, Swollen Neck, 6 In.	100.00

GUSTAVSBERG ceramics factory was founded in 1827 near Stockholm, Sweden. It is best known to collectors for its twentieth-century artwares, especially Argenta, a green stoneware with silver inlay. The company was sold in the 1990s.

Gustafsberg

Bowl, Cherub, Flowers, Wilhelm Kage, Marked, 2 ¾ In. *illus*	115.00
Box, Cover, Nude Females, Different Poses, Wilhelm Kage, Marked, 5 ¾ In. *illus*	403.00
Charger, Woman Riding Dolphin, Band Of Stars Rim, Wilhelm Kage, Marked, 13 ½ In. *illus*	345.00
Vase, Grazia, Flowers, Silver Overlay, White Ground, Rounded Cylinder, Pinched Waist, 5 ¾ In.	92.00
Vase, Puce, Children Picking Firewood Reserve, Inscribed 1887, 21 x 13 ¾ In.	369.00

HAEGER POTTERIES, INC., Dundee, Illinois, started making commercial artwares in 1914. Early pieces were marked with the name *Haeger* written over an *H*. About 1938, the mark *Royal Haeger* was used in honor of Royal Hickman, a designer at the factory. The firm is still making florist wares and lamp bases. See also the Royal Hickman category.

Bowl, Cover, Concentric Rings, Yellow, Orange, Black, Elongated Top, Royal Haeger, 8 In.	86.00
Compote, Gold Tweed, Foil Paper Label, 1960s, 6 x 7 x 4 In.	60.00
Jardiniere, Brown Drip Glaze, Textured, Label, 1950s, 5 ½ x 7 In.	30.00
Planter, Madonna Head, White Matte Glaze, c.1941, 6 x 5 In.	36.00
Sculpture, Cat, Seated, Head Turned, White Glaze, 21 x 10 ½ In.	425.00
Vase, Black Mistique, Swollen Neck, Footed, 16 In.	95.00
Vase, Tan & Brown Speckled Glaze, Cylindrical, Tooled Center, Royal Haeger, 14 In.	16.00
Vase, White Neck, Blue Base, Bottle Shape, Attached Stand, Marked Royal, c.1940, 15 ½ In.	34.00

HALF-DOLL, *see Pincushion Doll category.*

HALL CHINA COMPANY started in East Liverpool, Ohio, in 1903. The firm made many types of wares. Collectors search for the Hall teapots made from the 1920s to the 1950s. The dinnerware of the same period, especially Autumn Leaf pattern, are also popular. The Hall China Company merged with Homer Laughlin China Company in 2010. Autumn Leaf pattern dishes are listed in their own category in this book.

Ashtray, Brown Glaze, Square, Cigarette Rest In Center, 8 ½ In.	15.00

Blue Garden, Casserole, Lid, 8 In.	48.00 to 52.00
Clover, Casserole, Beefsteak, Oval	69.00
Golden Clover, Cookie Jar, Big Earred	289.00
Golden Glo, Casserole, Basket Weave, Lid, 8 ½ In.	95.00
Harlequin, Platter, 15 ⅛ In.	65.00
Harlequin, Platter, 17 ¼ In.	82.00
Medallion, Custard Cup, Olive Green, 6 Oz., Pair	16.00
Poppy, Bowl, Vegetable, Round, 9 In.	35.00
Poppy, Casserole, Oval	89.00
Poppy, Sugar & Creamer	90.00
Red Poppy, Pitcher, Milk, Ribbing, 1930s, 6 ¼ x 8 ½ In.	30.00
Rose Parade, Casserole, Tab Handles, Lid, 2 ½ Qt.	62.00
Rose Parade, Sugar & Creamer	200.00
Rose White, Salt	14.00
Royal Rose, Mixing Bowl, 6 ½, 7 ½, 8 ½ In., 3 Piece	99.00
Royal Rose, Salt & Pepper	41.00
Server, Iced Tea, Lipton, Stand, Black, Stamp Mark, 11 x 16 ½ In.	341.00
Teapot, Airflow, Cobalt Blue, Gold, Cover, 6 Cup	65.00
Teapot, Albany, Mahogany, 6 Cup	69.00
Teapot, Black & Gold, Handle, 4 Cup	27.00
Teapot, Boston, Gray, Gold, 6 Cup	41.00
Teapot, Crocus, 6 Cup	232.00
Teapot, Golden Clover, Windshield, 6 Cup	289.00
Teapot, Lipton, Maroon, Lid, 6 Cup	41.00
Teapot, Morning Glory, Aladdin	212.00
Teapot, Nautilus, Turquoise, Gold Trim, 6 Cup	96.00
Teapot, Parade Shape, Gold Acorns & Leaves, 6 x 6 In., 6 Cup	22.00
Teapot, Poppy, Melody, 6 Cup	399.00
Teapot, Steamline, Chinese Red, 6 Cup	39.00
Tom & Jerry, Mug, Black, Gold, 2 ½ In., 6 Piece	60.00
Tomorrow's Classic, Bowl, Cereal, 6 In.	12.00

HALLOWEEN is an ancient holiday that has changed in the last 200 years. The jack-o'-lantern, witches on broomsticks, and orange decorations seem to be twentieth-century creations. Collectors started to become serious about collecting Halloween-related items in the late 1970s. The papier-mache decorations, now replaced by plastic, and old costumes are in demand.

Bank, Clown, Plastic, Clown Smiling, Dressed As Pirate, Eye Patch, Rosbro, 1950s, 8 In.	675.00
Boot Scraper, Witch On Broom, Cast Iron, Paint, Albany Foundry Co, 10 x 7 In.	2645.00
Candy Box, Powerhouse Candy, Image Of Pumpkin, Black Cat, 9 x 5 In.	75.00
Centerpiece, Winking Cat, Die Cut, Sitting Atop A Honeycomb Base, 1940s, 12 x 6 In.	30.00
Costume, Archie Andrews, Jumpsuit Style, Blue & Red, Archie Comic Pub., Inc., 1969, Size 1 .	45.00
Costume, Bullwinkle The Moose, Rayon, Plastic Mask, Ben Cooper, Box, 1961	115.00
Costume, Bunny Rabbit, Boxing Bunny On Front, Ben Cooper, 1950s, Size 12 To 14	25.00
Costume, Doctor, Yankiboy, Box, Child, Size 6	55.00
Costume, George Jetson, Plastic Mask, Ben Cooper, Box, 1963, Size Small	115.00
Costume, Indian, Brave Eagle, Fringed Shirt & Pants, Headdress, Box, 1950s	115.00
Costume, Lucille Ball, Gold Fabric Dress, Plastic Mask, Box, Child's, 1960s, Medium .....*illus*	253.00
Costume, Smokey Bear Head, Molded Rubber, Wire Mesh Eyes, 16 x 18 In.	345.00
Costume, Witch, Orange & Black, Bells, Tambourine, Child's, Size 10-12	120.00
Costume, Yogi Bear, 1950s, Ben Cooper, Size 12-14	22.00
Figure, Bunny, Witch In Basket On Back, Porcelain, Papier-Mache, 7 In.	45.00
Game, Flaming Halloween Fortune Game, Beistle Co., c.1930	500.00
Horn, Cat's Head, Plastic, Bulb Shape, Squeeze Head, Fun World Inc., 1960s, 4 x 2 In.	34.00
Jack-O'-Lantern, Black Cat, Green Eyes, Paper Face, Candleholder, Handle, Germany, 4 In. *illus*	633.00
Jack-O'-Lantern, Candleholder, Green Paper Sides, Black Disc Eyes, Handle, 5 ¼ In.	720.00
Jack-O'-Lantern, Cardboard, 2-Sided, Crepe Paper Liner, Germany, 1930s, 4 x 3 In.	150.00
Jack-O'-Lantern, Cardboard, Accordion Design, Germany, 4 ½ In.	300.00
Jack-O'-Lantern, Composition, Round Eyes, Triangular Nose, Lid, 13 In. Diam.	120.00
Jack-O'-Lantern, Devil Ears, Grin, Paper Face, Candleholder, Germany, 3 In. ....*illus*	288.00
Jack-O'-Lantern, Eyeglasses, Large, Nose, Hair, Painted, Candleholder, 4 ½ In. ....*illus*	316.00
Jack-O'-Lantern, Papier-Mache, Wire Bail Handle, 1950s, 5 x 6 In.	65.00
Lantern, Foot, Figural, Composition, Painted, Insert, Debossed Ghosts On Toes, 7 ½ In. ... *illus*	4025.00
Lantern, Pumpkin Head, Bail Handle, Facial Expressions, Papier-Mache, Germany, 6 Piece ...	2703.00
Napkin, Pumpkin In Cart, Orange, Paper, Beach Products, 1940s, 36 Piece	54.00
Noisemaker, Horn, Clown, Paper, Plastic, Crepe Paper Streamers, Black, Orange, 1950s, 10 In.	28.00

Handel, Lamp, Desk, Mosaic Slag Glass Shade, Bronze Base, Adjustable Arm, c.1900, 16 x 7 ½ In.
$1715.00

Skinner, Inc.

Handel, Lamp, Domed Shade, Birch Trees, Bronze Base, Marked, c.1900, 23 x 18 In.
$5333.00

Skinner, Inc.

Handel, Lamp, Domed Shade, Hawaiian Sunset, Metal Overlay, 9 Panels, 3-Griffin Base, 68 In. $8050.00

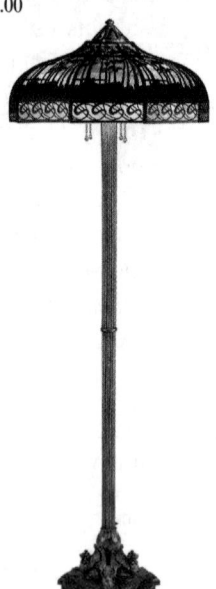

James D. Julia Inc.

Handel, Lamp, Landscape, Acid Etched Glass, Bronze, Signed, Julius Runge, 22 x 17 In. $6820.00

Rago Arts & Auction Center

Handel, Vase, Teroma, Autumn Mountain Landscape, Chipped Ice, Signed, Bedigie, 9 ¾ In. $1610.00

Cottone Auctions

Noisemaker, Party Blower, Pumpkin, Plastic, Celluloid, L. Glassner	45.00
Noisemaker, Ratchet, Tin, Witch, On Broom, US Metal Toy Mfg., c.1960	75.00
Noisemaker, Spinner, Witch, Die Cut Cardboard, Germany, 11 In. *illus*	115.00
Noisemaker, Wooden, Devil, Pumpkin, Cat, 9 ½ In., 3 Piece	210.00
Pin, Pumpkin In A Pear Tree, Jack-O'-Lantern, Creative Ideas, 1975, 2 ¼ In.	57.00
Postcard, Merry Halloween, Girl With Jack-O'-Lantern Head, Moves, Early 1900s, 5 x 3 In.	285.00
Postcard, Sailor Boy & Girl, Carrying Pumpkin, On Stick, 1909	30.00
Postcard, Vegetable Goblins In Car, Black Cat Sitting Shotgun, c.1900	30.00
Postcard, Woman Dressed As Clown, On Pine Branch, 4 Owls In Back, 1912	150.00
Pumpkin, Composition, Paper Inserts, Orange, Green, L. Glassner, 4 ½ In.	62.00
Roly Poly, Celluloid, Black Cat On Jack-O'-Lantern, Viscolid Co., 1900s, 4 x 2 In.	375.00
Toy, Pumpkin, Witch, Devil, Multicolor, Squeak, 9 In., 3 Piece	150.00
Vegetable Man, Moving Eyes, Papier-Mache, Internal Clockwork, c.1910, 16 In.	16520.00

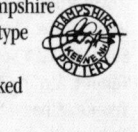

HAMPSHIRE pottery was made in Keene, New Hampshire, between 1871 and 1923. Hampshire developed a line of colored glazed wares as early as 1883, including a Royal Worcester–type pink, olive green, blue, and mahogany. Pieces are marked with the printed mark or the impressed name *Hampshire Pottery* or *J.S.T. & Co., Keene, N.H.* Many pieces were marked with city names and sold as souvenirs.

Bowl, Blue Mottled Matte Glaze, Marked, 5 ½ x 3 ¼ In.	120.00
Bowl, Leaf, Green Matte Glaze, Squat, Flattened, Rolled Rim, Leaf Design, Emoretta Mark	575.00
Ewer, Dark Green, 6 In.	331.00
Pitcher, Green Glaze, Leaf Design, Scalloped Rim, c.1905, 8 In.	184.00
Pitcher, Green Matte Glaze, Leaf Spout & Handle, Impressed Mark, c.1890, 8 ½ In. *illus*	415.00
Urn, Leaf, Green Matte Glaze, Marked, 5 ½ In.	354.00
Vase, Blue Matte Glaze, Bulbous, Marked, 3 ½ x 6 ¼ In.	270.00
Vase, Blue Matte Glaze, Flower Buds, Stems, Leaves, Oval, 7 In.	735.00
Vase, Blue Matte Glaze, Glazed Interior, Stylized, Bulbous, Marked, 3 ½ x 6 ¼ In.	270.00
Vase, Blue Matte Glaze, Stylized Design, Bulbous, Marked, 3 ½ x 6 ¼ In.	248.00
Vase, Buds, Leaves, Yellow Matte Glaze, Tapered, 6 In.	721.00
Vase, Corn, Green Matte Glaze, Bulbous, Marked, 6 x 5 ½ In.	300.00
Vase, Leaf, Blue Mottled Glaze, Squat Bottom, Long Narrow Neck, Flare Lip	633.00
Vase, Leaves, Buds, Green Matte Glaze, Elongated Oval, Pinched Rim, 7 ⅛ In.	805.00

HANDEL glass was made by Philip Handel working in Meriden, Connecticut, from 1885 and in New York City from 1893 to 1933. The firm made art glass and other types of lamps. Handel shades were made not only of leaded glass in a style reminiscent of Tiffany but also of reverse painted glass. Handel also made vases and other glass objects.

Bowl, Flowers & Scrolls, Frosted, Squat, Wide Rim, Curved In, Cameo Glass, Signed, 2 x 7 In.	920.00
Humidor, Indian's Head, Feathered Headdress, Green, Cylindrical, 7 In.	1438.00
Lamp, 3-Light, Art Deco Flower Design Glass Shade, Tapered Base, Signed, 18 x 22 In.	3163.00
Lamp, Boudoir, Domed Chipped Ice Shade, Winter Scene, Tree Trunk Base, 15 In.	2358.00
Lamp, Chipped Ice Shade, Green, Arts & Crafts Diamonds, Bronze Base, Chain, 11 In.	978.00
Lamp, Desk, Mosaic Slag Glass Shade, Bronze Base, Adjustable Arm, c.1900, 16 x 7 ½ In. *illus*	1715.00
Lamp, Desk, Sunset Palm Shade, 6 Slag Glass Panels, Scroll Border, Arched Arm, 14 In.	2655.00
Lamp, Domed Shade, Apple Blossoms, Butterflies, Pink, Green, 3 Scrolled Supports, 25 In.	7670.00
Lamp, Domed Shade, Birch Trees, Bronze Base, Marked, c.1900, 23 x 18 In. *illus*	5333.00
Lamp, Domed Shade, Chipped Ice, Bronze Bell-Shaped Harp, 56 In.	1438.00
Lamp, Domed Shade, Daffodils, Acid Etched, Bronze Urn Base, Signed, 24 x 18 In.	3720.00
Lamp, Domed Shade, Fiery Sunset Sky, Bamboo Overlay, Bronze Bamboo Base, 23 In.	5310.00
Lamp, Domed Shade, Hawaiian Sunset, Metal Overlay, 9 Panels, 3-Griffin Base, 68 In. *illus*	8050.00
Lamp, Domed Shade, Stylized Flower Band, Etched Milk Glass, Bronze Base, Signed, 23 x 16 In.	3720.00
Lamp, Domed Shade, Temple Ruins, Black, Brown, Green, Metal Base, Inscribed, c.1920, 25 x 18 In.	470.00
Lamp, Filigree Shade, Tropical Sunset, Slag Glass, 8 Panels, Textured Stem, Acorn Pulls, 23 In.	1593.00
Lamp, Geometric Shade, Leaded Glass, Bronze, 3-Footed, Marked, 56 x 12 ½ In.	11780.00
Lamp, Glass Shade, Basket Design, Harp Base, Signed, 11 x 7 x 18 In.	1800.00
Lamp, Hanging, Cherry Design Leaded Glass Shade, Chain, Cap, 25 x 14 In.	7700.00
Lamp, Hanging, Globe Shade, Obverse Flowers, Acid Etched, White Metal, 22 x 10 In.	744.00
Lamp, Hanging, Green Shade, Flowers, 6 x 19 In.	240.00
Lamp, Landscape, Acid Etched Glass, Bronze, Signed, Julius Runge, 22 x 17 In. *illus*	6820.00
Lamp, Leaded Glass Shade, Apple Blossom, Red, Green, Yellow, Acorn Pull Chain, c.1900, 26 x 23 In.	6457.00
Lamp, Leaded Glass Shade, Cherry Blossom, Tree Trunk Base, Acorn Pull Chain, 23 x 18 In.	3690.00
Lamp, Leaded Glass Shade, Flower, Orange, Green, 4 Handle Support, 18 x 24 In.	960.00
Lamp, Leaded Glass Shade, Wisteria, Purple, Lavender, Blue, Yellow, Leaves, Base, 31 In.	20125.00
Lamp, Molded Shade, Acorn Pull Chain, Metal Base, Electrified, 13 x 8 In.	414.00

H

Lamp, Oil, Teroma, Pulled Feathers, Yellow, Green, Brass Font, Clear Chimney, 22 x 12 In.		2604.00
Lamp, Shade, Birds Of Paradise, Acid Etched, Peter Broggi, c.1920, 22 x 18 In.		6573.00
Lamp, Shade, Field Scene, Bronze Bell Shape Base, 56 In.		1200.00
Lamp, Shade, Forest Scene, Elongated, Bronze Base, 14 ½ In.		275.00
Lamp, Shade, Landscape At Sunset, Bronze Base, 13 x 8 In.		4025.00
Lamp, Shade, Oak Leaves, Branches, Orange, Yellow, Green, Red Brown Base, 20 In.		4888.00
Lamp, Shade, Parrots, Butterflies, Flower Sprays, Signed, c.1900, 24 x 18 In.		7995.00
Lantern, Hanging, 6-Sided Slag Glass Shade, Acorn, Geometric Metal Overlays, 12 x 19 ½ In.		6000.00
Sconce, Copper, Hammered, Curved, Signed, 5 ½ x 5 In., Pair		660.00
Shade, Globe, Chipped Ice, Daisies, Black Stems, Arts & Crafts, 10 In.		413.00
Vase, Teroma, Autumn Mountain Landscape, Chipped Ice, Signed, Bedigie, 9 ¾ In.	*illus*	1610.00
Vase, Teroma, Autumn Trees, Frosted Ground, Pinched Waist, 4 ½ In.		518.00

HARDWARE, *see Architectural category.*

HARKER POTTERY COMPANY was incorporated in 1890 in East Liverpool, Ohio. The Harker family had been making pottery in the area since 1840. The company made many types of pottery but by the Civil War was making quantities of yellowware from native clays. It also made Rockingham-type brown-glazed pottery and whiteware. The plant was moved to Chester, West Virginia, in 1931. dinnerware were made and sold nationally. In 1971 the company was sold to Jeannette Glass Company, and all operations ceased in 1972. For more prices, go to kovels.com.

Alpine, Bowl, Vegetable, Round, 8 In.	18.00
Alpine, Chop Plate, 11 In.	20.00
Alpine, Plate, Dinner	9.00
Alpine, Platter, Serving, Oval, 13 In.	32.00
Amy, Cup & Saucer, Footed	16.00
Blue Dane, Cup & Saucer	10.00
Blue Mist, Cup & Saucer	28.00
Blue Mist, Sugar, Cover	18.00
Bouquet, Bowl, Vegetable	74.00
Bouquet, Cup & Saucer	14.00
Bouquet, Gravy Boat, Underplate	42.00
Bouquet, Plate, Bread & Butter	5.00
Bouquet, Platter, Oval, 13 In.	22.00
Bouquet, Sugar, Cover	28.00
Bridal Rose, Bowl, Fruit	10.00
Bridal Rose, Platter, Serving, Oval, 13 In.	32.00
Chesterton, Ashtray, Gray	7.00
Chesterton, Bowl, Vegetable, Round, Gray, 7 In.	18.00
Chesterton, Cake Plate, Handles, Gray	20.00
Chesterton, Gravy Boat, Gray	30.00
Chesterton, Platter, Serving, Oval, Gray, 13 In.	24.00
Chesterton, Salt & Pepper, Gray	20.00
Cock O'Morn, Creamer	18.00
Cock O'Morn, Cup & Saucer	9.00
Colonial Lady, Bowl, Fruit	9.00
Colonial Lady, Plate, Luncheon, 9 ¼ In.	41.00
Colonial Lady, Platter, Oval, 12 In.	142.00
Corinthian, Ashtray, Teal Green	8.00
Corinthian, Creamer, Teal Green	18.00
Corinthian, Cup & Saucer, Teal Green	10.00
Corinthian, Plate, Bread & Butter, Teal Green	4.00
Corinthian, Sugar, Cover, Teal Green	20.00
Coronet, Bowl, Vegetable, Round, 8 In.	18.00
Coronet, Casserole, Lid, 2 Qt.	48.00
Coronet, Plate, Bread & Butter	8.00
Currier & Ives, Plate, Bread & Butter	8.00
Currier & Ives, Plate, Dinner	24.00
Dainty Flower, Bowl, Fruit, Swirl	9.00
Dainty Flower, Bowl, Salad, Square, 6 In.	12.00
Dainty Flower, Bowl, Vegetable, Round, Swirl, 8 In.	28.00
Dainty Flower, Creamer	20.00
Dainty Flower, Cup & Saucer	38.00
Dainty Flower, Plate, Bread & Butter, Swirled	5.00
Dainty Flower, Platter, Oval, 13 In.	24.00 to 42.00

Hochst, Bowl, Embossed Flower Swags, Hand Painted Sprays, Square, Marked, c.1785, 3 ¼ x 8 In.
$259.00

James D. Julia Inc.

Hopalong Cassidy, Display, Figural, Hopalong Cassidy, Timex, Shock-Resistant Watches, Embossed, 1950s, 15 In.
$4175.00

Hake's Americana & Collectibles

Hopalong Cassidy, Ring, Compass, Removable Hat, Brass, Post Cereal Premium, Meadow Gold Dairy, 1952
$443.00

Hake's Americana & Collectibles

Horn, Drinking Horn, Silver Plated Stand, Set-On Lid, 23 ½ In. $690.00

The Stein Auction Co.

Horn, Figurine, Pu Tai, Surrounded By Children, Sack, Rhinoceros, Chinese, 4 ⅝ In. $71100.00

Skinner, Inc.

Howdy Doody, Barrettes, Plastic, Card, Howdy, Clarabell, Princess Summerfall-Winterspring, Kagran, 1956 $139.00

Hake's Americana & Collectibles

Howdy Doody, Flashlight Ring, Plastic Face Lights Up, Brass Ring, Battery Operated, Brownie, 1950s $115.00

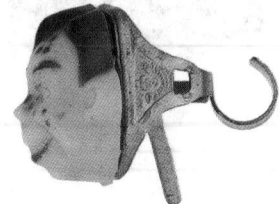

Hake's Americana & Collectibles

Dainty Flower, Salt & Pepper, Round	20.00
Dainty Flower, Utility Bowl, 4 In.	22.00
Dresden Duchess, Cup & Saucer, Footed	12.00
Dresden Duchess, Plate, Bread & Butter	8.00
Dresden Duchess, Plate, Salad	10.00
Godey, Ashtray	9.00
Godey, Bowl, Dessert	8.00
Godey, Plate, Dinner	9.00
Golden Dawn, Bowl, Vegetable, Oval, Divided	40.00
Golden Dawn, Creamer	10.00
Golden Dawn, Cup & Saucer	8.00
Golden Dawn, Sugar, Cover	16.00
Ivy, Bowl, Vegetable, Oval, Divided	38.00
Ivy, Bowl, Vegetable, Round, 8 In.	18.00
Ivy, Creamer	18.00
Ivy, Cup & Saucer	9.00
Ivy, Gravy Boat, Underplate	28.00 to 32.00
Ivy, Plate, Bread & Butter	6.00
Ivy, Plate, Dinner	10.00 to 24.00
Ivy, Plate, Salad	7.00
Ivy, Platter, Serving, Oval, 13 In.	24.00 to 30.00
Ivy, Soup, Dish, Coupe	9.00
Ivy, Soup, Dish, Rimmed	14.00
Ivy, Sugar, Cover	35.00
Lemon Tree, Creamer	16.00
Lemon Tree, Cup & Saucer	9.00
Lemon Tree, Platter, Serving, Oval, 13 In.	24.00
Magnolia, Bowl, Vegetable, Round, 8 In.	22.00
Magnolia, Plate, Bread & Butter	9.00
Magnolia, Sugar, Cover	18.00
Pate Sur Pate, Bowl, Fruit, Brown	7.00
Pate Sur Pate, Cup & Saucer, Brown	9.00
Peacock Alley, Bowl, Vegetable, Oval, Divided	45.00
Peacock Alley, Cup & Saucer	9.00
Persian Key, Creamer	12.00
Persian Key, Cup & Saucer	8.00
Persian Key, Plate, Bread & Butter	4.00
Persian Key, Plate, Dinner	10.00
Persian Key, Plate, Salad	8.00
Persian Key, Platter, Serving, Oval, 13 In.	18.00
Petit Point, Bowl, Cereal, Lugged	13.00
Petit Point, Bowl, Vegetable	80.00
Petit Point, Creamer	18.00
Petit Point, Plate, Bread & Butter, 6 In.	7.00
Petit Point, Plate, Dinner	20.00
Pine Cone, Bowl, Vegetable, Round, 8 In.	18.00
Pine Cone, Cup & Saucer	9.00
Rosebud, Bowl, Vegetable, Oval, Divided	24.00
Sea Fare, Bowl, Vegetable, Oval, Divided	26.00
Sweetheart Rose, Bowl, Vegetable, Round, 8 In.	28.00
Sweetheart Rose, Cup & Saucer	14.00
Sweetheart Rose, Platter, Serving, Oval, 13 In.	42.00
Sweetheart Rose, Sugar, Cover	18.00
Vintage, Gravy Boat, Underplate	48.00
Vintage, Plate, Dinner	30.00
Vintage, Plate, Salad	18.00
Vintage, Sugar, Cover	20.00
White Cap, Creamer	18.00
White Cap, Cup & Saucer	9.00
White Cap, Platter, Serving, Oval, 13 In.	24.00
White Clover, Bowl, Fruit	17.00
White Clover, Creamer	30.00
White Clover, Cup & Saucer	20.00 to 24.00
White Clover, Plate, Bread & Butter	8.00
White Rose, Platter, Serving, Oval, 13 In.	60.00
Wild Rose, Bowl, Vegetable, Round, 8 In.	32.99

H

Wild Rose, Platter, Serving, Oval, 13 In.	28.00
Wild Rose, Platter, Serving, Oval, 16 In.	60.00
Wild Rose, Sugar, Cover	24.00

HARLEQUIN dinnerware was produced by the Homer Laughlin Company from 1938 to 1964, and sold without trademark by the F. W. Woolworth Co. It has a concentric ring design like Fiesta, but the rings are separated from the rim by a plain margin. Cup handles are triangular in shape. Seven different novelty animal figurines were introduced in 1939. For more prices, go to kovels.com.

Chartreuse, Plate, Bread & Butter	8.00
Mauve Blue, Cup & Saucer	13.00
Mauve Blue, Pitcher, Water	45.00
Mauve Blue, Plate, Bread & Butter	8.00
Mauve Blue, Plate, Dinner	10.00
Medium Green, Cup, Homer Laughlin	10.00
Red, Cup & Saucer	13.00
Red, Plate, Dinner	13.00
Red, Soup, Dish, Cream	25.00
Rose, Bowl, Fruit	11.00
Rose, Plate, Dinner	13.00
Spruce Green, Cup & Saucer	78.00
Spruce Green, Plate, Dinner	26.00
Turquoise, Bowl, Fruit	11.00
Yellow, Ashtray	23.00
Yellow, Cup & Saucer	13.00
Yellow, Plate, Bread & Butter	8.00
Yellow, Plate, Dinner	11.00
Yellow, Platter, Serving, Oval, 11 ⅜ In.	15.00

HATPIN collectors search for pins popular from 1860 to 1920. The long pin, often over four inches, was used to hold the hat in place on the hair. The tops of the pins were made of all materials, from solid gold and real gemstones to ceramics and glass. Be careful to buy original hatpins and not recent pieces made by altering old buttons.

Brass, Teardrop, Art Nouveau, 1920s, 6 ½ In.	30.00
Porcelain Ends, Portrait Of Young Woman, 9 ¾ In., Pair	162.00
Silver, Bulbous, Incised Star, c.1880, 10 ½ In.	145.00
Silver, Octagonal, 10 In.	135.00

HATPIN HOLDERS were needed when hatpins were fashionable from 1860 to 1920. The large, heavy hat required special long-shanked pins to hold it in place. The hatpin holder resembles a large saltshaker, but it often has no opening at the bottom as a shaker does. Hatpin holders were made of all types of ceramics and metal. Look for other pieces under the names of specific manufacturers.

Carnival Glass, Orange Tree, Blue, Footed	105.00
Carnival Glass, Orange Tree, Marigold, Footed	120.00
Jadeite Green Glass, Grapes, Vines, 3-Footed, 6 ½ In.	26.00
Nippon, Flared Bottom, Gilt Bands, 6 ½ In.	109.00

HAVILAND china has been made in Limoges, France, since 1842. The factory was **HAVILAND & CO.** started by the Haviland Brothers of New York City. Pieces are marked *H & Co.,* *Haviland & Co.,* or *Theodore Haviland.* It is possible to match existing sets of dishes through dealers who specialize in Haviland china. Other factories worked in the town of Limoges making a similar chinaware. These porcelains are listed in this book under Limoges.

Bowl, Vegetable, Pink Flowers, Scalloped Edge, c.1910, 10 ¼ In.	50.00
Charger, Wild Roses, Leaves, Stems, c.1900, 14 In.	169.00
Coffeepot, Rosalinde, Gold Trim, 6 ⅜ In.	915.00
Cup & Saucer, Demitasse, Silver Anniversary, 1 ½ In.	80.00
Plate, Dinner, Golden Quail, 10 ⅜ In.	332.00
Plate, Dinner, Marie Antoinette, 10 ⅞ In.	138.00
Plate, Dinner, Ranson, 9 ¾ In.	48.00
Sauce Bowl, Underplate, Tight Crimp Scallop Rim, White Ground, Pink Flowers, c.1900, 8 ½ In.	50.00
Serving Bowl, Pink Flowers, Tight Crimp, Scalloped Rim, c.1905, 8 ½ In.	50.00
Soup, Cream, Saucer, Vieux Paris	188.00
Tray, 3 Tiers, Gothham, 10 ¼ In.	214.00

Howdy Doody, Marionette, Heidi Doody, Original Box, 12 In.
$150.00

Howdy Doody, Spoon & Fork Set, Display Box & Sleeve, 6 In.
$150.00

Hummel, Figurine, No. 16/1, Little Hiker, Full Bee, 5 ½ In.
$23.00

H

Hummel, Figurine, No. 23/111, Adoration, Missing Bee, 9 In. $196.00

The Stein Auction Co.

Hummel, Figurine, No. 47/0, Goose Girl, Prototype, Missing Bee, 4 ¾ In. $1150.00

The Stein Auction Co.

Hummel, Figurine, No. 64, Shepherd's Boy, Full Bee, 6 In. $161.00

The Stein Auction Co.

Tray, Flowering Vine, Gold Ribbon Handles, 1880s, 8 ½ In.	275.00
Vase, Fluted, Scalloped Rim, Holly, Berries, 5 ½ In.	30.00

HAWKES cut glass was made by T. G. Hawkes & Company of Corning, New York, founded in 1880. The firm cut glass blanks made at other glassworks until 1962. Many pieces are marked with the trademark, a trefoil ring enclosing a fleur-de-lis and two hawks. Cut glass by other manufacturers is listed under either the factory name or in the general Cut Glass category.

Bowl, Finger, 3 Fruits, American Brilliant, Marked, 12 Piece	275.00
Bowl, Flute, Scalloped Rim, American Brilliant, Marked, 3 ¾ x 8 In.	40.00
Bowl, Fruit, Grapevine Band, Lobed Bottom, 4 ¾ In., 12 Piece	177.00
Bowl, Hobstar, Split Vesica, Strawberry Diamond & Zipper, Square, Marked, 8 ½ In.	40.00
Bowl, Kohinoor, Blown-Out Mold, Fingers, American Brilliant, Marked, 4 x 10 In.	2100.00
Box, Cover, Hobstar, Strawberry Diamond, Round, American Brilliant, Marked, 2 ½ x 5 In.	160.00
Candelabrum, 2-Light, Scrolled, Pressed & Cut Glass, Prisms, c.1905, 17 ½ x 13 In., Pair	575.00
Cocktail Shaker, 19th Hole, Etched Glass, Sifter, Cover, c.1900, 10 x 4 In.	299.00
Cologne Bottle, Nautilus, Brilliant Cut, Ball Shape, Embossed Silver Stopper, 6 In.	2000.00
Compote, Cut Base, American Brilliant, Marked, 4 ¼ x 6 ¼ In.	50.00
Compote, Engraved, Pattern Cut Base, Marked, 4 x 6 ½ In.	120.00
Compote, Lid, Dome, Finial, Signed, 9 ½ In.	478.00
Cruet, Hobstar & Fan, Pedestal, American Brilliant, Marked, 8 ½ In.	125.00
Decanter, Wheel Cut, Thistle, Rye Stalk, Sterling Silver Top, c.1925, 9 ¾ x 4 ½ In., Pair	984.00
Ginger Jar, Cover, Engraved, Oriental Scene, American Brilliant, Marked, 5 ½ In.	75.00
Jam Jar, Cover, St. Regis, Ball Knop, American Brilliant, Marked, 4 ¼ In.	150.00
Nappy, Hobstar & Crosscut Diamond, American Brilliant, Marked, 5 ¾ In.	60.00
Pitcher, Water, Brunswick, American Brilliant, 8 ½ In.	300.00
Plate, Chrysanthemum, American Brilliant, 6 ¼ In.	75.00
Plate, Flower, Star, Marked, 1800s, 8 In.	1840.00
Tray, Lattice & Rosette, Round, American Brilliant, Marked, 9 ¾ In.	2900.00
Vase, Alice, Faceted Knob, Hobstar Foot, 20 In.	6495.00
Vase, Brunswick, Cut Glass, Trumpet Shape, 14 In.	345.00
Vase, Carnation, Gravic Glass, Pinched Waist, American Brilliant, 14 ¾ In.	250.00
Vase, Engraved Flower Basket, Pedestal, American Brilliant, Marked, 9 ¾ In.	300.00
Vase, Intaglio Cut, Clear, Flower Swags, Scrolling Fleur-De-Lis, Bulbous, Shouldered, 7 In.	173.00
Vase, Lorraine, Pinched Waist, American Brilliant, Marked, 14 In.	900.00

HEAD VASES, generally showing a woman from the shoulders up, were used by florists primarily in the 1950s and 1960s. Made in a variety of sizes and often decorated with imitation jewelry and other lifelike accessories, the vases were manufactured in Japan and the U.S.A. Less elaborate examples were made as early as the 1930s. Religious themes, babies, and animals are also common subjects. Other head vases are listed under manufacturers' names and can be located through the index in the back of this book.

Country Girl, Blue Eyes, Ruby Lips, Brinn, c.1940, 4 In.	45.00
Girl, Black Sleeveless Dress, Flower In Hair, Japan, 1960s, 7 In.	449.00
Girl, Nubian, Gold Accents, Bone In Hair	30.00
Girl, Red Hair, Green Cape, Hat, 6 In.	45.00
Glamour Girl, Hat, Heart Lips, c.1945, 4 x 3 ½ In.	45.00
Stewardess, Hat, Scarf, Japan, 1960s, 5 In.	165.00
Woman, Black & White Dress, Gray Hat, Pink Roses, Drop Pearl Earrings, 1960s	149.00
Woman, Black Dress, White Trim, Brimmed Hat, Bow, Marked Relpo, c.1960	775.00
Woman, Black Hair, Hat, Pearl Earrings & Necklace, Trimont Ware, 1960s, 7 In.	1399.00
Woman, Blond Hair, Scarf, Necklace, Marked, 7 In.	45.00
Woman, Blond Hair, Sundress, Floppy Hat, Sunglasses, Royal Crown, 1960s, 7 In.	3500.00
Woman, Eclectic Egyptian, Headdress, Royal Sealy Co., c.1940, 6 In.	95.00
Woman, Green Gloves, Holly, Red Hood, Blue Eyes, Marked Relpo, 1965, 7 ¼ In.	175.00
Woman, Hat, Morton Pottery, 1900s, 9 In.	50.00
Woman, Pioneer, Art Deco Style, White, Japan, 7 In.	50.00
Woman, Ruffled Green Dress, Pearls, Butterflies, 1960s	129.00
Woman, Silver Hair, Raised Collar, Tiara, Japan, 1950s	495.00

HEDI SCHOOP Art Creations, North Hollywood, California, started about 1945 and was working until 1954. Schoop made ceramic figurines, lamps, planters, and tablewares.

Hedi Schoop S

Bowl, Shell, Dark Rose To Pink, Ribbed, Gilt, Marked, 9 x 7 In.	50.00
Candleholder, Peasant Girl, Looking Up, 8 In.	45.00
Dish, Butterfly Shape, Pink, Gilt Trim, Marked, 5 x 4 In.	42.00

Figurine, Dutch Boy, Dutch Girl, Green, Marked, c.1946, 11 In., Pair	115.00
Figurine, Dutch Girl, Holding Apron, Yellow, Brown, White, 11 In.	45.00
Figurine, Oriental Man, Hat, 12 ½ In.	65.00
Figurine, Rooster, Greens, Browns, Marked, 13 In.	125.00
Planter, Horse, Pink & White, Green Saddle, Signed, 10 In.	60.00
Planter, Peasant Girl, Singing, Holding Basket, c.1940, 8 In.	45.00
Planter, Woman, Holding Book, Flowered Dress, Veil, 9 In.	49.00

HEINTZ ART METAL SHOP used the letters *HAMS* in a diamond as a mark. In 1902, Otto Heintz designed and manufactured copper items with colored enamel decorations under the name Art Crafts Shop. He took over the Arts & Crafts Company in Buffalo, New York, in 1903. By 1906 it had become the Heintz Art Metal Shop. It remained in business until 1930. The company made ashtrays, bookends, boxes, bowls, desk sets, vases, trophies, and smoking sets. The best-known pieces are made of copper, brass, and bronze with silver overlay. Similar pieces were made by Smith Metal Arts and were marked *Silver Crest*. Some pieces by both companies are unmarked.

Candlestick, Applied Orchid, Silver On Bronze, Impressed Mark, 5 ½ x 4 ½ In.	220.00
Compote, Applied Orchids, Double Handles, Silver On Bronze, Mark, 11 ½ x 5 ½ In.	240.00
Frame, Applied Linear Borders, Oval Opening, Silver On Bronze, Impressed Mark, 8 ½ x 10 ½ In.	193.00
Humidor, Silver On Bronze, Geometrics, Green, Impressed, 6 x 10 In.	360.00
Lamp, Applied Flowers, Silver On Bronze, 7 ½ x 11 ½ In.	900.00
Lamp, Applied Flowers, Silver, Geometric Designs, 9 x 12 ½ In.	1020.00
Lamp, Applied Organic Design, Silver On Bronze, 13 x 15 In.	990.00
Lamp, Applied Organic Design, Silver On Bronze, Patina, 13 x 15 In.	1080.00
Lamp, Art Deco, Domed Shade, Silver On Bronze, Flared Foot, 12 ½ In.	400.00
Lamp, Art Deco, Domed Shade, Silver On Bronze, Vine & Leaf, 11 In.	325.00
Lamp, Poppies, Silver On Bronze, Mica Cutout Shade, 9 ¾ x 8 ½ In.	1364.00
Vase, Applied Flowers, Silver On Bronze, Impressed Mark, 5 x 12 In.	420.00
Vase, Applied Rose Design, Silver On Bronze Impressed, 4 ¾ x 17 ¼ In.	900.00
Vase, Applied White Flowers, Silver On Bronze, Impressed Mark, 5 x 12 In.	385.00
Vase, Blossoms, Silver On Bronze, Flared Base, 8 In.	472.00
Vase, Bud, Applied Organic Design, Silver On Bronze, Impressed, 4 x 12 In.	360.00
Vase, Bud, Leaf, Berry, Silver On Bronze, Stamped, 11 ¾ In.	283.00
Vase, Flowers, Silver On Bronze, Trumpet Shape, 15 x 5 In.	230.00
Vase, Landscape, Flower Design Silver On Bronze, Cylindrical, 5 x 12 In.	720.00
Vase, Stylized Flowers, Silver On Bronze, Mottled Verdigris, 12 x 3 ½ In.	589.00
Vase, Stylized Flowers, Silver On Bronze, Stamped, 12 ¼ x 5 ¼ In.	589.00
Vase, Stylized, Flower, Silver On Bronze, Mark, 1900s, 10 ½ x 3 In.	155.00

HEISEY glass was made from 1896 to 1957 in Newark, Ohio, by A. H. Heisey and Co., Inc. The Imperial Glass Company of Bellaire, Ohio, bought some of the molds and the rights to the trademark. Some Heisey patterns have been made by Imperial since 1960. After 1968, they stopped using the *H* trademark. Heisey used romantic names for colors, such as Sahara. Do not confuse color and pattern names. The Custard Glass and Ruby Glass categories may also include some Heisey pieces.

Animal, Asiatic Pheasant, 10 ¼ In.	95.00
Animal, Clydesdale, 7 ¼ In.	65.00
Animal, Colt, Balking, 3 ¾ In.	40.00
Animal, Colt, Kicking, 4 ⅛ In.	55.00
Animal, Cygnet, 2 ⅛ In.	65.00
Animal, Fox, Sleeping, Ashtray, 6 ¼ In.	110.00
Animal, Gazelle, 11 In.	230.00
Animal, Goose, Wings Down, 10 ¼ In.	190.00
Animal, Goose, Wings Up, 6 ½ In.	30.00
Animal, Scottie, 3 ½ In.	35.00 to 55.00
Aristocrat, Candlestick, Cutting, 9 In., Pair	100.00
Beaded Swag, Butter, Cover	15.00
Beaded Swag, Butter, Cover, Gold	45.00
Beaded Swag, Nappy, Emerald, 9 In.	65.00
Beaded Swag, Toothpick Holder, Ruby	34.00
Cabochon, Juice, Footed, Sultana Base, 5 Oz.	65.00
Caitlin Rose, Puff Box, Metal Lid	15.00
Carcasonne, Champagne, Alexandrite	45.00
Carcasonne, Cocktail, Alexandrite, 3 Oz.	135.00
Carcasonne, Cordial, Alexandrite, Oz.	250.00
Carcasonne, Goblet, Short Stem, Alexandrite, 11 Oz.	65.00

Hummel, Figurine, No. 136/1, Friends, Three Line Mark, 5 ¼ In.
$41.00

DuMouchelles Art Gallery

Hummel, Figurine, No. 1530, Auf Wiedersehen, Boy With Hat, Full Bee, 5 ¼ In.
$546.00

The Stein Auction Co.

Hummel, Figurine, No. 183, Forest Shrine, New Mark, 9 In.
$84.00

DuMouchelles Art Gallery

As always, the edited listings in *Kovels' Antiques & Collectibles Price Guide* aren't available on any website, but readers should visit Kovels.com for information on trends, tips, reproductions, marks, old prices, and more!

Hummel, Figurine, No. 184, Latest News, Das Allerneuste, Three Line Mark, 5 In. $230.00

The Stein Auction Co.

Hummel, Figurine, No. 184, Latest News, The New York Times, Custom Title, Stylized Bee, 5 In. $276.00

The Stein Auction Co.

Hummel, Figurine, No. 315, Mountaineer, Master Sample, Arbeitsmuster Medal, Stylized Bee, 5 In. $2070.00

The Stein Auction Co.

> **TIP**
> Hummel figurines should be washed in liquid detergent and water, half and half.

Carcasonne, Goblet, Tall, Alexandrite, 11 Oz.	140.00
Carcasonne, Soda, Footed, Alexandrite, 12 Oz.	110.00
Circle Pair, Goblet, Flamingo	15.00
Coarse Rib, Plate, 4 In.	16.00
Cobel, Cocktail Shaker, 455 Sportsman Etch, Rooster Head Stopper, Qt.	95.00
Colonial, Basket, Anne Etch, Round	75.00
Colonial, Bowl, Round, Scalloped, Paneled, 9 x 3 In.	25.00
Colonial, Compote, Footed, Handles, 12 In.	25.00
Colonial, Dish, Pickle, Scalloped, Central Star, Oval, 5 x 10 In.	26.00
Colonial, Jug, ½ Gal.	30.00
Colonial, Syrup, Flower Cutting, 5 Oz.	25.00
Colonial, Toothpick Holder, Scalloped	450.00
Continental, Toothpick Holder	30.00
Corinthian, Goblet, 10 Oz.	15.00
Coronation, Tumbler, Soda, 498 Modern Polo Etch, 8 Oz.	45.00
Country Club, Tumbler, Soda, 517 Winchester 73 Etch, 18 Oz.	130.00
Creole, Champagne, Tall Stem, Sahara Bowl	15.00
Crysolite, Bowl, Flared, Ridged & Scalloped, 3 x 13 In.	69.00
Crystolite, Platter, 14 In.	10.00
Crystolite, Relish, Leaf, 9 In.	25.00
Daisy & Leaves, Nappy, 8 In.	30.00
Dolphin, Candlestick	45.00
Double Rib & Panel, Mustard, Cover, Moongleam	35.00
Duck, Ashtray	40.00
Empress, Ashtray, Cobalt Blue	70.00
Empress, Bowl, Flowers, Moongleam, 11 In.	45.00
Empress, Candlestick, Moongleam, 1-Light, Pair	45.00
Empress, Candlestick, Sahara, Pair	110.00
Empress, Compote, Crinoline Etch, Oval	35.00
Empress, Compote, Sahara, Round, 6 In.	30.00
Empress, Oil Cruet, Sahara	55.00
Empress, Platter, Old Colony Etch, Oval, 14 In.	60.00
Fancy Loop, Biscuit Jar, Metal Lid	55.00
Fancy Loop, Compote, Footed, 8 In.	70.00
Fancy Loop, Punch Glass, Footed, Cupped, Pair	65.00
Fancy Loop, Toothpick Holder	25.00
Fancy Loop, Vase, 10 In.	60.00
Fandango, Salt & Pepper, Metal Lid	25.00
Fandango, Toothpick Holder, Clear	65.00
Fish, Bookends	45.00
Fish, Candlestick, 5 In.	170.00
Fish, Match Holder, 3 In.	85.00
Flamingo Pink, Nut Dish, Octagonal, Square Handles, c.1930, 2 x 3 ½ In., 6 Piece	175.00
Flamingo, Basket, Pink, Double Rib, 6 Panel, 8 ½ In.	135.00
Flamingo, Ladle	40.00
Fleur-De-Lis, Plate, Square, 9 In.	35.00
Grape Cluster, Bowl, Flowers, Oval, Satin Handles	35.00
Grape Cluster, Candelabrum, 1-Light, Bobeches, Prisms, Pair	80.00
Greek Key, Nappy	15.00
Greek Key, Plate, 8 In.	20.00
Greek Key, Punch Bowl, Pedestal Base, Clear, 14 ½ x 15 In.	403.00
Greek Key, Sugar & Creamer, Debra Shape, Applied Handles, c.1930	45.00
Hexagon, Bowl, Salad, Flamingo, 10 In., 6 Piece	15.00
Kaylonal, Compote, Crimped, 9 In.	95.00
Kaylonal, Toothpick Holder	35.00
Kohinoor, Candelabrum, 2-Light, D Prisms	75.00
Lariat, Cake Plate, 14 In.	48.00
Liberty, Candlestick, 1-Light, Moongleam, Pair	210.00
Locket & Chain, Toothpick Holder, Footed, Ruby, 2 In.	4000.00
Lodestar, Cocktail, Dawn, 6 Piece	110.00
Lodestar, Plate, Party, Dawn, 13 ½ In.	75.00
McGrady, Syrup, Sahara, 7 Oz.	45.00
Monte Cristo, Cordial, Cutting, 1 Oz.	45.00
Narrow Flute, Jug, ½ Gal.	55.00
Narrow Flute, Jug, Qt.	40.00
New Era, Console Set, Floral Bowl, Candelabrum, 2-Light, Satin, 11 In., 3 Piece	150.00

H

Old Queen Ann, Toothpick Holder, Gold	55.00
Old Sandwich, Salt & Pepper, Flamingo	65.00
Old Williamsburg, Candelabrum, 2-Light, Hanging Prisms, Spear Finial, 10 ¾ x 13 In., Pair	148.00
Orchid, Bowl, Fluted, 12 x 4 In.	88.00
Orchid, Goblet, Water, Tyrolean, 10 Oz.	40.00
Paneled Cane, Toothpick Holder	30.00
Peerless, Goblet, Low, Flamingo, 7 Oz.	65.00
Peerless, Pitcher, ½ Gal.	50.00
Peerless, Toothpick Holder	5.00
Penguin, Decanter, Pt.	325.00
Petticoat Dolphin, Candlestick, Cupped Base, Sahara	3000.00
Pineapple & Fan, Spooner, Emerald	70.00
Pineapple & Fan, Toothpick Holder, Clear	60.00
Pineapple & Fan, Toothpick Holder, Green & Gold	160.00
Pinwheel & Fan, Jug, 3 Pt.	95.00
Plain Band, Pitcher, Qt.	45.00
Plantation, Bowl, Salad, 9 In.	155.00
Plantation, Candlestick, 1-Light, Pair	160.00
Plantation, Sherbet, 4 ¼ In.	30.00
Plantation, Tumbler, Iced Tea, Flared, Pair	160.00
Plantation, Tumbler, Juice, Footed, 5 ½ In.	68.00
Plantation, Vase, 9 ½ In.	160.00
Priscilla, Compote, Shallow, High Footed, Puntied Bottom, 10 In.	160.00
Priscilla, Oil Bottle, Stopper, 4 Oz.	25.00
Prism Band, Decanter, Moongleam	160.00
Prison Stripe, Toothpick Holder	100.00
Provincial, Punch, Cup	31.00
Puritan, Bowl, Footed, 7 In.	70.00
Puritan, Bowl, Footed, 9 In.	40.00
Puritan, Custard Cup, Shallow, Handles, 4 ½ Oz.	15.00
Puritan, Jug, Squat, Qt.	30.00
Puritan, Pitcher, Tankard	45.00
Puritan, Sugar & Creamer	55.00
Puritan, Toothpick Holder, Clear	85.00
Quator, Mustard, Cover	45.00
Queen Ann, Ice Bucket, Orchid Etch	75.00
Revere, Sauceboat, Footed, Square Handle, c.1950, 3 x 7 In.	65.00
Ridgeleigh, Ashtray, Square, 6 x 6 In.	15.00
Ridgeleigh, Cigarette Box, Cover, Oval	55.00
Ridgeleigh, Nappy, Square, 7 In.	20.00
Ridgeleigh, Relish, Oval, Divided, c.1940, 4 x 7 In.	23.00
Ridgeleigh, Tray Handles, Marked, c.1935, 7 x 3 ¾ In.	10.00
Ridgeleigh, Vase, Bud, 6 In.	43.00
Rooster Head, Cocktail Shaker, Silver Overlay, Stopper, Qt.	65.00
Rooster, Cocktail Shaker, c.1940, 13 x 3 ¼ In.	106.00
Sahara, Dish, Mayonnaise, Ladle	25.00
Saturn, Vase, Ball, Zircon Rim, 4 In.	60.00
Sparrow, 2 ¼ In.	35.00
Stanhope, Dish, Goblet, 490 Maytime Etch, 10 Oz.	65.00
Stanhope, Jelly, 490 Maytime Etch, No Knob, 3 Sections	15.00
Thumbprint & Panel, Candlestick, 2-Light, Sahara, Pair	75.00
Trident, Candlestick, 2-Light, Orchid Etch, Pair	20.00
Trojan, Comport, Flamingo, 7 In.	65.00
Tudor, Vase, 7 ½ In.	45.00
Twist, Plate, Marigold, 12 In.	20.00
Twist, Salt & Pepper, Glass Lid, Sahara	95.00
Warwick, Vase, Cornucopia	15.00
Warwick, Vase, Sahara, 9 In.	100.00
Waverly, Chocolate Box, Cover, Orchid Etch	80.00
Waverly, Compote, Footed, Rose Etch, 7 In.	15.00
Waverly, Goblet, 9015 English Ivy Etch, 10 Oz.	15.00
Waverly, Salt & Pepper, Orchid Etch	25.00
Waverly, Sugar & Creamer, Orchid Etch	25.00
Whaley, Mug, Beer, Golf Scene Etch, 12 Oz.	180.00
Whaley, Tankard, 674 Adams Cutting	45.00
Whirlpool, Sugar & Creamer, Tray	75.00

Icon, St. Florus & St. Laurus, Figures, Holding Crosses, Gilt Ground, Russia, c.1890, 8 ⅝ x 7 In.
$652.00

Skinner, Inc.

Imari, Charger, Central Flower, Figures, Ships, Flower & Dragon Cartouches, 15 ⅞ In.
$120.00

Neal Auction Co.

Imari, Vase, Bottle, 6-Sided Body, Panels Of Fans, Phoenixes, Dragons, c.1910, 12 ¼ In., Pair
$1888.00

Brunk Auctions

353

H

<table>
<tbody>
<tr><td>Wide Flat Panel, Cologne Bottle, Cutting</td><td>65.00</td></tr>
<tr><td>Wide Flat Panel, Sugar & Creamer, Sinclair Cutting</td><td>25.00</td></tr>
<tr><td>Williamsburg, Candlestick, 9 In., Pair</td><td>55.00</td></tr>
<tr><td>Winged Scroll, Cruet, Crystal Stopper, Gold Trim</td><td>65.00</td></tr>
<tr><td>Winged Scroll, Emerald, Toothpick Holder</td><td>35.00</td></tr>
</tbody>
</table>

HEREND, *see Fischer category.*

HEUBACH is the collector's name for Gebruder Heubach, a firm working in Lichten, Germany, from 1840 to 1925. It is best known for bisque dolls and doll heads, the principal products. The company also manufactured bisque figurines, including piano babies, beginning in the 1880s, and glazed figurines in the 1900s. Piano Babies are listed in their own category. Dolls are included in the Doll category under Gebruder Heubach and Heubach. Another factory, Ernst Heubach, working in Koppelsdorf, Germany, also made porcelain and dolls. These will also be found in the Doll category under Heubach Koppelsdorf.

<table>
<tbody>
<tr><td>Bust, Bisque, Girl Eating Candy, Bonnet, 16 In.</td><td>1750.00</td></tr>
<tr><td>Figurine, Boy With 2 Pups, Sailor Jacket & Hat, Snowy Ground, Bisque, c.1900, 15 In.</td><td>855.00</td></tr>
<tr><td>Figurine, Dog, Seated, Gray, Marked, 3 ½ x 3 ½ In.</td><td>100.00 to 200.00</td></tr>
<tr><td>Vase, Profile Portrait Medallion, Flowers, Multicolor, Blue Ground, c.1905, 6 In.</td><td>326.00</td></tr>
</tbody>
</table>

HISTORIC BLUE, *see factory names, such as Adams, Ridgway, and Staffordshire.*

HOBNAIL glass is a style of glass with bumps all over. Dozens of hobnail patterns and variants have been made. Clear, colored, and opalescent hobnail have been made and are being reproduced. Other pieces of hobnail may also be listed in the Duncan & Miller and Fenton categories.

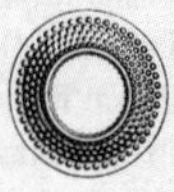

<table>
<tbody>
<tr><td>Pitcher, Cranberry, Applied Handle, Rippled Rim, 7 ½ In.</td><td>147.00</td></tr>
<tr><td>Sugar, Cover, White & Amber, Finial, Hobbs, Brockunier & Co., 5 x 6 In.</td><td>35.00</td></tr>
<tr><td>Syrup, White & Amber, Pewter Lid, Loop Handle, Hobbs, Brockunier & Co., 7 In.</td><td>81.00</td></tr>
</tbody>
</table>

HOCHST, or Hoechst, porcelain was made in Germany from 1746 to 1796. It was marked with a six-spoke wheel. Be careful when buying Hochst; many other firms have used a very similar wheel-shaped mark.

<table>
<tbody>
<tr><td>Bowl, Basket Weave, Arched Rim, Reticulated Handles, Flowers, Gold Mark, 12 x 9 In.</td><td>2200.00</td></tr>
<tr><td>Bowl, Embossed Flower Swags, Hand Painted Sprays, Square, Marked, c.1785, 3 ¼ x 8 In. ......illus</td><td>259.00</td></tr>
<tr><td>Figurine, Nude, Leaning On Tree Trunk, Red Cloth, Melchior, 1771, 6 ½ In.</td><td>1750.00</td></tr>
<tr><td>Figurine, Woman, Flowered Dress, Outstretched Hand, Marked, 19th Century, 4 ¾ In.</td><td>385.00</td></tr>
<tr><td>Urn, Swags, Cherubs, Tambourine, Sword, Marked, 18th Century, 5 ⅞ In., Pair</td><td>985.00</td></tr>
</tbody>
</table>

HOLLY AMBER, or golden agate, glass was made by the Indiana Tumbler and Goblet Company of Greentown, Indiana, from January 1, 1903, to June 13, 1903. It is a pressed glass pattern featuring holly leaves in the amber-shaded glass. The glass was made with shadings that range from creamy opalescent to brown-amber.

<table>
<tbody>
<tr><td>Butter, Dome Cover, Scalloped Tray, 7 ½ In.</td><td>450.00</td></tr>
<tr><td>Cake Plate, Rectangular, Pedestal Base, Saucer Foot, Beaded, Greentown, 7 In.</td><td>6325.00</td></tr>
<tr><td>Compote, Footed, Translucent, 4 ½ In.</td><td>325.00</td></tr>
<tr><td>Cruet, Original Stopper, 6 In.</td><td>550.00</td></tr>
<tr><td>Mug, Coffee, Opalescent, 3 ½ In.</td><td>125.00</td></tr>
<tr><td>Spooner, Cylindrical, Beaded Detail, Greentown, 4 In.</td><td>374.00</td></tr>
<tr><td>Tumbler, Beaded Detail, Greentown, 4 In.</td><td>173.00</td></tr>
</tbody>
</table>

HOLT-HOWARD was an importer that started working in New York City in 1949 and moved to Stamford, Connecticut, in 1955. The company sold many types of table accessories, such as condiment jars, decanters, spoon holders, and saltshakers. The figures shown on some of its pieces had a cartoon-like quality. The company was bought out by General Housewares Corporation in 1969. Holt-Howard pieces are often marked with the name and the year or *HH* and the year stamped in black. The *HH* mark was used until 1974. There was also a black and silver label. Production of Holt-Howard ceased in 1990. Similar pieces are being made today by Grant Holt, one of the founders, and are marked *GHA.*

<table>
<tbody>
<tr><td>Bottle, Russian Dressing</td><td>95.00</td></tr>
<tr><td>Cream Crock, 1950s</td><td>200.00</td></tr>
<tr><td>Ice Cream Sundae Set, Butterscotch Creamer, Chocolate Creamer, Strawberries Lid, 5 In.</td><td>135.00</td></tr>
<tr><td>Jar, Cherries</td><td>175.00</td></tr>
</tbody>
</table>

Imari, Vase, Figures In Landscape, Flowers, Fluted Flared Rim, Gilt, Underglaze, 42 In., Pair
$3444.00

New Orleans Auction Galleries, Inc.

Indian, Bag, Cheyenne, Elk Hide, Beaded, Sinew, Tin Cones, Horsehair, c.1885, 12 ½ x 20 In.
$5875.00

Cowan's Auctions

Indian, Bag, Lakota, Hide, Beaded, Multicolor, Geometric, Tin Cones, Horsehair, c.1885, 21 x 13 In.
$2370.00

Skinner, Inc.

Jar, Chili Sauce, 1959	325.00
Jar, Instant Coffee	225.00
Jar, Ketchup, 1958	30.00
Jar, Mustard	325.00
Jar, Mustard, Label, 1958	90.00
Jar, Olives	155.00
Jar, Onion	76.00
Ornament, Girl Holding Candy Cane, Red, Green, Gold, Red Feather Skirt, 3 x 4 In.	20.00
Salt & Pepper, Merry Mouse, 4 ½ In.	42.00

HOPALONG CASSIDY was a character in a series of twenty-eight books written by Clarence E. Milford, first published in 1907. Movies and television shows were made based on the character. The best-known actor playing Hopalong Cassidy was William Lawrence Boyd. His first movie appearance was in 1919, but the first Hopalong Cassidy film was not made until 1934. Sixty-six films were made. In 1948, William Boyd purchased the television rights to the movies, then later made fifty-two new programs. In the 1950s, Hopalong Cassidy and his horse, named Topper, were seen in comics, records, toys, and other products. Boyd died in 1972.

Blotter, Francis The Talking Mule, Promo, Francis Goes To Races, Spelter, 1930s, 6 In.	92.00
Coloring Book, Golden, 99 Pages, 1951, 11 x 8 ½ In.	27.00
Display, Figural, Hopalong Cassidy, Timex, Shock-Resistant Watches, Embossed, 1950s, 15 In. *illus*	4175.00
Doll, Cloth, Printed Features, Black & Yellow Cowboy Costume, 1940s, 31 In.	228.00
Doll, Cloth, Printed Features, Flocked Hair, Cowboy Costume, Chaps, 1940s, 22 In.	342.00
Doll, Rubber, Painted Features, Stuffed Head, Belt, Holster, Ideal, 1950s, 9 In.	345.00
Earmuffs, Red Plush, White, Tin Lithograph, Oval With Portrait, Child's	127.00
Game, Official Pony Express Toss, Masonite Board, 3 Holes, Toss Bag, Box, 18 In.	144.00
Holster & Belt, Black, Facsimile Signature, Metal Stud Accents	177.00
Jacket, Black Denim, White Stitching, Steer Heads, Snaps, Blue Bell, 16 In.	127.00
Jigsaw Puzzle, Hopalong Cassidy On Horseback, Black Attire, Box	23.00
Night-Light, Wall Plaque, Pinkish Beige, Aladdin	289.00
Poster, Movie, Bar 20 Justice, William Boyd, 1940, 80 x 40 In.	173.00
Ring, Compass, Removable Hat, Brass, Post Cereal Premium, Meadow Gold Dairy, 1952 *illus*	443.00
School Slate, 2-Sided, Pencil On 1 Side, Chalk On Other, 8 x 11 In.	50.00
Spurs, Metal, Leather Straps, Hoppy, George Schmidt, Box, 7 ½ In.	336.00
Tin, Potato Chip, Hopalong & Topper On Front, Kuchmann Foods, 1950, 15 Oz.	225.00
Toy, Cap Pistol, Nickel Finish, Ivory Plastic Grip, 7 In.	163.00
Toy, Figure, Hopalong On Topper, Hat, Plastic, Ideal, Box	153.00
Toy, Film Viewer, In The Heart Of The West, Display Box, 1950s, 11 x 10 In.	324.00

HORN was used to make many types of boxes, furniture inlays, jewelry, and whimsies.

Carving, 2 Frogs Holding Round Plaque, Chinese, 1800s, 2 ¼ In.	119.00
Carving, Stag Horn, Lotus, Leaf & Snail Shape, Carved, Chinese, 1800s, 5 In.	652.00
Cup, Libation, Carved, Scholars, Under Pine Tree, Chinese, 4 In.	179.00
Cup, Libation, Scholars, Attendants, Trees, Carved, Chinese, 1800s, 4 ¾ In.	306.00
Cup, Lotus Shape, Carved, Petal Layers, Leaves, Pods, 8 In.	1638.00
Drinking Horn, Silver Plated Stand, Set-On Lid, 23 ½ In. *illus*	690.00
Figurine, Creature, Bixie, Rhinoceros, Carved, 3 ¼ In.	649.00
Figurine, Pu Tai, Surrounded By Children, Sack, Rhinoceros, Chinese, 4 ⅝ In. *illus*	71100.00
Hackel, Copper, Strap, 11 In.	83.00
Inkwell, Clock, Penholder, 2 Ink Bottles, 15 In.	358.00
Paperweight, Bat, Carved, Round, Chinese, c.1910, 3 In.	735.00
Pendant, Hornbill, Carved, Fierce Dragon, Phoenix, In Clouds, Chinese, 2 ⅜ In.	1912.00
Perfume Bottle, Mirror, Cloth Rimmed, 7 x 7 x 4 In.	55.00
Snuff Bottle, Carved, Monkeys, Fruit Tree, Storage Box, 3 x 2 In.	2197.00
Stand, Round, Multiple Legs, Branch Shaped, Tan Color, 1 ⅞ In.	9760.00
Whimsy, Marbrie Loop, Opal, Rose, c.1870, 23 ½ x 2 ¼ In.	150.00

HOWARD PIERCE began working in Southern California in 1936. In 1945, he opened a pottery in Claremont. He moved to Joshua Tree in 1968 and continued making pottery until 1991. His contemporary-looking figurines are popular with collectors. Though most pieces are marked with his name, smaller items from his sets often were not marked.

Figurine, Cat, Crouching, Glossy, Marked, 6 x 4 In.	39.00
Head, Woman, African, Mottled Cream, Brown, Stamped California Studio, 7 ½ x 5 In.	185.00

Indian, Bag, Nez Perce, Corn Husk, Woven, Hourglasses, Diamonds, c.1910, 17 ½ x 11 ½ In.
$441.00

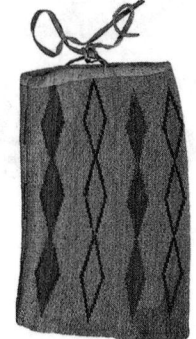

Cowan's Auctions

Indian, Bag, Ute, Hide, Beaded, Long Flap, Multicolor, Geometric, c.1885, 6 ¼ x 4 ½ In.
$1304.00

Skinner, Inc.

Indian, Basket, Chitimacha, Lid, Double Weave, Cane, Red, Black, c.1910, 5 ¾ x 6 In.
$2988.00

Neal Auction Co.

Indian, Basket, Chitimacha, Lid, Double Weave, Diagonal Bands, Geometrics, 4 ⅛ In.
$1652.00

Brunk Auctions

Indian, Basket, Hopi, Coiled, 4 Katsina Faces, Geometric Band, 1958, 9 x 12 In. $460.00

Allard Auctions

Indian, Basket, Jicarilla, Storage, Cylindrical, c.1930s, 18 x 14 In. $115.00

Allard Auctions

Indian, Basket, Northeast, Lid, Splint, Printed Wood, Synthetic Dye, 1800s, 14 x 10 ⅜ In. $1007.00

Skinner, Inc.

Indian, Basket, Pomo, Tight Weave, Stepped Design, c.1930, 1 ½ x 4 ¼ In. $431.00

Allard Auctions

HOWDY DOODY and Buffalo Bob were the main characters in a children's series televised from 1947 to 1960. Howdy was a redheaded puppet. The series became popular with college students in the late 1970s when Buffalo Bob began to lecture on campuses.

Barrettes, Plastic, Card, Howdy, Clarabell, Princess Summerfall-Winterspring, Kagran, 1956 ... *illus*	139.00
Bracelet, Howdy Doody Bust Charm, Goldtone, Spring Closure, 6 In.	25.00
Doll, Composition Head, Wood Segmented Body, Painted, Cameo, 1940s, 13 In.	228.00
Earmuffs, Celluloid Face, Fur, Metal Band, 4 ¾ In.	225.00
Figure, Pin, Bandanna, Lunch Box, 39 In.	480.00
Flashlight Ring, Plastic Face Lights Up, Brass Ring, Battery Operated, Brownie, 1950s ...... *illus*	115.00
Fun Book, Games, Jokes, Puzzles, Pictures To Color, Whitman, 1950s, 11 x 9 In.	15.00
Game, Howdy Doody's T.V. Game, Board, Spinner, Milton Bradley, c.1954, 9 x 19 In.	86.00
Marionette, Heidi Doody, Original Box, 12 In. ....*illus*	150.00
Marionette, Howdy Composite, Cloth, Multicolor, 16 In.	40.00
Spoon & Fork Set, Display Box & Sleeve, 6 In. ....*illus*	150.00
Toy, Howdy & Bob Smith, Piano, Tin Lithograph, Unique Art, 5 In.	863.00
Toy, Howdy & Clarabell, Piano, Clockwork, Linemar, Japan, 5 ¾ In.	1725.00
Toy, Race Car, Red, No. 3, Tin Lithograph, Windup, 9 ¼ In.	224.00
Wristwatch, Movable Eyes, Blue Band, Box, 1950s, 4 x 7 In.	319.00
Wristwatch, Silver Metal, Red Vinyl Strap, Die Cut Display Box, Ingraham, 1954	288.00

HULL pottery was made in Crooksville, Ohio, from 1905. Addis E. Hull bought the Acme Pottery Company and started making ceramic wares. In 1917, A. E. Hull Pottery began making art pottery as well as the commercial wares. For a short time, 1921 to 1929, the firm also sold pottery imported from Europe. The dinnerware of the 1940s (including the Little Red Riding Hood line), the high gloss artwares of the 1950s, and the matte wares of the 1940s are all popular with collectors. The firm officially closed in March 1986.

Banded, Mixing Bowl Set, Pink & Blue Bands, Nested, 3 ½ To 9 ¼ In., 6 Piece	47.00
Blossom Flite, Pitcher, Pink & Black, Rope Twist Handle, Elongated Spout, 8 ¾ In.	30.00
Bow Knot, Teapot, Pink Shaded To Cream Shaded To Blue, 6 ⅝ x 11 In.	115.00
Bow Knot, Vase, Blue Shaded To Cream Shaded To Blue, Baluster, Footed, Handles, 8 ½ In. ...	98.00
Candlestick, Spread Foot, Rolled Rim, Pink, Bird, Flowers, Marked, 7 In., Pair	29.00
Crabapple, Vase, Beige, Squat Bottom, Flared Top, 6 ¾ In.	18.00
Crabapple, Vase, White Matte Glaze, Rolled Lip, 1930s, 8 In.	125.00
Dogwood, Planter, Window Box, Cream, 3 ¼ x 10 ¾ In.	21.00
Ebb Tide, Vase, Fish, Shell Form, Pink, Green, 11 In.	18.00
Iris, Basket, Cream, Shaped Rim, Arched Handle, 7 x 7 ¾ In.	58.00
Iris, Ewer, Pink, Blue, Split Rim, Double Scroll Handle, 13 ¾ In.	161.00
Iris, Vase, Cream, Mauve, Oval, Flared Rim, 2 Handles, Footed, 11 In.	1109.00
Little Red Riding Hood, Bank, 1950s	499.00
Little Red Riding Hood, Cookie Jar, 13 In.	225.00
Little Red Riding Hood, Mustard, Spoon	329.00
Magnolia, Candleholder, Glossy Pink, 4 ¼ In., Pair	12.00
Magnolia, Ewer, Dusty Rose Matte Glaze, 13 ½ In.	63.00
Magnolia, Ewer, Footed, Matte Glaze, 13 ½ In.	40.00
Magnolia, Ewer, Pink Shaded To Blue, 13 ¾ In.	65.00
Magnolia, Pitcher, Cornucopia Shape, 8 ½ In.	28.00
Magnolia, Vase, Matte Glaze, 6 ½ In.	28.00
Marcrest, Pitcher, Footed, Red, 6 x 4 In.	29.00
Narcissus, Planter, Pink Over Blue Glaze, Hanging, c.1945	70.00
Open Rose, Ewer, White, Squat, Elongated Spout, 7 ¼ In.	40.00
Open Rose, Vase, Hand Holding Fan, Pink Shaded To Cream Shaded To Blue, 8 ¾ In.	138.00
Open Rose, Vase, Pink, Blue, Baluster, 2 Double Loop Handles, 6 ¼ In.	13.00
Orchid, Jardiniere, Cream, Pink, Shouldered, Wide Mouth, 6 x 10 In.	75.00
Parchment & Pine, Ashtray, Shaped Rim, 14 In.	22.00
Parchment & Pine, Vase, Cornucopia, 12 In.	24.00
Planter, Yellow, Ribbed, Marked, 1950s, 4 x 4 x 11 In.	55.00
Poppy, Basket, Cream Shaded To Pink, 9 ¼ In.	138.00
Poppy, Vase, Cream Shaded To Pink, Bulbous, Tapered, 2 Angular Handles, 10 ¾ In.	138.00
Rosella, Sugar & Creamer, Cover, Pink, 4 In.	12.00
Rosella, Wall Pocket, Heart Shape, Pink, 6 ¼ In.	15.00
Royal Butterfly, Lavabo, c.1950	110.00
Royal, Vase, Cornucopia, Blue Speckled, Gold Trim, Scalloped Foot, Swirl Handle, 6 x 11 In...	12.00
Sunglow, Pitcher, Footed, 6 x 7 In.	60.00
Swan, Planter, Yellow, Green, 6 x 6 x 7 In.	35.00
Tile, Sailboat, Water, Blue, White, Faience, 6 In.	978.00

H

Tokay, Basket, White, Green Branch Handle, 12 ¼ In.	21.00
Tokay, Bowl, Console, Pink, Green, Green Foot, Leaf & Branch Handles, 5 x 16 In.	52.00
Water Lily, Ewer, Glossy White, Footed, 5 ¾ In.	12.00
Water Lily, Vase, Dusty Rose, Shaded, Baluster, Footed, Buttressed Handles, 10 ½ In.	40.00
Wildflower, Basket, Dusty Rose, Flared, Scalloped Rim, 11 x 10 ⅜ In.	127.00
Wildflower, Candleholder, Footed, c.1942, 2 ¾ x 4 In.	45.00
Wildflower, Vase, Fan, Pink, Blue, 2 Angular Handles, 10 ⅝ In.	81.00
Wildflower, Vase, Pink, Brown, Flared, Scalloped Rim, 2 Handles, Footed, Series 61, 6 ¼ In. ..	40.00
Woodland, Ewer, Glossy Chartreuse & Cream, Pink Foot, 14 ¼ In.	63.00
Woodland, Tea Set, Glossy White, Gold Trim, Shaped Handles, 6 ½-In. Teapot, 3 Piece	58.00
Woodland, Vase, Double Cornucopia, Pink, Cream, Matte Glaze, 9 In.	22.00

HUMMEL figurines, based on the drawings of the nun M.I. Hummel (Berta Hummel), were made by the W. Goebel Porzellanfabrik of Oeslau, Germany, now Rodental, Germany. They were first made in 1935. The *Crown* mark was used from 1935 to 1949. The company added the *bee* marks in 1950. The *full bee* with variations was used from 1950 to 1959; *stylized bee*, 1957 to 1972; *three line mark*, 1964 to 1972; *last bee*, sometimes called *vee over gee*, 1972 to 1979. In 1979 the V bee symbol was removed from the mark. *U.S. Zone* was part of the mark from 1946 to 1948; *W. Germany* was part of the mark from 1960 to 1990. The Goebel *W. Germany* mark, called the *missing bee* mark, was used from 1979 to 1990; *Goebel, Germany*, with the crown and *WG*, originally called the *new mark*, was used from 1991 through part of 1999. The newest version of the bee mark with the word *Goebel*, the *current mark or Goebel with full bee*, was adopted in 2000. A special *Year 2000* backstamp was also introduced. Porcelain figures inspired by Berta Hummel's drawings were introduced in 1997. These are marked *BH* followed by a number. They were made in the Far East, not Germany. Goebel discontinued making Hummel figurines in 2008, but they continue to be made by Manufaktur Rodental GmbH. Hummel figurines made by Rodental are marked with a yellow and black bee on the edge of an oval line surrounding the words "Original M.I. Hummel Germany." The words "Manufaktur Rodental" are printed beneath the oval. Other decorative items and plates that feature Hummel drawings have been made by Schmid Brothers, Inc., since 1971.

Clock, No. 442, Chapel Time, Missing Bee, 11 ½ In.	649.00
Figurine, No. 3/1, Book Worm, Missing Bee, 5 ½ In.	94.00
Figurine, No. 10/111, Flower Madonna, Missing Bee, 11 ½ In.	118.00
Figurine, No. 16/1, Little Hiker, Full Bee, 5 ½ In. ....*illus*	23.00
Figurine, No. 23/111, Adoration, Missing Bee, 9 In. ....*illus*	196.00
Figurine, No. 47/0, Goose Girl, Prototype, Missing Bee, 4 ¾ In. ....*illus*	1150.00
Figurine, No. 56/B, Out Of Danger, Missing Bee, 6 ¾ In.	71.00
Figurine, No. 64, Shepherd's Boy, Full Bee, 6 In. ....*illus*	161.00
Figurine, No. 119/0, Postman, Last Bee, 5 ¼ In.	122.00
Figurine, No. 127, Doctor, Stylized Bee, 4 ¾ In.	145.00
Figurine, No. 136/1, Friends, Three Line Mark, 5 ¼ In. ....*illus*	41.00
Figurine, No. 142, Apple Tree Boy, Stylized Bee, 4 ¼ In.	265.00
Figurine, No. 153/0, Auf Wiedersehen, Boy With Hat, Full Bee, 5 ¼ In. ....*illus*	546.00
Figurine, No. 178, The Photographer, New Mark, 4 In.	192.00
Figurine, No. 183, Forest Shrine, New Mark, 9 In. ....*illus*	84.00
Figurine, No. 184, Latest News, Das Allerneuste, Three Line Mark, 5 In. ....*illus*	230.00
Figurine, No. 184, Latest News, The New York Times, Custom Title, Stylized Bee, 5 In. .....*illus*	276.00
Figurine, No. 315, Mountaineer, Master Sample, Arbeitsmuster Medal, Stylized Bee, 5 In. *illus*	2070.00
Figurine, No. 332, Soldier Boy, Three Line Mark, 6 In.	47.00
Figurine, No. 364, Supreme Protection, Missing Bee, 9 In.	177.00
Figurine, No. 414, In Tune, New Mark, 4 In.	196.00
Plate, Christmas, 1971, Angel, Holding Candle, Box, 10 In.	395.00

HUTSCHENREUTHER PORCELAIN FACTORY was founded by Carolus Magnus in Hohenburg, Bavaria, in 1814. A second factory was established in Selb, Germany, in 1857. The company made fine quality porcelain dinnerware and figurines. The mark changed through the years, but the name and the lion insignia appear in most versions. Hutschenreuther became part of the Rosenthal division of the Waterford Wedgwood Group in 2000. Rosenthal was bought by Sambonet Paderno Industries, headquartered in Orfento, Novaro, Italy, in 2009.

Bowl, Vegetable, Round, Fontaine, 9 In.	60.00
Charger, Roses, 13 In.	95.00
Figurine, Dogs, Running, Borzoi Hounds, K. Tutter, 12 x 14 In.	374.00
Figurine, Finch, Tilted Head, Base, c.1940, 3 ¼ In.	88.00
Figurine, Nude Woman, Blanc De Chine, Gold Ball, Carl Tutter, 8 ¾ In.	230.00
Figurine, Nude Woman, Prancing, 2 Leopards, Art Deco, Paper Label, 11 x 8 ½ In.	431.00
Figurine, Swans In Flight, 13 x 13 In.	354.00

Indian, Basket, Pomo, Twined, 2 Bands, Geometric Designs, 1900, 5 ½ x 6 In. $518.00

Allard Auctions

Indian, Belt, Navajo, Concha, Silver, c.1935, 36 In. $1320.00

Cowan's Auctions

Indian, Blanket, Navajo, Wool, Serrated Diamond Pattern, c.1890, 52 x 73 In. $1024.00

Garth's Auctions, Inc.

Indian, Boots, Comanche, Concha, German Silver, 18 In. $880.00

Old Barn Auction

Indian, Bowl, Santa Clara, Blackware, Oval, Flora Naranjo, c.1950, 3 x 6 x 5 In. **$161.00**

Allard Auctions

Indian, Bowl, Woodlands, Burl, Carved, Beaver Belly, Iron Tack Eyes, 1800s, 11 x 5 In. **$4730.00**

Old Barn Auction

Indian, Bracelet, Zuni, V-Shaped Band, Coral Needlepoint, Hallmark HH, 5 ¾ x ⅞ In. **$115.00**

Allard Auctions

Indian, Bust, Indian Brave, Plaster, Painted, Hiawatha, 27 ¾ x 18 In. **$59.00**

Conestoga Auction Co., Inc.

Plaque, Painted Cover, Woman's Portrait, Gilt Brass, Filigree, Palmette, 3 ¼ x 2 ½ In.	531.00
Plaque, Woman, Wearing Pearls, Brocade Dress, Stamped HR., Oval, 5 x 4 In.	472.00
Plate, Dinner, Apart, 10 ¼ In.	52.00
Plate, Dinner, Demoiselle, 10 ½ In.	20.00
Platter, Revere, Round, 12 ¾ In.	607.00
Platter, Sylvia, Oval, 15 In.	207.00
Sugar, Cover, Firenze	366.00
Teapot, Cover, Fleur On White	287.00
Tray, Blue, Pink Roses, Gold Trim, Square, Signed Koenig, 12 ½ In.	75.00
Urn, Cover, White, Cream, Green, Flowers, Gold Trim, 8-Sided, Marked, 22 In., Pair	250.00
Vase, Cobalt Blue, Silver Overlay, Bell Flowers, Trumpet Shape, Spread Foot, 7 ½ In.	173.00

ICONS, special, revered pictures of Jesus, Mary, or a saint, are usually Russian or Byzantine. The small icons collected today are made of wood and tin or precious metals. Many modern copies have been made in the old style and are being sold to tourists in Russia and Europe and at shops in the United States. Rare, old icons have sold for over $50,000. The riza is the metal cover protecting the icon. It is often made of silver or gold.

12 Feasts Of Russian Church, Multicolor, Gilt Ground, 28 x 24 In.	3437.00
12 Major Feasts, Saints In Rows, Liturgical Year, Multicolor, Russia, c.1875, 28 x 23 In.	10800.00
16 Major Church Feasts, Folding, Bronze, Enamel, 1800s, 7 x 16 In.	900.00
Akhtuirskaya Mother Of God, Mourning Virgin, Christ Crucified, Russia, c.1800, 13 x 10 In.	533.00
Angel, Wood, Painted, Rounded Edge, 46 x 15 In.	150.00
Apostle St. John In Silence, Fingers To Lips, Repousse Silver Metal Riza, Russia, 17 x 14 In.	780.00
Archangel Michael, Female Saint, Scroll, Sword At Feet, Gesso, Wood Panel, 1800s, 11 x 9 In.	359.00
Baptism Of Christ, Painted, Gilded Panel, c.1800, 10 ½ x 8 ¼ In.	403.00
Beheading Of St. John, Christ Blessing From Clouds, Salome Dancing, Russia, 1800s, 10 x 8 In.	735.00
Benjamin The Deacon, Holy Martyr, Book, Verso Inscription, Russia, 1800s, 4 x 3 In.	600.00
Birth Of Mary, Joakhim, Anna, Servants, Angels, Russia, c.1900, 12 ¼ x 10 ¼ In.	1320.00
Birth Of Mother Of God, Wide Gilt Border, Russia, 1800s, 12 ¼ x 10 ¼ In.	480.00
Chernigovskia Mother Of God, Jesus In Arms, Gold Border, Russia, c.1890, 7 x 5 ½ In.	480.00
Christ Lord Almighty, Bust, Blessing Hand, Gospels, Red Border, Russia, 1800s, 8 ¾ x 7 ½ In.	2400.00
Christ, Archangels Michael & Gabriel, Repousse Halos, Brass, Russia, c.1890, 12 x 11 In.	288.00
Christ, Blessing, Throne, Cast Bronze, Champleve Enamel, Slavic Text, 8 ¾ x 6 In.	2880.00
Christ, Child, Brass, Basma, Gilt, Halo Glass Insets, Russia, c.1780, 12 x 11 In.	4148.00
Christ, Cloth On Face, Image Not Made By Hands, Angel Corners, Gilt, 14 x 11 In.	444.00
Christ, Crown Of Thorns, Upward Glancing, Plaque, Painted, Frame, 10 x 9 In.	156.00
Christ, Crucifix, Carved Wood, Tortoiseshell, Ivory Inlay, U.S.A., 1800s, 24 In.	478.00
Christ, Crucifixion, Oil On Canvas, Frame, Signed, Jose Vizcarra, Mexico, 1929, 25 x 20 In.	330.00
Christ, Engraved & Silvered Metal, Enamel Work, Cyrillic Writing, Russia, 10 x 8 In.	600.00
Christ, Hand Raised, Book, Gilt, Paint, c.1890, 12 In.	1178.00
Christ, Healing Child, Painted, c.1900, Frame, 27 x 18 In.	180.00
Christ, Holding Scroll, Raised Flowers, Goblet, Silver, 1854	904.00
Christ, Ivory, Crucifix, Gilt & Wooden Cross, 1700s, 1734, 30 In.	2400.00
Christ, Lord Almighty, Incised Border, Giltwood Liner, Text, Russia, c.1890, 30 x 23 In.	3360.00
Christ, Pantocrator, Silver Plated Brass Riza, 9 x 7 In.	356.00
Christ, Pantocrator, Silver Riza, Russia, 5 x 4 In.	207.00
Christ, Pantocrator, Sterling Silver Riza, Russia, c.1912, 8 ¾ x 7 In.	344.00
Christ, Sculpted Wood, Crucifix, Lowered Head, Acrylic Stand, c.1800s, 11 In.	207.00
Christ, Seated, Biblical & Church Symbols, Gilt Ground, Russia, 1800s, 14 x 12 In.	3200.00
Christ, Throne, Virgin, John The Baptist, Faux Basma Border, Gilt, Russia, 1800s, 14 x 12 In.	1185.00
Christos, Spread Arms, Wood, Painted, Metal Stand, 1700s, 19 In.	508.00
Cross, Silvered Metal, Coptic, Staff Finial, Pierced Design, 25 x 19 In.	430.00
Crucifix, Gilded Frame, Arched Top, Red Ground, France, 12 ½ x 7 ½ In.	330.00
Crucifix, Wood, Carved & Painted, Jesus On Cross, 37 x 24 In.	625.00
Crucifixion, 14 Auxiliary Saints, Print, Frame, 1900s, 13 x 9 ½ In.	110.00
Crucifixion, Gilt Bronze Cross, Painted Panel, Saints, Silver Repousse, Russia, c.1825, 15 x 9 In.	4800.00
Face Of Christ, Painted Leather On Wood, Frame, c.1700, 18 x 15 In.	570.00
Holy Trinity, St. George & St. Dimitry, Greece, 1800s, 12 ½ x 9 In.	780.00
Holy Virgin, Christ Child, Gilded, Wooden, Metal Oklad, Russia, 19th Century, 5 x 4 In.	650.00
Isaiah, Face, Lithograph, Signed, Irving, c.1918, 18 x 14 In.	102.00
John The Baptist, Head On Platter, Filigre Halo, Seed Pearl Edging, Cloisonne, c.1900, 9 x 7 In.	11850.00
Kazan Mother Of God, Double Border, Gilt, Russia, 1700s, 12 x 10 ½ In.	2607.00
Kazan Mother Of God, Infant Jesus, Silver Plate Repousse Riza, Crown, Halo, 1800s, 16 x 14 In.	2040.00
Kazan Mother Of God, Jesus, Incised Gold Leaf Ground, 1800s, 11 ¼ x 8 ¾ In.	450.00
Kazan Mother Of God, Sterling Silver Riza, Mark, Russia, c.1900, 7 x 5 In.	504.00
Korsum Mother Of God, Black Border, Russia, 1800s, 14 x 12 In.	510.00

H

Madonna & Child, Christ, Temple, Annunciation, Carved Strapwork, Saints, c.1800, 22 x 16 In.	368.00
Madonna & Child, Crescent, Oil On Canvas, Spain, Frame, c.1785, 25 ½ x 19 ½ In.	676.00
Madonna & Child, Curved Wood Panel, Gold Surface, Cyrillic Writing, Russia, 14 x 12 In.	2300.00
Madonna & Child, Giltwood Frame, Spain, 11 x 8 In.	124.00
Madonna & Child, Painted Wood, Cross Shape Frame, Scrolls, Walnut, c.1800, 33 x 26 In.	540.00
Madonna & Child, Painted Wood, Red & Gold, Inscribed, Greece, 1800s, 14 x 12 In.	360.00
Madonna In Prayer, Oil On Canvas, Frame, Italy, 1800s, 16 ⅛ x 12 ¾ In.	459.00
Madonna, Joy Of All Who Suffer, Surrounding Angels, Coin Border, Russia, c.1890, 9 x 7 In.	504.00
Madonna, Wood, Painted, Gesso, 2 Folding Doors, Inner Compartment, 4 x 11 x 18 In.	86.00
Mary, Baby Christ, 10 Saints, Square, Brass, 20 x 16 In.	311.00
Mary, Rosary, Wood, Carved, Gesso, Multicolor, 19 ¾ x 8 In.	918.00
Metropolitan Alexia, Blessing, Holding Bible, Russia, 1700s, 12 ¼ x 10 ¼ In.	3600.00
Metropolitant Michael Of Kiev, Russia, c.1890, 5 ¼ x 4 In.	780.00
Month Of March, Saints' Feast Days, Old Slavonic Text, Russia, 1890, 17 x 14 ½ In.	1440.00
Mother & Child, Plaque, Enamel, Frame, Germany, c.1900, 5 x 7 In.	356.00
Mother & Child, Porcelain, Paint, Oval, Mounted, Gilt Carved Wood Frame, 9 x 6 In.	1003.00
Mother Of God, Jesus, Gilded Silver Repousse, Chased Riza, Stone Inset, c.1825, 13 x 11 In.	4560.00
Mother Of God, Passion, Tempera & Gesso, Wood Panel, Russia, 1800s, 16 x 12 In.	179.00
Mother Of God, Side Saints, Triptych, Carved, Gilt, Greece, c.1800, 17 ½ In.	2370.00
Mother Of God, St. George, St. Demetrius, Triptych, Gilt, Greece, 1700s, 12 x 15 In.	356.00
Mother Of God, Unfading Rose, Roses, Angels, Dedication In Greek, 1844, 17 x 12 In.	1960.00
New Testament Saints, Old Testament Figures, Paint, Multicolor, Russia, 1800s, 17 x 14 In.	8400.00
Our Lady Of Lourdes, Oil On Canvas, Standing, Blue Robe, Hands In Prayer, c.1900, 49 x 25 In.	228.00
Passion, 12 Passion, Resurrection, Feasts Images, Russia, 1800s, 28 x 23 In.	1800.00
Passion, Resurrection, Text, Multicolor, Russia, 1800s, 12 x 10 In.	5760.00
Pochaev Mother Of God, Gold Leaf Ground, Russia, c.1890, 5 x 4 ¼ In.	480.00
Prophet Elijah, Life Scenes, Silver Repousse Metal Riza, Russia, 1700s, 19 ½ x 15 ½ In.	780.00
Resurrection, 12 Orthodox Church Feasts, Gilt, Yellow Border, Russia, 1800s, 21 x 17 In.	2370.00
Resurrection, Empty Tomb, Descent Into Hades, Multicolor, Russia, 1700s, 12 ½ x 10 ½ In.	1320.00
Russia, Lord Almighty, Blessing, Gilded Silver Riza, Halo, c.1856, 12 ½ x 10 ½ In.	4556.00
St. Alexander Nevsky, Standing, Crown & Scepter, Russia, c.1890, 8 ⅝ x 6 ⅞ In.	5333.00
St. Barbara, Life Scenes, Saint, Sword Bearing Attacker, Gilt Border, Round, Painted, 10 In.	984.00
St. Basil, Standing, Paint, Greece, 1700, 9 x 7 In.	207.00
St. Benedict, Wearing Abbot's Robe, Holding Book, Carved Wood, Painted, Glass Eyes, 11 In.	508.00
St. Catherine, Gilt Ground, Life Scenes, Emperor Maximian, Russia, c.1880, 8 ⅝ x 7 In.	474.00
St. Eiljah, Seated, Life Scenes, Gilt, 1800s, 12 x 11 In.	830.00
St. Florus & St. Laurus, Figures, Holding Crosses, Gilt Ground, Russia, c.1890, 8 ⅝ x 7 In. ..illus	652.00
St. George & Alexandra, Arched Reserves, Faux Enamel Border, Russia, c.1900, 12 x 4 In.	780.00
St. George, Life Scenes, Dragon, Gold Leaf Field, Wood Panel., D. Arkhipova, Russia, 21 x 17 In.	2040.00
St. Jewel Encrusted Cross, Blue Robe, Halo, Oil On Oval Gilt Brass, 1800s, 28 x 22 In.	780.00
St. Job, Abbot Of Pochayiv Monastery, Hand, Blessing, Scroll, Gilt, Enamel, c.1900, 8 ⅝ x 7 In.	711.00
St. John The Apostle, Blessing, Holding Book, Slavic Text, Multicolor, 1700s, 11 ¾ x 10 In.	1680.00
St. John The Warrior, Life Scenes, Russia, 1800s, 14 x 12 In.	2133.00
St. Mark, Tempera, Gesso, Gilding, Wood Panel, Red Robe, Russia, 1800s, 12 x 10 In.	508.00
St. Michael, Assembly Of Angels, Gold Border, Russia, c.1800, 12 ¾ x 10 ¾ In.	1800.00
St. Michael, Red Horse, Trampled Devil, Russia, c.1800, 15 ¾ x 14 In.	660.00
St. Nicholas Of Mozhaisk, Sword, Church & Life Scenes, Gilt, Russia, 1800s, 35 x 29 In.	2489.00
St. Nicholas, Bishop, Blessing, Cyrillic Text, Multicolor, Russia, 1800s, 20 ¼ x 16 ¾ In.	3120.00
St. Nicholas, Blessing, Green Ground, Gilt Border, Russia, c.1850, 12 x 10 In.	780.00
St. Nicholas, Book, Christ, Mary Images, Orange Border, Russia, 1800s, 15 x 12 In.	237.00
St. Nicholas, Christ, Mother Of God, Russia, 1800s, 11 x 9 In.	1185.00
St. Nicholas, Oil On Panel, Old Believers Workshop, Russia, 1800s, 12 x 10 ½ In.	600.00
St. Panteleimon, Holding Medicine, Instrument, Gilt Ground, Russia, 17 ¼ x 14 In.	4320.00
St. Panteleimon, The Healer, Medicine Box, Spoon, Russia, 1800s, 12 x 11 In.	2963.00
St. Sergius, Life Scenes, Trinity Symbols, Russia, 1800s, 12 x 10 ½ In.	2489.00
St. Tikhon Of Zadonsk, Geometric Border, Gold Leaf Ground, Russia, c.1890, 7 x 5 ¾ In.	480.00
St. Vladimir & Dimitry, Christ Above Blessing, Turquoise Ground, Russia, 14 x 12 ¼ In.	960.00
Stations Of Cross, Bronze Plaque, Gilt Frame, Rectangular, France, c.1700, 6 In.	813.00
Sts. Cosmos & Damian, Arched Reserve, Gilt Ground, Russia, c.1890, 14 x 12 In.	1440.00
Sts. Damon, Guriv & Aviv, Guardian Angels, St. Anna In Border, Russia, c.1890, 21 x 10 In.	1440.00
Sts. Standing, Wide Gold Border, Multicolor, Russia, c.1890, 14 x 12 ¼ In.	2160.00
Sts. Zosim & Savvatiy, Holding Monastery Model, Text, Russia, 1700s, 12 ¾ x 11 In.	3360.00
Sweet Kissing Mother Of God, Puncture Work Halo, Gilt Ground, 1800s, 11 x 8 In.	6221.00
Transfiguration, Inscription, Porcelain, Round, Silver Frame, Cherub Suspension, 1848, 6 ½ In.	2040.00
Travel, Brass, 4 Panels, Painted Scenes, Russia, 1800s, 16 x 7 In.	415.00
Trinity Figures, Old Testament, Painted, Multicolor, 1800s, 29 x 20 In.	9600.00

Indian, Cradle, Mono, Willow, Basketry, Sunshade, Doll, Carved Wooden Face, 1950s, 8 x 3 ½ In.
$288.00

Allard Auctions

Indian, Cradle, Ute, Model, Hide, Beaded, Wood Frame, Pouch, Cloth Covered Doll, Fringe, c.1885, 20 In.
$4148.00

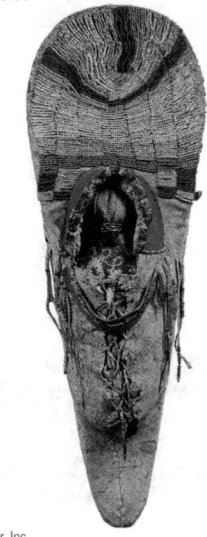

Skinner, Inc.

Indian, Doll, Mohawk, Corn Husk, Penciled Face, Silk, Wool Clothes, Beads, c.1910, 11 In., Pair
$115.00

Allard Auctions

Indian, Doll, Plains, Buckskin, Sinew Sewn, Beaded Features, c.1910, 17 In. $1955.00

Allard Auctions

Indian, Doll, Seminole, c.1950, 12 In. $66.00

Old Barn Auction

Indian, Dress, Crow, Red Felt, Ribbon Trim, Carved Bone Elk Teeth, Late 1900s, Girl's, 30 In. $345.00

Allard Auctions

Virgin Immaculate, Wood, Ivory, Gilt, Crown, Hands In Prayer, Portugal, 1700s, 28 In.	2375.00
Virgin Mary Praying, Radiating Nimbus, Wood, Carved, Painted, Spanish Colonial, 17 x 11 In.	400.00
Virgin Mary, Saints, Christ, Cathedral, Painted, Square, Russia, 13 x 11 In.	799.00
Virgin Of Kazan, Tempera On Panel, Russia, Dark Stain, c.1820, 17 x 14 In.	240.00
Weep Not For Me Mother, Christ, Mother, Metal, Repousse Riza, Russia, 1800s, 13 x 11 In.	1080.00

IMARI porcelain was made in Japan and China beginning in the seventeenth century. In the eighteenth century and later, it was copied by porcelain factories in Germany, France, England, and the United States. It was especially popular in the nineteenth century and is still being made. Imari is characteristically decorated with stylized bamboo, floral, and geometric designs in orange, red, green, and blue. The name comes from the Japanese port of Imari, which exported the ware made nearby in a factory at Arita. *Imari* is now a general term for any pattern of this type.

Bean Jar, Cover, Ball Finial, Iron Red, Cobalt Blue, Reserves, Japan, 1800s, 11 In.	300.00
Bowl, 6 Scenic Reserves, Flower, Leaf Center, Japan, 1800s, 9 In.	120.00
Bowl, Blue & White, Round Foot, Flowers, Late 1800s, 10 In. Diam.	24.00
Bowl, Blue Dragon, Chasing Bird Of Paradise, Gilt, Blue Characters, Japan, c.1900, 4 ¼ x 9 ¾ In.	196.00
Bowl, Cobalt Blue, Iron Red, Flowers & Leaves, Rolled Rim, Round Foot, 1700s, 10 In. Diam.	230.00
Bowl, Cobalt Blue, Red Flowers & Leaves, White Ground, Chinese, 1700s, 3 ½ x 10 ¼ In.	230.00
Bowl, Fan, Red, Gold, Blue Design, White Ground, 3-Footed, 12 ½ x 19 In.	230.00
Bowl, Fruit, Hexagonal, Landscapes & Flowers, Shaped Base, 5 In.	288.00
Bowl, Garden Scenes, Medallions, Multicolored, Wide Flare Rim, c.1900, 8 ⅝ In. Diam.	89.00
Bowl, Gilt Mounts, Handles, Brocade Ground, Flowers, Shishi, Phoenix Birds, Grapevines, 19 In.	2091.00
Bowl, Nautical Scenes, Rosewood Stand, c.1880, 7 ½ x 14 ½ In.	750.00
Bowl, Octagonal, Medallion, Ikibana In Basket, Peonies, Aster, Vase, Terrace, Gilding, 1800s, 13 In.	338.00
Bowl, Shaped Edges, Flower Basket Center, Flower Reserve Panels, 1800s, 12 x 12 In.	307.00
Bowl, White Ground, Birds, Flower Sprays, Peonies, Gilt, Footed, c.1800, 10 In. Diam.	690.00
Charger, 3 Flower Medallions, Cobalt Ground, Gilt, Hand Painted, c.1900, 15 ½ In.	60.00
Charger, Blue, White Flowers, 3 Shaped Panels, Gilt Deer, Trees, Fencing, Japan, 2 ¼ x 18 In.	117.00
Charger, Central Flower, Figures, Ships, Flower & Dragon Cartouches, 15 ⅞ In. ....*illus*	120.00
Charger, Flower Medallion Center, European Figures, Blue Underglaze, 1800s, 18 ¼ In.	492.00
Charger, Flower Medallion, Gilt, c.1900, 17 ¾ In.	403.00
Charger, Flowers, Birds, Reds, Blue, Green, 15 ½ In.	45.00
Charger, Gilded, Enamel, Panels Of Flowers, Garden Landscapes, 1800s, 18 ½ In.	184.00
Charger, Hawk, Red, White, Blue, c.1875, 18 In.	950.00
Charger, Iron Red, Cobalt Blue, Reserves, Flowers, Scalloped Edge, 1800s, 12 In.	360.00
Charger, Landscape, Crane, Flowers, Multicolor, 15 ¾ In. Diam.	119.00
Charger, Lion, Quail, Octagonal, 1800s, Japan, 13 ¾ In.	239.00
Charger, Mythical Animals, Immortals, Brocade Ground, Footed, 1800s, 20 In.	1422.00
Charger, Panels Of Flowers, Insects, Landscapes, Boats, Mountains, c.1900, 17 ⅞ In. Diam.	207.00
Charger, Queen Mother Of The West, Boy, Peach, Japan, 1900s, 21 ½ In.	358.00
Charger, Round, Lobed, Central Flower Medallion, Bamboo, Bird Panels, c.1900, 12 ½ In.	276.00
Charger, Roundel, Peacock, Banded Rim, Figures, Landscape, Cartouches, c.1900, 15 ½ In. Diam.	120.00
Charger, Scalloped Rim, Medallion, Asters, Garden, Peonies, Lion, Fretwork, Gilt, 1900s, 25 In.	861.00
Charger, Shaped Flower Reserves, Lion, Flower Ground, Pierced Border, 1900s, 14 ¾ In.	492.00
Charger, Shaped Reserve Flower Panels, Blue Underglaze, 1900s, 14 ¾ In.	461.00
Charger, Stand, Leaf Medallion, Rabbits, Plants, Birds, Japan, c.1920, 18 ½ In.	153.00
Charger, Women, Playing Instruments, Scalloped Rim, Multicolor, Japan, 1800s, 18 In.	150.00
Dish, Angular, Blue, Cranes, Phoenixes, Plants, Iron Red, Japan, 1800s, 12 x 10 In.	159.00
Dish, Fish Shape, Iron Red & Blue Glaze, Raised Scales, Gold Trim, 6 x 9 In., Pair	615.00
Fruit Cooler, Lid, Pineapple Finial, England, c.1820, 12 In., Pair	5192.00
Guglet, Flowering Trees, Flower Bands, Armorial Shield, Chinese, c.1880, 10 In., Pair	2415.00
Jar, Dome Lid, Baluster, Pointed Finial, Peonies, Leaves, Chrysanthemums, 11 In.	461.00
Jar, Lid, Women, Reading, Writing, c.1890, 37 In.	593.00
Jardiniere, Blue & White, 8 Panels, Figural Design, Cylindrical, 11 x 10 In.	509.00
Lamp, Double Gourd, Flowers, White, Red, Blue, Teakwood Footed Base, 15 In., Pair	2070.00
Lamp, Electric, Gilt, Brass Mounted, Carcel, Mid 1800s, 37 In., Pair	1476.00
Mug, Cobalt Blue, Iron Red, Gold, Round Foot, Loop Handle, Flowers, Branches, 6 x 4 In.	259.00
Mug, Red, Cobalt Blue, Gold Flowers, Chinese, c.1760, 6 x 3 ¾ In.	259.00
Plate, Cobalt Blue, Bamboo, Luna Moths, Birds, Scalloped Rim, 1800s, 7 x 5 In.	165.00
Plate, Figures, Landscape, Flower Border, Red, Blue, Gilt, Chinese, 1800s, 17 x 12 ¾ In.	593.00
Plate, Flowers, Red, Blue, Gilt, Chinese, 1700s, 8 ¾ In.	316.00
Plate, Shell, Flowers, Scalloped Rim, Red, Blue, Gold, Late 19th Century, 8 ½ In., Pair	71.00
Platter, Oval, Black Ship, Flowers, Figures, 1800s, 14 In.	538.00
Punch Bowl, Landscape, Pagoda, Flower & Leaf Border, 1800s, 12 In.	406.00
Umbrella Stand, Cylindrical, Iron Red & Blue, Leaf Band, Flower Sprays, 24 In.	711.00

Umbrella Stand, Cylindrical, Iron Red, Leaf Design, 1900s, 24 In.	889.00
Urn, Cover, Flowers, Pierced Handles, Orange, Blue, Gilt, Square Base, 18 x 6 ¾ In.	861.00
Vase, Birds Flowers, Boys Playing, Multicolor, Japan, 1800s, 12 In.	138.00
Vase, Bottle, 6-Sided Body, Panels Of Fans, Phoenixes, Dragons, c.1910, 12 ¼ In., Pair ...*illus*	1888.00
Vase, Bottle, Globular, Elongated Neck, Iron Red & Gold, Flowers, Figures, 1800s, 10 In., Pair	474.00
Vase, Bulbous, Flowers, Panels Of Cranes, 19th Century, 24 ½ In., Pair	1385.00
Vase, Children, Koi Pond, Flowers, Birds, Butterflies, Gilt Rim, Japan, 9 ¾ x 5 ½ In., Pair	196.00
Vase, Double Gourd, Reeding, Enamel, Leaves, Medallions, Aqua & Gold Accents, c.1900, 10 In., Pair	356.00
Vase, Exotic Birds, Flowers, Baluster, Multicolored, c.1900, 18 In.	118.00
Vase, Figures In Landscape, Flowers, Fluted Flared Rim, Gilt, Underglaze, 42 In., Pair ....*illus*	3444.00
Vase, Flared Lip, Flowering Plants, Plum Trees, Scrolling Leaves, 1800s, 19 In., Pair	738.00
Vase, Flowers, Birds, Gold, Red & Blue Enamel, 1800s, 18 In.	415.00
Vase, Flowers, Painted, Double Gourd Shape, Box, Cloth, 1600s, 3 x 7 In.	1210.00
Vase, Ho Ho Birds, Flower Cartouches, Baluster, Gilt, Chinese, 1800s, 10 ¼ In., Pair	316.00
Vase, Ribbed, Flared Rim, Flower, Leaf Shaped Pendant Reserves, 1800s, 11 ¾ In., Pair	1107.00

IMPERIAL GLASS CORPORATION was founded in Bellaire, Ohio, in 1901. It became a subsidiary of Lenox, Inc., in 1973 and was sold to Arthur R. Lorch in 1981. It was sold again in 1982, and went bankrupt in 1984. In 1985, the molds and some assets were sold. The Imperial glass preferred by the collector is freehand art glass, carnival glass, slag glass, stretch glass, and other top-quality tablewares. Tablewares and animals are listed here. The others may be found in the appropriate sections.

Animal, Horse, Caramel Slag, 4 ⅛ x 3 ½ In.	45.00
Candlewick, Basket, 6 ½ In.	50.00
Candlewick, Bowl, 9 ¾ In.	48.00
Candlewick, Bowl, Belled, 10 ½ In.	48.00
Candlewick, Bowl, Center, 11 In.	75.00
Candlewick, Cake Stand, Pedestal, 11 In.	85.00
Candlewick, Chip & Dip, 14 In.	400.00
Candlewick, Compote, 4 ¾ In.	38.00
Candlewick, Egg Plate, Center Heart Handle	175.00
Candlewick, Goblet, Water, 9 Oz., 7 ¼ In.	24.00
Candlewick, Muddler, 4 ½ In.	35.00
Candlewick, Pitcher, Ball Foot, 80 Oz.	255.00
Candlewick, Pitcher, Ball Handle, Pt.	275.00
Candlewick, Plate, 6 In.	9.00
Candlewick, Plate, Black, 2 Handles, Gold Trim, Beaded Rim, 10 In.	175.00
Candlewick, Relish, 5 Sections, Pinwheel, 10 In. Diam.	50.00
Candlewick, Sherbet, 6 Oz., 5 In.	20.00
Candlewick, Tray, Heart Handles, 7 In.	68.00
Candlewick, Tumbler, 5 Oz., 4 In.	16.00
Candlewick, Tumbler, 12 Oz., 5 In.	24.00
Cape Cod, Goblet, Water, Wafer Stem, Ritz Blue	44.00
Cape Cod, Sherbet, 4 In.	10.00
Cape Cod, Sherbet, Wafer Stem, Ritz Blue	34.00
Cape Cod, Vase, Flared Rim, Footed, 6 ¼ In.	48.00
Cathay, Bowl, Phoenix Dragon, c.1955, 8 ¾ In.	265.00
Chrysanthemum, Chop Plate, Marigold, Nuart	750.00
Frosted Lion, Dish, Reticulated Gallery, Cover, Patd. Aug. 6, 1889, 6 ½ x 7 ½ In.	34.00
Laced Edge, Bowl, Fruit, Katy Blue, 4 ½ In.	30.00
Laced Edge, Candlestick, Katy Green, 1930s, Pair	239.00
Laced Edge, Mayonnaise Set, Katy Blue, 1930s	179.00
Laced Edge, Soup, Dish, Katy Blue, Flat, 1930s	90.00
Open Rose, Bowl, Milk Glass, Flared Edge, c.1940, 3 x 8 In.	35.00
Open Rose, Dish, Footed, Gold, Purple, Blue, Ruffled Edge, c.1940	49.00
Perfume Bottle, Imperial Blue, 1940s	159.00
Pitcher, Spun Cobalt, Reeded, Ice Lip, 80 Oz.	150.00
Rose Bowl, Green, Gold Overlay, Marked, c.1940 3 ¾ x 6 In.	35.00
Vanity Set, Clear, Stylized Flowers, 2 Colognes, 2 Puff Boxes	139.00
Vanity Set, Forget-Me-Not Blue, 2 Bottles, Puff Box	129.00
Vase, Black Amethyst, Iridescent, 7 ¾ In.	50.00
Vase, Bulbous, Cylindrical, Marigold, Blue Hearts & Vines, 11 In.	550.00
Vase, Freehand, Footed, Cylindrical, Dark Cobalt With Orange Heart & Vines, 7 In.	325.00
Vase, Green, White Heart & Vine, 6 ¼ In.	425.00
Vase, Iridescent Orange, Freehand, Baluster, Flared Rim, 7 In.	58.00

Indian, Headdress, Northwest Coast, Cannibal Bird, Wood, Painted, Cedar Bark, 19 x 12 x 34 In.
$4740.00

Skinner, Inc.

Indian, Jar, Acoma, Curvy Designs, Brown, Black & White, c.1910, 9 x 11 In.
$863.00

Allard Auctions

Indian, Jar, Hopi, Black On Yellow, Zella Cheeda, 1960s, 7 x 9 In.
$403.00

Allard Auctions

Indian, Jar, San Ildefonso, Red Ground, Black Glaze, 1890, 9 ¼ x 11 ½ In.
$4183.00

Neal Auction Co.

Indian, Katsina, Hopi, Carved, Case Mask, Tablita, 1930s, 14 In. $1422.00

Skinner, Inc.

Indian, Katsina, Hopi, Cottonwood Root, Horns, 9 In. $183.00

Leslie Hindman Auctioneers

Indian, Katsina, Hopi, Sai Ast Asana, Carved, Painted, 1950s, 12 x 6 In. $374.00

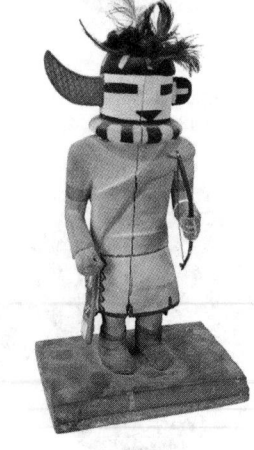

Allard Auctions

INDIAN art from North and South America has attracted the collector for many years. Each tribe has its own distinctive designs and techniques. Baskets, jewelry, pottery, and leatherwork are of greatest collector interest. Eskimo art is listed under Eskimo in this book.

Bag, Arapaho, Beaded, Buckskin, Fringe, Bearded Face, c.1950, 6 x 4 ½ In.	288.00
Bag, Athabascan, Woven Sinew, Moose Hide, Strap, Glass Beads, Alaska, c.1900, 9 x 8 In.	316.00
Bag, Cheyenne, Elk Hide, Beaded, Sinew, Tin Cones, Horsehair, c.1885, 12 ½ x 20 In. *illus*	5875.00
Bag, Iroquois, Glass Beaded, Wool, Calico Cat, Blue Eyes, Fringe, c.1900, 4 ½ In.	118.00
Bag, Lakota, Hide, Beaded, Multicolor, Geometric, Tin Cones, Horsehair, c.1885, 21 x 13 In. *illus*	2370.00
Bag, Mohawk Seneca, Beaded, Flowers, Hide, 6 ¼ In.	198.00
Bag, Mohawk, Beaded, Flower Design, Black Ground, c.1850, 6 ¼ In.	283.00
Bag, Nez Perce, Corn Husk, Bicolor Checker Board, Buckskin, c.1890, 20 x 25 In.	187.00
Bag, Nez Perce, Corn Husk, Woven, Geometric, Multicolor, Handles, 9 ¾ x 10 In.	472.00
Bag, Nez Perce, Corn Husk, Woven, Hourglasses, Diamonds, c.1910, 17 ½ x 11 ½ In. *illus*	441.00
Bag, Nez Perce, Geometric, Corn Husk Twist, Woven, Wool, c.1910, 11 ¾ x 10 In.	431.00
Bag, Northern Plains, Beaded, Pansies, Blue Ground, c.1950, 13 x 12 ½ In.	259.00
Bag, Plains, Beaded, Sinew Sewn, Geometric Designs, 17 In.	254.00
Bag, Plains, Buffalo Hide, Beaded, Fringe, 11 ¼ In.	452.00
Bag, Plains, Buffalo Hide, Beaded, Fringe, 15 x 4 ¼ In.	678.00
Bag, Plains, Tobacco, Buckskin, Beaded, Red, Blue, Yellow, c.1910, 6 x 3 In.	127.00
Bag, Plains, Woven, Wasco Root, Earth Tones, c.1910, 9 x 7 ½ In.	413.00
Bag, Plateau, Beaded, Buckskin, Fringe, Shield Shape, c.1950, 4 ½ x 4 ½ In.	316.00
Bag, Plateau, Beaded, Elk, Mountains, Multicolor, Purple Back Cloth, c.1950, 14 ½ x 13 In.	460.00
Bag, Plateau, Beaded, Federal Eagle, Fringe, Strap, Zipper, Red, White, Blue, 9 ½ x 12 In.	138.00
Bag, Plateau, Beaded, Red Rose, Geometric Symbols, Moosehide Fringe, 17 x 15 In.	288.00
Bag, Plateau, Beaded, Rose Design, Buckskin, c.1880, 12 x 9 In.	184.00
Bag, Plateau, Crescent, Star, Buckskin, Felt Trim, Beaded, Green Ground, 1900s, 12 x 11 In.	546.00
Bag, Seneca, Beaded, Hide, Fringe, Drawstring Closure, 7 ½ In.	79.00
Bag, Sioux, Buffalo Hide, Fringe, Beaded, c.1915, 10 ½ In.	283.00
Bag, Sioux, Buffalo Hide, Sewn, Beaded, Multicolor, c.1905, 15 x 20 ½ In.	2185.00
Bag, Sioux, Sinew Sewn, Lazy Stitch, Beaded, 15 x 20 In.	2185.00
Bag, Southern Plains, Beaded, Lazy Stitch, Strike-A-Light Flap, Geometric, c.1950, 7 x 4 In.	345.00
Bag, Tlingit, 8 Long Tabs, Flower Design, Red & Blue Cloth, c.1970, 20 x 12 In.	316.00
Bag, Tlingit, Octopus, 8 Tabs, Flowers, Beads, Blue & Red Cloth, c.1980, 22 x 10 In.	288.00
Bag, Ute, Hide Tail, Beaded, c.1875, 11 In.	1175.00
Bag, Ute, Hide, Beaded, Long Flap, Multicolor, Geometric, c.1885, 6 ¼ x 4 ½ In. *illus*	1304.00
Bag, Washo, Sally, Oval, Soft Woven, Figures, Animals, Buckskin Rim, c.1910, 6 ½ x 7 In.	1150.00
Bandolier, Woodlands, Beaded Front Panel Straps, Red Wool, Bead Tufts, c.1970, 41 x 13 In.	518.00
Basket, Achumawi, Burden, Cone Shape, Radiating Top Knot Design, c.1910, 18 x 19 In.	3163.00
Basket, Apache, Baluster, Crisscross Line Pattern, Animals, Figures, Golden, c.1890, 15 x 12 In.	3738.00
Basket, Apache, Burden, Buckskin Bottom, Tin Cone Suspensions, c.1950, 49 x 49 In.	316.00
Basket, Apache, Burden, Cone Shape, Geometric, c.1995, 13 ½ x 18 In.	403.00
Basket, Apache, Olla Shape, Figures, Animals, Geometric, Nellie Black, c.1990, 12 x 11 In.	316.00
Basket, Apache, Oval Diamond, c.1940, 3 ½ x 11 In.	633.00
Basket, Apache, Round Plaque, Silver Point Blossom Design, c.1950, 10 ½ In.	259.00
Basket, Apache, Stepped, Boxes, Crosses, Symbols, c.1930, 3 x 16 In.	2588.00
Basket, Apache, Tray, Coyote Tracks, Checkered Diamonds, c.1920, 14 x 3 ¾ In.	863.00
Basket, Apache, Tray, Geometric Designs, c.1905, 4 x 14 ½ In.	1495.00
Basket, Apache, Woven Tray, Repeated Radiating Stepped Design, 5 x 16 In.	1840.00
Basket, Attu, Cylinder, Wool & Silk, Bands, Multicolor, c.1900, 7 ½ x 9 ½ In.	575.00
Basket, Attu, Lid, Aleutian Wool, Russian Silk, Red, Pink Designs, c.1880, 8 x 7 In.	2300.00
Basket, Chehalis, Black Rim Design, 8 x 4 ½ In.	184.00
Basket, Chehalis, Indented Raised Border, 7 x 4 ½ In.	115.00
Basket, Cherokee, Gathering, River Cane, c.1950, 16 In.	531.00
Basket, Cherokee, River Cane, Diamonds, Hinged Handles, Wrapped Rim, c.1950, 17 ¼ In.	767.00
Basket, Cherokee, River Cane, Diamonds, Rowena Bradley, c.1950, 19 In.	1416.00
Basket, Cherokee, River Cane, Diamonds, Square To Round, c.1950, 15 ½ In.	1121.00
Basket, Cherokee, River Cane, Geometric Designs, c.1950, 15 In.	590.00
Basket, Cherokee, River Cane, Geometrics, Bentwood Lock Handle, Rectangular, 12 ¾ In.	295.00
Basket, Cherokee, River Cane, Square To Round, c.1950, 10 ¼ In.	590.00
Basket, Chitimacha, Lid, Double Weave, Cane, Red, Black, c.1910, 5 ¾ x 6 In. *illus*	2988.00
Basket, Chitimacha, Lid, Double Weave, Diagonal Bands, Geometrics, 4 ⅛ In. *illus*	1652.00
Basket, Chitimacha, Single Weave, Bowl Shape, Red, Black, Diagonal Design, c.1900, 4 x 9 ¾ In.	1195.00
Basket, Choctaw, Storage, Lid, 2 Handles, Spiral & Diamond Designs, c.1950, 27 ½ In.	1195.00
Basket, Coiled, Multicolor, Claw Design, 2 ¾ x 5 ¼ In.	561.00
Basket, Cowlitz, Checkered Columns, Sally Wakiacus, c.1905, 5 x 6 In.	184.00
Basket, Cowlitz, Zigzag Designs, Mary Kiona, 10 x 11 ½ In.	1380.00

Basket, Hopi, Coiled, 4 Katsina Faces, Geometric Band, 1958, 9 x 12 In. ....*illus*	460.00
Basket, Hupa, Bowl, Triangular, Crab Designs, c.1910, 4 x 7 In..	518.00
Basket, Hupa, Domed, Rhomboid Stars, c.1900, 3 ½ x 6 ¾ In...	518.00
Basket, Hupa, Flat Woven Basket Filled With Green, Bracken Fern Root Triangle, 4 x 20 In.	2185.00
Basket, Hupa, Geometric Designs, 8 x 7 ½ In..	690.00
Basket, Hupa, Hat, Geometric, Multicolor, c.1905, 3 ½ x 6 ½ In..	546.00
Basket, Hupa, Jump, Flat Woven Cylinder, Grass Bracken, Fern Root Triangles, c.1900, 4 x 20 In.	2185.00
Basket, Iroquois, Woven, Pedestal, Round, c.1950, 6 In.	115.00
Basket, Jicarilla, Storage, Cylindrical, c.1930s, 18 x 14 In. ....*illus*	115.00
Basket, Karok, Twined Hat, Raised Stitch Bands, c.1950, 4 x 7 In......................................	460.00
Basket, Kawaiisu, Bowl, Flared, Stepped Geometric, Red, 1900s, 6 x 14 ½ In.	1955.00
Basket, Klamath, Bowl, 3-Triangle Design, Top Knot Figure, c.1910, 4 ½ x 7 ½ In.	920.00
Basket, Klamath, Chevrons, Bowed Sides, Soft Woven, c.1910, 5 ¼ x 7 ½ In.	431.00
Basket, Klamath, Hat, Stacked Triangles, Yellow Quill Accents, c.1900, 4 x 7 In......................	460.00
Basket, Klickitat, 5 Open Loops On Rim, Geometric, Multicolor, 5 ½ In.	288.00
Basket, Koskimo, Bear Heads, Painted, Cedar Bark, Openwork Top, c.1880, 6 x 9 In.	2300.00
Basket, Maidu, Bowl, Coiled, Quail Plume & Redbud Design, c.1900, 3 ½ x 6 In.	690.00
Basket, Maidu, Burden, Cone Shape, Design Bands, Multicolor, c.1905, 16 ½ x 16 In.	546.00
Basket, Maidu, Game Tray, Central Figure, Corn Symbols, Red Fern, c.1900, 13 ¾ In.	2300.00
Basket, Mission, Bowl, Zigzag Pattern, c.1950, 4 x 12 ½ In.	138.00
Basket, Mission, Flower Design, c.1900, 2 x 10 ½ In..	546.00
Basket, Mono, Bowl, Flared, 2 Snake Design, Red Fern & Brackenroot, c.1950, 7 x 13 ½ In.	374.00
Basket, Mono, Bowl, Flared, Rattlesnake Diamonds, c.1900, 1 ½ x 5 In.	219.00
Basket, Nez Perce, Fez Shape, Woven Corn Husk, Black Wool Yarn, c.1950, 8 x 9 In.	920.00
Basket, Nisqually, Raised Undulating Rim, 8 ¼ In.	518.00
Basket, Nisqually, Stepped Zigzag Design, 14 ½ x 10 In..	1610.00
Basket, Nootka, Red & Green, Zigzag Rows, 5 x 3 ¾ In.	81.00
Basket, Northeast, Lid, Splint, Printed Wood, Synthetic Dye, 1800s, 14 x 10 ⅜ In. ....*illus*	1007.00
Basket, Northeast, Wrapped Wood, Felt, Round, Signed, 1919, 8 ¼ x 14 In..........................	186.00
Basket, Northwest Coast, Makah, 3 Ducks, Multicolor, 3 ½ In.	176.00
Basket, Nu Chah Nulth, Lid, Star Top, Duck Figures, 1940s, 3 ½ x 5 In.	66.00
Basket, Paiute, Beaded, Single Rod, Geometric Design, Blue Ground, c.1905, 3 ½ x 5 In........	316.00
Basket, Paiute, Bowl, Beading, Rod Coiled, Tan, Yellow, Blue, Red, c.1900, 2 x 3 ¼ In..............	374.00
Basket, Papago, Bowl, Flared, Repeating Bar Designs, c.1900, 8 x 12 In.............................	184.00
Basket, Papago, Bowl, Flared, Tan & Brown Geometric, c.1970, 8 ½ x 14 ½ In......................	259.00
Basket, Papago, Flared, Contrasting Zigzag Pattern, 3 x 4 ½ In.	33.00
Basket, Papago, Storage, Lid, Diamond X Pattern, 1880s, 24 x 24 In.	920.00
Basket, Papago, Storage, Lid, Squirrels, Eagles, Butterflies, Multicolor, 1880s, 27 x 25 In........	1150.00
Basket, Papago, Tight Weave, Oval Shape, c.1900, 7 ½ x 10 In..	44.00
Basket, Papago, Tray, Butterflies, c.1980, 4 ½ x 26 In...	1093.00
Basket, Piaute, Yucca, Willow Root, 9 x 4 ¼ In..	259.00
Basket, Pima, Bowl, Flared, Stepped Design, c.1940, 3 ½ x 7 ½ In.	99.00
Basket, Pima, Bowl, Key Design, Black Center, c.1940, 5 ½ x 16 ½ In.	1150.00
Basket, Pima, Bowl, Key Design, Black Center, c.1950, 6 x 16 In.	431.00
Basket, Pima, Cross Figures, Oval, c.1950, 3 ½ x 7 In..	66.00
Basket, Pima, Geometrics, Willow, Bear Grass, Devil's Claw, c.1930, 8 x 4 ¾ In.	184.00
Basket, Pima, Olla Shape, Checkerboard Design, c.1910, 9 ½ x 10 In.................................	1035.00
Basket, Pima, Oval, Checkerboard Pattern, c.1905, 4 ½ x 10 ½ In....................................	403.00
Basket, Pima, Squash Blossom, Stars, 4 ½ x 14 ½ In...	77.00
Basket, Pima, Tray, 2 Color Geometric, c.1950, 3 x 23 In..	1265.00
Basket, Pima, Tray, Fret Design, c.1910, 7 In..	489.00
Basket, Pima, Tray, Horsehair, Geometric Blossoms, c.1980, 5 In.....................................	518.00
Basket, Pima, Tray, Man In Maze, Tight Weave, c.1910, 1 ¾ x 7 In....................................	633.00
Basket, Pima, Tray, Tight Weave, Devil's Claw, Fret Pattern, c.1910, 3 ½ x 16 In.	460.00
Basket, Pima, Woven Wide Tray, Pedestal Base, c.1950, 5 ½ x 14 In.................................	219.00
Basket, Pit River, Globe Shape, Geometric Design, c.1910, 7 x 11 In.................................	1093.00
Basket, Pomo, Bamtush, Storage, Reverse Geometric Design, c.1905, 7 ½ x 10 In.................	1955.00
Basket, Pomo, Bowl, Diamonds, Closely Woven, Flared Rim, c.1910, 6 ½ x 8 In....................	403.00
Basket, Pomo, Bowl, Feathers, Shell Beads, Black, Yellow, Lydia Faught, c.1945, 1 ½ x 9 In. ...	2875.00
Basket, Pomo, Bowl, Flared, Feathers, c.1890, 2 ½ x 8 ½ In.	138.00
Basket, Pomo, Bowl, Flared, Feathers, Shell Beads, Multicolor, c.1910, 4 x 8 In.....................	1093.00
Basket, Pomo, Bowl, Flared, Fine Woven, X Design, Red Feathers, c.1900, 3 x 5 In.	345.00
Basket, Pomo, Bowl, Oval, Stepped Arrow Design, Red Feathers, c.1900, 2 x 7 ¼ In.	345.00
Basket, Pomo, Bowl, Round, Feathers, Beads, Yellow, Black, c.1905, 4 x 6 ½ In.	690.00
Basket, Pomo, Bowl, Round, Multicolor Top Knot Designs, c.1900, 1 ¼ x 3 In........................	978.00
Basket, Pomo, Coiled, 3 Rod, Stepped Design, Annie Lake, c.1950, 3 x 6 In............................	748.00

Indian, Mask, Iroquois, False Face, Painted, Copper Eyes, Horsehair, Wood, c.1890, 12 ½ x 4 ¼ In.
$518.00

Allard Auctions

Indian, Mask, Northwest Coast, Human Face, Cedar, Carved, Painted, c.1950, 11 x 8 x 5 In.
$633.00

Allard Auctions

Indian, Moccasins, Arapaho, Hard Sole, Beaded, Multicolor, Geometric, c.1885, 13 ½ In.
$3851.00

Skinner, Inc.

Indian, Moccasins, Beaded, Geometric
Pattern, c.1920, 8 ¼ In.
$440.00

Old Barn Auction

Indian, Moccasins, Cheyenne, Hide,
Beaded, Hard Soles, Multicolor,
Geometric, c.1885, 9 ½ In.
$919.00

Skinner, Inc.

Indian, Moccasins, Sioux, Beaded, Sinew
Sewn, Lazy Stitch, Rawhide Soles, 1900,
Child's, 5 In.
$748.00

Allard Auctions

Clean or Dirty

We like antiques dealers who
display their goods creatively,
have clean new price tags,
keep some candy in a bowl,
and don't tell us not to touch
anything. But then, we also
like dirty, confused, clut-
tered shops with unexpected
treasures under the table. We
expect to pay lower prices in
a dirty store. And we know
collectibles move faster in an
attractive setting—so we buy
what we want immediately.

Basket, Pomo, Feather, Shell Beads, 3 Rod Coil, Round, c.1950, 2 ¾ x 5 ¼ In.	748.00
Basket, Pomo, Flared Bowl, Stacked Diamonds & White Seed Bead Accents, 4 x 10 In.	1840.00
Basket, Pomo, Geometric, Single Rod Coil, Czech Seed Beads, Multicolor, c.1900, 2 x 4 In.	374.00
Basket, Pomo, Tight Weave, Stepped Design, c.1930, 1 ½ x 4 ¼ In. ....*illus*	431.00
Basket, Pomo, Twined, 2 Bands, Geometric Designs, 1900, 5 ½ x 6 In. ....*illus*	518.00
Basket, Quinault, Bowl, Plated Cedar Bark Bottom, Ring Loops, c.1950, 6 ½ x 11 In.	127.00
Basket, Quinault, Lid, Half Twist Weave, Multicolor, c.1905, 6 x 7 In.	230.00
Basket, Salish, Lid, Domed, Rectangular, Zigzag Design, c.1905, 5 x 5 ½ In.	316.00
Basket, Salish, Thompson River, X Designs, Multicolor, Olla Shape, c.1900, 7 x 7 In.	196.00
Basket, San Carlos Apache, Center Flower, Figures, Dogs, c.1900, 17 In.	6463.00
Basket, San Carlos Apache, Radiating Center Flower, Petals, Maltese Cross, c.1900, 17 In.	4700.00
Basket, Siletz, Storage, Gold Design Bands, c.1910, 5 ½ x 10 In.	184.00
Basket, Skagit, Zigzag, Multicolor, Mary Kionqa, c.1960, 11 ½ x 8 In.	1495.00
Basket, Skokomish, Berry, Cylindrical, Stepped Designs, c.1910, 8 x 7 In.	288.00
Basket, Skokomish, Bowl, Dogs Band, Geometric, Rim Loops, P. Charley, c.1940, 7 x 9 In.	1150.00
Basket, Southwest, Coiled, Multicolor Swags, Red Rings, c.1950, 6 ⅝ x 13 In.	127.00
Basket, Storage, Square, Round Top, Red & Blue Bands, Woven, New England, 14 x 19 In.	4313.00
Basket, Tlingit, Cap, Key & Triangles Design, Child's, c.1890, 2 ¼ x 5 ½ In.	920.00
Basket, Tlingit, Cylindrical, Key Designs, c.1920, 4 ½ x 5 In.	184.00
Basket, Tlingit, Diamonds, Black, Red, Yellow, Cylindrical, c.1890, 6 x 10 In.	1955.00
Basket, Tray, 2 Zigzag Rows, Round, Red Fern Woven, c.1910, 14 ½ In.	1150.00
Basket, Tribal, Tightly Woven Grass, Lightning Design, Round, Calif., 5 x 7 In.	489.00
Basket, Tulare, Cooking, Flared Sides, Zigzags, Red, Black, c.1902, 5 x 13 In.	489.00
Basket, Tulare, Zigzag, Triangle, Round, Woven, c.1900, 4 ½ x 7 In.	403.00
Basket, Washo, Bowl, Oval, 6-Point Stars, Red & Fern Root, c.1920s, 4 x 6 ½ In.	431.00
Basket, Washo, Burden, Cone Shape, 3 Rattlesnake, Diamond Designs, c.1900, 23 x 22 In.	1265.00
Basket, Washo, Sally Bag, Mule, Deer, Eagle, Figure Design, 5 ¾ x 4 In.	1495.00
Basket, Washo, Zigzag Design, c.1950, 5 x 8 ½ In.	173.00
Basket, Wintu, Encircling Geometric, Cone Shape, c.1910, 9 x 8 ½ In.	690.00
Basket, Yurok, Bowl, Reverse Geometric Design, Openwork Rim, c.1900, 5 x 8 In.	374.00
Basket, Yurok, Child's Hat, Geometric Designs, c.1902, 3 ½ x 6 ¾ In.	345.00
Belt, Concha, Sterling, 7 Ornaments, Butterflies, Leather, Buckle, Marked Herbert Begay, 40 In.	1652.00
Belt, Crow, Leather, Beaded, Tacked, c.1900, 83 In.	1058.00
Belt, Kiowa, Concha, Leather, German Silver, Side Drop, 1970s, Size 30-33 In., 28-In. Drop	316.00
Belt, Navajo, 9 Round Conchas, Figural Buffalo Buckle, c.1970 ¼ In.	316.00
Belt, Navajo, Concha, Adjustable Length, Size 40	66.00
Belt, Navajo, Concha, Silver, c.1935, 36 In. ....*illus*	1320.00
Belt, Navajo, Concha, Silver, Stamped, Diamond Cut, Buckle, c.1940, Ladies, Waist 30-32 In.	431.00
Belt, Navajo, Concha, Silver, Turquoise, 1975, 39 In.	353.00
Belt, Navajo, Silver, Blue Lapis, Thompson Piaso, Concha, c.1998, 34-44 Waist, 3 x 2 In.	863.00
Belt, Sterling, 3 Center Medallion, 34 In.	240.00
Blanket, Chilkat, Robe, Ceremonial, Figures, Woven, c.1800, 32 x 41 In.	48300.00
Blanket, Navajo, Black, White Zigzag, Red Ground, Germantown, c.1880, 79 x 57 ½ In.	5925.00
Blanket, Navajo, Broad Multicolor Bands, Natural Colors, 54 x 74 In.	3304.00
Blanket, Navajo, Chief's, Bands, Diamonds, Red, Gray, White, Black, c.1930, 64 x 52 In.	1840.00
Blanket, Navajo, Eye Dazzler, Center Track Design, Multicolor, 80 x 51 In.	715.00
Blanket, Navajo, Germantown, Wool, Crosses, Diamonds, Black, Purple, Red, 48 x 55 In.	3680.00
Blanket, Navajo, Transitional, Wool, Red, Indigo, Yellow, Green, c.1875, 76 x 51 In.	4406.00
Blanket, Navajo, Wool, Serrated Diamond Pattern, c.1890, 52 x 73 In. ....*illus*	1024.00
Blouse, Cheyenne, Girl's, Cowrie Shell Design, 13 ¾ x 13 ½ In.	198.00
Bolo, Navajo, Bisbee, Turquoise, Silver, 36 In.	154.00
Bolo, Navajo, Corals, Bear Claws, Turquoise, John Hummingbird, 1970s, 4 ½ x 3 ½ In.	403.00
Bolo, Navajo, Silver, Bear Claws, Coral Branches, Turquoise, Carlos White, c.1974, 4 x 3 In.	748.00
Bolo, Navajo, Turquoise, Silver, Katsina, Coral Eye, 36 In.	110.00
Bolo, Zuni, Channel Inlay Slide, Knife Wing Dancer, 1960s, 6 x 3 ½ In.	1150.00
Bolo, Zuni, Headdress, Shell Carved Face, c.1990, 2 ½ x 2 ½ In.	230.00
Bolo, Zuni, Inlaid Chief Dancer, Silver Tips, c.1980, 5 x 3 In.	403.00
Bonnet Case, Sioux, Parfleche, Fringe, Blue, Red, Yellow, c.1875, 34 In.	3819.00
Boots, Comanche, Concha, German Silver, 18 In. ....*illus*	880.00
Bottle, Pit River, Cap, Geometric Bands, c.1910, 14 x 3 In.	403.00
Bow, Apache, Double Recurve, Sinew Backed, c.1875, 43 In.	1058.00
Bow, Apache, Sinew String, Painted, 39 In.	1528.00
Bowcase & Quiver, Plains, Elk Hide, Beaded, Long Tails, Bow & Arrow, c.1990, 21 x 3 In.	546.00
Bowl, Acoma, Earthenware, Multicolor Geometric, Rectangular, c.1910, 9 In.	708.00
Bowl, Hopi, Birds, Geometric, Squat, J.P., c.1990, 4 ½ x 7 ½ In.	207.00
Bowl, Hopi, Round, Curled Rim, Interior Bird Figures, Earth Tones, c.1915, 3 ½ x 9 In.	1955.00

Bowl, Hopi, Shallow, Painted Geometric Design, 9 In. Diam.	1830.00
Bowl, Iroquois, Ash Burl, Cutout Handles, c.1800, 8 x 15 ½ In.	6695.00
Bowl, San Ildefonso, Blackware, Avanyu, Carved, c.1950, 4 ¼ x 7 ½ In.	374.00
Bowl, San Ildefonso, Blackware, Geometric Band, Maria & Santana Martinez, c.1945, 4 x 6 In.	805.00
Bowl, San Ildefonso, Blackware, Marie & Santana, c.1952, 11 ½ x 3 In.	1150.00
Bowl, San Ildefonso, Bulbous, Tapered, Red, Tan Glaze, Feather Design, Signed, 5 In.	565.00
Bowl, San Ildefonso, Seed, Blackware, Globular, Marie Poveka, c.1950, 4 x 4 ½ In.	1035.00
Bowl, Santa Clara, Blackware, Bulbous, Tapered, Incised Design, Signed, M. Tafoya, 5 In.	226.00
Bowl, Santa Clara, Blackware, Oval, Flora Naranjo, c.1950, 3 x 6 x 5 In. ....*illus*	161.00
Bowl, Santo Domingo, Dough, Geometric, c.1875, 7 x 17 In.	1880.00
Bowl, Woodlands, Burl, Carved, Beaver Belly, Iron Tack Eyes, 1800s, 11 x 5 In. ....*illus*	4730.00
Bowl, Zia, Curled Rim, Symbol Bands, Brown Ground, c.1910, 5 x 11 In.	345.00
Box, Iroquois, Beaded Box Spelled Out, c.1920, 4 ½ x 5 In.	77.00
Box, Northwest Coastal, Quill, Bark, Canister Shape, Flower Design, 2 ¼ x 2 ¾ In.	89.00
Box, Salishan, Woven Geometric Design, Tapered, c.1900, 14 x 22 In.	575.00
Bracelet, Hopi, Silver, Overlaid, Turquoise Stone, c.1970, 6 x 1 ½ In.	259.00
Bracelet, Navajo, 14K Gold, Turquoise Cabochons, Silver Interior, Marked A.Q., 1970, 6 x 1 In.	1495.00
Bracelet, Navajo, Cuff, 4 Bands, Turquoise, c.1970, 6 x 2 ½ In.	219.00
Bracelet, Navajo, Cuff, 8 Turquoise Stones, Coral, Stamped, c.1950, 6 x 1 In.	374.00
Bracelet, Navajo, Cuff, Silver Set, 14 Coral Stones, Filed Edge, c.1950, 6 ¼ x 1 In.	518.00
Bracelet, Navajo, Cuff, Silver, 5 Turquoise, 5 Coral Stones, c.1970, 6 x 2 ½ In.	489.00
Bracelet, Navajo, Cuff, Silver, Hollow Work, 3 Turquoise Stones, c.1970, 5 ½ x 1 ¼ In.	184.00
Bracelet, Navajo, Cuff, Silver, Sam Lovato, 1900s, 6 x 2 In.	316.00
Bracelet, Navajo, Cuff, Silver, Turquoise Stone, Leaves, c.1976, 5 ⅜ In.	489.00
Bracelet, Navajo, Cuff, Sterling Silver, Turquoise, Coral, Signed J. Nezzie, 5 ½ x 1 ½ In.	395.00
Bracelet, Navajo, Cuff, Sterling, Spider Web Turquoise Stones, c.1965, 5 ¼ In.	4025.00
Bracelet, Navajo, Cuff, Turquoise, Silver, 3 Oval Stones, Engraved Design Band, 1920s, 2 x 2 ½ In.	460.00
Bracelet, Navajo, Cuff, Turquoise, Silver, Signed R.C., c.1970, 6 x 1 In.	316.00
Bracelet, Navajo, Green Turquoise, Stamped Arrows, Whirling Logs, 1900-25, 6 ½ In.	353.00
Bracelet, Navajo, Silver, 2 Bands, 5 Turquoise Stones, c.1960, 5 ¼ x 1 ¼ In.	288.00
Bracelet, Navajo, Silver, Dot & Scrollwork, 2 Turquoise, c.1970, 5 ½ x 2 ⅝ In.	403.00
Bracelet, Navajo, Silver, Turquoise Stone, Leaf Applique, c.1950, 6 ½ x 2 In.	403.00
Bracelet, Navajo, Squash Blossoms, Turquoise Stones, Clyde Begay, c.1980, 26 x 3 In.	978.00
Bracelet, Navajo, Tufa Cast Silver, Turquoise, Signed, Morgan, Sterling, 1950-75, 6 ½ In.	150.00
Bracelet, Navajo, Turquoise, Silver, 3 Stones, c.1970, 5 ½ x 2 In.	187.00
Bracelet, Zuni, 3 Silver Bands, Turquoise, Petit Point Cluster, Oval, c.1950, 7 x 3 In.	460.00
Bracelet, Zuni, Cuff, 4 Silver Rows, 60 Tiny Coral Beads, Sharon Hustito, 1980s, 5 ¾ In.	316.00
Bracelet, Zuni, Cuff, Silver, Turquoise Cluster, c.1970, 5 x 3 In.	259.00
Bracelet, Zuni, Silver Knife Wing Dancer, Turquoise, Coral, Pearl, c.1970, 5 ¾ x 3 ¾ In.	489.00
Bracelet, Zuni, Silver, Turquoise, 10 Rows, Split Stamped Bands, 6 ⅝ x 3 ½ In.	1380.00
Bracelet, Zuni, V-Shape Band, Coral Needlepoint, Hallmark HH, 5 ¾ x ⅞ In. ....*illus*	115.00
Breastplate, Northern Plains, Bone, Hair-pipe, Harness Leather, c.1875, 20 x 9 In.	2233.00
Breastplate, Plateau, Beaded Bone, 3 Rows, c.1930, 11 x 12 ½ In.	248.00
Buckle, Navajo, Silver, 3 Spider Web Turquoise Stones, Jackie Adakie, 1970s	259.00
Buckle, Navajo, Turquoise, Repousse, c.1940, 2 ¾ x 1 ¼ In.	260.00
Bust, Indian Brave, Plaster, Painted, Hiawatha, 27 ¾ x 18 In. ....*illus*	59.00
Canteen, Cochiti, Pregnant Form, Handles, c.1875, 6 ½ x 7 ½ In.	823.00
Canteen, Navajo, Tobacco, Chain Cap, Feathers, Silver, Turquoise, c.1950, 3 ½ x 2 ½ In.	345.00
Case, Navajo, Silver, Green Turquoise Stones, Spring Clasp, c.1970, 7 x 3 ¼ In.	633.00
Case, Plains, Parfleche, Rawhide, Folding Container, Mineral Paint Symbols, 21 x 15 In.	575.00
Club, Eastern Plains, Gunstock, c.1850, 7-In. Blade, 29 In.	3055.00
Club, Northern Plains, Stone Head, c.1875, 34 ½ In.	1175.00
Coat, Northern Woodlands, Hide, Embroidered Flowers, c.1875, 42 x 38 In.	10575.00
Collar, Tlingit, Beaded Flowers, Stars, Whale, Red Cloth, c.1970, 10 ¾ x 16 ½ In.	173.00
Cradle, Flathead, Tradecloth, Buckskin, Blue Designs, Black Ground, c.1890, 15 x 7 In.	2300.00
Cradle, Mono, Willow, Basketry, Sunshade, Doll, Carved Wooden Face, 1950s, 8 x 3 ½ In. .....*illus*	288.00
Cradle, Sioux, Hide, Sinew Sewn, Beaded, c.1875, 25 In.	7638.00
Cradle, Ute, Model, Hide, Beaded, Wood Frame, Pouch, Cloth Covered Doll, Fringe, c.1885, 20 In. *illus*	4148.00
Cradleboard, Apache, Yellow Canvas, Bent, Carved Frame, Sunshade, Beading, 1970s, 38 x 15 In.	259.00
Cradleboard, Chippewa, Thread Sewn, Flowers, Bentwood Hoop, Beaded, c.1850, 31 In.	14400.00
Cradleboard, Mono, Woven, Willow, Red Fern, Sunshade, Finger Straps, c.1950, 28 x 16 ½ In.	748.00
Cradleboard, Osage, Pine, Carved, Painted, 1980s, 41 ½ x 10 In.	138.00
Cradleboard, Paiute, Bentwood, Willow, Buckskin, Beads, Sunshade, Mary Teton, 38 x 13 In.	920.00
Cradleboard, Pueblo, Wood Baby Carrier, Willow Sunshade Hoops, c.1910, 27 x 10 In.	403.00
Cradleboard, Sioux, Lazy Stitch Beading, Brass Tacked Boards, c.1970, 45 x 9 ½ In.	1725.00
Cross, Zuni, Brass, Turquoise Inlay, Ankh, Key Of Life, c.1970, 8 ½ x 4 ½ In.	150.00

Skookum

Skookum Indian dolls can be dated by the material used for the parts. The earliest dolls from the mid to late 1910s had apple heads, no feet, and a block of wood for a body. In the early 1920s, some apple-head dolls had composition shoes. In the 1930s, the feet were leather-over-wood moccasins. From the 1910s to the 1940s, dolls had composition masks, some marked "Germany." In the 1940s, plastic masks were used.

Indian, Necklace, Zuni, Fetish, Olivella Shell Heishi, Birds, Animals, 5 Strands, Tsikewa, c.1950, 15 In. $1998.00

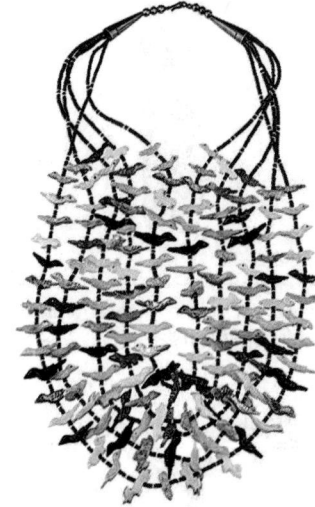

Cowan's Auctions

Indian, Olla, Acoma, Flowers, Geometric, Red, Orange, Black, c.1900, 10 x 11 ¾ In. $1763.00

Cowan's Auctions

INDIAN

Indian, Paddle, Haida, Wooden, Carved, 1820s, 52 ½ In.
$1870.00

Old Barn Auction

Indian, Pin, Hopi, Inlaid Snake, Signed, Charles Loloma, c.1985, 3 In.
$4113.00

Cowan's Auctions

Indian, Purse, Leather, Beaded Front, Shield Shape, Zippered Top, c.1930s, 5 x 6 In.
$150.00

Allard Auctions

Cuffs, Blackfoot, Buckskin, Fringed Sides, 6 x 4 In.	489.00
Cuffs, Crow, Beaded, Geometric Symbols, White Buckskin, Fringe, c.1950, 8 x 6 In.	259.00
Cuffs, Crow, Buckskin, Fringe, Beaded Designs, c.1950, Child's, 5 ½ x 4 In.	127.00
Doll Cradleboard, Crow, Strapped Front, Beaded Top, Canvas, 1880s, 20 x 7 In.	460.00
Doll, Mohawk, Corn Husk, Penciled Face, Silk, Wool Clothes, Beads, c.1910, 11 In., Pair ...... *illus*	115.00
Doll, Plains, Buckskin, Dress, Moccasins, Human Hair, Morning Star, 1890s, 15 In.	2185.00
Doll, Plains, Buckskin, Sinew Sewn, Beaded Features, c.1910, 17 In. ....*illus*	1955.00
Doll, Plains, Dress, Moccasins, Leggings, Human Hair, Beaded, Buckskin, c.1945, 10 ½ In.	345.00
Doll, Plains, Dress, Moccasins, Leggings, Thread Hair, Beaded Features, c.1960, 10 In.	259.00
Doll, Plains, Moccasins, Leggings, Belt, Human Hair, Sinew Sewn, Buckskin, c.1910, 12 In.	748.00
Doll, Plains, Rawhide, Buffalo Horn Headdress, Dentil Breastplate, Paint, 1900s, 10 In.	431.00
Doll, Seminole, c.1950, 12 In. ....*illus*	66.00
Doll, Sioux, Man, War Shirt, Leggings, Moccasins, Bag, Sinew Sewn, Buckskin, c.1910, 11 ½ In.	863.00
Doll, Skookum, Papier-Mache, Molded Face, Painted, Braided Hair, Blanket, c.1920, 40 In.	1150.00
Doll, Skookum, Woman, Papoose, Blanket Wrap, 14 In.	198.00
Dress, Cheyenne, Cowry Shell, Long Fringe, Ribbon Work, Size M/L	154.00
Dress, Crow, Red Felt, Ribbon Trim, Carved Bone Elk Teeth, Late 1900s, Girl's, 30 In. .....*illus*	345.00
Earrings, Zuni, Devil Dancer, Inlay, Screwback, 1 ¼ x ¾ In.	88.00
Earrings, Zuni, Teardrop, Turquoise, Clusters, Ladder Style, Pierced, c.1960, 4 In.	184.00
Effigy Stick, Angled Handle, Feathers At Top & Bottom, 43 In.	30500.00
Fetish, Sioux, Lizard, Beaded, Wood Frame, c.1890, 7 In.	452.00
Fetish, Zuni, Fish, Carved, Turquoise Chip Exterior, Edna Leika, c.1970, 9 x 9 In.	978.00
Gauntlets, Shoshone, Hide, Beaded, Flowers, Fringe, c.1900, 11 In.	470.00
Gloves, Plains, Hide, Beaded, 12 In., Pair	356.00
Gloves, Santee, Stars, Flowers, Buckskin, Rawhide Soles, Beads, Woman's, 11 x 5 In.	431.00
Hair Ornament, Navajo, Silver, Leaf, Scroll, Coral, Turquoise, Willie Singer, c.1970, 3 ½ x 2 In.	230.00
Handbag, Sioux, Beaded, Geometric Design, Snap Closure, c.1900	1875.00
Handbag, Sioux, Beaded, White, Stepped Design, Blue Border, c.1900, 9 x 12 In.	1500.00
Hat, Tlingit, Clan Iconography, c.1875, 14 x 6 In.	977.00
Hat, Yakima, Fez, Sun Symbols, Geometric, Beaded, c.1960, 6 ½ x 7 In.	748.00
Headdress Front, Haida, Cedar, Bear, Raven, Carved, Painted, c.1975, 8 ½ x 5 ½ In.	978.00
Headdress Front, Northwest, Alderwood, Faces, Wings, Abalone Inlay, 1980s, 7 x 5 In.	431.00
Headdress, Northwest Coast, Cannibal Bird, Wood, Painted, Cedar Bark, 19 x 12 x 34 In. .....*illus*	4740.00
Headdress, Pueblo, Deer Dancer, Buckskin, Painted Symbols, Antlers, c.1905, 18 x 30 In., 2 Piece	1150.00
Holster, Sioux, Beaded, Lazy Stitch Beaded, Elkhide, Geometric Design, 11 x 5 ½ In.	1840.00
Holster, Sioux, Geometric Designs, Elkhide, Beads, Sinew Sewn, c.1910, 11 x 5 ½ In.	1840.00
Horse Collar, Crow, Martingale, Beaded, Red & Blue Cloth, Brass Bells, c.1980, 41 x 18 In.	1035.00
Jacket, Apache, Hide, Beaded, Painted, Yellow, Green, Bib, Fringe, Copper Buttons, c.1875, 29 x 28 In.	7638.00
Jacket, Crow, Thread & Sinew Sewn, Beaded Flowers, Cuffs, c.1875, 34 x 38 In.	3600.00
Jar, Acoma, Curvy Designs, Brown, Black & White, c.1910, 9 x 11 In. ....*illus*	863.00
Jar, Acoma, Flute Playing Ants, Black On White, Lucy M. Lewis, 1980s, 3 ½ x 4 In.	460.00
Jar, Acoma, Geometric, Black On White, Fineline, Lucy M. Lewis, c.1970, 3 x 4 ½ In.	546.00
Jar, Acoma, Multicolor Geometric, Scalloped Rim, D. Patricio, 5 x 6 In.	44.00
Jar, Acoma, Olla, Parrot, Brown, White, Black, Virginia Lowden, 1970s, 9 x 10 In.	546.00
Jar, Hopi, Bird Design, Brown, Tan, Sadie Adams, c.1950, 8 x 4 ½ In.	575.00
Jar, Hopi, Birds, Geometric, Multicolor, Lena Charlie, c.1950, 12 ½ x 7 In.	28275.00
Jar, Hopi, Black On Yellow, Zella Cheeda, 1960s, 7 x 9 In. ....*illus*	403.00
Jar, Hopi, Cream Slip, Geometric Designs, c.1890, 4 ½ x 8 In.	805.00
Jar, Hopi, Frog Woman, Multicolor, 1880s, 10 x 7 In.	920.00
Jar, Hopi, Olla, Geometric, Black, Yellow, Zella Cheeda, c.1960, 7 x 9 In.	403.00
Jar, Hopi, Storage, Birds, Tadpoles, Feathers, Black, Red, White, Joffern Puffer, 12 x 14 In.	748.00
Jar, Laguna, Checkered, Geometric, Multicolor, White Ground, E. Cheramiah, c.1985, 12 x 13 In.	690.00
Jar, San Ildefonso, Blackware, Blue Corn, Avanyu Incised, c.1960, 8 x 6 ½ In.	863.00
Jar, San Ildefonso, Blackware, Serpent Carved, Christina Naranjo, c.1950, 11 x 8 In.	1035.00
Jar, San Ildefonso, Red Ground, Black Glaze, 1890, 9 ¼ x 11 ½ In. ....*illus*	4183.00
Jar, San Ildefonso, Wedding, Blackware, Double Spout, Handle, Maria Martinez, c.1935, 9 ½ In.	4720.00
Jar, Santa Clara, Blackware, Avanyu Incised, Milda Tafoya, c.1960, 9 x 7 ½ In.	748.00
Jar, Santa Clara, Wedding, Blackware, Double Neck, Serpent, Christina Naranjo, c.1960, 14 x 8 In.	805.00
Jar, Zuni, Deer Design, Heart Line, Squat, c.1885	14000.00
Jar, Zuni, Stylized Geometric Design, Cream, Black Squat, Concave Base, 10 In.	2585.00
Katsina, Hopi, Carved, Case Mask, Tablita, 1930s, 14 In. ....*illus*	1422.00
Katsina, Hopi, Cottonwood Root, Black Torso, O Shape Mouth, 9 In.	199.00
Katsina, Hopi, Cottonwood Root, Clown, Black & White, 16 In.	134.00
Katsina, Hopi, Cottonwood Root, Corn Cloud, Blue Mask, Rattle, 17 In.	134.00
Katsina, Hopi, Cottonwood Root, Dancer, Snake, 13 In.	149.00
Katsina, Hopi, Cottonwood Root, Eagle Dancer, 19 In.	122.00

Katsina, Hopi, Cottonwood Root, Feathered Headdress, 15 In.	171.00
Katsina, Hopi, Cottonwood Root, Horns, 9 In. ....*illus*	183.00
Katsina, Hopi, Cottonwood Root, Mudhead Koyemsi Shape, Carved, Painted, c.1960, 12 x 7 In.	126.00
Katsina, Hopi, Cottonwood Root, Patung Shape, Carved, Painted, c.1910, 8 x 4 ½ In.	161.00
Katsina, Hopi, Cottonwood, Yarn Mounted Feather, Necklace, Moccasins, c.1910, 8 In.	3068.00
Katsina, Hopi, Crippled Boy, Signed Geri Navasie Flores, 6 ¼ In.	141.00
Katsina, Hopi, Sai Ast Asana, Carved, Painted, 1950s, 12 x 6 In. ....*illus*	374.00
Katsina, Laguna, Large Tabletta, Buckskin Dress, 14 In.	55.00
Katsina, Zuni, Cottonwood Root, Carved, Painted Cloth, Sio Shalako Shape, c.1950, 2 x 3 In.	403.00
Ladle, Iroquois, Carved Maple, Stylized Bird Handle, 1800s, 9 In.	575.00
Ladle, Woodland, Maple, Bird Head Finial, Bird Claw, 1800s, 5 ¾ In.	1687.00
Leggings, Central Plains, Beaded, Hide, Blue, Yellow, Sinew Sewn, c.1875, 31 In.	2350.00
Leggings, Cheyenne, Buckskin, Sinew Sewn, Beads, Geometrics, Yellow, Child's, c.1890, 8 x 8 In.	690.00
Leggings, Kiowa, Buckskin, Yellow, Fringe, Sinew, Bead Trim, c.1905, 4 ½ x 30 In.	920.00
Leggings, Kiowa, Yellow Ocher Buckskin, Fringe, Sinew Beaded Rim, 35 x 15 In.	420.00
Leggings, Plains, Hide, Beaded, Blue, White, 8 ¼ x 16 In.	273.00
Leggings, Sioux, Beaded, Lazy Stitch, Buckskin Uppers, Chevrons & Fringe, 15 x 7 In.	863.00
Leggings, Sioux, Chevrons, Fringe, Sinew Sewn Beads, Yellow, Blue, White, c.1905, 15 x 7 In.	863.00
Mask, Iroquois, False Face, Painted, Copper Eyes, Horsehair, Wood, c.1890, 12 ½ x 4 ¼ In. ....*illus*	518.00
Mask, Iroquois, Wood, Horsehair, Copper, Painted, Signed, Todd Longboat, c.1985, 13 x 9 In.	431.00
Mask, Kwakiutl, Carved, Painted, Cedar, Bark Hair, Alex Hunt, c.1972, 7 ½ x 6 In.	374.00
Mask, Makah Indian, Red Cedar, Interior Coyote Features, Bark Hair, Painted, 45 x 24 In.	1380.00
Mask, Northwest Coast, Carved & Painted Cedar, Horsehair, Bark Brown Band, 10 x 8 In.	316.00
Mask, Northwest Coast, Cedar, Carved, White, Black, Green, Red, 13 x 8 In.	99.00
Mask, Northwest Coast, Human Face, Cedar, Carved, Painted, c.1950, 11 x 8 x 5 In. ....*illus*	633.00
Mask, Northwest, Face, Whalebone, Carved, 8 ¾ In.	565.00
Moccasins, Arapaho, Beaded, Buckskin, Hard Rawhide Soles, Blue, Green, c.1970, Size 11	259.00
Moccasins, Arapaho, Beads, Sinew Rawhide Soles, Multicolor, c.1900, Size 10	920.00
Moccasins, Arapaho, Hard Sole, Beaded, Multicolor, Geometric, c.1885, 13 ½ In. ....*illus*	3851.00
Moccasins, Arapaho, Lazy Stitch, Buckskin, Rawhide Soles, 10 In.	920.00
Moccasins, Arapaho, Sinew Sewn, Beads, Blue, Green, Buffalo Soles, c.1900, Size 11	690.00
Moccasins, Beaded, Geometric Pattern, c.1920, 8 ¼ In. ....*illus*	440.00
Moccasins, Cheyenne, Beaded, Green, Blue, White, Red, Tall Ankle, c.1880, 11 In.	1035.00
Moccasins, Cheyenne, Beaded, Sinew Sewn, Chevron Vamps, Rawhide Soles, c.1910, 11 In.	374.00
Moccasins, Cheyenne, Hide, Beaded, Hard Soles, Multicolor, Geometric, c.1885, 9 ½ In. .....*illus*	919.00
Moccasins, Cree, Buckskin, Cotton Trim, Lining, Cuffs, Geometric, Zigzag, 10 x 3 In.	1003.00
Moccasins, Crow, White Buckskin, Beaded, Leather Soles, Blue Ground, c.1970, 10 In.	259.00
Moccasins, Geometric Pattern, Green, Blue, Red, Child's, c.1920, 8 ¼ In.	452.00
Moccasins, Iroquois, Hide, Quilled & Beaded, c.1850, 10 In.	7050.00
Moccasins, Northern Plains, Beaded, White, Red, Black, Pink Chevrons, c.1910, 8 ¼ In.	400.00
Moccasins, Northern Plains, Flowers, Beaded, Lazy Stitch, Moosehide Trim, c.1970, Size 10	460.00
Moccasins, Osage, Buckskin, Puckered Vamps, Beaded Tabs, 1900s, 9 In.	978.00
Moccasins, Sioux Plains, Beaded, Green, White Dangle Beads, Red, Turquoise, c.1900, 7 In.	1500.00
Moccasins, Sioux, Beaded, Sinew Sewn, Lazy Stitch, Rawhide Soles, 1900, Child's, 5 In. ....*illus*	748.00
Moccasins, Sioux, Buckskin, Beaded, Sinew Sewn, Geometric, c.1950, 10 ½ In.	345.00
Moccasins, Sioux, Buckskin, Beaded, Sinew Sewn, Rawhide Sole, Child's, c.1900, Size 5	748.00
Moccasins, Sioux, Ceremonial, Beaded, c.1890, 10 In.	1074.00
Moccasins, Sioux, Elkhide, Quilled Flowers, Rawhide Soles, Sinew Sewn, c.1910, Size 10 ½	316.00
Moccasins, Sioux, Multicolor Beading, Tassels, Leather, 1800s, 10 In.	316.00
Moccasins, Ute, Sinew Sewn, Beads, Blue Ground, Rawhide Soles, c.1910, Size 9	316.00
Moccasins, Woodlands, Moose Hide, Beaded Vamps, Ankle Straps, c.1950, 10 In.	219.00
Model, Canoe, Birch Bark, Red Paint & Stitching, 56 x 10 ½ In.	575.00
Model, Canoe, Birch Bark, Wood Gunwale, Sawtooth Border, c.1900, 46 x 11 ¼ In.	978.00
Model, Canoe, Quileute, Sealing, Northwest Coast, 13 In.	170.00
Model, Totem Pole, Nootka, Alder, Acrobatic Figures, Whale, c.1825, 35 x 5 ½ In.	4600.00
Necklace, Navajo, Ghost Bead, Cedar, 36 In.	22.00
Necklace, Navajo, Silver Beaded Chain, Pendant, Coral Branch, Turquoise, 1970s, 24 In.	1265.00
Necklace, Navajo, Silver Beads, Bear Claw, Turquoise Stones, 1970s, 27 In.	748.00
Necklace, Navajo, Silver Squash Blossoms, Beads, Crescent Shape Pendant, c.1970, 22 In., 2 ¾ In.	489.00
Necklace, Navajo, Silver, Turquoise, Matrix, c.1950, 4-In. Pendant, 16 In.	431.00
Necklace, Navajo, Squash Blossom, Turquoise, 2 Silver Bead Strands, Mark Chee, c.1950, 15 In.	6463.00
Necklace, Navajo, Turquoise, Squash Blossom, Oval Cluster Pendant, c.1950, 28 x 3 ½ In.	518.00
Necklace, Pueblo, Beads, Heshi, Brown, Silver Cone Tips, 12 Strands, c.1980, 29 In.	288.00
Necklace, Pueblo, Disc Beads, Polished Turquoise, c.1980, 25 In.	460.00
Necklace, Pueblo, Olive Shell Heshi Beads, 9 Strands, c.1905, 30 In.	374.00
Necklace, Santo Domingo, Turquoise, Black Mosaic, Beads, Thunderbird Pendant, c.1930, 21 x 3 In.	403.00

Indian, Purse, Sioux, Beaded, Snap Closure, Lazy Stitch, Crosses, Triangles, c.1890, 5 ½ x 9 In. $863.00

Allard Auctions

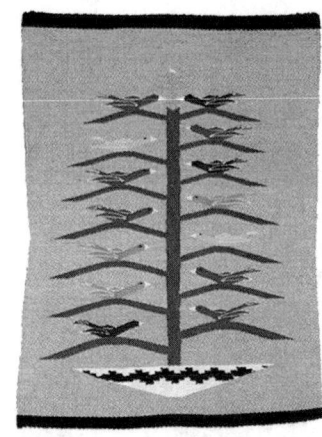

Indian, Rug, Navajo, Tree Of Life, Woven, Multicolor, Late 1900s, 31 x 23 In. $138.00

Allard Auctions

Indian, Snowshoes, Winnebago, Bentwood, Rawhide Webbing, Red Wool Tufts, 1900s, 33 In. $184.00

Allard Auctions

Indian, Snowshoes, Woodlands, Gut Weaving, Leather Straps, Painted Wood Frames, 42 In.
$402.00

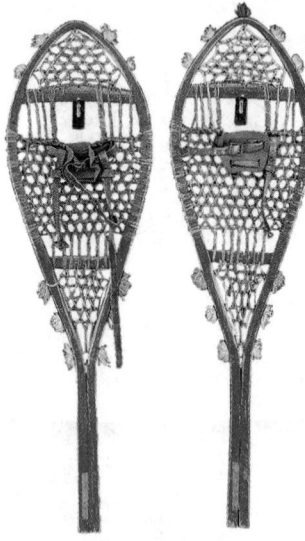

James D. Julia Inc.

Indian, Vase, Acoma, Squat, Geometric Design, Painted, Earth Tones, Signed, 6 ¾ In.
$244.00

Leslie Hindman Auctioneers

Indian, Vase, San Ildefonso, Blackware, Abstract Feather, Marie, 10 In.
$4288.00

Skinner, Inc.

Necklace, Silver, Squash Blossom Beads, Matching Pendant, Turquoise, 1960s, 26 In.	374.00
Necklace, Zuni, Fetish, Olivella Shell Heishi, Birds, 5 Strands, Tsikewa, c.1950, 15 In. ....*illus*	1998.00
Necklace, Zuni, Turquoise, 14 Squash Blossom, Beads, Crescent Pendant, c.1950, 23 x 2 In. ..	1093.00
Necklace, Zuni, Turquoise, Carved, Silver Leaf Tabs, Rolled Turquoise Heshi, c.1970, 22 x 2 In.	288.00
Necklace, Zuni, Turquoise, Squash Blossoms, Crowned Pendant, c.1964, 26 x 3 In.	345.00
Olla, Acoma, Flowers, Geometric, Red, Orange, Black, c.1900, 10 x 11 ¾ In. ....*illus*	1763.00
Olla, Acoma, Swollen, Pinched Neck, c.1900, 9 ¾ x 10 In.	1800.00
Olla, Hopi, Birds, Bees, Feathers, Geometric, Multicolor, Elva Nampeyo, 1980s, 6 ½ x 8 ½ In. .	633.00
Olla, Pueblo, Blackware, Snake, Rain Cloud, Matte Bands, Maria Martinez, c.1940, 9 In.	3840.00
Olla, San Juan, Blackware, c.1900, 11 ¼ In.	1541.00
Olla, Santo Domingo, Wide Mouth, Tan, Black Designs, V. Aguilar, c.1985, 14 x 11 In.	748.00
Olla, Zia, Bird, Flowers, c.1910, 11 ¼ In.	1778.00
Olla, Zia, Geometric, Pink, Black, c.1900, 11 In.	1007.00
Owl, Acoma, Multicolor, c.1960, 6 ½ x 5 In.	55.00
Paddle, Haida, Wooden, Carved, 1820s, 52 ½ In. ....*illus*	1870.00
Parfleche, Plains, Folded, Geometric, c.1910, 25 ½ x 13 In.	3680.00
Parfleche, Plains, Rawhide, Buckskin, Folded, Mineral Painted, c.1900, 21 x 15 In.	575.00
Pin, Hopi, Inlaid Snake, Signed, Charles Loloma, c.1985, 3 In. ....*illus*	4113.00
Pin, Iroquois, Boot Shape, Cotton, Turquoise, White & Red Beads, c.1900, 5 ½ x 3 In.	225.00
Pin, Zuni, Thunderbird, Jet, Shell Channel Work, c.1960, 2 ¾ x 2 ½ In.	184.00
Pin, Zuni, Turkey, Mother-Of-Pearl Inlay, Jet, Spiney Oyster, c.1960, 3 ½ x 1 ¾ In.	345.00
Pincushion, Iroquois, Glass Beaded, Wool, Cotton, Cat, Squirrel, Rabbit, c.1910, 10 ½ In.	705.00
Pincushion, Iroquois, Glass Beads, Velvet, Cotton, 3 Lobes, Bird, Beaver, c.1890, 11 In.	194.00
Pipe Bag, Cree, Felted Wool, Buckskin, Tab Closure, Fringe, Ties, Beaded Trim, 27 x 7 In.	472.00
Pipe Bag, Plateau, Flower Beaded Panel, Buckskin, Long Fringe, c.1995, Size 18 x 6 In.	460.00
Pipe Bag, Sioux, Geometric, Sinew, Beads, Fringe, Red, Yellow, White, Tan, c.1905, 26 x 8 In..	1380.00
Pipe Bowl, Cherokee, Steatite, Man's Head, Turban, Squirrel, c.1850, 3 In.	2585.00
Pipe, High Plains, Catlinite, Carved Buffalo, 3 ⅝ x 8 In.	711.00
Pipe, Plains, Catlinite Head, Wooden Stem, Quill Work, 30 In.	920.00
Pipe, Woodlands, Catlinite Bowl, Pewter Inlays, Carved Stem, Beads, c.1940s, 34 x 4 In.	575.00
Plaque, Hopi, Third Mesa, 4-Face Design, 1940s, 17 ½ In.	633.00
Plate, Pueblo, Blackware, Radiating Segments, Feathers, Ramona Gonzales, c.1960, 2 x 12 In.	660.00
Plate, San Ildefonso, Blue Corn, Geometric, Floral Slip, 1900s, 11 In.	2832.00
Plate, San Ildefonso, Feather, Bird Shape, Black Matte Glaze, Juanita Wo-Peen, c.1955, 3 x 15 In.	748.00
Pot, Pueblo, Blackware, Rounded Shoulder, Geometric, Maria Martinez, c.1980, 5 ½ x 6 ¾ In.	840.00
Pot, San Ildefonso, Blackware, Feather Border, c.1950, 4 ½ x 7 In.	1770.00
Pouch, Plateau, Flat Bag, Flower, Blue Ground, Beaded, Felt Trim, c.1910, 9 ¾ x 8 In.	316.00
Pouch, Plateau, Leather Flap, Flowers, Blue Ground, Beads, c.1950, 7 x 7 ½ In.	219.00
Pouch, Sioux, Buckskin, Quill Slats, Fringe, Beads, Brass Bells, c.1920, 14 x 7 In.	863.00
Pouch, Sioux, Hide, Beaded, 8 In.	533.00
Purse, Leather, Beaded Front, Shield Shape, Zippered Top, c.1930s, 5 x 6 In. ....*illus*	150.00
Purse, Sioux, Beaded, Snap Closure, Lazy Stitch, Crosses, Triangles, c.1890, 5 ½ x 9 In. ....*illus*	863.00
Rattle, Northwest Coast, Carved, Bear Figure On Front, 15 x 7 x 4 In.	863.00
Rattle, Northwest, Bird, Painted Wood Mask, Rich La Valle, c.1970, 10 x 4 ½ In.	863.00
Ring, Zuni, Turquoise, Silver, Horse Shape, c.1980	94.00
Rug, Navajo, 2 Diamond Pattern, Orange, Red, Yellow, c.1890, 87 x 58 In.	2875.00
Rug, Navajo, 2 Yeis, Cornstalk, Rainbow God, Natural Dye, Wool, Weaving, c.1960, 38 x 39 In.	460.00
Rug, Navajo, 4 Colors Klagetoh, Traditional Design, 31 x 42 In.	345.00
Rug, Navajo, Chinle, Diamond Bands, Amber Bands, Red Borders, 38 x 48 In.	118.00
Rug, Navajo, Crystal, Geometric, c.1940, 89 x 66 In.	1380.00
Rug, Navajo, Diamond, 2 Gray Hills, Earth Tones, Woven, c.1970, 60 x 36 In.	633.00
Rug, Navajo, Diamond, Brown, Cream, Crystal, Woven, c.1930, 59 x 36 In.	1840.00
Rug, Navajo, Diamond, Gray Ground, Multicolor, Wool, Woven, c.1940, 68 x 51 In.	2300.00
Rug, Navajo, Diamond, Storm Pattern, Tan, Brown, Gray, Woven, Susie Nez, c.1980, 64 x 38 In.	690.00
Rug, Navajo, Diamonds, Gray, Black, Pearl Henderson, c.1950, 52 x 31 In.	1725.00
Rug, Navajo, Diamonds, Serrated, Red Ground, Germantown, c.1900, 68 x 50 In.	2300.00
Rug, Navajo, Diamonds, Serrated, Red, Black, White, Gray, c.1930, 51 x 63 In.	3163.00
Rug, Navajo, Feathers, Bows, Arrows, Earth Tones, Woven, c.1940, 48 x 30 In.	690.00
Rug, Navajo, Klagetoh, Diamonds, Brown, Gray, Black, c.1950, 74 x 47 In.	489.00
Rug, Navajo, Klagetoh, Geometric, Blue, Black, Tan, 1980s, 53 x 35 In.	345.00
Rug, Navajo, Klagetoh, Line & Hook Designs, Gray Ground, Wool, c.1950, 48 x 36 ½ In.	690.00
Rug, Navajo, Red, White, Gray, Black, Geometric, 43 ½ x 32 ½ In.	311.00
Rug, Navajo, Sand Painting, Wool, Lucile Benally, c.1980, 48 x 47 In.	2185.00
Rug, Navajo, Storm, Crosses, Plants, Arrows, Gold Ground, c.1930, 60 x 31 In.	748.00
Rug, Navajo, Storm, Lightning Pattern, Black, White, Gray Ground, c.1950, 61 x 53 In.	1035.00
Rug, Navajo, Teec Nos Pos, Geometric, Figures, Earth Tones, c.1970, 69 x 80 In.	1955.00

Rug, Navajo, Tree Of Life, Woven, Multicolor, Late 1900s, 31 x 23 In. ....*illus*	138.00
Rug, Navajo, Valero Stars, Black, White, Gray, Crystal, Woven, Ruby Canton, c.1960, 37 x 55 In.	460.00
Rug, Navajo, Yei Figures, Earth Tones, Mae Williams, 1971, 31 x 42 In.	460.00
Rug, Navajo, Yei Figures, Multicolor, c.1970, 62 x 34 In.	303.00
Rug, Navajo, Yei Figures, Multicolor, c.1980, 42 x 30 In.	374.00
Saddle Blanket, Navajo, Soft Weave, Multicolor Stripes, Double, 32 x 64 In........................	110.00
Sash, Woodlands, Winnebago, Loom Beaded, c.1900, 32 x 2 ½ In.	275.00
Shirt, Blackfoot, Wool, Brass Beads, Thread Sewn, Fringe, c.1900, 25 x 44 In.	10575.00
Shirt, Seminole, Geometric, c.1900, 48 x 46 In.	2820.00
Skookum, Bully Good, With Papoose, Mohair Wigs, Composition Masks, 1930, 11 In.............	135.00
Sled Bag, Athabascan, Flap, Patchwork Sealskin, Bear, Moose Hide, Alaska, c.1905, 12 ½ x 12 In.	431.00
Snowshoes, Winnebago, Bentwood, Rawhide Webbing, Red Wool Tufts, 1900s, 33 In. ....*illus*	184.00
Snowshoes, Woodlands, Gut Weaving, Leather Straps, Painted Wood Frames, 42 In. ....*illus*	402.00
Spoon, Tlingit, Bears, Birds, Carved, Goat Horn, Alaska, c.1900, 12 x 12 In...........................	316.00
Spoon, Tlingit, Goat, Sheep Horn, Carved, Symbolic Figures, Brass Pins, c.1945, 18 x 2 ½ In.	1840.00
Staff, Kwakiutl, Eagle, Raven Figures, Carved, Painted, c.1980, 37 In...............................	403.00
Staff, Tlingit, Speaker's, Ceremonial, Cedar, Carved Figures, c.1940, 39 x 2 In......................	1495.00
Staff, Tonawanda Seneca, Hand Holding Face, Wrapped Snakes, Ferrule, 1841, 32 In...............	12925.00
Totem Pole, Haida, Bird, Wearing Shaman Headdress, c.1910, 17 x 3 ½ In.	3335.00
Totem Pole, Haida, Carved Argellite, Frog, Eagle, Raven, Bear, Man, c.1940, 15 In.	3450.00
Totem Pole, Haida, Figure, Black Argellite, Carved, McGuire, Skidegate, c.1970, 4 x 1 In........	173.00
Totem Pole, Northwest Coast, 3 Figures, Cedar, Carved, Painted, c.1920, 13 x 2 In..................	633.00
Totem Pole, Northwest Coast, Carved Bird, Faces, Paint, 1900s, 14 ¾ x 3 ½ In.....................	112.00
Totem Pole, Northwest Coast, Red Cedar, Man, Piggy Back Bear, c.1924, 13 x 2 In.................	288.00
Totem Pole, Tlingit, Carved Wood, Wooly Worm, Alaska, 71 In......................................	671.00
Tray, Apache, 5 Petal Flower, Upward Pointed Diamonds, Red Medallions, 4 x 17 In.	1035.00
Tunic, Northwest Coast, Button Blanket, Bear, Eagle Figures, Red Felt, 31 x 25 In.	460.00
Vase, Acoma, Oval Shape, Shoulder, Bird, Leaves, 10 In..	1736.00
Vase, Acoma, Squat, Geometric Design, Painted, Earth Tones, Signed, 6 ¾ In. ....*illus*	244.00
Vase, Hopi, Bird, Geometric, Brown, Tan, Cylindrical, Joy Navise, c.1960, 8 x 6 In.................	1035.00
Vase, Hopi, Olla, Birds, Geometric, Red, Yellow, Black, Frog Woman, P. Naha, c.1950, 10 In.....	1320.00
Vase, Pueblo, Painted Geometric Design, Slight Oval Shape, 1988, 6 In.............................	49.00
Vase, Round, Mottled Brown, Green Glaze, Grand Feu, Marked, 9 x 5 ¼ In..........................	2310.00
Vase, San Ildefonso, Blackware, Abstract Feather, Marie, 10 In. ....*illus*	4288.00
Vase, Santa Clara, Blackware, Bulbous, Carved Design, Signed, J.V. Gutierrez, 5 In.................	311.00
Vase, Santa Clara, Blackware, Bulbous, Figural Dog Handles, 11 ½ In..............................	978.00
Vase, Southwest, Marriage, Blackware, Double Spout, Strap Handles, 14 In., Pair	1298.00
Vest, Cheyenne, Geometric, Beaded, White, Lazy Stitch, Satin, c.1950, Man's, M/L, 21 x 19 In..	633.00
Vest, Cree, Quilled, Buckskin, Red Ribbon Trim, Leaf Symbols & Figures, 20 x 17 In...............	1380.00
Vest, Geometric, White, Lazy Stitch, Sinew Sewn, Beaded, Child's, c.1890, 18 x 16 In..............	1380.00
Vest, Menominee, Velvet, Flowers, Sequins, c.1884, Boy's, 16 x 12 In..............................	748.00
Vest, Plains, Lazy Stitch, Flags, Chiefs, Birds, Deer, Beaded, c.1985, Man's, XL	920.00
Vest, Plateau, Hide, Beaded, Multicolor, Animals, Flowers, Stars, Fringe, c.1920, 20 ½ In. .....*illus*	4740.00
Vest, Sioux, Beaded, Lazy Stitch, Sinew Sewn, Geometric, c.1890, Boy's, 18 x 16 In. ....*illus*	1380.00
Vest, Sioux, Beaded, Lazy Stitch, Stars, Flags, Geometric Symbols, Fringe, 20 x 18 In.............	4888.00
Vest, Sioux, Beaded, Sinew Sewn, Geometric, Striped Back, c.1890, Man's............................	3450.00
Vest, Sioux, Hide, Beaded, American Flags, c.1900, 14 x 17 In......................................	2520.00
Vest, Southern Plains, Beaded, Lazy Stitch, White, Red & Blue, c.1978, Man's, Medium	99.00
Wall Pocket, Tlingit, Apron Style, Eagles, Serpents, Stars, Black Wool, c.1970s, 20 x 10 In......	230.00
Wall Pocket, Tlingit, Sealskin Paw, Pouch, Beaded, c.1930s, 12 x 6 ½ In. ....*illus*	316.00
Watchband, Navajo, Silver Overlay, 5 Bisbee Stones, c.1970, 5 ½ x 1 In............................	288.00
Weaving, Navajo, Eyedazzler, Fringe, Germantown, c.1900, 53 x 35 ½ In. ....*illus*	1200.00
Weaving, Navajo, Peyote Bird, Wool, Cream, Brown & Black, 1930, 32 x 53 In.	2625.00
Weaving, Navajo, Stepped Cross, Whirling Log, Gray, Brown, c.1900, 85 ½ x 67 In. ....*illus*	711.00
Weaving, Navajo, Wool, Yei Figure, Ball Designs, Natural, Synthetic Dye, 1920s, 46 x 24 In. .....*illus*	652.00
Weaving, Yei, Wool, 6 Elongated Figures, Multicolor, c.1920, 40 x 73 ½ In. ....*illus*	470.00

INDIAN TREE is a china pattern that was popular during the last half of the nineteenth century. It was copied from earlier Indian textile patterns that were very similar. The pattern includes the crooked branch of a tree and a partial landscape with exotic flowers and leaves. Green, blue, pink, and orange were the favored colors used in the design. Coalport, Spode, Johnson Brothers, and other firms made this pottery.

Bell, Loop Handle, England, 6 In.	24.00
Cake Plate, Handle, Square, 10 ¼ x 10 ¼ In..	50.00
Coffeepot, Footed, Coalport..	100.00
Creamer, Coalport...	36.00

Indian, Vest, Plateau, Hide, Beaded, Multicolor, Animals, Flowers, Stars, Fringe, c.1920, 20 ½ In.
$4740.00

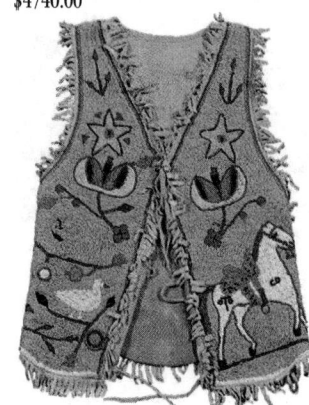

Skinner, Inc.

Indian, Vest, Sioux, Beaded, Lazy Stitch, Sinew Sewn, Geometric, c.1890, Boy's, 18 x 16 In.
$1380.00

Allard Auctions

Indian, Wall Pocket, Tlingit, Sealskin Paw, Pouch, Beaded, c.1930s, 12 x 6 ½ In.
$316.00

Allard Auctions

Indian, Weaving, Navajo, Eyedazzler, Fringe, Germantown, c.1900, 53 x 35 ½ In.
$1200.00

Cowan's Auctions

Indian, Weaving, Navajo, Stepped Cross, Whirling Log, Gray, Brown, c.1900, 85 ½ x 67 In.
$711.00

Skinner, Inc.

Indian, Weaving, Navajo, Wool, Yei Figure, Ball Designs, Natural, Synthetic Dye, 1920s, 46 x 24 In.
$652.00

Skinner, Inc.

Cup & Saucer, Aynsley	38.00
Cup & Saucer, Hammersley, c.1965	22.00
Cup & Saucer, Johnson Brothers	10.00
Cup & Saucer, Johnson Brothers, Demitasse	10.00
Eggcup, Double, Spode, 3 ⅝ In.	65.00
Grill Plate, Booths Silicon China, England, c.1950, 10 ½ In.	35.00
Mug, Spode	110.00
Plate, Bread & Butter, Salem China, 6 ½ In.	8.00
Platter, Myott, Staffordshire, 12 In.	9.00
Platter, Oval, Scalloped, Red Trim, Spode, 13 In.	120.00
Saucer, Johnson Brothers, 5 ¾ In.	4.00
Serving Bowl, Oval, Scalloped Rim, Coalport, 8 x 3 In.	34.00
Soup, Dish, Myott, Staffordshire, c.1936, 8 In.	8.00
Soup, Dish, Salem China, 8 ⅜ In.	9.00
Tea Set, Coalport, Miniature, 15 Piece	150.00
Teapot, Lid, Coalport	200.00
Teapot, Lid, Ribbed, Spode, 6 ⅞ In.	280.00

INKSTANDS were made to be placed on a desk. They held some type of container for ink, and possibly a sander, a pen tray, a pen, a holder for pounce, and even a candle to melt the sealing wax. Inkstands date to the eighteenth century and have been made of silver, copper, ceramics, and glass. Additional inkstands may be found in these and other related categories.

Brass, Neogothic, Round Inkwell, Leaf Pattern Lid, Tracery, c.1890, 13 x 5 In.	153.00
Brass, Well Inset, Embossed, Art Nouveau, 4 ¾ x 13 ¼ In.	127.00
Bronze, Agate, Pen Tray, Round Ball Shape, Ring Handles, Filigree, Overlay, 4 x 6 In.	170.00
Bronze, Bust Of Nymph, Flowing Hair, Pansy, Hinged Lid, Art Nouveau, 10 In.	2726.00
Bronze, Bust, Woman, Red Marble Base, Pen Tray, Oak Leaves, Flowers, Hinged Lid, 10 x 15 In.	396.00
Bronze, Casket Shape, Urns, Pen Tray, Footed, Lid, c.1900, 6 x 9 ½ In.	540.00
Bronze, Dog, Hinged Head, Cobalt Glass Pot, 5 ¾ In.	337.00
Bronze, Gilt, Louis XV Style, Scallop Shell Base, 2 Wells, Putto Holding Urn, 1800s, 14 In.	250.00
Bronze, Gilt, Swags, Ring Handle, Paw Feet, Clear Well, Sander, 1900s, 8 In.	354.00
Bronze, Marble, Voltaire, Robes, Hinged Lid, Front Pen Well, 16 In.	770.00
Bronze, Owl Shape, Victorian Style, Hinged Head, Glass Inkwell, c.1900, 4 x 9 ½ In.	625.00
Bronze, Painted, Tree Trunk, Squirrel Smoking Pipe, Hinged Lid, Austria, c.1900, 3 ¼ In.	1007.00
Bronze, Prone U.S. Marshall, Aiming Gun, Lidded Well Base, Marble, 4 ½ x 16 In.	555.00
Bronze, Rooster, On Rock, Leaves, Acorns, Wheat, 2 Wells, A. Marionnet, 10 x 14 In.	508.00
Bronze, Smelter, Wearing Apron, Gloved Arm To Head, Swivel Front Lid, 9 ¾ x 6 In.	380.00
Cut Glass, Silver Mounted Bottles, Box, Pen Tray, c.1829, 12 In.	717.00
Famille Rose, Women, Birds, Flowers, Bamboo, Characters, 19th Century, 5 x 3 x 7 In.	300.00
Gilt Bronze, Dolphin, Cast Urn, Glass Liner, Bronze Tray, France, 1800s, 10 x 6 In.	3540.00
Ivory, Faux Chryselephantine, Fashionable Woman, Flowers, Umbrella, Descending Steps, 8 x 9 In.	492.00
Pewter, Lidded Pot, Drawer, 4 Quill Holes, c.1780	250.00
Porcelain, 2 Doves, Blue Wings, Flowers, 4 Wells	68.00
Porcelain, Gilt, Louis XV Style, 3 Tiers, Pen Rest, Shell Shape Recess, Late 1800s, 6 x 12 In.	250.00
Pressed Glass, Silver Plated Stand, Drawer, Hinged Cap, 4 ½ In.	45.00
Pug Dog Head, Plated Cast Metal, Hinged, Bib Desk Tray, Glass Eyes, 3 ¾ In.	215.00
Redware, Heart Shape, Green, Brown, Yellow, Hearts Design, Pa.	28750.00
Silver Plate, Center Quill Urn, Leaf Feet, 2 Wells, Josiah Adams & Sons, c.1890	288.00
Silver Plate, Pen Rest, Ball Feet, Roberts & Belk, c.1880, 6 x 4 In.	295.00
Silver, 4 Sections, Glass Sander & Well, Scrolls, Gadroon, Aldridge, Stamper, c.1759, 8 In.	711.00
Silver, Oblong, Inkwell, Fitted Sander, Scroll Feet, Germany, c.1728, 8 ½ In.	1185.00
Silver, Pierced Gallery, 4 Paw Feet, 2 Cut Glass Ink Pots, Dated 1898, 10 x 7 In.	1410.00
Silver, Rectangular, Lidded Wells, Glass Interior, Ball Feet, JHS Mark, 1923, 11 In.	1541.00
Silver, Rectangular Tray, 2 Glass Inkwells, Pen Supports, 1938, 8 x 5 In.	325.00
Silver, Reticulated Gallery, Shell, Leaf, C-Scroll, Lift Lid, Monogram, Gorham, 7 ¾ In.	450.00
Silver, Rococo Style, Shell & Scrolls, Pierced, Table Gong, Figural Finial, c.1895, 7 x 12 In.	885.00
Walnut, Shaped Plaque Base, Pierced Back, Recessed Pen Trough, 2 Glass Wells, 12 In.	154.00

INKWELLS, of course, held ink. Ready-made ink was first made about 1836 and was sold in bottles. The desk inkwell had a narrow hole so the pen would not slip inside. Inkwells were made of many materials, such as pottery, glass, pewter, and silver. Look in these categories for more listings of inkwells.

Aluminum, Crab Shape, Baltimore Brewmaster's Convention, 1907, 6 x 5 In.	255.00
Brass, Flowers, Butterfly Finial, 6 x 4 In.	35.00

Brass, Traveling, Hinged, Latch, 1900, 2 x 2 x 1 ¾ In.	150.00
Bronze, 2 Owlets, Branch, Rhubarb Leaf, Gilt Glass Ink Bottles, 1800s, 7 x 18 In.	1230.00
Bronze, Bird On Nest, 19th Century, 3 ½ x 5 In.	354.00
Bronze, Gilt, Bust Of Napoleon, 2 Ink Pots, Marble Stand, Scroll Feet, c.1885, 12 ½ In.	399.00
Bronze, Lion's Head, Red Eyes, Slate Base, Milk Glass Well, c.1870, 4 x 3 ½ In.	144.00
Bronze, Louis XV Style, Landscape, Base, 5 ½ x 10 ½ x 12 ½ In.	100.00
Bronze, Rat Hiding Well In Stack Of Books, Soapstone Base, 4 x 7 In.	424.00
Cast Metal, Boy Pushing Hand Cart, Barrel Has Well, Sander, Black, 6 x 7 In.	147.00
Cut Glass, Jar Shape, Brass Band, c.1860, 4 ½ x 3 In.	324.00
Cut Glass, Silver Top, 5 ¼ x 3 ½ In.	825.00
Enamel, Bronze, 2 Lovers, Seated In Garden, Signed, France	480.00
Figural, Black Man, Bust, Hinged Head, Bottle, Spelter, 5 ¾ x 5 In.	489.00
Glass, Bull's-Eye, Square, Blue Cut To Clear, Rayed Base, Top, Square, 5 In.	225.00
Glass, Green, Waisted, Saratoga Glassworks, c.1850, 5 In.	288.00
Glass, Silver Plate, Hinged Cover, Faceted, c.1870, 4 ½ x 3 In.	120.00
Glass, Swirls, Brockwitz Glass, Germany, c.1930	45.00
Hercules, Wrestling Snake, Marble Base, 3 Paw Feet, 6 ½ In.	248.00
Inkstand, Napoleon III, Goat, Gilt, Patinated Bronze, Sander, Penholders, 5 ¼ x 4 ¾ In.	359.00
Jade, Carved Oval Plaque, Figures Amongst Leaves, Urn Shape Well, Stylus, 1900s, 6 In.	200.00
Maiden, Resting In Vessel, Holding Pitcher, Signed H. Gauquie, 1800s, 5 x 7 In.	431.00
Nickel Plate, Gun Shape, Milk Glass Reservoir, 8 x 2 x 5 In.	280.00
Paperweight Base, Millefiori, Red, White, Blue, Bell Shape, Roll Rim, Dome Stopper, 7 In.	460.00
Pewter, Native American, Bust, 4 x 4 x 4 ½ In. ....*illus*	165.00
Pewter, Round, Hammered, Organic, A. Knox, Liberty & Co., 1905, 4 ½ x 3 In.	840.00
Porcelain, Famille Verte, Ormolu Mounts, Corner Holes, Flower Finial, 1800s, 4 ¾ In.	590.00
Porcelain, Imari Style, Blue, Red, Gilt, Pinched Sides, Drip Pan, c.1900, 4 In.	118.00
Porcelain, Phrenology, Head Shape, Gilt Labeling, Brain's Regions, 1800s, 5 ½ In. ....*illus*	288.00
Porcelain, Snail Shape, Imari Pattern, 3 ½ x 6 In.	345.00
Pottery, Green Over Blue Matte Glaze, Lid, Cone Finial, Square, 1909, 3 In.	1035.00
Silver, Cut Glass, Rococo Style Repousse Lid, Bulbous, Spread Foot, 1894, 6 In.	650.00
Silver, Elephant Head, Monkey On Top, Stamped, Meriden, 4 x 6 ½ x 4 In. ....*illus*	1364.00
Silver, Helmet Shape, Acorns, Oak Leaves, Royal Crown Badge, England, c.1877	6192.00
Spelter, Camel, Resting, Hinged Saddle, c.1900, 5 ¾ In.	356.00
Spelter, Pug Dog Head, Turned Wood Base, 4 In.	147.00
Tortoiseshell, Red, Cased, Oval, Hinged Lid, England, c.1800, 1 ⅝ In.	980.00
Wood, Ivory, Skull Shape, Serpent, Toad, Japan, Early 1900s, 3 ⅜ In.	1599.00
Wood, Treen, Black, Red, c.1800, 2 ¾ x 3 ¾ In.	441.00

INSULATORS of glass or pottery have been made for use on telegraph or telephone poles since 1844. Thousands of different styles of insulators have been made. Most common are those of clear or aqua glass; most desirable are the threadless types made from 1850 to 1870.

Boston Bottle Works, Green Aqua, Hexagonal Dome, Tapered Skirt, 4 Threads, 4 In.	497.00
No Name, Yellow Green, Threadless, Wire Groove, c.1860, 3 ⅝ In.	176.00
S.P. & Co., Stoneware, Red, Glossy, 2 In.	77.00

IRISH BELLEEK, *see Belleek category.*

IRON is a metal that has been used by man since prehistoric times. It is a popular metal for tools and decorative items like doorstops that need as much weight as possible. Items are listed here or under other appropriate headings, such as Bookends, Doorstop, Kitchen, Match Holder, or Tool. The tool that is used for ironing clothes, an iron, is listed in the Kitchen category under Iron and Sadiron.

Ashtray, Brothel, Reclining Woman, Fan, Painted Black, White, Cast, 6 ½ x 5 In.	55.00
Bell Ringer, Frog, Glass Eyes, Open Mouth, Impressed, R. E. Rich, 6 ½ In.	1150.00
Boot Jack, Bull Dog, John Harvin Moore, Box, Houston, Tex., 8 ½ x 3 ¼ In.	112.00
Boot Jack, Woman's Form, Cast, Marked, 8 ½ In.	47.00
Bust, Woman, Classical, Cast, 28 ½ x 16 In.	431.00
Candle Snuffer, Mahogany Handle, Carved Snake Head, Bone Eyes, Flowers, Leaves, c.1800, 8 In.	2252.00
Canteen, Drum Type, Threaded Neck, Stamped, 4 ¼ In.	11.00
Cross, Cemetery, Cast, France, 1800s, 61 ½ In.	420.00
Family Crest, Double Eagle, Lion, Crossed Axes, c.1900, 13 ¾ x 12 ¾ In.	173.00
Figure, Bear, On All Fours, Growling, Late 1800s, 8 x 16 In.	563.00
Figure, Cat, Resting, Hubley c.1910, 5 ¾ x 10 ¼ In.	61.00
Figure, Court Official, Standing, Robe, Cap, Clasped Hands, Chinese, 1800s, 6 ¾ In.	215.00
Figure, Dog, Sniffing, Signed Anne Law, c.1970, 29 x 34 In.	155.00

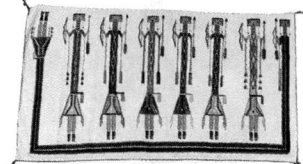

Indian, Weaving, Yei, Wool, 6 Elongated Figures, Multicolor, c.1920, 40 x 73 ½ In.
$470.00

Cowan's Auctions

Inkwell, Pewter, Native American, Bust, 4 x 4 x 4 ½ In.
$165.00

Showtime Auction Services

Inkwell, Porcelain, Phrenology, Head Shape, Gilt Labeling, Brain's Regions, 1800s, 5 ½ In.
$288.00

Leland Little Auction

Inkwell, Silver, Elephant Head, Monkey On Top, Stamped, Meriden, 4 x 6 ½ x 4 In.
$1364.00

Rago Arts & Auction Center

Iron, Gate Weight, Sun Face, Cast, Stand, c.1790, 12 ½ x 9 In. $8295.00

Skinner, Inc.

Iron, Plaque, Theodore Roosevelt Bust, Applied Patina, James Earl Fraser, 1920, 13 x 10 In. $575.00

Leland Little Auction

Iron, Windmill Weight, Rooster, Elgin Wind Power & Pump Co., c.1880, 19 x 18 In. $1185.00

Skinner, Inc.

Ironstone, Pitcher, Presentation, Railroad House, Con Daly. Prop., Purple, Gilt, c.1885, 9 In. $316.00

James D. Julia Inc.

Figure, Dog, Terrier, Hubley, 1 ¾ x 1 ½ In.	35.00
Figure, Eagle, Outstretched Wings, Rocky Plinth, Gilded, 28 x 34 In., Pair	550.00
Figure, Face, Base Mounted, 26 ½ x 8 ½ In., Pair	677.00
Figure, Guanyin, Seated, Flame Shape Halo, Long Robe, Round Foot, Korea, 14 In.	150.00
Figure, Hitchhiker, Thumb Up, Yellow, Brown Paint, 3 ½ In.	57.00
Figure, Horse Head, Mounted On Plaque, 1900s, 30 x 15 In.	650.00
Figure, Horse, Painted Brown, Black Mane, Tail, Walnut Base, 8 In.	47.00
Figure, Hunting Hound, Seated, Black Paint, Oval Stand, 36 x 34 In., Pair	1400.00
Figure, Pheasant, Orange, Yellow, Brown, Paint, 2 ¾ In.	136.00
Finial, Urn Shape, Scrolled Base, 16 x 8 In., Pair	225.00
Gate Weight, Sun Face, Cast, Stand, c.1790, 12 ½ x 9 In. ....*illus*	8295.00
Handcuffs, Engraved Bernville, Peter Derr, Berks County, c.1800	2309.00
Hanger, Standing, Adjustable, Heart Shape, Hooks, Tripod Base, 1800s, 33 In.	441.00
Lamp, Oil Can, Banded, Square Handle, Fluted Spout, Turned Wood Stopper, 4 Gal., 21 In.	130.00
Plaque, Theodore Roosevelt Bust, Applied Patina, James Earl Fraser, 1920, 13 x 10 In. ...*illus*	575.00
Safe, Chest Shape, Black, Painted, Milner Coat-Of-Arms Medallion, Key, 13 ½ x 20 In.	531.00
Safe, Mosler Safe Co., Black Door, Painted Landscape, Combination, M 417, c.1910, 32 x 20 In.	748.00
Shade Pull, Mayflower Ship Shape, Double-Sided, 1930s, 2 x 1 ⅝ In.	75.00
Shield, Bronzed, Classical Figures, Battle Scene, Embossed 1800s, 26 ½ In.	889.00
Shield, Half Helmet, 16th Century Style, Cast, Tear Shape, Embossed, Bronze, 37 In.	531.00
Shooting Gallery Birds, Revere Beach, Mass., 1920s, 4 x 3 In., Pair	66.00
Statue, Saint, Multicolor Paint, Hollow, Label N. Serf. Manufacturers, 70 x 20 In.	1495.00
Urn, Lid, Oval Finial, Swags, 22 In., Pair	900.00
Utensil Rack, Jamb Style, Wrought, 5 Hooks, Riveted Demilune, Spade Points, 9 x 8 In.	142.00
Utensil Rack, Jamb Style, Wrought, 5 Hooks, Riveted Scrolls, Heart, 12 ¾ In.	153.00
Vase, Komei Inlays, Landscape, Phoenix, Bulbous, Japan, Late 1800s, 5 In.	674.00
Weight, Clasped Hands, 1800s, 9 ½ In.	889.00
Windmill Weight, Bird, Painted, Official Emblem G.O.F.P.O.P., 12 In.	900.00
Windmill Weight, Bull, Red Paint, Stand, Cast, 26 x 18 ½ In.	776.00
Windmill Weight, Crescent, Eclipse, 10 ½ In.	230.00
Windmill Weight, Horse, Short Tail, Black Paint, Stand, 18 x 16 In.	345.00
Windmill Weight, Horse, Silver Paint, Dempster Mill Mfg., c.1910, 16 ½ In.	323.00
Windmill Weight, Rooster, Black Paint, Hummer, Cast, 10 x 8 ½ In.	460.00
Windmill Weight, Rooster, Elgin Wind Power & Pump Co., c.1880, 19 x 18 In. ....*illus*	1185.00
Windmill Weight, Star, Building, Cast, 11 ½ In.	23.00

IRONSTONE china was first made in 1813. It gained its greatest popularity during the mid-nineteenth century. The heavy, durable, off-white pottery was made in white or was decorated with any of hundreds of patterns. Much flow blue pottery was made of ironstone. Some of the decorations were raised. Many pieces of ironstone are unmarked, but some English and American factories included the word *Ironstone* in their marks. Additional pieces may be listed in other categories, such as Chelsea Grape, Chelsea Sprig, Flow Blue, Gaudy Ironstone, Mason's Ironstone, Moss Rose, Staffordshire, and Tea Leaf Ironstone.

Bowl, Footed, Rolled Rim, Round Pedestal Foot, Ivory Colored, Marked, 7 ½ x 11 ½ In.	118.00
Cup & Saucer, King's Rose, Melon Shapes, Green	51.00
Footbath, Gilded Rope Twist Handles, Hamlet Scene, Flowers, Oval, 1890s, 9 x 22 In.	225.00
Footbath, White, Gold Band, Applied Handles, Oval, 8 ½ x 19 In.	220.00
Mold, Elephant, Standing, Curled Trunk, Reeded Border, Oval, Late 1800s, 7 In.	58.00
Pitcher & Basin, Prunus Decoration, Blue & White, Royal Crownford, 12-In. Pitcher	74.00
Pitcher, Blue Floral Spray, Octagonal Body, 5 ½ In.	12.00
Pitcher, Oak Pattern, Brown Handle, 6 In.	59.00
Pitcher, Patriotic, Fraternal Vignettes, William S. Ping, Clark Servering & Co., 7 ¼ x 9 In.	1121.00
Pitcher, Presentation, Inscribed Mollie, Sailboat, Seagulls, Bristol Slip Glaze, c.1900, 8 ½ In.	403.00
Pitcher, Presentation, Railroad House, Con Daly. Prop., Purple, Gilt, c.1885, 9 In. ....*illus*	316.00
Pitcher, White, Ribbed, Leaf Terminal Handle, Pankhurst, 3 In.	75.00
Plate, Blue Transfer, Abbey On Water Center & Border, 10-Sided Rim, Marked, 8 ¼ In.	12.00
Plate, Buffalo Ranch Oklahoma, Western Scenes, 1950s, 10 In.	35.00
Plate, Chinoiserie, Rippled Rim, Gold Trim, Marked, Kirkee, J. Meir & Son, 10 ¼ In. ......*illus*	24.00
Plate, Mauve Transfer, Castle, Canal & Water Fountain, Harbor Scene, 10-Sided Rim, 9 In.	12.00
Plate, School House Pattern, Blue, Red House, Yellow Roof, 8 ½ In.	201.00
Platter, Black Transfer, River, Houses, Octagonal, Marked, John Alcock, 11 x 15 In.	90.00
Platter, Blue & White, Columbia Pattern, Rectangular, Angled Corners, 18 In.	69.00
Platter, Blue & White, Flowers, Pagoda, c.1850, 21 In.	489.00
Platter, Corinth, Blue Transfer, Flowers, Leaf Rim, G. Phillips, Longport, Octagonal, 20 x 16 In.	35.00
Platter, Corinthia Pattern, Purple Transfer, E. Challinor, Octagonal, 9 x 12 In.	51.00
Platter, Meat, Well, Tree, Orange, Blue, F. Morley & Co., 21 x 17 In.	288.00

Platter, Pomona, Classical Women, Black Transfer, 1800s, 12 x 15 In.	61.00
Sauceboat, Blue Transfer, Molded Handle, Shell Mount, Pedestal Foot, Marked, 8 ¾ In.	47.00
Soup, Dish, Flowers, Red, Blue, Green, Scalloped Rim, 1900s, 10 ½ In., Set Of 10.	58.00
Teapot, Paneled Grape, White, Embossed Leaf, Grapes, c.1860, 11 In.	310.00
Teapot, Wheat In The Meadow, White, Embossed Flowers, Powell & Bishop, c.1860, 10 In.	325.00
Tureen, Cover, Stand, Blue, Iron Red, Gilding, Flowers, Chinese, 1900s, 11 x 15 In.	738.00
Urn, Domed Cover, Gilt Lion, Leaves, Blossoms, Hexagonal, Baluster Base, 16 In., Pair	2400.00
Vase, Swirl, Baluster Shape, B.B. Craig, Vale, N.C., 13 In.	649.00

ISPANKY figurines were designed by Laszlo Ispanky, who began his American career as a designer for Cybis Porcelains. In 1966, he established his own studio in Pennington, New Jersey; since 1976, he has worked for Goebel of North America. He works in stone, wood, or metal, as well as porcelain. The first limited edition figurines were issued in 1966.

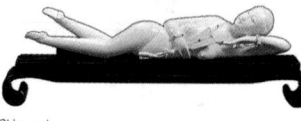

Figurine, Ballet Couple, 12 ¾ In.	225.00
Figurine, Bust, Hair Up, Blue Bow, 9 In.	300.00
Figurine, Bust, Moses, Holding 10 Commandments, 12 ½ In.	895.00
Figurine, Dog, Cat Up Tree, 9 ½ In.	650.00
Figurine, Girl, Holding Wheat, 9 In.	350.00
Figurine, Girl, Seated, Painting, 1967, 10 ½ In.	650.00
Figurine, Nude, With Baby, 10 ¼ In.	300.00
Figurine, Otter Couple, Holding Hands, 13 In.	1950.00
Figurine, Young Girl, Gathering Flowers, Holding Hat, 9 In.	250.00
Figurine, Young Lady, Sitting On Stool, Wrapped In Drape, 11 In.	575.00
Vase, Seminudes, Raised, Panels, 11 In.	200.00

IVORY from the tusk of an elephant is thought by many to be the only true ivory. To most collectors, the term *ivory* also includes such natural materials as walrus, hippopotamus, or whale teeth or tusks, and some of the vegetable materials that are of similar texture and density. Other ivory items may be found in the Scrimshaw and Netsuke categories. Collectors should be aware of the recent laws limiting the buying and selling of elephant ivory and scrimshaw.

African Elephant Tusk, Base, c.1950, 68 x 58 In., Pair	11950.00
Apple, Open Worm Holes, Figures, Landscape Scene, Painted, 2 In.	460.00
Ball, Carved, Intertwined Elephants, Cats, Gilt Painted Eyes, 2 ½ In.	761.00
Basket, Dome Cover, Panel Sides, Peach Finials, Carved Bail Handle, Chinese, c.1805, 5 ¾ In.	1659.00
Belt Slide, Carved, Dragon, Pearl Of Wisdom, Rings, Square, 1 ½ x 1 ⅝ In.	522.00
Belt, Link, Square, 30 In.	71.00
Boat, Carved, Chinese, 3 ½ x 12 ½ In.	2360.00
Boat, Dragon, Horns, Scales, Waves, Tiered Pavilion, Mast, Wood Stand, 1900s, 25 x 29 In.	7995.00
Boat, Junk, Pierced, Carved, Flags, White, Wood Stand, Chinese, 3 ¾ x 4 ¼ In.	230.00
Boat, Phoenix Head Bow, Wings, Mast, 2 Sails, Movable Rudder, c.1910, 17 ½ x 18 In.	3690.00
Box, Applied Lizard Grip, White, 7 In.	565.00
Box, Carved, Flowers, Bud Finial, Round, 3 ½ x 4 In.	460.00
Box, Cover, Carved Dragon, Serpent, Removable Medallion, Round, 2 x 4 In.	173.00
Box, Cover, Carved, Flowers, Cylindrical, Round Wood Stand, 7 In.	1130.00
Box, Cover, Carved, Tree Branch, Flowers, Round, Signed, Yoshi Nobu, Japan, 2 ⅛ x 3 In.	115.00
Box, Cover, Elephant Tusk, Round, Dragon Supporting Sphere, Japan, Late 1800s, 4 ¼ In.	1600.00
Box, Incised Branches, Peony, Landscape, Text, Round, Chinese, 1 ½ x 2 In.	4148.00
Box, Lid, Carved, Shaped Medallions, Flowers, Rectangular, Chinese, 1800s, 10 In.	1554.00
Box, Tobacco, Figures, Courtyard, Hot Air Balloon, 3 ½ In.	403.00
Brush Holder, Bitong, Phoenix Birds, Chinese, 5 ¾ In.	657.00
Brush Holder, Carved, Dragons, Animals, Landscape, Oval, Wood Base, Chinese, 5 ½ x 3 ¾ In.	3163.00
Brush Holder, Carved, Serpent, Pierced, Wood Base, Chinese, 5 In.	460.00
Brush Holder, Dragons, Flaming Pearl, Clouds, Waves, Keyfret Border, Cylindrical, 8 In., Pair	2271.00
Brush Holder, Figures, Garden, Scroll, Leaf Openwork Foot, Cylindrical, Chinese, 1800s, 4 ¾ x 3 In.	4740.00
Brush Holder, Women Picking Flowers, Children, Man, Monkey, Cylindrical, Japan, 9 ½ In.	2032.00
Brushpot, Carved, Dragon, Cylindrical, Signed, 6 ¼ In.	2280.00
Brushpot, Carved, Figure, Cylindrical, Wood Base, Japan, 7 ½ In.	840.00
Brushpot, Carved, Figures, Lappet Border, Dragons, Flaming Pearl, Pierced, Wood Stand, 10 In.	4216.00
Brushpot, Figures, Scrolling Clouds, Silver Lid, Chrysanthemum Finial, 6 In.	1342.00
Bust, African Woman, Headpiece, Round Base, Carved, 9 ½ x 3 ½ In.	546.00
Bust, African Woman, Wearing Headpiece, Round Wood Base, 6 x 2 In.	60.00
Bust, Buddha, Ivory, Carved, Painted Eyes, Hair, Green Forehead Stone, Wood Base, Japan, 7 In.	546.00
Bust, Guanyin, Crown, Buddha Resting Atop Her Head, Wooden Base, 6 In.	823.00
Bust, Socrates, Cylindrical Column, Square Base, Late 1800s, 7 ½ In.	531.00
Bust, Woman, Carved, Glass Stand, African Elephant Tusk, 63 x 18 In.	920.00

Ironstone, Plate, Chinoiserie, Rippled Rim, Gold Trim, Marked, Kirkee, J. Meir & Son, 10 ¼ In.
$24.00

Conestoga Auction Co., Inc.

Ivory, Doctor's Doll, Nude Woman, Reclining, Holding Fan, Inlaid Necklace, Chinese, 16 In.
$3200.00

Skinner, Inc.

Ivory, Figurine, Boy, On Buffalo, Base, Japan, 6 ⅜ In.
$1098.00

Leslie Hindman Auctioneers

Ivory, Figurine, Goddess, Prunus, Insects, Rosewood Stand, Lotus Pedestal, 1700s, 25 ⅜ In.
$50363.00

Skinner, Inc.

Ivory, Figurine, Hotei, Sack On Back, Auspicious Symbols, Scroll, Chinese, 7 ¾ In.

$504.00

Skinner, Inc.

Ivory, Figurine, Immortal, Standing, Holding Branch, Long Robes, Headdress, Chinese, 12 In.

$1135.00

Sloans & Kenyon

Ivory, Figurine, Lan Tsai Ho, Standing, Robe, Flowers, Painted, Gilt, Chinese, 1800s, 12 In.

$1593.00

Skinner, Inc.

Bust, Woman, Vertical Braid, African Elephant Carving, Wood Base, 11 In.	316.00
Cabinet, Lacquer, Gold, Red, Black, 3 Interior Drawers, Japan, 3 ½ x 3 ¼ In.	2530.00
Candy Dish, 3 Legs, Scalloped Edge, Riveted Handle, Rotating Bowl, Hexagonal, 7 x 8 In.	1410.00
Card Case, Carved, Birds, Flowers, Chinese, 3 ¼ In.	717.00
Card Case, Carved, Cross, Enclosing Court Scene, Chinese, 1800s, 4 ½ In.	657.00
Card Case, Carved, Figural Landscape, Rectangular, Canton, 1800s, 4 In.	900.00
Card Case, Carved, Figures, Buildings, Leaves, 4 x 2 In.	1159.00
Card Case, Carved, Figures, Landscape, Leaves, Chinese, 4 x 3 In.	2480.00
Card Case, Carved, Figures, Trees, Pagoda, Rectangular, Chinese, 1800s, 4 ³⁄₁₆ In.	956.00
Card Case, Figural Scenes, Trees, Pagodas, Oval Medallion, 1800s, 4 x 3 In.	767.00
Card Case, Figures, Courtyard, Flowering Branches, Chinese, 19th Century, 4 x 2 x ¾ In.	2400.00
Card Case, Figures, Flowers, Shaped Rectangular, 1800s, 5 In.	3466.00
Carte De Visite, Chinese, Figures, Landscape, 1800s, 3 ¾ x 2 ⅛ In.	2963.00
Case, Playing Cards, Rectangular, Flag, Steamboat, Leaf Border, 3 x 6 In.	248.00
Censer, Animal Mask, Ring Handles, Dragons, Geometric, 3 Claw & Ball Feet, 12 ¼ In.	3904.00
Censer, Cover, Dragon, Clouds, C-Shape Handles, Domed Top, Foo Dog Finial, Tripod, 1900s, 12 In.	2629.00
Censer, Dragons, Flaming Pearl, Dome Lid, Ring Handles, Tripod, Chinese, c.1905, 7 In., Pair	2607.00
Censer, Foo Dog Shape, Lid, Pierced Craving, Curled Tail, 4 Squat Legs, 6 In.	1464.00
Censer, Lid, 2 Foo Dog Finial, Ring Handles, Beast Masks, Dragon Handles, 3 Legs, 12 In.	4216.00
Censer, Lid, Foo Dogs, 4 Rings, Dragon Masks, Handles, Tripod Wood Base, Chinese, 1900s, 9 x 8 In.	3884.00
Charm, Good Luck, Gourd Shape, Leaf Tendrils, Hanging Fruit, Scrolling, 4 In.	92.00
Cigar Tip Cutter, Tusk Shape, 7 In.	165.00
Cigarette Holder, Dragonfly, Flaming Pearl, 1920s, 2 ⅝ In.	85.00
Crab Cage, Crabs, White, Carved, Wood Base, 7 ¼ In.	1610.00
Doctor's Doll, Nude Woman, Arm Across Chest, Fitted Stand, Chinese, 8 In.	978.00
Doctor's Doll, Nude Woman, Reclining On Wood Bench, 9 In.	2390.00
Doctor's Doll, Nude Woman, Reclining, Holding Fan, Inlaid Necklace, Chinese, 16 In. ...... *illus*	3200.00
Doctor's Doll, Nude Woman, Wood Stand, Chinese, 1900s, 6 ½ In.	799.00
Doctor's Doll, Reclining Nude, Chinese, c.1900, 4 ½ In.	294.00
Dragon, Resting, Ray Crest, Openwork Wood Stand, Chinese, c.1900, 13 In.	1793.00
Dressing Set, Lady's, Shibayama Decoration, Flowers, Birds, 14-In. Fitted Case, 6 Piece	1107.00
Ewer, Carved, Feathers, Cylindrical Spout & Legs, Loop Handle, Lid, 1800s, 9 ¼ In.	3553.00
Fan, Carved, Embroidered Silk & Leather, Box, Chinese, 7 ½ In.	717.00
Fan, Carved, Pierced Design, Framed Glass Case, 18 x 9 ½ In.	300.00
Fan, Carved, Pierced, Figural Landscape Scene, 1800s, 7 ½ In.	1195.00
Fan, Pierced, Plaque, Cranes, Rocks, Blue Cabochon, Silk Tassel, Wood Stand, Chinese, 25 In.	4428.00
Figurine, 2 Foo Dogs, Leg Raised, Ball In Mouth, Curved Wood Stand, 2 In.	461.00
Figurine, 2 Performers, Flowing Scarves, 10 In.	2196.00
Figurine, 2 Women, Holding Flowering Lotus Branch, Hoe, Fan, 9 In., Pair	2728.00
Figurine, Ancestral, Emperor & Empress, Seated, Throne, Dragon, Bird, c.1900, 6 In., Pair	708.00
Figurine, Andromeda, Sacrificed To Sea Monster, Dieppe, 1800s, 12 ¼ In.	11250.00
Figurine, Armorer, Couched, Striking Blade, Black Cap, Anvil, Water Bucket, 1800s, 6 In.	690.00
Figurine, Asian Woman, Windblown Dress, Painted Hair, Flowers, Wood Base, Chinese, 7 In.	1560.00
Figurine, Basket Of Flowers, Pierced, Geometric Design, Chinese, 22 In.	4960.00
Figurine, Bearded Man, Standing Over Dragon & Dog, 8 In.	384.00
Figurine, Begger, Sack, White, Wood Plinth, Germany, 1700s, 8 ½ In.	3600.00
Figurine, Bijin With Child, Standing, Wearing Long Robes, Signed, 1800s, 13 ½ In.	3250.00
Figurine, Bird Catcher, Fowl, White, Carved Base, Germany, c.1800, 10 In.	4800.00
Figurine, Boy, On Buffalo, Base, Japan, 6 ⅜ In. ......*illus*	1098.00
Figurine, Boy, Reaching, Glass Eyes, Wood Robes, Rocky Base, Germany, 1700s, 7 In.	4080.00
Figurine, Buddha Head, Reticulated Crown, Round Wood Base, 7 x 4 In.	1200.00
Figurine, Buddha Hotoi, Standing, Holding Fan, Sack Of Good Fortune, Signed, 5 x 5 In.	259.00
Figurine, Buddha, Laughing, Ruyi Scepter, Polished, 2 ¼ x 2 ¼ In.	196.00
Figurine, Buddha, Maitreya, Holding Child, Beads, Stand, Chinese, 1900s, 10 In.	2868.00
Figurine, Buddha, Seated, Dhyanasana, Raised Hand, Double Lotus Throne, 1900s, 5 In.	325.00
Figurine, Buddha, Standing, Smiling, Wearing Beaded Necklace, Wooden Base, 1900s, 5 In.	118.00
Figurine, Buddha's Hand, Carved, Dyed Yellow, Wood Stand, Chinese, c.1910, 7 ¼ In.	13035.00
Figurine, Carpenter, Seated On Timber, Uplifted Arm Mallet, Chisel, Saw, Wood, Iron, c.1900, 9 In.	1150.00
Figurine, Carved, Horse, Reclining, Fitted Base, Scrolling Band, 5 In.	1364.00
Figurine, Cavalier, Standing, 18th Century Costume, Round Base, c.1890, 12 In.	3438.00
Figurine, Child Samurai, Brocade Robes, Hat, Sword, Wood Stand, Japan, 1900s, 8 ½ In.	1230.00
Figurine, Classical Woman, Holding, Flowers, Continental, 7 x 2 In.	660.00
Figurine, Court Attendant, Woman, Brocade Robes, Obi, Flat Hat, Japan, c.1900s, 7 In.	123.00
Figurine, Court Entertainer, Standing, Robes, Holding Tasseled Fan, Wood Stand, 10 In.	2460.00
Figurine, Court Lady & Throne, Seated, Wearing Long Robes, Chignon, Chinese, 6 In.	837.00
Figurine, Court Musician, Standing, Brocade Robes, Peaked Hat, Drum, Japan, 1900s, 8 In.	553.00

Figurine, Court Musician, Standing, Robes, Holding Instrument, Hand Raised, 10 In.	1845.00
Figurine, Court Official, Beard, Mandarin's Hat, Dragon Robe, Sword, Octagonal Base, 1900s, 9 In.	3444.00
Figurine, Cranes, Pine Trees, Flower Buds, Rockery, Rectangular Wood Base, 7 In.	657.00
Figurine, Cricket, Lettuce Leaf, Trailing Pineapple, Peppers, Wood Base, Chinese, 7 In.	595.00
Figurine, Deity, Figure In Lap, Coral, Double Lotus Petal Base, Wood Stand, Hindu, 6 In.	1708.00
Figurine, Deity, Seated, Holding Flowers, Wood Pedestal, Chinese, 5 In.	266.00
Figurine, Double Dragon, Spiraling, Chasing Ball, Flower Heads, Stand, Chinese, 1800s, 6 In.	1725.00
Figurine, Dragon, Clouds, White, Round Stand, Chinese, 10 In.	489.00
Figurine, Dragon, Horned, Scaly, Open Mouth, Pearl Of Wisdom, Wood Stand, 1900s, 21 In.	984.00
Figurine, Dragon, Swirling Through Sea, Japan, 1800s, 6 ¾ In.	593.00
Figurine, Drunken Poet, Seated, Upturned Knees, Holding Wine Jar, Grinning, 2 ½ x 2 In.	366.00
Figurine, Duck, Incised Feathers, Turquoise Bead Detail, Wood Stand, Chinese, 4 ¾ x 7 ½ In.	7170.00
Figurine, Ear Of Corn, Partially Shucked, Hardwood Stand, Japan, c.1890, 15 In.	3623.00
Figurine, Elderly Man, Fan, Red Inked Mark, Mounted To Wood Stand, 8 In.	561.00
Figurine, Elderly Man, Wearing Leafy Hat, Holding Fish & Basket, c.1900, 9 In.	590.00
Figurine, Elephant, Applied Abalone, Metal, Coral, Crystal Ball, Japan, 4 x 5 In.	1650.00
Figurine, Elephant, Curled Trunks, Walking, Wood Stand, Chinese, 1900s, 7 ½ In., 3 Piece	1845.00
Figurine, Elephant, Figure On Top, Seated, Mantra, 5 In.	1364.00
Figurine, Elephant, Mirror Images, Saddle Cloth, Scenic, Chinese, 2 ¼ x 8 In., Pair	854.00
Figurine, Elephant, Raised Trunk, White, Carved Wood Stand, 2 ½ x 6 ½ In.	489.00
Figurine, Emperor & Empress, Throne, Dragon, Birds, Necklace, Stand, c.1900, 10 In., Pair	2360.00
Figurine, Emperor, Carved, Hardwood Stand, Chinese, 1900s, 12 ¾ In.	1434.00
Figurine, Emperor, Empress, Carved, Holding Peonies, Symbols, Chinese, 1900s, 18 In., Pair.	6765.00
Figurine, Emperor, Empress, Formal Court Dress, Rosewood Stand, Chinese, 1900s, 13 In., Pair	3690.00
Figurine, Emperor, Empress, Standing, Robes, Wood Base, 11 In., Pair	3472.00
Figurine, Emperor, Empress, White, Black Inked Detail, Wood Base, Chinese, 9 In., Pair	1200.00
Figurine, Emperor, Standing, Court Robes, Tiered Cap, Holding Tablet, c.1910, 12 ¼ In.	1353.00
Figurine, Entertainer, Woman, Brocade Kimono, Court Hat, Fan, Drum, Japan, 1900s, 11 ½ In.	1168.00
Figurine, Farmer, Wide Brimmed Hat, Holding Dragon Headed Staff, Flower Basket, 10 In.	992.00
Figurine, Female Deity, Holding Lotus Blossom Basket, Phoenix, 1900s, 34 In.	5412.00
Figurine, Fertility, Woman, Seminude, Seated, Child In Lap, Legs Crossed, 13 In.	625.00
Figurine, Fish, Carved, 5 Boys, 7 ¼ x 2 ¾ In.	403.00
Figurine, Fisherman, Fish Basket, Lotus Leaf Hat, Bamboo Rod, Chinese, 1800s, 5 In.	922.00
Figurine, Fisherman, Holding 2 Tortoises, Basket, Japan, 1800s, 6 In.	896.00
Figurine, Fisherman, Holding Rod, 19th Century, 9 ¼ In.	200.00
Figurine, Fisherman, Robed, Palm Raised, Fishing Pole, Wood Stand, Chinese, 13 In.	1968.00
Figurine, Fisherman, Standing, Signed Hidegetsu, Japan, 1800s, 18 ¾ In.	1304.00
Figurine, Flower Basket, Beetles, Finches, Chain, Wooden Stand, Chinese, 1900s, 15 In.	6000.00
Figurine, Flower, Carved, Plaque, Japan, 28 x 18 In., Pair	992.00
Figurine, Flying Bird, Basket, Bamboo Branches, Wood Base, 11 In.	3346.00
Figurine, Foo Dog, Carved, Wood Stand, c.1890, Pair	5451.00
Figurine, Foo Lions At Play, 19th Century, 2 In.	225.00
Figurine, Fredrick The Great, Brown Marble Base, Germany, 1800s, 10 ¼ In.	2640.00
Figurine, Frogs, Snake, Resting On Lotus Leaf, 3 In.	613.00
Figurine, Gama Sennin, Standing, String Of Coins, Toad, Wave Shape Wood Stand, Japan, 6 In.	1195.00
Figurine, Ganesha, Lord Of All Existing Beings, Elephant Head, 4 Arms, India, 4 ¼ In.	98.00
Figurine, Geisha, Incised Robe, Wood Stand, Japan, 7 ¾ In.	429.00
Figurine, Geisha, Seated On Table Top, Sea Set, Holding Fan, c.1900, 5 In.	885.00
Figurine, Goat Herder, Bearded Man, Holding Hook, Standing, Goat, Round Base, 6 In.	219.00
Figurine, God Of Literature, Standing, Robes, Sword, Brush, Incised, Chinese, 1900s, 12 In.	1722.00
Figurine, Goddess Of Creative Sciences, On Lotus Blossom, India, 6 ¾ In.	584.00
Figurine, Goddess Of Harvest, White, France, Stained Wood Base, 1800s, 8 ½ In.	4800.00
Figurine, Goddess, Guanyin, Flame Halo, Carved, Wood Stand, Chinese, c.1910, 16 In.	7703.00
Figurine, Goddess, Guanyin, Standing, Lotus Stand, Chinese, 1800s, 11 In.	13475.00
Figurine, Goddess, Prunus, Insects, Rosewood Stand, Lotus Pedestal, 1700s, 25 ⅜ In. ......illus	50363.00
Figurine, Goddess, Sitting On Foo Dog, Plinth Base, Wooden Stand, Chinese, 1900s, 15 x 10 In.	7200.00
Figurine, Guandi, God Of War & Literature, Military Armor, Holding Halberd, Stand, 12 In.	2337.00
Figurine, Guanyin, Atop Lotus Base, 8 In.	1860.00
Figurine, Guanyin, On Horse, Robe, Sword, Wooden Footed Stand, 7 In.	960.00
Figurine, Guanyin, Seated, Thousand Hands, Triple Lotus Throne, Chinese, 8 In.	3675.00
Figurine, Guanyin, Stained, Lotus Throne, Holding Bottle, Flowering Spray, Wooden Base, 7 In.	266.00
Figurine, Guanyin, Standing, Holding Fan, Upswept Hair, Flower Robe, Signed, 12 In.	2280.00
Figurine, Heroine Soldier, Sword, Carved, Rosewood Stand, Chinese, 1800s, 10 In.	2151.00
Figurine, Horse, Prancing, Carved, Tinted, Stand, Box, 5 x 6 In., Pair	627.00
Figurine, Horse, Raised Hoof, Elephant Ivory, Chinese, 11 x 14 ¼ In., Pair	7703.00
Figurine, Horse, Saddle, Raised Leg, Ruby Eyes, Wood Stand, Chinese, 5 ½ In., Pair	799.00

Ivory, Figurine, Old Man, With Child & Rooster, Japan, 1800s, 6 ½ In.
$521.00

Skinner, Inc.

Ivory, Figurine, Samurai, Embracing Child, Signed, Japan, 1800s, 7 ⅜ In.
$889.00

Skinner, Inc.

Ivory, Okimono, Man, Child On Shoulder, Holding Rooster, Signed, Japan, 15 ½ In.
$1135.00

Sloans & Kenyon

As always, the edited listings in *Kovels' Antiques & Collectibles Price Guide* aren't available on any website, but readers should visit Kovels.com for information on trends, tips, reproductions, marks, old prices, and more!

Ivory, Portrait, Child, John Carl I, Oval, Frame, Miniature, 2 ¼ x 1 ½ In. $300.00

DuMouchelles Art Gallery

Ivory, Portrait, Woman, Tortoiseshell Comb, Leather Case, James Dyer, c.1825, 2 ⅝ x 3 ⅛ In. $294.00

Garth's Auctions, Inc.

Ivory, Puzzle Ball, Figural Stand, Carved, Dragons, 3 Layers, Pierced, 7 ⅛ In. $154.00

Neal Auction Co.

Figurine, Horses, Crown, Gold, Jeweled, Coral, Rubies, Lapis Lazuli, c.1900, 7 ½ x 5 In.	4740.00
Figurine, Hotei, Both Hands Raised, Wearing Beaded Necklaces, Robes, Chinese, 8 In.	4960.00
Figurine, Hotei, Sack On Back, Auspicious Symbols, Scroll, Chinese, 7 ¾ In. *illus*	504.00
Figurine, Huntsman, Crossbow, Boy At His Side, Round Pedestal, 7 In.	919.00
Figurine, Immortal Figure, Li Tieh-Kuai, In Robe, Holding Gourd, Staff, Wood Stand, 8 In.	460.00
Figurine, Immortal, Chinese, Woman, Riding Phoenix, Flowers, Stand, Chinese, c.1950, 15 In., Pair	7072.00
Figurine, Immortal, Lame Leg, Staff, Leaf Coat, Carved, Wood Stand, Japan, 7 ¾ In.	861.00
Figurine, Immortal, Long Beard, Robes, Official's Hat, Belt, Holding Yuanbao, 1800s, 7 ¼ In.	956.00
Figurine, Immortal, Red Tassel, Chinese, 31 ½ In.	5975.00
Figurine, Immortal, Seated, Dragon Cane, Fly Whisk, Wood Stand, Chinese, c.1910, 6 In.	3081.00
Figurine, Immortal, Standing, Amber Color, Chinese, 12 In.	589.00
Figurine, Immortal, Standing, Holding Branch, Long Robes, Headdress, Chinese, 12 In. *illus*	1135.00
Figurine, Iris, Raised In Bulb Dish, Stained, Japan, 10 In.	2232.00
Figurine, Kannon, Standing, Wheel Shape Mandala, Pierced, Necklaces, Lotus Base, 24 In.	5456.00
Figurine, Krishna, Standing, Lotus Blossom, Flute, Wood Base, India, c.1875, 9 ½ In.	650.00
Figurine, Krishna & Radha, Round Wood Base, India, 6 x 2 In.	266.00
Figurine, Laborer, Smiling, Basket, Tool, 7 In.	327.00
Figurine, Lan Tsai Ho, Standing, Robe, Flowers, Painted, Gilt, Chinese, 1800s, 12 In. *illus*	1593.00
Figurine, Lion, Stalking, White, c.1890, 5 In.	153.00
Figurine, Lohan, Carved, Wood Base, Chinese, 5 In.	207.00
Figurine, Lohan, Monk, Staff, Scrolls, Textured Robes, Cap, Wood Plinth, Japan, 10 In.	600.00
Figurine, Lohan, Openwork, Throne, Holding Eyebrow, Ruyi Scepter, 6 x 6 ½ In., Pair	5976.00
Figurine, Lohan, Standing, Holding Fly Whisk, Staff, Chinese, 1800s, 9 In.	15405.00
Figurine, Lu Dongbin, Bearded Immortal, Standing, Flowing Robes, Holding Whisk, Pearl, 9 In.	1912.00
Figurine, Maiden, Standing, Long Robes, Holding Flower Basket, Wood Stand, 14 In.	2684.00
Figurine, Man & Boy, Smiling, Holding Cups, Wearing Robes, Chinese, 5 ⅜ In.	1016.00
Figurine, Man & Dragon, Pine Trees, Wood Base, 14 In.	2390.00
Figurine, Man, Bearded, Sitting, Knees Up, Arms Over Rock, Resting Head, 3 ¼ In.	295.00
Figurine, Man, Bucket, Child, Carved, 6 ½ In.	660.00
Figurine, Man, Goose In Basket, Stick, Incised Flower, 11 In.	1380.00
Figurine, Man, Hat On Back, Gourd, Leaning Over Hinged Box, c.1900, 2 In.	266.00
Figurine, Man, Peddler, Carrying Baskets, Smiling, Inked Detail, Japan, 4 ¾ In.	330.00
Figurine, Man, Playing Flute, Dark Barrel Base, 8 ¾ In.	472.00
Figurine, Man, Seated, Parasol, Pots, Wood Base, Red Seal, 4 ½ x 4 In.	880.00
Figurine, Man, Smiling, Performing Monkey, Carved, Painted, 7 ¼ In.	403.00
Figurine, Man, Standing, Carrying Big Fish & Basket, Duck, c.1900, 5 ⅝ In.	237.00
Figurine, Man, Standing, Holding Basket Of Vegetables, Robes, Oval Base, 10 x 4 ½ In.	575.00
Figurine, Man, Standing, Walking Stick, Carved, Red Seal, Japan, 2 ½ x 8 In.	880.00
Figurine, Man, Standing, Wearing Hat, Holding Puppet, Box, 8 In.	657.00
Figurine, Man, Tool Over Shoulder, Jug, Signed, c.1960, 5 ¼ In.	295.00
Figurine, Man, Woman, Standing, Wood Plinth, Holding Hoe, Carrying Jar, Africa, 8 In., Pair	598.00
Figurine, Mask Maker, Signed, Japan, 1800s, 2 In.	178.00
Figurine, Mountainous Landscape, Pagoda, Pine Trees, Figures, 7 x 4 In.	299.00
Figurine, Mulan, Warrior Heroine, Standing, Wearing Robes, Sword, Wood Stand, 11 In.	2390.00
Figurine, Musician, White, Germany, Wood Plinth, 1700s, 9 In.	3600.00
Figurine, Mythical Beast, Seated, Rocks, White, Wood Stand, Chinese, c.1900, 4 In., Pair	900.00
Figurine, Napoleon, Base, 19th Century, 5 In.	708.00
Figurine, Old Man, With Child & Rooster, Japan, 1800s, 6 ½ In. *illus*	521.00
Figurine, Owl, Incised Feathers, Inset Eyes, On Log, Continental, 1800s, 3 ¼ In.	984.00
Figurine, Parakeet, Perched, Flowering Branch, Wood Stand, 12 In., Pair	2760.00
Figurine, Peddler, Carrying Basket On Back, Pipe, Japan, 10 ½ In.	1200.00
Figurine, Pekinese, Ribbon Bow Tie, Frolicking, Abalone Eyes, Signed, Japan, c.1890, 3 x 4 In.	1725.00
Figurine, Phoenix Bird, On Tree Stump, Square Wood Base, Chinese, 7 & 8 In., 2 Piece	540.00
Figurine, Plant, Flowers, Birds, Bug, Wood Base, Chinese	300.00
Figurine, Poultry Farmer, Man, Bird, Woman, Basket On Back, Stand, 8 In., Pair	1410.00
Figurine, Quail, Male, Female, Painted, Paper Label, Japan, c.1910, 2 x 2 In., Pair	767.00
Figurine, Queen, Braided Hair, Standing, Wearing Crown, Clasping Hand To Chest, 5 In.	533.00
Figurine, Rabbit, Baby, Coiled, Signed, Japan, 1 ½ x 1 ¼ In.	207.00
Figurine, Ram, Tucked In Legs, Fur, Curled Horns, Wood Stand, Chinese, 5 x 7 ½ In.	1673.00
Figurine, Rice Farmer, Hat, Sheaf, Woman, Fan, Basket, Chinese, c.1935, 10 ½ In., Pair	2460.00
Figurine, Samurai, Embracing Child, Signed, Japan, 1800s, 7 ⅜ In. *illus*	889.00
Figurine, Samurai, Standing, Brocade Coat, Swords, Topknot, Carved, 1900s, 12 ¼ In.	1845.00
Figurine, Samurai, Sword, Brocade Coat, Topknot, Carved, Wood Stand, Japan, 8 ½ In.	922.00
Figurine, Scholar, Standing, Flowing Robes, Rectangular Wood Base, Chinese, 12 In., Pair	5208.00
Figurine, Skull, Disarticulated Jaw, Lift-Off Cranium, Attached Springs, Hooks, 4 ½ In.	6641.00
Figurine, St. Francis, White, Carved, Wood Plinth, 8 ¾ In.	4080.00

Figurine, Tantric Demon, Bare Chest, Crown, Scepter, Seated, Gold Lion, 1900s, 8 x 6 In. 430.00
Figurine, Toy Seller, Puppet, Japan, c.1905, 8 In. 735.00
Figurine, Vase Of Flowers, Pierced, Ring Handles, Carved, 1900s, 20 In. 7800.00
Figurine, Vendor, Tunic, Carrying, Baskets, Masks, Wood Stand, Japan, c.1950, 9 In. 922.00
Figurine, Village, Figures, Animals, Trees, Pierced Openwork, Wood Base, 7 x 8 In. 173.00
Figurine, Virgin Mary, Standing, Hands In Prayer, Round Base, Putti, Bone, 1800s, 8 In. 1875.00
Figurine, Virgin, White, Leather Case, Italy, 1700s, 7 In. 2400.00
Figurine, Warrior, Standing, 2 Swords, Headpiece, Round Rosewood Stand, 10 In. 2520.00
Figurine, Wise Man, Flowing Robes, Holding Stick & Bamboo, Wood Base, 8 In. 805.00
Figurine, Woman, Asian Dress, Holding Branch, Sash Ornaments, Wood Base, 9 In. 5950.00
Figurine, Woman, Bird On Shoulder, Carved, 1800s, 15 In. 3081.00
Figurine, Woman, Child On Back, Parasol, Japan, c.1900, 4 ½ x 9 ½ In. 1800.00
Figurine, Woman, Fan, Flowers, Multicolor, Chinese, 8 ½ In. 900.00
Figurine, Woman, Feeding Bird, White, Ivory Column Base, Dieppe, c.1875, 6 ¾ In. 2400.00
Figurine, Woman, Holding Basket Of Flowers & Fruit, Inked, Wood Stand, 1800s, 12 In., Pair 2360.00
Figurine, Woman, Holding Fan & Flower, Wood Base, 6 In. 774.00
Figurine, Woman, Holding Flowers, Child, Holding A Peach, 10 x 3 In. 930.00
Figurine, Woman, Holding Flowers, Draped Robes, 14 x 5 In. 3904.00
Figurine, Woman, Holding Lotus Flower, Square Base, c.1900, 7 In. 384.00
Figurine, Woman, Holding Rose, Long Robe, Large Knot Hairdo, 1900s, 6 In. 148.00
Figurine, Woman, Immortal, Seated, Flower Basket, Rosewood Stand, 9 In. 3555.00
Figurine, Woman, Meiren, Robe, Open Book, Stand, Chinese, 13 ¼ In. 3227.00
Figurine, Woman, Small Child, Holding Hands, Robes, Japan, 1800s, 3 ¾ In. 276.00
Figurine, Woman, Standing, Draped Gown, Holding Fan, Flowers, Chinese, Wood Stand, 14 In. 1380.00
Figurine, Woman, Standing, Grasping Scroll, Long Robes, Black Hair, Wood Stand, Early 1900s, 8 In. 1100.00
Figurine, Woman, Standing, Holding Flower Basket, Robe, c.1900, 7 In. 725.00
Figurine, Woman, Standing, Nude, Long Hair, Earrings, Hand Up, Wood Stand, 13 In. 1708.00
Figurine, Zhong Kui, Demon Queller, Carrying Demon Heads, Stand, Chinese, 10 ½ In. 1046.00
Figurines, Immortals, Attendants Scene, Carved, White, Chinese, Cylinder, c.1920, 3 In. 390.00
Group, 2 Children, Holding Peach, Wood Stand, Chinese, 3 ¼ In. 460.00
Group, 2 Farmers, Holding An Axe & Basket, 1800s, 4 In. 598.00
Group, 2 Women, Flutist, String Player, Wood Stand, Japan, 7 ¾ In. 593.00
Group, 4 Elephants, Leaf Carved Pedestal, India, c.1905, 9 In. 533.00
Group, 4 Figures, Pine Tree, Conical, Chinese, 1800s, 5 In. 796.00
Group, 5 Immortals, Nan Shan Wu Lao, Standing Under Tree, Holding Scroll, Chinese, 11 In. 2151.00
Group, 6 Immortals, Boat, Dragon Shape, White, Wood Stand, Japan, 1800s, 13 x 3 In. 796.00
Group, Fisherman, 2 Children, Basket Over Shoulder, Stick, Japan, 1800s, 9 ¾ x 8 In. 593.00
Group, Geisha, Robe, Straw Hat, Pole Ax, Vase With Brooms, Painted, Japan, 1900s, 7 ½ In. 799.00
Group, Man, Standing, Lotus Hat, Backpack, Staff, 2 Children, Japan, 1900s, 9 In. 1230.00
Group, Official, Dancing Boy, Kneeling Geisha, Flowers, Fan, Drum, Carved, Japan, c.1910, 15 ¾ In. 5658.00
Group, Street Entertainers, 2 Men, Standing In Waraji, Smoking, Monkey, Boy, Japan, 7 In. 777.00
Group, Vendor, Peach Baskets, Pipe, Pouch, Japan, 1900s, 5 ½ x 5 In. 1476.00
Group, Water Buffalo, Resting, Boy Climbing On, Hat, Stand, Chinese, 1900s 5 ½ In., Pair 1476.00
Group, Woman, Riding Reindeer, Carved, Signed, c.1900, 5 x 3 In. 443.00
Group, Woman, With Umbrella, Child, Wood Stand, Etched, Inked, 1900s, 10 In. 885.00
Handle, Dog, Greyhound, Glass Eyes, Hand Carved, 2 ¾ x 5 ½ In. 362.00
Hunter's Horn, Serpent's Head, Hunters, Horses, Flower, Cameos, Stand, Germany, c.1800, 50 In. 29520.00
Incense Holder, Bone, Laminated, Bird, Lotus, Trees, Rockwork, Stand, c.1910, 3 ⅝ In. 86.00
Jar, Cover, Cylinder, Birds, Vining, Wood Base, Foo Dogs, Flowers, c.1890, 9 ½ In. 2868.00
Jar, Foo Dog, Figures, House, Trees, Ring Handles, Cylindrical, Hardwood Stand, 10 In. 2588.00
Letter Holder, Openwork, Rounded Rectangular Back, 5 Stands, Canton, Early 1800s, 10 In. 2900.00
Letter Opener, Carved Wood Handle, Sheath, Chinese, 13 In. 598.00
Lion, Curled Mane, Seated On Plinth Base, Turquoise, Coral Accents, 6 In., Pair 1968.00
Mirror, Hand, Silver Plaque, Tree, Coral, Malachite, Amethyst, Carnelian, Chinese, 1800s, 10 In. 2083.00
Model, Pagoda, 5 Tiers, Gallery, Rail, Panel Doors, Sloped Roof, Gourd Finial, 1900s, 26 ¼ In. 2952.00
Necklace, Doctor's Doll, Nude, Lapis Beads, Chinese, c.1900, 3 In. 470.00
Okimono, Barefoot Fisherman, Trident, Rope, Signed, Japan, 5 ¼ In. 403.00
Okimono, Basket Seller, Japan, 1800s, 10 ¼ In. 1793.00
Okimono, Buddha, Seated, Lotus Throne, Japan, 1900s, 2 ½ In. 210.00
Okimono, Chrysanthemum, Hakusui Co., Japan, 8 ¾ x 10 In. 1725.00
Okimono, Figures Climbing On Each Other, Mark, Japan, 2 ½ x 3 In. 1210.00
Okimono, Fisherman, Smiling, Holding Net, Large Fish, 11 Wicker Baskets, c.1900, 4 ½ In. 307.00
Okimono, Fisherman, Standing On Crag, Waves, Holding Net, Signed, Japan, 7 ½ In. 717.00
Okimono, Fisherman, Woven Hat, Fishnets, Basket, Seashells, 6 In. 238.00
Okimono, Geisha, Kneeling, Maple Leaf Pattern Kimono, Arranging Flowers, Japan, 6 In. 657.00
Okimono, Geisha, Raised Arm, Japan, 8 In. 717.00

Ivory, Puzzle Ball, Twisting Dragons In Fixed Ring, Stand, Pierced, Chinese, 16 ½ In.
$4216.00

Leslie Hindman Auctioneers

Ivory, Tusk, Phoenix, Peonies, Prunus, Birds, Pine Tree, Carved, Marked, Chinese, 39 In.
$3081.00

Skinner, Inc.

Jade, Box, Lid, Relief Carved, Raised Designs, Loop Finial, Jump Ring, Chinese, 1800s, 2 x 2 ⅞ In.
$4740.00

Skinner, Inc.

Jade, Carving, Mountain, Scholars, White Celadon, Markings, Wood Stand, Chinese, 6 ½ x 5 In.
$3063.00

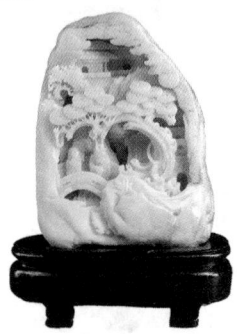

Skinner, Inc.

Jade, Censer, Cover, Lobed, Pale Green White, Ring Handles, Chinese, 7 x 6 ½ In.
$16590.00

Skinner, Inc.

Jade, Dish, Leaf, Chi Dragon, Crawling, Gray Celadon, Chinese, 5 ¾ In.
$2252.00

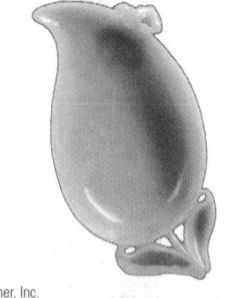

Skinner, Inc.

Jade, Figurine, Horse, Costume, Wood Stand, Chinese, 17th Century, 2 ¾ x 3 ¾ In.
$11850.00

Skinner, Inc.

Okimono, Man, Basket, Woman, Reading Scroll, Tinted Attire, Wood Base, Japan, 6 ½ x 6 In.	431.00
Okimono, Man, Bearded, Holding Harvest Hoe, Lotus Stalks, Wood Stand, 6 In.	1785.00
Okimono, Man, Child On Shoulder, Holding Rooster, Signed, Japan, 15 ½ In. ......*illus*	1135.00
Okimono, Old Man, Beaded, Bent Back, Official's Hat, Long Robes, Japan, 8 In.	837.00
Okimono, Old Man, Carrying Child, Spinning Top, Mother-Of-Pearl Inlays, Japan, 6 In.	1265.00
Okimono, Samurai, Wearing Armor, Helmet, Katana, Japan, c.1900, 8 In.	6573.00
Okimono, Seashell Gatherer, Standing, Carrying Basket Of Shells, c.1900, 7 ½ In.	676.00
Orb, Opens To Carved Religious Scenes, c.1890, 1 ½ x 2 ¼ In.	307.00
Page Turner, Carved, Curved, Vining Roses, Leaves, c.1935, 14 In.	461.00
Page Turner, Immortal, Lotus Finial, Brocade Surface, Chinese, 1800s, 11 ¼ In.	3553.00
Pagoda, 5 Tiers, Reticulated Doors, Dragon Design Base, Chinese, 42 x 14 In.	21510.00
Panel, Carved, Figures, Landscape, Pagodas, Flowers, 2-Sided, 6 ½ x 3 In.	389.00
Panel, Scholar, Reading, Multicolor, Wood Frame, Indo-Persian, c.1800s, 6 x 3 In.	230.00
Pendant, Pierced, Bird, Plum Blossoms, Lattice Work, Endless Knot, Rectangular, 5 In.	553.00
Planter, Iris, Carved, Multicolor, Chinese, c.1910, 8 ¾ In.	4444.00
Plaque, Figures In Boat, Pierce Carved Wood Frame, 8 x 10 In.	2976.00
Plaque, Hunting Scene, Painted, Persia, 13 In.	508.00
Plaque, Marriage Of King Louis XIV & Maria Theresa, France, Blue, White, Etched, 1800s, 7 x 5 In.	5280.00
Plaque, Seated Figure, On Carpet, Flying Dragon, Chinese, 14 x 10 In.	744.00
Plaque, St. Sebastian, Tree, Angel, Wood Frame, Continental, 1800s, 4 x 3 In.	600.00
Portrait, Child, John Carl I, Oval, Frame, Miniature, 2 ¼ x 1 ½ In. ....*illus*	300.00
Portrait, Woman, Tortoiseshell Comb, Leather Case, James Dyer, c.1825, 2 ⅝ x 3 ⅛ In. .....*illus*	294.00
Prayer Beads, 4 Green, Dyed, Carved Characters, Chinese, c.1890, 26 In.	521.00
Puzzle Ball, Dragons, Clouds, Openwork, Immortal Shaped Stand, Chinese, c.1890, 2 x 8 In.	504.00
Puzzle Ball, Figural Stand, Carved, Dragons, 3 Layers, Pierced, 7 ⅛ In. ....*illus*	154.00
Puzzle Ball, Figures, Scrolls, Designs, Chinese, 13 In.	2844.00
Puzzle Ball, Flower Design, 5 Layers, Pedestal Stand, Phoenix, 8 ½ In.	307.00
Puzzle Ball, Reticulated Stand, Dragon, Flowers, Stand, Chinese, c.1900, 9 ½ In.	1554.00
Puzzle Ball, Twisting Dragons In Fixed Ring, Stand, Pierced, Chinese, 16 ½ In. ....*illus*	4216.00
Screen, Table, 4 Women, Scholars, Musical, Pavilion, Wood Stand, Chinese, c.1890, 12 x 5 In.	4900.00
Screen, Table, 4-Panel, Wood Frame, Carved Taoist Plaques, 14 x 13 ½ In.	3063.00
Screen, Table, Angel, Child, Village, Leaves, Moonlit Sky, Carved, c.1800, 15 ¾ In.	5629.00
Screen, Table, Etched Landscape, Inscriptions, Reticulated Black Frame, Chinese, c.1895, 7 In.	7200.00
Seal, Foo Dog Shape, Chinese, c.1910, 4 x 2 In.	1912.00
Seal, Square, 2 Dragons, Clouds, Pearl, Carved, Chinese, 1800s, 3 x 2 ½ In.	1659.00
Shell, Half Open, Figures, Landscape, Man Playing Zither, Wood Stand, Chinese, 1800s, 2 ¾ x 1 In.	326.00
Shell, Half Open, Figures, Rustic Landscape, Signed, Japan, 1800s, 2 ¾ In.	296.00
Shrine, Carved, Phoenix, Dragon, Flowers, Pagoda Shape, Japan, c.1910, 9 In.	359.00
Snuff Bottle, Birds, Flowering Trees, Oblong, Stopper, Chinese, c.1900, 3 In.	551.00
Snuff Bottle, Figural, Reclining Man, Foot Stopper, Spoon, 1800s, 3 ½ x 1 In.	605.00
Snuff Bottle, Lid, Carved, White, Signed Yang Shi Hui, Chinese, c.1930, 3 ½ In.	11950.00
Stand, Puzzle Ball, Figures, Flowers, Carved, Chinese, 3 ¾ x 3 In.	259.00
Tankard, Battles, Flowers, Fruits, Scroll Handle, Hinge Lid, Silver Gilt, Germany, 1800s, 14 In.	21600.00
Tankard, Lid, Classical Figures, Boar, Silver Plate Handle, Base, Germany, 1800s, 9 In.	10073.00
Teapot, Lotus Flower Shape, Turtle Finial, Dragonfly Spout, 3 ½ In.	2938.00
Toothpick Holder, Bodkin, Nude Woman, Standing, Hand Finial, Horn Pick, c.1850, 5 In.	590.00
Totem, Indian Head, Eagles, Owls, Wolves, Native American, Base, 6 In.	7500.00
Tray, Fan Shape, Canted Corners, Magnolia Tree, Plants, 1800s, 4 ⅜ x 7 ⅛ In.	2460.00
Triptych, Knighting Of Sir Francis Drake, Carved, Continental, 19th Century, 7 In.	826.00
Triptych, Mary Queen Of Scots, Robe Open, Interior Attendants, White, France, 1800s, 7 ¾ In.	4080.00
Triptych, Saint, Standing, Hands In Prayer, Hinged, Nativity Scene, Dieppe, 1800s, 10 In.	2350.00
Tusk, 3 Figures, Under Pine Tree, Carved, Inked, Signed, 1900s, 8 x 5 In.	1062.00
Tusk, 8 Immortals, Carved, Pierce Design, Wood Stand, 21 In.	2976.00
Tusk, 9 Graduated Elephants, Train Of Animals, Bridge, Chinese, 22 In.	1793.00
Tusk, Animals In Conflict, Carved, 29 In.	2520.00
Tusk, Battle Scene, Carved, Chinese, 45 In.	8060.00
Tusk, Bridge, 9 Graduated Elephants, Palm Leaves, Africa, 33 In.	1121.00
Tusk, Bust, Woman, Carved, Marble Base, Africa, 25 In.	920.00
Tusk, Carved, Curved, 2 Confronting Dragons, Flaming Pearl, Wooden Stand, 25 In.	3936.00
Tusk, Dragon, Wooden Stand, c.1900, 16 In.	885.00
Tusk, Dragons, Chasing Flaming Pearl Of Wisdom, Carved, 23 In.	2390.00
Tusk, Elephant Bridge, 5 Striding Animals, Graduated Sizes, 12 ½ In.	527.00
Tusk, Elephant Bridge, Carved, Wood Base, Chinese, 11 In.	1320.00
Tusk, Face, Carved, Square Wood Base, Africa, 11 x 2 ½ In., Pair	150.00
Tusk, Fisherman, 2 Boys, Man On Tree, Boy In Basket, Fish, Rope, Stacked, Japan, 12 In.	657.00
Tusk, Guanyin, Standing On Rock, Waves, Dragon, Lotus Flowers, Carved, c.1900, 13 In.	2950.00

Tusk, Hunter, Carved, Japan, Late 1800s, 8 ¼ In.		1185.00
Tusk, Immortal, Symbols, Tan, Rosewood Stand, Chinese, c.1890, 16 In., Pair		4428.00
Tusk, Immortals, Carved, Chinese, c.1900, 29 In.		7170.00
Tusk, Mary Of Heaven, Period Attire, Portugal, 1700s, 8 ⅛ In.		3540.00
Tusk, Musician, Dancer, Flowering Tree, 13 In.		1612.00
Tusk, Phoenix, Peonies, Prunus, Birds, Pine Tree, Carved, Marked, Chinese, 39 In. ....*illus*		3081.00
Tusk, Phoenix, Seated, Peony, Birds, Blossoms, Cylindrical, Curved, 14 In.		5456.00
Tusk, Pierced Figures, Wood Village, Carved, Stand, 12 x 5 In.		575.00
Tusk, Pot, Painted, Japan, Late 1800s, 7 ½ In.		1896.00
Tusk, Samurai, Seated, Sword, Servant, Wood Stand, Japan, 6 ½ In.		799.00
Tusk, Samurai, White, Carved, Japan, Late 1800s, 8 ½ In.		1701.00
Tusk, Segment Of Bamboo, Pierced Carved Cranes, Pine Trees, Wood Stand, 20 In.		3968.00
Tusk, Village Scene, Temple, Pagodas, Figures, Carved, Wood Base, Chinese, 27 In.		2185.00
Urn, Lid, Dragons, Ring Handles, Figures In Garden, Carved, Marked, 21 In.		12000.00
Vase, Beast Face, Dragons, 4 Rings At Base, Cylindrical, Carved, Chinese, 1800s, 15 In.		14340.00
Vase, Bottle Shape, Flared & Waisted Neck, Carved, Rabbit With Carrot, Dragon Handles, 6 In.		992.00
Vase, Buddhist Figures, Dragon Scroll Lugs, Pierced Foot, Flowers, Bats, Octagonal, c.1890, 11 In.		1960.00
Vase, Ceremonial, Dragon Lid, Dragons, 2 Handles, Ring Drops, 3 Ball & Claw Feet, 12 In.		3173.00
Vase, Cover, Figures, Carved, Foo Dog Finial, Cylinder, Chinese, 5 ½ In.		508.00
Vase, Dragon, Clouds Cartouches, Text, Carved, Wood Stand, Chinese, c.1905, 8 ¾ In., Pair		5629.00
Vase, Figural Carvings, Scroll Ground, Finial, Cylinder, Chinese, c.1905, 10 In.		1778.00
Vase, Frogs, Serpent, Carved Cylindrical, Stand, 4 ½ x 8 In., Pair		3080.00
Vase, Lid, Figures, Garden, Foo Dog Finial, Key Fret Border, Ring Handles, 15 In., Pair		9300.00
Vase, Lid, Foo Dog Supports, Brocade Ground, Double Gourd, Finial, Chinese, c.1905, 14 In.		5925.00
Vase, Pagodas, Figures On Verandas, Dragon's Head Handles, Rings, Oval, 1700		1035.00
Vase, Rolled Rim, Etched, Ink Stained, Scenes, Cylinder, Box, Asia, c.1905, 6 In., Pair		384.00
Vase, Scholars, Symbols, Landscape, Petal Collar Mouth, Double Gourd, Chinese, 1800s, 4 ¾ In.		2328.00
Wrist Rest, Book, Engraved, Picture Of 2 Women, Garden, Text, Signed, 1900s, 4 x 4 In.		1845.00
Wrist Rest, Carved, Warriors, High Relief, Rectangular, 10 In.		17328.00

JACK-IN-THE-PULPIT vases, shaped like trumpets, resemble the wildflower named jack-in-the-pulpit. The design originated in the late Victorian years. Vases in the jack-in-the-pulpit shape were made of ceramic or glass.

Vase, Iridescent Beige, Light Blue Stringing, c.1900, 7 In.		144.00
Vase, Iridescent Blue, White, Wide Flared Rim, Slender Stem, Onion Knob, 17 In.		489.00
Vase, Iridescent, Long Stem, Footed, Lundberg Studios, 7 ¾ x 5 In.		230.00
Vase, Lavender, Enamel Highlights, 5 ½ In.		400.00
Vase, Purple, Drizzled With Vines, Tricorner Ruffle Rim, 7 ⅛ In.		316.00
Vase, Vaseline Glass Body, Applied Pink Petal Rim, 11 ½ In.		120.00
Vase, Violet Iridescent, Ribbed, 7 In.		72.00

JADE is the name for two different minerals, nephrite and jadeite. Nephrite is the mineral used for most early Oriental carvings. Jade is a very tough stone that is found in many colors from dark green to pale lavender. Jade carvings are still being made in the old styles, so collectors must be careful not to be fooled by recent pieces. Jade jewelry is found in this book under Jewelry.

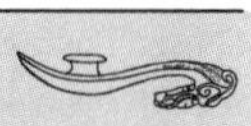

Abacus, 13 Rows, 65 Beads, Bronze Rods, Hardstone Figure Shoulao, 3 x 8 In.		682.00
Amulet, Round, Cloud Design, Scholar's Tool, Bronze Mount, Gilt Spiders, Chinese, 4 x 2 In.		1150.00
Ashtray, Round, Cigarette Rest, Circle Handle, Swastika, Gilt Accents, 1900s, 3 ¼ In. Diam.		91.00
Belt Buckle, Deer, Leaves, Scrolls, Cream, Carved, Chinese, 1900s, 2 x 5 In.		738.00
Belt Buckle, Dragon, White, Apple Green, Carved, Square Shape, Chinese, 3 ½ In.		448.00
Belt Buckle, Dragons, Carved, 2 Parts, Celadon Green, Chinese, 4 ½ In.		418.00
Belt Hook, Dragon, Raised Head, Carved, Round Knob, 1800s, 5 In.		1845.00
Belt Toggle, Dragons, Phoenix, Carved Creamy White, Chinese, 3 In.		461.00
Boulder, Scholar, Attendant, Bridge, Rocks, Pines, Green, Russet, Wood Stand, Chinese, 6 x 4 In.		356.00
Bowl, Bell Curve, Wide Rim, Round Foot, Spinach Green, Carved Wood Base, 8 In. Diam.		4464.00
Bowl, Bell Shape, Carved Characters, Vines, Flowers, Dark Green, Chinese, 2 ½ x 7 In.		2832.00
Bowl, Chrysanthemum Petals, Wide Rim, Dyed Green Ivory Stand, 1 ⅝ x 4 In.		7110.00
Bowl, Chrysanthemum, Mughal, Ridged Rim, Chinese, 1800s, 7 In.		1793.00
Bowl, Cover, Carved, 8 Precious Objects, Ba Bao, Chinese, 5 ⅜ In.		4780.00
Bowl, Dome Lid, Knob, Strap Handles, Round, Yellow White, Chinese, 3 ¾ x 5 ⅛ In.		8295.00
Bowl, Dragon, Carved, Round Wood Base, Spinach Green, 12 In.		388.00
Bowl, Dragon, Flaming Pearl, Clouds, Flowers, Green, Stand, Seal, Chinese, 1800s, 6 In.		3936.00
Bowl, Dragons, Carved, Mask Handles, Key Fret Ground, Gray, Oval, Chinese, 1800s, 4 ¾ x 3 ¼ In.		7110.00
Bowl, Flowers, Bamboo, Rocks Carved Sides, Spinach Green, Chinese, 7 x 2 ¾ In.		3021.00
Bowl, Lotus Leaf Shape, 3 Bats, Translucent Olive Green, 7 ½ x 7 In.		593.00

Jade, Vase, Square, Low Relief, Mask & Chrysanthemum Handles, Rings, Chinese, 5 ¾ In.
$2607.00

Skinner, Inc.

Jewelry, Bracelet, 18K Gold, Rose Cut Diamonds, 8 Textured Panels, Anton Fruhauf, 1960s, 7 ⅜ In.
$7110.00

Skinner, Inc.

Jewelry, Bracelet, Agates, Shaped, Engraved Gold Terminals, Ball Charm, Scotland, Victorian, 7 ½ In.
$1422.00

Skinner, Inc.

Jewelry, Bracelet, Bangle, Hinged, Turquoise Beads, 14K Gold, 6 ½ In.
$1067.00

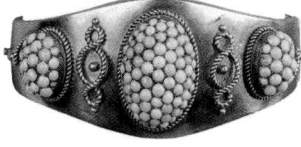

Skinner, Inc.

Jewelry, Bracelet, Beads, 5 Strands, Tumbled, Emeralds, Pearls, Gold, Engraved Clasp, c.1825, 7 ⅛ In. $1422.00

Skinner, Inc.

Jewelry, Bracelet, Cuff, Hinged, Bombe Shape, Textured Diamonds, 18K Gold, David Webb, 6 ¼ In. $8295.00

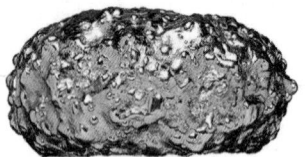

Skinner, Inc.

Jewelry, Bracelet, Cuff, Overlapping Bands, 18K Gold, Tiffany & Co., 1980, 1 In. $2607.00

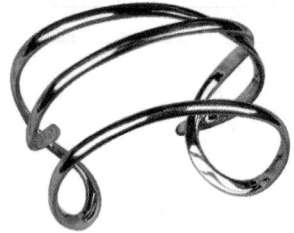

Skinner, Inc.

Jewelry, Bracelet, Earrings, Ring, Sterling, Enamel Panels, Screwback, Doris Hall, c.1950, 3 Piece $2800.00

M. Schon Gallery

TIP

Don't let metal jewelry touch chlorine bleach. It may pit or discolor.

Bowl, Lotus Scrolls, Sprigs, Carved, Flared, Footed, White, Chinese, 1800s, 5 x 2 In.	6518.00
Bowl, Mossy Spinach, Wide Rim, Inclusions, Round Foot, 6 In. Diam.	279.00
Bowl, Open Chrysanthemum Shape, Buddha, Yellow Green Color, 2 ½ x 4 ¼ In.	3185.00
Bowl, Rice, Flared Bell Shape, Lip Rim, Wood Stand, 1900s, 7 In., Pair	861.00
Bowl, Rice, Round, Raised Foot Rim, Mottled Green, Black, Wood Stand, 6 In., Diam.	399.00
Bowl, Spinach Green, Engraving, Boy, Crane, Peaches, Woman, Bamboo, Lotus, Footed 8 In., Pair	1845.00
Bowl, Turned Out, Lip Rim, Splayed Foot Rim, White, 4 Engraved Characters, Gilt, 6 In.	553.00
Bowl, Wedding, Relief Carved, Shou Characters, Dragon, Clouds, Flaming Pearl, 3 x 7 ½ In.	1599.00
Bowl, White, Pale Green & Brown Veining, Chinese, 5 ½ In.	593.00
Box, 2 Parts, Dragons, Scroll Carved, Compartments, Gray, Chinese, 1800s, 1 ½ x 2 ¾ In.	11850.00
Box, Cube Shape, 2 Sections, Carved, Shou Character, 2 Bats, White, Striated, 4 In.	9225.00
Box, Lid, Relief Carved, Raised Designs, Loop Finial, Jump Ring, Chinese, 1800s, 2 x 2 ⅞ In. ....*illus*	4740.00
Brush Holder, Rounded Square Shape, Gilt Calligraphy, Bamboo Design, Green, Chinese, 6 In.	538.00
Brush Washer, Chi Dragons, Celadon, Carved, Chinese, 8 In.	1673.00
Brush Washer, Chi Dragons, Gray, Green, Russet, Chinese, 3 ¼ In.	448.00
Brush Washer, Double Gourd Shape, Leafy Stem, Wood Stand, White, Chinese, 1 x 3 In.	1195.00
Brush Washer, Double Gourd, Carved, Pine Tree Branches, Spider, Wood Stand, 1900s, 5 In.	615.00
Brush Washer, Elongated Oval, Carved Dragons, Scrolling Clouds, Flaming Pearl, 7 In.	13420.00
Brush Washer, Frog, Seed, Flower, Carved, Lotus Shape, Pale Green, Chinese, 5 x 4 In.	1103.00
Brush Washer, Round, Curved-In Rim, 2 Snails, Carved Feet, Feelers, Shells, Green, 1700s, 7 In.	8302.00
Brushpot, Bamboo Shoot Shape, Pine, Prunus, Bamboo, Friends Of Winter, Carved, 6 ½ In. .	3437.00
Brushpot, Double, Bamboo Shape, 2 Boys, Branches, Chinese, 1800s, 2 x 4 In.	1125.00
Brushpot, Sages, Forest, Rocks, Pine Trees, Bamboo, Prunus, Crane, Key Fret Border, 6 In.	11685.00
Brushpot, Twisting Tree Trunk Shape, Vines, Root Stand, 4 ¼ In.	4800.00
Buckle, 2 Square Sections, Carved Beasts, Loose Ring, White, 3 In.	232.00
Buckle, Dragon, Divided Tail, Head Finial, Pale Green, Chinese, 4 ⅜ In.	474.00
Buckle, Dragon, Holding Flowers, Foo Dog Clasp, White, Chinese, 1800s, 3 In.	5333.00
Buckle, Dragon, Pale Celadon, Chinese, 1800s, 4 ⅞ In.	2963.00
Buckle, Foo Dog, Head Backward, Green, Oval, Brass Mounts, Chinese, 2 x 2 In.	1067.00
Candlestick, Pricket, Column, Splayed Base, Lotus Blossom Cup, Dragons, Spinach Green, 9 In., Pair	2460.00
Cane Handle, Coiled Snake, Ruby Colored Eyes, Gold Mounted, Marked, E.S., Russia, 3 x 4 In.	8125.00
Carving, Cylinder, Rounded Top, Phoenixes, Flowering Trees, Dark Green, Chinese, 1900s, 6 In., Pair	267.00
Carving, Lotus Blossom, Fish, Apple Green, Lavender, White, Chinese, 4 ½ In.	478.00
Carving, Mountain, Scholars, White Celadon, Markings, Wood Stand, Chinese, 6 ½ x 5 In. ...*illus*	3063.00
Carving, Pagoda, Green, Celadon, Wood Stand, 19 x 20 In.	12548.00
Carving, Panda, Cub, Base, 1 ½ x 1 In.	1350.00
Carving, Pumpkin, Vines, Spinach, Chinese, Carved Rosewood Base, 5 ¼ In.	5346.00
Censer, Bombe Body, Stylized Dragon, 2 Phoenix Handles, Calligraphy Rim, 3-Footed, 7 x 3 In.	8963.00
Censer, Bulbous, 3 Openwork Handles, Cartouches, Pine Trees, Pale Celadon, 4 ¾ x 5 ⅜ In. ..	5629.00
Censer, Cover, Globe Shape, Animal Masks, Foo Dog Finial & Handles, Rings, Wood Stand, 1800s	1035.00
Censer, Cover, Lobed, Pale Green White, Ring Handles, Chinese, 7 x 6 ½ In. ....*illus*	16590.00
Censer, Cover, Tripod, Gray Celadon, Mythical Beast Finial, Foo Dog Handles, 5 ¾ In.	777.00
Censer, Dome Flower, Lid, Strap Handles, Green, Chinese, 1800s, 4 In.	1659.00
Censer, Dome Lid, Masks, Mythical Birds, Gray, Flat Globe Shape, Chinese, 1800s, 4 x 4 ½ In.	9480.00
Censer, Foo Dog Finial, Round Body, Animal Mask, Ring Handles, 3 Squat Legs, Green, 6 In. .	4216.00
Censer, Lid, Squat, Dragon Handles, Rings, Footed, Scrolling, 6 In.	510.00
Censer, Roses, Leaves, 2 Rose Handles, Loose Rings, Dome Lid, Flower Finial, 3 Feet, 4 In.	980.00
Censer, Round, S-Shape Handles, Dome Cover, Round Foot, Celadon Green, Chinese, 1800s, 8 In.	19120.00
Censer, Silver Lid, Openwork Cash Coin Design, Cylindrical, Lavender, Chinese, 1800s, 2 x 3 In.	1838.00
Censer, White, Baluster, Lid Chained To Carved Flower Spray, Bird, Chinese, 1900s, 3 x 3 In.	15340.00
Cup, Carved Scrolls, Incised Dragons, Green, Russet Inclusions, Chinese, 10 In.	593.00
Cup, Carved, Fluted, Cylindrical, Carved Wood Stand, Footed, 3 In., Pair	4712.00
Cup, Chi Dragon, Lotus, Carved, Chinese, 1600s, 1 ¾ x 4 In.	2988.00
Dish, Leaf, Chi Dragon, Crawling, Gray Celadon, Chinese, 5 ¾ In. ....*illus*	2252.00
Dish, Round, Squat, Wavy Rim, Leave & Vines, Green & Amber, 1800s, 2 x 6 In.	1725.00
Disk, Pi, Center Circular Opening, Carved, Cream & Brown, 6 In. Diam.	338.00
Document Holder, Cylindrical, White, Bronze Screw, Incised Calligraphy, 1700s, 14 In.	4674.00
Ewer, Dome Lid, Mountains, Pines, Loop Handles, Gray, Pear Shape, Chinese, 7 In.	1778.00
Figurine, Beast, Crouched, Green & Russet, Wings, Fangs, Chinese, c.1880, 1 x 2 ¼ In.	3360.00
Figurine, Beast, Sitting, Defined Spine, Grayish White, 1700s, 1 ½ x 2 ¼ In.	1200.00
Figurine, Bird, Celadon & Russet, Long Tail, Head Turned Back, Nesting, c.1800s, 5 In.	12915.00
Figurine, Bird, Flowers, Spread Wings, Oval Wood Stand, Chinese, 12 x 12 In.	896.00
Figurine, Bird, Mottled Green, Carved, On Rock, Wood Stand, Chinese, 1800s, 7 In., Pair	2988.00
Figurine, Bird, On Mythical Animal, Yellowed White, Russet Inclusions, Chinese, 1 ¾ In.	398.00
Figurine, Boy, Crouching, Deer, Russet & White, Chinese, c.1890, 3 x 2 ½ In.	4200.00
Figurine, Boy, Fishing, Raft, Gray, White, Russet, Chinese, 7 x 4 ¾ In.	214.00
Figurine, Boy, Holding Fan, Chinese, c.1925, 2 ¾ In.	100.00

Figurine, Boy, Mushrooms Over Back, Ram, Pale Green, Chinese, 5 ½ In.	16500.00
Figurine, Boy, On Ox, Carved, Rosewood Stand, 4 x 6 In.	431.00
Figurine, Boy, Standing, Yellow, White, Chinese, 2 In.	830.00
Figurine, Boys, Resting, Rocks, Lotus, Bats, Openwork, Carved, Pale Green, Chinese, 4 x 4 In.	490.00
Figurine, Buddha, Laughing, Seated, Bare Chested, Loose Robes, Lotus Leaf, 7 ¼ In.	307.00
Figurine, Buddha, Seated, Crowned & Jeweled, Double Lotus Throne, 7 ½ In.	11025.00
Figurine, Buddha, Seated, Hands In Lap, Gilt Accents, 1800s, Chinese, 4 ½ In.	1265.00
Figurine, Buddha, Seated, Laughing, Holding Branch, Peaches Overhead, 1900s, 9 x 5 In.	525.00
Figurine, Buddha, Seated, White, Wood Stand, 1800s, 8 x 6 In.	1356.00
Figurine, Buddha's Hand, Citron, Leaf, Wood Stand, White, Chinese, 1800s, 2 In.	4740.00
Figurine, Bull, Standing, Spinach Green, Carved Wood Base, Chinese, 5 ½ In., Pair	538.00
Figurine, Camel, Reclining, Opening At Top, Incense Stick, Spinach Color, 10 In.	1116.00
Figurine, Camel, Standing, Open Mouth, Mottled Celadon, 1700s, 5 ¼ x 4 ¾ In.	1320.00
Figurine, Children Playing, Celadon, Chinese, 2 ½ x 5 In.	1016.00
Figurine, Cicada, White, Folded Legs, Archaic Symbols, Chinese, 2 ⅜ In.	4720.00
Figurine, Courtier, Mottled Green, Holding Vase, Lotus, Fly Whisk, Wood Stand, 1900s, 8 In.	1353.00
Figurine, Crab & Shrimp, Green, Carved Wood Base, Chinese, 5 In.	209.00
Figurine, Crane, Upward Stretched Neck, Branch Of Linghzhi Fungus, 7 In., Pair	397.00
Figurine, Cranes, Russet, Apple Green, Mounted, Ruyi Banded Gilt Stand, c.1900, 9 In., Pair	1293.00
Figurine, Cub, Crawling, Foo Dog, White, Brocade Ball, Chinese, 1800s, 1 x 2 x 2 In.	925.00
Figurine, Deer, Resting, White Inclusions, Chinese, 3 ½ x 5 In.	1298.00
Figurine, Dog, Pekingese, Resting, White, Dark Inclusions, Chinese, 3 ⅜ In.	153.00
Figurine, Dog, Seated, Gray, Brown, Chinese, c.1890, 6 ½ In.	1800.00
Figurine, Dog, Sleeping, Bird On Back, White, Russet Veining, Chinese, 1800s, 3 x 4 In.	17250.00
Figurine, Dragon, Green, Carved, Chinese, 8 x 13 In.	122.00
Figurine, Dragon, Horned, Mottled White, Green, Russet, Chinese, c.1970, 9 ¾ In.	184.00
Figurine, Dragon, Tortoise & Lion Body, Olive, Yellow Inclusions, Chinese, 1800s, 4 ¾ In.	430.00
Figurine, Duck, Holding Sprig, Gray, Chinese, 2 ⅜ In.	214.00
Figurine, Duck, Mandarin, White, Russet Veining, Chinese, 1700s, 2 ½ In.	1715.00
Figurine, Duck, Seated, Fungus Spray In Mouth, Olive, Brown, Chinese, 1800s, 3 In.	215.00
Figurine, Elephant, Mottled Apple & Spinach, Carved Symbol, Stand, Chinese, 3 x 5 In.	748.00
Figurine, Elephant, Standing, With Baby At Rear, White, 3 In.	4216.00
Figurine, Elephant, Washed By 2 Riders, Pouring Water, Broom, White, 3 In.	3224.00
Figurine, Fish, Tiger Face, Chinese, c.1925, 3 ½ x 7 In.	975.00
Figurine, Foo Dog, Backwards Head, Divided Tail, White, Chinese, 2 ½ In.	770.00
Figurine, Foo Dog, Pup, Seated, On Haunches, Light Green, Footed Wood Base, 6 In.	589.00
Figurine, Foo Dog, Seated, Russet, Celadon, Wood Base, Chinese, 4 ½ In.	43020.00
Figurine, Foo Dogs, Playing With Ball, Chinese, c.1900, 3 ¾ x 4 ½ x 17 In.	225.00
Figurine, Guanyin, Flowing Cloak, Hair In Bun, Holding Scepter, Lotus Stand, 8 ¼ In.	11992.00
Figurine, Guanyin, Goddess Of Compassion, Holding Scroll, Nephrite, Chinese, 1900s, 8 ¾ In.	777.00
Figurine, Guanyin, Mottled Green To White, On Lotus Throne, Flattened Shape, c.1900, 7 In.	207.00
Figurine, Guanyin, Royal Pose, Lotus Stand, White, Wood Stand, Chinese, 5 ¼ In.	490.00
Figurine, Guanyin, Seated On Lotus Throne, Aureole Behind, Mottled Green To White, c.1900, 7 In.	354.00
Figurine, Guanyin, Standing, Lotus Plinth, Holding Vase & Pearl, Wood Base, Chinese, 8 In.	203.00
Figurine, Guanyin, Standing, Pouring Water From Bottle, Holding Jewel, Gray, Chinese, 4 ½ In.	368.00
Figurine, Guanyin, Standing, Wearing Long Robes, Beaded Jewelry, Apple Green & White, 16 In.	3227.00
Figurine, Horse, Costume, Wood Stand, Chinese, 17th Century, 2 ¾ x 3 ¾ In. ....*illus*	11850.00
Figurine, Horse, Rolling On Back, In-Curved Tail, Mottled White & Russet, Wood Stand, 4 In.	7995.00
Figurine, Horse, Standing, Lowered Head, White, Brocade Box, Chinese, 1900s, 3 ½ x 7 In.	3444.00
Figurine, Horse, Standing, Turned Head, Mottled Green, Lavender, Base, 1900s, 8 In.	676.00
Figurine, Horseman, Small Attendant Pulling, Gray, Wood Stand, Chinese, 1800s, 4 x 4 In.	10665.00
Figurine, Ibex, Resting, Pale Green, Russet, Chinese, 2 x 3 In.	1800.00
Figurine, Immortal, Attendants, Bat On Shoulder, Holding Peach, Celadon Green, 7 In.	3585.00
Figurine, Immortal, Deity Shou Lao, God Of Longevity, Staff, Double Gourd, Peach, 12 In.	470.00
Figurine, Immortal, In Long Robes, Celestial Scarf, Holding Blossoms, Chinese, 8 ½ In.	538.00
Figurine, Immortal, Woman, Long Robes, Celestial Scarf, Holding Fan & Cup, Chinese, 6 In.	329.00
Figurine, Immortal, Woman, Standing, Holding Flywhisk, Robe, Wood Base, Green, 5 ½ In.	359.00
Figurine, Kylin, Standing, Round Wood Base, White, Chinese, c.1900, 3 In.	1840.00
Figurine, Landscape, Pavilion, Mountains, Pine Tree, Carved, 2-Sided, Chinese, 9 x 10 ¾ In.	16605.00
Figurine, Lion, Seated, Front Legs Raised, Green, 2 In., Pair	366.00
Figurine, Lotus Blossom, Squirrel, Peanut, Celadon Color, Fitted Wood Base, 2 In.	3416.00
Figurine, Lotus Branch, Dragonfly, Wood Stand, 11 ½ In.	6000.00
Figurine, Lotus Pond Scene, Flower, Leaves, Semitranslucent White, Chinese, 5 x 3 In.	1348.00
Figurine, Lotus, Half Opened, Bee, Dragonfly, Carved, Semitranslucent, Chinese, 1800s, 2 ½ In.	3555.00
Figurine, Maiden, Standing, Flowing Robes, Holding Peach & Flowers, Wood Stand, 4 ¾ In.	246.00
Figurine, Maiden, Standing, Holding Flower Bouquet, Pale Green, Lavender, 7 ½ In.	6200.00

Jewelry, Bracelet, Enamel, Gold Metal, Bezel Set Stones, Ciner, 1 ½-In. Wide
$59.00

Ivey-Selkirk Auctioneers

Jewelry, Bracelet, Horse's Head, Snake Link, 15 Brilliant Cut Diamonds, Red & Blue Enamel, 18K Gold
$4425.00

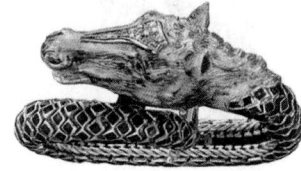

Ivey-Selkirk Auctioneers

Jewelry, Bracelet, Link, Geometric, Agate, Multicolor, 18K Gold, Tiffany & Co., 7 ¼ In.
$2489.00

Skinner, Inc.

Jewelry, Bracelet, Link, Leaves, Silver, Lapis Cabochon, Georg Jensen, 7 ⅛ In.
$1778.00

Skinner, Inc.

J

JADE

Jewelry, Bracelet, Snake, Gold, Garnet, Enamel, Flexible Body, Victorian, 7 In.
$1960.00

Skinner, Inc.

Jewelry, Bracelet, Snake, Gold & Enamel, Rose-Cut Diamond Head, Hinged, 6 In.
$5333.00

Skinner, Inc.

Jewelry, Chatelaine, Notebook, Silver, Birds, Flowers, 6 Celluloid Day Cards, Victorian, 2 ¾ x 1 ¾ In.
$148.00

Ivey-Selkirk Auctioneers

Jewelry, Cuff Links, Fish, Tortoiseshell Inlay, Silver, William Spratling, Mexico, 1 In.
$593.00

Skinner, Inc.

Figurine, Man, Kneeling, Ram's Head, White, Russet, Chinese, 2 In.	356.00
Figurine, Man, On Horseback, Reclining Horse, Oval Wood Base, Chinese, 4 In.	1195.00
Figurine, Man, Seated, Holding Staff, Toad, Pale Green, Chinese, 9 In.	337.00
Figurine, Mei Tree, Flowering, Bronze Planter, Hardstone & Coral Buds, 1800s, 15 x 8 In.	1121.00
Figurine, Money Toad, Light Celadon Green, Chinese, 3 In.	329.00
Figurine, Mongolian Pony, Celadon, Chinese, 4 x 6 In.	799.00
Figurine, Monk, Seated, Carved, Wood Stand, Chinese, c.1890, 3 ¼ In.	7170.00
Figurine, Monkey, Climbing Gourd, Gray, Chinese, 3 ½ In.	267.00
Figurine, Monkey, Fruit Branch, Translucent White, Russet Marks, Chinese, 2 ⅛ x 1 ½ In.	770.00
Figurine, Monkey, Mother Holding Baby By Scruff Of Neck, Olive Green, 2 In.	399.00
Figurine, Monkey, On Resting Horse, Gray, Russet, Chinese, 1800s, 4 In.	2450.00
Figurine, Mouse, Head Backwards, Green, Chinese, 2 ½ In.	237.00
Figurine, Mouse, On Buddha's Hand, Carved, Celadon, White, Chinese, 3 ¼ In.	179.00
Figurine, Mythical Animal, Antlers, Boar Face, Tortoise Body, Green, 1800s, 1 ¼ x 1 ¼ In.	858.00
Figurine, Mythical Animal, Resting, Flowers In Mouth, Yellow, Green, Russet, 1700s, 2 x 1 ¾ In.	6518.00
Figurine, Mythical Figure, Resting, Dragon, Cloud Pattern Base, Green, Russet, 4 x 2 ¼ In.	7350.00
Figurine, Mythological Lion, Bixie, Mushrooms, Carved, Gray Green, Chinese, 1800s, 2 In.	368.00
Figurine, Mythological Lion, Bixie, Resting, White, Chinese, 2 In.	613.00
Figurine, Mythological Lion, Celadon, Reclining, Pearl Of Wisdom, Late 1700s, 4 In.	984.00
Figurine, Pebble, Dragon, Riding On Leafy Scrolls, Carved, Celadon, Russet, 2 ⅛ In.	2573.00
Figurine, Phoenix Birds, Carved, Chinese, 4 ¾ In., Pair	413.00
Figurine, Phoenix, Lidded Vase On Back, Flowing Tail Feathers, Wood Base, 8 In.	9150.00
Figurine, Pig, Carved Design On Back, Round Shape, Standing, Ears Down, 6 x 9 In.	813.00
Figurine, Pig, White, Resting, Legs Tucked Under, 1700s, 1 x 1 ½ In.	2880.00
Figurine, Ram, Resting, Carved, Light Green, Wood Stand, Chinese, 6 x 3 In.	356.00
Figurine, Ram, Resting, Carved, White, Russet, Chinese, 3 ¾ x 2 ½ In.	4444.00
Figurine, Rooster, Double Gourd, Trees, Lavender & Apple Green, Footed Wood Base, 17 x 13 In.	4541.00
Figurine, Sage, Seated, Bamboo Chair, Holding Dog, Flute-Playing Child, Cloud Shape Base, 4 In.	4920.00
Figurine, Shoe, Mottled Brown, Elongated, Cicada Head, Peonies, Wooden Stand, 1600s, 3 In.	307.00
Figurine, Sleeping Figure On Top, Gray, White, Chinese, 2 ¾ x 3 In.	1126.00
Figurine, Taoists, Happy Marriage Symbols, Puppy, Carved, Chinese, c.1800, 2 ¾ In.	2390.00
Figurine, Tiger, Crouching, Carved, Olive Green, Brown, 4 x 1 ½ In.	311.00
Figurine, Tiger, Reclining Under Tree, Box, 4 In.	30.00
Figurine, Unicorn, Resting, White, Chinese, 4 x 2 In.	2083.00
Figurine, Water Buffalo, Gray, White, Chinese, 5 ¾ In.	478.00
Figurine, Water Buffalo, Resting, Clenched Teeth, Dimpled, Green, 2 x 4 ¾ In.	308.00
Figurine, Water Buffalo, Resting, Gray-Green, Brown, 3 ½ x 7 ¾ In.	6458.00
Figurine, Woman, Holding Flowers, Phoenix, Blooming Rose Branches, Chinese, 1900s, 8 In.	266.00
Flask, Lid, Immortals, Attendants, Landscape, Bird Lugs, Flat Hu Shape, Gray, Chinese, 7 In.	3851.00
Flower Shape, Overlapping Petals, Round Footed Base, White, c.1900, 1 ¼ x 7 x 4 ½ In.	489.00
Group, 2 Boys, Seated, Lotus Leaf, Celadon, Russet, 2 ⅛ In.	711.00
Group, 2 Dogs, Resting, Pale Green, 2 x 1 ¾ In.	474.00
Group, 2 Horses, Resting, Pale Green, Chinese, 2 ½ x 1 ½ In.	337.00
Group, 2 Taoist Figures, Symbol Of Happy Marriage, Carved, Chinese, 1900s, 2 ½ x 3 In.	1793.00
Group, 5 Birds, Perched In Branches, Prunus Tree, Buds & Flowers, 1900s, 12 In.	676.00
Group, Cranes, Magnolia Tree, Pine Tree, Dark Green & White, 1900s, 8 In.	246.00
Group, Foo Dog, Flowers, Pale Green, 1 ¾ In.	368.00
Group, Foo Dogs, Contesting Mushroom, Pale Green, Chinese, 2 ¼ In.	593.00
Group, Foo Dogs, Mother, Pup, Mottled Green, Wood Stand, Chinese, 1900s, 6 ½ In.	338.00
Group, Lotus Scepter, Pines, Plums, Bats, Dragons, Openwork, Green, White, Chinese, 6 In.	830.00
Group, Lotus Seed Pods, Leaves, Openwork Carved, Chinese, 2 ½ x 2 In.	674.00
Group, Mandarin Ducks & Fish, White, Chinese, 6 In.	956.00
Group, Mountain, Immortals, Attendants, Rocks, Pines, Green, Russet, Chinese, 1800s, 8 x 6 ½ In.	3063.00
Group, Mountain, Scholar, Attendant, Pine, Pavilions, Waves, Green, Brown, Wood Stand, 6 x 9 In.	4740.00
Group, Quail, Nesting, Grasses, Pebble Shape, White, Chinese, 1800s, 2 x 2 ¼ In.	276.00
Group, Ram, Resting, Clouds, Pale Green, Chinese, 5 ½ In.	1659.00
Group, Rams, Mushroom Sprigs, Gray, Green, Chinese, 5 ¼ In.	3553.00
Group, Scholar, Attendant, Pine Tree, Mountain Shape, Pale Green, Chinese, 3 x 3 ¼ In.	613.00
Group, Scholar, Boat, Rocks, Pines, Gray, White, Chinese, 9 x 3 In.	1541.00
Hairpin, Pumpkins, Squirrels, Carved, Chinese, c.1750, 11 In.	2629.00
Handle, Nilgai Head, Curved Neck, Mughal Celadon, Black Base, 1700s, 5 ¼ In.	6405.00
Hat Ornament, Carved Cranes, Lotus, Gray, Rosewood Stand, Chinese, 1800s, 1 ¼ x 1 ⅛ In.	7703.00
Hook, Garment, Dragon, Holding Mushroom, Finial, Curved, Pale Green, Chinese, 1800s, 6 In.	796.00
Hook, Garment, Dragon's Head Facing Chi Dragon, 19th Century, 4 ¼ In.	2000.00
Hook, Garment, S-Shape, Relief Carved, Dragon Finial, Yellow, Chinese, 5 In.	444.00
Incense Burner, 3 Lion Head Feet, Dragon Head Handles & Finial, Pierced Cover, c.1905, 6 In.	1168.00

Incense Holder, Stick, Squared Shape, Slight Tapering, Carved, Pierced, Dragon, Leaves, 4 In.	2952.00
Jar, Cover, Tapered, Ram's Head Handles, Rope Design, Pale Yellow, c.1900, 5 In.	1838.00
Jar, Snuff, Green, Cream, Silver, Globe Shape, Stone Stopper, 1700s, 2 ¼ x 3 ¼ In.	1430.00
Jar, Snuff, Green, White, Round, Metal, Amethyst Stopper, 1800s, 2 ¼ x 2 ¼ In.	880.00
Jar, Snuff, Purple, White, Carved Birds, Flowers, Stopper, Attached Spoon, 1800s, 3 ¾ x 4 In.	715.00
Jardiniere, Quatrefoil Shape, 3 Squat Legs, Spinach Green, 3 In.	992.00
Mirror, Flower Basket Plaque, Dragon Handle, White, Silver Mounts, Chinese, 1800s, 8 ¾ In.	8365.00
Mirror, Hand, Hairpin & Pierced Roundel, Enamel & Gilt Mount, Celadon Color, 8 In.	1342.00
Mountain, Interior Carved, Deer, White, Wood Stand, Chinese, 2 ¾ x 2 ⅜ In.	1067.00
Mountain, Scholar On Ledge, Tree Groves, Waves, Moss Green, Chinese, 1800s, 10 In.	2337.00
Mountain, Scholars, Boat, Pines, Dark To Light Green, Nanyang, Chinese, 6 ½ In.	1845.00
Mountain, Scholars, Bridge, Pavilion, Clouds, Gnarled Trees, Branch Stand, 15 In.	2952.00
Mountain, Scholars, Pale Green, Lavender, Peak, Pine Trees, Rockwork, Bridge, Stream, 9 ½ In.	1845.00
Mountain, Scholars, Pine & Prunus Trees, Chinese, 5 x 8 ½ In.	676.00
Mountain, Scholars, Toe-Skin, Landscape, Boat, Bridge, Waterfall, Chinese, 1800s, 6 x 7 ½ In.	9560.00
Pendant, Carved, Tree, Calligraphy, White, 2 ½ In.	657.00
Pendant, Carved, Vase, Scrolling Leaves, Openwork, Spinach Green Color, Chinese, 3 In.	269.00
Pendant, Dragon, Apple Green, Celadon, Chinese, 2 ¼ In.	179.00
Pendant, Layered Fretwork, Ribbed Sides, Scrolling, Chinese, 1700s, 2 x 1 ½ In.	1035.00
Pendant, Lozenge Shaped, Carved, Dragons, Crashing Waves, Brass Mounting, Chinese, 1 ⅝ In.	214.00
Pendant, Mottled Black, Archaic Ax, Stylized Leaves, Taotie Mask, 2 Dragon Handle, 3 In.	615.00
Pendant, Red & White, Leaping Carp, Waves, Spray, Lotus Leaf, Chinese, 3 ⅛ x 1 ⅝ In.	307.00
Pitcher, White, Brown Veining, Footed, Phoenix Handle, 1700s, 4 In.	38340.00
Plaque, 2 Boys, Playing, Bats, Peach, Carved, Pierced Borders, White, Round, Chinese, 2 In.	593.00
Plaque, 2 Cranes, Pine Tree, Gray, Chinese, 2 ¼ x 1 ¾ In.	474.00
Plaque, 2 Hornless Dragons, Carved, White, Russet, Round, Wood Stand, Chinese, 3 ⅜ In.	6518.00
Plaque, 2 Wild Geese Flying, Round, Carved, Pierced, Gray, Chinese, 1800s, 2 ¼ In.	4740.00
Plaque, Bamboo Joints, Rocks, Scroll Borders, Text, White, Chinese, 2 ¼ x 2 In.	652.00
Plaque, Birds, Boys, Playing Flute, Trumpet, White, Chinese, 2 x 2 In.	674.00
Plaque, Birds, Flying, Fruit, Arched Scroll Border, Inscriptions, White, Chinese, 2 x 1 ½ In.	1164.00
Plaque, Boy, Picking Fruit, Inscriptions, Carved, Pale Green, Chinese, 2 ¾ x 2 In.	415.00
Plaque, Boy, Riding Foo Dog, Cloud Scrolls, Treasures, Pale Green, Pierced, Chinese, 2 ¾ In.	2607.00
Plaque, Boy, Water Buffalo, Willow Tree, Wavy Border, Gray, Chinese, 2 ¼ x 2 In.	652.00
Plaque, Celestial Landscape, Bats, Clouds, Fish, Scroll Borders, Wood Stand, Chinese, 5 x 2 ¼ In.	1699.00
Plaque, Child Holding Vase, Vapors, Lotus, Pond, 2 Opposing Dragons, 1800s, 3 x 2 ⅜ In.	246.00
Plaque, Dragon Carved, Bat Pierced, Coins, Scrolls, Pale Green, Chinese, 2 ¾ x 1 ¾ In.	533.00
Plaque, Female Immortal, Attendant, White, Chinese, 3 x 1 ½ In.	267.00
Plaque, Immortal, Playing Zither, Tree, Yellow White, Chinese, 2 ¼ x 1 ½ In.	613.00
Plaque, Man, Riding Serpent, Carved, Wood Stand, Chinese, 2 x 3 ¼ In.	5451.00
Plaque, Monkey, Peach Tree, Bat, Carved Lotus Blossoms, White, 3 x 2 In.	615.00
Plaque, Mythical Animals, Carved, Pale Green, Chinese, 3 ½ x 2 In.	415.00
Plaque, Oval, Carved, Buddhist Emblems, 2 Umbrellas, Wheel, Waves, White, 4 x 3 In.	3904.00
Plaque, Round, Carved, Children At Play, White, 5 x 6 In.	688.00
Plaque, Round, White, 2 Dragons, Landscape Scene, Marked, 3 In.	1220.00
Plaque, Scholar, Attendant, Inscriptions, Pale Green, Chinese, 2 x 1 In.	674.00
Plaque, Scrolling Serpent, Pale Stone, Opaque Inclusions, 5 In.	110.00
Plaque, Translucent Green, Oval, Curved, Carved, Silver Surround, Embossed, Chinese, 3 ½ x 5 In.	2400.00
Plume Holder, Peacock Feather, Cylindrical, Narrow, Arched Top, Loop, Hole, White, 3 In.	7440.00
Pomander, Lid, Pierced Design, Animals, Scrolling Leaves, Green & Brown, 4 In.	10540.00
Pot, Cover, Carved, Round, Pale Yellow, 1 ½ x 2 In.	153.00
Scepter, Ruyi, Bronze, Gnarled Branch, Leaves, 2 Peaches, Celadon Plaque, 11 In.	2337.00
Scepter, Ruyi, Carved Design, Silk Tassels, Opaque White, Wood & Glass Case, 17 In.	14880.00
Scepter, Ruyi, Celadon & Russet, Chinese, 13 In.	657.00
Scepter, Ruyi, Dragons, Lotus Shape, Carved, Celadon, 1800s, 15 ½ In.	38850.00
Scepter, Ruyi, Entwined, Blue, Gray, Openwork Rosewood Stand, Chinese, 1800s, 6 ½ In.	1722.00
Scepter, Ruyi, Green, 3 Carved White Plaques, Fitted Box, Chinese, c.1945, 10 ½ In.	2337.00
Scepter, Ruyi, Inset Hardwood, Carved, 2 Cranes Under Pine Tree, Chinese, 14 ½ In.	389.00
Scepter, Ruyi, Multi Stemmed, Fungus Heads, Celadon, Russet Inclusions, 11 In.	799.00
Scepter, Ruyi, Twin Fish Heads, Shell, Parasol, Carved, Yellow Green, Chinese, 13 In.	1126.00
Screen, Dragons, Hugging Roundel, White, Oval, Rosewood Stand, Chinese, 4 ½ x 2 ¾ In.	2370.00
Screen, Table, Dragons, Scrolls, Carved, Openwork Wood Stand, Chinese, 1800s, 5 x 8 In.	2963.00
Screen, Table, Figure, Tree, Mountain, Spinach, 14 ½ x 16 In.	452.00
Screen, Table, Flowers, Branches, Rocks, Carved, Gray, Wood Stand, Chinese, 1800s, 4 x 3 In.	7963.00
Scroll Weight, Shen Yeh, God Of Wealth, Holding Silver Ingot, Rosary, 5 x 3 ½ In.	2706.00
Seal, Calligraphy, Foo Dog Finial, White, Chinese, 4 ½ In.	2390.00

Jewelry, Cuff Links, Glass, Reverse Painted, Horse's Head, Double Link, 14K Gold
$1422.00

Skinner, Inc.

Jewelry, Cuff Links, Playing Cards, 4 Aces, Black & Red Enamel, 14K Gold, Marked
$2762.00

Skinner, Inc.

Jewelry, Cuff Links, Ram's Head, Ruby Eye, 18K Gold, Kurt Wayne
$1422.00

Skinner, Inc.

Jewelry, Cuff Links, Snail Shell, Silver, Gold, Georg Jensen, No. 52
$770.00

Skinner, Inc.

J

Jewelry, Earrings, Cameo, Lion's Head, Citrine, Sunburst Border, Enamel, 18K, Gage, 1 ¼ In.
$3555.00

Skinner, Inc.

Jewelry, Earrings, Cameo, Winged Figure, Putti, Shell, 18K Gold Mount, 2 ¾ In.
$1304.00

Skinner, Inc.

Jewelry, Earrings, Coral, Button, 18K Gold, Tiffany & Co., 1 ¼ In.
$3555.00

Skinner, Inc.

Jewelry, Earrings, Coral, Cameo, Faceted Drop, 18K Gold Mounts, 2 ¾ In.
$1348.00

Skinner, Inc.

Seal, Chimera Finial, Carved, Green, White Inclusions, Chinese, 1800s, 2 ¼ x 2 ¼	735.00
Seal, Double Dragon Finial, Square, Olive Color, Russet, Black Trim, Chinese, 3 ¾ x 3 ¾ In.	1896.00
Seal, Dragon Head, Ram's Antlers, Foo Dog Body, Characters, White, Chinese, 1800s, 2 x 2 In.	14220.00
Seal, Dragon, Square, Chinese, 4 In.	3884.00
Seal, Dragons, Semitranslucent, Opaque, Russet, Square, 2 x 2 ¼ In.	415.00
Seal, Dragon-Tortoise, Celadon & Russet, Chinese, 3 In.	239.00
Seal, Square, Double Dragon Shape Finial, Dark Green, 4 ¼ In.	1554.00
Teapot, Cover, Globular, Lotus Blossom Finial, Scrolling Leaf Tip, Celadon Green, c.1855, 4 x 7 In.	23000.00
Teapot, Lotus, Scrolls, Carved, Domed Lid, Translucent White, Chinese, 4 ¾ x 7 In.	6125.00
Teapot, Scholar, Bridge, Mushrooms, Mountains, Scroll Handle, Carved, Gray, Chinese, 3 ¾ In.	3675.00
Urn, Cover, Vines, Ring Handles, Paw Feet, Carved, 9 ½ x 8 ½ In.	362.00
Vase, Applied Dragon, Mythical Animals, Carved, Chinese, Translucent, c.1900, 4 ½ In.	575.00
Vase, Bird On Shoulder, Wave Lid, Carved, Double Fish Shape, Green, Chinese, 1800s, 9 In.	306.00
Vase, Celadon, Square, Flared Rim, Ribbed Edges, Square Foot, Carved, 5 In.	4636.00
Vase, Cover, 3 Tiers, Carved, Loose Ring Handles, White, Chinese, 9 x 7 In.	366.00
Vase, Cover, Apple Green, Russet, Flattened Shape, Phoenix Birds, Peonies, Rose Handles, 5 In.	307.00
Vase, Cover, Birds, Flowers, Inscriptions, Short Neck, Scroll Lugs, Green, Chinese, 5 ½ In.	1896.00
Vase, Cover, Carved, Prunus Tree Design, Oval Shape, Wood Base, Green, Chinese, 7 In.	3884.00
Vase, Cover, Engraved, Loop Handles, Lion Finial, Carved Wood, Chinese, 6 x 3 In.	472.00
Vase, Cover, Lion's Head Handles, Rings, Deer, Bridge, Pavilions, White, c.1900, 8 ¼ In.	4674.00
Vase, Cover, Stylized, Green, Lions, Chimera, Flattened Rectangle, Dragon Handles, 14 In.	2952.00
Vase, Cover, Urn Shape, Ring Handles, Foo Dog Finial, Round Base, Spinach Green, 7 In.	1315.00
Vase, Dome Lid, 5 Carved Dragons, Yellow, Chinese, 5 ½ In.	3675.00
Vase, Double, Rectangular, Bat, Ring Handles, Spinach Green, Wood Base, 1950, 11 In.	956.00
Vase, Dragons, Side Rings, Elephant Handles, Flared-Spinach Green, 1900s, 12 x 7 In., Pair	4780.00
Vase, Flower Group, Carved, Green Mottled, Brown, Double Gourd Shape, Wood Stand, 7 ½ In.	307.00
Vase, Fruit, Scrolling Leaves, Flower Shape, Wood Stand, Carved, 1800s, 4 In.	4888.00
Vase, Lid, Lion Finial, Compressed Flask Shape, Ram's Head Handles, Gray, Russet, 9 In., Pair	6200.00
Vase, Mythical Animals, Ring Handles, Chinese, 19th Century, 2 ¼ In.	425.00
Vase, Mythical Creatures, Carved, Pale Green, Chinese, 1900s, 7 ¾ In.	1593.00
Vase, On Kneeling Ram, Ruffled Rim, Ring Handles, Gray & Green, Wood Base, Chinese, 6 ½ In.	538.00
Vase, Round Foot, Elongated, Rounded Bottom, Flared Rim, 4 In., Pair	780.00
Vase, Square, Low Relief, Mask & Chrysanthemum Handles, Rings, Chinese, 5 ¾ In. ....*illus*	2607.00
Vase, Square, Trumpet Top, Cutout Design, Chinese, 4 In.	837.00
Vase, Tapered, Turned-Out Lip, Fretwork, Flowering Branches, Icy Mint, 1800s, 6 ½ In.	738.00
Vase, White, Chrysanthemums, Ring Handles, 19th Century, 9 x 3 In.	10100.00
Water Coupe, 3 Flower Blossoms, Joining Branch, Bird, Child, Yellow Tan, 1800s, 9 x 5 ¼ In.	3981.00
Water Coupe, 4 Sides, Lotus Shape, White, Gilt Mark, Chinese, 1800s, 3 ¼ x 2 ½ In.	4740.00
Water Coupe, Boys, Playing, Pond, Pale Green, Carved, Woven Basket Shape, Chinese, 3 ½ x 8 In.	3981.00
Water Coupe, Carved, Lotus Blossoms, Branches, Leaves, Raised Wood Stand, Celadon, 6 In.	12200.00
Water Coupe, Curled Lotus Leaf, Bug, Carved, Green, White, Chinese, 1700s, 3 ½ In.	858.00
Water Coupe, Dragon, Incised Patterns, Swirling Water, White, Green, Chinese, 2 ¼ x 2 ¼ In.	796.00
Water Coupe, Pine Tree, Gray, Russet Veining, 1800s, 5 x 3 ½ In.	4740.00
Wrist Rest, Carved, Flowers, Leaves, Relief, Cartouche, Calligraphy, Rectangular, 4 ¼ In.	598.00
Wrist Rest, Scroll Feet, Rectangular, Pale Green, Chinese, 6 x 1 In.	356.00

JAPANESE CORALENE is a ceramic decorated with small raised beads and dots. It was first made in the nineteenth century. Later wares made to imitate coralene had dots of enamel. There is also another type of coralene that is made with small glass beads on glass containers.

Ewer, Flowers, Gilt Handle, 5 ½ In.	383.00
Jar, Flowers, Ferns, Blue, Cover, 5 In.	75.00
Sugar & Creamer, Flower, Blue, Gilt Trim	55.00
Vase, Chrysanthemum, Gray, Footed, Handles, 9 In.	625.00
Vase, Cylinder, Rose, 8 x 3 In.	995.00
Vase, Green, 3-Footed, c.1920, 4 ¾ In.	251.00
Vase, Iris, 2 Handles, Cylinder, Gilt, c.1900, 14 In.	525.00
Vase, Medallions, Ribbons, Shouldered, Scrolled Handles, 1909, 14 In.	1995.00

JAPANESE WOODBLOCK PRINTS *are listed in this book in the Print category under Japanese.*

JASPERWARE can be made in different ways. Some pieces are made from a solid-colored clay with applied raised designs of a contrasting colored clay. Other pieces are made entirely of one color clay with raised decorations that are glazed with a contrasting color. Additional pieces of jasperware may also be listed in the Wedgwood category or under various art potteries.

Bell, Dark Green, Angels, Cherubs, Playing Instruments, 4 ½ In.	54.00
Bowl, Blue, White, Hunting Scene, Silver Rim, c.1900, 5 x 9 In.	125.00

J

Box, Blue, Lady, Holding Parrot & Vase, Roses, c.1890, 3 ¾ In. Diam.	125.00
Cheese Dish, Plate, Domed, Inverted Acorn Finial, Classical Relief Figures, Vines, 11 x 11 In.	119.00
Plaque, Portrait, Beethoven, Blue, White, c.1880, 7 ½ In. Diam..	98.00
Teapot, Green, White, Classical Figures, Flower Border, 1940s, 5 In.	128.00
Trinket Box, Bird, On Branch, 2 ¾ In.	28.00
Vase, Blue, White, Woman, Holding Mirror, 3 ¼ In.	25.00
Vase, White, Blue Palm Leaves, Cylindrical, c.1926, 8 ½ In.	88.00

JEWELRY, whether made from gold and precious gems or plastic and colored glass, is popular with collectors. Values are determined by the intrinsic value of the stones and metal and by the skill of the craftsmen and designers. Victorian and older jewelry has been collected since the 1950s. More recent interests are Art Deco and Edwardian styles, Mexican and Danish silver jewelry, and beads of all kinds. Copies of almost all styles are being made. American Indian jewelry is listed in the Indian category. Tiffany jewelry is listed here.

Belt Buckle, Bakelite, Round, 1940s, 2 ½ In..................................	20.00
Belt Buckle, Enameled, Flowers, Green, Red, 4 ¼ In..................................	360.00
Bracelet, 4 Plaques, Rome Scenes, Burgundy Glass, Flora & Fauna Oval Plaques, c.1850, 7 ¼ In.	6083.00
Bracelet, 18K Gold, Rose Cut Diamonds, 8 Textured Panels, Anton Fruhauf, 1960s, 7 ⅜ In. ..... *illus*	7110.00
Bracelet, Agates, Shaped, Engraved Gold Terminals, Ball Charm, Scotland, Victorian, 7 ½ In. *illus*	1422.00
Bracelet, Aluminum, Hammered, Chased, Dots, Sunburst, Marked, FHB, Retro, 6 ¼ & 6 ¼ In., Pair	125.00
Bracelet, Angel Skin Coral, Blossoms, Leaves, 14K Gold, c.1945, 7 ¾ In.	1895.00
Bracelet, Aurora Borealis Crystal, 2 Strands, Box Clasp, Silvertone, 1950s........................	17.00
Bracelet, Bakelite, Marbled Evergreen, Brass Filigree, Chunky, c.1950, 6 ¾ x 2 ½ In.	195.00
Bracelet, Band, Textured, Flower Head, Tassels, Gold, 1950s, 7 In..................................	6083.00
Bracelet, Bangle, 14K Gold, Enamel, Marked, Hermes, Austria, 2 ⅝ In..................................	510.00
Bracelet, Bangle, Bakelite, Black, White Rhinestones, c.1955, 1 x 2 ¼ In..................................	185.00
Bracelet, Bangle, Bakelite, Carved Rose, Yellow, 1930s..................................	225.00
Bracelet, Bangle, Bakelite, Yellow, Diamonds, 1950s..................................	75.00
Bracelet, Bangle, Cameo, Shell, Cherub Scene, 14K Gold Band, Engraved 1854, 7 In.	1035.00
Bracelet, Bangle, Catalin, Basket Weave Pattern, 1920s, 7 ½ In..................................	250.00
Bracelet, Bangle, Celluloid, Blue, Rhinestones, c.1925, ½ In..................................	45.00
Bracelet, Bangle, Celluloid, Green, Carved Tropical Leaves, 1930s..................................	140.00
Bracelet, Bangle, Diamonds, Onyx Bars, 14K Gold, Foldover Safety, 1970s, 2 ½ In....................	546.00
Bracelet, Bangle, Flowers, Pearl, 10K Gold, Victorian, 6 ¼ x 2 In..................................	475.00
Bracelet, Bangle, Hinged, 23 Round Diamonds, 18K Gold, Scott Keating..................................	1003.00
Bracelet, Bangle, Hinged, Ball & Claw, Etruscan Style, Victorian, 1 ¾ x 2 ¼ In.	378.00
Bracelet, Bangle, Hinged, Carved Metal Bird, 15K Gold, Castellani..................................	1888.00
Bracelet, Bangle, Hinged, Turquoise Beads, 14K Gold, 6 ½ In. ....*illus*	1067.00
Bracelet, Bangle, Leaves, Engraved, 3 Sapphires, 14K Gold, Art Nouveau, 7 ½ In.	1659.00
Bracelet, Bangle, Lucite, Black, c.1970, ½ In..................................	33.00
Bracelet, Bangle, Sapphires, Rose Gold, Notched Edges, Teardrop Shape, 1880s	750.00
Bracelet, Bangle, Silver Polished Wave Design, Georg Jensen..................................	236.00
Bracelet, Bangle, Sweetheart, 14K Gold, Etched, c.1910..................................	525.00
Bracelet, Beads, 5 Strands, Tumbled, Emeralds, Pearls, Gold, Engraved Clasp, c.1825, 7 ⅛ In. *illus*	1422.00
Bracelet, Beads, Carnival Glass, Marigold, Pearls, Judy Lee, 7 ½ In.	155.00
Bracelet, Beads, Immortals, Celadon, Chinese, 8 Piece..................................	269.00
Bracelet, Bohemian Garnet Cabochon, 10K Gold, Hinged, c.1890, 6 In..................................	525.00
Bracelet, Cameo, Profile, 4 Strands, Orange Coral, 14K Gold, c.1890, 6 ½ In..................................	690.00
Bracelet, Chatons, French Blue Glass, Rhinestones, Silver Metal, DeLizza & Elster, 1950s, 7 ¼ In.	155.00
Bracelet, Cuff, 3 Little Pigs, Who's Afraid Of The Big Bad Wolf, Enameled Silver, c.1933..........	215.00
Bracelet, Cuff, Cable, 14K Gold, White Gold, Overlaid X, David Yurman, c.1985, 7 In.	3286.00
Bracelet, Cuff, Diamond Swirl, Triple Cable, 14K Gold, David Yurman, c.1980, 7 ½ In.	4183.00
Bracelet, Cuff, Hinged, Bombe Shape, Textured Diamonds, 18K Gold, David Webb, 6 ¼ In. ......*illus*	8295.00
Bracelet, Cuff, Hinged, Copper, Scrolls, Renoir, 1960s, 2 x 8 ½ In..................................	215.00
Bracelet, Cuff, Hinged, Silver, Inset Stone, Eagle Mark, Taxco, c.1960	97.00
Bracelet, Cuff, Hinged, Watch, Silver, Cone-Shaped Quartz, Torun Bulow-Hube, 6 In.............	2133.00
Bracelet, Cuff, Overlapping Bands, 18K Gold, Tiffany & Co., 1980, 1 In. ....*illus*	2607.00
Bracelet, Cuff, Silver, Applied Coil, Marked, Antonio Pineda, 2 ¼ In..................................	1265.00
Bracelet, Cuff, Silver, Engraved, Flowers, Marked, S. Kirk & Son, 2 x 1 In., Pair	167.00
Bracelet, Cuff, Silver, Engraved, Lines, Ecco, c.1900..................................	79.00
Bracelet, Cuff, Silver, Geometric, Turquoise Stone, Dino, Santo Domingo, c.1990, 5 ½ x 1 In.	431.00
Bracelet, Cuff, Silver, Glass, Lalique Cabochons, 5 ¼ x 2 ½ In..................................	1185.00
Bracelet, Cuff, Silver, Marked, G. Jensen, Denmark, 2 ¾ x 2 ½ In..................................	450.00
Bracelet, Cuff, Silver, Raised Vine, B. Goodspeed, Mexico, Men's, 8 x 1 ¾ In..........................	268.00
Bracelet, Cuff, Silver, River Of Life, William Spratling, Mexico, c.1935................................	546.00
Bracelet, Cuff, Silver, Tapered, Paul Lobel, 1950s, 2 ⅛ x ⅝ In.	795.00

Jewelry, Earrings, Etruscan Revival, Urn Shape Drop, Applied Beads, Ropework, 18K Gold, 2 ⅞ In.
$5629.00

Skinner, Inc.

Jewelry, Earrings, Hoop, Hinged, Sodalite Beads, 22K Gold, Lalaounis, 1 In.
$948.00

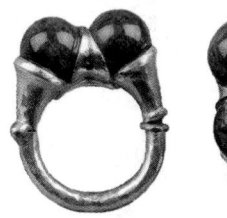

Skinner, Inc.

Jewelry, Earrings, Rock Crystal, Intarsia, Domed Oval, 18K Gold, Angela Cummings, c.1986, 1 In.
$3555.00

Skinner, Inc.

Jewelry, Earrings, Stylized Shell, Applied Beads, Earwire, 18K Gold, John Paul Miller
$2252.00

Skinner, Inc.

J

Jewelry, Earrings, Textured, 18K Gold, Full Cut Diamonds, Judith Ripka, 1 ⅝ In. $1422.00

Skinner, Inc.

Jewelry, Locket, Bicolor Gold, Oval, Ribbed Links, 14K Gold Chain, Victorian, 1 ½ In., 16-in. Chain $1304.00

Skinner, Inc.

Jewelry, Necklace & Earrings, Flower & Leaf Swags, 18K Gold, Empire, c.1810, 15 ⅜ In. $4148.00

Skinner, Inc.

Bracelet, Cuff, Zodiac, Silver, Rhodium Plate, Tortolani, 1970s, 2 ⅜ In.	425.00
Bracelet, Diamonds, Round, Brilliant Cut, 14K Gold, 1900s, 8 x 7 ½ In.	7170.00
Bracelet, Earrings, Ring, Sterling, Enamel Panels, Screwback, Doris Hall, c.1950, 3 Piece ...*illus*	2800.00
Bracelet, Enamel, Gold Metal, Bezel Set Stones, Ciner, 1 ½-In. Wide ...*illus*	59.00
Bracelet, Feathers, Pink Enamel, Gold, Marked, ART, 1950s, 7 ¾ In.	85.00
Bracelet, Flowers, Rose Montees, Art Glass Beads, Miriam Haskell, c.1950, 8 ½ In.	195.00
Bracelet, Geometric, 8K Gold, Engraved, Art Deco, c.1930, 7 x 2 ½ In., Pair	245.00
Bracelet, Green Turquoise Cabochon, 14K Gold, Edwardian, c.1900, 7 In.	645.00
Bracelet, Harlequin, Black Celluloid, Silver Rhinestone, Art Deco, 1930s, 8 ¼ In.	145.00
Bracelet, Hinged, 14K Gold, Twisted, Topaz, Tourmaline Terminals, David Yurman, c.1985, 6 ½ In.	2032.00
Bracelet, Horse's Head, Snake Link, 15 Brilliant Cut Diamonds, Red & Blue Enamel, 18K Gold ..*illus*	4425.00
Bracelet, Leaf, Textured, 18K Gold, Van Cleef & Arpels, 6 ¾ In.	2250.00
Bracelet, Link, 6 Rectangular, Oval Gemstone, Cabochons, 14K Gold, Maria Regnier, 7 In.	708.00
Bracelet, Link, Amethyst Tubes, Silver, Antonio Pineda, 6 ¼ In.	1304.00
Bracelet, Link, Bookchain, Flattened Circles, Stars, Silver, c.1865, 7 x ¾ In.	245.00
Bracelet, Link, Bronze, Embossed, Carved Sunstone, Toggle Clasp, Marked Stephen Dweck, 8 In.	299.00
Bracelet, Link, Cameos, 14K Gold, Slide In Clasp, Victorian, c.1910, 7 In.	891.00
Bracelet, Link, Crested, Platinum, Diamond, Sapphire, Art Deco, c.1920, 7 ¼ In.	4830.00
Bracelet, Link, Diamond Melee, 2 Blue Stones, 14K Gold, L. Fritschze & Co., c.1930, 7 In.	518.00
Bracelet, Link, Diamond, Round Cut, Platinum.Art Deco, 7 In.	5520.00
Bracelet, Link, Enamel, Cobalt Blue, White, David Andersen, Norway, 8 x ½ In.	195.00
Bracelet, Link, Figural, Beaded & Open, Silver, Victoria, Taxco, Mexico	429.00
Bracelet, Link, Geometric, Agate, Multicolor, 18K Gold, Tiffany & Co., 7 ¼ In. ...*illus*	2489.00
Bracelet, Link, Gold, Tiffany, 7 ¼ In.	336.00
Bracelet, Link, Greek Key, Turquoise Enamel, Silver, Margot De Taxco, 7 ¼ In.	130.00
Bracelet, Link, Jet, Stretch, Rectangular, Cabbage Rose, Faceted Beads, Whitby, 6 ¼ In.	295.00
Bracelet, Link, Leaves, Silver, Lapis Cabochon, Georg Jensen, 7 ⅛ In. ...*illus*	1778.00
Bracelet, Link, Openwork, Step Cut Aquamarine, Diamonds, Meister, 7 In.	7096.00
Bracelet, Link, Panel, Silver, Villads Nielsen, Denmark, c.1930, 7 In.	173.00
Bracelet, Link, Quatrefoil, Rope Twist, 6 Opals, Seed Pearls, 14K Gold, Art Nouveau, 7 In.	1007.00
Bracelet, Link, Silver, Round Enameled Discs, Garnet Cabochons, Modernist, 1960s, 7 In.	525.00
Bracelet, Link, Square Diamond, Sapphire, Bezel Set, Platinum, 7 In.	4140.00
Bracelet, Link, Turquoise, 18K Gold, Tiffany & Co., 7 In.	1298.00
Bracelet, Link, Venetian, Silver, Round Charm, Tiffany & Co., Pouch & Box, 7 ½ In.	148.00
Bracelet, Link, Vertical Openings, Diamonds, 14K Gold, Russia, c.1910, 8 ½ In.	1800.00
Bracelet, Link, Woman's Portrait On Porcelain, Bezel Set Coral, 14K Gold, Victorian, 7 In.	944.00
Bracelet, Loveknots, Gold-Washed Silver, 19th Century, 8 In.	225.00
Bracelet, Mesh Strap, Buckle, Engraved Scrolls, 14K Gold, Carter, Howe & Co.	1007.00
Bracelet, Mod, Black, 5 Beads, Plastic, 1960s, 6 x 1 ½ In.	155.00
Bracelet, Necklace & Earrings, Black & Gold Copper, Lucite, Bruce Tolman, 8 & 4 ¾ In.	195.00
Bracelet, Necklace & Earrings, Leaves, Gold, Pearls, Marked, Trifari, Avon, 1971, 7 ¼ In. & 1 In..	85.00
Bracelet, Necklace & Earrings, Link, Tank Track, Silver Rhodium, Coro Pegasus, 1950s, 7 & 1 In..	85.00
Bracelet, Panels, Alternating Polished & Pierced, Silver, G. Jensen, No. 62, 7 ⅜ In.	504.00
Bracelet, Pearls, 6 Strands, Silver Filigree Clasp, c.1918, 7 In.	225.00
Bracelet, Plaques, Rectangular 14K White Gold, Sapphire, Diamond, Art Deco, 7 ½ In.	2460.00
Bracelet, Platinum, 18K Rose Gold, Diamond, Quatrefoil, Charles Krypell, 6 ¾ In.	8625.00
Bracelet, Porcelain, Painted Roses, Filigree Mount, Silver, Russia, 1980s, 7 ¼ In.	95.00
Bracelet, Ram's Head, Silver, Aries, Modernist, 1900s, 2 x 3 In.	129.00
Bracelet, Silver, Blue Rhinestone, Diamond Bar, Art Deco, 1930s, 6 ¾ In.	145.00
Bracelet, Silver, Embossed, Marked, Hector Aguilar, Mexico, c.1955, 7 ½ In.	489.00
Bracelet, Snake, Gold, Garnet, Enamel, Flexible Body, Victorian, 7 In. ...*illus*	1960.00
Bracelet, Snake, Gold & Enamel, Rose-Cut Diamond Head, Hinged, 6 In. ...*illus*	5333.00
Bracelet, Snake, Hinged, Emerald & Diamond Head, 14K Gold, 1910	2875.00
Bracelet, Snake, Silver, Etruscan Revival Style, c.1875, 6 ¾ In.	265.00
Bracelet, Stylized Flowers, Art Nouveau, Ella Lily, 7 In.	225.00
Bracelet, Thermoplastic, Blue Rhinestone, Glass Beads, 1960s, 6 ¼ In.	125.00
Charm, Berlin Opera House, 18K Gold	205.00
Charm, Globe, Ivory, 14K Gold, Rotates, Etched Continents, 1 In.	259.00
Charm, Roman Coliseum, 18K Gold	270.00
Charm, St. Paul's Cathedral, London, 18K Gold	151.00
Chatelaine, Notebook, Silver, Birds, Flowers, 6 Celluloid Day Cards, Victorian, 2 ¾ x 1 ¾ In. ...*illus*	148.00
Cigarette Case, Silver, Engraved Exotic Bird, Purple Stone On Closure, Russia, 5 In.	194.00
Cigarette Case, Silver, Painted, Seminude Woman, W. Neale & Son, 1936, 5 ¾ In.	420.00
Clip, Dress, Celluloid, Roses, Leaves, Pink, Green, c.1925, 2 ¼ x 1 In.	25.00
Clip, Dress, Diamonds, Platinum Shield Mount, Art Deco, 2 In., Pair	2733.00
Clip, Dress, Feathers, Fan Spray, Flower, Marbled Turquoise, Silver Over Brass, Filigree, c.1935, 2 ¼ In.	75.00

Jewelry, Necklace & Earrings, Leaves & Berrries, Silver, Arts & Crafts, Kalo, 15-In. Necklace
$830.00

Skinner, Inc.

Jewelry, Necklace, Carnelian, Pendant & 3 Tablets, Pierced, Mouse, Berries, Lampl, 1930s, 15 ½ In.
$1541.00

Skinner, Inc.

Jewelry, Necklace, Coral, Cameo, Maiden, Putti, Roses, Suspended Drops, Beads, Gold Chain, 13 In.
$2963.00

Skinner, Inc.

Jewelry, Necklace, Jadeite, Beads, Pierced & Carved, 14K Gold, Chinese, 18 ½ In.
$6820.00

Leslie Hindman Auctioneers

Jewelry, Necklace, Millefiori, Chevron Trade Beads, Gold Colored Spacers, 27 In.
$44.00

Old Barn Auction

Jewelry, Necklace, Pendant, Abstract, Silver, Link Chain, Salvador Teran, Mexico, 15 ¾ In.
$711.00

Skinner, Inc.

Jewelry, Necklace, Pendant, Glass, Insect, Flowers, Ivy Frame, Glass Beads, Link Chain, 18 In.
$1067.00

Skinner, Inc.

Jewelry, Necklace, Scarab, Faience, Lotus Blossoms, Ball & Link Chain, 14K, F.G. Hale, 1 ¾ In.
$5036.00

Skinner, Inc.

Jewelry, Necklace, Zipper Shape, Adjustable, Full Cut Diamonds, 18K Gold, 26 In.
$23700.00

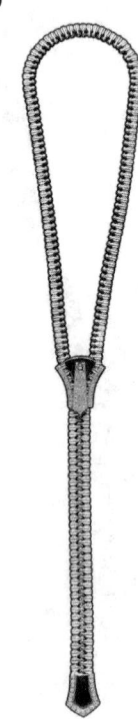

Skinner, Inc.

Jewelry, Pendant, Amethyst, Diamonds, Enamel, 18K, Marcus & Co., Edwardian, 1 ⅜ In.
$4148.00

Skinner, Inc.

Jewelry, Pendant, Aquamarines, Rubies, Chain Swags, Tassels, 14K Gold, c.1875, 3 ¼ In.
$1968.00

New Orleans Auction Galleries, Inc.

Clip, Dress, Flower, Milk Glass, Opalescent, 2 x 3 In.	65.00
Clip, Dress, Flower, Rose Gold Petals, Red Glass, 1940s, 1 ½ In.	65.00
Clip, Dress, Flower, Rose Gold, Pink Crystal Center, 1930s, 1 ½ In., Pair	165.00
Clip, Dress, Insect, Rhinestones, Marked, Eisenberg, Box, 1940s, 3 ¾ x 2 In.	345.00
Clip, Dress, Pearl Cluster, Champagne, Layered, Brass Leaves, Art Nouveau, 1920s, 1 ⅝ In.	55.00
Clip, Fur, Camelia, Trembler, Gold Plated, Emerald Crystals, Coro, 1940s, 1 ½ x 1 ½ In.	145.00
Clip, Fur, Climbing Rose, Gold, Crystals, Alfred Philippe, Trifari, 1940s, 2 x 1 ½ In.	145.00
Clip, Leaf, 18K Gold, Marked M. Buccellati, 1 ¼ In.	536.00
Clip, Shoe, Rhinestone, Rhodium Plated, Marked, Art Deco Style, S.G.D'Or, 1 ¼ x 1 In.	45.00
Compact, Cream Perfume, Elephant, Gold, Red Rhinestone Eyes, Max Factor	40.00
Cuff Links, 14K Gold, Reeded, Cylindrical, H-Shape, Van Cleef & Arpels	1554.00
Cuff Links, 18K Gold, Sapphire Pyramid Terminals, Box, Cartier	2133.00
Cuff Links, Bird & Berries, Silver, Georg Jensen, No. 43	385.00
Cuff Links, Bull, Bear, 14K Gold, Textured	915.00
Cuff Links, Citrine, Herkimer Crystal Shape, Twisted Double Link, 18K Gold, Verdura	2726.00
Cuff Links, Disc, Iridescent, Silver Toggle Back, 1960s	42.00
Cuff Links, Double Link, Diamond Melee, Emerald Edges, Platinum, Art Deco	2133.00
Cuff Links, Double Link, Garland, Engraved Lines, 14K Gold, Blue Enamel, Edwardian	356.00
Cuff Links, Double Link, Platinum Over Gold, Emerald, Blue Enamel Tracery, Garrigus	899.00
Cuff Links, Fish, Silver, Green Onyx Cabochon, Georg Jensen, No. 14	711.00
Cuff Links, Fish, Tortoiseshell Inlay, Silver, William Spratling, Mexico, 1 In. ....*illus*	593.00
Cuff Links, Fishing Fly, Neon Green, Anson, 1940s, 1 x ½ In.	95.00
Cuff Links, Flower, 8 Petals, Bead Center, Silver, Rafael Melendez, Taxco, ⅝ In.	43.00
Cuff Links, Flowers, Blue, Enamel, 14K Gold, c.1950	150.00
Cuff Links, Glass, Reverse Painted, Horse's Head, Double Link, 14K Gold ....*illus*	1422.00
Cuff Links, Horse's Head Chess Piece, Checkerboard Ground, Gold, Square, 1950s, ¾ In.	75.00
Cuff Links, Jade, Oval Cabochons, Gold Metal Frame, 1950s, 1 x ¾ In.	85.00
Cuff Links, Jasper, Polished Square, Openwork Frame, Anson, 1950s, ¾ In.	95.00
Cuff Links, Mother-Of-Pearl, Rhodium, Shadow Box, Raised Geometrics, 1950s, 1 x ½ In.	65.00
Cuff Links, Mother-Of-Pearl, Silver Rhodium, Split Design, Diamond Medallion, 1950s, ¾ x ¾ In.	65.00
Cuff Links, Music Notes, Goldtone, Enamel, Swank, c.1950, 1 In.	27.00
Cuff Links, Painted Dogs, Glass, Marked, Edwardian, ⅝ In.	165.00
Cuff Links, Persian Turquoise, Oval, 18K Woven Chain Ground, 1 x ⅝ In.	513.00
Cuff Links, Pheasants, Flying, Silver, 1950s, 1 In.	85.00
Cuff Links, Platinum, Diamonds, Square Openwork Panel, Link, Chain Edwardian	538.00
Cuff Links, Playing Cards, 4 Aces, Black & Red Enamel, 14K Gold, Marked ....*illus*	2762.00
Cuff Links, Ram's Head, Ruby Eye, 18K Gold, Kurt Wayne ....*illus*	1422.00
Cuff Links, Reverse Painted Glass, Dogs, Silver, Edwardian ⅝ In.	165.00
Cuff Links, Rock Crystal, Purple, Oval Cabochons, 14K Gold, Art Nouveau, 1 ¾ In.	415.00
Cuff Links, Round, Shield Insert, M Monogram, 14K Rose Gold	431.00
Cuff Links, Ruby Glass Dome, Gold, Swank, 1940s, ⅝ In.	75.00
Cuff Links, Silhouettes, Dancing, Silver, Mexico, c.1955, 1 ⅞ In.	495.00
Cuff Links, Silver Disc, Lapis Orb, Joseph Vastano, c.1956, 1 In.	110.00
Cuff Links, Silver, Etched, Swank, 1950s, ¾ In.	65.00
Cuff Links, Silver, Marked, Elsa Peretti, Tiffany & Co., ½ In.	127.00
Cuff Links, Silver, Oval, Filigree, Konstantino	118.00
Cuff Links, Snail Shell, Silver, Gold, Georg Jensen, No. 52 ....*illus*	770.00
Cuff Links, Tiger's Eye, Gold Metal Mount, Spyro Gyro 1960s, ¾ In.	60.00
Dress Set, Man's, Mother-Of-Pearl Tablet, 18K Gold, Double Link, 4 Studs, Tiffany & Co.	11126.00
Dress Set, Man's, Pink Resin Tablet, Round, Diamond Melee Border, Platinum, Cartier	5333.00
Earrings, 2 Rectangles, Bubbles, Copper, Brass, H. Harmon, Mexico, 1950s, 1 ½ In.	106.00
Earrings, Amethyst, Cable Wrap, Faceted, Diamonds, 14K Gold Accents, Clip-On, Yurman, 1 In.	472.00
Earrings, Amethyst, Multicolored, Sapphire Border, Clip-On, Marked, Elke Berr, France	7096.00
Earrings, Amethyst, Seed Pearls, Wirework, Gold, Screwback, Edwardian, c.1900, 1 ½ In.	285.00
Earrings, Basket Weave, Square, 18K Gold, Clip-On, Webb, ¾ In.	1298.00
Earrings, Beetle, Silver, Rhinestones, Turquoise, Marked, Clip-On, 1940s, 2 x 1 In.	395.00
Earrings, Blossom, Hand Wrought, Silver, Marked, Morris Robinson, c.1950, 1 ½ In.	173.00
Earrings, Blue Enamel, 23K Gold Center, J. Kimmel & Co., ⁹⁄₁₆ In.	600.00
Earrings, Butterflies, Pink Enamel, Openwork, Gold, Clip-On, Trifari, 1960s, 1 ½ In.	60.00
Earrings, Cameo, Lion's Head, Citrine, Sunburst Border, Enamel, 18K, Gage, 1 ¼ In. ......*illus*	3555.00
Earrings, Cameo, Three Graces, Onyx, Black & White, 18K Oval Mount, Victorian	461.00
Earrings, Cameo, Winged Figure, Putti, Shell, 18K Gold Mount, 2 ¾ In. ....*illus*	1304.00
Earrings, Cat's-Eye Agate, Silver, Ed Wiener, 1 ⅞ x 1 ½ In.	595.00
Earrings, Chandelier, Black Glass, Red Discs, 6-Sided, Clip-On, Laura Vogel, 1980s, 4 x 1 In.	125.00
Earrings, Chandelier, Rhinestones, Baguettes, Silver, 1950s, 2 ⅜ x 1 In.	95.00
Earrings, Chandelier, Rhinestones, Waterfall, Clip-On, 1950s, 2 In.	110.00

J

Earrings, Chandelier, Silver, Pastes, Screwback, Art Deco, 1930s, 2 ½ In.	135.00
Earrings, Chandelier, Silver-Flashed Crystals, Pearls, Gold Filigree, Hattie Carnegie, 1950s, 2 In.	120.00
Earrings, Circle, 23K Gold, Green Enamel Rectangle, J. Kimmel & Co., ⅜ In.	300.00
Earrings, Citrine, Yellow, Emerald Cut, Faceted, Screwback, Austria, 1930s, ¾ x ¾ In.	95.00
Earrings, Copper, Abstract, Almond Shape, Renoir, 1950s, 1 ½ x 1 In.	45.00
Earrings, Copper, Mixed Metal, Los Castillo, 1 In.	120.00
Earrings, Copper, Silver Plated, Abstract, Monet, 1950s, 1 ½ x 1 In.	50.00
Earrings, Copper, Spiral, Marked, Art Smith, 1 ½ In.	480.00
Earrings, Coral, Button, 18K Gold, M. Buccellati, ¾ In.	2489.00
Earrings, Coral, Button, 18K Gold, Tiffany & Co., 1 ¼ In. ....illus	3555.00
Earrings, Coral, Cameo, Faceted Drop, 18K Gold Mounts, 2 ¾ In. ....illus	1348.00
Earrings, Coral, Diamond, 18K Gold, Van Cleef & Arpels, 1 ⅛ In.	9440.00
Earrings, Dangling Grapes, Ivory, 14K Gold, Pierced, c.1900, 1 ⅜ In.	195.00
Earrings, Diamond Lines, Ruby Drops, Diamond Pave Mount, Clip-On, Michele Della Valle...	9732.00
Earrings, Diamond, 14K Gold, 1900s, ⁵⁄₁₆ In.	5975.00
Earrings, Doorknocker, White Enamel, 18K Gold Stripes, David Webb, 1 ⅝ In.	7406.00
Earrings, Double Teardrop, 18K Gold, Marina B.	1416.00
Earrings, Drop, Baroque Pearl, Rose Montee, Clip-On, Marked, Miriam Haskell, 2 In.	165.00
Earrings, Drop, Coin, Gypsy, Gilt Metal, Yves Saint Laurent, c.1990, 3 ⅝ In.	738.00
Earrings, Drop, Gray Pearl, 14K White Gold, Yamashita	148.00
Earrings, Drop, Hoop, Fleur-De-Lis, Gold, 1940s, 2 ¼ x ⅝ In.	60.00
Earrings, Enameled Woman's Portrait, Diamond, 14K Gold, Pierced, France, Victorian, ⅝ In.	295.00
Earrings, Etoile, Diamonds, 18K Gold, Platinum, Tiffany & Co., ⅜ In.	1007.00
Earrings, Etruscan Revival, Urn Shape Drop, Applied Beads, Ropework, 18K Gold, 2 ⅞ In. .....illus	5629.00
Earrings, Faux Emeralds, Christian Dior	118.00
Earrings, Feather, Gray Crystal, Baguettes, Marquise, Clip-On, Kramer, 1950s, 1 ½ x 1 ¼ In.	85.00
Earrings, Feather, Sapphire, Rhinestones, Textured Gold Metal, Clip-On, Selini, 1950s, 1 ¼ x ¾ In.	45.00
Earrings, Firework, Rhinestones, White Celluloid, Clip-On, Weiss, 1950s, 1 ⅛ In.	55.00
Earrings, Fleur-De-Lis, Gold, Blue Domed Glass Cabochons, Screwback, Marino, 1950s, 1 ¾ In.	65.00
Earrings, Flower, 8 Petals, Clear & Turquoise Rhinestones, Clip-On, Hobe, 1 In.	55.00
Earrings, Flower, Baroque Pearls, Rhinestones, Brushed Gold, Miriam Haskell, 2 ½ In.	141.00
Earrings, Flower, Ginkgo Leaf, Satin Gold, Pastel Crystal Stem, Screwback, 1950s, 1 x ¾ In.	65.00
Earrings, Flower, Mosaic, Red, White & Cobalt Glass, Gilt Brass, Italy, 1940s, 1 In.	75.00
Earrings, Flower, Sapphire & Ruby Petals, Diamond Center, Clip-On, Marked Sabbadini	8110.00
Earrings, Flowers, Blue & Yellow Enamel, Green To White Leaves, Silver, Art Nouveau, 1 ⅜ x ½ In.	245.00
Earrings, Freshwater Pearls Cluster, 14K Gold Ear Hoop, 2 x 1 ½ In.	195.00
Earrings, Garnet, Silver, Dangling, Clip-On, Victorian, 1 ½ In.	145.00
Earrings, Geometric, Black Resin, Silver Dangling, Modernist, c.1950, 4 In.	125.00
Earrings, Geometric, Elongated Oval, 18K Bicolor Gold, Clip-On, Bulgaria, 1 ⅛ In.	2124.00
Earrings, Hawaii, Cascade, Wirework Rings, 18K Gold, Buccellati, 2 ⅝ In.	5096.00
Earrings, Hearts, Nested, 18K White & Rose Gold, Bulgari, Italy, 1 ¼ In.	1180.00
Earrings, Hoop, Etched Puffed Pillows, Satin Gold, 1960s, 1 ⅝ x 1 ⅝ In.	45.00
Earrings, Hoop, Hinged, Sodalite Beads, 22K Gold, Lalaounis, 1 In. ....illus	948.00
Earrings, Intaglio, Green Glass, 18K Gold, Omega Clip-On, Elizabeth Locke	984.00
Earrings, Kidney Shape, Black Resin, Gerda Lynggaard, c.1980, 1 ⅝ In.	75.00
Earrings, Leaf, Iridescent, Crystal, Pearls, Oval, Rhinestone Chatons, Clip-On, 1980s, 1 ⅝ x 1 ½ In.	65.00
Earrings, Orbs, Topaz Carnival Glass, Gold Rays, Clip-On, Sarah Coventry, 1960s, 1 ½ x 1 In.	35.00
Earrings, Pendant, Alternating Cubes, Spheres, Open Disks, 18K Gold, Bulgaria, Box	1476.00
Earrings, Pendant, Fish, Silver, Ruth Berridge, c.1950, 1 ⅜ x ¾ In.	195.00
Earrings, Pendant, Green Enamel Oval, Square Mount, 23K Gold, J. Kimmel & Co., 1 ⅛ In.	540.00
Earrings, Pendant, Green Paste, Diamond Melee Center, Kite Shape, Art Deco, 1 ⅝ In.	889.00
Earrings, Pendant, Onyx, Jadeite, Diamond, Platinum, Art Deco, c.1925, 2 ⅞ In.	9760.00
Earrings, Pink Cabochon, Rhinestones, Silver Rope Twist Wirework, Hobe, 1 In.	75.00
Earrings, Pink Sapphire, Spring Clasp Miriam Haskell, 1930s	45.00
Earrings, Pod, Domed, 18K Gold, Clip-On, David Webb	2500.00
Earrings, Portrait On Ivory, Woman, Red Drape, 14K Gold, Beaded Frame, Pearls, Victorian	472.00
Earrings, Portrait, Pearl Drops, 14K Gold, Victorian, 1 ¼ In.	288.00
Earrings, Quartz Crystal, Pools Of Light, Rhinestone Chatons, Brass, Clip-On, 1940s, ½ In.	95.00
Earrings, Rhinestones, Red, Blue, Green Crystal, Ciner, c.1960, 1 In.	65.00
Earrings, Rock Crystal, Intarsia, Domed Oval, 18K Gold, Angela Cummings, c.1986, 1 In. ......illus	3555.00
Earrings, Rose Mosaic, Glass, Round, Gilt Brass, Italy, 1940s, ⅝ In.	55.00
Earrings, Sapphires, Oval, Aquamarine, Diamonds, Bombe Shape, Clip-On, Michele Della Valle	8180.00
Earrings, Shell, Blue Enamel, Ruby Melee, 18K Gold, Clip-On, Schlumberger, Tiffany, ¾ In.	2607.00
Earrings, Shrimp, 18K Gold, Polished, Hammered, Henry Dunay, 1 ⅛ In.	2242.00
Earrings, Silver, 14K Gold, Diagonal Ribs, David Yurman, ¾ x ⅔ In.	98.00
Earrings, Silver, Free-Form, Center Link, Marked, Art Smith, 5 x 2 ½ In.	900.00

Jewelry, Pendant, Cameo, Maiden, Hardstone, Beaded Border, 18K Gold, 3 In.
$652.00

Skinner, Inc.

Jewelry, Pendant, Cross, Pearls, 14K Gold, Beaded Edges, 2 ⅜ In.
$2963.00

Skinner, Inc.

Jewelry, Pendant, Pin, Caddis Worm, 18K, Enamel, Woven Cord, John Paul Miller, 1950, 2 ½ In.
$11258.00

Skinner, Inc.

Jewelry, Pendant, Pin, Cameo, Bacchus, Hardstone, Enamel, Ropework Frame, 18K Gold, 2 ⅛ In.
$3200.00

Skinner, Inc.

J

Jewelry, Pendant, Pin, Cameo, Marianne, Agate, Diamonds, Pearls, 18K Bicolor, Vever, c.1880, 2 ¼ In. $4977.00

Skinner, Inc.

Jewelry, Pendant, Pin, Flower, Enamel, Diamond Melee Center, 14K Gold, Art Nouveau, 1 ½ In. 652.00

Skinner, Inc.

Jewelry, Pendant, Stylized Flowers, 2 Baroque Pearls, Enamel, 14K Gold, Chain, Art Nouveau, 1 ½ In. $504.00

Skinner, Inc.

Jewelry, Pin & Earrings, Brass Wire, Marked, Claire Falkenstein, 4 ⅛ x 1 ½-In. Pin $2133.00

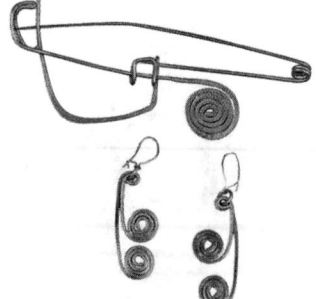

Skinner, Inc.

Earrings, Silver, Geometric, Screwback, Paul Lobel, 2 ¼ x ⅞ In.	375.00
Earrings, Silver, White Agate Cabochons, Omega Back, Tiffany & Co.	46.00
Earrings, Silver, Wooden Drop, Screwback, c.1950, 1 ⅜ x ¼ In.	75.00
Earrings, Squash Bead Pearls, Chain Dangles, Pink, 1970s, 3 ½ In.	24.00
Earrings, Stylized Flower, 5 Petals, 3 Marquise-Shaped Rubies, 18K Gold, Chaumet, ¾ In.	889.00
Earrings, Stylized Flower, 5 Petals, Green Melon Glass, Rhinestones, Miriam Haskell, 1 In.	155.00
Earrings, Stylized Grasshopper, 18K Gold, Onyx, Clip-On, Shakudo, 1 ¼ In.	444.00
Earrings, Stylized Shell, Applied Beads, Earwire, 18K Gold, John Paul Miller ......*illus*	2252.00
Earrings, Textured, 18K Gold, Full Cut Diamonds, Judith Ripka, 1 ⅝ In. ......*illus*	1422.00
Earrings, Thermoplastic, Blue Leaves, Silver Tone Stems, Clip-On, c.1970, 1 x ⅞ In.	35.00
Earrings, Tortoiseshell, Dangling, Pierced, Victorian, 2 x 1 ⅜ In.	65.00
Earrings, Triangle, Silver, Clip-On, Maria Regnier	177.00
Earrings, Tulips, Domed Shape, Diamonds, 18K Gold, Clip-On, Marked Bulgari	1100.00
Earrings, V Rope, 6 Twisted Strands, 18K Gold, J. Schlumberger, Tiffany & Co., 1 ¼ In.	1067.00
Earrings, Woman's Profile, Copper, Pierced, Art Nouveau Style, 1970s, 1 ½ x 2 ½ In.	75.00
Earrings, X Design, Silver, 14K Gold Accents, Yurman	531.00
Fob, Silver, Shield Shape, Monogram, England, 1917	65.00
Hair Clip, Butterfly, 18K Textured Gold, Diamond Melee, Ruby Eyes, Buccellati, 2 In.	4740.00
Hair Comb, Jade, White Stylized Roundels, Rectangular, Chinese, 1800s, 12 In.	1960.00
Hair Comb, Phoenix, Flowers, Kingfisher Feathers, Jadeite, Stones, Frame, Chinese, 1800s, 4 ½ In.	3555.00
Hair Comb, Scrolling Flowers, Pearl Blossoms, Beaded, 14K Gold, Day, Clark & Co.	444.00
Hair Comb, Silver, Chased, Flower Urn, Medallion, Shaped, 9 Teeth, Victorian, 5 In.	76.00
Hairstick, Bone, Pineapple Design, Carved, 4 ½ In., Pair.	24.00
Hatpins are listed in this book in the Hatpin category.	
Lipstick Case, 18K Gold, Sapphires, Engraved, Van Cleef & Arpels, c.1978	4720.00
Locket, Bicolor Gold, Oval, Ribbed Links, 14K Gold Chain, Victorian, 1 ½ In., 16-in. Chain .....*illus*	1304.00
Locket, Bird In Flight, Flowers, Swag, Silver, Etched, Bookchain, c.1870, 18 ½ In.	595.00
Locket, Blue Cottage Rose, Guilloche, Domed, Silver Twist Chain, 1950s, 2 x 1 ½ In.	110.00
Locket, Crescent Moon, Star, Diamonds, Embossed Leaves, Scrolls, Round, c.1870, 1 ¼ x 24 In.	845.00
Locket, Flowers, Enamel & Pearls, 12K Gold, c.1875, 1 x ¾ In.	425.00
Locket, Flowers, Etched, Silver, Art Nouveau, 2 Frames, c.1900, 2 x 1 In.	160.00
Locket, Heart, Engraved, Lines, Flowers, Serpentine Chain, 12K Gold, c.1920, 1 x ¾ In.	145.00
Locket, Heart, Turquoise, Diamond, Star Shape, Child Portrait, On Ivory, Gold Chain, c.1850, 16 In.	8516.00
Locket, Muses, Repousse, Lyre Bail, 18K Gold, Renaissance Revival, Tiffany, 2 In.	5925.00
Locket, Pendant, Mourning, 10K Gold, Black Enamel, Seed Pearls, Victorian	649.00
Locket, Strawberry Plant, Silver, Art Nouveau, c.1905, 1 ¼ In.	226.00
Locket, Woman's Face, Flowing Hair, 9 Inset Stones, Gilt Metal, Art Nouveau, 1 In.	108.00
Medal, Cavalry, First City Troop, Shield Shape, Crossed Swords, 12 Panels, c.1909, 5 ¼ In.	650.00
Necklace & Bracelet, Fleur-De-Lis, Silvered Gold, Aquamarine Gemstones, Louis Stern, 15 & 7 In.	225.00
Necklace & Earrings, Bead Clusters, Pink, Yellow, Blue, Green, Miriam Haskell, 29 In.	106.00
Necklace & Earrings, Beads, Orange Iridescent, Large & Small, 2 Strands, Marvella	25.00
Necklace & Earrings, Beads, Peacock Glass, 4 Strands, Blue, Green, Clip-On, 1950s, 17 & 1 ⅜ In.	165.00
Necklace & Earrings, Blue Bauble Crystal, 2 Strands, Clip-On, Vendome, 1950s, 20 & 1 In.	165.00
Necklace & Earrings, Flower & Leaf Swags, 18K Gold, Empire, c.1810, 15 ⅜ In. .....*illus*	4148.00
Necklace & Earrings, Leaves & Berrries, Silver, Arts & Crafts, Kalo, 15-In. Necklace ......*illus*	830.00
Necklace & Earrings, Leaves, Yellow Green Lucite, Gold Metal, Marvella, 16 In.-Necklace	23.00
Necklace & Earrings, Link, 18K Gold, Angela Cummings, Tiffany, 18 & 1 ¼ In.	4255.00
Necklace, Amethyst, Graduated Stones, 10K Gold, Link, Chain, Victorian, 26 In.	495.00
Necklace, Amethyst, Lapis, Carnelian, Jade, 14K Gold, Van Ness, 16 ½ In.	575.00
Necklace, Amethysts, 18 Graduated, Bezel Set, Wire Twist Frames, c.1880, 16 ¼ In.	5629.00
Necklace, Baroque Pearls, Rose Montees, Rondelle Spacers, Miriam Haskell, 1975, 16 ½ In.	215.00
Necklace, Barrel Crystal, Graduated, Faceted, Art Deco, 1930s, 17 x ⅜ In.	165.00
Necklace, Beads, Barrel, Etched, Satin Gold, Napier, c.1960, 22 In.	85.00
Necklace, Beads, Blue & Yellow Glass, Graduated, Chrome Set, Machine Age, 1930s, 16 In.	125.00
Necklace, Beads, Cherry Amber, Faceted, Oval, Graduating, c.1860, 31 In.	279.00
Necklace, Beads, Clear, Faceted, Graduated, 3 Strands, Marvella, 16 In.	135.00
Necklace, Beads, Czech Glass, Each Bead Unique, Art Deco, 1920s, 20 In.	245.00
Necklace, Beads, Czech Glass, Rhinestone, Carnelian, Brass Chain, Tortoise Tubes, 1950s, 46 In.	145.00
Necklace, Beads, Fossilized Coral, Marbleized, Blue, 1970s, 21 ½ In.	110.00
Necklace, Beads, Glass, Multicolor, Chinese, 1800s, 34 In.	674.00
Necklace, Beads, Gold, Ribbed, 3 Strands, Button Clasp, Sarah Coventry, 1960s, 15 ½ In.	55.00
Necklace, Beads, Jade Peking Glass, Multicolored Spacers, Art Deco, c.1925, 65 In.	295.00
Necklace, Beads, Milk Glass, Metal Caps, 6 Strands, Miriam Haskell, 18 In.	37.00
Necklace, Beads, Millefiori, Metal, 1950s, 16 ¾ In.	65.00
Necklace, Beads, Sandalwood, Jade, Glass, Quartz, Celadon Jade, Pendant, Chinese, 50 In.	214.00
Necklace, Bib, Clear & Red Crystals, Gold Metal Band, France, Art Nouveau, 27 x 8 In.	900.00

Necklace, Bracelet & Earrings, Link, Alternating Leaves & Beads, Silver, Georg Jensen	2015.00
Necklace, Carnelian, Pendant & 3 Tablets, Pierced, Mouse, Berries, Lampl, 1930s, 15 ½ In. *illus*	1541.00
Necklace, Cascade, Silver, Bead & Chain, Marked, Espo Sig, 18 In.	177.00
Necklace, Celluloid, Graduated Beads, Carved, France, 16 In.	85.00
Necklace, Choker, Diagonal Links, Brushed Gold Rectangular Panels, Hobe, 14 In.	75.00
Necklace, Coin, Spanish Silver, Double Pierced, c.1810, 23 In.	288.00
Necklace, Coins, 6 Strands, Repousse, Goldtone, 1960s, 20 In.	69.00
Necklace, Collar, 24 Pyramidal Drops, Frosted Glass, Silver Mounts, France, Art Deco	108.00
Necklace, Collar, 6 Overlapping Rings, Bezel Set Opals, 18K Gold Filled, Grosse, 1971	59.00
Necklace, Collar, Diamonds, Brilliant Cut, 18K Gold, 1900s, 19 In.	4481.00
Necklace, Coral, Cameo, Maiden, Putti, Roses, Suspended Drops, Beads, Gold Chain, 13 In. *illus*	2963.00
Necklace, Diamond, 14K Gold Twisted, Italy, 1900s, 19 In.	478.00
Necklace, Diamond, Pear Shape, Surround, 14K Gold Chain, Italy, 1900s, 18 In.	2390.00
Necklace, Diamond, Tapered & Straight Baguettes, 14K Gold Chain, Italy, 1900s, 28 In.	1673.00
Necklace, Diamonds, Brilliant Cut, Sapphire, Marquis Cut, 14K Gold Chain, 1900s, 19 In.	956.00
Necklace, Diamonds, Round & Brilliant Cut, 14K Gold, 1900s, 17 ½ In.	777.00
Necklace, Dogwood Blossom, Diamond Melee, 18K Gold Chain, Tiffany & Co., 16 In.	1470.00
Necklace, Festoon, Jadeite, Oval Cabochons, 14K Gold, Oval Links, Walter Lampl, 14 In.	3792.00
Necklace, Floating Heart, Chain, Peretti, Tiffany & Co., 1 ½ & 30 In.	236.00
Necklace, Gold Scallop & Graduated Fringe, Diamond Highlights, c.1950, 16 In.	4866.00
Necklace, Gray Pearl Beads, Lucite, Hematite Rounds, Gold Hammered Book Chain, 35 In.	75.00
Necklace, Iridescent, Graduated Bubbles, Miriam Haskell, 1970s, 30 In.	345.00
Necklace, Ivory, Graduated Beads, Carved, Dorothy Chase, Saks 5th Avenue, 23 ½ In.	354.00
Necklace, Jadeite, Beads, Pierced & Carved, 14K Gold, Chinese, 18 ½ In. *illus*	6820.00
Necklace, Keshi Pearls, 2-Tone, 14K Gold Clasp, 17 ½ In.	1534.00
Necklace, Lavaliere, Diamond Pendant, Platinum Filigree, 18-In. Link Chain, c.1905, 2 ¾ In.	2070.00
Necklace, Lavaliere, Feather, Rhinestone, Black Navettes, 1950s, 2 ½ x 17 In.	145.00
Necklace, Lavaliere, Openwork Swag, Rhinestones, Pididdly Winks, Art Deco Style, 1970s, 8 x 1 ½ In.	110.00
Necklace, Link, Arched Tubes, Beads, 18K Bicolor Gold, Marina B, 16 ½ In.	5333.00
Necklace, Link, Chain, Oval, Polished, 18K Gold, Cartier, 28 In.	1298.00
Necklace, Link, Geometric Beads, Silver, Marked, Kalo, 28 In.	1800.00
Necklace, Link, Gold, Givenchy, 1980s, 15 In.	165.00
Necklace, Link, Graduated Orange Pendants, 1930s, 16 In.	195.00
Necklace, Link, Organic Shapes, Silver, Marked, Mexico, 1934, 15 In.	240.00
Necklace, Link, Ribbed, 18K Gold, Caplain Paris, 16 In.	1298.00
Necklace, Link, Silver, Fluted, 14K Gold Center Hook, Citrine, Garnet, Yurman	1003.00
Necklace, Link, Silver, Organic Design, Mexico, 1934, 15 In.	220.00
Necklace, Link, Square, Black, White & Copper Red Enamel, Silver, M. De Taxco, 15 In.	679.00
Necklace, Link, Wavy Bars, 18K Gold, Platinum, Diamonds, Tiffany & Co., 1977, 18 In.	1770.00
Necklace, Link, Wheat Chain, 14K Gold, Marked Tiffany & Co., 17 In.	1150.00
Necklace, Mesh, 18K Gold, Elsa Peretti, Tiffany & Co., 38 In.	4594.00
Necklace, Mesh, Goldtone, Bergere, 1940s, 14 ½ x ½ In.	39.00
Necklace, Micro Mosaic, Roses, Lime Green, Turquoise, Teardrop Shape, Italy, c.1935, 3 x 1 ½ In.	195.00
Necklace, Millefiori, Chevron Trade Beads, Gold Colored Spacers, 27 In. *illus*	44.00
Necklace, Moonstone, Gray Brown, 7 Domed Cabochons, 14K Gold, 1970s, 18 In.	140.00
Necklace, Native Figure, Coiled Link Chain, Silver, G. Laffi, Peru, 15 In.	97.00
Necklace, Owl, Segmented, Textured Pewter, White Lucite Eyes, 1960s, 5 ½ x 2 ½ & 21 In.	85.00
Necklace, Pearl Beads, Champagne Gold, Pink Crystals, Gold Filigree, Vendome, 1950s, 26 In.	145.00
Necklace, Pearls, 2 Strands, Champagne, Baroque, Round Moonstone Lucite, 1950s, 19 In.	65.00
Necklace, Pearls, Clusters, Goldtone Metal Mount, Marvella, 17 x ½ In.	25.00
Necklace, Pendant, Abstract, Cabochon Sapphires, Rubies, Emerald, Diamonds, Boucheron, 16 ½ In.	8110.00
Necklace, Pendant, Abstract, Silver, Link Chain, Salvador Teran, Mexico, 15 ¾ In. *illus*	711.00
Necklace, Pendant, Cross, Rhinestones, Elliptical Sections, Paper Clip-On Chain, Hobe, 2 ½ In.	139.00
Necklace, Pendant, Flower, Enamel, Rhinestones, Round, 1960s	35.00
Necklace, Pendant, Glass, Insect, Flowers, Ivy Frame, Glass Beads, Link Chain, 18 In. *illus*	1067.00
Necklace, Pendant, Kilimanjaro, Silver, Acrylic, Bjorn Weckstrom, 1970s, 28 In.	506.00
Necklace, Pendant, Lotus, Bell, Pink Tourmaline, Enamel On Bronze, Chinese, 1800s, 24 In.	2573.00
Necklace, Pendant, Parentesi, Band, 18K Gold, Bulgari, 17 x 15 In.	1064.00
Necklace, Pendant, Peridot, Split Pearl, Shield Shape, 14K, Platinum Chain, Edwardian, 16 In.	1185.00
Necklace, Pendant, Sapphire, Drop, Diamond Frame, 14K White Gold Chain, c.1910, 16 In.	1093.00
Necklace, Pendant, Scarab, Isis Wings, Glass, Enamel, Egyptian Revival, Trifari, 1970s, 2 ½ x 2 In.	140.00
Necklace, Pendant, Zodiac, Silver Rhodium Plated, Tortolani, 1970s, 35 ½ In.	195.00
Necklace, Rhinestones, Marquise, Silver, Dangling Faux Pearls, Hattie Carnegie, 16 In.	89.00
Necklace, Scarab, Faience, Lotus Blossoms, Ball & Link Chain, 14K, F.G. Hale, 1 ¾ In. *illus*	5036.00
Necklace, Seed Pearls, 14K Gold, Angular, Chain, Art Nouveau, 22 x 1 In.	365.00
Necklace, Seed Pearls, 18K White Gold, Diamond Drop, Box Clasp, Edwardian, 20 In.	1438.00

Jewelry, Pin, Abstract Flower, Diamond Melee Accents, 18K Gold, 3 In.
$1185.00

Skinner, Inc.

Jewelry, Pin, Arrow, Diamonds, Old Mine Cut & Rose Cut, Platinum, 18K Gold, Edwardian, 4 ¼ In.
$4148.00

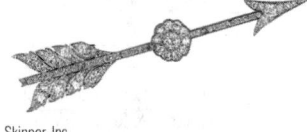

Skinner, Inc.

Jewelry, Pin, Bakelite, 3 Pears, Brown, Celluloid Bar, 2 ¼ In.
$75.00

Hake's Americana & Collectibles

Jewelry, Pin, Bakelite, Pineapple, Carved, 3 In.
$75.00

Hake's Americana & Collectibles

TIP
Keep basement windows locked at all times.

391

Jewelry, Pin, Bar, Etruscan Revival, Applied Bead & Wiretwist Accents, 2 ⅜ In. **$415.00**

Skinner, Inc.

Jewelry, Pin, Beetle, Green, Red Rhinestones, Coro, Stamped **$12.00**

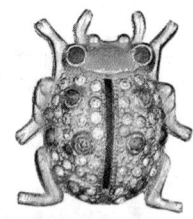

Cowan's Auctions

Jewelry, Pin, Beetle, Micro Mosaic, Gold Frame, Applied Barrel & Ropework, 1 ¾ In. **$1126.00**

Skinner, Inc.

Jewelry, Pin, Branch, Amethyst, Ruby, Aquamarine, Sapphires, 14K Gold, Edward Oakes, 2 ¾ In. **$4977.00**

Skinner, Inc.

Jewelry, Pin, Butterfly, Rubies & Sapphires, Silver Over Gold Mount, 1 ½ In. **$770.00**

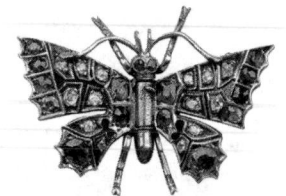

Skinner, Inc.

Necklace, Silver, Blister Pearls, Green Onyx, Paper, Clip-On Chain, Georg Jensen, c.1920, 34 In.	2252.00
Necklace, South Sea Pearls, Diamonds, 18K Gold Chain, 1900s, 16 In.	1076.00
Necklace, Stylized Ribbon, Hinged & Folded, Silver, A. Cummings, c.1985, 16 In.	1304.00
Necklace, Tutti-Frutti, Plastic Beads, Orange, Pink, White, 3 Strands, Germany, 1960s, 18 In.	65.00
Necklace, V-Form, Overlapping Links, Riveted, Beaded, Silver, Margot De Taxco, 15 x 1 In.	525.00
Necklace, Zipper Shape, Adjustable, Full Cut Diamonds, 18K Gold, 26 In. *illus*	23700.00
Necklace, Zuni, Squash Blossom, Turquoise, Red Coral, Beads, Marked, C. Haley, 1900s, 18 In.	288.00
Pendant, 14K Gold, Open Design, Suspended Keshi Pearl, Edwardian, 1 ¾ In.	104.00
Pendant, Agate, Sparrow, Mushroom, Leaves, Openwork, Carved, Chinese, 1800s, 2 In.	4444.00
Pendant, Amethyst, 2 Male Figures, 1 Winged, 1 Buck, Gold, Greek, 2 ⅛ In.	3000.00
Pendant, Amethyst, Diamonds, Enamel, 18K, Marcus & Co., Edwardian, 1 ⅜ In. *illus*	4148.00
Pendant, Ant, 10 Suspended Geometric Shapes, Silver, Lalaounis, 7 In.	770.00
Pendant, Aquamarines, Rubies, Chain Swags, Tassels, 14K Gold, c.1875, 3 ¼ In. *illus*	1968.00
Pendant, Archer, Silver Frame, Round, 18K Gold Trim, Fred Of Paris, 1 ⁷⁄₁₆ In.	1652.00
Pendant, Aztec Figure, Silver, Green Stone, Jaimez, Emma Melendez, Mexico, 1960s, 2 ½ In.	355.00
Pendant, Bat, Carp, White, Chinese, 3 In.	896.00
Pendant, Blue, Green Enamel, Pewter, Chain, Art Nouveau, 1 x 1 ½ In.	310.00
Pendant, Cameo, Classical Girl, Amethyst, Seed Pearl Rim, White Gold Mount, c.1915, 1 In.	1007.00
Pendant, Cameo, Maiden, Citrine, Oval, Seed Pearl Border, 4 Diamonds, c.1915, 1 ¾ In.	4029.00
Pendant, Cameo, Maiden, Hardstone, Beaded Border, 18K Gold, 3 In. *illus*	652.00
Pendant, Coin, In 3 Concentric Hoops, 14K Gold, Maria Regnier, 2 ½ In.	472.00
Pendant, Cross, Amethysts, Oval & Heart Shaped, Sapphire Rim, Michael Youssoufian	7705.00
Pendant, Cross, Pearls, 14K Gold, Beaded Edges, 2 ⅜ In. *illus*	2963.00
Pendant, Cross, Silver, Scroll Border, Inset Wood, Spratling, 2 In.	243.00
Pendant, Dragon, Jade, Gray Green, Pear Shape, Ribbed Edge, Black Cord, Chinese, 2 ½ x 2 In.	236.00
Pendant, Drop, 2 Pearls, 18K Gold, Art Nouveau Style, c.1910	160.00
Pendant, Flames, Openwork, 18K Gold, Round Stainless Steel Frame, Bulgari, 1 ⅔ x 1 ¼ In.	397.00
Pendant, Heart, Diamonds, 14K Gold, 1900s, 1 x 1 In.	836.00
Pendant, Horseshoe On Shamrock, Diamonds 1900s, 1 ¾ In.	3286.00
Pendant, Jade, 3 Chi Dragons, Carved, White, Russet Veining, Chinese, 1700s, 3 x 1 ¾ In.	7350.00
Pendant, Jade, Bird, Seed Pearls, Black Enamel, Oval, 14K Gold, Art Deco, 2 x 1 ½ In.	863.00
Pendant, Jade, Dragon, 3 Claws, Clouds, Suns, White, Carved, Chinese, 1800s, 3 ½ In.	307.00
Pendant, Jade, Dragon, Carved & Pierced, 19th Century, Chinese, 2 ⅞ In.	525.00
Pendant, Jade, Dragon, Cloud, Relief, White, Rectangular, Chinese, c.1925, 4 x 2 In.	461.00
Pendant, Jade, Dragon, Leaf Carved, Domed, Chinese, 1800s, 3 ¼ In.	1353.00
Pendant, Jade, Entwined Lotus Leaves, Ridged, 14K Gold, Marked, Cartier, 2 ¼ x 1 ¼ In.	2691.00
Pendant, Jade, Flowers, Longevity Symbol, Awabi Bats, Oval, Reticulated, Chinese, 3 ½ x 2 ¾ In.	529.00
Pendant, Jade, Spinach, Carved Immortal, Chinese, 3 ¼ In.	329.00
Pendant, Jade, White, Lion, Playing With Cub, Symbols, Woven Silk Strap, Chinese, 1800s, 3 ½ In.	799.00
Pendant, Key, 18K White Gold, Diamonds, Marked Tiffany & Co., 16 In.	932.00
Pendant, Moses Holding 10 Commandments In Hebrew, 18K Gold, A. Tillander, Russia	649.00
Pendant, Pencil, 14K Gold Case, Ball End, Tiffany & Co., 2 ½ In., Extends To 4 In.	472.00
Pendant, Pin, Caddis Worm, 18K, Enamel, Woven Cord, John Paul Miller, 1950, 2 ½ In. *illus*	11258.00
Pendant, Pin, Cameo, Bacchus, Hardstone, Enamel, Ropework Frame, 18K Gold, 2 ⅛ In. *illus*	3200.00
Pendant, Pin, Cameo, Marianne, Agate, Diamonds, Pearls, 18K Bicolor, Vever, c.1880, 2 ¼ In. *illus*	4977.00
Pendant, Pin, Flower, Enamel, Diamond Melee Center, 14K Gold, Art Nouveau, 1 ½ In. *illus*	652.00
Pendant, Quartz, Hollowed, Carved, Applied Dragons, Chinese, 1800s, 1 ½ x 2 In.	550.00
Pendant, Rectangular, Star Of David Inside, White Gold, Baraka, Italy	595.00
Pendant, Scholar, Attendant, Boat, Text, White, Rectangular, Chinese, 1800s, 2 x 1 ½ In.	6125.00
Pendant, Silver, 3 Geometric Open Dangling Links, Tiffany & Co., Pouch & Box	177.00
Pendant, Silver, Angular, Blue & Green Enamel, Blister Pearls, Arts & Crafts, c.1900, 2 ½ x 1 In.	325.00
Pendant, Stylized Flowers, 2 Baroque Pearls, Enamel, 14K Gold, Chain, Art Nouveau, 1 ½ In. *illus*	504.00
Pendant, Stylized Poppies, Diamond Accents, 14K Gold, Round, Art Nouveau, 1 ⅛ In.	385.00
Pendant, Tablet, 10 Commandments, 14K Gold, Engraved, 1967, 1 ⅛ In.	140.00
Pendant, Topaz, Diamond Teardrop, Bow & Garland Surround, Black, Starr, Frost, 1 ¾ In.	7703.00
Pendant, Triangle, Green Enamel, 23K Gold Square Mount, J. Kimmel & Co., 2 ½ In.	4080.00
Pin & Earrings, Beads, Crystal, Scrolling Floral Pattern, Schiaparelli, 5 x 3 ½ & 1 ¾ In.	395.00
Pin & Earrings, Brass Wire, Marked, Claire Falkenstein, 4 ⅛ x 1 ½-In. Pin *illus*	2133.00
Pin & Earrings, Floral Spray, 10K Gold, Screwback, Forstner, 2 ¼ x 1 ¾ In.	222.00
Pin & Earrings, Flowers, Gold, Glass Pearl, Petal Edges, Clip-On, Napier, 3 ¼ x 1 ½ In.	145.00
Pin & Earrings, Gold Plate Leaves, Glass Pearls, Screwback, Jomaz, 1950s, 3 x 1 ½ & 1 In.	95.00
Pin & Earrings, Leaf, Rhinestones, Turquoise Glass Cabochon, Jomaz, 2 x 1 ¾ In.	165.00
Pin & Earrings, Stylized Leaves, Johan Rohde, Georg Jensen, 2 ¼-In. Pin	1896.00
Pin, 2 Flowers, Pink & Violet Rhinestones, Silver Openwork, Hobe, 1940, 2 In.	250.00
Pin, 2 Stylized Mushrooms, Coral, Fluted, Diamond Caps, Textured Gold Grass, 1950s	7096.00
Pin, 25 Amethysts, 20 Seed Pearls, Cross, Silver, Gold, Enamel, c.1850, 1 ¾ x 1 ¾ In.	274.00

Pin, 3 Hearts, Silver, Marcasite, c.1945, 1 ⅜ x 1 In.	95.00
Pin, Abstract Flower, Diamond Melee Accents, 18K Gold, 3 In. ....*illus*	1185.00
Pin, Abstract Shape, 2 Shaped Cutouts, Silver, Henning Koppel, 2 In.	356.00
Pin, Abstract Shape, Textured, 14K Gold, Stamped, Ed Weiner, 2 ½ x 2 ¼ In.	1200.00
Pin, Abstract, Silver, 18K Gold, Enamel, Faceted Stones, Earl Pardon, 3 x 1 In.	2500.00
Pin, Agate, Gilt Copper Frame, Scrolling, c.1855, 3 x 2 In.	229.00
Pin, Amethyst, Diamonds, 14K Folded Triangle Frame, Russia, 1 ¼ In.	1200.00
Pin, Amethyst, Seed Pearls, Ribbon Border, Edwardian, 1 x 1 In.	175.00
Pin, Aquamarine, Diamonds, Platinum Openwork Mount, Edwardian, 1 ½ In.	2370.00
Pin, Arrow, Diamonds, Old Mine Cut & Rose Cut, Platinum, 18K Gold, Edwardian, 4 ¼ In. ....*illus*	4148.00
Pin, Arrowhead, Silver, Henning Koppel, Georg Jensen, 2 In.	184.00
Pin, Art Deco, Bakelite, Horse Head, Green, Brass Mane, c.1940, 2 ¼ x 2 ½ In.	155.00
Pin, Art Nouveau Woman, Butterfly, Poppies, Celluloid, Oval, 1920s, 2 ¼ In.	75.00
Pin, Aztec Design, Silver, William Spratling, 1 ½ x 1 ½ In.	105.00
Pin, Azurite, Blue, Green, Silver Frame, 1970s, 1 ½ x 1 ¾ In.	45.00
Pin, Bakelite, 3 Pears, Brown, Celluloid Bar, 2 ¼ In. ....*illus*	75.00
Pin, Bakelite, Bird, Flying, Green, Painted Eyes, Clear Lucite Beak, Wings, Feathers, 4 In.	75.00
Pin, Bakelite, Deer, Butterscotch, Glass Eye, 1940s, 3 ⅜ x 2 In.	125.00
Pin, Bakelite, Fruit Salad, 1900s, 2 In.	150.00
Pin, Bakelite, Pineapple, Carved, 3 In. ....*illus*	75.00
Pin, Bakelite, Rhinestones, Dangle, Domed Bar, 1930s, 1 ¾ x 1 ¼ In.	35.00
Pin, Bar, Diamond, Edwardian, 2 ½ In.	88.00
Pin, Bar, Diamonds, 14K Bicolor Gold, Art Deco, 2 In.	334.00
Pin, Bar, Diamonds, Sapphire Ends, Platinum, Beaded, Tiffany & Co., 2 In.	2370.00
Pin, Bar, Etruscan Revival, Applied Bead & Wiretwist Accents, 2 ⅜ In. ....*illus*	415.00
Pin, Bar, Marcasite, Silver, Openwork Medallion, Leaves, Geometric, Edwardian Style, 1920s, 2 In.	145.00
Pin, Bar, Navette, Filigree, 14K White Gold, Oval Mine Cut Diamond, c.1940, 2 In.	246.00
Pin, Bar, Purple Stone, Cutout, Krementz, 1930s, 2 ¼ In.	55.00
Pin, Bar, Rosette, Single & Rose Cut Diamonds, Diamond Column, Case, Russia, c.1900, 1 ¼ In.	2640.00
Pin, Bar, Trefoil Ends, Gold Metal, Applied Clear Stones, Victorian, 2 ½ In.	108.00
Pin, Bar, Turquoise Arches, Diamond Melee, White Enamel Edge, Raymond Yard, 2 In.	2963.00
Pin, Bear, Deer Antlers, Jointed Arms & Legs, Silver, Napier, 2 x 1 ⅛ In.	38.00
Pin, Bee, 18K Gold, Engraved Wings, 19 Round Diamonds, Rosenthal, 1 ⅜ In.	2714.00
Pin, Beetle, Green, Red Rhinestones, Coro, Stamped ....*illus*	12.00
Pin, Beetle, Micro Mosaic, Gold Frame, Applied Barrel & Ropework, 1 ¾ In. ....*illus*	1126.00
Pin, Bird In Flight, Elongated Features, Silver, Coro, Mexico, 3 x 3 ¼ In.	16.00
Pin, Bird In Flight, White & Blue Rhinestones, Red Rhinestone Eyes, 1940s, 3 ¼ x 2 In.	135.00
Pin, Bird, Blue Enamel, Mardi Gras Carnival Krewe Favor	150.00
Pin, Bird, Leaves, Silver, Moonstone, Round, Georg Jensen, 2 ¼ In.	1250.00
Pin, Birds, Nest, Pearls, 18K Gold, Enamel, C Clasp, Italy, 1 x 1 In.	489.00
Pin, Black Dancer Warrior, Goldtone Metal, Enamel, Ankle Stones, 1950s, 2 ½ In.	130.00
Pin, Bow, Diamond, 18K Gold, Cartier, 2 In.	4830.00
Pin, Bow, Multiple Loops, Plastic, Red, c.1947, 3 x 2 In.	20.00
Pin, Bow, Rhinestones, Filigree, Silvertone Metal, 1930s, 2 ⅜ In.	15.00
Pin, Bow, Rhinestones, Trifari, c.1950, 2 In.	47.00
Pin, Bow, Rubies, 14K Gold, 1950s, 2 In.	320.00
Pin, Bow, Sapphire Cluster, 14K Rose Gold, Marked, Cartier, c.1945	2750.00
Pin, Bow, White Paste, Rhinestones, Trifari, c.1941	150.00
Pin, Branch, Amethyst, Ruby, Aquamarine, Sapphires, 14K Gold, Edward Oakes, 2 ¾ In. *illus*	4977.00
Pin, Branch, Leaves, C-Shape, Goldtone Metal, Sarah Coventry, 1 ¾ x 1 ⅝ In.	6.00
Pin, Buddha, Seated, Clouds, Ivory, 2 ¼ In.	196.00
Pin, Bumblebee, Gold Cloisonne, Rhinestone, Gold Metal, Domed Body, 1 ¾ x 1 ¼ In.	55.00
Pin, Butterfly, 18K Gold Rigato, Rubies, Emeralds, Sapphires, Buccellati, 2 ⅜ In.	7080.00
Pin, Butterfly, 18K Gold, Diamonds, Tiffany & Co., 1 ⅜ In.	3245.00
Pin, Butterfly, 18K Gold, Silver, Steven Lagos, Box, c.1990, ⅝ x 1 ⅜ In.	110.00
Pin, Butterfly, Enameled, Neon Rainbow, Gold Metal, 1970s, 2 ½ x 1 ½ In.	45.00
Pin, Butterfly, Goldtone Metal, Textured, Marked, 1960s, 3 ¼ x 2 In.	40.00
Pin, Butterfly, Plique-A-Jour, Teal, 14K Gold, Navette, Burmese Ruby, c.1965, 1 ⅜ x 1 ½ In.	345.00
Pin, Butterfly, Rubies & Sapphires, Silver Over Gold Mount, 1 ½ In. ....*illus*	770.00
Pin, Butterfly, Yellow Satin Glass, Rhinestones, Monet, 3 x 2 In.	55.00
Pin, Cameo, Bacchante, Coral, 14K Gold, Beaded & Ropework Frame, 2 In. ....*illus*	711.00
Pin, Cameo, Day & Night, Shell, 18K Gold Frame, 2 ½ In. ....*illus*	796.00
Pin, Cameo, Gorgon Medusa, Shell, Scrolling Mount, 14K Gold, 2 ¼ In. ....*illus*	1067.00
Pin, Cameo, Helios, In Horse-Pulled Cart, Over Clouds, Shell, 18K Gold Mount, 1 ¾ In.	1304.00
Pin, Cameo, Helmeted Man, Hardstone, 18K Gold Ropework Frame, Seed Pearls, 2 In.	889.00
Pin, Cameo, Jupiter, Flowing Curls, Oak Leaf Crown, Shell, 14K Gold Ropework Frame, 1 ⅝ In.	415.00

Jewelry, Pin, Cameo, Bacchante, Coral, 14K Gold, Beaded & Ropework Frame, 2 In.
$711.00

Skinner, Inc.

Jewelry, Pin, Cameo, Day & Night, Shell, 18K Gold Frame, 2 ½ In.
$796.00

Skinner, Inc.

Jewelry, Pin, Cameo, Gorgon Medusa, Shell, Scrolling Mount, 14K Gold, 2 ¼ In.
$1067.00

Skinner, Inc.

J

TIP
The ladies pictured on old cameos often have long thin noses. The cute turned-up nose is seen on modern cameos.

Jewelry, Pin, Cameo, Winged Angel, Child, Shell, 14K Gold Frame, Engraved E.J. May, 2 x 2 In.
$531.00

James D. Julia Inc.

Jewelry, Pin, Citrine, European-Cut Diamonds, 18K Gold, Tiffany & Co., 1 ½ In.
$1185.00

Skinner, Inc.

Jewelry, Pin, Crescent, 15 Inset Diamonds, Straight Pin Back, 14K Gold, 1890s, 1 ½ In.
$323.00

Cowan's Auctions

Jewelry, Pin, Enameled, Swirl, Yellow Metal, Wekstein, J. Hansen, Marked, c.1989, 3 In.
$119.00

Skinner, Inc.

Pin, Cameo, Medusa, Shell, 15K Gold Frame, Applied Wire & Braid Trim, 2 ⅜ In.	830.00
Pin, Cameo, Shell Carved, Male Profile, Wings In Hair, Snake, 14K Gold Frame, 1 ¾ x 1 ⅞ In.	652.00
Pin, Cameo, Winged Angel, Child, Shell, 14K Gold Frame, Engraved E.J. May, 2 x 2 In. .....*illus*	531.00
Pin, Cameo, Woman, Ivory Casein, Book Frame, Bakelite, c.1920, 2 ¼ x 1 ¾ In.	245.00
Pin, Cameo, Woman's Profile, Shell, 10K Gold, c.1890, 1 ½ In.	489.00
Pin, Cat, Lucite, Googly Eyes, Art Deco, 1950s, 2 x 2 In.	45.00
Pin, Celluloid, Basket Of Flowers, Yellow, Pink, Carved, c.1925, 2 ¼ x 1 ½ In.	45.00
Pin, Celtic, Carnelian, Pewter, Marked, Jacobite, 1950s, 1 ⅝ In.	85.00
Pin, Christmas Lantern, Goldtone Metal, Rhinestone, Green Enamel, Citrine, 1960s, 2 ¼ x 1 ⅜ In.	45.00
Pin, Christmas Tree, Clear Crystal, Gold Plated, 1960s, 2 x 1 ⅝ In.	75.00
Pin, Christmas Tree, Enamel, Rhinestones, Hedy, c.1960, 2 ½ x 1 ½ In.	28.00
Pin, Circle, 18 Fluted & Folded Over Curls, Goldtone Metal, Marvella, 2 In.	9.00
Pin, Circle, Divided, Brass, Ebony, Rosewood, Ivory Inlay, Peter Macchiarini, 2 x 3 ¼ In.	1800.00
Pin, Circle, Leaf, 18K Gold, Tiffany & Co., 1 ⅝ In.	531.00
Pin, Circle, Pink Coral, Tulips, 10K Gold Braid, 1950s, 1 ¼ In.	120.00
Pin, Circle, Silver, Alternating Crystals, Pearls, Edwardian, 1 ⅛ In.	275.00
Pin, Citrine, European-Cut Diamonds, 18K Gold, Tiffany & Co., 1 ½ In. ....*illus*	1185.00
Pin, Clover, Pearls, Diamonds, Flared Terminals, Cabochons, Russia, c.1900, 1 ¾ In.	1440.00
Pin, Comet, Amethyst, 9K Gold, c.1900, 2 ½ In.	235.00
Pin, Cowgirl, Lasso, Plastic, Art Deco, 1920s, 4 In.	185.00
Pin, Crab, Jadeite Cabochon, Diamonds, Ruby Eyes, Shreve & Co., 1 ¼ In.	2963.00
Pin, Crescent, 15 Inset Diamonds, Straight Pin Back, 14K Gold, 1890s, 1 ½ In. ....*illus*	323.00
Pin, Daisy, Elephant Ivory, Layered Yellow Petals, Green Stem, Marked, 1940s, 1 x 3 In.	135.00
Pin, Diamond, 14K Gold, Swirled Flower, Marked, KGJ, 1 ½ In.	690.00
Pin, Diamond, Blue Enamel Sunburst, 14K Gold Frame, Shaped, Russia, c.1910, 1 ½ In.	1800.00
Pin, Diamond, Old Mine Cut, Textured 10K Gold, Black Enamel, Victorian, 1 ½ In.	1150.00
Pin, Diamond, Pearl, Black Enamel, Filigree, 18K Gold, Tiffany & Co., c.1910, 1 In.	575.00
Pin, Diamonds, Platinum Branches, c.1950, 3 ¼ In.	3450.00
Pin, Dirk, Scottish Agate, Jasper, Citrine Accents, Engraved Silver Mount, Victorian, 3 In.	711.00
Pin, Dog, Schnauzer, On Arched Lead, Silver, Red Enamel Collar & Grip, Art Deco, 2 In.	474.00
Pin, Dogwood, Pearl Center, 12K Gold, Marked, Wells, 1950s, 1 ½ In.	165.00
Pin, Doll Shape, Silver, Blue & White Enamel Dress, Bonnet, Margot De Taxco, 2 In.	129.00
Pin, Donkey, 18K Gold, Ruby Eye, Marked, Cartier, 2 In.	1470.00
Pin, Donkey, Silver, Gold, Sapphire Eye, Marked, Tiffany, 1 ½ x 1 ¾ In.	173.00
Pin, Dragonfly, Rhinestone, Kenneth Lane, 4 ¾ In.	413.00
Pin, Enamel On Copper, Gold Foil Design, 1950s, 1 ½ In.	135.00
Pin, Enamel, Diamond, Maiden, Flowers, 18K Gold, Scalloped Border, Tiffany & Co., c.1880, 1 In.	6710.00
Pin, Enameled, Swirl, Yellow Metal, Wekstein, J. Hansen, Marked, c.1989, 3 In. ....*illus*	119.00
Pin, Fan, Open, Textured Goldtone, Miriam Haskell, 2 In.	2 5.00
Pin, Feather, Prince Of Wales, Black Jasper, Wedgwood, 14K Gold, 1 ¼ x 1 In.	184.00
Pin, Fish, Articulated, Blue, Green & Orange Enamel, Silver, Margot De Taxco, 2 In.	133.00
Pin, Fish, Brass, Coral, Ivory, Tag, Peter Macchiarini, 4 ½ x 1 ¼ In.	1800.00
Pin, Fleur-De-Lis, Enameled, Red, Green, Blue, Black, Art Nouveau, c.1910, 2 ¼ x 2 ¼ In.	245.00
Pin, Florentine Woman, Enamel, 14K Gold, Krementz, Art Nouveau, 3 x ⅜ In.	425.00
Pin, Flower Basket, Carved Amethyst, Silver, William Spratling, Mexico, 2 ⅜ In. ....*illus*	356.00
Pin, Flower Basket, Moonstone & Carnelian Blossoms, Onyx Basket, Art Deco, 1 ¼ In.	4385.00
Pin, Flower Basket, Rubies, Diamonds, Emerald Basket, 18K Gold, Edwardian, 1 ⅝ In.	7406.00
Pin, Flower Bouquet, Green & Purple Gemstones, 14K Gold Bow, Hobe, 3 In.	250.00
Pin, Flower Petals, Diamond, 14K Gold, c.1950, 2 ½ In.	460.00
Pin, Flower Spray, Diamonds Platinum Mount, 14K Gold, c.1930, 1 ⅝ x 1 In., Pair	3105.00
Pin, Flower Spray, Diamonds, Single, Marquise & Baguette, Platinum, Garrard, 2 ½ In.	3200.00
Pin, Flower Spray, Moonstones & Cabochons, Sapphires, 14K Bicolor Gold, 2 ½ In. ....*illus*	889.00
Pin, Flower Spray, Platinum, Diamond, Emerald, Double Clip, Art Deco, 3 ½ In.	4481.00
Pin, Flower, 14K Gold, Purple Enamel, Diamond Drop, Art Nouveau, 1 ¾ In.	652.00
Pin, Flower, 5 Petals, Gold, Diamonds, Center Bombe Cluster, 1950s	5069.00
Pin, Flower, Bow, 7 Sapphires, 18K Gold, Marked, Tiffany, 2 ¼ In.	774.00
Pin, Flower, Diamond, Pearls, Enamel, Green, Pink, 14K Gold, Art Nouveau, 1 In.	546.00
Pin, Flower, Leaf, Green Rhinestones, Goldtone Metal, 1940s, 2 x 1 In.	20.00
Pin, Flower, Milk Glass, Blue Lobelia, Pink Forget-Me-Nots, Leaf Frame, 1950s, 2 ¼ x 1 ¾ In..	85.00
Pin, Flower, Moonstone Center, Pearls, Carnelian Petals, Gold Metal, 1950s, 2 ¾ In.	160.00
Pin, Flower, Sapphire Cluster, 18K Gold, Marked, Marianne Ostier, c.1950	2750.00
Pin, Flower, Scalloped Silver Petals, Lapis Center, 1 ¼ In.	625.00
Pin, Flower, Stem, Enamel, Metal Base, 1950s, 3 ½ In.	40.00
Pin, Flower, Yellow Enamel Petals, 1960s, 2 x 2 In.	34.00
Pin, Flower, Yellow, 4 Guilloche Enamel Petals, Diamonds, Boucheron	7502.00

Pin, Flowers, Diamond, Blue Gem, Peach Enamel Ground, Flattened Oval, Russia, c.1900, 2 ½ In.		2880.00
Pin, Flowers, Leaves, Rhinestone, Enamel, Pot Metal, Swivel Pin, c.1930, 2 ¼ x 1 ⅝ In.		44.00
Pin, Flowers, Stems, Round Cut Diamond Centers, 18K Gold, Hammerman, 1 ¾ x 2 In.		3335.00
Pin, Flowers, Turquoise, 14K Gold, Engraved, A.J. Bauer, Kalo, 2 In.		1440.00
Pin, Flowers, Women's Profiles, Art Nouveau, 3 In.		208.00
Pin, Flying Cherubs, Woman, Flowing Hair, Flowers, Vines, Silver, Art Nouveau, 1 ¼ x 1 ¼ In.		165.00
Pin, Fox, Diamonds, Garnet Eyes, Platinum Over Gold, 1 ⅝ In.		3318.00
Pin, Giraffe, Polished Gold Metal, Rhinestones, Black Enamel, 1980s, 3 ½ x 1 ½ In.		65.00
Pin, Giraffe, Sapphire Eyes, Full Cut Diamonds, 18K Gold, Tiffany & Co., 1989, 3 In. ......*illus*		2133.00
Pin, Girls Dancing, Celluloid, c.1930, 1 x 2 In.		82.00
Pin, Grape & Leaf Design, Silver, Georg Jensen, 2 ½ In.		420.00
Pin, Grasshopper, Demantoid Garnets, Diamonds, Ruby Eye, 18K Gold, Edwardian, 1 ½ In. .....*illus*		4385.00
Pin, Hat, Emerald Rhinestones, Gold, Round Medallion, DeLizza & Elster, 1 ¾ In.		75.00
Pin, Heart, Turquoise Cabochons, Beaded Silver Frame, c.1925, 1 ⅛ x 1 In.		75.00
Pin, Horseshoe, Good Luck, Rose Cut Diamonds, Split Pearls, 14K, Registry Mark, 1 ¼ In. *illus*		593.00
Pin, Interlocking Squares, 18K Gold Domes, Lapis Tablets, Spritzer & Fuhrmann, 2 In.		1067.00
Pin, Jester, Lying Down, Holding Book, Mardi Gras, Elves Of Oberon Krewe ....*illus*		1016.00
Pin, Knot, 3 Lobes, Tortoiseshell, Silver Edges, William Spratling, 2 In.		889.00
Pin, Knot, Loop Chain, Inset Wire Flowers, Diamonds, 18K Gold, Cartier, France, c.1950		6500.00
Pin, Lapel, Armor Bearer, Sword, Diamond, 14K Gold, Bales Jewelers, 1 ¼ In.		118.00
Pin, Lapel, Pug Dog Face, Copper, Die Struck, Silver Pin, 3 ½ In.		11.00
Pin, Leaf, 14K Gold, Diamond, 11 Rubies, 1946, 2 In.		443.00
Pin, Leaf, Folded, 18K Gold, Tiffany & Co., c.1987, 2 In. ....*illus*		948.00
Pin, Leaves, Swirls, Brass, Turquoise Glass Bead Clusters, Frank Hess, 1930s, 3 x 1 ½ In.		115.00
Pin, Locket, Dangling, Blue & White Rhinestones, Filigree, Sandor Goldberger, 1940-50s, 1 ¾ In.		207.00
Pin, Lucite, Butterfly, Yellow, Green Enamel, c.1940, 3 x 2 ½ In.		175.00
Pin, Lucite, Turtle, c.1970s, 2 x 2 ½ In.		75.00
Pin, Lyre, Scrolled Plaque, Beaded, Silver, Aztec Style, Spratling, Mexico, c.1940, 1 ½ In.		151.00
Pin, Mama & Baby Bear, 18K Gold, Ruby Eyes, Diamond, Tiffany & Co., 1989, ⅞ In.		600.00
Pin, Man On High-Wheel Bicycle, Composition, Marked, Made In W. Germany, 2 ½ In.		25.00
Pin, Man, Sombrero, Blanket Over Shoulder, Silver, Enamel, Margot De Taxco, 2 In.		247.00
Pin, Marcasite, Chrysoprase Cabochon, Silver, Germany, c.1920, 2 In.		59.00
Pin, Micro Mosaic, Flowers, Multicolor, Italy, c.1900, 1 ¼ In.		78.00
Pin, Micro Mosaic, Roman Forum, Malachite, 14K Gold, Twisted Border, 1 ½ In. ....*illus*		767.00
Pin, Modernist, Amethyst Cabochon, Black Enamel, Silver Border, Denmark, 1950s, 1 ¾ In.		185.00
Pin, Molded Cherries, Leaves, Silver, Kalo, 2 In.		217.00
Pin, Moth, 14K Gold Openwork, Emerald, Diamonds, Rubies, Sapphires, Russia, Victorian		2655.00
Pin, Mother-Of-Pearl, Square, Carved, C-Clasp, c.1930, 2 x 2 In.		28.00
Pin, Mourning, Dried Flowers, Porcelain, 14K Gold, Twisted Rope Rim, c.1860, 2 ¼ x 1 ¾ In.		215.00
Pin, Mourning, Weeping Willow, Monument, Woven Hair, Oval Locket, Gilt, 2 x 1 ¼ In.		850.00
Pin, O Douce Fantaisie, Enamel, Mother-Of-Pearl, Malachite, Gold, Max Papart, 1980s, 2 In. .*illus*		1541.00
Pin, Owl, Sitting On Branch, Coral, Carved, 14K Gold, 2 In. ....*illus*		652.00
Pin, Pansy, Purple Enamel, Diamond, 14K Gold, Marked Bohm, Victorian, 1 ¼ In.		518.00
Pin, Paste, Amethyst Stones, Gilt Metal, Safety Chain, 1930s, 1 ¼ x 1 In.		98.00
Pin, Pendant, Cameo, Shell Carved, Three Graces, 14K Gold Frame, 2 ⅛ In. ....*illus*		385.00
Pin, People At Cafe, Awning, Satin Gold Metal, Polished Accents, 1970s, 2 x 1 ½ In.		55.00
Pin, Phone, 24 Rhinestones, Silver Metal, 1930s, 2 x 1 In.		39.00
Pin, Pinwheel, Multicolor Glass Beads, Frank Hess, Miriam Haskell, 1940s, 2 x 3 In.		165.00
Pin, Portrait, Gentleman, Mother-Of-Pearl, 19th Century		226.00
Pin, Renaissance Revival, Helmeted Figure, Enamel, Gold Mount, Split Pearl, Limoges, 1 ⅛ In. ... *illus*		474.00
Pin, Repeating S, 18K Gold, Hammered, Henry Dunay, 4 In.		826.00
Pin, Rooster, Clear Rhinestones, Red Stone Eye, c.1945, 2 In.		65.00
Pin, Rose, Enamel, Goldtone Metal, 1950s, 3 ½ In.		15.00
Pin, Ruskin Pottery Center, Silver Mounted, England, 1880s, 2 ⅛ In. ....*illus*		300.00
Pin, Scorpion, Chain Linked Segments, Rhinestones, 1980s, 5 x 2 In.		85.00
Pin, Scroll, Diamonds, Emeralds, Platinum, Openwork, Canted Rectangle, c.1900, 2 In. ...... *illus*		5078.00
Pin, Seahorse, Lucite, Metal Stud Eye, c.1960, 2 ½ In.		26.00
Pin, Silver, Bird, In Leafy Scroll, G. Jensen, 1 ½ x 1 ¾ In.		390.00
Pin, Silver, Oval, Domed, Open Center, Flowers, Georg Jensen, 1 ½ In.		295.00
Pin, Silver, Red Baguette Rhinestone, Round, c.1950, 1 ⅜ In.		48.00
Pin, Snake, Green Enamel, Mardi Gras, Mistick Krewe Of Comus Ball ....*illus*		717.00
Pin, Snake, Intertwined, Gold Plate, Emerald Rhinestone Eyes, Denicola, 1960s, 2 x 1 ¼ In. ..		95.00
Pin, Songbird, On Branch, Silver, Georg Jensen, 2 In.		296.00
Pin, Squirrel, 14K Gold, Ruby Eye, Pearl Belly, c.1950, ¾ In.		125.00
Pin, St. Michael's Hospital School Of Nursing, 10K Gold, Engraved, 1920, 1 In.		345.00

Jewelry, Pin, Flower Basket, Carved Amethyst, Silver, William Spratling, Mexico, 2 ⅜ In.
$356.00

Skinner, Inc.

Jewelry, Pin, Flower Spray, Moonstones & Cabochons, Sapphires, 14K Bicolor Gold, 2 ½ In.
$889.00

Skinner, Inc.

Jewelry, Pin, Giraffe, Sapphire Eyes, Full Cut Diamonds, 18K Gold, Tiffany & Co., 1989, 3 In.
$2133.00

Skinner, Inc.

Jewelry, Pin, Grasshopper, Demantoid Garnets, Diamonds, Ruby Eye, 18K Gold, Edwardian, 1 ½ In.
$4385.00

Skinner, Inc.

Jewelry, Pin, Horseshoe, Good Luck, Rose Cut Diamonds, Split Pearls, 14K, Registry Mark, 1 ¼ In.
$593.00

Skinner, Inc.

Jewelry, Pin, Jester, Lying Down, Holding Book, Mardi Gras, Elves Of Oberon Krewe
$1016.00

Neal Auction Co.

Jewelry, Pin, Leaf, Folded, 18K Gold, Tiffany & Co., c.1987, 2 In.
$948.00

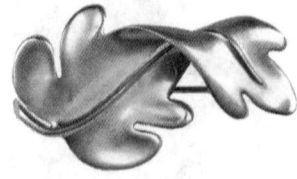

Skinner, Inc.

Jewelry, Pin, Micro Mosaic, Roman Forum, Malachite, 14K Gold, Twisted Border, 1 ½ In.
$767.00

Ivey-Selkirk Auctioneers

Pin, Star Shape, Silver, Paloma Picasso, Tiffany & Co., 2 ¾ In.	296.00
Pin, Starry Host, Atlanteans, Silver, Enamel, Mardi Gras, Krewe Favor, 1910	120.00
Pin, Steer's Head, Plastic, Painted, c.1940, 1 ¾ x 1 In.	28.00
Pin, Stylized Feather, 18K Gold, Paloma Picasso, Tiffany & Co., 2 In.	533.00
Pin, Stylized Fireworks, 18K Gold, 18 Diamonds, Tiffany & Co.	3068.00
Pin, Stylized Flower Basket, Gilt Bronze, Blue Enamel, Line Vautrin, 1960s, 2 x 1 ½ In. *illus*	1054.00
Pin, Stylized Flower, Wire, Diamonds, Oval Ruby, 18K Gold, Cartier, c.1950	9000.00
Pin, Stylized Insect, Amber Stone Body & Eyes, Silver Legs, Tono, Taxco, c.1950, 3 In.	54.00
Pin, Stylized Sunburst, Carved Mask, Silver, Amethyst Quartz, H. Harmon, 7 In.	2200.00
Pin, Sun, Smiley Face, Enamel On Metal, c.1960, 2 x 2 In.	65.00
Pin, Sunflower, Enamel, Pearls, Goldtone Metal, 1940s, 3 ½ In.	40.00
Pin, Swan, Celluloid, Black On Yellow, c.1930, 1 In.	45.00
Pin, Target, Silver, Malachite, Cusped Edges, c.1855, 2 In.	140.00
Pin, Thistle, Sapphires, Emeralds, 18K Gold, Schlumberger, Tiffany & Co., 2 In.	7703.00
Pin, Tiger, Diamonds, Green Chalcedony Eyes, Enamel Stripes, 18K Gold, Cartier, 2 In. *illus*	5333.00
Pin, Toucan On Branch, Diamond, Sapphire, Turquoise, 18K Gold, 20th Century, 2 ½ In. *illus*	4140.00
Pin, Turquoise Glass, Square Cabochon, Gold Veins, Portugal, Edwardian, c.1930, 1 ¾ x 1 ¼ In.	145.00
Pin, Turtle, Head Swivels, Amethyst, Emerald, Diamond, 18K Gold, Cartier, c.1960	3750.00
Pin, Watermelon Rhinestones, Purple, Green, Juliana, 1950s, 2 x 1 ⅝ In.	75.00
Pin, Woman, Bird, Flower, White Enamel Ground, Copper, Koloman, Moser, c.1909, 1 ½ x 1 ¼ In.	1736.00
Pin, Woman, Wearing Turban, Ceramic, Elzac, 2 x 1 In.	68.00
Pin, Wood, Orange Flowers, 3 Leaves, Painted, c.1935, 3 ½ In.	30.00
Ring & Earrings, Turquoise Cabochon, Rows Of Diamonds & Sapphires, 1960s	8296.00
Ring, 2 Diamonds, Platinum, 18K Gold, Prong Set, Tiffany & Co., Size 6	6900.00
Ring, 3 Diamonds, 14K Gold, Scrolled Setting, c.1975, Size 8 ¼	720.00
Ring, 3 Sapphires, White Gold, Filigree Mount, c.1930, Size 5 ¾	600.00
Ring, 4 Aquamarines, Baguette Cut, 18K Gold Rectangular Mount, P. Picasso, Tiffany	1511.00
Ring, 5 Coral Buttons, 14K Gold Leaf Mount, Size 7	593.00
Ring, 6 Black Pearls, 2 Diamonds, 14K Gold Mount, Mikimoto, Size 8	649.00
Ring, 7 Diamonds, 14K Gold, Concave Setting, c.1975, Size, 4 ¾	480.00
Ring, 10 Diamonds, 14K Gold, c.1980, Size 9 ¼	480.00
Ring, 18K Gold, Baguette Diamonds, Paloma Picasso, Tiffany & Co., Size 6 ¼	1778.00
Ring, 32 Diamonds, Bead, Channel Set, Platinum Mount, Art Deco, Size 6 ½	748.00
Ring, Amethyst, 14K Gold, Art Deco, c.1925, Size 9	695.00
Ring, Amethyst, Cushion Cut, Faceted, Silver, 14K Gold Accent, Yurman, Size 5	472.00
Ring, Amethyst, Filigree, 18K Gold, Edwardian, Size 10 ½	575.00
Ring, Amethyst, Gold, Victorian, Size 4 ¼	81.00
Ring, Amethyst, Pearls, 14K Gold, Victorian, 1880s, Size 8	450.00
Ring, Amethyst, Round, Step Cut, 18K Gold, Mario Buccellati, Size 5 ½	6000.00
Ring, Amethyst, Seed Pearls, 14K Gold, Oval Mount, Braid Border, Size 6 ½	184.00
Ring, Aquamarine Cabochon, 18K Gold, Paloma Picasso, Tiffany & Co., Size 6 ½	1854.00
Ring, Aquamarine, 18K White Gold Filigree, Art Deco, c.1930, Size 7	285.00
Ring, Aquamarine, Diamond Starburst, Austria, 1960s, Adjustable Size 6 ½ To 8	65.00
Ring, Azurite, Domed, Gadrooned, Diamond Melee Rim, 18K Gold, David Webb, Size 8	5333.00
Ring, Baroque Pearl, 18K Gold, Elsa Peretti, Tiffany & Co., Size 4	550.00
Ring, Bishop's, Amethyst, Diamonds, Gold, Man's, Size 14	1220.00
Ring, Black Diamond, Brilliant Cut, 14K Gold, 1900s, Size 6 ½	837.00
Ring, Blue Enamel, 18K Gold, Hidalgo, Size 6 ½, Pair	472.00
Ring, Blue Topaz, Diamonds, 18K Gold, Bulbous, Oval, 1950s, Man's, Size 6 ½	435.00
Ring, Bombe, Alternating Lapis Tablets & Diamond Melee, Van Cleef & Arpels, Size 6	3555.00
Ring, Bombe, Diamond Melee, Pave Set, 18K Gold, Cartier, Size 6 ¼	8295.00
Ring, Cameo, Classical Maiden Bust, Shell, Gold Band, Size 8 ¼	243.00
Ring, Cameo, Hardstone, Nude Male Figure, Holding Lion Skin & Staff, 14K Gold, Size 6 *illus*	2252.00
Ring, Caviar, Silver, 18K Gold, Beaded, Cabochons, Lagos, Size 6 ¼	75.00
Ring, Cerchi, Shield, Swivel, 18K Gold, Bulgari, Size 6	1064.00
Ring, Citrine, 14K Gold, Openwork, Charles Loloma, c.1995, Size 7 ½	2185.00
Ring, Citrine, Diamond, 14K Gold, Victorian, Size 7	595.00
Ring, Cocktail, 3 Rows Diamonds, Platinum, Scalloped, Edwardian	3107.00
Ring, Cocktail, Amethyst, Diamonds, Ballerina Set, 14K Gold, 1900s, Size 7 ½	597.00
Ring, Cocktail, Diamonds, Princess Cut, Rectangular, 14K White Gold, 1900s, Size 7	1554.00
Ring, Cocktail, Opal Cabochon, Opalescent Glass Chatons, Brass Rim, 1950s, Size 7	75.00
Ring, Cocktail, Sapphire Glass, Round, Faceted, Adjustable, 1950s, ⅝ In.	60.00
Ring, Coral, Jadeite, Opal, Onyx, Tiger's Eye, Gold, 1960s, Size 7 ½	75.00
Ring, Diamond, 14K Gold, c.1960, Size 8 ½	600.00
Ring, Diamond, 14K Gold, Free-Form Mount, c.1975, Size 9 ¼	900.00

Ring, Diamond, 14K Gold, Gold Shank, c.1950, Size 6 ¼ 1195.00
Ring, Diamond, 18K Gold, c.1975, Man's, Size 11 .... 2880.00
Ring, Diamond, Art Deco, Size 3 ½ 497.00
Ring, Diamond, Cluster, Brilliant Cut, 14K Gold, c.1950, Size 6 .... 856.00
Ring, Diamond, Emerald Cut, 14K Gold, c.1950, Size 6 .... 1560.00
Ring, Diamond, Emerald Cut, Platinum, Etienne Perret, Size 6 ½ 5175.00
Ring, Diamond, Emerald Cut, Smaller Diamond Surround, Size 4 ½ 575.00
Ring, Diamond, Emerald, Rectangular, Step Cut, 14K Gold, 1900s, Size 6 .... 1554.00
Ring, Diamond, Round Cut, 14K White Gold, Art Deco, Size 7 ½ 345.00
Ring, Diamond, Round, Brilliant Cut, Platinum, 18K Gold, 1900s, Size 4 .... 2748.00
Ring, Diamond, Ruby, 14K Gold, Filigree, Oval Mount, Art Deco, Size 5 ¾ 270.00
Ring, Diamond, Sapphires, Platinum, Gold, Art Deco, Woman's, Size 7 ½ 437.00
Ring, Diamond, Solitaire, Baguette Sides, Platinum, 1930s, Size 6 ½ 2070.00
Ring, Diamond, Solitaire, Gold, c.1955, Size 7 ¾ 780.00
Ring, Diamond, Synthetic Sapphire, 18K White Gold, Scalloped Setting, Edwardian, Size 6 ½ ... 239.00
Ring, Diamond, White Gold, Filigree Mount, c.1930, Size 8 ¾ 1320.00
Ring, Diamonds, 14K Gold, Flower Shaped Mount, c.1970, Size 8 ¼ 600.00
Ring, Diamonds, Amethyst, 14K Gold, 1930s, Size 4 .... 395.00
Ring, Diamonds, Brilliant Cut, 10K Gold, 1900s, Size 7 .... 298.00
Ring, Diamonds, Brilliant Cut, 14K Gold, Nugget Style, c.1980, Size 8 ¾ 720.00
Ring, Diamonds, Emerald Cabochon, 18K Bicolor Gold, David Webb 4481.00
Ring, Diamonds, Emeralds, Textured 18K Gold, Mauboussin, Size 6 ....*illus* 1185.00
Ring, Diamonds, Filigree, 18K Gold, 1920s, Size 6 ½ 978.00
Ring, Diamonds, Round Cut, Bead Set, Platinum, 14K Gold, David Webb, Size 5 .... 1093.00
Ring, Diamonds, Synthetic Ruby Cabochon, Platinum, Edwardian, Size 5 ½ 956.00
Ring, Edwardian, Flower, Gold Open Petals, Pastel Enamel, Edwardian, Size 8 .... 155.00
Ring, Emerald, 18 Small Diamonds, 18K White Gold, Size 9 .... 460.00
Ring, Emerald, 4 Side Brilliant Diamonds, 14K Gold, 1900s, Size 6 ½ 598.00
Ring, Emerald, Bezel Set, 14K Gold, Wide Beaded Band, Size 6 ½ 1725.00
Ring, Emerald, Diamond, Rectangular, Step Cut, 18K Gold Band, 1900s, Size 6 ½ 5378.00
Ring, Emerald, Oval, 2 Triangular Diamonds, 18K White Gold Mount, 1900s, Size 7 ... 1075.00
Ring, Flower Cluster, Sapphires, Gold Plate, 1960s, Adjustable Size 6 To 9 .... 75.00
Ring, Flower, Opal, Diamond, 18K Gold, Box, 1960s, Size 6 ¼ 75.00
Ring, Garnet, Seed Pearls, Square, 14K Gold, Scrolls, Victorian, 7 ½ 135.00
Ring, Grid, 18K Gold, Ruby, Round, Diamonds, Man's, Size 13 ¼ 366.00
Ring, Hematite, Oval Cabochon, Bezel Set, Silver, Georg Jensen, Size 5 .... 199.00
Ring, Jade, Mottled Green, Gold, Man's, Size 13 ¾ 1037.00
Ring, Jadeite, Carved, Qing, Chinese, 1800s, Size 7 .... 478.00
Ring, Kinetic, 3 Beads In Cage, Silver, Ed Weiner, Man's Size 9 .... 1680.00
Ring, Lion's Head Crest, Oval, Relief, Garnet Eyes, 14K Gold, Cartier, Size 11 .... 1770.00
Ring, Love, Diamond, 18K Bicolor Gold, Sliding, Cartier, Size 12 .... 2360.00
Ring, Micro Mosaic, Flower Medallion, Multicolored Glass, Diamond, Italy, 1950s, 1 ½ x 1 In. ... 85.00
Ring, Mourning, Woman, Willow, Ivory, Inkwork, 10K Gold, Navette, c.1790, Size 8 ½ ... 613.00
Ring, Opal, Diamond, Gold, Victorian, Size 6 ½ 561.00
Ring, Pearl & Diamond, Cluster, Bezel Set, Platinum, Tiffany & Co., Size 4 ½ 1416.00
Ring, Pearl Cluster, 2 Diamonds, 18K Gold Mount, Mikimoto, Size 7 .... 472.00
Ring, Pearl, Amethyst Cluster, 14K Gold, Size 7 ¼ 431.00
Ring, Rubies, Channel Set, Diamond Melee, 18K Gold, Van Cleef & Arpels, Size 6 ¼ ... 5629.00
Ring, Ruby, 15K White Gold, c.1925, Art Deco, Size 8 .... 195.00
Ring, Sapphire, Cushion-Cut, 18K Textured Gold, Ed Wiener, Size 4 ¼ ....*illus* 770.00
Ring, Sapphire, Diamond, 14K Gold Square Leafy Mount Oakes, Size 5 ¾ 5629.00
Ring, Sapphire, Oval, Diamonds, Bezel Set, 18K Gold, Ted Hendrickson, Size 6 ½ 633.00
Ring, Serpent, 18K Gold, Coiled, Diamond Eyes, Gemstone, c.1890, Size 9 .... 239.00
Ring, Serpent, 18K Gold, Green Enamel Eyes, David Webb, Size 4 .... 1304.00
Ring, Silver Pearl, Leafy Mount, Georg Jensen, Size 5 .... 296.00
Ring, Silver, Cigar Band, Beads, Mexico, Size 8 ½ 58.00
Ring, Silver, Inlaid Lapis, Turquoise, Marked Charles Loloma, c.1985, Size 7 .... 2875.00
Ring, Snake, Coiled, 14K Gold, Diamond Head, c.1910, Size 6 ½ 650.00
Ring, Spoon, Grand Baroque Pattern, Silver, Marked Wallace, 1970s, Size 6 ½ 65.00
Ring, Stones, Red, Green, Blue, Silvertone Metal, Adjustable, Sarah Coventry, 1970s, 1 x 1 In. ... 12.00
Ring, Tahitian Pearl, Diamond Surround, Brilliant Cut, 14K Gold, 1900s, Size 7 .... 1195.00
Ring, Textured, Diamond, 18K Gold, Abstract Mount, 1960s, Size 6 .... 948.00
Ring, Thistle, Sapphires, Emeralds, 18K Gold, Schlumberger, Tiffany & Co., Size 7 ..... 6125.00
Ring, Trinity, 18K Tricolor Gold, 3 Ribbed Bands, Cartier, Size 4 .... 415.00
Ring, Turquoise, Silver, Sunshine Reeves, Size 9 .... 89.00

Jewelry, Pin, O Douce Fantaisie, Enamel, Mother-Of-Pearl, Malachite, Gold, Max Papart, 1980s, 2 In.
$1541.00

Skinner, Inc.

Jewelry, Pin, Owl, Sitting On Branch, Coral, Carved, 14K Gold, 2 In.
$652.00

Skinner, Inc.

Jewelry, Pin, Pendant, Cameo, Shell Carved, Three Graces, 14K Gold Frame, 2 ⅛ In.
$385.00

Skinner, Inc.

The Tango Compact
A compact with a chain and finger ring or loop is called a "tango." It was a popular style in the 1920s and '30s. A tango was meant to be carried on the dance floor and often held powder and lipstick.

Jewelry, Pin, Renaissance Revival, Helmeted Figure, Enamel, Gold Mount, Split Pearl, Limoges, 1 ⅛ In.
$474.00

Skinner, Inc.

Jewelry, Pin, Ruskin Pottery Center, Silver Mounted, England, 1880s, 2 ⅛ In.
$300.00

Jewelry, Pin, Scroll, Diamonds, Emeralds, Platinum, Openwork, Canted Rectangle, c.1900, 2 In.
$5078.00

Sloans & Kenyon

Jewelry, Pin, Snake, Green Enamel, Mardi Gras, Mistick Krewe Of Comus Ball
$717.00

Neal Auction Co.

Jewelry, Pin, Stylized Flower Basket, Gilt Bronze, Blue Enamel, Line Vautrin, 1960s, 2 x 1 ½ In.
$1054.00

Rago Arts & Auction Center

Jewelry, Pin, Tiger, Diamonds, Green Chalcedony Eyes, Enamel Stripes, 18K Gold, Cartier, 2 In.
$5333.00

Skinner, Inc.

Jewelry, Pin, Toucan On Branch, Diamond, Sapphire, Turquoise, 18K Gold, 20th Century, 2 ½ In.
$4140.00

Leland Little Auction

Jewelry, Ring, Cameo, Hardstone, Nude Male Figure, Holding Lion Skin & Staff, 14K Gold, Size 6
$2252.00

Skinner, Inc.

Jewelry, Ring, Diamonds, Emeralds, Textured 18K Gold, Mauboussin, Size 6
$1185.00

Skinner, Inc.

Jewelry, Ring, Sapphire, Cushion-Cut, 18K Textured Gold, Ed Wiener, Size 4 ¼
$770.00

Skinner, Inc.

Jewelry, Stickpin, American Indian Head, Stone, Carved, Mounted On Yellow Gold
$660.00

William H. Bunch Auctions

Stickpin, American Indian Head, Stone, Carved, Mounted On Yellow Gold ....*illus*	660.00
Stickpin, Cameo, Rectangular, 10K Gold, c.1950, 2 In.	30.00
Stickpin, Dragon, Gold Filled, Art Nouveau, c.1905, 3 In.	35.00
Stickpin, Elephant's Head, Pear On Trunk, 14K Yellow Gold ....*illus*	480.00
Stickpin, Fox, Running, Diamond Melee, Ruby Eyes, Platinum, Tiffany & Co., 1 In.	830.00
Stickpin, Star, Pearls, Coral Cabochon, 14K Gold, Victorian, c.1900, 2 In.	75.00
Stickpin, Woman, Flowing Hair, Open Work Heart Frame, Art Nouveau, c.1900, 2 x 1 ¾ In. ...	245.00
Stud Set, Gold, Ruby Cabochon, Square, Chain Links, Fitted Box, Man's, 4 Piece...................	448.00
Tie Clasp, Bar, 18K Gold Basket Weave, Tiffany & Co., 2 ⅛ In.	590.00
Watches are listed in their own category.	
Watch Chain, Platinum, Figaro Link, 3 Spring Ends, T-Bar End, 22K Gold, ¾ In.	1521.00
Watch Key, Brass, Ivory, Shells, Central Ship Medallion, French Flag, c.1775, 3 In..................	881.00
Wristwatches are listed in their own category.	

JOHN ROGERS statues were made from 1859 to 1892. The originals were bronze, but the thousands of copies made by the Rogers factory were of painted plaster. Eighty different figures were created. Similar painted plaster figures were produced by some other factories. Rights to the figures were sold in 1893, and the figures were manufactured for several more years by the Rogers Statuette Co. Never repaint a Rogers figure because this lowers the value to collectors.

Group, The Council Of War, Abraham Lincoln, Ulysses S. Grant, Edwin M. Stanton, 1868, 24 In..	2950.00
Group, The Photographers, The Sitter, Plaster, 1878, 19 In., Pair.........................	3540.00
Group, The Traveling Magician, Plaster, 1877, 23 In..	3245.00
Plate, Christening, Flower Border, Hannah, c.1820, 7 ⅛ In...............................	500.00

JOSEF ORIGINALS ceramics were designed by Muriel Joseph George. The first pieces were made in California from 1945 to 1962. They were then manufactured in Japan. The company was sold to George Good in 1982 and he continued to make Josef Originals until 1985. The company was then sold to Southland Corporation. The name is now owned by Applause, and the Birthday Girl series is still being made.

Figurine, Birthday Angel, Age 9, Pale Blue Gold Accents, Carrying Star Wand, 5 1/16 In.	42.00
Figurine, Carol, Incised 53, 4 ¼ In.	50.00
Figurine, Cat, Orange Tabby, Back & Tail Up, Sticker, 4 x 3 ¾ In.	22.00
Figurine, Down To Sleep, Young Girl, Pajamas, Sticker, c.1945, 3 In.	35.00
Figurine, Ring Bearer, Boy, 3 In.	39.00
Lipstick Holder, Figural, Girl, Pink Dress, 4-Holder, Sticker, 1960s, 3 ½ In.	64.00
Music Box, Boy Caroling, Santa Suit, Japan, c.1955, 8 In.	22.00
Planter, Lady, White & Blue Dress, Sticker, 6 ¼ In.	75.00

JUDAICA is any memorabilia that refers to the Jews or the Jewish religion. Interests range from newspaper clippings that mention eighteenth- and nineteenth-century Jewish Americans to religious objects, such as menorahs or spice boxes. Age, condition, and the intrinsic value of the material, as well as the historic and artistic importance, determine the value.

Candleholder, Sabbath, Silver, Fluted Column, Round Base, Poland, 15 In., Pair...................	891.00
Cup, Kiddush, Silver, Food Symbols, 13 ½ x 6 In.	537.00
Finial, Torah, Silver, Crown Top, Hexagonal Arched Body, Bells, Filigree Base, 9 ½ In., Pair....	489.00
Goblet Set, Silver, Etched, Star Of David, Stamped, 4 x 2 In., 12 Piece.....................	518.00
Knife, Bread, Sabbath Day, Silver Plate, Mother-Of-Pearl, Hebrew Letters, Hinged, 5 In.	400.00
Menorah, 7-Light, Brass, Stepped Base, c.1910, 11 x 9 In.	89.00
Menorah, Brass, Arched Wood Backing, Cups, Symbols, c.1800, 14 ¾ x 10 ¼ In.	4600.00
Menorah, Modernist, Brass, Jerusalem, 1900s, 13 ½ x 9 ½ In.	185.00
Menorah, Silver, 4 Double, 2 Single Arm Branches, Capital Nozzles, Stepped Base, c.1905, 28 In.	3851.00
Menorah, Silver, Embossed, Germany, 6 ½ x 7 In..	748.00
Menorah, Silver, Filigree Scrolls, Thistle Shape Sconce, Hexagonal Stem, Base, Israel, 16 x 14 In.	3081.00
Menorah, U-Shape Arms, Pierced Base, Hebrew Quote, Israel, c.1980, 13 ½ In.	1422.00
Pitcher, Incised Cobalt Blue Star Of David, Banded Base & Collar, 1800s, 6 In.	489.00
Pitcher, Tankard, Stoneware, Cobalt Blue Star Of David, Symbols, Westerwald, c.1825, 10 In.	1093.00
Ring, Marriage, Spice Tower, Compartment, Hebrew Lettering Mazel Tov, 18K Gold, Size 7 ¼ ... *illus*	2370.00
Ring, Silver, Square Top, Torah, Lions, Rabbi, Warrior, Marked, 1900s, ⅝ x ⅝ In. ....*illus*	178.00
Shofar, Horn, Ram's, Silver Mounted End Cup & Cap, 6 ½ In..................................	115.00
Spice Box, Besamim, Silver, Filigree, Openwork Base, Stylized Snakes, Continental, c.1810, 6 In. .*illus*	356.00
Spice Box, Besamim, Silver, Scrolls, Octagonal, Flared Stem, Tiered Domed Foot, c.1850, 8 ½ In.	490.00
Spice Box, Besamim, Silver, Tower Shape, Turret, Square, Filigree, 4 Bells, Russia, c.1890, 10 In..	237.00

Jewelry, Stickpin, Elephant's Head, Pear On Trunk, 14K Yellow Gold
$480.00

Bob Courtney Auctions

Judaica, Ring, Marriage, Spice Tower, Compartment, Hebrew Lettering Mazel Tov, 18K Gold, Size 7 ¼
$2370.00

Skinner, Inc.

Judaica, Ring, Silver, Square Top, Torah, Lions, Rabbi, Warrior, Marked, 1900s, ⅝ x ⅝ In.
$178.00

Skinner, Inc.

Judaica, Spice Box, Besamim, Silver, Filigree, Openwork Base, Stylized Snakes, Continental, c.1810, 6 In.
$356.00

Skinner, Inc.

J

Jugtown, Vase, Mottled, Blue Glaze, Red Runs, Impressed Mark, c.1935, 9 In. $413.00

Brunk Auctions

Kate Greenaway, Napkin Ring, Silver Plate, Figural, Girl, On Toboggan, Wilcox Silver Plate Co., 4 ¼ In. $1080.00

Morphy Auctions

Kelva, Humidor, Enameled Flower Blossoms, Cigars, Green Mottled Ground, Marked, 5 ¾ x 4 In. $690.00

James D. Julia Inc.

Kew Blas, Vase, Green & Gold Pulled Feather, Ivory Ground, Gold Collar, Marked, 4 In. $518.00

James D. Julia Inc.

Spice Box, Besamin, Silver, Fish Shape, Hinged Mouth, Glass Eyes, Germany, c.1890, 5 In.	227.00
Spice Box, Besamin, Silver, Tower Shape, Filigree, Twisted Wirework Legs, Hungary, c.1925, 6 ½ In.	429.00
Spice Box, Besamim, Tower, Silver, Tiered Cylinder Lid, Pierced, Bell, Germany, 1700s, 9 ½ In.	2133.00
Spice Box, Silver, Modern, 2 Scoop Opening, Joined Base, Hans Christiansen, 1964, 12 x 6 In.	19000.00
Spice Tower, Silver, Flags, Star Of David, Footed, Austria, 9 ¾ x 2 ¾ In.	283.00
Torah Pointer, Chain, 9 ¼ In.	430.00
Torah Pointer, Silver, Filigree Handle, Plaques, 2 Knops, Tapered Stem, Loop & Chain, 11 ½ In.	356.00
Torah Pointer, Wood Shaft, Silver & Brass Pommel, Red & Turquoise Cabochons, 20 In.	590.00
Tray, Ceremonial, Chased, Silver, Oval, 9 x 12 ½ In.	1440.00

JUGTOWN POTTERY refers to pottery made in North Carolina as far back as the 1750s. In 1915, Juliana and Jacques Busbee set up a training and sales organization for what they named Jugtown Pottery. In 1921, they built a shop at Jugtown, North Carolina, and hired Ben Owen as a potter in 1923. The Busbees moved the village store where the pottery was sold to New York City. Juliana Busbee sold the New York store in 1926 and moved into a log cabin near the Jugtown Pottery. The pottery closed in 1959. It reopened in 1960 and is still working near Seagrove, North Carolina.

Candlestick, Black Glaze, Flared, Impressed, c.1950, 12 ½ In., Pair	1298.00
Chicken, Pedestal, Incised, Al Powers, c.1962, 6 ¾ x 7 ¾ In.	201.00
Crock, Black Salt Glaze, Pinched Handles, 8 In.	119.00
Pitcher, Brown Glaze, 6 ½ x 4 ½ In.	65.00
Vase, Egg Shape, Runny Blue Ground, Red Swirl Glaze, 5 ⅞ In.	354.00
Vase, Mottled, Blue Glaze, Red Runs, Impressed Mark, c.1935, 9 In. *illus*	413.00
Vase, Narrowed Bottom, Tab Handles, 6 ¼ In.	165.00
Vase, Oval, Chinese Blue, Green, Footed, 4 ⅛ In.	395.00
Vase, Red Glaze, Blue Mottling, c.1930, 8 In.	1180.00
Vase, Red, Chinese Blue Glaze, Squat, c.1930, 5 ½ In.	354.00

JUKEBOXES play records. The first coin-operated phonograph was demonstrated in 1889. In 1906 the Automatic Entertainer appeared, the first coin-operated phonograph to offer several different selections of music. The first electrically powered jukebox was introduced in 1927. Collectors search for jukeboxes of all ages, especially those with flashing lights and unusual design and graphics.

Packard, Play-More, Walnut Case, Art Deco, Waterfall Design, 24 Selections, 35 x 61 In.	1380.00
Seeburg, Select-O-Matic, Rectangular, Wood, Gold, c.1940, 59 x 35 In.	2700.00
Seeburg, Select-O-Matic 100, c.1950, 59 x 35 In.	1046.00
Wurlitzer, Model 700, Keys, c.1940	4200.00
Wurlitzer, Model 850, Peacock, Water Bubbler, Chrome, Burled Walnut, 78S, c.1941, 64 x 36 In.	15530.00
Wurlitzer, Model 1015, One More Time, 45 RPM Records, Keys	3850.00
Wurlitzer, Model 1100, Walnut Case, Chrome, Multicolor, 24 Selections, 58 x 30 In.	2358.00
Wurlitzer, One More Time, Reproduction 45 Model 1015 300, Plays 45S, 60 x 33 In.	3910.00

KATE GREENAWAY, who was a famous illustrator of children's books, drew pictures of children in high-waisted Empire dresses. She lived from 1846 to 1901. Her designs appear on china, glass, and other pieces.

Book, April Baby's Book Of Tunes, Hardcover, 1901, 7 x 7 In.	125.00
Book, Marigold Garden, Wood Block Designs, Hardcover, 9 x 7 In., 56 Pages	57.00
Bowl, Silver Plate, Boys, Girls, Raised Flowers, Leaves, Reed & Barton, 6 x 4 In.	165.00
Box, Enamel On Copper, Girls, Holding Umbrellas, Round, England, 1 ⅝ In.	225.00
Button, Children, On Fence, Holding Umbrella, Loop Shank	49.00
Button, Children, Sitting On Fence, Holding Umbrella, 1 In.	49.00
Mug, Alphabet, Child's, 1885, 2 ¼ In.	40.00
Napkin Clip, Reclining Boy, Flower Medallions, James Tufts Co., c.1885	600.00
Napkin Ring, Silver Plate, Figural, Boy On Bench, Holding Baton, c.1885	700.00
Napkin Ring, Silver Plate, Figural, Boy, Eating Cookie, Wm. Rogers & Son	225.00
Napkin Ring, Silver Plate, Figural, Girl, On Toboggan, Wilcox Silver Plate Co., 4 ¼ In. *illus*	1080.00
Napkin Ring, Silver Plate, Figural, Girls Climbing Ladder, 1880s	2600.00
Pitcher, Glass, Children, Leaves, Flowers, Blue, 9 In., Pair	1300.00
Plate, Children Playing, Multicolor, Wedgwood, 10 In.	66.00
Toothpick Holder, Silver Plate, Child, Barrel, c.1885, 4 ¾ In.	580.00
Tray, Tin, Girls, Garden, Cottage, Scalloped Rim, Yellow, 17 x 13 In.	60.00
Tumbler, Children Holding Hands, 3 ½ In.	15.00
Washbasin, 2 Parts, Children Playing, 4 ½ x 15 x 10 ¾ In.	245.00

KAY FINCH CERAMICS

KAY FINCH CERAMICS were made in Corona Del Mar, California, from 1935 to 1963. The hand-decorated pieces often depicted whimsical animals and people. Pastel colors were used.

Kay Finch CALIFORNIA

Bank, Pig, Smiley, Raised Ears, 6 ¼ x 8 In.	350.00
Centerpiece, Turkey Shape, 10 x 10 In.	325.00
Figurine, Angel, Blue Wings, Blond, Arms Up, 4 ¼ In.	48.00
Figurine, Bird, Mr. Blue Bird, 3 In.	85.00
Figurine, Bird, Singing, Stand, Pink, Mauve, Gold, 4 In.	195.00
Figurine, Cat, Jezebel, Cream, Pink, Blue, Closed Eyes, 6 In.	175.00
Figurine, Couple, Godey, Cream & Pink Outfits, Marked, 7 ¾ In., 2 Piece	110.00
Figurine, Dog, Doggie, Sitting, Tilted Head, Blue Collar, 5 In.	450.00
Figurine, Elephant, Peanuts, Trunk Up, Leg Up, 8 ¼ In.	285.00
Figurine, Grumpy Pig, 6 In.	399.00
Figurine, Kitten, Muff, Closed Eyes, Tilted Head, 3 ¼ In.	65.00 to 75.00
Figurine, Kitten, Puff, 3 ¼ In.	65.00
Figurine, Madonna, Kneeling, Blue Shawl, 6 In.	110.00
Figurine, Owl, Toot, Big Eyes, 5 ¾ In.	35.00
Figurine, Peanut Elephant, 8 ¼ In.	399.00
Figurine, Pig, Grumpy, Flowers, Squinty Eyes, 10 In.	295.00
Figurine, Rooster, Chanticleer, 11 In.	325.00
Figurine, Woman, Cape, Muff, Head Down, 7 In.	56.00
Toby Jug, Santa Claus, 4 In.	130.00

KAYSERZINN, *see Pewter category.*

KELVA

KELVA glassware was made by the C. F. Monroe Company of Meriden, Connecticut, about 1904. It is a pale, pastel-painted glass decorated with flowers, designs, or scenes. Kelva resembles Nakara and Wave Crest, two other glasswares made by the same company.

KELVA

Box, Pink, White Flowers, Mottled Green Ground, Silver Plated Collar, Marked, 4 x 2 ¾ In.	266.00
Humidor, Enameled Flower Blossoms, Cigars, Green Mottled Ground, Marked, 5 ¾ x 4 In. .... *illus*	690.00
Pin Dish, Green Mottled Ground, Pink Flowers, Gilt Metal Rim, Handle, 6-Sided, Handle, 3 ½ In.	125.00

KEMPLE

KEMPLE glass was made by John Kemple of East Palestine, Ohio, and Kenova, West Virginia, from 1945 to 1970. The glass was made from old molds. Many designs and colors were made. Kemple pieces are usually marked with a *K* on the bottom. Many milk glass pieces were made with or without the mark.

John E. Kemple

Banana Boat, Milk Glass, Heart Pattern, Sticker, 10 x 6 x 3 In.	48.00
Bonbon, Milk Glass, Sunburst, 2 Handles, Footed, Marked	25.00
Candleholder, Milk Glass, Octagonal Foot, Marked, 1950s, 3 ¼ In., Pair	30.00
Candlestick, Milk Glass, White Jewel Dewdrop, Ovals, Flowers, c.1946, 4 ¼ In.	17.00
Cup & Saucer, Milk Glass, Ivy Leaves	10.00
Goblet, Water, Lace & Dewdrop, Green	15.00
Pitcher, Milk Glass, Lace & Dewdrop, 4 ½ In.	19.00
Plate, Milk Glass, Pheasants, Branches, Panel Peg Open Edge, 1940s, 7 ½ In.	22.00
Plate, Milk Glass, Windmill, Lacy Edge, Pierced Heart Edge, 7 ¼ In.	20.00
Relish, Sunbursts, Trailing Stars, Amber, Scalloped Rim, 7 x 5 In.	35.00
Sherbet, Lacy Dew Drop, Amber, 4 x 2 In.	5.00
Sugar, Milk Glass, Lace & Dew Drop, 4 ⅛ In.	9.00
Tankard, Milk Glass, 5 ½ In.	9.00
Toothpick Holder, Milk Glass, Coal Bucket Shape, Ribbed, 2 ¼ In.	8.00
Vase, Milk Glass, Beaded Jewel, Ruffled Rim, 4 ¾ In.	12.00

KENTON HILLS POTTERY

KENTON HILLS POTTERY in Erlanger, Kentucky, made artwares, including vases and figurines that resembled Rookwood, probably because so many of the original artists and workmen had worked at the Rookwood plant. Kenton Hills opened in 1939 and closed during World War II.

Vase, Yellow Matte Ground, String Banding Design, Shouldered, 8 ½ In.	403.00

KEW BLAS

KEW BLAS is the name used by the Union Glass Company of Somerville, Massachusetts. The name refers to an iridescent golden glass made from the 1890s to 1924. The iridescent glass was reminiscent of the Tiffany glass of the period.

KEW-BLAS

Candlestick, Gold Iridescent, Twisted Shaft, c.1900, 8 In., Pair	399.00
Vase, Green & Gold Pulled Feather, Ivory Ground, Gold Collar, Marked, 4 In. .... *illus*	518.00
Vase, Iridescent Blue, Pulled Feather Design, Squat Pear Shape, c.1900, 10 In.	492.00
Vase, Iridescent Gold, Urn Shape, Slight Flared Rim, Round Foot, Marked, 8 In.	144.00

TIP

A paste of baking soda and water can be used to clean old enameled cast-iron pots.

Kitchen, Broiler, Revolving, Wrought Iron, Star Center, Lizard Form Base, 1800s, 25 In.
$382.00

Garth's Auctions, Inc.

Kitchen, Chest, Feed, Pine, Paint, Slant Lid, Dovetailed, Lebanon County, Pa., 1800s, 36 x 47 In.
$1469.00

K

Conestoga Auction Co., Inc.

Kitchen, Churn, Cobalt Stencil, Salt Glaze, Handles, Albany Slip, Catlettsburg Pottery, c.1884, 4 Gal.
$1495.00

Rock Island Auction Company

As always, the edited listings in *Kovels' Antiques & Collectibles Price Guide* aren't available on any website, but readers should visit Kovels.com for information on trends, tips, reproductions, marks, old prices, and more!

Kitchen, Coffeepot, Lid, Graniteware, Mottled Gray, Biggin, Basket, Weld Handle, 8 x 3 ½ In.
$59.00

Conestoga Auction Co., Inc.

Kitchen, Eggcup, Wood, Turned, Painted, Pomegranates, Joseph Lehn, 3 In.
$561.00

Conestoga Auction Co., Inc.

Kitchen, Mold, Cheese, Tinned Sheet Iron, Herringbone Band, Pierced, Handles, Coil Feet, 4 ¼ In.
$41.00

Conestoga Auction Co., Inc.

Kitchen, Mold, Turk's Head, Manganese Slip, Redware, Spiral Post, 9 ⅜ In.
$47.00

Conestoga Auction Co., Inc.

K

KEWPIES, designed by Rose O'Neill, were first pictured in the *Ladies' Home Journal*. The figures, which are similar to pixies, were a success, and Kewpie dolls and figurines started appearing in 1911. Kewpie pictures and other items soon followed. Collectors search for all items that picture the little winged people.

Bank, At Barrel, Tin Lid, Borgfeldt & Co., 3 In.	92.00
Bisque, Hottentot, Black Complexion, Side-Glancing Eyes, Loop Jointed, Starfish Shape Hands, 4 ½ In..	58.00
Bisque, Jointed, Wings, Rose O'Neill, 4 ½ In.	95.00
Bisque, Painted Face, 2 In.	19.00
Bisque, Painted Side-Glancing Eyes & Curls, Molded Topknot, Germany, 1912, 11 In.	3990.00
Bisque, Uncle Sam, Loop Jointed, Painted Hair, Jacket, Hat, O'Neill Mark, c.1915, 6 In.	63.00
Book, Paper Doll, In Kewpieville, 1966	25.00
Candy Container, Standing By Barrel, Slotted	30.00
Chalkware, Carnival, Yellow Dress, 12 In.	65.00
Composition, Cameo, 1930s, 12 In.	160.00
Composition, Side-Glancing Eyes, Curly Wig, Flapper Dress, Rose O'Neill, c.1920, 14 In.	1083.00
Dish, Carrying Flag, Marked, c.1970, 4 In.	12.00
Head Vase, Lefton, 1950s, 7 x 4 In.	28.00
On Pillow, Poodle, Piano Baby, 4 ¾ In.	18.00
Paperweight, Kewpie Doll, Cast Metal, 1920s, 1 ½ In.	35.00
Papier-Mache, Pink Checkered Sun Dress, c.1945, 7 In.	45.00
Perfume Bottle, Sitting, Germany, 1920s, 2 ½ In.	59.00
Pigeon-Toed, Orange Bow Tie, Japan, c.1925, 4 ½ In.	65.00
Plastic, Sleep Eyes, Jointed Head, Arms & Legs, Rose O'Neill, 12 In.	295.00
Plate, Milk Glass, Carrying Flowers, Turtle, Lattice, 8 ½ In.	15.00
Porcelain, Crawling, Glancing Upward, Lefton, c.1960, 4 x 3 In.	42.00
Tray, Fairmont's Ice Cream, Kewpie Eating Ice Cream, Red, 15 x 10 In.	195.00
Twins, Hugging, Germany, c.1910, 2 ½ In.	55.00
Vase, Bisque, Striped Swimsuit, Arms Up, Fearful Face, Bee On Stomach, c.1910, 6 In.	456.00
Vinyl, Devil, Cameo, Marked, 7 ½ In.	35.00
Vinyl, The Thinker, Marked, Rose O'Neill, 4 In.	25.00

KING'S ROSE, *see Soft Paste category.*

KITCHEN utensils of all types, from eggbeaters to bowls, are collected today. Handmade wooden and metal items, like ladles and apple peelers, were made in the early nineteenth century. Mass-produced pieces, like iron apple peelers and graniteware, were made in the nineteenth century. Also included in this category are utensils used for other household chores, such as laundry and cleaning. Other kitchen wares are listed under manufacturers' names or under Advertising, Iron, Tool, or Wooden.

Apple Corer, Bone, Engraved, 1741	350.00
Apple Corer, Silver, Ivory, Marked, Joseph Wilmore, c.1842, 6 In.	495.00
Apple Tub, Wood, Staves, Banded Top & Bottom, Open Tab Handles, 1800s, 9 x 21 In.	1035.00
Board, Cutting, Maple, Groove, Carved Bread, Round, 1800s, 10 In.	130.00
Board, Slaw, Tiger Maple, Lollipop End, Pa., 1800s, 48 x 14 In.	178.00
Bowl, Burl, 1800s, 5 x 18 In.	2242.00
Bowl, Burl, Extended Handle, Old Patina, 7 ½ x 20 x 12 In.	3795.00
Bowl, Burl, Old Green & Blue Paint, Molded Rim, Flared, 19th Century, 6 x 20 In.	4485.00
Bowl, Burl, Organic Shape, Dan Karner, 20th Century, 2 ½ x 14 In.	368.00
Bowl, Butter Paddle, Burl, 1800s, 3 x 9 & 8 ½ In.	1058.00
Bowl, Cover, Wood, Round, Flared Tube Handles, c.1960, 6 x 15 In.	1000.00
Bowl, Dough, Wood, Raised Sided, Handles, 17 x 40 In.	150.00
Bowl, Pine, 4 x 20 In.	121.00
Bowl, Pine, Carved, Rounded Corners, 1800s, 21 x 14 In.	180.00
Bowl, River Birch, Lathe Turned, 6 ¾ x 11 In.	1416.00
Bread Box, Porcelain, Wood, Hinged Lid, Enamel, Pink & Blue Flowers, 1900s, 6 x 15 In.	123.00
Broiler, Revolving, Wrought Iron, Star Center, Lizard Form Base, 1800s, 25 In. ....*illus*	382.00
Broiler, Wrought Iron, Revolving, Scrolled Tulip Design, 1800s, 22 ½ In.	411.00
Broom Holder, Ives, Seated Figure, Raised Arms, Wall Mount, 1890s, 4 ½ In.	805.00
Broom Holder, Wire, Round, c.1895, 16 In.	91.00
Butcher's Block, Chamfered, Splayed Legs, 1800s, 28 x 70 In.	881.00
Butter Box, Wood, Fingered Construction, Blue Paint, Marked, Chasbry, 7 x 16 In.	1610.00
Butter Mold, look under Mold, Butter in this category.	
Butter Stamp, Heart, Leaf, Crosshatched, Carved, 2 ½ In.	236.00
Butter Stamp, Insect, Carved, Handle, 2 ¼ In.	562.00
Butter, Cover, Artillery Shell, Patriotic Emblem, Tapered, Glass, 1890s, 5 ½ x 7 In.	86.00

Butter, Napkin Holder, White, Orange Butterfly, Flowers, Plastic, 1970s, 7 ¾ x 2 ¾ In.............	35.00
Cabbage Cutter, Wood, Diagonal Blade, Heart Shape End, 22 In.........................	374.00
Cake Board, Man, Woman, Elaborate Dress, Headwear, 1800s, 53 x 14 In., Pair	1058.00
Cheese Strainer, Heart Shape, Punched Tin, 1800s, 15 ½ x 14 ½ In.........................	1126.00
Cheese Strainer, Tin, Heart Shape, Punched Pinwheel, 1800s, 14 In.........................	1024.00
Chest, Feed, Pine, Paint, Slant Lid, Dovetailed, Lebanon County, Pa., 1800s, 36 x 47 In. ..... *illus*	1469.00
Chopper, Herb, Gondola, Cast Iron, Shape, Splayed Legs, Round Cutter, Wood Handle, 18 x 7 In.	354.00
Churn, Cobalt Stencil, Salt Glaze, Handles, Albany Slip, Catlettsburg Pottery, c.1884, 4 Gal. *illus*	1495.00
Churn, Dasher, Staves, Metal Bands, Stave Handle, 29 ½ In.........................	35.00
Churn, Dazey, Glass, Pinched Sides, Crank Handle On Screw Lid.........................	36.00
Churn, Dazey, Glass, Wood Paddles, Crank Handle On Screw Lid.........................	98.00
Churn, Standard Churn Co., Lid, Dasher, Staves, Stenciled Label, Wapakoneta, 23 In.........................	176.00
Churn, Wood, Cross Type Plunger, Staved Barrel Shape, Bands, Lid, 23 In.........................	113.00
Churn, Wood, Staved, Bands, Lid, Carved Batten, Wood Agitator, Iron Crank, 17 x 14 In.	83.00
Churn, Wood, Staved, Carved Agitator, Iron Crank, Bands, Oval Lid, Handles, 15 ¾ In.	59.00
Churn, Wood, Staved, Cone Shape, Metal Bands, Pierced Lid, Agitator, Painted Blue, 18 x 34 In.	106.00
Coffeepot, Lid, Graniteware, Mottled Gray, Biggin, Basket, Weld Handle, 8 x 3 ½ In. ......*illus*	59.00
Coffee Grinders are listed in the Coffee Mill category.	
Coffee Mills are listed in their own category.	
Coffee Urn, Chrome, Globular, Plastic Mounts, Chase Brass & Copper, 12 In.........................	86.00
Colander, Brass, Handles, Copper Riveted Body, c.1815, 7 ½ x 12 In.........................	215.00
Cookie Board, Pine, 2-Sided, Horse, Masonic Compass & Square, Vines, 1800s, 5 x 9 In.	904.00
Cookie Cutter Set, Farm Theme, Tinned Sheet Iron, Handles, 6 ⅛ To 3 ½ In., 9 Piece	24.00
Cookie Cutter, Man, Woman, Shaped Figures, Tin Panel, Handle, U.S.A., 1800s, 6 x 4 In.......	148.00
Corncob Holder, Bakelite, Diamond Shape, Box, S.J. Schneider Co., 1940s, 2 In., 8 Piece.......	125.00
Dipper, Wood, Carved, Hooked Handle, Initials A.H., Blue Paint, 4 ¾ In.........................	575.00
Dough Box, Cover, French Provincial, Oak, Carved, Apron, Stretcher, 37 x 42 In......................	1037.00
Dough Box, Cover, Softwood, Dovetailed, Turned Legs, 1800s, 23 x 31 x 14 In.........................	102.00
Dough Box, Fruitwood, Lid, Demilune Trough, Trestle Base, 1800s, 46 x 22 In.........................	155.00
Dough Box, Pine, Lift Lid, Stand, Stretcher, 33 x 47 x 18 In.........................	270.00
Dough Box, Pine, Poplar, Dovetailed, 1-Board Lid, Gray Paint, 1800s, 15 x 26 In.........................	734.00
Dough Box, Sliding Dovetail Battens, Splayed Legs, Scrubbed Lid, c.1840, 28 x 18 In............	316.00
Dough Box, Softwood, Turned Legs, 19th Century, 22 x 31 x 16 In.........................	170.00
Dough Box, Stand, Poplar, Pine, Lift Top, Red Paint, Splayed Legs, c.1790, 29 x 46 In............	2607.00
Dough Box, Stand, Walnut, Carved, France, 33 x 60 In.........................	244.00
Dough Box, Walnut, Chestnut, Hinged Lid, Canted, Drawer, Incised Diamond, 1800s, 28 x 49 In.	230.00
Dough Scraper, Iron, Brass, Stamped Peter Derr, 1845, 3 ½ In.	948.00
Dough Scraper, Wrigglework Flowers, Wrought Iron, Impressed G. Conrad, c.1830, 3 x 4 In.	652.00
Drip Pan, Iron, 8-Point Star Design, Oval, M & H Schrenkeisen, New York, 2 x 8 In.	11.00
Dry Measure, Lap Joint, Iron Nails & Bands, Painted, 9 x 13 In.........................	136.00
Egg Timer, Humpty Dumpty, Cast Iron, Glass Vial, Painted, 3 ¼ In.........................	144.00
Eggbeater, Aluminum Beauty, 1920s, 10 In.	68.00
Eggcup, Wood, Turned, Painted, Pomegranates, Joseph Lehn, 3 In. ....*illus*	561.00
Firkin, Stave Construction, Red Paint Over Green, Lapped Finger Bands, 14 x 11 In................	345.00
Funnel, Flint, Glass, Diagonal Cut Spout Lip, 13 x 7 ½ In.........................	12.00
Grater, Nutmeg, Monitor, Wood, Tin, 1889, 4 ½ In.........................	95.00
Griddle, Cast Iron, Round, Twisted Handle, Hook, 10 x 15 In.........................	94.00
Gridiron, Cast Iron, Channeled, Attached Drip Pan, Handles, 18 x 14 In.........................	153.00
Gridiron, Cast Iron, Curved, Channeled Grill, Drip Pan, Handle, 6 ½ x 14 ½ In.........................	189.00
Gridiron, Wrought, 3 Legs, Channeled Grill, Drain Holes, Strap Handle, 6 ½ x 23 In.............	83.00
Grinder, Herb, Cast Iron, Pine Frame, Grooved Legs, Floor Model, 19 ½ x 26 In.........................	1410.00
Hook, Pot, S-Hook, Long Links, Wrought Iron, 71 In.........................	590.00
Hoosier Cabinet, Flour Sifter, Meat Grinders, Oak, Cast Iron.........................	605.00
Hoosier Cabinet, Oak, Doors, Drawers, Slide Shelf, Hoosier Mfg. Co., c.1920, 72 x 41 In........	219.00
Ice Chest, Golden Oak, Hinged Top, Door, 43 x 24 In.	403.00
Icebox, Industrial Metal, 2 Doors, Brass Latches, 52 x 33 In.	650.00
Icebox, Oak, Dark Finish, Aluminum Lined Fitted Interior, 3 Doors, 42 x 32 In.........................	488.00
Icebox, Walnut, String Inlay, Enamel Interior, Shelf, Sample, McKee Refrigerator Co., 19 x 13 In.	208.00
Iron, Archaic Shape, Hardwood Bronze, Jade Handle, Carved, Chinese, c.1900, 2 ¾ x 7 In.	89.00
Iron, G.E., Hotpoint, Wood Handle, c.1900, 8 ½ In.........................	90.00
Iron, Slug, Victor Combination, Revolving, Flat, Polishing, Handle Release.........................	94.00
Kettle Stand, Brass, Adjustable Tripod, Snake Feet, England, 16 ½ x 28 ½ In.........................	708.00
Kettle, Cast Iron, c.1920, 10 ¼ In.	115.00
Kettle, Footed, Iron, 10 ½ x 18 In.........................	50.00
Kettle, Hot Water, Cast Iron, Hinged Lid, Swing Handle, Soutard & Co., 7 ½ x 9 In.........................	47.00
Kettle, Lid, Iron, Oval, Embossed A. Kendrick & Sons, 12 x 12 In.........................	66.00

Kitchen, Percolator Funnel, Collar, Loop Handle, Gray, Extra Agate, L & G Mfg. Co., 7 x 5 In.
$47.00

Conestoga Auction Co., Inc.

Kitchen, Pie Crimper, Wheel Is 1848 Coin, Copper, Iron, Looped Handle, c.1850, 6 ½ In.
$241.00

Garth's Auctions, Inc.

Kitchen, Rolling Pin, Stoneware, Cobalt Blue Design, Wood Handles, 16 ½ In.
$53.00

Conestoga Auction Co., Inc.

Kitchen, Spit, Georgian, Brass, Iron, Wood Tower, Clockwork, c.1750, 18 x 20 In.
$3335.00

James D. Julia Inc.

New Iron Is Rough
Vintage cast-iron pans were hand-cast in sand, while modern pieces are made by a different method that leaves a rough surface. Old ones bring the highest prices.

Kitchen, Stringholder, Pearl Pureheart, Mighty Mouse Girlfriend, Plaster, Marked, 1950s, 7 ½ x 8 In.
$863.00

Hake's Americana & Collectibles

Kitchen, Washing Machine, New Becker, Wooden, Salesman's Sample, Pat. 1885 & 1887, 15 x 12 ½ In.
$2420.00

Wm Morford Antiques

Knife, Throwing, Ingessana Tribe, Incised, Scorpion, Leather Grip, Sudan, c.1900, 29 In.
$173.00

Leland Little Auction

Kosta, Vase, Amber Interior, 11 x 3 ½ In.
$72.00

DuMouchelles Art Gallery

Kettle, Molasses, Cast Iron, Knopped Rim, 1800s, 22 Gal., 15 x 27 In.	488.00
Kettle, Sugar, Cast Iron, 1800s, 20 x 54 In.	1912.00
Kettle, Sugar, Stamped Kehoe Iron Works Savannah, Georgia, c.1890, 15 x 47 In.	2151.00
Masher, Stainless Steel, Red Bakelite Handle, c.1907, 8 x 4 In.	22.00
Match Holders can be found in their own category.	
Match Safes can be found in their own category.	
Measure, Bentwood Carrier, Lapped Seams, Painted, River Edge Farm, c.1894, 6 ½ x 11 In.	512.00
Measure, Bentwood, Steel Tacks, Blue Paint, New Hampshire, c.1890, 4 ½ x 10 ½ In.	151.00
Measure, Liquid, Tin, Tapering Shape, Raised Middle Raised Handle, c.1900, 6 ½ In.	143.00
Meat Fork, Iron, Brass, Maple, 3 Prong, Turned Handle, Marked JD, 18th Century, 17 In.	1058.00
Meat Tenderizer, Cobalt Blue Design, Sawtooth, Squared, Stoneware, c.1875, 8 ½ In.	834.00
Milk Can, Dome Cover, Green, White, Swirl, Black Rim, White Interior, Handle, 12 x 6 In.	266.00
Mixing Bowl, Carved, Wide Rim Band, 5 ½ x 16 ¼ In.	94.00
Mixing Bowl, Green, Spout, Lip, Hazel Atlas Glass, 1900s	40.00
Mixing Bowl, Wood, Carved, 7 x 20 In.	83.00
Molds may also be found in the Pewter and Tinware categories.	
Mold, Butter, Heart, Leaf Border, 4 ½ In.	506.00
Mold, Butter, Lollipop Shape, Philpot Design, 6 ¾ In.	1422.00
Mold, Butter, Oak Leaf, Acorns, Square, 3 x 3 In.	101.00
Mold, Butter, Swan, Carved, 4 In.	113.00
Mold, Cake, Horse & Wagon, Wood, Wax, Dated 1744	165.00
Mold, Candle, see Tinware category.	
Mold, Cheese, Tinned Sheet Iron, Herringbone Band, Pierced, Handles, Coil Feet, 4 ¼ In. *illus*	41.00
Mold, Cheese, Tinned Sheet Iron, Perforated Heart Shape, Handle, Round Feet, 4 In.	106.00
Mold, Crown, Raised Foot, Redware, 2 ½ x 4 In.	117.00
Mold, Ice Cream, Boy & Girl, Hugging, Anton Reiche, Germany, Painting, 7 x 4 In.	325.00
Mold, Ice Cream, Boy, Playing Bagpipes, Anton Reiche, Germany, 5 x 3 In.	250.00
Mold, Ice Cream, Policeman, Anton Reiche, Germany, 7 x 4 In.	235.00
Mold, Ice Cream, Rabbit Golfer, Anton Reiche, Germany, 7 x 4 In.	375.00
Mold, Ice Cream, Swan, Anton Reiche, Germany, 8 x 9 In.	445.00
Mold, Jelly, Tin, c.1890, 7 x 5 x 5 In.	65.00
Mold, Pug Dog, Tinned Steel, 2 ½ x 3 In.	45.00
Mold, Springerle, 2-Sided, Dog, Horse, Sheep, Deer, Swan, Rooster, Hawk, Hen, 5 x 22 In.	531.00
Mold, Turk's Head, Manganese Slip, Redware, Spiral Post, 9 ⅜ In. *illus*	47.00
Mold, Turk's Head, Salt Glaze Interior, Green Slip Glaze Exterior, Tab Handles, Redware, 4 x 9 In.	24.00
Mortar & Pestle, Bronze, Bands Scrolling Leaves, Squares, Shields, Handle, 4 In., Pair	830.00
Mortar & Pestle, Cylindrical, Pinched Waist, Molded Line, Lignum Vitae, 1800s, 7 x 6 In.	115.00
Mortar & Pestle, Log Stump, Cone Shape, Tapered Log Pestle, Angle Handle, 23 x 3 ¼ In.	295.00
Oven, Reflector, Iron Spit, Tinned Sheet Iron, Semi-Circular Shell, Skewer, 20 x 21 In.	224.00
Pan, Ebelskiver, Apple Turnover, Japanned Wood Handle, c.1875, 16 ¼ In.	875.00
Pan, Tin, Round, Handles, Pa., 3 ½ x 18 In.	77.00
Pan, Warming, Copper, Peter Derr, Pa., Stamped P.D., 1854, 12 x 16 In.	1007.00
Pantry Box, Ash, Gray Paint, Round, Lapped Seams, Cut Nails, c.1800, 6 x 16 In.	490.00
Pantry Box, Bentwood, Oval, Harvard Fingers, Tacks, Blue, Green, 2 ½ x 6 ½ In.	470.00
Pantry Box, Bentwood, Tack, Wood Pin Construction, Green, Yellow, c.1880, 2 ½ x 6 In.	403.00
Pantry Box, Green Paint, Gold Stenciled Design, Leaves, Grapes, Round, Lid, 3 x 5 In.	52.00
Pantry Box, Maple, Bentwood, Glued Seam, Red, White, Blue, 1800s, 5 ¼ In.	323.00
Pantry Box, Maple, Pine, Bentwood, Fruit Basket, Black Ground, 1800s, 6 ¼ In.	572.00
Pantry Box, Mixed Woods, Vinegar Decoration, Brown, Yellow, c.1835, 12 ½ In., Diam.	294.00
Pantry Box, Oak, Painted, Pumpkin, Blue, Round, Bail Handle, c.1890, 9 ½ x 5 ½ In., Pair	1380.00
Pantry Box, Pine, Semicircular Lids, Ship, Gray, Green, Hinged, c.1800, 9 ¼ In.	353.00
Pantry Box, Red, Round, Lid, New England, 1800s, 4 x 8 ½ In.	115.00
Peeler, Apple, Forged Iron, Free-Form Cut Foot Attachment, 5 ½ x 30 In.	153.00
Peeler, Apple, Mechanical, Cast Iron, Table Clamp, Wood Handle, Gear Crank, 1856, 7 In.	59.00
Peeler, Apple, Pine, Stenciled Eagle, Christian Hostetter, Pa., 1842, 24 In.	1541.00
Peeler, Apple, Walnut, Chip Carved Edges, Pa., 1800s, 10 ½ x 12 ½ In.	593.00
Peeler, Apple, Wood, Paddle Shape Base, Framework, Crank, Iron Fork, 32 ¾ In.	12.00
Pepper Bin, Tin, Demilune, Painted Red, Sheet Iron, Hinged, Gold Stencil, 7 ¼ x 7 In.	130.00
Percolator Funnel, Collar, Loop Handle, Gray, Extra Agate, L & G Mfg. Co., 7 x 5 In. *illus*	47.00
Pie Crimper, Wheel Is 1848 Coin, Copper, Iron, Looped Handle, c.1850, 6 ½ In. *illus*	241.00
Pitcher, Lemonade, Farm Scene, Ice Lip, 9 ¾ In.	35.00
Posset Pot, 3-Footed, Cast Iron, 1800s, 11 In.	23.00
Pot Hanger, Iron, Figure 8 Shape Platform, Curved Supports, Swing Handle, 14 x 14 In.	71.00
Pot Pusher, Scrolled Heart, Hook, Wrought Iron, 1800s, 3 x 7 ¾ In.	187.00
Pot, Aluminum, Avocado Green, Lid, 1960s, 4 Qt.	34.00

Pot, Copper, Dovetailed, Riveted Handle, 10 ¼ In.	79.00
Rack, Utensil, Yew, Stepped, Shaped Skirt, Cutouts, Hanging, 1800, 13 x 15 In.	119.00
Reamers are listed in their own category.	
Recipe Holder, Wood, Mushroom, Little Man, Woodpecker, Painted, Italy, 2 ½ x 2 ¾ In.	45.00
Roaster, Chestnut, Perforated Sheet Iron Box, Riveted Wrought Iron Handles, 34 ½ In.	71.00
Roaster, Coffee, Iron, Free Standing, Drum Type, Slide Door, Crank, Loop Handles, 19 x 20 In.	94.00
Roasting Stand, Adjustable Fork Heads, Tripod Base, Handle, Iron, c.1790, 29 ½ In.	472.00
Rolling Pin, Blue & White, Flowers, Bands, Stoneware, 8 In.	86.00
Rolling Pin, Blue Vines, Turned Wooden Handle, Stoneware, 15 ½ In.	79.00
Rolling Pin, Glass, Amber, 2 Drawn Handles, Pontil, 14 ½ In.	115.00
Rolling Pin, Glass, Blue, 2 Knob Handles, Pontil, 17 ½ In.	81.00
Rolling Pin, Glass, Cobalt Blue, Sailor's Farewell, Knob Handles, England, c.1850, 28 In.	83.00
Rolling Pin, Glass, Green, Bubbles, Ball Shape Handles, 15 ½ In.	130.00
Rolling Pin, Stoneware, Cobalt Blue Design, Wood Handles, 16 ½ In. ....*illus*	53.00
Rolling Pin, Wood, c.1950, 17 x 2 ½ In.	10.00
Rolling Pin, Wood, Red Handles, c.1950, 17 x 1 ¾ In.	7.50
Rotisserie, Clockwork, Free Standing, Brass, Sheet Iron, Brass Bail Handle, Crank, 15 In.	384.00
Salt & Pepper Shakers are listed in their own category.	
Sausage Press, Wood, Mechanical, Crank Screw Press, Slide Top Box, 1800s, 32 x 15 x 41 In.	173.00
Scoop, Ice Cream, Heart Shaped, Wood Handle, c.1925, 11 In.	7800.00
Scoop, Mahogany, Pierced Handle, Flat Bowl, Gouge Carved, 35 x 13 ½ In.	30.00
Seed Chest, Green Paint, 11 Rows Of 5 Segmented Drawers, Turned Pulls, 14 x 12 In.	2691.00
Seed Chest, Pine, Brown, Red, Drawers, 1800s, 61 x 84 In.	4503.00
Seed Chest, Pine, Red Stain, 12 Drawers, 1800s, 18 x 15 In.	1304.00
Sifter, Wood, Painted, The Clipper, 14 x 22 In.	1875.00
Skillet, Iron, Griswold Erie No. 6, Heat Ring On Bottom, 3 Pour Spouts, 1907-12, 9 In.	50.00
Skillet, Wrought Iron, Stamped David Rohrer, Pa., c.1835, 18 ½ In.	1185.00
Skimmer, Sheet Brass, 25 In.	17.00
Slicer, Cheese, Oak Handle, 8 ¾ In.	25.00
Slicer, Crinkle Cut, Plastic, Stainless Steel, 1950s	6.00
Spatula, Iron, Brass, Cut Pinwheels, Hearts, Wrigglework Tulip Handle, Pa., c.1850, 19 In.	8888.00
Spatula, Wrought Iron, Punched Holes, Shaped Handle, Marked, J.H., 22 In.	11.00
Spice Box, Baroque, Walnut, Vargueno Style, Fall Front, Drawers, Bail Handle, c.1700, 7 x 9 In.	768.00
Spice Box, Hanging, Poplar, Oak, 11 Drawers, Mustard Over Red Paint, c.1900, 25 x 10 In.	176.00
Spice Box, Pine, Red Paint, Apothecary Shape, 9 Drawers, Cutout Feet, c.1855, 9 In.	705.00
Spice Box, Walnut, Drawers, Spinning Tin Drum, Compartments, Lift Lid, 8 ½ x 11 ¾ In.	705.00
Spice Box, Wood, Flower Shape, 5 Compartments, Lid Slides To Side, 3 x 6 In.	158.00
Spice Chest, Pine, Drawers, Blue & Gray, Brass Pulls, 1800s, 15 x 11 x 4 In.	529.00
Spit, Bird, Wrought Iron, Tripod Base, Urn Finial, Handled Bracket, Spring, Hooks, 29 In.	325.00
Spit, Georgian, Brass, Iron, Wood Tower, Clockwork, c.1750, 18 x 20 In. ....*illus*	3335.00
Strainer, Aluminum, Cone Shape, Handle, Wear-Ever, c.1950, 9 ¾ In.	13.00
Strainer, Cobalt Blue Handle, Oval Body, Punched Drain Holes, Stoneware, 5 ¾ x 5 ½ In.	86.00
Stringholder, Brass, Urn, Finial Blade, John Ewing Tea Merchant, c.1820, 12 In.	177.00
Stringholder, Heinz Pickles, Pickle Shape, 57 Varieties, Hanging Chains, 17 x 17 x 7 In.	12100.00
Stringholder, Pearl Pureheart, Mighty Mouse Girlfriend, Plaster, Marked, 1950s, 7 ½ x 8 In. ..*illus*	863.00
Stringholder, Pirate, Majolica, 5 ½ In.	59.00
Sugar Nips, Iron, 1700s, 8 ½ x 3 In.	325.00
Sugar Nips, Steel, Wood Base, Brass Post, c.1800, 13 In.	382.00
Syrup, White Frosted Glass, Green Ivy, Bakelite Handle, c.1935, 5 ½ In.	30.00
Tagine, Cooking Pot, Flowers, Leaves, Brass, Middle Eastern, 26 x 17 In.	177.00
Toaster, Heart Handle, Wrought Iron, Pa., 1800s, 11 In.	889.00
Toaster, Wrought Iron, Hinged Handle, Wood Grip, 2 Fences, Footed, 22 x 14 In.	130.00
Toaster, Wrought Iron, Stationary Handle, 3 Leg Frame, Serpentine Fencing, 6 ½ x 19 In.	118.00
Tongs, Sugar, Brass, c.1750	250.00
Tongs, Waffle, Cast Iron, Wrought Iron Handles, Square Molds, Marked, 28 In.	47.00
Tongs, Waffle, Wrought Iron, Shape Grip Blades, Curled Terminus, Ring, 28 In.	35.00
Trammel, Twisted Link, 3 Sections, 4 Links Twisted Together, Wrought Iron, 75 In.	142.00
Tray, Utensil, Softwood, Kidney Pierced Handle, Divider, Applied Sawtooth, 11 ½ x 9 ¼ In.	118.00
Trivet, see Trivet category.	
Waffle Iron, Belgian Type, Cast & Wrought Iron, 29 In.	34.00
Washboard, Saw Tooth, Stepped Agitation Teeth, Tombstone Top, 27 ¾ In.	189.00
Washing Machine, New Becker, Wooden, Salesman's Sample, Pat. 1885 & 1887, 15 x 12 ½ In. *illus*	2420.00
Washing Machine, Oak, Iron, Brass, Barrel, Stretcher Shelf, Crank, 42 x 34 In.	314.00
Washtub, Wood, Staved, Metal Bands, Painted Blue, Wood Agitator, Turned, 18 x 26 In.	189.00
Wonder Shredder, Aluminum, Pat. Oct. 21, 1929, 8 x 4 In.	7.00

A Lot of Bread
A Griswold No. 28 bread pan can be worth $25,000.

KPM, Plaque, Marguerite, Wreath Of Daisies, Marked, Marked, Wagner, Frame, 1800s, 10 x 10 In.
$600.00

Cowan's Auctions

KPM, Plaque, Queen Louise, Marked, Paper Label, Frame, 1800s, 10 ½ x 8 ¾ In.
$3900.00

K

Cowan's Auctions

KPM, Plaque, Roman Empress, Messalina, Frame, Marked, Wagner Wien, 1800s, 10 x 15 ¾ In.
$15340.00

Brunk Auctions

Ku Klux Klan, Staff, Skull Terminal, Carved Wood, 36 In.
$236.00

Conestoga Auction Co., Inc.

Ku Klux Klan, Uniform, White Robe, Embroidered Blood Patch, Cape, Hood With Tassel, c.1920
$384.00

Conestoga Auction Co., Inc.

Kutani, Urn, Helmet Shape, Flower & Butterfly, Fired Gold Accents, 9 ½ x 9 ¼ In.
$210.00

DuMouchelles Art Gallery

KNIFE collectors usually specialize in a single type. In the 1960s, the United States government passed a law that required knife manufacturers to mark their knives with the country of origin. This seemed to encourage the collectors, and knife collecting became an interest of a large group of people. All types of knives are collected, from top quality twentieth-century examples to old bone- or pearl-handled knives in excellent condition.

Crooked, Iron, Maple, Hearts, c.1875, 8 ½ In.	482.00
Dagger, Curved Steel Blade, Celadon Jade Hilt, Carved Leaves & Flower Heads, 13 ¼ In.	1016.00
Dagger, Silver Mounted Ivory, Iron, Case, Tibet, 12 In.	478.00
Fighting, British Sykes, Ribbed Handle, 6 ½ In.	161.00
Presentation, Great Western Steamer, Deer Foot Handle, Moore Tichbornes, c.1840, 19 In.	588.00
Tanto, Black Lacquer, Silver Mounted, Japan, 7 ½ In.	4780.00
Throwing, Ingessana Tribe, Incised, Scorpion, Leather Grip, Sudan, c.1900, 29 In. ....*illus*	173.00

KNOWLES, *Taylor & Knowles items may be found in the KTK and Lotus Ware categories.*

KOREAN WARE, *see Sumida.*

KOSTA, the oldest Swedish glass factory, was founded in 1742. During the 1920s through the 1950s, many pieces of original design were made at the factory. Kosta and Boda merged with Afors in 1964 and created the Afors Group in 1971. In 1976, the name Kosta Boda was adopted. The company merged with Orrefors in 1990 and is still working.

KOSTA

Bowl, Centerpiece, White, Black Horizontal Rings, Blue Green Diagonal Swathes, 6 x 13 In.	83.00
Ewer, Transparent Green Blue, Stripes, Orange Handle, Stepped Base, Kosta Boda, 14 In.	59.00
Vase, Amber Interior, 11 x 3 ½ In. ....*illus*	72.00
Vase, Clear, Etched, Marked, 13 In.	71.00

KPM refers to Berlin porcelain, but the same initials were used alone and in combination with other symbols by several German porcelain makers. They include the Konigliche Porzellan Manufaktur of Berlin, initials used in mark, 1823–1847; Meissen, 1723–1724 only; Krister Porzellan Manufaktur in Waldenburg, after 1831; Kranichfelder Porzellan Manufaktur in Kranichfeld, after 1903; and the Krister Porzellan Manufaktur in Scheibe, after 1838.

K.P.M

Bowl, Wild Flowers, Butterflies, 2 Seated Putti, Pinched Rim, Marked, 1800s, 8 x 16 In.	1645.00
Compote, Bisque Cherubs & Fish, Relief, 19th Century, 14 x 12 In.	944.00
Cup & Saucer, Cover, Landscape, Gilt, Marked, 1800s, 5 ¼ x 6 ½ In.	259.00
Cup & Saucer, German Landscapes, Houses, Blue Ground, Gilt Interior, c.1890, 7 In.	3851.00
Cup & Saucer, Portrait, Imperial German Officer, Scroll Handle, Gilt, 5 In.	390.00
Figurine, Boy, Flute, Hat, Lace Trimmed Cloth, c.1900, 6 In.	177.00
Figurine, Europa & The Bull, Seminude, Seated On Bull, Lavender Blanket, Marked, 1900s, 16 In.	708.00
Figurine, Hercules, Seated, Draping, Lion's Pelting, Round Base, Marked, c.1900, 16 In.	900.00
Figurine, Ram, White Glaze, Germany, c.1900, 4 ½ In.	295.00
Figurine, Woman, Dancing, Marked, 1800s, 8 In.	345.00
Figurine, Woman, Stepping, Cape, Marked, 1800s, 8 In.	316.00
Group, 3 Geese, Base, 7 x 5 In.	125.00
Group, Apollo, Medusa's Head, Chariot, 4 Horses, Wave Stand, 1800s, 15 x 18 In.	1185.00
Lithophane, see also Lithophane category.	
Plaque, Allegory Of Ambition, Skeleton Horseman, Angels, Wagner, 12 ½ In.	4025.00
Plaque, Beauty, Red Headscarf & Vest, Necklaces, Jeweled, c.1900, 8 x 6 In.	984.00
Plaque, Classical Woman, Oval, Frame, 7 x 9 In.	354.00
Plaque, Cupid Breaking His Bow, Seated On Rocky Step, Woodland, Marked, 9 x 6 In.	2800.00
Plaque, Dauphin, Oval, Young Boy, Blond Hair, Brown Coat, Hand Painted, 1800s, 10 In.	613.00
Plaque, Dutch Scenes, Giltwood Frame, c.1890, 10 x 12 ½ In., Pair	3555.00
Plaque, Girl, Holding Purple Flowers, Dark Wavy Hair, Oval, Frame, 6 ½ x 4 ½ In.	974.00
Plaque, Girl, Leaning On Chair, Impressed, Frame, Mark, J. Ahne, c.1875, 4 x 5 ¾ In.	861.00
Plaque, Girl, With Hands Clasped, Oval Shape, 11 In.	948.00
Plaque, Infant Moses, Basket, Reeds, c.1890, 6 ½ In.	1035.00
Plaque, Kiss Of The Wave, Nude, On Water, Kissing Man, Ship, Frame, c.1900, 11 x 13 In.	9225.00
Plaque, Lisette, Woman, Holding Candle, Giltwood Frame, Crest, Signed Knoller, 10 x 7 ½ In.	3042.00
Plaque, Lorelei, Seminude, Flowing Hair, Pink Robes, Perched On Rocks, 1800s, 9 x 6 In.	2607.00
Plaque, Madonna & Child, Oval Shape, Enameled, Giltwood Frame, Germany, 1800s, 9 In.	652.00
Plaque, Madonna, Looking Up, Blue Drape, Oval, Pierced Gilt Wood Frame, 17 x 13 In.	5750.00
Plaque, Marguerite, Wreath Of Daisies, Marked, Marked, Wagner, Frame, 1800s, 10 x 10 In. .... *illus*	600.00
Plaque, Moses, Baby In Basket, Pharaoh's Daughter Peeking Through Reeds, 1800s, 9 x 6 In.	5629.00
Plaque, Queen Louise, Marked, Paper Label, Frame, 1800s, 10 ½ x 8 ¾ In. ....*illus*	3900.00
Plaque, Roman Empress, Messalina, Frame, Marked, Wagner Wien, 1800s, 10 x 15 ¾ In. ..*illus*	15340.00

Plaque, Ruth, Maiden Harvesting Grain, Carved Giltwood Frame, 1800s, 8 x 13 In. 4148.00
Plaque, Siren Lorelei, Flaxen Hair, Rocky Cliff, Seminude, Scarf, Scroll Frame, 14 x 17 In. 4025.00
Plaque, Woman, Seated, Infant In Basket, Rolling Waves, Beach, Frame, c.1900, 15 x 17 In. 2706.00
Plaque, Woman, White Dress, Holding Bouquet, Pink Roses, Oval, Giltwood Frame, 1800s, 6 ½ In. 1422.00
Plaque, Young Gypsy Girl, Rectangular, Necklace, Gilt Frame, 12 x 10 In. 2000.00
Plaque, Young Man, Portrait, Oval, Enamel, Marked, c.1900, 6 ⅞ In. 474.00
Plate, Flower Rim, Peasant Women, Water Scenes, Gilt Ground, 1840, 10 In., Pair 2300.00
Plate, Fruit Clusters, Hand Painted, Raised Gilt Borders, Germany, 1800s, 8 ½ In., 12 Piece 944.00
Plate, Painted, Scenic, Flower Edge, 8 ¾ In., 12 Piece 720.00
Salt, Figural, Open, Cherub, Exotic Birds, Germany, c.1870, 6 x 5 In., Pair 240.00
Salt, Putto, 2 Birds, Bowl, 6 In., Pair 199.00
Sconce, 2-Light, Oval, Flower Plaque, Bronze Mounts, Bow Swag Crest, Mark, 14 x 11 In., Pair 1785.00
Sugar, Cover, Flowers, White Ground, Gilt, Marked, 1800s, 5 x 4 In. 92.00
Teapot, Lid, Bulbous, Ruffled Rim, Doves, Lovebirds, Lavender, 11 In. 35.00
Tile, Aurora & The Chariot, Gilt Frame, Painted, Marked, c.1870, 12 ½ x 15 ½ In. 3565.00
Urn, Cover, Enamel, Crackled Teal, Jeweled, Scepter Mark, Germany, 5 In. 1304.00
Urn, Cover, White, Blue Swags, Flowers, Butterflies, Maiden Handles, Pinecone Finial, 1800s, 15 In. 510.00
Vase, Cover, Couples Panels, Pink, Cherub, Grapes Finial, Ram's Head Handles, c.1885, 18 In., Pair 1126.00
Vase, Flowers, Woman, Mourning, Mask Handles, Multicolor, Gilt, Mark, c.1890, 12 In. 415.00
Vase, Potpourri, Cover, Oval Reserves, Cottage Scene, White, Violet, Tint, Gold Trim, 10 In. 246.00

KU KLUX KLAN items are now collected because of their historic importance. Literature, robes, and memorabilia are seen at shows and auctions. Laws passed in 1870 and 1871 caused the decline of the Klan. A second group calling itself the Ku Klux Klan emerged in 1915. There are still local groups using the name.

Pin, National Anti-Klan Network, White Hooded Figure, Red Border, Slash, 1 ¾ In. 10.00
Staff, Skull Terminal, Carved Wood, 36 In. *illus* 236.00
Uniform, White Robe, Embroidered Blood Patch, Cape, Hood With Tassel, c.1920 *illus* 384.00

KUTANI porcelain was made in Japan after the mid-seventeenth century. Most of the pieces found today are nineteenth-century. Collectors often use the term *Kutani* to refer to just the later, colorful pieces decorated with red, gold, and black pictures of warriors, animals, and birds.

九谷

Bowl Set, Red, Gilt Phoenix, Blue Decor, Serrated Rim, c.1900, 4 x 6 ¾ In., 4 Piece 489.00
Bowl, Mountainscape, Pheasants, Flowers, Multicolor, Gilt, 3 x 7 In. 58.00
Compote, Red & White, Gold Accents, Stork, Mountain, Stylized Border, Marked, 10 x 2 In. 138.00
Figurine, Dogs, 2 Pugs, Wrestling, One Yellow, One Brown, Marked, 5 In. 11.00
Ginger Jar, Landscape Scenes, Gold Highlights, c.1900, 8 x 7 In. 48.00
Ginger Jar, Lid, Chrysanthemums, Multicolor, Gold Geometrics, Marked, 1960s, 5 x 4 ½ In. 75.00
Plate, Calligrapher, Chrysanthemum Design, Round, Footed, Flared Border, 8 ¼ In. 219.00
Urn, Helmet Shape, Flower & Butterfly, Fired Gold Accents, 9 ½ x 9 ¼ In. *illus* 210.00
Vase, Bottle Shape, Painted Sparrows, Pine Forest, Gilt Mums, 9 ½ x 4 ½ In. 63.00
Vase, Bottle Shape, Rust & White, Birds, Insects, Flowers, Gilt, 8 In., Pair 575.00
Vase, Red & White, Cranes, Baluster, 2 Loop Handles At Neck, Loose Rings, Flared Rim, 16 In., Pair 478.00
Vase, Scholars, Pupils, Seated On Koi, Gilt, Marked, 14 ¼ In. *illus* 374.00

L.G. WRIGHT Glass Company of New Martinsville, West Virginia, started selling glassware in 1937. Founder "Si" Wright contracted with Ohio and West Virginia glass factories to reproduce popular pressed glass patterns, like Rose & Snow, Baltimore Pear, and Three Face, and opalescent patterns, like Daisy & Fern and Swirl. Collectors can tell the difference between the original glasswares and L.G. Wright reproductions because of colors and differences in production techniques. Some L.G. Wright items are marked with an underlined *W* in a circle. Items that were made from old Northwood molds have an altered Northwood mark—an angled line was added to the *N* to make it look like a *W*. Collectors refer to this mark as "the wobbly W." The L.G. Wright factory was closed and the existing molds sold in 1999.

Aqua Crest, Epergne, 4 Horns, c.1940, 16 ¾ x 10 ½ In. 550.00
Argonaut Shell, Sugar & Creamer, Chocolate, 7 x 5 In. 108.00
Beaded Shell, Mug, Amethyst, 1970s, 4 x 2 In. 28.00
Blue Opalescent, Barber Bottle, Eye Dot, 8 ½ In. 245.00
Coin Dot, Cruet, Cranberry, 6 x 3 ⅜ In. 148.00
Cranberry Opalescent Swirl, Tumbler, Iced Tea, c.1955, 5 ¼ x 2 ⅜ In., Pair 50.00
Cranberry Opalescent, Creamer, Honeycomb, 5 ½ In. 125.00
Cranberry Opalescent, Cruet, Honeycomb, Clear Stopper, 7 x 3 In. 230.00
Daisy & Button, Bowl, Crimp, Light Green, c.1965, 3 ¼ In. 15.00
Daisy & Button, Bowl, Fruit, Amberina, 4-Footed, c.1945, 10 x 8 ½ In. 58.00

Kutani, Vase, Scholars, Pupils, Seated On Koi, Gilt, Marked, 14 ¼ In.
$374.00

Leland Little Auction

Lalique, Figurine, Trophee, Stylized Olympic Skater, 13 x 9 In.
$1920.00

DuMouchelles Art Gallery

Lalique, Plaque, Masque De Femme, Frosted, Stand, 12 ½ x 12 ½ In.
$3245.00

Ivey-Selkirk Auctioneers

TIP
If you are having a piece restored, get a written estimate first.

L

Lamp, Advertising, Figural, Dog, Spuds MacKenzie, Bud Light, Plastic, Counter, 1970s
$240.00

Victorian Casino Antique Auction

Lamp, Aladdin, Reverse Painted, Shade, Landscape, Water View, Ribbed Standard, 20 ½ In.
$1164.00

Skinner, Inc.

Lamp, Bouillotte, 2-Light, Louis Philippe, Gilt Bronze, Leafy Scrolled Base, c.1840, 21 ½ In.
$598.00

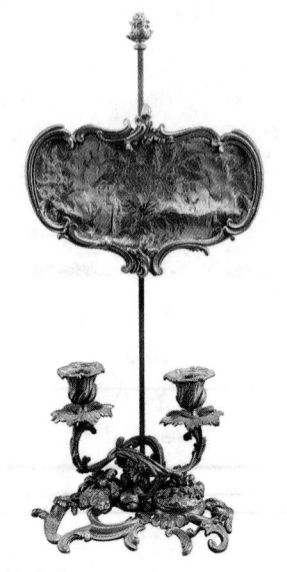

Neal Auction Co.

Daisy & Button, Goblet, Thumbprint Vaseline, Opalescent, 3 ¼ x 6 In.	49.00
Daisy & Fern, Barber Bottle, Blue, Metal Stopper, 8 ½ In.	230.00
Daisy & Fern, Barber Bottle, Cranberry, Porcelain Stopper, 8 ½ In.	166.00
Daisy & Fern, Pitcher, Blue Opalescent, Ruffled Rim, 5 ½ In.	80.00
Daisy & Fern, Pitcher, Cranberry Opalescent, Ruffled Rim	375.00
Daisy & Fern, Sugar Shaker, Cranberry Opalescent, 1970s, 4 ½ x 3 ¾ In.	190.00
Eye Winker, Goblet, Ruby, c.1965, 6 x 3 ⅜ In., Pair	30.00
Honeycomb, Tumbler, Blue Opalescent, c.1940, 3 ¾ x 3 In.	50.00
Maple Leaf, Water Set, Blue, Pitcher, 6 Tumblers, 1982, 7 Piece	500.00
Moon & Star, Bowl, Blue, c.1950, 10 x 5 ½ In.	75.00
Moon & Star, Creamer, Red, 6 ¼ In.	40.00
Moon & Star, Jelly, Ruby, 8 x 4 ½ In.	90.00
Moon & Star, Spooner, Red, c.1950, 5 ¼ In.	49.00
Moon & Star, Toothpick Holder, Amethyst, 2 ½ In.	25.00
Moon & Star, Toothpick Holder, Light Green, 2 ¼ x 2 In.	10.00
Moon & Star, Tumbler, Amber, 2 ⅝ x 2 ½ In.	15.00
Moon & Star, Vase, Footed, Amber, 13 x 2 In.	20.00
Moss Rose, Lamp, Ruffled Rim, Brass Leaf Base, c.1960, 22 x 6 ¾ In.	300.00
Panel Grape, Goblet, Ice Blue, Wine, c.1972, 4 In.	12.00
Panel Grape, Goblet, Ruby Red, 6 ¼ In.	15.00
S Ruby, Goblet, c.1965, 6 x 3 ¼ In., Pair	30.00
S Ruby, Toothpick Holder, 2 ½ In.	20.00
Spiral Optic, Jug, Cranberry Satin, 6 ¼ In.	230.00
Spiral, Pitcher, Cranberry Opalescent, 5 ½ x 4 In.	250.00
Strawberry & Current, Compote, Amethyst, 1950s, 5 ½ In.	48.00
Strawberry & Current, Goblet, Red, 1970s, 3 ½ x 6 ½ In., Pair	39.00
Swirl, Syrup, Cranberry Opal, 1973, 5 x 6 ½ In.	300.00
Thumbprint, Apothecary Jar, Cranberry, Footed, 1970s, 10 ¼ x 6 ½ In.	250.00
Thumbprint, Apothecary Jar, Cranberry, Ruby Overlay, 9 ¾ x 6 ¾ In.	79.00

LACQUER is a type of varnish. Collectors are most interested in the Chinese and Japanese lacquer wares made from the Japanese varnish tree. Lacquer wares are made from wood with many coats of lacquer. Sometimes the piece is carved or decorated with ivory or metal inlay.

Bench, Spring, Red, Recessed, Rounded Legs, Chinese 1800s, 43 x 11 In.	236.00
Box, Animal, Flower Carved, Gilt, Black, Japan, Fitted Interior, c.1905, 6 x 16 In.	354.00
Box, Couple, Greeting Guests, Drinks In Hand, Black Ground, Rectangular, Russia, c.1890, 7 In.	267.00
Box, Cover, Rectangular, Camellia Blossoms, Japan, Late 1800s, 9 ½ x 2 In.	153.00
Box, Figural Landscape, Paint, Rectangular, Russia, c.1905, 6 ⅜ In.	119.00
Box, Game, Figure Scenes, Fitted Interior, Chamfered, Rectangular, 4 ½ x 15 In.	234.00
Box, Mother-Of-Pearl Inlay, Flower, Geometric Designs, Oval, Chinese, c.1690, 1 ½ x 1 ⅜ In.	8575.00
Case, Mirror, Wood, Hinged Doors, Birds Flowers, Interior Couple, Paint, Persia, c.1800, 23 x 17 In.	444.00
Case, Pen, Papier-Mache, Birds, Butterflies, Flowers, 1896, 7 ½ In.	1007.00
Cigar Case, 2 Corona, Red, Brown, Gold Trim, S.T. Dupont Maduro, Chinese, 8 In.	330.00
Humidor, Scenic, Pewter Lining, Chinese, 1800s, 6 ½ x 11 In.	330.00
Inro, Mother-Of-Pearl Inlay, 5 Compartments, Seeding Grass Bunches Design, 3 ½ In.	2196.00
Inro, Turtle, Single Case, 2 Parts, Animal, Gilt, 2 ⅝ In.	248.00
Pedestal, Black, Birds, Branches, Leafy Plants, Cylindrical, Plinth Base, 36 x 12 In., Pair	154.00
Pen Box, Scenic, Flowers, Persian, 19th Century, 9 ½ In.	270.00
Tray, Scrolls, Carved, Red, Black, Chinese, 1800s, 7 ¾ In.	504.00
Tray, Stand, Victorian, Red, Gilt Flowers, Leaves, Gallery, Bamboo Turned Stand, 22 x 30 In.	468.00
Vase, 4 Cartouches, Peonies & Antiques, Carved, Red, Chinese, c.1800, 22 In.	8888.00
Vase, Gold Luster, Baluster, Japan, Late 1800s, 17 ½ In.	593.00

LADY HEAD VASE, *see Head Vase.*

LALIQUE glass was made by Rene Lalique in Paris, France, between the 1890s and his death in 1945. The glass was molded, pressed, and engraved in Art Nouveau and Art Deco styles. Pieces were marked with the signature *R. Lalique*. Lalique glass is still being made. Pieces made after 1945 bear the mark *Lalique*. After 1980 the registry mark was added and the mark became *Lalique ® France*. In the prices listed here, this is indicated by Lalique (R) France. Some pieces that are advertised as ring dishes or pin dishes were listed as ashtrays in the Lalique factory catalog and are listed as ashtrays here. Jewelry made by Rene Lalique is listed in the Jewelry category.

R.LALIQUE

Ashtray, Gao, Overlapping Leaves, Scalloped, Round, 4 In.	88.00
Ashtray, Lion Head, Round, 8 In.	132.00
Bookends, Reverie, Kneeling Nude, Frosted, 9 x 5 ¼ In.	1033.00

Bookends, Tete D'Aigle, Eagle Head, Tiffany Silver Base, 1900s, 5 In.	1380.00
Bowl, Caviar, Igor, 10 In.	357.00
Bowl, Compiegne, Leaves, 3 ¾ x 7 ¾ In.	300.00
Bowl, Faisons, Pheasant, Clear, Frosted, R. Lalique, 4 x 4 ¼ In.	180.00
Bowl, Fish, Bubbles, Opalescent, c.1932, 2 ½ x 14 In.	2356.00
Bowl, Moissac, Overlapping Leaves, Amber, Clear, Frosted, 1900s, 5 ⅛ In.	840.00
Bowl, Nemours, Flower Heads, 4 x 10 In.	472.00
Bowl, Nemours, Flower Heads, Black Centers, R. Lalique, c.1930, 10 x 4 In.	444.00 to 610.00
Bowl, Ormeaux, Elm Leaves, Frosted, Molded, c.1930, 3 ¼ x 8 ¼ In.	323.00
Bowl, Pinsons, Finches, Round, Etched, R. Lalique, 9 In. Diam.	219.00
Bowl, Raisins, Stylized Grapes, Finger, Hexagonal, Flared, R. Lalique, c.1950, 2 x 5 In.	123.00
Bowl, Serpents, Snakes, Clear, Amber Opalescent, Tapered, 3 x 9 In.	690.00
Bowl, Yeso, 2 Stylized Fish, Opalescent Green, Clear, 9 In.	443.00
Box, Cover, Canards, Ducks, Frosted, 2 ½ x 4 In.	118.00
Box, Cover, Coppelia, Roses In Relief, Round, 7 In.	540.00
Box, Cover, Daphne, Nude Woman, Round, 2 x 3 In.	354.00
Box, Cover, D'Orsay, Trois Figurines, 3 Nudes Dancing, Round, 3 ⅝ In. Diam.	173.00
Box, Dresser, Cover, Dahlia, Marked, 3 ⅛ x 5 ½ In.	230.00
Ceiling Light, Coquilles, Shells, Frosted, 24 x 11 ½ In.	1364.00
Charger, Beliers, Rams' Heads, 15 ½ In.	590.00
Clock, Naiades, Water Nymphs, Clear & Frosted, Arched, Silvered Dial, 9 In.	920.00
Compote, Nogent, Moineaux, 4 Sparrows Frosted Base, 3 ½ In.	325.00
Decanter, Barsac Pattern, Tapered, Frosted Stopper, 10 In.	310.00
Decanter, Cut Leaves, Shaped Stopper, Baluster Shape, Engraved, France, 10 x 6 In.	360.00
Figurine, Ara, Cockatoo, Frosted, Clear, Etched R. Lalique, 11 ½ x 10 ¼ In.	2006.00
Figurine, Buffalo, Frosted, Enamel Tag, France 3 ¾ x 4 ¾ In.	336.00
Figurine, Chat A Satoilette, Cat, Grooming, Square Base, Etched, 6 In.	384.00
Figurine, Chat Assis, Sitting Cat, 8 ¼ In.	590.00
Figurine, Coq Nain, Rooster, Frosted, Clear, Lalique France, 8 In.	238.00
Figurine, Coq Nain, Rooster, Tail Up, Round Base, Lalique France, 8 In.	313.00
Figurine, Crested Bird, Marked, Late 1900s, 14 In.	522.00
Figurine, Cygne, Swan, Frosted, 10 x 12 In.	2074.00
Figurine, Deux Danseus, 2 Dancers, Clear, Frosted, Etched, 10 ½ x 5 ½ In.	661.00
Figurine, Deux Poissons, 2 Fish, Intertwined, Clear, Frosted, Etched, 11 In.	1225.00
Figurine, Elephant, Standing, Raised Trunk, 6 In.	248.00
Figurine, Gran Goura, Exotic Bird, Engraved Lalique France, Sticker, c.1990, 11 In.	657.00
Figurine, Gregorie, Toad, Seated, 4 In.	310.00
Figurine, Luxembourg, 3 Cherubs, Holding Swags, Frosted, 8 In.	655.00
Figurine, Rhinoceros, Standing, Black, Lalique France, 5 x 10 In.	563.00
Figurine, Tete De Coq, Rooster Head, Scalloped Comb, Round Base, Lalique France, 7 ½ In.	219.00
Figurine, Trophee, Stylized Olympic Skater, 13 x 9 In. ....*illus*	1920.00
Hood Ornament, Chrysis, Kneeling Nude Woman, Frosted, Etched, 5 In.	460.00
Hood Ornament, Sirene, Opalescent Glass, Blue Patina, Signed R. Lalique, c.1920, 4 In.	2988.00
Hood Ornament, Tete D'Aigle, Eagle Head, Clear & Frosted, 1928, 4 ½ In.	325.00
Luminaire, Fauvettes, Warblers, Clear & Frosted, Illuminated Base, c.1930, 11 ½ x 15 In.	5270.00
Luminaire, Suzanne, Nude, Arms Extended, Fabric Draped, Frosted, Lighted Base, 11 x 10 In.	9775.00
Paperweight, Faucon, Falcon, 3 ¼ x 2 In.	180.00
Paperweight, Tete De Coq, Rooster's Head, Turned Steel Base, c.1928, 7 In.	896.00
Perfume Bottle, Claire Fontaine, Lily-Of-The-Valley, 4 ½ In.	330.00
Perfume Bottle, Claire Paris, Oree, Maidens, Clear, Frosted, Sepia, Stopper, 1930, 3 ⅛ In.	3450.00
Perfume Bottle, D'Orsay, Flacon Ambre, 4 Maidens, Gowns, Sepia, Pebbled Stopper, 5 ¾ In.	1495.00
Perfume Bottle, D'Orsay, Le Succes, Frosted, Spiral, Mermaid Stopper, 1914, 3 ½ x 2 ½ In.	4650.00
Perfume Bottle, Glass, Molded, Nudes, Amber Tint, Molinard, Gold Metal Atomizer, 5 In.	432.00
Perfume Bottle, L'Air Du Temps, Swirling Ribbed, Stopper, 2 Birds In Flight, 12 In.	590.00
Plaque, Masque De Femme, Frosted, Stand, 12 ½ x 12 ½ In. ....*illus*	3245.00
Plate, Berries, Frosted Center Roundel, Clear Border, 10 In.	199.00
Plate, Chasse Chiens, Hunting Hounds, Sepia Tint, Leaves, Bird Border, Engraved R. Lalique, 8 In.	805.00
Tumbler, Hesperides, Ferns, Honey Amber, Frosted, R. Lalique, 5 In.	230.00
Vase, Actinia, Serrated Swirls, Opalescent, Flared, Signed R. Lalique, c.1935, 8 ⅝ In.	2950.00
Vase, Avallon, Birds & Grapes, Clear, Frosted, c.1927, 5 ¾ x 6 ¼ In.	708.00 to 1240.00
Vase, Bacchantes, Frieze Of Female Nudes, 9 ¾ x 7 ½ In.	2300.00 to 4800.00
Vase, Bagatelle, Sparrows, Branches, Frosted, 6 x 5 In.	480.00
Vase, Berries, Birds, Squat, Trumpet, Opalescent Base, Signed, 8 x 9 In.	2825.00
Vase, Birds, Berries, Frosted, Cylindrical, Wide Rim, 6 x 6 In.	590.00
Vase, Camees, Cameos, Nude Women, Blue, Frosted, Triangular, Signed, 6 x 10 In.	2040.00
Vase, Campanule, Bellflower, Frosted, Molded, Flared, c.1926, 5 ½ In.	294.00

Lamp, Chandelier, 3-Light, Brass, Glass, Mottled Red, Swirls, Brass, France, c.1910, 34 x 15 ¾ In.
$1599.00

New Orleans Auction Galleries, Inc.

Lamp, Chandelier, Paavo Tynell, Pendant, Counter Balance, Brass, Rattan, Linen, 1950s, 10 x 18 In.
$3100.00

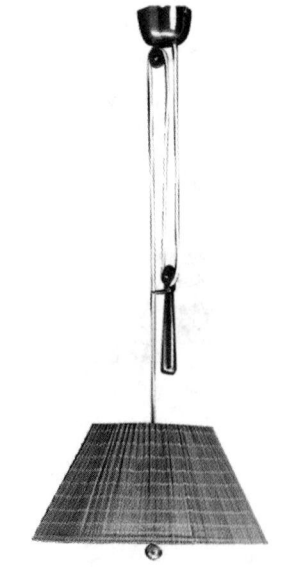

Rago Arts & Auction Center

Lamp, Chandelier, Wood, Horn, Carved, Painted, Metal Brackets, Lusterweipschen
$2760.00

Fox Auctions

Lamp, Electric, 2-Light, Moe Bridges, Reverse Painted, Woodland, Metal Base, c.1920, 22 ½ x 15 ¾ In. **$896.00**

Sloans & Kenyon

Lamp, Electric, Bergman, Arab Rug Seller, Bronze, Cold Painted, Marked, c.1900, 20 ¾ In. **$4594.00**

Skinner, Inc.

Lamp, Electric, Bigelow & Kennard, Leaded Shade, Leaves, Acorn Pulls, Grueby Pottery Base, 15 In. **$8050.00**

James D. Julia Inc.

Vase, Chevreuse, Daisies, Vertical Bands, Frosted, Clear, 1900s, 14 In.	420.00
Vase, Coquilles, Scallops, Shells, Frosted, Trumpet Shape, Leaves, Footed, c.1951, 10 In.	1195.00
Vase, Courges, Pears, Pale Staining, Gourd Shape, Engraved, France, c.1914, 7 ½ x 8 In.	4200.00
Vase, Dampierre, Protuding Birds, Clear & Frosted, Pedestal, c.1950, 5 In.	399.00
Vase, Doves Among Leaves, Marked, 7 In.	279.00
Vase, Elisabeth, Birds & Leaves, Clear, Frosted, Square Base, 5 ½ In.	240.00
Vase, Formose, Swirling Carp, Yellow Opalescent, Globular, 6 ¾ In.	6000.00
Vase, Gui, Mistletoe & Berries, Frosted, Sepia Patina, c.1920, 6 ¾ In.	575.00 to 956.00
Vase, Luxembourg, 3 Cherubs, Clear & Frosted, 8 ½ In.	1673.00
Vase, Monnaie Du Pape, Money Plant, Amber, Frosted, Bronze Base, c.1914, 9 ¼ x 6 ½ In.	4650.00
Vase, Oleron, Little Fish, c.1927, 3 ½ In.	1016.00 to 1298.00
Vase, Oleron, Little Fish, Opalescent, Ball Shape, R. Lalique, 4 In.	1265.00
Vase, Ormeaux, Overlapping Elm Leaves, Round, Signed R. Lalique, 7 In.	1074.00
Vase, Renoncules, Buttercups, Molded, Opalescent, Impressed Rene Lalique, c.1935, 6 In., Pair	764.00
Vase, Saint-Francois, Finches, On Branches, Frosted, Opalescent, Signed, c.1930, 7 x 6 ½ In.	2108.00
Vase, Sylvie, 2 Birds Entwined, Flower Frog Insert, Frosted, Signed, Label, 8 ½ x 7 In.	472.00
Vase, Sylvie, 2 Birds Entwined, Frosted & Clear, Extended Wings, Engraved, 8 ½ x 7 In.	293.00
Vase, Tourterelles, Turtle Doves, Frosted, Signed, 8 x 6 In.	425.00
Veilleuse, Night Light, Amours, Cupids, Frosted, Black Bakelite Base, Masks, 8 ½ In., Pair	35850.00

LAMPS of every type, from the early oil-burning Betty and Phoebe lamps to the recent electric lamps with glass or beaded shades, interest collectors. Fuels used in lamps changed through the years; whale oil (1800–40), camphene (1828), Argand (1830), lard (1833–63), turpentine and alcohol (1840s), gas (1850–79), kerosene (1860), and electricity (1879) are the most common. Other lamps are listed by manufacturer or type of material.

Advertising, Figural, Dog, Spuds MacKenzie, Bud Light, Plastic, Counter, 1970s *illus*	240.00
Advertising, Hamm's Beer, Take Home Cool Refreshment, Metal, 12 x 51 In.	130.00
Aladdin, B-12, 4 Post, Hanging, Cottage, Windmill	525.00
Aladdin, B-23, Brass, 9-Sided Shade, Morning Glory	160.00
Aladdin, B-53, Washington Drape, Clear, Bell Stem, Burner, 11 ¼ In.	85.00
Aladdin, B-81, Beehive, Green, Nu-Type, Burner, 12 In.	79.00
Aladdin, B-100, Venetian, Burner, c.1932, 12 ½ In.	165.00
Aladdin, B-105, Corinthian, Burner, Clear, 12 ½ In.	175.00
Aladdin, Electric, Light Green, Alacite, 1940s, 14 ½ In.	75.00
Aladdin, Electric, Porcelain, Bouquet, Cloth Shade, Tassels, Table, 1950s, 28 In.	179.00
Aladdin, G-244, Alacite, Ivory, Footed, Wing-Like Scrolls, Electric, 16 ½ In.	150.00
Aladdin, G-257, Alacite, Opal Scrolled Feet, Leaves, Finial, 1940s, 20 In.	80.00
Aladdin, Lincoln Drape, Cobalt Blue, Kerosene, Burner, 24 In.	200.00
Aladdin, Reverse Painted, Shade, Landscape, Water View, Ribbed Standard, 20 ½ In. *illus*	1164.00
Aladdin, Rose & White Moonstone, Diamond Quilt, c.1937, 13 In.	650.00
Argand, Gilt & Patinated Bronze, Brass Plate, Eagle, Etched Glass Shade, Gothic Style, 18 In., 3 Piece	1968.00
Argand, Gilt Brass, Bronze, Stepped Pedestal, Cut & Etched Glass Shade, c.1850, 19 In., Pair	1434.00
Argand, Gilt Brass, Patinated Bronze, Cut Glass, Mark, B. Gardiner, c.1830, 21 ½ In.	259.00
Astral, Brass, Reeded Column, Tulip Shade, Intaglio Cut Grapes, Flowers, Marble Base, 26 In.	413.00
Astral, Gilt Brass, G. Washington, Eagle, Etched Glass Shade, Prisms, Marble Base, 26 In.	1380.00
Betty, Copper, Wrought Iron, Hanger, Wick Pick, Peter Derr, Berks County, c.1835, 6 ½ In.	2703.00
Betty, Wrought Iron, Adjustable, Stand, 1800s, 16 ½ In.	353.00
Bouillotte, 2-Light, Gilt Bronze, Screen, Classical Woman Reading, Alabaster Base, France, 16 In.	595.00
Bouillotte, 2-Light, Louis Philippe, Gilt Bronze, Leafy Scrolled Base, c.1840, 21 ½ In. *illus*	598.00
Bouillotte, 3-Light, Gilt Brass, Flowers, Adjustable Tole Shade, France, c.1925, 26 x 13 In.	2091.00
Bradley & Hubbard lamps are included in the Bradley & Hubbard category.	
Bronze, Birds & Flowers, Relief Design, Narrow, Bulbous Sections, Japan, 63 In.	354.00
Chandelier, 1-Light, Bronze, Glass, Snowflake Pendants, Scrolls, 21 x 11 In.	240.00
Chandelier, 2-Light, Billiard, Bronze, Center Sphere, 2 Figural Arms, Shades, 48 x 60 In.	400.00
Chandelier, 3-Light, Antlers, Chains, Turned Wood Ceiling Cap, Brass Sockets, c.1900, 39 x 33 In.	826.00
Chandelier, 3-Light, Arts & Crafts, Copper, Urn Shape, Iridescent Pendant Shades, 12 In.	854.00
Chandelier, 3-Light, Arts & Crafts, Domed, Woven Willow Shade, 21 x 36 In.	660.00
Chandelier, 3-Light, Blue Crystal Drops, Clear Swags, 24 x 13 In., Pair	387.00
Chandelier, 3-Light, Brass, Glass, Mottled Red, Swirls, Brass, France, c.1910, 34 x 15 ¾ In. *illus*	1599.00
Chandelier, 3-Light, Brass, Glass, Trumpet Shape, 1900s, 25 In.	239.00
Chandelier, 3-Light, Directoire, Gilt Metal, Greek Key Frame, Link Chain, 35 x 11 In.	878.00
Chandelier, 3-Light, Glass, Beaded Garlands, Branches, Baccarat, France, c.1900, 38 x 32 In.	1304.00
Chandelier, 3-Light, Ram's Head Figures, Chains, c.1890, 28 ½ x 23 In.	2952.00
Chandelier, 3-Light, Wrought Iron, Victorian, Scrolls, Leaves, Vines, Cherubs, c.1900, 48 x 36 In.	518.00
Chandelier, 4-Light, 4 Animals, Round, Chains, Wrought Iron, c.1915, 27 In.	2500.00

Chandelier, 4-Light, Empire Style, Bronze, 2 Rings, 4 Rope Twist Chains, c.1910, 32 x 30 In..	800.00
Chandelier, 4-Light, Fontana Arte Style, Brass, Downswept Arms, c.1970, 30 x 14 In.	677.00
Chandelier, 4-Light, Gilt Metal, Porcelain, Column, Ball, Flower, Chain, Sevres, 1800s, 17 In.	613.00
Chandelier, 4-Light, Louis XVI Style, Gilt, Glass, Flowers, Amethyst, Pendants, c.1900, 17 x 12 In.	922.00
Chandelier, 4-Light, Neoclassical, Cut Glass, Ruby, Gilt, Beads, Cut Spears, Shades, 21 x 18 In.	738.00
Chandelier, 4-Light, Wrought Iron, Tole, Gold Leaf, Hot Air Balloon Shape, France, 21 x 11 In.	1450.00
Chandelier, 5-Light, Art Deco, Iron, Strapwork, Milk Glass Inserts, c.1910, 53 x 27 In............	615.00
Chandelier, 5-Light, Black Painted Metal, Green & Yellow Opalescent Drops, Italy, 20 x 20 In.	327.00
Chandelier, 5-Light, Brass, 8 Panels, Inverted Pyramid Form, Leaves, Gold Bell Shades.........	1416.00
Chandelier, 5-Light, Georgian Style, Glass, S-Shaped Arms, Pendants, 1900s, 24 x 23 In.	203.00
Chandelier, 5-Light, Iron, Flowers, Oak Leaves, c.1905, 19 ½ x 18 In.....................................	495.00
Chandelier, 5-Light, Sinumbra, Oil, Gilt Bronze, Acanthus Frame, Shades, c.1845, 46 ½ In. ..	8365.00
Chandelier, 5-Light, Walnut, Barley Twist Stems, 30 x 29 ½ In..	122.00
Chandelier, 6-Light, Blue Opaline Glass, Cage Shape, Prisms, Shaped Drops, France, 20 In. ..	3416.00
Chandelier, 6-Light, Blue Opaline Glass, S-Scroll Arms, Candle Shape Lights, 20 x 15 In........	875.00
Chandelier, 6-Light, Brass Arms, Cobalt Hurricane Shades & Bowl, 34 In...............................	1722.00
Chandelier, 6-Light, Brass, Frosted Lobed Globes, Elbow Shaped Arms, Stilnovo, c.1955, 35 x 25 In.	183.00
Chandelier, 6-Light, Bronze, Acanthus, Grotesque Masks, Flower Collars, Italy, c.1860, 43 In.	4183.00
Chandelier, 6-Light, Bronze, Porcelain Cups & Finial, Flowers, Spain, 1900s, 24 x 21 In.	155.00
Chandelier, 6-Light, Cast Metal, Pierced Flowers, Rose Medallion Mounts, 40 In.	1180.00
Chandelier, 6-Light, Cut Glass, Brass, Centerl Green Vase, Pendant Canopy, c.1800, 35 In. ...	3690.00
Chandelier, 6-Light, Empire Style, Glass, Faux Candles, Pendants, 1800s, 21 x 24 In.	299.00
Chandelier, 6-Light, Empire Style, Ormolu, Patinated, 28 x 18 ½ In..	702.00
Chandelier, 6-Light, Frosted Glass, Love Birds, 6-Sided Dome, Tapered Shades, Muller Freres, 32 In.	1180.00
Chandelier, 6-Light, George III, Cut Glass, Beaded Chains, Prisms, Baluster Pendant, 38 In...	11800.00
Chandelier, 6-Light, Gilt Brass, Draped Cut Glass Chains, Drops, Spears, 35 x 20 In...............	676.00
Chandelier, 6-Light, Gilt Bronze, Cut Glass, Faceted Bead Swags, Spears, France, 44 x 26 In. .	1476.00
Chandelier, 6-Light, Gilt Metal, Cage Shape, Leaves, Frosted Glass Pendants, 36 In.	1830.00
Chandelier, 6-Light, Gilt Metal, Drop Prisms, 38 x 28 In.	978.00
Chandelier, 6-Light, Gilt Metal, Porcelain, Cage Shape, Flowers, Tole Leaves, 26 In..............	2318.00
Chandelier, 6-Light, Gilt Metal, Serpentine Arms, Pinecone Finial, Chains, Teardrop Lustres, c.1900..	2133.00
Chandelier, 6-Light, Glass, Frosted, 2 Tiers, Leaves, Flower, Electrified, c.1950, 39 x 52 In.......	1230.00
Chandelier, 6-Light, Hanging Prisms, Beaded Swags, Teardrops, 43 In.	553.00
Chandelier, 6-Light, Hexagonal Arms, Baluster Stem, Hanging Spears, Globe Shades, c.1875, 45 In.	4182.00
Chandelier, 6-Light, Iron, Dagger Shaped Holders, France, 1800s, 23 x 31 In.	180.00
Chandelier, 6-Light, Louis XVI Style, Gilt, Brass, Cut Glass, Bead, Chains, Shaped Pendants, 23 In.	676.00
Chandelier, 6-Light, Murano Glass, Multicolor Glass, Fruit Pendants, 24 x 23 In.	657.00
Chandelier, 6-Light, Neoclassical, Brass, Jewel Cut Glass, Link Chains, c.1835, 42 x 27 In.	1353.00
Chandelier, 6-Light, Oil, Wrought Iron, Welded, Strap Iron Ring, Hooks, Electrified, 30 In.....	24.00
Chandelier, 6-Light, Parcel Gilt, Ram's Head Masks, Electrific, 30 x 29 In.............................	714.00
Chandelier, 6-Light, Pendant Drops, Inverted Bowl Shape, S-Scroll Arms, Waterford, 29 In....	538.00
Chandelier, 6-Light, Porcelain, Cage Shape, Courtier, Squirrel, Leaves, 1900s, 24 x 21 In.......	676.00
Chandelier, 6-Light, Prisms, Cut Glass, 2 Tiers, Swags, Cranmore, Waterford, 30 x 28 In.	1380.00
Chandelier, 6-Light, Rococo Revival, Brass, Etched Glass Shades, Cornelius & Co., 71 x 52 In.	7995.00
Chandelier, 6-Light, Tin, Witch's Hat Cone, Chain, Candle Cups, c.1850, 37 x 26 In.	1840.00
Chandelier, 6-Light, Tole Black Globe, Figure Of Abundance, Linen Shades, France, 38 In.	1722.00
Chandelier, 6-Light, Tole, Scrolling Candle Arms, Leafy Standard, 28 In.	723.00
Chandelier, 6-Light, Troubadour, Bronze Gilt, Chocolate Patina, Hexagonal, c.1835, 62 x 22 In.	1968.00
Chandelier, 6-Light, Wrought Iron, Glass, Branch Shape, Center Column, c.1940, 26 x 22 In. ..	861.00
Chandelier, 8-Light, Brass, Cut Glass, Multicolor Fruit, Pendants, France, c.1935, 33 x 23 In.	922.00
Chandelier, 8-Light, Bronze, Faceted Crystal Pendants, Icicles, 33 ½ x 28 In.........................	275.00
Chandelier, 8-Light, Cut Glass, Fluted Arms, Circlets, Spear Prisms, Pendant Ball, 1900s, 28 x 27 In.	1195.00
Chandelier, 8-Light, Gilt Metal, Crystal Prisms, Leaf Shaped Pendants.................................	1534.00
Chandelier, 8-Light, Gilt Metal, Tiers, 3 Prisms, Scrolling Supports, 32 x 24 In.......................	1180.00
Chandelier, 8-Light, Louis XVI Style, Bronze, Glass, Bead Swags, Cage Shape, Drops, c.1900, 31 In.	738.00
Chandelier, 8-Light, Neoclassical, Basket Shape, Gilt Metal Leaves, Prisms, 37 x 30 In............	2706.00
Chandelier, 8-Light, Neoclassical, Gilt Gesso, Leaves, Swans, Scroll Base, 1900s, 38 x 34 In....	598.00
Chandelier, 8-Light, Prisms, Waterfall, Spears, S-Shape Arms, Bronze Crown, c.1900, 31 In...	2952.00
Chandelier, 8-Light, Tiered Prisms, Flower Bands, England, c.1900, 32 ½ In., Pair	8888.00
Chandelier, 8-Light, Tin, Cone Shape, Crimped Bobeches, Red Faux Candles, 32 x 20 In.	492.00
Chandelier, 8-Light, Tole Paint, Turned Baluster Stem, Leaf Candle Cups, 32 In.....................	671.00
Chandelier, 8-Light, Wrought Iron, Scrolls, France, 30 ½ x 35 In...	366.00
Chandelier, 9-Light, Glass, Pendant Drops, Victorian, 26 x 19 In...	777.00
Chandelier, 9-Light, Wrought Iron, 3 Tiers, Scrolled Arms, 53 x 49 In.	1968.00
Chandelier, 10-Light, Bronze, Glass, 3 Chains, Pendant, Frosted Shade..................................	1225.00
Chandelier, 10-Light, Bronze, Glass, Luster Ropes, Basket Form, Leaf Corona, c.1900, 48 x 34 In.	6573.00

Lamp, Electric, Brass, Figural, Woman In Bloomers, End Of Day Glass Globe Shade, 21 ½ In.
$590.00

Lamp, Electric, Bronze, Leaded Glass, Tulip Border, Attributed To Goodwin & Kintz, 27 In.
$1035.00

L

Lamp, Electric, Chicago Mosaic Lamp Co., Flowers, Cat's-Paw Glass, Metal Tree Trunk, 29 In.
$5175.00

Lamp, Electric, Chicago Mosaic Lamp Co., Flowers, Reeded Bronze Base, Paw Feet, 65 In.
$1150.00

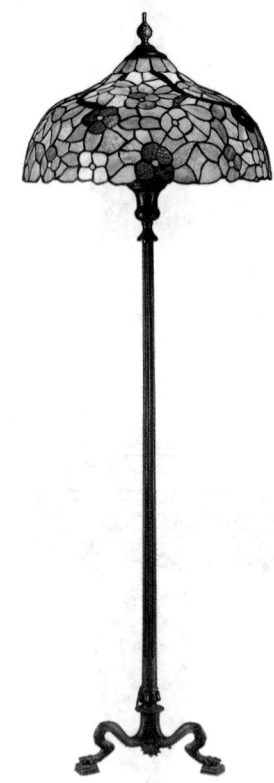

James D. Julia Inc.

Lamp, Electric, Figural, Art Nouveau, Woman, Copper Shade, Glass Nuggets, Fringe, 21 ½ In.
$1470.00

Skinner, Inc.

Chandelier, 10-Light, Candle, Turned Shaft, Steel Candle Cups, c.1805, 18 x 31 In.	2760.00
Chandelier, 10-Light, Louis XVI Style, Gilt Brass, Glass, Reeded Arms, Faceted Drops, c.1900, 29 In.	1968.00
Chandelier, 12-Light, 2 Tiers, Glass, Faux Wax Drip Candles, Electrified, 36 In.	359.00
Chandelier, 12-Light, Brass, Faceted Vase Standard, 2 Tiers, Scrolled Arms, 1800s, 35 x 34 In.	1315.00
Chandelier, 12-Light, Brass, Glass, Tiered Prism Drops, 31 x 30 In.	976.00
Chandelier, 12-Light, Brass, Pressed Glass, Scrolled Arms, Prisms, 24 In. Diam.	125.00
Chandelier, 12-Light, Brass, Stepped Tiers, Ball Finial, c.1920, 34 x 30 In.	1045.00
Chandelier, 12-Light, Bronze, Crystal Drops, Spires, Shades, France, c.1940, 36 x 24 In.	523.00
Chandelier, 12-Light, Empire, Bronze, Glass, Ormolu, Chariots, Scrolled Arms, c.1810, 43 x 35 In.	21240.00
Chandelier, 12-Light, George II Style, Brass, 2 Tiers, 28 x 27 In.	553.00
Chandelier, 12-Light, Gothic Revival, Wrought Iron, Green Paint, Chain, c.1910, 48 x 36 In.	420.00
Chandelier, 12-Light, Sputnik, Brass Tone Metal, 20 x 17 In.	413.00
Chandelier, 12-Light, Wood, Gilt, Carved, 46 x 38 In.	488.00
Chandelier, 14-Light, Curved Metal Rods, c.1955, 28 x 21 In., Pair	1046.00
Chandelier, 15-Light, Brass, 2 Tiers, Scrolled, Stepped Bowls, 26 x 30 In.	922.00
Chandelier, 15-Light, Brass, Chrome, Geometric, Scholari, Italy, 29 x 17 In.	780.00
Chandelier, 15-Light, Maria Theresa Style, Gilt Metal, Tiered, Prisms, 45 x 26 In.	1098.00
Chandelier, 16-Light, Bronze, Gilt, Fluted Urn, Scrolls, Rosettes, c.1890, 50 x 23 In.	4780.00
Chandelier, 18-Light, Belle Epoque, Gilt Bronze, Scrolling Leaves, Pendant, c.1900, 41 x 33 In.	1554.00
Chandelier, 18-Light, Brass, Alabaster Globe, Tiered, 56 x 43 In.	2214.00
Chandelier, 18-Light, Bronze, Glass, 5 Tiers, Faceted Drops, 45 In.	1225.00
Chandelier, 18-Light, Bronze, Scrolled Flower Arms, Patina, c.1900, 34 x 32 In.	3318.00
Chandelier, 18-Light, Glass, Prisms, Beaded Swags, Pear Shaped Drops, 27 x 32 In.	1353.00
Chandelier, 18-Light, Ormolu, Cut Glass, Tiered Drops, Prisms, c.1890, 49 x 28 In.	8050.00
Chandelier, 18-Light, Wrought Iron, Flower Scrolled Arms, Faux Candles, Glass Drops, 70 x 60 In.	2952.00
Chandelier, 24-Light, 3 Tiers, Chrome, Steel, Prisms, Italy, c.1960, 32 x 38 In.	2300.00
Chandelier, 36-Light, Chrome, Aluminum, Rubber, 29 ½ x 20 In.	1364.00
Chandelier, Afra & Tobia Scarpa, Chrome, Enameled Steel, Italy, 1960s, 11 x 17 In.	1860.00
Chandelier, Alabaster, Amber, Dome Shape, Rope Hanger, c.1920, 19 x 14 In.	138.00
Chandelier, Art Deco Style, Camphor Glass, Bronzed Metal, Flower Shades, 36 x 27 In.	538.00
Chandelier, Art Deco, Brass, Cut Glass, Waterfall, Octagonal Beads, 36 x 24 In.	1476.00
Chandelier, Art Deco, Gilt Metal, Glass, Grapes & Pansies, Mesh Wire, 26 x 24 In.	863.00
Chandelier, Art Deco, Nickel Plated Frame, Pleated Fabric Shade, Dutch, c.1920, 47 x 25 In.	806.00
Chandelier, Blue Globe, White Cable, Ceiling Cap, Italy, 12 x 13 In.	434.00
Chandelier, Bronze, Glass, Etched, Leaves, Flowers, Chain, c.1805, 14 ½ x 14 In.	1912.00
Chandelier, Camer, Brushed Steel, Pulegoso Glass Shades, Italy, 1970s, 15 x 37 In.	2728.00
Chandelier, Camer, Glass, Enameled Steel, Tiers, Italy, 1960s, 65 x 73 In.	4030.00
Chandelier, Empire Style, Porcelain, Pink & Yellow, Flowers, Glass Prisms, 26 x 14 In.	300.00
Chandelier, Fer Forge, Frosted Glass Panels, Flowers, France, c.1920, 22 x 31 In.	677.00
Chandelier, Frosted & Cut Glass, Prisms, Spears, Vase Shape, 1800s, 34 In.	2952.00
Chandelier, Gaetano Sciolari, Chromed Steel, Italy, 1970, 13 ½ x 21 In.	620.00
Chandelier, Gilt Brass, Cut Glass, Bead Chains, Prisms, France, c.1900, 29 ½ x 12 In.	738.00
Chandelier, Glass, Beads, Prisms, Swags, Blue Pendants, Brass, Globe Finial, 29 x 23 In.	1107.00
Chandelier, Glass, Grape Clusters, Murano, Italy, 1900s, 20 x 29 In.	3163.00
Chandelier, Glass, Smiling Devil Masques, 4 Chains, Cap, 8 x 20 In.	298.00
Chandelier, Max Ingrand, Dahlia, Glass, Brass, Fontana Arte, c.1955, 20 x 43 In.	8680.00
Chandelier, Max Sauze, Orion, Aluminum, Zinc Plated Steel, France, 1967, 16 x 18 In.	3224.00
Chandelier, Neoclassical Style, Oval, Tiered Prisms, Gilt Metal Bands, c.1890, 11 x 16 In.	976.00
Chandelier, Paavo Tynell, Pendant, Counter Balance, Brass, Rattan, Linen, 1950s, 10 x 18 In. . *illus*	3100.00
Chandelier, Rococo, Brass, Leaf Molded, Baluster Standard, Milk Glass Globes, Spain, 25 x 14 In.	676.00
Chandelier, Vistosi, Red, Frosted Glass Discs, Chrome Steel Frame, Italy, 1960s, 32 x 13 ½ In.	682.00
Chandelier, Wood, Horn, Carved, Painted, Metal Brackets, Lusterweipschen ....*illus*	2760.00
Electric, 2-Light, Art Deco, Wrought Iron, Trellis Stem, Roses, Purple Shades, 1900s, 19 In.	1067.00
Electric, 2-Light, Chipped Ice Shade, Gold & Red Iridescent, Metal Leaf Base, 12 x 17 In.	345.00
Electric, 2-Light, Gilt Metal, Leaves, Wings, Flower Shades, Iridescent Yellow, 28 In.	384.00
Electric, 2-Light, Moe Bridges, Reverse Painted, Woodland, Metal Base, c.1920, 22 ½ x 15 ¾ In. .*illus*	896.00
Electric, 2-Light, Neoclassical, Urn, Patinated Metal, Marble Base, Paw Feet, 14 In., Pair	416.00
Electric, 2-Light, Renaissance Style, Bronze, Angels, Paw Feet, Black Paint, c.1900, 40 ½ In., Pair	2400.00
Electric, 3-Light, Lily Shades, Yellow Iridescent, Bronze Base, Buffalo Metal Works, 11 x 12 In.	374.00
Electric, 4-Light, Bronze, Barefoot Woman, Arms Up, Stalks, Leaves, c.1920s, 41 In.	2588.00
Electric, 8-Panel Shade, Caramel & Green Slag Glass, Metal Base, Pat'd Oct 20, 08, 14 x 21 In.	748.00
Electric, A. Fraser, Nastro, Plastic Neck, Multicolor Wires, Black Shade, Base, Stilnovo, 24 x 20 In.	1140.00
Electric, A. Hart, Cherry Blossom Shade, Mottled Green Ground, Spread Foot, 16 In.	5900.00
Electric, Acrylic, Aluminum, Enameled, Domed Shade, Italy, 17 ½ x 14 ½ In., Pair	248.00
Electric, Aphrodite, Nautilus Shell Shade, Mother-Of-Pearl, 21 x 10 In.	288.00
Electric, Arredoluce, Triennale, 3-Light, Chromed Brass, Enameled Aluminum, c.1950, 62 x 25 In.	3720.00

Electric, Arredoluce, Triennale, Chrome, Black Leather, 3 Arms, Marble Base, Italy, 70 In.......	4600.00
Electric, Art Deco, Black Glass Base, Dome Green Shade, c.1935, 11 ½ In.............	627.00
Electric, Art Deco, Brass, Copper, Pink Lucite Finial, Kurt Versen, 16 ½ x 13 ½ In..............	527.00
Electric, Art Deco, Bronze, Cream Paneled Glass Shade, Metal Trim, 24 x 16 In., Pair............	183.00
Electric, Art Deco, Gilt Metal, Spindle Support, Outstretched Arm, Pierced Foot, 21 x 10 x 13 In.	120.00
Electric, Art Deco, Porcelain, Urn, Woman's Portrait, Bronze Mounts, Handles, Sevres, France, 14 In..	384.00
Electric, Art Nouveau, 10-Light, Thistle, Bronze, Cold Painted, Maurice Bouval, c.1900, 73 In.	9660.00
Electric, Art Nouveau, Bronze, Lily Pad, Woman's Head, Lily Shade, Leonard, c.1920, 20 x 11 In.	3680.00
Electric, Art Nouveau, Corinthian Column, Umber Onyx, Pierced Metal Mount, 17 ½ In., Pair	374.00
Electric, Art Nouveau, Glass, Fiery Amber, Fish, Wave Border, Footed Base, A. Hunebelle, 13 x 9 In.	708.00
Electric, Art Nouveau, Leaded Glass Shade, Bronze, Maiden, Flowing Gown, c.1900, 19 In......	940.00
Electric, Arteluce, Triennale, 3 Arms, Stainless Steel, Marble Base, Cone Shades, 1955, 77 In..	2844.00
Electric, Arts & Crafts, Bronze Tree Trunk, Overlay Shade, Caramel, Amber, Panels, 19 x 23 In.	840.00
Electric, Astrolabe, Bronze, France, 1960s, 18 x 11 ½ In..........	496.00
Electric, Bergman, Arab Rug Seller, Bronze, Cold Painted, Marked, c.1900, 20 ¾ In. ......illus	4594.00
Electric, Bigelow & Kennard, Domed Shade, Greek Key, Mottled Amber, Bronze Base, 23 In....	4720.00
Electric, Bigelow & Kennard, Domed Shade, Stylized Leaf Border, Green Slag, 20 In.	2489.00
Electric, Bigelow & Kennard, Domed Shade, Stylized Leaves & Flowers, Green & Rose Slag, 21 In.	2818.00
Electric, Bigelow & Kennard, Leaded Shade, Leaves, Acorn Pulls, Grueby Pottery Base, 15 In. illus	8050.00
Electric, Borghese, Figural, Man & Woman, Carrying Basket, Terra-Cotta, 24 In., Pair..........	246.00
Electric, Brass Frame, Square, Adjustable, Burlap Shade, Laurel, 1960s, 67 In.........	540.00
Electric, Brass, 2 Pillars, Black Metal & Glass Top, Italy, 15 x 17 In.	118.00
Electric, Brass, Alternating Large & Small Glass Spheres, Hexagonal Stepped Base, 26 In.......	369.00
Electric, Brass, Arched Base, Round White Glass Shade, Laurel, 13 x 13 In............	450.00
Electric, Brass, Column Shaft, Tiered Square Base, Paw Feet, Gilt Ebonized Shade, 66 In........	799.00
Electric, Brass, Figural, Woman In Bloomers, End-Of-Day Glass Globe Shade, 21 ½ In. ....illus	590.00
Electric, Brass, Steel, Paint, Pole Shape, Tripart Base, France, c.1940, 56 In.	738.00
Electric, Brass, Tripod Base, Acorn Finials, Fabric Shade, c.1925, 65 In., Pair.........	489.00
Electric, Brass, Tripod Base, Paw & Leaf Feet, 66 In........	633.00
Electric, Bronze, Bird, Pine, Embossed, Urn Shape, Cream Shade, Japan, 32 x 15 In., Pair	854.00
Electric, Bronze, Cactus Shape, Patinated, France, 1960s, 17 ½ x 6 In.	279.00
Electric, Bronze, Child, Basket On Head, Drum Base, Children Frieze, France, 1900s, 17 In....	237.00
Electric, Bronze, D. Giacometti, Chien Et Faucon, Dog & Falcon, Patina, c.1965, 13 x 8 ½ In., Pair	35850.00
Electric, Bronze, Lantern Shape, Amber Glass Panels, Finial, 1900s, 23 x 6 In., Pair...........	122.00
Electric, Bronze, Leaded Glass, Tulip Border, Attributed To Goodwin & Kintz, 27 In. ......illus	1035.00
Electric, Bronze, Metal Mesh, Shade In Harp, Splayed Feet, Adjustable, L.H. Nash, 64 x 12 In., Pair	2232.00
Electric, Bronze, Pinched Neck, Bird Scene, Wood Base, Elephant Handles, Japan, c.1890, 32 In.	492.00
Electric, Bronze, Stork, Birds, Turtle, Bulbous, Waisted, Wood Base, Silk Shade, Japan, 1800s, 31 In.	1230.00
Electric, C. Hartman, Brass, Swivel Shade, Adjustable, 47 ½ In........	1920.00
Electric, C. Jere, Steel, Stacked, Wood Base, Chromed Steel Drum Shade, Artisan House, 18 x 39 In.	780.00
Electric, Candlestick, Brass, Acanthus Leaf Capitals, Marble Base, Purple Shade, 37 In., Pair.	655.00
Electric, Candlestick, Brass, Dolphins, Sphere, Trefoil Base, Shade, Chapman, 38 In., Pair.....	417.00
Electric, Candlestick, Silver Plate, Cream & Parcel Gilt Demilune Tole Shade, c.1905, 10 ½ In..	246.00
Electric, Castiglioni, Taccia, Chromed Steel, Aluminum, Glass, Flos, 21 x 20 In., Pair............	2728.00
Electric, Ceiling, Aluminum Spheres, Cluster, 1972, 28 x 17 In., Pair.	750.00
Electric, Ceramic, Corinthian Column, Cherubs, Gilt Shade, Ball Finial, 31 ½ In., Pair	299.00
Electric, Chicago Mosaic Lamp Co., Flowers, Cat's-Paw Glass, Metal Tree Trunk, 29 In. ......illus	5175.00
Electric, Chicago Mosaic Lamp Co., Flowers, Reeded Bronze Base, Paw Feet, 65 In. ....illus	1150.00
Electric, Chrome, Stone Base, 63 In., Pair..........	322.00
Electric, Copper, Revere, Pine Needle Overlay, Green Slag Glass, 18 In.	633.00
Electric, Crystal, Brass, Fontana Art, Milan, Italy, 1980s, 70 x 13 In........	682.00
Electric, Cut Glass, Globular Shade, Prisms, American Brilliant, 22 ½ In.	293.00
Electric, Czech Glass, Clear, Wine, Red, Flowers, Vase Shape, Shade, 32 In., Pair..........	230.00
Electric, Danish Modern, Bentwood Teak, Iron Curved Base, Caprani, Denmark, 57 x 12 In...	550.00
Electric, Desk, D. Deskey, Aluminum, Nickel Plated Brass, Wood, Deskey Vollmer, 1930s, 15 x 9 In.	13640.00
Electric, Desk, Eileen Gray, Metal, Stripped, V-Shape Support, Jumo, France, 1930s, 18 x 16 In.	800.00
Electric, Domed Shade, Dogwood, Leaded Slag Glass, Giltwood Base, Carved, 75 x 25 In........	1860.00
Electric, Driftwood, Free-Form, Speckled Shade, 41 In., Pair........	748.00
Electric, Duffner & Kimberly, Domed Shade, Autumn Leaves, Slag Glass, Bronze Base, 25 x 19 ¾ In.	13640.00
Electric, Duffner & Kimberly, Domed Shade, Geometric Band, Slag Glass, Bronze Base, 23 x 19 In.	2604.00
Electric, Duffner & Kimberly, Leaded Glass, Arrowhead, Green, Orange, Amber, Panels, 17 In.	4720.00
Electric, Duffner & Kimberly, Louis XV, Leaded Glass, Shade, Gilt Bronze, c.1910, 29 x 21 In...	23000.00
Electric, Duffner & Kimberly, Wavy Grid Work, Striated Green Glass, Bellflowers, Shaped Rim, 21 In...	4444.00
Electric, E. Martinelli, Serpent, Polished Steel, Plastic Domed Shade, Italy, c.1968, 16 x 15 In.	840.00
Electric, Eileen Gray, Tube, Chrome, Pole, Tubular Bulb, c.1994, 41 In.............	502.00
Electric, Electrolier, Glass, Ruby Over Clear, Etched Chimney, Bobeche, Prisms, c.1940, 22 In...	120.00

Lamp, Electric, Figural, Dancer, Marble, Gilt Accents, Art Deco, 26 In. $3851.00

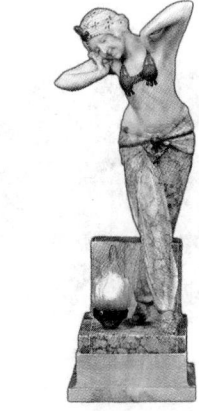

Skinner, Inc.

Lamp, Electric, Figural, Hula Girl, Copper Flash Finish, Lamp Base Motion, 17 In. $495.00

Showtime Auction Services

Lamp, Electric, Figural, Nymph, Silver Plate, Nautilus Shell Shade, WMFB, c.1900, 14 In. $2252.00

Skinner, Inc.

L

Lamp, Electric, Figural, Peacock, Brass, Czech, Beaded Feathers, Marble Base, 1900s, 20 ½ In.
$948.00

Skinner, Inc.

Lamp, Electric, G.N. Bennett, In Oakland, Copper, Brass, Oak, Signed, 1995, 20 ½ x 13 In.
$2480.00

Rago Arts & Auction Center

Lamp, Electric, Hanging, Tobia Scarpa, Nictea, Brass, Glass, Flos, Italy, 1961, 12 x 19 In.
$1500.00

Los Angeles Modern Auctions

Electric, Elephant Seated, Trunk Up, Bronze, Round Faux Marble Base, 21 x 10 In.	90.00
Electric, Elizabeth Burton, Hylas, Copper, Patinated, Hammered, Abalone Shell Shade, 27 x 18 In.	52700.00
Electric, Emeralite, 2 Green Glass Shades, Prairie School Metal Base, 14 x 8 ½ In.	450.00
Electric, Emeralite, Green Cased Glass Shade, Adjustable Metal Base, 14 In.	230.00
Electric, Empire Style, Brass Column, Black Fabric Shade, 70 x 23 In.	600.00
Electric, Empire Style, Bronze, Urn, Sculpted Faces, Flowers, Glass Shade, France, 31 x 12 In.	4181.00
Electric, Empire Style, Gilt Metal, Patinated, Campana Urn, Figures, 23 x 8 In., Pair	338.00
Electric, Empire Style, Gilt Metal, Patinated, Oval Bowl, 3 Sphinx Head Supports, Footed, 36 x 20 In.	439.00
Electric, F. Ligtelijin, Chrome, White Marble Base, 2 White Glass Globes, c.1960, 64 x 24 In.	1150.00
Electric, Figural, Art Nouveau, Woman, Copper Shade, Glass Nuggets, Fringe, 21 ½ In. *illus*	1470.00
Electric, Figural, Curtis Jere, Bird Of Paradise, 60 In.	518.00
Electric, Figural, Dancer, Bronze, Ivorine Face, Marble Base, Millefiori Shade, 1920s, 9 In.	431.00
Electric, Figural, Dancer, Marble, Gilt Accents, Art Deco, 26 In. *illus*	3851.00
Electric, Figural, Doughboy, Hand Raised, Bronze, Shade, Viquesney, 1920, 18 x 10 In.	244.00
Electric, Figural, Goddess, Guanyin, Hardstone, Brass, Petal Silk Shade, Chinese, 12 ½ In.	259.00
Electric, Figural, Hula Girl, Copper Flash Finish, Lamp Base Motion, 17 In. *illus*	495.00
Electric, Figural, Jester, Ivorine Face, Glass Millefiori Globe, Marble Base, France, 9 In.	1003.00
Electric, Figural, Maiden, Carrying Two Baskets, 2 Red Glass Flower Lights, Cast Metal, 13 x 8 In.	184.00
Electric, Figural, Nymph, Silver Plate, Nautilus Shell Shade, WMFB, c.1900, 14 In. *illus*	2252.00
Electric, Figural, Peacock, Brass, Czech, Beaded Feathers, Marble Base, 1900s, 20 ½ In. *illus*	948.00
Electric, Figural, Putto, Holding Snake Socket, Gilt Metal, Wood Base, 1900s, 9 ½ x 4 ½ In., Pair	122.00
Electric, Figural, Seminude Dancer, Brass Base, Peach & Gold Iridescent Shade, 24 In.	575.00
Electric, Figural, Venus, Resting In Clamshell, Putti Supports, Alabaster, Italy, c.1900, 25 In.	1800.00
Electric, Figural, Woman, Asian, Parasol, Rose Quartz, Bronze Base, c.1920, 21 x 13 In.	492.00
Electric, Figurine, Parrot, Green, Brown Rock, Porcelain, Brass Base, Shade, Chinese, 1800s, 17 In.	553.00
Electric, Frosted Glass Shade, Tole Stem & Base, Black, Gilt, 26 In.	633.00
Electric, G. Stickley, Copper, Hammered, Handle, Wicker Shade, 20 x 14 In.	4340.00
Electric, G. Stickley, Copper, Hammered, Woven Shade, 18 x 25 In.	3900.00
Electric, G.N. Bennett, In Oakland, Copper, Brass, Oak, Signed, 1995, 20 ½ x 13 In. *illus*	2480.00
Electric, Gerald Thurston, Brass, 3 Legs, Wood Sleeve, 3 Shades, 64 x 13 In.	660.00
Electric, Gilt Bronze, Abstract Design, Rectangular, Painted Shade, Prago, 1970s, 10 x 22 In.	600.00
Electric, Gilt Metal, Iridescent Glass, Swirled Silk Shade, Gilt & Glass Finial, c.1920, 27 In.	272.00
Electric, Giltwood, Eglomise, Urn, Painted, Putti, Medallions, Blue, 27 x 6 In., Pair	984.00
Electric, Glass White, Frosted, Bulbous Base, Tapered Cylindrical Shade, 30 In.	1304.00
Electric, Glass, 6 Textured Stylized Leaves, Elliptical Nickel Shade, 34 x 20 ¼ In.	1247.00
Electric, Glass, Clear, Bottle Shape, Brass Mount, Label, Marbro Lamp Co., 1950s, 44 x 8 ½ In., Pair	1116.00
Electric, Glass, Frosted Shade, Abstract, Flower Head, Fluted Rim, Domed Base, 23 In.	770.00
Electric, Glass, Millefiori, Red, White, Gilt, Mushroom, Baluster Base, 17 In., Pair	529.00
Electric, Hanging, 6-Light, Leaded Glass, Feather Design, Cone Shape, Scalloped Border, Finial, 26 In.	9200.00
Electric, Hanging, Antlers, Elk, Blacktail Deer, Entwined, Tapered Rawhide Shade, 63 x 22 In.	554.00
Electric, Hanging, Art Deco, Bronze Overlay, 8 Zigzag Panels, White Glass, Tapered, 38 In.	2360.00
Electric, Hanging, Art Deco, Marble Bowl, 4 Chains, 17 ½ x 6 ½ In.	127.00
Electric, Hanging, Art Deco, School House, Brass, Glass, 28 x 9 In.	69.00
Electric, Hanging, Billiard, 2-Light, Milk Glass Globe, Green Shade, 41 x 46 In.	180.00
Electric, Hanging, Brass, Pierced, Scalloped Edge, Fringe, c.1870, 7 x 16 In.	92.00
Electric, Hanging, C. & H. Greene, Bronze, Glass, Linen, Rectangular, 1907, 26 ½ x 14 In.	21080.00
Electric, Hanging, G. Nelson, Ball, Sticker, Herman Miller	384.00
Electric, Hanging, G. Nelson, Bubble, Mottled, Lobed, Pull Cord, Howard Miller, c.1948, 7 x 18 In.	370.00
Electric, Hanging, Gino Sarfatti, Brass, Tubes, Nested, Italy, 1960s, 32 x 25 In.	2726.00
Electric, Hanging, Killark, Steel Cage, Teardrop Globe, Industrial, c.1950, 12 x 8 In.	195.00
Electric, Hanging, Louis XVI Style, Brass, Etched Glass Panels, Flowers, 39 x 15 In., Pair	1434.00
Electric, Hanging, Poul Henningsen, Artichoke, Enameled Aluminum, 1958, 24 In.	4148.00
Electric, Hanging, Pressed Bouquets, Tin, Black, Frosted Hanging Amber Panes, 15 x 13 ½ In.	259.00
Electric, Hanging, Slag Glass, Caramel, Tile Panels, Multicolor, Fruit, 16 ½ x 22 In.	288.00
Electric, Hanging, Tobia Scarpa, Nictea, Brass, Glass, Flos, Italy, 1961, 12 x 19 In. *illus*	1500.00
Electric, Hanging, Vistosi, Glass Loops, Matte Chromed Steel, Italy, 1960s, 24 ½ x 34 In. *illus*	3224.00
Electric, Hula Dancer, Figural, Countertop	440.00
Electric, Iron, Bridge Arm, White Paint, Blown-Out Grape Shade, c.1920, 58 x 17 In.	58.00
Electric, J. Royere, Persane, Gilt Wrought Iron, Vellum Shades, France, 1950s, 72 x 21 In.	14880.00
Electric, James Mont, Camouflage, Gold, Bronze, Silver Leaf, Shade, 1950s, 41 x 20 In., Pair *illus*	1488.00
Electric, Jean De Bro, Glass Tube Column, Iron Base, 68 x 19 In., Pair	1046.00
Electric, Jefferson, Reverse Painted Shade, Hollyhocks, 2-Socket Hexagonal Base, 18 In.	3245.00
Electric, Jefferson, Reverse Painted, Scenic, Woodland Sunset, Baluster Standard, 22 In.	948.00
Electric, Karl Kipp, Copper, Leaded Glass, 16 x 10 In. *illus*	26040.00
Electric, L. Sullivan, Bronze, Adjustable Arm, Square Base, Suspended Glass Shade, c.1908, 17 ½ In.	5676.00
Electric, Lampada, Silver, 2 Sections, Oval, Copper Liner, Cross Finial, Greece, 1900s, 9 In.	444.00

Electric, Leaded Glass Shade, Blue, Green & Lavender Panels, Metal Frame, 28 In.	2000.00
Electric, Leaded Glass Shade, Flowers, Scalloped Edge, Bronze Standard, 23 ½ In. ....*illus*	4425.00
Electric, Leaded Glass Shade, Geometric, Multicolor, Bronze Leaf Base, Wilkinson, 18 x 24 In.	2070.00
Electric, Leaded Glass Shade, Poinsettia, Attributed To Unique Art Glass & Metal Co., 24 In. ....*illus*	3565.00
Electric, Leaded Glass Shade, Wisteria, Purple, Green, Caramel Glass Brickwork, Brass Base, 70 In.	7375.00
Electric, Leaded Glass, Green & Amber, Lily, Bronze Tree Trunk Base, 21 In...........................	1020.00
Electric, Leaded Glass, Hibiscus, Pink, Green, Ribbed Stem, Stepped Square Base, 31 In.	6785.00
Electric, Leaded Glass, Pink Hollyhocks, Leaves, Caramel Ground, Domed, Reeded Base, 31 In.	1265.00
Electric, Leaded Slag Glass, Yellow Flowers, Bronze Base, Suess, 7 ¼ x 24 In. ....*illus*	8680.00
Electric, Leather Covered Shaft, Tripod Base, Upturned Milky Shade, c.1940, 69 ½ In.	861.00
Electric, Lightolier, Frosted Glass, Egg Shape, Steel Base, Painted, 18 ½ x 15 In.....................	527.00
Electric, Limbert, Caramel Slag Glass, Hammered Copper, 60 x 25 In. ....*illus*	10540.00
Electric, Lucite, 4 Tapered Panels, Brass Knobs, Tapered Shade, 28 ½ In.	119.00
Electric, Luminaire, Fan, Cast Metal, c.1910, 59 In. ....*illus*	813.00
Electric, M.D. Lucchi Tolomeo, Aluminum, Adjustable, White Shade, Artemide, 70 x 90 In.....	780.00
Electric, Marble, Campana Shape, Turned Support, Round Base, 20 In.	325.00
Electric, Marcello Fantoni, Pottery, Glazed, Brass Shaft, Wood Base, Shade, 1960s, 38 x 21 In., Pair	1860.00
Electric, Max Bill, Aluminum, Enameled, Flaring Shade, Round Foot, 1960s, 65 x 11 In., Pair	1984.00
Electric, Metal, Blue Glass, c.1960, 41 x 14 In.	71.00
Electric, Metal, Circle Pattern Base, c.1960, 64 ½ x 14 In.	584.00
Electric, Metal, Scroll, Openwork, Wood, Marble Plinth, Cream Shade, 39 x 10 In., Pair.........	183.00
Electric, Miller, Reverse Painted, Landscape, Sheep, Bronze Base, Flowers, c.1910, 22 ½ In. *illus*	1645.00
Electric, Moe Bridges, Reverse Painted, Scenic, Lake At Sunset, Orange, Flower Foot, 21 In....	2065.00
Electric, Mosaic Glass, Pink Blossoms, Green Leaves, Blue Ground, Tree Trunk Base, 23 In....	1715.00
Electric, Murano Glass, Globe, Clear Center Band, Metal Base, Italy, 15 x 15 In.	480.00
Electric, Murano Glass, Green, Faceted, White Drum Shade, 7 x 15 In., Pair	4800.00
Electric, Oak & Walnut, Bulbous Standard, Barley Twist Support, Bun Feet, c.1905, 62 In.	338.00
Electric, Oak, Art Glass Shade, Inlaid, Geometric, Aurora Studio, 61 ½ In.	1092.00
Electric, Oggetti, Black Glass, Gold Inclusions, Frosted Glass Shade, Brass Rods, 16 x 22 In.....	240.00
Electric, Opalescent Glass, Black Enamel Base, 20 ½ x 19 ½ In..	1054.00
Electric, P. Henningsen, PH3, White Enameled Aluminum, Louis Poulsen, 1980s, 6 x 16 In., 4 Piece	1054.00
Electric, P. Henningsen, Snowball, Hanging, Enameled Metal, Louis Poulsen, 1960s, 15 x 17 In.	1364.00
Electric, Pagoda, Enameled, Fruited Vines, Pierced Medallions, Chinese, 16 x 8 In.	104.00
Electric, Parking Meter, Duncan Miller, 29 In...	354.00
Electric, Parrot, Glass, Multicolor, Base, 13 ¼ In.	113.00
Electric, Parzinger, Fluted Standard, Brass Balls, Fabric Shade, c.1962, 72 In., Pair ....*illus*	11025.00
Electric, Pendant, Bronze, Stained Glass, National Farmer's Bank, L. Sullivan, c.1908, 23 x 8 In.	13145.00
Electric, Pendant, Massimo Vignelli, Blown Glass, Single Sockets, Venini, 14 x 6 In., 3 Piece..	4650.00
Electric, Pendant, Robert Sonneman, Chrome, Brass, 1970s, 26 x 11 ½ In............................	1116.00
Electric, Phoenix Glass, Katydid, Brown, Etched, White Shade, c.1930, 7 In...........................	123.00
Electric, Pittsburgh Lamp Co., Call Of The Wild, Woodland Lake, Teepee, Leafy Gourd Base, 18 In.	2950.00
Electric, Pittsburgh Lamp Co., Reverse Painted Shade, Winter Woodland, Prisms, 26 In.	944.00
Electric, Pittsburgh Lamp Co., Reverse Painted, River Scene, Gilt Brass Base, c.1910, 10 In. *illus*	1298.00
Electric, Pole, P. Evans, Steel, Multicolor, Silk Shade, 1966, 94 x 14 ½ In. ....*illus*	6820.00
Electric, Porcelain, Painted, Landscape, Cobalt Ground, Gilt, L. Morin, Sevres, c.1900, 19 In., Pair.	748.00
Electric, Porcelain, Sang De Boeuf Glaze, Bean Jar, Brass Fittings, Chinese, c.1920, 9 In........	3600.00
Electric, Porcelain, Woman, Man, 18th Century, Pleated Shade, D. Polouitoto, Italy, 47 x 23 In., Pair.	345.00
Electric, Porcelli Studios, Leaded Glass, Orchid Bouquet, Green, Metal Base, 22 x 30 In..........	16100.00
Electric, Prairie School, Oak, Tapered Buttress Base, Flared Slag Glass Shade, 23 x 15 In.	806.00
Electric, R. Sonneman, Chrome Ball Shade, Black Cast Iron, Adjustable, 1960s, 26 x 5 ¾ In..	500.00
Electric, R. Sonneman, Chrome Supports, White Enamel Shade, 1960s, 58 x 14 In................	600.00
Electric, Radio, Rocket Shape, Lighted Dial, Lumitone Mfg. Co., 1940s, 16 In.	175.00
Electric, Reverse Painted Shape, Winter Landscape, Brass Lyre Base, Lightolier Co., 14 x 22 In.	633.00
Electric, Reverse Painted, Winter Landscape, Lighted Metal Base, Pittsburgh Lamp Co., 23 x 19 In.	268.00
Electric, Robertson, Pottery, Glazed, Leaded Slag Glass Butterflies, F.H.R., 15 x 12 In. ....*illus*	28520.00
Electric, Rococo Style, Lantern, Gilt, Paint, Dome Top, Scrolling, Italy, Early 1900s, 23 In......	764.00
Electric, Rococo, Gilt, Patinated Brass, 2 Scroll Arms, Leaf Feet, Shade, c.1930, 64 In..............	633.00
Electric, Rose Medallion, Urn, Lid, Round Base, Cream Shade...	90.00
Electric, Sconce, Venini, Etched Glass Discs, Brass Mount, 1950s, 7 x 13 In., Pair	434.00
Electric, Silvered Glass, Metal, Rocket Shape, Red, Amber Star Base, Eng., 1950s, 10 x 5 ½ In.	500.00
Electric, Slag Glass, Filigree Overlay, Illuminated Base, c.1910, 21 ½ In. ....*illus*	522.00
Electric, Spelter, Cold Painted, Arab Man, Seat, Smoking Pipe, Austria, c.1890, 13 x 6 In. .....*illus*	764.00
Electric, Spiral Staircase, Fluted Columns, Metal Base, Penshell Dome Shade, 32 x 18 In.......	1500.00
Electric, Stain Glass Flower Shade, Metal Twist Standard, Onyx Base, 64 ½ x 11 In................	374.00
Electric, Student, Green Damascene Shades, Bronze Canister, Coil Base, c.1900, 29 ½ In. ......*illus*	7703.00
Electric, Suess, Leaded Glass Shade, Bronze Base, Parasol, 3 Sockets, 22 In. ....*illus*	2588.00

Lamp, Electric, Hanging, Vistosi, Glass Loops, Matte Chromed Steel, Italy, 1960s, 24 ½ x 34 In.
$3224.00

Rago Arts & Auction Center

Lamp, Electric, James Mont, Camouflage, Gold, Bronze, Silver Leaf, Shade, 1950s, 41 x 20 In., Pair
$1488.00

Rago Arts & Auction Center

Lamp, Electric, Karl Kipp, Copper, Leaded Glass, 16 x 10 In.
$26040.00

Rago Arts & Auction Center

L

Lamp, Electric, Leaded Glass Shade, Flowers, Scalloped Edge, Bronze Standard, 23 ½ In.
$4425.00

Ivey-Selkirk Auctioneers

Lamp, Electric, Leaded Glass Shade, Poinsettia, Attributed To Unique Art Glass & Metal Co., 24 In.
$3565.00

James D. Julia Inc.

Lamp, Electric, Leaded Slag Glass, Yellow Flowers, Bronze Base, Suess, 7 ¼ x 24 In.
$8680.00

Rago Arts & Auction Center

Electric, Suess, Leaded Glass Shade, Tulips, Caramel Glass Border, Metal Base, 20 x 24 In.	5175.00
Electric, Terra-Cotta, Nude, Buildings, Pedestal, Animals, Fritz Albert, c.1920, 13 x 11 In.	3900.00
Electric, Turquoise Opaline Glass, Gilt Bronze, Ormolu, Swag Handles, Laurel Wreath, 32 x 13 In.	449.00
Electric, Tusk, Ivory, Round Black Base, 12 ½ In.	640.00
Electric, Umbrella Shade, Leaded Glass Panels, Mottled Metal Base, Gorham, 16 x 21 In.	1840.00
Electric, Unique Art Glass & Metal Co., Leaded Glass, Periwinkle, Metal Base, 22 x 31 In.	4600.00
Electric, Victorian Style, Chrome, Brass, Glass Chimney, Shade, c.1960, 33 x 10 In.	495.00
Electric, W. Haines, Celadon, Urn Shape, 2 Handles, Cylindrical Shade, c.1948, 29 x 11 In., Pair	813.00
Electric, W. Haines, Figural, Bird, Green Parrot, Perched, Ceramic, Round Base, c.1948, 27 In., Pair	2500.00
Electric, W. Haines, Urn, Glazed Composition & Wood Pedestal, c.1948, 69 In., Pair	5000.00
Electric, W. Von Nessen, Brass, Adjustable Arm, 22 x 26 In.	510.00
Electric, W. Von Nessen, Brass, Counter Weight, Lucite Diffuser, Adjustable, 52 ½ In.	1140.00
Electric, W. Von Nessen, Brushed Aluminum, Spaced Discs, Mica Shade, 1935-40, 21 In. ....*illus*	2820.00
Electric, W. Von Nessen, Marble Base, Rectangular, Metal Support, Tapered Shade, 29 In., Pair.	237.00
Electric, Wall, Baluster, Green Paint, Gilt Band, Bell Shades, 28 In., Pair	246.00
Electric, Wall, Brass, Satin Finish, Round, Pierced, Mirror, 26 In.	369.00
Electric, Wall, Sheet Iron, Painted Black, Trapezoidal Beveled Panes, 14 In., Pair	47.00
Electric, Walnut Shaft, Stepped Base, Studio, 69 x 20 In.	527.00
Electric, Wilkinson, Trumpet Vine Shade, Black Metal Base, Impressed Shells, 21 ½ In. ....*illus*	5750.00
Fairy, Diamond Quilted, Blue, Domed, Frosted, Dish, Ruffled Edge, American Glass, 1880s, 4 ¾ In.	89.00
Fat, Brass, Copper, Iron, Gimbaled, Painted, c.1840, 7 ½ In.	385.00
Fat, Brass, Wrought Iron, Hanger, Peter Derr, Pennsylvania, 1856, 5 ½ In.	3081.00
Fat, Copper, Iron, Stamped, Peter Derr, Pennsylvania, 1842, 5 ¼ In.	4029.00
Fat, Copper, Iron, Turned Gilt & Stand, Penn., c.1835, 14 In.	593.00
Fat, Copper, Wrought Iron, Stamped, Peter Derr, 1849, Pennsylvania, 5 ½ In.	4266.00
Fat, Redware, Berks Co., Pennsylvania, 1800s, 7 In.	3081.00
Fat, Sheet Brass, 2 Opposing Wicks, Lidded Canister, Footed, 2 Troughs, Handle, 7 x 10 In.	83.00
Fat, Tin, Pennsylvania, 1800s, 18 In.	1304.00
Fat, Tinned Sheet Iron, Open Canister, Brass Wick Holder, Loop Handle, 8 x 7 In.	106.00
Fluid, Overlay Glass, Amethyst, Pear Shape, Brass Shaft, Square Marble Base, 1800s, 11 In.	563.00
Fluid, Overlay Glass, Blue, Brass Standard, Marble Base, Glass Font, Eagle Burner, c.1870, 11 In.	489.00
Gas, Chandelier, 2-Light, Pulls Down, Cast Bronze, Faces, Wreaths, Chains, Prisms, 1880, 46 x 34 In.	1150.00
Gas, Chandelier, 8-Light, Gilt Bronze, Scrolls, Swans, Leaves, France, 1800s, 53 x 29 In.	4320.00
Gas, Shade, Pink Swirl, Pinched Edge, c.1880, 5 ½ x 7 ½ In.	92.00
Gasolier, 6-Light, Rococo Revival Style, Lacquered Brass, Etched Glass Globes, 67 x 35 In.	3936.00
Grease, Redware, Albany Slip Glaze, 2 Spouts, Saucer Base, Handle, S. Routson, 7 In.	353.00
Grease, Redware, Albany Slip Glaze, 2 Spouts, Saucer Base, Handle, S. Routson, c.1840, 6 In.	588.00
Handel lamps are included in the Handel category.	
Kerosene, Adlams Burner, Monitor, String Wick Lip, Ring Handle, 1862, 2 ½ In.	633.00
Kerosene, Banquet, Dietz, Pink Opaline, Paneled, Pear-Shaped Font, Gilt, Marble Base, 24 ¾ In.	2990.00
Kerosene, Bear Paw, Opaque White Cut To Cranberry Pear-Shaped Font, Brass, Marble, 19 ¾ In.	9200.00
Kerosene, Bethesda Under Glass, Periwinkle Blue, Brass, Scalloped Chimney, 10 In.	863.00
Kerosene, Blue Opalescent Glass, Enamel Flowers, Gold Coralene, Melon Ribbed, 4 ½ In.	40.00
Kerosene, Blue Satin Glass, Diamond Quilted, Clear Ruffled Shade, 10 In.	300.00
Kerosene, Brass, Patinated Zinc, Column, Putti Masks, Glass Font, Globe, c.1850, 23 x 7 In., Pair.	717.00
Kerosene, Bulging Loop, Opaque White, Gilt, Orange Enamel Band, Brass, c.1860, 9 In.	403.00
Kerosene, Cahoon Burner, Cottage Dirigo, Swirled Ribs, Ring Handle, Lip Chimney, 3 ½ In.	259.00
Kerosene, Cinnabar, Circular Panels, Peonies, 19th Century, 10 ½ In.	300.00
Kerosene, Cut Glass, Blue To White To Clear, Bands Of Ovals, White 8-Sided Base, 13 In.	518.00
Kerosene, Cut Glass, Blue To White, Star, Flower & Punty, Brass & Marble Stand, 12 In.	690.00
Kerosene, Cut Glass, Green To Clear, Geometric, Punty & Oval Cuttings, Brass Stem, 13 In.	633.00
Kerosene, Cut Glass, Luster Form, Faceted Shaft, Scalloped Bobeche, Spear Prisms, 29 In., Pair	246.00
Kerosene, Dietz, Lighthouse No. 1 Lip Burner, 2 Arms, Finger, Ripley & Co., 3 x 3 In.	1150.00
Kerosene, Finger, Banded Font, Applied Handle, Footed, Dillaway Patent, c.1870, 5 ¼ In.	374.00
Kerosene, Finger, Opalescents, Font, Clear Foot & Handle, 6 ½ In.	181.00
Kerosene, Finger, Petal Rim, Applied Handle, Thumbrest, Dillaway Patent, 1876, 3 x 4 In.	150.00
Kerosene, Finger, Vines, Stippled, Taplin-Brown Collar, Slip Chimney, Ripley, 5 x 3 ¾ In.	259.99
Kerosene, Glass, Ribbed, Pink Tint, Applied Handle, Star Mark On Thumbwheel, 3 x 2 ¾ In.	92.00
Kerosene, Gone With The Wind, Glass, Pink Roses, Brass Font & Burner, 26 ½ In. ....*illus*	295.00
Kerosene, Gone With The Wind, Pink & White Flowers, Shaded Green, Ball Shade, 19 ½ In.	192.00
Kerosene, Gone With The Wind, White Globe, Flowers Bands, Bronze Base, Medallions, 23 In.	354.00
Kerosene, Gone With The Wind, Yellow, White Chrysanthemums, Ball Shade, 23 In.	181.00
Kerosene, L'Ange Guardien, Cobalt, Beehive Chimney, Handle, String Burner, 5 x 2 ½ In.	184.00
Kerosene, Latticinio Font, Blue & White Stripes, Pear Shape, Brass & Marble Base, 10 In.	978.00
Kerosene, Latticinio Font, Green Cut To Clear, Punty Stem, Pear-Shaped Font, 10 In.	2185.00
Kerosene, Little Favorite Improved, Star On Base, Applied Handle, Opaque White Shade, 4 ¾ In.	92.00

Lamp, Electric, Limbert, Caramel Slag Glass, Hammered Copper, 60 x 25 In. $10540.00

Lamp, Electric, Luminaire, Fan, Cast Metal, c.1910, 59 In. $813.00

Lamp, Electric, Miller, Reverse Painted, Landscape, Sheep, Bronze Base, Flowers, c.1910, 22 ½ In. $1645.00

Lamp, Electric, Pittsburgh Lamp Co., Reverse Painted, River Scene, Textured, Gilt Brass Base, c.1910, 10 In. $1298.00

Lamp, Electric, Pole, P. Evans, Steel, Multicolor, Silk Shade, 1966, 94 x 14 ½ In. $6820.00

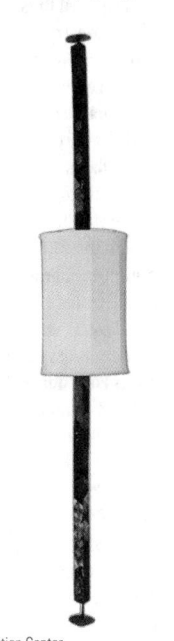

Lamp, Electric, Robertson, Pottery Glazed, Leaded Slag Glass Butterflies, F.H.R., 15 x 12 In. $28520.00

Lamp, Electric, Slag Glass, Filigree Overlay, Illuminated Base, c.1910, 21 ½ In. $522.00

Lamp, Electric, Spelter, Cold Painted, Arab Man, Seat, Smoking Pipe, Austria, c.1890, 13 x 6 In. $764.00

L

Lamp, Electric, Student, Green Damascene Shades, Bronze Canister, Coil Base, c.1900, 29 ½ In.
$7703.00

Skinner, Inc.

Lamp, Electric, Suess, Leaded Glass Shade, Bronze Base, Parasol, 3 Sockets, 22 In.
$2588.00

James D. Julia Inc.

Lamp, Electric, Parzinger, Fluted Standard, Brass Balls, Fabric Shade, c.1962, 72 In., Pair
$11025.00

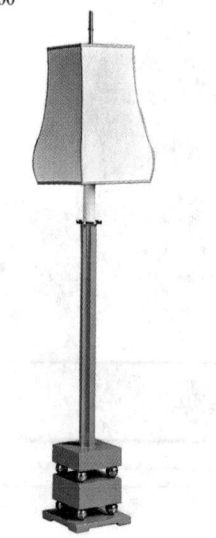

Skinner, Inc.

Kerosene, Milk Glass, Artichoke, Lavender & Green Accents, Ribbed Base, 9 ¾ In. ....*illus*	177.00
Kerosene, Paneled Spears Under Glass, Clear Font, White Base, Brass, Slip Burner, 10 In.	805.00
Kerosene, Piano, Brass, Milk Glass Shade, Ostrich Feet, Adjustable, 64 To 81 In. ....*illus*	403.00
Kerosene, Porcelain, Milk Glass, Puttie, Gold, Importe All Allf Magne HS Burner, 13 In. *illus*	148.00
Kerosene, Pressed & Cut Glass, Brass Burner, New England Glass Co., 12 x 3 ½ In.	531.00
Kerosene, Pressed Glass, Atterbury Loop, Opaque Lavender, Brass Collar, Petal Rim, 8 ¼ In...	460.00
Kerosene, Pressed Glass, Clambroth Font, Gem Base, Drummond Burner, 10 ¼ In.	575.00
Kerosene, Pressed Glass, Flame Bull's-Eye, Clear Font, Translucent Base, E.F. Jones Burner, 9 ¾ In. ..	460.00
Kerosene, Pressed Glass, Moorish Windows, White To Yellow, Black Baroque Base, 12 In.	1955.00
Kerosene, Pressed Glass, Prism With Diamond Point, Marbled Teal Base, Brass Collar, 9 x 3 ¾ In.	633.00
Kerosene, Pressed Glass, Reeded Oval, Green, White Threads, Opaque White Base, 8 ½ In.	863.00
Kerosene, Pressed Glass, Ring Punty, Yellow Font, Black, Brass Connector, 8 ⅜ In................	863.00
Kerosene, Pressed Glass, Shield & Star, Turquoise Baroque, Brass, Merrill's Patent, 8 ¾ In.....	374.00
Kerosene, Pressed Glass, Triple Flute & Bar, Clear, Fluted Green Alabaster Base, 13 In.	230.00
Kerosene, Pressed Glass, Tulip & Star, Fiery Opalescent, Cobalt Blue, Brass Burner, 18 In......	5463.00
Kerosene, Satin Glass Shade & Base, Yellow Cased, Bulbous Swirls, 8 x 5 In................	295.00
Kerosene, Scallop & Fan, Engraved Flowers, Mottled Blue, Baroque Base, Brass, 12 In...........	345.00
Kerosene, Student, Brass, Shade Ring, Green & White Cased Glass Shade, c.1884, 22 ½ In.....	295.00
Kerosene, Student, Double, Brass, Cylinder Font, Opaque Glass Shades, c.1890, 30 x 28 In.....	700.00
Kerosene, Washington Cutting, Quatrefoils, Amethyst To Clear, Brass, Marble, 11 ½ In...........	3450.00
Lard, Sheet Iron, Rectangular Tube, Strap Handle, Saucer Base, 2 Wicks, 7 In.	58.00
Lard, Tinned Sheet Iron, Oval Font, Wick Holder, Brass Cap & Vent Tube, 6 ¼ x 6 ½ In.	118.00
Lard, Tinned Sheet Iron, Oval Font, Wick Holder, Kinnear Patent, 6 ½ In........	30.00
Oil, 2-Light, Brass, Pink Cased Ribbed Shades, 2 Milk Glass Fonts, Adjustable, 21 In..........	565.00
Oil, Blown Glass Font, Knopped Stem Leaf Base, 7 ¼ In.........	863.00
Oil, Blown Glass, Bulbous Top, Faceted Stem, 11 ½ x 5 In., Pair.........	805.00
Oil, Blue Glass Cut To Clear, Grapes, Leaves, Ovals, Inverted Pear Shape, Marble Base, 14 In. ...	90.00
Oil, Brass, Globe, Prism Ring, Boy On Triangular Base, Cornelius & Baker, c.1845, 32 x 9 ½ In.	1586.00
Oil, Carcel, Louis Philippe Style, Gilt Bronze, Glass Globe, Chimney, Pump, Marked, 27 In....	610.00
Oil, Copper, Iron Handle, Double Wick, 3 x 3 ¼ In.................	45.00
Oil, Cranberry Opalescent Spatter Glass, Redware Base, White Lobed Shade, Ruffled, 23 In.	432.00
Oil, Cut Glass, Butterfly & Pinwheel, Tapered, Duplex Burner, Globe Shade, 32 In...........	9775.00
Oil, Czech Glass, Alternating White & Blue, Red Flowers, Embossed Base, 19 In............	200.00
Oil, Egret, Standing On 1 Leg, Majolica............	1298.00
Oil, Etched Glass Shade, Boy Standard, Star & Snowflake Prisms, Marble Base, c.1850, 22 In.	800.00
Oil, Figural, 3-Light, Maiden Holding Urn, Metal Chains, Marble Base, 19 x 4 ½ In., Pair.......	288.00
Oil, Fostoria, Blue Opaque Glass, Flowers On Lattice Work, Relief, Brass Burner, 4 In..............	45.00
Oil, Globe, Brass, Hinged, Pierced, Flowers, Bird Engraved, 5 In.	316.00
Oil, Gothic Revival, Glass, White, Enamel Overlay, Palmer Patent, Electrified, c.1850, 32 In. *illus*	3198.00
Oil, Green Opaque Glass, Leaves, Flowers, Beaded Rim, Loop Handle, 4 ¼ In...........	34.00
Oil, Hanging, Cranberry Opalescent Swirl, Font, Embossed Brass, Prisms, 20 In. ....*illus*	863.00
Oil, Hanging, Gilt & Lacquered Brass, Etched Glass Shade, 3 Chains, 1800s, 25 x 6 ½ In.	837.00
Oil, Hurricane Shade, Cranberry Glass, Etched Vignettes, Flared, Brass Base, 16 x 4 In., Pair ..	123.00
Oil, Kettle, Brass, Wrought Iron, Stamped, Peter Derr 1837, Berks Co., Penn., 10 ½ In.	11850.00
Oil, Milk Glass, Clematis Leaves, Stippled Ground, C Scrolls, 13 x 8 In.	28.00
Oil, Milk Glass, Flowers, Painted, Loop Handle, 3 In.	17.00
Oil, Miner's, Round, Heart Cover, Thumbscrew, Cast Iron, 1800s, 17 x 5 In.	198.00
Oil, Opalescent Glass, Bulbous, Pinched Foot, 4 In..............	57.00
Oil, Peg, Candlestick, Brass, Convex Saucer, Raised Rim, 3-Footed, 7 In.	83.00
Oil, Peg, Candlestick, Pewter, Tubular Brass Burner, Victor, 9 ¾ x 22 In., Pair............	472.00
Oil, Peg, Clear Cut, Diamonds, Ribs, Oval, Single Tube Burner, c.1830, 4 In.	1035.00
Oil, Peg, Rainbow Satin Glass, Brass, 11 In. ....*illus*	1438.00
Oil, Peg, Yellow Glass Globe Font & Base, Brass Mount, Paw Feet, P & A Mfg. Co., 20 In.	531.00
Oil, Porcelain, Green Glaze, Cylindrical, Geometric Design, 4 x 4 In.	150.00
Oil, Pottery Stem, Flowers, Brass Burner, 1880s, 22 ¼ In.............	225.00
Oil, Pressed Glass, Clear Font, Tapered, Cup Plate Base, 6 In.............	345.00
Oil, Pressed Glass, Daisy & Sunburst, Blue Stepped Base, Clear Font, 10 In.............	136.00
Oil, Pressed Glass, Fluted Font, Jade Green Hexagonal Base, Brass Collar & Burner, 4 In.	269.00
Oil, Pressed Glass, Opaque Robin's-Egg Blue, Hexagonal Font & Base, 4 In........................	211.00
Oil, Rainbow Mother-Of-Pearl, Ruffled Rim, Clear Rigaree Collar, Foot, 10 In. ....*illus*	6670.00
Oil, Redware, Pennsylvania, 1800s, 2 ½ x 7 In.	948.00
Oil, Ruby Satin Glass, Beaded Drape, Brass Base, Ball Shade, Oval Bottom, 25 In., Pair..........	920.00
Oil, Skull Font, Burner, Silvered Metal, Bronze Bone-Form Shaft, Resin Grip, 9 In.	1348.00
Oil, Triple Stem & Feathered Arches, Flange Burner, Frosted, Findlay, c.1900	200.00
Pairpoint lamps are in the Pairpoint category.	

L

Sconce, 1-Light, Bronze, Sunburst, Wall, 17 x 19 x 8 ½ In.	90.00
Sconce, 1-Light, Figural, Parcel Gilt, Putto, Holding Candle Arm, 11 In., Pair	458.00
Sconce, 2 Scrolled Arms, Center Torch, Flowers, France, c.1900, 18 ½ In.	889.00
Sconce, 2-Arm, Brass, Etched, Hurricane Shade, Applied Blue Rim, c.1850, 15 In., Pair	705.00
Sconce, 2-Light, Art Deco, Cast Metal, Running Deer, Electrified, 10 x 9 ½ In., Pair	295.00
Sconce, 2-Light, Bague, Gilt Bronze, Porcelain, Famille Verte, Flowers, Flattened Urn, 15 In., Pair	1625.00
Sconce, 2-Light, Brass, Round Backplate, Scrolled Candle Arms, Prisms, 13 In., Pair	122.00
Sconce, 2-Light, Bronze Dore, Porcelain, Guanyin, Wheat, Ribbon, Scrolled Arms, 1900s, 24 In., Pair	448.00
Sconce, 2-Light, Bronze, Inset Transfer Porcelain Plate, Ribbon Top, France, 31 x 12 In., Pair	518.00
Sconce, 2-Light, Bronze, Lyre Shape, Feather Finial, c.1940, 21 x 10 In., Pair	738.00
Sconce, 2-Light, Bronze, Lyre Shape, Palmette Crest, Masks, Scrolled Arms, 1800s, 20 x 12 In., Pair	1434.00
Sconce, 2-Light, Bronze, Putto, Seated, Holding Stem Candle Arms, Garlands, c.1900, 17 In., Pair	3851.00
Sconce, 2-Light, Empire Style, Gilt Bronze, Oval Leaf, Patinated Arms, 7 ½ x 8 In., Pair	878.00
Sconce, 2-Light, Empire Style, Gilt, Woman Holding Sockets, Leaves, Scrolls, 21 x 6 In., Pair	375.00
Sconce, 2-Light, French Style, Brass, 12 x 11 In., Pair	120.00
Sconce, 2-Light, Gilt Brass, Bronze, Ribboned Back, Leaf, Horn Arms, France, 17 x 9 In., Pair	738.00
Sconce, 2-Light, Gilt Brass, Empire Style, Woman, Standing, Globe, 23 x 14 In., Pair	420.00
Sconce, 2-Light, Gilt Brass, Glass, Etched Fruit & Leaves, Czechoslovakia, 15 x 10 In., Pair	553.00
Sconce, 2-Light, Gilt Bronze, Anthemion Backplate, Scrolled Arms, Swags, Pendants, 18 x 12 In.	738.00
Sconce, 2-Light, Gilt Bronze, Classical Woman, Obelisk, Mahogany Mount, France, c.1875, 32 In.	1180.00
Sconce, 2-Light, Gilt Bronze, Scrolled, Tapered, Reeded, France, c.1910, 20 In., Pair	531.00
Sconce, 2-Light, Gilt Bronze, Urn Shaped Back Plate, c.1940, 16 x 11 In., Pair	492.00
Sconce, 2-Light, Gilt Metal, Leaf Shaped Arms, Hanging Prisms, 17 x 12 In., Pair	246.00
Sconce, 2-Light, Gilt Metal, Pierced Back Panel, Cylindrical Arms, E.F. Caldwell, 11 x 10 In., Pair	4387.00
Sconce, 2-Light, Gilt, Rectangular, Mirror, Leaf Crest, Glass Prisms, France, 21 In., Pair	100.00
Sconce, 2-Light, Giltwood, Mirror, Leaf & Flower Border, Italy, c.1890, 27 In.	711.00
Sconce, 2-Light, Glass, Metal, Louis XVI Style, Birds, Leaves, Scroll, 20 x 11 In.	3936.00
Sconce, 2-Light, Louis XVI Style, Tassel, Ribbon, ScrollLeaves, Ram's Head, 21 x 10 In., Pair	531.00
Sconce, 2-Light, Louis XVI Style, Woman, Rose Wreath, Scrolling Leaves, Gilt, 20 x 15 In., Pair	3438.00
Sconce, 2-Light, Neoclassical, Gilt, Wheat Sheaves, Italy, c.1900, 28 In., Pair	4230.00
Sconce, 2-Light, Neoclassical, Giltwood, Oval Medallion, Dancing Muse, 12 ½ In.	199.00
Sconce, 2-Light, Regency Style, Giltwood, Convex Mirror, Fleur-De-Lis, Eagle, 1900, 39 In.	178.00
Sconce, 2-Light, Silver Plate, Mirror, Pillar, Lion's Head, Paws Supports, 19 x 13 In., Pair	770.00
Sconce, 2-Light, Silver, Flowers & Grapes, 15 x 12 In., Pair	123.00
Sconce, 2-Light, Silver, Stepped, Shaped Mirror, Portugal, 1700s, 16 x 7 In., Pair	7998.00
Sconce, 2-Light, Tole, Painted, Mirror, Scrolls, 1950s, 28 x 14 In.	250.00
Sconce, 2-Light, Wood, Carved, Pierced, Flower Basket, Leaves, Scrolled Arms, Italy, 20 In., Pair	279.00
Sconce, 2-Light, Wrought Iron, Steel, Blown Glass Hurricane Shades, 24 x 23 In., Pair	1230.00
Sconce, 3-Light, Brass, Mirrored Shaped Back, Mask Designs, Prisms, 16 x 10 In., Pair	119.00
Sconce, 3-Light, E. Mottheau, Gilt Bronze, Paris, c.1900, 25 In., Pair	4025.00
Sconce, 3-Light, Empire Style, Bronze, Cone Shape, Scrolled Leaf Arms, 17 x 11 In., Pair	125.00
Sconce, 3-Light, Empire, Gilt Bronze, Pierced, Leaf Back, Cherub, Patinated, 13 x 7 ½ In.	1638.00
Sconce, 3-Light, Gilt Brass, Scrolled Branch Arms, 18 x 6 ½ In., Pair	183.00
Sconce, 3-Light, Gilt Bronze, Black Lion Mask Mounts, Oval, France, 1900s, 9 ¼ In., Pair	593.00
Sconce, 3-Light, Gilt Bronze, Grotesque Mask, Blossoms, Prisms, Electrified, France, 27 In.	259.00
Sconce, 3-Light, Gilt Metal, Mirror Back, Crystal Drops, 30 x 22 In., Pair	984.00
Sconce, 3-Light, Louis XVI Style, Acanthus Leaves, Scrolls, Painted, Italy, 1900s, 24 In.	767.00
Sconce, 3-Light, Louis XVI Style, Gilt, Tassel, Trumpet Arms, Acorns, Leaves, 38 x 23 In.	1375.00
Sconce, 3-Light, Maison Bagues, Gilt Bronze, Ribbon & Tassel, Leaves, c.1880, 30 x 12 In.	2390.00
Sconce, 3-Light, Metal, Lemon Branch Shape, c.1950, 22 x 10 In., Pair	338.00
Sconce, 3-Light, Neoclassical, Strings Of Glass Prisms, Amber, Hanging, 22 x 17 In., Pair	1045.00
Sconce, 3-Light, Silver, Repousse Flowers, Sheffield, 11 ½ x 7 ¾ In., Pair	431.00
Sconce, 3-Light, Tin, Punched Circle Over Oval, Flowers, Reeded Rim, 1900s, 12 x 9 In., Pair	178.00
Sconce, 3-Light, Wrought Iron, Vertebrae Scrolls, c.1940, 34 x 12 In., Pair	523.00
Sconce, 4-Light, Charles X Style, Arrow Quiver, Mask Head, C-Scroll Arms, 16 x 14 In., Pair	1170.00
Sconce, 4-Light, Charles X Style, Medallion, Flame Finial, Greek Key Arm, 13 x 14 In., Pair	1845.00
Sconce, 4-Light, Empire Style, Brass, Sunburst, Woman's Head, Lion's Head, Electrified, 25 In.	1840.00
Sconce, 4-Light, Empire Style, Bronze, Winged Maidens, Scrolled Leaf Tip Arms, 20 In., Pair	2370.00
Sconce, 4-Light, Louis XV, Bronze, Lyre Shape, Cabriole Branches, Leaves, Grapes, 31 x 17 In., Pair	861.00
Sconce, 4-Light, Louis XV, Giltwood, Scrolling Leaves, 38 x 29 In.	767.00
Sconce, 5-Light, Black & Gilt, Wheat, Bow Knot, Sword Handle Finial, Reeded Cups, Arms, 38 x 20 In.	184.00
Sconce, 5-Light, Bronze, Drapery Swags, Grapevines, France, 21 x 13 In., Pair	690.00
Sconce, 5-Light, Bronze, Fan Shaped Back, Putti, 1800s, 23 ¾ In., Pair	735.00
Sconce, 5-Light, Empire Style, Giltwood, Acanthus Arms, Trumpet Cups, 1800s, 26 x 21 In., Pair	4594.00
Sconce, 5-Light, Gilt Bronze, Cut Glass, Faceted Pendants, c.1950, 25 x 19 In., Pair	1045.00

Lamp, Electric, W. Von Nessen, Brushed Aluminum, Spaced Discs, Mica Shade, 1935-40, 21 In.
$2820.00

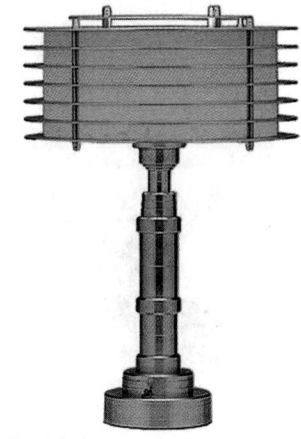
Cowan's Auctions

Lamp, Electric, Wilkinson, Trumpet Vine Shade, Black Metal Base, Impressed Shells, 21 ½ In.
$5750.00

James D. Julia Inc.

L

Lamp, Kerosene, Gone With The Wind, Glass, Pink Roses, Brass Font & Burner, 26 ½ In.
$295.00

Conestoga Auction Co., Inc.

419

Lamp, Kerosene, Milk Glass, Artichoke, Lavender & Green Accents, Ribbed Base, 9 ¾ In.
$177.00

Lamp, Kerosene, Piano, Brass, Milk Glass Shade, Ostrich Feet, Adjustable, 64 To 81 In.
$403.00

Lamp, Kerosene, Porcelain, Milk Glass, Puttie, Gold Trim, Importe All Allf Magne HS Burner, 13 In.
$148.00

Lamp, Oil, Gothic Revival, Glass, White, Enamel Overlay, Palmer Patent, Electrified, c.1850, 32 In.
$3198.00

Lamp, Oil, Hanging, Cranberry Opalescent Swirl, Font, Embossed Brass, Prisms, 20 In.
$863.00

Lamp, Oil, Peg, Rainbow Satin Glass, Brass, 11 In.
$1438.00

Lamp, Oil, Rainbow Mother-Of-Pearl, Ruffled Rim, Clear Rigaree Collar, Foot, 10 In.
$6670.00

Lamp, Solar, Cornelius & Co., Gilt Lacquer, Leaves, Shells, Trumpet Glass Shade, Prisms, c.1850, 24 In.
$861.00

Lamp, Solar, Kerosene Font, Gilt Standard, Frosted & Clear Glass Shade, Prisms, c.1850, 28 In.
$837.00

Sconce, 5-Light, Gilt Bronze, Scrolled Leaf Arms, Drapery Swags, Ribbon Crest, 32 In.	674.00
Sconce, 5-Light, Gilt Metal, Scrolled Arms, Faux Candles, Teardrop Prisms, 18 In., Pair	295.00
Sconce, 5-Light, Louis XV Style, Gilt Bronze, Chased Flowers, Spiral Twist Arms, 20 x 15 In., Pair	352.00
Sconce, 6-Light, Gilt Metal, Scrolls, Black Putto, Holding Branch, 18 x 13 In.	366.00
Sconce, 6-Light, Wrought Iron, Leafy Scrolls, 17 In., Pair	885.00
Sconce, Acrylic, Enamel, Chrome Steel, 20 x 7 In., Pair	1074.00
Sconce, Art Deco, Bronze, Frosted Glass, Geometric, Fans, 1929, 13 x 16 In.	1250.00
Sconce, Baroque Style, Iron, Twisted Standard, Fleur-De-Lis Finial, c.1900, 32 In., Pair	246.00
Sconce, Blackamoor, Chest Length, Round Plaque, Holding Dish, Leaves, Birds, 16 In.	1298.00
Sconce, Blackamoor, Hand Painted, Red, Black & Gold, Stripes, 13 x 10 x 6 In.	300.00
Sconce, Brass, Cut Glass, Scalloped Rim, Leaves, Star, Arch, Geometric, 1800s, 13 In., Pair	770.00
Sconce, Brass, Glass Globes, 10 In., Pair	83.00
Sconce, Brass, Mirror, Glass, Obelisk Shape, 22 x 6 ½ In., Pair	310.00
Sconce, C. & H. Greene, Cedar, Ebonized Wood, Glass & Silk Shade, 1907, 19 x 14 In.	17360.00
Sconce, Candle, Pieced Mirrors, Tinned Sheet Iron Frame, Oval, Leafy Sockets, 13 ¾ In., Pair	1003.00
Sconce, Classical Style, Plaster, France, Electrified, 1970s, 19 x 12 In., Pair	4030.00
Sconce, Figural, Blackamoor, Bust, Plaque, Leaves, Birds, Painted, 16 x 13 In.	1180.00
Sconce, G. Pesce, Fish Designs, Resin, Metal Rods, Fluorescent Tubes, Italy, 1980s, 7 x 29 In.	3100.00
Sconce, Gaetano Sciolari, Chromed Steel, Italy, 1970s, 24 x 13 In., Pair	806.00
Sconce, Gas, Ormolu, Putti, Grapes, Fruit, Gilt Arms, Etched Shade, c.1859, 12 x 17 In., Pair	717.00
Sconce, Gilt Bronze, Blackamoor, Fruit Tray, Taupe & Fringe Shade, Round Plate, 36 In., Pair	1599.00
Sconce, Gilt Metal, Sheaf Of Wheat, 2 Tulip Shaped Sockets, 1900s, 27 In., Pair	1062.00
Sconce, Glass, Cast Metal, Baluster Shape, Scrolling Candle Arms, Fruit Prisms, 17 In., Pair	671.00
Sconce, Jarvie Shop, Candle, Brass, Hammered, Embossed, Stamped, 13 ¾ x 6 ½ In.	1116.00
Sconce, Jean Louis Dimecq, Metal, Industrial Design, France, 1950s, 14 x 6 ½ In., Pair	680.00
Sconce, Louis XV Style, Gilt Bronze, Scrolled, France, c.1900, 15 ½ In., Pair	236.00
Sconce, Louis XVI Style, Gilt Metal, Center Torchere, Leaves, Crest, 24 In., Pair	500.00
Sconce, Meissen, 2-Light, Bronze, Flowers, Putto, Mark, c.1900, 6 x 19 In., Pair	1195.00
Sconce, Queen Anne Style, Chinoiserie, Mirror Back, Candleholder, 28 x 9 In., Pair	460.00
Sconce, Tole, Red, Gilt, Lacquered, Brass Disc Reflector, Rectangular, 1800s, 10 In., Pair	1912.00
Sconce, Wood Carved, Man On Swing, Holding Metal Lantern, Brittany, 15 x 6 ½ In., Pair	396.00
Scone, Metal, Accordion Shaped Arm, Christian Dell Kaiser, Germany, 1920s, 50 x 7 In.	520.00
Sinumbra, Brass, Gilt Accents, Tapered, Squat Shade, Grapes, 23 ½ In.	2185.00
Sinumbra, Brass, Gilt Bronze, Donut Tank, Squat Glass Shade, Clark, Coit & Cargill, 27 In.	3565.00
Solar, Bronze, Gilt Lacquer, Turned Standard, Etched Shade, Converted To Kerosene, c.1845, 33 In.	1673.00
Solar, Cornelius & Co., Gilt Lacquer, Leaves, Shells, Trumpet Glass Shade, Prisms, c.1850, 24 In. *illus*	861.00
Solar, Gilt Lacquered Brass, Bronze, Leafy Standard, Cut Glass, Etched, Prisms, c.1845, 29 In.	1195.00
Solar, Kerosene Font, Gilt Standard, Frosted & Clear Glass Shade, Prisms, c.1850, 28 In. *illus*	837.00
Tiffany Lamps are listed in the Tiffany category.	
Torchere, 4 Reeded Columns, Ram's Head Festoon, Sphinx, Bronze Bowl, Tripod, 68 In.	1035.00
Torchere, 7-Light, Gothic Revival, Brass, Hexagonal, Baluster Stem, 3-Sided Base, 61 In.	1612.00
Torchere, Gilt, Blackamoor, Red Pants, Venice, c.1825, 81 x 23 In., Pair	3350.00
Torchere, Iron, Alabaster, Grapevines, Octagonal Base, Ball Feet, 74 In., Pair	793.00
Torchere, Iron, Brass, 4 Cups, Applied Flowers, Scrolls, c.1910, 60 In., Pair	775.00
Torchere, Milk Glass, Cast Metal, Bellflower & Greek Key, Fluted Stem, 66 In., Pair	244.00
Torchere, Neoclassical, Silver, Fluted, Baluster Shape, Tripartite Base, 70 In., Pair	1488.00
Torchere, Regency Style, Bronze, Patinated, X-Form, Leaded Glass Globe, 74 In., Pair	7872.00
Torchere, Tommi Parzinger, Chrome Plated Brass, Steel, Lightolier, 1940s, 61 x 7 In., Pair	3720.00
Whale Oil, Blown, Pressed, Urn Shape Font, Swag & Tassel, 7-Panel Stem, 8 ½ x 3 ½ In., Pair	345.00
Whale Oil, Brass, Gimbal, Demilune Font, Hinged, Baluster Stem, Handle, 6 In.	71.00
Whale Oil, Clear, Cone Font, Bear Paw Base, Button Feet, 8 ¾ In.	138.00
Whale Oil, Cone Shape, Tin, Handle, Wood Stopper, 1800s, 8 In.	100.00
Whale Oil, Fiery Opalescent Glass, Squat Cone Shape, Footed, Curled Handle, 2 ½ In.	161.00
Whale Oil, Globular Font, Double-Button Stem, Folded Rim, Saucer Base, 7 ¾ In.	748.00
Whale Oil, Hand, Diamond, Amethyst, Bell Shape, Handle, Pewter Cap, c.1850, 5 In.	1007.00
Whale Oil, Hexagonal, Wafer Construction, Brass Collar, Sandwich Glass, c.1860	147.00
Whale Oil, Olive Green Streaks, Cone Shape, Domed Foot, Cup Plate Base, 6 In.	1380.00
Whale Oil, Opaque White Glass, Globe, 6 Wafers, Lion's Head & Flower Basket Base, 12 In.	920.00
Whale Oil, Peg, Blown Glass, 16 Panels, Umbrella Form, Pewter Collar, 4 In.	81.00
Whale Oil, Peg, Blown Glass, Split Flutes, 15 Upper & Lower, Globular, 4 ½ In., Pair	431.00
Whale Oil, Peg, Cut Glass, Diamond Band, Globular, 4 In.	46.00
Whale Oil, Peg, Cut Glass, Strawberry Diamond, Flashed Roundel & Fan, Globular, 4 In.	69.00
Whale Oil, Pressed Glass, Bulb Font, Scrolling 3-Feet, Pewter Collar, Boston & Sandwich, 11 x 5 In.	431.00
Whale Oil, Pressed Glass, Waisted Loop, Canary Yellow, Hexagonal Font & Stem, 8 ¾ In.	219.00
Whale Oil, Pressed, Loop & Leaf, Amethyst, Dome Top, Baluster Standard, 9 ½ x 3 In.	173.00
Whale Oil, Sinumbra, Brass, Bronze, Gilt, Cut & Etched Shade, 1800s, 18 ½ In. *illus*	2440.00
Whale Oil, Sparking, Blown, Pressed, Globe Font, Scalloped Base, Tin, Cork, c.1835, 3 x 2 ¼ In.	219.00

Lamp, Whale Oil, Sinumbra, Brass, Bronze, Gilt, Cut & Etched Shade, 1800s, 18 ½ In.
$2440.00

Neal Auction Co.

Lantern, Bicycle, Nickel Plated Brass, Flip-Up Side Lights, Oil, Marked, M & W, Pat. 1897, 5 ¾ In.
$71.00

Conestoga Auction Co., Inc.

TIP
A piece of ribbon can be "pressed" by pulling it across a warm light bulb.

Le Verre Francais, Vase, Birds, Flowering Bush, Brown Mottled, Red, Cameo, Signed, c.1925, 11 ½ In. $3185.00

Skinner, Inc.

Le Verre Francais, Vase, Red & Black Butterflies, Handles, Cameo, Signed, 10 ½ In. $3063.00

Skinner, Inc.

Le Verre Francais, Vase, Yellow, Orange Mottled, Red Flowering Vine, Cameo, Signed, 13 ½ In. $1150.00

Early Auction Co.

LAMPSHADE

Art Glass, King Tut, Green & Blue Iridescent, Yellow Ground, Flared Rim, 5 x 10 In.	575.00
Globe, Acid Etched, Farm Scene, Sheep, Boston & Sandwich, c.1900, 7 x 4 In.	104.00
Hurricane, Glass, Dahlia Blossoms, Stems, c.1820, 23 ¼ In.	3450.00
Leaded Glass, Pink Flowers, Leaves, Honeycomb Ground, Duffner & Kimberly, 24 In.	5310.00
Mosaic, Multicolor, 8 ½ x 15 In.	148.00
Slag Glass, Tiles, Pinecone Border, Bronze Base, Bigelow & Kennard, 2 8 x 22 In.	7440.00

LANTERNS are a special type of lighting device. They have a light source, usually a candle, totally hidden inside the walls of the lantern. Light is seen through holes or glass sections.

Bicycle, Nickel Plated Brass, Flip-Up Side Lights, Oil, Marked, M & W, Pat. 1897, 5 ¾ In. ...... *illus*	71.00
Brass, Aesthetic Movement, Leaded & Stained Glass, White, Green & Red, 25 ¼ x 10 In.	682.00
Candle, Tin, Red Paint, Half Round, Hinged Door, Pierced Chimney, Ring Handle, 1800s, 15 In.	711.00
Candle, Tinned Sheet Iron, Glass, 9-Sided, Cone Shape Cap, Loop Handle, 10 ½ In.	224.00
Candle, Tinned Sheet Iron, Square, Cross Guarded Glass Lenses, Hinged Door, 16 In.	266.00
Candle, Tole, Glass, 18 x 6 In.	34.00
Carriage, Brass, Eagle Finials, 19th Century, 31 In., Pair	750.00
Carriage, Copper, Brass, Nickel Plated, Electric, 19th Century, 35 ½ In., Pair	800.00
Coach, Swag & Tassel, Glass Panes, Bulbous Finial, 1800s, 38 ½ In., Pair	1200.00
Dietz Fire Dept., Nickel Plated Brass, Red Globe, Pat. Aug. 12, 1907, 14 In.	990.00
Famille Rose, Hexagonal, Reticulated, Flowers, Porcelain, Late 1800s, 12 In., Pair	1230.00
Glass, Brass, 2-Tier Top, Eagle Finial, Pole, Victorian, 26 In., Pair	156.00
Glass, Scrolled Arm, Gilt Leaf, Swag, Electric, c.1930, 17 x 11 In., Pair	590.00
Globe, Onion Shape, Tole, Glass, Green, Gold Paint, France, 23 In.	2242.00
Gothic Style, Tole, Etched Glass, Hexagonal, Chains, Flowers, c.1840, 20 x 11 In.	717.00
Hall, 4-Light, Gilt Bronze, Etched Glass, Dome Top, 4 Leaf Finials, Urn, c.1905, 35 x 19 In., Pair	2460.00
Hall, Regency Style, Glass, Engraved, Grapes, Flowers, Chains, 29 x 12 In.	492.00
Hanging, Brass, Glass, 2 Electric Candles, Shaped Drop, 1900s, 20 x 9 In.	239.00
Hanging, Cranberry Swirl Glass, Gold Tone Metal Frame, Scrolling, c.1870, 12 In.	210.00
Hanging, Dore Bronze, Scroll Arms, Etched Frosted Glass, 31 x 14 In., Pair	3000.00
Hanging, Gilt Bronze, Cloisonne, Pagoda Shaped, Flowers, Pierced Hook, c.1900s, 12 In., Pair	1348.00
Hanging, Iron, Pagoda Shape, Pierced, 4-Footed, Japan, 11 ½ In.	418.00
Iron, Hinged Lid, Door, Glass, Strap Handle, Covered Chimney, Loop Handle, 8 In.	142.00
Iron, Spanish Provincial, Cage Shape, Scrolled Bracket, 39 x 24 In.	461.00
Kerosene, Oval Lens, Black, Vented Cap, Collar, Finger Ring, Swing Bail, c.1854, 12 ½ In.	266.00
Mahogany, Ebonized, Roof Top, Carved Lattice Sides, Chinese, Electric, 1900s, 33 x 13 In., Pair	397.00
Parcel Gilt, Jewels, Globe Shade, Chains, Embossed Brass Canopy, Late 1800s, 24 x 10 In.	338.00
Porcelain, Cover, Bronze, Pierced, Flowers, Handles, Footed, 6-Sided, Chinese, 1800s, 15 ½ In.	3944.00
Porcelain, Pierced, Enameled Cartouche, Leaves, Chinese, 16 In., Pair	558.00
Skater's, Brass, Shaped Glass Globes, Adjustable Wick Holders, 7 In., Pair	142.00
Skater's, Cobalt Blue Shade, Brass Hardware, Bail Handle, 7 In.	403.00
Tin, Oil Font, Glass Chimney, Paw Feet, France, c.1850, 13 ½ In.	206.00
Wood Frame, Glass Panes, Iron Ring, Tin Candleholder, Octagonal, 1800s, 18 In.	1528.00
Wood, 12 Reverse Painted Panels, Figures, Flowers, Dragon Finial, Electric, Chinese, c.1905, 17 In.	240.00
Wrought Iron, Tole, Twists, Arched Window, Quatrefoil Panels, Fleur-Di-Lis, Chain, 51 x 23 In.	1195.00
Wrought Iron, Triangular, Amber Shade, 1900s, 8 x 10 ½ In., Pair	217.00

LE VERRE FRANCAIS is one of the many types of cameo glass made by the Schneider Glassworks in France. The glass was made by the C. Schneider factory in Epinay-sur-Seine from 1918 to 1933. It is a mottled glass, usually decorated with floral designs, and bears the incised signature *Le Verre Francais*.

Compote, Footed, Flared, Orange, Crimson To Rose Stemmed Flowers, Signed, 9 In.	1500.00
Fernery, Orange Leaves, Pink Ground, Swollen Rectangular Shape, 4 x 7 x 3 In.	561.00
Lamp, Electric, Blue, Orange, 3 Twisted Metal Columns, 41 In.	2034.00
Pitcher, Urn Shape, Applied Purple Handles, Pink Mottled, Stemmed Flowers, Signed, 10 In.	1100.00
Vase, Birds, Flowering Bush, Brown Mottled, Red, Cameo, Signed, c.1925, 11 ½ In. ......*illus*	3185.00
Vase, Bulbous, Orange & Green Design, Fougeres, Cameo, Signed, 7 In.	450.00
Vase, Flowers, Orange, Black Foot, Signed, 19 In.	1547.00
Vase, Green Neck, Red, Yellow Body, Cameo, Signed, 14 In.	893.00
Vase, Orange, Yellow, Purple, Cameo, Footed, c.1920, 8 In.	826.00
Vase, Pink & Burgundy, Etched Flowers, Squat, Bulbous, Rolled Rim, Signed, 3 In.	230.00
Vase, Purple, Art Deco Stemmed Flowers, Round Foot, Trumpet Shape, Signed, 14 In.	1553.00
Vase, Red & Black Butterflies, Handles, Cameo, Signed, 10 ½ In. ......*illus*	3063.00
Vase, Rhododendron, Mottled Pink, Cylindrical, Flared Rim, Round Foot, 9 In.	2013.00

Vase, Urn Shape, Yellow, Orange & Green Cameo, Coqueret, Footed, 12 In.	700.00
Vase, Yellow Mottled, Tree Design, Blue To Orange, Cameo, Footed, Signed, 8 In.	350.00
Vase, Yellow, Crimson & Orange Flowers, Footed, Cylindrical, Signed, 10 In.	950.00
Vase, Yellow, Orange & Green Design, Footed, Urn Shape, Signed, 12 In.	700.00
Vase, Yellow, Orange Mottled, Red Flowering Vine, Cameo, Signed, 13 ½ In. ....illus	1150.00

LEATHER is tanned animal hide and has been used to make decorative and useful objects for centuries. Leather objects must be carefully preserved with proper humidity and oiling or the leather will deteriorate and crack. This damage cannot be repaired.

Briefcase, Satchel Style, Alligator, Black, Foldover, Metal Clasp, Thailand, 13 x 16 ½ In.	305.00
Bucket, Black, Copper Bands, Tacks, 1800s, 10 In.	121.00
Bucket, Ice, Royal Crest, Metal, Handle, 9 ½ x 9 ¾ In.	275.00
Bucket, Painted Shield, Strap Handle, Fabric Interior, England, 1900s, 28 In.	413.00
Cigarette Case, Wood Lining, 14K Gold, Dunhill, Germany, 1 ½ x 4 In.	92.00
Panel, Stamped, Chinoiserie Figure Scenes, Gold Ground, Carved Giltwood, 43 x 25 In., Pair.	995.00
Saddle, Western, Eddleman Brothers, Texas, c.1950, 15 In.	259.00

LEEDS pottery was made at Leeds, Yorkshire, England, from 1774 to 1878. Most Leeds ware was not marked. Early Leeds pieces had distinctive twisted handles with a greenish glaze on part of the creamy ware. Later ware often had blue borders on the creamy pottery. A Chicago company named Leeds made many Disney-inspired figurines. They are listed in the Disneyana category.

LEEDS POTTERY.

Bowl, 4 Colors, Flowers & Leaves, 4 ¾ x 10 ½ In.	118.00
Bowl, Leaf & Berry Rim, Rum Center, Footed, c.1800, 6 ¼ In.	353.00
Charger, Blue Feather Edge, 2 Handles, Vase With Flowers, c.1800, 14 ½ In.	529.00
Jardiniere, Embossed Stylized Flowers & Leaves, Faience, Blue, Green, Brown, 11 In.	708.00
Loving Cup, Reeded Handles, Round Foot, Figures Holding Parasols, Flowers, c.1780, 7 In.	1770.00
Mug, Flowers, Leaves, Loop Handle, Soft Paste, 4 ¾ In. ....illus	106.00
Pitcher, Cream, Helmet Form, Blue Bud & Leaf Banding, 5 In.	53.00
Pitcher, Farm Landscape, Baluster Shape, Make-Do Handle & Spout, Pa.	3900.00
Pitcher, Stoneware, Smear Glazed, Hunters, Shooting Quail, Hounds, House, c.1790, 6 In.	1062.00
Plate, Painted Fruit Border, Leaves, Blue Rim Ring, Paste, 8 ¼ In.	177.00
Platter, American Eagle Border, Feather Edge, White, Blue Trim, Elongated Oval, 1800s, 16 In.	403.00
Platter, Blue Ruffled Edge, 17 x 13 In.	325.00
Sugar, 5 Colors, Geometric & Leafy Design, Open Handle, 4 In.	153.00
Sugar, Pearlware, Multicolor Flower Garland, Applied Handles, Oblong, c.1800, 4 ¾ In.	176.00
Sugar, Pearlware, Round, Fruit, Flowers, c.1800, 4 In.	206.00
Teapot, Blue Flowers, Child's, 4 ¼ In.	47.00
Teapot, Shell Spout, Twist Reeded Handle, Prince William V Bust, c.1785, 4 In.	2703.00

LEFTON is a mark found on pottery, porcelain, glass, and other wares imported by the Geo. Zoltan Lefton Company. The company began in 1941. George Lefton died in 1996 and the company was sold in 2001. The company mark has changed through the years, but because marks have been used for long periods of time, they are of little help in dating an object.

Bank, Poodle, White With Blue, Gold Necklace, 7 ½ In.	87.00
Butter, Figural, Bluebird, Big Eyes, Eyelashes, Pink Flowers, Burgundy Bow, 1960s, 5 In.	55.00
Figurine, Lady, Pink, White Trim, Hat, Parasol, Bonnet, Marked, 1960s, 7 In.	89.00
Jewelry Box, Chintz, Pink, Purple Roses, Gold Trim, Heart Shape, Sticker, 1992, 3 ¾ x 2 In.	55.00
Mug, Yellow Rose Pattern, Green Leaves, Yellow Background, 3 x 2 ⅞ In.	10.00
Salt & Pepper, Pink Roses, Beige Ground, Cork Stopper, 3 In.	24.00

LEGRAS was founded in 1864 by Auguste Legras at St. Denis, France. It is best known for cameo glass and enamel-decorated glass with Art Nouveau designs. Legras merged with Pantin in 1920 and became the Verreries et Cristalleries de St. Denis et de Pantin Reunies.

Legras

Vase, 3 Sheep, Mountain Top, Orange Sky, Trees, Narrow, Square Shape, Flared Foot, Cameo, 7 In.	431.00
Vase, Barrel Shape, Mottled Purple With Winter Scene, Bear Trees, Signed, 4 ½ In.	450.00
Vase, Bud, Tapered, Flared Rim, River Scene, Bridge, Trees, Cameo, c.1910, 7 ½ In.	885.00
Vase, Cylinder, Mottled Orange, Basket Of Fruit On Scrolling Blue Chain, Signed, 9 In.	150.00
Vase, Enamel, Winter Scene, 9 ¾ In.	425.00
Vase, Lake, Shoreline, Trees, Peach & Cream Ground, Rectangular, Signed, 3 x 8 In.	748.00
Vase, Mottled Yellow, Orange, Flower Medallion, Scrolling Tendrils, 4 x 8 In.	345.00
Vase, Onion Form, Green Leaves & Branches, Yellow Shaded To Pink Ground, 12 ½ In.	1180.00
Vase, Stick Form, Green To Pink & Blue, Stemmed Willow, Signed, 12 In.	300.00
Vase, Urn, Caramel, Red & Green Water Scene, Shells & Plants, Cameo, Signed, 22 In.	600.00
Vase, White, Peach, Pink Ivy, Cameo, Signed, 5 ¾ In.	475.00

Leeds, Mug, Flowers, Leaves, Loop Handle, Soft Paste, 4 ¾ In. $106.00

Conestoga Auction Co., Inc.

Lenox, Stein, Golfer, Green, Sterling Silver Rim, ½ Liter $633.00

Fox Auctions

Libbey, Bowl, Cut Glass, Scalloped Rim, Signed, Acid Etched Mark, 4 x 8 In. $58.00

James D. Julia Inc.

Libbey, Vase, Peachblow, Pinks, Gilt Enameled Flowers, World's Fair 1893, 5 ¼ In. $230.00

Early Auction Co.

L

Lighter, Cigar, Winston Churchill Likeness, England, Tallent, 8 ½ In. $300.00

DuMouchelles Art Gallery

Lighter, Tinder, Flintlock, Candle Socket, Knob Handle, Steel, 1700s, 3 x 7 ⅜ In. $1185.00

Skinner, Inc.

Limoges, Chocolate Pot, Cranberry Flowers, Gold Trim, Gerard, Dufraisseix & Abbot, c.1900, 12 In. $120.00

DuMouchelles Art Gallery

Limoges, Chocolate Pot, Roses, Gilded Handle & Rim, Gerard, Dufraisseix & Abbott, c.1900, 11 ½ In. $150.00

DuMouchelles Art Gallery

LENOX porcelain is well-known in the United States. Walter Scott Lenox and Jonathan Coxon Sr. founded the Ceramic Art Company in Trenton, New Jersey, in 1889. In 1906, Lenox left and started his own company called Lenox. The company makes porcelain that is similar to Irish Belleek. In 2009, after a series of mergers, Lenox became part of Clarion Capital Partners. The marks used by the firm have changed through the years, so collectors can date the ceramics. Related pieces may also be listed in the Ceramic Art Co. category.

Compote, Footed, Pedestal, Gold Trim, c.1925, 7 In.	35.00
Dinner Service, Hayworth, Cream, Gold Rim, 12 Settings, 48 Piece	540.00
Pitcher, Autumn, 7 ¾ In.	394.00
Place Setting, Cretan, Dinner, Cup, Saucer, Bread, Salad, 5 Piece	145.00
Plate, Dinner, Ashley, 10 ⅞ In.	39.00
Plate, Dinner, Autumn, 10 ½ In.	66.00
Plate, Dinner, Embossed Gold Band, White Center, 10 ¼ In., 12 Piece	259.00
Stein, Golfer, Green, Sterling Silver Rim, ½ Liter ....*illus*	633.00
Vase, Bottle Shape, Incised Black Outline Design, Pale Green, Flare Rim, Round Foot, 10 In.	150.00
Vase, Cylinder, Blue & Gray, Cascading Purple Wisteria, Belleek Type, Signed, 16 In.	275.00
Vase, Flowers, Leaves, Scalloped Lip, Fluted Base, Cylindrical, Ribbed, Stamped, 16 x 10 In.	240.00
Vase, Yellow Iris, Hand Painted, Signed J. Nosek, 16 In.	268.00

LETTER OPENERS have been used since the eighteenth century. Ivory and silver were favored by the well-to-do. In the late nineteenth century, the letter opener was popular as an advertising giveaway and many were made of metal or celluloid. Brass openers with figural handles were also popular.

3 People, Spray Of Flowers, Pagoda, Mixed Metal, c.1890, 12 In.	265.00
Asian Soldier, Ivory, 10 ⅛ In.	100.00
Bird's Head Handle, Steampunk Viking Style, Ornate, Brass, 1890s, 9 In.	349.00
Crown, Flag, Spreading Flower, Silver, 6 ½ In.	75.00
Cutout Work Handle, Silver, Mexico, 1950s, 8 In.	225.00
Duck, Wood, Amber Glass Eye, c.1950, 7 ½ In.	17.00
Eagle, Copper, Embossed, c.1920, 11 In.	90.00
Ear Of Corn, John Deere, Brass, 3 ½ In.	25.00
Elephants, Marching, Petal Flowers, Openwork, Celluloid, 7 In.	14.00
George Washington, Celluloid, Japan, 1920s, 7 ½ In.	90.00
Hedgehog, Mother-Of-Pearl, Silver Collar, 5 In.	42.00
Indian Head, 3-D, Celluloid, Niagara Falls, 7 ¾ In.	95.00
Magnifying Glass, Plastic, Marbled, 9 In.	24.00
Mother-Of-Pearl, Silver, 19th Century, 4 In.	115.00
Owl, Bronze, Orange Glass Eyes, 9 ¾ In.	295.00
Porcelain Handle, White Ground, Pink Flowers, 9 In.	39.00
Prehistoric Fish Handle, Ivory, Pierced Blade, c.1850, 8 ½ In.	236.00
Ruler Marks, Lion's Paw, Silver, c.1945, 5 ½ In.	75.00
Seal Handle, Ivory, Signed, 7 ⅝ In.	178.00
Serpent, Silver, Tortoiseshell, 1895, 8 In.	495.00
Sword Style, Nickel Plated Brass, Naples, Italy, 1946, 9 In.	49.00
Talon, Faux Pearl, Silver Metal, c.1870, 4 In.	158.00
Tunbridgeware, Mosaic Geometric Patterns, 1880s, 9 In.	175.00
Turkey Foot, Feather, Cast Iron, 9 In.	48.00
Victorian Woman, 14K Rose Gold, Dagger Style, Scrolls, c.1885, 8 In.	400.00
Whaler, Boats, Scrimshaw, Whale Baleen, 12 In.	150.00

LIBBEY Glass Company has made many types of glass since 1888, including the cut glass and tablewares that are collected today. The stemwares of the 1930s and 1940s are once again in style. The Toledo, Ohio, firm was purchased by Owens-Illinois in 1935 and is still working under the name Libbey Inc. Maize is listed in its own category.

Basket, American Brilliant Cut Glass, 13 x 9 In.	138.00
Bowl, American Brilliant, Signed, 3 x 7 In.	387.00
Bowl, Colonna, American Brilliant, Signed, 3 ½ x 9 In.	150.00
Bowl, Corinthian, American Brilliant, 4 x 9 In.	40.00
Bowl, Cut Glass, Scalloped Rim, Signed, Acid Etched Mark, 4 x 8 In. .....*illus*	58.00
Bowl, Gem, Signed, 3 ¾ x 8 In.	150.00
Bowl, Gloria, American Brilliant, Round, 3 ½ x 8 ¾ In.	150.00
Bowl, New Brilliant, Deep Edge Scallops, Signed, 3 ½ x 8 In.	40.00
Box, Cover, Engraved, Thistle & Bee, Signed, 4 x 5 ½ In.	50.00
Bread Tray, Neola, Scalloped Notched Edge, 7 ¾ x 11 ¾ In.	246.00

Carafe, Ellsmere, American Brilliant, 8 ¾ In.	375.00
Compote, Cranberry To Clear, Round Foot, Narrow Stem, Flare Rim, Signed, 11 In., Pair	1800.00
Decanter, Empress, Flower Center, American Brilliant, 6 x 8 In.	268.00
Decanter, Princess, Snake Handle, American Brilliant, 12 In.	80.00
Ice Bucket, Hobstar, Nailhead Diamond, Strawberry Diamond, Vesica, Cattail, Shooting Star, 5 In.	55.00
Nappy, Gem, Cut Glass Handle, Sawtooth Rim, American Brilliant, Signed, 6 In.	30.00
Nappy, Hobstar, Handle, 7 ½ In.	47.00
Perfume Bottle, Amberina, Ribbed, Dabber Stopper, 8 ⅜ In.	1380.00
Pitcher, Florence, 7 ¾ x 8 ¼ In.	138.00
Plate, Checkerboard & Hobstar, 7 In. Diam.	135.00
Relish, Hobstar, 7 ½ In.	30.00
Rose Bowl, Corinthian, Signed, 7 In.	445.00
Salt Dip, Harvard, American Brilliant, 3 Piece	50.00
Serving Bowl, Ellsmere Pattern, 8 x 3 In.	495.00
Sugar Shaker, Maize, Pewter Lid, Corncob Design, Blue Husks, 5 ½ In.	115.00
Tray, Lenox, American Brilliant, Round, Signed, 9 ¾ In.	1300.00
Vase, Agata, Tulip Shape, Round Foot, Stem, Ruffled Rim, Fuchsia, Gold Specks, 6 In.	345.00
Vase, Amberina, Flower Shape, Signed, 11 In.	1000.00
Vase, Amberina, Ribbed, Fuchsia To Amber Top, Tapered, Footed, 14 ¼ In.	1150.00
Vase, Engraved Vine, Cone Shape, Signed, American Brilliant, 12 In.	60.00
Vase, Peachblow, Pinks, Gilt Enameled Flowers, World's Fair 1893, 5 ¼ In. ....*illus*	230.00
Wine, Stem, Silver Leaf Pattern, 6 ¼ In., 8 Piece	40.00

LIGHTERS for cigarettes and cigars are collectible. Cigarettes became popular in the late nineteenth century, and with the cigarette came matches and cigarette lighters. All types of lighters are collected, from solid gold to the first of the recent disposable lighters. Most examples found were made after 1940. Some lighters may be found in the Jewelry category in this book.

18K Bicolor Gold, Wavy Lines, Platinum Frame With 36 Diamonds, Cartier	3540.00
Brass, Elsa Peretti, Tiffany, Blue Drawstring Pouch, N.Y., 1982, 2 ½ In.	153.00
Cigar, Devil, Claw Feet Base, Bronze, 8 ¾ In.	330.00
Cigar, Duck Shape, Silver Plate, 5 x 5 x 3 In.	413.00
Cigar, Joker, Punch On Pedestal, Gas Run, Bronze Patina, 9 ¼ In.	2700.00
Cigar, Jump Spark, Midland, Wood Case	605.00
Cigar, Man In Suit, Smoking Cigarette, Railroad Conductor, Round Base, Metal, 7 ¼ In.	180.00
Cigar, Pistol, Cast Iron Handle, Copper Flashed Barrel, Ideal, 10 ½ In.	1232.00
Cigar, Shaped As Roman Oil Lamp, Scrolling, Loop Handle, Silver, 1859, 5 ½ In.	239.00
Cigar, Silver, Samovar Shape, Hardstone Accents, Marked, Russia, c.1908-26, 5 In.	8125.00
Cigar, Winston Churchill Likeness, England, Tallent, 8 ½ In. ....*illus*	300.00
Cigarette, W.C. Fields' Head, Cast Metal, Bronze Patina, Protruding Red Nose, 1920s, 5 In.	171.00
Dunhill, Gold Tone, Box, 2 ½ In.	115.00
Hans Hansen, Silver, Rosewood, 6 Sides, Metal Plaque, Denmark, 2 x 4 In.	60.00
Kool Penguin, Cast Metal, Willie, Light Up A Kool, Hinged Head, 1930s	250.00
Pistol, Walnut, Brass, Steel, Flintlock, Engraved, Leaves, c.1780, 4 x 5 In.	1067.00
Pistol, Walnut, Brass, Steel, Flintlock, Scrolled Brass, c.1780, 5 x 9 In.	980.00
Ronson, Figural, Black Bartender, Bar, Barware, 1930s, 7 x 6 In.	1895.00
Salem Cigarettes, By Penguin, 1950s	25.00
Tinder, Flintlock, Candle Socket, Knob Handle, Steel, 1700s, 3 x 7 ⅜ In. ....*illus*	1185.00
Zippo, Brushed Chrome, Red Coca-Cola Logo, Japan, 1970s	25.00
Zippo, Chrome, Stripped, Flowers, c.1964, 2 ½ x 1 In.	10.50

LIGHTNING RODS AND LIGHTNING ROD BALLS are collected. The glass balls were at the center of the rod that was attached to the roof of a house or barn to avoid lightning damage. The balls were made in many colors and many patterns.

LIGHTNING ROD

Arrow, Twisted Rod, Violet Glass Globe, 1930s, 51 In.	217.00
Blue Arrow Tail, Spiral Shaft, 3-Sided Tip, Milk Glass Ball, 54 x 17 In.	162.00
Cast Iron, Arrow, Red Slag Glass Tail, Milk Glass Ball, 1920s, 16 x 18 In.	245.00
Cast Iron, Brass, Moon, Star, Clear Glass, c.1950, 36 In.	239.00
Tail Feather Insert, Flashed Ruby Red To Clear Ball, Star Finial, Kretzer, 36 In.	300.00

LIGHTNING ROD BALL

9-Sided, Blue Milk Glass, Copper Caps, D & S Company, c.1920	129.00
Blue Slag Glass, Moon & Stars, Diamond Pattern, c.1900	159.00
Emerald Green, Quilted, George Thompson, c.1930, 5 In. Diam.	188.00

Limoges, Pitcher, Yellow, Red Mums, Double Waist Gilt Band, Gold Handle, Marked, 14 ½ In.
$230.00

Early Auction Co.

Lindbergh, Toy, Airplane, Lindy, Gray Paint, Embossed, Nickel Propeller, Cast Iron, Hubley, c.1928, 9 In.
$863.00

Bertoia Auctions

Lladro, Figurine, Balloon Seller, No. 5141, 10 In.
$84.00

DuMouchelles Art Gallery

Lladro, Figurine, Dreams Of A Summer Past, No. 6401, 9 In.
$90.00

DuMouchelles Art Gallery

L

Lladro, Figurine, Pensive Clown, No. 5130, 11 In. $120.00

DuMouchelles Art Gallery

Lladro, Figurine, Pet Me, No. 5114, 3 ½ In. · $148.00

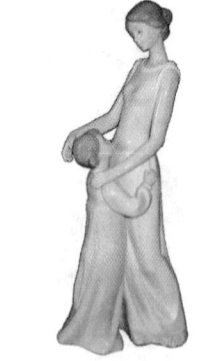

DuMouchelles Art Gallery

Lladro, Figurine, Someone To Look Up To, No. 6771, 13 ¾ In. $295.00

DuMouchelles Art Gallery

Lladro, Figurine, Summer Stock, No. 1407, 10 In. $300.00

Milk Glass, Raised Mark, WC Shinn, c.1930, 4 x 4 ½ In.	129.00
Milk Glass, White, Copper Caps, U.S.A.	119.00
Sky Blue Milk Glass, c.1930, 4 In. Diam.	149.00
Swirling Amethyst, Copper Caps, c.1920, 4 ½ In.	144.00
Transparent Orange, Oval, c.1940	168.00
White Milk Glass, 1930s	119.00

LIMOGES porcelain has been made in Limoges, France, since the mid-nineteenth century. Fine porcelains were made by many factories, including Haviland, Ahrenfeldt, Guerin, Pouyat, Elite, and others. Modern porcelains are being made at Limoges and the word *Limoges* as part of the mark is not an indication of age. Haviland, one of the Limoges factories, is listed as a separate category in this book.

Bowl, Spider Web, Lily Pad Design, Gilt Handles, Scalloped Rim, Jean Pouyet, c.1892, 13 x 4 ½ In.	173.00
Box, Porcelain Flowers, Garlands, Bronze Mounts, Hinged, Shaped, Marked, 3 x 10 In.	238.00
Cachepot, Gold Borders, Scenic, Victorian Couple, 8 In.	50.00
Cake Plate, Daffodils, Leaves, Scalloped Edge, Signed, c.1896, 10 In.	195.00
Centerpiece, Pedestal, Round Foot, Wavy Rim, Leaves, Acorns, Gilt Accents, 1907-19, 4 x 9 ½ In.	475.00
Charger, Courting Scene, Gold Scalloped Edge, 13 In.	395.00
Charger, Painted, Leaping Trout, Square Gilt Frame, Early 1900s, 17 In.	275.00
Charger, Peasant Maiden, Marked, 1900s, 13 In.	279.00
Chocolate Pot, Cranberry, Flowers, Gold Trim, Gerard, Dufraisseix & Abbot, c.1900, 12 In. ....*illus*	120.00
Chocolate Pot, Roses, Gilded Handle & Rim, Gerard, Dufraisseix & Abbott, c.1900, 11 ½ In. .....*illus*	150.00
Chocolate Set, Blue Purple Berries On Vines, Gold, Rust, 9 Piece	825.00
Chop Plate, Klingenberg Dwenger, Pink Flowers, c.1905, 13 In.	175.00
Cup & Saucer, Lily Pattern, Signed, 1890s	175.00
Dessert Set, Mistletoe Sprigs With White Berries, Green Ground, Gold Trim, 6 Piece	399.00
Dish, Divided, 3 Sections With Flowers, 11 x 11 In.	125.00
Dish, Mayonnaise, Underplate, Rust Gooseberry, Signed, 6 In.	50.00
Dresser Bottle, Flower Canes, Red, White, Blue, Oval, Stopper, 1900s, 5 ½ In.	431.00
Dresser Box, Cover, Woman, Red Shawl, Round, c.1900, 5 ½ In.	489.00
Ewer, Pink Flowers, White Ground, Gilt, Footed, Figural Handle, 14 In.	546.00
Ginger Jar, Dome Lid, Blue, Gilt, Scrolls, Flowers, Acorn Finial, Signed, c.1915, 16 In., Pair ...	1045.00
Jardiniere, Art Nouveau, Pale Blue Flower Band, Cobalt Blue Base, Gold Trim, 11 x 9 In.	102.00
Jardiniere, Cream, Orchids, Gold Highlights, Serpent Handles, Footed, 6 ¾ x 11 ½ In.	225.00
Jardiniere, Roses, Gilt Trim, Paw Feet, 11 In.	3995.00
Mug, Portrait, Young Girl, Highlighted, Dragon Handle, Signed, 5 In., 5 Piece	30.00
Oyster Plate, 5 Wells, Ferns, Gold Detail, Rim, 8 In.	83.00
Oyster Plate, Green & White, Gold Trim, 8 In.	85.00
Pitcher, Art Deco, Paneled, Gilt Detail, c.1920, 8 ½ In.	47.00
Pitcher, Yellow, Red Mums, Double Waist Gilt Band, Gold Handle, Marked, 14 ½ In. ......*illus*	230.00
Plaque, Amourous Couple, Hand Painted, France, 1800s, 9 x 6 In.	948.00
Plaque, Beach Scene, Cupid, Woman Holding Fishing Pole, Bowl, Pierced Metal Frame, 14 x 9 In.	690.00
Plate Set, Green, Flower Border, c.1920, 9 ½ In., 11 Piece	531.00
Plate, Cabbage Rose, Gold Highlights, Scalloped Rim, Delinieres D & C Mark, 8 ½ In.	145.00
Plate, Gilt Borders, Central Medallion, Shreve, Crump & Low, 11 In., 12 Piece	863.00
Plate, Luncheon, Pink, Blue Flower Border, Charles Ahrenfelt, B.B. & B., 8 ¾ In., 12 Piece	92.00
Plate, Violets, 24K Gold Trim, Fluted Rim, Signed, 6 In.	60.00
Platter, 2 Ducks In Flight, Gold Scrolls, Pink Border, Shaped Rim, Signed, 17 x 12 In.	230.00
Platter, Flower Swags, Gold Trimmed Rim, 13 x 12 In.	207.00
Punch Bowl, Green Ground, Family Scene Rondels, Gilt, Flower & Leaf Interior, Transfer, 7 x 16 In.	657.00
Punch Bowl, Painted, Fruit, Leaves, Gilt Accents, Shaped Rim, Round Foot, 7 x 14 In.	486.00
Tankard, Blue, Green, Brown, Gold Highlights, Dragon Handle, 14 ½ In.	100.00
Tankard, Dragon Design, Blue, Green & Brown Tones, Gold Highlights, 14 ½ In.	100.00
Tankard, Grape & Vine Design, Signed Seidel, Mark Guerin, c.1915, 14 ¾ In.	184.00
Tankard, Green Tones, Leaf Design, 6 Mugs, 12 In.	150.00
Tea Set, Blue & White, Flowers, Gilt Highlights, Creamer, Sugar, Teapot, 1800s, 4 ½ In.	360.00
Tea Set, Flowers, Blue Edge, Red Lined Case, c.1900, Miniature, 8 Piece	180.00
Tea Set, Green, Pink Rose, 4 Piece	175.00
Teapot, Creamer, Sugar, T & V, c.1910	118.00
Tray, Egg, Cream Ground With Violet Design, Gold Trim, 10 In.	70.00
Tray, Painted, Grapes, Gold Trim, Signed, c.1880, 13 x 16 In.	144.00
Tray, White, Blue Border, Pink Rose Garland Highlights, Handles, 16 In.	30.00
Tray, Yellow With Apple Design, Gold Border, Round, Signed, 12 ¾ In.	50.00
Trinket Box, Round, Gilt, Transfer, White, Blue, Flowers, 5 x 13 In.	63.00
Tureen, Soup, Tray, Cover, Pink Flowers, Burgundy, Green & Yellow Scroll, 12 In.	1995.00
Urn, Ram's Head Handles, Flower Swags, Gilt, Signed, 1900s, 6 In., Pair	215.00

L

Vase, 3 Blue Birds, Berry Bush, Signed Gardner, H. Balleroy, c.1920, 12 ½ In. 127.00
Vase, Bowed Cylindrical Shape, Flared Rim & Foot, Roses, Signed, 22 In. 2108.00
Vase, Elongated Oval, Round Foot, Rolled Rim, Flowers, Leaves, Green, Purple, Pink, 5 In. 1770.00
Vase, Flowers, Baluster, Hand Painted, Gilt, White, Blue, Flared Rim, 17 x 8 In., Pair 144.00
Vase, Flowers, Pink, Peach, Yellow, Gilt Accents, Rolled Rim, c.1890, 21 ¾ In. 5635.00
Vase, Flowers, Raised Details, Multicolor, Pink Ground, Gilt Neck Handles, 12 x 9 ½ In., Pair. 183.00
Vase, Globular, Trumpet Neck, Flowers, Gold Rim, c.1895, 10 ⅜ In. 177.00
Vase, Hunt Theme, Gilt, Deer, Mother Bird, Nest, Fox, c.1850, 14 ¼ x 10 ½ In., Pair 1230.00
Vase, Pillow, Bulbous, Handles, Flowers, Pink, Purple, Gold Trim, c.1900, 9 x 8 ½ In. 1295.00
Vase, Pink & Purple Orchids, Green Ground, Gold Handles, Tressemann & Vogt, 1917, 11 x 8 In. 173.00

LINDBERGH was a national hero. In 1927, Charles Lindbergh, the aviator, became the first man to make a nonstop solo flight across the Atlantic Ocean. In 1932, his son was kidnapped and murdered, and Lindbergh was again the center of public interest. He died in 1974. All types of Lindbergh memorabilia are collected.

Airplane, Spirit Of St. Louis, Buffalo Airport, Aluminum, c.1928, 5 ½ In. 375.00
Bank, Charles A. Lindbergh, Bronzed Aluminum, Marked N. Tregor, 1928, 6 In. 75.00
Button, Photograph Portrait, Civilian Clothes, Celluloid, 1 ¼ In. 144.00
Button, Welcome Col. Charles Lindbergh, Minnesota's Own, Photograph, 1927, 1 ¾ In. 158.00
Button, Welcome To Boston, Quadgate, Lindbergh & 3 Other Men, Celluloid, 1 ¼ In. 147.00
Clock, Alarm, Portrait, Airplane Over Water, Square, 5 In. 500.00
Doll, Composition Head, Molded Features, Intaglio Eyes, Muslin Body, Regal, 27 In. 1083.00
Doll, Lucky Lindy, Composition Head, Molded Hair, Muslin Body, Aviator Costume, 14 In. 228.00
Plaque, High Relief Bust, New York, Paris, 33 1/12 Hours, Metal, 7 x 5 In. 275.00
Toy, Airplane, Lindy, Gray Paint, Embossed, Nickel Propeller, Cast Iron, Hubley, c.1928, 9 In. ... *illus* 863.00
Toy, Airplane, Spirit Of St. Louis, Metalcraft, c.1927 .... 250.00

LITHOPHANES are porcelain pictures made by casting clay in layers of various thicknesses. When a piece is held to the light, a picture of light and shadow is seen through it. Most lithophanes date from the 1825–75 period. A few are still being made. Many lithophanes sold today were originally panels for lampshades.

Lamp, Fairy, 2 Parts, Molded, Gilt Highlights, Little Miss Muffett, Saucer Base, 5 In. 230.00
Lampshade, Porcelain, Cone Shape, 8 Panels, Cartouche, American Views, Gilt, c.1850, 12 x 3 ¾ In. 4600.00
Panel, Nativity Scene, Baby In Manger, Shaped Wood Frame, 9 ½ x 7 ¼ In. 266.00

LIVERPOOL, England, has been the site of many pottery and porcelain factories since the eighteenth century. Color-decorated porcelains, transfer-printed earthenware, stoneware, basalt, figurines, and other wares were made. Sadler and Green made print-decorated wares from 1756. Many of the pieces were made for the American market and feature patriotic emblems, such as eagles, flags, and other special-interest motifs. Liverpool pitchers are always called Liverpool jugs by collectors.

Jug, Ecru Body, Applied Loop Handle, Black Transfer, Religion, 8 ¼ In. 83.00

LLADRO is a Spanish porcelain. Juan, Jose, and Vicente Lladro opened a ceramics workshop in Almacera in 1951. They soon began making figurines in a distinctive, elongated style. In 1958 the factory moved to Tabernes Blanques, Spain. The company makes stoneware and porcelain figurines and vases in limited and unlimited editions. Dates given are first and last years of production.

LLADRÓ®

Figurine, A Happy Encounter, Horse, Car, No. 1523, 13 In. .... 1062.00 to 1770.00
Figurine, A Sunday Drive, No. 1510, 14 ½ In. 944.00
Figurine, Baby Holding Bottle, No. 5103, 5 In. 89.00
Figurine, Baby's Outing, No. 4938, 12 ½ In. 345.00
Figurine, Balloon Seller, No. 5141, 10 In. .... *illus* 84.00
Figurine, Basket Of Goodies, No. 4501, 13 In. 225.00
Figurine, Beautiful Rhapsody, No. 6319, 9 ¼ In. 265.00
Figurine, Biking In The Country, No. 5272, 10 In. 472.00
Figurine, Bird Watcher, No. 4730, 6 ¼ In. 345.00
Figurine, Bison, Resting, No. 5312, 1 ½ In. 250.00
Figurine, Boy Meets Girl, No. 1188, 8 ½ In. 375.00
Figurine, Boy With Teddy Bear, No. 6974, 7 In. 24.00
Figurine, Car In Trouble, No. 1375, Car, Geese, 16 ½ In. 1416.00
Figurine, Country Ride, No. 5958, 10 ¼ In. 590.00
Figurine, Dalmatian, No. 1260, 2 ½ In. 500.00
Figurine, Days Of Yore, Fisherman In Boat, No. 2248, 21 ½ In. 502.00

Lladro, Figurine, Tailor Made, No. 6489, 8 In.
$78.00

DuMouchelles Art Gallery

Lladro, Figurine, The Flirt, No. 5789, 9 ½ In.
$236.00

DuMouchelles Art Gallery

Lladro, Figurine, Three Sisters, No. 1492, 12 In.
$960.00

DuMouchelles Art Gallery

Loetz, Rose Bowl, Pink Iridescent, Ruffled Rim, Blue Iridescent, Leaf Base, 3 ½ In.
$920.00

Early Auction Co.

L

LLADRO

Loetz, Vase, Federzeichnung, Mother-Of-Pearl, Brown, Gilt Branches, White, Flowers, Signed, 9 ¾ In.
$4600.00

Early Auction Co.

Loetz, Vase, Federzeichnung, Octopus, Mother-Of-Pearl, Gold Enameled Flowers, Leaves, Signed, 9 In.
$3163.00

James D. Julia Inc.

Loetz, Vase, Gold Iridescent, Spreading Scalloped Rim, Trumpet Shape, Footed, 12 In.
$259.00

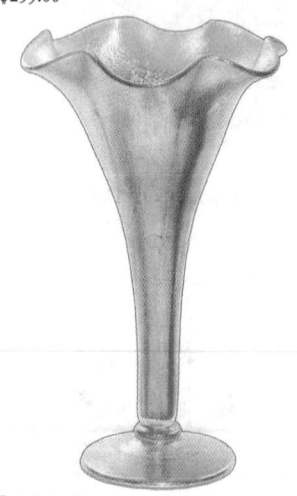

Early Auction Co.

Figurine, Death Of The Swan, Ballerina, No. 4855, 5 In.	225.00
Figurine, Devotion, No. 1278, 9 In.	165.00
Figurine, Doctor, No. 4602, 15 ¾ In.	207.00
Figurine, Dog & Cat, No. 5032, 7 In.	325.00
Figurine, Don't Forget Me, No. 5743, 8 In.	195.00
Figurine, Doves Group, No. 1335, 21 In.	502.00
Figurine, Dreams Of A Summer Past, No. 6401, 9 In. ......illus	90.00
Figurine, Ducklings, No. 1307, I4 In.	48.00
Figurine, Easter Fantasy, No. 1810, 12 ¾ In.	885.00
Figurine, Enchanted Lake, No. 7679, 15 ½ In.	354.00
Figurine, Eskimo Boy & Girl, No. 2038, 13 In.	675.00
Figurine, Far Away Thoughts, No. 1798, 15 ½ In.	1800.00
Figurine, Feed Me Cat, No. 5113, 5 ½ In.	125.00
Figurine, First Date, No. 1393, 16 ¼ In.	826.00
Figurine, Fishing With Gramps, No. 5215, 7 ½ In.	383.00
Figurine, Flowers Of The Season, No. 1454, 11 In.	1180.00
Figurine, Follow Me, No. 5722, 4 In.	83.00
Figurine, Girl Ceramic Seller, No. 5081, 11 ¾ In.	180.00
Figurine, Girl With Child, No. 4636, 7 ¾ In.	235.00
Figurine, Girl With Doll, No. 1211, 9 In.	198.00
Figurine, Girl With Goose, No. 5034, 9 ½ In.	90.00
Figurine, Girl With Lamb, No. 4505, 10 ½ In.	200.00
Figurine, Girl With Puppies, No. 1311, 9 ³⁄4 In.	103.00
Figurine, Girl With Toy Wagon, No. 5044, 11 In.	365.00
Figurine, Girl, Basket, Dog, No. 1034, 10 ½ In.	185.00 to 195.00
Figurine, Golfer, No. 4824, 10 ½ In.	259.00 to 350.00
Figurine, Gras Eskimo Boy, No. 2007.3, White Design, 10 ¼ In.	400.00
Figurine, Gras Eskimo Girl, No. 2008.3, White Design, 11 ½ In.	400.00
Figurine, Guardian Angel, No. 6352, 20 In.	375.00
Figurine, Heather, Ballerina, No. 1359, 5 In.	225.00
Figurine, Hebrew Student, No. 4684, 11 ½ In.	115.00
Figurine, Ingenue, No. 5487, 8 In.	60.00
Figurine, Innocence In Bloom, No. 7644, 9 ¾ In.	118.00
Figurine, Landau Carriage, No. 1521, 11 ¾ In.	1534.00
Figurine, Laura, Ballerina, No. 1360, 8 ½ In.	60.00
Figurine, Little Duck, No. 4551, 3 ¾ In.	65.00
Figurine, Little Pals, Clown, Puppies, Box, No. 7600, 8 ¾ In.	375.00
Figurine, Monkey, Seated, Baby, No. 2000, 12 ¼ In.	240.00
Figurine, Moses, No. 5170, 16 In.	295.00
Figurine, Motoring In Style, Man, Woman, In Car, No. 5884, 7 ¾ In.	826.00
Figurine, My Cuddly Puppy, No. 6463, 10 In.	59.00
Figurine, Nurse, No. 4611, 13 ½ In.	240.00
Figurine, Oration, No. 5357, 8 ½ In.	375.00
Figurine, Peace Offering, No. 3559, 19 ¾ In.	413.00
Figurine, Pensive Clown, No. 5130, 11 In. ......illus	120.00
Figurine, Pet Me, No. 5114, 3 ½ In. ......illus	148.00
Figurine, Phyllis, Ballerina, No. 1356, 6 In.	225.00
Figurine, Pierrot With Puppy, No. 5277, 4 ¼ In.	180.00
Figurine, Quixote, Horse, Windmill, No. 1497, 22 In.	708.00
Figurine, Rabbit's Food, No. 4826, 9 In.	275.00
Figurine, Rebirth, No. 6571, 16 ½ In.	510.00
Figurine, Reclining Angel, No. 4541, 5 ½ In.	150.00
Figurine, Rescue, Rowboat, Crew, Dog, Girl, No. 3504, 17 In.	2065.00
Figurine, Rey De Copas, King, No. 5366, 10 ½ In.	237.00
Figurine, Rey De Espadas, King, No. 5368, 11 In.	271.00
Figurine, Rey De Oros, King, No. 5367, 11 In.	237.00
Figurine, Rickshaw, No. 1383, 11 x 14 In.	492.00 to 633.00
Figurine, Romeo & Juliet, No. 4750, 17 ¾ In.	210.00
Figurine, Serenade, Couple, Pond, Swans, No. 5381, 11 In.	288.00
Figurine, Serenade, Man, Lute, Woman, Balcony, No. 5381, 10 In.	238.00
Figurine, Shepherdess, Dove, No. 4660, 6 ½ In.	95.00
Figurine, Skye Terrier, No. 4643, 6 ½ In.	425.00
Figurine, Someone To Look Up To, No. 6771, 13 ¾ In. ......illus	295.00
Figurine, Songbird, No. 6093, 9 In.	177.00
Figurine, Spring Recital, No. 6452, 8 In.	472.00
Figurine, Star Struck, No. 5610, 8 In.	219.00

Figurine, Statue Of Liberty, No. 7563, 20 In.	472.00
Figurine, Stormy Sea, No. 3554, 20 In.	708.00
Figurine, Summer On The Farm, No. 5285, 10 In.	236.00
Figurine, Summer Serenade, No. 6193, 12 In.	238.00
Figurine, Summer Stock, No. 1407, 10 In. ....*illus*	300.00
Figurine, Sweet Song, No. 6408, 8 ¼ In.	182.00 to 207.00
Figurine, Sweety, No. 1248, 7 ½ In.	300.00
Figurine, Tailor Made, No. 6489, 8 In. ....*illus*	78.00
Figurine, Teasing The Dog, No. 5078, 10 ½ In.	184.00
Figurine, The Flirt, No. 5789, 9 ½ In. ....*illus*	236.00
Figurine, The Quest, No. 5224, 10 In.	136.00
Figurine, Three Sisters, No. 1492, 12 In. ....*illus*	960.00
Figurine, Turtle Dove, No. 4550, 11 In.	148.00
Figurine, Violin Sonata, No. 1804, 15 ½ In.	245.00
Figurine, Voyage Of Columbus, No. 5847, 9 In.	531.00
Figurine, Where Love Begins, No. 7649, Woman, Child, 14 In.	438.00
Figurine, Where To Sir, Chauffeur, Woman, Car, No. 5952, 13 ¾ In.	1062.00
Figurine, Winter, No. 5220, 8 In.	41.00 to 94.00
Figurine, Young Bach, No. 1801, 11 ½ In.	236.00
Figurine, Young Mozart, No. 5915, 6 ½ In.	266.00
Group, A Happy Encounter, No. 1523, 13 In.	1416.00
Plate, Mother's Day, 1973, Dia De La Madre, 8 In.	110.00

LOETZ glass was made in many varieties. Johann Loetz bought a glassworks in Klostermuhle, Bohemia (now Klastersky Mlyn, Czech Republic), in 1840. He died in 1848 and his widow ran the company; then in 1879, his grandson took over. Most collectors recognize the iridescent gold glass similar to Tiffany, but many other types were made. The firm closed during World War II.

Loetz Austria

Biscuit Jar, Art Nouveau, Iridescent Cranberry To Clear, Brass Cover, Bail Handle, 6 ¾ In.	150.00
Biscuit Jar, Iridescent Cranberry To Clear, Brass Lid & Bail, 6 ¾ In.	15.00
Bowl, 2 Handles, Squatty, Honey Brown Circles, 7 In.	650.00
Bowl, Amethyst, Shallow, Crimped Edges, c.1900, 2 x 10 In.	307.00
Bowl, Gold Iridescent, Papillon Pattern, Speckled, Pulled Rim, Scalloped, 2 ½ x 9 ¼ In.	403.00
Bowl, Gold Iridescent, Red & Violet Highlights, Round, Squat, c.1910, 5 x 2 In.	230.00
Bowl, Red Iridescent, Enamel Flowers, Ruffled, 10 ½ In.	350.00
Bowl, Verre De Soie, Gold Iridescent Snails, Appliques, 6 In.	75.00
Centerpiece, Bowl, 3 Storks, Standing, Green Iridescent, Scalloped Rim, Gold Accents, 8 In.	518.00
Compote, Footed, Yellow With Red Flowers, Pavot Pattern, Signed, 6 In.	125.00
Compote, Green Oil Spot, Iridescent Bowl, Ruffle Rim, Metal Stand, Spread Foot, 1900s, 9 In.	176.00
Compote, Green, Pearly White Bowl, Scalloped Rim, Ornate Metal Standard & Base, 14 ½ x 10 In.	518.00
Compote, Green, Threaded Design, Gilt Metal Mounts, Handles, Footed, 7 ½ x 10 In.	460.00
Decanter, Papillon Pattern, Blue Iridescent, Pinched Waist, Applied Tadpoles, 11 ½ In.	1400.00
Figurine, Conch Shell, Gold Iridescent, Orange, Wave Shape Base, 4 ½ x 7 ½ In.	460.00
Inkwell, Cover, Papillion Pattern, Blue Iridescent, Round Spread Base, 3 x 6 In.	920.00
Inkwell, Glass, Squat, Dark Green, Gold Swirls, Flip Lid, Signed, 2 ½ x 5 ¼ In.	431.00
Rose Bowl, Pink Iridescent, Ruffled Rim, Blue Iridescent, Leaf Base, 3 ½ In. ....*illus*	920.00
Shade, Candlestick, Gold Iridescent, Red Orange Vine, Leaves, Ruffled, 3 ½ In.	322.00
Sugar & Creamer, Amethyst Iridescent, Wild Threaded Design, Brass Lid, Spout, Handles	130.00
Vase, 3 Leaves, Green, Pink, Pinched, Bulbous, 4 In.	288.00
Vase, Aubergine, Green, Silver Overlay, Tapered, 11 In.	3600.00
Vase, Beige, Luster, Raised Swirled Design, Flared Base, Max Ritter Von Spaun, 12 x 6 ½ In.	1984.00
Vase, Blue Iridescent, Gold Highlights, Silver Overlay, Flowers & Vines, Baluster, Swollen Top, 4 In.	230.00
Vase, Blue Iridescent, Silver Overlay, Pinched Neck, 4 ¾ In.	1534.00
Vase, Blue Iridescent, Vine Design, Bulbous Stick Shape, Flared Ruffle Rim, 11 In.	1035.00
Vase, Blue Swags, Orange, Pink Ground, Scalloped Rim, 3 ½ x 6 In.	385.00
Vase, Bottle Neck, Iridescent, Teardrop Designs, Ridges, 11 ½ In.	690.00
Vase, Bulbous, Ruffled Fold Down Rim, Cobalt Blue Interior, Iridescent Green, Silver Swirls, 5 In.	2185.00
Vase, Cameo, Footed, Cylindrical, Pink, Cascading Crimson Branches, 5 Red Apples, 8 In.	700.00
Vase, Candia Silberiris, Gold Iridescent, Ball Shape, Ruffled Top, 3-Footed, 6 In.	350.00
Vase, Cobalt Pampas, Rainbow Iridescent, Urn Shape, Flared Rim, 6 ½ In.	1495.00
Vase, Coupe Form, Yellow With Brown Leafy Stems, Signed, 4 ¾ In.	250.00
Vase, Creta Chine, Green, Ribbed, Threaded, Ball Shape Bottom, Stick Neck, Flared Lip, 14 ½ In.	403.00
Vase, Creta Dispora, Bronze Mount, Curling Vines, Swollen Mouth, Flared Rim, 15 ½ In.	690.00
Vase, Creta Pampas, Green, Blue Iridescent, Vines, 3 Loop Handles, Smokestack, 5 ½ In.	690.00
Vase, Creta Pampas, Green, Blue, Yellow Iridescent, Globe Shape, Scallop Edge, Pedestal Base, 8 In.	460.00
Vase, Creta Silberiris Neptune, Blue, Green Iridescent, Baluster, Pinched Shoulder, Flared Rim, 5 In.	345.00
Vase, Crete Rusticana, Green Iridescent, Magenta, Gourd Shaped, Round Foot, 4 ½ In.	173.00

Loetz, Vase, Gold Luster, Heart & Vine, 7 x 4 In.
$1240.00

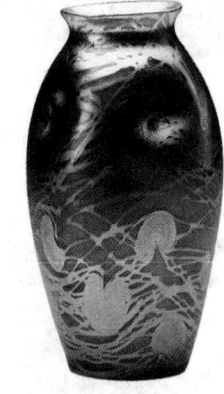

Rago Arts & Auction Center

Lone Ranger, Bracelet, Silvered Metal, Enameled, Lone Ranger In Oval, Premium, T.L.R. Inc., 1938, 2 In.
$380.00

Hake's Americana & Collectibles

Lone Ranger, Display, Standee, Lone Ranger On Silver, Cardboard, General Mills, 1957, 48 x 74 In.
$1380.00

Hake's Americana & Collectibles

L

Lunch Box, Gunsmoke, Matt Dillon U.S. Marshal, Metal, Aladdin, 1959
$115.00

Hake's Americana & Collectibles

Luster, Copper, Mug, Blue Zigzag, Scroll Handle, Raised Foot, 4 3/8 x 4 5/8 In.
$24.00

Conestoga Auction Co., Inc.

Luster, Copper, Pitcher, Sailing Ship Transfer, Verse, The Sailors Tear, Waves, 1800s, 8 1/2 In.
$354.00

Brunk Auctions

Lustres, Bohemian Glass, Green, Portraits & Flowers Panels, White Overlay, Gilded Trim, 1800s, 12 In.
$2607.00

Skinner, Inc.

Vase, Cytisus, Baluster, Flared Rim, Yellow Ground, Flower Silver Overlay, 5 In.	3163.00
Vase, Cytisus, Pedestal, Pinched Waiste, Orange To Blue Iridescent, Oil Spot, Silver Overlay, Iris, 8 In.	550.00
Vase, Elongated Neck, Snake Coil, Buttons, Pontil, c.1900, 9 1/2 In.	510.00
Vase, Emerald Green, Ribbing, Flower Silver Overlay, Baluster, Trumpet Neck, 5 7/8 In.	575.00
Vase, Enamel Tapestry, Turquoise, Iron Red, Green, Marbled Look, Squat, Bulbous, 6 In.	690.00
Vase, Enamel, Gray & Gold Irises, Leaves, Amber Iridescent Oil Spots, Footed, Baluster, 11 In., Pair.	1003.00
Vase, Federzeichnung, Mother-Of-Pearl, Brown, Gilt Branches, White, Flowers, Signed, 9 3/4 In. . *illus*	4600.00
Vase, Federzeichnung, Octopus, Mother-Of-Pearl, Gold Enameled Flowers, Leaves, Signed, 9 In. *illus*	3163.00
Vase, Formosa, Iridescent, Trifold, Peach With Gold Coil, 9 In.	300.00
Vase, Gloria, Opalescent, Threading All Over, 5 Applied Gold Iridescent Leaves, c.1906, 11 In. .	613.00
Vase, Gold Iridescent, Blue Highlights, Footed, Elongated Compote Shape, Foldover Rim, 8 In.	288.00
Vase, Gold Iridescent, Pink, Crackle Finish, Melon Shape, 4 In.	259.00
Vase, Gold Iridescent, Rose Highlights, Green Reeded, Rolled Rim, 7 x 4 3/4 In.	345.00
Vase, Gold Iridescent, Spreading Scalloped Rim, Trumpet Shape, Footed, 12 In. *illus*	259.00
Vase, Gold Luster, Heart & Vine, 7 x 4 In. *illus*	1240.00
Vase, Gold Oil Spot, Blue Iridescent, Green, Double Gourd Shape, Candia Papillon, 6 In.	259.00
Vase, Gold, Opalescent White & Pink Pulled Swirls, Flower Form, Waisted, 9 3/8 In.	504.00
Vase, Gold, Rose Accents, Mushroom Shape, 6 3/4 x 5 1/2 In.	345.00
Vase, Gourd Bottle Form, Yellow With Green Leafy Stemmed Red Flowers, Signed, 11 In.	500.00
Vase, Green & Gold Iridescent, Red Highlights, 3 Handles, Pear Shape, c.1900, 3 In.	219.00
Vase, Green Iridescent Mushroom, Top, Brown Textured Body, c.1920, 8 1/2 In.	362.00
Vase, Green Iridescent, Blue Highlights, Oil Spot, Bulbous Stick Shape, Flared Ruffle Rim, 12 In.	460.00
Vase, Green Iridescent, Blue Tortoiseshell, Smokestack, Shouldered, Brass Collar, 7 1/2 In.	345.00
Vase, Green Iridescent, Cylindrical, Ribbing, 5 1/2 In.	58.00
Vase, Green Iridescent, Draping, Signed, 7 In.	350.00
Vase, Green Iridescent, Jar Shape, Pinched, Tadpole Prunts, 3 1/4 x 4 In.	201.00
Vase, Green Iridescent, Pulled Feather Design, Cylindrical, Tapering, Flared Rim, 7 In.	1380.00
Vase, Green Iridescent, Textured Crackle, Globular, Jack-In-The-Pulpit Mouth, c.1900, 10 In.	430.00
Vase, Green Iridescent, Textured, Iris Overlay, Footed, Pinched Base, Pear Shape Top, c.1900, 4 In.	984.00
Vase, Green, Oil Spot, Tapering Slender Neck, Bulbous Base, 9 In.	368.00
Vase, Iridescent, Gold Papillon, Silver Geometric Overlay, Squat, Raised Rim, 3 5/8 In.	980.00
Vase, Iridescent, Silver Overlay, Lapierre Mark, 10 1/4 x 6 In.	633.00
Vase, Ivory Iridescent, Gold Pulled Feathers, Signed, 4 3/4 In.	345.00
Vase, Lavender, Cream Spatter, Maroon Up From Base, Round Foot, Swollen Top, 9 In., Pair ..	115.00
Vase, Medici, Shouldered, Iridescent, Applied Silver Overlay, 5 x 7 1/2 In.	2400.00
Vase, Mottled Iridescent, Folded Rim, 11 In.	385.00
Vase, Neptune, Blue Iridescent, Golden Accents, Cylindrical, Pinched Waist, 9 1/4 In.	345.00
Vase, Oil Spot, Honey Gold, Corona Highlights, Smokestack Shape, Candia Papillon, 5 In.	316.00
Vase, Oil Spots, Leaves, Green, Blue, Opal, Fuchsia, Cylindrical, Tapered Bottom, Shouldered, 12 In.	316.00
Vase, Oil Spots, Textured, Magenta Iridescent, Gold, Green, Blue, Baluster Shape, 10 In.	633.00
Vase, Orange, Gold, Tree Bark Texture, Triple Dimpled, Round, Cylindrical Neck, Flared Lip, 4 In.	219.00
Vase, Phanomen, Blue & Gold Oil Spot, Pinched Waist, Pulled Ears, Signed, 6 3/4 In.	3200.00
Vase, Pinched Waist, Orange To Blue Iridescent, Silver Overlay With Iris Design, 8 In.	650.00
Vase, Purple, Iridescent Swirls, Bulbous, Lobed, Flared Rim, 4 In.	59.00
Vase, Ruffled Bulbous Top, Waisted Stem, Round Foot, Red Iridescent, Green, 10 In.	305.00
Vase, Salmon, Pulled Feathers, Oil Spots, 3 Pinched Lobes, 5 3/4 x 3 3/4 In.	1674.00
Vase, Shouldered, Cylindrical, Threading, Pontil, c.1900, 14 1/2 In.	499.00
Vase, Silvery Gold Butterfly Wings, Orange, Tapered Cylinder, Triple Pinched, Rolled Rim, 5 7/8 In.	1775.00
Vase, Swollen Body, Silver Overlay, Vines, Flowers, Art Nouveau, c.1900, 5 3/4 In.	944.00
Vase, Tango, Lime Green, Dark Blue, 3 Cobalt Blue Square Handles, 5 In., Pair	196.00
Vase, Titania, Blue, Green, 9 1/2 x 5 In.	2232.00
Vase, Twisted Cylinder, Bronzed Color, Iridescent, 10 In.	294.00
Vase, Twisted Square Shape, Ruffle Rim, Dark Green, Bark Effect, Gilt Highlights, c.1890, 13 In.	288.00
Vase, Urn Shape, Foldover Rim, Blue, Green Stripes, Ausfuhrung, c.1914, 9 1/2 In.	259.00
Vase, Yellow Glass, Applied Blue Iridescent Threads, 5 1/4 In., Pair	236.00
Vase, Yellow Iridescent, Bottle Neck, Rolled Lip, Drip Design, 11 1/2 In.	1150.00

LONE RANGER, a fictional character, was introduced on the radio in 1932. Over three thousand shows were produced before the series ended in 1954. In 1938, the first Lone Ranger movie was made. Television shows were started in 1949 and are still seen on some stations. The Lone Ranger appears on many products and was even the name of a restaurant chain for several years.

Bracelet, Silvered Metal, Enameled, Lone Ranger In Oval, Premium, T.L.R. Inc., 1938, 2 In. ....*illus*	380.00
Display, Standee, Lone Ranger On Silver, Cardboard, General Mills, 1957, 48 x 74 In. ....*illus*	1380.00
Flashlight, Signal, Siren, Silver Bullet Secret Code Brochure, Usalite, Box, 7 In.	89.00
Game, Legend Of The Lone Ranger, Board, Milton Bradley	85.00

Game, Ring-Toss, Amusing, Thrilling, Rosebud Art Co., 1946, 10 x 12 In.	283.00
Guitar, Jefferson Of Philadelphia, 1950s, 30 In.	65.00
Gun, Cap, Cast Iron, Kilgore, 8 ½ In.	57.00
Pencil, Mechanical, Floater, Pistol Drawn, 1940s, 5 ½ In.	125.00
Poster, Lone Ranger, Tonto, Wheaties Premium, Envelope, 75 x 25 In., Pair	345.00
Record Album, Lone Ranger Original Broadcast, 1972	25.00
Ring, 6-Gun, Plastic Gun, Horseshoe Around LR, Branding Iron, Saddle, Adjustable, Kix Cereal, 1947	114.00
Shirt, Red, Repeating Pattern, Hi-Yo Silver, Collar, Button Front, 1949, Boys' Size 10	115.00
Toy, Lone Ranger, Hi-Yo Silver, Lasso, Tin Litho, Windup, Box, Marx, 7 In.	225.00 to 690.00
Watch, Lapel, Gun Holster Fob, New Haven Clock Co., Box, 1939, 4 In.	411.00

LONGWY WORKSHOP of Longwy, France, first made ceramic wares in 1798. The workshop is still in business. Most of the ceramic pieces found today are glazed with many colors to resemble cloisonne or other enameled metal. Many pieces were made with stylized figures and Art Deco designs. The factory used a variety of marks.

Charger, Hotel De Ville, Black Glaze, Triangular, Foil Label, 10 In.	65.00
Figurine, Lion, On Cliff, White, 14 x 11 ½ In.	185.00
Gravy Boat, Blue & White, Twisted Handles, Squared, c.1850, 9 x 6 x 4 In.	85.00
Plate, Octagonal, Flowers, Leaves, Multicolor, 7 In.	165.00
Plate, Whimsical, Village, People, Marked, c.1875, 8 In.	86.00
Tea Caddy, Flowers, Vines, Lid, Marked, c.1892, 5 In.	220.00
Tile, Flying Swallows, Blue & White, Transfer, c.1910, 8 x 8 In.	145.00
Vase, Cherry Blossoms, Turquoise Ground, 1920s, 4 In.	150.00
Vase, Stylized Flowers, Crackle Glaze, Flower Panels, Multicolor, 1920s, 6 In.	1200.00

LONHUDA POTTERY COMPANY of Steubenville, Ohio, was organized in 1892 by William Long, W. H. Hunter, and Alfred Day. Brown underglaze slip-decorated pottery was made. The firm closed in 1896. The company used many marks; the earliest included the letters *LPCO*.

Jug, Bull Head, Brown Glaze, Handle, Signed Charles Upjohn, 3 ¼ x 5 ¼ In.	275.00
Vase, 3 Fish, Caught, Stringer & Cork Bobber, Tapered, Wide Shoulder, Narrow Rim, c.1895, 8 In.	1150.00

LOTUS WARE was made by the Knowles, Taylor & Knowles Company of East Liverpool, Ohio, from 1890 to 1900. Lotus Ware, a thin porcelain that resembles Belleek, was sometimes decorated outside the factory. Other types of ceramics that were made by the Knowles, Taylor & Knowles Company are listed under KTK.

Barrel, Biscuit, Pink & Blue, Raised Pink Flowers, Gold Acorns, Marked, 7 In.	600.00
Bowl, Crimped Edge, 1890s, 5 x 2 In.	130.00
Bowl, Flowers, Oval, Gilt Handles, c.1890, 6 x 4 In.	675.00
Pitcher, Gilded, Fishnet, KTK, c.1891, 5 In.	300.00
Vase, Flower Vines, Scalloped & Hobnail Beaded Rim, White, c.1894, 4 ¾ In.	250.00

LOW art tiles were made by the J. and J. G. Low Art Tile Works of Chelsea, Massachusetts, from 1877 to 1902. A variety of art and other tiles were made. Some of the tiles were made by a process called "natural," some were hand-modeled, and some were made mechanically.

Tile, Allover Flowers, Green, Marked, 3 x 3 In.	65.00
Tile, Entwined Circles, Blue, Marked, c.1890, 6 x 6 In.	115.00
Tile, Mistletoe, Gun Metal Blue, Marked, 6 In., 2 Piece	100.00
Tile, Mother Holding Baby, Men Playing Game, Dog, Green, c.1890, 4 ½ x 4 ½ In.	250.00
Tile, Old Jewish Man, Shylock, Brown, c.1890, 6 x 6 In.	175.00
Tile, Plaque, Eureka, Mule Scene, Green, Wood Frame, Signed A. Osbourne, 7 ½ x 24 In.	2480.00
Tile, Spiral, Yellow, Marked, c.1890, 4 x 4 In.	85.00

LOY-NEL-ART*, see McCoy category.*

LUNCH BOXES and lunch pails have been used to carry lunches to school or work since the nineteenth century. Today, most collectors want either early tobacco advertising boxes or children's lunch boxes made since the 1930s. These boxes are made of metal or plastic. Boxes listed here include the original Thermos bottle inside the box unless otherwise indicated. Movie, television, and cartoon characters may be found in their own categories. Tobacco tin pails and lunch boxes are listed in the Advertising category.

Alvin & The Chipmunks, Vinyl, King Seeley, 1963	121.00 to 153.00
American Scenes, Metal, American Thermos, 1958, 8 ¾ In.	68.00

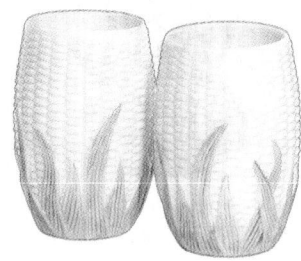

Maize, Tumbler, Pressed Glass, Custard Glass, Green, Ear Of Corn, 4 In., Pair
$201.00

Early Auction Co.

Majolica, Asparagus Server, Attached Undertray, 10 x 8 ¼ In.
$489.00

Strawser Auction Group

Majolica, Cheese Keeper, Kingfisher, Pond Lily, Turquoise, George Jones, 14 In.
$5060.00

Strawser Auction Group

LUNCH BOX

Majolica, Compote, Boy On Shell, Enameled, Impressed Mark, Minton, c.1873, 15 In.
$5333.00

Skinner, Inc.

Majolica, Jardiniere, Bird & Flowers, Footed, Turquoise, George Jones, 14 x 14 In.
$2300.00

Strawser Auction Group

Majolica, Pitcher, Figural, Pig Waiter, Frie Onnaing, 1900s, 10 ¾ x 5 In.
$132.00

Gray's Auctioneers LLC

Astronaut, Metal, Dome, King Seeley, 1960	121.00
Bazooka Bubble Gum, Red, White & Blue, Topps, 1970s, 8 x 6 In.	40.00
Bullwinkle, Vinyl, King Seeley, 1963	614.00
Care Bears, Embossed Images, Aladdin, 1984	50.00
Carnival, Castle, Balloons, Roller Coaster, Metal, Universal, 1959, 8 ¾ In.	102.00
Central Fire Station, Domed, American Thermos, 1959, 9 x 6 ½ In.	96.00
Disneyland, Monorail, Submarine Voyage, Metal, Thermos, Aladdin, 1960, 7 x 8 In.	326.00
Dr. Seuss, The Cat In The Hat, Horton The Elephant, Aladdin Industries, 1970	289.00
Fall Guy, Aladdin, 1981	22.00
Flag-O-Rama, Flags Of The United Nations, Metal, Universal, c.1954, 8 ¾ In.	79.00
Get Smart, Agent 99, Agent 86, K-13, King Seeley, 1966	380.00 to 462.00
Guns Of Will Sonnett, Metal, King Seeley, 1968	176.00
Gunsmoke, Matt Dillon U.S. Marshal, Metal, Aladdin, 1959 ....*illus*	115.00
Heathcliff The Cat, Canadian Issue, Aladdin Industries, 1982	39.00
Hometown Airport, Dome, Metal, King Seeley, c.1960, 9 In.	283.00
Jetsons, Dome, Metal, Aladdin, 1963, 9 x 4 ½ In.	678.00
Knight In Armor, Metal, Universal, c.1959, 8 ¾ In.	90.00
Land Of The Giants, Non-Raised Images, Aladdin, 1968	150.00
Lost In Space, Dome, Metal, King Seeley, 1967, 9 In.	520.00
Mod Flowers, Metal, Okay Industries, 1975	44.00
NFL Quarterback Football, Chicago Bears, Green Bay Packers, Aladdin, 1964	135.00
Orbit, Astronaut Inside Space Capsule, King Seeley, 1963	295.00
Pac-Man, Soft Puffy Vinyl, Aladdin Industries, 1981	79.00
Pathfinder, Cowboys & Indians, Metal, Universal, c.1959, 8 ¾ In.	96.00
Porky's Lunch Wagon, Dome, American Thermos, 1959	565.00
Satellite, Metal, King Seeley, c.1960, 8 ¾ x 4 In.	107.00
Tarzan, Tarzan With Knife Fighting Lion, Raised Images, Aladdin, 1966	159.00
The Black Hole, Sci-Fi, Image Of Spaceship, Aladdin, 1979	125.00
The Flying Nun, Brunch Bag, Aladdin Industries, 1968	500.00
The Osmonds, 5 Brothers On Front, Tour Bus, Instruments, Aladdin, 1973	100.00
The Pink Panther, Vinyl, White With Pink Panther & Inspector Clouseau, United Artists, 1980	139.00
Tom Corbett Space Cadet, Red Version, Aladdin, 1952	189.00
Travelers, Blue Ground, Red Border, Trains, Boats, Airplanes, Ohio Art, 1962	50.00
Voyage To The Bottom Of The Sea, Sub & Giant Octopus, Aladdin, 1967	350.00
Yankee Doodles, George Washington, Minutemen Crossing Delaware, King Seeley, 1975	50.00
Zorro, Red Sky & Red Border, Zorro Rearing Up On Horse, Aladdin, 1966	179.00

LUNEVILLE, a French faience factory, was established about 1730 by Jacques Chambrette. It is best known for its fine biscuit figures and groups and for large faience dogs and lions. The early pieces were unmarked. The firm was acquired by Keller and Guerin and is still working.

Basket, Flower, Bird On Branch, Fan Shape, Gilt Trim, c.1890, 8 In.	296.00
Vase, Black Overlay, Flowers, Cameo, Signed Muller Freres, 14 In.	476.00
Vase, Cameo, Orange, Black Overlay, Flowers, Signed, Muller Freres, 14 In.	506.00
Vase, Rampart Eagle, Scrolled Patterns, Red Glaze Ground, Gilt, France, c.1910, 14 ¼ In., Pair	1093.00

LUSTER glaze was meant to resemble copper, silver, or gold. The term *luster* includes any piece with some luster trim. It has been used since the sixteenth century. Some of the luster found today was made during the nineteenth century. The metallic glazes are applied on pottery. The finished color depends on the combination of the clay color and the glaze. Blue, orange, gold, and pearlized luster decorations were used by Japanese and German firms in the early 1900s. Tea Leaf pieces have their own category.

Blue, Dish, Striated, Marbled, Gold Trim, Shaped Rim, Stretched Handles, 20 x 16 In.	212.00
Cobalt Blue Shaded To Green, Candlestick, Tapered, 2 High Angular Handles, 14 ½ In.	41.00
Copper, Creamer, Lafayette & Cornwallis, 1800s, 3 ¾ In.	267.00
Copper, Goblet, Blue Band, Footed, 4 ½ In.	34.00
Copper, Mug, Blue Zigzag, Scroll Handle, Raised Foot, 4 ⅜ x 4 ⅝ In. ....*illus*	24.00
Copper, Pitcher, Cherubs, Relief, Footed, 5 ½ In.	40.00
Copper, Pitcher, Flowers, Hand Painted, 7 ½ In.	18.00
Copper, Pitcher, Sailing Ship Transfer, Verse, The Sailors Tear, Waves, 1800s, 8 ½ In. .....*illus*	354.00
Fairyland luster is included in the Wedgwood category.	
Fairyland, see Wedgwood	
Pink Pitcher, Setter, Pointer, Leaves & Berries, Footed, 8 In.	895.00
Pink, Enameled Flowers, Gilding, Cut Glass Hanging Prisms, Pointed Arches, 14 In., Pair	522.00
Pink, Pitcher, Volunteer Soldier, Rifle, Round Foot, c.1850, 8 In.	115.00
Sunderland luster pieces are in the Sunderland category.	

L

LUSTRE ART GLASS Company was founded in Long Island, New York, in 1920 by Conrad Vahlsing and Paul Frank. The company made lampshades and globes that are almost indistinguishable from those made by Quezal. Most of the shades made by the company were unmarked.

Vase, Flared, Long Neck, 8 ¾ x 4 In.	279.00
Vase, Green, White Enamel, Gilt Designs, 13 ¼ In., Pair	118.00

LUSTRES are mantel decorations or pedestal vases with many hanging glass prisms. The name really refers to the prisms, and it is proper to refer to a single glass prism as a lustre. Either spelling, luster or lustre, is correct.

Bohemian Glass, Cobalt Blue, 2 Crystal Prism Tiers, Floral Enameling, c.1910, 14 In., Pair..	472.00
Bohemian Glass, Flowers, Green, Rose, Marked Czechoslovakia, Lusters 13 In., Bowl, 6 ½ In., 3 Piece	506.00
Bohemian Glass, Gilt, Flowers, Women, 1800s, 12 ¼ In., Pair	2695.00
Bohemian Glass, Green, 2 Tiers, Prisms, Enamel Design Body, c.1905, 14 In., Pair	413.00
Bohemian Glass, Green, Gilded Trim, Raised Gold Panels, Flowers, 1800s, 12 ⅛ In., Pair	1659.00
Bohemian Glass, Green, Portraits & Flowers Panels, White Overlay, Gilded Trim, 1800s, 12 In. ..*illus*	2607.00
Clear Prisms, Ruffled Rim, Cranberry Glass, Early 20th Century, 10 x 6 ½ In., Pair	118.00
Cranberry Glass, Clear, Open Diamond Shape Top, Crystal Prisms, 12 In., Pair	1035.00
Cranberry Glass, Flower Design, Enamel, Prisms, 11 ½ x 6 ¾ In., Pair	196.00
Cut Glass, Amber, Hanging Prisms, Foldover Petal Rim, Round Foot, c.1850, 12 ½ In.	326.00
Cut Glass, Blue Hanging Prisms, Foldover Rim, Round Foot, c.1850, 12 In.	235.00
Cut Glass, Clear, Hanging Prisms, Foldover Petal Rim, Round Stepped Foot, c.1850, 10 ¼ In..	265.00
Etched Glass, Double Knotted Stem, Flaring Urn Top, Domed Foot, 8 Prisms, 1900s, 11 ½ In., Pair	118.00
Green & Cut Glass, Flower Bouquets, Hanging Prisms, Medallions, Bohemian, Overlay, 13 In., Pair	2124.00
Opaline, Green, Gilt, Ogee Arches, Leaves, Back Cut Prisms, c.1850, 9 ½ In., Pair	215.00
Ruby Glass, Gold, White Accents, Cut Crystal Prisms, c.1880, 13 x 7 In., Pair	1495.00
Ruby Red, Enameled, Goblet Shape, Faceted Hanging Prism Drops, c.1900, 15 In., Pair	518.00
White Cased Glass, Cut To Clear, Oval Classical Portraits, Flowers, Prisms, 13 In., 3 Piece	1169.00
White Cut To Cranberry, Medallions, Spots, Scalloped Edge, Spear Prisms, 10 In., Pair	797.00

MACINTYRE, *see Moorcroft category.*

MAIZE glass was made by W.L. Libbey & Son Company of Toledo, Ohio, after 1889. The glass resembled an ear of corn. The leaves were usually green, but some pieces were made with blue or red leaves. The kernels of corn were light yellow, white, or light green.

Shaker, Muffineer Pattern, Corncob, Ribbed Leaves, Metal Top, c.1890s, 5 ¾ In.	325.00
Tumbler, 2-Tone Leaves, 4 In.	175.00
Tumbler, Pressed Glass, Custard Glass, Green, Ear Of Corn, 4 In., Pair ...*illus*	201.00
Vase, Milk Glass, Impressed White Kernels, Green Husks, 6 ½ In.	144.00

MAJOLICA is a general term for any pottery glazed with an opaque tin enamel that conceals the color of the clay body. It has been made since the fourteenth century. Today's collector is most likely to find Victorian majolica. The heavy, colorful ware is rarely marked. Some famous makers include Minton; Griffen, Smith and Hill (marked *Etruscan*); and Chesapeake Pottery (marked *Avalon* or *Clifton*). Majolica made by Wedgwood is listed in the Wedgwood category.

Asparagus Server, Attached Undertray, 10 x 8 ¼ In. ...*illus*	489.00
Bank, Hen On Nest, 4 ½ In.	16.00
Bowl, Leaf Shape, Flowers, Multicolor, Open Handle, 9 In.	81.00
Bowl, Lettuce Leaf, Wannoppe, 9 In., Pair	71.00
Box, Cover, Bird In Nest, Multicolor, Minton, 4 In.	1380.00
Bust, Black Banjo Player, Green Jacket, Crumpled Top Hat, Flowers, Austria, 30 In.	4385.00
Cachepot, Dragon, Cobalt Blue, 7 ½ In.	47.00
Cachepot, Picket Fence, Flowers, Square, 8 x 7 In.	165.00
Candlestick, Monkey, Climbing Tree Trunk, Cauldon, 1800s, 7 In.	360.00
Centerpiece, Bowl, Scalloped Rim, Curved Cylindrical Support, Wavy Feet, Flowers, 14 In.	30.00
Centerpiece, Figural, Man & Woman Satyr, Nautilus Shell, Mask, Lion, c.1880, 14 In., Pair	1195.00
Centerpiece, Lily Pad Plate, Molded Stork Base, Joseph Holdcroft, c.1875, 9 x 10 In.	418.00
Centerpiece, Peacock Form, Flared Tail Side Panels, Sky Blue Interior, 10 x 17 In.	338.00
Charger, Commemorative, French Town, Coat Of Arms, Signed, 15 In. Diam.	89.00
Charger, Holly, Putti Panels, Mistletoe, Lavender, Minton, 15 ½ In.	1180.00
Cheese Bell, Dome Lid, Berry & Leaf Design, Branch Handle, Brown, Green Leaves, 11 x 10 In.	345.00
Cheese Keeper, Albino Bird, Branch, 7 In.	30.00
Cheese Keeper, Kingfisher, Pond Lily, Turquoise, George Jones, 14 In. ...*illus*	5060.00

Majolica, Stein, Cherubs & Bacchus, Capo-Di-Monte Style, 1 Liter
$325.00

Fox Auctions

Malachite, Obelisk, Neoclassical, Square Base, 29 x 6 In., Pair
$3884.00

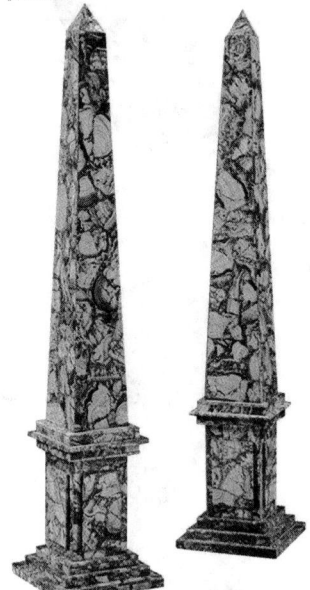
Neal Auction Co.

TIP
Marble is porous and will absorb water vapors into the stone up to 6 inches deep. Airborne pollutants will also be absorbed, and eventually, when the marble dries, the dirt will erode or stain the surface of the marble. Avoid humidity.

Map, Atlantic Ocean, Double Page, Hand Colored, German Text, J. Joannes, c.1650, 20 x 24 In.
$948.00

Skinner, Inc.

Map, Globe, 12 Gores, Ebonized Stand, J.W. Schermerhorn & Co., c.1860, 5-In. Globe
$490.00

Skinner, Inc.

Map, Globe, Aesthetic Revival Stand, A.H. Andrews, c.1860, 43 x 26 In.
$5288.00

Cowan's Auctions

Map, Globe, Celestial, Brass Meridian, Zodiac, Cherry Stand, Wilson's, Albany, N.Y., 1845, 13 In.
$3851.00

Skinner, Inc.

Cheese Keeper, Swan, Water Lily, Estruscan, 7 ½ In.	518.00
Chestnut Server, Spoon, Pond, Leaves, Scallop Shell Shape, Minton, 10 & 8 In.	1208.00
Compote, Basket Weave Bowl, Flowers, Child Figural Stem, Scroll Tripod, c.1862, 36 In.	11850.00
Compote, Blue Shell Shape Bowl, On Coral Stand, Rocky Base, Shells, c.1870, 8 x 11 In.	2133.00
Compote, Boy On Shell, Enameled, Impressed Mark, Minton, c.1873, 15 In. ....*illus*	5333.00
Compote, Daisies, Leaves On Base, 9 In.	102.00
Compote, Griffin Handles, Palissy Ware, 13 ½ In.	59.00
Cup & Saucer, Earthenware, Gold, Brown Drip Glaze, Raised Leaves, Flowers, 3 x 4 ¾ In., Pair	80.00
Cup & Saucer, Pineapple	59.00
Dish, Corn Shape, Green, Yellow, France, c.1900, 5 ½ x 13 ¾ In.	289.00
Dish, Dog Chasing Deer, 8 In.	57.00
Dish, Oval, Blue, Cherry Sprays, Twig Rims, Handles, 2 Birds, Twig Feet, c.1900, 6 x 17 In.	177.00
Dish, Rider On Safety Bicycle, Clair Duckham, 19th Century, 7 ¾ In.	40.00
Dish, Sweetmeat, Putti, Barrel, Vines, Wheat, Cobalt Base, Minton, 1859, 11 x 10 In.	1495.00
Ewer, Applied Amphibians, Insects, Textured Sand Ground, Palissy Ware, 9 ¼ In.	472.00
Ewer, Lid, Applied Amphibians, Insects, Green Ground, Palissy Ware, Portugal, c.1860, 12 ½ In.	944.00
Ewer, Lizards, Shells, Leaves, Ferns, Snake Handle, Palissy Ware, 17 In.	3450.00
Figurine, Blackamoor, Man, Basket On Knee, Cotton Bale, 1800s, 26 In.	668.00
Figurine, Rooster, Running, France, 15 x 9 In.	649.00
Figurine, Senorita, Seated On Settee, Impressed, 18 ½ In.	345.00
Figurine, Young Boy, Sitting On Conch Shell, Lobster Pinching Finger, Tears, 15 In.	2760.00
Garden Seat, Birds, Flowers, 19 In.	24.00
Humidor, Frog, Red, Yellow Attire, 1800s, 7 In.	182.00
Humidor, Indian Chief, 8 In.	141.00
Humidor, Monkey, On Melon, 5 In.	153.00
Jardinere, Floral Reserves, Turquoise Interior, Handles, Oval, France, 18 x 8 In.	219.00
Jardiniere Stand, Iris, Turquoise, Pink, George Jones, 8 ¼ In.	161.00
Jardiniere, Bird & Flowers, Footed, Turquoise, George Jones, 14 x 14 In. ....*illus*	2300.00
Jardiniere, Mottled Green, Brown, 12 In.	24.00
Jardiniere, Pedestal, Pink, Green, c.1900, Planter 16 In., Pedestal 37 In.	700.00
Jardiniere, Pedestal, Yellow, Flowers, 41 ½ In.	106.00
Jardiniere, Shell & Seaweed, 4-Sided, Plankton, 11 In.	245.00
Jardiniere, Stand, White, Dark Green, Julius Dressler, c.1900, 28 In.	1180.00
Jardiniere, Turquoise Ground, Peacocks, Cherry Branches, Shaped Feet, Ring Handles, 15 In.	245.00
Jardiniere, Window Box, Painted Panel, Hunting Dogs, Flushing Birds, France, 17 ½ x 5 In.	184.00
Jug, Figural, Pig, Ham, Orchies, France, 9 In.	115.00
Jug, Frogs, Green, Cream, c.1870, 6 ½ In.	1385.00
Jug, Fruit, Aqua Scroll, Yellow, Looped Handle, Italy, 20 x 19 ½ In.	305.00
Jug, Pineapple Shape, Green Glaze Leaves, Yellow Body, c.1872, 9 In.	474.00
Jug, Turquoise, Brown, Cobalt Blue Cameo, 6 ½ In.	83.00
Lavabo, Multicolor, Insects, Reptiles, Palissy Ware, 16 x 8 In., 2 Piece	1440.00
Match Striker, Elephant, Figural, 5 ½ In.	212.00
Match Striker, Monk, Figural, Standing On Stone With Cup, 8 ½ In.	300.00
Matchbox, Cobalt Blue, Tied With Yellow Rope, George Jones, 3 In.	1150.00
Nut Dish, Applied Squirrel Figure, Holding Nut, Leaf Design Dish, Late 1800s, 12 In.	173.00
Oyster Plate, 4 Wells, Basket Ground, Minton, 9 x 7 ½ In.	2124.00
Oyster Plate, 6 Wells, Lavender, Minton	3658.00
Oyster Plate, 6 Wells, Starfish Center, France, 9 ¾ In.	165.00
Oyster Plate, 7 Wells, Shell, Seaweed, Turquoise, Fielding, 9 ¼ In.	413.00
Oyster Plate, 12 Wells, Fish Head, Blue Ground, Palissy Ware, 11 ½ In.	826.00
Oyster Server, 4-Tier, Revolving, Minton, 11 In.	5074.00
Pedestal, Tapering Columns, Masks, Scrolls, Flowers, Gold Accents, c.1890, 46 x 12 ¾ In., Pair	2390.00
Pitcher, Bamboo, Fern, Multicolor, Wardle & Co., c.1880, 7 ¾ x 4 ½ In.	138.00
Pitcher, Corn, 6 ¼ In.	192.00
Pitcher, Cylinder Shape, Protruding Rim, Applied Handle, Multicolor, 9 ¼ x 7 ½ In.	115.00
Pitcher, Fern, Etruscan, 6 ½ In.	173.00
Pitcher, Figural, Cat, Mouse, Blue, Minton, 10 ½ In.	708.00
Pitcher, Figural, Fish, 10 ½ In.	130.00
Pitcher, Figural, Owl, 8 ½ In.	226.00
Pitcher, Figural, Pig Waiter, Frie Onnaing, 1900s, 10 ¾ x 5 In. ....*illus*	132.00
Pitcher, Flowers, White Panels, Blue Border, Shaped Handle, Baluster, Wide Spout, 15 In.	161.00
Pitcher, Game, Hound Handle, Portugal, 8 ½ In.	130.00
Pitcher, Green Fern, Pink Interior, Marked, Etruscan, 8 ½ In.	181.00
Pitcher, Gurgling Fish, Green & Brown, Tail Curled Up, England, 10 In.	236.00
Pitcher, Lizard Shape, Monk's Robes, Mouth Is Spout, Handle Shape By Tail, c.1900, 13 In.	674.00
Pitcher, Morning Glory, Yellow Ribbon, Bow, Fielding, 7 ½ In.	92.00

Pitcher, Pineapple, 7 In.	130.00
Pitcher, Pug Dog Shape, Seated, Open Head & Mouth, 8 ¾ In.	34.00
Pitcher, Rat, With Umbrella, France, 7 ¾ In.	546.00
Pitcher, Stork In Marsh, Cobalt Blue, Turquoise, Bamboo Handle, Trim, Forestor, 9 ¼ In.	316.00
Pitcher, Stork, Cobalt Blue, 8 ½ In.	94.00
Pitcher, Underplate, Applied Insects, Lizard Handle, Palissy Ware, Portugal, c.1900, 1 ½ x 9 ½ In.	354.00
Plaque, Lobster, Palissy Ware, 13 In.	83.00
Plaque, Madonna & Child, Seated, Tiled Chair, Holding Christ, Roses, Frame, 1800s, 23 x 14 In.	1067.00
Plaque, Pan With Pipe, Seated, Ram's Head, Medallions, Palmettes, Bellflowers, 1800s, 25 x 19 In.	553.00
Plaque, Renaissance Procession, Prince On Horseback, G. Castellini, c.1900, 12 x 15 In., Pair	3107.00
Plate, Butterflies, Flowers, Multicolor, France, 8 ½ In., 7 Piece	154.00
Plate, Choisy, Rabbits, Vegetable Garden, France, c.1900, 8 ⅝ In., 6 Piece	1778.00
Plate, Cottage, Multicolor, Lattice Border, Portugal, 8 ½ In.	120.00
Plate, Enamel, Rabbits Around Vegetable Garden, 6 Scenes, c.1900, 8 In Diam., 11 Piece	1422.00
Plate, Lobed, Yellow Scalloped Edge, Raised Cherub Center, Dutch, 1600s, 6 ¾ In.	748.00
Platter, Dog, Doghouse, 11 In., Pair	130.00
Platter, Fruit, Snake Handles, 14 In.	150.00
Platter, Leaf Shape, Loop Handle, Marked, 12 In.	124.00
Platter, Multicolor, Mottled Center, c.1880, 10 ½ x 14 In.	81.00
Platter, Pears, 12 x 10 In.	207.00
Platter, Salmon, Bed Of Ferns, Seaweed, 23 ½ In.	633.00
Platter, Snake, 2 Frogs, Crayfish, Lizard, Leaves, Palissy Ware, 1600s, 22 ½ In.	3068.00
Pot, 3 Handles, Flower Draped Sides, Footed, Mottled Green, Squat, 6 x 5 In., Pair	184.00
Sardine Box, Basket Weave, Shell Finial	94.00
Sardine Box, Lid, Fish, Basket Weave	154.00
Sardine Box, Lid, Flowers, Leaves, Red Ground, Yellow Trim, Seashell Finial, 4 x 8 In.	188.00
Stand, Sweetmeat, Cherub Riding Dolphin, Shell On Head, 4 Shell Shape Dishes, c.1880, 15 In.	5925.00
Stein, Cherubs & Bacchus, Capo-Di-Monte Style, 1 Liter *illus*	325.00
Sugar, Cauliflower, Multicolor, Estruscan, Marked, Griffin, Smith & Hill, 5 x 4 In.	184.00
Syrup, Pewter Top, Leaves, Ferns, Green, Pink, 1800s, 6 In.	240.00
Syrup, Pewter Top, Turquoise, Dogwood, Holdcroft, 5 In.	165.00
Tazza, Basket Weave, Leaf, Etruscan, 5 x 9 ⅛ In.	92.00
Teapot, Flowers, Cobalt Blue Rim, Flower Finial, Octagon, Footed, T.C. Brown Westhead Moore	374.00
Teapot, Isle Of Man, 3-Legged Sailor, Blue, Brown, Willaim Brownfield & Sons, 9 ½ x 10 ½ In.	230.00
Teapot, Monkey Shape, Seated, Cone Shape Hat, Snake Shape Spout, 9 In.	459.00
Teapot, Monkey Sitting Astride Coconut Shape Pot, 11 In.	237.00
Teapot, Shell, Coral, Fish Handle, 9 ½ In.	472.00
Teapot, Shell, Seaweed, Multicolor, Shell Finial, Estruscan, c.1880, 6 ¼ x 5 ½ In.	259.00
Tray, Applied Bird, On Branches, Turquoise Ground, 5 ½ x 9 In.	288.00
Tray, Asparagus, Flower Shape, Multicolor, c.1890, 9 ¾ x 17 In.	138.00
Tray, Basket Weave, Cobalt Blue Accent, Minton, 9 x 7 ½ In.	153.00
Tray, Fish Shape, Orange, Green, Yellow, Minton, 9 ½ In.	138.00
Tray, Sunflower, Open Side Handles, Yellow, Green, Brown, Continental, c.1910, 11 In., Pair	518.00
Tray, Tobacco Leaf Shape, Green, Mottled Detail, George Jones, 20 ½ In.	1093.00
Trivet, Tea, Bamboo Border, 9 In.	95.00
Tureen, Cover, Castle, Horse, Rider Cartouche, Yellow Ground, Footed, c.1790, 16 ½ In.	531.00
Tureen, Duck, Duck Head Ladle, Duckling Finial, 1900s, 6 ¼ x 12 ½ In.	196.00
Tureen, Mussel, Clam Shell, Undertray, Minton, 13 ½ In.	8260.00
Tureen, Pie, Cover, Game Birds, Grape Swags, Vines, c.1900, 7 ½ In.	177.00
Umbrella Stand, Flared Base, Ferns, Cherry Branches, Brown Mottled Ground, c.1875, 21 x 9 In.	478.00
Urn, Cover, Purple Ground, Bud Finial, 4 Vine Handles, Minton, 11 ½ In.	489.00
Urn, Lion Handles, Masques, Pedestal Foot, Narrow Neck, Multicolor, 1900s, 32 In.	837.00
Urn, Stand, Neoclassical Style, 3 Lion's Heads, Bellflowers, 3 Paw Feet, Red, Green, 69 x 32 In.	1776.00
Urn, White Glaze, Mottled, S-Curve Handles, Applied Lion Masks, Swags, 31 x 15 In., Pair	1179.00
Vase, Angels, Cream Glaze, Brown, Green Accents, Laurel Garlands, 1930s, 5 x 3 ½ In.	30.00
Vase, Bacco E Ariana, Landscapes, Winged Masks, Snake Handles, Ginori, Italy, 1900s, 12 In.	1673.00
Vase, Calla Lily, Minton, 6 In.	295.00
Vase, Calla Lily, Turquoise, Mottled Coiled Snake Base, Minton, 7 ¼ In.	230.00
Vase, Cover, Eagle, Men Chained To Scroll Handles, Pedestal Foot, 1800s, 49 In.	27070.00
Vase, Cover, Flowers, Palmettes, Pedestal Foot, 4 Double Handles, Enamel, c.1862, 11 In.	613.00
Vase, Dolphin, Shells, Scroll, Fruit Medallions, Cantagalli, Italy, 1800s, 15 ½ In.	593.00
Vase, Hand, Ear Of Corn, 7 In.	130.00
Vase, Leaf, Berry, Gold Luster Collar, Snake Handles, Cantagalli, Florence, c.1890, 13 ¼ In.	649.00
Vase, Portrait Medallions, Dolphins, Shells, Scrolls, Fruit, Masks, Italy, 1800s, 15 ½ In.	237.00
Vase, Portrait, Musical Instruments, Dishes, Scrolls, Italy, 1800s, 10 In.	385.00
Vase, Stylized Branches, Flower Crown, Dutch Boy, Girl, Gathering Flowers, c.1900, 13 In., Pair	148.00

Map, Globe, Celestial, Turned Maple Base, J. Wilson Sons, Albany St., N.Y., 1826, 12-In. Globe
$2300.00

Cottone Auctions

Map, Globe, Celestial, Zodiac Horizon Ring, Cherry Stand, Loring, Boston, 1841, 17 x 17 In.
$1645.00

Garth's Auctions, Inc.

M

Map, Globe, George III, Mahogany Stand, T.M. Bardin, London, 1807, 18 x 18 In.
$944.00

Ivey-Selkirk Auctioneers

Numismatic Collectibles

Numismatic collectors want anything that was ever used in place of money. This includes trade dollars, wooden nickels, tokens, shells, or stones used for barter by Indians and twentieth-century phone, charge, debit, and credit cards.

Map, Globe, Library, Turned Maple Stand, Gilman Joslin, Boston, 14 In. $1896.00

Skinner, Inc.

Map, Northern Europe, Atlantic Ocean, Canada, Ortelius, Abraham, c.1590, 15 x 20 In. $1185.00

Skinner, Inc.

M

Map, United States, Southern Dominions, Indian Countries, La. & Fl., Frame, c.1794, 18 x 24 In. $861.00

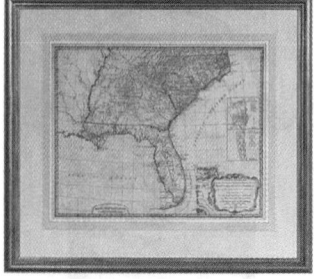

New Orleans Auction Galleries, Inc.

Map, Western Hemisphere, Visscher, Nicolaus, Double Page, Hand Colored, c.1680, 23 x 20 ⅜ In. $1541.00

Skinner, Inc.

Vase, Symbols, Yellow Ground, Chinese, 14 x 7 In., Pair	61.00
Vase, Wraparound Handles, Swollen Bottom, Multicolor, 6 x 3 ½ In.	69.00

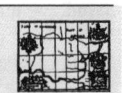

MALACHITE is a green stone with unusual layers or rings of darker green shades. It is often polished and used for decorative objects. Most malachite comes from Siberia or Australia.

Ashtray, 8 x 6 In.	98.00
Bowl, 3 Winged Bronze Figures, Cylindrical Base, Swan Feet, 6 Candles, 22 In.	3444.00
Bowl, Carved, Oval, Handle, Chinese, 2 ⅜ x 3 In.	48.00
Box, Gilt, Silver, Cloverleaf Shape, Florence, Italy, c.1970, 7 ¾ In.	295.00
Box, Lid, Removable, Figured Stones, Polished, 3 x 6 In.	676.00
Box, Lift Top, Wedged Panels, Hexagonal, 1 ⅝ x 2 ⅝ In.	369.00
Figurine, Bird, On Stone, 2 x 2 In.	206.00
Figurine, Birds, Pine Trees, Wood Stand, Inscribed, Chinese, c.1905, 5 ¾ In.	521.00
Figurine, Buddha, Seated, Lotus Position, Robe, Opalescent, c.1950, 8 x 6 In.	369.00
Figurine, Elephant, Trunks Raised, 1900s, 6 ¾ x 10 ¾ In., Pair	777.00
Figurine, Hippopotamus, Carved, 4 ½ x 8 ½ In., Pair	861.00
Frame, Picture, Silver, Octagonal, 9 ½ x 7 In.	1000.00
Jewelry Box, Brass, Metal Frame, Block Feet, Tufted Silk Lining, Russia, c.1925, 5 x 11 In.	854.00
Obelisk, Inlays, Triple Step Plinth, Grand Tour, 1800s, 23 x 8 In., Pair	1107.00
Obelisk, Neoclassical Style, 4 Sides, Spire Top, Square Base, 10 In., Pair	1599.00
Obelisk, Neoclassical, Square Base, 29 x 6 In., Pair ....*illus*	3884.00
Obelisk, Stepped Base, 1900s, 17 ¼ In.	1016.00
Table, Round, Brass, Steel Pedestal, 1900s, 29 x 60 In.	1770.00
Thermometer, Obelisk, Pietra Dura, Registers Blood Heat, Summer Heat, c.1850, 15 In.	708.00
Urn, Mask Handles, Pinecone Finial, Gilt Swags, Putto Supports, Plinth, 24 x 11 In., Pair	6457.00

MAPS of all types have been collected for centuries. The earliest known printed maps were made in 1478. The first printed street map showed London in 1559. The first road maps for use by drivers of automobiles were made in 1901. Collectors buy maps that were pages of old books, as well as the multifolded road maps popular in this century.

Atlantic Ocean, Double Page, Hand Colored, German Text, J. Joannes, c.1650, 20 x 24 In. .....*illus*	948.00
Atlas, Caldwell's Illustrated Combination Centennial Atlas, Washington Co., Pa., c.1876	253.00
Atlas, Greene, Washington, Allegheny Counties, Mat, Gilt Frame, 1800s, 16 x 20 In., 7 Piece	118.00
Baja Peninsula, Copperplate Engraved, Le Nouveau Mexique, Paris, 1781, 10 x 14 In.	584.00
Canada, Newfoundland, Copperplate Engraved, Paper, Frame, Germany, 1700s, 26 x 22 In.	546.00
Caribbean, England, 18th Century, 1756, 20 x 14 In.	201.00
Charleston, South Carolina, British Attack, Life Of George Washington, c.1807, 10 x 15 In.	118.00
Globe, 12 Gores, Ebonized Stand, J.W. Schermerhorn & Co., c.1860, 5-In. Globe ....*illus*	490.00
Globe, Aesthetic Revival Stand, A.H. Andrews, c.1860, 43 x 26 In. ....*illus*	5288.00
Globe, Black, Plaster, Chicago, 1920s, 12 In.	820.00
Globe, Brass Meridian, Engraved, Mahogany Tripod Stand, Crutchley, 47 x 21 In.	18750.00
Globe, Brass Ring Circle, Zodiac, Calendar, Walnut Base, Turned Legs, Kittinger, 38 In.	2133.00
Globe, Cast Iron Base, Johnston, Hammett Publisher, England, 1920, 20 x 12 In.	580.00
Globe, Celestial, Brass Meridian, Zodiac, Cherry Stand, Wilson's, Albany, N.Y., 1845, 13 In. ...*illus*	3851.00
Globe, Celestial, Husun Star, Mahogany, Brass Frame, Calibration Markers, 1920, 11 x 10 ½ In.	590.00
Globe, Celestial, Turned Maple Base, J. Wilson Sons, Albany St., N.Y., 1826, 12-In. Globe ......*illus*	2300.00
Globe, Celestial, Zodiac Horizon Ring, Cherry Stand, Loring, Boston, 1841, 17 x 17 In. ......*illus*	1645.00
Globe, Cut Glass, Chrome Stand, Round Base, Waterford, 12 ¼ In.	593.00
Globe, George III, Mahogany Stand, T.M. Bardin, London, 1807, 18 x 18 In. ....*illus*	944.00
Globe, Iron Half Ring, Wood Base, C.S. Hammond Co., c.1930, 21 x 13 In.	184.00
Globe, Iron Stand, C.S. Hammond & Co., c.1920, 12 In.	795.00
Globe, Library, Turned Maple Stand, Gilman Joslin, Boston, 14 In. ....*illus*	1896.00
Globe, Oak Floor Stand, Cheney, Seneca Falls, c.1890, 12 x 47 In.	353.00
Globe, Stand, Rand McNally & Gutton, 59 In.	2607.00
Globe, Turned Walnut Stand, Thos. & Greares, After Merzbach & Falk, 23 x 11 In.	418.00
Globe, Walnut Stand, Replogle Globes, Inc., 36 x 12 In.	110.00
Globe, Wood Stand, George F. Cram, 1930, 9 x 7 In.	121.00
Globe, Zodiac, Calendar, Wood Sphere, Stand, 12 Gores, Murdock & Co., c.1835, 5 In.	948.00
Kentucky, Tennessee, Engraved, Cyrus Harris, Thomas & Andrews, Boston, 1700s, 8 x 13 In.	460.00
New Orleans, Engraved, Hand Colored, Acanthus Frame, S. Augustus Mitchell, 10 x 12 In.	215.00
Niagara Falls, Folding, Tourist Guide Book, Parsons, c.1835, 3 ¾ x 5 ¾ & 14 x 12 In.	339.00
Northern Europe, Atlantic Ocean, Canada, Ortelius, Abraham, c.1590, 15 x 20 In. ....*illus*	1185.00
Ohio, Indiana, Illinois, Michigan Territory, Anthony Finley, c.1826, Frame, 18 x 22 In.	499.00
Pennsylvania, Geographical, Statistical, Historical, Hand Colored, Carey & Lean, c.1822, 24 x 28 In.	294.00
Pennsylvania, Nova Jersey, Et Nova York, Engraved, Hand Colored, Frame, 32 x 28 In.	2340.00

Port Royal, South Carolina, British Naval, Frame, 18th Century, 34 x 24 In.	2070.00
Quebec, Glazed & Mat, Frame, 18th Century, 31 x 24 In.	2250.00
Scotland, 17th Century, Parts Of England, Ireland, Nicholaum Visscher, c.1680, 22 x 19 In.	354.00
Sharon, Farrell, Sharpsville & Wheatland, Pa., Street, 1943, 16 x 22 In.	15.00
United States, Railroad & County, Colton, 1875, 32 x 42 In.	173.00
United States, Southern Dominions, Indian Countries, La. & Fl., Frame, c.1794, 18 x 24 In. ..*illus*	861.00
Virginia, Engraved, Hand Color, Tourist's, S. Augustus Mitchell, c.1845, 13 x 15 In.	690.00
Virginia, Mid-Atlantic States, Engraved, Hand Colored, Johann Baptiste Homann, c.1710, 19 x 23 In.	1840.00
Western Hemisphere, Visscher, Nicolaus, Double Page, Hand Colored, c.1680, 23 x 20 ⅜ In. ..*illus*	1541.00

MARBLE collectors pay highest prices for glass and sulphide marbles. The game of marbles has been popular since the days of the ancient Romans. American children were able to buy marbles by the mid-eighteenth century. Dutch glazed clay marbles were least expensive. Glazed pottery marbles, attributed to the Bennington potteries in Vermont, were of a better quality. Marbles made of pink marble were also available by the 1830s. Glass marbles seem to have been made later. By 1880, Samuel C. Dyke of South Akron, Ohio, was making clay marbles and The National Onyx Marble Company was making marbles of onyx. The Navarre Glass Marble Company of Navarre, Ohio, and M. B. Mishler of Ravenna, Ohio, made the glass marbles. Ohio remained the center of the marble industry, and the Akron-made Akro Agate brand became nationally known. Other pieces made by Akro Agate are listed in this book in the Akro Agate category. Sulphides are glass marbles with frosted white figures in the center.

Akro Agate, Blue, Yellow, White, Clear, ⅝ In.	39.00
Akro Agate, Corkscrew, Blue, Red Prize Name, 1 In.	80.00
Akro Agate, Corkscrew, Christmas Tree, Red, Green, ¹³⁄₁₆ In.	15.00
Akro Agate, Corkscrew, Ketchup & Mustard, ¹⁵⁄₁₆ In.	9.00
Akro Agate, Corkscrew, Multicolor, Superman Prize Name, ¾ In.	30.00
Akro Agate, Moonie, Opalescent, ⅝ In.	12.75
Akro Agate, Patch, Multicolor, ⅞ In.	10.00
Akro Agate, Purple, White, Swirl, ⅞ In.	13.00
Akro Agate, Slag, Orange, ⅝ In.	30.00
Clambroth, Black, White & Black, ¹⁹⁄₃₂ In.	40.00
Joseph's Coat, Swirl, Olive, Peach, White Bands, ⅝ In.	45.00
Lutz, Blue, Copper, White Swirl Bands, ¹⁹⁄₃₂ In.	107.00
Lutz, Copper, Red Bands, ⅝ In.	181.00
Lutz, Copper, Yellow Bands, ¹³⁄₁₆ In.	136.00
Lutz, Green Swirls, ⅝ In.	192.00
Lutz, Green, Copper Bands, ¹⁷⁄₃₂ In.	113.00
Lutz, Onionskin, Brown, Blue Swirls, ²³⁄₃₂ In.	96.00
Lutz, Onionskin, Gold, Brown Vertical Bands, Blue Ground, ⅞ In.	90.00
Lutz, Onionskin, White, Copper, Green Bands, ¾ In.	203.00
Lutz, Solid Core, Red, Gold Bands, 1³⁄₁₆ In.	57.00
Onionskin, Multicolor, 1 ⅜ In.	17.00
Onionskin, Pink, White, Blue Swirl, 1 In.	23.00
Ribbon Core Swirl, Blue, Pink, Yellow, Aquamarine Edge, Germany, c.1880, 1 ⅝ In.	47.00
Swirl, Red, Green, White, Latticinio, Germany, 2 In. *illus*	115.00
Swirl, Ribbon Core, Green, Red, Blue, Pontil, 1 ½ In.	54.00

MARBLE CARVINGS, such as large or small figurines, groups of people or animals, and architectural decorations, have been a special art form since the time of the ancient Greeks. Reproductions, especially of large Victorian groups, are being made of a mixture using marble dust. These are very difficult to detect and collectors should be careful. Other carvings are listed under Alabaster.

Bust, 3 Children, Huddled Together, Looking Over Wall, Oak Plinth, c.1890, 9 ½ x 14 In.	805.00
Bust, Antonius As Dionysius, Carrara, Pedestal, Inscribed, Emma Stebbins, 16 In. *illus*	5629.00
Bust, Apolla, Signed Pietro Bazzanti, 16 ½ In.	1534.00
Bust, Apollo, Diana, Carrara, Socle Base, 24 ¾ & 23 ½ In., Pair	4780.00
Bust, Augustus, White, 1800s, 17 In.	850.00
Bust, Beatrice, Micro Mosaic Detail, 1800s, 22 ½ x 21 In.	3900.00
Bust, Benjamin Franklin, Early 19th Century, 14 In.	3000.00
Bust, Boy, Curly Hair, Cross Around Neck, Rose Garland, Italy, 28 In. *illus*	1722.00
Bust, Constanza Bonarelli, White, Waisted Socle, Italy, 1800, 23 In.	3200.00
Bust, Dante Alighieri, Laurel Wreath Crown, Green Marble, 18 In.	208.00
Bust, Evangeline, Cross Necklace, Downward Glancing, Pedestal Base, c.1881, 21 In.	9560.00
Bust, Evangeline, William Couper, Signed, 20 In.	4661.00
Bust, Gentleman, Long Curls, Socle, White, 1800s, 19 In.	1180.00

Marble, Swirl, Red, Green, White, Latticinio, Germany, 2 In.
$115.00

Hake's Americana & Collectibles

Marble Carving, Bust, Antonius As Dionysius, Carrara, Pedestal, Inscribed, Emma Stebbins, 16 In.
$5629.00

Skinner, Inc.

M

Marble Carving, Bust, Boy, Curly Hair, Cross Around Neck, Rose Garland, Italy, 28 In.
$1722.00

Neal Auction Co.

TIP
The best time to buy an antique is when you see it.

MARBLE CARVING

Marble Carving, Bust, Young Man In A Toga, Signed, J. Steell, R.S.A., 1865, 28 In. $2440.00

Neal Auction Co.

Marble Carving, Statue, Woman, Standing, Holding Rose, Urn, Pedestal, Stepped Base, 34 In. $2963.00

Skinner, Inc.

Marble Carving, Urn, Empire Style, Cover, Gilt Bronze, Entwined Branches, Ram's Head Handles, 20 In., Pair $1599.00

Neal Auction Co.

Bust, George Washington, White, Round Socle, Paris, 21 In.	4015.00
Bust, Girl, Bonnet, Hand On Cheek, Signed, Fratelli, Italy, 14 In.	385.00
Bust, Girl, Reading Book, Ribbon In Hair, Ponytail, Round Stand, 14 In.	325.00
Bust, Guanyin, Scrolling Headdress, Birds, Eyes Closed, White, c.1800, 16 In.	748.00
Bust, Hermes From Olympia, c.1890, 26 x 20 In.	1776.00
Bust, Madame Recamier, Upswept Hair, Draped, France, 1800s, 20 x 10 In.	1107.00
Bust, Madame Recamier, Upswept Hair, Wearing Wrap, Italy, c.1900, 26 In.	2963.00
Bust, Maiden, Head Draped, White, Tapered Square Column Pedestal, 50 x 19 In.	2000.00
Bust, Marie Antoinette, White, Alabaster Pedestal, France, 1800s, 24 In.	1410.00
Bust, Roman Emperor, Downward Glancing, Bearded, Draped Clothing, 36 x 31 In.	1500.00
Bust, Roman Senator, Rouge Robe, Black Base, 1900s, 19 ¾ In.	1320.00
Bust, Roman Soldier, Rouge Robe, Black Base, 1900s, 20 In.	1320.00
Bust, Urchin, Smoking Pipe, Green, Waisted Stand, Italy, 16 x 10 In.	527.00
Bust, Venus, Aphrodite, Downward Glancing, Italy, c.1890, 26 ½ In.	3286.00
Bust, Woman, Art Nouveau, Carrara, Signed A. Piazza, 21 In.	1309.00
Bust, Woman, Neoclassical, Incised, Rhinehart, 1874, 27 In.	4750.00
Bust, Woman, Renaissance Style, White, Ottavio Scheggi, Inscribed, 1800s, 14 x 14 In.	598.00
Bust, Woman, Victorian Attire, Lace Bonnet, Round Socle, c.1900, 27 x 16 In.	1342.00
Bust, Young Man In A Toga, Signed, J. Steell, R.S.A., 1865, 28 In. ....*illus*	2440.00
Bust, Young Man, Glancing Down, Ivory Color, Round Pedestal Base, 1800s, 15 In.	550.00
Cassolette, Gilt Bronze, Ram's Head Handles, Swags, Plinth, c.1890, 16 x 9 In., Pair	1599.00
Obelisk, Engraved Hieroglyphics, Grand Tour, c.1850, 10 ½ In.	1315.00
Pedestal, Art Deco, Turned Capital, Honey Mottled, 40 x 16 In.	660.00
Pedestal, Black, Column Shape, 34 x 14 In.	489.00
Pedestal, Black, Round, Turned, 36 x 13 In.	660.00
Pedestal, Green Scagliola Column, Black Base, 46 x 15 In., Pair	3936.00
Pedestal, Neoclassical, Black Top & Plinth, Speckled Tan Column, 40 In.	1230.00
Pedestal, Neoclassical, Octagonal Top, Corinthian Column, Cast Metal, 1900s, 47 x 13 In.	805.00
Pedestal, Octagonal Top & Base, Spiral Column, Ivy Band, Italy, 1800s, 41 ¾ In.	652.00
Pedestal, Octagonal Top, Doric Capital, Spiral Standard, Greek Key Band, c.1905, 39 x 15 In.	374.00
Pedestal, Round Banded Top, Leaf Carved, Lobed Column, Gilt, Italy, 36 x 12 In., Pair	500.00
Pedestal, Round Top, Cylindrical Column, Round Base, Green, 31 x 12 In., Pair	127.00
Pedestal, Round Top, Ring Turned Support, Floral Band, Octagonal Base, Carrara, 40 In.	236.00
Pedestal, Square Top & Base, Column, Green Onyx, 1900s, 39 In.	1541.00
Pedestal, Turned Stem, Stepped Base, 55 In.	489.00
Pedestal, Victorian, Bronze, Corinthian Column, c.1890, 49 x 13 In.	1673.00
Pedestal, White, Square Top, Spiral Twist Column, Round Stepped Plinth, c.1950, 43 In.	690.00
Pedestal, White, Twisted Stem, 23 x 13 In.	458.00
Plaque, Figures Of Women, Neoclassical, Signed Francois Duquesnoy, c.1892, 17 x 6 In.	1121.00
Plaque, Venus, Chastisement, Italy, 16th Century, 15 ¼ In.	1875.00
Statue, Ariadne On Panther, Nude Woman, H. Dannecker, 24 x 19 In.	1770.00
Statue, Buddha, Seated On Lotus Flower, White, Chinese, 24 In.	502.00
Statue, Buddha, Seated, Tranquil Position, White, Chinese, 19 In.	207.00
Statue, Crouching Venus, Marble Pedestal, Nude, Italy, Early 1900s, 53 x 18 In.	10755.00
Statue, Daydreaming, Nude Woman Against Rocks, C. Verona, Italy, c.1900	390.00
Statue, Dolphin, Rock Base, Italy, 38 x 10 In.	3159.00
Statue, Farm Boy, Baby, Wheelbarrow, Italy, c.1910, 17 ¾ x 21 In.	308.00
Statue, Fisherman, Day's Catch, Pole, c.1880, 41 x 14 In.	2952.00
Statue, Fisherman, Net & Gourd, Pietro Barzanti, Italy, 1800s, 41 x 17 In.	1725.00
Statue, Foo Dogs, Draped Plinth, White, Chinese, 1900, 18 In., Pair	738.00
Statue, Girl, Winter Coat, Hat & Boots, Leaning On Stump, 19 In.	1003.00
Statue, Goddess, Guanyin, Carved, Chinese, 36 ½ In.	729.00
Statue, Horse, Full Figure, Trotting, 18 x 20 In.	1180.00
Statue, Hunter, Nude, Standing Against Tree Trunk, Arrows, Neoclassical Style, 60 x 22 In.	2250.00
Statue, Idylle, Boy, Playing Flute, Gilt Bronze Goat, After Joaquin Angles, 37 In.	4182.00
Statue, Lion, Paw On Ball, Mottled Green, Italy, 9 x 13 In.	1755.00
Statue, Lovers, Man & Woman, Embracing, Oval Base, Italy, 1800s, 23 x 20 In.	770.00
Statue, Mother, Child With Serpent Head, Signed J. De Creeft, c.1970, 27 x 12 In.	460.00
Statue, Navajo Woman, Holding Baby In Lap, Papoose, G. Johnson, 14 In.	59.00
Statue, Nude, Resting, Signed Parera, 1986, 8 x 18 In.	345.00
Statue, Saint Joseph, Holding Christ Child, Lilies, Continental, c.1900, 61 In.	4674.00
Statue, Venus, Holding Robe, Italy, c.1890, 22 x 7 In.	598.00
Statue, Woman, Classically Robed, Standing, 1800s, 23 In.	593.00
Statue, Woman, Nude, Dolphin, 2 Cherubs, Tapering Octagonal Pedestal, 28 In.	1062.00
Statue, Woman, Nude, Reclining On Panther, Wreath In Hair, Italy, 23 x 22 In.	4266.00
Statue, Woman, Standing, Holding Rose, Urn, Pedestal, Stepped Base, 34 In. ....*illus*	2963.00

M

Urn, Empire Style, Cover, Gilt Bronze, Entwined Branches, Ram's Head Handles, 20 In., Pair ....*illus*	1599.00
Urn, Empire Style, Green, Bronze Pineapple Finial, Swan Handles, c.1900, 18 In., Pair	2640.00
Urn, Louis XVI Style, Gilt Bronze, Garland, Loop Handles, Fitted As Lamp, 21 In., Pair ....*illus*	1230.00
Urn, Mottled Gray & White, Ormolu Mounts, France, 1800s, 20 In., Pair......................	920.00
Urn, Neoclassical Style, Flared Egg & Dart Rim, Ram's Heads, Socle Base, Italy, 43 In., Pair ...	2390.00
Urn, Ring Handles, Banded, Square Marble Base, Rolled Rim, 26 x 14 In.	196.00
Urn, Rolled Rim, Etched, Round Pedestal Base, 36 x 23 In., Pair	1000.00
Vase, Pierced, Flowering Prunus, Pine Trees, Bamboo, Hollow Tree Trunk, c.1905, 5 In..........	215.00

MARBLEHEAD POTTERY was founded in 1905 by Dr. J. Hall as a rehabilitative program for the patients of a Marblehead, Massachusetts, sanitarium. Two years later it was separated from the sanitarium and it continued operations until 1936. Many of the pieces were decorated with marine motifs.

Bowl, Acorns, Oak Leaves, Painted, Ship Mark, HT, 2 x 7 ¼ In........................	1240.00
Bowl, Yellow Crackle Glaze, Flared, 6 x 2 ½ In..................................	56.00
Bowl, Yellow Matte Glaze, Flared, Signed AEB, 5 x 8 In...........................	1364.00
Candlestick, Geometric Pattern, Sarah Tutt, Ship Mark, HJH, 7 ¼ x 3 ¾ In............	3596.00
Tile, Ship, White, Blue Matte Glaze, Marked, 6 ½ In..............................	178.00
Vase, Blue Matte Glaze, Bulbous, Marked, 11 ½ x 10 ½ In.........................	258.00
Vase, Blue Matte Glaze, Red Clay, Beaker Shape, Marked, 7 In.....................	460.00
Vase, Blue Matte Glaze, Stylized Flowers, Green, Red, Impressed Mark, 3 ¼ x 3 ½ In..........	1320.00
Vase, Blue Matte Glaze, Tapered, 3 x 7 ¾ In..................................	220.00
Vase, Blue Matte Glaze, Tapered, Cabinet, Marked, 5 In..........................	230.00
Vase, Brown Matte Glaze, Squat, Round, 5 ¼ x 2 ½ In...........................	605.00
Vase, Budding Branches, Painted, Ship Mark, HT, 5 x 3 ½ In.......................	6820.00
Vase, Fish, Painted, Stamped, Ship Mark, 4 ½ x 5 In............................	17360.00
Vase, Flowers, Painted, Stamped, Ship Mark, 4 ¼ x 2 In..........................	1860.00
Vase, Glasgow Roses, Rolled Rim, Blue, Red Matte Glaze, 3 ½ x 3 ¾ In................	2108.00
Vase, Green Matte Glaze, Speckled Glaze, Oval, Stamped, 7 x 4 In..................	230.00
Vase, Green Matte Glaze, Textured Ground, 2 Handles, Ship Mark, Paper Label, 5 x 6 ½ In.....	527.00
Vase, Lavender Matte Glaze, Bulbous, Marked, 6 x 4 ¼ In..........................	360.00
Vase, Red, Green Flowers, Blue Matte Glaze, Cylindrical, 3 ¼ x 3 ½ In................	1210.00
Vase, Slender Flare, Blue Matte Glaze, Marked, 3 x 7 ½ In.........................	240.00
Vase, Stylized Flowers, Incised, Painted, Marked, 6 x 5 In........................	2356.00
Vase, Stylized Flowers, Incised, Painted, Stamped, Ship Mark, 6 x 5 In...............	2356.00
Vase, Stylized Leafy Branches, Green & Blue Matte Glaze, Cylindrical, Tapered, 11 In.	3200.00
Vase, Yellow Matte Glaze, Cylindrical, Inverted Rim, 4 x 4 ¼ In.....................	360.00
Vase, Yellow Matte Glaze, Cylindrical, Marked, 4 x 4 ¼ In.........................	330.00

MARTIN BROTHERS of Middlesex, England, made Martinware, a salt-glazed stoneware, between 1873 and 1915. Many figural jugs and vases were made by the three brothers. Of special interest are the fanciful birds, usually made with removable heads. Most pieces have the incised name of the artists plus other information on the bottom.

Martin Bro/ London

Jug, Barrister, 2-Sided, Stoneware, c.1880, 6 ¾ In...............................	5975.00
Jug, Fish & Eels, Eel Form Handle, Blue & Brown Glazes, 1887, 9 ¼ In. ....*illus*	4148.00
Spoon Holder, Grotesque, Crab-Like Creature, Clawed Feet, Gaping Mouth, c.1880, 3 ½ In....	19620.00
Tobacco Jar, Bird, Glazed Stoneware, Signed, 1897, 9 ¼ x 5 In. ....*illus*	28520.00
Vase, Bottle Shape, Dragons, Winged, Blue, Dark Metallic Ground, c.1931, 10 ¾ In.	1865.00
Vase, Bud, Fish, Incised, Oval, 1914, 3 ¾ x 2 ¼ In..............................	1612.00
Vase, Gourd Shape, Tobacco Brown Glaze, Incised Mark, 4 ⅝ In. ....*illus*	460.00
Vase, Snails, Incised, 4-Sided, Signed, 1903, 9 x 4 In. ....*illus*	4030.00

MARY GREGORY is the name used for a type of glass that is easily identified. White figures were painted on clear or colored glass as the decoration. The figures chosen were usually children at play. The first glass known as Mary Gregory was made about 1870. Similar glass is made even today. The traditional story has been that the glass was made at the Sandwich Glass works in Boston by a woman named Mary Gregory. Recent research says that none was made at Sandwich. In fact, all early Mary Gregory glass was made in Bohemia. Beginning in 1957, the Westmoreland Glass Co. made the first Mary Gregory–type decorations on glassware in the United States. These pieces had simpler designs, less enamel paint, and more modern shapes. France, Italy, Germany, Switzerland, and England, as well as Bohemia, made this glassware. Children standing, not playing, were pictured after the 1950s.

Biscuit Jar, Blue, Scenic, Girl, Gold Stencil Highlights, Silver Plate Lid, Bail Handle, 9 ½ In...	300.00
Bottle, Barber, Cobalt, Boy, Girl, Flowers, Enameled, Pontil, 7 ½ & 7 ⅞ In., Pair ....*illus*	140.00
Pitcher, Clear, Gold Trim, Man, Carrying Oars, 1800s Clothes, Applied Handle, 9 ½ In.	28.00

Marble Carving, Urn, Louis XVI Style, Gilt Bronze, Garland, Loop Handles, Fitted As Lamp, 21 In., Pair
$1230.00

Neal Auction Co.

Martin Brothers, Jug, Fish & Eels, Eel Form Handle, Blue & Brown Glazes, 1887, 9 ¼ In.
$4148.00

Skinner, Inc.

M

Martin Brothers, Tobacco Jar, Bird, Glazed Stoneware, Signed, 1897, 9 ¼ x 5 In.
$28520.00

Rago Arts & Auction Center

Martin Brothers, Vase, Gourd Shape, Tobacco Brown Glaze, Incised Mark, 4 ⅝ In.
$460.00

Humler & Nolan

439

Martin Brothers, Vase, Snails, Incised, 4-Sided, Signed, 1903, 9 x 4 In. $4030.00

Rago Arts & Auction Center

Mary Gregory, Bottle, Barber, Cobalt, Boy, Girl, Flowers, Enameled, Pontil, 7 ½ & 7 ⅞ In., Pair $140.00

Norman C. Heckler & Company

Massier, Vase, Twist, Fern, Metallic Glaze, Signed, 3 ⅝ In. $805.00

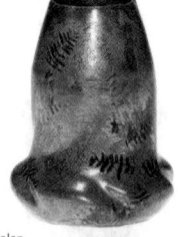

Humler & Nolan

Match Holder, Joan Of Arc, Well For Cigars, Ashtray, Bottom Striker, Porcelain, 5 x 8 x 5 In. $69.00

Showtime Auction Services

Vase, Green, Woman's Bust, Surrounded By Flowers, Tapered, Ruffled, 8 In.	59.00
Water Set, Frosted Cranberry, Boy, Girl, Ruffled Rim, Clear Handle, 5 Piece	201.00
Water Set, Pitcher, Girl, Flower Basket, 6 Tumblers, 3 Boys & 3 Girls, Green, 14 In., 7 Piece	201.00

MASONIC, *see Fraternal category.*

MASON'S IRONSTONE was made by the English pottery of Charles J. Mason after 1813. Mason, of Lane Delph, was given a patent for this improved earthenware. He usually called it *Mason's Patent Ironstone China*. It resisted chipping and breaking, so it became popular for dinnerware and other table service dishes. Vases and other decorative pieces were also made. The ironstone was decorated with orange, blue, gold, and other colors, often in Japanese-inspired designs. The firm had financial difficulties but the molds and the name *Mason* were used by many owners through the years, including Francis Morley, Taylor Ashworth, George L. Ashworth, and John Shaw. Mason's joined the Wedgwood group in 1973 and the name is still found on dinnerware.

Ashtray, Cigarette Holder, Chartreuse, Green, Gold, 3 ½ x 3 ½ & 2 ¼ x 1 In., 2 Piece	57.00
Bowl, Oriental Flowers, Wrigglework Border, Brown Band, c.1850, 15 ½ x 5 ¼ In.	345.00
Cake Plate, Strathmore, Green, Rust, Ochre, Maroon, Pierced Handle, 11 x 9 ¼ In.	45.00
Cake Plate, Vista, Pink, Square Handle, 1940s, 11 x 9 In.	45.00
Chamber Pot, Blue & White, Blue Willow, c.1840, 9 x 5 ½ In.	355.00
Charger, Dragon, Yellow Ground, Copper, Blue, White Striated Edge, 10 ½ In.	275.00
Compote, Oval Top, Ruffled Edge, Pedestal Stand, 1800s, 6 x 15 In.	540.00
Cup & Saucer, Demitasse, Vista, Pink, 2 ¼ x 2 ⅝ In.	22.00
Cup & Saucer, Flowers, Blue, Orange, Yellow, 1820-40, 10 Piece	60.00
Cup & Saucer, Nell Gwyn, Garlands, Leaf Handle, Octagonal Shape, 1920s, 4 ¾ x 5 ¾ In., Pair	120.00
Cup, Vista, Blue & White, 2 ¼ x 4 In.	10.00
Ginger Jar, Chartreuse, Green, Yellow Transfer, Flowers, Gilt Tracery, c.1920, 9 ¼ x 8 In.	170.00
Gravy Boat, Underplate, Regency, Flowers, Grasshopper, 1930s, 8 x 5 In.	40.00
Jug, Bandana Ware, Blue, Red, Orange, Yellow, Chinese Mythical Beast, 5 ¾ In.	195.00
Jug, Red Scale Hydra, Octagonal, Applied Dragon Handle, 1830-40, 5 ¼ In.	225.00
Jug, Water, Japanese Pagoda, Octagonal, Flowers, 11 ½ x 10 In.	750.00
Milk Jug, English Park Scene, Cathedral, Gilding, Marked, 7 In.	165.00
Pitcher, Mandarin, Oriental Style, Snake Head Handle, 6 x 7 In.	95.00
Plate, Ascot, Navy Blue, Center Bouquet, Flower Border, c.1950, 9 ¾ In.	25.00
Plate, Asiatic Pheasants, In Tree, Flow Blue, 9 In.	129.00
Plate, Dessert, Chinese Peacock, 6 ¼ In.	14.00
Plate, Imari, Puce, Orange, Green, Shaped Rim, c.1830, 8 In., 5 Piece	345.00
Plate, Iron Red, Cobalt Blue, Gilt Highlights, Inscribed, 9 ½ In., 12 Piece	431.00
Plate, Ironstone, Derby Design, 10 ¼ In., 8 Piece	489.00
Plate, Mogul, Chinoiserie Transferware, Impressed Mark, c.1818, 8 In.	195.00
Plate, Niagara Falls, Canada, Scenic, Maple Leaf Border, Coat-Of-Arms, 10 ¾ In.	20.00
Plate, Oriental Style, Painted Flowers, 1820-30, 8 ½ In.	25.00
Plate, Soup, Chinese Peacock, 9 ½ In.	35.00
Plate, Turner's Willow, Blue, White, c.1820, 9 ½ In.	125.00
Platter, Chinese Peacock, c.1830, 12 ½ In.	105.00
Platter, Imari, Cobalt Blue, Iron Red, Scalloped Edge, 1800s, 10 ½ x 9 ½ In.	895.00
Sugar, Cover, Chinese Peacock, 5 ¾ x 5 ½ In.	80.00
Tea & Coffee Service, Butterfly, Coffeepot, Teapot, Creamer, Sugar, 5 Cup & Saucers, 9 ½ In.	125.00
Tea Set, Vista, Teapot, Sugar, Creamer, Pink, Square, Pre 1940	395.00
Teapot, Chinese Peacock, 1830s, 8 ¾ x 6 ½ In.	125.00
Thimble, Oriental Flowers, 1 In.	13.00
Toothpick Holder, Mandalay, 2 ¼ x 2 ½ In.	80.00
Tureen, Sauce, Lid, Underplate, Mikado, Painted Flowers, 6 x 8 In.	125.00

MASSIER, a French art pottery, was made by brothers Jerome, Delphin, and Clement Massier in Vallauris and Golfe-Juan, France, in the late nineteenth and early twentieth centuries. It has an iridescent metallic luster glaze that resembles the Weller Sicardo pottery glaze. Most pieces are marked J. Massier. Massier may also be listed in the Majolica category.

Bowl, Flower Shape, Footed, Majolica, 9 ½ In.	413.00
Jardiniere, Monkey Holding 2-Handled Tub, 17 x 9 In.	196.00
Jardiniere, Swan, White, Black, Yellow, c.1905, 12 In.	180.00
Pitcher, Red Glaze, Nude Handle, Art Nouveau, 8 In.	1200.00
Vase, Homme Enleve Par Morphee, Art Nouveau, Iridescent Glaze, James Vibert, c.1900, 19 In.	1380.00
Vase, Hoopee Bird, 9 ½ In.	2070.00
Vase, Iris, Majolica, 12 ½ In.	59.00

Vase, Mottled Green, Bat Wing Handles, Gilt Leaves, Gilt, 10 In.		925.00
Vase, Twist, Fern, Metallic Glaze, Signed, 3 ⅝ In.	*illus*	805.00

MATCH HOLDERS were made to hold the large wooden matches that were used in the nineteenth and twentieth centuries for a variety of purposes. The kitchen stove and the fireplace or furnace had to be lit regularly. One type of match holder was made to hang on the wall, another was designed to be kept on a tabletop. Of special interest today are match holders that have advertisements as part of the design.

Bronze, Barrel Shape, Cat Hanging On Rim, Austria, 3 ⅛ In.		459.00
Cigar Holder, Bear, Red Jeweled Eyes, Metal, 10 x 6 In.		345.00
Cigar Holder, Champagne Bottle, Pairpoint Mfg., c.1921, 10 ¾ In.		115.00
Climax Horse Collars, Tin, H.H. Bunker Agent, Miranda, S.D., Multicolor, 3 ½ x 5 In.		532.00
Diamond Matches, Toilet, Wood Tank, Lid, Base, 3 ¾ x 5 In.		1093.00
Dr. Pepper, Tin, 3 x 5 In.		144.00
Elk, Bronze, 9 x 10 In.		303.00
Fly, Cast Iron, Hinged, Painted, Embossed, Simpson Iron Co., 4 ½ In.		2588.00
Fly, Gold Mine Flours, Brass, Sheffield Milling Co., 3 x 4 ½ In.		489.00
Fly, Sheffield Milling Co., Gold Mine Flour, Figural, Cast Iron, 2 ½ x 4 ½ In.		448.00
Hat & Gloves, Black & Tan, Bisque, Mark Gardner, Russia, c.1890, 5 In.		720.00
Hog, White Metal, Patina, 4 x 7 x 3 In.		908.00
Joan Of Arc, Well For Cigars, Ashtray, Bottom Striker, Porcelain, 5 x 8 x 5 In.	*illus*	69.00
Man, Large Head, Seated, Metal, 4 x 2 In.		44.00
Man, Smoking Pipe, Striker On Both Sides, Cast Iron, Wall, 9 ¼ In.		360.00
Man's Head, Open Mouth Smile, Ruby Eye, Brass, 4 ¼ x 2 ¾ x 2 ¾ In.	*illus*	110.00
Mother's Worm Syrup, Gooch Co., Tin Lithograph, 6 ⅞ x 2 ⅛ In.	*illus*	1705.00
Moxie, Learn To Drink, Very Healthful, Bottle Shape, Tin, c.1910, 7 In.		300.00
Old Judson, Girl Giving Bottle To Dad, Tin Litho, Early 1900s, 5 x 3 In.		163.00
Police Officer, Uniform, Painted, Cast Iron, 5 In.	*illus*	118.00
Puss-In-Boots, 7 In.		275.00
Turtle, Grand Rapids Brass Co., Hinged, Brass, 5 x 2 x 1 ¼ In.		253.00
Woman, Holding Candle, Metal, Hinged Hat, Zimmerman, 4 x 2 In.		253.00

MATCH SAFES were designed to be carried in the pocket. Early matches were made with phosphorus and could ignite unexpectedly. The matches were safely stored in the tightly closed container. Match safes were made in sterling silver, plated silver, or other metals. The English call these "vesta boxes."

Advertising Club House, 5 Cent Cigar, Wichita, Kan., Celluloid, 1 ⅜ x 2 ⅜ In.		403.00
Allyn & Blanchard, Coffees & Spices, Shaped Top, Tin, Black & Yellow, c.1885, 7 In.		270.00
Bayardo, Horse & Jockey, 2 ¼ In.		330.00
Boots Cash Chemists, At Your Service, Horse, Celluloid, 1 ½ x 2 ¼ In.		280.00
Brass, Stag Head, Hanging Game, In Hunting Bag, Initials, c.1890, 11 In.		29.00
Buffalo Pitts Steam Rollers, Standing Buffalo, 2 ¾ In.		420.00
Cawston Ostrich Farm, Man Riding Ostrich, Trees, Ostriches, 2 ¾ In.		210.00
Celluloid, Blue Bell Binder Twine, Belfast Ropework Co., 1 ½ x 2 ¼ In.		708.00
Celluloid, Ironside Co., Columbus, Oh., 2 ¾ x 1 ½ In.		468.00
Chocolat-Menier, Little Girl Writing On Wall, Braids, Umbrella, 2 ¾ In.		270.00
Dance Hall Girl, Celluloid, Felix Bros., Lorain News Agency, 1 ½ x 2 ⅝ In.		220.00
German House Whiskey, Woman, Long Black Hair, Pure Rye Whiskey, 2 ⅜ In.		330.00
Gold Lizard, Flowers, Rounded, 2 ¼ In.		60.00
Gold Medal Flour, Washburn, Crosby Co., Celluloid, 1 ½ x 2 ¼ In.		201.00
Gold Quartz Inlay, Multicolor Diamond Pattern, Green, Pink, White, 1 ⅛ x 2 ¼ In.		10620.00
Junket Tablets, Have Some Junket, Girl, Holding Trays, 10 Tablets, 10 Cents, 2 ⅞ In.		240.00
Lamb Lumber Co., Steer Head, The Best Lumber Yard, 2 ¾ In.		480.00
Mermaid With Flowers, Art Nouveau, Sterling, 2 ¾ In.		120.00
Modern Climax Stove, Taplin Rice & Co. Akron, O., Celluloid, 1 ½ x 2 ¼ In.	*illus*	345.00
Nude, Tiger, Nickel Plated Brass, Celluloid Cameo, 1 ½ x 3 In.		90.00
Old Judson, Rectangular, Wall, J.C. Stevens, Figures, Tin, 5 In.		180.00
Round Oak, Standard Of America, Indian, Stove, 2 ⅞ In.		570.00
Shortsville Wheel Co., Devil, Not To Scare You But, Celluloid, 2 ¾ In.		540.00

MATT MORGAN, an English artist, was making pottery in Cincinnati, Ohio, by 1883. His pieces were decorated to resemble Moorish wares. Incised designs and colors were applied to raised panels on the pottery. Shiny or matte glazes were used. The company lasted less than two years.

Jug, Corn Design, Blue Glaze, Gilt Trim, Marked, 6 ¼ In.		130.00

Match Holder, Man's Head, Open Mouth Smile, Ruby Eye, Brass, 4 ¼ x 2 ¾ x 2 ¾ In.
$110.00

Match Holder, Mother's Worm Syrup, Gooch Co., Tin Lithograph, 6 ⅞ x 2 ⅛ In.
$1705.00

Match Holder, Police Officer, Uniform, Painted, Cast Iron, 5 In.
$118.00

Match Safe, Modern Climax Stove, Taplin Rice & Co. Akron, O., Celluloid, 1 ½ x 2 ¼ In.
$345.00

M

Pitcher, Incised Leaves, Bulbous, Signed, 7 ½ x 6 ½ In.	110.00
Pitcher, Modeled Green Glaze, Flowers, Stamped, 6 ½ In.	425.00

McCOY pottery was made in Roseville, Ohio. Nelson McCoy and J.W. McCoy established the Nelson McCoy Sanitary and Stoneware Company in Roseville, Ohio, in 1910. The firm made art pottery after 1926. In 1933 it became the Nelson McCoy Pottery Company. Pieces marked McCoy were made by the Nelson McCoy Pottery Company. Cookie jars were made from about 1940 until December 1990, when the McCoy factory closed. Since 1991 pottery with the McCoy mark has been made by firms unrelated to the original company. Because there was a company named Brush-McCoy, there is great confusion between Brush and Nelson McCoy pieces. See Brush category for more information.

Bank, Seaman, Sailor Carrying Duffel Bag, Coin Slot, White, Box, 5 ¾ In. ....*illus*	230.00
Bowl, Brown Drip, 5 ¼ In.	6.00
Bowl, Pink Trim, Butterflies, c.1945, 3 x 8 In.	92.00
Candlestick, Cleo, Pink, White, Green, Low Angular Handles, Brush, 9 In.	345.00
Compote, Swirl, Green, Signed, 1960s, 4 ½ In.	29.00
Cookie Jar, Bobby The Baker, White, 10 In.	23.00
Cookie Jar, Happy Bunny, Marked Brush, 12 ¾ In.	17.00
Cookie Jar, Mammy, Figure, Red & White, 1930-40s, 11 In.	120.00
Cookie Jar, Mammy, White Dress, Red Head Scarf, Marked, 11 ¼ In.	51.00
Crock, Stoneware, Brown, White, Cylindrical, 8 Gal., 16 x 14 In.	29.00
Dispenser, Iced Tea, El Rancho, Barrel Shape, Western Decoration, Tan, Brown, 11 In.	1173.00
Dutch Boy Clog, Yellow, Flower, 1940s, 3 ½ x 2 ½ In.	19.00
Jardiniere, Aqua, Zigzag, White Matte Glaze, 5 x 5 In.	112.00
Jardiniere, Pedestal, Grapevine, Green, Brown, 17 ¾ x 12 ½ In.	230.00
Jardiniere, Pedestal, Yellow Flowers, Green, Spread Base, Loy-Nel-Art, 5 ⅞ In.	104.00
Jardiniere, Yellow Flowers, Brown Ground, Standard Glaze, Flared Rim, 9 ¾ x 12 In.	81.00
Mug, Morning Glory, Basketweave, c.1925, 4 In.	32.00
Mug, Strawberry Country, 3 ⅛ x 2 ¾ In.	12.00
Oil Jar, Glossy Blue Glaze, White Striations, Oval, 11 ¾ In.	46.00
Oil Jar, Speckled White, Maroon Ground Glaze, 18 ¼ In.	81.00
Pitcher, Brown, Cream, Fruit, Marked, 5 ½ In.	18.00
Pitcher, Donkey, White Matte Glaze, 6 ⅜ In.	69.00
Sugar & Creamer, Dark Brown Bands, 1970s	40.00
Vase, Bird, Perched, Side Pockets, 8 ½ In.	78.00
Vase, Blossoms, Burgundy Glaze, Footed, 6 In.	81.00
Vase, Chrysanthemum, Lavender, 8 ⅛ In.	58.00
Vase, Chrysanthemum, Yellow, Mark, 8 In.	40.00
Vase, Hyacinth, Blue, Green, 7 ⅞ In.	69.00
Wall Pocket, Gray, Flat Iron, Metallic Trivet, c.1953	80.00
Water Set, Glossy Burgundy, Ball Shape Pitcher, Ice Lip, 7 ½-In. Pitcher, 5 Piece	58.00

McKEE is a name associated with various glass enterprises in the United States since 1836, including J. & F. McKee (1850), Bryce, McKee & Co. (1850 to 1854), McKee and Brothers (1865), and National Glass Co. (1899). In 1903, the McKee Glass Company was formed in Jeannette, Pennsylvania. It became McKee Division of the Thatcher Glass Co. in 1951 and was bought out by the Jeannette Corporation in 1961. Pressed glass, kitchenwares, and tablewares were produced. Jeannette Corporation closed in the early 1980s. Additional pieces may be included in the Custard Glass and Depression Glass categories.

Bowl, Cereal, Canister, Cover, Jade Green, Black Block Lettering, c.1950, 5 In.	100.00
Bowl, Flower, Clear Rock Crystal, c.1935, 12 x 2 ¾ In.	65.00
Bowl, Jade Green, Embossed Flowers, Scroll Handles, Oval, Footed, 1930s, 10 x 5 ¾ In.	90.00
Bowl, Rock Crystal, Clear, Scalloped Edge, c.1925, 10 ¼ In.	25.00
Bowl, Vegetable, Delphite, Scalloped Rim, Impressed Exterior, c.1955	26.00
Box, Storage, Lid, Seville Yellow, 5 x 9 In.	85.00
Butter, Cover, Croesus, Green, Amethyst, Gold Trim, c.1900, 6 x 7 ½ In.	125.00
Butter, Cover, Sultan, Flower, Frosted Green Ground, Child's, 3 ¾ x 5 In.	285.00
Cake Stand, Doric Feather, 8 ½ In.	85.00
Cake Stand, Yale, Crow Foot, Long Stem, Rum Ring, c.1894, 7 x 10 In.	110.00
Candlestick, Rock Crystal, Blue Frosted, c.1925, 8 ½ In.	295.00
Canister, Flour, Chalaine Blue, Square, Block Black Lettering, Metal Lid, 7 ½ x 4 In.	445.00
Casserole, Cover, Queen Anne, Glasbake, Footed, c.1935, 4 x 10 In.	32.00
Celery Vase, Deer & Pine Tree, Diamond Bands, c.1888, 7 ½ x 4 In.	115.00
Compote, Sunbeam, c.1900, 8 ¾ x 8 ½ In.	78.00
Creamer, Laurel, French Ivory, Red Trim, 1930s, 2 ½ In.	40.00

Mccoy, Bank, Seaman, Sailor Carrying Duffel Bag, Coin Slot, White, Box, 5 ¾ In. $230.00

Bertoia Auctions

Medical, Cabinet, Apothecary, Pine, 40 Drawers, Metal Brackets, c.1890, 48 ½ x 24 x 8 ½ In. $531.00

James D. Julia Inc.

Cruet, Monarch, c.1902, 4 ½ x 7 In.	85.00
Grill Plate, Jade Green, Embossed Rim, 1930s	30.00
Jar, Coffee, Green Jade, Metal Screw Lid, Black Block Lettering, 1930s	250.00
Measuring Cup, Handle Spout, 2 Cups	29.00
Mug, Glasbake, Seville Yellow, c.1955, 4 ¾ x 2 ⅜ In.	25.00
Nappy, Etched, Innovation Series, c.1920, 2 x 6 In.	20.00
Pitcher, Rock Crystal, c.1925, 7 ½ In., 54 Oz.	125.00
Plate, Luncheon, Rock Crystal, Clear, c.1925, 8 ½ In.	15.00
Plate, Salad, Crackle Pattern, Clear, 1920s, 8 In.	10.00
Platter, Milk Glass, Scale Textured, Fish Shape, Glasbake, Sticker, 18 x 8 ½ In.	20.00
Punch Bowl & Cups Set, Metal Hangers, 12 Cups, Scalloped, Clear, Footed, 12 ¾ x 7 In.	195.00
Reamer, Custard Glass, Yellow, c.1925	55.00
Refrigerator Dish, Jade Green, 6 ¾ In.	76.00
Refrigerator Dish, Red Sailboat, Anchor, Wheel, White Ground, Lid, 4 x 5 x 2 ¾ In.	50.00
Relish, Pink, Oval, Signed, 9 ¼ x 5 ¼ In.	28.00
Relish, Rock Crystal, 5 Sections, Flowers, Clear, c.1930, 11 ½ In.	35.00
Rose Bowl, Innovation, Cut Flowers, 3-Footed, 7 ¼ x 8 In.	98.00
Salt & Pepper, Milk Glass, Black Watering Can Lady, Black Block Lettering, 4 ¾ x 2 ⅜ In.	80.00
Salt & Pepper, Roman Arch, Black, White Script Lettering, 4 ¼ In., Pair	68.00
Salt & Pepper, Seville Yellow, Black Block Lettering, Metal Lid, c.1930, 5 ½ In., Pair	115.00
Shaker, Flour, Seville Yellow, Black Block Lettering, 5 In.	85.00
Shaker, Jade Green, 4 ¾ x 2 ¼ In.	75.00
Shaker, Jade Green, Block Lettered Pepper, 5 In.	51.00
Shaker, Jade, Square, 4 ¾ In.	45.00
Shaker, Light Jade Green, Block Lettering, 5 In.	45.00
Spooner, Croesus, Green Amethyst, Gilt Trim, c.1900, 4 ½ In.	95.00
Sugar Shaker, Roman Arch, Black, White Script Lettering, c.1935	45.00
Sugar, Seville Yellow, Black Block Lettering, 5 ½ In.	145.00
Toothpick Holder, Peek-A-Boo, Blue, Cherub At Sides, 1904, 3 ⅝ In.	65.00
Tray, Hand Shape, Milk Glass, Painted Wrist Flower, 5 In.	13.00
Tumbler & Coaster, Bottoms Up, Seville Yellow	150.00
Tumbler, Bottoms Up, Seville Yellow, 3 ¼ x 2 ⅜ In.	100.00
Tumbler, Marked Pres Cut, c.1910, 4 In.	25.00
Vase, Rock Crystal, Green, Bulbous Top, Footed, 11 x 6 In.	100.00
Vase, Sarah, Seville Yellow, Scalloped Rim, 1930s, 8 In.	90.00

MECHANICAL BANKS *are listed in the Bank category.*

MEDICAL office furniture, operating tools, microscopes, thermometers, and other paraphernalia used by doctors are included in this category. Veterinary collectibles are also included here. Medicine bottles are listed in the Bottle category. There are related collectibles listed under Dental.

Apothecary Case, Traveling, Mahogany, Brass Mouth, Lift Top, 14 Bottles, Scales, 8 x 7 In.	472.00
Birthing Stool, 3 Hand Holds, Tripod Base, Wrought Iron Brace, Wooden, Continental, 1800s, 32 In.	176.00
Bleeding Cup, Brass Bleeder, Pump, Hose, Walnut, Mon. Charriere Collin, Paris, 1800s, 4 x 11 In.	1175.00
Bolo Knife, Hospital Corps, Walnut Grip, Brass Fittings, Leather Scabbard, Model 1904, 12 In.	345.00
Box, Apothecary, Mahogany, Square, Compartments, Bottles, Drawer, Weights, c.1865, 8 x 8 In.	246.00
Cabinet, Apothecary, 30 Drawers, Scalloped Feet, Glass Pulls, Gilt Borders, 1800s, 64 x 35 In.	920.00
Cabinet, Apothecary, Mahogany, 2 Doors, Interior Fitted Drawers, England, 1800s, 18 x 12 In.	5750.00
Cabinet, Apothecary, Mahogany, 9 Drawers, Gilt Label, Glass Pulls, England, c.1905, 26 x 34 In.	546.00
Cabinet, Apothecary, Mahogany, 13 Drawers, Stand, c.1910, 41 x 43 In.	978.00
Cabinet, Apothecary, Mahogany, Dovetailed, Drawers, 40 x 44 x 11 In.	1035.00
Cabinet, Apothecary, Mahogany, Drawers, Central Compartment, 41 x 45 In.	1035.00
Cabinet, Apothecary, Pine, 17 Drawers, Turned Wood Knobs, Mushroom Feet, 1800s, 39 x 45 In.	1380.00
Cabinet, Apothecary, Pine, 24 Drawers, Green Paint, c.1900, 35 x 28 In.	326.00
Cabinet, Apothecary, Pine, 40 Drawers, Metal Brackets, c.1890, 48 ½ x 24 x 8 ½ In. ....*illus*	531.00
Cabinet, Apothecary, Pine, Dovetailed Case, 15 Drawers, 1800s, 20 ¼ x 43 In.	588.00
Cabinet, Apothecary, Rolling Lip, 46 Drawers, Cupboard Doors, Korea, 33 x 32 In.	561.00
Cabinet, Mahogany, Door, 21 Drawers, White Knobs, Backsplash, 48 x 36 In.	688.00
Cabinet, Multidrawer, 3 Drop Front Doors, Inset Glass Shelf, c.1900, 61 x 45 In.	1046.00
Chart, Anatomy, Pull Down, Rudolf Schick, Canada, 1944	165.00
Chest, Apothecary, Mahogany, 6 Compartments, 8 Bottles, Arthur J. Wells, Gloucester, 1800s ......*illus*	546.00
Chest, Apothecary, Mahogany, Brass, 6 Compartments, Bottles, Tops, England, 1800s, 8 x 10 In.	546.00
Chest, Apothecary, Mahogany, Fitted Case, Swing-Out Drawers, c.1810, 11 x 11 In.	470.00
Chest, Apothecary, Walnut, Lift Top, Bottles, Fitted Drawer, England, c.1900, 9 ½ x 12 In.	273.00
Chest, Apothecary, Wood, 47 Drawers, Wood Knobs, 1800s, 36 x 42 In.	690.00

Medical, Chest, Apothecary, Mahogany, 6 Compartments, 8 Bottles, Arthur J. Wells, Gloucester, 1800s
$546.00

Leland Little Auction

Medical, Model, Optometrist's Eye, Anatomy, Plaster, Glass, Name Plate, Continental, c.1950, 9 x 10 In.
$460.00

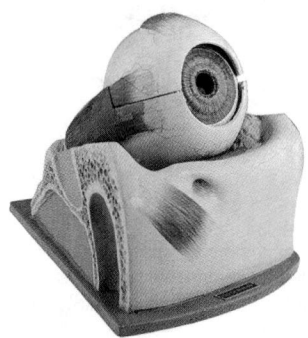

Leland Little Auction

M

Medical, Water Bottle, St. Paul Rubber Co., The Revelation Guaranteed, Embossed Label, 10 In.
$35.00

Showtime Auction Services

Roll-Top Desks
The first American patent for a horizontal tambour roll-top desk was issued to Abner Cutler in 1850. He worked in Buffalo, New York.

Meissen, Figurine, Cherub, Broken Heart, Tree Stump, Marked, 8 ⅛ In. $1103.00

Skinner, Inc.

Meissen, Figurine, Gardener, Man, Standing, 20 x 9 In. $4200.00

DuMouchelles Art Gallery

Meissen, Figurine, Woman, Flower Basket, Urn, Round Base, Marked, 7 ¾ In. $490.00

Skinner, Inc.

Meissen, Group, Cherubs Around Easel, Leafy Base, Blue Crossed Swords, c.1910, 7 ⅜ x 7 In. $3705.00

Neal Auction Co.

Chest, George II, Mahogany, Brass Mounts, Lock, 2 Door, Handle, c.1730, 11 x 11 In.	1135.00
Counter, Pharmacy, Art Nouveau, Wood, White Panel Sides, 8 Drawers, Shelf, c.1900, 41 x 67 In.	1722.00
Cupboard, Apothecary, Pine, 13 Drawers, Bootjack Feet, 1700s, 50 x 36 ½ In.	4740.00
Divider Unit, Pharmacy, Wood, Arched Opening, 2 Glass Doors, Carved, Painted, 15 x 13 Ft.	5166.00
Doctor's Bag, Alligator Skin, Satchel Shape, 12 x 20 In.	875.00
Electrostatic Machine, Pine, Cherry, Cloth, Wire, Blown Glass Jar, Shaker, c.1840, 18 x 23 In.	527.00
Instrument, Davidson Pneumothorax Apparatus, Black Enamel, Nickel Plate, Bottles, 4 x 17 In.	211.00
Leech Jar, Blown Glass, Folded Rim, c.1850, 7 x 7 ½ In.	88.00
Model, Anatomic, Removable Organs, Easel Back, Germany, c.1890, 14 ½ x 10 In.	413.00
Model, Optometrist's Eye, Anatomy, Plaster, Glass, Name Plate, Continental, c.1950, 9 x 10 In. *illus*	460.00
Mold, Suppositories, Tin, 6 Forms	68.00
Mortar & Pestle, Bronze, 2 Handles, 1800s, 4 In.	118.00
Mortar & Pestle, Cast, Brass, 3 x 4 ¾ & 7 ½ In.	118.00
Phrenology Head, Plaster, Cast, Impressed, Tooled Lines, American, 1850-1900, 11 ¾ In.	382.00
Pill Crusher, Pharmacist, Cast Iron, 28 In.	266.00
Psychogalvano Meter, Lie Detector, Wood Case Model No. 100, 1940s, 8 x 17 In.	165.00
Pump Kit, Brass, Ivory Handle, Hinged Mahogany Case, Signed, Dr. Shaw, c.1800s, 12 ¼ In.	264.00
Pump, Electrical, Bottles, Wood Base, Label, Physicians Supply Co., Kansas City, c.1900, 12 In.	211.00
Pump, Hand, Brass, Seamed, Bone Handles, Fitted Mahogany, c.1850, 1 ½ x 9 In.	121.00
Scalpel Kit, 7 Labeled Instruments, Ebonized Handles, Oak Case, A. Boreux Bale, 7 ½ In.	118.00
Show Globe, Apothecary, Filigree Detail, Griffin Bracket, 22 In.	4675.00
Slide Box, 65 Prepared Slides, 7 Trays, Pine Case, c.1900, 3 ¼ x 8 ½ In.	235.00
Surgeon's Kit, Mahogany Case, S. Maaw & Son & Thompson, London, 3 x 10 ½ In.	593.00
Surgical Kit, Gilt Leather Case, Tortoiseshell Handles, Charriere, France, 1800s, 3 ½ x 5 ½ In.	176.00
Surgical Kit, Pocket, Rosewood Case, Brass Plate, Velvet Lining, Geo. Tiemann & Co., 1 ½ x 8 In.	295.00
Surgical Kit, Tools, Rosewood Case, Brass Trim, G. Tiemann & Co., N.Y., c.1850, 4 x 14 ½ In.	2938.00
Trephine Kit, 5 Instruments, Ivory Handles, Wood, Metals, Fitted Rosewood Case, 8 x 5 In.	823.00
Urethratome, Steel, Adjustable, Leather Covered Case, 11 ½ In.	60.00
Vapo-Cresoline, Lamp, Metal, Scroll Arm, Font, Chimney, Bottle Of Cresoline, Box, 6 ½ In.	34.00
Water Bottle, St. Paul Rubber Co., The Revelation Guaranteed, Embossed Label, 10 In. *illus*	35.00

MEISSEN is a town in Germany where porcelain has been made since 1710. Any china made in the town can be called Meissen, although the famous Meissen factory made the finest porcelains of the area. The crossed swords mark of the great Meissen factory has been copied by many other firms in Germany and other parts of the world. Pieces of Meissen dinnerware in the Onion pattern are listed in their own category in this book.

Bowl, Blue & White Flowers, Reticulated Rim, Signed, 9 ¼ In.	259.00
Bowl, Center, Gilt Scrolling Leaves, White Ground, Marked, 12 In.	134.00
Bowl, Flower Center, Gold Accents, 12 x 2 ½ In.	161.00
Bowl, Flowers, Oval, Reticulated Basket Weave Sides, 2 Branch Handles, c.1900, 9 ½ In.	708.00
Bowl, Fruit, Oval, Pierced Body, Branch Feet, Gilt Trim, Flowers, c.1890, 14 ¼ In.	237.00
Bowl, Gilt Flowers, Panels, Maroon, Hand Painted Flowers Center, Shaped Rim, 12 In.	374.00
Bowl, Outdoor Banquet Scene, Gilt Bronze Base, Rim, Raised Base, Germany, 1700s, 9 ½ x 13 ½ In.	4248.00
Bowl, Shaped, Gold Flower Center, Gold Rim, Pink Flowers, Handles, 13 ¾ x 8 In.	138.00
Box, Green, Landscapes, Courting Couple, Fan Shape, Crossed Swords Mark, 1700s, 4 x 2 ½ In.	403.00
Candelabrum, 2-Light, Man Playing Guitar, Woman Playing Hurdy-Gurdy, 1800s, 8 In., Pair	1185.00
Candelabrum, Man, Woman, Carrying Instruments, Marked, 17 ½ x 7 ¾ In., Pair	748.00
Candlestick, Enamel & Gilt, Entangled Babe, Dolphin With Sconce In Mouth, 11 In., Pair	1185.00
Candlestick, Figures, Woman, Man, Standing In Arbor, c.1930, 9 x 6 In., Pair	1298.00
Centerpiece, Flower, Man & Woman Standard, Scrolled Rocky Base, c.1890, 23 x 14 In.	2749.00
Chocolate Pot, Rococo Style, Shell, Leaves, Gilt, Baluster Shape, c.1850, 9 ¾ In.	118.00
Clock, Draped Drum Case, Putto, Seated, Reading, Cock Atop Dial, 11 x 10 In.	2925.00
Clock, Figural, Seasons' Cherubs, Leaf, Scroll Case, Enamel, Gilt, Tripart Base, c.1890, 18 ¾ In.	8888.00
Coffee Set, Pot, Sugar, Cover, Cream, Tray, Flower Bouquets, Gilding, 1800s, 7 In.	660.00
Cologne Bottle, Flowers, Butterflies, White, Double Gourd Shape, Rose Blossom Finial, 4 In.	69.00
Compote, Figural, 8 Putti, Flowers, Vines, Onion, Handles, Stand, 1800s, 22 In.	4740.00
Compote, Reticulated Basket, Flowers, 4 Seasons' Cherubs, Handles, Stand, c.1890, 22 In.	5925.00
Compote, Reticulated Lattice Panels, Pedestal Foot, Onion, Multicolor, Gilt, 1900s, 8 x 9 In.	431.00
Cup & Saucer, Indian Flower, Box, c.1890, 2 ¼ x 4 ¼ In., 6 Piece	518.00
Dish, Flowers, Gilt Trim, Oval, c.1900, 10 In.	106.00
Dish, Oval, Gilt Flower Relief, Oak Leaf Handles, White Ground, Marked, 1800s, 14 x 10 In.	207.00
Dish, Sweetmeat, Reclining Man, Figural, 8 x 12 In.	177.00
Dresser Box, Cover, Gilt Mounted, Flowers, Hand Painted Interior, 4 x 6 In., Pair	345.00
Egg, Cover, Applied Flowers, Multicolor, Gilt Trim, 3-Footed, Signed, 1800s, 6 In.	489.00
Figurine, Atlanta, Woman, Scantily Draped, Bent Over, 14 ½ In.	2006.00
Figurine, Bird, Black, Tail Up, Crossed Swords Mark, 21 In.	621.00

Figurine, Bird, Perched, Round Natural Base, 5 x 6 In., Pair	620.00
Figurine, Boy & Girl, Playing Horn, Round Base, Marked, 6 x 5 In.	806.00
Figurine, Boy, 18th Century Costume, Flower Garland Around Shoulders, 6 ½ x 4 In.	826.00
Figurine, Boy, Basket On Back, Grapes, 5 ¾ In.	265.00
Figurine, Boy, Fancy Pants, Crossed Swords Mark, 6 ¾ In.	324.00
Figurine, Cherub, Broken Heart, Tree Stump, Marked, 8 ⅛ In. ....*illus*	1103.00
Figurine, Cherub, Holding Flower, Torch, Sunflower, Bird, 1800s, 14 ½ In.	2370.00
Figurine, Cherub, Making Tea, Signed, 1800s, 4 ½ In.	489.00
Figurine, Child, Seated, Wearing Apron, Holding Basket Of Apples On Head, Marked, 1800s, 6 ½ In.	266.00
Figurine, Cupid, Arrows, Arms Raised, 8 x 3 ½ In.	690.00
Figurine, Cupid, Gardener, Foot On Spade, Flowerpots, 4 ½ x 4 ¾ In.	585.00
Figurine, Cupid, Seated, Shoemaker, Hammering Sole, Workbench, 4 ¾ x 4 In.	878.00
Figurine, Cupid, Sharpening Arrows, 4 ¾ x 4 In.	575.00
Figurine, Cupid, Stoking The Flame, Kneeling Before Flaming Pot, Heart, Mallet, Arrow, 5 x 4 In.	936.00
Figurine, Dog, Bolognese Terrier, Sitting, White & Brown, c.1800, 8 In.	944.00
Figurine, Dog, Retriever, Standing, Tree Stumps, Flowers & Leaves, 1900s, 9 ½ In.	459.00
Figurine, Elephant, Raised Trunk, 1800s, 7 ½ In.	354.00
Figurine, Embracing Couple, Young Woman Weeping, Flowers, Gilt, Oval Base, 1800s, 13 In.	2450.00
Figurine, Flower Gatherer, Lace Bodice, Necklace, Pink Shapes, Marked, 6 ¾ In.	345.00
Figurine, Flute Player On Stump, 6 In.	431.00
Figurine, Fruit Seller, Woman, Standing, Hat, Fruit In Apron, Round Base, c.1840, 6 ¾ x 2 ½ In.	676.00
Figurine, Gardener, Man, Standing, 20 x 9 In. ....*illus*	4200.00
Figurine, Girl, Holding Doll, Pink Dress, Crossed Swords Mark, Late 1800s, 5 ½ In.	805.00
Figurine, Girl, Holding Flower Garland, 1800s, 7 In.	976.00
Figurine, Girl, Holding Tambourine, 5 ½ In.	1098.00
Figurine, Girl, Playing Ball, Lilac Dress, Outstretched Arm, Gilt Bowl, 1900s, 12 In.	1534.00
Figurine, Girl, Playing Tambourine, Marked, 5 In.	796.00
Figurine, Girl, Seated, Holding Book & Clock, Round Base, c.1865, 5 ¾ x 3 In.	615.00
Figurine, Goat Herder, 3 Goats, Marked, c.1908, 15 In.	558.00
Figurine, Goat, Brown & White, Horns, Standing On Rocky Base, Oval, 1800s, 6 In.	948.00
Figurine, Horse & Arab Handler, Rearing Horse, Feathered Turban, c.1885, 10 In.	2271.00
Figurine, Horse, Reclining, Bent Front Leg, Glancing Sideways, Marked, 1900s, 5 x 9 In.	227.00
Figurine, Hunter, Dog, Blanc De Chine, Impressed X8A, 7 In.	184.00
Figurine, Lemon Seller, Standing, Flower Vest, Lemons In Apron, Round Base, 1700s, 7 In.	3068.00
Figurine, Little Girl, Red Stripe Cap, Doll, Signed, 1800s, 5 ½ In.	920.00
Figurine, Maid, Seated, Taking Inventory, Signed, 1800s, 7 In.	1265.00
Figurine, Malabar, Man, Woman, Holding Instrument, Multicolor, Marked, c.1865, 6 ¾ In., Pair	984.00
Figurine, Man & Woman, Man Holds Woman Over Shoulder, 8 In.	567.00
Figurine, Man & Woman, Wheat Stalks, Man With Bouquet Behind Back, 8 In.	1134.00
Figurine, Man, Blue Coat, Holding Cane, 6 ¼ In.	767.00
Figurine, Man, Rustic Country Outfit, Flower Basket, 14 In.	8260.00
Figurine, Man, Seated, Reading Book, Pink Jacket, 1800s, 5 In.	748.00
Figurine, Man, Woman, Feathered Hat, Flowers, Dog At Feet, Lamb, Round Base, c.1855, 13 In., Pair.	3163.00
Figurine, Muse, Bare-Breasted, Cherub With Harp, 12 In.	2242.00
Figurine, Putto, Saluting, Bow & Arrows, Marked, c.1900, 6 In.	502.00
Figurine, Rooster, Resting, 4 ½ x 4 ½ In.	236.00
Figurine, Satyr, Bagpipe, 1800s, 6 ¼ In.	1298.00
Figurine, Sculptress, Mallet In Hand, Working On Bust, 8 ½ x 3 ¾ In.	354.00
Figurine, Triumph Of Venus, Stand, Gilt, Seminude, Cherubs, Mermaids, 1800s, 22 x 20 In. ..	22050.00
Figurine, White Horse, Moor, Germany, c.1934, 9 ½ In.	1880.00
Figurine, Wolverine, 5 ½ x 8 In.	443.00
Figurine, Woman, 18th Century Dress, Holding Birdcage, 11 In.	3000.00
Figurine, Woman, Barefoot, Sun Hat, Basket, Rose, Marked, 4 ¼ In.	144.00
Figurine, Woman, Basket, Vegetables, Signed, 1800s, 6 ¾ In.	460.00
Figurine, Woman, Bavarian National Dress, Hat, Marked, c.1928, 5 ½ In.	472.00
Figurine, Woman, Flower Basket, Urn, Round Base, Marked, 7 ¾ In. ....*illus*	490.00
Figurine, Woman, Full Skirt Of Flowers, Marked, 1800s, 6 In.	793.00
Figurine, Woman, Lamb, Period Attire, Signed, 1800s, 11 ¾ In.	1150.00
Figurine, Woman, Man, Period Dress, 1800s, 19 In., Pair	7080.00
Figurine, Woman, Napping, Chair, Table, Enamel, Gilt, c.1895, 7 ½ In.	1778.00
Figurine, Woman, Rustic Country Dress, Flower Basket, 14 In.	590.00
Figurine, Woman, Seated, Sense Of Touch, Holding Bird, Cage, c.1885, 6 x 3 ¾ In.	1230.00
Figurine, Woman, Standing, Carrying Muff, Reading Pamphlet, Shaped Base, 8 In.	796.00
Figurine, Woman, Standing, Wearing Peasant Dress, Playing Hurdy-Gurdy, 1800s, 13 In.	1007.00
Figurine, Young Girl, Carrying Harvest In Cloth, On Head, Marked, 5 ¼ In.	472.00
Figurine, Young Man, With Letter, Lamb, 7 ¾ In.	649.00

Meissen, Group, Man & Woman, Flowers, Dog, Blue Crossed Swords, 6 ¼ In.
$1180.00

Brunk Auctions

Meissen, Platter, Panels, Courting Scenes, Bouquets, Gilt Rim, Blue Crossed Swords, c.1900, 16 In.
$176.00

Cowan's Auctions

Meissen, Salt, Double, Woman, Man, Crossed Swords Mark, 5 ½ In., Pair
$854.00

Leslie Hindman Auctioneers

Meissen, Tray, Insects, Gilt Borders, Oval, Crossed Swords Mark, 17 ¼ In.
$1364.00

Leslie Hindman Auctioneers

M

TIP

An unglazed rim on the bottom of a plate usually indicates it was made before 1850.

Merrimac, Pitcher, Green Matte Glaze, 8 ½ x 4 ¾ In. $868.00

Rago Arts & Auction Center

Mettlach, Humidor, No. 646, Barrel, Weasel On Lid, 9 In. $318.00

Fox Auctions

Mettlach, Plaque, No. 7026, Phanolith, Norse Gods, 16 x 12 In. $748.00

The Stein Auction Co.

Mettlach, Punch Bowl, No. 1121, Lid, Underplate, PUG, H. Schlitt, 5 ½ Liter $403.00

The Stein Auction Co.

Group, Birds, Tufted, White Stump, Germany, c.1930, 10 ¼ In.	787.00
Group, Boy & Girl, 1700s Dress, Birdcage, Bird, Flowers, c.1900, 6 In.	978.00
Group, Boy & Girl, 1700s Dress, Playing Lute, Sitting On Wheat Sheaf, c.1890, 5 ¾ In.	805.00
Group, Boy & Girl, Sheep, Crossed Swords Mark, 6 In.	708.00
Group, Broken Bridge, Man, 2 Putti Helping Woman Across Brook, Roses, 1800s, 10 In.	1838.00
Group, Cherubs Around Easel, Leafy Base, Blue Crossed Swords, c.1910, 7 ⅜ x 7 In. *illus*	3705.00
Group, Children, Barefoot, Musical Horn, Rocky Base, Mark, 6 x 4 ¾ In.	460.00
Group, Courting Couple, Woman Seated, Holding Book, Round Gilt Base, Marked, c.1900, 8 In.	1410.00
Group, Courting Couple, Woman Standing, Man Kneeling, 12 In.	4403.00
Group, Dancing Couple, Round Base, c.1865, 6 x 5 In.	1599.00
Group, Diana & Minerva, Cupid, 19th Century, 13 x 13 In.	5900.00
Group, Europa The Bull, 8 ½ x 8 In.	2070.00
Group, Europa, Seated On Bull, Figures, Flowers, Oval Base, 1800s, 8 ¼ In.	2133.00
Group, Girl Goat Herder, Goats, 10 ½ x 17 In.	1416.00
Group, Lover Discovered, Blanc-De-Chine, Couple, Seated On Bed, Cupid, Wife's Lover, 6 x 9 In.	590.00
Group, Lovers, Man, Sharing Snuff, Gilt, Enamel, c.1890, 4 ⅞ In.	652.00
Group, Man & Woman, 1700s Dress, Wine Flask, Flower Basket, c.1870, 6 ½ In.	805.00
Group, Man & Woman, Flowers, Dog, Blue Crossed Swords, 6 ¼ In. *illus*	1180.00
Group, Man, Playing Horn, Girl Seated On Goat, c.1890, 6 In.	889.00
Group, Man, Woman, Lamb, Period Attire, 1800s, 8 In.	767.00
Group, Man, Woman, Playing Instruments, 9 x 7 ½ In.	590.00
Group, People Working In Garden, Flowers, Rocky Base, Enamel & Gilt, 1800s, 9 In.	1715.00
Group, Putti With Emblems, 5 Senses, Marked, 1800s, 5 In.	767.00
Group, Putti, Playing With Flowers, Holding Wreath Over Head, Marked, c.1900, 4 ¾ In.	443.00
Group, Putti, Playing, Flowers, Multicolor, Mark, c.1800, 5 In.	420.00
Group, Rooster, Hen, Chicks, 8 ½ x 9 In.	2832.00
Group, Sculptor's Workshop, c.1890, 8 x 7 In.	1920.00
Group, Silenus, Donkey, Attendants, Rocky Base, 8 x 8 In.	978.00
Group, Tailor's Wife, Woman, Nursing Baby, Goat, Nursing Goat Kid, 7 x 6 ½ In.	1770.00
Group, Triumph Of Venus, Nude Venus, Putti, Mermaids, Flowers, Shells, Stand, 22 x 20 In.	21330.00
Group, Woman, Attending To Cherub, Book, Women, Children, Rocky Base, Germany, 1800s, 11 In.	3553.00
Group, Women, Children, Cherub, Writing In Book, Flowers, Multicolor, 1800s, 11 In.	5036.00
Inkstand, Reclining Mastiff, Shell Cartouche, Scroll Legs, 1800s, 10 In.	533.00
Paperweight, Pug Dog, Reclining, Base, Flowers, Gold Highlights, 7 ½ In.	170.00
Plate, Blue Ground, Woman Cameo, Scrolling, Pate-Sur-Pate, c.1890, 9 ½ In.	2151.00
Plate, Portrait, Woman, Wearing Purple, Pink, Yellow, Draped In Pearls, c.1895, 7 In. Diam.	123.00
Plate, Putti, Flower Border, Multicolor, Gilt, Marked, 1800s, 9 In., 10 Piece	3674.00
Plate, Soup, Hand Paint, Flowers, Insect Border, c.1850, 10 In. Diam., 12 Piece	492.00
Plate, White Ground, Flowers, Butterflies, Insects, Wavy Rim, 9 ½ In. Diam., 12 Piece	1610.00
Platter, Birds & Butterflies, Oval, Gold Trim, Shell Handles, 18 In.	561.00
Platter, Game, Pheasants, 21 In.	767.00
Platter, Oval, Flowers, Couples Panels, Blue White Ground, Gilt Trim, 1800s, 18 ¼ x 13 ¼ In.	240.00
Platter, Panels, Courting Scenes, Bouquets, Gilt Rim, Blue Crossed Swords, c.1900, 16 In. *illus*	176.00
Ring Holder, Seated Woman, Double Basket, Holding Bouquet, Marked, 1800s, 5 x 6 In.	345.00
Salt, Double, Seated Boy, Hat, Girl, Nosegay, Basket, Blue, White, c.1885, 5 x 5 ½ In., Pair	492.00
Salt, Double, Woman, Man, Crossed Swords Mark, 5 ½ In., Pair *illus*	854.00
Salt, Man, Woman, Lying Next To Bowl, Flowers, Insects, 8 x 12 In., Pair	2440.00
Serving Bowl, Flower Bouquet, Cartouches, Birds, Enameled, 13 In. Diam.	460.00
Serving Bowl, Leaf Shape, Twig Handles, Flowers, Germany, c.1910, 9 ¾ In.	472.00
Soup, Dish, Birds, Gilt Trim, c.1900, 9 ½ In.	118.00
Soup, Dish, Blue & White, 2 Handles, Underplate, Blue Danube, 4 In.	39.00
Tea Service, Teapot, Cups, Saucers, Jar, Rose Finial, Dragon Pattern, c.1930	300.00
Teapot, Bombe Shape, Children Scenes, Swing Handle, Blue, Marked, 1800s, 6 In.	750.00
Tray, Center Flower Spray, Cobalt Reserves, Heavy Gilding, 2 Handles, 4 x 14 x 8 In.	459.00
Tray, Insects, Gilt Borders, Oval, Crossed Swords Mark, 17 ¼ In. *illus*	1364.00
Tray, Shell, Flower, Border, Cobalt Trim, Pierced Handle, New Gold, Germany, c.1890, 16 In.	474.00
Tray, Square Handles, Flower Spray, Gilt Border, 16 In.	682.00
Tray, Square, Flowers, Gilt Accents, Cutout Handles, Mark, Germany, 16 In.	531.00
Tureen, Cover, Footed, Putto Finial, Applied Flowers, c.1900, 11 In.	525.00
Tureen, Full Green Vine Pattern, Cover, 20th Century, 10 x 9 x 14 In.	209.00
Tureen, Soup, Cover, Oval, Putti, Scroll Handles, Flowers, Cornucopia, 1700s, 11 x 15 In.	805.00
Tureen, Swan, Flowers, Mermaid Handles, Maid & Dolphin Cover, Germany, 1800s, 16 In.	3318.00
Tureen, Underplate, Flower, Couple Panels, Yellow, Gilt Handles, Swirled Finials, c.1860, 10 x 18 In.	1020.00
Urn, Baluster, Flowers, Gilt, Marked, 10 In.	122.00
Urn, Baluster, Fruit Design, White Ground, Gilt, Snake Handles, 10 ¾ In., Pair	518.00
Urn, Cover, Finial, Flowers, Cherubs, Handles, 1800s, 5 ½ In., Pair	275.00

M

Urn, Cover, Flowers, Scenic Cartouche, Bronze Mounts, Handles, Finial, Marked, 13 In., Pair	1265.00
Urn, Cover, Painted, Applied Flowers, Swags, Figures, Stand, 24 In.	7670.00
Urn, Cover, Reticulated, White, Applied Flowers, 1800s, 21 In.	14160.00
Urn, Empire Style, Molded, Double Coiled Snake Handles, Pink, Gilt, c.1900, 14 ¾ In.	590.00
Vase, Beethoven, White, Gilt Detail, 13 ½ In.	295.00
Vase, Cobalt Blue, Gilt Borders, Enamel Flowers, Snake Handles, Marked, c.1890, 10 ½ In.	563.00
Vase, Lobed Pedestal Base, Blue, Gilt, Banding, Swan's Head Handles, 19 In., Pair	1528.00
Vase, Pedestal Foot, Ball Shape, Ruffled Rim, Applied Flowers, Gilt Highlights, 1900s, 3 ⅝ In., Pair	236.00

MERCURY GLASS, or silvered glass, was first made in the 1850s. It lost favor for a while but became popular again about 1910. It looks like a piece of silver.

Candlestick, Baluster Form, Stepped Domed Foot, Pontil, c.1860, 11 In., Pair	69.00
Globe, On Stand, 2 Sections, Tapered Knop, Spread Foot, c.1860, 12 In.	690.00
Kugel, On Stand, Cobalt Blue, Flared & Footed Stand, Rolled Rim, 8 In.	115.00
Ornament, Ball, Stem, 1800s, 5 In.	415.00
Salt, Silvered, Round, Spread Foot, New England Glass Co., c.1860, 3 ¼ x 3 ¼ In.	92.00
Shade, Quilted Offset, 6 x 8 In., Pair	450.00
Vase, Peacock Blue, Optic Rib, Painted Butterfly, Flowers, Flared Rim, Footed, 8 In.	35.00
Vase, Stars, Swirls, Incised, 17 ½ x 14 In.	400.00
Vase, Stylized Flowers, Melon Shape, Pedestal Foot, 17 x 12 In., Pair	584.00

MERRIMAC POTTERY Company was founded by Thomas Nickerson in Newburyport, Massachusetts, in 1902. The company made art pottery, garden pottery, and reproductions of Roman pottery. The pottery burned to the ground in 1908.

Jardiniere, Squat, Water Lilies, Green Matte Glaze, 4 ¾ x 8 ½ In.	2604.00
Pitcher, Green Matte Glaze, 8 ½ x 4 ¾ In. ....*illus*	868.00
Vase, Veined Green Matte Glaze, Spherical, 10 x 8 ½ In.	2728.00

METLOX POTTERIES was founded in 1927 in Manhattan Beach, California. Dinnerware was made beginning in 1931. Evan K. Shaw purchased the company in 1946 and expanded the number of patterns. Poppytrail (1946-89) and Vernonware (1958-80) were divisions of Metlox under E.K. Shaw's direction. The factory closed in 1989.

Antique Grape, Baker, Oval, 10 ⅛ In.	41.00
Antique Grape, Bowl, Cereal, 7 ¼ In.	11.00
Antique Grape, Bowl, Vegetable, Cover, 2 Qt.	25.00
Antique Grape, Cup & Saucer	8.00
Antique Grape, Pitcher, 1 ½ Qt.	40.00
Antique Grape, Plate, Dinner, 10 ½ In.	14.00
Antique Grape, Platter, 14 ⅜ In.	20.00
Antique Grape, Sugar & Creamer	35.00
Bandero, Plate, Dinner, 10 ½ In.	16.00
California Apple, Plate, Luncheon, 9 ¼ In.	20.00
California Contempora, Saltshaker, Black	16.00
California Ivy, Bowl, Cereal, 6 In.	17.00
California Ivy, Chop Plate, 13 ¼ In.	28.00
California Ivy, Jam Dish, Divided, 7 ½ In.	21.00
California Rose, Plate, Dinner, 10 ⅜ In.	14.00
California Strawberry, Bowl, Vegetable, Cover, 6 ¾ In., 2 Qt.	21.00
California Strawberry, Plate, Dinner, 10 ¼ In.	12.00
California Strawberry, Relish, 2-Part	35.00
Central Park, Plate, Dinner, 10 ¼ In.	16.00
Colonial Heritage, Plate, Dinner, 10 In.	15.00
Colorstax, Bowl, Cereal, Aqua, 6 ⅜ In.	14.00
Colorstax, Bowl, Cereal, Brick, 6 ⅜ In.	14.00
Colorstax, Bowl, Cereal, Canary, 6 ⅜ In.	8.00
Colorstax, Bowl, Cereal, Sand, 6 ¼ In.	10.00
Colorstax, Bowl, Vegetable, Apricot, 9 ⅛ In.	25.00
Colorstax, Butter, Cover, Apricot	21.00
Colorstax, Plate, Dinner, Apricot, 10 ¾	21.00
Colorstax, Plate, Dinner, Aqua, 10 ¾ In.	15.00
Colorstax, Plate, Dinner, Brick, 10 ¾ In.	12.00
Colorstax, Plate, Dinner, Sand, 10 ¾ In.	10.00
Country Side, Plate, Dinner, 10 In.	42.00

Mettlach, Punch Bowl, No. 2341, Cover, Underplate, Banners, Inscription, Villeroy & Boch, 18 ¼ In.
$403.00

James D. Julia Inc.

Mettlach, Stein, No. 1212-1909, ½ Liter, Bowling, Pewter Lid, PUG
$265.00

The Stein Auction Co.

Mettlach, Stein, No. 2140, ½ Liter, Bicycle & Train, Inlaid Lid, PUG
$288.00

The Stein Auction Co.

Mettlach, Stein, No. 2190, ½ Liter, Bicycle, Etched, Pewter Lid
$345.00

The Stein Auction Co.

METTLACH

Milk Glass, Syrup, Raised Design, Woman & Child, Silver Plated Top & Handle, 6 ¾ In.
$81.00

Glass Works Auctions

Minton, Cachepot, Stand, Atlas Figure On Corners, Medallions, Thornwaldsen, c.1870, 11 ½ In., Pair
$2370.00

Skinner, Inc.

Minton, Group, Cupid & Psyche, Standing Figures, Embracing, Parian, c.1851, 16 ½ In.
$356.00

Skinner, Inc.

METTLACH, Germany, is a city where the Villeroy and Boch factories worked. Steins from the firm are marked with the word *Mettlach* or the castle mark. They date from about 1842. *PUG* means painted under glaze. The steins can be dated from the marks on the bottom, which include a date-number code. Other pieces may be listed in the Villeroy & Boch category.

Beer Tap, No. 2672, Deer, Etched, 18 In.	2645.00
Biscuit Jar, Browns, Blue & Green Pineapple Style, Barrel Shape, Silver Plate Lid, Handle, 8 In.	175.00
Charger, Pictorial, Elf, Sitting In Tree, Gilt Rim, Marked, 16 In.	489.00
Humidor, No. 646, Barrel, Weasel On Lid, 9 In. ....*illus*	318.00
Pitcher, Beer, No. 2332, Pewter Lid, Baluster, Square Handle, Bearded Dwarves, 10 In.	230.00
Pitcher, No. 2541, Metal Overlay, Marked Orivit, 13 In.	431.00
Plaque, Gnome, Sitting In Nest, Grapevines, Wine Bottles, Gilt Rim, 16 In.	657.00
Plaque, No. 1044-1105, Farm Couple With Hay-Cutting Tools, PUG, 17 In.	230.00
Plaque, No. 1044-1122, Swan, Child, PUG, 17 In.	358.00
Plaque, No. 1044-9022, Boar, PUG, 17 ¼ In.	259.00
Plaque, No. 2070, Dogs Chase Elk, Signed Stocke, Etched, 15 In.	690.00
Plaque, No. 2148, Snow White & 7 Dwarfs, Etched, 16 In.	748.00
Plaque, No. 2149, Papagano, Etched, 16 In.	805.00
Plaque, No. 2533, Godesburg Castle, Etched, 17 In.	518.00
Plaque, No. 2899, Woman, Carrying Wheat, Etched, 18 In.	2530.00
Plaque, No. 5078, Town Of Mettlach, Delft, 17 ½ In.	805.00
Plaque, No. 7026, Phanolith, Norse Gods, 16 x 12 In. ....*illus*	748.00
Punch Bowl, No. 418, Underplate, Figural Handles, Vines, Medallions, 14 In.	300.00
Punch Bowl, No. 1121, Lid, Underplate, PUG, H. Schlitt, 5 ½ Liter ....*illus*	403.00
Punch Bowl, No. 2341, Cover, Underplate, Banners, Inscription, Villeroy & Boch, 18 ¼ In. ......*illus*	403.00
Punch Bowl, No. 3037, Undertray, Portrait, Eagle, 2 Handles, Loop Finial, 14 In.	474.00
Stein, Newport, Scenic, Pewter Thumblift, Earthenware, Villeroy & Boch, c.1895, 8 In.	708.00
Stein, No. 227, 3 Liter, Hand Painted & Enameled, Strassburg, Pewter Lid	46.00
Stein, No. 591-1526, ½ Liter, Lovers, PUG, Pewter Lid	69.00
Stein, No. 715-1090, ½ Liter, Drunken Revelers, PUG, Pewter Lid	176.00
Stein, No. 1038-1526, 3 Liter, PUG, Pewter Lid	690.00
Stein, No. 1107-2271, ½ Liter, Men Around Pot, PUG, Pewter Lid	311.00
Stein, No. 1109-1526, 1 Liter, PUG, Pewter Lid	391.00
Stein, No. 1212-1909, ½ Liter, Bowling, Pewter Lid, PUG ....*illus*	265.00
Stein, No. 1282-1526, ½ Liter, Hunter & Peasant, PUG, Pewter Lid	242.00
Stein, No. 1467, ½ Liter, Harvest Scenes, Relief, Inlaid Lid	115.00
Stein, No. 1494, 5 Liter, Man, Sits On Top Of Large Barrel, Etched, Pewter Lid	1035.00
Stein, No. 1526, ½ Liter, Komp. Vrendenb Train, Pewter Lid	300.00
Stein, No. 1526, ½ Liter, Munich Child, Pewter Lid	98.00
Stein, No. 1526, ½ Liter, PUG, Von Hotzendorf, Inlaid Lid	607.00
Stein, No. 1526, 3 ½ Liter, Transfer & Enameled, Pewter Lid	184.00
Stein, No. 1527, ½ Liter, Card Playing, Pewter Lid	138.00
Stein, No. 1527, ½ Liter, Outdoor Gathering, Inlaid Lid	288.00
Stein, No. 1794, ½ Liter, Bismarck In Uniform, Inlaid Lid	288.00
Stein, No. 1863, ½ Liter, City Scene Of Stuttgart, Inlaid Lid	403.00
Stein, No. 1909, ½ Liter, Drunken Gentlemen, Pewter Lid, PUG	161.00
Stein, No. 1909, ½ Liter, Kaiser Wilhelm's Wife, Pewter Lid, PUG	690.00
Stein, No. 1909, 1236, ½ Liter, Dutch Children, With Cat, Pewter Lid, PUG	259.00
Stein, No. 1947, ½ Liter, Innkeeper, Inlaid Lid	288.00
Stein, No. 2018, ½ Liter, Pug Dog, Stoneware Lid	978.00
Stein, No. 2025, ½ Liter, Cherubs, Etched, Inlaid Lid	288.00
Stein, No. 2069, ½ Liter, Monkey Holding Fish, Stoneware Lid	2200.00
Stein, No. 2075, ½ Liter, Telegrapher Occupational, Etched, Inlaid Lid	1380.00
Stein, No. 2090, 3 Liter, Tavern Scene, Etched, Inlaid Lid	184.00
Stein, No. 2093, ½ Liter, Suites Of Cards, Etched, Inlaid Lid	575.00
Stein, No. 2097, ½ Liter, Bars Of Music, Etched, Inlaid Lid	345.00
Stein, No. 2107, 2 ½ Liter, Gambrinus On Throne, Etched, Inlaid Lid	805.00
Stein, No. 2140, ½ Liter, Bicycle & Train, Inlaid Lid, PUG ....*illus*	288.00
Stein, No. 2190, ½ Liter, Bicycle, Etched, Pewter Lid ....*illus*	345.00
Stein, No. 2206, 3 Liter, Tavern Scene, Etched, Inlaid Lid	776.00
Stein, No. 2231, ½ Liter, Cavalier Drinking, Etched, Inlaid Lid	276.00
Stein, No. 2384-1035, 2 ¼ Liter, Musical Scene, Pewter Lid, PUG	488.00
Stein, No. 2384-1036, 2 ¼ Liter, Woman & Cherubs Play Music, Pewter Lid, PUG	460.00
Stein, No. 2388, ½ Liter, Character, Pretzels, Inlaid Lid	219.00
Stein, No. 2401, ½ Liter, Tannhouser In The Venusberg, Etched, Inlaid Lid	295.00
Stein, No. 2530, 1 Liter, Boar Hunt, Cameo, Inlaid Lid	578.00
Stein, No. 2635, ½ Liter, Girl Holding Bicycle, Inlaid Lid	431.00

Stein, No. 2652, ½ Liter, Knights Drinking, Inlaid Lid	368.00
Stein, No. 2724, ½ Liter, Mason, Occupational, Lid Of Mason Tools, Etched, Inlaid Lid	2070.00
Stein, No. 2727, ½ Liter, Printer, Occupational, Etched, Inlaid Lid	1925.00
Stein, No. 2745, ½ Liter, Bavarian Man, Etched, Inlaid Lid	220.00
Stein, No. 2796, 3 Liter, Heidelberg, Etched, Inlaid Lid	460.00
Stein, No. 2823, 1 Liter, Woman Target Shooter, Pewter Lid	394.00
Stein, No. 2936, ½ Liter, Elks Club, Inlaid Lid	259.00
Stein, No. 3034, 1 Liter, Portrait Of Friedrick Schiler, Cameo, Inlaid Lid	570.00
Stein, No. 3137, ½ Liter, Art Nouveau, Inlaid Lid	518.00
Tureen, Underplate, Lid, Figural Handles, Grapevine, Blue & Cream, Squat, 14 In.	300.00
Vase, No. 1220, Mosaic, 13 In.	201.00
Vase, No. 1537, Children, 4-Panel, Etched, 14 ½ In.	207.00
Vase, No. 2414, Etched, 17 In.	132.00
Vase, No. 2537, Flowers, Engraved, Glazed, T. Adam, 13 ½ In.	805.00

MILK GLASS was named for its milky white color. It was first made in England during the 1700s. The height of its popularity in the United States was from 1870 to 1880. It is now correct to refer to some colored glass as blue milk glass, black milk glass, etc. Reproductions of milk glass are being made and sold in many stores. Related pieces may be listed in the Cosmos, Vallerysthal, and Westmoreland categories.

Atomizer, Hobnail, 1950s, 3 ½ In.	15.00
Basket, Ruffled, Hobnail, Handle, 7 In.	44.00
Bowl, Open Lattice, Tri-Stemmed Ribbed, Open Edged Base, c.1890, 7 x 12 In.	288.00
Cake Stand, Flowers, Stripes, 5 ¾ x 9 In.	11.00
Candleholder, Acanthus Leaves, c.1950, 5 In., Pair	10.00
Candy Dish, Hen On Nest, Cover, 7 x 5 In.	24.00
Candy Dish, Opaque White, Hobnail With Fluted Edge, 6 In.	18.00
Cup, Tom & Jerry, McKee, 3 ½ In.	5.00
Decanter, Eagle, Boston Tea Party, Stopper, 1968, 9 In.	40.00
Dish, Dove In Hand, Green Rhinestone, c.1889, 6 x 8 In.	140.00
Egg, Chick, Painted, 5 In.	23.00
Jar, Ivy, Quilted, Gold Beads, c.1950, 8 In.	45.00
Jug, Flowers, Applied Handle, Open Pontil, c.1840, 2 In.	45.00
Lamp, Impressed Drapery Design, Turquoise & White, 10 In.	118.00
Lamp, Pineapple Shade, Basket Weave Base, White & Green, 8 In.	118.00
Lamp, White, Blue Flowers, Leaves, Vertical Ribbing, Double Round Base, Domed Shade, 8 In.	81.00
Pitcher, Chocolate, Feathered, c.1925, 8 In.	825.00
Punch Bowl, Tom & Jerry, McKee, 11 In.	42.00
Reamer, Sunkist, USA, 3 In.	43.00
Shaker, Pepper, Square, Red Lid, 3 ⅛ In.	8.00
Syrup, Raised Design, Woman & Child, Silver Plated Top & Handle, 6 ¾ In. ...*illus*	81.00
Vanity Jar, Screw Cap, Ribbed, Anchor Hocking, c.1925, 2 ¾ x 2 In.	18.00

MILLEFIORI means, literally, a thousand flowers. Many small pieces of glass resembling flowers are grouped together to form a design. It is a type of glasswork popular in paperweights and some are listed in that category.

Vase, Paperweight, Signed, 1993, 7 In.	124.00
Vase, Stretched, Swirled Glass, Solid Blue Interior, 10 x 6 ½ In.	138.00

MINTON china has been made in the Staffordshire region of England from 1793 to the present. The firm became part of the Royal Doulton Tableware Group in 1968, but the wares continued to be marked *Minton*. In 2009 the brand was bought by KPS Capital Partners of New York and became part of WWRD Holdings. Many marks have been used. The word *England* was added in 1891. Minton majolica is listed in this book in the Majolica category.

Bowl, Footed, Persian Blue, Black Transfer, Flowers, Leaves, c.1872, 7 ½ In., Pair	563.00
Bowl, Gold Border & Accents, Leaves, Stylized Flowers, Turquoise Ground, 4 x 9 ½ In.	819.00
Cachepot, Cupid Panels, Blue Ground, Pate-Sur-Pate, Openwork Rim, 8 x 9 In., Pair	7705.00
Cachepot, Stand, Atlas Figure On Corners, Medallions, Thornwaldsen, c.1870, 11 ½ In., Pair ..*illus*	2370.00
Candlestick, Figural, King Of Spades, Queen Of Hearts, 14 x 8 ½ In., Pair	1521.00
Centerpiece, Open Latticework Bowl, 2 Kneeling Winged Putti, Turquoise, White, 1873, 8 In.	705.00
Charger, Portrait Of Young Woman, Hand Painted, Impressed, 1887, 13 ½ In.	288.00
Compote, Lid, Basket Weave Bowl, Turquoise & White, 3 Boys, Seated, 1900s, 10 In., Pair	940.00
Compote, Round, Shallow, Turquoise Band, Reticulated Border, Gilt, Round Base, c.1872, 10 In.	352.00
Dish, Game Pie, Liner, Majolica, Raised Hare, Duck Cover, 1800s, 7 x 12 In.	780.00
Eggcup, White & Gold, 1880s, 2 ⅜ In.	95.00

Minton, Jardiniere, Dragon, Elephant Handles, Footed, Christopher Dresser, Stamped, 20 x 27 In. $1612.00

Rago Arts & Auction Center

Minton, Vase, Classical Style Landscape, Gilt Accents, Hand Painted, c.1815, 3 x 3 In. $120.00

DuMouchelles Art Gallery

Mocha, Mug, Brown Band, Blue Seaweed, Applied Handle, 3 ¼ x 3 ½ In. $158.00

Conestoga Auction Co., Inc.

Mocha, Mug, Cat's-Eye, Blue, Light & Dark Brown Bands, 3 In. $561.00

Conestoga Auction Co., Inc.

M

As always, the edited listings in *Kovels' Antiques & Collectibles Price Guide* aren't available on any website, but readers should visit Kovels.com for information on trends, tips, reproductions, marks, old prices, and more!

Monmouth, Jug, Cobalt Blue Leaf, Monmouth, Ill., Strap Handle, 1890s, 1 Gal.
$1093.00

Rock Island Auction Company

Moorcroft, Ginger Jar, Eventide, Landscape, Trees, Marked, c.1920, 10 ¾ In.
$18300.00

Neal Auction Co.

Moorcroft, Vase, Cornflowers, 2 Handles, Macintyre, c.1902, 10 x 7 ½ In.
$1736.00

Rago Arts & Auction Center

Flask, White, Gilt, Dots, Pate-Sur-Pate, Leaves, Nymph, Bouquet, Henry Hollins, c.1884, 10 ½ In.	3004.00
Group, Cupid & Psyche, Standing Figures, Embracing, Parian, c.1851, 16 ½ In. ....*illus*	356.00
Jardiniere, Dragon, Elephant Handles, Footed, Christopher Dresser, Stamped, 20 x 27 In. .....*illus*	1612.00
Jug, Blue & Pink Azaleas, Spout, Angled Handle, c.1842-48, 18 In. Diam.	120.00
Jug, Green Glaze, Molded Cherubs, Twist Handle, England, c.1840, 7 In.	72.00
Jug, Milk, Cat Shape, Tail Forms Handle, Peering, Mouse, 1873, 10 In.	2832.00
Oyster Plate, 9 Wells, Flow Blue, Bamboo, Cranes, 9 ¼ In.	201.00
Pitcher, Blue Glaze, Pear Shape, Scroll Handle, Leaves, Greek Key Band, c.1872, 10 In.	326.00
Plate Set, Cobalt Blue & Gold Border, Classical Symbols, J.E. Caldwell, 1900s, 10 ½ In., 12 Piece	489.00
Plate Set, Fish, Aquatic Scene, Gilt Border, c.1905, 9 In., 12 Piece	920.00
Plate Set, Flower & Berry Border, Fruit Filled Bowl Center, c.1920, 10 ½ In., 12 Piece	207.00
Plate Set, Flower Sprays, Light Blue Border, Gilt, 1900s, 10 In., 12 Piece	150.00
Plate Set, White, Gold Flowers, Rim, Tiffany & Co., 9 In., 6 Piece	252.00
Plate, Chief Personage Of An Argive Feast, Cobalt Blue Border, Figure Reclining, c.1878, 9 In.	118.00
Plate, Flower Centers, Reticulated Edge, Hand Painted, Signed Pillsbury, 9 ¼ In., Pair	805.00
Plate, Jeweled Gilding, Turquoise Enamel, Birds, Butterflies, Desire Leroy, c.1878, 9 ½ In., Pair.	1802.00
Plate, Painted, Scenic, Fish, Blue Border, Gold Discs, c.1910, 10 In.	295.00
Plate, Underwater Scene Of Sea Urchin & Plants, Green Border, Octagonal, c.1880, 9 In.	135.00
Platter, Asian Style, Flowering Twigs, Pheasant, Leaves, Medallions, Stand, 1881, 19 x 15 In. .	207.00
Platter, Blue & White Transfer, Chinese Pattern, Gadrooned Rim, Dragon, 1843, 20 x 16 In. ...	148.00
Urn, Cover, White, Gold Filigree Decoration, Handles, Footed, 16 In., Pair	660.00
Vase, Classical Style Landscape, Gilt Accents, Hand Painted, c.1815, 3 x 3 In. ....*illus*	120.00
Vase, Figure, Courtyard, Flower Bouquet, Elephant Handles, Scroll Feet, Gilding, c.1878, 12 In., Pair	2726.00
Vase, Moon Flask Shape, Bird On Branch, Crackled Turquoise, 1872, 7 In., Pair	5800.00
Vase, Pink, Round Body, Footed, Circular Reserve, Painted Winter Scene, c.1900, 6 x 4 ¾ In., Pair	310.00

MIRRORS *are listed in the Furniture category under Mirror.*

MOCHA pottery is an English-made product that was sold in America during the early 1800s. It is a heavy pottery with pale coffee-and-cream coloring. Designs of blue, brown, green, orange, black, or white were added to the pottery and given fanciful names, such as Tree, Snail Trail, or Moss. Mocha designs are sometimes found on pearlware. A few pieces of mocha ware were made in France, the United States, and other countries.

Bowl, Conical, Rolled Foot, Curly Bands, 5 ¼ In.	79.00
Bowl, Earthworm, Zigzag Band, Brown Stripes, 4 In.	236.00
Chamber Pot, Cover, Wide White Ornamented Band, Seaweed Splotches, 1800s, 9 In.	178.00
Crock, Butter, White Band, Blue Seaweed, Foot Rim, 2 x 4 In.	102.00
Cup, Seaweed, Cone Shape, Blue Bands, Turned Beading, Orange Band, 3 ¾ In.	83.00
Mixing Bowl, Seaweed, Footed, White Band, Cobalt Blue, 7 x 14 In.	201.00
Mug, Brown Band, Blue Seaweed, Applied Handle, 3 ¼ x 3 ½ In. ....*illus*	158.00
Mug, Cat's-Eye, Blue, Light & Dark Brown Bands, 3 In. ....*illus*	561.00
Pitcher, Applied Handle, Earthworm, 6 In.	40.00
Pitcher, Brown, Blue Slip Bands, Green Herringbone, Pearlware, 8 x 7 ½ In.	748.00
Pitcher, Earthworm & Cat's-Eye Bands, Tan, Chocolate & Blue Glazes, 7 In.	644.00
Pitcher, Slip Inlaid Banding, Reeded Blue Rim, Bulbous, Leaf Patterned Bands, c.1800, 9 In.	889.00
Pitcher, Slip Marbled, Barrel Shape, Green Reeded Rim, Handle With Leaf Terminals, 1700s, 7 In.	1896.00
Shaker, Pepper, Blue Tree Seaweed, Footed, 4 In.	113.00
Tankard, Multicolor Bands, Varied Width, Molded Foot, Loop Handle, 6 In.	345.00

MONMOUTH POTTERY COMPANY started working in Monmouth, Illinois, in 1892. The pottery made a variety of utilitarian wares. It became part of Western Stoneware Company in 1906. The maple leaf mark was used until 1930. If *Co.* appears as part of the mark, the piece was made before 1906.

Jug, Cobalt Blue Leaf, Monmouth, Ill., Strap Handle, 1890s, 1 Gal. ....*illus*	1093.00
Vase, Blue Glaze, Cylindrical, 10 In.	95.00

MONT JOYE, *see Mt. Joye category.*

MOORCROFT pottery was first made in Burslem, England, in 1913. William Moorcroft had managed the art pottery department for James Macintyre & Company of England from 1898 to 1913. The Moorcroft pottery continues today, although William Moorcroft died in 1945. The earlier wares are similar to the modern ones, but color and marking will help indicate the age.

Biscuit Jar, Florian Macintyre, Oval, Scrolling Medallions, Blue Poppies, 7 In.	700.00
Bowl, Footed, Moonlit Blue Landscape, Signed, Impressed, 7 x 5 ½ In.	2160.00

Bowl, Fruit, Pomegranates, Footed, Marked, 5 x 9 In.	930.00
Bowl, Pansy, Dark Blue Ground, 2 Handles, Footed, Signed, 3 ½ x 10 In.	432.00
Bowl, Pomegranate, 2 Handles, Footed, Signed, 4 ¾ x 12 ½ In.	1188.00
Box, Freesia, Cobalt Blue Ground, Green Inside, Lid, 2 x 5 x 3 ½ In.	118.00
Candlestick, Pears, Plums, Leaves, Cylindrical, Spread Foot, Rolled Rim, 8 In., Pair	240.00
Compote, Silver Base, 2 Handles, 5 x 11 ½ In.	1240.00
Ginger Jar, Eventide, Landscape, Trees, Marked, c.1920, 10 ¾ In. ....*illus*	18300.00
Jar, Blue Stopper, Multicolor Flower, Bulbous, Marked W.M., 6 In.	295.00
Jug, Lamia, Flowers, Rachel Bishop, 9 In.	518.00
Lamp Base, Cornflower, Red Glaze, Signed, 12 x 7 In.	2852.00
Lamp, Peacock Feather, Blue To Green, Brass Finish, Cloth Shade, Signed, 65 In.	944.00
Pitcher, Cone Shape, Applied Handle, Speckled Blue Glaze, Marked, 7 In.	45.00
Soup, Coupe, Pomegranate, Pewter Base, England, 8 x 5 In.	69.00
Vase, Anemone, Cinched Waist, Stamped, 5 In.	310.00
Vase, Anemone, Flambe Glaze, Impressed Mark, 4 ¼ x 6 In.	510.00
Vase, Anemone, Orange Flower, Blue Ground, Stamped, 9 ¼ x 5 ½ In.	279.00
Vase, Chrysanthemum Flame, Bulbous, Stamped, 12 ¼ x 8 In.	6820.00
Vase, Clematis, Green Ground, Oval, 7 In.	324.00
Vase, Clematis, Red, Deep Blue Ground, Round, Stamped, 1 ¾ x 2 In.	120.00
Vase, Columbine, Rusty Red Ground, Signed W. Moorcroft, 7 ¼ In.	372.00
Vase, Cornflowers, 2 Handles, Macintyre, c.1902, 10 x 7 ½ In. ....*illus*	1736.00
Vase, Eventide Landscape, Tapered, Tudric Pewter Foot, Hammered, Mark, c.1925, 4 ½ x 7 In.	2400.00
Vase, Fish, Red Flambe Glaze, Bulbous, Signed, 9 x 11 In.	4200.00
Vase, Flowers, Cobalt Blue Ground, Marked, 4 ¾ In.	144.00
Vase, Grape Leaf & Berry, Green Ground, Impressed Mark, 4 ¾ x 6 ¾ In.	420.00
Vase, Grape Leaf & Berry, Impressed Mark, Signed, 2 ½ x 3 ½ In.	240.00
Vase, Hazeldene, Moonlit Blue Glaze, Stamped, 8 ¼ In.	2473.00
Vase, Hibiscus, Indigo Glaze Ground, Stamped, 12 ½ In.	465.00
Vase, Landscape, Pearl Glaze, Blue, White, Signed, 11 ¾ x 7 ½ In.	5270.00
Vase, Magnolia, Green Glaze, Stamped, 12 ½ In.	341.00
Vase, Moonlit Blue Landscape, Dark Ground, Flared Rim, Signed, Impressed, 4 x 4 ½ In.	1680.00
Vase, Moonlit Blue, Green, Trees, Tapered Cylinder, Shouldered, Flared Rim, 10 In.	2875.00
Vase, Orange Glaze, Waisted, 8 ¾ In.	173.00
Vase, Orchid, Blue To Green Gloss Glaze, Multicolor Flowers, 1918, 3 ½ In.	299.00
Vase, Orchid, Flambe Glaze, Impressed Mark, 4 ½ x 5 In.	600.00
Vase, Orchid, Flowers, Multicolor, Blue Ground, Bulbous, Impressed, 10 ½ x 11 In.	1440.00
Vase, Orchid, Yellow, Black, Paper Label, 2 ½ x 3 In.	300.00
Vase, Pansies, Footed, Flared Rim, c.1902, 9 ½ x 5 ½ In.	1736.00
Vase, Pansy, Multicolor, Deep Red Ground, Printed Mark, 3 ¼ In.	390.00
Vase, Polar Bears, Cream Ground, Signed J. Moorcroft, 6 ¾ In.	620.00
Vase, Pomegranate & Birds, Green Ground, Round, Impressed, 6 ½ x 6 ½ In.	450.00
Vase, Pomegranate, Black Ground, Shouldered, Impressed, 2 ¼ x 4 In.	240.00
Vase, Pomegranate, Blue Ground, Hammered Tudric Pewter Top, Impressed, 3 ¼ x 6 In., Pair	840.00
Vase, Pomegranate, Dark Green Ground, Cylindrical, Impressed, 4 ½ x 10 ½ In.	720.00
Vase, Pomegranate, Dark Ground, Paper Label, 2 ¼ x 4 In.	210.00
Vase, Pomegranate, Long Neck, Signed, 8 ½ x 4 In.	1116.00
Vase, Pomegranate, Signed, Liberty Co., 7 ½ x 5 ½ In.	2108.00
Vase, Poppies, 2 Handles, Marked, c.1902, 10 x 7 In.	4650.00
Vase, Poppies, Bulbous, Footed, Marked, 12 ¼ x 5 ½ In.	868.00
Vase, Poppy, Green Ground, Impressed, Paper Label, 4 x 5 ¼ In.	330.00
Vase, Poppy, Large Orange Flowers, Dark Blue Ground, Signed, 14 ½ x 8 ½ In. ....*illus*	3596.00
Vase, Poppy, Red, Black Ground, Impressed Mark, 6 x 9 ¼ In.	2160.00
Vase, Purple Orchid, Mottled Blue Ground, Impressed, 10 ¾ x 7 ½ In.	2070.00
Vase, Red Poppies, Stamped, Moorcroft Made In England, 1920s, 8 x 4 ½ In. ....*illus*	2356.00
Vase, Wisteria, Dark Ground, Impressed, 3 x 7 In.	510.00
Vase, Wisteria, Multicolor, Dark Blue Ground, Impressed Mark, 4 ½ x 8 ¹⁄₃₂ In.	480.00

MORGANTOWN GLASS WORKS operated in Morgantown, West Virginia, from 1900 to 1974. Some of their wares are marked with an adhesive label that says *Old Morgantown Glass*.

Champagne, Cupped, Churchill, Ruby, 6 ⅛ In.	40.00
Champagne, Monroe, Red, 6 ¼ In.	35.00
Champagne, Red, 6 ¼ In.	35.00
Champagne, Reverse Twist Stem, Red, 6 ⅛ In.	50.00
Cocktail, Monroe, Ruby, 5 ¼ In.	30.00
Cocktail, Plantation, Red, 5 ⅝ In.	30.00
Cocktail, Red Empress, 5 In.	30.00

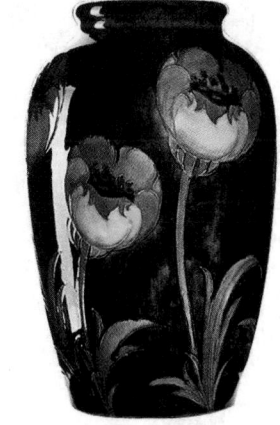

Moorcroft, Vase, Poppy, Large Orange Flowers, Dark Blue Ground, Signed, 14 ½ x 8 ½ In.
$3596.00

Rago Arts & Auction Center

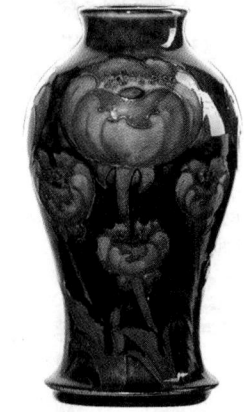

Moorcroft, Vase, Red Poppies, Stamped, Moorcroft Made In England, 1920s, 8 x 4 ½ In.
$2356.00

Rago Arts & Auction Center

Moriage, Pitcher, Flowers, Leafy Scrolls, Jade Green, Japan, c.1900, 16 In.
$230.00

Leland Little Auction

Moriage

Moriage became a popular decoration on Japanese ceramics about 1900. A white clay thinned to look like toothpaste was put on the piece to make a raised decoration.

Moser, Ewer, Green, Enamel, Horn Of Plenty, Applied Scrolling Vines, Stemmed Foot, c.1900, 11 In.
$492.00

Neal Auction Co.

Moser, Goblet, Green Grapes, Leaves, Coral Band, Jeweled Flowers, Rosettes, 8 In., Pair
$920.00

Early Auction Co.

Decanter, Pink, Drape Loop, Handle, 9 ⅝ In.	250.00
Goblet, Water, Empress, Ruby, 7 ¼ In.	40.00
Jug, Berry, Belton, Etched Black Foot & Handle, 9 ¼ In.	295.00
Sherbet, Empress, Ruby, Low, 3 ½ In.	25.00
Sherbet, Red, 6 ⅛ In.	50.00
Wine, Cobalt Blue, 5 ⅝ In.	60.00

MORIAGE is a special type of raised decoration used on some Japanese pottery. Sometimes pieces of clay were shaped by hand and applied to the item; sometimes the clay was squeezed from a tube in the way we apply cake frosting. One type of moriage is called Dragonware by collectors.

Ashtray, Flowers, Bird, Orange, Black Border, Japan, 5 ⅜ In.	45.00
Biscuit Jar, Paneled, 6-Footed, Leaves, Flowers, Beading, Finial, Nippon, c.1900, 6 In.	265.00
Bowl, Dragon Handles, Wooded Scene, Footed, Nippon, c.1800, 8 x 6 x 4 ½ In.	600.00
Cheese Dish, Cover, Gold Design, Nippon, 1910, 7 ½ x 5 ¾ In.	75.00
Chocolate Pot, Nippon, Green Ground, Leaves, Violets, 10 In.	225.00
Cup & Saucer, Demitasse, Dragonware, Geisha, Gray	40.00
Ewer, Daisies, Multicolor, RS Prussia, 7 In.	250.00
Figurine, Hotei & Boy, Japanese Kutani, 6 ½ x 8 ½ In.	375.00
Pin Holder, Nippon, Blue Ground, Lotus Flowers, Dots, 5 In.	125.00
Pitcher, Flowers, Jade Green Ground, Hand Painted, Japan, 16 In.	230.00
Pitcher, Flowers, Leafy Scrolls, Jade Green, Japan, c.1900, 16 In. ....*illus*	230.00
Tea Caddy, Beaded, Flowers, Gilt Trim, Lid, Nippon, 4 ⅞ In.	75.00
Vase, Daffodils, Raised Gilt Highlights, Mark RS Japan, c.1940, 5 x 4 In.	244.00
Vase, Dragonware, Gray, White, Shouldered, Footed, c.1940, 7 In.	135.00
Vase, Flowers, Ruffled Rim, Bulbous, Nippon, 4 ½ In.	259.00
Vase, Green Ground, Brown Border, Flowers, 8 ½ In.	95.00
Vase, Open Work Neck, Handles, Flared, Serpentine Rim, Gilt, Sparrow, Lilies, 23 x 13 In.	173.00
Vase, Plum Blossom, Bulbous, Painted, Vines, Pink Flowers, Chinese, 5 x 5 In.	690.00
Vase, Scenic, Desert, Stork, Handles, Nippon, 12 In.	75.00
Wall Pocket, Blue, Dragonware, 5 In.	119.00

MOSER glass is made by a Bohemian (Czech) glasshouse founded by Ludwig Moser in 1857. Art Nouveau–type glassware and iridescent glassware were made. The most famous Moser glass is decorated with heavy enameling in gold and bright colors. The firm, Moser Glassworks, is still working in Karlovy Vary, Czech Republic. Few pieces of Moser glass are marked.

Biscuit Jar, Green, Enamel Flowers, Applied Gilt Bee Highlights, Metal Lid, Bail Handle, 6 In.	275.00
Bowl, Blue Art Glass, Applied Salamander, Clear Ruffled Rim, Gilt, 9 x 3 In.	150.00
Bowl, Cranberry, Gilt Flowers, Bees, 2 Handles, 7 ½ In.	575.00
Bowl, Light Purple, Shaded, Yellow Enamel Flowers, Gold Beading, Swollen, 5 In.	118.00
Bowl, Prussian Blue, Multicolor Leaves, Clear Handle With Pewter Bird, Oblong, Shaped Rim, 9 In.	230.00
Cruet, Cranberry, Urn Form, White Enameled Moorish Pattern, 9 In.	69.00
Cup, Presentation, Game Birds, Multicolor, Paper Label, Case, 11 x 7 In., 6 Piece	196.00
Ewer, Green, Enamel, Horn Of Plenty, Applied Scrolling Vines, Stemmed Foot, c.1900, 11 In. ..... *illus*	492.00
Goblet, Cobalt Blue, Baluster, Oak Leaves & 5 Acorn Jewels, 7 In.	300.00
Goblet, Green Grapes, Leaves, Coral Band, Jeweled Flowers, Rosettes, 8 In., Pair ....*illus*	920.00
Oyster Plate, 5 Wells, Cobalt Blue, Glass, Majolica, 9 ¾ In.	9145.00
Perfume Bottle, Ruby Glass, Enamel Flowers & Leaves, Shouldered, Ball Stopper, 4 In.	460.00
Pitcher, Blue, Enamel Flower Overlay, Ball Shape, 6 ¼ In.	450.00
Pitcher, Cornucopia Shape, Amber, Applied Blue Feet, Handle, Leaves, Insects, Jewels, 13 In.	600.00
Pitcher, Crested Bird, Branches, Oak Tree, Leaves, Acorns, Enamel, Loop Handle, 6 ¾ In.	2530.00
Rose Bowl, Cranberry, Enameled Peacock, 3 Rigaree Feet, Yellow Jade Handles, Ball Shape, 3 ½ In.	58.00
Saltshaker, Amber, Applied Glass Fish, Enameled Flowers, 4 In.	450.00
Saltshaker, Cranberry Glass, Embossed, Enamel, Fish, Cattail, 4 ¼ In.	900.00
Toothpick Holder, Egg Form, Prussian Blue, Autumn Oak Leaves, Gold Scrolling Feet, 3 In.	425.00
Tumbler, Amberina, Oak Leaves, Insects, Raised Acorns, 4 In. ....*illus*	776.00
Tumbler, Cranberry, Multicolor Oak Leaves, Raised Acorns, 4 In.	288.00
Vase, Amber, Gold Filigree Band, Inverted Teardrop, Flared Rim, Flattened Foot, 9 x 7 In.	118.00
Vase, Art Nouveau, Cut Glass, Engraved Yellow Cased, Tapering, Signed, c.1900, 11 ½ In.	179.00
Vase, Bud, Cranberry, Cornucopia Form, Oak Leaves, Raised Acorn Jewel, 6 ½ In.	150.00
Vase, Cranberry, Multicolor Leaves, Gold Scrolling, Genie Bottle Shape, Round Foot, 8 In.	144.00
Vase, Crystal, Ribbed, Enameled, Pink Flowers, Yellow, Gold Band Rim, Circles, Beaker, 16 ¾ In.	115.00
Vase, Cut & Engraved, Yellow Glass, Flowers & Leaves, c.1900, 11 ½ In.	175.00
Vase, Cylindrical, Dark Green, Etched Gilt Palm Tree Design, Beveled, 10 ½ In.	173.00
Vase, Gold, Enameled, Green Leaves, Red Berries, 4 Lobes, 3 ¾ x 2 ¾ In.	130.00

Vase, Ruffled Rim, Stick, Green, Flowers, 8 In.	550.00
Vase, Sapphire Blue, Flowers, Gold & Pink Leaves, Footed, Elongated Oval, 12 ½ In.	748.00

MOSS ROSE china was made by many firms from 1808 to 1900. It has a typical moss rose pictured as the design. The plant is not as popular now as it was in Victorian gardens, so the fuzz-covered bud is unfamiliar to most collectors. The dishes were usually decorated with pink and green flowers.

Bonbon, Raised Scalloped Edges, Pierced, Embossed, 1950, 5 In.	20.00
Bowl, Vegetable, Cutout Handles, Rosenthal, 10 In.	80.00
Bowl, Vegetable, Oval, Sango China, Japan, 10 ½ In.	32.00
Bowl, Vegetable, Scalloped, Ironstone, Grindley, 9 x 9 In.	100.00
Condiment Pot, Lid, Salem, c.1950, 3 ¾ In.	9.00
Cup & Saucer, Lusterware, Japan, Label, c.1960	5.50
Cup & Saucer, Rubbed Cup, Ruffled Foot, Scroll Handle, Staffordshire	25.00
Eggcup, Footed, England, 2 ¼ x 1 ¾ In.	12.00
Ladle, Soup, Ironstone, 9 In.	60.00
Lamp, Oil, Aladdin Style, 4 ½ x 6 In.	9.50
Lighter, Square, c.1960, 2 ½ x 2 x 2 In.	12.50
Nappy, Grindley Favorite, 5 Piece	30.00
Pitcher, Hot Water, Cable Etruria Pottery Co., 8 In.	140.00
Pitcher, Sterling Base, Rosenthal, 40 Oz.	160.00
Plate, Luncheon, 7 ¼ In.	8.00
Plate, Lusterware, Gilt Trim, c.1960, 10 ½ In.	8.50
Plate, Salad, 22K Gold Trim, Nasco, c.1950, 7 ⅝ In.	5.00
Platter, Meat, Open Handles, Raised Scroll Design, Gilt Trim, England, c.1875, 13 x 9 In.	75.00
Platter, Oval, Wallace & Chetwynd, 9 x 13 In.	30.00
Salt & Pepper, Bulbous, Universal Pottery	18.00
Sugar & Creamer, Sango China, Japan	24.00
Teapot, Lid, Diamond China, Japan	60.00
Trinket Box, Gilt Trim, Curved Feet, Japan, 2 x 3 x 4 In.	12.00

MOTHER-OF-PEARL GLASS, or pearl satin glass, was first made in the 1850s in England and in Massachusetts. It was a special type of mold-blown satin glass with air bubbles in the glass, giving it a pearlized color. It has been reproduced. Mother-of-pearl shell objects are listed under Pearl.

Biscuit Jar, Raspberry Satin, Gold Flowers, White Interior, Silver Plated Collar, Handle, 9 In.	805.00
Card Case, Quilted Diamond Design, c.1885, 4 x 2 ¾ In.	215.00
Corncob Picks, Steel, Wide Handles, Black Box, c.1975, 5 ¾ x 4 ¾ In.	123.00
Ewer, Pink Satin, Diamond Quilted Pattern, Melon Ribbed, Camphor Handle, 7 In.	58.00
Perfume Bottle, Yellow, Oval, Drape Swag Pattern, Enhanced With Flower, 5 In.	745.00
Pitcher, Diamond Quilted, Ribbon Edge, Coralene Beading, 3 ½ x 5 In.	119.00
Pitcher, Water, Amber, Rain Drop Pattern, Reeded Handle, Bulbous, Shaped Rim, 6 In.	150.00
Pitcher, Water, Blue, Herringbone, Melon Ribbed, Loop Handle, 9 In.	224.00
Sugar & Creamer, Diamond Quilted Pink Camphor, Handles, Finial, 4 ½ In. ....*illus*	345.00
Vase, Blue Glass, Herringbone Pattern, Urn Shape, Round Foot, 7 In.	29.00
Vase, Butterscotch, Diamond Quilted, Matsu-No-Kee Branch, Flowers, 5 In. ....*illus*	805.00
Vase, Herringbone Pattern, Pink, Shouldered, Cylindrical Neck, In Turned Ruffle Rim, 10 In.	58.00
Watch Holder, Helmet Shape, Brass, Elgin Pocket Watch Inside, Alabaster Base, 5 In.	345.00

MOTORCYCLES and motorcycle accessories of all types are being collected today. Examples can be found that date back to the early twentieth century. Toy motorcycles are listed in the Toy category.

Aeramacchi Ala D'Oro Corsa, 1966	16800.00
Ariel, 250cc, Single Cylinder, 1936	5040.00
Benelli, Tornado, 1968	10640.00
Blotter, Indian Scout Motorcycle, Red Cycle, 1920s, 3 ½ x 6 In.	225.00
BMW, R50, 1960	4760.00
BSA Victor GP, Round Barrel, 1967	4256.00
BSA, A50, 500cc, Sidecar, 1968	6272.00
BSA, A65F, Firebird Scrambler, 1971	4144.00
Catalog, Harley-Davidson, 1917, 8 ¼ x 12 In., 8 Pages	375.00
Cleveland, Single Cylinder, 2 ½ Horsepower, 1916	8960.00
Excelsior V-Twin, 3 Speed, Tank Shaft, Claxon Horn, Side Car, 1917	33600.00
Harley-Davidson, Model B, Head & Tail Lights, 3 Speed, Tank Shaft, Foot Clutch, 1926	12880.00

Moser, Tumbler, Amberina, Oak Leaves, Insects, Raised Acorns, 4 In.
$776.00

Early Auction Co.

Mother-Of-Pearl, Sugar & Creamer, Diamond Quilted Pink Camphor, Handles, Finial, 4 ½ In.
$345.00

Early Auction Co.

Mother-Of-Pearl, Vase, Butterscotch, Diamond Quilted, Matsu-No-Kee Branch, Flowers, 5 In.
$805.00

Early Auction Co.

Movie, Mobile Dangler, Casino Royale, 007, Tattooed Woman, Cardboard, 2-Sided, 1967, 12 x 18 In.
$563.00

Hake's Americana & Collectibles

Mt.Washington, Vase, Sicilian Lava, Black, Multicolor Shards, Reeded Handles, 9 In. $6038.00

Early Auction Co.

Muller Freres, Vase, Cameo, Trumpet, Yellow, Red Mums, Leaves, Signed, 15 In. $1778.00

Early Auction Co.

Music, Banjo, American Tenor, Silver Bell Symphony, Bacon Mfg. Co., Case, 1922, 11 In. $1126.00

Skinner, Inc.

Harley-Davidson, Single Strap Tank, 1905	39200.00
Harley-Davidson, V-Twin, 3 Speed, 45CI, Rear Box, 3 Wheeler, 1934	15000.00
License Plate, California, Steel, 1963, 8 x 5 In.	150.00
License Plate, Texas, Galvanized, 1975, 7 In.	75.00
Parts Manual No. 640, Indian, Military, 11 x 8 ½ In., 60 Pages	65.00
Pin, Harley-Davidson, 25000 Mile Club, Brass, 1 ½ x 1 In.	770.00
Pin, Harley-Davidson, Logo, Canton Motorcycles, c.1920, ⁹⁄₁₆ In.	702.00
Pin, Indian Motocycles, Hendee Manufacturing Co., c.1905, ⅞ In.	86.00
Sign, Harley-Davidson, Yellow, Blue, Black, Heavy Paper Stock, c.1916, 53 x 19 In.	1380.00
Sign, Indian Motorcycles, Neon, Metal Frame, 21 x 47 In.	1808.00
Sign, Palmer Motorcycle Tires, Paper, 19 x 27 In.	1295.00
Sign, V-Twin, Replacement Parts, Yellow, Black, Tin, 18 x 24 In.	70.00
Vest, Leather, Skull, Cobra, Star, Harley-Davidson Patch, c.1950, 40-In. Chest	150.00

MOUNT WASHINGTON, *see Mt. Washington category.*

MOVIE memorabilia of all types are collected. Animation Art, Games, Sheet Music, Toys, and some celebrity items are listed in their own section. A lobby card is usually 11 by 14 inches, but other sizes were also made. A set of lobby cards includes seven scene cards and one title card. An American one sheet, the standard movie poster, is 27 by 41 inches. A three sheet is 40 by 81 inches. A half sheet is 22 by 28 inches. A window card, made of cardboard, is 14 by 22 inches. An insert is 14 by 36 inches. A herald is a promotional item handed out to patrons. Press books, sent to exhibitors to promote a movie, contain ads & lists of what is available for advertising, i.e., posters, lobby cards. Press kits, sent to the media, contain photos and details about the movie, i.e., stars' biographies and interviews.

Color Transparency, Splendor In The Grass, Natalie Wood, Warren Beatty, 1961, 8 x 10 In.	50.00
Doll, John Wayne, Cowboy Clothing, Effanbee, 1981, 17 In.	40.00
Lobby Card, Abbott & Castello Meet The Mummy, Universal, 1955, 11 x 14 In.	58.00
Lobby Card, Adventures Of Robin Hood, Errol Flynn, Warner Brothers, 1938, 11 x 14 In.	53.00
Lobby Card, African Queen, Humphrey Bogart, Katharine Hepburn, 1952, 11 x 14 In.	56.00
Lobby Card, Alias Boston Blackie, Chester Morrie, Columbia, 1942, 11 x 14 In.	59.00
Lobby Card, Blithe Spirit, Rex Harrison, United Artists, 1945, 11 x 14 In.	155.00
Lobby Card, Cry Wolf, Errol Flynn, Barbara Stanwyck, 1947, 11 x 14 In.	30.00
Lobby Card, Down To Earth, Rita Hayworth, Columbia, 1947, 11 x 14 In., 8 Piece	286.00
Lobby Card, Goldfinger, Sean Connery, 1964, 11 x 14 In.	131.00
Lobby Card, How The West Was Won, Gregory Peck, James Stewart, 1970, 11 x 14 In., 8 Piece	96.00
Lobby Card, Son Of Frankenstein, Boris Karloff, Basil Rathbone, Realart, 1953, 11 x 14 In.	275.00
Magazine, Motion Picture, Shirley Temple On Cover, 1942	18.00
Magazine, Picture Play, Debunking The Cinderella Myth, Dorothy Sebastian, 1928	56.00
Magazine, Screen Play, Joan Bennett, December, 1931	32.00
Mobile Dangler, Casino Royale, 007, Tattooed Woman, Cardboard, 2-Sided, 1967, 12 x 18 In. *illus*	563.00
Photo, Modern Times, Paulette Goddard, 1936, 8 x 10 In., 2 Piece	53.00
Photo, Robert Mitchum, Portrait, Signed, 1940s, 9 ¾ x 13 ¼ In.	84.00
Pin, Wizard Of Oz, Bert Lahr As Lion, No. 9103, Orange Border, 1939, 1 ¼ In.	230.00
Poster, Alice In Wonderland, 20th Century Fox, 1933	326.00
Poster, All That Jazz, 20th Century Fox, 1979, 27 x 41 In.	39.00
Poster, American Graffiti, Richard Dreyfus, Ron Howard, Universal, 1973, 27 x 41 In.	120.00
Poster, Apocalypse Now, Martin Sheen, Marlon Brando, 1979, 27 x 41 In.	203.00
Poster, Barbarella, Jane Fonda, Paramount, 1968, 27 x 41 In.	239.00
Poster, Big Pond, Maurice Chevalier, 1930, 27 x 41 In.	627.00
Poster, Black Bird, George Segal, Columbia, 1975, 27 x 41 In.	15.00
Poster, Black Castle, Universal International, 1952, 27 x 41 In.	119.00
Poster, Blood Of Dracula, American International, 1957, 27 x 41 In.	95.00
Poster, Boom Town, Clark Cable, Spencer Tracy, 1940, 27 x 41 In.	115.00
Poster, Braveheart, Mel Gibson, Patrick McGoohan, 1995, 27 x 41 In.	26.00
Poster, Brides Of Dracula, Peter Cushing, AIP, 1960, 27 x 41 In.	119.00
Poster, Cabaret, Liza Minnelli, Michael York, Joel Grey, 1972, 27 x 41 In.	21.00
Poster, Carousel, Gordon MacRae, Shirley Jones, 1957, 27 x 41 In.	23.00
Poster, Chinese Cat, Charlie Chan, Sydney Toler, 1944, 22 x 28 In.	113.00
Poster, Christmas Story, Melinda Dillon, Peter Billingsley, Darren McGavin, 1983, 27 x 41 In.	227.00
Poster, Curse Of The Mummy's Tomb, Terrance Morgan, 1964, 27 x 41 In.	336.00
Poster, Custer's Last Fight, 1912, 41 x 81 In.	900.00
Poster, Docks Of New Orleans, Roland Winters, 1948, 22 x 28 In.	120.00
Poster, Empire Strikes Back, Mark Hamill, 1980, 27 x 41 In.	86.00
Poster, For A Few Dollars More, Clint Eastwood, 1967, 27 x 41 In.	310.00
Poster, Forever Amber, Linda Darnell, 1947, 22 x 28 In.	42.00

Poster, Giant, Elizabeth Taylor, Rock Hudson, James Dean, 27 x 41 In.	113.00
Poster, Godfather, Marlon Brando, 1972, 27 x 41 In.	84.00
Poster, Gone With The Wind, France, Reissue 1969, 62 x 46 In.	720.00
Poster, Green Hornet, Bruce Lee, 20th Century Fox, 1974, 27 x 41 In.	149.00
Poster, Half Angel, Frances Dee, Brian Donlevy, 1936, 41 x 81 In.	283.00
Poster, Hellcats Of The Navy, Ronald Reagan, Nancy Davis, 1957.	400.00
Poster, Idol Of The Crowds, John Wayne, 1937, 14 x 36 In.	295.00
Poster, Jane Marny, Woman's Face, Actress, M. Chachoin, Paris, 62 x 46 In.	1150.00
Poster, Lassie Come Home, Elizabeth Taylor, Roddy McDowall, 1943, 47 x 63 In.	220.00
Poster, Life & Adventures Of Buffalo Bill, Riverside Printing, 28 x 42 ½ In.	2200.00
Poster, Life Of Buffalo Bill, 3 Reels, White Horse, Indians, Pawnee Bill Film Co., 28 x 42 In.	990.00
Poster, Lucky Ghost, Mantan Moreland, 1941, 27 x 41 In.	79.00
Poster, Mistinguette, Dress, Entertainer, Frame, G.K. Benda, Phillip G. Dryfus, Paris, 65 x 50 In.	2070.00
Poster, Monty Python & The Holy Grail, Cinema 5, 1975, 27 x 41 In.	144.00
Poster, Muscle Beach Party, Annette Funicello, Frankie Avalon, Don Rickles, 1964, 27 x 41 In.	69.00
Poster, Night Of The Living Dead, Duane Jones, 1968, 27 x 41 In.	1434.00
Poster, One Million Years B.C., Raquel Welch, 1966, 27 x 41 In.	286.00
Poster, Redskin, Richard Dix, Paramount, 1921, 27 x 41 In.	275.00
Poster, Rocky, Sylvester Stallone, 1977, 27 x 41 In.	119.00
Poster, Sheik, Rudolph Valentino, Reissue, 1938, 41 x 27 In.	570.00
Poster, The Babe Comes Home, Babe Ruth, Linen Backed, 1927, 14 x 36 In.	2640.00
Poster, The Sting, Paul Newman, Robert Redford, Universal, 1974, 27 x 41 In.	180.00
Press Book, Drums, Sabu, 1938, 12 x 18 In., 24 Pages.	36.00
Press Book, Gun Crazy, United Artists, 1949, 11 x 17 In., 16 Pages	597.00
Program, Moulin Rouge, Joe Ferrer, Zsa Zsa Gabor, Toulouse-Lautrec Cover, 1953, 14 Pages.	115.00
Shoes, Platform, Herman Munster, Fred Gwynn	700.00
Window Card, Doctor Zhivago, Omar Sharif, 1965, 17 x 24 In.	18.00
Window Card, Soft Boiled, Tobacco Cutter Tom Mix, 1923, 14 x 22 In.	266.00

MT. JOYE is an enameled cameo glass made in the late nineteenth and twentieth centuries by Saint-Hilaire Touvier de Varraux and Co. of Pantin, France. This same company made De Vez glass. Pieces were usually decorated with enameling. Most pieces are not marked.

Basket, Strawberry Design, Green Ground, Metal Mounts, Handle, 5 ¾ x 5 ½ In.	345.00
Biscuit Jar, Acid Cut Ground, Enamel Iris, Embossed Gilt Metal Lid, Bail Handle, 7 In.	250.00
Ewer, White Satin Glass, Enamel Poppy, Gilt Metal, Curved Handle, 10 ½ In.	175.00
Rose Bowl, Gold Enamel Design, 5 ½ In.	40.00
Vase, 3 Purple Irises, Gold Leaves, Frosty Texture, Bulbous, Wide Ruffle Rim, 8 In.	546.00
Vase, Bud, Bulbous Base, Narrow Neck, Ruffled Rim, Emerald Green, Flowers, 10 In.	100.00
Vase, Enamel Iris Blossoms, Gold Leaves, Clear Chipped Ice Ground, Cylindrical, 7 In., Pair	460.00
Vase, Gold Enamel Flowers, 6-Sided Top, 5 In.	80.00
Vase, Green, Fish Scale Ground, Poppy, Gold Highlights, 16 In.	750.00
Vase, Opaque Green, Gilt Enamel Design, Flower, Marked, 10 ½ In.	403.00
Vase, Textured Crystal Body, 2 Colorful Leafy Stemmed Thistles, 12 In.	350.00

MT. WASHINGTON Glass Works started in 1837 in South Boston, Massachusetts. In 1870 the company moved to New Bedford, Massachusetts. Many types of art glass were made there until 1894, when the company merged with Pairpoint Manufacturing Co. Amberina, Burmese, Crown Milano, Cut Glass, Peachblow, and Royal Flemish are each listed in their own category.

Basket, Camphor Thorn Handle, Loop, Crimped Rim, Green & White, Satin Finish, 8 x 5 In.	633.00
Biscuit Jar, Blue Flowers, White Ground, Gilt, Silver Plated Lid, 9 In.	413.00
Biscuit Jar, Bulbous, White Opal Glass, Gold & Green Lilies, Bail & Lid, 9 x 7 In.	345.00
Biscuit Jar, Green & White, Blue Violets, Embossed Lid & Bail, 6 In.	150.00
Biscuit Jar, Lid, Cream, Multicolor Flowers, Silver Plate, Egg Crate Mold, 7 ½ In.	60.00
Biscuit Jar, Melon Ribbed, Green, Yellow, Pansies, Embossed Floral Lid, Butterfly Finial, 5 In.	200.00
Biscuit Jar, Melon Ribbed, White, Pink, Blue Pansies, Silver Plate Lid, Bail, 7 In.	125.00
Biscuit Jar, Melon Ribs, Green & White, Gold Enamel Sunflower, Silver Lid, 7 In.	150.00
Biscuit Jar, Melon Shape, Glass, Silver Plate, Painted Acorn Branches, Turtle, 1900s, 7 In.	413.00
Biscuit Jar, White & Blue Melon Ribbed Panels, Cherub Medallions, Silver Lid & Bail, 7 In.	450.00
Box, Melon Ribbed, Covered, Blue & White Blossoms, 3 ½ x 5 In.	110.00
Condiment Set, 4 Bottles, Flowers, Hand Painted, Silver Plated Stand, c.1890, 6 ½ x 4 ½ In.	115.00
Creamer, Glossy Finish, 3 ½ In.	144.00
Dish, Sweetmeat, Green, Tapestry Flowers, Melon Ribbed, Silver Plated Lid, Bail, 4 x 5 In.	500.00
Dish, Sweetmeat, Holly Leaves, Ruby Beads, Diamond Quilting, Silver Cover, Twig Finial, 5 In.	431.00
Dish, Sweetmeat, Melon Ribbed, Pink, White, Flowers, Embossed Silver Plate Lid, Handle, 4 x 5 In.	175.00
Ewer, Duck Bill Shape, 2 Gray Dragons, Flower Medallions, Gold Applied Handle, 12 In.	4250.00

Music, Box, Celestina Organette, Paper Roll, Mechanical Orguinette Co., New York, 9 Rolls, c.1900
$1619.00

Auction Team Breker

Music, Box, Criterion, Mahogany, Double Comb, 11 Discs, Marked, 9 x 15 x 14 In.
$1410.00

Cowan's Auctions

Music, Box, Cylinder, Walnut, Flower Inlay, 8 Airs, 56-Note Comb, Lever Wind Movement, 16 ¾ In.
$368.00

Skinner, Inc.

M

Music, Box, Regina, Mahogany, 12 Disc, 27-In. Disc Changer, Coin-Operated, c.1900, 66 x 25 In.
$10073.00

Skinner, Inc.

Music, Box, Regina, Style 63, Mahogany, Double Comb, Courting Scene, Landscape, c.1910, 37 x 31 In.
$17038.00

Cowan's Auctions

Music, Box, Singing Bird, Cage, 2 Birds, Continental, 16 In.
$488.00

Leslie Hindman Auctioneers

Music, Box, Singing Bird, Feathers, Brass Cage, Gilded Wood Base, Reuge, Switzerland, 19 ½ In.
$1967.00

Auction Team Breker

Flower Holder, Mushroom Shape, White, Purple Flowers, 5 ½ In.	345.00
Humidor, Cream Tones, Leaves, Acorns, Gold Enamel Cigars Written On Front, 6 ¼ In.	550.00
Inkwell, Square Black Glass Case, Clear Lip, Nickel Plunger, 1887, 3 ¼ In.	58.00
Lemonade Set, Pitcher, 6 Tumblers, Round, Bulbous, Square Handle, Pink, Yellow, 7 In.	1035.00
Mustard, Melon Ribbed, Panels, Flower, Spoon, Metal Lid & Handle, 3 In.	259.00
Pickle Insert, Embossed Scrolling, Enamel Branch, Flowers, Pairpoint Frame, 10 In.	950.00
Pincushion, Mushroom Shape, Enameled Flowers, White Ground, 5 In.	201.00
Pitcher, Water, Oval, Perched Owl, Shakespeare Verse, Applied Amber Handle, 7 In.	3500.00
Powder Box, Cream Ground, Pink Highlights, Round, Hinged, 2 x 5 In.	200.00
Rose Bowl, Blue, White, Satin, c.1900, 3 x 3 In.	35.00
Rose Bowl, Yellow, White, Globular, Crimped Edge, 1940s, 4 In.	39.00
Sugar & Creamer, Cream, Green, Pink Flowers, Pink Enamel Highlights, Silver Plate	150.00
Sugar Shaker, Fig, Cinnamon Colored With White Clusters Of Daises & Leaves, 4 ¼ In.	1000.00
Sugar, Squat, Scalloped Rim, Optic Ribbed, Clusters Of White Daisies, 4 In.	345.00
Toothpick Holder, 2 Dancing Brownies, Opal, Blue Shading, Squat, 2 ¼ In.	633.00
Toothpick Holder, Ferns, Silver Plate Pedestal Holder, Figural Bird Design, 6 In.	662.00
Toothpick Holder, Tricornered, Enameled Pansies, 2 In.	350.00
Vase, Blue Shaded To White, Satin Glass, 11 ½ x 7 ¼ In.	207.00
Vase, Globular Stick Form, Gilt Fern Branches, Cream, Scrolling, 9 In.	1650.00
Vase, Jack-In-The-Pulpit, Crimped Rim, Round Mirror Base, Iris Blossom, 16 In.	431.00
Vase, Jack-In-The-Pulpit, Crimped Ruffled Rim, Narrow Stem, Peach & Yellow, 7 In.	316.00
Vase, Jack-In-The-Pulpit, Footed, Green & Pink, Dainty Flowers, 11 In.	250.00
Vase, Lava, Black Matte, Red, Blue, Green, Orange Glass Shards, 4 ¾ In.	1610.00
Vase, Lava, Opaque Black, Blue, Pink, White Shards, Hexagonal, Round Foot, Flared Rim, 7 In.	2875.00
Vase, Lava, Pink, Green & Blue Geometrics, Bell Shape, Flared Rim, 6 In.	3218.00
Vase, Lily, Salmon Pink, Pale Blue, Flower Shape, Ruffle Fold-Down Rim, Round Foot, 10 In.	863.00
Vase, Napoli, Jack-In-The-Pulpit Form, Ribbed, Flower Cluster, Signed, 3 ½ In.	650.00
Vase, Oak Leaves, Acorns, Limbs, Gourd Shape, Pinched Neck, Ruffled Rim, 9 In.	690.00
Vase, Peach Shaded To White, Satin Glass, 11 ¼ x 7 In.	295.00
Vase, Sicilian Lava, Black, Multicolor Shards, Reeded Handles, 9 In. ....*illus*	6038.00

MULBERRY ware was made in the Staffordshire district of England from about 1850 to 1860. The dishes were decorated with a reddish brown transfer design, now called mulberry. Many of the patterns are similar to those used for flow blue and other Staffordshire transfer wares.

Bowl, Vegetable, Corean, White, Podmore, Walker & Co., 7 ½ x 9 ½ In.	207.00
Coffeepot, Corean, On White, Pedestal, Podmore, Walker & Co., 9 ½ x 6 In.	345.00

MULLER FRERES, French for Muller Brothers, made cameo and other glass from about 1895 to 1933. Their factory was first located in Luneville, then in nearby Croismare, France. Pieces were usually marked with the company name.

Bowl, Cameo, Purple Over Frosted, Lake Scene, Round Foot, Oval, Shaped Rim, Signed, 7 In.	403.00
Bowl, Orange, Lavender, Silver Mica Highlights, Luneville, 14 ¾ In.	400.00
Tile, Farmer, Multicolor, Arts & Crafts Style Frame, 6 x 12 ½ In.	420.00
Vase, Cameo, Frosted, Cascading Green Fern, Trumpet Shape, 4 ½ In.	230.00
Vase, Cameo, Glossy Rose, Blooming Anemone, Footed Urn, Signed, 12 ½ In.	1265.00
Vase, Cameo, Trumpet, Yellow, Red Mums, Leaves, Signed, 15 In. ....*illus*	1778.00
Vase, Cylindrical, Frosted Pink & Amethyst, Long-Stemmed Green Flowers, Signed, 10 In.	1300.00
Vase, Cylindrical, Mottled Blue, Yellow & Rust, 12 Colorful Butterflies, Signed, 11 In.	2300.00
Vase, Flame Red & Orange To Yellow, Jar Shape, c.1920s, 9 In.	431.00
Vase, Flask, Purple Mottled, Blue Flowers, Leafy Vines, Footed, 10 In.	1300.00
Vase, Mottled Amber, Gold, Orange, Swollen Baluster, Narrow Rim, Signed, 11 x 6 In.	270.00
Vase, Pink, Green & White, Flowers, Leaves, Signed, 2 ¼ In.	550.00

MUNCIE Clay Products Company was established by Charles Benham in Muncie, Indiana, in 1922. The company made pottery for the florist and giftshop trade. The company closed by 1939. Pieces are marked with the name *Muncie* or just with a system of numbers and letters, like *1A.*

Bowl, Gunmetal Black, Wavy Rim, Oblong, Marked, 12 In.	28.00
Pitcher, Blue & Green Crystalline Glaze, Shaped Mouth, Marked, 4 In.	39.00
Vase, Green Matte, Pumpkin Orange, Marked, 7 ⅛ In.	86.00
Vase, Gunmetal, Pillow, High Handles, 6 In.	69.00
Vase, Pillow, Rose Glaze, Drippy White Foam, 4 Lobes, Marked, 6 x 5 In.	49.00
Vase, Ruba Rombic, Green Matte Glaze, Star Shaped Mouth, Marked, 4 x 5 ½ In.	253.00

MURANO, *see Glass-Venetian category.*

MUSIC boxes and musical instruments are listed here. Phonograph records, jukeboxes, phonographs, and sheet music are listed in other categories in this book.

Banjo, 4-String, Tenor, Mother-Of-Pearl Fingerboard Inlay, Case, 23 x 9 ½ In.	201.00
Banjo, 5-String, Cherry Neck, Rosewood Fingerboard, S.S. Stewart, c.1890, 10 ½-In. Head	316.00
Banjo, 5-String, Chrome, Mother-Of-Pearl Inlay, Hardshell Case, Ibanez, c.1970s	489.00
Banjo, American Tenor, Silver Bell Symphony, Bacon Mfg. Co., Case, 1922, 11 In. ....*illus*	1126.00
Banjo, Cherry, Rosewood, Schooner, Full Sail, 5-String, c.1890	316.00
Bass, Maple, Ebony, Arch Back, Cremona, ¾ Size, 74 In.	236.00
Baton, Conductor's, Ivory, Brass Mounted, Victorian, c.1890, 19 In.	269.00
Box, 6 Bells, Bumblebees, Etouffoirs, En Acier, 1800s, 22 ½ x 11 ¼ In.	1413.00
Box, Bass Violin, Silver Plate, Engraved, Back Opens, Cigarette Box, 15 In.	565.00
Box, Birdcage, Singing Birds, Brass, Move, 11 ½ In.	442.00
Box, Bird's-Eye Maple, Marquetry, Love Story, Tray, Paw Feet, Italy, 1970s, 14 x 16 In.	244.00
Box, Burl Walnut, Hinged Lid, Lion's Mask, Birds, Branches, 12 Disc, c.1885, 9 x 20 In.	885.00
Box, Burl, Ebonized, Cylinder, 30 Airs, English Crest On Lid, 26 In.	915.00
Box, Celestina Organette, Paper Roll, Mechanical Orguinette Co., New York, 9 Rolls, c.1900 .....*illus*	1619.00
Box, Criterion, Mahogany, Double Comb, 11 Discs, Marked, 9 x 15 x 14 In. ....*illus*	1410.00
Box, Cylinder, Bells, Burl Veneer, Ebonized, 11-In. Cylinder, Bremond, 25 x 16 In.	3539.00
Box, Cylinder, Brass, Marquetry Rosewood Lid, Swiss, 12 ¾-In. Cylinder, 1800s, 22 In.	360.00
Box, Cylinder, Ebony & Walnut, Inlaid Border, 8 Tunes, Single Spring Motor, 24 x 8 In.	431.00
Box, Cylinder, Ebony Case, Walnut, String Inlay, 2 Brass Handles, 17 ½ In.	374.00
Box, Cylinder, Jaycot, Grain Painted, Flower Inlay, Single Comb, Mermod Freres, 18 x 22 In. ..	565.00
Box, Cylinder, Mahogany, Banded Base, 20 Airs, Sea Captain Association, 1890s	1380.00
Box, Cylinder, Mermod Swiss 10, Glass Window, Flower Inlay, Ebony Case, 31 x 10 In.	1725.00
Box, Cylinder, Oak, Flip Lid, Molded Edge, Crank Handle, 6 Tunes, 14 x 7 ½ In.	360.00
Box, Cylinder, Rosewood, Swiss Inlay, Musical Instruments, 10 Tunes, 1800s, 7 x 25 In.	546.00
Box, Cylinder, Walnut, Abalone Inlay, Bells, Drum, Zither, 8 Tunes, 12 x 34 ½ In.	1770.00
Box, Cylinder, Walnut, Flower Inlay, 8 Airs, 56-Note Comb, Lever Wind Movement, 16 ¾ In. .....*illus*	368.00
Box, Cylinder, Walnut, Mother-Of-Pearl Inlay, Crossbanded, Single Comb, 1800s	1800.00
Box, Disc, Olympia, Oak Case, Carved, Double Comb, Crank, 10 Discs, 22 x 12 In.	2300.00
Box, Disc, Regina, Oak Case, Carved, Moldings, Double Comb, 22 Discs, 15 ½ In.	2013.00
Box, Disc, Rosewood, Inside Putti, Instruments, Scene, Windup, Swiss, c.1900, 9 ¼ In.	540.00
Box, German Village, Dancing Figures, Erzeberg, 8 ½ x 9 ½ In.	1495.00
Box, Grain Painted Case, 12 Discs, Britannia St. Croix, Swiss, c.1910, 17 ½ x 10 ¾ In.	708.00
Box, Harmonia, Double Comb, Crank Operated, 3 Discs, 16-In. Cylinder, 25 x 10 ½ In.	1120.00
Box, Kalliope, Upright, Glass Front, Walnut, Columns, Coin-Operated, 10 Discs, 90 x 33 In.	8625.00
Box, Kalliope, Walnut, 6 Bell, 9 Discs, Comb	1610.00
Box, Mandarin, Inlaid Lid, Chinese Bell Striker, 6 Tunes, 6 Swiss Cylinders, Crank, 16 x 11 In.	2588.00
Box, Olympia, Carved Cherrywood, Olympia, Metal Discs, Single Comb, 1898, 9 x 16 In.	575.00
Box, Piano, Silver Plate, Engraved, Keyboard & Lid Lift, Wood Lined Cigarette Box, 10 In.	537.00
Box, Polyphon, 22 ½-In. Disc, 16 Orchestra Bells, Double Comb, Coin-Operated	2750.00
Box, Polyphon, Carved Crest, Glazed Door, Drawer, Bun Feet, 20 Discs, Coin-Operated, 19 In..	4148.00
Box, Regina, Disc, Double Comb, Oak Case, Carved, 15 ½ In.	2860.00
Box, Regina, Mahogany, 12 Discs, 27-In. Disc Changer, Coin-Operated, c.1900, 66 x 25 In. .....*illus*	10073.00
Box, Regina, Model 19, Table Model, Double Comb, 16 Discs, Carved Case, Lithograph	2750.00
Box, Regina, Oak Case, Double Comb, Crank, 46 Discs, Coin Operated, 15 ½ In.	1035.00
Box, Regina, Serpentine, Double Comb, 20 Discs, c.1897, 13 x 22 In.	3055.00
Box, Regina, Single Comb, Oak, 18 ½ x 20 ¾ In.	2242.00
Box, Regina, Style 9, 15 ½-In. Disc, Press Carved Case, Crank	2750.00
Box, Regina, Style 63, Mahogany, Double Comb, Courting, c.1910, 37 x 31 In. ....*illus*	17038.00
Box, Regina, Twist Columns, Carved Pediment, Cabriole Legs, 34 Discs, 67 x 25 In.	5750.00
Box, Reginaphone, Style 155, Double Comb, Serpentine Cabinet, 9 Panel Horn, 2 Discs	8250.00
Box, Rosewood, Inlay, Table Top, 12 Songs, Swiss, c.1876, 5 x 22 In.	705.00
Box, Rosewood, Marquetry, Leaf & String Inlay, 10 ½-In. Cylinder, Swiss, 7 x 20 x 10 In.	677.00
Box, Singing Bird, Cage, 2 Birds, Continental, 16 In. ....*illus*	488.00
Box, Singing Bird, Cage, Feathered, Yellow, Moves & Whistles, Brass Cage, Germany, 9 In.	420.00
Box, Singing Bird, Double, Reuge Movement, Sainte-Croix, Swiss, 11 x 6 ½ In.	935.00
Box, Singing Bird, Enamel, Silver, Amethyst Panels, Oval Medallion, Ivory Feet, 4 x 2 ¾ In.	7190.00
Box, Singing Bird, Enameled, 1700s Scenes, Woman On Swing, 2 Men, Germany, 1900s, 2 x 4 In.	4484.00
Box, Singing Bird, Feathered, Rectangular Cage, Key Wind, Switch, 11 In.	345.00
Box, Singing Bird, Feathered, Round Cage, Key Wind, Switch, France, 11 In.	230.00
Box, Singing Bird, Feathers, Brass Cage, Gilded Wood Base, Reuge, Switzerland, 19 ½ In. .....*illus*	1967.00
Box, Singing Bird, Filigree, Round Lid, Red Feathers, Drawer, Bun Feet, 3 x 4 ¼ In.	2530.00
Box, Singing Bird, Flaps Wings, Gilt Brass, Hinged Lid, Cabochons, Red, Rotates, 1900s, 2 x 5 In.	4148.00
Box, Singing Bird, On Branch, Bronze, Natural Rock Base, Cold Painted, Continental, 6 In.	598.00
Box, Singing Bird, Red, Blue, Green, Gilt, c.1880, 25 x 15 In.	2990.00

Music, Concertina, Paper Covered Bellows, Mahogany Case, Mother-Of-Pearl Keys, c.1850, 10 ½ In. $353.00

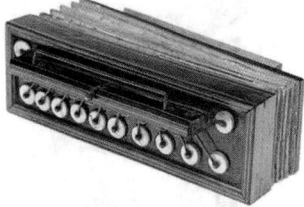

Garth's Auctions, Inc.

Music, Coronet, Carrying Case, Yamaha $84.00

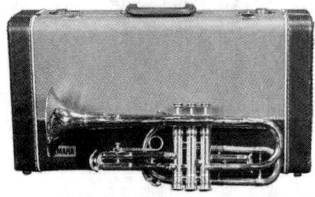

Victorian Casino Antique Auction

TIP
Do not moisten a rye straw basket. If it gets too wet, it may mold.

M

Music, Harp, Chicago Concertino, Lyon & Healy, Neoclassical Style, Patd Sept 14, 1915, 70 x 39 In. $6038.00

Bob Courtney Auctions

Music, Harp, Lyon & Healy, Style 22 Gold, 45 Strings, Chicago, Canvas Cover, c.1905, 70 In.
$7110.00

Skinner, Inc.

Music, Mandolin, Gibson, Unusual Spindle Openings, Original Case, 27 In.
$3231.00

Cowan's Auctions

Music, Mandolin, Raphael Ciani, Scrolling Leaves, Angels, Label, N.Y., c.1910, 12 ¾ In.
$444.00

Skinner, Inc.

Box, Singing Bird, Red, Yellow, Brass, c.1880, 22 x 11 In.	2185.00
Box, Stella, Mahogany, Hinged Lid, Carved Frieze, Drawer, Key, 18 Discs, 30 x 21 In.	1778.00
Box, Stella, Mahogany, Single Comb, 20 Discs, 14 x 25 In.	2640.00
Box, Stella, No. 1272, Mahogany, Lift Top, Comb Disc, Carved, Mermod, Swiss, c.1900, 14 x 30 In.	4600.00
Box, Symphonion, Oak, Carved, Religious Lithograph, Push Button, 12 Discs, 23 x 20 In.	2015.00
Box, Symphonion, Oak, Carved, Scrolling, Putti, Double Combs, 6 Discs, Crank, 13 x 20 In.	2607.00
Box, Walnut, Burl, 12 Tunes, Banded Inlay, Ormolu Handles, 12 Airs, Victorian, 29 x 14 In.	1265.00
Bugle, Marked Regulation, USA, 17 In.	50.00
Concertina, Paper Covered Bellows, Mahogany Case, Mother-Of-Pearl Keys, c.1850, 10 ½ In. *illus*	353.00
Coronet, Carrying Case, Yamaha *illus*	84.00
Drum, African Ceremonial, Carving, Wood, Figures, Round Base, 29 In.	250.00
Drum, Bentwood, American Eagle, Spread Wings, Stars, 1800s, 13 x 17 In.	237.00
Drum, Brass, British Royal Air Force, Multicolor, A.F. Matthews, c.1946, 14 ½ x 15 In.	316.00
Drum, Brass, Wood, Swiss, 1900s, 10 x 12 In.	180.00
Drum, Hand, Round, Rawhide, Hardwood Frame, Open Bottom, c.1910, 2 ½ x 10 In.	127.00
Drum, Metal, Wood, Painted, Rope, Leather, Liberty Or Death, Drumsticks, 1800s, 21 x 13 In.	431.00
Drum, Parade, Hide, Rope Ties, Royal Coat Of Arms, Union Jacks, Victorian, 16 ½ x 33 In.	251.00
Drum, Rain, Bronze, Cylindrical, Splayed Base, Strap Handles, Starburst, Asia, 21 x 13 In.	956.00
Drum, Rain, Bronze, Round Top, 4 Frog Shaped Handles, Bands, 17 In.	3172.00
Drum, Rain, Bronze, Waisted, Ring Top, Star, Frogs, Shan Tribe, Burma, 24 x 16 In.	345.00
Drum, Rain, Spread Foot, Round Overlapping Top, Black, Southeast Asia, 19 x 25 In.	299.00
Drum, Rushworth & Dreaper, Painted, Red, White, England, 29 In.	472.00
Drum, Snare, Gold Paint, Lithographs, 5 Pointed Stars, c.1863, 14 x 17 In.	1668.00
Drum, Wood, 2-Sided, Bentwood Bands, Jute Handles, c.1890, 11 x 28 In.	1495.00
Drum, Wood, Leather, String, Copper, Painted, 1800s, 15 In.	413.00
Drum, Wood, Rope Binding, Bentwood Body, P.R. Winn Field, Boston, 1800s, 10 ½ x 9 In.	127.00
Guitar, Dean Electric, Signed Jerry Cantrel	294.00
Guitar, Electric, Gibson, Les Paul Jr., Mahogany, Sunburst, Case, 1956, ¾ Size	3450.00
Guitar, Fender, Deluxe, 6 Lap Steel, Case, 1950s, 28 ¾ In.	575.00
Guitar, Gibson, 6-String, Acoustic, Dot Neck, Rosewood, Spruce, Marked, c.1925, 41 In.	881.00
Guitar, Gibson, Acoustic, Sunburst, Mahogany, Case, String, Picks, c.1961	1554.00
Guitar, Gibson, Hummingbird Flat Top, Hardshell, 1965	2530.00
Guitar, Gibson, Hummingbird Flat Top, Kalamazoo Label, 1965	2530.00
Guitar, Gibson, Hummingbird Flat Top, Kalamazoo Label, 1974	1380.00
Guitar, Gibson, Les Paul Jr., Electric, Mahogany, Sunburst Top, 1958, ¾ Scale	3450.00
Guitar, Resonator, Dobro, No. D8255, Square Neck, Hardshell Case, 1970s	403.00
Harp Case, Wood, Lyon & Healy, Chicago, Ill., 74 ½ In.	836.00
Harp, Chicago Concertino, Lyon & Healy, Neoclassical Style, Patd Sept 14, 1915, 70 x 39 In. *illus*	6038.00
Harp, Gilt Wood, Reeded Upright, Female Capital, J.F. Browne & Co., 19th Century, 67 In.	2655.00
Harp, Lyon & Healy, Style 22 Gold, 45 Strings, Chicago, Canvas Cover, c.1905, 70 In. *illus*	7110.00
Mandolin, Gibson, Unusual Spindle Openings, Original Case, 27 In. *illus*	3231.00
Mandolin, Ivory Turning Pin, Inlaid Mother Of Pearl, Vega Co.	189.00
Mandolin, Raphael Ciani, Scrolling Leaves, Angels, Label, N.Y., c.1910, 12 ¾ In. *illus*	444.00
Organ, Band, Wurlitzer Style 105, Painted Scenes, c.1926, 75 x 85 In. *illus*	12500.00
Organ, Monkey, Tremolo, Barrel, 9 Songs, 26 Key, Cart, 23 x 24 In.	5600.00
Organ, Roller, Casket Shape, Crank Bellows, Walnut, Mechanical Orguinette Co., 9 x 12 In.	424.00
Organ, Roller, Chautauqua, Oak Case, Crank, 14 Wooden Pin Rolls, 12 ½ x 18 In. *illus*	295.00
Organ, Roller, Gem, 9 Cobs, Walnut, Stenciled	403.00
Organ, Walnut Panel Box, Worm Screw Cogged Roll, Bellows, Pipes, Crank, 6 x 11 In.	236.00
Piano, Baby Grand, Chickering, Cabriole Legs, Scroll Feet, c.1930	36000.00
Piano, Baby Grand, Chickering, Walnut Veneer, Art Case, 58 Music Rolls, c.1935, 64 In.	10755.00
Piano, Baby Grand, Samick, Hepplewhite Style, Square Legs, Hinged Bench, 4 Ft. 9 In.	4720.00
Piano, Baby Grand, Steinway & Sons, Mahogany, Bench, c.1929, 67 In.	5000.00
Piano, Baby Grand, Steinway & Sons, Mahogany, Tapered Legs, Spade Feet, Bench, 39 x 56 In.	5040.00
Piano, Baby Grand, Steinway, Model M, Black Lacquer, Bench, c.1978, 38 x 65 In.	14938.00
Piano, Baby Grand, Wissner Piano Co., Ebony, Bench, 39 ½ x 57 ½ In.	1265.00
Piano, Barrel Automaton, Classical, Mahogany, George Hicks, N.Y., c.1840, 92 x 17 In. *illus*	6875.00
Piano, Georgian, Mahogany, Square, 6 Legs, John Broadwood, London, 1808, 31 x 66 In.	593.00
Piano, Grand, Howard, Black Walnut, 38 x 54 In.	575.00
Piano, Grand, Kimball, Ebony, Bench, 1974, 38 x 35 In.	1342.00
Piano, Grand, Starr Piano Co., Black Lacquer, Bench, Richmond, 1902, 40 x 75 In.	1035.00
Piano, Grand, Steinway & Sons, Model M 313081, Mahogany, Bench, c.1942, 37 x 57 x 64 In.	2988.00
Piano, Grand, Steinway, Model M, Mahogany, Bench, 1917, 67 In.	4600.00
Piano, Grand, Steinway, Wood, Black Lacquer, Bench, 1969, 39 x 67 In.	8340.00
Piano, Regency, Mahogany, Ebony, Square, 6 Legs, J. Broadwood, London, c.1900, 32 x 66 In.	830.00
Piano, Spinet, Fiddelback Maple, Carved, Turned Column Legs, c.1940, 46 x 58 ½ In.	230.00

M

Music, Organ, Band, Wurlitzer Style 105, Painted Scenes, c.1926, 75 x 85 In.
$12500.00

Bonhams & Butterfields

Music, Organ, Roller, Chautauqua, Oak Case, Crank, 14 Wooden Pin Rolls, 12 ½ x 18 In.
$295.00

Conestoga Auction Co., Inc.

Music, Piano, Barrel Automaton, Classical, Mahogany, George Hicks, N.Y., c.1840, 92 x 17 In.
$6875.00

Bonhams & Butterfields

Music, Ukulele, Samuel Kamaka, Pineapple Pattern, Hawaii, 1927, 9 ¾ In.
$3200.00

Skinner, Inc.

Music, Violin, Maple, Spruce, Mother-Of-Pearl, String Inlay, Ebony, Paper Label, c.1890, 21 ½ In.
$177.00

Brunk Auctions

Music, Violin, Richard Henry Knopf, N.Y., 1905, 14 In.
$4148.00

Skinner, Inc.

Nailsea, Bowl, Yellow, White Looping, Pink Overshot Bands, Ruffled Rim, c.1840-80, 4 ⅛ In.
$316.00

Glass Works Auctions

Nailsea, Flask, Milk Glass, Cobalt Blue Looping, Tooled Mouth, Pontil, c.1840-60, 6 ¼ In.
$173.00

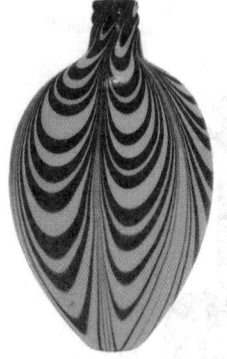

Glass Works Auctions

Nakara, Broom Holder, Pink & White Blossoms, Gold Wash Metal, Cloth Interior, 10 x 7 x 3 In.
$920.00

James D. Julia Inc.

Napkin Ring, Silver Plate, Figural, Sphinx, Meriden Britannia, 3 ¼ In.
$840.00

Morphy Auctions

Piano, Steinway & Sons, Rosewood, Cabriole Legs, c.1878, 38 x 81 In.	863.00
Piano, Steinway, L Style, Mahogany, Bench, 39 x 70 In.	6490.00
Piano, Upright, Mozart Medallion, Walnut, 2 Candle Sconces, Germany, 50 x 53 In.	390.00
Piano, Upright, Steinway & Sons, Rosewood, Octagonal Legs, Casters, c.1864, 38 x 78 In.	633.00
Piano, Upright, Steinway, Figured Wood, Recessed Panels, Ivory Keys, Column Base, c.1898	1955.00
Pianoforte, Clementi & Co., Mahogany, Brass Banding, Turned Legs, Brass Casters, 34 x 68 In.	600.00
Saxophone, Gold Plate Brass, Naked Woman Medallion, Marked C.G. Conn Ltd, 1933, 32 In.	960.00
Saxophone, Gold, Case, Pan American	73.00
Sitar, Inlaid, Painted Figures, 1800s, 39 ½ In.	395.00
Stringed Instrument, Rectangular, Wooden, Strings, Southeast Asia, Mid 1900s, 75 In.	89.00
Trumpet, Mendez, Model N 10, Mouthpiece, Mutes, Case, Olds & Sons, c.1955	806.00
Trumpet, Silver, Engraved Parker Elington, 20 ½ x 7 In.	397.00
Ukelin, Hardwood, 32 Strings, Box Style, Bow, Label, 1926, 25 x 5 In.	115.00
Ukulele, C.F. Martin & Co., c.1920, 21 x 6 ¼ In.	690.00
Ukulele, C.F. Martin & Co., Mahogany Body, Rosewood Fingerboard, Inlays, c.1916, 21 In.	748.00
Ukulele, Samuel Kamaka, Pineapple Pattern, Hawaii, 1927, 9 ¾ In. ....*illus*	3200.00
Viola, Stroh, Decal	495.00
Violin, Heinrich T. Heberlein Jr., Tiger Maple, 1927, 23 In.	1353.00
Violin, Maple, Spruce, Mother-Of-Pearl, String Inlay, Ebony, Paper Label, c.1890, 21 ½ In. ..... *illus*	177.00
Violin, Maple, Spruce, String Inlay, Ebonized Tuners, Case, 1900s, 28 x 8 In.	236.00
Violin, Richard Henry Knopf, N.Y., 1905, 14 In. ....*illus*	4148.00

MUSTACHE CUPS were popular from 1850 to 1900 when the large, flowing mustache was in style. A ledge of china or silver held the hair out of the liquid in the cup. This kept the mustache tidy and also kept the mustache wax from melting. Left-handed mustache cups are rare but are being reproduced.

Barber Pole, Hand Painted, Lefton, Saucer, c.1950, 3 ½ In.	45.00
Flowers, Gilt, Victorian	55.00
Hunt Scene, Gold Trim, Hammersley & Co., c.1950, 3 ¾ In.	65.00
Roses, Pink, Yellow, Leaves, Gold Netting, 3 x 3 ½ In.	40.00
Triple Silver Plate, Flowers, Engraved, Simpson, Hall & Miller Co.	60.00
Yellow Violets, Metallic Gold, 4-Footed, 3 ⅜ In.	95.00

MZ AUSTRIA is the wording on a mark used by Moritz Zdekauer on porcelains made at his works in Altrolau, Austria, from 1884 to 1909. The mark was changed to MZ *Altrolau* in 1909, when the firm was purchased by C.M. Hutschenreuther. The firm operated under the name Altrolau Porcelain Factories from 1909 to 1945. It was nationalized after World War II. The pieces were decorated with lavish floral patterns and overglaze gold decoration. Full sets of dishes were made as well as vases, toilet sets, and other wares.

MZ Austria

Bowl, Pink Roses, Fan Shape, Footed, 7 x 4 In.	32.00
Cake Plate, Gold Border, Handles, 10 ½ In.	65.00
Cup & Saucer, Gold Leaves & Trim	41.00
Dish, Yellow, White, Pink Flowers, Handles, Gold Trim, 8 x 3 In.	28.00
Plate, Flowers, Leaves, Gold Trim, 8 ½ In.	25.00
Plate, Pink & Red Roses, 8 In.	25.00
Plate, Pink Roses, Gold Trim, Pointed Rim, 9 ¾ In.	30.00
Plate, Red Roses, Branches, Thorns, Gold Trim, 8 ½ In.	89.00
Plate, Roses, On Vine, 8 In.	23.00
Tray, Violets, Yellow, Green Ground, 11 x 8 In.	39.00
Vase, Bulbous, Red Roses, Green Ground, Gold Top & Bottom, 10 In.	425.00

NAILSEA glass was made in the Bristol district in England from 1788 to 1873. The name also applies to glass made by many different factories, not just the Nailsea Glass House. Many pieces were made with loopings of either white or colored glass as decoration.

Basket, Pink Cased, Clear Thorn Twist Handle, 8 ½ x 7 ½ In.	75.00
Bottle, Cruet Shape, Red, White Swags, Pedestal, 6 ½ In.	20.00
Bowl, Yellow, White Looping, Pink Overshot Bands, Ruffled Rim, c.1840-80, 4 ⅛ In. ......*illus*	316.00
Decanter, Olive Green, White Splotch, Applied Seal, Alloa Glass Works, Scotland, c.1826, 10 x 4 In.	8050.00
Dish, Sweetmeat, Green, Blue, Orange, Silver Plate Lid, Bail Handle, 5 ½ In.	125.00
Fairy Lamp, Cranberry, Clear Insert, 6 In.	175.00
Fairy Lamp, White Looping, Frosted Yellow Ground, Ruffled Rim Base, Domed Shade, 6 In.	690.00
Flask, Milk Glass, Cobalt Blue Looping, Tooled Mouth, Pontil, c.1840-60, 6 ¼ In. ....*illus*	173.00
Lamp, White Loopings, Clear, Pink, Yellow Threading, Shell Shape Rigaree Base, 11 ⅜ In.	460.00
Pitcher, Water, Pink, White Cased, Clear Applied Handle, 8 ½ In.	100.00

NAKARA is a trade name for a white glassware made about 1900 by the C. F. Monroe Company of Meriden, Connecticut. It was decorated in pastel colors. The glass was very similar to another glass, called Wave Crest, made by the company. The company closed in 1916. Boxes for use on a dressing table are the most commonly found Nakara pieces. The mark is not found on every piece.

NAKARA

Bowl, Pale Blue, Blue, Purple Flowers, Yellow Centers, Octagonal, Signed, 3 x 3 ½ In.	518.00
Box, Glove, Green Opaque, Red Flowers, Rectangular, Signed, 10 In.	518.00
Broom Holder, Pink & White Blossoms, Gold Wash Metal, Cloth Interior, 10 x 7 x 3 In. ..... *illus*	920.00
Dresser Box, Blue, Stemmed Pink Mums, Bishop's Hat Shape, Stamped, 8 In.	690.00
Dresser Box, Pink To Amber, Daisies, Round, Swollen Center, Collars & Cuffs, Verse, Cover, 8 In.	633.00
Ferner, White Opal Glass, Purple, White Flowers, Green, Footed, Metal Trim, Signed, 8 x 6 In.	460.00
Humidor, Indian Chief Bust, Feathered Headdress, Swollen Shape, Pipe Handle, 7 In.	863.00
Jewelry Bowl, Green & Pink Scene Of Young Girl's Tea Party, Pink Rose Design, Signed, 3 x 5 In.	500.00
Jewelry Box, Green, Pink, Scenic, Girl's Tea Party, Pink Roses, Hinged, Signed, 3 x 5 ½ In.	500.00
Jewelry Box, Hinged, Embossed Pansy Lid, Pink, Marked, 7 ½ In.	85.00

NANKING is a type of blue-and-white porcelain made in China from the late 1700s to the early 1900s. It was shipped from the port of Nanking. It is similar to Canton wares listed in that category, but it is of better quality. The blue design was almost the same, a landscape, building, trees, and a bridge. But a person was sometimes on the bridge on a Nanking piece. The "spear and post" border was used, sometimes with gold added. Nanking sells for more than Canton.

Chocolate Pot, White & Blue, Handle, S-Scroll Spout, Foo Dog Finial, Lid, 8 In.	1121.00

NAPKIN RINGS were in fashion from 1869 to about 1900. They were made of silver, porcelain, wood, and other materials. They are still being made today. The most popular rings with collectors are the silver plated figural examples. Small, realistic figures were made to hold the ring. Good and poor reproductions of the more expensive rings are now being made and collectors must be very careful.

Art Glass, Purple, Oval, Cut To Clear, c.1970, 2 ¼ In.	24.00
Ivory, Leaves, Scalloped & Reticulated Flared Rim, c.1890, 1 ¾ In.	38.00
Porcelain, Pearl Luster, Roses, Leaves, Raised Gold Bands, 2 ¼ In.	45.00
Silver Plate, Chinoiserie Carnival Performers, Cats, Jester, Juggler, c.1895, 2 In.	504.00
Silver Plate, Clovers, Flanged Edge, Engraved, c.1900, 1 ¾ In.	40.00
Silver Plate, Figural, 2 Rabbits, Pairpoint, 3 In.	208.00
Silver Plate, Figural, Bird, Meriden, 3 In.	208.00
Silver Plate, Figural, Doe, Cherub, Leaf Feet, Reed & Barton, 3 In.	119.00
Silver Plate, Figural, Dog, Bone In Mouth, 3 ½ In.	117.00
Silver Plate, Figural, Dog, Dachshund, 3 In.	119.00
Silver Plate, Figural, Giraffe, 4 In.	367.00
Silver Plate, Figural, Mother Owl, Babies, Simpson, Hall, Miller & Co., 4 In.	357.00
Silver Plate, Figural, Owl, Glass Eyes	850.00
Silver Plate, Figural, Sphinx, Meriden Britannia, 3 ¼ In. *illus*	840.00
Silver Plate, Figural, Tennis Player, Meriden Britannia, 3 ¾ In. *illus*	960.00
Silver Plate, Figural, Turtle, Meriden Brittannia, 2 ½ In. *illus*	210.00
Silver Plate, Figural, Wheat Sheaf, Cow, Wilcox, 3 In.	149.00
Silver Plate, Figural, Wolf, Ball Feet, Barbour, 3 In.	179.00
Silver Plate, Gilt Wash, Coin, Stippled Ground, Engraved Monogram, 2 x 2 In., Pair	418.00
Silver Plate, Mother-Of-Pearl, Paneled, 1930s, 1 ½ In.	22.00
Silver Plate, Ostrich, Kangaroo, With Ring, Leaf Base, Stuart Dawson & Co., Australia, 2 x 5 In.	201.00
Silver Plate, Pedestal, Leaves, James Tuft, c.1880, 2 ¾ In.	80.00
Sterling Silver, Alternating Circles, Atkin Bros., Box, England, c.1935, 1 ¼ x 2 In., Pair	132.00
Sterling Silver, Basket Weave, 1 ¾ In.	126.00
Sterling Silver, Figural, Lion's Head, Engraved, Marion Knox, Beaded, c.1900, 1 ½ In.	30.00
Sterling Silver, Figural, Squirrel, 2 ¾ In.	356.00
Sterling Silver, London, 1946, 3 ¾ In., 4 Piece	115.00
Sterling Silver, Scalloped, Oblong, 1902, 2 ½ In.	73.00

NASH glass was made in Corona, New York, from about 1928 to 1931. A. Douglas Nash bought the Corona glassworks from Louis C. Tiffany in 1928 and founded the A. Douglas Nash Corporation with support from his father, Arthur J. Nash. Arthur had worked at the Webb factory in England and for the Tiffany Glassworks in Corona.

NASH

Bowl, Gold Iridescent, Ruffled, Flared & Flattened Rim, Crackle Edge, 4 ½ x 13 In.	944.00
Bowl, Underplate, Pink Opalescent, Ruffled Edge, Footed, 6 x 3 In.	132.00
Vase, Gold Aurene, 4-Sided Rim, 6 ¾ x 3 ¼ In.	270.00

Napkin Ring, Silver Plate, Figural, Tennis Player, Meriden Britannia, 3 ¾ In. $960.00

Morphy Auctions

Napkin Ring, Silver Plate, Figural, Turtle, Meriden Brittannia, 2 ½ In. $210.00

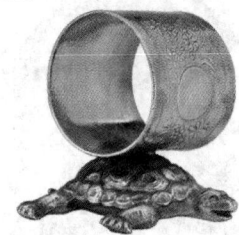

Morphy Auctions

Nautical, Canoe, Birch Bark, Laced Construction, Woven Seats, 1900s, 12 Ft. 6 In. $2006.00

Brunk Auctions

Nautical, Canoe, Model, Mahogany, Steam Bent Ribs, Canvas, Copper, Pine Stand, c.1915, 52 x 10 In. $3680.00

James D. Julia Inc.

TIP
Dip polishes remove all the oxidation that blackens crevices in the designs on silver and often leaves the finish looking more like tin than silver.

N

Nautical, Clock, Chelsea, Ship's Bell, 8-Day, Brass Movement, Mahogany Desk Stand, 9 ½ In.
$385.00

Skinner, Inc.

Nautical, Compass, Brass, Silvered Dial, Adjustable Sighting Frame, Leather Case, c.1890, 2 ½ In.
$207.00

Skinner, Inc.

Nautical, Pond Boat, Wood, Cloth Sails, Marked, Seifert-Boot, Schutzmarke, Germany, 48 x 37 In.
$588.00

Garth's Auctions, Inc.

Vase, Gold Aurene, Paneled Body, 10-Crimp Scalloped Edge, Saucer Foot, 4 x 2 ½ In.	243.00
Wine, Opalescent, Squirrel Stem, c.1930, 4 In.	59.00

NAUTICAL antiques are listed in this category. Any of the many objects that were made or used by the seafaring trade, including ship parts, models, and tools, are included. Other pieces may be found listed under Scrimshaw.

Anchor, Brass, 2 Hooks	124.00
Bell, Ship's, Bridge, RMS Queen Mary, Clapper, Hanging Thread, In.	2510.00
Bell, Ship's, Dolphin Supports, 17 x 16 In.	400.00
Binnacle, Brass Hood, Compass, C. Plath, Mark, Hamberg, Germany, c.1910, 52 ½ In.	460.00
Binnacle, McLeod & Sons, Teak, Brass Housing, Cylindrical, Spheres, England, 54 x 26 In.	1035.00
Canoe, Birch Bark, Laced Construction, Woven Seats, 1900s, 12 Ft. 6 In. ....*illus*	2006.00
Canoe, Model, Mahogany, Steam Bent Ribs, Canvas, Copper, Pine Stand, c.1915, 52 x 10 In. .... *illus*	3680.00
Chest, Camphorwood, Dovetailed, Molded Top, Canted Sides, Handles, Chinese, 1800s, 18 x 36 In.	711.00
Chest, Nantucket, Red, Stencil, Ships, Flags, Captain McCullugh, Plymouth, c.1860, 17 x 35 In.	403.00
Chest, Pine, 6-Board, Becket Handles, Henry Gardner First Voyage, April 6th, 1809, 19 x 44 In.	353.00
Chest, Pine, Mahogany, Dovetailed, Rope Handles, 9 Drawers, 1800s, 24 x 37 In.	826.00
Chest, Sailor's, Sweetheart, Mixed Wood, 5 Drawers, Carved, 1800s, Miniature, 15 x 13 In.	237.00
Chronometer, Hamilton, Model 22, Double Case, Walnut, Leather	1074.00
Chronometer, Hamilton, Wood Box, 6 ¾ In.	565.00
Chronometer, Hamilton, Wood Case, U.S. Navy Plaque, Lancaster, Pa., World War II	738.00
Chronometer, Victor Kullberg, Brass, Mahogany, Case, 2 ½ In.	633.00
Chronometer, Waltham, Hinged Lid, Glass Top, Marked, Case, 5 x 5 In.	460.00
Clock, Banjo, Chelsea, Federal Style, Mahogany, Constitution Vs. HMS Guerriere, c.1930, 34 In.	767.00
Clock, Chelsea, Ship's Bell, 8-Day, Brass Movement, Mahogany Desk Stand, 9 ½ In. ....*illus*	385.00
Clock, Round, Metal Case, Red Star, Anchor, Russia, 8 In.	58.00
Clock, Ship's Bell, Brass, Round, Ball Base, 30-Hour, Seth Thomas, Early 1900s, 10 ½ In.	403.00
Clock, Ship's Bell, Bronze, Silvered Dial, Pierced Hands, Chelsea Clock Co., 18 x 17 In.	15930.00
Clock, Ship's Bell, Wall, Yacht Wheel, Brass, Bronze, Hinged Bezel, 1919, 15 In.	1185.00
Clock, Ship's Wheel, Brass, Seth Thomas, 9 In.	124.00
Clock, Ship's, Mahogany Case, Fusee, Charles Frodsham, London, 1825, 7 x 6 In.	1840.00
Compass, Brass, Silvered Dial, Adjustable Sighting Frame, Leather Case, c.1890, 2 ½ In. ...... *illus*	207.00
Compass, Perko, Binnacle, Star Of Boston, 5 x 8 In.	270.00
Diorama, Ship, Flying Dragon, Carved Wood, American Flag, Shadow Box, c.1950, 17 x 23 In.	88.00
Easel, Crossed Oars, Holding Turned Ship's Wheel, Boat Hull Support, 76 x 22 In.	2185.00
Figurehead, Knight, Beard, Red Robe, Sword, Hands, Wood, Painted, 1800s, 64 In.	6900.00
Figurehead, Woman, Blue Dress, Softwood, Early 1900s, 46 x 16 In.	3450.00
Gong, Cory & Son, Engine Room, Brass, 2 Walnut Tip Hammers, c.1900, 16 In.	431.00
Half-Model, Crosby Cat Sea Hound, White & Green Paint, 1975, 25 ½ In.	460.00
Half-Model, Yellow Pine, 10 Sections, Black Paint, Backboard, Half Hull, 12 x 64 In.	345.00
Harpoon, Whaling, Iron, Toggle Head, Rope Lashing, c.1850, 33 ½ In.	499.00
Kayak, Luan, Mahogany, Fiberglass, 20th Century, 11 Ft. 9 In.	590.00
Kayak, Model, Animal Skin, Hand Sewn, Wood Frame, 3 Openings, Alaska, c.1890, 4 x 48 In.	540.00
Lantern, Brass, Cabin Light, England, 20 In.	147.00
Lantern, Brass, Metal, Green, J.H. Peters & Bey, Hamburg, 19 x 11 In.	70.00
Lantern, Copper, Handle, Norway, c.1910, 21 x 9 In., Pair	650.00
Lantern, Ship's, Brass, Hinged Top, Fresnel Glass Lens, Cylindrical, 12 In.	161.00
Life Jacket, SS Andrea Doria, Final Voyage Survivor, Orange, c.1956, 44 In.	717.00
Life Ring, El Presidente, c.1939, 30 In.	448.00
Life Ring, RMS Queen Elizabeth, Red, White, Liverpool, 20 In.	2032.00
Long Boat, Wood, Carved, Multicolor, High Bow, Stern, Rudder Support, Mast, 1900s, 48 In.	41.00
Model, Boat, Ivory, Carved, Multi Deck, Figures, Wave Shape Base, 13 ⅜ In.	4636.00
Model, Boat, Rosewood, Zelkova, Deities, Sail, Oval Base, Rooster Head Bow, Japan, 9 In.	956.00
Model, Constitution, Copper Tile, Lifeboat, Hand Tied Rigging, 1900s, 47 x 63 In.	2350.00
Model, Greek Sailboat, Dingys, Ladders, 7 In.	904.00
Model, Sailboat, 3 Masts, Rigging, Cream, Burgundy, Stand, France, 17 x 22 In.	275.00
Model, Sailboat, Cream, Green, 3 Masts, Sails, Stand France, 19 x 28 In.	244.00
Model, Sailboat, Cruising Yawl, Valkyrie, Plaster Water, Plexiglas Case, Early 1900s, 21 x 22 In.	403.00
Model, Sailboat, Mesh Sails, Flags, Glass Paneled Base, Sterling, Gilt, Chinese, 17 ½ x 12 In.	1315.00
Model, Sailboat, Star Yacht, Endeavour 1, Painted, Rigging, Sails, Birkenhead, c.1910, 17 In.	151.00
Model, Schooner Atlantic, Sails, Rectangular Base, 74 x 97 In.	625.00
Model, Schooner, Yacht Meteor, Planked Deck, Sails, Mahogany, Glass Case, 30 x 35 In.	1725.00
Model, Ship, 3 Masts, British Man Of War, Gun Ports, Cannons, Life Boats, 1900s, 36 x 48 In.	207.00
Model, Ship, 3 Masts, Wood, Painted, Inscribed E. LeClerc, 1900s, 46 In.	550.00
Model, Ship, Bone, Baleen, Planked, Pinned Hull, Carved, Maple, Plexiglas Cover, 14 x 22 In.	1422.00

N

Model, Ship, Fredericus Quartus, Pine, Pierced For 100 Guns, Denmark, c.1900, 63 x 68 In. ...	10350.00
Model, Ship, In Bottle, 5 Masts, American Flag, Guaranteed Full Quart, 10 In.	58.00
Model, Ship, Katy Of Norfolk, Green & White Hull, Case, 1900s, 25 x 26 In.	288.00
Model, Ship, Mermaid, Wood, White, Green Paint, Base, Plexiglas Case, c.1900, 25 x 35 In.	490.00
Model, Ship, Normandie, c.1939, 32 In.	472.00
Model, Ship, Pactolus, Glass Dome, Wood, Spun Glass, Mahogany, 1800s, 19 In.	711.00
Model, Ship, Wood, Sails, Painted, Carved Base, c.1950, 19 ½ In.	59.00
Pond Boat, 2 White Sails, Red Hull, Jacrim Hollow, 19 ½ In.	89.00
Pond Boat, Peter Pan Mfg., Majestic, Sailor, Mahogany Laminate, Maple, Brass Mounted, 53 In.	413.00
Pond Boat, Wood, Cloth Sails, Marked, Seifert-Boot, Schutzmarke, Germany, 48 x 37 In. ..... *illus*	588.00
Pond Boat, Wooden, Metal Fittings, Removable Masts, Cloth Sails, c.1910, 55 In.	588.00
Pond Boat, Yacht, Steam Powered, Wood, Grooved Decking, Removable Top, 35 ½ In.	767.00
Sailor's Box, Maple, Pine, Bentwood, Carved Joint, Hearts, 1800s, 9 ¼ In. Diam.	1116.00
Sailor's Mat, Canvas, Geometric, Red, White, Blue, Fringe, Painted, 1800s, 23 x 49 In.	999.00
Sailor's Valentine, Octagonal, Shell Work, Anchor Within Star, Gilt Frame, 18 In. Diam.	590.00
Sailor's Valentine, Shells, Multicolor, Lift Lid, 8 x 12 In.	403.00
Sea Chest, Pine, 6-Board, Black Paint, Pinwheel Design, Tombstone Panel, 1700s, 14 x 40 In.	805.00
Sextant, Brass, Ross, Leather Case, London, c.1900, 4 ¾ In.	81.00
Ship model, see Nautical, Model.	
Ship's Wheel, Maple, Iron Bands, Ocher Yellow Paint, 38 ½ In.	413.00
Ship's Wheel, Teakwood, 10 Turned Spokes, Brass Hub, 60 In.	127.00
Ship's Wheel, Turned Spokes, Salvaged, 41 In.	144.00
Table, Ship's Telegraph, Round, Brass, Red Cast Iron Dial, 4 Black Metal Legs, 22 x 14 In.	58.00
Telegraph, Ship's, A. Robinson & Co., Engine Speed, Brass, Wood Handles, Bell, 36 ½ In.	575.00
Telegraph, Ship's, Bendix, Brass, 47 In.	875.00
Telegraph, Ship's, Brelco Brass & Enamel, Bulkhead Mounted, 1900s, 16 In.	150.00
Watch Hutch, Sailor's, Wood, Mother-Of-Pearl, Scrimshaw, Whale, Checkerboard, 8 x 5 In.	705.00
Yacht Cannon, L.T. Snow, Signal, Bronze, Mahogany Carriage, Marked, 1800s, 23 x 12 In.	4313.00

NETSUKES are small ivory, wood, metal, or porcelain pieces used as toggles on the end of the cord that held a Japanese money pouch or inro. The earliest date from the sixteenth century. Many are miniature carved works of art. This category also includes the ojime, the slide or string fastener that was used on the inro cord.

Boxwood, Ashinaga & Tenaga, Long Legs, Long Arms, Elongated, Octopus, 6 In.	732.00
Ivory, Amorous Couple, Embracing, Coupling, Erotic, Signed, 2 ¼ In.	399.00
Ivory, Bird & Flowers, Carved, Walnut Shape, c.1885, 2 ½ In.	1050.00
Ivory, Boy Under Hat, Chinese, 1 ⅛ x 2 ⅛ In. *illus*	472.00
Ivory, Chick, Hatching, Signed, 1 ¼ In.	368.00
Ivory, Chinese Official, Napping, 1700s, 2 In.	323.00
Ivory, Conch, Stippled Design, 1 ¾ In.	915.00
Ivory, Dog, Seated, Ball, 1 ½ In.	671.00
Ivory, Elephant, Standing, Carved Blanket Over Back, Oval Base, 1 x 2 In.	310.00
Ivory, Fighting Skeleton & Wolf, Warrior, 2 ½ In., Pair.	74.00
Ivory, Foreign Emissary, Holding Chicken, 3 ¼ In.	237.00
Ivory, Horse, Bending, c.1900, 2 ¾ In.	400.00
Ivory, Jurojin, God Of Longevity, Signed Tompmasa, 2 In.	214.00
Ivory, Man, Carrying Gourd On Back, c.1900, 2 In.	250.00
Ivory, Man, Seated, Holding Brush, Incised Robes, 1800s, 1 ⅞ In.	148.00
Ivory, Man, Seated, Smoking Pipe, Holding Fan, 19th Century, 2 ½ x 2 x 2 In.	150.00
Ivory, Man, Smoking Pipe, Seated, c.1940, 1 ¾ In.	150.00
Ivory, Man, With Fish, Signed, 2 In.	121.00
Ivory, Mice, Cheese, Carved, Chinese, Signed, 1 ⅝ x 1 ¼ In.	236.00
Ivory, Monkeys, On Rocks, Carved, Chinese, 2 ½ In.	207.00
Ivory, Mystical Animal, Biting Human Skull, 19th Century, 1 ¾ x 1 ½ In.	175.00
Ivory, Oni Face, 14K Gold Setting, Chrysoberyl, Curved Back, Signed, 1800s, 2 ¾ In. *illus*	354.00
Ivory, Scholar, Seated, Cleaning Brush, 2 ¾ x 2 ⅛ In.	184.00
Ivory, Shoki, Demon Slayer, Seated, Oni, Demon, Fierce Figure, Signed, 1 ¼ In.	1586.00
Ivory, Warrior, Sea Serpent, 19th Century, 2 In.	600.00
Mother-Of-Pearl, Bird, Carved Leaf, 1 ¾ In.	549.00
Papier-Mache, Lacquer, Toy Dog, Painted, 1 ¼ In. *illus*	336.00
Wood, 2 Nio Wrestlers, On Large Sandal, Signed, 2 In.	948.00
Wood, Daruma, Buddhist Preacher, Seated, Signed Masayama, 1800s, 1 ⅞ In.	305.00
Wood, Haniwa Bear, Black Persimmon, Red Lacquer Ring, 1 ½ In.	223.00
Wood, Man, Wrestling Tiger, c.1880, 2 In.	350.00

Netsuke, Ivory, Boy Under Hat, Chinese, 1 ⅛ x 2 ⅛ In.
$472.00

DuMouchelles Art Gallery

Netsuke, Ivory, Oni Face, 14K Gold Setting, Chrysoberyl, Curved Back, Signed, 1800s, 2 ¾ In.
$354.00

Brunk Auctions

Netsuke, Papier-Mache, Lacquer, Toy Dog, Painted, 1 ¼ In.
$336.00

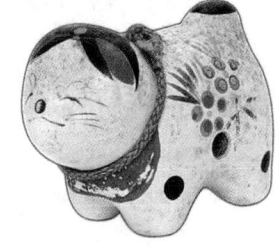

Leslie Hindman Auctioneers

Newcomb, Candlestick, Jasmine, Relief Carved, Semimatte Glaze, Marked, A.F. Simpson, 1929, 3 ½ In.
$738.00

Neal Auction Co.

Newcomb, Jardiniere, Pear Tree Blossoms, Buff Body, Marked, Joseph Meyer, 1908, 5 x 6 ⅜ In.
$7768.00

Neal Auction Co.

Newcomb, Plaque, Landscape, Trees, Country Road, Relief Carved, Henrietta Bailey, 1917, 10 ¼ x 6 In.
$7170.00

Neal Auction Co.

Newcomb Pottery Designs

Newcomb Pottery was usually blue green with incised decorations emphasized with black from 1900 to 1910. Molded designs and dull matte glaze were used from about 1910 to 1930. Newcomb made vases, mugs, tea sets, candlesticks, and lamps. Designs often included trees dripping moss and full moons.

NEW MARTINSVILLE Glass Manufacturing Company was established in 1901 in New Martinsville, West Virginia. It was bought and renamed the Viking Glass Company in 1944. In 1987 Kenneth Dalzell, former president of Fostoria Glass Company, purchased the factory and renamed it Dalzell-Viking. Production ceased in 1998.

Moondrops, Ashtray, Ruby, 4 In.	36.00
Moondrops, Candleholder, Ruffled, Ruby, 2 In.	35.00
Moondrops, Cocktail Shaker, Ruby, Chrome Lid	78.00
Moondrops, Cordial, Amber, 3 In.	25.00
Moondrops, Cup & Saucer, Ruby	26.00
Moondrops, Goblet, Ruby, 4 In.	28.00
Moondrops, Plate, Dinner, Ruby, 9 In.	34.00
Moondrops, Whiskey, Cobalt Blue, 2 ¾ In.	15.50
Moondrops, Wine, Ruby, 4 ⅝ In.	30.00
Radiance, Platter, Ruby, 14 In.	85.00

NEWCOMB POTTERY was founded at Sophie Newcomb College, New Orleans, Louisiana, in 1895. The work continued through the 1940s. Pieces of this art pottery are marked with the printed letters *NC* and often have the incised initials of the artist and potter as well. A date letter code was printed on pieces made from 1901 to 1941. Most pieces have a matte glaze and incised decoration.

Bowl, Blue Ground, Daisies, 1914, 7 ½ In.	1720.00
Bowl, Green, White Flowers, Painted, Low Shape, H. Bailey, 8 x 2 ½ In.	1540.00
Bowl, Low, Animal Frieze, Green, White, Blue, Mary Summey, 1910, 2 x 5 ½ In.	5270.00
Bowl, Matte Glaze, Relief Freesia Band, A.F. Simpson, c.1927, 6 x 11 ⅜ In.	7170.00
Bowl, Painted Green, White Flowers, Blue Ground, Henrietta Bailey, 8 x 2 ½ In.	1680.00
Bowl, Semimatte Blue Glaze, Louisiana Irises, Marked, 1912, 8 ½ In.	950.00
Candlestick, Flowers, Blue Ground, Trumpet Base, Signed, A.F. Simpson, 1925, 7 ½ In., Pair .	2478.00
Candlestick, Freesia, Trumpet Bottom, Marked, 1922, 7 ⅜ In.	1353.00
Candlestick, Jasmine, Relief Carved, Semimatte Glaze, Marked, A.F. Simpson, 1929, 3 ½ In. ...*illus*	738.00
Candlestick, Lilies, Blue, Green, Yellow, Flared Foot, Matte Glaze, 1926, 7 In., Pair	3466.00
Candlestick, Matte Glaze, Relief Carved Butterfly, Sadie Irvine, c.1926, 9 ¾ x 10 In., Pair	5079.00
Charger, Cactus Blossoms, Yellow, Blue, White, E. Elliott, 1904, 12 ¾ In.	12400.00
Chocolate Pot, Scenic, Transitional, Lid, A.F. Simpson, 1912, 10 ½ In.	9300.00
Flower Frog, Fruits & Vegetables, Basket, c.1915, 1 ⅞ In.	288.00
Inkwell, Pink, White Flowers, Blue, Bell Shape, Knob Finial, A.F. Simpson, 3 ½ x 3 ½ In.	660.00
Jar, Cover, African Violets, Green & Blue, Mary Sheerer, 1906, 4 ¼ x 3 In.	9920.00
Jardiniere, Pear Tree Blossoms, Buff Body, Marked, Joseph Meyer, 1908, 5 x 6 ⅜ In. ......*illus*	7768.00
Pitcher, Milk, Flowers, Blue, Sabrina Wells, 1904, 5 ¼ x 5 ½ In.	3720.00
Pitcher, Violets, Blue, Green, White, Loop Handle, 1918, 6 In.	2875.00
Plaque, Landscape, Trees, Country Road, Relief Carved, Henrietta Bailey, 1917, 10 ¼ x 6 In. ..*illus*	7170.00
Plaque, Pine Trees, Moon, Blue, Green, Matte Glaze, 1915, 10 x 6 In.	11378.00
Plate, Rooster, Grapevines, Green, Yellow, 1907, 9 In.	4960.00
Teapot, Matte Glaze, Relief Carved Eggplant, Sadie Irvine, c.1932, 5 x 8 ½ In.	3690.00
Tile, Landscape, Green Trees, Blue Ground, Katherine Kopman, c.1910, 10 ½ x 4 ¾ In.	2530.00
Tile, Scenic, Moss Covered Oaks, Camp, Sailboat, Blue, Green, Matte Glaze, 1918, 4 x 4 In.	11950.00
Vase, Band Of Blossoms In Relief, Blue, Green, Cream Matte Glaze, S. Irvine, 1917, 6 In.	1659.00
Vase, Band Of Flowering Vines, Blue, Turquoise, Pear Shape, 1929, 6 ½ In.	1725.00
Vase, Blue Matte Glaze, Paperwhites, Green Stems, Alma Mason, c.1914, 6 In.	2151.00
Vase, Bud, Embossed, Glossy, 10 ¾ In.	4130.00
Vase, Bud, Flowers, Blue, Green, White, Cabinet, H. Bailey, 4 ¾ x 2 In.	2480.00
Vase, Bud, Painted Pink Flowers, Blue Ground, A.F. Simpson, 2 ¾ x 5 ¾ In.	960.00
Vase, Bulbous, Squat, Moon & Moss, Pale Green, Blue Matte Glaze, Marked, 1927, 6 ⅜ In.	13145.00
Vase, Dogwood Flowers, Encircling Shoulder, Blue, Cylindrical, Slight Taper, 1915, 6 ⅜ In.	2415.00
Vase, Dogwood, White, Green Flowers, Anna Mason, 7 ¼ x 4 ¼ In.	3224.00
Vase, Elongated Oval, Irises, Blue, Green, Yellow, Matte Glaze, 1915, 11 In.	11950.00
Vase, Elongated Oval, Moon & Moss Landscape, Green, Blue Matte Glaze, 1922, 12 ¾ In.	9560.00
Vase, Green, Blue, Cameo, Sadie Irvine, c.1929, 2 x 31 In.	532.00
Vase, High Glaze, Joseph Fortune Meyer, Signed, Marie Odell Delavigne, c.1901, 6 x 4 In.	3075.00
Vase, Incised Flower Bud, Blue Green Underglaze, Marie L. Benson, 1908, 9 x 3 ½ In.	3690.00
Vase, Leaves, Green Matte Glaze, Cream Accents, Baluster, Rolled Lip, Marked, 1901-20, 6 x 4 In.	1265.00
Vase, Leaves, Painted, Marie De Hoa LeBlanc, 9 x 6 ¼ In. ....*illus*	5890.00
Vase, Live Oaks, Spanish Moss, Blue, Green, A.F. Simpson, 1918, 3 ½ x 4 In.	2480.00
Vase, Narcissus, Matte Glaze, Henrietta Bailey, 1919, 7 ⅞ In. ....*illus*	3884.00
Vase, Narcissus, Yellow Green Matte Glaze, Shouldered, A.F. Simpson, 1926, 12 x 3 In.	1353.00
Vase, Oaks, Spanish Moss, Blue, Green Ground, Sadie Irvine, 8 x 6 ¾ In.	2852.00

N

Vase, Pink Flowers, Blue Ground, Painted, Anna F. Simpson, 2 ¾ x 5 ¾ In.	880.00
Vase, Relief Carved Moon, Live Oak, Sadie Irvine, c.1930, 6 x 6 In.	2509.00
Vase, Roses On Trellis, Harriet Coulter Joor, 12 In. ....*illus*	92000.00
Vase, Roses, White, Blue Ground, Alma Mason, 1921, 6 ¾ x 5 In.	2480.00
Vase, Roses, White, Green Ground, Bulbous, Alma Mason, 1913, 8 ¾ x 5 In.	3472.00
Vase, Scenic, Full Moon, Live Oaks, Shouldered, Sadie Irvine, 1918, 7 ¼ x 4 In.	4340.00
Vase, Scenic, Live Oaks, Spanish Moss, Anna Simpson, 1930, 6 x 5 ½ In.	4340.00
Vase, Scenic, Live Oaks, Spanish Moss, Full Moon, Sadie Irvine, 1927, 8 x 4 In.	5890.00
Vase, Spanish Moss, Oak Trees, Sadie Irvine, 1916, 3 ¼ x 3 In. ....*illus*	2232.00
Vase, St. Tammany Pines, Matte Glaze, 2 Handles, Sadie Irvine, Signed, 1931, 9 x 4 In.	9225.00
Vase, Swollen, Tapered, Irises, Blue & Green Glaze, Marked, 1910, 11 ¾ In.	4880.00
Vase, Trees, Spanish Moss, Yellow Moon, Blue & Green, c.1918, 7 ½ In. ....*illus*	3851.00
Vase, Urn Shape, Velum Glaze, Moon Moss & Live Oak Design, Blue, Inscribed, 1930, 8 In.	5658.00
Vase, Vellum Glazed, Gardenias, Marked, 2 ⅜ x 2 ⅞ In.	553.00

NILOAK POTTERY (*Kaolin* spelled backward) was made at the Hyten Brothers Pottery in Benton, Arkansas, between 1910 and 1947. Although the factory did make cast and molded wares, collectors are most interested in the marbleized art pottery line made of colored swirls of clay. It was called Mission Ware. By 1931 the company made castware, and many of these pieces were marked with the name *Hywood*.

Head Vase, Southern Belle Pattern, Green & Pink Glaze, 7 ¼ x 5 In.	108.00
Planter, Burma Camel, Tan, Marked, c.1940, 5 x 3 In.	28.00
Vase, Cornucopia, Tan Matte Glaze, c.1935, 7 In.	60.00
Vase, Footed, Handles, Flattened Rim, Marked, Label, 5 ¾ In.	65.00
Vase, Mission Ware, Swirl, Hourglass, Impressed, 6 In.	50.00

NIPPON porcelain was made in Japan from 1891 to 1921. *Nippon* is the Japanese word for "Japan." A few firms continued to use the word *Nippon* on ceramics after 1921 as a part of the company name more than as an identification of the country of origin. More pieces marked *Nippon* will be found in the Dragonware, Moriage, and Noritake categories.

Biscuit Jar, Green, Pink Flowers, Moriage Floral Highlights, 7 In.	90.00
Bowl, Cobalt Blue Border, Pale Green Center, Pink Rose Design, 10 In.	75.00
Bowl, Cream Ground, Gold Highlights, Pink Rose, Scalloped, 11 ½ In.	100.00
Bowl, Cream, Blue, Pink Flowers, Gold Tapestry Highlights, 10 In.	75.00
Bowl, Green Center, Pink Rose, Cobalt Blue Border, Gold Highlights, 10 In.	75.00
Bowl, Hand Painted, Gilt Accents, 10 In. Diam.	80.00
Bowl, Handles, Castle, Lake, Dot Inner Border, c.1920, 8 ¼ x 7 ³⁄₁₆ In.	170.00
Candy Dish, Acorn, Pinched Edge, Signed, 6 x 6 ½ In.	23.00
Charger, Native American Warrior, Full Headdress, Rifle, On Horse, 10 In. Diam.	207.00
Chocolate Pot, Cobalt Blue, Gold Tapestry Ground, Pink Flowers, 12 ½ In.	150.00
Cider Jug, Green With Cobalt Blue Trim, Pink Flowers, White Enamel Highlights, 7 ¼ In.	80.00
Cider Jug, Green, Cobalt Blue Trim, Pink Flowers, White Enamel Highlights, Gold Trim, 7 In.	80.00
Dish, Mayonnaise, Ladle, 3-Footed, 5 In. Diam.	40.00
Dish, Roses, Cobalt Blue Border, Raised Gold Scrolling, Coral Jewels, 8 x 4 In.	58.00
Dresser Box, Lid, Flowers, White Ground, 4 In., Pair	62.00
Ewer, Cobalt Blue, Pink Roses, Red Rose Highlights, Ball Shape, Handle, 9 ½ In., Pair	175.00
Ewer, Pyramid Shape, Cobalt Blue With Gold Ground, Pink Roses, Handle, 10 ½ In.	200.00
Hair Receiver, Cobalt Blue, Flower Highlights, Gold, Footed, 4 ½ In.	50.00
Mustard, Underplate, Cover, Cobalt Blue, Gold, Rose, 4 ½ In.	50.00
Pitcher, Blue, Multicolor Flowers, Gold Highlights, 8 ¾ In.	80.00
Plate, Cream Center With Pink Flowers, Cobalt Blue Border, Scalloped, Pierced, 11 In.	70.00
Plate, Cream, Pink Flowers, Cobalt Blue Border, Gold, Scalloped, Pierced, 11 In.	70.00
Punch Bowl, Riverfront Scene, Greek Key Interior, Handles, Pedestal Base, 9 ¼ x 13 In.	259.00
Sugar Shaker, Cobalt Blue, Cherry Blossoms, Flowers, Bulbous, c.1875, 4 In.	36.00
Sugar, Gold Grapevine, Pink Ground, White Interior, Footed, 4 x 2 In.	12.00
Tankard, Cobalt Blue, Pink, Yellow Rose, Gold Stencil Highlights, 9 In.	150.00
Tankard, Corset Shape, Green With Pink Rose Design, Cobalt Blue Border, 10 In.	175.00
Tankard, Turquoise Ground, Pink Rose, Gold Enamel Tapestry Netting, 15 ½ In.	175.00
Tea Strainer, White, Green, Pink Roses	90.00
Urn, Cream With Pink Rose Design, Pedestal, Covered, 2 Handles, 14 In.	150.00
Vase, Bulbous Oval, 5 Swans In Flight, Gray Ground, Green Grass, Maple Leaf Mark, c.1891, 6 In.	413.00
Vase, Double Vertical Handles, Indian Designs, Paint, Stamped Imperial, 11 ½ In.	181.00
Vase, Elongated Oval, Round Foot, Ribbon Handles, Azaleas, Calla Lilies, 24K Gold Accents, 10 In.	475.00
Vase, Fish, Water Design, Green Ground, Shaped Handles, 15 ½ x 8 ½ In.	80.00
Vase, Flared Bottom, Roses, Gilt Trim, Marked, 9½ In.	1200.00

Bullet, the Pottery Maker
The founder of the Niloak Pottery, Charles Hyten, was nicknamed Bullet. He was born in 1877 in Benton, Arkansas. He died in 1944.

Newcomb, Vase, Leaves, Painted, Marie De Hoa LeBlanc, 9 x 6 ¼ In.
$5890.00

Rago Arts & Auction Center

Newcomb, Vase, Narcissus, Matte Glaze, Henrietta Bailey, 1919, 7 ⅞ In.
$3884.00

Neal Auction Co.

Newcomb, Vase, Roses On Trellis, Carved, Harriet Coulter Joor, 12 In.
$92000.00

Cottone Auctions

Newcomb, Vase, Spanish Moss, Oak Trees, Sadie Irvine, 1916, 3 ¼ x 3 In. $2232.00

Rago Arts & Auction Center

Newcomb, Vase, Trees, Spanish Moss, Yellow Moon, Blue & Green, c.1918, 7 ½ In. $3851.00

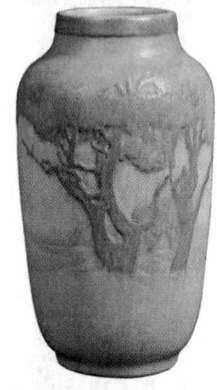

Skinner, Inc.

N

Who's Huck?
"Huck" is the mark used by Flora Cable Huckfield on North Dakota School of Mines pottery. She worked there from 1924 to 1949.

Nodder, Figurine, Chinese Man, Seated, Smiling, Ruffle Collar, Germany, c.1885, 7 ½ In. $3690.00

New Orleans Auction Galleries, Inc.

Vase, Flowers, Multicolor, Green Ground, High Gilt Handles, 12 x 6 In.	122.00
Vase, Green, Cobalt Blue Trim, Gold Tapestry Highlights, Egg Shape, Footed, 7 ¼ In.	50.00
Vase, Green, Cobalt Blue, Pink Flowers, Ball Shape, Handles, Footed, 7 In.	70.00
Vase, Green, Pink Rose, Cobalt Blue Border, Gold Highlights, Fish Shape, Handles, 9 In.	175.00
Vase, Orchids, Cobalt Blue Ground, Gilt, Hand Painted, Morimura Bros., 9 ½ In.	374.00
Vase, Painted, Gilt Detail, Flowers, Shaped Handles, c.1900, 7 In.	148.00
Vase, Pillow, Cobalt Blue, Gold Ground, Pink Rose Design, Handles, 7 In., Pair	275.00
Vase, Square Open Handles At Top, Windmill, Gilt Enamel, Early 1900s, 16 In.	144.00

NODDERS, also called nodding figures or pagods, are figures with heads and hands that are attached to wires. Any slight movement causes the parts to move up and down. They were made in many countries during the eighteenth, nineteenth, and twentieth centuries. A few Art Deco designs are also known. Copies are being made. A more recent type of nodder is made of papier-mache or plastic. These often represent sports figures or comic characters. Sports nodders are listed in the Sports category.

Big Boy, Standing, Checkerboard Overalls, Round Base, Papier-Mache, 1960s, 7 ¾ In.	510.00
Cat, Lying Down, Red, Yellow, Black, c.1895, 6 In.	764.00
Figurine, Chinese Man, Seated, Smiling, Ruffle Collar, Germany, c.1885, 7 ½ In. ....*illus*	3690.00
Mandarin, Seated, Flower Robe, Green Velvet Cushion, Gold Fringe, Porcelain, Germany, 9 x 10 ¼ In.	896.00
Red Goose, Red & Yellow, Round Base, Red Goose Shoes, Papier-Mache, 1960s, 6 ½ In.	120.00
Salt & Pepper Shakers are listed in the Salt & Pepper category.	
Set, Our Gang Characters, Nodding Heads, Painted, Bisque Box, 2 To 4 In., 7 Piece	2280.00
Soldier, Reaching For Sword, Porcelain, Portugal, 1900s, 10 ¼ In.	18.00

NORITAKE porcelain was made in Japan after 1904 by Nippon Toki Kaisha. The best-known Noritake pieces are marked with the *M* in a wreath for the Morimura Brothers, a New York City distributing company. This mark was used until the early 1950s. There may be some helpful price information in the Nippon category, since prices are comparable. Noritake Azalea is listed in the Azalea category in this book.

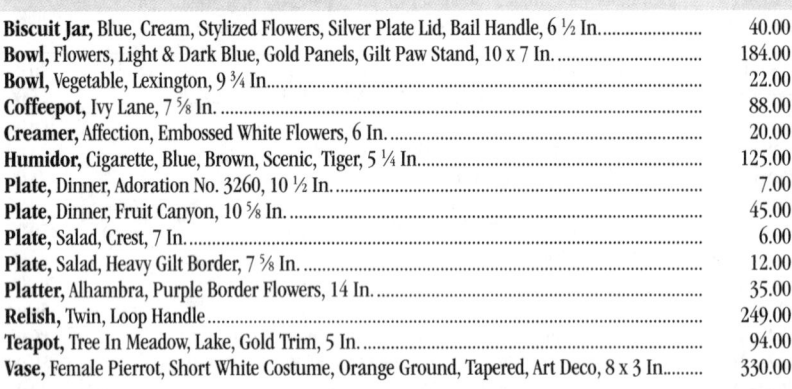

Biscuit Jar, Blue, Cream, Stylized Flowers, Silver Plate Lid, Bail Handle, 6 ½ In.	40.00
Bowl, Flowers, Light & Dark Blue, Gold Panels, Gilt Paw Stand, 10 x 7 In.	184.00
Bowl, Vegetable, Lexington, 9 ¾ In.	22.00
Coffeepot, Ivy Lane, 7 ⅞ In.	88.00
Creamer, Affection, Embossed White Flowers, 6 In.	20.00
Humidor, Cigarette, Blue, Brown, Scenic, Tiger, 5 ¼ In.	125.00
Plate, Dinner, Adoration No. 3260, 10 ½ In.	7.00
Plate, Dinner, Fruit Canyon, 10 ⅝ In.	45.00
Plate, Salad, Crest, 7 In.	6.00
Plate, Salad, Heavy Gilt Border, 7 ⅝ In.	12.00
Platter, Alhambra, Purple Border Flowers, 14 In.	35.00
Relish, Twin, Loop Handle	249.00
Teapot, Tree In Meadow, Lake, Gold Trim, 5 In.	94.00
Vase, Female Pierrot, Short White Costume, Orange Ground, Tapered, Art Deco, 8 x 3 In.	330.00

NORSE POTTERY COMPANY started in Edgerton, Wisconsin, in 1903. In 1904 the company moved to Rockford, Illinois. The company made a black pottery, which resembled early bronze relics of the Scandinavian countries. The firm went out of business in 1913.

Jug, Rolled Rim, Sea Serpents, C-Shape Handle, Logo, 7 x 5 ½ In.	295.00
Vase, Black, Gold, Tapered Cylinder, 9 In.	40.00
Vase, Cylindrical, Tapered, Geometric Designs, c.1910, 9 x 3 In.	195.00
Vase, Geometric Design, Black Glass Stand, Marked, 6 x 4 In.	210.00

NORTH DAKOTA SCHOOL OF MINES was established in 1892 at the University of North Dakota. A ceramic course was included and pieces were made from the clays found in the region. Students at the university made pieces from 1909 to 1949. Although very early pieces were marked *U.N.D.,* most pieces were stamped with the full name of the university.

Humidor, Carved Medallion, Figure, Animal, Lorene Mennie Jasper, 1946, 7 ½ x 5 In. ...*illus*	4650.00
Vase, Brown, Matte Glaze, Daffodil Design, Signed Ruth Skyberg, 1949, 5 ½ x 7 ¾ In.	900.00
Vase, Cover Lamp, Portraits Of Dacotah Territory, Carved, Brown, L. Jasper, 1947, 8 x 6 In.	5580.00
Vase, Covered Wagon, Pulled By Oxen, White, Turquoise, Bell Shape, 3 ¼ In.	748.00
Vase, Cowboy On Horse, Lasso, Cream, Blue, Marked, 4 ½ x 3 In.	4650.00
Vase, Daffodils, Carved, Brown Glaze, Lorene Mennie Jasper, 1944, 5 ½ x 6 ¼ In. ....*illus*	1240.00
Vase, Foals, Trees, Blue, Cream, L. Jasper, 1945, 7 x 6 ½ In.	5270.00
Vase, Geometric Design, Blue, Black, Yellow, Bulbous, Squat, 1940, 3 ½ In.	546.00
Vase, Green, Ivy Leaves, Incised, Black Outline, Jensen, 1943, 5 ½ In. ....*illus*	546.00

Vase, Horizontal Bands, Cream, Brown Ground, Mattson, Marked, 4 ½ In.	106.00
Vase, Mottled Brown, Green Glaze, Oval, Blue Stamp, 4 ½ x 4 In.	248.00
Vase, Native American Design Bands, Yellow, Tan, Brown, Bell Bottom, Round Foot, 4 In.	489.00
Vase, Prairie Rose, Rose Matte Glaze, Amber Color, Banding, Bulbous, Squat, 2 ¾ In.	230.00
Vase, Speckled Ocher & Green Matte Glaze, Squat, Signed Julia Mattson, 4 ½ x 5 ¼ In.	341.00
Vase, Stylized Design Band, Bentonite Clay, Brown, L. Jasper, 1945, 6 ¾ x 6 ½ In.	3472.00
Vase, Terra-Cotta Glaze, Horizontal Bands, Tapered, Cabinet, Marked, 2 ¾ In.	39.00

NORTHWOOD glass was made by the H. Northwood Co., founded in Wheeling, West Virginia, in 1901 by Harry Northwood. He worked for the Hobbs-Brockunier and LaBelle firms in the 1880s before operating his own glass plants in Martins Ferry, Ohio, and Ellwood City and Indiana, Pennsylvania. At the Wheeling factory, Harry Northwood and his brother Carl manufactured pressed and blown tableware and novelties in many colors that are collected today as custard, opalescent, goofus, carnival, and stretch glass. Pieces made between 1905 and about 1915 may have an underlined *N* trademark. Harry Northwood died in 1919, and the plant closed in 1925.

Basket, Wavy Pull-Up Design, Melon Ribs, Twist Loop Handle, Footed, Ruby, Amber, Pink, 14 In.	690.00
Chrysanthemum Sprig, Butter, Cover, Blue Opaline, Shaped Round Base, 7 In.	316.00
Chrysanthemum Swirl, Butter, Cover, Opalescent Cranberry, Ball Finial, 6 In.	259.00
Chrysanthemum Swirl, Pitcher, Water, Canary, Speckled, Smokestack Shape, 9 In.	230.00
Chrysanthemum Swirl, Syrup, Blue, Speckled Design, 7 In.	403.00
Corn, Vase, Ice Green, Stalk Base	180.00
Daisy & Fern, Sugar Shaker, Apple Blossom Mold, Blue Opalescent, 4 In.	132.00
Diamond Point, Vase, Purple, 10 ½ In.	70.00
Good Luck, Bowl, Ice Blue, Horseshoe, Ruffled, 2 ½ x 9 In.	1062.00
Grape & Cable, Hatpin Holder, Amethyst, 6 ½ In.	150.00
Grape & Cable, Water Set, Iridescent Amethyst, 1920s, 8 Piece	201.00
Jewel Threaded Swirl, Pitcher, Clear To Cranberry, Bulbous, Loop Handle, 8 In.	115.00
Leaf Mold, Butter, Cover, Cranberry Amber Spatter Finish, 5 ½ In.	550.00
Leaf Mold, Cruet, Cranberry Cased Finish, Crystal Stopper, 7 In.	400.00
Leaf Mold, Cruet, Red Spatterware, Bulbous, Faceted Ball Stopper, Handle, 7 In., Pair	201.00
Leaf Mold, Pitcher, Opal Cased Red Spatter, Silver Flakes, Bulbous, Loop Handle, 8 In.	460.00
Leaf Mold, Pitcher, Water, Cranberry & Amber Spatterware, 8 In.	250.00
Leaf Mold, Pitcher, Water, Frosted Cranberry, Applied Frosted Handle, 8 In.	650.00
Leaf Mold, Water Set, Cased Cranberry Finish, Pitcher & 4 Tumblers, 8 In.	300.00
Leaf Umbrella, Berry Bowl, Cased Blue, Bulbous, Squat, 5 In., Pair	288.00
Leaf Umbrella, Condiment Set, Cranberry Glass, Double Holder, 4 ¾ In.	225.00
Leaf Umbrella, Pitcher, Water, Blue Cased, 9 In.	300.00 to 450.00
Leaf Umbrella, Sugar Shaker, Pink Cased, Bulbous, Round Foot, Dome Lid, 5 In.	374.00
Leaf Umbrella, Syrup, Pink Cased, 7 In.	662.00
Leaf Umbrella, Water Set, Cased Yellow, 7 Piece	600.00
Leaf Umbrella, Water Set, Cranberry Spatter, Bulbous, Round Foot, Wide Spout, 9 In.	920.00
Leaf Umbrella, Water Set, Cranberry, Bulbous Pitcher, Loop Handle, 5 Tumblers, 9 In.	259.00
Leaf Umbrella, Water Set, Vaseline, Pink, White Spatter, 6 Tumblers, 1890s, 7 ¾ In.	1400.00
Louis XV, Cruet, Cream Custard Glass, Gilt Rose, Stopper, 6 In., Pair	86.00
Memphis, Table Set, Gold Detail, Emerald Green, Butter, Creamer, Spooner	50.00
Opaline Brocade, Pitcher, Water, Blue Opalescent, Ruffled Rim, 9 In.	650.00
Poinsettia, Compote, Custard Glass, Blue Ground, 3 Scrolled Custard Feet, 9 In.	295.00
Poinsettia, Tankard, Blue Opalescent, 13 ¼ In.	350.00
Rose Bowl, Footed, Ruffled Rim, Opalescent, Ribbed, c.1900, 4 ½ In.	35.00
Royal Ivy, Butter, Cover, Cranberry & Amber Spatterware, Frosted, 5 ½ In.	425.00
Royal Ivy, Condiment Set, Cranberry & Amber Spatterware, 3 Piece	400.00
Royal Ivy, Cruet, Cranberry & Amber Spatterware, Frosted, Craquelle Finish, 7 In.	400.00
Royal Ivy, Sugar Shaker, Red Spatter Design, Cylindrical, Metal Lid, 5 In., Pair	345.00
Spanish Lace, Butter, Cover, Cranberry, Clear, Ruffled Rim, 8 In.	431.00
Swirl, Punch Cup, Red & Yellow, Opalescent, Loop Handle, Pull Up, 3 In.	115.00
Twist, Sugar Shaker, Green Opalescent, Spread Foot, Metal Lid, 5 In., Pair	460.00

NU-ART, *see Imperial category.*

NUTCRACKERS of many types have been used through the centuries. At first the nutcracker was probably strong teeth or a hammer. But by the nineteenth century, many elaborate and ingenious types were made. Levers, screws, and hammer adaptations were the most popular. Because nutcrackers are still useful, they are still being made, some in the old styles.

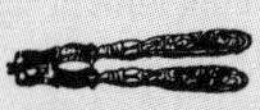

Alligator, Nickel Finish, Headford Bros. & Hitchins Foundry, 13 In.	295.00
Parrot, Cast Iron, Painted, 10 In.	518.00

North Dakota School of Mines, Humidor, Carved Medallion, Figure, Animal, Lorene Mennie Jasper, 1946, 7 ½ x 5 In. $4650.00

Rago Arts & Auction Center

North Dakota School of Mines, Vase, Daffodils, Carved, Brown Glaze, Lorene Mennie Jasper, 1944, 5 ½ x 6 ¼ In. $1240.00

Rago Arts & Auction Center

N

North Dakota School of Mines, Vase, Green, Ivy Leaves, Incised, Black Outline, Jensen, 1943, 5 ½ In. $546.00

Humler & Nolan

TIP
Big dogs seem scary, but small dogs bark more. It's the bark that discourages a burglar.

Ohr, Cup & Saucer, Folded Rim, Green Glaze, Marked, 1 ⅞-In. Cup, 4 ½-In. Saucer
$944.00

Brunk Auctions

Ohr, Inkwell, Figural, Log Cabin, Variegated Green Glaze, Stamped, c.1895
$2875.00

Rock Island Auction Company

Ohr, Pitcher, Pinched, Green Mottled Glaze, Marked, 4 x 6 ½ In.
$2728.00

Rago Arts & Auction Center

Pirate Captain, Wood, Patch, Germany, Steinbach, 1980s, 15 In.	125.00
Squirrel, Iron, 5 ¼ In.	79.00
Woman, Head, Peasant, Black Forest, 8 In.	39.00

NYMPHENBURG, *see Royal Nymphenburg.*

OCCUPIED JAPAN was printed on pottery, porcelain, toys, and other goods made during the American occupation of Japan after World War II, from 1947 to 1952. Collectors now search for these pieces. The items were made for export. Ceramic items are listed here. Toys are listed in the Toy category in this book.

Bank, Pig, Pink, Purple Flowers, 2 ¾ In.	40.00
Bank, Pig, Smiling, Flowers, 2 x 3 ½ In.	45.00
Basket, White, Painted Flower, Gold Trim, Pico, 1940s, 2 In.	10.00
Bear, Brown Fur, Felt Ears, Foot Pads, Mechanical, Windup, 8 In.	125.00
Box, Porcelain, Painted, Birds, Golden Bamboo, 5 x 4 In.	22.00
Cigarette Dispenser, Marquetry, Dog, Rolling Tambour Top, 1940s, 4 x 3 ⅞ In.	85.00
Cup & Saucer, Demitasse, Regal, Flowers, Rose, Gold, Laurel Wreath & Crown Mark, 2 ⅜ In.	20.00
Cup & Saucer, Raised Gold Design, Green, 22K Gold, 2 ¼ x 2 ½ In.	23.00
Eggcup, Bunny, Dancing, White, Green Jacket, Gold Band, 2 x ½ In.	19.00
Fan, Paper, Wood, Blue, White Ground, Flowers, 14 x 8 ½ In.	18.00
Figurine, Airedale Terrier, Porcelain, c.1945, 3 ½ x 4 In.	35.00
Figurine, Angel, Bisque, Holding Harp, Music Scroll, Flowers, 2 ¾ x 4 In., Pair	25.00
Figurine, Black Boy On Bedpan, 3 ¼ x 3 ½ In.	35.00
Figurine, Boy, Playing Tuba, Wearing Tuxedo Jacket, Multicolor, 5 In.	45.00
Figurine, Cherubs, Butterfly, Grapes, Porcelain, Painted, 1940s, 3 ¼ x 2 ⅝ In., Pair	35.00
Figurine, Colonial Couple, Seated, Multicolor, Marked, 3 ¾ In., Pair	24.00
Figurine, Colonial Man, White, 1945, 4 ⅛ In.	15.00
Figurine, Courting Couple, Gathering Flowers, c.1948, 6 In.	45.00
Figurine, Flirty Girl, Hiked Ruffled Skirt, Tilted Wide Brimmed Hat, 5 ½ In.	26.00
Figurine, Football Player, Red Football, Hat, Orange Jersey, Strung Arms, 6 ¼ In.	77.00
Figurine, French Bulldog, Standing, White, Brown Splotches, Collar, 4 ½ x 3 ½ In.	12.00
Figurine, Frog, Sitting, Reclining, Wearing Jacket, 4 ¼ In., Pair	42.00
Figurine, Lady, Gentleman, Courting, 1700s Dress, Marked, 5 x 5 ¼ In.	12.00
Figurine, Man, Woman, Peasant Dress, Flower Basket, Stamped, 6 In., Pair	43.00
Figurine, Oriental Man, Holding Weapon, Green Robe, 6 In.	17.00
Figurine, Oriental Man, Yellow Robe, Black Hat, 6 ¾ In.	14.00
Figurine, Swan Planter, Cherub Playing Instrument, Bisque, Ucagco, c.1950, Pair	145.00
Figurine, Victorian Lady, Shelf Sitter, Porcelain, Painted, Gold Highlights, 2 ½ x 3 ¼ In.	20.00
Figurine, Wedding Cake Couple, Stamped, 1940s, 3 ⅝ In.	45.00
Lighter, Car Shape, Chrome, Push Button, Hood Pops Up, 1940s, 3 x 1 In.	125.00
Lighter, Cornucopia, 2 ¾ x 4 In.	35.00
Marmalade, Lid, Underplate, Basket Weave, Flowers, Green Edging, Marked, 2 ¾ x 4 In.	15.00
Nodder, Scottie Dog, Painted, Pink Sweater, Green Bug, Celluloid, Windup, Key, 5 In.	75.00
Nut Dish Set, Porcelain, Painted, White, Pink Roses, 3 x 1 ½ In., 6 Piece	12.00
Pitcher, Tomato Shape, Painted Red, Green, Leaf Handle, Maruhan Ware, 6 ¼ x 7 ½ In.	35.00
Planter, Cow, Pulling Cart, Painted, Marked, 7 ¾ x 3 In.	18.00
Plaque, Colonial Couple, Multicolor, 6 ¼ x 5 ½ In.	20.00
Plate, Aiyo, White, Violets, Reticulated Gilded Border, Edge, 8 ¼ In.	9.00
Plate, Painted, Green Fruit, Gilt Rim, Ohata	10.00
Plate, Painted, White, Violets, Gold Trim, Scalloped Edge, Handle, 4 ½ x 3 In., Pair	20.00
Plate, Pink Flowers, Blue Ground, Gold Edge, Ucagco, 7 ¼ In.	28.00
Salt & Pepper, Boy, Girl, Tray, Multicolor, 2 In.	25.00
Salt & Pepper, Oranges, In Green Basket, 4 ½ x 2 ½ In.	35.00
Tray, Metal, Atlantic City, N.J., 3 ½ x 5 In.	18.00

OFFICE TECHNOLOGY includes office equipment and related products, such as adding machines, calculators, and check-writing machines. Typewriters are in their own category in this book.

Bank Punch, Automatic, No. 5060, Brady Mfg. Co., Brooklyn, N.Y., Original Advertising	226.00
Desk Organizer, Wood, Painted, Rectangular, Drawer, Rooster, Carrot, Chick, 10 x 14 In.	92.00

OHR pottery was made in Biloxi, Mississippi, from 1883 to 1906 by George E. Ohr, a true eccentric. The pottery was made of very thin clay that was twisted, folded, and dented into odd, graceful shapes. Some pieces were lifelike models of hats, animal heads, or even a potato. Others were decorated with folded clay "snakes." Reproductions and reworked pieces are appearing on the market. These have been reglazed, or snakes and other embellishments have been added.

O

Bowl, Body Twist, Amber Glaze, Stamped, 2 ½ x 4 In.		992.00
Bowl, Brown Mottled Glaze, Bulbous, Squat, Signed, 4 x 2 ½ In.		600.00
Bowl, Dimpled, Green & Gunmetal Glaze, Stamped, 2 ¼ x 3 ½ In.		1736.00
Bowl, Low, Pink Blister Glaze, Stamped, 2 ¼ x 4 ½ In.		2108.00
Bowl, Mottled Brown Glaze, Signed, 4 x 2 ½ In.		550.00
Bowl, Raspberry & Green Glaze, Ruffled, Low, Signed, 2 ¼ x 5 In.		3720.00
Bowl, Red, Blue, White, Green Mottled Glaze, In-Body Twist, Stamped, 2 ¾ x 3 ½ In.		4650.00
Bowl, Speckled Amber Glaze, Folded, Slanted Rim, Stamped, 3 ¼ x 5 In.		3472.00
Cup & Saucer, Folded Rim, Green Glaze, Marked, 1 ⅞-In. Cup, 4 ½-In. Saucer ....*illus*		944.00
Cup, Sponged Red Glaze, 3 Ear-Shaped Handles, Twisted Body, Signed, 4 x 5 ½ In.		6880.00
Inkwell, Figural, Log Cabin, Variegated Green Glaze, Stamped, c.1895 ....*illus*		2875.00
Mug, Brown, Green Glaze Cutout Handle, Signed, 4 x 4 In.		1100.00
Mug, Dark Brown, Joe Jefferson, Snake Handle, Stamped, 1896, 3 ¾ x ³⁄₃¾ In.		7440.00
Mug, In-Body Twist, Brown Glaze, Red Inclusions, Joe Jefferson, 1896, 3 ¼ x 4 ½ In.		2556.00
Mug, Mottled Brown & Green, Snake, Signed, 4 x 5 In.		3720.00
Mug, Puzzle, Brown Glaze, Signed, 3 ½ x 3 ½ In.		682.00
Pitcher, Bisque Fired, Cream, Pinched, Signed, 3 ¾ x 6 ½ In.		1364.00
Pitcher, Bisque Fired, Squat, Script Signature, 3 ¼ x 7 ¾ In.		496.00
Pitcher, Brown, Green Glaze, Amorphic Shape, Cutout Handle, Signed, 4 x 4 In.		1200.00
Pitcher, Folded, Dimpled, Speckled Brown & Gunmetal Glaze, Signed, 3 ¼ x 3 ¾ In.		3224.00
Pitcher, Green & Gunmetal Glaze, Lobed, Pinched, Signed, 3 ½ x 5 In.		4030.00
Pitcher, Mottled, Deep Green Glaze, Pinched Rim, Marked, 3 ¼ x 5 ½ In.		2108.00
Pitcher, Pinched, Green Mottled Glaze, Marked, 4 x 6 ½ In. ....*illus*		2728.00
Pitcher, Raspberry Volcanic Glaze, Signed, 7 ¼ x 6 ¾ In.		5270.00
Pitcher, Squat, Mottled Amber & Green Glaze, Stamped, 3 x 5 In.		1240.00
Urn, Runny Gunmetal & Raspberry Glaze, Scroll Handles, Stamped, 7 x 5 ½ In.		16120.00
Vase, Bisque Fired, Russet, Folded, Signed, 5 x 5 ½ In.		2480.00
Vase, Bisque Fired, White, Dimples, Narrow Neck, Signed, 4 ¼ x 4 ¼ In.		1488.00
Vase, Bud, Sponged-On Indigo & Raspberry Glaze, Marked, 4 ½ x 2 ½ In.		1860.00
Vase, Bulbous, In-Body Twist, Sponged Black & Amber Glaze, 7 ¼ x 4 ½ In.		4960.00
Vase, Green, Yellow, Smokestack Shape, Round Foot, Glazed, 3 In.		920.00
Vase, Gunmetal & Green Glaze, Ruffled Rim, Signed, 3 x 3 ¼ In.		1860.00
Vase, Lobed, Green & Teal Glaze, Stamped, 5 ½ x 4 ½ In.		3100.00
Vase, Mottled Amber & Gunmetal Glaze, Ribbon Handles, Stamped, 9 x 5 In.		6820.00
Vase, Mottled Green & Red Glaze, Ruffled Rim, Marked, 4 ½ x 4 ¼ In. ....*illus*		5270.00
Vase, Mottled Green Glaze, Yellow Interior, Squat, Stamped, 2 ¾ x 4 In.		682.00
Vase, Pinched Rim, Flambe Green & Amber, Gunmetal Glaze, Stamped, 3 ½ x 3 ¼ In.		1736.00

OLD IVORY china was made by the Ohme Porcelain Works in Silesia, Germany, a factory working from 1882 to 1928. The china had an ivory matte background and was usually decorated with flowers or fruit. Dinner sets, fish sets, mustache cups, and souvenir pieces were made. Pieces were marked with a crown, the cipher *OH*, and the word *Silesia*. Some pieces are also marked with the words *Old Ivory*. The pattern numbers appear on the base of many pieces.

OLD IVORY
84

Chop Plate, No. 201, 12 ½ In.		150.00
Mustard, No. 15		121.00
Nappy, No. 16, 6 ¼ In.		65.00
Plate, No. 118, 7 ½ In.		45.00
Plate, Salad, Elysee Pattern, Scalloped, Gilt, 8 In., 4 Piece		225.00
Sugar, Lid, 2 Handles, Rosebud Pattern, 4 ½ In.		55.00

OLD PARIS, *see Paris category.*

OLD SLEEPY EYE, *see Sleepy Eye category.*

ONION PATTERN, originally named bulb pattern, is a white ware decorated with cobalt blue or pink. Although it is commonly associated with Meissen, other companies made the pattern in the late nineteenth and the twentieth centuries. A rare type is called *red bud* because there are added red accents on the blue-and-white dishes.

Berry Bowl, Blue & White, Meissen, 5 In.		25.00
Butter, Blue & White, Round, Cover, Underplate, Meissen, 8 In.		225.00
Pitcher, Blue & White, Meissen, 6 x 5 In.		125.00
Platter, Blue & White, Scalloped Edge, Oval, Meissen, 13 ¾ In.		110.00
Tureen, Cover, Scrolling Leaf Finial, Squat, Leaf Shape Handles, Meissen, 13 In.		519.00

Ohr, Vase, Mottled Green & Red Glaze, Ruffled Rim, Marked, 4 ½ x 4 ¼ In. $5270.00

Rago Arts & Auction Center

Opaline, Pitcher, Water, Brocade, Blue, Northwood, 10 In. $230.00

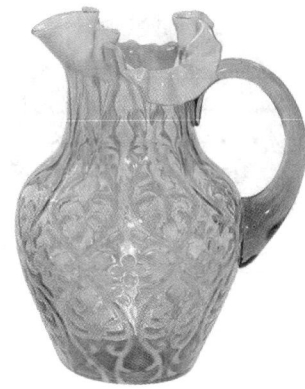

Early Auction Co.

Opaline, Vase, Rose & White, Applied Flower Bouquet, Crimped Top, Amber Glass, 8 ¾ In. $89.00

Ivey-Selkirk Auctioneers

O

Opera Glasses, Brass, Enamel, Flowers, Applied Beads, Mother-Of-Pearl Eye Rests, Signed, 4 x 2 ¾ In.
$461.00

New Orleans Auction Galleries, Inc.

Orphan Annie, Pin, Annie & Sandy, Silver On Blue Metallic, Lithograph, Geraghty, Chicago, 1930s, 1 ⅜ In.
$460.00

Hake's Americana & Collectibles

Orphan Annie, Toy, Annie On Tin Platform, Pulls Sandy, Celluloid, Clockwork, Japan, Box, 6 ½ In.
$920.00

Bertoia Auctions

Orphan Annie, Toy, Sandy, Press Tail Down For Rolling Motion, Tin Lithograph, Marx, 7 ½ In.
$230.00

Bertoia Auctions

OPALESCENT GLASS is translucent glass that has the tones of the opal gemstone. It originated in England in the 1870s and is often found in pressed glassware made in Victorian times. Opalescent glass was first made in America in 1897 at the Northwood glassworks in Indiana, Pennsylvania. Some dealers use the terms *opaline* and *opalescent* for any of these translucent wares. More opalescent pieces may be listed in Hobnail, Northwood, Pressed Glass, and other glass categories.

Acanthus Leaf, Salt, Powder Blue, Round, 16-Scallop Foot, 2 ½ x 2 In.	92.00
Baby Windows, Jelly, Cover, Cranberry, Silver Caddy, 12 Spoons, 11 In.	489.00
Basket, Blue, Mottled, Ribbed Swirl Mold, Blue Thorn Handle, 7 In.	125.00
Buttons & Braids, Pitcher, White, Baluster, Ruffled Rim, Loop Handle, Blue Accents, 10 In.	132.00
Candlestick, Hexagonal, Thistle Socket, Orbs, Wafer, 9 ½ In., Pair	546.00
Cheese Dome, Pink & Amber, Clear Ball Finial, Round Wood Base, 8 In.	58.00
Coin Spot, Pitcher, Water, Green, 9 ¼ In.	175.00
Coin Spot, Pitcher, Water, Green, Bell Shape Bottom, Ruffled Rim, Loop Handle, 11 In.	155.00
Cornucopia & Scroll, Salt, Scallop Rim, Oval, 1830-50, 2 ¼ x 3 ¼ In.	316.00
Daisy In Crisscross, Pitcher, Water, Tumbler, Green, Beaumont, 9 In.	1840.00
Diamond Point & Leaf, Nappy, Blue, Lead, Beaded Rim, c.1875, 4 ¼ In.	46.00
Eggcup, 8-Panel, Banded Rim, Domed Foot, 3 ⅝ In., 6 Piece	104.00
Fern, Cruet, White, Clear Faceted Stopper, 7 In., Pair	115.00
Fern, Pitcher, Water, Cranberry, Baluster, Shaped Rim, Loop Handle, 10 In.	690.00
Gothic Arch, Sugar, Cover, 8-Sided, 6-Sided Finial, Footed, 5 In.	460.00
Herringbone, Pitcher, Water, Ribbed, Cranberry, 9 In.	2760.00
Lattice, Pitcher, Ribbed, White, Conical, Loop Handle, Narrow Spout, Hobbs, 10 In.	115.00
Lattice, Toothpick Holder, Cranberry, Ribbed, 2 In.	127.00
Maple Leaf, Chalice, White, c.1905, 6 In.	65.00
Poinsettia, Pitcher, White, Round Foot, Narrow Body, Loop Handle, Hobbs, Brockunier, 14 In.	115.00
Polka Dot, Tumbler, Ribbed, Blue, Cylindrical, 4 In.	460.00
Punty & Ellipse, Spoon Holder, Hexagonal Bowl, Round Foot, 5 x 3 ¾ In.	374.00
Scottish Moor, Cruet, Opalescent, 6 In.	863.00
Stars & Stripes, Bottle, Barber, Cranberry, Bulbous, Stick Neck, 9 In.	431.00
Stars & Stripes, Pitcher, Tumbler, c.1890, 8 ½ & 3 ¾ In., 2 Piece	390.00
Stripe, Tankard, Prussian Blue, Cylindrical, Tapered, Round Foot, Loop Handle, 10 In.	575.00
Swirl, Butter, Cover, Cranberry, Clear Finial, Flattened Circular, 6 In.	173.00
Swirl, Jar, Cover, Cranberry, 7 In.	173.00
Swirl, Vase, Cranberry, Ribbed, Ruffled Rim, Shouldered, 5 In.	58.00
Swirl, Vase, White, Ruffled Rim, 9 ½ In.	40.00
Toothpicks are listed in the Toothpick category.	
Vase, Cascading Light Blue Hooked Feather Design, Pear Shape, 1973, 8 In.	345.00
Vase, Pink To White, Hobnail, Ruffled, Pinched Edge, c.1900, 5 x 5 ½ In.	80.00
Water Set, Blue, Fluted Scrolls, Enamel Floral, 6 Tumblers, 8 ¼ In.	500.00

OPALINE, or opal glass, was made in white, green, and other colors. The glass had a matte surface and a lack of transparency. It was often gilded or painted. It was a popular mid-nineteenth-century European glassware.

Biscuit Barrel, Enameled Flowers, Tiara Style Handle, 9 In.	100.00
Box, Lime Green, Gilt, Rectangular, Beveled Corners, Hinged Top, France, 4 ⅛ x 5 ⅛ In.	1003.00
Compote, Ruffled Rim, Trumpet Stem, Applied Rope Design, Round Foot, Gilt, 15 In.	183.00
Dish, Ruffled Rim, Pulled Design, Round Foot, 9 In. Diam.	122.00
Flask, Enameled, Young Girl, c.1900, 6 ⅞ In.	415.00
Girandole, Baluster, Hung With Prisms, 12 In., Pair	744.00
Jardiniere, Squat, Leaf Gilt Mounts, Gilt Grass Design, Footed, Art Nouveau, 10 In.	2684.00
Lamp, Pricket Shape, 15 In.	580.00
Pitcher, Water, Brocade, Blue, Northwood, 10 In. *illus*	230.00
Punch Bowl, Blue, Column Base, Round Foot, 8 x 14 In.	144.00
Punch Bowl, White, Satin, Gilt Trim, Flower Open Finial, France, 17 ½ In.	35.00
Tureen, Cover, Undertray, Melon Shape, Gilt & Enamel Design, S Handle, Ruffle Rim, 15 In.	2728.00
Urn, Cover, Baluster, Classical Profiles, Gilt Banding, Bell Shape Base, Cone Finial, 15 In.	244.00
Vanity Set, 2 Boxes, Lids, Round, Dish, Footed, Painted, France, c.1900, 4 x 1 ¾ In., 3 Piece	118.00
Vase, Cream To Peach, Raised Gold Enamel, Flowers, Scrolling Leaves, 1800s, 14 In., Pair	444.00
Vase, Enameled Flower Design, Mounted As Lamp, 14 In., Pair	793.00
Vase, Enameled Portrait & Gilt Design, 13 In.	183.00
Vase, Gilt Metal Mounts, Raised Enamel Grapevines, Flowers, 13 ½ x 9 ½ In.	259.00
Vase, Pink Flowers, Amber Branches, Cream, Green Glow, Globular, Crimped Rim, 5 ⅞ In., Pair	89.00
Vase, Rose & White, Applied Flower Bouquet, Crimped Top, Amber Glass, 8 ¾ In. *illus*	89.00
Vase, White To Rose, Pink Leaves, Twigs, Crimped Rim & Base, Swollen Center, 10 ¼ In.	148.00
Vase, White, Blue, Amber Branches, Leaves, Square Handle, Long Neck, Crimped Rim, Footed, 11 In.	177.00

O

OPERA GLASSES are needed because the stage is a long way from some of the seats at a play or an opera. Mother-of-pearl was a popular decoration on many French glasses.

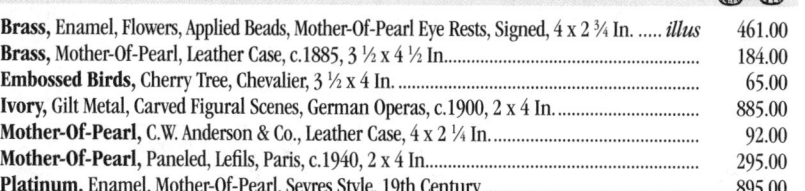

Brass, Enamel, Flowers, Applied Beads, Mother-Of-Pearl Eye Rests, Signed, 4 x 2 ¾ In. ..... *illus*	461.00
Brass, Mother-Of-Pearl, Leather Case, c.1885, 3 ½ x 4 ½ In.	184.00
Embossed Birds, Cherry Tree, Chevalier, 3 ½ x 4 In.	65.00
Ivory, Gilt Metal, Carved Figural Scenes, German Operas, c.1900, 2 x 4 In.	885.00
Mother-Of-Pearl, C.W. Anderson & Co., Leather Case, 4 x 2 ¼ In.	92.00
Mother-Of-Pearl, Paneled, Lefils, Paris, c.1940, 2 x 4 In.	295.00
Platinum, Enamel, Mother-Of-Pearl, Sevres Style, 19th Century	895.00

ORPHAN ANNIE first appeared in the comics in 1924. The last strip ran in newspapers on June 13, 2010. The redheaded girl, her dog Sandy, and her friends were on the radio from 1930 to 1942. The first movie based on the strip was produced in 1932. A second movie was produced in 1938. A Broadway musical that opened in 1977, a movie based on the musical and produced in 1982, and a made-for-television movie based on the musical produced in 1999 made Annie popular again, and many toys, dishes, and other memorabilia have been made.

Book, Pop-Up, Jumbo The Elephant, Pleasure Books, 1935	525.00
Bracelet, Brass, Enamel Portrait, Die Cut, Hinged, Box, 1930s, 2 ⅞ In.	190.00
Dime Bank, Annie, Sandy, Save A Dime A Day, Tin, 3 In.	244.00
Game, Little Orphan Annie Travel Game, Board, Spinner, Markers, Milton Bradley, 13 In.	95.00
Pin, Annie & Sandy, Silver On Blue Metallic, Lithograph, Geraghty, Chicago, 1930s, 1 ⅜ In. ..... *illus*	460.00
Ring, Secret Society, Silver Star, Roa, Compartment, No. 1793, 1938	403.00
Toothbrush Holder, Annie & Sandy, Bisque, 1940s, 3 ⅝ x 3 ½ In.	150.00
Toy, Annie On Tin Platform, Pulls Sandy, Celluloid, Clockwork, Japan, Box, 6 ½ In. ....*illus*	920.00
Toy, Sandy, Press Tail Down For Rolling Motion, Tin Lithograph, Marx, 7 ½ In. ....*illus*	230.00
Watch, Sun, Brass, Inset Compass, Hinged Lid, Egyptian Symbols, 1939, 1 ½ In.	158.00
Wristwatch, Sport, Annie, Blue Leather Band, Green Box, New Haven Watch Co., 1935, 2 x 4 In. *illus*	230.00

ORREFORS Glassworks, located in the Swedish province of Smaaland, was established in 1898. The company is still making glass for use on the table or as decorations. There is renewed interest in the glass made in the modern styles of the 1940s and 1950s. In 1990, the company merged with Kosta Boda. Most vases and decorative pieces are signed with the etched name *Orrefors*.

Orrefors

Bowl, Cobalt Blue, Round Foot, Flared Rim, Rolled Lip, c.1950, 8 x 15 In.	799.00
Bowl, Multi-Eye, Signed, 6 ½ In.	30.00
Bowl, Onion Pattern, 5 ½ In.	69.00
Bowl, Transparent Green & Blue Fish, Flowers, Clear Ground, Vertical Cutting, Wide Rim, 8 In.	354.00
Champagne, Rhapsody, Smoke, 5 ¼ In.	10.00
Cordial, Claire, 5 ¾ In.	28.00
Goblet, Coronation, 6 ⅛ In.	35.00
Goblet, Water, 8 ¼ In.	35.00
Goblet, Water, Prelude, Clear, 6 ⅞ In.	27.00
Goblet, Water, Prelude, Clear, 8 ¼ In.	40.00
Vase, Cylindrical, Leaves, Sprigs, Etched, 5 In.	45.00
Vase, Egg Shape, Ariel, Profile, 7 ½ x 5 In.	2480.00
Vase, Engraved, Man, Woman, Child, c.1937, 10 ½ x 7 In.	1240.00
Vase, Engraved, Siren, Woman, Raised Arms, c.1934, 10 x 6 ¼ In.	1240.00
Vase, Gondolier, Elongated Oval, Royal Blue, Gold, c.1950, 7 x 5 In.	4000.00
Vase, Nude Swimmer, 11 ½ x 6 ¼ In., Pair	1240.00
Vase, Romeo & Juliet, Etched, 8 x 5 In.	60.00
Vase, Square, Nils Landberg, 1950s, 6 In.	47.00
Wine, Esprit, 6 In.	30.00

OTT & BREWER COMPANY operated the Etruria Pottery at Trenton, New Jersey, from 1871 to 1892. It started making belleek in 1882. The firm used a variety of marks that incorporated the initials *O & B*.

Bust, Abraham Lincoln, Parian, 1876, 9 In.	2000.00
Oyster Plate, 6 Wells, Crescent Shape, Ironstone, 9 ¾ In.	94.00

OVERBECK POTTERY was made by four sisters named Overbeck at a pottery in Cambridge City, Indiana. They started in 1911. They made all types of vases, each one-of-a-kind. Small, hand-modeled figurines are the most popular pieces with today's collectors. The factory continued until 1955, when the last of the four sisters died.

Figurine, Elephant, Grotesque, Multicolor, Marked, 2 ¼ In. ....*illus*	230.00
Figurine, Goose, Long Outstretched Neck, Marked, 4 ½ x 3 ¼ In.	480.00

Orphan Annie, Wristwatch, Sport, Annie, Blue Leather Band, Green Box, New Haven Watch Co., 1935, 2 x 4 In. $230.00

Hake's Americana & Collectibles

Overbeck, Figurine, Elephant, Grotesque, Multicolor, Marked, 2 ¼ In. $230.00

Humler & Nolan

Overbeck, Figurine, Robin, Blossoms, Green Leaves, Marked, 2 ¾ In. $288.00

Humler & Nolan

O

TIP

Look in your hardware store for the new glues that can fix almost anything. Buy the proper one to fix transparent glass, porous pottery, or nonporous metals. There will be one that will work.

Retired Plates

When a limited edition figurine or plate is "retired," it is no longer made and will never be made again. When the figurine or plate is "suspended," it is not currently in production but may be at a later date.

Owens, Vase, Lotus, Stork, Standing, Raised Foot, Charles Chilcote, 7 ½ In.
$259.00

Humler & Nolan

Oyster Plate, 5 Wells, Majolica, Crescent Shape, Purple, Green Plant, Footed, 10 In.
$316.00

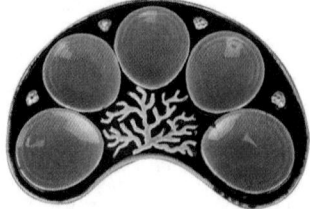

Strawser Auction Group

Oyster Plate, 5 Wells, Majolica, White Basket Weave, Shells In Wells, Wedgwood, 9 In.
$690.00

Strawser Auction Group

Figurine, Grotesque Cockatoo, Perched, Curly Tail, White, Yellow, Green, Marked, 4 ¾ In.	345.00
Figurine, Hen, 4 Chicks, Grassy Patch, Brown, Pink, Green, Marked, 3 In.	316.00
Figurine, Mad Duck, Beak Open, Spread Wing, White, Yellow, Marked, 2 ¼ In.	431.00
Figurine, Robin, Blossoms, Green Leaves, Marked, 2 ¾ In. ....*illus*	288.00
Figurine, Skunk, Black, White, Impressed Mark, 4 ½ x 3 ½ In.	413.00 to 450.00
Figurine, Southern Belle, Wide Hat, High Yellow Gloves, Incised, 4 ¾ In.	224.00

OWENS POTTERY was made in Zanesville, Ohio, from 1891 to 1928. The first art pottery was made after 1896. Utopian Ware, Cyrano, Navarre, Feroza, and Henri Deux were made. Pieces were usually marked with a form of the name *Owens*. About 1907, the firm began to make tile and discontinued the art pottery wares.

Ewer, Utopian, Orange Flower, Tan Leaves, Brown Glaze, Ruffled Rim, 10 ½ In.	119.00
Jardiniere, Bird Creatures, Green To Brown Base, 7 ¾ x 6 ½ In.	35.00
Jardiniere, Griffins, Green, Yellow & Brown Blended Glaze, Shield Mark, 11 ¾ x 10 In.	40.00
Jug, Lightweight, Blue Flowers, Squat, Signed, 3 x 5 ¾ In.	104.00
Jug, Utopian, Yellow Corn, Brown Glaze, Neck Handle, 7 ½ In.	115.00
Mug, Oxblood, Copper Red Glaze, Round Foot, Loop Handle, 6 In.	184.00
Tile, Seascape, Ship, Painted, Carved, Arts & Crafts Style Frame, 18 x 12 In.	1920.00
Vase, Chicks, Yellow, Brown Glaze, Signed CL Leffler, Marked, 10 ½ In.	662.00
Vase, Green Ground, Nasturtium Vine, Edith Bell, c.1900, 8 ¾ In.	311.00
Vase, Gunmetal Black, Squat, Handles, 9 ¾ x 3 ½ In.	336.00
Vase, Lotus, Stork, Standing, Raised Foot, Charles Chilcote, 7 ½ In. ....*illus*	259.00
Vase, Lotus, Tulip Designs, Signed Chilcote, Marked, 7 ½ In.	121.00
Vase, Opalescent Flowers, Butterflies, Green Leaves, Cream Ground, 8 ⅛ In.	345.00
Vase, Underwater Scene, Fish, Blue, Green, Cream, Oval, Flared, Chilcote, 10 ⅜ In.	735.00
Vase, Utopian, Irises, Green & Orange, Brown Ground, Round, Stamped, 12 ½ x 10 In.	1116.00
Vase, Utopian, Poppy, White Glaze, Swollen Cylinder, Signed Denny, 11 In.	432.00
Vase, Utopian, Stick Neck, Swollen, Marked, 12 ½ In.	142.00

OYSTER PLATES were popular from the 1880s. Each course at dinner was served in a special dish. The oyster plate had indentations shaped like oysters. Usually six oysters were held on a plate. There is no greater value to a plate with more oysters, although that myth continues to haunt antiques dealers. There are other plates for shellfish, including cockle plates and whelk plates. The appropriately shaped indentations are part of the design of these dishes.

5 Wells, 5 Dolphins, 5 Sea Plants, Multicolor, Wedgwood, c.1900, 9 In.	1275.00
5 Wells, Acorn & Oak Leaf, Gilt Center, Rim, T & V, Limoges, France, 8 ¼ In.	300.00
5 Wells, Blue, Cream, Raised Gilt Design, Strauss, France, c.1890, 8 ½ In.	225.00
5 Wells, Blue, White Shells, Ball Footed, Salt Cup, France, c.1850, 9 In.	395.00
5 Wells, Chrysanthemums, Central Salt Cup, Gilt, Haviland, Limoges, c.1890, 8 In.	195.00
5 Wells, Clam Shape, Violets, Salt Cup, T. Haviland, Limoges, c.1890, 8 ½ In.	225.00
5 Wells, Cobalt Blue, Gold, Creamy Depressions, Charles Haviland, c.1895, 11 In.	475.00
5 Wells, Dolphin Dividers, Cobalt Blue, Turquoise Center, 9 In.	2760.00
5 Wells, Flowers, Burgundy Trim Ruffled Rim, Salt Cup, Haviland, Limoges, c.1890, 9 In.	295.00
5 Wells, Flowers, Leaves, White, Scalloped, Center Cup, Haviland, Limoges, c.1900, 9 In.	195.00
5 Wells, Gold Detail, Turkey, Haviland, Limoges, c.1880, 8 ½ In.	700.00
5 Wells, Green Roses, Scalloped Gilt Rim, Salt Cup, Tressemann & Vogt Limoges, c.1900, 9 ½ In.	200.00
5 Wells, Green, Gold Accents, Haviland, 8 ½ In.	83.00
5 Wells, Majolica, Crescent Shape, Purple, Green Plant, Footed, 10 In. ....*illus*	316.00
5 Wells, Majolica, White Basket Weave, Shells In Wells, Wedgwood, 9 In. ....*illus*	690.00
5 Wells, Medallions, Green, Gilt, Haviland, Limoges, 9 In.	125.00
5 Wells, Painted Shells, Scalloped, Center Salt Cup, Haviland, 9 In.	125.00
5 Wells, Pink, Gilt Flower Border, Scalloped, Center Salt Cup, Signed Gutherz, 9 In.	115.00
5 Wells, Pink, Gilt, Embossed, Limoges, 8 ½ In.	185.00
5 Wells, Pink, White, Ribbon Design, Side Salt Cup, 8 Sides, 8 In.	185.00
5 Wells, Red Roses, Blue Forget-Me-Nots, Haviland, c.1887, 7 ¾ In.	399.00
5 Wells, Salmon Ground, Gold Wells, c.1890, 8 ¾ In.	275.00
5 Wells, Sea Creatures, Turkey, Haviland, Limoges, c.1882, 8 ½ In.	750.00
5 Wells, White Porcelain, Gilt Accents, Haviland Limoges, c.1882, 8 ½ In.	180.00
6 Wells, Blue Flowers, Cream Ground, Center Salt Cup, Germany, 10 In.	125.00
6 Wells, Blue Flowers, White Ground, Center Salt Cup, Victoria Austria, 8 ½ In.	145.00
6 Wells, Cream, Gold, Fan Shape, Sauce Cup, 9 x 11 In.	425.00
6 Wells, Flowers, Gilt Rim, White Ground, Center Salt Cup, Germany, 8 ½ In.	125.00
6 Wells, Flowers, Sealife, Kutani, 9 In.	219.00
6 Wells, Flowers, White Ground, Charles Ahrenfeldt, Limoges, c.1915, 9 In.	145.00
6 Wells, Flowers, White Ground, Gilt, Salt Cup, C. Ahrenfeldt, Limoges, 9 In.	185.00

O

6 Wells, Gold Fish Design, Minton, England, c.1880, 8 ½ In.	375.00
6 Wells, Leaf Shape Wells, Square, 8 ½ x 8 ½ In.	189.00
6 Wells, Magenta, White Ground, Gilt, Central Salt Cup, V. Karlsbad, Austria, c.1890, 9 In.	165.00
6 Wells, Majolica, Black, Turquoise, Center Salt Cup, England, 8 ½ In.	200.00
6 Wells, Majolica, Blue, Magenta, Gilt, Haviland, Limoges, 9 In.	225.00
6 Wells, Majolica, Blue, Yellow, Keller, Guerin St. Clement, c.1900, 10 ½ In.	275.00
6 Wells, Majolica, Pink, Blue, Green, Salt Cup, 1970, 9 ¼ In.	65.00
6 Wells, Majolica, Pink, Green, Center Salt Cup, England, 10 In.	285.00
6 Wells, Marguerite Pattern, Brown, Royal Staffordshire, 1907, 9 ½ In.	485.00
6 Wells, Marine Symbols, Pink Ground, Center Salt Cup, Haviland, Limoges, c.1880, 9 In.	450.00
6 Wells, Martha Design, Center Cup, Cambridge Glass c.1945, 10 ¼ In.	20.00
6 Wells, Mint Green Ground, Center Salt Cup, Haviland, Limoges, c.1880, 9 In.	250.00
6 Wells, Pastel Flowers, White Ground, Scalloped Rim, Depose, France, 9 In.	175.00
6 Wells, Shell Shapes, Pink Ground, Royal Worcester, c.1910, 8 ½ In.	450.00
6 Wells, Turkey, Flowers, 8 ¾ In.	47.00
6 Wells, White, Gilt, Center Salt Cup, Haviland Limoges, 9 In.	125.00

PADEN CITY GLASS MANUFACTURING COMPANY was established in 1916 at Paden City, West Virginia. The company made over twenty different colors of glass. The firm closed in 1951. Paden City Pottery may be listed in Dinnerware.

Black Ebony, Tray, Center Handle, 10 x 10 In.	30.00
Old Rose, Plate, Bread & Butter, 6 ¼ In.	3.00
Old Rose, Plate, Dinner, 9 ½ In.	7.50
Old Rose, Plate, Salad, Square, 7 ¼ In.	6.50
Peacock & Wild Rose, Dish, Mayonnaise, Underplate, Pink, Paden City	135.00

PAINTINGS listed in this book are not works by major artists but rather decorative paintings on ivory, board, or glass that would be of interest to the average collector. Watercolors on paper are listed under Picture. To learn the value of an oil painting by a listed artist, you must contact an expert in that area.

Acrylic On Board, Planter Box, Flowers, Frame, 23 x 25 In.	250.00
Acrylic On Canvas, Winter Landscape, Railway Station, Village, R. Smith, 23 x 27 In.	283.00
Ink On Paper, Imperial Pair, Ancestor Portraits, Multicolor, Chinese, Frame, 1800s, 76 x 47 In.	1845.00
Ink On Paper, Votive, Avatar Of Shiva, Beggars, Glazed, India, Frame, c.1900, 22 x 17 ¼ In. ...... *illus*	1126.00
Oil On Board, A Good Smoke, Pipe, Tobacco, Frame, A. Telbisz, Hungary, 14 x 12 In.	316.00
Oil On Board, Antelope Jack, Cowboy, 1984, 9 x 12 In.	510.00
Oil On Board, Black Figures, Landscape, Cabin, Catherine Stockwell, Frame, 12 x 15 In.	403.00
Oil On Board, Campfire Scene, Travelers, Cooking Fire, Frame, 26 x 37 In.	452.00
Oil On Board, Children Playing With Bubbles, Genevieve Reckling, 1930, 12 x 16 In.	60.00
Oil On Board, Coastal Landscape, Ocean, Rocky Land, Trees, Frame, 1800s, 4 x 9 In.	230.00
Oil On Board, Dutch Canal Scene, Gilt Frame, c.1890, 10 x 13 In.	213.00
Oil On Board, Evening At The Beach, Ocean Shore, England, Frame, 16 x 20 In.	230.00
Oil On Board, Fall Birches By The Lake, Bertram R. Wilson, Canada, 1900s, 12 x 15 In.	239.00
Oil On Board, Fall Pastures, Hillside, Trees, Roger E. Gilson, Frame, 1900s, 18 x 22 In.	288.00
Oil On Board, Fishing Boats, Docks, Wharf, John Cuthbert Hare, Frame, 23 x 29 In.	345.00
Oil On Board, Flower Garden, Buildings, Trees, M.D. Elwell, Frame, 1914, 16 x 12 In.	184.00
Oil On Board, Lake Quinsigamond, W.J. Robinson, Frame, 1890, 9 x 14 In.	201.00
Oil On Board, Lake, Sailing Ship, Blue Sky, Green Water, Wood Frame, 1800s, 12 x 17 In.	122.00
Oil On Board, Landscape With Cows Crossing Stream, C. Raschen, Frame, 16 x 20 In.	403.00
Oil On Board, Landscape, Forest, Blooming Flowers, Mountains, Frame, Signed, 10 x 13 In.	633.00
Oil On Board, Landscape, Trail In Woods, Wilbur Adam, c.1898, 9 x 12 In.	588.00
Oil On Board, Ocean, Waves, Sea Plane, A.F. Gerstmayer, Frame, 1900s, 28 x 20 In.	230.00
Oil On Board, Pastoral Landscape, P. Tubbecke, Germany, Frame, 14 x 20 ½ In.	210.00
Oil On Board, Plaque, Spanish Heraldry, Banners, Painted Wood Frame, c.1868, 23 x 28 In.	1200.00
Oil On Board, Red Barn, Bridge, Creek, Trees, Ken Gore, U.S.A., Frame, 1900s, 8 x 10 In.	239.00
Oil On Board, Rocky Pasture, Distant House, DeHaven, U.S.A., Frame, 8 x 10 In.	748.00
Oil On Board, Ship, Moorings, Sails Up & Down, Gulls, E. Adair '96, 21 x 13 ½ In.	173.00
Oil On Board, St. Augustine, Street Scene, Shops, Eldor Gathman, 1900s, 25 x 31 In.	920.00
Oil On Board, Still Life, Bowl Of Strawberries, Frame, 1900, 12 x 18 ¾ In. .... *illus*	176.00
Oil On Board, The Mother, Ewe, Sheep, James Crawford, Frame, 20 x 18 In.	410.00
Oil On Board, Vue De Notre-Dame, Signed, Julian Brosius, France, Frame, 1900s, 5 ½ x 7 In.	239.00
Oil On Board, Winter Sport, Frame, Signed Marion Gray Traver, 1938, 22 x 26 ¼ In.	936.00
Oil On Board, Woman, Standing, 3 Children, Red Robe, Pedro Lapa, 1800s, 63 x 22 In.	600.00
Oil On Canvas, 2 Cabins At Lakeside, Trees, Rowboat, Folk Art, Frame, Late 1800s, 22 x 31 In.	230.00
Oil On Canvas, 2 Peacocks, Trees, Blue Sky, Clouds, T. William, Gilt Frame, 24 x 20 In.	210.00

Painting, Ink On Paper, Votive, Avatar Of Shiva, Beggars, Glazed, India, Frame, c.1900, 22 x 17 ¼ In.
$1126.00

Skinner, Inc.

Painting, Oil On Board, Still Life, Bowl Of Strawberries, Frame, 1900, 12 x 18 ¾ In.
$176.00

Garth's Auctions, Inc.

Painting, Reverse On Glass, General Harrison, Portrait, Stars, Flag, Frame, c.1835, 5 ¾ x 8 In.
$1687.00

Garth's Auctions, Inc.

P

Most Expensive Painting
In 2011 over $250 million was paid for the famous Cezanne painting, *The Card Players.* It is one of five versions of the picture. The buyer is the royal family of Qatar, a country on the border of Saudi Arabia. It is a record price for any work of art.

PAINTING

Early Auction Co.

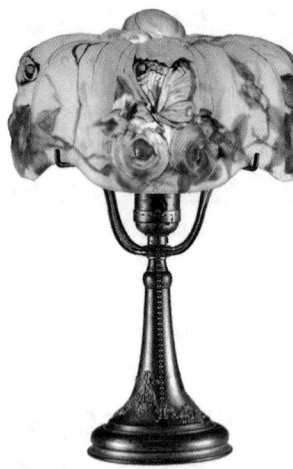

James D. Julia Inc.

TIP

*Check the hooks
holding your paintings
and photographs
every few years.
Eventually, a heavy
picture will loosen
the nail and hook and
the painting will fall.
Also check the wire
holding the picture.*

Oil On Canvas, 3 Bull Cows, 3 Sheep, Landscape, W.W. Moor, Frame, 12 x 18 In.	690.00
Oil On Canvas, 4-Masted Schooner, On High Seas, Francis Glusing, 1929, 32 x 48 In.	956.00
Oil On Canvas, Abstract In Red, Andre Elbaz, Morocco, Frame, 1934, 40 x 32 In.	1195.00
Oil On Canvas, Adam & Eve, Multicolor, Giraffes, Garden, G. Abelard, Haiti, 1922, 24 x 30 In.	1434.00
Oil On Canvas, Alpine Landscape, Waterfall, Francis Snowe, Frame, 1876, 25 x 31 In.	690.00
Oil On Canvas, Angel Presenting Wreath To Martyred Child, Austria, c.1800, 72 x 48 In.	1680.00
Oil On Canvas, Bacchanale, Nude Figures, Water, Z. Molnar, Hungary, 1932, 33 x 23 In.	236.00
Oil On Canvas, Ballerina, Pink Tutu, Blue Bow, A. Balogh, Hungary, 1900s, 31 x 23 In.	345.00
Oil On Canvas, Blue Day, Rocky Coastal Scene, Waves, A.J. Shelton, Frame, 12 x 16 In.	288.00
Oil On Canvas, Boy With Ball, S. Bradbury, Frame, 1909, 18 x 13 In.	249.00
Oil On Canvas, Boy, Seated, Wearing Buster Brown Outfit, Tennis Racquet, c.1910	460.00
Oil On Canvas, Boy, Whittling With Pocket Knife, F. Buicard, Gesso Frame, 45 x 33 In.	590.00
Oil On Canvas, Carnival, Street Scene, William Jacobs, c.1945, 30 x 36 In.	540.00
Oil On Canvas, Cathedral Interior, Frame, c.1950, 19 x 16 In.	629.00
Oil On Canvas, Child By Pond With Iris, Arthur Johnson, Frame, 25 x 30 In.	230.00
Oil On Canvas, Child Spooning Liquid Into Pocket Watch, Hungary, c.1900, 30 x 20 In.	216.00
Oil On Canvas, Christus, Scourged Christ, 25 ¼ x 20 ½ In.	2223.00
Oil On Canvas, Clown, Frowning, Multicolor, Meshoko, 1968, 24 x 20 In.	180.00
Oil On Canvas, Cows In Landscape, 1800s, 20 x 16 In.	518.00
Oil On Canvas, Cows, Sheep, Pasture, Frame, 19th Century, 19 x 14 In.	212.00
Oil On Canvas, Curly Headed Toddler With Ball, H.E. House, Gilt Frame, 24 x 30 In.	81.00
Oil On Canvas, Death Of A Poet, Figure Releasing Birds, Leonard Maurer, 40 x 52 In.	269.00
Oil On Canvas, Desolate Building, Sand Dunes, H. Kruuse, Denmark, Frame, 20 x 26 In.	196.00
Oil On Canvas, Dock Scene, Cannery, Patsee Parker, Frame, 1900s, 24 x 48 In.	316.00
Oil On Canvas, Dream Of Arcadia, Trees, Mountains, Lake, 1800s, 27 x 36 In.	1185.00
Oil On Canvas, Duty Calls, World War II, Soldier, Leaving Woman, Gold Frame, 15 x 19 In.	69.00
Oil On Canvas, Feeding Doves, Birds Hovering, E. Hausmann, Germany, c.1900, 21 x 28	1750.00
Oil On Canvas, Flowers In Vase, Fruit, Waterfall, 48 x 36 In.	240.00
Oil On Canvas, Gentleman In Elaborate Wig, Frame 38 x 33 In.	2340.00
Oil On Canvas, Girl, Lace Collar, Horseback, Boys Playing, Spain, 1800s, 23 x 18 In.	3105.00
Oil On Canvas, Girl, On Dock, Water Fowl, Gilt Frame, 34 x 27 In.	283.00
Oil On Canvas, Girl, Red Dress, Holding Kitten, c.1840, 33 x 23 In.	1960.00
Oil On Canvas, Girl, Seated, Blue Dress, Frame, Late 1800s, 39 x 29 In.	345.00
Oil On Canvas, Girl, With Dog, Colonial Clothing, Standing, 1700s, 29 x 24 In.	2703.00
Oil On Canvas, Glorious Nature, Fall Trees On Hill, Lee Winslow Court, Frame, 1900s, 18 x 26 In.	374.00
Oil On Canvas, Harbor Scene, Frame, c.1950, 20 x 40 In.	312.00
Oil On Canvas, Harbor Scene, Sailboats, Buildings, Water, Signed, LL, 1947, 20 x 24 In.	281.00
Oil On Canvas, Hillside With Minarets, Blowing Wheat, Frame, 1904, 18 x 26 In.	478.00
Oil On Canvas, Horse, Stable Yard Dog & Cat, Carved Gilt Frame, 19 x 24 In.	2489.00
Oil On Canvas, House In The Valley, Yellow, Blue Shutters, Philip Koch, 1984, 40 x 60 In.	780.00
Oil On Canvas, Hudson River Valley Landscape, Frame, Late 1800s, 22 x 35 In.	518.00
Oil On Canvas, Hunting Dog, Brown, Long Floppy Ears, Tall Grass, Dark Sky, 1900s, 24 x 20 In.	438.00
Oil On Canvas, Indian Campground, Frame, 16 x 22 In.	2468.00
Oil On Canvas, Lady In Gown, Roses In Delft Urn, Frame, c.1900, 49 x 32 In.	960.00
Oil On Canvas, Laid On Board, Hudson River, J.G. Durand, Frame, 25 x 39 In.	960.00
Oil On Canvas, Lake, People In Boat, Woods, Gilt Frame, 31 x 43 In.	424.00
Oil On Canvas, Lakeshore, Rocks, Trees, Hills, L.C. Earle, Frame, 12 x 20 In.	690.00
Oil On Canvas, Landscape With Bridge At Sunset, Frame, Dusk, Bervin, 1900s, 20 x 27 In.	896.00
Oil On Canvas, Landscape With Cows & Distant City, Henri J. Pieron, Frame, 14 x 20 In.	478.00
Oil On Canvas, Landscape With Haystacks, Lake, Frame, 16 x 20 In.	431.00
Oil On Canvas, Landscape, Farm, Stream, Birds, Bridge, Houses, Folk Art, 1800s, 24 x 29 In.	494.00
Oil On Canvas, Landscape, Snow, Stream, Covered Bridge, Trees, c.1941, 22 x 30 In.	764.00
Oil On Canvas, Little Smoker, Young Boy With Pipe, Hat, Miklos, Frame, 39 x 29 In.	173.00
Oil On Canvas, Log Bridge, Creek, Stone Fence, Lake, Frame, 24 x 31 In.	961.00
Oil On Canvas, Lucretia, Seminude, Knife To Chest, Green Robe, Frame, 1800s, 29 x 23 In.	472.00
Oil On Canvas, Madonna & Child, Seated, Italy, 1700s, 49 x 37 In.	575.00
Oil On Canvas, Madonna With Angels, Cherubs, Spain, Frame, 1923, 12 x 16 In.	1020.00
Oil On Canvas, Madonna With Halo Of Stars, Italy, Silver Frame, 1700s, 12 x 9 In.	805.00
Oil On Canvas, Male, Standing, Gordy, 35 x 19 In.	676.00
Oil On Canvas, Man, Black Suit, Neck Stock, Holding Ruler, 34 x 26 In.	311.00
Oil On Canvas, Messenger Of Salem, 3-Masted Ship, J. Hardcastle, Frame, 21 x 31 In.	460.00
Oil On Canvas, Moody Seascape, Ocean Waves, Jansen, Frame, c.1951, 20 x 16 In.	259.00
Oil On Canvas, Mother & Her Young Child, Flowers, Bonnet, Frame, c.1845, 30 x 25 In.	2607.00
Oil On Canvas, Mother Prepares Son & Daughter For School, Frame, c.1887, 21 x 18 In.	403.00
Oil On Canvas, Mountain Waterfall, John Hammerstad, c.1915, 16 x 24 In.	600.00
Oil On Canvas, Mysterious Depths, Orange Sky, Waves, J. Einerssen, Frame, 1949, 25 x 29 In.	230.00

Oil On Canvas, Mythological Scene, Women, Gods, Frame, 53 x 63 In.	6435.00
Oil On Canvas, Off Yorkshire, Sailboats, Sea, Bluff, Alex Beattie, 1800s, 10 ¾ x 15 In.	236.00
Oil On Canvas, Oil Town By Night, Saloon, Horses, Buggy, Men, Towers, R.R. Runcel, 24 x 36 In.	240.00
Oil On Canvas, Old Man By The Sea, May S. Clinedinst, Frame, 29 x 25 In.	144.00
Oil On Canvas, Old Woman, Germany, 19 x 15 In.	470.00
Oil On Canvas, Outermost House, Cliff Edge, Ocean, R. Woodhouse Barbour, 1945, 18 x 22 In.	90.00
Oil On Canvas, Paris Street, Frame, 19 x 23 In.	434.00
Oil On Canvas, Parlor Scene, 19th Century, Frame, 19 x 22 In.	446.00
Oil On Canvas, Penitent Magdalene, Italy, c.1820, 35 ½ x 27 ½ In.	738.00
Oil On Canvas, Philip's Church, Dock Street, Theater Facade, Frame, 1954, 18 x 16 In.	288.00
Oil On Canvas, Primitive Mountain Landscape, Frame, c.1900, 24 x 32 In.	431.00
Oil On Canvas, Reflection, Woman, Mirror, Frame, 32 ½ x 25 ½ In.	819.00
Oil On Canvas, River Landscape With Factory Building, Frame, 1800s, 18 x 28 In.	184.00
Oil On Canvas, Rocky Coastal Scene, Waves, Frame, 1900s, 20 x 36 In.	115.00
Oil On Canvas, Rough Waters, Sailboat On Ocean, Large Waves, France, 1700s, 10 x 13 In.	646.00
Oil On Canvas, Russian Landscape, Building, Steeple, Trees, Snow, River, Signed, 1893, 15 x 18 In.	960.00
Oil On Canvas, Sailboat At Sea, Dark Skies, William F. Halsall, Frame, 18 x 24 In.	805.00
Oil On Canvas, Sandy Beach, Allan Gay, Frame, 14 x 24 In.	2760.00
Oil On Canvas, Seascape, Waves, Rocky Shore, A. Casay, Frame, 1900s, 24 x 36 In.	1725.00
Oil On Canvas, Ship, Castillian Of Newburyport, Frame, 28 x 34 In.	920.00
Oil On Canvas, Ship, Great Western, Shortening Sail, 1852, 30 x 42 In.	11560.00
Oil On Canvas, Spring Landscape, Leafy Trees In Bloom, R. Feuer, 1900s, 28 x 22 In.	227.00
Oil On Canvas, Steam Yacht, Waves, Clouds, Columbia, Frame, 1900s, 20 x 36 In.	575.00
Oil On Canvas, Still Life With Apples & Head Of Cabbage, A. Ribard, 1900s, 22 x 25 In.	538.00
Oil On Canvas, Stone Bridge, Building, Frame, Gilt, 25 x 35 In.	170.00
Oil On Canvas, Stone Canyon, Jack Laycox, U.S.A., Frame, 1900s, 24 x 30 In.	431.00
Oil On Canvas, Strings Section, Men Playing String Instruments, S. Heller, 1900s, 36 x 46 In.	181.00
Oil On Canvas, Sunlight & Shade, Farm House, Fence, W.R. Watkins, Frame, 31 x 36 In.	345.00
Oil On Canvas, Sunset Gold, Oregon Coast, Joyce Clark, Gilt Frame, 1900s, 16 x 20 In.	575.00
Oil On Canvas, Tea Time, People Seated, Stephen Lewin, Frame, c.1890, 34 ¼ x 43 ¼ In.	1404.00
Oil On Canvas, The Blacksmith's Shop, Standing Man, Window, Frame, 1900s, 23 x 17 In.	250.00
Oil On Canvas, The Lagoon, Pond, Green Plants, Flowers, Floating In Water, 1900s, 30 x 38 In.	156.00
Oil On Canvas, The Mandolin Player, Figures Seated Around Table, 18 x 23 ½ In.	640.00
Oil On Canvas, The River, View From Potomac, John Sitton, Frame, 1907, 32 x 37 In.	345.00
Oil On Canvas, The Smokehouse, Field Landscape, Rene Ovyn, Frame, c.1900, 16 x 12 In.	179.00
Oil On Canvas, Traveler Along A Country Road, G. Lovati, France, 1900s, 24 x 48 In.	625.00
Oil On Canvas, Travelers At Rest, Snowcapped Mountains, B.R. Catalan, 20 x 22 In.	173.00
Oil On Canvas, Trees, Field Of Flowers, Multicolor, R. Feuer, 1900s, 24 x 30 In.	359.00
Oil On Canvas, Tuscan Hill Town, Multicolor, Nancy W. Sheppard, 15 x 24 In.	149.00
Oil On Canvas, Veduta Di Venezia, Waterfront, Boats, Frame, 24 x 48 In.	2151.00
Oil On Canvas, View Of Rolling Waves, C. Haliberg, Frame, 1915, 18 x 39 In.	920.00
Oil On Canvas, Winter Landscape, House, Wiktor Korecki, Poland, c.1950, 24 x 36 In.	499.00
Oil On Canvas, Winter Scene, Skaters, Canal, Village, Blacksmith, Frame, 1800s, 22 x 27 In.	690.00
Oil On Canvas, Woman In White Seated In Salon, Scharf, Austria, c.1900, 31 x 24 In.	2880.00
Oil On Canvas, Woman Sewing In Kitchen, Hugh Newell, Frame, 12 x 16 In.	633.00
Oil On Canvas, Woman Wearing Pearls, Spain, Frame, 1700s, 26 x 20 In.	805.00
Oil On Canvas, Woman With Fan, Turtle, Kimono, Frame, Cuba, 1900s, 75 x 32 In.	2390.00
Oil On Canvas, Woman, Seated In Chair, Green Dress, W. Adam, c.1898, 35 x 28 In.	588.00
Oil On Canvas, Woman, Seated, Flowers, Red Gown, E. Edward, Frame, 1900s, 16 x 12 In.	150.00
Oil On Canvas, Young Beauty, Playing Double Flute, Signed, France, 99 x 49 In.	11258.00
Oil On Canvas, Young Boy With Dog, England, Frame, 36 ¾ x 32 In.	2574.00
Oil On Canvas, Young Couple On Lake Shore, Trees, Oval Frame, 1800s, 12 x 10 In.	345.00
Oil On Canvas, Young Girl Resting, Orange Suit, R. Philipp, Frame, c.1900, 19 x 27 In.	2875.00
Oil On Canvas, Young Woman In Green Dress, Somber, N. Cikovsky, Frame, 12 x 10 In.	259.00
Oil On Canvas, Young Woman Seated By Stream, Leo Malempre, 1904, 24 x 20 In.	474.00
Oil On Canvas, Young Woman, Lace Collar, Frame, 1800s, 13 x 10 In.	978.00
Oil On Cardboard, Tiger Cat, Oak Frame, c.1900s, 12 x 12 In.	235.00
Oil On Masonite, Farmscape, Rew Hocker, c.1945, 28 x 38 In.	4500.00
Oil On Masonite, Mallards In Flight, 3 Dimensional, J. Howes, Frame, 1955, 8 x 20 In.	374.00
Oil On Masonite, Still Life, Apples, Grapes, Glass Of Champagne, J. Howes, 11 x 14 In.	288.00
Oil On Masonite, Yucca San Gabriel Canyon, F. M. Moore, c.1900, 23 x 30 In.	1440.00
Oil On Metal, Lady In Black, Leaning Against Wall, Long Dress, A. Hadoon, 11 x 9 In.	240.00
Oil On Panel, Ducks By A Stream, Max Hanger Sr., Germany, Frame, 10 x 15 In.	575.00
Oil On Panel, Figural Winterscape, J. Beekhout, Dutch, 1900s, 20 x 24 In.	182.00
Oil On Panel, Hannan Harrison Park, Woman, Bonnet, Dress, Frame, c.1800, 11 x 13 In.	230.00
Oil On Panel, Harbor Scene, Frame, 11 x 13 ½ In.	760.00

Pairpoint, Lamp, Puffy, Pansies & Roses, Reverse Painted, Metal Base, Signed, 27 x 15 x 11 ½ In.
$3730.00

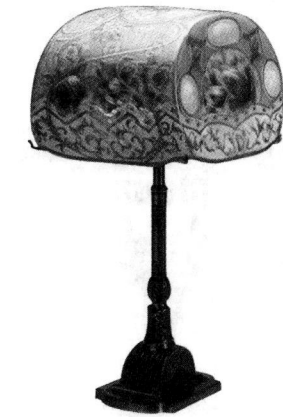

Rago Arts & Auction Center

Pairpoint, Lamp, Puffy, Stratford Shade, Yellow, White Lattice, Bronze Footed Base, Signed, 16 In.
$920.00

Early Auction Co.

P

Pairpoint, Lamp, Reverse Painted, Autumn Landscape, Harvest Scene, Signed, 23 In.
$2070.00

Cottone Auctions

Paper, Cutwork, Scherenschnitte, Birds, Watercolors, Rosanna Witmer, June 11, 1815, Frame, 12 x 13 In.
$904.00

Garth's Auctions, Inc.

Paper, Cutwork, Scherenschnitte, Watercolor, Hearts, Handwriting, Frame, 1823, 16 ¼-In. Square
$353.00

Garth's Auctions, Inc.

Scrapbooking

Scrapbooking is nothing new. It was a popular hobby in England, France, and Germany in the late 1700s.

Oil On Panel, Horses, Ducks & Pigeon, John F. Herring, Frame, 15 ¾ x 17 ¾ In.	2340.00
Oil On Panel, Hunter, Horse, Dog, England, Hunt Scene, c.1835, 25 x 36 In.	2607.00
Oil On Panel, Landscape With Bridge & Figures, Frame, 1800s, 7 x 14 In.	1035.00
Oil On Panel, Rooster, Multicolor, J.H. Click, Frame, 1950, 20 x 16 In.	173.00
Oil On Panel, Still Life Poppies, Hermione Von Preuschen, Germany, Frame, 16 x 12 In.	575.00
Oil On Panel, Sunset Harbor Scene, Ships & Shoreline, Frame, Late 1800s, 6 x 9 In.	184.00
Oil On Panel, Woman & Children, Outside, Leu Caillet, France, Frame, 20 x 16 In.	920.00
Oil On Panel, Woman Praying, Open Window, Joh Makloth, Frame, 1882, 8 x 6 In.	316.00
Oil On Panel, Woman, Eastman Johnson, Frame, c.1890, 15 ½ x 13 ½ In.	3217.00
Oil On Panel, Work Horses Pulling Wagon, Otto Von Thoren, 1800s, 13 x 23 In.	230.00
Oil On Silk, The Fish Bowl, Kittens, Nahui Olin, Mexico, Frame, 8 ½ x 12 ½ In.	1195.00
On Ivory, Woman, Flowers In Hair, Oval Gilt Louis XVI Frame, 4 ½ In.	98.00
On Tin, Hudson River, Boy, Girl, Walking Dog, c.1840, 17 x 22 In.	288.00
Reverse On Glass, General Harrison, Portrait, Stars, Flag, Frame, c.1835, 5 ¾ x 8 In. ...*illus*	1687.00
Reverse On Glass, Girl, Playing, Kitten, Drapery, Shell, Leaf Border, France, 1800s, 14 x 12 In.	179.00

PAIRPOINT Manufacturing Company started in 1880 in New Bedford, Massachusetts. It soon joined with the glassworks nearby and made glass, silver-plated pieces, and lamps. Reverse-painted glass shades and molded shades known as "puffies" were part of the production until the 1930s. The company reorganized and changed its name several times but is still working today. Items listed here are glass or glass and metal. Silver-plated pieces are listed under Silver Plate.

Biscuit Jar, Gold Water Lily, Green Lily Pads, Pale Green Ground, Silver Plate Collar, 8 ½ x 6 ½ In.	148.00
Biscuit Jar, Round Ball Shape, Enameled Scrolls, Colonial Couple, Shaped Handle, 6 In.	431.00
Biscuit Jar, White, Embossed Windows, Multicolor Flowers, Silver Plate Lid, Bail, Signed, 7 In.	100.00
Biscuit Jar, White, Pink, Sailboat Scene, Silver Plate Lid, Handle, 16-Sided, Marked, 6 ¼ In.	200.00
Bottle, Perfume, 6-Panel, Cranberry Ribbons, Flower Stopper, c.1940, 5 In.	235.00
Bowl, Myrtle, Rolled Rim, Hobstar Base, 3 ½ x 9 In.	495.00
Bowl, Oranges, Hobstar, Fan & Cane Bowtie, Oval, Snowflake Foot, 7 x 10 In.	246.00
Bowl, Oval, Etched, Gilt Metal Cherub Stand, 8 ½ x 13 ¼ In.	115.00
Bowl, Scalloped Rim, Savoy, Hobstar Base, 9 In.	575.00
Candelabrum, 4-Arm, Art Nouveau, Silver Plate, Center Finial, Marked, 19 ½ In.	345.00
Case, Green Vertical Waves, Gargoyle Brass Tripod Frame, White Alabaster Base, 5 ½ In., Pair	403.00
Cologne Bottle, Ramona, 7 ¾ In.	340.00
Dish, Cover, Silver Plate Base, Green, Enamel Flowers, Gold Stencil Highlights, Oval, 6 x 9 In.	125.00
Dresser Box, Gilt Flowers, Green Leaves, Molded, Signed PMC, 7 x 2 ¾ In.	230.00
Jewelry Box, Embossed Gilt Metal, Garlands, Maroon, White Lid, Flowers, Footed, Marked, 3 x 5 In.	75.00
Lamp, Farm Scene, Wood Baluster Base, Signed, 20 In. ...*illus*	1035.00
Lamp, Puffy Stratford Shade, Flowers, 4 Lobes, Frosted, Closed Top, Gilt Metal Base, 21 In.	3851.00
Lamp, Puffy, Butterflies, Roses, Scalloped Edge, 2-Socket Molded Base, 21 In.	3245.00
Lamp, Puffy, Candle, Opaline Glass Base, 20th Century, 8 x 4 In.	369.00
Lamp, Puffy, Dogwood, Stratford, Pink Satin Ground, Molded Base, 14 ½ In.	1770.00
Lamp, Puffy, Double, Puffy, Pansies, Pinched Waist Base, 9 x 11 In.	2185.00
Lamp, Puffy, Flowers, Butterfly, Rounded Corners, Brass, Signed, 13 ½ In. ...*illus*	3163.00
Lamp, Puffy, Pansies & Roses, Reverse Painted, Metal Base, Signed, 27 x 15 x 11 ½ In. ...*illus*	3730.00
Lamp, Puffy, Reverse Painted, Stratford Shed, Yellow & White Roses, 2 Birds, Signed, 14 In.	5000.00
Lamp, Puffy, Rose Bouquet, Trumpet Base, Molded Leaves, 4 Iris Arms, 21 In.	3540.00
Lamp, Puffy, Roses, Frosted, Green Leaves, Ribbed Stem, Relief Flowers On Base, 21 In.	7110.00
Lamp, Puffy, Stratford Shade, Yellow, White Lattice, Bronze Footed Base, Signed, 16 In. ...*illus*	920.00
Lamp, Puffy, Yellow Lotus, Green Leaves, Lotus Base, Serpentine Supports, 18 x 10 In.	6785.00
Lamp, Reverse Painted Shade, Landscape, Silver Plate Base, 16 x 20 In.	510.00
Lamp, Reverse Painted, Autumn Landscape, Harvest Scene, Signed, 23 In. ...*illus*	2070.00
Lamp, Sailboats, Seashells, Etched Glass Shade & Base, Stamped, Signed H. Fisher, 25 x 19 ¾ In.	2356.00
Lampshade, Reverse Painted, Soft Pink Ground, Blue & Yellow Flowers, Leaves, Birds, 16 In.	649.00
Powder Jar, Pearl Pattern, Silver Plated Collar, Hinge, 4 ½ x 2 ¾ In.	144.00
Vase, Boston, Hobstar Base, Green Cut To Clear, Bowling Pin Shape, 12 In.	550.00
Vase, Chalice Shape, Clear, Monroe Pattern, Bubble Ball Connector, Round Foot, 12 In.	75.00
Vase, Cobalt Blue, Cylindrical, Tapered, Wide Rim, Silver Plated, Leaves, Square Foot, 12 In.	69.00

PALMER COX, *Brownies, see Brownies category.*

PAPER collectibles, including almanacs, catalogs, children's books, some greeting cards, stock certificates, and other paper ephemera, are listed here. Paper calendars are listed separately in the Calendar category. Paper items may be found in many other sections, such as Christmas and Movie.

Advertisement, 1903 Shredded Wheat, 6 ½ x 9 ½ In.	15.00
Book, Pop-Up, New Adventures Of Tarzan, Pleasure Books, 1935	850.00

P

Catalog, Montgomery Ward, 1927, 55th Anniversary, 600 Pages	85.00
Cutwork, Scherenschnitte, Birds, On Pedestals, Cut Work, Inlaid Frame, 11 x 13 In.	118.00
Cutwork, Scherenschnitte, Family, Boy Holding Flag, Frame, Pa., c.1800, 16 x 19 ¾ In.	2607.00
Cutwork, Scherenschnitte, Birds, Watercolors, Rosanna Witmer, June 11, 1815, Frame, 12 x 13 In. *illus*	904.00
Cutwork, Scherenschnitte, Panel, Watercolor, On Paper, Symbols, Velvet Mount, Frame, 1800s	359.00
Cutwork, Scherenschnitte, Watercolor, Hearts, Handwriting, Frame, 1823, 16 ¼-In. Square *illus*	353.00
Family Record, Abraham Moore, Ink, Watercolor, Arches, Births, Deaths, 1813, 12 x 15 In.	1380.00
Family Record, Watercolor, Albert Swank, Lottie Shrader, Signed, K.K. Emmett, Oh., 23 x 19 In.	151.00
Fraktur, Alphabet, Ink & Watercolor, Vorschift, Frame, 1836, 8 x 11 In.	948.00
Fraktur, Birth & Baptism, Watercolor, Ink, Daniel Doub, Black Children, Frame, c.1771, 12 x 15 In.	1122.00
Fraktur, Birth Record, Tulip, Bird, Ink, Watercolor, Rachel Gaff, 1808, 13 x 16 In.	5451.00
Fraktur, Birth Record, Tulips, Hearts, Birds, Ink, Watercolor, Elizabeth Riegel, 1825, 13 x 8 In.	11258.00
Fraktur, Birth, Angels, Flowers, Ink, Watercolor, Margaret Walbert, 1806, 12 ¾ x 15 ½ In.	608.00
Fraktur, Birth, Building, Bird, Maria Elizabeth Troutman, Ink, Watercolor, 1789, 12 ½ x 14 ¾ In.	972.00
Fraktur, Birth, Durck Groff, Birds, Snakes, Flowers, c.1822, 12 ½ x 15 ½ In.	77025.00
Fraktur, Birth, Flowers, Scrolls, Ink, Watercolor, Catharina Vilmaenn, 1761, 8 x 13 In.	593.00
Fraktur, Birth, Heart, Flowers, Angels, Ink, Watercolor, Rubin Kruger, 1825, Pa., 8 x 12 ½ In.	1215.00
Fraktur, Birth, Watercolor, Ink, Catharina Kinig, Flowers, Tulips, Lancaster Cnty., 13 x 7 In.	940.00
Fraktur, Birth, Watercolor, Ink, Drapes, Angel, Heart Reserve, Salvinus Roller, c.1820, 8 x 10 In.	10350.00
Fraktur, Birth, Watercolor, Ink, Parrots, Floral Vines, Jacob Miller, Frame, 1791, 8 x 13 In.	1725.00
Fraktur, Metamorphosis, Life's Journey, 4 Panels, Ink, Watercolor, c.1910	15405.00
Fraktur, Watercolor, Ink, Martin Brechall, 1810, Northampton County, Pa., Frame, 11 x 16 In.	529.00
Fraktur, Watercolor, Tulips, Multicolor, Adam Hiester, 1856, 7 ½ x 9 In.	588.00
Indenture, Philadelphia, Signed William Allen, William Webb, Sam Powell, Frame, 1739, 13 x 31 In.	148.00
Lunch Set, Crepe Paper, Violet Pattern, Plates, Napkins, Table Cloth, Dennison, Box, 8 x 14 ½ In.	30.00
Magazine, Playboy, 1st Issue, Marilyn Monroe, Nude, Full Color, December 1953 *illus*	3000.00
Map, South West Virginia & Contiguous Territory, Dated 1891, 30 x 51 In.	345.00
Poster, Motorcycle Racing, Readville, Mass., October 12th, 1925, White & Red, 27 x 18 In.	385.00
Program, Ringling Brothers & Barnum & Bailey Circus, 1951, 8 ½ x 11 In.	40.00
Scrapbook, Elbert Hubbard's, Ribbon Bound, Hardcover *illus*	102.00
Stock Certificate, Euro Disneyland, 10 Shares, French Francs, Mickey, Globe, c.1989, 11 ½ x 8 In.	55.00
Stock Certificate, Kinner Airplane & Motor Corp., 1936	100.00
Stock Certificate, Lehman Brothers, Holdings Specimen, 1 Share, May 1994, 8 x 12 In.	32985.00
Textbook, American Red Cross First Aid, 114 Photos & Drawings, 1940, 12 In.	1.00
Wallpaper, Grape Clusters, Leaves, Lattice Ground, Purple, Green, 1930s, 28 x 18 In. *illus*	2000.00
Wedding Certificate, Engraved, Ink, On Paper, Decorated Frame, Wyandot County, 16 x 12 In.	59.00

PAPER DOLLS were probably inspired by the pantins, or jumping jacks, made in eighteenth-century Europe. By the 1880s, sheets of printed paper dolls and clothes were being made. The first paper doll books were made in the 1920s. Collectors prefer uncut sheets or books or boxed sets of paper dolls. Prices are about half as much if the pages have been cut.

Amy Carter, Sealed In Box	35.00
Ann Sothern, 2 Dolls, 16 Outfits, Saalfield, 1956, 11 ½ x 8 ½ In., Uncut	55.00
Dancer, Pierced Crepe, Tulle, Satin Dress, Hand Colored, France, 1860, 15 ½ In.	413.00
Esther Williams, Look-Thru Book, 20 Outfits, Dog Angie, Merrill, 1950s, 13 x 11 In.	175.00
Family Affair, Uncle Bill, Jody, Mr. French, Buffy, Whitman	25.00
Green Acres, Oliver & Lisa, Whitman, 1968	35.00
Itsy Bitsy Baby Beans, Whitman, 1973, 6 Pages, Uncut	22.00
Kellogg's Cereal, Doll, Stand, Outfit, 1942, 9 ½ In.	35.00
Lennon Sisters, 4 Dolls, Uncut Clothing Sheet, Whitman Publishing, 1959	60.00
Margaret O'Brien, Fun On The Farm, 2 Dolls, Clothes By Hedwigjo Meinner, 5 Pages	175.00
Marilyn Monroe, 2 Dolls, Wearing Underwear, Wardrobe, Saalfield, 1954, Uncut, 12 ½ In. *illus*	114.00
Millie Fay, 3 Dolls, 3 Pages Of Dresses, McLaughlin Bros., 1880, 7 x 4 In., Uncut	55.00
Ricky Nelson, 2 Dolls, 6 Sheets Of Outfits Plus Guitar, Whitman, 1959, 10 x 12 In.	170.00
Ronald & Nancy Reagan, First Family, Book, Dell Inc., Uncut	90.00

PAPERWEIGHTS must have first appeared along with paper in ancient Egypt. Today's collectors search for every type, from the very expensive French weights of the nineteenth century to the modern artist weights or advertising pieces. The glass tops of the paperweights sometimes have been nicked or scratched, and this type of damage can be removed by polishing. Some serious collectors think this type of repair is an alteration and will not buy a repolished weight; others think it is an acceptable technique of restoration that does not change the value. Baccarat paperweights are listed separately under Baccarat.

AC, Coiled Brown & Yellow Snake Ready To Strike, Earth Ground, Signed, 2 x 2 ⅜ In.	402.00
Advertising, Brass Over Steel, R.C. Remmey Son Co., 2 ¾ In. Diam.	203.00

Paper, Magazine, Playboy, 1st Issue, Marilyn Monroe, Nude, Full Color, December 1953
$3000.00

Victorian Casino Antique Auction

Paper, Scrapbook, Elbert Hubbard's, Ribbon Bound, Hardcover
$102.00

DuMouchelles Art Gallery

Paper, Wallpaper, Grape Clusters, Leaves, Lattice Ground, Purple, Green, 1930s, 28 x 18 In.
$2000.00

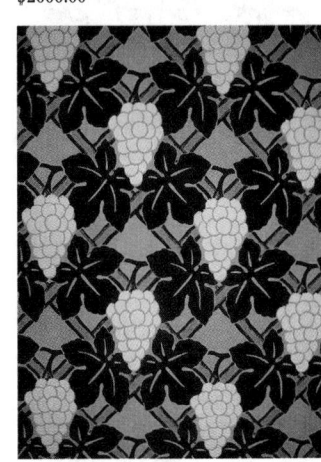

Paper Doll, Marilyn Monroe, 2 Dolls, Wearing Underwear, Wardrobe, Saalfield, 1954, Uncut, 12 ½ In.
$114.00

Serious Toyz

Advertising, Dice Game, Belleville Glass Co., 4 ¼ x 2 ¾ In.		69.00
Advertising, Independent Stove Co., Elephant, Cast Iron, 3 ½ x 2 In.		68.00
Advertising, K.W. Hexter & Co., Everlasting Finish Linings, Celluloid, Ohio, 2 ¾ In. Diam.	*illus*	47.00
Advertising, Kellogg, Child In Basket, Oh Look Who's Here, Milk Glass, 5 In.		120.00
Advertising, Kellogg, Girl Holding Box, Milk Glass, Fired Image, 5 x 3 In.		231.00
Advertising, Mirror, Dutch Boy, National Lead & Oil Co., Pa., Celluloid, 4 In.		115.00
Advertising, Mirror, J.T. Hinton & Son, Finest Ambulance In The World, 3 ½ In.		308.00
Advertising, Murphy Varnishes, Pug Dog Head, Ceramic, White Ground, 3 x 3 In.		34.00
Advertising, Packard Car Co., Ask The Man Who Knows, Bronze, Car, 4 x 3 x ½ In.		4400.00
Advertising, Parker Vises, Figural, Bear, White, Paint, Cast Iron, 3 ½ In.		73.00
Advertising, Whale, Figural, Knox Stove Works, Cast Metal, Early 1900s, 4 In.		230.00
Ayotte, Blueberries, Flowers, Leaves, Signed, 1989, 3 x 5 In.		961.00
Ayotte, Pansies, Lady Bug, Flowers, 6 & 1 Faceting, Signed, 1988, 3 x 4 In.		537.00
B, Pink Rose, 5 Pink & White Morning Glories, Green Leaves, Signed, 2 ⅞ x 2 ¼ In.		531.00
Bakelite, Variegated, Red, Brown, Orange, 3 ½ In.		225.00
Bronze, Figural, Group Of Fisherman, Boat, Nets, Japan, 1900s, 2 x 5 In.		354.00
Caithness, Multicolor Trefoil Design, Pink, White Double Overlay, 6-Sided, 1982, 2 ¾ x 2 In.		115.00
Caithness, Pink, White Flowers, Green Stem, Multifaceted Pyramid Shape, 3 x 4 In.		118.00
Caithness, Single Pink Blossom, Pale Blue Pad, Blue, Yellow Millefiori Surround, 1950, 2 ½ x 2 In.		58.00
Caithness, Whitefriars, Faceted Body, Cane Base, Green Ground, Box, 2 ¾ x 2 In.		144.00
Cast Iron, Bear, Black, Paint, 3 ¼ In.		96.00
Cast Iron, Dog, Afghan, Tan, Brown, Paint, 2 ½ x 4 ½ In.		113.00
Cast Iron, Dog, Boston Bull Terrier, Black, White Paint, 3 In.		74.00
Cast Iron, Double Quail, Paint, 2 ¼ In.		158.00
Cast Iron, Duck, Purse, Yellow, Blue, Paint, 2 ¼ In.		57.00
Cast Iron, Embracing Couple, Civil War Attire, Paint, 3 In.		57.00
Cast Iron, Here's A Pal For You, 3 ½ In.		62.00
Clichy, Central Pink Cane, Maroon, Pink Green Canes, Blue Millefiori Garland, White Ground, 3 In.		6038.00
Clichy, Chequer, Center Rose, 16 Millefiori Canes, White Latticinio Twists, 2 ¾ x 2 ½ In.		2013.00
Clichy, Garland, Rose Surrounded By 2 Rows Of Millefiori Cane, Muslin Ground, 2 x 2 ¾ In.		1725.00
Clichy, Millefiori, Close Pack, Multicolor, White Stave Basket, 2 ⅞ In.		9200.00
Clichy, Millefiori, Multicolor Canes, Latticinio Ground, Mark, France, c.1845, 3 In.		690.00
Clichy, Pink, Green Millefiori Rings, Central Blue Cane, Green, White Stave Basket Frame, 3 x 2 In.		8050.00
Comolera, Paul, Bronze, Flat Back, Sparrow, Marked 1 ½ In.		676.00
Copper, Commemorative, Pax Mfg., 1967, 2 ¾ In.		5.00
Donofrio, Jim, Indian, Campfire, Pots, Bows, Signed, 1999, 3 ¾ x 2 ⅝ In.		590.00
DT, Blossoms, Blue, White, Red & Orange, Green Leaves, Signed, 2 x 3 In.		920.00
Eicholt, R., Glass, Blue Iridescent, Green, Swirls Design, Round Ball, 1982, 3 In.		81.00
Figural, Black, Dandy, Green, Cream, Paint, Cast Iron, 3 In.		113.00
Fote, Andrew, White Swirl, Applied Metal Exterior, Globe, Signed, 3 ¼ x 3 In.		115.00
G., Blue Over White Double Overlay, Red, White & Blue Floral Bouquet, Signed, 2 ½ x 2 ¾ In.		632.00
G., Bunches Of Chardonnay Grapes Hanging From Brown Stems, Signed, 2 ¼ x 3 In.		413.00
Glass, Abstract, Rock Shape, Blue, Black Drizzle Design, Signed, Nourot, c.1986, 3 In.		23.00
Glass, Anchor, Shield, Shape, Stars, Brass, 5 x 4 In.		48.00
Glass, Blue & White Crown Weight In Red & White Crown, Large Facet On Top, 2 x 3 In.		632.00
Glass, Bouquet Of Daises, Yellow Center, Purple Blossoms, Brown Leaves, Signed, 2 x 2 ¾ In.		1121.00
Glass, Bouquet Of White Flowers, Yellow Blossoms, Purple & White Flowers, Signed, 2 x 2 ¾ In.		460.00
Glass, Central Silhouette Of Rooster Surrounded By Silhouette Canes, Signed, 2 ¼ x 3 In.		345.00
Glass, Dome Shape, 8-Sided, Internal Multicolor Lilies, 1900s, 4 In.		30.00
Glass, Ducks Swimming On Pond, Shoreline, Mushrooms, Flowers, Signed, 3 x 3 ¾ In.		1437.00
Glass, Goose, Yellow Matte Glaze, 1930s, 5 In.		575.00
Glass, Gray & White Bird Sits On Branch, Magnolia Blossom, Green Leaves, Signed, 2 x 3 ⅜ In.		1150.00
Glass, Green & Yellow Turtle Rests On Earth Ground, Yellow & White Flowers, Signed, 3 x 4 In.		2185.00
Glass, Horse, Beige, Jockey, Green & Brown Ground, White Fence, 2 ½ x 3 In.		767.00
Glass, Magnum, 6-Bubble, Ribbon Joiners, Aqua Jasper Ground, 1900s, 5 x 6 In.		58.00
Glass, Micro Mosaic, Bouquet, Roses, Flowers, c.1880, 3 x 3 In.		380.00
Glass, Millefiori & Silhouette Canes, Blue Crosshatch Lines, Signed, 2 x 2 ¾ In.		460.00
Glass, Millefiori, Incased In Crystal, Surrounded By White Latticinio Basket, Signed, 2 x 2 ⅜ In.		517.00
Glass, Millefiori, Latticinio Faceted Base, Mushroom Shape Top, Multicolor, Signed, 1990, 4 x 4 In.		594.00
Glass, Millefiori, Star Of David, 3 ¼ In.		59.00
Glass, Mountain, Orbiting Satellite, Signed, 5 ½ x 5 In.		460.00
Glass, Our Martyred Presidents, Lincoln, McKinley, Garfield, 4 x 2 In.		45.00
Glass, Plaque Shape, Flower Bouquet, Pulled Glass, Diamond Cut Edges, 6 x 4 In.		1469.00
Glass, Powdered Frit White Boat With Blue Water & Red Flag, Clear Foot, 4 In.		805.00
Glass, Stump, Loren, Butterflies, Orange Flower, Brown Leaves, Nude Fairy, Gold Egg Half, 4 In.		2300.00
Glass, Uprooted Chicory Plant With 2 Blue Flowers, Leaves, Stems, Says Seeds Pollen, 2 x 3 In.		1121.00

Glass, Vase, Red Headed Woodpecker, Perched, Oak Tree, Acorns, Mottled Blue Sky, 6 In.	150.00
Glass, Venetian, End Of Day, 4 In. Diam.	45.00
Glass, Yellow & White Pulled Wisteria, Aventurine Mushroom, Ball Shape, 1973, 5 In.	460.00
Green, Yellow, Blue Striped Lizard, Skeleton Of Lizard, Desert Flower, Sand, 2 x 3 ¼ In.	805.00
Horn, Water, Buffalo, Lotus Plants Shaped, Chinese, 4 ½ x 3 ⅜ In.	326.00
Jablonski, Adam, Teardrop, Bubbles, Red Center, Signed	28.00
Jade, Coiling Dragon, Pearl, Translucent White, Green, Orange, Round, Chinese, 1 ¼ x 1 ¾ In.	296.00
JD, American Bald Eagle, Spread Wings, Hovering Over Earth, Signed, 2 ⅝ x 3 ⅜ In.	944.00
Kaziun, Bottle, Pulled Glass, Yellow Flower, Red, Green, White, Turquoise, Flecked Goldstone, 3 x 2 In.	509.00
Kaziun, Charles, Clematis, Blue & Green, Red, Green Ground, 1900s, 2 ¼ In.	259.00
Kaziun, Snake & Rose, Leaves, Red & Yellow Pulled Glass, Turquoise, Flecked Goldstone, 2 x 3 In.	791.00
Lotton, C., Opalescent, Blue, Cobalt Pulled Feather Design, Oval Shape, Signed, 1973, 3 In.	115.00
Lotton, Cobalt Blue Glass, Iridescent Hooked Feather, Ball Shape, 1972, 3 In.	144.00
Lotton, Dark Amber, Red Flowers, Blue Vines, Flowers, Heart Shape Leaves, Ball Shape, 1974, 3 In.	345.00
Lotton, John, Glass, Ruby Flowers, Khaki Green Vines, Cobalt Blue, Round, 1990, 3 ½ x 5 In.	288.00
Lotton, Opal Glass, Iridescent Blue Hooked Feather, Ball Shape, Signed, 1973, 3 In.	201.00
Lotton, Opal Glass, Iridescent Turquoise Hooked Feather, Ball Shape, Signed, 1972, 3 In.	230.00
Lotton, Translucent Blue, Red, Blue, Green, Round, Signed, 1983, 2 ½ In.	144.00
Lotton, Translucent Glass, Blue & White Pulled Feather, Central Aventurine Mushroom, Ball, 5 In.	489.00
Lotton, Translucent, Central Mushroom, Variegated Amber, Signed, 1971, 3 In.	92.00
Manson, William, Strawberries, Branch, Blue Overlay, 12-Side Facets, 6-Side Flutes, 3 ½ x 2 ⅜ In.	177.00
McDougal, Peter, Magnum, Red, White Barber Poles Chequer, Blue Canes, Signed, 4 ½ x 3 In.	518.00
Millefiori, Black & White Silhouette Of Whistler's Mother, Signed, 1 ½ x 2 In.	488.00
Millefiori, Blue, Pink & White, On Blue Ground, Signed, 1 ¾ x 2 ½ In.	287.00
Millefiori, Double Pentagon, 3 In.	295.00
Millefiori, Scattered Cane On Ground, Muslin Ground, Signed, 2 ⅛ x 3 In.	345.00
Murano, Ribbon Pattern, Multicolor, Ball Shape, Italy, 3 ½ In.	59.00
Paley, Albert, Steel, Forged, Fabricated, Abstract Design, Stamped, 1994, 8 ¼ x 4 In.	155.00
Parabelle, Central Rose Cane, Multicolor Radiating Twists, Signed, 2 ¾ x 2 In.	1033.00
Parabelle, Close Pack Millefiori, Flowers, Magnum, Translucent Red Ground, Signed, 1999, 4 x 3 In.	1265.00
Parabelle, Flower Millefiori, Red, White Twist Handle, Signed 1989, 3 x 2 In.	590.00
Parabelle, Multicolor Loose Pack Millefiori, Blue, White Basket, Signed 1986, 3 x 2 ½ In.	413.00
Parabelle, Triple Stacked, Close, Concentric & Miniature Millefiori Orbs, Signed 1994, 4 ¾ In.	2530.00
Parsley, John, Yellow, White, Blue, Pink Flowers, Translucent Blue Ground, Signed 1997, 2 ½ x 2 In.	1380.00
Perthshire, Blue, Green Concentric Millefiori Rings, Signed, 1970, 3 ¾ x 2 ⅜ In.	345.00
Perthshire, Close Millefiori, Purple & White Double Overlay, 16-Sided Facets, 1974, 2 ¾ x 2 In.	345.00
Perthshire, Clown, Standing On Ball, Hollow, Cranberry Overlay, 16-Sided, 1998, 3 x 2 ¾ In.	575.00
Perthshire, Lampwork Eagle, Ball, Hollow Blown, Pink Overlay, 16 Facets, 1987, 3 ¼ x 2 ¾ In.	413.00
Perthshire, Millefiori, Locomotive, Colored Canes, 1983, 1 ¾ x 2 ⅞ In.	230.00 to 500.00
Perthshire, Millefiori, Red, White Barber Pole Twists, 1993, 2 ½ x 2 In.	148.00
Perthshire, Pattern Millefiori Garland, 5 Picture Canes, White Ground, Signed 1980, 3 x 2 ¼ In.	207.00
Perthshire, Picture Canes, Blue Rod Checks, White, Blue Muslin Ground, 1991, 2 ⅞ x 2 In.	403.00
Perthshire, Triple Stack, Millefiori Canes, White Muslin Ground, 5 In.	1062.00
Perthshire, Yellow, Blue, Pink, Green Millefiori, Black Ground, Signed 1997, 3 x 2 ⅛ In.	144.00
Pottery, Woman, Nude, Reclining, Square Base, Green Glaze, 1928, 4 In.	288.00
R, Purple & Yellow Blossoms, Bud & 8 Yellow, Orange & Green Berries, Signed, 2 ¾ x 3 In.	230.00
Red Rose Blossoms, Cobalt Blue Ground, Swirl Spiral Of Black & White, 4 x 4 In.	1955.00
Rosenfeld, Ken, Yellow, Blue, Pink 2-Sided Bouquet, Green Leaves, Pale Blue Ground, 3 ⅜ In.	805.00
Saint Louis, Fruit Basket, 2 ½ x 2 ½ In.	542.00
Salazar, Daniel, Snow Covered Orange Fruit, Branch, Clear Surround, Signed, 1999, 3 ½ x 3 ⅛ In.	236.00
Sautner, Barry, Yellow, White Daffodils, Caterpillars, Yellow Gems, Signed, 1995, 3 ⅜ x 1 ¾ In.	1955.00
Seccombe, Grace, Blue, Orange & Yellow Fish, Coral & White Ground, Signed, 2 ⅛ x 3 In.	1652.00
Seccumbe, G., 5 Red Strawberries, 2 Green Strawberries, 1 Bud, Signed, 2 x 3 In.	1725.00
Silver, Horseshoe & Stirrup, Green Serpentine Base, Marked, England, c.1908, 5 x 4 In.	489.00
St. Louis, 4 Gridel Silhouettes, 11 Millefiori Canes, White Carpet, Signed, 3 x 3 In.	1840.00
St. Louis, Blue Dahlia, Green Leaves, Ruby, Jasper Ground, 2 ¾ In.	531.00
St. Louis, Blue, Purple White, Green Close Pack Millefiori, Signed, 1993, 3 x 2 ⅜ In.	633.00
St. Louis, Conch Shape, France, 6 x 2 x 2 In.	69.00
St. Louis, Dahlia, Faceted, Lime Green, Pulled Glass, Signed, 1970, 2 x 3 In.	311.00
St. Louis, Diamond Shaped Millefiori Patterns, Red, White, Blue, Green, Signed, 1996, 3 x 2 ¼ In.	1121.00
St. Louis, Green, White Cross, Red, White Twists, Millefiori Sections, Signed, 1981, 3 x 2 In.	1323.00
St. Louis, Horizontal Rows Of Millefiori Canes, Pink, Blue, Green & Chartreuse, Signed, 2 x 2 ¾ In.	575.00
St. Louis, Large Blue Dahlia, Yellow Stamen, Green Leaves, 3 x 2 ¼ In.	16100.00
St. Louis, Latticinio Basket, Millefiori Canes, Green, White Twist Trim, Handleless, 1981, 3 ⅞ In.	690.00
St. Louis, Millefiori & Latticinio Rod Chequer, Red Ground, Signed, 3 ½ x 2 ⅝ In.	460.00
St. Louis, Millefiori, Latticinio Coils, Star, Cog, Bull's-Eye Canes, Blue, Signed, 1972, 3 x 3 In.	215.00

Paperweight, Advertising, K.W. Hexter & Co., Everlasting Finish Linings, Celluloid, Ohio, 2 ¾ In. Diam.
$47.00

Showtime Auction Services

Papier-Mache, Lap Desk, Hinged Lid, Mother-Of-Pearl, Architectural Scene, Felt Inset, Victorian, 17 x 13 In.
$183.00

Leslie Hindman Auctioneers

P

TIP

If using a glass shelf to display a paperweight collection, be sure it is strong enough. The ideal size is 18 inches long, 4 inches deep, ¼ inch thick. Paperweights are very heavy, and collectors tend to add "just one more," which overloads the shelf. Glass will become more brittle with age.

Papier-Mache, Milliner's Model, Painted Face, Hair & Bodice, Applied Kidskin Cap, Silk Hat, c.1820, 15 ½ In.
$1896.00

Skinner, Inc.

St. Louis, Multicolor Dahlias, Green Leaves, Rectangular, Signed, 1980, 6 ¾ x 1 ¾ In.	2185.00
St. Louis, Multicolor Flowers, White Latticinio, Red Twists, 6-Sided Facets, 2 ⅞ x 2 ⅜ In.	413.00
St. Louis, Multicolor, Close Packed Millefiori, Signed, 1981, 2 ⅞ x 1 ⅞ In.	708.00
St. Louis, Mushroom, Double Cased, Millefiori, Red & White Double Overlay, Signed, 1978, 4 x 3 In.	1668.00
St. Louis, Mushroom, Pink & White Stave Basket Surrounded By Blue & White Torsade, 2 x 2 ¾ In.	1207.00
St. Louis, Obelisk, Tree Shape, Lampwork Flowers, Multicolor, 1995, 7 ½ In.	2300.00
St. Louis, Piedouche, Concentric Millefiori Rings, Multicolor, Signed, 1989, 3 ¾ In.	1840.00
St. Louis, Piedouche, Concentric Millefiori Rings, White Starburst Ground, Signed, 1992, 3 x 3 In.	1955.00
St. Louis, Pink, Blue Cane, Green, Red Crown Twists, White Latticinio, 2 ¾ x 2 In.	2588.00
St. Louis, Red, Green, Yellow, Blue Crowns, White Latticinio, Signed Can, 1973, 3 x 2 ½ In.	472.00
St. Louis, Sphere, Mounted To Brass Base, Millefiori Canes, Latticinio Ground, 1985, 7 x 3 In.	1500.00
St. Louis, Spiral Latticinio Basket, Lampwork Fruit, Signed, 1993, 4 ¼ x 3 ½ In.	1150.00
St. Louis, Spray Of Bleeding Hearts, Leaves, Pink, Green, Blue, Faceted, Signed, 1986, 2 x 3 In.	367.00
St. Louis, Star Pattern Millefiori, Blue Pad, Red, White Double Overlay, 5-Sided, 1971, 3 x 2 ⅛ In.	431.00
St. Louis, Upright Blue, Pink, White, Green Flowers, Multiple Faceted Egg, Signed, 1991, 3 x 3 ⅞ In.	805.00
St. Louis, Vase On Round Base, Multicolor Circle Design, Signed, Cane, 1985, 6 x 2 In.	750.00
St. Louis, Wafer Dish, Millefiori Base, Green Bowl, White Latticinio Rim, Signed, 1983, 4 x 4 In.	1438.00
St. Louis, White, Blue, Green, Red, Chartreuse Swirl, Central Cane, Signed, 1971, 3 x 2 ⅛ In.	403.00
St. Louis, Zinnia, Pedestal, Red & White Canes, Petals, 1977, 5 x 4 In.	565.00
Stankard, Bellwort Flowers, Blue Flowers, 3 Buds, Glass Ball, Signed, 1986, 2 x 3 In.	452.00
Stankard, Paul, Water Lily, Cobalt Ground, S Cane, 1984, 3 x 2 In.	633.00
Stankard, Paul, Wild Rose, S Cane, 3 x 1 ½ In.	575.00
Stankard, Squash Plant, Vines & Leaves, Glass Ball, 1987, 2 x 4 In.	904.00
Stoneware, Lamb, Sleeping, Brown Glaze, c.1870	875.00
Stoneware, Turtle, Salt Glaze, Cobalt Blue, c.1920, 3 ½ In.	248.00
Strawberries & Blossoms, Honeybee Resting On Ground, Cube Shape, Signed, 2 ¾ x 2 ¾ In.	1610.00
Sulphide, Rooster, Green, Internal Bubbles, 4 In.	115.00
Tarsitano, 5 Tiers Of Blue & Amethyst Petals, Green Leaves, Signed, 1 ⅞ x 2 ¼ In.	747.00
Tarsitano, Blue Flowers, Latticinio Ground, St. Louis, Signed, 1982, 3 In.	489.00
Tarsitano, D., Flower Crescent Bouquet, Flowers, Yellow, Pink, Blue, Amethyst & Red, Signed, 2 x 4 In.	1770.00
Tarsitano, D., Strawberries & Blossoms, Spider Resting On Ground, Signed, 2 x 3 ¼ In.	1725.00
Tarsitano, D., Strawberry, White Blossoms, Leaves, Muslin Ground, Signed DT, 2 ⅜ x 3 ½ In.	1150.00
Tarsitano, Debbie, Pink Blue Flowers, Green Leaves, Clear, Faceted, Magnum, 1986, 4 ¼ In.	920.00
Tarsitano, Debbie, Pink, Blue, Purple Flowers, Opaque Blue Ground, Signed, 3 ½ x 2 ½ In.	1150.00
Tarsitano, Debbie, Yellow, Pink, Blue Flowers, White Basket Ground, 1992, 2 ½ x 1 ½ In.	502.00
Tarsitano, Delmo, Central Pink Flower, Millefiori Surround, Signed, 3 ½ x 2 ½ In.	1495.00
Tarsitano, Delmo, Green Zucchini Plant, Green, Jasper Ground, 1978, 2 ⅝ In.	288.00
Tarsitano, Delmo, Red, White Strawberry Flowers, Blue Millefiori Base, Fruit, 3 In.	1150.00
Trabucco, V., Red Raspberries, Blossom, Buds, Green Leaves, Signed, 3 ⅜ x 3 ½ In.	805.00
Trabucco, Victor, Faceted, Red Flower, Branches, Wavy Circle Shape, Signed, 1987, 3 x 5 In.	469.00
Trabucco, Victor, Pink Flower, 2 Buds, Green Leaves, Gray Ground, Signed, 2 x 1 ¾ In.	92.00
Trabucco, Victor, Red, Blue Berries, Pink Flower, Leaves, White Lace Ground, 1997, 3 ¾ x 3 ½ In.	633.00
Ward, Mayauel, Blueberries, Pink, Purple, Blue Flowers, Black Ground, Signed, 1997, 3 x 3 In.	531.00
Yaffa, Paul, Todd, Yellow Purple Upright Flowers, Butterflies, Memories, Signed, 1988, 3 ½ x 3 ¼ In.	177.00
Ysart, Flower Bouquet, Blue Ribbon, Lavender, Signed, 2 x 3 In.	565.00
Ysart, Paul, Blue, White, Pink, Green Millefiori, Snowflake Pattern, Cobalt Blue Ground, 3 In.	649.00
Ysart, Paul, Dragonfly, White & Gold Wings, Pink Pulled Glass, Blue Millefiori, Brown, Signed, 3 In.	283.00

PAPIER-MACHE is made from paper mixed with glue, chalk, and other ingredients, then molded and baked. It becomes very hard and can be painted. Boxes, trays, and furniture were made of papier-mache. Some of the nineteenth-century pieces were decorated with mother-of-pearl. Papier-mache is still being used to make small toys, figures, candy containers, boxes, and other giftwares. Furniture made of papier-mache is listed in the Furniture category.

Dog, Salon, White Fur, Kid Cover, Amber Glass Eyes, France, c.1900, 3 & 5 In., 2 Piece	69.00
Figurine, Box, Mother-Of-Pearl Inlays, Flower Sprays, Black Ground, 1800s, 11 x 11 In.	58.00
Figurine, Buddha, Gilt, Lacquer, Seated, Lotus Pedestal Base, Knotted Hair, 1800s, 22 ½ x 16 In.	246.00
Frame, Victorian, Cartouche Shape, Mounted Shelf, Hand Painted Flowers, 1800s, 13 x 10 In.	59.00
Inkstand, Mother-Of-Pearl Inlay, Black Lacquer, Drawer, 3 ¼ x 12 In.	59.00
Lap Desk, Hinged Lid, Mother-Of-Pearl, Architectural Scene, Felt Inset, Victorian, 17 x 13 In. *illus*	183.00
Mask, Black Man's Head, Wearing Top Hat, Painted, c.1900, 16 In.	521.00
Mask, Scarlet & Black Lacquer, Gilt, Signed, Japan, c.1900, 14 In.	326.00
Milliner's Model, Painted Face, Hair & Bodice, Applied Kidskin Cap, Silk Hat, c.1820, 15 ½ In. *illus*	1896.00
Punch Head, Face, Jester Hat, Red & Yellow, c.1900, 15 In.	575.00
Tray, Black, Gilt & Mother-Of-Pearl, Bridge, 5 Pagodas, Shaped Edges, 1800s, 13 x 18 In.	148.00
Tray, Boston Terrier, Oval, c.1880, 16 In.	1600.00
Tray, Chinoiserie, Inlaid Mother-Of-Pearl, Jennens & Bettridge, 15 x 19 In.	418.00

Tray, Dish Top, Shaped Edge, Gilt, Mother-Of-Pearl, X-Stretcher Stand, England, 1800s, 32 In.	948.00
Tray, Flowers, Birds, Gold Border, Black Ground, England, 1800s, 18 ½ x 24 In.	474.00
Tray, Gilt, Ebonized Stand, Splayed Legs, c.1850, 23 x 33 In.	296.00
Tray, Lobed, Oval, Scenic, Lake Kilarney, Gilt Border, Ireland, c.1850, 24 x 19 In.	704.00
Tray, Ogee Shape Rim, Oval, Waterway Landscape, Trees, Leaves, Chinoiserie, c.1800, 24 x 32 In.	889.00
Tray, Terrier, Scalloped Rim, c.1870, 14 x 16 In.	2800.00
Tray, Winter Coach Scene, Oval, Clay, London, England, c.1850, 30 ¾ In.	385.00

PARASOL, *see Umbrella category.*

PARIAN is a fine-grained, hard-paste porcelain named for the marble it resembles. It was first made in England in 1846 and gained in favor in the United States about 1860. Figures, tea sets, vases, and other items were made of Parian at many English and American factories.

Bust, Abraham Lincoln, c.1876, 9 In.	711.00
Bust, Angel, Winged Cherub, Square Plinths, 9 In., Pair	711.00
Bust, Apollo Belvedere, 2 Parts, Sideward Glancing, England, 1861, 13 ½ x 9 ½ In.	645.00
Bust, Henry Wadsworth Longfellow, Impressed, England, c.1850, 9 In.	123.00
Bust, Oliver Wendell Holmes, Square Base, c.1875, 10 In.	184.00
Bust, President James A. Garfield, Impressed James Wilson London, c.1890, 12 In.	375.00
Bust, Princess Diana, Gold Base, Signed, 30 In.	6500.00
Bust, Woman, Rococo Dress, Elaborate Hairstyle, Straw Hat, Flowers, Socle Base, 43 ¼ In.	861.00
Figurine, Benjamin Franklin, Rectangular Cut Corner Base, c.1825, 8 In.	950.00
Figurine, Bisque, Boy, With Dog, 1800s, 15 x 9 In.	240.00
Figurine, Children, Carrying Basket, Grapes, Leaves, Wheat, c.1865, 10 x 10 In.	850.00
Figurine, Maiden, Standing, Pink Enamel, Gilt Trim, Against The Wind, c.1865, 10 In.	296.00
Figurine, Peter & Cornelius, c.1855, 14 ¼ x 11 ½ In.	338.00
Figurine, Poison'd Wound Edward I, 2 Women, Attending To Wound, c.1850, 22 x 15 In.	1599.00
Figurine, Poodle, Standing, Side-Glancing, Basket Of Fruit In Mouth, 1850-58, 9 In., Pair	5333.00
Figurine, Sappho, Grecian Beauty, Turtleback Lyre, c.1873, 32 In.	154.00
Figurine, Woman, Feeding Hound, Man, Bowl Of Water, Oval Base, Fluted, 1800s, 16 In., Pair	889.00
Figurine, Young Woman, Standing, Hand To Cheek, France, c.1900, 13 ¾ In.	59.00
Group, 2 Soldiers, Civil War Era Attire, One More Shot, c.1900, 9 ½ In.	2574.00
Group, 3 Classical Women, Child, Doves, Flowers, White, Column, 12 x 11 In.	470.00
Group, Man, Woman, Child, 1860s Attire, Taking The Oath & Drawing Rations, c.1900, 19 x 13 In.	2340.00
Group, Rock Of Ages, Draped Woman, Singing To Cross, c.1875, 17 ½ x 10 ½ In.	430.00
Pitcher, 8-Panel, White Ground, Vines & Flowers, 1853, 5 In.	119.00
Pitcher, Fern, Flowers, 1880s, 8 ½ In.	220.00
Pitcher, Mulberry, Cast, Classical Style, White Body, Molded Spout, Handle, 8 ¾ In.	24.00
Pitcher, Water, Renaissance Revival, Knights, Maidens, 1860, 10 In.	431.00
Syrup, Vertical Scrolled Leaf Pattern, Stippled Ground, c.1853, 6 In.	61.00

PARIS, Vieux Paris, or Old Paris, is porcelain ware that is known to have been made in Paris in the eighteenth or early nineteenth century. These porcelains have no identifying mark but can be recognized by the whiteness of the porcelain and the lines and decorations. Gold decoration is often used.

Bowl, Vegetable, Dome Lid, Octagonal Shape, Enamel Flower, Gilt Highlights, 1800s, 7 x 10 In.	89.00
Clock, Rococo Style, Flowers, Multicolor Enamel, Stand, Mark, 1800s, 15 In.	326.00
Clock, Shelf, Bronze Flame Finial, Flowers, Green, Gilt, Movement, Jacob Petit, c.1850, 14 x 10 In.	1434.00
Coffeepot, White, Gilt, Leaf Decoration, Griffon Spout, 7 In.	86.00
Compote, Pink Coral Border, Romantic Landscape Center, 9 In., Pair	69.00
Jar, Dome Lid, Fruit Shape Finial, White, Green Vertical Stripes, Flower Reserve, Gilt, 7 ½ In.	98.00
Jardiniere, Flaconer, Peasant Family, Cylindrical, Gilt Black Ground, c.1825, 6 ½ x 6 ¾ In., Pair	246.00
Perfumer, Figural, 1400s Bearded Nobleman, Holding Portrait, Multicolor, Gilt, c.1875, 14 In.	369.00
Platter, Great Seal Of The United States, Burgundy Border, Oval, c.1825, 10 In.	700.00
Tureen, Lid, Underplate, Boat Shape, Leaves, Berries, Gilt, Green, Red, c.1820, 4 x 11 In., Pair	676.00
Urn, Castle Landscape, White, Gold Trim, Flared-Out Rim, Dish & Pedestal Base, 11 In., Pair.	345.00
Urn, Classical Scene, Raised Gilt Scrolls, Winged Woman Handles, c.1850, 17 In., Pair	1610.00
Urn, Italy Landscapes, Artist In Tavern Panel, Multicolor, Gilt, Campana Shape, c.1825, 10 In.	861.00
Urn, Landscape, Gilt Rim, Handles, 1800s, 7 ½ In., Pair	152.00
Vase, 1600s Couple, By Window Reserves, Relief Mask Handles, 12 ½ In., Pair	293.00
Vase, Baluster, Oval Scene Panels, Gilt Flower Cartouche, Magenta Ground, c.1890, 26 ¾ In., Pair	861.00
Vase, Campana Shape, Italy Country House Panels, Gilt Handles, Base, c.1825, 12 ¾ x 9 ½ In.	184.00
Vase, Couple Fishing Cartouche, Blue, Gilt Rim, Borders, Handles, c.1890, 13 In., Pair	374.00
Vase, Flared, Applied Nymphs, Garden Panels, Multicolor, Gilt, Enamel, 1800s, 17 In., Pair	1778.00
Vase, Flower Cartouche, Blue & Cafe Au Lait, Scroll Handles, Jacob Petit, c.1850, 16 ¾ In., Pair	3286.00
Vase, Flowers & Fruit, Relief Molded Leaves, Painted Flowers, Gilt, c.1860, 14 In., Pair .... *illus*	403.00

Paris, Vase, Flowers & Fruit, Relief Molded Leaves, Painted Flowers, Gilt, c.1860, 14 In., Pair
$403.00

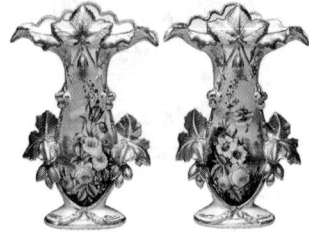

James D. Julia Inc.

Paris, Vase, Spill, Classical Landscape, Gilt Borders, Removable Base, c.1825, 9 ½ In., Pair
$1673.00

Neal Auction Co.

P

Patent Model, Wheel Plow, No. 220701, Wood, Iron, Brass, P.L. Case, Oct. 21, 1879, 4 ¾ x 12 x 8 ¾ In. $1121.00

Conestoga Auction Co., Inc.

Pate-Sur-Pate, Vase, Stags, Woodland, Butterflies On Reverse, Snake Base, Signed, E. Steele, 1800s, 8 ¾ In. $826.00

Brunk Auctions

Paul Revere, Tile, Hull Street Galloupe House, Frame, Fannie Levine, S.E.G., 1909, 3 ½ x 3 ½ In. $1240.00

Rago Arts & Auction Center

Paul Revere, Vase, Landscape, Yellow Ground, Initials, S.E.G., 1917, 10 x 4 ½ In. $4650.00

Rago Arts & Auction Center

Vase, Garniture, Daisies, Gilt Butterfly, Periwinkle Ground, Flared, Scalloped, 8 In., Pair	277.00
Vase, Garniture, Flower Cartouche, Green Ground, Gilt, Scrolled Arms, c.1850, 15 ½ In., Pair	369.00
Vase, Painted Country Landscape, Hourglass Neck, Ebonized Base, Gilt Handles, 17 In.	74.00
Vase, Period Couple Medallion, Pink Ground, Applied Gold Vines & Fruit, Scalloped Rim, 17 In.	259.00
Vase, Potpourri, Neoclassical, Couple, Black, Mask Handles, Reticulated, Gilt, c.1825, 8 In., Pair	184.00
Vase, Spill, Classical Landscape, Gilt Borders, Removable Base, c.1825, 9 ½ In., Pair ....*illus*	1673.00
Vase, Spill, Landscapes, Gilt Bands, c.1820, 6 ⅜ x 5 ⅞ In., Pair	538.00
Vase, Woman's Portrait Panel, Blue, Griffin, Metal Base, Handles, 20 In., Pair	622.00

PATE-DE-VERRE is an ancient technique in which glass is made by blending and refining powdered glass of different colors into molds. The process was revived by French glassmakers, especially Galle, around the end of the nineteenth century.

Lamp, Mushroom, Yellow Mottled, Orange, Blue, White, 1900s, 21 In., Pair	478.00
Sculpture, Venus, Female Nude, Russet, Engraved George Despret, 12 x 3 In.	1116.00

PATENT MODELS were required as part of a patent application for a United States patent until 1880. In 1926 the stored patent models were sold as a group by the U.S. Patent Office and individual models are now appearing in the marketplace.

Bill File, Metal Document Spike, No. 223546, James Shannon, 1879	6500.00
Billiard Cushion, Rubber, Wood, No. 118288, 1871	895.00
Card Rack, No. 119995, 1871	995.00
Curtain Fixture, No. 152271, 1874	895.00
Door Securer, No. 103068, Brass, 1870	745.00
File Folder, Metal, No. 284534, John Blankman, Applied 1883	675.00
Furniture Spring, Metal, Wood, No. 147048, William T. Doremus, 1874	795.00
Hydraulic Elevator, Wood, Brass Screws, Tag, Karl Fletcher, Jan. 28, 1879, 12 x 6 In.	944.00
Inkstand, No. 22582, George M. Prentiss, c.1858	1225.00
Iodine Distiller, From Seaweed, Wood, Brass, Copper, No. 167410, July 20, 1875	299.00
Liquid Meter, No. 107769, Brass, 1870	1495.00
Lithographic Press Damping Apparatus, Wood, Steel, Brass, Rubber, No. 151688, P. Ehrogott, 1874	99 5.00
Marine Propeller, Brass, Original Tag, Signed Wm. D. Smith, Mar., 1874, 7 x 7 ½ In.	826.00
Mercurial Pressure Regulator, Iron, Steel, No. 102464, Matthew, 1870	1125.00
Pen Rack, Wood, Metal, Spring, No. 73448, James M. Keep, Applied 1866	625.00
Pocket Writing Desk, Metal, Wood, No. 35781, A. Ritter, July 1, 1862	1275.00
Printing Press Fly Frame, Wood, Metal, No. 087695, Theodore Mead, 1869	1125.00
Racing Boat Steering Device, No. 148434, Charles Elliott, 1874	2095.00
Smoke Burning Furnace, Tin, Paint, No. 141574, C. McGinniss, W. Naylor, 1873	1345.00
Steam Gauge, No. 68849, Brass, 1867	1195.00
Wheel Plow, No. 220701, Wood, Iron, Brass, P.L. Case, Oct. 21, 1879, 4 ¾ x 12 x 8 ¾ In. .....*illus*	1121.00
Whirligig, Jockey & Horse, Cast Iron, Steel, 8 Paddle Blades	4600.00

PATE-SUR-PATE means paste on paste. The design was made by painting layers of slip on the ceramic piece until a relief decoration was formed. The method was developed at the Sevres factory in France about 1850. It became even more famous at the English Minton factory about 1870. It has since been used by many potters to make both pottery and porcelain wares.

Jar, Cover, Cylindrical, Gilt Trim, Leafy Pinecones, Dark Teal Ground, c.1900, 5 In.	1896.00
Pitcher, Brown Glaze, Young Man, Bird, Smokestack Bottom, Twisted Square Handle, 7 In.	518.00
Plaque, Nude, Cobalt Blue, Embossed Silver & Gilt Frame, Limoges, France, 1900s, 9 ¾ x 7 In.	240.00
Plaque, Round, 3 Musical Cherubs, Blue Ground, Limoges, c.1900, 5 In. Diam	98.00
Plaque, Veiled Nude Woman, Water's Edge, Tambourine, Brass Frame, 1900s, 8 x 5 In., Pair	399.00
Teapot, Dome Lid, Baluster, Lavender & Ivory Glaze, Gilt, S-Scroll Handle, Figures, 11 In.	633.00
Vase, Baluster, Greek Woman, Cupid's Basket, Gilt Garland, Handles, Heubach, 9 x 5 In.	316.00
Vase, Bulbous, Faceted, Terra-Cotta, Branch Shape Handles, Grapevines, Putti, Footed, 8 In.	403.00
Vase, Classical Maiden, Basket Of Flowers, 1900s, 5 In.	338.00
Vase, Drape Green, Flattened Oval, Applied Enamel Classical Figures, 9 ¼ In.	173.00
Vase, Louis XVI Style, Gilt Bronze Mounts, Celadon Bowl, Flowers, Husk Handles, 11 In., Pair	351.00
Vase, Stags, Woodland, Butterflies On Reverse, Snake Base, Signed, E. Steele, 1800s, 8 ¾ In. .....*illus*	826.00

PAUL REVERE POTTERY was made at several locations in and around Boston, Massachusetts, between 1906 and 1942. The pottery was operated as a settlement house program for teenage girls. Many pieces were signed *S.E.G.* for Saturday Evening Girls. The artists concentrated on children's dishes and tiles. Decorations were outlined in black and filled with color.

Bookends, Woodland Scene, Cottage, Curved Panel, S.E.G., 1923, 4 x 5 In.	1778.00
Bowl, Centerpiece, Blossom, Blue Green Matte Glaze, Leaf Rim, S.E.G., 1926, 13 In.	326.00
Bowl, Triple Chick, Green Border, Albina Mangini, S.E.G., 1911, 6 x 1 ¾ In.	420.00

Bowl, Water Lilies, Cuerda Seca, Sarah Gelner, 1914, 2 x 8 ½ In.		1612.00
Breakfast Set, Rabbit, Green, Cream, Blue, Inscribed, Victoria, Her Plate, 3 Piece		521.00
Jar, Lid, Globular, Mottled Blue, c.1920, 6 ½ In.		200.00
Pitcher, Blue & Ocher Streaks, Oval, Tapered, Wide Rim, 7 In.		326.00
Pitcher, Gunmetal Black, Marked, 3 In.		95.00
Plate, Duck, Blue Band, Freddy His'n, S.E.G., 6 ¼ In.		504.00
Tile, Hull Street Galloupe House, Frame, Fannie Levine, S.E.G., 1909, 3 ½ x 3 ½ In. *illus*		1240.00
Vase, Brown Matte Glaze, Paneled, S.E.G., 7 ½ x 8 ½ In.		120.00
Vase, Cylindrical, Satin Blue, Speckled, 10 ½ In.		495.00
Vase, Landscape, Yellow Ground, Initials, S.E.G., 1917, 10 x 4 ½ In. *illus*		4650.00

PEACHBLOW glass was made by several factories beginning in the 1880s. New England peachblow is a one-layer glass shading from red to white. Mt. Washington peachblow shades from pink to bluish-white. Hobbs, Brockunier and Company of Wheeling, West Virginia, made Coral glass that they marketed as Peach Blow. It shades from yellow to peach and is lined with white glass. Reproductions of all types of peachblow have been made. Related pieces may be listed under Gundersen and Webb Peachblow.

Biscuit Jar, Rose Shaded Ground, Gilt Flowers, Silver Plate Collar, Handle, 8 In.	460.00
Celery Vase, Coralene Coral Overlay, 6 ¼ In.	400.00
Cruet, Enameled Fish, Amber Handle & Stopper, 7 In.	403.00
Cruet, Wheeling, Teepee Shape, Faceted Stopper, Loop Handle, 7 In.	489.00
Paperweight, Apple Shape, New England, 2 ½ In. *illus*	460.00
Pitcher, Baluster, Ruffled Rim, Amber Loop Handle, Deep Red To Butter, 5 In.	403.00
Pitcher, Deep Pink, White, Smokestack, Loop Handle, Ruffled Rim, Ribbed, 4 ½ In.	443.00
Pitcher, Wheeling, Bulbous, Baluster, Shaped Rim, Amber Handle, Glossy, 8 In.	460.00
Salt & Pepper, Stand, Rose Shaded To Pale Pink, Silver Plated Stand, Wm Rogers, c.1886	575.00
Sugar & Creamer, Optic Ribbed, Applied Loop Handles, Libbey, 2 ½ In. *illus*	920.00
Toothpick Holder, Pink Satin, Cylinder, Ruffled Tricornered Rim, 2 ¼ In.	374.00
Toothpick Holder, Wheeling, Bulbous, Round Foot, 2 ½ In.	201.00
Vase, Amber Glass Griffin Holder, Hobbs, Brockunier, 9 In. *illus*	633.00
Vase, Bud, Rose, Glossy, 8 In.	197.00
Vase, Coral, Hobbs, Brockunier, 6 ¼ x 6 In.	700.00
Vase, Footed, Quadrafold Rim, Robin's-Egg Blue To Pink, Mt.Washington, 7 In.	3250.00
Vase, Glossy, Peach To Red, Narrow Neck, 8 In.	837.00
Vase, Lily, Rose Pink, White, Rolled Ruffled Rim, 9 In.	403.00
Vase, Morgan, Amber Satin Glass, Griffin Base, New England, 10 In.	1300.00
Vase, Pink Shaded To Blue White, Shaped Neck, Victorian, 9 In. *illus*	690.00
Vase, Satin, Porcelain Griffin Base, Morgan, Hobbs, Brockunier, 9 ½ In.	1000.00
Vase, Shaded, Rows Of Coralene Beading, Bulbous, 7 x 4 ¼ In.	119.00
Vase, Stick, Bulbous Bottom, Mahogany Red To Blush Red To Soft Butter, Acid Finish, 9 In.	920.00
Vase, Trumpet, Tricorn Top, Spread Foot, 9 x 4 In.	270.00
Vase, Wheeling, Morgan, Fuchsia Neck, Yellow Body, 8 In.	460.00
Water Set, Blossom & Branch Enamel, 2 Tumblers, 8 In.	175.00

PEANUTS is the title of a comic strip created by cartoonist Charles M. Schulz (1922–2000). The strip, drawn by Schulz from 1950 to 2000, features a group of children, including Charlie Brown and his sister Sally, Lucy Van Pelt and her brother Linus, Peppermint Patty, and Pig Pen, and an imaginative and independent beagle named Snoopy. The Peanuts gang has also been featured in books, television shows, and a Broadway musical.

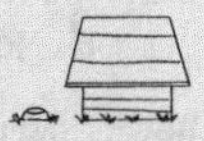

Activity Book, Snoopy, Doghouse, Kohl's Department Store, Landoll, Inc., 10 x 8 In.	10.00
Bank, Snoopy Asleep, Doghouse, Determined Productions, 1969, 4 ½ x 4 ½ In.	14.00
Bank, Snoopy Sailor, Rowboat, Composition, Paint, c.1965, 5 In.	25.00
Bank, Snoopy, Resting Atop Rainbow, Multicolor, Ceramic, 1966, 5 x 5 ¼ In.	20.00
Book, Christmas Is Time Together, Comic Strip Characters, Charles Schulz, 1st Edition, 1964	32.00
Book, The Joy Of A Peanuts Christmas, Charles Schulz, Hallmark Cards, 2000, 120 Pages	19.00
Bookends, Snoopy, Woodstock, Heart Shape, Red, White, Yellow, 1972, 4 ½ x 4 ¼ In.	34.00
Canister, Lid, Glass, Snoopy, Woodstock, Rainbows, Peanuts Character Corp., 1958, 8 ½ x 4 In.	20.00
Cookie Cutter, Snoopy, Charlie Brown, Heart Shape, United Feature, 1958, 4 ½ x 4 ¾ In., Pair	16.00
Date Book, Lettered Peanuts, Orange, Blue, Red Spiral Bound, 1972, 13 x 10 In.	24.00
Doll, Charlie Brown, Soft Plastic, United Features Syndicate Inc., 1966, 6 In.	11.00
Handkerchief, Let's Make Bread, Characters, Ingredients, Japan, Hallmark, c.1966, 11 x 10 ½ In.	9.00
Jigsaw Puzzle, Snoopy Superstar Baseball Player, Wood, Playskool, 6 Piece	12.00
Lunch Box, Charlie Brown, Snoopy, Lucy, Tree, King-Seeley Thermos Co., 9 x 7 In.	25.00

Peachblow, Paperweight, Apple Shape, New England, 2 ½ In.
$460.00

Peachblow, Sugar & Creamer, Optic Ribbed, Applied Loop Handles, Libbey, 2 ½ In.
$920.00

Peachblow, Vase, Amber Glass Griffin Holder, Hobbs, Brockunier, 9 In.
$633.00

P

TIP

Wood-boring beetle larvae sometimes find their way into furniture in a house. The adult beetles emerge in July or August and fly to other pieces of furniture. Watch for signs of pinhead-size holes or sawdust. Spray immediately and treat with appropriate bug-killing chemicals.

Peachblow, Vase, Pink Shaded To Blue White, Shaped Neck, Victorian, 9 In. $690.00

James D. Julia Inc.

Peanuts, Pin, The In Crowd, Peanuts Characters, United Features Syndicate, 1966, 3 In. $108.00

Hake's Americana & Collectibles

Peking Glass, Vase, Snowflake, Red, Pavilions, Peacocks, Pine, Clouds, Figures, Chinese, 9 ½ In. $8295.00

Skinner, Inc.

Pen, Wipe, Owl, Felt, c.1890, 6 In. $121.00

Garth's Auctions, Inc.

Mug, Irish Coffee, Snoopy, Yellow Woodstock, Golfing, c.1960, 4 ¼ In.	25.00
Mug, Lucy, Pink Ground, Musical, Schmid, Japan, United Features Syndicate, 1971, 4 ¼ In.	35.00
Mug, Snoopy, Woodstock, Life Is Pure Joy, White, Fire-King, Anchor Hocking, 4 x 4 In.	30.00
Music Box, Schroeder, Baby Grand Piano, Wood, Carved, Paint, Anri, Italy, 1968, 5 ¼ x 4 ¼ In.	150.00
Music Box, Snoopy Red Baron, In Plane, Wood, Metal, Schmid Co., 1968, 9 In.	94.00
Music Box, Snoopy, Top Hat, Plays Happy Days Are Here Again, Porcelain, Metal, 1979, 7 ½ In.	98.00
Nodder, Lucy, Red Dress, Composition, 1952, 3 ½ In.	49.00
Nodder, Snoopy, Joe Cool Shirt, Composition, 1960s, 4 ¼ In.	45.00
Ornament, Snoopy, Carrying Christmas Tree, 3 In.	22.00
Ornament, Snoopy, Ice Skating, Glass, Waterford, Box, Cloth Bag, 3 x 3 ½ In.	26.00
Ornament, Snoopy, Santa Sack, Holy, Ceramic, Black, White, 2 ½ In.	25.00
Ornament, Snoopy, Tennis Player, Made In Korea, United Features Syndicate, 1966, 3 In.	25.00
Ornament, Snoopy, Woodstock, Embossed, Round, Metal, United Features Inc., c.1965, 2 ¼ In.	30.00
Ornament, Snoopy, Woodstock, Glitter Hats, Candy Canes, Hallmark, 1989, 2 ¾ In.	22.00
Ornament, Spike, Snoopy's Brother, Ceramic, Japan, c.1970, 2 ¾ In.	39.00
Ornament, Woodstock, Fire Engine, Santa Cap, Ceramic, Determined Prod., 1979, 2 ½ x 2 ½ In.	18.00
Ornament, Woodstock, Yellow, Red, Ceramic, Gold Hanger, 2 ⅞ In.	20.00
Pajama Holder, Charlie Brown, Cotton, Felt, Hanger, Simon Simple Originals, 1956, 28 x 17 ½ In.	75.00
Pin, Snoopy Hugging Charlie Brown, Metal, United Features, 1972, 1 ½ x 1 ¼ In.	14.00
Pin, Snoopy Hugging Woodstock, Metal, United Features Syndicate, 1972, 1 ½ x 1 In.	14.00
Pin, The In Crowd, Peanuts Characters, United Features Syndicate, 1966, 3 In. ....*illus*	108.00
Planter, Snoopy, 4 Alphabet Panels, Square, Ceramic, Peanuts Character Corp., c.1965, 3 In.	25.00
Planter, Snoopy, Suitcase, Dish On Head, Woodstock On Nose, Ceramic, 7 ½ In.	25.00
Poster, Snoopy Come Home, Snoopy, Woodstock, Runaways, Blue, Movie, 27 x 41 In., 1972	80.00
Snow Cone Machine, Snoopy, Lucy, Unused, Box, Kid Dimension, 1991	49.00
Thermos, Lucy, Charlie Brown, Linus, Playing Baseball, 1959, 6 ¾ In.	16.00
Tie, Snoopy, Joe Cool Gridlock, Diamond Plaid, Burgundy, United Features, 1980s, Width 4 In.	10.00
Toy, Rattle, Snoopy Asleep, Pink, Green Ground, c.1966, 4 x 3 In.	20.00
Toy, Snoopy, As Astronaut, Rubber Head, Plastic Body, 1969, 9 In.	100.00
Toy, Snoopy, Cowboy Attire, Rubber, Made In Taiwan, United Features, c.1970, 5 ½ In.	14.00
Toy, Snoopy, Woodstock, On Skateboard, Plastic, Peanuts Characters Corp., c.1970, 4 In.	15.00
Toy, Woodstock, Flying Trapeze, Paper Label, Avia Toy Co., Hong Kong, c.1970, 5 ½ In.	24.00
Tumbler, Snoopy, Vote For The American Beagle, Red, White, Blue, Anchor Hocking, 6 x 2 ½ In.	30.00
Wastebasket, Snoopy, Charlie Brown, Lucy, Dark Green Ground, Cheinco, 1970, 13 x 11 ¾ In.	36.00
Wristwatch, Lucy On Face, Windup, Suede Band, 1 x 6 ¾ In.	35.00

PEARL items listed here are made of the natural mother-of-pearl from shells. Such natural pearl has been used to decorate furniture and small utilitarian objects for centuries. The glassware known as mother-of-pearl is listed by that name. Opera glasses made with natural pearl shell are listed under Opera Glasses.

Tray, Inlay, Damascus, 15 ½ In.	47.00

PEARLWARE is an earthenware made by Josiah Wedgwood in 1779. It was copied by other potters in England. Pearlware is only slightly different in color from creamware and for many years collectors have confused the terms. Wedgwood pieces are listed in the Wedgwood category in this book. Most pearlware with mocha designs is listed under Mocha.

Pearl

Bowl, Flowers, Branches, c.1806, 4 x 9 In.	436.00
Creamer, Cow Mottled Brown, c.1820, 6 x 7 ¾ In.	413.00
Cup & Saucer, Raindrop Style, Brown, Handleless, c.1800	118.00
Figurine, Dog, Dalmatian, Wood Base, Staffordshire, 5 In., Pair	119.00
Figurine, Dog, Spaniel, Seated, Staffordshire, c.1805, 4 ¾ x 8 ¾ In.	2607.00
Figurine, Lion, Front Paw Resting On Lavender Ball, Rectangular Base, 10 x 14 In.	1150.00
Figurine, Lion, Paw On Orb, Paint, Staffordshire, 8 ¾ x 11 In.	1458.00
Figurine, Spring, Woman Holding Garland, c.1820, 12 ¼ In.	167.00
Flowerpot, Stand, Sponged In Design, Green Reeded Rim, Flower Garland, c.1785, 6 In.	590.00
Jug, Bacchus & Pan, Green Dolphin, Monkey Forming Handle, Wood Family, c.1785, 13 In.	2242.00
Jug, Bacchus & Pan, Lion's Skin, Grapevine, Dolphin Spout, Monkey Handle, c.1795, 13 In.	2242.00
Jug, Figural, Snuff Taker, Seated, Hat, Cream, Scrolling Blue, Marked, 10 ½ In.	115.00
Jug, Milk, Little Jockey, Footed, c.1840, 2 ¾ In.	110.00
Jug, White, Black Transfer, Boy, Gun, Dog, 1800, 2 ½ x 2 In.	184.00
Jug, Woman Standing In Rowboat, Distant Ship, Multicolor, Transfer Printed, c.1815, 11 In.	400.00
Lamp, Fluid, Figural, Atlas, World On Shoulders, Staffordshire, 11 In.	889.00
Loving Cup, Farm Implements, Wheat Sheaf, Jonathan Warrington, 1802, 4 ½ In.	132.00
Mold, Jelly, Gillyflower, Flower Sprigs, Grape Bunch Shape, Oval, Rounded Underside, c.1780, 7 In.	760.00

Mug, Christening, A Present For Mary, Staffordshire, c.1830, 2 ½ In.		550.00
Pitcher, Black & White Transfer, Buckingham Palace, c.1790, 12 ¾ In.		418.00
Plaque, Circular, 2 Cows, Dairy Maid, Winged Putto, Flowers, 1810-20, 7 In.		413.00
Plaque, Round, Black Monkey, Cobalt Blue Coat, Vine Border, c.1820, 7 In.		265.00
Plate, Christmas Day, Scalloped Rim, Staffordshire, Molded Flower Border, c.1850, 5 In.		325.00
Plate, Name, Mary, Octagonal, Staffordshire, c.1830, 4 ½ In.		295.00
Sugar, Cover, White Ground, Pink Flowers, Green Leaves, Ball Finial, 1800s, 5 In.		60.00
Tankard, America Independent 1776, Raised Letters, Floral Band, Curved Stripes, 5 In.		2950.00
Tankard, Cylindrical, Loop Handle, Dotted Fish Scale Design, Bits Of Clay, c.1795, 6 In.		590.00
Teapot, Oblong, Octagonal, Molded Decoration, Swan Finial, c.1800, 5 ½ In.		147.00
Vase, Hand Shape, 5 Cylindrical Nozzles, Blue & White, Flowers, Leaves, 7 In., Pair		590.00

PEKING GLASS is a Chinese cameo glass first made popular in the eighteenth century. The Chinese have continued to make this layered glass in the old manner, and many new pieces are now available that could confuse the average buyer.

Bottle, Bowl Shape, White, Domed Jadeite & Brass Stopper, Chinese, 1800s, 2 ¼ In.		207.00
Bottle, Ruby Red, Crane In Trees, Flowers, Butterfly, Coral Stopper, 4 ½ In.		497.00
Bowl, Lobed, Carved Flower Relief, Yellow, Raised Wood Stand, 1900s, 2 ½ x 6 In., Pair		299.00
Bowl, Quatrefoil Shape, Blue, Marked, 8 In.		12200.00
Bowl, Sparrows, Prunus Branches, Yellow, Wood Stand, Chinese, 3 x 7 In.		296.00
Bowl, White, Green Leaf, Wood Base, 2 ½ x 4 ½ In.		180.00
Bowl, Yellow, Carved, Lotus Flowers, Ducks, Wood Stand, 2 ½ x 6 In.		500.00
Bowl, Yellow, Dragon Design, Wooden Stands, Flared Rim, 3 x 8 In., Pair		7050.00
Bowl, Yellow, Hand Cut, Embossed Design, 1800s, 6 ¼ In.		1800.00
Censer, Dome Lid, Round Dragon Finial, Lion's Head Handles, 3 Legs, Indigo Blue, 1800s, 9 In.		11500.00
Jar, Lid, Cobalt Blue, Iridescent Ground, Blooming Trees, Birds, Wave Design, Overlay, 5 In.		89.00
Jar, Lid, Figures, Houses, Landscape, Red, White, 1900s, 6 ½ In., Pair		1075.00
Saucer, Ash Pink, Chinese, 3 ½ In.		153.00
Snuff Bottle, Amber, 19th Century, 2 ½ In.		100.00
Snuff Bottle, Beige To Opaque White, Metal Wire Cap, Spoon, 2 ¾ x 2 In.		195.00
Snuff Bottle, Birds, Blossoms, Spattered Gold Ground, Brown Scrolls, Masks, 3 In.		295.00
Snuff Bottle, Blue, Round, White Rose Quartz Stopper, 2 ¼ x 2 ¾ In.		385.00
Snuff Bottle, Blue, Silver & Cork Stopper, Inset Green Stone, 1 ½ x 2 ¾ In.		110.00
Snuff Bottle, Figures, Landscape, Flat, Green Stopper, 1 ½ x 3 In.		550.00
Snuff Bottle, Flattened Oval, Carved Brown To Orange To White, Flowers, 2 ½ x 1 ½ In.		178.00
Snuff Bottle, Globular, Golden Hue, Bubbles, 19th Century, 2 ¼ In.		100.00
Snuff Bottle, Pink, Black To White, Branches, Butterflies, 2 ¼ x 1 ⅔ In.		408.00
Snuff Bottle, Rectangular, Orange Hue, 19th Century, 3 ¼ In.		250.00
Snuff Bottle, Red, Amethyst Stopper, Bulbous, 1800s, 1 ¾ x 2 ½ In.		248.00
Snuff Bottle, Translucent White, Red Fruit Branches, Monkeys, Jade Stopper, 3 In.		236.00
Snuff Bottle, White Ground, Multicolor Animals, Flattened, 2 ¾ x 1 ¾ In.		178.00
Snuff Bottle, Woman, Nude, Resting, Enamel, Signed, 3 In.		104.00
Vase, 2 Birds, Cherry Tree, Fruit, Blue, Opaque White Overlay, Chinese, 11 ½ In.		240.00
Vase, Cameo, Engraved Flowers, Blue To White, Bowling Pin Shape, 7 ¼ In.		125.00
Vase, Coral, Flared Rim, Carved Leaves, Strapwork, Cutout Ivory Stands, Pair		14100.00
Vase, Enamel, Flowers, Turquoise, Yellow, Round Foot, Bulbous, Narrow Neck, Pair		508.00
Vase, Enamel Design, Iron Red Dragons, 8 ½ In.		310.00
Vase, Flowers, Ducks, Shoulder, Yellow Hue, 19th Century, 8 In., Pair		600.00
Vase, Guanyin, Immortals, Landscape, Etched, Yellow, Chinese, 8 ⅛ In.		1007.00
Vase, Lotus, Butterfly, Phoenix, Blue, Opaque White Overlay, Chinese, 1900s, 11 ¾ In.		210.00
Vase, Pear Shape, Flaring Mouth, Turquoise Ground, San Duo, Phoenixes, c.1900, 10 In.		1225.00
Vase, Red, White, Birds, Flowers, Baluster, Narrow Neck, Flared Rim, Wood Stand, 7 In., Pair		1880.00
Vase, Snowflake, Red, Pavilions, Peacocks, Pine, Clouds, Figures, Chinese, 9 ½ In. ....*illus*		8295.00
Vase, Yellow, Carp & Duck, Water Plants, Pilgrim Shape, c.1900, 7 ¾ In.		354.00
Vase, Yellow, Ducks, Water Lilies, Butterflies, Flowers, Baluster, 1900s, 9 In., Pair		294.00
Vase, Yellow, Phoenix, Flying, Peonies, Wood Stand, Chinese, 1800s, 9 In.		770.00
Water Droppers, White, Red Overlay, Precious Object, Fish, 3 In., 2 Piece		658.00

PELOTON glass is a European glass with small threads of colored glass rolled onto the surface of clear or colored glass. It is sometimes called spaghetti, or shredded coconut, glass. Most pieces found today were made in the nineteenth century.

Dish, Sweetmeat, Multicolor, Ribbed, Morning Glory Finial, Silver Plate Lid, Bail Handle, 3 ¾ x 5 In.		450.00
Pitcher, Water, Pink, White, Blue, Yellow, Clear Crackle Handle, Square, 8 ½ In.		150.00

Pencil, Tiffany & Co., Mechanical, Ivory, Accent Beads, 18K Gold, Schlumberger, 1960s, 5 In.
$1348.00

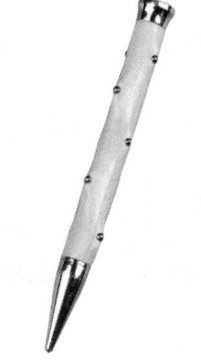

Skinner, Inc.

Pepsi-Cola, Toy, Truck, Delivery, Green Paint, Silver Roof, Wood, Railroad Express, Buddy L, 16 In.
$460.00

Bertoia Auctions

Perfume Bottle, Enamel On Copper, Cylindrical, Victorian Woman, Forest Background, 2 ¼ In.
$173.00

Early Auction Co.

Perfume Bottle, Porcelain, Figural, Sultan & Sultana, Seated, c.1835, 10 ¾ x 6 In., Pair
$2091.00

New Orleans Auction Galleries, Inc.

P

485

Perfume Bottle, Porcelain, Woman With Flowers, Man With Bagpipe, Gilt, Marked, c.1850, 9 ¼ In., Pair
$590.00

Brunk Auctions

Peters & Reed, Vase, Chromal, Abstract Design, 8 ½ In.
$230.00

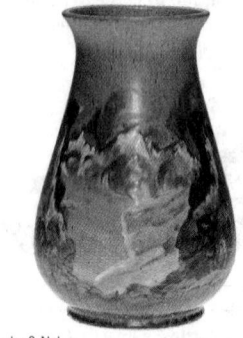

Humler & Nolan

Pewabic, Vase, Gray Iridescent, Turquoise Blue, Signed W.J. Smale, 4 ¾ x 4 ½ In.
$225.00

DuMouchelles Art Gallery

Pewabic, Vase, Luster, Blue Over Copper Glaze, Impressed, 6 In.
$575.00

Humler & Nolan

PENS replaced hand-cut quills as writing instruments in 1780, when the first steel pen point was made in England. But it was 100 years before the commercial pen was a common item. The fountain pen was invented in the 1830s but was not made in quantity until the 1880s. All types of old pens are collected. Float pens that feature small objects floating in a liquid as part of the handle are popular with collectors. Advertising pens are listed in the Advertising section of this book.

14K Gold, Ebony Handle, E.S. Johnson, Dip, Box, c.1880	120.00
Ballpoint, Kiss, Ace Frehley Portrait, Facsimile Signature, Retractable, On Card, 7 ¾ In.	86.00
Dupont, Fountain, Taj Mahal	3000.00
Faber-Castell, Fountain, Rollerball, Silver	625.00
Fountain, Concealed Shotgun, Steel, Late 19th Century, 5 In.	1250.00
Fountain, Hundertwasser, Edition 100	14375.00
Montblanc, Ballpoint, Hemingway	625.00
Montblanc, Fountain, 4th Of July Edition 56	18750.00
Montblanc, Fountain, Brandenburger Tor, Edition 89	16875.00
Montblanc, Rollerball, Generation, Orange, Papers, Box	300.00
Tiffany & Co., 18K Yellow & White Gold, Basket Weave, Parker Stylus, Pocket Clip	1534.00
Wipe, Owl, Felt, c.1890, 6 In. ....*illus*	121.00

PEN & PENCIL

A. Morton & Co., 14K Gold, Black Barrel, Rolled Gold Finish, Box, N.Y., c.1800s, 6 ⅜ In.	150.00
Remington, Fountain Pen, Mechanical, Gold Plated, Box, 5 ½ In.	56.00
Tiffany & Co., 18K Yellow & White Gold, Basket Weave, 3 ¾ In.	413.00

PENCILS were invented, so it is said, in 1565. The eraser was not added to the pencil until 1858. The automatic pencil was invented in 1863. Collectors today want advertising pencils or automatic pencils of unusual design. Boxes and sharpeners for pencils are also collected. Advertising pencils are listed in the Advertising category. Pencil boxes are listed in the Box category.

Mechanical, Crown Shape Top, Gold Plate, Rolled, Yellow Crystal Jewel, 4 ½ In.	120.00
Mordan & Co., Mechanical, Machined Design, Black Crystal Cap, Signed, 1830s, 4 ½ In.	120.00
Tiffany & Co., Mechanical, 18K Yellow Gold, Basket Weave, 5 ⅜ In.	767.00
Tiffany & Co., Mechanical, Ivory, Accent Beads, 18K Gold, Schlumberger, 1960s, 5 In. ...... *illus*	1348.00

PENCIL SHARPENER

Automatic, Automatic Pencil Sharpening Co., Patent Oct. 15, 1907, 3 x 4 ½ x 3 ½ In.	141.00
Baker's Chocolate Girl, Metal, Painted, 1950s, 2 x 1 In.	65.00
Cash Register, Metal, Box, Hong Kong, 2 ¼ x 2 x 1 ⅝ In.	12.00
Chick In Hat, Celluloid, Painted, 2 ⅝ In.	30.00
Clown Face, Pot Metal, Painted, Germany, 1 ¾ In.	32.00
Covered Wagon, Die Cast, Brass & Copper Finish, Plastic, Hong Kong, 2 In.	21.00
Dog Head, Metal, Painted, Japan, c.1930, 2 In.	175.00
Donald Duck, Bakelite, Scalloped Edge, 1 ⅜ In., Diam.	60.00
Duck Head, Brass, 2 In.	65.00
Egg Shape, Retro, Plastic, Orange, Boston, c.1950	75.00
Fireplace Hearth, Pot Metal, Brass Finish, 3 x 2 In.	16.00
Globe, Stand, Pot Metal, Hong Kong, 3 In.	22.00
Gun, Cast Iron, Eraser Handle, Germany, 1930s, 1 ½ In.	30.00
Harp, Metal, Hong Kong, 4 In.	23.00
Jiminy Cricket, Tipping Hat, Catalin, Decal, 1 ¾ In.	78.00
Pelican, Metal, Japan, 3 ⅛ In.	110.00
Peter Pan, Wolf, Bakelite, 1 ½ In., Diam.	10.00
Pluto, Graduation Cap, Tin Lithograph, Hong Kong, 1960s, 2 ½ In.	14.00
Saddle, Metal, 3 ¼ In.	6.00
Santa Claus, Raised Hand, Sack, Celluloid, Japan, 2 ½ In.	235.00
Sewing Machine, Brass Tone, 2 x 1 x 2 In.	26.00
Statue Of Liberty, Antique Finish, Box, Hong Kong, 3 ½ In.	9.00
Telephone, Copper Tone, Cord, Cast Iron, 2 x 2 ½ In.	52.00
Tortoise, Black, Green, Plastic, 3 In.	20.00
Traffic Light, Green, Hong Kong, c.1950, 3 ¾ In.	10.00

PENNSBURY POTTERY worked in Morrisville, Pennsylvania, from 1950 to 1971. Full sets of dinnerware as well as many decorative items were made. Pieces are marked with the name of the factory.

Thanksgiving Harvest, Cake Stand, Amish Couple, Turkey, Pumpkins, 11 x 4 In.	225.00

PEPSI-COLA, the drink and the name, was invented in 1898 but was not trademarked until 1903. The logo was changed from an elaborate script to the modern block letters in 1963. Several different logos have been used. Until 1951, the words *Pepsi* and *Cola* were separated by 2 dashes. These bottles are called "double dash." In 1951 the modern logo with a single hyphen was introduced. All types of advertising memorabilia are collected, and reproductions are being made.

Can, Cone Top	259.00
Clock, Bubble Face, Say Pepsi Please, Yellow Ground, 16 In. Diam	330.00
Cooler, Countertop, Ice Cold Pepsi-Cola, Sold Here, 5 Cents, Red, White, Blue, 1940s, 27 x 15 In.	960.00
Cup Holder, Bakelite, Embossed Lettering, Enjoy Pepsi-Cola, 1943, 6 ½ x 4 In.	250.00
Door Pull, Bigger-Better, Dark Blue, Tin, 1940s, 12 In.	420.00
Hanger, String, Double Dash, Die Cut, Flange, Frame, 9 x 16 In.	1210.00
Matchbook, Double Dash, Logo, Red, White & Blue, Bottle Cap Logo, 1939, Full Book	10.00
Poster, Refresh Without Filling, Girl Reaching For Bottle, Cap, Cardboard, c.1955, 36 ½ x 24 ½ In.	180.00
Radio, Bottle Shape, Plastic, Countertop	275.00
Radio, Ice Cold, Bottle Cap Knob, Plastic, Pale Blue, Red, White, 1950s, 6 x 7 ½ In.	270.00
Sign, 2 Cops With Pepsi Carton, Cardboard, Die Cut, 2-Sided, R. Goldberg, c.1940, 21 In.	380.00
Sign, 5 Cents, A Sparkling Beverage, Bottle, Tin, 1930s, 44 ½ In.	900.00
Sign, 5 Cents, Enjoy, America's Biggest Nickel's Worth, Red, Blue, Yellow, Tin, 1940s, 30 x 10 In.	390.00
Sign, 5 Cents, Refreshing, Healthful, Nickel Drink-Worth A Dime, Celluloid, Tin, 1930s, 12 ½ In.	420.00
Sign, Arrow Shape, Sold Here, Beverage Dept., Hanging, Wood, c.1940, 15 x 15 In.	403.00
Sign, Bottle Cap Shape, Die Cut, 2-Sided, Flange, Masonite, 13 x 12 In.	390.00 to 480.00
Sign, Bottle Cap Shape, Die Cut, Embossed, Tin, 38 x 30 In.	240.00
Sign, Bottle Cap, Red, White, Blue, 42 In.	358.00
Sign, Bottle, Cap, Porcelain, Self-Frame, 9 x 19 In.	330.00
Sign, Bottle, Company Of Canada Ltd., Tin, 1940, 16 x 48 In.	266.00
Sign, Die Cut, Bigger Better, 5 Cents, 6 Bottles, Cardboard, c.1936, 19 x 15 In.	316.00
Sign, Drink Pepsi, Cap, Rectangular, Plastic, Metal, Light-Up, 1950s, 19 ¼ x 14 ¼ In.	240.00
Sign, Drink Pepsi-Cola Iced, Bottle, Ice, Yellow, Red, Tin, 1940s, 17 x 53 In.	570.00
Sign, Drink Pepsi-Cola, Delicious-Delightful, Tin, Black, White, Red, 1910-15, 14 x 27 ½ In.	1080.00
Sign, Drink Pepsi-Cola, Red, White, Blue, Plastic, Metal, Light-Up, 1950s, 11 x 17 In.	360.00
Sign, Girl Holding Bottle, Looking Over Shoulder, Flowers, Cardboard, 1940s, 34 x 24 ¾ In.	1080.00
Sign, Have A Pepsi, Light Refreshment, Bottle Cap, Yellow, Embossed Tin, 1960s, 17 ½ x 54 In.	210.00
Sign, More Bounce To The Ounce, Bottle, Cap, Aluminum, Pale Blue, Red, White, 1940s, 36 x 14 In.	330.00
Sign, Pepsi, Cap, Oval, Revolving, Round Metal Base, White, Black, Red, Blue, Light-Up, 1950s, 15 In.	660.00
Sign, Round, Glass Face, Electric, Le Breuvage Leger, Light Refreshment, Light-Up, 15 In., Pair	230.00
Sign, Tops, Bottle Caps, Aluminum, Red, White, Blue, 1950s, 36 x 19 In.	360.00
Statue, Sparkling Quality, Girl, Standing, Red Gown, Bottle, Cap, Plaster, 1950s, 11 In.	2160.00
Toy, Hog Dog Vendor Wagon, Detachable Man, Umbrella, Pepsi Bottles, Ideal, 1945, 8 x 9 In.	675.00
Toy, Pull, Drink Pepsi-Cola, Hot Dogs, 5 Cents, Dog, Pushing, Cart, Bell, Wood, 1950s, 10 In.	120.00
Toy, Truck, Delivery, Green Paint, Silver Roof, Wood, Railroad Express, Buddy L, 16 In. *illus*	460.00
Vending Machine, Bottle, V-81, 10 Cents, Keys, 1950s	4500.00

PERFUME BOTTLES are made of cut glass, pressed glass, art glass, silver, metal, enamel, and even plastic or porcelain. Although the small bottle to hold perfume was first made before the time of ancient Egypt, it is the nineteenth- and twentieth-century examples that interest today's collector. DeVilbiss Company has made atomizers of all types since 1888 but no longer makes the perfume bottle tops so popular with collectors. These were made from 1920 to 1968. The glass bottle may be by any of many manufacturers even if the atomizer is marked *DeVilbiss*. The word *factice*, which often appears in ads, refers to store display bottles. Glass or porcelain examples may be found under the appropriate name such as Lalique, Czechoslovakia, Glass-Bohemian, etc.

14K Gold, Yellow, Glass, Etched Shells, Flowers, Quatrefoils, Oval Stopper, c.1905, 4 ⅝ In.	474.00
Art Glass, Flowers, Green Leaves, Narrow Bottom, Bulbous Top, Clear Stopper, 6 In.	230.00
Art Glass, Orange, Iridescent Green Leaves, Bulbous, Ruffle Rim, Stopper, C. Lotton, 12 In.	1093.00
Blue Aurene Feather Design, Cobalt Blue, Footed, Teardrop Stopper, Lundberg, 1982, 8 ¾ In.	173.00
Blue Opalescent, Cosmos Pattern, DeVilbiss, 1941, 4 In.	65.00
Cameo Glass, Ferns, White To Blue, Silver Hinged Cap, Tapered, Laydown, 5 In.	1495.00
Cameo Glass, Flowers, Butterfly, Green, White, Silver Cap, Tapered, Laydown, 10 In.	1610.00
Cased Glass, Glossy Coral Shaded To Yellow, Globular, Silver Cap, 4 In.	150.00
Cologne, Cobalt Blue, Reeded Sides, Ringed Neck, Blown Stopper, 6 In.	136.00
Corday Toujours Moi, Cut Glass Stopper, Art Deco Box, 1930s, ½ Oz.	125.00
Cranberry Glass, Gold Enamel, Bell Lily, 4 ½ In.	100.00
Cut Glass, Octagonal, Green, Fan Stopper, 1940s, 6 In.	32.00
Enamel On Copper, Cylindrical, Victorian Woman, Forest Background, 2 ¼ In. *illus*	173.00
Etched Glass, Horse, Trees, Tapered Triangular Shape, Flared Lip, 10 x 4 In.	98.00

Pewabic, Vase, Multicolor Iridescent, Impressed Medallion Mark, Paper Label, c.1920, 6 ½ x 6 ½ In. $1320.00
DuMouchelles Art Gallery

Pewabic, Vase, Squat, Yellow & Iridescent Green Glaze, Stamped, Paper Label, 5 ½ x 5 ½ In. $2852.00
Rago Arts & Auction Center

Pewter, Basin, Marked Watts & Harton, London, c.1820, 8 ⅞ In. $59.00
Conestoga Auction Co., Inc.

Pewter, Biscuit Jar, Liberty & Co., Archibald Knox, Tudric, Enameled Design, c.1910, 4 ¾ In. $1416.00
DuMouchelles Art Gallery

TIP
You cannot fix a cracked snowdome paperweight.

Pewter, Box, Cover, Enamel Flowers, Compartments, Liberty & Co., Marked, England, 3 x 7 ¼ In.
$1020.00

Treadway Toomey Galleries

Pewter, Charger, Johann Georg Neeff, Scalloped Edge, Lions, Shield, Frankfurt, c.1774, 13 ⅝ In.
$35.00

Conestoga Auction Co., Inc.

Pewter, Charger, Zunst Zinn, Flowers, Geese, Relief, Art Nouveau, Marked, c.1890, 13 In.
$18.00

Conestoga Auction Co., Inc.

Faceted, Octagonal, Iridescent Gold, Flat Stopper With Molded Flowers, 5 In.	518.00
Glass, Houbigant, Presence, Paneled, Green Moire Fitted Box, c.1937, 4 ¼ In.	119.00
Glass, Schiaparelli, Candle Shape, Fluted Base, Gold Trim, Red Flame Stopper, 6 In.	54.00
Gold, Butterfly Pattern, Round Foot, Teardrop, Spear Shape Stopper, Lundberg, 10 In.	259.00
Peachblow, Gold Tip, Tapered, Laydown, Silver Cap, England, 1887, 4 In.	460.00
Porcelain, Figural, Sultan & Sultana, Seated, c.1835, 10 ¾ x 6 In., Pair ....*illus*	2091.00
Porcelain, Lavender, Blue, Green, Raised Gilt, Tasseled Cushion, Scimitar, c.1835, 8 ½ x 5 ½ In.	676.00
Porcelain, Woman With Flowers, Man With Bagpipe, Gilt, Marked, c.1850, 9 ¼ In., Pair ......*illus*	590.00
Presentation, Arrow Shape, Frosted, Cardboard Quiver, Lancome, 1950s, 7 In.	37200.00
Prince Matchabelli, Crown Shape, Metal Mount, Maltese Cross Stopper, 7 In.	104.00
Satin Glass, Diamond Quilted, Mother-Of-Pearl, Shaded Blue, Tapered, Laydown, 7 In.	575.00
St. Louis, Paperweight, White Spiral, Blue Rim, Stopper, Spaced Millefiori Base, SL 1985, 7 ½ In.	708.00
Sterling Silver, Cylindrical, Embossed Flowers, Flip Lid, Twist-Off Bottle, 2 In.	201.00
Topaz, Faceted, Chrome Finish, Atomizer, 3 ⅛ x 2 ½ In.	75.00
Translucent Glass, Blue Flowers, Green Leaves, Cylindrical, Footed, Ball Stopper, 1974, 7 In.	662.00
Yellow Jade, Bulbous, Flared Rim, Stopper, 4 In.	920.00

PETERS & REED POTTERY COMPANY of Zanesville, Ohio, was founded by John D. Peters and Adam Reed in 1897. Chromal, Landsun, Montene, Pereco, and Persian are some of the art lines that were made. The company, which became Zane Pottery in 1920 and Gonder Pottery in 1941, closed in 1957. Peters & Reed pottery was unmarked.

Flower Frog, Landsun Mushroom, c.1920, 3 ¾ In.	150.00
Flower Frog, Landsun, Blue Over Green, 3 ¾ In.	50.00
Flower Frog, Pereco, Green, Lily Pad Shape, 3 ¾ In.	125.00
Flowerpot, Hanging, Ivory, 5 x 8 ½ In.	185.00
Flowerpot, Moss Aztec, 2 ¼ x 3 In., Pair	95.00
Jar, Flower Panels, Multicolor, Ivory Gloss Ground, 15 ½ In.	265.00
Jardiniere, Garland, Lion's Heads, 3-Footed, 6 ¾ x 10 In.	159.00
Jardiniere, Pereco Grape Design, Raised Rim, 5 ½ x 6 ¾ In.	275.00
Jug, Squat, Standard Ware, Brown Glaze, Sprig Flowers, Lobed, 2 ¾ x 4 ¾ In.	95.00
Jug, Standard Ware Brown Glaze, Grape, Lion, Yellow, Green, 4 x 4 ½ In.	125.00
Mug, Grape Pattern, Brown Glaze, c.1920, 5 ¼ In.	89.00
Vase, Brown Glaze, 3 Flower Sprigs, c.1910, 4 x 4 ½ In.	100.00
Vase, Brown Glaze, Flower Sprigs, 4 Panels, Octagonal, 5 In.	100.00
Vase, Chromal, Abstract Design, 8 ½ In. ....*illus*	230.00
Vase, Chromal, House Scene, Blue, Brown, Ivory, Shouldered, 1915, 5 ½ x 4 ½ In.	575.00
Vase, Embossed Leaves, Ivory, Flared, 8 In.	150.00
Vase, Marbleized, Lobed, Maroon, Black, Gold, 9 x 4 In.	195.00
Vase, Mirror Black, Cold Painted Design, 7 ¾ In.	185.00
Vase, Mirror Black, Pastel Flowers, Lobed, 9 In.	175.00
Vase, Montene, Green, Round, 6 ½ In.	250.00
Vase, Moss Aztec, Embossed Roses, 16 ½ In.	500.00
Vase, Shadow Ware, Salmon, Black Drip, 6 ⅞ In.	400.00
Vase, Standard Ware, Brown Glaze, Pink Flower Sprigs, Handle, 4 ¼ In.	85.00
Vase, Velvet Blue Matte, c.1916, 4 ½ In.	45.00
Vase, Wilse Blue, Slightly Flared, 10 In.	195.00
Wall Pocket, Egyptian, Portrait In Panel, Pereco Glaze, Wood Support, c.1922, 4 x 8 In.	175.00

PETRUS REGOUT, *see Maastricht category.*

PEWABIC POTTERY was founded by Mary Chase Perry Stratton in 1903 in Detroit, Michigan. The company made many types of art pottery, including pieces with matte green glaze and an iridescent crystalline glaze. The company continued working until the death of Mary Stratton in 1961. It was reactivated by Michigan State University in 1968.

Ashtray, Bronze Crystalline Glaze, Rectangular, Canted Corners, 2 Platforms, 4 ½ In.	150.00
Cigarette Box, Green Gold Glaze, Deer On Cover, c.1940, 2 x 3 ¾ In.	210.00
Plate, Painted Orange, Peaches Border, 10 ¾ In.	150.00
Tile Set, Emerald Green Crystalline Glaze, 1 ¾ x 3 ¾ In., 48 Piece	1020.00
Tile, Alice In Wonderland, Iridescent Glazes, Green Border, Rectangular, Marked, 4 ¾ In.	3105.00
Tile, Boy, On Fish, Marked, 4 x 4 In.	65.00
Tile, Cat Profile, Purple Matte Glaze, 1990, 7 ¾ x 7 ¾ In.	1020.00
Tile, Face, Sad & Scrunched, Sea Green Matte Glaze, Marked Detroit, 1991, 6 ¼ In.	123.00
Tile, Luster, Red Swirls, Wood Frame, 11 In.	246.00
Trivet, Hexagonal, Multicolor, 9 In.	413.00
Vase, Blue Iridescent, Footed, Globular, Stamped, 10 ½ x 9 In.	4340.00

Vase, Blue Luster Glaze, Silver Iridescence, Yellow, Baluster, 9 ¾ In.	575.00
Vase, Blue, Purple, Metallic Iridescent Glaze, Cylindrical, 2 x 2 ½ In.	4123.00
Vase, Brown, Blue, Lobed, Pinched Neck, Metallic Iridescent Glaze, Bulbous, 6 x 10 In.	1760.00
Vase, Chinese Calligraphy, Black, Brown Glaze, 3 ½ x 3 ½ In.	330.00
Vase, Famille Rose Matte Glaze, Green, Genie Bottle Shape, 4 ⅞ In.	518.00
Vase, Gray Iridescent, Turquoise Blue, Signed W.J. Smale, 4 ¾ x 4 ½ In. illus	225.00
Vase, Green Matte, Bulbous, Handles, 6 In.	365.00
Vase, Green Mottled Glaze, Narrow Neck, c.1920, 8 ½ x 6 ½ In.	540.00
Vase, Luster, Blue Over Copper Glaze, Impressed, 6 In. illus	575.00
Vase, Multicolor Iridescent, Impressed Medallion Mark, Paper Label, c.1920, 6 ½ x 6 ½ In. . illus	1320.00
Vase, Squat, Bulbous, Multicolor Green Glaze, c.1915, 3 ½ x 6 ½ In.	540.00
Vase, Squat, Yellow & Iridescent Green Glaze, Stamped, Paper Label, 5 ½ x 5 ½ In. illus	2852.00
Vase, Swollen, Rolled Rim, Marked, 5 x 3 In.	65.00
Wall Pocket, Flower, Green, Marked, 1907, 6 x 7 In.	75.00

PEWTER is a metal alloy of tin and lead. Some of the pewter made after 1840 has a slightly different composition and is called Britannia metal. This later type of pewter was worked by machine; the earlier pieces were made by hand. In the 1920s pewter came back into fashion and pieces were often marked *Genuine Pewter*. Eighteenth-, nineteenth-, and twentieth-century examples are listed here.

Ashtray, Art Nouveau Style, Embracing Angels, 4 ¾ In.	24.00
Basin, Benjamin & Joseph Harbeson, c.1780, 1 ¾ x 6 ⅝ In.	533.00
Basin, Marked Robert Palethorp, Philadelphia, c.1820, 11 In.	444.00
Basin, Marked Watts & Harton, London, c.1820, 8 ⅞ In. illus	59.00
Basin, Single Beaded Rim, Initials, Marks, Crown, N.D. In Arches, Tudor Rose, 2 ¼ x 13 In.	94.00
Basket, Organic Design, Blue Enamel Center, England, 9 ½ x 6 In.	275.00
Beaker, Thomas Boardman, Hartford, Conn., c.1835, 5 In., Pair	770.00
Bedpan, Thomas Boardman, c.1835, 10 ¾ In.	119.00
Biscuit Jar, Archibald Knox, Liberty, Tudric, Geometrics, England, 5 ¼ x 5 ¼ In.	1116.00
Biscuit Jar, Liberty & Co., Archibald Knox, Tudric, Enameled Design, c.1910, 4 ¾ In. illus	1416.00
Bowl, Clover, Double Handles, Partial Reticulated Rim, Marked, England, 11 x 2 In.	60.00
Bowl, Double Handle Shape, Clover, England, 11 In.	55.00
Box, Cover, Enamel Flowers, Compartments, Liberty & Co., Marked, England, 3 x 7 ¼ In. illus	1020.00
Bread Tray, Hatfield Meat Packing Co., Pig Wearing Hat, 6 x 9 In.	22.00
Chalice, Attribution Johann Christoph Heyne, Lancaster, Pa., c.1760, 8 ⅝ In.	5688.00
Charger, Johann Georg Neeff, Scalloped Edge, Lions, Shield, Frankfurt, c.1774, 13 ⅝ In. illus	35.00
Charger, Parks Boyd, c.1805, 13 ½ In.	356.00
Charger, Robert Palethorp Jr., c.1820, 12 In.	711.00
Charger, Samuel Hamlin, Rhode Island, c.1780, 15 In.	1304.00
Charger, Thomas Badger, Boston, 12 ¼ In.	356.00
Charger, Wrigglework Design, Engraved, 1821, 22 In. Diam.	735.00
Charger, Zunst Zinn, Flowers, Geese, Relief, Art Nouveau, Marked, c.1890, 13 In. illus	18.00
Coffee Service, Zeister, Coffeepot, Teapot, Sugar, Creamer, Waste Bowl, Tray, 6 ¾ x 12 ¼ In.	475.00
Coffeepot, Allen Porter, c.1845, 11 ¼ In.	237.00
Coffeepot, William Will, Scroll Treen Handle, Beaded Bands, Gooseneck Spout, 1775, 15 ¾ In.	45030.00
Creamer, Philadelphia, Attribution Parks Boyd, c.1800, 5 ¼ In.	5925.00
Cup, Cover, Ostrich Egg, Overlay, Female Supports, Flowers, Leaves, Germany, c.1800, 18 In. illus	385.00
Dish, Deep, Robert Palethorp Jr., c.1920, 13 In.	1215.00
Flagon, Hinged Lid, Engraved, Carpenter's Herald, 1845, 7 ½ In.	215.00
Flagon, Hinged Lid, Kayserzinn Laurel Leaf, Embossed, Flared Base, 16 x 10 In.	115.00
Flagon, Lid, Scroll Handle, Boardman & Co, New York, c.1835, 12 ½ In.	1541.00
Flask, Johann Christoph Heyne, Pa., 1757, 5 ¼ In.	37920.00
Flask, Porcelain Plaque, Fox Hunt Scene, England, 3 ¼ In.	89.00
Frame, Art Nouveau Flower Panels, WMF, c.1905, 6 ¼ x 9 In.	440.00
Ladle, Scoop, Whalebone Handle, 14 ½ In. illus	470.00
Mold, Candle, 24 Tubes, Pine, Stamped W. Wenn, Penn., 17 ¾ x 22 In.	948.00
Mug, 2 Handles, Thomas Boardman Mark, 5 In., Pair	3081.00
Mug, James Edward, Raised Rings, Scroll Handle, Camden Town, England, 6 In.	180.00
Mug, Joseph Danforth, Connecticut, c.1785, 5 ¾ In.	2607.00
Mug, Love, Philadelphia, 4 ¼ In.	5346.00
Pitcher, Hinged Lid, William McQuilkin, Pa., c.1845, 8 ¾ In.	178.00
Pitcher, Hinged Lid, William McQuilkin, Philadelphia, c.1845, 10 ¼ In.	563.00
Pitcher, Kayserzinn, Figural, Satyr's Mask, Germany, 12 ½ In.	120.00
Pitcher, Paul Evans, Oval, Tapered, Squared Handle, Rosewood Plaque Inset, 12 In.	1126.00
Plate, Benjamin & Joseph Harbeson, 1 ¾ x 6 ⅝ In.	533.00
Plate, Danforth, Flat Rim, Marked, 7 ¾ In. Diam.	173.00

Pewter, Cup, Cover, Ostrich Egg, Overlay, Female Supports, Flowers, Leaves, Germany, c.1800, 18 In. $385.00

Skinner, Inc.

Pewter, Ladle, Scoop, Whalebone Handle, 14 ½ In. $470.00

Cowan's Auctions

Pewter, Plate, Plain Rim, 1700s, 9 ¼ In. $106.00

Conestoga Auction Co., Inc.

Pewter, Plate, Samuel Ellis, Single Reeded, London, 1700s, 8 ½ In. $24.00

Conestoga Auction Co., Inc.

P

Pewter, Porringer, Crown Handle, Spline Back Strap, Attributed To Jo. Belcher, c.1780, 5 In.
$472.00

Conestoga Auction Co., Inc.

Pewter, Porringer, Samuel Hamlin, Reticulated Handle, Touchmark, 1800s, 5 ¼ In.
$354.00

Conestoga Auction Co., Inc.

Pewter, Syrup, Homan & Co., Cincinnati, c.1850, 6 In.
$53.00

Conestoga Auction Co., Inc.

Plate, Marked Johann Christopher Heyne, c.1765, 6 ¼ In.	8295.00
Plate, Plain Rim, 1700s, 9 ¼ In. .... *illus*	106.00
Plate, Round, Engraved Center Design, Rolled Rim, c.1800, 9 ½ In. Diam.	30.00
Plate, Samuel Ellis, Single Reeded, London, 1700s, 8 ½ In. .... *illus*	24.00
Plate, Thomas Danforth, c.1810, 8 ⅞ In.	385.00
Platter, Fish, Kayserzinn, Lion Fish & Octopus Design, Oval, 23 ½ In.	219.00
Porringer, 2 Openwork Flower & Crown Handles, c.1800, 7 x 8 In., 4 Piece	59.00
Porringer, Crown Handle, Spline Back Strap, Attributed To Jo. Belcher, c.1780, 5 In. ....*illus*	472.00
Porringer, David Melville, Deep Dish, Crown Handle, c.1770, 4 ¼ In.	1304.00
Porringer, David Melville, Flower Handle, Rhode Island, 5 ⅛ In.	770.00
Porringer, Dolphin Handle, Connecticut, c.1800, 5 ½ In.	1896.00
Porringer, Samuel Hamlin, Flower Handle, Rhode Island, 4 ¼ In.	652.00
Porringer, Samuel Hamlin, Reticulated Handle, Touchmark, 1800s, 5 ¼ In. .... *illus*	354.00
Porringer, Samuel Hamlin, Rhode Island, c.1825, 5 ½ In.	356.00
Porringer, Scroll Handles, Foot Ring, 1600s, 8 ½ x 5 ½ In.	24.00
Porringer, Simon Pennock, Tab Handle, Chester Co., Pa., c.1825, 5 ½ In.	5103.00
Pot, Handle, Joshua Graves, c.1850, 11 ¼ In.	147.00
Rose Bowl, Archibald Knox, Liberty, Tudric Handle Stand, Flower Design, 5 ¾ x 11 ½ In.	1984.00
Sugar & Creamer, Cover, Wooden Wafer Finial, c.1850, 7 ¼ x 6 In.	176.00
Sugar, Cover, Attr. William Will, Phil., c.1775, 4 ¾ In.	10073.00
Syrup, Homan & Co., Cincinnati, c.1850, 6 In. ....*illus*	53.00
Tankard, Coat Of Arms, Ear Handle, Reeded Thumbpiece, 3 Spherical Feet, Sweden, c.1900, 8 In.	119.00
Tankard, Lid, William Will, Wrigglework, Phil., 1775, 7 In.	17010.00
Tantalus, Wine, Screw Lids, Shaped Handle, Round Top Handle, Baluster, Cylindrical Spout, 11 In.	87.00
Teapot, Federal Style, Touchmark, 1800s, 8 ½ In.	89.00
Teapot, James Yates, Footed, Shell Thumbprint, c.1850, 7 ½ In.	155.00
Teapot, Painted Cartouches, Bail Handle, Chinese, 6 ½ In.	269.00
Teapot, Robert Bush, Scrolled Wood Handle, England, c.1775, 6 ¼ In.	296.00
Teapot, William Will, Squat, Scrolled Wood Handle, 6 ¼ In.	30810.00
Tray, 2 Nude Maidens, Reclining Beside Water, 11 x 9 ¼ In.	219.00
Tray, Sweetmeat, Inlaid, Enameled Metal Trays Inset, Lotus Pond, 14 ¾ In.	187.00
Vase, Cover, Double Gourd, Fruit, Flowers, Cartouches, Poems, Mythical Beast Finial, 8 In.	299.00
Vase, Just Andersen, Fish Shape, Patinated, Denmark, 5 x 3 In., Pair	58.00

PHOENIX GLASS Company was founded in 1880 in Pennsylvania. The firm made commercial products, such as lampshades, bottles, and glassware. Collectors today are interested in the "Sculptured Artware" made by the company from the 1930s until the mid-1950s. Some pieces of Phoenix glass are very similar to those made by the Consolidated Lamp and Glass Company. Phoenix made Reuben Blue, lavender, and yellow pieces. These colors were not used by Consolidated. In 1970 Phoenix became a division of Anchor Hocking, which was sold to the Newell Group in 1987. The factory is still working.

Fishbowl, Ruba Rhombic, Vaseline Glass, Metal Tripod Stand, c.1928, 32 x 13 In.	21510.00
Fishbowl, Ruba Rhombic, Vaseline, Triangles, Ruben Haley, 1928, 15 x 8 In.	6000.00
Lamp, Reverse Painted, Lake Scene, Embossed Metal Flower Base, 6 ½ x 15 ¾ In.	288.00
Vase, Blue Iridescent, Silver Heart, Millefiori Highlights, Signed, 1984, 11 In.	225.00
Vase, Cameo, Leaves, Berries, Oval, 1930s, 10 In.	125.00
Vase, Cameo, Peonies, White Matte Glaze, Yellow, Tendrils, Shouldered, 1930s, 12 In.	139.00
Vase, Cameo, Poppies, Applied Gold, 1930s, 11 In.	179.00
Vase, Molded Blooms, Sinewy Stems, Center Bands, 7 x 3 x 5 In.	175.00
Vase, Urn Shape, Iridescent Gold, Crisscross Design, Signed C. Roelke, 6 x 6 In.	115.00

PHONOGRAPHS, invented by Thomas Edison in 1877, have been made by many firms. This category also includes other items associated with the phonograph. Jukeboxes and Records are listed in their own categories.

Berliner, Disc, Side Brake, Record Screw, Crank, Brass Horn, J Reproducer, c.1895	3850.00
Bing, Kiddyphone, Horn, Reproducer, Needles, Circus Graphics, Box, Child's	484.00
Brunswick, Panatrope, Radiola, Model PR-17-8, Floor Model	55.00
Brunswick, Ultonia, Disk, Floor Model, Door, Crank	104.00
Busy Bee, Grand, Disc, Red Morning Glory Horn	550.00
Columbia Graphophone, Model AK, Reproducer, Crank, Aluminum Support, Tone Arm	330.00
Columbia Graphophone, Model AU, Disc, Black Bell Horn, Crank, Quick Release Reproducer	495.00
Columbia, Coin-Operated, Cylinder, Nickel Horn	4255.00
Columbia, Graphophone, Model B, Horn, c.1900, 11 ¾ In.	240.00
Columbia, Graphophone, Model BKT Cylinder, Flower Painted Horn, Crank	863.00
Columbia, Home Grand, Cylinder, Mandrel, Reproducer, Crank, Brass Horn	2750.00
Disc, Victor, Record Player, Floor Model, 2 Doors	920.00

P

Edison, Fireside, Model A, Cylinder, Metal Cygnet Horn, Lid, Crank	489.00
Edison, Fireside, Model A, Cylinder, Oak Case, Crank	184.00
Edison, Fireside, Model B, Cylinder, Metal Cygnet Horn, Crank	715.00
Edison, Gem, Black Cylinder, C Reproducer, Conical Gold Band Horn, Crank, Cover	132.00
Edison, Gem, Cylinder, Reproducer, Key, Cover	330.00
Edison, Home, Cylinder Shaver, Table Top	431.00
Edison, Model 130, Disc, Long Play Reproducer, Floor Model	403.00
Edison, Model A, Flat Top, Cylinder, c.1899	413.00
Edison, Model A-275, Mahogany, Disc, Floor Model, Door, Crank	345.00
Edison, Model C, Oak, Domed, Top Handle, Crank, 9 Rolls	356.00
Edison, Music Master, Oak, Grain Painted Metal, Cygnet Horn, 1906	2295.00
Edison, Standard, Banner, Morning Glory Horn, Chicago Easy Style Horn Crane, Babson Bros.	605.00
Edison, Standard, Model B, Cylinder, Crane, Black Horn	460.00
Edison, Standard, Oak, Newest Patent Date 1903, 10 ½ x 12 ¾ In. *illus*	472.00
Edison, Standard, Type 2, Model C Reproducer, 4 Cylinders, c.1905 *illus*	567.00
Edison, Triumph, Model A, Cylinder, Lid, Crank	325.00
Edison, Triumph, Model D, Cylinder, O Reproducer, Crank, Oak Cygnet Horn, Crane	2310.00
Heywood-Wakefield, Disc, Wicker, Floor Model	546.00
Nifty Nirona, Decals, Crank, Germany, Child's	230.00
Phono-Lamp, Model D, Interior Base Phonograph, Shade Frame, Cloth Shade Panels, Embossed	2640.00
Portetec, Horn & Reproducer Unit, 78 RPM Only, Crank, c.1948	81.00
Radio, Capehart Amperion, Model 140-18H, Combination, Instructions, Records	4730.00
Regina, Disc, Mahogany, Floor Model, Door	374.00
Reginaphone, Style 246, Mahogany, Duplex Combs, 50 15 ½-In. Discs, 47 In.	47420.00
Talkophone, Disk, Front Mount Horn, Crank	374.00
Victor, 50, Portable, Mahogany Case	138.00
Victor, D, Disc, Oak Spear Tip Horn	1540.00
Victor, I, Humpback, Rear Mount Victor Horn, Exhibition Reproducer, Crank	715.00
Victor, II, Black & Brass Bell Horn, Disc, Crank	489.00
Victor, II, Disc, Exhibition Reproducer, Brass Bell Horn	770.00
Victor, II, Disc, Outside Black Horn, Crank	1035.00
Victor, II, Humpback, Exhibition Reproducer, Brass Bell Horn, Crank	715.00
Victor, IV, Disc, Mahogany Horn, Exhibition Reproducer, Crank	1955.00
Victor, M, Disc, Exhibition Reproducer, Smooth Oak Horn, Crank	1980.00
Victor, Monarch Special, Oak Horn, c.1903	2200.00
Victor, MS, Rigid Arm, Brass Bell Horn, Threaded Elbow, Record Screw, Concert Reproducer, Crank	2475.00
Victor, No. 3, Disc, Outside Nickel Horn, Table Model, Crank	690.00
Victor, R, Metal Tone Arm, Exhibition Junior Reproducer, Black Bell Horn, Crank, 14 x 10 In.	121.00
Victor, Reproducer, Eldridge Johnson, A, Disc, Horn, Slotted Crank, Leather Elbow	2200.00
Victor, V, Oak, Stencils, Paneled Horn, 32 x 17 x 21 In.	4130.00
Victor, Victoria Record Player, Victor Talking Machine, Oak, Crank, c.1910, 17 x 20 In.	895.00
Victor, Victrola, No. 627, Oak Cabinet, 22 D Metal Horn, c.1910	633.00
Victor, W-XII, Table Model, Disc, Mahogany, Crank	546.00
Victor, W-XVII, Disc, Mahogany, Floor Model, 4 Doors	460.00
Victrola, Disc, No. XIV, 41479, Cabinet, Oak, Horn Speaker, 2 Doors, c.1915, 46 x 22 In.	400.00
Victrola, Victor Talking Machine, VV-XIV, Oak, Floor Model	440.00
Victrola, VV-XVI, Walnut, Hinged Lid, Gilt Hardware, Doors, c.1915, 50 x 24 x 25 In.	1652.00
Victrola, XIV, Oak Cabinet, Built-In Horn, c.1912, 46 x 22 In.	288.00
Wondrola, Hand Crank, Instruction, Box, Wilkins Toy Co., Child's	528.00
Zon-O-Phone, Horn Support, Rod Tone Arm, Reproducer, 25-In Brass Bell Horn, Crank	3300.00
Zon-O-Phone, Oak Horn, Square Oak Case, Gold Lettering, c.1910	575.00

PHONOGRAPH NEEDLE CASES of tin are collected today by music and phonograph enthusiasts and advertising addicts. The tins are very small, about 2 inches across, and often have attractive graphic designs lithographed on the top and sides.

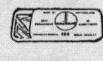

RCA Victor, Chromium, Box	154.00
Victor, 1000 HMV, Tin	72.00
Zon-O-Phone, Papier-Mache, 2 Compartments	121.00

PHOTOGRAPHY items are listed here. The first photograph was a view from a window in France taken in 1826. The commercially successful photograph started with the daguerreotype introduced in 1839. Today all sorts of photographs and photographic equipment are collected. Albums were popular in Victorian times. Cartes de visite, popular after 1854, were mounted on 2 ½-by-4-inch cardboard. Cabinet cards were introduced in 1866. These were mounted on 4 ¼-by-6 ½-inch cards. Stereo views are listed under Stereo Card. Stereoscopes are listed in their own section.

Albumen Print Set, Southwestern Dwellings, Hayden Expedition, W.H. Jackson, 6 Piece	1800.00

Digital Date
The first digital or "film-less" camera was invented in 1975 by Steven Sasson of Eastman Kodak.

Phonograph, Edison, Standard, Oak, Newest Patent Date 1903, 10 ½ x 12 ¾ In.
$472.00

Conestoga Auction Co., Inc.

Phonograph, Edison, Standard, Type 2, Model C Reproducer, 4 Cylinders, c.1905
$567.00

Auction Team Breker

Photography, Ambrotype, Girl, Tinted, Gilt Necklace, Union Case, Littlefield & Parsons & Co., ¼ Plate
$245.00

Skinner, Inc.

P

Photography, Ambrotype, Portrait, Blacksmith, Gilt Watch Fob, Leather Case, ¼ Plate
$2252.00

Skinner, Inc.

Photography, Ambrotype, Portrait, Girl, Holding Chalkware Cat, Single Pear, Union Case, ⅑ Plate
$770.00

Skinner, Inc.

Photography, Camera, Luzo, Rollfilm, J.J. Redding & Gyles, London, No. 664, Mahogany, 1896
$2006.00

Auction Team Breker

Photography, Camera, Rolleiflex T, Franke & Heidecke, No. T2108086, Tessar 3, Leather Case, 1958
$435.00

Auction Team Breker

Photography, Carte De Visite, Sojourner Truth, Portrait, Imprinted Message, Inscription, 1878
$881.00

Cowan's Auctions

Photography, Daguerreotype, Gold Miner, Beard, Bulky Coat, 10 Gallon Hat, ⅙ Plate
$999.00

Cowan's Auctions

Photography, Daguerreotype, Militia Officer, Shako & Sword, Leather Case, c.1850, ¼ Plate
$940.00

Cowan's Auctions

Photography, Daguerreotype, Portrait, Architect At Work, Pressed Paper, Leather Case, ½ Plate
$15405.00

Skinner, Inc.

Photography, Daguerreotype, Portrait, Young Man, Beaver Top Hat, Leather Case, ⅙ Plate
$1067.00

Skinner, Inc.

P

Albumen Print Set, Yellowstone, Hayden Expedition, W.H. Jackson, 6 Piece	1320.00
Albumen Print, Boy In Gray Uniform, Hat, Belt, Bayonet, Civil War, Staunton, Va., 12 x 10 In.	104.00
Albumen Print, Chief Joseph, Nez Perce Leader, Holding Tomahawk, 6 ½ x 8 ¼ In.	7638.00
Albumen Print, Field Gun & Crew, Union Artillery, Brady, c.1862, 2 ¾ x 4 In.	176.00
Albumen Print, General Grant At Lookout Mountain, Royan Linn, 1863, 7 ¾ x 4 ¾ In.	1175.00
Albumen Print, Harvest Of Death, Timothy O'Sullivan, Gettysburg, Civil War, 7 ½ x 9 In.	1410.00
Albumen Print, Wounded Zouave, Fredericksburg, Civil War, 4 x 8 In.	1645.00
Ambrotype, Early Frontiersman, Posed With Whip, Hat, Colt Revolver, ½ Case, ½ Plate	3819.00
Ambrotype, Girl, Tinted, Gilt Necklace, Union Case, Littlefield & Parsons & Co., ¼ Plate *illus*	245.00
Ambrotype, Mexican Officer, Pre-Maximillan Uniform, c.1860, ¼ Plate	1020.00
Ambrotype, Portrait, Blacksmith, Gilt Watch Fob, Leather Case, ¼ Plate *illus*	2252.00
Ambrotype, Portrait, Girl, Holding Chalkware Cat, Single Pear, Union Case, ⅑ Plate *illus*	770.00
Ambrotype, Western Surveyor, Pierre L. Gibbs, Panama, c.1848, ½ Plate	2115.00
Cabinet Card, Annie Oakley, Little Sure Shot, Elliott & Fry, London	3055.00
Cabinet Card, Curley, Custer's Scout, D.F. Barry	823.00
Cabinet Card, Geronimo, Blanket Over Shoulder, 1904, 6 ½ x 4 ¼ In.	926.00
Cabinet Card, Sitting Bull, Holding Pipe, Bailey, Dix & Mead, 1882	646.00
Camera, Leica Leitz M3, Lens, Ranger, No. 962455, 1959	1380.00
Camera, Leica Leitz, M4, 35 mm Rangefinder, 1969	2588.00
Camera, Leica, IIIG, 1957	567.00
Camera, Luzo, Rollfilm, J.J. Redding & Gyles, London, No. 664, Mahogany, 1896 *illus*	2006.00
Camera, Rolleiflex T, Franke & Heidecke, No. T2108086, Tessar 3, Leather Case, 1958 *illus*	435.00
Carte De Visite, George A. Custer, Autographed, Mathew Brady, 1864	8225.00
Carte De Visite, Lincoln's Funeral Catafalque, Cleveland, Oh., J.F. Ryder	499.00
Carte De Visite, Portrait, Rufus Ingalls, 16th Quartermaster General, R.W. Addis	441.00
Carte De Visite, Sojourner Truth, Portrait, Imprinted Message, Inscription, 1878 *illus*	881.00
Daguerreotype, Black Nursemaid, Holding Sleeping White Infant, Paper Case, 3 ¼ x 2 ¾ In.	2006.00
Daguerreotype, Fireman, Bowtie, Cap, Hose 2, ⅑ Plate, Case	750.00
Daguerreotype, Gold Miner, Beard, Bulky Coat, 10 Gallon Hat, ⅙ Plate *illus*	999.00
Daguerreotype, Jenny Lind, Portrait, Hand Colored, With Ambrotype, ⅙ Plate	1763.00
Daguerreotype, Locket, Man, Wife With Son, 2-Sided, Gold, Hinged, 2 In.	475.00
Daguerreotype, Militia Officer, Shako & Sword, Leather Case, c.1850, ¼ Plate *illus*	940.00
Daguerreotype, Niagara Falls, Men & Women, Babbit, Half Tint, 1858, ½ Plate	2585.00
Daguerreotype, Portrait, Architect At Work, Pressed Paper, Leather Case, ½ Plate *illus*	15405.00
Daguerreotype, Portrait, Young Man, Beaver Top Hat, Leather Case, ⅙ Plate *illus*	1067.00
Daguerreotype, Post Mortem, Baby, Brass Mat, Ball & Thomas, c.1860, ½ Plate	2160.00
Daguerreotype, Post Mortem, Mother Holding Deceased Child, Inscribed, 1853, ⅙ Plate *illus*	652.00
Daguerreotype, Violinist, Holding Violin & Bow, Music On Table, ⅙ Plate, Case	1750.00
Daguerreotype, Young Girl, Nellie McCallum, Brass Mat, Ball & Thomas, c.1860, ⅙ Plate	294.00
Graphoscope, Burl, 3-Part Folding Frame, Lens, Ring, 1800s, 8 ½ x 5 ½ In.	345.00
Magic Lantern, Brass Lens Apparatus, Tin Smoke Cap, Newton & Co., 13 x 14 ½ In.	118.00
Magic Lantern, Brass, Paper Covered Box, Vulcan Figure, Embossed Tin, Schoenner, 13 In.	472.00
Magic Lantern, Mechanical, Oil Lamp Insert, Box	525.00
Photograph, Cabinet Card, Apache Scout, Baker & Johnston, Evanston, 1880s *illus*	919.00
Photograph, Cemetery Marble Monument Samples, 4 ½ x 9 ½ In., 4 Piece	141.00
Photograph, Civil War Color Bearer, Kady Brownell, Zouave Uniform, Holding Carbine	1410.00
Photograph, Portrait, Robert E. Lee, Brady, Vignette, Oval, Frame, c.1866, 6 x 7 In.	1293.00
Photograph, Terminal Tower, View In Arch, Black, White, M. Bourke-White, 29 x 22 In.	351.00
Photograph, U.S.S. Akron, Signed, Margaret Bourke-White, 1930s, 17 x 23 In.	2160.00
Tintype, Civil War, 8th Maine Drum & Bugle Corps, Glass Negative, 3 x 3 ¾ In., ½ Plate	1410.00
Tintype, Civil War, Armed Virginia Volunteer, ½ Case, c.1860, ⅙ Plate	1645.00
Tintype, Union Soldier, Standing, Inscribed, Isaac Grant My Soldier Boy, Leather Case, ⅙ Plate *illus*	533.00

PIANO BABY is a collector's term. About 1880, the well-decorated home had a shawl on the piano. Bisque figures of babies were designed to help hold the shawl in place. They range in size from 6 to 18 inches. Most of the figures were made in Germany. Reproductions are being made. Other piano babies may be listed under manufacturers' names.

Baby, Crying, Norcrest, 1960s, 5 In.	27.00
Baby, Seated, Holding Doll, Paint, 12 In.	207.00
Boy, Crawling, Thumb In Mouth, 6 ½ x 8 In.	100.00
Boy, Playing With Toes, Marked, 4 ½ In.	20.00
Girl, Holding Bowl & Spoon, Marked, Royal Crown, 4 ½ In.	30.00
Girl, Playing With Cat, Marked, Royal Crown, 4 ½ In.	20.00
Twins, Boys, Bird's Nest, Heubach, 1800s, 5 ¼ In.	1200.00

Photography, Daguerreotype, Post Mortem, Mother Holding Deceased Child, Inscribed, 1853, ⅙ Plate
$652.00

Skinner, Inc.

Photography, Photograph, Cabinet Card, Apache Scout, Baker & Johnston, Evanston, 1880s
$919.00

Skinner, Inc.

TIP
Put felt pads on the bottom corners behind a hanging picture frame to protect the wall and to let air circulate.

Photography, Tintype, Union Soldier, Standing, Inscribed, Isaac Grant My Soldier Boy, Leather Case, ⅙ Plate
$533.00

Skinner, Inc.

Picture, Memorial, Paper, Embossed, Cutout, Gilt, Inscription, Windsor, Frame, 1857, 17 x 20 In.
$147.00

Garth's Auctions, Inc.

Picture, Memorial, Watercolor, Simulated Needlework Stitches, Inscription, Frame, c.1825, 22 x 25 In.
$4113.00

Garth's Auctions, Inc.

Picture, Needlework, Mourning, Woman At Grave, Silk, Frame, 1800s, 14 x 11 ½ In.
$295.00

Brunk Auctions

Picture, Portrait, Woman, Oval, Gilt Metal Frame, England, 1800s, 2 ⅝ In.
$184.00

Skinner, Inc.

PICKARD China Company was started in 1893 by Wilder Pickard. Hand-painted designs were used on china purchased from other sources. In the 1930s, the company began to make its own china wares in Chicago, Illinois. The company now makes many types of porcelains, including a successful line of limited edition collector plates.

Bowl, Cover, Underplate, Forest Pattern, Gilded, Signed, Yeschek, Bowl 5 ½ x 9 ⅜ In.	173.00
Cake Plate, Cream Ground With Pheasant Design, 2 Handles, 10 ½ In.	125.00
Cup & Saucer, Brocade, 3 ⅜ x 3 ⅛ In.	34.00
Pitcher, Fruit, Leaves, Gilt Border, Scrolled Handle, 11 In.	678.00
Place Setting, Bracelet, Cream, Silver Rim, 4 Piece	60.00
Plate, Dinner, Athena, 10 ⅞ In.	33.00
Plate, Dinner, Crescent, 10 ¾ In.	124.00
Plate, Salad, Nocturne, 8 ¼ In.	88.00
Plate, Service, White, Wide Gold Rim, 10 ½ In., 12 Piece	420.00
Sugar & Creamer, Green, Floral Blossoms, Gold Trim, Signed	10.00
Sugar & Creamer, Light Green With Blossom Design, Gold Trim, Signed	10.00

PICTURES, silhouettes, and other small decorative objects framed to hang on the wall are listed here. Some other types of pictures are listed in the Print and Painting categories.

Beadwork, Flower, Metallic Thread, Glass Beads, Silk Ground, Vines, Wood Frame, 1600s, 10 x 9 In..	2015.00
Calligraphy, Pen, Ink, Watercolor, German Text, Birds, Tulip Border, Frame, c.1818, 11 x 9 In.	353.00
Charcoal, On Paper, 4 Hands, Reaching, Pointing, Edmund Quincy, U.S.A., 1900s, 19 x 25 In..	60.00
Charcoal, On Paper, Deux Avocats En Conversation, Initialed, H.D., 9 x 8 In.	563.00
Charcoal, On Paper, Nude Study, Raphael Soyer, Frame, 25 x 21 In.	322.00
Drawing, Ink, At The Well, France, Frame, 14 x 20 In.	380.00
Drawing, On Paper, Silhouette, Kaufman Family, Samuel Metford, Frame, 1838, 8 x 9 In.	1300.00
Dried Flowers, Farmer's Wreath, Seeds, Shadowbox Frame, c.1870, 21 x 17 In.	120.00
Fish, Diorama, Rainbow Trout, Wood, Charles A. Lawrence, Shadowbox Frame, 1940, 14 x 11 In.	353.00
Memorial, Paper, Embossed, Cutout, Gilt, Inscription, Windsor, Frame, 1857, 17 x 20 In. ....*illus*	147.00
Memorial, Watercolor, Simulated Needlework Stitches, Inscription, Frame, c.1825, 22 x 25 In. *illus*	4113.00
Memorial, Watercolor, Urn, 2 Children, Rebecca & Capt. Jonathan Foster, c.1813, 13 x 17 In.	1410.00
Needlepoint, Wool, Red Tailed Hawk, On Branch, Frame, c.1900, 8 ¼ x 8 ½ In.	354.00
Needlework, 7 Rows Of Alphabets, House, 2 Dogs, Girl, Peacock, Bird, Bush, c.1827, 11 x 17 In.	237.00
Needlework, Books, Fence, Pond, Wool, Velvet, Silk, Frame, c.1875, 16 x 20 In.	764.00
Needlework, Courting Scene, Sheep, Pastor, 41 x 30 In.	750.00
Needlework, Crewel, Basket, Cherries, Red, Brown, Yellow, Frame, Signed C. Petty, c.1900, 16 x 20 In.	124.00
Needlework, Dragons, Waves, Glazed, Frame, Chinese, c.1890, 13 x 12 In., Pair	858.00
Needlework, Floral Wreath, Yarn Sculptured, Black Felt, Black Painted Frame, 22 x 22 In.	165.00
Needlework, Floral Wreath, Yarn Sculptured, Black Velvet, Brown Painted Frame, 22 x 23 In.	130.00
Needlework, Flower Bouquet, Yarn Sculptured, Black Velvet, Gold Painted Frame, 18 ½ x 18 ½ In.	153.00
Needlework, Holy Family Fleeing To Egypt, Biblical Verse, Frame, 1800s, 17 x 13 In.	460.00
Needlework, Landscape, Figures, Panel, Silk, Chinese, Frame, 22 In., 4 Piece	239.00
Needlework, Memorial, Woman Under Weeping Willow, Oval, On Silk, 1806, 13 x 11 In.	3163.00
Needlework, Mourning, Maiden Placing Flowers At Tomb Of Shakespeare, Gilt Frame, 15 x 12 In.	440.00
Needlework, Mourning, Woman At Grave, Silk, Frame, 1800s, 14 x 11 ½ In. ....*illus*	295.00
Needlework, Portrait, George Washington, 13 Stars, Eagle, Flags, Flowers, Frame, 16 x 27 In.	470.00
Needlework, Potted Plants, Vines, Animals, Trees, Hearts, Crowns, Birds, Frame, 1797, 19 x 13 In.	889.00
Needlework, RMS Lusitania, On Water, Stumpwork, Wool, Frame, 21 x 31 In.	950.00
Needlework, Salute The Flag, Sailor Holding American Flag, Frame, Early 1900s, 14 x 17 In.	288.00
Needlework, Still Life, Wool Felt, Embroidery Thread, Birds, Berry Baskets, Gilt Frame, 19 x 23 In.	1058.00
Needlework, Urn, Flowers, Distant Castle, On Silk, Frame, c.1815-25, 10 x 14 In.	115.00
Pastel, On Paper, Portrait Of Young Woman In Feathered Headpiece, 1777, 17 ¼ x 14 In.	263.00
Pastel, Portrait Of Girl In Pink, Frame, France, 33 x 25 In.	2340.00
Phoenix, Flowers, Panel, Embroidered, Silk, Frame, 1800s, 18 x 28 ½ In.	150.00
Plaque, Landscape, Metal, Painted, 5 ¾ x 4 ¾ In.	210.00
Portrait, Wax, Dr. Ray, Oak, Frame, England, 1800s, Miniature, 2 In.	120.00
Portrait, Woman, Oval, Gilt Metal Frame, England, 1800s, 2 ⅝ In. ....*illus*	184.00
Silhouette, Husband, Wife, Master Hubbard, Watercolor, Maple Frame, c.1835, 14 x 10 In., Pair *illus*	764.00
Silhouette, Lucy & Benjamin, Clilverd, Cut Paper, Inked Names, Aged 7 & 12, 1840, 8 In.	690.00
Silhouette, Major General Josef Edson, Hollowcut, Black Oval Frame, Conn., 1778, 6 x 5 In..	58.00
Silhouette, Man, Standing, Checked Trousers, Top Hat, A. Edouart, Frame, c.1835, 14 x 12 In. *illus*	499.00
Silhouette, Man, Waistcoat, Hat, Wood Frame, Signed, A. Edouart, 1828, 14 x 10 ¼ In.	51800.00
Silhouette, Portrait, George & Martha Washington, Tan Paper Mat, Frame, 5 ½ x 4 ¼ In., Pair	46.00
Silhouette, Woman, Man, Cut By Moses Chapman, Danvers, Frame, 1808, 4 ¾ x 3 ¼ In., Pair	138.00
Stumpwork, Elizabethan Style, Elijah, Fed In Desert, Embroidered, Silk, 10 ½ x 13 ½ In.	94.00

P

Stumpwork, Elizabethan Style, Moses Brings Forth Water, Embroidered, Silk, 11 x 14 In.......	83.00
Theorem, Gouache, On Linen, Watermelon, Frame, 21 ½ x 25 ½ In.	1404.00
Theorem, Gouache, On Velvet, Flowers, Frame, 22 ½ x 26 ¾ In..........................	497.00
Theorem, On Velvet, Basket, Strawberries, David Ellinger, Blue Frame, 1900s, 7 ½ x 8 ¼ In. ...	356.00
Theorem, On Velvet, Hunter, Wife On Horseback, Dog, House, Trees, 1828, 18 x 22 In.	14900.00
Theorem, Watercolor, On Moire, Green Fruit, Frame, Applied Half Turnings, 11 x 13 In.	206.00
Theorem, Watercolor, On Velvet, 2 Cats, Playing With Ball, Painted Frame, 12 x 16 In...........	4888.00
Theorem, Watercolor, On Velvet, Basket Of Fruit, Frame, c.1840, 13 ½ x 17 In. ....*illus*	542.00
Theorem, Watercolor, On Velvet, Basket Of Fruit, Gilt Frame, c.1800s, 15 x 17 ½ In.	558.00
Theorem, Watercolor, On Velvet, Child's Silhouette, Stencil, Frame, Aug. 18, 1827, 18 x 17 ½ In. *illus*	588.00
Theorem, Watercolor, On Velvet, Fruit Still Life, Compote, Multicolor, Signed, Frame, 9 ½ x 11 ½ In...	236.00
Theorem, Watercolor, On Velvet, Rooster Crowing, Terrence Graham, Frame, 26 x 26 In.	353.00
Theorem, Watercolor, Paper, Wild Rose, Buds, Violets, E.A. Shipler, c.1834, 5 x 7 In...............	288.00
Tinsel, Reverse Painted Glass, Urn Of Flowers, Mary Hull, Frame, 23 x 17 In...............	90.00
Watercolor, 3 Kittens, 1 On Red Stool, Mahogany Frame, 10 x 14 In......................	288.00
Watercolor, At The Track, Horses, Paul Maze, c.1890, 4 ½ x 8 In......................	293.00
Watercolor, Autumn Cattails, Barn, Stream, Trees, Signed, Martin Banke, Frame, 1900s, 24 x 37 In. ..	173.00
Watercolor, Balloon Seller In The Park, John C. Pellew, U.S.A., Frame, 1900s, 20 x 26 In........	660.00
Watercolor, Bird Of Paradise, Multicolor, Patricia Burlin, Frame, 1900s, 15 x 18 In...............	173.00
Watercolor, California Seascape, Coastal Village, Guy McCoy, Frame, 1900s, 15 x 22 In.	69.00
Watercolor, Cape Cod Marsh, J. Grasso, Frame, 10 x 18 In.	196.00
Watercolor, Child, Hoop Toy, Landscape Background, Frame, 6 x 6 ½ In......................	201.00
Watercolor, Clovelly Herring Boat, 2 Boats, River Scene, L.R. O'Brien, 10 ½ x 14 ¾ In............	1118.00
Watercolor, Daisy, Calico Cat, Black Eye, Sitting On Rug, Wood Frame, 7 x 9 In.................	920.00
Watercolor, Early Morning Mist, Provincetown, Sailboat, John Hare, Frame, 8 x 7 In.	460.00
Watercolor, Family Record, Tree With Fruit, New England, Gilt Frame, c.1810, 10 ½ x 9 In. ... *illus*	646.00
Watercolor, Flowers, Urn, Applied Paper, Other Materials, Diederichs, 1845, 16 ½ x 13 In. ..*illus*	353.00
Watercolor, Fresh Air In Hampstead, J. Shaw Crompton, Frame, 20 x 23 In.	293.00
Watercolor, Girl Standing, Wearing Blue Dress, Frame, 1800s, 9 x 7 In.	633.00
Watercolor, Harbor Scene, Ships, Sailboats, J. Dull, Frame, 9 x 13 In.......................	173.00
Watercolor, In The Jemez Indian Pueblo, J.N. Darling, 1926, 13 x 10 In......................	173.00
Watercolor, Lady, Profile, Hair Comb, Frame, 5 x 4 In.......................	2468.00
Watercolor, Lake, Tree Line, Frame, c.1930, 23 x 18 ¾ In.	195.00
Watercolor, Landscape, Church & Cart, George Nattress, Frame, 13 x 9 In......................	403.00
Watercolor, Landscape, Crypt, Trees Form Napoleon Outline, Gilt Frame, c.1840, 11 x 9 In. ....*illus*	294.00
Watercolor, Landscape, J.L. Sangster, c.1926, 9 ¾ x 7 ¼ In.	325.00
Watercolor, Mourning, Ink, Gold Foil, Woman Grieving, Monument, Oval, Frame, 1835, 13 x 10 In.	2844.00
Watercolor, Niagara, J. Wells, 1896, Frame, 23 x 27 In.	556.00
Watercolor, On Board, After Dinner, Women, Table, R. Moretti, Italy, 1800s, 20 x 14 In........	480.00
Watercolor, On Ivory, Mourning, Woman, Urns, Incised Frame, 1 ¾ x 1 ½ In. ....*illus*	236.00
Watercolor, On Porcelain, Ruth, Standing, Holding Wheat, Gilt Wood Frame, 5 x 4 In.	863.00
Watercolor, Portrait, Child, Red Dress, Holding Whip, Frame, 11 ½ x 9 In.	382.00
Watercolor, Portrait, Young Girl, Coral Beaded Necklace, c.1800, 3 x 2 In......................	118.00
Watercolor, River Landscape, Cattle, Distant Farm, Sunset, B.H. Martin, Frame, 14 x 26 In....	161.00
Watercolor, Rooster, Frederick Chatterton, England, Frame, 12 x 8 In.	237.00
Watercolor, Rooster, Yellow, Red Comb, Wood Frame, 1800s, 4 x 3 In.	259.00
Watercolor, Satire Of Jamaican Medicine, Captain William Frazer, Frame, 1801, 10 x 15 In......	5925.00
Watercolor, Screech Owl, Perched On Tree Branch, V. Stieler, Frame, 1900s, 32 x 26 In.	144.00
Watercolor, Sketch Of 2 Women, Standing Close, I.R. Wiles, Frame, 1883, 10 x 7 In..............	374.00
Watercolor, View Of Barnet Centre, Church, Hillside, Wood Frame, c.1830, 12 x 15 In.	2015.00
Watercolor, Winter Scene, Mt. Monadnock, Ralph W. Gray, Frame, 1931, 17 x 22 In.	230.00
Watercolor, Woman In Blue Dress, Holding Book, Nosegay, Frame, c.1830, 17 x 16 In.............	547.00
Watercolor, Woman, Seated At Table, Hat, Flowers, I. Tarkay, Frame, 16 x 11 In.............	1063.00
Watercolor, Yellow Bearded Iris, A.E. Sherer, Frame, 27 ¾ x 21 In........................	380.00
Watercolor, Young Man, Well Dressed, Holding Hat, Frame, 1800s, 12 x 10 In.	374.00

PICTURE FRAMES *are listed in this book in the Furniture category under Frame.*

PIERCE, *see Howard Pierce category.*

PIGEON FORGE POTTERY was started in Pigeon Forge, Tennessee, in 1946. Red clay found near the pottery was used to make the pieces. Molded or thrown pottery with matte glaze and slip decoration was made. The pottery closed in 2000.

Candleholder, Green Glaze, Marked, E. Ownby, 2 ½ In..........................	34.00
Jug, Green Matte Glaze, Foamy White Drip Top, 5 In........................	6.00
Mug, Blue Crystalline Glaze, Brown Drip Top, Tapered, D. Ferguson, 4 In................	5.00

Picture, Silhouette, Husband, Wife, Master Hubbard, Watercolor, Maple Frame, c.1835, 14 x 10 In., Pair
$764.00

Garth's Auctions, Inc.

Picture, Silhouette, Man, Standing, Checked Trousers, Top Hat, A. Edouart, Frame, c.1835, 14 x 12 In.
$499.00

Garth's Auctions, Inc.

Picture, Theorem, Watercolor, On Velvet, Basket Of Fruit, Frame, c.1840, 13 ½ x 17 In.
$542.00

Garth's Auctions, Inc.

Picture, Theorem, Watercolor, On Velvet, Child's Silhouette, Stencil, Frame, Aug. 18, 1827, 18 x 17 ½ In.
$588.00

Garth's Auctions, Inc.

Picture, Watercolor, Family Record, Tree With Fruit, New England, Gilt Frame, c.1810, 10 ½ x 9 In.
$646.00

Garth's Auctions, Inc.

Picture, Watercolor, Flowers, Urn, Applied Paper, Other Materials, Diederichs, 1845, 16 ½ x 13 In.
$353.00

Garth's Auctions, Inc.

Picture, Watercolor, Landscape, Crypt, Trees Form Napoleon Outline, Gilt Frame, c.1840, 11 x 9 In.
$294.00

Garth's Auctions, Inc.

Vase, Black, Cream Vertical Striations, Baluster, B. Summers, 6 In.	38.00
Vase, Free-Form, Marked, 7 ⅝ x 7 In.	125.00
Vase, Striped, Pinched Waist, 5 ½ In.	95.00

PILKINGTON TILE AND POTTERY COMPANY was established in 1892 in England. The company made small pottery wares, like buttons and hatpins, but soon started decorating vases purchased from other potteries. By 1903, the company had discovered an opalescent glaze that became popular on the Lancastrian pottery line. The manufacture of pottery ended in 1937. Pilkington's Tiles Ltd. has worked from 1938 to the present.

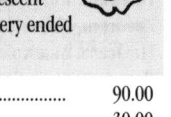

Tile, Mountain, Lake, Tree, 1930s, 8 x 4 In.	90.00
Tile, Yellow Flowers, Green Leaves, Art Nouveau, c.1900, 6 x 6 In.	30.00
Vase, 2-Horned Deer, Leaves, Shouldered, Richard Joyce, 8 In.	4500.00
Vase, Abstract Flower Design, Luster Glaze, Green, Yellow, Blue, Urn Shape, 1918, 13 ½ In.	920.00
Vase, Holly, Berries, Iridescent, Squat, Royal Lancastrian, c.1906, 3 ¼ In.	29.00

PILLIN pottery was made by Polia (1909–1992) and William (1910–1985) Pillin, who set up a pottery in Los Angeles in 1948. William shaped, glazed, and fired the clay, and Polia painted the pieces, often with elongated figures of women, children, flowers, birds, fish, and other animals. Pieces are marked with a stylized Pillin signature.

W+P
Pillin

Bowl, Fishing Scene, Signed, 6 ½ x 10 ½ In.	1612.00
Bowl, Multitoned Brown, White Glaze, Signed Polia Pillin, 12 ¼ x 4 ¼ In.	220.00
Bowl, Round Foot, Wide Rim, Volcanic Glaze, Turquoise Color, Signed, 4 x 9 In.	316.00
Cup, Bird Design, Yellow Ground, Signed Polia Pillin, 3 x 3 ¼ In., 6 Piece	303.00
Plaque, Horses, Painted, Blue, Signed Polia Pillin, Frame, 11 x 5 ½ In.	1020.00
Plaque, Tile, Horses, Paint, Blue, Pink, Signed Polia Pillin, Frame, 11 x 5 ½ In.	935.00
Tray, 2 Women, Under Tree, 1 Playing Lute, Bird, Marked, 7 x 6 In.	489.00
Vase, 2 Women, Gazelle, Brown Tones, Marked, 9 ½ In. *illus*	531.00
Vase, 3 Figures, Multicolor, Tapered, Polia Pillin, 2 ¾ x 9 ¼ In.	523.00
Vase, 3 Horses, Painted, Green, Brown Glaze, Long Neck, Signed Polia Pillin, 5 ¼ x 6 ¾ In.	385.00
Vase, Bottle Shape, Bulbous, Redheaded Woman, Bird, Black Ground, Signed, 4 In.	460.00
Vase, Brown Tones, White Volcanic Glaze, Bulbous, Signed Polia Pillin, 6 x 21 In.	385.00
Vase, Figure, Animals, Blue Ground, Bulbous, Signed Polia Pillin, 4 ½ x 4 ¾ In.	440.00
Vase, Multitone Brown, White Volcanic Glaze, Tall, Bulbous, Polia Pillin, 6 x 21 In.	420.00

PINCUSHION DOLLS are not really dolls and often were not even pincushions. Some collectors use the term "half-doll." The top half of each doll was made of porcelain. The edge of the half-doll was made with several small holes for thread, and the doll was stitched to a fabric body with a voluminous skirt. The finished figure was used to cover a hot pot of tea, powder box, pincushion, whiskbroom, or lamp. They were made in sizes from less than an inch to over 9 inches high. Most date from the early 1900s to the 1950s. Collectors often find just the porcelain doll without the fabric skirt.

Bonnet Woman, Painted, Dresden Flowers, Ernst Bohne, c.1900, 7 In. *illus*	952.00
Elegant Hat, Curls, Hard Stuffed Skirt, Porcelain Upper, Germany, c.1900, 7 ½ In.	210.00
Nude Woman With Hair Ornaments, Porcelain, Dresden Rose, Germany, c.1900, 5 ½ In. *illus*	224.00
Nude Woman, Bisque, Mohair Wig, Painted Mask, Goebel, Germany, c.1915, 4 ½ In. *illus*	672.00
Nude Woman, Porcelain, 18th Century Hair, Germany, c.1915, 5 In. *illus*	280.00
Nude Woman, Porcelain, Textured Gold Turban, Turquoise Beads, Germany, c.1910, 4 In. *illus*	1456.00
Pierrette, Porcelain, Painted Curls, Parasol Skirt, Wood Handle, Germany, 1920, 11 In.	228.00
Renaissance Woman, Painted, Gilt Cap, Herend, Hungary, c.1920, 6 In. *illus*	616.00
Woman In Plumed Bonnet, Porcelain, Sculpted Hair, Dresden Flower, Germany, c.1900, 6 In. *illus*	280.00
Woman, Flapper, Arms Closed, Orange Buttons, Marked 5857, Germany, 2 ¾ In.	100.00
Woman, Molded Hair, Silk & Lace Dress, Germany, c.1900, 5 In.	145.00
Woman, Tilted Head, Bent Arms, Sculpted Hair, Wide-Brim Hat, Flower, Germany, c.1900, 7 In.	662.00

PINK SLAG pieces are listed in this book in the Slag Glass category.

PIPES have been popular since tobacco was introduced to Europe by Sir Walter Raleigh. Carved wooden, porcelain, ivory, and glass pipes may be listed here.

Applewood, Black Man, Stick, Poking Alligator, Carved, Painted, Southern, c.1900, 9 ¾ In.	531.00
Birchwood, Hand Carved, Man's Head, Bead Eyes, Folk Art, c.1900, 6 x 5 In.	29.00
Briarwood, Carved, Bust Of Devil, Feathered Cap, Glass-Eyed Dragon Shank, Amber Bit, 18 In.	1067.00
Burlwood, Carved, American Eagle Bowl, 6 ¼ In.	207.00
Clay, Glazed, Bust Portrait, Martha Washington, c.1850	212.00
Hookah, 3-Piece, Porcelain, Flowers, Medallions Of Persian Men, 27 In.	2640.00

P

Meerschaum, Baseball Players, Swinging Bat, Catcher, Gold Band, Case, 10 ¼ x 4 ⅛ In.........	1896.00
Meerschaum, Celluloid Stem, Horse Head, 14K Gold Presentation, Osage Chief, Case, c.1900	1150.00
Meerschaum, Figural, Woman Jockey, Leather Covered Case, 5 In................................*illus*	209.00
Meerschaum, Scantily Clad Woman, Leaves, Branches, Carved, 1900, 9 ¾ In.....................	207.00
Meerschaum, Turk's Head, Dark Face, Headdress, Silver Band, Half Fitted Case, 6 ⅞ x 3 In....	674.00
Opium, Metal, Scrolling Dragon, Leaves, Chinese, 11 In...	122.00
Opium, Tortoiseshell, Jade Mouthpiece, 21 In...	671.00
Stone, Tube, 8 In..	533.00
Tamper, Iron, Lovers Under Tree, c.1750...	295.00
Chrysanthemum, Wood Carving, 8 ⅛ In..	336.00
Stag Antler, Kirin, Geometric Cartouche, Wood Carving, 1800s, 8 ⅜ In..........................	671.00
Stag Antler, Leaf & Bamboo Design, Wood Carving, 7 ⅞ In......................................	244.00

PIRKENHAMMER is a porcelain manufactory started in 1802 by Friedrich Holke and J. G. Lilst. It was located in Bohemia, now Brezova, Czechoslovakia. The company made tablewares usually decorated with views and flowers. Lithophanes were also made. The mark of the crossed hammers is easy to remember as the Pirkenhammer symbol.

Bowl, Vegetable, Louise Shape, Flowers, Handles, c.1920.	45.00
Plate, Cupid, Flowers, Beads, Ribbed Border, Gilt Reticulated Rim, c.1910, 8 ¾ In.	295.00
Plate, Peach Roses, Violet To Yellow Ground, Gilt Rim, Marked, c.1910, 9 In.	115.00
Plate, Reticulated Rim Panels, Gold, Blue, Beige Ground, Marked, 9 ½ In.	195.00

PISGAH FOREST POTTERY was made in North Carolina beginning in 1926. The pottery was started by Walter B. Stephen, who had been making pottery in that location since 1914. The pottery continued in operation after his death in 1961. The most famous kinds of Pisgah Forest ware are the cameo type with designs made of raised glaze and the turquoise crackle glaze wares.

Lamp Base, Pale Blue Ground, Westward Ho, Marked Stephen, 1940s, 12 ¼ In.	708.00
Pitcher, Westward Ho, Blue Matte Glaze, White Glossy Glaze, W.B. Stephen, 1949, 5 ¾ In. ....*illus*	354.00
Teapot, Green & Brown, Stamped, 5 ¼ x 7 ¾ In...	18.00
Vase, Aubergine Glaze, Cream Inside, Baluster, Flared Rim, W. Stephen, 1930s, 11 In.	194.00
Vase, Blue Mottled Glaze, Baluster, Stamped, 6 ½ x 4 In..	112.00
Vase, Covered Wagon, Mottled Turquoise, Marked, W.B. Stephen, 1939, 7 In. ....*illus*	4012.00
Vase, Crackled Blue Glaze, Stephen, 1940, 18 In. ....*illus*	2832.00
Vase, Cream, Green, Blue, Crystalline Glaze, Marked, 6 ¾ In. ....*illus*	345.00
Vase, Gray, Pink Interior, Crystalline Glaze, Bands, 5 In.	259.00
Vase, Green, Beige Ground, Crystalline Glaze, Impressed W.B. Stephen, 1936, 9 ¼ In.	4248.00
Vase, Pioneer Scene Neck Band, Blue, Baluster, Stamped, 1931, 7 x 5 ½ In.	341.00
Vase, Runny Red Glaze, Green Rim, Impressed, W.B. Stephen, 1932, 13 ¾ In........................	590.00
Vase, Turquoise Gloss Exterior, 1940s, 6 ¾ In...	45.00

PLANTERS PEANUTS memorabilia are collected. Planters Nut and Chocolate Company was started in Wilkes-Barre, Pennsylvania, in 1906. The Mr. Peanut figure was adopted as a trademark in 1916. National advertising for Planters Peanuts started in 1918. The company was acquired by Standard Brands, Inc., in 1961. Standard Brands merged with Nabisco in 1981. Some of the Mr. Peanut jars and other memorabilia have been reproduced and, of course, new items are being made.

Ad, Magazine, Girl Juggling Nuts Atop Peanut Jar, 1962, 10 x 13 ½ In.........................	7.00
Bowl Set, Embossed Tin, Mr. Peanut Graphics, 1938, 6 In., 4 Bowls, 3 In., 5 Piece	15.00
Can, 10 Lb. Of Wholesome Whole Peanuts, Logo, Red, Green, 9 ¾ x 8 ¼ In........................	50.00
Can, Oil, Novola Brand, Mr. Peanut, Tin, Graphics On 4 Sides, Green, Red, Black, 8 x 14 In., Gal.	34.00
Case Cutter, Supermarket Premium, Metal, Retractable Razor, Yellow, Blue, c.1980, 4 In.......	6.00
Clock, Electric, Mr. Peanut On Face, Red Letters, Neon, c.1940, 18 In.	384.00
Coloring Book, 12 Months, c.1970, 8 ½ x 5 In.	12.00
Coloring Book, Story Of Company, c.1950, 13 Pages, 10 x 6 ¾ In................................	45.00
Cookbook, Cooking The Modern Way, Planters Edible Oil Company, 1948, 39 Pages	10.00
Costume, Mr. Peanut, Top Hat, Black, Yellow, Papier-Mache, 1930s................................	390.00
Dish, Cover, Peanut Shape, Squirrel Finial, Mr. Peanut Inside, 8 ¾ In.	25.00
Doll, Mr. Peanut, Wood, Painted, Segmented Limbs, Top Hat, c.1935, 9 In.......................	285.00
Figure, Fence Post Sitter, Mr. Peanut, Cast Iron, Painted, 1920s, 38 In.	5933.00
Figure, Mr. Peanut, Bendable, Planters Life Savers, 1991, 6 In.	9.00
Figure, Mr. Peanut, Blinking Eye, Base, 1939, 12 In.	5060.00
Figure, Mr. Peanut, Metal, Base, 1930s, 7 x 2 x 2 In.	715.00
Game, Planters, Mr. Peanut Punch-Out, 5 Cent To Select Winner, Board, 1930s	125.00
Glass, Premium, Mr. Peanut, Waving, Black, Yellow, 5 ½ x 2 ¾ In................................	26.00

Picture, Watercolor, On Ivory, Mourning, Woman, Urns, Incised Frame, 1 ¾ x 1 ½ In.
$236.00

Brunk Auctions

Pillin, Vase, 2 Women, Gazelle, Brown Tones, Marked, 9 ½ In.
$531.00

Brunk Auctions

Pincushion Doll, Bonnet Woman, Painted, Dresden Flowers, Ernst Bohne, c.1900, 7 In.
$952.00

Theriault's

Pincushion Doll, Nude Woman With Hair Ornaments, Porcelain, Dresden Rose, Germany, c.1900, 5 ½ In.
$224.00

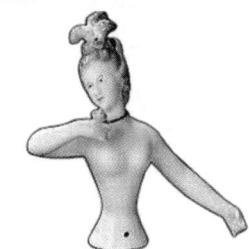

Theriault's

P

PLANTERS PEANUTS

Pincushion Doll, Nude Woman, Bisque, Mohair Wig, Painted Mask, Goebel, Germany, c.1915, 4 ½ In.
$672.00

Pincushion Doll, Nude Woman, Porcelain, 18th Century Hair, Germany, c.1915, 5 In.
$280.00

Pincushion Doll, Nude Woman, Porcelain, Textured Gold Turban, Turquoise Beads, Germany, c.1910, 4 In.
$1456.00

Pincushion Doll, Renaissance Woman, Painted, Gilt Cap, Herend, Hungary, c.1920, 6 In.
$616.00

Golf Set, Metal Divot, Plastic Ball Marker, Wood Tee, Golf Tournament Premium, 1970	12.00
Jar, Lid, 5 Cents, Clear Glass, Square Shape, Round Foot, 12 In.	120.00
Jar, Lid, Clear Glass, Impressed Mr. Peanut, 75th Anniversary, 1981, 8 x 3 ¼ In.	13.00
Jar, Lid, Peanut Finial, Hexagonal, Clear Glass, 12 ½ In.	150.00
Jar, Lid, Planters 5 Cent Pennant Salted Peanut, 8-Sided, Embossed Mr. Peanut, 12 ½ In.	45.00
Knife, Premium, Mr. Peanut Handle, Red, Plastic, c.1955, 6 ¾ In.	9.00
Lighter, Mr. Peanut, Blue Ground, Bic, c.1970, 3 ¼ In.	8.00
Ornament, Mr. Peanut, Chenille Arms & Legs, 5 ¼ In.	3000.00
Patch, Cloth, c.1970, 2 ½ In.	8.00
Pen, Mechanical, Mr. Peanut On Top, Barrel Ad Text, c.1980, 5 ¼ In.	15.00
Pen, Old Planters Mr. Peanut Bic Ballpoint, c.1980, 6 In.	10.00
Salt & Pepper, Black, Yellow, Plastic, c.1950, 4 In.	28.00
Salt & Pepper, Blue, Plastic, c.1930, 3 In.	18.00
Salt & Pepper, Monocle, Cane, Top Hat, 4 In.	20.00
Salt & Pepper, Pink, Plastic, 4 In.	18.00
Salt & Pepper, Rhinestone Monocle, Black Top Hat, Porcelain, Beige, 1958	150.00
Stringholder, Mr. Peanut, Holding Scissors, Chalk, 6 In., 1950s	295.00
Tin, Planters Salted Peanuts, Clean Crisp, Litho, Planters Nut & Chocolate Co., c.1915, 10 Lb. *illus*	231.00
Toy, Walker, Mr. Peanut, Plastic, Windup, 8 ½ In.	124.00 to 341.00
Vending Machine, Mr. Peanut, 10 Cent, Tin, 36 In.	181.00

PLASTIC objects of all types are being collected. Some pieces are listed in other categories. Celluloid is in its own category.

Barrette, Art Deco, Celluloid, Black Teardrop, Applied To Wavy Cream Base, 3 In.	45.00
Frame, Art Deco, Light Green, Black, c.1935, 8 x 11 In.	120.00
Nail Kit, Art Deco, Bakelite, Carved Cylinder, Elephant Head Top, Austria, c.1930, 3 ½ In.	125.00
Rattle, Holiday Lamb, Jumping Over Green Fence, Irwin Plastic, 4 ½ x 4 ½ In.	15.00
Salt & Pepper, Bell Shape, Red, 3 ¾ In.	10.00
Salt & Pepper, Figural, Toaster, Chromed, c.1950, 4 ¼ x 3 In.	8.00
Salt & Pepper, Washer, Dryer Shape, c.1960, 3 ½ In.	14.00
Sprinkler, Bottle, Figural, Woman, Yellow, c.1950, 6 ¾ In.	42.00
Syrup, Aunt Jemima, Red, F & F Plastics, Dayton, c.1935, 5 ¼ In.	45.00

PLATED AMBERINA was patented June 15, 1886, by Joseph Locke and made by the New England Glass Company. It is similar in color to amberina, but is characterized by a cream colored or chartreuse lining (never white) and small ridges or ribs on the outside.

Creamer, Amber Yellow To Rose, Applied Amber Handle, 4 ¼ In. ...*illus*	3738.00
Punch Cup, Ribbed, Amber Handle, 3 In. ...*illus*	2070.00
Syrup, Silver Plate, Ribbed, New England	500.00
Tumbler, Ribbed, Mahogany To Amber, c.1886, 3 ¾ x 2 ⅜ In.	1999.00

PLIQUE-A-JOUR is an enameling process. The enamel is laid between thin raised metal lines and heated. The finished piece has transparent enamel held between the thin metal wires. It is different from cloisonne because it is translucent.

Bowl, Flowers, Clear Ground, 4 In.	145.00
Bowl, Leaves, Flowers, Multicolor, 3 ¼ x 4 ¼ In.	350.00
Bowl, Lid, Copper, Open Framework, Chrysanthemums, Blue, 2 x 4 In.	140.00
Bowl, Paneled, Flowers, 7 x 3 ¾ In.	395.00
Ladle, Silver, Green & Red, Shell Shape Bowl, 5 ⅝ In.	165.00
Spoon, Sterling Silver, Pointed Tip, Rope Handle, 5 ½ In.	76.00
Vase, Butterflies, Red, Yellow, White Ground, 4 ¾ In.	350.00

POLITICAL memorabilia of all types, from buttons to banners, are collected. Items related to presidential candidates are the most popular, but collectors also search for material related to state and local offices. Memorabilia related to social causes, minor political parties, and protest movements are also included here. Many reproductions have been made. A jugate is a button with photographs of both the presidential and vice presidential candidates. In this list a button is round, usually with a straight pin or metal tab to secure it to a shirt. A pin is brass, often figural, sometimes attached to a ribbon.

Album, Bobby Kennedy, Interview With David Frost, Unopened, 12 ½ In.	30.00
Ashtray, John F. Kennedy, Ich Bin Ein Berliner, Wolfram Wiesau, Bavaria, 1963, 6 x 6 In. ...*illus*	109.00
Badge, McKinley, Brass, Gold & Silver Luster, Eagle, Suspended Black & White Photo, 2 ¼ In. ..*illus*	82.00
Badge, Theodore Roosevelt, Our Next President, Celluloid, Brass Back, 1912, 2 ½ In. ...*illus*	661.00
Bandanna, Adlai Stevenson, Blue Trim, Red, White, 1956, 28 x 28 In.	43.00

Bandanna, Benjamin Harrison, Protection Vs. Free Trade, Pension For Soldiers, 1888, 20 In.	122.00
Bandanna, Cleveland, Stevenson, Tariff Reform, Red, White Ground, Frame, 1892, 21 x 22 In.	258.00
Bandanna, Cleveland, Thurman, Horseshoe, Eagle, 1888, 18 x 19 In.	161.00
Bandanna, Garfield, Arthur, Red, White, Frame, 1880, 26 x 27 In.	258.00
Bandanna, Garfield, Arthur, The Union & The Constitution Forever, Jugate, Red, 19 x 21 In.	230.00
Bandanna, Grover Cleveland, Allen Thurman, Jugate, Red, White, 26 x 27 In.	225.00
Bandanna, Harrison, Reid, Eagles, Blue, 1892, 20 x 20 In.	207.00
Bandanna, Parker, Davis, Stars, Stripes, Red, White, Blue, 1904, 24 x 21 In.	280.00
Bandanna, We Want Willkie, Elephant Border, 1940, 22 x 22 In.	137.00
Bank, Full Dinner Pail, Metal, Gold Letters, Rectangular, Shaped Handle, Key, 3 In.	1500.00
Bank, Theodore Roosevelt Bust, Rear Slot, Glazed Plaster, 14 In.	575.00
Banner, Douglas, Johnson, Grand National, Jugate, Currier & Ives, Frame, 1860	2500.00
Banner, Printed, Grand Army Of The Republic, Muslin, 41 ½ x 24 ¼ In.	385.00
Banner, Welcome General MacArthur, Picture, Cloth, 56 x 34 In.	400.00
Bell, Figural, Suffragette, Woman Yelling, Other Side Pretty Woman, Acadian Crested, 4 In.	85.00
Blotter, Roosevelt, New Deal, Blue, Red, White, Streator Drain Tile Co., Celluloid, 7 ¾ In.	232.00
Bottle Opener, Taft, Elephant, Engraved T, Metal, 3 In.	44.00
Bottle, Pour Spout, Figural, Winston Churchill Head, Cigar In Mouth	90.00
Bumper Sticker, Ford, Dole, 1976, 11 ½ In.	8.00
Bust, Abraham Lincoln, Macerated United States Currency, Cardboard Plaque, 6 ½ x 3 ½ In.	182.00
Bust, Grover Cleveland, Public Office Is A Public Trust, Parian, 1884, 11 ½ x 7 ½ In.	275.00
Button, Adlai & Estes, The Bestest, Winning Team, 4-Leaf Clover, Celluloid, 1956, 3 In. *illus*	420.00
Button, Al Smith, Up From The Street, Photograph, Celluloid, 1928, 1 In.	201.00
Button, Alaskan Independence Party, Peroutka, Celluloid, Yellow, Black, 2004, 2 ½ In.	13.00
Button, Alben W. Barkley For Vice President, Portrait, Attached Ribbon, 1948, ⅞ In.	417.00
Button, Alf Landon, Picture, Double Sunflower Border, Celluloid, 1 ¼ x 2 ¾ In.	345.00
Button, Alfred E. Smith, For President, Photograph, Celluloid, 1928, 2 ½ In.	253.00
Button, Alfred Smith, President, Attached Brown Derby Hat, Celluloid, Plastic, 1 ½ In.	45.00
Button, Alton B. Parker, Portrait, Covered Metal, Bar Pin, 2 ⅛ In. *illus*	115.00
Button, Beware Hidden Hippies, Psychedelic Lettering, Black Rim, 1960s, 1 ¼ In.	52.00
Button, Bryan, Watson, Celluloid, Jugate, 1896, ⅞ In.	253.00
Button, Bush, Quayle Team, Oval, c.1988, 2 ¾ In.	7.00
Button, Bush, Trick Or Treat, 4 More Wars, Wearing Flight Suit, Celluloid, 3 In.	15.00
Button, Carter For Governor, Unflattering Caricature, Black & White, 1976, 2 ¼ In.	40.00
Button, Carter For President, Smiling Peanut, c.1976, 3 In.	9.00
Button, Carter, For President '76, Green, White, 1 ½ In.	5.00
Button, Charles Hughes, Red, White, Blue, 7 ⅛ In.	7.00
Button, Clenched Fist, Number On Wrist, Remember In Hebrew Letters, 1 ½ In.	52.00
Button, Clinton, Saxophone, New Tune For America, Celluloid, 2 ¼ In.	18.00
Button, Congress Of Racial Equality, Break The Noose, Yellow Ground, Black, 1 In.	200.00
Button, Coolidge Again, Red, White, Blue, Celluloid, 2 ½ In.	569.00
Button, Coolidge Again, Red, White, Blue, Celluloid, 4 In.	468.00
Button, Daniel Ellsberg, We Love You, Red, White & Blue, Celluloid, 2 ¼ In. *illus*	114.00
Button, Dewey, Warren, Celluloid, Jugate 3 ½ In.	35.00
Button, Dukakis, Bentsen, Stars, Stripes, 1988, 1 ¾ In.	6.00
Button, Eisenhower, Nixon, Jugate, Michigan Party Ribbon, 1952, 1 ¾ In.	1708.00
Button, Eisenhower, Sign Language, Celluloid, 1 ¼ In. *illus*	235.00
Button, Elect Kennedy President, Portrait, Blue Tones, 1960, 2 ½ In.	748.00
Button, Experience Counts, Vote Nixon, Lodge, Yellow, Blue, 1960	3.50
Button, FDR, A Pauper For Roosevelt, 1932, 1 ¼ In.	30.00
Button, FDR, Photograph, He's Good Enough For My Buck, ⅞ In.	30.00
Button, FDR, Sweeping The Depression Out, Black, White, 1932, 1 ¼ In.	30.00
Button, Fight University Bosses, Ally With Campus Workers, SDS, 1960s, 1 ¾ In.	75.00
Button, Fill The Faith Gap In '68, Bobby Kennedy, Psychedelic Style, 3 In.	52.00
Button, Flasher, Win With Nixon, 1960	11.00
Button, For President, Convict No. 9653, Eugene Debs Photograph, 1920	822.00
Button, For Truman In '48, Celluloid, White, Blue Letters, ⅞ In.	850.00
Button, Fourth Of July, Uncle Sam, Firecracker, Celluloid, Whitehead & Hoag, 1 ⅜ In.	259.00
Button, Franklin D. Roosevelt, For State Senator, Photograph, 1910, ⅞ In.	5816.00
Button, Franklin Roosevelt, Photograph, A Gallant Leader, c.1935, ⅞ In.	12.00
Button, Free The Knoxville 22, Red Fist, 1970, 1 ¼ In.	62.00
Button, Gen. John Pershing, He's All Right, Who's All Right?, Ribbon, Huntzinger, 1920, 1 ¼ In.	230.00
Button, General Ulysses S. Grant, Image, Multicolor, ¾ In.	10.00
Button, George McGovern, Autograph, On Stationary, Celluloid, 1972, 6 In.	246.00
Button, George Wallace, Photograph, Stand Up For America, 1968, 3 In.	12.00
Button, Goldwater, For Halloween, Black Ground, Gold Lettering, Celluloid, 1 ½ In.	30.00

Pincushion Doll, Woman In Plumed Bonnet, Porcelain, Sculpted Hair, Dresden Flower, Germany, c.1900, 6 In. $280.00

Theriault's

Pipe, Meerschaum, Figural, Woman Jockey, Leather Covered Case, 5 In. $209.00

Wm Morford Antiques

Pisgah Forest, Pitcher, Westward Ho, Blue Matte Glaze, White Glossy Glaze, W.B. Stephen, 1949, 5 ¾ In. $354.00

Brunk Auctions

Pisgah Forest, Vase, Covered Wagon, Mottled Turquoise, Marked, W.B. Stephen, 1939, 7 In. $4012.00

Brunk Auctions

As always, the edited listings in *Kovels' Antiques & Collectibles Price Guide* aren't available on any website, but readers should visit Kovels.com for information on trends, tips, reproductions, marks, old prices, and more!

Pisgah Forest, Vase, Crackled Blue
Glaze, Stephen, 1940, 18 In.
$2832.00

Brunk Auctions

Pisgah Forest, Vase, Cream, Green,
Blue, Crystalline Glaze, Marked, 6 ¾ In.
$345.00

Humler & Nolan

Planters Peanuts, Tin, Planters Salted
Peanuts, Clean Crisp, Litho, Planters Nut
& Chocolate Co., c.1915, 10 Lb.
$231.00

Wm Morford Antiques

Plated Amberina, Creamer, Amber
Yellow To Rose, Applied Amber Handle,
4 ¼ In.
$3738.00

Early Auction Co.

Button, Gone But Not Forgotten, Black, Glass Beer Mug Pendant, c.1919, 1 ¼ In.	127.00
Button, Gore, Bush As Scarecrow, Saying If Only I Had A Brain, Celluloid, 2 ¼ In.	17.00
Button, Gore, Soccer Moms, Celluloid, White, Black, Red, 2000, 2 ¼ In.	17.00
Button, GW Bush, Cheney, Flasher, 3 In. ....*illus*	10.35
Button, Harry S. Truman For President, Portrait, Union Bug On Reverse, 1948, ⅞ In.	557.00
Button, Harry S. Truman, Truman Eight-Ball, Tin Lithograph, 1 ¼ In.	9560.00
Button, Harvey Milk, For Supervisor, Picture, White Ground, Celluloid, c.1977, 1 ½ In.	93.00
Button, Herbert C. Hoover, For President, Portrait, Celluloid, 3 ½ In. ....*illus*	487.00
Button, Herbert Hoover Photograph, Black & White, 1928, 1 ¾ In.	230.00
Button, Hoo But Hoover, Poppy, A.G. Trimble Back Paper, ⅞ In.	2128.00
Button, Hoover, Stars & Stripes, Red, White & Blue, Celluloid, ¾ In. ....*illus*	22.00
Button, Humphrey & Muskie, HHH, Capitol City, Capitol Idea, St. Paul, Celluloid, 2 ¼ In. ....*illus*	76.00
Button, I Like Ike, Hebrew, White, Red, Blue, 1 ¼ In.	168.00
Button, Ike & Dick, Don't Change The Team, Red, White & Blue, Celluloid, 1956, 3 ½ In. ....*illus*	168.00
Button, Ike, I Hate Everybody, Celluloid, 1 ¼ In.	11.00
Button, Ike, I Work For Dick, Junior Club, Lithograph, 3 In.	22.00
Button, Ike's For Dick, & So Am I, Red, Blue, White Lettering, Celluloid, 1 In.	15.00
Button, I'm For Dick Nixon, Lithograph, 1960	4.50
Button, Irish Nationalists, Annual Outing, Robert Emmet, Cleveland, O., 1901, 1 ½ In.	139.00
Button, It's Gotta Be McG, Blue, Celluloid, 1 In. ....*illus*	12.65
Button, Jesse Jackson, 1988, 3 In.	7.00
Button, JFK, Mamie Start Packing, The Kennedys Are Coming, Celluloid, Red, White, Blue, 3 ½ In.	30.00
Button, John F. Kennedy, Hologram, The Man For The 60's, 2 ½ x 2 ½ In.	75.00
Button, John Glenn, U.S. Senate, Photograph, 1974, 1 ¾ In.	5.00
Button, John W. Davis, Farm Relief & Teapot Dome, Oil Cans, Celluloid, 1924, 1 ½ In.	750.00
Button, Kennedettes Girls For Kennedy, White Ground, Blue, Red, Celluloid, 1960, 3 ½ In.	290.00
Button, Kennedy For President, White, Blue Letters, 2 ¼ In.	86.00
Button, Kennedy, Humphrey, Freeman, Matthews, Capitol Dome, 2 ¼ In.	253.00
Button, LBJ, Light Bulb, Johnson, Turn Him Out In November, 2 ½ In.	40.00
Button, Let Well Enough Alone, Theodore Roosevelt, Celluloid, 1900, 1 In.	190.00
Button, Let's Get Out Of UN, Yellow Ground, ½ In.	2.00
Button, Lincoln, Ferrotype, ⅞ In.	840.00
Button, Make Hoover President, Photograph, 1928, ⅞ In.	95.00
Button, McCain, Palin, Geezer & Gidget, Celluloid, Color, 2 ¼ In.	24.00
Button, McCarthy, Blue, White, 1968, 1 ¾ In.	7.00
Button, McCarthy, For Peace, Anti War, Celluloid, Green Rim, Black, Photo, 1 In.	17.00
Button, McGovern 72, Superman Cartoon, 1 ½ In. ....*illus*	115.00
Button, McGovern, Concert, James Taylor, Carole King, Barbra Streisand, Celluloid, 3 ½ In.	224.00
Button, McGovern, Don't Blame Me, I Voted For McGovern, Celluloid, 1 ¼ In.	7.00
Button, McGovern, Vote A Hawk Out Of Office, Celluloid, ⅞ In.	34.00
Button, McKinley & Roosevelt, Gold, Rough Rider At Bottom, Jugate, 1 ½ In.	399.00
Button, McKinley Hobart National Wheelmen's Club, Jugate, Celluloid, Whitehead & Hoag, 1 ¼ In.	504.00
Button, McKinley Sweeper Cigars, Picture On Broom, Celluloid, ⅞ In.	102.00
Button, McKinley, Hobart, National Wheelmen's Club, Jugate, Celluloid, 1896, 1 ¼ In.	259.00
Button, McKinley, Portrait, Black & White Ray Background, Celluloid, Baltimore Badge, 1 ¼ In.	45.00
Button, McKinley, Roosevelt, Blue, Gold Beaded Ovals, Jugate, 1900, 1 ¼ In.	108.00
Button, McKinley, Roosevelt, Commerce & Industries, Jugate, 1900, 1 ¼ In.	316.00
Button, McKinley, Roosevelt, Ribbon, Celluloid, W & H Back Paper, Jugate, 2 ⅛ In. ....*illus*	114.00
Button, Nixon, Bugs Me, Ladybug, Celluloid, White, Black, 1 ½ In.	7.00
Button, Nixon, Jailhouse, Watergate, White, Black, Celluloid, 1 ¼ In.	10.00
Button, Nixon, Lodge, Experience Counts, Jugate, Easel Back, 1960, 9 In.	75.00
Button, Nixon, Watergate, 4 More Years Mr. Nixon, Then 10 To 20, Celluloid, 1 ½ In.	8.00
Button, No Oil On Al, Teapot Dome Scandal Reference, 1928, 1³⁄₁₆ In.	234.00
Button, Obama Inauguration, Triple Layers, 2009, 2 ¼ In.	28.00
Button, Our Choice, Parker & Davis, Flag & Ribbon Design, Jugate, 1904, 1 ¼ In.	538.00
Button, Our Next President, JFK Portrait, American Flag, 1960, 4 In.	139.00
Button, Parker, Davis, Lady Liberty Holding Flag, Jugate, Celluloid, 1904, 1 ¼ In.	978.00
Button, Parker, Davis, Shure Mike, Patriotic Rooster, Celluloid, 1904, 1 ¼ In.	627.00
Button, Peace, Jobs, Education, 5 Fists, Dove, Young Workers Liberation League, 2 ¼ In.	40.00
Button, Perot, 1996, Blue Ground, 1 ⅝ In.	5.00
Button, President Roosevelt, Rough Rider On Horseback In Horseshoe, 1 ¼ In.	998.00
Button, Reagan, Women For Reagan, Dancing White Elephant In Tutu, 2 ½ In.	34.00
Button, Reagan-Mania Sweeps N.J., Hoboken Dems For Reagan, Portrait, 1984, 2 ¼ In.	75.00
Button, Re-Elect Ronald Reagan, Our Choice, Barrett's Tavern, Portrait, 2 ¼ In.	86.00
Button, RFK, 68, Celluloid, Blue Ground, Red, White, 1 In.	235.00
Button, Richard M. Nixon, Photograph, 1968	7.00

Button, Richard Nixon, For President, Portrait, Celluloid, 1960, 9 In.	350.00
Button, Robert Kennedy, A Return To Greatness, Kennedy For President, 3 ⅔ In.	1540.00
Button, Ronald Reagan Is Watching You, Pyramid With Eye, 1984, 2 ½ In.	40.00
Button, Roosevelt, Fairbanks, Pince Nez, Pictures, Tinted Sepia, 1 ⅝ In.	193.00
Button, Roosevelt, Friend Of The People, Blue, Red, White, ⅞ In.	17.00
Button, Roosevelt, Garner, Jugate, Photo, 1 ¼ In.	520.00
Button, Roosevelt, Johnson, Progressive Party, Bull Moose, Liberty Bell, 1912, 1 ¼ In.	4480.00
Button, Roosevelt, Johnson, Progressives, Sepia Images, 1912, 1 ¼ In.	2550.00
Button, Roosevelt, Labor's Choice, Portrait, 1932, 1 ¾ In.	221.00
Button, Roosevelt, Mead, Stars & Stripes, Jugate, 1904, 1 ¼ In.	173.00
Button, Roosevelt, Rose-Velt, Rebus, Celluloid, Whitehead, Hoag, Back Paper, 1 ¼ In. ....illus	308.00
Button, Roosevelt, Truman, Jugate, Black & White, 1944, 1 ½ In.	316.00
Button, Ross Perot, 1992, 3 In.	5.00
Button, Salute Or I Shoot, Wilson, U.S. & Mexico Crisis, 1914, 1 ¼ In.	765.00
Button, Slovaks For Ford, 1976, 1 ½ In.	5.00
Button, Socialism, Hand Holding Torch, c.1917, ⅝ In.	63.00
Button, Spanish American War, One Country, One Flag, Whitehead & Hoag, Celluloid, 1 ¼ In.	23.00
Button, Stevenson, For President, Photograph, c.1952, ¾ In.	10.00
Button, Stevenson, Shoe With Hole In The Sole, For '56, Celluloid, 3 ½ In. .....illus	57.00
Button, Suffrage, Votes For Women, Celluloid, Gold, Black, ¾ In.	17.00
Button, Taft, Sherman, Jugate, Hearts, Art Nouveau Style, BB Backpaper, Celluloid, 1 ¼ In. ...	276.00
Button, Ted Kennedy, Celluloid, Photo, Printed Signature, 1 ¼ In.	27.00
Button, Teddy Roosevelt, Horseshoe, Celluloid, Arcade Co. Sewing Machines, 1904, 1 ¼ In. illus	748.00
Button, Teddy Roosevelt, Progressive, Moose Head, Celluloid, 1912, ⅞ In.	24.00
Button, Teddy Roosevelt, Rough Riders Campaign, American Flag Top, Celluloid, 1904, 2 In.	375.00
Button, The Allies, 5 Nation Flags, Celluloid, Mirror Back, Bastian, 2 ¾ In. .....illus	52.00
Button, Treehuggers For Kerry, Bear Cub In Tree, Paw Prints, Border, Celluloid, 2004, 3 ½ In.	17.00
Button, Truman, Barkley, Stars, Jugate, 1 ¼ In.	383.00
Button, Vietnam Pax, Peace, Celluloid, Black Ground, Turquoise, 1 In.	12.00
Button, Vietnam, Peter Max, Peace, Celluloid, Multicolor, 2 ½ In.	68.00
Button, Vietnam, Send John Wayne To Vietnam, Celluloid, Red, Black, 1 ¼ In.	25.00
Button, Vote Dry, Safety First, Ohio, Red Ground, Blue Umbrellas, White State, Celluloid, ¾ In.	7.84
Button, Vote Republican For Dewey & Warren, Jugate, Easel Back, Philadelphia Badge, 9 In..	104.00
Button, Votes For Women, Yellow, Blue Border, 12 White Stars, Ehrman Back Paper, Celluloid, 1 In.	230.00
Button, Wallace, For President, Photograph, 2 ⅞ In.	16.00
Button, Warren G. Harding, Portrait, Celluloid, 1 ¼ In.	275.00
Button, We Want Bobby K, Portrait Of Bobby Kennedy, 1968, 3 ½ In.	52.00
Button, White Elephant, Parker, Davis, 1 ½ In.	371.00
Button, Will-Key, For President, Celluloid, Lithograph, Attached Silver Metal Key, 1 In.	19.00
Button, Willkie, Better A Third Termer Than A Third Rater, Celluloid, 3 ½ In. .....illus	101.00
Button, Willkie, For Us, 1940, ¾ In.	4.00
Button, Winning Team, Nixon, Agnew, Black, Light Blue	5.00
Button, Wm. H. Taft, Colors, Celluloid, 1 ¼ In. .....illus	69.00
Button, Womanpower For Eisenhower, Female Elephant, GOP Banner, 1 ½ In.	75.00
Candy Container, Suffragette, Button, Votes For Women, Plaster, Composition, 5 In.	1950.00
Card, Election, Anti Alcohol, California, Vote Yes On Amendments 1 & 3, 7 In.	28.00
Cartoon, Such Is Life, Politician, Ice Cream Cones, V. Shoemaker, 1966, 15 x 13 In.	100.00
Chamber Pot, William Gladstone Portrait On Bottom, Ironstone, 9 In.	475.00
Cigarettes, Willkie, Cardboard Case, 1 ¾ x 2 ¾ In.	142.00
Clock, FDR, Man Of The Hour, Bartender Clock Face, 5:00 Shaker Arm, 1934, 10 x 14 x 4 In..	207.00
Cup & Saucer, Garfield & Wife, Porcelain, Sepia Photographic Transfer Portraits	575.00
Doily, Votes For Women, White Lace, 3 ½ x 5 In.	300.00
Doll, Winston Churchill, Pressed Felt, Cloth, Painted, Cigar, Fingers In V, 1940s, 17 In.	456.00
Doorstop, F.D. Roosevelt, Relief Image, Crossed Flags, Eagle, Brass, Shaped, 12 In.	675.00
Earrings, Dewey, H-Club, Help Hustle Harry Home, Celluloid, ⅞ In.	128.00
Envelope, Fremont & Wife, We Stand By The Union, Jugate, Crossed Flags, 3 x 5 ½ In.	127.00
Fan, Sunflower, Alf Landon, Paper Petals, Fabric, Wood, 1936, 15 x 11 In.	204.00
Figure, Donkey, Victory With Roosevelt 1932, Words In Relief, Cast Aluminum, 2 ½ x 3 In.	65.00
Figure, Elephant, Dirksen, Raised Trunk, White, Morton Pottery, 1950s, 2 ½ x 3 In.	25.00
Figure, George Washington, Cast Iron, Painted, c.1910, 36 In.	600.00
Figure, Hanging, Frederick Cook & Admiral Peary, Hugging Globe, Bisque, c.1910, 5 In.	570.00
Figure, JFK, Exaggerated Features, Gray Suit, Wood, Carved, J. Erickson, 8 ¼ In.	253.00
Flask, Figural, Club, Amber, Relief Letters, Big Stick, 7 In.	950.00
Flask, Whiskey, Statue Of Liberty, Holding Bottles, Raising Toast, Porcelain, Relief, 6 In.	500.00
Handkerchief, Hoover, Curtis, Linen, Embroidered, Elephant, 16 ½ In.	48.00
Hatchet, George Washington, Portrait, Silver, Metal, c.1940, 13 x 5 ½ In.	350.00

Plated Amberina, Punch Cup, Ribbed, Amber Handle, 3 In.
$2070.00

Early Auction Co.

Political, Ashtray, John F. Kennedy, Ich Bin Ein Berliner, Wolfram Wiesau, Bavaria, 1963, 6 x 6 In.
$109.00

Hake's Americana & Collectibles

Political, Badge, McKinley, Brass, Gold & Silver Luster, Eagle, Suspended Black & White Photo, 2 ¼ In.
$82.00

Hake's Americana & Collectibles

Political, Badge, Theodore Roosevelt, Our Next President, Celluloid, Brass Back, 1912, 2 ½ In.
$661.00

OUR NEXT PRESIDENT

Hake's Americana & Collectibles

P

Political, Button, Adlai & Estes, The Bestest, Winning Team, 4-Leaf Clover, Celluloid, 1956, 3 In.
$420.00

Anderson Americana

Political, Button, Alton B. Parker, Portrait, Covered Metal, Bar Pin, 2 ⅛ In.
$115.00

Hake's Americana & Collectibles

Political, Button, Daniel Ellsberg, We Love You, Red, White & Blue, Celluloid, 2 ¼ In.
$114.00

Anderson Americana

Political, Button, Eisenhower, Sign Language, Celluloid, 1 ¼ In.
$235.00

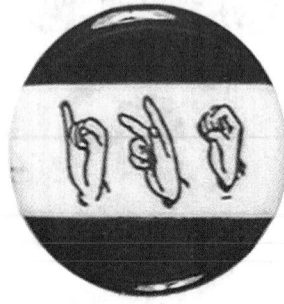

Anderson Americana

Lamp, Electric, Candlestick, FDR Seated, A New Deal, NRO Logo, Metal, Embossed, 7 x 5 In.	190.00
Lantern, Dinner Bucket Shape, Punched, McKinley, Roosevelt, 1900, 8 In.	1375.00
License Plate Attachment, Drive Ahead With Roosevelt, FDR, Uncle Sam, Rubber, 1936, 8 x 11 In.	230.00
License Plate Attachment, Landon, Knox, Sunflower, Letters On Petals, 1936, 3 ¾ x 5 In. ... *illus*	173.00
License Plate Attachment, Nixon, Wallace, Caricature Images, By George, I'm Worried, 1972	75.00
License Plate Attachment, Willkie, McNary, People's Choice, Jugate	650.00
License Plate Attachment, Win With Willkie, Metal, 4 ½ x 10 In.	85.00
License Plate Reflector, Landon, Knox, Sunflower, 4 In.	93.00
Lighter, Goldwater, Stylized Portrait, Elephant, 2 ⅛ In.	56.00
Mask, Barry Goldwater, I Go For Goldwater, Paper, Multicolor, 10 ¾ In.	25.00
Mask, Theodore Roosevelt, Die Cut, Cardboard, Cord, Eye Holes, Fold-Out Nose, c.1904, 4 x 5 ½ In. *illus*	173.00
Match Safe, McKinley, Metal, Embossed Profile, 2 ¾ In.	103.00
Medal, Rutherford B. Hayes, Indian Peace, Bronze, Oval, George T. Morgan, c.1877	1652.00
Mirror, Lafayette, Portrait, Commemorative, Nickel Plated, Hanger Loop, c.1824	2662.00
Mirror, Parker, Davis, Jugate, 1904, Celluloid, Glass, 1 In.	173.00
Mold, Candy, 3 Theodore Roosevelt Busts, Rough Rider Uniform, Metal, 2 Halves, 6 In.	225.00
Mug, Elephant Shape, Blue, Frankoma, c.1970, 4 x 5 In.	36.00
Mug, Lincoln, Garfield, Country's Martyrs, Clear Glass, Adams, c.1881, 2 ⅝ x 2 ⅝ In.	90.00
Mug, William Henry Harrison, Tippecanoe-Thames, Eagle, Union, Copper Luster, 4 In.	5750.00
Necktie, We Want Roosevelt, 1940 ....*illus*	139.00
Oyster Plate, 5 Wells, Rutherford Hayes, White House China, Limoges, c.1880, 8 ¾ In. .... *illus*	1793.00
Pamphlet, Al Gore, Jr. For U.S. Senate	6.50
Paperweight, Figural, Eagle Holding NRA, We Do Our Part, Cast Iron, Red, Blue, 4 In.	275.00
Paperweight, Harrison & Reid, Top Hat, One Good Term Deserves Another, 1892, 3 In.	173.00
Pass, House Of Representatives, 1953, Green, Black	16.00
Pennant, Elect Thomas E. Dewey President, White On Green, 1944, 29 ½ In.	45.00
Pennant, Inauguration January 20th, 1937, President F.D. Roosevelt, White & Blue, 28 In.	49.00
Pennant, NRA, We Do Our Part, Eagle, White, Red & Blue, 3-Sided, Streamers, c.1933, 23 In.	90.00
Pennant, Stonewall Texas, Home Of L.B.J., White Letters, Gold Border, House, 12 In.	7.00
Pennant, Vote Goldwater, American Needs A Change, Red & Blue, Photo, 1964, 29 ½ In.	35.00
Pennant, Woodrow Wilson, Felt, Cardboard Image, Eagle, Souvenir, 1913, 26 In.	364.00
Pillow, FDR, Churchill, Bombers, Battleships, WWII Slogans, Cloth, Fringe, 1941, 16 In.	133.00
Pin, Bryan, Silver Bug, Mechanical, Wings Open, Reveal Picture, 16 To 1, 1 ½ In.	123.00
Pin, Carter, Eagle, Spread Wings, Cloth, Sequins, Painted, 3 In.	98.00
Pin, Donkey, I'm So Wild About Harry, 1948, 2 ⅛ In. ....*illus*	224.00
Pin, Elephant, Enameled, Election Night, Nov. 6-84	9.50
Pin, FDR, Flag, Rhinestone, Pinback, 1 ¼ In.	39.00
Pin, FDR, Kick Out Depression, Mechanical, Donkey Kicking Elephant, Litho, 1932, 2 ¼ In.	157.00
Pin, FDR, V For Victory, Portrait On Panel, Goldtone Metal, 1944, 1 ½ In.	63.00
Pin, Goldwater, Elephant Shape, Black Glasses, 1 ¼ x 1 In.	48.00
Pin, Goldwater, Gold Elephant Head, Black Glasses, Clutch Back, 1 In.	14.00
Pin, GOP Elephant, 1960s, ⅞ In.	5.00
Pin, Grover Cleveland, Bar Pin, Name Spelled Out, Brass, 1 ¾ In.	39.00
Pin, Harding, Figural, Elephant, Enamel, ⅞ In.	68.00
Pin, Harrison, Gun, Brass, 1 ⅜ In.	111.00
Pin, JFK, Rocking Chair, Goldtone, ⅚ In.	30.00
Pin, Landon, Sunflower, Enamel, 9/16 In.	54.00
Pin, LBJ, For The USA, Vari-Vue Flasher, c.1964, 2 ½ In. .... 12.00 to 17.00
Pin, McKinley, Gold Bug, Gold Tone Metal, 6 In.	202.00
Pin, McKinley, Sound Money, Metal Bag Of Gold, Ribbon, Dinner Bucket, 2 ¼ In.	34.00
Pin, Mondale, Ferraro, Eviction Notice, Donkey Kicking Elephant, Celluloid, 2 ¼ In.	39.00
Pin, Nixon, As Cockroach, Watergate Bug, Celluloid, White, Black, 1 ¾ In.	11.00
Pin, Our Shirt For Roosevelt, Gray Cloth Shirt, Red, White, Blue Ribbon, 1 In.	46.00
Pin, Pitchfork Ben Tillman, U.S. Senator, S.C., Silver, 3 Speared Goldbugs, 2 In.	500.00
Pin, Sure Bet Reagan, Nevada, Sleeping Elephant, Enamel, Red, Blue, White, 1980, 2 ¼ In.	364.00
Pin, Taft, Name Spelled, Rhinestones, 1 ½ x ¾ In.	42.00
Pin, William Jennings Bryan, Mechanical, Pull Jaw, Mouth Opens, 16 To 1, 1 In.	504.00
Pitcher, Andrew Jackson In Cartouche, Hero Of New Orleans, Copper Luster, Shaped Handle, 7 In.	3750.00
Pitcher, John Kennedy, Jackie, Images, White Ground, Porcelain, 1960s, 4 ¾ In.	25.00
Pitcher, Portraits, Teddy Roosevelt, G. & M. Washington, Greek Key, Royal Doulton, 7 In.	1250.00
Pitcher, Reward Of Temperance, Family Scene, Eagle, Shield, Porcelain, 7 In.	500.00
Pitcher, Temperance Association, Flowers, Gilt, Porcelain, 6-Sided, 1840s, 8 ½ In.	1350.00
Plate, Bush, Quayle, White Ground, Red Border, 1989, 6 ½ In.	15.00
Plate, Dewey, Portrait, Crossed Flags, Eagle Above, Red & Blue Bands, 8 ½ In.	135.00
Plate, Ulysses S. Grant In Medallion, Flags, Capitol, Swords, Palm Fronds, 1885, 9 In.	1000.00
Playing Cards, Spiro T. Agnew, Vice President, Cleveland, Ohio, June 20, 1970 ....*illus*	10.00

P

Political, Button, GW Bush, Cheney, Flasher, 3 In.
$10.35

Political, Button, Herbert C. Hoover, For President, Portrait, Celluloid, 3 ½ In.
$487.00

Political, Button, Hoover, Stars & Stripes, Red, White & Blue, Celluloid, ¾ In.
$22.00

Political, Button, Humphrey & Muskie, HHH, Capitol City, Capitol Idea, St. Paul, Celluloid, 2 ¼ In.
$76.00

Political, Button, Ike & Dick, Don't Change The Team, Red, White & Blue, Celluloid, 1956, 3 ½ In.
$168.00

Political, Button, It's Gotta Be McG, Blue, Celluloid, 1 In.
$12.65

Political, Button, McGovern 72, Superman Cartoon, 1 ½ In.
$115.00

Political, Button, McKinley, Roosevelt, Ribbon, Celluloid, W & H Back Paper, Jugate, 2 ⅛ In.
$114.00

Political, Button, Roosevelt, Rose-Velt, Rebus, Celluloid, Whitehead, Hoag, Back Paper, 1 ¼ In.
$308.00

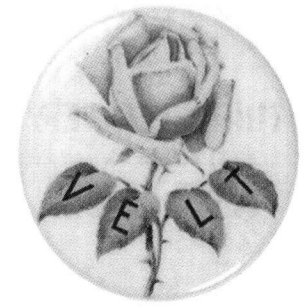

Political, Button, Stevenson, Shoe With Hole In The Sole, For '56, Celluloid, 3 ½ In.
$57.00

Political, Button, Teddy Roosevelt, Horseshoe, Celluloid, Arcade Co. Sewing Machines, 1904, 1 ¼ In.
$748.00

Political, Button, The Allies, 5 Nation Flags, Celluloid, Mirror Back, Bastian, 2 ¾ In.
$52.00

P

Political, Button, Willkie, Better A Third Termer Than A Third Rater, Celluloid, 3 ½ In.
$101.00

Political, Button, Wm. H. Taft, Colors, Celluloid, 1 ¼ In.
$69.00

Political, License Plate Attachment, Landon, Knox, Sunflower, Letters On Petals, 1936, 3 ¾ x 5 In.
$173.00

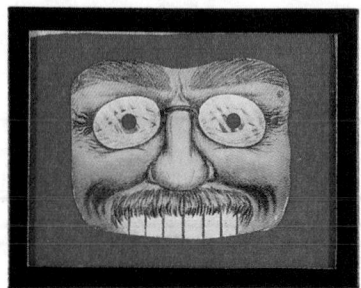

Political, Mask, Theodore Roosevelt, Die Cut, Cardboard, Cord, Eye Holes, Fold-Out Nose, c.1904, 4 x 5 ½ In.
$173.00

Political, Necktie, We Want Roosevelt, 1940
$139.00

Political, Oyster Plate, 5 Wells, Rutherford Hayes, White House China, Limoges, c.1880, 8 ¾ In.
$1793.00

Political, Pin, Donkey, I'm So Wild About Harry, 1948, 2 ⅛ In.
$224.00

Political, Playing Cards, Spiro T. Agnew, Vice President, Cleveland, Ohio, June 20, 1970
$10.00

Political, Poster, America Needs Roosevelt, Portrait, Framed Under Glass, 10 x 13 ½ In.
$83.00

Political, Poster, We're Going To Win, Vote For Al Smith, Rooster, 1928, 24 x 36 In.
$139.00

Political, Poster , Zachary Taylor, People's Candidate For 12th President, Frame, N. Currier, 1848, 12 x 16 In.
$288.00

P

Postcard, Abraham Lincoln, Martyred President, Centennial, 3 ½ x 5 ½ In.	18.00
Postcard, Barry Goldwater, For President, 10 Reasons Why, c.1964, 5 ½ x 3 ½ In.	6.00
Postcard, George Washington, On White Horse, 3 ½ x 5 ½ In.	20.00
Postcard, Ronald Reagan, Photograph, Jelly Beans, 3 ½ x 5 ½ In.	8.00
Postcard, Washington Birthday Greeting, Portrait, 3 ½ x 5 ½ In.	18.00
Poster, America Needs Roosevelt, Portrait, Framed Under Glass, 10 x 13 ½ In. ......illus	83.00
Poster, Birthday Ball For The President, FDR, Christy Girl, January 30, 1935, 22 x 12 In.	670.00
Poster, Cartoon, Free The Watergate 500, Nixon & Others In Jail Stripes, 1973, 22 x 35 In.	127.00
Poster, Elephant's Job, No Time For Donkey Business, Vote Republican, 1932, 16 x 35 In.	146.00
Poster, Hon. Wm. McKinley, Our Next President, Picture, Heavy Paper, 24 x 18 In.	115.00
Poster, Hubert Humphrey, Some Talk Change, Others Cause It, Signature, 1968, 34 x 22 In.	115.00
Poster, Kennedy For President, A Time For Greatness, Picture, JFK, 1960, 28 x 18 In.	285.00
Poster, LBJ, U.S. Senator, Unite, Defense, Red, White, Blue, Cardboard, 1941, 14 x 11 In.	158.00
Poster, McGovern, Stylized Letters, Black, Red, Blue, Autograph, A. Calder, 1972, 34 In.	474.00
Poster, McGovern, Stylized Peace Dove, Glossy Paper, Autographed, 35 x 23 In.	506.00
Poster, Re-Elect Kennedy, U.S. Senator, Picture, Red, White, Blue, 1958, 45 x 29 In.	4750.00
Poster, Spiro Agnew, Photograph, Black & White, c.1970, 22 ½ x 34 In.	125.00
Poster, Wanted, Watergate Conspirators, 20 Pictures With Apprehended, 29 x 23 In.	99.00
Poster, We're Going To Win, Vote For Al Smith, Rooster, 1928, 24 x 36 In. ......illus	139.00
Poster, Zachary Taylor, People's Candidate For 12th President, Frame, N. Currier, 1848, 12 x 16 In. illus	288.00
Print, Lewis Cass, For 12th President, Kellogg & Comstock, Frame, 1848, 13 x 17 In. .....illus	601.00
Program, Cleveland, Hendricks, Inauguration Ball, March 4, 1885, Jugate	125.00
Purse, Willkiette, No Third Term, Shoulder Bag, Cloth, 1940, 12 In. ......illus	106.00
Razor, Straight, Etched, Abraham Lincoln, Union & Freedom	2000.00
Ribbon, Bell, Everett, Union Badge, For The Campaign Of 1860, Silk, Jugate ......illus	9400.00
Ribbon, Franklin Roosevelt, Blue, 6 ¾ In.	34.00
Ribbon, Grover Cleveland, Tammany Hall, Flag, Tiger, Capitol, 1893, 10 ¾ In.	235.00
Ribbon, Henry Clay, Harry Of The West, The Honest Statesman, Picture, 1844, 7 In.	397.00
Ribbon, McKinley, Photo Button, Celluloid, Will Lead Column To Victory, 1896, 6 ¼ In. ......illus	431.00
Ribbon, National Suffrage Convention, 60th Anniversary, Elizabeth Cady Stanton Shell, 1908, 13 In.	2352.00
Roly-Poly, Bill The Beamer, President Taft Baseball Themed Figure, White, c.1910, 4 In.	230.00
Scarf, Warren Harding, Capitol, Flowers, Greetings, Washington DC, Silk, 10 In.	1250.00
Sheet Music, President Lincoln's Grand March, Helmsmuller, Color, Frame, 1962, 15 x 19 In. illus	360.00
Shield, Patriotic, Lincoln Portrait, Wood, Painted, Interchangeable Photos, c.1909, 18 x 24 In.	960.00
Sign, Liberty Bonds, Sheet Metal, Shield Shape, Painted, c.1918, 18 x 17 ½ In.	400.00
Silhouette, William Henry Harrison, Black & Gray On White Linen, 1845, 11 ⅝ x 8 ¼ In.	175.00
Snuffbox, William Henry Harrison, Pewter, Log Cabin, Cider Barrel, Embossed, Oval, 3 x 2 In.	826.00
Soup, Dish, Lincoln White House, Eagle, Gilt, Haviland, Limoges, c.1861, 9 In. ......illus	13200.00
Spoon, General "Spoons" Ben Butler, Sterling Silver, Head On End, 1884, 5 ¾ In.	244.00
Spoon, National Women's Suffrage Convention, 1912, Philadelphia Scenes, Silver, 4 In.	700.00
Spoon, Soup, William Henry Harrison, Silvered Brass, Log Cabin, c.1840, 8 In.	649.00
Stickpin, Benjamin Harrison, 1892, Portrait On Flag, Tin Lithograph, 2 In.	386.00
Stickpin, Bryan, Silver Bug, On Bicycle, ⅝ In.	75.00
Stickpin, Hatchet, Carry A Nation, Die Cut Metal, Early 1900s, 2 ¼ In.	75.00
Stickpin, R.B. Hayes, Photograph, Cardboard, Embossed Brass Frame, 1 In.	380.00
Stickpin, Taft, Silver, Painted Red Rose, ¾ In.	47.00
Stickpin, Vermont Bell, Gold Tone, 1904, ¾ In.	21.00
Straight Razor, Bryan, Kern, Jugate, Etched, 6 ¼ In.	202.00
Stud, Big Bill Thompson, Chicago Mayor, Hat Shape, Gold Tone	11.00
Stud, McKinley, 4-Leaf Clover, Enamel, White, Blue, Red, Stud Back, ¾ In.	34.00
Stud, Teddy Roosevelt, Figural, Bull Moose, 1 In.	19.00
Teapot, Wm. Henry Harrison, Portrait, Log Cabin, Flag, Barrel, Staffordshire, 7 x 11 In.	1200.00
Thimble, Nixon, He's The One, Elect Nixon In '68, Red, Cream, Plastic	9.00
Tie Clasp, FDR, Profile, Metal, 2 ¾ In.	25.00
Tie Tack, Barry Goldwater, Elephant, Black Glasses, 1 x 1 In.	48.00
Tie, Adlai Stevenson, Yellow, Elect Stevenson, 1950s	59.00
Tray, Roosevelt Bears, Bear Border, Verse, Tin, Edward Stern & Co., 1906, 3 ¼ x 5 In. ......illus	209.00
Tray, Taft, Sherman, Republican Candidates Border, Tin, Round, 1909, 9 ½ In. ......illus	199.00
Tray, Teddy Roosevelt Portrait, Yours Truly, Fred. W. Peterson, Oval, 1905, 16 In.	1100.00
Tray, Teddy Roosevelt, Rough Rider, Portrait, Tin, Oval, 16 In.	1000.00
Trolley Card, 6 Pretty Women, Vote Yes On Woman Suffrage, Poem, 12 x 22 In.	475.00
Vase, Bud, Portrait, Ulysses S. Grant, Presidential Campaign, 7 ½ In. ......illus	1320.00
Vase, Jackie Kennedy, Head, Gloved Hand, Inarco, 1964, 6 In.	600.00
Watch Fob, James H. Cox, Best Ever Clothes, Chicago, Shield, 2 Donkeys, Celluloid, 1 ¾ In.	2750.00
Watch Fob, John F. Kennedy, 10 ¼ In.	8.00
Watch Fob, Taft, Figural, Billy Possum, Embossed, Metal, 1908, 2 ¼ x 1 ⅝ In. ......illus	187.00

Political, Print, Lewis Cass, For 12th President, Kellogg & Comstock, Frame, 1848, 13 x 17 In.
$601.00

Hake's Americana & Collectibles

Political, Purse, Willkiette, No Third Term, Shoulder Bag, Cloth, 1940, 12 In.
$106.00

Anderson Americana

Political, Ribbon, Bell, Everett, Union Badge, For The Campaign Of 1860, Silk, Jugate
$9400.00

Cowan's Auctions

Political, Ribbon, McKinley, Photo Button, Celluloid, Will Lead Column To Victory, 1896, 6 ¼ In.
$431.00

Anderson Americana

505

Political, Sheet Music, President Lincoln's Grand March, Helmsmuller, Color, Frame, 1962, 15 x 19 In. $360.00

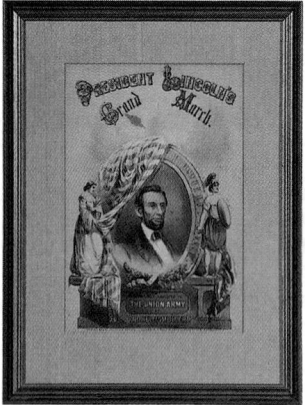

Cowan's Auctions

Political, Soup, Dish, Lincoln White House, Eagle, Gilt, Haviland, Limoges, c.1861, 9 In. $13200.00

Cowan's Auctions

Political, Tray, Roosevelt Bears, Bear Border, Verse, Tin, Edward Stern & Co., 1906, 3 ¼ x 5 In. $209.00

Hake's Americana & Collectibles

Watch Fob, Taft, Sherman, Jugate, Celluloid, Leather, 1 ½ In.	154.00
Window Card, President Ford, Vice President Rockefeller, Iowa, 1976, 22 In.	86.00
Wristwatch, Nixon, I Am Not A Crook, Caricature, Stainless Steel Back, 1970s, 1 ¼ In.	115.00

POMONA glass is a clear glass with a soft amber border decorated with pale blue or rose-colored flowers and leaves. The colors are very, very pale. The background of the glass is covered with a network of fine lines. It was made from 1885 to 1888 by the New England Glass Company. First grind was made from April 1885 to June 1886. It was made by cutting a wax surface on the glass, then dipping it in acid. Second grind was a less expensive method of acid etching that was developed later.

Pickle Castor, Blue Cornflowers, Amber Leaves, Reticulated Meriden Holde, 11 In.	575.00
Pitcher, Cornflower, Amber Rigaree Feet, 7 ½ In. ....*illus*	1438.00
Pitcher, Satin, Cornflower, Loop Handle, Scalloped Spout, 5 ¼ In.	115.00
Toothpick Holder, Fan Shape, Ruffled Rim, Round Foot, 2 In.	115.00

PONTYPOOL, *see Tole category.*

POOLE POTTERY was founded by Jesse Carter in 1873 in Poole, England, and has operated under various names since then. The pottery operated as Carter & Co. for several years and established Carter, Stabler & Adams as a subsidiary in 1921. The company specialized in tiles, architectural ceramics, and garden ornaments. Tableware, bookends, candelabra, figures, vases, and other items have also been made. The name *Poole Pottery Ltd.* was taken in 1963. The company went bankrupt in 2003, but is in business today with new owners.

Dish, Delphis, Spear, Abstract, Orange Ground, 16 In.	123.00
Dish, Green, c.1935, 11 ½ In.	47.00
Plate, Aegean, Spear, 17 In.	55.00

POPEYE was introduced to the Thimble Theatre comic strip in 1929. The character became a favorite of readers. In 1932, an animated cartoon featuring Popeye was made by Paramount Studios. The cartoon series continued and became even more popular when it was shown on television starting in the 1950s. The full-length movie with Robin Williams as Popeye was made in 1980. KFS stands for King Features Syndicate, the distributor of the comic strip.

Ashtray, Holder, Figural, Wooden, Painted, 36 In.	403.00
Bag, Trick Or Treat Bag, Popeye & Olive Oyl, Orange Cloth	49.00
Bank, Dime Register, Tin, Popeye, Bank Windows, Marked, King Features, 1929, 3 In.	90.00
Bank, Popeye, Daily Dime, Tin Lithograph, 1936, 2 ½ x 2 ½ In.	62.00
Clock, Alarm, Popeye & Swee'Pea, Animated, Smiths, London	181.00
Doll, Popeye, Stuffed, Felt, Plastic Buttons, Leather Belt, 1930s, 15 ½ In. ....*illus*	820.00
Game, Adventures Of Popeye, Shadowbox Style Box, Transogram, Board, 1950s	107.00
Game, Tiddlywinks, Popeye, Olive Oyl, Wimpy, Box, 1930s, 6 x 10 ½ In.	383.00
Lunch Box, Popeye & Brutus Arm Wrestling, Aladdin, 1980	85.00
Lunch Box, Popeye Ties Up Boat As Olive Oyl Watches, King Seeley, 1964	45.00
Toy, Boxer, Shadow, Tin Lithograph, Boxing Gloves, Windup, 7 In.	575.00
Toy, Brutus & Cart, Celluloid, Tin Lithograph, Windup, Marx, 7 In. ....*illus*	403.00
Toy, Brutus, Dippy Dumper, Dump Truck, Tin Lithograph, Marx, Celluloid, Marx, 9 In.	489.00
Toy, Popeye & Baggage, Wheelbarrow, Parrot, Tin Lithograph, Marx, 8 ½ In.	431.00
Toy, Popeye & Olive Oyl, Dancing On Roof, Tin Lithograph, Windup, 1930s, 9 In.	506.00
Toy, Popeye & Olive Oyl, Handcar, Spring Bodies, Key Wind, Tin Lithograph, Linemar, Japan, 7 In.	863.00
Toy, Popeye, Bag Puncher, Canopy, Wire Frame, Tin Lithograph, Celluloid, Chein, 1930s, 9 ½ In.	1725.00
Toy, Popeye, Barrel Walker, Tin Lithograph, Clockwork, Chein, 7 In.	403.00
Toy, Popeye, Basketball Player, Tin Lithograph, Continuous Action, Linemar, Japan, 9 In. ....*illus*	805.00
Toy, Popeye, Boom-Boom, Drum, Platform, Wheels, No. 491, Fisher-Price, c.1937, 9 In. ....*illus*	316.00
Toy, Popeye, Bubble Blowing, Tin Lithograph, Can, Pipe, Battery Operated, Linemar, 11 3/4 In.	518.00
Toy, Popeye, Champ, Fights Brutus In Boxing Ring, Tin, Celluloid, Marx, Box, 1930s, 8 In.	1048.00
Toy, Popeye, Cyclist, Tin Lithograph, Windup, Linemar, Japan, 5 x 7 In. ....*illus*	633.00
Toy, Popeye, Drummer, Tin Lithograph, Hand Held, Plunger, Chein, Box, 7 ½ In.	1093.00
Toy, Popeye, Floor Puncher, Tin Lithograph, Clockwork, Chein, 7 In.	863.00
Toy, Popeye, Heavy Hitter, Key Wind, Tin Lithograph, Chein, c.1932, 11 In.	1725.00
Toy, Popeye, In Rowboat, Tin Lithograph, Pressed Steel, Decal, Windup, Hoge, 1935, 14 In.	4025.00
Toy, Popeye, Parrot Cages, Tin Lithograph, Windup, Marx, 6 ½ In.	193.00
Toy, Popeye, Parrots, Cages, Carrying, Tin Lithograph, Windup, 8 ¼ In.	189.00
Toy, Popeye, Pilot, Monoplane, Tin Lithograph, Clockwork, Marx, 7 In.	690.00
Toy, Popeye, Riding Tricycle, Tin Lithograph, Cloth Clothes, Clockwork, Box, King Features, 6 ¼ In.	1495.00
Toy, Popeye, Roller Skater, Holding Platter, Tin Lithograph, Linemar, 6 ½ In. ....*illus*	460.00

Toy, Popeye, Rowboat, Pressed Steel, Clockwork, Hoge Mfg., 14 In.		1265.00
Toy, Popeye, Rowboat, Tin Lithograph, Running Motor, Rowing, 1930s, 15 In.		518.00
Toy, Popeye, Speedboat, Lithograph Sheet Metal, Windup, Hoge Mfg., 1930s, 15 In.		460.00
Toy, Popeye, Spins Olive Oyl In Chair, Tin Lithograph, Clockwork, Linemar, 9 In.		1265.00
Toy, Popeye, Walker, Stand-Up, Tin Lithograph, 6 In.	*illus*	316.00
Toy, Walker, Metal, Windup, Marx, Box, 1930s		395.00
Wristwatch, Popeye Walking, Arms Are Hands, Leather Band, New Haven Clock Co., Box, 1935		1645.00

PORCELAIN factories that are well known are listed in this book under the factory name. This category lists pieces made by the less well-known factories. Additional pieces of porcelain are listed in this book in the categories Porcelain-Contemporary, Porcelain-Midcentury, and under the factory name.

Barrel, Wine, Mythological Figures, Grapes, Gilt, Multicolor, Carl Thieme, Germany, c.1890, 14 In.	1007.00
Basket, Sweetmeat, Reticulated, 2 Dolphin Masques, Blue Plinth, Paw Feet, c.1800, 6 x 9 In. .	276.00
Biscuit Jar, White, Blue, Pink Flowers, Silver Plate Lid, Handle, W. Wood & Son, 6 ½ In.	70.00
Bottle, Cover, Blue & White, Lotus, Green Highlights, Square, 6 ½ In.	187.00
Bough Pot, Demilune Shape, Malahide Castle, Bun Feet, England, c.1790, 6 ½ x 8 ¼ In.	1000.00
Bowl, Blanc De Chine, Gilt Metal Footed Base, Portugal, 6 x 18 x 11 In.	115.00
Bowl, Blue & White, Landscape, Figures, 6 ¾ x 17 ¼ In.	923.00
Bowl, Blue & White, Peony Blossoms, Brown Rim, Footed, 3 x 6 In.	230.00
Bowl, Center, Oval, Footed, Reticulated Basket, Fruit, Nut Swags, Germany, 11 x 14 In.	199.00
Bowl, Dome Lid, Cylindrical, Blue & White, Scrolling Lotus Vines, Blossoms, Wood Base, 9 In.	2440.00
Bowl, Fruits, Painted, Gilt Rim, Base, Tressemanes & Vogt, Limoges, France, 6 ½ x 14 In.	397.00
Bowl, Grotesque Horned Masks, Snake Rings, Shell Shape, Flowers, Gilt, Bronze, 9 x 18 In.	655.00
Bowl, Incised Red Dragons, Turtle, Pheasant, White Glaze Ground, 1700s, 7 ¼ In.	2280.00
Bowl, White, Lily-Of-The-Valley, Gold Rim, Handle, Scalloped Edge, Silesia, c.1900, 2 x 8 ¾ In.	60.00
Box, Paste, Dome Shape, Peach Blossom Glaze, 5 In. Diam.	434.00
Box, Sugar, Cover, Round, Monogram, Garlands, Multicolor, Tettau, Germany, c.1800, 4 In.	230.00
Bust, Boy, Girl, Pedestal, Square Base, France, 1800s, 8 In., Pair	235.00
Butter Pot, Figural, Flapper On Lobster, Orange, Germany, 1920s	150.00
Cask, Rum, Black, Yellow, Gilt Letters, Spigot, Oval, England, Cork Lined, 12 ½ x 12 In.	124.00
Centerpiece, Courting, Landscape Reserves, Cobalt Blue Ground, c.1935, 16 ½ x 19 In.	1554.00
Centerpiece, D-Shape Ends, Young Musicians, Ribbons, Flowers, Germany, c.1900, 7 x 10 In.	236.00
Centerpiece, Figural, Maiden, Holding Poppies, Art Nouveau, RstK, c.1900, 28 ½ In.	1315.00
Charger, Flowering Branches, Enameled, 14 In.	161.00
Charger, Louis XVI, Royal Dress, Multicolor, Blue L Mark, c.1900, 20 In.	1315.00
Charger, Porcelain, Cavalier Portrait, Signed, 2 ¼ In., Pair	316.00
Charger, Round, Portrait, Seminude Woman, Long Hair, T & V Limoges, L.F. Patten, 1907, 23 In. *illus*	1348.00
Coffeepot, Cover, Basket Weave Ground, Scroll Handle, Courting Couple, Flowers, Gilt, 8 In.	590.00
Coffeepot, Tapered, Loop Handle, Blue, Royalty Child, Holding Plate, Gilt, Germany, c.1900, 8 In.	325.00
Coffeepot, Tobacco Leaf, Cross Strap Handle, Domed Spout, c.1890, 10 In.	805.00
Compote, Golden Bramble, Painted Flowers, Center, Edge, Royal Stafford, 5 x 9 In., Pair	60.00
Compote, Pedestal, Scalloped Edge, Footed, Cobalt Blue, Orange, Teal, Gilt, 1800s, 6 x 13 In. .	357.00
Compote, Tan Border, Gilt Rims, Painted Flower Bouquet, 1800s, 4 In., Pair	177.00
Cruet, Olive Branch, Bulbous, Cylindrical Neck, Loop Handle, c.1881, 5 In.	2530.00
Cup, Fish Head, Gilt Trim, The Angler's Delight, England, 1800s, 4 ¾ In.	2489.00
Cup, Handleless, White, Green Vining Leaves, 2 x 3 In.	150.00
Decanter, Figural, Cossack, Red, Black Trim, Mustache, Cap Stopper, Robj, France, 10 ½ x 4 In.	1100.00
Dish, 6-Sided, Reticulated, Roses, Germany, 8 In.	20.00
Dish, Butterfly Shape, Multicolor, Hand Painted, Gold Highlights, Germany, c.1900, 8 x 11 In.	207.00
Dish, Flared, Landscape, Fishermen, Blue Leafy Scrolls, Iron Red Flowers, c.1800, 4 x 9 In.	1298.00
Dish, Lid, Young Boy, Seated On Chair, Book, Grandpapa Banner, Blue & White, 7 x 4 In.	60.00
Dresser Box, Shaped Oval, 1700s Scenes, Gilt, Gilman, Collamore & Co., c.1890, 4 x 13 In.	2990.00
Eggcup, Horse Race, Boy Jockey, 2 ⅝ In.	38.00
Ewer, Wine, Blue & White, Ming Style Shape, Straight 4-Sided Spout, Chinese, 9 x 7 In.	2415.00
Figurine, 2 Grouses, Brown, Gold, 7 x 5 ½ In.	153.00
Figurine, Bulldog, White, Black, Gold Metal Chain, Fornasetti, Milano, Italy, 15 In.	796.00
Figurine, Cook & Peary Climbing Globe Towards North Pole, 5 In.	50.00
Figurine, Dancer, Woman, Green Gown, Fasold & Stauch, Germany, c.1925, 11 In.	590.00
Figurine, Geese, White, Leafy Base, France, c.1950, 11 ¾ x 8 ¾ In., Pair	460.00
Figurine, Gentleman, Colonial, Holding Nest Of Birds, Flower Base, 9 In.	181.00
Figurine, Knight, Standing, Armor, Blue Robe, Jacob Petit, c.1890, 19 ¼ x 7 ½ In.	598.00
Figurine, Lady On Draissine, Luigi Fabris, Italy, 1930s, 6 ¼ In.	350.00
Figurine, Man, Woman, Standing, Whispering, Gilt Accents, Red Roses, 1900s, 7 In., Pair	89.00
Figurine, Mansion House Dwarf, Grotesque Punch, 6 ¾ In.	92.00

Political, Tray, Taft, Sherman, Republican Candidates Border, Tin, Round, 1909, 9 ½ In.
$199.00

Hake's Americana & Collectibles

Political, Vase, Bud, Portrait, Ulysses S. Grant, Presidential Campaign, 7 ½ In.
$1320.00

Cowan's Auctions

Political, Watch Fob, Taft, Figural, Billy Possum, Embossed, Metal, 1908, 2 ¼ x 1 ⅝ In.
$187.00

Wm Morford Antiques

Pomona, Pitcher, Cornflower, Amber Rigaree Feet, 7 ½ In.
$1438.00

Early Auction Co.

PORCELAIN

Popeye, Doll, Popeye, Stuffed, Felt, Plastic Buttons, Leather Belt, 1930s, 15 ½ In.

$820.00

Hake's Americana & Collectibles

Popeye, Toy, Brutus & Cart, Celluloid, Tin Lithograph, Windup, Marx, 7 In.

$403.00

Bertoia Auctions

Popeye, Toy, Popeye, Basketball Player, Tin Lithograph, Continuous Action, Linemar, Japan, 9 In.

$805.00

Bertoia Auctions

Popeye, Toy, Popeye, Boom-Boom, Drum, Platform, Wheels, No. 491, Fisher-Price, c.1937, 9 In.

$316.00

Bertoia Auctions

Figurine, Matador, Red Cape, Germany, 11 In.	210.00
Figurine, Napoleon, Hand In Waistcoat, Gilt Trim, 9 ¼ In.	615.00
Figurine, Nude On White Horse, Bisque Woman, Schaubach Kunst, Germany, 11 In. *illus*	336.00
Figurine, Nude Woman, Arms Outstretched, Gold Sphere, Flower Shape Bowl, Germany, 7 In.	259.00
Figurine, Parrots, 2, Perched On Tree Trunk, Multicolor, c.1890, 13 ¼ In.	115.00
Figurine, Putti, Winged, Molded Flower Base, Blue & White Pedestal, 11 In., Pair	215.00
Figurine, Rabbit, Seated On Hind Legs, Eating Grapes, Long Ears, c.1900, 7 In.	920.00
Figurine, Red Basket, 4 Cats & Kittens, Hand Painted, 3 ½ x 8 x 4 In.	90.00
Figurine, Rooster, White, Red, Brown, 1900s, 14 In., Pair	450.00
Figurine, Spaniel, Bird In Mouth, Keramos, Austria, 9 x 9 In.	106.00
Figurine, Woman, Beating Kneeling Figure, 6 In.	351.00
Figurine, Woman, Colonial Dress, Pug Dogs, Ludwigsburg, Germany, 9 ¾ In.	236.00
Figurine, Woman, Provincial Clothing, Gathering Flowers, Luigi Fabris, 5 ½ x 5 ¾ In.	236.00
Fish Set, Fish, Green Border, Floral Medallions, Gold Trim, 22-In. Oval Platter, 7 Piece	492.00
Fish Set, Marine Scenes, Purple, Gilt Border, Platter, 12 Plates, Sauceboat, Undertray, 23 In.	1007.00
Flask, Regimental, 3. Esc., Husar Regt. Nr. 9, Trier 1893-96, Res. Blum, ¼ Liter *illus*	92.00
Group, Courting Couples, Palm Tree, Latticework Base, Blanc De Chine, 14 x 6 In.	214.00
Group, Figures, Playing Checkers, 1800s Attire, France, 1900s, 13 ½ x 22 In.	944.00
Group, Man, Woman, Dancing, Bisque, Gilt, Multicolor, Germany, 1800s, 18 In.	770.00
Group, Man, Woman, On Monument, Garlands Base, Ludwigsburg, Germany, c.1915, 9 ¾ In.	178.00
Group, Seated & Standing Figures, Oval Base, Dresden Style, Village Granted, Germany, 9 x 15 In.	360.00
Ice Bucket, Pink, Blue, Pink Flowers, Silver Plate Lid, Bail Handle, 7 ½ In.	50.00
Jar, Cover, Bronze Mounts, Bearded Man Handles, Flowers, 17 In.	575.00
Jar, Cover, Dresden Style, Urn Shape, Applied Flowers, Bird Finial, Schneeballen, 23 In., Pair .	1793.00
Jar, Cover, Red Ground, Enamel Classical Cartouche, Pineapple Finial, Austria, c.1890, 13 In.	1007.00
Jar, Dome Lid, Blue, Gilt, Phoenix Roundels, Hawk, Pine Tree, Baluster, 17 x 17 In., Pair	610.00
Jardiniere, Pheasants, Peonies, Wood Stand, 19 x 18 In.	325.00
Jug, Cover, Rectangular, Short Neck, Painted Reserve, Classical Child, Flowers, 1900s, 6 ½ In.	89.00
Jug, Hot Water, Woman & Gallant, Man & Son, Trees, Flowers, Gilt, c.1770-80, 6 In.	708.00
Jug, Seltzer, 2 Parts, Mix As Poured, France, 1800s, 8 In.	184.00
Monkey, White Glaze, On Tree Stump, Eating Bananas, Eagle Mark, Germany, 17 ⅝ In.	356.00
Mustard, Airplane Shape, Head, White, Blue, Germany, 6 ¾ In.	236.00
Pail, Chamber, Neoclassical Style, White, Parcel Gilt Trim, France, c.1875, 9 ¼ In., Pair	799.00
Pitcher, Baluster Shape, Molded Leaves, Painted Flowers, Multicolor, 9 ½ x 7 ¾ In.	2574.00
Pitcher, Figural, Friar, Smiling, Tricornered Hat, Red Robe, Marked, 9 In.	51.00
Pitcher, Figural, Spaniel, Black, Russet, Gold, 10 x 4 In.	98.00
Pitcher, Molded Corn, White, Gilt Medallion, Caroline Sewell, 10 x 5 ¾ In.	104.00
Planter, Famille Jaune, Scalloped Oval, Lotus & Buddhist Symbols, Yellow Ground, 12 In.	738.00
Planter, Male, Female Bust Terminals, Gilt, Blue, White, 1900s, 13 x 11 ½ In., Pair	1195.00
Plaque, Cherub, Chin Resting On Hand, Germany, 3 x 2 ¼ In.	270.00
Plaque, Empress Josephine, Multicolored, Roundel, Signed, O. Brun, France, 1800s, 8 ½ In. *illus*	504.00
Plaque, Enamel, Landscape, Figures, Raging Rapids, Giltwood Frame, 1800s, 15 ¼ x 22 In.	337.00
Plaque, Garden, 2 Couples, Musical Instrument, Multicolor, Hand Paint, Frame, 1900s, 19 x 11 In.	531.00
Plaque, Gypsy Woman, Scrolling, Wood Frame, Germany, 18 x 25 In.	805.00
Plaque, Marie Antoinette, Hand Paint, Roundel, Signed, O. Brun, France, 1800s, 10 In.	504.00
Plaque, Monk, Wine Cellar, Paint, Gilt Frame, Signed, W.H. Nolker, Germany, 10 x 11 In.	413.00
Plaque, Paint, Maidens, Putto, Nude Man, Hammer, Sheath, Frame, Germany, 1874, 7 x 5 In., Pair	3444.00
Plaque, Painted, Shipwreck, Naked Woman, Kissing Lover, Frame, Germany, 1900s, 5 x 7 In.	800.00
Plaque, Portrait, Old Woman, Bronze Frame, Ribbon Tied Finial, Stand, 4 ¼ In.	150.00
Plaque, Princess Louise, Enamel Design Portrait, Frame, Germany, c.1900, 4 x 6 In.	521.00
Plaque, Rest On The Flight Into Egypt, Enameled, Putti, Richard Ginori, Italy, 12 x 14 In.	861.00
Plaque, Scholars Under Plantain Tree, Enameled, 15 x 10 In.	527.00
Plaque, Songbirds, Flowers, Oval, 14 x 13 In.	595.00
Plaque, Woman, Flowers, Paint, 6 ½ x 4 ¾ In.	1243.00
Plaque, Woman, Statue Of Nike, Signed, 6 x 4 ⅛ In.	214.00
Plaque, Young Girl, Bedroom, Admiring Locket, Giltwood Scrolling Frame, 11 x 13 In.	1035.00
Plaque, Young Woman, Braiding Hair, Hand Painted, Oval Frame, 6 ¾ In.	360.00
Plaque, Young Woman, White Dove, Perched On Shoulder, Frame, France, 1900s, 4 x 3 In.	184.00
Plate, Basket Of Flowers, Dark Blue Rim, 1900s, 11 In. Diam., 12 Piece	207.00
Plate, Blue & White, Barbed, Flowers, Radiating Lotus On Cavetto, Border, c.1710, 8 ¾ In.	388.00
Plate, Blue & White, Flowers, Bamboo, Octagonal, 18th Century, 8 ¾ In., Pair	369.00
Plate, Blue Transfer, Table Rock, Niagara, Enoch Wood & Sons, England, c.1830, 10 In., Pair	540.00
Plate, Burgundy, Gilt Highlights, Figural Scenes, Germany, 1900s, 10 In., 12 Piece	354.00
Plate, Cobalt Blue, Gilt Rim, Panels, View, Flowers, Leaves, Boyer, c.1845, 9 In., Pair	1416.00
Plate, Dessert, Center Reserves, Birds, Flowers, 8 ¼ In., 6 Piece	523.00
Plate, Dessert, Green Rim, Flower Center, Tirschenreuth, Bavaria, 8 ¼ In., 15 Piece	240.00

P

Plate, Edgerton Pattern, Flower Bouquet Center, Gilt Rim, Heinrich & Co., 1900s, 11 In., 12 Piece...	443.00
Plate, Gilt, Monogram, Blue Border, Gilt Lights, Imperial Mark, Russia, c.1800s, 9 ¾ In.	1150.00
Plate, Green Rim, Gold, Heirich & Co., 11 In., 12 Piece...	502.00
Plate, Hammer, CCC Design, Border, Marked, Hammer & Sickle, Russia, 1930s, 9 ½ In. ....*illus*	413.00
Plate, Medallion Center, Russian Scene Border, Gilt, Kornilov, c.1890, 9 ½ In., 12 Piece	9000.00
Plate, Mother & Child, Raised Gilt, Blue Underglaze, Vienna, c.1890, 9 ½ In. ....*illus*	427.00
Plate, Salad, Golden Heron, Signed, Fritz & Floyd, c.1978, 7 ½ In.....................................	35.00
Plate, Service Of The Order Of St. Andrew First Called, Russia, c.1780, 9 ½ In.	6875.00
Plate, Service, Black Knight, Germany, c.1925, 10 ½ In., 11 Piece.....................................	960.00
Plate, Service, Black Knight, Gold, Germany, c.1925, 10 ½ In., 11 Piece...............................	420.00
Plate, White, Gilt Rim, Monogram, Marked Upsala Ekeby, Sweden, 9 ½ In., 12 Piece...............	148.00
Platter, Blue Transfer, Kenmount Dumfriesshire, Enoch Wood & Sons, England, c.1830, 16 In.	240.00
Platter, Ontario Lake Pattern, Blue & White, J. Heath, England, 13 In..................................	79.00
Platter, Plymouth 1622, Blue Transfer, England, 17 In..	102.00
Pot De Creme Set, Dome Lid, Flowers, Gold Transfer, 10-In. Underplate, 13 Piece	74.00
Potpourri, Ormolu Mounts, Blue, White Leaf Design, Flower Handles, Scrolled Feet, 13 x 13 In.	2390.00
Punch Bowl, Stand, Footed, 2 Gilt Handles, Hand Painted Flowers, Blue Iridescent, 1900s, 13 In.	207.00
Saucer, Blue & White, Courtesan, Official, Garden Pavilion, Underglaze, 1700s, 5 ¾ In.	984.00
Serving Dish, Flower Stem, Cobalt Blue Border, Gilded Rim, Cartouche Corners, 9 ¼ x 9 ¼ In.	123.00
Soup, Cream, Saucer, Ambassador Ware, Foudeville, 35 Piece	390.00
Tankard, Flowers, Multicolor, Gilt Border, Hinged Pewter Lid, Germany, 1800s, 7 ¼ In.	5629.00
Teapot, Applied Flowers & Birds, Bulbous, Loop Handle, Gilt, 1800s, 5 In............................	472.00
Teapot, Blue Transfer, Castle Shape, England, c.1800, 6 ¾ In..	150.00
Teapot, Bulbous, Figural Spout, Shaped Handle, Berry Finial, Putti, White, Pink, Blue, 4 In...	230.00
Teapot, Cover, Cafe-Au-Lait, Blue & White, Flowers, Cockerel, Loop Handle, Straight Spout, 5 In.	239.00
Teapot, Trivet, White, Raised Design, Dudson Bros., Hanley, England, 6 x 7 & 6 In...................	35.00
Tray, Painted, Flowers, 4 Recessed Sections, Center Handle, 1930s, 8 ½ x 5 In.	55.00
Tureen, Cover, Platter, Oval, 2 Handles, Footed, Gilt Flower, France, 1900s, 20 x 14 In.	443.00
Tureen, Cover, Underplate, Tobacco Leaf, Pinecone Finial, Pomegranate Handles, c.1890, 9 x 12 In.	1840.00
Tureen, Underplate, Roses, Magenta Ground, Gilt, Hand Painted, France, 13 ½ x 9 In.	244.00
Urn, Birds, Flowers, Fruit, Painted, Gilt, Blue, White, Pierced Lid, Handles, England, 1800s, 15 In.	720.00
Urn, Campana Shape, Landscape, Figures, Pedestal Base, Flared Rim, Germany, 1920s, 16 ⅜ In.	354.00
Urn, Campana Shape, Scenes, Balcony, Open Window, Mask Handles, 1800s, 8 In., Pair..........	276.00
Urn, Cobalt Blue, White, Gilt Accents, Snake Handles, Pedestal Foot, Meissen Style, 15 In........	326.00
Urn, Cover, Baluster, Reticulated Neck, Scroll Handles, Robed Woman Archer, 2 Soldiers, 24 In.	519.00
Urn, Cover, Classical Figures, Cherubs, Von Schierholz, c.1910, 31 x 16 In.	1800.00
Urn, Cover, Classical Scene, Portrait, Handles, Signed, C. Forster, Vienna, c.1890, 16 In. .*illus*	919.00
Urn, Cover, Pink Flowers, Cream Ground, Gold Scroll Handles, Square Base, 14 In., Pair	1476.00
Urn, Cover, Turquoise, Painted Reserves, Amorous Couple, Scroll Handles, c.1900, 17 In., Pair	900.00
Urn, Cylindrical, Pierced Rim, Loop Handles, Leaf Feet, Gilt, Figures, 1900s, 15 In., Pair.........	750.00
Urn, Gilt, Flower, Bird Reserves, Green, Scalloped Rim, Masque Handles, Base, France, 15 x 9 In.	492.00
Urn, Pastoral Reserve, Hand Painted, Gilt Rim, Handles, Base, c.1900, 15 In., Pair	2640.00
Urn, Rococo, Applied Flowers, Putti, Figural Handles, Maidens, Pierced Lids, 24 x 12 In., Pair	4920.00
Urn, Rose Ground, Gilt, Hand Painted, Allegory Of Love, Bronze Base, 29 In.........................	1494.00
Urn, Seated Couple, Trees, Flowers, Snake Handles, Pedestal Foot, Meissen Style, 19 In.	444.00
Urn, Sevres Style, Pink, Scenic Reserves, Open Handles, 1900s, 18 x 10 In., Pair.....................	676.00
Urn, Viennese Style, Figures, Gilt, Footed, 2 Angular Handles, Germany, c.1900, 11 In.	207.00
Urn, Women, Harp, Flowers, Bronze, Sevres Style, E. Grisard, France, c.1900, 37 In................	2596.00
Vase, 4 Swan Feet, Leda & Swan, Irises, Gilt, Cobalt Blue, Handles, Baluster, 1800s, 22 In........	1400.00
Vase, 6 Pipe Opening, Bright Green, 18 ½ x 15 In.	248.00
Vase, Aesthetic, Landscape, Cranes, Signed Gustave Leonce, c.1875, 23 ½ In.	568.00
Vase, Amorphic Design, Squat, Oxblood Glaze, 4 x 5 In.	308.00
Vase, Art Nouveau, Gilt Leaves, Branches, Iridescent, Round, Carl Knoll, Karlsbad, 8 In..........	268.00
Vase, Bag Shape, Red, Gold, Tie Neck, 9 x 5 In..	480.00
Vase, Baluster, Swan Shape Handles, Gilt, Landscape, Square Base, 9 In., Pair.....................	244.00
Vase, Bat & Cloud, Elephant Shape Handles, Pear Shape, Clair-De-Lune, Molded, 12 ½ In. ...	2988.00
Vase, Bird, Flowers, Lavender Ground, Gilt Handles, 11 In., Pair	327.00
Vase, Bottle Shape, Copper Red Glaze, Chinese, 1800s, 7 ⅜ In.	209.00
Vase, Chinese Courtyard Scenes, Mounted As Lamp, c.1910, 24 In., Pair	443.00
Vase, Country Scene, Naturalistic Gilt Handles, Applied Flowers, Baluster, 19 In., Pair	2006.00
Vase, Courting Couple, Garden, Square Pedestal, Cobalt Blue, Gilt, 8 ½ In..............................	207.00
Vase, Cover, Sevres Style, Gilt Bronze, Fruit Finial, Pierced Collar, Mask Handles, 20 x 8 In., Pair	1793.00
Vase, Cover, Urn Shape, Acorn Finial, Ormolu, White, High Waist Handle, 21 x 11 In., Pair	3355.00
Vase, Cover, White Ground, Applied Multicolor Flowers, Garlands, 9 ¾ x 6 ¾ In.	360.00
Vase, Crackled Glaze, Flowers, Butterflies, Blue & White, Oval, 6 In...................................	239.00

Popeye, Toy, Popeye, Cyclist, Tin
Lithograph, Windup, Linemar, Japan,
5 x 7 In.
$633.00

Bertoia Auctions

Popeye, Toy, Popeye, Roller Skater,
Holding Platter, Tin Lithograph,
Linemar, 6 ½ In.
$460.00

Bertoia Auctions

Popeye, Toy, Popeye, Walker, Stand-Up,
Tin Lithograph, 6 In.
$316.00

Bertoia Auctions

Porcelain, Charger, Round, Portrait,
Seminude Woman, Long Hair, T & V
Limoges, L.F. Patten, 1907, 23 In.
$1348.00

Skinner, Inc.

PORCELAIN

Porcelain, Figurine, Nude On White Horse, Bisque Woman, Schaubach Kunst, Germany, 11 In.
$336.00

Theriault's

Porcelain, Flask, Regimental, 3. Esc., Husar Regt. Nr. 9, Trier 1893-96, Res. Blum, ¼ Liter
$92.00

The Stein Auction Co.

Porcelain, Plaque, Empress Josephine, Multicolored, Roundel, Signed, O. Brun, France, 1800s, 8 ½ In.
$504.00

Skinner, Inc.

Porcelain, Plate, Hammer, CCC Design, Border, Marked, Hammer & Sickle, Russia, 1930s, 9 ½ In.
$413.00

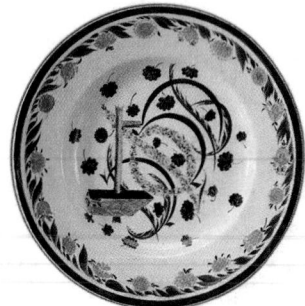

Brunk Auctions

Vase, Cylinder, Gilt Border, Neo-Grec Design, Central Flowers & Vines, Brass Lip, 10 In., Pair	123.00
Vase, Double Gourd, Figures, Lavender & Gilt, Flower Bouquets, Berry Knop, 1800s, 8 In., Pair	633.00
Vase, Figural Scene, Flare Rim, White, Baluster, Chinese, 17 In.	478.00
Vase, Figural Scene, Putti, Beige Ground, Baluster, Spread Foot, 2 Gilt Handles, Germany, 1900s, 12 In.	148.00
Vase, Figural, Elephant, Vase On Back, Teadust Yellow Glaze, 13 x 11 In.	767.00
Vase, Figures, Rolled Rim, Iron Red, Turquoise, Yellow, Baluster, Silver Metal Mounts, 11 In.	236.00
Vase, Flared Gilt Banded Lip, Winged Caryatid Mount, Square Base, 1800s, 14 In., Pair	1912.00
Vase, Flower Cartouches, Green, Scroll Handles, Jacob Petit, France, c.1890, 16 x 8 In., Pair	2868.00
Vase, Flowers, Animal, Blue & White, Baluster, Pierced Handles, c.1890, 23 In.	345.00
Vase, Flowers, Bird, Blue & White, Neck Knob, Bulbous, Late 1800s, 9 In.	540.00
Vase, Garniture, Flowers In Oval Reserves, Cobalt Blue Ground, Gilt Shaped Rim, 17 In., Pair	984.00
Vase, Geometric Calligraphy, Blue & White, 7 ½ x 4 ⅝ In.	443.00
Vase, Gilt, Green, Figures, Country Scene, Baluster, 2 Dolphin Handles, France, 1800s, 11 In.	130.00
Vase, Gold Leaves, Red Berries, Green Ground, England, 7 In., Pair	201.00
Vase, Green Chicken Skin, Raised Pink, Green, Yellow Flowers, 1800s, 11 ¼ In., Pair	3220.00
Vase, Handles, Fluted, Gilded, Birds, Flowers, Sevres Style, France, 1800s, 11 ⅞ In., Pair	368.00
Vase, Heart Shape, Mountain Landscape, Flowers, Handles, Footed, 8 ¼ x 5 In.	120.00
Vase, Immortals, Iron Red, Gilt Scroll Handles, Footed, Pear Shape, Rolled Rim, c.1930s, 6 ¼ In.	337.00
Vase, Lid, Couples, Landscape, Blue, Flower Finial, Lion's Head Handles, Bronze, France, 18 In.	492.00
Vase, Louis XV Style, Green, Medallions, Courtly Women, Rural Scenes, 22 In., Pair *....illus*	1265.00
Vase, Lovers Scenes, Cobalt Blue Ground, Gold Flowers, Winged Handles, Bronze, 28 In.	4444.00
Vase, Molded Figures, Landscape, Turquoise Glaze, Garlic Mouth, Strap Handles, 8 ¼ In.	214.00
Vase, Mottled Purple Flambe, Elephant Handles, 14 In.	7660.00
Vase, Orange Flowers, Man, Woman, Child, Gilt Rings, Baluster, France, 1800s, 13 In., Pair	770.00
Vase, Pear Shape, Blue & White, Footed, 10 In.	142.00
Vase, Pear Shape, Trumpet Rim, Handles, Platinum, Blue Flowers, Gilt, 1878, 10 In., Pair	2271.00
Vase, Potpourri, Shepherd Scenes, Shell Mounts, Plum Ground, Gilt, England, 1800s, 8 In., Pair	385.00
Vase, Rectangular, Landscape, Nomads, France, 1800s, 11 ¼ In.	245.00
Vase, Sages, Children, Flowers, Melon Shape, Blue & White, England, 1800s, 12 In.	430.00
Vase, Spill, Cornucopia Shape, Square Pierced Base, Ruffled, Flowers, Blue, 1800s, 8 In., Pair	472.00
Vase, Spill, Cylinder, Flared Rim, 3 Paw Feet, Cobalt, Beading, Gilt Trim, 1800s	275.00
Vase, Urn Shape, Seminude, Running, Woods, Green Alabaster Pedestal Base, France, 9 In.	288.00
Vase, Waves, Flowers, Leaves, Faux Handles, Squat, Baluster, Cobalt Blue & White, 15 In.	2185.00
Vase, Woman & Child, Under Tree, Blue & White, Baluster, 19th Century, 11 In.	200.00
Vessel, Drinking, Squat, Hibiscus Flowers, Scrolls, Leaves, Doucai, Mark, 3 ½ In.	178.00
Water Pot, Globular, Lid, Footed, Claire De Lune Glaze, Marked, Chinese, c.1900, 4 In.	245.00
Wig Stand, Blue & White, Figures, Cylindrical, Pierced, 1800s, 11 ¾ In., Pair	2640.00

PORCELAIN-ASIAN includes pieces made in China, Japan, Korea, and other Asian countries. Asian porcelain is also listed in Canton, Chinese Export, Imari, Japanese Coralene, Moriage, Nanking, Occupied Japan, Satsuma, Sumida, and other categories.

Biscuit Jar, Cover, Outdoor Scene, Woman, Red Edge, Handle, Japan, c.1910, 7 ½ In.	84.00
Bowl, 9 Dragons, Waves, Iron Red Paint, Blue & White Stem, Mark, Chinese, 5 x 6 In.	1470.00
Bowl, Blue & White, Figures, Landscape, Round, Chinese, 8 x 17 In.	1920.00
Bowl, Blue & White, Flowers Scrolling Leaves, Stem Pedestal, Chinese, 4 ½ In.	179.00
Bowl, Blue & White, Narrow Base, Chinese, 5 x 7 In.	480.00
Bowl, Blue & White, Quatrefoil Shape, Lotus Leaf Reserves, Warriors, Brocade, 7 ½ In.	2032.00
Bowl, Blue & White, Ring Foot, Leaves, Bird, Flower Interior Center, Chinese, 7 x 3 ½ In.	92.00
Bowl, Blue & White, Round Foot, Flared Rim, Dragons, Wave Borders, Chinese, 1800s, 8 In. Diam.	1960.00
Bowl, Blue & White, Scalloped, Cafe-Au-Lait Glaze, Flowers, Scrolling Leaves, Chinese, 9 In.	191.00
Bowl, Blue Designs, White Ground, Gilt, Chinese, 2 ½ x 4 ½ In., Pair	690.00
Bowl, Blue, Crackle Glaze, Footed, Chinese, 3 ¼ x 7 In.	1265.00
Bowl, Brush Water, Painted, Faux Wood Grain, Chinese, 4 x 5 ½ In.	480.00
Bowl, Chickens, Roosters, Cranes, Flowers, Rolled Rim, Chinese, 3 ½ x 9 ¾ In.	4830.00
Bowl, Cover, Foo Dog Finial, Plum Branches, Blue, White, Lugs, Chinese, 1800s, 7 x 7 In., Pair	398.00
Bowl, Cover, Winged Beast, Scrolling, Round Foot, Pink, Green, White Ground, Chinese, 4 In.	310.00
Bowl, Cover, Winter Scene, Oval, Loop Handles, Chinese, 1936, 7 ½ In.	214.00
Bowl, Cylindrical, Blue & White, Dragons, Clouds, Pagoda, Lotus Blossom, 10 In.	122.00
Bowl, Dragon, Iron Red Dragons, Blue Waves, White Ground, Chinese, 7 x 3 In.	899.00
Bowl, Enameled, Ming Style Dragon, Famille Rose, Key Fret Ground, c.1900, 8 In.	1045.00
Bowl, Fish, Waves, Sea Green Glass Ground, Silver Rim, Flared, Chinese, 2 ½ x 7 ¼ In.	593.00
Bowl, Flared Sides, Dark Blue, Chinese, 1800s, 3 x 6 ¾ In., Pair	674.00
Bowl, Flared, Amber, Yellow White Flowers, Green Ground, Chinese, c.1720, 8 ¾ x 2 ⅝ In.	2726.00
Bowl, Flared, Attendant, Teacups, Immortal Sleeping, Blue, White, Chinese, 1800s, 7 x 2 In.	296.00
Bowl, Flared, Blue Cranes, Clouds, White Ground, Yongzheng Mark, Chinese, 7 In.	830.00
Bowl, Flowering Branch, Flower Sprays, Scrolls, Mint Green Ground, Chinese, 8 In. Diam.	682.00

Bowl, Flowers, Butterflies, Red, Yellow, Purple, Gilt, Chinese, 1800s, 5 x 12 In.	237.00
Bowl, Flowers, Gilt, Grisaille, Chinese, c.1735, 11 ¼ In.	1380.00
Bowl, Flowers, Leaves, Encre-De-Chine, Iron Red, Yellow Ground, Cixi Seal, Chinese, c.1900, 5 ¾ In.	522.00
Bowl, Flowers, Ling-Chih Fungus, Multicolor, Blue Trim, Chinese, c.1940, 8 In.	1230.00
Bowl, Flying Crane, Enamel, Red Rim, Japan, 4 x 9 In.	177.00
Bowl, Geese, Cranes, Turtles, Brown, White, Black, Red Rim, Japan, c.1920, 3 x 10 ½ In.	288.00
Bowl, Green, Purple Dragons, Pearls, Exterior Fruit, Yellow Ground, Chinese, 5 In.	1541.00
Bowl, Iron Red, Blue, Reserves, Japan, 5 x 10 In.	47.00
Bowl, Iron Red, White, Bamboo Trunks, Leaves, Round Foot, Chinese, 5 In.	2091.00
Bowl, Juno & Peacock Pattern, Birds, Swags, Flowers, Grisaille, Chinese, c.1735, 10 In.	920.00
Bowl, Leaf & Scroll Roundels, Multicolor Enamels, Lemon Ground, Chinese, 3 ⅝ In.	178.00
Bowl, Lemon Yellow Glaze, Slight Flare Rim, Carved Wood Stand, Chinese, 7 In., Pair	3172.00
Bowl, Lotus Shape, Lobed Rim, Iron Brown, White, Wood Lotus Shape Stand, 8 In.	5856.00
Bowl, Lotus, Scrolls, Blue, Red, Green, White, Doucai, Chinese, 5 ½ In., Pair	1063.00
Bowl, Molded, Round Foot, Flared Rim, Clouds, Ice Blue Glaze, Chinese, 8 In.	360.00
Bowl, Painted, Coiled & Flying Dragons, White Ground, 1900s, 13 In. Diam.	236.00
Bowl, Pavilions, River, Grisaille Landscapes, Magenta Ground, Chinese, 2 ¾ x 5 ¾ In.	490.00
Bowl, Pink & Yellow, Birds, Flowers, Round Foot, Chinese, 9 In. Diam.	2280.00
Bowl, Rice, Phoenixes, Lotuses, Leaves, Round, Pastels, Chinese, c.1850, 5 ½ In.	584.00
Bowl, Roundels, Lanterns, Antiques, Double Gourd Vines, Yellow, Chinese, c.1940, 8 x 4 In., Pair	1103.00
Bowl, Rust Scroll Design, Gilt Highlights, Blue & White Flower Interior, Chinese, 6 In. Diam.	480.00
Bowl, Squat, Round, Fish, Plants, Signed, Teng Pi Shan, Chinese, 1926	858.00
Bowl, Vegetable, Flowers, Central Rose, Indented Corners, Pink, White, Chinese, 1800s, 10 x 10 In.	492.00
Bowl, Yellow, Bird, Prunus, Gilt, Flared Rim, Ring Foot, Chinese, 3 x 7 ½ In.	759.00
Box, Face Shape Cover, Round, Hirado, Japan, 1800s, 4 In. ....illus	178.00
Brush Holder, Basket Weave Ground, Butterfly, Pink, Blue Flowers, Oval, Chinese, 4 x 3 In.	780.00
Brush Holder, Cylindrical, Crackled Design, Cream Ground, Chinese, 1800s, 5 In.	179.00
Brush Rest, Mountain Peak Shape, Water Bowl At End, Giltwood Stand, Chinese, 1800s, 3 ¾ In.	184.00
Brush Rest, Mountain, Blue Underglaze, Scholar, Landscape, Water Horses, Chinese, 7 ½ x 4 In. ...illus	245.00
Brush Washer, Foo Dog, Green, Beige, Qianlong Seal Mark, Chinese, 4 ½ In.	1554.00
Brush Washer, Lotus Shape, Blue, White, Inturned, Shaped Rim, Signed, Chinese, 2 x 6 In.	120.00
Brush Washer, Robin's-Egg Blue, Chinese, 7 ½ In.	369.00
Brush Washer, Squat, Round Foot, Wide Rim, Light Green Ground, Crackled, Chinese, 5 In.	388.00
Brushpot, Blue & White, Bamboo, Plum & Pine Trees, 1800s, 5 ¼ x 5 In.	100.00
Brushpot, Blue & White, Cylindrical, Chinese, 6 ¼ x 7 ½ In.	520.00
Brushpot, Blue & White, Diamond Shape, Pierced Panels, Flowers, Chinese, c.1875, 7 x 8 x 4 In.	1325.00
Brushpot, Blue & White, Figures, Landscape, Cylindrical, Chinese, 1700s, 6 ½ x 8 In.	374.00
Cachepot, Flowers, Chinese, c.1700, 6 ½ x 9 In., Pair	1701.00
Case, Dragon, Phoenix, Flaming Pearls, Multicolor, c.1900, 13 In.	633.00
Censer, Blue & White, Landscape, Tripod Feet, Chinese 1800s, 4 x 10 In.	550.00
Censer, Bombe Body, Loop Upright Handles, 3 Cylindrical Feet, Chinese, 4 In.	239.00
Censer, Flowers, Raised Feet, Red, Coral, Gilt, Scrolls, Dragon Handles, Pierced Lid, Chinese, 9 ½ In.	1416.00
Charger, Armorial, Cherubs, Flower Ring, Chinese, 13 ¾ In.	293.00
Charger, Blue & White, Flowers, Insects, River Scenes, Chinese, 16 In.	345.00
Charger, Blue & White, Flowers, Meadow, Japan, c.1900, 18 In. Diam.	59.00
Charger, Blue Flowers, Leaves, Mark, Chinese, 15 In.	889.00
Charger, Blue, Shishi, Brocade Patterns, Arita Ware, Japan, 16 ½ In.	148.00
Charger, Dragon & Phoenix, Flaming Pearl, 5 Bats, Red, Chinese, 19th Century, 16 ⅞ In. .....illus	956.00
Charger, Horses, Dragons, Yellow Ground, Teal Border, Chinese, c.1910, 16 ¼ In.	288.00
Charger, Interior Peony & Rock Roundels, Iron Mounts, Chinese, c.1885, 14 ½ In.	245.00
Charger, Landscape, Man, Horseback, Mount Fuji, Flowers, Foo Dogs, Geometric Rim, Japan, 16 In.	266.00
Cider Jug, Flowers, Armorial Design, White Ground, Chinese, 1900s, 9 In.	161.00
Compote, Brown Matte Glaze, Blue & White Flower Interior, Pedestal, Square, Chinese, 6 In.	240.00
Creamer, Dome Lid, Mandarin Pattern, Domestic Scenes, Chinese, 1800s, 5 ½ In.	228.00
Cup, 2 Dragons, Waves, Pearls, Iron Red, Mark, Chinese, 1800s, 2 ½ x 3 ¾ In., Pair	593.00
Cup, Double Dragon Roundels, Magenta, Chinese, 2 x 3 In., Pair	652.00
Cup, Molded Magnolia Flowers, Purple, Chinese, 1800s, 2 ½ In.	153.00
Cup, Round Foot, Turquoise, Stylized Lotus Scrolls, Bats, Gilt, Chinese, 1800s, 3 ½ In., Pair	1470.00
Cup, Wine, Enamel Kingfisher, Lotus, Yellow Ground, Chinese, c.1940, 3 ¼ In., Pair	307.00
Dish, Blue & White, Painted Crane, Pine Tree, Chinese, 6 In.	239.00
Dish, Dome Lid, Cup Shape, 2 Handles, Rose Medallion, Birds, Crab Finial, Chinese, 1800s, 5 x 7 In.	89.00
Dish, Doucai, Painted, Mandarin Duck, Lotus, Chinese, 7 In.	508.00
Dish, Dragon, Flames, Blue & White, Marked, 1700s, 6 ¾ In. ....illus	4920.00
Dish, Guan Style, Blue White Crackle Glaze, Lobed Rim, Foot Rim, 6 In.	410.00
Dish, Reticulated, Central Cylinder, Raised Upon Dish, Vines, Blossoms, Scalloped, Chinese, 9 In.	915.00
Dish, Warrior Scene, Mountains, Footed, Gilt Edge, Chinese, c.1865, 2 ½ x 8 ½ In.	259.00

Porcelain, Plate, Mother & Child, Raised Gilt, Blue Underglaze, Vienna, c.1890, 9 ½ In.
$427.00

Porcelain, Urn, Cover, Classical Scene, Portrait, Handles, Signed, C. Forster, Vienna, c.1890, 16 In.
$919.00

Porcelain, Vase, Louis XV Style, Green, Medallions, Courtly Women, Rural Scenes, 22 In., Pair
$1265.00

P

TIP
*Never touch the front
of a photograph.
Fingers leave oil.*

Porcelain-Asian, Box, Face Shape Cover, Round, Hirado, Japan, 1800s, 4 In. $178.00

Skinner, Inc.

Porcelain-Asian, Brush Rest, Mountain, Blue Underglaze, Scholar, Landscape, Water Horses, Chinese, 7 ½ x 4 In. $245.00

Skinner, Inc.

Porcelain-Asian, Charger, Dragon & Phoenix, Flaming Pearl, 5 Bats, Red, Chinese, 19th Century, 16 ⅞ In. $956.00

Neal Auction Co.

Porcelain-Asian, Dish, Dragon, Flames, Blue & White, Marked, 1700s, 6 ¾ In. $4920.00

New Orleans Auction Galleries, Inc.

Item	Price
Ewer, Chicken Head, Spout, Handle, Carved Lotus Scrolls & Petals, Chinese, 8 ½ In.	415.00
Ewer, Fruit, Flower Panels, Cobalt Leather, Scrolled Gilt Handle, c.1895, 11 ¾ In., Pair	236.00
Ewer, Round Lobed Body, Arched Spout, Loop Handle, Flared Rim, Narrow Neck, Chinese, 6 ½ In.	368.00
Figurine, Blanc-De-Chine, Immortal, Sitting On Elephant, Mounted As Lamp, 12 In.	359.00
Figurine, Boy, Seated, Flower Apron, Holding Bird Toy, Open Mouth, Japan, 1800s, 8 In.	118.00
Figurine, Chinese Elder, Bottle Hanging From Cord Around Neck, Chinese, c.1920, 18 In. ......*illus*	300.00
Figurine, Dancer, Posed, Fan Raised To Side Of Face, Japan, 8 In., Pair	123.00
Figurine, Dog, On Haunches, Snarling, Multicolor, Japan, 1900s, 9 In., Pair	461.00
Figurine, Elderly Man, Staff, Multicolor Robe, Chinese, c.1900, 24 ½ In.	420.00
Figurine, Foo Dog, Male, Female, Cub, Kangxi Style, Famille Verte, Chinese, 15 ¾ In., Pair ....*illus*	836.00
Figurine, Foo Dog, Rectangular Base, Pierce Carved Design, Multicolor, 13 In., Pair	305.00
Figurine, Guanyin, Blanc De Chine, Seated, Hands On Knee, Chinese, c.1905, 10 In.	1422.00
Figurine, Guanyin, Kneeling, Child Sitting On Knee, Robes, Chinese, 8 In.	598.00
Figurine, Mythological Animal, Enamel Plinth, Multicolor, Japan 1800s, 8 In., Pair	430.00
Figurine, Parrot, Deep Turquoise Glaze, Mouth Open, Perched, Chinese, 1800s, 15 In., Pair	474.00
Fishbowl, Blue & White, Vining Flowers, Yongzheng, Chinese, 20 x 22 In.	478.00
Flask, Moon, Blue Bat, Branch Panels, Blue Neck Ruyi Handles, Chinese, 10 In.	1103.00
Footbath, Painted, Landscape, Handles, Gilt, Chinese, 8 x 22 In.	270.00
Ginger Jar, Blue & White, Flowers, Scenic, Chinese, 7 x 6 In.	84.00
Ginger Jar, Bulbous, Green Glaze, Flower & Geometric Design, Chinese, 7 In.	89.00
Ginger Jar, Cover, Blue & White Foo Dog, Flowers, Chinese, 1800s, 9 In.	456.00
Ginger Jar, Cover, Blue & White, Scrolling Leaves, Vines, Flower Medallions, Chinese, 9 In.	89.00
Ginger Jar, Cover, Multicolor Pastel, Enameled, 17 In.	187.00
Ginger Jar, Lotus Scrolls, Characters, Oval, Blue, White, Wood Cover, Stand, Chinese, 7 In.	385.00
Hook, Garment, Dragon Finial, Officials, General, Butterflies, Scrolls, Chinese, c.1910, 4 In.	237.00
Inkstone, Blue & White, Scrolling Lotus, Round, Chinese, Marked, 1800s, 5 ½ In.	7350.00
Jar, Baluster Shape, Birds, Flowering Branch, Giltwood Lid, Ormolu Finial, 20 In.	2887.00
Jar, Baluster, 3 Dragons, Clouds, Rocks, Multicolor, Wucai, Chinese, 15 In.	3068.00
Jar, Baluster, Multicolor, Wurcai, Chinese, 1600s, 16 In.	7800.00
Jar, Blue & White, Globular, Straight Rim, Leaves, Insects, Chinese, c.1900, 7 x 7 In.	138.00
Jar, Blue & White, Scrolling Flowers, Figures, Baluster, Chinese, 17 ¾ In.	207.00
Jar, Blue Glaze, Red Design, Cranes, Clouds, Korea, 1700s, 10 In.	652.00
Jar, Blue, White, Cylindrical, Metal Handles, Plum Flowers, Vase, Chinese, 1800s, 6 x 5 In.	150.00
Jar, Cover, Baluster Shape, Blue & White, Foo Dogs, Mark, 20 In.	388.00
Jar, Cover, Baluster, Chartreuse, Famille Rose, Flowers, Chinese, 1800s, 19 In. ....*illus*	2940.00
Jar, Cover, Blue & White, Flowering Prunus Branches, Cracked Ice Ground, 6 ½ In., Pair	269.00
Jar, Cover, Blue & White, Prunus Blooms, Cracked Ice Ground, 1800s, 9 ½ In.	78.00
Jar, Cover, Carved Lotus Petals, Bulbous, Round Foot, 6 ½ In.	582.00
Jar, Cover, Dragons, Clouds, Waves, Wucai, 5 Enamels, Chinese, 1600s, 18 ½ In., Pair	6518.00
Jar, Cover, Landscape, Cottages, Blue, White, 6-Sided, Chinese, 9 ¾ In., Pair	398.00
Jar, Dome Lid, Warrior, Conquering Dragon, Waves, Blue White, Chinese, 21 In.	429.00
Jar, Dragons, Clouds, Blue & White, Mallet Shape, Mark, Chinese, 1800s, 7 In.	178.00
Jar, Dragons, Pearls, Clouds, Bulbous, Chinese, 15 x 18 ½ In.	5925.00
Jar, Famille Rose, Green Foo Dog Finial, Chinese, 24 ½ In., Pair	430.00
Jar, Flowering Tree, Blue & White, Chinese, c.1720, 9 ¾ In.	1126.00
Jar, Globular, Lotus Leaves, Geometric Pattern, Dragons, River, Mountains, Chinese, 6 In.	150.00
Jar, Landscape, Dancing Figures, Playing Instruments, Chinese, 10 ½ x 12 In.	328.00
Jar, Pink, Green, Mark, Yongzheng, 4 In., Pair	407.00
Jar, Scaly Dragon, Phoenix, Flaming Clouds, Blue & White, Chinese, 7 ¼ In.	119.00
Jar, Storage, Cover, Peonies, Butterflies, Bulbous, Chinese, c.1790, 10 In.	922.00
Jar, Water, Figure & Landscape Cartouches, Orange Base, Rim, Squat, Chinese, 1800s, 2 x 2 ½ In.	711.00
Jar, Yellow Glaze, Wood Stand, Chinese, 1800s, 9 ½ In., Pair	720.00
Jardiniere, Blue Underglaze, Dragon Roundels, Chinese, 1800s, 10 In. ....*illus*	652.00
Jardiniere, Globular, Fishbowl, Blue & White, Flowers, Birds, Insects, Chinese, 1800s, 14 In.	345.00
Jardiniere, Painted, Butterflies, Blossoms, Chinese, 12 x 16 In.	180.00
Jardiniere, Painted, Flowers, Bands, Chinese, 14 x 15 ½ In.	780.00
Jardiniere, Painted, Phoenix, Lotus, Trees, Square, Raised Lip, Chinese, 8 x 14 ½ In.	60.00
Jardiniere, Rectangular, Dragons, Flaming Pearl, Waves, Bracket Feet, Base, 14 In.	519.00
Jardiniere, Scenic Reserves, Earth Colors, Japan, 11 x 15 In.	71.00
Jardiniere, Yellow Ground, Birds Of Paradise, Black Ground Rim Band, Chinese, 11 x 12 In.	69.00
Opium Burner, Painted, Dragon, Chinese, 3 ½ x 3 In.	150.00
Pillow, Blue & White, Women, Courtyards, Baths, Pierced, Chinese, 1800s, 2 x 5 x 2 In.	225.00
Planter, Blue & White, Birds, Dragon, Zigzag Edge, Chinese, 7 x 15 In.	960.00
Planter, Branching Peonies, Blue Key Fret Rim, Square, Tai He Di An, Chinese, 9 ½ In. .....*illus*	2083.00
Planter, Clair De Lune, Blue, Ring Handles, Drum Shape, Seal Mark, c.1930, 71 ½ In.	369.00
Planter, Famille Verte, Flowers, Lotus Scroll Ground, Chinese, 1800s, 12 x 14 In.	2370.00

Plaque, Peonies, Rocks, Butterfly, Famille Verte, Frame, Chinese, c.1910, 9 x 6 In.		276.00
Plaque, River Valley, Mountains, Figures, Boats, Fishermen, Frame, Chinese, 10 x 15 In.		854.00
Plaque, Village Landscapes, Giltwood Frame, Chinese, 37 ½ x 21 In.		1230.00
Plaque, Winter Scene, Openwork Stand, Frame, Zhu Shan, Chinese, c.1905, 21 x 11 In.		1348.00
Plaque, Women, Boys, Garden, Wood Frame, Chinese, 1900s, 20 ½ x 15 In., Pair		3120.00
Plate, 100 Flowers, Black Ground, Mark, Chinese, c.1910, 10 In.		214.00
Plate, Antique Objects, Reticulated Border, Wavy Blue Rim, Chinese, 1700s, 10 In.		948.00
Plate, Bats, Iron Red, Gilt Rim, Chinese, 1800s, 7 In.		652.00
Plate, Blue & White, Dragon, Flames, Rosewood Stand, Chinese, 1700s, 11 In.		325.00
Plate, Blue Scrolls, Medallion, Yellow Ground, 5 Bats, Mark, Chinese, 7 ¾ In.		2015.00
Plate, Dark Blue Glaze, Gilt Mark, Chinese, 7 ¾ In.		385.00
Plate, Doucai, 100 Boys, Mark, Chinese, 6 In.		919.00
Plate, Dragon, Phoenix Roundels, Flowers, Butterflies, Mark, Chinese, 1800s, 6 ¾ In., Pair		1126.00
Plate, Dragons, Pearls, Clouds, Green Enamel, Chinese, 1800s, 9 In.		474.00
Plate, Famille Rose, Rose Medallion, Symbols, Landscapes, Chinese, 9 ¾ In., 6 Piece		1845.00
Plate, Figures, Garden, Cottages, Multicolor, Inscriptions, Chinese, c.1910, 9 In.		980.00
Plate, Flowering Branches, Peonies, Peacock Roundel, Chinese, 1800s, 15 In.		429.00
Plate, Interior Iron Red 5 Bats, Exterior Flowering Branches, Chinese, 1800s, 7 ¼ In.		1304.00
Plate, Lotus Flowers, Scrolls, Red, Yellow, Green Paint, Mark, Chinese, 8 ⅛ In.		1304.00
Plate, Lotus Interior, Pink & Yellow, 5 Bats Exterior, Iron Red, Chinese, 8 In.		1541.00
Plate, Mythological Scenes, Gilt, Grisaille, Chinese, 9 In.		259.00
Plate, Open Lotus Flower Shape, Yellow Glaze, Yongzheng Mark, Chinese, 1900s, 8 In.		551.00
Plate, Painted, Cranes, Butterflies, Marsh Landscape, Gilt, Footed, 9 x 7 In.		23.00
Plate, Thousand Faces, Japan, 7 ¼ In.		48.00
Plate, Yellow Glaze, Dragons, Aubergine, Green, Chinese, 5 In.		1139.00
Platter, Ship Design, Iron Red Border, Gilt Trim, Oblong, Chinese, 1900s, 14 ¾ In.		345.00
Platter, Tobacco Leaf, Enamel Birds, Landscapes, Multicolor, Chinese, 1900s, 15 x 12 ½ In.		127.00
Punch Bowl, Blue & White, Painted Birds, Flowers, Chinese, c.1800, 13 ½ In.		657.00
Sauce, White, Blue Floral Center, Rim, Chinese, 5 ⅛ In.		266.00
Saucer, Fruits, Vegetable Paint, Box, Chinese, 1700s, 6 In.		1838.00
Teapot, Cadogan, Puzzle, Chinese, 6 ¼ x 8 ¼ In.	*illus*	266.00
Teapot, Cover, Blue & White, Scenic, Flowers, Chinese		508.00
Teapot, European Figures, Gilt, Grisaille, Chinese, 5 ½ In.		633.00
Temple Jar, Wedding, Lid, Blue & White, Leaves, Double Happiness Symbol, Chinese, 20 In.		266.00
Umbrella Stand, Dragon & Tiger, Forest Green, Japan, c.1890, 24 ½ In.		267.00
Urn, Cover, Blue & White, Women, In Courtyard, Chinese, 10 x 11 In., Pair		207.00
Urn, Crackle Glaze, Tan, Green, Brown Bands, Chinese, c.1900, 24 In., Pair		3318.00
Urn, Lid, Garden, Red, Basket Finial, Bronze, Putto Handles, Chinese, 27 x 11 In., Pair		396.00
Urn, Swollen Body, Flared Rim, Flowers, Chinese, c.1950, 34 x 15 In., Pair		826.00
Vase, 3 Monkeys, Climbing Cypress Tree, Multicolor, Mark, Chinese, 14 In.		948.00
Vase, 100 Boys Design, Neck Dragon Lugs, Baluster, Chinese, 1800s, 18 In., Pair		3200.00
Vase, 100 Children Design, Bats, Symbols, Chinese, c.1940, 8 In.		2370.00
Vase, Antique Objects, Iron Red, Blue Brocade Ground, Chinese, 1800s, 18 ¼ In.		14220.00
Vase, Apple Green Glaze, Chinese, 1800, 5 ¾ In.		237.00
Vase, Applied Pomegranate, Leaves, Bulbous, Red, Blue, Flambe, Chinese, 22 In.		2133.00
Vase, Archaic Style, Fish Shape Handles, Turquoise Glaze, Chinese, 1900s, 8 In.		207.00
Vase, Baluster, Gray Matte Glaze, Silver Speckles, Chinese, 15 In.		900.00
Vase, Baluster, Warriors On Horseback, Castle, Blue & White, Rolled Rim, Chinese, 18 In.		508.00
Vase, Beaker Shape, Petals, Vines, Blue & White, Chinese, 1600s, 7 ½ In.		840.00
Vase, Blue & White, Dragons, Animal Mask Lug Handles, Baluster, Chinese, 15 In., Pair		732.00
Vase, Blue & White, Landscape, Flying Birds, Red Sky, Baluster, Japan, c.1905, 6 In.		177.00
Vase, Blue Landscape, White Ground, Chinese, 1700s, 17 ½ In.		2607.00
Vase, Blue Scrolling Leaves, Grass, Calligraphic Inscription, Baluster, Japan, 6 In.		195.00
Vase, Bottle Shape, Dragons & Fire, Blue & White, Chinese, 23 In.		354.00
Vase, Bottle Shape, Horned Dragon, Blue, Brown, Seal Mark, Chinese, 1900s, 6 ¾ In.		2460.00
Vase, Bottle Shape, Lotus, Flowering Sprays, Crane, Art Nouveau Style, Chinese, 1900s, 13 In.		325.00
Vase, Bottle Shape, Peaches, Leaves, Pink, Gilt, Cobalt Blue, Chinese, 1900s, 12 In.		178.00
Vase, Bottle Shape, Ruffled Rim, Dragon, Blue & White, Black, Gold, Red, Brown, Chinese, 49 In.		1180.00
Vase, Bottle Shape, White Ground, Gilt Highlights, Flowers, Wood Foot, Japan, c.1980, 20 In., Pair		448.00
Vase, Bottle Shape, Yellow Glaze, Round Foot, Plantain Leaves, Chinese, 9 In.		366.00
Vase, Bottle Shape, Yellow, Mythical Figures Repousse, Chinese, 28 In.		403.00
Vase, Bulbous, White Cranes, Pink Ground, Silver Rim, Makuso Kozan, Japan, 6 x 9 ½ In.		1100.00
Vase, Children At Play, Double Gourd Shape, Blue, White, Chinese, 10 ¼ In.		674.00
Vase, Children Playing, Tapered Neck, Blue & White, Chinese, 16 x 12 In.		122.00
Vase, Compressed Oval, Flared Lip, 2 Sinuous Dragons, Yellow & Iron Red, 7 In.		2091.00
Vase, Cover, Pilgrim Flask Shape, Birds, Flowers, Dragon Handles, Green, 1800s, 12 In.		1126.00

Porcelain-Asian, Figurine, Chinese Elder, Bottle Hanging From Cord Around Neck, Chinese, c.1920, 18 In. $300.00

DuMouchelles Art Gallery

Porcelain-Asian, Figurine, Foo Dog, Male, Female, Cub, Kangxi Style, Famille Verte, Chinese, 15 ¾ In., Pair $836.00

Neal Auction Co.

P

Porcelain-Asian, Jar, Cover, Baluster, Chartreuse, Famille Rose, Flowers, Chinese, 1800s, 19 In. $2940.00

Skinner, Inc.

Porcelain-Asian, Jardiniere, Blue Underglaze, Dragon Roundels, Chinese, 1800s, 10 In.
$652.00

Skinner, Inc.

Porcelain-Asian, Planter, Branching Peonies, Blue Key Fret Rim, Square, Tai He Di An, Chinese, 9 ½ In.
$2083.00

Skinner, Inc.

Porcelain-Asian, Teapot, Cadogan, Puzzle, Chinese, 6 ¼ x 8 ¼ In.
$266.00

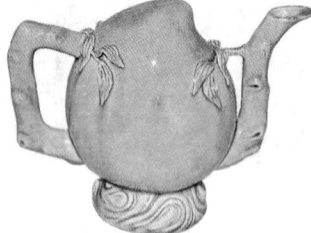

DuMouchelles Art Gallery

Porcelain-Asian, Vase, Double Gourd, Red, Straw Shade Mouth, Flambe, Chinese, 1800s, 8 ¼ In.
$144.00

Leland Little Auction

Vase, Cylindrical, Figures, Landscape, Blue & White, Chinese, c.1900, 18 x 7 In.	1169.00
Vase, Deer, Grassland, Pines, Paint, Orange Elephant Head Lugs, Chinese, 19 In.	4900.00
Vase, Dome Lid, Dragon, Magnolia Branches, Foo Dog Finial, Yellow, Chinese, 8 ¾ In., Pair	306.00
Vase, Dome Lid, Lotus, Scrolls, Blue, White, Paint, Chinese, 25 ¾ In.	1896.00
Vase, Double Gourd, Figures, Landscape, Scholar, Moon, Blue, White, Chinese, c.1905, 13 In..	2963.00
Vase, Double Gourd Figures, Mountain Scene, Blue, White, Chinese, 1800s, 8 In.	237.00
Vase, Double Gourd, Herd Of Deer, Chinese, 1929, 7 ½ In.	796.00
Vase, Double Gourd, Red, Straw Shade Mouth, Flambe, Chinese, 1800s, 8 ¼ In. ....*illus*	144.00
Vase, Double Gourd, S-Handles, Iron Red, Gilt, Medallions, Dragons, Phoenixes, c.1930, 9 In.	119.00
Vase, Double Gourd, Stylized Dragon Handles, Winter Scene, Chinese, 1934, 8 ½ In.	184.00
Vase, Dragon, Beige, Chocolate, Chinese, 10 In.	209.00
Vase, Dragon, Blue, White, Flared, Chinese, 17 ¾ x 8 In.	615.00
Vase, Dragon, Round Foot, Flared Rim, Handles, Blue & White, Chinese, 1800s, 24 In.	956.00
Vase, Dragons, Flowers, Scrolls, Blue & White, Chinese, 12 In.	119.00
Vase, Egg & Spinach Glaze, Conical, Radiating Petal Tips, Applied Dragon, Multicolor, 5 In.	2988.00
Vase, Figures & Flowers, Chinese, 30 In.	519.00
Vase, Figures, Landscape, Multicolor, Eggshell Finish, Chinese, 9 In., Pair	127.00
Vase, Fish, Reeds, Water Lilies, Chinese, Late 1800s, 6 In.	3220.00
Vase, Flared Mouth, Pale Blue, Wood Stand, Chinese Republic, c.1935, 4 ½ In., Pair	717.00
Vase, Flower & Symbol Bands, Pierced Handles, Multicolor, Chinese, c.1850, 23 x 9 In.	3000.00
Vase, Flowers, Birds, Scalloped Rim, Gold Band, Signed, Chinese, 49 ½ x 15 ½ In.	201.00
Vase, Flowers, Garlic Bulb Shape, Blue & White, Chinese, 11 x 5 In.	900.00
Vase, Flowers, Iron Red, Gilt, Turquoise Interior, Base, Mark, 3 ½ In.	1255.00
Vase, Flowers, Leaves, Iron Red, White, Paint, Chinese, 1800s, 5 ½ In.	385.00
Vase, Flowers, Turquoise Ground, Double Gourd Shape, Chinese, 13 x 7 In.	92.00
Vase, Foo Dog, Baluster, Blue & White, Crackle Glaze, Handles, Chinese, 1800s, 25 In.	1434.00
Vase, Foo Dog, Cloud, Hexagonal, Blue & White, Chinese, 1800s, 24 In.	1076.00
Vase, Foo Dogs, Iron Red, Applied Handles, Calligraphy, Wood Base, Chinese, 18 ½ In., Pair	322.00
Vase, Gilt Dragon, Silver Clouds, Coral Ground, Eiraku, Japan, c.1890, 14 ½ In.	900.00
Vase, Globular, 3 Spouts, Teadust Glaze, Chinese, 8 In.	1952.00
Vase, Green Dragon, Flaming Clouds, Yellow Ground, Wood Stand, Chinese, 5 ¼ In.	490.00
Vase, Hawks, Waves, Peonies, Plums, Bamboo, Lotus Border, Blue, White, Japan, 1800s, 38 In. *illus*	674.00
Vase, Hexagonal, Relief Design, Dragons, Chinese, c.1900, 13 ¾ In.	119.00
Vase, Landscape, Blue & White, Pear Shape, Flared Mouth, Chinese, 1800s, 13 In.	237.00
Vase, Landscape, Leaves, Baluster, Shaped Cartouches, Chinese, c.1800, 11 In., Pair	1054.00
Vase, Landscape, Man, Handles, White Ground, Baluster, Japan, 14 ¼ In., Pair	230.00
Vase, Lid, Overall Figures, Flowers Pattern, Applied Gold Designs, Chinese, 36 x 14 In.	800.00
Vase, Molded Plum Branch, Meiping Shape, Buff Glaze, Chinese, 10 In.	490.00
Vase, Moon Flask, Blue Underglaze, Plum Blossoms, Neck Dragons, Mark, Chinese, 1800s, 10 In.	1593.00
Vase, Moon Flask, Stylized Scrolls, Dragon Lugs, Blue, White, Chinese, 20 ½ x 14 ½ In.	5925.00
Vase, Mountain Scene, Figures, Pierced Gilt Handles, Chinese, 23 x 9 In.	150.00
Vase, Mt. Fuji, Lake Kawaguchiko, Osa Kamon, Chrysanthemum, Japan, 1900s, 15 In.	863.00
Vase, Oval Flower Cartouche, Bird, Insects, Flowers, Baluster, Marked, Chinese, 11 In.	465.00
Vase, Oval, Dragon, Flaming Pearl, Clouds, Creamy White, Mark, Chinese, 1800s, 5 ¼ In.	5036.00
Vase, Palace, Satsuma Style, Figures, Flowers, Handles, Multicolor, Gilt, Japan, 1900s, 72 In., Pair	2440.00
Vase, Panels, European Scenes, Blue Lotus Ground, Mark, Chinese, 7 ¾ In.	385.00
Vase, Pear Shape, Flared Rim, Round Foot, White, Red Dragon, Chinese, c.1900, 10 ¾ In.	459.00
Vase, Pheasants, Flower Scrolls, Carved, Yellow Glaze, Flared, Chinese, 11 ¾ In.	660.00
Vase, Pine Tree Shape, Male & Female, Brown, Blue, Hirado, Japan, 1800s, 11 ½ In. ......*illus*	119.00
Vase, Purple Ground, Gilt Medallions, Banded Neck, Shoulder, Chinese, 15 x 9 In.	4130.00
Vase, Red, Apple Green Spots, Wood Stand, Chinese, 1800s, 6 In.	551.00
Vase, Red, Blue Enameled Clouds, Cranes, Marked, Chinese, 1820-50, 7 ¾ In. ....*illus*	830.00
Vase, Red, Multicolor Leaves, Scrolling, Chinese, 14 x 9 ¾ In.	1888.00
Vase, Rickshaws, Animals, Flared Rim, Chinese, Da Ming, 17 ½ In.	735.00
Vase, Robin's-Egg Blue, Bands, Gilt, Masks, Archaic Designs, Chinese, c.1890, 8 ½ In. ....*illus*	1838.00
Vase, Rouge De Ver, Symbols, Allover Pattern, Tapered Neck, Chinese, c.1890, 15 ½ In.	460.00
Vase, Round, Blue, Red Birds, Plum Flowers, Chinese, 13 ¾ In.	296.00
Vase, Sack Shape, Wall, Hexagonal Pattern, Yellow Ground, Chinese, c.1910, 10 In.	337.00
Vase, San Duo, 3 Fruits, Yellow Sgraffito Ground, Chinese, c.1910, 8 ½ In. ....*illus*	1225.00
Vase, Scenic, Warriors, Bats, Clouds, Baluster, High Shoulders, Trumpet Neck, 37 In., Pair	1708.00
Vase, Scholarly Objects, Scrolled Bands, Mirror Black Ground, Gilt, Chinese, 1800s, 8 ¼ In.	110.00
Vase, Seated Monk, Symbols, Pink, Cylindrical, Mark, Chinese, 5 In.	267.00
Vase, Sparrow, Willow Branches, Inscribed, Wood Stand, Chinese, 5 In., Pair	245.00
Vase, Trees, Buildings, Pear Shape, Round Foot, Blue & White, Marked, Chinese, 7 In.	183.00
Vase, Turquoise Glaze, Bulbous, Rounded Mouth, Mark, Chinese, c.1890, 8 ½ In.	178.00

Vase, Turquoise Glaze, Flower Design, Baluster, Chinese, 7 In.	460.00
Vase, Turquoise, Yellow, Double Gourd, Handles, Chinese, 11 x 7 In.	413.00
Vase, Urn Shape, Gilt, Cranes, Wooden Round Base, Japan, 24 In., Pair	1195.00
Vase, Water Chestnut Shape, Red, 9 Peaches, Branch, Chinese, 6 ¾ In.	593.00
Vase, White Flowers, Rock, Sapphire Blue Ground, Lobed Mouth, Mark, Chinese, 12 In.	153.00
Vase, Woman, Flared Rim, Chinese, 11 ½ In.	64.00
Water Coupe, Molded Dragon, Turquoise, Pale Blue, 6-Sided, Chinese, 3 x 1 ½ In.	178.00
Water Coupe, Squat, Narrow Sunken Neck, Green Tea Dust Glaze, Chinese, 1800s, 3 ½ x 2 ½ In.	1593.00
Water Dropper, Butterfly Shape Mouth, White, Square, Animal Shape Finial, Korea, 5 ½ In.	1135.00
Water Pot, Dragon Molded, Head Over Rim, Beehive Shape, Flambe Glaze, Chinese, 2 In.	178.00

PORCELAIN-CONTEMPORARY lists pieces made by artists working after 1975.

Bowl, Check Carved, White, Signed Arnse, Norway, 1980, 6 ¼ x 5 ¾ In.	279.00
Figurine, Peasant Mother & Child, Black, Yellow, Russia, c.1955, 9 ¾ In.	1080.00
Figurine, Ruffles, Pierrot, Daisies, Giuseppe Armani, Box, 1991	173.00
Figurine, Woman, Figure Skater, White Skating Dress, Gloves, West Germany, 7 In.	120.00
Figurine, Woman, Long Hair, Awakening, No. 591, Giuseppe Armani, Box, Italy, 1990	403.00
Figurine, Woman, Swan, Dahl Jensen, Denmark, 8 ½ In.	237.00
Moonpot, Rattle, Blue Glaze, Toshiko Takaezu, 6 ¾ x 5 ½ In.	5270.00
Moonpot, Rattle, Brown Glaze, Toshiko Takaezu, 5 ¾ x 5 ½ In.	4340.00
Moonpot, Rattle, Brown Glaze, Toshiko Takaezu, 9 x 8 ½ In.	4960.00
Vase, Euphrates, Stacked Forms, Marked, E. Sottsass, Memphis, 1983, 15 ¾ In. ....*illus*	676.00

PORCELAIN-MIDCENTURY includes pieces made from the 1940s to about 1975.

Bowl, White, Pink Rose, Open Lattice Sides, Scalloped, Gold Trim, Handles, Georg Jensen	71.00
Bowl, Yellow, Transfer Images, Mao Zedong At Different Ages, 1968, 8 In. ....*illus*	179.00
Bust, Lady, Curled Hair, Closed Eyes, Cloak, Stars, Art Deco, USA, c.1940, 6 In.	75.00
Figurine, Flamingo, Pink, Head In Grass, USA, c.1950	45.00
Figurine, Ice Skater, Mark, Russia, c.1970, 6 In.	120.00
Ginger Jar, Dome Lid, White Prunus, Hawthorn, Blue Crackled Ice Ground, c.1900, 7 ⅝ In.	177.00
Group, Dog Trainer, Man, Ball Behind Back, Poodle, Borsato, Italy, 9 x 6 ¼ In.	196.00

POSTCARDS were first legally permitted in Austria on October 1, 1869. The United States passed postal regulations allowing the card in 1872. Most of the picture postcards collected today date after 1910. The amount of postage can help to date a card. The rates are: 1872 (1 cent), 1917 (2 cents), 1919 (1 cent), 1925 (2 cents), 1928 (1 cent), 1952 (2 cents), 1958 (3 cents), 1963 (4 cents), 1968 (5 cents), 1971 (6 cents), 1973 (8 cents), 1975 (7 cents), 1976 (9 cents), 1978 (10 cents), March 1981 (12 cents), November 1981 (13 cents), 1985 (14 cents), 1988 (15 cents), 1991 (19 cents), 1995 (20 cents), 2001 (21 cents), 2002 (23 cents), 2006 (24 cents), 2007 (26 cents), 2008 (27 cents), 2009 (28 cents), 2011 (29 cents), 2012 (32 cents). While most postcards sell for low prices, a small number bring high prices. Some of these are listed here.

Alphabet Animals, T Is For Turtle, 1910	6.00
Ashland, Wisconsin, Ellis Avenue, Houses, Tree Lined Street, Linen, 1942	6.00
Baseball, New York Giants Vs. Boston Red Sox, World Series, Panoramic, 1912, 27 x 4 ¾ In.	1528.00
Bunny, Playing Accordion, Easter Eggs, 1930	10.00
Cat Theme Set, Grade School, Alfred Mainzer, Marked Max Kunzli, 3 ½ x 5 ½ In., 6 Piece	30.00
Cherubs, Church Clock Tower, Hummel, 1939	18.00
Coney Island, Cincinnati, Ohio, Flower Clock, 1950s, 5 x 8 In.	12.00
Dog, Hat & Cigar, Cat, Wearing Glasses, Black & White, c.1910	10.00
Equitable Building, New York City, 1913	18.00
Funchase & Roller Coaster, Wildwood, New Jersey, Linen Type, c.1953	4.95
Gillette Safety Razor, Baby With Razor, Begin Early, Shave Yourself, 1908	100.00
Girl, Dog, I Don't Love You Anymore, Black & White, 1910	14.00
Kewpie, Suitcase, G & B, Chicago, 1919	22.00
Kewpies, Giant Easter Egg, 1920	17.00
Kitten, Candle, Megaphone, 1909	20.00
Kittens, In Basket, 1940s, 5 x 8 In.	2.75
Lord Street, London Square, Southport, U.K., 1920s	8.99
Miami, Florida, Linen Type, 1 Cent Stamp, 1949	5.00
New Year's, 2 Girls, Grandfather Clock, 1907	8.00
Puppies, In Basket, Daisies, 1900s	9.00
Rabbit Couple, Sitting On Bench, 1907	10.00
San Francisco Seals, Pacific Coast League Championship, 1909	1410.00
Sitting Woman, Man Handing Rose, 1908	12.00

Porcelain-Asian, Vase, Hawks, Waves, Peonies, Plums, Bamboo, Lotus Border, Blue, White, Japan, 1800s, 38 In. $674.00

Skinner, Inc.

Porcelain-Asian, Vase, Pine Tree Shape, Male & Female, Brown, Blue, Hirado, Japan, 1800s, 11 ½ In. $119.00

Skinner, Inc.

Porcelain-Asian, Vase, Red, Blue Enameled Clouds, Cranes, Marked, Chinese, 1820-50, 7 ¾ In. $830.00

Skinner, Inc.

P

Porcelain-Asian, Vase, Robin's-Egg Blue, Bands, Gilt, Masks, Archaic Designs, Chinese, c.1890, 8 ½ In. $1838.00

Skinner, Inc.

Porcelain-Asian, Vase, San Duo, 3 Fruits, Yellow Sgraffito Ground, Chinese, c.1910, 8 ½ In. $1225.00

Skinner, Inc.

Porcelain-Contemporary, Vase, Euphrates, Stacked Forms, Marked, E. Sottsass, Memphis, 1983, 15 ¾ In. $676.00

New Orleans Auction Galleries, Inc.

Porcelain-Midcentury, Bowl, Yellow, Transfer Images, Mao Zedong At Different Ages, 1968, 8 In. $179.00

Sloans & Kenyon

Teddy Roosevelt, Bear, Real Fur, 3 ½ x 5 ¼ In.	*illus*	70.00
Thanksgiving Greeting, Girl With Wings Cooking, 1909		5.00
Thomas Edison, Phonograph, We've Come A Long Way, 1905		40.00
Ty Cobb, Standing With Bat, Sepia, 1910		4113.00
Valentine Greetings, Embossed, Woman In Heart, 1910		6.00

POSTERS have informed the public about news and entertainment events since ancient times. Nineteenth-century advertising and theatrical posters and twentieth-century movie and war posters are of special interest today. The price is determined by the artist, the condition, and the rarity. Other posters may be listed under Movie, Political, and World War I and II.

6 Days Of Sound, The Doors, Chuck Berry, Salvation, Dec. 26-30, 1967, 14 x 21 In.	*illus*	515.00
101 Ranch Real Wild West, Rodeo Parade, c.1911, Vertical ½ Sheet, 57 x 20, In.		3525.00
Alexander Calder Design, Perl Gallery Exhibition, Feb. 8-Mar. 12, 1966, Lithograph, 29 In.		593.00
Bal Du Grand Prix, Color Lithograph, M. Dobuzinski, Frame, Opera Le 29 Juin, 1929, 21 x 14 In.		1416.00
Bob Marley & The Wailers, Image, Greek Theater, U.C. Berkeley, July 21, 1978, 18 x 12 In.		230.00
Broadside, Auction, Isaac F. Hite, Horses, Farming Tools, Frame, Frederick Co., 1885, 19 x 13 In.		345.00
Broadside, Public Sale, Sorrel Mare, 6 Cows, Household Goods, Denver, Pa., Feb. 19, 1919, 40 x 26 In.		354.00
Brotherhood Of Locomotive Firemen, Vignettes, Stone Lithograph, Frame, c.1885, 22 x 28 In.		58.00
Brothers Byrne, 8 Bells, Carriage Theater, Acrobats, Horse, Frame, 28 x 42 In.		330.00
Bulletin, Mardi Gras, Carnival Parade, Rex Edition, 4 Elements, Weekly Budget, 1880		538.00
Bulletin, Mardi Gras, Carnival Parade, Rex Edition, Fantasy Of The Sea, Searcy & Pfaff, 1923		149.00
Bulletin, Mardi Gras, Carnival Parade, Rex Edition, Realm Of Flowers, Times Democrat, 1888		299.00
Bull's-Eye, Rock Concert, Creedence Clearwater Revival, Black Pearl Lights, 1968, 14 x 22 In.		180.00
Carter The Great, World's Weird Wonderful Wizard, Otis Litho, Frame, 1935, 3 Sheets, 77 x 40 In. *illus*		563.00
Circus, Adam Forepaugh & Sells Brothers, Hippos, Polar Bear, Seal, Multicolor, 40 x 30 In.		767.00
Circus, Barr Brothers Circus & Wild West Show, 2-Sided, 1910s, 9 x 24 In.		60.00
Circus, Bertram Mills Circus At Olympia, Open Dec. 17th, 1935, Tiger On Front, 37 x 22 In.		163.00
Circus, Cole Brothers, Children's Favorite Circus, Kids On Hippopotamus, 1930s, 30 x 40 ½ In.		263.00
Circus, Hagenbeck-Wallace, Jeanette May, Aerial Ballet, Temple Litho, 1930s, 28 x 41 In.		79.00
Circus, Jack Hoxie, Big 3 Ring Circus, Horses, Dogs, Attached Title Snipe, Color, 29 x 41 In.		74.00
Circus, Ringling Bros. & Barnum & Bailey, Circus Kings Of All Time, c.1935, 28 x 51 In.		358.00
Circus, Ringling Bros & Barnum & Bailey, Elephant With Girl In Mouth, 1930, 28 x 41 In.		150.00
Circus, Ringling Bros. & Barnum & Bailey, Frank Buck, Nepal, Elephant, c.1938, 41 x 28 In.		1955.00
Circus, Ringling Bros. & Barnum & Bailey, Portraits, 1936, 26 ¾ x 41 ½ In.		263.00
Circus, Ringling Bros. & Barnum & Bailey Circus, Greatest Show On Earth Lion, 1942, 28 x 42 In.		127.00
Circus, Tom Mix, Chimpanzee In Tuxedo On High Wire, 1937, 40 x 14 In.		152.00
Cocose, Color Lithograph, A. Cometti, Frame, 60 x 43 In.		2832.00
Dartmouth Winter Carnival, Saturday, Feb. 6, 1937, Paper, 34 x 22 In.		5280.00
Doors, Avalon Concert, San Francisco, June 1-4, 1967, 14 x 20 In.		407.00
Draft, Register, June 5th, Uncle Sam, Red, White, Blue, 37 x 24 In.		23.00
Fallout Shelter, The Who, North American Tour, Fallout Shelter Symbol, 1973, 53 x 40 In.		974.00
Grateful Dead, Carousel Ballroom, Feb. 14, 1968, Heart, Be Mine, 11 x 11 In.		452.00
Grateful Dead, Concert, Worcester, Mass., April 7-9, 1988, Psychedelic, 15 ½ x 23 In.		192.00
Hendrix & Zeppelin, California Folk Rock Concert, May 23-25, 1969, 14 x 20 In.		1695.00
Herbie Hancock, Concert, McGonigle Hall, Phila., Pa., Jan. 26, 1974, 30 x 22 In.		173.00
Indiana, Have Fun, Burger Beer, Race Car, c.1955, 25 x 21 In.		1680.00
Italian Bakery, Red Open Top Touring Car, 3 Women, Driver, Paper, 1908, 22 ½ x 17 In.		360.00
Jimi Hendrix, Photograph, Playing Guitar, Stars & Stripes, Early 1970s, 33 x 23 In.		158.00
John & Yoko, Nude, Headshop, Two Virgins Album, 1970, 22 x 28 In.		85.00
L'Andalouise Exposition 1900, Lithograph, Woman, Sagot, 51 x 37 In.		649.00
MG, Series T.F., Safety First, J. Pelling, Green Roadster On Dirt Track, 1953, 25 x 35 In.		707.00
Missouri Girl, Daisy All Dressed Up, Donaldson Litho Co. Newport, Ky., Frame, 18 x 28 In.		550.00
Monterey Pop, Black Ground, Neon Multicolor Flower Graphic, 1968, 27 x 41 In.		155.00
Nirvana, U.K. Tour, Orange, 1991, 30 x 40 In.		192.00
Opera, Esclarmonde, Alfred Choubrac, Color, F. Appel, Paris, Frame, c.1889, 46 x 31 In.		767.00
Overland Mail Route To California, Wells Fargo, 1930s, 19 x 13 In.		532.00
Playbill, Held By The Enemy, Union Soldier, Horse, Springer Lithograph Co., c.1890, 82 x 42 In.		254.00
Queen, German Concert, Black & White, 1979, 24 ¼ x 33 ½ In.		180.00
Ring It Again, Buy U.S. Gov't Bonds, Third Liberty Loan, April 15th, 1918, 20 x 30 In. *illus*		180.00
Salon Des Humoristes, Laughing Woman, Grinning Bear, Auguste Roubille, c.1905, 46 x 30 In.		1476.00
Slaves Of The Mine, Comedy Drama, Up With That Hand, Enquirer Job Printing, 42 x 29 In.		193.00
Tiger God, Horace Goldin, Lithograph, Mounted, Moody Bros., 6 Sheets, 85 x 78 ½ In. *illus*		1500.00
Vine Of Liberty, Revolutionary War, Root To Fruit, Litho, William Rankin, 1849, 40 x 32 In.		118.00
Western Ammunition, Bob White, Lynn Bogue Hunt, Paper, 15 ½ x 24 In.		791.00
Yoga, Positions, Paper, On Cloth, Multicolor, Jogasan India, Wood Frame, c.1955, 29 x 19 In.		200.00

POTLIDS are just that, lids for pots. Transfer-printed potlids had their heyday from the 1840s to the early 1900s. The English Staffordshire potteries made ceramic containers with decorative lids for bear's grease, shrimp or meat paste, cold cream, and toothpaste. Printed advertising and pictures of historical events, portraits of famous people, or scenic views were designed in black and white or color. Reproductions have been made.

Cherry Toothpaste, Patronized By The Queen	56.00
Cold Cream, Drippy Letters, 2 ¾ In.	45.00
Parfumerie Brunier, Blue Transfer, Farmyard Scene, Cows, Trees, Building, Paris, 2 ⅜ In.	518.00
Saponaceous Tooth Powder, Dr. Bowditch, B.B. Thayer & Co., San Francisco, 3 ¼ In.	728.00
Worsley's Saponaceous Shaving Compound, Philadelphia, c.1870, 3 ⅞ In. ....*illus*	585.00

POTTERY and porcelain are different. Pottery is opaque; you can't see through it. Porcelain is translucent. If you hold a porcelain dish in front of a strong light, you will see the light through the dish. Porcelain is colder to the touch. Pottery is softer and easier to break and will stain more easily because it is porous. Porcelain is thinner, lighter, and more durable. Majolica, faience, and stoneware are all pottery. Additional pieces of pottery are listed in this book in the categories Pottery-Art, Pottery-Contemporary, Pottery-Midcentury, and under the factory name. For information about pottery makers and marks, see *Kovels' Dictionary of Marks—Pottery & Porcelain: 1650–1850* and *Kovels' New Dictionary of Marks—Pottery & Porcelain: 1850 to the Present.*

Basin, Pitcher, Painted, White, Blue Flowers, Carved Bow, Ruffled Rim, England, c.1880	48.00
Basket, Mottled Green, Footed, Handle, 6 x 5 In.	38.00
Biscuit Jar, Rectangular Form, Cream Color, Ferns, 7 In.	200.00
Bowl, Blue, Monkey, Hare, Persia, 16th Century, 7 ¼ In. Diam.	237.00
Bowl, Bubble, Turquoise, Interior Purple Splash, Footed, Jun Ware, 5 ¼ In. ....*illus*	610.00
Bowl, Dragonfly, Green Purple, 1957, 12 In.	69.00
Bowl, Olive Gray Glaze, Ring Foot, Wide Rim, Earthenware, 6 In. Diam.	30.00
Bowl, Olive Green, Conical, Molded Flower Design, Wave Pattern, Chinese, 7 ⅜ In. Diam.	118.00
Bowl, Pale Green Glaze, Flower Shaped, Wide Petal Rim, Asia, 5 ⅝ In. Diam.	59.00
Bowl, Shallow, Birds & Leaves, Blackware, Signed, 9 In. Diam.	171.00
Bowl, Squat, Figural & Geometric Design, Blackware, 9 In.	110.00
Brushpot, Scholars, Poetry, White Beaded Borders, 6-Sided, Chinese, 1900s, 6 ¾ In. ......*illus*	582.00
Bust, Stylized Male Head, Blackware, Mexico, 11 In.	310.00
Card Caddy, Scottie Dog, Cornflower Blue, Art Deco, USA Original Pottery, c.1935, 2 x 3 In.	35.00
Censer, Purple, Gray Glaze, Squat, Bulbous, Tripod Feet, Squared Rim, Chinese, 3 ⅝ x 6 ⅜ In.	177.00
Cricket Cage, Jumping Frog, Japan, c.1890, 3 x 6 In.	750.00
Crock, Cobalt Blue Stencil 3, Salt Glaze, Ottawa Pottery, Brown Albany Slip, 1884, 3 Gal. ....*illus*	632.00
Crock, Millers Department Store, Cobalt Blue Stamp, Bristol Glaze, Alexis Pottery, 5 Gal. ......*illus*	1265.00
Cup, Bottoms Up, Bent Over Figure, White Cloud Pottery, N.Y., 3 In.	28.00
Ewer, Oval, Dragon Shape Handle, Spout, Mottled Amber, Green, Ribbed Neck, Chinese, c.1900, 18 In.	173.00
Figurine, Camel, 2 Bags On Saddle, Square Base, 15 In.	598.00
Figurine, Dancer, Arm Raised, Long Robes, Full Sleeves, Chignon Hairstyle, Tang Style, 13 In.	244.00
Figurine, Dancer, Headdress, 2 Open Loops, Red & Green Pigments, Tang Style, 15 In.	5368.00
Figurine, Deity, Standing, Scholar's Robes, Hat, Holding Ruyi Scepter, Chinese, 16 In.	492.00
Figurine, Dog, Pug, Glass Eyes, Gray Paint, Earthenware, Germany, 1800s, 8 In.	652.00
Figurine, Horse, Head Down, Leg Raised, Square Base, Tang Style, 19 In., Pair ....*illus*	9760.00
Figurine, Horse, Standing, Leg Up, Saddle, Square Base, Chinese	269.00
Figurine, House, Rectangular, Doors, Shutters, Iridescent Green Glaze, 4 Stilt Legs, Chinese, 18 In.	1830.00
Figurine, Man, Standing, Moving Head, Open Hands, Green Glaze, Ming Style, 27 In., Pair	2928.00
Figurine, Winston Churchill, Standing, Bovey, 8 In.	150.00
Figurine, Woman, Seated, Black Hair, 6 In., Pair	305.00
Figurine, Woman, Standing, Flowing Robes, 2 Loops In Hair, Tang Style, 15 In.	4880.00
Figurine, Woman, Standing, Flowing Robes, Gilt Accents, Tang Style, 15 In.	6100.00
Flask, Potato Shape, Mottled Matte Brown Glaze, 7 In.	98.00
Jar, Blue & White, Carved Wood Cover, Blossoms, Leaves, Cracked Ice, Chinese, 8 ½ In. ...*illus*	2607.00
Jar, Flowers, Incised, M. Dustin, 6 Gal.	8500.00
Jar, Matte Black, Swirl Design, Handles, Chinese, 13 In.	1220.00
Jar, Olive Green, Round, 4 Handles, 3 Legs, Lion Mask Terminals, Lid, Foo Dog, c.1900, 14 In.	118.00
Jar, Sake, Cover, Ribbed Sides, Open Handles, Pink Flowers, Cobalt Blue Calligraphy, 16 In.	104.00
Jar, Water, Urn Shape, Orange, Brown, Rolled Lip, 2 Handles, Indonesia, 23 ½ x 20 x 20 In.	180.00
Jardiniere, Pedestal, Grape & Leaf Design, Impressed, 29 In.	119.00
Jardiniere, Stand, Bulbous Top & Foot, Mottled Green & Blue, Square Design, 28 In.	68.00
Jardiniere, Stand, Cream & Tan, Vertical Line Design, Flowers, Leaves, 29 In.	91.00
Jardiniere, Stand, Goblet Shape, Green Matte Glaze, 30 In.	125.00
Jardiniere, Stand, Green & Purple Iridescent, Embossed Art Nouveau Flowers, 44 In.	277.00
Jardiniere, Stand, Rose & Green, Arrow Shape Design, Pedestal Bottom, Bowl Top, 28 In.	68.00

Postcard, Teddy Roosevelt, Bear, Real Fur, 3 ½ x 5 ¼ In.
$70.00

Anderson Americana

Poster, 6 Days Of Sound, The Doors, Chuck Berry, Salvation, Dec. 26-30, 1967, 14 x 21 In.
$515.00

Hake's Americana & Collectibles

Poster, Carter The Great, World's Weird Wonderful Wizard, Otis Litho, Frame, 1935, 3 Sheets, 77 x 40 In.
$563.00

P

Bonhams & Butterfields

Poster, Ring It Again, Buy U.S. Gov't Bonds, Third Liberty Loan, April 15th, 1918, 20 x 30 In. $180.00

Victorian Casino Antique Auction

Poster, Tiger God, Horace Goldin, Lithograph, Mounted, Moody Bros., 6 Sheets, 85 x 78 ½ In. $1500.00

Bonhams & Butterfields

Potlid, Worsley's Saponaceous Shaving Compound, Philadelphia, c.1870, 3 ⅞ In. $585.00

Norman C. Heckler & Company

Pottery, Bowl, Bubble, Turquoise, Interior Purple Splash, Footed, Jun Ware, 5 ¼ In. $610.00

Leslie Hindman Auctioneers

Pickle Jar, Cobalt Blue Stencil, Fancy Pickles, Peoria Pickle Works, Salt Glaze, 5 Gal. ......*illus*	1840.00
Pillow, Cat Shape, Reclining, Turned Head, Brown Glaze, Ribbed Plinth, Chinese, 10 In.	430.00
Pitcher, Brown Slip Fuchsia Design, Geneva, c.1850, 9 ¼ In.	852.00
Pitcher, Cockatoo, White, 12 In.	634.00
Pitcher, Figural, Woman Handle, White, Blue, Red, Pierre Adrien Dalpayrat, 11 ½ x 9 In.	6200.00
Pitcher, Green, Red, Purple, Blue, Black Glaze, Art Nouveau Shape, Handle, Dalpayat, 9 In....	720.00
Pitcher, Manganese Glaze, Applied Loop Handle, Shouldered, 9 In.	34.00
Pitcher, Salt Glaze, Linear Shoulder Band, Angled Handle, c.1870, 11 In.	201.00
Planter, Pink Roses, Buds, Green Leaves, Cobalt Blue Ground, 1931, 4 x 8 ½ In.	460.00
Plate, Carved Geometric Patterns, Cobalt Blue Glaze, Persia, 1600s, 8 ¼ In. Diam.	237.00
Sculpture, 2 Intertwined Figures, Glazed, Stoneware, Signed Walter Sinz, Ohio, 1930s, 10 x 9 In.	1116.00
Serving Dish, White, Red Diamonds, Black Rim, Oblong, 5 ¼ x 11 ¼ In.	12.00
Teapot, Dome Lid, Ball Finial, Brick Red, Straight Spout, Loop Handle, Silver Design, Chinese, 5 In.	191.00
Tureen, Elves, Wine, Bacchus, Transfer, Marked Geschutzt, Germany, c.1905, 11 ¾ x 16 In.	259.00
Urn, 2 Tulips, Flared Rim, Earthenware, Marked, J. Eberly Bro., Va.	8100.00
Urn, Cover, Agate Ware, Scroddled, Early 1800s, 8 In., Pair	180.00
Vase, African Dancers, Bird, Multicolor, Lenci Ceramic Studio, Italy, 1930, 4 ½ In.	920.00
Vase, Applied Flowers & Leaves, Glazed, Pear Shape, Rust, Yellow, Green, Signed, 1800s, 10 x 9 In.	360.00
Vase, Art Deco, Green, Red & Gold Decorated Band, Figural Handles, Austria, c.1920, 6 x 10 In.	472.00
Vase, Art Deco, Green, Red, Black Abstract Design, Rene Buthad, France, 1930s, 9 ¾ x 6 ½ In.	1116.00
Vase, Art Nouveau, Blue, Green, Gourd Shape, Silver Handles & Casing, France, c.1900, 6 x 6 ½ In.	1020.00
Vase, Art Nouveau, Raised Beetle, Pinched Shape, Metallic Luster, J. Barol, Montiers, 4 ¾ In...	750.00
Vase, Blue, Green, Red Glaze, Squat, Large Handles, Dalpayrat, 3 In.	605.00
Vase, Bottle Shape, Phlox & Bird, Painted, Signed, J. Bennett, 8 x 5 In. ......*illus*	3100.00
Vase, Brown Runny Glaze, Green, Squeezebag Shape, Incised A. Rhead, c.1920, 4 ¾ x 5 ½ In.	806.00
Vase, Bulbous, Tapered Bottom, Loop Handles, Geometric Design, Chinese, 18 In.	1434.00
Vase, Cabinet, 3 Handles, Frackelton, 3 ½ x 3 In.	3596.00
Vase, Carved Leaves, Buds, Yellow Matte Glaze, Marked Arts & Clay Co., 1988, 4 x 9 ½ In.	330.00
Vase, Cylindrical, Gold Crater Luster, J. Haggerty, Haggerty Ceramics, 6 x 8 In.	420.00
Vase, Flattened Heart Shape, Figure On Horseback, Rocky Coast, Green, Albinoware, 1896, 9 In.	1067.00
Vase, Flowers, Faux Jewels, Triangle Design Border, Urn Shape, Hadsburg, Austria, 11 ⅜ In.	403.00
Vase, Globular, Pereny, American, 1935, 9 ½ In., Diam.	324.00
Vase, Green, Carved Tree Design, Max Kandern, Germany, c.1910, 8 ½ In.	920.00
Vase, Junyao Style, Mottled Strawberry Glaze, Interior Gray, Incised Mark, Chinese, 12 ½ In. ..*illus*	354.00
Vase, Kaikemon Pattern, Ho Ho Bird, Tree, England, c.1780, 11 In., Pair	246.00
Vase, Marigolds & Butterflies, Bottle Shape, Green Ground, John Bennett, 11 x 7 ½ In.	3224.00
Vase, Mirror Black, Bulbous, Paper Label, Clifwood, 7 ¼ In.	22.00
Vase, Mottled Purple, Scalloped Rim, Horizontal Ribs, Handles, Burley Winter, 6 In.	45.00
Vase, Multicolor Fish, Green Seaweed Ground, Round, France, 9 x 9 In.	122.00
Vase, Pink Ground, Gilt Handles, Japan, c.1900, 22 ¼ In.	214.00
Vase, Pink, Mottled, Burley & Winter, 11 In.	50.00
Vase, Poppies, Vellum Green Glaze, Denaura, 1903, 8 ½ x 6 In.	1054.00
Vase, Raised Design, Blue, Glazed, Lappet Border At Base, Chinese, 11 In. ......*illus*	558.00
Vase, Trees, Lake, Gray, Tan, White, Marked Fraunfelter, 6 ¼ In.	150.00
Vase, Wedding, Globular, Avanyu Serpent, Twisted Handle, Blackware, Signed, 1900s, 9 In......	764.00

POTTERY-ART Art pottery was first made in America in Cincinnati, Ohio, during the 1870s. The pieces were hand thrown and hand decorated. The art pottery tradition continued until the 1930s when studio potters began making the more artistic wares. American, English, and Continental art pottery by less well-known makers is listed here. Most makers listed in *Kovels' American Art Pottery*, such as Arequipa, Ohr, Rookwood, Roseville, and Weller, are listed in their own categories in this book. More recent pottery is listed under the name of the maker or in another pottery category.

Bank, Rabbit Shape, Gold Yellow Glaze, Nicodemus, 4 ½ x 2 ½ In.	146.00
Bowl, Blue Landscapes, Glazed, 3 Handles, Susan Frackelton, 3 ¼ x 9 ½ In. ......*illus*	5580.00
Bowl, Blue, Drip Glaze, Round, Brydcliffe, 12 ½ x 6 In.	1140.00
Bowl, Green Matte Glaze, Round, Arts & Crafts, Mark Shawsheen, 6 ½ x 3 In.	184.00
Bowl, Iron Red Flower Design, Yellow Ground, Blue Interior, Clear Glaze, T. Deck, 7 x 5 In.	518.00
Bowl, Low Shape, Mottled Brown Crystalline Glaze, Grand Feu, 5 ¾ In.	523.00
Bowl, Matador, Yellow, Black, Fletcher Martin, Stonelain, 12 ¾ In.	112.00
Bowl, Mustard Glaze, Incised Laura Anderson, 1949, 2 x 5 ¼ In.	124.00
Bowl, Sea Gulls, Incised, Squat, Stamp, Rhead Pottery, 2 ¾ x 7 ½ In.	11160.00
Candleholder, Green Matte Glaze, Vance Avon Faience Co., 8 In.	112.00
Incenser, Foo Dog, Yellow, Brown, Green Glaze, Pierced Plinth, Tubular Holder, c.1900, 8 In.	430.00
Jar, Lion Heads, Blue Drip Glaze, Shoulder Handles, Burley Winter, 20 ½ In.	460.00
Jardiniere, Glorious Summer's Symphony, Squeezebag, Signed, Avon, 1903, 8 ¼ x 12 ½ In. ...*illus*	2728.00

P

Pottery, Brush Pot, Scholars, Poetry, White Beaded Borders, 6-Sided, Chinese, 1900s, 6 ¾ In.
$582.00

Skinner, Inc.

Pottery, Crock, Cobalt Blue Stencil 3, Salt Glaze, Ottawa Pottery, Brown Albany Slip, 1884, 3 Gal.
$632.00

Rock Island Auction Company

Pottery, Crock, Millers Department Store, Cobalt Blue Stamp, Bristol Glaze, Alexis Pottery, 5 Gal.
$1265.00

Rock Island Auction Company

Pottery, Figurine, Horse, Head Down, Leg Raised, Square Base, Tang Style, 19 In., Pair
$9760.00

Leslie Hindman Auctioneers

Pottery, Jar, Blue & White, Carved Wood Cover, Blossoms, Leaves, Cracked Ice, Chinese, 8 ½ In.
$2607.00

Skinner, Inc.

Pottery, Pickle Jar, Cobalt Blue Stencil, Fancy Pickles, Peoria Pickle Works, Salt Glaze, 5 Gal.
$1840.00

Rock Island Auction Company

Pottery, Vase, Bottle Shape, Phlox & Bird, Painted, Signed, J. Bennett, 8 x 5 In.
$3100.00

Rago Arts & Auction Center

Pottery, Vase, Junyao Style, Mottled Strawberry Glaze, Interior Gray, Incised Mark, Chinese, 12 ¼ In.
$354.00

Brunk Auctions

Pottery, Vase, Raised Design, Blue, Glazed, Lappet Border At Base, Chinese, 11 In.
$558.00

Leslie Hindman Auctioneers

Pottery-Art, Bowl, Blue Landscapes, Glazed, 3 Handles, Susan Frackelton, 3 ¼ x 9 ½ In.
$5580.00

Rago Arts & Auction Center

Pottery-Art, Jardiniere, Glorious Summer's Symphony, Squeezebag, Signed, Avon, 1903, 8 ¼ x 12 ½ In.
$2728.00

Rago Arts & Auction Center

Pottery-Art, Plate, Botanicals, Multicolor, Glazed, Henry Varnum Poor, 8 ½ In.
$806.00

Rago Arts & Auction Center

P

519

Pottery-Art, Vase, Geometric Design, Signed, A. Bohrod, F.C. Ball, 1950s, 15 x 6 ¾ In.
$2000.00

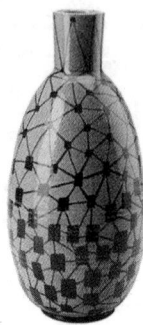

Rago Arts & Auction Center

Pottery-Art, Vase, Goose In Flight, Shoulder Band, Incised, Jervis, 3 ⅞ In.
$1840.00

Humler & Nolan

Pottery-Art, Vase, Grapes, Embossed, Matte & Crystalline Glaze, Marked, Dressler Castle, Austria, 16 ⅛ In.
$184.00

Humler & Nolan

Pottery-Art, Vase, Green & Brown Matte Crystalline Glaze, Charles Binns, 1915, 9 x 6 ½ In.
$3100.00

Rago Arts & Auction Center

Pottery-Contemporary, Charger, Carved Scribble Design, Foldover Edge, Peter Voulkos, Signed, 1981, 20 In. Diam.
$10665.00

Skinner, Inc.

Pottery-Contemporary, Figurine, Gourd With Rabbits, Signed, Sergio Bustamante, c.1983, 7 x 10 ½ In.
$593.00

Skinner, Inc.

Pottery-Contemporary, Jar, Lily, Chinese Red, Handles, Ben Owen III, 2000, 12 In.
$690.00

Leland Little Auction

Pottery-Contemporary, Moonpot, Glazed, 3 Openings, Toshiki Takaezu, Signed, 10 x 7 In.
$4340.00

Rago Arts & Auction Center

Pottery-Contemporary, Vase, Mottled, Iridescent Oxblood Glaze, Ojai, Calif., Signed, Beato, 4 ¼ x 4 ¾ In.
$2375.00

Rago Arts & Auction Center

Pottery-Contemporary, Vase, Raised Figure, Glazed, Beatrice Wood, Signed Beato, 6 ½ x 3 ½ In.
$2232.00

Rago Arts & Auction Center

Pottery-Contemporary, Vase, Stone, Linear Sgraffito, Narrow Rim, Claude Conover, 16 In.
$3308.00

Skinner, Inc.

Pottery-Contemporary, Vase, Verdigris Volcanic Glaze, Signed Natzler, Paper Label, 1977, 7 ½ x 4 ½ In.
$2852.00

Rago Arts & Auction Center

P

Jug, Cat Shape Handle, Yellow, Signed Myott, c.1939, 8 x 10 In.	155.00
Mug, Hillbilly, Woman Handle, Multicolor, Paul Webb, Imperial Porcelain, 1947, 4 In.	28.00
Pitcher, Green, Red, Purple, Blue, Black Glaze, Dalpayrat, 9 In.	660.00
Pitcher, Red, Turquoise, Bronze Glaze, Organic Cylinder Shape, Dalpayrat, 5 ½ x 10 In.	523.00
Plate, Botanicals, Multicolor, Glazed, Henry Varnum Poor, 8 ½ In. ....illus	806.00
Plate, Etched Flower Design, Inscription, Metallic Glaze, Jacques Sicardo, France, 1901, 9 In.	1320.00
Teapot, Birds & Bamboo In Relief, Flattened Sides, Bamboo Handle, c.1875, 7 In.	296.00
Vase, Abstract Leaf Design, Blue, Green, Brown, Tapered, Signed Vontury, 1947, 13 ¾ In.	56.00
Vase, Applied Bat, Green Matte Glaze, Mark, Freiwald, 6 ½ x 13 In.	330.00
Vase, Atomic, Northern Lights, Green Matte Glaze, Neck Lug Handles, Door Pottery, 6 ½ In.	67.00
Vase, Beige & Black Flowers, Gray Ground, Carved, Avon, 6 ½ x 6 ½ In.	930.00
Vase, Black High Glaze, Pear Shape, Squared Rim, Strobl, c.1908, 10 In.	489.00
Vase, Blue Crystalline Glaze, Oval, 2 Handles, Pierrefonds, Early 20th Century, 12 In.	593.00
Vase, Blue Gloss, High Shoulder Handles, 28 ¼ In.	431.00
Vase, Bronzeware, Bottle Shape, 11 ¾ In.	112.00
Vase, Brown Matte Glaze, Balloon Shaped, Pinched Neck, Narrow Rim, 6 ⅛ In.	173.00
Vase, Bud, Arts & Crafts, Holes In Top, Green Matte Glaze, Tapered, William Walley, 5 ½ In.	246.00
Vase, Bulbous, Narrow Neck, Flare Rim, Blue Flambe Glaze, Saturday Evening Girls, Signed, 10 In.	345.00
Vase, Cobalt Blue Iridescent, Pink, Green, Pewter Mounts, Pear Shape, Squared Handles, 6 In.	316.00
Vase, Denver Denaura, Raised Flowers, Green Matte Glaze, Marked, 6 x 5 ½ In.	1680.00
Vase, Egg Harbor, Misty Blue Matte Glaze, Oval, Marked Door Pottery, 7 ½ In.	50.00
Vase, Enamel Lily Design, Tan, Brown Ground, St. Cloud, France, 12 In.	374.00
Vase, Floor, Green, Orange Glaze, Applied Handles, Burley Winter, 22 ½ In.	403.00
Vase, Geometric Design, Signed, A. Bohrod, F.C. Ball, 1950s, 15 x 6 ¾ In. ....illus	2000.00
Vase, Goose In Flight, Shoulder Band, Incised, Jervis, 3 ⅞ In. ....illus	1840.00
Vase, Grapes, Embossed, Matte & Crystalline Glaze, Marked, Dressler Castle, Austria, 16 ⅛ In. ..illus	184.00
Vase, Green & Brown Matte Crystalline Glaze, Charles Binns, 1915, 9 x 6 ½ In. ....illus	3100.00
Vase, Green Matte Glaze, Koi, Marked Freiwald, 10 ¾ x 10 ¾ In.	259.00
Vase, Green Matte Glaze, Tapered, Organic Design, Marked Valentien, 3 ¼ x 7 ½ In.	1200.00
Vase, Mottled Green & Brown Glaze, Cylindrical, Marked, 2 ½ x 6 In.	540.00
Vase, Oval, Feelie, Narrow Rim, Golden Yellow Glaze, Signed, Rose Cabat, 3 In.	179.00
Vase, Pastoral, Vines, Lattice, Ram Head Handles, Green, I. Broome, c.1900, 18 x 10 In.	26040.00
Vase, Pine Needle, Green, Marked Max Lauger, 14 ½ x 9 In.	3472.00
Vase, Sang De Boef, Hardwood Plinth, Chinese, 19 ½ x 19 ¾ In., Pair	316.00
Vase, Shoulder Monkey Masks, Yellow Drip, Green Gourd Body, William Woodward, 1914, 5 ⅜ In.	1673.00
Vase, Speckled Blue Glaze, Flowers Around Base, Urn Shape, Textured Rim, c.1940, 8 ¼ In.	184.00
Vase, Yellow Crocuses, Bottle Shape, Frederick Rhead, Wardle, 13 ¾ x 7 In.	310.00

POTTERY-CONTEMPORARY lists pieces made by artists working about 1975 and later.

Bowl, Footed, Blue Striped Glaze, H. McIntosh, 5 x 5 ¼ In.	744.00
Bowl, Mottled Brown, Yellow Crystalline Glaze, Flared, Signed Rose Cabat, 6 ¼ x 3 ½ In.	468.00
Bowl, Pedestal, Pastel Glaze, Signed Larry Spears, c.1990, 10 ¼ x 3 In.	22.00
Bowl, Ribbed, Cream, Brown Glaze, Paper Label, Harrison McIntosh, 3 ¼ x 8 ¼ In.	372.00
Bowl, Salt Glaze, Black, Orange, White Geometrics, Denmark, 1989, 8 x 14 In.	434.00
Box, Lid, Earth Tone Glazes, 5-Sided, Mark, Warren McKenzie, 6 x 4 In.	265.00
Charger, Carved Scribble Design, Foldover Edge, Peter Voulkos, Signed, 1981, 20 In. Diam. ......illus	10665.00
Figurine, Gourd With Rabbits, Signed, Sergio Bustamante, c.1983, 7 x 10 ½ In. ....illus	593.00
Jar, Lily, Chinese Red, Handles, Ben Owen III, 2000, 12 In. ....illus	690.00
Jug, Indian Portrait, Incised, Brown Ground, Signed Rick Wisecarver, Marked, 13 ¼ In.	150.00
Lamp Base, Brown, Black, Round, Signed Peter Voulkos, 13 ½ x 8 ½ In.	1736.00
Moonpot, Glazed, 3 Openings, Toshiki Takaezu, Signed, 10 x 7 In. ....illus	4340.00
Vase, Black Matte Glaze, Bulbous, 3 x 2 In.	248.00
Vase, Blackware, Casa Granda, Embossed Salamanders, Signed Rosa Quezada, 7 x 10 In.	863.00
Vase, Blue, Brown Glaze, Tapering Cylinder, Loops, Stoneware, Heino, c.1990, 8 ¼ In.	299.00
Vase, Bottle Shape, Mottled Blue & Brown Matte Glaze, Signed McIntosh, 7 ½ x 3 In.	930.00
Vase, Brown Iridescent Glaze, Signed Beatrice Wood, 3 ¼ In.	550.00
Vase, Brown, Black, Squat, Signed Vivika & Otto Heino, 1995, 3 ¾ In.	280.00
Vase, Bulbous, Tan Shoulder, Brown Shaded Body, Paul Chaleff, 1980, 15 x 15 In.	217.00
Vase, Calla Lilies, Tan Ground, Signed Eric Olson, 7 ¼ In.	179.00
Vase, Cat Portrait, Multicolor, Shaped Sides, Signed Rick Wisecarver, 1989, 13 In.	403.00
Vase, Chinese Red Drip, Terra-Cotta Body, Bulbous, Signed Ben Owen, 1987, 8 ½ In.	134.00
Vase, Cover, Green & Blue Crystalline Glaze, Bulbous, Signed Rose Cabat, 5 ½ x 6 ½ In.	550.00
Vase, Earth Tone Glazes, Marked, Warren McKenzie, 6 ¼ x 3 ½ In.	69.00
Vase, Feelie, Green, Oval, Signed, Rose Cabat, 3 ¼ In.	246.00
Vase, Gold Metallic Glaze, Bulbous, Signed Beatrice Wood, 4 ¼ x 3 ¼ In.	880.00
Vase, Incised Frontiersman, Pillow Shape, Marked Rick Wisecarver, 1981, 4 ½ In.	58.00

Pottery-Contemporary, Wall Pocket, Mask, Man's Face, Mustache, Curled Hair, Collar, Nick Kelly, 1976, 11 ¼ x 8 In. $130.00

Conestoga Auction Co., Inc.

Pottery-Midcentury, Bowl, Brown & Ocher Glaze, Folded Rim, G. & O. Natzler, 2 x 7 In. $6875.00

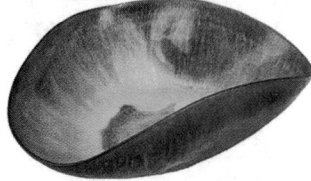

Los Angeles Modern Auctions

Pottery-Midcentury, Bowl, Glazed, Imitation Letters, Signed, Gambone Italy, c.1960, 2 ¾ x 7 ½ In. $875.00

Los Angeles Modern Auctions

Pottery-Midcentury, Bowl, Green Glaze, G. & O. Natzler, c.1965, 3 ¾ x 4 In. $3125.00

Los Angeles Modern Auctions

P

Pottery-Midcentury, Bowl, Oval, Turquoise Glaze, Gertrud & Otto Natzler, Signed, c.1964, 9 ¼ x 6 ½ In. $3750.00

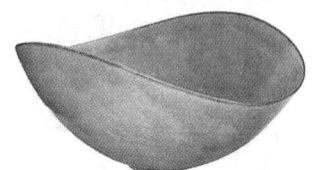

Los Angeles Modern Auctions

Pottery-Midcentury, Charger, Blue & White, Lion & Cub Design, Prunus Blossoms, Chinese, c.1950, 16 ¾ In. $748.00

Leland Little Auction

Pottery-Midcentury, Dish, Pablo Picasso, Bird On Branch, Glazed, 1952, 6 ¼ x 2 ¼ In. $1125.00

Los Angeles Modern Auctions

Pottery-Midcentury, Dish, Picador, Inscribed, Pablo Picasso, Madoura, 1952, 6 In. $1062.00

DuMouchelles Art Gallery

Vase, Indian Brave, On Horse, Tapered, Slanted Mouth, Signed Rick Wisecarver, 1995, 17 In. .	316.00
Vase, Indian Chief Head, Bulbous, Pink, Teal, Purple Ground, Wisecarver, 8 In.	115.00
Vase, Indian Maiden, Pink Ground, Signed Rick Wisecarver, 1986, 10 ¾ In.	299.00
Vase, Iridescent Curdled Glaze, Long Neck, Beatrice Wood, 7 In.	1540.00
Vase, Iridescent Glaze, Signed Beatrice Wood, 3 ¼ In.	600.00
Vase, Iridescent Volcanic Glaze, Short Neck, Bulbous, Beatrice Wood, 7 In.	935.00
Vase, Magnesium Brown Glaze, Tapering Cylinder, Loops, Stoneware, Heino, 7 ¼ In.	359.00
Vase, Mottled, Iridescent Oxblood Glaze, Ojai, Calif., Signed, Beato, 4 ¼ x 4 ¾ In. ....*illus*	2375.00
Vase, Nude Woman, Leaping Deer, Mottled Green, Gold, White Crackle, Flat Circle, c.1935, 12 ½ In.	2875.00
Vase, Raised Figure, Glazed, Beatrice Wood, Signed Beato, 6 ½ x 3 ½ In. ....*illus*	2232.00
Vase, Squat, Mottled Brown, Signed Vivika & Otto Heino, 3 ¾ x 4 ¾ In.	341.00
Vase, Stone, Linear Sgraffito, Narrow Rim, Claude Conover, 16 In. ....*illus*	3308.00
Vase, Tan & Black Matte Glaze, Bulbous, Signed Rose Cabat, 3 ¼ x 3 In.	440.00
Vase, Tan, Black Matte Glaze, Bulbous, Signed Rose Cabat, 3 ¼ x 3 In.	480.00
Vase, Tan, Brown Glaze, Free-Form, Ewen Hendersen, 1985, 5 ½ x 17 In.	1054.00
Vase, Turquoise, Blue, Tan Matte Glaze, Bulbous, Rose Cabat, 2 ¾ x 3 ¼ In.	240.00
Vase, Verdigris Volcanic Glaze, Signed Natzler, Paper Label, 1977, 7 ½ x 4 ½ In. ....*illus*	2852.00
Wall Pocket, Mask, Man's Face, Mustache, Curled Hair, Collar, Nick Kelly, 1976, 11 ¼ x 8 In. ...*illus*	130.00

POTTERY-MIDCENTURY includes pieces made from the 1940s to about 1975.

Bowl, Brown & Ocher Glaze, Folded Rim, G. & O. Natzler, 2 x 7 In. ....*illus*	6875.00
Bowl, Brown, Glazed, Footed, Carl-Harry Stalhane, Sweden, c.1950, 3 ½ In.	200.00
Bowl, Glazed, Imitation Letters, Signed, Gambone Italy, c.1960, 2 ¾ x 7 ½ In. ....*illus*	875.00
Bowl, Green Glaze, G. & O. Natzler, c.1965, 3 ¾ x 4 In. ....*illus*	3125.00
Bowl, Oval, Turquoise Glaze, Gertrud & Otto Natzler, Signed, c.1964, 9 ¼ x 6 ½ In. ....*illus*	3750.00
Bowl, Speckled Brown, Matte Gray, Round, Straight-Sided, P. Voulkos, 5 x 9 In.	735.00
Bust, Maxwell Stuart Simpson, Glazed, Wood Base, Signed Waylande Gregory, 1960, 18 x 11 In.	1178.00
Candlestick, Brown Ware, Flared Base, Large Round Handle, Marked Wannopee, 8 ¼ In.	45.00
Charger, Blue & White, Lion & Cub Design, Prunus Blossoms, Chinese, c.1950, 16 ¾ In. *illus*	748.00
Dish, Pablo Picasso, Bird On Branch, Glazed, 1952, 6 ¼ x 2 ¼ In. ....*illus*	1125.00
Dish, Picador, Inscribed, Pablo Picasso, Madoura, 1952, 6 In. ....*illus*	1062.00
Figurine, Bird, Earthenware, Wood, Metal Rods, Inlaid, John Risley, c.1957, 11 x 25 In.	1364.00
Figurine, Bobcat On Watch, Signed Betty Davenport Ford, 1950s, 5 x 2 ½ In.	310.00
Figurine, Zebra, White, Wood Base, Waylande Gregory, 10 ¾ x 11 ¾ In. ....*illus*	161.00
Jug, Red, White Spatter, Tapered, Raymor, Italy, 18 ½ x 9 In.	27.00
Pitcher, Owl Shape, Blue, White, Picasso, Madoura, 10 In.	1840.00
Pitcher, Owl, Black & White, Glazed, Picasso, Madoura, c.1951, 11 ¾ x 8 ½ In. ....*illus*	5270.00
Pitcher, Stylized Lines & Dots, Black, Striated Pink Ground, J. Dediego, 11 In.	296.00
Plate, Flower Pot, Flowers, Fruit, White & Blue, Glazed, Picasso, Madoura, c.1956, 9 ¾ In. ....*illus*	2232.00
Plate, Relief Goat's Head, Gray, White, Picasso, Madoura, 10 In.	1610.00
Plate, Shield Design, Blue, Green, Brown, Yellow, Signed Fritz Scholder, c.1970, 13 In.	920.00
Plate, Visage No. 0, Stylized Face, Picasso, Madoura, 1963, 10 In. ....*illus*	11875.00
Plate, Yellow, Green Glaze, Ribbed, Signed Maija Grotell, 9 ½ In.	620.00
Platter, Hawaiian, Figures, Pink & White Sponge, 3-Sided, M. Bellaire, 14 In.	22.00
Platter, Still Life, Knife Engraved, Picasso, Madoura, Stamped, 1953, 12 x 15 In. ....*illus*	9480.00
Platter, Stylized Owl, Picasso, Madoura, 1955, 15 ¼ x 12 ¼ In. ....*illus*	17500.00
Tray, Primitive Figures, Glazed, Stoneware, Paul Bogatay, 1962, 11 x 20 In.	620.00
Tray, Stylized Flower, Leaves, Pink Spatter, 3-Sided, Marc Bellaire, 20 In.	38.00
Vase, Abstract Nudes, Glazed, Stoneware, Incised, Peter Voulkos, 1955-58, 14 ¾ x 8 ½ In. ....*illus*	4650.00
Vase, Bellflower, Gray Orange Peel Glaze, Cylindrical, W. Germany, 18 In.	38.00
Vase, Cover, Tenmoku Glaze, Incised Crosshatching, Bernard Leach, 11 In.	593.00
Vase, Cylindrical, Rectangular Double Handle, Black Gloss, Mottled Blue Glaze, c.1955, 9 x 6 In.	17.00
Vase, Etched Stylized Native American, Oval, Tapered, M. Bellaire, 20 In.	108.00
Vase, Fat Lava Glaze, Red & Blue Over Brown, Bottle Shape, Rings, 10 In.	16.00
Vase, Flambe Glaze, Mauve, Maroon, Gold, Blue, Otto & Vivika Heino, Marked, 5 ⅝ In. ....*illus*	345.00
Vase, Green Glaze, Dripped Over Tan, Squat, Paul Cox, 3 ⅛ In.	138.00
Vase, Lava Glaze, White, Brown & Blue Drippy Bands, Swollen, W. Germany, 15 In.	22.00
Vase, Mosaic, Star Banding, Flower Ground, Multicolor, c.1950, 8 ½ x 8 ½ In.	492.00
Vase, Mottled Green & Brown Glaze, Signed Natzler, 1960s, 4 x 3 In. ....*illus*	682.00
Vase, Nude Female, Glazed, Signed, K. Price, 1950s, 18 ½ x 6 In. ....*illus*	2000.00
Vase, Plants, Flowers, Glazed, Scroll Handles, Vally Wieselthier, c.1920, 13 ½ x 7 ½ In. ....*illus*	1984.00
Vase, Production Ware, Ribbed Green, Gold, Red, Mottled Gray Ground, P. Voulkos, c.1950, 5 In.	1100.00
Vase, Red Stalactites, Foamy Brown & White Glaze, W. Germany, 7 ½ In.	16.00
Vase, Tall, Green Crystalline, Stamped, Pierrefonds, 17 x 8 In.	1984.00
Vase, Tiger Lilies, Blue Ground, Signed Osif, Atwill, Santa Barbara Ceramic Design, 9 ½ In.	150.00

Vase, Women, Fantoni, Raymor, Marked, Black Slip, 9 ½ In. ....*illus*	196.00
Vase, Yellow, Textured Band, Flared Base, Marked Gambone, Italy, c.1955, 4 ½ x 4 ¼ In..........	217.00

POWDER FLASKS AND POWDER HORNS were made to hold the gunpowder used in antique firearms. The early examples were made of horn or wood; later ones were of copper or brass.

POWDER FLASK

Brass, Man, On Horse, Dog, James Dixon & Son's, Sheffield, 10 ½ In......................................	254.00
Brass, Quatrefoil Design, Round, 17th Century	340.00
Copper, Brass, Thumb Tab, 3 ¾ In..	100.00
Copper, Flags, Crossed Rifles, Cannon, Embossed, c.1900, 7 In...	95.00
Copper, Flask, Ribbed, 19th Century, 7 ¼ x 2 ½ In.	100.00
Copper, Shell Design, Embossed, Bag Shape, c.1850, 9 x 4 ¼ In.	50.00
Horn, Leather Cover, Leaves & Geometric Design, Rolled Brass Cap, 6 ½ In.	225.00
Leather, Brass, Pear Shape, 19th Century, 8 x 3 In.	165.00
Wood, Carved, Moroccan Design, Footed, Leather Strap, 12 x 7 x 4 In.	275.00
Wood, Eagle, Shaking Hands, Spout, Suspension Rings, Batty, 1850	625.00

POWDER HORN

Carved, Pouring Spout, Wooden Plug, Rings, 1700s, 16 In.	1898.00
Cow, Beehive Screw Tip, Strap, 12 In...	396.00
Engraved, Carved, Vines, Samuel Staples, Leaping Stag, c.1775, 16 ½ In.	7188.00
Engraved, Indian, Birds, Fish, Sun, Angel, Vines, Spout, Wavy Plug End, c.1773, 20 In...........	5629.00
Urns Of Flowers, Carved, Painted, 19th Century, 9 ½ In..	1293.00

PRATT ware means two different things. It was an early Staffordshire pottery, cream-colored with colored decorations, made by Felix Pratt during the late eighteenth century. There was also Pratt ware made with transfer designs during the mid-nineteenth century in Fenton, England. Reproductions of the transfer-printed Pratt are being made.

PRATT
FENTON

Figurine, Eagle, Sponged, c.1800, 7 In.	1100.00
Figurine, Lion, Lying Down, Brown & Tan Spots, Humanistic Facial Features, 2 ¾ x 4 ⅜ In. ...	460.00
Mug, Bacchus, Smiling, Grape & Vine Circlet, Curved Handle, 4 x 5 In.	167.00
Potlid, Harriet Beecher Stowe, Holding Uncle Tom's Cabin, Painted, 5 In.................................	1400.00
Toby Jug, Man, Standing, Full Figure, Holding Snuff Box, 8 ¼ In. ....*illus*	57.00
Urn, Potpourri, Lid, Matte Black, Classical Figures, Pierced Lid, Gilt Handles, c.1890, 28 In. ......*illus*	732.00
Vase, Ginko Leaf, Yellow Matte Leaves, White Body, Sawtooth Rim, Signed, 5 In.	213.00

PRESSED GLASS, or pattern glass, was first made in the United States in the 1820s after the invention of glass pressing machines. Hundreds of patterns of pressed glass were made in complete table settings. Although the Boston and Sandwich Works was the most famous of the pressed glass factories, there were about sixteen other factories making pressed glass from 1830 to 1850, and still more from 1850 to 1900, when pressed glass reached its greatest popularity. It is now being widely reproduced. The pattern names used in this listing are based on the information in the book *Pressed Glass in America* by John and Elizabeth Welker. There may be pieces of pressed glass listed in this book in other categories, such as Lamp, Ruby, Sandwich, and Souvenir.

1000-Eye pattern is listed here as Thousand Eye.
Acanthus pattern is listed here as Ribbed Palm.

Arched Panel, Tumbler, Cobalt Blue, Footed, 8-Petal Foot, c.1865, 5 x 3 ½ In..........................	161.00
Argus, Compote, 8 In...	63.00
Ashburton, Compote, Green, Dolphin, Hexagonal Base, 7 ½ x 7 In., Pair.................................	83.00

Banded patterns may also be listed under the name of the basic pattern: e.g., Banded Honeycomb is called Honeycomb, Banded.

Beaded Scroll, Salt, Cover, Basket Of Flowers, Pinecone Finial, Interior Rim Beads, 10 x 19 In.	748.00
Bellflower, Jar, Ribbed Ground, Pedestal Foot, 9 In., Pair	144.00
Bicycle Girl, Pitcher, Molded Relief, Dalzell, Gilmore & Leighton, 11 In.	325.00

Candlewick as a pressed glass pattern is properly named Banded Raindrop. There is also a pattern called Candlewick, which has been made by Imperial Glass Corporation since 1936. It is listed in this book in the Imperial Glass category.

Clambroth, Candlestick, Ringed Column, Hexagonal, 8 In...	226.00

Coin Spot pattern is listed in this book in its own category.
Cosmos pattern is listed in this book as its own category.

Daisy & Button, Condiment Set, Salt & Pepper, Mustard, Cruet, Glass Stand, 1890s, 9 In.	58.00
Daisy & Button, Sleigh, Pink, 7 x 11 ¼ x 7 In...	192.00
Daisy & Button, Syrup, Canary Yellow, Applied Handle, Embossed Top, 8 ⅛ In........................	127.00
Diamond Quilted, Salt, Double Ogee Form, 6-Petal Foot, c.1830, 2 ⅜ In.	69.00
Diamond Quilted, Salt, Light Green, Double Ogee Bowl, Footed, 3 In..	115.00

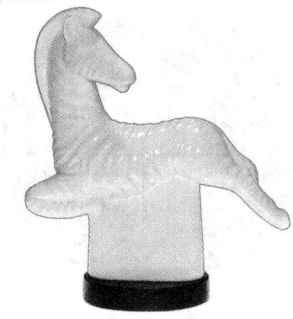

Pottery-Midcentury, Figurine, Zebra, White, Wood Base, Waylande Gregory, 10 ¾ x 11 ¾ In.
$161.00

Humler & Nolan

Pottery-Midcentury, Pitcher, Owl, Black & White, Glazed, Picasso, Madoura, c.1951, 11 ¾ x 8 ½ In.
$5270.00

Rago Arts & Auction Center

Pottery-Midcentury, Plate, Flower Pot, Flowers, Fruit, White & Blue, Glazed, Picasso, Madoura, c.1956, 9 ¾ In.
$2232.00

Rago Arts & Auction Center

Pottery-Midcentury, Plate, Visage No. 0, Stylized Face, Picasso, Madoura, 1963, 10 In.
$11875.00

Los Angeles Modern Auctions

P

PRESSED GLASS

Pottery-Midcentury, Platter, Still Life, Knife Engraved, Picasso, Madoura, Stamped, 1953, 12 x 15 In. $9480.00

Skinner, Inc.

Pottery-Midcentury, Platter, Stylized Owl, Picasso, Madoura, 1955, 15 ¼ x 12 ¼ In. $17500.00

Los Angeles Modern Auctions

Pottery-Midcentury, Vase, Abstract Nudes, Glazed, Stoneware, Incised, Peter Voulkos, 1955-58, 14 ¾ x 8 ½ In. $4650.00

Rago Arts & Auction Center

Pottery-Midcentury, Vase, Flambe Glaze, Mauve, Maroon, Gold, Blue, Otto & Vivika Heino, Marked, 5 ⅝ In. $345.00

Humler & Nolan

Diamond Scroll, Lily, Cup & Saucer, Violet Blue, Rope Ring, 1 x 1 ¾ In.	1035.00
Double Circles, Spoon Holder, Amethyst, Hexagonal Bowl, Petal Rim, Round Foot, 5 ¾ x 3 ¾ In.	207.00
Eagle, Cup, Flint, Serrated Rim, Leaf Border, Heart, Scallop, Dart, Dot Rim, 3 ½ In., 7 Piece	41.00
Eagle, Salt, Clear, Empire Sofa Form, 4 Scrolled Feet, 2 x 2 ⅝ x 3 ¾ In.	374.00
Flower Basket, Salt, Rope Twist Frame, Opaque White, 4-Footed, 2 x 2 x 3 In.	259.00
Four Printie Block, Vase, Cobalt Blue, Cone Shape Bowl, Ruffled Rim, Hexagonal Knop, 12 x 5 In.	1495.00
Frosted patterns may also be listed under the name of the main pattern.	
Gothic Arch, Sugar, Cover, Cobalt Blue, 8-Sided, Scalloped Foot, 5 ¼ In.	633.00
Grape & Cable pattern is listed in this book in the Northwood category.	
Hobnail pattern is in this book as its own category.	
Horn Of Plenty, Creamer, Applied Handle, 8-Scalloped Foot, c.1875, 6 ¼ x 3 ¼ In.	138.00
Inverted Thumbprint, Syrup, Turquoise, White Thumbprints, Bird Thumb Pull, 6 ¾ In.	219.00
Jewel & Dew Drop, Jewelry Box, Domed Lid, Fluted Base, Ribbed Panels, c.1907, 4 ¼ x 2 ¼ In.	55.00
Jeweled Moon & Star, Butter, Cover, Scalloped Rim, Star Finial, 1890s, 6 ¾ x 6 In.	110.00
Kansas pattern is listed here as Jewel & Dewdrop.	
Lacy Beehive & Thistle, Dish, Scallop Rim, Rope Table Ring, Octagonal, 9 In., 5 Piece	161.00
Lacy Gothic Arch, Sugar, Sapphire Blue, Octagonal, 8-Petal Foot, 1840-50, 3 ½ x 5 In.	92.00
Lacy Hairpin, Dish, Leafy Quatrefoil, Blossom, Diamond In Square Ground, 7 ¼ x 7 ¾ In.	2875.00
Lacy Medallion, see the related pattern Princess Feather.	
Lacy, Candlestick, Beaded Socket, Plain Rim, Tri-Part Knop, 6 Step Base, 6 ¾ In., Pair	489.00
Lacy, Salt, Washington & Lafayette Medallions, 1 ⅞ x 3 In.	2478.00
Loop, Vase, Sapphire Blue, Cone Shape Bowl, Petal Rim, Hexagonal Baluster Standard, 11 x 4 In.	1380.00
Maltese Cross, Plate, 12-Petal Flower, Chevrons, 7 ¼ In.	259.00
Monkey, Butter, 7 In.	575.00
Monkey, Pitcher, Tankard Form, 9 In.	2250.00
Morning Glory, Syrup, Opaque Milk Glass, Applied Handle, Metal Top, 7 ⅛ In.	46.00
Mount Vernon, Salt, Aquamarine, 1835-1850, 2 x 3 In.	518.00
New York Honeycomb, Candlestick, Deep Cobalt Blue, Tapered Stem, 2 Knops, 9 In., Pair	230.00
One-Thousand Eye pattern is listed here as Thousand Eye.	
Peacock, Salt, Sapphire Blue, Round, Scalloped Openwork Rim, 1 ½ x 4 In.	2990.00
Peacock's Eye & Scale, Vase, Citron, 6-Petal Rim, 2 Knop Stem, Hexagonal Base, 9 In., Pair	1093.00
Pittsburgh Steamboat, Salt, Medium Blue, Embossed, Rope Ring, Stourbridge, 2 x 3 ½ In.	1955.00
Plume, Nappy, Rays, Stippling, Beaded Bull's-Eye Foot, Scalloped Edge, 5 x 7 In.	1150.00
Princess Feather, Pitcher, Blue, Gilt, Footed, Ruffle Rim, Loop Handle, US Glass, 9 In.	460.00
Quilted Phlox, Syrup, Green Opaque, Applied Handle, Tin Top.	173.00
Ribbed Palm, Creamer, Elongated Spout, 6 ½ In.	69.00
Rochelle pattern is listed here as Princess Feather.	
Rose In Snow, Compote, Cover, 10 x 8 In.	56.00
Sandwich Star, Spoon Holder, Electric Blue, Hexagonal Rim, Pontil, c.1875, 5 x 3 ¾ In.	460.00
Sawtooth, Creamer, Footed, Child's	72.00
Scroll, Salt, Blue Green, OG-4B, 1 ⅝ x 2 x 3 In.	805.00
Sheaf of Wheat pattern is listed here as Wheat Sheaf.	
Stippled Scroll pattern is listed here as Scroll.	
Strawberry Diamond & Rosette, Bowl, Cross Shape Center, Fan Border, 11 In.	196.00
Strawberry Diamond, Fan, Compote, Clear, Knop Stem, Star Cut Foot, 6 ¾ In.	345.00
Swirl, Pitcher, Water, Yellow, Bulbous, Loop Handle, Narrow Spout, Hobbs, Brockunier, 8 In.	230.00
Thousand Eye, Dish, Sweetmeat, Cover, Reeded Oval Finial, Trumpet Foot, c.1890, 15 In.	1304.00
Three Printie, Vase, Deep Peacock Green, 6-Petal Rim, Hexagonal Base, 9 ⅝ In.	748.00
Three Printie, Vase, Electric Blue, 6-Petal Rim, Hexagonal Base, 10 In., Pair	1150.00
Tulip, Vase, Amethyst, Octagonal Bowl, Flared Rim, Wafer Base, Boston & Sandwich, 10 x 5 In.	805.00
Wheat Sheaf, Dish, Strawberry Diamond, Serrated Edge, Scallops, Oval, 6 x 9 ½ In.	127.00
Wildflower, Syrup, Yellow Amber, Applied Handle, Embossed Top, 8 ⅛ In.	92.00

PRINT, in this listing, means any of many printed images produced on paper by one of the more common methods, such as lithography. The prints listed here are of interest primarily to the antiques collector, not the fine arts collector. Many of these prints were originally part of books. Other prints will be found in the Advertising, Currier & Ives, Movie, and Poster categories.

Audubon bird prints were originally issued as part of books printed from 1826 to 1854. They were issued in two sheet sizes, 26 ½ inches by 39 ½ inches and 11 inches by 7 inches. The quadrupeds were issued in 28-by-22-inch prints. Later editions of the Audubon books were done in many sizes, and reprints of the books in the original size were also made. The words *After John James Audubon* appear on all of the prints, including the originals, because the pictures were made as copies of Audubon's original oil paintings. The bird pictures have been so popular they have been copied in myriad sizes by both old and new printing methods. This list includes originals and later copies because Audubon prints of all ages are sold in antiques shops.

J.W.Audubon

Audubon, American Crow, Havell, Frame, 1833, 38 x 25 In. ....*illus* 3525.00

Audubon, American Red Fox, Imperial Folio, J.T. Bowen, 21 ⅝ x 27 In.	1298.00
Audubon, Blue Jay, Chromolithograph, Bien Edition, Large Folio, Frame, c.1859, 38 x 26 In.	353.00
Audubon, Brown Pelican, Chromolithograph, Oak Frame, 39 x 26 In. ....*illus*	1725.00
Audubon, Canada Lynx, Imperial Folio, Lithograph, 20 ¾ x 27 In.	3068.00
Audubon, Chuck-Will's-Widow, 37 ½ x 25 ¾ In.	4481.00
Audubon, Grey Rabbit, 21 ½ x 27 In.	1220.00
Audubon, Harlequin Duck, Whatman, Frame, J., 1836, 24 x 36 ½ In. ....*illus*	4183.00
Audubon, King Duck, Engraved, Aquatint, Havell, c.1836, 25 x 37 ⅝ In.	3186.00
Audubon, Long Billed Curlew, Lithograph, Frame, 24 ½ x 37 ½ In.	269.00
Audubon, Nuttal's Starling, Yellow-Headed Troopial, Bullock's Oriole, 38 ½ x 26 ½ In.	2032.00
Audubon, Purple Grackle, Chromolithograph, Frame, c.1860, 38 x 25 ¾ In.	295.00
Audubon, Purple Martin, Chromolithograph, Bien Edition, Frame, c.1860, 38 x 26 In.	646.00
Audubon, Red-Shouldered Hawk, 1829, 36 ¾ x 24 ½ In.	4112.00
Audubon, Red-Tailed Squirrel, J.T. Bowen, 1844, 26 ½ x 19 ½ In. ....*illus*	504.00
Audubon, Sanderling, 26 x 38 ½ In.	1195.00
Audubon, Whip-Poor-Will, 38 ¼ x 25 ½ In.	5378.00
Audubon, White Ibis, 1834, 18 ¾ x 23 ¾ In.	4406.00
Audubon, Yellow-Billed Magpie, Frame, 32 x 25 ½ In.	4270.00
Audubon, Yellow-Throated Vireo, Engraved, Aquatint, Havell, Frame, 38 ½ x 28 ½ In. ......*illus*	2510.00
Berthon, Paul, Queen Wilhelmina, Lithograph, Color, Gilt Frame, c.1901, 15 x 14 In.	443.00
Bodine, A. Aubrey, Wheels Of Industry, Gelatin Silver, Signed, Frame, 19 ½ x 15 ½ In.	1135.00
Brown, W.H., Andrew Jackson, Lithograph, Linen, Sewn Accents, c.1900, 12 x 8 ½ In.	369.00
Edwards & Gerard, Flowers, Engraved, Frame, 11 x 9 In., 5 Piece	478.00
Erte, Bath Of The Marquise, Serigraph, Signed, Frame, 19 x 13 In.	472.00
Gearhart, Frances, Now The Moon, Linoleum Block, Color, Signed, 1924, 6 ½ x 3 ½ In. *illus*	1736.00
Gurshner, Herbert, Tirol, Woodblock, Rice Paper, Multicolor, Mat, 1931, 9 ¼ x 10 ¼ In.	1364.00
Hurley, E.T., Marsh Scene, Signed, My 1st Attempt At Etching, 1896, Frame, 6 x 9 In.	600.00

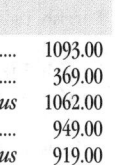

Icart prints were made by Louis Icart, who worked in Paris from 1907 as an employee of a postcard company. He then started printing magazines and fashion brochures. About 1910 he created a series of etchings of fashionably dressed women and he continued to make similar etchings until he died in 1950. He is well known as a printmaker, painter, and illustrator. Original etchings are much more expensive than the later photographic copies.

Icart, Flower Seller, Woman, Flower Cart, Frame, c.1928, 23 ½ x 19 ¼ In.	1093.00
Icart, Le Menuet, Etched, Aquatint, Blind Stamp, Pencil Signed, Mat, Frame, 21 x 15 In.	369.00
Icart, Lilies, Etching, Signed, Frame, 1934, 27 ½ x 19 In. ....*illus*	1062.00
Icart, Storyteller, Pan, Woman, Frame, c.1926, 22 x 25 In.	949.00
Icart, Symphony In Blue, Seated Woman, Hat, Flowers, Frame, 23 ½ x 19 ½ In. ....*illus*	919.00
Icart, Tennis, Etching, Aquatint, Signed, Frame, 1928, 18 x 15 In.	837.00
Jacobs, Monkeys, Engraving, Frame, c.1812, 15 x 11 In., 6 Piece	837.00

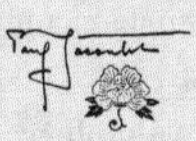

Jacoulet prints were designed by Paul Jacoulet (1902–1960), a Frenchman who spent most of his life in Japan. He was a master of Japanese woodblock print technique. Subjects included life in Japan, the South Seas, Korea, and China. His prints were sold by subscription and issued in series. Each series had a distinctive seal, such as a sparrow or butterfly. Most Jacoulet prints are approximately 15 x 10 inches.

Jacoulet, Fumees De Santal Mandchoukuo, Sandalwood Smoke, Woman Resting, Frame, 21 x 24 In..	325.00

Japanese woodblock prints are listed as follows: Print, Japanese, name of artist, title or description, type, and size. Dealers use the following terms: Tate-e is a vertical composition. Yoko-e is a horizontal composition. The words Aiban (13 by 9 inches), Chuban (10 by 7 ½ inches), Hosoban (13 by 6 inches), Koban (7 by 4 inches), Nagaban (20 by 9 inches), Oban (15 by 10 inches), Shikishiban (8 by 9 inches), and Tanzaku (15 by 5 inches) denote approximate size. Modern versions of some of these prints have been made. Other woodblock prints that are not Japanese are listed under Print, Woodblock.

Japanese, Azechi, Umetaro, Calling To The Mountain, Woodblock, Signed, 15 ¼ x 9 ½ In.	239.00
Japanese, Hiroshige, Festival At Itsukushima Shrine, Aki, 1905, Mat, 9 x 6 In.	60.00
Japanese, Hiroshige, Tenno Festival At Tsushima, Mat, 1905, 9 x 6 In.	90.00
Japanese, Kunihiro, Utagawa, Portrait Of Arashi Tomisaburo, Woodblock, Signed, c.1816	448.00
Japanese, Kunisada, Utagawa, Actor, With Straw Hat, Woodblock, Frame, 14 ½ x 9 ¾ In.	148.00
Japanese, Saito, Kiyoshi, Village With Persimmon Tree, Woodblock, Frame, 11 ½ x 17 ½ In.	253.00
Japanese, Saito, Kiyoshi, Winter In Aizu, Woodblock, Color, Signed, Frame, 9 ¾ x 15 In.	388.00
Japanese, Sekino, Jun-Ichiro, Rooftops, Woodblock, Signed, 12 ¾ x 18 In.	717.00
Japanese, Sharaku, Kabuki Actor, Red Robes, Woodblock, 14 ⅜ x 9 ⅜ In.	183.00
Japanese, Steamship With Sails, Blue & Beige, Frame, Woodblock, 1800s, 13 x 18 In.	150.00
Japanese, Toyonara, Story Of Genji, Various Scenes, Woodblock, 53 Sheets, 14 x 9 In.	1220.00

Pottery-Midcentury, Vase, Mottled Green & Brown Glaze, Signed Natzler, 1960s, 4 x 3 In.
$682.00

Rago Arts & Auction Center

Pottery-Midcentury, Vase, Nude Female, Glazed, Signed, K. Price, 1950s, 18 ½ x 6 In.
$2000.00

Rago Arts & Auction Center

Pottery-Midcentury, Vase, Plants, Flowers, Glazed, Scroll Handles, Vally Wieselthier, c.1920, 13 ½ x 7 ½ In.
$1984.00

P

Rago Arts & Auction Center

PRINT

Pottery-Midcentury, Vase, Women, Fantoni, Raymor, Marked, Black Slip, 9 ½ In.
$196.00

Humler & Nolan

Pratt, Toby Jug, Man, Standing, Full Figure, Holding Snuff Box, 8 ¼ In.
$57.00

Conestoga Auction Co., Inc.

Pratt, Urn, Potpourri, Lid, Matte Black, Classical Figures, Pierced Lid, Gilt Handles, c.1890, 28 In.
$732.00

Neal Auction Co.

Japanese, Triptych, 3 Women, Attendant, Playing Cards, Woodblock, Frame, 16 x 30 In.	59.00
Japanese, Utamaro, Geisha, Woodblock, Frame, 19th Century, 9 x 14 In.	75.00
Japanese, Utamaro, Kitagawa, Women Abalone Divers, Triptych, Frame, 11 x 41 In.	384.00
Japanese, Woodblock, Choki, Eishosai, Tsukasa-Dayu, Courtesan, Osaka, Frame, 24 x 18 In.	86.00
Laurier, Art Nouveau Woman, Mucha, Alphonse, Lithograph, Color, c.1901, 24 x 18 In.	767.00
Lichtenstein, Finger Pointing, Silkscreen, Color, c.1973, 12 x 9 In.	4130.00
McKenney & Hall, Asseola, Seminole Leader, Litho, J.T. Bowen, c.1842, 21 ½ x 15 In. ....*illus*	2160.00
McKenney & Hall, Not-Chi-Mi-Ne, Lithograph, Frame, c.1840, 15 x 11 ½ In. ....*illus*	956.00

Nutting prints are now popular with collectors. Wallace Nutting is known for his pictures, furniture, and books. Nutting prints are actually hand-colored photographs issued from 1900 to 1941. There are over 10,000 different titles. Wallace Nutting furniture is listed in the Furniture category.

Nutting, Braiding A Straw Hat, Frame, c.1916, 13 x 11 In.	225.00
Nutting, Country Scene, Signed, Frame, c.1900, 13 x 10 In.	95.00
Nutting, Larkspur, Woman In Flower Beds, Signed, Frame, 17 x 14 In.	150.00
Nutting, Meeting Of The Ways, Frame, c.1920, 17 x 11 In.	75.00
Nutting, Steam, Flowers, Signed, c.1900, 6 x 5 In.	125.00
Nutting, Village Dale, Signed, 9 ½ x 4 In.	119.00
Nutting, Woman, Braiding Rug, Fireplace, Frame, Signed, c.1900, 7 x 9 In.	89.00
Ottaviani, Giovanni, Loggia Di Rafaele, Vatican, Etching, c.1810, 32 x 19 ½ In., Pair	598.00

Parrish prints are wanted by collectors. Maxfield Frederick Parrish was an illustrator who lived from 1870 to 1966. He is best known as a designer of magazine covers, posters, calendars, and advertisements. His prints have been copied in recent years.

Parrish, Arizona, Mountains, Blues, Frame, c.1960, 11 ¼ x 8 ½ In.	199.00
Parrish, Child, Old Man, c.1900, 7 x 9 ½ In.	90.00
Parrish, Daybreak, Figures, Under Trees, Frame, c.1923, 34 x 22 In.	1200.00
Parrish, Evening, Stream, Barn, Trees, Calendar Print, 10 x 7 ½ In.	250.00
Parrish, Florentine Fete, People On Steps, c.1925, Frame, 13 x 15 In.	375.00
Parrish, King Of The Black Isles, P.F. Collier, Frame, c.1907, 14 x 19 In.	295.00
Parrish, King Presented With Tarts, c.1925, 10 x 12 In.	95.00
Parrish, Ladies Home Journal, Women On Steps, Flowering Tree, May 1913, 11 x 16 In.	125.00
Parrish, Solitude, Girl On Rock, Signed, Frame, 16 x 13 In.	225.00
Parrish, The King Presented With Tarts, c.1925, 10 x 12 In.	95.00
Parrish, When Day Is Dawning, Calendar Print, Frame, 1954, 12 x 16 In.	250.00
Peirce, Gerry, Arizona, Etching, Signed, Frame, c.1946, 3 ¾ x 3 In.	120.00
Roberts, David, Karnac, Holy Land & Egypt, Lithograph, Louis Haghe, c.1820, 20 x 14 In.	329.00
Whinnery, H.P., Horseracing, Southern Ohio Fair Grounds, Lithograph, Frame, 1874, 34 x 42 In.	294.00

Woodblock prints that are not in the Japanese tradition are listed here. Most were made in England and the United States during the Arts and Crafts period. Japanese woodblock prints are listed under Print, Japanese.

Woodblock, Baumann, Gustave, A Lilac Year, Signed, Frame, 12 x 13 In. ....*illus*	14880.00
Woodblock, Eckmann, Otto, Night Herons, Mat, Frame, 1896, 5 ¼ x 9 ¼ In. ....*illus*	2976.00
Woodblock, Esherick, Wharton, January, 1922, 9 x 8 ¼ In.	992.00
Woodblock, Esherick, Wharton, Man In The Snow Storm, 1923, 8 ½ x 7 ¾ In.	744.00
Woodblock, Esherick, Wharton, Nude In Bed, 1923, 10 x 9 In.	1116.00
Woodblock, Esherick, Wharton, September Corn, Signed, Frame, c.1922, 9 x 8 ½ In.	2232.00
Yoshida, Hiroshi, Morning Of Abuto, Woodblock, Color, c.1930, 9 ⅝ x 14 ¾ In.	538.00

PURINTON POTTERY COMPANY was incorporated in Wellsville, Ohio, in 1936. The company moved to Shippenville, Pennsylvania, in 1941 and made a variety of hand-painted ceramic wares. By the 1950s Purinton was making dinnerware, souvenirs, cookie jars, and florist wares. The pottery closed in 1959.

Apple, Bowl, Fruit, 4 In.	12.00
Apple, Chop Plate, 11 ⅝ In.	38.00
Apple, Creamer	18.00
Apple, Plate, Dinner, 9 ¾ In.	24.00
Apple, Plate, Salad, 6 ¾ In.	14.00
Apple, Sugar, Cover, 3 ¼ In.	14.00
Apple, Teapot, Lid, 4 ½ In., 3 ½ Cup	70.00
Fruit, Creamer, 3 In.	18.00
Fruit, Jug, 12 Oz.	18.00
Fruit, Pitcher, 5 In.	20.00
Intaglio, Butter, Brown	16.00

P

Intaglio, Chop Plate, Brown, 11 In.	44.00
Intaglio, Cup & Saucer, Brown	9.00
Intaglio, Dish, Pickle, Brown, 6 ¼ In.	18.00
Intaglio, Jug, Brown, 16 Oz., 4 ½ In.	28.00
Mountain Rose, Chop Plate, 12 In.	112.00
Mountain Rose, Teapot, Lid, Individual, 2 ⅞ In., 1 Cup	18.00
Normandy Plaid, Creamer	28.00
Normandy Plaid, Cup & Saucer	9.00
Shooting Star, Vase, 5 ⅝ In.	24.00

PURSES have been recognizable since the eighteenth century, when leather and needlework purses were preferred. Beaded purses became popular in the nineteenth century, went out of style, but are again in use. Mesh purses date from the 1880s and are still being made. How to carry a handkerchief and lipstick is a problem today for every woman, including the Queen of England.

Alligator, Adjustable Handle, Cuba, 10 x 8 In.	75.00
Alligator, Brown, Brass Clasp, Handle, c.1950, 10 ¾ x 12 In.	154.00
Alligator, Cognac, Leather Lined, Inside Pockets, Clutch, Gilt Stamp, Cuba, 4 ½ x 9 ¼ In. *illus*	679.00
Bakelite, Black, Rhinestones, Recessed Clock, Art Deco Clasp, Tassel, Wrist Cord, c.1920, 4 x 2 ½ In.	184.00
Basket, Nantucket, Carved Whale, Oval Mahogany Plaque, Bentwood Handle, c.1969, 7 x 11 In..	575.00
Basket, Nantucket, Ivory Scrimshaw Medallion, Ship, Handle, Signed, Jose Formosa Reyes, 1969, 8 In.	2350.00
Basket, Nantucket, Ivory Sea Gull, Hinged, Bail Handle, Wood Base, Jose Formoso Reyes, 11 x 6 In.	1610.00
Basket, Nantucket, Scrimshaw, Harbor, Walnut, Handle, Farnum, c.1988, 7 x 11 x 7 In. ...*illus*	885.00
Basket, Nantucket, Sea Gull, Signed, Jose Formoso Reyes, 7 In.	2587.00
Basket, Nantucket, Whale, Signed, Jose Formoso Reyes, 9 In.	2875.00
Basket, Nantucket, Wood Lid, Ivory Whale, Swing Handle, 6 ½ x 8 In.	460.00
Basket, Nantucket, Woven, Whalebone, Faux Ivory, Wood Disc Base & Lid, 6 ½ x 9 In.	147.00
Beaded, Black, Glass Seed Beads, Handle, 1960s, 7 x 6 x 12 In.	40.00
Beaded, Blue Cabochon Stones, Rectangular, Fringe Bottom, Gilt Clasp, Chain Handle, France	118.00
Beaded, Fringe, Purple, Blue, Black, Signed, Mandalian, 7 ½ x 3 ¼ In.	130.00
Beaded, Gilt Metal, Peach Satin Interior, Evening, Spritzer & Fuhrmann, France, 7 ¼ x 7 ½ In.	153.00
Beaded, Gold Carnival Glass Beads, Curb Chain Handle, Reticule, Tassel, c.1900, 6 In.	95.00
Beaded, Mesh, Steel Frame, Yellow & Blue, Art Nouveau Design, Fringe, Clasp, 1900s, 7 In.	69.00
Beaded, Pansies, Leaves, Multicolor, Pear Shape, Celluloid Clasp, c.1890, 10 x 7 ½ In.	115.00
Beaded, Scrolls, Cream, France, c.1920, 5 x 7 In.	79.00
Beaded, Sequins, Flowers, Silvertone Metal, Chain Link Handle, 5 x 6 In.	35.00
Beaded, Silver, Fringe, Fan Shape, France, c.1920	359.00
Beaded, Silvered, Scrolling Design, Fringe, Victorian	118.00
Beaded, White, Pastel Flowers, Beaded Handles, Label, Jorelle, Belgium, 1940s, 7 x 8 In.	110.00
Calf, Navy Blue, Gilt Brass, Red Leather Interior, Hobo, 9 ¾ x 11 In.	461.00
Carpetbag, Needlepoint, Blue, Roses, 1800s, 14 ½ x 13 In. *illus*	118.00
Clutch, Foldover, Satin, Black, Black Sequins, 7 x 5 In.	28.00
Coin, Patent Leather, Goldtone Metal, GG Logo Clasp, Gucci, 1960s	118.00
Coin, Suede, Brown, Judith Leiber, Saks Fifth Avenue	354.00
Compact, Clip-On Hinged Lid, Mirror, Coin Holders, Chain, Sterling Silver, 1900s, 3 ½ x 2 ⅜ In.	89.00
Crocodile, Black, Art Deco Clasp, Handle, Coin Purse, France, c.1945, 6 ½ x 9 In.	307.00
Crocodile, Brown, Gold Fittings & Clasp, Outside Pocket, Handles, c.1945, 10 x 13 ½ In.	153.00
Crocodile, Foldover, Hidden Pocket, Inside Pockets, Chain Handle, c.1945, 9 ½ x 13 In. *illus*	307.00
Crocodile, Fuchsia, Suede Interior, Pocket, Clutch, Bow, Nancy Gonzales, 5 x 10 ¾ In.	598.00
Crocodile, Navy Blue, Zippered Pocket, Flap Pouch, Morabito, 7 ½ x 13 In.	657.00
Crocodile, White, Goldtone Metal Chain Link Handles, Coin Purse, Morabito, France	826.00
Crystals, Black, Silver Leather Lining, Shoulder Strap, Judith Leiber, 3 ½ x 6 ½ In.	269.00
Crystals, Lucky Cat, Garnet Eyes, Coin Purse, Comb, Mirror, Judith Leiber, 5 ¼ In. ....*illus*	1195.00
Crystals, Penguin, Red, Black, Goldtone Metal, Pillbox, Judith Leiber, 2 In.	269.00
Embroidered, Flame Stitch, Geometric, Red, Blue, Green, Gold, Flap, 1800s, 9 In.	920.00
Embroidered, Phoenix, Flowers, Birds, Bats, Chinese, 1800s, 15 ½ In.	86.00
Fretwork, Clouds, Celluloid Bars, Dragons, Silk Tassels, Cord Strap, Chinese, c.1815, 8 ¾ x 8 ½ In..	553.00
Glass Beads, Blue Silk, Victorian, c.1910, 5 x 4 In.	85.00
Lambskin, Mustard Yellow, Tassel, Zipper Top, Chain, Box, Chanel, 7 ½ x 5 ½ In.	600.00
Leather, Black & White, Geometric, Foldover, Clutch, Textured, Magnetic Closure, Carlos	369.00
Leather, Black Epi, Handles, Louis Vuitton, France, 9 x 10 In.	345.00
Leather, Black, Beige Suede Interior, Zippered Pocket, Fendi, 8 ½ x 12 In.	179.00
Leather, Black, Brown & White, Tote, Canvas Interior, Pochette, 11 x 19 In.	418.00
Leather, Black, Gilt Brass, Structured, Celine Black, 7 ¼ x 10 ¾ In.	799.00
Leather, Black, Goldtone Metal, Kelly, c.1950, 9 x 4 x 8 In.	56.00
Leather, Black, Quilted, Pouch, Gilt Metal Clasp, Multi-Strap, Chanel, c.1985, 26 ½ x 8 ½ In.	615.00

Print, Audubon, American Crow, Havell, Frame, 1833, 38 x 25 In.
$3525.00

Cowan's Auctions

Buy a Magazine, Get a Purse
Mesh purses were given as gifts with fashion magazine subscriptions before 1917.

Print, Audubon, Brown Pelican, Chromolithograph, Oak Frame, 39 x 26 In.
$1725.00

James D. Julia Inc.

P

Print, Audubon, Harlequin Duck, Whatman, Frame, J., 1836, 24 x 36 ½ In.
$4183.00

Neal Auction Co.

Print, Audubon, Red-Tailed Squirrel, J.T. Bowen, 1844, 26 ½ x 19 ½ In.
$504.00

Skinner, Inc.

Print, Audubon, Yellow-Throated Vireo, Engraved, Aquatint, Havell, Frame, 38 ½ x 28 ½ In.
$2510.00

Neal Auction Co.

Print, Gearhart, Frances, Now The Moon, Linoleum Block, Color, Signed, 1924, 6 ½ x 3 ½ In.
$1736.00

Rago Arts & Auction Center

Leather, Black, Satchel, Silver Closure, Handles, External Pockets, Coach, 15 x 17 In.	118.00
Leather, Brown, Sac Plat Tote, Monogram, Leather Straps, Louis Vuitton, 15 x 14 In.	717.00
Leather, Burgundy, Woven, Lucite Frame, Shoulder, Bottega Veneta, Italy, c.1990, 8 ½ x 9 In.	522.00
Leather, Camel, Woven Design, Brown Suede Interior, Bottega Veneta, 11 x 11 In.	299.00
Leather, Clutch, Onyx, Cameo Medallion, Gold Trim, Strap, J. Leiber, Neiman Marcus, c.1985, 9 ½ In.	305.00
Leather, Constance, Goldtone Hardware, Shoulder Strap, Magnetic Closure, Hermes, 9 In. *illus*	1541.00
Leather, Embossed, Navy Blue, Gilt Metal Logo, Shoulder Strap, Hermes, 6 ½ x 10 In.	837.00
Leather, Fabric, Leopard Print, Trapezoidal, Foldover, Turn Clasp, La Bagagerie, France, 5 x 8 In.	369.00
Leather, Light Blue, White, Cloth Bag, Salvatore Ferragamo	325.00
Leather, Quilted, Gilt Brass Chain Handles, Ball Clasp, Stamped, Chanel, France, 6 ½ x 10 In.	1045.00
Leather, Red, Triangular, France, 1950s, 11 x 10 In.	60.00
Leather, Red, Woven, Shoulder Handles, Gold Metal, Coin Purse, Koret, Saks Fifth Avenue, 1970s	325.00
Lizard, Brown, Glasses Case, Bergdorf Goodman, France	30.00
Lizard, Gathered, Satin Lined, Clutch, Chain Drop, Judith Leiber, 6 x 9 In.	369.00
Lizard, Gold Stamp, Palizzio, 1960s	149.00
Lizard, Quilted, Goldtone Hardware, Shoulder Strap, Inside Pockets, Chanel, 7 x 9 ½ In. *illus*	770.00
Lizard, Turquoise, Gilt Metal, Round Mirror, Coin Purse, Box, Judith Leiber	443.00
Lucite, Gray, Clear Lid, Etched Flower, Lucite Latch, Clear Handle, 7 x 4 In.	49.00
Lucite, Light Brown, Oval, Straight Sides, Clear Lid, Etched, Hinged, Lucite Latch, 7 x 4 x 9 In.	151.00
Lucite, Marbleized, Box Shape, Round Mirror Inside, Double Handle, 1960s, 7 x 4 In.	49.00
Lucite, White Pearl Oyster, Demilune Shape, Handle, c.1950, 7 ¾ x 4 In.	259.00
Mesh, 14K Gold, Engraved Crest, Shield, Sapphire Cabochon Closure, Compact, Victorian	4012.00
Mesh, Art Deco Style, Black Stylized Clasp, Rectangular, Scalloped Bottom, Chain Handle	177.00
Mesh, Chinese Lantern Shape, 3 Tiers, Flowers, Whiting & Davis, 1922, 4 In.	425.00
Mesh, Enameled, Geometric Art Deco Design, Pin, Green & Brown, Whiting & Davis, 1920s, 6 In.	110.00
Mesh, Enameled, Swirls, Half Moons, Silvertone Frame & Chain, Mandalian, 3 x 7 In.	195.00
Mesh, Goldtone Metal, Glass Beads, Flowers, Fringe, Olette, France, c.1890, 5 ½ x 10 ½ In.	86.00
Mesh, Goldtone, Whiting & Davis, c.1930, 7 In.	75.00
Mesh, Metal, Enameled, Gilt Clasps, Blue Cabochon Stones, Chain Handle, 6 In.	89.00
Mesh, Multicolor, Silver Plated Frame, Chain Link Handle, Whiting & Davis Co., 7 In.	113.00
Mesh, Silver, Rectangular, Cable Chain, 5 In.	120.00
Mesh, Silvertone Metal, Whiting & Davis, c.1900, 5 In.	45.00
Mesh, Sterling Silver Rim, Monogram Medallion, Chain, 6 ½ In.	180.00
Mesh, Sterling Silver, Pierced, Engraved, Cornucopia, Birds, Scrolls, Germany, c.1900, 5 ½ In.	119.00
Mesh, White, Scalloped Frame, 1950s, 7 x 5 In.	48.00
Minaudiere, Marguerite, Gold, Diamonds, Mirror, Van Cleef & Appels, 1950s, 6 x 5 In.	22303.00
Mink, Brown, Hobo Style, Leather Rope Handles, Laura Biagiotti, 11 x 21 In.	203.00
Needlepoint, Bird, Silver Chain, c.1910, 7 x 7 x In.	44.00
Needlework, Pearl, Amethyst, Flowers, Foldover, Marked, Paris, c.1945, 5 x 8 ¼ In.	307.00
Nylon, Black, Leopard Print, Reversible, 2 Zippered Pockets, Square Tote, Bottega Veneta, 12 x 20 In.	144.00
Ostrich Skin, Brown, Chain Link Handles, Morabito, Paris, 1960s	1298.00
Patent Leather, Black, Brown Suede, Kelly, Shoulder Strap, Serapian, 9 ½ x 12 ½ In.	191.00
Patent Leather, Brown, Enameled Design, Square	148.00
Patent Leather, Tote, Braided Handles, Guarantee Tape, Label, Jean Paul Gaultier, France, 16 x 14 In.	153.00
Plastic, Leather, Zipper, Louis Vuitton, Saks Fifth Avenue, c.1990, 12 x 15 In.	720.00
Satin, Black, Monogram, Zippered Pocket, Silver Metal Studs, Clutch, Christian Dior, 4 x 8 In.	227.00
Silk Brocade, Battle Scene, Plum Velvet Trim, Cartier, 7 x 9 In.	1007.00
Silk, Blue, Beaded, Gold Tone Metal, Chain Link Handle, 1920s, 5 x 6 In.	65.00
Silk, Embroidered, Birds, Flowers, Chinese, Frame, 19th Century, 10 x 19 In.	225.00
Silk, Satin, Bag, Embroidered, Foldover, Pockets, Chere Souvenance, c.1786, 5 ¾ x 4 ¾ In.	215.00
Silk, Signature, Geometric Print, Multicolor, Gold Tassel, Silver Cord Handle, Pucci, 5 ½ x 9 In.	143.00
Silver, Mesh, Bow Tie Laurel Leaves Clasp, Ball Embellishment, Chain, Germany, 6 In.	60.00
Silver, Reticulated Embossed Flowers, Hinged, 2 ¼ x 4 ½ In.	230.00
Sterling Silver, Embossed Flowers, Pierced, Hinged, Rounded Rectangle, 2 x 5 In.	230.00
Straw, Leather, Metal Closure, 1960s, 10 x 4 x 11 In.	36.00
Taffeta, Purple, Ruffle Trim, Interior Pocket, Clutch, Christian Dior, 5 ½ x 8 ½ In.	167.00
Tapestry, Needlepoint, Flowers, Vinyl Trim & Handle, 1970s, 12 x 6 In.	52.00
Tapestry, Needlepoint, Vinyl Accents, Goldtone Metal, 1960s, 14 x 4 x 7 In.	42.00
Velvet, Beaded, Goldtone Stitching, Faux Emeralds, Compartments, Clutch, 8 x 5 In.	52.00
Velvet, Red, Black, Geometrics, Shoulder Strap, Roberta Di Carmerino, Venice, 7 x 11 In.	775.00
Velvet, Silver Bouillon Embroidery, Crest, Leather Pocket Inside, c.1765, 8 x 5 In.	1495.00
Vinyl, Brown, Goldtone Metal, Kelly, 1950s, 11 x 3 x 5 In.	40.00
Wallet, Leather, White, Goldtone Metal Clasp, Gucci	148.00
Wallet, Leather, Yellow, Pierced, Prince Gardner	30.00
Wallet, Lizard, Brown, Box, Lederer	106.00
Wood, Decoupage, Victorian Market Scene, Box Form, Anton Pieck, 9 x 6 In.	125.00

QUEZAL glass was made from 1901 to 1924 at the Queens, New York, company started by **Quezal** Martin Bach, Sr. Other glassware by other firms, such as Loetz, Steuben, and Tiffany, resembles this gold-colored iridescent glass. Martin Bach died in 1921. His son-in-law, Conrad Vahlsing Jr., went to work at the Lustre Art Company about 1920. Bach's son, Martin Bach Jr., worked at the Durand Art Glass division of the Vineland Flint Glass Works after 1924.

Bowl, Gold, Wide Flared Rim, 2 ½ x 10 In.	177.00
Bowl, Nut, Gold Iridescent, Green, Magenta, Ribbed, Squat, 1 x 2 ½ In.	316.00
Bowl, Pulled Feather, Gold Iridescent Inside, Flaring Rim, Footed, Wood Stand, 14 x 4 ½ In.	2657.00
Compote, Blue Hues, Gold Footed, Iridescent, Signed, 5 In.	300.00
Lamp Shade, Gold, Facetted, Bell Shape, White Opaline Interior, c.1900, 5 ¼ x 5 ⅛ In.	598.00
Lamp Shade, Iridescent, Stepped, Hanging, c.1920, 10 ¼ In.	896.00
Lamp, 4-Light, Gold Iridescent Bell Shades, Pulled Threading, Hammered Copper	2065.00
Lamp, 4-Light, Metal Fixture, White Iridescent Shades, 17 In. .....*illus*	2489.00
Lamp, Bronze, Flower Shape, Lily Pad, Gold, Purple & Green Iridescent Shade, c.1900, 16 In.	1968.00
Lamp, Gold Iridescent Shade, Pulled Feather, Harp Shape, Electrified, 10 In.	1000.00
Plate, Iridescent Gold, Stretch Mark Border, Halos, Green & Pink Accents, 6 In. Diam.	374.00
Salt, Shiny Gold, Ribs, Blue, Pink, Yellow, Wide Rim, Tapered, 1 x 3 In.	316.00
Shade, Blue, Yellow, Opal White, Leaves, Gold Iridescent, Frilly Ruffled Rim, Signed	288.00
Shade, Flared, Ribbed Body, Gold Aurene, Signed, 5 ¼ In., 4 Piece	483.00
Shade, Glass, Lobed, Scalloped, Iridescent, Signed, 7 ½ In.	259.00
Vase, Amber, Iridescent Ground, Footed, 8 ¼ In.	826.00
Vase, Blue Aurene, Satin Finish, Spread Foot, Swollen Top, 7 In.	460.00
Vase, Blue King Tut Design, Gold Iridescent, Elongated Oval, Rolled In Mouth, Signed, 7 In.	2300.00
Vase, Flower Form, Green, Gold Feathering, Gold Iridescent Inside, Ruffled Rim, c.1910, 6 x 6 In.	1195.00
Vase, Flower Form, Iridescent, Green Pulled Feathers, Ruffled Rim, 6 ¾ In.	1315.00
Vase, Globular Form, Flared Rim, Translucent Amber, Green, Pulled Feather Design, c.1907, 10 In.	2813.00
Vase, Gold & Green, Pulled Decoration, Pink Shaded Flower, Bulbous, Flared, 4 ¼ In.	1554.00
Vase, Gold Iridescent, Silver Flower Overlay, Carafe Shape, Signed, 8 In.	300.00
Vase, Green Leaves, Gold Tipped, Pulled, Gold Iridescent, Morning Glory, Trumpet Shape, 7 In.	1093.00
Vase, Green Pulled Feather, Iridescent, Gold Interior, Trumpet, Scalloped Rim, Oval, Signed, 7 In.	1955.00
Vase, Green, Gold Pulled Feather, Iridescent Gold Interior, Bowling Pin Shape, 10 ¾ In.	1800.00
Vase, Green, Gold Pulled Feather, Iridescent Gold Interior, Paper Label, 9 ¼ x 7 ½ In.	1800.00
Vase, Jack-In-The-Pulpit, Gold Iridescent, Green Pulled Hooked Feathers, Scalloped Rim, 11 In. *illus*	6613.00
Vase, Jack-In-The-Pulpit, Green & Gold Iridescent, Pulled Feather Design, c.1900, 9 In.	1599.00
Vase, Pulled Feather Design, Green, Gold, Iridescent, Flared Base, Signed, 5 ¼ x 9 In.	3500.00
Vase, Rainbow Iridescent, Magenta Accents, Ribbed, Flared, Scalloped Rim, 2 ⅛ In.	431.00
Vase, Silver Overlay, Bulbous, Gold With Silver Overlay, Flowers, Signed, 5 ½ In.	550.00
Vase, Silver Overlay, Gold Iridescent, Art Nouveau Flowers, Leaves, Signed, 5 ½ In. .....*illus*	1035.00

QUILTS have been made since the seventeenth century. Early textiles were very precious and every scrap was saved to be reused. A quilt is a combination of fabrics joined to a filler and a backing by small stitched designs known as quilting. An appliqued quilt has pieces stitched to the top of a large piece of background fabric. A patchwork, or pieced, quilt is made of many small pieces stitched together. Embroidery can be added to either type.

Album, 16 Blocks, Floral Wreath, Swag Border, Red, Green, Yellow, Cream, 90 x 87 In.	1600.00
Amish, Patchwork, Center Diamond, Green, Maroon, Violet, Early 1900s, 71 x 74 In.	374.00
Amish, Patchwork, Diamond In Square, Pieced Cotton, 1900s, 81 x 84 In.	2196.00
Amish, Pieced, Sunshine & Shadow, Flower Basket Border, Multicolor, Initials L.S., 72 X73 ½ In.	400.00
Amish, Postage Stamp, Double Borders, Cotton, Sateen, Wool, c.1850, Crib, 39 x 46 In.	411.00
Appliqued, 9 Wreaths, Red & Green, Leaf Vine Border, 1800s, 89 x 90 In.	940.00
Appliqued, Album Trapunto, 25 Block, Flowers, Eagle, Flag Center, Balt., 1846, 101 x 102 In.	33180.00
Appliqued, Album, 16 Block, Flower Wreaths, Swag, Red, Green, Yellow, Cream, 1800s, 91 x 87 In.	1680.00
Appliqued, Cherry Blossom, Sawtooth Border, Pa., c.1890, 90 x 76 In.	415.00
Appliqued, Concentric Shells, Circles, Shelly Zegart, 1800s, 67 x 77 In.	944.00
Appliqued, Coxcomb, Sawtooth Borders Cotton, Muslin Back, c.1925, 79 x 79 ½ In. .....*illus*	470.00
Appliqued, Crib, Center Leaf Panel, Ohio Star Blocks, Flowers, Vines, White, Red, c.1890, 38 x 41 In.	2370.00
Appliqued, Flower Wreaths, Narrow Sashing, Floral Vine Border, Cotton, c.1850, 86 x 90 In.	499.00
Appliqued, Flowers, Tulip Border, Cream, Red, 86 x 72 In.	115.00
Appliqued, Fruit Trees, Red, Yellow Birds, Flowers, Grapevine Border, c.1890, 74 x 71 In.	2185.00
Appliqued, Fruits, Birds, Flowers & Yellow Birds Center, 1880s, 72 x 60 In.	2185.00
Appliqued, Medallion, Eagle, Olive Branch, Swag Border, Yellow, White, Cotton, 80 x 92 In.	235.00
Appliqued, Patchwork, Chintz, Embroidered, Margaret M. Allsher Ballygawley, 1800s, 80 x 83 In.	1000.00
Appliqued, Patchwork, Presentation, Flowers, Birds, Scallop Border, Cotton, c.1844, 98 x 103 In.	32500.00
Appliqued, Patchwork, Princess Feather, Yellow, Red, Olive, White, 1860, 82 x 82 In.	295.00
Appliqued, Presentation, Flowers, Birds, Scallop Border, July 19, 1844, 97 x 103 In.	40000.00

Print, Icart, Lilies, Etching, Signed, Frame, 1934, 27 ½ x 19 In. $1062.00

Ivey-Selkirk Auctioneers

Print, Icart, Symphony In Blue, Seated Woman, Hat, Flowers, Frame, 23 ½ x 19 ½ In. $919.00

Skinner, Inc.

Print, McKenney & Hall, Asseola, Seminole Leader, Litho, J.T. Bowen, c.1842, 21 ½ x 15 In. $2160.00

Gray's Auctioneers LLC

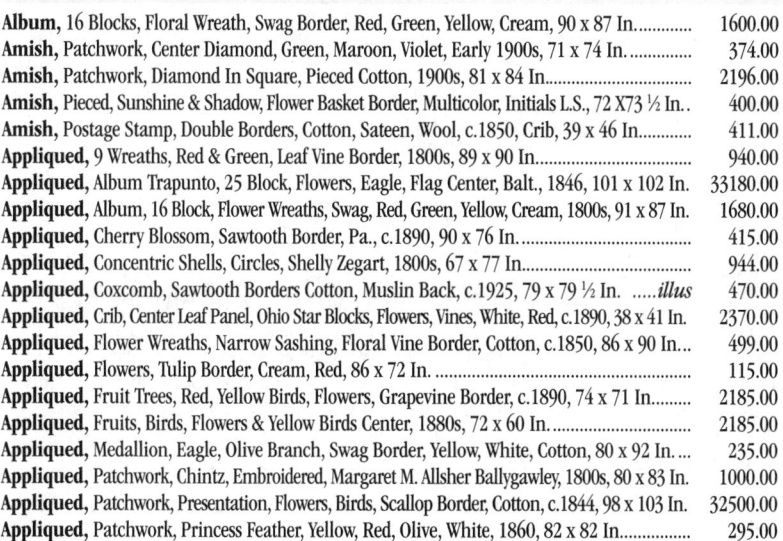

Print, McKenney & Hall, Not-Chi-Mi-Ne, Lithograph, Frame, c.1840, 15 x 11 ½ In. $956.00

Neal Auction Co.

Print, Woodblock, Baumann, Gustave, A Lilac Year, Signed, Frame, 12 x 13 In. $14880.00

Rago Arts & Auction Center

Print, Woodblock, Eckmann, Otto, Night Herons, Mat, Frame, 1896, 5 ¼ x 9 ¼ In. $2976.00

Rago Arts & Auction Center

Appliqued, Red & Green, White Ground, 19th Century, 89 x 94 In.	144.00
Appliqued, Rising Sun, Red Sashing, Diamond Border, Cotton, c.1880, 74 x 96 In.	823.00
Appliqued, Roses, Buds, Alternating Block Pattern, Chain Border, c.1910, 74 x 75 In.	316.00
Appliqued, Starburst, Red, Green, Yellow, Red Border, Early 1900s, 71 x 86 In.	489.00
Appliqued, Triangles, Memorial Hall Handkerchief Center, Lancaster, Pa., 1876, 92 x 92 In.	9480.00
Appliqued, Tulips, Green Borders, Feather Wreath Quilting, c.1870s, 74 x 96 In.	294.00
Appliqued, Vine Border, Birds, Whig Rose, Red, Green, Pa., c.1890, 78 x 74 In.	2370.00
Appliqued, Wandering Foot, Red Diamond, White Ground, Signed Mary J. Sips 1891, 80 x 67 In.	600.00
Appliqued, Whig Rose, Flowers, Pink, Red, Green, 1800s, 87 x 89 In.	3792.00
Appliqued, Whig Rose, Red, Pink, Yellow, Green, Cotton, 87 x 78 In.	388.00
Bride's, White On White, Geometric, Flowers, Monogram, SSH, Pa., 1914, 78 x 83 In.	1896.00
Crazy, Embroidered, Silk, Velvet, Hand Painted, c.1900, 65 ½ x 56 ½ In. *illus*	143.00
Crazy, Embroidered, Silk, Velvet, Pink Taffeta Backing, Signatures, c.1897, 71 x 71 In.	418.00
Crazy, Embroidered, Silk, Velvet, Yellow Silk Backing, 12 Block, c.1880, 80 x 68 In.	269.00
Crazy, Silk, 9 Patch, 3-D Dimensions, Green & Purple, 1860s, 67 x 63 In.	1285.00
Friendship, Pinwheel Star, Red, White, Stitched Names, Cotton, 84 x 68 In.	254.00
Patchwork, 9 Patch, Alternating Blocks, Cotton, Signed L.G.M., 1943, 32 x 22 In.	47.00
Patchwork, 9 Patch, Red Border, Cotton, 76 x 86 In.	136.00
Patchwork, 9 Patch, Signatures, Cotton, c.1850, 91 x 76 In.	351.00
Patchwork, Amish Star, Blue, Green, Magenta, Mary D. Stutzman, Feb. 1913, 74 x 74 In.	690.00
Patchwork, Appliqued, Flowers, 12 Block, Sawtooth Border, c.1885, 79 x 89 In. *illus*	331.00
Patchwork, Appliqued, Mariner's Compass, Flower, Vine Border, 1800s, 84 x 84 In. *illus*	264.00
Patchwork, Barn Raising, Calico, Brown Print Backing, Cotton, 86 x 84 In.	177.00
Patchwork, Basket, Red & Yellow, Green Ground, 1800s, 86 x 84 In.	119.00
Patchwork, Checkerboard, Cotton Signed, Eliza. P. Mohler, 1911, 80 x 82 In.	1243.00
Patchwork, Diamond In Square, Red & Yellow, Bars, On Back, Cotton, 1900s, 75 x 75 In. *illus*	470.00
Patchwork, Diamonds, Red, White, Blue Rays, Hanging Sleeve, c.1900, 58 x 68 In.	236.00
Patchwork, Double Wedding Ring, Purple Binding, Scalloped Border, Cotton, 1911, 79 x 76 In.	136.00
Patchwork, Drunkard's Path, Red & Orange, c.1850, 68 x 83 In.	588.00
Patchwork, Feathered Star, Red & White, Sawtooth Borders, Cotton, c.1900, 80 x 96 In.	512.00
Patchwork, Flower Basket, Border, Corner Blocks, Tan, Paisley, Cotton, 52 x 41 In.	153.00
Patchwork, Friendship, 13 Block, Names, Flower, Red, Yellow, Green, Cotton, 104 x 98 In.	826.00
Patchwork, Houses, Red, Blue, Gray, Cotton, 76 x 64 In.	452.00
Patchwork, Lemoyne Star, Calico Border, Printed, Blue Back, Cotton, 85 x 84 In. *illus*	295.00
Patchwork, Log Cabin, Brown, Black, White, Pennsylvania, c.1890, 87 x 88 In.	207.00
Patchwork, Log Cabin, Calico, Multicolor, Blue Back, Cotton, 82 x 80 In. *illus*	142.00
Patchwork, Monkey Wrench, Cotton, Signed, Eliza. P. Fautt, Mohler, 1908, 80 x 80 In.	1130.00
Patchwork, Multicolor, Flowers, Round Wreaths, 2 Birds, Fan Tails, Cotton, 86 x 99 In.	203.00
Patchwork, Ocean Wave, Red, Black, Double Border, Lancaster Co., c.1900, 74 x 74 In.	444.00
Patchwork, Ocean Waves, Cotton, 75 x 79 In.	283.00
Patchwork, Olive, Gold, Navy Blocks, Pennsylvania, 1800s, 12 ¼ x 12 In.	273.00
Patchwork, Red, White Sawtooth Design, Blue Ground, Pennsylvania, c.1905, 72 x 86 In.	178.00
Patchwork, Roses, Leaves, Feather Quilting, Zigzag, Cotton, 79 x 101 In.	147.00
Patchwork, Serpentine Fan, Multicolor, Red Border, Cotton, 74 x 66 In.	181.00
Patchwork, Star, Dress Prints, Diamond Quilting, c.1850, 72 x 92 In.	211.00
Patchwork, Star, Red, Yellow, Cream Ground, c.1890, 69 x 65 In.	89.00
Patchwork, Stars, Green, Red Tulip Border, White Ground, Pennsylvania, 1800s, 84 x 92 In.	148.00
Patchwork, Sunflower Star, Quilted Wreaths, Zigzag Border, c.1880, 82 x 84 In.	230.00
Patchwork, Sunshine & Shadow, Navy, Pink, White, Blue, Yellow, Beige, 1940s, 78 x 92 In.	525.00
Patchwork, Touching Stars, Red, White, Cotton, 80 x 80 In.	489.00
Patchwork, Yellow Circles, Red Print Ground, Sawtooth Border, Crib, c.1910, 26 ½ x 26 ½ In.	356.00
Ribbon, Grover Cleveland, U.S. Centennial, Indiana Commandery, c.1890, 77 x 78 In. *illus*	570.00

QUIMPER pottery has a long history. Tin-glazed, hand-painted pottery has been made in Quimper, France, since the late seventeenth century. The earliest firm was founded in 1708 by Pierre Bousquet. In 1782, Antoine de la Hubaudiere became the manager of the factory and the factory became known as the HB Factory (for Hubaudiere-Bousquet), de la Hubaudiere, or Grande Maison. Another firm, founded in 1772 by Francois Eloury, was known as Porquier. The third firm, founded by Guillaume Dumaine in 1778, was known as HR or Henriot Quimper. All three firms made similar pottery decorated with designs of Breton peasants and sea and flower motifs. The Eloury (Porquier) and Dumaine (Henriot) firms merged in 1913. Bousquet (HB) merged with the others in 1968. The group was sold to an American holding company in 1984. More changes followed, and in 2011 Jean-Pierre Le Goff became the owner and the name was changed to Henriot-Quimper.

HR. Quimper

Bowl, Shell Shape, Footed, Breton Woman, Signed, 4 x 5 In.	65.00
Coffeepot, Minstral Blue Design, Squared Handle, Finial, 10 In.	150.00
Jug, Woman, Flowers, Footed, 7 ½ In.	38.00

Q

Oyster Plate, 6 Wells, Multicolor, 8 ½ In.	59.00
Oyster Plate, 7 Wells, Multicolor, Flowers, 8 In.	45.00
Oyster Plate, Scalloped Edge, Starfish, c.1925, 9 In.	95.00
Pitcher, Geometric, Brown, Orange, Yellow, Green, Loop Handle, Bulbous, 9 ¼ In.	230.00
Plate, Octagonal, Breton Man, Flower Border, 5 In.	125.00
Vase, Portrait, Breton Man, Bulbous, 8 In.	75.00
Water Can, Child On Boat, 6 x 9 In.	59.00

RADFORD pottery was made by Alfred Radford in Broadway, Virginia; Tiffin and Zanesville, Ohio; and Clarksburg, West Virginia, from 1891 until 1912. Jasperware, Ruko, Thera, Radura, and Velvety Art Ware were made. The jasperware resembles the famous Wedgwood ware of the same name. Another pottery named Radford worked in England and is not included here. *RADURA.*

Bowl, Grapevine, Jasperware, Cameo, Marked, 9 ¼ x 3 In.	62.00
Vase, Thera, Pelican, Albert Haubrich, Marked, 13 ½ In.	806.00

RADIO broadcast receiving sets were first sold in New York City in 1910. They were used to pick up the experimental broadcasts of the day. The first commercial radios were made by Westinghouse Company for listeners of the experimental shows on KDKA Pittsburgh in 1920. Collectors today are interested in all early radios, especially those made of Bakelite plastic or decorated with blue mirrors. Figural advertising radios and transistor radios are also collected.

Advertising, 7-Up, Figural, Push Button In Bottom, Made By Enterprise, 6 ½ In.	40.00
Advertising, Duracell Battery, Figural, Push Button On Bottom, Made By Cameo, 6 ½ In.	45.00
Advertising, Labatt Beer Can, Figural, Push Button On Bottom, Made By Cameo, 6 ¼ In.	45.00
Advertising, Sylvania Radio & TV Tubes, Clock, Round, 15 In.	141.00
Airline, Super Heterodyne, Cathedral, Tube, Counter, 1930s ....*illus*	224.00
Bluebird, Walter Dorwin Teague, Blue Glass, Chrome, Sparton, 1934, 14 ½ x 14 ½ In. .*illus*	2500.00
Fada, Model 1000, Butterscotch Bakelite, 6 ½ x 10 ½ In.	950.00
General Electric, Model 401, Ivory Plastic, AC/DC, Super Heterodyne, 1955, 6 x 7 In.	60.00
Monkey Shape, Band Leader Hat & Coat, Blinking Eyes, AM, 1970s, 7 In.	25.00
Novelty, Owl, Red, Holding Baby Bottle, Wearing Cap, Blinking Eyes, AM, 1970s, 7 In.	25.00
Philco, Cathedral, Wood Case, AM & SW Band, 4 Knobs, 1935, 17 x 12 In.	225.00
Sign, Motorola Audio Radio, Neon, Lighted, Reverse Painted Panel, 12 x 26 In.	904.00
Westinghouse, Little Jewel, H-125, Countertop, c.1945	110.00
Westinghouse, Little Jewel, Refrigerator Shape, H-125, c.1945	240.00

RAILROAD enthusiasts collect any train memorabilia. Everything is wanted, from oilcans to whole train cars. The Chessie system has a store that sells many reproductions of its old dinnerware and uniforms.

Bowl, Ice Cream, AT & SF Santa Fe, Mimbreno Pattern, 6 In.	192.00
Bowl, Norwalk Southern Railway, Flowers, Gilt Handles, Oval, 2 ½ x 9 ¼ In.	367.00
Broadside, Pioneer Fast Line Train, Philadelphia, 1837, 16 ¼ x 12 In.	127.00
Butter Chip, Florida East Coast, Rococo Pattern, Buffalo China, 1943, 3 ½ In.	192.00
Cap, Pullman Conductor, Black Silk, Gilt Badge, Gold Braid, Marshall Fields, Size 6 ½.	65.00
Carafe, Water, Etched PRR, Pennsylvania Railroad, International Silver Co., 1957, 10 In.	550.00
Cup & Saucer, Demitasse, Tennessee Central Railroad, Nashville, Inca Ware, Shenango, 2 x 3, 4 ¾ In.	170.00
Glass, Cordial, NYC Crest, Libbey, 3 ½ In.	84.00
Lamp, Switch, Yellow, Green Targets, Handle, Marked Adlake Non Sweating Lamp, 16 x 10 ½ In.	173.00
Lantern, American Express, Blue Etched Globe, Bail Handle, Star Head Light Co., 16 In.	531.00
Lantern, Kerosene, Searchlight, Green, Ribbed Glass, Domed Copper Hanger, c.1900, 21 In.	115.00
Map Timetable, American Overland Central Pacific, Rates, Scenic Views, 1875, 36 x 14 In.	158.00
Medallion, Lackawanna Railroad, Road Of Anthracite, Hand On Reverse, Brass, c.1920, 1 In.	40.00
Menu Holder, Fred Harvey, Cutout Initials, Gorham Co.	283.00
Mustard Pot & Lid, AT & SF, Mimbreno Pattern, Syracuse China, 2 ¼ x 2 ¼ In.	452.00
Picture Booklet, Fred Harvey Old Santa Fe, 12 Views, Colored	90.00
Pin, Cartoon Engineer, Safety First, That's For Me, Pennsylvania, Eastern Division, Celluloid, 1 ¼ In.	13.00
Pin, New England Assoc. Of R.R. Veterans, Locomotive, Ribbon, 16th Annual Outing	95.00
Plate, Baltimore & Ohio Railroad, Blue Transfer, 10 In.	590.00
Plate, Baltimore & Ohio Railroad, Blue, Enoch Wood & Sons, 10 ¼ In.	948.00
Plate, New York Central, Commodore Turquoise, 10 ¾ In.	57.00
Platter, Reading, Central Railroad Of New Jersey, Bethlehem Pattern, Oval, 8 ½ x 12 ½ In.	124.00
Sign, Crossing, Shield Shape, X-Mark, Cast Iron, 10 x 16 In.	330.00
Sign, Overland Route, Union Pacific, Porcelain, Shield Shape, Blue, White, Red Stripes, 9 x 9 ½ In.	1430.00
Sign, Railway Express Agency, Tin Over Cardboard, Frame, 19 x 13 In.	767.00
Sign, Rock Island Railroad, Reverse Glass, Multicolor, Frame, 1906, 99 x 24 In.	71500.00

Purse, Alligator, Cognac, Leather Lined, Inside Pockets, Clutch, Gilt Stamp, Cuba, 4 ½ x 9 ¼ In.
$679.00

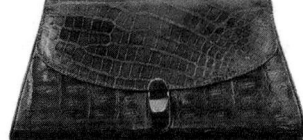

New Orleans Auction Galleries, Inc.

Purse, Basket, Nantucket, Scrimshaw, Harbor, Walnut, Handle, Farnum, c.1988, 6 x 10 x 7 In.
$885.00

James D. Julia Inc.

Purse, Carpetbag, Needlepoint, Blue, Roses, 1800s, 14 ½ x 13 In.
$118.00

James D. Julia Inc.

Purse, Crocodile, Foldover, Hidden Pocket, Inside Pockets, Chain Handle, c.1945, 9 ½ x 13 In.
$307.00

New Orleans Auction Galleries, Inc.

R

Purse, Crystals, Lucky Cat, Garnet Eyes, Coin Purse, Comb, Mirror, Judith Leiber, 5 ¼ In.
$1195.00

Sloans & Kenyon

Purse, Leather, Constance, Goldtone Hardware, Shoulder Strap, Magnetic Closure, Hermes, 9 In.
$1541.00

Skinner, Inc.

Purse, Lizard, Quilted, Goldtone Hardware, Shoulder Strap, Inside Pockets, Chanel, 7 x 9 ½ In.
$770.00

Skinner, Inc.

R

Mesh for Purses
A machine that made metal mesh was invented in 1909. Before that, mesh purses were made from individual pieces assembled by hand.

Sign, Union Pacific, American Buffalo, Sepia Tone, Cardboard, Frame, 30 x 26 In.	403.00
Sugar, Burlington Route Railroad, Galesburg Pattern, 3 ¾ x 4 ½ In.	875.00
Sugar, Louisiana & Arkansas, Silver, Engraved Logo, Reed & Barton, 2 ¾ x 6 In.	1469.00
Sugar, Tongs, Western Pacific, Silver, International Silver Co., 4 ¼ x 5 In.	180.00
Timetable, Missouri Pacific Railway System, 1891	45.00
Transit, Engraved Hendry Corp., Keuffek & Esser, Case, 13 ½ x 11 ¾ In.	259.00
Tumbler, Missouri Kansas & Texas Market Railroad, Etched Logo, 5 In.	45.00
Water Can, D & H Railroad, Lid, Spout Cap, Tin, 11 x 13 In.	45.00

RAZORS were used in ancient Egypt and subsequently wherever shaving was in fashion. The metal razor used in America until about 1870 was made in Sheffield, England. After 1870, machine-made hollow-ground razors were made in Germany or America. Plastic or bone handles were popular. The razor was often sold in a set of seven, one for each day of the week. The set was often kept by the barber who shaved the well-to-do man each day in the shop.

Cut Throat, R.M.S. Lusitania, Black, Ivory Celluloid Handle, Steel Blade, Box, 9 ¾ In.	287.00
Mustache, Celluloid Handle, 1 ½ In.	34.00
Our Pet, Silver Inlay Handle, Johnson Bros.	140.00
Straight, Double Bladed, Naval, Bone Handle, Etched Blade	328.00
Straight, Ebony Handle, Finck's Golden Gate, Germany, San Francisco	207.00
Straight, Ivory Handle, Inlaid Pique, Carved, Checkered, c.1825	408.00
Strap, Leather Tag, Reppenhagen, Will & Finck, San Francisco, 27 In.	1045.00

REAMERS, or juice squeezers, have been known since 1767, although most of those collected today date from the twentieth century. Figural reamers are among the most prized.

Aluminum, Foley, Mpls. Minn., Handle, 8 ¼ In.	7.99
Aluminum, Handle, Foley, c.1955, 2 x 4 x 8 In.	15.00
Custard Glass, Handle	7.00
Custard Glass, McKee, Loop Handle, c.1940, 3 ¼ In.	45.00
Depression Glass, Rose, 1930s	11.00
Glass, Cobalt Blue, Handle, Duboe, c.1970, 5 x 3 In.	38.00
Glass, Delphite Blue, Paneled, 2 Piece, 3 ½ In.	38.00
Glass, Easley's Pat. July 10, 1888, 4 x 2 ¾ In.	55.00
Glass, Footed, Cambridge, Pat. Jan 6, 1909	19.00
Glass, Green, Anchor Hocking	15.00
Glass, Green, Clear, Tab Handle, 4 ½ In. Diam.	18.00
Glass, Green, Footed, 2 Cup	30.00
Glass, Green, Loop Handle, 2 ½ In.	35.00
Glass, Jadite, Fire-King, 7 In.	35.00
Glass, Sunkist, Green, Embossed, 1920s	41.00
Glass, Vertical Ribbing, Seed Catcher, Clear, 5 In.	11.00
Lusterware, Figural, Duck, Green Head, Japan, Marked, 1940s, 3 ½ In.	155.00
Metal, Spout, Footed, Handle, Paul Revere	23.00
Milk Glass, Sunkist, Handle, Embossed, 8 ½ x 5 ¾ In.	8.00
Opalescent, Fry, c.1940, 2 ½ x 6 ½ In.	40.00
Porcelain, Child's Face, Red, Japan, 3 In.	165.00
Porcelain, Citrus Face, Handle, Japan, 1940s, 5 ¼ In.	210.00
Porcelain, Clown, Mikori Ware, Japan, 7 x 6 In.	92.00
Porcelain, Duck, Japan, 2 ½ In.	165.00
Porcelain, Figural, Puddinhead, Japan, 6 x 5 ½ In.	75.00
Porcelain, Flowers, Moriyama, Japan, 2 Piece	10.00
Porcelain, Flowers, White Ground, Gold Trim, 2 Piece, 1930s, 3 ¾ In.	50.00
Porcelain, Sad Clown, Jester Hearts, Bavaria, 5 ½ x 5 ½ In.	80.00
Pottery, Autumn Leaf, Hall, Tab Handle	250.00
Pottery, Hall, Silhouette, Taverne, Platinum Trim, Decals, 2 ⅜ x 6 ¼ In.	80.00
Pottery, Pitcher Style, Clown, Japan	35.00
Pressed Glass, Crisscross, Footed, 1950s, 2 ¼ In.	27.00
Vaseline Glass, Green, Handle	9.00

RECORDS have changed size and shape through the years. The cylinder-shaped phonograph record for use with the early Edison models was made about 1889. Disc records were first made by 1894, the double-sided disc by 1904. High-fidelity records were first issued in 1944, the first vinyl disc in 1946, the first stereo record in 1958. The 78 RPM became the standard in 1926 but was discontinued in 1957. In 1932, the first 33 ⅓ RPM was made but was not sold commercially until 1948. In 1949, the 45 RPM was introduced. Compact discs became available in the U.S. in 1982 and many companies began phasing out the production of phonograph records.

Basin Street & Sugar Blues, Vogue Picture Record, Detroit, Mich., 78 RPM, c.1946, 10 In.	65.00

Beatles, Ain't She Sweet, Nobody's Child, 45 RPM, Atco, 1964	225.00
Beatles, Yellow Submarine, Eleanor Rigby, 45 RPM, Capitol, 1966	75.00
Bob Dylan, Freewheelin' Bob Dylan, Folk Album, Mono LP, 1963	60.00
Bob Dylan, Highway 61 Revisited, Folk Album, Columbia, Mono LP, 1965	60.00
Count Basie, Basie In London, Jazz Album, Verve Record, Hi-Fi Mono, 1957	40.00
David Allen Narrator, Little Red Riding Hood, Colet Lithograph Cover, 78 RPM, 1947	75.00
Dolly Parton, Heartbreaker, Country, RCA, Vinyl LP, 1978	20.00
Fisherman & The Genie, Treasure Tales For Children, Picture Tone Record, Cardboard	36.00
Gene Autry, South Of The Border, Cowboy Songs, Bulldog Label, c.1960	22.00
Gertie Narrator, E.T. Record, Read-A-Long Book, Buena Vista Record, Universal City, 1982	12.00
Harry Bellafonte, Best Of Bellafonte, RCA Victor Record, 7 LPS, 1956	35.00
Harry James, The Mellow Horn, 2 Records, Pickwick Record, LP, c.1970	20.00
Liberace, Photo, Turquoise Ground, Pop Album, 33 ⅓ RPM, 1979	29.00
Mel Blanc Narrator, Bugs Bunny & The Tortoise, 25 Page Book, 78 RPM	25.00
Otis Redding, Live In Europe, Volt Record, Stereo LP, 1967	40.00
Prince, U Got The Look, Paisley Park Record, 45 RPM, 1987	8.00
Ronald McDonald Alphabet, Talking Book, Kid Stuff Record, 45 RPM, 1980s	20.00

RED WING POTTERY of Red Wing, Minnesota, was a firm started in 1878. The company first made utilitarian pottery, including stoneware jugs and canning jars. In the 1920s art pottery was introduced. Many dinner sets and vases were made before the company closed in 1967. Rumrill pottery made by the Red Wing Pottery for George Rumrill is listed in its own category. For more prices, go to kovels.com.

Advertising, Crock, Lid, Metal Handles, Red Wing Union Stoneware, c.1915, 4 Gal.	198.00
Advertising, Jug, 3 Orphans Saloon, Bristol Glaze, Higgins Aske Co., Moorhead, Minn.	1955.00
Advertising, Jug, Petty's Tonic, Hog Remedy, Stamped, Bristol Glaze, Sioux City, Iowa, 2 Gal.	1725.00
Ash Receiver, Donkey, Aqua, 3 In.	107.00
Beige Fleck, Platter, 12 ½ In.	24.00
Beige Fleck, Relish, 5 Sections, 12 ½ In.	32.00
Blue Shadows, Cup & Saucer	15.00
Blue Shadows, Plate, Dinner, 10 ⅜ In.	12.00
Bob White, Casserole, Lid, 1 Qt.	50.00
Bob White, Casserole, Lid, 4 Qt.	100.00
Bob White, Creamer, 7 ¼ In.	20.00
Bob White, Pitcher, Spout, Lid, 15 In.	90.00
Bob White, Plate, Bread & Butter, 6 In.	8.00
Bob White, Relish, 3 Sections	30.00
Bob White, Salt & Pepper	35.00
Brittany, Plate, Bread & Butter, 6 In.	9.00
Brittany, Plate, Salad, 7 ¼ In.	12.00
Centerpiece, Bronzed Deer Flower Frog, Turquoise & Bronze Bowl, 10 x 13 In.	50.00
Churn, Cobalt Blue 3, Birch Leaf, Table Relishes, Mennig & Slater, 3 Gal. ....*illus*	1955.00
Cookie Jar, Dancing Peasants, Flowers, 10 In.	85.00
Damask, Plate, Dinner, 10 ⅜ In.	10.00
Lotus Bronze, Cup & Saucer	12.00
Lotus Bronze, Plate, Dinner, 10 ⅜ In.	8.00
Lotus Bronze, Soup, Dish, Squared	10.00
Stoneware, Jug, Beehive, Gal.	19.00
Stoneware, Jug, Presentation, Van Deuson, Wreath, Doves, Olive Branch, Anchor, Shepard, Sun, 12 In.	17250.00
Stoneware, Water Cooler, Spigot, Lid, 9 ½ x 14 In.	330.00
Vase, Egyptian Style, Green, White, Marked, c.1920, 12 In.	145.00
Vase, Nokomis, 2 Wide Handles, Squat, Narrow Neck, Round Foot, Green, Brown Glaze, 8 In.	460.00
Vase, Ribbon, Tan, Green, Marked, c.1955, 7 In.	40.00

REDWARE is a hard, red stoneware that originated in the late 1600s and continues to be made. The term is also used to describe any common clay pottery that is reddish in color.

Bank, 2 Incised Shoulder Lines, Round, Pennsylvania, 1800s, 3 In.	474.00
Bank, Bulbous, Green Mottled Design, Penn., 1800s, 4 In., Pair	4740.00
Bank, Dog Finial, Penn., 1800s, 7 In.	2015.00
Bank, Hen On Nest, Inscribed Save A Penny Today Have Money Some Day, 4 ¾ In.	474.00
Bank, Hen, Chick, Glazed, Incised, Penn., 1800s, 5 x 6 ¾ In.	575.00
Bank, Jug Shape, Manganese Streaks, Pennsylvania, 1800s, 5 In.	889.00
Bank, Round, Yellow, Green Slip, Penn., 1800s, 2 ½ In.	1778.00
Bank, Spire Finial, Round Center, Pedestal Spread Foot, Terra-Cotta Speckled Glaze, 8 In.	805.00

Quezal, Lamp, 4-Light, Metal Fixture, White Iridescent Shades, 17 In.
$2489.00

Skinner, Inc.

Quezal, Vase, Jack-In-The-Pulpit, Gold Iridescent, Green Pulled Hooked Feathers, Scalloped Rim, 11 In.
$6613.00

Early Auction Co.

R

Quezal, Vase, Silver Overlay, Gold Iridescent, Art Nouveau Flowers, Leaves, Signed, 5 ½ In.
$1035.00

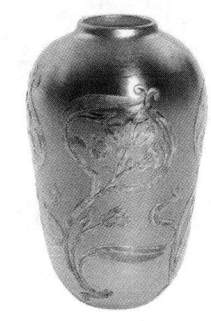

Early Auction Co.

Quilt, Appliqued, Coxcomb, Sawtooth
Borders Cotton, Muslin Back, c.1925,
79 x 79 ½ In.
$470.00

Garth's Auctions, Inc.

Quilt, Crazy, Embroidered, Silk, Velvet,
Hand Painted, c.1900, 65 ½ x 56 ½ In.
$143.00

Sloans & Kenyon

Quilt, Patchwork, Appliqued, Flowers,
12 Block, Sawtooth Border, c.1885,
79 x 89 In.
$331.00

Garth's Auctions, Inc.

Quilt, Patchwork, Appliqued, Mariner's
Compass, Flower, Vine Border, 1800s,
84 x 84 In.
$264.00

Cowan's Auctions

Item	Price
Basket, Rope Twist Handle, Penn., 1800s, 4 x 6 In.	830.00
Batter Pitcher, Slip Glaze, Green, Orange, Cream, Strap Handle, Boston Merchant's Stamp, 7 ¼ In.	2300.00
Batter Pitcher, Sponged Manganese, Glazed, Applied Strap, 1800s, 7 In.	259.00
Bean Pot, Sponged Manganese, 19th Century, 6 ½ In.	147.00
Bottle, Manganese Dots, Stamped J.S. Henne, Penn., c.1850, 9 In.	1304.00
Bowl, Bread, Slip Wave, Branch Design, Cobbled Rim, 3 x 7 ½ In.	936.00
Bowl, Circle, Dot Slip, Yellow, 1800s, 8 ⅞ In.	2844.00
Bowl, Incised American Eagle, Tulips, I.S. Stahl 1947, 10 ¼ In.	1304.00
Bowl, Loaf, Yellow Slip, Pennsylvania, 1800s, 8 x 12 In.	889.00
Bowl, Mottled Slip Glaze, Footed, 1823, 4 ¼ x 6 In.	89.00
Bowl, Multicolor Flower Slip, Brown, Red, Green, Dutch, 1700s, 2 ¾ x 11 ¾ In.	316.00
Bowl, Sgraffito, I.S. Stahl, 2 ½ x 8 ¼ In.	356.00
Bowl, Slip Glaze, 2 x 6 ½ In.	115.00
Bowl, Tub Shape, 2 Manganese Bands, Handles, 1800s, 6 x 10 In.	830.00
Bowl, White, Green Slip Bands, Manganese Splotched Interior, 2 ½ x 8 ¼ In.	889.00
Bowl, Yellow Circle, Wavy Slip Bands, c.1810, 2 ¾ x 11 ½ In.	474.00
Bowl, Yellow Slip Star, Shallow, Moravian, 1800s, 9 ½ In.	2015.00
Bowl, Yellow, Brown Slip Lattice, Penn., 1800s, 11 In.	296.00
Charger, 2 Men In Sword Fight, 1714, Tulip & Vine Border, Incised, Tin Glaze, 16 In.	1750.00
Charger, Bird, Tulips, Leaves, Scraffito, Henry Roudebush, c.1810, 13 ¾ In.	18960.00
Charger, Brown, Green Slip Flowers, Cream Glaze Ground, c.1810, 3 ¼ x 15 ½ In.	1610.00
Charger, Compass Star, Amber Slip Glaze, Black, Green, Sgraffito, Breininger, 12 ½ In.	212.00
Charger, Peacock, Tulip, Verse, Scraffito, Signed, George Hubener, 1792, 14 In.	1541.00
Charger, Tulip, Pinwheel Flower, Squiggle Border, Dots, Sgraffito, Penn., c.1800, 13 ¾ In.	4266.00
Charger, Tulips, Circles, Green, Yellow Slip, John Leidy, Bucks County, c.1800, 13 ½ In.	10073.00
Charger, Yellow Glaze, Green Spots, Swag Rim, Flowers, Leaves, Breininger, 15 ½ In.	130.00
Charger, Yellow Loop Slip, 1800s, 12 In.	711.00
Charger, Yellow Radiating Star Slip, Penn., 1800s, 13 In.	516.00
Charger, Yellow Slip Ground, Sgraffito Flower Heads, Green Leaves, Coggle Rim, 12 ¾ In.	177.00
Charger, Yellow Slip Horse, Jacob Medinger, Penn., 12 ¾ In.	830.00
Charger, Yellow Slip Tulip, Dots, Penn., 1800s, 11 ½ In.	652.00
Charger, Yellow Slip, 1800s, 11 In.	326.00
Charger, Yellow Slip, Inscribed Charlotte, Penn., 1800s, 12 ¼ In.	1541.00
Charger, Yellow Slip, Penn., 11 ½ In.	1422.00
Charger, Yellow, Green, Black, Slip Tulip, Penn., 13 ¼ In.	1422.00
Chimney Flue Liner, Cylindrical, Tooled Base, Flattened Rim, John W. Bell, c.1880, 10 ¾ In.	115.00
Colander, Glazed, Ribbed Handles, Punched Drain Holes, 3-Footed, 1800s, 8 In.	489.00
Colander, Pail Shape, Lead Glaze, Rounded Rim, Incised Band, Drain Holes, 5 x 7 ½ In.	316.00
Creamer, Green Mottled, Brown, Cream Glaze, Shenandoah Valley, 1800s, 3 ⅞ In.	1541.00
Creamer, Manganese Design, 1800s, 3 ¼ In.	563.00
Crock, Blue Glaze, Rolled Rim, Incised Lines, Flared Foot, Stahl, 4 ½ In.	170.00
Crock, George Washington Bust, U.S. Seal, Painted, 12 ¼ In.	326.00
Crock, Green Glaze, Manganese Splash, 4 ⅞ In.	2844.00
Crock, Lid, Brown Mottled Glaze, Penn., 1800s, 7 In.	563.00
Crock, Oval, Manganese Splash Design, Lug Handles, New England, c.1820, 11 ½ In.	356.00
Crock, Oval, Manganese Splotch Design, Everted Base Rim, Crescent Handles, 9 ¾ x 7 ½ In.	920.00
Crock, Spotted Flowers, Yellow Brown, Handles, 6 ½ In.	2015.00
Crock, Tulip, Emerging From Heart, Stars, Dots, Solomon Grimm, Marked 1816, 9 ½ In.	37920.00
Crock, Yellow Mottled, Green, Brown, 7 ¼ In.	1659.00
Cup, Blue, Green Designs, Mottled, Henry Varnum Poor, 1958, 3 ¼ In.	434.00
Cuspidor, Hexagonal, Manganese Glaze, Molded, Footed Base, P. Sipe, Lewisbery, 2 ¾ x 4 ½ In.	1380.00
Cuspidor, Marked Willoughby Smith, Penn., c.1900, 3 ½ x 7 In.	504.00
Custard Cup, Green Glaze Interior, Incised Lines, Stahl, 1941, 2 ½ In.	23.00
Dish, Salt Glaze Slip, Tulips, Yellow, Green Borders Rings, Manganese Spatter, Breininger, 11 In.	106.00
Dish, Yellow Serpentine Slip Design, Coggled Rim, Early 1800s, 9 In. Diam.	296.00
Dish, Yellow Slip Ground, Heart, Flowers, Tulip, Incised, Drip Edge Rim, 9 ¼ In.	12.00
Eggcup, Multiglaze, Stepped Pedestal, Strasburg, Va., c.1890, 3 ¼ In.	345.00
Figurine, Bird, Whistle, Red & Yellow Mottled, Flared Round Base, c.1855, 6 x 5 ¾ In.	115.00
Figurine, Cat, Sitting, Green Glaze, Stahl, 1950, 4 In.	192.00
Figurine, Dog, Curled Tail, 19th Century, 3 ¾ In.	7110.00
Figurine, Dog, Resting, Base, Paint, Inscribed Towser, 1800s, 4 ½ x 7 In.	2252.00
Figurine, Dog, Seated, Fruit Basket In Mouth, Brown, Orange, 4 ¾ In.	17775.00
Figurine, Dog, Seated, Green Gold Lead Glaze, Orange Accents, 10 x 7 In. .... *illus*	1265.00
Figurine, Dog, Seated, Incised Flower Base, 1800s, 8 In.	6518.00
Figurine, Dog, Seated, Incised Flowers, Oval Base, Penn., 5 ¼ In.	1067.00
Figurine, Dog, Spaniel, Green Glaze, 1800s, 6 ½ In., Pair	593.00

Figurine, Dog, Spaniel, Signed EM 1861, Penn., 10 In.	1896.00
Figurine, Dog, Standing, Basket In Mouth, Bell Pottery, Penn., 1800s, 9 ⅞ In.	23700.00
Figurine, Dog, Standing, Oval Incised Flower Base, 4 x 3 ¾ In.	830.00
Figurine, Goose, 1800s, 2 ¼ In.	948.00
Figurine, Lion, Standing, Oval Base, c.1870, 5 ¾ x 9 In.	2370.00
Figurine, Mother, Child, Glazed, Penn., c.1890, 4 ¾ In.	316.00
Figurine, Stag, Standing, Incised Flowers, Oval Base, Penn., 6 ½ In.	1422.00
Flowerpot, Attached Tray, Brown Mottled, Red, Shenandoah, 1800s, 9 x 8 In.	770.00
Flowerpot, Oval, Applied Decoration, Pedestal Base, Myrtle E. Bell, 1874, 6 ½ In., 2 Piece	4830.00
Flowerpot, Underplate, Scalloped Rim, c.1895, 2 ¼ In.	563.00
Flowerpot, Undertray Attached, Red, Green, White Mottling, Shenandoah, 6 x 6 In.	593.00
House, Incised Bricks, Shingles, 2 Chimneys, Glazed, 7 x 5 ¾ x 8 ¾ In.	6900.00
Humidor, Acorn Shape, 3-Footed Sawed Log Base, Painted, c.1890, 6 ½ In.	403.00
Jar, Canister Shape, Coggle Design, Rows, Brown Glaze, Splotch Manganese, 8 x 5 ½ In.	460.00
Jar, Canister Shape, Manganese Drip, Mottled, Olive To Cream Glaze, 7 ¾ x 4 ¼ In.	518.00
Jar, Canister Shape, Manganese Splotch Design, Golden Brown, 8 x 5 In.	633.00
Jar, Cover, Incised Squiggle Waist Band, Inscribed S.B., Sept 9th 1840, Penn., 4 ½ In.	770.00
Jar, Cover, Lead Glaze, Manganese Splotches, Flared Collar, Tab Handles, 11 ½ In.	748.00
Jar, Cream, Lead Glaze, Oval, Stamped V. Rudolph, Shippensburg, Pa., c.1875, 7 ¼ In.	173.00
Jar, Cream, Splashed Manganese, Green, Yellow, Orange, Lead Glaze, 4 In.	173.00
Jar, Cream, Tan, Arches, Dots, Lug Handles, North Carolina, c.1850, 6 In.	2530.00
Jar, Cylindrical, Manganese Splotches, Red, Brown, Flared Rim, Incised Lines, 10 ½ x 7 In.	460.00
Jar, Cylindrical, Manganese Sponging, Olive, Orange Spots, Tooled Foot, 10 ¼ In.	1610.00
Jar, Flared Mouth, Incised Lines, 9 x 6 In.	11.00
Jar, Lobed Body, Manganese Splash, Rope Twist Handle, 1800s, 5 In.	711.00
Jar, Manganese Splash, Lug Handles, Mass., c.1830, 13 In.	1422.00
Jar, Oval, 2 Incised Wavy Lines, Brown Splotches, Lug Handles, Early 1800s, 13 In.	1185.00
Jar, Oval, Glazed, Handles, Heart & Croft, c.1870, 5 In.	920.00
Jar, Oval, Shaped Rim, Light Olive Green Glaze, Orange Halos, 1800s, 10 In.	533.00
Jar, Storage, Lid, Bulbous, Green On Yellow Slip, Manganese Strokes, Flared Rim, Footed, 7 ½ In.	59.00
Jar, Storage, Straight-Sided, Shouldered Mouth & Incised Rope Line, 6 In.	24.00
Jar, Swollen Shape, Green Glaze, Tan Streaks, Flared Rim, Maine, 7 ¾ x 4 In.	322.00
Jar, Tooled Shoulder, Rounded Rim, Olive, Orange Mottled, Lead Glaze, Gonic, N.H., 4 ¼ In.	201.00
Jar, Vase Shape, Green, Copper Glaze, Tooled Shoulder, Ribbed Open Handles, 8 ½ In.	690.00
Jug, Brown Mottled, Tan Glazes, John Bell, Waynesboro, Pennsylvania, c.1860, 12 In.	2223.00
Jug, Green Mottled, Orange Glaze, Stamped J.S. Henne, c.1860, 10 ½ In.	1458.00
Jug, Manganese Splash Design, Penn., 2 ⅝ In.	1541.00
Jug, Oval, Green, Orange, Manganese Glaze, Rounded Foot, Ribbed Handle, 8 ½ In.	2875.00
Jug, Oval, Incised Design, Green, Orange Mottled Glaze, Flared Spout, Handle, 8 ¾ x 6 In.	403.00
Jug, Oval, Moon, Yellow Glaze, 8 Decorations, Applied Strap Handle, 2 Gal.	748.00
Jug, Puzzle, Pierced Rectangles, Circles, Tall Collar, c.1810, 5 In.	690.00
Jug, Yellow, Green Splotch, New England, 1843, 11 ½ In.	1185.00
Loaf Pan, Birds, Tulips, Pinwheel, Sgraffito, Penn., c.1810, 15 ¾ x 11 In.	4977.00
Loaf Pan, Green, Cream, Brown, Orange, Marbled Glaze, Goggled Edge, 15 In.	489.00
Loaf Pan, Yellow Ground, Incised, Serrated Edge Scallops, Green Slip, Flowers, 7 x 6 In.	47.00
Loaf Pan, Yellow Slip Design, Penn., 1800s, 10 x 16 In.	770.00
Loaf Pan, Yellow Waves & Ferns, Orange Red Glaze, 15 x 11 In.	1053.00
Loaf Pan, Yellow Wavy Line Design, 11 x 16 ½ In.	3318.00
Mug, Barrel Shape, Brown, Loop Handle, c.1735, 6 In.	178.00
Mug, Manganese Speckles, Salt Glaze Interior, Yellow Slip, Incised Stars, Becky Mummert, 3 ½ In.	12.00
Mug, Manganese Vertical Stripes, 1800s, 3 ¾ In.	830.00
Mug, Yellow Squiggle Design, Loop Handle, Date 1805 In Yellow Slip, 5 x 5 In.	863.00
Pie Plate, Coggled Rim, Brown Glaze, 3-Line Slip Waves, 8 ¾ In.	266.00
Pie Plate, Green Wavy Lines, Penn., 1800s, 7 ¼ In.	1007.00
Pie Plate, Heart, Smiley Face, Penn., 1800s, 8 In.	3081.00
Pie Plate, Slip Glaze, Eagle, Liberty In Banner, Olive Branches, Stars, Coggled Rim, 1800s, 8 In. *illus*	1955.00
Pie Plate, Wavy Yellow Slip, Coggled Rim, 8 In.	264.00
Pie Plate, Yellow Clef, 1800s, 9 ¾ In.	948.00
Pie Plate, Yellow Slip Wavy Line, Pennsylvania, 1800s, 8 In., Pair	504.00
Pie Plate, Yellow Slip, 1800s, Pa., 8 In.	119.00
Pitcher, Flared Rim, Loop Handle, Pinched Spout, Footed, 6 ¾ In.	136.00
Pitcher, Green & White, Footed, 19th Century, 7 ½ In.	382.00
Pitcher, Incised Rings, Green Mottled Glaze, 19th Century, 7 In.	940.00
Pitcher, Manganese, Flared Rim, Pulled Spout, Applied Loop Handle, Footed, 6 ¾ In.	59.00
Pitcher, Milk, Olive Green, Manganese Splotch, Turned Out Rim, Shaped Spout, Side Handle, 4 x 5 In.	403.00
Pitcher, Milk, Pear Shape, Green Mottled Glaze, Shaped Spout, Strap Handle, 7 x 5 In.	1783.00

Quilt, Patchwork, Diamond In Square, Red & Yellow, Bars, On Back, Cotton, 1900s, 75 x 75 In.
$470.00

Garth's Auctions, Inc.

Quilt, Patchwork, Lemoyne Star, Calico Border, Printed, Blue Back, Cotton, 85 x 84 In.
$295.00

Conestoga Auction Co., Inc.

Quilt, Patchwork, Log Cabin, Calico, Multicolor, Blue Back, Cotton, 82 x 80 In.
$142.00

Conestoga Auction Co., Inc.

Quilt, Ribbon, Grover Cleveland, U.S. Centennial, Indiana Commandery, c.1890, 77 x 78 In.
$570.00

Cowan's Auctions

Radio, Airline, Super Heterodyne, Cathedral, Tube, Counter, 1930s $224.00

Victorian Casino Antique Auction

Radio, Bluebird, Walter Dorwin Teague, Blue Glass, Chrome, Sparton, 1934, 14 ½ x 14 ½ In. $2500.00

Los Angeles Modern Auctions

TIP

Never wash vintage silk, satin, banners, flags, or embroideries. The delicate fabrics may fade or the colors may run and the lightweight fabrics wear out very quickly. Unglazed earthenware and terra-cotta, creamware, and other unglazed ceramics should not be washed. Never put them in the dishwasher, the heat will harm the clay body.

Pitcher, Orange, Cream Slip Stars, Brown Ground Glaze, c.1810, 10 ½ In.	3440.00
Pitcher, Oval, Multiglaze, Ribbed Handle, Flared Foot, Strasburg, Va., 6 ½ In.	1035.00
Pitcher, Paneled Sides, New Hampshire, 1800s, 4 ¾ In.	122.00
Pitcher, Putti, Mottled Glaze, Stamped John Bell, Waynesboro, Penn., 1800s, 10 In.	889.00
Pitcher, Squat, Oval, Glazed, William Washington Cline, Indiana, c.1906, 2 ¾ In.	403.00
Pitcher, Yellow Slip Lines, Flared Rim, Raised Foot, Applied Loop Handle, 5 In.	311.00
Pitcher, Yellow, Green Slip, Berks Co., Penn., c.1820, 7 ½ In.	2133.00
Plate, 3-Line Slip Waves, 1800s, 9 ½ In.	948.00
Plate, 3-Line Yellow Slip Waves, 1800s, 4 In.	444.00
Plate, 4-Line Yellow Wavy Slip, 1800s, 4 In.	1580.00
Plate, Flowers, Rim Blossoms, Swags, Brown, Green, Cream, N.C., c.1905, 11 In.	5750.00
Plate, Green, Yellow Slip, J. Henne, Penn., 1800s, 6 ¾ In.	4266.00
Plate, Incised Slip Star, c.1820, Penn., 10 ½ In.	474.00
Plate, Octagonal, Yellow, Black Squiggles, Herestine Pottery, Bucks Co., 1800s, 6 x 7 In.	2607.00
Plate, Safety Cyclists, Bushes, 13 In.	100.00
Plate, Slip Decorated, Leaves, Wavy Lines, Coggled Edge, 5 ½ x 7 ¾ In.	288.00
Plate, Tulip Center, Banded Swag Border, Tan, Cream, Brown, c.1800, 2 ¾ x 13 ¾ In.	4600.00
Plate, Yellow Line, Raised Rim, Impressed Willoughby Smith, c.1900, 8 In.	1185.00
Plate, Yellow Slip Sprig, Pennsylvania, 1800s, 4 In.	711.00
Plate, Yellow Slip Stripes, 1800s, 4 In.	3159.00
Plate, Yellow Slip, Dots, Squiggles, Coggle Rim, 10 ½ In.	130.00
Plate, Yellow Slip, Pennsylvania, 6 In.	652.00
Plate, Yellow Slip, Stamped Johnsonville, Penn., 6 ¾ In.	2133.00
Plate, Yellow, Green Slip Tulip, Diehl Pottery, 1800s, 8 ½ In.	8888.00
Plate, Yellow, Green Sprig Slip, 4 ¼ In.	4029.00
Pot, Bulbous, Hens & Chickens, Manganese Glaze, Penn., 9 ¼ In.	593.00
Rattle, Goose, Seated, Oval Base, Pennsylvania, 1800s, 2 In.	326.00
Rundlet, Semi-Oval, Yellow Green Ground, Orange, Lead Glaze, Tooled Bands, Bung Hole, c.1825	345.00
Sugar, Cover, Dots, Yellow, Black Slip, 4 ½ In.	8295.00
Sugar, Cover, Yellow, Black Slip Dots, Penn., c.1820, 4 ½ x 4 ½ In.	8295.00
Urn, Cover, Ring Handles, 1800s, 8 In.	207.00
Urn, Lined Shoulder, Applied Strap Handles, Marked, 14 In.	107.00
Urn, Medallion, Putti, Seated On Lion's Head Handles, Round Base, c.1875, 33 In.	2963.00
Vase, Bulbous, Turquoise Glaze, Side Rings, Collar Neck, c.1950, 8 ½ In., Pair	420.00
Vase, Bulbous, Yellow Slip Ground, Manganese, Green Drip, Footed, Marked, 8 In.	24.00
Vase, Face, Man With Moustache & Unibrow, Ears, Crimped Rim, c.1900, 6 ½ In.	288.00
Vase, Incised Eagle, Handles, Jacob Medinger, Penn., c.1900, 6 In.	2370.00
Vase, Manganese Splash, Yellow Ground, Impressed AB, Penn., 1827, 7 ¾ In.	1896.00
Vase, Pear Shape Bottom, Clay Color, Dragon, Gilt Accents, Bottle Neck, Japan, 12 In.	115.00
Vase, Round, Squat, Incised Design Top Band, Signed, Pearl Talachy, New Mexico, 3 ½ x 4 In.	138.00
Wall Pocket, Basket, Yellow Slip, Manganese Splash, 6 ⅞ x 6 ¾ In.	4977.00
Wall Pocket, Glazed, Tooled Bands, Pointed Finial, Splashed Manganese, 8 In.	288.00
Waterer, Bulbous, 2 Handles, Smokestack Base, Finial, 1800s, 22 In.	89.00
Well Post, Slip Inscribed, John Ing May Town, Penn., 1835, 15 In.	1659.00
Whistle, Bird-On-Pot, Spread Wings, Oval Jar, Glazed, Ohio, c.1855, 2 ¼ x 2 ¾ In.	518.00
Whistle, Rooster, Penn., 1800s, 4 In.	1304.00

REGOUT, *see Maastricht category.*

RICHARD was the mark used on acid-etched cameo glass vases, bowls, night-lights, and lamps made by the Austrian company Loetz after 1918. The pieces were very similar to the French cameo glasswares made by Daum, Galle, and others.

Vase, Brown Leaves & Buds, Green Ground, Pinched Mouth, Signed, 3 ½ In. ....*illus*	368.00
Vase, Orange, Red Flowering Branch, Stems, Footed, Swollen, Flared Rim, Cameo, Signed, 7 In.	230.00

RIDGWAY pottery has been made in the Staffordshire district in England since 1808 by a series of companies with the name Ridgway. Ridgway became part of Royal Doulton in the 1960s. The transfer-design dinner sets are the most widely known product. Other pieces of Ridgway may be listed under Flow Blue.

Eggcup, Double, Buildings, Transfer, c.1900, 3 ½ In.	35.00
Plate, City Hall, New York, Flower Border, Blue Transfer, Beauties Of America, 9 ¾ In. ...*illus*	106.00
Plate, Giraffe Pattern, Blue & White Transfer, Shaped Rim, 10 In.	236.00

RIFLES *that are firearms are not listed in this book. BB guns and air rifles are listed in the Toy category.*

RIVIERA dinnerware was made by the Homer Laughlin Co. of Newell, West Virginia, from 1938 to 1950. The pattern was similar in coloring and in mood to Fiesta and Harlequin. The Riviera plates and cup handles were square. For more prices, go to kovels.com.

Green, Casserole, Cover	45.00
Green, Casserole, Cover, 8 ¾ x 7 In.	46.00
Mauve Blue, Platter, Meat	23.00
Mauve Blue, Sugar, Cover	19.00
Orange, Plate, Luncheon	15.00
Red, Gravy Boat	26.00
Red, Sugar & Creamer	56.00
Turquoise, Butter, Cover	115.00
Yellow, Platter	20.00
Yellow, Salt & Pepper	20.00

ROCKINGHAM, in the United States, is a pottery with a brown glaze that resembles tortoiseshell. It was made from 1840 to 1900 by many American potteries. Mottled brown Rockingham wares were first made in England at the Rockingham factory. Other types of ceramics were also made by the English firm. Related pieces may be listed in the Bennington category.

Bank, Spaniel, 1800s, 2 ½ x 3 ¼ In.	178.00
Bowl, Glaze, Flared Rim, Footed, 3 ¼ x 7 ½ In.	24.00
Bowl, Keeler, Molded Staves, Hoops, Tab Handles, Mottled Brown, 4 ½ x 7 ½ In.	184.00
Bowl, Nesting, Mottled Brown, Flared Rim, Oval, c.1850, 3 Piece	138.00
Candlestick, Mottled Brown, Molded Flowers, 5 x 3 ¼ In.	196.00
Cup, Shaving, Applied Plaques, Urn With Flowers, Greek Key Border, 4 ¼ In.	30.00
Figurine, Dog, Seated, Glazed, Domed, Gothic Arch, Base, 1800s, 12 In., Pair	325.00
Figurine, Dog, Spaniel, Seated, 10 ½ In.	243.00
Flask, Clenched Fist, Glazed, c.1850, 5 In.	119.00
Flask, Mermaid, Brown, Curled Tail, c.1850, 7 ½ x 4 In.	150.00
Flask, Shoe, Lacing, Mottled Brown, 6 ½ x 7 In.	92.00
Inkwell, Pen Holder, Sheep, Reclining, Oval Base, 1800s, 3 x 4 In.	214.00
Loving Cup, Applied Frog, 2 Handles, Smoking Figure, 1800s, 4 In.	115.00
Mixing Bowl, Mottled Brown, Banded Rim, Shallow Foot, c.1860, 7 ¼ x 15 ¼ In.	115.00
Mold, Mottled Brown, Daisies, Englert, 2 ⅜ x 6 ⅛ x 4 ¼ In. ....*illus*	47.00
Mug, Mottled Brown, Waisted, Strap Handle, c.1860, 4 ½ x 4 ¾ In.	184.00
Pie Pan, Mottled Brown, Slanted Side, c.1860, 1 ¾ x 12 ¼ In.	46.00
Pitcher, Blossoms, Griffins, Obelisk, c.1850, 9 In.	237.00
Pitcher, Corn Stalk, c.1850, 9 In.	83.00
Pitcher, Cupid & Psyche, Molded Design, Acanthus Leaf Spout, c.1850, 9 In.	59.00
Pitcher, Figural, Dog, Pug, Raised Letter S On Collar, Comrade, Edwin Bennett, Md., c.1854, 10 In.	102.00
Pitcher, Fireman, Pulling Hand Pumper, Relief Molded, 1800s, 9 In.	1126.00
Pitcher, Horseman, Dogs, Mottled Brown Glaze, Twig Handle, Frog On Bottom, 1800s, 9 In.	546.00
Pitcher, Hounds Chasing Stag, Grapevines, Spout Collar, Hound Handle, 10 ¼ In.	767.00
Pitcher, Hunting Scene, Stag & Boar, Grapevines, Wide Spout, Hound Handle, c.1848, 12 In.	245.00
Pitcher, James Garfield Silhouette, Relief Molded, 8 In.	600.00
Pitcher, Leaf Design, Brown Glaze, Lava Drip, 8-Sided, Marked, 5 ⅜ In.	490.00
Pitcher, Spaniel, Begging, Rust, Hat Shaped Spout, Lid, 1800s, 9 In.	115.00
Planter, Tree Stump, Cut Branch Openings, Incised, Glazed, c.1875, 25 ¼ In. ....*illus*	356.00
Shaving Mug, 12-Sided, Inset Soap Cup, Loop Handle, 3 ½ In.	90.00
Teapot, 8-Panel Body, Scrolling Leaves, Glazed, c.1875, 7 In.	178.00
Teapot, Ribbed, Squat, Reeded Pewter Spout, Acorn Finial, c.1870, 7 In.	296.00
Tobacco Jar, Barrel, Mottled Brown, Tortoiseshell, 5 x 4 ½ In.	45.00
Water Cooler, Columns, Figures, Instruments, Molded, 8-Sided, Distin Family On Band, 1850, 16 In.	3081.00

ROGERS, *see John Rogers category.*

ROOKWOOD pottery was made in Cincinnati, Ohio, from 1880 to 1960. All of this art pottery is marked, most with the famous flame mark. The *R* is reversed and placed back to back with the letter *P*. Flames surround the letters. After 1900, a Roman numeral was added to the mark to indicate the year. The company went bankrupt in 1941. For several years various owners tried to revive the pottery, but by 1967 it was out of business. The name and some of the molds were bought by a collector in 1984. In 2005, Christopher Rose and his brother, Patrick, bought the company and 3,700 original molds, the name, and trademark. Today they make architectural tile, art pottery, beer steins, bookends, and limited edition items.

Ashtray, Frog, Brown Matte Over Green Glaze, 3-Sided, 1926, 1 ¼ x 6 In.	115.00
Ashtray, Owl, Blue Matte Crystalline Glaze, 1931, 4 ⅛ In.	288.00

Red Wing, Churn, Cobalt Blue 3, Birch Leaf, Table Relishes, Mennig & Slater, 3 Gal.
$1955.00

Rock Island Auction Company

TIP
Don't use gummed labels on colored paint or gilding.

Redware, Figurine, Dog, Seated, Green Gold Lead Glaze, Orange Accents, 10 x 7 In.
$1265.00

Rock Island Auction Company

Redware, Pie Plate, Slip Glaze, Eagle, Liberty In Banner, Olive Branches, Stars, Coggled Rim, 1800s, 8 In.
$1955.00

James D. Julia Inc.

R

Richard, Vase, Brown Leaves & Buds, Green Ground, Pinched Mouth, Signed, 3 ½ In.
$368.00

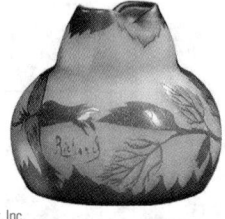

Skinner, Inc.

Ridgway, Plate, City Hall, New York, Flower Border, Blue Transfer, Beauties Of America, 9 ¾ In.
$106.00

Conestoga Auction Co., Inc.

Rockingham, Mold, Mottled Brown, Daisies, Englert, 2 ⅜ x 6 ⅛ x 4 ¼ In.
$47.00

Conestoga Auction Co., Inc.

Rockingham, Planter, Tree Stump, Cut Branch Openings, Incised, Glazed, c.1875, 25 ¼ In.
$356.00

Skinner, Inc.

Bookends, Owls, Golden Brown, Perched, Base, 1945	115.00
Bookends, Parrot, Blue, Pink, Green, Yellow Glaze, Wings Up, 1927, 7 ⅛ In.	3220.00
Bookends, Rook, Turquoise, Purple Glaze, 1946, 5 ½ x 5 ½ In.	165.00 to 180.00
Bookends, Tree, Coromandel Glaze, Red, Amber, Yellow, 1930, 5 ⅝ In.	690.00
Bowl, 2 Turtles, Green Matte Glaze, Footed, Wavy Rim, 1901, 5 In.	633.00
Bowl, Dragon, Green Matte Glaze, 1906, 3 In.	460.00
Bowl, Green Matte Glaze, Red Highlights, Squat, Rolled Rim, 3-Footed, 1913, 2 In.	92.00
Bowl, Green Matte Glaze, Squat, Round, 2 Handles, 1915, 2 x 7 In.	104.00
Bowl, Poppies, Red, Green Stem, Red Brown Glaze, Squat, Rolled Rim, 1903, 2 x 7 In.	374.00
Box, Green Ground, Flower Border, Hexagonal, Lid, 1928, 2 x 5 In.	546.00
Compote, Elephant Base, Green Interior, 1922, 11 x 16 In.	978.00
Compote, Ivory Glaze, Long Stem, 1915, 14 ¼ In.	196.00
Corbel, Cream Glaze, Scrolls, Leaves, 22 x 12 In., Pair	470.00
Ewer, 2 Crabs, Glossy Brown Glaze, Bulbous, Elongated Neck & Handle, 1884, 8 In.	368.00
Ewer, Butterflies, Orange, Gold Band, Stick Neck, Ruffled Rim, Loop Handle, 1886, 8 ½ In.	288.00
Ewer, Carnations, Standard Glaze, Clara Newton, 9 x 3 In.	341.00
Ewer, Clover, Green, Amber, Brown, Ruffled Rim, Loop Handle, 1898, 5 ½ In.	115.00
Ewer, Dragonfly, Blue, Flowers, Grass, Brown, Rust, Dull Finish, Loop Handle, 1884, 12 In.	3565.00
Ewer, Flowers, Leaves, Green, Amber, Yellow, Stick Neck, Ruffled Spout, 1890, 12 ⅞ In.	1093.00
Ewer, Flowers, Standard Glaze, Artus Van Briggle, 1892, 8 ½ In.	230.00
Ewer, Leaves, Green, Red, Orange, Long Neck, Ruffled Rim, 1899, 9 ⅝ In.	460.00
Ewer, Mahogany Glaze, Bulbous, Shaped Handle, 1888, 8 In.	207.00
Ewer, Oak Leaves, Orange, Amber, Brown, Ruffled Edge, 1899, 11 ¼ In.	518.00
Ewer, Orange, Gold, Round, Bottom, Stick Neck, Ruffled Rim, Loop Handle, 1886, 9 In.	345.00
Figurine, Ballerina, Ivory Matte Glaze, Round Pedestal Base, c.1934, 8 In.	805.00
Figurine, Cockatoo, Red Glaze, Green, Round Base, 1945, 9 ½ In.	173.00
Figurine, Pheasant, Multicolor, 1949, 8 ⅞ In.	288.00
Flower Frog, Pelican, Marked, 1925, 7 In.	36.00
Flower Frog, Turtle, Green Matte Glaze, Marked, 1930, 2 ¾ In.	300.00
Flower Holder, Dolphin, Cobalt Blue, Round Base, Wavy Rim, 1917, 3 x 5 In.	92.00
Fountain, Nude Woman, Seated, Frog, Green Matte Glaze, 26 ½ x 18 In.	6900.00
Frieze, Bacchus, Grapes, Leaves, Faience, 25 x 24 ½ In., Pair ....*illus*	1116.00
Ginger Jar, Cover, Cherry Blossoms, Birds, Blooms, Black Opal Glaze, 1925, 10 In.	2875.00
Grate, Openwork, Flowers In Urns, Scrolls, Mills Restaurant, c.1921, 42 x 22 In., 3 Piece	1645.00
Humidor, Pipes, Cigars, Matches, Standard Glaze, Harriet Wilcox, 1894, 6 x 5 ½ In.	150.00
Incense Burner, Butterfly, Morning Glory, Blue Matte, Reversible Lid, Matt Daly, 8 In. ..... *illus*	633.00
Jar, Cover, Pansies, Red, Yellow To Orange, 1885, 4 ¼ In.	690.00
Jar, Pink, 2 Covers, 1928, 4 In.	107.00
Jardiniere, Pomegranates, Leaves, Green, Yellow, Red, Squat, Flared Flattened Rim, 1889, 11 ¼ In.	1150.00
Jardiniere, Sea Green Glaze, Fluted, Round, 1926, 8 ½ In.	184.00
Jug, Aventurine Glaze, Urn Shape, Dragon Handle, Spout, 1926, 8 ¾ In.	259.00
Jug, Bird, Grasses, Tan Ground, Gold Trim, Oval, Flattened Sides, 4 ⅜ In.	276.00
Jug, Birds, Grasses, Limoges Glaze, Handle, 1883, 3 ½ x 4 ¾ In.	330.00
Jug, Geometric Pattern, Incised, Brown Matte Glaze, Square, Garlic Mouth, 1901, 7 ½ In.	345.00
Jug, Portrait, Man, Standard Glaze, Harriette R. Strafer, c.1895, 7 In.	413.00
Lamp, Flowers, Raised, Mottled Glaze, 4-Footed, 29 ½ In.	177.00
Match Holder, Devil Face, Green Over Rose Matte Glaze, Oval, 1880s, 2 ¼ x 4 ½ In.	748.00
Mug, Ben Johnson, African-American Boy, Standard Glaze, Olga Reed, 1899, 5 In.	853.00
Mug, Berry, Leaves, Green, Standard Glaze, Sadie Markland, 1895, 4 x 6 In.	173.00
Mug, Cherries, Standard Glaze, Applied Handle, Caroline F. Steinle, c.1900, 6 In.	413.00
Mug, Fish, Carved, Green Matte Glaze, 3 Handles, Sallie Toohey, 1905, 7 x 9 In.	1860.00
Mug, Lion, Standard Glaze, E.T. Hurley, 1899, 5 ½ x 4 ¾ In.	372.00
Mug, Monk, Drinking Beer, Standard Glaze, Bruce Horsfall, 1895, 5 ½ x 5 In.	440.00
Mug, Monkey, Clothed, Holding Mug Of Beer, Green Standard Glaze, 1892, 5 x 4 ¾ In.	825.00
Mug, Standing Buffalo, Ponca, Native American, Standard Glaze, S. Lawrence, 1898, 5 In.	1200.00
Panel, Copper, Embossed, Fish, Crab, Jeweled Eyes, Rectangular, c.1915, 18 x 11 In.	3525.00
Panel, Copper, Embossed, Fish, Sea Creatures, Jeweled Eyes, Frame, c.1913, 19 x 18 In.	6463.00
Paperweight, Bird, White Opal Glaze, Base, 1936	288.00
Paperweight, Blackbird, Glancing Downward, Rectangular Base, Purple Matte Glaze, 1921, 2 ⅞ In.	316.00
Paperweight, Cat, Chestnut Brown Matte Glaze, 1930, 6 ¾ In.	690.00
Paperweight, Cat, Seated, Ivory Matte Glaze, 1946, 6 ⅝ In.	575.00
Paperweight, Chimpanzee, Seated, Blue Matte Glaze, 1929, 4 ¼ x 4 In.	270.00
Paperweight, Gazelle, Burnt Orange Matte Glaze, Standing, Rectangular Base, 1930, 6 In.	345.00
Paperweight, Rabbit, Seated, Ears Straight Up, Ivory Matte Glaze, 1965, 3 In.	207.00
Paperweight, Rooster, Mottled Gray Glaze, Square Base, 1958, 5 In.	316.00
Paperweight, Shell Shape, Faience, 4 ½ x 2 In.	56.00

R

Paperweight, Turtle, Blue Matte Glaze, 1921, 2 ¼ In.	575.00
Pencil Holder, Rooks, Pale Blue Matte Glaze, Square, 1945, 4 ⅝ In.	184.00
Pitcher, Bees, Grass, Mottled Blue Green & White Ground, Albert Valentien, 1883, 8 In.	415.00
Pitcher, Blue Matte Glaze, Pear Shape, Footed, Loop Handle, 1965, 9 In.	115.00
Pitcher, Cherries, Standard Glaze, Tricorn Rim, Mae Timberlake, 6 x 7 In.	270.00
Pitcher, Flowers, Bird, Fish, White, Rust, Baluster, Loop Handle, 1943, 9 In.	978.00
Pitcher, Geisha, Standard Glaze, Teardrop Shape, Ruffled Rim, c.1891, 13 In.	1314.00
Pitcher, Gremlins, Tapping Liquor Barrel, Drinking, Brown, Orange, Handle, 1894, 9 ¼ In.	4600.00
Pitcher, Iris, Brown Standard Glaze, Anna Marie Valentien, 8 ½ x 4 In.	403.00
Pitcher, Jellyfish, Sea Urchin, Yellow, Green, Standard Glaze, Ribbed, 1886, 8 ½ In.	403.00
Planter, Papyrus Leaves, Embossed, Dark Blue Glaze, 4 x 8 In.	45.00
Plaque, Along The Shore, Vellum Glaze, Label, Sallie Coyne, Frame, 1920, 9 x 12 In.	2604.00
Plaque, Close Of Day, Venice, Sailboats, Water, Carl Schmidt, Frame, 1916, 9 x 14 ½ In.	6200.00
Plaque, Landscape, Edge Of The Woods, Fred Rothenbusch, Frame, 1921, 12 ½ x 10 ½ In.	3080.00
Plaque, Landscape, Edge Of The Woods, Vellum Glaze, Fred Rothenbusch, 1921, 8 x 6 In.	3360.00
Plaque, Landscape, Late Autumn, Vellum Glaze, F. Rothenbusch, Frame, 1915, 14 x 10 In.	2640.00
Plaque, Landscape, Vellum Glaze, F. Rothenbusch, 1917, 20 x 17 In.	3900.00
Plaque, Landscape, Water Scene, Vellum Glaze, Green, Ed. Diers, Frame, 1919, 8 ½ x 11 In.	3348.00
Plaque, Scenic, Harbor, Sailboats, Vellum Glaze, E.T. Hurley, Frame, 1945, 9 x 12 In. ....*illus*	5405.00
Plaque, Scenic, Snow Covered Mountain, Vellum Glaze, Sara Sax, Frame, 1912, 10 ¾ x 13 In.	1736.00
Sign, Dealer, Tan High Glaze, Rectangular, Scroll, 3 ¾ x 13 In.	1035.00
Teapot, Crocus, Blue & Yellow, Standard Glaze, Squat, 1899, 5 ⅛ In.	288.00
Tile, Abstract Design, Pink, Green, Brown, Faience, Oak Frame, 6 ½ x 6 ½ In.	168.00
Tile, Flower In Pot, Faience, Oak Frame, 9 x 9 In.	189.00
Tile, Flowers, Pink, Green, Faience, Dard Hunter, Frame, 9 ¼ In.	134.00
Tile, Herschede Clock Co., 3 Molded Clocks, Round, Light Blue Glaze, 6 In.	79.00
Tile, Jardinere On Pedestal, Green, Tan, Faience, Wood Frame, 8 ¾ x 10 ¼ In.	146.00
Tile, Lion Crest, Green, Pink Matte Glaze, 9 In.	390.00
Tile, Sailing Ship, Shell Corners, Tan, Blue, Brown, Faience, 12 x 12 In.	1200.00
Tile, Ship, Shell, Blue, Green, Tan, Faience, Marked, 12 In.	1100.00
Tile, Wreath, Faience, Frame, 9 x 9 In.	224.00
Tray, Flowers, Yellow Matte Glaze, Blue Highlights, Rectangular, 1903, 3 x 13 In.	288.00
Tray, Rook, Ivory High Glaze, 1946, 7 ¾ x 4 In.	180.00
Trivet, Crown Prince, Frog Wearing Crown, Green, Cream, Brown, 1915, 4 In.	431.00
Trivet, Grapes, Purple, Green Leaves, Blue Border, 1927, 6 x 6 In.	90.00
Trivet, Grapevine, Brown Glaze, c.1950, 6 In.	56.00
Trivet, Parrot, Pink, Yellow, Light Blue, Square, 1925, 5 ¾ In.	115.00
Trivet, Southern Belle, Woman, Full Skirt, Flowers, Blue, Red, 1927, 5 ¾ In.	173.00
Urn, Garden, Green Matte Glaze, Faience, 1905	316.00
Vase, 2 Birds, Blossoms, Green, White, Blue, Baluster, Flared Rim, 1933, 7 ¼ In.	575.00
Vase, 2 Black Cranes, Sea Green Glaze, Cylindrical, Ball Bottom, Flared Rim, 1899, 10 In.	3565.00
Vase, 2 Figures On Rim, Blue Green, A.M. Valentien, 1901, 6 ½ x 4 In.	2356.00
Vase, 2 Irises, Blue To Green Ground, Tapered, Shouldered, 1904	7480.00
Vase, 2 Mice, Gold, Brown, Standard Glaze, Crescent Shape, B. Horsfall, 1894, 4 ¾ x 5 In.	440.00
Vase, 2 Rooks, Branch, Moon, Aerial Blue Glaze, Shouldered Oval, Flared Rim, 1946, 7 ⅛ In.	1580.00
Vase, 2 Swimming Fish, Iris Glaze, Peach, Green, Pinched Waist, 1906, 8 In.	1150.00
Vase, 3 Figures In Relief, Blue Crystalline Glaze, 1923, 6 x 12 ½ In.	440.00
Vase, 3 Honeybees, Clover, Cylindrical, Shouldered, Rolled Rim, 1900	2875.00
Vase, 3 Peacock Feathers, Black, Green, Cobalt Blue, Yellow, Cylindrical, 1910, 7 In.	4255.00
Vase, 3 Rubenesque Nude Women, Flowers, Bulbous, Rolled Rim, 1931, 7 In.	8050.00
Vase, 3 Swallows, Yellow Ground, Elongated Oval, 1905, 6 In.	805.00
Vase, Abstract Design, Ombroso, Textured, Elongated Oval, 2 Up Turned Handles, 1901, 5 In.	748.00
Vase, Abstract Flowers, Elongated Oval, Pinched Neck, Flared Rim, 1919, 25 In.	2990.00
Vase, Abstract Flowers, Mustard & Black Matte Glaze, 1920, 7 In.	518.00
Vase, Apple Blossoms, Pink, Blue To Turquoise, Vellum, Swollen, Flared Rim, Footed, 1926, 9 ¾ In.	575.00
Vase, Apple Blossoms, White, Ginger Clay, Cylindrical, Tapered, 1886, 13 In.	1380.00
Vase, Art Deco Design, Deep Blue High Glaze, Bulbous, Rolled Rim, 1931, 4 ½ In.	161.00
Vase, Band Of Cows, Cream & Tan, Wide Flared Rim, 1944, 5 In.	690.00
Vase, Bearded Man, Green, Brown, Yellow, Glazed, Baluster Shape, Flared Rim, 1894	1035.00
Vase, Bellflowers, Blue, Orange, Elongated Oval, 1918, 10 ½ In.	978.00
Vase, Berries, Leaves, Branch, Brown To Gold, Elongated Oval, 1901, 7 In.	558.00
Vase, Birds, Flowers, Grapes, Cream, Baluster, 1946, 13 In.	1495.00
Vase, Birds, Grass, Limoges Glaze, High Shoulders, Gold Trim, A. Valentien, 1883, 10 x 17 In.	1650.00
Vase, Birds, Trees, Flowers, Vellum Glaze, Sara Sax, 14 In.	5310.00
Vase, Black Iris Glaze, Sara Sax, 1900, 3 x 8 ½ In.	13200.00
Vase, Black-Eyed Susans, Brown To Green To Orange, Edith Regina Felton, 7 In.	322.00

Rookwood, Frieze, Bacchus, Grapes, Leaves, Faience, 25 x 24 ½ In., Pair
$1116.00

Cowan's Auctions

Rookwood, Incense Burner, Butterfly, Morning Glory, Blue Matte, Reversible Lid, Matt Daly, 8 In.
$633.00

Early Auction Co.

Rookwood, Plaque, Scenic, Harbor, Sailboats, Vellum Glaze, E.T. Hurley, Frame, 1945, 9 x 12 In.
$5405.00

Humler & Nolan

Rookwood, Vase, Bleeding Hearts, Jewel Porcelain Glaze, Shirayamadani, 1927, 7 x 5 ½ In.
$1860.00

Rago Arts & Auction Center

R

Rookwood, Vase, Bluebirds, Snow Covered Tree, Night Sky, Albert Valentien, 1882, 13 ⅛ In.
$9200.00

Humler & Nolan

Rookwood, Vase, Flowers, White, Blue Ground, Squat, E.T. Hurley, 1928, 5 In.
$764.00

Cowan's Auctions

Rookwood, Vase, Indian Man, Suriap, Standard Glaze, Grace Young, 1900, 12 In.
$29900.00

Humler & Nolan

Vase, Bleeding Hearts, Jewel Porcelain Glaze, Shirayamadani, 1927, 7 x 5 ½ In. ....*illus*	1860.00
Vase, Blue Bellflowers, Leaves, Pink & Gray Ground, 2 Low Handles, Flared Rim, 1929, 8 ½ In.	863.00
Vase, Blue Grapevines, Yellow To Green, Round, Narrow Neck, 1901	518.00
Vase, Blue Ground, White Flower Band, Green Stems, c.1915, 10 ¼ In.	1195.00
Vase, Blue, Green, Cream, Iris Matte Glaze, Tapered Oval, 1905, 12 ¼ In.	1304.00
Vase, Blue, Incised Lines, Shoulder, 8 ½ In.	203.00
Vase, Bluebirds, Snow Covered Tree, Night Sky, Albert Valentien, 1882, 13 ⅛ In. ....*illus*	9200.00
Vase, Branches, Leaves, Berries, Vellum, Pink & Blue Ground, 1929, 7 ¼ In.	646.00
Vase, Brave In War Dress, Black Ground, Standard Glaze, A. Sehon, 1901, 8 x 4 In.	5225.00
Vase, Brown Drip Glaze, Over Aventurine, Baluster, Flared Rim, 1938, 7 ⅜ In.	374.00
Vase, Brown Glaze, Silver Overlay, 3 Handles, Fred Rothenbusch, 5 ½ x 4 ¾ In.	1860.00
Vase, Bulbous, Folded Rim, Leona Van Briggle, c.1899, 5 In.	384.00
Vase, Bulbous, Narrow Neck, Flared Rim, Matthew A. Daly, c.1890, 11 In.	1770.00
Vase, Butterflies, Green To Gold To Brown, L. Asbury, c.1897, 10 ¾ In.	1076.00
Vase, Checkerboard Band, Yellow Matte Glaze, 1927, 5 ¼ In.	403.00
Vase, Cherry Blossom Band, Peach, Gray, Vellum Glaze, C. McLaughlin, 7 x 4 ¼ In.	403.00
Vase, Cherry Blossoms, Geometrics, Vellum Glaze, Bulbous, E.T. Hurley, 1914, 4 x 5 In.	825.00
Vase, Cherry Branch, Standard Glaze, Cylindrical, Handles, Lenore Asbury, 1902, 8 In.	551.00
Vase, Chicks, Mahogany Glaze, Tiger Eye, Bulbous, Squat, Narrow Neck, 1894, 5 ¼ In.	2070.00
Vase, Chrysanthemums, Bulbous, L. Epply, 1932, 5 ½ x 5 ½ In.	495.00
Vase, Clover, Leaves, Baluster Shape, McDonald, c.1893, 8 ¾ x 6 In.	657.00
Vase, Clover, Tiger Eye Glaze, Squat, Square Handles, 1892, 4 In.	345.00
Vase, Crane, Standing On One Leg, Sea Green Glaze, E.T. Hurley, 1901, 4 x 8 ¾ In.	6600.00
Vase, Crocus, Blue, Iris Glaze, Carl Schmidt, 1908, 4 ¼ x 9 ¾ In.	2200.00
Vase, Crocus, Green, Yellow, Painted Matte Glaze, K. Shirayamadani, 1934, 4 x 5 ½ In.	605.00
Vase, Crocuses, Pink, White, Green Ground, Carl Schmidt, 1914, 11 x 4 In.	1488.00
Vase, Cyclamen, Orange Matte Glaze, Harriet Wilcox, 1905, 8 ¼ x 3 ¼ In.	5667.00
Vase, Daffodil, Blue, Cylindrical, Shouldered, 12 In.	150.00
Vase, Daffodils, Orange, Yellow, Green, Brown Glaze, Baluster, Rolled Rim, 1900	1150.00
Vase, Daisies, Orange Matte Glaze, Monogram, Margaret Helen McDonald, 8 ¼ In.	322.00
Vase, Daisy Band, Ivory, 1944, 5 ½ In.	124.00
Vase, Daisy, Iris Glaze, Fred Rothenbusch, 1904, 3 ½ x 8 In.	825.00
Vase, Dandelions, Blue Ground, Ed Diers, 7 x 3 ½ In.	1364.00
Vase, Dandelions, Carved, Standard Glaze, Silvered Bronze Overlay, K. Shirayamadani, c.1910, 10 In.	6600.00
Vase, Dogwood, Persimmon Gloss Glaze, Harriet Wilcox, 8 ½ In.	472.00
Vase, Dogwood, White & Peach, Oval, Flared Rim, 1800s, 5 In.	230.00
Vase, Dragonflies, Raised, Green Matte Ground, Albert Pons, 1907, 4 ½ In.	767.00
Vase, Drip Glaze, Green & Blue Over Maroon, Baluster, Flared Rim, 1932, 6 ⅞ In.	259.00
Vase, Drip Glaze, Pale Blue Over Dark Gray, Baluster, Flared Rim, 1932, 6 ⅞ In.	173.00
Vase, Fans, Impressed, Pink, Green Matte Glaze, 1930, 6 In.	115.00
Vase, Firebird, Mahogany Glaze, Tiger Eye Effect, Baluster, Narrow Neck, 1893, 7 In.	633.00
Vase, Flower Band, Pink, Cylindrical, Marked C.M., 1915, 6 In.	92.00
Vase, Flower Panels, Impressed Pink, Green Matte Glaze, 1934, 7 ¼ In.	92.00
Vase, Flower, Iris Glaze, Bulbous, Sara Sax, 4 x 8 In.	840.00
Vase, Flowering Vine On Shoulder, Blue, Dark Blue Ground, L. Epply, 1918, 6 ½ In.	830.00
Vase, Flowering Vine, Light Green, Squat, Shouldered, 1920, 3 In.	207.00
Vase, Flowers, Blue Matte Glaze, 1904, 5 ¼ x 4 ½ In.	620.00
Vase, Flowers, Blue, Black Border, Green Ground, Trumpet Shape, Wide Rim, 1917, 5 In.	219.00
Vase, Flowers, Blue, Green, Bowling Pin Shape, Marked, 7 ¾ In.	300.00
Vase, Flowers, Blue, Purple, Double Vellum Glaze, Katherine Jones, 1927, 7 ½ In.	546.00
Vase, Flowers, Blue, White, Green, Jewel Porcelain Glaze, Arthur Conant, 1918, 11 x 5 In.	1240.00
Vase, Flowers, Brown, Sage Green, Elongated Oval, Rolled Rim, Footed, 1931, 6 In.	374.00
Vase, Flowers, Double Vellum Glaze, Mottled Gray Ground, Katherine Jones, 1924, 7 ½ In.	489.00
Vase, Flowers, Embossed, Pink Glaze, 1934, 5 ½ In.	63.00
Vase, Flowers, Green, Blue, White, Vellum Glaze, Tapered, L. Ashbury, 1930, 6 x 11 ½ In.	2750.00
Vase, Flowers, Lavender, Green, Tapered, Shouldered, Rolled Rim, Shirayamadani, 1926, 13 In.	5875.00
Vase, Flowers, Leaves, Blue, Green, Lavender, 1926, 13 In.	5875.00
Vase, Flowers, Light Green Matte Glaze, Flared Neck, 1940, 5 ½ In.	73.00
Vase, Flowers, Painted, Pink & Red Ground, Matte Glaze, Harriet Wilcox, 1902, 5 ¾ x 15 In.	2520.00
Vase, Flowers, Pink & Red, Matte Glaze, Tapered, H. Wilcox, 1902, 5 ¾ x 15 In.	2415.00
Vase, Flowers, Pink Matte Glaze, Tapered, 1927, 6 ¼ In.	84.00
Vase, Flowers, Plum Ground, Red, Yellow, Green Matte Glaze, Cylindrical, 10 In.	1035.00
Vase, Flowers, Purple, Peach Ground, Matte Glaze, K. Shirayamadani, 1938, 7 ¼ In.	744.00
Vase, Flowers, White, Blue Ground, Squat, E.T. Hurley, 1928, 5 In. ....*illus*	764.00
Vase, Forget-Me-Nots, Cobalt Blue To Maroon Ground, Elongated Oval, 1925, 5 ¼ In.	1610.00
Vase, Fruit, Leaves, Cream Ground, Urn Shape, 2 Loop Handles, Footed, 1928, 13 In.	10638.00

R

Vase, Geometric Band, Blue Matte Glaze, 1937, 5 ¼ In.		276.00
Vase, Geometric, Blue Glossy Glaze, Oval, 1940, 5 ½ In.		98.00
Vase, Geometric, Blue, Black Ovals, Vellum Glaze, Jens Jensen, 1930, 6 ¼ x 3 ½ In.		930.00
Vase, Geometric, Brown Matte Glaze, Green, Shouldered, Rolled Rim, 1906, 8 In.		518.00
Vase, Geometric, Embossed, Teal Green Matte Glaze, Impressed, 5 ⅞ In.		115.00
Vase, Geometric, Green Matte Glaze, c.1900, 6 x 4 In.		245.00
Vase, Grapes, Vines, Purple, Blue To Turquoise, Bulbous, Tapered, 1918, 4 ⅝ In.		403.00
Vase, Grapevine, Blue, Green Vellum Glaze, Edward Hurley, 7 ¼ In.		368.00
Vase, Grapevine, Turquoise Matte Glaze, Tapered, Shouldered, Rolled Rim, 1914, 13 In.		1380.00
Vase, Gray Gloss Glaze, Flared, Fish Handles, 10 In.		138.00
Vase, Greek Key Rim, Mauve, Gray, Embossed, 1913, 6 ¼ x 4 ¼ In.		201.00
Vase, Greek Key Rim, Pink To Sage Green, Urn Shape, 1913, 6 x 4 In.		201.00
Vase, Green Matte Glaze, Squat, Rolled Wide Rim, 1921, 4 In.		115.00
Vase, Harbor Scene, Sailboats, Moon, Turquoise Ground, Vellum Glaze, c.1910, 9 ¼ In.		2032.00
Vase, Hawthorne Branch, Vellum Glaze, Ed Diers, 1931, 5 In.		633.00
Vase, Holly & Berries, Purple Matte Glaze, Impressed, 6 ½ In.		184.00
Vase, Holly, Mauve Matte Glaze, 1920s, 6 ½ In.		207.00
Vase, Hollyhocks, White, Green Leaves, Iris Glaze, Spread Base, 1910, 12 In.		8050.00
Vase, Hops, Vines, Amber To Rust, Globular, Wide Neck, Flared Rim, 1889, 8 ¼ In.		1093.00
Vase, Hyacinth, Blue Tinted Glaze, Purple, Tapered, Footed, 1922, 11 In.		748.00
Vase, Hydrangea, Vellum Glaze, Cylindrical, Katherine Van Horne, c.1913, 8 ¼ In.		616.00
Vase, Indian Man, Suriap, Standard Glaze, Grace Young, 1900, 12 In. ....*illus*		29900.00
Vase, Iris Glaze, Shouldered, Fred Rothenbusch, 1904, 8 ½ x 5 In.		1488.00
Vase, Iris, Blue, Bud, Black, White, Iris Glaze, Cylindrical, 1906, 11 In.		13800.00
Vase, Iris, Blue, Caramel, Cylindrical, 5 In.		125.00
Vase, Iris, Blue, Iris Glaze, C. Schmidt, c.1909, 3 x 7 In.		2420.00
Vase, Iris, Blue, Mint Green Ground, Flattened Oval, 1907, 5 ⅛ In.		518.00
Vase, Iris, Brown, Gold, Green, Standard Glaze, M.A. Daly, 1889, 3 ½ x 7 In.		550.00
Vase, Iris, Bud, Iris Glaze, Flared, Carl Schmidt, 1923, 7 ½ x 3 ½ In.		2970.00
Vase, Iris, Molded, Turquoise, 7 In.		50.00
Vase, Iris, Pink, Black Iris Glaze, Sara Sax, 1900, 3 x 8 ½ In.		12100.00
Vase, Japanese Irises, Pink Green Glaze, Elongated Oval, 1902, 9 In.		2185.00
Vase, Landscape, Blue Ground, Vellum Glaze, Fred Rothenbusch, 1919, 4 x 7 ½ In.		990.00
Vase, Landscape, Blue, Green, Painted, Vellum Glaze, F. Rothenbusch, 1910, 7 x 16 In.		2200.00
Vase, Landscape, Blue, Green, Vellum Glaze, Carl Schmidt, 1917, 5 ¼ x 13 ¼ In.		2200.00
Vase, Landscape, Blue, Green, Vellum Glaze, Carl Schmidt, 1920, 4 ¼ x 10 ¼ In.		2310.00
Vase, Landscape, Blue, Green, Vellum Glaze, Sallie Coyne, 1921, 4 ½ x 6 In.		715.00
Vase, Landscape, Blue, Vellum Glaze, Bulbous, Sallie Coyne, 1923, 3 x 5 ½ In.		935.00
Vase, Landscape, Shouldered, Vellum Glaze, Ed Diers, 1915, 11 In.		2124.00
Vase, Landscape, Vellum Glaze, Sallie Coyne, 1921, 4 ½ x 6 In.		780.00
Vase, Landscape, Vellum Glaze, Sallie Coyne, 1923, 3 x 5 ½ In.		1020.00
Vase, Leaf & Berry, Copper Ground, Scalloped Rim, Silver Braided Overlay, 9 x 8 In.		518.00
Vase, Leaves, Avocado Green, Brown, Baluster, 1946, 6 ½ In.		94.00
Vase, Leaves, Berries, Yellow, Green, Standard Glaze, Bulbous, 4 ½ x 10 ¼ In.		1045.00
Vase, Leaves, Blue & Purple, Oval, 1929, 4 ½ In.		600.00
Vase, Leaves, Blue Over White, Urn Shape, 1940s, 7 In.		58.00
Vase, Leaves, Blue, Green, Maroon, Shouldered, Rolled Rim, 1915, 9 In.		1380.00
Vase, Leaves, Brown, Orange, Square, Pinched Neck, Flared Rim, Branches, 1896, 10 In.		588.00
Vase, Leaves, Mottled Blue, Green, Elizabeth Barrett, 8 ¾ In.		1315.00
Vase, Leaves, Pale Pink Ground, Bulbous, Rolled Rim, 1942, 4 ¾ In.		259.00
Vase, Leaves, Standard Glaze, H.R.S., 1893, 7 ⅛ In. ....*illus*		295.00
Vase, Lilies, Orange, Leaves, Bottle Shape, A. Sehon, 1902, 8 In.		288.00
Vase, Lily Of The Valley, White, Green Leaves, Vellum Glaze, Elongated Oval, 8 In.		431.00
Vase, Lily Pads, Green Matte Glaze, Red Hazing, Stick Neck, 1911, 13 In.		1150.00
Vase, Magnolias, Red, Brown Glaze, Green Leaves, Bulbous, 1946, 7 ¼ In.		316.00
Vase, Man's Portrait, Yellow, Amber, Brown, Standard Glaze, Pillow Shape, Footed, 1895, 7 x 7 In.		1150.00
Vase, Matte Glaze, Blue, Green, Rust, Pink, Baluster, Footed, 1930, 6 In.		978.00
Vase, Mottled Pink, Multicolor Designs, Vellum Glaze, Charles Todd, 1920, 6 ½ In.		275.00
Vase, Mountain Ash Branches, Berries, Green, Amber, 1890, 10 ½ In.		2185.00
Vase, Mushrooms, Iris Glaze, Carl Schmidt, 1904, 9 In.		3835.00
Vase, Mustard, Black, Beech Leaves, Green, Urn Shape, 1895, 13 In.		1725.00
Vase, Nasturtiums, Brown, Green, Cream, Iris Glaze, Rose Fechheimer, 1899, 7 ½ x 3 In.		2356.00
Vase, Native American Portrait, Bear Claw Necklace, Moss Green, Amber, Yellow, 1900, 9 ½ In.		7763.00
Vase, Oak Leaves, Painted Matte Glaze, Harriet Wilcox, 6 ½ In.		868.00
Vase, Orchids, Brown To Amber, Green Leaves, Bottle Shape, Trumpet Rim, 1891, 14 In.		3680.00
Vase, Organic Design, Embossed, Turquoise Matte Glaze, Round, 1940, 6 x 4 ½ In.		450.00

Rookwood, Vase, Leaves, Standard Glaze, H.R.S., 1893, 7 ⅛ In.
$295.00

Conestoga Auction Co., Inc.

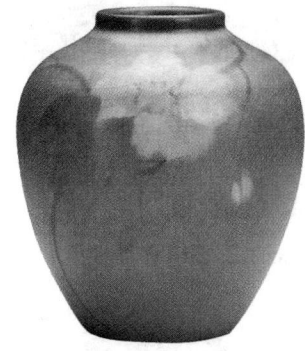

Rookwood, Vase, Roses, Vellum Glaze, Ed Diers, 1912, 6 x 5 ¼ In.
$868.00

Rago Arts & Auction Center

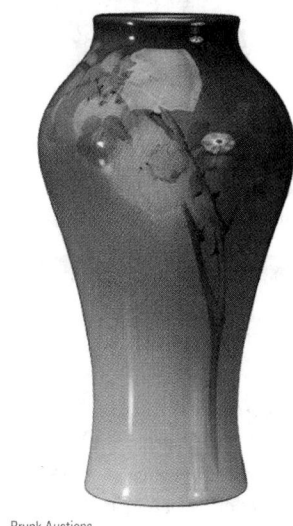

Rookwood, Vase, Roses, Yellow, Buff Shaded To Brown, Rose Fechheimer, 1903, 9 ¾ In.
$649.00

Brunk Auctions

R

Rookwood, Vase, Spider's Web, Bats, Moon, Clouds, Green Ground, Maria Longworth Nichols, 1882, 12 ¾ In. $4140.00

Humler & Nolan

Rose Mandarin, Bowl, Vegetable, Cover, Raised Enamel, Fired Gold Accents, Signed, 1800s, 4 x 9 ½ x 11 In. $270.00

DuMouchelles Art Gallery

Rose Mandarin, Coffeepot, Strap Handle, Strawberry Knop, 1800s, 9 In. $1495.00

James D. Julia Inc.

Recent Marks
Modern inventions have made new marks needed on dishes. "Cooking ware" was first used about 1923, "craze proof" about 1960, "dishwasher proof" after 1955, "freezer-oven-table" in the 1960s, "microwave safe" after 1970, "ovenproof" in 1934, and "oven-to-table" in 1978.

Vase, Pansies, Vellum Glaze, Round, Ed Diers, 1931, 4 ½ x 4 In.	468.00
Vase, Peacock Feathers, Ombroso, Yellow, Green, Pinched Waist, 1910, 11 In.	489.00
Vase, Peacocks, Red, Blue, Yellow Feathers, Turquoise Ground, Baluster, Flared Rim, 1921, 9 In.	1955.00
Vase, Peonies, Gold, Orange, Brown Glaze, Urn Shape, Rolled Rim, 1896, 11 In.	5520.00
Vase, Pinecones, Needles, Brown Matte Glaze, Cylindrical, Tapered, 1911, 7 In.	460.00
Vase, Pink Over Green Drip Glaze, Reeded, Bottle Shape, 1952, 13 In.	575.00
Vase, Pink, Purple, Brown, Blue, Bulbous, Shouldered, 1932, 3 In., Pair	610.00
Vase, Poppies, Green Brown Standard Glaze, E.T. Hurley, 7 In.	472.00
Vase, Poppies, Iris Glaze, Pink, Black, Green, Squat, Rose Fechheimer, 1904, 6 x 7 In.	1430.00
Vase, Poppies, Red, Black & Gray Ground, Stick Neck, Flared Rim, 1899, 19 In.	4370.00
Vase, Poppies, Red, Green, Lavender Matte Glaze, Cylindrical, Flared Foot, 1940, 7 In.	1150.00
Vase, Poppy, Glossy Glaze, Cylindrical, Rolled Rim, 1916, 9 x 5 In.	2645.00
Vase, Poppy, Iris Glaze, Oval, Olga Reed, 6 ½ x 3 ¾ In.	1116.00
Vase, Pussy Willow Stems, Red, Gray, Green, Deep Purple Ground, Swollen, 1920, 7 ¼ In.	1265.00
Vase, Raised Flowers, Oval, Openwork Handles, Katherine Jones, 1929, 9 ½ In.	885.00
Vase, Red Carnations, Pale Green Flowing Glaze, Gourd Shape, 1900, 5 ⅜ In.	4140.00
Vase, Red Flower Band, Yellow Matte Glaze, Oval, 1925, 6 In.	400.00
Vase, Red Hot Poker Flowers, Green Matte Glaze, Baluster, 1929, 14 In.	1840.00
Vase, Red Roses, Embossed, Blue Matte Glaze, Vera Tischler, 1922, 6 ½ x 6 ½ In.	992.00
Vase, Rook, Molded Band, Orange Brown, Cylindrical, 1926, 6 ¾ In.	184.00
Vase, Rooster, Flowers, Trees, Flattened Rim, Arthur Conant, 1922, 24 ¾ In.	5015.00
Vase, Rose Band, Ombroso Glaze, Golden Honey, Red, Baluster, 1914, 12 In.	3220.00
Vase, Rose Branch, Urn Shape, Glazed, Sara Sax, c.1894, 6 In.	896.00
Vase, Rose Hips, Painted Yellow Matte, Red, Mustard, Tapered, Wide Mouth, 1902, 5 In.	460.00
Vase, Rose Hips, Red, Green To Black Ground, Cylindrical, Shoulder, Rolled Rim, 1899, 8 ½ In.	575.00
Vase, Rose, Green Matte Glaze, 1924, 5 ¼ In.	92.00
Vase, Roses, Black Opal, Glaze, Oval, Pinched Neck, Footed, 1928, 11 ¼ In.	2300.00
Vase, Roses, Embossed, Green Matte Glaze, Katherine Jones, 1929, 7 ½ x 6 ½ In.	1116.00
Vase, Roses, Pink, Green Leaves, White, Blue, Urn Shape, Rolled Rim, 1938, 6 In.	863.00
Vase, Roses, Vellum Glaze, Ed Diers, 1912, 6 x 5 ¼ In. *illus*	868.00
Vase, Roses, Yellow, Buff Shaded To Brown, Rose Fechheimer, 1903, 9 ¾ In. *illus*	649.00
Vase, Sailboat Band, Gray, Cream, Vellum Glaze, Lenore Asbury, 1909, 8 ½ In.	575.00
Vase, Scenic River Landscape, Vellum Glaze, Ed Diers, 1914, 4 ½ x 8 In.	960.00
Vase, Scenic Rolling Wooded Hills, Blue, Green, Sallie Coyne, c.1918, 7 ½ In.	1165.00
Vase, Scenic, Snowy Landscape, Vellum Glaze, E.T. Hurley, 1913, 9 ½ x 4 In.	868.00
Vase, Scenic, Woodland, Blue, Green, Vellum Glaze, Cylindrical, S. Coyne, 1922, 5 ¾ In.	840.00
Vase, Silver Overlay, Shouldered, Handles, 7 In.	2950.00
Vase, Sparrow, Hawthorn Tree, Blue, Pink, Tan, Swollen Shape, 1918, 14 In.	3335.00
Vase, Speckled Blue Matte Glaze, Cylindrical, 1923, 7 In.	374.00
Vase, Spider's Web, Bats, Moon, Clouds, Green Ground, Maria Longworth Nichols, 1882, 12 ¾ In. *illus*	4140.00
Vase, Squash & Vine, Black Opal Glaze, K. Shirayamadani, 1925, 9 ¾ x 6 ¼ In.	1240.00
Vase, Stylized Cactus, Carved, Green High Glaze, Baluster Shape, 1948, 12 In.	173.00
Vase, Stylized Flowers, Green, Blue, White, Tapered, Lenore Asbury, 1930, 6 x 11 ½ In.	3000.00
Vase, Stylized Flowers, Red, Green Matte Glaze, Charles Todd, 7 ½ x 10 ½ In.	450.00
Vase, Stylized Flowers, Turquoise, Cylindrical, Tapered, Flared Rim, 1921, 7 ⅞ In.	518.00
Vase, Stylized Irises, Ombroso Glaze, Yellow, Blue, Globular, Narrow Neck, 10 In.	1840.00
Vase, Stylized Leaves, Embossed, Purple Matte Glaze, Bulbous, Hentchel, 1927, 5 ½ x 7 In.	660.00
Vase, Stylized Nudes, Flowers, Deer, Green, Tan, Bulbous, Rolled Rim, J. Jensen, 1946, 7 In.	2070.00
Vase, Stylized Petals, Bottle Shape, 9 In.	137.00
Vase, Stylized Poppies, Yellow Ground, Wax Matte Glaze, Katherine Jones, 1924, 18 x 8 In.	2420.00
Vase, Stylized Roses, Deep Red, Pinched Waist, 1918, 10 ¼ In.	2875.00
Vase, Sung, Plum, Cobalt Blue, Black, Thumbprint Design, Squat, Handles At Neck, 1937, 6 ⅛ In.	3450.00
Vase, Thistles, Iris Glaze, Ed Diers, 1903, 5 x 9 ½ In.	1210.00
Vase, Tree, Water's Edge, Blue Vellum, Rothenbusch, c.1930, 6 ¼ In.	633.00
Vase, Trio Of Nudes, Musical Pursuits, Deep Purple Glaze, Pinched Waist, 1921, 10 ½ In.	345.00
Vase, Tulips, Glossy Aqua Blue, High Shoulders, 1939, 10 In.	67.00
Vase, Tulips, Lilies, Wisteria, Dogwood, Square, Panels, Shouldered, 1938, 14 In.	5750.00
Vase, Tulips, Red, Green Leaves, Stems, Shouldered, Tapered, Shirayamadani, 1927, 11 In.	10925.00
Vase, Tulips, Standard Glaze, M.A. Daly, 1901, 5 ½ x 10 In.	900.00
Vase, Tulips, Yellow, Leaves, Sea Green Glaze, Elongated Oval, 1884, 12 In.	2300.00
Vase, Venetian Harbor, Vellum Glaze, Light Blue, Pear Shape, Flared Foot & Rim, 1921, 6 In.	920.00
Vase, Venetian Scene, Vellum Glaze, Ed Diers, 1931, 4 ½ x 9 In.	5400.00
Vase, Violet Gray Glaze, Cylindrical, Flared Rim, 1954, 12 ½ In.	173.00
Vase, Violets, Branches, Blue, Brown, Green Glaze, Genie Bottle, Footed, 1898, 7 ¼ In.	403.00
Vase, Violets, Purple, Carved, Green Ground, John Dee Wareham, 1901, 6 x 4 ½ In.	5580.00
Vase, Vista Blue Glaze, White Highlights, Tan Rim, Handkerchief Shape, 1959, 7 ⅞ In.	150.00

Vase, Water Lilies, Sea Green Glaze, Bulbous, Narrow Neck, 1901, 7 In.	1380.00
Vase, Water Lilies, Shaded Blue, High Glaze, Oval, 6 In.	173.00
Vase, Water Lily, Iris Glaze, Silver Plated Bronze Foot, Dragonflies, J.D. Wareham, 1903, 20 x 10 In.	66000.00
Vase, Wheat, Brown, Orange Ground, Shouldered, Rolled Rim, 1927, 12 ⅝ In.	230.00
Vase, Wild Rose, Pink, Orange, Yellow, Fan Shape, Footed, 1892, 6 In.	207.00
Vase, Winter Landscape, Vellum, Cylindrical, Waisted, L. Epply, 1911, 7 In.	415.00
Vase, Winter Scene, Trees, Snow, Vellum Glaze, Cylindrical, Rolled Lip, 1905, 11 In.	6325.00
Vase, Wisteria Band, Blue, Turquoise, Vellum Glaze, Pear Shape, 1923, 14 In.	3450.00
Vase, Wisteria, Blue, Green, Iris Glaze, E. Lincoln, 1910, 3 x 8 In.	1320.00
Vase, Wisteria, Blue, Red, Green Matte Glaze, Trumpet Shape, Flared Foot, 1923, 9 In.	748.00
Vase, Woodland Landscape, Blue, Green, Beige, Vellum Glaze, Oval, 1920, 13 ⅜ In.	1041.00
Vase, Woodland Landscape, Blue, White, E. Hurley, 1928, 12 ¾ In.	649.00
Vase, Woodland Landscape, Cream, Blue, Vellum Glaze, Tapered, E. Diers, 1930, 12 In.	2133.00
Vase, Yellow Matte Glaze, Tapered, Spread Base, Vertical Lines, 1910, 7 In.	219.00
Wall Pocket, Molded Leaves, Blue, Brown Matte Glaze, 1915, 6 x 8 In.	248.00
Water Jug, Lobster, Yellow, Green, Top Handle, Bulbous, Spout, 1885	748.00

RORSTRAND was established near Stockholm, Sweden, in 1726. By the nineteenth century Rorstrand was making English-style earthenware, bone china, porcelain, ironstone china, and majolica. The company is still working and is now owned by Fiskars Sweden. The three crown-mark has been used since 1884.

Bowl, Fish, Emerging, Green, Pink, White Ground, 6 ½ x 4 In.	300.00
Bowl, Hand Painted, 1 Eye, Cream, Blue, Black, Marked, 9 In. Diam.	92.00
Bowl, Pansy Shape, Pastels, 5 ½ In.	650.00
Coffeepot, Cup & Saucer, Isolde, 3 x 5 ⅜ In.	20.00
Creamer, Isolde, 2 ⅜ In.	20.00
Cup & Saucer, Claire De Lune, White	25.00
Cup & Saucer, White Windowpane, Black, Gold Trim, c.1915, 2 ½ x 4 ½ In.	500.00
Dish, Flowers, Applied Nightcrawler, Art Nouveau, 5 In.	125.00
Figurine, Boy, Kneeling, Fish, White, 4 ¾ In.	120.00
Figurine, Boy, Shell, White, 5 In.	120.00
Figurine, Mermaid, Holding Ears, White, Marked HS, 4 ½ x 5 In.	125.00
Plate, Dinner, 9 ¼ In.	75.00
Urn, Lid, Daffodils, 8 ½ In.	450.00
Vase, Art Nouveau, Green Openwork Clover, White Ground, 9 ½ In.	850.00
Vase, Art Nouveau, Tulip, Blue, White, Faience, Marked, 14 In.	300.00
Vase, Carved Factory Scene, Mustard Yellow, Flared, 4 ¼ In.	60.00

ROSALINE, *see Steuben category.*

ROSE BOWLS were popular during the 1880s. Rose petals were kept in the open bowl to add fragrance to a room, a popular idea in a time of limited personal hygiene. The glass bowls were made with crimped tops, which kept the petals inside. Many types of Victorian art glass were made into rose bowls.

Amber Glass, Flowers, Gold Leaf, Silver Stencil, 7 In.	75.00
Blue Satin Glass, Diamond Quilted, 3 ¼ In.	60.00
Blue Satin Glass, Embossed Shell, Coral, Gold, Enamel Flowers, 5 In.	90.00

ROSE CANTON china is similar to Rose Mandarin and Rose Medallion, except that no people or birds are pictured in the decoration. It was made in China during the nineteenth and twentieth centuries in greens, pinks, and other colors.

Bowl, Blue, Leaves, Border Rain, Clouds, Oval, Footed, c.1840, 15 x 11 ½ In.	1000.00
Bowl, Square, Gilt, Silver Center, Flowers, Bugs, Scrolls, c.1845, 9 ½ x 9 ½ In.	595.00
Bowl, Vegetable, Cover, Diamond Shape, c.1820, 11 ½ x 3 ½ In.	595.00
Charger, 4 Panels, Birds, Butterflies, Rose Center, 1800s, 13 In.	289.00
Cup & Saucer, Birds, Fruits, Flowers, Scalloped Border, c.1890, 3 ¾ x 5 ½ In.	145.00
Ewer, Blue, Tobacco, Leaves, c.1820, 5 ½ In.	2500.00
Jar, Dresser, Green Leaves, Pink, Red Roses, c.1875, 2 x 1 ¾ In.	245.00
Mug, Child's, Blue, Pagoda, Trees, c.1840, 2 ½ x 2 ½ In.	395.00
Pitcher, Green Leaves, Pink Roses, c.1870, 7 In.	495.00
Pitcher, Lid, Fluted, Scalloped, c.1870, 9 x 4 ¾ In.	295.00
Pitcher, Rose Cartouches, Footed, Gilt, 3 ¼ In.	155.00
Tureen, Soup, Cover, Double Strap Handles, c.1880, 9 ¾ x 13 In.	2000.00
Underplate, Blue, Reticulated, Basket Weave Border, c.1840, 11 x 9 ¾ In.	495.00

Rose Mandarin, Garden Seat, 6-Sided, Figures, Flowers, Butterflies, c.1840, 18 x 10 In. $1320.00

DuMouchelles Art Gallery

Rose Mandarin, Platter, Reserve Panels, Domestic Scenes, Flowers, Butterflies, 1800s, 18 ¼ In. $420.00

DuMouchelles Art Gallery

Rose Medallion, Bowl, 6 Panels, Flowers, Scenes, 11 x 14 In. $270.00

DuMouchelles Art Gallery

Roseville, Blackberry, Jardiniere, Handles, 4 ⅛ In. $345.00

Humler & Nolan

Heir Apparent

Be sure your important—and unimportant—antiques and collectibles are accounted for in your will. Make a list and tell everyone who gets the Fiesta dishes, who gets the Tiffany lamp, and who gets the Stickley desk. But don't forget the emotional family mementos, like photos, family paintings, and the Bible. An Ohio judge had to decide what to do with a 125-year-old family Bible that was wanted by both the children after Mother died. He ruled that the Bible must be sold and the proceeds split between the children. Mother would be sad to know her Bible led to a family feud and hard feelings—and that it could be lost to the family.

Roseville, Fujiyama, Vase, Flowers, Leaves, Gray Matte, Ink Stamp, 11 ½ In. $460.00

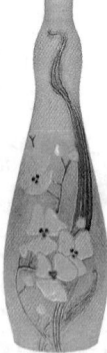

Humler & Nolan

TIP

A vase that has been drilled for a lamp, even if the hole for the wiring is original, is worth 30% to 50% of the value of the same vase without a hole.

ROSE MANDARIN china is similar to Rose Canton and Rose Medallion. If the panels in the design picture only people and not birds, it is Rose Mandarin.

Bottle, Cover, Painted Reserves, Court Scenes, Flower Bands, Chinese, 1800s	960.00
Bowl, 4 Lobes, Figures, Enameled, c.1770, 3 ¾ In.	165.00
Bowl, Court Scene, Fluted Body, Round Foot, Chinese, 10 In.	568.00
Bowl, Figures, c.1820, 5 ½ In.	235.00
Bowl, Figures, Flowers, Hand Painted, Chinese, c.1860, 13 ½ x 5 ½ In.	863.00
Bowl, Vegetable, Cover, Raised Enamel, Fired Gold Accents, Signed, 1800s, 4 x 9 ½ x 11 In. ...*illus*	270.00
Charger, 4 Reserves, Flowers, Court Scenes, Chinese, 1800s, 13 In.	420.00
Charger, Figural Decoration, Chinese, c.1840, 15 In.	1434.00
Cider Jug, Enamel, Figures In Landscape, 2 Part Handle, Chinese,1800s, 9 In.	711.00
Coffeepot, Strap Handle, Strawberry Knop, 1800s, 9 In. ...*illus*	1495.00
Garden Seat, 6-Sided, Figures, Flowers, Butterflies, c.1840, 18 x 10 In. ...*illus*	1320.00
Mug, Cylindrical Shape, Bamboo Shape Handle, Gilt Rim, Garden Scene, 5 x 4 In.	150.00
Mug, Pavilion, Women Talking, Sewing, Shaped Handle, 4 ¼ In.	120.00
Pitcher, Courtyard, Interior Scenes, c.1890, 5 x 6 In.	175.00
Pitcher, Painted, Court Scene, Chinese, 7 x 6 In.	210.00
Plate, Courtyard Scene, Chinese, c.1820, 8 In.	443.00
Plate, Paneled Scenes, Figures, Flowers, 7 ½ In.	25.00
Platter, Painted, Generals Of Yang Clan, Oval, 18 ½ In.	1912.00
Platter, Reserve Panels, Domestic Scenes, Flowers, Butterflies, 1800s, 18 ¼ In. ...*illus*	420.00
Serving Bowl, 4 Reserves, Landscape, Flowers, Oval, Chinese, 1800s, 10 x 8 In.	210.00
Teapot, Cartouches, c.1880, 10 In.	375.00
Teapot, People, Flowers, 1800s, 10 In.	269.00
Teapot, People, Plants, Birds, 1920s, 5 In.	130.00
Tureen, Sauce, Stand, Courtyard Scenes, Gilt, Enamel, Chinese, 1800s, 8 In., Pair	1126.00
Urn, Court, Garden Scenes, Pistol Handles, c.1810, 15 In., Pair	7000.00
Urn, Cover, Figures In Courtyard Scenes, c.1835, 15 In., Pair	3540.00
Vase, 3 Sections, Women, Court Officials, Flowers, Symbols, Impressed Feathers, c.1800	2500.00
Vase, 8 Treasures Panels, Applied Foo Dogs, Dragons, Chinese, 1800s, 25 In., Pair	2415.00
Vase, Baluster, Painted, Court Scenes, Animal Head Handles, 1800s, 10 In., Pair	600.00
Vase, Baluster, Scalloped Rim, Chinese, 1800s, 12 In., Pair	500.00
Vase, Court Scene, Flowers, Figural Handles, 18 In.	266.00

ROSE MEDALLION china was made in China during the nineteenth and twentieth centuries. It is a distinctive design with four or more panels of decoration around a central medallion that includes a bird or a peony. The panels show birds and people. The background is a design of tree peonies and leaves. Pieces are colored in greens, pinks, and other colors. It is similar to Rose Canton and Rose Mandarin.

Basket, Fruit, Stand, Oval, Pierced Vertical Bands, Raised Handles, 9 x 10 In.	923.00
Bottle, Pavilion, Women Talking, 8 In.	150.00
Bowl, 6 Panels, Flowers, Scenes, 11 x 14 In. ...*illus*	270.00
Bowl, Centerpiece, White Ground Center, Gold Ground Rim, Flowers, 9 In.	180.00
Bowl, Deep U-Shape, 1800s, 12 In.	650.00
Bowl, Figures, Flowers, Multicolor, c.1850, 11 ½ In.	431.00
Bowl, Key Fret Borders, Butterflies, Flowers, 1 ½ x 6 ½ In., Pair	461.00
Bowl, Multicolor, Figures, Flowers, Pagodas, 25 In.	3792.00
Bowl, Scenic Reserves, Flowers, 4 ½ In., 4 Piece	210.00
Candlestick, Foo Dog, Painted, 1800s, 3 x 6 ¼ In.	510.00
Dish, Cover, Underplate, c.1840, 10 x 11 In.	295.00
Fishbowl, Famille Rose, Oval Shape, Yellow, Flowers, 6 x 9 In.	345.00
Ginger Jar, Lid, Figures, Leaves, Chinese, c.1900, 11 In.	294.00
Jar, Cover, Gold Finial, Figural, Landscape Panels, 1800s, 18 In., Pair	2706.00
Platter, 6 Reserves, Painted, Flowers, Oval, Chinese, 1800s, 16 In.	390.00
Platter, Gathering Of Officials, Pavilion, Flowers, Vines, 19 x 16 In.	2006.00
Platter, Round, Divided Scenes, Chinese, 1800s, 9 x 16 In.	920.00
Platter, Scenic, Floral Reserves, Chinese, 1800s, 11 In.	180.00
Platter, Scenic, Floral Reserves, Chinese, 1800s, 13 ¼ In.	210.00
Punch Bowl, Courtyard Landscape, Flower & Bird Panels, Chinese, c.1890, 13 In.	1126.00
Punch Bowl, Figures, Flowers, Multicolor, Chinese, 1800s	3107.00
Punch Bowl, Footed, Palace Life Scenes, Chinese, 1800s, 5 x 13 In.	600.00
Serving Dish, Oval, Fruit, Flowers, Pinecone Finial, 1800s, 5 x 11 In., Pair	345.00
Teapot, Wicker Handle, Flower Reserves, c.1890, 5 In.	210.00

Tureen, Cover, Underplate, Bird, Butterflies, Gilt Twist Handles, 11 x 14 In.	1521.00
Urn, Cover, Foo Dog Finial, Parcel Gilt, Purple, Flowers, Wood Stand, 28 In.	316.00
Vase, Applied Lizards, Gilt Foo Dog Handles, Chinese, c.1890, 24 In.	1067.00
Vase, Baluster, Flared Lip, Foo Dog Handles, Dragons, Flowers, Chinese, 1800s, 10 In.	110.00
Vase, Birds, Flowers, Figures, Chinese, c.1890, 35 In.	1840.00
Vase, Bowl, Scalloped Edge, Gilt, 9 ¾ x 3 ¾ In.	161.00
Vase, Cover, Foo Dog Finial, Tapered, Shoulder Ring Handles, Chinese, 1800s, 15 ¾ In., Pair	1495.00
Vase, Cover, Scenic, Gilt Detail, Mounted As Lamps, 32 In., Pair	2280.00
Vase, Cylindrical, Figures On Balcony, Chinese, 1800s, 9 ¼ In.	104.00
Vase, Dragons, Antique Objects Panels, Baluster, Chinese, 16 ¼ In.	306.00
Vase, Flared, Scalloped Rim, Applied Gilt Dragons, Chinese, 1800s, 24 ½ In.	863.00
Vase, Moon Shape, Flat Sides, 2 Handles, Flowers, Scrolls, Chinese, 16 In., Pair	460.00
Vase, Painted, Dragons Applied To Neck, Gilt, Multicolor, 12 In.	132.00
Vase, Palace, Scenic Cartouches, Flowers, Chinese, 45 x 14 In.	122.00

ROSE O'NEILL, *see Kewpie category*

ROSE TAPESTRY porcelain was made by the Royal Bayreuth factory of Tettau, Germany, during the late nineteenth century. The surface of the porcelain was pressed against a coarse fabric while it was still damp, and the impressions remained on the finished porcelain. It looks and feels like a textured cloth. Very skillful reproductions are being made that even include a variation of the Royal Bayreuth mark, so be careful when buying.

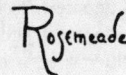

Basket, Pink & Yellow Roses, 4 ½ In.	90.00
Basket, Scenic, Blue Mark, 4 ½ In.	75.00
Chocolate Set, Pink & Cream Roses, 6 Piece	316.00
Pitcher, Castle, Mountains, Lake, 6 In.	259.00
Plate, Woodland Scene, Deer In Stream, Scrolled Edge, Gilt Trim, c.1890s, 11 In.	115.00

ROSEMEADE POTTERY of Wahpeton, North Dakota, worked from 1940 to 1961. The pottery was operated by Laura A. Taylor and her husband, R.I. Hughes. The company was also known as the Wahpeton Pottery Company. Art pottery and commercial wares were made.

Rosemeade

Candleholder, Blue, Square, Sticker, 3 x 3 x 1 In., Pair	82.00
Dish, Black, 4 Sections, Figural Pheasant Center, 5 x 9 In.	54.00
Flower Holder, Heron, Foil Label, 1950s, 6 ¾ In.	87.00
Salt & Pepper, Black Cat, Sitting, Cork Stopper, 3 In.	89.00
Salt & Pepper, Corncob, Cork Stopper, Tray, Ink Stamp, 2 ½ In.	72.00
Salt & Pepper, Dog Head, Terrier, Brown & White, Sticker, 3 In.	81.00
Salt & Pepper, Kangaroo, Looking Up, Brown, Marked, c.1950, 3 In.	72.00
Salt & Pepper, Pelican, Pink, Sticker, 3 In.	71.00
Shaker, Pheasant, Multicolor, Sticker, 3 In.	15.00
Sugar & Creamer, Corn, Yellow, Stamped, 2 ½ In.	49.00

ROSENTHAL porcelain was made at the factory established in Selb, Bavaria, in 1880. The factory is still making fine-quality tablewares and figurines. A series of Christmas plates was made from 1910. Other limited edition plates have been made since 1971. In 1998 Rosenthal was acquired by the Waterford Wedgwood Group. Rosenthal was bought by Sambonet Paderno Industries, headquartered in Orfento, Novaro, Italy, in 2009. Rosenthal china is still being produced in Bavaria.

MARKE
Rosenthal

Bowl, Green, Pink Roses, Gold Trim, Scalloped, Pierced Handle, 10 In.	170.00
Figurine, Angora Cat, Lying, Pale Green Eyes, Long Hair, 1920s, 9 ¾ In.	425.00
Figurine, Birds, On Branch, Bisque, 11 ½ In.	266.00
Figurine, Borzoi Hounds, Fritz Heidenreich, 6 x 8 In.	266.00
Figurine, Lion, Lioness, On Boulder, Marked, c.1880, 20 x 8 ½ In.	1840.00
Figurine, May, Woman, Blowing Horn, Over Snake, Gray Base, 8 x 5 In.	207.00
Figurine, Nude Woman, Blue Drape, Standing On Blue Ball, Wenck, 12 In.	489.00
Figurine, Nude, Kneeling, Die Hockende, Matte Glaze, Fritz Klimsch, 14 In.	431.00
Figurine, Peacock, Fritz Heidenreich, 7 x 9 In.	177.00 to 295.00
Figurine, Turkish Warrior, On Bended Knee, Hat, Round Base, Marked, Selb, c.1950, 6 In.	177.00
Plate, Dinner, White, Gold Brocade Trim, Flower Border, 10 ¼ In., 12 Piece	170.00
Sugar, Cover, Donatello, Blue Cherries, Leaves	100.00
Vase, Blue, Gilt, Konigsblau, Round, 7 In.	119.00
Vase, Crinkled Olive Lava Glaze, Concentric Enamel Rings, Cylindrical, 12 x 5 In.	43.00

Roseville, Jonquil, Strawberry Pot, Handles, Foil Sticker, 7 ¼ In.
$489.00

Humler & Nolan

Roseville, Juvenile, Plate, Rabbits, Rolled Rim, 7 ½ In.
$288.00

Humler & Nolan

R

Roseville, Luffa, Vase, Green & Gold, Leaves, Ribbed, Molded, 2 Handles, 8 ¼ In.
$200.00

Morphy Auctions

Roseville, Pauleo, Vase, Chrysanthemums, 18 ¼ In.
$690.00

Humler & Nolan

Roseville, Rozane, Vase, Olympic, Persia & Ionia Yoked To The Chariot Of Xerxes, Signed, 14 x 6 In.
$5580.00

Rago Arts & Auction Center

ROSEVILLE POTTERY COMPANY was organized in Roseville, Ohio, in 1890. Another plant was opened in Zanesville, Ohio, in 1898. Many types of pottery were made until 1954. Early wares include Sgraffito, Olympic, and Rozane. Later lines were often made with molded decorations, especially flowers and fruit. Most pieces are marked *Roseville*. Many reproductions made in China have been offered for sale the past few years.

Roseville U.S.A.

Apple Blossom, Basket, Circle Handles, Marked, 8 ½ In.	460.00
Apple Blossom, Basket, Green, Branch Handle, 7 ½ x 11 ½ In.	374.00
Apple Blossom, Ewer, Pink, Mauve, Brown Branch Handle, Marked, 8 ¼ In.	184.00
Apple Blossom, Teapot, Green	79.00
Apple Blossom, Vase, Angular Shape, 2 Branch Handles, Fan Rim, Square Foot, Pink, 7 In.	80.00
Apple Blossom, Vase, Flattened, Pointed Bottom, Square Foot, Branch Handles At Foot, 12 In.	68.00
Apple Blossom, Window Box, Blue, Handles, 15 x 4 In.	22.00
Artwood, Planter, 8 ¾ x 6 In.	86.00
Aztec, Pitcher, Light Blue, Signed L, 4 ¾ x 7 ¾ In.	112.00
Aztec, Vase, Squeezebag, Iridescent Green, 10 ¼ In.	109.00
Baneda, Bowl, Flowers, Pink, 2 Handles, 9 x 3 In.	138.00
Baneda, Vase, Flower Band, Plum, Pink, Handles, 6 In.	253.00
Baneda, Vase, Footed, 2 High Shoulder Handles, Green, Blue, 7 x 7 In.	523.00
Baneda, Vase, Footed, High Handles, Green, Blue, Orange, 6 x 7 In.	440.00
Baneda, Vase, Green, Double Handle, Bulbous, 7 ½ x 6 ½ In.	450.00
Baneda, Vase, Green, Green Glaze, Footed, Handles, Round, 5 In.	649.00
Baneda, Vase, Leaves, Flowers, Green, Bulbous, High Handles, 7 ½ x 6 ½ In.	413.00
Baneda, Vase, Pink, Double Handles, 4 ½ x 9 ¼ In.	330.00
Baneda, Vase, Plum, High Handles, 6 In.	288.00
Baneda, Vase, Plum, Shoulder Flowers, Handles, Foil Label, 6 ¼ x 6 ½ In.	259.00
Baneda, Wall Pocket, Fan Shape, 2 Upper Handles, Blue, Green, Leaves, Flowers, 8 In.	1840.00
Bittersweet, Basket, Gray, Shaped Rim, Brown Handle, 10 ½ x 6 ¾ In.	69.00
Bittersweet, Basket, Yellow, Orange, Stem Handle, Marked, 7 In.	95.00
Bittersweet, Bookends, Gray, Rose, Branches, Leaves, Marked, 5 ½ In.	57.00
Bittersweet, Jardiniere, Round, 4-Scallop Rim, 2 Angular Handles, 5 In.	47.00
Bittersweet, Vase, Elongated Oval, 2 Uneven Branch Handles, Green, Flowers, 8 In.	92.00
Blackberry, Console, 2 Handles, 13 ½ In.	324.00
Blackberry, Jardiniere, Green, 4 x 5 ½ In.	207.00
Blackberry, Jardiniere, Handles, 4 ⅛ In. ....*illus*	345.00
Blackberry, Vase, Cylindrical, Narrow Rim, 2 Handles, Leaves, Green, Brown, 12 In.	978.00
Blackberry, Vase, Mottled Green, Handles, 6 In.	184.00
Bleeding Heart, Basket, Blue, High Arched Handle, 9 ½ x 9 ¾ In.	299.00
Bleeding Heart, Rose Bowl, Blue, 2 Handles, 4 ¼ x 7 In.	69.00
Bleeding Heart, Vase, Bulbous, Shaped Rim, Triangular Handles, Round Foot, Turquoise, 4 In.	51.00
Bunny, Plate, Child's, 7 ½ In.	40.00
Burmese, Candlestick, Mint, 7 ½ In.	35.00
Bushberry, Basket, Brown, 11 ¼ In.	354.00
Bushberry, Bookends, Tree Trunk, Leaf, Berries, c.1941, 5 x 4 In.	360.00
Bushberry, Creamer, Blue	51.00
Bushberry, Jar, Brown, Small Square Handles, Squat	45.00
Bushberry, Vase, Brown, Footed, Large Square Handles	85.00
Bushberry, Vase, Brown, Handles, Marked, 6 In.	52.00
Bushberry, Vase, Bud, Double, Blue, Green, Cylindrical, Round Foot, Leaves, Intertwined, 5 In.	68.00
Bushberry, Vase, Leaves, Textured, Round Foot, Tapered, Triangular Branch Handles, 9 ½ In.	70.00
Bushberry, Wall Pocket, Blue, Asymmetrical Handles, 8 In.	235.00
Carnelian I, Bowl, Centerpiece, Green, Cream, Flared, Footed, 4 x 9 ¾ x 7 In.	70.00
Carnelian I, Wall Pocket, Blue Matte Drip Glaze, 8 In.	130.00
Carnelian II, Bowl, Horizontal Ripples, Blue Green, Footed, Marked, 9 In.	34.00
Carnelian II, Vase, Cylindrical, Pinched Neck, Rolled Rim & Foot, Mottled Green, 6 In.	46.00
Carnelian II, Vase, Green Matte Glaze, Neck Handles, 9 ¼ x 7 ¼ In.	62.00
Carnelian II, Vase, Mottled Blue, Handles, 8 ¼ In.	84.00
Carnelian II, Vase, Pine, Purple & Gold Glazes, 1930s, 12 In.	950.00
Carnelian II, Vase, Rose, Runny Gray Drip, 8 In.	112.00
Carnelian II, Vase, Urn Shape, 2 Handles At Neck, Mottled Green, Round Foot, 10 In.	170.00
Cherry Blossom, Basket, Hanging, Brown, White Flowers, 7 ¾ x 5 In.	265.00
Cherry Blossom, Bowl, Brown, Oblong, 10 ¾ x 3 In.	213.00
Cherry Blossom, Candlestick, Brown, Flared Base, Handles, 4 ¼ In.	69.00
Cherry Blossom, Jardiniere, Pink, Blue, 14 ½ x 10 In.	460.00
Cherry Blossom, Vase, Brown, Cylindrical, Flared Rim, 2 Handles At Neck, 12 In.	604.00
Cherry Blossom, Vase, Globular, Tapered, 2 Handles, 5 In.	270.00

R

Chloron, Vase, 2 High Loop Handles, Green Matte Glaze, Stamped, 5 ½ x 5 ¼ In.	496.00
Chloron, Vase, Green Matte Glaze, Raised Panels, 5 ½ In.	324.00
Clematis, Basket, Yellow Flowers, Brown, 10 x 9 ¾ In.	69.00
Clematis, Bookends, Brown, 5 ⅛ In.	86.00
Clematis, Ewer, Bottle Shape, Angled Handle, Spread Spout, Round Foot, Brown, 15 In.	79.00
Clematis, Ewer, Green, Marked, 10 ½ In.	104.00
Clematis, Flowerpot, Hanging, Brown, Handles, 8 In.	45.00
Clematis, Jar, Yellow, 3 In., Pair	96.00
Clematis, Jardiniere Stand, White Flower, Green Leaves, Blue, Spread Foot, 17 In.	57.00
Clematis, Pitcher, Green, Square Handle, 6 In.	28.00
Clematis, Planter, Brown, Rectangular, 8 In.	50.00
Clematis, Vase, Brown, Jug Handles, 6 In.	102.00
Clematis, Vase, Brown, Marked, 10 ¼ In.	24.00
Clematis, Vase, Cornucopia, 6 In.	71.00
Clematis, Vase, Green, Peach, Angled Handles, Tapered, 7 In.	40.00
Clematis, Window Box, Brown, 11 x 3 ¼ In.	46.00
Columbine, Vase, Blue, Waist Handles, Marked, 12 In.	207.00
Columbine, Vase, Brown, 3 In.	40.00
Columbine, Vase, Handles, 12 In.	127.00
Columbine, Vase, Pink To Green, Handles, 14 ½ In.	253.00
Columbine, Vase, Rose, Green, Footed, Handles, 6 ¼ In.	75.00
Corinthian, Vase, Elongated Oval, Vertical Ribbing, Band Of Fruit, Green, Round Foot, 11 In.	57.00
Cornucopia, Vase, Brown, 6 In., Pair.	147.00
Cosmos, Bowl, Brown, 8 In.	62.00
Cosmos, Bowl, Egg Shape, Brown Glaze, Handles, 3 x 4 In.	95.00
Cosmos, Console, Purple, White, Blue, 1940s, 11 x 6 x 3 In.	145.00
Cosmos, Ewer, Blooms, Lavender, Textured, Multi-Point Spout, 10 In.	295.00
Cosmos, Rose Bowl, Blooms, Lavender, Scalloped Rim, Handles, 4 In.	135.00
Cosmos, Vase, Flowers, 2 Handles, Tan, 1940, 4 In.	109.00
Cosmos, Vase, Green, Pink Flowers, Handles, Footed, 8 ¼ In.	63.00
Cosmos, Window Box, 10 ½ x 4 In.	81.00
Cremo, Vase, Bulbous, 4-Footed, 7 ½ x 5 In.	2728.00
Cremona, Vase, Footed, Square, 6 ¼ In.	200.00
Crocus, Vase, Blue & Yellow Flowers, Green, Pinched Waist, 9 In.	258.00
Crocus, Vase, Light Blue, Squeezebag Shape, Yellow, White, 4 ½ x 7 In.	450.00
Crystalis, Vase, 3 Handles At Top, Tan, Brown Glaze, 5 ½ x 14 ½ In.	1200.00
Daffodils, Urn, Dark Green, 3-Footed, 11 In.	102.00
Dahlrose, Bowl, Flared Rim, 2 Handles, 4 ⅝ x 10 ½ In.	127.00
Dahlrose, Vase, Orange, White, Flowers, 4 In.	69.00
Dawn, Vase, Urn Shape, Square Handles & Base, Yellow Matte Glaze, Green Design, c.1937, 6 In.	69.00
Della Robbia, Mug, Tan Glaze, Carved, Painted Flowers, Poem, Initials, Rozane, 5 ½ x 6 In.	540.00
Dish, Feeding, 4 Rabbits, Rolled Edge, 6 ½ In.	81.00
Dogwood I, Jardiniere, Bulbous, Green, Flowers, Branches, 12 In.	57.00
Dogwood I, Vase, Yellow Flowers, Green, 11 ½ In.	288.00
Dogwood II, Vase, Green, 8 In.	161.00
Dogwood II, Wall Pocket, Horn Shape, Squared Handle, White Flowers, Green, 10 In.	374.00
Donatello, Jardiniere, Stand, Ribbed, Green & Brown, 28 In.	204.00
Dutch, Mug, Girl Holding Flowerpot, Creamware, 4 In.	92.00
Earlam, Vase, Blue, Green, Tan, Mottled Glaze, Handles, 7 ½ In.	224.00
Earlam, Vase, Green Matte Glaze, Blue, Tan, 7 x 8 ¾ In.	276.00
Egypto, Vase, Squat, 3 Handles, Rolled Rim, Green Textured Glaze, Feather Design, 5 In.	288.00
Falline, Vase, Cylindrical, 2 Loop Handles, Round Foot, Rolled Rim, Brown, Orange, Green, 6 In.	374.00
Falline, Vase, Dark Brown Glaze, Pea Pods Design, 2 Handles At Shoulder, 8 In.	236.00
Falline, Vase, Wavy Corn Design, Brown, Green, Blue, Handles, 5 x 6 In.	303.00
Ferella, Candlestick, Mottled Red, Wide Drip Cup, Black Paper Label, 4 In.	184.00
Ferella, Vase, Brown, Green Border, Handles, 9 In.	374.00
Ferella, Vase, Pink, Green, 2 Handles Shape, Openwork Rim & Base, 4 ½ x 6 ½ In.	495.00
Florentine, Basket, Handle, Marked, 8 ¾ In.	127.00
Florentine, Compote, Impressed, Tapered Base, Footed, Marked, 4 ¼ x 6 ¼ In.	22.00
Florentine, Urn, Brown, High Square Handles, 8 ½ In.	68.00
Florentine, Vase, Brown, 6 ½ In., Pair.	96.00
Foxglove, Basket, Blue, Pink Flowers, Wide Rim, 10 x 9 ½ In.	115.00
Foxglove, Ewer, Blue, Pink Flowers, Marked, Arched Handle, 10 ¼ In.	69.00
Foxglove, Jardiniere Stand, Pink, Green Leaves, Spread Foot, Handles, Flared Rim, 22 In.	91.00
Foxglove, Jardiniere, Blue, Square Handles, White Flowers, 10 In.	147.00
Foxglove, Jardiniere, Stand, Mocha, Narrow Square Handles, 30 In.	424.00

Roy Rogers, Jacket, Suede, Fringe, Zipper Front, Graphic Label, 1950s, 17 In. $115.00

Hake's Americana & Collectibles

Lunch Box Collecting
Lunch box collecting started in earnest after the publication in the 1960s of a book about lunch boxes and values.

Roy Rogers, Lunch Box, Roy Rogers, Dale Evans, Chow Wagon, Dome Top, Thermos, c.1955, 4 ¼ x 8 ¾ In. $239.00

Hake's Americana & Collectibles

R

Royal Bayreuth, Pitcher, Cow, Black & Orange, Marked, c.1900, 4 x 6 In. $71.00

DuMouchelles Art Gallery

Royal Bayreuth, Sugar, Cover, Devil & Cards, Diamond Shape, 4 ½ In. $104.00

Humler & Nolan

R

Foxglove, Vase, Pink, Handles, 4 In.	45.00
Foxglove, Vase, Pink, Yellow, Blue, 2 Handles, Footed, 15 ½ In.	295.00
Foxglove, Vase, Shaded Pink, Flared Rim, Stepped Angular Handles, c.1942, 6 In.	71.00
Foxglove, Vase, Tapered, Swollen Center, 2 Elongated Handles, Round Foot, Pink, 15 In.	215.00
Freesia, Cookie Jar, Dome Lid, Bulbous, Squared Handles, Brown, Yellow, 8 In.	158.00
Freesia, Pitcher, Purple & White Flowers, Dark To Light, Marked, 10 ½ In.	51.00
Freesia, Vase, Blue Handles, Stamped, 15 ½ In.	127.00
Freesia, Vase, Cornucopia, 8 In.	35.00
Freesia, Vase, Cornucopia, Brown, 9 In.	50.00
Freesia, Vase, Green, 15 ½ x 9 ½ In.	367.00
Freesia, Vase, Green, Marked, c.1900, 8 ½ x 6 In.	92.00
Freesia, Vase, Green, Pink Flowers, Marked, 10 ½ In.	138.00
Freesia, Vase, Yellow Flowers, Brown, Orange, Low Handles, Marked, 7 ¼ In.	84.00
Fuchsia, Jardiniere, Pedestal, Cornflower Blue, Rolled Rim, 27 In.	490.00
Fuchsia, Vase, Brown, Marked, Handles, 6 ¼ In.	81.00
Fuchsia, Vase, Green, Pink Flowers, High Handles, Marked, 6 ¼ In.	109.00
Fujiyama, Vase, Flowers, Leaves, Gray Matte, Ink Stamp, 11 ½ In. *illus*	460.00
Futura, Jardiniere, Handles, 13 ½ x 9 In.	75.00
Futura, Vase, 4-Ball, 4-Sided, Tapered, Square Base, 12 In.	675.00
Futura, Vase, Ball Shape, Bamboo Leaf Design, Narrow Rim, Square Base, Blue, Green, White, 8 In.	518.00
Futura, Vase, Balloon, Blue Matte Glaze, 1920s, 8 ½ In.	780.00
Futura, Vase, Geometric, Flared, Footed, Brown, Green Paper Label, 5 x 8 In.	385.00
Futura, Vase, Green, Footed, Paper Label, 5 ½ x 3 ½ In.	1240.00
Futura, Vase, Little Blue Triangle, Stepped Foot, 8 In.	350.00
Futura, Vase, Mauve Thistle, Rose, 8 In.	288.00
Futura, Vase, Pillow Shape, Blue Sunray, 5¼ In.	236.00
Futura, Vase, Red Vee, Pink, Green, Round Base, 7 ⅛ In.	190.00
Futura, Vase, Squat Round Bottom, Telescoping Neck, Pink & Green Glaze, Round Foot, 8 In.	104.00
Futura, Vase, Triangular, Stepped Foot, 2-Tone Blue, 8 ¼ In.	142.00
Futura, Window Box, Rectangular, Matte Glaze, Tan, Blue, Green, 5 x 16 In.	460.00
Gardenia, Basket, Green, Marked, 8 ½ x 8 In.	115.00
Gardenia, Candlestick, Green, 1 ¾ In., Pair	123.00
Gardenia, Ewer, Gray, Tan, Footed, Handle, 10 ¼ In.	115.00
Gardenia, Urn, Handle, Footed, 15 In., Pair	120.00
Gardenia, Vase, Cup Shape, Beige, White, Green, Round Foot	34.00
Holly, Bowl, Fern, Creamware, Marked, 8 ¾ x 3 In.	350.00
Imperial I, Jardiniere, Wide Rim, Round Shape, Stamped, RV, 1924, 11 x 10 In.	288.00
Imperial II, Vase, Blue Matte Glaze, Ivory Over Glaze, Marked, 7 In.	184.00
Imperial II, Vase, Drip Glaze, Flared, 5 ¼ In.	118.00
Imperial II, Vase, White Mouth, Pale Blue Base, Foil Label, 7 ¼ In.	230.00
Iris, Bowl, Blue, High Handles, 7 In.	86.00
Ivory Tint, Box, Lid, Green & Tan Designs, Round, 3 x 4 In.	50.00
Ixia, Vase, Green Glaze, Oval, Flared Rim, 2 Raised Handles, Footed, 9 ½ x 6 In.	194.00
Ixia, Vase, Pink Green, Footed, Handles, Marked, 7 ¼ In.	81.00
Ixia, Vase, Yellow, Tan, High Lug Handles, Marked, 7 ¼ In.	75.00
Jonquil, Strawberry Pot, Handles, Foil Sticker, 7 ¼ In. *illus*	489.00
Jonquil, Vase, Brown, White Flowers, Handles, 9 ¼ In.	69.00
Jonquil, Vase, Bud, Bottle Shape, Flared Rim, 2 Lower Elongated Handles, Flower, 7 In.	173.00
Jonquil, Vase, Bulbous, 2 Handles, 5 x 6 ½ In.	173.00
Juvenile, Pitcher, Dog, Cream, Marked, 3 ½ In.	73.00
Juvenile, Plate, Rabbits, Rolled Rim, 7 ½ In. *illus*	288.00
Lombardy, Wall Pocket, Green Glaze, 8 In.	118.00
Luffa, Vase, Green & Gold, Leaves, Ribbed, Molded, 2 Handles, 8 ¼ In. *illus*	200.00
Magnolia, Ashtray, Brown, 7 x 2 In.	46.00
Magnolia, Basket, Wide Mouth, Blue, Marked, 13 ¼ x 9 ¾ In.	63.00
Magnolia, Blue, 7 In., Pair	62.00
Magnolia, Blue, Basket, Angled Handle, Marked, 13 ½ x 9 ¾ In.	109.00
Magnolia, Bookends, Brown, 5 ¼ In., Pair	115.00
Magnolia, Bowl, c.1940, 14 x 11 In.	69.00
Magnolia, Bowl, Green, Low Handles, 6 In.	35.00
Magnolia, Candlestick, Cylindrical, Triangular Handles, Round Foot, 5 In., Pair	40.00
Magnolia, Cookie Jar, 2 Square Handles, Bulbous, Green, Flowers, Branches, 9 In.	40.00
Magnolia, Cookie Jar, Brown, 2 Angular Handles, 10 ½ In.	161.00
Magnolia, Cookie Jar, Bulbous, Square Handles, Multicolor, 8 In.	68.00
Magnolia, Pitcher, Brown, Ball Shape, Ice Lip, 9 In.	196.00
Magnolia, Vase, Blue, White Flowers, Handles, 9 ¼ x 9 ¾ In.	86.00

Magnolia, Vase, Blue, White, Yellow Flowers, Handles, 12 ½ In.	150.00
Magnolia, Vase, Brown, Handles, 15 ½ In.	127.00
Magnolia, Vase, Brown, Handles, 6 In.	45.00
Magnolia, Vase, Bud, Globular, Square Handles, Cone Neck, Tan, 8 In., Pair	68.00
Magnolia, Wall Pocket, Brown, 8 ½ x 8 ¼ In.	98.00
Matte Green, Jardiniere, 5 x 7 ½ In.	75.00
Matte Green, Jardiniere, Classical Frieze, Round, 8 ½ x 10 In.	155.00
Matte Green, Jardiniere, Marked, 5 ¾ x 4 In.	67.00
Matte Green, Umbrella Stand, Flowers, Panels, Wavy Rim, 24 In.	374.00
Matte Green, Vase, Feathered, Marked, 5 In.	104.00
Ming Tree, Vase, Blue, Asymmetrical Branch Handles, Marked, 10 ¼ In.	150.00
Ming Tree, Vase, Blue, Stylized Trees, Asymmetric Branch Handles, 8 ¼ In.	103.00
Ming Tree, Vase, Mint Green, Pink Trees, Branch Handle, Footed, 6 ½ In.	58.00
Mock Orange, Basket, Green, Marked, 10 ¼ In.	207.00
Mongol, Vase, Oxblood Red Glaze, 3-Footed, 11 In.	805.00
Mongol, Vase, Red, Long Tapered Neck, Flared Foot, 14 x 4 ½ In.	992.00
Monticello, Vase, 2 Handles, Egg Shape, 7 ½ In.	354.00
Monticello, Vase, Green, Brown, Squat, Handles, 4 ¼ In.	138.00
Monticello, Vase, Urn Shape, 2 Loop Handles Below Rim, Tan, Yellow, Orange, 6 In.	259.00
Morning Glory, Basket, Flowers, Leaves, Vines, Multicolor, 10 In.	413.00
Morning Glory, Basket, Lavender Blue & Yellow, White, 10 In.	365.00
Morning Glory, Vase, Footed, Flared, Green, 7 x 8 ½ In.	468.00
Morning Glory, Vase, Green, Handles, 10 In.	345.00
Morning Glory, Vase, Green, Tapered, Footed, 12 ¼ In.	403.00
Moss, Bowl, Blue, Green, Shaped Rim, 11 ¾ x 3 ¼ In.	138.00
Moss, Vase, Pink, Green, 12 In.	518.00
Moss, Wall Pocket, Blue Green Matte Glaze, Handles, 9 In.	165.00
Mostique, Bowl, 6 ¾ x 2 ¾ In.	81.00
Mostique, Bowl, Stylized Flowers & Band, Tan, 9 ¼ In.	22.00
Mostique, Jardiniere, Stand, White, Blue, Geometric Design, 18 In.	102.00
Mostique, Vase, Cylindrical, Trumpet Rim, Flared Foot, Green, Yellow, Blue, 10 In.	460.00
Panel, Vase, Orange Leaves, Green, 10 ¼ In.	161.00
Pauleo, Vase, Bulbous, Burgundy Metallic Glaze, 6 ½ x 9 ½ In.	605.00
Pauleo, Vase, Chrysanthemums, 18 ¼ In. ....*illus*	690.00
Peony, Basket, Hanging, Green Ground, White Flowers, Small Handles, 7 ¼ x 4 ¾ In.	75.00
Peony, Bowl, Pink, Green, 9 x 3 In.	46.00
Peony, Vase, Cornucopia, Green, Yellow, Brown, 8 In.	40.00
Peony, Vase, Flattened, Rounded Bottom, Fan Rim, Triangular Handles, Round Foot, Turquoise, 8 In.	40.00
Peony, Vase, Pink, Handles, 15 In.	170.00
Persian, Vase, Creamware, Multicolor Stylized Base, Tapered, 10 ½ In.	190.00
Persian, Wall Vase, Creamware, Yellow Flowers, Cone Shape, 14 ¼ In.	840.00
Pine Cone, Basket, Blue, Footed, 10 ½ In.	383.00
Pine Cone, Bookends, Brown, 5 x 5 ¼ In.	398.00
Pine Cone, Double Tray, 2 Bowls, Green Intertwined Loop Center Handle, Orange, 6 x 13 In.	161.00
Pine Cone, Ewer, Brown, Marked, 15 ¼ In.	403.00
Pine Cone, Jar, Brown, 3 In.	180.00
Pine Cone, Jardiniere, Stand, Cobalt Blue, Brown Accents, Shaped Handles, 17 In.	170.00
Pine Cone, Pitcher, Brown, Ice Lip, Marked, 7 ¾ x 8 ¾ In.	196.00
Pine Cone, Pitcher, Cylindrical, Flare Rim, Shaped Twig Handle, Round Foot, Brown, Yellow, 15 ¾ In.	518.00
Pine Cone, Vase, Blue, Small Handles, 6 ½ In.	136.00
Pine Cone, Vase, Brown Baluster, Elongated, Round Foot, Branch Shaped Handles, Pair	255.00
Pine Cone, Vase, Brown Matte, Orange, Yellow, Branch Shape Handles, 1931, 11 In.	316.00
Pine Cone, Vase, Green, Footed, Twig Shape Handle, 8 ½ x 10 ½ In.	303.00
Pine Cone, Vase, Green, Handles, Footed, 8 ½ x 10 ½ In.	330.00
Pine Cone, Vase, Orange, Green Branch Handle, Marked, 7 ½ In.	207.00
Poppy, Bowl, Shaped Elongated Oval, 2 Loop Handles, Flowers, Leaves, Peach, Yellow, 12 In.	68.00
Poppy, Ewer, Gray, Marked, 10 ¼ In.	242.00
Poppy, Vase, Blue, Green, Pink Yellow, Bulbous, Scrolled Handles, 9 ¼ In.	150.00
Poppy, Vase, Flattened, Round Bottom, Shaped 3-Hole Top, Loop Handles, Flower, Light Green, 8 In.	57.00
Primrose, Vase, Blue, Round, 5 In.	45.00
Primrose, Vase, Elongated Oval, Triangular Handles, Round Foot, Rust, Yellow, 14 In.	136.00
Raymor, Plate, Dinner, Gray Matte Glaze, 12 In.	28.00
Rosecraft, Vase, Black, Vertical Handles, 11 ½ In.	109.00
Rosecraft, Vase, Blue, High Shoulder, 13 ½ In.	84.00
Rosecraft, Vase, Burnt Orange, Brown, 5 ¾ In.	63.00
Rosecraft, Vase, Tan & Orange Vines, Flowers, Black, Marked, 10 In.	213.00

Royal Bonn, Clock, Ansonia, La Plata, Gong, 8-Day, Open Escapement, c.1904, 12 ½ In.
$360.00

Cowan's Auctions

Royal Bonn, Vase, Art Nouveau Flowers, Silver Overlay, Signed, 4 ½ In.
$45.00

Conestoga Auction Co., Inc.

TIP

If you are looking for collectibles in old warehouses, abandoned houses, or other old and dirty buildings, always wear long pants, long sleeves, sturdy shoes, gloves, and, if possible, a face mask. Old chemicals, animal droppings, and rusty nails can kill. If you get a cut during a foraging trip or become sick right after one, call your doctor. Most of the illnesses can be cured if treated quickly with the correct antibiotic.

R

Royal Bonn, Vase, Flowers, Painted, Applied Angular Handles, Marked, c.1910, 16 In.
$148.00

Ivey-Selkirk Auctioneers

Royal Bonn, Vase, Flowers, Wine Colored Ground, Gilt Highlights, Dolphin Handles, Scroll Feet, c.1900, 17 In.
$915.00

Neal Auction Co.

Rozane Royal, Vase, Purple Flowers, Cylindrical, J. Imlay, 12 ½ In.	190.00
Rozane Royal, Vase, Roses, Wide Base, Josephine Imlay, 6 x 8 ¼ In.	364.00
Rozane, Ewer, Trefoil, Rose Design, Signed, Marked, 8 In.	173.00
Rozane, Jug, Cardinal Profile, Painted, Brown Glaze, Signed Dunlavy, 6 x 5 In.	495.00
Rozane, Mug, Flowers, Poem, Tan Glaze, Della Robbia, 5 ½ x 6 In.	495.00
Rozane, Planter, Rectangular, Cream Textured, Roses, Leaves, 6 In.	46.00
Rozane, Vase, Horse Portrait, Stamped, Signed Charles Leffler, 13 In.	992.00
Rozane, Vase, Indian, Stamped, Signed Arthur Williams, 21 x 11 In.	3224.00
Rozane, Vase, Olympic, Persia & Ionia Yoked To The Chariot Of Xerxes, Signed, 14 x 6 In. *...illus*	5580.00
Rozane, Vase, Pansy Design, Signed Virginia Adams, 9 In.	79.00
Rozane, Vase, Tulips, Brown Glaze, Oval, Pinched Neck, Flared Rim, 8 In.	173.00
Rozane, Vase, Woodland, Poppies, Garlic Mouth, Spread Foot, 10 ⅞ In.	690.00
Rozane, Vase, Yellow Roses, Brown, Marked, c.1908, 8 ¼ In.	138.00
Sign, Roseville Pottery, Light Green Matte Glaze, Raised Lettering, 9 ½ x 4 In.	1440.00
Silhouette, Basket, Rose, Blue, 6 In.	50.00
Silhouette, Vase, Fan Shape, Nude, Blue, Green, Marked, 7 ¼ In.	235.00
Silhouette, Vase, Maroon, Nudes, Shaped Rim, 10 ¼ In.	345.00
Silhouette, Vase, Squat Bottom, Trumpet Shape, Ruffled Rim, Mustard Color, Leaf, 14 In.	125.00
Snowberry, Basket, Pink, Mauve, Marked, 10 ½ In.	121.00
Snowberry, Ewer, Flowers, Pink, Mauve, Handle, Marked, 15 ¾ In.	489.00
Snowberry, Tea Set, Teapot, Sugar, Creamer, 3 To 7 In.	240.00
Snowberry, Vase, Floor, Blue, 18 ½ In.	265.00
Snowberry, Vase, Green, Orange, Low Handles, Footed, Marked, 9 ¼ In.	161.00
Snowberry, Vase, Green, Orange, Ruffled Rim, Signed, c.1900, 12 ½ x 8 ½ In.	58.00
Snowberry, Vase, Pink, Clipped Rim, 2 Low Angular Handles, 12 ¾ In.	184.00
Snowberry, Wall Pocket, Green, Brown, Triangular Handles, Marked, 5 x 7 ¾ In.	112.00
Snowberry, Wall Pocket, Pink, Mauve, Marked, 8 x 5 ¼ In.	52.00 to 92.00
Sunflower, Bowl, Mottled Green, 7 ¾ x 4 In.	403.00
Sunflower, Jardiniere, Pedestal, Brown, Green, Blue, Marked, 14 x 28 ½ In.	4200.00
Sunflower, Vase, Angled Handles, Green, 6 In.	431.00
Sunflower, Vase, Green, Handles, 5 In.	431.00
Sunflower, Vase, Handles, 8 ¼ In.	489.00
Sunflower, Vase, High Loop Handles, Brown, Green, Blue, 6 x 4 In.	358.00
Sunflower, Vase, Shouldered, Brown, Green, Blue, 6 ½ x 5 In.	495.00
Sunflower, Vase, Squat, Bulbous, 2 Loop Handles, Green, Yellow, 4 ⅛ In.	374.00
Sunflower, Wall Pocket, 6 ½ x 5 x 3 In.	744.00
Sunflower, Wall Pocket, Basket Shape, Arched Pierced Top, Yellow, Green, Glazed, 7 In.	690.00
Sylvan, Jardiniere, Pedestal, Hunting Dogs, Cream, Brick Red, 32 ½ In.	805.00
Teasel, Vase, Tan Speckled Glaze, 2 Vertical Tab Handles, Clipped Rim, Footed, c.1938, 6 In.	65.00
Thorn Apple, Bowl, Blue, Handles, 6 In.	40.00
Thorn Apple, Vase, Blue, Flared Rim, Footed, Apple, 10 ¼ In.	184.00
Thorn Apple, Vase, Pale Yellow Flowers, Blue, Handles, Marked, 10 ½ In.	179.00
Topeo, Vase, Blue, 9 ½ In.	158.00
Topeo, Vase, Bulbous, Oxblood Red, 9 ¼ In.	178.00
Tourmaline, Vase, Baluster, Bulbous Bottom, 2 Handles At Neck, Blue, Green, 9 In.	51.00
Tourmaline, Vase, Blue Shading, Foil Label, 8 In.	115.00
Tourmaline, Vase, Blue, High Handles, 6 In.	40.00
Tourmaline, Vase, Pillow, Turquoise, Square, Tapered Center, Handles At Waist, 7 In.	29.00
Tuscany, Vase, Blue Gray, 6-Sided, Footed, 2 Buttressed Handles, 5 ¼ In.	46.00
Velmoss, Vase, Double Cornucopia, Bottle Blue Glaze, Pink Interior, 8 ½ In.	219.00
Velmoss, Vase, Green Matte Leaves, Tan, 5 ¾ In.	316.00
Venetian Line, Vase, Blue, Ed Diers, 1931, 4 ½ x 9 In.	4950.00
Victorian Art, Vase, Impressed Leaves, Yellow Fruit, Blue, Cylindrical, 7 ¾ In.	90.00
Vista, Vase, Shaded Green, Tapered, 14 ¾ In.	690.00
Water Lily, Basket, Blue, Peaked Handle, Marked, 8 x 8 In.	104.00
Water Lily, Basket, Hanging, Brown, Yellow Flower, Small Handles, 9 x 5 In.	81.00
Water Lily, Basket, Hanging, Flowers, Matte Glaze, Peaked Handles, Rose To Green, c.1943, 5 x 9 In.	295.00
Water Lily, Bookends, Open Book Shape, White Lilies, Blue Green Book, 5 x 5 In.	57.00
Water Lily, Bowl, 10 In.	48.00
Water Lily, Ewer, Blue, Marked, 15 ¼ x 8 ¼ In.	230.00
Water Lily, Ewer, Brown Base, Pumpkin Orange Spout, Handle, Marked, 15 ¼ In.	173.00
Water Lily, Jardiniere, Cobalt Blue, Yellow Flowers, Green Leaves, Handle, Squat, 8 In.	125.00
Water Lily, Vase, Blue, Green, Large Handles, 7 In.	173.00
Water Lily, Vase, Brown, Handles, Marked, 8 ¼ In.	58.00
Water Lily, Vase, Green Glaze, Blue Band, Footed, 18 ½ In.	590.00
Water Lily, Vase, Green Shaded To Terra-Cotta, Cylindrical, 2 Angular Handles, c.1943, 6 In.	153.00

Water Lily, Vase, Handles, c.1940, 7 x 6 In.	69.00
Water Lily, Vase, Pink & Green, Waist Handles, 10 ¼ x 8 ¾ In.	127.00
Water Lily, Vase, Pink, Green, Handles, Marked, 8 In.	77.00
White Rose, Bowl, Green, Orange, Signed, c.1900, 5 x 8 In.	58.00
White Rose, Bowl, Pink & Green, Marked, 8 ¾ x 2 ½ In.	24.00
White Rose, Vase, Blue, Asymmetrical Handles, 7 In.	219.00
White Rose, Vase, Squat, Bulbous, Round Handles, Notched Rim, Pale Pink, White, Green, 7 In.	79.00
White Rose, Vase, White Flowers, Blue, High Handles, 8 ½ x 8 ¼ In.	230.00
White Rose, Window Box, Pink, Green, 10 ½ x 3 ½ In.	58.00
Wincraft, Basket, Blue Green, Elongated End & Handle, 8 x 14 In.	65.00
Wincraft, Basket, Blue, Asymmetrical Mouth, Marked, 8 x 9 ½ In.	92.00
Wincraft, Planter, Green & Brown Glaze, Canoe Form, Shaped Rim, 5 x 11 In.	65.00
Wincraft, Vase, Curved, Shaped Triangle, Fan Top, Flowers, Leaves, Square Base, 8 In., Pair	68.00
Wincraft, Vase, Globular, Green Glaze, Shaped Rim, 4-Sided Brown Foot, 8 x 8 In.	86.00
Wincraft, Vase, Pinecone, Blue, Low Brown Handles, 8 ¼ In.	104.00
Windsor, Vase, Fern, Large Handles, Blue, 7 ¼ In.	431.00
Wisteria, Vase, Blue Glaze, Sticker, 1933, 6 x 5 In.	196.00
Wisteria, Vase, Blue, Hip Handles, Foil Label, 9 ¼ In.	288.00
Wisteria, Vase, Brown, Blue, Double Handles, 6 x 7 In.	480.00
Wisteria, Vase, Elongated Oval, Open Handles, Narrow Neck, Mid 1900s, 15 In.	288.00
Wisteria, Vase, High Handles, Blue, Brown, 7 x 8 In.	660.00
Wisteria, Vase, Mottled Blue, Handles, 8 In.	604.00
Wisteria, Vase, Squat, Blue, Foil Label, 4 x 6 ½ In.	230.00
Zephyr Lily, Bowl, Brown, Green, 7 x 2 In.	46.00
Zephyr Lily, Bowl, Cobalt Blue, Boat Shape, 2 Handles, 8 In.	46.00
Zephyr Lily, Candlestick, Brown, Green, Marked, 4 ¾ In., Pair	63.00
Zephyr Lily, Ewer, Brown Shaded To Green, Elongated Spout, Handle, 15 ⅝ In.	207.00
Zephyr Lily, Jar, Brown, 4 In.	40.00
Zephyr Lily, Vase, Brown, Green, Marked, 7 ¼ In.	63.00
Zephyr Lily, Vase, Brown, Green, Marked, 9 ½ In.	52.00
Zephyr Lily, Vase, Cornucopia, Square Foot, Blue, Yellow Flowers, 8 In., Pair	80.00
Zephyr Lily, Vase, Elongated Oval, Shouldered, 2 Handles, Round Foot, Blue, 19 In.	226.00
Zephyr Lily, Vase, Elongated Oval, Shouldered, Round Handles, Rust, Cream, Round Foot, 20 In.	215.00
Zephyr Lily, Vase, Hanging, Green, Pink & Yellow Lilies, Handles, 7 ½ In.	40.00
Zephyr Lily, Vase, Orange, Green, Marked, Signed, 13 ½ x 9 In.	138.00

ROWLAND & MARSELLUS COMPANY is part of a mark that appears on historical Staffordshire dating from the late nineteenth and early twentieth centuries. *Rowland & Marsellus* is the mark used by an American importing company in New York City. The company worked from 1893 to about 1937. Some of the pieces may have been made by the British Anchor Pottery Co. of Longton, England, for export to a New York firm. Many American views were made. Of special interest to collectors are the plates with rolled edges, usually blue and white.

Cup & Saucer, Auld Lang Syne, Blue & White, 3 x 5 ½ & 7 x 1 ¼ In.	100.00
Plate, American Poets, Blue Transfer, Round Portraits, Roses, 10 In.	85.00
Plate, Bridgeport, Conn., Flow Blue, Local Landmarks, 10 ¼ In.	119.00
Plate, Charles Dickens, Flow Blue, Book Landmarks, 10 In.	48.00
Plate, Hartford, Conn., Blue & White, Local Landmarks, 1903, 10 In.	135.00
Plate, Niagara Falls, Flow Blue, Local Landmarks, Rolled Edge, 10 In.	100.00
Plate, Pilgrim Hall, Blue & White, Rolled Edge, Fruit & Flower Border, 10 In.	24.00
Plate, Plymouth, Mass., Blue & White, Local Landmarks, 1907, 10 In.	95.00
Plate, St. Louis, Mo., Blue & White, Local Landmarks, 10 In.	75.00
Plate, William Shakespeare, Flow Blue, Local Landmarks, 10 In.	48.00
Plate, Zanesville, Ohio, Flow Blue, Local Landmarks, 10 ¼ In.	108.00
Toothbrush Holder, White, Blue Flowers, Ribbed, c.1890, 5 ½ In.	64.00

ROY ROGERS was born in 1911 in Cincinnati, Ohio. In the 1930s, he made a living as a singer; in 1935, his group started work at a Los Angeles radio station. He appeared in his first movie in 1937. From 1952 to 1957, he made 101 television shows. The other stars in the show were his wife, Dale Evans, his horse, Trigger, and his dog, Bullet. Roy Rogers memorabilia, including items from the Roy Rogers restaurants, are collected.

Bank, Boot Shape, Cast Metal, Box	225.00
Binoculars, Logo Of Roy & Trigger On Both Sides, Herbert George Co., 1950s	85.00
Binoculars, Roy & Trigger On Front, Manufactured By Herbert George Co., 1950s	65.00
Camera, Telescope Sight, Box	250.00
Canteen, Plastic, White, Straw, Strap	15.00

Royal Copenhagen, Plate, Mother's Day, 1980, 6 In. $48.00

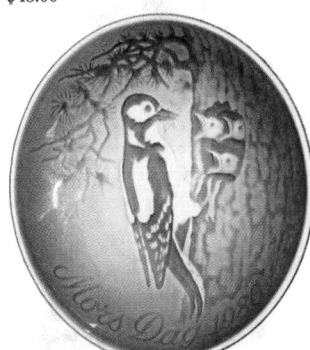

DuMouchelles Art Gallery

R

Royal Copenhagen, Vase, Wavy Woven Design, Matte Brown Glaze, Axel Salto, 6 ¼ x 3 In.
$1240.00

Rago Arts & Auction Center

Royal Crown Derby, Vase, Enameled, Gilt, Oval, Flared Neck, Socle Foot, Leaves, 1900s, 9 ¼ In., Pair
$830.00

Skinner, Inc.

Royal Doulton, Character Jug, 'Ard Of Hearing, D 6588, 7 ½ In.
$835.00

Potteries Specialist Auctions

Cap Gun, Die Cast, 8 ½ In., Pair	124.00
Coloring Book, Dale Evans, Ranch Tales, 1953, 11 x 8 ½ In.	17.00
Cup, Figural, Head, Plastic, F & F Mold & Die Works, 4 ½ In.	25.00
Doll Set, Roy & Dale, Cloth, Stuffed, Painted, Round Eyes, Autographed, 1950s, 14 In., Pair	114.00
Doll, Dale Evans, Hard Plastic, Sleep Eyes, Cowgirl Costume, Boots, 1950s, 13 In.	627.00
Double Holster, Leather, Jewels, Wood Bullets, Die Cast, Plastic Horse Head Grips, 1950s	225.00
Figure, Dale Evans On Buttermilk, Green & White Outfit, Hartland, 1950s, 9 In.	150.00
Figure, Roy On Trigger, Hartland, 1950s, 10 In.	175.00
Figure, Trigger, Trigger Jr., Nellybelle, Horse Trailer, Tin Lithograph, Marx, 15 In.	236.00
Flashlight, Signal, Siren, Box, Usalite, 7 In.	55.00
Game, Rodeo, 4 In 1 Game, 1949	200.00
Harmonica, King Of The Cowboys, 1943, 4 In.	15.00
Hat, Double R Bar Ranch, Wool, Ribbon Trim, Pull Cord, Box, 1959, Size Junior Medium	95.00
Hat, Felt, Red	150.00
Holster Set, Double, Leather, Jewels, Studs, Wood Bullets, Horse Head Grips, 1950s, 26 In.	225.00
Holster Set, Double, Roy & Trigger, Cap Guns, Hand Tooled, Embossed Belt Buckle	660.00
Holster Set, Gun, Dale Evans, Queen Of The West, Box	1050.00
Holster Set, Guns, Schmidt Guns, Box	1200.00
Jacket, Suede, Fringe, Zipper Front, Graphic Label, 1950s, 17 In. .... *illus*	115.00
Lantern, Ohio Art, 1950s, 8 In.	40.00
Lunch Box, Chow Wagon, Oval, Dome Top, 1955, 9 x 4 x 6 In.	125.00
Lunch Box, Dale Evans, Flat Steel, RR Brand, American Thermos, Blue Panels, c.1953, 6 x 3 In.	25.00
Lunch Box, Roy Rogers, Dale Evans, Chow Wagon, Dome Top, Thermos, c.1955, 4 ¼ x 8 ¾ In. . *illus*	239.00
Lunch Box, Trigger, Metal, American Thermos, 1956	198.00
Modeling Clay Set, Standard Toycraft Products, 17 ½ x 11 In.	28.00
Pedal Car, Nellybelle, Blue, Red Wheels, Decal, Garton, Pat Brady, Restored, 1950s, 39 In.	715.00
Photograph, With Dale Evans, Frame, 8 x 10 In.	30.00
Pin, Tab, Roy Rogers, King Of The Cowboys, Nebraska State Fair, 1958, Metal, 2 ¼ In.	77.00
Poster, Movie, Along The Navajo Trail, Republic, 1945, 27 x 41 In.	131.00
Poster, Movie, Under Western Stars, Roy, Smiley Burnette, Signed, 1938, 41 x 27 In.	3919.00
Rocker, Red Vinyl, Roy On Trigger, Wood Platform & Arms, Child's, 17 x 22 In.	403.00
Thermos, Roy Riding Trigger, American Thermos Bottle Co., 7 ½ In.	75.00
Toy, Covered Wagon, Wood, Fabric Cover, Painted Metal Wheels, N.N. Hill, 11 x 20 In.	173.00
Toy, Jeep, Nellybelle, Deputy Badge On Window, Cast Steel, Marx, 1950s, 12 In.	285.00
Toy, Jeep, Peep Hole For Gun, Mechanic's Legs Protruding, Garton, 39 In.	385.00
Toy, Roy Astride Trigger, Wood, Paper Design, Red Metal Wheels, Pull Toy, c.1950, 10 In.	285.00
Toy, Stagecoach Wagon Train, Plastic Stagecoach, 3 Cars, Box, Marx, 3 x 15 In.	158.00
Toy, Stagecoach, Horses, Plastic, Ideal, Box, 1955	250.00
Toy, Trigger, Double R Bar Ranch, Musical, Coin-Operated, 10 Cents, 1955	15000.00
Toy, Trigger, Hollywood Horses Series, Breyer, Box, VHS Golden Stallion, 14 x 11 In.	165.00
View Finder, Box, c.1955	85.00

ROYAL BAYREUTH is the name of a factory that was founded in Tettau, Bavaria, in 1794. It has continued to modern times. The marks have changed through the years. A stylized crest, the name Royal Bayreuth, and the word *Bavaria* appear in slightly different forms from 1870 to about 1919. Later dishes may include the words *U.S. Zone,* the year of the issue, or the word *Germany* instead of *Bavaria.* Related pieces may be found listed in the Rose Tapestry, Sand Babies, Snow Babies, and Sunbonnet Babies categories.

Bowl, Cornucopia, Brown & Pink Tones, Scene Of Young Woman, 12 ½ In.	100.00
Bowl, Poppy Shape, Scarlet Red, Marked, c.1910, 9 ½ In.	115.00
Box, Green & Brown, Horn Of Plenty Scene, Covered, Square, Green Mark, 2 ½ In.	30.00
Candleholder, Devil & Cards, c.1900, 3 x 5 In.	266.00
Cigarette Box, Violet Pattern, c.1960, 2 In.	17.78
Creamer, Cat, Black Matte, Orange Accents, Handle, Marked, 5 In.	150.00
Creamer, Elk, Blue Mark, c.1910, 4 ½ x 5 ½ In.	85.00
Creamer, Fox Head, 4 ½ x 5 ¼ In.	2110.00
Creamer, Gold & Roses, Bavaria	65.00
Creamer, Rabbit, 4 ½ x 3 In.	1003.00
Hatpin Holder, Penguin, c.1900, 5 x 3 In.	325.00
Match Holder, Devil & Cards, c.1919, 6 x 4 In.	1003.00
Pitcher Set, Lemon, c.1900, 7 Piece	885.00
Pitcher, Alligator, c.1900, 4 ½ x 3 ¾ In.	336.00
Pitcher, Bear, c.1900, 4 ½ x 4 ½ In.	531.00
Pitcher, Butterfly, 4 x 6 In.	106.00
Pitcher, Cockatoo, White, Yellow, c.1900, 5 x 5 ¼ In.	472.00
Pitcher, Cow, Black & Orange, Marked, c.1900, 4 x 6 In. .... *illus*	71.00

R

Pitcher, Devil & Cards, c.1900, 7 ½ x 7 ¾ In.	266.00
Pitcher, Devil, Seated, c.1900, 3 ¾ x 5 In.	236.00
Pitcher, Duck, Mallard, Blue Head, 6 ¾ x 6 ¾ In.	207.00
Pitcher, Elk, c.1900, 5 x 6 ½ In.	148.00
Pitcher, Frog, Green, 2 ½ x 3 x 4 ¾ In.	83.00
Pitcher, Geranium, c.1900, 5 x 5 In.	266.00
Pitcher, Lobster, Red, Green Loop Handle, c.1900, 7 In.	144.00
Pitcher, Lobster, Shell, 2 ¾ x 5 ¼ In.	83.00
Pitcher, Milkmaid, c.1900, 4 ½ x 5 In.	266.00
Pitcher, Monkey, Brown, 4 x 4 ¼ In.	118.00
Pitcher, Monkey, Green, c.1900, 4 ¼ x 4 In.	266.00
Pitcher, Orange, c.1900, 3 ¼ x 5 In.	348.00
Pitcher, Parrot, Red, White c.1900, 6 ¾ x 5 In.	266.00
Pitcher, Shell, Seahorse Handle, Pearl Coloring, c.1910, 7 ½ In.	525.00
Pitcher, Spiky Shell, Boot Shape, 4 x 5 In.	35.00
Pitcher, Squirrel, Gray, 8 x 7 In.	2950.00
Pitcher, Trout, Standing, c.1900, 4 ½ x 3 ¾ In.	207.00
Pitcher, Water Buffalo, c.1900, 4 x 6 In.	71.00
Salt & Pepper, Cherries, 3 x 2 ½ In.	118.00
Salt & Pepper, Purple Grapes, c.1900, 3 x 2 ¾ In.	71.00
Sauceboat, Poppy, Scarlet Red, Matching Underplate, c.1910, 4 ¾ In.	165.00
Sugar, Cover, Devil & Cards, Diamond Shape, 4 ½ In. ....illus	104.00
Sugar, Tomato, 2 ¾ In.	75.00
Tea Set, Yellow Rose, c.1900, 7 Piece	590.00
Teapot, Strawberry, White Flowers, Leaves, Gold Handles, Sugar & Creamer, 5 In.	550.00
Vase, Hunt Scene Band, Green Bottom, Cylindrical, Flared Rim, 6 ½ x 2 ½ In.	89.00
Vase, Mother, Child, Blue & White, Handles, c.1900, 9 ⅝ x 4 ½ In., Pair	384.00
Vase, Portrait, Girl, With Muff, Cobalt Blue, Brocaded Gold, Rose, 8 ½ In.	120.00
Vase, Woman, On Horse, Sidesaddle, 6 ½ x 2 ½ In.	94.00

ROYAL BONN is the nineteenth- and twentieth-century trade name used by Franz Anton Mehlem, who had a pottery in Bonn, Germany, from 1836 to 1931. Porcelain and earthenware were made. The factory was purchased by Villeroy & Boch in 1921 and closed in 1931. Many marks were used, most including the name Bonn, the initials FM, and a crown.

Biscuit Jar, Embossed, Pink, Blue, White, Flowers, Scrolls, Silver Plated Lid, Bail, 7 ¼ In.	120.00
Biscuit Jar, Green, Yellow, Red Flowers, Scrolls, Gilt Silver Plated Lid, Handle, 6 ½ In.	70.00
Clock, Ansonia, La Blois, Flowers, Cobalt Blue, Gilt, Pendulum Case, Marked, 11 x 8 ¾ In.	518.00
Clock, Ansonia, La Layon, Painted Flowers, Pink, Blue, Magenta, Scrolls, 14 x 15 In.	837.00
Clock, Ansonia, La Palma, Shaded Green, Flowers, Gold Trim, c.1905, 12 x 14 In.	378.00
Clock, Ansonia, La Plata, Gong, 8-Day, Open Escapement, c.1904, 12 ½ In. ....illus	360.00
Clock, Ansonia, La Rambla, Flowers, Blue Shaded To Yellow & Pink, 12 In.	141.00
Clock, Ansonia, La Vergne, Pendulum, Curvy Shaped, Scrolls, Shell, Flowers, 11 x 14 In.	188.00
Clock, Ansonia, Porcelain, Gilt Trim, Pendulum, Late 1800s, 11 x 14 x 5 In.	384.00
Clock, Flowers, Pendulum, Key, 11 In.	383.00
Clock, Mantel, La Bonita, Blue & White, Flowers, Red Stamp, 10 x 7 ½ x 4 In.	120.00
Clock, Shelf, Delft Blue & White, Windmill, Sailboat, Flowers, c.1880, 13 ½ x 8 In.	431.00
Dish, Sweetmeat, White, Flowers, Silver Plate Lid, Bail Handle, Square, 4 ½ x 4 ½ In.	75.00
Jardiniere, Tapestry, Mountain Scene, Floral Highlight, 7 x 10 In.	150.00
Urn, Cover, 2 Handles, Round Foot, Flowers, Gold Highlights, 24 In.	316.00
Urn, Cover, Baluster, Molded Leaves, Gilt, Painted Flowers, c.1900, 15 ¼ In.	177.00
Urn, Cover, Flowers, Gold Accents, White Ground, Handles, Germany, 24 In.	259.00
Urn, Delft Style, Sailing Ship, Harbor, Scroll & Flower Borders, c.1910, 29 ½ In.	236.00
Vase, Art Nouveau Flowers, Silver Overlay, Signed, 4 ½ In. ....illus	45.00
Vase, Cover, White, Cobalt Blue, Gilt, Pedestal Foot, 16 In.	118.00
Vase, Cream Ground, Cactus Blossoms, 9 ½ In.	90.00
Vase, Flowers, Painted, Applied Angular Handles, Marked, c.1910, 16 In. ....illus	148.00
Vase, Flowers, Wine Colored Ground, Gilt Highlights, Dolphin Handles, Scroll Feet, c.1900, 17 In. illus	915.00
Vase, Green, Yellow, Flowers, Square Neck, Bun Base, 2 Square Handles, Marked, 16 x 10 In.	120.00

ROYAL COPENHAGEN porcelain and pottery have been made in Denmark since 1775. The Christmas plate series started in 1908. The figurines with pale blue and gray glazes have remained popular in this century and are still being made. Many other old and new style porcelains are made today.

Bowl, Flora Danica, Domed Cover, Oval, Crabstock Handle, Flowers, 6 In.	1067.00
Bowl, Flora Danica, Oval, Branch & Flower Handle, Gilt, c.1970, 8 ¾ In.	1673.00

Royal Doulton, Figurine, Hostess Of Williamsburg, HN 2209, 7 ⅜ In. $47.00

Conestoga Auction Co., Inc.

R

Royal Doulton, Figurine, Moor, Flambe, HN 3642, c.1952, 17 ⅛ In. $1185.00

Skinner, Inc.

Royal Doulton, Figurine, Napoleon At Waterloo, HN 3429, 11 ½ In. $1200.00

DuMouchelles Art Gallery

R

TIP

If there are traces of glue on the back of a label, soak the label and carefully scrape the glue off under water. Then dry flat.

Bowl, Salad, Flora Danica, Blue Wave Mark, 1969-74, 9 In.	1075.00
Bowl, Salad, Flora Danica, Oval, Botanical Orchids, 1969, 11 In.	976.00
Cup & Saucer, Botanical, Straight-Sided, Angular Handles, 5 ½ In., 10 Piece	4481.00
Dish, Centerpiece, White, Leaves, Gold Trim, Triangular, Round Pedestal Base, 5 x 8 ½ In.	780.00
Figurine, 2 Girls Reading, 7 In.	95.00
Figurine, 2 Playful Ducks, Mottled Brown & Tan Glaze, 9 In.	98.00
Figurine, Boy & Calf, 7 In.	120.00
Figurine, Boy, On Side, Holding Leg, 4 ½ In.	400.00
Figurine, Boy, Seated, Whittling, Christian Thomsen, 7 ¼ In.	104.00
Figurine, Brown Bear Cub, 4 x 6 In.	71.00
Figurine, Cat, Seated, Sung Glaze, Incised Knud Kyhn, Denmark, 5 In.	298.00
Figurine, Dog, Pointer, Seated, 5 x 10 In.	127.00
Figurine, Dog, Pug, Seated, Marked, 3 ¼ In.	68.00
Figurine, Europa, The Bull, Star Studded Gown, 6 ¾ x 7 In.	878.00
Figurine, Faun, Pulling Bear's Ear, 1925, 7 ¼ In.	1800.00
Figurine, Fish, Cod, Green, Pin, White, Marianne Hoest, 1890, 10 In.	1500.00
Figurine, Flight To America, Couple, Standing, Man, Arm Around Woman, 8 In.	173.00
Figurine, Girl Feeding Calf, 6 ½ In.	250.00
Figurine, Girl Milking Cow, 9 In.	300.00
Figurine, Girl, Lamb, Kneeling, White, Blue, 1925, 6 ⅜ In.	600.00
Figurine, Man, Backpack, Geese, Rock Base, Multicolor, 7 In.	761.00
Figurine, Milkmaid, Cow, 5 ¼ x 7 ¼ In.	936.00
Figurine, Pheasant, 7 ½ In.	115.00
Figurine, Rooster, Hen, 9 ½ In.	147.00
Figurine, Siamese Cat, Sitting, 7 ½ In.	190.00
Figurine, Snowy Owl, 16 In.	500.00
Figurine, Tabby Cat, Gray, 7 ½ In.	190.00
Figurine, Wave & Rock, Nudes Kissing, 18 In.	826.00 to 1440.00
Figurine, Woman, Holding Hen, Egg Basket, Multicolor, 6 In.	702.00
Figurine, Woman, Holding Skirt Out, Hat, Ruffled Collar, 1865, 7 In.	550.00
Figurine, Woman, Kneeling, Braids, Hat, Blanc De Chine, 5 ½ In.	350.00
Figurine, Young Lovers, Seated, Tree, Dog, 6 x 5 ¼ In.	556.00
Group, Bacchus, Bacchante, Child Satyr, Tub, Tiger, Glass Dome, 13 x 9 ½ In.	4095.00
Group, Hercules, Battling Lion, Blue Cloak, Swags, Ram's Heads, 9 x 5 ½ In.	1404.00
Plate, Bread, Flora Danica, 6 ¾ In., 12 Piece	2963.00 to 3750.00
Plate, Bread, Floral Danica, Reticulated, Gilt, 1900s, 9 In., 6 Piece	3437.00
Plate, Christmas, 1908, Madonna & Child, 6 In.	2655.00
Plate, Christmas, 1909, Winter Scene, 6 In.	295.00
Plate, Christmas, 1910, Wise Men, 6 In.	177.00
Plate, Dinner, Flora Danica, Reticulated, 11 In., Pair	2000.00
Plate, Mother's Day, 1980, 6 In. ....*illus*	48.00
Plate, Tropical Fish, Basket Weave Border, Green Glaze, Gilt, 1900s, 9 ⅞ In., 12 Piece	1067.00
Platter, Flora Danica, Oval, Violet Plant, c.1970, 14 ¼ In.	2868.00
Platter, Flora Danica, Serrated Rim, 16 ¼ In.	1000.00
Platter, Serving, Flora Danica, Oval, Flowers, Gilt Edge, 1900s, 18 x 14 In.	5036.00
Sauceboat, Flora Danica, Underplate, Handle, Flower Heads, Gilt Rim, 1900s, 6 x 9 In.	1185.00
Serving Platter, Flora Danica, Lobster Design, Oval, Gilt Rim, 1900s, 18 x 14 In.	4444.00
Soup Tureen, Flora Danica, Oval, Dome Lid, Handles, Flower Heads, 1900s, 12 x 9 In.	3851.00
Tray, Flora Danica, Round, Botanical Painting, Dentil Border, c.1970, 9 ½ In.	2806.00
Tray, Flora Danica, Waisted Rectangle, Botanical Salix, Gilt, 11 ¾ In.	2562.00
Vase, Stoneware, Warty, Cream, Brown, Green, Stamp, 4 ¾ x 3 ¾ In.	4340.00
Vase, Wavy Woven Design, Brown Matte Glaze, Axel Salto, 6 ¼ x 3 In. ....*illus*	1240.00

ROYAL COPLEY china was made by the Spaulding China Company of Sebring, Ohio, from 1939 to 1960. The figural planters and the small figurines, especially those with Art Deco designs, are of great collector interest.

Head Vase, Pirate Head, Dark Hair, Gray Head Covering, Green Shirt, Yellow Collar, 8 In.	55.00

ROYAL CROWN DERBY COMPANY, LTD., is a name used on porcelain beginning in 1890. There is a complex family tree that includes the Derby, Crown Derby, and Royal Crown Derby porcelains. The Royal Crown Derby mark includes the name and a crown. The words *Made in England* were used after 1921. The company became part of Allied English Potteries Group in 1964. It was bought in 2000 and is now privately owned.

Bowl, Salad, Red Aves, 1943, 4 ½ x 11 ½ In.	461.00
Candlestick, Imari, Porcelain, Gilt, 11 In., Pair	720.00

Candlestick, Imari, Porcelain, Square Base, Red, Blue, Gilt, 10 ½ In., Pair	400.00
Ewer, Urn Shape, Footed, Gilt Flower Design, Salmon Ground, Long Neck, Handle, 1894, 10 In.	207.00
Figurine, Lamb, Resting, Cobalt Face, Blue Swirls, Gilt, 1990, 3 x 2 ½ In.	175.00
Paperweight, Tom Tabby Cat, White, Blue & Red Stripes, 5 ¾ In.	175.00
Plate, Chinese Birds, Pate-Sur-Pate, Blue Ground, White, 10 ½ In., 11 Piece	590.00
Plate, Dessert, Old Imari, Fluted, 8 ½ In.	456.00
Plate, Dinner, Blue Mikado, Scalloped, 10 ¼ In.	87.00
Plate, Dinner, Mandarin, 10 ½ In.	165.00
Plate, Enamel, Leaf Banded Border, Monogrammed Crest, Gilt, 1800s, 8 In., 12 Piece	889.00
Plate, Flower Urns, C-Scrolling, Leaf Tips, Blue, Ivory, Gilt, 1893, 10 In., 12 Piece	2596.00
Plate, Olde Avesbury, Frame, 10 ½ In.	236.00
Plate, Urns, Fruit, Scrolling Leaf Tips, Cinnabar Ground, Gilt, c.1900, 9 In., 12 Piece	2185.00
Platter, Fish, Lily, Gilt Rim, Cobalt Blue, White, 23 ¼ In.	230.00
Platter, Imari Style, c.1877-90, 11 x 13 In.	276.00
Soup, Dish, Blue Mikado, Scalloped, 8 ⅛ In.	214.00
Urn, 2 Handles, Amphora, Pedestal, Gilded, Flowers, c.1898, 5 ⅞ x 4 In.	700.00
Urn, Cobalt Blue, Gilt Design, Cartouche, Flowers, Signed, 14 In., Pair	652.00
Urn, Imari Pattern, Gold, Red, White, Black, High Scroll Handles, 1900s, 17 In, Pair	575.00
Vase, Cover, Raised Tooled Gold, Swags, Blue Ground, Urn Shape, Square Foot, c.1891, 15 In., Pair	2403.00
Vase, Enameled, Gilt, Oval, Flared Neck, Socle Foot, Leaves, 1900s, 9 ¼ In., Pair ....*illus*	830.00

ROYAL DOULTON is the name used on Doulton and Company pottery made from 1902 to the present. Doulton and Company of England was founded in 1853. Pieces made before 1902 are listed in this book under Doulton. Royal Doulton collectors search for the out-of-production figurines, character jugs, vases, and series wares. Some vases and animal figurines were made with a special red glaze called flambe. Sung and Chang glazed pieces are rare. The multicolored glaze is very thick and looks as if it were dropped on the clay. In 2005 Royal Doulton was acquired by the Waterford Wedgwood Group, which was bought by KPS Capital Partners of New York in 2009 and became part of WWRD Holdings.

Animal, Bull Dog, British, Union Jack Drape, D 5913, 5 ½ In.	250.00
Animal, Bull Dog, Helmet, Haversack, HN 146, 6 ½ In.	650.00
Animal, Cat, Persian, Seated, DA 129, 4 In.	125.00
Animal, Tiger, Rock, HN 2639, 10 x 12 In.	374.00
Biscuit Jar, Brown Tortoiseshell Ground, Gold Sea Turtle & Seaweed Design, Silver Lid & Bail, 6 ½ In.	90.00
Bowl, Flambe, Red Floral Blossom Interior, Signed, 4 x 9 ¾ In.	60.00
Bowl, Golfing Scene, Painted, Verse, He That Always Complains Is Never Pitied, 8 In.	104.00
Bowl, Mottled Brown, Wave Design, Signed Vera Huggins, c.1925-50, 11 In.	237.00
Bowl, Red Flambe Glaze, Gold Wash Sterling Rim, Pierced Flowers, Gorham, 1902, 12 In.	1422.00
Bowl, Round Foot, Berry Branches, Leaves, White Ground, 13 In.	178.00
Bucket, Slop, Removable Inset, Scene Of Girl With Balloon, Bamboo Handle, 10 x 11 In.	2300.00

Royal Doulton character jugs depict the head and shoulders of the subject. They are made in four sizes: large, 5 ¼ to 7 inches; small, 3 ¼ to 4 inches; miniature, 2 ¼ to 2 ½ inches; and tiny, 1 ¼ inches. Toby jugs portray a seated, full figure.

Character Jug, Air Raid Precaution Warden, D 7209, 5 ½ In.	203.00
Character Jug, 'Ard Of Hearing, D 6588, 7 ½ In. ....*illus*	835.00
Character Jug, Bacchus, D 6499, 7 ¼ In.	110.00
Character Jug, Beatles, Caricature, S.T. Taylor, 1984, 6 In., 4 Piece	285.00
Character Jug, Cleopatra & Antony, D 6728, 2-Sided, 7 ½ In.	65.00
Character Jug, Country Cousin, Straw In Teeth, D 6295, Small	180.00
Character Jug, General Custer & Sitting Bull, D 6712, 2-Sided, 7 ½ In.	65.00
Character Jug, Rip Van Winkle, D 6463, 4 ¾ In.	50.00
Character Jug, Toby Philpots, D 5737, 3 ¼ In.	50.00
Ewer, 3 Stag Medallions, Hannah Barlow, 15 x 6 In.	1364.00
Ewer, Burslem, Flower, Hand Painted, 9 x 5 ½ In.	90.00
Figurine, A Courting, HN 2004, 1946, 7 ¼ In.	260.00
Figurine, Anniversary, HN 3625, 8 ¾ In.	249.00
Figurine, As Good As New, HN 2971, 1981, 6 ½ In.	73.00
Figurine, Autumn Breezes, HN 1913, 7 ⅝ In.	53.00
Figurine, Balloon Girl, HN 2818, 6 ⅜ In.	135.00
Figurine, Balloon Man, HN 1954, 7 ¼ In.	47.00 to 51.00
Figurine, Bedtime Story, HN 2059, 4 ¾ In.	165.00
Figurine, Beggar, HN 2175, 6 ¼ In.	226.00
Figurine, Bernice, HN 2071, 8 In.	224.00
Figurine, Biddy Penny Farthing, HN 1843, 9 In.	240.00
Figurine, Biddy, HN 1513, 1946, 5 ½ In.	79.00

Royal Doulton, Figurine, Old Balloon Seller, HN 1315, 7 ½ In. $120.00

DuMouchelles Art Gallery

Royal Doulton, Figurine, Rhapsody, HN 2267, 6 ¾ In. $59.00

Conestoga Auction Co., Inc.

Sunlight Is Bad

Be careful where you display valued collectibles. Keep them out of direct sunlight. Sunlight can damage all kinds of rugs, photographs, upholstery, fabrics, even wood. It fades colors and weakens materials. Three elements in the light spectrum cause the problems. Ultraviolet (UV) causes 40 percent of the fading and over 50 percent of the deterioration. Visible light causes 25 percent of the fading. Infrared (solar heat) causes the other 25 percent of the fading. Other environmental factors cause 10 percent of the fading. Heat will also cause dryness, warping, and deterioration in wood, paper, and natural fibers.

Royal Doulton, Jug, Kingsware, Huntsman Fox, Dewar's, Brown Glaze, c.1900, 4 In.
$207.00

Glass Works Auctions

TIP

When packing a piece of pottery for shipping, look at the shape. If it has a hollow space larger than one inch across, fill the space with sponge foam or bubble wrap.

Figurine, Blithe Morning, HN 2065, 7 In.	35.00
Figurine, Bluebeard, HN 2105, 1952-92, 11 In.	59.00
Figurine, Bonnie Lassie, HN 1626, 5 ¼ In.	328.00
Figurine, Captain Cook, HN 2889, 8 In.	237.00
Figurine, Captain, HN 2260, 9 ½ In.	180.00
Figurine, Carrie, HN 2800, c.1980, 6 In.	30.00
Figurine, Country Love, HN 2418, 8 In.	136.00
Figurine, Cup Of Tea, HN 2322, 6 ¾ In.	175.00
Figurine, Dancing Years, HN 2235, 6 ¾ In.	147.00
Figurine, Duke Of Wellington, HN 3432, 12 In.	678.00
Figurine, Elegance, HN 2264, 7 ¼ In.	48.00
Figurine, Eventide, HN 2814, 1976, 7 ¾ In.	96.00
Figurine, Falstaff, HN 2054, 7 In.	71.00 to 83.00
Figurine, Field Marshal Montgomery, HN 3405, 11 ¾ In.	565.00
Figurine, Flower Seller's Children, HN 1342, 8 ¼ In.	180.00
Figurine, Foaming Quart, HN 2162, 5 ¾ In.	71.00
Figurine, Good King Wenceslas, HN 3262, 9 In.	295.00
Figurine, Goody Two Shoes, HN 2037, 1975, 5 ¼ In.	47.00
Figurine, Goose Girl, HN 2419, 8 In.	136.00
Figurine, Granny's Heritage, HN 2031, 6 ¾ In.	339.00
Figurine, Gretchen, HN 1397, 8 In.	497.00
Figurine, H.M Queen Elizabeth, HN 2882, 1980, 8 In.	339.00
Figurine, H.M Queen Elizabeth, HN 3944, 10 ¾ In.	136.00
Figurine, Heart To Heart, HN 2276, 1960, 5 ½ In.	339.00
Figurine, Hold Tight, HN 3298, 8 ½ In.	294.00
Figurine, Home Guard, HN 4494, 8 ¾ In.	192.00
Figurine, Hostess Of Williamsburg, HN 2209, 7 ⅜ In. ....*illus*	47.00
Figurine, Jack Point, HN 2080, 16 ½ In.	960.00
Figurine, Janet, Green, HN 1737, 6 ½ In.	249.00
Figurine, Janet, Pink, HN 1916, 5 ¼ In.	102.00
Figurine, Janet, Purple, M 75, 4 ¼ In.	249.00
Figurine, Jean, HN 1878, 8 In.	170.00
Figurine, Joan Of Arc, HN 3681, 10 In.	237.00
Figurine, Kate Hardcastle, HN 1719, 8 In.	339.00
Figurine, Kate Hardcastle, HN 2028, 8 ¼ In.	189.00
Figurine, King Charles, HN 2084, 16 In.	767.00
Figurine, Kirsty, HN 2381, 1971-96, 7 ½ In.	175.00
Figurine, Lady & The Unicorn, HN 2825, 8 ¾ In.	1074.00
Figurine, Lady Charmain, HN 1948, 8 In.	72.00
Figurine, Land Girl, HN 4361, 8 ¾ In.	158.00
Figurine, Le Bal, HN 3702, 8 ½ In.	158.00
Figurine, Leda & The Swan, HN 2826, 9 ¾ In.	1130.00
Figurine, Lydia, Green, HN 1907, 4 ¾ In.	192.00
Figurine, Lydia, Red, HN 1908, 4 ¾ In.	50.00
Figurine, Make Believe, HN 2225, 1961, 5 ¾ In.	50.00
Figurine, Marietta, Green, HN 1446, 8 ¼ In.	678.00
Figurine, Marietta, Red, HN 1341, 8 ¼ In.	735.00
Figurine, Mary Queen Of Scots, HN 3142, 9 In.	283.00
Figurine, Master, HN 2325, 6 ½ In.	90.00
Figurine, Meditation, HN 2330, 5 ¾ In.	113.00
Figurine, Mendicant, HN 1365, 8 In.	147.00
Figurine, Midsummer Noon, HN 1899, 4 ¾ In.	362.00
Figurine, Miss Muffet, Green, HN 1937, 5 ½ In.	147.00
Figurine, Monica, HN 1467, c.1975, 4 In.	83.00
Figurine, Moor, Flambe, HN 3642, c.1952, 17 ⅛ In. ....*illus*	1185.00
Figurine, Moor, HN 4646, 16 ½ In.	1062.00
Figurine, Moor, HN 2082, 17 In.	735.00
Figurine, Napoleon At Waterloo, HN 3429, 11 ½ In. ....*illus*	1200.00
Figurine, Officer Of The Line, HN 2733, 9 In.	249.00
Figurine, Old Balloon Seller, HN 1315, 7 ½ In. ....*illus*	120.00
Figurine, Old Balloon Seller, HN 3737, 7 ½ In.	300.00
Figurine, Pantalettes, Green, HN 1362, 8 In.	226.00
Figurine, Pantalettes, Pink, HN 1412, 8 In.	203.00
Figurine, Pensive Moments, HN 2704, 5 In.	47.00
Figurine, Pretty Lady, HN 565, 10 In.	622.00
Figurine, Pretty Polly, HN 2768, 1983, 6 In.	102.00

Figurine, Queen Anne, HN 3141, 9 In.	180.00
Figurine, Queen Elizabeth I, HN 3099, 9 In.	226.00
Figurine, Rag Doll Seller, HN 2944, 1983, 7 In.	147.00
Figurine, Railway Sleeper, HN 4418, 7 In.	203.00
Figurine, Rest Awhile, HN 2728, 8 In.	124.00
Figurine, Rhapsody, HN 2267, 6 ¾ In. ....*illus*	59.00
Figurine, Rustic Swan, HN 1746, 5 ¼ In.	1017.00
Figurine, Sailor, HN 4632, 8 ¼ In.	158.00
Figurine, Save Some For Me, HN 2959, 1982, 7 ¼ In.	62.00
Figurine, Sir Walter Raleigh, HN 2015, 11 ½ In.	430.00
Figurine, Sir Winston Churchill, HN 3057, 1984, 10 ½ In.	96.00
Figurine, Solitude, HN 2810, 5 ½ In.	158.00
Figurine, Sophie, HN 2833, 6 In.	30.00
Figurine, Spring Flowers, HN 1807, 7 In.	130.00
Figurine, Squire, HN 1814, 9 ¾ In.	1752.00
Figurine, Symphony, HN 2287, 5 ¼ In.	100.00 to 126.00
Figurine, Territorial Service, HN 4495, 8 ¾ In.	180.00
Figurine, Tete-A-Tete, HN 799, 6 In.	1356.00
Figurine, Tootles, HN 1680, 4 ¼ In.	30.00
Figurine, Valerie, HN 2107, 4 ¾ In.	45.00
Figurine, Vice Admiral Lord Nelson, HN 3489, 12 ½ In.	537.00 to 678.00
Figurine, Wardrobe Mistress, HN 2145, 5 ¾ In.	260.00
Figurine, Willy Won't He, HN 2150, 5 ½ In.	170.00
Figurine, Winston Churchill, HN 3433, 12 In.	339.00
Figurine, Women's Auxiliary Air Force, HN 4554, 8 ¼ In.	170.00
Figurine, Women's Royal Navy Service, HN 4498, 9 In.	180.00
Figurine, Young Love, HN 2735, 10 In.	237.00
Humidor, Cover, Greek Key Border, Figures, c.1900, 8 In.	711.00
Jug, Bands Of Flowers, Scroll Leaves, Loop Handle, Round Foot, Hinged Lid, c.1875, 9 In.	356.00
Jug, Cobalt Blue, Gray, Scrolled Leaves, Bottle Shape, Loop Handle, Flare Rim, 9 In.	356.00
Jug, Kingsware, Huntsman Fox, Dewar's, Brown Glaze, c.1900, 4 In. ....*illus*	207.00
Jug, Servant, Presenting Plate Of Fruit To Cavalier, Fence, Roses, Castle, Gilt Sky, 8 In.	123.00
Pitcher, Kingsware, Golf Scene, Multicolor, c.1940, 9 ¼ In.	299.00
Plate Set, Fish Design, Gilt Bellflower Swag Border, Joseph Hancock, 9 ⅛ In., 12 Piece	345.00
Plate, 3 Men, Carrying Coach, Woman Inside, Gilt Border, 12 ½ In.	11.00
Plate, Hiding In The Primroses, 8 In.	13.00
Plate, Nursery Rhymes, Cat & Fiddle, 1905, 8 In.	130.00
Plate, Scalloped Rim, Gilt Flower Design, Multicolor, England, 1900s, 10 ½ In., 10 Piece	1541.00
Tobacco Jar, Lid, Owl Shape, Blue, Brown, Silicon Line, Lambeth, c.1900, 7 ¾ In.	575.00
Toby Jug, Cardinal, 6 In.	89.00
Urn, The King's Speech, 2 Handles, Coronation Of George VI, 1937, 11 In.	600.00
Vase, Berry & Leaf, Tile Design, Incised, Signed, Lambeth, 15 In.	374.00
Vase, Blue, Brown Glaze, Beaded Flower, Flower Cartouches, c.1915, 10 In., Pair	173.00
Vase, Cobalt Blue, Squares Design Around Neck, Swirls, Tapered, Rolled Rim, 10 In.	207.00
Vase, Cylindrical, Barkis, 2 Handles, 1931, 4 ½ In.	105.00
Vase, Cylindrical, Blue Design, Multicolor Art Deco Design, Stamped, 10 In.	125.00
Vase, Cylindrical, Tapered Neck, Band Of Fruit, Multicolor, 1900s, 12 In., Pair	296.00
Vase, Duck Medallions, Carved Stoneware, Lambeth Stamp, 14 x 5 ¾ In., Pair	2332.00
Vase, Flambe, Shouldered, 11 ½ In.	140.00
Vase, Flambe, Veined, 16 In.	2232.00
Vase, Flambe, Woodcut, Fisherman, Landscape, Castle, Bottle Shape, 13 In.	150.00
Vase, Fruit & Leaves, Upturned Loop Handles, Eliza Simmance, c.1910, 7 In., Pair ....*illus*	306.00
Vase, Mottled Blue Glaze, Mermaid, Crashing Waves, Round Foot, Urn Shape, 1900s, 8 In.	296.00
Vase, Sung, Red Glaze, Black, Blue, Amber, 5 ⅝ In.	518.00
Vase, Turquoise, White Enamel, Stippled Gold, Blue Flared Neck, c.1920, 6 ½ In.	115.00
Vase, Woman Seated, Courtyard, Flowers, Gilt, Baluster, Flare Rim, 1800s, 10 In.	1126.00

ROYAL DUX is the more common name for the Duxer Porzellanmanufaktur, which was founded by E. Eichler in Dux, Bohemia (now Duchov, Czech Republic), in 1860. By the turn of the twentieth century, the firm specialized in porcelain statuary and busts of Art Nouveau–style maidens, large porcelain figures, and ornate vases with three-dimensional figures climbing on the sides. The firm is still in business.

Bowl, Shell Shape, Barefoot Woman, Standing, Wearing Robes, Flowers, Marked, 10 x 9 In.	288.00
Centerpiece, Maiden, Gold Gown, Holding Fishnet, Shell Shape Bowls, Pedestal, Waves, 14 In.	518.00
Centerpiece, Maiden, Leaf Form Side Bowls, Folded Leaf Vase, Marked, 22 In.	144.00
Figurine, Blacksmith & Family, Wife Kneeling, Child Reaching, 25 In.	213.00

Royal Doulton, Vase, Fruit & Leaves, Upturned Loop Handles, Eliza Simmance, c.1910, 7 In., Pair
$306.00

Skinner, Inc.

Royal Flemish, Biscuit Jar, Lid, Golden Earth Tones, Roses, Gilt Branches, Rope Handle, 8 In.
$1725.00

Early Auction Co.

R

Royal Flemish, Vase, Cover, Raised
Section, Romanesque Coins, Crown
Finial, 7 In.
$2013.00

Early Auction Co.

Royal Nymphenburg, Figurine, Stag,
Branch In Mouth, Marked, c.1940, 21 In.
$649.00

Brunk Auctions

558

Figurine, Boy On Donkey, 15 x 12 In.	83.00
Figurine, Couple Sitting At Table, Tea, Dog Under Chair, Cobalt Blue, Gold, Marked, 13 x 15 In.	288.00
Figurine, Dancer, 23 In.	413.00
Figurine, Rebecca, Sitting, Painting Urns, Matte Glaze, 8 x 6 x 4 In.	108.00
Vase, Iris, 2 Angled Handles, 2 Loop Handles, c.1910, 13 In.	147.00
Vase, Pink Hollyhocks, Green Leaves, Ground, Baluster, 16 ½ In.	173.00
Vase, Smokestack Shape, 2 Handles, Rolled Rim, Seed & Leaf, Marked, 22 In.	201.00

ROYAL FLEMISH glass was made during the late 1880s in New Bedford, Massachusetts, by the Mt. Washington Glass Works. It is a colored satin glass decorated with dark colors and raised gold designs. The glass was patented in 1894. It was supposed to resemble stained glass windows.

Biscuit Jar, Gold Earth Tone Panels, 4 Roman Coin Medallions, 8 In.	900.00
Biscuit Jar, Lid, Golden Earth Tones, Roses, Gilt Branches, Rope Handle, 8 In. ....*illus*	1725.00
Ewer, 3 Multicolor Segments, Rampant Lion, Lance, Banner, Crest, Gold, 11 ¾ In.	3250.00
Ewer, Double Lion Crest, Crown On Front, 4-Color Panels, 12 In.	2200.00
Vase, Bulbous, Stick Form, Earth Tones, 3 Griffins, Gilt Rim, 11 In.	3000.00
Vase, Bulbous, Trifold Rim, Blue & Crimson Design, Dragon, 14 In.	1900.00
Vase, Cover, Raised Section, Romanesque Coins, Crown Finial, 7 In. ....*illus*	2013.00

ROYAL HAEGER, *see Haeger category.*

ROYAL IVY, *see Northwood, Royal Ivy.*

ROYAL NYMPHENBURG is the modern name for the Nymphenburg porcelain factory, which was established at Neudeck-ob-der-Au, Germany, in 1753 and moved to Nymphenburg in 1761. The company is still in existence. Marks include a checkered shield topped by a crown, a crowned *CT* with the year, and a contemporary shield mark on reproductions of eighteenth-century porcelain.

Figurine, Leopard, Reclining, Ears Upright, 5 x 12 In.	813.00
Figurine, Parrot, White, Red, Blue, Green, Yellow Crown, c.1890, 7 ½ x 6 In.	2360.00
Figurine, Stag, Branch In Mouth, Marked, c.1940, 21 In. ....*illus*	649.00
Group, Couple, Under Apple Tree, Glazed, Round Grass Design Base, 1900s, 9 x 9 In.	89.00
Group, Venus Blindfolding Cupid, 15 In. ....*illus*	1652.00
Jar, Lid, Baluster, Applied Pale Flowers, Cream Ground, Germany, 1900s, 12 In.	120.00

ROYAL RUDOLSTADT, *see Rudolstadt category.*

ROYAL VIENNA, *see Beehive category.*

ROYAL WORCESTER is a name used by collectors. Worcester porcelains were made in Worcester, England, from about 1751. The firm went through many different periods and name changes. It became the Worcester Royal Porcelain Company, Ltd., in 1862. Today collectors call the porcelains made after 1862 "Royal Worcester." In 1976, the firm merged with W.T. Copeland to become Royal Worcester Spode. The company was bought by the Portmeirion Group in 2009. Some early products of the factory are listed under Worcester. Related pieces may be listed under Copeland, Copeland Spode, and Spode.

Basket, Branch Shape Handle, Shells, Fruit, 4-Footed Base, c.1840, 6 x 9 In.	1725.00
Bowl, Flowers, Scalloped Rim Applied Stem Lotus Bud, Stem, Seed Pod, Frog, c.1870, 7 x 12 In.	923.00
Candle Snuffer, Boy, Wearing Nightshirt, Pompom Hat, 4 In.	160.00
Compote, Shell, Cream, Molded Seaweed & Round Base, Gilt & Brown Accents, c.1890, 8 In.	207.00
Decanter, Yellow Ground, Gilt Leaves, Buds, Handles, 14 ½ In.	176.00
Dish, Leaf Shape, White, Brown Veins, Green Rim, 10 In., Pair	300.00
Dish, Sweetmeat, Figural, Man, On Tree Branch, White, Gold, 1880, 7 In.	95.00
Ewer, Gilded Enamel Flowers, Butterflies, Ivory Ground, Bronze Dragon Handle, c.1885, 12 In.	178.00
Figurine, Water Carrier, White Body, Gold, Multicolor, Mounted As Lamp, 1800s, 21 x 35 In.	540.00
Flask, Moon, Circle, Footed, Black & Gilt, Asian Landscapes, Birds, 1877, 16 In., Pair	3760.00
Jug, Flowers, Gold Trim & Handle, c.1889, 6 ½ In.	175.00
Jug, Hot Water, Oval, Molded Mask, Woman, Ivory Ground, Gilt Trim, Flowers, c.1887, 10 In.	276.00
Pitcher, Water, Cream Color, Gold Leaf, Handle Highlights, 8 In.	125.00
Planter, Figural, Swan, 7 ¼ x 9 ½ In.	225.00
Plaque, Silhouette, Mother & Child, White, Terra-Cotta, Frame, 14 x 9 In.	443.00
Plate, Dessert, Fruits, Blossoms, Scalloped Border, 1918, 8 ¾ In., 11 Piece	1495.00
Plate, Floral Sprigs, Leaf Shape, Pink Veining, c.1800, 7 ½ x 10 In.	460.00

R

Potpourri, Parcel Gilt Lobed Body, Handley Rose Design, Gilt Cover, c.1920, 4 ½ x 3 ½ In......		460.00
Vase, Blackberries, A. Davis, 3 In. ....*illus*		520.00
Vase, Bottle Shape, Dolphin Handles, Gilt Trim, Landscape, Cottage, Signed, c.1903, 9 In........		1715.00
Vase, Bottle Shape, Jeweled, Ivory Ground, Flowers, Raised Gold, 1800s, 15 ⅛ In.......................		474.00
Vase, Campana Shape, Leaf Scroll Handles, Flared Rim, Cattle Scene, Signed, 1900s, 22 In. ...		9500.00
Vase, Cover, Fruit, Handles, H.H. Price, 9 ½ In. ....*illus*		741.00
Vase, Elongated Pear Shape, Lattice Carved, Light Blue Glaze, Pheasants, Signed, 11 In..........		2200.00
Vase, Flowers, Long Neck, Gold Rim, Yellow Ground, Handles, 15 ½ In...............................		196.00
Vase, Monkey Holding Hexagonal Vase, Cranes, England, 1872, 7 In....................................		184.00
Vase, Royal Swan & Shells, Posy, 8 ½ In. ....*illus*		2013.00
Vase, White Glaze, Raised Carp, Greek Key Border, Urn Shape, 11 x 8 In...............................		1265.00
Wall Pocket, Slipper Orchid Shape, 1884, 8 ½ In..		978.00

ROYCROFT products were made by the Roycrofter community of East Aurora, New York, in the late nineteenth and early twentieth centuries. The community was founded by Elbert Hubbard, famous philosopher, writer, and artist. The workshops owned by the community made furniture, metalware, leatherwork, embroidery, and jewelry. A printshop produced many signs, books, and the magazines that promoted the sayings of Elbert Hubbard. Furniture by the Roycroft community is listed in the Furniture category.

Andirons, Iron, Scrolled, Chain, 27 x 13 In..		992.00
Bookends, Brass, Hammered, Stylized Geometric Design, Marked, 5 In.		354.00
Bookends, Copper, Flowers, Orb & Cross Mark, 5 ½ x 5 In............................		744.00
Bookends, Relief Quatrefoil, Open Panels, Copper, Hammered, Orb, 8 ½ x 5 In.		237.00
Candlestick, Copper, Hammered, Impressed Mark, 3 ½ x 8 In., Pair		360.00
Desk Set, Hammered, Bronze Patina, Over Brass, Letter Holder, Blotter, Corners, 3 x 5 ½ In...		173.00
Lamp, Copper, Hammered, Brass Washed, Marked, 14 x 6 In............................		992.00
Lamp, Copper, Hammered, Helmet Shade, Signed, 6 x 14 In.		1440.00
Lamp, Copper, Hammered, Mica Shade, 13 ½ x 10 In............................		3720.00
Tabouret, Square Top, Drawer, Marked, 19 x 11 In.		1860.00
Vase, Bud, Glass, Brass Base With Orb, 2 ½ x 8 In.		264.00
Vase, Copper, Hammered, Dogwood, Cylindrical, Marked, 10 x 3 In.		1054.00
Vase, Copper, Hammered, Long Neck, Marked, 11 ½ x 5 ½ In.		2108.00

ROZANE, *see Roseville category.*

ROZENBURG worked at The Hague, Holland, from 1890 to 1914. The most important pieces were earthenware made in the early twentieth century with pale-colored Art Nouveau designs.

Lamp Base, High Glaze, Bulbous, Round Base, Botanical Design, c.1899, 16 In.		296.00
Plate, Wall, High Glaze, Enamel, Flowers & Leaves, c.1894, 9 & 11 In., Pair........................		711.00
Vase, Bud, Eggshell Porcelain, Handles, Brown, White, Green, Marked Den Haag, 7 x 3 ½ In..		3720.00
Vase, Bud, Iris, Pinched Waist, Footed, 1903, 3 ¼ x 1 ¼ In...		1116.00
Vase, Bud, Sunflower, Spider In Web, Square Rim, Footed, Marked, 1903, 4 x 3 In..................		4650.00
Vase, Fish, Stick Neck, Bulbous, Footed, Marked, 1900, 16 x 9 ½ In..................................		4030.00
Vase, Flowers, Gourd Shape, Signed, 13 x 9 In...		1860.00
Vase, Paneled, Parrot, Signed, 1902, 8 x 4 In..		2356.00
Vase, Parrot, Flowers, Plants, Eggshell Porcelain Handles, Huyvenaar, 1904, 17 x 5 ½ In. .....*illus*		5580.00

RRP, or RRP Roseville, is the mark used by the firm of Robinson-Ransbottom. It is not a mark of the more famous Roseville Pottery. The Ransbottom brothers started a pottery in 1900 in Ironspot, Ohio. In 1920, they merged with the Robinson Clay Product Company of Akron, Ohio, to become Robinson-Ransbottom. The factory closed in 2005.

R. R. P.Co. U.S.A. Roseville. O.

Biscuit Jar, Point & Clover, White Satin, Pink & White Roses, 7 ½ In.		300.00
Bowl, Iris Mold, White, Peach & Lavender Tones, Pink Poppies, Satin Finish, 10 ¼ In.		200.00
Pitcher, Aqua, Tan & White Drip Glaze, Baluster, Square Handle, Marked, RRP Co., 21 In.		35.00
Tea Set, Yellow, Green & Brown, Flowers, Pedestal, 3 Piece		100.00

RS GERMANY is part of the wording in marks used by the Tillowitz, Germany, factory of Reinhold Schlegelmilch from 1914 until about 1945. The porcelain was sold decorated and undecorated. The Schlegelmilch families made porcelains marked in many ways. See also ES Germany, RS Poland, RS Prussia, RS Silesia, RS Suhl, and RS Tillowitz.

Bowl, Oval, Pink, Cream Roses, Gilt, Cut-In Handles, c.1910, 9 ¼ x 4 In.		360.00
Bowl, Pink Carnation Center, Gold Pierced, Scalloped Rim, 10 In.....................................		129.00
Bowl, Portrait, Woman, Brown Hair Piled High, Brown Scalloped Rim, 10 In..........................		195.00

Royal Nymphenburg, Group, Venus Blindfolding Cupid, 15 In.
$1652.00

DuMouchelles Art Gallery

Royal Worcester, Vase, Blackberries, A. Davis, 3 In.
$520.00

Potteries Specialist Auctions

Royal Worcester, Vase, Cover, Fruit, Handles, H.H. Price, 9 ½ In.
$741.00

Potteries Specialist Auctions

R

Royal Worcester, Vase, Royal Swan & Shells, Posy, 8 ½ In. $2013.00

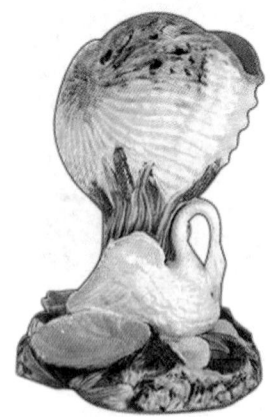

Strawser Auction Group

Embezzler Turned Artist

Karl Kipp (1881–1954) started working in copper at the Roycroft community in 1908 and by 1910 he was designing and making many important pieces of silver. But what is rarely told is that Kipp had been in prison for three years before he came to the Roycroft Copper Shop. He was a convicted embezzler who was found guilty of grand larceny. Kipp was one of many former prisoners hired by Elbert Hubbard, who had a theory about prison reform. Kipp went on to open his own Tookay shop, named for his initials (two *K*s). Later he worked again for Roycroft, then opened the Karl Kipp Shops to produce pewter, then designed for Daystrom Corporation, manufacturers of chrome and steel dinette sets.

Cake Plate, Pink Roses, 10 ⅞ In.	80.00
Candy Basket, White Green Poppies, Pastel Ground, Shaped, Gilt, Marked, c.1910, 7 x 3 ¾ In.	90.00
Celery Dish, 3 Roses, Peach, White, Cut-In Handles, c.1910, 12 ½ x 5 In.	45.00
Chocolate Set, Pink Roses, Green Leaves, Taupe Band, c.1932, 9 In. Pot, 4 Cups, Saucers 3 x 5 In.	165.00
Plate, Salmon Lilies, Green Leaves, Transferware, c.1915, 8 ¼ In.	25.00
Plate, Serving, White, Green California Poppies, Cut-In Handles, Gilt, c.1915, 9 ¾ In.	40.00
Plate, White Magnolias, Green Leaves, Cut-In Handles, Gilt, 10 x 9 ½ In.	200.00
Relish, Dahlias, White, Peach, Shaped, Marked, c.1915, 8 x 4 In.	60.00
Serving Bowl, Gold & Flower Border, Center, Marked, 9 ½ x 2 In.	70.00
Serving Bowl, White & Peach Dahlias, c.1910, 9 ¼ x 2 ¼ In.	75.00
Serving Bowl, Yellow, Peach Flower Border & Center, Scalloped Gilt Rim, Marked, 9 ½ x 2 In.	85.00
Sugar & Creamer, White, Peach Magnolias, Marked, c.1910, 3 ¾ In.	95.00
Teacup, Saucer, Peach Roses, White Ground, Gilt Rim.	95.00
Toothbrush Holder, 3 Openings, Triangular, Pink Roses, Painted, Marked, c.1870, 3 ¾ In.	175.00
Toothpick Holder, Rose, 3 Handles, c.1910, 2 ¼ In.	80.00
Tray, Orange Poppies, Gilt, c.1910, 14 x 6 ½ In.	95.00

RS POLAND (German) is a mark used by the Reinhold Schlegelmilch factory at Tillowitz from about 1946 to 1956. After 1956, the factory made porcelain marked *PT Poland*. This is one of many of the RS marks used. See also ES Germany, RS Germany, RS Prussia, RS Silesia, RS Suhl, and RS Tillowitz.

Cup & Saucer, Cabbage Rose Design, Gilt, Pedestal Cup, 1930s, 2 x 3 ¼ In.	98.00
Plate, Large White Flowers, Scalloped Gilt Rim, c.1935, 7 ½ In.	37.00
Vase, Homecroft Scene, Gilt Handles, Rim, Marked, 9 ½ In.	580.00

RS PRUSSIA appears in several marks used on porcelain before 1917. Reinhold Schlegelmilch started his porcelain works in Suhl, Germany, in 1869. See also ES Germany, RS Germany, RS Poland, RS Silesia, RS Suhl, and RS Tillowitz.

Berry Bowl, White, Lavender, Peach Satin Finish, Summer Portrait, Iris Mold, 5 ½ In.	275.00
Biscuit Jar, Green, Yellow, Pink, Glass Bowl, 8-Sided, 7 In.	225.00
Bowl, Carnation, Pink, Yellow, Roses, 10 ½ In.	150.00
Bowl, Cream Center, Green Border, Pink Poppy, Gold, Mauve, Green, Iris Mold, 10 ¼ In.	150.00
Bowl, Lily, Turquoise Border, Lavender Medallions, Wild Flowers, Gold Detail, 10 ½ In.	260.00
Bowl, Salad, Flowers, Green Shaped Rim, Gilt, 2 ⅝ x 10 ⅜ In.	184.00
Bowl, Scalloped, Yellow, Blue & Lavender, Violet, 10 ½ In.	150.00
Bowl, White, Iridescent Green, Lavender Border, Pink, Yellow Roses, 10 In.	125.00
Bowl, Yellow, Green, Lavender, Fruit, Ruffled Edge, 10 ½ In.	100.00
Bowl, Yellow, Green, Scenic, Fruit, Wine, Scalloped, 10 In.	175.00
Cake Plate, Hidden Image, White, Pink, Green, Flowers, 2 Handles, 12 In.	175.00
Celery Dish, Turquoise & Rose Medallion, 2 Pierced Handles, Oval, 12 In.	525.00
Celery Dish, Yellow, Green, Flowers, 12 In.	150.00
Chocolate Pot, Cover, Pink, White, Cream, Roses, 4 Cups & Saucers, 9 ½ In.	400.00
Coffeepot, Cream, White, Pink Rose, Gold Highlights, Buttressed Handle, 9 In.	70.00
Ewer, Portrait, Summer Season, Pedestal, Footed Base, 1900s, 9 ⅛ In.	950.00
Hatpin Holder, Calla Lily, Leaves, Green To Tan, 1930s, 4 ½ In.	33.00
Sugar & Creamer, Green, Roses, Morning Glory Mold	25.00
Sugar & Creamer, Green, White, Flowers, Acorn Mold	100.00
Tankard, Yellow, Brown, Pink Roses, 13 ¾ In.	250.00
Toothpick Holder, Green, Roses, Medallion Mold, 2 Handles	60.00
Tray, Bun, Scenic, Castle, Yellow, Green, Pink, 13 In.	225.00

RS SILESIA appears on porcelain made at the Reinhold Schlegelmilch factory in Tillowitz, Germany, from the 1920s to the 1940s. The Schlegelmilch families made porcelains marked in many ways. See also ES Germany, RS Germany, RS Poland, RS Prussia, RS Suhl, and RS Tillowitz.

Bowl, Cover, Cabbage Roses, Handles, Gilt	62.00
Bowl, Opalescent, Footed, Oval, Handles, 8 In.	30.00
Bowl, Orange Poppies, Oval, Pierced Gilt Rim Handles, Marked, 10 ¼ x 6 ¾ In.	85.00
Cake Plate, Flowers, Leaves, White, Green, Three Handles, c.1930, 8 In.	24.00
Celery Dish, Flowers, Green Ground, Oval, c.1925, 9 ¼ x 1 ½ In.	47.00
Plate, Springtime, Maiden, Green Band, Blue Check Rim, Signed Y.R. Oubrem, c.1920, 12 In.	747.00
Sugar & Creamer, Cover, Sage Green, Peach Fuchsia Blossoms, Sugar 5 ½ In., Creamer 4 ¾ In.	55.00
Syrup, Underplate, Lily Of The Valley, Pastel Green, c.1910, 5 ½ x 3 ½ In.	95.00
Tidbit, White Flowers, Gilt Set-In Handles, Rim, Marked, 1940s, 6 ¾ In.	40.00
Tray, Old Ivory Pattern, Roses, 6 ¼ In.	75.00

RS SUHL is a mark used by the Reinhold Schlegelmilch factory in Suhl, Germany, between 1900 and 1917. The Schlegelmilch families made porcelains in many places. See also ES Germany, RS Germany, RS Poland, RS Prussia, RS Silesia, and RS Tillowitz.

Bowl, Cream, Red, Kaufmann Courting Scene, Gold Detail, Prussia Mold, 10 In.	100.00
Vase, Castle Cartouche, Wide Pink, Yellow Rose Bands, Gilt, 4 ½ In.	450.00
Vase, Melon Eaters Cartouche, Mountain Scene Reverse Side, 5 In.	675.00

RS TILLOWITZ was marked on porcelain by the Reinhold Schlegelmilch factory at Tillowitz from the 1920s to the 1940s. Table services and ornamental pieces were made. See also ES Germany, RS Germany, RS Poland, RS Prussia, RS Silesia, and RS Suhl.

Bowl, 6 Lobed Hawthorn Flowers, Gray Matte, Border, Gilt Edge, c.1938, 9 ¾ x 2 ½ In.	62.00
Dresser Set, Tray, 2 Covered Cups, Pink Flowers, Green Ground, Gilt	135.00
Jam Jar, Underplate, Cover, Salmon Roses, Buds, Gilt, Jar 4 x 3 ½ In., Plate 5 ½ In.	145.00
Plate, Pheasant Scene, Flower Border, Octagonal, Gilt, 8 In.	30.00
Plate, Yellow Roses, Gilt Border, Mark, 8 ½ In.	12.00
Relish, White Lilies, Lily Of The Valley, Cut-In Handles, Gilt, 1920s, 8 x 3 ¾ In.	42.00
Vase, Pheasant Scene, Mark, 4 ⅜ In.	155.00

RUBINA is a glassware that shades from red to clear. It was first made by George Duncan and Sons of Pittsburgh, Pennsylvania, about 1885. This coloring was used on many types of glassware. The pressed glass patterns of Royal Ivy and Royal Oak are listed under Northwood.

Cheese Dome, Thumbprint Pattern, Daisy & Button Canary Base, 7 In.	144.00
Condiment Set, 3 Bottles, Silver Plated Ivy-Leaf Stand, New England Glass Co., c.1890, 6 In.	295.00
Cruet, Raindrop, Opalescent, Multicolor Enamel Flowers, 8 ½ In. *illus*	690.00
Mug, 2 Daffodils, Leaves, Crystal Handle, Fuchsia & Gold, 5 In.	173.00
Pitcher, Coin Spot, Enamel Flowers, Ribbed Handle, 5 ½ In.	100.00
Pitcher, Water, Acid Etched Bird, Flowers, 9 In.	150.00
Pitcher, Water, Hobnail, Polished Pontil, 8 ½ In.	150.00
Punch Bowl, Opalescent, Optic Diamond Pattern, Wide Rim, 16 In.	403.00
Reamer, Tab Handles, Marked, 3 ½ In., 2 Piece	75.00
Syrup, Coin Spot, Ring Neck, Pear Shape, Loop Handle, Metal Lid, Hobbs, Brockunier, 7 In., Pair	173.00

RUBINA VERDE is a Victorian glassware that was shaded from red to green. It was first made by Hobbs, Brockunier and Company of Wheeling, West Virginia, about 1890.

Cruet, Teepee Shape, Thumbprint Pattern, Flowering Pussy Willow, 7 In.	475.00
Pitcher, Water, Coin Spot, 7 ¾ In.	200.00

RUBY GLASS is the dark red color of a ruby, the precious gemstone. It was a popular Victorian color that never went completely out of style. The glass was shaped by many different processes to make many different types of ruby glass. There was a revival of interest in the 1940s when modern-shaped ruby table glassware became fashionable. Sometimes the red color is added to clear glass by a process called flashing or staining. Flashed glass is clear glass dipped in a colored glass, then pressed or cut. Stained glass has color painted on a clear glass. Then it is refired so the stain fuses with the glass. Pieces of glass colored in this way are indicated by the word *stained* in the description. Related items may be found in other categories, such as Cranberry Glass, Pressed Glass, and Souvenir.

Compote, Round Dish, Cut Rim, Gold & Platinum Leaves, Silver Base, c.1900, 8 ¼ In.	267.00
Epergne, 2 Tiers, Triple Camel Brass Base, 1800s, 16 In.	690.00
Jar, Dome Cover, Gilded, Flared Rim, Tapered, 3 Bun Feet, Leafy Vines Design, 7 ¾ In.	123.00
Stirrup Cup, Cut Glass, Overlay, c.1890, 13 ¾ In.	72.00
Vase, Enameled Flowers, c.1900, 15 x 5 In.	144.00
Vase, Flared Scalloped Rim, Flower Spray, Twisting Vines & Leaves, c.1900, 6 ¾ In., Pair	399.00
Vase, Golf Scene, Sterling Overlay, c.1940, 8 In.	311.00

RUDOLSTADT was a faience factory in the Thuringia region of Germany from 1720 to about 1791. In 1854, Ernst Bohne began working in the area. From about 1887 to 1918, the New York and Rudolstadt Pottery made decorated porcelain marked with the RW and crown familiar to collectors. This porcelain was imported by Lewis Straus and Sons of New York, which later became Nathan Straus and Sons. The word *Royal* was included in their import mark. Collectors often call it "Royal Rudolstadt." Most pieces found today were made in the late nineteenth or early twentieth century. Additional pieces may be listed in the Kewpie category.

Figurine, 1800s Aristocratic Dress, Marked Germany RW, 19 x 5 ½ In., Pair	461.00
Oyster Plate, 5 Wells, Flower, 8 ¾ In.	59.00
Plate, 5 Frolicking Kewpies, Gold Trim, Rose O'Neill Wilson, 6 ¼ In.	49.00

R

Rozenburg, Vase, Parrot, Flowers, Plants, Eggshell Porcelain Handles, Huyvenaar, 1904, 17 x 5 ½ In. $5580.00

Rago Arts & Auction Center

Rubina, Cruet, Raindrop, Opalescent, Multicolor Enamel Flowers, 8 ½ In. $690.00

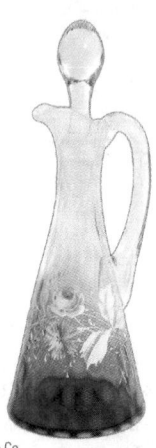

Early Auction Co.

Rug, Chinese, Flowers, Vines, Lavender Ground, c.1935, 8 Ft. x 9 Ft. 8 In. $2006.00

Brunk Auctions

R

Vase, Flowers, Gilt Feet, Handles, 5 ¾ x 4 In.	65.00
Vase, Pink, Cream, Wild Flowers, Pedestal, Handles, 10 ½ In.	200.00

RUGS have been used in the American home since the seventeenth century. The oriental rug of that time was often used on a table, not on the floor. Rag rugs, hooked rugs, and braided rugs were made by housewives from scraps of material. American Indian rugs are listed in the Indian category.

Afshar, Animal Medallions, Red, Turquoise, Navy Blue Ground, Persia, c.1910, 9 Ft. 6 In. x 6 Ft. 10 In.	4148.00
Afshar, Ivory, Blue, Gold, Red Medallions, Red Ground, Wool, Cotton Weft, 5 Ft. 5 In. x 6 Ft. 5 In.	242.00
Agra, Allover Boteh, Multicolor, Green Field, Ivory Palmette Border, 13 Ft. x 12 Ft. 7 In.	1875.00
Andy Warhol Design, Figures, Moon, Orange, Red, Gray, Sphinx Weavers, Polypropylene, 10 ½ x 8 Ft.	830.00
Art Deco, Cream Ground, Stylized Radiating Flowers, Wool, c.1945, 8 Ft. 9 In. x 9 Ft. 8 In.	2868.00
Aubusson, Flowers, Medallions, Black, Cream, Pink, Fringe, Chinese, 11 Ft. 6 In. x 18 Ft.	2040.00
Aubusson, Needlework, Flowers, Red Medallion, Vine, Green Field, 5 Ft. 10 In. x 9 Ft.	177.00
Bakhtiari, Meandering Flower Palmettes, Medallions, Black Ground, Wool, 6 Ft. x 9 Ft. 2 In.	391.00
Bidjar, Trees, Flowers, Blues, Yellow, Red, Multiple Borders, Persia, c.1875, 12 Ft. 8 In. x 8 Ft.	8295.00
Bokhara, Beige, Red Medallions, Blue Field, Multiple Borders, 3 Ft. 3 In. x 3 Ft. 6 In.	148.00
Bokhara, Geometric, Brown, Tan, Silk, Wool, 14 Ft. 5 In. x 10 Ft. 7 In.	9000.00
Caucasian, Black, Red, Beige, Geometric Design, Fringe, Runner, 3 Ft. 9 In. x 9 Ft. 6 In.	805.00
Chinese, 11 Scholars, Standing On Cloud Of Flowers, Characters, 3 x 5 Ft.	154.00
Chinese, Art Deco, Flowers, Fans, Cobalt Blue, Green Border, Peking Wool, 11 Ft. x 14 Ft. 5 In.	960.00
Chinese, Art Deco, Flowers, Pagoda, Red, Wool, c.1930, 9 x 9 Ft.	1599.00
Chinese, Flowers, Vines, Lavender Ground, c.1935, 8 Ft. x 9 Ft. 8 In. ....*illus*	2006.00
Chinese, Purple Ground, Flowers, Diagonal Lined Border, 2 Ft. 6 In. x 4 Ft. 2 In.	266.00
Chinese, Red Field, Flowers & Butterflies, Green Border, c.1900, 2 Ft. 6 In. x 4 Ft. 5 In.	413.00
Dazkiri, Red, Flower, Geometric, Stepped Medallion, Red, Green, Turkey, c.1870, 5 Ft. 2 In. x 4 Ft. 5 In.	14220.00
Gabbeh, Art Deco Style, Red Ground, Abstract Gold, Pink, Blue, Wool, 5 Ft. 8 In. x 8 Ft. 6 In.	311.00
Gabbeh, Art Deco, Round, Rectangular Shapes, Ivory, Gold, Brown, Wool, 5 Ft. 6 In. x 7 Ft. 9 In.	425.00
Gabbeh, Red Ground, Crenellated Design, Scattered Designs, 9 Ft. 2 In. x 7 Ft. 2 In.	2988.00
Geometric, Woven Cipher, Ivan Da Silva Bruhn, Wool, 1920s, 4 Ft x 6 Ft. 2 In.	5580.00
Hamadan, Camel, Diamonds, Lattice, Flower, Geometric Border, c.1915, 11 Ft. 6 In. x 3 Ft. 7 In. . .*illus*	1035.00
Hamadan, Flowers, Ivory Ground, Blue & Black Borders, Persia, c.1970, 3 Ft. 8 In. x 6 Ft. 3 In.	295.00
Hamadan, Ivory Medallion, Herati Design, Red, Green, Blue, 7 Ft. 2 In. x 11 Ft. 4 In.	690.00
Hereke, Leaf Panels, Ivory Ground, Salmon Border, Flowers, Silk, 2 Ft. 2 In. x 3 Ft. 2 In.	708.00
Heriz, Arabesque Medallion, Red Ground, 1900s, 14 Ft. 2 In. x 9 Ft. 3 In.	465.00
Heriz, Central Medallion, Brick Red Ground, c.1950, 6 Ft. x 9 Ft. 4 In. ....*illus*	1416.00
Heriz, Geometric, Leafy Medallions, Red Field, Multiple Borders, Runner, 3 x 7 Ft.	384.00
Heriz, Ivory, Blue, Red Medallion, Spandrels, Blue Center Field, Red Border, 9 Ft. x 12 Ft. 3 In.	2596.00
Heriz, Medallion, Red, Dark Blue, Green, Ivory Spandrel, Vines, 6 Ft. 9 In. x 9 Ft. 7 In.	489.00
Heriz, Vegetable Dyes, Geometric, Red Border, Wool, c.1930, 8 Ft. 6 In. x 12 Ft.	2185.00
Hooked, Abstract Geometric Design, Multicolored, 74 ½ x 24 In. ....*illus*	200.00
Hooked, Beaver, On Log, Stumpwork Style, Fringe, 29 x 48 In.	5062.00
Hooked, Blue, Striated Center, Leaves, Vines, Flowers, c.1900, 55 x 73 In.	121.00
Hooked, Concentric Ovals, Pink, Red, Black Outline, Mounted, c.1925, 19 x 36 In. ....*illus*	118.00
Hooked, Cottage On Lake, Rowboat, Bridge, Acanthus Scrolls, 1900s, 31 x 51 In.	184.00
Hooked, Cow, Red, 14 x 18 In.	562.00
Hooked, Cream Colored Cottage, Trees, Flowers, Fence, Black, Beige, 1880s, 24 x 15 In.	245.00
Hooked, Diamond Pattern, Black, Cream, c.1900, 87 x 76 In.	1778.00
Hooked, Dog, Blue & Green Ground, Scalloped Border, Mounted, 25 x 45 In.	720.00
Hooked, Dog, Brown & White, Gray Ground, Flowers, Zigzag Border, 26 x 43 In.	79.00
Hooked, Dog, Lying Down, Tan & Brown, Frost Design, 31 x 55 In.	431.00
Hooked, Dog, Multicolored, Scalloped & Line Borders, Mounted, Wood Frame, c.1890, 28 x 46 In. *illus*	1185.00
Hooked, Dog, Scottie, Airedale, Green Lawn, Blue Sky, Wool, Knits, c.1930, 34 ½ x 50 In.	264.00
Hooked, Flower Basket, Oak Leaf Corners, 34 x 66 In.	365.00
Hooked, Flowerpots, Red, Orange & Yellow Flowers, c.1910, 27 x 38 In. ....*illus*	844.00
Hooked, Flowers, Checkerboard Corners, Diamond Shape Field, Frame, c.1890, 24 x 40 In.	81.00
Hooked, Flowers, Multicolor, Oval, Mounted, c.1910, 44 ½ x 27 In.	29.00
Hooked, Flowers, Pastel, 1900s, 114 x 164 In.	118.00
Hooked, Flowers, Pomegranates, Bud & Blossom Border, Wool, Frame, c.1910, 34 x 63 In. ...*illus*	1896.00
Hooked, Geese, In Pond, Lilies, Trees, Woven Tape Edge, 23 x 43 In.	170.00
Hooked, Geometric Design, Braided Border, Mounted, Wood Frame, c.1900, 24 x 40 In. ....*illus*	415.00
Hooked, Geometric Designs, Multicolor, Mounted, 31 x 51 In.	311.00
Hooked, Gray Tiger Cat, Leaves, Wool, Burlap, c.1930, 24 x 43 In.	499.00
Hooked, Hearts & Lovebirds, Black Border, 32 x 27 In.	1100.00
Hooked, Hens, Chicks, Multicolor, Black Ground, 27 ½ x 42 In.	1126.00
Hooked, Horse, Gray Ground, Black & Red Border, 17 ½ x 39 In.	226.00

Hooked, House, Wool, Cotton, Velvet Strips, Abstract Border, Frame, c.1910, 30 x 41 In. *illus*	1126.00
Hooked, Ice Skaters, Dog, Holly Leaves, The Ice Is Thin, c.1890, 30 x 47 In.	1093.00
Hooked, Lion, Reclining, Flower, Leaf Border, c.1900, 29 x 54 In.	2950.00
Hooked, Mat, Goose Flying Over Pine Trees, Grenfell, 1900-35, 16 ½ x 21 ½ In.	126.00
Hooked, Multicolor Striations, Framed Diamonds, Wool, Burlap, 45 x 57 In.	176.00
Hooked, Nantucket Harbor, Ships, Shoreline, Signed Cynthia McAdoo, 1900s, 37 x 54 In.	184.00
Hooked, Pot Of Roses Center, Gold Border, Red Roses, Green Stems, 75 x 82 In.	173.00
Hooked, Potted Tulip, Star, Flowers, Red, Green, Black, Lancaster Co., c.1930, 87 x 38 In.	1896.00
Hooked, Quatrefoil Flowers, Diamond, Striped Ground, Wool, Cotton, Burlap, 40 x 43 In.	235.00
Hooked, Rigged Ship, Sails, Early 1900s, 30 x 53 In.	403.00
Hooked, Still Life, Compote, Multicolor, Oval Shape, Maine, 39 x 48 In.	2760.00
Hooked, Stripes, Multicolor, c.1900, 144 x 118 In.	4688.00
Hooked, Stylized Tree, Striped Curved Shapes, Wool, Cotton, Burlap, Frame, 30 x 39 In.	382.00
Hooked, Wedding, House, Flowers, Tree, Initials, Henry, Wool, Cotton, Frame, c.1910, 33 x 40 In. *illus*	3081.00
Hooked, Welcome, Leaf Border, 31 x 60 In.	4200.00
Hooked, Wool, Duck, 2 Ducklings, Flowers, Multicolor Border, Wool, Burlap, c.1900, 23 x 39 In.	441.00
Isfahan, Flowers, Red, Navy, Tan, Fringe, 5 Ft. 3 In. x 7 Ft. 9 In.	720.00
Karaja, Navy, Ivory Medallion, Red Field, Ivory Border, Blue Guard Borders, 4 Ft. 10 In. x 6 Ft.	531.00
Kasham, Allover Flowers, Multicolor, Burgundy Field, Blue Palmette, 17 Ft. 6 In. x 10 Ft. 6 In.	2000.00
Kasham, Floral, Burgundy Ground, Ivory Borders, Persia, c.1950, 12 Ft. 4 In. x 18 Ft. 4 In.	1416.00
Kasham, Ivory Ground, Gold, Blue Scrolling Flowers, Multiple Borders, 8 Ft. 4 In. x 11 Ft. 10 In.	767.00
Kazak, Blue Ground, Red, Green Medallions, Red Border, c.1880, 4 Ft. 9 In. x 7 Ft. 5 In.	1652.00
Kazak, Cartouches, Multicolor, Geometric Border, Caucasus, c.1885, 7 Ft. 2 In. x 4 Ft. 2 In.	6518.00
Kazak, Double Prayer, Ivory Border, Blue Ground, 4 x 7 Ft.	2115.00
Kazak, Flowers, Stars, Crosses, Blue, Red, Tan Ground, Caucasus, c.1890, 8 Ft. 5 In. x 5 Ft. 3 In.	5333.00
Kazak, Indigo Field, 3 Multicolor Stepped Medallions, Ivory Border, 7 Ft. 10 In. x 4 Ft. 4 In.	1750.00
Kerman Laver, Multicolor Scrolling & Leaves, c.1920, 11 Ft. 6 In. x 17 Ft. 8 In.	1770.00
Kerman, Blue Field, Spruce Trees, Curved Archway, Ivory Border, 13 Ft. 11 In. x 9 Ft. 9 In.	4063.00
Kerman, Cream, Rust Ground, Flowers, Geometric, Red, Blue, Vine Border, 16 Ft. 6 In. x 12 Ft.	5378.00
Kerman, Ivory Ground, Flowering Urns, Leaf Bouquets, Blue, Red, Navy Borders, 2 Ft. 10 In. x 6 Ft.	384.00
Kerman, Meditation, Tree, Flowers, Garden, Olive Ground, Blue, Red, 6 Ft. 10 In. x 10 Ft. 5 In.	1770.00
Kerman, Palace, Flowers, Ivory Ground, Vines, Leaf Medallion, Border, 13 Ft. 4 In. x 23 Ft. 11 In.	2655.00
Konya, Prayer, Geometric, Flowers, Figure, Stepped, Red, Blue, Turkey, c.1870, 5 Ft. x 3 Ft. 8 In.	6518.00
Kurd, Bag Face, Diamonds, Geometric Design, Red, Blue, Peach, Ivory, 2 Ft. 10 In. x 3 Ft. 5 In.	489.00
Kurdish, Repeating Boteh Designs, Blue Black Diagonal Borders, 1900s, 2 Ft. 10 In. x 8 Ft. 10 In. *illus*	649.00
Laver, Geometrics & Flowers, Black, Tan, Red, Persia, c.1900, 13 Ft. 10 In. x 11 Ft. 8 In.	13035.00
Lillihan, Mat, Red Ground, Flowers, Navy Border, 1 Ft. 10 In. x 2 Ft. 7 In.	266.00
Mahal, Flowers, Red, Olive Green, Blue Cream, 11 Ft. x 17 Ft. 3 In.	1150.00
Mahal, Garden, Square Panels, Leaves, Red Border, Blue Guard Borders, 4 Ft. 9 In. x 6 Ft. 10 In.	384.00
Mahal, Meandering Flower Palmettes, Red Ground, Round, Wool, 6 Ft. x 6 Ft. 2 In.	316.00
Marasali, Prayer, Geometric, House Shape, Red, Black, Tan, Caucasus, c.1885, 5 Ft. 3 In. x 3 Ft. 5 In.	4740.00
Mashad, Ivory, Red Leaf Medallion, Spandrels, Navy Field, Red Border, Ivory Guard, 10 x 13 Ft.	1180.00
Mihrab, Prayer, Stepped Pendant, Blue Ground, Turkey, 3 Ft. 4 In. x 5 Ft. 5 In.	295.00
Moroccan, Diamonds, Beige, Black, Wool, 1950s, 101 x 60 In. *illus*	4688.00
Oriental, Geometric Medallion, Blue, Yellow, Red, Anchor Pendants, 3 Ft. 4 In. x 4 Ft. 9 In.	184.00
Oushak, Flowers, Scroll Border, Cream, Beige, Fringe, Pakistan, 13 Ft. 8 In. x 9 Ft. 10 In.	3300.00
Oushak, Salmon Medallion, Blue Ground, Flowers, Leaves, Turkey, 10 Ft. x 14 Ft. 2 In.	1298.00
Oushak, Yellow Field, Floral Medallion, Palmette, Vine Border, 12 Ft. 5 In. x 10 Ft. 11 In.	5313.00
Penny, Appliqued Plant, Red Blooms, Multiple Rooms, Wool, Felt, Burlap, c.1890, 26 ½ x 46 In. *illus*	690.00
Persian, Geometric, Navy Ground, Wide Blue Border, c.1930s, 4 Ft. 4 In. x 6 Ft. 6 In.	649.00
Persian, Geometric, Red, Ivory, Navy, Red Panels, Borders, 3 Ft. 3 In. x 4 Ft. 6 In.	325.00
Persian, Navy Blue Field, Elongated Medallion, c.1920, 3 Ft. 6 In. x 5 Ft.	230.00
Persian, Red Ground, Navy Border, Leafy Vines, 3 Ft. 5 In. x 5 Ft. 1 In.	148.00
Persian, Red Ground, Navy Medallions, Flowers, Navy, Ivory Borders, 7 Ft. 7 In. x 9 Ft. 9 In.	384.00
Persian, Red Ground, Orange & Red, Navy Geometric Medallions, 3 Ft. 4 In. x 9 Ft. 10 In.	413.00
Persian, Scrolling Flowers, Leaves, Black Ground, Tan, Rust, Border, 11 x 14 Ft. *illus*	276.00
Qashqai, Flowers, Medallions, Geometrics, Red, Blue, Yellow, Persia, c.1890, 10 Ft. x 5 Ft. 10 In.	5925.00
Rag, Braided, Flower Head Center, Circles, Scalloped Border, Multicolor, 11 x 9 Ft.	2100.00
Rag, Joined Panels, Random Color Strips, Shenandoah Valley, 82 x 158 In.	115.00
Rag, Oval, Multicolor, 20th Century, 163 x 112 In.	750.00
Rag, Single Panel, Tied Fringe, Shenandoah Valley, Runner, 123 x 190 & 82 In., 2 Piece	374.00
Sarouk, Flowers, Leaves, Medallion, Red Ground, Borders, Wool, 11 Ft. 7 In. x 8 Ft. 9 In. *illus*	1220.00
Sarouk, Mat, Medallion, Red Ground, Flowering Vines, Blue Spandrels, 2 Ft. 2 In. x 2 Ft. 6 In.	207.00
Sarouk, Medallion, Flower Arabesques, Border, Black Ground, Multicolor, 10 Ft. 4 In. x 14 Ft.	920.00
Sarouk, Red Field, Flowers, Cobalt Blue Border, 6 Guard Borders, 16 Ft. 10 In. x 10 Ft. 3 In.	1053.00
Serapi, Blue, Red Ground, Floral Medallion, Vine Border, 13 Ft. 8 In. x 10 Ft. 5 In.	6573.00

Rug, Hamadan, Camel, Diamonds, Lattice, Flower, Geometric Border, c.1915, 11 Ft. 6 In. x 3 Ft. 7 In. $1035.00

James D. Julia Inc.

Rug, Heriz, Central Medallion, Brick Red Ground, c.1950, 6 Ft. x 9 Ft. 4 In. $1416.00

R

Brunk Auctions

Rug, Hooked, Abstract Geometric Design, Multicolored, 74 ½ x 24 In.
$200.00

Conestoga Auction Co., Inc.

Rug, Hooked, Concentric Ovals, Pink, Red, Black Outline, Mounted, c.1925, 19 x 36 In.
$118.00

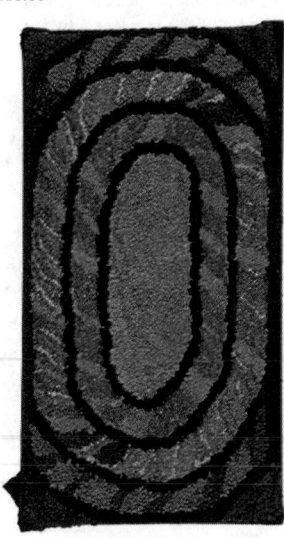

Garth's Auctions, Inc.

Serapi, Flowers, Red, Orange, Gold, Brown, Persia, 4 Ft. 1 In. x 6 Ft. 2 In.		450.00
Serapi, Medallion, Pendants, Red Ground, Green, Persia, 9 Ft. 2 In. x 12 Ft. 10 In.		4720.00
Sewan Kazak, Stylized Green Cross, Red Ground, Caucasus, c.1880, 8 Ft. 5 In. x 5 Ft. 6 In.		3555.00
Seychour, Triangular Panels, Flower, Leaf Borders, Red, Green, Caucasus, 1871, 10 Ft. 6 In. x 3 Ft. 5 In.		3851.00
Shiraz, Red Ground, Ivory, Blue, Pole Medallion, Ivory Border, c.1930, 5 Ft. 4 In. x 6 Ft. 3 In.		266.00
Shiraz, Scatter, Multicolor, Geometric Design, Diamond Shapes, 5 Ft. 3 In. x 10 Ft.		1150.00
Shirvan Baku, Cross Medallions, Geometrics, Red, Yellow, Caucasus, c.1875, 5 Ft. 6 In. x 3 Ft. 9 In.		4444.00
Shirvan, Blue Ground, Medallions, 3 Borders, c.1900, 3 x 4 Ft.		805.00
Tabriz, Black, Gold, Ivory Medallions, Red Ground, Wool, Cotton Weft, 3 Ft. 10 In. x 6 Ft. 6 In.		219.00
Tabriz, Blue Ground, Burgundy Medallion, Salmon Border, c.1940, 9 Ft. 3 In. x 12 Ft. 3 In.		823.00
Tabriz, Flower Bouquets, Vines, Diamond Lattice, Red Ground, 9 Ft. 7 In. x 13 Ft. 4 In.		7670.00
Tabriz, Flowers, Horses, Leaves, Gold, Orange, Green, Fringe Trim, Persia, 9 Ft. 4 In. x 12 Ft. 8 In.		660.00
Tabriz, Medallion, Flowers, Vines, Blue, Green, Red, Ivory, 8 Ft. 2 In. x 9 Ft. 9 In.		1265.00
Tabriz, Medallions, Blue, Gold, Ivory, Lattice, Terra-Cotta, Wool, 2 Ft. 7 In. x 2 Ft. 10 In.		667.00
Tabriz, Open Field, Red Ground, Blue Borders, c.1930, 7 Ft. 5 In. x 10 Ft. 8 In.		470.00
Turkish, Arabesque Medallion, Red, Cotton, c.1950, 12 x 8 Ft.		575.00
Turkoman, Gold Geometric, Red, Gray, Black Borders, Wool, 10 Ft. x 6 Ft. 4 In.		357.00
Yazd, Red Ground, Beige & Blue Medallion, Borders, c.1940s, 9 Ft. x 12 Ft.		1003.00

RUMRILL POTTERY was designed by George Rumrill of Little Rock, Arkansas. From 1933 to 1938, it was produced by the Red Wing Pottery of Red Wing, Minnesota. In January 1938, production was transferred to the Shawnee Pottery in Zanesville, Ohio. It was moved again in December of 1938 to Florence Pottery Company in Mt. Gilead, Ohio, where Rumrill ware continued to be manufactured until the pottery burned in 1941. It was then produced by Gonder Ceramic Arts in South Zanesville until early 1943.

RumRill

Bowl, White Glaze, Ribbed, 8 x 3 In.		30.00
Console, Beige Glaze, Pulled Down Corners, 13 x 8 In.		45.00
Cornucopia, Tan Matte Glaze, Footed, 1930s, 8 x 5 x 3 In.		25.00
Ewer, Grapes, Relief, Bulbous Base, Grapevine Handle, 10 ½ In.		95.00
Flower Frog, Brown Glaze, Deer Shape, 10 In.		39.00
Jug, Blue Gray Glaze, Globe Shape, Stopper, c.1930, 6 In.		52.00
Pitcher, Ball, Blue, Marked, 8 In.		95.00
Pitcher, Green, White, Mottled, Globe Shape, c.1937, 8 In.		34.00
Planter, Cadet Blue Glaze, Fan Shape, c.1940, 6 In.		21.00
Vase, 2-Tone, Fluted, Footed, Handles, c.1938, 12 In.		31.00
Vase, Dessert Rose, Basket Shape, Weave, c.1938, 6 x 9 x 6 In.		40.00
Vase, Dutch Blue, Fan Shape, c.1935, 6 x 6 In.		38.00

RUSKIN is a British art pottery of the twentieth century. The Ruskin Pottery was started by William Howson Taylor, and his name was used as the mark until about 1899. The factory, at West Smethwick, Birmingham, England, stopped making new pieces in 1933 but continued to glaze and sell the remaining wares until 1935. The art pottery is noted for its exceptional glazes.

RUSKIN POTTERY WEST SMETHWICK

Vase, Blue Mottled Glaze, Bulbous, c.1920, 9 In.		349.00
Vase, Blue Mottled Glossy Glaze, Marked, c.1920, 9 In.		240.00
Vase, Flared Rim, Round Foot, Pink, Opalescent Glaze, Globe Shape, Stamped, 1925, 9 ¼ In.		150.00
Vase, Mauve Mottled Glaze, Blue Grapevines, Grapes Around Shoulder, Marked, 8 ¾ In.	*illus*	920.00

RUSSEL WRIGHT designed dinnerware in modern shapes for many companies. Iroquois China Company, Harker China Company, Steubenville Pottery, and Justin Tharaud and Sons made dishes marked *Russel Wright*. The Steubenville wares, first made in 1938, are the most common today. Wright was a designer of domestic and industrial wares, including furniture, aluminum, radios, interiors, and glassware. A new company, Bauer Pottery Company of Los Angeles, is making Russel Wright's American Modern dishes using molds made from original pieces. The pottery is made in Highland, California. Pieces are marked *Russel Wright by Bauer Pottery California USA*. Dinnerware and other pieces by Wright are listed here. For more prices, go to kovels.com.

Russel Wright MFG. BY STEUBENVILLE

Aluminum, Bowl, Fruit, Rattan Handle, 1930s, 11 In.		500.00
Aluminum, Bun Warmer, Swivel Cover, Wood Handle, 10 In.		200.00
Aluminum, Canape Tray, Ball, Hoop, 13 ¾ In.		350.00
Aluminum, Tea Set, Teapot, Sugar & Lid, Creamer, Bowl & Lid, Pitcher, Tray, c.1935	*illus*	3750.00
Aluminum, Tray, 2 Tier, Rattan, Canape Tray, Handle, 13 ½ In.		190.00
American Modern, Bowl, Divided, Black Chutney, 13 ½ In.		135.00
American Modern, Bowl, Salad, Cedar Green, 11 In.		95.00
American Modern, Bowl, Salad, Coral, 11 In.		85.00
American Modern, Bowl, Salad, Granite Gray, 11 In.		85.00

R

American Modern, Casserole, Cover, Chartreuse, 4 Qt.	265.00
American Modern, Casserole, Cover, Handle, Granite Gray, 12 In.	38.00
American Modern, Celery Dish, Rolled Edges, Coral, 13 In.	22.00
American Modern, Chop Plate, Square, Chartreuse, 13 In.	45.00
American Modern, Compote, Seafoam Green, 4 In.	20.00
American Modern, Creamer, Coral, 7 In.	19.00
American Modern, Creamer, Seafoam Green, 7 In.	15.00
American Modern, Cup & Saucer, After Dinner, Coral, 4 ½ In., Pair	24.00
American Modern, Cup & Saucer, Bean Brown, 3 ¾ In.	25.00
American Modern, Cup & Saucer, Black Chutney, 3 ¾ In.	20.00
American Modern, Cup & Saucer, Coral, 3 ¾ In.	15.00
American Modern, Cup & Saucer, Granite Gray, 3 ¾ In.	20.00
American Modern, Gravy Boat, Chartreuse, 10 ½ In.	10.00
American Modern, Gravy Boat, Coral, 10 ½ In.	15.00
American Modern, Gravy Boat, Free-Form, Granite Gray, 5 ½ In.	50.00
American Modern, Gravy Boat, Underplate, Black Chutney	65.00
American Modern, Gravy Boat, Underplate, Chartreuse, 10 ½ In.	45.00
American Modern, Pitcher, Coral, 10 ½ In.	75.00 to 90.00
American Modern, Pitcher, Granite Gray, 10 ½ In.	78.00 to 85.00
American Modern, Plate, Bread & Butter, Seafoam Green, 6 In.	10.00
American Modern, Plate, Dinner, Coral, 10 In.	14.00
American Modern, Plate, Oval Handle, Coral, 10 In.	50.00
American Modern, Platter, Chartreuse, 13 ¼ In.	24.00
American Modern, Platter, Oval, Seafoam Blue, 13 ½ In.	36.00
American Modern, Platter, Rectangular, Chartreuse, 13 ½ In.	38.00
American Modern, Platter, Rectangular, Granite Gray, 13 ½ In.	25.00
American Modern, Salt & Pepper, Coral, 2 In.	18.00 to 24.00
American Modern, Salt & Pepper, Granite Gray, 2 In.	10.00
American Modern, Salt & Pepper, Seafoam Green	20.00
American Modern, Serving Bowl, Divided, Bean Brown, 11 ¼ In.	16.00
American Modern, Serving Bowl, Rolled Sides, Black Chutney, 10 x 7 In.	55.00
American Modern, Soup, Dish, Lug Handle, Bean Brown, 7 In.	25.00
American Modern, Teapot, Granite Gray, 10 In.	110.00
Imperial Pinch, Tumbler, Clear, 3 In.	28.00
Iroquois Casual, Bowl, Divided, Nutmeg Brown, 10 ¼ In.	18.00
Iroquois Casual, Butter, Pinched, Charcoal, 8 In.	50.00
Iroquois Casual, Casserole, Cover, Charcoal Gray, 4 Qt.	75.00
Iroquois Casual, Casserole, Cover, Nutmeg Brown, 2 Qt.	38.00 to 55.00
Iroquois Casual, Casserole, Cover, Pink Sherbet, 2 Qt.	59.00
Iroquois Casual, Casserole, Cover, Sugar White, 2 Qt.	68.00
Iroquois Casual, Creamer, Avocado	43.00
Iroquois Casual, Creamer, Sugar White.	11.00
Iroquois Casual, Cup & Saucer, Ripe Apricot	9.75
Iroquois Casual, Cup & Saucer, Sugar White.	5.00
Iroquois Casual, Gravy Boat, Avocado, 5 ¼ In.	85.00
Iroquois Casual, Gravy Boat, Pinch Top Handle, Charcoal Gray, 5 ¼ In.	42.00
Iroquois Casual, Plate, Dinner, Aqua, 10 In.	65.00
Iroquois Casual, Plate, Dinner, Sherbet Pink, 10 In.	16.00
Iroquois Casual, Plate, Luncheon, Ice Blue, 9 In.	10.00
Iroquois Casual, Plate, Luncheon, Ripe Apricot, 9 In.	10.00
Iroquois Casual, Platter, Nutmeg Brown, Oval, 15 In.	40.00
Iroquois Casual, Platter, Sherbet Pink, Oval, 13 In.	24.00
Iroquois Casual, Platter, Sugar White, Oval, 15 In.	25.00
Iroquois Casual, Salt & Pepper, Stacking, Charcoal Gray, 3 ¼ In.	34.00
Iroquois Casual, Sugar & Creamer, Pink Sherbet, 4 ¾ In.	38.00
Iroquois Casual, Teapot, Ripe Apricot, 11 In.	90.00
Oceana, Bowl, Free-Form, 4 ½ x 12 ½ In.	1054.00
Oceana, Bowl, Wood, Carved, Divided, 13 x 11 ½ In. ....*illus*	1488.00
Plate, Wild West Design, Indian Symbols, Brown, Harold's Club, Sterling China, 11 In.	50.00
Polynesian, Coffeepot, Blue, Green, White Lid, Sterling China, 9 In.	215.00
Queen Anne's Lace, Creamer	35.00
Queen Anne's Lace, Pitcher, White, Gold Stars, 9 ½ In.	125.00
Queen Anne's Lace, Plate, Bread & Butter	22.00
Tablecloth, Bold Geometric Grid, Yellow, Blue, 48 x 54 In.	30.00
Theme Informal, Bowl, Cereal, Dune, 5 ½ In.	125.00

Rug, Hooked, Dog, Multicolored, Scalloped & Line Borders, Mounted, Wood Frame, c.1890, 28 x 46 In. $1185.00

Skinner, Inc.

Rug, Hooked, Flowerpots, Red, Orange & Yellow Flowers, c.1910, 27 x 38 In. $844.00

Garth's Auctions, Inc.

Rug, Hooked, Flowers, Pomegranates, Bud & Blossom Border, Wool, Frame, c.1910, 34 x 63 In. $1896.00

Skinner, Inc.

Rug, Hooked, Geometric Design, Braided Border, Mounted, Wood Frame, c.1900, 24 x 40 In. $415.00

Skinner, Inc.

R

TIP
*Use castor cups
under the legs
of chairs to
protect carpets.*

Rug, Hooked, House, Wool, Cotton, Velvet Strips, Abstract Border, Frame, c.1910, 30 x 41 In.
$1126.00

Skinner, Inc.

Rug, Hooked, Wedding, House, Flowers, Tree, Initials, Henry, Wool, Cotton, Frame, c.1910, 33 x 40 In.
$3081.00

Skinner, Inc.

Rug, Kurdish, Repeating Boteh Designs, Blue Black Diagonal Borders, 1900s, 2 Ft. 10 In. x 8 Ft. 10 In.
$649.00

Brunk Auctions

SABINO glass was made in the 1920s and 1930s in Paris, France. Founded by Marius-Ernest Sabino (1878–1961), the firm was noted for Art Deco lamps, vases, figurines, and animals in clear, colored, and opalescent glass. Production stopped during World War II but resumed in the 1960s with the manufacture of nude figurines and small opalescent glass animals. Pieces made in recent years are a slightly different color and can be recognized. Only vintage pieces are listed here.

Sabino France

Bowl, Shell, Opalescent, Signed, 4 ¾ x 2 In.	135.00
Figurine, Escargot, Opalescent, Signed, 1 ¼ x 3 In.	60.00
Figurine, Isadora Duncan, Nude, Flowing Cape, 9 ¼ x 6 ½ In.	2045.00
Figurine, Kingfisher, Art Deco, Opalescent, Molded, Signed, c.1930, 4 ½ In.	145.00
Figurine, Libellule, Dragonfly, Opalescent, Signed, 6 In.	495.00
Figurine, Saint George's Fish, Poisson, Blown, Opalescent, 4 ½ x 4 In.	165.00
Figurine, Silhouette, Nude Woman, Paper Mark, Signed, 7 x 2 ½ In.	450.00
Figurine, Sparrow, Opalescent, Signed, 2 x 2 x 1 ½ In.	65.00
Lamp, Art Deco, Opalescent, Puffy Flowers, Nickel Base, Electric, 20 x 21 ½ In.	6500.00
Perfume Bottle, Frivolities, Art Deco Nudes, Swan, Opalescent, 6 ½ In.	210.00
Perfume Bottle, Opalescent Glass, Satin, Nudes, Flower Vines, Pinecone Stopper, Box, 6 In.	225.00
Perfume Bottle, Orchidees, Beveled Crystal Stopper, Paper Mark, 4 ½ x 1 ½ In.	130.00
Pin Tray, Violets, Leaves, Opalescent, ¾ x 4 ½ In.	89.00
Sign, Dealer's, Opalescent, Triangular Block, Logo In Block Letters, 1940s, 5 x 1 In.	125.00
Tray, Oyster Shell, Opalescent, Signed, 5 ¾ x 3 ½ In.	95.00
Tray, Rosace, Opalescent, Signed, 1 ½ x 5 ¼ In.	80.00
Vase, Art Deco Floral, Amber, Spherical, Pedestal Base, Signed, 6 In.	550.00
Vase, Fish, Flared, Square Base, Signed, 5 ¼ x 5 In., Pair	895.00
Vase, La Danse, Neoclassical Woman Dancers, Amethyst, Molded, Signed, c.1925, 8 x 6 In.	5900.00

SALOPIAN ware was made by the Caughley factory of England during the eighteenth century. The early pieces were blue and white with some colored decorations. Another ware referred to as Salopian is a late-nineteenth-century tableware decorated with color transfers.

Salopian

Coffeepot, Dome Lid, Round Foot, Curved Spout, Loop Handle, c.1800, 13 In.	230.00
Cup & Saucer, Handleless, Fruit, Flowers, Bird, 2 ⅛-In. Cup, 5 ⅜-In. Saucer ....*illus*	71.00
Waste Bowl, Transfer, Countryside, Cows, Sheep, Boy, Woman, 3 x 6 ⅛ In. ....*illus*	165.00

SALT AND PEPPER SHAKERS in matched sets were first used in the nineteenth century. Collectors are primarily interested in figural examples made after World War I. Huggers are pairs of shakers that appear to embrace each other. Many salt and pepper shakers are listed in other categories and can be located through the index at the back of this book.

Aunt Jemima & Uncle Mose, Plastic, F & F Mold & Die Works, 2 x 5 x 2 In.	90.00
Bakelite, Red, Black, 1 ½ In.	125.00
Bear, Cream, Red, Blue, American Bisque, Cork Stopper, 4 In.	36.00
Boy & Girl Kneeling, Praying, c.1950, 3 In.	10.00
Dog, Terrier, Black, Red Bow, Japan, 3 In.	18.00
Flamingo, Octagonal, Florida, 2 ¾ In.	10.00
Glass, Bluerina, Amethyst Shaded To Blue, Bull's-Eye, Stanley, 1880s, 2 ½ In.	2530.00
Glass, Green, Opaque, Tapered, 2 ½ In.	575.00
Green, Paneled, Hazel Atlas, 3 In.	36.00
Kewpie, Cupid, Japan, 1930s, 3 In.	19.00
Kewpie, Japan, 2 In.	100.00
Little Red Riding Hood, Hull, 5 ¼ In.	125.00
Metal, Enamel Plaques, Atlantic City, Japan, 2 In.	25.00
Porcelain, Versailles Pattern, Germany, Gilt Over White, Rosenthal	60.00
Swan, Cork Plug, 1960s	7.00
Tombstone, Japan.	26.00
Violin, Cobalt Blue, Plastic Lid, Maryland Glass Co., 1930s, 4 In.	40.00

SALT GLAZE has a grayish white surface with a texture like an orange peel. It is a method of decoration that has been used since the eighteenth century. Salt-glazed pieces are still being made.

Bottle, Bulbous, Flared Spout, Hunting Scenes, Maidens, Birdcages, Leaves, c.1745-60, 9 In.	375.00
Bowl, Fruit, Reticulated Oval Basket Shape, 2 Handles, Openwork Design, c.1760, 4 x 9 In.	325.00
Cistern, Cover, Bear Shape, Seated, Holding Object, Chain, Clay Chips, Brown Glaze, c.1760, 9 In.	4750.00
Coffeepot, Lid, Enamel Paint, Baluster, Loop Handle, House, Figures, Round Foot, c.1760, 8 In.	2000.00
Figurine, Spaniel, Incised, Oblong Fox Hunt Scene Base, 1800s, 15 In., Pair	4503.00
Pitcher, Raised Flower Design, Loop Handle, Round Foot, Marked, c.1858, 7 In.	58.00

Stirrup Cup, Fox Head Shape, England, c.1745-69, 4 In.	1100.00
Teapot, Lid, Round, Bulbous, Loop Handle, Round Foot, Clay Chips & Gilt Design, c.1745-60, 4 In.	600.00
Tureen, Lid, Oval, Bulbous Shape, Scrolling Handles, Oval Foot, c.1745-60, 10 x 14 In.	325.00

SAMPLERS were made in America from the early 1700s. The best examples were made from 1790 to 1840. Long, narrow samplers are usually older than square ones. Early samplers just had stitching or alphabets. The later examples had numerals, borders, and pictorial decorations. Those with mottoes are mid-Victorian. A revival of interest in the 1930s produced simpler samplers, usually with mottoes.

AB CDE

Adam & Eve, Flowers, Verse, Mary Sumption, 1853, Silk On Linen, 15 ½ x 9 In.	243.00
Alphabet, Animals, Flowers, Verse, Elizabeth Lowe, Silk On Linen, Age 12, 1802, 26 x 22 In.	1920.00
Alphabet, Birds, Flowers, Martha Long, 12 Yrs Old, Frame, 1847, 10 x 16 In.	460.00
Alphabet, Bouquet, Mary Eliza Atkinson, Wool On Linen, 18 ½ x 16 ½ In.	152.00
Alphabet, Clarissa Curtis, Age 9, Silk On Linen, 1837, Frame, 12 ¼ x 12 ¼ In.	243.00
Alphabet, Deer, Trees, Wreath, Flower Border, Mary McCord, Silk On Linen, c.1805, 18 x 14 In.	147.00
Alphabet, Federal House, Fence, Levinea Campbell, Aged 14, Silk On Linen, c.1824, 18 x 17 In.	34500.00
Alphabet, Figures, Birds, Elizabeth Ambridge, Age 9 Years, 1836, Silk On Linen, Frame, 13 x 12 In.	207.00
Alphabet, Flower Bands, Birds, Alphabet, Verse, Silk On Linen, 1700s, 9 x 8 In.	326.00
Alphabet, Flower Basket, Mariar L. Fuller, Frame, Cape Vincent, c.1810, 21 x 21 ½ In.	646.00
Alphabet, Flower Border, Elizabath Zeiglers, March 11, 1825, 16 x 16 In.	201.00
Alphabet, Flowering Vine, Tree, Plant, Silk On Linen, c.1821, 17 x 18 In.	1185.00
Alphabet, Flowers, Birds, Houses, Mary A. Hull, 1833, 16 ¼ x 17 In.	413.00
Alphabet, Flowers, Trees, Birds, Jane Steel, 1831, Silk On Linen, Frame, 11 ½ x 10 ¼ In.	152.00
Alphabet, Home Landscape, Ann Marie Ray, Wool On Linen, Frame, 1833, 16 x 12 ½ In.	243.00
Alphabet, Hope Poem, Eliza Hawkins, Born October 10th 1813 Aged 9 Years, 16 x 17 In.	593.00
Alphabet, House, Landscape, H. Bulman, Wool On Linen, Frame, 1856, 17 x 14 ½ In.	273.00
Alphabet, House, Trees, Sheep, Mary Jackson Moody, Age 10, Silk On Linen, c.1801, 21 x 19 In.	1293.00
Alphabet, Lebanon Shakers, Harriet Hazlin, Frame, c.1869	9000.00
Alphabet, Lucy Morie, 1796, Linen, Green Wool Thread, Frame, 11 x 11 In.	248.00
Alphabet, Marie Cornelia Wadsworth, Canfield, 1840, Silk, Cotton, Frame, 12 x 22 In.	6228.00
Alphabet, Numbers, Crowns, Blue, Gold, Signed B.S., 1751, Silk On Linen, Frame, 21 x 17 In.	362.00
Alphabet, Numbers, House, Trees, Rebecca Sherrell, Age 9, Wool On Linen, c.1839, 19 x 19 In.	470.00
Alphabet, Numbers, People, Trees, Dog, Birds, Frame, 1844, 8 x 10 In.	748.00
Alphabet, Numbers, Verse, Lorinda Hodley, Aged 11 Years, Yarn, Cotton, c.1844, 8 x 8 ½ In.	5265.00
Alphabet, Numbers, Verse, Silk On Linen, Mary Burch, 1863, Frame, 7 x 8 In.	207.00
Alphabet, Peacock Border, Katty Wright Crize, 1785, Frame, 7 ½ x 21 In.	316.00
Alphabet, Prayer, Landscape, Annabella Moffat, Age 9 Years, Wool, Linen, Frame, 1828, 22 x 17 In.	243.00
Alphabet, Sarah E. Decou, 1835, Linen, Brown, Frame, 9 ½ x 19 In.	308.00
Alphabet, Verse, Basket, Fruit, Flowers, Silk On Linen, Frame, 1840, 17 x 18 In.	1126.00
Alphabet, Verse, Charlotte C. Burnham, Canterbury, 13 Years, 1835, 14 x 15 In.	431.00
Alphabet, Verse, Flower Border, Eliz. Wallace, Departed Life, 1838, Aged 15, Silk On Linen, 21 x 19 In.	558.00
Alphabet, Verse, Flowers, C.J. Francis, Age 8 Years, Silk On Linen, Frame, 1802, 19 x 17 In.	237.00
Alphabet, Verse, Number, Family Names, Designs, Red Thread, 1800s, 17 ½ x 8 In.	73.00
Alphabet, Verse, Trees, Birds, Hanna Beney, Silk On Linen, Frame, 1814, 22 x 13 In.	243.00
Alphabet, Zilphia Philbrook, June 11, 1826, Linen, Frame, 18 ¼ x 8 ¾ In.	399.00
Bible Verse, Silk, Metallic, Chenille, Silk Ground, Faces, Frame, 1809, 16 x 18 In.	3851.00
Birds, Animals, Flower Basket, Elizabeth Rosson, Wool, Frame, c.1874, 29 x 23 In.	294.00
Birds, Flowers, Baskets, Wreath, Strawberry Border, Rachel Lewis, Silk, Linen, 31 x 21 In.	411.00
Birds, Flowers, Clover Leaf Border, Sarah Smith, Silk On Wool, c.1805, 15 ½ x 20 In.	705.00
Bluebirds, Trees, Floral Baskets, Gunship, Silk On Linen, Arts & Crafts, Frame, 17 x 9 ½ In.	121.00
Crowns, Tulips, Birds, E.W., Age 14 Years, Silk On Linen, Frame, 1820, 11 ½ x 9 In.	243.00
Darning, Stitch Samples, Silk On Linen, Frame, 1700s, 12 x 9 In.	533.00
Family Record, Flowers, Blue Bowknots, Statistics, Silk On Linen, Frame, 1830, 18 x 24 In.	3437.00
Family Record, Names, Dates, Verse, Patty Milton, 10 Yrs., Silk On Linen, 1821, 19 x 16 In. *illus*	734.00
Family Record, Temple, Columns, Statistics, Silk On Linen, 1833, 17 x 18 In.	1422.00
Flower Baskets, Hills, Trees, Plumes, Harriet McCoy, Born 1821, Silk On Linen, 19 x 17 In.	823.00
Flowers, Animals, Letters, Louise Dumet, San Jose, 1876, Wool On Canvas, 29 x 23 In.	2160.00
House, Adam & Eve, Garden, Ark, Eagle, Henrietta Morrison, Danville, 1826, 17 x 17 In.	920.00
House, Birds, Verse, Flowers, Sarah Griffin, Age 10, 1818, Silk On Linen, Frame, 12 x 12 ½ In.	835.00
House, Flowers, Animals, Clementa M. Bolton, 1860, Wool On Linen, Frame, 26 x 25 In.	296.00
House, Sheep, Trees, Flowers, Phebe Ann Rogers, Silk On Linen, Frame, 22 x 17 In.	4000.00
Mourning, Silk, Chenille, Painted Ground, Juliet Allen, Frame, 1811, 20 x 24 ½ In. *illus*	2370.00
Pilgrim Couple, Trees, Flowers, Elizabeth Walker, Silk On Linen, Frame, 1824, 13 x 11 In.	334.00
Red House, Flowers, Mary Griffiths, Age 12 Years, 1896, Wool On Linen, 25 x 24 ½ In.	213.00
Sprays, Basket, Flower Border, Deborah Knabb, Woolwork, Frame, c.1846, 18 x 18 In.	130.00
Verse, Adam & Eve, Rebecca Maidmen, 11 Years, 1833, Silk On Linen, Frame, 16 x 12 In.	456.00

Rug, Moroccan, Diamonds, Beige, Black, Wool, 1950s, 101 x 60 In.
$4688.00

Los Angeles Modern Auctions

Rug, Penny, Appliqued Plant, Red Blooms, Multiple Rooms, Wool, Felt, Burlap, c.1890, 26 ½ x 46 In.
$690.00

James D. Julia Inc.

Rug, Persian, Scrolling Flowers, Leaves, Black Ground, Tan, Rust, Border,

New Orleans Auction Galleries, Inc.

Rug, Sarouk, Flowers, Leaves, Medallion, Red Ground, Borders, Wool, 11 Ft. 7 In. x 8 Ft. 9 In.
$1220.00

Leslie Hindman Auctioneers

S

Ruskin, Vase, Mauve Mottled Glaze, Blue Grapevines, Grapes Around Shoulder, Marked, 8 ¾ In.
$920.00

Humler & Nolan

Russel Wright, Aluminum, Tea Set, Teapot, Sugar & Lid, Creamer, Bowl & Lid, Pitcher, Tray, c.1935
$3750.00

Los Angeles Modern Auctions

Russel Wright, Oceana, Bowl, Wood, Carved, Divided, 13 x 11 ½ In.
$1488.00

Rago Arts & Auction Center

Verse, Alphabet, Hearts, Dogs, Mary Ann Nunn, Born 1821, Silk On Linen, Frame, 17 x 13 In.	486.00
Verse, Alphabet, Numbers, E.M. Lancaster, Loretto, A.D., 1837, Silk, Linen, Frame, 18 x 18 In.	2115.00
Verse, Animals, House, Silk On Linen, Frame, 1814, 22 x 13 In.	356.00
Verse, Birds, Crowned Lions, Flowers, Trees, Jane Routh, Aged 9, Frame, c.1818, 14 x 19 ¼ In.	354.00
Verse, Birds, Trees, Flowers, Man, Cat, M. Williams, Silk On Linen, 1835, Frame, 18 x 13 In.	1185.00
Verse, Cat Climbing Weeping Willow, Figures, Mary Rigby, 1852, Silk On Canvas, 20 x 22 In.	1024.00
Verse, Couple, Farm Animals, Sarah Ellen Whitley, 1847, Wool On Linen, 23 x 22 In.	207.00
Verse, Flowers, Adam & Eve, Sarah Brown, Silk On Linen, Frame, 1822, 13 x 10 In.	304.00
Verse, Flowers, Birds, Emeline Mayer, 1833, Silk On Linen, Berks Co., Frame, 16 ¾ x 17 ½ In.	425.00
Verse, Flowers, Farm Animals, Sarah Brown Ruddington, Silk On Linen, 1800s, 20 ½ x 16 In.	300.00
Verse, Flowers, House, Palm Trees, Mary Gano, Silk On Linen, New Jersey, c.1838, 25 x 32 In.	940.00
Verse, Flowers, Mary-Ann Howes, 1823, Silk On Linen, Wood Frame, 12 ½ x 13 ¼ In.	148.00
Verse, Heart Bands, Crown, Diamonds, Flowers, Theodosia Cavston, Frame, 1752, 16 ½ In.	603.00
Verse, House, Landscape, Ann Smith, 1824, Silk On Linen, Frame, England, 19 x 12 ½ In.	385.00
Verse, House, Trees, Emblem Of Love, Beulah Rulon, Age 11, 1816, Silk On Linen, 22 x 17 In.	1093.00
Verse, Loving Couple, Flower Border, Elizabeth Barlow, 1852, Wool On Linen, Frame, 22 x 24 In.	148.00
Verse, Mary Ann Harris, 1822, Silk On Linen, Frame, 16 ¾ x 12 ½ In.	207.00
Verse, Mary Ann Hyde, 1839, Silk On Linen, Frame, 15 ½ x 11 ¼ In.	385.00
Verse, Pagoda, Deer, Butterflies, Flowers, Elizabeth Ainge, 1841, Silk On Wool, Frame, 21 x 17 In.	558.00
Verse, Sarah Corderoy, 1852, Silk On Linen, Frame, 16 ½ x 12 ½ In.	243.00
Verse, Scroll Border, Fanny Clark, 1842, Woven Silk, Glass Bead Stitched, Frame, 21 x 20 In.	578.00
Verse, Solomon's Temple, Mary Ann Edwards, 1847, Wool On Linen, 25 x 23 In.	243.00
Verse, Stylized Trees, Vines, Martha Ward, Silk On Linen, Frame, c.1810, 17 x 16 In.	356.00
Verse, Trees, Dogs, Flowers, Anne Kirtley, 1843, Silk On Linen, Frame, 15 x 17 ½ In.	395.00

SAMSON and Company, a French firm specializing in the reproduction of collectible wares of many countries and periods, was founded in Paris in the early nineteenth century. Chelsea, Meissen, Famille Verte, and Chinese Export porcelain are some of the wares that have been reproduced by the company. The firm used a variety of marks on the reproductions. It closed in 1969.

Bowl, Flowers, Multicolor, Gilt Trim, 11 ½ In.	107.00
Figurine, Napoleon, White Glaze, Parcel Gilt, Laurel Crown, Imperial Robes, 13 ½ x 9 In.	234.00
Figurine, Parrot, White, Blue, Green, Yellow Crown, c.1890, 11 x 8 In.	649.00
Ginger Jar, Cover, Armorial, Flowers, Gilt Foo Dog Finial, 18 ½ In., Pair	644.00
Jar, Louis XVI Style, Gilt Bronze Mounted, Famille Verte, c.1900, 10 ½ In., Pair	1375.00

SANDWICH GLASS is any of the myriad types of glass made by the Boston and Sandwich Glass Works in Sandwich, Massachusetts, between 1825 and 1888. It is often very difficult to be sure whether a piece was really made at the Sandwich factory because so many types were made there and similar pieces were made at other glass factories. Additional pieces may be listed under Pressed Glass and in related categories.

Bird Waterer, Colorless, 5-Sided, Protruding Trough, Ball Finial, 1882-1855, 5 ¼ In.	46.00
Bowl, Openwork, 22 Vertical Staves, Flared, Low Foot, 2 ¼ x 6 In.	81.00
Candlestick, Dolphin, Single Step, Translucent Blue Over Clambroth, 10 ¼ In.	748.00
Candlestick, Hexagonal, Acanthus Leaf, Blue Starch Over Clambroth, 8 In., Pair	460.00
Candlestick, Hexagonal, Deep Cobalt Blue, Urn Socket, 3 Knops, Wafer, 9 In.	288.00
Candlestick, Petal & Hexagonal, Electric Blue, 6-Petal Socket, Wafer, 7 ¼ In.	345.00
Candlestick, Petal & Loop, Starch Blue Over Clambroth, 6-Petal Socket, 7 In., Pair	920.00
Cologne Bottle, Amethyst, Square, Tapered, Thumbprint Panels, Sawtooth Corners, 6 In.	468.00
Cologne Bottle, Clambroth, 10 Lobes, Beads, Squat, Starch Blue Umbrella Stopper, 5 In.	431.00
Cologne Bottle, Cobalt Cut To Clear, Panel-Cut Neck, Stepped Shoulder, Cylindrical, 7 In.	518.00
Cologne Bottle, Diamond Thumbprint, Ruby Cut To Clear, Elongated Pear Shape, 11 In.	1380.00
Cologne Bottle, Star & Punty, Canary Yellow, 8-Sided, Panel Cut Stopper, 6 ¾ In.	127.00
Cologne Bottle, Vintage Grape, Ruby Stain, Etched Grapevines, Faceted Neck, 8 In.	489.00
Creamer, Acanthus Leaf & Shield, 8-Sided, Shaped Handle, Scalloped Foot, 4 In.	35.00
Creamer, Diamond Diaper, Vertical & Swirled Ribs, Curled Handle, 3 In.	259.00
Decanter, Brandy, Embossed, Swirled Ribs, Flutes, Swirled Ball Stopper, Qt., 11 In.	288.00
Decanter, Diamond Diaper, Vertical Ribs, Rigaree Rings, Wheel Stopper, 7 In., Pair	207.00
Dish, Cover, Lacy, Princess Feather Medallion & Basket Of Flowers, c.1835, 10 ½ x 9 ¾ In.	978.00
Dish, Hen On Nest, Cover, Clambroth, Straw Rim, Drape Sides, Waffle Base, 6 x 7 In.	1150.00
Dish, Openwork, Apple Green, Flared, Scallop Rim, Footed, 6 x 3 In.	1955.00
Figurine, Bear, Black, On Haunches, 3 ¾ In., Pair	413.00
Figurine, Bear, Blue, Embossed X. Bazin Philada, 3 ½ In.	345.00
Figurine, Dolphin, Double Step, Canary Yellow, 6-Petal Socket, Square Base, 9 ½ In.	184.00
Flat Iron, Canary Yellow, Boston & Sandwich, 1800s, 1 x 1 ⅜ In.	374.00
Jar, Chained Bear, Opaque Black, 4 ⅝ In.	316.00

S

Jar, Muzzled Bear, Deep Amethyst, 3 ¾ In.	230.00
Jar, Muzzled Bear, Opaque White, 5 ⅛ In.	150.00
Lamp, Blown Font, Grape, Vine Design, Frosted, Pewter Collar, Stepped Base, 15 ¾ In., Pair	4830.00
Lamp, Kerosene, Blue To White To Clear, Cut Quatrefoils, Starch Blue Base, 10 In.	575.00
Lamp, Kerosene, Green Cut To Clear, Pear Shaped, Brass Stem, Marble Base, 11 In.	748.00
Lamp, Peg, Kerosene, Ruby Cut To Clear, Trefoils, Brass Collar, 5 ¼ In.	196.00
Lamp, Whale Oil, Pressed Loop, Clear, Bulb Shaped Font, Monument Base, 11 In.	230.00
Lamp, Whale Oil, Sandwich Star, Clear, Hexagonal, Domed Lid, 11 In., Pair	115.00
Mustard, Cover, Lacy Peacock Eye, Beaded Ring, Spoon Slot, 3 x 3 In.	196.00
Nappy, Colorless, Ribbed Band, Swirled To Left, Rayed Base, 1 ½ x 5 In.	104.00
Nappy, Cover, Divided Petal, Canary Yellow, 8-Petal Rim, Hexagonal Finial, 4 In.	345.00
Nappy, Fleur-De-Lis & Thistle, Stippled Scalloped Rim, Roped Table Ring, 9 In.	46.00
Nappy, Heart & Sheaf, Strawberry Diamond Band, Footed, Ovals & Darts, 5 x 6 In.	2990.00
Pitcher, Overshot, Cranberry Cased, Bulbous, Tapered, Icer, Clear Handle, 11 In.	575.00
Salt, Basket Of Flowers, Fiery Opalescent, 4-Footed, 2 x 1 ¾ x 3 In.	403.00
Salt, Basket Of Flowers, Opaque Blue Mottled, Footed, 2 x 1 ¾ In.	633.00
Salt, Cover, Beaded Scroll & Basket, Colorless, Pinecone Finial, Rayed Base, 3 In.	978.00
Salt, Eagle & Shield, Colorless, 4-Footed, 2 x 2 x 3 ¼ In.	104.00
Salt, Hat, Sunburst, Folded Rim, Rayed Base, 2 ¼ In.	127.00
Salt, Horizontal Ring Pattern, Wide Rim, Drawn Foot, Rayed Base, c.1830, 3 x 2 In.	230.00
Salt, Lafayette, Steamboat, Fiery Opalescent Blue, BT-8, 2 x 3 In.	633.00
Salt, Lafayette, Steamboat, Purple Blue, B. & S. Glass Co. On Stern, BT-4D, 2 x 3 In.	127.00
Salt, Strawberry Diamond, Blue, Scallop & Point Rim, 4-Footed, 2 x 2 x 3 In.	345.00
Spooner, Star & Punty, Canary Yellow, Hexagonal Bowl, Round Foot, 4 ⅞ In.	173.00
Sugar, Cover, Gothic Arch, Clambroth, 8-Sided, 6-Sided Finial, Footed, 5 In.	184.00
Sugar, Cover, Gothic Arch, Electric Blue, 8-Sided, 6-Sided Finial, Footed, 5 In.	805.00
Sugar, Cover, Gothic Arch, Starch Blue, 8-Sided, 6-Sided Finial, Footed, 5 In.	863.00
Tray, Pineapple & Gothic Arch, 8-Sided, Scallop & Point Rim, 6 x 9 In.	219.00
Tumbler, Diamond Sunburst, Colorless, Barrel Form, Rayed & Ringed Base, 2 ⅝ In.	150.00
Tumbler, Gray Tint, Diamond Diaper, Swirled Flutes, Ribs, c.1830, 4 ½ In.	127.00
Undertray, Lacy Heart, Scallop & Point Rim, Rope Table Ring, 4 ½ x 7 In.	58.00
Vase, 4-Printie Block, Canary Yellow, 6-Petal Rim, Hexagonal Base, 11 ½ In.	207.00
Vase, Beehive Form, Flared & Tooled Rim, Footed, 10 In.	761.00
Vase, Pressed Loop, Fluted Rim, 8-Sided Standard, Emerald Green, Pontil, c.1850, 9 In. .... *illus*	2223.00
Vase, Tulip, Amethyst, Octagonal Bowl & Base, Flared Scalloped Rim, 10 In., Pair	1955.00
Vase, Tulip, Knob Stem, c.1850, 8 In.	532.00
Vase, Twisted Loop, Deep Cobalt Blue, Conical Bowl, Flared Rim, Square Base, 11 In.	863.00
Witch's Ball, Cranberry, Ruby, Rough Pontil, 1860-90, 4 In.	150.00

SARREGUEMINES is the name of a French town that is used as part of a china mark. Utzschneider and Company, a porcelain factory, made ceramics in Sarreguemines, Lorraine, France, from about 1775. Transfer-printed wares and majolica were made in the nineteenth century. The nineteenth-century pieces, most often found today, usually have colorful transfer-printed decorations showing peasants in local costumes.

Bowl, Cobalt Blue Interior, Gold, Bronze Mounts, Handles, Marked, 7 x 20 ½ In.	230.00
Candleholder, Figural, Poodle, 5 ½ In., Pair	1062.00
Ewer, Brown Ware, Marked, 9 ½ In.	11.00
Jug, Figural, Griffin, 20 In.	863.00
Jug, Figural, Scottish Man, Long Sideburns, 7 ½ In.	81.00
Pitcher, Figural, Foo Dog, Blue, White, 13 In.	472.00
Pitcher, Relief, Figures, Feast, Green Glaze, 1 ½ Liter	138.00 *illus*
Planter, Hanging, Multicolor, Majolica, 11 In.	590.00
Tureen, Cover, Basket Of Fruit, 8 ½ In.	59.00

SASCHA BRASTOFF made decorative accessories, ceramics, enamels on copper, and plastics of his own design. He headed a factory, Sascha Brastoff of California, Inc., in West Los Angeles, from 1953 until about 1973. He died in 1993. Pieces signed with the signature *Sascha Brastoff* were his work and are the most expensive. Other pieces marked *Sascha B.* or with a stamped mark were made by others in his company. Pieces made by Matt Adams after he left the factory are listed here with his name.

Cigarette Box, Copper, Enameled, Flowers, Green, 5 x 3 In.	100.00
Coffeepot, Lid, Surf Ballet	440.00
Figurine, Bear, Amber, Resin, Signed, 7 ¼ x 4 ¼ In.	40.00
Lamp, Stylized Leaves, Cylindrical, Gunmetal Gray, Brushed Aluminum, 28 In.	173.00
Plate, Dinner, Surf Ballet, 10 ⅜ In.	73.00

Salopian, Cup & Saucer, Handleless, Fruit, Flowers, Bird, 2 ⅛-In. Cup, 5 ⅜-In. Saucer
$71.00

Conestoga Auction Co., Inc.

Salopian, Waste Bowl, Transfer, Countryside, Cows, Sheep, Boy, Woman, 3 x 6 ⅛ In.
$165.00

Conestoga Auction Co., Inc.

Sampler, Family Record, Names, Dates, Verse, Patty Milton, 10 Yrs., Silk On Linen, 1821, 19 x 16 In.
$734.00

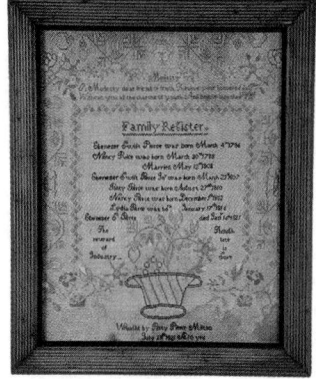

Garth's Auctions, Inc.

Sampler, Mourning, Silk, Chenille, Painted Ground, Juliet Allen, Frame, 1811, 20 x 24 ½ In.
$2370.00

Skinner, Inc.

Sandwich Glass, Vase, Pressed Loop, Fluted Rim, 8-Sided Standard, Emerald Green, Pontil, c.1850, 9 In.
$2223.00

Norman C. Heckler & Company

Sarreguemines, Pitcher, Relief, Figures, Feast, Green Glaze, 1 ½ Liter
$138.00

Fox Auctions

Satsuma, Censer, Dome Lid, Lion Handles & Finial, Tripod Feet, Chinese Figures, c.1900, 29 ½ In.
$1121.00

Brunk Auctions

Plate, Flowers, Gilt Highlights, Frame, Signed Sascha Brastoff, 10 ¼ In.	81.00
Platter, Fish, Blue, Orange Streaks, Black Ground, Wavy Rim, Signed, 13 ¾ In.	6.00

SATIN GLASS is a late nineteenth-century art glass. It has a dull finish that is caused by hydrofluoric acid vapor treatment. Satin glass was made in many colors and sometimes has applied decorations. Satin glass is also listed by factory name, such as Webb, or in the Mother-of-Pearl category in this book.

Basket, Blue Herringbone, Ruffled Top, Frosted Thorn Handle, 8 x 8 ½ In.	75.00
Basket, Blue, Tricornered, Frosted Thorn Handles, 4 x 6 In.	350.00
Biscuit Jar, Beaded Drape, Silver Plated Lid, Bail Handle, 7 ½ In.	80.00
Biscuit Jar, Floret, Pink, Silver Plate, Embossed Lid, Rim, 6 ½ In.	90.00
Bowl, Blue Satin, White Opalescent, Ruffled, 3 ¾ x 8 In.	40.00
Bowl, Blue, Ruffled White Opalescent Rim, Pie Plate Shape, 2 ¼ x 9 In.	60.00
Bowl, Pink, Diamond-Quilted, Ruffled, Pie Crust Edge, Petal Feet, 12 In.	300.00
Dish, Sweetmeat, Blue, Ribbon, Mother-Of-Pearl, Silver Plate, Lid, Bail Handle, 4 ½ In.	325.00
Ewer, Pink, Applied Blossoms, Branches, Handle, 6 In.	35.00
Ewer, Rainbow Swirl, Ruffled Rim, 8 ½ In.	150.00
Ewer, Rose Overlay, Blue, Footed Oval, Loop Handle, Foldover Rim, 14 ⅛ In.	59.00
Lamp, Raindrop, Ball Base & Shade, White, Mother-Of-Pearl, Frosted Glass Feet, 9 In.	1380.00
Lamp, Raspberry, Diamond Pattern, Squat Base, Ruffled Rim, Round Foot, Mother-Of-Pearl, 6 In.	1725.00
Lamp, Red, Lattice, Scroll, Beaded Shell, 8 ½ In.	150.00
Lamp, Shouldered Cylinder Base, Frosted Crystal Feet, Yellow, White, Ruffled Rim Shade, 10 In.	920.00
Lamp, Squat Oval Base, Raspberry Diamond Point Design, Ruffled Ball Shade, 8 In., Pair	1955.00
Perfume Bottle, Pink, Enamel Flowers, 3 ¼ In.	100.00
Rose Bowl, Rainbow, Diamond-Quilted, 4 In.	90.00
Spooner, Pink Herringbone, Square, 4 ½ In.	100.00
Toothpick Holder, Blue, Ribbon, Pinched Waist, 2 ¾ In.	300.00
Vase, Baluster, Flared Rim, Pink Overlay, White Opaline, Enamel, Owls, Leaves, 7 In., Pair	148.00
Vase, Blue Shaded, Ribbed, Cased, England, 13 ⅜ In.	1093.00
Vase, Blue, Ribbed, Enameled Flower Design, 9 In.	40.00
Vase, Bulbous Stick, Yellow To Caramel, Enameled White Flowers, 8 In.	58.00
Vase, Bulbous Stick, Yellow, Gilt Sun Bursts, Rectangular Design, 13 In.	460.00
Vase, Jack-In-The-Pulpit, Frosted, Applied Petal Feet, 5 ½ In.	25.00
Vase, Light Amber, Raindrop Pattern, Bulbous Body, Ruffled Rim, 10 In.	115.00
Vase, Pink, Bowling Pin Shape, Enameled Branch, Blossom, 11 ¾ In.	25.00
Vase, Pink, Diamond-Quilted, Melon Shape, 8 In.	400.00
Vase, Pink, Trumpet Shape, Scalloped, Face Medallion Silver Base, c.1875, 15 ¼ In., Pair	596.00
Vase, Pink, Zigzag Pattern, Bulbous Ribbed Body, Long Slight Flare Neck, 7 In.	29.00
Vase, White, Blue, Pink, Yellow, Gourd Shape, Thorn Handles, 7 ¾ In.	50.00
Water Set, Yellow, Gilt Leafy Branch, Flowers, Ruffle Rim, Ribbed, Reeded Handle, 6 Tumblers, 8 In.	259.00

SATSUMA is a Japanese pottery with a distinctive creamy beige crackled glaze. Most of the pieces were decorated with blue, red, green, orange, or gold. Almost all Satsuma found today was made after 1860, especially during the Meiji Period, 1868–1912. During World War I, Americans could not buy undecorated European porcelains. Women who liked to make hand-painted porcelains at home began to decorate plain Satsuma. These pieces are known today as "American Satsuma."

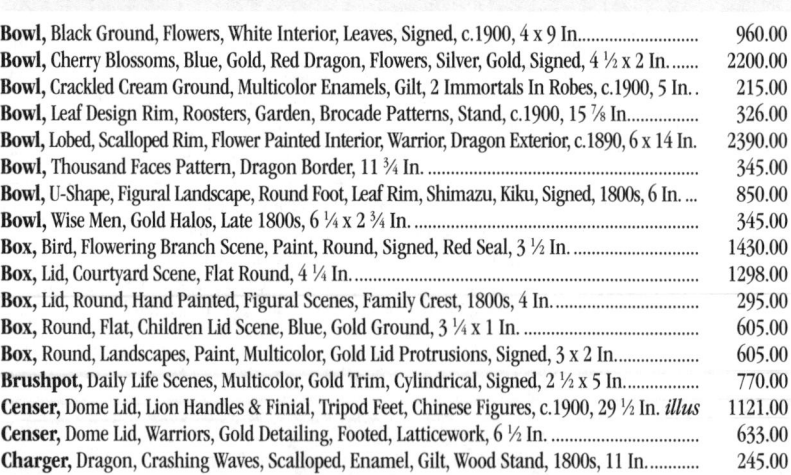

Bowl, Black Ground, Flowers, White Interior, Leaves, Signed, c.1900, 4 x 9 In.	960.00
Bowl, Cherry Blossoms, Blue, Gold, Red Dragon, Flowers, Silver, Gold, Signed, 4 ½ x 2 In.	2200.00
Bowl, Crackled Cream Ground, Multicolor Enamels, Gilt, 2 Immortals In Robes, c.1900, 5 In.	215.00
Bowl, Leaf Design Rim, Roosters, Garden, Brocade Patterns, Stand, c.1900, 15 ⅞ In.	326.00
Bowl, Lobed, Scalloped Rim, Flower Painted Interior, Warrior, Dragon Exterior, c.1890, 6 x 14 In.	2390.00
Bowl, Thousand Faces Pattern, Dragon Border, 11 ¾ In.	345.00
Bowl, U-Shape, Figural Landscape, Round Foot, Leaf Rim, Shimazu, Kiku, Signed, 1800s, 6 In.	850.00
Bowl, Wise Men, Gold Halos, Late 1800s, 6 ¼ x 2 ¾ In.	345.00
Box, Bird, Flowering Branch Scene, Paint, Round, Signed, Red Seal, 3 ½ In.	1430.00
Box, Lid, Courtyard Scene, Flat Round, 4 ¼ In.	1298.00
Box, Lid, Round, Hand Painted, Figural Scenes, Family Crest, 1800s, 4 In.	295.00
Box, Round, Flat, Children Lid Scene, Blue, Gold Ground, 3 ¼ x 1 In.	605.00
Box, Round, Landscapes, Paint, Multicolor, Gold Lid Protrusions, Signed, 3 x 2 In.	605.00
Brushpot, Daily Life Scenes, Multicolor, Gold Trim, Cylindrical, Signed, 2 ½ x 5 In.	770.00
Censer, Dome Lid, Lion Handles & Finial, Tripod Feet, Chinese Figures, c.1900, 29 ½ In. *illus*	1121.00
Censer, Dome Lid, Warriors, Gold Detailing, Footed, Latticework, 6 ½ In.	633.00
Charger, Dragon, Crashing Waves, Scalloped, Enamel, Gilt, Wood Stand, 1800s, 11 In.	245.00
Charger, Priests, Dragons, White Enamel & Gilt Ground, 12 In.	450.00

Charger, Ribbon Design, 1000 Cranes, Signed, 14 ½ In.	127.00
Charger, Round, U-Shape Design, Figural Landscape, Earthenware, Early 1900s, 14 In., Pair	500.00
Charger, Scalloped Rim, Village Scenes, Elders, Gilt, 12 In. Diam.	600.00
Compote, Blue, Gold, Blue Accents, Painted River, Rowers, Signed, c.1900, 4 ¾ x 2 ½ In.	960.00
Compote, River Scene, Painted, Blue, Gold Accents, Footed, 5 x 3 In.	880.00
Cricket Cage, Vented Lid, Male Figures, Flowers, Butterflies, Handle, Footed, Signed, 3 ¼ x 4 ¾ In.	1980.00
Dish, Scenic, 7 Chinese Characters, 3 ½ In.	40.00
Figurine, Man, Seated, Holding Censer, Enamel, Gilt, 19th Century, 3 ½ In.	316.00
Incense Burner, Cover, Guardian Dog Finial, Shishi Handles, Footed, Gilt & Enamel, 33 x 22 In.	690.00
Incense Burner, Dome Lid, Flowers, Multicolor, Gold Accents, Round, Footed, Signed, 3 ¾ x 2 ½ In.	600.00
Incense Burner, Dome Lid, Reticulated, Flowers, Gold Accents, Round, Footed, 4 x 2 ½ In.	550.00
Incense Burner, Handle, Buildings, Figures, Foo Dog Finial, Gold Footed, Signed, 2 ¾ x 4 ¼ In.	605.00
Incense Burner, Pierced Cover, Warrior Scenes, Round, Footed, Handles, Signed, 10 x 8 In.	366.00
Incense Burner, Scenes, Gold, Red Trim, Carved, Foo Dog Finial, Handles, 2 ½ x 4 In.	1870.00
Jar, Cover, 6-Sided, Immortals In Landscapes, Wood Base, 18 x 13 In.	403.00
Jar, Cover, Enamel & Gilt, Male Figures, Dragon, 3 Splayed Supports, Marked, c.1880, 14 In. *illus*	1058.00
Jar, Cover, Footed, Ball Shape, Immortals, Gold Detailing, Dragon Wrapping Rim	489.00
Jardiniere, Brass Filigree Scrolled Handles, Rim, Women Seated, 1800s, 12 x 17 In.	366.00
Jardiniere, Tiger Hunt, Sages, Scrolls, Bulbous, 3 Bird Feet, Gilt, Bronze Stand, Late 1800s, 7 x 5 In.	444.00
Plate, Landscape & Figural Rondel, Children, Flower Border, Enamel, Gilt, 1800s, 9 In.	948.00
Tray, Buildings, Figures, Snow Scene, 4 ¾ x 7 ¼ In.	523.00
Tray, Sake, Hand Painted, Figures, Butterflies, Birds, Signed, 10 x 7 In.	230.00
Urn, Raised Enamel, Females In Village Landscape, Dragon Handles, c.1920, 37 x 18 In. *illus*	1920.00
Vase, 3 Cartouches, Deities, Geisha, Dignitaries, Flowers, Reticulated, Painted, 1800s, 12 In.	1554.00
Vase, Animal & Landscape Scenes, Painted, Red, Gold Trim, Flared, Signed, 1 ¾ x 3 In., Pair	2200.00
Vase, Animal & Ring Handles, Enameled Flying Birds, Gilt, Baluster, c.1900, 9 ½ In.	118.00
Vase, Bird, Trees, Flowers, Moon Shape, 19 In.	296.00
Vase, Black Matte Glaze, Gold Stencil Flowers, 4 ½ In.	60.00
Vase, Cartouche, Figures, Court Scene, Gilt Accents, Baluster, 18 In., Pair	868.00
Vase, Chicken & Flower, Mother & Child Panels, Gold & Blue Ground, Bulbous, 3 x 5 In.	1650.00
Vase, Chrysanthemum, Beaker Shape, Flare Rim, Gilt, Flowers, Marked, 1800s, 16 x 10 In., Pair	2645.00
Vase, Courtyard, Flowering Trees, Women, Flared, Shouldered, Signed, 4 x 6 ½ In.	1210.00
Vase, Cylinder, Samurai, Water Scenes, Birds, Signed, 12 In.	115.00
Vase, Cylinder, Splay Feet, Dome Top, Multicolor, Immortals, Brocade Ground, c.1900, 7 ½ In., Pair	430.00
Vase, Double Gourd Shape, Gold Cranes, White & Black, 1800s, 12 x 7 In.	575.00
Vase, Ecru, Gold Floral Decoration, 1800s, 16 In.	2151.00
Vase, Everyday Life Scene Panels, Blue & Gold Ground, Tapered, Signed, 3 ½ x 6 ¼ In.	880.00
Vase, Figures, Brocade Neck, Key Border, Gilding, Applied Foo Dog Handles, c.1890, 14 ¾ In. *illus*	1093.00
Vase, Figures, Dragon, Oval Shape, 7 In.	159.00
Vase, Figures, Dragon, Phoenix, Leaf Designs, Enamel, Ruffles, Foo Dog Handles, c.1910, 48 In. *illus*	767.00
Vase, Figures, Gold Accents, White Ground, Late 1800s, 13 In.	92.00
Vase, Figures, Outdoor Scenes, Shaped Cartouches, Gilt Highlights, Baluster, c.1900, 10 In., Pair	177.00
Vase, Figures, Seated, Multicolor, Long Neck, Signed, Bulbous, Late 1800s, 2 ¼ x 4 ¾ In.	770.00
Vase, Figures, Symbols, Tapered, Ribbed, Gilded, Foo Dog Handles, 19th Century, 14 ¾ In.	1093.00
Vase, Flower, Bird Panels, Latticework, Red, Orange, White, Gilt, 23 ½ x 8 ½ In., Pair	183.00
Vase, Flowering Trees, Baluster, Gilt, Gold, Red Enamel, White Ground, c.1905, 18 x 9 In.	690.00
Vase, Group Scenes, Flowers, Miniature, Gold Ground, Oval Ring Shape, Signed, 3 x 5 In.	880.00
Vase, Handles With Tassels, Warriors Design, Floor, Baluster, 36 ¾ In.	1984.00
Vase, Landscape & Figures Panels, Gold Flowers, Leaves, Black Ground, Signed, 2 x 5 In.	1100.00
Vase, Landscape & Market Scenes, Gold, Red Trim, Late 1800s, 2 x 3 ¾ In.	880.00
Vase, Landscape, Figure Scene Panels, Flower Ground, Gilt Detail, Signed, 2 ¼ x 3 ¾ In., Pair	1540.00
Vase, Landscape, Figured, Interior Scene Cartouche, Gold Accents, Bulbous, 5 ½ x 7 ½ In.	550.00
Vase, Lions, Landscape, Gold, Flowers, Water, Rocks, Relief Peonies, Brocade Bands, 1800s, 9 ⅝ In. *illus*	474.00
Vase, Lobed, Elephant Shape Handles, 1000 Faces, Gold, Baluster, 6 In., Pair	295.00
Vase, Millefleur, Oval, 1960s, 10 ¼ In., Pair	403.00
Vase, Mountains, Village, Figures, Flowers, Blue Ground, Tapered, 4 x 7 ½ In., Pair	1430.00
Vase, Multicolor, Cobalt Blue Rolled Rim, Urn Shape, Seated Figures, Marked, 1800s, 16 x 10 In.	180.00
Vase, Musician, Scholar Scenes, Foo Dog Handles, 7 ½ x 4 In., Pair	316.00
Vase, Musicians, Scholars, Foo Dog Handles, Earthenware, Signed, Baluster, 8 x 4 In., Pair	316.00
Vase, Priests, Raised Enamels, Gilt, c.1910, 9 ¾ In.	360.00
Vase, Raised Crane, Signed, 7 ½ x 3 ¾ In.	115.00
Vase, Samurai, Bulbous, Tapered Neck, Flared Rim, Enameled, Mountain Landscape, 6 x 4 In.	161.00
Vase, Scenic, Cascading Wisteria, Butterflies, Bulbous, Signed, 7 x 6 ¼ In.	480.00
Vase, Scenic, Wisteria, Cherry Blossoms, Women, Pavilion, Gold Detail, Flared, Signed, 4 x 6 ½ In.	1320.00
Vase, Soldiers, Mt. Fuji, Drum Shape, 5 In.	240.00

Satsuma, Jar, Cover, Enamel & Gilt, Male Figures, Dragon, 3 Splayed Supports, Marked, c.1880, 14 In.
$1058.00

Cowan's Auctions

Satsuma, Urn, Raised Enamel, Females In Village Landscape, Dragon Handles, c.1920, 37 x 18 In.
$1920.00

DuMouchelles Art Gallery

Satsuma, Vase, Figures, Brocade Neck, Key Border, Gilding, Applied Foo Dog Handles, c.1890, 14 ¾ In.
$1093.00

S

Leland Little Auction

Satsuma, Vase, Figures, Dragon, Phoenix, Leaf Designs, Enamel, Ruffles, Foo Dog Handles, c.1910, 48 In. $767.00

Satsuma, Vase, Lions, Landscape, Gold, Flowers, Water, Rocks, Relief Peonies, Brocade Bands, 1800s, 9 ⅝ In. $474.00

Scale, Candy, Fairbanks, Cast Iron, Decals, Brass Pan, 11 x 5 x 11 In. $113.00

Vase, Travelers Scene, Wide Mouth, Painted, 1800s, 7 ½ x 6 In.	1920.00
Vase, Urn Shape, Rolled Rim, Figural Handles, Faces, Gilt Highlights, 9 In.	179.00
Vase, Urn Shape, Warrior Multicolor, Black Ground, Gilt Bands, 1800s, 7 ½ x 7 ½ In.	183.00
Vase, Warrior Scenes, Flowers, Patchwork Gold Designs, Handles, 2 ½ x 4 ½ In., Pair	1540.00
Vase, Warrior Training Tea Ceremony, Flared, Key Handles, Bulbous, Paint, Gilt, 2 x 3 ½ In.	220.00
Vase, Warriors, Women, Landscape Scenes, Phoenix Handles, c.1920, 43 In.	748.00
Vase, Wisteria, Butterflies, Bulbous, Signed, Red Seal, 4 x 6 ¼ In.	440.00

SATURDAY EVENING GIRLS, *see Paul Revere Pottery category.*

SCALES have been made to weigh everything from babies to gold. Collectors search for all types. Most popular are small gold dust scales and special grocery scales.

Balance, Brass Dish, Porcelain Plate, Marble Base, Parnell & Sons, Bristol, 11 x 26 ½ In.	62.00
Balance, Brass, Cast Construction, Wood Base, Christian Becker Inc., 49 ½ x 39 ½ In.	5500.00
Balance, Brass, Pole Mounted, Wood Base, Bartlett & Son, c.1890, 23 x 20 In.	104.00
Balance, Fairbanks, Knott, Milk Glass Plates, Boston Cast Iron Scale, 2 Lb., 7 ¾ x 14 In.	57.00
Candy, Brass, Removable Weigh Dish, Metal Base, Painted Green, Jacobs Bros., c.1900, 10 In.	480.00
Candy, Dayton, 3 Lb., Counter	770.00
Candy, Fairbanks, Cast Iron, Decals, Brass Pan, 11 x 5 x 11 In. ....*illus*	113.00
Candy, Stimpson No. 40, Leaner, Maroon, Cream, Nickel Trim	1582.00
Candy, Victory V Gum & Lozenges, Tin, Faux Wood, 20 Lb. Max., Rear Door, Eng., c.1920, 16 In. ..*illus*	144.00
Fortune, 1 Cent, American Scale Mfg. Co., Washington, D.C., 51 x 24 In.	260.00
Gas, Rectangular, Glass Case, Brass Plaque, Measures Weight Of Gases, c.1895, 15 ½ x 25 ½ In.	173.00
Jewelers, Oak, Brass, Drawer, Portable, c.1880, 2 ½ x 11 x 6 In.	147.00
Jockey, W. & T. Avery, Mahogany, Cast Iron, Upholstered, England, 37 x 22 In. ....*illus*	4148.00
Letter, Brass, Wood, c.1900, 5 x 9 In.	118.00
Opium, Hanging Weight, Wood Case, c.1860, 6 ½ x 8 ½ In.	295.00
Paper, Fred Baker, To 100 Lbs., 2 Scales, Velvet Case, Pillar Support, Box, c.1900, 4 x 6 In.	83.00
Postal, Edwardian, Sterling Silver, Birmingham, c.1908, 2 ¾ In.	960.00
Postal, Salter No. 30, Red, Gold, Britain, 9 ½ In.	60.00
Postal, Weight Set, Cast Iron, Gold Color, 9 x 3 ½ In.	58.00
Produce, Molen, Jan Molenschotz & Zn. Breda-Holland, 21 x 43 In. ....*illus*	325.00
Single Beam, Cast Iron, Turkey's Foot, 3 Weights, Red Paint, 9 ½ In.	68.00
Store, National Store Specialty Company, Black, Silver, 10 ½ In.	540.00
Table, Brass, Black Transfer Print, Earthenware Pan, Royal Coat Of Arms, London, 31 ½ In.	119.00
Weighing, 1 Cent, Lollipop Shape, Porcelain, White, Your Doctor Says Weigh Yourself Daily, c.1920	720.00
Weighing, 1 Lb., Detect-O-Gram, Pan, 6 Weights, Jacobs Bros., Co., 16 ½ x 16 In.	79.00
Weighing, 2 Lb., Cast Iron, Scoop, Tray, National Store Specialty Co., Counter	189.00
Weighing, Ace, Detecto, Jacob's Bros. Co.	55.00
Weighing, Angldile, Open Face, Red & Black, Brass, Electric, Counter ....*illus*	3000.00
Weighing, Coin, How Much Do You Weigh, Metal, Paint, Black Face, Watling, 1928, 73 x 24 In.	830.00
Weighing, Correct Weight, Cast Iron, Floor Model, Porcelain Face, Specialty Scale Co.	2280.00
Weighing, Dayton, Barrel, Light Up, Model 146, Counter	1100.00
Weighing, Enamel Iron, Brushed Steel, Linoleum, Fairbanks Morse & Co., 1940s, 45 x 20 In.	99.00
Weighing, Gold, Brass, Wm. Ainsworth & Sons, Inc., Glass & Wood Cabinet, Wilson & Anderson, 19 In.	158.00
Weighing, Honest Weight, Porcelain, Peerless, Lollipop, Floor Model, 1 Cent	385.00
Weighing, Peerless Junior, Porcelain, White, Floor Model, 1 Cent	440.00
Weighing, Toledo, Black, Metal, 14 ¾ x 14 In.	325.00

SCHAFER & VATER, makers of small ceramic items, are best known for their amusing figurals. The factory was located in Volkstedt-Rudolstadt, Germany, from 1890 to 1962. Some pieces are marked with the crown and *R* mark, but many are unmarked.

Bottle, Baby, Bottle Nipple From Old Whiskey, Brown Glaze, 4 ½ In.	128.00
Bottle, Baseball Player, 5 ½ In. ....*illus*	380.00
Bottle, Devil, Brown Tree Bark Ground, Cannon, 5 In.	125.00
Bottle, Girl In Wineglass, Long Stemmed, Girl Holding Pink Rose, 6 x 2 In.	228.00
Creamer, Black Mummy Boy, Polka Dot Robe, Long Black Fingernails, 3 ⅜ In.	170.00
Creamer, Cow, Plaid Suit, Hat With Feather, Shoes, 3 ½ x 5 ¾ In.	145.00
Creamer, Dutch Girl, Holding Duck, Multicolor, 4 ¾ In.	250.00
Creamer, Goat, Orange Jacket, Flowers On Lapel, Green Pants, Shoes, 5 ¼ In.	180.00
Creamer, Witch, With Fan, Blue, 4 ⅛ In.	90.00
Figurine, Dutch Boy & Shoe, Marked, 5 ½ In. ....*illus*	58.00
Match Holder, Jasperware, Green, White Slip Flowers, Fairies	225.00

Match Holder, Mother Cat, Kitten, Don't Scratch Me Scratch Mother, Multicolor, 3 ¾ In........	118.00
Match Holder, Nodder, Egyptian Woman, Holding Up Hands, c.1900..................................	200.00
Pin Tray, Embossed Black Children, Mule, 1890s, 5 x 4 In.	266.00
Pitcher, Cow, Wearing Dress, Lace Collar, Blue Bow, 5 ¼ x 3 ½ In.......................	145.00
Pitcher, Dutch Girl, 5 In. ....*illus*	81.00
Pitcher, Jester, Marked, 5 ¾ In. ....*illus*	207.00
Pitcher, Milk Maid, Holding Vase, Blue, c.1900	59.00
Plaque, Jasperware, Pink, Brown, White, Fairies, 6 In.	350.00
Toby Jug, Boy's Head, Green Turtle Neck Sweater, Purple Hat, 4 ¾ In.	150.00

SCHEIER POTTERY was made by Edwin Scheier (1910–2008) and his wife, Mary (1908–2007). They met while they both worked for the WPA, and married in 1937. In 1939, they established their studio, Hillcrock Pottery, in Glade Spring, Virginia. From 1940 to 1968, Edwin taught at the University of New Hampshire and Mary was artist-in-residence. They moved to Oaxaca, Mexico, in 1968 to study the arts and crafts of the Zapotec Indians. When the Scheiers moved to Green Valley, Arizona, in 1978, Ed returned to pottery, making some of his biggest and best-known pieces.

Bowl, Brown, White Matte Band, Figural Sgraffito, 4 x 5 In.	2015.00
Bowl, Cover, Mother & Child Finial, Runny Gray Glaze, Baluster, c.1959, 21 ¼ x 12 In.	4030.00
Bowl, Fish, Brown, Yellow Ground, Round, 1950s, 3 ½ x 17 ½ In............	4340.00
Bowl, Incised Designs, Glazed, Signed, 1950s, 4 ½ x 6 ½ In. ....*illus*	1860.00
Bowl, Incised Faces, Pink Glaze, Signed, 7 ½ x 14 ¼ In........................	7440.00
Bowl, Mottled Brown, Tan & Cream Matte Glaze, Footed, Inscribed, 4 ¾ x 7 In. ....*illus*	326.00
Bowl, Sgraffito Faces, Blue, Brown Matte Glaze, Round, Footed, 4 x 6 In.	1348.00
Charger, Abstract Figures, Yellow Matte Glaze, 1950s, 11 In.	4030.00
Charger, Intersecting Sgrafitto Faces, Taupe Matte Glaze, 16 In.	2370.00
Plate, Stylized Sgraffito Figures, White Outlines, Blue Glaze, 10 In.	919.00
Vase, 6 Men Holding Fish, Waves, Incised, 9 In. ....*illus*	4025.00
Vase, Families, Mottled Gray Glaze, Gold, Orange Flecks, 1966, 21 x 9 In.......	11160.00
Vase, Full-Length Figures, Tan, Black Glaze, Signed, 1950s, 24 ¼ x 8 In.	7440.00
Vase, Mothers & Children, Etched, Gray, White, Mottled, Tapered Base, 1960s, 19 ¼ x 9 ½ In..	8680.00

SCHNEIDER GLASSWORKS was founded in 1917 at Epinay-sur-Seine, France, by Charles and Ernest Schneider. Art glass was made between 1917 and 1930. The company still produces clear crystal glass. See also the Le Verre Francais category.

Bowl, Amethyst, Blue, Amethyst Stem, Figural Leaf, Glass Bead, 6 ¾ x 15 In.	800.00
Bowl, Metal Base, Figural Leaf & Beaded, Amethyst Stem, Blue Bowl, 15 In.	800.00
Vase, Footed, Coupe, Purple To Yellow & Orange Rim, Signed, 7 ¼ In..............	100.00
Vase, Grape Clusters, Purple, Orange Ground, Inverted Teardrop, Bulbous Foot, 7 In.......	502.00
Vase, Mottled Purple & Blue, Blown Through Wrought Iron Frame, Handles, 12 In.	443.00
Vase, Orange, Red Trees, Flared, Cameo, Incised, Le Verre Francais, 14 x 6 ¼ In.	4340.00
Vase, Orange Shaded To Dark Orange, Swirls, Elongated Neck, Rigaree Handles, 14 In., Pair .	1470.00
Vase, Red, White, Orange, Mottled, Encased On Metal, 7 x 6 In. ....*illus*	720.00

SCIENTIFIC INSTRUMENTS of all kinds are included in this category. Other categories such as Barometer, Binoculars, Dental, Medical, Nautical, and Thermometer may also price scientific apparatus.

Astrolabe, Planetarium, Wood, Metal, Spherical, 23 x 16 In.	180.00
Calculating Machine, Millionar, Wood Case, 1895 ....*illus*	3884.00
Calculator, Royal Typewriter, Model 80K, UA 119, Vacuum Fluorescent Display, c.1972..........	15.00
Chemist Apparatus, Distilling Water, Copper, Brass, 8 x 13 In.........................	89.00
Chronometer, 1 Wheel, Brass, Jeweled Lever, Components, c.1895, 5 In.	13035.00
Chronometer, Marine, 8-Day, Brass Dial, Seconds Dial, Case, 5 In. Diam............	2370.00
Chronometer, Waltham Watch Co., Mahogany Box, 3 Tiers, Brass Gimbals	593.00
Chronometer, William Gerard, Gimbal, Adjustable, Brass Frame, c.1910, 7 ½ x 7 In.	826.00
Compascope, Gordon Roberts, Brass, Wood Box, 9 In..............................	69.00
Compass Set, Mueller, Pink, Purple Tile, Green Arrow, Frame, 21 x 21 In...........	644.00
Compass, Brass, Ivory Handle, Curved Arm, Microscope, England, 1700s, 6 In.......	2607.00
Compass, Brass, Ivory Handle, Sliding Specimen Holder, Microscope, 1700s, 6 In.............	1715.00
Compass, Brass, Turned Wood Handle, 3 Magnifier Arms, Microscope, 1800s, 8 In.	3437.00
Compass, Nautical, Brass, Folding, Needle Ring, Mahogany Box, 2 ½ In...............	95.00
Compass, Ship's, Kelvin & White, Brass, Gimbal Mount, Hardwood Block, 7 In.........	148.00
Compass, Surveying, Painted Birch Frame, Fleur-De-Lis, c.1800, 16 In...............	337.00
Compass, Surveyor's, Vernier, Brass, Wooden Box, Leather Strap, 6 x 15 In.........	353.00
Compass, Surveyor's, Walnut, Fleur-De-Lis, Star Pattern, Schooner, 1700s, 12 In..........	1185.00

Scale, Candy, Victory V Gum & Lozenges, Tin, Faux Wood, 20 Lb. Max., Rear Door, Eng., c.1920, 16 In.
$144.00

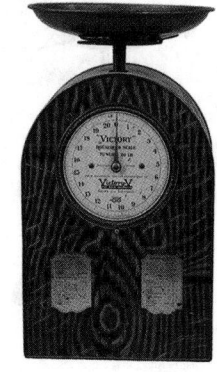

Bertoia Auctions

Scale, Jockey, W. & T. Avery, Mahogany, Cast Iron, Upholstered, England, 37 x 22 In.
$4148.00

Skinner, Inc.

Scale, Produce, Molen, Jan Molenschotz & Zn. Breda-Holland, 21 x 43 In.
$325.00

Showtime Auction Services

Scale, Weighing, Angldile, Open Face, Red & Black, Brass, Electric, Counter
$3000.00

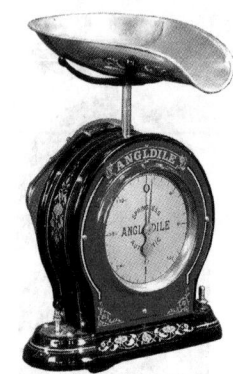

The Stein Auction Co.

Victorian Casino Antique Auction

Schafer & Vater, Bottle, Baseball Player, 5 ½ In.
$380.00

The Stein Auction Co.

Schafer & Vater, Figurine, Dutch Boy & Shoe, Marked, 5 ½ In.
$58.00

The Stein Auction Co.

Schafer & Vater, Pitcher, Dutch Girl, 5 In.
$81.00

The Stein Auction Co.

Galvanometer, Darsonval, Central Scientific Co., Chicago, Oak Case, 14 In.	58.00
Graphoscope, Burl Veneer, Folding Case, Magnifying Lens, 1800s, 8 ½ x 5 ½ In. ....*illus*	345.00
Lamp, Standing, Surveyor's, Metal, Wood Legs, c.1920, 73 In.	492.00
Magnifying Glass, Bamboo Handle, Carved, Curved, 11 x 3 ½ In.	122.00
Magnifying Glass, Elephant Ivory, Perusal Handle, Dog Head, Lady Liberty, c.1880, 5 In.	150.00
Magnifying Glass, Parasol Handle, Sterling, c.1890, 11 In.	225.00
Magnifying Glass, Partridgewood, Porcelain, Parasol Handle, c.1880, 8 In.	125.00
Magnifying Glass, Walrus Ivory, Totem Pole, c.1875, 4 ½ In.	195.00
Microscope Illuminator, Collins London Brockett Microscope Lamp, Brass, c.1910, 9 In. .*illus*	431.00
Microscope, Botanical, Mahogany, Pivoting Eyepiece, Knife, Point, 1800s, 5 In.	3437.00
Microscope, Botanist's, Lacquer, Brass, Circular Stage, Leather Case, c.1800, 2 In.	889.00
Microscope, Browning's Miniature, Silver, Forceps, Clips, Mirror, c.1880, 3 In.	2726.00
Microscope, Compound, Brass, Rackwork Coarse, Micrometer Fine Focus, 1800s, 13 ½ In. *illus*	153.00
Microscope, Compound, Monocular, Williams Brown & Earle, Wood, Metal, 75 x 30 In.	118.00
Microscope, Compound, Pocket, Brass, Tripod, Pillar, Detachable Legs, 1800s, 5 In.	2844.00
Microscope, Monocular, J. Swift, Fitted Mahogany Case, Brass Handles, 12 x 8 ½ In.	441.00
Microscope, Naturalist's, Brass, Hinged Box, Fixed Arm, Eyepieces, Clip, 1800s, 6 In.	533.00
Microscope, Naturalist's, Brass, Mahogany Box, Drawer, France, 1800s, 7 In.	652.00
Microscope, Wood, Turned Handle, Spherical Lens, Ebony Mount, 1800s, 3 In.	119.00
Slide Rule, Keuffel & Esser Co., 1900s, 85 x 8 In.	444.00
Telegraph Register, Fire Alarm, Brass Case, Tape Reel, Gamewell, c.1900, 10 In.	207.00
Telescope Gauge, Wood Box, C.J. Lusk Co., 7 x 1 ¾ In.	65.00
Telescope, Bardou & Son, Brass, 36 In. Barrel, Tripod Oak Stand, France, 1800s, 51 In.	633.00
Telescope, Brass, Almer Coe & Co., Walnut Tripod, Case, c.1900, 50 In.	2963.00
Telescope, Brass, Broadhurst, Clarkson & Co., England, 77 x 73 In.	5310.00
Telescope, Brass, Refracting, Ebonized Folding Tripod, 62 In.	1348.00
Telescope, Decagonal, Mahogany Tube, Brass Draw, 35 In.	1067.00
Telescope, Surveyor's, Ambluco Chicago, 12 x 9 In.	295.00
Transit, Surveyor's, Compass, Wood, Metal, Adjustable Base	277.00
Transit, Surveyor's, Marked W. & L.E. Gurley, Wood Case, 1800's 9 ½ x 23 In. .... 230.00 to 395.00	
Water Magnifying Glass, Clear Receiver, Cast Iron Stand, Adjustable, c.1870, 14 In.	403.00
Weather Station, Clock, Thermometer, Barometer, Hydrometer, Brass Base, c.1951	531.00

SCRIMSHAW is bone or ivory or whale's teeth carved by sailors and others for entertainment during the sailing-ship days. Some scrimshaw was carved as early as 1800. There are modern scrimshanders making pieces today on bone, ivory, or plastic. Other pieces may be found in the Ivory and Nautical categories.

Belt Buckle, Sterling, Sailboat, Choppy Seas, Mounted, Teak Stand, c.1990, 1 ¾ x 1 ½ In.	86.00
Busk, Bone, Scalloped Top, Incised, Inked, Flowers, Cross, Peacock, Portrait, 1800s, 12 ¾ In.	764.00
Busk, Whalebone, Woman, Man With American Flag, 25 Stars, Eagle, Shield, 1800s, 12 In.	6325.00
Frame, Carved, Heart, 19th Century, 5 ¼ x 3 ⅛ In.	422.00
Knife, Bone Handle, Cabin Scene, Folding, ¾ x 1 In.	17.00
Knife, Bone, Elk Design, Folding, 3 x ¾ In.	17.00
Ostrich Egg, Spread Wing Eagle Design, c.1900, 6 In.	431.00
Penguin, Carved Whale's Tooth, Standing, Outstretched Beak, Oval Plinth, c.1900, 6 ¾ In., Pair.	518.00
Pie Crimper, Bone & Wood, Mahogany Handle, Hen Head, Tail, 3 Tine Fork, 1800s, 8 In.	3450.00
Pie Crimper, Bone, Inlaid Abalone Shell, Angled Support, Square Handle, 1800s, 6 In.	1610.00
Pie Crimper, Tapered Carved Handle, Scalloped Edge, Heart Cutout, 1800s, 6 In.	920.00
Powder Horn, Pictures, Daniel Boone, Liberty, Rifle, Marked, Fred W. Glasier, Mass., 1885	1093.00
Rolling Pin, Whalebone & Ebony, 1800s, 17 In.	711.00
Rolling Pin, Whalebone & Wood, Tapered End, Carved Line Design, 1800s, 12 In.	863.00
Ruler, Whalebone, Squared Ends, 1 Edge Angled, 1800s, 24 In.	633.00
Stool, Whale Vertebrae Seat, 3 Whalebone Legs, 23 x 14 In.	288.00
Tooth, Whaling Ship, Fortune, Flag, Banner, Scroll, c.1895, 7 In.	2013.00
Tusk, Eskimo, Kayak, Rifle, 2 Seals, Man, Dog, Hut, 6 Men In Canoe, Whale, Walrus Ivory, 15 In.	575.00
Whale Panbone, Engraved, Rectangular Panel, Whaling Ship, Dead Whale, Men, 1800s, 5 x 15 In.	8295.00
Whale's Tooth, Elizabethan Woman, Riding Horse, Woman Holding Wheat Basket, 1800s, 8 In.	2645.00
Whale's Tooth, Engraved, Sailing Vessels In Battle, American & British Flags, 1800s, 6 In.	1185.00
Whale's Tooth, Engraved, Spreadwing Eagle, Shield, Ship, Woman & Daughter, 1800s, 6 In.	2489.00
Whale's Tooth, Man With Mutton Chop Sideburns, Wearing Suit, Engraved, 1800s, 5 In.	518.00
Whale's Tooth, Portrait, 2 Women, 1800s, 5 In.	1410.00
Whale's Tooth, Scrollwork, 3-Masted Ship, Engraved, 1800s, 7 In.	374.00
Whale's Tooth, Sperm & Right Whale, Spouting, Engraved, 1800s, 6 In.	1150.00
Whale's Tooth, USS Columbia, Flags, Shield, Eagle, Banner, Wheat, Garlands, c.1855, 7 In. ..	7188.00
Whale's Tooth, Young Couple, Lovebirds, Clutching Heart, Flag, England, c.1840s, 3 ½ In.	382.00

SEBASTIAN MINIATURES were first made by Prescott W. Baston in 1938 in Marblehead, Massachusetts. More than 400 different designs have been made and collectors search for the out-of-production modes. The mark may say *Copr. P.W. Baston U.S.A.*, or *P.W. Baston U.S.A.*, or *Prescott W. Baston*. Sometimes a paper label was used.

Santa Claus, Jell-O A Fine Treat For All, P.W. Baston, Copr. 1955, 3 x 4 In. ....*illus* 115.00

SEG, *see Paul Revere Pottery category.*

SEVRES porcelain has been made in Sevres, France, since 1769. Many copies of the famous ware have been made. The name originally referred to the works of the Royal Porcelain factory. The name now includes any of the wares made in the town of Sevres, France. The entwined lines with a center letter used as the mark is one of the most forged marks in antiques. Be very careful to identify Sevres by quality, not just by mark.

Bowl, Ormolu, Flowers, Straw Hat, Insects, Scroll Handles, Oval Base, 4-Footed, 1800s, 19 ½ In....	4740.00
Box, Hinged Lid, Figures, Landscape, Lake Panels, Shaped, Gilt Cobalt, Signed Lancry, c.1900, 5 x 13 In.	2596.00
Cake Stand, Cobalt Blue, Gilt, Round Top, Leaf Borders, Molded Legs, Paw Feet, c.1833, 3 ¼ x 9 ¼ In.	245.00
Casket, Jewelry, Painted Porcelain Panels, Jewels, Gilt Bronze, Women, Birds, 6 x 11 In.	7015.00
Cup & Saucer, Cover, Central Flower Spray, Gilt & Blue Scrolling Leaf Borders, c.1754, 3 x 6 In., Pair	748.00
Cup & Saucer, Marie Antoinette, Enameled, Garlands, Blue Ground, France, 1780, 2 ⅝ In.....	858.00
Cup, Art Nouveau, Yellow, Flowing Vines, Multicolor, c.1903, 4 ¾ x 4 In.	1434.00
Dresser Box, Lid, Lobed Flower Shape, Flowers, Gold Foil Ground, c.1900, 3 x 6 In................	276.00
Dresser Box, Lid, Oval, Courting Couple, Chalet & Forest, Gold Scrolls, Marked, 8 In. ...*illus*	633.00
Figurine, Art Deco, Golden Locks, Nude Woman, Frosted Crystal, Etched, 9 In.	138.00
Garniture, Red, Bronze Mounted, Garlands, Footed, Signed, 7 To 18 In., 3 Piece	900.00
Gravy Boat, Notched Lid, Flowers, Courting Scene, Liner Plate, Leaf Finial, 8 ½ x 5 ½ In.	155.00
Jar, Cover, Art Nouveau, White, Painted, Yellow Flowers, Sinuous Blue Stems, c.1900, 3 x 4 In...	508.00
Plaque, Round, White Classical Relief, Woman, Cherub, Blue Ground, 1800s, 17 ¾ In., Pair..	948.00
Plate, Flower Garlands, Blue Ribbon, Scattered Bouquets, Gilt, 10 In., 12 Piece	2124.00
Plate, Portrait, Gilt, Flowers, Pink, Shaped, c.1790, 9 In., Pair	649.00
Plate, Portrait, Hand Painted, Gold To Green Border, Princesse De Lamballe, 1800s, 9 ⅝ In. ..	123.00
Serving Bowl, Chateau De Fontainbleau, Animal, Diamond, Star Border, France, c.1846, 12 In...	119.00
Tureen, Cover, Lemon Finial, Flowers, Bouquets, Butterflies, Cobalt & Gilt Accents, 1800s, 9 ¾ x 14 In.	7670.00
Urn, Acorn Finial, Flowers, Birds, Cobalt Blue, Bronze Mounts, 17 ¾ In., Pair	1074.00
Urn, Cover, Champleve Mounted, Fashionable Woman, Landscape, France, 1800s, 8 ½ In.	429.00
Urn, Cover, Shepherdess, Lamb, Couple, Pink, Fired Gold, Signed S. Buleau, 23 In. ....*illus*	2040.00
Urn, Dining Scene, Garden Scene, Cobalt Ground, Gilt Highlights, Handles, 29 ½ In. ....*illus*	2242.00
Urn, Dome Lid, Cylindrical, Pedestal Foot, Pineapple Finial, Handles, 1800s, 18 In., Pair........	1380.00
Urn, Lid, Art Nouveau, 2 Women, Fanciful Settings, Footed, Signed Collinet, c.1905, 29 In.	4012.00
Urn, Lid, Artichoke Bronze Finials, Courting Scene, Cobalt Ground, France, c.1900, 39 In., Pair...	23600.00
Urn, Lid, Bronze Dore Handles, Bacchus Head Mount, Tavern Scenes, D. Teniers, 11 ¾ In., Pair ...	3540.00
Urn, Napoleon Transfer Design, Blue, 2 Loop Handles, Pedestal Foot, Flowers, 1800s, 6 In.	59.00
Urn, Painted, Reserve, Classical Women, Fired Gold, Signed Bock, 1800s, 28 In........................	4800.00
Urn, Peaked Lid, Acorn Finial, Courting Couple, Flower Spray, Flared Foot, Stamped, 14 In. ...	521.00
Urn, Turquoise, Painted Scenes, Angular Handles, Cover, 6 ½ x 5 ½ In..	1200.00
Urn, Women, Fans, Courtyard, Landscape Panels, White, Bronze Mounts, Signed Petit, c.1915, 33 In.	4956.00
Urn, Women, Landscape Panels, Bronze Handles, Signed G. Poiterin, 1800s, 23 In., Pair.........	3540.00
Vanity Box, Ormolu Mounted, Blue Glaze, Portrait Medallion, Paul Milet, c.1940, 3 ½ x 5 ½ In...	708.00
Vase, Baluster, Enamel, Violets, Gold Foil Ground, Leaves, Signed, c.1900, 6 In...................	584.00
Vase, Baluster, Round Foot, Red, Flambe Glaze, Dark Mottling, Signed, c.1950, 14 In.	369.00
Vase, Baluster, Turquoise To Cobalt, Gilt Collar, Lily-Of-The-Valley Handles, 1900s, 4 In., Pair	430.00
Vase, Bleu Celeste Ground, Ormolu Swags, Base, Flared, White Interior, 7 In., Pair	1380.00
Vase, Canal Scenes, Bottle Shape, Gold Scrolls, Flowers, Handles, c.1900, 11 In.	593.00
Vase, Children In Cartouche, Goat, Dog, Cart, Blue, Gilt Bronze Mount, Handles, 20 In., Pair .	8050.00
Vase, Cobalt Glaze, Bronze Gilt Shell Rims & Base, c.1910, 12 In., Pair	885.00
Vase, Cover, Cobalt Blue Glaze, Gilt Bronze Mounts, Mark, France, 1800s, 14 In.	1067.00
Vase, Cover, Ivory, Blue, Gilt Bronze Mounts, Winged Female Handles, 1800s, 22 ½ In.............	2607.00
Vase, Cover, Nymphs, Cupids, Raised Gold Borders, Bronze Base, 1800s, 40 ¾ In. ....*illus*	2695.00
Vase, Cover, Urn Shape, 2 Handles, Gilt, Green, Couple, Octagonal Base, c.1774, 17 ¾ In.	674.00
Vase, Dome Lid, Acorn Finial, Medallions, 2 Putti, Garden, Flowers, Flared Base, c.1785, 16 In......	674.00
Vase, Enamel, Cylindrical, Shouldered, Dragonflies, Irises, Gold Foil Ground, Signed, c.1900, 7 In....	799.00
Vase, Lid, Cobalt Blue, Putti In Medallion, Applied Garlands, Female Handles, c.1785, 17 In. ..*illus*	735.00
Vase, Peaked Lid, Champleve, Pineapple Finial, Courting Couple, Square Base, 1800s, 15 ¾ In.....	1164.00
Vase, Silver Mount, Enameled, Urn, Acorn Band, 4 Dolphins, Gold Foil, Leaves, c.1900, 6 In...	1353.00

Schafer & Vater, Pitcher, Jester, Marked, 5 ¾ In.
$207.00

The Stein Auction Co.

Scheier, Bowl, Incised Designs, Glazed, Signed, 1950s, 4 ½ x 6 ½ In.
$1860.00

Rago Arts & Auction Center

Scheier, Bowl, Mottled Brown, Tan & Cream Matte Glaze, Footed, Inscribed, 4 ¾ x 7 In.
$326.00

Skinner, Inc.

Scheier, Vase, 6 Men Holding Fish, Waves, Incised, 9 In.
$4025.00

Humler & Nolan

As always, the edited listings in *Kovels' Antiques & Collectibles Price Guide* aren't available on any website, but readers should visit Kovels.com for information on trends, tips, reproductions, marks, old prices, and more!

Schneider, Vase, Red, White, Orange, Mottled, Encased On Metal, 7 x 6 In. $720.00

DuMouchelles Art Gallery

Scientific Instrument, Calculating Machine, Millionar, Wood Case, 1895 $3884.00

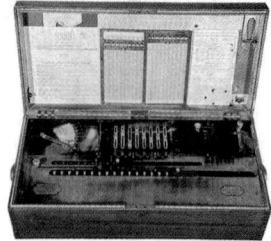

Auction Team Breker

Scientific Instrument, Graphoscope, Burl Veneer, Folding Case, Magnifying Lens, 1800s, 8 ½ x 5 ½ In. $345.00

Leland Little Auction

Scientific Instrument, Microscope Illuminator, Collins London Brockett Microscope Lamp, Brass, c.1910, 9 In. $431.00

Leland Little Auction

SEWER TILE figures were made by workers at the sewer tile and pipe factories in the Ohio area during the late nineteenth and early twentieth centuries. Figurines, small vases, and cemetery vases were favored. Often the finished vase was a piece of the original pipe with added decorations and markings. All types of sewer tile work are now considered folk art by collectors.

Birdhouse, Tree Bark, Tooled, c.1910, 9 In.	*illus*	235.00
Chimney Cap, Paneled, Scalloped Rim, Ohio, c.1900, 29 ½ In.		353.00
Doorstop, Spaniel, Seated, Incised Details, Red Brown Glaze, c.1900, 10 In.		173.00
Figure, Bulldog, Seated, Collar, Ohio, c.1910, 7 ½ In.		323.00
Figure, Deer, Reclining, Ohio, c.1910, 12 ½ In.		59.00
Figure, Dog, Spaniel, Molded, Tooled, c.1900, 7 ½ In.		499.00
Figure, Dog, Spaniel, Seated, Incised Details, Collar, Inscribed Roy Blind, 9 ¾ In.		118.00
Figure, Football, Marked EJE, Life-Size		1200.00
Figure, Frog, Incised Feet, Mouth, Eyes, Lyman Clark, c.1931, 6 ½ In.		173.00
Figure, Lion, Reclining, Incised Details, Oval Base, c.1900, 7 x 14 In.		264.00
Figure, Winged Lion, Seated, Curly Mane, Green Glaze, Chinese, Late 1800s, 11 x 11 In.		366.00
Paperweight, Frog, Seated, Bulging Eyes, Red Brown Glaze, 4 ½ In.		201.00
Planter, Oak Leaves, Protuding Tree Trunks, Glazed, 1800s, 8 ½ x 11 In.	*illus*	201.00
Roof Tile, Seated Dragon, Green Glaze, Yellow Accents, 8 ½ x 4 ¼ In.		259.00
Tobacco Jar, Tree Stump, Cover, Seated Dog Knob, Impressed Whatcher, c.1910, 4 x 7 In.		588.00
Umbrella Stand, Tree Bark, St. Louis Sewer Pipe Co., Anheuser-Busch, c.1880, 26 x 13 In.	*illus*	7475.00

SEWING equipment of all types is collected, from sewing birds that held the cloth to tape measures, needle books, and old wooden spools. Sewing machines are included here. Needlework pictures are listed in the Picture category.

Basket, Reed, Wood Bottom, Lid, Milk Glass Knob, c.1915, 4 x 8 In.	45.00
Basket, Wicker, Flowers, Handle, Dritz, 10 In.	40.00
Bird, Velvet Pincushion, Clamp, Iron, c.1810, 6 ½ x 3 In.	325.00
Box, 5-Point Star, Contrasting Colors, Narrow Notch Cut, Padded Calico, 3 ¾ x 13 In.	24.00
Box, Banded Geometric Parquetry Design, Tray, 11 Compartments, c.1875, 7 ⅝ x 12 In.	150.00
Box, Bentwood, 4-Finger, Silk Lining, Bentwood Handle, Oval, Label, 1800s, 3 ¼ x 9 In.	118.00
Box, Chest Of Drawers, Hearts, Stars, 6 Drawers, Lift Pincushion Top, 1800s, 19 x 17 In.	920.00
Box, Curly Maple, Tiered Thread Caddy, Pincushion Top, Drawer, Ohio, c.1850, 13 In. *illus*	558.00
Box, George IV, Rosewood, Ivory Inlays, 6 ¼ x 13 In.	652.00
Box, Hinged Lid, Removable Fitted Interior, England, 1800s, 6 x 18 x 11 In.	177.00
Box, Lacquer, Chinoiserie, Rectangular, Domed & Hinged Top, 1800s, 5 ½ In.	337.00
Box, Lacquer, Courtyard Scene, Gold & Enamel Design, Ivory, Chinese, 1800s, 14 ¼ In.	459.00
Box, Lehnware, Painted, Decals, Stripping, Flowers, Lock, Turned Feet, 6 x 11 In.	904.00
Box, Lid, Mahogany, Satinwood, Bombe Shape, Fitted Tray, Brass Paw Feet, 6 x 10 In.	148.00
Box, Lid, Painted, Multicolor, 1800s, 11 x 7 In.	489.00
Box, Mahogany, Ivory Inlay, Piano Shape, Paper Lined, France, c.1904, 6 ¼ x 11 ½ In.	354.00
Box, Marquetry, 1800s, 7 x 14 ¾ In.	119.00
Box, Olive Wood, Ivory, Star, c.1880, 18 x 18 In.	206.00
Box, Pasteboard, Gold Stamped Foil, Pincushion, Mirror, Flowers, Heart, c.1875, 3 ½ In. *illus*	60.00
Box, Pine, Maple, Lapped Swing Handle, Silk Lined, Pincushion, Round, Wax, c.1890, 4 x 8 In.	326.00
Box, Poplar, Dovetailed Drawer, Openwork, Shoe Feet, c.1875, 6 x 7 x 5 In.	1645.00
Box, Stand, Black Lacquer, Brass Inlay, Fitted Interior, Victorian, 30 x 15 In.	748.00
Box, Victorian, Hunting Dog, Gilt, Black Lacquer, Mother-Of-Pearl Spools, Marked Evening	1150.00
Box, Wood, Drawer, Shaped Feet, Diamond Inlay, Mid 1800s, 7 x 7 In.	353.00
Cabinet, Spool, Oak, 6 Drawers, 22 x 12 ½ In.	192.00
Cabinet, Spool, Walnut, 18 Glass Drawers, 18 Panel Drawers, 36 x 42 In.	633.00
Cabinet, Spool, see also the Advertising category under Cabinet, Spool.	
Darning Egg, Blown Glass, Amber, c.1875, 5 ½ In.	101.00
Darning Egg, Glass, Green, Ball Shape, Handle, 6 ⅜ In.	35.00
Darning Set, Sterling Silver, Case, 3 ½ In., 3 Piece	79.00
Embroidery Frame, Hand Carved, Bird's-Eye & Tiger Maple, 1800s, 24 x 17 In.	796.00
Etui, Grand Piano Shape, Walnut, Brass, Mother-Of-Pearl Keyboard Music Box, 7 ¾ x 12 In.	2875.00
Lacemaker's Lamp, Blown Glass, Globe, Hourglass Stem, Applied Handle, Round Foot, 8 x 3 ½ In.	81.00
Loom, Table Top, Mixed Wood, Warp In Wool, 12 ¼ x 14 ¾ x 15 ½ In.	35.00
Machine, Singer, Model 66-14, 1940	48.00
Machine, Singer, Model 221-1, Featherweight, Portable, c.1949	535.00
Necessaire, Tan Kidskin, Silk Ribbon Bands, 4 Brass Feet, Fitted Interior, c.1875, 5 In.	684.00
Needle Case, Fleur-De-Lis, Brass, Avery Golden, England, c.1870, 2 ¾ In.	295.00
Needle Case, Rolling Pin Case, Celluloid, Roses, c.1900, 4 ½ In.	58.00
Needle Threader, Cast Iron, Painted, Table Model, 8 x 6 In.	374.00
Needlebook, Family Scene By Lake, Assorted, Vintage Royal Sewing Needle, Japan, 1940s, 5 x 3 In.	12.95

S

Pattern, Evening Gown, Simplicity, c.1948, 34 Bust	22.00
Pattern, McCalls, No. 12/32, Dress	8.00

Pincushion Dolls are listed in their own category.

Pincushion, Bonnet, Crocheted, Posies	15.00
Pincushion, Dog, Lying, On Cushion, Velvet, Glass Eyes, 19th Century, 3 ¼ In.	50.00
Pincushion, Figural, Pig, Silver Plate, Burgundy Cushion On Back, 2 x 2 In.	27.00
Pincushion, Hanging, Leather, Velvet, 2 Hearts, 2 Birds, Pa., 1800s, 10 x 10 In. ....*illus*	1939.00
Pincushion, Hedgehog Shape, Pierced Back, Silver, c.1900, 5 x 2 ½ In.	598.00
Pincushion, Kewpie, Plastic Satin, Pink, Green	32.00
Pincushion, Maple Pedestal, Screw Clamp Base, Purple Velvet, 9 In.	28.00
Pincushion, Milk Glass, Pedestal, Beaded Swag	51.00
Pincushion, Needlepoint, Star Shape Chip Carved Hanger, Round Finial, 14 x 8 In.	94.00
Pincushion, Shoe Shape, Rope Work, c.1800	225.00
Pincushion, Silk, Needlework, Chenille Thread, Flowers, Tassels, Aug. 1840, 4 x 6 ½ x 8 ½ In. .*illus*	948.00
Pincushion, Squash, Fabric, 2 ¾ In.	35.00
Pincushion, Velvet, Carrot Shape, Orange, 1800s, 11 ½ x 14 ½ In., Pair	1304.00
Pincushion, Wool, Silk, Velvet Ends, Drum Shape, Pa., c.1900, 3 ½ x 3 In.	325.00
Pinking Shears, Joseph Rodgers, Box, 1960s	32.00
Pocketbook, Canvaswork, Leather Lined, Pincushions, Needle Holder, 1800s, 5 x 10 In.	889.00
Purse, Ladies Maid's, Leather, Fitted For Tools, c.1850, 3 ½ x 6 In.	1750.00
Roll-Up, Beaded Needlework, Cotton, Linen, Flowers, Birds, Branches, 1800s, 4 x 11 In.	148.00
Scissors, Embroidery, Silver, Ornate Design, 3-In. Span	114.00
Snap Fasteners, Flapper Lady, W.T. Grant Co., 1930s, Size 4 Snaps, 5 x 3 Card	12.95

Spool Cabinets are listed here or in the Advertising category under Cabinet, Spool.

Spool, Thread Caddy, Mahogany, 2 Tiers, Octagonal Base, Bracketed Shaft, 16 In.	45.00
Tape Loom, Dovetailed Frame, Foot Pedal, Carved Base Frame, 31 x 16 In.	649.00
Tape Loom, Poplar, Dovetailed Box, Warp Comb, Padded Warp Spool, Weft Shuttles, 20 x 6 In.	708.00
Tape Measure, Coffee Mill Shape, Crank Handle, c.1950, 1 ¼ x 1 ¼ In.	95.00
Tape Measure, McCormick Harvesting Machine Co., Machine On Back, Celluloid, 1 ¾ x ½ In. *illus*	242.00
Tape Measure, Owl, Branch, Embossed, Tin, Germany, ½ x 1 ½ In.	65.00
Tape Measure, Priscilla Maid Of New England, Celluloid, Image Of Building, 1 ⅜ In.	95.00
Thimble Holder, Chester, Sterling, Leather Case, c.1918, 1 ¼ In.	101.00
Thimble Holder, Swashbuckler, Etched, My Favorite Thimble, Nickel Plated, 2 x 3 In.	58.00
Thimble, Gold, Scrolled Edge, Engraved, Size 8	100.00
Thimble, Horseshoe, 4 Leaf Clovers, Stern Bros., c.1910, Size 9	105.00
Thimble, Silver, Blue Enamel, Russia, ⅞ In.	115.00
Thimble, Sterling, Faceted Border, Size 12	60.00
Thimble, Sterling, Stars, Engraved, Size 8	55.00
Thread Winder, Cross Shape, Wood, Tunbridge, 5 x 5 In.	186.00
Yard Winder, 6 Maple Arms, Scrimshaw, 1800s, 9 x 17 ½ In.	650.00
Yarn Winder, Ash Block, Chip Carved, Through Tenon Support, Worm Gear, 47 x 14 In.	106.00
Yarn Winder, Barrel Style, Crank, 8 Spokes, 4 Arms, 29 x 20 In.	24.00
Yarn Winder, Ivory, Rosewood, Maple, Carved Standard, Round Base, 15 ¾ In.	911.00
Yarn Winder, Mahogany, 4 Arms, Crank, Lathe Turned Shaft, Worm Gear, 35 x 27 In.	59.00
Yarn Winder, Mixed Wood, Pennsylvania, 19th Century, 41 In.	34.00
Yarn Winder, Turned Cup, Adjustable Slat Winder, Turned Clamp, Expanding, 1800s, 22 In.	613.00
Yarn Winder, Walnut Block, Pine, Double Squirrel Cage, Adjustable, 43 x 15 In.	295.00
Yarn Winder, Wood, Paint, 1800s, 32 In.	173.00

SHAKER items are characterized by simplicity, functionalism, and orderliness. There were many Shaker communities in America from the eighteenth century to the present day. The religious order made furniture, small wooden pieces, and packaged medicines, herbs, and jellies to sell to "outsiders." Other useful objects were made for use by members of the community. Shaker furniture is listed in this book in the Furniture category.

Basket, Berry, Wood Staves & Bail Handle, Pumpkin Wash, Stars, 3 ½ x 4 ½ In.	173.00
Basket, Cheese, Oak Splint, Double Wrapped Contour Rim, c.1850, 7 x 23 In.	322.00
Basket, Drying, Black Ash Splint, Round Top, Square Open Weave Base, 5 ½ x 14 ½ In.	293.00
Basket, Fancy Works, Black Ash Splint, Needle Case, Pincushion, 2 ½ x 5 ½ In.	2105.00
Basket, Kindling, Wrapped Rim, Ticking Lining, 3 Slat Runners, Signed MW 83, 19 x 23 In.	322.00
Basket, Picket Fence, Stave Construction, 2 Bail Handles, 11 ½ x 20 In.	646.00
Basket, Sewing, Cardboard, Plaid Silk, Swing Handle, Pockets, Needle Case, Pincushion, 4 ⅜ x 7 ⅜ In.	234.00
Basket, Splint, Ash, Notched Hardwood Handle, Enfield, Conn., c.1820, 8 x 11 x 8 In.	537.00
Basket, Stays, Joined By Metal Bands, Side Wire Handles, c.1900, 28 In.	300.00
Bonnet, Sister's, Winter, Blue, Gray Silk, Quilted, Puffed, Cotton, Ribbon Ties, c.1880, 10 x 8 In.	70.00
Box, 3-Finger, Oval, Lid, Pine, Maple, Brick Red Paint, Signed Ural Williamson, 3 x 7 In.	3159.00
Box, 3-Finger, Oval, Lid, Red Paint, Pine & Maple, Copper Tacks, c.1890, 2 x 4 In.	5036.00

Scientific Instrument, Microscope, Compound, Brass, Rackwork Coarse, Micrometer Fine Focus, 1800s, 13 ½ In. $153.00

Skinner, Inc.

Sebastian Miniatures, Santa Claus, Jell-O A Fine Treat For All, P.W. Baston, Copr., 1955, 3 x 4 In. $115.00

Hake's Americana & Collectibles

Sevres, Dresser Box, Lid, Oval, Courting Couple, Chalet & Forest, Gold Scrolls, Marked, 8 In. $633.00

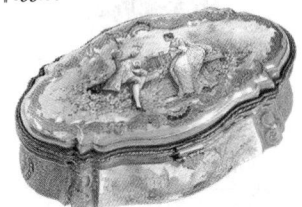

Early Auction Co.

TIP
Mayonnaise can be used to remove old masking tape, stickers, or labels from glass or china.

Sevres, Urn, Cover, Shepherdess, Lamb, Couple, Pink, Fired Gold, Signed S. Buleau, 23 In.
$2040.00

DuMouchelles Art Gallery

Sevres, Urn, Dining Scene, Garden Scene, Cobalt Ground, Gilt Highlights, Handles, 29 ½ In.
$2242.00

Brunk Auctions

TIP

Plastic bubble wrap can ruin the glaze on old ceramics. If the wrap touches the piece for a long time in a hot storage area, it may discolor the glaze or adhere to the surface in an almost permanent glob.

Box, 3-Finger, Oval, Maple, Pine, Red Stain, c.1825, 1 ¾ x 3 ¾ In.	819.00
Box, 4-Finger, Oval, Lid, Maple, Pine, Copper Tacks, c.1840, 4 ⅞ x 11 ⅝ In. *illus*	1755.00
Box, 4-Finger, Oval, Lid, Maple, Pine, Cranberry Paint, c.1835, 3 ⅝ x 9 ¼ In.	2457.00
Box, 4-Finger, Oval, Lid, Pine & Maple, Blue Paint, c.1830, 4 ½ x 11 ¼ In.	3218.00
Box, 4-Finger, Oval, Maple, Pine, Red Paint, Pincushion On Lid, c.1845, 6 ¾ x 10 In.	1287.00
Box, 4-Finger, Oval, Pine, Maple, Copper Tacks, Red Paint, c.1840, 4 ½ x 11 ⅜ In.	2574.00
Box, 5-Finger, Oval, Maple, Pine, Red Walnut Stain, Copper Tacks, c.1835, 6 x 15 In.	5042.00
Box, Dark Green Paint, Oval, 2 ¼ x 5 ¾ In.	226.00
Box, Desk, Maple, Hinged Lift Lid, Blind Dovetailed, Felt Lined Surface, 6 Wells, 24 x 9 ½ In.	351.00
Box, Desk, Slanted Breadboard Lid, Pine Brass Hinges, Shaped Gallery, 4 Wood Pens, 10 x 11 In.	1170.00
Box, Kindling, Poplar, Oak, Maple Handle, L Brackets, Signed, c.1840, 17 ½ x 11 ½ In.	1170.00
Box, Seed, Hinged Lid, Pine, Divided Interior, Mount Lebanon, N.Y., 3 ¼ x 23 x 11 ½ In. *illus*	4680.00
Box, Sewing, Cover, 3-Finger, Pine, Maple, Silk Lining, Cushion, Needle Holder, Oval, 3 x 13 In.	2328.00
Box, Sewing, Dome Lid, Pressboard, Paper Covered, Applied Heart, c.1900, 2 ½ x 4 In.	1483.00
Box, Sewing, Hinged Lift Lid, Butternut, Pine, Turned Feet, Medial Scribe Line, c.1830, 8 x 12 In.	5616.00
Box, Sewing, Pine, Yellow Stain, Heart Shape Ivory Escutcheon, c.1850, 11 x 7 In.	322.00
Box, Sewing, Slide Lid, Pine, Poplar, Brown Stain, Brass Pull, Interior Till, Signed, c.1845, 18 x 10 In.	468.00
Box, Storage, Chamfered Lid, Poplar, Dovetailed, Brass Hook & Eye Clasp, c.1850, 11 x 7 In.	205.00
Box, Storage, Fitted Sliding Lid Figured Birch, Dovetailed, c.1835, 6 ¾ x 12 In.	1404.00
Box, Storage, Hinged Lid, Poplar, Walnut Stain, Double Beveled Molding, 24 x 17 In.	702.00
Box, Storage, Lift Lid, Pine, Red Stain, Turned Pull, 3-Section Interior, c.1825, 3 ¾ x 8 ½ In.	529.00
Box, Storage, Poplar, Blue Paint, 2 Dovetailed Drawers, c.1835, 11 x 17 In.	2457.00
Box, Storage, Slide Lid, Pine, Blue Paint, Carved Finger Holes, A.K.P. Meserve, c.1845, 10 x 14 In.	1521.00
Box, Utility, Butternut, Red Stain, Dovetailed, 13 x 101 ½ In.	819.00
Bucket, Lid, Pine, Bittersweet Red Stain, Wire Bail, Birch Handle, Steel Bands, 9 ¾ x 12 In.	1838.00
Bucket, Lid, Pine, Mustard Yellow Paint, Birch Handle, Wire Bail, c.1840, 11 x 9 In.	5850.00
Carrier, Birch & Pine, Divided, Dovetailed, Canted Sides, Cutout Handle, c.1840, 7 ¼ x 13 ¼ In.	2223.00
Carrier, Butternut, Hickory Hoop Handle, Arrow Ends, Copper Tacks, 5 ½ x 3 ½ In.	1053.00
Carrier, Double Lid, Maple, Pine, Brass Hinges, Swing Handle, c.1890, 8 ½ x 8 ¾ In.	585.00
Carrier, Seed Packet, Pine, Slanted, Hinged Lids, Center Divider, Raised Handle, 25 x 16 In.	1287.00
Cloak, Wool, Blue, Gray Silk Lined Hood, Collar, Child's, 22 In.	1170.00
Cloak, Wool, Blue, Silk Ribbon Ties, Interior Pockets, 48 In.	468.00
Cloak, Wool, Pink, Silk Ribbon Ties, Interior Pockets, Oak Hanger, 47 & 39 In.	322.00
Dipper, Fruitwood Burl, Carved, Bird's Beak Handle, 2 ½ x 4 ¼ In.	1638.00
Dipper, Maple, Tiger Maple, Carved, Curved Handle, c.1840, 3 ⅝ x 6 In.	1053.00
Doll, Porcelain Head, Gray Cloak, Silk Lined Hood, Bonnet, Gray Wool Dress, c.1900, 12 In.	468.00
Drying Rack, Cherry, Center Turned Shaft, 3 Tiers, 8 Arms, Snake Legs, c.1850, 73 x 18 In.	1872.00
Hat Brush, Maple Handle, Brown Horsehair, c.1860, 12 In.	263.00
Herb Press, Birch, Dovetailed Pegged Side Arms, Iron Support & Turn Screw, 1830-40, 10 x 8 ½ In.	585.00
Instrument Holder, Cherry, Pine, Cylinder Top, Pivoting, 8-Sided Nut, Base, 61 In.	283.00
Kerchief, White, Blue Double Line Border, Bonnets Label, Frame, Shadowbox, c.1850, 16 x 25 In.	176.00
Measuring Stick, Tiger Maple, Red Stain, Stamped Numerals, Stamped LLT, Alfred, 28 In.	1287.00
Peg Board, Pine, 3 Large, 2 Small Turned Pegs, Walnut Stain, c.1840, 12 ½ x 43 In.	2691.00
Peg Board, Pine, Cherry, 4 Pegs, Walnut Hanger, T-Shape, 18 & 12 ½ x 12 In.	263.00
Peg Rail, Hanging, Pine, Ocher Paint, 4 Pegs, 2 In. To 3 ½ In., 2 Vertical Struts, 56 x 17 In.	585.00
Pill Roller, Walnut, Cast Brass, Sliding Arm, Base, Brass Cutters, 14 ½ x 13 In.	585.00
Pincushion, Tabletop, Maple, Velvet, Cotton, Wood Clamp, Painted Yellow, c.1855	293.00
Rug Whip, Steel Wire, Turned Maple Handle, Spring Base, Brass Collar, Levi Shaw, 31 In.	322.00
Rug, Wool & Cotton, Crocheted Foundation, Multicolored, Maine, c.1920, 39 x 92 In. *illus*	1404.00
Sewing Kit, Shoe Shape, Bronzed Leather, Brown Silk Ribbon, Fitted Interior, Compartments, 5 In.	1170.00
Shovel, Grain, Carved From Single Piece Of Wood, Beveled Edge, 36 ½ x 11 ¼ In. *illus*	604.00
Sieve, Adjustable, Paper Label, A.S. Clough, Meredith, N.H., c.1890, 18 x 18 In.	181.00
Sieve, Herb, Maple, Ash, Woven Silk Tread Mesh, Copper Nails, 3 ¾ & 3 ⅝ In., 2 Piece	234.00
Sieve, Herb, Pine, Maple, Turned Handle, Double Scribe Line, Pegged Hoop, Horsehair Mesh.	702.00
Spool, Maple, Yellow Stain, White Thread, c.1825, 1 ¾ x 1 ½ In.	468.00
String Winder, Maple, Half Circle Cutout Ends, Pivots On Steel Rod, c.1870, 4 ½ x 8 ½ In. *illus*	995.00
Swift, Maple, Yellow Paint, Yarn Cup, Expandable Arms, Adjustable Screws, c.1870, 21 In., Pair	410.00
Toy, Top, Birch, Cherry, Carved, Control Stick, Plumb-Bob Spinner, c.1860, 4 x 6 ½ In.	205.00
Tray, 2-Finger, Band Box Handle, Stained Red, Copper Tacks, Oval, 5 x 7 In.	295.00
Washtub, Pine, Blue Paint, Wire, Wood Handles, Iron Bands, c.1850, 13 x 23 In.	322.00
Yarn Winder, Maple, Yellow Stain, 5-Spoke Clock Reel, Turned Handle, c.1825, 42 x 21 In.	702.00

SHAVING MUGS were popular from 1860 to 1900. Many types were made, including occupational mugs featuring pictures of men's jobs. There were scuttle mugs, silver-plated mugs, glass-lined mugs, and others.

Bird & Butterflies, Pink Flowers, A.S. Zebley, 3 ½ In.	60.00
Family Crest, Fac Et Spera, R.H. Caldwell, France, 3 ⅞ In.	150.00

Main Street Scene, Lakota, N.D., Color Transfer Print, Gold Trim, Limoges	450.00
Man, Drinking From Bottle, James Jordan, Limoges, 3 ¾ In.	720.00
Occupational, Baseball Game In Progress, Sebastiano Mancuso, 4 In. *illus*	1610.00
Occupational, Blacksmith, F.C. Prugh, 3 ½ In.	360.00
Occupational, Bricklayer, Henry B. Kelley, 3 ½ In.	1080.00
Occupational, Calligraphy, Hand Writing With Quill Pen, Gold Trim, 3 ½ x 3 ½ In. *illus*	165.00
Occupational, Carpenter, Chisel, Plane, Saw, Compass, Hammer, Bert Samm, 3 ¾ In.	120.00
Occupational, Cavalryman Leading Charge, Tim Reus, Gold Trim	600.00
Occupational, Clerk, Grocery Store, Waiting On Woman, Stonebraker, 4 In.	120.00
Occupational, Conductor, Brakeman, Madison Ave., N.C. Burroughes, 3 ¾ In.	1140.00
Occupational, Delivery Man, Wagon, Fruits & Vegetables, James Werner, 3 ½ In.	780.00
Occupational, Fire Ladder Wagon, Gold Trim, W. Emerick, Stamped CFH, CDM, 3 ¾ In.	173.00
Occupational, Fireman, Helmet, Ladder, Ax, Fire Nozzle, Lantern, F.V. Woodington, Limoges	570.00
Occupational, Fisherman, 2 Men, Rowboat, Displaying Catch, C.D. Bach, 4 In.	780.00
Occupational, Glassblowers, Working At Furnace, Thos. Jack, 3 ¾ In. *illus*	1035.00
Occupational, Ice Wagon, 2 Horses, Driver, Block Of Ice, G.M. Hallenbeck, 3 ½ In.	540.00
Occupational, Man Driving Horse Drawn Buggy, W.Y. Harlan, A. Kern B.S. Co., 3 ⅞ In.	92.00
Occupational, Pawn Broker, Chas. Livingston, Gold Trim, Limoges	600.00
Occupational, Plumber, Tools, Working On Sink, W.H. Murphy, 3 ½ In.	240.00
Occupational, Police Officer, Standing, Baton, Uniform, Charles McKie	210.00
Occupational, Printing Press, Purple Wrap, P. Giannett, 3 ¾ In.	173.00
Occupational, Rugby Players, Pink Wrap, Fred K. Whitney, 3 ⅝ In.	1955.00
Occupational, Shoemaker, Geo. H. Barber, 3 ½ In.	120.00
Occupational, Tailor, B. Rosenthal, 3 ¾ In.	180.00
Occupational, Undertaker, Coffin, 2 Pedestals, Gilt Handles, Says Dead, 3 ½ In.	1080.00
Occupational, Woman Examining Roll Of Cloth, Salesman, D.C. Jones, T.&V., 3 ⅝ In. *illus*	230.00
Odd Fellows, L.L. Irish, Limoges, 3 ½ In.	120.00
Orange, Green Glaze, Dotted Band, Redware, Penn., 3 In.	533.00
Panama Canal, Photographic Transfer, Roll Rim, Gilt Trim, F.H. Peck, Flared Foot, 4 x 5 In.	8775.00
Portrait, Kendall House, Fred B. Jenkins, 3 ¾ In.	1920.00
Redware, Inscribed John C. Geiger, Mahoney City, Penn., 1879, 5 ¼ In.	4740.00
Sailboat, Setting Sun, Island, Flowers, M.A. O'Mara, 3 ¾ In.	60.00
Statue Of Liberty, Boats, N.Y. Harbor, Fred D. Kline, 2 ½ In.	210.00

SHAWNEE POTTERY was started in Zanesville, Ohio, in 1937. The company made vases, novelty ware, flowerpots, planters, lamps, and cookie jars. Three dinnerware lines were made: Corn, Lobster Ware, and Valencia (a solid color line). White Corn pattern utility pieces were made in 1945. Corn King was made from 1946 to 1954; Corn Queen, with darker green leaves and lighter colored corn, from 1954 to 1961. Shawnee produced pottery for George Rumrill during the late 1930s. The company closed in 1961.

Basket, Yellow, Flowers, Embossed, Marked, c.1940, 3 In.	45.00
Bean Pot, Lobster, Covered, c.1954	229.00
Butter, Corn King, Cover	90.00
Casserole, Corn King, Cover, Oval, 1 ½ Qt.	60.00
Casserole, Corn King, Marked, Individual	195.00
Cookie Jar, Corn King, 12 In.	250.00
Cookie Jar, Dog, Muggsy, Gilt Trim, Decals, Blue Bow, 1940s	995.00
Cookie Jar, Drum, Drummer, Pink, Blue, 10 x 6 In.	225.00
Cookie Jar, Smiley Pig, Red Bib, Chrysanthemum Decals, 10 In.	375.00
Creamer, Elephant, 4 ½ In.	199.00
Creamer, Elephant, Marked, c.1945, 3 x 3 In.	55.00
Creamer, Puss 'n Boots, Gold Trim, 4 ½ In.	289.00
Creamer, Smiley Pig, Closed Eye, c.1950, 4 ½ In.	75.00
Figurine, Donkey, 6 x 4 In.	45.00
Figurine, Muggsy, Curly Hair, Brown, 6 ¼ In.	31.00
Figurine, Tumbling Bear, Sticker, 3 In.	95.00
Jug, Chanticleer, Gold Trim, 1940s	289.00
Jug, Smiley Pig, Gold Trim	289.00
Pie Bird, Pastels, 1950s, 5 ¼ In.	33.00
Pitcher, Bo Peep, Gold Trim	439.00
Pitcher, Milk, Bo Peep, Yellow, Red, Blue, 7 In.	140.00
Planter, Boy, Fishing, Pink, Yellow, Marked, 6 In.	28.00
Planter, Elf, Sitting On Green Shoe, Yellow Outfit, Brown Flower-Shape Hat, 6 x 6 In.	30.00
Planter, Elf, Wheel Barrel, Marked, 1950s, 5 ¼ x 4 In.	20.00
Planter, Piano, Yellow, Orange, 5 x 5 x 3 In.	35.00
Planter, Seashell, Blue & White, 3-Footed, Marked, 2 x 6 x 5 ¼ In.	18.00

Shawnee
USA

Sevres, Vase, Cover, Nymphs, Cupids, Raised Gold Borders, Bronze Base, 1800s, 40 ¾ In.
$2695.00

Skinner, Inc.

Sevres, Vase, Lid, Cobalt Blue, Putti In Medallion, Applied Garlands, Female Handles, c.1785, 17 In.
$735.00

Skinner, Inc.

Sewer Tile, Birdhouse, Tree Bark, Tooled, c.1910, 9 In.
$235.00

Garth's Auctions, Inc.

Sewer Tile, Planter, Oak Leaves, Protuding Tree Trunks, Glazed, 1800s, 8 ½ x 11 In. **$201.00**

Cottone Auctions

Sewer Tile, Umbrella Stand, Tree Bark, St. Louis Sewer Pipe Co., Anheuser-Busch, c.1880, 26 x 13 In. **$7475.00**

Rock Island Auction Company

Sewing, Box, Curly Maple, Tiered Thread Caddy, Pincushion Top, Drawer, Ohio, c.1850, 13 In. **$558.00**

Garth's Auctions, Inc.

TIP

Small collectibles can be used as window-shade pulls.

Planter, Shoe, White, Dog On Toe, 7 x 4 In.	40.00
Salt & Pepper, Dutch Boy & Girl, Cork Stopper, c.1940s, 5 In.	70.00
Salt & Pepper, Muggsy, White, Black Bows, Paws Up	245.00
Salt & Pepper, Puss 'n Boots, White, Pink Neck Ribbon, 3 ¼ In.	30.00
Shaker, Chanticleer, White Body, Sticker, c.1950, 3 ¼ In.	21.00
Sugar, Corn King, c.1950, 5 x 4 In.	27.00
Teapot, Corn King, Marked No. 75, 7 x 9 In.	80.00
Teapot, Granny Ann, White, Blue Trim Cape, Marked, 8 ½ In.	165.00
Teapot, Rosette, Burgundy, 6 In.	24.00
Vase, Aqua, Ribbed, Flared, Footed, 8 x 6 In.	45.00
Vase, Bamboo Style, Marked, 4 x 7 In.	30.00
Vase, Bulbous, Ruffled Rim, Yellow, Bud, 1950s, 9 In.	55.00
Vase, Confetti, 1950s, 6 In.	32.00
Vase, Green, Pink Roses, 2 Handles, Ribbed Base, 10 In.	48.00
Vase, Pedestal, 2 Handles, Peach, 8 In.	34.00
Vase, Swan, Yellow, Gilt Trim, Marked, 6 x 3 In.	48.00
Vase, White Spattered Drips, Pale Green, Ruffled Rim, Marked, 10 x 3 In.	20.00

SHEARWATER POTTERY is a family business started by Mr. and Mrs. G.W. Anderson, Sr., and their three sons. The local Ocean Springs, Mississippi, clays were used to make the wares in the 1930s. The company was damaged by Hurricane Katrina in 2005 but was rebuilt and is still in business.

Bowl, Eagle, Sgraffito, Walter Anderson, Impressed Mark, c.1950, 5 ¼ In.	2749.00
Figurine, Bull, Green Rutile Glaze, Marked, 6 ½ x 3 In.	95.00
Figurine, Puss In Boots, Signed, 1993, 7 In.	179.00
Figurine, Woman, Caribbean Attire, Multicolor, Walter Anderson, Marked, 10 In.	29.00
Pitcher, Turquoise Fleck Glaze, Bulbous, Loop Handle, Calif., 1940s, 5 ½ In.	173.00

SHEET MUSIC from the past centuries is now collected. The favorites are examples with covers featuring artistic or historic pictures. Early sheet music covers were lithographed, but by the 1900s photographic reproductions were used. The early music was larger than more recent sheets, and you must watch out for examples that were trimmed to fit in a twentieth-century piano bench.

Bell Bottom Trousers, Moe Jaffe, 1944, 9 x 12 In.	9.95
Bess, You Is My Woman, From Porgy & Bess, George Gershwin, 1935, 9 x 12 In.	20.00
Deep In The Heart Of Texas, June Hershey, 1941, 9 x 12 In.	6.95
Feudin' & Fightin', Al Dublin & Burton Lane, 1947, 9 x 12 In.	6.96
Hail, Hail, The Gang's All Here, Theodore Morse, Arthur Sullivan, 1917, 10 x 13 In.	12.00
Home On The Range, Dick Jurgens Orchestra, 1935, 9 x 12 In.	14.95
I'd Like To Be In Texas For The Round Up, Nick Manoloff, 1935, 9 x 12 In.	5.95
I'm Getting So Now I Don't Care, Richard Howard, 1923, 9 x 11 ½ In.	6.96
In My Arms, Donna Reed & Robert Walker, Fred Loesser, 1943, 9 x 12 In.	6.95
Life & Love Seem Sweeter After The Storm, Jack Nelson, 1924, 9 ¼ x 12 In.	6.96
Mambo Jambo, Que Rico El Mambo, Perez Prado, 1950, 9 x 12 In.	5.95
Meet Me In Blossom Time, George Moriarty, 1914, 10 ¾ x 13 ¾ In.	8.95
Old Cape Cod, Patti Page, 1956	10.00
Pistle Packin' Mama, Al Dexter, 1943, 9 x 12 In.	5.95
Prisoner Of Lover, Perry Como, Leo Robin, Russ Columbo, 1931, 9 x 12 In.	5.95
Roll Along Prairie Moon, Ted Lewis & Orchestra, Harry MacPherson, 1935, 9 x 12 In.	6.95
Somebody Loves You, Tommy Tucker & Californians, Peter De Rose, 1932, 9 x 12 In.	6.95
Take Your Girlie To The Movies, Words By Edgar Leslie & Bert Kalmer, 1919	6.95
White Christmas, Irving Berlin, 1940	25.00

SHEFFIELD *items are listed in the Silver Plate and Silver-English categories.*

SHELLEY first appeared on English ceramics about 1912. The Foley China Works started in England in 1860. Joseph Ball Shelley joined the company in 1862 and became a partner in 1872. Percy Shelley joined the firm in 1881. The company went through a series of name changes and in 1910 the then Foley China Company became Shelley China. In 1929 it became Shelley Potteries. The company was acquired in 1966 by Allied English Potteries, then merged with the Doulton group in 1971. The name Shelley was put into use again in 1980. A trio is the name for a cup, saucer, and cake plate set.

Butter, Maytime Chintz, Cover, 3 x 7 x 5 In.	110.00
Butter, Rose Pansy, Forget-Me-Not, Cover, White Body, Green Leaves, Pink Roses	229.00
Butter, Stocks, Dainty, Round, Cover.	169.00
Butter, Stocks, Dainty, Round.	169.00

Cake Plate, Honeysuckle Pink, Tab Handle, c.1955, 9 x 9 ½ In.	60.00
Cake Plate, Melody, Chintz, Handles, 9 x 8 In.	66.00
Coffeepot, Rose, Pansy, Forget-Me-Not, 6 ¼ In.	299.00
Creamer, Harebell, 2 ½ In.	179.00
Cup & Saucer, Blue Daisy, Ripon, c.1950, 3 x 5 ⅝ In.	75.00
Cup & Saucer, Blue Rock	79.00
Cup & Saucer, Blue Rock, Demitasse	79.00
Cup & Saucer, Burgundy, Fruit, c.1960	75.00
Cup & Saucer, Melody, Chintz	89.00
Cup & Saucer, Melody, Chintz, Demitasse	89.00
Cup & Saucer, Paisley Green Chintz	440.00
Cup & Saucer, Rock Garden, Demitasse, 1945	89.00
Cup & Saucer, Rose Spray, White Body, Green Leaves, Miniature	229.00
Cup & Saucer, Rose, Pansy, Forget-Me-Not, Dainty, c.1950	110.00
Cup & Saucer, Rosebud, Demitasse	64.00
Cup & Saucer, Stocks, Dainty, Demitasse, 1940s	72.00
Hot Water Pot, Rambler Rose, Lid, Finial, 7 x 5 In.	121.00
Luncheon Trio, Bluebell Wood, Plate, Cup, Saucer	58.00
Plate, Bread & Butter, Harebell, 6 In.	94.00
Plate, Dinner, Rose Trousseau, 10 ⅞ In.	145.00
Plate, Rock Garden, 8 In., Pair	66.00
Sugar & Creamer, Begonia	189.00
Sugar & Creamer, Blue Rock, Dainty, c.1950	50.00
Sugar & Creamer, Cover, Begonia	189.00
Teapot, Begonia	549.00
Teapot, Blue Delft, Footed, Lid, 5 ½ x 6 ¾ In.	550.00
Toast Stand, Art Deco, 4 Slice, Green, Red, 2 ¼ x 7 In.	33.00
Vase, Harmony, Footed, Flared Rim, Orange, Brown, 4 ½ In.	51.00
Vase, Orange, Brown, Footed, c.1930, 4 ½ x 3 ½ In.	48.00

SHIRLEY TEMPLE, the famous movie star, was born in 1928. She made her first movie in 1932. Thousands of items picturing Shirley have been and still are being made. Shirley Temple dolls were first made in 1934 by Ideal Toy Company. Millions of Shirley Temple cobalt blue glass dishes were made by Hazel Atlas Glass Company and U.S. Glass Company from 1934 to 1942. They were given away as premiums for Wheaties and Bisquick. A bowl, mug, and pitcher were made as a breakfast set. Some pieces were decorated with the picture of a very young Shirley, others used a picture of Shirley in her 1936 Captain January costume. Although collectors refer to a cobalt creamer, it is actually the 4 ½-inch-high milk pitcher from the breakfast set. Many of these items are being reproduced today.

Bowl, Cobalt Blue, 4-Footed, Scalloped, Portrait, 4 ½ In.	43.00
Bust, Terra-Cotta, Antiqued Finish, Curly Hair, Dimples, F. Coffio, 1930s, 12 In.	399.00
Doll, Celluloid, Brown Glass Eyes, Molded Bob, Jointed, Tulle Dress, France, 21 In.	399.00
Doll, Celluloid, Felt, Glass Eyes, Muslin Body, Sailor Suit, Lenci, 1940s, 20 In.	1254.00
Doll, Composition, Baby, Cloth, Teeth, Ringlets, Dress, Bonnet, Ideal, c.1935, 26 In.	855.00
Doll, Composition, Flirty Eyes, Lashes, Teeth, Ringlets, Dress, Molly-'Es, 13 In.	627.00
Doll, Composition, Sleep Eyes, Teeth, Ringlets, Short Dress, Ideal, c.1935, 18 In.	627.00
Doll, Composition, Sleep Eyes, Texas Ranger Costume, Ideal, c.1938, 17 In.	2166.00
Doll, Waxed Papier-Mache, Cotton & Lace Dress, Lewis Sorensen, 1961, 45 In.	2736.00
Movie Banner, Heidi, Cloth, 1937, 37 x 53 In.	2500.00
Pitcher, Cobalt Blue, Portrait, 4 ½ In.	35.00
Pitcher, Portrait, Decal, Teal Blue, Applied Handle, 12 x 3 In.	185.00
Plate, Cobalt Blue ABC, Scalloped, 7 In.	25.00
Playing Cards, United States Playing Card Co., Double Deck, 1935	135.00
Soap Doll, Box, 1930s, 5 ¼ In.	44.00
Stringholder, Chalk, c.1940, 6 ¾ In.	295.00

SHRINER, *see Fraternal category.*

SILVER DEPOSIT glass was first made during the late nineteenth century. Solid sterling silver is applied to the glass by a chemical method so that a cutout design of silver metal appears against a clear or colored glass. It is sometimes called silver overlay.

Cologne Bottle, Oval Body, Stick Neck, Flower Scrolls, Top Shape Stopper, 14 In.	276.00
Cruet, Repousse Flowers, Clear Glass, Marked, Japan, Talon Shape Stoppers, 13 x 5 In.	230.00
Decanter, Flowers, Triangular Shape, Stopper, Stamped, 12 In.	259.00

Sewing, Box, Pasteboard, Gold Stamped Foil, Pincushion, Mirror, Flowers, Heart, c.1875, 3 ½ In.
$60.00

Garth's Auctions, Inc.

Sewing, Pincushion, Hanging, Leather, Velvet, 2 Hearts, 2 Birds, Pa., 1800s, 10 x 10 In.
$1939.00

Garth's Auctions, Inc.

Sewing, Pincushion, Silk, Needlework, Chenille Thread, Flowers, Tassels, Aug. 1840, 4 x 6 ½ x 8 ½ In.
$948.00

Skinner, Inc.

Sewing, Tape Measure, McCormick Harvesting Machine Co., Machine On Back, Celluloid, 1 ¾ x ½ In.
$242.00

Wm Morford Antiques

581

SILVER DEPOSIT

Shaker, Box, 4-Finger, Oval, Lid, Maple, Pine, Copper Tacks, c.1840, 4 ⅞ x 11 ⅝ In. $1755.00

Willis Henry Auctions, Inc.

Shaker, Box, Seed, Hinged Lid, Pine, Divided Interior, Mount Lebanon, N.Y., 3 ¼ x 23 x 11 ½ In. $4680.00

Willis Henry Auctions, Inc.

Shaker, Rug, Wool & Cotton, Crocheted Foundation, Multicolored, Maine, c.1920, 39 x 92 In. $1404.00

Willis Henry Auctions, Inc.

Shaker, Shovel, Grain, Carved From Single Piece Of Wood, Beveled Edge, 36 ½ x 11 ¼ In. $604.00

James D. Julia Inc.

Pitcher, Cylindrical, Tapered, Reeded, Loop Handle, Silver Scrolling Leaves Collar, c.1900, 7 In.	338.00
Sugar, Cover, 2 Handles, Openwork, Cobalt Blue Glass, Scroll Feet, France, 1800s 3 x 8 In.	450.00
Vase, Art Nouveau, Cobalt Blue Glass, Iridescent Blue & Green, 9 ¼ In. ....*illus*	2573.00
Vase, Bud, Emerald Glass, Smokestack, Flared Rim, Flowers, Trellises, c.1900, 6 x 3 In.	584.00
Vase, Flared Stick Neck, Round Base, Green Glass, Overlay Blossoms, Leaves, c.1900, 14 In.	1250.00
Vase, Flowering Vines, Amethyst Glass, Swollen Shoulder, Flared Rim, 10 ½ In.	1103.00
Vase, Gold Iridescent, Waisted, Bulbous Top, Rim, Rainbow Effect, c.1900, 5 x 3 In.	522.00
Vase, Gourd Shape, 3 Handles, Orange Poppies, Brown, Yellow, 1900, 5 ½ In.	2070.00
Vase, Leafy Vine, Gold Iridescent Glass, Pulled Feathers, Bulbous Neck, Austria, 13 In.	1422.00
Vase, Tapered Oval, Emerald Green Glass, Pierced Sterling Overlay, Flared Neck, c.1900, 10 In.	533.00

SILVER FLATWARE includes many of the current and out-of-production silver and silver-plated flatware patterns made in the past eighty years. Other silver is listed under Silver-American, Silver-English, etc. Most silver flatware sets that are missing a few pieces can be completed through the help of one of the many silver matching services listed on our website, www.kovels.com.

SILVER FLATWARE PLATED

Adam, Jelly Server, Onieda, Community, 1900s, 6 ⅛ In.	10.00
Alhambra, Carving Set, Anchor Rogers International, 2 Piece	438.00
Anniversary, Dinner Knife, Rogers, 1923	12.00
Apollo, Cake Fork, Oneida	33.00
Arbutus, Sauce Ladle, Wm. Rogers, 6 In.	13.00
Berkeley, Salad Servers, Peerless, 1929	50.00
Berkshire, Gravy Ladle, Rogers, 1847, 8 ½ In.	31.00
Bridal Rose, Cold Meat Fork, Niagara, 1911, 8 ¼ In.	40.00
Bridal Wreath, Gravy Ladle, Tudor Plate, 7 ¼ In.	25.00
Casino, Cocktail Fork, Marked, Vernon Oneida, c.1931, Pair	10.00
Chester, Gravy Ladle, Towle, 7 ¼ In.	30.00
Coronation, Sugar Spoon, Community, 1936	6.00
Corsican, Fish Knife, Reed & Barton, c.1926, 8 ⅛ In.	6.00
Daffodil, Pickle & Olive Fork, Rogers, 1950, 6 ⅛ In.	14.00
Enchantment, Jelly Knife, Oneida, 1960, 6 ¼ In., 4 Piece	40.00
English Georgian, Teaspoon, Lunt, 1980, 6 In.	23.00
Evening Star, Olive Fork, Oneida, 6 ⅜ In.	20.00
Fantasy, Pastry Server, Tudor Oneida, 1941, 9 ⅝ In.	18.00
First Love, Cream Soup Spoon, Rogers International, 1937, 7 In.	12.00
Flair, Gravy Ladle, William Rogers, c.1956, 6 ¼ In.	28.00
Gentle Rose, Pastry Server, Oneida, 1960, 9 ¼ In.	22.00
Georgian, Gravy Ladle, Community, 6 ¾ In.	16.00
Hanover, Bouillon Spoon, Wm. Rogers, c.1900, 5 ¼ In., 6 Piece	45.00
Haverford, Gravy Ladle, Lunt, 1980	132.00
Hawthorne, Meat Fork, Marked, Rockford Oneida, 1908, 7 ½ In.	15.00
Interlude, Fork, International Silver Co., c.1970, 9 ⅜ In.	13.00
Joan, Soup Spoon, Wallace, 1896, 7 In.	10.00
Juliette, Serving Spoon, Pierced, Rogers International, 1980s, 8 ⅜ In.	18.00
Lady Esther, Butter Spreader, Lunt, 1935	17.00
Leona, Salad Fork, Williams, 1910, 6 ⅞ In.	20.00
Longfellow, Olive Fork, Rogers	18.00
Longwood, Serving Spoon, Pierced, Reed & Barton, 8 ¾ In.	14.00
Lorne, Sugar Spoon, Rogers, 1978, 5 ⅞ In.	5.00
Martinique, Fish Fork, Monarch, 6 In.	12.00
Mary Stuart, Sugar Spoon, Tudor Plate, 1927, 5 ¾ In.	19.00
Moselle, Meat Fork, American Silver, c.1915, 8 In.	65.00
Primrose, Butter Knife, Oneida, 1915, 5 ¾ In.	5.00
Princess Royal, Teaspoon, National Silver Co., 6 In.	5.00
Queen Bess, Iced Tea Spoon, Betty Crocker Premium, Oneida Community, 1946	8.00
Queen Bess, Serving Spoon, Pierced, Tudor Plate, 1924, 8 In.	49.00
Queen Elizabeth, Nut Server, Williams, 6 ⅛ In.	24.00
Raphael, Dinner Knife, Rogers & Hamilton International, c.1900, 8 ¾ In.	44.00
San Diego, Sauce Ladle, Rogers, c.1889, 6 ¼ In.	1800.00
Saratoga, Teaspoon, Marked, Anchor Rogers International	18.00
Silver Arbor, Butter Knife, Oneida, 7 In.	19.00
South Seas, Salad Fork & Spoon, Oneida Community, 1955, 11 In., Pair	40.00
Springtime, Serving Spoon, Pierced, Rogers, 1957, 8 ½ In.	12.00
Wild Rose, Lemon Fork, Marthinsen, Norway, 4 In.	10.00

S

SILVER FLATWARE STERLING

Acanthus, Salad Servers, Georg Jensen, 9 In., 2 Piece	326.00
Acanthus, Salad Serving Spoon, Georg Jensen, c.1920, 8 In.	224.00
Arlington, Cocktail Fork, Towle, 6 In., 12 Piece	330.00
Art Nouveau, Pickle Fork, Baird-North Co., c.1920, 5 ¾ In.	40.00
Blossom, Cream Ladle, Lobed Bowl, Gilt, c.1908, 5 ¾ In.	40.00
Blossom, Sugar Tongs, Georg Jensen, c.1920, 3 ¾ In.	97.00
Bridal Rose, Salad Servers, Gold Washed Bowl & Tines, Monogram, Alvin, c.1910, Pair	296.00
Buttercup, Fork, Gorham, 7 ½ In., 12 Piece	594.00
Canterbury, Cream Soup Spoon, Towle, 5 In., 15 Piece	330.00
Chambord, Lettuce Fork, Reed & Barton, c.1909, 9 ½ In.	75.00
Chrysanthemum, Bonbon Spoon, Pierced Vermeil Bowl, Imperial, 8 In.	173.00
Dresden, Lettuce Fork, Whiting, c.1900, 9 ¼ In.	145.00
Early Colonial, Dinner Knife, Lunt, 8 ½ In.	39.00
Easter Lily, Teaspoon, Watson, 6 In.	49.00
Elizabeth I, Spoon, Queen, Shield Stem, Gorham, c.1920, 9 In.	385.00
Emperor, Pie Server, Knowles & Ladd	379.00
Fountainebleu, Fish Set, Gorham, 11 ½ In., 2 Piece	1035.00
Francis I, Soup Ladle, Reed & Barton, c.1907, 12 ¼ In.	472.00
Francis I, Stuffing Spoon, Button, Reed & Barton, c.1907, 13 ¾ In.	207.00
Granada, Pickle Fork, Hammered, Old Newbury Crafters, 6 ⅝ In.	125.00
Grecian, Pudding Spoon, Gorham, 9 ⅜ In.	339.00
Grecian, Salt Spoon, Gorham, 5 ¼ In.	115.00
Intaglio, Server, Gold Washed Bowl, Tines, Reed & Barton, c.1905, 9 ¾ x 10 In., Pair	326.00
King, Knife, Fork, Salad Fork, Teaspoon, Dominick & Haff, c.1880, 4 Piece	289.00
Kings Court, Salad Servers, Gold Washed, F.M. Whiting, 9 In., 2 Piece	225.00
La Marquise, Salad Servers, Gold Washed, Reed & Barton, Box, c.1905, 8 ¾ x 9 In.	207.00
Labors Of Cupid, Dessert Spoon, Gold Washed Bowl, Dominick & Haff, 7 In., 12 Piece	1007.00
Lexington, Berry Spoon, Knowles, Ribbed Bowl, c.1900, 7 In.	90.00
Lily, Berry Spoon, Vermeil Fluted Bowl, Whiting Mfg. Co., c.1902, 9 In.	425.00
Love Disarmed, Salad Servers, Art Nouveau, Reed & Barton, c.1900	800.00
Madam Jumel, Knife, Fork, Salad Fork, Teaspoon, Whiting, 1908, 4 Piece	269.00
Medallion, Salad Servers, Gorham, c.1870, 9 In., 2 Piece	443.00
Medallion, Teaspoon, Gorham, c.1900, 5 Piece	425.00
Morning Glory, Serving Spoon, Leaf Shape Bowl & Terminal, Gorham, 1800s, 11 In.	325.00
Norfolk, Asparagus Server, Pierced Scrolls, Gorham, 1904, 9 In.	338.00
Old Colonial, Cocktail Fork, Towle, c.1930, 9 Piece	522.00
Old English, Soup Ladle, Georgian, Rounded Terminal, Engraved Crest, c.1828, 13 In.	239.00
Palm, Fruit Spoon, Scalloped Edge, F.M. Whiting, 8 In.	165.00
Palm, Sugar Tongs, Claw Finials, F.M. Whiting, 4 ½ In.	59.00
Poppies, Serving Spoon & Fork, Reed & Barton, c.1900, 8 ½ & 9 In.	288.00
Raphael, Demitasse, Spoon, Gorham, Case, 1800s, 12 Piece	180.00
Regent, Sauce Ladle, Openwork Leaves, Flowers, Durgin, c.1905, 7 ¼ In.	296.00
Renaissance, Cheese Scoop, Dominick & Haff, 6 ⅛ In.	255.00
Repousse, Berry Spoon, Jenkins & Jenkins, c.1910, 10 ¼ In., 2 Piece	295.00
Strawberry, Spoon, Round Bowl, Reticulated, Gorham, c.1909	207.00
Tara, Serving Spoon, Reed & Barton, 1955, 8 ½ In.	149.00
Tuscan, Pudding Spoon, John C. Farr, Philadelphia, 12 ⅝ In.	695.00
Venetian, Soup Ladle, Wood & Hughes, N.Y., 1875, 13 In.	118.00
Virginiana, Salad Servers, Spoon, Fork, Art Nouveau Design, Gorham, 8 ¾ In.	345.00
Wadefield, Serving Fork, Samuel Kirk & Son, 12 In.	308.00

SILVER PLATE is not solid silver. It is a ware made of a metal, such as nickel or copper, **E P S N S** that is covered with a thin coating of silver. The letters EPNS are often found on American and English silver-plated wares. Sheffield is a term with two meanings. Sometimes it refers to sterling silver made in the town of Sheffield, England. Sometimes it refers to an old form of plated silver.

Barrel, Cover, 2 Loop Handles, Etched Design, Finial, G. Richmond Collis, England, 13 x 14 In.	219.00
Biscuit Box, 3-Part, Coquille Shape, Oak Branch Frame, Spherical Finial, c.1885, 10 x 9 In.	246.00
Biscuit Box, Greyhound Finial, Flowers, Oval, Pierced Base, Ball & Claw Feet, c.1900, 7 x 9 In.	177.00
Biscuit Jar, Dome Lid, Footed, 8 x 14 In.	120.00
Bowl, Flattened Spherical, Scroll Bands, Flowers, 2 Handles, 4 Openwork Scroll Feet, c.1885, 14 ½ In.	98.00
Bowl, Lobed Body, Chased Bows, Flower Swags, Footed, Mappin & Webb, Sheffield, 1900, 7 x 12 In.	1380.00
Bowl, Strawberry, Cover, Round, Waisted Stem, Domed Foot, Openwork Berries, c.1885, 7 ¼ In.	215.00
Bowl, Vegetable, Gadroon Cover, George V, Ivory Button, Paw Footed, Oval, c.1925, 14 ½ x 9 ¾ In.	215.00
Box, Collar Button, Embossed, Finial, Round, Victorian, 2 ½ In.	23.00

Shaker, String Winder, Maple, Half Circle Cutout Ends, Pivots On Steel Rod, c.1870, 4 ½ x 8 ½ In.
$995.00

Willis Henry Auctions, Inc.

Shaving Mug, Occupational, Baseball Game In Progress, Sebastiano Mancuso, 4 In.
$1610.00

Glass Works Auctions

Shaving Mug, Occupational, Calligraphy, Hand Writing With Quill Pen, Gold Trim, 3 ½ x 3 ½ In.
$165.00

Wm Morford Antiques

Shaving Mug, Occupational, Glassblowers, Working At Furnace, Thos. Jack, 3 ¾ In.
$1035.00

Glass Works Auctions

S

Shaving Mug, Occupational, Woman Examining Roll Of Cloth, Salesman, D.C. Jones, T.&V., 3 ⅝ In. $230.00

Glass Works Auctions

Silver Deposit, Vase, Art Nouveau, Cobalt Blue Glass, Iridescent Blue & Green, 9 ¼ In. $2573.00

Skinner, Inc.

Silver Plate, Cake Basket, Shell & Scroll Rim, Swing Handle, Sheffield, c.1830, 10 ½ x 13 ⅝ In. $269.00

Neal Auction Co.

Box, Cover, Rococo Style, Bacchantes Playing, Grape Border, Oval, Continental, c.1905, 12 In...	356.00
Cake Basket, Shell & Scroll Rim, Swing Handle, Sheffield, c.1830, 10 ½ x 13 ⅝ In. ......*illus*	269.00
Cann, Cup, Baluster, Applied Foot, Handle, c.1800, 5 ¾ In.	403.00
Castor Set, 7 Bottles, Oval, Scroll Supports, Hallmark, D&S, c.1890, 12 ½ In. ....*illus*	598.00
Centerpiece, Egyptian Revival, Boat, Curved Ends, Chimera Supports, Gorham, c.1869, 9 x 13 In..	593.00
Centerpiece, Embossed Gold Colored Bird, Flower Rim, 8-Sided, Elkington & Co., 2 ¼ x 12 ¾ In.	173.00
Centerpiece, Fern Shape, Cut Glass Bowl, Scalloped Rim, Star & Diamond Design, c.1865, 19 ½ In..	1722.00
Centerpiece, Glass, Stylized Lines, Raised Stem, Scrolled Base, Putti, Sea Creatures, c.1900, 18 ⅜ In..	474.00
Centerpiece, Gondola, Putto Gondolier, Swan, Oval Base, Waves, Feet, c.1900, 11 x 22 In.......	1888.00
Chafing Dish, Convertible, Oblong, Handles, Fitted Dish, Belted Ball Feet, Sheffield, c.1820, 14 In., Pair	474.00
Chafing Dish, Dome Lid, Lion, Shield Finial, Shell Border, Scroll Feet, Bone Handles, 21 In...	717.00
Chalice, Gilt Overlay, Applied Swags, Medallions, 1800s, 11 x 6 In.	458.00
Champagne Bucket, Towle, 12 x 10 In.	41.00
Claret Jug, Etched Glass, Lion Shape Finial, Loop Handle, Round Foot, 12 In.	458.00
Cocktail Shaker, Screw-On Lid, Lighthouse Shape, 1900s, 14 In.	944.00
Coffee & Tea Set, Cartouches, Scrolls, Bird Finial, Mappin & Webb, 5 Piece	1134.00
Coffee & Tea Set, Coffeepot, Teapot, Sugar, Creamer, Tray, Elkington & Co.	236.00
Coffee & Tea Set, Viners Of Sheffield, Coffeepot, Teapot, Sugar, Creamer, Tray...................	177.00
Coffee Urn, 2 Scroll Leaf Handles, Wood Accents, Flower Finial, Paw Feet, 15 In.	288.00
Coffee Urn, 4 Maidens, Draped In Capes, Hoof Supports, Beading, Ball Foot, Handles, 22 In. .	345.00
Coffee Urn, Burner, 2 Handles, Engraved Flowers, 4-Footed, 15 x 10 x 10 In.	173.00
Coffeepot, Hinged Lid, Victorian, Oval, Ivory Crested Handle, Reeded Gooseneck Spout, c.1885, 12 In.	215.00
Coffeepot, Lamp Stand, Lobed Body, Wood Handle, Sheffield, c.1820, 11 x 11 In.	538.00
Coffeepot, Restauration, Fused, Oval, Gadrooning, Hound's Head Spout, Paw Feet, 14 x 9 In.	461.00
Compote, Banded Moses Life Scenes, Grape, Star Rondel, Israel, 12 x 12 In...................	1170.00
Cover, Entree, Engraved Coat Of Arms, Instaurator Ruinae, Oval, Loop Top Handle, 15 x 10 In.....	150.00
Cover, Meat, Medallion, Flowers, Monogram, Walker & Hall, England, c.1910, 9 x 12 In.	81.00
Cover, Meat, Oval, Gadroon, Beaded Rim, Reeded Handles, Martin, Hall & Co., 10 x 12 In.	399.00
Cover, Meat, Oval, Lobed, Etched Leaves, Stag, Dog, Medallion, Finial Handle, c.1811, 12 x 17 ¾ In....	384.00
Cover, Meat, Regency, Oval, Gadroon Banding, Reeded Handle, Crest, c.1815, 8 ½ x 15 ½ In..	430.00
Dish, Bacon, Oval, Roll Top, 4 Reeded Paw Legs, Repousse Flowers, Ivory Handle, c.1900, 7 ¾ x 11 In.	89.00
Dish, Bacon, Rotating Cover, Pierced, Footed, Victorian, 9 In.................................	84.00
Dish, Entree, Cover, Round, 2 Handles, c.1900, 4 ¾ x 13 ⅛ In.	325.00
Dish, Entree, Cover, Scroll Handles, Footed, Round, c.1900, 7 ½ x 14 In.	266.00
Dish, Entree, Cover, Sheffield, c.1900, 8 ½ x 12 ½ In.	354.00
Dish, Entree, Oval, Gadroon Edge, Gorham, 11 ¼ In., Pair	179.00
Dish, Meat, Cover, 2 Handles, Gadroon Shell Border, Crest, Sunburst, 14 x 26 In.	4575.00
Dish, Shell Shape, Putti On Rim, Footed, Italy, 8 x 16 In.	156.00
Dome, Game Bird, Edwardian, Oval, Annulated Rim, Handle, Sheffield, 8 ½ x 12 ¼ In.	110.00
Dome, Poultry, Oval, Molded Rim, Reeded Handle, Monogram, Jos. Rodgers & Son, c.1875, 10 x 14 In.	184.00
Dresser Box, Lid, Scene, Woman With Flowers, Trumpeting Boy, France, 3 x 7 In.................	244.00
Egg Cooker, Spiral Gadroon Lid, 4 Holders, Oval, Burner, Mappin & Webb, c.1920, 8 ½ x 5 In..	246.00
Epergne, 4 Arms, 5 Cut Glass Bowls, Etched Royal Brierley, England, c.1905, 13 x 14 ½ In......	660.00
Epergne, Candlestick Shape Base, Trumpet Glass Vase, Shaped Rim, 19 ¾ In.	378.00
Epergne, Figural, 3 Glass Dishes, Draped Chains, Tray, 19 In.	565.00
Epergne, Rococo, Flowers, Leaves, Scroll Arms, Glass Bowls, c.1890, 25 x 24 In.................	554.00
Epergne, Trumpeting Standard, Round Knop, Lobed Foot, 4 Scrolling Reeded Arms, c.1865, 10 x 20 In.	522.00
Ewer, Flared Pouring Lip, Cupid On Loop Handle, Satyr Mask, Putto, Round Base, 22 In.	438.00
Ewer, Ivory Shaped Handle, Sheffield, c.1910, 12 In.	120.00
Figurine, Young Boy, Knickers, Jacket, Hat, Carrying Tray, Round Base, 7 In.	86.00
Fruit Bowl, Reticulated, Lobed, Oval, Oak Branch Handles & Rim, Scroll Feet, 1800s, 5 x 17 In....	184.00
Garniture, Epergne, Candelabrum, 4-Light, Dolphin Supports, 22 x 17 In., 3 Piece	3690.00
Honey Pot, Bee Shape, Red Glass, Silver Spoon, 6 ¼ In.	316.00
Hot Water Urn, Dome Lid, Acanthus Scrolls, Engraved, Elkington & Co., c.1890, 24 In. ......*illus*	796.00
Hot Water Urn, Dome Lid, Regency, Ball Finial, Ribbed, Loop Handles, Plinth, Sheffield, 19 In...	418.00
Hot Water Urn, Dome Lid, Wooden Handles, 4 Shell & Scroll Feet, c.1875, 16 x 14 In. .....*illus*	430.00
Hot Water Urn, George III, Palmette Handles, Ivory Spigot, Annular Ball Feet, c.1785, 23 x 10 ½ In.	399.00
Hot Water Urn, Lid, Greek Key Band, Bird's Head Handles, Sphinx, Pilasters, 1900s, 16 x 15 In..	225.00
Humidor, 2 Pug Dogs On Lid, 2 Compartments, Marked, 5 ½ x 6 ¼ x 6 In.	254.00
Humidor, Ball Feet, Mounted Hounds, Hinged Cover, Flowers, Birds, Leaves, c.1900, 11 ½ In..	1659.00
Humidor, Punch & Judy, Figural, 7 In...	177.00
Jardiniere, Boat Shape, Seated Cherub, Playing Flute, Pierced Body, Leaf Feet, 1800s, 8 ½ x 15 ½ In.	561.00
Jardiniere, Bulbous, Oval, Whiplash Lines, 4-Footed, Openwork Handles, c.1900, 9 x 22 In....	307.00
Jardiniere, Globular Bowl, Dolphin Supports, Ball Feet, Pierced Flowers, Leaves, 12 In..........	875.00
Kettle, Stand, Rococo Style, Pear Shaped, Chased Design, Scroll Handle, Marked, c.1800, 14 ½ In.....	177.00
Kettle, Tilting, Repousse, Stand, 4-Footed, Tumbler, c.1905, 13 In..............................	180.00

Label Set, Liquor Bottle, Bourbon, Scotch, Gin, Vodka, Brandy, 2 In., 5 Piece	180.00
Letter Holder, Handle, 2-Sided, Sheffield, c.1900, 5 In.	59.00
Martini Shaker, Lid, Cylindrical Spout, Loop Handle, Shouldered, 1900s, 7 In.	59.00
Mirror, Hand, Derby Silver Co., c.1900, 10 x 6 In.	118.00
Nut Dish, Squirrel Mounted, Melon Shape, Floral & Scroll Feet, E.G. Webster, 7 x 7 ½ In.	538.00
Oyster Plate, 6 Wells, Copper, Reed & Barton, 10 In.	118.00
Pitcher, Hammered, Green Parrot Handle, Stamped, Spain, 14 x 8 In.	153.00
Pitcher, Water, Flip Lid, Engraved Flowers, Porcelain Liner, Loop Handle, 8 ½ In.	75.00
Pitcher, Water, Floral Bands, Shell, Under Spout, Etched, Flower, Wheat, Fern, c.1850, 12 In. .. *illus*	150.00
Pitcher, Water, Hinged Lid, Bear Finial, Round Foot, Engraved Design, 1868, 13 x 10 In.	115.00
Pitcher, Water, Lid, 3 Graces Medallion, Parker & Casper Co., c.1875, 13 x 7 In.	307.00
Pitcher, Water, Tropical Farm, House, Bridge, Leaf Scroll Handle, Grape Finial, 12 x 11 In.	138.00
Plateau, Flower Scroll, Round Mirror, England, c.1900, 3 ½ x 17 ½ In.	538.00
Plateau, Mirror, Baroque Style, Wallace, 1900s, 16 ½ In.	96.00
Plateau, Mirror, Neoclassical, Rounded Ends, Gallery, Swag, Bowknot Apron, 3 x 71 In.	1912.00
Plateau, Mirror, Oblong, 3 Sections, Acanthus Leaves, Scroll Feet, France, 46 x 17 In.	3520.00
Plateau, Mirror, Oval, Shell & Scroll Borders, Footed, c.1900, 26 ½ x 16 ½ In.	502.00
Platter, Cover, Lobster Shape, Oval, U.S.A., 1900s, 26 ½ In.	800.00
Platter, Victorian Pattern, Well & Tree, Oval, Scroll Border, Feet, Reed & Barton, 16 x 22 In.	307.00
Punch Bowl, Molded Rim, Footed, 9 ½ x 16 In.	176.00
Punch Bowl, Monteith, Lion Head & Swan Neck Handles, Reeded Round Foot, 1900s, 15 In., Pair ..	2360.00
Punch Bowl, Pedestal, Round Foot, Gilt Banding, Art Deco, International Silver Co., 11 x 17 In.	500.00
Punch Bowl, Repousse Grapes, Rolled Rim, Domed Foot, India, 11 x 17 In.	153.00
Salt & Pepper, Footed, Urn Shape, Peerless Silver Co., 5 ½ In.	19.00
Salver, Repousse Flower Rim, Engraved Crest, Motto, Raised Paw Feet, c.1835, 12 In.	598.00
Salver, Scalloped Edge, Leaf Design, Center Griffin, 3 Scrolled Feet, England, 12 In.	403.00
Salver, Serpentine, Hexagonal, Flower Scroll Rim, 3 Acanthus Scroll Feet, Victorian, 16 ½ In. Diam.	184.00
Salver, Serpentine, Lobed, Round Shape, Palmette Banding, 3 Ball & Claw Feet, 13 In. Diam.	184.00
Shaving Stand, Lavabo Shape, Spout, Basin, Round Mirror, Scrolling Supports, c.1915, 30 x 21 In.	1722.00
Silver Plate, Spoon, Souvenir, see Souvenir category.	
Sucrier, Cover, Empire, Faceted Glass Bowl, Lobed Borders, Acorn Finial, Ball Feet, 11 In.	956.00
Tankard, Classical Figure Frieze, Scroll Handle, Acorn Finial, Elkington & Co., 1880, 11 x 10 In. .	836.00
Tankard, Drunken Peasants Frieze, Scroll Handle, Thumb Lift, Gilt, Elkington, c.1890, 8 x 10 In.	1434.00
Tazza, Cut Glass Dish, Woven Fronds, Grapevines, C-Scroll Feet, Elkington & Co., c.1876, 20 In. *illus*	735.00
Tea Caddy, Fitted Lid, Harvesters, Scenic Views Design, Rectangular 1900s, 6 In.	148.00
Tea Urn, Georgian Style, Handles, Shield Shape Cartouche, Ball Footed Base, 19 x 11 ½ In.	518.00
Tea Urn, Repousse Bands, Flowers, Handles, Spigot, Heraldic Crest, Motto, 18 x 9 In.	776.00
Toast Rack, Arched Uprights, Ring Handle, Rectangular Base, 4 Ball Feet, 1890, 4 x 3 ½ In.	153.00
Tray, 3-Part, Raised, Paw Feet, Rectangular With Rounded Ends, Pierced Gallery, 4 x 50 In.	1750.00
Tray, Castleton Pattern, Oval, Beaded Rim, International Silver, c.1975, 24 ½ x 15 ¼ In.	399.00
Tray, Chased Rim, Footed, Mappin & Webb, 2 x 17 x 29 In.	150.00
Tray, Floral Embossed Rim, Round, Sheffield, 20 ½ In.	150.00
Tray, Gadroon, Rococo Shells, Rectangular, Handles, Ellis-Barker Co., c.1920, 25 x 17 In.	307.00
Tray, Gallery, Scalloped, Reticulated Masks, Medallions, Handles, Oval, England, c.1910, 3 ½ x 22 In..	575.00
Tray, Meat, Dome Lid, Shield, Scalloped, Well & Tree, Old Sheffield, c.1810, 24 x 17 ½ In. .....*illus*	1298.00
Tray, Oval, 2 Handles, Chased Leaf Scrolls, Flowers, Flare Rim, 4 Scroll Feet, 29 ¾ x 20 In.	717.00
Tray, Oval, 2 Satyr Mask Handles, Engraved, 4 Supports, Gorham, c.1865, 38 x 22 ½ In.	1434.00
Tray, Oval, Galleried Rim, 2 Handles, Gadroon Shaped Rim, Ball Feet, c.1900, 2 ⅞ x 15 In.	177.00
Tray, Pierced Gallery, Wavy Gadroon Rim, Handles, Oval, c.1990, 24 ½ x 17 In.	430.00
Tray, Rectangular, Gadroon, Shell Rim, Leaf Handles, Armorial, Scroll Feet, Sheffield, c.1830, 24 In. .	356.00
Tray, Rectangular, Reticulated Rim, Scrolls, Leaf Handles, Crown Silver Co., c.1950, 29 x 19 In.	276.00
Tray, Remembrance, Rogers Brothers, 1948, 16 ¾ x 28 ¾ In.	307.00
Tray, Rococo, Rectangular, Shaped Rim, Band Of Cartouches & Scroll, 30 x 18 In.	153.00
Tray, Rococo, Round, Rocaille Engraved, Openwork Border, Animals, c.1900, 20 In. Diam.	499.00
Tray, Tea, 2 Handles, Rectangular, Rolled Rim, Christofle, Marked, 29 In., Pair	823.00
Tray, Tea, Beaded Handles, Border, Chased Field, James Deakin & Sons, 1800s, 29 In.	717.00
Tray, Tea, Octagonal, Beaded Borders, Renaissance Revival Chasing, 23 ½ x 18 ½ In.	359.00
Tray, Tea, Octagonal, Leaf Handles, Gadroon Border, Scroll Feet, c.1880, 29 ½ x 17 ¾ In.	837.00
Tray, Vintage Pattern, Applied Border, Shell, Scroll Handles, Engraved, c.1950, 30 x 18 In.	98.00
Trophy, Urn Shape, 3 Serpentine Handles, Flowers, Round Base, Inscribed, 1912, 18 In.	173.00
Trophy, Vase, Horn Handles, Automobile Club, Williamsport, Pa., 1908, 6 ½ x 8 ½ In.	138.00
Tureen, Cover, Embossed Flowers, Raised Handles, Chased & Reeded Feet, 10 x 15 In.	615.00
Tureen, Cover, Rolled, Scroll Handles, Oval, Sheffield, c.1800, 12 ½ x 11 x 15 In.	502.00
Tureen, Cover, Stag Finial, Stag Head Handles, Armorial, Elkington & Co., 1865, 13 In.	1896.00
Tureen, Dome Lid, Rococo Style, Lobed, 2 Leaf Handles, Leaf Finial Handle, Coat Of Arms, c.1800	148.00
Tureen, Sauce, William IV, Lobed Oval Shape, Acanthus Handle, Sheffield, 7 x 6 In., Pair	1045.00

Silver Plate, Castor Set, 7 Bottles, Oval, Scroll Supports, Hallmark, D&S, c.1890, 12 ½ In.
$598.00

Neal Auction Co.

Silver Plate, Hot Water Urn, Dome Lid, Acanthus Scrolls, Engraved, Elkington & Co., c.1890, 24 In.
$796.00

Skinner, Inc.

Silver Plate, Hot Water Urn, Dome Lid, Wooden Handles, 4 Shell & Scroll Feet, c.1875, 16 x 14 In.
$430.00

S

New Orleans Auction Galleries, Inc.

585

Silver Plate, Pitcher, Water, Floral Bands, Shell, Under Spout, Etched, Flower, Wheat, Fern, c.1850, 12 In. $150.00

DuMouchelles Art Gallery

Silver Plate, Tazza, Cut Glass Dish, Woven Fronds, Grapevines, C-Scroll Feet, Elkington & Co., c.1876, 20 In. $735.00

Skinner, Inc.

Silver Plate, Tray, Meat, Dome Lid, Shield, Scalloped, Well & Tree, Old Sheffield, c.1810, 24 x 17 ½ In. $1298.00

Brunk Auctions

S

> **TIP**
> When buying silver with bright cut designs, avoid worn pieces. Best prices are paid for silver with clear, crisp designs.

Tureen, Soup, Cover, Navette Shape, Pedestal, Fluted Sides, Loop Handles, c.1900, 8 ⅝ x 14 ¾ In.	418.00
Vase, Art Deco, Geometric Shape, Handles, Tapered, Spiked Relief Designs, 14 In.	265.00
Vase, Repousse, Hammered, Long Neck, High Handles, Barbour, c.1900, 17 ½ In., Pair	120.00
Warming Stand, Oval, 2 Handles, 4 Leaf Feet, Christofle, c.1910, 4 ½ x 10 In.	234.00
Warming Stand, Round, Wood Finial & Handle, England, 17 In.	134.00
Wine Bottle Pourer, Cable Handle, Attached Collar, Victorian, 11 ½ In.	154.00
Wine Bucket, Cylindrical, Tapering, Stag Handles, Greek Key Bands, 10 ¾ In., Pair	1230.00
Wine Bucket, Tapering Body, Greek Key Border, Stag Handles, Inserts, 11 x 8 In., Pair	1476.00
Wine Coaster, Grapevines, Swags, Lion Masks, Pierced, Mahogany Base, c.1850, 4 In., Pair	237.00
Wine Coaster, Scalloped Openwork Sides, Wood Base, 1900s, 2 x 4 ¾ In.	295.00
Wine Cooler, 2 Twig Handles, Leaf Shape Base, Grapevine Supports, 11 In.	345.00
Wine Cooler, Campagna Shape, Gadroon Rim, Handles, Sheffield, 1800s, 11 ½ In. *illus*	598.00
Wine Cooler, Campagna Shape, Grapevine, Handles, Pedestal, Stepped Foot, c.1900, 11 In., Pair.	944.00
Wine Cooler, Campagna Shape, Lion Mask, Ring Handles, 10 ¼ In., Pair	180.00
Wine Cooler, Campagna Shape, Regency Style, Lobed, Reeded Border, Loop Handles, 10 In., Pair	1793.00
Wine Cooler, Gadroon, Mask Ring Handles, Eagle, Coronet Shield, Sheffield, 1800s, 8 ½ In., Pair	1150.00
Wine Cooler, Stand, Cylindrical, Round Foot, Banded, Ring Handles, 35 In., Pair	1293.00
Wine Cooler, Urn Shape, Handle, Grape & Vine Design, 12 In., Pair.	1984.00
Wine Trolley, Georgian Style, T-Shape Handle, Gadroon Rimmed Coasters, c.1915, 2 ¾ x 13 In.	215.00

SILVER-AMERICAN. American silver is listed here. Coin and sterling silver are included. Most of the sterling silver listed in this book is subdivided by country. There are also other pieces of silver and silver plate listed under special categories, such as Candelabrum, Napkin Ring, Silver Flatware, Silver Plate, Silver-Sterling, and Tiffany Silver. Silver prices in 2011 and 2012 became so high many pieces were worth more in meltdown value than as decorative silver. These prices are based on current silver values. For information about makers and marks, see *Kovels' American Silver Marks: 1650 to the Present.*

Asparagus Tongs, Repousse Pattern, Pierced Top, Marked S. Kirk & Sons, 7 ¾ In.	219.00
Baby Cup, Hammered, Dominick & Haff, c.1890, 3 In.	478.00
Basin, Washstand, Round, Ribbed Border, A. Rasch & Co., Inscribed, c.1795, 12 ½ In.	7000.00
Basket, Chased Chrysanthemums, Reticulated Base, Scroll Feet, Handle, Whiting, 22 x 14 In.	6325.00
Basket, Elongated Oval, Applied Leaves Design, Entwined Handle, Reed & Barton, 6 In.	425.00
Basket, Footed, Handle, Gorham, 1855-60, 3 ½ x 10 In.	780.00
Basket, Fruit, Oval, Upright Wirework Handle, Applied Grapevines, Gorham, 1874, 9 x 11 In.	1778.00
Basket, Lobed Oval Shape, Pierced Leaf & Ribbon Border, Putti, Sheep, 10 In.	275.00
Basket, Ornate Flower & Fruit Design, Ball & Claw Feet, Gorham Mfg., Co., 7 ½ x 7 ½ In.	546.00
Basket, Reticulated, Band Handle, Frank W. Smith Silver Co., 5 ¾ x 6 ½ In.	180.00
Basket, Reticulated, Handle, Footed, Redlich & Co., 20th Century, 14 x 14 In.	885.00
Basket, Reticulated, Lotus Petals, Octagonal Foot, Towle, 13 In.	1020.00
Basket, Round Foot, William Gale & Son, c.1860, 9 x 11 ½ In.	1080.00
Basket, Shaped Rim, Ribbed Handle, Footed, Monogram, Gorham, 5 ½ In.	158.00
Beaker, Curved Cylindrical, Engraved Script, 1825, 3 ⅛ In.	299.00
Berry Spoon, Chrysanthemum Pattern, H Monogram, Durgin, 8 ¼ x 5 ½ In.	489.00
Berry Spoon, Embossed, Engraved, Coin, Haddock, Lincoln, Box, c.1950, 10 In.	356.00
Berry Spoon, Les Six Fleurs Pattern, Gilt Bowl, Monogram, Reed & Barton, 1901, 10 In.	215.00
Berry Spoon, Strawberries, Flowers, Stamped Stieff, 8 x 2 ½ In.	107.00
Blotter Corners, Jenkins & Jenkins, c.1910, 3 In., 4 Piece	531.00
Bonbon Spoon, Leaf & Berry Interior, Handle, Gold Washed, Gorham, c.1910, 8 In.	178.00
Bonbon, Round, Chased, Embossed Flowers, Fruits, Gilt Repousse, S. Kirk & Son, c.1950, 6 In.	178.00
Bottle Stand, Flower Repousse Border, Round, S. Kirk & Sons, 7 In.	259.00
Bowl, 2 Intersecting Flowers, Relief, Petal Border, Marked, Wallace Sterling, 2 x 10 In.	518.00
Bowl, Art Nouveau, Repousse, Scalloped Rim, Gorham, 10 In.	420.00
Bowl, Art Nouveau, Repousse, Theodore Starr, 9 ½ In.	417.00
Bowl, Bicentennial, Applied Patriotic Figures Border, Franklin Mint, c.1976, 7 x 14 In.	5750.00
Bowl, Center, Boat Shape, Curved Base, Peter Muller-Munk, c.1939, 5 x 19 In.	26250.00
Bowl, Center, Chased & Engraved Rim, Clover Design, Tiffany & Co., c.1900, 10 x 3 In.	920.00
Bowl, Center, Flared Rim, Meandering Leaf Pattern, Lebkuecher & Co., 12 ½ In.	713.00
Bowl, Center, Flared, Oval, Applied Elk, Scroll, Trumpet Foot, Whiting Mfg., c.1860, 5 x 13 ½ In.	1541.00
Bowl, Center, Ribbed, Wide Flared Rim, Round Foot, Marked, Gorham, 12 In.	1058.00
Bowl, Center, Round, Acanthus Leaf Supports, Round Foot, Gorham, 10 In.	930.00
Bowl, Center, Round, Lobed, Chased Fruit, Flowers, Flower Frog, Reed & Barton, c.1910, 8 x 19 ½ In.	8917.00
Bowl, Child's, Chased Rim Animals, William Kerr, c.1900, 6 In.	136.00
Bowl, Chippendale Style, Gorham, 1 ½ x 10 In.	330.00
Bowl, Cover, Flower, Repousse, 2 Central Cartouches, Finial Handle, Gorham, 1896, 6 x 12 In., Pair.	4248.00
Bowl, Cover, Round, Repousse, Cartouches, Shell, Flowers, Handles, Gorham, 1896, 6 x 12 In., Pair.	5280.00
Bowl, Deep, Square Rim, Fluted Foot, Marked, 6-Petal Blossom, M. Craver, 3 In.	1593.00

Bowl, Dome Lid, Flared Oval, Chased, Embossed Flowers, Leaf Handles, T.B. Starr, c.1890, 10 In...	1778.00
Bowl, Elongated Oval, Reeded Edge, Monogram, Towle, 12 x 7 In.	345.00
Bowl, Engraved Flower Cover, Top Ring Handle, Kirk & Sons, c.1915, 10 In., Pair	2133.00
Bowl, Engraved Geometric Band, Flowers, Low Foot, Monogram, Gorham, 1878, 5 In.	267.00
Bowl, Flared Rim, Openwork Stem, Leaves, Grapes, Woodside Sterling Co., c.1920, 6 x 9 In.	711.00
Bowl, Flared Rim, Repousse Flowers, 3 Splayed Feet, S. Kirk & Son, 3 x 5 In.	155.00
Bowl, Floral Repousse Rim, S. Kirk & Co., 4 ½ x 9 ½ In.	590.00
Bowl, Florenze, Flared, Scrolls, Flowers, Vines, Satyr Masks, Footed, Gorham, 1925, 4 x 13 In.	1093.00
Bowl, Flowers, Embossed, Towle, 9 In.	265.00
Bowl, Footed, Beaded Rim, Monogram, Coin, Haddock, Lincoln & Foss, c.1850, 4 ⅞ In.	385.00
Bowl, Footed, Oval Shape, Pierced, Shaped Rim, Flat Handles, Gorham	646.00
Bowl, Fruit & Leaf Relief, 4 Ball Feet, S. Kirk & Son, 2 ½ x 9 ½ In.	633.00
Bowl, Fruit, 4 Sections, Scroll, Shell Rims, Openwork, Theodore B. Starr, c.1905, 12 In.	770.00
Bowl, Fruit, 8-Sided, Molded Rim, Interior Skyscraper Design, Durgin-Gorham, 1930, 3 x 10 In.	553.00
Bowl, Fruit, Chased, Embossed Flowers, Leaf Tip Base, Baltimore Silversmiths, c.1910, 8 ¼ In.	1541.00
Bowl, Fruit, Fluted, Beaded Rim, Gorham, 1897, 8 ½ In.	356.00
Bowl, Fruit, International, Meriden Brittania, 8 In.	210.00
Bowl, Fruit, Ogee, Pierced Scrolls, Cherubs, Garlands, Bailey, Banks & Biddle Co., c.1905, 14 x 5 In.	830.00
Bowl, Fruit, Oval, C-Scroll Rim, Chased, Embossed, Dominick & Haff, 1892, 11 In.	948.00
Bowl, Fruit, Pierced, Engraved, Howard & Co, 1902, 12 In.	474.00
Bowl, Fruit, Round, Ball Feet, Chased Fruit, Flowers, S. Kirk & Son, c.1890, 2 ½ x 9 ½ In.	615.00
Bowl, Fruit, Vertical Fluting, Scrolled Rim, Shreve, Crump & Low, c.1890, 11 In.	474.00
Bowl, Gadroon Base, Reticulated Rim, Oval, Gorham, c.1925, 4 x 12 x 8 In.	1230.00
Bowl, Grande Baroque Pattern, Repousse Flowers, Swags, Scrolls, Shallow, 10 ¾ In.	354.00
Bowl, Hammered, Engraved Leaves, Cabochon Buds, Whiting, 3 x 8 ½ In.	5750.00
Bowl, Ice Cream, Flared Base, Watson Co., 2 ½ x 3 ¼ In., 12 Piece	575.00
Bowl, Lady Constance, Footed, Towle, c.1925, 3 ½ x 10 ½ In.	450.00
Bowl, Lobed, Scalloped Border, Windsor Pattern, Reed & Barton, 8 ½ In.	403.00
Bowl, Oblong, Raised, 4-Footed, Wavy Rim, Graff, Washbourne & Dunn, 13 x 6 In.	259.00
Bowl, Octagonal, Leaf, Flower Designs, Marked J.E. Caldwell, 1900s, 2 ¾ x 11 ½ In.	590.00
Bowl, Oval, Flat Rim, Rolled Edge, Waisted Foot, Hammered, Lebolt & Co., c.1900, 4 x 8 In.	399.00
Bowl, Oval, Repousse Wavy Rim, Kirk & Sons, 10 ½ In., Pair	960.00
Bowl, Oval, Ridged Rim, Reed & Barton, 10 ½ In.	295.00
Bowl, Pedestal, Stepped Round Foot, 2 C-Scroll Handles, Leaves, F.M. Whiting, 11 ¾ In.	1135.00
Bowl, Persian Style, Round, Tapering, Trumpet Foot, Vines, Birds, Shreve & Co., c.1900, 6 ½ In.	613.00
Bowl, Pierced Brass Flower Frog, Footed, Round, Hamilton, 4 x 10 In.	316.00
Bowl, Pierced, Relief, Scrolling, Swags, Birds, Crystal Liner, Scalloped Rim, 9 x 8 In.	955.00
Bowl, Presentation, Hammered, Chased Rim, Marked, Hammer, A. Stone, 1913, 8 In.	1185.00
Bowl, Race Trophy, Paul Revere Shape, Poole Silver, 4 ¼ x 8 In.	350.00
Bowl, Raised Rim, Flaring Body, Kirk & Son, 8 In.	427.00
Bowl, Repousse Flower Band, Round, H Monogram, S. Kirk & Son, 9 In.	345.00
Bowl, Repousse Flowers, Flared Wavy Rim, Art Nouveau, Marked, Gorham, 11 In.	403.00
Bowl, Repousse, Chased Flower, Lobed, Monogram, S. Kirk & Son, 9 In.	334.00
Bowl, Repousse, Flowers, Scrolling, Gorham, c.1953, 11 ½ In.	690.00
Bowl, Reticulated, Embossed Rim, Pedestal, Wallace, 4 x 10 In.	417.00
Bowl, Revere Style, Ringed Foot, Inscribed, 1913-38, 5 ¾ x 11 In.	1121.00
Bowl, Revere, Gorham, Footed, 7 ¼ In.	450.00
Bowl, Ribbed Sides, Rectangular, Reed & Barton, 2 x 10 In.	444.00
Bowl, Ribbed, Pedestal Base, Dunkirk Silversmiths, 4 ½ x 9 In.	690.00
Bowl, Rolled Rim, Engraved, George W. Shiebler & Co., c.1910, 6 x 2 ⅛ In.	237.00
Bowl, Round, Flared Rim, Openwork Leaf Stem, A. La Paglia, International, c.1950, 5 x 5 In.	474.00
Bowl, Round, Footed, Molded Shell Border, Randahl Shop, c.1920, 3 ½ x 10 In.	777.00
Bowl, Round, Lobed, Bead & Dart Rim, Monogram, 1898, 1 ¾ x 8 In.	123.00
Bowl, Round, Lobed, Randahl Shop, c.1925, 9 In.	1016.00
Bowl, Round, Lobed, Rolled Rim, Monogram, Lebolt & Co., c.1900, 3 x 8 In.	369.00
Bowl, Round, Plain Body, Squat Foot, Monogram, Gorham, 1900s, 9 ¾ In.	700.00
Bowl, Round, Ribbed, Gorham, 8 In., Pair	610.00
Bowl, Round, Ruffled Rim, Flowers & Leaves, Towle, 12 x 3 In.	489.00
Bowl, Salem, Rectangular, Reed & Barton, 1941, 6 ¾ x 10 ⅜ In.	390.00
Bowl, Scalloped Rim, Fluted Body, Whiting Sterling Co., 3 x 9 ½ In.	345.00
Bowl, Scalloped, Flared, Stamped Reed & Barton, 11 ¾ x 7 ¾ In.	791.00
Bowl, Scalloped, Lobed, Monogram, Dominick & Haff, c.1880, 3 x 12 ½ In.	633.00
Bowl, Scalloped, Lobed, Reed & Barton, 9 x 15 In.	460.00
Bowl, Scalloped, Openwork Sides, Shells & Scrolls, Dominik & Haff, 1900s, 4 x 13 In.	660.00
Bowl, Scrolls, Flowers, George W. Shiebler & Co., c.1905, 3 ¾ x 9 ½ In.	652.00
Bowl, Shaped, Applied Daisies, Round, Monogram EJM, William Kerr, 8 In.	316.00

TIP

You can clean the inside of a silver teapot by filling it with warm water and adding a five-minute denture-cleaning tablet for every two cups of water. Rinse after 10 minutes. If a residue remains, use a soft brush to clean it off.

Silver Plate, Wine Cooler, Campagna Shape, Gadroon Rim, Handles, Sheffield, 1800s, 11 ½ In.
$598.00

Neal Auction Co.

Silver-American, Butter, Cover, Oval, Chased, Embossed, Flowering Vines, Handles, Gorham, c.1850, 6 ¼ In.
$2015.00

Skinner, Inc.

Silver-American, Centerpiece, Florenz, Flower Frog, Gorham, 1925, 4 ½ x 12 ¾ In.
$1800.00

DuMouchelles Art Gallery

S

Silver-American, Chalice, Beaded Rim, Etched Monogram, Krider & Co., c.1850, 6 ¾ x 4 In.
$330.00

DuMouchelles Art Gallery

Silver-American, Coffeepot & Sugar, Monogram, Liberty Browne, Phila., 18th Century, 11 In. & 11 In.
$7935.00

Cottone Auctions

Silver-American, Ewer, Repousse, Chased, Buildings, Plants, Coat Of Arms, Motto, S. Kirk, 1830-46, 14 In.
$3555.00

Skinner, Inc.

Bowl, Shaped, Art Nouveau, Chased Flowers, Monogram, Gorham, 9 ¾ In.	374.00
Bowl, Shell, Flower Bands, Boat Shape, Cock Figural Handles, 6 ¼ x 12 ¾ In.	1521.00
Bowl, Tulip, 8-Sided, Shaped, Flared Rim, Footed, Worden-Munnis Co., c.1975, 4 ¾ x 9 In.	615.00
Bowl, Underplate, Louis XIV Pattern, Flared, Towle, 1927, 12-In. Bowl	1476.00
Bowl, Wildflower Cartouches, Diapered Edges, Redlich & Co., c.1900, 14 In.	1659.00
Bowl, Windsor Design, Monogram, Reed & Barton, c.1941, 8 ⅞ In.	259.00
Bowl, Windsor, Double Scalloped Rim, Square, Reed & Barton, 1 ½ x 8 ½ In.	403.00
Box, Bail Handle, Mahogany Liner, Williamsburg Reproduction, c.1960, 2 x 9 In.	805.00
Brandy Warmer, Bulbous, Squat, Turned Wood Handle, Hinged Spout, Cover, 1800s, 5 ⅜ x 11 In.	6871.00
Bread Tray, Crimped Edge, Meriden Co., Monogram, c.1900, 12 In.	295.00
Bread Tray, Oblong, Shaped, Monogram, Engraved, Gorham, 1904, 14 x 7 In.	438.00
Bread Tray, Ornate, Pierced Rim, Flowers, Scrolls, Oval, Ferdinand Fuchs & Bros., 2 x 14 ½ In.	863.00
Butter Spreader, Dominick & Haff, 5 ¾ In., 6 Piece	210.00
Butter, Cover, Goddess Finial, Handles, Beaded, Chased, Wood & Hughes, Coin, c.1850, 6 In.	1422.00
Butter, Cover, Oval, Chased, Embossed, Flowering Vines, Handles, Gorham, c.1850, 6 ¼ In. *illus*	2015.00
Butter, Cover, Ram's Head Finial, Engraved, Profile Medallions, Round, Gorham, 1869, 6 In.	2015.00
Cake Basket, Beaded Swing Handle, Reticulated Footed Shape, J.E. Caldwell & Co., c.1849, 11 In.	1016.00
Cake Basket, Engraved Flowers, Wavy Rim, Boat Shape, Swing Handle, 8 ¾ x 12 ½ In.	819.00
Cake Plate, Engraved Flowers, Band Handle, Watson Co., c.1910, 7 ½ x 10 In.	450.00
Cake Plate, Griffin Scrolls, Putti, Stamped, Pierced, Bailey, Banks & Biddle, c.1920, 11 In.	652.00
Cake Plate, Pierced Rim, Scrolls, Fronds, Lyres, Flowers, Engraved, Theodore B. Starr, c.1900, 10 In.	830.00
Cake Plate, Repousse, S. Kirk & Sons, 12 ⅛ In.	920.00
Cake Plate, Reticulated Edge, Applied Scrolls, Shells, Handles, Black, Starr & Frost, c.1905, 13 In.	770.00
Cake Plate, Reticulated Handle, Gorham, 1932, 5 x 9 ½ In.	330.00
Candelabra are listed in the Candelabrum category.	
Candlesticks are listed in their own category.	
Candy Dish, Baroque Style, Scrolling, Leaves, Handles, Footed, Dominick & Haff, 11 x 9 In.	518.00
Cann, Cup, Scroll Handle, Engraved, Coin, Woodward & Grosjean, Boston, c.1848, 6 ½ In.	652.00
Card Case, Presentation, Engraved, Leather Hinge, Albert Coles & Co., 3 ¾ x 2 ½ In.	354.00
Card Tray, Mother Of Pearl, FBO Monogram, Kalo, 8 ¼ x 4 ½ In.	3348.00
Cart, Arba, 2-Wheel, Detachable Guard Rails, Stamped, Cartier, 3 ½ x 8 ¼ In.	293.00
Case, Dance Card, Openwork Scrolls, Hinged, Chain, R. Blackington, 3 ½ In.	108.00
Centerpiece, Bacchus Masks, Square Handles, Spread Foot, Gorham, c.1870, 6 x 9 ¼ In.	708.00
Centerpiece, Florenz, Flower Frog, Gorham, 1925, 4 ½ x 12 ¾ In. *illus*	1800.00
Centerpiece, Footed Bowl, Monogram, Meriden Britannia Co., 11 In. Diam.	767.00
Centerpiece, Oval, Lobed, Randahl Shop, c.1920, 3 ¾ x 10 In.	1135.00
Centerpiece, Strawberry Pattern, Mauser, c.1900, 16 ½ x 13 ¾ In.	2486.00
Chalice, Beaded Rim, Etched Monogram, Krider & Co., c.1850, 6 ¾ x 4 In. *illus*	330.00
Cheese Scoop, Carved, Twisted, Stem, Gold Wash Blade, Whiting, c.1890, 9 In.	237.00
Cheese Scoop, Cluny, Antoine Heller, Gorham, c.1883, 8 In.	205.00
Cheese Scoop, Whiting, 8 In.	104.00
Chocolate Pot, Jacobi & Jenkins, c.1900, 8 In.	1770.00
Chop Set, 2-Tine Fork, Elongated Spoon Bowl, Porter Blanchard, 10 In.	214.00
Christening Cup, 2 Leaf Design Handles, Pedestal Stepped Base, Reed & Barton, 6 x 5 In.	184.00
Cigarette Box, Humidor, Hinged Lid, Mahogany Liner, Monogram, Schroth's, 6 x 4 In.	299.00
Claret Spoon, Spiral Twist Shaft, Dominick & Haff, 13 ¼ In.	595.00
Claret Spoon, Twisted Center, Grape Leaf Handle, Gorham, 1875, 15 ½ In.	267.00
Clothes Brush, Gold Washed, Repousse Flowers & Leaves On Handle, Shiebler, 6 In.	119.00
Cocktail Shaker, Bucket Shape, Domed Cap, Weidlich Sterling Spoon Co., c.1935, 10 ½ x 4 In.	615.00
Cocktail Shaker, Hand Hammered, Foot Ring & Finial, Webster Co., 9 ½ In.	374.00
Cocktail Shaker, Inscribed, J.E. Caldwell & Co., c.1900, 20 Oz.	750.00
Cocktail, Wrought, Kalo Shop, 5 ½ In., 12 Piece	1920.00
Coffee Set, Coffeepot, Teapot, Creamer, Sugar, Cover, Tray, International Silver Co., c.1950	7638.00
Coffee Set, Donatello, Coffeepot, Teapot, Sugar, Creamer, Chased Flowers, Amston	2875.00
Coffee Set, Spring Glory, Coffeepot, Sugar, Cover, Creamer, 2 Trays, International, 1942	2645.00
Coffeepot & Sugar, Monogram, Liberty Browne, Phila., 18th Century, 11 & 11 In. *illus*	7935.00
Coffeepot, Baluster, Gooseneck, Scrolled Handle, Wilcox & Eversten, c.1935, 10 x 5 In.	861.00
Coffeepot, Flower Repouse, Ivory Heat Shields, Ram's Head Handle, Bailey & Co., 8 ½ x 6 ¾ In.	1438.00
Coffeepot, Gadroon Pattern, Fisher Silversmiths, c.1965, 11 ¾ x 10 ½ In.	676.00
Coffeepot, Repousse, Flowers, Shaped Handle, Ram's Head Terminal, S. Kirk & Son, 8 ¼ In.	1315.00
Compote, Engraved, Pierced, Vine & Husk Rim, Black, Starr & Frost, c.1920, 7 ½ x 3 In.	593.00
Compote, Flared Rim, Gadroon, Winged Paw Feet, Whiting Mfg., 5 ¼ x 7 In.	497.00
Compote, Francis I, Footed, Reed & Barton, 4 ¼ x 11 ½ In.	944.00
Compote, Francis I, Fruit Garlands, Leaf Rim, Reed & Barton, 1950, 5 x 8 In.	504.00
Compote, Pierced Flower Border, Conforming Foot, Black, Starr & Frost, 7 In., Pair	854.00
Compote, Raised Pedestal, Flower Design Openwork, Mauser, Mount Vernon, 5 x 11 In.	575.00

S

Compote, Repousse Rim, Black, Starr & Frost, c.1925, 4 ¾ x 10 ¼ In.		720.00
Compote, Repousse Rim, Footed, Graff, Washbourne & Dunn, c.1925, 4 ¾ x 10 ¼ In.		660.00
Compote, Repousse, Kirk & Son, c.1930, 6 ¼ x 3 In.		374.00
Compote, Round, Embossed Rim, Pedestal Base, Gorham, 1903-06, 3 ¼ x 9 ½ In.		1435.00
Compote, Urn Shape, Lid, Beaded, Flower Rim, Marked, Gorham, 8 ¼ In.		1920.00
Compote, Wavy Flower Openwork Rim, Marked Mauser, Mount Vernon, 4 ½ x 10 ¾ In.		575.00
Compote, Wavy Rim, Stamped, Gorham, 10 x 4 ½ In.		452.00
Cracker Scoop, Olive Stem, Curved Bowl, Coin, Case, c.1825, 9 In.		178.00
Creamer, Engraved Flowers, Village Scenes, 3 ¼ In.		184.00
Creamer, Impressed Border, Rim, Bulbous, Coin, c.1835, 6 x 6 ¾ In.		177.00
Crumber, Repousse, Jenkins & Jenkins, c.1910, 12 ½ In.		177.00
Cup, Beaker Shape, Footed, Reeded, 1840s, 4 In.		646.00
Cup, Footed Urn, Scroll Handle, Flowers, Engraved, c.1850, 3 ⅜ In.		1230.00
Cup, Repousse, Footed Urn, Scroll Handle, Fruit, Flowers, Birds, Armorial, c.1840, 4 ½ In.		598.00
Cup, Vining Flowers & Leaves, Rolled Rim & Foot, C-Scroll Handle, Marked, c.1851, 4 In.		382.00
Cuspidor, Concave Funnel Top, Coin, Inscribed Jane Williams, c.1810, 2 ½ x 3 ¼ In.		1003.00
Decanter, Sterling Over Glass, Geometric Pierced Design, Black, Star & Frost, 1900s, 11 ½ In.		354.00
Decanter, Whiskey, Glass, Flatted Sphere, Fluted Neck, Handle, Alvin, c.1900, 8 x 6 In.		553.00
Demitasse Pot, Dome Lid, Tapered, Ear Handle, Bigelow, Kennard & Co., c.1900, 7 ½ In.		504.00
Demitasse Pot, Grape, Repousse, Twig Handle, Baltimore Silversmiths Mfg. Co., c.1904, 10 In.		633.00
Dish Cross, Adjustable Arms, Center Heater, Shell Feet, T. Shields, c.1770, 4 ½ x 12 In.		9200.00
Dish, 3 Interconnected Leaves Shape, Bun Feet, Reed & Barton, 1932, 7 x 7 In.		334.00
Dish, Entree, Cover, Leaf Finial, Oval, Beaded Rim, Low Foot, Gorham, 11 In.		1067.00
Dish, Entree, Cover, Leaf Handle, Redlich & Co., 1900s, 5 x 11 In.		960.00
Dish, Flower Heads, Footed, Elongated Oval, Lobes, Round Foot, Art Nouveau, Gorham, 1904, 9 ¾ In.		326.00
Dish, Francis I, Chased Flowers, Shaped Edge, Reed & Barton, 8 In.		554.00
Dish, Hostess, Reed & Barton, 8 x 8 In.		295.00
Dish, Oval, Cover, Reeded Handles, Monogram, Gorham, 11 ¾ x 7 ½ In., Pair		1783.00
Dish, Scalloped Edge, Art Nouveau, Wm. B. Kerr Co., c.1900, 6 ½ In.		295.00
Dish, Scrolling, Round, Monogram, Alvin Hallmark, 7 In.		150.00
Dish, Shell Shape, Script Monogram, Ball Feet, Gorham, c.1932, 9 x 9 In.		598.00
Dish, Sweetmeat, Cover, Oval Urn, 2 Loop Handles, Prick Dot Design, 1790, 5 x 9 In.		850.00
Dish, Vegetable, Repousse, Oval, Boar's Head Finial, S. Kirk & Son, 11 ½ In.		3835.00
Dish, Windsor, Scalloped, Everted Serpentine Rim, Reed & Barton, 1950, 11 x 8 In.		575.00
Dresser Box, Filigree, Star & Bird Design, Repousse, Oval, Gilt Interior, Paw Feet, 4 x 3 In.		489.00
Dresser Set, Beaded Edge, Monogram, Gorham, Brushes, 13-In. Mirror, 3 Piece		184.00
Dresser Set, Mirror, Brush, Tray, Comb, Letter Opener, Bootjack, File, Repousse, S. Kirk & Son, 7 Piece		431.00
Ewer, Beaded Wide Spout, Urn Body, Scroll Handle, Leaves, Round Foot, Reeded, c.1835		5676.00
Ewer, Communion, Bulbous, Hinged Lid, Cross Finial, S-Handle, Engraved, 1800s, 15 In.		700.00
Ewer, Oval Body, Gadroon, Loop Handle, Whiting Manufacturing, c.1907, 15 In.		1304.00
Ewer, Repousse, Chased, Buildings, Plants, Coat Of Arms, Motto, S. Kirk, 1830-46, 14 In. *illus*		3555.00
Ewer, Rim Beading, Scroll Handle, Coin, Philadelphia, c.1840, 12 ¾ In.		830.00
Ewer, Scroll & Flower Repousse, Hinged Lid, Eagle Finial, Openwork Base, c.1900, 11 ½ In. *illus*		1003.00
Figurine, Pheasant, Standing, Hinged Wings, Removable Head, Marked, Wyler, 7 ¾ x 15 In., Pair		2070.00
Fish Set, Kenilworth, Pierced, Engraved, Coin, Albert Coles, c.1850, 11 In., 2 Piece *illus*		575.00
Flagon, Repousse Top, Cut Glass Flower Design Base, Theodore B. Starr, 13 ½ In.		920.00
Flask, Engraved, Ahrendt, & Taylor Co., c.1936, 8 ⅞ x 5 ¼ In.		652.00
Flask, Perfume, Oval, Chased, Embossed Daisies, Leaves, Gorham, 1890, 4 ¾ In.		385.00
Flask, Repousse, Flowers, Gorham, c.1890, 4 ½ x 2 ¼ In.		345.00
Flask, Stripes, Watrous Mfg. Co., 1900s, 5 ¾ In.		330.00
Flower Frog, Footed, Weighted Base, Brass, Hamilton, 4 x 10 In.		316.00
Fork Set, Repousse, Jacobi & Jenkins, c.1900, 7 In., 10 Piece		472.00
Fruit Knife Set, Mother-Of-Pearl Handle, c.1910, 6 ½ In.		72.00
Goblet, Flower Repousse, Marked, Stieff, 1900s, 7 In, 6 Piece		4720.00
Goblet, Grape Repousse, Coin, Inscribed, Savannah, c.1850, 6 x 3 In., Pair		1888.00
Goblet, Marked Wallace, 6 ¾ In., 8 Piece		1150.00
Goblet, Pattern 14, M Monogram, Wallace Sterling, 6 ½ In., 8 Piece		1495.00
Goblet, Victorian, Oval, Waisted Stem, Round Foot, Engraved, Bamboo, Crane, Crest, c.1877, 7 ½ In.		215.00
Gravy Boat, Repousse, Flowers, Leaves, Gorham, 1895, 6 x 4 In.		840.00
Gravy Boat, Underplate, Loop Handle, Ribbed, Wide Shaped Spout, Wallace, 8 x 5 In.		345.00
Gravy Boat, Underplate, Scrolled Handle, Reed & Barton		345.00
Hair Receiver, Stieff Rose, Monogram, c.1925, 3 ¾ x 4 ½ In.		288.00
Holy Water Sprinkler, Jacobi & Jenkins, 1897, 5 In.		590.00
Hot Water Urn, Dome Lid, 2 Handles, Openwork Grapevines, Round, Footed, 1800s, 18 In.		2468.00
Hot Water Urn, Repousse Castles, Flowers, 2 Handles, S. Kirk & Son, 16 In.		7670.00
Ice Bowl, Iceberg Shape, 2 Polar Bear Mounts, Footed, Ford & Tupper, c.1870, 7 x 10 In.		9261.00

Silver-American, Ewer, Scroll & Flower Repousse, Hinged Lid, Eagle Finial, Openwork Base, c.1900, 11 ½ In.
$1003.00

Ivey-Selkirk Auctioneers

Silver-American, Fish Set, Kenilworth, Pierced, Engraved, Coin, Albert Coles, c.1850, 11 In., 2 Piece
$575.00

Leland Little Auction

Silver-American, Ice Cream Knife, Hizen, Carp, Water Swirls, Bamboo Leaves, Hollow Handle, Gilt, c.1880, 12 In.
$2440.00

Neal Auction Co.

Silver-American, Juicer, Citrus, Gilt Wash, Decorated Rim, Ring Handle, Ferdinand Fuchs & Bros., N.Y., c.1890
$288.00

Leland Little Auction

S

Silver-American, Julep Cup, Coin, c.1850-60, 3 ½ In. $837.00

Neal Auction Co.

Silver-American, Julep Cup, Tapered Sides, Reeded Borders, Monogram, Coin, E. Kinsey, 1800s, 3 ½ x 3 In. $413.00

Brunk Auctions

Silver-American, Pastry Server, Flower Stems, Gold Washed, Presentation, N.G. Wood & Son, c.1886, 9 ⅝ In. $267.00

Skinner, Inc.

Silver-American, Pitcher, 8-Sided, Straight Neck, Double Scroll Handle, Hyde & Goodrich, c.1850, 7 ⅜ In. $2032.00

Neal Auction Co.

Ice Cream Knife, Hizen, Carp, Water Swirls, Bamboo Leaves, Hollow Handle, Gilt, c.1880, 12 In. *illus*	2440.00
Ice Tongs, Eleder-Hickok, c.1925, 7 ½ In.	173.00
Jam Pot, American Aesthetic, Wooden Bucket Shape, Swing Handle, c.1885, 4 In.	1422.00
Jam Pot, Dome Lid, Barrel Shape, Loop Handle, Applied Butterfly, Gorham, 1869, 4 In.	652.00
Jewelry Box, Turned, Engraved Monogram, Shreve & Co., c.1895, 5 x 3 In.	215.00
Juicer, Citrus, Gilt Wash, Decorated Rim, Ring Handle, Ferdinand Fuchs & Bros., N.Y., c.1890 ..*illus*	288.00
Julep Cup, Coin, c.1850-60, 3 ½ In. .*illus*	837.00
Julep Cup, Cylinder, Flared Rim, J. Scearce, Shelbyville, Ky., 4 In., 4 Piece	1553.00
Julep Cup, Plain, Molded Rim, Wallace, 20th Century, 5 ¾ In., 8 Piece	900.00
Julep Cup, Tapered Sides, Reeded Borders, Monogram, Coin, E. Kinsey, 1800s, 3 ½ x 3 In. ....*illus*	413.00
Julep Cup, Tapered, Molded Rims, Beading, Script Monogram, c.1850, 3 ⅝ In.	1230.00
Kettle, Hot Water, Stand, Lobed Cover, Mushroom Finial, Leaves, Howard & Co., c.1890, 8 In..	1422.00
Kettle, Hot Water, Stand, Repousse Flowers, Bulbous, Shaped Handle, Whiting, 1890-1900, 8 In..	1121.00
Kettle, Stand, Bullet Shape, Fruitwood Swing Handle, Engraved Coat Of Arms, c.1935, 13 In..	1689.00
Kettle, Stand, Oval, Beaded Rim, Fruitwood Handle, Ball Feet, Gorham, 1896, 12 ½ In.	1304.00
Kettle, Stand, Presentation Inscription, c.1940, 54 In.	1912.00
Kettle, Stand, Squat, Gadroon Rim, Wood Handle, Monogram, Anthemion Feet, 10 In.	1554.00
Knife Set, Repousse, Jacobi & Jenkins, c.1900, 10 ½ In., 12 Piece	295.00
Ladle, Condiment, Engraved Handle, Farrington & Honeywell, Boston, 5 ¼ In.	125.00
Ladle, Engraved Border, Sabine, George B. Sharp, c.1850, 14 ½ In.	250.00
Ladle, Marked J.M. Freeman, 1800s, 10 x 3 In.	646.00
Ladle, Monogram, Oval Cartouche, Gold Wash Bowl, Arabesque, Whiting, 10 ½ In.	144.00
Ladle, Shaped Handle, Coin, 1800s, 13 In.	236.00
Ladle, Shell Shape, Threaded Handle, Coin, Zadek & Caldwell, c.1850, 10 In.	326.00
Ladle, Theodore Dunosq, Phil., c.1835, 11 ½ In.	148.00
Ladle, TMM Monogram, Deforest & Co., N.Y., c.1827-28, 13 ¼ In.	269.00
Loving Cup, Cylinder, 3 Ear Handles, Rococo Revival, Whiting Manufacturing Co., c.1905, 8 In..	1067.00
Macaroni Server, Repousse, Jacobi & Jenkins, c.1900, 9 ½ In.	177.00
Mirror, Dressing, Rectangular, Incised Stripes, Elder-Hickok Co., c.1930, 17 x 14 In.	474.00
Mirror, Hand, Cupids, Flowers, Scrolled, Repousse, Unger Bros., c.1890, 9 In.	395.00
Muffineer, Baluster Shape, Dome Foot, Monogram, Bailey, Banks & Biddle, c.1885, 8 In.	356.00
Mug, Chased Flowers, Bailey & Co., Philadelphia, c.1800s, 5 ½ In.	1080.00
Mug, Cylindrical, Applied Ovolo Rim, Leaf Handle, Gold Wash, Gorham, 1906, 3 ½ In.	296.00
Mug, Flower Repousse, Scroll Handle, Tapered, Coin, Wilmot, c.1960, 4 x 4 ½ In.	354.00
Mug, Ivy Leaves, Shamrock Banding, Shallow Flutes, Ear Handle, N.Y., c.1950, 4 ¼ In.	296.00
Mug, Repousse, Signed Durgin, 1887, 5 ½ In.	460.00
Mug, Tapered, 2 Profile Medallions, Flowers, Angular Handle, Coin, Gorham, 1866, 3 ½ In. ...	474.00
Mug, Tapered, Cylindrical, Applied Rim, Flower Swags, Scroll Handle, Shreve & Co., c.1890, 4 In..	267.00
Mug, Tapered, Cylindrical, Flared Base, Leaves, Shells, Whiting, c.1876, 3 ¾ In.	237.00
Mug, Tree, Bridge, Shrine Repousse, Scrolled Rim, Coin, c.1847, 3 ¼ x 4 ¼ In.	177.00
Mug, U.S. Army, Presentation, Soldier, Armed, Kneeling, Reed & Barton, 1916, 4 In.	125.00
Mustard Pot, Stippled Texture, Cylindrical, Tapered, Ivory Finial, M. Craver, 3 In.	980.00
Napkin Rings are listed in their own category.	
Nut Dish, Greek Key Rim, Footed, Gorham, 4 x 2 ¾ In., 10 Piece	403.00
Oyster Ladle, Shell Bowl, Hinge Lidded Oyster Shell, Back Tipt Stem, Ball, Black & Co., c.1865, 13 In..	3851.00
Pastry Server, Flower Stems, Gold Washed, Presentation, N.G. Wood & Son, c.1886, 9 ⅝ In. ...*illus*	267.00
Perfume Bottle, Ruffled Rim, Stopper, Repousse Flowers, Redlich & Co., 6 x 3 In.	334.00
Pill Box, Lid, Round, Cherubs, Gilded Rim, Buccellati	185.00
Pitcher, 8-Sided, Straight Neck, Double Scroll Handle, Hyde & Goodrich, c.1850, 7 ⅜ In. .... *illus*	2032.00
Pitcher, Aesthetic Style, Repousse, Leaves, Flowers, Butterflies, Dominick & Haff, Marked, 8 In. *illus*	10350.00
Pitcher, Aesthetic, Copper Accent, Gorham, Repousse Rim, Handle, Gorham, c.1880, 6 ¼ In..	2160.00
Pitcher, Angular, Tapered, Neoclassical Bands, Whiting Mfg. Co., 10 ¼ In.	760.00
Pitcher, Art Deco, Engraved, Monogram, Schofield Co., c.1910, 8 x 8 In.	837.00
Pitcher, Baltimore Rose Pattern, Chased Flowers, Schofield, Baltimore, 9 In.	1169.00
Pitcher, Cylindrical, Strainer Spout, Wood Handle, Porter Blanchard, 1930-60, 7 ½ In. ....*illus*	3318.00
Pitcher, Embossed Flowers, Monogram, Coin, Lincoln & Foss, 8 ½ x 4 ¾ In.	259.00
Pitcher, Engraved, Soldiers, Eagle, Banner, c.1861, 12 In.	3585.00
Pitcher, Etched Flowers, Scroll Handle, Acanthus Feet, Gorham, 10 ½ In.	3600.00
Pitcher, Flower Repousse, Bulbous, Marked, Kirk, 1900s, 8 ¼ x 8 ¼ In.	1180.00
Pitcher, Flower Repousse, Faux Bois Handle, Jacobi & Co., 9 In.	1989.00
Pitcher, Fruit, Cornucopia, Chased, Repousse, Frank Whiting Co., 1962, 10 ½ In.	760.00
Pitcher, Hampton Court Shield, Melon Ribbed, Shells, Footed, Reed & Barton, 9 In.	1121.00
Pitcher, Paneled, Swag Design, Durgin, c.1920, 8 In.	920.00
Pitcher, Panels, Monogram, MKH, 1923, Pinched Neck, Wm. Durgin Co., 8 In.	783.00
Pitcher, Pear Shape, Flower Scroll Handle, Stepped Pedestal Base, Marquand & Co., c.1835, 16 In.	3075.00
Pitcher, Pear Shape, Stepped Base, 1959, 8 In.	819.00

Pitcher, Renaissance Style, Lion's Head On Handle, Lobed Lip, Engraved, Coin, c.1859, 13 x 9 In.		3321.00
Pitcher, Repousse Flowers, Leaves, Thumb Rest, Coin, Harris & Hoyt, c.1850, 13 ¼ In. ..*illus*		5700.00
Pitcher, Rose Bouquet, Bombay Shape, Leaf Handle, Footed, T. Starr, Gorham, 11 In.		3894.00
Pitcher, Urn Shape, Scroll Handles, Watrous, 9 ¼ In.		480.00
Pitcher, Water, Baluster, Scroll Handle, Integral Spout, Fisher Silversmiths, c.1975, 9 x 5 In.		922.00
Pitcher, Water, Cartier, Lord Saybrook Pattern, Scroll Handle, Stepped Base, Cartier, 8 ¾ In....		1353.00
Pitcher, Water, Chased Flowers, Jennings Silver Co., c.1925, 9 ¼ In.		1035.00
Pitcher, Water, Classical, Flared Lip, C-Scroll Handle, Reeded Stepped Baluster Shape, 9 In....		1952.00
Pitcher, Water, Fourteenth Century, Tapered, Strainer Spout, Swing Handle, Shreve, c.1900, 6 In.		3318.00
Pitcher, Water, George II, Chased, Engraved, Scroll Handle, Tuttle Silver Co., c.1929, 9 ½ In..		1440.00
Pitcher, Water, Hepplewhite, Engraved, Monogram, Reed & Barton, c.1910, 9 ¾ In.		1062.00
Pitcher, Water, Leaves, Scrolls, Flowers, Wide Spout, Ear Handle, Durgin, c.1910, 9 In.		1126.00
Pitcher, Water, Loop Handles, Flared Foot, Monogram, Wallace, 1900s, 10 In.		711.00
Pitcher, Water, Paneled Pear Shape, Scroll Handle, Reed & Barton, 10 x 8 In.		1121.00
Pitcher, Water, Pear Shape, Chase, Embossed Flowers, Leaves, Scrolls, Gorham, 1892, 8 In......		4148.00
Pitcher, Water, Plymouth, Angular Handle, Engraved, Gorham, 1943, 10 In.		889.00
Pitcher, Water, Repousse, Flowers, Leaves, S-Shape Handle, Ribbed Spout, c.1860, 11 In........		2585.00
Pitcher, Water, Repousse, Jacobi & Jenkins, c.1900, 8 ¼ In.		2006.00
Pitcher, Water, Rose Point, Raised Flowers, Gadroon Base, Wallace, 9 x 9 In.		943.00
Plate, Bread & Butter, Lobed, Gadroon Edge, Plateau, Redlich & Co., c.1975, 6 ⅜ In., 8 Piece.		1845.00
Plate, Bread & Butter, Rose Point, Reticulated Flower Border, Wallace, 6 ¾ In., 12 Piece........		1524.00
Plate, Bread & Butter, Square, Flowers, Swags Panels, Wallace & Sons, c.1925, 5 ⅝ In., 12 Piece...		1045.00
Plate, Dinner, Medallion, Swag Border, Monogram, AKE, Baldwin & Miller, c.1920, 11 In., 12 Piece ...		7480.00
Plate, Flowers, Scrolls, Monogram, Theodore Neuhaus & Co., 1900s, 6 In., 12 Piece............		1440.00
Plate, Round, Key Border Decoration, Gorham, 1900s, 11 In., 4 Piece....................		2000.00
Plate, Service, Francis I, Reed & Barton, 1901, 11 In., 6 Piece		5166.00
Platter, Oval, Quail Handles, Hammered, Dominick & Haff, 1903, 19 x 11 In.		2032.00
Platter, Oval, Rolled Rim, Monogram, Whiting, 1919, 20 In...................		1304.00
Platter, Oval, Scalloped, Monogram, Dominick & Haff, 18 ¼ x 11 ½ In.		1150.00
Platter, Repousse, Jacobi & Jenkins, c.1900, 19 In.		1416.00
Platter, Rosepoint, Round, Pierced Rim, Stamped Flower Rondels, Wallace, 1900s, 17 In.		1304.00
Platter, Scrolled Engraving, Gadroon Edge, Whiting & Co., 14 ½ x 11 In.		575.00
Platter, Scrolling, Reticulated Border, Putti, Swag, Mount Vernon Co., c.1920, 11 ½ In.		538.00
Porringer, Carved Ivory Handle, Engraved Flowers, Gorham, c.1915, 2 x 7 In.		359.00
Porringer, Coin, Openwork Handle, Coin, Monogram, J. Clarke, c.1740, 7 ½ In.		1304.00
Porringer, Colonial Style, Pierced Keyhole Handle, Lunt, c.1910, 6 In.		118.00
Porringer, Embossed Garland Rim, Pierced Handle, Bigelow & Kennard, 1877, 1 ¾ x 7 ¾ In....		259.00
Porringer, Pierced Handle, Monogram, T. Coverly, Rhode Island, c.1760, 8 ¼ In.		1422.00
Porringer, Pierced Shaped Handle, Whiting & Co., c.1900, 1 ½ x 6 ⅞ In.		89.00
Porringer, Reticulated Handle, Monogram, Coin, c.1830, 7 ⅞ In.		326.00
Porringer, Round Bowl, 2 Elephants On Handle, Engraved, Arthur Stone Assoc., c.1923, 7 ¾ In..		1659.00
Pudding Spoon, Birds Nest, Eggs, Gold Washed Bowl, Cast Claw, Gorham, 1865, 10 ½ In......		1955.00
Punch Bowl, Flattened Spherical Body, Reticulated Wavy Rim, Gorham, 1901, 8 x 15 In.		2460.00
Punch Bowl, Flower Rim, 3 Scroll Handles, Engraved, Graff, Washbourne & Dunn, c.1918, 12 In.....		1778.00
Punch Bowl, Marked, Exemplar Paul Revere 1768, Watson, c.1950, 5 ½ x 11 In.		1422.00
Punch Bowl, Monogram, Graff, Washbourne & Dunn, 1900s, 7 x 14 In.		2300.00
Punch Ladle, Adams, Frank M. Whiting, 13 ½ In............		148.00
Punch Ladle, Antique Pattern, Engraved, Spout, Gorham, c.1890, 11 ¼ In.		119.00
Punch Ladle, Chantilly, Gorham, 15 In.		201.00
Punch Ladle, Curved & Flattened End, Monogram, W. Ball, 13 ½ In.......		502.00
Punch Ladle, Double Pouring, Repousse, S. Kirk & Son, 14 ¼ In.		374.00
Punch Ladle, Engraved SR, c.1790, 14 In.		275.00
Punch Ladle, Fiddle Thread, Monogram, Wood & Hughes, c.1890, 12 ⅞ In.		246.00
Punch Ladle, Figural Handle, Shield, Gilt Bowl, Mark, Wood & Hughes, c.1860, 15 In............		944.00
Punch Ladle, Fontainebleau, Gentleman On Handle, Gilt Wash Bowl, Gorham, c.1885, 13 In..		385.00
Punch Ladle, King's, Gold Wash Interior, John R. Wendt, c.1850, 13 ⅝ In.		296.00
Punch Ladle, Les Cinq Fleur, Back Tipt Stem, Double Spouted Bowl, Reed & Barton, c.1900, 12 ½ In.		296.00
Punch Ladle, Oliver Pattern, Bailey, Kettell & Chapman, 11 ½ In.		138.00
Relish, Shell Shape, 2 Sections, 2 Scroll Handles, Claw Feet, Reed & Barton, 4 x 11 In.		384.00
Salad Servers, Francis I, Gold Washed Bowl, Tines, Reed & Barton, 9 In., Pair......................		474.00
Salad Servers, Gold Wash Bowl, Pinecone Handles, Gorham, c.1890, 11 In.....................		770.00
Salad Servers, Tipt Fiddleback Handle, Hammered, Porter Blanchard, c.1910, 10 ½ In., Pair .		1304.00
Salt & Pepper, Heavily Chased Flowers & Leaves, Teardrop Shape, Kirk, 5 In.		531.00
Salt & Pepper, Roman Soldier In Medallion, Urn Shape, Ivory Finial, JLW, c.1830, 5 ½ In. ....*illus*		600.00
Salver, Card, Round, Flower, Fern Repousse Rim, 3 Ball & Claw Feet, Welsh & Bro., 1885, 6 In.		267.00
Salver, Diapered Acanthus Demilunes Rim, Monogram, Gorham, 1927, 12 In. Diam..............		474.00

Silver-American, Pitcher, Aesthetic Style, Repousse, Leaves, Flowers, Butterflies, Dominick & Haff, Marked, 8 In.
$10350.00

James D. Julia Inc.

Silver-American, Pitcher, Cylindrical, Strainer Spout, Wood Handle, Porter Blanchard, 1930-60, 7 ½ In.
$3318.00

Skinner, Inc.

Silver-American, Pitcher, Repousse Flowers, Leaves, Thumb Rest, Coin, Harris & Hoyt, c.1850, 13 ¼ In.
$5700.00

DuMouchelles Art Gallery

Silver-American, Salt & Pepper, Roman Soldier In Medallion, Urn Shape, Ivory Finial, JLW, c.1830, 5 ½ In.
$600.00

DuMouchelles Art Gallery

Silver-American, Spoon, Elongated Oval Bowl, Husk Pendant, Monogram, Paul Revere, c.1790, 5 In.
$590.00

Early American History Auctions, Inc.

Silver-American, Strainer Ladle, King George, Enameled, Gold Fleur-De-Lis, Gold Washed, Gorham, 6 In.
$119.00

Skinner, Inc.

Sandwich Server, Round, Poppy Flower, Embossed, Wallace Silversmiths, c.1980, 10 ¼ In....	461.00
Sauceboat, Underplate, Plymouth, Square Handle, Scalloped Rims, 1926.	354.00
Server, Cover, Repousse, Handles, Leaves, Flowers, Dominick & Haff, 9 ½ x 14 In.	5000.00
Server, Pierced & Chased, Scrolls, Ivory Handle, Whiting, 10 ¾ In.	207.00
Server, Presentation, Bright Cut, Case, Silk Liner, 8 ¾ In.	121.00
Serving Bowl, Grape Leaf Shape, Twig Handle, Redlich & Co., c.1899, 8 ½ In.	1185.00
Serving Bowl, Oblong, Grape Handles, Acanthus Feet, Durham, c.1950, 15 In.	948.00
Serving Dish, Boat Shape, Relief Flowers, Applied Shaped Leaf Border, S. Kirk, 15 ½ x 8 ½ In.	748.00
Serving Fork, Hammered, Kalo Shop, 9 ⅞ In.	119.00
Serving Spoon, Arabesque, Wide Oval Bowl, Whiting Mfg., c.1895, 12 ½ In.	356.00
Serving Spoon, Ivy, Oval, Pierced Shoulders, Monogram, Gorham, c.1870, 10 In.	207.00
Serving Spoon, Oyster Shell Shape, Bamboo Design Handle, Gorham, 10 In.	1304.00
Sherbet & Spoon Set, Wallace, 3 x 3 In., 12 Piece	480.00
Sherbet, Footed, Wallace, 2 ½ In., 6 Piece	328.00
Sherbet, Monogram, Frank W. Smith Silver Co., c.1920, 3 x 4 In., 12 Piece	1035.00
Shoehorn, Black, Starr & Frost, 7 In.	120.00
Shoehorn, Jacobi & Jenkins, c.1900, 6 ½ In.	177.00
Soup Ladle, Burnett & Rigden, Washington, D.C., c.1840, 14 In.	300.00
Soup Ladle, Cottage, Gorham, c.1890, 11 ¼ In.	119.00
Soup Ladle, Fiddle Thread Pattern, Engraved, 1800s, 12 ¾ In.	837.00
Spoon, Aesthetic, Sunflower Finial, Gorham, Case, c.1890, 12 Piece	185.00
Spoon, Coin, South Carolina, Duffel, c.1800, 5 ⅛ In.	240.00
Spoon, Elongated Oval Bowl, Husk Pendant, Monogram, Paul Revere, c.1790, 5 In. ......*illus*	590.00
Spoon, Stirring, Jenkins & Jenkins, c.1910, 12 ½ In.	118.00
Strainer Ladle, King George, Enameled, Gold Fleur-De-Lis, Gold Washed, Gorham, 6 In. ....*illus*	119.00
Strawberry Fork Set, Monogram, R. Blackinton & Co., c.1890, 6 Piece	161.00
Sugar & Creamer, Art Moderne, Teak Handle, Redlich, 4 ¼ In.	620.00
Sugar & Creamer, Caramel, Oval, Hammered, Angular Handles, Wallace, c.1904, 2 ¼ In.	207.00
Sugar & Creamer, Cover, 4 Quadrant Body, Leaf Band, Monogram, c.1845, 7 & 9 ½ In.	805.00
Sugar & Creamer, Parcel Gilt, Flared Oval, Twig Loop Handles, Engraved, Whiting, c.1875, 4 ½ In.	563.00
Sugar & Creamer, Scroll Handle, Bud Finial, Beaded, Coin, Philadelphia, c.1840, 10 x 9 In..	1080.00
Sugar & Creamer, Squat, Oval, Wheeled Rims, Loop Handles, Gorham, c.1874, 3 x 2 In.	474.00
Sugar Sifter, Florentine Decoration, J. Wendt, 7 ⅝ In.	365.00
Sugar Urn, Goblet Shape, Peaked Lid, Beaded Rim, Trumpet Foot, Square Base, c.1795, 9 In., Pair...	2083.00
Sugar, Cover, Bird Finial, Footed, Coin, R & W Wilson, 10 In.	1380.00
Sugar, Cover, Repousse Flowers, Monogram, Footed, Berry Finial, A.E. Warner, 9 In.	1062.00
Sugar, Cover, Vase Shape, Dome Lid, Strawberry Finial, Branch Handles, c.1850, 10 In.	3585.00
Table Casket, Peacock Finial, Scrolling Leaves, Scrolled Toes, Lion Masks, 5 In.	366.00
Tazza, Lobed, Flared Rim, Chased Repousse Flowers, Scrolls, Gorham, 1891, 4 x 9 In., Pair....	1968.00
Tazza, Round, C-Scrolls, Pine Needles, Pinecones, J.E. Caldwell & Co., 3 ¾ In.	650.00
Tea & Coffee Set, Beaded, Geometric Borders, C Monograms, Gorham, c.1870, 5 Piece	2185.00
Tea & Coffee Set, Coffeepot, Teapot, Sugar, Creamer, Waste Bowl, Tray, Gorham, 32-In. Tray.	10030.00
Tea & Coffee Set, Kettle, Stand, Coffeepot, Teapot, Gorham, Kettle 10 ½ In., 3 Piece	1495.00
Tea & Coffee Set, Old Silver Pattern, Renaissance Revival, Gorham, c.1865, 5 Piece	5605.00
Tea & Coffee Set, Oval, Serpentine, Leaf & Scroll, Egg Finials, Grogan, 6 Piece	4000.00
Tea & Coffee Set, Puritan, Gorham, Coffeepot, Teapot, Sugar, Creamer, Bowl	2006.00
Tea & Coffee Set, Repousse, Footed Vase Shape, Scroll Handles, c.1855	9261.00
Tea & Coffee Set, Squat Pear Shape, Ball Finials, Leaves, Gorham, 8 ½ In., 6 Piece	6000.00
Tea & Coffee Set, Stems & Tendrils, Hammered, Globular, Peer Smed, 1935, 4 Piece	13035.00
Tea & Coffee Set, Talisman Rose Pattern, Frank Whiting, c.1948, 6 Piece	2214.00
Tea Canister, Round Cap, Tapered Body, Engraved Flowers, Stepped Foot, Gorham, 1895, 5 In.	356.00
Tea Set, 6 Panels, Stepped Rim & Foot, Angular Handle, Wallace, 4 Piece	1566.00
Tea Set, Fairfax, Hot Water Pot, Covered Sugar, Waste Bowl, Tray, Gorham, 7 In.	1600.00
Tea Set, Repousse, Neoclassical Vase Shape, Ram's Head Handles, A.E. Warner, 4 Piece	7380.00
Tea Set, Teapot, Coffeepot, Creamer, Sugar, Cover, Signed Mulholland, 9 x 4 In.	2160.00
Tea Set, Teapot, Hot Water Pot, Sugar, Creamer, Waste Bowl, Tray, Fisher Cape Cod, 6 Piece...	2023.00
Tea Strainer, Boat Shape, Griffin Heads, Gorham, 2 ½ In.	295.00
Tea Strainer, Swing Handle, Double Prong, Cut Design, c.1900, 2 x ¾ In.	65.00
Tea Tray, Rectangular, Rolled Rim, Demilune Handles, Monogram, Watson, 1900s, 26 In.	3555.00
Teapot, Creamer, Oval, Ball Finial, Pinched Neck, John B. Jones, c.1825, 8 In.	800.00
Teapot, Hinged Lid, Ebony Finial, Embossed, Marked Birks, 5 ½ x 11 ½ In.	575.00
Teapot, J.E. Caldwell & Co., Philadelphia, 8 ½ In.	444.00
Teapot, Lid, Lobed Body, Die-Rolled Borders, Coin, J. Ewan, 1800s, 10 ½ In. ......*illus*	3540.00
Teapot, Old Baltimore, Chinoiserie, Inverted Pear Shape, Repousse, c.1830, 7 ½ In.	1845.00
Teapot, Relief Landscape, Buildings, Cow, Bridge, Globular, S. Kirk & Son, 9 In.	2006.00
Teapot, Ribbed, Oval Urn Finial, Gadroon Chased Rim, Jos. Shoemaker, c.1798, 7 ½ In.	2800.00

Teaspoon, Candlelight, Tapered Handle, Flowers, Marked Towle, c.1934, 6 In., 12 Piece	334.00
Teaspoon, Contest Award, Pretty Baby, Sterling, Whiting, c.1900, 4 ¾ In.	191.00
Teaspoon, Fiddle Shape Handle, Pointed Tip Bowl, James Watts, c.1850, 6 In., 12 Piece	213.00
Tongs, Flat & Claw Ends, A.E. Warner, 9 ½ In.	443.00
Tongs, Neo-Grec Claw Bowls, George B. Sharp, Philadelphia, 1847, 8 ½ In.	185.00
Tongs, Sheaf-Of-Wheat Decoration, Shell Finial, J. Wendt, 6 ⅞ In., Pair	395.00
Tongs, Shell Terminal, Coin, Marked Peabody, c.1840, 6 ½ In.	720.00
Tray, 2 Handles, Flower Design, Beaded Rim, Rectangular, 1900s, 26 In.	2585.00
Tray, Bud, Scroll & Berry Design, Caldwell & Co., c.1900, 21 x 15 In.	3360.00
Tray, Chantilly Grand Pattern, Oval, Handles, Marked Gorham, 1900s, 29 x 18 In.	4130.00
Tray, Chippendale Style, Shaped Rim, 3 Paw Feet, Dominick & Haff, 10 In.	518.00
Tray, Chippendale, Round, Piecrust Edge, Gorham, 1946, 14 In.	1304.00
Tray, Commemorative, Chippendale, Gorham, 1947, 12 In.	1020.00
Tray, Flared Rim, Molded Edge, Black, Starr & Gorham, c.1950, 13 x 8 ½ In.	799.00
Tray, Flowers, Stippled Ground, Oval, Double Handles, Gorham, c.1925, 22 ¼ x 16 In.	2530.00
Tray, Footed, Shaped Corners, Cartier, 1900s, 11 ¾ In.	1003.00
Tray, Grape & Leaf Border, Round, Barbour, c.1930, 16 In.	125.00
Tray, Hanover, Reed & Barton, 1928, 28 In.	4200.00
Tray, Heart Shape, Openwork, Gorham, 3 In.	57.00
Tray, Kidney Shape, Scrolled Leaves, Oval Reserve, Gorham, 1917, 17 In.	1422.00
Tray, Old Newbury Crafters, Lobed, 5 ¾ x 7 ¾ In.	259.00
Tray, Oval, Bud, Scroll & Berry Design, Caldwell & Co., c.1900, 24 x 10 In.	2880.00
Tray, Oval, Chased Flower Scrolls, Fleur-De-Lis Border, Handles, Dominick & Haff, 25 x 18 In.	2415.00
Tray, Oval, Grapevines, 4 Cartouches, Birds, Stags, Handles, Ball, Black & Co., c.1850, 26 In. .... *illus*	3851.00
Tray, Plymouth, Monogram, Gorham, c.1930, 14 ⅜ In.	1121.00
Tray, Roll, Monogram, Repousse Roses Along Rim, Oval, Stieff Co., 1922, 13 In.	588.00
Tray, Round, Embossed Edge, Gorham, 10 In.	238.00
Tray, Round, Gorham, c.1909, 16 x 11 In.	1035.00
Tray, Round, Pierced Rim, Monogram, Redlich & Co., 11 In.	403.00
Tray, Round, Reeded Banding Around Rim, Gorham, c.1971, 12 In.	531.00
Tray, Round, Repousse Border, Loop, Dart & Garlands, Flower, Gorham, 17 In.	950.00
Tray, Round, S. Kirk & Sons, 11 In.	690.00
Tray, Round, Stepped Border, Monogram, J.E. Caldwell & Co., c.1900, 16 In.	1200.00
Tray, Scroll Molded Openwork Border, Howard Sterling, c.1900, 17 In.	900.00
Tray, Square Shape, Shallow, Blossoms & Tendril Rim, Round Stepped Foot, 3 x 14 ¾ In.	1875.00
Trivet, Oval, Reticulated, Engraved, Flower Garland, Gadroon Rim, Ball Feet, Gorham, 1909, 11 In.	711.00
Tumbler, Tapered Cylindrical, Reeded Rim, Officer On Horseback, Inscribed, c.1795, 3 ¼ In.	1067.00
Tureen, Cover, Handles, Monogram, Gorham, 15 In. .... *illus*	823.00
Tureen, Cover, Oval, Vines, Grapes, Twisted Vine Handles, Spread Foot, c.1855, 15 ½ In.	35850.00
Tureen, Soup, Dome Lid, Fruitwood Finial, Reeded, Oval, Angular Handles, Gorham, 1903, 14 ½ In.	1304.00
Vase, Bud, Trumpet Shape, Applied Lily Of The Valley, c.1875, 6 In.	474.00
Vase, Flared, Spiral Design, Round Foot, Tuttle Silver Co., c.1943, 7 ½ x 8 In.	780.00
Vase, Flower Basket Shape, Weighted, Footed, Clarence A. Vanderbilt, 15 In.	148.00
Vase, Fluted, Smooth Neck, Flared Rim, Round Foot, Mueck-Cary Co., c.1950, 9 In.	531.00
Vase, Pedestal Base, Cylindrical Body, Scalloped Rim, Monogram, U.S.A., 7 x 10 In.	196.00
Vase, Pierced Below Lip, Flower Accents, Monogram, Meriden Britannia, 14 In. .... *illus*	240.00
Vase, Repousse, Baluster Shape, Flared Rim, Round Foot, A.G. Schultz & Co., 11 In.	1100.00
Vase, Scalloped, Repousse Pierced Rim, Chased, Footed, Reed & Barton, c.1925, 12 x 11 In.	5078.00
Vase, Triple Bud, Applied Vines & Leaves, Engraved, Gorham, 6 In.	316.00
Vase, Trumpet Shape, Lead Base, Hardy & Hayes, c.1920, 12 In.	186.00
Vase, Trumpet, Cement Filled Base, Black, Starr & Gorham, c.1940, 12 In.	266.00
Waiter, Chippendale Pattern, Round, Shaped, Poole & Co., c.1900, 13 ½ In.	944.00
Waiter, Oval, Molded Rim, Engraved, Rococo Scrolls, Bigelow Bros., 7 x 10 In.	676.00
Waiter, Round, Applied Scrolls, Shells, 3 Claw & Ball Feet, Coin, J. Howell, c.1805, 8 ⅞ In., Pair	1659.00
Waste Bowl, Cover, Serrated, Monogram, Marked, Hyde & Goodrich, c.1855, 4 x 6 In. ..*illus*	8066.00
Wine Coaster, Repousse, Flowers, Cupid, Shaped Edge, Black, Starr & Frost, c.1890, 2 ½ x 5 In. ..	330.00
Wine, Bell Shape Bowl, Trumpet Foot, Tuttle, 1969-74, 7 In., 8 Piece	1422.00

SILVER-ANGLO-INDIAN

Sculpture, Carriage, Cupola, Peacocks, Rearing Horses, Filigree, Base, 12 x 11 In.	610.00

SILVER-AUSTRALIAN

Teapot, Derby Trophy, Sterling, Wood Handle, Finial, Footed, W.J. Sanders, c.1970, 6 x 10 In.	649.00

SILVER-AUSTRIAN

Basket, Octagonal, Fixed Handle, Openwork, Wiener Werkstatte, 1900s, 7 x 6 In.	18800.00
Box, Flowers, Leaves, Branches, Twig Shape Handle, Rectangular, Footed, 1920s, 4 ¼ x 3 ½ In.	374.00
Compote, Pedestal, Round Foot, Ruffled Rim, Filigree Design, 14 Oz.	563.00

Silver-American, Teapot, Lid, Lobed Body, Die-Rolled Borders, Coin, J. Ewan, 1800s, 10 ½ In.
$3540.00

Brunk Auctions

Silver-American, Tray, Oval, Grapevines, 4 Cartouches, Birds, Stags, Handles, Ball, Black & Co., c.1850, 26 In.
$3851.00

Skinner, Inc.

Silver-American, Tureen, Cover, Handles, Monogram, Gorham, 15 In.
$823.00

Cowan's Auctions

Silver-American, Vase, Pierced Below Lip, Flower Accents, Monogram, Meriden Britannia, 14 In.
$240.00

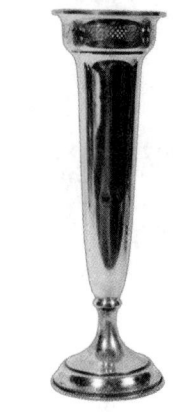

DuMouchelles Art Gallery

S

SILVER-AUSTRIAN

Silver-American, Waste Bowl, Cover, Serrated, Monogram, Marked, Hyde & Goodrich, c.1855, 4 x 6 In.
$8066.00

Neal Auction Co.

Silver-Chinese, Cigarette Case, Engraved Both Sides, Buildings & Landscapes, Monogram, 1900s, 5 ½ In.
$385.00

Skinner, Inc.

Silver-Chinese, Tea Set, Teapot, Covered Sugar, Creamer, Chased, Embossed, Scenes, c.1890, 5 ⅝ In., 3 Piece
$10413.00

Skinner, Inc.

Silver-Continental, Beaker, Ceremonial, Tapered Octagon, Chased, 7 Panels, Hebrew Letters, c.1890, 4 In.
$474.00

Skinner, Inc.

Compote, Repousse Flowers, Pink Embossed Glass Top, 8 ¼ x 11 ⅝ In.	184.00
Ewer, Ornate Embossed Jungle Animals, Birds, Leaves, Hinged Lid, 9 ½ x 5 ½ In.	1035.00
Parasol Handle, Enamel, Tortoiseshell Stem, Leaves, Cabochon Green Hardstone, c.1890, 2 ½ In.	245.00
Salt Stand, Double, Center Baluster Standard, 2 Side Cellars, c.1920, 6 x 6 In.	153.00
Tea Caddy, Hinged Lid, Oval, Leaf Design, Berry Finial, Handles, 4 Paw Feet, 1800s, 5 x 7 In.	1000.00
Tray, Pierced Corners, Stylized Flowers, Stamped, Singer, c.1900, 20 x 11 In.	1000.00
Wine Cooler, Flared, Reeded Rim, Ring Handles, Crown Monogram, 1827, 6 ¼ x 7 In.	1521.00

SILVER-AUSTRO-HUNGARIAN

Box, Dome Lid, Lobed, Flowers, Scroll Handle, Rectangular, c.1900, 6 x 4 In.	460.00
Chalice, Marble, 3-Tone, Art Deco, Tem, Birds, Mythical Beasts, K.K., c.1925, 6 In.	750.00
Cigarette Case, Enameled, Butterflies, Ladybug, 1900s, 4 x 3 In.	1188.00
Pitcher, Lobed, Circular Foot, C-Scroll Handle, Ivory Insulators, c.1922, 6 ½ In.	508.00

SILVER-BURMESE

Bowl, Rice, Bands Of Leaves, Figures, Repousse Design, 13 ½ In.	2356.00
Bowl, Rice, Repousse Design, Prisoner Capture, Archers, Chariots, 5 x 9 ½ In.	671.00
Box, Cover, Repousse Figures, Leaf Borders, Animal Masks, 1800s, 6 ¾ x 3 ¾ In.	1960.00

SILVER-CANADIAN

Mug, Tyg, Staghorn Handles, Presentation Inscription, Roden Bros., c.1910, 7 x 11 In.	837.00
Sugar & Creamer, Lobed Globular Shape, Flat Engraving, Henry Birks & Son, c.1930, 4 x 7 In.	598.00

SILVER-CHINESE

Bowl, Hammered, Scalloped Rim, 3 Dragons, Flaming Pearl, Footed, 10 ½ In.	8963.00
Bowl, Openwork Flowers, Ring Base, c.1895, 4 ¾ x 8 In.	1888.00
Bowl, Scalloped Rim, Panels, Flowers, Round Foot, 6 In. Diam.	1830.00
Box, Cover, 2 Dragons, Flowers, Animals, Repousse, Octagonal, Lobed, c.1905, 1 ⅝ x 2 ⅛ In.	551.00
Box, Cover, Enameled Flowers, Carnelian Cabochon, Rectangular, c.1950, 2 ½ x 2 ½ In.	738.00
Box, Figures, Lions, Insects, Chased, 1800s, 2 x 1 ¾ In.	354.00
Cigarette Case, Engraved Both Sides, Buildings & Landscapes, Monogram, 1900s, 5 ½ In. *illus*	385.00
Condiment Set, Man, Frame, Basket Salt, Mustard Pot, Pepper, Wheel Base, Zee Wo, c.1905, 4 In.	1778.00
Cup, Cover, Dragon Head Finial, Urn Shape, Embossed, Loop Handles, A. Lock, c.1905, 11 In.	8295.00
Ewer, Cover, Double Gourd, Dragons & Flowers, S-Shape Handle, 9 In.	5975.00
Fan, Parcel Gilt, Blue Cloisonne Scenes, Embossed Figures, Filigree Wheels, Case, c.1890, 10 In.	8295.00
Sauce Bowl, Round, Dragon Band, 5 ⅛ In., 12 Piece	3081.00
Tea Caddy, Lid, Enameled Flowers, Leaves, Stones, c.1875, 7 In.	1880.00
Tea Set, Teapot, Covered Sugar, Creamer, Chased, Embossed, Scenes, c.1890, 5 ⅝ In., 3 Piece *illus*	10413.00
Tea Set, Teapot, Creamer, Sugar, Chased, Embossed, Bamboo, Pear Shape, Hoching, c.1860, 5 ½ In.	4444.00
Tea Set, Teapot, Sugar & Creamer, Dragon, Flaming Pearl, Bamboo Shape Handles, 3 Piece	6573.00
Tray, Dragons, Characters, Chased, Embossed, c.1905, 18 x 11 In.	3555.00
Tray, Dragons, Flower Handles, Pierced Border, Chased, c.1900, 16 x 12 In.	4780.00
Tray, Warriors, Horses, Square Bamboo Shaped Handles & Border, 23 x 16 In.	11950.00
Vase, Trumpet Shape, Pierced Bamboo, Birds, Handles, Luen Wo, Shanghai, c.1900, 4 ½ In., Pair	2015.00
Vase, Trumpet Shape, Scalloped Rim, Chrysanthemums, Round Foot, 1800s, 11 In., Pair	1434.00

SILVER-CONTINENTAL

Basket, Oval, Repousse Flowers, Cherubs, Pierced, Handle, Flaring Base, c.1900, 6 ⅝ x 5 ¾ In.	118.00
Beaker, Ceremonial, Tapered Octagon, Chased, 7 Panels, Hebrew Letters, c.1890, 4 In. *illus*	474.00
Beaker, Chased, Bands, Persian Style Flowers, Hebrew Inscription, 1907-17, 4 ⅜ In. *illus*	711.00
Belt, Link, Repousse Cherubs, Fleur-De-Lis, Grapes, 37 In.	173.00
Bowl, Ecuelle, Dome Lid, Louis XV Style, Bowl, Handles, Fruit, Flowers, Cabbage Finial, c.1890, 11 In.	711.00
Bowl, Reeded, Crimped Rim, 6 Medallions, Cabochon, Scroll Feet, c.1900, 10 In. Diam.	337.00
Centerpiece, Nef, 3-Masted Ship, Blue Enameled Sails, Garnets, Pearls, c.1900, 13 x 10 In. *illus*	8850.00
Centerpiece, Oval, Openwork, Infants, Scroll Handles, Putto, Flowers, 1800s, 16 In.	1900.00
Centerpiece, Swan, Head Lowered, Hinged Wings, Upright Tail Feathers, 8 x 11 In., Pair	3125.00
Chalice, Ceremonial, Multicolor Semiprecious Stones, Wirework, Beaded, 1900s, 7 ⅝ In. *illus*	479.00
Claret Jug, Stand, Bottle Shape, Pouring Lip, Grapes, S-Shape Handle, c.1900, 13 In.	1500.00
Collar Box, Serpentine Oval, Battle Scenes, Scrolls, Flowers, Stippled Ground, 1900s, 9 In.	1304.00
Dresser Box, Chased, Embossed, Putti Panels, Hanau, c.1900, 5 x 3 In.	415.00
Fruit Basket, Oval, Lobed Body, Applied Double Handles, Stepped Foot, c.1800, 7 ½ x 11 In.	863.00
Ice Bucket, Urn Shape, Scroll Handles, Knopped Lid, Repousse Design, 13 x 12 In.	4025.00
Incense Boat, Scrolled Finials, Hinged Lid, Baluster Stem, Dome Foot, 1700s, 6 ½ In.	674.00
Muffineer, Domed Lid, Repousse, Baluster Shape, Scrolling Leaves, Fruit, 4 ¾ In.	209.00
Punch Ladle, Strainer Spout Bowl, Wood Handle, 1800s, 20 ½ In.	237.00
Salad Servers, Spoon, Fork, Openwork Handles, Sailboat Terminals, 12 In., 2 Piece	325.00
Soup Ladle, Parcel Gilt Oblong Bowl, Monogram, 1800s	115.00
Spoon, Anointing, Teardrop Shape Bowl, Slender Stem, Engraved Vine, c.1600, 6 ⅛ In.	385.00
Spoon, Tapered Stem, Scrolls, Vines, Monogram, c.1632, 7 In.	444.00

S

Tea Caddy, Ornate Repousse, Cherubs, Courting Couples, c.1890, 4 ½ In.	316.00
Teapot, Tete-A-Tete, Germany, c.1860, 4 ½ x 7 In.	418.00
Tureen, Hammered, Dome Lid, Urn Finial, Square Handles, Round Foot, 13 x 18 In.	2233.00
Tureen, Underplate, Oval, Artichoke Finial, Leaves, Flowers Engraved, c.1990, 13 x 17 In.	4029.00
Tussie Mussie, Corsage Holder, Grapes, Leaf Tips, Scroll Handle, Chain & Ring, c.1895, 6 In.	356.00
Urn, Cover, 3 Cherubs At Base, Dragon Handles, Swan Finial, 6 ½ In.	288.00
Wine Fountain, Grape Bunches, 8 Branches, Holding Cups, Center Cup, 1900s, 17 In.	1500.00

SILVER-DANISH

Beaker Set, Hammered, Tapered, Beaded, Engraved, Georg Jensen, c.1936, 6 In., 12 Piece	11950.00
Beaker, Tapered, Cylindrical, Embossed Fruit & Flowers, c.1890, 3 ¼ In.	178.00
Bowl, 4 Lobes, 4 Openwork Designs, Monogram, International Royal Danish, 12 In.	595.00
Bowl, Flared, Hammered, Openwork Stem, Georg Jensen, c.1915, 4 x 7 In.	1422.00
Bowl, Openwork Standard, Footed, G. Jensen, c.1910, 5 ½ In.	911.00
Bowl, Oval, Circular Foot, Grape Cluster Handles, 1948-58, 6 ½ x 6 ¼ In.	478.00
Butter Chip, People, Trading In Market, 3 ¼ In.	34.00
Cake Server, Blossom & Bead Handle End, O. Morgensen, 10 In.	237.00
Chalice, 12 Apostles, Jesus, Followers Silhouette Base, Hans Christensen, 1963, 10 x 5 In.	2678.00
Chalice, Interfaith, Lobed, Tapered Stem, Hans Christensen, 1975, 8 ½ x 4 ¾ In.	1751.00
Cigarette Box, Double Bud Feet, Hinged, Leaf Wreath, Georg Jensen, c.1920, 8 In.	3483.00
Cocktail Shaker, Art Deco Style, Melon Ribbon Handles, Evald Nielsen, c.1935, 7 ¾ In.	1840.00
Coffee Set, Oval, Hammered, Coffeepot, Creamer, Sugar, Cover, Hansen, c.1936, 7 ⅜ In., 3-Piece	1659.00
Compote, Applied Grapes, Twisted Stem, Georg Jensen, c.1930, 5 x 5 In.	1035.00
Compote, Grapevine Pattern, Georg Jensen, 5 In., Pair	3164.00
Compote, Signed Georg Jensen, 5 x 2 ½ In.	420.00
Dish, Flared & Flattened, Hammered, Short Cylindrical Foot, Georg Jensen, 7 In.	474.00
Dressing Spoon, Threaded Handle, Egg Shape Bowl, Engraved Initials, 15 In.	149.00
Fish Platter, Oval, Applied Rim Flowers, Vines, Georg Jensen, c.1930, 23 In.	5629.00
Fork & Spoon, Cactus Pattern, Marked Demark, Georg Jensen, 6 ½ In.	630.00
Jewelry Box, Rosewood Inset, Oval, Hans Christensen, 1954, 5 x 6 ¾ In.	4250.00
Knife, Folding, 2 Blades, Box, Georg Jensen, 6 In.	288.00
Ladle, Acorn, Georg Jensen, 7 ½ In.	239.00
Ladle, Curved End, Engraved Leaves, Graduated Beads, Georg Jensen, 6 ½ In.	307.00
Ladle, Pattern No. 21, Georg Jensen, c.1904, 5 ½ In.	199.00
Pie Server, Cactus Pattern, Georg Jensen, 10 In.	115.00
Pie Server, Georg Jensen, Sterling Silver Handle, 9 In.	240.00
Pitcher, Chocolate, Rosewood Straight Handle, Finial, H. Christensen, 1950, 6 x 4 In.	2800.00
Pitcher, Grape, Ebonized Handle, Georg Jensen, c.1930, 9 In.	4830.00
Pitcher, Hammered, Wood Handle, Engraved, Hans Hansen, 1950, 5 ⅝ In.	760.00
Pitcher, Water, Lobed, Tilted, Rosewood Handle, Hans Christensen, 1959, 13 x 7 In.	14000.00
Plate, Shallow, Round, Hammered Borders, Beaded Rim, Georg Jensen, c.1926-32, 14 In.	2500.00
Salad Servers, Fork & Spoon, Hollow Handle, Leaf Bud Finials, Georg Jensen, c.1920, 8 ¾ In.	504.00
Salad Servers, Stylized Flower, Pierced Handle, Georg Jensen, c.1948, 9 ⅝ In., Pair *illus*	1185.00
Salad Set, Ornamental, G. Jensen, c.1933, 7 In.	590.00
Saltcellar & Spoon, Cactus, Cobalt Blue Interior, Georg Jensen, c.1950, 2 ½ In.	110.00
Sauce Ladle, Hammered, Geometric Handle, Georg Jensen, c.1946, 7 ¾ In.	359.00
Sauceboat, Grape Bunches, Oval Bowl, Pedestal Foot, Georg Jensen, 7 x 9 In.	2988.00
Sauceboat, Short Spout, Curved Tapered Handle, Oval, Georg Jensen, c.1920, 5 In.	1304.00
Sculpture, Drill In Ocean Stabile, Abstract, Smooth, Textured, Base, H. Christensen, 1975, 6 x 6 ¼ In.	1700.00
Sculpture, Hearing Stabile, Abstract Spiral, Wood Base, H. Christensen, 1975, 6 x 4 ½ In.	1300.00
Sculpture, Speed Stabile, Aeronautic Abstract, Wood Base, H. Christensen, 1975, 5 x 10 ¼ In.	2200.00
Serving Fork, 3 Tines, Openwork Handle, Flower Terminal, Georg Jensen, 10 In.	830.00
Serving Spoon, Cactus, Georg Jensen, c.1940, 8 ⅞ In.	296.00
Serving Spoon, Leaf Bowl, Curled Beaded Handle, Georg Jensen, 1915, 8 In.	178.00
Tazza, Pierced Leaf, Pineapple Stem, Impressed, Georg Jensen, 2 ½ x 7 In.	1287.00
Tomato Server, Horn Bowl, Shell Shape Terminal, Georg Jensen, c.1910, 8 ¾ In.	119.00
Tray, Pyramid, Oval, Stepped Curved Handles, Georg Jensen, 14 x 7 ¾ In.	5617.00

SILVER-DUTCH

Basket, Sweetmeat, Tray, Oval, Ornate, Pierced, Bird, Flower Panels, Ball & Claw Feet, 7 x 5 ¾ In.	662.00
Bowl, Footed, Oval, 2 Handles, Repousse Scroll & Flowers, 9 x 7 In.	633.00
Bowl, Lobed, Oval, Beast Masks, Shield, Scroll Handles, 1752, 8 x 4 In.	948.00
Coffeepot, Lid, Berry Finial, Oval, Chased Shells, Rondels, Cherubs, Crabstock Feet, c.1890, 7 In.	444.00
Cruet Stand, Central Handle, Coiled Snake, 2 Glass Cruets, Reeded Ring Frame, c.1900, 10 In.	443.00
Salad Servers, Figural Handles, Windmills, Figures On Bowl, c.1910, 10 ½ In. *illus*	177.00
Salad Serving Tongs, Spoon & Fork Ends, Den Bosch, 1839, 11 ½ In.	338.00
Spoon, Marriage, Oval, Engraved With Armorial, Openwork Stem, 1895, 12 ¾ In.	125.00
Tea Caddy, Cover, Square Shape, Reeded Banding, Fluted Ball Finial, Marked, 1819, 5 In.	767.00

Silver-Continental, Beaker, Chased, Bands, Persian Style Flower, Hebrew Inscription, 1907-17, 4 ⅜ In. $711.00

Skinner, Inc.

Silver-Continental, Centerpiece, Nef, 3-Masted Ship, Blue Enameled Sails, Garnets, Pearls, c.1900, 13 x 10 In. $8850.00

Ivey-Selkirk Auctioneers

Silver-Continental, Chalice, Ceremonial, Multicolor Semiprecious Stones, Wirework, Beaded, 1900s, 7 ⅝ In. $479.00

Skinner, Inc.

S

Silver-Danish, Salad Servers, Stylized Flower, Pierced Handle, Georg Jensen, c.1948, 9 ⅝ In., Pair $1185.00

Skinner, Inc.

Silver-Dutch, Salad Servers, Figural Handles, Windmills, Figures On Bowl, c.1910, 10 ½ In.
$177.00

Ivey-Selkirk Auctioneers

Silver-English, Box, Hinged Lid, Engraved, Hallmark, Samuel Pemberton, Birmingham, 1798, 1 ¾ In.
$308.00

DuMouchelles Art Gallery

Silver-English, Cruet Set, 5 Cut Glass Bottles, Stand, F. Purton & T. Johnson, London, 1793-94, 8 In.
$960.00

DuMouchelles Art Gallery

Silver-English, Dish, Entree, Edwardian, Gadroon Borders, Removable Handle, Sheffield, 1903, 11 x 8 In.
$1793.00

Neal Auction Co.

SILVER-EGYPTIAN

Bowl, Cover, Turned Finial, Engraved Crown Initials, Raised Handles, c.1925, 6 In., Pair 1126.00

SILVER-ENGLISH. English sterling silver is marked with a series of four or five small hallmarks. The standing lion mark is the most commonly seen sterling quality mark. The other marks indicate the city of origin, the maker, and the year of manufacture. These dates can be verified in many good books on silver. Silver prices in 2011 and 2012 became so high many pieces were worth more in meltdown value than as decorative silver. These prices are based on current silver values.

Asparagus Tongs, George III, Pierced, Chased, Wriggle Work Border, c.1809, 11 In.	598.00
Asparagus Tongs, George III, Squared Ends, Smith & Fears, 1795, 9 ½ In.	400.00
Asparagus Tongs, George III, Tapered Rectangular Arms, Engraved Crest, c.1795, 12 In.	356.00
Basket, Boat Shape, Reeded Rim, Swing Handle, Engraved, P. & A. Bateman, 1798, 13 ½ In.	1896.00
Basket, Boat Shape, Scrolled Cutwork Flowers, Swing Handle, Edward VII, 1905, 14 In.	1541.00
Basket, Floral Repousse, Scalloped Edge, Pierced Handle, Raised Feet, Martin Hall & Co., 14 x 11 In.	2988.00
Basket, George III, Oval, Reeded Swing Handle, Swags, Trophies, Engraved, Footed, 1786, 17 x 10 In.	1793.00
Basket, Repousse Flowers, Lobed, Openwork Border, Masks, Snakes, Oval, c.1898, 2 x 10 In.	325.00
Basket, Repousse, Gadroon, Swing Handle, Waterhouse, Hudson & Co., 1824, 13 ½ x 11 In.	2868.00
Berry Spoon, Chased Vine Pattern, Coquille Bowl, Eagle, c.1835, 10 ¼ In., Pair	1599.00
Berry Spoon, Hanovarian, Engraved, William Robertson, 1791, 8 ½ In.	207.00
Berry Spoon, King's Pattern, c.1810	127.00
Biscuit Box, Lobed Shape, Wood Finial, London, c.1914, 6 x 5 ¼ In.	920.00
Bottle Tag, Sherry, Port, Madeira, c.1838, 3 Piece	120.00
Bowl, Center Band, C-Curve Handles, Footed, Martin Hall & Co., c.1904, 5 x 9 In.	360.00
Bowl, Flared Rim, Flat Sphere, Mappin & Webb, Sheffield, c.1903, 6 x 10 In.	1476.00
Bowl, George VI, Volute Leaf Tip Ends, Pierced Scrollwork, Oval Foot, 1942, 6 ¼ x 11 In.	593.00
Bowl, Monteith, Round, Monogram, Molded Rim, Cherub Masks, Stepped Round Foot, 1895, 9 In.	3055.00
Bowl, Round, Chased, Embossed, Scrolled, 3 Bead & Leaf Feet, Lambert, 1891, 4 ½ In., Pair	504.00
Bowl, Round, Ruffle Rim, Pierced Design, Flowers, 4 Oz.	188.00
Bowl, Shaped Rim, Pierced, Birmingham, 1896, 8 x 10 ½ In.	230.00
Bowl, Shell Shape, Gadroon Rim, Female Bust, Fish, Kelp, Shells, 3 Dolphin Feet, Handle, 1945, 8 In.	3081.00
Box, Dome Lid, Hinged, Lion Mask & Ring Side Handles, Rectangular, 5 ½ In.	85.00
Box, Hinged Lid, Engraved, Hallmark, Samuel Pemberton, Birmingham, 1798, 1 ¾ In. *illus*	308.00
Box, Lid, Engraved Flowers, Monogram, Gilt Interior, Shaped Square, 1914, 3 ¼ x 4 ⅛ In.	236.00
Box, Oval, Dome Lid, Leaves, Coiled Snake Handles, Chrichton Brothers, George V, 1912, 8 In.	2105.00
Box, Slant Top, Hinged Lid, 4 ½ In.	271.00
Brandy Warmer, George I, George Wickes, London, c.1723, 8 ¾ In.	615.00
Brandy Warmer, George III, Round Treen Handle, Monogram, 4 x 11 In.	538.00
Brandy Warmer, George III, Wood Handle, T. Robins, 1803, 13 x 6 ½ In.	1380.00
Brandy Warmer, Oval, Armorial, Spire & Wood Finial, Hands & Sons, c.1880, 4 ½ In.	711.00
Bread Fork, Embossed Tines, Mother-Of-Pearl Handle, C.E. Williams, 1908, 5 ½ In.	165.00
Bugle, Hunting, Presentation, East Essex Hunt Club, Leather Case, c.1881, 9 ½ In.	1793.00
Cake Basket, Round, Lobed Panels, Flowers, Serpentine Rim, Swing Handle, William IV, 13 In.	2032.00
Cake Basket, Swing Handle, Beaded Top, Pierced Rim, Shield Crest, W. Abdy, 1781, 3 ½ x 14 In.	1912.00
Cake Basket, Swing Handle, Pierced Sides, Grapevine Rim, George II, Ball & Claw Feet	15275.00
Cake Server, Gothic Revival, Pierced Blade, Armorial Crest, Ivory Handle, 1809, 10 ½ In.	191.00
Candelabra are listed in the Candelabrum category.	
Candlesticks are listed in their own category.	
Card Caddy, Bridge, Lion's Heads, Footed, 8 x 2 x 1 In.	299.00
Chafing Dish, Stand, George III, Armorial, Reeded, Fluted, Fruit Finial, London, c.1825, 9 x 13 In.	2574.00
Chalice, Edwardian, Walker & Hall, Sheffield, c.1903, 12 In.	777.00
Charger, George I, Cartouche, Eagle, Fruit & Flowers, 1725, 9 ½ In. Diam.	521.00
Charger, William IV, Shaped Gadroon Rim, Engraved, 2 Crests, 1834, 9 ¾ In., Pair	1304.00
Cigar Box, Rectangular, Hinged Lid, Monogram, Wood Lined Interior, c.1878, 9 In.	488.00
Cigarette Box, Monogram, Stepped Lid, Cedar Lined, 2 x 7 In.	281.00
Coffee Set, Coffeepot, Open Sugar, Creamer, John Aldwinkle, James Slater, 1880	1265.00
Coffee Set, Coffeepot, Sugar, Creamer, Lobed, Mistletoe Handles, Crichton Bros., c.1905, 8 In.	861.00
Coffeepot, Acorn Finial, Domed, Hinged, Engraved Coat Of Arms, Thomas Parr, c.1750, 9 ½ In.	4183.00
Coffeepot, Cover, George III, Baluster, Flowers, Leaves, Scroll Wood Handle, 1771, 14 In.	1800.00
Coffeepot, Crested, Motto Macte, Gadroon Borders, Chased, c.1754, 11 ½ In.	956.00
Coffeepot, George II, Tapered, Ring Foot, Mark John Swift, 1742, 9 ¾ In.	1180.00
Coffeepot, George III, Baluster Shape, Swan Spout, Swirl Finial, William Grundy, c.1775, 10 In.	1265.00
Coffeepot, George III, Oval, Wood Finial, Engraved Swag, Bateman, 1799, 7 x 10 ¾ In.	590.00
Coffeepot, Lighthouse, Applied Leaf Spout, Fruitwood Handle, E. Feline, George II, c.1740, 9 In.	1185.00
Coffeepot, Scrolled Wood Handle, Twisted Oval Finial, 11 In.	950.00
Coffeepot, Swollen Cylindrical Shape, Acorn Finial, Treen Handle, c.1750, 10 In.	1375.00

Coffeepot, Urn Shape, Beaded Base, Shoulder & Lip, Round Foot, Loop Handle, 1785, 13 In. .	978.00
Compote, Lobed, Scalloped Rim, Flaring Domed Base, Crichton Bros., 4 x 8 In., Pair.............	563.00
Creamer, Dome Lid, George III, Reeded Rim, Angular Handle, Ball Finial, 1804, 4 ⅜ In.	356.00
Creamer, Flowers, Swag, Beaded Rim, High Handle, Helmet Shape, Mark, Charles Hougham, 5 In.....	230.00
Creamer, George II, Oval, 3 Hoof Feet, Elongated C-Scroll Handle, Ayme Videau, c.1737, 4 In...	896.00
Creamer, Helmet Shaped, Swags, Garlands, Square Base, Marked, Anne Bateman, c.1813, 6 In....	353.00
Creamer, Reeded Rim, Helmet Shape, Monogram, 4 ½ In.	138.00
Cruet Set, 5 Cut Glass Bottles, Stand, F. Purton & T. Johnson, London, 1793-94, 8 In. ....*illus*	960.00
Cruet Stand, George III, Double Diamond Shape, Pierced Gallery, William Abdy, 8 ¼ In........	118.00
Crumber, Ivory Handle, Robert Pringle & Sons, Sheffield, 1925, 12 ¾ In...................	96.00
Cup, 2 Handles, Trophy Style, Shaped Rim, Round Base, Inscribed, c.1915, 7 x 10 In......	531.00
Cup, Barrel Shape, Ribbed, Child's, c.1790, 3 In.....................................	411.00
Cup, Christening, William IV, Reeded Body, Scroll Handle, Joseph & John Angell, 3 In.............	598.00
Cup, Lid, Oval, Entwined Serpent Handles, Nike Finial, c.1790, 19 x 13 In...................	19680.00
Cup, Presentation, Cover, Mansion Grammar School, Chased, Globe Finial, c.1863, 14 In.......	2629.00
Cup, Urn Shape, Loop Handles, c.1790, 5 ½ In..	359.00
Dish Cross, Oval Front, Rococo Reeds, Flowers, Openwork Supports, H. Bailey, 1770, 10 In. ...	1541.00
Dish, Entree, Edwardian, Gadroon Borders, Removable Handle, Sheffield, 1903, 11 x 8 In. ......*illus*	1793.00
Dish, Entree, Lid, Leaf Finial, Gadroon Border, Dragon Crest, W. Elliot, 1817, 5 x 12 In., Pair..	7170.00
Dish, Shell Shape, Openwork Handle, 3 Dolphin Feet, 1909, 6 x 7 In.	443.00
Dish, Square, Flared Rim, Reticulated, Cartouches, Cherubs, C-Scrolls, Openwork Feet, 1888, 8 In.....	551.00
Dish, Sweetmeat, Boat Shape, Latticework, Swags, Goldsmith & Silversmiths Co., c.1900, 4 x 8 In.	522.00
Dish, Sweetmeat, Boat Shape, Rococo Flowers, Charles Stuart Harris, c.1890, 10 ½ x 8 In.	399.00
Dish, Warming, Cover, George III, Oval, Armorial, Engraved, Paul Storr, 1793-94, 15 In.	2360.00
Dish, Warming, Hinged Drop Ring Handles, Scroll Supports, Round Base, Sheffield, 4 x 11 In..	149.00
Dresser Box, Enameled Dog Hunt Scene Lid, c.1875, 1 ¾ x 5 ½ In., Pair...................	2133.00
Dresser Box, Lid, Chased, Embossed Couple, Scrolls, Mark, George III, 1801, 5 In..............	593.00
Dresser Box, Tortoiseshell Lid, 4 Applied Feet, Mappin & Webb, Birmingham, c.1911, 5 x 1 ¾ In.	575.00
Epergne, Pierced Scalloped Bowl, 4 Flared Arms, 4 Baskets, S. Dawson, c.1913, 11 x 12 In.......	3335.00
Ewer, Baluster, Cylindrical Neck, Ovolo Band, Twisted Reed Handle, 9 In.....................	6773.00
Ewer, Wine, Repousse Leaves, Medallions, Ribbed Waist, Applied Handle, 1902, 11 ½ In.........	3738.00
Figurine, Knight, Detailed Face, Armor, Shield, Sword, Mark, Charles Boyton, 10 In.............	4025.00
Fish Set, Column & Flowers, 12 Forks, 12 Knives, Charles Ellis & Co., c.1900	207.00
Fish Slice, Crested, Pierced & Curved, Wood Handle, 1772, 14 ¼ In...................	269.00
Fish Slice, Fiddle & Shell, Pierced Openwork, Entwined Strapwork, WK Mark, c.1825, 12 In...	267.00
Fish Slice, Fiddle & Shell, Threaded Blade, Pierced Flowers, Scrolls, J. Hayne, c.1830, 12 In. ..	207.00
Fish Slice, Fiddle Handle, Crest, Pierced Scimitar Blade, P. Bateman, W. Bateman, 1810, 12 In. .*illus*	299.00
Fish Tongs, Oval, Reticulated Blades, Threaded Handle, Monogram, 1810, 11 ¼ In.	326.00
Frame, Art Nouveau, Flowers, 11 x 10 In..	238.00
Frame, Grapevine Repousse Border, Birmington, c.1990, 9 ½ x 7 ¼ In.....................	127.00
Goblet, George III, Samuel Hennell, London, c.1802, 5 ⅜ In.............................	837.00
Gravy Boat, George V, Oval, Ogee Rim, C-Scroll Handle, Shell Topped Pad Feet, 1926, 4 ⅝ In...	237.00
Group, Horse Race, 3 Mounts, London, 1880, 5 x 6 ¾ In................................	1534.00
Hot Water Urn, Acanthus Cast Knop, Loop Handles, Sheffield, 20 In.......................	1875.00
Hot Water Urn, Regency, Dome Lid, Gadroon, Crested Handles, Old Sheffield, c.1925, 16 x 13 In.	615.00
Humidor, Wood Liner, Divider, Engraved Dedication, Harman Brothers, c.1934, 9 x 4 In.	196.00
Jewelry Box, Hinged Dome Lid, Chased Flowers & Leaves, 1921, 3 x 13 In...................	472.00
Jug, Hinged Lid, Wood Handle, Chased, Thomas Bradbury & Sons, 1898, 7 ¾ In.	478.00
Jug, Milk, Winged Cupid, Scrolls, Flowers, Marked, Beresford, 1889, 9 In. ....*illus*	767.00
Jug, Serpentine Handle, Flowering Vines, Domed Foot, John Jones, 1735, 7 ½ In. ....*illus*	3675.00
Julep Cup, Engraved Stag, John Harris, c.1803, 2 ⅝ In., Pair.........................	652.00
Kettle, Hot Water, Stand, Lobed, Scrolled, Dolphin Feet, R. Garrard, c.1842, 15 x 11 In.	3965.00
Ladle, Back Tipt Handle, London, 1898, 13 In..	259.00
Ladle, Downturned Fiddle Handle, Mark Lias, London, 1837, 13 In.	236.00
Ladle, Victorian, Fiddle Pattern, George Adams, c.1890, 13 In.	307.00
Lemon Strainer, Round, Pierced Bowl, 2 Cast Shape Handles, c.1780, 9 ½ In..................	478.00
Loving Cup, George III, 2 Handles, Pedestal Base, Marked, 1811-12, 5 In..............	460.00
Medallion, Speed Trials, Yorkshire Automobile Club, Malcolm Campbell, c.1922, 3 In.........	2629.00
Milk Pot, George II, Swollen Shape, Acorn Knop, Leaf Cast Spout, c.1754, 9 ¼ In.	960.00
Muffineer, Smokestack Shape, Openwork Top, Pedestal Foot, 1910, 8 In.	150.00
Mug, George III, Baluster Shape, Serpentine Handle, Spread Foot, 1762, 4 ⅞ In......................	474.00
Mug, George III, Loop Handle, Repousse Scrolling Leaves, c.1785, 5 In.	688.00
Mug, George III, Tapered, Cylindrical, Reeded, Ear Handle, Gold Wash Interior, 1800, 3 ⅜ In.	385.00
Mug, Incised, Lion, Swags, Leaf Capped Scroll Handle, Marked, Hester Bateman, 1783, 5 x 5 ¼ In. *illus*	2832.00
Mug, Repousse, Handle, Leafy Scroll Design, 1726-27, 4 ½ In........................	356.00
Mustard Pot, Dome Lid, George III, Oval, Openwork, Flower Heads, Leaf Tips, 1815, 4 x 4 In.	450.00

Silver-English, Fish Slice, Fiddle Handle, Crest, Pierced Scimitar Blade, P. Bateman, W. Bateman, 1810, 12 In.
$299.00

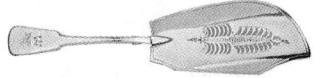

Neal Auction Co.

Silver-English, Jug, Serpentine Handle, Flowering Vines, Domed Foot, John Jones, 1735, 7 ½ In.
$3675.00

Skinner, Inc.

Silver-English, Jug, Milk, Winged Cupid, Scrolls, Flowers, Marked, Beresford, 1889, 9 In.
$767.00

Brunk Auctions

Invisible Mark

A new technique called acoustical imaging can be used to make rubbed-out hallmarks on silver visible again. A special type of image similar to an ultrasound can show the slight compression of the metal where the silver was stamped with the hallmark. Sounds like a good tool for museums and the very, very serious collector.

Silver-English, Mug, Incised, Lion, Swags, Leaf Capped Scroll Handle, Marked, Hester Bateman, 1783, 5 x 5 ¼ In.
$2832.00

Brunk Auctions

Silver-English, Sauceboat, George III, Beaded Rim, Charles Wright, 1777, 5 ½ x 7 ⅞ In.
$837.00

Neal Auction Co.

Silver-English, Sugar Castor, George III, c.1779, 8 ⅝ In.
$538.00

Neal Auction Co.

Mustard Pot, Ornate Pierced Body, Figures, Birds, Hinged, Glass Liner, 2 ¾ In.	374.00
Nail Buffer, Scrolls, Repousse, c.1909, 2 ¼ In.	75.00
Napkin Rings are listed in their own category.	
Nutmeg Grater, George III, Barrel Shape, Ribbed Design, 1795, 1 ⅞ In.	398.00
Papboat, George II, c.1736, 1 ¼ x 4 ½ In.	288.00
Pastry Fork, Blue Enamel Terminal, Box, Liberty & Co., 1928, 5 ⅛ In., 6 Piece	1600.00
Pitcher, Water, Scroll Handle, Acanthus Thumb, Bellflower Swag, Gilt Interior, c.1899, 7 ¾ In.	1298.00
Plate, Portrait, Queen Charlotte, George II, Repousse, 8 ½ In.	299.00
Platter, George II, Oval, Gadroon Edge, Peter Taylor, c.1752, 21 In.	2813.00
Platter, George III, Oval, Shell, Scroll Border, Thomas Robins, c.1811, 27 In., 4 Piece	18750.00
Platter, Oval, Gadroon, Leaves, Engraved Border, Armorial, George III, c.1825, 23 ½ In.	5036.00
Platter, Well & Tree, Gadroon, Scalloped Rim, Engraved Crest, Motto, 1805, 23 x 17 In.	5676.00
Punch Bowl, Gadroon Body, Footed, William Gibson, John Langman, c.1891, 9 x 16 In.	4183.00
Punch Ladle, Fiddle Thread & Shell, Coquille Bowl, Crest Of Holt, Squirrel, c.1812, 13 ¼ In.	492.00
Punch Ladle, Georgian, Stag Head Crest, W. Eley, W. Fearn, c.1800, 13 In.	219.00
Punch Ladle, Hanoverian Pattern, Monogram, London, 1803, 13 ¼ In.	230.00
Punch Ladle, Rampant Lion, Crown Coat Of Arms, Adey Bellamy Savory, 1829, 13 In.	288.00
Rattle, Victorian, Coral, Embossed, Leaves & C-Scrolls, 7 Bells, Whistle, c.1850, 5 ½ In.	474.00
Salt & Pepper, Chased Flowers, Bulbous Base, Domed, 3 Spade Feet, I. Freeman, 1956	325.00
Salt Set, Waved Bow & Shell Canopy, Viking Ship Shape, 1904, 2 ⅜ x 4 ¼ In., 4 Piece	497.00
Salt, Queen Anne, Open Footed, London, c.1742, 2 ½ x 1 ½ In., Pair	196.00
Salver, Engraved Armorial, Gadroon, Leaves, Shells, Claw & Ball, R. Rogers, 1770, 6 In., Pair	1067.00
Salver, Footed, Engraved Flower Border, Ball & Claw Feet, c.1730, 9 In.	896.00
Salver, Gadroon Rim, Round, 4 Ball & Claw Feet, H. Lambert, London, c.1930, 8 In.	345.00
Salver, George II, Round, Flared Serpentine Border, Applied Shells, Scrolling, Crest, c.1758, 17 In.	2868.00
Salver, George III, Gadroon Border, Engraved Crest, P. Storr, London, 1808, 9 In.	3585.00
Salver, George III, Scroll, Shell Border, Flower, Crest Engraving, John Mewburn, 1800, 16 ¼ In.	4183.00
Salver, Henry Brind, Shaped Rim, c.1750, 7 In.	443.00
Salver, Molded Edge, Scroll, Shell Rim, Coat Of Arms, 3 Pad Feet, John Carter, 1759, 13 In.	1778.00
Salver, Molded Rim, Beaded Edge, Monogram, Ball & Claw Feet, R. Rugg, 1798, 8 ¼ In., Pair	1304.00
Salver, Monogram In Shield, Shell & Scroll Rim, Pad Feet, J. Robinson, 1749, 12 In.	2655.00
Salver, Octagonal Lobed, Round, Reticulated Rim, Beaded, Henry Holland, 14 In.	2214.00
Salver, Round, Shaped Openwork Rim, Berries, Vines, Masks, 3-Footed, 1748, 8 In.	1500.00
Salver, Round, Shaped, Leaf Cast Border, 3 Scroll Feet, 1901, 20 In.	3660.00
Salver, Round, Stepped, Flaring Serpentine Rim, 3 Scroll Feet, 8 In.	418.00
Salver, Scalloped Border, Shells, Engraved, Pad Feet, Mark, William Peaston, c.1750, 9 ¾ In.	1180.00
Salver, Scalloped Rim, Engraved Crest, 3-Footed, Ebenezer Coker, 1759, 12 ¼ In.	1793.00
Salver, Scrolled Border, Engraved Motto, Hoof Feet, John Carter II, 1769, 12 In.	2031.00
Salver, Shaped Rim, Scroll Feet, Engraved Crest, Wreath, Swag, c.1735, 14 In.	1770.00
Salver, Shell, Scroll Border, Engraved Griffin Head, Tripod Hoof Base, c.1798, 9 x 9 In.	1955.00
Salver, Shell, Scroll Border, Scalloped, Crest, London, c.1750, 13 ¼ In.	2706.00
Sauceboat, Crimped Edge, 3 Shell Feet, Leaf Thumbguard, Crichton & Co., Ltd., 1908, 4 x 8 In.	259.00
Sauceboat, George III, Beaded Rim, Charles Wright, 1777, 5 ½ x 7 ⅞ In. ....*illus*	837.00
Sauceboat, George III, Oval, Elongated Spout, Loop Handles, Lion, 1804, 3 ⅛ In.	178.00
Sauceboat, George III, Scroll Handle, Footed, Wm. Chawner, c.1790, 10 ¾ In.	179.00
Sauceboat, Horse Head Crest, 1700s, 8 In.	316.00
Sauceboat, Lobed, Chased, Applied Leaf Handle, Ball Feet, Emes & Barnard, London, c.1826, 4 x 6 In.	366.00
Sauceboat, Oval Shape, Flared Rim, Leaf Handle, 3 Shell Feet, Engraved, 1770, 5 x 8 In.	800.00
Sauceboat, Oval, 3-Footed, Flared Serpentine Rim, C-Scroll Handle, 1918, 2 x 5 In., Pair	227.00
Sauceboat, Oval, Ogee Rim, Leaf Carved Handle, Monogram, George II, 1755, 3 In.	207.00
Sauceboat, Scroll Handle, Shell Design Feet, Birmingham, 1913, 4 x 6 ½ In.	173.00
Serving Spoon, King's Pattern, 1827, 12 In.	201.00
Sewing Egg, Hinged, Gilt Interior, Thread Holder, Needle Case, Thimble, c.1868, 1 ¾ x 1 ¼ In.	354.00
Shoe Buckle, George III, Pierced, Chased, c.1790, 2 ¼ x 3 In., Pair	207.00
Skewer, George III, Loop Terminal, Shell Collar, Tapered, 1761, 13 In.	380.00
Skewer, Meat, George III, Engraved Script Initials, Bateman, 14 ½ In.	149.00
Skewer, Meat, George III, Engraved, Crest, 1819, 14 ½ In.	296.00
Skewer, Tapered, Loop Top, Hester Bateman, London, 1830, 9 In.	162.00
Soup Ladle, Back Tipt, Engraved Crest, George III, T. Northcote, 1796, 13 ¼ In.	356.00
Soup Ladle, George IV, Fiddle Handle, Engraved Crest, London, c.1828, 12 ½ In.	230.00
Soup Ladle, Monogram, George Angell, Victorian, 1877, 12 ¾ In.	296.00
Soup Ladle, Monogram, WE Mark, 1832, 13 In.	356.00
Soup Ladle, Pointed Back Tipt, Monogram, WA Mark, George III, 1804, 14 ¼ In.	326.00
Soup Ladle, Round Tipt Handle, Mark, Peter & Ann Bateman, 14 In.	316.00
Spoon, Anointing, Engraved, Cast, Birmingham, c.1902, 9 In.	81.00
Spoon, Golf, Wood Shape, Marked, Goldsmiths & Silversmiths Co., c.1929, 8 In.	84.00

S

Spoon, Hester Bateman, London, 1785, 8 ½ In...	345.00
Spoon, Strainer, George III, Old English Pattern, c.1796, 12 In.	246.00
Stirrup Cup, Victorian, Fox Mask, Ears Up, Open Mouth, Marked, 1864-65, 4 ⅝ In.	8850.00
Strainer, Punch, George III, Scroll Handles, 1763, 12 In.............................	613.00
Stuffing Spoon, Engraved Crest, HS Mark, George III, 1794, 11 In., Pair	326.00
Stuffing Spoon, Geo. Smith & W.M. Fearn, London, c.1792, 12 In.................	120.00
Stuffing Spoon, Round Back Tipt Handle, Mark Thomas Wallis, London, c.1815, 12 In.	150.00
Sugar & Creamer, Squat, Bulbous, Shield, Sheffield, 1875, Creamer 2 ½ In., Sugar 3 In.	246.00
Sugar Basket, George III, Boat Shaped, Trumpet Foot, Beaded Rims, Swing Handle, 1789, 7 ⅛ In.	429.00
Sugar Castor, George III, c.1779, 8 ⅝ In. ....*illus*	538.00
Sugar Castor, Pierced Dome Lid, Octagonal, Birmingham Mark, 1907, 7 ½ In.	403.00
Sugar Castor, Pierced Dome Lid, Octagonal, Monogram S, Mark, London, 1908, 6 ¾ In.	259.00
Sugar Castor, Pierced Dome Lid, Urn Shape, George Hope, Sheffield, c.1910, 8 ¼ In.	431.00
Sugar Castor, Pierced Lid, Pedestal Foot, Hallmarks, HB, Hester Bateman, 1787, 8 ¼ In. .....*illus*	353.00
Sugar Nips, George II, Lion Passant, c.1760	450.00
Sugar Nips, Wakely & Wheeler, London, 4 ¼ In.	43.00
Sugar Shaker, Turned Finial, Pierced Top, Repousse Body, S. Walton, Smith, 1889, 8 ½ In. ...	356.00
Sugar Sifter, Gilt, Chased Vine, Serpentine Lobed Bowl, Pierced, Eagle, c.1835, 6 ¼ In.	1045.00
Sugar Tongs, Engraved, Acorn Nips, Monogram, H. Bateman, 5 In., Pair	119.00
Sugar Tongs, Harlequin Shape, 2 Circle Snake Handles, 4 In.	474.00
Tankard, Dome Lid, Tapered, Girdle Band, Monogram, H. Payne, George II, 1732, 7 In.	3851.00
Tankard, George III, Dome Lid, Coat Of Arms, c.1746, 7 ½ In.	3525.00
Tantalus, Chased Grapevines, 2 Rotating Doors, Fitted Interior, Bottles, 21 In.	1845.00
Tea Caddy, George III, Oval, Scrolling Vine, Beaded Borders, Ivory Knop, 1794-95, 6 In.	2242.00
Tea Stand, Oval, Engraved Leaves, Armorial, Splayed Feet, H. Chawner, George III, 1790, 7 In.	178.00
Tea Urn, Cover, Fluted, Upswept Scroll Handles, Spread Foot, 1785, 14 In.	1500.00
Teakettle, Stand, Oval Shape, Paneled Sides, Fixed Ivory Handle, c.1932, 12 In.	1250.00
Teakettle, Stand, Squat, Half Rib Design, Leaf Handle, 4 Paw Feet, Ebony Finial, 11 In.	920.00
Teakettle, Warming Stand, Squat, Geometric & Flower Design, Scroll Feet, c.1900, 14 In.......	144.00
Teapot Stand, George III, Oval, Engraved Crest, Swag, Flower Garland, Pierced Feet, 1786, 7 ⅜ In.	415.00
Teapot Stand, Shaped Lozenge Shape Body, Engraved, Footed, 8 In.............	411.00
Teapot & Coffeepot, Ebonized Mushroom Finial, Baluster, Barraclough & Sons, c.1940, 5 & 6 ¾ In..	1304.00
Teapot, Cylindrical, Straight Spout, Rattan Ear Handle, Ivory Oval Finial, E. Darvill, 1773, 5 In...	1007.00
Teapot, Flower Repousse, Figural Finial, Marked, c.1822, 4 ¾ In.	532.00
Teapot, Fluted, Engraved Flower Border, Wood Handle & Finial, J. Deakin, 1891, 7 In.	531.00
Teapot, George III, Chased Flowers, Elongated Handle, Spout, c.1810, 7 In........	717.00
Teapot, George III, Crest, Acanthus Chasing, Paw Feet, Joseph Angell, c.1819, 6 ½ In. .....*illus*	1075.00
Teapot, George III, Navette Shape, Angular Spout, Scalework, C-Scrolls, Leaves, 1790-91, 11 In...	504.00
Teapot, George III, Wood Handle, Andrew Fogelberg, London, c.1797, 6 In..........	649.00
Teapot, Georgian, Leaf Finial, Wood Handle, JCE, London, c.1792, 5 ½ In.	633.00
Teapot, Hinged, Repousse Body, Wood Handle, Solomon Hougham, 1806, 6 ½ x 11 In.	920.00
Teapot, Ivory Pineapple Finial, Angled Body, Spout, Engraved Flowers, C. Fuller, c.1795, 6 In.	830.00
Teapot, Lobed Base, Wood Handle, E. Viner, Sheffield, 1931, 8 ½ In.	518.00
Teapot, Lobed Lower Body, Wood Handle, Finial, G. Gordon & Co., c.1810, 6 In.	1380.00
Teapot, Pricked Designs, Wood Handle, Ivory Final, c.1800, 6 ½ x 11 ½ In.	546.00
Teapot, Square Wood Handle, Upright Spout, Reeded, Ball Feet, Finial, 1807-08, 6 In.	547.00
Teapot, Wood Handle & Finial, John Schofield, 6 ¼ x 10 ¾ In.......................	474.00
Toast Rack, Scalloped Handle, Gadroon Base, Scrolled Feet, 1742, 7 In.	450.00
Tray, George II, Shaped, Scrolls, Leaves, Flower Feet, 1742, 14 In.	1062.00
Tray, George III, Scalloped Rim, Gadroon Rim, Crest, Motto, R. Garrard, 1804, 17 x 12 In.	1793.00
Tray, George III, Wavy Scroll, Shell Border, Pad Feet, Marked John Carter, 1772, 6 ½ In..........	236.00
Tray, George IV, Shell Cast, Scroll Rim, Tripod Scroll Feet, 1829, 8 ¼ In.	380.00
Tray, Molded Border, Pinched Corners, Rectangular, J. Robinson, 28 In..............	7375.00
Tray, Oval, 2 Handles, Scrolling Leaves Border, Acanthus Feet, 1830, 26 In.	4148.00
Tray, Oval, Applied Leaves, Scrolls, Snake Handles, HA & S, George V, 1915, 29 In....................	4740.00
Tray, Oval, Pierced Gallery, 2 Handles, Etched Flowers & Leaves, Copper, 1900s, 3 x 21 x 14 In..	177.00
Tray, Rounded Rectangle, Gadroon Scroll, Shell Border, Handles, 1898, 30 x 17 In.................	4248.00
Trophy, George III, Plashing The Greatest Length Of Fence, Thomas Buckley, c.1798, 10 In. ..	2629.00
Tureen, Cover, Blackamoor Finial, Oval, Gadroon Border, Sheffield, 1833, 9 ½ x 15 In...........	10030.00
Tureen, Cover, Edwardian, Round, Rococo Scroll Handles, Tent Shape Lid, 1909, 8 In.	1600.00
Tureen, Cover, Loop Handles, Navette Shape, Oval Pedestal Base, c.1785, 5 ¼ x 8 ¾ In.	956.00
Tureen, Sauce, Cover, Fruit Finial, Reed Rim, Handles, Masks, W. Burwas, R. Sibley, 1807, 6 ½ In.	3318.00
Urn, Flowers, Campana Shape, 2 Handles, Footed, Cover, Finial, 1827, 7 ½ In.	767.00
Vase, Condiment, Engraved Coat Of Arms, John Swift, c.1755, 6 ¼ In.	615.00
Vase, Oval, Flared Rim, Gadroon, Blossoms, Birds, Round Foot, c.1897, 10 In., Pair.................	2500.00
Vinaigrette, Castle Scene, Scrolled Edge, Flowers, Gold Wash, 1 ¼ x 2 ½ In..........................	920.00

Silver-English, Sugar Castor, Pierced Lid, Pedestal Foot, Hallmarks, HB, Hester Bateman, 1787, 8 ¼ In.
$353.00

Cowan's Auctions

Silver-English, Teapot, George III, Crest, Acanthus Chasing, Paw Feet, Joseph Angell, c.1819, 6 ½ In.
$1075.00

Neal Auction Co.

Silver-French, Pitcher, Hot Milk, Hinged Lid, Ebonized Handle, Rosette Supports, Marked AS, 1838, 6 ¼ In.
$418.00

Neal Auction Co.

Silver-Irish, Game Fork, Stamped Cartouche, M. West, Hallmark, Date Letter 1821, 8 In., Pair
$374.00

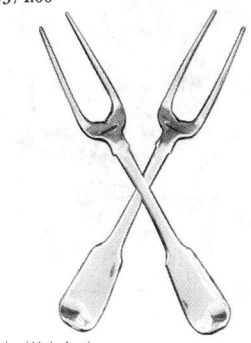

Leland Little Auction

Silver-Irish, Loving Cup, Gadroon Design, Half Ribs, Scrolled Handles, E. Johnson, Dublin, 1962, 6 ¾ In. **$1380.00**

James D. Julia Inc.

Silver-Mexican, Ice Bucket, Applied Ball Decoration, Pedestal Base, Marked, Tane, 1900s, 11 x 9 In. **$5192.00**

Brunk Auctions

Silver-Mexican, Kettle, Stand, Center Spout, Angular Rosewood Handle, Bernice Goodspeed, c.1950, 14 ¼ In. **$2133.00**

Skinner, Inc.

Vinaigrette, George III, Thimble Shape, Cut Glass Bottle, Stopper, Leather Case, c.1780, 1 ½ In.	538.00
Vinaigrette, Rectangular, Gilt Interior, Openwork Compartment, 1823, 0.3 Oz.	100.00
Vinaigrette, Repousse Flowers, William Hall, London, 1817, 1 ½ In.	420.00
Waiter, George III, Flower & Shell Rim, Engraved Border, Crest, Richard Peston, 1761, 7 In.	2032.00
Waiter, George III, Round, Beaded Scalloped, Lion Crest, Mark, John Carter, London, 1774, 6 In.	358.00
Waiter, George III, Scalloped Shell Rim, Flower Border, Monogram, Ebenezer Coker, 1762, 7 In.	717.00
Waiter, George III, Shell & Scroll Border, Engraved Crest, Hoof Feet, Hugh Mills, 1775, 8 In.	1195.00
Waiter, Round, Molded, Engraved Stampwork, Monogram, 3 Scrolled Feet, J. Hunt, 1855, 11 In.	711.00
Waiter, Shaped, Rocaille Edge, Leaves, Scrolls, 4-Footed, James Morrison, George II, 1751, 24 In.	8888.00
Wine Coaster, Embossed, Raised Rim, c.1920, 5 In.	180.00
Wine Coaster, George III, Reticulated, Husk Swags, Urns, Mahogany Base, 1775, 5 ½ In., Pair	1896.00
Wine Coaster, Plated Wirework, Treen, Sheffield, 5 ¼ In., Pair	531.00
Wine Coaster, Shells & Leaves, Turned Treen Base, 6 ¼ In., Pair	896.00
Wine Cooler, Plated, Urn Shape, Gadroon Rim, Scroll Handles, 1800s, 9 ½ In., Pair	1216.00
Wine Funnel, Strainer, Engraved, Serpent, Crown, Crest, Monogram, 1817, 6 In.	764.00
Wine Funnel, Tray, Crowned Lion, Inscribed, 1700s, 5 ½ In.	431.00

SILVER-FRENCH

Beaker, Cylindrical Shape, Flared Rim, Engraved, c.1819-38, 4 ⅛ In.	123.00
Bowl, Cover, Artichoke Finial, Pierced Flower Handles, Monograms, Odiot, Prevost & Cie, 8 x 15 In.	2988.00
Bowl, Repousse, Maids & Satyrs, Nude, Flowers, Shell Handles, Ball Feet, 1800s, 13 x 9 In.	863.00
Carving Set, Knife, Fork, Steel Blade, Hoofed Leg Handle, Minerva Mark, 1800s, 13 & 11 In.	148.00
Centerpiece, Flower Frame, Griffin Supports, 4 Scrolled Candle Arms, Veyrat, c.1890, 14 In.	3555.00
Chalice & Paten, Bands, Knob, Cup & Base Religious Rondels, Gold Wash, c.1890, 5 ¾ In.	1541.00
Chocolate Pot, Flared Fluted Bowl, Lateral Wood Handle, Bracket Spout, Reeded Rim, 8 ½ In.	526.00
Claret Jug, Etched Glass, Baluster, Flower Swags, Leaf Finial, Loop Handle, c.1895, 13 In., Pair	4740.00
Coffeepot, Acorn Finial, Eagle Mask Spout, Treen Handle, 3 Paw Feet, 1800s, 10 ¼ In.	2125.00
Coffeepot, Dome Lid, Baluster, Acorn Finial, C-Scroll Treen Handle, c.1809, 8 ¼ In.	538.00
Cosmetics Pot, Etched Glass, Enamel, Round, Flower Border, Roundel, Vine, c.1900, 5 ¾ x 6 ¾ In.	504.00
Creamer, Baluster Shape, 3 Stepped Feet, Hinged Cover, Chased, Armorial Crest, c.1800, 4 ½ In.	329.00
Dresser Box, Hinged Lid, Cut Glass, Reeded Rims, Star Cut Base, c.1895, 6 ⅝ x 4 ¼ In.	368.00
Ewer, Etched Glass Body, Scroll & Flower Overlay, Marks E. Tetard, c.1900, 12 x 6 In.	900.00
Pitcher, Hot Milk, Hinged Lid, Ebonized Handle, Rosette Supports, Marked AS, 1838, 6 ¼ In. *illus*	418.00
Plateau, Mirror, Rectangular, Molded Edges, J.E. Caldwell & Co., c.1930, 21 ½ x 16 In.	830.00
Salt & Pepper, Fish Shape, Petrossian Of Paris, 3 ¼ In.	590.00
Soup Ladle, Dip Bowl, Long Handle, Marked, c.1809, 14 ½ In.	148.00
Spoon, Sifting, Oval Bowl, Pierced, Engraved Village Scene, Chased Handle, c.1750, 7 In.	207.00
Taster, Grape Design, Hammered, Round, Engraved, Bousion, 1800s, 3 In.	288.00
Tray, Palm, Dart Border, Oval, c.1825, 9 ¼ x 5 ¼ In.	177.00
Wine Taster, Circular, Repousse Grapevine Design, Loop Handles, Marked, 3 ½ In., Pair	239.00

SILVER-GERMAN

Basket, Repousse, Openwork Handle, Marked, 10 x 9 In.	527.00
Basket, Reticulated, Flowers, Swing Handle, Tapered, Hanau, 1890, 5 x 5 ½ In.	403.00
Boat, Repousse, Cherub, c.1900, 5 ¼ In.	191.00
Bowl, 8-Lobed, Flared Rim, Dome Foot, 6 x 9 In.	380.00
Bowl, Fruit, Reticulated, Pierced Flowers, Love Birds, C-Scrolls, Scroll Feet, c.1900, 7 ¼ x 9 In.	980.00
Bowl, Fruit, Square, Serpentine Sides, Scroll Rim, Flower Swags, Putti, c.1900, 3 x 12 In.	399.00
Bowl, Hammered, Lobed, Scalloped Rim, Footed, J. Hoffman, Stamped Wiener Werkstatte, 5 x 6 In.	8680.00
Bowl, Pierced, Repousse, Woman, Sleeping Cherub, G. Roth & Co., c.1890, 8 ½ In.	374.00
Box, Hinged Lid, Vermeil Interior, 4 Applied Feet, 3 ½ x 4 ½ In.	230.00
Centerpiece, 6-Sided, Openwork Rococo Designs, Family Crest, Hanau, 3 x 11 In.	578.00
Centerpiece, Pierced, Swags, 4 Fluted Columns, Side Reserves, Glass Liners, W. Binder, 15 x 24 In.	7170.00
Centerpiece, Woman Standing, Column, Ram's Heads, Flowers, Cherubs, c.1860, 25 In.	5750.00
Chalice, Parcel Gilt, Round Bowl, Cylindrical Stem, Ball Feet, Old Coins, Stippled, 4 ½ In.	533.00
Cigarette Case, White Enamel Checkered Grid, Blue Sapphires, Hinged Lid, 3 ½ x 2 ¾ In.	148.00
Claret Jug, Cut Glass, Ewer Shape, Flip Top, Scroll Handle, Round Body, Marked, 15 In.	1300.00
Compote, Pierced, Bird Flower Swags, Repousse Figures, Raised Foot, c.1890, 6 ¾ x 10 ¼ In.	1075.00
Cup, Wine, Ceremonial, Bell Shape, Slender Stem, Domed Foot, Grapevines, 4 ⅞ In., Pair	711.00
Dish, Entree, Cover, Rococo Style, Oval, Embossed Flowers, Loop Top Handle, c.1900, 12 In.	1058.00
Fish Serving Set, Vermeil, c.1900, 10 ¾ In., 2 Piece	94.00
Frame, Oval, Openwork Borders, Scrolling Leaves, Chickens, Easel Back, c.1900, 10 ¾ In.	368.00
Goblet, Trellis Openwork, Rocaille Reserves, Cherub Stem, c.1910, 5 In., Pair	385.00
Grape Scissors, Calla Lily Repousse, Art Nouveau, Marked, Germany, 6 ½ x 3 In.	90.00
Jardiniere, Navette Shape, Scrolls, Latticework, C-Scroll Handles, Putto, Scroll Feet, c.1915, 7 x 15 In.	1353.00
Mirror, Hand, Engraved Flowers & Feathered Scrolls, Shaped, c.1925, 4 x 8 In.	185.00
Muffineer, Urn Shape, Berry Finial, Husk Bands, Flower Garland, Trumpet Stem, c.1900, 7 In.	326.00

S

Sauceboat, Fish Shape, Head Spout, Tail Handle, 3 Fin Feet, Red Stone Eyes, c.1890, 11 x 5 In.....	2726.00
Sauceboat, Underplate, Divided Flower Handle, Royal Prussian, H.J. Wilm, c.1900, 5 x 8 In., Pair	7766.00
Serving Dish, Oval, Hammered Surface, Arts & Crafts Style, c.1900, 12 ¼ In.	459.00
Soup Ladle, Gilt Bowl, Reeded Handle, Leaf Design, c.1900, 13 In..	177.00
Sugar, Glass Lined, Pierced, Flower Swags, Grapevine Scrolls, Footed, c.1900, 4 ¾ In. Diam. ..	178.00
Tazza, Round, Repousse, 4 Bernini Twist Columns, Flowers, Ruffled Rim, Round Base	920.00
Tea Caddy, Oval Shape, Armorial, Engraved Cover, Shield, c.1800, 5 In.	885.00
Tea Set, Coffeepot, Teapot, Sugar, Creamer, Oval Tray, Chased Flower Design, 1900s..............	4140.00
Tea Set, Repousse Flowers, Teapot, Coffeepot, Creamer, Sugar, Tray, Strainer, Hanau City, 6 Piece	4313.00
Tea Strainer, Rococo Style, Round, Tavern Scenes On Rim, Rocaille Handles, c.1900, 4 x 7 In.	184.00
Wedding Cup, Woman Wearing Long Dress, Holding Swiveling Cup Overhead, c.1967, 5 In....	236.00
Wedding Cup, Woman, Holding Basket Over Head, 7 In.	540.00

SILVER-INDIAN

Cigarette Case, Rectangular, Lid, Stalking Lion, Lioness, Map Of India, c.1900, 5 ⅜ In.	153.00
Salver, Embossed, Band Of Deities, Roundels, Leaf Tip Banding, Scrollwork, c.1900, 8 ⅜ In. Diam.	533.00
Teapot, Oval, Ruffled Rim, Ear Handle, Elephant Finial, Serpentine Spout, Farmers, c.1900, 5 ½ In..	1422.00
Tray, Molded Rim, Rounded, Engraved Persian Design, Marked, 1900s, 18 ¼ x 13 In.	1298.00

SILVER-IRISH

Bowl, Pedestal, George III, 3-Footed, Repousse, 1818, 6 x 3 In..	978.00
Bowl, Scalloped, Flared, Animal, House Repousse, Tripod Paw Feet, Marked, 5 ¾ x 9 ¾ In......	1638.00
Box, Glove, George III, Curved Corners, Hinged Lid, Engraved, 1791, 8 x 4 In.....................	900.00
Fish Server, Arching Blade, Dolphin, Openwork Vines, Celluloid Handle, 1780, 13 In.............	299.00
Game Fork, Stamped Cartouche, M. West, Hallmark, Date Letter 1821, 8 In., Pair ....*illus*	374.00
Ladle, George II, John Hamilton, 1700s, 14 ½ In.	316.00
Ladle, Terminal, Armorial Crest, George III, 13 In..	269.00
Loving Cup, Gadroon Design, Half Ribs, Scrolled Handles, E. Johnson, Dublin, 1962, 6 ¾ In. . *illus*	1380.00
Loving Cup, Urn Shape, Round Foot, 2 Handles, Coat Of Arms, 1774, 6 x 8 In., Pair.............	1495.00
Sauceboat, George III, Chased, Beaded, Reeding, Stepped Hoof Feet, Scroll Handle, c.1790, 4 x 8 In..	478.00
Spoon, Strainer, Engraved Crest, R Sawyer, Dublin, 1816, 12 ¾ In.....................................	533.00
Sugar, Punchwork Rim, Chased Birds, Trees, Figures, Crest, 3 Hoof Feet, c.1780, 2 ¾ x 2 ¾ In..	460.00
Tea Set, George III, Ruffle Rim, Chasing Scrolling Leaves, Paw Footed, c.1814, 3 Piece..........	1673.00
Waiter, Flowers, Scrolls Shell Border, Matthew West, Dublin, c.1780, 7 In.	896.00

SILVER-ITALIAN

Basket, Fruit, Scrolls, Openwork Weave, Handle, Marked Grand, 1900s, 19 x 26 In.	11800.00
Bowl, Oval, Scalloped Swirls, Footed, c.1990, 3 ¾ x 10 In...	360.00
Bowl, Shell Shape, Shell Feet, Buccellati, 6 ½ In..	660.00
Box, Flat Hinged Lid, Textured Finish, Tiffany & Co., c.1970, 1 ¼ x 3 ¾ In.......................	738.00
Ice Cream Set, Knife, 6 Spoons, Gold Wash Black, Bowls, Case, 11 & 6 ¾ In., 7 Piece	207.00
Ornament, Eagle, Evergreens, Oval, Buccellati, 4 ½ In.	150.00
Plaque, Saint Martin, Scalloped Shell, 1800s, 8 In.	425.00
Platter, Oval, Ogee Reeded Rim, c.1945, 18 ¾ In..	1126.00
Soup Ladle, Threaded Coffin Handle, Oval Bowl, Monogram, c.1775, 13 ¾ In.	207.00
Tureen, Flower Repousse, Bouquet Handles, Gilt Liner, Wavy Underplate, 1900s, 14 x 17 In.....	10620.00

SILVER-JAPANESE

Bowl, Enamel Flowers, Butterflies, Signed Masaharu, 1800s, 3 x 6 In...........................	2607.00
Bowl, Tulip, 6 Lobes, Shaped Rim, Applied Enamel Flowers, 3 x 6 In., Pair	2460.00
Bucket, Water, Branch Formed Handle, Bamboo Shoots, Japan, c.1880, 9 In.	1320.00
Cigarette Case, Rectangular, Lid, Navette, Tiger, Engraved Lines, Leafy Scrolls, c.1900, 6 ⅜ In.	184.00
Jewelry Box, Cover, Chased, Flowers, Fitted Interior, Rectangular, Signed Miyamoto, 9 x 6 In...	1778.00
Pipe, Bamboo Body, Monk, Fan, Tree Carved, Signed, 7 ¾ In...	237.00
Teapot, Persimmon Shape, Domed Cover, Swing Strap Handle, Spout, 6 ¾ In........................	1708.00
Vase, Enamel Accents, Baluster, Prunus Branch, Flowers, Birds, Script, c.1972, 8 ¼ In.	735.00

SILVER-LATVIAN

Chalice, Flared Rim, Ring Stem, c.1895, 10 In..	413.00

SILVER-MEXICAN

Bowl, Dome Lid, Beaded Petals, Leaf Handles, Footed, Fitted Ladle, Sanborns, 10 In.	3200.00
Bowl, Fruit, Round, Flaring Rim, Leaf Band, Lobed Body, Handles, 13 In.	1000.00
Bowl, Fruit, Round, Lobed Border, Openwork Scroll Base, 1900s, 9 In.	500.00
Bowl, Openwork, Scroll Feet, Swan Shape, Marked, P.S. Gonzalez, c.1900s, 7 x 15 ¾ In.	1180.00
Bowl, Oval, Cast Rococo Scroll Rim, Reticulated Foot, c.1965, 3 ¼ x 14 ½ In.	861.00
Bread Tray, Rounded Rectangular, Outscrolled Gadroon Tab Handles, Beehive Feet, 2 x 14 ¼ In.	676.00
Caviar Spoon, Ebony Accents, William Spratling, Marked, 6 In.	184.00
Coffeepot, Dome Lid, Gooseneck, Incised Hexagonal Panels, Sanborns, c.1980, 10 x 6 In.......	1476.00

Silver-Portuguese, Vase, Baroque Style, Embossed, Fluted, Scalloped, Scrolled Base, Stamped, 1900s, 13 ¾ x 6 ½ In. $1320.00

Gray's Auctioneers LLC

Silver-Russian, Letter Opener, Grape Pattern, St. Petersburg Mark, c.1847, 8 ½ In. $1035.00

James D. Julia Inc.

Silver-Russian, Tea Caddy, 4 Engraved Panels, Silver Mounted Cork Stopper, Marked, BTC, c.1900, 5 ¾ In. $2124.00

James D. Julia Inc.

Silver-Russian, Vodka Bucket, Ribbed Bands, Engraved Scrolls & Leaves, Swing Handle, Marked, c.1908, 8 ¼ In.
$978.00

Leland Little Auction

Silver-South American, Mate Pot, Cover, Figural, African Bust, Swirl Fluted Body, Ring Handles, 1800s, 16 ½ In.
$4183.00

Neal Auction Co.

Silver-Sterling, Cigar Case, Pocket, 3 Tubes, Embossed Flowers, Monogram, Marked, 5 ½ In.
$201.00

Early Auction Co.

Coffeepot, Dome Lid, Sphere Finial, Cylinder Base, Fruitwood Handle, Spratling, c.1950, 9 In.	1067.00
Cup, Flared Body, Banded Neck, Leaf Base, W. Spratling, c.1935, 2 ¾ x 3 ¼ In.	360.00
Frame, Engraved Leaves, Easel Back, Sanborn, 18 x 15 In.	299.00
Gravy Boat, Undertray, Scroll Handle, Beaded Edges, 1900s, 8 In.	881.00
Ice Bucket, Applied Ball Decoration, Pedestal Base, Marked, Tane, 1900s, 11 x 9 In. *illus*	5192.00
Julep Cup, Cylindrical, Tapered, Reeded Rim, c.1950, 3 ⅞ In., 10 Piece	1896.00
Kettle, Stand, Center Spout, Angular Rosewood Handle, Bernice Goodspeed, c.1950, 14 ¼ In. *illus*	2133.00
Pitcher, Abalone Plaques, Cylindrical, Disc Foot, Rosewood Handle, Taxco, 11 In.	296.00
Pitcher, Baluster Shape, 3 Leafy Feet, Scroll Rim, C-Scroll Handle, 9 ¾ In.	1016.00
Pitcher, Bulbous, Footed, Wide Spout, Ear Handle, Marked, Eagle, Sanborns, 7 In.	652.00
Plate, Reeded, Double Rim, Monogram, Diego Gonzales De La Cueva, c.1770, 9 In.	770.00
Platter, Oval, Shaped, Handles, Gadroon Border, 26 In.	3416.00
Punch Bowl, Handles, Footed, Engraved, Lion Crest, 1900s, 14 ½ In.	2800.00
Salad Servers, P. Lopez, Mexico, 10 In.	238.00
Salad Servers, Spoon, Fork, Curved Up Handle, Bowl Hook, 11 ¼ In.	368.00
Sauceboat, Underplate, Bombe Form, Shaped Scroll Handle & Rim, 9 In.	443.00
Spurs, Horseman's, Wheel, Peso Coin, Chains, Buckles, 1800s, Pair.	492.00
Sugar, Cover, Bulbous, Squat, Strap Handles, Flower Finial, T. Jimenes, 5 In.	326.00
Tea Set, Ribbed Melon Shape, Squat Urn Finials, Openwork Scroll Base, 26 In., 6 Piece	4500.00
Tea Set, Teapot, Creamer, Sugar, Cover, Stamped J. Torres, c.1950, 8 In.	1422.00
Tray, 3 Leaf Form Sections, Center Curled Handle, Prieto, 11 In.	354.00
Tray, Oval Shallow Well, Scalloped Corners, 30 x 18 In.	3884.00
Tray, Oval, Chiseled Rim, Marked, Sanborns, 23 x 15 In.	2415.00
Tray, Oval, Line Stepped Border, 2 D-Shaped Handles, Leaves, Marked, 26 x 16 In.	2990.00
Vase, Mother-Of-Pearl Band, Globular, Round Foot, Los Castillo, 5 In.	219.00

SILVER-PERSIAN

Bowl, Underplate, Engraved Flowers, Leaves, Scalloped Rim, Round, c.1900, 9 ¼ In., 12 In.	1150.00
Box, Tobacco, Engraved Flowers, Leaves, Square, 4 ¾ x 4 ¾ In.	403.00
Creamer, Engraved Flowers & Leaves Panels, 1900s, 4 ½ In., Pair	345.00
Mug, Cylindrical, Landscape Scene, Farmers, Elephants, Ear Handle, Domed Foot, c.1900, 5 ⅜ In.	593.00
Stirrup Cup, Bridled Horses Head, Plush Case, Arabic Hallmarks, 1900s, 8 In.	1800.00
Tray, Rectangular, Engraved Birds, Flowers, Animals, c.1905, 14 ¼ x 10 In.	690.00

SILVER-PERUVIAN

Bowl, Aztec Design Band, Applied Handles, 6 x 7 ½ In.	690.00
Tray, Gadroon Edge, Open Handles, Square, 18 ½ x 13 In.	1035.00
Tray, Molded Rim, J. Porclee, 16 ½ In.	1073.00
Tray, Rectangular, Shaped, Leaf Border, 2 Square Handles, 22 In.	1708.00

SILVER-PORTUGUESE

Bowl, Flower Shape, Gold Washed, Poppy, Fluted Leaves, c.1950, 8 In. Diam.	711.00
Platter, Round, Basket Weave Border, Flowers, Leaves, 3 Scroll Feet, 1959, 14 In.	657.00
Salver, Round, Engine Turned, Anthemia Banding, Ball & Paw Feet, c.1805, 10 ¼ In. Diam.	533.00
Salver, Round, Fleur-De-Lis Reticulated Gallery, 4 Ball & Claw Feet, c.1814, 13 ¾ In. Diam.	1185.00
Vase, Baroque Style, Embossed, Fluted, Scalloped, Scrolled Base, Stamped, 1900s, 13 ¾ x 6 ½ In. *illus*	1320.00

SILVER-RUSSIAN. Russian silver is marked with the Cyrillic, or Russian, alphabet. The numbers 84, 88, or 91 indicate the silver content. Russian silver may be higher or lower than sterling standard. Other marks indicate maker, assayer, or city of manufacture. Many pieces of silver made in Russia are decorated with enamel. Silver prices in 2011 and 2012 became so high many pieces were worth more in meltdown value than as decorative silver. These prices are based on current silver values. Faberge pieces are listed in their own category.

Beaker, Cylindrical, Roundels, Tree, Hound, Bird, Strapwork, 3 Ball Feet, c.1780, 3 ¾ In.	858.00
Bowl, Engraved Flowers, Footed, Moscow, 2 x 3 In.	531.00
Box, Hinged, Engraved Design, Cigar Band, Marked, c.1896-1908, 2 ¼ x 7 In.	3450.00
Cake Basket, 10-Sided, Molded Rim, Swing Handle, Lobed Interior, Mark, St. Petersburg, 3 x 10 In.	936.00
Cigarette Case, Enameled, 2 Swans, Riverscape, Flowering Branches, Purple Stone Clasp, 4 In.	1470.00
Cigarette Case, Geometric Design, Push Button Clasp, N. Zverev, Moscow, 4 In.	1150.00
Cigarette Case, Lion Slayer, Hinged, Red Cabochon Thumbpiece, Gilt Interior, c.1927, 4 ¼ In.	480.00
Cigarette Case, Rectangular, Scrolling Leaves, Moscow In Cartouche, c.1850, 3 x 5 In.	329.00
Cigarette Case, Warrior Attacking Bear, Hinged, Green Stone Thumbpiece, c.1911, 4 ¼ In.	1200.00
Claret Jug, Nicholas II, Cut Glass, Vertical Diamond, Starburst Band, c.1900, 13 x 9 In.	3936.00
Coin Case, Enamel, Flower Scrolls, Multicolor, Rectangular, Blue Stone Latch, c.1915, 3 ¾ In.	889.00
Creamer, Bulbous, Repousse Handle & Rim, Scrolling Leaves, Flowers, 1800s, 4 In.	650.00
Creamer, Gilt, Rectangular, Engraved Sides, Armorial Crest, Square Handle, 1850, 3 In.	750.00

S

Cross, Altar, Crucifixion Front, Passion Terminals, Double Eagle Mark, 1877, 12 In.	1440.00
Cup & Saucer, Engraved Flowers & Leaves, c.1888	420.00
Cup, Loop Handle, Mounted With Scene Of Troika, Early 1900s, 4 ½ In.	875.00
Cup, Vodka, Enameled, Multicolor Flowers, Cylindrical, Round Foot, 1800s, 3 In.	213.00
Dessert Spoon, Gilt, Cloisonne, Scrolling Flowers, Multicolor Enamel, 7 In.	98.00
Figure, Gnome, Holding Hammer, On Pink Sapphire, Fitted Case, 1889, 3 In.	826.00
Frame, Pierce Work Classical Figures, Garlands, Mark, c.1900, 3 x 2 ¼ In.	920.00
Kovsh, Boat Shape, Double Headed Eagle, Chased, Embossed, Gold Wash Interior, 1900s, 16 x 9 In. ..	770.00
Lamp, Hanging, Gold Wash, Wirework Filigree, Tapered Oval, 6 Clear Stones, Link Chain, c.1844, 4 In.	1007.00
Letter Opener, Grape Pattern, St. Petersburg Mark, c.1847, 8 ½ In. ....*illus*	1035.00
Punch Bowl, Lid, Silver Top, Swags, Leaves, Diamond & Star Cut Crystal Bowl, 13 In.	5400.00
Salt Cellar, Spoon, Triangular, Anchor, Crossed Sword, 2 Headed Eagle, Box, c.1908-26, 1 In. ..	5000.00
Salt, Flared Foot, Raised Panel, Reserves, Punchwork, Gilt Interior, Inscribed, 3 ¾ In.	1440.00
Salt, Master, Imperial, C-Scroll & Shell Border, 6 Panel Body, Footed, 3 ½ x 1 ¾ In.	161.00
Sculpture, Bear Atop Walrus, Paw Up, Rock Crystal Iceberg Base, Marked, 7 ½ x 9 ¼ In.	10350.00
Sugar, Cover, Oblong, Reeded, Scrolls, Vines, Birds, 2 Handles, Ivory Finial, 1834, 5 In.	796.00
Sugar, Military Helmet Shape, Romanov Eagle Crest, Handle, c.1910, 2 ¾ x 3 ½ In.	805.00
Sugar, Shovel, Flower Rim, Shaped Swing Handle, 1911, 4 ½ In.	403.00
Tea Caddy, 4 Engraved Panels, Silver Mounted Cork Stopper, Marked, BTC, c.1900, 5 ¾ In. *illus*	2124.00
Tea Strainer, Cloisonne, Stylized Flower Stem, Beaded Enameling, Gold Washed, 1894, 5 ⅞ In. ..	652.00
Tea Strainer, Gilt, Cloisonne, Enamel Inlaid Handle, 1900s, 6 In.	374.00
Vase, Elongated Oval, Flared Beaded Rim, Chased, Herons, Leaves, Scrolling Vines, 1800s, 6 In. ..	295.00
Vodka Bucket, Ribbed Bands, Engraved Scrolls & Leaves, Swing Handle, Marked, c.1908, 8 ¼ In. *illus*	978.00

SILVER-SCANDINAVIAN

Cross, Basket Weave, Looped Finial, Knops, 2 ½ In.	237.00

SILVER-SCOTTISH

Basket, George III, Oval Shape, Flower Swags, Garland, Urns, Swing Handle, 1786, 5 x 7 In. ...	400.00
Ladle, George IV, Glasgow, c.1828, 6 ½ In.	89.00
Ladle, King's Pattern, Crest, Monogram, Robert Gray & Sons, c.1828, 4 In.	246.00
Loving Cup, Pedestal Shape, C-Curved Handles, Robert Gey & Sons, c.1810, 8 ¼ In.	805.00
Serving Spoon, Fiddle & Thread Design, Applied Medallion, Edinburgh, 1805, 12 ¾ In.	288.00
Teapot, Flowers, Leaves, Scrolls, Squat, Marked, J. McKay, 1828, 4 x 8 In.	590.00
Toast Rack, Divided Uprights, Handle, Ball Feet, DH Mark, George IV, 1829, 5 ½ x 6 ¾ In.	474.00
Teapot, Thai Nakon, Sterling, Fluted Body, Buddha Rosettes, Elephant Finial, 5 x 9 In.	708.00

SILVER-SOUTH AMERICAN

Mate Pot, Cover, Figural, African Bust, Swirl Fluted Body, Ring Handles, 1800s, 16 ½ In. .... *illus*	4183.00

SILVER-SPANISH

Brasier, Oval, Reeded Body, Fruitwood Handles, Dolphin Supports, Oval Foot, c.1830, 3 In.....	652.00
Plate, Colonial, Hot Forged, Serpentine Lobes, Threaded Rim, 1800s, 10 In.	369.00

SILVER-STERLING. Sterling silver is made with 925 parts silver out of 1,000 parts of metal. The word *sterling* is a quality guarantee used in the United States after about 1860. The word was used much earlier in England and Ireland. Pieces listed here are not identified by country. Silver prices in 2011 and 2012 became so high many pieces were worth more in meltdown value than as decorative silver. These prices are based on current silver values. Other pieces of sterling quality silver are listed under Silver-American, Silver-English, etc.

Bacon Fork, Marked W In Circle, 8 In...	35.00
Basket, George III, Oval, Swing Handle, Reticulated, Lion's Masks, Swags, 1777, 4 x 14 In......	7500.00
Basket, Handle, Chased, Footed, Frank M. Whiting & Co., 8 ½ x 10 In.	360.00
Basket, Oval, Reticulated Sides, Shaped Rim, Leaves, Flowers, Monogram, 1868-1908, 3 x 12 In. .	590.00
Basket, Round, Filigree Design, Fixed Bail Handle, Wavy Rim, 9 x 9 In.	281.00
Basket, Round, Rolled Rim, Quarter Lobed, Openwork Strap Handle, Hammered, c.1900, 7 x 10 In..	676.00
Basket, Sweetmeat, George III, Openwork Body, Swing Handle, Scroll Feet, 1761, 6 In.	499.00
Basket, Sweetmeat, Oval Shape, Flared Reticulated Sides, Strap Handle, c.1935, 4 ½ x 4 In., Pair...	153.00
Basket, Swing Handle, Footed, Whiting, c.1910, 12 ½ x 9 ¾ In...	720.00
Basket, Urn Shape, Swing Handle, Glass Liner, Piercework, Birds, Leaves, Flowers	1668.00
Berry Spoon, Engraved Butterfly, Leaves, Gold & Copper Highlights, Scalloped Edge, c.1885, 9 In. ...	215.00
Blotter Corner Set, Repousse, Textured Edge, 4 x 2 ¼ In., 4 Piece...............................	120.00
Bonbon Scoop, Enamel, Oval Bowl, Openwork, Grapevines, Bunches, c.1890, 5 In.	119.00
Bonbon, Chased Flower Design, Swirls, Wavy Rim, Art Nouveau, c.1895, 6 In. Diam., Pair	148.00
Bonbon, Repousse Reticulated Bowl, Roses, Grecian Woman, c.1900, 9 In.	518.00
Bowl, 3 Compartments, Acanthus Bud Finial, 1 ¾ x 9 ¾ In..	550.00
Bowl, Allover Flower Repousse, Stippled, Footed, c.1910, 3 ¾ x 9 In...................................	863.00

Silver-Sterling, Serving Spoon, Calla Lily Stem, Parcel Gilt, Openwork Leaves, c.1860, 8 ½ In. $326.00

Skinner, Inc.

Silver-Sterling, Tea & Coffee Set, Sugar & Creamer, Tray, Ebony Finials, Angular Handles, c.1970, 12 x 18 In. $5310.00

Ivey-Selkirk Auctioneers

S

Sleepy Eye, Textile, American Indian Trademark, Background Indian Scene, Frame, 25 x 25 In.
$1760.00

Wm Morford Antiques

Smith Brothers, Jar, Sweetmeat, Embossed Lid, Melon Ribbed, Flowers, Leaves, Red Lion Trademark, 5 ½ In.
$403.00

Early Auction Co.

Soapstone, Seal, Head, Relief Carved, Daoist God Of Wealth & Prosperity, Chinese, 3 ½ In.
$615.00

Neal Auction Co.

Soapstone, Seal, Rectangular, Carved, Calligraphic Inscription, Chinese, 2 ¼ In.
$178.00

Skinner, Inc.

Bowl, Basket Frame, Glass Insert, 2 Handles, 4-Footed, 7 x 6 In.	173.00
Bowl, Beaded Rim, Round Beaded Foot, Pedestal, c.1880, 5 x 9 In.	767.00
Bowl, Bird Crest, Banner, Leaves, Round, Wide Rim, Banding Design, 1892, 6 In.	1175.00
Bowl, Center, Fluted Body, Scalloped Rim, Marked, Monogram, 3 x 10 In.	345.00
Bowl, Center, Lobed Oval Body, 2 Scroll Handles, 4 Ball Feet, Marked, c.1887, 4 x 14 In.	1175.00
Bowl, Center, Round Flared Rim, Molded Leaves, Edge Scroll, 1900s, 7 ½ In.	1200.00
Bowl, Flared Rim, Chased Flowers, Monogram, Oval, 1903, 2 x 15 In.	748.00
Bowl, Flower, Round, Bulbous, Scroll Rim, 4 Cast Feet, Monogram, 1898, 4 x 8 ½ In.	553.00
Bowl, Footed, Tripod, Round, Paneled, Chased Flowers, Scroll Feet, c.1900, 2 x 3 ½ In.	118.00
Bowl, Fruit, Clover Pattern, Lobed Octagonal, Openwork Rim, Monogram, 12 In.	1045.00
Bowl, Fruit, Flared Rim, Elongated Acanthus Scrolls, Flower Heads, Scroll Feet, 1901, 11 ½ In.	1007.00
Bowl, Fruit, Oval, Steeply Flared Sides, Reticulated Scrolling Whiplash Lines, c.1900, 5 x 12 In.	492.00
Bowl, Lid, Navarre Pattern, Pierced, Pedestal, Flared Rim, Monogram, c.1900, 5 x 13 In.	885.00
Bowl, Lobed, Embossed Roses Rim, Monogram, c.1925, 3 x 10 ½ In.	615.00
Bowl, Lobed, Roses & Scrolls, Shaped High Relief Rim, Monogram, 2 ¾ x 7 ¾ In.	236.00
Bowl, Oval, 6 Rim Lobes, Rounded Rim, Flower & Leaf Design, Monogram, 3 ¼ x 10 In.	472.00
Bowl, Oval, Monogram, Foldover Rim, c.1932-61, 2 x 10 x 7 In., Pair	885.00
Bowl, Oval, Ogee Rim, Hammered Interior, 10 ¾ In.	533.00
Bowl, Pierced & Chased Fern & Flowers, Lobed Rims, 1897, 10 In.	944.00
Bowl, Plateau, Urn Shape, Flared Rim, Scrolling, c.1890, 9 ¾ x 13 ¾ In.	4780.00
Bowl, Repousse Flowers & Fruit, Monogram, Round Foot, c.1870, 3 ¾ x 10 In.	1840.00
Bowl, Repousse, Gilt Interior, Boat Shape, Scrolled Handles, Footed, Nisan, 9 ½ x 4 ½ In.	259.00
Bowl, Rococo Style, Scroll Feet, Rocaille, Lobed, Handles, 7 x 5 x 4 In.	363.00
Bowl, Round, Lobed Panels, Trailing Chrysanthemum Rim, Mauser, 12 ½ In.	478.00
Bowl, Round, Squared Projections, Rolled Rim, Hammered, 4 Bracket Feet, c.1900, 4 x 9 In.	861.00
Bowl, Shells, Rosettes, Scrolls, Lobed, Art Nouveau, 1898, 2 ⅜ x 8 ¾ In.	295.00
Bread Basket, Elongated, Pierced Leaf Scrolling, Low Handle, 13 ½ x 7 In.	259.00
Bread Tray, Pierced Rim, Oval, c.1900, 2 x 11 In.	325.00
Bucket, Cut Glass Liner, Openwork Diamond Design, 5 In.	215.00
Butter, Dome Lid, Square, Leaves, Flowers & Butterflies, Flower Finial, 1881, 4 x 7 In.	3690.00
Cake Basket, George II, Oval, Pierced Scrolls, Leaves, Swing Handle, Stepped Base, 15 In.	2510.00
Cake Basket, George III, Flared Openwork Rim, Dolphin Head, Footed, 1762, 24 In.	4230.00
Cake Basket, Oval Shape, Scroll & Lattice Rim, Monogram, Swing Handle, Round Foot, 1900s.	1230.00
Cake Basket, Pierced, Swing Handle, Flared Rim, Grapevine, Leaves, Claw Feet, 1744	15275.00
Cake Plate, Pierced Rim, 4 Acanthus Pendants, Reeded, Low Foot, c.1900, 9 ⅞ In.	368.00
Candelabra are listed in the Candelabrum category.	
Candlesticks are listed in their own category.	
Carving Set, Repousse, Roses, Knife, Fork, Steel, Marked, 12 To 15 In., 3 Piece	115.00
Celery Dish, Scroll & Flower Design, 4 Shell Feet, 2 Handles, c.1897, 12 ½ In.	345.00
Centerpiece, Geometrically Pierced Sides, Round, Footed, Foldover Rim, c.1911, 2 ¾ x 11 In.	443.00
Centerpiece, Repousse, Oval, Scalloped Edge, Rose Garland, Classical Figures, 17 x 11 In.	1200.00
Centerpiece, Round, Flared Rim, Elk Head Handles, Columnar, Circular Foot, 9 In.	1750.00
Chalice, Gothic, Dome Lid, Ogee Bands, Pointed Arches, Ogee Foot, Diamond, c.1935, 10 ⅞ In.	948.00
Charger, Shaped Rims, Chased Flowers, Leaves, 15 In. Diam., Pair	2124.00
Chocolate Pot, Hinged Lid, Wide Spout, Turned Wood Handle, Monogram, c.1900, 8 In.	295.00
Chocolate Set, Pot, Creamer, Sugar, Inscribed October 23, 1948 From All Of Us, 3 Piece	714.00
Cigar Case, 3 Shaped Compartments, c.1900, 2 x 5 In.	420.00
Cigar Case, Pocket, 3 Tubes, Embossed Flowers, Monogram, Marked, 5 ½ In. ....*illus*	201.00
Cigarette Case, Art Nouveau, Flowers, c.1900, 3 ⅜ x 2 ⅝ In.	472.00
Coffee Spoon, Mayflower Pattern, Monogram, Satin Lined Taupe Case, c.1900, 4 In., 12 Piece	153.00
Coffeepot, Curved Spout, Squared Handle, Round Foot, c.1905, 11 In.	460.00
Coffeepot, Cylindrical, Tapered, Lid, Pineapple Finial, Ivory Handle, c.1895, 8 ½ In.	1185.00
Coffeepot, Demitasse, Tapered Cylindrical Shape, Angular Handle & Spout, c.1935, 7 ½ In.	356.00
Coffeepot, Shaped Handle, Upright Spout, Scrolling, Ball Finial, 9 In.	415.00
Compote, Leaf Shape Bowl, Curved Handle, Berry Clusters, Round Foot, 1900s, 8 In., Pair	3125.00
Compote, Lobed, Scalloped, Serpentine Handles, Reeded, Hammered, 1907, 7 ⅝ x 10 In., Pair.	1422.00
Compote, Monogram, Footed, Flared Scalloped Rim, Morning Glory Vine, 8 x 15 In.	3450.00
Compote, Navette Pierced Sides, Shaped Rim, Rocaille Scrolls, Trumpet Base, c.1900, 12 In.	770.00
Compote, Pedestal Foot, Serpentine Border, Gadroon, Shells, 1950s, 4 x 12 In.	1016.00
Compote, Pedestal, Stepped Circular Foot, Flowers, Anthemion Banding, 1884, 6 ½ In.	956.00
Compote, Repousse Leaves, Scrolls, Flowers, Flared Shaped Rim, Round Foot, 6 ½ In.	390.00
Compote, Round Bowl, Leaf Design Border, Tapered Stem, Round Foot, 6 In., Pair	199.00
Compote, Round Reeded Pedestal Base, Repousse Flowers & Leaves, c.1930, 6 x 3 In.	230.00
Creamer, Underplate, Oval, Crested Square Handle, Flared Spout, Round Foot, 1955, 4 ¼ In.	184.00
Cup, 2 Handles, Urn Shape, Copper Body, Dome Foot, Serpentine Handles, c.1900, 6 ¼ In.	178.00

Cup, Christening, Cylindrical, Bulbous, Herringbone Design, Reeded Handle, c.1885, 3 3 ¼ In.	215.00
Cup, Dome Lid, 2 Scroll Handles, Campana Shape, Serpents, c.1776, 15 ½ x 10 ½ In.	15990.00
Cup, Trophy, 2 Scroll Handles, Round Pedestal Foot, c.1905, 7 In.	764.00
Demitasse Spoon, Floral Repousse, Marked, 3 ¾ In., 12 Piece	104.00
Dish, Cover, Oval, 2 Handles, Hot Water Chamber, Reeded Borders, Strapwork, c.1780, 5 ½ x 14 In.	1708.00
Dish, Footed, Chased Repousse, Putto, Bows & Arrows, Clouds, Shaped Rim, c.1900, 2 ⅝ x 10 In.	472.00
Dish, Footed, Shaped Oval, Lion's Head, Loop Pulls, Sphinx Shape Feet, 3 x 10 In.	1528.00
Dish, Reticulated Scroll Border, Round, Hammered, 10 In.	242.00
Dish, Round, Shaped Rim, Molded Leaf Border, 15 ½ In.	1300.00
Dish, Scalloped Shell Shape, Marked, 8 ¼ x 5 ¾ In.	155.00
Dish, Sweetmeat, Pierced Rim, Carnation Stems, N.Y., c.1895, 7 In.	178.00
Dresser Bottle, Lid, Undulating Shape, Chased Poppies, 5 In.	690.00
Dresser Set, Floral Pattern, Fitted Box, Marked Simons Brothers, c.1900, 9 x 12 In., 8 Piece	316.00
Ewer, Footed, Wide Spout, S-Shape Handle, Bulbous Body, Marked, c.1860, 9 In.	3163.00
Figurine, Dog, Airedale Terrier, Seated Pose, Floppy Ears, 5 ¾ In.	625.00
Figurine, Pug Dog, Playful, Marked, 1 ¾ In.	57.00
Figurine, Rabbit, Seated, c.1905, 4 ½ In.	230.00
Fish Serving Set, Parcel Gilt, Etched Flowers, Leaves, Textured, c.1890, Knife, 11 ½ In., Fork, 9 ½ In.	563.00
Flask, Rectangular, Hammered, Engraved Polo Player, Winged Mercury Foot, c.1910, 10 ¼ In.	711.00
Flower Basket, Round Foot, Trumpet Shape, Flared Rim, Pierced Stationary Handle, 23 In.	1315.00
Fork, B Engraved, W In Circle, 2 Birds, 6 ½ In.	35.00
Grape Stand, Pierced Rim, Band Of Daffodils, Low Foot, Over Arching Support, c.1900, 10 ½ In.	770.00
Ice Bucket, Cylindrical, Low Flared Foot, 2 Handles, Reeded Rim, Peak Lid, c.1950, 10 ½ In.	613.00
Ice Cream Spoon, Crystal Handle, c.1910, 10 In.	390.00
Jug, Wine, Pear Shape, Applied Bull, Hay Bale, Branches, Engraved, 1983, 13 In.	878.00
Julep Cup, Cylindrical, Monogram, Beaded Band At Top & Bottom, 1800s, 4 In.	690.00
Julep Cup, Marked Old Friend, Monogram, 5 ¼ In., 6 Piece	1434.00
Kettle, Hot Water, Stand, Flowers, Finial, Scroll Feet, Round Base, Engraved, 15 In.	3738.00
Ladle, Round Bowl, Slashed Drop, Down Turned Handle Tip, Engraved Bellflower, Marked, 14 ¼ In.	444.00
Loving Cup, Trophy, Red Enamel, Engraved, Monogram ERL, c.1903	604.00
Mirror, Snow White & 7 Dwarfs, Easel Stand, 15 ½ x 13 In.	1150.00
Mirror, Vanity, Openwork Filigree, Flowers, Red Velvet Backing, Fox, 16 In.	242.00
Muddler, Wood Base, 6 ½ In.	73.00
Mug, Engraved Design, Handle, c.1850, 3 ½ In.	210.00
Mustard Pot, Hinged Lid, Reticulated Surround, Bun Feet, Spoon, c.1800s, 19 x 21 ¼ In.	239.00
Napkin Rings are listed in their own category.	
Perfume Bottle, Trivet Set, Art Nouveau, Overlay, 4 ½ & 4 In., 6 Piece	600.00
Pitcher, Bulbous, Stepped Round Foot, Repousse Flowers, 9 ¼ In.	717.00
Pitcher, Chased Panels, Flower Garlands, Baluster, Angular Handle, Wide Spout, 1915, 7 ¼ In.	885.00
Pitcher, Cocktail, Baluster, Wide Spout, Lid, Ear Handle, Chased Leaves & Flowers, c.1950, 11 ⅜ In.	830.00
Pitcher, Flower Embossed, Footed, 7 ½ In.	480.00
Pitcher, Globular, Flare Spout, Loop Handle, Footed, Shield, Melon Design, c.1949, 9 In.	920.00
Pitcher, Helmet Shape, Bellflower Border, 1900s, 8 ½ x 9 ½ In.	720.00
Pitcher, Oval, Waisted Foot & Collar, Flowers, Whiplash Leaves, Arched Handle, c.1900, 10 In.	1476.00
Pitcher, Urn Shape, Spread Foot, Scrolling Flowers, C-Scroll Handle, Flared Spout, 9 In.	657.00
Pitcher, Water, Fish & Seagrass Design, c.1900, 9 In.	2875.00
Pitcher, Water, Oval, Round Foot, Waisted Collar, Shaped Spout, C-Scroll Handle, 1946, 9 x 9 ½ In.	1353.00
Pitcher, Water, Oval, Serpentine Handle, Short Spout, Tiered Foot, c.1900, 9 ½ In.	652.00
Pitcher, Water, Oval, Waisted Collar, Integral Spout, S-Scroll Handle, Beaded Banding, 1898, 6 ½ In.	522.00
Pitcher, Water, Shaped Spout, Reeded Round Foot, Square Handle, Monogram, 10 In.	863.00
Plaque, Round Classical Design, Seated Woman, Floral Corners, 7 x 7 In.	180.00
Plate, Bellflower, Scroll & Leaf, 1900s, 11 ¼ In.	660.00
Platter, Oval, Gadroon Edge, Flower Rim, 14 ½ x 11 In.	575.00
Platter, Round, Molded Rim, Monogram Center, c.1915, 14 In. Diam.	922.00
Platter, Round, Quarter Lobed, Recessed Plateau, Hammered Finish, c.1900, 14 In.	1045.00
Porringer, Bulbous, Chased, Embossed Flowers, Pierced Handle, 1895, 7 ¼ In.	237.00
Porringer, Colonial Revival, Reticulated Handle, c.1955, 7 ⅛ In.	337.00
Punch Ladle, Enamel & Gold Wash, 3 Lobes, Neptune Figure, Masked Figure, 14 In.	708.00
Punch Ladle, Flowers, Stippled Ground, Gold Wash Bowl, c.1880, 13 ¾ In.	326.00
Salver, George II, Round, Coat Of Arms, Cupid Masks, Shells, Scroll Feet, 1749, 17 In.	6500.00
Salver, Oval, Gadroon, Raised Borders, Serpentine Rim, Monogram, 14 x 10 In.	621.00
Sauce Ladle, Morning Glory, Blossoms & Leaves, Cast Handle, 1865, 7 In.	288.00
Serving Bowl, Cut Glass Liner, Footed, Monogram, 3 ½ x 6 ¼ In.	201.00
Serving Bowl, Repousse Flowers & Leaves, Lobed Top, Gilt Interior, 8 ½ In. Diam.	472.00
Serving Bowl, Round, Gadroon Rim, 9 ⅝ In. Diam.	354.00

Souvenir, Sand Picture, Bottle, Needles Rocks, Alum Bay, Isle Of Wight, W. Carpenter, c.1850, 4 ⅞ In.
$770.00

Skinner, Inc.

Spatterware, Cup & Saucer, Peafowl, Blue Sponge Rims, Handleless Cup, 2 ½ x 5 In.
$94.00

Conestoga Auction Co., Inc.

Spatterware, Cup & Saucer, Thistle, Yellow, Red, Green, Handleless Cup, 6 In.
$649.00

Morphy Auctions

Spatterware, Pitcher & Bowl, Blue & Green, Sponge, Blue Bands, 8-In. Pitcher, 11 ½-In. Bowl
$83.00

Conestoga Auction Co., Inc.

S

Spatterware, Pitcher, Blue & White, Sponge, Applied Handle, 9 In. $396.00

Conestoga Auction Co., Inc.

Spatterware, Pitcher, Blue & White, Sponge, Pinch Spout, Applied Handle, 7 x 5 ¼ In. $142.00

Conestoga Auction Co., Inc.

Spatterware, Plate, 3 Acorns, Leaves, Blue Paneled Border, 9 ¼ In. $472.00

Conestoga Auction Co., Inc.

Pottery Padded the Price

Old Sleepy Eye stoneware pitchers were put in bags of flour sold by the Sleepy Eye Milling Company. But the government made the company stop the practice because the pottery was so heavy the customer did not get the full weight of flour paid for.

Serving Dish, Cover, Oval, Double Ogee Rim, c.1900, 11 ½ In.	1304.00
Serving Dish, Dome Lid With Reeded Handle, 2 Handles, Elongated Octagon, c.1801, 5 x 15 In.	1298.00
Serving Dish, Floral Repousse, Engraved Diamond Pattern, Cartouche, 12 ½ x 7 In.	529.00
Serving Dish, Leaf Shape, Loop Handle, c.1950, 10 ⅝ In.	385.00
Serving Dish, Oblong, Shaped Sides, Molded Flower Rim, Engraved Center, c.1900, 15 ½ In.	1470.00
Serving Spoon, Calla Lily Stem, Parcel Gilt, Openwork Leaves, c.1860, 8 ½ In. *illus*	326.00
Serving Spoon, Cast Hibiscus Flowers, Gold Wash Blade, c.1920, 9 ½ In.	296.00
Serving Spoon, Good Luck, Shaped Stem, 4-Leaf Clover Ground, c.1895, 9 In.	356.00
Smoking Set, Square Shape, Miniature Oil Lamp Lighter, Hammered, 1907-37, 8 In.	748.00
Soup Ladle, Olive Stem, Monogram, c.1950, 12 ¾ In.	207.00
Spoon, Souvenir, see Souvenir category.	
Stuffing Spoon, Scallop Shell Handle, Arrow, c.1820, 12 In., Pair	805.00
Sugar & Creamer, Curved Strap Handles, Flower Shape Rim, Bulbous Body, Pad Feet, 6 In.	305.00
Sugar & Creamer, Flattened Spherical Shape, Handle, 3 In.	244.00
Sugar & Creamer, Helmet Shape, Footed, Loop Handles, Flower Rim, Marked, 4 ½ In.	259.00
Sugar & Creamer, Helmet Shape, Reeded Rim, Lion, Feet, Strapwork, c.1850, 4 ⅜ In.	563.00
Sugar & Creamer, Undertray, Loop Handles, Bulbous, Wide Spout, 9 In.	519.00
Sugar Basket, Navette Shape, Oval Base, Leaf & Flowers, Reeded Swing Handle, c.1793, 5 ¾ In.	1185.00
Sugar Basket, Oval Shape, Round Foot, Reeded Edge, Swing Handle, Cobalt Glass, c.1907, 5 x 4 In.	338.00
Sugar Bowl, Sack Shape, Gold Washed Wire Tie, Interior, Marked AK, c.1903, 5 In.	504.00
Sugar Castor, 8 Paneled Sides, Footed, Finial, c.1932, 8 In.	413.00
Sugar Castor, Flower Basket Finial, 5 ½ In.	113.00
Sugar Tongs, Bow Style, Acorn Grips, c.1810-18, 5 ⅜ In.	123.00
Tankard, C-Shape Handle, Raised Heart, Cylindrical, Footed, Thumblift Lid, c.1773, 7 In.	1770.00
Tankard, Scroll Handle, Thumb Lift, Band Trim, Marked, 6 In.	1495.00
Tankard, Trophy, Hinged Lid, Cylindrical, Ear Handle, Thumbpiece, Birds, c.1887, 6 ¾ In.	2252.00
Tantalus Set, 3 Cut Crystal Decanters, Footed, 12 x 12 In.	390.00
Tazza, Chased Gadroon, Acanthus, Flower Heads, Monogram, 2 ¾ x 6 ½ In., Pair	384.00
Tazza, Pierced Design, Monogram, Pedestal Foot, Shell Feet, Shaped Rim, c.1895, 13 In.	502.00
Tazza, Swan Handles, Footed, 5 ½ x 4 ½ In.	173.00
Tea & Coffee Set, Plymouth, Gorham, 13 ½ In., 1900s, 7 Piece	3250.00
Tea & Coffee Set, Rococo, Embossed, Coffeepot, Teapot, Creamer, Sugar, Tray, 1900s, Tray, 27 ¾ In.	1920.00
Tea & Coffee Set, Sugar & Creamer, Tray, Ebony Finials, Angular Handles, c.1970, 12 x 18 In. *illus*	5310.00
Tea Tray, Plymouth, Oval, Reeded Rim, Cutout Handles, 1900s, 25 In.	3911.00
Teapot, Hinged Lid, Urn Shape, Wood Handle, c.1885, Miniature, 7 ¾ x 7 In.	418.00
Teapot, Oval Urn Shape, Angular Square Handle, R Monogram, S-Spout, Lid, c.1885, 8 In.	472.00
Teapot, Repousse Roses, Leaves, Round Foot, Loop Handle, Curved Spout, 1880-90, 7 In.	1293.00
Teapot, Tilting, Stand, Embossed, Ivory Insulators On Handles, 11 ½ In.	575.00
Toothpick Holder, Pendant, Engraved, Silver Bail, 2 ½ In.	118.00
Tray, Oval, Gadroon Design Rim, Central Inscription, c.1972, 12 ½ In. Diam.	563.00
Tray, Round, Footed, Repousse Flowers & Leaves, Scrolling, Marked, 1712, 12 In.	1763.00
Tray, Round, Greek Key Edge, Stylized Flower Border, 11 In.	339.00
Tray, Round, Reticulated Gallery, Gadroon Band, 4 Spherical Feet, Mirrored, 12 In. Diam.	738.00
Trophy, Bowl, Applied Fish, Lily Pads, Seaweed, Bear Head Handles, 1873-91, 5 x 11 In.	5875.00
Trophy, Urn Shape, Half Rib Design, Flowers, New York Yacht Club, c.1907, 7 In.	460.00
Tureen, Dome Lid, Round, Rope Twist Border, Ebony Finial, c.1945, 5 x 9 In.	2125.00
Urn, Potpourri, Pierced Lid, Spiral Finial, Loop Handles, Engraved Husks, Trumpet Foot, c.1900, 8 In.	385.00
Vase Holder, Etched Glass Insert, Openwork, Cone Shape, Ruffled Rim, 16 In.	456.00
Vase, Cone Shape, Flared Scalloped Rim, Round Foot, Engraved Flowers, 1900s, 10 In.	160.00
Vase, Round, Serpentine, Molded Rim, Flower Vignettes, Engraved, Quatrefoil Base, 15 In.	1100.00
Waiter, Forget-Me-Not Swags, Beaded Shaped Rim, Round, Footed, Marked, 1900s, 14 ¼ In. Diam.	1062.00
Waiter, Oval, Beaded Greek Key Rim, Engraved, Leaf Scrolling, Scroll Feet, 1859, 9 x 11 In.	1107.00
Wine Coaster, Crested, Pierced Side, Engraved, Reeded Rims, 1 ½ In., Pair	1912.00
Wine Coaster, Pierced & Repousse, Turned Wood Bottom, c.1895, 2 x 4 In. Diam., Pair	472.00
Wine Cooler, Stand, Urn Shape Foot, C-Scroll Handles, Leaves, Pedestal Base, c.1885, 23 ½ x 12 In.	531.00

SILVER-SWEDISH

Beaker, Applied Silver Eagle, Blue Banner, Tapered, Flared, Footed, 1945, 6 ¾ x 4 ½ In.	518.00
Cup, Betrothal, Stippled, Ribbed Base, Monogram, 1779, 4 x 3 ½ In.	173.00
Platter, Applied Ripple Rim, Button Feet, Marked K. Anderson, 19 x 13 In.	1755.00
Tea Urn, Applied Leaves, Pomegranate Finial, Oval, Raised Feet, G. Mollenborg, 1838, 15 ½ In.	4600.00
Wreath, Wedding, Leaf & Flower Design, Set In Shadowbox, Sweden, 9 In.	232.00

SILVER-SWISS

Double Cup, Tapered, Animals, Masks, Spreading Foot, Coat-Of-Arms, 13 In.	23220.00
Platter, Fish, Oval, Molded Edge, 1900s, 25 ⅝ In.	1659.00

SILVER-THAI
Tray, Oval, 10 Figures, Flower Ground, Intertwined Serpent Border, 14 In.................................. 1037.00

SILVER-TURKISH
Cup, Parcel Gilt, Engraved Flowers, Footed, Pink, Gold Russian Porcelain Liner, c.1905, 2 x 2 In., Pair 474.00

SINCLAIRE cut glass was made by H.P. Sinclaire and Company of Corning, New York, between 1904 and 1929. He cut glass made at other factories until 1920. Pieces were made of crystal as well as amber, blue, green, or ruby glass. Only a small percentage of Sinclaire glass is marked with the *S* in a wreath.

Basket, Hiawatha, Triple Notched Handle, Hobstar Base, Pedestal, Oval, American Brilliant, 11 ½ In. 800.00
Bowl, Assyrian, Star Cut Buttons, Sterling Silver Rim, American Brilliant, 4 ½ x 10 In. 550.00
Bowl, Silver Thread, Floral Medallions, Crosscut Diamond, Window Border, 4 x 9 ¼ In........... 300.00
Bowl, Snowflake & Holly, Square, Signed, American Brilliant, 7 ¼ In........................ 600.00
Compote, Translucent Green Foot & Bowl, Amber Stem, Foldover Rim, Etched Flowers, 7 In.. 58.00
Sugar & Creamer, Clear, Green Feet & Handles, 5 In. 58.00
Tray, Star & Pillar, Round, Signed, American Brilliant, 10 In. 1800.00
Vase, Iridescent, Etched Flower Design, Gilt Accents, Cylindrical, Signed, 10 In. 374.00
Vase, Optic Rib, Etched, Meandering Flowers, Leaves, Intaglio, 8 ½ In...................... 63.00
Vase, Trumpet Shape, Wavy Rim, Flowers, Round Foot, Etched Mark, 12 In. 81.00

SKIING, *see Sports category.*

SLAG GLASS resembles a marble cake. It can be streaked with different colors. There were many types made from about 1880. Caramel slag is the incorrect name for chocolate glass. Pink slag was an American product made by Harry Bastow and Thomas E.A. Dugan at Indiana, Pennsylvania, about 1900. Purple and blue slag were made in American and English factories in the 1880s. Red slag is a very late Victorian and twentieth-century glass. Other colors are known but are of less importance to the collector. New versions of chocolate glass and colored slag glass are being made.

Blue, Bell, Southern Woman, 5 In.. 23.00
Blue, Candy Dish, Horse, Lying Down, 4 x 5 In.. 43.00
Blue, Compote, Rose Pattern, Ruffled Rim, Scalloped, Footed, 6 ½ In...................... 45.00
Blue, Dish, Hen On Nest Cover, 6 ½ x 5 ½ In... 41.00
Blue, Salt, Hen On Nest Cover, 2 ¾ x 2 ¼ x 2 In... 27.00
Pink, Compote, Inverted Fan & Feather, c.1900, 5 x 4 In.................................. 650.00
Pink, Tumbler, Inverted Fan & Feather, 4 In.. 300.00
Purple, Box, Cover, Bee Finial, 5 In... 125.00
Purple, Creamer, Wreathed Cherry, 5 In... 55.00
Purple, Dish, Cover, Kitten, 5 In... 40.00
Purple, Toothpick Holder, Forget-Me-Not, 3-Footed.. 36.00
Red, Bell, Figural, Melanie, 1970s, 5 In... 25.00
Red, Compote, Crimped.. 50.00
Red, Nappy, Scalloped Rim, Handle, c.1970, 5 x 2 In. 35.00

SLEEPY EYE collectors look for anything bearing the image of the nineteenth-century Indian chief with the drooping eyelid. The Sleepy Eye Milling Co., Sleepy Eye, Minnesota, used his portrait in advertising from 1883 to 1921. It offered many premiums, including stoneware and pottery steins, crocks, bowls, mugs, and pitchers, all decorated with the famous profile of the Indian. The popular pottery was made by Weir Pottery Co. from c.1899-1905. Weir merged with six other potteries and became Western Stoneware in 1906. Western Stoneware Co. made blue and white Sleepy Eye from 1906 until 1937, long after the flour mill went out of business in 1921. Reproductions of the pitchers are being made today. The original pitchers came in only five sizes: 4 inches, 5 ¼ inches, 6 ½ inches, 8 inches, and 9 inches. The Sleepy Eye image was also used by companies unrelated to the flour mill.

Butter Carton, Chief Sleepy Eye, Sleepy Eye Creamery Butter 5.00
Calendar, 1904, Indian, Sleepy Eye Flour & Cereals.. 130.00
Pitcher, Blue, White, No. 1, 4 In. .... 70.00 to 225.00
Pitcher, Blue, White, No. 3, 6 ½ In.. 120.00
Pitcher, Blue, White, No. 5, 9 In.. 225.00
Pitcher, Blue Rim, No. 3, 6 ½ In.. 2650.00
Pitcher, Blue Rim, No. 4, 8 In.. 100.00
Pitcher, Blue Rim, No. 5, 9 In.. 240.00
Sign, Flour & Cereal Products, Tin, Frame, 25 x 33 In... 9350.00
Stein, Blue, White, Teepee.. 425.00
Textile, American Indian Trademark, Background Indian Scene, Frame, 25 x 25 In. ....*illus* 1760.00

Spatterware, Plate, Peafowl, Blue, Yellow, Red, 8 ¼ In.
$177.00

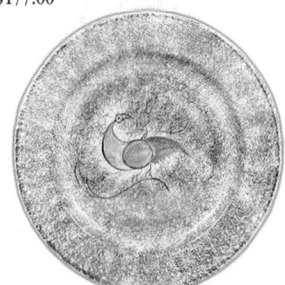

Conestoga Auction Co., Inc.

Spatterware, Plate, Schoolhouse, Ironstone, 8 ½ In.
$189.00

Conestoga Auction Co., Inc.

Spatterware, Plate, Schoolhouse, Red, Blue, Green, c.1820, 8 ¼ In.
$708.00

Morphy Auctions

S

607

Not the Babe

Beware of a baseball that is autographed "Sincerely, Babe Ruth." The Sinclair Oil Company gave signed baseballs as prizes in 1947. The balls were stamped "Sinclair Oil." It is now known that the autograph was signed by a secretary.

Spelter, Sculpture, Caesar Augustus, Standing, Holding Scroll, 1800s, 22 ¼ In.
$245.00

Skinner, Inc.

Spode, Plate, Soup, Partridge, Grasshopper, Flower & Insect Border, Marked, 9 ¾ In.
$12.00

Conestoga Auction Co., Inc.

TIP

To clean old golf clubs, use Liquid Wrench (an oil found in the hardware store) and 0000-grade steel wool. The oil should not discolor the shaft.

SLOT MACHINES *are included in the Coin-Operated Machine category.*

SMITH BROTHERS glass was made after 1878. Alfred and Harry Smith had worked for the Mt. Washington Glass Company in New Bedford, Massachusetts, for seven years before going into their own shop. They made many pieces with enamel decoration.

Biscuit Jar, Blue Opaque Ground, Birds, Medallion Church Scene, Silver Plate, 7 ½ In.	110.00
Biscuit Jar, Melon Ribbed, Cream Color, Autumn Colors, Stamped, 7 In.	200.00
Biscuit Jar, Melon Ribbed, Cream, Autumn Oak Leaves & Acorns, Stamped, 7 In.	250.00
Biscuit Jar, Melon Ribbed, Cream, Green Mottled Ground, Gold Enamel, Applied Jewels, 6 ¼ In.	150.00
Biscuit Jar, Melon Ribbed, Squat, Pink, Green & Gold Leaves, Silver Plate Lid, Handle, 8 In.	173.00
Biscuit Jar, Square, Cream With Crab, Fish & Seaweed Design, Embossed Lid & Bail, 6 In.	300.00
Dish, Sweetmeat, Melon Ribbed, Green, Pink Mottled Ground, Gold Enamel, Silver Plate, 4 ½ In.	110.00
Jar, Sweetmeat, Embossed Lid, Melon Ribbed, Flowers, Leaves, Red Lion Trademark, 5 ½ In. *illus*	403.00
Powder Jar, Babs II, Pink Satin, c.1920s	129.00
Powder Jar, Cinderella's Coach, Green Satin	249.00
Powder Jar, Jackie, Jade Green, 1920s	289.00
Powder Jar, Jackie, Pink Satin, 1920s	149.00
Powder Jar, Kissing Elephants, Pink, Transparent, c.1920s	229.00
Powder Jar, Rin Tin Tin, Green Satin	289.00
Powder Jar, Sailboat, Cobalt Blue	299.00
Powder Jar, Scottie Dog, Cobalt Blue, 1930s	289.00
Powder Jar, Terrier, Standing, Green Satin, Miniature	129.00
Powder Jar, Twins, Green Satin, c.1920s	149.00
Vase, Purple Iris, Long Green Leaves, Clear Body, Ribbed, Ruffled Rim, 10 ½ In.	201.00
Vase, Swirl Mold, Cream Ground, Enamel Daisy, Gold Stencil, Marked, 6 ¾ In.	375.00

SNOW BABIES, made from bisque and spattered with glitter sand, were first manufactured in 1864 by Hertwig and Company of Thuringia. Other German and Japanese companies copied the Hertwig designs. Originally, Snow Babies were made of candy and used as Christmas decorations. There are also Snow Babies tablewares made by Royal Bayreuth. Copies of the small Snow Babies figurines are being made today and a line called "Snowbabies" was introduced by Department 56 in 1987. Don't confuse these with the original Snow Babies.

Figurine, Snow Baby On Raft, Blue Water, Black Dog, Rust Mast & Boots, Marked, 2 ½ In.	295.00

SNUFF BOTTLES *are listed in the Bottle category.*

SNUFFBOXES held snuff. Taking snuff was popular long before cigarettes became available. The gentleman or lady would take a small pinch of the ground tobacco or snuff in the fingers, then sniff it and sneeze. Snuffboxes were made of many materials, including gold, silver, enameled metal, and wood. Most snuffboxes date from the late eighteenth or early nineteenth centuries.

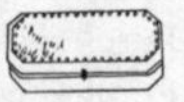

Boxwood, Carved, Mandarin Shape, Hinged, Tortoiseshell Lined, 1800s, 4 ½ In.	420.00
Brass, Copper, Engraved, Oblong, Dutch, 1700s, 7 In.	207.00
Burl, Inset Stylized Star, Oval, Tortoiseshell Liner, 19th Century, 3 ¼ x 2 In.	27.00
Enamel, Copper, Hinged Lid, Round, Cobalt Blue, Man, Woman, Blade Grinder, 1700s, 2 In.	385.00
Enamel, Hound Head Shape, Stone Lid, Paint, England, 2 ¾ In.	486.00
Gold & Diamond, Roundel, Photo, Scrolls, Flower Heads, Lion Mask, c.1840, 4 x 3 In.	14220.00
Hinged Lid, Niello, Rose Cartouche, Checkered Ground, c.1860, 4 In.	652.00
Lacquer, Metamorphic Portrait Man & Woman, Round, 19th Century, 2 ¾ In.	235.00
Papier-Mache, Hinged Lid, Monkey & Dog, Don't You Wish You May Get It, 2 ½ In.	230.00
Papier-Mache, Hinged, Monkey, Dog, Multicolor, 19th Century, ¾ x 2 x 1 In.	230.00
Porcelain, Mennecy Style, Cat, Kittens, Flowers, Hinged Lid, France, c.1890, 2 ¼ In.	474.00
Porcelain, Terrior Head, Hinged Flower Decorated Lid, Gilt Metal Mounts, England, 3 x 2 ½ In.	234.00
Silver Gilt, Gold Trim, Enamel Portrait Of Gainsborough's Blue Boy, Mark London, 1926, 3 ¼ x 2 In.	575.00
Silver Plate, Black Boy On Barrel, Ship, My Massa Sells De Best Tobacco	600.00
Silver, 2 Lids, Gold Wash, Oblong, Leafy Scrolls, Ivory, Cherubs, Lovebird, Cornucopia, 1928, 3 In.	1185.00
Silver, Chinoiserie, George III, Rectangular, Rounded Corners, Asian Script, Gold Wash, 1805, 3 ⅝ In.	337.00
Silver, Geometric Case, Niello Russian City Oval, Clasp, 2 ½ x 1 ½ In.	240.00
Silver, George III, Armorial, Scrolled, Shell Shape, Inscribed Francis Knapp, 2 ¾ x 4 ¼ In.	760.00
Silver, Hinged Lid, Blank Cartouche, 1 ⅛ x ⅞ In.	125.00
Silver, Hinged Lid, Engraved Flowers, Geometrics, Vermeil Interior, Austria, 3 ¼ x 2 In.	127.00
Silver, Hinged Lid, George IV, Rectangular, Engine Turned, 1829, 3 ¼ In.	418.00
Silver, Lid, Rectangular, Copper Enamel Roundel, Cherubs, Faux Lapis Detail, c.1900, 3 ⅛ In.	593.00
Silver, Ogee Edge, Gray Enamel Shield, Black & Gray Ground, Engraved, c.1885, 3 In.	593.00
Tin, General Eleazar Ripley, Bust, Name Above Image, Painted, Cut Corners, 3 In.	2500.00

Tortoiseshell, Hinged Lid, Egg Shape, Gold Inlay, Field Of Stars, England, c.1840, 3 In.	830.00
Tortoiseshell, Lid, Oval Shape, Plaque, Coiled Fierce Dragon, 1900s, 3 ¾ In.	307.00
Tortoiseshell, Silver, Gold Inlay, Kidney Shape, Mother-Of-Pearl, Rooster, c.1800, 3 In.	368.00
Vermeil, Mother-Of-Pearl, Oval, England, 1700s, 3 x 2 In..........	2160.00

SOAPSTONE is a mineral that was used for foot warmers or griddles because of its heat-retaining properties. Soapstone was carved into figurines and bowls in many countries in the nineteenth and twentieth centuries. Most of the soapstone seen today is from China or Japan. It is still being carved in the old styles.

Brush Bowl, Squat, Round, Travelers, Bridge, Men, Mountains, Trees, 1700s, 3 x 6 In.	10925.00
Brushpot, Figures, Landscape, Green, Cylindrical, Chinese, c.1900, 4 ¾ x 4 ⅛ In.	613.00
Brushpot, Green, Amber, Sages, Mountains, Bridges, Village, Buddha, Carved, 1800s, 6 x 6 In..	23000.00
Carving, Bitter Melon, Chinese, 11 ½ In.	329.00
Carving, Dragon, Pearl Ball, Stand, Chinese, 19th Century, 2 x 4 In.	325.00
Carving, Dragons, Clouds, 5 ½ x 5 ½ In.	330.00
Carving, Dragons, Rounded Triangle, Coral Color, Square Base, 8 In.	478.00
Carving, Figure, Monk, Lohan, Kneeling, 6 In.	107.00
Carving, Mountain Landscape, 2 ¼ In.	568.00
Carving, Mountain, Iris Branches, Wood Stand, Chinese, 3 ½ In.	429.00
Carving, Mythological Creature, Head Backwards, Rosewood Stand, Chinese, 5 x 3 ¼ In.	1541.00
Censer, Foo Dogs, Carp, Carved, Chinese, 12 ½ x 11 In.	259.00
Censer, Taotie Mask Design, Carved, Tripod Feet, 2 Handles, Ball Finial, Red, Cream, 9 In.	568.00
Figurine, 8 Immortals, Crossing Sea On Turtle Back, Carved, Footed Base, Rust, Green, 21 ½ In..	538.00
Figurine, Bodhidharma, Seated, Waves, Foo Dog, Incised, Yellow, Red, Wood Stand, Chinese, 6 x 7 In.	5036.00
Figurine, Buddha, Carved, Hardwood Stand, c.1790, 6 In.....	17000.00
Figurine, Buddha, Seated, Foo Dog, Attendants, Waves, Rosewood Stand, 7 x 5 In.	3200.00
Figurine, Dragons, 5 Lohans, Monks, Wood Stand, 6 ½ x 9 ½ In.	1428.00
Figurine, Guanyin On Foo Dog Back, Holding Scepter, Robes, Red, Wood Base, 1900s, 5 In.	4481.00
Figurine, Guanyin, Bronze Mounts, Jade Plaque Finial, Chinese, 13 ½ In.....	123.00
Figurine, Guanyin, Seated, Cross-Legged, Celadon, Robes, Chinese, 13 In.	568.00
Figurine, Horse, Reclining, Green, Carved Wood Base, 5 In., Pair.....	179.00
Figurine, Immortal, Carrying Tree Sprig, Cloud, Flower Robes, Chinese, 1700s, 11 x 14 In....	13035.00
Figurine, Immortal, Standing, Holding Peach, Wood Stand, Chinese, c.1800, 4 ¾.....	980.00
Figurine, Lohan, Seated, Drunk, Holding Wine Jar, Wood Stand, 5 In.....	1470.00
Figurine, Lohan, Seated, Emaciated, Holding Bowl To Chin, 5 ¾ In.	468.00
Figurine, Monk, Lohan, Seated, Gray, Chinese, 3 In.	613.00
Figurine, Mountainous Landscape, People, Chinese, c.1900, 6 In.	9560.00
Figurine, Shao Lao, Holding Staff & Peach, Stand, Chinese, c.1900, 11 In.....	184.00
Group, Melons, Leaves, Dragons Crawling, Wood Stand, Chinese, 3 ¾ x 2 In.	415.00
Group, Water Buffalo, Boy, Child On Top Of Animal, Chinese, 8 In.	239.00
Plaque, Inuit, Walrus, Iceberg, 7 x 5 In.....	15.00
Scarab, Hieroglyphics, Egypt, 2 ½ x 3 ¾ In.....	153.00
Seal, 4 Chi Dragons, Waves, Carved, Orange Ocher, Chinese, 2 ¾ In.....	237.00
Seal, Bear, Fighting, 1968, 7 ½ In.....	68.00
Seal, Birds, Rockery, Coral Color, 2 In.....	478.00
Seal, Dragons, Pearl Finial, Spinach Green, Chinese, 3 ½ x 2 ¾ In.	178.00
Seal, Foo Dog, Calligraphy, Chinese, 4 ⅜ In.....	448.00
Seal, Foo Dog, Puppies, Etched Flower Panels, Columns, 1900s, 6 In., Pair.....	59.00
Seal, Head, Relief Carved, Daoist God Of Wealth & Prosperity, Chinese, 3 ½ In. ....*illus*	615.00
Seal, Horned Dragon, Flared Whiskers, Pearl Of Wisdom, Square Base, Trees, c.1905, 10 ¼ In..	2214.00
Seal, Landscape, Pines, Cottage, Carved, Rectangular, Wood Stand, Chinese, 2 ½ In.	3437.00
Seal, Landscape, Rectangular, Chinese, c.1900, 2 ⅛ x ⅞ In.....	356.00
Seal, Lohan Finial, Hat, Chinese, c.1800.....	214.00
Seal, Mountain Landscape, 7 ½ In.....	388.00
Seal, Mythical Animal, Sleeping, Rectangular, Wood Stand, Chinese, 2 ¼ In.....	178.00
Seal, Rectangular, Carved, Calligraphic Inscription, Chinese, 2 ¼ In. ....*illus*	178.00
Seal, Tortoise, Etched Animal Bones, Characters, Chinese, 2 x 2 In.....	338.00
Snuff Bottle, Female Immortal, Elephant, Waves, Hu Shape, Stopper, Chinese, c.1910, 2 In...	474.00
Stand, Rocky Mountain & Clouds Shape, Chinese, 1800s, 7 x 10 ½ In.....	184.00
Vase, Cover, Baluster, Carved, Taotie Mask Design, Animal Shape Handles, 10 ½ In..............	179.00
Vase, Double Gourd Shape, Grapevine Design, 9 In.	389.00
Vase, Double, Applied Flowers, Branches, Birds, Green, Red, Brown, Black, Chinese, 1900, 8 In.	120.00
Vase, Dragon Carved Body, Tan & Brown Neck, Stand, Chinese, c.1880, 4 ½ x 7 ½ In..............	1210.00
Vase, Flowers & Animals, Carved, Chinese, 8 In.....	104.00
Vase, Stand, Carved, Amber Colored, Dragons, Chinese, c.1880, 4 ½ x 7 ½ In.....	1320.00

Sports, Baseball, Button, Baltimore Welcomes All Star Game, Union Bug, 1958, 1 ¼ In.
$75.00

Hake's Americana & Collectibles

Sports, Baseball, Nodder, New York Mets, 1962
$73.00

Philip Weiss Auctions

Sports, Football, Figure, Chicago Bears, Running Back, No. 18 Decal, Hartland, 1960s, 7 ½ In.
$190.00

Hake's Americana & Collectibles

Sports, Football, Nodder, St. Louis Cardinals, Composition, 1960s, 7 In.
$48.00

Serious Toyz

S

Sports, Horse Racing, Trophy, Pitcher, Silver, Fleetwood Driving Park, Gorham, 1896, 9 ½ In.
$1476.00

Neal Auction Co.

Sports, Pool, Cue Rack, Oak, Marble, Brass Mounts, Fluted Columns, Rotating, c.1900, 87 x 20 In.
$1968.00

New Orleans Auction Galleries, Inc.

Vase, Urn Shape, Flowers, Birds, Footed, c.1940, 6 ½ In.	65.00
Weight, Scroll, Scholars, Rocky Landscape, Rectangular, Chinese, c.1900, 7 ¾ x 1 In., Pair	563.00

SOFT PASTE is a name for a type of pottery. Although it looks very much like porcelain, it is a chemically different material. Most of the soft-paste wares were made in the early nineteenth century. Other pieces may be listed under Gaudy Dutch or Leeds.

Bowl, Blue Willow, Blue & White, 9 ¾ x 7 ¼ In.	150.00
Bowl, Reticulated, Flowers, Octagonal, 9 ¼ x 2 In.	250.00
Cup & Saucer, Fruit, Flowers, 1800s	50.00
Dresser Doll, Blue Dress, Blonde, Bow, 5 In.	95.00
Mug, Canary Yellow, Silver Trim, Flowers, Leaves, 4 ⅜ In.	495.00
Plate, Feather, Blue & Yellow Flowers, Scalloped Rim, c.1850, 10 ½ In.	80.00
Plate, King's Rose, Oyster Variant, Pink Border, c.1830, 7 ½ In.	82.00
Plate, Queen's Rose, Feathered Border, 1830s, 8 ⅜ In.	95.00
Sugar, King's Rose, 2 Handles, Flower Finial, Creamware, 4 ¾ x 4 ¾ In.	150.00

SOUVENIRS of a trip—what could be more fun? Our ancestors enjoyed the same thing, and souvenirs were made for almost every location. Most of the souvenir pottery and porcelain pieces of the nineteenth century were made in England or Germany, even if the picture showed a North American scene. In the twentieth century, the souvenir china business seems to have gone to the manufacturers in Japan, Taiwan, Hong Kong, England, and America. Another popular souvenir item is the souvenir spoon, made of sterling or silver plate. These are usually made in the country pictured on the spoon. Related pieces may be found in the Coronation and World's Fair categories.

Book Cover, Alaska, Satin, Roses, Mountains, Dog Sled, 1930s, 16 x 11 In.	10.00
Bowl, Custard Glass, Ohio Valley Expo, 1910, 2 ½ In x 3 ¼ In.	50.00
Charm, Washington, D.C., Capitol, Flags, Sterling, Rosecraft, 1960s, 1 In.	19.00
Compact, Disneyland, Metal, Mirror, Square, Box	31.00
Compact, New Jersey, Metal, Engraved, Lois B, Mirror	50.00
Compact, Niagara Falls, Canada, Metal, Mirror, Square, Push Opener, Box	32.00
Compact, Vero Beach, Florida, Pink Flamingo, Plastic	68.00
Creamer, Billy Possum, Figural, Souvenir Of Washington, Gold Trim, 5 ½ In.	500.00
Creamer, Men On Horse, Widecombe Fair, Yellow, c.1850, 3 ⅜ In.	45.00
Glass, Kentucky Derby, 1960, Mint Julep, 5 ⁵⁄₁₆ In.	45.00
Glass, Kentucky Derby, 1970, Mint Julep 5 ⁵⁄₁₆ In.	70.00
Glass, Kentucky Derby, Swag Of Red Roses, 112th Race, 1986, 5 ¼ In.	13.00
Life Belt, R.M.S. Titanic, Olympic, Painted Ship Panels, Flags, Shadowbox, 8 ½ In., Pair	10158.00
Pennant, Astronaut John Glenn, 1st American In Orbit, Felt, Photo, 1962, 17 ½ In.	115.00
Pennant, Coney Island, Parachute Jump Ride, Blue Green, 3-Sided, 1930s, 30 In.	128.00
Pig In Cup, Kingston, N.Y., Germany, 2 ½ In.	23.00
Pillbox, A Trifle From New York, Enamel Insert, Filigree Border, Silver, 1780s, 2 In.	2500.00
Pillow Cover, Adirondacks, Stag, Satin, Embroidered, 1923, 17 x 17 In.	35.00
Pin, America's Astronauts, Men Of The Year, Glenn, Shephard, Grissom, 1962	323.00
Pin, Astronaut John Glenn, Man Of The Year, New Frontier, Portrait, 1962, 6 In.	86.00
Pin, Atlanta, G-E-O-R-G-I-A, Watermelon Sliced In Two Pieces, 1 ¼ In.	58.00
Pin, Atlantic City For Mine, Photograph Of Beach Scene, 1909, 2 ⅛ In.	97.00
Pin, Bar, Stand Up For Kansas, Suspended Sunflower, Brass, Embossed, Early 1900s, 2 In.	57.00
Pin, Chicago, The World's Greatest Convention City, Woman I Will, Scenes, 2 In.	115.00
Pin, Meet Me At The Abilene Carnival, Oct. 3, 1900, Man In Devil Costume, 1 ¾ In.	109.00
Pin, Playboy Club, VIP With Logo, Oval, Yellow, Black, Litho, 1960s, 2 ⅜ In.	40.00
Pin, Saltwater Summer Resort, Devil's Lake, N. Dak., Vacation Couple, 1898, 1 ¼ In.	52.00
Pin, Tulsa, Photograph Of City, 1926, 2 ⅜ In.	83.00
Pin, Visit Cave Of The Winds, Cyclone Of Fun, Woman, Blowing Hair, 1901, 1 ¼ In.	82.00
Pin, Wichita Carnival & Fall Festival, Oct. 1 To 6, 1900, Woman In Gauzy Veil, 1 ¾ In.	424.00
Pin, Wichita Carnival, Sept. 30 To Oct. 5-01, I'm Glad I Came, Art Nouveau Woman, 1 ½ In.	52.00
Plate, Clambroth, Buffalo, N.Y., Daisies, Leaves, Lacy Edge, 5 ½ In.	25.00
Plate, Conneaut Lake Exposition, White China, Violets, Leafy Plant, 1900, 5 ½ In.	50.00
Plate, Empire State Building, Black Border, Gilt Trim, c.1950, 10 ¾ In.	35.00
Plate, The Alamo, Texas, Japan, 8 In.	12.00
Powder Jar, Niagara Falls, Medal Lid. Canadian Falls At Night, Ribbed Glass, 1930s, 3 In.	45.00
Ring, Yellowstone Park, Bear, Pine Trees, Old Faithful, Silvered Brass, Adjustable, 1930s	52.00
Sand Picture, Bottle, Needles Rocks, Alum Bay, Isle Of Wight, W. Carpenter, c.1850, 4 ⅞ In. ...*illus*	770.00
Sculpture, Dog, TAMCB Guggenheim, Handmade Boxwood Display, Resin Base, Spain, 1992, 8 x 8 In.	900.00
Spoon, Birmingham, England, Sterling Silver, 1905, 5 ¾ In.	128.00
Spoon, Pittsburgh, Castle, Sterling Silver, Twisted Handle, 1764, 5 ½ In.	17.00
Toothpick Holder, Solon, Maine, Ring Band, Custard, Gold, Heisey	45.00

S

Toothpick Holder, Mug, Ruby Flash Glass, Coney Island, 1905, 2 In.	20.00
Tumbler, Atlantic City Boardwalk, Ruby Glass, 1904, 4 In.	35.00
Tumbler, Glass, Green, Prospect Point, Niagara Falls, Decal, Enamel Flowers, Gilt, c.1900, 4 In. ..	50.00

SPANGLE GLASS is multicolored glass made from odds and ends of colored glass rods. It includes metallic flakes of mica covered with gold, silver, nickel, or copper. Spangle glass is usually cased with a thin layer of clear glass over the multicolored layer. Similar glass is listed in the Vasa Murrhina category.

Bowl, Crimped Rim, Ruffled, Pink, 3 ⅛ In.	165.00
Bowl, Melon Shape, 5 x 5 ½ In.	295.00
Pitcher, Pink, Amber Twisted S-Shape Handle, Amber Round Foot, 7 In.	58.00
Vase, Jack-In-The-Pulpit, Twisted, 7 In.	60.00
Vase, Pinched Feet, 6 In.	150.00
Vase, Pink, Globular, Ribbed, 4-Footed, c.1875, 4 ⅞ In.	100.00
Vase, Stick Neck, Swirled Ribs, c.1890, 5 In.	290.00

SPANISH LACE *is listed in the Opalescent category as Opaline Brocade.*

SPATTER GLASS is a multicolored glass made from many small pieces of different colored glass. It is sometimes called End-of-Day glass. It is still being made.

Bowl, 3-Footed, 8 ½ x 4 In.	79.00
Pitcher, Clear Handle, 4 In.	104.00
Toothpick Holder, Leaf Mold, Northwood, 1 ¾ In.	150.00
Vase, Bulbous, Ruffled Rim, Hobbs, Brockunier, 1880s, 6 In.	75.00
Vase, Green, Pink, Flowers, Leaves, Ebony Vines, Gourd Shape, 7 In.	431.00
Vase, Pink, Blue Iridescent, Orange Glow, Lava, Pea Fowl Feathers Design, 4 ⅜ In.	460.00
Vase, Swirled, Pinched Rim, 8 In.	178.00

SPATTERWARE and spongeware are terms that have changed in meaning in recent years, causing much confusion for collectors. Some say that *spatterware* is the term used by Americans, *sponged ware* or *spongeware* by the English. Spatterware is creamware or soft paste dinnerware decorated with colored spatter designs. The earliest pieces were made in the late eighteenth century, but most of the spatterware found today was made from about 1800 to 1850. Early spatterware was made in the Staffordshire district of England for sale in America. Collectors also use the word *spatterware* to refer to kitchen crockery with added spatter made in America during the late nineteenth and early twentieth centuries. Spongeware is very similar to spatterware in appearance. Designs were applied to ceramics by daubing the color on with a sponge or cloth. Many collectors do not differentiate between spongeware and spatterware and use the names interchangeably. Modern pottery is being made to resemble old spongeware, but careful examination will show it is new.

Bowl, Green, Brown, Tan, Incised Swirls, Scalloped Band At Top, 10 In.	5.15
Creamer, Green, Red, Brown, Schoolhouse, c.1820, 4 ½ In.	2360.00
Creamer, Loop Handle, Multicolor Splotches, 4 In.	57.00
Cup & Saucer, Crisscross Design, Handleless	53.00
Cup & Saucer, Dove, Blue, Yellow	1652.00
Cup & Saucer, Peacock, Red Spatter, Handleless Cup, 5 ¾-In. Saucer	86.00
Cup & Saucer, Peafowl, Blue Sponge Rims, Handleless Cup, 2 ½ x 5 In. ....*illus*	94.00
Cup & Saucer, Peafowl, Red, Green, Blue, Yellow, c.1820	324.00
Cup & Saucer, Red, Blue & Yellow Rooster On Front, Spatter Border	118.00
Cup & Saucer, Thistle, Yellow, Red, Green, Handleless Cup, 6 In. ....*illus*	649.00
Cuspidor, Blue, White, Paper Label, 5 ½ In.	95.00
Jug, Cream, Bulbous, Blue & Manganese, Applied Loop Handle, 4 ⅞ In.	153.00
Mug, Baseball Players, 4 ½ In.	156.00
Mug, Stick, Tapered, Flowers, Rabbit & Frog Border, Applied Handle, 5 ½ In.	1074.00
Pitcher & Bowl, Blue & Green, Sponge, Blue Bands, 8-In. Pitcher, 11 ½-In. Bowl ....*illus*	83.00
Pitcher, 5 Colors, Scalloped Rim, Flared Spout, Scroll Handle, Round Foot, 10 In.	1725.00
Pitcher, Blue & White, Sponge, Applied Handle, 9 In. ....*illus*	396.00
Pitcher, Blue & White, Sponge, Pinch Spout, Applied Handle, 7 x 5 ¼ In. ....*illus*	142.00
Pitcher, Blue Sponge, Bombe Base, Applied Loop Handle, Pinch Spout, 9 x 5 ½ In.	71.00
Pitcher, Lady Liberty, Blue Sponging, Baluster, Loop Handle, U.S.A., c.1850, 9 ¼ In.	118.00
Plate, 3 Acorns, Leaves, Blue Paneled Border, 9 ¼ In. ....*illus*	472.00
Plate, Acorn Center Design, Purple, 1800s, 9 In.	1007.00
Plate, Blue, Green Rainbow, Bull's-Eye, 1800s, 8 ¼ In.	2252.00
Plate, Blue, Sunburst & Star, Paneled Border, 9 ¼ In.	236.00
Plate, Peafowl, Blue, Yellow, Red, 8 ¼ In. ....*illus*	177.00

Sports, Pool, Table, Arts & Crafts, Accessories, Monarch, Brunswick-Balke-Collender, c.1910, 110 x 60 In. $4425.00

Ivey-Selkirk Auctioneers

Staffordshire, Casserole, Hen On Nest Cover, Painted, 3 ¾ x 4 In. $59.00

Conestoga Auction Co., Inc.

Staffordshire, Coffeepot, Dome Lid, Castle Ruins, Blue Transfer, Footed, 11 ¼ In. $130.00

Conestoga Auction Co., Inc.

Is the Day Old?
Old Staffordshire figurines have slightly concave bottoms, not flat ones like new figurines. Old bottoms have a small hole that lets steam escape while in the hot kiln. Fakes often have large holes. The gold trim on new Staffordshire figurines is very bright and shiny. Old figurines have worn gold trim that is dull.

S

Staffordshire, Figurine, Man & Woman, Seated, 1800s, 13 In., Pair
$300.00

DuMouchelles Art Gallery -Du1111-2465

Staffordshire, Figurine, Sheep Standing In Front Of Tree, c.1850, 4 ½ x 4 In.
$108.00

DuMouchelles Art Gallery

Staffordshire, Figurine, Zebra, Bridles & Reins, Grassy Ground, 1800s, 9 x 8 ¼ In., Pair
$299.00

Neal Auction Co.

Staffordshire, Group, Androcles & Lion, Seated, Flowing Robe, Holding Paw, c.1850, 10 ½ In.
$633.00

Leland Little Auction

Plate, Primrose Pattern, Blue, 8 ¾ In.	71.00
Plate, Rainbow, Red, Green, 1800s, 8 ½ In.	889.00
Plate, Rose & Leaves, Blue Spatter Border, c.1835, 7 In.	86.00
Plate, Schoolhouse Pattern, House, Green Tree & Ground, Red Spatter Border, 8 ½ In.	106.00
Plate, Schoolhouse, 3 Colors, Green Border, 1800s, 8 ½ In.	1018.00
Plate, Schoolhouse, Ironstone, 8 ½ In. ......*illus*	189.00
Plate, Schoolhouse, Red, Blue, Green, c.1820, 8 ¼ In. .....*illus*	708.00
Plate, Toddy, Acorn Center, Red Paneled Border, c.1810, 5 In.	588.00
Platter, Peafowl, Red Spatter Border, Octagonal, c.1820, 14 x 11 In.	708.00
Sugar, Cover, Blue, Red, Bulbous, Flared Rim, Raised Molded Foot, 6 ½ x 5 ¾ In.	118.00
Sugar, Covered, Red & Green Tulip Design	47.00
Teapot, Blue With Yellow, Blue & Red 2-Sided Rooster, Matching Lid With Finial, 1840	295.00
Teapot, Blue, Rooster, 2-Sided, Lid, Finial, c.1840, 5 ¼ In.	295.00
Umbrella Stand, Cylindrical, Blue Sponging Over White, Late 1800s, 21 In.	40.00

SPELTER is a synonym for a zinc alloy. Figurines, candlesticks, and other pieces were made of spelter and given a bronze or painted finish. The metal has been used since about the 1860s to make statues, tablewares, and lamps that resemble bronze. Spelter is soft and breaks easily. To test for spelter, scratch the base of the piece. Bronze is solid; spelter will show a silvery scratch.

Candleholder, Gilt, Verdigris, Stocky Man In Tights, Holding Sword, Round Base, 8 In., Pair.	237.00
Candlestick, Figural, Man, Holding Cigar, Woman, Lap Dog, Opera Glasses, c.1900, 18 In., Pair.	385.00
Cordial Set, Camel Shape Holder, Enamel Glass, 6 Cups, 1800s, 15 In.	652.00
Sculpture, Apotheose Des Arts, 2 Mythological Figures, Signed Bruchon, 36 In.	387.00
Sculpture, Arab, Camel, Holding Rifle, Red, White, Green Paint, Gilt, Square Base, c.1900, 11 In.	207.00
Sculpture, Bird Grouping, 2 Doves In Conflict, Ebonized Wood Stand, Early 1900s, 13 x 11 In.	175.00
Sculpture, Caesar Augustus, Standing, Holding Scroll, 1800s, 22 ¼ In. .....*illus*	245.00
Sculpture, Dog, Crouched, Tongue Out, Germany, c.1910, 3 x 8 In.	125.00
Sculpture, Elephant, Walking, 8 ½ In., Pair	113.00
Sculpture, Mercury, Base, 26 In.	237.00
Sculpture, Napoleon, Hands Behind Back, L. Hottot, 27 In.	714.00
Sculpture, Tiger, Ferocious Snarl, 1900s, 13 In.	490.00

SPINNING WHEELS in the corner have been symbols of earlier times for the past 100 years. Although spinning wheels date back to medieval days, the ones found today are rarely more than 200 years old. Because the style of the spinning wheel changed very little, it is often impossible to place an exact date on a wheel.

Flax, Oak, Maple, Punched Scallop Decorations, 1835, 51 x 21 In.	127.00
Mixed Wood, Tripod Stand, Wheel 44 In.	127.00
Oak, Turned Tripod Legs, 36 x 30 In.	63.00
Saxony Style, Oak, Maple, Lathe Turned, Carved Wool Wheel, Foot Treadle, 37 x 36 In.	47.00
Walking, Maple, Oak, Red Stain, Adjustable Flyer, Pewter Band, Shaker, c.1840, 61 x 70 In.	146.00

SPODE pottery, porcelain, and bone china were made by the Stoke-on-Trent factory of England founded by Josiah Spode about 1770. The firm became Copeland and Garrett from 1833 to 1847, then W.T. Copeland or W.T. Copeland and Sons until 1976. It then became Royal Worcester Spode Ltd. The company was bought by the Portmeirion Group in 2009. The word *Spode* appears on many pieces made by the factories. Most collectors include all the wares under the more familiar name of Spode. Porcelains are listed in this book by the name that appears on the piece. Related pieces may be listed under Copeland, Copeland Spode, and Royal Worcester.

Bowl, Blue Luster, Gilt Transfer, Chinese Landscape, c.1900, 10 In. Diam.	207.00
Bread Plate, Aster Red, 6 ½ In.	9.00
Bread Plate, Fleur-De-Lis, Gold, 6 ½ In.	22.00
Coffeepot, Lid, Gloucester Blue, 7 ¼ In.	108.00
Cup, Cowslip, Flat, Flowers	34.00
Flowerpot, Stand, Red Flower Band, Yellow Ground, c.1820, 4 ¼ In.	115.00
Ice Pail, Red Design, Gold Trim, Dolphin Head Handles, 1800s, 4 x 4 In., Pair	200.00
Jardiniere, Tapered, Flared Rim, Gilt Dolphin Handles, 3 Lion Feet, Stand, c.1810, 5 ½ In.	841.00
Loving Cup, Goblet Shape, Twin Handles, Painted, Sheep, Kiln, Flowers, Birds, c.1820, 7 ¾ In.	1602.00
Plate, Fleur-De-Lis, Gold, 10 ¾ In.	90.00
Plate, Imperial Plate Of Persia, 10 In.	295.00
Plate, Soup, Partridge, Grasshopper, Flower & Insect Border, Marked, 9 ¾ In. .....*illus*	12.00
Plate, Soup, Rome, Blue Transfer, c.1830, 9 ¾ In., 4 Piece	120.00
Plate, Virginia, White Flower Center, Honeycomb Border, 10 ¾ In.	27.00

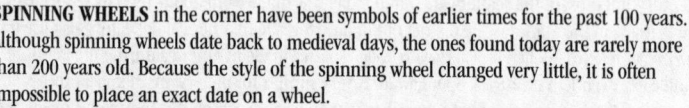

Platter, Bridal Rose, White, Rose Center, Gilt Rim, 16 ¾ In.......................................	89.00
Potpourri, Cover, Diced Design, Flower Border, Entwined Handles, Blue, Green, c.1805, 8 In.	443.00
Warming Dish, Multicolor Flowers, Shaped Rim, Impressed, c.1800, 10 ¼ In.	35.00

SPORTS equipment, sporting goods, brochures, and related items are listed here. Items are listed by sport. Other categories of interest are Bicycle, Card, Fishing, Sword, Toy, and Trap. Kentucky Derby glasses are listed in the Decorated Tumblers category.

Baseball, Autograph, On Paper, Thurman Munson..	1652.00
Baseball, Ball, Autographed, Brooklyn Dodgers, 1938, Babe Ruth On Sweet Spot...................	2596.00
Baseball, Ball, Autographed, Jackie Robinson, 1950	1293.00
Baseball, Ball, Autographed, Jimmie Foxx, Winner Ball, 1937.........................	26438.00
Baseball, Ball, Autographed, Joe DiMaggio, Rawlings	234.00
Baseball, Ball, Autographed, Joe DiMaggio, Retirement Day, Inscribed To Del Webb, 1951	4994.00
Baseball, Ball, Autographed, N.Y. Yankees, 1935..	4720.00
Baseball, Ball, Autographed, N.Y. Yankees, 1953, 27 Signatures	288.00
Baseball, Ball, Autographed, N.Y. Yankees, Joe McCarthy On Sweet Spot, Late 1940s................	885.00
Baseball, Ball, Autographed, Stan Musial, 1960s	115.00
Baseball, Ball, Autographed, Ted Williams, Rawlings, American League......................	238.00
Baseball, Bat, Autographed, Pete Rose, Louisville Slugger 125, Ash, 34 ¾ In.	460.00
Baseball, Bat, Autographed, Roberto Clemente, All-Star Game, Adirondack, 1967, 36 In........	7050.00
Baseball, Book, Autographed, Babe Ruth Story, 1948..	2596.00
Baseball, Button, Baltimore Orioles, Champions, 1894, 1895, 1896, Stud Back, Blue, Orange	2644.00
Baseball, Button, Baltimore Welcomes All Star Game, Union Bug, 1958, 1 ¼ In. ....*illus*	75.00
Baseball, Button, Casey Stengel Testimonial Dinner, Jan. 14th, 1959, 3 ½ In...................	460.00
Baseball, Button, Charlie Grimm Eats Ward's Sporties, 1930s, 1 ¼ In.....................	75.00
Baseball, Button, Cleveland Indians, Old Stadium, Celluloid, 1993, 3 In.	10.00
Baseball, Button, Leroy Satchel Paige, 1948, 1 ¼ In.	106.00
Baseball, Button, Official American League Ball, Ball Design, A.J. Reach Co., c.1901, 1 ¼ In..	75.00
Baseball, Button, Stonewall Jackson Day, Fenway Park, Aug. 29, 1931, Picture, Tassel, 1 ¼ In..	84.00
Baseball, Charm Bracelet, Babe Ruth, Baseball, Bat, Glove, Quaker Oats, 1935-36, 6 ½ In.	127.00
Baseball, Game, Mickey Mantle's Backyard Baseball Set, Ball On String, Bat, 1960s, 25 In.	127.00
Baseball, Gate Pass, New York Giants, Silver, Warner F. Russell, Marked, 1924, 1 ¼ x ¾ In......	403.00
Baseball, Jersey, Nolan Ryan, Houston Astros, 1989, Size 44.................................	208.00
Baseball, Nodder, New York Mets, 1962 ....*illus*	73.00
Baseball, Pen, Philadelphia Athletics, Bat Form, Logo, Bakelite, Yellow, Nib, c.1920, 6 In......	275.00
Baseball, Pennant, All-Star Game, 1948, St. Louis, Red, White Star & Letters, 9 In..............	86.00
Baseball, Pennant, Boston Red Sox, 1916, World's Champions, Red Felt, 32 In.	940.00
Baseball, Pennant, New York Yankees, 1921, World Series, Blue Felt, 28 In.	11750.00
Baseball, Photograph, Boston Red Sox, 1912, Panoramic, Glines, 10 x 27 In.	600.00
Baseball, Photograph, Lou Gehrig, At Home Plate On The Day He Retired, 1939, 13 x 10 In...	1416.00
Baseball, Photograph, The Babe Bows Out, Ruth's Last Game, June 13, 1948, Nat Fein, 10 ½ x 13 In.	1046.00
Baseball, Pillow Case, Baseball Players, Helmar & Turkey Red Tobacco Silks, 1912.............	6463.00
Baseball, Postcard, Chicago American Giants Negro League Team Photo, c.1917, 5 x 3 ½ In.	16303.00
Baseball, Postcard, Maud Nelson, 1911 Postmark, 3 ⅜ x 5 ⅜ In...............................	170.00
Baseball, Press Badge, Brooklyn Dodgers, 1941 World Series, ⅞ In..........................	230.00
Baseball, Press Badge, N.A.P.B.L., 1941, Jacksonville, Fla., Enamel On Brass, 1 In.	115.00
Baseball, Press Pin, Brooklyn Dodgers, World Series, 1916, Blue, White Enamel, Gold	3525.00
Baseball, Press Pin, St. Louis Cardinals, World Series, 1942, Paper, Cardboard......................	2644.00
Baseball, Program, Baltimore Orioles, 1896, Sepia Portrait, Jack Doyle, Pepsin Gum Ad.........	1293.00
Baseball, Ring, Centennial, Jack Armstrong, Raised Image, 1839-1939	230.00
Baseball, Ring, Newark Eagles, 1946, World Championship, Negro League	1763.00
Baseball, Scorer, Celluloid, Centennial 1839/1939, Quaker Oats Premium, 1 ¾ In.	287.00
Baseball, Season Pass, Polo Grounds, 1920, Giants Bid You Welcome, Silver, Octagonal	607.00
Baseball, Sheet Music, Between You & Me, A Home Run Song, Tinker & Evers, 1908...............	675.00
Baseball, Sneakers, Roberto Clemente Model, Red, White Canvas Bottom, 1970s, Size 9	400.00
Baseball, Stadium Seat, Crosley Field, Cincinnati Reds, No, 12, 1934-1970, 27 ½ In.............	130.00
Baseball, Stadium Seat, Yankee Stadium, Blue, No. 5 & 15, 31 x 25 In., Pair..........................	1984.00
Baseball, Trunk, New York Yankees, Equipment, Steiner, 1930s, 41 x 19 x 24 In.	2644.00
Baseball, Uniform, Pete Rose, Cincinnati Reds, White, Red, Home, 1970	15275.00
Basketball, Ball, Autographed, University Of North Carolin, Michael Jordan, Team, 1983-84 .	1763.00
Boxing, Ring, Joe Louis, Raised Image & Facsimile Signature, Silver Metal, Size 11	765.00
Boxing, Trophy, 17th Infantry Brigade Competition, c.1919, 9 ½ In.	2151.00
Canoeing, Paddle, Old Town, Monogram, 54 x 7 In...	94.00
Exercise, Medicine Ball, Leather, Germany, 8 ½ In...	140.00
Football, Ball, Autographed, Syracuse University, 1959, National Champs, Cotton Bowl.........	1239.00

Staffordshire, Loving Cup, John Bull Engine, Brown Transfer, Red, Green, Applied Loop Handles, 4 ¼ In. $71.00

Conestoga Auction Co., Inc.

Staffordshire, Pastille Burner, House Shape, Red & Black, Cottage Cheese Roof, 5 ¼ In. $40.00

Conestoga Auction Co., Inc.

Staffordshire, Pitcher, White Figures, Tall Plants, Blue, 9 ¼ In. $48.00

DuMouchelles Art Gallery

Staffordshire, Plate, Florentine Fountains, Butterfly & Flowers, Rippled Rim, Red Transfer, Marked, 10 ¼ In. $24.00

Conestoga Auction Co., Inc.

S

Staffordshire, Plate, Grecian Urn, Seashells & Maids, Blue Transfer, 10-Sided, Mycene, H.N. & A., 8 ¼ In.
$12.00

Conestoga Auction Co., Inc.

Staffordshire, Plate, Landing Of General Lafayette, Blue Transfer, Clews, 8 ¾ In.
$153.00

Conestoga Auction Co., Inc.

Staffordshire, Sugar, Cover, Countryside, Castle, Fruit, Flowers, Blue Transfer, 2 Handles, Marked, 5 ¼ x 8 In.
$94.00

Conestoga Auction Co., Inc.

Staffordshire, Teapot, Figural, Camel, Howdah, Serpent Handle, Salt Glaze, c.1750, 8 x 9 ½ In.
$2990.00

James D. Julia Inc.

Football, Betting Handicap Card, NCAA, 2-Sided, 1944, 3 x 5 In.	20.00
Football, Button, Red Grange, Ice Man Of Chicago Bears, Photo, Ribbon, 1950s, 1 ¾ In.	633.00
Football, Figure, Chicago Bears, Running Back, No. 18 Decal, Hartland, 1960s, 7 ½ In. ...*illus*	190.00
Football, Nodder, St. Louis Cardinals, Composition, 1960s, 7 In. ...*illus*	48.00
Golf, Pin Holder, Clubs, Crossed, Silver Plate, Base, Mesh Insert, 11 Golf Club Pins, 11 ¾ In.	299.00
Golf, Pocket Comb, Putter Medallion, Sterling, Enamel, A.R. Blackinton & Co., c.1900, 3 ⅛ In.	96.00
Golf, Putting Set, Parlor, Cast Iron, 3 Wood-Shaft Clubs, Side Opening Hole, 35 In.	990.00
Golf, Score Keeper, Pocket, Sterling, c.1920, 3 ¼ In.	203.00
Golf, Sports Illustrated, Ben Hogan Cover, Autographed, March 11, 1957, 68 Pages	127.00
Golf, Trophy Cup, Silver, Lion, Tree, Thistle, Repousse, Scroll Handle, J. Hall & Co., c.1925, 5 In.	478.00
Hockey, Program, Boston Bruins Victory Dinner, 1939, World Champions, Bear, Stanley Cup.	300.00
Horse Racing, Button, Derby Day, Horse & Jockey, Sept. 13, 1904, Topeka, Kan., 2 ¼ In.	115.00
Horse Racing, Pendant, Race Horse, Metal, Moss Agate Medallion, Beaded Edge, 1890s, 1 In.	52.00
Horse Racing, Trophy, Pitcher, Silver, Fleetwood Driving Park, Gorham, 1896, 9 ½ In. ...*illus*	1476.00
Hunting, Ammunition, Brick, Remington Kleanbore, 22 Caliber, Winchester	535.00
Hunting, Bear Trap, Oneida Newhouse, 1880s, 43 Lbs.	3491.00
Hunting, License, Fort Geo. G. Mead, Maryland, No. 107, 1958, 2 In.	52.00
Juggling, Club, Maple, Blue Paint, c.1875, 15 In., Pair	176.00
Juggling, Pin, Wood, Narragansett Machine Co., 15 ¼ x 3 In., Pair	110.00
Pool, Cue Rack, Oak, Marble, Brass Mounts, Fluted Columns, Rotating, c.1900, 87 x 20 In. ...*illus*	1968.00
Pool, Cue Rack, Walnut, Burled, Ebonized, Holds 12, c.1870, 68 x 18 In.	1093.00
Pool, Cue Set, Wood, Ivory, c.1880, 55 In., 9 Piece.	1840.00
Pool, Table, Arts & Crafts, Accessories, Monarch, Brunswick-Balke-Collender, c.1910, 110 x 60 In. *illus*	4425.00
Pool, Table, Hardwood, Adjustable Turned Legs, Balls, Skittles, Cues, Brush	2510.00
Pool, Table, Mother-Of-Pearl Inlay, Shaped Legs, Leather Pockets, Tassels, F. Schwikert, 110 In.	4720.00
Pool, Table, Walnut, Mahogany, Lion's Head, Leather Pockets, Regulation	1760.00
Skating, Ice Skates, Curled Iron Blades, Shaped Back, Wood Platform, Maine, 1960s, 17 In.	633.00
Skating, Roller Skates, Metal, Rubber Tires, Wing Nut Adjustment, 1930s, 16 x 5 In.	85.00
Snowshoes, Bentwood, Woven Rawhide, Leather Harness, Straps, 1800s, 46 x 13 In.	118.00
Snowshoes, Wood, Yellow Paint, 60 In., Pair	35.00
Tennis, Photograph, Bill Tilden, Holding Rackets, Frame, c.1930, 12 ½ x 10 ¼ In.	173.00
Tennis, Presentation Plaque, George V, Chased, Engraved, Celtic Borders, Scotland, 20 x 14 In.	1434.00
Yacht Racing, Button, Shamrock III, America's Cup Challenger, 1903, 1 ¾ In.	63.00

STAFFORDSHIRE, England, has been a district making pottery and porcelain since the 1700s. Hundreds of kilns are still working in the area. Thousands of types of pottery and porcelain have been made in the many factories that worked and still work in the area. Some of the most famous factories have been listed separately, such as Adams, Davenport, Ridgway, Rowland & Marsellus, Royal Doulton, Royal Worcester, Spode, Wedgwood, and others. Some Staffordshire pieces are listed under categories like Fairing, Flow Blue, Mulberry, Shaving Mug, etc.

Bonbonniere, Pigeon, Puffed Up, Hunter With Bird, Woman, c.1765	6160.00
Bowl, Cathedral & Fisherman, Scenic View Blue, Transfer, 1800s, 6 In. Diam.	89.00
Bowl, Vegetable, Mycene, Blue Transfer, Oval, 10 ½ In.	45.00
Box, Hen On Nest Cover, Multicolor, Shaw & Sons, 7 ½ x 8 ½ In.	403.00
Cann, Cup, Acanthus, Double Handles, Molded Foot, Marked, 4 ¾ In.	24.00
Casserole, Hen On Nest Cover, Painted, 3 ¾ x 4 In. ...*illus*	59.00
Coffeepot, Dome Lid, Castle Ruins, Blue Transfer, Footed, 11 ¼ In. ...*illus*	130.00
Coffeepot, Dome Lid, Ship, In Shell Grotto, Blue Transfer, Flower Border, c.1890, 12 In.	422.00
Coffeepot, Lid, Horse Drawn Chariot, Red Transfer, Scroll Handle, 1800s, 12 In.	173.00
Coffeepot, Lid, Hunting Scene, Marked, 9 In.	245.00
Coffeepot, Woman, Man, Reading Book, Building, 11 ½ In.	124.00
Creamer, Cottage Shape, White, Red Trim, Green Leaves, Twig Handle, c.1835-45, 6 In.	29.00
Cup & Saucer, Spotted Dog Design, Girl & Dog, Well, c.1830, 2 ½ x 6 In.	86.00
Cup Plate, George Washington, Linked States Border, Dark Blue Transfer, 1820s, 3 ½ In.	300.00
Cuspidor, Oriental Scenes, Blue Transfer, Handle, Lady's Spout, 3 x 5 In.	28.00
Dish, Leaf Shape, Stem Handles, Veining, Tortoiseshell Glaze, 1760-70, 6 ½ In.	1652.00
Figurine, Angel, Great Britain, Harp, Ireland, Shield, England, c.1890, 13 x 10 In.	161.00
Figurine, Anthony, Cleopatra, Reclining, Marbleized Rectangular Base, 13 In., Pair	1896.00
Figurine, Autumn, Man, Wheat, Sickle, c.1830, 9 ¼ In.	230.00
Figurine, Bird, Yellow, Base, 5 ½ In.	297.00
Figurine, Britannia, Shield, Lion, c.1820, 14 In.	304.00
Figurine, Cat, Tabby, Black, Gray, Yellow Ribbon, Seated On Green Base, c.1825, 14 ½ In.	9007.00
Figurine, Child, Autumn, Wheat Sheaf, Sickle, 1830s, 9 ¼ In.	230.00
Figurine, Dog, Curly Mane, Black Base, c.1820, 8 ¾ In.	207.00
Figurine, Dog, Dalmatian, Tasseled Pillow, 9 ¾ In.	153.00
Figurine, Dog, Greyhound, Resting, Base, c.1820, 4 x 6 ½ In.	385.00

Figurine, Dog, Hound, Resting, Tan, c.1820, 3 ½ x 6 In.		486.00
Figurine, Dog, King Charles Spaniel, Resting On Pillow, 1800s, 7 x 12 ½ In.		1067.00
Figurine, Dog, Poodle, Seated, White Ground, Rust & Red Spots, c.1900s, 11 In., Pair		118.00
Figurine, Dog, Pug, Seated, White, c.1890, 10 ½ In., Pair		385.00
Figurine, Dog, Pug, Standing, 1800s, 9 x 9 ½ In., Pair		1007.00
Figurine, Dog, Seated, Black, White, c.1820, 7 In.		790.00
Figurine, Dog, Spaniel, Brown Spots, Yellow Eyes, Gold Accents, 8 ½ In., Pair		161.00
Figurine, Dog, Spaniel, Pipe In Jaw, 1800s, 14 ¼ In., Pair		1659.00
Figurine, Dog, Spaniel, Red & White, 10 x 6 In.		230.00
Figurine, Dog, Spaniel, Red & White, Chain Collar, Lock, 10 In., Pair		90.00
Figurine, Dog, Spaniel, White, 1800s, 13 x 11 In.		173.00
Figurine, Dog, Spaniel, White, Gilt Lock & Chain Collars, 12 ½ In., Pair		288.00
Figurine, Dog, Whippet, Seated, Black Spots, Gilt, Cobalt Base, England, 1800s, 8 In., Pair		237.00
Figurine, Elijah, 2 Ravens & Bocage, Early 1800s, 10 ½ In.		138.00
Figurine, Emperor Napoleon III, Multicolor, Gilt, c.1850, 15 x 7 ¼ In.		104.00
Figurine, Hector MacDonald, On Horseback, White, Gilt, 12 In.		113.00
Figurine, Horse, Standing, Brown Spots, Green & Brown Oblong Base, 1800s, 9 x 12 In.		593.00
Figurine, Hunters, Man, Gun, Dog, Dead Bird, Multicolor, 10 & 10 ½ In.		138.00
Figurine, King Richard, Seated, Flag, 1800s, 15 x 7 In.		240.00
Figurine, Lion, Brown Glaze, Glass Eyes, Gold Highlights, c.1900, 10 x 13 x 5 In.		459.00
Figurine, Lion, Reclining, Brown, 13 In., Pair		73.00
Figurine, Lion, Striding Pose, 14 In., Pair		244.00
Figurine, Man & Woman, Seated, 1800s, 13 In., Pair	*illus*	300.00
Figurine, Scottish Lad & Lass, Black & White Tall Dog, Marked, 10 x 10 In., Pair		2013.00
Figurine, Sheep Standing In Front Of Tree, c.1850, 4 ½ x 4 In.	*illus*	108.00
Figurine, W.E. Gladstone, Union Jack, Multicolor, Gilt, c.1890, 13 ½ x 6 In.		81.00
Figurine, Woman, Young, Hat, Coat, Muff, c.1850, 8 ½ x 3 ½ In.		81.00
Figurine, Wombell's Menagerie, Animal Park Scene, People, 8 ½ x 7 In.		150.00
Figurine, Zebra, Bridles & Reins, Grassy Ground, 1800s, 9 x 8 ¼ In., Pair	*illus*	299.00
Figurine, Zebra, Prancing, Oval Base, Grass, 1800s, 5 x 5 In., Pair		374.00
Flask, Dogs, 2-Sided, 1800s, 7 In.		593.00
Garniture, Mansion, Gold Face, Potash Farm, 5 ½ In.		47.00
Group, Androcles & Lion, Seated, Flowing Robe, Holding Paw, c.1850, 10 ½ In.	*illus*	633.00
Group, Dog, Greyhound & Rabbit, 1800s, 10 ½ In., Pair		593.00
Group, Dog, Whippet, Rabbit, 1800s, 9 ¾ x 8 In.		236.00
Group, Dogs, 2 Greyhounds, Black, White, 1800s, 7 ¼ In.		1126.00
Group, Queen Victoria, Prince Albert, Multicolor, Gilt, 10 ½ x 5 ½ In., Pair		92.00
Jug, Milk, Shanghai Pattern, Pheasant, Flowers, Blue Transfer, c.1920, 5 ⅞ In.		177.00
Jug, Octagonal, Swans, Flower Sprays, Blue Fish Scale Design, 1790-1810, 7 In.		472.00
Jug, Snuff Taker, Gentleman, Right Hand To Mouth, Hat Lid, 1800s, 13 ¾ In.		144.00
Loving Cup, John Bull Engine, Brown Transfer, Red, Green, Applied Loop Handles, 4 ¼ In.	*illus*	71.00
Mug, Frog, Double Handles, Mid 1800s, 5 ½ x 8 In.		120.00
Pastille Burner, House Shape, Red & Black, Cottage Cheese Roof, 5 ¼ In.	*illus*	40.00
Pastille Burner, Lilac, Octagonal, Oval Base, Flowers, Gilded Trim, Finial, 1800s, 5 ½ In.		184.00
Pitcher, Basin, Canova, Blue & White, Thomas Mayer, c.1840, 10 ¼ x 13 ½ In.		375.00
Pitcher, Blue, Lafayette At Franklin's Tomb, 11 In.		1422.00
Pitcher, Botanical, Green, Red & Yellow, Loop Handle, 6 ¼ In.		24.00
Pitcher, Copper Luster, Beaded Rim, Molded Flowers, c.1850, 14 ½ In.		1100.00
Pitcher, Franklin, Flying Kite, Cityscape, Brown Transfer, c.1835, 10 ¾ In.		475.00
Pitcher, Great Erie Canal, Boats, Blue, c.1870, 6 ¾ In.		558.00
Pitcher, Kneeling Slave, Figure Of Justice, Loop Handle, Anti-Slavery, Blue, c.1837, 7 In.		345.00
Pitcher, Salt Glaze, Enameled, Pear Shape, Loop Handle, Flowers, Banding, c.1760, 7 In.		3894.00
Pitcher, Sportsman, Purple Transfer, Footed, 7 ¼ In.		124.00
Pitcher, Wasp Boarding The Frolic, Green Transfer, Pink Trim, c.1840		1265.00
Pitcher, Water, Flowers, Applied Handle, 8 ¼ In.		71.00
Pitcher, Welcome Lafayette, Blue, 1800s, 7 In.		1185.00
Pitcher, White Figures, Tall Plants, Blue, 9 ¼ In.	*illus*	48.00
Plaque, 2 Lions Reclining, Dotted, Blue Mane, Leaf Sprays, Flowers, Oval, 9 ⅝ In.		531.00
Plate, 1st Amendment, Anti Slavery, Scalloped Rim, Eagles Border, Shields, 1800s, 9 In.		356.00
Plate, Arms Of Rhode Island, Blue Transfer, Thomas Mayer, c.1870, 8 ½ In.		512.00
Plate, Blenheim, Oxfordshire, Blue Transfer, 10 ½ In.		79.00
Plate, Blue, Eastern Street Scene, Marked, 8 ½ In.		12.00
Plate, Boat Dancing Scene, Scalloped Edge, Red Transfer, 8 ½ In.		45.00
Plate, Castle Garden Battery, Blue Transfer, Impressed Wood, c.1810, 3 ¾ In.		235.00
Plate, Castle On Mount With Sheepherder & Woman, Blue Transfer, Marked, 8 ½ In.		56.00
Plate, Castle Ruins, Blue Transfer, 10 In.		47.00

Staffordshire, Watch Stand, 3 Women, Period Dress, 1800s, 10 x 7 In.
$120.00

DuMouchelles Art Gallery

Stein, Burl, Lid, c.1950s, 12 In.
$92.00

The Stein Auction Co.

Stein, Character, Bud Man, Budweiser, Pottery, ½ Liter
$151.00

Fox Auctions

Stein, Character, Chinese Man, Merkelbach & Wick, ½ Liter
$295.00

Fox Auctions

S

Stein, Character, Clown, Pottery, Diesinger, ½ Liter
$1380.00

Fox Auctions

Stein, Character, Fox, Head, Porcelain, Marked, Musterschutz, Schierholz, ½ Liter
$276.00

The Stein Auction Co.

Stein, Character, Ludwig, Porcelain, Musterschutz, Schierholz, ½ Liter
$207.00

The Stein Auction Co.

Stein, Character, Man With Pipe, Pottery, Relief, Pewter Lid, Marked 663, 1 Liter
$374.00

The Stein Auction Co.

Plate, Church Spire & Building, Couple In Background, Floral Border, 9 ¾ In.	71.00
Plate, Commodore MacDonnough, Dark Blue Transfer, Marked, 1815, 9 In.	235.00
Plate, Couple & Child, Building, Blue Transfer, 10 ⅜ In., Pair	124.00
Plate, Dinner, Fair Mount Near Philadelphia, Eagle & Flowers Border, Blue Transfer, c.1800, 10 In.	123.00
Plate, Florentine Fountains, Butterfly & Flowers, Rippled Rim, Red Transfer, Marked, 10 ¼ In. *illus*	24.00
Plate, Grand Erie Canal, Blue Transfer, c.1830, 10 ¼ In.	288.00
Plate, Grecian Urn, Seashells & Maids, Blue Transfer, 10-Sided, Mycene, H.N. & A., 8 ¼ In. . *illus*	12.00
Plate, Jefferson, Lafayette, View Of Aqueduct Falls, Blue Transfer, 8 ¼ In.	7708.00
Plate, Lamb Tavern, Flower Border, Blue Transfer, c.1895, 9 In.	118.00
Plate, Landing Of General Lafayette & La Grange, Dark Blue Transfer, 1800s, 10 In., Pair	316.00
Plate, Landing Of General Lafayette, Blue Transfer, 6 ⅝ In.	91.00
Plate, Landing Of General Lafayette, Blue Transfer, Clews, 8 ¾ In. *illus*	153.00
Plate, Lute Players, Scalloped Edge, Red Transfer, Dillon, 10 ¾ In.	68.00
Plate, Marine Hospital, Louisville, Shell Border, Blue Transfer, c.1870, 9 ¼ In.	118.00
Plate, Oriental Temple Scene, Floral Border, Blue Transfer, Scalloped, Marked, 9 ¾ In.	36.00
Plate, Pagodas On A Lake, Floral Border, Scalloped Rim, Blue Transfer, Impressed Mark, 8 In.	71.00
Plate, Pastoral Scene Wild Rose Border, Scalloped Rim, Europa, Marked, 7 In.	24.00
Plate, People Picnicking, Fishing, Cathedral, Blue Transfer, 10 In.	115.00
Plate, Quebec View, Blue Transfer, 9 In.	334.00
Plate, Salt Glaze, Pierced Trellis Diaperwork Rim, Basket Weave, Flowers, 10 In. Diam.	708.00
Plate, Ship Cadmus, Flower Border, Blue Transfer, 1800s, 9 In. Diam.	184.00
Plate, Soup, Arms Of New York, Blue Transfer, Impressed T. Mayer, c.1870, 10 ¼ In.	235.00
Plate, Troy Line, Ship, Blue Transfer, 1800s, 10 In.	161.00
Plate, View Near Conway, New Hampshire, Red Transfer, 8 ⅞ In.	47.00
Plate, W. Penn's Treaty, 2 American Indians, Purple Transfer, c.1834-54, 10 ½ In.	144.00
Plate, Washington, Lafayette, Entrance Of Canal Into Hudson At Albany, Blue Transfer, 1800s, 9 In.	7110.00
Platter, Boatmen On Lake, Cottage Border, Blue Transfer, 15 x 12 In.	35.00
Platter, Catskill Mountains, Hudson River, Blue Transfer, Impressed Wood & Sons, 8 ½ x 10 ¾ In.	1659.00
Platter, Chinese Marine Pattern, Boats, Bridges, Well & Tree, Blue Transfer, c.1835, 14 ¼ x 11 ½ In.	98.00
Platter, Highlands Castle, Flower Border, Blue Transfer, Scalloped Rim, Burgess & Leigh, 9 ¾ In.	83.00
Platter, Italian Scenery, Well & Tree, 18 ¼ In.	178.00
Platter, Landing Of General Lafayette, Blue Transfer, 11 ¾ x 15 ¼ In.	668.00
Platter, Oblong Shape, East View Of La Grange, Blue Transfer, 1819-46, 8 x 10 In.	398.00
Platter, Peace & Plenty, Flowers, Leaves, Blue Transfer, 15 In.	2150.00
Platter, Pennsylvania Hospital, Blue Transfer, Phil., 14 x 18 ½ In.	1541.00
Platter, Pickett's Charge, Gettysburg, 9 ½ x 12 In.	1659.00
Platter, Siam, Blue Transfer, Brown-Westhead Moore & Co., 14 x 17 In.	115.00
Platter, State House, Boston, Blue Transfer, Impressed Rogers, 16 x 21 In.	1778.00
Platter, States Design, George Washington, Scalloped Edge, Blue Tranfer, c.1830, 16 ½ In.	1093.00
Platter, Trident, Black Transfer, Green, Flower Border, c.1845, 12 ½ x 15 ½ In.	288.00
Platter, Upper Ferry Bridge Over The River Schuylkill, Blue Transfer, 1800s, 19 x 15 In.	1150.00
Platter, View Of Detroit, Blue Transfer, Marked, c.1850, 20 x 16 In.	3173.00
Platter, Zebra Design, Asian Family & Child, On Zebra, Blue & White, c.1825, 17 In.	259.00
Punch Bowl, Dolphin Base, Putti Bacchus & Pan, Band Of Grapes, Vines, 1880s, 8 In.	374.00
Quill Holder, Dog, Whippit, Reclining, Blue Oval Base, 5 ½ x 8 In., Pair	460.00
Sauceboat, Woman, Flowers, Salt Glaze, Scalloped Rim, Loop Handle, Round Foot, c.1755, 7 In.	4130.00
Scent Bottle, Figural, Girl's Head, Plaid Dress, Makeup, Classical Ruins, c.1765	6160.00
Soup, Dish, Castle Water, Couple, Garden, Castle Border, Blue Transfer, Marked, 9 ¾ In.	12.00 to 18.00
Soup, Dish, Fair Mount Near Philadelphia, Floral Rim, Blue Tranfer, 10 In.	165.00
Spill Vase, Dog, Greyhound, Standing, Tree Stump, 10 x 9 In., Pair	390.00
Spill Vase, Figural, Scottish Dressed Woman, Basket Of Vegetables, 8 In.	40.00
Spill Vase, Hunting Scene, Dog Taking Down Buck, 9 x 7 In.	120.00
Stirrup Cup, Hound Head, Tan, 7 In.	1659.00
Sugar & Creamer, Cover, Landing Of Gen. Lafayette, Battery Park, Ships, Blue Transfer, 1800s, 7 In.	413.00
Sugar, Cover, Countryside, Castle, Fruit, Flowers, Blue Transfer, 2 Handles, Marked, 5 ¼ x 8 In. . *illus*	94.00
Sugar, Cover, Landing Of Gen. Lafayette At Castle Garden, Blue Transfer, c.1819, 6 In.	490.00
Tankard, Shakespeare, Cylindrical, Blue Transfer, Commemorative, Late 1700s, 6 In.	178.00
Tankard, View Of Erie Canal, Blue Transfer, 1800s, 6 In.	1541.00
Teapot, Christmas Eve, Footed, Blue Transfer, Clews, 8 ¼ In.	198.00
Teapot, Cover, Flowering Branches, Leaves, Salt Glaze, Crabstock Handle & Spout, 4 In.	708.00
Teapot, Cover, Fruit Vines, Salt Glaze, Compressed Spherical, Blue, 3 Hooved Feet, 5 In.	1062.00
Teapot, Cover, Spherical, Aubergine, Flower Spray, Leaves, Salt Glaze S-Scroll Handle, 5 In.	3658.00
Teapot, Cover, Tortoiseshell Glaze, Hexagonal, Reeded Spout, Griffin Knop, c.1765, 6 In.	3776.00
Teapot, Figural, Camel, Howdah, Serpent Handle, Salt Glaze, c.1750, 8 x 9 ½ In. ....*illus*	2990.00
Teapot, Sleigh Rider, Horses, Woods, Deer, Flower Borders, Octagonal, Blue Transfer, 8 x 11 In.	142.00

S

Tobacco Jar, Cover, Grooms Carousing, Groom Keeled Over Knop, c.1790, 7 In.	1888.00
Toby Jugs are listed in their own category.	
Toothbrush Holder, Reclining Stag, Cover, Blue Transfer, 8 ¼ In.	68.00
Tray, Bun, Flowers, Pastoral, Blue Transfer, Scalloped Rippled Rim, 11 x 14 In.	203.00
Tray, Prepare To Meet Thy God, Rectangular, Gabriel, Gold Luster Border, c.1830, 9 In.	144.00
Tureen, Ben Franklin, Blue Transfer, Child's, 2 ½ x 3 ¼ In.	115.00
Tureen, Cover, Underplate, Curved Handles, Shaped Knop, Marked, Clews, 10 ½ x 13 ½ In.	472.00
Tureen, Soup, Cover, Undertray, India Flowers Design, Flower Finial, 1800s, 11 x 16 In.	345.00
Tureen, Soup, Tournay Pattern Blue & White Transferware, 11 ¾ In.	190.00
Underplate, Peace, Plenty, Blue Transfer, England, c.1870, 8 ¼ In.	294.00
Vase, Rocky Hillside, 3 Spotted Sheep, c.1800-10, 5 In.	1121.00
Vase, Tree, Cow Nursing Calf, Oval Base, Multicolor, 1800s, 11 In.	259.00
Watch Stand, 3 Women, Period Dress, 1800s, 10 x 7 In. ....illus	120.00

STANGL POTTERY traces its history back to the Fulper Pottery of New Jersey. In 1910, Johann Martin Stangl started working at Fulper. He left to work at Haeger Pottery from 1915 to 1920. Stangl returned to Fulper Pottery in 1920, became president in 1926, and changed the company name to Stangl Pottery in 1929. Stangl acquired the firm in 1930. The pottery is known for dinnerware and a line of bird figurines. Martin Stangl died in 1972 and the pottery was sold to Frank Wheaton Jr. of Wheaton Industries. Production continued until 1978, when Pfaltzgraff Pottery purchased the right to the Stangl trademark and the remaining inventory was liquidated. A single bird figurine is identified by a number. Figurines made up of two birds are identified by a number followed by the letter *D* indicating Double.

Bird, Cockatoo, Jacob, Multicolor, Marked, 11 ¾ In.	104.00
Bird, Cockatoo, No. 34055, Pinks, Blue, Yellow, Brown & Green, 6 ⅜ In.	75.00
Bird, Hummingbird, No. 3629, Marked, K.D., 5 x 3 ½ x 6 ½ In.	38.00
Bird, Hummingbirds, No. 3599, On Flower, Ink Stamp, E.S., 8 ¾ x 11 In.	205.00
Country Garden, Gravy Boat, Underplate	65.00
Fruits & Flowers, Bowl, Vegetable, Oval, 8 In.	40.00
Spongeware, Pitcher & Bowl, Blue, Marked, c.1950.	76.00
Terra Rose, Bowl, Vegetable, Yellow, Round, 8 ¾ In.	40.00
Thistle Rose, Plate, Green, Pink Flowers, 5 Piece, 10 In.	50.00
Vase, Pillow, White Matte Glaze, Flower Shape, 7 x 3 x 7 In.	25.00

STAR TREK AND STAR WARS collectibles are included here. The original *Star Trek* television series ran from 1966 through 1969. The series spawned an animated TV series, three TV sequels, and a TV prequel. The first Star Trek movie was released in 1979 and ten others followed, the most recent in 2009. The movie *Star Wars* opened in 1977. Sequels were released in 1980 and 1983; prequels in 1999, 2002, and 2005. All six episodes are being converted to 3D and will be re-released beginning in 2012. Other science fiction and fantasy collectibles can be found under Batman, Buck Rogers, Captain Marvel, Flash Gordon, Movie, Superman, and Toy.

STAR TREK

Action Figure, Commander La Forge Moc, Playmates, 1993, 5 In.	3.95
Action Figure, Commander William Riker, Playmates, 1999, 12 In.	30.00
Action Figure, Klingon Warrior, Worf Moc, Playmates, 1993, 5 In.	3.95
Action Figure, Lt. Commander Data, Playmates, 1993	15.00
Action Figure, Lt. Tash Yar, Paramount Pictures, 1988, 1 ¼ x 3 ½ In.	24.50
Comic Book, Dynabrite Whitman, Western Publishing, 1978, 48 Pages	25.00
Comic Book, Enterprise Logs, Vol. 2, Golden Press, 1976	34.00
Cookie Jar, Spock & Kirk Heads, Blue, Gold, Treasure Craft, Star Jars, 1996, 14 x 12 ½ In.	325.00
Figure, Cadet Data, Paramount, 1997, 5 ½ In.	13.50
Figure, Cardassian Soldier, 1998, 6 In.	9.00
Figure, Dr. Noonian Soung, 1994, 4 ½ In.	5.00
Figure, Lieutenant Commander Data, Flexible, Paramount, 1988, 3 ½ In.	24.00
Figure, Lieutenant Tasha Yar, Flexible, Paramount, 1988, 3 ½ In.	24.00
Figure, Tellante Alien, Blue & White Suit, Green Base, Enesco, c.1993, 4 In.	8.00
Game, Target, Tin, Spring-Loaded Pistol, 3 Suction Cup Darts, On Card, Hasbro, 13 In.	173.00
Key Chain, Enterprise Ship, Polyvinyl, Enesco, c.1993, 1 ½ In.	5.00
Lunch Box, The Enterprise, Mr. Spock, Capt. Kirk, Dome, Metal, Aladdin, 1968, 9 x 4 ½ In.	452.00
Mug, Captain Kirk, Ceramic, Applause, 5 ½ In.	30.00
Mug, Mr. Spock, Ceramic, Applause, 5 ½ In.	30.00
Ornament, Dr. McCoy, Inside Transporter Room, Anita Rogers, Hallmark, 1997, 5 ¼ In.	32.00
Ornament, Romulan Warbird, Lynn Norton, Hallmark, 1995	10.00
Ornament, Star Ship Enterprise, Red, Green Blinking Lights, Plug In, Hallmark, 1991	250.00
Patch, Planet Saturn, Sew On, 2 ⅞ x 2 In.	5.00
Plate, Captain Kirk, Yellow Shirt, Susie Morton, R.J. Ernst, 9 In.	50.00

Stein, Character, Munich Child, Inlaid Lid, Pottery, Marked, 1880, ½ Liter
$334.00

The Stein Auction Co.

Stein, Glass, Blown, Enameled, Zum Andenken, Pewter Lid, ½ Liter
$35.00

The Stein Auction Co.

Stein, Military, Feldmarschall V. Hindenburg, Transfer, Enamel, Metal Lid, ½ Liter
$92.00

The Stein Auction Co.

S

TIP
Don't hide all your valuables in one place. Burglars may miss some hiding places.

Stein, Military, Third Reich, Komp., Pionier Batl. 34, Koblenz, Pewter Lid, Relief Helmet, ½ Liter
$345.00

The Stein Auction Co.

Stein, Occupational, Schweizer, Cheese Maker, Pewter Lid, Porcelain, ½ Liter
$109.00

The Stein Auction Co.

Stein, Pewter, Women In Relief, Art Nouveau, WMF, 2 Liter
$2530.00

Fox Auctions

Plate, Counselor Deanna Troi, Blue Shirt, Blackshear, Hamilton, 1994, 8 ¼ In.	48.00
Plate, Lieutenant Worf, Orange Shirt, Blackshear, Hamilton, 1994, 8 ¼ In.	48.00
Poster, Spock, Kirk, Enterprise, Paramount, 1992, 17 ¾ x 11 ¾ In.	15.00
Poster, Voyage Continues, Signed Sonia Hillios, 22 x 34 In.	28.00
Toy, Communicators, Pair Of Walkie-Talkies, Blue Plastic, On Card, Mego, 1974, 5 In.	221.00
Toy, Klingon Cruiser, Die Cast, Metal, Dinky, 1979	33.00
Toy, Next Generation Micro Machine, Galoob, 1993	20.00
Toy, Transporter, Playmate, 1993, 9 x 10 In.	25.00
Trading Card, Time's Arrow Scene, Black Mounting, Sonia Hill	20.00
Tumbler, Enterprise Destroyed, 1984, 5 ¾ In.	8.00

STAR WARS

Action Figure, Clone Trooper Officer	5.00
Action Figure, Han Solo Millennium Falcon, Gunner Station, Kenner, 1997	13.00
Action Figure, Han Solo, Trench Coat, 1984	12.00
Action Figure, Princess Leia, Vinyl, Box, Kenner, 1977, 11 ½ In.	125.00
Action Figure, Qui-Gon Jinn, Comm Tech Chip, Hasbro, 1998	15.00
Action Figure, Sand People, Jointed, Vinyl, 4 In.	22.00
Action Figure, Stormtrooper, Power Of The Force Collection, Kenner, 1995	10.00
Book & Record, Droid World, Lucas Film Ltd, 1983, 7 In., 33 ⅓ Record	19.00
Book, Empire Strikes Back, Del Ray, 1980	47.00
Book, Ewoks Join The Fight, Random House, Lucas Films, 1983, 32 Pages	20.00
Calendar, 1979, May The Force Be With You, Complete, Ballentine Book Co.	22.00
Cookie Jar, C-3PO Robot, Gold Paint, 1977	395.00
Cookie Jar, Chewbacca, Star, 16 x 10 In.	160.00
Display, Drink, Jar Blinks, Episode I, Rubber, Straw Insert, 1999, 7 In.	3.00
Display, Force Lightsaber, Graphics, Cardboard, 3 Lightsabers, Kenner, 1982, 39 In.	209.00
Doll, C-3PO, Star Wars, Robot, Gold, Soft Fabric, 1997, 10 In.	15.00
Doll, Darth Vadar, Cloth Cape, Applause, 1996, 11 In.	20.00
Figure, Luke Skywalker, Display Base, In Package, Kenner, 6 ½ In.	20.00
Figure, R2-D2, Hasbro, 1997, 2 ½ In.	12.00
Game, Electronic Laser Battle, Death Star, Lights, Sound, Kenner, 1977, 20 x 7 In.	86.00
Game, Escape From Death Star, Kenner, 1977	18.00
Game, Escape From Death Star, Kenner, Box, 1977	25.00
Game, Escape The Death Star, 2-4 Players, Unused, 1998	25.00
Jigsaw Puzzle, Aboard The Millennium Falcon, Crew, 1977, 1000 Piece	145.00
Jigsaw Puzzle, R2-D2, Star Wars Episode I, Complete, Electronic Voice Box, Batteries, 708 Piece.	17.00
Key Chain, Darth Vadar, 20th Century Fox, 1977, 2 ¾ x 1 ¼ In.	48.00
Lunch Box, King Seeley Thermos Company, 1977	49.00
Lunch Box, Metal, Plastic Thermos, King Seeley, 1977	143.00
Model Kit, Return Of The Jedi Speeder Bike, Box, 1983, 12 In.	32.00
Movie Poster, Luke, Leia, Darth Vader, 1977, 41 x 27 In.	210.00
Movie Poster, Return Of The Jedi, 3 Cast Autographs, 41 x 27 In.	115.00
Mug, Figural, Darth Vadar, Applause, 1996, 5 In.	7.00
Mug, Figural, Emperor, Palpati, Applause, 1996, 5 In.	7.00
Ornament, Darth Vadar, Light, Sound, Dill Thodus, 5 x 2 ½ In.	25.00
PEZ, Darth Vadar, Lights, Plays Theme Song, Lucas Films Ltd., 12 x 5 In.	25.00
Plate, Luke Skywalker & Darth Vadar, Hamilton, 1987, 8 ½ In.	110.00
Plate, Princess Leia, Gold Rim, Hamilton, 1987, 8 ½ In.	75.00
Poster, Harrison Ford, Peter Cushing, 20th Century Fox, 1977, 27 x 41 In.	250.00
Record, Sleeve, 45 RPM, Millennium Records, Cantina Band & Funk Galactic, 1977	12.00
Soap, Yoda, Impressed, Unused, 1983, 2 x 3 ½ In.	5.00
Toy, Action Fleet Vehicle, Y Wing Starfighter, Galoob, Original Box, 1996	20.00
Toy, Jawa Sand Crawler, Unused, Die Cast Metal, Galoob, 1996	14.00

STEINS have been used by beer and ale drinkers for over 500 years. They have been made of ivory, porcelain, stoneware, faience, silver, pewter, wood, or glass in sizes up to nine gallons. Although some were made by Mettlach, Meissen, Capo-di-Monte, and other famous factories, most were made by less important German potteries. The words *Geschutz* or *Musterschutz* on a stein are the German words for "patented" or "registered design," not company names. Steins are still being made in the old styles. Lithophane steins may be found in the Lithophane category.

Basket Weave, Pewter Lid, Handle & Footring, Korbmacherei, 1750, 9 In.	5750.00
Burl, Gourd Shape, 3 Ball Feet, c.1800, 7 ½ In.	1431.00
Burl, Lid, c.1950s, 12 In. ....*illus*	92.00
Burl, Peg Tankard, Scandinavia, 9 ¼ In.	1062.00

Character, Bison, Porcelain, E. Bohne Sohne, ½ Liter	2300.00
Character, Black Robed Munich Child, Holds Stein & Radishes, 1 Liter	374.00
Character, Bud Man, Budweiser, Pottery, ½ Liter ....*illus*	151.00
Character, Cat, On Book, Inlaid Lid, Porcelain, E. Bohne & Sohne, ½ Liter	1840.00
Character, Chinese Man, Merkelbach & Wick, ½ Liter ....*illus*	295.00
Character, Clown, Pottery, Diesinger, ½ Liter ....*illus*	1380.00
Character, Fox, Head, Porcelain, Marked, Musterschutz, Schierloz, ½ Liter ....*illus*	276.00
Character, Frog Plays Squeezebox, ½ Liter	1150.00
Character, Ludwig, Porcelain, Musterschutz, Schierloz, ½ Liter ....*illus*	207.00
Character, Man With Pipe, Pottery, Relief, Pewter Lid, Marked 663, 1 Liter ......*illus*	374.00
Character, Monkey, Pottery, Inlaid Lid, Diesinger, ½ Liter	834.00
Character, Mother-In-Law, Pottery, Inlaid Lid, ½ Liter....................	288.00
Character, Munich Child, Holds Stein & Radish, ¼ Liter	375.00
Character, Munich Child, Holds Stein & Radish, 1 Liter	690.00
Character, Munich Child, Inlaid Lid, Pottery, Marked, 1880, ½ Liter ....*illus*	334.00
Character, Munich Child, Wears Barrel, Holds Large Stein & Radishes, ½ Liter	632.00
Character, Rhinoceros, Pottery, ½ Liter	403.00
Character, Smoking Pig, Porcelain, Inlaid Lid, ½ Liter	431.00
Character, Stag, Porcelain, Musterschutz, ½ Liter	1553.00
Character, Von Molte In Military Uniform, No. 584, Stoneware, ½ Liter...........	288.00
Faience, Bowling Scene, Pewter Lid, Leobersdorfer Birnkrug, c.1775, 9 In.	1380.00
Faience, Buildings, Dresdener Walzenkrug, Pewter Lid & Footring, c.1775, 10 In.	2760.00
Faience, Cherub On Horse, Pewter Footring & Lid, 1 Liter	1495.00
Faience, Gardener, Muffle Fired, Pewter Lid & Footring, c.1800, 9 In..........	2990.00
Faience, Rebecca & Elizar, Pewter Lid & Footring, c.1750, 9 In.............	1840.00
Glass, Blown, Defregger Scene, Amber, Enameled, Pewter Lid, ½ Liter...........	299.00
Glass, Blown, Enameled, Zum Andenken, Pewter Lid, ½ Liter ....*illus*	35.00
Glass, Blown, Farmer's Tools, Enameled, Late 1700s, ½ Liter..............	345.00
Glass, Blown, Man Drinking, Relief Pewter Lid, F. Ringer, ½ Liter	431.00
Glass, Egg Shape, Etched Flowers, Leaves, Cone Shape Lid, Clear Handle, Pewter Rim, 8 In. ...	207.00
Mettlach steins are listed in the Mettlach category.	
Military, Battleship Hessen, Commissioned In 1905, Pottery, ½ Liter...........	300.00
Military, Feldmarschall V. Hindenburg, Transfer, Enamel, Metal Lid, ½ Liter ......*illus*	92.00
Military, No. 1828, Naval Sailor On Front, Stoneware, 1914, ½ Liter	250.00
Military, Soldiers, Target Shooting, Pottery, Pewter Lid, Relief, ½ Liter..........	230.00
Military, Third Reich, Komp., Pionier Batl. 34, Koblenz, Pewter Lid, Relief Helmet, ½ Liter ....*illus*	345.00
Occupational, Schweizer, Cheese Maker, Pewter Lid, Porcelain, ½ Liter ....*illus*	109.00
Pewter, Women In Relief, Art Nouveau, WMF, 2 Liter ....*illus*	2530.00
Porcelain, Flowers, Applied Handle, Pewter Lid, 9 ¼ In.	68.00
Porcelain, Golfing Scene, Gilt, Pewter Lid, Figural Thumblift, Royal Bonn, c.1890, 9 In........	1315.00
Porcelain, Lithophane Bottom, Flowers, Hinged, Pewter Lid, ½ Liter	68.00
Porcelain, Man On High Wheel, All Heil, Footed, 19th Century, ½ Liter, 7 In.	250.00
Porcelain, Man On High Wheel, Germany, Marked, KK, 19th Century, ½ Liter, 6 ¼ In...........	150.00
Porcelain, Royal Vienna Style, Transfer, Enamel, Inlaid Lid, Kaufmann, ½ Liter ....*illus*	207.00
Porcelain, Transfer, Enameled, Scene, Marked, GG. Leykauf, Nurnberg, ½ Liter ....*illus*	247.00
Pottery, Bowling Ball Shape, Hinged, Germany, 8 ½ In........................	170.00
Pottery, Frisch Auf, Standard Bicycle, Relief, Pewter Lid, ½ Liter ....*illus*	184.00
Pottery, Gnomes, Animals, Etched, Hauber & Reuther, Pewter Lid, ½ Liter.............	230.00
Pottery, Train, River, Relief, Elberfeld, Pewter Lid, Marked, No. 1530, c.1900, ½ Liter ....*illus*	322.00
Pottery, Washington, Capitol, Relief, Inlaid Lid, ½ Liter....................	265.00
Regimental, 3 Comp., Regt. Erzhg., 2-Sided Scene, Prism Lid, ½ Liter..........	633.00
Regimental, 4-Sided, St. Hubert Thumblift, 1903, 6 ½ In., ½ Liter..........	777.00
Regimental, 4th Regt., Fish Handle, Footed, Hinged, No. 1464, 1903-1906, 12 In.	124.00
Regimental, Field Artillery, Scenic, Pewter Lid, Handle, Cannon Finial, Germany, c.1911, 11 In. .	540.00
Regimental, Inft., Regt. Nr. 113, 2 Scenes, Griffin Thumblift, ½ Liter, 9 In.	431.00
Regimental, Kgl. 4, Chev., Ret. Konig 3, Helmet Lid, ½ Liter................	369.00
Regimental, Kgl. Vayr 10, Feld At., Regt 2F, Raised Acorns, ½ Liter	288.00
Regimental, Roster, 1 Comp., Bad, Fuss. Art. Regt No. 14, ½ Liter.............	345.00
Regimental, Roster, 2 Esk., 3 Bad. Drag. Regt., 4-Sided Scene, ½ Liter	460.00
Regimental, Roster, 2. Kgl., Sachs Jager Bat. Nr. 13, ½ Liter	380.00
Regimental, Roster, 3 Battr., Felld Art. Regt. No. 51, 2 Side Scenes, ½ Liter............	259.00
Regimental, Roster, 3 Comp., Inft. Regt. Nr. 87, Mainz, Lion Thumblift, Porcelain, c.1909, ½ Liter *illus*	403.00
Regimental, Roster, 4 Eskadr., Drag., Regiment No. 19, ½ Liter.............	300.00
Regimental, Roster, 6 Comp., 23 Inft. Regt., Reservist Schwarz, ½ Liter............	259.00
Regimental, Roster, 6 Comp., Nass, Pion, Batl. No 21, Bridge Building, ½ Liter	804.00
Regimental, Roster, 7 Comp., Bayr. Inft. Leib Regt., Munchen, Lion Thumblift, 1911-13, ½ Liter *illus*	288.00

Stein, Porcelain, Royal Vienna Style, Transfer, Enamel, Inlaid Lid, Kaufmann, ½ Liter
$207.00

The Stein Auction Co.

Stein, Porcelain, Transfer, Enameled, Scene, Marked, GG. Leykauf, Nurnberg, ½ Liter
$247.00

The Stein Auction Co.

Stein, Pottery, Frisch Auf, Standard Bicycle, Relief, Pewter Lid, ½ Liter
$184.00

The Stein Auction Co.

S

Stein, Pottery, Train, River, Relief, Elberfeld, Pewter Lid, Marked, No. 1530, c.1900, ½ Liter
$322.00

The Stein Auction Co.

Stein, Regimental, Roster, 3 Comp., Inft. Regt. Nr. 87, Mainz, Lion Thumblift, Porcelain, c.1909, ½ Liter
$403.00

The Stein Auction Co.

Stein, Regimental, Roster, 7 Comp., Bayr. Inft. Leib Regt., Munchen, Lion Thumblift, 1911-13, ½ Liter
$288.00

The Stein Auction Co.

Regimental, Roster, 8 Comp., Inft.-Regt., Photo Transfer Of Owner, ½ Liter	403.00
Regimental, Roster, 10 Comp., Rus. Reft. V. Gersdoff, ½ Liter	288.00
Regimental, Roster, 20 Inft. Regt. 10, Unteroffizer Kommel, ½ Liter	460.00
Regimental, Sanitats Comp., Munchen, Horse Drawn Ambulance Scene, Pewter Lid, ½ Liter	2070.00
Regimental, Scenic, Pewter Lid, Handle, Soldier Finial, c.1910, 11 In.	330.00
Regimental, Zur Erinnerung, A.M., Naval Soldier Finial, Anchor Thumblift, ½ Liter	978.00
Stoneware, Freiberger Birnkrug, Gray, Black & White Enamel, Pewter Lid, c.1650, 8 In.	8625.00
Stoneware, Golf Scene, Salt Glaze, Pewter Lid, Gerz, Germany, c.1900, 7 ½ In.	448.00

STEREO CARDS that were made for stereoscope viewers became popular after 1840. Two almost identical pictures were mounted on a stiff cardboard backing so that, when viewed through a stereoscope, a three-dimensional picture could be seen. Value is determined by maker and by subject. These cards were made in quantity through the 1930s.

Amherst College Library, Massachusetts, J.L. Lovell	39.00
Blue Room, White House, Washington, D.C., J.F. Jarvis	19.00
Gas Well, Brookville, Pennsylvania	49.00
Nantucket Harbor, Massachusetts, Kilburn Brothers	89.00
New Hampshire State House, H.A. Kimball	29.00
Renwick Castle, Syracuse, New York, Gates & Co.	29.00
Teddy Roosevelt, Hunters, Camping, 1907, 7 x 3 ½ In.	90.00
White Mountains, New Hampshire, Indian Craft Tent, Boat House	59.00

STEREOSCOPES were used for viewing stereo cards. The hand viewer was invented by Oliver Wendell Holmes, although more complicated table models were used before his was produced in 1859. Do not confuse the stereoscope with the stereopticon, a magic lantern that used glass slides.

Burl Wood, Focusable Oculars, Box, c.1890	290.00
Graphoscope Style, Bust, Swags, Torches, Folding, Union Case, 1880s, 10 x 7 x 4 In.	550.00
James Davis, 21 Washington Place, N.Y., Wood, Aluminum, c.1896, 13 In.	85.00
Keystone View Co., Wood, Metal, Model 40, 15 x 7 In.	110.00
Pocket Rotoscope, Green, Yellow, Art Nouveau Tinplate, c.1910, 3 x 1 x 5 In.	581.00

STERLING SILVER, *see Silver-Sterling category.*

STEUBEN glass was made at the Steuben Glass Works of Corning, New York. The factory, founded by Frederick Carder and T.G. Hawkes, Sr., was purchased by the Corning Glass Company. Corning continued to make glass called Steuben. Many types of art glass were made at Steuben. Schottenstein Stores Inc. bought 80 percent of the business in 2008. The factory closed in 2011 and no more of this quality glass will be made. Additional pieces may be found in the Cluthra and Perfume Bottle categories.

Bowl, Amethyst, Round, Flared Rim, 3 x 11 In.	115.00
Bowl, Apple Shape, 8 In.	240.00
Bowl, Aureen Strap, Calcite Interior, Pedestal, Flared Rim, Round Foot, 5 x 12 In.	326.00
Bowl, Blue Jade, Flared, Footed, 12 In. Diam.	2645.00
Bowl, Blue, Flared, Carder, Aurene, 5 x 12 In.	881.00
Bowl, Blue, Round Foot, Flared Rim, Aurene, 5 ½ x 12 In.	920.00
Bowl, Blue, Round Pedestal Foot, Wide Flare Rim, Signed, Aurene, 4 In.	748.00
Bowl, Blue, Ruffled Rim, Iridescent, Aurene, 10 In. Diam.	764.00
Bowl, Calcite, Gold, Pink Highlights, Aurene, c.1900, 10 In. Diam., Pair	676.00
Bowl, Centerpiece, Iridescent Interior, White Exterior, Compressed, Aurene, F. Carder, 12 In.	299.00
Bowl, Clear, Covered, Goat Head Figural Lid, Marked, 5 In.	173.00
Bowl, Clear, Flared Rim, 4 Applied Scrolls, Domed Foot, 1984, 7 x 9 In.	267.00
Bowl, Florentia, Broad Green Leaf Set On Aventurine Satin Finish, 12 In.	1500.00
Bowl, Florentia, Cinnamon Leaf, Aventurine Satin Ground, Scalloped Rim, 12 In.	2990.00
Bowl, Footed, Optic Ribbed, Applied Leaves, Red Wrap, 10 In.	400.00
Bowl, Fruit, Gold, Calcite, Rolled Rim, Aurene, 15 In.	230.00
Bowl, Glass, Jade Green Color, Round Foot, Flared Rim, c.1900, 12 In. Diam.	492.00
Bowl, Gold Calcite, Round Foot, Flared Rim, Aurene, 10 In.	173.00
Bowl, Gold Iridescent, Ruffle Rim, Aurene, c.1900, 2 x 5 In.	307.00
Bowl, Gold, Calcite, Aurene, 12 In.	173.00
Bowl, Gold, Puce, Green, Aurene, Marked, 8 ¼ x 7 ¾ In.	667.00
Bowl, Gold, Scalloped Edge, Applied Branch & Leaf Handles, Marked, 5 x 13 In.	3163.00
Bowl, Gold, Trumpet Shape, 3 Loop Handles, Aurene, Marked, 7 In. ....*illus*	1265.00
Bowl, Gold, White Exterior, Lavender Iridescent Flashes, Footed, Aurene, 2 ½ x 9 ¾ In.	184.00
Bowl, Green Over Alabaster, Acid Cut Design, Flowers, Scrolls, Round Foot, Flared Rim, 13 In.	1093.00

Bowl, Green, Clear, Flower Shape, 4 Sections, 1900s, 7 In.	236.00
Bowl, Light Blue Jade, Footed, Flaring Rim, 6 In.	345.00
Bowl, Light Blue Jade, Translucent, Polished, Egg Shape, 2 x 8 x 6 In.	177.00
Bowl, Oriental Jade, Turquoise, Opalescent Ribbing, Squat, Bulbous, 6 In.	230.00
Bowl, Plum Jade, Acid Cut, Medallions, Flowers, Curly Q Design, Squat, Bulbous, 8 In. Diam.	2300.00
Bowl, Rosaline Center, Flared, Carder, c.1920, 5 x 15 In.	294.00
Bowl, Rosaline Pink, Rolled Wide Rim, Marked, 9 In.	230.00
Bowl, Rosaline, Rosy Purple, 14 ½ x 5 In.	295.00
Bowl, Shallow, Verre De Soie, Frosty White, Wide Rim, Rounded Inward, c.1900, 2 x 12 In.	399.00
Candleholder, Clear, Black Thread Highlights, Marked, 6 In., Pair	225.00
Candlestick, Blue, Double Ring, Swollen Neck, Aurene, Marked, 12 In.	2480.00
Candlestick, Blue, Twisted Standard, Aurene, c.1925, Pair	1528.00
Candlestick, Celeste Blue, Swollen, Flemish Blue Lip Wrap, 10 In.	144.00
Candlestick, Clear, Twist Stem, Flared Foot & Rim, Mirror Black Wrap, 10 In.	316.00
Candlestick, Flaring Ruffled Rim, Calcite Glass, Squat, 4 In.	250.00
Candlestick, Gold, Twist Stem, Iridescence, Signed, Aurene, 8 In., Pair	805.00
Candlestick, Twist Stem, Optic Ribbed, Amethyst Foot & Rim Separated With Blue Stem, 12 In.	425.00
Candlestick, White, Applied Blue Twist On Stem, Flared Rim, Round Foot, Aurene, 8 In.	201.00
Candy Dish, Translucent, Covered, Urn Form, 2 Handles, Teardrop Finial, Marked, 11 In.	450.00
Centerpiece, Calcite, Jadeite, 6 Graduated Triangular Flutes, 15 x 7 ½ In.	1770.00
Charger, Rouge Flambe, Tomato Red, 11 In. Diam.	1380.00
Cocktail Set, Flared Rim, 3 ¾ In., 12 Piece	590.00
Cocktail Shaker, Bottle Shape, Flared Stopper, 2 Spouts, c.1950, 8 In.	369.00
Cocktail, Footed, Teardrop, c.1950, 4 In., 4 Piece	522.00
Cocktail, Teardrop, George Thompson, 4 x 3 ½ In., Pair	399.00
Cologne Bottle, Blue, Melon Ribbed, 3 Scrolling Feet, Aurene, Marked, 4 In.	1200.00
Compote, Aurene On Calcite, Cone Shape Foot, Flared Rim, Lilies & Leaves, 6 ½ In.	150.00
Compote, Blue, Long Stem, Aurene, c.1920, 7 ¾ In.	2390.00
Compote, Bronze, Scrolling Grape Leaves, Calcite Bowl, Marked, 7 ½ In.	2000.00
Compote, Celeste Blue, Pedestal, Faceted & Oval Cut Accents, 10 In.	259.00
Compote, Gold Calcite, Spread Foot, Pedestal, 3 ½ x 9 ⅞ In.	259.00
Compote, Gold Iridescent, Pedestal, Flower Shape Foot, Flared Rim, Aurene, 5 ½ x 12 In.	920.00
Compote, Oriental Poppy, Opalescent Pink, Accented With Green Stem, 6 In.	700.00
Compote, Oriental Poppy, Twist Stem, Pomona Standard, 7 In. .....*illus*	575.00
Compote, Pomona Green, Topaz Standard, Optic Ribbed Foot & Tray, 8 In.	144.00 to 200.00
Compote, Ribbed, Covered, Baluster Form, Pear Shape Finial, 10 In.	450.00
Compote, Rosaline, Alabaster, Flower, Full Bloom, Pedestal Foot, Ruffled Rim, 4 ½ x 13 In.	460.00
Compote, Underplate, Pink Rosaline, Cone Shape, Calcite Foot, 6-In. Underplate	354.00
Compote, Yellow & Orange, Cintra Stem & Foot, Wide Rim Bowl, 7 x 7 In.	1150.00
Console Set, Flemish Blue, Oval Bowl, 2 Side Candlesticks, 11 ½ In.	316.00
Console Set, Green, Yellow Conical Foot, Fleur-De-Lis, Candlesticks, 12 In., 3 Piece	805.00
Cruet, Stopper, Gooseneck Spout, Blue Iridescence, 5 In.	2607.00
Dish, Rosaline, Apple Shape, Alabaster Leaf, 5 In.	150.00
Dish, Shrimp, Blue, Rolled Rim Bowl, Sauce Dish, 3-Footed, Aurene, Marked, 11 In. .....*illus*	2070.00
Dresser Jar, Blue, Cover, Flower, Triangle Finial, Aurene, Carder, 5 ¾ In.	2115.00
Figurine, Apple, Marked, 7 In.	330.00
Figurine, Beaver, Clear, Red Glass Eyes, Signed Lloyd Atkins, c.1975, 9 In.	276.00
Figurine, Cat, Clear, Pale Green Eyes, Donald Pollard, c.1973, 4 ½ x 4 ½ In.	253.00
Figurine, Dolphin, Diving, Clear, 7 x 12 In.	138.00
Figurine, Elephant, Standing, Trunk Up, 7 In.	510.00
Figurine, Owl, Clear, Frosted, Signed Donald Pollard, c.1955, 5 ¼ x 3 ½ In.	362.00
Figurine, Penguin, Clear, George Thompson, c.1957, 6 ¼ In.	408.00
Figurine, Porpoise, 3 ¾ x 6 ¼ In.	295.00
Figurine, Porpoise, Clear, Lloyd Atkins, Engraved, c.1964, 9 ¼ In.	311.00
Figurine, Song Birds, George Thompson, c.1963, 4 ¾ In., Pair	414.00
Figurine, Squirrel, Clear, George Thompson, 6 ¼ In.	397.00
Figurine, Swan, 8 ½ In., Pair	330.00
Flower Frog, 2 Tiers, Clear, Frosted Figural Insert Of Kneeling Woman, 8 In.	748.00
Flowerpot, Bristol Yellow, Applied Green Rings, 6 ½ In.	300.00
Goblet, Celeste Blue, Topaz Standard, Silver Mica Accents, 5 In.	161.00
Goblet, Clear, Rosa Twist Stem, Etched Cup, 8 ½ In.	230.00
Goblet, Gold Aurene & Calcite, 6 In.	75.00
Goblet, Gold, Twist Stem, Flared Rim, Aurene, 5 In., 10 Piece	1725.00
Goblet, Oriental Jade, Opalescent Stem, Rolled Rim, 6 In.	403.00
Goblet, Oriental Poppy, Green Foot, Striated Pink Cup, Marked, 8 In.	500.00
Goblet, Rosaline Pink, Clear Wide Twist Stem, Round Foot, Flared Rim, 6 In.	58.00

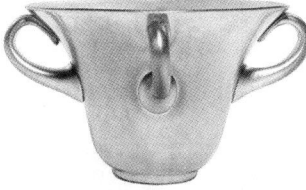

Steuben, Bowl, Gold, Trumpet Shape, 3 Loop Handles, Aurene, Marked, 7 In. $1265.00

Early Auction Co.

Steuben, Compote, Oriental Poppy, Twist Stem, Pomona Standard, 7 In. $575.00

Early Auction Co.

Steuben, Dish, Shrimp, Blue, Rolled Rim Bowl, Sauce Dish, 3-Footed, Aurene, Marked, 11 In. $2070.00

Early Auction Co.

Steuben, Lampshade, Intarsia, Brown Aurene, Gold Border, White, Brown Zigzags, 5 In. $403.00

Early Auction Co.

S

Steuben, Perfume Bottle, Atomizer, Aurene, Gold, Bulbous, Footed, 7 In. $288.00

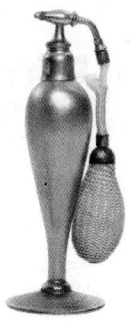

Early Auction Co.

Steuben, Vase, Acid Cut Back, Flowers, Curling Leaves, Mountains, Greek Key Border, 12 In. $3910.00

Humler & Nolan

Steuben, Vase, Blue, Tree Trunk Shape, Disk Foot, 3 Trunk Prongs, Aurene, Marked, 6 ¼ In. $920.00

Early Auction Co.

Goblet, Rosaline, Alabaster Foot & Chain Linked Stem, Conical Glass, 7 In.	230.00
Goblet, Selenium Red, Decorated With Etched Grape Pattern, 5 In.	86.00
Goblet, Water, Cyprian, Aquamarine With Applied Celeste Blue Rigaree, Standard Prunts	115.00
Goblet, Water, Oriental Poppy, Green Stem, 8 In.	690.00
Goblet, Water, Teardrop, 8 Piece	540.00
Jam Jar, Cover, Celeste Blue, Fruit Finial, 4 In.	100.00
Jar, Mirror Black, Domed Gold Aurene Stopper, Threading, Footed, Urn Shape, Flared Rim, 6 In.	2185.00
Jar, Straw, Opal Glass, Vertical Stripes, Pedestal Foot, Black Amethyst Pointed Stopper, 7 In.	719.00
Lamp Base, Alexandrite, Flemish Blue Swag, Acid Cut, 12 In.	2500.00
Lamp Base, Blue, Platinum, Pulled Feather Design, Brass Foot, Shouldered, Aurene, 23 In.	1380.00
Lamp Base, Double Etched, Green Jade, Mounted In Metal Fittings, 12 In.	690.00
Lamp Base, Green Jade, Alabaster Threading, Globe Bottom, Stick Neck, 22 In.	230.00
Lamp Base, Green Jade, Urn Form, Black Handles, 23 In.	288.00
Lamp Base, Iris Flowers & Stems, Pink & White, Acid Cut, Urn Shape, Paw Foot Stand, 28 In.	1265.00
Lamp Base, Mansard Pattern, Gold Aurene Over Green Jade, Acid Cut, 12 In.	4000.00
Lamp Base, Moss Agate, Urn, Footed, Aventurine Blue, Flowing Amber Accents, 12 In.	863.00
Lamp Base, Urn, Textured Yellow, Green Leaves, Gilt Metal Fittings, 12 In.	1150.00
Lamp Base, Urn, Yellow Jade Cut Back In Sculptured Chrysanthemum, 12 In.	1000.00
Lamp, Blue Jade, Swirled Urn Form, Marked, Fleur-De-Lis, 11 In.	600.00
Lamp, Hanging, 4-Light, Gold Aurene Glass Shades, Bronze Fittings, 21 x 25 In.	1240.00
Lamp, Hanging, Calcite Design, Acid Cut Band, Chain, 26 In.	300.00
Lamp, Mirror Black, Urn, Flying Griffin In Medieval Pattern, 19 In.	1265.00
Lampshade, Gold, Ribbed Body, Aurene, 4 In.	50.00
Lampshade, Gold, Ribbed, Flared Rim, Aurene, 6 x 5 ½ In.	109.00
Lampshade, Intarsia, Bell Form, Marigold To White, Iridescent, Aurene, 5 In.	400.00
Lampshade, Intarsia, Brown Aurene, Gold Border, White, Brown Zigzags, 5 In. ....*illus*	403.00
Nappy, Gold, Footed, Heart Form, Ring Finger Holder, Aurene, Marked, 4 In.	150.00
Perfume Bottle, Atomizer, Aurene, Blue, Embossed Metal Fittings, Footed, 9 In.	450.00
Perfume Bottle, Atomizer, Aurene, Gold, Bulbous, Footed, 7 In. ....*illus*	288.00
Perfume Bottle, Blue Aurene, Melon Ribbed Form, Teardrop Stopper, Marked, 5 In.	374.00
Perfume Bottle, Gold, Garlic Bulb Form, Flame Finial, Aurene, 6 In.	590.00
Perfume Bottle, Gold, Round Foot, Tapered, Teardrop Stopper, Aurene, c.1900, 8 In.	461.00
Perfume Bottle, Verre De Soie, Bulbous, Melon Ribbed, Blue Teardrop Stopper, 4 In.	115.00
Perfume Bottle, Yellow, Cylindrical Form, Optic Ribs, Teardrop Stopper, 10 In.	425.00
Pitcher, Cocktail, Art Deco, Black Glass Stopper, Handle, 11 In.	208.00
Sauce, Gold, Oval Shape, Scalloped Rim, 3 Reeded Feet, Signed, Aurene, 5 In.	288.00
Shade, Mushroom Form, Calcite Design, Scrolling Leaves, Flowers & Waves, 9 ½ In.	125.00
Sherbet, Underplate, Amethyst, Cintra Lip Wrap, 6 In.	125.00
Sherbet, Underplate, Gold Aurene On Calcite, 6 In.	100.00
Sherbet, Underplate, Gold, Calcite, Flare Rim, Footed Bowl, Aurene, 6 In., Pair	173.00
Sugar & Creamer, Celeste Blue, Footed, Ribbed, Applied Handles, 5 ¼ In.	250.00
Tobacco Jar, Blue, Covered, Aurene, Stamped, 5 ½ In.	1725.00
Tumbler, Iced Tea, Oriental Poppy, Pomona Green Foot, 6 In.	403.00
Urn, Alabaster, Black Handles, Stepped Base, 11 ¾ x 12 In., Pair	1488.00
Urn, Alabaster, High Black Handles, 12 x 9 ¾ In.	682.00
Urn, Cover, Teardrop, 2 Handles, Marked, c.1950, 11 x 9 In.	369.00
Urn, Greek Shape, Striated & Bubbled Cobalt, Clambroth Handles, Rolled Rim, 11 x 8 In.	1725.00
Vase, 3-Prong Stump, Translucent Amethyst, Marked, 6 ¾ In.	300.00
Vase, 3-Prong Stump, Translucent Topaz, Marked, 6 ¼ In.	225.00
Vase, Acid Cut Back, Flowers, Curling Leaves, Mountains, Greek Key Border, 12 In. ....*illus*	3910.00
Vase, Acid Cut, Shouldered, Pink Cintra, Green Lattice & Flowers, Arrow Design, Label, 14 In.	3000.00
Vase, Alabaster, Cylindrical, Shouldered, 8 ½ In.	150.00
Vase, Alabaster, Gold Aurene Vine, Leaf, 6 ¼ In.	400.00
Vase, Amber Glass, Blue Vertical Ribbing, Flaring Ruffled Rim, Pinched Waist, Spread Foot, 8 In.	345.00
Vase, Aquamarine, Translucent, Flared Rim, Short Stem, Flared Foot, c.1900, 11 In.	230.00
Vase, Art Deco, Emerald Green Uranium, Etched, Baluster, Flared Rim, 11 x 5 ½ In.	167.00
Vase, Art Deco, Glass, Green Jade, Jar Shape, Acid Cut, Flowers, c.1925-30, 10 x 10 In.	1610.00
Vase, Baluster, Narrow Neck, Flared Rim, Clear, Marked, 9 x 4 In.	83.00
Vase, Blue Iridescent, Platinum Heart & Vine Design, Purple, Bulbous, Tapered, Aurene, 5 x 5 In.	11500.00
Vase, Blue Iridescent, Trumpet Shape, Flare Rim, Aurene, 5 ⅛ In.	460.00
Vase, Blue Ribs, Flaring Shade, Shaped, Round Foot, Signed, Aurene, 6 In.	575.00
Vase, Blue, 3 Handles, Reverse Corset Form, 3 Applied Handles, Aurene, Marked, 5 In.	625.00
Vase, Blue, 3-Prong Stump, Aurene, Marked, 6 In.	800.00
Vase, Blue, Basket Shape, Scalloped Rim, Handle, Aurene, c.1925, 12 ½ In.	1998.00
Vase, Blue, Bud, Aurene, c.1925, 12 In.	353.00
Vase, Blue, Purple Highlights, Cylindrical, Stick, Round Foot, Aurene, c.1900, 8 x 3 In.	430.00

Vase, Blue, Tapered, Shouldered, Rolled Lip, Aurene, c.1900, 12 x 8 In.	1045.00
Vase, Blue, Tree Trunk Shape, Disk Foot, 3 Trunk Prongs, Aurene, Marked, 6 ¼ In. ....*illus*	920.00
Vase, Blue, Trumpet Shape, Flared Rim, Tapering Body, Round Disc, Aurene, 8 In.	976.00
Vase, Blue, Urn, 2 Handles, Aurene, 10 In.	2000.00
Vase, Bristol Yellow, Diagonal Swirl Design, Flared Rim, 10 In.	201.00
Vase, Bristol Yellow, Fan Shape, Black Threading, 9 In.	259.00
Vase, Bud, Green, Tree Trunk Shape, 3-Prong, Marked, 6 In.	300.00
Vase, Calcite, Spread Foot, White Ground, Cobalt Blue Ribbon Design, Aurene, 9 In.	395.00
Vase, Corintha Pattern, Oval Shape, Green Cintra, Rose Crystal Flowers, Arrow Points, 8 In.	2760.00
Vase, Cornucopia, Pedestal, While Opaque Foot With Pink Swirl, 15 ½ In.	125.00
Vase, Cyprian, Footed, Urn, Aqua Marine With Blue Wrap, 7 In.	175.00
Vase, Double Corset Shape, French Blue, Ribbing, Flared Rim, 6 In.	230.00
Vase, Fan Shape, French Blue, S-Curved Design, Marked, 8 ½ In.	403.00
Vase, Fan Shape, Topaz, Etched Polynesian Scene, 9 In.	86.00
Vase, Flared Rim, Applied Stem Design, 7 In.	115.00
Vase, Gold Calcite, Morning Glory Blossom Shape, Ruffled Rim, Round Foot, 6 In.	259.00
Vase, Gold Iridescent, Cranberry Highlights, Urn, Aurene, 7 x 6 In.	518.00
Vase, Gold Iridescent, Long Narrow Neck, Dark Amber, Aurene, 12 In.	1495.00
Vase, Gold Iridescent, Purple, Blue Highlights, Bulbous Top, Narrow Base, Footed, Aurene, 3 x 3 In.	403.00
Vase, Gold Ruby Threading, Optic Diamond, 6 ½ In.	50.00
Vase, Gold Ruby, Fan Shape, Swirled Pattern, Clear Foot, 9 In.	374.00
Vase, Gold, Alabaster, Peacock Eyes, Feather Highlights, Scalloped Rim, Aurene, 7 In. ...*illus*	6325.00
Vase, Gold, Bulbous, Pinched Sides, Narrow Neck, Quadrafold Rim, Signed, Aurene, 4 In.	804.00
Vase, Gold, Bulbous, Shouldered, Rolled Rim, Aurene, c.1900, 11 In.	1107.00
Vase, Gold, Extended Ribs, Aurene, Marked, 5 In.	400.00
Vase, Gold, Flaring Trumpet, Ruffle Rim, Spread Foot, Blue Accents, Aurene, Signed, 8 ½ In.	633.00
Vase, Gold, Footed Trumpet Vase, Ruffled Rim, Signed, Aurene, 11 In.	1265.00
Vase, Gold, Jack-In-The-Pulpit, Flower Shape, Teardrop Face, Footed, Aurene, Signed, 9 In. ..*illus*	1725.00
Vase, Gold, Optic Rib, Coupe, Footed, Scalloped Rim, Aurene, Marked, 5 ½ In.	345.00
Vase, Gold, Rainbow Of Iridescent Colors, Aurene, Marked, 1920s, 12 In.	2300.00
Vase, Gold, Squat Bottle Shape, Iridescent Green Hooked Feather, Aurene, Marked, 4 In.	805.00
Vase, Gold, Trumpet, Red Hues, Footed, Aurene, Marked, 12 In.	450.00
Vase, Green Crackle, Amber Lion Head Handles, 9 ¼ In.	153.00
Vase, Green Grotesque, Translucent With Free-Form Ruffled Rim, 5 In.	125.00
Vase, Green Over Yellow Jade, Indian Pattern, Footed Urn, Marked, 9 In.	2185.00
Vase, Green, Cylinder, 4 Green Leaves At Base, Heart & Vine Pattern, Aurene, Marked, 7 In.	8625.00
Vase, Grotesque, Purple To Clear, 5 ¼ In.	177.00
Vase, Iridescent Gold, Aurene, c.1900, 8 In.	86.00
Vase, Iridescent Gold, Openwork Metal Frame, Footed, Ruffled Rim, Aurene, 10 In.	575.00
Vase, Ivory, Footed Helmet Shape, Ruffled Rim, 9 In.	115.00
Vase, Ivory, Footed, Helmet Shape, 6 ½ In.	50.00
Vase, Ivory, Grotesque, Handkerchief Flaring Rim, 12 In., 10 In., Pair	288.00
Vase, Ivrene, Optic Ribbed, Fan, Round Foot, 10 In.	345.00
Vase, Ivrene, Urn, M-Shape Handles, Round Foot, Rolled Rim, 11 In.	1035.00
Vase, Jack-In-The-Pulpit, Ivrene, White, Slight Ribbing, Flared Foot, Marked, 7 In.	259.00
Vase, Jade Over Alabaster, Flared Foot & Rim, Bulging Waist, Oriental Design, 10 In.	1610.00
Vase, Jade, Oval, Flared Neck, Applied Twisted Loop Handles, c.1920, 10 ½ In.	4196.00
Vase, Jade, Urn, Alabaster M-Shape Handles, Round Foot, Rolled Rim, 11 In.	1208.00
Vase, Lace, Bulbous, Flaring Rim, Alternating Black & White Lace, 8 In.	1750.00
Vase, Lamp Base, Aurene Over Black, Dresden Pattern, Acid Cut, Flowers, Swirls, 12 In.	920.00
Vase, Lotus, Clear, Trumpet Shape, Applied Elements, George Thompson, Marked, 13 In.	767.00
Vase, Medieval Pattern, Mirror Black Glass, Baluster, 12 In.	1150.00
Vase, Morning Glory, Blue, Purple, 10 Ribs, Flared Rim, Round Foot, 5 ½ In.	518.00
Vase, Moss Agate, Green, Red, Turquoise, Orange, Gray Mottled, Aventurine Amber, Marked, 6 In. ..*illus*	5750.00
Vase, Optic Ribbed, Wisteria, Purple To Blue, Marked, 6 In.	200.00
Vase, Oval, Acid Cut, Green Jade Over Alabaster, Oriental Pattern, 4 ½ In.	275.00
Vase, Oval, Mirror Black, Gold Pattern Of Grape Leaves, Norfolk Pattern, 8 In.	12000.00
Vase, Pink & Jade, Flowers, Branches, Round, Cameo, Stamped Mark, 7 x 7 ½ In.	1116.00
Vase, Plum Jade, Acid Cut Back, Cased Purple, Chang Pattern, 8 In. ....*illus*	2070.00
Vase, Plum, Etched Water Lilies, Bulbous, F. Carder, c.1926, 7 In.	3884.00
Vase, Pomona Green, Rosa, Fan Shape, Footed, 9 x 7 In., Pair	944.00
Vase, Purple, Gold Iridescent, Pulled Feather Design, c.1900, 7 In.	492.00
Vase, Red, Scalloped Rim, Opal, Red Pulled Feathers, Gold Hearts, Vines, Aurene ....*illus*	17250.00
Vase, Rosaline & Alabaster, Trumpet, Footed, 2 Ring Handles, 6 In.	230.00
Vase, Rosaline, Round Alabaster Foot, Urn, Rolled Rim, 11 x 8 ¼ In.	920.00
Vase, Rosaline, Trumpet, Footed, 2 Alabaster Ring Handles, 8 In.	374.00

Steuben, Vase, Gold, Alabaster, Peacock Eyes, Feather Highlights, Scalloped Rim, Aurene, 7 In.
$6325.00

Steuben, Vase, Gold, Jack-In-The-Pulpit, Flower Shape, Teardrop Face, Footed, Aurene, Signed, 9 In.
$1725.00

Steuben, Vase, Moss Agate, Green, Red, Turquoise, Orange, Gray Mottled, Aventurine Amber, Marked, 6 In.
$5750.00

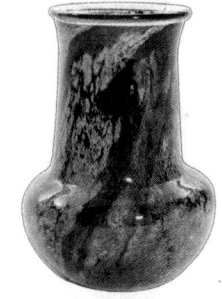

Steuben, Vase, Plum Jade, Acid Cut Back, Cased Purple, Chang Pattern, 8 In.
$2070.00

S

Steuben, Vase, Red, Scalloped Rim, Opal, Red Pulled Feathers, Gold Hearts, Vines, Aurene
$17250.00

Early Auction Co.

Steuben, Vase, Tree Trunk, Iridescent Amber & Blue, Signed, Aurene, 5 ¾ In.
$708.00

Brunk Auctions

Steuben, Vase, Trumpet, Etched Floral, Rosaline Over Alabaster, Footed, 12 In.
$1265.00

Early Auction Co.

Vase, Round Bottom, Trumpet Neck, Gold, Red & Violet Highlights, Aurene, c.1900, 12 In.......	799.00
Vase, Sea Holly, Bulbous, Oval, Opal, Black Leaves, 7 In.	1380.00
Vase, Selenium Red, Flask Form, Ribbed Ball, Rigaree Collar, Footed, 14 In.	1300.00
Vase, Selenium Red, Vertical Ribbing, Cylindrical, Flared Rim, Round Foot, 7 x 7 In.	288.00
Vase, Tapered, Loop Pedestal, Round Foot, 11 In.	150.00
Vase, Tapered, Pedestal, Square Base, 12 x 7 ½ In.	240.00
Vase, Tree Trunk, Iridescent Amber & Blue, Signed, Aurene, 5 ¾ In. ....*illus*	708.00
Vase, Trumpet, Etched Floral, Rosaline Over Alabaster, Footed, 12 In. ....*illus*	1265.00
Vase, Trumpet, Footed, Bristol Yellow, Internal Silverina, 12 In.	1000.00
Vase, Trumpet, Footed, Ribbed Pomona Green, 8 In.	75.00
Vase, Trumpet, Pale Amber, Ribbing, Dangling Braided Rings, Cobalt Blue Trim, 12 In. *illus*	403.00
Vase, Trumpet, Ribs, Gold Pulled Feather Over Red Ground, Aurene, Marked, 9 ½ In.	22500.00
Vase, White Fan Shape Top, Stem, Round Foot, Swirl Design, Aurene, 8 ½ In.	413.00
Vase, White Opaque Drop Design, Jar Shape, c.1920, 10 x 10 In.	920.00
Vase, Wisteria, Corset Shape, Optic Ribbing, Round Foot, 5 In.	316.00
Vase, Wisteria, Optic Ribbed Form, Blue To Amethyst, 8 In.	250.00
Wine, Oriental Jade, Opalescent Twist Stem, Green Opalescent Bowl, 6 In.	325.00

STEVENGRAPHS are woven pictures made like fancy ribbons. They were manufactured by Thomas Stevens of Coventry, England, and became popular in 1862. Most are marked *Woven in silk by Thomas Stevens* or were mounted on a cardboard that tells the story of the Stevengraph. Other similar ribbon pictures have been made in England and Germany.

Building, Crystal Palace, Frame, England, 1851, 8 x 6 In.	300.00
Horse Scene, The Start, c.1860, Frame, 11 x 9 In.	245.00
Horseracing, The Start, The Finish, Jacquard Woven, Silk, Mat, Frame, 2 x 6 In., Pair	413.00
Men On Horseback, The Struggle, Frame, c.1860, 11 x 9 In.	245.00
Postcard, R.M.S. Titanic, Silk, 3 ½ x 5 ½ In.	3585.00

STEVENS & WILLIAMS of Stourbridge, England, made many types of glass, including layered, etched, cameo, and art glass, between the 1830s and 1930s. Some pieces are signed *S & W*. Many pieces are decorated with flowers, leaves, and other designs based on nature.

Basket, Conjoined Horns, Flowers, Ruffled Rim, Arched Thorn Handle, Footed, 7 In.	259.00
Biscuit Jar, Cranberry Cut To Clear, Alternating Swirls, Ivy, Wheat, Silver Plate, 6 ¼ In.	525.00
Bowl, Pompeiian Swirl, Ruffled Rim, Amber To Blue, 2 In.	201.00
Dish, Sweetmeat, Cream, Pink Interior, Applied Leaves, Multicolor, Silver Plated Lid, Handle, 4 x 6 In.	150.00
Finger Bowl, Underplate, Pompeiian Swirl, Red To Butterscotch, 5 In. ....*illus*	805.00
Goblet, Green Cut To Clear, Scrolling & Grapes, 6 In.	50.00
Jar, Cover, Blue, Amber Overlay, Cut Flowers, Squat Finial, Signed, 6 In.	1955.00
Mustard, Cylinder, Vertical Ribs, Pink, Mother-Of-Pearl, 3 ½ In.	460.00
Perfume Bottle, Pompeiian Swirl, Green Shading To Rose, Embossed Swirl, 5 In.	920.00
Perfume Bottle, Pompeiian Swirl, Green, To Salmon, Repouse Silver Stopper, 4 ½ In.	690.00
Rose Bowl, Bulbous, Ruffled Rim, Blue, Cascading Gingko Branches, Mother-Of-Pearl, 2 In.	288.00
Vase, Aventurine, Green, Pink, Sparkly Silver, Combed Design, Slender, Swollen Mouth	230.00
Vase, Blue, Amber Applied Thorn Feet, Applied Strawberries, 3-Footed, 4 In.	650.00
Vase, Bud, Orange Cased, Flowers, Leaves, Bulbous Bottom, 10 In.	177.00
Vase, Cameo Glass, Blue & White, Flowers, 14 In. ....*illus*	5310.00
Vase, Cameo, Rose Du Barry, Flower Garden, Scrolling, 8 ¾ In. ....*illus*	259.00
Vase, Cameo, Stick Form, Pink With White Poppies, Butterfly, 8 ¾ In.	2750.00
Vase, Double Gourd, Genie Bottle Shape, Amber To Rose, Dogwood, Butterfly, Signed, 10 In....	8050.00
Vase, Pink Cased Glass, Applied Amber Branch, White Blossom, 5 ½ In.	30.00
Vase, Pink Ruffled Rim, Applied Amber Feet, Wheat, 9 ½ In.	550.00
Vase, Pink, Amber Glass, Oak Branch, Leaves, Acorns, Frilly Ruffled Rim, Squat Bottom, 10 In.	173.00
Vase, Pompeiian Swirl, Bottle Form, Purple & Rose, 9 ½ In. ....*illus*	1725.00
Vase, Pompeiian Swirl, Rose Shaded To Amber, 8 ¼ In. ....*illus*	259.00
Vase, Stick Shape, Blue, Cascading Raspberry Branch, Flowers, Cameo, 10 In.	3220.00

STIEGEL TYPE glass is listed here. It is almost impossible to be sure a piece was actually made by Stiegel, so the knowing collector refers to this glass as "Stiegel type." Henry William Stiegel, a colorful immigrant to the colonies, started his first factory in Pennsylvania in 1763. He remained in business until 1774. Glassware was made in a style popular in Europe at that time and was similar to the glass of many other makers. It was made of clear or colored glass and was decorated with enamel colors, mold blown designs, or etching.

Flask, Diamond Pattern, Molded, Amethyst, c.1760, 5 ¼ In. ....*illus*	3450.00

STONE includes those articles made of stones, coral, shells, and some other natural materials not listed elsewhere in this book. Micro mosaics (small decorative designs made by setting pieces of stone into a pattern), urns, vases, and other pieces made of natural stone are listed here. Stoneware is pottery and is listed in the Stoneware category. Alabaster, Jade, Malachite, Marble, and Soapstone are in their own categories.

Basket, Fruit, Twisted Wire Rope, Painted Green, Wax, Plaster, 6 In., 19 Piece	529.00
Basket, Overflowing Flowers, Shellwork, Bell Jar, c.1870, 15 ½ In.	150.00
Box, Cover, Geometrics, Flowers, Lapis Lazuli Inset, 1 ¾ x 6 In.	492.00
Brush Rest, Agate, 5 Crested Mountains, 4 x 2 ½ In.	711.00
Brush Washer, Agate, Gray, Black, Brown Mottled, Lotus Leaf, Branches, Crab, Fish, 2 x 4 In.	239.00
Brush Washer, Hardstone, Pines, Inscriptions, Carved, Wood Stand, Chinese, 7 x 6 ¼ In.	1896.00
Carving, Hardstone, Carved Horses, Immortals, Rocky Landscapes, Ocher, Rounded, 12 ½ x 5 In.	3318.00
Chalice, Rock Crystal, Ruby Bands, Flared Rim, 5 ¾ x 6 ¼ In.	1422.00
Conch Shell, Cameo, Carved, 3 Graces, 6 In.	150.00
Figure, Agate, Phoenix Bird, Holding Vine In Mouth, Rocks, Green Quartz Base, 7 ½ In.	538.00
Figure, Apple, Yellow, Red Paint, 20th Century, 4 In.	118.00
Figure, Beast, White, Scrolling Metal Design, Carved Bat, 4 ⅝ In.	279.00
Figure, Bharma, Hindu God, 4 Faces, Khmer, Metal Base, 10 x 8 In.	805.00
Figure, Bird, Amethyst, Carved, Perched, Rosewood Footed Stand, 10 x 6 x 5 ½ In.	180.00
Figure, Boat, 2 Top Sails, Dragon Heads & Tails, Green, Carved, Wooden Stand, Chinese, 29 x 25 In.	230.00
Figure, Boat, Oarsman, Coral, c.1900, 4 ½ In.	777.00
Figure, Buddha Head, Limestone, Downcast Eyes, Chinese, 13 ½ In. *illus*	2185.00
Figure, Buddha, Seated, Amber, Hardwood Stand, 4 ½ In.	796.00
Figure, Carnelian, Female Deity, Standing, Round Pierced Base, Carved, Chinese, 7 In.	359.00
Figure, Carved, Fish, Wood Base, Chinese, 7 x 6 In.	207.00
Figure, Carved, Hindu Deity, Pale Yellow, Multi Armed Figure, Seated, Lotus Blossom Base, 9 In.	275.00
Figure, Coral, Carved, Female Deity, Robes, Standing, Rockwork Base, Flute, Phoenix, 6 In.	9532.00
Figure, Coral, Carved, Woman, Standing, Seminude, Leaves, Wood Stand, Chinese, 6 In.	2000.00
Figure, Coral, Woman, Musician, Stringed Instrument, Child Attendant, c.1905, 6 ¾ In.	6457.00
Figure, Crane, Quartz, Glass Eyes, Patinated Silver Metal Legs, 1970s, 6 ½ x 5 ¼ In.	604.00
Figure, Dancing Russian Peasant, Red, Black, Faberge Style, Hardstones, c.1975, 5 ¾ In.	3600.00
Figure, Dove, White, Wood Base, Cleo Hartwing, c.1970, 9 x 7 ½ In.	780.00
Figure, Dragon, Agate, Chinese, 1 ½ x 3 In.	360.00
Figure, Dragons, Carved, Red & Cream, Chinese, 1800s, 2 ½ x 3 In.	605.00
Figure, Duck, Pink Quartz, Incised Details, Wood Stand, 5 ½ x 3 ¼ In., Pair	253.00
Figure, Egyptian Bust, Woman, Ruler, Crown, Royal Headdress, Black, 3 ⅜ In.	522.00
Figure, Flower, Bud, Feathery Petals, White, Square Scroll Legged Base, 2 x 9 In.	563.00
Figure, Foo Dog, Seated On Lotus Throne, White, 12 ½ In., Pair	190.00
Figure, Gargoyles, Outstretched Wings, Perched On Ball Base, 13 ½ x 9 ½ x 8 In., Pair	90.00
Figure, Lapis Lazuli, Carved, 2 Immortals, Clouds, Pavilion, Crane, Deity, Deer, 1900s, 12 In.	2706.00
Figure, Lion, Crouching, Open Mouth, White, Russet Veining, Agate, Chinese, c.1790, 1 ¾ x 3 In.	1200.00
Figure, Monk, Gray, Praying Hands, Korea, 5 ½ In.	717.00
Figure, Old Testament Prophet, Carved, Romanesque Style, Limestone, 13 In.	450.00
Figure, Onyx, Bok Choy, Fluted Leaves, Layered Stone, Wood Stand, 1900s, 10 ½ In.	2337.00
Figure, Parrots, Amethyst, Geode, Silver Metal Legs, Quartz, 8 x 2 x 6 In.	426.00
Figure, Ram, Pine Tree, Pear Shape, Inkstone, Chinese, 2 x 5 ¾ In.	296.00
Figure, Rooster, Standing, Translucent Green, Hardstone, Wood Stand, Chinese, 1900s, 5 In., Pair	420.00
Figure, Temple Dragon, Open Mouth, Walking Pose, Carved, 7 x 11 In., Pair	444.00
Figure, Ukranian Man, Smoking Pipe, Standing, Faberge Style, Hardstone, c.1975, 6 In.	3600.00
Figure, Walrus, Purple Hardstone, White Tusks, Red Stone Eyes, Quartz Base, c.1880, 5 x 8 In.	3840.00
Figure, Water Buffalo, Reclining, Russet, White, 1800s, 5 x 10 In.	646.00
Figure, Woman, Standing, Rock Crystal, Flowering Branch, 6 In.	148.00
Floral Study, Berry Plant, Crystal Blooms, Diamond, Agate, 18K Gold, Jade, Cartier, c.1967, 8 ¼ In.	2211.00
Floral Study, Lily, Crystal, Diamond, 18K Gold Stem, Jade Leaves, Rock Crystal Base, Cartier, 7 ¼ In.	2629.00
Fruit, Apples, Oranges, Bananas, Grapes, Figs, Lemons, Pomegranate, Painted, 1900s, 30 Piece	294.00
Fruit, Grape Bunches, Rose Quartz, Serpentine, Chinese, 6 Piece	108.00
Geode, Amethyst, 28 x 18 In.	837.00
Group, Coral, Dragons, Clasping Pearl, Clouds, Flames, Wood Stand, c.1905, 5 x 10 ¼ In.	2460.00
Group, Female Immortal, Coral, Standing, Boat, Resting Boy, Plant, Carved, Wood Stand, 5 In.	4740.00
Head, Guanyin, Variegated Brown, Serene Expression, Topknot, Chinese, Wood Plinth, 8 x 15 In.	388.00
Incense Burner, Carved, 8 Tiers, Round, Ring Handles, Scrolling, 2-Tier Teak Stand, 44 In.	1304.00
Incense Burner, Quartz, Green, Squat Shape, Handles, Rings, Wood Base, Chinese, 1800s, 3 x 6 In.	531.00
Lingzhi Fungus, Speckled Black & White, Carved Wood Stand, 3 In.	854.00
Obelisk, Rock Crystal, Stepped Plinth, 17 ½ In.	1230.00
Ornament, Agate, Koi Fish, Lotus Flower, Carved, Banded, Chinese, 2 ¼ x 1 ½ In.	155.00

Steuben, Vase, Trumpet, Pale Amber, Ribbing, Dangling Braided Rings, Cobalt Blue Trim, 12 In.
$403.00

Humler & Nolan

Stevens & Williams, Finger Bowl, Underplate, Pompeiian Swirl, Red To Butterscotch, 5 In.
$805.00

Early Auction Co.

Stevens & Williams, Vase, Cameo Glass, Blue & White, Flowers, 14 In.
$5310.00

Ivey-Selkirk Auctioneers

As always, the edited listings in *Kovels' Antiques & Collectibles Price Guide* aren't available on any website, but readers should visit Kovels.com for information on trends, tips, reproductions, marks, old prices, and more!

Stevens & Williams, Vase, Cameo, Rose Du Barry, Flower Garden, Scrolling, 8 ¾ In.
$259.00

Early Auction Co.

Stevens & Williams, Vase, Pompeiian Swirl, Bottle Form, Purple & Rose, 9 ½ In.
$1725.00

Early Auction Co.

Stevens & Williams, Vase, Pompeiian Swirl, Rose Shaded To Amber, 8 ¼ In.
$259.00

Early Auction Co.

Picture, Bouquet, Stones, Black Lacquer Board, Tortoiseshell Frame, 26 x 23 In. ....*illus*	944.00
Planter, Limestone, Relief Lion Mask Frieze, c.1905, 10 x 38 In.	180.00
Plaque, Birds, On Bowl, Water Reflection, Pietra Dura, Italy, c.1875, 7 x 5 In.	1230.00
Plaque, Hardstone, Scholar, Pine Tree, Water Buffalo, Boat, Green, Round, Stand, Chinese, 8 In.	3200.00
Sculpture, Buddha, Seated, Down Cast Eyes, Elongated Earlobes, Quartz Striations, 25 x 12 In.	288.00
Sculpture, Mephistopheles, Carved, c.1950, 24 In.	1560.00
Seal, Agate, Flattened Pebble, Ocher Skin, 3 Bats, Ruyi Scepter, Green, Orange, 2 In.	246.00
Seal, Domed Top, Scholar, Mountains, 4 x 1 ⅞ In.	5904.00
Seal, Hardstone, Carved Recluse, Landscape, Boulder Shape, Chinese, 2 ½ x 4 ¼ In.	237.00
Seal, Lion, Resting, Atop Boulder, Open Mouth, Backward Glancing, Teeth, 4 In.	584.00
Seal, Tianhuang, Square Base, Winged Dragons, Pearl Of Wisdom, 5 In.	3444.00
Table, Limestone Slab Top, Wrought Iron Trestle Stretcher, Red Paint, c.1905, 30 x 59 In.	1440.00
Teapot, Carnelian, Ribbed Body, Gourd Shape, Cover, 6 ½ In.	388.00
Trough, 4 Carved Relief Panels, Oval, 17 x 45 x 25 In.	738.00
Trough, Hardstone, Roughhewn, 1800s, 9 x 22 In.	441.00
Urn, Neoclassical Style, Round, Emanating Flame, Leaf Bands, Waisted Ribbed Base, 27 x 16 In., Pair.	430.00
Vase, Cover, Suspended, Carved Chain, Carved Hardwood Stand, Chinese, 10 In. ....*illus*	6820.00
Vase, Cover, Turquoise, Carved, Taotie Mask, Rose Quartz Stand, Chinese, 9 ⅜ In ....*illus*	4481.00
Vase, Double, Flower Shape, Opaque, 2 Blossoms, Vines, Insect, Wood Stand, 6 ½ In.	1178.00
Vase, Green Quartz, Cover, Carved Wood Base, Chinese, 8 In.	207.00

STONEWARE is a coarse, glazed, and fired potter's ceramic that is used to make crocks, jugs, bowls, etc. It is often decorated with cobalt blue decorations. In the nineteenth and early twentieth centuries, potters often decorated crocks with blue numbers indicating the size of the container. A 2 meant 2 gallons. Stoneware is still being made. American stoneware is listed here.

Bank, Pig, Bristol Glaze, Cobalt Blue Forehead Spot, A.D. Ruekel & Sons Pottery, 3 ½ x 8 In.	2185.00
Batter Basket, Oval, Pouring Spout, Bail Handle, New York State, c.1870, 9 In.	173.00
Batter Jug, Cobalt Blue Highlights, Impressed N.A. White & Co., Wire Bail Handle, 8 ½ In.	118.00
Batter Jug, Manganese Glaze, Applied Handle Ears, Crescent Handle, 11 In.	118.00
Batter Jug, Metal Lids, Blue Man In Moon, Flowers, Impressed Cowden & Wilcox, 1800s, 9 In.	7703.00
Bean Pot, Dome Lid, Flowers & Leaves, Teal Blue, Brown Speckles, Handles, 7 x 8 ½ In.	65.00
Bean Pot, Incised Lines, Red Glaze, Bulbous, Applied Crescent Tab Handle, 8 x 10 In.	59.00
Bottle, Wine, Cream Color Glaze, Sgraffito Lotus Scrolls, Chinese, 17 In.	2607.00
Bottle, Wine, Pale Celadon, Crackling, Korea, 1700s, 11 ¼ In.	337.00
Bottle, Wine, Shouldered, Narrow Neck, Roll Rim, Purple, Turquoise Glaze, 1700s, 11 In.	889.00
Bowl, Milk, Salt Glaze, Stencil, A.P. Donaghho, Parkersburg, W. Va., Tapered, 5 x 10 In.	1495.00
Bowl, Tulips, Cobalt Blue, Applied Handles, 12 ½ In.	203.00
Bowl, Verdigris & Mottled Brown, Semimatte Glaze, Signed Natzier, 1 ¾ x 6 ½ In.	341.00
Chamber Pot, Applied Lions, Medallion, Curved Rim, Westerwald, 4 ½ x 5 ½ In.	173.00
Chicken Waterer, Cylindrical, Footed, Bristol Slip Glaze, Red Wing, Union, 1885, 8 ¼ In.	58.00
Chicken Waterer, Flowers, Blue, Domed, Applied Handles, Thos Haig, Philadelphia, 7 ¾ In.	633.00
Churn, Bird, Flower Spray, Cobalt Blue, Lug Handles, Rolled Rim, c.1850, 2 Gal., 14 x 8 In.	288.00
Churn, Cobalt Blue Detail, Narrow Oval Shape, Lunate Handles, c.1850, 18 In.	617.00
Churn, Dasher, Bands & Stencil, Cobalt Blue, L.L. Pottery, Amory, Miss., 4, 16 x 10 In.	86.00
Churn, Flowers, Blue, 1800s, 13 In.	259.00
Churn, Flowers, Cobalt Blue, 2 Handles, Rolled Rim, Ottman Bros. & Co., N.Y., 16 In.	288.00
Churn, Fuchsia Blossoms, Cobalt Blue, Wm Porter, Oil Creek, c.1815, 15 In.	353.00
Churn, Leaves, Flowers, Cobalt Blue, Cylindrical, Lug Handles, Rolled Rim, 18 In.	345.00
Churn, Stylized Leaf Design, Cobalt Blue, Lug Handles, 1900s, 15 In.	276.00
Churn, Swags, Cobalt Blue, Flared Collar, Lug Handles, Remmey, Philadelphia, 11 In.	201.00
Churn, Tulips, Cobalt Blue, c.1850, 16 In.	323.00
Churn, Turkey, On Branch, Cobalt Blue 5, Lug Handles, Rolled Rim, c.1850, 16 ½ In.	1528.00
Colander, Molded, Beige Exterior, White Interior, Oval Panels, 5 x 11 In.	41.00
Cooler, Spigot Socket, Cobalt Blue, Impressed Albany, N.Y., 16 ½ In.	502.00
Cream Jar, Flowers, Cobalt Blue, Oval, Flattened Rim, Lug Handles, 1800s, 7 In.	201.00
Cream Pot, Salt Glaze, Oval, Wide Mouth, Incised Ring, Flat Rim, Cobalt Blue Tulip, Gal.	81.00
Crock, 2-Stemmed Plant, Swags, Cobalt Blue, Handles, 4 Gal., 16 In.	201.00
Crock, Applied Handles, Sponge Decoration, White Glaze, 14 ½ In.	79.00
Crock, Bird & Flower Stem, 2 Handles, Flared Rim, 1700s, 8 Gal., 17 In.	2415.00
Crock, Bird On Stump, Cobalt Blue, Salt Glaze, 4 Gal., 14 In.	522.00
Crock, Bird, Cobalt Blue, 2 Applied Handles, Marked, W. Roberts, 3, 1800s, 13 In.	374.00
Crock, Bird, Cobalt Blue, c.1870, 9 In.	354.00
Crock, Bird, Cobalt Blue, Straight-Sided, 3, Applied Crescent Handles, 11 x 11 In.	177.00
Crock, Bird, Cylindrical, Rounded Rim, Lug Handles, Stamped, Hudson Pottery, c.1875, 10 In.	230.00
Crock, Bird, Sprig, Cobalt Blue, Incised, Lug Handles, Rolled Rim, N.Y., c.1855, 11 ¼ x 11 ¾ In.	173.00

Crock, Brown Lead Glaze, Applied Lug Handles, Impressed 5, Mineral Point, Wisc., 14 x 12 In..	489.00
Crock, Butter, Raised Design Of 4 Swastikas, Blue, 4 ¾ x 7 In.	12.00
Crock, Butter, Stripes, Cobalt Blue, Rolled Rim, c.1875, 3 x 2 In.	127.00
Crock, Cake, Flowers, Cobalt Blue, Applied Handles, 9 In. Diam.	254.00
Crock, Cake, Lid, Flowers, Cobalt Blue, Handles, Round, 7 x 12 In.	339.00
Crock, Cake, Lid, Leaves, Clovers, Cobalt Blue, 2 Handles, c.1850, 5 x 9 In.	499.00
Crock, Cake, Lid, Leaves, Cobalt Blue, Ribbed Lug Handles, Remmey, Phila., c.1875, 10 ½ In.	259.00
Crock, Cake, Lid, Leaves, Tulips, Handles, c.1850, 7 x 11 In.	499.00
Crock, Cake, Stripes, Stenciled Flowers, Rolled Rim, Lug Handles, c.1875, 9 In.	127.00
Crock, Cake, Vinery, Cobalt Blue, Reeded Band, C-Scroll Handles, Salt Glaze, c.1885, 4 ½ x 8 In.	230.00
Crock, Canning, Freehand Design, Marked Graham & Stone, 10 In.	189.00
Crock, Cobalt Blue Label, 3, Hamilton & Jones, Greensboro, Pa., c.1860, 14 In.	558.00
Crock, Cobalt Blue Stencil, H.B. & G.B. Pfaltzgraff, 3, Heavy Rim, 11 ½ In. ....illus	94.00
Crock, Cobalt Blue, Design, Applied Loop Handle, Marked New York Stoneware Co., 11 In.	94.00
Crock, Cobalt Blue, Stencil, Brown Slip, E.H. Miller & Co., Danville, Va., 11 x 8 In.	196.00
Crock, Cream, Sprig, Cobalt Blue, Wide Rolled Rim, Pa., Late 1800s, 10 In.	173.00
Crock, Curved Sides, Flower, Freehand, Cobalt Blue, P.S. Co., 2 Pfaltzgraff, 10 ½ In.	130.00
Crock, Cylindrical, Rolled Rim, Stamped, E.J. Miller & Son Alexandria, Va., 1800s, 8 In.	395.00
Crock, Daisy, Cobalt Blue, White's, Utica, c.1870, 13 ½ In.	58.00
Crock, Deer Tracks, Cobalt Blue, Incised Line Around Shoulder, 8 In.	83.00 to 142.00
Crock, Double Birds, Cobalt Blue, Applied Lug Handles, Ottman Bros., c.1880, 4 Gal., 11 ½ In..	403.00
Crock, Eagle, 3, Cobalt Stencil, A. Conrad, New Geneva, Fayette Co., Pa., c.1875, 13 ½ In. illus	1410.00
Crock, Eagle, Flag, 2 Swans, Blue, Rolled Rim, Lug Handles, c.1885, 13 ¼ x 13 ½ In.	230.00
Crock, Flourishes, 20, Cobalt Blue, Stenciled Label, C.I. Williams & Co., 26 In.	1175.00
Crock, Flower, Cobalt Blue, Rolled Rim, Hog Ear Handles, 6 ¾ x 9 In.	254.00
Crock, Flowers, 1, Cobalt Blue, Salt Glaze, Conical, Handles, Mt. Crawford, 8 x 9 In.	219.00
Crock, Flowers, 2, Cobalt Blue Straight-Sided, Applied Crescent Handles, 9 x 9 ¾ In.	94.00
Crock, Flowers, Bird, Hamilton & Jones Greensboro, Pa, Stenciled, 8 In.	509.00
Crock, Flowers, Cobalt Blue, 2 Handles, Marked, Frank B. Norton, No. 2, 1800s, 12 In., 2 Gal.	219.00
Crock, Flowers, Cobalt Blue, Applied Lug Handles, Albany Slip Glaze, 1869, 14 ½ x 12 ½ In.	863.00
Crock, Flowers, Cobalt Blue, Incised 4, c.1850, 12 ½ In.	294.00
Crock, Flowers, Cobalt Blue, Molded Collar, 11 In.	153.00
Crock, Flowers, Cobalt Blue, Rolled Rim, Hog Ear Handles, Yeager & Co., 7 In.	250.00
Crock, Flowers, Cobalt Blue, Salt Glaze, 2 Handles, High Rim, c.1850, 9 x 13 In.	165.00
Crock, Flowers, Flaring Collar, Oval, Joseph Remmey, South Amboy, N.J., 1823, 11 ½ In.	748.00
Crock, Flowers, Semi-Rounded Rim, Lug Handles, F.B. Norton, Worcester, Mass., 3 Gal., 10 ½ In..	316.00
Crock, Freehand, 6, Cobalt Blue, Williams & Reppert, Greensboro, Pa., Handles, 15 x 12 In. illus	142.00
Crock, Freehand Roses, Cobalt Blue Stencil, Jas. Hamilton Co., Greensboro, Pa., c.1851-80 .... illus	1293.00
Crock, House, Flower, Cobalt Blue, Cylindrical, Rolled Rim, 12 In.	711.00
Crock, Incised Lines, Lead Glaze, Beaded Foot, Semi-Oval, Coffman, 8 ½ x 6 ¾ In.	173.00
Crock, Knox, Haught & Co., Stenciled, Cobalt Blue, 2 Handles, 14 In.	1116.00
Crock, Leaves, Blue Slip Design, 2 Ear Shape Handles, Rolled Rim, Marked, 16 In.	531.00
Crock, Leaves, Flowers, Cobalt Blue, Stamped H.C. Smith, Alexa., c.1840, 6 ½ x 7 In.	575.00
Crock, Lid, Jewel Tea Company, 75th Anniversary, Salesman, Wagon, c.1974, 4 ½ x 6 ¼ In.	85.00
Crock, Lid, Leaves, Cobalt Blue, Squat, 2 Handles, Emerick & Hopkins, 1800s, 6 x 8 In.	1541.00
Crock, Lid, Sprig, Flower, Cobalt Blue 2 Applied Handles, Marked, Ballard Vale, 14 In., 4 Gal..	460.00
Crock, Lugs, Blue Slip, S. Risley Norwich, 1800s, 12 In.	89.00
Crock, Ribbon, Numbers, Cobalt Blue, Blue Ribbon Brand, Buckeye Pottery Co., 10 Gal.	68.00
Crock, Roses, Cobalt Blue Label, Hamilton & Jones, c.1870, 14 ½ In.	964.00
Crock, Salt Glaze, Cobalt Blue Stencil Stamp, E.P. Munson, Albany Slip Glaze, Lug Handles, 4 Gal..	690.00
Crock, Salt Glaze, Cobalt Blue Stencil, 20, Lug Handles, Ottawa Stoneware Co., 21 x 19 In.	978.00
Crock, Salt Glaze, Gray, Peach Spots, Lug Handles, Dubuque Iowa Pottery, 3 Gal., 11 x 11 In.	2185.00
Crock, Shaped Collar, Springs, Cobalt Blue, Straight-Sided, 15 In.	226.00
Crock, Snowflake, Stripes, Cobalt Blue, 7 ¾ In.	537.00
Crock, Sprout, Leaves, 2, Cobalt Blue, Bulbous, Applied Crescent Handles, 9 ¾ In.	106.00
Crock, Star, Rays, Roses, Stripes, Stenciled, Hamilton & Jones, c.1875, 16 ¼ In.	863.00
Crock, Storage, Wreath, Cobalt Blue, Lid, Applied Crescent Handles, Union Pottery, Newark, 13 In.	177.00
Crock, Stripes, Eagle, Banner, Eagle Pottery, 8 In.	2034.00
Crock, Stylized Flower, Daubed Cobalt Blue, Impressed 4, c.1870, 15 In.	470.00
Crock, Tree Of Life, Cobalt Blue, Signature, Lowndes, Petersburg, Va., ½ Gal., 7 ¾ In.	2300.00
Crock, Tulip, Cobalt Blue, c.1870, 12 In.	203.00
Crock, Tulips, Cobalt Blue, Impressed 3, Oval, c.1870, 14 In.	646.00
Crock, Tulips, Cobalt Blue, Impressed, J. Weaver, 3, 2 Handles, c.1850s, 13 In.	353.00
Crock, Tulips, Cobalt Blue, Incised 4, c.1870, 12 In.	294.00
Crock, Tulips, Cobalt Blue, Label, Hamilton & Jones, Single Bead Molded, 7 x 8 ¼ In.	130.00
Cuspidor, Cobalt Blue, U.S.A., c.1865, 4 ½ In.	323.00

Stiegel Type, Flask, Diamond Pattern,
Molded, Amethyst, c.1760, 5 ¼ In.
$3450.00

James D. Julia Inc.

Stone, Figure, Buddha Head, Limestone,
Downcast Eyes, Chinese, 13 ½ In.
$2185.00

Leland Little Auction

Stone, Picture, Bouquet, Stones,
Black Lacquer Board, Tortoiseshell
Frame, 26 x 23 In.
$944.00

S

Brunk Auctions

Stone, Vase, Cover, Suspended, Carved Chain, Carved Hardwood Stand, Chinese, 10 In.
$6820.00

Leslie Hindman Auctioneers

Stone, Vase, Cover, Turquoise, Carved, Taotie Mask, Rose Quartz Stand, Chinese, 9 ⅜ In
$4481.00

Sloans & Kenyon

Stoneware, Crock, Cobalt Blue Stencil, H.B. & G.B. Pfaltzgraff, 3, Heavy Rim, 11 ½ In.
$94.00

Conestoga Auction Co., Inc.

Fat Lamp, 2 Fonts, Saucer Base, High Glaze, 8 ¼ In.	770.00
Figurine, Cow & Calf, Bennington Glaze, Bristol Accents, Beveled Rim, 5 x 6 ¼ In.	2875.00
Figurine, Dog, Freestanding Front Legs, White, Newcomerstown, Tucarawas County, c.1870, 10 In.	470.00
Figurine, Dog, Lying Down, Molded, Impressed Eyes, Incised, c.1890, 7 ½ In.	259.00
Figurine, Girl, Seated, White, Brown, Blue, Red, Signed M. Kovacs, Hungary, c.1950, 7 ¼ In.	294.00
Figurine, Lion, Reclining, Olive Glaze, Mogadore, Oh., 1800s, 14 ¼ In.	805.00
Figurine, Mother & Child, Seated On Bench, Glazed, U.S.A., 1900s, 10 x 6 In.	115.00
Figurine, Pig, Bristol Glaze, Cobalt Blue Stamp, Monmouth Pottery Co., 3 ½ x 7 ½ In.	863.00
Figurine, Rabbit, White, c.1890, 5 In.	356.00
Figurine, Rooster, Alkaline Glaze, Inscribed E. Meaders, 7/14/1987, 15 ½ In.	978.00
Figurine, Rooster, Black, Backward Glancing, Round Base, Initialed, Edwin Meaders, 14 In.	2309.00
Figurine, Rooster, Dark Blue Glaze, Green Splashes, 1900s	1770.00
Figurine, Rooster, Mottled Blue Glaze, Edwin Meaders, 1990s, 16 In., Pair	1121.00
Flagon, Drinking Party, Relief, April 23, 1877, Hinged Pewter Lid, 9 In.	102.00
Flask, Incised Band On Shoulder & Base, Cobalt Blue Leaf, Flattened Circle Shape, 1800s, 6 In.	830.00
Flask, Pig, Gray & Blue Glaze, Cork Tail Stopper, 2 ¼ x 6 ½ In.	1778.00
Flowerpot, Copper, Manganese, Lead Glaze, Conical, Crimped Rim, Eberly	1725.00
Flowerpot, Impressed 4, White, Albany Slip, Ohio, c.1900, 7 In.	59.00
Holy Water Font, Crucifixion, Hearts, Ferns, Cobalt Blue Relief, Westerwald, 6 In.	127.00
Honey Jar, Bronze Glaze, Zoomorphic, Round, Squat, Lid, Handle, Khmer, 8 In. Diam.	478.00
Inkwell, Cobalt Blue Detail, Tooled Rim, Base, Quill Holes, C. Crolius, 1 ¾ x 4 ¼ In.	1035.00
Jar, Birds, Incised, Oval, Flared Rim, c.1821, 7 ¼ In.	690.00
Jar, Canner, Salt Glaze, Cylindrical, Rounded Shoulder, Cobalt Blue, Mt. Crawford, 2 ½ In.	259.00
Jar, Canning, Albany Slip Glaze, Frogskin, Oval, c.1860, 10 ¼ In.	330.00
Jar, Canning, Galena, Hand Turned, Green Base, Gold Speckled Spots, c.1875, 1 Gal.	748.00
Jar, Canning, Galena, Multicolor, Green Glaze Ground, Orange Spots, ½ Gal., 8 x 6 ½ In.	2300.00
Jar, Canning, Stripes, Cobalt Blue, Stenciled Flower, Wax Sealer Interior, c.1875, 8 ¼ In.	288.00
Jar, Canning, Tapered, Tooled Shoulder, Rolled Rim, Stencil, A. Conrad, c.1875, 8 ½ In.	144.00
Jar, Canning, Wax Sealer Rim, Stencil, Richey & Hamilton, Palatine, W.V., c.1875, 9 ¾ In.	259.00
Jar, Canning, Wax Sealer, Painted, Over Glaze, Moon Distlry, Ky., 12 In.	92.00
Jar, Churn, Rounded Shoulder, Salt Glaze, Wood Top, Dasher, Mid Atlantic, 11 x 6 In.	104.00
Jar, Cobalt Blue Design, Salt Glaze, Lug Handles, Hamilton & Jones, Pa., c.1875, 20 Gal. .... *illus*	4113.00
Jar, Cobalt Blue Swat, Morgan & Amoss, Makers, Baltimore, Ear Handles, 1820, 15 In.	4600.00
Jar, Coconut Oil, Glazed, Handles, Thailand, c.1600, 4 ½ x 5 In.	120.00
Jar, Cow, Cobalt Blue, Incised, Semi-Oval, Tall Collar, Strap Handle, Salt Glaze, c.1870, 15 x 10 In.	2588.00
Jar, Cream, Flower, Cobalt Blue, Sipe & Sons, Williamsport, Pa., c.1880, Gal., 7 ¾ In.	173.00
Jar, Cylindrical, Squared Rim, Handles, Cobalt Blue Flowers, 3, 13 x 9 In.	150.00
Jar, Double Blown Rockingham Tulip, Manganese, Arched Handles, 2 Gal.	1380.00
Jar, Double Copper Glaze, Coggle Wheel Decoration, Round Hill Pottery, c.1930, 8 x 4 In.	633.00
Jar, Double Copper Glaze, Coggle Wheel Neck, Shouldered, Winchester, Va., 8 In.	633.00
Jar, Double Wing, Cobalt Blue, Salt Glaze, Squared Rim, Ear Handles, Virginia, 10 In.	173.00
Jar, Eagle On Branch, Cobalt Blue, Salt Glaze, Oval, Rolled Handles, Connecticut, 3 Gal., 15 In.	863.00
Jar, Eagle, On Branch, 3, Cobalt Blue, Salt Glaze, Oval, Incised Rings, Galleried Rim	863.00
Jar, Fern, Cobalt Blue, Cylindrical, Rolled Rim, Richmond, Va., Gal., 10 x 6 In.	259.00
Jar, Flower & Bird, Cobalt Blue, Barrel Shape, Lug Handles, Reeded Neck, c.1800, 13 In.	6518.00
Jar, Flowers, Cobalt Blue, Applied Lug Handles, White's, Utica, c.1860, 2 Gal., 11 ¼ In.	201.00
Jar, Flowers, Cobalt Blue, Oval, Flared Rim, Baltimore, c.1850, 4 Gal., 14 In.	374.00
Jar, Flowers, Fern, Cobalt Blue, Rolled Rim, Ear Handles, John P. Schermerhorn, Gal.	805.00
Jar, Lid Cutouts, Blue Swirl Glaze, Signed Edna Arrow, 7 x 6 ¾ In.	90.00
Jar, Lid, Animal Mask Handles, Rings, Squat, Footed, Olive Glaze, 10 x 8 ½ In.	119.00
Jar, Lid, Brown Drip High-Glaze, Cream Ground, Warren MacKenzie, 8 x 12 In.	360.00
Jar, Lid, Handkerchief Top, Mottled Gray, Raku Fired, Signed Paul Soldner, 10 x 11 In.	1080.00
Jar, Lid, Morning Glories, Footed, J. Bennett, 1880, 7 x 6 ¾ In.	4340.00
Jar, Lid, Underglaze, Flowers, 5, Blue, Handles, Wands, Olean, N.Y., 17 ¾ In.	439.00
Jar, Loopety Loop Design On Shoulder, c.1850, 10 ¼ In.	550.00
Jar, Manganese Tulip, 2, Oval, Straight Collar, Arched Handles, Coffman, Rockingham	1380.00
Jar, Mottled Pale Alkaline Glaze, Edgefield, c.1850, 9 ¼ In.	354.00
Jar, Pine, Prunus, Bamboo, Brown Glaze, Molded, c.1900, 22 In.	178.00
Jar, Rattlesnake, Applied, Slithering Through Body, Dark Glaze, Signed Otis Norris, 10 ¼ In.	236.00
Jar, Runny Alkaline Glaze, Lug Handles, Edgefield, 1800s, 16 In.	780.00
Jar, Split Head Tulip, Cobalt Blue Oval, Arched Handles, Gal.	230.00
Jar, Split Tulip & Leaf, Cobalt Blue, Squared Rim, Ear Handles, Coffman, 10 x 6 In.	230.00
Jar, Stencil, E.J. Miller & Son, Dealers, China & Glass Ware, Alexandria, Va., 10 In.	575.00
Jar, Stephen H. Ward, Stenciled, Cobalt Blue, Stars, c.1870, 11 ¾ In.	3408.00
Jar, Swag & Tassel, Cobalt Blue, Oval, Tooled Foot, Commeraws, c.1810, 3 Gal., 11 ½ In.	2530.00
Jar, Triple Blown Rockingham Tulips, High Flared Collar, Arched Handles, 14 x 7 In.	863.00

S

Jar, Vine, Cobalt Blue, Salt Glaze, Oval, Squat, Beaded Neck, Arched Handles, 6 In.	2070.00
Jar, Vine, Tornado & Stripes, Cobalt Blue, Cylindrical, Rolled Rim, Ear Handles, 3 Gal., 14 In.	575.00
Jug, 8-Point Quilt Star, Cobalt Blue, Applied Loop Handle, 11 In.	94.00
Jug, Albany Glaze, Compliments Of Wheat & Summerson, Staunton, Va., 3 In.	259.00
Jug, Applied Dome Top, Loop Handle, White Glaze, Cobalt Blue Stencil, H. Free & Co., 9 In.	24.00
Jug, Applied Flowers, Manganese, Cobalt Blue, Incised, Westerwald, c.1690, 7 ¾ In.	489.00
Jug, Bird & Leaves, Cobalt Blue, Bulbous Oval, Narrow Rim, Strap Handle, 1800s, 14 In.	2233.00
Jug, Bird On Branch, Cobalt Blue, Fort Edward, N.Y., 16 In.	561.00
Jug, Bird, Blue, West Troy, N.Y. Pottery, Tan Glaze, Straight-Sided, 10 ¼ x 6 ¾ In.	556.00
Jug, Bird, Cobalt Blue, Incised, Perched On Branch, Reeded Neck, 9 ½ In.	1960.00
Jug, Bird, Cobalt Blue, Salt Glaze, Beidinger & Caire, Poughkeepsie, 3 Gal., 16 x 10 In.	460.00
Jug, Bitters, Hubert Deuster, Dealer In Wines & Liquors, Handle, Salt Glaze, c.1890, 12 ¾ In. *illus*	2070.00
Jug, Blue Bird, Flower Sprig, Handle, White's, Utica, N.Y., Salt Glaze, c.1885, 14 In.	288.00
Jug, Blue Slip Design, S. Risley Norwich, 1800s, 13 In.	119.00
Jug, Blue Slip, Tan Ground, Tyler Pottery, Albany New York, 1800s, 14 ½ In.	59.00
Jug, Blue, Flower, Tan Glaze, Oval, 14 x 9 ¾ In.	410.00
Jug, Bottle Neck, Flowers, Cobalt Blue, Incised Rings, 13 In.	24.00
Jug, Branch Of 5 Flowers, Evan R. Jones, Cobalt Blue, 14 In.	71.00
Jug, Bristol Glaze, Cobalt Blue Stamp, Giglin & Walsh, Fine Old, Bourbon & Rye, Springfield, ½ Gal.	1150.00
Jug, Brown Alkaline Glaze, Green Runny Glaze, J.F. Seagle, c.1875, ½ Gal., 9 In.	2645.00
Jug, Brown Salt Glaze, Applied Handle, Incised M.W. Owen, 1800s, Qt., 7 In.	460.00
Jug, Chas. D. Moul, Wines & Liquors, York, Pa., Manganese Shoulder, Strap Handle, 8 ¼ In. *illus*	94.00
Jug, Clover, Cobalt Blue, Impressed 6, Applied Handles, c.1850, 18 In.	940.00
Jug, Cobalt Blue Label, Applied Finger Loop Handle, Gamble Bros., Newark, N.J, 11 In.	130.00
Jug, Crush Glass Glaze, Olive, Applied Snake, Cord Handle, 9 ¾ In.	715.00
Jug, Dutchman's Breeches Flower, Cobalt Blue, Applied Strap Handle, Oval, 10 ½ In.	130.00
Jug, Face, Alkaline Glaze, Broken China Teeth, Stamped, B.B. Craig, c.1985, 11 In.	590.00
Jug, Face, Alkaline Glaze, Ceramic Teeth, Signed Lanier Meaders, c.1985, 10 ½ In.	1062.00
Jug, Face, Brown, China Teeth, Blue, Cream Swirl, N.C., 12 ½ In.	173.00
Jug, Face, Cream & Blue Swirl, Alkaline Glaze, China Teeth, Wavy Line, Burlon Craig, 13 ¼ In.	374.00
Jug, Face, Mottled Green Glaze, Ceramic Eyes, Teeth, Signed Lanier Meaders, c.1950, 9 ½ In.	889.00
Jug, Face, Snake, Brown, Blue Cream Swirl, Double Handle, China Teeth, Burlon Craig, 12 ¼ In.	316.00
Jug, Flower Blossom, 3, Cobalt Blue, Loop Handle, 1800s, 3 Gal.	317.00
Jug, Flower Spray, Cobalt Blue, Buff, Salt Glaze, Rolled Rim, Loop Handle, c.1885, 10 In.	115.00
Jug, Flower, 2, Leaves, Cobalt Blue, Applied Loop Handle, Pfaltzgraff, P.S. Co., 14 In.	94.00
Jug, Flower, Cobalt Blue, Semi-Oval, A.L. Hyssong, Bloomsburg, Pa., c.1900, 2 Gal., 12 ¾ In.	259.00
Jug, Flowers On Front, 4, 17 ½ In.	502.00
Jug, Flowers, 2, Applied Loop Handle, Cowden & Wilcox, 13 ¾ In.	443.00
Jug, Flowers, Blue, Frank B. Norton, Worcester, Mass., 13 ½ In.	178.00
Jug, Flowers, Cobalt Blue, Applied Loop Handle, West Roy Pottery, 13 In.	106.00
Jug, Flowers, Cobalt Blue, H.B. Pfaltzgraff, Penn., 1800s, 16 In.	504.00
Jug, Flowers, Cobalt Blue, Impressed, D.P. Shenfelder, Reading, Penn., 13 ½ In.	326.00
Jug, Flowers, Cobalt Blue, Incised Rings Around Neck, 13 In.	177.00
Jug, Flowers, Cobalt Blue, McDonald & Benjamin, Cincinnati, c.1870, 3 Gal., 15 ½ In.	460.00
Jug, Flowers, Cobalt Blue, Salt Glaze, Beehive Shape, Paneled Handle, Signed D.W. Graves, 11 In.	207.00
Jug, Freehand Flower, Cobalt Blue, Applied Hog Ear Handle, Impressed, H.B. Pfaltzgraff, 10 ½ In. *illus*	94.00
Jug, Freehand Flower, Ring Neck, Applied Strap, 11 ¼ In.	130.00
Jug, Glass Melt, Oval, Tooled Lines, Ridge Top Handle, c.1855, 17 In.	3740.00
Jug, Grape Cluster, Stylized, Cobalt Blue, Oval Shape, Loop Handle, 1800s, 14 In.	306.00
Jug, Grape Clusters, Cobalt Blue, Salt Glaze, Handle, Oval, c.1850, 13 In.	121.00
Jug, Gray Salt Glaze, Applied Handle, Impressed J.A. Craven, N. Car., c.1850, Qt., 7 ¾ In.	375.00
Jug, Harvest, Albany Slip Glaze, Molded Acanthus, Leaves, Twist Handle, 9 ¼ In.	316.00
Jug, Heinz, White Pickling & Table Vinegar, Label, 7 ¼ In. *illus*	303.00
Jug, Lead Glaze, Oval, Ringed Mouth, Strap Handle, Footed, Coffman, 12 ½ In.	633.00
Jug, Liquor Dealer, Cobalt Blue Flower, Tooled Shoulder, Brooklyn, c.1860, 3 Gal., 15 ½ In.	86.00
Jug, Merchant, G.A. Straub Quakertown Pa., Cobalt Blue Lettering, 8 In.	181.00
Jug, Monkey, Crushed Glass Glaze, Double Spouted, Strap Handle, 1930s, 11 In.	1155.00
Jug, Parrot, Between Leaves, Blue, Narrow Rolled Rim, Handle At Rim, c.1855, 15 In.	230.00
Jug, Poppy Sprig, Blue, Narrow Rim, Round Handle, N.A. White & Son, c.1885, 14 ½ In.	173.00
Jug, S. Scheuer & Co., Bloomfield, N.J., Cream, Sloping Collar, Handle, Gal.	250.00
Jug, Saddle, Wave Decoration, Flat Handle, Thumb Press, Olive, c.1800, 7 ⅝ In.	330.00
Jug, Salt Glaze, Oval, Incised Shoulder Ring, Collared Mouth, 2, H.C. Smith	460.00
Jug, Schmidt & Friday, Wines & Liquors, Oval, 2 Handles, Cobalt Blue, c.1865, 18 In.	823.00
Jug, Slave, Crossed Branches, Cobalt Blue, Salt Glaze, Westhafer & Lambright, 1865, 20 ½ In. *illus*	1495.00
Jug, Slave, Flowers, Cobalt Blue, Double Handles, Impressed Block Stamp, 6, N. Tracy, 1864, 19 x 12 In.	1955.00
Jug, Slave, Water Cooler, Flowers, Cobalt Blue, 6, Thomas Commeraw, Strap Handles, 1800s	2300.00

Stoneware, Crock, Eagle, 3, Cobalt Stencil, A. Conrad, New Geneva, Fayette Co., Pa., c.1875, 13 ½ In.
$1410.00

Garth's Auctions, Inc.

Stoneware, Crock, Freehand, 6, Cobalt Blue, Williams & Reppert, Greensboro, Pa., Handles, 15 x 12 In.
$142.00

Conestoga Auction Co., Inc.

Stoneware, Crock, Freehand Roses, Cobalt Blue Stencil, Jas. Hamilton Co., Greensboro, Pa., c.1851-80
$1293.00

Garth's Auctions, Inc.

TIP

If your old cast-iron pan without a wooden handle is dirty, clean it in a self-cleaning oven.

STONEWARE

Stoneware, Jar, Cobalt Blue Design, Salt Glaze, Lug Handles, Hamilton & Jones, Pa., c.1875, 20 Gal.
$4113.00

Cowan's Auctions

Stoneware, Jug, Bitters, Hubert Deuster, Dealer In Wines & Liquors, Handle, Salt Glaze, c.1890, 12 ¾ In.
$2070.00

Glass Works Auctions

Stoneware, Jug, Chas. D. Moul, Wines & Liquors, York, Pa., Manganese Shoulder, Strap Handle, 8 ¼ In.
$94.00

Conestoga Auction Co., Inc.

Jug, Snake, Open Mouth, Alkaline Glaze, Signed, Crocker, 1997, 13 ¼ In. ....*illus*	1298.00
Jug, Snakes, Intertwined, Albany Slip Glaze, Incised Leaves, Pt., 5 ½ x 4 ½ In.	1955.00
Jug, Snow Brand Horse Radish, Beige, Brown Tapered Top & Handle, Gal.	102.00
Jug, Souvenir, Compliments Of Wheat & Summerson, Staunton, Va., c.1890, 3 In.	259.00
Jug, Spread Eagle, 2, Applied Loop Handle, Molded Spout, Gt. F. Reppert, 14 In.	384.00
Jug, Spread Eagle, 2, Cobalt Blue, Applied Loop Handle, Marked, 14 In.	385.00
Jug, Stetzenmeyer, Cobalt Blue Slip Trailed Flowers, c.1850, 3 Gal., 15 ½ In.	2530.00
Jug, Stork, Blue, Impressed, White's, Utica, 11 In.	480.00
Jug, Stylized Tree, Cobalt Blue, Beehive Form, D.W. Graves, Westmoreland, N.Y., 11 In.	207.00
Jug, Sweet Mash Corn, Atlantic Coast Distilling Co., Bristol Glaze, c.1875, 2 ⅞ In.	66.00
Jug, Tooled Spout, Open Strap Handles, J.D. Craven, c.1870, 16 ¾ In.	403.00
Jug, Tulip, Cobalt Blue, Applied Loop Handle, Pfaltzgraff, 11 ½ In.	212.00
Jug, Tulip, Cobalt Blue, Applied Strap Handle, Oval, 13 In.	83.00
Jug, Watson Littell Franklin Furnace, N.J., Brown Albany Glaze, Handle, c.1900, 8 ⅝ In. *illus*	207.00
Milk Pan, Tulip, Cobalt Blue, Tab Handles, Pour Spout, c.1840, 5 ¼ x 9 ¾ In.	144.00
Mixing Bowl, Cobalt Blue Design, Flared Sides With Foot, 4 x 9 In.	47.00
Mixing Bowl, Molded Arch Design, Blue, 6 x 11 ¾ In.	71.00
Mixing Bowl, Yellow Glaze, 3 White Bands, Flared, Rolled Rim, 10 ½ In.	21.00
Mortar, Wood Pestle, Tooled Bands, Salt Glaze, Rounded Foot, Flared Body, 5 ¾ In.	201.00
Mug, Albany Slip Glaze, Applied Handle, Incised, Yale Courant, c.1894, 5 ½ In.	316.00
Mug, Cobalt Blue, Pewter Lid, Wingender, Haddonfield, c.1880, 8 In.	235.00
Mug, GR Seal, Tooled Bands, Leaves, Cobalt Blue Detail, Westerwald, 5 ½ In.	288.00
Mug, Lead, Copper, Manganese Glaze, Barrel Shape, Incised Ring, Handle, Ebery, 5 x 4 In.	748.00
Pear Canner, Stencil, Wing, Palatine Pottery Co., W. Va., Tapered, c.1875, 8 In.	748.00
Pitcher, Apostles, Paneled, Salt Glaze, 7 ¾ In.	68.00
Pitcher, Batter, Mottled Copper & Manganese Glaze, Bulbous, Strap Handle, 9 x 6 In.	403.00
Pitcher, Batter, Stylized Flower, Tan, Blue, J.S. Taft & Co., Keene, N.H., 12 In.	1053.00
Pitcher, Double Flowers, Cobalt Blue, Shouldered, Incised Rings, Footed, ½ Gal.	403.00
Pitcher, Flower & Feather, Cobalt Blue, Stand-Up Rim, Strap Handle, Rolled Foot, ½ Gal.	518.00
Pitcher, Flower, Cobalt Blue, Salt Glaze, Oval, Incised Shoulder Ring, Shenandoah Valley, ½ Gal.	518.00
Pitcher, Flower, Cobalt Blue, Triple Blossom, Heatwole, Silber, Medial Shoulder, ½ Gal.	690.00
Pitcher, Flower, Leaves, Cobalt Blue, Remmey, Philadelphia, Gal., 10 ½ In.	460.00
Pitcher, Flowers, Blue, Elongated Neck, Incised Rings, Philadelphia, ½ Gal., 9 In.	403.00
Pitcher, Flowers, Cobalt Blue, Rolled Rim, Spout, 1800s, 12 In.	652.00
Pitcher, Frog, Crouching, Monkey Shape Handle, Frogs Mouth Spout, c.1880, 13 ½ In.	17825.00
Pitcher, Green Glaze, Band Design, Loop Handle, Narrow Spout, Burlon Craig, 1900s, 19 In. ..	294.00
Pitcher, Lead, Copper & Manganese Glaze, Incised Ring, Flared Rim, 9 ¼ In.	1495.00
Pitcher, Medium Olive Alkaline Glaze, Light Green Drips, B.B. Craig 1900s, 19 ½ In.	531.00
Pitcher, Painted, Oyster Sponge Design, Cream, Green, Loop Handle, Scallop Rim, 1900s, 7 In.....	115.00
Pitcher, Red & Orange Glaze, Loop Handle, Elongated Oval, 16 ½ In.	58.00
Pitcher, Rooster, Cobalt Blue, Bottle Shape, Loop Handle, 1800s, 14 In.	385.00
Pitcher, Sunflower, Cobalt Blue, Loop Handle, Marked ½ Inside, 8 In.	316.00
Pitcher, Tulip, Swags, Cobalt Blue, Rounded Foot, Tooled Collar, c.1865, 10 ¾ In.	403.00
Planter, Oval, Loop Design, Mark Hewitt, 24 x 24 In.	2070.00
Planter, Tree Stump Shape, Vines, Cut Branches, Bird's Nest, Openings, N. Rockingham, 1800s, 19 In.	385.00
Planter, Tree Trunk Shape, Brown Glaze, Turquoise Markings, 3 ¾ x 6 ½ In.	490.00
Sugar & Creamer, Applied Bird On Branch, Dogwood Blossom, 1930s, 3 In.	121.00
Tankard, Leaf Design, Brown & Green Enamel, 3 Handles, 1800s, 7 In.	178.00
Tankard, Lid, Squat Neck, Bulbous Body, Lion Head Medallions, Strap Handle, Germany, 7 In. ..	735.00
Teapot, Crushed Glass Glaze, Cord Handle, Footed, c.1952, 5 ¾ In.	248.00
Tobacco Jar, Lid, Lead, Octagonal, Swords, Slave's Bust, 4 ½ x 5 In.	179.00
Tobacco Jar, Oval, Tooled Lid, Red Brown Slip Glaze, Verse, Yale University, 7 ¾ In.	748.00
Umbrella Stand, Couple, Under Umbrella, Cylindrical, Oh., 20 ½ In.	719.00
Umbrella Stand, Water Lilies, Art Nouveau, Green, Brown, 10 x 19 ¼ In.	124.00
Urn, Flowers, Cobalt Blue, Impressed 4, Applied Ribbed Lug Handles, 4 Gal.	920.00
Urn, Flowers, Cobalt Blue, Swags, Eared Handles, Rolled Rim, Stamped, 1850-75, 12 In.........	201.00
Vase, Albany Slip Glaze, Footed, Chocolate, c.1890, 9 ¾ In.	77.00
Vase, Crystalline Hare's Fur Glaze, Globular, Lid, 1916, 7 x 6 ¼ In.	10540.00
Vase, Double Gourd, Celadon Ground, White & Black, Cranes, Clouds, 1900s, 15 ½ In............	119.00
Vase, Dragon, Cloud, Blue, Chinese, 8 ¾ x 7 ¼ In.	1955.00
Vase, Figural, Stump, Birds, Nest, Snake, c.1920, 7 ½ In.	193.00
Vase, Green, Brown Swirl, White Base Glaze, C.B. Masten, No. Car., c.1935, 6 ¼ In.	633.00
Vase, Mottled Blue Glaze, Foo Dog Head Handles, Chinese, 14 ½ x 12 In.	1845.00
Vase, Parakeets, Salt Glaze, Marked, Charles Graham, 1885, 7 ½ x 5 ½ In.	1240.00
Vase, Salt Glaze, Cobalt Blue, 4 Handles, Groove Top Handles, Thumb Press, 1910s, 16 In.......	605.00
Vase, Tan, Black Stripes, Solid Neck, Glazed, Inscribed Harrison McIntosh, 8 x 5 In.	806.00

S

Wall Pocket, Copper, Manganese, Lead Glaze, Slip Wash, Conical, Arched Hanger, Eberly, 8 In.	3335.00
Water Cooler, 2 Top Handles, Narrow Rim, Cobalt Blue Stencil, Wreath, 24 In.	1175.00
Water Cooler, Cast Iron Lid, Light Blue Ground, Oval, Man At Well Cartouche, c.1910, 10 x 20 In.	360.00
Water Cooler, Flowers, Blue, Nichols & Boynton, Burlington, Vt., c.1859, 3 Gal., 12 In.	86.00
Water Cooler, Flowers, Cobalt Blue, Lug Handles, Penn., c.1860, 13 In.	1185.00
Water Cooler, Flowers, Cobalt Blue, Salt Glaze, Rings, Rope Twist Handles, Bung Hole, 16 In.	1495.00
Water Cooler, Pedestal, Drip Pan, Lug Handles, 2 Birds, Acanthus Leaf, Wood Spout, 1890s, 19 In.	4113.00
Water Cooler, Salt Glaze, Oval, Collared Rim, Twisted Rope Handles, Bung Hole, Cobalt Blue Flowers	1495.00
Water Cooler, Spout, Gold Salt Glaze, Albany Slip Glaze Interior, Cobalt Blue Flowers, 19 x 13 In.	489.00
Wine Cask, Barrel Shape, Bands, Platinum Overlay, Grapevines In Relief, Spigot, Lid, 17 x 16 In.	531.00

STORE fixtures, cases, cutters, and other items that have no advertising as part of the decoration are listed here. Most items found in an old store are listed in the Advertising category in this book.

Bag Filler, Stringholder, Tin Funnel, Adjustable, Jacoby & Co., 25 In.	330.00
Bell, Figural, Turtle Shape, Cast Iron Flash Finish, 3 ½ x 2 ½ x 7 In.	518.00
Bill Spindle, Hardwood, Iron, Semi-Spherical, Flowers, Black Ground, 1800s, 5 ¾ In.	121.00
Bin, Grain, Pine, Divided Interior, 34 x 40 In.	150.00
Bin, Grain, Pine, Lift Top, Planks, Bracket Feet, Pa., 1800s, 35 x 29 In.	119.00
Carving, Parrot On Bar, Holding Sign, Wood, Condotti & Co., 35 x 26 In.	1265.00
Case, Display, Canes, Edwardian, Oak, Curved Glass, Mounted Grid, 50 Slots, 48 x 36 In.	777.00
Case, Display, Oak, Taylor Bros., Crawford's Delightful Biscuits, c.1910, 35 x 62 In.	1298.00
Case, Wood, Ogee Cornice, Brass Gallery, Glass Door, Plaques, c.1950, 56 x 27 In.	3444.00
Chair, Beautician, Metal, Vinyl Flower Upholstery, Adjustable, 42 x 26 In.	1000.00
Cigar Cutter, Brass, Figural, Nude, Art Nouveau Style, 3 ½ x 4 In. ....*illus*	253.00
Cigar Cutter, Guillotine, Walnut, Ivory, Carved, Tilting Platform, 1800s, 17 ¾ In. ....*illus*	1464.00
Cigar Cutter, Indian Shape, Warrior, Holding Club, Raised Hand, Plinth Base, Owl, Bird, 18 In.	3290.00
Clothes Hanger, Girl's Head & Shoulders, Modelo Garment Hanger Co., Greenber & Picker, 1917 *illus*	295.00
Coffee Grinders are listed in the Coffee Mill category.	
Container, Chocolate, Mother, Children, Roof Lifts, Shingles, Tin Litho, Germany, 6 x 7 In. *illus*	86.00
Display, Cigar Store, Cuban Flower & Card Receiver, Black Man, Holding Basket, 28 x 16 In.	920.00
Display, Man, Profile, Carrying Walking Stick, Tin, Paint, 1800s, 19 In.	770.00
Display, Mannequin Shoes, High Top, Iron, Victorian, Frankel DF Co. N.Y., 5 x 6 In.	99.00
Display, Pie Safe, Screen Stencil, Rushton's Famous Fresh Pies, 21 x 21 In.	385.00
Rack, Printer's, Adjustable Leaves, Scrolled Feet, Stretcher, Early 1900s, 46 x 32 In.	104.00
Seed Chest, Painted, Brown Faux Grain, 22 Drawers, Porcelain Knobs, Signed, 22 ½ x 19 In.	1180.00
Shop Figure, Jack Tar, Sailor, Uniform, Wooden Leg, Hat, Holding Box, Beard, 1900s, 64 In.	4600.00
Sign, Antique Shop, Highboy, Brown Paint, 62 ½ x 30 In.	711.00
Sign, Antiques, Pointing Finger, Tin, White Paint, 24 In.	58.00
Sign, Apothecary, Mortar & Pestle, Red, Sheet Metal, Chain, 15 x 19 In.	1150.00
Sign, Apothecary, Zinc, c.1890, 33 In.	1126.00
Sign, Butcher Shop, Bull's Head, Zinc, Mounted, c.1880, 27 In.	3055.00
Sign, Butcher's, Crossed Tools, Bull, Gloeklers Patent, Paint, Iron, 1887, 25 x 20 In.	820.00
Sign, Carved, Pretzel, Gold Paint, c.1890, 13 x 22 ½ In. ....*illus*	823.00
Sign, Colorado Springs, Denver 72.4 Mi., Pueblo 42.7 Mi., White, Blue Paint, 104 x 12 In.	3575.00
Sign, Eye Doctor, Glasses, Eyes, 11 x 15 In.	456.00
Sign, General Store, Poplar Board, Breadboard Ends, Cream, c.1895, 34 x 22 ½ In.	863.00
Sign, Gun Trade, Gun, Pine, Words, Guns, Ammunition, Paint, c.1890, 30 ½ In.	2370.00
Sign, Haberdashery, Sheet Metal, Man's Bust, In Wide Brimmed Hat, Black, Gray, Kansas, 24 In.	2703.00
Sign, Hardware, Black Ground, White Lettering, Lime Green Shading, 122 x 13 ¾ In.	1380.00
Sign, Night Hawks, Neon, Blue Ground, White, Red, 120 x 67 In.	880.00
Sign, Novelties, Rounded Ends, White & Black Paint, c.1900, 60 x 8 In.	504.00
Sign, Nursery, Letters, Stacked Blocks, Boy, Girl, Playing, Metal, Paint, 1940s, 48 x 54 In.	1150.00
Sign, Oculist, Spectacles Shape, Eyes, Zinc, Painted, 1800s, 14 x 36 In.	9988.00
Sign, Optician, Pair Of Glasses, Eyes, Paint, Metal, 37 ½ x 11 In.	575.00
Sign, Optometrist, R.A. Esslinger Opt. D., Glasses, Hicksville, N.Y., c.1920, 11 x 30 In.	6888.00
Sign, Painter's, Wood Panel, Eagle, Shield, Banner, New York, c.1900, 13 x 18 In.	7800.00
Sign, Pawn Shop, Wood, Carved, Shaped, Paint, 2-Sided, 50 x 26 In.	1035.00
Sign, Pawn, 3 Metal Balls, Scrolled Iron Support, Wood, Paint, 1800s, 34 x 36 In.	1265.00
Sign, Pocket Watch Shape, Round, 2-Sided, Pine, Iron Ring, c.1890, 21 ½ x 14 In.	1265.00
Sign, Pocket Watch, Painted Zinc Dial, Cast Iron, 17 ¾ x 22 ¾ In.	1495.00
Sign, Saddlery, Molded Zinc, Wall Mount, Horse Head, c.1800s, 19 x 15 In.	2573.00
Sign, Sanitary Restrooms, Porcelain, Flange, 2-Sided, 30 x 15 In.	115.00
Sign, Straight Razor, Folding Blade, Wood, Inscribed SRD 18, 29 In.	510.00
Sign, Tavern, Bird-In-Hand, Bagshot, Victorian Couple From Behind, Metal, Painted, 53 x 41 In.	1003.00

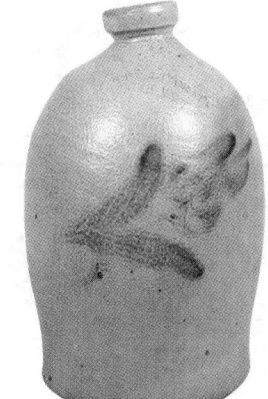

Stoneware, Jug, Freehand Flower, Cobalt Blue, Applied Hog Ear Handle, Impressed, H.B. Pfaltzgraff, 10 ½ In.
$94.00

Conestoga Auction Co., Inc.

Stoneware, Jug, Heinz, White Pickling & Table Vinegar, Label, 7 ¼ In.
$303.00

Wm Morford Antiques

Stoneware, Jug, Slave, Crossed Branches, Cobalt Blue, Salt Glaze, Westhafer & Lambright, 1865, 20 ½ In.
$1495.00

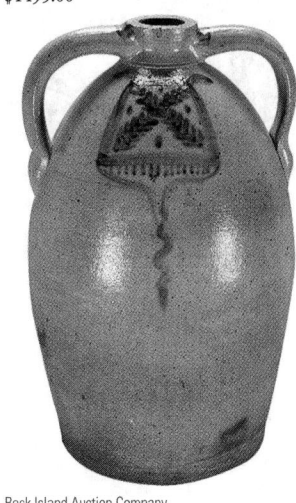

Rock Island Auction Company

S

Stoneware, Jug, Snake, Open Mouth, Alkaline Glaze, Signed, Crocker, 1997, 13 ¼ In.
$1298.00

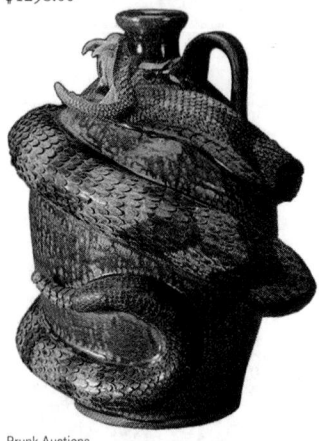

Brunk Auctions

Stoneware, Jug, Watson Littell Franklin Furnace, N.J., Brown Albany Glaze, Handle, c.1900, 8 ⅝ In.
$207.00

Glass Works Auctions

Store, Cigar Cutter, Brass, Figural, Nude, Art Nouveau Style, 3 ½ x 4 In.
$253.00

Wm Morford Antiques

Sign, Tavern, Duke Of Clarence, Full Military Dress, Black Frame, 48 x 36 In.	443.00
Sign, Tavern, King Charles, Whitbread, Wood, Painted, 2-Sided, White Frame, 33 x 25 In.	590.00
Sign, Tourists, Red Arrow, Painted, Black & Gold, 16 x 42 In.	326.00
Sign, Trade, Horse Head, Brown Paint, Stand, Victorian, 35 In.	444.00
Sign, Warning Bad Bull, Standing Bull, Paint, 33 x 30 In.	748.00
Sign, Whale Shape, Tin, Painted, 37 ½ In.	558.00
Sign, Whale Trade, Sperm Whale, 2-Sided, Glass Eyes, Open Mouth, Nail Teeth, 11 x 36 In.	805.00
Strawholder, Greek Key, Glass, 10 In.	61.00
Strawholder, Pressed Glass, Flower Knob, Flared Bottom, 12 x 4 x 4 In.	935.00
Tobacco Cutter, Bird, Shamrock, Canada, 19th Century	731.00
Tobacco Cutter, P.J. Sorg & Company, Spear Head Plug, Metal, 18 In.	60.00
Tobacco Cutter, Planked, Wrought Iron, Bolted Hinge, Serpentine Cutter, Wood Handle, 16 x 8 In.	24.00
Tobacco Cutter, Plug, Cast Iron, Relief Cast, John Finzer & Bro's., Louisville, Ky., 6 ¾ x 18 In.	35.00
Tobacco Cutter, Plug, Figural, Cast Iron, Geared, Leaf Handle, Boy Thumbing Nose, 7 ½ x 12 ½ In.	106.00
Tobacco Cutter, Plug, K. Lauber Wangeheim Co., Los Angeles, Patent 1914, 15 In.	303.00
Tobacco Cutter, Turtle, Figural, Press Head Down, Trapdoor, Under Tail, 6 In. ....*illus*	880.00

STOVES have been used in America for heating since the eighteenth century and for cooking since the nineteenth century. Most types of wood, coal, gas, kerosene, and even some electric stoves are collected.

Base, Trestle Style, Cast Iron, Oval Keyhole Ends, Rosettes, Stretcher, Black, 13 In.	219.00
Bronze, 3 Legs, Masks, Bas Relief Panels, Cranes, Finches, Rooster, Ornate, Chinese, 11 x 12 x 8 In.	147.00
Cast Iron, 3 Tiers, Raised, Spayed Legs, France, 1800s, 48 x 21 In.	275.00
Cook, Colebrook, 10 Plate, Cast Iron, 36 x 14 x 37 In.	203.00
Cook, Keeley Stove Co., Iron, 6 Plate, Fire Box, Enamel, Nickel Plated, c.1926, 56 x 48 In. *illus*	1298.00
Cook, M. & H.P. Robeson Manada Furnace, 10 Plate, Stand, c.1800, 24 ½ In.	770.00
Cook, Tinnerman, Gas, Porcelain, 1935.	1200.00
Foot, Sheet Iron, Perforated, Riveted Metal Box, Wire Bail Handle, Wood Frame, Wire Door, 7 x 9 ½ In.	47.00
Gas, Iron & Enamel, Green Marbled, Cream Front & Sides, 1920s, 37 x 27 In.	435.00
Heating, N.P. Richardson, Open Hearth, Cast Iron, Portland, Me., No. 5, 28 x 35 x 25 In.	203.00
Heating, Potbelly, B & O Railroad, No. 1, Cast Iron, 50 x 31 x 35 In.	283.00
Parlor, Antoine Venet Chambon-Frugerolles, Porcelain Tiles, Cast Iron, Art Nouveau, Flowers, France	863.00
Parlor, Ludwigs Bitte, Pierced Arched Door, Winged Figure, Swan, Germany, c.1880, 73 x 26 In.	3936.00
Parlor, Roberts & Mander Stove Co., Metal, Porcelain, Gas, Pat. Feb. 24, 1925	270.00
Parlor, Victorian, Cast Iron, Filigree, Marble Accents, 24 ¾ x 15 ½ In.	184.00
Parlor, Warnick B. Leibrandt, Cast Iron, Union Air Tight Patent, 25 x 23 x 17 In.	124.00
Stove Plate, Berkshire Furnace, John Patton, Cast Iron, c.1785, 25 x 30 ½ In.	593.00
Stove Plate, G. Egemount Hope Furnace, Urn, Scrolls, Cast Iron, P. Grubb, c.1790, 17 x 23 In.	889.00
Stove Plate, Impressed Flower Basket, Tulip Flanked, Cast Iron, Elizabeth Furnace, 1765, 20 x 21 In.	2607.00
Stove Plate, Impressed Water Running Into Wine, Cast Iron, 28 ½ x 22 ¾ In.	385.00
Stove Plate, Stiegel Of 1758, Stylized Tulips, Cast, Iron, 23 ½ x 25 ½ In.	2252.00
Stove Plate, Stiegel Of 1769, Cast Iron, Flowering Vines, 19 In.	1126.00
Stove Plate, Stylized Tulips, Jacob Huber 1st Der Erste, Cast Iron, 1755, 26 ½ x 19 In.	2133.00
Stove Plate, W.J. Loth Stove Co., Cast Iron, Center Torch, Scrolled Frame, c.1880, 15 x 13 In.	115.00

STRETCH GLASS is named for the strange stretch marks in the glass. It was made by many glass companies in the United States from about 1900 to the 1920s. It is iridescent. Most American stretch glass is molded; most European pieces are blown and may have a pontil mark.

Bowl, Amber Iridescent, Black Foot, Flared, Jeannette, 12 x 3 ½ In.	65.00
Bowl, Amber Iridescent, Low Foot, c.1930, 10 In.	51.00
Bowl, Blue Iridescent, Black Foot, Flared, Northwood, 4 x 10 In.	65.00
Bowl, Celeste Blue, Flared Rim, Sticker, Fenton, 3 ½ x 7 ¾ In.	35.00
Bowl, Florentine Green, Basket Weave, Fenton, c.1920, 2 ½ x 6 ¾ In.	175.00
Bowl, Green, Gold Iridescent, Pedestal, 7 ¼ x 4 In.	55.00
Bowl, Iridized, Inverted Rim, Footed, Fenton, 8 ½ x 2 ½ In.	49.00
Bread Tray, Celeste Blue, Onion Skin, U.S. Glass, Early 1900s, 12 ¼ x 7 ⅜ In.	125.00
Candleholder, Sky Blue, Scalloped Base, Tiffin, 9 In., Pair	162.00
Candlestick, Green Iridized, 1920s, 3 ½ In.	32.00
Candy Dish, Cover, Marigold, Onionskin, Pointed Star Shape Finial, 1916-35, 7 x 5 In.	30.00
Candy Dish, Marigold, Iridescent, Onion Skin, Ribbed, Scalloped, 5 ¾ x 3 In.	22.00
Compote, Celestial Blue, Iridescent, Pedestal, 4 ¼ x 7 ½ In.	45.00
Compote, Mother-Of-Pearl Crystal, Ruffled Rim, 1920s, 6 ¾ x 6 ¾ In.	115.00
Console, Pink, Rolled Rim, Channeled, Tiffin, 10 ¼ In.	80.00
Console, Vaseline, Wide Rim, Low, 10 ½ x 2 In.	85.00

S

Mug, Vaseline, Blue Handle, 5 ¼ x 2 ⅜ In.	125.00
Plate, Green Uranium, Footed, 8 In.	22.00
Rose Bowl, Blue Milk Glass, Inverted Rim, 6 ½ x 2 ½ In.	60.00
Tray, Sandwich, Handle, Rose Ice Iridescent, Imperial, 4 ½ x 10 ⅝ In.	70.00
Vase, Diamond, Red, Ruffled, Flared, Ruffled Rim, 6 x 7 ¼ In.	45.00

SULPHIDES are cameos of unglazed white porcelain encased in transparent glass. The technique was patented in 1819 in France and has been used ever since for paperweights, decanters, tumblers, marbles, and other type of glassware. Paperweights and Marbles are listed in their own categories.

Bottle, Portrait, Emperor Napoleon, Marie & Napoleon III, c.1820, 3 In.	885.00
Plaque, Bust, Benjamin Franklin, Faceted Rim, Hanging Loop, Desprez, Paris, 3 In.	3250.00

SUMIDA is a Japanese pottery that was made from about 1895 to 1941. Pieces are usually everyday objects—vases, jardinieres, bowls, teapots, and decorative tiles. Most pieces have a very heavy orange-red, blue, brown, black, green, purple, or off-white glaze, with raised three-dimensional figures as decorations. The unglazed part is painted red, green, black, or orange. Sumida is sometimes mistakenly called Sumida gawa, but true Sumida gawa is a softer pottery made in the early 1800s.

Bowl, Figures, Branches, Leaves, Flowers, c.1900, 11 ½ x 3 In.	1100.00
Bowl, Monkeys Hanging Over Rim, Dark Green, 2 x 4 In.	195.00
Humidor, Crouching Men, Applied Figures, Marked, 6 x 3 ¾ x 4 ½ In. ....*illus*	288.00
Pitcher, Gawa, 2 Multicolor Applied Figures, Brown, Red Ground, 12 ½ In.	201.00
Sugar, Lid, Monkey, Playing Children, Red, c.1935, 3 ½ x 4 In.	175.00
Teapot, Dragon Spout, Applied Figures, Marked, 5 ½ x 4 ½ In. ....*illus*	184.00
Vase, 3 Figures, Footed, Black Ground, Circular Handle, 5 ¾ In.	368.00
Vase, 3 Monkeys, Basket Handle, Blue, Red, Brown, Japan, 9 In.	260.00
Vase, Boy, Rock, Red, Shouldered, c.1900, 6 In.	100.00

SUNBONNET BABIES were introduced in 1900 in the book *The Sunbonnet Babies*. The stories were by Eulalie Osgood Grover, illustrated by Bertha Corbett. The children's faces were completely hidden by the sunbonnets. The children had been pictured in black and white before this time, but the color pictures in the book were immediately successful. The Royal Bayreuth China Company made a full line of children's dishes decorated with the Sunbonnet Babies. Some Sunbonnet Babies plates have been reproduced, but are clearly marked.

Ashtray, Wednesday, Mending, Blue Mark, 4 x 4 In.	60.00
Bowl, Monday, Washing, 2 In.	65.00
Candlestick, Friday, Sweeping, 4 ½ In.	175.00
Candlestick, Sunday, Fishing, 5 In.	175.00
Creamer, Friday, Sweeping, Blue Mark, 3 In	145.00
Creamer, Monday, Washing, 3 In.	80.00
Creamer, Sunday, Fishing, 2 ½ In.	95.00
Mug, Friday, Sweeping, Blue Mark, 2 ½ In.	80.00
Nappy, Friday, Sweeping, 2 x 9 In.	80.00
Nappy, Wednesday, Mending, 5 ½ In.	60.00
Pitcher, Tuesday, Ironing, 5 In.	60.00 to 110.00
Pitcher, Wednesday, Mending, Blue Mark, 4 In.	90.00
Plate, Friday, Sweeping, 7 ¼ In.	200.00
Plate, Monday, Washing, 7 ¼ In.	200.00
Plate, Playtime Series, Swinging, 7 In.	225.00
Plate, Saturday, Baking, 7 ¼ In.	200.00
Plate, Sunday, Fishing, 7 ¼ In.	190.00 to 200.00
Plate, Thursday, Scrubbing, 7 ¼ In.	195.00 to 225.00
Plate, Wednesday, Mending, 7 ¼ In.	190.00
Rug, Hooked, Girl & Cat, Black Fabric Border, c.1925, 16 x 22 In.	90.00
Slipper, Monday, Washing, Blue Mark, 5 ¼ In.	225.00
Teapot, Friday, Sweeping, 4 In.	130.00
Vase, Monday, Washing, Oval, 5 ¾ In.	110.00

SUNDERLAND luster is a name given to a special type of pink luster made by Leeds, Newcastle, and other English firms during the nineteenth century. The luster glaze is metallic and glossy and appears to have bubbles in it. Other pieces of luster are listed in the Luster category.

Jug, Pink Luster, Transfer, Northumberland, Pearlware, Verse Under Spout, Marked, 8 ½ In. ..*illus*	531.00

Store, Cigar Cutter, Guillotine, Walnut, Ivory, Carved, Tilting Platform, 1800s, 17 ¾ In.
$1464.00

Neal Auction Co.

Store, Clothes Hanger, Girl's Head & Shoulders, Modelo Garment Hanger Co., Greenber & Picker, 1917
$295.00

Showtime Auction Services

Store, Container, Chocolate, Mother, Children, Roof Lifts, Shingles, Tin Litho, Germany, 6 x 7 In.
$86.00

Bertoia Auctions

Store, Sign, Carved, Pretzel, Gold Paint, c.1890, 13 x 22 ½ In.
$823.00

Garth's Auctions, Inc.

Store, Tobacco Cutter, Turtle, Figural, Press Head Down, Trapdoor, Under Tail, 6 In.
$880.00

Showtime Auction Services

Stove, Cook, Keeley Stove Co., Cast Iron, 6 Plate, Shelves, Fire Box, Enamel, Nickel Plated, c.1926, 56 x 48 In.
$1298.00

Conestoga Auction Co., Inc.

Mug, George, Applied Loop Handle, Luster, c.1830, 2 ½ x 2 ⅝ In.	500.00
Soap Dish, Cover, Black & White Ships Medallion, Pink Starburst Ground, 1800s, 6 x 3 ¾ In.	119.00
Tea Caddy, Flying Cloud, Sailors Farewell, Flower Wreath, 4 x 6 In.	150.00

SUPERMAN was created by two seventeen-year-olds in 1938. The first issue of Action comics had the strip. Superman remains popular and became the hero of a radio show in 1940, cartoons in the 1940s, a television series, and several major movies.

Action Figure, Mr. Mxyzptlk, Posable, Mego, Box, 1973, 8 In.	97.00
Action Figure, Posable, On Card, Mego, 1976, 8 In.	173.00
Action Figure, Superman, Bend 'N Flex, Mego, Blister Card, Copyright 1972, 5 In. ....*illus*	158.00
Ballpoint Pen, White Ground, DC Comics Inc., 1978	9.00
Bank, Bust, Plastic, 8 In.	20.00
Bank, Dime Register, Superman Breaking Chain, Tin Lithograph, Yellow, 2 ½ x 2 ½ In. *illus*	176.00
Belt & Buckle, S In Shield Logo, Red Vinyl, Aluminum, 27-In. Belt, 3-In. Buckle	86.00
Cake Pan, Bust, Wilton, DC Comics, 1977	15.00
Charm, Superman Flying, Sterling Silver, On Tan Cardboard, 1 In.	949.00
Comic Book, DC Comics, No. 133, Nov. 1959	25.00
Cookie Jar, Phone Booth, Ceramic, 1978, 13 ½ In.	398.00
Figure, Christopher Reeves, Box, 1978, 12 In.	176.00
Figure, Cutout, Jointed, Cardboard, 72 In.	50.00
Figure, Mattel, Box, 30 In.	280.00
Figure, Superman, Composition Head, Wood Arms & Legs, Cloth Cape, Ideal, 13 In. .....*illus*	431.00
Game, Superman Speed Game, Markers, Board, Milton Bradley, 1940s, 15 In........ 40.00 to	127.00
Horseshoe Set, Rubber, Red, Blue, Box, Super Swim Inc., c.1954	48.00
Kryptonite, Metal Chain	60.00
Lunch Box, Superman Vs. The Robot, Metal, Universal, 1954, 8 ¾ In.	791.00
Lunch Box, Under Fire, Flying Through Sky, Thermos Co., 1967	950.00
Matches, Safety, Superman Brand, Registered Trade Mark, 1940s, 1 ½ x 2 ¼ In. ....*illus*	288.00
Muscle Building Set, Hand Grippers, Bungees, Chart, Box, 18 x 11 In., 1954	280.00
Ornament, Clark Kent Shirt With Blazer, Hanger, Hallmark	13.00
Ornament, In A Single Bound, Hallmark, Box	60.00
Paperweight, S-Shape, Gold & Silver Plating, 6 x 6 In.	40.00
Patch, Supermen Of America Action Comics, Premium, c.1940, 5 ½ In. ....*illus*	2300.00
Pendant, S Logo, Gold Metal, ¾ x ½ In.	85.00
Phonograph, Action Images, Solid State, Model SP-19, Dejay Corp., Box, 1978, 12 In.	233.00
Pin, Lapel, S, Gold Metal, 1977	15.00
Pin, Superman, Block Letters, Action Comics, 1942, ⅞ In.	95.00
Pin, Superman, Cartoon Image, Lithograph, 1939, ⅞ In.	177.00
Radio, AM, Phone Booth, Battery, Box, Vanity Fair, 1978	195.00
Ring, Crusader, Portrait With S Chest Logo, Silver Plated Brass, 1946	115.00
Ring, S Logo, FX & 95 On Sides, Sterling Silver, 1994	177.00
Ring, Superman Flying, Silver Plated Brass, Coded Symbols, 1940s	949.00
Sign, Man Of Steel, Tin, DC Comics, 16 x 25 In.	38.00
Telephone, Figural Superman, Hands On Hips, Push Button, Plastic, 1981, 17 In.	345.00
Telephone, Figural Superman, Hands On Hips, Rotary Dial, Plastic, 1979, 17 x 10 In.	506.00
Toy, Daisy Cinematic Picture Pistol, Pressed Steel, Filmstrip, Box, 1940s, 6 In.	380.00
Toy, Inflatable Flying Superman, Vinyl, Ideal, 1966, 17 x 7 In.	115.00
Toy, Krypton Rocket Gun, Blue Plastic, Prototype, Marx, 1953, 23 ½ In.	1837.00
Toy, Superman, Action Figure, Bend 'N Flex, 1972, 9 ¾ x 5 In.	158.00
TV Guide, Vol. 1, No. 26, George Reeves, Man & Superman, Article, Sept. 25, 1953	153.00
Wallet, Brown Leather, Raised Figure, Art Deco Geometrics, Zipper, Pioneer, 1940s, 4 In.	200.00
Watch, Adult, Men's, Box, Mechanical, 1977	269.00

SUSIE COOPER began as a designer in 1925 working for the English firm A.E. Gray & Company. In 1932 she formed Susie Cooper Pottery, Ltd. In 1950 it became Susie Cooper China, Ltd., and the company made china and earthenware. In 1966 it was acquired by Josiah Wedgwood & Sons, Ltd. The name *Susie Cooper* appears with the company names on many pieces of ceramics.

Coffeepot, Black Fruit, Apple, Peach, White Ground, Cylindrical, Loop Finial, c.1950, 8 x 4 ⅜ In.	40.00
Coffeepot, Saturn, White, Golden Trim, Cylindrical, S-Spout, Loop Finial, 9 x 9 In.	149.00
Dish, Cornpoppy, Square, White Ground, Red Flower, Green Leaves, c.1972, 4 In.	25.00
Pitcher, Cubist, Multicolor, Round Foot, C-Handle, Art Deco, 1930s, 4 ¾ In.	550.00
Tray, Crescents, Green, Round, Handles, 11 ⅛ x 10 ⅛ In.	39.00

S

SWANKYSWIGS are small drinking glasses. In 1933, the Kraft Food Company began to market cheese spreads in these decorated, reusable glass tumblers. They were discontinued from 1941 to 1946, then made again from 1947 to 1958. Then plain glasses were used for most of the cheese, although a few special decorated Swankyswigs have been made since that time. For more prices, go to kovels.com.

Bustling Betsy, Yellow	23.00
Cornflower No. 2, Dark Blue	23.00
Cornflower No. 2, Light Blue	23.00
Daisy, Red & White	23.00
Forget-Me-Not, Light Blue, 3 ½ In.	4.00 to 15.00
Jonquil, Yellow	20.00
Red Tulips, Clear, 4 ½ In.	18.00

SWORDS of all types that are of interest to collectors are listed here. The military dress sword with elaborate handle is probably the most wanted. A tsuba is a hand guard fitted to a Japanese sword between the handle and the blade. Be sure to display swords in a safe way, out of reach of children.

Artillery, Brass, Model 1832, Ames Foot, Marked, 1835, 18 ¾-In. Blade	316.00
Bayonet, Police, Third Reich, P.D. Lunerschlon, 19 ½ In.	776.00
Bayonet, Saber, Brass Fish Scale Design, Yataghan Shape Blade, Red Copper Patina Hilt, 21 ½ In.	1265.00
Bayonet, Snell, Fits 1841 Rifle, Steel Locking Lug, Steel Ring, Brass Pommel, 21 ¾ In.	1920.00
Cavalry, Curve Blade, Leather Grip, Marked, US J.C.W. 1865, Ames Mfg Co., Model 1860, 35 In.	518.00
Confederate, Short, Concentric Rig, 2 Blade, Triangular Stopped Fuller, 19 In.	5175.00
Cut Steel Hilt, Etched Triangular Glade, Adams Urn Pommel, c.1790, 36 ¾ In.	123.00
Cutlass, Naval, Model 1860, Brass Guard, Wire Wrapped Grip, Leather Scabbard, c.1862, 26 In.	663.00
Cutlass, Navy, Hortsmann M1841, Brass Hilt, Riveted Grip, Civil War Era, 21 In.	1438.00
Dagger, Army Officer, Third Reich, Paul Seilheimer, 15 ½ In.	265.00
Field Officer's, Rounded Spine & Back Of Blade, 2 Inscriptions, 1800s, 31 In.	9775.00
Foot Soldier's, Scabbard, Ames, Military Designs, 1850, 30 ½ In.	780.00
Hilt, Dagger, Leaf Patterns, Flowers, Rubies, White, Green Jade, Silver, Chinese, 1700s, 5 ¾ In.	11850.00
Hunting, Antler Grip, Brass Mounts, Engraved Blade, Double Fullers, Marked Vivat, 1700s, 29 In.	531.00
Imperial, Openwork Brass Guard, Regimental Marks, Wire Wrapped Shagreen Grip, 37 ¾ In.	295.00
Imperial, Wurttemberg Infantry Officer, 38 ½ In.	374.00
Officer's, 3-Branch Brass Hilt, Iron Scabbard, Leather Grip, Twisted Wire Wrap, c.1863, 34 In.	575.00
Officer's, Navy, Fouled Anchor, Eagle, Dolphin Head Finial, Sharkskin Grip, 1852	657.00
Officer's, World War II, Shin Gunto, Type 98, Gilt Copper, Metal Scabbard, Japan, 42 In.	2832.00
Saber Bayonet, Scabbard, Fits Harpers Ferry Rifle Or Mississippi Rifle, c.1850, 22 In.	392.00
Saber, Cavalry, 3 Lines On Hilt, Unstopped Fuller, 34 In.	4313.00
Saber, Cavalry, Double Edge Blades, General Wade Hampton, KG & K, 3 Branches Handle, 38 In.	27025.00
Saber, Cavalry, Model 1840, Palmetto, Leather Wrapped Grip, Stamped, Columbia SC, 35 ½ In. *illus*	4025.00
Saber, Cavalry, Single Wire Wrap Grip, 40 In.	3450.00
Saber, U.S. Cavalry, War Of 1812, Spread Eagle, Shield, Ribbed Bone Grip, Gilt, 1800s, 35 In.	708.00
Steel, 2 Fullers, Curved Blade, Gold Koftgari Hilt, India, Cover, 1800s, 35 In.	368.00
Wakizashi, Blade With 2 Fullers, Cover, Signed, Japan, 20 ½ In.	2963.00

SYRACUSE is a trademark used by the Onondaga Pottery of Syracuse, New York. The company was established in 1871. The name became the Syracuse China Company in 1966. Syracuse China closed in 2009. It was known for fine dinnerware and restaurant china.

SYRACUSE
China

Bombay, Sugar & Creamer, c.1960	55.00
Canterbury, Bowl, Dark Blue, Rust Flowers, 1930s, 4 ½ In.	14.00
Cascade, Plate, 9 In.	8.00
Cinnamon, Platter, Oval, Embossed, 9 ⅝ x 7 ⅞ In.	16.00
Coventry, Plate, 8 In.	12.00
Greenbrier Hotel, Plate, Pink Rhododendron, Dorothy Draper, 10 ½ In.	58.00
Lyric, Bowl, Round, 9 In.	35.00
Lyric, Bread Plate, 6 ¼ In.	10.00
Lyric, Platter, 14 In.	50.00
Monticello, Platter, 14 In.	50.00
Nimbus Platinum, Platter Oval, 16 x 11 In.	35.00
Ox Head, Cup	15.00
Pine Cones & Boughs, Bowl, Rim Stripe, Lake Placid Club, 1937, 3 x 4 ½ In.	75.00
Pine Cones & Boughs, Cup & Saucer, c.1960	29.00
Raleigh, Bowl, Oval, 1930s	20.00
Red Leaf, Plate, Scalloped Rim, 6 ½ In.	8.00

Sumida, Humidor, Crouching Men, Applied Figures, Marked, 6 x 3 ¾ x 4 ½ In. $288.00

Jeffrey S. Evans & Assoc.

Sumida, Teapot, Dragon Spout, Applied Figures, Marked, 5 ½ x 4 ½ In. $184.00

Jeffrey S. Evans & Assoc.

Sunderland, Jug, Pink Luster, Transfer, Northumberland, Pearlware, Verse Under Spout, Marked, 8 ½ In. $531.00

James D. Julia Inc.

S

635

Superman, Action Figure, Superman, Bend 'N Flex, Mego, Blister Card, Copyright 1972, 5 In.
$158.00

Hake's Americana & Collectibles

Superman, Bank, Dime Register, Superman Breaking Chain, Tin Lithograph, Yellow, 2 ½ x 2 ½ In.
$176.00

Wm Morford Antiques

Superman, Figure, Superman, Composition Head, Wood Arms & Legs, Cloth Cape, Ideal, 13 In.
$431.00

Bertoia Auctions

Superman, Matches, Safety, Superman Brand, Registered Trade Mark, 1940s, 1 ½ x 2 ¼ In.
$288.00

Hake's Americana & Collectibles

Rose Trellis, Plate, Dinner, 11 In.	12.00
Strawberry Hill, Bowl, 4 ⅝ In.	9.00
Suzanne, Gravy Boat, Scalloped, Federal Shape, Underplate, 9 ½ In.	29.00
Syralite, Platter, Lime Green, c.1970, 12 x 10 ½ In.	20.00
Tropical Floral, Cup & Saucer, 1951	12.00

TAPESTRY, *Porcelain, see Rose Tapestry category.*

TEA CADDY is the name for a small box made to hold tea leaves. In the eighteenth century, tea was very expensive and it was stored under lock and key. The first tea caddies were made with locks. By the nineteenth century, tea was more plentiful and the tea caddy was larger. Often there were two sections, one for green tea, one for black tea.

Burl Walnut, Dome Lid, Brass & Ivory Straps, 5 x 5 In.	238.00
Burl, Barber Pole Inlays, Boat Shape, England, c.1790, 4 ½ In.	1770.00
Burl, Brass Mounts, Flat Top, Fitted Interior, c.1820, 5 ½ x 9 In.	259.00
Burl, Bronze, Hinged Lid, Porcelain Plaque, Galleried Shelf, Cabriole Legs, 29 x 15 In.	1007.00
Burl, Coffin Shape, Bun Feet, Fitted Interior, c.1845, 6 ½ x 11 ½ In.	480.00
Cherry Bark, Jade Finial, Boy, Cylindrical, 6 ½ In.	2684.00
Cloisonne, Turquoise Ground, Flowers, Cylindrical, Chinese, c.1900, 3 x 3 In.	121.00
Creamware, Prince William V, Verse, c.1775, 3 x 4 In.	1175.00
Curly Maple, Mahogany Inlaid Oval Panels, Herringbone Inlay, Federal, 1800s, 6 x 12 In.	546.00
Enamel Lacquer, Troika Scene, Paint, Gilt, Russia, 1800s, 5 In.	180.00
Faux Tortoise & Abalone Shell, Coffin Shape, Fitted Interior, Ivory Feet, 1800s, 5 x 8 In.	690.00
Fruitwood, 2-Color Stain, 6 Incised Lines, Ivory Knop, Paper Interior, George III, 5 x 4 ½ In.	878.00
Fruitwood, Apple Shape, Foil Lined, Hinged Lid, England, 1800s, 4 ¼ In. ....*illus*	590.00
Fruitwood, Apple Shape, Metal Escutcheon, Foil Lining, George III, c.1800, 4 In. ....*illus*	1778.00
Fruitwood, George III Style, Apple Shape, c.1885, 6 In.	246.00
Fruitwood, George III Style, Pear Shape, 6 ½ In.	399.00
Fruitwood, Ivory Escutcheon, George III, Pear Shape, Early 1800s, 8 In.	708.00
Fruitwood, Octagonal, Inlaid Fan Patera, Banded Edges, George III, 1800s, 6 x 5 In.	531.00
Fruitwood, Rolled Paper, Hexagonal, Brass Handle, George III, 6 x 7 In.	550.00
Gilt Metal, Pastoral Scenes, Pink Border, Staffordshire, c.1770, 3 Piece	32725.00
Hardwood, Parquetry, Hinged Square Lid, Silver Plaque, George III, 5 x 5 In.	250.00
Ivory Veneered, Silver Mounted, George III, Rectangular Top, 5 x 4 In.	1500.00
Ivory, Green Tortoiseshell, Harlequin, Decagon Shape, Horn Foot Rim, c.1800, 4 x 4 In.	11850.00
Lacquer, Black, Birds, Flowers, Gold, Pewter Container, Chinese, 1800s, 8 ¼ x 5 ¼ In.	796.00
Lacquer, Black, Gilt, Dragon Head Feet, Garden Scenes, Casket Shape, Lock & Key	2990.00
Lacquer, Black, Gilt, Hinged Lid, Pewter Canisters, Wing Paw Feet, Octagonal, Chinese, 5 x 7 ½ In.	940.00
Lacquer, Black, Wood, Tin Overlay, Bronze Ship, c.1890, 4 x 4 x 3 In.	395.00
Lacquer, Dome Lid, Pewter Lined, Footed, Canton, 1800s, 6 x 8 In.	700.00
Lacquer, Flower Framed Panels, Hexagonal, 3 Paw Feet, Chinese, c.1800, 7 ¾ In.	1541.00
Lacquer, Mother-Of-Pearl Inlay, Victorian, Chinoiserie Scenes, Square, 5 In.	122.00
Lacquer, Red, Chinoiserie, Gold, Figures, Courtyard Scenes, 4 Ivory Ball Feet, 1800s, 11 x 7 In.	267.00
Lacquer, Red, Octagonal, Gilt Design, Footed, Fitted Compartments, 1800s, 6 x 10 In.	1534.00
Lacquer, Wood, Lid, Paper Veneer, Red, Orange Designs, c.1890, 11 In., Pair	177.00
Mahogany & Oak, George III, Stepped Lid, Brass Handle, Bats Wing Escutcheon, c.1785, 6 x 10 In.	369.00
Mahogany, Bowfront, Carved Pilasters, Scalloped Skirt, Inlays, Fitted, England, 1800s, 8 x 12 In.	1020.00
Mahogany, Brass Hardware, Key & Lock, Compartment Tray, 6 x 15 x 9 In.	1610.00
Mahogany, Casket Shape, Button Feet, 5 x 8 In.	195.00
Mahogany, George III, Marquetry, Satinwood, Oval, Flower Medallion, Ivory Knop, 4 ¾ x 6 In.	263.00
Mahogany, George III, Molded Edge, Brass Handle, 3 Compartments, Bats Wing, 5 ¼ x 9 ¼ In.	215.00
Mahogany, George III, Oval Bee Medallion, Conch Shell, Paper Interior, 4 ½ x 4 ¾ In.	497.00
Mahogany, George III, Oval Urn Panel, Shell, c.1785, 4 ¼ x 4 ¾ In.	338.00
Mahogany, Hinged Lid, Brass Escutcheon, Early 1800s, 6 x 12 In.	356.00
Mahogany, Hinged Lid, Coiled Shell Medallions, Brass Ball Feet, 1800s, 6 ⅛ x 11 ⅜ In.	118.00
Mahogany, Hinged Lid, Fitted Interior, Handle, England, c.1790, 7 ½ In.	236.00
Mahogany, Hinged Lid, Regency, Coffin Shape, Brass Ball Feet, 8 x 12 In.	118.00
Mahogany, Inlaid, Hinged Lid, Brass Handle, Crossbanded, Shield, Bird, 7 x 12 In.	356.00
Mahogany, Quillwork, England, c.1800, 6 ½ In.	415.00
Mahogany, Regency, Coffin Shape, Tapering Rectangular Case, Brass Ball Feet, 4 x 8 In.	153.00
Mahogany, Regency, Ebonized Ring Handles, Coffin Shape, Footed, 12 In.	236.00
Mahogany, Shell Inlay, Georgian, Octagonal Shape, England, c.1790, 5 ⅞ In.	652.00
Mahogany, Shell Inlay, Octagonal, England, 1700s, 6 ⅜ In.	919.00
Mahogany, String Inlay, Brass, 3 Compartments, Velvet Lining, George III, c.1800, 6 x 9 ½ In.	239.00
Mahogany, Tambour Doors, Brass Bail Handle, Paw Feet, George III, England, 6 x 8 In.	1840.00
Metal, Lift Lid, Green Tea Stencil, Paint, 1800s, 19 ½ x 13 ½ In.	280.00

Oyster Shell Burl Inlay, Brass Lion's Head & Ring Handles, Ball Feet, Fitted Interior, Regency, 7 In.	288.00
Papier-Mache, Mother-Of-Pearl Flower Inlays, Coffin Shape, England, 1800s, 11 x 6 In.........	504.00
Papier-Mache, Mother-Of-Pearl Inlay, Extended Feet, 5 ¼ x 8 ½ In..................................	187.00
Porcelain, Blue & White, Central Flower, Vines, Rosewood Lid & Base, 1700s, 6 x 2 x 6 In.	175.00
Porcelain, Blue & White, Vines, Rosewood Stand, 18th Century, 5 x 3 In.	350.00
Porcelain, Figures, Flowers, Blue & White, Triangular Ends, Footed, Chinese, 10 x 7 In.........	863.00
Porcelain, Figures, Landscape, Blue & White, Diamond Shape, Chinese, 1900s, 12 x 7 In., Pair...	1076.00
Porcelain, Octagonal, Imari Flower Sprays, Iron Red, Cobalt Blue, 4 In.	510.00
Porcelain, Tole Lid, Baluster, England, 16 In...	232.00
Pottery, Yixing, Hexagonal, Flowers, Chinese, c.1865, 9 In., Pair	1195.00
Rosewood Veneer, Swing Handle, Monogrammed Oval Plaque, Inlaid Escutcheon, 4 ½ x 8 ½ In.	189.00
Rosewood, Banded, Canted Hinged Top, 2 Tin Canisters, Elongated Octagon, 1830s, 4 x 8 In.	460.00
Rosewood, Cherry, Banded, Coffin Shape, 2 Compartments, Gilt Metal Paw Feet, 10 In.	236.00
Rosewood, Fitted Interior, Coffin Shape, Regency, 1800s, 7 x 14 In.	120.00
Rosewood, Hinged Lid, Crossbanded Border, Ivory Escutcheon, 6 ¼ x 12 In.	119.00
Rosewood, Hinged Lid, Interior Compartments, Bowl, William IV, Coffin Shape, c.1835, 8 x 13 In.	594.00
Rosewood, Hinged Lid, Mother-Of-Pearl Inlay, Coffin Shape, Regency, Handles, c.1820, 5 ⅞ x 8 ½ In. .	236.00
Rosewood, Hinged, Dome Lid, Waste, Bowl, Regency, Coffin Shape, 8 x 14 In.	226.00
Rosewood, Regency, Coffin Shape, Tapering Body, 2 Lidded Compartments, c.1815, 5 ¼ x 8 In.....	214.00
Rosewood, Rounded Lid, Banding Design, Interior Compartments, 1800s, England, 4 x 8 In.	119.00
Rosewood, Satin Inlays, Triangular Ivory Escutcheon, Ring Handles, Fitted Interior, c.1825, 6 x 8 In.	345.00
Satinwood, George III, Canted Corners, Inlaid Leaves, Ebonized, c.1800, 5 x 5 In..................	235.00
Satinwood, George III, Penwork, Coffin Shape, Maritime Scene, Flowers, Lid, 6 x 9 In.	400.00
Satinwood, Herringbone Strip, Fan Inlay, Hepplewhite, Ball Feet, 3 Compartments, 7 x 12 In..	354.00
Silver, Crest, Garland, Knop Top, Goodnow & Jenks, Octagonal, c.1900, 5 ¾ In.	330.00
Silver, Cylindrical Lid, Chrysanthemum Stems, Leaves, Urn Shape, Japan, c.1890, 6 ½ In.......	1778.00
Silver, Flowering Vines, Cylindrical Lid, Inverted Pear Shape, Spread Foot, c.1900, 5 ½ In.	356.00
Silver, Lid, Flower Head, Flower Bands, George IV, Oval Cylindrical, England, 1821, 5 In.........	425.00
Silver, Lobed, Hinged, Gadroon Lip, Ball Feet, London, 1810, 5 In.	1150.00
Silver, Sliding Lid, Canted Corner, George I, Rectangular, Stepped Foot, Marked, 1720, 5 In....	1293.00
Silver, Wave Design, Art Nouveau Style, Round, c.1895, 3 ¼ x 2 In.	295.00
Tin, Flowers, Blue Ground, Japan, c.1950, 3 ¼ In...	25.00
Tin, Slanted Lift Lid, Red Dragon, Bell Conrad & Co., Japan, 20 x 18 In................................	91.00
Tortoiseshell, Banded Lip, Compartments, Ivory Feet, c.1815, 4 x 6 ¾ In. ....illus	1722.00
Tortoiseshell, Coffin Shape, England, c.1810, 6 x 6 ¾ In.	2400.00
Tortoiseshell, Dome Lid, Brass Segmented, Ball Finial, Fitted Interior, c.1825, 5 ½ x 6 ¾ In..	1722.00
Tortoiseshell, Dome Lid, Inlaid Mother-Of-Pearl, Canted, c.1815, 3 ¼ x 4 ½ In....................	984.00
Tortoiseshell, Double, Ivory Inlaid, Column Supports, Silver, Birds, Hinged Top, c.1810, 8 x 6 In.....	2252.00
Tortoiseshell, Hinged Lid, 2 Compartments, Pearl Escutcheon, Regency, 6 ¾ x 3 ¾ In.	794.00
Tortoiseshell, Ivory, England, c.1800, 6 ¾ In.	790.00
Tortoiseshell, Lid, Bowed Coffin Shape, Regency, Ivory Handles, c.1825................................	1495.00
Tortoiseshell, Pagoda Top, Silver Piping, Ivory Handles & Feet, Cartouche, c.1830, 8 ¾ x 12 ½ In...	2450.00
Tortoiseshell, Stepped Lid, Fitted Interior, 2 Compartments, Bun Feet, Regency, 6 x 6 ½ In.....	3198.00
Tortoiseshell, Stepped Lid, Regency, Pagoda Shape, Gilt Bun Feet, 1800s, 6 x 7 In..................	2091.00
Tortoiseshell, Stepped Lid, Tapering Rectangular, Bone Knop & Bun Feet, 6 x 7 In.	2214.00
Walnut, Cove Molded Lid, Post & Ball Handle, Bracket Feet, Compartments, c.1785, 5 ¼ x 9 In.....	184.00
Walnut, Dome Lid, Stringing, Regency, Diamond Shape Escutcheon, c.1815, 5 x 4 ¾ In.	153.00
Walnut, Lid, Inlaid Satinwood Stringing, Ivory Escutcheon, George III, c.1785, 4 ½ x 5 In.	153.00
Wood, Arched Handle, Men, Smoking, Drinking, Cockfight, Capstan Feet, 1790-1800, 7 x 7 In.	1003.00
Wood, Chinoiserie, Hinged Lid, 2 Pewter Lined Compartments, Elongated Octagon, Chinese, 11 In...	372.00
Wood, Parquetry, Inlaid Zigzag Borders, Loop Handles, Regency, 6 x 13 In.	1298.00
Wood, Treen, Cored & Peeled Apple Shape, Finial, England, 1800s, 6 In.	1416.00
Wood, Tunbridgeware, Dome Lid, Geometric Border, c.1850, 9 x 5 x 5 In.	1795.00

TEA LEAF IRONSTONE dishes are named for their decorations. There was a superstition that it was lucky if a whole tea leaf unfolded at the bottom of your cup. This idea was translated into the pattern of dishes known as "tea leaf." By 1850 at least twelve English factories were making this pattern, and by the 1870s it was a popular pattern in many countries. The tea leaf was always a luster glaze on early wares, although now some pieces are made with a brown tea leaf. There are many variations of tea leaf designs, such as Teaberry, Pepper Leaf, and Gold Leaf. The designs were used on many different white ironstone shapes, such as Bamboo, Lily of the Valley, Empress, and Cumbow.

Basin, Ewer, Lily-Of-The-Valley, Anthony Shaw...	170.00
Basin, Morning Glory, Crystal Shape, Elsmore & Forster, 14 In.	180.00
Bowl, Apple, Scalloped, Pedestal, Wedgwood, 10 In..	350.00
Bowl, Vegetable, H. Burgess, 9 x 6 ½ In..	33.00
Butter Pat, White, Gold, 14 Piece	136.00
Butter, Cover, Insert, Lily-Of-The-Valley, Anthony Shaw...	120.00

Superman, Patch, Supermen Of America Action Comics, Premium, c.1940, 5 ½ In.
$2300.00

Hake's Americana & Collectibles

Sword, Saber, Cavalry, Model 1840, Palmetto, Leather Wrapped Grip, Stamped, Columbia SC, 35 ½ In.
$4025.00

James D. Julia Inc.

Tea Caddy, Fruitwood, Apple Shape, Foil Lined, Hinged Lid, England, 1800s, 4 ¼ In.
$590.00

Brunk Auctions

Tea Caddy, Fruitwood, Apple Shape, Metal Escutcheon, Foil Lining, George III, c.1800, 4 In.
$1778.00

Skinner, Inc.

T

TEA LEAF IRONSTONE

Tea Caddy, Tortoiseshell, Banded Lip, Compartments, Ivory Feet, c.1815, 4 x 6 ¾ In.
$1722.00

New Orleans Auction Galleries, Inc.

Teco, Vase, Tulip, Buttressed, Green Matte Glaze, Marked, 11 ½ x 4 ½ In.
$2108.00

Rago Arts & Auction Center

Teco, Wall Pocket, Leaves, Green Matte Glaze, Marked, 16 ½ x 6 ½ In.
$1736.00

Rago Arts & Auction Center

Cake Plate, Augusta, J. Clementson	425.00
Cake Plate, Berry Cluster Botanical, Jacob, Furnival	1200.00
Cake Plate, Fig Cousin, Davenport	450.00
Cake Plate, Rose, Washington Shape, Powell & Bishop	200.00
Cake Plate, Simple Pear, Alfred Meakin, 10 In.	140.00
Chamber Pot, Cable, Anthony Shaw	40.00
Chamber Pot, Lid, Cable, Anthony Shaw	100.00
Coffeepot, Lid, Paneled Grape, 5 Sided	80.00
Coffeepot, Lid, Teaberry, Grand Loop	160.00
Compote, Scroll, Oval, Alfred Meakin, 10 In.	600.00
Creamer, Bamboo, V-Shape Spout, Alfred Meakin	20.00
Creamer, Chelsea, Alfred Meakin, 5 In.	60.00
Creamer, Fanfare, Tobacco Leaf, Elsmore & Forster, 5 ½ In.	270.00
Creamer, Grape Octagon, Pinwheel, 5 ¼ In.	70.00
Creamer, Lily-Of-The-Valley, Anthony Shaw, 5 ¼ In.	150.00
Creamer, Sunburst, Wilkinson	40.00
Cup & Saucer, White, Gold, 4 In., 6 Piece	100.00
Dish, Pickle, Mitten, Desoto Shape, Anthony Shaw, 9 x 5 ½ In.	170.00
Gravy Boat, Crewel, Alfred Meakin, 4 ½ In.	65.00
Ladle, Sauce, Lily-Of-The-Valley, Anthony Shaw	700.00
Mug, Cable, Furnival, 4 In.	80.00
Mug, Tulip, Cobalt Blue Plumes, Elsmore & Forster	80.00
Nappy, Paneled Grape, Pinwheel, 4 Piece	44.00
Pitcher, Hot Water, Bow Knot, Wilkinson, 8 In.	400.00
Pitcher, Morning Glory, Portland Shape, Elsmore & Forster, 8 In.	225.00
Pitcher, Teaberry, New York Shape, Clementson Bros., 8 ½ In.	275.00
Plate, Bread & Butter, Classic Shape, Fluted Edges, Adams, 6 In., 2 Piece	30.00
Plate, Niagara Fan, Anthony Shaw, 8 ¼ In., 4 Piece	36.00
Plate, Soup, Lily-Of-The-Valley, Anthony Shaw, 9 ⅝ In.	25.00
Plate, Soup, Plain, Round, Alfred Meakin, 9 In., 6 Piece	60.00
Platter, Chinese Shape, Anthony Shaw, 14 In.	30.00
Platter, Niagara Fan, Anthony Shaw	25.00
Saucer, New York Shape, White, Clementson, 6 In.	60.00
Sugar, Cable, Anthony Shaw, 5 x 4 ½ In.	25.00
Sugar, Cover, Chelsea, Alfred Meakin, 5 In.	20.00
Sugar, Cover, Fishhook, Alfred Meakin	25.00
Sugar, Cover, Hexagon, Anthony Shaw	40.00
Sugar, Cover, Lily-Of-The-Valley, Anthony Shaw, 7 ½ In.	70.00
Tea Set, Portland, Elsmore & Foster, 7, 7 ½, 10 In., 3 Piece	238.00
Teapot, Fig, White, Embossed, 9 ¼ x 10 In.	275.00
Teapot, Lid, Chinese Shape, Anthony Shaw, 10 In.	50.00
Teapot, Lid, Laurel Wreath, Elsmore & Forster, 9 ½ In.	100.00
Toothbrush Holder, Arthur J. Wilkinson, 5 In.	70.00
Tureen, Cover, Lily-Of-The-Valley, 2 Piece	450.00
Tureen, Cover, Lily-Of-The-Valley, Anthony Shaw, 10 In.	100.00
Tureen, Cup, Posset, Plain, Round, 3 In.	275.00
Tureen, Sauce, Lid, Ladle, Underplate, Fishhook, Alfred Meakin, 4 Piece	225.00
Tureen, Vegetable, Lid, Bamboo, Alfred Meakin, 11 In.	20.00
Vase, Brush, Bamboo, Alfred Meakin	35.00

TECO is the mark used on the art pottery line made by the American Terra Cotta and Ceramic Company of Terra Cotta and Chicago, Illinois. The company was an offshoot of the firm founded by William D. Gates in 1881. The Teco line was first made in 1885 but was not sold commercially until 1902. It continued in production until 1922. Over 500 designs were made in a variety of colors, shapes, and glazes. The company closed in 1930.

Ashtray, Tan, Green Matte Frog & Bowl, Marked, 4 ½ x 2 In.	280.00
Bookends, Nude Man, Bow & Arrow, Gold Gloss Glaze, Prairie Style, Marked Filbert	1380.00
Bowl, Low, Squat, Flattened, Green Matte Glaze, Embossed Flowers, 9 In. Diam.	230.00
Bowl, Salad, Green Matte Glaze, White Interior, 4-Footed, Holmes Smith, 12 x 6 In.	6000.00
Jardiniere, Green Matte Glaze, Ribbed, Scalloped Rim, Fritz Albert, 12 x 8 In.	3000.00
Vase, Aventurine, Brown, Yellow, Red Flame Glaze, Shouldered, Stamped, 13 ½ x 5 In.	1240.00
Vase, Aventurine, Deep Brown, Baluster, Stamp, 11 x 9 In.	3720.00
Vase, Bulbous Bottom, Cylindrical Neck, Square Handles, Green Matte Glaze, 6 In.	1035.00
Vase, Flared, Aventurine, Cabinet, Stamped, 4 In.	279.00
Vase, Green Matte Glaze, 4 Long Handles, Stamped, 14 x 8 ½ In.	3720.00
Vase, Green Matte Glaze, Flared Rim, Octagonal Foot, Paneled, 12 ¼ In.	2124.00
Vase, Green Matte Glaze, Long Neck, Impressed Marks, 7 x 13 In.	6000.00

T

Vase, Green Matte Glaze, Prairie Weed Design, W.D. Gates, 6 x 18 In.	3600.00
Vase, Green Matte Glaze, Ribbed, Impressed Hugh Garden, 7 x 12 In.	3000.00
Vase, Green Matte Glaze, Stylized Flowers, William Jenney, 8 x 10 ½ In.	9600.00
Vase, Green Trunk, Shaped 4 Corner Rim, Circular Base, Marked, 16 In.	1955.00
Vase, Green, 2 Handles, Stamped, 11 x 5 In.	2108.00
Vase, Green, Charcoal Matte Glaze, Bulbous, W. Gates, 3 x 4 ½ In.	480.00
Vase, Green, Round 4-Footed, 4 Handles, Stamped, 12 x 10 In.	19840.00
Vase, Green, Ruffled Rim, Long Neck, Footed Stamped, 13 ¾ x 8 In.	1860.00
Vase, Light Green Matte Glaze, 4 Open Handles, Marked, 11 ½ In.	1840.00
Vase, Lobed, Cutout, 3-Footed, Green Matte Glaze, Marked, 9 ¼ x 6 ¾ In.	1612.00
Vase, Textured, Green Matte Glaze, High Shouldered, 6 In.	403.00
Vase, Tulip, Buttressed, Green Matte Glaze, Marked, 11 ½ x 4 ½ In. ....*illus*	2108.00
Vase, Tulips, Signed, 10 x 7 In.	3720.00
Wall Pocket, Green Matte Glaze, Impressed Marks, W. Gates, 5 ½ x 6 ½ In.	570.00
Wall Pocket, Leaves, Green Matte Glaze, Marked, 16 ½ x 6 ½ In. ....*illus*	1736.00

TEDDY BEARS were named for a president of the United States. The first teddy bear was a cuddly toy said to be inspired by a hunting trip made by Teddy Roosevelt in 1902. Morris and Rose Michtom started selling their stuffed bears as "teddy bears" and the name stayed. The Michtoms founded the Ideal Novelty and Toy Company. The German version of the teddy bear was made about the same time by the Steiff Company. There are many types of teddy bears and all are collected. The old ones are being reproduced. Other bears are listed in the Toy section.

Mohair, Blond, Shaved Muzzle, Embroidered, Swivel Head, Disc-Jointed, Germany, 1950s, 23 In...*illus*	112.00
Mohair, Jointed, Hump Back, Pads On Feet, 19 In.	144.00
Mohair, Shaded Brown, Swivel Head, Blue Glass Eyes, Disc-Jointed, Felt Paws, 10 In.	2394.00
Steiff, Black, Shoebutton Eyes, Excelsior Stuffing, Swivel Limbs, 11 In.	3738.00
Steiff, Cinnamon, Shoebutton Eyes, Hump, Ear Button, 18 In.	1150.00
Steiff, Clown, Glass Eyes, Pompom Hat, Jointed, Ear Button, 10 In.	2300.00
Steiff, Glass Eyes, Stitched Nose, Mouth & Claws, Jointed, Ear Button, c.1950, 11 In.	230.00
Steiff, Mohair, Gold, Glass Eyes, Stitched Nose, Ear Button, Swivel Neck, 16 In.	1062.00
Steiff, Mohair, Gold, Jointed, Swivel Head, Button Ear, c.1910, 20 In.	3658.00
Steiff, Mohair, White, Shoebutton Eyes, Stitched Nose, Mouth, Claws, Hump, Ear Button, 24 In.	2242.00
Steiff, White, Felt Paw Pads, Ear Button, 15 In.	978.00
Steiff, Zotty, Growler Voice, Tag, 19 In.	63.00

TELEPHONES are wanted by collectors if the phones are old enough or unusual enough. The first telephone may have been made in Havana, Cuba, in 1849, but it was not patented. The first publicly demonstrated phone was used in Frankfurt, Germany, in 1860. The phone made by Alexander Graham Bell was shown at the Centennial Exhibition in Philadelphia in 1876, but it was not until 1877 that the first private phones were installed. Collectors today want all types of old phones, phone parts, and advertising. Even recent figural phones are popular.

American Telephone & Telegraph Co., Candlestick, Black, Patented July 9, '89, 11 In.	79.00
Con Tel, Wall, Oak, c.1925, 16 In.	213.00
Crest Toothpaste, Figural, Translucent, Plastic, 1980s	50.00
Elektrisk Bureau Kristiania De Luxe, Nickel Plated, Metal, Gold Colored Flowers, Norway, c.1895	9427.00
Ericsson, Coffee Mill Shape, Rolled Tin Lithograph Case, Crank Inductor, Sweden, 1895	29893.00
Ericsson, Tin Case, Wood Base, Desk, c.1902	352.00
Hand Crank, Oak, Wall Mount	240.00
Keebler Elf, Figural, Full Figure, 1980s	50.00
Kellogg, Wall, Oak, Crank, 2 Gold Bells, 26 x 8 x 11 ½ In.	102.00
L.M. Ericsson, Model BC 2050, Table, Nickel Plated, Sweden, c.1892 ....*illus*	667.00
North Electric Co., Wall, Oak, 26 In.	324.00
Paperweight, Western Electric, Figural, Bell, Glass, Deep Blue, 3 ¼ x 3 ⅜ In. ....*illus*	44.00
Pin, Pioneer Telephone, When In Doubt, Telephone & Find Out, Woman, c.1901, 2 In.	316.00
Rotary Phone, French Provincial, Brass, Faux Ivory, France, 8 x 9 In.	122.00
Sign, Bell Logo, Stainless Steel, Plywood, Saul Bass, 25 x 25 In.	395.00
Sign, Bell System Public Telephone, Arrow, 2-Sided, Porcelain, 5 ½ x 12 In.	158.00
Sign, Bell System, Mountain States, Porcelain, Flange, 2-Sided, 12 x 11 In. ....*illus*	275.00
Sign, Independent Local & Long Distance, Shield Logo, Porcelain, Flange, 18 x 17 In.	170.00
Sign, Independent Public Telephone, Porcelain, Flange, 18 x 18 In.	170.00
Sign, Independent Telephone, Porcelain, 2-Sided, Flange, 18 x 17 In. ....*illus*	132.00
Sign, Public Telephone, Bell System, Logo, Flange, Porcelain, 1930s, 11 x 11 In.	115.00
Sign, Public Telephone, Bell Systems, Porcelain Flange, 12 x 12 In.	283.00
Sign, Public Telephone, Green & White, Round, Bell, Flange, Porcelain	150.00
Sign, Telephone Bell System, Arrow, 2-Sided, Porcelain, 8 ½ x 34 In.	226.00
Sign, Western Union Telegrams May Be Telephoned From Here, Porcelain, Flange, 9 x 18 In.	396.00

Teddy Bear, Mohair, Blond, Shaved Muzzle, Embroidered, Swivel Head, Disc-Jointed, Germany, 1950s, 23 In.
$112.00

Theriault's

Telephone, L.M. Ericsson, Model BC 2050, Table, Nickel Plated, Sweden, c.1892
$667.00

Auction Team Breker

Telephone, Paperweight, Western Electric, Figural, Bell, Glass, Deep Blue, 3 ¼ x 3 ⅜ In.
$44.00

Wm Morford Antiques

T

Telephone, Sign, Bell System, Mountain States, Porcelain, Flange, 2-Sided, 12 x 11 In.
$275.00

Showtime Auction Services

Telephone, Sign, Independent Telephone, Porcelain, 2-Sided, Flange, 18 x 17 In.
$132.00

Wm Morford Antiques

Television, Philips, TX400, Wood Case, 4 Channel Tuner, Desk, 1951, 9-In. Screen
$810.00

Auction Team Breker

Societe Des Telephones Gramont, Candlestick, Wood Case, 1 Push Switch, France, c.1925, 14 In.	1231.00
StarKist Tuna, Charlie Tuna, Figural, Push Button, Royal Blue, 10 In.	55.00
Telephone Mfg. Co., Wall, Imperial, Oak, c.1900, U.S.A., 29 x 14 In.	144.00
Wall, Model No. 305, Bell-Type Receiver, c.1890	816.00
Wincrantz Model, Metal Case & Cradled Receiver, Desk, Art Deco, c.1930	879.00

TELEVISION sets are twentieth-century collectibles. Although the first television transmission took place in England in 1925, collectors find few sets that pre-date 1946. The first sets had only five channels, but by 1949 the additional UHF channels were included. The first color television set became available in 1951.

Philips, TX400, Wood Case, 4 Channel Tuner, Desk, 1951, 9-In. Screen ....*illus*	810.00
Pin, I Love Lucy, Lucille Ball, 1911-1989, Photo, 1989, 3 ½ In.	52.00 Pin,
New RCA Victor Television, Ask About The Big Change, Nipper, Logo, 1950s	66.00
Sign, Stewart-Warner United Radio Television AM-FM, Reverse Painted, Neon, 12 x 31 In.	311.00
Sign, TV Service, We Use RCA Tubes, Logo, Lighted, 10 x 21 In.	57.00

TEPLITZ refers to art pottery manufactured by a number of companies in the Teplitz-Turn area of Bohemia during the late nineteenth and early twentieth centuries. Two of these companies were the Alexandra Works founded by Ernst Wahliss, and The Amphora Porcelain Works, run by Riessner, Stellmacher, and Kessel.

Bowl, Applied Woman, Lily, Amphora, 14 x 12 In.	429.00
Bowl, Ceramic Teardrops Rim, Footed, Double Handles, Gilt, Paul Dachsel, Amphora, 5 ½ x 15 ½ In.	2356.00
Bowl, Yellow Flower Rim, Blue, Red Mottled Body, Pedestal, Stamped, Amphora, 6 ½ x 8 In.	68.00
Bust, Gypsy, Long Hair, Scarf, Green, Tan, Ernst Wahliss, Amphora, 13 ½ x 11 In.	372.00
Bust, Maiden, Enameled & Gilded, Ribbon Inscribed 1830, Austria, c.1900, 17 ½ In.	858.00
Ewer, Persian Style, Brown Mottled Glaze, Green Dots, Gilt Bubbles, 17 ½ In.	259.00
Figurine, Woman, Holding Flower, Garland, Flowing Gown, Bowl Base, Women Heads, 27 In.	863.00
Jug, Wine, Flowers, Raised Gilt, Dragon Shape Handles, Narrow Neck, Ruffle Rim, c.1900, 14 In.	413.00
Pitcher, Free-Form, Pierced Cabochons & Branching Handles, Signed, 8 In.	125.00
Teapot, Rooster, Applied Mythological Winged Creatures, Gold Highlights, Signed, 10 In. ...*illus*	805.00
Vase, Applied Juniper Branches, Bulbous, Paul Dachsel, Amphora, 7 ½ x 12 ¾ In.	1815.00
Vase, Art Nouveau, Tree Shape, Purple Mark, Austria, c.1905, 9 In.	708.00
Vase, Basket Weave Ground, Applied Leaves, Geraniums, Amphora, Handles, 8 x 8 In.	259.00
Vase, Bulbous, Scroll Feet, Climbing Dragon Handles, Hand Painted, 10 x 12 In.	460.00
Vase, Cream, Green Shading, Leaves, Handle Twists Around Body, Amphora, 6 In.	158.00
Vase, Crows Flying, Field, Incised, Painted, Handles Campina Series, Amphora, c.1910, 8 x 13 In.	345.00
Vase, Cylindrical, Bulbous Mouth, Handles At Rim, Sun, Lilac Clouds, Amphora, c.1900-05, 16 In.	1125.00
Vase, Double Handle, Riessner & Kessel, Impressed Crown Mark, Amphora, 1905-10, 7 ½ In.	115.00
Vase, Dragonflies, Looped Handles, Paul Dachsel, Amphora, 5 ¾ x 4 ½ In.	1488.00
Vase, Edda, Impressed Crown Mark, Amphora, 9 In.	431.00
Vase, Egyptian Revival, Women, Green Ground, Signed Julius Dressler, Amphora, c.1915, 20 x 12 In.	2450.00
Vase, Elongated Oval, Grape Cluster, Leaves, Wavy Rim, 2 Upper Handles, 11 In.	460.00
Vase, Flowers, Berries, Multicolor, Handles, Amphora, 14 ¾ x 9 In.	201.00
Vase, Flowers, Gilt, Enamel, Blue Ground, Round, 8 ½ In.	207.00
Vase, Forest Scene, Rising Sun, Flowers, Wasps, Gilt Accents, c.1900, 13 x 6 In.	369.00
Vase, Forest Surprise, Applied Bug, Flowers, Painted Landscape, Amphora, 5 ½ x 12 In.	825.00
Vase, Frog, Insect, Water Lilies, Stamped Austria, c.1905, 21 In.	2360.00
Vase, Gold Rim, Double Handle, 2-Headed Dragon, Grape Design, Gourd Shape, Amphora, 8 In.	58.00
Vase, Grape Clusters, Blue & White Iridescent, Bulbous Shoulder, Ribbed Protrusions, 14 In.	674.00
Vase, Lady Slipper Orchids, 3 Handles, Paul Dachsel, Amphora, 4 ½ x 6 In.	372.00
Vase, Lobed, Organic Shape, Mottled Green, Amphora, Paul Dachsel, c.1900, 6 ½ In.	675.00
Vase, Organic Raised Branches, Metallic Glaze, Amphora, Ernst Wahliss, 7 x 10 In.	480.00
Vase, Organic Shape, Applied Crayfish, Green Glaze, E. Stellmacher, Amphora, c.1900, 7 x 9 ½ In.	660.00
Vase, Pear Shape, Overflow Lip, Grapes & Vines, Amphora, 9 x 7 In.	115.00
Vase, Pine Tree, Applied Cones, Flared, Paul Dachsel, Terex Amphora, 11 In.	2200.00
Vase, Praying Mantis, Applied Cyclamen, Red, Green Mottled Glaze, Gold, Amphora, 8 x 16 In.	9900.00
Vase, Rectangular, Basket Weave Design, Cherries, Leaves, Marked, Amphora, 19 x 9 In.	230.00
Vase, Sculpted Applied Octopus, Crab, Amphora, Eduard Stellmacher, 6 ½ x 19 ½ In.	10800.00
Vase, Trees, Blooming Irises, Yellow, Blue, Green, Gilt, Urn Shaped, Garlic Mouth, 5 ½ In.	196.00
Vase, White & Black Grapes, Cylindrical, 4 Swooping Handles, Iridescent, 11 ⅝ In.	259.00
Vase, White Birds, Black Outlines, Mottled Mauve Iridescent, Gold Trim, Amphora, 13 In.	593.00
Vase, Woman's Portrait, Multicolor, Painted, Tapered, Signed, Amphora, 3 ½ x 6 ¾ In.	825.00

TERRA-COTTA is a special type of pottery. It ranges from pale orange to dark reddish-brown in color. The color comes from the clay, which is fired but not always glazed in the finished piece.

Ashtray, Frog, Impressed, 2 In. ....*illus*	138.00

T

Brushpot, 3-Claw Dragon, Clouds, Key Fret Rim, Cylindrical, Chinese, c.1950, 4 ¼ In.	110.00
Bust, Diana, Diadem, Moon Emblem, Cast, Continental, c.1890, 17 ½ In.	239.00
Bust, Lady, Curled Hair, Draped Grapevines, Marble Base, 27 x 18 ½ In.	2106.00
Bust, Little Girl, Round Base, c.1815, 16 In.	805.00
Bust, Marie Antoinette, Upswept Hair, Draped Gown, Pedestal Base, 1800s, 27 x 17 In.	1845.00
Bust, Socrates, Raised, Round Base, Italy, 27 In.	279.00
Column, Classical, Stop Fluting, Stepped Base, 38 x 12 ½ In., Pair	308.00
Confit Jar, Ocher Glazed Buff, 2 Handles, France, c.1915, 12 In.	184.00
Creamer, Stylized Draped Robe, Sleeping Man, Hinged Lid, 4 x 5 In.	24.00
Figurine, Apostle, Open Book, Italy, 8 ¾ x 4 In.	354.00
Figurine, Bacchante & Putto, Albert-Ernest Carrier-Belleuse, c.1900, 24 In.	5975.00
Figurine, Bear, Serrated, Painted, K.W. Lane, Weems, 1971, 6 ¾ x 7 ¼ In.	575.00
Figurine, Bulldog, Glass Eyes, Docked Ears, Painted, England, 1800s, 20 In.	1298.00
Figurine, Gnome, Multicolor, c.1890, 28 x 10 In.	1265.00
Figurine, Hens, On Basket, Multicolor, France, 11 In., Pair	430.00
Figurine, Madonna & Child, Crown, Halo, Painted, Signed Professor E. Pattarino, Italy, c.1930, 21 In.	1200.00
Figurine, Man, Suit, Fisher Austin Productions, 1987, 22 x 14 ½ In.	750.00
Figurine, Mary, Standing, Angel At Feet, Painted, 20 In.	84.00
Figurine, Monkey, Playing Instrument, Cone Hat, White Glaze, Square Base, 46 In., Pair	2706.00
Figurine, Pan, Nymph, 2 Putti, Cream Paint, Signed Caron, France, 1900s, 19 ½ In.	600.00
Figurine, Primitive, Seated, Bowl On Lap, Headdress, Square Base, 16 x 8 In.	156.00
Figurine, Putti, Inscribed Coyzevoc, France, 1798, 11 In.	830.00
Figurine, Putto, Flared Case, Signed Lebroc, 20 x 12 In.	403.00
Figurine, Sphinx, Woman's Head, Tasseled Shawl, Base, c.1850, 4 ½ x 6 ½ In., Pair	1195.00
Figurine, Temple Guardian, Cloud Stand, Multicolor, Paint, Chinese, 1800s, 11 ½ In.	214.00
Figurine, Venus, Cupid, Roses, 13 ¼ x 10 ¾ In.	369.00
Figurine, Virgin, Flowing Gown, Cherubs, Glass Eyes, Multicolor, Naples, 1700, 34 ½ In.	5040.00
Figurine, Warrior, Standing, Square Base, 17 In.	248.00
Figurine, Young Maiden, Crowned, Oak Leaf Wreath, Carrying Basket Of Kindling, 27 In.	211.00
Figurine, Young Woman, Painted, c.1890, 25 x 9 In.	805.00
Jar, Olive, Etruscan Style, Oval, 3 Handles, Turned Highlights, 41 ¾ In.	325.00
Jar, Storage, Provincial, Ribbed, Teardrop Shape, 3 Handles, c.1890, 38 x 26 In.	584.00
Mask, Bacchus, Majolica, 21 x 21 In.	431.00
Planter, Brown Dragon, Sea Green, Glazed, Chinese, Graduated Sizes, 4 Piece	649.00
Plaque, Chief Sitting Bull, Metal Stand, 27 x 19 In.	2990.00
Urn, Draped Garland, Acanthus Leaf Rim, Swirl Base, c.1940, 43 x 31 In.	1230.00
Urn, Green & Blue Speckled Glaze, Galloway, 1920s, 41 x 18 In. ....*illus*	2000.00
Urn, Green Paint, Faux Marble Base, Italy, 12 In.	649.00
Urn, Lid, Flowers, Scrolls, Painted, 34 x 14 In., Pair	554.00
Vase, Applied Carved Dragons, Glass Eyes, Blue, Cream, Rust, Asia, 25 x 14 In.	520.00
Vase, Atelier Primavera, Guitar Players, Incised, c.1930, 18 In.	1793.00
Vase, Blue Glaze, Rolled Rim, Banded, Galloway, c.1930, 18 ½ x 12 In., Pair	1599.00
Vase, Classical Figures, Flowers, Hearts, Urn Shape, Handles, 12 ½ In.	119.00
Vase, Garniture, Roman Emperor, Empress & Attendants, Pyriform, 2 Handles, 7 In., Pair	738.00

TEXTILES listed here include many types of printed fabrics and table and household linens. Some other textiles will be found under Clothing, Coverlet, Rug, Quilt, etc.

Banner, Centennial, Illinois State Seal, Canvas, American Flag, Wood Rod, 1876, 62 x 45 In. ..*illus*	3555.00
Banner, Centennial, Seal Of Virginia, American Flag, Canvas, Gilt, Wood Rod, 1876, 62 x 45 In.	4444.00
Banner, Circus Sideshow, Strange Girl-Alive, Spider, Woman's Head, Canvas, c.1910, 104 x 80 In. *illus*	1175.00
Banner, White Ground, Immaculate Virgin, Flower Border, Embroidered, Silk, 56 ½ x 34 ¾ In.	369.00
Bedspread, Chenille, 2 Peacocks In Center, Blue, Red & Yellow Flowers, 100 x 91 In.	295.00
Blanket, Beaver State, Woodsman Symbols, Black Ground, Wool, Pendleton, 6 ½ x 5 ½ Ft.	230.00
Blanket, Indian Trade Pattern, Multicolor, Wool, Pendleton Co., 73 x 60 In.	403.00
Blanket, Saddle, Geometric Stripe Design, Fringe, Germantown, 1890s	2800.00
Blanket, Wool, Red Field, Sawtooth Medallion, Red, Green, Ivory, Fringe, Mexico, 1800s, 42 x 77 In.	354.00
Blanket, Wool, Twill, Embroidered, Blue, Natural Windowpane, Flowers, 60 x 82 In.	470.00
Canopy, Embroidered, 4 Lobed Panel, 4 Dragons, 5 Taloned Claws, Chinese, 52 x 57 In.	976.00
Curtain, Arts & Crafts, Brown, Blue & Green Stylized Flowers, Linen, 47 x 95 In., Pair	2880.00
Drapery Swags, Drops, Tasseled, Gold Brocade Print, Ivory Ground, 70 x 53 In., 4 Piece	2091.00
Flag, American, 20 Stars, Hand Sewn, Wool Gauze, 1819, 70 x 115 In.	3185.00
Flag, American, 38 Stars, 1877-99	288.00
Flag, American, Army, Red, White, 7, Letter A, Cotton, Pennant, 7th Cavalry, c.1900, 75 In.	259.00
Flag, Battle, Confederate, Virginia Infantry, Wool, Cotton, Red, Blue & White Saltire, 47 x 50 In.	82860.00
Flag, Confederate, 13 Stars, 3 Bands, Red, White, Cotton, Captured Dec. 1861, 36 x 56 In.	17625.00
Flag, Mourning, Lincoln's Assassination, 34 Stars In Star Formation, 13 Stripes, 5 x 7 In.	2350.00
Mat, Hooked, Moose, Landscape, Multicolor Striped Border, Folk Art, c.1915, 33 x 35 In.	144.00

Teplitz, Teapot, Rooster, Applied Mythological Winged Creatures, Gold Highlights, Signed, 10 In.
$805.00

James D. Julia Inc.

Terra-Cotta, Ashtray, Frog, Impressed, 2 In.
$138.00

Humler & Nolan

Terra-Cotta, Urn, Green & Blue Speckled Glaze, Galloway, 1920s, 41 x 18 In.
$2000.00

Rago Arts & Auction Center

T

TIP
Gold or silver lace may tarnish. Sometimes it can be cleaned by rubbing it with a brush dipped in warm white wine.

Textile, Banner, Centennial, Illinois State Seal, Canvas, American Flag, Wood Rod, 1876, 62 x 45 In.
$3555.00

Skinner, Inc.

Textile, Banner, Circus Sideshow, Strange Girl-Alive, Spider, Woman's Head, Canvas, c.1910, 104 x 80 In.
$1175.00

Garth's Auctions, Inc.

Textile, Panel, Embroidered, American Eagle, E Pluribus Unum, Flags, Frame, c.1900, 22 x 25 In.
$411.00

Garth's Auctions, Inc.

Panel, Altar, Silk Embroidered, Dragon, Cream Ground, Case, Chinese, 18 x 64 In.	310.00
Panel, Apotheosis Of Washington & Franklin, Cotton, c.1800, 32 x 27 In.	225.00
Panel, Brocade, Bolt, Shou Characters, Objects, Yellow, Chinese, 290 x 29 In.	2083.00
Panel, Damask, Applique, Rose Ground, Scrolling, Acanthus, Urns, Italy, 1700s, 70 x 87 In.	3245.00
Panel, Dragons, Vase, Peonies, Chinese, 1800s, 30 x 36 In.	2450.00
Panel, Embroidered, 2 Smiling Figures, Multicolor, Inscribed, Signed, c.1910, 65 x 28 In.	2573.00
Panel, Embroidered, 3 Literary Figures, Multicolor, Gray Ground, Chinese, c.1900, 48 x 10 In.	429.00
Panel, Embroidered, American Eagle, E Pluribus Unum, Flags, Frame, c.1900, 22 x 25 In. *illus*	411.00
Panel, Embroidered, Dragons, Dragon & Cloud Ground, Yellow, Chinese, 35 x 28 In.	6738.00
Panel, Embroidered, Shoulao, Immortal, Crane, Silk, Frame, Chinese, c.1910, 66 x 36 In. *illus*	1593.00
Panel, Embroidered, Silk, Crane, Waves, Green Ground, Black Border, Chinese, c.1710, 36 x 24 In.	1041.00
Panel, Embroidered, Silk, Eagle, Flags, Banner, Silk & Metallic Thread, c.1900, 23 ½ x 27 ½ In. *illus*	294.00
Panel, Embroidered, Silk, Immortals, Symbols, Gold, Silver, Frame, Chinese, c.1860, 64 x 25 In., Pair	1599.00
Panel, Embroidered, Traditional Designs, Black Border, Uzbek Suzani, c.1900, 72 x 77 In.	127.00
Panel, Embroidered, Velvet, Burgundy, Scrolling Flower, Heraldic Crest, 53 ½ x 142 In.	144.00
Panel, George Washington, Horse, Oval Reserve, Shields, Stars, Stripes, c.1876, 18 x 24 In.	1200.00
Panel, Hair Embroidery, Buddhist Figures, Blue Dragon Border, Chinese, 38 x 21 In.	5333.00
Panel, Silk, Embroidered, 2 Roosters, Leaves, Bamboo Frame, Chinese, 21 x 22 In.	179.00
Panel, Silk, Embroidered, Birds, Ducks, Flowering Peony Tree, Frame, Chinese, 48 x 15 In.	359.00
Panel, Silk, Embroidered, Crane, Trees, Hexagonal Boxes, Gold Thread, Japan, 1800s, 24 x 23 In.	239.00
Panel, Silk, Tapestry, Flower Design, 40 x 21 In.	6100.00
Panel, Tapestry, Figural Scenes, Gilt, Frame, 39 ½ x 10 ¾ In., Pair	1464.00
Panel, Tea Ceremony, Embroidery, Silk, Multicolor, Flowering Branches, Frame, 10 ½ x 5 In.	89.00
Panel, Velvet, Elephant, Carrying Objects, Peony Scrolls, Frame, Chinese, 36 x 31 In.	5036.00
Panel, Virgin, Children, Altar, Needlework, Multicolor, Continental, c.1825, 10 x 9 In.	720.00
Panel, Wool, Embroidered, Stylized Flowers, Hand Woven, 1800s, 2 Strips, 55 x 22 In.	29.00
Piano Shawl, Black Silk, Embroidered, Gold Metallic Thread, Flowers, Fringe	155.00
Piano Shawl, Paisley, Scotland, 63 x 133 In.	380.00
Pillow Cover, Linen, She's My Idol, She's My Queen, Smoking, Mat, Frame, 22 In. *illus*	330.00
Pillow, Chintz, Glazed, Central Flower Urn, Vine Border, 24 ½ x 16 In., Pair	1304.00
Pillow, Embroidered Flowers, Leaves, Cream, Pink, Fringe, Aubusson Style, 22 x 22 In., Pair	360.00
Rank Badge, Silk, Embroidered, Metallic Thread, Chinese, Frame, 1800s, 11 x 12 In.	1495.00
Scroll, Gold, Black, Silk, Velvet, Rosewood Hanger, Chinese, Late 1800s, 43 x 25 In.	1094.00
Tablecloth, Black On Red, Thin Red Lines, Signed Vera, 1960s, 52 x 70 In.	75.00
Tablecloth, Linen, White, Embroidered, Cutwork, Round, c.1915	35.00
Tapestry, Basket, Flowers, Scrolling, Green, Orange, Pink, 42 x 51 In.	60.00
Tapestry, Butterfly, Abstract, Multicolor, Wool, Woven, Wood Frame, c.1970, 33 x 48 In.	237.00
Tapestry, Couple In Fishing Boat, Flower Border, France, Flanders, 1600s, 105 x 86 In.	2813.00
Tapestry, Figures, Wooded Landscape, Aubusson Style, 55 x 65 In.	864.00
Tapestry, Flemish Style, Forest Landscape, Cottage, Stream, Goat, Floral Border, 80 x 83 In.	1062.00
Tapestry, Forest, Deer, Trees, Rocks, Distant Castle, Blue & Tan, Wall, Italy, 53 x 79 In.	270.00
Tapestry, Geometric, Wool, Embroidered, Frank Stella, c.1976, 9 Ft. 10 In. *illus*	3720.00
Tapestry, King & Queen, On Horseback, Entourage, Belgium, Flanders, c.1700, 92 x 68 In.	6250.00
Tapestry, Leaves, Stork & Owl, Armorial Medallions, 17th Century, 8 Ft. 9 In. x 10 Ft.	4130.00
Tapestry, Magicscope Weave, Blue, Gray Circles, Feliciano Bejar, Mexico, 1973, 28 ½ x 37 In.	744.00
Tapestry, Medieval Landscape, Castle, Velvet, Tassel Fringe, 17th Century, 78 x 47 ½ In.	777.00
Tapestry, Mother & Child, Figures, Hand Woven, Gilt Gesso Frame, 1800s, 58 x 46 In.	767.00
Tapestry, Panel, Heron, Wooded Landscape, Village, Continental, c.1800, 57 x 44 In.	1195.00
Tapestry, Panel, Wooded Landscape, Bird, Town, Aubusson, c.1700, 93 x 73 In.	5000.00
Tapestry, Turquoise, Alexander Calder, Maguey Fiber, Bon-Art, c.1975, 57 x 84 In.	7440.00
Tapestry, Woman, Unicorn, Flowers, Wool, Mounted, Wood Stretcher, Multicolor, 71 x 78 In.	448.00
Towel, Show, Red, Blue Deer, Flowerpots, Hanging Loops, Margaret Grubb, 1834, 56 x 18 In.	121.00
Valance, Embroidered, Taupe Silk Band, Orange Panels, Couched, Dragons, Clouds, 43 x 37 In.	184.00
Wall Hanging, ABC Nursery Alphabet, Dean's Rag Book Co., London, c.1916, 30 x 19 In. *illus*	775.00
Wall Hanging, Wheeled Cart, Flowers, Leaves, Silk, Chinese, 8 x 5 In.	3600.00

THERMOMETER is a name that comes from the Greek word for heat. The thermometer was invented in 1731 to measure the temperature of either water or air. All kinds of thermometers are collected, but those with advertising messages are the most popular.

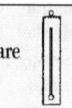

Auto King Motor Oil Still Flows When Temperature Gets Down There, Wood, 21 x 8 In.	339.00
Bireley's, Bottle, Orange Soda, Cap, Tin, 1950s, 13 ½ In.	210.00
Booster, Refreshing Drink, Bottle, Round, 1940s, 9 In. Diam.	210.00
Cheer Up, Round, Pam-Style, A Sparkling Refresher, Bottle, White, Blue, Red, c.1945, 12 In. Diam.	240.00
Cloverdale, Ginger Ale, Stays Lively Longer, Round, Pam-Style, Clover, 12 In. Diam.	150.00
Crescent Wall Paper Cleaner, Wood, Painted, 4 x 15 In.	110.00
Delco Batteries, Tin, White, 1950s, 8 x 38 In.	138.00

Dr Pepper, When Hungry, Thirsty Or Tired, Good For Life, Bottle, Yellow, Red, Tin, c.1945, 25 In..		300.00
Drink Barq's Its Good, Bottle Graphics, Tin, 26 x 10 In.		170.00
Drink Wishing Well Orange, Orange, Bottle, Arched Top, 1960s, 40 ½ In.		360.00
Esso Service Station, Dial Type, Aluminum, Glass, 17 x 17 In.		330.00
Eveready Prestone Anti-Freeze Does Not Boil Away Tin, 36 x 8 In.		198.00
Exide Batteries, Logs, Round, 12 In.		311.00
Ex-Lax, Light Blue, Red & White, 36 x 8 In.		150.00
Fleet-Wing Gasoline Motor Oil, White, Glass Front, Round, 12 In.		283.00
Gilbey's Whiskey, Multicolor, Under Glass, 9 In. Diam.		40.00
Ginger Ale, Take Home A-Treat, Finer Beverages, Bottle, Tin, Round Top, 1950s, 39 In.		360.00
Golden Sun Drop, Goodness, Relax & Enjoy Every Golden Drop, Bottle, Green, Tin, 1960s, 27 In.		300.00
Green Spot Fruit Drinks, Tin, 24 x 8 In.		226.00
Gulf Oil Co., No-Nox Gasoline, Metal, 26 x 7 In.		495.00
King Midas Flour, Minneapolis, Minn., Porcelain, 7 x 27 In.	*illus*	1100.00
L.S. Congdon & Sons, Funeral Directors, Wallingford, Vermont, Metal, 1800s, 38 In.		288.00
Lowe's Kitty Litter, Round, Multicolor, 12 In.		354.00
Maxwell House Coffee, Cup, Drip, Round, White, Black, Pale Blue, 1940s-50s, 12 In.		330.00
Mobil Freezone, Mobil Perma Zone, Pegasus, Tin, 36 x 8 In.		226.00
Mobiloil, All Weather Protection, Pegasus, Can, Round, 12 ¼ In. Diam.		450.00
Nature's Remedy, NR To-Night Tomorrow Alright, 25 Cents A Box, Blue & White, Porcelain, 27 In..		360.00
Nesbitts, Orange Soda Bottle, Tin, 1950s, 17 ¼ In.		180.00
Orange Crush, Tin, Bottle Shape, 1950s, 28 ½ In.		210.00
Pocket, Compass, Bone Scale, Round, Hinged Red Leather Case, 1800s, 3 In.		1126.00
Polar Bear Ice Cream, Bears Watching Plane Flying, 10 x 8 In.		288.00
Prestone Anti-Freeze Magnetic Film, Porcelain, 36 x 9 In.		198.00
Prestone Anti-Freeze You're Safe & You Know It, Porcelain, 36 x 9 In.		311.00
Quaker State Motor Oil, It's A Lucky Day For Your Car, Tin, 39 x 8 In.		125.00
Ramon's Brownie Pills, Little Doctor, Real Laxative, Yellow, Green, Tin, 1940s, 21 x 9 In.		450.00
Raybestos Fan Belt, Tin, 31 x 10 In.		339.00
Red Crown Gasoline, Porcelain, Red, White, Blue, Wood Frame, 19 x 72 In.		1680.00
Sauer's Pure Vanilla, Wood, 1918, 8 x 22 In.		532.00
Squirt, Tin, Bottle, Boy, Green, Yellow, 1961, 13 ½ In.		150.00
Trico Wiper Blades & Solvent, Red, Glass, Metal, Round, 12 In.		170.00
Valvoline, The World's First Motor Oil, Yellow, Glass Front, Round, 12 In.		424.00
Vess Cola, In Your Favorite Flavors, Bottle, Boy, Round, Dial, 1950s, 12 In. Diam.		420.00
Whatever You Do Read The Daily News, Porcelain, 8 x 39 In.		413.00
Whistle, Tin, Bottle, 2 Elves, Arched Top, Thirsty? Just Whistle, Orange, Navy, 1940s, 21 In.		270.00
Wiper Blades, Solvent, Round, 12 In.		226.00
Zodiac, Medallions, Interlaced Design, Signed, Tiffany, 8 x 4 In.		1438.00

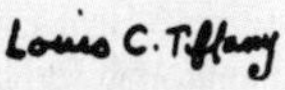

TIFFANY is a name that appears on items made by Louis Comfort Tiffany, the *Louis C. Tiffany* American glass designer who worked from about 1879 to 1933. His work included iridescent glass, Art Nouveau styles of design, and original contemporary styles. He was also noted for stained glass windows, unusual lamps, bronze work, pottery, and silver. Tiffany & Company, often called "Tiffany," is also listed in this section. The company was started by Charles Lewis Tiffany and Teddy Young in 1837 in New York City. In 1853 the name was changed to Tiffany & Company. Louis Tiffany (1848-1933), Charles Tiffany's son, started his own business in 1879. It was named Louis Comfort Tiffany and Associated American Artists. In 1902 the name was changed to Tiffany Studios. Tiffany & Company is still working today and is best known for silver and fine jewelry. Louis worked for his father's company as a decorator in 1900 but at the same time was working for his Tiffany Studios. Other types of Tiffany are listed under Tiffany Glass, Tiffany Gold, Tiffany Pottery, or Tiffany Silver. The famous Tiffany lamps are listed in this section. Tiffany jewelry is listed in the Jewelry and Wristwatch categories. Some Tiffany Studio desk sets have matching clocks. They are listed here. Clocks made by Tiffany & Co. are listed in the Clock category. Reproductions of some types of Tiffany are being made.

Blotter Ends, Pine Needle, Bronze, c.1910, 8 In.		185.00
Bookends, Grapevine, Bronze Dore, Caramel Slag Glass, Expandable, 6 ¼ x 19 In.		770.00
Bookends, Pine Needle, Adjustable, Green Striated Glass, Bronze Overlay, Signed, 14 x 19 In.	*illus*	4313.00
Bookends, Religious Symbols Panels, Bronze, Parcel Gilt, 1920s, 6 x 4 ¾ In.		1364.00
Bookends, Seashell, Bronze, Dark Patina, Tiffany Studios, 4 ¾ x 4 ½ In.		593.00
Bookrack, Grapevine, 2 Hinged Plates, Green Slag Glass, Expands, 6 x 14 In.		1298.00
Bowl, Bronze, Favrile Gilt, Clipper Ship Medallion, Footed, Marked, Tiffany Furnaces, 3 ¾ x 8 ¼ In.		230.00
Bowl, Bronze, Gold Dore Patina, Signed Tiffany Studios, 10 x 3 ¾ In.		413.00
Bowl, Spun Metal, Bronze Finish, Jeweled Edge, 9 ½ In.		270.00
Box, Bronze, Pine Needle, Square, Hinged Top, Spherical Feet, 3 x 7 In.		519.00
Box, Grapevine, Bronze Dore, Caramel Slag Glass, Hinged Lid, 3 x 4 x 6 In.		490.00
Box, Stamp, Bronze, Greek Key Design, Hammered, Arts & Crafts, Signed, 4 x 2 x 1 In.		805.00

Textile, Panel, Embroidered, Shoulao, Immortal, Crane, Silk, Frame, Chinese, c.1910, 66 x 36 In.
$1593.00

Skinner, Inc.

Textile, Panel, Embroidered, Silk, Eagle, Flags, Banner, Silk & Metallic Thread, c.1900, 23 ½ x 27 ½ In.
$294.00

Garth's Auctions, Inc.

Textile, Pillow Cover, Linen, She's My Idol, She's My Queen, Smoking, Mat, Frame, 22 In.
$330.00

Showtime Auction Services

T

Textile, Tapestry, Geometric, Wool, Embroidered, Frank Stella, c.1976, 9 Ft. 10 In.
$3720.00

Rago Arts & Auction Center

Textile, Wall Hanging, ABC Nursery Alphabet, Dean's Rag Book Co., London, c.1916, 30 x 19 In.
$775.00

Aleph-Bet Books

Thermometer, King Midas Flour, Minneapolis, Minn., Porcelain, 7 x 27 In.
$1100.00

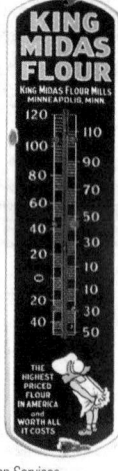

Showtime Auction Services

Tiffany, Bookends, Pine Needle, Adjustable, Green Striated Glass, Bronze Overlay, Signed, 14 x 19 In.
$4313.00

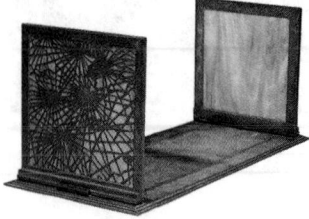

James D. Julia Inc.

Box, Venetian, Gold Dore, Wood Liner, Signed, No. 1680, 5 ½ x 4 In.	1140.00
Bust, Woman, Surrounded By Flowers, Art Nouveau, Bronze, Marked, c.1900, 9 x 5 In.	1440.00
Calendar Holder, Pine Needle, Signed, c.1900, 4 ½ x 6 ¼ In.	690.00
Candelabrum, 3-Light, Bronze, Blown Glass Candle Supports, Snuffer, Signed, 14 In. *...illus*	5463.00
Candelabrum, 3-Light, Flowers, Fluted Branches, Monogram, Tiffany & Co., 13 x 13 In., Pair	2300.00
Candelabrum, 6-Light, Green Favrile, Bronze Frame, Fitted Center Snuffer Post, 15 ½ x 21 In.	9490.00
Candelabrum, 6-Light, Patinated Bronze, Green Favrile Glass Cup Insets, Stamped, 15 x 22 In.	3720.00
Candelabrum, 8-Light, Bronze, Cup Favrile Glass Insets, Center Stem, Marked, 1910, 15 x 29 In..	19840.00
Candlestick, 2-Arm, Jeweled, Turtleback, Bulbous Cups, Handle, Shaped Base, Green Patina, 3 x 7 In.	5463.00
Candlestick, 3-Arm, Bronze, Brown Patina, Urn Holder, Bobeche, Marked, 21 In., Pair	1093.00
Candlestick, Bronze, Bamboo Design Stem, Round Foot, Cutout, Early 1900s, Marked, 10 In., Pair.	1875.00
Candlestick, Bronze, Gold Dore, Urn Support, Double Knopped Stem, Swirled Foot, Marked, Pair *illus*	1840.00
Candlestick, Bronze, Reticulated, Glass Socket, Flower Shape, Knopped Stem, 1900s, 20 In., Pair.	1250.00
Candlestick, Enameled, Peacock Blue, Green Highlights, Inverted Saucer Foot, 9 In., Pair.....	3450.00
Candlestick, Green Inserts, Iridescent Hanging Prisms, Pierced Bronze Cap, 30 In.	9200.00
Candlestick, Snuffer, Favrile Glass, Pulled Feather, Marked, 9 ½ x 5 In. ....*illus*	2604.00
Casket, Jewelry, Grapevine, Green Glass Inserts, Verdigris Patina, Hinged, 9 ½ x 6 ½ In.	1179.00
Chandelier, 6-Light, 88 Gold Iridescent Prisms, Shaped Hammered Bronze Base, 33 x 28 In.	10030.00
Charger, Favrile, Purple Iridescent, Bronze Mounted, 17 In. Diam.	2091.00
Cigarette Box, Zodiac, Bronze, Enameled, 6 Medallions On Sides, Marked, 2 x 4 ½ In. ......*illus*	1380.00
Desk Calendar, Torch, Medallions, Dragons, Gilt Bronze, 1935, 6 In.	1793.00
Desk Set, Abalone, Bronze, 5 Piece	3163.00
Figure, Goat, Bronze, Textured, Russian Inscription, 5 ½ x 5 In.	1652.00
Frame, Abalone, Bronze, Gold Dore Patina, Marked, 7 x 9 In.	2280.00
Frame, Chinese Pattern, Bronze, No. 1757, Marked, 8 ¾ x 7 ½ In.	960.00
Frame, Grapevine, Mottled Turquoise Glass, 2 Ovals, Beaded Edge, 7 x 10 In.	2006.00
Frame, Modeled Pattern, Bronze, Marked Tiffany Studios, 11 x 9 In.	952.00
Frame, Pine Needle, Bronze Dore, Caramel Slag, Easel Back, 14 x 12 In.	2489.00
Frame, Pine Needle, Bronze, Green Slag Glass, 7 x 8 ½ In.	506.00
Frame, Zodiac, Gold Color, Square, Marked, 7 x 8 In.	1553.00
Humidor, Grapevine, Green Striated Glass, Ball Feet, Bronze Beading, Signed, 4 x 7 In.	1035.00
Inkwell, Blown Glass, Melon Panels, Bronze, Hammered, Hinge Lid, Signed, 5 ½ In.	4629.00
Inkwell, Bronze, Favrile Glass Inclusions, Round, Footed, Marked, 4 x 4 In.	7440.00
Inkwell, Bronze, Grapevine, Cup Shape, Flare Rim, 2 x 2 In.	91.00
Inkwell, Bronze, Pine Needle, Round, Green Striated Glass, Signed, 2 x 4 In.	978.00
Inkwell, Grapevine, Hinged, Filigree Over Slag Glass, Impressed, 2 ¾ x 3 In.	345.00
Inkwell, Pine Needle, Caramel Slag Glass, Round, Squat, Hinged Lid, 3 ½ x 7 In.	563.00
Inkwell, Zodiac, Bronze, Gold Dore, 6-Sided, Glass Insert, 6 ½ x 3 ½ In.	401.00
Lamp, 3-Light, Bronze, 12 Spine Stem Standard, 4-Footed Base, Marked Tiffany Studios, 20 x 9 In.	4972.00
Lamp, 3-Light, Hexagonal Bronze Stem, Shade Amber Favrile Fabrique, c.1905, 23 x 20 In.	11500.00
Lamp, 3-Light, Lily Glass, Bronze Artichoke Base, Signed, 9 In.	3163.00
Lamp, Arabian, Shade, Green Favrile, Gold Iridescent Highlights, Signed L.C.T., 14 In.	6500.00
Lamp, Ashtray, Removable Magazine Rack, Footed Base, Floor, N.Y., 1920s	27500.00
Lamp, Base Only, Blue Favrile, Swirl Base, Cord Ready, Marked L.C.T. Favrile, 5 ½ In.	403.00
Lamp, Base Only, Gold Favrile, 3 Applied Button Medallions, Acorn Pull, Marked, 13 In.	426.00
Lamp, Base, Bronze, Patinated, Cabochon Glass, Fluted Foot, c.1900, 18 In.	5079.00
Lamp, Bronze Base, Leaf & Vine Glass Shade, Signed, 16 x 19 ½ In.	1440.00
Lamp, Bronze, 3 Arched Arms, Tendrils, Ribbed Base, Flower-Form Amber Shades, 25 In.	8888.00
Lamp, Bronze, Amphora Shape, 3 Supports, Round Base, Stamped, 26 In.	4636.00
Lamp, Bronze, Weight-Balance, Eggplant Weight, Signed, 13 x 15 ½ In.	2006.00
Lamp, Candle, Gold Favrile, Twist Stem, Green Pulled Feather, Scalloped, Signed, 12 ½ In. *illus*	1150.00
Lamp, Ceiling, Flower Shade, Favrile Glass, Gilt Metal Mount, Round, c.1910, 12 In.	5975.00
Lamp, Chandelier, 8-Light, Gold Favrile Inverted Shades, Bronze Fittings, Signed, 53 ½ x 29 In....	25040.00
Lamp, Colonial Shade, Yellow, Leaded, Bronze, Footed, Marked, 7 ¼ x 15 ½ In.	6200.00
Lamp, Daffodil, Green, Yellow, Bronze Stick Base, c.1915, 21 ½ In.	56763.00
Lamp, Desk, Adjustable, Bell Shape, Green, Gold Shade, Signed L.C.T., Tiffany Studios, 5 ½ x 9 ½ In.	3575.00
Lamp, Desk, Blue Turtleback Glass Panels, Bronze Leaf & Bead Base, Glass Cabochons, 14 In..	14160.00
Lamp, Desk, Bronze, Gold Dore, Gold Damascene Shade, Harp, Etched, L.C.T., 19 In.	4720.00
Lamp, Desk, Damascene Design, Gold, Ivory, Domed Shade, Opalescent, Bronze 3-Arm Base, 13 In.	4720.00
Lamp, Desk, Green Damascene Shade, Favrile, Bronze Base, Stamped, 13 x 7 In.	4960.00
Lamp, Desk, Weight-Balance, Adjustable Arm, Pedestal Base, Gold Favrile Shade, 14 In.	7110.00
Lamp, Desk, Weight-Balance, Brass, Adjustable Scroll Arm, Lobed Base, Marked, 17 x 15 ½ In.	1755.00
Lamp, Domed Pomegranate Shade, Leaded Slag, Bronze Base, Stamped, 22 ½ x 16 In.	11780.00
Lamp, Dragonfly Shade, Blue, Green Ground, Favrile, Metal Base, 25 x 20 In.	11500.00
Lamp, Fairy, Green & Blue Shade, Blue Favrile, Swirl Base, Marked L.C.T., 9 x 7 In.	776.00
Lamp, Floor, Bronze, Gold Iridescent Glass Shade, Flower Shape, 5 Point Feet, 53 In. .....*illus*	1652.00
Lamp, Floor, Domed Yellow Geometric Shade, Within Harp, Bronze, Marked, 57 ½ x 14 In.	21080.00

Lamp, Floor, Weight-Balance, Bronze, Etched Damascene Shade, Favrile Glass, L.C.T., 55 x 17 In. *illus*	9300.00
Lamp, Floor, Weight-Balance, Green Favrile Shade, No. 468, Signed L.C. Tiffany, 10 x 52 In....	19200.00
Lamp, Glass Shade, Cream Ground, Green Pulled Feather Design, Harp, Bronze Footed Base, 14 In.	5750.00
Lamp, Gold Iridescent Bell Shade, Bronze Base, Signed, 57 In.	2200.00
Lamp, Greek Key Shade, Green, Hammered Bronze Leafy Base, Curled Feet, 24 In.	26550.00
Lamp, Green Linenfold Shade, Inverted Mushroom Base, Signed, 13 x 19 In.	32400.00
Lamp, Green, Amber, White Glass Shade, Bronze Base, Signed No. 532, 18 x 25 ½ In.	32400.00
Lamp, Kerosene Tank Base, 3 Arms, Footed, Green, Yellow, Geometric Glass Shade, Signed, 16 x 22 In.	9900.00
Lamp, King Tut, 3-Light, Green, Silver Iridescent, Artichoke Base, Rope Twist, 26 In.	17700.00
Lamp, Leaded Glass, Acorn Shade, Green, Gold, Mottled Earthenware Base, c.1915, 20 x 16 In.	5676.00
Lamp, Leaded Glass, Spider Web Shade, Gilt Bronze, Urn Shape Base, c.1915, 32 x 15 In.	15535.00
Lamp, Lily, 3-Light, Favrile Shades, Gilt Bronze, Stamped Tiffany Studios, 12 ¾ In.	5980.00
Lamp, Lily, 3-Light, Gold Favrile Shades, Bronze Base, Round Foot, Signed, 13 In.	1495.00
Lamp, Lily, 3-Light, Gold Favrile Shades, Ribbed Bronze Base, 13 In.	5925.00
Lamp, Lily, 18-Light, Favrile Glass, 18 Bronze Stem Supports, Leaf & Pod Base, 22 ½ x 9 In.	8190.00
Lamp, Mosaic Glass, Egyptian Scene, Beaded Fringe, Bronze Base, 26 x 17 In.	6900.00
Lamp, Nautilus, Shell Shade, Bronze Base, Inlaid Shell Border, c.1910, 12 ½ In.	8963.00
Lamp, Peony Shade, Red, Jacob's Ladder Base, Marked, c.1910, 32 x 22 In.	101200.00
Lamp, Piano, Zodiac, Bronze, Copper Color Patina, Signed, Tiffany Studios, 11 ½ x 7 ½ In.	1800.00
Lamp, Piano, Zodiac, Bronze, Signed Tiffany Studios, 11 ½ x 7 ½ In.	1650.00
Lamp, Striated Glass Panels, Yellow, Bronze Twisted Leading, Inverted Saucer Foot, 18 In.	920.00
Lamp, Student, Brass, Copper Plated, Lithophane Shade, Scenic Waterfalls, c.1910, 21 In.	2562.00
Lamp, Student, Double, Acorn Shades, 2 Supports, Arched Handle, Pedestal Base, 29 In.	4720.00
Lamp, Trumpet Shade, Gold Iridescent, Bronze Candlestick Base, c.1900, 23 In.	4930.00
Lamp, Tulip Shade, Yellow, Green Leaves, Mottled Enamel Base, Iridescent, Smokestack, 16 In.	28750.00
Lamp, Weight-Balance, Green Glass Shade, Yellow, & Red Rim, Signed L.C.T. Favrile, 7 x 16 In.	9000.00
Lamp, Zodiac, Turtle Back Tiles, Iridescent, Bronze Base, Adjustable Domed Shade, 10 x 14 ½ In.	9600.00
Lantern, Favrile Glass, Bronze, Round Stepped Foot, Pierced Domed Cap, 17 In.	8625.00
Letter Holder, Nautical, Parcel Gilt Bronze, Stamped, 7 ½ x 11 In.	2728.00
Letter Holder, Nautical, Waves, Dolphins, Shell, 2 Slots, 1849, 7 x 11 x 2 In.	1728.00
Letter Holder, Venetian, Minks Along Border, 4 ½ x 6 ½ In.	550.00
Magnifying Glass, Band Of Ornaments, Carved, Strapwork, 9th Century Pattern Handle, 9 x 4 In.	1298.00
Paperweight, Sphinx, Bronze, Gold Dore, 2 ⅜ x 1 ½ In.	590.00
Pen Rack, Upright, 3 Layers, Bronze Overlay, Grapevine, Green Striated Glass, Signed, 4 x 5 In.	944.00
Plaque, Fairy, Smelling A Flower, Dancing On Water, Crescent Moon, Stars, Bronze, Signed, 19 In.	1955.00
Plate, Wide Flower Border, Gold, Pink, Blue, Yellow, 9 In., 12 Piece	374.00
Postage Scale, 9th Century Pattern, Carved, Cut Strapwork, 8 Applied Jewels, Signed, 3 x 3 In. *illus*	1955.00
Powder Jar, Grapevine, Gilt Bronze, Silvered Copper Insert, Tiffany Studios, 3 In.	429.00
Sconce, 2-Arm, Bronze, Glass Shade, c.1910, 12 x 12 In., Pair	4830.00
Thermometer, Desk, Zodiac Pattern, Gilt Bronze, Easel Stand, 8 x 4 In.	830.00
Tray, Figural, Rooster, Standing On Rim, Bronze, Cold Painted, 6 x 7 ½ In.	472.00
Tray, Metal, Raised Geometric & Floral Rim, Inlaid Abalone Discs, Tiffany Studios, 12 In.	245.00
Trivet, Mosaic, Iridescent, Blue Bolt, Bronze Base, Stamped, 7 In.	11960.00
Vase, Bud, Favrile, Enameled Bronze Base, Circular Foot, Signed, 1920, 11 ½ In.	1840.00
Vase, Gilt Bronze, Flaring, Footed, Stamped, c.1920, 12 ½ x 13 In.	657.00

TIFFANY GLASS

Ashtray, Favrile, Elephant Foot Shape, Gilt Rim, Cigar Rest, Signed, 2 x 4 In.	345.00
Bowl, Aqua Iridescent Glass, Opalescent Leaf Design, Favrile, Round Foot, Signed, c.1900, 8 In. *illus*	398.00
Bowl, Blue Favrile, Footed, Flaring Scalloped Rim, Ribbed Convex Sides, c.1900, 2 ¾ x 6 ¾ In.	1353.00
Bowl, Blue, Iridescent Purple Highlights, Gold, 10 Ribs, Slight Curl, Wavy Rim, 3 x 7 In.	575.00
Bowl, Centerpiece, Blue Favrile, Leaves, Etched, 1925, 3 ½ x 12 In.	992.00
Bowl, Centerpiece, Gold Iridescent, Green Trailing Vines, Columnar Flower Frog, 13 In.	674.00
Bowl, Favrile, Iridescent Cobalt Blue, Round, Petal Rim, Signed, 2 x 6 In.	688.00
Bowl, Favrile, Oval, Scalloped Rim Shading From Purple To Royal Blue, 12 In.	920.00
Bowl, Favrile, Pink & Opalescent Striped, Signed, 5 In.	662.00
Bowl, Flower Frog, Gold Iridescent Favrile, Green Leaves, Vines, Signed, c.1917, 14 ¾ In. *illus*	2588.00
Bowl, Footed, Gold, Favrile, Amber Iridescent, Signed, 6 In.	600.00
Bowl, Fruit, Favrile, Gold Iridescent, Wide Rim, Round Foot, Signed, 8 x 2 In.	460.00
Bowl, Gold Favrile, Flat Rim, 1 ¾ x 4 ½ In.	472.00
Bowl, Gold Favrile, Footed, Paper Label, Ruffles, c.1900, 5 In.	500.00
Bowl, Gold Favrile, Oval, Ribbed Form, Scalloped Rim, 7 ¼ In.	259.00
Bowl, Gold Favrile, Scalloped Rim, Swirling Ribs, Signed, c.1900, 6 In. Diam.	553.00
Bowl, Gold Iridescent, Curled Prunts, Dimples, 2 In.	295.00
Bowl, Gold, Rose, Violet Iridescent, Ruffled Rim, Signed L.C.T. Favrile, 9 ¼ x 2 ¾ In.	546.00
Bowl, Green & Opalescent, Quilted Design, Flared, Crackle Edge, Yellow Base, 12 In.	1770.00
Bowl, Green Leaf & Vine Design, Gold Iridescent, Round, Signed L.C. Tiffany Favrile, 12 x 3 In.	440.00
Bowl, Laurel Leaf, Purple Opal, Gold Iridescent, Wide Ruffle Rim, 2 ⅝ x 6 ½ In.	374.00

Tiffany, Candelabrum, 3-Light, Bronze, Blown Glass Candle Supports, Snuffer, Signed, 14 In.
$5463.00

James D. Julia Inc.

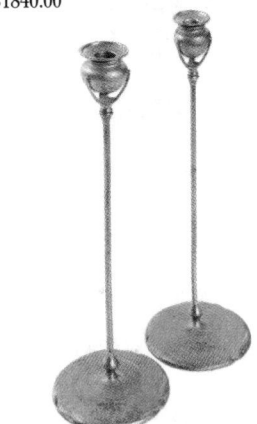

Tiffany, Candlestick, Bronze, Gold Dore, Urn Support, Double Knopped Stem, Swirled Foot, Marked, Pair
$1840.00

Early Auction Co.

Tiffany, Candlestick, Snuffer, Favrile Glass, Pulled Feather, Marked, 9 ½ x 5 In.
$2604.00

Rago Arts & Auction Center

Tiffany, Cigarette Box, Zodiac, Bronze, Enameled, 6 Medallions On Sides, Marked, 2 x 4 ½ In.
$1380.00

James D. Julia Inc.

Tiffany, Lamp, Candle, Gold Favrile, Twist Stem, Green Pulled Feather, Scalloped, Signed, 12 ½ In.
$1150.00

Early Auction Co.

Tiffany, Lamp, Floor, Bronze, Gold Iridescent Glass Shade, Flower Shape, 5 Point Feet, 53 In.
$1652.00

Ivey-Selkirk Auctioneers

Bowl, Laurel Leaves, Opal, Blue, Lavender, Flared Rim, 4 x 12 In.	1150.00
Bowl, Rainbow Iridescent, Gold Intaglio Grapevines Inside, Scalloped, 8 In.	1888.00
Bowl, Ribbed Body, Optic Feathering, Random Intaglio Vines, Signed, 8 In.	450.00
Candle Lamp, Blue Iridescent, Ruffled Shade, Twisted Base, c.1900, 12 ½ In.	3884.00
Candleholder, Gold Favrile, Bowl, Scalloped Rim, Signed, 5 In.	546.00
Candlestick, Clear Stem, White Ribbons, Pink Holder, Ruffled Rim, Signed, 15 ¾ In.	1725.00
Candlestick, Green Pastel, Opalescent Foot, O-Ring, Green, Signed, 6 In.	1300.00
Candlestick, Opalescent, Purple Scalloped Holder, Wide Scalloped Rim, Signed, 1927, 4 In.	863.00
Case, Tapered, Footed, Lily Pads, Gold Iridescent, Signed L.C. Tiffany Favrile, 3 ½ x 9 In.	3120.00
Chalice, Scalloped Rim, Gold Favrile, Signed L.C.T., 7 ½ In.	403.00
Champagne, Gold Favrile, Acanthus Leaves, Signed, 6 In.	288.00
Charger, Gold Favrile, Scalloped Rim, Signed, 10 In.	259.00
Compote, Blue Pastel, Alabaster Stem, Flowers, Butterfly, Etched L.C.T., 4 ½ x 5 ½ In.	2950.00
Compote, Favrile, Footed, Balled Stem, Onionskin Rim, Signed, 3 ½ In.	325.00
Compote, Gold Favrile, Conical Foot, Knopped Stem, Signed, 9 In.	700.00
Compote, Gold Favrile, Flower Shape, Scalloped Rim, Round Foot, Signed, 5 In.	920.00
Compote, Gold Iridescent, Flared & Ruffled Edge, 7 In., Pair	1135.00
Compote, Iridescent Halo, Gold, Scarab Beetle, Ribbed Base, Pedestal Foot, 3 ¼ x 5 ⅞ In.	316.00
Compote, Pastel Yellow Favrile, Flared, Foil Label, 5 x 7 In., Pair	1240.00
Compote, Pedestal Base, Scarab Beetle, Diamond Quilted, Stout Stem, Amber, 3 In.	403.00
Compote, Round Foot, Wide Rippled Rim, Iridescent Blue, Purple, 12 In. Diam.	920.00
Compote, Vine Of Leaves, Gold Favrile, Scalloped Rim, Signed, 6 In.	500.00
Compote, White Opalescent Feathers, 2 Intaglio Flower Stems, Signed, 3 In.	400.00
Cordial, Favrile, Cut Faceted Stem, Bowl, c.1900, 4 ⅝ x In., 19 Piece	5975.00
Cordial, Grapevine, Gold Favrile, Stemmed, Round Foot, Signed, 4 In.	115.00
Cordial, Grapevine, Gold Favrile, Stemmed, Signed L.C.T., 4 ¾ In., Pair	247.00
Decanter Set, Gold Favrile, Etched Flowers, Footed, Stick Neck, 12 Cordials, Signed, 10 In.	1955.00
Decanter, Favrile, Gold Iridescent, Stopper, Signed L.C. Tiffany, 9 In.	950.00
Decanter, Gold Iridescent, Pinched Sides & Stopper, Favrile, 11 In.	2032.00
Figurine, Apple, Signed, 1900s, 3 In.	123.00
Finger Bowl, Underplate, Gold & Blue Iridescent, Ruffled Edge, Pair, 2 ¼ In.	777.00
Finger Bowl, Underplate, Gold Favrile, Scalloped Rim, Pigtail Prunts, Signed, 6 In.	288.00
Flower Bowl, Favrile, Cobalt Blue Iridescent, Round, Molded Center, Signed, c.1919, 10 In.	1875.00
Flower Frog, 2 Layers, Favrile, Signed L.C. Tiffany, 3 ½ x 3 In.	226.00
Flower Frog, Blue Iridescent, Loops, 2 Layers, Favrile, 3 ¼ x 2 ½ In.	243.00
Flower Frog, Green Iridescent, 2 Layers, Lily Pads, Vines, Favrile, Signed, c.1900, 4 x 9 ¾ In. ..*illus*	1541.00
Goblet, Gold Favrile, Flared Rim, Double Molded Tapering Bowl, Round Foot, c.1900, 8 ¼ In.	430.00
Goblet, Gold Iridescent, Shaped Stem With Knop, Flared Rim, 6 ½ In.	508.00
Goblet, Green, Etched Leaves & Berries, Flared Rim, Favrile, 6 ¼ In.	478.00
Goblet, Water, Favrile, Green Iridescent, Cut Cherries & Leaves, Signed, 6 In.	460.00
Loving Cup, Favrile, Green Leaf & Vine, 3 Iridescent Handles, Signed, 5 In.	2300.00
Nut Cup, Gold Iridescent, Violet Highlights, Ruffle Rim, c.1900, 2 ½ In., Pair	345.00
Nut Dish, Blue Iridescent, Vertical Ribs, Wavy Rim, Favrile, 3 x 7 In.	826.00
Paperweight, Coin Dot, Amber Base, Impressed Favrile, 2 ¾ x 3 In.	403.00
Perfume Bottle, Iridescent Gold, Blue Rim, Stopper, Signed L.C. Tiffany, 4 ½ x 4 ¼ In.	431.00
Plate, Gold Iridescent, Rose & Blue Highlights, Raised Rim, Signed, L.C.T.	161.00
Rose Bowl, Violet Iridescent, Ruffled Rim, Signed L.C.T., 4 ½ x 2 ¼ In.	345.00
Salt, Favrile, 3-Footed, Flared Rim, Marked, 1 ¼ x 2 In.	226.00
Salt, Gold Favrile, Inward Ruffle Rim, Signed, 3 In.	201.00
Salt, Gold Favrile, Iridescent, Turquoise, Witch's Caldron Shape, 2 Pulled Handles, Signed, 2 x 1 In.	460.00
Salt, Gold Favrile, Scalloped Rim, Signed, 4 In.	230.00
Salt, Gold Favrile, Squat, Round, Pulled Glass Pigtail Design, Signed, 2 In.	148.00
Salt, Gold Iridescence, Pinched Rim, Favrile, Signed L.C.T., 3 In.	179.00
Salt, Gold Iridescence, Pinched Ruffled Rim, Signed L.C.T., c.1900, 2 ½ In.	196.00
Salt, Gold Iridescent, Octagonal, Pinched Neck, 1 ½ In., 6 Piece	1135.00
Salt, Gold Iridescent, Ruffled Rim, Favrile, 1 x 2 ½ In.	108.00
Salt, Master, Oval, Ribbed, Scalloped Rim, Favrile, 4 In.	150.00
Salt, Pinched Ruffled Rim, Gold Iridescent, Signed L.C.T., c.1900, 2 ½ In.	207.00
Shade, Domed, Cased Blue, Iridescent Gold Damascene, Signed, 7 In.	4550.00
Shade, Gold Favrile, Pink Iridescent, Flower Shape, Signed L.C.T., 3 x 7 In.	541.00
Shade, Gold Iridescent, Etched L.C.T., 5 ½ x 6 ½ In.	177.00
Shade, Green Damascene Design, Iridescent, Signed, 9 x 5 In.	7200.00
Shade, Green Damascene, Gold Iridescent, Signed L.C.T. Favrile, 9 x 5 In.	7150.00
Shade, Green, Yellow, White, Geometric Tiles, Leaded, 8 ½ x 20 ½ In.	11780.00
Shade, Leaded Glass, Conical Shape, Flowers, Leaves, Beaded Edge, 14 x 28 In.	65000.00
Shade, Oak Leaf & Acorn, Yellow, Leaded Slag, Stamped, 7 ½ x 18 In.	11160.00
Shade, Stalactite, Favrile, Gold Iridescent, Pulled Feathers, Fixture, c.1903, 10 ½ In.	5400.00

Sherbet, Gold Favrile, Conical Foot & Bowl, Pigtail Prunts, Signed, 3 ½ In.		230.00
Sherbet, Green, Lappet Design, Pedestal Foot, Iridescent Inside, Signed, 3 ¼ In., 4 Piece		552.00
Sugar & Creamer, Royal Blue Opalescent, Clear & Opaque, Pinched, Footed		1003.00
Tazza, Blue Iridescent, Flared & Flattened Rim, Crackle Edge, Trumpet Foot, 2 x 8 In.		2006.00
Toothpick Holder, Gold Favrile, 1 ¾ In.		206.00
Toothpick Holder, Gold Favrile, Pinched Sided, Signed, 2 In.		173.00
Toothpick Holder, Lily Pad, Favrile, Gold Iridescent, Marked L.C.T., c.1900, 2 ³⁄₁₆ In.		316.00
Vase, Amber, Blue, Trailing Vines, Tapered Undulating Sides, 9 In.		50788.00
Vase, Baluster, Round Foot, Iridescent Blue, Hooked Design On Neck, 8 In.		1150.00
Vase, Blue Agate Glass, Gold Iridescent, Silver Spatter, Favrile, Signed, c.1899, 5 ½ In.	*illus*	1150.00
Vase, Blue Favrile, Ribbed, Scalloped Rim, Footed, Signed, c.1918, 15 In.	*illus*	2128.00
Vase, Blue Iridescent, 5 Feathery Plumes, Stick Shape, Spread Foot, 8 In.		1610.00
Vase, Blue, Green Iridescent, Waisted, 2 In.		240.00
Vase, Bud & Flower Form, Gold Iridescent, Elongated Stem, Footed, 1900, 10 In.		2868.00
Vase, Bud, Cobalt Blue Iridescent, Leaves, Bulbous Base, Stick Neck, Favrile, c.1919, 6 In.		2125.00
Vase, Bud, Flared Rim, Yellow, Pedestal Foot, Favrile, 10 x 3 ¼ In.		1495.00
Vase, Bud, Gourd Shape, Leaf Pattern, Favrile, Signed, 8 ½ In.		1612.00
Vase, Bud, Trumpet Shape, Favrile, Signed L.C.T., c.1920, 11 ¾ In.		1680.00
Vase, Bud, Trumpet, Yellow Shaded To Opalescent, Bulb & Disk Foot, Favrile, 6 In.		735.00
Vase, Bulbous, Platinum Gold, Green Striated Heart & Vine, 4 ½ In.		600.00
Vase, Cameo Cut, Favrile, Rounded Shape, Grape Leaf Design, Paper Label, Signed, 8 ¼ In.		1208.00
Vase, Carved Yellow & White Flowers, Leaf & Vines, Bulbous, Squat, Gold Favrile, Signed, 6 x 6 In.		6038.00
Vase, Cobalt Blue Iridescent, Urn Shape, Flared Rim, Favrile, Signed, c.1918, 9 In.		875.00
Vase, Corona Flower Shape, Iridescent Gold, Ruffled Rim, Pulled Feather Tip, 14 In.		1150.00
Vase, Corset Shape, Iridescent Gold, Engraved, 4 In.		196.00
Vase, Corset Shape, King Tut, Opal Glass, Swirling Green & Gold Favrile, 4 In.		805.00
Vase, Corset Shape, Reticulated, Pinch Sided Rim, Geometric Openings, Gold Favrile, Signed, 4 In.		805.00
Vase, Cream Iridescent, Green Pulled Feather, Curved Ribbing, Slender Stem, Flower Shape, 14 In.		8625.00
Vase, Cypriot, Green, Blue, Purple, Platinum, Egyptian, Rolled Rim, Gold Dore Stand, 8 In.		10925.00
Vase, Dimpled Oval Shape, Gold Iridescent, Favrile, Signed, 5 In.		549.00
Vase, Double Bulbous, Frosted, Ribbed Neck, Bubbles Design, Light Green, Signed, 20 In.		1035.00
Vase, Double Gourd, Gold Hooked Feather, Green, Signed, 8 In.		2000.00
Vase, Dragon Fly, Flowers, Paperweight, Favrile, Signed, 12 ¼ x 5 ½ In.		5060.00
Vase, Elongated Cup, Band Of Gold Threading, Tadpoles, Conical Base, Gold Favrile, 6 In.		518.00
Vase, Flattened Neck, Bulbous, Spreading Disc Foot, Gold Favrile, 5 ¾ x 6 ½ In.		148.00
Vase, Flower Shape Chalice, Citron Yellow, Molded Stem, Leaf Blades, 9 In.		1093.00
Vase, Flower Shape, Favrile, Green, Gold Iridescence, White Striations, c.1905, 17 In.		8625.00
Vase, Flower Shape, Footed, Bulb Form, Gold, Striated Green Vines, 19 Green Hearts, Signed, 9 In.		2500.00
Vase, Flower Shape, Footed, Coupe Form, Scalloped Onionskin Rim, Signed, 1910, 6 In.		1700.00
Vase, Flower Shape, Gold Favrile, Ribbed, Footed, Tulip Form, Scalloped Rim, Signed, 1913, 15 In.		2588.00
Vase, Flower Shape, Ruffled Rim, Round Foot, Blue Favrile, Signed, c.1909, 5 In.		1495.00
Vase, Flower Shape, White, Green Pulled Feathers, Crackle Edge, Gold Foot, 6 In.		2065.00
Vase, Free-Form, Gold, Oval, Double Band Of Dimples, Label, 4 In.		500.00
Vase, Gold Favrile, Green Leaf Design, Flower Shape, Signed, 3 ¾ x 12 ½ In.		10800.00
Vase, Gold Favrile, Iridescent, Hooked Designs, Gourd Shape, Signed, 6 In.		1200.00
Vase, Gold Iridescent Pulled Feathers, Cinched Neck, Wide Mouth, Favrile, 7 In.		1673.00
Vase, Gold Iridescent, Bulbous, Folded & Pinched, 4 x 3 ½ In.		405.00
Vase, Gold Iridescent, Bulbous, Pinched Form, Favrile, c.1900, 8 ½ In.		956.00
Vase, Gold Iridescent, Green, Leaves, Vines, Bulbous Base, Stick Neck, Favrile, c.1913, 6 In.		1625.00
Vase, Gold Iridescent, Tapered, Favrile, 10 ¼ In.		648.00
Vase, Gold Iridescent, Threaded Center, Magenta Highlights, Beaker Shape, 3 In.		489.00
Vase, Gold Iridescent, Trailing Leafed Vines, Favrile, c.1900, 10 In.		2032.00
Vase, Gold Shaded To Pink Shaded To Blue Iridescent, Drippy Prunts, Cinched, 4 In.		708.00
Vase, Golden Leaves, Green Edged, Trumpet Shape, Pineapple Stem, Round Foot, 12 In.		1495.00
Vase, Green & Gold Pulled Feather Design, 3-Sided Shape, Opalescent Top, Signed L.C.T., 4 x 13 In.		4400.00
Vase, Green Iridescent, Pulled Chain & Swirls, Bulbous Base, Long Neck, Favrile, 7 In.		7703.00
Vase, Green Leaves, Rounded, Coved Rim, Gold Favrile, Signed L.C. Tiffany, 6 ½ x 6 In.		2818.00
Vase, Green, Pulled Feather, Flared, Peach Favrile, Etched Bronze Base, 14 ¼ x 5 ½ In.		1612.00
Vase, Heart & Vine Design, Etched, Blue Favrile, 9 x 4 ½ In.		6200.00
Vase, Hooked Design, Iridescent, Gourd Shape, Gold Favrile, Signed L.C. Tiffany, 6 In.		1100.00
Vase, Iridescent Cobalt Blue & Gold, Tapered, Shouldered, Ruffled Rim, Favrile, c.1900, 4 In.		531.00
Vase, Iridescent Gold, Band Of Favrile Waves, Opal, Blue, Green, Squat, Cylindrical Neck, 3 In.		1265.00
Vase, Iridescent Gold, Inverted Trumpet Shape, Stick Neck, Blue Ring On Foot, 14 In.		920.00
Vase, Iridescent Gold, Pulled Feathers, Opal Rim, Cobalt Blue Base, Favrile, Signed, 9 ½ In.	*illus*	6900.00
Vase, Iridescent Gold, Square Mouth, Gourd Shape, Ribbed, Favrile, Signed, c.1905, 3 In.		563.00
Vase, Iridescent Gold, Tri-Columnar, Open Bowl Rim, Signed, 5 In.		1380.00
Vase, Iridescent Orange, Yellow, Pink Highlights, Swollen Center, Molded Ringed Design, 9 In.		2128.00

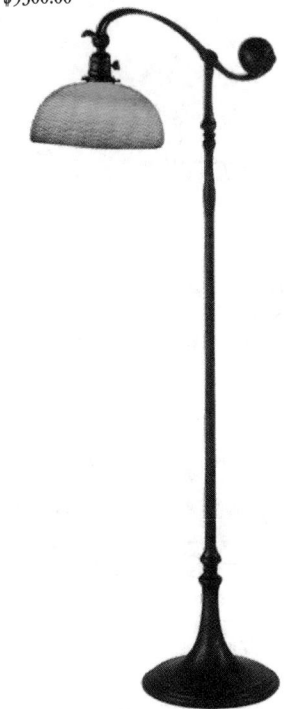

Tiffany, Lamp, Floor, Weight-Balance, Bronze, Etched Damascene Shade, Favrile Glass, L.C.T., 55 x 17 In.
$9300.00

Rago Arts & Auction Center

Tiffany, Postage Scale, 9th Century Pattern, Carved, Cut Strapwork, 8 Applied Jewels, Signed, 3 x 3 In.
$1955.00

James D. Julia Inc.

Tiffany Glass, Bowl, Aqua Iridescent Glass, Opalescent Leaf Design, Favrile, Round Foot, Signed, c.1900, 8 In.
$398.00

T

Skinner, Inc.

TIFFANY GLASS

Tiffany Glass, Bowl, Flower Frog, Gold Iridescent Favrile, Green Leaves, Vines, Signed, c.1917, 14 ¾ In.
$2588.00

Early Auction Co.

Tiffany Glass, Flower Frog, Green Iridescent, 2 Layers, Lily Pads, Vines, Favrile, Signed, c.1900, 4 x 9 ¾ In.
$1541.00

Skinner, Inc.

Tiffany Glass, Vase, Blue Agate Glass, Gold Iridescent, Silver Spatter, Favrile, Signed, c.1899, 5 ½ In.
$1150.00

Early Auction Co.

Tiffany Glass, Vase, Blue Favrile, Ribbed, Scalloped Rim, Footed, Signed, c.1918, 15 In.
$2128.00

Early Auction Co.

Vase, Iridescent Purple, Blue, Flower Shape, Vertical Ribbing, Scalloped Top, Saucer Foot, 15 In.	3450.00
Vase, Iridescent, Green, Purple, Blue, Bulbous, Platinum Design, Gold Favrile, Signed, 9 In....	4025.00
Vase, Jack-In-The-Pulpit, Conical Foot, Ribbed, Onionskin, Face Features, Blue, 1906, 14 In. .	5250.00
Vase, Jack-In-The-Pulpit, Favrile, Gold Iridescent, Signed L.C. Tiffany, 18 In.....................	6500.00
Vase, Jack-In-The-Pulpit, Gold Iridescent, Etched, L.C. Tiffany Favrile, 19 ¾ In. ....*illus*	7380.00
Vase, King Tut, Squatty Form, Caramel Iridescent, Gold Hooked Feather, Favrile, 5 In.	900.00
Vase, Mauve, Blossoms, Hearts, Vines, Favrile, Signed, 9 ¾ x 4 In...	23560.00
Vase, Millefiori Flowers, Leaves On Vines, Blue Iridescent On Green, Oval, 9 In......................	37950.00
Vase, Opal Gold Over Green Pulled Feathers, Oval, Pinched Sides, 6 In...............................	1560.00
Vase, Opal Neck, Green Ribbed Body, Hook Design, Rolled Rim, Signed, Gold Favrile, 7 In.	1955.00
Vase, Opalescent, Green, Gold, Flower Shape, Stem, Round Foot, Favrile, Signed, c.1908, 12 In.	2125.00
Vase, Opalescent, Red Flowers, Green Leaves, Paperweight Design, Orange, Signed, 10 In.......	1725.00
Vase, Orange & Gold Iridescent, Clear Stem, Pinched Flower Shape, Signed L.C.T., 11 In........	1725.00
Vase, Organic Shape, Protrusions, Gold Iridescent Favrile, Signed L.C.T., 3 x 2 ½ In.	413.00
Vase, Oval, Dimpled Sides, Gold Over Green Pulled Feathers, Label, 6 In..............................	1300.00
Vase, Peach, Coral, Ribbed, Green Transparent Stem, Iridescent, Flower Shape, Gold Favrile, 13 In.	4025.00
Vase, Peach, Gold Favrile, Dimpled, Iridescent, Cylindrical, 8 In.	649.00
Vase, Pear Shape, Rolled Rim, Ribs, Thumbprint Depressions, Amber, Gold, 5 In.	690.00
Vase, Pinched Gourd Shape, Gold Iridescent, Signed L.C. Tiffany, Favrile, 4 ½ In................	550.00
Vase, Platinum Design, Vertical Ribbing, Sapphire Blue Favrile, Flower Shape, Signed, 12 In.	2875.00
Vase, Prunt, Yellow Favrile, Ruffled Rim, Signed L.C.T., 8 In...	719.00
Vase, Pulled Designs, Yellow Favrile, Bulbous, Signed L.C.T., 6 x 6 In.................................	1200.00
Vase, Pulled Feather, Iridescent Pink, Blue, Swollen Center, Flare Rim, Gold Favrile, Signed, 3 x 4 In.	920.00
Vase, Pulled Feathers, Green, White, Yellow, Flower Shape, Scalloped Rim, Signed, 5 x 14 In. .	6050.00
Vase, Pulled Green Leaf & Vine, Gold Iridescent, Flared, Footed, Signed L.C. Tiffany Favrile, 6 x 11 ¾ In.	1150.00
Vase, Pulled Green Leaves, 3 Handles, Pink, Gold Favrile, Signed L.C. Tiffany, 5 ¾ x 6 In.........	935.00
Vase, Pulled Prunts, Iridescent Blue, Green, Purple, Vertical Ribbing, Swollen, Favrile, 6 In....	2013.00
Vase, Red Favrile, Yellow, c.1927, 3 ½ x 2 ½ In...	3224.00
Vase, Ribbed, Flower Shape, Iridescent Orange, Green, Ruffled Onionskin Rim, c.1900, 14 In...	10350.00
Vase, Ruffled Flower Shape, Green Stem, Folded Foot, Gold Iridescent, Label, 14 In.	8400.00
Vase, Shouldered, Scalloped Rim, Ribbed, Gold Favrile, Signed, 3 ½ In.	518.00
Vase, Slender, Green, Pulled Feather Design, Footed, Signed L.C.T., 3 x 9 ½ In.	6600.00
Vase, Stopper, Bottle Shape, Gold Favrile, Signed, c.1900, 8 In.	960.00
Vase, Striated Pastel Purple, Trumpet Shape, Round Clear Foot, Signed, 1881, 7 In.	1265.00
Vase, Tel El Amarna, Egyptian Collar, Peacock Blue Iridescent, Pulled Zigzag, c.1910, 5 In.	4083.00
Vase, Trumpet Shape, Footed, Green Opalescent, Flaring Rim, Signed, 9 In.	600.00
Vase, Trumpet, Gold Iridescent, Knop, Domed Foot, Favrile, 14 In......................................	1434.00
Vase, Trumpet, Pulled Feather, Bronze Base, Signed, 16 ¾ x 6 In.	690.00
Vase, Tulip, Gold Iridescent, Fluted Sides, Undulating Rim, Domed Foot, 15 In.....................	1912.00
Vase, Turquoise Blue Iridescent, Green Trailing Vine & Leaves, Baluster, 9 In.	7469.00
Vase, Vertical Ribs, Long Neck, Scalloped Rim, Gold Favrile, Iridescent, Signed, 4 ½ x 8 ½ In. .	935.00
Vase, Yellow Favrile, Gold Pulled Designs, Iridescent, Bulbous, Signed, 6 x 6 In.....................	1320.00
Vase, Yellow Pastel, Footed, Trumpet Form, Signed, 1873, 6 ½ In.	335.00
Vase, Yellow, Gold Pulled Feather, Green Tips, Oval, 3 In. ....*illus*	690.00
Vase, Yellow, Green Favrile, Flower Shape, Long Stem, Etched, 11 x 4 In..............................	3596.00
Whiskey, Gold Iridescent, Dimpled Sides, 2 In., 6 Piece..	613.00
Window, Blue, Green River Landscape, Mottled, Rippled, Frame, Signed, 1916, 38 ½ x 38 In. ..	132000.00
Window, Stained Glass, Center Double Handle Urn, Ribbons, Garland, Jewels, c.1880, 21 x 24 In.	11500.00
Window, Stained Glass, Horizontal Tiles, Flower Center, Turtleback Tiles, 21 x 36 In., Pair	5975.00
Window, Stained Glass, Medallion, Stylized Trailing Vines, Turtleback Tiles, Frame, c.1890, 27 x 51 In.	1912.00
Wine, Acanthus Leaves, Lily Pad Foot, Gold Favrile, Signed, 6 In.......................................	345.00
Wine, Acanthus Leaves, Lily Pad Foot, Gold Favrile, Signed, 7 In.......................................	460.00
Wine, Green Iridescent, Free-Form Favrile Swirl Design, Ribbed Cup, Opalescent Swags, c.1896, 8 In.	1610.00
Wine, Iridescent, Swirling Favrile Design, Ribbed Cup, Wispy Opalescent Highlights, c.1896, 8 In.	1380.00
Wine, Long Stemmed, Ribbed, Favrile Swirling, Green To Iridescent, Signed, 1896, 7 ½ In......	1380.00
Wine, White Opalescent, Ribbed, Gold Inside, Flared, Disc Foot, Favrile, 5 ⅜ In.	184.00
TIFFANY GOLD	
Pencil Ruler, Measurements, 14K Gold, Extends 2 ½ To 6 In..	510.00
TIFFANY POTTERY	
Vase, Jack-In-The-Pulpit, Molded Leaves, Blue, Red, Green, Yellow, Leaf Handles, 1906, 13 In.	1770.00
Vase, Old Ivory Glaze, Inscribed L.C.T., 1909, 9 ½ x 3 ½ In. ....*illus*	2852.00
TIFFANY SILVER	
Asparagus Dish, Liner, Repousse Border, Shaped Flared Rim, Paw Feet, 13 x 10 In................	3220.00
Asparagus Dish, Scrolls, Acanthus, Shells, Paw Feet, Openwork Strainer, 13 x 10 In..............	2124.00
Asparagus Server, Olympian, Pierced, Engraved Scrolls, c.1935, 8 In.	830.00
Asparagus Server, Richelieu, Monogram, c.1892, 7 ¼ In...	657.00

T

Asparagus Tongs, Grapevine, Leaf Pierced Blade, c.1935, 8 In. 1422.00
Asparagus Tongs, Renaissance, c.1910, 7 ¾ In. 1067.00
Basket, Cartouche Shape, Openwork Sides, Scroll & Acanthus Border, 8 x 10 In. 826.00
Basket, Pierced Sides, Flowers, Oval, Swing Handle, Scrolled Feet, c.1900, 7 ½ x 10 In. 863.00
Basket, Shaped Oval, Pierced Sides, Swing Handle, Marked, Tiffany & Co., 7 ½ x 10 ¼ In. 863.00
Berry Spoon, Berry, Blackberry, Kidney Shape, c.1905, 9 ½ In. 652.00
Berry Spoon, Renaissance, Gold Wash, Scallop Shell Bowl, c.1906, 9 In. 830.00
Bonbon Scoop, Vine, Monogram, c.1890, 6 ⅜ In. 474.00
Bookmark, Open Book, Tiffany & Co., 2 ⅝ x 2 ¼ In. 79.00
Bowl, 12-Sided, Scalloped, Tapered, Round, c.1940, 7 In. 497.00
Bowl, Center, Lobed, Embossed Roses, Footed, Bailey, Banks & Biddle, c.1925, 4 ½ x 12 In. 1168.00
Bowl, Center, Round, Upright Leaf Handles, Round Foot, Tiffany & Co., c.1865, 7 x 9 In. 1375.00
Bowl, Center, Seamed, Scalloped Rim, Applied Vertical Leaf Bands, 3 ⅜ x 9 ¼ In. 1920.00
Bowl, Chrysanthemum Border, Flared, Tiffany & Co., 9 In. 546.00
Bowl, Clover Design Rim, Monogram Center, c.1914, 10 In. Diam. 885.00
Bowl, Condiment, Boat Shape, Crescent Leaf, Ball Feet, c.1890, 7 In. 178.00
Bowl, Flower Cartouches, Engraved Swags, Footed, c.1920, 7 ¾ In. 830.00
Bowl, Flower Shape, Scalloped, Round, 5 In. 540.00
Bowl, Fruit, Clover, c.1907, 10 In. 830.00
Bowl, Fruit, Round, Convex Bottom, Pierced Geometric Banding, c.1914, 9 In. Diam. 369.00
Bowl, Fruit, Squat, Hemispheric Shape, Molded Rim, Band, Round Foot Ring, 1925, 9 ¼ In. 1230.00
Bowl, Gilt Interior, Scroll Handles, Egg Border, Pedestal, 1800s, 6 ¾ x 13 In. 1180.00
Bowl, Hammered, Applied Lotus Blossoms, Reeds, c.1876, 2 ¼ x 8 ⅕ In. 6333.00
Bowl, Hammered, Lobed Rim, Tiffany & Co., 1880s, 9 x 2 ½ In. *illus* 1150.00
Bowl, Heart Shape, Pierced, Quatrefoil Diapering, Flowering Vine, C-Scrolls, c.1891, 10 In. 1422.00
Bowl, Lobed Edge, Monogram, Marked, 9 ¼ In. 570.00
Bowl, Lotus Shape, Monogram, Scalloped, Melon Ribbing, 9 In. 575.00
Bowl, Monteith, Scalloped Rim, Lobed, Leaf Design, Ball & Claw Raised Feet, c.1900, 6 x 11 In. 2070.00
Bowl, Reeded Sides, Monogram, Low Flared Foot, c.1880, 6 ½ In. 267.00
Bowl, Ribbed Edge, Panels, Signed, 9 ½ In. 774.00
Bowl, Rose, Footed, Flared & Lobed Rim, Engraved, Hammered, 1949. 1265.00
Bowl, Scalloped Rim, Lobed, Engraved Flowers, Monogram, 11 ¼ In. 660.00
Bowl, Shell Shape, Chased, Leaf, Scroll Handle, 3 Dolphin Feet, Tiffany & Co., 1959, 9 x 11 ½ In. 3081.00
Bowl, Silver Plated Lid, Oval, Applied Flowers, Flower Handles, c.1880, 5 In. 444.00
Bowl, Thistle, Clover Pierced Border, 12 ½ In. 952.00
Bowl, Underplate, Engraved Nesting Birds, Pines, Arts & Crafts, 2 ½ x 6 ½ In. 1035.00
Bowl, Underplate, Hammered, Round, Rolled Rim, Bowl 4 ¾ In., 6 ½ In. 2015.00
Box, Square, Fitted Lid, Applied Rope, Engraved, c.1967, 2 ¼ x 2 ¼ In. 219.00
Box, Vanity, Repousse, Flowers, Domed, c.1890, 5 x 1 ¾ In. 745.00
Bread Tray, Oblong, Cut Corners, Reeded Rim, 1907-38, 11 In. 474.00
Butter Chip, Round Scrolls & Leaves, 1910, 3 ½ In. 178.00
Cake Plate, Acid Etched Classical Scenes, Shells, Husk Swags, Monogram, 11 In. 948.00
Cake Plate, Etched Rim, Footed, c.1928, 3 ¼ x 10 In. 1035.00
Cake Plate, Pierced Rim, Quatrefoil, Leaves, Monogram, c.1910, 10 In. 593.00
Cake Plate, Round, Classical Design, Pierced Rim, Gadroon Edge, A Monogram, c.1920, 11 In. 863.00
Cake Plate, Round, Reeded Rim, 1947-56, 9 ⅞ In. 474.00
Cake Plate, Square, Egg & Dart Border, Scrolls, Flowers, Center Monogram, c.1915, 1 ¼ x 10 ¼ In 920.00
Candlestick, Pierced Cup, Applied Bows, Swags, 5 ¼ In., Pair 374.00
Candlestick, Round Base, Spiral Rope Edge, 6-Sided Shaft, Drip Design Neck, 16 ½ In., Pair. 16100.00
Carving Set, Winthrop, 1907-38, 2 Piece 77.00
Centerpiece, Round, Trumpet Base, Leafy Strapwork, Polar Bear Handles, c.1865, 9 ¼ In. 17775.00
Cigarette Case, Grooved Etching, Signed, 3 ½ In. *illus* 173.00
Cocktail Shaker, Oval Lid, Engraved Crest, Motto, Tapered, Cylindrical, c.1910, 11 In. 2133.00
Coffeepot, Repousse, Pear Shaped, Serpentine Handle, Leaves, Fluting Terminals, c.1875-91, 9 ¼ In. 2015.00
Compact, Medallion, Banded Ribbon Border, Gold Washed Inside 354.00
Compote, Conical, Openwork Dolphin Stem, c.1940, 2 ½ x 5 In. 267.00
Compote, Flower Repousse, Footed, c.1890, 5 x 13 In. 2151.00
Compote, Fruit, Round Bowl, Chased Crosshatch, Oval, Flowers, c.1910, 9 In. 425.00
Compote, Shallow, 3 Strap & Ball Feet, Monogram, 3 ¼ x 11 ¾ In. 711.00
Cup, Cordial, Signed, 1 ½ x 2 In., 8 Piece 660.00
Cup, Travel, 4 Collapsible Layers, Beaded Foot, 4 In. 338.00
Dish, Cover, Beaded Rim, Oval Handles, Monogram, c.1860, 11 In., Pair 3081.00
Ewer, Leafy Scroll Handle & Spout, Applied Leaves, Berries, Female Head, c.1880, 20 In. 9184.00
Ewer, Oval, Embossed, Maidens, Curved Rim, Arched Handle, Tiffany & Co., c.1865, 10 In. 1845.00
Flask, Oval, Chased Butterflies, Cornucopias, Flowers, c.1890, 4 In. 1541.00
Gravy Boat, Neo-Grec Style, Monogrammed EMS, Tiffany & Co., 1870-75, 5 ¾ In. *illus* 657.00
Gravy Spoon, Renaissance, Stem With Button To Reverse, 1907, 12 ½ In. 889.00
Ice Bucket, Cover, Barrel Shape, 2 Handles, Wood Grain Design, Tiffany & Co., 7 x 11 In. 8000.00

Tiffany Glass, Vase, Iridescent Gold, Pulled Feathers, Opal Rim, Cobalt Blue Base, Favrile, Signed, 9 ½ In.
$6900.00

Early Auction Co.

Tiffany Glass, Vase, Jack-In-The-Pulpit, Gold Iridescent, Etched, L.C. Tiffany Favrile, 19 ¾ In.
$7380.00

New Orleans Auction Galleries, Inc.

Tiffany Glass, Vase, Yellow, Gold Pulled Feather, Green Tips, Oval, 3 In.
$690.00

Early Auction Co.

As always, the edited listings in *Kovels' Antiques & Collectibles Price Guide* aren't available on any website, but readers should visit Kovels.com for information on trends, tips, reproductions, marks, old prices, and more!

Tiffany Pottery, Vase, Old Ivory Glaze, Inscribed L.C.T., 1909, 9 ½ x 3 ½ In. $2852.00

Rago Arts & Auction Center

Tiffany Silver, Bowl, Hammered, Lobed Rim, Tiffany & Co., 1880s, 9 x 2 ½ In. $1150.00

Leland Little Auction

Tiffany Silver, Cigarette Case, Grooved Etching, Signed, 3 ½ In. $173.00

Early Auction Co.

Tiffany Silver, Gravy Boat, Neo-Grec Style, Monogrammed EMS, Tiffany & Co., 1870-75, 5 ¾ In. $657.00

Neal Auction Co.

Ice Bucket, Stave & Band Construction, 3 Pt., 8 In.	2124.00
Ice Bucket, Tongs, Signed, Numbered, 5 ½ x 9 In.	1560.00
Ice Cream Server, Dolphin Pattern, 13 In.	1725.00
Ice Cream Server, Wave Edge, Oyster Shell Shaped, Monogrammed, 9 ½ In.	345.00
Kettle, Stand, Faceted Spire Finial, Tapered, Scrolled Supports, Splayed Feet, c.1910, 12 In.	2015.00
Key Chain, Dangling Globe Disc	30.00
Lamp, Jeweler's, Alcohol, Garlands, Bulbous Font, Hinged Lid, Trumpet Base, 7 In.	767.00
Lamp, Spirit, Reeded Scrolled Waist, Wick Lid, Loop Handles, Copper Body, c.1895, 4 ½ In.	1541.00
Letter Opener, Paul Revere Pattern, c.1958, 9 ¼ In.	300.00
Loving Cup, Scrolling Leaf Medallion, Hourglass Shape, 3 Serpentine Handles, 7 In.	1003.00
Loving Cup, Urn Shape, Leaf Capped Scroll Handle, Stepped Base, c.1892, 5 x 7 In.	413.00
Mirror, Round, Frame, Beveled, c.1930, 15 In.	2726.00
Mug, Cylinder, Tapered, Beaded Rim, Lappets, Vines, Ear Handle, Greek Key Foot, c.1860, 4 In.	521.00
Mug, Cylinder, Tapered, Beaded Rim, Scroll Handle, Poseidon, c.1865, 2 ¾ In.	267.00
Nut Dish, Leaf Shape, c.1910, 5 ¾ In.	120.00
Nut Dish, Scalloped, Lobed, Marked, Round, 4 In.	161.00
Pitcher, Cylindrical, Angled Handle, Seaweed, Swimming Fish, Tiffany & Co., 9 In.	17250.00
Pitcher, Pour Spout, Globular, Round Footed Base, Tiffany & Co., N.Y., 7 ¼ In.	510.00
Pitcher, Water, Jug Shape, Flower Garland, Reeded Handle, Paw Feet, c.1891-1902, 9 In.	6573.00
Pitcher, Water, Short Spout, Leaf Engraved, Handle, Trumpet Foot, Monogram, 1855, 13 ¾ In.	4148.00
Pitcher, Water, Shoulder Rim, Monogram, c.1947-56, 6 ¾ In.	1062.00
Pitcher, Water, Urn Shape, Pedestal Base, Scroll Handle, Acanthus, Monogram, 12 In.	1062.00
Pitcher, Wide Spout, Square Handle, Round Foot, Marked, Monogram, 1917, 9 x 9 In.	1380.00
Plate, Stepped Rim, Monogram, Marked, Tiffany & Co., 10 In.	575.00
Plate, Youth, Round, Engraved Inscription, Ivy Vine, 1875-91, 6 ⅞ In.	267.00
Salt, Master, Tripod Base, Lion Mask & Ring, Bowl, Gilt Interior, Spoon, 3 ¼ In., 8 Piece	4371.00
Salver, Molded Wave Edge, Monogram, c.1880, 13 ½ In.	1778.00
Salver, Round, Raised Rim, Engraved Center, Presentation, 1962, 10 ⅞ In. Diam.	461.00
Serving Fork, Grecian, Pierced, 5 Slender Tines, Tiffany & Co., c.1862, 10 In.	215.00
Serving Fork, Serving, San Lorenzo, 9 In.	420.00
Smoking Tray, Matchbox Stand, 2 Compartments, Hand Hammered, 11 x 5 In.	374.00
Stand, Dessert, Clover, Marked, 1935, 4 x 11 In.	1670.00
Stuffing Spoon, Persian, Monogrammed, c.1873-91, 11 ¼ In.	711.00
Stuffing Spoon, Turkey Over Cornucopia, Harvest Bounty, 12 ¼ In., Pair	563.00
Sugar, Basket, Oval, Waisted, Flared Rim, Greek Key Trim, Swing Handle, Parcel Gilt, c.1890, 6 x 4 In.	307.00
Sugar, Round, Rolled Rim, Beaded, Engraved, Rope Twist Swing Handle, c.1850, 4 In.	385.00
Tablespoon, Broom Corn, Monogram, c.1890, 7 ⅛ In., 12 Piece	652.00
Tazza, Round, Shaped, Shell Design, Tiffany & Co., U.S.A., 1914, 10 In.	854.00
Tea & Coffee Set, Engraved Flowers, Scroll Band, Dome Lids, Squat, Oval, c.1890, 5 Piece	3444.00
Tea Set, Kettle, Stand, Burner, Sugar, Creamer, Pointed Lambrequins, Monogram, 1907, 11 ¾ In. *illus*	2370.00
Tray, Art Deco Style, Flat Rim Handles, 11 ½ x 9 ¾ In.	1440.00
Tray, Canted Rectangle, Twin Handles, Monogram, 24 In.	3250.00
Tray, Elongated Oval, Shaped Rim, Monogrammed MSW, Marked, 20 In.	2006.00
Tray, Round, Flower Repousse, Open Work, C-Scroll, c.1900, 10 In., Pair	1300.00
Tray, Round, Footed, Egg, Dart, Tassel Border, John C. Moore, 1 ⅛ x 12 In.	748.00
Tray, Round, Raised Rim, Sterling, Signed, 12 In.	540.00
Tray, Stepped Trim, c.1907-47, 13 In.	1093.00
Tray, Vanity, Rectangular, Unfurling Ferns & Flowers, Scalloped Rim, 1875-91, 6 ⅞ In.	306.00
Tureen, Cover, Rectangular, 2 Handles, Repousse Flower Borders, Leaves, Shells, 11 In.	3658.00
Vase, Art Deco, Flared, Lobed, Tapered, Weighted, 9 In.	127.00
Vase, Bud, Cylinder, Leaves, Flared Foot & Rim, Scalloped, 3 Low Paw Feet, 1875-91, 4 ¾ In.	398.00
Vase, Bud, Scalloped Edge, Monogram, Marked, 10 ¼ x 3 ¾ In.	219.00
Vase, Bud, Trumpet Shape, Round Foot, Scalloped Edge, Monogram, Tiffany & Co., 10 In.	219.00
Vase, Embossed Leaf Design, Tapered, Wavy Rim, Marked, 1908, 11 ¼ x 3 ¾ In.	5300.00
Vase, Flowers, Fan Shape, Tapered, Lobed, Pierced, Flower Base, Paw Feet, c.1905, 11 ½ In.	5629.00
Vase, Oval, Engraved Strapwork, Flowers, Leaves, Loop Handles, Monogram, c.1905, 17 x 7 ½ In.	3393.00
Vase, Trumpet, Acid Etched Leaves, Monogram, c.1920, 12 In.	948.00
Vase, Trumpet, Octagonal, Stepped Base, c.1935, 11 ½ In.	920.00
Waiter, Square, Round Corners, Chased Leaves, Flower Heads, Scroll Feet, 1875-91, 10 In.	1659.00

TIFFIN Glass Company of Tiffin, Ohio, was a subsidiary of the United States Glass Co. of Pittsburgh, Pennsylvania, in 1892. The U.S. Glass Co. went bankrupt in 1963, and the Tiffin plant employees purchased the building and the inventory. They continued running it from 1963 to 1966, when it was sold to Continental Can Company. In 1969, it was sold to Interpace, and in 1980, it was closed. The black satin glass, made from 1923 to 1926, and the stemware of the last twenty years are the best-known products.

Cherokee Rose, Champagne, c.1950, 5 In.	12.00

Franciscan, Cocktail, 4 ⅝ In.	19.00
Franciscan, Wine, 5 ½ In.	23.00
June Night, Goblet, Water, 10 Oz.	34.00
June Night, Tumbler, Iced Tea, Footed, 12 Oz.	34.00
Killarney, Tumbler, Green, Gold Trim, 2 ¾ In.	35.00
King's Crown, Plate, Salad, Cranberry, c.1955, 7 ½ In., 10 Piece	90.00
Royal Thumbprint, Sherbet, Clear, Red, c.1955, 3 In., 10 Piece	55.00

TILES have been used in most countries of the world as a sturdy building material for floors, roofs, fireplace surrounds, and surface toppings. The cuerda seca (dry cord) technique of decoration uses a greasy pigment to separate different glaze colors during firing. In cuenca (raised line) decorated tiles, the design is impressed, leaving ridges that separate the glaze colors. Many of the American tiles are listed in this book under the factory name.

Abstract Landscape, Wood Mount, Harris Strong, 6 x 18 In., 3 Piece,	162.00
Art Nouveau, 3 White Flowers, Green Leaves, Blue Ground, Wood Frame, Tropico Pottery, 6 In.	101.00
Bird, Flower Spray, Yellow Ground, Wood Frame, 11 ½ In.	56.00
Blue Stepped Design, Yellow Ground, Copper Frame, California Faience, 6 ½ In.	138.00
Cat, Stylized, Seated, Whiskers, Gold Ground, Wood Frame, La Mirada, c.1935, 11 x 15 In.	112.00
Cowboy, White Hat, Blue Chaps, Brown Ground, Round, Signed Harding Black, 1944, 5 ½ In.	179.00
Don Quixote, Sancho Panza, Multicolor, 5 ½ In.	28.00
Farmer, Sewing Seed, Multicolor, Square, Arts & Crafts Oak Frame, Signed Mueller, 6 x 12 ½ In.	385.00
Flower, Mosaic, Hexagonal Shape, 4 ½ In., Pair	28.00
Flowers, Multicolor, Black Ground, Square, Claycraft, 7 ¾ In.	138.00
Griffin, Green Matte Glaze, Brown, Marked Edison, 5 ½ In.	22.00
Hay Field, Yellow, Wood Frame, 5 ¾ In.	24.00
Landscape, Incised, Arts & Clay Co., Signed Art Accardi, Paper Label, Frame, 11 x 17 In.	330.00
Landscape, Incised, Marked, Arts & Clay Co., Signed Art Accardi, Frame, 4 ¾ x 10 ½ In.	360.00
Lavender Flower & Buds, Glass Black Border, Impressed, Flint Faience Tile Co., 6 ⅛ In. .....illus	259.00
Mallard, In Flight, Water, Blue, Green, Impressed, Hartford Faience, 12 x 9 In.	7200.00
Man On Horseback, Feeding Phoenix, Brown, Blue, c.1935, 8 ½ x 6 ½ In., Pair	215.00
Man, Stylized, Tadzio, David Plant, c.1958, 61 ½ x 16 In. ....illus	3438.00
Mission San Jose, White Church, Green Ground, Wood Frame, 9 ¼ In.	123.00
Native American, Looking At Blanket, Multicolor, Square, San Jose, Texas, 8 In.	440.00
Peacock, Pear, Raised, Gretchen Kramp, 5 In.	24.00
Plaque, Street In Normandy, Sheep, Buildings, Green, Frame, Signed Arthur Osborne, 11 x 10 In.	2852.00
Roof, Figural, Man, Standing, Giltwood Frame, Chinese, 12 x 4 In.	489.00
Roof, Figural, Mythical Bird, Rider, Multicolor, Chinese, 11 x 13 In., Pair	316.00
Sea Gulls, White, Blue, Orange Ground, Black Frame, 9 ¾ In.	39.00
Stork, Flowers, Butterflies, 2-Tile Design, Shadowbox Frame, 17 x 10 ½ In.	86.00
Stylized Picnic Scene, Multicolor, Wood Mount, Harris Strong, 12 x 24 In., 8 Piece	119.00
Thunderbird, Brown, Tan, c.1930, 7 ¼ x 7 ½ In.	978.00
Tin Glazed, 8-Point Star, Lion, Mountains, Moorish Arches, Flowers, 1800s, 10 x 10 In., Pair.	1107.00
Victorian Couple, Multicolor, Blue Ground, Mueller, Wood Frame, 7 ½ In.	78.00
Wall Hanging, Woman, Mosaic, Multicolor, Harris Strong, 17 ¾ x 11 ⅘ In.	496.00
Woman, Green Profile, Black Ground, Round, Beaver Falls, 3 ⅛ In.	81.00
Woman, Washing Clothes, Tub, Blue Green Glaze, 6 x 6 In.	180.00

TINWARE containers for household use have been made in America since the seventeenth century. The first tin utensils were brought from Europe, but by 1798, tin plate was imported and local tinsmiths made the wares. Painted tin is called tole and is listed separately. Some tin kitchen items may be found listed under Kitchen. The lithographed tin containers used to hold food and tobacco are listed in the Advertising category under Tin.

Biscuit Tin, Woven Basket Style, Painted, 7 In.	35.00
Bowl, Angel, Cymbal, Pierced Wide Border & Foot, Paint, White Ground, c.1825, 10 In.	1230.00
Candlestick, Push-Up, Red Paint, Columnar Shape, Square Base, 3 In., Pair	1659.00
Canister, Tea, Painted Black, Armorial Crest, Pro Tanto Quid Retribulamus, 17 In.	59.00
Chest, Hinged Top Flowers, Brown Ground, Paint, Drop Lock Plate, 15 ¾ x 24 In.	59.00
Churn, Dasher, Slight Splayed Sides, Wood Plunger, 1800s, 23 In.	230.00
Coffeepot, Barrel Shape, Lid, 8 ½ In.	68.00
Coffeepot, Dome Lid, Gooseneck, Cone Shape, Hinged, Finial, 10 In.	34.00
Coffeepot, Gooseneck, Fruit, Flowers, Red Ground, c.1800, 10 ¼ In.	18960.00
Coffeepot, Gooseneck, Punched Tulip Design, Penn., 12 In.	395.00
Coffeepot, Lighthouse, Painted, Stylized Leaves & Fruit, Black Mottled Ground, c.1850, 9 In. ..illus	1067.00
Coffeepot, Punched, Peacocks, Tulips, Willoughby Shade, F. Ehrenfried, c.1835, 10 In. ..illus	940.00
Coffeepot, Punched, Tulips, Brass Finial, Gooseneck Spout, c.1850, 11 ½ In.	470.00
Coffeepot, Wrigglework, Eagle, American Flag, Flowers, Swag, 1800s, 10 In.	7110.00

Tiffany Silver, Tea Set, Kettle, Stand, Burner, Sugar, Creamer, Pointed Lambrequins, Monogram, 1907, 11 ¾ In. $2370.00

Skinner, Inc.

Tile, Lavender Flower & Buds, Glass Black Border, Impressed, Flint Faience Tile Co., 6 ⅛ In. $259.00

Humler & Nolan

Tile, Man, Stylized, Tadzio, David Plant, c.1958, 61 ½ x 16 In. $3438.00

Los Angeles Modern Auctions

Tinware, Coffeepot, Lighthouse, Painted, Stylized Leaves & Fruit, Black Mottled Ground, c.1850, 9 In.
$1067.00

Skinner, Inc.

Tinware, Coffeepot, Punched, Peacocks, Tulips, Willoughby Shade, F. Ehrenfried, c.1835, 10 In.
$940.00

Garth's Auctions, Inc.

Tinware, Sconce, Wall, Stylized Flower, Candle Cup, 1800s, 8 ½ In.
$646.00

Garth's Auctions, Inc.

Tobacco Jar, Cobalt Blue, Cover, Stork Type Birds, Trees, Spanish Moss, Carlton, 6 x 5 In.
$84.00

DuMouchelles Art Gallery

Figure, Bird, Stylized, Full Body, Painted, 1800s, 34 x 24 In.	1528.00
Fountain, Wine, Figural, Drunken Putti, Cup, Flask, Wine Casket, Lid, 23 x 14 In.	430.00
Jug, Water, Figural, Dog, Brown, Green, Yellow, Tail Curled Handle, c.1780, 6 ½ In.	461.00
Lockbox, Book Shape, Inscribed Ladies Cabinet 1843, Painted, 6 x 4 ½ In.	365.00
Mold, Candle, 8 Tube, Square, Strap Handle, 11 In.	62.00
Mold, Candle, 20 Tube, Sheet Iron, Double Loop Handles, Base Tray, 11 In.	106.00
Mold, Candle, 36 Tube, Maple Frame, Red Wash, 1800s, 12 x 13 In.	1998.00
Mold, Cheese, Punched, Irregular Shape, Pennsylvania, 1800s, 8 ¼ In.	1067.00
Rattle, Whistle, For A Good Child, Drum Shape, c.1850, 1 x 4 In.	150.00
Rattle, Whistle, Gavel Shape, c.1860, 5 ¼ In.	100.00
Sconce, Octagonal Light Box, Glass Panels, William Spratling, c.1935, 15 x 10 In., Pair	920.00
Sconce, Tulip Shape, Crimped Edges, 10 ½ x 8 ¾ In., Pair	805.00
Sconce, Tulip Shape, Crimped Edges, American, 10 x 8 In., Pair	805.00
Sconce, Wall, Stylized Flower, Candle Cup, 1800s, 8 ½ In. ....*illus*	646.00
Squirrel Cage, Church Shape, c.1895, 15 x 12 ¼ In.	770.00
Stove Cover, Campbell's Tomato Soup, 2 Piece	95.00
Tray, Circus Clowns & Animals, Lithographed, Multicolor, c.1890, 12 x 9 In.	150.00
Tray, Scalloped Shape, Star, Flowers, Mark W. Spratling, Mexico, c.1935, 14 x 12 In.	240.00
Trunk, Dome Top, Painted, Hinged Lid, Wire Bail, Flowers, Leaves, 1800s, 7 x 10 In.	533.00
Water Cooler, Flowers, Red Ground, Handles, Liner, 1800s, 25 In.	107.00

TOBACCO CUTTERS *may be listed in either the Advertising or Store categories.*

TOBACCO JAR collectors search for those made in odd shapes and colors. Because tobacco needs special conditions of humidity and air, it has been stored in special containers since the eighteenth century.

7 Lucky Gods, Bearded Man Lid, Multicolor, Majolica, Humidor, 7 ½ In.	250.00
Alpine Hunter, Rifle, Game Bird, Terra-Cotta, 1800s, 9 In.	165.00
Alpine Man, Roly-Poly, Bisque, Humidor, 5 ⅛ In.	145.00
Austrian Soldier, Red Coat, Blue Hat, Mustache, 1890, 6 ½ In.	295.00
Barrel Shape, Bakelite, Marble Brown, England, c.1920, 5 ¼ x 3 ¼ In.	65.00
Barrel Shape, Cast Bronze Country Scenes, Lined Interior, France, c.1860	295.00
Barrel Shape, Green Jasperware, White Letters, Pewter Rim, Finial, Humidor, 5 x 3 ¼ In.	250.00
Barrel Shape, Smoking Paraphernalia Designs, Blue, White, Porcelain, 7 In.	75.00
Barrel Shape, Will Rogers Finial, Pottery, 7 x 5 In.	62.00
Black Gentleman, Straw Hat, Bowtie, Bisque, c.1910, 7 In.	155.00
Black Gentleman, White Hat, Red Bowtie, 5 ¼ x 3 ½ In.	550.00
Black Girl, Yellow Bonnet, Porcelain, 1930s, 5 x 6 In.	98.00
Black Hat, Cobalt Blue Coat, Pottery, Toby, England, c.1845, 5 In.	145.00
Blue, Cartouche, Indians, Holland, Delft, 1700s, 9 ⅞ In.	356.00
Burl, Brass Mounts, Hinged Top, Base Drawer, Stand, Humidor, 11 ½ x 11 ½ In.	497.00
Clown, Boy, Bisque, Humidor, Heubach, 5 ½ x 3 ½ In.	650.00
Cobalt Blue, Cover, Stork Type Birds, Trees, Spanish Moss, Carlton, 6 x 5 In. ....*illus*	84.00
Coconut Shell Barrel, Ebony, Elephants, Carved, Burma, 1930s, 10 In.	154.00
Cowboy, Hat, 4 ½ x 9 In. ....*illus*	303.00
Devil, Red, Black Horns, Humidor, Germany, 5 x 5 ½ In.	575.00
Diana, Stag, Deep Blue Ground, Acorn Finial, Barrel Shape, Wedgwood Jasper, 1882, 7 ½ x 8 In.	169.00
Dog, Bonzo, Calico, Multicolor, Porcelain, Japan, c.1930, 5 ¾ In.	315.00
Dog, Bonzo, Orange, Porcelain, Art Deco, c.1925, 5 x 4 ¾ In.	310.00
Dog, Boxer, Head, 1800s, 9 x 7 ¾ In.	1245.00
Dog, Bulldog, Pink Jacket, White Pipe, Majolica, Humidor, Germany, c.1890, 7 ½ In.	365.00
Dog, Hat, Sucking Pipe, Edwardian, Staffordshire, 1905, 5 x 3 In.	245.00
Dog, Pug, Yellow Exterior, Pink Interior, Majolica, Humidor, c.1890, 8 In.	945.00
Doghouse, Dog, Borzoi Saluki, 1890s, 8 x 6 In.	750.00
Enamel Flowers, Black Ground, Gold Bands, England, 1800s, 4 x 6 In.	60.00
Female Portrait, Gray Hat, Flowers, Humidor, Stellmacher Teplitz, c.1900, 6 x 3 ½ In.	325.00
Gentleman, Brown Face, Coat, Horn, Wm. Schiller, c.1890, 8 ½ x 8 ½ In.	495.00
Glass, Fenton Favrene, Grape, Cable Design, Silvery Blue, 7 In.	375.00
Glass, John Middleton, Blenders Of Fine Tobaccos, Lid, Gold, Humidor, Duraglass, 5 x 5 ½ In.	20.00
Gleaners, Gypsies Design, Humidor, S. Wilson, Royal Doulton, c.1909, 5 ½ x 3 In.	249.00
Hippopotamus, Floor Length Coat, Belt, Plumed Hat, Humidor, c.1930, 5 ¾ x 3 ½ In.	75.00
Hooded Face, Majolica, Humidor, c.1890, 4 ½ x 3 ½ In.	75.00
Indian Chief, Pottery, Humidor, 7 x 6 In.	125.00
Inscriptions, George VI, Yellow Crown, Green Ground, Moorcroft, 1937	975.00
Kaiser Wilhelm I, Seated, c.1871, 10 ½ x 6 ¾ In.	195.00

King, Mug In Hand, Crown On Lap, Bernhard Bloch, Bohemia, c.1900, 10 x 7 In.	950.00
Man Smoking, Swirl Of Smoke Shape, Blue, Cream Porcelain, 4 ½ In.	125.00
Man, Pottery, Deep Brown Suit, 13 In.	475.00
Man, Smiling, Gray Hat, Terra-Cotta, Humidor, Signed Bernhard Bloch, 6 In.	325.00
Man, Wearing Fez, Smoking Cigar, Green Suit, Majolica, 5 In.	75.00
Man's Head, Eerie Expression, Terra-Cotta, Signed FG, 9 In.	375.00
Men Sitting, Smoking, Yellow Ground, Royal Winton Grimwades, Humidor, 5 ½ x 5 ½ In.	79.00
Monk, Black Cap, Smiling, Bisque, 4 ½ x 3 ¾ In.	95.00
Monk, Torch In Hand, Wood, Black Forest Carved, c.1880, 9 ½ In.	1395.00
Monkey Head, Wearing Feather Hat, Terra-Cotta	*illus*	460.00
Monkey, Sitting On Melon, Humidor, Majolica, Germany, 5 In.	225.00
Nude Women, Cartouche, Cobalt Blue, Gilt, Twist Finial, Humidor, Rosenthal & Co., 6 x 5 In.	650.00
One Man Band, Barrel Shape, Multicolor, Conte & Boehme, Germany, c.1875, 8 ½ x 5 In.	125.00
Pierrot Clown Head, Pointed Hat, Gray, Cream, Pottery, Marked FD, France, Art Deco, 12 In.	475.00
Pierrot Clown, Peeking From Box, Old Paris Porcelain, 12 In.	575.00
Pipe Smoking Man, Bas Relief, Stoneware, Mocha, Scotland, c.1850, 7 x 6 In.	275.00
Porcelain, Pansies, Green Leaves, Brown Ground, Hand Painted, Woman's, 5 In.	384.00
Porcelain, Priest, Glasses, Holding Book, 10 In.	475.00
Rabbit, Top Hat, Glass Eyes, Wood, 8 ½ In.	58.00
Redware, Cover, Finial, Wm Hill Tobacco, N.Y., 1856.	4600.00
Redware, Incised Bands, Wavy Lines, Manganese Glaze, Applied Handles, 5 ¾ x 6 ¼ In.	144.00
Roosters, Barrel, Wood, Black Forest Carved, 1800s, 8 x 8 In.	395.00
Rosewood, Treen Turned, c.1880, 5 x 4 ¾ In.	300.00
Stoneware, Bristol Glaze, Oval, Beaded, Peach, Ocher, Metal Cover, c.1870, 8 ½ x 3 ½ In.	81.00
Tavern Scene, Pink, Green Jasperware, Barrel Shape, Humidor, Schafer & Vater, c.1910, 3 x 3 In.	250.00
Theodore Roosevelt, Rough Rider Hat, Monocle, Squat, Bisque, Germany, c.1900, 4 ¾ x 3 In.	135.00
Tiger, Green Hat, Majolica, Humidor, 5 In.	125.00
Woman, Flowers In Hair, Marked Royal Floretta Ware, Austria, c.1900, 6 x 5 In.	110.00
Woman, Holding Cup, Terra-Cotta, Marked, 10 In.	*illus*	265.00

TOBY JUG is the name of a very special form of pitcher. It is shaped like the full figure of a man or woman. A pitcher that shows just the top half of a person is not correctly called a toby. More examples of toby jugs can be found under Royal Doulton and other factory names.

Man, Black Face, Standing, Holding Pitcher Of Ale, Lid, Staffordshire, 1800s, 10 In.	1185.00
Man, Monocle, Umbrella, Majolica, France, 7 ¼ In.	94.00
Man, Seated, Pitcher, Wineglass In Hand, Figural Handle, Pratt, 1800s, 9 ½ In.	*illus*	236.00
Man, Woman, Seated, Flower Design Clothing, Hinged Lid, Metal Thumbpiece, 12 In., Pair	385.00

TOLE is painted tin. It is sometimes called japanned ware, pontypool, or toleware. Most nineteenth-century tole is painted with an orange-red or black background and multicolored decorations. Many recent versions of toleware are made and sold. Related items may be listed in the Tinware category.

Basket, Openwork, Ribbed, Leaf, Rope Design, White, Blue Paint, France, 1800s, 8 x 10 In.	472.00
Box, Document, Gold Ground, Red, Green, White Band, Tin Hasp, Wire Handle, 3 ½ x 6 In.	84.00
Box, Document, Japanned, Flowers, Red, Blue, c.1850, 6 x 10 In.	88.00
Box, Document, Stencil Designs, Red Paint, House Shape, 1800s, 10 x 7 In.	115.00
Box, Dome Lid, Japanned Ground, White Band, Berries, Wire Hoop Handle, c.1870, 2 ½ x 4 ¼ In.	84.00
Box, Dome Lid, Stenciled Basket Of Flowers, Black Ground, 1800s, 2 x 6 ½ In.	88.00
Box, Flowers, Black Ground, Ring Handle, 5 ½ x 9 In.	106.00
Box, Sgraffito Decoration, Gilt Enamel, Oval, We May Never Know Sorrow, c.1850, 7 In.	60.00
Coal Bin, Victorian, Flower Sprigs, Black Ground, Mask & Ring Handles, 25 In.	219.00
Coal Scuttle, Black, Red Detail, Brass Handles, Footed, 14 x 12 x 11 In.	180.00
Coffeepot, Handle, Side Spout, Black Ground, Red Tulips, Yellow, c.1870, 8 ½ In.	331.00
Coffeepot, Yellow, Green, Blue Fruit, Red Ground, c.1900	3318.00
Tray, Black Ground, Flowers, Leaves, Gilt Stripe, Shaped Edge, 16 x 20 ½ In.	63.00
Tray, Black Ground, Raised Shaped Lip, Warriors, Pagodas, Garden, Chinoiserie, England, 33 In.	326.00
Tray, Cloisonne, Black Ground, Stand, Bamboo Turned Legs, 1800s, 16 x 29 In.	359.00
Tray, Figures, Garden, Handles, Ebonized Faux Bamboo Stand, 20 x 24 In.	356.00
Tray, Flowering Basket, Raised Edge, Red, Yellow, Black, Handles, 1800s, 24 x 18 In.	201.00
Tray, Flowers, Classical Scene, Red Ground, Oval, England, 1800s, 29 ½ In.	889.00
Tray, Flowers, Red Ground, Open Handles, Oval, 3 x 10 x 6 In.	17775.00
Tray, Fruit Compote & Flower Border, Multicolor, Black Ground, Stand, 30 x 22 In.	317.00
Tray, Fruit, Gold Ground, Cut Handles, c.1945, 22 x 15 In.	27.00
Tray, Gold Design Banding On Rim, Cutout Handles, 1800s, 22 x 31 In.	89.00
Tray, Grape, Leaves, Rolled Edge, Oval, c.1920, 30 x 24 In.	325.00
Tray, Landscape, Swags, Doves, Pierced Frame, Green Ground, Signed Hayden Wells, 22 ½ x 17 In.	179.00

Tobacco Jar, Cowboy, Hat, 4 ½ x 9 In. $303.00

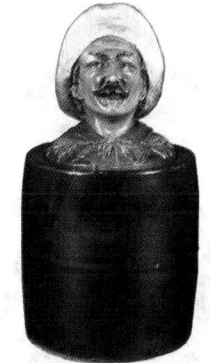

Tobacco Jar, Monkey Head, Wearing Feather Hat, Terra-Cotta $460.00

Tobacco Jar, Woman, Holding Cup, Terra-Cotta, Marked, 10 In. $265.00

TIP
Restring beads on dental floss.

TOLE

Toby Jug, Man, Seated, Pitcher, Wineglass In Hand, Figural Handle, Pratt, 1800s, 9 ½ In.
$236.00

James D. Julia Inc.

Tool, Hatchel Flax, Incised, Round Spike Bed, Wood Base, Marked, A.M.S.T. 1834, 22 ½ In.
$173.00

Conestoga Auction Co., Inc.

Toothpick, Opaque Glass, Green, Amethyst, Gold Staining, New England, 2 In.
$633.00

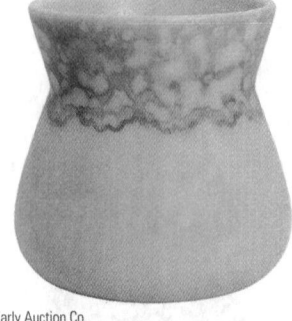

Early Auction Co.

Toy, 3 Little Pigs, Each With Instrument, Felt Outfits, Clockwork, Schuco, Germany, 5 In., 3 Piece
$978.00

Bertoia Auctions

Tray, Mixed Flowers, Gold Trim, Black Ground, Pierced Rim, Oval, 1940s, 22 x 16 In.	156.00
Tray, Red Ground, Gold Stenciling, Cutout Handles, c.1900, 11 x 22 In.	118.00
Tray, Red, Swag Painted Border, Cutout Handles, Octagonal, 1800s, 21 x 30 In.	175.00
Tray, Reticulated Gallery, Handles, Gilt Strapwork, Dido & Aeneas, Oval, 1800s, 23 x 32 In.	1434.00
Tray, Tulip, Fruit Band, Octagonal, c.1890, 16 x 22 In.	176.00
Urn, Chestnut, Fruit Finial, Scrolled Handles, Fishermen, Boats, Outswept Sides, 9 x 11 In., Pair.	4183.00
Urn, Cover, Neoclassical Style, Red, Yellow Oval, Flowers, Ring Handles, 16 In., Pair	690.00

TOOLS of all sorts are listed here, but most are related to industry. Other tools may be found listed under Iron, Kitchen, Tinware, and Wooden.

Ax, Slater's, Hand Forged Iron, Wood Handle, 13 ¾ x 6 In.	24.00
Bench, Mixed Woods, Vises, Drawer, Red Paint, c.1900, 33 x 83 In.	960.00
Berry Comb, Wire Tooth, Dust Pan Shape, Internal Wood Handle, Sheet Iron Hopper, 13 x 10 In.	24.00
Bolt, Star Expansion, New Jersey, Pat. Apr1-02, 2 ¾ In.	25.00
Bootjack, Mahogany, Folding Iron Pulls, Brass Fittings, 1800s, 12 In.	165.00
Box, Softwood, Dovetailed, Open Till, Snipe Hinges, Iron Lock, Blue Over Red, 9 x 21 In.	130.00
Box, Tool, Gershner, Oak, Drop Front, 11 Drawer, Green Felt Lines, 16 x 20 In.	389.00
Box, Tool, Open Style, Wood, Paint, 20 ½ x 12 In.	38.00
Box, Wood, Red Paint, Divided Interior, Iron Hinges, Lock, Hasp, Molded Edge, Footed, 9 x 23 In.	106.00
Brush, Rhino, Wright Bernet, Whitewash Cold Paint, Wood Handles, Straw Bristles, 11 ½ x 8 ½ In.	22.00
Bucket, Apple Picker's, Galvanized, Canvas, 2 Web Straps, 16 x 8 ½ In.	40.00
Bullet Mold, Enfield, Marked 26, c.1853, 8 ½ In.	147.00
Chest, Machinist, Oak, Fitted Interior, 1900s, 13 x 20 In.	237.00
Chest, Pine, Top Handle, Hardware, Painted, 1800s, 8 x 17 In.	210.00
Chest, Red Oak, H. Gersther & Sons, 70 Drawer, c.1986, 20 x 14 In.	375.00
Clamp, Jorgensen, Adjustable, Wood, Chicago, 15 x 7 In.	49.00
Clothes Washer, Plunger Type, Metal, 39 x 8 In.	40.00
Corn Husker, Boss Mfg., Leather, Cloth Metal Buckles, c.1920	39.00
Drafting Set, Eugene Dietzgen Co., Dependo, Case, c.1930, 11 Piece	37.00
Drill, Seed, American Seeding Machine Co., Planting Machine, Ohio, c.1900, 9 x 13 In.	7050.00
Drill, Wood Handle, c.1900, 13 In.	42.00
Flint Powder Tester, Candle Socket, Iron, Carved Oak Grip Handle, Storage Door, 7 In.	649.00
Funnel Strainer, Copper, Screen Inside, 9 x 5 ½ In.	39.00
Funnel, Copper, Spout V-Notch, 13 x 6 In.	65.00
Glass Cutter, Fletcher Terry Co., Box, Gold Tip, Bronze Bearings, c.1960, 5 In.	20.00
Glass Cutter, Oak Leaf, 6 Rotating Wheels, 5 ¼ In.	22.00
Grass Clipper, Chadwick Miller, Battery Operated, 1950s, 11 ¼ In.	55.00
Hammer, Blacksmith, Swage Block Face, Allard Forged, 16 ½-In. Handle	35.00
Hammer, Blacksmith, Swage Block, Forged, 14 ½-In. Handle, ⅝-In. Head	35.00
Hammer, Slater's, Hand Forged Head, Puller, Pick, Layered Leather Handle, 12 ¼ x 8 ⅝ In.	41.00
Hammer, Sugar, Wrought Iron, Brass, England, 19th Century, 7 ¼ In.	241.00
Hatchel, Flax, Battens, Mounting Holes, Painted Black, Wood Spike Bed, 4 ¾ x 22 In.	47.00
Hatchel, Flax, Incised, Round Spike Bed, Wood Base, Marked, A.M.S.T. 1834, 22 ½ In. .....*illus*	173.00
Hatchel, Flax, Iron Spike Bed, Wood Plate, Cherry Baseboard, Mounting Holes, 4 ¾ x 23 In.	47.00
Hatchel, Lollipop Hanger, Iron, Pine, Penn., 17 In.	267.00
Hayfork, Iron, 14 x 20 In.	55.00
Hedge Trimmer, Electric, Sunbeam, A-1-A, 1950s	54.00
Hex Nut Driver Set, Spinite Stevens Walden Inc., Wood Handles, Display, 11 x 8 In., 7 Pieces	62.00
Hod, Coal, Walnut Veneer, Metal Liner, Shoe Shape, Lift Lid, Iron Handles, Knob, 12 x 13 In.	71.00
Ice Chipper, Wood, Cast Iron Tines, 1800s	30.00
Labeler, Better Packages Inc., Cast Iron, Water Table, No. 202, 4 ½ x 2 ½ In.	25.00
Ladder, Wood, Folding, 7 Rungs, 93 x 14 ½ In.	72.00
Level, Carpenter's, E. Preston & Sons, Wood, Brass Fittings, England, c.1915	75.00
Level, Stanley, No. 3, Brass, Mahogany, 1910, 24 x 3 In.	55.00
Level, Surveyor's, Dietzgen, Black, Steel Tripod, Wood Case, Box, 18-In. Telescope, 20 x 11 In.	207.00
Marking, Wood, W. Johnson, Marked, Newark, N.J., 8 In.	125.00
Measure, Oak, Pine, Lap Joint, Iron Nails, Painted, 5 ½ x 9 In.	124.00
Measuring Gauge, Ebony, Brass, c.1890, 6 ½ In.	120.00
Nail Puller, Wood Handle, Steel Collar, 8 In.	15.00
Nail Ripper, Slater's, Hand Forged Iron, 28 In.	12.00
Nail Ripper, Slater's, Hand Forged, Wood Handle, 22 In.	5.40
Notcher, Sheet Metal, Whitney Metal Tool Co., Steel, No. 1412, c.1911, 8 ½ x 5 In.	35.00
Padlock, Key, Brass, Property Of Wells Fargo Co., Express San Francisco Div., Swivels, 7 In.	124.00
Padlock, Tube & Half Loop Form, Embossed Brass Sheath, Iron, Key, 9 x 4 ½ In.	79.00
Pipe Tongs, Blacksmith Made, Iron, 18th Century, 6 ½ In.	185.00
Pipe Tongs, Brass, c.1750	495.00

Pitchfork, Oak, Acorn, 65 ½ In..	124.00
Plane, Blade, L. Sorby, Blade Guard, 17 x 3 In.	40.00
Plane, Block, Walnut, Carved, Boat Tail, Contoured Horn, 9 ½ x 2 ¾ In...........	18.00
Plane, Bull Nose Shoulder, Stanley, No. 90, 1909, 5 x 2 ¼ In.	125.00
Plane, Fence, C. Failey, Walnut, Adjustable, Wedged Rails, Diamond Escutcheons, 9 x 10 In. ..	41.00
Plane, Gouge Plow, Stamped F.W. Pennell, D. Hinkle, 14 In.	12.00
Plane, Plow, Carpenters, Wood, Wedged, Depth Adjuster, 1820....................	175.00
Plane, Rabbet, Carved, Assembled, Adjustable Fence Plow, Thumbscrews, 13 ¾ x 8 In...........	24.00
Plane, Rabbet, Wood, Adjustable Fence Plow, Wedge, 14 x 8 In.	18.00
Plane, Smoothing, Craftsman, No. 37054, 9 ½ In., 2-In Cutter	30.00
Plane, Toothing, Kendrick, Domed, Loaf Shape, Oak, Stamped, 5 ½ In.	18.00
Plane, Wood, Auburn Tool Co., Dado, Robert, 1880, 14 In.	100.00
Plane, Wood, Erbschloe & Sohne, 1800s, 10 ¾ In.	79.00
Plow, Champion, Carved Rosewood, Marked, ¾ Scale, 1880s, 78 In.	9200.00
Press Wringer, Wood, 1800s, 27 x 31 In.	115.00
Protractor, Bass, Stamped Peter Derr, Berks Co., Penn., 1848, 5 x 10 In.	5688.00
Pump, Water, C. Blatchley, Wood, Paint, Stamped, 73 x 12 ½ In.	468.00
Rope Maker, New Era, Cast Iron, Minneapolis, Patented 1911, 7 x 9 In.	495.00
Router, Double Handle, Adjustable, Carved, Brass Back Plate, 12 In.	12.00
Rule, Folding, Rustless Rule Co., Zigzag, Aluminum, Brass Tips, 1930s	45.00
Rule, Folding, Wooden, Czechoslovakia, 6 Ft.	12.50
Rule, Folding, Zigzag, Stanley SW, 7-Fold, Patent 7-13-09, 48 In.	47.00
Saw, Compass, Hand, Marked, William Conway, Phila., Open Wood Grip, 20 ½ In.	12.00
Saw, Pit, Wood Frame, Wrought Iron Yoke, 3-In. Blade, 59 x 19 In.	47.00
Scissors, Candlewick, Black Metal, c.1890, 5 ¼ In.	28.00
Scratch Awl, Stanley, No. 117, Metal, USA, 6 ⅝ In.	50.00
Sharpening Stone, Ohio Knife Co., Celluloid, 3 ½ In.	67.00
Shaver, Wood Spoke, Brass Fittings, Guide Plates, 10 ¾ In.	75.00
Shoe Rest, Cobbler's, Cast Iron, 1868 Patent.	36.00
Shovel, Grain, Log Carved, Painted Blue, D Shape Grip, Round Shaft, Flat Blade, 36 x 15 In. .	236.00
Shovel, Grain, Wood, 36 ¼ x 11 In.	150.00
Shovel, Grain, Wood, c.1800, 35 ½ x 15 In.	675.00
Surveyor Kit, F.W. & R. King, Brass Compass, Verticals, Spirit Level, Tripod, Chains, 15 In.	153.00
Tape Measure, Crank, Brass Case, 1897, 25 Ft., 2 ½ x 1 In.	20.00
Tape Measure, Leather, Constantis Chesterman, Sheffield, England, 66 In.	80.00
Tape Measure, Stanley Defiance, Red, Gray, White Blade, Box, c.1952, 10 In.	25.00
Tongs, Pipe, Wrought Iron, Spring Activated Handle, Hook, Scrape & Tamp, 1700s, 18 In.	563.00
Tool, Painter's, Wood, Rubber Grain Pad, c.1900, 3 x 7 In.	20.00
Tray, Typesetting, Wood, England, c.1895, 32 x 16 ½ In.	125.00
Trencher, Log, Long Grain Pine, Carved, Tab Handles, 9 x 76 In.	189.00
Vacuum, Leather Bellows, Success Hand Vacuum Cleaner, No. 15177, 1910, 51 In.	300.00
Vise, Cast Iron, Wilton Company, c.1950, 6 x 10 In.	10.00
Vise, Jeweler's, Adjustable, Deck Clamp, 7 x 6 ¾ In.	41.00
Voltmeter, Norton Electrical Instrument Co., Die Cast Metal Faceplate, c.1900, 6 x 4 In.	295.00
Wagon Jack, Conestoga, Wood, Orange, Wrought Iron, Cogged Gear, 1855, 20 x 35 In.	130.00
Wallpaper Hanging Kit, Warner Mfg., Knife, Blades, Roller, Brushes, Box, 13 x 7 In., 7 Piece	14.00
Wheelbarrow, Pine, Stencil Designs, Paint, 1800s, 54 In.	245.00
Wood Scribe, Rosewood, Brass, c.1880, 6 ½ In.	145.00
Wrench, Pipe, Ridge Tool Co., Adjustable, Alloy Steel, Green Paint, Elyria, 1929, 15 In.	29.00
Wrench, Plumber's, Bathtub, Schofield Strainer, Pat. 1954, 8 x 2 ½ In.	20.00

TOOTHBRUSH HOLDERS were part of every bowl and pitcher set in the late nineteenth century. Most were oblong covered dishes. About 1920, manufacturers started to make children's toothbrush holders shaped like animals or cartoon characters. A few modern toothbrush holders are still being made.

Andy Gump & Min, Bisque, Japan, 1930s, 4 In.	95.00
Donkey, Multicolor, Sitting, Japan, 1940s, 6 ¼ In.	125.00
Kitten, Pottery, Black, White, Japan, 1930s, 5 In.	48.00
Moon Mullins & Kayo, Bisque, Japan, c.1930, 4 In.	75.00
Skeezix, Uncle Walt, Bisque, Japan, 1930s, 4 In.	85.00

TOOTHPICK HOLDERS are sometimes called *toothpicks* by collectors. The variously shaped containers used to hold small wooden toothpicks are made of glass, china, or metal. Most of the toothpick holders are made of Victorian pressed glass. Additional items may be found in other categories, such as Bisque, Silver Plate, Slag Glass, etc.

3 Monkeys, Glass, Stump, c.1880, 2 ½ In.	115.00

Toy, Acrobats, Gravity Moves Clowns Down Wire Support, Tin, Painted, France, 16 ⅜ In.
$575.00

Bertoia Auctions

Toy, Action Figure, Incredible Hulk, Parkdale Novelties, Canada, Blister Card, MCG, 1978, 8 In.
$228.00

Hake's Americana & Collectibles

Toy, Action Figure, Iron Man, Posable, Fabric Outfit, Mego, Hong Kong, Box, 1974, 8 In.
$235.00

Hake's Americana & Collectibles

T

Toy, Action Figure, Spider-Man, Polyester Costume, Mego, Blister Card, MCG Copyright, 1978, 8 In.
$173.00

Hake's Americana & Collectibles

Toy, Airplane, America, Embossed Red Letters, Tri-Motor, Cast Iron, Aluminum, Hubley, 14 In.
$1265.00

Bertoia Auctions

Toy, Airplane, Bremen Junkers, Painted, Embossed Lettering, Gold Trim, Cast Iron, 6 ½-In. Wingspan
$633.00

Bertoia Auctions

Toy, Airplane, Gyro, Tin Lithograph, Prop On Top Wing, Spain, 8 ½ In.
$518.00

Bertoia Auctions

Alexis	10.00
Athenia, Handle, Footed, Gold Spray, 3 ½ In.	22.00
Banded Portland, Clear, Maiden Blush	40.00
Basket, Pressed, Translucent Blue Base, Clambroth Cover, Molded Handles, 3 ¾ x 2 In.	150.00
Bead & Scroll, Clear	45.00
Beatty Rib, Blue Opal	20.00
Blocked Thumbprint, Clear, Ruby, State Fair, 1907	35.00
Button & Star	12.00
Button Panel	40.00
Button Panel, Clear	30.00
Button Star Panel, Clear	25.00
Columbia, Clear, Gold	40.00
Croesus, Green & Gold	55.00
Daisy & Button, Hat Shape, Milk Glass, 2 ¾ In.	14.00
Diamond Peg, Ivory, Enamel & Gold	55.00
Diamond Pyramid, Clear	20.00
Diamond Sawtooth Honeycomb, Clear	40.00
Diamond Spearhead, Clear Opalescent	40.00
Dog, Pug, Silver Plate, Glass Eyes, 2 In.	138.00
Donkey With Cart, Glass, Clear, 4 ½ x 2 ¼ In.	8.00
Empress, Clear, Engraved	45.00
Esther, Enamel Dots	145.00
Eureka, Ruby	95.00
Fan & Hobnail, Pedestal, Fostoria, 2 ¾ In.	50.00
Fancy Loop, Emerald Green, Gold	25.00
Fandango, Clear	75.00
Feather, Clear	45.00
Forget-Me-Not, Green, Boyd Glass, 4-Footed	25.00
Georgia Gem	20.00
Glass, Flashed Gold Rim, Ruffled, 2 Handles, c.1910, 2 ½ In.	30.00
Horseshoe, Clover, Opal	35.00
Idyll, Green, Gold	140.00
Illinois, Clear	8.00
Juno, Clear	20.00
Kentucky, Emerald Green, Gold	35.00
King's Crown, Clear, Ruby	20.00
Ladder With Diamonds, Clear, Gold	55.00
Lone Star, Clear	40.00
Long Buttress, Clear	15.00
Lower Manhattan, Amethyst, Gold	50.00
Maiden's Blush, Intaglio Sunflower	75.00
Milk Glass, Cylindrical, Curved Design, 1950s, 2 ¾ In.	16.00
Myrtle, Clear	15.00
Opaque Glass, Green, Amethyst, Gold Staining, New England, 2 In. ....*illus*	633.00
Orinda	15.00
Panama, Clear	12.00
Pennsylvania, Clear	8.00
Pride, Beveled Star	20.00
Pug Dog Head, Wood, Brass Eyes, Brass & Leather Collar, 2 ¾ In.	113.00
Punty Band, Clear, Ruby	25.00
Purple Slag, Forget-Me-Not, 3-Footed, Marked, Degenhart	36.00
Rabbit, Cream, Signed	35.00
Rib & Bead, Clear, Ruby	30.00
Ribbed Spiral, Yellow Opalescent	95.00
Scallop Six Point, Clear, Vase Shape	40.00
Scalloped, Rim, 3 Handles, Westmoreland Glass Co.	36.00
Sunbeam, Clear	12.00
Sunk Daisy	15.00 to 20.00
Teepee, Clear	45.00
Thumbprint, Clear, Gold, Enamel	35.00
Tokyo, Clear & Gold	35.00
Toltec, Clear	25.00
Union Railroad Station, Rhode Island, Germany, 2 In.	35.00
Verona, Clear	40.00
Wedding Bells, Clear	40.00
Wellsburg, Clear	45.00
Zippered Swirl Diamond, Clear, Gold	40.00

T

TORQUAY is the name given to ceramics by several potteries working near Torquay, **TORQUAY** England, from 1870 until 1962. Until about 1900, the potteries used local red clay to make classical-style art pottery vases and figurines. Then they turned to making souvenir wares. Items were dipped in colored slip and decorated with painted slip and sgraffito designs. They often had mottoes or proverbs, and scenes of cottages, ships, birds, or flowers. The Scandy design was a symmetrical arrangement of brushstrokes and spots done in colored slips. Potteries included Watcombe Pottery (1870–1962); Torquay Terra-Cotta Company (1875–1905); Aller Vale (1881–1924); Torquay Pottery (1908–40); and Longpark (1883–1957).

Bowl, Motto, Ill Blows The Wind That Profits Nobody, Cottage, c.1940, 4 x 2 ½ In.	78.00
Candleholder, Sgrafitto, Motto, Snore & You Sleep Alone, Cottage Design, c.1920, 3 x 4 In.	110.00
Creamer, Motto, Fresh From The Dairy, 2 ¼ In.	68.00
Dish, Motto, Ilka Dog Has His Day, Leaf Pattern, Longpark, c.1905, 5 In.	68.00
Figurine, Toothache Kitty, Torquay Arms, 1950s, 3 ½ In.	45.00
Inkwell, Motto, Us Be Always Glad Tu Yer Frum E, Longpark, c.1950, 2 x 1 ¾ In.	56.00
Plate, Motto, Come What Come May, c.1970, 9 ¼ In.	125.00
Teapot, Burns' Cottage, Alloway, 3 ½ x 6 In.	135.00
Vase, 4 Openings, Flowers, Multicolor, Marked, Longpark, 5 ⅞ In.	50.00

TORTOISESHELL is the shell of the tortoise. It has been used as inlay and to make small decorative objects since the seventeenth century. Some species of tortoise are now on the endangered species list, and old or new objects made from these shells cannot be sold legally.

Box, Hinged Dome Lid, Silver Piping & Medallion, Ivory Trim, Rectangular, c.1825, 5 ⅜ In.	368.00
Box, Lid, Baroque, Brass, Ivory Inlays, Doors, Fitted Interior, Side Handles, 19 x 21 In.	17550.00
Box, Lid, Figures, Landscape, Pavilions, Trees, Chinese, c.1800, 3 In.	1896.00
Box, Oval Angel, Guarding Children Brass Medallion, 1800s, 11 ½ x 5 ½ In.	649.00
Brush Holder, Cylindrical, Black, Brown, Tan, 4 ½ In.	478.00
Cabinet, Marble, Gilt Metal Mounts, Flat Cornice, 3 Drawers, 2 Drawers, Stand, 61 x 46 In.	2457.00
Card Case, Leaf & Flower Design, Ivory Trim, c.1800, 2 ¾ x 4 In.	398.00
Card Case, Mother-Of-Pearl & Gold Inlay, Timepiece, Ivory Note Card, c.1850, 2 ¾ x 4 In.	1304.00
Card Case, Silver Stringing, Ivory, Red Cloth Lining, c.1880, 3 ½ In.	568.00
Case, Burl, Rectangular, Mother-Of-Pearl Inlaid Star Center, England, 1800s, 4 ⅛ In.	356.00
Cigar Case, Inlaid, Victorian, c.1850, 5 In.	295.00
Cosmetic Case, 2 Women, Carved Ivory Plaque, Chinese, 1800s, 3 x 2 ½ In.	948.00
Desk, Lap, Brass Overlay, Curved Top, Fitted Bird's-Eye Maple Interior, c.1860, 15 ¾ x 11 ¾ In.	1150.00
Dominoes, Case, Rectangular, Silver Inlay, England, c.1875, 5 ¼ In., 28 Pieces	948.00
Game Box, Silver Cartouche, Ivory Trim, 2 Decks Cards, Signed, c.1870, 4 ½ x 3 ½ In.	2370.00
Ink Case, Silver Mounted, Rectangular, Hinged Lid, 2 Wells, Pen, Seal, England, c.1800, 2 ⅞ In.	1470.00
Letter Opener, Silver Mount, Green Ivory Lion's Head Handle, Saber Shape, c.1900, 20 In.	500.00
Match Safe, William IV, Rectangular, Rounded Corners, Gold Inlay, England, c.1835, 2 ½ In.	368.00
Necessaire, Pagoda Top, Gilt Border, Landscape, Ivory Inlaid, England, 1800s, 3 x 6 ½ In.	1838.00
Necessaire, Sewing, Barrel Shape, Mother-Of-Pearl Bands, Gilt Garlands, c.1865, 4 In.	855.00
Notebook, Pencil, Carved, Celluloid Pages, Clip, 4 x 2 ½ In.	225.00
Pin Box, Pagoda Top, Silver Piping, Ivory Feet, c.1800s, 2 ⅝ x 1 ⅞ In.	368.00
Pipe, Opium, Blue Mouthpiece, Silver, Copper, Glass Mounts, c.1900, 23 In.	1180.00
Purse, Coin, Steel, Gold Inlay, Shell Sides, Inlaid Stars, Shield Cartouche, c.1800, 2 ¾ In.	368.00
Snuffbox, Cover, Pressed Basket Weave Top, Silver Beading, c.1800s, 1 ½ x 2 ⅜ In.	504.00
Trinket Box, Round, Carved, Figures, Buildings, Landscape, 1800s, 4 In.	550.00

TORTOISESHELL GLASS was made during the 1800s and after by the Sandwich Glass Works of Massachusetts and some firms in Germany. Tortoiseshell glass is, of course, named for its resemblance to real shell from a tortoise. It has been reproduced.

Compote, Clear To Green, Brown Splashes, 8 In.	125.00
Jar, Silver, Shell Cover, Medallion, Leaves, England, c.1930, 4 ¼ In.	504.00
Lamp Globe, Brown, Red, Orange, 1930s, 5 x 5 In.	150.00

TOY collectors have special clubs, magazines, and shows. Toys are designed to entice children, and today they have attracted new interest among adults who are still children at heart. All types of toys are collected. Tin toys, iron toys, battery-operated toys, and many others are collected by specialists. Dolls, Games, Teddy Bears, and Bicycles are listed in their own categories. Other toys may be found under company or celebrity names. This year there were several auctions of major collections of toys and records were set.

3 Little Pigs, Each With Instrument, Felt Outfits, Clockwork, Schuco, Germany, 5 In., 3 Piece .. *illus*	978.00
Acrobat, Tin Lithograph, Windup, Metal, Tin Base, Marx, Box, 1930s, 7 ½ x 1 3 ½ In.	237.00
Acrobats, Gravity Moves Clowns Down Wire Support, Tin, Painted, France, 16 ⅜ In. ..... *illus*	575.00

Toy, Airplane, Lindy Sirius, Cast Iron, Painted, Single Nickel Prop, Hubley, 8 In. $1725.00

Bertoia Auctions

Toy, Airplane, Pilot, Gyro, Tin Lithograph, Red & Silver, Prop On Fuselage, Windup, Cierva, 6 In. $633.00

Bertoia Auctions

Toy, Airplane, U.S. Mail, Tri-Motor, Steel, Decal, Nickel Props, Steelcraft, c.1929, 26 ½-In. Wingspan $863.00

Bertoia Auctions

Toy, Badge, Captain Video, Clip-On, Metal, Post's Raisin Bran, Prototype, Premium, 1950s, 7 x 10 In. $320.00

Hake's Americana & Collectibles

Toy Prices
Toys often go through a cycle of collecting and rising prices, then a lack of interest and falling prices. The cycle for Beanie Babies took only five years, from 1995 to 2000.

Toy, Bell, Mr. Flip, Figure, Little Nemo Series, Nickel Spoke Wheels, Painted, Iron, Watrous, 6 ½ In.
$1093.00

Bertoia Auctions

Toy, Bellhop, Black Man, Carrying Suitcases, Legs Move, Wood, Pull, Hustler, c.1927, 6 ¾ x 7 ¾ In.
$173.00

Hake's Americana & Collectibles

Toy, Bicyclist, Rolls Along String, Tin Lithograph, Die Cut, Center Weight, A.C. Gilbert, 8 ¼ In.
$115.00

Bertoia Auctions

Action Figure, Amazing Spider-Man, World's Greatest Superheroes, On Card, Mego, 1979, 8 In.	100.00
Action Figure, Aquaman, Posable, Mego, Box, 1972, 8 In.	230.00
Action Figure, Captain America, Removable Shield, Case, Mego Superheroes, 1972, 8 In.	2981.00
Action Figure, Incredible Hulk, Case, Mego Superheroes, 1978, 8 In.	228.00
Action Figure, Incredible Hulk, Parkdale Novelties, Canada, Blister Card, MCG, 1978, 8 In. *illus*	228.00
Action Figure, Incredible Hulk, Plastic, Posable, On Card, Mego, 1979, 8 In.	86.00
Action Figure, Incredible Hulk, World's Greatest Superheroes, On Card, Mego, 1970, 8 In.	83.00
Action Figure, Iron Man, Belt, Boots, Chest Button, Mego Superheroes, Box, 1974, 8 In.	235.00
Action Figure, Iron Man, Posable, Fabric Outfit, Mego, Hong Kong, Box, 1974, 8 In. *illus*	235.00
Action Figure, Josh Randall & Horse, Wanted Dead Or Alive, Plastic, Hartland, 1956-61, 9 ½ In.	291.00
Action Figure, Lucas McCain & Horse, Rifleman, Plastic, Hartland, 1960, 9 ½ In.	173.00
Action Figure, Spider-Man, Case, Mego Superheroes, 1978, 8 In.	173.00
Action Figure, Spider-Man, Polyester Costume, Mego, Blister Card, MCG Copyright, 1978, 8 In. *illus*	173.00
Action Figure, Supergirl, Removable Shoes, Belt & Cape, Mego Super Gals, 1973, 8 In.	696.00
Action Figure, Wonder Woman, Removable Boots, Mego Super Gals, 1973, 8 In.	696.00
Airplane Set, Plane, Hanger, Transformer, Aerco & Ritco Decals, 9 x 18 In., 3 Piece	208.00
Airplane Spiral, Tin Lithograph, 2 Planes, Center Support, Penny Toy, 7 ¼ In.	575.00
Airplane, Air Mail, Embossed, Cast Iron, Disc Wheels, 7 x 7 In.	690.00
Airplane, America, Embossed Red Letters, Tri-Motor, Cast Iron, Aluminum, Hubley, 14 In. *illus*	1265.00
Airplane, American Airlines, Passenger, Flagship Carolyn, Tin, Battery Operated	450.00
Airplane, Biplane, Pilot, Tin, Yellow & Red Paint, Cardboard Propeller Blades, Windup, 16 x 12 In.	4600.00
Airplane, Biplane, Tin, Pilot, Celluloid Propeller, Clockwork, Gunthermann, Germany, 6 In.	460.00
Airplane, Boeing B-29 Superfortress, Decals, Cast Metal, Base, Desk Model, 23 x 17 ½ In.	889.00
Airplane, Bremen Junkers, Painted, Embossed Lettering, Gold Trim, Cast Iron, 6 ½-In. Wingspan *illus*	633.00
Airplane, C-133, U.S. Air Force, Cast Aluminum, 4 Propellers, Curved Steel Stand, 34 x 35 In.	863.00
Airplane, Do-X, Blue & Red Paint, Propellers On Top, Rubber Tires, Cast Iron, Hubley, 8 In.	5750.00
Airplane, Friendship, Embossed, Single Prop, Pontoons, Cast Iron, Hubley, c.1929, 12 In.	3163.00
Airplane, Gyro, Tin Lithograph, Prop On Top Wing, Spain, 8 ½ In. *illus*	518.00
Airplane, Junkers F13, Doors Open, Corrugated Metal, Rubber Tires, Disc Wheels, 28 x 15 In.	8260.00
Airplane, Lindy Sirius, Cast Iron, Painted, Single Nickel Prop, Hubley, 8 In. *illus*	1725.00
Airplane, Lindy, Iron, Painted, Raised Letters On Wing, Nickel Plated Wheels, Hubley, 10 x 9 ½ In.	441.00
Airplane, Little Jim, Ford Tri-Motor, Pressed Steel, Painted, Hard Rubber Tires, Steelcraft, 29 x 23 In.	708.00
Airplane, Mail, Pilot, Tin Lithograph, Windup, Strauss, 7 In.	374.00
Airplane, Monoplane, Air Ford, Hubley, 3 ¾ In.	225.00
Airplane, Pan-American Airline, China Clipper, 4 Engines, Pressed Steel, Wyandotte, 13 In.	259.00
Airplane, Pilot, Gyro, Tin Lithograph, Red & Silver, Prop On Fuselage, Windup, Cierva, 6 In. *illus*	633.00
Airplane, Pontoon, Coast Guard, Windup, Ohio Art, 1950, 10 In.	150.00
Airplane, Right Plane, Propeller, Disc Wheels, Pilot, Passengers, Tin Lithograph, Schieble, 27 In.	403.00
Airplane, Seaplane, Beach Patrol, Orange Plastic, Battery Operated, Box, 1960s, 10 In.	126.00
Airplane, Single Engine, Pressed Steel, Painted, Turner, c.1930, 24 In.	431.00
Airplane, Spiral Post, Hand Painted, Tin Litho Pilots, 2 Planes Spin Down, Turnover, 18 In.	1035.00
Airplane, U.S. Mail, Stars, Green, Red, NX-130, Steelcraft, 22 ½ x 24 In.	518.00
Airplane, U.S. Mail, Tin Lithograph, Windup, Marx, 18 In.	230.00
Airplane, U.S. Mail, Tri-Motor, Steel, Decal, Nickel Props, Steelcraft, c.1929, 26 ½-In. Wingspan *illus*	863.00
Airship, Shenandoah, Tin Lithograph, Celluloid Props, Clockwork, Lehmann, Box, 7 In.	590.00
Alabama Coon, Jigger, Black Men Dance On Top Of Box, Windup, Lehmann, Germany, 10 In., Pair	690.00
Ambulance, 340, White, Wyandotte, 12 In.	50.00
Ambulance, Army, M.D. War Dept., Tin Lithograph, Pressed Steel, Windup, Graphics, Marx, 14 In.	316.00
Ambulance, Electric Lights, Fender Flag, Clockwork, Hausser, Germany, 11 In.	1840.00
Ambulance, Horse Drawn, Rider, Tin Lithograph, Penny Toy, Meier, 4 ½ In.	546.00
Ambulance, Pressed Steel, Decal, Wyandotte, 11 In.	275.00
Ambulance, Pressed Steel, Siren, Lights, Painted, Clockwork, 1930s, 14 In.	431.00
Ambulance, Tin Lithograph, Friction, Japan, c.1960, 3 In.	14.00
Art-By-Numbers, Bonanza, Stardust Touch Of Velvet, Hasbro, 1965, 14 x 11 In.	50.00
Badge, Captain Video, Clip-On, Metal, Post's Raisin Bran, Prototype, Premium, 1950s, 7 x 10 In. *illus*	320.00
Ball Toss, Black Man, Ball In Open Mouth, Out Bottom, Wheels, France, 1920s, 26 In.	1265.00
Barney Google, Riding Sparkplug, Galloping, Tin Lithograph, Clockwork, Fischer, 7 In.	346.00
Bears are also listed in the Teddy Bears category.	
Bear, On Wheels, Shoebutton Eyes, Sewn Mouth, Lips, Ear Button, Steiff, 14 In.	460.00
Bear, Polar, Rabbit Fur, Glass Eyes, Clockwork Mechanism, Decamps, c.1910, 9 ½ In.	1035.00
Bear, Ride On, Full Bodied, Brown, Glass Eyes, Metal Wheel Frame, Steiff, 41 x 32 In.	345.00
Bear, Riding, Glass Eyes, Brown, Steiff, 40 x 28 ½ In.	472.00
Beetle, Flapping Wings, Tin Lithograph, Clockwork, Lehmann, 3 ¾ In.	288.00
Beetle, Painted, Flapping Wings, Tin, Clockwork, Gunthermann, Germany, 6 In.	288.00
Bell, Black Child, Raccoon, Entering Hollowed Log, Wheels, Roll To Ring Bell, Cast Iron, 9 In.	1150.00
Bell, Mr. Flip, Figure, Little Nemo Series, Nickel Spoke Wheels, Painted, Iron, Watrous, 6 ½ In. *illus*	1093.00
Bellhop, Black Man, Carrying Suitcases, Legs Move, Wood, Pull, Hustler, c.1927, 6 ¾ x 7 ¾ In. *illus*	173.00

T

Toy, Black Man, Bee Bop Dancer, On Drum, Plastic Jointed Limbs, Windup, Tin Litho, 9 x 4 ⅜ In.
$231.00

Wm Morford Antiques

Toy, Boat, Canoe, Rower, Celluloid Head, Cloth, Oars, Wood, Windup, Auto-Rameur, France, 22 In.
$4888.00

Bertoia Auctions

Toy, Boat, Gun, Upper Cabin, Tall Stack, Figure On Bow, Painted, Tin, Spoke Wheels, 10 In.
$259.00

Bertoia Auctions

Toy, Boat, Ocean Liner, Smokestack, Deck, Tin Litho, Windup, Arnold, Germany, Box, 6 In.
$374.00

Bertoia Auctions

Toy, Boat, Paddlewheel, Red & Blue, Side Wheels, Single Stack, Clockwork, Bing, Germany, 8 ½ In.
$460.00

Bertoia Auctions

Toy, Boat, Racing Scull, Clockwork, Tin, Painted, Bing, 1909, 20 In.
$5014.00

Auction Team Breker

Toy, Boat, Tugboat, Pressed Steel, Green Paint, Decal, Buddy L, 27 ½ In.
$9200.00

Toy, Boat, Warship, Masts, Battle Guns, Lifeboats, Anchors, Painted, Fleischmann, 20 In.
$1840.00

Bertoia Auctions

Toy, Boy, Cart, Galloping Horse, Painted, Spoke Wheels, George Brown, c.1870, 17 In.
$2300.00

Bertoia Auctions

Toy, Boy, Scooter, 3 Wheels, Heini 507, Tin Lithograph, Windup, Key, 1930s, 6 In.
$374.00

Bertoia Auctions

Bertoia Auctions

T

Toy, Bus, Double-Decker, Inter-State, Bench Seats, Tin Litho, Clockwork, Strauss, 10 In. **$489.00**

Bertoia Auctions

Toy, Bus, Double-Decker, Kenton City, Rear Stairway, Green, Red, Cast Iron, 6 In. **$633.00**

Bertoia Auctions

Toy, Bus, Greyhound, Century Of Progress, Chicago, Cast Iron, Tandem, 1934, 10 ¼ In. **$230.00**

Bertoia Auctions

Toy, Busy Lizzie, Woman Pushing Mop, Tin Lithograph, Clockwork, Germany, 7 In. **$345.00**

Bertoia Auctions

Toy, Camel, Bell, Figure, Seated, Side Baskets, Painted, Pull Toy, c.1874, 9 x 9 In. **$1265.00**

Bertoia Auctions

Bicycles that are large enough to ride are listed in their own category.

Bicyclist, Rolls Along String, Tin Lithograph, Die Cut, Center Weight, A.C. Gilbert, 8 ¼ In. .... *illus*	115.00
Big Bill Pelican, Blue Wheels, Red Bill & Feet, Walks, Opens & Closes Bill, Moise, 1961, 7 x 5 In...	75.00
Big Show Circus Cage Truck, Cage, Wagon Body, Lion Tamer, Clockwork, Strauss, 9 In.	748.00
Billiards Player, Tin Lithograph, Brown & Green Table, Penny Toy, Kellerman, 4 In.	230.00
Bird, Pick-Pick, Mechanical, Windup, Schuco, 1950	250.00
Birds, Father Tuck's, Mechanical, Chromolithograph Paper, 6 Different Birds, Box..................	800.00
Black Child, Vest, Clockwork Eyes, Windup, Germany, c.1905, 12 In.	1380.00
Black Dandy, Cast Iron, Walks, Box, Browers, c.1865...	1017.00
Black Man, Bee Bop Dancer, On Drum, Plastic Jointed Limbs, Windup, Tin Litho, 9 x 4 ⅜ In. *illus*	231.00
Black Man, Pushing Wheelbarrow, Tin, Windup, c.1900, 6 ¼ In..	176.00
Blocks, Cardboard Lithograph, Buildings, Cars, Shrubbery, Keystone, Box, 15 x 22 In., 16 Piece	518.00
Boat, Canoe, Rower, Celluloid Head, Cloth, Oars, Wood, Windup, Auto-Rameur, France, 22 In. *illus*	4888.00
Boat, Chinese Junk, Wood, Carved, Painted, Model, c.1910, 20 x 25 In.........................	444.00
Boat, Chinese Trading Junk, Wood, Carved, c.1940, 32 ½ x 28 In...............................	474.00
Boat, Gun, Tin Litho, Wood, Indiana, Sailors, Cannons, Anchor, 4 Wheels, American Shield, 30 In..	805.00
Boat, Gun, Upper Cabin, Tall Stack, Figure On Bow, Painted, Tin, Spoke Wheels, 10 In. ....*illus*	259.00
Boat, Lake, Painted, Plank Deck, Portholes, Lifeboats, Smokestacks, Clockwork, Marklin, 20 In..	10350.00
Boat, Ocean Liner, 2 Masts & Funnels, Lifeboats, Clockwork, Fleischmann, Germany, 12 ¾ In..	575.00
Boat, Ocean Liner, Painted, Masts, Funnel, Tin, Fleischmann, 19 In............................	1610.00
Boat, Ocean Liner, Railed Stern & Bow, 4 Funnel, Rope Ladder Mast, Clockwork, Carette, 16 In.	1265.00
Boat, Ocean Liner, Smokestack, Deck, Tin Litho, Windup, Arnold, Germany, Box, 6 In. ...*illus*	374.00
Boat, Paddlewheel, Enameled, Side Wheel, Niagara Decal, Mermaid, Windup, Uebelacker, Box, 13 In.	4140.00
Boat, Paddlewheel, Red & Blue, Side Wheels, Single Stack, Clockwork, Bing, Germany, 8 ½ In. ..*illus*	460.00
Boat, PT 107 Navy Patrol, Tin Lithograph, Linemar, 11 In.......................................	124.00
Boat, Racing Scull, 8 Man, Orange, Green, Articulated Action, Spoke Wheels, Cast Iron, 1890s, 14 In.	3738.00
Boat, Racing Scull, Clockwork, Tin, Painted, Bing, 1909, 20 In. ....*illus*	5014.00
Boat, Riverboat, Ocean Queen, Wood, Paper Lithograph, Pilot House, Smokestacks, Reed, 23 In..	885.00
Boat, Riverboat, Puritan, Wood, Lithograph, Cardboard, Multicolor, Cutouts, Instructions, Reed, 36 In.	1888.00
Boat, Rowboat, Motor, Pressed Steel, Painted, Bench Seating, 13 ½ In.........................	259.00
Boat, Speedboat, Outboard Motor, Red, Rubber Tires, Hubley, 4 ¾ In.........................	450.00
Boat, Speedboat, Pleasure Craft, Tin Clockwork, Lionel, c.1935, 18 In......................	316.00
Boat, Speedboat, Static, Cast Iron, Embossed, Driver, Hubley, 10 In.........................	2875.00
Boat, Speedboat, Tin, Crank Operated, Japan, 1950s, 9 ¼ In...................................	120.00
Boat, Speedboat, Tin, Driver, Clockwork, Germany, 6 ½ In....................................	431.00
Boat, Steam Launch, Wood, Pond Vessel, 2 Propellers, Stained Deck, Motor, Stand, Boucher, 48 In.	5900.00
Boat, Steamboat, Wood, Propeller, Red & Cream Hull, Open Top, Live Steam, Funnel, 42 x 9 In...	3450.00
Boat, Torpedo, Gray, Red Pinstripes, 2 Lifeboats, Flag Masts, Clockwork, 20 In.	2875.00
Boat, Tugboat, B & O Railroad, Smokes, Whistles, Lights, Lionel, Box........................	118.00
Boat, Tugboat, Green Paint, Search Light, Propel Mechanism, Buddy L Navigation Co., 27 In...	17250.00
Boat, Tugboat, Pressed Steel, Brass Rails, Decal, Buddy L Navigation Co., 27 In.............	6900.00
Boat, Tugboat, Pressed Steel, Green Paint, Decal, Buddy L, 27 ½ In. ....*illus*	9200.00
Boat, Warship, Masts, Battle Guns, Lifeboats, Anchors, Painted, Fleischmann, 20 In. ......*illus*	1840.00
Boat, Whaling, Moby Dick, Tin, Lights, Siren, Linemar, 1950s, 4 ½ x 3 In.	300.00
Boob McNutt, Walker, Tin Lithograph, Clockwork, Strauss, 8 In...............................	403.00
Boy, Cart, Galloping Horse, Painted, Spoke Wheels, George Brown, c.1870, 17 In. ....*illus*	2300.00
Boy, On Rocking Horse, Metal, Japan, Windup, 1950s..	120.00
Boy, On Tricycle, Tin Lithograph, Clockwork Pedal Action, Ringing Bell, Unique Art, 8 In.	207.00
Boy, Riding Hand Cart, Tin Lithograph, Seated In Open Car, Windup, Strauss, 5 In............	259.00
Boy, Scooter, 3 Wheels, Heini 507, Tin Lithograph, Windup, Key, 1930s, 6 In. ....*illus*	374.00
Bucky Burro, Donkey Cart, Yellow Wheels, Yellow Ears, Spring Tail, Kicks, 1955, 13 x 7 In. ...	130.00
Buffalo Hunter, Animated Rocking, Tin, Painted, Embossed Lettering, Pull Cord, Fallows, 9 ½ In.	7670.00
Building, Garage, Paper Lithograph Over Tin, Embossed Roof, Car, Gas Pump, Gibbs, 15 In. .	489.00
Bump Ball, Instructions, Milton Bradley, Box, 1968..	35.00
Bus Terminal, Metal, Marx, 1930s, 24 In..	395.00
Bus Terminal, Tin Lithograph, Stop Signs, Gas Pumps, Marx, 11 ¾ In......................	288.00
Bus, Blue Line, Tin Lithograph, Disc Wheels, Bench Seating, Chein, 18 In.	690.00
Bus, Deluxe, Tin Lithograph, Die Cast Curtains, Clockwork, Driver, Strauss, 13 ½ In.	805.00
Bus, Double-Decker, Cast Iron, Rubber Tires, Passenger, Arcade, 7 ¾ In...................	403.00
Bus, Double-Decker, Driver, Tin Lithograph, Clockwork, Main Street, Germany, c.1930, 9 ¾ In.	863.00
Bus, Double-Decker, Inter-State, Bench Seats, Tin Litho, Clockwork, Strauss, 10 In. ....*illus*	489.00
Bus, Double-Decker, Kenton City, Rear Stairway, Green, Red, Cast Iron, 6 In. ....*illus*	633.00
Bus, Double-Decker, Red, Yellow, Stairway, Spoke Wheels, Driver, Lithograph, Lehmann, Box, 9 In.	4600.00
Bus, Electric Lights, Bench Seats, Pressed Steel, Cor-Cor Toys, c.1929, 24 In.............	403.00
Bus, Green Paint, Gold Stripes, Pressed Steel, Buddy L Transportation Co., 29 In..........	5750.00
Bus, Greyhound, Century Of Progress, Chicago, Cast Iron, Tandem, 1934, 10 ¼ In. ....*illus*	230.00
Bus, Greyhound, Scenicruiser, Cragston, Box, 9 In...	195.00

Bus, Greyhound, Scenicruiser, Tootsietoy, Box, 9 In.	195.00
Bus, Greyhound, World's Fair, Cast Iron, Painted, Rubber Wheels, N.Y., 1939, 8 x 2 In.	74.00
Bus, Little Jim, Pressed Steel, Painted, Bench Seats, Steelcraft, c.1929, 25 In.	345.00
Bus, School, Yellow, Rubber Tires, New Era, 26 ½ In.	283.00
Bus, Windup, Strauss, 1920s, 11 In.	675.00
Busy Bunny Egg Cart, Wood, Pull, Aqua Wagon, Fisher-Price, 1941, 8 In.	125.00
Busy Lizzie, Woman Pushing Mop, Tin Lithograph, Clockwork, Germany, 7 In. ......illus	345.00
Button, Bart Simpson, Underachiever & Proud Of It, Metal, Bar Pin, 1989, 20th Century Fox, 1 ¾ In.	40.00
Buzz Buzz Whirligig, Windup, Box, 1950s	375.00
Cackling Hen, White, Legs & Wings Go Up & Down, Clucks, Fisher-Price, 1958, 8 x 10 In.	85.00
Camel, Bell, Figure, Seated, Side Baskets, Painted, Pull Toy, c.1874, 9 x 9 In. ....illus	1265.00
Camera, Fred Flintstone, Box	28.00
Camera, Merry Matic, Flash, Battery Operated, Silver Ring Around Lens, Red Letters, 1960s, 4 x 4 In.	30.00
Cannon, Big Bang Carbide, Black, Red Wheels, Conestoga Co., 8 ¾ x 25 In.	113.00
Cap Bomb, Dog's Head Shape, Cast Iron, c.1900, 2 x 1 In.	92.00
Cap Bomb, Figural, Oscar Wilde, Embossed, 2 ¼ In.	1150.00
Cap Gun, Hip, Spitfire, Box, 1950s, 9 In.	49.00
Cap Gun, Monkey & Coconut, Japanned Finish, Cast Iron, J. & E. Stevens, c.1890, 4 In.	345.00
Cap Gun, Pony Boy, 1950s, 10 ½ In.	45.00
Cap Gun, Sea Serpent Shape, Cast Iron, Stevens, c.1890, 7 ½ In.	575.00
Cap Gun, Shoot The Hat, Japanned, Cast Iron, Ives, c.1885 ....illus	460.00
Cap Gun, Texan Gold Plated Deluxe Pistol, White Steer Head Grips, Hubley, Box, c.1950, 9 In...	288.00
Cap Gun, Texan, 50-Shot Repeating Pistol, Cowboy, Cast Iron, Hubley, Box, c.1940, 9 In.	190.00
Cap Gun, Wild Bill Hickock, Nickel Plated, Engraved Scrolls, Horseshoes, Horse, c.1955, 9 In.	115.00
Car Repair Shop, Wood Frame, Windows, Door, Tools, Equipment, Lift, Schuco, c.1955, 20 x 11 In.	29.00
Car, 2 Door, Driver, Tin, Blue, Rubber Tires, Arnold, 10 In. ....illus	259.00
Car, 4002 Tacho Examico, Windup, Key, Schuco, Box	283.00
Car, AMC, Sedan, Marlin, White, 1966, 9 In.	158.00
Car, AMC, Sedan, White, 1965, 9 In.	57.00
Car, Andy Gump, Andy At Wheel, Disc Wheels, Iron, Arcade, 7 In. .... 489.00 to 519.00	
Car, Aston Martin, Secret Agent's Action Car, Tin Lithograph, Battery Operated, Box, 11 In......	417.00
Car, Austin Healy, Tin, Friction, Japan, Box, 1950s, 8 ¼ In.	195.00
Car, BMW Isetta, Door On Front Opens, Tin Lithograph, Bandai, Japan, 1950s, 6 ½ In. ...illus	173.00
Car, Boat, Trailer, Tin, Friction, Japan, 1950s, 13 In.	295.00
Car, Buick, Century, 2 Door, Friction Motor, Asahi, Japan, 1958, 14 In.	1450.00
Car, Buick, Coupe, Lewis, Cast Iron, Teal, Black, Arcade, 8 ¼ In.	259.00
Car, Buick, Tin, Friction, Japan, 1954, 7 ½ In.	110.00
Car, Cadillac, Convertible, Box, Japan, 1962, 11 ½ In.	275.00
Car, Cadillac, Metal, Friction, Japan, 1954, 9 ½ In.	295.00
Car, Cadillac, Tin, Friction, Black, Red, Japan, 1954, 10 In.	195.00
Car, Capitol Hill Racer, Tin, Windup, Unique Art, 16 In.	175.00
Car, Chevrolet, 1956 Model, Battery Operated, Ichiko, Japan, 9 ¼ In.	395.00
Car, Chevrolet, Camaro, Tin, Battery Operated, Japan, 1967, 13 ½ In.	345.00
Car, Chevrolet, Coupe, Gray, Black, Arcade, 1929, 8 ¼ In.	1850.00
Car, Chevrolet, Impala, Hub Caps, Tin, Friction, Japan, 1959	175.00
Car, Chevrolet, Impala, Red, Box, 1961, 9 In.	79.00
Car, Chevrolet, Sedan, Green, 1937, 9 In.	68.00
Car, Chevrolet, Superior, Sedan, Spoke Wheels, Nickel Plated Driver, Iron, Arcade, 7 In. ....illus	1380.00
Car, Chevrolet, Tin, Friction, Japan, 1956, 9 ½ In.	175.00
Car, Chrysler, Airflow, Kingsbury, Pressed Steel, Clockwork, Rubber Tires, Tan, 1936, 14 In......	374.00
Car, Chrysler, Airflow, Orange, Cast Iron, 1934, 6 ½ In.	1725.00
Car, Chrysler, Airflow, Rubber Tires, Battery Operated Lights, Hubley, c.1934, 7 ½ In. ......illus	489.00
Car, Chrysler, Airflow, Sedan, Pressed Steel, Electric Lights, Rubber Tires, Kingsbury, 1934	288.00
Car, Chrysler, Imperial, 1962 Model, Blue, Tin, Embossed Seating, Asahi Toys, Japan, 15 In. .....illus	6900.00
Car, Chrysler, Tin, Friction, Japan, 1954, 10 In.	375.00
Car, Convertible, 2 Seats, Tin, Windup, Distler, 10 In.	460.00
Car, Convertible, Gray, Franklin Mint, 9 In.	68.00
Car, Corvette, Convertible, Brown, Franklin Mint, 1955, 8 ½ In.	57.00
Car, Coupe, 3 Windows, Red, Tin Lithograph, Push Down Friction, 13 In.	124.00
Car, Coupe, Headlights, Steering, Battery Operated, Tin, Japan, 1950s, 9 ½ In.	175.00
Car, Coupe, Pressed Steel, Rubber Tires, Clockwork, Rumble Seat, Kingsbury, 1927, 13 In.	345.00
Car, Coupe, Red, Tin Lithograph, Windup, Marx, 14 In.	226.00
Car, Coupe, Rumble Seat, Nickel Spoke Wheels, Cast Iron, Arcade, 1932, 5 ⅞ In.	173.00
Car, Coupe, Rumble Seat, Painted, Cast Iron, 1930s, 6 ¼ In.	115.00
Car, Coupe, Tin Lithograph, Red With Brown Roof, Windup, Marx, 7 ½ In.	230.00
Car, Driver, Movable Arm, Tin, Friction, Japan, 1950s, 7 ½ In.	195.00
Car, Driver, Passenger, Embossed Luggage Rack, Rubber Tires, Cast Iron, Arcade, 8 In.	115.00

Toy, Cap Gun, Shoot The Hat, Japanned, Cast Iron, Ives, c.1885
$460.00

Toy, Car, 2 Door, Driver, Tin, Blue, Rubber Tires, Arnold, 10 In.
$259.00

Toy, Car, BMW Isetta, Door On Front Opens, Tin Lithograph, Bandai, Japan, 1950s, 6 ½ In.
$173.00

Toy, Car, Chevrolet, Superior, Sedan, Spoke Wheels, Nickel Plated Driver, Iron, Arcade, 7 In.
$1380.00

Toy, Car, Chrysler, Airflow, Rubber Tires, Battery Operated Lights, Hubley, c.1934, 7 ½ In.
$489.00

Toy, Car, Chrysler, Imperial, 1962 Model, Blue, Tin, Embossed Seating, Asahi Toys, Japan, 15 In.
$6900.00

Bertoia Auctions

Toy, Car, Jalopy, Sedan, Driver, Slogans, Windup, Sheet Iron, Tin Litho, Marx, 4 x 7 In.
$212.00

Conestoga Auction Co., Inc.

Toy, Car, Racing, Pee-Wee, Bunch Engine, Aluminum, Painted Trim, Dooling, 11 In.
$1035.00

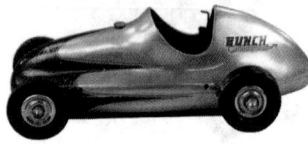

Bertoia Auctions

Toy, Car, Racing, Red Devil, Embossed 5, Nickel Plated, Red Paint, Rubber Tires, Hubley, 9 ½ In.
$1035.00

Bertoia Auctions

Toy, Car, Studebaker, Roadster, Spare Rubber Tire, Cast Iron, Nickel, Hubley, c.1935, 6 ½ In.
$863.00

Bertoia Auctions

Car, Driver, Windup, Tin, Louis Marx, 15 In.	113.00
Car, Fire Chief, Lupor, Metal, Friction, 1950s, 10 ½ In.	145.00
Car, Ford, 2-Tone Green, Japan, 1957, 12 In.	295.00
Car, Ford, Convertible, Tin, Friction, Box, Japan, 1957, 12 In.	275.00
Car, Ford, Falcon, Sprint, Gray, 1968, 9 In.	79.00
Car, Ford, Highway Patrol, Friction, Japan, Box, 1959, 9 In.	175.00
Car, Ford, Model T, 2 Door Sedan, Cast Iron, Gold Stripe, Driver, Spoke Wheels, Arcade, 6 ½ In.	374.00
Car, Ford, Model T, 4 Door, Cast Iron, Spoke Wheels, Driver, Arcade, 1920s, 6 ⅝ In.	288.00
Car, Ford, Model T, Coupe, Black Paint, Cast Iron, Arcade, 6 ½ In.	124.00
Car, Ford, Model T, Sedan, Blue, Black Paint, Cast Iron, Arcade, 7 In.	79.00
Car, Ford, Thunderbird, Hardtop, Red, Box, 1956, 9 In.	51.00
Car, Ford, Touring Sedan, 1923 Model, Cast Iron, Black, Spoke Wheels, Arcade, 6 ¼ In.	345.00
Car, Funny, Widowmaker, Gas Engine, Cox, 17 In.	68.00
Car, G-Man Pursuit, Driver Shoots From Front Window, Tin Lithograph, L. Marx, 14 In.	565.00
Car, Graham Paige, No. 3, Tin, Windup, Japan, Box, 1930s, 6 ½ In.	575.00
Car, Green Hornet, Corgi, 1965	125.00
Car, Highway Patrol, Speed Meter, Black, White, Tin Lithograph, Pusher, 13 In.	85.00
Car, Hi-Way Henry, Clockwork, Tin Lithograph, Moves, Rocks, Fischer, Germany, 10 In.	767.00
Car, Hi-Way Henry, Tin Lithograph, Auto Picturing Clothesline On Roof, 8 In.	345.00
Car, Hot Rod No. 7, Tin, Friction, Box, Japan, 1950s, 8 ½ In.	395.00
Car, Irwin Hot Rod For Barbie, Turquoise, Mattel, 1963	113.00
Car, Jaguar XKE, Coupe, Tin, Friction, Bandai, Japan, 8 In.	95.00
Car, Jaguar, Light Blue, Doepke, 1956, 18 In.	425.00
Car, Jaguar, Tin, Friction, Bandai, Japan, 1950s, 9 ½ In.	195.00
Car, Jalopy, Sedan, Driver, Slogans, Windup, Sheet Iron, Tin Litho, Marx, 4 x 7 In. ....*illus*	212.00
Car, Kommando Anno 2000, Red, Tin Lithograph, Windup, Schuco, 6 In.	113.00
Car, Limousine, Clockwork, Tin Lithograph, Driver, Rear Door Opens, Bub, 7 In.	413.00
Car, Limousine, Clockwork, Tin Lithograph, Rear Doors Open, Rubber Tires, Bing, 10 In.	1061.00
Car, Limousine, Die Cut Passengers, Roof Rack, Clockwork, Penny Toy, Distler, 4 ¼ In.	518.00
Car, Limousine, GMC, Flat Top, Arcade, No. 5, 8 ¼ In.	3500.00
Car, Limousine, Tin Lithograph, Lass Windows, Driver, Clockwork, Gunthermann, Germany, 9 ¾ In.	2588.00
Car, Limousine, Tin Lithograph, Luggage Rack, Driver, Clockwork Driven, Carette, Germany, 6 In.	1093.00
Car, Limousine, Tin, Open Side, Blue & Black, Wood Front Seat, Running Boards, Hafner, 1900, 10 In.	1093.00
Car, Lincoln Zephyr, Sedan, Cast Iron, Rubber Tires, Hubley, 7 In.	546.00
Car, Lincoln, Tin, Friction, Japan, 1950s, 11 ½ In.	145.00
Car, Mercedes-Benz, 230SL, Tekno, Box, 1955	125.00
Car, Mercedes-Benz, Tin, Friction, Removable Top, Japan, 1950s, 8 ½ In.	195.00
Car, MG TD, Leather Door Panels, Tonneau Cover, Burgundy, Doepke, 1955, 15 In.	325.00
Car, Monkeemobile, Corgi, 1965	100.00
Car, Oldsmobile, Deluxe, Battery Operated, Tin, Japan, 15 In.	295.00
Car, Police, Chevrolet, Battery Operated, Japan, 1963, 14 In.	275.00
Car, Police, Comic, Tin, Battery Operated, Bandai, Box, 9 ½ In.	34.00
Car, Police, Oldsmobile, Japan, Tin Lithograph, Friction, 7 ¼ In.	95.00
Car, Porsche, Blue, Dinky Toys, 1962	75.00
Car, Racing, Blue Bird, Metal, Land Speed Car, Friction, U.S. Zone Germany, 9 In.	85.00
Car, Racing, Blue Bird, Pressed Steel, Clockwork, Aerodynamic, Driver, 1928, 19 In.	489.00
Car, Racing, Blue Bird, Tin, Spiral Rod Activation, Buffalo Toys, 21 In.	413.00
Car, Racing, Cast Iron, Folding Roof, Figures, Spoke Wheels, Kenton, c.1900, 9 In.	690.00
Car, Racing, Champion, No. 8, Tin, Friction, Japan, 1950s, 9 In.	195.00
Car, Racing, Ford, Lotus, Battery Operated, Tin, Okuma, 12 In.	135.00
Car, Racing, Indy Style, Gas Engine, Box, Cox, 13 In.	113.00
Car, Racing, Midget, No. 4, Tin Lithograph, Windup, Marx, 5 In.	150.00
Car, Racing, No. 1, Tin, Friction, Japan, 1950s, 9 In.	175.00
Car, Racing, Open Wheel, Die Cast, Pusher, Thimble Drome, 10 In.	124.00
Car, Racing, Painted, Driver, Articulated Pistons, Nickel Disc Wheels, Cast Iron, Hubley, 8 ½ In.	805.00
Car, Racing, Pee-Wee, Bunch Engine, Aluminum, Painted Trim, Dooling, 11 In. ....*illus*	1035.00
Car, Racing, Plastic Driver, Tin Lithograph, Marx, Box, 11 ¼ In.	633.00
Car, Racing, Red Devil, Embossed 5, Nickel Plated, Red Paint, Rubber Tires, Hubley, 9 ½ In. ...*illus*	1035.00
Car, Racing, Turns Over, Tin, Friction, Japan, Box, 1950, 8 ½ In.	575.00
Car, Roadster, Driver, License Plate, Clockwork, Kingsbury, c.1924, 10 ½ In.	1495.00
Car, Roadster, Drive-Ur-Self, Streamline, Tin Lithograph, Clockwork, Marx, 13 ½ In.	207.00
Car, Roadster, Minister Delux, Mechanical, Automatic, Box, 10 In.	46.00
Car, Roadster, Open, Cast Iron, Blue, Nickel Passengers, Kilgore, 6 In.	805.00
Car, Roadster, Stutz Style, Open, Cast Iron, Running Boards, Yellow, Kilgore, 10 In.	805.00
Car, Roadster, Turner Packard, Pressed Steel, Rubber Tires, Tool Box, Bumper, c.1924, 27 In.	1093.00
Car, Rodeo Joe, Trick Car, Windup, Unique Art	275.00
Car, Rumble Seat, Blue, Black, White Walls, Kingsbury, 14 In.	283.00

Car, Runabout, Woman Driver, Open Seating, Spoke Wheels, Cast Iron, Ives, 7 In.	518.00
Car, Scarab, Streamlined, Pressed Steel, Painted Red, Clockwork, Decals, Buddy L, 10 ½ In.	323.00
Car, Sedan, Pressed Steel, Orange, Neff Moon, 11 ½ In.	115.00
Car, Sedan, Streamlined, Tin, Painted Green, Wood Wheels, Wyandotte, c.1940, 15 In.	236.00
Car, Sedan, Take Apart, Rubber Tires, Nickel Hubs, Cast Iron, A.C. Williams, 7 In.	316.00
Car, Station Wagon, Woodie, Celluloid Windows, Buddy L, 1940s, 18 In.	863.00
Car, Studebaker, Convertible, Blue, 1962, 9 In.	141.00
Car, Studebaker, Roadster, Spare Rubber Tire, Cast Iron, Nickel, Hubley, c.1935, 6 ½ In. *illus*	863.00
Car, Stutz Bearcat, Racing, Tin, 2 ½ x 3 x 7 In.	385.00
Car, Tin, Clockwork, U.S. Zone Germany, Distler, 9 ½ In.	115.00
Car, Tin, Windup, France, 1950s, 6 ½ In.	175.00
Car, Touring, 2 Seat, Crank, Inertia Wheel, Spoke Wheels, Driver, Passenger, Tin Lithograph, Hess, 6 In.	1265.00
Car, Touring, Hillclimber, Wood, Cast Iron, Steel, Painted, Inertia Wheel Friction, 7 In.	205.00
Car, Town & Country, Convertible, Woody Model, Trunk Opens, Buddy L, 18 ½ In. *illus*	805.00
Car, Trik-Auto, Open Top, Driver, Tin Lithograph, Windup, Strauss, 7 ¾ In.	230.00
Car, Turbo Jet Nib, Plastic, Metal, Ideal, 15 In.	124.00
Car, Tut-Tut, Man Riding, Clockwork, Tin Lithograph, Painted, Lehmann, 7 In.	943.00
Car, Uncle Wiggly, At Wheel, Holding Cane, Tin Litho, Distler, Germany, c.1928, 9 In.	1840.00
Car, Uncle Wiggly, Tin Lithograph, Clockwork, Driver, Marx, 10 ½ In.	748.00
Car, Vis-A-Vis, Tin Lithograph, Rubber Tires, Spoke Wheels, Gunthermann, c.1895, 9 ¾ In. *illus*	1035.00
Car, Volkswagen, Beetle, Dinky Toys, 1959	50.00
Car, Volkswagen, Karmann Ghia, Celluloid Windows, Friction, Tin Lithograph, 1960s, 9 ¾ In. *illus*	345.00
Car, Whoopee, Tin, Windup, Louis Marx, 8 ½ In. *illus*	196.00
Car, Zigzag, Rocking, 2 Men, Tin Lithograph, Painted, Clockwork, Lehmann, 4 ¼ In.	1955.00
Carnival Car Ride, 2 Level, Tin Lithograph, Windup, Box, Germany, c.1950	350.00
Carnival, Mechanical, Tin Lithograph, Germany, Box, 1950s	750.00
Carousel, Tin Lithograph, Plink-Plunk Music, Painted, Germany, 12 In.	443.00
Carousel, Wood, Figures, Seated, Germany, Pull, 8 ½ In.	1035.00
Carriage, Doll's, Tin, Cream, Pink, Gold Trim, Scroll Edge, Silk Shade, Marklin, 1890, 9 In.	2166.00
Carriage, Giltwood, Metal Wheels, Red & Gold Interior Upholstery, c.1940, 9 ½ x 6 In.	461.00
Carriage, Horseless, Steel, Wood, Tin, Rear Driver's Seat, Spoke Wheels, D.P. Clark, c.1900, 11 In.	201.00
Cart, Horse Drawn, Mohair, Wood, Brown Horse, Green Card, Pull Toy, 1800s, 18 In.	178.00
Cart, Horse, Trots, Black Driver, Striped Cap, Tin, Windup, Gunthermann, c.1888, 8 In.	1368.00
Case, Barbie Goes Traveling, Vinyl, Pink, Blue & Yellow, Standard Plastics, 1965, 10 x 15 In.	110.00
Case, Barbie, Blue, Figures, Mattel, 1961	50.00
Cash Register, Pressed Steel, Play Money, Buddy L, c.1930, 11 x 9 In.	115.00
Cat, Felix Flex Doll, Wood Jointed, Black & White Features, Pat Sullivan, 1922, 7 ½ In.	173.00
Cat, Felix, Figure, Wood, Jointed, Schoenhut, Felix Copyright 1922, 8 ½ In.	201.00
Cat, Felix, Handcar, Gunthermann	895.00
Cat, Felix, Riding Scooter, Tin Lithograph, Orange Scooter, Clockwork, Chein, 1922, 7 ¼ In.	460.00
Cat, Felix, Walking, Composition, Wood Feet, Segmented Tail, 1924, 5 In.	407.00
Cat, Mohair, Glass Eyes, Standing, Iron Wheels, Painted Stripes, Pull Toy, 1800s, 11 x 6 In.	652.00
Cat, Sleeping, Tan Mohair, Tabby, Embroidered Eyes, Nose, Mouth, Ribbon, Tag, Steiff, 9 ½ In.	178.00
Cat, White Fur, Purring, Green Glass Eyes, Clockwork Mechanism, Decamps, 17 In.	345.00
Chair, Folding, Pinky Lee, Image Of Laughing Pinky With Balloons, Fritze Toys, 1950s, Pair	115.00
Chest, Cast Iron, Black, Gray, 3 Drawers, Mirror On Top, Stevens & Brown, c.1875, 10 x 4 In.	237.00
Chest, Doll's, Empire, Mahogany, Wavy Backsplash, 3 Drawers, Porcelain Knobs, 13 x 14 ½ In.	230.00
Chick Cart, Red Cart, Blue Wheels, Pull String, Chick Hatches From Egg, Fisher-Price, 1950, 6 In.	65.00
Chick, Wood Body, Composition Head, Dressed, Basket On Back, Platform, Windup, 7 In.	460.00
Chickmobile, Handcar, Peter Rabbit, Basket, Steel, Painted, Composition, Circle Of Track, 10 In.	500.00
Child On Skis, Ski Pole, Pressed & Spun Cotton, Celluloid Face, Fur Hat, 5 In. *illus*	144.00
Child, In Highchair, Folding, Tin Lithograph, Penny Toy, Meier, 2 ⅞ In.	173.00
Chuck Wagon, Ralston Purina, Squeak, 1975, 8 x 3 ¾ In.	45.00
Circus Cars, Tin, Windup, Japan, Penny Toy, Prewar, 6 ½ In.	2295.00
Circus Rider, Standing On Mare, Tin Horse, Prancing, Spinning, Clockwork, 1880s, 15 In.	3450.00
Circus Set, Humpty Dumpty, Flags, Figures, Animals, Tent, Schoenhut, c.1920, 37 x 52 In., 34 Piece	5750.00
Clarinetist, Man Bobs Head, Arms, Horn Move, Whistling Noise, Clockwork, Gunthermann, 8 In.	885.00
Clock, Graf Zeppelin, Enameled Tin Face, Graphics, Dummy Weights, Hour Hand, 4 x 2 ½ In.	71.00
Clock, Take Apart, Square, Bell, Multicolor, Doepke, 1957, 8 In.	95.00
Clown, Harp, Plink-Plunk, Music, Tin, Metal, Celluloid Head, Clockwork, Germany, 12 ¼ In. *illus*	1725.00
Clown, Hitting Donkey, Tin Lithograph, Articulated Action, Penny Toy, Meier, 4 In.	489.00
Clown, Hoky Poky, Clowns On Handcar, Clockwork, Tin Litho, Wyandotte, 6 In.	144.00
Clown, In Box, Composition, Papier-Mache, Hobo, In Box, Automation, Electric, 20 x 28 In.	834.00
Clown, On Donkey, Bucking, Tin Litho, Clockwork, Germany, 6 In.	690.00
Clown, Plays Violin, Felt Suit & Hat, Clockwork, Schuco, Germany, 5 In. *illus*	86.00
Coast Defense, 3 Anti-Aircraft Guns, Airplane, Hanger, Tin Lithograph, Marx, 8 In.	374.00
Constructor Car, Pressed Steel, Clockwork, Meccano, England, Box, 7 ¾ In.	403.00

Toy, Car, Town & Country, Convertible, Woody Model, Trunk Opens, Buddy L, 18 ½ In.
$805.00

Bertoia Auctions

Toy, Car, Vis-A-Vis, Tin Lithograph, Rubber Tires, Spoke Wheels, Gunthermann, c.1895, 9 ¾ In.
$1035.00

Bertoia Auctions

Toy, Car, Volkswagen, Karmann Ghia, Celluloid Windows, Friction, Tin Lithograph, 1960s, 9 ¾ In.
$345.00

Bertoia Auctions

Toy, Car, Whoopee, Tin, Windup, Louis Marx, 8 ½ In.
$196.00

Showtime Auction Services

T

Toy, Child On Skis, Ski Pole, Pressed & Spun Cotton, Celluloid Face, Fur Hat, 5 In. $144.00

Bertoia Auctions

Toy, Clown, Playing Harp, Plink-Plunk, Music, Tin, Cast Metal, Celluloid Head, Clockwork, Germany, 12 ¼ In. $1725.00

Bertoia Auctions

Toy, Clown, Plays Violin, Felt Suit & Hat, Clockwork, Schuco, Germany, 5 In. $86.00

Bertoia Auctions

Toy, Dog, Bulldog, Nodder, Pull Leash, He Barks & Nods, 18 In. $1652.00

Showtime Auction Services

Cow, Composition, Glass Eyes, Mooing Mechanism, Wood Platform, Wheels, Pull, 17 x 10 ½ In.	354.00
Cow, Hide Covered, Glass Eyes, Brass Bell, Wood Platform, Wheels, Pull Toy, Germany, c.1905, 16 In...	345.00
Crane, Red & Black Paint, Pulley System Moves Crane, Metal, Windup, Buddy L, c.1929, 43 x 24 In.	2300.00
Crib, Stick Figure, Bakelite, Shaped Segments, Orange, Brown, Cord, 6 In.	253.00
Dandy Digger, Pressed Steel, Hand Operated, Seat, Painted, Buddy L, 1940, 29 In.	58.00 to 144.00
Dare Devil Motorcycle, Tin Lithograph, Driver, Jumping Cyclist, Unique Art, 1930s, 8 In......	345.00
Desk, Roll Top, Wood, Drawers Open, 5 ½ x 7 In..........	54.00
Digger, Cast Iron, Treads, Nickel Shovel, Figure, Hubley, 5 ½ In.	431.00
Digger, Kenton Fairfield Ditcher, Chain Drive, Embossed, c.1930, 9 ½ In.	1093.00
Dirigible, Pressed Steel, Pull Handle, Clockwork, 4 Props, Rubber Tires, Kingsbury, c.1929, 20 In..	2070.00
Dizzy Donkey, Pop-Up, Gray & Black, Blue Paddle, Fisher-Price, 1932, 11 In.	65.00
Dog, Brown Mohair, Embroidered Nose, Bead Eyes, Felt Hunting Suit, Ear Button, Steiff, 9 In.	114.00
Dog, Bulldog, Nodder, Pull Leash, He Barks & Nods, 18 In. ....*illus*	1652.00
Dog, Cocker Spaniel, White Mohair, Painted Detail, Glass Eyes, Stitched Nose, Steiff, 1950s, 12 In.	58.00
Dog, French Bulldog, Nodding, Glass Eyes, Hinged Mouth, Papier-Mache, Pull Toy, c.1900, 15 x 19 In.	1470.00
Dog, Patchwork Fabric, Stuffed, Metal Wheels, Pull Toy, Late 19th Century, 9 x 12 x 4 In.........	98.00
Dog, White Mohair, Black, Brown, Lying Down, Front Paws Extended, Raised Head, Arco, 1950s, 31 In.	115.00
Dolls are listed in their own category.	
Dollhouse, 2 Story, Paper Lithograph, Wood, Porch, Celluloid, Open Back, 11 x 13 In. ....*illus*	259.00
Dollhouse, 2 Story, Red Roof, Balcony, Windows, Front Porch, Gottschalk, 32 x 29 x 13 In.....	1355.00
Dollhouse, 4 Rooms, Rooftop Gazebo, 2 Front Open Panels, Hand Carved Accents, 32 x 33 In.	1035.00
Dollhouse, Blue Roof, 2 Porches, Painted Stairs, Paper Lithograph, Gottschalk, 19 ½ In........	2358.00
Dollhouse, Bungalow, Porch, Brickwork, Wood, 13 x 12 In.......................	115.00
Dolly's Nurse Kit, Tin, Nurse, Red, Toyville, 1940s, 9 x 5 In.	34.00
Donkey, On Wheels, Stuffed, Red & White Leather Bridle, Steiff, Germany, 1940s, 33 x 39 In. .	460.00
Dozer, Yellow, Doepke, 1953, 15 In.	395.00
Drum, Lithograph Pattern, Drum Stick, Ohio Art, 1950s, 6 ¼ x 4 In......	55.00
Duck, Rocking, Wood, Saddle Seat, Waddles, Opens, Beak, Happyland, 1920s-30s, 37 x 23 In.	201.00
Elephant, Clown Rider, Celluloid, Japan, 7 ½ In........	201.00
Elephant, Ivory Tusks, Glass Eyes, Downcurved Trunk, 4 Wheels, Windup, c.1905, 10 In.	531.00
Elephant, Musical, Floppy Ears, Spring Tail, 4 Red Wheels, Pull Toy, Fisher-Price, 13 In.	102.00
Elephant, On Wheels, Mohair, Felt, Wood, Growler, Steiff, 19 x 16 In.	518.00
Elephant, On Wood Wheels, Head Moves Side To Side, Makes Noise, Fisher-Price, 1948, 12 x 8 In..	175.00
Elephant, Painted, Wheeled Platform, Tin, Pull Toy, Fallows, 8 In. ....*illus*	460.00
Elephant, Rider In Howdah, Clockwork, Tin, Painted, Gunthermann, 6 ¼ In.	944.00
Elephant, Tin, Painted, Wheeled Platform, Friction, Republic, 9 In.......	176.00
Elephant, Wood, Painted, Red, Yellow, Pull Toy, 11 x 16 In........	30.00
Elevator, Remote Control, Box, Lionel No. 97, 11 ½ x 12 In........	230.00
Engine House, Tin Lithograph, Embossed Brick, Bing, 6 ¼ x 10 ¼ In.	374.00
Erector Set, American Model Builder No. 1, Instruction Booklet, Box, 13 ½ In.	57.00
Erector Set, Skyscraper, No. 5, Metal, Lithograph Panels, Booklet, A.C. Gilbert, Box, 18 x 10 In.	2950.00
Ferris Wheel, Clockwork, Cast Iron, Pressed Steel, Gondolas, Figures, Painted, 17 In.............	2300.00
Ferris Wheel, Clown Face, Tin Lithograph, Windup, Gondolas, Amusement Park, Chein, 16 In. .	460.00
Ferris Wheel, Hercules, Tin Lithograph, Windup, J. Chein, 16 ½ In...........	248.00
Ferris Wheel, Tin, 9 Riders, Painted, Circling, Plink Plunk Music, Windup, c.1910, 15 In.......	690.00
Field Cannon, Cast Iron, Brass Barrel, Painted, Rivet Frame, Marklin, 12 ¼ In.	345.00
Figure, Bellhop Pushing Suitcase, Travel Decals, Tin, Windup, Gestha, Germany, 1930s, 3 In.	183.00
Figure, Harold Lloyd, Tin Lithograph, Big Head & Feet, Mechanical, 1920s, 11 In..............	456.00
Figure, Indian, Crawling, Tin, Windup, Ohio Art, 1950s, 8 ½ In..........	120.00
Figure, Man, Safari Outfit, Composition Head, Wood Feet & Arms, Moustache, Schoenhut, 8 In.	2070.00
Figure, Porky Pig, Cowboy Outfit, Lasso, Windup, Marx, c.1949, 8 In.	36.00
Figure, Seth Adams & Horse, Wagon Train, Plastic, Hartland, 1958-61, 9 ½ In.........	139.00
Figure, Turf King & Jockey, No. 811, Plastic, Hartland, Box, Late 1950s, 9 x 8 In.......	173.00
Finnegan's Baggage Cart, Flat Cap, Clockwork, Tin Lithograph, 1950s, 13 ½ In.......	140.00
Finnegan's Baggage Cart, Visor Cap, Clockwork, Tin Lithograph, 11 In........	195.00
Fire Pumper, Steam, Nickeled Boiler, Hubley, 5 In........	250.00
Fire Truck, 2 Firemen, Rubber Tires, Spoke Wheels, Hubley Mfg. Co., 8 ½ x 12 ½ In. ......*illus*	266.00
Fire Truck, Aerial Ladder, Ladder Rigging, Model L Mack, 1952, 36 In........	525.00
Fire Truck, Aerial Ladder, Ladders Move, Brass Bell, CFD, Buddy L, 28 In........	1955.00
Fire Truck, Big Boy, Aerial Ladder, Pressed, Bell, Kelmet, c.1926, 29 In.	978.00
Fire Truck, Hook & Ladder, Headlights, Siren, Pressed Steel, Tonka, 1960s, 32 In.	168.00
Fire Truck, Hook & Ladder, Wood, Trailer, Decals, Buddy L, 37 ½ In.........	978.00
Fire Truck, Ladder, Big Boy, Crank, Open Cab, Working Wheel, Red, Steel, Kelmet, c.1930, 7 ½ x 8 In.	805.00
Fire Truck, Ladder, Big Boy, Red Paint, Aerial White, Pressed Steel, Kelmet, c.1930, 9 x 26 ½ In..	575.00
Fire Truck, Ladder, Driver, Hose Reel, Pressed Steel, Wilkins, 13 In....................	1610.00
Fire Truck, Ladder, L Mack, Die Cast, Red, Tootsietoy, Box, 8 In........	145.00
Fire Truck, Ladder, Mack, Pressed Steel, Painted, Bell, Steelcraft, c.1928, 26 In........	575.00

T

Fire Truck, Ladder, Tin Litho, Figures, Penny Toy, Meier, 3 ½ In.	403.00
Fire Truck, Open Cab, Mack, Driver, Spoke Wheels, Cast Iron, 17 ¾ In.	805.00
Fire Truck, Open Cart, Boiler, Fireman, Tin Lithograph, Penny Toy, Fischer, 3 ¼ In.	288.00
Fire Truck, Pumper, Cast Iron, 2 Seated Drivers, Rubber Tires, Hubley, 10 In.	201.00
Fire Truck, Pumper, Cast Iron, Driver, Spoke Wheels, Horses, Pratt & Letchworth, 17 In.	1380.00
Fire Truck, Pumper, No. 5, Tonka, 18 In.	62.00
Fire Truck, Pumper, Pressed Steel, Open Cab, Bell, Structo, c.1928, 2 In.	748.00
Fire Truck, Pumper, Red Paint, Search Light, Nickel Bumper, Squirts Water, Boiler, Buddy L, 23 In.	1553.00
Fire Truck, Pumper, Steam, Boiler, Spoke Wheels, Bench Seat, Union, 10 In.	2300.00
Fire Truck, Pumper, Texaco, Box, 1957	107.00
Fire Truck, Pumper, White, Suburban, 1959, 18 In.	57.00
Fire Truck, Steel, Open Bench Seat, Rubber Tires, Clockwork, Kingsbury, c.1926, 24 In.	1150.00
Fire Truck, Water Tower, Red, Press Steel, Sturditoy, 34 In.	622.00
Fire Truck, Winky-Blinky, Firemen's Heads With Red Hats, Bell, Eyes Roll, Fisher-Price, 12 In.	125.00
Fire Wagon, 2 Horses, Japanned, 4 Ladders, Firemen, Cast Iron, Phoenix, 26 In.	885.00
Fire Wagon, Chief Fire Dept., Horse, Seated Driver, Wagon, Embossed, Ives, 15 ½ In. ......illus	2185.00
Fire Wagon, Hook & Ladder, 2 Horses, 2 Firemen, Gongbell, Pratt & Letchworth, 1885, 28 In.	2095.00
Fire Wagon, Pumper, 3 Horses, Fireman, Yellow & Gold Paint, Cast Iron, Wilkins, 17 In.	345.00
Fire Wagon, Pumper, Horse Drawn, Triple Team, Painted, Iron, c.1900, 7 ½ x 18 ¾ In.	415.00
Fireman, Climbing, Yellow Ladder, Clockwork, Tin Lithograph, Marx, 21 In.	288.00
Flashlight Gun, Shiny Chrome, Battery Operated, 1936, 4 x 5 In.	230.00
Fork Lift, Tow Motor, Electric, Pressed Steel, Rubber Tires, Scale, 10 x 13 In.	316.99
Freddie Fireplug, Take Apart, Plastic, Red, White, Blue, Doepke, 1957, 8 In.	75.00
Fuel Station, Tin Building, Wood Pumps, Electric Lights, Marklin, 5 x 8 In.	201.00
Gabby Goose, Pull, Paper On Wood, Rolls Head, Neck Extends, Quacks, All-Fair Toy, 1930s, 8 In.	100.00
Games are listed in their own category.	
Gas Pump, Red, Gold Foot, Embossed Gas, Cast Iron, Arc Arcade Label, 6 ¼ In. ......illus	259.00
Gas Pump, Tin Lithograph, Red, Black, Bell, Celluloid Globe, Electric Light, Gong Bell Mfg., 13 In.	173.00
Gas Station, Shell, Car, Truck, Windup, Box, Germany, 1950s	325.00
Gazelle, Carved Wood, Glass Eyes, Schoenhut, 6 In.	1534.00
Gilbert, Electric Eye, Tin Box, Decal, 8 x 12 In.	86.00
Giraffe, Ride On, Glass Eyes, Steerable Metal Wheels, Steiff, 38 x 48 In.	531.00
Girl, In Stroller, Tin Lithograph, Movable Wheels, Penny Toy, Fisher, c.1920, 2 ⅝ In. ......illus	139.00
Glider, Spider-Man, Fleetwood Toys, Styrofoam, 1978, 4 x 9 ½ In.	13.00
Gnomes, Hitting Anvil, Tin Lithograph, Penny Toy, Meier, 4 In.	518.00
Goat, Kid, Tan Mohair, Painted, Green Glass Eyes, Felt Horns, Ribbon, Bell, Steiff, 1950s, 12 In.	259.00
Goose, Nodding, Tin Lithograph, Jointed, Wheels, Penny Toy, Distler, 3 ½ In.	345.00
Graf Zeppelin, Pressed Steel, Rubber Tires, Propellers, Painted, Silver, Steelcraft, c.1930, 25 In.	374.00
Grasshopper, Spring Antennae, Pull Cord, Rear Leg Move, Iron, Aluminum, Hubley, 10 In.	531.00
Guitar, Monkees Music Box Ge-Tar, Caricature Images, Plastic, Crank, Box, Mattel, 14 In.	529.00
Gump Deluxe Auto, Iron, Red, Green, Driver, Balloon Wheels, License Plate, Arcade, 7 In.	690.00
Gun & Holster, Swivelshot Trick Holster & Fanner 50 Smoking Cap Pistol, Mattel, Box, 11 In.	190.00
Gun, G-Man Automatic, Pressed Steel, Painted, Popping Noises, Sparks, Marx, Box, 1930s, 5 In.	230.00
Gun, G-Man, Attached Siren, Pressed Steel, Portrait Decal, Marx, 1934, 8 In. ......illus	145.00
Gun, Johnny Ringo, Die Cast, Holster, Marx, 10 In.	316.00
Ham & Sam Minstrel Band, Tin Lithograph, Clockwork, Piano, Strauss, 6 ½ In.	489.00
Hansom Cab, Coachman, Lila, 2 Women Passengers, Umbrella, Dog, Tin, Germany, Lehmann, 6 In.	920.00
Hansom Cab, Horse, Driver, Paint, Cast Iron, Hubley, c.1900, 11 ¾ In.	1080.00
Happy Hooligan, Tin Lithograph, Hooligan In Suit, Windup, Chein, 1932, 6 In.	230.00
Happy Hooligan, Walker, Tin Lithograph, Windup, Chein, 1932, 6 In. ......illus	403.00
Harold Lloyd, Walker, Arms Swing, Eyes Raising, Grin, Windup, Marx, 10 ½ In. ......illus	374.00
Harris Tiller, Cast Iron, Black With Red Sides, Open Seat, Driver, 4 In.	201.00
Heavy Swell, Man, Coat, Metal Body, Cane, Tin Litho, Key, Box, Lehmann, Germany, 8 ¾ In. ...illus	4600.00
Helicopter, Air Rescue Helicopter Service, Plastic, Pull Cord, Box, 1950s, 6 ½ In.	86.00
Helicopter, Spider-Man, Plastic, Decals, Empire Toys, Box, 1978, 14 In.	115.00
Hen, Katy Klucker, Wood, Paper Lithograph, Pull Toy, Fisher-Price, No. 140, 9 x 8 In.	68.00
Hillclimber, Cast Iron, Blue With Black Motor, Driver's Jacket Embossed, Hubley, 6 ½ In.	431.00
Hobbyhorse, Texas Stallion, Red Vinyl Head, Vinyl Ears, Nu-Cushion, 1950s, 36 In.	75.00
Hobbyhorse, Wood, Buck Teeth, Fiber Man, Tail, Rockers, On Wheels, 1900s, 23 x 33 In.	59.00
Holster Set, Sheriff, Double, Leather, Gold Foil Wrapping, Brass Plated Trim, Box, Arrow, 1950s	115.00
Honeymoon Express, Tin Lithograph, 3 Tunnels, Conductor, Hand Signal, Train, Windup, 9 ½ In.	173.00
Honeymoon Express, Tin Lithograph, Train, Track, 3 Tunnels, Clockwork, Marx, 9 ½ In.	144.00
Hoppy Marvel Bunny, Plush Body, Velveteen, Composition Hands & Feet, Fawcett, 1946, 21 ½ In. illus	3956.00
Horse & Carriage, Top Hat Driver, Dent Hanson, 1905, 10 In.	325.00
Horse & Rider, Military Figure, Tin Lithograph, Gold Finished Base, Japan, 2 In. ......illus	690.00
Horse & Wagon, 2-Wheeled Platform, Slanted Walls, Wood, Carved, 29 x 16 In.	345.00
Horse & Wagon, Driver, Maple, Carved, c.1890, 18 In.	830.00

Toy, Dollhouse, 2 Story, Paper Lithograph, Wood, Porch, Celluloid, Open Back, 11 x 13 In.
$259.00

Bertoia Auctions

Toy, Elephant, Painted, Wheeled Platform, Tin, Pull Toy, Fallows, 8 In.
$460.00

Bertoia Auctions

Toy, Fire Truck, 2 Firemen, Rubber Tires, Spoke Wheels, Hubley Mfg. Co., 8 ½ x 12 ½ In.
$266.00

Conestoga Auction Co., Inc.

Toy, Fire Wagon, Chief Fire Dept., Horse, Seated Driver, Wagon, Embossed, Ives, 15 ½ In.
$2185.00

Bertoia Auctions

T

Toy, Gas Pump, Red, Gold Foot, Embossed Gas, Cast Iron, Arc Arcade Label, 6 ¼ In.
$259.00

Bertoia Auctions

Toy, Girl, In Stroller, Tin Lithograph, Movable Wheels, Penny Toy, Fisher, c.1920, 2 ⅝ In.
$139.00

Hake's Americana & Collectibles

Toy, Gun, G-Man, Attached Siren, Pressed Steel, Portrait Decal, Marx, 1934, 8 In.
$145.00

Hake's Americana & Collectibles

Toy, Happy Hooligan, Walker, Tin Lithograph, Windup, Chein, 1932, 6 In.
$403.00

Bertoia Auctions

Horse & Wagon, Stake, Cast Iron, Painted, Kenton, 15 In.	431.00
Horse, Dexter, On Wheels, Painted, Red Saddle, George Brown, Late 1880s, 9 In. *illus*	748.00
Horse, Glider, Stuffed Horsehide Body, Leather Saddle, Wood, Painted, c.1905, 36 x 43 ½ In.	115.00
Horse, Mechanical, Tin, Leather Saddle, Harness, Platform, Spoke Wheels, c.1860, 8 In.	920.00
Horse, Mobo Bronco, Gallops, Steel Body, Enamel, Sebel Products, Rubber Wheels, 30 x 27 In. *illus*	283.00
Horse, Mohair, Galloping Pose, Green Saddle Blanket, Beige, Steiff, Mid 1900s, 26 x 33 In.	178.00
Horse, On Wheels, Painted, Tan & Black, Embossed Platform, Tin, Fallows, 6 In. *illus*	201.00
Horse, On Wheels, Wood Handle, Expert Doll & Toy Co., New York, 1940s, 18 x 22 In.	150.00
Horse, Platform, Carved & Painted, Wood, Germany, 1850s, 8 x 8 In.	259.00
Horse, Push Along, Walker, Mohair, Metal, Wood Footrests, Wheels, Lines Bros., Ireland, 24 x 24 In.	115.00
Horse, Rocking, Board Sided, Painted, Chamfered Edges, 44 In.	71.00
Horse, Rocking, Carousel, Prancing, Painted, Leather Saddle, Heubner, Germany, c.1900, 50 x 32 In.	3835.00
Horse, Rocking, Carved, Applied Saddle Back, Double Horn, Painted Orange, Red, Green, 23 x 44 In.	1003.00
Horse, Rocking, Dapple Gray, Saddle, Tin Eyes, 42 x 29 In.	177.00
Horse, Rocking, Mixed Woods, Leather Saddle, Horsehair Mane & Tail, c.1875, 24 x 48 In.	1326.00
Horse, Rocking, Mohair, Saddle, Stirrups, 1800s, 14 ½ In.	119.00
Horse, Rocking, Painted Gray & White, Red Base, Early 1900s, 22 x 30 In.	127.00
Horse, Rocking, Wood, Painted, White, Blue, Red, Landscape On Base, c.1900, 29 x 57 In.	411.00
Horse, Sparkplug, Jointed, Leather Ears, Blanket With Name, King Features, Schoenhut, c.1920s, 9 In.	115.00
Hotdog Wagon, Puppy Driver, Wood, Paper, Pull Toy, No. 750, Fisher-Price, 9 ¾ x 12 In.	102.00
Humphrey Mobile, Tin Lithograph, Riding An Outhouse Shape Bike, Wyandotte, 6 In.	316.00
Humpty Dumpty, Rolling & Rocking Action, Fisher-Price, Pull, 1971, 7 x 5 In.	45.00
Hyena, Glass Eyes, Schoenhut, 6 ¾ In.	2124.00
Ice Cream Cart, Seller, Tin, Friction, Japan, 1950s, 5 ½ In.	375.00
Icebox, Metal, Green Paint, 4 Doors, Nickel Latches, 4-Footed, 25 x 18 x 6 In.	216.00
Ignatz Mouse, Stuffed, Rubber Tail, Metal Eyes, Knickerbocker, 1930s, 12 In. *illus*	1646.00
Jazzbo Jim, Dancer On Roof, Tin Lithograph, Windup, Strauss, 10 In.	271.00 to 316.00
Jeep, Army, Soldiers, Tin Lithograph, Battery Operated, Modern Toys, Japan, Box, 11 In.	518.00
Jeep, Jumpin', 4 Figures, Windup, Marx, 6 In.	175.00
Jeep, Sedan, Brown Body, Red Stripes, Tin Wheels, License Plates, Clockwork, 13 In.	978.00
Jeep, Tin, Friction, Plastic Top, Bandai, 7 In.	195.00
Jeep, Tin, Push, France, 1930s, 5 In.	145.00
Jockey & Horse, Tin Lithograph, 3-Wheel Support, Windup, 5 ¾ In.	489.00
Jocko The Golfer, Tin Lithograph, Swings, Tee Area, Metal Balls, 6 ½ x 6 ½ In.	316.00
Joe Penner & His Duck Goo Goo, Tin Lithograph, Windup, Marx, Box.	650.00
Johnny Mouse, Gray Felt, Pointy Nose, Button Eyes, Shirt, Pants, Cap, Gruelle, c.1921, 10 In.	230.00
Jolly Jumper, Frog, Bug Eyes, Red Wheels, Green Feet, Pull String, Jumping Motion, 1954, 6 x 5 In.	50.00
Joy Rider, Car, Funny Car, Driver, Tin Litho, Clockwork, Marx, 1929, 7 ½ In.	201.00 to 425.00
Kaleidoscope, Painted Cardboard, Brass, Ship's Wheel Rotator, Mahogany Stand, G.C. Bush, 13 In.	825.00
Kid Flyer Scooter, Boy On Box Scooter, Tin Litho, Pull Cord, U.S.A., 1920, 8 In.	288.00
Kiddy Cyclist, Boy On Tricycle, Tin Litho, Windup, Unique Art, 8 ¾ In.	144.00 to 189.00
Kiddy Cyclist, Child Ringing Bell, Tin Litho, Windup, Unique Art, 1950s, 9 In.	173.00
Kitchen Set, Cardboard, Walls, Folding, Alcove, Iron Furniture, Arcade, 32 x 16 In.	889.00
Krazy Kat, Chasing Mice, Wheeled Platform, Tin Lithograph, Nifty, 7 ¼ In. *illus*	546.00
Leaping Lena, Jalopy, Tin Litho, Clockwork, Strauss, 8 In.	115.00
Li'l Abner Dogpatch Band, Tin Lithograph, Windup, Unique Art.	345.00
Lincoln Tunnel, Allows Traffic To Flow, Tin Litho, Clockwork, Unique Art, 23 ¾ In.	259.00
Lion, Clockwork, Nodding, Papier-Mache, Fabric, Glass Eyes, Moving Lower Jaw, 25 In.	944.00
Lion, Sitting, Steiff, c.1910, 29 x 21 In.	690.00
Little Lulu Cleaning Set, Metal Sweeper, Dustpan, Broom, Apron, Box, 1947, 27 x 10 In.	361.00
Loader, Hough, Red, Ny-Lint, 1955, 18 In.	85.00
Locomotive, Niagara, Clockwork, Tin, Wood, Iron Wheels, Stenciled, George Brown, 10 In.	1121.00
Luggage Trailer, Moon Mullins, Red Cap, Green, Arcade, 1936, 3 ½ In.	375.00
Machinery, Hauler, Low Boy Trailer, Nickel, Kilgore, 12 ¼ In.	2070.00
Magic Set, Silks, Rings, Tubes, Slates, Red Wood Box, Metal Hinges, A.C. Gilbert, 21 x 8 In.	264.00
Magician, Sitting, Top Hat, Disappearing Ball, Windup, Tin Lithograph, Germany, 6 ¾ In.	489.00
Mail Cart, Pulled By Ostrich, Black Driver, Flywheel, Tin Litho, Lehmann, 7 In.	649.00
Main Street, Tin Lithograph, Clockwork, Marx, 24 In.	316.00
Man, Carved, Painted, Dancing, Metal Wire, c.1875, 13 In.	1150.00
Man, Eats Watermelon, Exaggerated Features, Mouth Moves, Composition, 1930s, 5 In.	354.00
Man, Motorcycle, Tin Litho, Engine, Clockwork, Spoke Wheels, M & K, Germany, 8 In.	2300.00
Mary & Her Little Lamb, Tin Lithograph, Windup, Kuramochi, Box.	375.00
Mego Man, Tin Lithograph, Windup, Sy, Japan, 7 In.	85.00
Merry Mason, Sand, Wolverine, Box.	350.00
Merry-Go-Round, Clockwork Bell Ringer, Children Riding Horses, Swans, Tin Litho, 11 x 10 In.	471.00
Merrymakers Band, Mice, Conductor, 3 Musicians, Tin Litho, Clockwork, Marx, 9 In. *illus*	748.00
Milliner's Shop, Doors, Gilt Stencil, Cupboards, Mirror, Christian Hacker, c.1880, 24 x 12 In. *illus*	5985.00

T

Toy, Harold Lloyd, Walker, Arms Swing, Eyes Raising, Grin, Windup, Marx, 10 ½ In. $374.00

Toy, Heavy Swell, Man, Coat, Metal Body, Cane, Tin Litho, Key, Box, Lehmann, Germany, 8 ¾ In. $4600.00

Toy, Hoppy Marvel Bunny, Plush Body, Velveteen, Composition Hands & Feet, Fawcett, 1946, 21 ½ In. $3956.00

Toy, Horse & Rider, Military Figure, Tin Lithograph, Gold Finished Base, Japan, 2 In. $690.00

Toy, Horse, Dexter, On Wheels, Painted, Red Saddle, George Brown, Late 1880s, 9 In. $748.00

Toy, Horse, Mobo Bronco, Gallops, Steel Body, Enamel, Sebel Products, Rubber Wheels, 30 x 27 In. $283.00

Toy, Horse, On Wheels, Painted, Tan & Black, Embossed Platform, Tin, Fallows, 6 In. $201.00

Toy, Ignatz Mouse, Stuffed, Rubber Tail, Metal Eyes, Knickerbocker, 1930s, 12 In. $1646.00

Toy, Krazy Kat, Chasing Mice, Wheeled Platform, Tin Lithograph, Nifty, 7 ¼ In. $546.00

Toy, Merrymakers Band, Mice, Conductor, 3 Musicians, Tin Litho, Clockwork, Marx, 9 In. $748.00

Toy, Milliner's Shop, Doors, Gilt Stencil, Cupboards, Mirror, Christian Hacker, c.1880, 24 x 12 In. $5985.00

Toy, Model Kit, Frankenstein, Universal Pictures, Aurora, Box, 1961, 13 ¼ x 5 ¼ In. $540.00

Toy, Monkey Playing Guitar, Moves Head, Mohair & Celluloid Head, Fabric On Tin, 1930s, 9 ½ In.
$116.00

Serious Toyz

Toy, Motorcycle Cop, Rollover, Tips Over, Corrects Position, Tin Lithograph, Marx, 1930s, 9 In.
$460.00

Bertoia Auctions

Toy, Motorcycle, Hillclimber, Rider, Embossed, Rubber Tires, Cast Iron, Hubley, 6 ½ In.
$633.00

Bertoia Auctions

Toy, Motorcycle, Policeman, Rubber Tires, Red Wood Centers, Electric Headlight, Iron, Hubley, 6 In.
$575.00

Bertoia Auctions

Toy, Motorcycle, Rider, Front Light, Tin Lithograph, Windup, Arnold, Germany, 7 ¼ In.
$546.00

Bertoia Auctions

Minstrel, Tin Lithograph, Jointed, Hand Held, Lehmann, Germany, 7 ¾ In.	460.00
Mirror, Doll's, Psyche, Walnut, String Inlay, Hinged Frame, Spindled Brackets, France, c.1875, 11 In.	230.00
Model Kit, Frankenstein, Universal Pictures, Aurora, Box, 1961, 13 ¼ x 5 ¼ In. *illus*	540.00
Model, Flying Car, Chitty Chitty Bang Bang, Die Cast Metal, 1967, 4 In.	195.00
Monkey Playing Guitar, Moves Head, Mohair & Celluloid Head, Fabric On Tin, 1930s, 9 ½ In. *illus*	116.00
Monkey, Cymbals, Japan, 1950s	50.00
Monkey, Cymbals, Red Cap, Windup, West Germany, 7 In.	85.00
Monkey, Gibbon, Dangly Arms & Legs, Brown Felt Pad, Long Mohair, Steiff, 1962, 6 x 12 In.	60.00
Monkey, Jocko, Stuffed, Ear Button, Jointed, Steiff, 7 In.	30.00
Monkey, Pops Up, Fabric, Wire Frame, Wood Wheels, Squeak Box, Pull Toy, Steiff, 10 ¼ In.	295.00
Mork From Ork Egg Ship, 1979, 5 x 3 In.	25.00
Mother Goose, On Nodding Duck, Composition Face, Painted Wood, Cloth Clothes, 15 In.	1770.00
Motor Drome, Dare Devil, Plastic, Tin Lithograph, Marx, 9 In.	288.00
Motorcycle Cop, Rollover, Tips Over, Corrects Position, Tin Lithograph, Marx, 1930s, 9 In. *illus*	460.00
Motorcycle, Boy Rider, Feet Turn Pedals, Tin, Chain Drive, Windup, Gunthermann, Germany, 8 In.	1610.00
Motorcycle, Crash Car, Rider, Cast Iron, Painted, 3 Wheels	79.00
Motorcycle, Harley-Davidson Style, Blue, Black, Tin Lithograph, Windup, Japan, 1958, 5 In.	115.00
Motorcycle, Harley-Davidson, Rider, Cast Iron, Embossed, Painted, Champion, 5 ¼ In.	144.00
Motorcycle, Hillclimber, Rider, Embossed, Rubber Tires, Cast Iron, Hubley, 6 ½ In. *illus*	633.00
Motorcycle, Indian, Sidecar, Cast Iron, Red, Armored Shield, Passenger In Sidecar, Hubley, 8 In.	805.00
Motorcycle, Policeman, Attached Sidecar, Tin Lithograph, Windup, Marx, 1950s, 5 x 8 In.	201.00
Motorcycle, Policeman, Cast Iron, Rubber Tires, Champion, 7 In.	144.00
Motorcycle, Policeman, Painted, Rubber Tires, Cast Iron, Champion, 7 In.	201.00
Motorcycle, Policeman, Rubber Tires, Red Wood Centers, Electric Headlight, Iron, Hubley, 6 In. *illus*	575.00
Motorcycle, Policeman, Tin Lithograph, Windup, Marx, 8 ½ In.	173.00
Motorcycle, Rider, Front Light, Tin Lithograph, Windup, Arnold, Germany, 7 ¼ In. *illus*	546.00
Motorcycle, Rider, Tin Lithograph, Friction, Cafe Racing, 8 In.	68.00
Motorcycle, Rider, Tin Lithograph, Windup, Multicolor, Technofix, U.S. Zone, Germany, 7 In.	170.00
Motorcycle, Rider, V-Twin, Century Of Progress, Red, Cast Iron, Hubley, 5 In.	124.00
Motorcycle, Rookie Cop, Tin Litho, Yellow Cycle, Red Uniform, Clockwork, Marx, 8 ½ In.	230.00
Motorcycle, Sidecar, Police, France, Penny Toy, 4 In. *illus*	173.00
Motorcycle, Sidecar, Police, Harley-Davidson, Cast Iron, Hubley, 9 In.	1265.00
Motorcycle, Sidecar, Police, Tin Lithograph, Windup, Marx, 1930s, 8 ½ x 6 In.	362.00
Motorcycle, Speed Boy Delivery, Mechanical, Marx, Box, 1940s	575.00
Motorcycle, Tin, Boy Rider, Painted, Windup, Germany, 9 x 8 In.	2183.00
Motorcycle, Touring, Rider, Sidecar, Tin Lithograph, License Plate, SFA, France, 1950s, 6 In. *illus*	238.00
Mouse, In Cage, Tin Lithograph, Articulated Action, Penny Toy, Meier, 4 ¾ In.	374.00
Mr. Potato Head, Face Kit, Hassenfeld Bros., Box, 1952, 10 ¼ x 7 ½ In. *illus*	54.00
Murphy Bed, Doll's, Wardrobe, Doors, Drawer, Fold-Down Bed, c.1895, 12 In.	95.00
Music Box, Teddy Bears Picnic, Plastic, Fisher-Price, 4 x 5 In.	12.00
Mutt & Jeff, Tin, Windup, Piggyback Ride, Gunthermann, 6 In.	3680.00
Noah's Ark, Wood, Bird Motif, Painted, 24 Animals, 16 In.	115.00
Noah's Ark, Wood, Painted Windows, Full Bottom, Hinged Roof, Animals, Germany, 25 x 15 In.	1438.00
Noah's Ark, Wood, Painted, Barge Bottom, Hinged Roof, Interior Stalls, Over 70 Figures, 23 x 13 In.	5015.00
Noah's Ark, Wood, Papier-Mache, Canvas, 12 Animals, Steiff, Button In Ear, 34 In.	863.00
Noisemaker, Clown, Multicolor, Tin	36.00
One Horse Open Sleigh, Horse Drawn, Figure, Barclay, Box	225.00
Ostrich, Rudy, Tin Lithograph, Debeck, Germany, 8 ½ In. *illus*	2070.00
Paddy & Pig, Tin, Irishman, Riding Pig, Pipe In Hat, Windup, Germany, Lehmann, 6 In.	863.00
Pail, Cedar Point, Tin Lithograph, Wood Handle, Beach, Rides, 5 x 6 In.	1265.00
Pail, Seaside, Eagles, Stars, Stripes, Tin Lithograph, Wire Handle, 1890s, 3 In.	204.00
Pail, Shovel, Tin, Children Playing, Chein, c.1945, 4 ¼ In.	50.00
Panda, Smoking, Shoe Shining, Plush, Nods, Pipe Lights, Battery Operated, Alps, Japan, 1950s *illus*	127.00
Passenger Coach, Tin, Cast Iron Spoke Wheels, Painted, Multicolor, c.1890, 4 In.	266.00
Peacock, Paper Bellows, Tin Lithograph, Clockwork, Eberl, 10 ½ In.	295.00
Pedal Bike, Good Humor Ice Cream, Chain Drive, Murray, 1951-61, 38 In.	1003.00
Pedal Car, Airplane, U.S. Army Pursuit, Propeller, Gray, 48 In.	259.00
Pedal Car, Atomic Missile, Pressed Steel, Open, Chain Driven, Gold, Murray, 1950s, 46 In.	660.00
Pedal Car, Buick, Pressed Steel, Open, Deep Burgundy, c.1938, 40 In.	1140.00
Pedal Car, Buick, Pressed Steel, Open, Red Paint, Original Seat, 1938, 38 In.	1200.00
Pedal Car, Cadillac, Pink & Black, Garton, Restored, 1950, 45 In. *illus*	1652.00
Pedal Car, Chevrolet, Pressed Steel, Open, 2-Tone Blue, 42 In.	1320.00
Pedal Car, Chrysler, Convertible, Green, Black Running Boards, Red Wheels, 37 In.	590.00
Pedal Car, Chrysler, Pressed Steel, Open, Green, Bumpers, c.1941, 38 In.	660.00
Pedal Car, Dump Truck, Pressed Steel, Sand & Gravel, Orange, Murray, 40 In.	120.00
Pedal Car, Dump Truck, Sad Face, Decals, Sand Gravel, No. 742, Jet Flow Drive, Murray, 42 In.	990.00
Pedal Car, Fire Engine, Chief, Pressed Steel, Open, Red, Late 1920s, 36 In.	1020.00

Pedal Car, Fire Truck, Ladder, Buddy L, 1934..	2900.00
Pedal Car, Ford, Fire Truck, Hook & Ladder, Pressed Steel, Red, 1940s, 48 In.	510.00
Pedal Car, Ford, Roadster, Open, Light & Dark Blue, c.1935, 55 In.	1320.00
Pedal Car, Ford, Wagon, Pressed Steel, Open, Woodwork, Burgundy, Garton, 1940s, 48 In.	540.00
Pedal Car, Highway Patrol, Pressed Steel, Open, Windshield, Decals, Blue, 1950s, 38 x 28 In..	480.00
Pedal Car, Jet Flow Drive Suburban, Red, Metal, 1950s........................	660.00
Pedal Car, Lincoln Pioneer, American National, Tandem, Upholstered, 64 In.	4313.00
Pedal Car, Mobile Home Shape, Wood, Metal, Chain Driven, Robbie Barber, 33 x 98 In.	1035.00
Pedal Car, Mustang, Convertible, Red, Restored, 40 In................................	935.00
Pedal Car, Oldsmobile, Pressed Steel, Open, Green & Pale Yellow, Late 1930s, 40 In.	1560.00
Pedal Car, Oscar Meyer Wienermobile, Yellow, Orange, 1970s, 48 In.	311.00
Pedal Car, Packard, Green, Canvas Convertible Top, Searchlight, Horn, Rubber Tires, 50 In. .	6325.00
Pedal Car, Pierce Arrow, Pressed Steel, Open, Green & Gold Paint, Steelcraft, 1930s, 44 In......	1020.00
Pedal Car, Police Chief, Running Boards, Upholstered, American National, 53 In.	5175.00
Pedal Car, Pontiac, Blue, Restored, 1949 ....*illus*	1017.00
Pedal Car, Pontiac, Pressed Steel, Open, Tan & Orange, Murray, 1940s, 40 In.	480.00
Pedal Car, Pontiac, Station Wagon, Woody, Red, White, Restored, 1948-55, 44 In.	880.00
Pedal Car, Pressed Steel, Disc Wheels, Brown, Red, Delahaye, 40 In.	1093.00
Pedal Car, Pressed Steel, Open, Handbrake, Green & Red, Gendron Jordan, 1920s, 40 In.	1080.00
Pedal Car, Racing, BMC 8-Ball, Pressed Steel, Open, Yellow, c.1950, 40 In.	1680.00
Pedal Car, Racing, Pressed Steel, Open, Hood Ornament, Hubcaps, Green, 1936, 34 In.	360.00
Pedal Car, Royal Deluxe, Pressed Steel, Open, Motor Tone Shift, Cream, Orange, c.1950s, 34 In...	1440.00
Pedal Car, Scooter, Skippy Racer, Steel, Art Deco, Fenders, Stenciling, Handle, 1940s, 44 x 32 In.	480.00
Pedal Car, Space Cruiser, Pressed Steel, Painted, 3-Wheel, Gar-Ton, c.1953, 47 In.	589.00
Pedal Car, Tractor, Ford, Model 8000, 1968, 25 x 38 In..................................	220.00
Pedal Car, Tractor, Inland Tractall, 27 x 45 In..................................	220.00
Pedal Car, Tractor, International Harvester, Model 66, 1971, 38 In.	193.00
Pedal Car, Tractor, John Deere, Model 20, Trailer, Paint, 1960s, 42 In.	303.00
Pedal Car, Tractor, John Deere, Model 20, Trailer, Star Rims, 1965, 27 x 40 In.	303.00
Pedal Car, Tractor, John Deere, Model 40, Trailer, 1973, 25 x 40 In.	220.00
Pedal Car, Tractor, John Deere, Model 55, Industrial, c.1990, 25 x 40 In.	248.00
Pedal Car, Tractor, Tractall, Inland Mfg. Co., 26 x 42 In.	275.00
Pedal Car, Truck, Open Body, Tilt Lever, Side Horn, Yellow, Green, Steelcraft, 60 In..................	2588.00
Pedal Car, U.S. Air Mail, Spoke Wheels, Rubber Tires, 1920s, 42 In.	1955.00
Pedal Car, Windshield, Disc Wheels, Pioneer Line, Gendron Jordon, 50 In.	3738.00
Pedal Car, Wood, Tin, Metal Spoke Wheels, Lift Seat, Pioneer, 37 In.	748.00
Pencil Box, Jackie Cooper, Image Of Jackie On Lid, 12 Pencils, Wallace Pencil Co., 1930, 2 x 7 In.	35.00
Phonograph, Tin Lithograph, Meier, Penny Toy, c.1900, 3 ¼ In.	209.00
Pig, Mechanical, Composition, Glass Eyes, Painted Snout, Walks, Nods Head, Squeals, 13 In...	707.00
Pile Driver, On Treads, Red, Black, Buddy L, 18 x 24 In................................	2588.00
Planetarium, Junior, Spitz, Box, 1950, 15 In..	45.00
Playset, Soldiers Of Fortune, Tin, Box, Marx, 1930s	650.00
Police Patch, Red & Golden Orange, Embroidered, Security, Fisher-Price Toys, 1950s, 3 In....	75.00
Poodle, On Wheels, Glass Eyes, Mohair, Cast Iron, Steiff, c.1910, 15 x 15 ½ In.	590.00
Pool Player, Table, Tin Lithograph, Penny Toy, Kellermann, Germany, 4 In...........................	259.00
Pop Gun, Cork, Wood, Markham Air Rifle Co., 1909, 14 In.	66.00
Porky Pig, Umbrella, Windup, Multicolor, Tin Lithograph, 8 In....................	158.00
Porky Pig, Wearing Blue Jacket, Evan Show For Warner Bros., 1940s, 7 In...........	49.00
Powerful Katrinka, Jimmy, Wheelbarrow, Tin Litho, Windup, Borgfelldt, 1923, 7 In. 863.00 to 1035.00	
Quacky Doodles, Family, Wood, Jointed Legs, Swivel Neck, Painted Clothes, Schoenhut, 11 In., 4 Piece.	173.00
Rabbit, Babies, Rear Lever, Tin Lithograph, Penny Toy, Meier, 3 ⅜ In.	805.00
Rabbit, Tin, Celluloid, Windup, Holding Rattles, c.1930, 9 In.	78.00
Radio Music Box, Pocket, Do Re Me Song, Carry Handle, 1969..................	33.00
Ranger Basketball, Tin Lithograph, Ranger Steel Products, Box, 1950s, 14 In.	195.00
Reindeer, On Wheels, Cast Iron, Felt, Leather, Steiff, c.1910, 19 x 18 In................	748.00
Road Grader, Orange, Rubber Tires, Pressed Steel, Ny-Lint, 18 In.	79.00
Road Grader, Tonka, State Highway Dept. 975, 18 In.	45.00
Road Roller, Green, Red, Hubley, 15 In...	3500.00
Road Roller, Pressed Steel, Canopy Roof, Spoke Wheels, Decals, Buddy L, 1930s, 18 In..........	2070.00
Road Roller, Pressed Steel, Canopy Roof, Spoke Wheels, Roller, Buddy L, c.1930, 20 In..........	2875.00
Road Roller, Pressed Steel, Green, Red, Fly Wheel, Chains, Buddy L, 1920s, 20 In.	978.00
Road Roller, Steel, Black & Red, Steelcraft, 11 x 16 In.	178.00
Robot, Atomic Robot Man, Tin Lithograph, Cast Aluminum Arms, Windup, Japan, c.1948, 5 In. *illus*	190.00
Robot, X-2, Tin Lithograph, Dome Head, Antenna, Windup, 7 In.	345.00
Rocket Fighter, Pilot, Spaceship, Tin Litho, Clockwork, Marx, 12 In.	345.00
Rocking Bell, Jack & Jill, Cast Iron, Double Bell, Spoke Wheels, Watrous, c.1884, 7 ½ In.......	633.00
Rocking Chair, Child Holding Bunny, Tin, Painted, Penny Toy, Meier, 2 ½ In. ....*illus*	805.00

Toy, Motorcycle, Sidecar, Police, France, Penny Toy, 4 In.
$173.00

Toy, Motorcycle, Touring, Rider, Sidecar, Tin Lithograph, License Plate, SFA, France, 1950s, 6 In.
$238.00

Toy, Mr. Potato Head, Face Kit, Hassenfeld Bros., Box, 1952, 10 ¼ x 7 ½ In.
$54.00

Toy, Ostrich, Rudy, Tin Lithograph, Debeck, Germany, 8 ½ In.
$2070.00

T

Toy, Panda, Smoking, Shoe Shining, Plush, Nods, Pipe Lights, Battery Operated, Alps, Japan, 1950s
$127.00

Hake's Americana & Collectibles

Toy, Pedal Car, Cadillac, Pink & Black, Garton, Restored, 1950, 45 In.
$1652.00

Showtime Auction Services

Toy, Pedal Car, Pontiac, Blue, Restored, 1949
$1017.00

Victorian Casino Antique Auction

Toy, Robot, Atomic Robot Man, Tin Lithograph, Cast Aluminum Arms, Windup, Japan, c.1948, 5 In.
$190.00

Hake's Americana & Collectibles

Rocking Chair, Red & Blue Paint, Scrolled Openwork Back, Cast Iron, J. & E. Stevens	45.00
Rocking Girl, Girl Rocks In Rocker, Under Umbrella, Bird, Celluloid, Tin, Windup, Japan	213.00
Rollo-Chair, Riding On Boardwalk, Black Porter, Walks, Tin Litho, Strauss, 1921, 8 In.	855.00
Rolly Dolly, Black, Papier-Mache, Painted, Weighted, Exaggerated Features, 7 ½ In.	264.00
Roly Poly, Jester, Painted, Weighted, Holding Jester Stick, 9 ½ In.	649.00
Rooster, On Wheels, Felt, Wire, Wood, Steiff, 7 ½ In.	748.00
Rooster, Pulling Rabbit On Egg Cart, Clockwork, Tin Lithograph, Lehmann, 7 ½ In.	944.00
Roosters, Pecking, Tin Litho, Basket Candy Container, Penny Toy, Meier, Germany, 3 ¾ In. *illus*	288.00
Rub-A-Dub-Dub, 3 Men In A Tub, Stuffed Bears, Wood Tub, Steiff, Box, 9 In.	51.00
Sailor, Dancing, Clockwork, Cloth Clothes, Tin, Painted, Box, Lehmann, 7 ¾ In.	1003.00
Sand Loader, Chain Treads, Flat Cab, Scoop, Figure, Arcade, 8 ½ In.	1265.00
Scooter, Tin, Boy Rider, Oh Boy, Legs Pump Floor Boards, Windup, Fisher, Germany, 6 x 8 In.	776.00
See-Saw Circus, Monkeys On Seesaw, Tin, Windup, Lewco, Box, 1930	175.00
Service Station, Sunny Side, Marx, Battery Operated, Tin Litho, Pump, Car, 10 x 14 In.	1265.00
Sewing Machine, Cast Iron, Black Paint, Gilt Stencils, Late 19th Century, 6 In. *illus*	224.00
Sewing Machine, Little Mary Mix-Up, Joseph Schneider, 1930s, 7 In.	200.00
Sewing Machine, Tin, Black Paint, Gilt & Red Stencils, Germany, c.1910, 5 In. *illus*	112.00
Sheep, On Platform, Wool Covered, Glass Eyes, Pull Toy, 13 ¼ In. *illus*	575.00
Ship, Destroyer, Tin, Guns, Lifeboat, Clockwork, Fleischmann, 19 In.	920.00
Sink, 2 Faucets, Metal Stopper, Divided Reservoir, Drain Pipe, Enamel, Tin, Marklin, 6 x 4 In.	590.00
Ski Jumper, Tin, U.S.A. Wolverine, Box, 26 In.	275.00
Ski Rolf, Blue Ski Suit, Yellow Skis, Poles In Hands, Clockwork, Tin Litho 5, Lehmann, 7 In. *illus*	3450.00
Skittles Set, Soldiers, Old Guard, Cannon, Wood, Lithograph, 10-In. Figures	177.00
Sky Rangers, Lighthouse, Zeppelin, Windup, Saybird, Monoplane, Box, Unique Art Mfg., 27 In.	173.00
Sled, Black Flyer, Painted Wood, Rounded Back, Shaped Front, Child's, Inscribed, 1800s, 48 x 12 In.	948.00
Sled, Doll's, Wood, Raised Sides, Double Runner Trucks, Red, Steerable, Pull Handles, 26 In.	502.00
Sled, Green Paint, Stencil, Scrolling Cartouches, Dog, Steel Runners, Wood, 11 ½ x 32 In.	518.00
Sled, Metal, Rounded Ends, Elongated Oval Shape, Art Deco Style, 1940s, 48 In.	180.00
Sled, Pine, White Paint, 57 In.	148.00
Sled, Wood, Handmade, Contoured, Iron Stock Runners, 28 x 11 In.	35.00
Sled, Wood, Horse, Blue Ground, F.H.D. Wolf, 19th Century, 16 In.	2938.00
Sled, Wood, Metal Rear Runners, Spring Control, Slatted, 18 x 8 In.	3105.00
Sled, Wood, Painted Green, Stencils, Garibaldi, 19th Century, 44 x 11 In.	86.00
Sled, Yankee Clipper, Oak, Etal Runners, Name On Control Arm, 1950s, 30 x 14 In.	90.00
Sleigh, Child's, Wood, Flowers Scroll Design, Paint, 1800s, 30 x 12 In.	267.00
Sleigh, Child's, Wood, Paint, Salmon Body, Mustard Rails & Runners, 1800s, 23 x 41 In.	748.00
Slipping Sam, Fireman, Climbing Ladder, Tin Lithograph, Windup, Box, 7 ½ In.	403.00
Snoop Sniffer Dog, Black & White, Spring Tail, Legs Move, Tail Wiggles, Fisher-Price, 1957, 5 ⅓ In.	95.00
Snow Plow, Bing, Fan, 8 Wheels, Side Doors, O Gauge, Germany, 8 In.	978.00
Soldier Set, U.S. Band, 14 Navy, 12 Marine, Boxes, 26 Piece	149.00
Soldier, 5 Different Uniforms, 34 Figures, Trees, Wood, Painted, Erzgebirge, Frame, 30 x 9 In.	413.00
Soldier, Arming Shell, Lead, Paint, Manoil	125.00
Soldier, Bicycle Dispatcher, Lead, Paint, Manoil	85.00
Soldier, Cook's Helper, Ladle, Lead, Manoil	90.00
Soldier, Crawling, Lead, Barclay	55.00
Soldier, Dog, Lead, Barclay	185.00
Soldier, Firing From Behind Wall, Lead, Barclay	125.00
Soldier, Gas Mask, Flare, Manoil	65.00
Soldier, Lying, Long Binoculars, Lead, Barclay	65.00
Soldier, Nurse, Kneeling, Lead, Barclay	60.00
Soldier, Pigeon Dispatcher, Lead, Barclay	60.00
Soldier, Running, Rifle, Lead, Barclay	60.00
Soldier, Stretcher Bearer, Lead, Barclay	40.00
Soldier, U.S. Marines, 3 Stances, Lead, W. Britain, London, 3 In., 27 Piece	58.00
Somstepa Coon Jigger, Tin Lithograph, Dancing Figure On Base, Clockwork, Marx, 8 In.	518.00
Speed Boy, Delivery Cycle, 3-Wheel, Open Bed, Clockwork, Marx, 9 ¾ In. *illus*	489.00
Speed Racer, Mechanical, Indy 500, Windup, Marx, Box, 1948, 12 In.	950.00
Spinning Rope Lasso, Tom Mix, Premium From Ralston Cereal Straight Shooters Club, 1935, 88 In.	125.00
Steam Roller, Huber, Driver, Cast Iron, Nickel Roller, Hubley, 7 ½ In.	1380.00
Steam Roller, Steel, Ride On Wood Handle, Keystone, 19 ½ In.	170.00
Steam Shovel, Pressed Steel, Green, Boiler, Sturditoy, c.1926, 19 In.	201.00
Steam Tractor, Model, Horizontal Cylinder, Boiler, Spoke Wheels, Green, Red, 18 x 8 In.	5175.00
Steam Van, Tin Litho, Rubber Tires, Clockwork, Box, Triang, 8 ¾ In.	518.00
Stove, Cook, Quick Meal Range, Silver Painted Doors, 6 Burner, St. Louis, 27 x 17 In.	460.00
Stove, Crescent, Cast Iron, Black, Openwork, Scrolls, Gold Letters Logo On Door, 11 x 13 In.	57.00
Stove, Empire Metal Ware Corp., Metal, Green Paint, c.1920, 17 x 20 x 8 ½ In.	119.00
Stove, Iron, Swirling Design, Nickel Plated Doors, Bucks Head, 16 x 22 In.	354.00

T

Stove, Jemco, Steel, Cast Iron, Chrome Plated, 21 ½ x 10 ½ In. ....*illus*	770.00
Stove, Jewel Range Jr., Detroit Stove Works, Iron Oven Rack, Copper Drip Pan, 16 x 18 In. ...*illus*	3540.00
Stove, Karr Range Co., Red, Nickel Plated, Lifter, Crank, Rack, Accessories, 21 x 13 In. ...*illus*	4366.00
Stove, Kenton, Cast Iron, Vine Embossed, 6 Burner, Shelves, Backsplash, 15 x 18 In.	1265.00
Stove, Lionel, Electric Range & Oven, Porcelain, Steel, No. 455, 4 Legs..........................	362.00
Street Sweeper, Driver, Brushes, Hubley, Pull, c.1930, 8 ½ In.	1725.00
Street Sweeper, Driver, The Elgin, Iron, Turning Sweeper Brush, Gray Paint, Hubley, 9 In.....	2655.00
Streetcar, Center Door, Pressed Steel, Lever Operated Doors, Battery Operated, 21 In.	266.00
Submarine, Hardwood, Carved, Teardrop Shape, Brass Propeller, Cutout Open Top, Boucher, 26 x 8 In.	1062.00
Sulky, Driver, Cast Iron, Painted, Kenton, 7 In.	136.00
Sunny Bunny, Look-Alike, White Mohair, Pink Eyes, Felt Costume, Hat, Shoes, 1940s, 12 In. .	403.00
Superior Service Station, T. Cohen, Box, 1950s, 25 ½ x 15 In. ....*illus*	274.00
Surrey, Driver, White Prancing Horse, Simulated Fringe, Tin, George Brown, 15 In.	1150.00
Suzie Seal, Pull, Wood & Paper, Spinning Plastic Ball & Ringing Bell, Fisher-Price, 1961, 9 In.....	75.00
Sweeper, Suzy Goose, Image Of Suzy & Goose Riding Broom To The Moon, Red Sweeper, 1940s.	45.00
Sweeper, Wood & Metal, Bissell's Jr., 1930s, 3 x 9 In.	145.00
Tailspin Tabby, Pop-Up Kritter, Cat, Stands, Sits, Bows, Wiggles, Fisher-Price, 1931, 11 In.	75.00
Tambourine, Monkees, Box, Chein, 1967, 8 ½ In.	173.00
Tank, 99-32, Green, Tin Lithograph, Windup, Gama Gigant, 8 In.	113.00
Tank, Caterpillar Wippet, Pressed Steel, Gun Turret, Chain Treads, Structo, c.1930, 11 ½ In. ..	345.00
Tank, Circling Airplane, Soldier In Hatch, Binoculars, Friction, Japan, 5 ⅛ In. ....*illus*	489.00
Tank, Turnover, Flintstones, Fred Lifts & Rolls It Over, Tin Lithograph, Linemar, Box, 1961, 4 x 3 In..	536.00
Tap Tap Porter, Clockwork, Tin Lithograph, 6 ½ In.	412.00
Taxi, Amos 'N' Andy, Fresh Air, Tin Lithograph, Comical Jalopy, Dog In Front, Marx, 8 In.	690.00
Taxi, Check-A-Cab, Driver, Disc Wheels, Spare Tire, Tin Litho, Clockwork, Strauss, 8 ¼ In. ......*illus*	403.00
Taxi, Metal, Orange & Black, Driver, Flat Top, Rubber Tires, Spare, Arcade, 8 x 4 In.	3680.00
Taxi, Metal, Press Down To Go, U.S.A. Wolverine, 1950s, 13 In.	345.00
Taxi, Orange, Black, Driver, Clockwork, Tin Lithograph, Germany, Orobr, 5 ¾ In.	316.00
Taxi, Yellow Cab, Driver, Stenciled Doors, Mesh Grille, Disc Wheels, Iron, Arcade, 8 ½ In. ......*illus*	460.00
Taxi, Yellow Cab, Flat Top, Orange & Black, Cast Iron, Nickel Lights, Disc Wheels, Arcade, 8 In. ..*illus*	920.00
Taxi, Yellow Cab, Meter, Tin, Friction, Japan, 1950s, 6 ¼ In.	95.00
Taxi, Yellow Cab, Plymouth Fury, 1961, 9 In.......................	85.00
Teddy Bears are also listed in the Teddy Bear category.	
Teddy Bear, Balloon Blowing, Tin, 6 Actions, Alps, Japan, 1950s, 11 In.	200.00
Terminal, Railroad Freight, Lithograph, Marx, 10 ¾ x 28 ¾ In.	34.00
Theater, Opera House, Wood, Painted, Garlands, Curtains, Gesso, Gottschalk, c.1885, 30 x 31 In.	1026.00
Theater, Paper, Lithograph, Wood Box Base, Cloth Curtain, Scene Panels, 28 x 24 x 26 In.	589.00
Theater, Wood, Paper Litho, Cloth Curtain, J.F. Schreiber, 1893, 24 x 26 In.........................	912.00
Theater, Wood, Paper Lithograph, Renaissance Style, Drapes, J.F. Schreiber, 1891, 26 In.........	1140.00
Tombo, Alabama Coon Jigger, Lithograph, Sheet Steel, Ferdinand Strauss, c.1910, 10 In........	413.00
Tool Box, Little Jim, Removable Tray, Tools, A.C. Gilbert, 27 x 12 In.	106.00
Toonerville Trolley, Skipper Turns & Moves, Tin Litho, Windup, Nifty, Box, 5 x 7 In.	1093.00
Top, Spinning, Kids Playing, Tin Lithograph, 1950s, 7 In.........................	32.00
Top, Spinning, Space Theme, Tin, c.1950, 5 In.........................	28.00
Tower Tramway, Aerial, Latticework, Gear Box, Bucket, Buddy L, c.1928, 33 In........	3450.00
Tractor, Caterpillar, Driver, Red, Yellow, Marx, Box, 1930s, 9 In.	195.00
Tractor, Caterpillar, Yellow, Plated Cast Iron, Decals, Arcade, 1930s, 5 x 8 In.	664.00
Tractor, John Deere, Metal, Green, Yellow, 8 Wheels, 13 In.........................	34.00
Tractor, Nickel Plated, Red Wheels, Marx, 1931, 11 In.	150.00
Tractor, Open Bed Trailer, Clockwork Motor, Kingsbury, 1920s, 11 In.	431.00
Tractor, Pressed Steel, Caterpillar, Kingsbury, Green, Orange, Windup, 8 ½ In.	316.00
Tractor, Pressed Steel, Chain Tracks, Wood Wheels, Clockwork, Wilkens, 7 In.........................	460.00
Tractor, Structo, Pressed Steel, Windup, Shut Off Gear, 8 In.	173.00
Tractor, Ten Caterpillar, Painted, Spoke Wheel, Nickel Chain Treads, Iron, Arcade, 6 ¾ In. ....*illus*	805.00
Tractor, Trailer, Boat, John Deere Model 8530, Pedal, Green, Yellow	1413.00
Traffic Car, Indian, Driver, Bobble Head, Red, Blue, Hubley, 9 In.	750.00
Traffic Car, Indian, Red, Blue, 3 Wheels, Driver, Bobble Head, Hubley, 9 In.	850.00
Trailer, Lonesome Pine, Tin Lithograph, Multicolor, Marx, 8 In.........................	170.00
Trailer, Military, Open, Red Hub Caps, Marx, 1940s, 5 In., 2 Piece	95.00
Trailer, Sunshine Fruit Growers, Lithograph, Phone Number, Pineapple Photo, Red, Marx, 13 In.	460.00
Train Accessory, Central Station, Marklin, Gilt Roof Trim, Flag, Arched Window, c.1910, 14 x 8 In.	5175.00
Train Accessory, Station, Tin Lithograph, Painted, Embossed Tile Roof, Issmayer, Bub, 9 In..	83.00
Train Accessory, Station, Wood, Painted, Embossed Composition Board, Schoenhut, 17 x 13 In.	118.00
Train Accessory, Transformer, American Flyer, Twin, 350 Watt, A.C. Gilbert Co......................	124.00
Train Car, American Flyer, Club Car, No. 4340, Pocohontas, Green & Yellow	203.00
Train Car, Aster Hobby Co., Locomotive, Live Steam, Green & Black, Glaskasten, Box, 10 In...	1380.00
Train Car, Buddy L, Caboose, Outdoor, Pressed Steel, Painted Red, 18 In.	382.00

Toy, Rocking Chair, Child Holding Bunny, Tin, Painted, Penny Toy, Meier, 2 ½ In. $805.00

Bertoia Auctions

Toy, Roosters, Pecking, Tin Litho, Basket Candy Container, Penny Toy, Meier, Germany, 3 ¾ In. $288.00

Bertoia Auctions

Toy, Sewing Machine, Cast Iron, Black Paint, Gilt Stencils, Late 19th Century, 6 In. $224.00

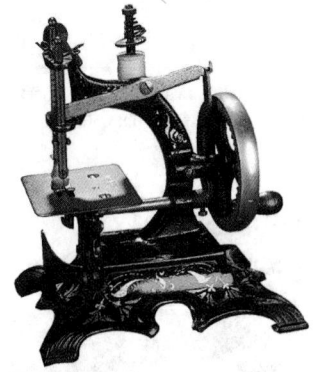

Theriault's

Toy, Sewing Machine, Tin, Black Paint, Gilt & Red Stencils, Germany, c.1910, 5 In. $112.00

Theriault's

Toy, Sheep, On Platform, Wool Covered, Glass Eyes, Pull Toy, 13 ¼ In. $575.00

Bertoia Auctions

Toy, Ski Rolf, Blue Ski Suit, Yellow Skis, Poles In Hands, Clockwork, Tin Litho 5, Lehmann, 7 In. $3450.00

Bertoia Auctions

Toy, Speed Boy, Delivery Cycle, 3-Wheel, Open Bed, Clockwork, Marx, 9 ¾ In. $489.00

Bertoia Auctions

TIP

Keep lead soldiers away from fresh paint, oak and other fresh wood, paper, and cardboard. All of these emit acidic vapors that attack the lead and cause corrosion.

Train Car, Buddy L, Coal Car, Steel, Embossed, Decal, c.1920s, 22 ½ In. ....*illus*	144.00
Train Car, Buddy L, Tanker, Yellow, Steel, Decals, 20 In. ....*illus*	1265.00
Train Car, Ives, Locomotive, Orion Stencil, Tall Stack, Cowcatcher, Tin, Painted, c.1885, 8 In. ..*illus*	920.00
Train Car, Ives Whistler, Locomotive, Paint, Clockwork Mechanism, Tin, May 2, 1876 Pat'd., 11 ½ In.	3738.00
Train Car, Lionel, Locomotive, No. 42 NYC, Center Cab, 8 Wheels, Standard Gauge, 13 ½ In. ....*illus*	316.00
Train Car, Lionel, Locomotive, No. 252, Olive 0-4-0, Box	136.00
Train Car, Lionel, Locomotive, No. 380E, Green, Metal	215.00
Train Car, Lionel, Milk Car, No. 3662, Platform, Cans, Box..........	271.00
Train Car, Lionel, U.S. Marines Mobile Missile Launcher, 4 Missiles, c.1950	102.00
Train Car, Locomotive, Wide Gauge, Red, White, 24 In.	960.00
Train Car, Marklin, Engine, No. RS66, Electric, Tin Lithograph, O Gauge, Germany, 7 ⅜ In. ....*illus*	518.00
Train Car, Marklin, Locomotive, 0-4-0, Electric, Overhead Pantographs, Tin Litho, Germany, 8 In.	460.00
Train Car, McCoy, Locomotive, Steam, Fuel Tablets, Green Loco, England	124.00
Train Car, Radiquet, Locomotive, Steam, 0-6-0 Wheel Configuration, France, Box, 22 x 11 In.	8050.00
Train Car, Rail King, Steam Engine, Union Pacific Big Boy, Box..........	378.00
Train Set, American Flyer, Freight, Locomotive, Tender, Copper, Brass Trim, 1930s, 7 Piece....	950.00
Train Set, Carl Bub, Tender, 3 Passenger Cars, Box, c.1950	450.00
Train Set, Issmayer, Locomotive, Tender, 2 Passenger Coaches, Tin Lithograph, Painted, 23 In.	826.00
Train Set, Lionel, No. 390-E, Locomotive, Tender, Bild-A-Loco Motor, 2-4-2 Steam Profile, 22 In.	382.00
Train Set, Magic Cross Road, Tin, Windup, Japan, 1950s, 9 ½ In.	95.00
Train Set, Marvel Super Hero, Locomotive, 3 Cars, Tin Litho, Plastic, Windup, Marx, 1960, 12 In....	3226.00
Train Set, Pioneer Express, Pressed Steel, Marx, 27 In..........	115.00
Train Set, Pratt & Letchworth, Steam Engine, Coal Car, 2 Freight Cars, Cast Iron, Figures, 1890s	750.00
Traveling Sam, Peace Corps Man, Tin Litho, World Map Wheels, Windup, Japan, c.1963, 6 ¾ In. *illus*	86.00
Tricycle, Spider-Man, Bell, Tin Lithograph, Vinyl Figure, Celluloid Feet, Windup, Marx, 4 In. .	291.00
Trik-Auto, Zeppelin, Figure, Tin Lithograph, Windup, Strauss, 9 In........	403.00
Trolley, Bell, Tin, Friction, Germany, 1930s, 12 In.	225.00
Trolley, City, Tin, Lever Operated, Japan, Box, 7 ½ In........	175.00
Trolley, Comic Express, Tin, Friction, Japan, 1950s, 7 ½ In........	75.00
Trolley, Electric, Bench Seats, Clockwork, Converse, 15 In........	1150.00
Trolley, Embossed Conductors, Cast Iron, Painted, Wilkins, 7 In........	805.00
Trolley, Peace, Tin, Friction, Japan, Box, 1950s.........	75.00
Trolley, Pennsylvania, Tin, Friction, Japan, Box, 6 ½ In........	95.00
Trolley, Rapid Transit, Green, Steel, Electric Lights, Rubber Tires, Schieble, 21 In.	460.00
Truck, Aristocrat Ice Cream, Yellow, Steel, 35 In.	4294.00
Truck, Armored, Pressed Steel, Die Cast, Decals, Bank Of America, Smith Miller, 13 ½ In........	235.00
Truck, Army Cannon, Windup, Marx, U.S.A., 1920s, 8 In........	225.00
Truck, Army Supply, Tan, Tootsietoy, c.1938, 4 ½ In........	125.00
Truck, Army, Dinky Toys, Box, 1955	50.00
Truck, Army, Pressed Steel, Canvas Top, Disc Wheels, Rubber Tires, c.1926, 26 In.	518.00
Truck, Bell Telephone, Cast Iron, Painted, Open Top, Embossed, Hubley, 4 In........	201.00
Truck, Bell Telephone, Green, Embossed, Open Top, Rubber Tires, Iron, Nickel, Hubley, 9 In. *illus*	230.00
Truck, Bell Telephone, Hydraulic Lift, Boom, Green, Steel, Buddy L, 14 In.	113.00
Truck, Car Carrier, 3 Cars, Cast Iron, Arcade, 18 ¾ In........	460.00
Truck, Car Carrier, 4 Cars, 2 Tiers, Cast Iron, 1938, 10 ¼ In.	316.00
Truck, Car Carrier, Bedford, Blue, Dinky Toys, 1952	95.00
Truck, Cattle Trailer, Rear Doors, Bogy Wheels, Structo, 1950s.........	95.00
Truck, Cement Mixer, Jaeger, Cast Iron, Aluminum Drum, Kenton, 9 ¼ In. ....*illus*	460.00
Truck, Cement Mixer, Jaeger, Cast Iron, Nickel Plated Drum, Rubber Tires, Kenton, 6 ½ In. ....*illus*	259.00
Truck, Cement Mixer, Jaeger, Yellow, 1949, 15 In........	225.00
Truck, Cement Mixer, Mack, Hercules Ready Mixed, Revolving Drum, Tin Litho, Chein, 16 ½ In. *illus*	1955.00
Truck, Cement Mixer, Pressed Steel, Buddy L, No. 280, 1926, 17 ¾ In........	900.00
Truck, Cement Mixer, Pressed Steel, Drum, Chute, Buddy L, 1930s, 14 x 15 In.........	690.00
Truck, Cement Mixer, Red & Yellow, Axle Driven Gear, Structo, 1956	225.00
Truck, Cement Mixer, Revolving Drum, Driver, Cast Iron, Hubley, 1930s, 7 ¾ In.	4600.00
Truck, Cement, Cast Iron, Open Body, Scoop, Kenton, 8 In........	1035.00
Truck, Circus, 6 Animal Cages, Tin, Paper Lithograph, Flip Down Sides, 26 In.	4543.00
Truck, Circus, Big Show, Driver, Lion & Tamer, Clockwork, Strauss, 9 In. ....*illus*	863.00
Truck, Circus, Semi-Trailer, Tin Lithograph, Pressed Steel, Wood Wheels, Wyandotte, 18 In....	460.00
Truck, City, Windup, 2 Tin Firemen, France, 1950s, 10 In.	245.00
Truck, Coal, Open Cab, Driver, Cast Iron, Embossed, Painted, 8 In. ....*illus*	546.00
Truck, Covered Back, J.D., Tin Lithograph, Distler, Germany, Penny Toy, c.1920, 3 ½ In.	139.00
Truck, Crane, Pressed Steel, Yellow, Magnetic, Marx, 17 In........	158.00
Truck, Delivery, Ballantine's Ale, Dark Green, Steel, New Era, 35 In.........	848.00
Truck, Delivery, Coaster, Pressed Steel, Red, Gold Trim, Friction, Dayton, 1928, 16 In.	265.00
Truck, Delivery, Dugan's Bakers, Tin, Friction, Japan, 1950s, 7 In.	375.00
Truck, Delivery, Express Parcels, Tin Lithograph, Embossed, Penny Toy, Distler, 4 In.	118.00

Toy, Stove, Jemco, Steel, Cast Iron, Chrome Plated, 21 ½ x 10 ½ In.
$770.00

Wm Morford Antiques

Toy, Stove, Jewel Range Jr., Detroit Stove Works, Iron Oven Rack, Copper Drip Pan, 16 x 18 In.
$3540.00

Conestoga Auction Co., Inc.

Toy, Stove, Karr Range Co., Red, Nickel Plated, Lifter, Crank, Rack, Accessories, 21 x 13 In.
$4366.00

Conestoga Auction Co., Inc.

Toy, Superior Service Station, T. Cohen, Box, 1950s, 25 ½ x 15 In.
$274.00

Serious Toyz

Toy, Tank, Circling Airplane, Soldier In Hatch, Binoculars, Friction, Japan, 5 ⅛ In.
$489.00

Bertoia Auctions

Toy, Taxi, Check-A-Cab, Driver, Disc Wheels, Spare Tire, Tin Litho, Clockwork, Strauss, 8 ¼ In.
$403.00

Bertoia Auctions

Toy, Taxi, Yellow Cab, Driver, Stenciled Doors, Mesh Grille, Disc Wheels, Iron, Arcade, 8 ½ In.
$460.00

Bertoia Auctions

Toy, Taxi, Yellow Cab, Flat Top, Orange & Black, Cast Iron, Nickel Lights, Disc Wheels, Arcade, 8 In.
$920.00

Bertoia Auctions

Toy, Tractor, Ten Caterpillar, Painted, Spoke Wheel, Nickel Chain Treads, Iron, Arcade, 6 ¾ In.
$805.00

Bertoia Auctions

Toy, Train Car, Buddy L, Coal Car, Steel, Embossed, Decal, c.1920s, 22 ½ In.
$144.00

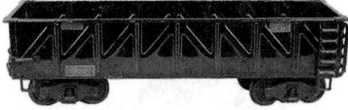

Bertoia Auctions

Toy, Train Car, Buddy L, Tanker, Yellow, Steel, Decals, 20 In.
$1265.00

Bertoia Auctions

Toy, Train Car, Ives, Locomotive, Orion Stencil, Tall Stack, Cowcatcher, Tin, Painted, c.1885, 8 In.
$920.00

Bertoia Auctions

T

Toy, Train Car, Lionel, Locomotive, No. 42 NYC, Center Cab, 8 Wheels, Standard Gauge, 13 ½ In.
$316.00

Bertoia Auctions

Toy, Train Car, Marklin, Engine, No. RS66, Electric, Tin Lithograph, O Gauge, Germany, 7 ⅜ In.
$518.00

Bertoia Auctions

Toy, Traveling Sam, Peace Corps Man, Tin Litho, World Map, Wheels, Windup, Japan, c.1963, 6 ¾ In.
$86.00

Hake's Americana & Collectibles

Toy, Truck, Bell Telephone, Green, Embossed, Open Top, Rubber Tires, Iron, Nickel, Hubley, 9 In.
$230.00

Bertoia Auctions

Truck, Delivery, Parcel Post, Pressed Steel, Painted, Screen Sides, Sonny, 26 In.	825.00
Truck, Dump, A-Frame, Open Cab, Pressed Steel, Black & Red Paint, Raises & Lowers, Buddy L, 24 In.	575.00
Truck, Dump, Driver, Bumper, Windup, Marx, 1930s, 10 ½ In.	245.00
Truck, Dump, Electric Lights, Metal Wheels, Steelcraft, c.1934, 23 In.	863.00
Truck, Dump, Giant, Raises, Lowers, Orange & Green Paint, American National, 26 In.	1898.00
Truck, Dump, Hi-Lift, Windup, Structo, 1950s, 12 In.	95.00
Truck, Dump, Hydraulic, Decals, Buddy L, 1928, 24 In.	595.00
Truck, Dump, Hydraulic, Pressed Steel, Painted, Aluminum Disc Wheels, Buddy L, 24 In.	353.00
Truck, Dump, International, Open Bed, Iron, Decals, Rubber Tires, Arcade, 11 In.	115.00
Truck, Dump, Orange, Buddy L, 15 In.	45.00
Truck, Dump, Pressed Steel, Blue, Bench Seat, Disc Wheels, GMC, Steelcraft, 25 ½ In.	489.00
Truck, Dump, Pressed Steel, Red, Running Board, Clockwork, Kingsbury, c.1927, 14 In.	575.00
Truck, Dump, Pressed Steel, Rubber Wheels, Decals, Buddy L, c.1934, 24 In.	374.00
Truck, Dump, Red, Side Levers, Pressed Steel, Decal, Structo, 17 ½ In.	303.00
Truck, Dump, Side Lever, Disc Wheels, Sturditoy Construction Co., c.1926, 24 In.	1725.00
Truck, Dump, Steel, Lumar, 19 In.	85.00
Truck, Dump, Toyland Construction Company, Windup, Structo, 1951, 12 ½ In.	95.00
Truck, Dump, Toyville, Tin, Windup, Nonpareil Toy Co., 3 ¾ x 4 ¼ x 8 ¾ In.	220.00
Truck, Dump, Wooldridge, 5 Ribs, Yellow, Metal, Doepke, 1946, 25 In.	450.00
Truck, Farm, Trailer, Cow, Tin Lithograph, Battery Operated, Box, Japan, 11 In.	173.00
Truck, Flat Bed Coaster, Pressed Steel, Open Cab, Keystone, c.1927, 26 In.	460.00
Truck, Flat Bed, 5-Ton, Corgi	50.00
Truck, Flat Bed, Koaster, Pressed Steel, Painted, Rubber Tires, Hoisting Rope, Keystone, 25 ½ In.	500.00
Truck, Flat Bed, Leyland, Octopus, Chains, Dinky Toys, 1960	75.00
Truck, Flat Bed, State Highway Dept., Yellow, 38 In.	170.00
Truck, Garbage, Red, White, No. 500, Structo, 1953, 21 In.	160.00
Truck, Gas, Red, Gray, Pressed Steel, Wyandotte, 22 In.	113.00
Truck, Hauler, International, Harvester, Die Cast, Open Body, Yellow, 19 In.	230.00
Truck, Ice, Embossed, Ice, Rubber Tires, Cast Iron, Arcade, 7 In.	259.00
Truck, Ice, Orange & Green Paint, C-Cab, Mack Bulldog, City Ice Co., 3 Ice Cubes, Steelcraft, 27 In.	1725.00
Truck, Jiffy Painting & Decorating, Buckets, Ladders, Red, White, Tin Lithograph, Plastic, 9 ½ In.	107.00
Truck, Junior, Tin, Push, 1930s, 8 ½ In.	145.00
Truck, Ladder, Pressed Steel, Open Frame, Clockwork, Driver, 18 In.	173.00
Truck, Ladder, Windup, Box, Germany	300.00
Truck, Lumber, Aluminum Wheels, Buddy L, c.1926, 24 In.	1035.00
Truck, Lumber, Pressed Steel, Stake Sides, Painted, Buddy L, 24 In.	1265.00
Truck, Mack, Hercules, Motor Express, Stake Sides, Balloon Wheels, Litho, Chein, c.1928, 19 In.	978.00
Truck, Moving Van, Pressed Steel, Open Cab, Green, Black, Decals, Steelcraft, c.1925, 24 In.	1150.00
Truck, Moving Van, Red, Steel, Con-Cor, 1920s, 24 In.	248.00
Truck, Moving, Decals, Black & Red Paint, Pressed Steel, Keystone, c.1935, 11 x 8 In.	748.00
Truck, Oil, Richfield, Disc Wheels, American National, Steelcraft, c.1926, 26 ½ In.	1495.00
Truck, Open Bed, Baggage Line, Yellow, Black, Pressed Steel, Buddy L, c.1940, 12 x 9 In.	460.00
Truck, Payloader, Pressed Steel, Orange, Rubber Tires, Ny-Lint, 18 In.	45.00
Truck, Pickup, Chevrolet, Tin, Friction, Japan, 9 ½ In.	145.00
Truck, Pickup, Tool Box, Yellow, Buddy L, 13 In.	23.00
Truck, Pile Driver, Decals, Red, Cast Iron, Hubley, 12 x 15 In.	208.00
Truck, Police Patrol, Pressed Steel, Closed Cab, Screen Side, Keystone, 27 In.	1495.00
Truck, Police Patrol, Pressed Steel, Decals, Blue Paint, Structo, 16 In.	325.00
Truck, Popsicle, Wood, Painted, Bell, Buddy L, 17 ½ In.	805.00
Truck, Railway Express Agency, Steel, Removable Roof, Doors Open, Decal, Buddy L, c.1940, 24 In. *illus*	489.00
Truck, Semi-Trailer, Gulf, Tin, Orange, Blue, Retractable String Hose, Friction, Courtland, 12 ¾ In.	460.00
Truck, Semi-Trailer, Red Ball Express, Friction, Japan, Box, 1950s, 12 ½ In.	110.00
Truck, Semi-Trailer, Sunshine Service Fruit Growers, Tin Lithograph, Marx, 14 In.	113.00
Truck, Service Wrecker, Steel, Red & White, Wyandotte, 1938, 22 In.	110.00
Truck, Shovel, Clamshell Digger, Open Cab, Red, Black, Spoke Wheels, Big Boy, Kelmet, 26 In.	2415.00
Truck, Shovel, Michigan, Yellow, Pressed Steel, Ny-Lint, 1956, 30 In.	225.00
Truck, Side Dump, Rubber Tires, Disc Wheels, Sturditoy Co., Paint, c.1926, 24 In.	1035.00
Truck, Side, Dump, Mack, Cast Iron, Green, Red, Disc Wheels, 11 In.	690.00
Truck, Son-Ny Railway Express Co., Green & Black, Pressed Steel, Dayton, c.1935, 12 x 7 In.	633.00
Truck, Stake, Black Cab, Yellow Bed, Chain, Baggage Line, Buddy L, 26 In.	3680.00
Truck, Stake, Coast To Coast Cartage Co., Model A Cab, Iron, A.C. Williams, 10 In. *illus*	374.00
Truck, Stake, Kingsbury, Decals, Disc Wheels, Clockwork, c.1927, 10 ½ In.	431.00
Truck, Stake, Open Cab, 5 Removable Stakes, Red & Black Paint, Buddy L, 24 In.	1955.00
Truck, Stake, Red & Blue, Hubley, 5 ¼ In.	275.00
Truck, Stake, Take-Apart, Yellow, Black, Iron, Rubber Tires, A.C. Williams, 7 ¼ In. *illus*	345.00
Truck, Sunshine Biscuits, Embossed, Red, Yellow, Pressed Steel, Metalcraft, 12 In.	345.00

Truck, Swing Loader, Pettibone Mulliken, Steel, Orange, Black, Ny-Lint, 1955......	113.00
Truck, Tanker, Black Cab, Water Tank, Brass Spigot, Metal Cans, Red, Silver Wheels, 23 In.	2473.00
Truck, Tanker, Black, Red Wheels, Pressed, Steel, Buddy L, c.1920, 25 In..........	706.00
Truck, Tanker, Gasoline, Esso, Decal, Red, Gray Plastic Wheels, Matchbox, Box, 1958 ..... *illus*	50.00
Truck, Tanker, Gasoline, Mack Bulldog, Nickel Wheels, A.C. Williams, 5 In.	225.00
Truck, Tanker, Gasoline, Shell Oil, Plastic, Tin Lithograph, Friction, Japan, 1950s, 4 In........	45.00
Truck, Tanker, Gasoline, Tin, Yellow, Red, Nickel Grille, Windup, Marx, 14 ½ In......................	489.00
Truck, Tanker, Oil, Black, Red, Green, Buddy L, 1925, 24 In..........	1450.00
Truck, Tanker, Oil, Hercules, Mack, C-Cab, Balloon Wheels, Paint, Chein, 19 In.	1840.00
Truck, Tanker, Shell, Yellow, Red, Decals, Pressed Steel, Buddy L, c.1930, 6 x 6 In.	489.00
Truck, Tanker, Standard Oil, Red & White, Tin Grill, Spigot, Buddy L, 25 In........	2300.00
Truck, Tanker, Standard Oil, Tin, Red Closed Cab, Electric Headlights, Spigot, 26 In...........	1495.00
Truck, Tanker, Texaco, Paint, Decals, Parking Lights, Buddy L, 1959, 24 In........	95.00
Truck, Tanker, Texaco, Pressed Steel, Buddy L, 1960s, 25 In........	395.00
Truck, Telephone, Mack, Cast Iron, Nickel Water Tank, Painted, Hubley, 9 In........	345.00
Truck, Timber, Tin Litho, Wood Trailer, Driver, Windup, Strauss, 18 In.......	633.00
Truck, Tow, Big Bruiser Super Highway Service, Wrench, Marx, 26 x 10 In.......	30.00
Truck, Tow, Black & Red, Rubber Tires, Buddy L, 27 In..........	5175.00
Truck, Tow, Cast Iron, Rubber Tires, Arcade, 6 In.......	115.00
Truck, Tow, Ford, Die Cast, Hubley, Box, 1953, 6 ½ In.......	135.00
Truck, Tow, Goodrich, Metalcraft, Box, 9 In........	950.00
Truck, Tow, Mack, Rail, Crane, Decal, Painted, Cast Iron, Arcade, 10 ½ In........	863.00
Truck, Tow, No Cab, Open Bench, Crane, Decals, Red, Buddy L, 27 In.......	1093.00
Truck, Tow, Red Paint, Rubber Tires, Sturditoy Trucking Company, Tow Bar, 31 In........	4313.00
Truck, Tow, Red, Blue Chassis, Nickel Grille, Champion, c.1934, 4 ½ In. .... *illus*	805.00
Truck, Tow, Roadster, Orange, Hubley, 5 In.......	250.00
Truck, Tow, Winch, Pressed Steel, Structo, 22 In.......	74.00
Truck, Tow, Yellow, Wyandotte, 1939, 18 In........	225.00
Truck, Toy Town Express Van Lines, Tin Lithograph, L. Marx, 6 x 12 In........	79.00
Truck, U.S. Army, Covered Trailer, Red Hub Caps, Marx, 1940s, 11 & 5 In., 2 Piece........	150.00
Truck, U.S. Army, Pressed Steel, Disc Wheels, Headlights, Canopy, c.1926, 27 In.	1093.00
Truck, U.S. Army, Steel, Canvas Tarp, Balloon Wheels, Structo, c.1928, 17 In........	403.00
Truck, U.S. Mail, Pressed Steel, Mesh Sides, Rubber Tires, Sturditoy .... *illus*	7475.00
Truck, U.S. Mail, Pressed Steel, Screen Panels, Disc Wheels, Decal, Black, Olive, Keystone, 20 In...	1035.00
Truck, Van, Horse, Dinky Toys, Box, 1953	250.00
Truck, Water Tower, Pressed Steel, Painted, Lift-Up Hood, Pump Reservoir, Siren, Keystone, 30 In..	472.00
Truck, Wrigley's Spearmint Chewing Gum, Pressed Steel, Electric Lights, Buddy L, c.1935, 24 In..	805.00
Tucky Turkey, Mohair, Metal Feet, Felt Tail Feathers, Steiff, 1950s, 5 x 4 ½ In.......	200.00
Typewriter, Junior, Tin Lithograph, Turn Dial To Letter, Red & Black, Marx, 1940s, 11 x 8 In.	50.00
Universal Freight Station, Tin, Box, Marx, 12 x 3 ¼ x 7 In........	138.00
Van, Coast To Coast, Mack Semi, Tootsietoy, Box	250.00
Van, Federal, Boggs & Buhl, Die Cast, Tootsietoy, c.1927, 3 In........	350.00
Van, Ford Thames, Light Green, Gray Plastic Wheels, Matchbox, Box, 1958 .... *illus*	44.00
Van, U.S. Mail, Tin Litho, Simulated Panel, Driver, Spring Barrel Mechanism, 1930s, 8 In.......	345.00
Velocipede With Boy, Tin, Stevens & Brown.......	1187.00
Violinist, Tin, Windup, Arms Move, Body Vibrates, T.P.S. Japan, 1956, 5 ¼ In.......	385.00
Wagon, Amish, Open Back, Driver, 2 Horses, Barrels, Cotton, Iron, J. & E. Stevens, c.1900, 15 In. ..	1200.00
Wagon, Barrel, Wood, Lithograph Horses, Jointed, Gibbs Gray Beauty Pacers, Pull, c.1900, 19 In. ..	300.00
Wagon, Circus, Calliope, Overland Circus, Cast Iron, Embossed, Kenton, 9 In. .... *illus*	748.00
Wagon, Circus, Overland, Red Cage, Polar Bear, Driver, Outriders, Iron, Painted, Kenton, 14 ½ In.	205.00
Wagon, Circus, Polar Bear, Horses, Hubley, 1915, 12 In.......	495.00
Wagon, Dairy, Horse, Wood, Printed, Decals, Bottle Carrier, 6 Glass Bottles, Sheffield, 21 ½ In. .	944.00
Wagon, Delivery, Horse Drawn, White, Mar Farm, 10 In........	107.00
Wagon, Drummer's Wagon 1892, Wood, Metal, Gray, Yellow, Model, 31 ½ x 10 In.......	230.00
Wagon, Farm, 2-Wheel Cart, Mule, Welker & Crosby, 1885	1295.00
Wagon, Ice, Driver, 2 Horses, Red, White Wheels, Cast Iron, Hubley, c.1900, 12 In.......	600.00
Wagon, Milk, Horse Drawn, Tin, Windup, Marx, 11 In.	195.00
Wagon, Milk, Horse, Wood, Hood's Grade A Milk, Spoke Wheels, Cow Decal, Schoenhut, 23 In..	633.00
Wagon, Tin, Stenciled, Red, Curved Wood Handle, c.1890, 14 ½ x 23 ½ In........	237.00
Wagon, Water Tank, Motorized, Tin, Enameled, Striping, Rubber Tires, Marklin, 15 In.	12980.00
Waltzing Couple, Tyrolean Costume, Clockwork, Tin, Wire, Painted, 6 ½ In........	502.00
Wheelbarrow, Wood, Painted, Trotting Horse, Light Green, Yellow, Late 1800s, 30 In........	207.00
Whistle, Ferris Wheel, Tin Lithograph, Penny, France, 3 ¾ In........	139.00
Woman, Washing Clothes, Windup, Martin, France, 8 In. .... *illus*	1840.00
Woodcutters' Camp, Wood, Figures, Trees, Horses, Cart, Box, Erzgebirge, c.1880s, 14 x 9 In..	766.00
Zeppelin, Akron, Pressed Steel, Silver, Metal Wheels, Hitch, Steelcraft, 24 In........	1150.00

Toy, Truck, Cement Mixer, Jaeger, Cast Iron, Aluminum Drum, Kenton, 9 ¼ In. $460.00

Bertoia Auctions

Toy, Truck, Cement Mixer, Jaeger, Cast Iron, Nickel Plated Drum, Rubber Tires, Kenton, 6 ½ In. $259.00

Bertoia Auctions

Toy, Truck, Cement Mixer, Mack, Hercules Ready Mixed, Revolving Drum, Tin Litho, Chein, 16 ½ In. $1955.00

Bertoia Auctions

Toy, Truck, Circus, Big Show, Driver, Lion & Tamer, Clockwork, Strauss, 9 In. $863.00

Bertoia Auctions

Toy, Truck, Coal, Open Cab, Driver, Cast Iron, Embossed, Painted, 8 In. $546.00

Bertoia Auctions

Toy, Truck, Railway Express Agency, Steel, Removable Roof, Doors Open, Decal, Buddy L, c.1940, 24 In. $489.00

Bertoia Auctions

Toy, Truck, Stake, Coast To Coast Cartage Co., Model A Cab, Iron, A.C. Williams, 10 In. $374.00

Bertoia Auctions

Toy, Truck, Stake, Take-Apart, Yellow, Black, Iron, Rubber Tires, A.C. Williams, 7 ¼ In. $345.00

Bertoia Auctions

Toy, Truck, Tanker, Gasoline, Esso, Decal, Red, Gray Plastic Wheels, Matchbox, Box, 1958 $50.00

Serious Toyz

Toy, Truck, Tow, Red, Blue Chassis, Nickel Grille, Champion, c.1934, 4 ½ In. $805.00

Bertoia Auctions

Zeppelin, Tin Lithograph, Celluloid Propellers, Clockwork, Germany, 10 ½ In.	403.00
Zilotone, Tin, Figure Plays Tunes, 2 Discs, Multicolor, Windup, Wolverine, 8 x 8 In.	345.00
Zoetrope, 9 2-Sided Lithographed Animation Strips, Bradley, 12 ½ x 12 In.	500.00

TRADE CARD, *see Card, Advertising*

TRAMP ART is a form of folk art made since the Civil War. It is usually made from chip-carved cigar boxes. Examples range from small boxes and picture frames to full-sized pieces of furniture.

Bank, Cottage, 2-Story Building, White Framed Windows, Lace Curtains, Shingles, 9 x 8 In.	224.00
Bank, Cottage, Applied Wood, Gilt Nail, Coin Slot, 9 x 10 In.	71.00
Bank, Cottage, White With Red & Green Accents, Coin Slot On Roof, 3 x 4 In.	130.00
Box, 10 Layer Feet, 7 Layer Sides, 13 Layer Lid, Handle, Lined, 8 x 10 In.	325.00
Box, 12 Layer Hinged Lid, 8-Step Foot, Fabric Lined Interior, Shenandoah Valley, 6 x 10 In.	173.00
Box, 3 Layer Chip Carved Central & Border Design, Dark Stained Shellac, 5 x 14 In.	118.00
Box, Cathedral Shape, Crucifix Imbedded In Top, Flowers, Leaves, Flowers, 20 x 6 In.	153.00
Box, Chip Carved, 6 Layers, Lift Lid, Hexagonal Legs, Peanut Shape Handle, 7 x 10 In.	59.00
Box, Crucifix, 8-Tack Diamond & Triangle Panel, Metal, 15 x 6 In.	47.00
Box, Cube Shape, 5 Layer Pyramid Side, Brass Tack Design, 5-Point Star, 5 x 5 In.	94.00
Box, Lid, Geometric, Pierced, Hearts, Painted, Inside Mirror, 7 ½ x 12 ½ In. ....*illus*	94.00
Box, Pine, Castle Cover, Crisscross Slats, C.M. Barnes, Dobbs, Indiana, 1930, 9 ½ In. ....*illus*	264.00
Box, Pyramids, 62 Layer, Lock Box, Hinged, Brass Lion Handle, Picture, 6 x 8 In.	325.00
Box, Sewing, Hinged Lid, Red Velvet Pincushion Top, 7 x 10 In.	173.00
Box, Sewing, Painted Red, Layered Chip Carved Strips Frame, Recessed Panels, Hinged Lid, 4 x 10 In.	47.00
Box, Sewing, Triangles & Rectangles, Padded Pincushion, Hinged, 7 x 10 In.	295.00
Box, Sewing, Wood, Hinged Lid, Pincushion, Carved Bead Design, 7 x 10 In.	173.00
Box, Wall, Crossbar Crests, Applied Bird Cutouts, Mirror, 38 x 17 In.	88.00
Chest, Chip Carved, 3 Drawers, Layers, Pyramids, Finial, 22 x 12 ¾ In.	561.00
Cigar Box, 3 & 5 Layer Geometric Shapes, Shaped Feet, Paper Lining, Hinged, 4 x 10 In.	35.00
Cigar Box, 6 Layer, Pyramids, Chip Carved, Hinged Lid, 17 Layer, Brass Knob, 6 x 10 In.	41.00
Cigar Box, Old Original Plantation, Hinged, Bracket Feet, 5 x 13 In.	118.00
Cigar Box, Pyramid Side, Hinged Lid, Lock & Hasp, 1891, 5 x 9 In.	59.00
Clock Case, Chip Carved, Triangular Pediment, Rosettes, Hinged Door, 36 x 17 In.	83.00
Clock Case, Shellac Case, Layered, Brass Tacks, Porcelain Button, 10 x 8 ¾ In.	142.00
Crucifix, Christ Figure, Layered Box, Mounted, 17 x 10 In.	59.00
Dresser Box, 5 Layer Lid, Brass Knob, 2 Drawer, Square Feet, Signed Bell, 9 x 10 In.	649.00
Dresser Box, 5 Layer, Chip Carved, Geometric Shapes, Lock, 6 x 11 x 8 In.	147.00
Dresser Box, Chip Carved, Hinged Lid, Bicolor Strips Of Wood, Compartment, 5 x 7 ½ In.	59.00
Dresser, 2 Drawers, Serpentine Trim, Corner Blocks, Shaped Backboard, 7 ½ x 5 ¾ In. ..*illus*	384.00
Frame, 3 Layers, Geometrical Ornaments, Shenandoah Valley, c.1910, 11 x 9 In.	288.00
Frame, 5 Layer Pyramids, Chip Carved, Crisscrossed Frame, Lithographs, Sailor Boys, 8 ¾ x 11 In.	71.00
Frame, Crossed Style, 5 Layer, Photo, German Soldiers Drinking Beer, c.1902, 12 x 14 In.	173.00
Frame, Heart Shape, Double Image, 5 Raised Panels, Lined With Black Velvet, 10 x 10 In.	30.00
Frame, Home Sweet Home, Needlepoint, 4 Long Pyramids, 10 x 12 In.	71.00
Frame, House Shape, Chip Carved, Green, Silver, Gold Strips, Cowboy, Bull, Gable, 13 x 14 In.	47.00
Frame, House Shape, Rosette Finials, 4 Photo Slots, Velvet Lined Triangles, 10 ¾ x 11 In.	165.00
Frame, Openings, 3 Crosses, Porcelain Buttons, Brass Backs, 41 x 25 In. ....*illus*	384.00
Frame, Picture, 17 Religious Images, Brass Collared Milk Glass Buttons, Cross, 34 x 17 In.	325.00
Frame, Picture, 3 Layer, Horizontal Framing, 2 Layer, Nun With Cross, 4 x 11 In.	69.00
Frame, Picture, Multiple Layers, Flat Frame, Flowers, Needlepoint Corner Blocks, 20 x 18 In.	165.00
Frame, Picture, Stained, 5 Layer Design At Corners, 3 Layer Design Between, 10 x 8 In.	35.00
Frame, Printed Church Confirmation Dated 1875, Crossed Corner, 21 x 17 In.	83.00
Frame, Stand-Up, Pierced, Chip Carved, Octagonal, Moonlit Indian Princess, 14 x 14 In.	130.00
Ink Bottle Stand, Dark Stain 3 Layers, 2 Bottles, Pen Rest, 4 x 6 ¾ In.	201.00
Jewelry Box, 3 Layers, Carved, Brown Velvet Lined Panels, Embossed Tape, 6 x 5 In.	71.00
Jewelry Box, Pyramid Shape Sides, Elongated Handle, Hinged, Satin Lining, 6 ½ x 10 ½ In.	142.00
Jewelry Box, Stained Finish, Layered Carving, Crescent Moon, Bird, 2 Doors, 9 x 13 In.	472.00
Match Packet, Walnut & Acorn Design, Porcelain Button, Sandpaper Striker, 9 x 6 In.	47.00
Match Safe, Chip Carved Grid, Diamond Shape, Divided Pocket, Parquet Pieces, 12 x 7 In.	36861.00
Matchbox, Open, Stained 5 Layers, Star Rosettes, 2 ½ x 3 ½ In.	59.00
Mirror, 2 Layer Frame, Lap Jointed, Corner Rosettes, Pedestal, Adjustable, 15 x 9 In. ....*illus*	153.00
Mirror, Chip Carved, Dark Stain, Scallops, Leaves, Crescent, 19 x 8 In.	142.00
Mirror, Frame, Dark Stained, Perpendicular Borders, 23 x 17 In.	94.00
Mirror, Pedestal, Chip Carved, 5 Layer Round Base, Oval 2 Layer Mirror, 9 ½ x 4 ¼ In.	94.00
Mirror, Wall Pocket, Chip Carved, X-Carved Molding, 3 Layer Pyramids, 16 x 12 In.	201.00
Mirror, Wall, Dark Stain, Layered Chip Carved Design, Half Round Top, 49 x 18 In.	153.00

Model, Church, Carved Pyramid, 2 Griffin Doors, 11 Windows, Steeple, Red Roof, 43 x 16 In..	649.00
Mountain Cabin, Rail Fence Border, Levels, Attached Doghouse, Hinged Roof, 10 x 15 In......	212.00
Pencil Box, Multilayer, Carved Sides, Divided Interior, Lock, Catch, Signed, 3 x 9 In............	106.00
Pincushion, Wall Hanging, Chip Carved Backboard, Round, Geometric Shapes, 7 x 4 In.	71.00
Shadow Box, Chip Carved Hearts, Rosettes, Crosses, Crown Shape Finial, 20 x 13 In...............	165.00
Shelf, 2 Shelves, 4 Layer Carved Design, 21 x 22 In.	35.00
Shelf, Wall, 3 Shelves, 11 Layers Of Zigzag Carving, 8 Inset Mirrors, 28 x 28 In.	153.00
Spice Cabinet, Zigzag & Diamond Cut Design, Velvet Liner, Porcelain Knob, 15 x 11 In.........	1118.00
Trinket Box, 3 Pyramid Layers, Recessed Lid, Lock & Key, 4 Brass Knobs, 5 x 10 In.	531.00
Trinket Box, 4 Recessed Sides, Red Velvet Inserts, Hinged, X Pattern, 7 x 7 In....................	142.00
Trinket Box, 5 Layer Base, 6 Chip Carved Layers, 3 ¾ x 5 In....................	71.00
Trinket Box, 5 Layer Pyramids On 4 Sides, 3 Layer Feet & Lid With Pyramids, 4 x 5 In.	71.00
Trinket Box, Chip Carved, Applied Diamond Shapes, Hinges, Lined, 2 ¾ x 5 In.................	59.00
Trinket Box, Chip Carved, Painted Gold, Spool Knob, Inside Painted, 4 ½ x 3 ½ In................	283.00
Trinket Box, Cube Shape, Footed, Framed Panels, 6 Layer Lift Lid, Acorn Finial, 6 x 6 In.......	384.00
Trinket Box, Multilayered Carving, 2 Drawers, 5 Layer Round Feet, Round Knobs, 8 x 6 In....	708.00
Trinket Box, Red Painted Chip Carving, Blue Panels, Square Black Feet, Lift Lid, 4 x 8 In.	35.00
Trinket Box, Slide Lid, 4 Layer Pyramid Sides, 6 Layer Lid, Red Chief Cigar Label, 3 x 6 In......	47.00
Trinket Box, Slide Lid, Felt Lined, Layered Pyramids, Splayed Feet, Wallpaper, 4 x 11 In.......	53.00
Trinket Box, Stained, 3 & 5 Layer Carved Design, Velvet Lined, Lid, 4 x 9 In.................	83.00
Trinket Box, Stars, Diamonds, Triangles In Layers, 9 Sides, Hinged, 3 Layer Feet, 7 x 12 In....	325.00
Wall Bracket, Chip Carved, Demilune Shelf, 7 ¾ x 8 ¾ In	83.00
Wall Bracket, Dark Stain, Triangular, Layers, Chip Carved, Pyramid Feet, 6 ¾ x 7 ½ In.	118.00
Wall Bracket, Diamond Shape, Cross Pierced In Backboard, Shield Shape, 8 x 7 In...............	12.00
Wall Pocket, 6 Layer Splayed Base, 5-Sided Back, Diamond Shape Finial, 1902, 9 x 10 In......	142.00
Wall Pocket, Dark Stain, Carved Backboards, Pocket, Rosettes, 10 x 8 In.	142.00
Wall Pocket, Half Round Backboard, Wedge Shape, Painted Maple Leaves, Star, 9 x 6 In.......	47.00
Wall Pocket, Mirror Back, Chip Carved, Elongated Pyramid, 6 & 7 Layers, 16 x 10 ½ In........	295.00
Wall Pocket, Stained & Varnished 2 Color Diamond Shaped Design, Chain Hanger, 11 x 7 In..	118.00
Watch Safe, Chip Carved, Backboard, 4 Layer, 6 Layer Heart, Wall, 10 x 4 In.	590.00

TRAPS for animals may be handmade. One of the most unusual is the mousetrap made so that when the mouse entered the trap, it was hit on the head with a mallet. Other traps were commercially manufactured and often are marked with the name of the manufacturer. Many traps were designed to be as humane as possible, and they would trap the live animal so it could be released in the woods.

Bear, Iron, Wrought, 3 Tooth Jaws, Springs, 29 In........................	189.00
Bear, Kodiak, No. 41-A-X, Cast Iron, Herter's Inc....................	1560.00
Bear, Oneida Newhouse No. 6, 1880s	3491.00
Bee, Amber Glass, Stopper, Raised Center Base, Wire Bail Handle, 8 ¾ x 5 ½ In.	35.00
Critter, Cage, 15 x 7 ¾ In.	69.00
Fish, Woven Bamboo, Japan, 1900s, 12 x 3 In.	70.00
Fly Catcher, Etched, Engraved Bamboo, Scroll Feet, 1800s, 7 ½ x 10 In.....................	657.00
Minnow, Wire, Hinged Lid, Ring, c.1900, 15 x 9 In.	65.00
Rat, 4-Way, Can't Miss Spring, McGill Metal Products, 1940s.......................	14.00
Rat, Cage, Ramp, Tin, Paint, Germany, 4 ¾ x 1 ½ In...........................	275.00
Snare, Small Game, Self Locking Steel, No. 00, Thompson, 1960s, 30 In........................	22.00

TREEN, *see Wooden category.*

TRENCH ART is a form of folk art made by soldiers. Metal casings from bullets and mortar shells were cut and decorated to form useful objects, such as vases.

Bracelet, Cuff, RGH Monogram, Star Circle, Pierced, Metal, 5 ¼ x 1 ½ In................................	158.00
Letter Opener, World War I Bullet Shell, Dove Holding Flower, c.1916, 7 ¾ In........................	110.00
Vase, Artillery Shell, Leaves, FN St. 124, Aug. 1918 & Juni 1918, 9 In., Pair ....*illus*	230.00
Vase, Shell Case, Bronze, Silver, Copper Moorish Designs, Hebrew Text, c.1918, 11 In.............	682.00
Vase, Shell Casing, Brass, Holly Design, Reims France, World War I, 13 In., Pair	435.00
Vase, Shell, Brass, Torch Design, c.1915, 7 ½ x 3 ¾ In.................................	175.00

TRIVETS are now used to hold hot dishes. Most trivets of the late nineteenth and early twentieth centuries were made to hold hot irons. Iron or brass reproductions are being made of many of the old styles.

Brass, Reticulated, Iron Stand, 3 Shaped Legs, 11 x 14 In.................................	118.00
Cast Iron, Heart, Rope Twist, 1800s, 26 In........................	323.00
Cast Iron, Round, Spoked, Center Cross, Footed, 16 ¼ In........................	118.00

Toy, Truck, U.S. Mail, Pressed Steel, Mesh Sides, Rubber Tires, Sturditoy
$7475.00

Bertoia Auctions

Toy, Van, Ford Thames, Light Green, Gray Plastic Wheels, Matchbox, Box, 1958
$44.00

Serious Toyz

Toy, Wagon, Circus, Calliope, Overland Circus, Cast Iron, Embossed, Kenton, 9 In.
$748.00

Bertoia Auctions

Toy, Woman, Washing Clothes, Windup, Martin, France, 8 In.
$1840.00

Bertoia Auctions

Tramp Art, Box, Lid, Geometric, Pierced, Hearts, Painted, Inside Mirror, 7 ½ x 12 ½ In.
$94.00

Conestoga Auction Co., Inc.

Tramp Art, Box, Pine, Castle Cover, Crisscross Slats, C.M. Barnes, Dobbs, Indiana, 1930, 9 ½ In.
$264.00

Garth's Auctions, Inc.

Tramp Art, Dresser, 2 Drawers, Serpentine Trim, Corner Blocks, Shaped Backboard, 7 ½ x 5 ¾ In.
$384.00

Conestoga Auction Co., Inc.

Tramp Art, Frame, Openings, 3 Crosses, Porcelain Buttons, Brass Backs, 41 x 25 In.
$384.00

Conestoga Auction Co., Inc.

Copper, Pierced Brass Overlay, Reptile Design, 6 In.	17.00
Redware, Round, Hammer, Heart, Linked Chains, Stenciled Snuff, 8 ¼ In.	152.00
Wrought Iron, Heart Shape, 3 Legs, Penny Feet, 7 In.	236.00
Wrought Iron, Hearth Pot, 3 Legs, Boots On 2 Legs, Hanging Loops, 9 x 6 ½ In.	118.00

TRUNKS of many types were made. The nineteenth-century sea chest was often handmade of unpainted wood. Brass-fitted camphorwood chests were brought back from the Orient. Leather-covered trunks were popular from the late eighteenth to mid-nineteenth centuries. By 1895, trunks were covered with canvas or decorated sheet metal. Embossed metal coverings were used from 1870 to 1910. By 1925, trunks were covered with vulcanized fiber or undecorated metal. Suitcases are listed here.

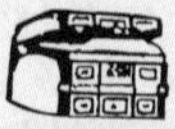

American Tourister, Tiara, Scarlet Red, 1960s, 6 Piece	275.00
Basswood, Dovetailed Box, Painted, New England, c.1820, 10 ½ x 28 In.	382.00
Bird & Flower Design, Black & Brown, Metal Lock & Hinges, 1800s, 6 x 9 In.	230.00
Briefcase, Crocodile, Black, Hard Case, Brass Locks, Latches, Pigskin, c.1970, 17 x 12 In.	1554.00
Camphorwood, Brass Bound, Lock & Key, 1800s, 9 x 22 In.	489.00
Copper, Hammered Scene Of Dutch Family, Riverside, Lift Top, 15 x 20 x 14 In.	150.00
Dome Top, Decorated, Multicolor Vines, Leaves, Newspaper Lined, c.1868, 14 x 23 In.	353.00
Dome Top, Hinged, Pierced Strap Work, Painted Scrolling Highlights, c.1780, 30 x 50 In.	325.00
Dome Top, Leather, Black, Brown, Fitted Interior, c.1880, 23 x 34 In.	207.00
Dome Top, Leather, Embossed, Scroll Design, Bracket Feet, Spain, 1700s, 11 x 18 In.	441.00
Dome Top, Mixed Wood, Dovetailed, Flowers, Leaves, 19th Century, 16 x 26 x 17 In.	181.00
Dome Top, Pine, Dovetailed, Black, Red & Yellow, New England, c.1825, 9 x 24 In. *illus*	499.00
Dome Top, Pine, Dovetailed, Grain Painted, Yellow, Green Accents, c.1850, 11 x 24 In.	353.00
Dome Top, Pine, Paint, Flower Panel, c.1900, 8 x 17 ¼ In.	235.00
Dome Top, Pine, Painted, Red, Wavy Black Lines, Dashes, Hinged Lid, 1800s, 7 x 16 In.	563.00
Dome Top, Red, Yellow & Green, Decorations, c.1830, 8 x 16 x 6 In.	16100.00
Dome Top, Wood, Metal, Fitted Decoupage, Interior, 26 ½ x 34 ¼ In.	201.00
Goyard, Cloth, Leather Bound, Hinged Lid, Lift Out Tray, Monogram, France, c.1900, 18 x 20 In.	2963.00
Iron, Gilt Brass Paneled Front, Peacocks & Horses, Lift Top, 40 x 56 x 33 In.	720.00
Leather Covered, Brass Studded, 1812	95.00
Louis Vuitton, Backpack, Leather, Classic Pattern	649.00
Louis Vuitton, Beechwood Slat, Leather Trim, c.1900	6613.00
Louis Vuitton, Brass Tacks, Latches, Leather Strips, Wood, Steel, Label, c.1910, 23 x 36 In. *illus*	5664.00
Louis Vuitton, Briefcase, Canvas, Monogram, 11 x 16 In. *illus*	600.00
Louis Vuitton, Ebonized Canvas, Imprinted Brass Nail Heads, Lined, 11 x 36 x 22 In.	900.00
Louis Vuitton, Garment Bag, Folding, Brown Leather Accents, Monogram, 17 x 23 x 10 In.	325.00
Louis Vuitton, Garment Bag, Foldover, Brown, Tan Leather Trim, Monogram, 36 x 22 In.	388.00
Louis Vuitton, Leather Bands, Handles, Early 1900s, 28 x 36 In.	7500.00
Louis Vuitton, Steamer, Wood, Cloth, 37 x 21 In.	2726.00
Louis Vuitton, Suitcase, Leather, Brown, Tan Trim, Linen Interior, Soft Sides, 21 x 31 In.	359.00
Louis Vuitton, Suitcase, Leather, LV Monogram, Belted Strap, Casters, 22 x 24 In.	6573.00
Louis Vuitton, Suitcase, Leather, Paper Label, France, c.1925, 6 ¾ x 26 ½ In.	1955.00
Louis Vuitton, Suitcase, Logo, Leather Straps, Buckles, Brass Fittings, Pockets, 32 x 20 In. *illus*	676.00
Louis Vuitton, Suitcase, Logos, Key, Initials FJG, Label, 24 x 14 x 7 In.	1475.00
Louis Vuitton, Suitcase, Soft Sides, 2 Leather Straps, 18 x 27 x 10 In.	502.00
Louis Vuitton, Suitcase, Soft Sides, 2 Leather Straps, Medium, 21 x 31 x 10 In.	384.00
Louis Vuitton, Travel Bag, Canvas, Soft Sides, Monogram, 18 x 27 x 8 In.	720.00
Louis Vuitton, Travel Bag, Soft Side, 24 x 25 x 10 In.	826.00
Louis Vuitton, Trunk, Flat Top, Canvas, Wood Staves, Fitted Interior, c.1890, 14 x 44 In.	8050.00
Louis Vuitton, Trunk, Flat Top, Canvas, Wood Staves, Fitted Interior, c.1895, 20 x 39 In.	3738.00
Oak, Carved Panels, Lift Top, c.1790, 26 x 52 In.	366.00
Pigskin, Domestic Life Scenes, Metal Loop Handles, Chinese, c.1935, 9 x 12 In.	153.00
Plank, Embossed Metal Panels & Corners, Brackets, Leather Handles, 14 x 26 In.	270.00
Seaman's, Painted Wood, Ship Painting, Inside Lid, Flip Top, Bail Handles, 1800s, 17 x 30 In.	178.00
Softwood, Red Ground, Leaves, Flowers, Bail Handles, Iron Strap Hinges, c.1900, 14 x 32 In.	254.00
Wood, Grain Painted, Brass Handles, 30 x 42 x 20 In.	800.00

TUTHILL Cut Glass Company of Middletown, New York, worked from 1902 to 1923. Of special interest are the finely cut pieces of stemware and tableware.

Vase, Sweetpea, Tiger Lily, Engraved, American Brilliant, 4 ½ x 5 ¾ In.	100.00

TYPEWRITER collectors divide typewriters into two main classifications: the index machine, which has a pointer and a dial for letter selection, and the keyboard machine, most commonly seen today. The first successful typewriter was made by Sholes and Glidden in 1874.

AT&T, Model 6510, Electronic, Black, Cover, Cord, Ribbon, Correcting Tape, Receipt, c.1988	25.00

Award Pin, 30 Words Per Minute, Commercial Award Pin Co., Chicago, 1930s, ½ x ¾ In.	11.00
Facit, Model 1620, Leatherette Case, Sweden, c.1969	95.00
Font Elements, IBM Selectric I & II, c.1961, 5 Piece	98.00
Hammond, Multiplex, Portable, Case, Ohio, c.1913, 14 x 13 x 10 In.	935.00
Hermes Baby Rocket, Portable, Subcompact, Aqua, Hard Case, Swiss, 11 ½ x 11 ½ In.	90.00
Hermes Rocket, Sea Green, Portable, Case, 2 ¾ x 11 ¼ x 11 ¼ In.	59.00
Musicwriter, R.C. Allen Business Machines, c.1954 ....*illus*	194.00
Olympia, Deluxe SM, Manual, Case, West Germany	250.00
Olympia, Manual, Wood Case, Early 1950s, 13 x 12 x 5 In.	95.00
Remington, Compact, Portable, Case, 1937	145.00
Royal, Model 10, Round Glass Keys, Beveled Glass Panel, Manual, 1924-25	90.00
Simplex, Model G, Tin Lithograph, Original Box, c.1924, 8 ⅛ x 6 ½ x 2 ½ In.	90.00
Smith-Corona, Skyriter, Green Keys, Manual, Portable, Case, 1950s	350.00
Tom Thumb, Junior, Red, White Space Bar, Plastic, Box, Instructions, c.1960, 10 x 7 ½ In.	45.00
Underwood, Leader, Manual, Green Carry Case, 1950s, 12 x 11 x 6 In.	110.00

TYPEWRITER RIBBON TINS are now being collected. The lithographed tin containers have been used since the 1870s. Most popular with collectors are tins with pictorial graphics.

A.P. Little, Black Boy Image, Satin Finish, Underwood, 2 ½ In.	148.00
Allied, Sea Gull, Flying Over Ocean Wave, Gray, Black, White, 2 ½ In.	30.00
Benjamin Franklin, Portrait, Tin Lithograph, Round, 2 ½ In.	15.00
Butterfly, Trees, Yellow, Orange, Black, Codo Mfg., Round, 2 ½ In.	24.00
Carter's Ideal, Green, Yellow, Square, 1 ⅞ In.	29.00
Carter's, Five O'Clock, Woman Powdering Nose, Gold, Black, White, Round, 2 ½ In.	30.00
Carter's, Woman's Silhouette, Navy Blue, Round, 2 ⅜ In.	22.00
Challenge, Knight In Armor, Green, Black, For Underwood Med., 2 ¼ In.	30.00
Commercial, Silver, Blue, Secretary Silhouette, Stenno Ribbon & Carbon Mfg., 2 ½ In.	28.00
Crusader Brand, Blue, Silver, Red, c.1900, 2 ¾ In.	50.00
Degan Publishing Co., Longwearing, Woman Typing, 2 ⅝ x ⅞ In. ....*illus*	176.00
Elk, Smith Corona, Black, Yellow, White, Tin	22.00
Fie Service, Airplane Graphic, For Underwood Black & Red Med, 2 x 2 In.	18.00
Flint, Royal No. 10, Black Record, Mustard Yellow, Red, Keelox, 2 ½ x 2 ½ In.	11.00
Old English, Horse Drawn Carriage, In Snow, Round, Waters Mfg. Co., 2 ½ In.	35.00
Panama, Canal Image, Orange, Yellow, Blue, Manifold Supplies, 2 ½ x 2 ½ In.	22.00
Panama, Map, Airplane Flying Over Panama, Blue, Yellow, Red, L.C. Smith, 2 ½ x 3 In.	15.00
Pinnacle, Stripes, Mauve, Yellow, Gold, Columbia Ribbon & Carbon Mfg., 2 ½ In.	28.00
Underwood, Jumping Horse, Rider, Gold Ground, Blue, 2 ½ In.	18.00

UHL POTTERY was made in Evansville, Indiana, in 1854. The pottery moved to Huntingburg, Indiana, in 1908. Stoneware and glazed pottery were made until the mid-1940s.

Crock, Knife Sharpener Edge, Acorn Mark, ½ Gal.	48.00
Figure, Boot, Star, 4 In.	130.00
Pitcher, Blue, White, Grapes, Leaves, 9 In.	220.00
Pitcher, Globular, Red, Flowers, Marked, 5 In.	54.00
Stein, Brown, Lattice, Grapes, Leaves, 5 ¼ In.	80.00

UMBRELLA collectors like rain or shine. The first known umbrella was owned by King Louis XIII of France in 1637. The earliest umbrellas were sunshades, not designed to be used in the rain. The umbrella was embellished and redesigned many times. In 1852, the fluted steel rib style was developed and it has remained the most useful style.

Gold Filled Handle, Engraved, F.C. & Co., 12 In.	207.00
Malacan Shaft, Dog Head Handle, Glass Eye, c.1920	300.00
Parasol, Carved Ivory Handle, Nautical Robes, Lace Shade, England, 1800s, 23 ½ In. ....*illus*	206.00
Wood Handle, Cotton, Monogram Logo, Louis Vuitton, 35 In.	120.00
Wood Shaft, Rayon, Plaid, Japan, c.1945, 17 In.	24.00

UNION PORCELAIN WORKS was originally William Boch & Brothers, located in Greenpoint, New York. Thomas C. Smith bought the company in 1861 and renamed it Union Porcelain Works. The company went through a series of ownership changes and finally closed about 1922. The company made a fine quality white porcelain that was often decorated in clear, bright colors. Don t confuse this company with its competitor, Charles Cartlidge and Company, also in Greenpoint.

Oyster Plate, 4 Wells, Multicolor, White Ground, Sea Life, Shell Cup, c.1881, 9 x 6 In.	375.00
Oyster Plate, 5 Wells, Orange, Pink, Sea Life, Oval, 1881, 8 ½ x 6 ½ In.	395.00
Oyster Plate, 6 Wells, Nautical Symbols, Multicolor, c.1885, 9 ¼ In.	595.00

Tramp Art, Mirror, 2 Layer Frame, Lap Jointed, Corner Rosettes, Pedestal, Adjustable, 15 x 9 In.
$153.00

Conestoga Auction Co., Inc.

Trench Art, Vase, Artillery Shell, Leaves, FN St. 124, Aug. 1918 & Juni 1918, 9 In., Pair
$230.00

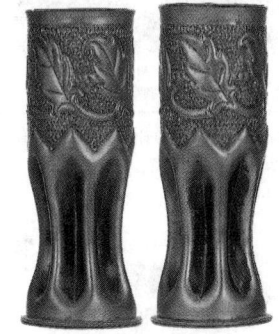

The Stein Auction Co.

Trunk, Dome Top, Pine, Dovetailed, Black, Red & Yellow, New England, c.1825, 9 x 24 In.
$499.00

Garth's Auctions, Inc.

Trunk, Louis Vuitton, Brass Tacks, Latches, Leather Strips, Wood, Steel, Label, c.1910, 23 x 36 In.
$5664.00

U
V

Brunk Auctions

Trunk, Louis Vuitton, Briefcase, Canvas, Monogram, 11 x 16 In.
$600.00

DuMouchelles Art Gallery

Trunk, Louis Vuitton, Suitcase, Logo, Leather Straps, Buckles, Brass Fittings, Pockets, 32 x 20 In.
$676.00

New Orleans Auction Galleries, Inc.

Typewriter, Musicwriter, R.C. Allen Business Machines, c.1954
$194.00

Auction Team Breker

TIP

Never fold old paper.

Typewriter Ribbon Tin, Degan Publishing Co., Longwearing, Woman Typing, 2 ⅝ x ⅞ In.
$176.00

Wm Morford Antiques

Pitcher, Dog Handle, Pioneer, Indian, Eagle, c.1888, 9 ¼ In. 1860.00
Pitcher, Glaze, Jasperware, Heathen Chinee, Karl Mueller, c.1880, 9 ¾ x 10 ½ In. .... *illus* 6820.00
Water Cooler, Stone Filter, Ribbed Lid, Marked, c.1883, 17 x 9 ½ In. 310.00

UNIVERSITY CITY POTTERY, of University, Missouri, worked from 1909 to 1915. Well-known artists, including Taxile Doat, Adelaide Alsop Robineau, and Frederick Hurten Rhead, worked there.

Vase, Blue & Amber Matte Glaze, Spherical, Signed, 5 x 5 In. 1240.00

UNIVERSITY OF NORTH DAKOTA, *see North Dakota School of Mines category.*

VAL ST. LAMBERT Cristalleries of Belgium was founded by Messieurs Kemlin and Lelievre in 1825. The company is still in operation. All types of table glassware and decorative glassware have been made. Pieces are often decorated with cut designs.

Box, Cranberry Cut To Clear, Flashed Hobstar, Crosscut Diamond & Fan, 3 x 8 In. 100.00
Candlestick, Galatee, 5 In. 25.00
Champagne, Glamour, 4 ⅜ In. 28.00
Dresser Set, Cornflower Blue, Geometrics, Floral Band, Stopper, 4-6 In., 3 Piece 161.00
Glass, Juice, Empire, 5 ⅛ In. 40.00
Goblet, Water, Kussnacht, 6 In. 55.00
Inkwell, Cranberry To Green, Cameo Cut, Brass Flip Top, Flowers, 5 In. 650.00
Spoon Rest, Shaped Rim, ¾ x 2 ½ In., 8 Piece 122.00
Vase, Cobalt Blue Cut To Clear, Gold Classical Greek Design, Signed, 10 ¼ In. 100.00
Vase, Flowers, Cobalt Blue, Cut To Clear, Signed, 6 ½ In. 316.00
Vase, Green To Clear, Double Cut, Overlay, Signed Label, 6 ⅜ In. 115.00
Vase, Irises, Acid Etched, Cameo, Cylinder, Signed, 12 ¼ x 3 ½ In. 1054.00
Wine, Berncastel, Light Green, 7 ¼ In. 90.00
Wine, Red Cut To Clear, 7 ½ In. 325.00

VALLERYSTHAL GLASSWORKS was founded in 1836 in Lorraine, France. In 1854, the firm became Klenglin et Cie. It made table and decorative glass, opaline, cameo, and art glass. A line of covered, pressed glass animal dishes was made in the nineteenth century. The firm is still working.

Bowl, Argonaut Shell, Shells, Dolphin Feet, Lid, Finial, Blue, 1900s, 6 x 5 In. 145.00
Candleholder, Bambous Pattern, Yellow, Opaline, 21 ¼ In., Pair 960.00
Decanter, Portieux, Bulbous, Long Neck, Blue, Stopper, Sticker, 11 In. 65.00
Dish, Cover, Artichoke, Milk Glass, White, Footed, 1880s, 6 In. 43.00
Dish, Cover, Fish, Milk Glass, White, Orange, c.1875, 7 ½ In. 135.00
Dish, Cover, Turtle & Snail, Blue, 5 ½ x 7 ½ In. 280.00
Dish, Hen On Nest Cover, Milk Glass, Signed, 2 In. 22.00

VAN BRIGGLE POTTERY was started by Artus Van Briggle in Colorado Springs, Colorado, after 1901. Van Briggle had been a decorator at Rookwood Pottery of Cincinnati, Ohio. He died in 1904 and his wife took over managing the pottery. One of the employees, Kenneth Stevenson, took over the company in 1969. He died in 1990 and his wife and son ran the pottery. She died in 2010 and her children are trying to sell the company. The wares usually had modeled relief decorations and a soft, dull glaze.

Bookends, Owl, Figural, Dark Mulberry Glaze, 5 x 4 ¼ In. 130.00
Bookends, Owl, Spread Wings, Mountain Crag Brown Glaze, 1915, 5 x 5 x 3 In. 1364.00
Bookends, Peacock, Swirled Fan, Shaped Base, Turquoise, 5 ½ x 5 ¾ In. 108.00
Bowl, Brown, Green Overspray, 1915, 6 ¾ x 2 ¾ In. 213.00
Bowl, Flower Frog, Oak Leaf, Ming Turquoise, Marked, 14 ½ x 5 ¼ In. 127.00
Bowl, Mottled Pink Matte Glaze, Marked, 1907, 6 ½ x 2 ½ In. 84.00
Bowl, Shell Maiden, Seated, Mauve Matte Glaze, Marked, 7 ½ In. 132.00
Bowl, Yucca, Brown & Green Matte Glaze, Squat, Marked, 4 ¼ In. 138.00
Candlestick, Lizards, Blue Shaded To Green Glaze, Tapered, Swollen Top, 1930s, 11 In., Pair. 324.00
Humidor, Lid, Tomahawks, Green Matte Glaze, Marked, 1902, 6 x 5 In. .... *illus* 4650.00
Lamp, Maiden Holding Jug, Dried Butterflies & Flowers On Shade, 24 In. .... *illus* 109.00
Letter Holder, Mountain Craig Brown Glaze, Impressed Design, 4 ½ x 5 ¾ In. 351.00
Pitcher, Purple, Blue Accents, Marked, 5 ½ In. 45.00
Planter, Elephant, Ming Turquoise, Mark, 1985, 11 x 8 ½ In. 46.00
Plate, Grapes, Leaves, Blue, Green Glaze, Paper Label, 8 In. 1116.00
Toast Cup, Footed, Blue & Turquoise Glaze, 10 ½ x 5 ½ In. 3596.00
Urn, Maroon Matte Glaze, Shouldered Incised Marks, c.1905, 6 ½ x 5 In. 450.00
Vase, 2 Loop Handles, Bell Shape, Daisies, Mulberry Glaze, 9 ¾ In. 316.00

Vase, 4 Handles, Cylindrical, Swelled, Peacock Feather, Mulberry Glaze, 14 ⅜ In.	489.00
Vase, Arrow Leaf Plants, Light Brown & Beige Glaze, Incised, 1906, 9 ¼ x 8 ½ In. ....*illus*	3100.00
Vase, Bats, Persian Rose Glaze, Flared Bottom, 1916, 10 ¾ x 4 In.	992.00
Vase, Birds In Flight, Pink Glaze, c.1906, 4 x 4 ¾ In.	124.00
Vase, Blue Matte Glaze, Dragonfly Handles, Marked, c.1910, 10 In.	476.00
Vase, Blue Matte Glaze, Lavender, Marked, 1917, 5 ½ In.	345.00
Vase, Bud, Swirl Lobed, Green Matte Glaze, Incised, 1902, 6 x 2 In.	2356.00
Vase, Bulbous, Blue Glaze, 1905, 7 x 3 ½ In.	868.00
Vase, Bulbous, Moth Design, Blue Matte Glaze, Sea Green, 2 ¾ In.	104.00
Vase, Bulbous, Purple, Blue Accents, Relief Lotus, 4 ½ In.	57.00
Vase, Bulbous, Squat, Pinecones, Mulberry Matte Glaze, Blue Hazing, 5 ¾ x 10 ½ In.	259.00
Vase, Climbing For Honey, Bears, Mountain Craig Brown Glaze, Marked, 1919, 14 ½ x 5 In. *illus*	6200.00
Vase, Columbines, Blue Glaze, Incised, 1906, 10 ¾ x 4 ½ In.	2232.00
Vase, Cornflowers, Curdled Green & Purple Glaze, Squat, 1904, 5 x 9 ¼ In.	2356.00
Vase, Crabs, Slip Design, Pink Ground, Textured, Marked, c.1884, 7 ¼ In.	834.00
Vase, Cylinder, Aqua Matte Glaze, Marked, 9 ½ In.	135.00
Vase, Cylinder, Slight Taper, Round Foot, Mulberry Glaze, 1917, 8 In.	230.00
Vase, Daffodil, Dusty Rose, Marked, 9 ⅓ In.	115.00
Vase, Daffodils, Green Glaze, 1902, 10 ¾ x 4 In.	1860.00
Vase, Daisies, Maroon, Blue Matte Glaze, Incised Marks, Post 1920s, 7 ½ x 4 ½ In.	90.00
Vase, Daisies, Maroon, Blue Matte Glaze, Incised, c.1928, 7 ½ x 9 In.	385.00
Vase, Dandelions, Squared, Persian Rose Glaze, 1903, 10 x 3 ¾ In.	1984.00
Vase, Despondency, Nude Female, Blue Over Green Matte Glaze, 1920s, 13 x 5 ½ In. ....*illus*	5270.00
Vase, Dogwood Flower, Blue Matte Glaze, Neck Handles, Impressed, c.1910, 10 ½ In.	558.00
Vase, Dragonflies, Purple Matte Glaze, Over Rose, Marked, c.1925, 7 In.	253.00
Vase, Elongated Oval, Raised Design, 5 In.	124.00
Vase, Embossed Coneflower Design, Mulberry Glaze, Marked, 9 ¼ In.	633.00
Vase, Figure Of Woman, Gown, Mottled Pink Matte Glaze, Shaped Rim, Marked, 1916, 8 In.	3565.00
Vase, Green & Mottled Brown Matte Glaze, Oval, Signed, 1903, 6 ¼ In.	589.00
Vase, Green Matte Glaze, Arts & Crafts, Footed, 1915, 4 ½ In.	354.00
Vase, Heart Shape Leaves, Brown Glaze, c.1906, 9 ½ x 5 In.	1984.00
Vase, Irises, Deep Purple Glaze, c.1910, 9 x 4 ¼ In.	1054.00
Vase, Leaves, Blue & Green Glaze, c.1910, 5 x 4 In.	868.00
Vase, Leaves, Blue Green Glaze, Squat, 1920, 4 ½ x 7 ½ In.	465.00
Vase, Leaves, Swirling, Green Glaze, Squat, c.1910, 4 ¼ x 5 In.	682.00
Vase, Lorelei, Mountain Craig Brown, 1920s, 9 ½ x 4 ¼ In.	1116.00
Vase, Moths, Blue Green Glaze, Oval, c.1910, 6 ¾ x 3 ¾ In.	868.00
Vase, Mulberry Matte Glaze, Metallic Glaze, Tapered, 1920s, 6 In.	550.00
Vase, Peacock Feather, Bright Green Glaze, Cylinder, 1903, 12 x 3 ¾ In.	4960.00
Vase, Pear Shape, 2 Handles At Neck, Embossed Leaves, Brown Glaze, 9 In.	259.00
Vase, Pine Boughs, Brown Glaze, Squat, 1915, 6 x 9 ¾ In.	2232.00
Vase, Poppies, Blue & Green Glaze, 1907, 7 x 4 ½ In.	1364.00
Vase, Poppies, Brown Mottled Matte Glaze, Incised Mark, 1915, 7 ½ In.	483.00
Vase, Poppies, Curdled Blue Glaze, Paneled, 1907, 8 ¾ x 3 ½ In.	1364.00
Vase, Poppies, Green Matte Glaze, 1903, 8 ¼ x 3 In.	1364.00
Vase, Smokestack Shape, Band Of Leaves, Mulberry Matte Glaze, Blue Hazing, 8 ¾ In.	345.00
Vase, Stylized Flowers, Yellow, Cream Matte Glaze, Signed, c.1906, 4 ½ x 9 In.	1140.00
Vase, Stylized Leaves, Shaded Mulberry Glaze, 4 ½ x 8 In.	194.00
Vase, Stylized Leaves, Shouldered, Brown Glaze, c.1915, 13 ¼ x 6 In.	1116.00
Vase, Swirling Leaves, Mulberry Glaze, Squat, Tapered, 1922-26, 4 ½ x 6 ½ In.	243.00
Vase, Swollen Shoulder, Cylinder, Flowers, Gray Over Pink Matte Glaze, c.1910, 3 ¼ In.	403.00
Vase, Tulips, Yellow & Glaze, Paper Label, c.1909, 5 x 5 In.	930.00
Vase, Turquoise Glaze, Flared, 1906, 10 x 4 In.	465.00
Vase, Turquoise, Globular, 2 Handles, 1930s, 7 ½ x 8 ½ In.	243.00
Vase, Virginia Creepers, Rose & Green Glaze, 2 Handles, Incised, 1905, 8 x 9 In. ....*illus*	2108.00
Vase, Yucca Covered, Mountain Craig Brown Glaze, 1920, 17 In.	496.00
Vessel, Indigo Glaze, 1905, 3 ½ x 4 ½ In.	186.00

VASA MURRHINA is the name of a glassware made by the Vasa Murrhina Art Glass Company of Sandwich, Massachusetts, about 1884. The glassware was transparent and was embedded with small pieces of colored glass and metallic flakes. The mica flakes were coated with silver, gold, copper, or nickel. Some of the pieces were cased. The same type of glass was made in England. Collectors often confuse Vasa Murrhina glass with aventurine, spatter, or spangle glass. There is uncertainty about what actually was made by the Vasa Murrhina factory. Related pieces may be listed under Spangle Glass.

Pitcher, Water, Coin Spot, Tricorner Top, Amber Ribbed Handle, 8 ½ In.	250.00

Umbrella, Parasol, Carved Ivory Handle, Nautical Robes, Lace Shade, England, 1800s, 23 ½ In.
$206.00

Cowan's Auctions

Union Porcelain Works, Pitcher, Glaze, Jasperware, Heathen Chinee, Karl Mueller, c.1880, 9 ¾ x 10 ½ In.
$6820.00

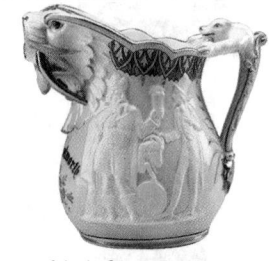

Rago Arts & Auction Center

Van Briggle, Humidor, Lid, Tomahawks, Green Matte Glaze, Marked, 1902, 6 x 5 In.
$4650.00

Rago Arts & Auction Center

Van Briggle, Lamp, Maiden Holding Jug, Dried Butterflies & Flowers On Shade, 24 In.
$109.00

James D. Julia Inc.

U
V

Van Briggle, Vase, Arrow Leaf Plants, Light Brown & Beige Glaze, Incised, 1906, 9 ¼ x 8 ½ In.
$3100.00

Rago Arts & Auction Center

Van Briggle, Vase, Climbing For Honey, Bears, Mountain Craig Brown Glaze, Marked, 1919, 14 ½ x 5 In.
$6200.00

Rago Arts & Auction Center

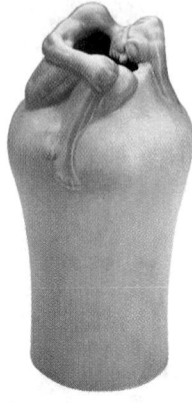

Van Briggle, Vase, Despondency, Nude Female, Blue Over Green Matte Glaze, 1920s, 13 x 5 ½ In.
$5270.00

Rago Arts & Auction Center

U
V

TIP
Never put old pictures or papers in a "cling" album page.

Vase, Black, Multicolor Highlights, Pedestal, Sandwich Glass Co., c.1875, 6 ½ In., Pair	75.00
Vase, Pink, Yellow, Blue, Red, Swirled, Applied Clear Rim, 12 In.	350.00
Vase, Trifold Ruffled Rim, Red Mottled, Green Spatter, Gold Aventurine, 10 ½ In. ....*illus*	115.00

VASELINE GLASS is a greenish-yellow glassware resembling petroleum jelly. Pressed glass of the 1870s was often made of vaseline-colored glass. Some vaseline glass is still being made in old and new styles. Additional pieces of vaseline glass may also be listed under Pressed Glass in this book.

Basket, Applied Pink Flowers, Fan Shape, Crimped Rim, Twist Handle, Footed, Opalescent, 11 In.	177.00
Basket, Red Flower Shape Fringe Rim, Bulbous, Twist Handle, 6 ¾ In.	89.00
Ewer, Pink Flowers, Striated, Footed Jug, Amber Square Handle, Opalescent, 8 ⅜ In.	59.00
Pitcher, Measuring, Green, Marked T&S Handimaid, 16 Oz.	30.00
Vase, Applied Pink Flowers, Striated, Globular, Crimped Rim, Opalescent, 5 ¼ In., Pair	89.00
Vase, Bell Shape, Pink Flowers, Star Shaped Top, Leaf Feet, Loop Handles, 11 ⅛ In., Pair	177.00
Vase, Tulip Shape, Opalescent Top, Light Green, 10 x 4 In.	83.00

VENETIAN GLASS, *see Glass-Venetian category.*

VENINI GLASS, *see Glass-Venetian category.*

VERLYS glass was made in Rouen, France, by the Societe Holophane Français, a company that started in 1920. It was made in Newark, Ohio, from 1935 to 1951. The art glass is either blown or molded. The American glass is signed with a diamond-point-scratched name, but the French pieces are marked with a molded signature. The designs resemble those used by Lalique.

Verlys

Vase, Blackberries, Orange, Protrusions, Swirling Leaves, Tapered, 6 ¾ In.	118.00
Vase, Frosty Prussian, Leaves, Berries Design, Ball Shape, 10 ½ In.	374.00

VERNON KILNS was the name used by Vernon Potteries, Ltd. The company, which started in 1931 in Vernon, California, made dinnerware and figurines until it went out of business in 1958. The molds were bought by Metlox, which continued to make some patterns. Collectors search for the brightly colored dinnerware and the pieces designed by Rockwell Kent, Walt Disney, and Don Blanding. For more prices, go to kovels.com.

Beverly, Honey Jar, Elongated Oval, Round Foot, Flower Finial, c.1942, 4 ½ x 3 In.	49.00
Bouquet, Chop Plate, Round, 12 ¼ In.	15.00
Constellation, Coffee Urn, Ball Shape, 7 Blue Star, Bakelite Handle, c.1938, 7 ⅞ x 19 ⅜ In.	347.00
Figurine, Hippo Ballerina, Fantasia, Porcelain, 1940, 5 ¼ In.	158.00
Figurine, Nubian Centaurette, Fantasia, Ceramic, 1940, 8 In.	742.00
Figurine, Sprite, Fantasia, Head On Hands, Colors, No. 7, 4 ½ In. ....*illus*	411.00
Figurine, Sprite, Fantasia, Seated, Colors, No. 12 ....*illus*	115.00
Hawaiian Flowers, Salt & Pepper, White & Maroon, 2 ¼ x 2 ⅜ In.	65.00
Hibiscus, Relish, Elongated Oval, 2 Handles, Cream, Yellow, Green, 10 ¼ In.	16.00
Homespun, Salt & Pepper, Plaid, Yellow, Green, Rust, Bulbous, c.1948, 3 In.	18.00
Melody Lane, Plate, Cream & Blue, Deep In The Heart Of Texas, c.1941, 10 ½ In. Diam.	20.00
Monterey, Teapot, White Ground, Maroon & Blue, Leaf Design, 7 x 10 ¼ In.	33.00
Raffia, Bowl, Divided, Green Ground, Rust Plaid Brushing, c.1953, 11 ¼ x 6 ½ In.	32.00
Tam O'Shanter, Bowl, Vegetable, Plaid, Rust, Yellow, Green, c.1949, 8 ⅞ In., Pair	45.00
Vernonware, Teapot, Coffee Carafe, Cup, Saucer, Green, 8 ¼ In.	24.00
Winchester 73, Cup & Saucer, Demitasse, c.1950, 1 ¾ x 5 ¼ In.	64.00

VERRE DE SOIE glass was first made by Frederick Carder at the Steuben Glass Works from about 1905 to 1930. It is an iridescent glass of soft white or very, very pale green. The name means "glass of silk," and it does resemble silk. Other factories have made verre de soie, and some of the English examples were made of different colors. Verre de soie is an art glass and is not related to the iridescent, pressed, white carnival glass mistakenly called by its name. Related pieces may be found in the Steuben category.

Bowl, Frosty White, Squat, c.1900, 6 In. Diam.	123.00
Sherbet & Underplate, Light Blue Jade Lip Trim, 6 In.	75.00
Vase, Etched Berries, Flaring & Fluted Shape, Ruffled Rim, Clear, 7 In.	58.00
Vase, Iridescent, Etched, Flared Rim, Marked Hawkes, 8 ½ In.	173.00
Vase, Pink Shoulder Threading, Flared Mouth, 9 In.	443.00
Vase, Tapered, Shouldered, Frosty White, Blue Iridescent Rim, c.1900, 12 x 8 In.	738.00

VIENNA, *see Beehive category.*

VILLEROY & BOCH POTTERY of Mettlach was founded in 1836. The firm made many types of wares, including the famous Mettlach steins. Collectors can be confused because although Villeroy & Boch made most of its pieces in the city of Mettlach, Germany, the company also had factories in other locations. The dating code impressed on the bottom of most pieces makes it possible to determine the age of the piece. Additional items, including steins and earthenware pieces marked with the famous castle mark or the word *Mettlach*, may be found in the Mettlach category.

Cup & Saucer, Vivian, Yellow, Red Bands, Mug, Tobacco, 4 ⅝ In.	30.00
Dessert Set, Turquoise, Pink Flowers, 6 Plates, 2 Footed Dishes, c.1885, 8 Piece	359.00
Platter, Cannes, Round, 12 In.	80.00
Tureen, Cover, Underplate, Jardiniere, Footed, Scroll Handles, Gilt, Mark, 11 x 11 In.	149.00
Vase, Mottled, Orange, Tan, Green, Shouldered, Rolled Rim, Marked, 11 ½ In.	73.00

VOLKMAR POTTERY was made by Charles Volkmar of New York from 1879 to about 1911. He was associated with several firms, including the Volkmar Ceramic Company, Volkmar and Cory, and Charles Volkmar and Son. He was hired by Durant Kilns of Bedford Village, New York, in 1910 to oversee production. Volkmar bought the business and after 1930 only the Volkmar name was used as a mark. Volkmar had been a painter, and his designs often look like oil paintings drawn on pottery.

VOLKMAR
Corona N.Y

Lamp Base, Green, Yellow, Squat, Electrified, 12 In.	80.00

VOLKSTEDT was a soft-paste porcelain factory started in 1760 by Georg Heinrich Macheleid at Volkstedt, Thuringia. Volkstedt-Rudolstadt was a porcelain factory started at Volkstedt-Rudolstadt by Beyer and Bock in 1890. Most pieces seen in shops today are from the later factory.

Ewer, Applied Cherubs, Flowers, Gilded, Scrolled, Germany, c.1880, 14 ½ In., Pair	504.00
Figurine, 2 Putti, Walking On Each Side Of Goat, Holding Basket, Grape Clusters, 9 x 12 In.	173.00
Figurine, Dancer, Lacy Dress, Pink, Hand Raised, 12 x 8 In.	144.00
Figurine, Frederick The Great, Uniform, Walking Stick, 2 Dogs, White, Oval Plinth, c.1910, 30 In.	655.00
Group, Courting Couple, Rose Bouquet, Fan, 6 ⅞ In.	309.00
Group, Family, Harpsichord, 13 x 22 In.	1200.00
Incense Burner, Dragon, Foo Dog, Lion Finial, c.1900, 7 ¾ In.	95.00

WADE pottery is made by the Wade Group of Potteries started in 1810 near Burslem, England. Several potteries merged to become George Wade & Son, Ltd., early in the twentieth century, and other potteries have been added through the years. The best-known Wade pieces are the small figurines given away with Red Rose Tea and other promotional items. The Disney figures are listed in this book in the Disneyana category.

WADE
c.1936+

Box, Harvest Ware, Plum, Leaves, Cover, 5 x 3 ¼ In.	18.00
Coffeepot, Art Deco, Green, Yellow, Ribbed, Marked, 7 ½ In.	90.00
Figurine, Bird, Blue & White, 1 ¼ In.	12.00
Figurine, Butterfly, Tan, Brown, 1 ¾ In.	13.00
Figurine, Camel, Tan, 1 ¾ In.	4.00
Figurine, Cat & Fiddle, Brown, 3 In.	40.00
Figurine, Cockatoo, White, c.1960, 3 In.	24.00
Figurine, Cocker Spaniel, 1 ¼ In., Pair	4.00
Figurine, Dr. Foster, White, 1 ¾ In.	25.00
Figurine, Edward Fox, Winking, 4 ¾ In.	60.00
Figurine, Fawn, 1 ¼ In.	5.00
Figurine, Giraffe, Seated, Tan, Brown, 1 ¼ In.	4.00
Figurine, Jack Horner, White, 1 ½ In.	20.00
Figurine, Larry The Gnome, 4 In.	30.00
Figurine, Laughing Bunny, Green Ground, 6 ¼ In.	65.00
Figurine, Lion, Reclining, 1 ½ In.	6.00
Figurine, Man, Camera, Brown, Blue, Gold, Buffalo Fair Special, 4 In.	62.00
Figurine, Marie, My Fair Ladies, 3 ½ In.	40.00
Figurine, Mary Had A Little Lamb, Brown, 3 In.	38.00
Jar, Cover, Paisley Pattern, Gold Trim, 8 In.	75.00
Jug, Art Deco, Ribbed, Orange, Yellow Black, 5 ¼ In.	115.00
Jug, Art Deco, Swirled Mottled Green, Gold, 5 In.	45.00
Mug, 1925 MG Car, Mustard Yellow, 5 In.	22.00
Mug, 1933 Duesenberg Car, Mustard Yellow Ground, 4 ⅝ In.	22.00
Pipe Holder, Alsatian Dog, Green, Brown, 3 ¼ In.	45.00
Pitcher, Bramble, Red, Purple Summer Berries, 5 In.	50.00
Pitcher, Copper Luster, Bold Flowers, 4 ½ In.	45.00
Pitcher, Copper Luster, Enameled Flowers, 6 ½ In.	45.00
Pitcher, Copper Luster, Running Deer, Embossed, Marked, 7 In.	45.00

Van Briggle, Vase, Virginia Creepers, Rose & Green Glaze, 2 Handles, Incised, 1905, 8 x 9 In.
$2108.00

Rago Arts & Auction Center

Vasa Murrhina, Vase, Trifold Ruffled Rim, Red Mottled, Green Spatter, Gold Aventurine, 10 ½ In.
$115.00

Early Auction Co.

Vernon Kilns, Figurine, Sprite, Fantasia, Head On Hands, Colors, No. 7, 4 ½ In.
$411.00

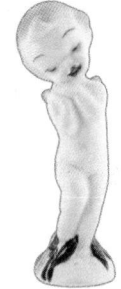

Hake's Americana & Collectibles

Vernon Kilns, Figurine, Sprite, Fantasia, Seated, Colors, No. 12
$115.00

Hake's Americana & Collectibles

W

Walrath, Vase, Squat, Stylized Leaves,
Matte, 3 ¼ x 4 In.
$3348.00

Rago Arts & Auction Center

Walrath, Vase, Stylized Flowers Form
Handles & Lip, Semimatte Glaze, Marked,
1919, 5 ⅜ In.
$1912.00

Neal Auction Co.

Watch, Chaumet, Pendant, Edwardian,
Enamel, Emeralds, Diamonds, 18K,
Pearl Chain, c.1910
$9480.00

Skinner, Inc.

Pitcher, Majolica, Oak Tree Shape, Rabbit At Base, Flower, Green Ground, 8 In.	111.00
Pitcher, Rabbit Shape, Orange, 4 In.	45.00
Salad Set, Bowl, 2 Serving Utensils, Golden Turquoise, Pebbled, Marked, 6 ¾ x 4 ¼ In.	90.00
Salt & Pepper, Green, Marked Irish Porcelain, 2 ½ In.	35.00
Sugar, Paisley Pattern, Flowers, 5 In.	30.00
Trinket Box, Turtle, 4 ¼ x 1 ¾ In.	26.00
Whimsey, Brown Bear, Ball, Hat, 1 ½ In.	6.00
Whimsey, Clown, Green, 1 ¾ In.	3.00 to 9.00
Whimsey, Cottage, Barley Mow, 3 In.	45.00
Whimsey, Girl Chimpanzee, 1 ½ In.	6.00
Whimsey, Gold Fish, Pet Shop Friends, 1 ½ In.	5.00
Whimsey, Goosey Gander, 2-Tone Brown, 1 ⅜ In.	9.00
Whimsey, Koala Bear, Tan, 1 ½ In.	4.00
Whimsey, Lion, Seated, Brown, 1 In.	4.00
Whimsey, Little Bopeep, Multicolor, 1 ¾ In.	9.00
Whimsey, Merryweather Farm, No. 19, Copper Roof, L Shape, 4 x 3 In.	20.00
Whimsey, Mongrel, 1 ⅜ In.	7.00
Whimsey, Old King Cole, 1 ½ In.	9.00
Whimsey, Old Woman In A Shoe, Multicolor, 1 ½ x 1 ½ In.	9.00
Whimsey, Owl, Brown, 1 ⅜ In.	4.00 to 14.00
Whimsey, Palamino Colt, Eating Grass, 1 ⅜ In.	150.00
Whimsey, Panther, Seated, Tan, 1 ⅜ In.	4.00
Whimsey, Pied Piper, Multicolor, 2 In.	9.00
Whimsey, Poodle, White, 1 ½ In.	40.00
Whimsey, Queen Of Hearts, Beige, Pink, 1 ¾ In.	10.00
Whimsey, Rhino, 1 In.	3.00
Whimsey, Three Bears, Brown, 1 ½ x 1 ½ In.	45.00
Whimsey, Tiger, Tan, Brown, 1 In.	4.00
Whimsey, Wee Willie Winkie, Yellow, 1 ¾ In.	20.00

WAHPETON POTTERY, *see Rosemeade category.*

WALLACE NUTTING *photographs are listed under Print, Nutting. His reproduction furniture is listed under Furniture.*

WALRATH was a potter who worked in New York City; Rochester, New York; and at the Newcomb Pottery in New Orleans, Louisiana. Frederick Walrath died in 1920. Pieces listed here are from his Rochester period.

Walrath
Pottery

Vase, Cylindrical, Lilies, Signed, 8 x 3 ½ In.	21080.00
Vase, Lemon Trees, Green, Yellow, Cylindrical, Pinched Rim, Marked, 6 ¾ In.	3565.00
Vase, Squat, Stylized Leaves, Matte, 3 ¼ x 4 In. .....*illus*	3348.00
Vase, Stylized Flowers Form Handles & Lip, Semimatte Glaze, Marked, 1919, 5 ⅜ In. .....*illus*	1912.00
Vase, Stylized Green Matte Leaves, Flowers, Brown Ground, Incised, 9 ¼ x 4 ¼ In.	6900.00

WALT DISNEY, *see Disneyana category.*

WALTER, *see A. Walter category.*

WARWICK china was made in Wheeling, West Virginia, in a pottery working from 1887 to 1951. Many pieces were made with hand painted or decal decorations. The most familiar Warwick has a shaded brown background. The name *Warwick* is part of the mark and sometimes the mysterious word *IOGA* is also included.

Cup & Saucer, Demitasse, Cherries, Leaves, c.1900	15.00
Pitcher, Monk, Gilt Trim, Marked, 8 In.	127.00
Pitcher, Poinsettias, Brown Ground, Footed, Scroll Handle, c.1900, 10 ½ In.	145.00
Tankard, Elk, Full-Length Handle, Marked, 11 In.	174.00
Urn, Flowers, 2 Handled, Scalloped Rim, Marked, 12 In., Pair	200.00
Vase, Flowers, Triple Cylinder, Footed, c.1900, 10 In.	150.00
Vase, Fuchsia, Flared & Scalloped Rim, 13 In.	120.00
Vase, Portrait, Woman, Roses, Flared Bottom, Handles, 10 ½ In.	115.00

WATCH pockets held the pocket watch that was important in Victorian times because it was not until World War I that the wristwatch was used. All types of watches are collected: silver, gold, or plated. Watches are listed here by company name or by style. Wristwatches are a separate category.

14K Yellow Gold, Hunt Scene, White Dial, Arabic Numbers, Waltham, Pocket	575.00
18K Gold, Hunting Case, Moon Style Hands, 15 Jewel, England, Pocket, Chain	1495.00
18K Gold, Joseph Johnson, 2 ¼ In.	1872.00
18K Gold, Lapis Flowers, Woman's, 1 ¼ In.	497.00
18K Yellow Gold, Open Face, English Key Wind, Marked, 1821	885.00
Alton, 14K Rose Gold, 6 Diamonds, 2 Square Rubies, Snake Chain Bracelet, 6 ½ In.	354.00
Audemars Piquet & Co., Open Face, Chronometro, 18K Gold, 2 In.	1840.00
Ball Watch Co., Hunting Case, 14K Yellow Gold, Rose Gold Crest, Flowers, White Dial	1298.00
Baume & Mercier, 14K Yellow Gold, 17 Diamonds, Leaf Design Links, Woman's, 6 ⅝ In.	767.00
Borel & Courvoisier Neuchatel, Hunting Case, 14K Yellow Gold, Monogram, Chain	885.00
Cartier, Travel, 18K Gold, Sliding Case, Silvertone Dial, Arabic Numerals, 17 Jewel	1896.00
Chaumet, Pendant, Edwardian, Enamel, Emeralds, Diamonds, 18K, Pearl Chain, c.1910 ....*illus*	9480.00
Dunand, 14K Gold, Open Face, Arabic Numerals, Quarter Hour Repeater, Red Minutes Dial, Pocket	1185.00
Elgin, Dueber Watch Co., Railroad, Coin Silver Case, Lever Set, Cincinnati, c.1890, Size 18	295.00
Elgin, Gold, 19 Jewel, Wadsworth Case, No. 10689, c.1930, Size 12, Pocket	460.00
Elgin, Hunting Case, 10K Gold Filled, Spade Style, Woman's, 1899, Pocket	249.00
Elgin, Hunting Case, 14K Yellow Gold, Engraved, Scrolling, Chain, 1 ⅔ & 12 In.	932.00
Elgin, Hunting Case, 14K Yellow Gold, Monogrammed, 1884	2006.00
Elgin, Hunting Case, Engraved Bird, Flowers, 14K Gold, 7 Jewel Movement, c.1905	460.00
Elgin, Train, Engraved Engine On Tracks, Double Sunk Dial, Spear Hands	90.00
Gunmetal Case, Silver Easel Frame, Triple Calendar, Enamel Dial, Moon Phases, c.1900, Pocket	711.00
Hamilton, Chronometer, Satin Finish Metal, Arabic Numeral Dial, Signed, Pa., Pocket, 2 ⅜ In.	660.00
Hampden, Hunting Case, Coin Silver, 1800s, 2 In., Pocket	115.00
Hunting Case, Yellow Gold, Blue Enamel, 2 Headed Eagle, Roman Numerals, Signed, Russia, Pocket	3750.00
J. Allan & Co., Hunting Case, Flower, Engraved, 18K, White Enamel Dial, Charleston, 1899, 1 ½ In.	1093.00
Longines, Open Face, 18K Gold, 21 Jewel, Charm Monogram, Fob, 16 In.	748.00
Mathey Tissot, 14K Gold, Square Face, 1970s, 8 In.	999.00
Mauboussin, Pendant, Tutti Frutti, Flowerpot, Emeralds, Rubies, Sapphire, 18 Jewel, 3 ⅛ In. *illus*	33180.00
Omega, 14K Yellow Gold, Presentation Box, Gold Case, Hallmarked, Wadsworth Case Co., Size 12	575.00
Omega, Pendant, Bow, Ruby & Diamond, 14K Gold, Woman's, 2 In. ....*illus*	649.00
Open Face, 11 Jewel, Pearls, 18K Gold, c.1890, 1 ¼ In.	575.00
Patek Philippe, 18K Gold, 20 Jewel, Open Face, c.1916, 1 ¾ In. Diam., Pocket	2938.00
Patek Philippe, Nautilus, Stainless Steel, 18K Gold, Black Ribbed Dial, Baton Numerals	15405.00
Patek Philippe, Satin Face, 18 Jewel, 18K Gold, 1 ¾ In.	1888.00
Rolex, 18K Gold, Yellow, President, Diamond Bezel, 44 Diamonds, 3 Carat, Brown Dial, c.1973	6500.00
Seth Thomas, Hunting Case, 14K Yellow Gold, Engraved, Landscape, Flowers, 1 ½ In.	483.00
Southbend, Hunting Case, Engraved Shield & Leaves, Black Hills Tricolor Gold Pin Fob	170.00
Tiffany & Co., Satin Face, 17 Jewel, 18K Gold, 1 ¾ In.	1298.00
Tiffany, Sterling Silver, Inscription, Pocket, 1 ⅞ In., 14 In. Chain	420.00
Waltham, 14K Gold, 15 Jewel, Engraved Scene, c.1902, 2 In., Pocket	881.00
Waltham, Crescent Street Railroad, 21 Jewel, Montgomery Dial, Gold Filled Case, 2 In., Pocket	201.00
Waltham, Hunting Case, Embossed Stag & Flowers, 14K Gold, c.1905, Size 6	1380.00
Waltham, Open Face, 14K White Gold, 2 In.	460.00
Waltham, Open Face, 14K Yellow Gold, 17 Jewel, 2 In., Pocket	920.00
Waltham, Railroad, No. 21J Crescent St., Steel Case, Double Dial	136.00
Waltham, Stag Head & Acorn Engraved, Monogram, 13 Jewel Movement, 2 ⅛ In.	1092.00
Zodiac, 14K Yellow Gold, Mesh Bracelet, Woman's, 7 ⅛ In.	1770.00

WATCH FOBS were worn on watch chains. They were popular during Victorian times and after. Many styles, especially advertising designs, are still made today.

Bloodstone, 9K Yellow Gold, Carnelian Bezel, 1 x 1 In.	395.00
Caterpillar Tractor, Beckwith Machinery, 1 x 1 In.	18.00
Cricket Player, Sterling Silver, Engraved, T. Dowe Royal, 1907	100.00
Elk Tooth, Silver, Diamond, Clock Face, c.1900, 1 In.	269.00
Glass, Goldtone, Black Onyx, Oriental Scene, Etched, 1940s, 1 ⅛ In.	95.00
Goldtone, Mother-Of-Pearl, Shell Shape, John Deere Logo, c.1930	950.00
Harley-Davidson Motorcycle, Sterling Silver, 1 ½ In.	158.00
Offaly Waltz Competition, Sterling Silver, Shield, J.T. Dublin, c.1948, 1 x 1 In.	118.00
One Cent Coin, Goldtone Frame, 1 ½ In.	74.00
Racehorse, Jockey, Horseshoe, Goldtone, c.1910, 1 ½ x 1 ½ In.	245.00
Schoolmaster Club, Sterling Silver, 10K , Golf Clubs, c.1950	139.00
Shield, Cartouche, Sterling Silver, W.A. Birmingham, c.1935, 1 x 1 In.	98.00
Sterling Silver, Box, Reticulated, c.1900	225.00

Watch, Mauboussin, Pendant, Tutti Frutti, Flowerpot, Emeralds, Rubies, Sapphire, 18 Jewel, 3 ⅛ In.
$33180.00

Skinner, Inc.

Watch, Omega, Pendant, Bow, Ruby & Diamond, 14K Gold, Woman's, 2 In.
$649.00

Ivey-Selkirk Auctioneers

Wave Crest, Humidor, American Indian, Cigars Painted On Lid, Footed, 6 x 6 ½ x 3 ¾ In.
$2688.00

Showtime Auction Services

W

TIP
Store cuff links or earrings in foam egg cartons.

WATERFORD

Wave Crest, Vase, Mold Blown Opal, Medallion Panel, Daisies, Bronze Base, Dolphin Handles, 15 In.
$633.00

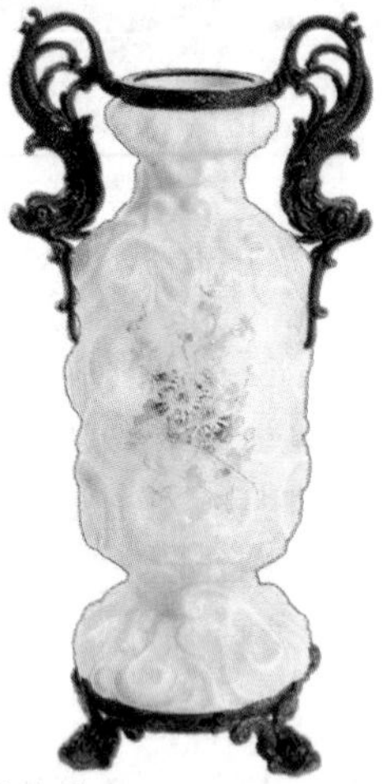

Early Auction Co.

Weapon, Knuckle Duster, Cast Iron, 4 In.
$345.00

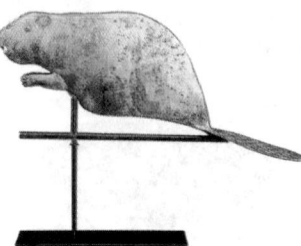

Showtime Auction Services

Weather Vane, Beaver, Sheet Metal Ears, Crosshatch On Copper Tail, c.1900, 13 x 32 x 24 In.
$17250.00

James D. Julia Inc.

Weather Vane, Cow, Standing, Full Body, Copper, Molded, Gilt, Applied Ears, Tail, Stand, c.1900, 17 ½ x 28 In.
$3081.00

Skinner, Inc.

W

WATERFORD type glass resembles the famous glass made from 1783 to 1851 in the Waterford Glass Works in Ireland. It is a clear glass that was often decorated by cutting. Modern glass is being made again in Waterford, Ireland, and is marketed under the name Waterford. Waterford merged with Wedgwood in 1986 to form the Waterford Wedgwood Group. Most Waterford Wedgwood assets were bought by KPS Capital Partners of New York in 2009 and became part of WWRD Holdings.

Bowl, Centerpiece, Crystal, Henry Ford Commemorative, 6 x 10 In.	180.00
Bowl, Fruit, Reeded Shaped Rim, Pedestal Base, Round Foot, Water Mark, 9 In.	403.00
Bowl, Glencar, Flared Rim, Footed, 10 In.	177.00
Bowl, Hatch Cut, Fluted Rim, 4 x 8 In.	150.00
Bowl, Lismore, Cut, Signed, Michael Vereker, 1900s, 6 x 13 In.	708.00
Bowl, Monteith, Scalloped Rim, Footed, 7 x 10 In.	230.00
Brandy Snifter, Colleen, 5 In., 6 Piece	207.00
Brandy, Lismore, 5 ¼ In.	55.00
Bucket, Champagne, Millennium, Flared, Footed, 10 ½ x 9 ¾ In.	230.00
Candlestick, Oceana, Seahorse Shape, 11 ½ In.	460.00
Champagne, Colleen, Flute, 6 In., 14 Piece	944.00
Champagne, Flute, Lismore, 1960s, 7 ½ x 2 ½ In., 6 Piece	295.00
Champagne, Flute, Tramore, 6 ¼ In., 8 Piece	266.00
Champagne, Fluted, Dungarvin, 8 ½ In.	78.00
Champagne, Kylemore, 4 ¾ In.	25.00
Compote, Crystal, Red Rim, 7 x 5 In.	150.00
Cordial, Boyne, 3 ¼ In.	32.00
Decanter, Clear, Diamond Cut, Signed, 9 x 5 ¾ In.	110.00
Decanter, Ship's, Silver Neck, Signed, Ireland Mark, 6 ½ In.	161.00
Fixture, Ceiling, 2-Light, Dome Glass Shade, Round Crystal Finial, Signed, 13 x 10 In., Pair	374.00
Goblet, Water, Glenmore, 7 In.	49.00
Goblet, Water, Lismore, 6 ¾ In., 6 Piece	219.00
Goblet, Water, Tyrone, 7 In.	50.00
Jar, Canning, Lid, Alana, 4 ¾ In.	63.00
Lamp, Hurricane, Brass, Marble Base, 17 In., Pair	446.00
Pitcher, Crystal, 1969, 6 x 8 In.	150.00
Plate, 3 French Hens With Holly Berries & Leaves, Original Box, 1986, 8 In.	50.00
Sherbet, Alana, 4 ⅛ In.	36.00
Sherbet, Merano, Stemmed, 3 ½ x 3 ⅛ In.	85.00
Sherbet, Sheila, 4 ¾ In.	25.00
Tumbler, Clarendon Cobalt, Blue, 4 In., 3 Piece	1793.00
Tumbler, Iced Tea, Saxony, 8 ⅛ In.	45.00
Tumbler, Lismore, Flat, 3 ½ In.	63.00
Tumbler, Old Fashioned, Kinsale, 3 ½ In., 8 Piece	209.00
Wine, Clarendon Cobalt, Blue, 8 In., 3 Piece	1434.00
Wine, Claria, 8 In.	27.00
Wine, Kinsale, 6 In., 7 Piece	89.00
Wine, Lismore, 1950s, 7 ½ x 3 In., 8 Piece	413.00
Wine, Lismore, 5 In., 6 Piece	472.00
Wine, Lismore, 6 In., 6 Piece	360.00
Wine, Port, Kathleen, 4 In.	38.00

WATT family members bought the Globe pottery of Crooksville, Ohio, in 1922. They made pottery mixing bowls and tableware of the type made by Globe. In 1935 they changed the production and made the pieces with the freehand decorations that are popular with collectors today. Apple, Starflower, Rooster, Tulip, and Autumn Foliage are the best-known patterns. Pansy, also called Rio Rose, was the earliest pattern. Apple, the most popular pattern, can be dated from the leaves. Originally, the apples had three leaves; after 1958 two leaves were used. The plant closed in 1965. For more prices, go to kovels.com.

Apple, Baker, Cover, No. 600, Ribbed, 7 ¾ In.	65.00
Apple, Baker, Cover, No. 601, Ribbed, 8 ¾ In.	95.00
Apple, Bean Cup, No. 75, 2 ⅜ In.	49.00
Apple, Cookie Jar, No. 91, 2-Leaf, Dome Lid	100.00
Apple, Creamer, No. 62	65.00
Apple, Creamer, No. 62, 3-Leaf	100.00
Apple, Ice Bucket, Lid, 7 In.	175.00
Apple, Mixing Bowl, No. 63, 3-Leaf, 6 ½ In.	60.00
Apple, Mixing Bowl, No. 64, Ritze Feed & Supplies, Lafayette, Iowa, 7 ¾ In.	32.00
Apple, Pitcher, No. 15, 16 Oz., 5 ⅜ In.	52.00

Cherry, Pitcher, No. 15, 5 ¾ In.	79.00
Cherry, Saltshaker, Barrel Shape, No. 45, 4 In.	30.00
Double Apple, Bowl, No. 5, Ribbed	25.00
Double Apple, Pitcher, No. 15, 5 ¼ In.	30.00
Pansy, Pitcher, No. 15, 16 Oz.	325.00
Rio Rose, see Pansy.	
Rooster, Casserole, Cover	50.00
Rooster, Casserole, Handle	40.00
Rooster, Mug, Batman Grain	65.00
Rooster, Pitcher, No. 15, 5 ½ In.	27.00 to 125.00
Rooster, Pitcher, No. 16, 6 ½ In.	35.00
Rooster, Pitcher, No. 62, ½ Pt., 4 ¼ In.	65.00
Starflower, Bowl, Cereal, 5 ½ In.	25.00 to 35.00
Starflower, Bowl, Spaghetti, Maroon	280.00
Starflower, Casserole, Lid, Handle	75.00
Starflower, Creamer, 5-Petal, 4 In.	60.00
Starflower, Mug, 4-Petal, 5 In.	50.00
Starflower, Pitcher, No. 16	40.00
Starflower, Platter, No. 49, 12 In.	30.00
Tulip, Casserole, Cover, No. 18	50.00
Tulip, Creamer, No. 62, 4 ¼ In.	125.00

WAVE CREST glass is an opaque white glassware manufactured by the Pairpoint Manufacturing Company of New Bedford, Massachusetts, and some French factories. It was decorated by the C.F. Monroe Company of Meriden, Connecticut. The glass was painted in pastel colors and decorated with flowers. The name Wave Crest was used after 1898.

WAVE CREST WARE

Biscuit Jar, Corset Shape, Lavender, Flowers, Berries, Silver Plated Lid, Handle, 8 In.	60.00
Biscuit Jar, Cream, Brown, Pink Roses, Egg Crate Shape, Silver Plated Lid, Bail Handle, 8 In.	70.00
Biscuit Jar, Embossed Fleur-De-Lis, Yellow With Pink Flowers, Lid & Bail, 7 In.	150.00
Biscuit Jar, Embossed Pewter Lid, 7 In.	800.00
Biscuit Jar, Leaf Shape, Blue, Poppies, Beaded, Barrel Shape, Silver Plated Lid, Bail, 8 In.	170.00
Biscuit Jar, Yellow, White, Pink Blossoms, Scroll, Silver Plated Lid, Bail, 7 In.	150.00
Box, Bishop's Hat, Green, Pink Apple Blossoms, White Scrolls, Footed Base, 6 x 10 In.	413.00
Box, Collars & Cuffs, Blue, Orchids, Enamel Beads, Marked, Nakara, 7 ¼ x 5 ¼ In.	280.00
Box, Collars & Cuffs, Egg Crate, Pink Flowers, Metal Collar, 5 ¾ x 6 ½ In.	395.00
Box, Cover, Blue, White, Pink Flowers, Embossed Flower, Marked, 4 x 4 ½ In.	150.00
Box, Cover, Collars & Cuffs, Wild Roses, Vines, Enameled Berries, 5 ⅞ x 6 ½ In.	345.00
Box, Egg Crate Shape, White & Yellow, Flowers, Hinged, Marked, 3 x 3 In.	200.00
Box, Puffy, Pink Honeysuckle, Enamel Beads, Footed, Satin Lining, 5 x 5 ¾ In.	168.00
Box, Ring, Blue, Pink & White Apple Blossoms, Hinged Lid, Gilt Collar, 2 ½ x 4 In.	148.00
Box, Round, Enameled Flowers, Ribbed, Swirled Ground, Metal Band & Latch, 5 In.	58.00
Cardholder, Cream, Egg Crate, Pink Flowers, Gold Metal Collar, 4 ½ x 6 x 3 In.	443.00
Cigar Box, Egg Crate, Cream With Flowers, Humidor Lid Inside, 5 x 6 In.	650.00
Dish, Sweetmeat, Pink, White, Flowers, Reticulated Silver Plated Lid, Handle, 6 ¼ In.	225.00
Dish, Sweetmeat, Silver Plated Frame, Pink & White, Flowers, 6 ¼ In.	225.00
Dresser Box, Bishop's Hat, Pink, White Flowers & Beading, Hinged Lid, 3 x 4 ½ In.	384.00
Dresser Box, Blue, Pink Tapestry, Egg Crate Shape, Hinged, 7 In.	325.00
Dresser Box, C.F. Monroe, c.1900, 4 ½ In. Diam.	236.00
Dresser Box, Egg Crate Shape, White, Blue, Yellow Tiger Lily, Square, 6 ¼ x 6 1 ½ In.	450.00
Dresser Box, Swirl, Pink, White, Blue Flowers, Hinged, Metal Footed, 7 In.	350.00
Fernery, Olive Gloss Glaze, Ferns, Blown-Out, Marked, Nakara, 7 x 7 In.	112.00
Fernery, White Opal Glass, Yellow Flower Blossoms, Leaves, Metal Rim, Molded, Round Foot, 7 x 4 In.	115.00
Humidor, American Indian, Cigars Painted On Lid, Footed, 6 x 6 ½ x 3 ¾ In. *illus*	2688.00
Jewelry Box, Green Frosted Glass, Embossed Flower, Scroll, Enameled, C.F. Monroe, 4 x 5 In.	475.00
Jewelry Box, Hinged, Embossed Flowers, Pink & White With Blue Flowers, 4 In.	200.00
Jewelry Box, Square, Egg Crate Shape, White & Yellow, Floral, 3 x 3 In.	200.00
Pin Dish, Green, Raised Enamel, c.1875, 3 ½ x 1 ½ In.	125.00
Plaque, White Opal Glass, Molded Scrolls, Metal Gold Wash Frame, 13 x 8 In.	2875.00
Plate, Pink Chrysanthemums, Royal Blue Ground, Pierced Brass Frame, 11 ½ In.	1652.00
Sugar & Creamer, Blue & White, Cherub Scene, Silver Plated Lid, Handle, Spout	60.00
Vase, Blue, White Scroll, Pink Flowers, Gold Highlights, Gilt Metal Handles, Rim, Feet, 13 ½ In.	800.00
Vase, Mold Blown Opal, Medallion Panel, Daisies, Bronze Base, Dolphin Handles, 15 In. *illus*	633.00
Vase, Painted Flowers, Raised Gilt, Scroll Feet, Brass Mounted, 9 ¼ x 6 In.	717.00
Vase, Painted, Cherub, Pine Trees, Raised Rococo Box, Marked, 4 x 2 In.	144.00
Vase, Pink, White, Blue Flowers, Molded Scrolls, Scroll Metal Handles, Tapered, Dolphin Base, 15 In.	518.00
Vase, Urn, Opalescent, Green Scrolling Panels, Red Flowers, 2 Handles, Marked, 12 In.	600.00

Weather Vane, Ewe, Flattened Body, Sheet Copper, Molded, Copper Rod, Verdigris, c.1900, 21 x 25 In.
$4444.00

Skinner, Inc.

Weather Vane, Fish, Open Mouth, Copper, Molded, Verdigris, Wood Stand, c.1900, 12 x 25 ⅝ In.
$2607.00

Skinner, Inc.

Weather Vane, Horse, Running, Full Body, Copper, J. Harris & Co., Boston, c.1885, 25 x 36 In.
$15525.00

James D. Julia Inc.

Weather Vane, Horse, Running, Full Body, Copper, Molded, Zinc Head, A.E. Jewell & Co., c.1865, 16 ¾ x 28 ½ In.
$5750.00

James D. Julia Inc.

Weather Vane, Peacock, Full Body, Copper & Zinc, Gilt, Embossed, c.1900, 17 x 32 ½ In.
$8295.00

W

Skinner, Inc.

Weather Vane, Ram, Full Body, Flattened, Applied Ears & Horns, Copper, Stand, c.1910, 33 x 35 In.
$7703.00

Skinner, Inc.

Weather Vane, Rooster, Full Body, Flattened, On Arrow, Copper, Gilt, Verdigris, c.1910, 22 x 24 In.
$1541.00

Skinner, Inc.

Webb, Perfume Bottle, Fish Shape, Blue, Silver Aventurine, Gold Scales, Silver Tail, Box, 6 In.
$6900.00

Early Auction Co.

Webb, Perfume Bottle, Teardrop Shape, Leaves, Flowers, Morning Glory, Cameo, 4 In.
$2530.00

Early Auction Co.

Vase, White Opal Glass, Blue, White Flowers, Metal Hardware, 2 Handles, Footed, Urn, 13 x 9 In... 2243.00
Vase, White Opal, Molded Scrolls, Pink, Blue Flowers, Leaves, Square, Dolphin Feet, 14 In. 518.00
Vase, White, Pink, Brown, Flowers, Gilt Metal Rim, Handles, Footed, 12 ½ In. 1200.00
Wall Plaque, Burgundy Border, Indian Portrait, Signed, 10 In. 6000.00

WEAPONS listed here include instruments of combat other than guns, knives, rifles, or swords and clothing worn in combat. Firearms are not listed in this book. Knives and Swords are listed in their own categories.

Ax, Australian Aboriginal, Wood, Wrought Iron, 19th Century, 21 In. 235.00
Billy Club, Turned Wood Handle, 21 ¾ In. 95.00
Blackjack, Leather, Lead Weighted, Pear Shape, c.1925 ..... 85.00
Boomerang, Mulga Wood, Australia, 1930s, 29 ½ In. 152.00
Canteen, Metal, 2 Compartments, 2 Screw Caps, Japanese Marks, c.1900, 2 ½ x 2 ¾ In. 65.00
Knuckle Duster, Cast Iron, 4 In. ..... *illus* 345.00
Shell Casing, Brass, Nordenfeldt, Stamped N, 1880s, 6 ½ In. 85.00
Shield, Bronze, Battle Scenes, Warriors, Castle, 19th Century, 25 x 17 x 5 In. 3500.00
Truncheon, Hardwood, Royal Cypher Of King George V, Coat Of Arms, c.1916, 15 In. 375.00
Truncheon, Wood, Center Turnings, New Zealand, c.1885, 23 ¾ In. 155.00
War Club, Chief's, Root Stock, Fiji Islands, c.1880, 44 In. 1800.00
Whip, Slave, Elephant Hide, Twisted, Knotted Grip, c.1875, 62 In. 285.00

WEATHER VANES were used in seventeenth-century Boston. The direction of the wind was an indication of coming weather, important to the seafaring and farming communities. By the mid-nineteenth century, commercial weather vanes were made of metal. Many were shaped like animals. Ethan Allen, Dexter, and St. Julian are famous horses that were depicted. Today's collectors often consider weather vanes to be examples of folk art, even though they may not have been handmade.

Angel, Gabriel, Horn, Holding Brass Ring, Gilt Metal, 20 x 14 ½ In. 184.00
Arrow, Man Driving Automobile, Copper, 26 x 5 In. 523.00
Automobile, Touring Car, Driver, Cream Color, 20th Century, 30 In. 382.00
Banner, Copper & Iron, Pierced, Geometric, Iron Rod Roof Mount, Scrolls, U.S.A., c.1890, 88 x 51 In. 2489.00
Banner, Cutout, Copper, Verdigris, Paint Traces, c.1870, 36 In. 2115.00
Banner, Pierced Geometric Shapes, Copper, Tall Post, Verdigris, c.1900, 43 In. 470.00
Beaver, Full Body, Copper, Verdigris, Stand, c.1900, 16 x 37 In. 14950.00
Beaver, Sheet Metal Ears, Crosshatch On Copper Tail, c.1900, 13 x 32 x 24 In. ..... *illus* 17250.00
Billy Goat, Cutout Silhouette, Sheet Metal, Brown Over Red Paint, c.1910, 25 x 31 In. 265.00
Black Hawk, Flattened, Copper, c.1890, 20 x 25 In. 8295.00
Codfish, Full Body, Copper, Gilt, Molded, Crimped Fins, Stand, 1800s, 14 x 25 In. 3851.00
Cow, Full Body, Copper, Molded, Red Paint, Zinc Ears, Rod, c.1900, 24 x 23 In. 4444.00
Cow, Full Body, Sheet Iron, Silver Paint, Stand, c.1900, 22 x 38 In. 2133.00
Cow, Standing, Full Body, Copper, Molded, Gilt, Applied Ears, Tail, Stand, c.1900, 17 ½ x 28 In. *illus* 3081.00
Directional, Wrought Iron, Scrolls, Black Paint, 48 In. 90.00
Dog, Hunting, Sheet Iron, Cutout, Painted Red, c.1930, 10 ½ x 24 ½ In. 3105.00
Dog, Setter, Full Body, Copper, Pointing Position, Stand, c.1950, 15 x 33 In. 1725.00
Eagle, Copper, Wrought Iron, 1800s, 52 x 36 In. 2520.00
Eagle, Directionals, Metal, 62 In. 95.00
Eagle, Partly Spread Wings, On Ball, Copper, Gilt, 32 x 43 In. 1840.00
Eagle, Spread Wings, Copper, Open Mouth, Ball, Black Stand, c.1890, 20 x 13 In. 354.00
Ewe, Flattened Body, Sheet Copper, Molded, Copper Rod, Verdigris, c.1900, 21 x 25 In. ..... *illus* 4444.00
Fish, Full Body, Copper, Gilt, c.1960, 21 In. 1645.00
Fish, Full Body, Copper, Verdigris, Gilt, Stand, c.1900, 27 In. 1175.00
Fish, Hollow Body, Tin, 19th Century, 16 In. 2700.00
Fish, Open Mouth, Copper, Molded, Verdigris, Wood Stand, c.1900, 12 x 25 ⅝ In. ..... *illus* 2607.00
Fish, Open Mouth, Full Body, Scales, Fins, Molded Copper, Verdigris, Gilded, Stand, c.1900, 12 x 26 In.. 4600.00
Fish, Pike, Copper, Green Verdigris, 36 x 12 In. 16415.00
Fish, Sheet Iron, Stand, 23 x 16 In. 259.00
Fish, Wood, Multicolor, Paint, Base, 28 In. 413.00
Fish, Wood, Sheet Tin Fins, Stand, 34 In. 1035.00
Fox, Running, Full Body, Copper, Rod, Wood Stand, c.1950, 18 x 32 In. 1422.00
Grasshopper, Full Body, Copper, c.1870, 27 ½ In. 764.00
Horse, Full Body, Copper, Cast Zinc, Iron Strap Base, c.1860, 16 x 20 In. 5333.00
Horse, Galloping, Full Body, Copper, J. Harris & Co., c.1890, 24 x 37 In. 5175.00
Horse, Galloping, Full Body, Copper, Stand, c.1890, 15 x 25 In. 4313.00
Horse, Hackney, Trotting, Full Body, Steel, Stand, 21 x 24 In. 1725.00
Horse, Jockey, Sheet Copper, Metal Stand, U.S.A., 19th Century, 20 x 31 In. 3851.00

Horse, Jumping Fence, Rider, Hounds, Fox, Cutout, Copper, Iron, c.1900, 41 In.	2242.00
Horse, Prancing, Cast Iron, Sheet Iron Tail, Rochester Iron Works, c.1880, 26 x 36 In.	11850.00
Horse, Prancing, Full Body, Copper, Gilt, Copper Rod, c.1940, 37 x 28 In.	4740.00
Horse, Running, Cutout, Sheet Metal, Silhouette, Painted Salmon, 17 In.	470.00
Horse, Running, Dexter, Full Body, Copper, Molded Rod, U.S.A., Late 1800s, 17 x 37 In.	3981.00
Horse, Running, Full Body, Copper, J. Harris & Co., Boston, c.1885, 25 x 36 In. ....*illus*	15525.00
Horse, Running, Full Body, Copper, Molded, Zinc Head, A.E. Jewell & Co., c.1865, 16 ¾ x 28 ½ In. *illus*	5750.00
Horse, Running, Full Body, Copper, Verdigris, Stand, 21 x 43 In.	4888.00
Horse, Running, Full Body, Copper, Verdigris, Stand, Ethan Allen, c.1890, 20 In.	2013.00
Horse, Running, Full Body, Wood & Iron, Flat Panel Figure, U.S.A., c.1900, 26 x 29 In.	474.00
Horse, Running, Sheet Metal, Red Paint, Stand, 37 x 20 In.	316.00
Horse, Sulky, Full Body, Molded, Copper, Cast Zinc, Painted Gold, c.1880, 50 x 24 In.	6900.00
Horse, Sulky, Galloping, Large Spoked Wheels, Copper, Molded, c.1900, 19 x 36 In.	9200.00
Horse, Sulky, Rider, Copper, Molded, Painted Black, Harris & Co., c.1885, 17 ¾ x 33 In.	7080.00
Horse, Trotting, Arabian, Full Body, Copper, c.1890	1928.00
Hunting Dog, Standing, On Point, Full Body, Arrow, N & S, Rust, Wood Base, 26 x 27 In.	236.00
Indian Chief, Drawing Bow, Quiver Of Arrows On Back, Gilt Metal, Composition, 21 x 14 In.	184.00
Indian, Bow & Arrow, Sheet Iron, U.S.A., c.1910, 24 x 22 In.	763.00
Indian, Massasoit, Archer, Bow Drawn, 3 Feather Headdress, Arrow, c.1900, 35 x 42 In.	29900.00
Indian, With Bow, Silhouette, Sheet Metal, Painted Black, c.1910, 34 In.	999.00
Lady Liberty, Flag, Wood, Carved, Flat Relief, Painted, 1900s, 36 In.	723.00
Lion, On Incline, Sheet Steel, Painted, Black, Orange, White, 1900s, 34 ½ In.	472.00
Locomotive, Articulated, Sheet Metal, Patina, 8 x 15 In.	978.00
Peacock, Full Body, Copper & Zinc, Gilt, Embossed, c.1900, 17 x 32 ½ In. ....*illus*	8295.00
Quill, Arrow, Copper, Dark Verdigris, Stand, 36 x 17 In.	1610.00
Ram, Full Body, Flattened, Applied Ears & Horns, Copper, Stand, c.1910, 33 x 35 In. ....*illus*	7703.00
Rooster, Bull Body, Zinc, Copper, Gilt Iron Bar, Stand, c.1860, 31 x 26 In.	24885.00
Rooster, Crowing, Full Body, On Ball, Copper, Stand, c.1890, 24 x 16 ½ In.	2588.00
Rooster, Full Body, Copper, Molded, Mounted On Arrow, Stand, U.S.A., c.1900, 31 In.	796.00
Rooster, Full Body, Copper, Mustard Color Paint, Stand, c.1900, 29 x 32 In.	2300.00
Rooster, Full Body, Copper, Verdigris, Rectangular Base, 1800s, 22 x 20 In.	2530.00
Rooster, Full Body, Flattened, On Arrow, Copper, Gilt, Verdigris, c.1910, 22 x 24 In. ....*illus*	1541.00
Rooster, Full Body, Gilt, On Cast Zinc Arrow, Stand, 1800s, 26 x 30 In.	1955.00
Rooster, Full Body, Pressed Tail, Copper, Wood Stand, 51 ½ x 24 In.	345.00
Rooster, Long Beak, 3 Tail Feathers, Iron, Red Paint, Stand, c.1890, 12 In.	1150.00
Rooster, Sheet Iron, Rivets, Stand, U.S.A., c.1800, 10 x 11 In.	948.00
Rooster, Sheet Iron, Variegated, c.1900, 17 ½ In.	529.00
Rooster, Standing, Full Body, Copper, Late 1800s, 19 x 17 In.	3450.00
Rooster, Stylized Detail, Tin, Wood Base, c.1850, 31 In.	14100.00
Stag, Leaping Over Fallen Tree, Full Body, Gilt, Rod Mounted, c.1890, 24 x 28 In.	12650.00
Stag, Leaping, Full Body, Copper, Gilt, Molded, Rod, c.1900, 26 x 29 In.	5036.00
Stag, Leaping, Full Body, Copper, Verdigris, c.1890, 28 In.	3643.00
Stallion, Full Body, Copper, c.1890, 30 x 31 In.	4288.00
Swordfish, Full Body, Carved Wood, Iron Fins, 1800s, 40 In.	5463.00
Trolley, Copper, Red, c.1910, 18 ½ x 45 In.	5688.00
Whale, Full Body, Copper, Molded, Flattened, Verdigris, 1900s, 21 x 36 In.	1185.00
Young Couple, Dancing, Moon Face, Painted, Cutout Directionals, 11 x 30 In.	403.00

WEBB glass was made by Thomas Webb & Sons of Ambelcot, England. Many types of art and cameo glass were made by them during the Victorian era. Production ceased by 1991 and the factory was demolished in 1995. Webb Burmese and Webb Peachblow are special colored glasswares of the Victorian era. They are listed at the end of this section. Glassware that is not Burmese or Peachblow is included here.

Webb

Atomizer, Melon Ribbed, Etched Flowers, Leaves, Stems, Amber To Green, 5 In.	288.00
Biscuit Jar, Blue, White, Diamond Quilted, Mother-Of-Pearl, Gold Flowers, Silver Plated Cover, 7 In.	300.00
Biscuit Jar, Salmon Pink, Yellow, Green Ivy Leaves, Metal Bail & Lid, 9 In.	288.00
Biscuit Jar, Silver Plated Cover, Pink & White, Meadow Flowers, Wheat, Leaves, 7 In.	173.00
Bowl, Blue Satin, Foldover, Rim, Clear Feet, Raspberry Prunt, Mother-Of-Pearl, Signed, 7 In.	403.00
Bowl, Pink, White, Geometric Stars, Opalescent Foot, Signed, 4 In.	207.00
Cup & Saucer, Rose Overlay, White Ground, Oriental Scene, Couple, Garden, Pagodas, 5 In.	1265.00
Decanter, Daisy, Button Pattern, Flower Medallions, Bird's Nest, Stick Neck, Ball Stopper, 11 In.	575.00
Dish, Sweetmeat, Cascading Gingko, Kangaroo Finial, 5 In.	201.00
Fairy Lamp, Dome Shade, Amber, Metal Base, Marked, 7 In.	150.00
Finger Bowl, Alexandrite, Crimped Rim, Amber To Purple To Blue, 5 In.	625.00
Finger Bowl, Underplate, Blue Satin, Gold Draped Collar, Gilt Flowers, Scalloped Rim, 6 In.	920.00
Ginger Jar, Cover, Flowering Vines, Butterfly, c.1890, 4 ⅜ x 3 ⅜ In.	1195.00

Webb, Rose Bowl, Globe Shape, Yellow, White Over Blue Branch, Ivy, Cameo, 2 ¼ In.
$460.00

Early Auction Co.

Webb, Tobacco Jar, Satin Glass, Gold Edged Roses, Pierced Collar, Embossed Lid, 9 In.
$5750.00

Early Auction Co.

Webb, Vase, Flowering Branch, White Cut To Blue, Vertical Band, Cameo, Marked, 5 ¼ In.
$978.00

Early Auction Co.

TIP
Can't hook the catch on your bracelet? Tape one end of the bracelet to your wrist, then close the catch.

W

Webb, Vase, Prussian Blue, White, Intaglio Carved, Flowers, Leafy Stems, Cameo, Acid Stamp, 5 In. **$518.00**

Early Auction Co.

Webb Burmese, Rose Bowl, Mother-Of-Pearl, Peacock Eye, Scalloped Rim, Red Mums, Insects, 5 ½ In. **$10925.00**

Early Auction Co.

Wedgwood, Barber Bottle, Cover, Leaves, Gilt, Bacchus Mask & Horn Handles, Marked, c.1880, 10 ⅝ In. **$948.00**

Skinner, Inc.

Wedgwood, Bowl, Fairyland Luster, 8-Sided, Dana Castle On A Road, Marked, c.1920, 10 ¼ In. **$5333.00**

Skinner, Inc.

Mustard, Cylinder, Cascading Gingko Branch, Round Foot, 3 In.		431.00
Perfume Bottle, Elongated Teardrop, Laydown, Blue, Flowers, Butterflies, Cameo, 7 In.		1725.00
Perfume Bottle, Fish Shape, Blue, Silver Aventurine, Gold Scales, Silver Tail, Box, 6 In.	*illus*	6900.00
Perfume Bottle, Oval, Cascading Gingko Branches, 2 ¾ In.		863.00
Perfume Bottle, Oval, Red With Leafy Branch, 5 Blooming Day Lilies, 2 ½ In.		1400.00
Perfume Bottle, Rolled Rim, Red Glass, Lattice, Swirled Opaline Stopper, Cameo, 8 In.		1495.00
Perfume Bottle, Sapphire Blue, White, Poppy, Leaves, Laydown, Silver Lid, Glass Stopper, 4 In.		2875.00
Perfume Bottle, Teardrop Shape, Leaves, Flowers, Morning Glory, Cameo, 4 In.	*illus*	2530.00
Perfume Bottle, Teardrop, Yellow, White Flowers & Leaves, Butterfly, Metal Stopper, Cameo, 3 In.		805.00
Pitcher, Yellow, Gingko Branch, Butterfly, Elongated Oval, Round Foot, Loop Handle, 4 In.		115.00
Rose Bowl, Citrine Yellow Ground, Blue, White Leaf Overlay, Cameo, 2 ½ In.		600.00
Rose Bowl, Footed, Yellow, Red Over White, Rose, Leaves, Butterfly, Cameo, Signed, 3 ½ In.		690.00
Rose Bowl, Globe Shape, Yellow, White Over Blue Branch, Ivy, Cameo, 2 ¼ In.	*illus*	460.00
Rose Bowl, Hexagonal Shape, Hawthorn Pattern, 3 In.		173.00
Rose Bowl, Ivory Ground, Dogwoods, Leaves, Butterfly In Flight, Signed, Cameo, 3 In.		288.00
Tazza, Verre De Soie, Water Lily Leaves, Green Stem Base, Ruffled Rim, 5 x 6 ½ In., Pair		69.00
Tobacco Jar, Satin Glass, Gold Edged Roses, Pierced Collar, Embossed Lid, 9 In.	*illus*	5750.00
Tumbler, Mauve Design, Wild Flowers, Green Stems, Signed, 3 ¼ In.		2400.00
Vase, Blue Ground, White Flowers, Cameo, 3 x 5 In.		600.00
Vase, Blue, Leafy Stalk, Flowers, Buds, Butterfly, Marked, 6 ¾ In.		863.00
Vase, Bronze, Mirror Blue Finish, Elongated Oval, Flared Rim, 12 In., Pair		374.00
Vase, Bulbous, Peach Satin, Gold Enamel Flowers & Butterfly, Flared Rim, 5 ¼ In.		236.00
Vase, Bulbous, Scalloped Rim, Red Berries On Autumn Colored Branches, 3 ½ In.		173.00
Vase, Bulbous, Squat, Vines, Leaves, Berries, Hexagonal Rim, Pink To Cream, 3 In.		345.00
Vase, Bulbous, Stick, Cinnamon To Peach, Garden Of Stemmed Foxgloves, 12 In.		6000.00
Vase, Flowering Branch, White Cut To Blue, Vertical Band, Cameo, Marked, 5 ¼ In.	*illus*	978.00
Vase, Flowers, Birds, Butterfly, Fuchsia To Pink, Ruffle Rim, Swirl Handles, 10 In.		403.00
Vase, Flowers, Lavender, Blue, Brown & Green Leaves, Hexagonal Rim, 3 In.		207.00
Vase, Flowers, Leaves, Butterflies, Red Ground, Cameo, c.1900, 6 In.		1004.00
Vase, Flowers, Vine, Ball Shape Bottom, Narrow Neck, Frilly Top, Pink To Cream, 4 In.		207.00
Vase, Gourd Shape, Blue To Pink, Carved Poppy, Cameo, 7 In.		3600.00
Vase, Muted Red To Peach, Flowers, Butterfly, Rolled Rim, Cameo, 6 In.		431.00
Vase, Oxblood, Gilt & Silver Flowers, Vines, Opal Interior, 5 In.		230.00
Vase, Pink & White, Clear, Grapes, Leaves, Branches, Flared Rim, Round Foot, Cameo, 18 In.		3835.00
Vase, Pink, White, Oriental Poppies, Leaves, Butterfly, Flared Lip, White Band, 6 In.		1298.00
Vase, Pink, White, Trumpet Vine, Butterfly, Yellow Ground, Teardrop Shape, Cameo, c.1890, 10 In.		2645.00
Vase, Prussian Blue, White, Intaglio Carved, Flowers, Leafy Stems, Cameo, Acid Stamp, 5 In.	*illus*	518.00
Vase, Red Ground, White Flowers, Butterfly, Bulbous, Elongated Neck, Round Foot, Banding, 5 In.		1121.00
Vase, Red, Peach Ground, White Flowers, Butterfly, Cameo, 6 ¼ In.		431.00
Vase, Stick Shape, Blue Glass, Purple Over White Cascading Flowers, Dragonfly, 3 In.		1265.00
Vase, Stick, Frosted Red, White Leafy Stemmed Foxglove, Round Foot, Cameo, 12 In.		2760.00
Vase, Stick, Scalloped Rim, Enameled Leafy Branch, 7 In.		366.00

WEBB BURMESE is a shaded Victorian glass made by Thomas Webb & Sons of Stourbridge, England, from 1886. Pieces are shades of pink to yellow.

Fairy Lamp, Domed Satin Shade, Piecrust Edge, Ribbed Base, Stamped Clarke, 5 In.		173.00
Fairy Lamp, Domed Shade, Ruffled Rim Base, Footed, Clear Inset, 5 ¾ In.		403.00
Lampshade, Brown Birds, Butterflies, Leaves, Scalloped, 5 ½ x 8 ¾ In.		805.00
Rose Bowl, Mother-Of-Pearl, Peacock Eye, Scalloped Rim, Red Mums, Insects, 5 ½ In.	*illus*	10925.00
Rose Bowl, Sprig, Blossoms, Green To Cream To Pink, Ball Shape, In-Turned Scalloped Rim, 2 ¾ In.		115.00
Vase, Lavender Flowers, Green Leaves, Cream To Pink, Star Shape Collar, Ball Bottom, 2 ¾ In.		184.00

WEBB PEACHBLOW is a shaded Victorian glass made by Thomas Webb & Sons of Stourbridge, England, from 1885.

Biscuit Jar, Quilted, Silver Plate Handle & Lid	325.00
Perfume Bottle, Oval, Cascading Flowering Branch, Blue Butterfly, 3 ½ In.	431.00
Vase, Glossy Amber To Rose, Cascading Gingko Branch, 4 In., Pair	345.00
Vase, Stick, Gold, Silver Enamel Flowers, Birds, Marked, 9 ¼ In.	200.00

WEDGWOOD, one of the world's most successful potteries, was founded by Josiah Wedgwood, who was considered a cripple by his brother and was forbidden to work at the family business. The pottery was established in England in 1759. The company used a variety of marks, including Wedgwood, Wedgwood & Bentley, Wedgwood & Sons, and Wedgwood's Stone China. A large variety of wares has been made, including the well-known jasperware, basalt, creamware, and even a limited amount of porcelain. There are two kinds of jasperware. One is made

WEDGWOOD

from two colors of clay, the other is made from one color of clay with a color dip to create the contrast in design. In 1986 Wedgwood and Waterford Crystal merged to form the Waterford Wedgwood Group. Most Waterford Wedgwood assets were bought by KPS Capital Partners of New York in 2009 and became part of WWRD Holdings. Some manufacturing will be transferred to Germany, Indonesia, and Slovakia. Other Wedgwood pieces may be listed under Flow Blue, Majolica, Tea Leaf Ironstone, or in other porcelain categories.

Barber Bottle, Cover, Leaves, Gilt, Bacchus Mask & Horn Handles, Marked, c.1880, 10 ⅝ In. ..*illus*	948.00
Basket, Sweetmeat, Underplate, Shaped, Pierced, 10 In.	588.00
Biscuit Jar, 3 Colors, Pedestal, Classical Scene, Dark Blue, Yellow Border, 6 ¾ In.	115.00
Biscuit Jar, Cover, Jasperware, Purple, Goldtone Mounts, Underplate, Impressed, 8 ¼ x 7 ½ In. ..	201.00
Bowl, Apple Green, Slip Glaze, Rings Around Rim & Pedestal Base, c.1935, 10 In.	296.00
Bowl, Cauliflower, Cobalt Blue Rim, 11 In.	95.00
Bowl, Center, Luster Melba, Mottled Orange & Red, Gilt Butterfly, Pedestal Foot, c.1920, 8 In.	830.00
Bowl, Dragon Luster, Octagonal, Enamel, Gilt, Mottled Blue, Mother-Of-Pearl, Interior, 7 In.	533.00
Bowl, Fairyland Luster, 8-Sided, Dana Castle On A Road, Marked, c.1920, 10 ¼ In. ....*illus*	5333.00
Bowl, Fairyland Luster, Asian Inspired Scenes, Butterflies, Gold Accents, Footed, 8 x 5 ½ In.	720.00
Bowl, Fairyland Luster, Pagoda, Toads, Fairies, Leaves, Gnomes, Pedestal, Flared Rim, 10 In..	13800.00
Bowl, Fairyland Luster, Woodland Bridge, Black Sky, Interior Day Lit Sky, c.1920, 10 In.	5333.00
Bowl, Fairyland Luster, Woodland Elves VII-Toadstool, 8-Sided, c.1920, 4 ½ x 9 ½ In. ....*illus*	2360.00
Bowl, Hummingbird Luster, Mottled Blue Exterior, Mottled Orange Interior, c.1920, 9 In.	1041.00
Bowl, Jasper Dip, Yellow, Upturned Handles, Black Medallions, Ribbon, Vine, c.1930, 6 In.	1778.00
Bowl, Moonstone, Hand Painted, Springtime Design, Flowers, c.1938, 10 In.	245.00
Bowl, Rolled In-Rim, Dragon Design Interior, Footed, Luster, 5 In.	199.00
Bowl, Salad, Jasper Dip, Green Ground, Lilac Border, White Figures, 1800s, 9 In.	245.00
Bowl, Sinuous Dragon, Blue, Green, Gilt, Round Foot, 5 In.	220.00
Box, Cover, Creamware, Game Birds, Rabbit Shape Finial, 8 In.	199.00
Bust, Mercury, Black Basalt, Waisted Round Base, England, 1800s, 18 In.	1778.00
Bust, Prior, Black Basalt, Waisted Round Base, England, 1800s, 13 In.	1067.00
Bust, Seneca, Black Basalt, Marked, 1800s, 10 ⅛ In. ....*illus*	296.00
Bust, Venus, Black Basalt, Waisted, Round Base, 1800s, 10 In.	415.00
Cachepot, Jasperware, Applied Greek Muses, 1900s, 5 ¼ x 6 ¼ In.	99.00
Cachepot, Ruffled Leaf Rim, Red, White Flowers, Ball Feet, 8 In.	633.00
Candlestick, Jasper Dip, Dark Blue, Cylindrical, White Figures, Flower Band, c.1900, 8 In., Pair..	119.00
Candlestick, Stoneware, Red, Flowers, Impressed, Rosso Antico, England, c.1870, 7 ¾ In., Pair..	345.00
Charger, Moonstone, Cream, Platinum Luster, Flowers & Leaves Design, c.1939, 12 ½ In.	207.00
Cheese Dish, Cover, Jasper Dip, Dark Blue, White Figures, Oak Leaf Border, 1800s, 11 In.	533.00
Cheese Keeper, Jasperware, Dome Lid, Tray, Blue, Women, Children, Flowers, 8 x 10 In. ....*illus*	189.00
Cheese Plate, Cover, Pale Blue, 1800s, 8 x 10 In.	580.00
Coffee Cup, Saucer, Jasper Dip, Lilac, Green Medallions, Figures, Ram's Heads, 1800s, 5 In....	770.00
Compote, Ivy, Wicker, Reticulated Rim, Hoof Footed, 9 In.	138.00
Compote, Luster, Fish, Blue Ground, Pedestal Round Foot, 4 In. Diam.	310.00
Cruet Set, Queen's Ware, Leaves, Berries, Central Crest, Round Stand, Footed, 1700s, 7 In.	1185.00
Dessert Set, Black Basalt, 6 Plates, 6 Cups, 6 Saucers, Creamer, Teapot, 7 In.	124.00
Dish, Niobe, Flow Blue, c.1895, 6 In.	27.00
Ewer, Wine & Water, Black Basalt, Triton Seated, Bacchus Seated, 1800s, 15 ¼ In., Pair ...*illus*	4148.00
Figurine, Sphinx, Rosso Antico, Basalt Hieroglyphs, c.1859, 4 x 6 ½ In.	3107.00
Flower Holder, Black Basalt, Bamboo, Simulated Stalks, c.1850, 4 ¾ In. ....*illus*	2015.00
Jar, Cover, Black Jasperware, Terra-Cotta, Hieroglyphs, Zodiac Symbols, Egyptian Head, 1978, 9 In.	1715.00
Jar, Cover, Jasper Dip, Black, Cylindrical, White Figures, Acorn Finial, Oak Leaves, c.1876, 8 In.	474.00
Jug, Etruscan, Jasper Dip, Crimson, White Figures, Flower Banded Border, c.1920, 6 In.	237.00
Jug, Jasper Dip, Crimson, White, Classical Figures, Flower Festoon Border, Marked, c.1920, 6 In. ..*illus*	711.00
Jug, Roger Williams, Greeting Indians, Providence, White, Red Floral Rim, 7 ½ In.	285.00
Letter Box, Ormolu, Brass, Florentine Design, Blue Jasper Medallions, 1800s, 6 x 7 In.	881.00
Loving Cup, Vine Border, 2 Loop Handles, Round Foot, 1790-1800, 5 In.	354.00
Medallion, Jasperware, Portrait, Linnaeus, Oval In Circle, Blue, White, 1700s, 3 ½ In.	770.00
Medallion, Silhouette, Man Kneeling, Am I Not A Man & A Brother, c.1800	1200.00
Oyster Plate, 5 Wells, Diving Dolphin, Shells, Majolica, 9 ½ In.	3304.00
Oyster Plate, 6 Wells, Chrysanthemum, Majolica, 9 ¼ In.	590.00
Oyster Plate, 6 Wells, Shells, Waves, Majolica, 7 ¼ In.	266.00
Pitcher, Jasperware, Blue, Oval George Washington, Ben Franklin Medallions, 5 ½ In.	385.00
Planter, Blue Ground, White Swags, Classical Scenes, Marked, c.1900, 6 ½ In., 4 Piece	590.00
Plaque, Jasper Dip, 3 Colors, Achilles, Dragging Hector, Troy, 1800s, 6 x 18 In.	2015.00
Plaque, Jasper Dip, Black, Discovery Of Achilles, 1800s, 7 x 22 In.	4740.00
Plaque, Jasperware, Blue & White, Achilles, Chiron, Centaur, 1800s, 8 x 21 In.	2844.00
Plaque, Jasperware, Blue, White Portraits, Ovals, Ribbons, Flowers, Leaves, 1800s, 8 x 11 In. .	1126.00
Plaque, Jasperware, Blue, White, Bacchus & The Panther, Oval, 1800s, 8 ½ In. ....*illus*	2607.00

Wedgwood, Bowl, Fairyland Luster, Woodland Elves VII-Toadstool, 8-Sided, c.1920, 4 ½ x 9 ½ In.
$2360.00

Ivey-Selkirk Auctioneers

Wedgwood, Bust, Seneca, Black Basalt, Marked, 1800s, 10 ⅛ In.
$296.00

Skinner, Inc.

Wedgwood, Cheese Keeper, Jasperware, Dome Lid, Tray, Blue, Women, Children, Flowers, 8 x 10 In.
$189.00

Conestoga Auction Co., Inc.

Wedgwood, Ewer, Wine & Water, Black Basalt, Triton Seated, Bacchus Seated, 1800s, 15 ¼ In., Pair
$4148.00

Skinner, Inc.

W

Wedgwood, Flower Holder, Black Basalt, Bamboo, Simulated Stalks, c.1850, 4 ¾ In.
$2015.00

Skinner, Inc.

Wedgwood, Jug, Jasper Dip, Crimson, White, Classical Figures, Flower Festoon Border, Marked, c.1920, 6 In.
$711.00

Skinner, Inc.

Wedgwood, Plaque, Jasperware, Blue, White, Bacchus & The Panther, Oval, 1800s, 8 ½ In.
$2607.00

Skinner, Inc.

Wedgwood, Platter, Queen's Ware, Flower Sprigs, Heron, Insects, Butterfly Border, Impressed, c.1800, 18 ½ In.
$1610.00

James D. Julia Inc.

Plaque, Lord Nelson, Black Basalt, Oval, Frame, 5 ¼ x 4 In.	403.00
Plate, 3-Masted Sailboat, Blue & White Flower Border, 10 ½ In., 10 Piece	805.00
Plate, Bamboo Pattern, Woven, Blue Leaves, Yellow Ground, 1790-1800, 8 ½ In.	826.00
Plate, Cutler Hall, Old View, Ohio University, Green, Transfer, 1970, 10 ⅜ In.	30.00
Plate, Dinner, Cobalt Blue Band, 6 Gold Medallions, Gold Rim, 10 ½ In., 12 Piece	920.00
Plate, Dinner, Creamware, Armorial, Gilt, Ocher Diaper Banding, Griffin Crest, 9 ¾ In., 12 Piece	956.00
Plate, Dinner, Gilt Rosette, Classical Figure, White Center, Green Border, 10 ½ In., 12 Piece	984.00
Plate, Flower Center, Border, Cobalt Blue Ground, Gilt, 1900s, 11 In., 12 Piece	593.00
Plate, Queen's Ware, 3 Autumn Leaves, Gilt Berry Vine Border, Mid 1800s, 8 In., Pair	354.00
Plate, Queen's Ware, Embossed Flower Rim, 10 ¾ In., 12 Piece	144.00
Plate, Ventnor, 10 ½ In., 12 Piece	270.00
Platter, Majolica, Sunflower, Leaf, On Wicker, 11 In.	236.00
Platter, Niobe, Flow Blue, Oval, c.1895, 14 x 10 In.	50.00
Platter, Queen's Ware, Flower Sprigs, Heron, Insects, Butterfly Border, Impressed, c.1800, 18 ½ In. *illus*	1610.00
Platter, Seafood, Majolica, Ocean, Oval, 19 ¼ In.	413.00
Platter, Salmon, Argenta, 25 ¼ In.	165.00
Potpourri, Cover, Jasper Dip, Classical Figures, Loop Handles, Marked, c.1850, 9 ½ In. *illus*	184.00
Potpourri, Stand, Jasper Dip, Pierced, Flowers, Figures, 2 Handles, Drum Base, 1800s, 23 In.	830.00
Tazza, Jasper Dip, Ormolu, Rope Trim, Portrait Medallions, Ram's Head, Flowers, 1800s, 13 In.	1007.00
Tazza, Majolica, Tripod Foot, Basket Weave Pattern, Green, Flower Border, 3 x 8 ½ In.	552.00
Teapot, Cover, Clay Color, Black Strapwork, Sphinx, Urns, Alligator Knop, 1805-10, 4 In.	826.00
Teapot, Cover, Jasperware, Blue & White, Seated Figures, Cylindrical, Loop Handles, 5 In.	1304.00
Tray, Black Basalt, Playing Cart Suits, Clubs, Hearts, Spades & Diamonds, 4 ¾ In.	175.00
Urn, Cover, Base, Jasperware, Black, Handles, White Classical Relief, 10 In.	1434.00
Urn, Cover, Fairyland Luster, Bubbles, Purple, Green, Blue, Fairies, Grass, Trees, 8 In.	33925.00
Urn, Cover, Jasperware, Blue & White, Footed, Handles, Rose Swags, Square Base, 1957, 12 In.	207.00
Urn, Cover, Jasperware, Brass Finial, Classical Figures, Marble Base, 16 ¾ In.	308.00
Urn, Stand, Jasper Dip, Light Blue, White Scroll Handles, Leaf Border, Trophy Drops, 7 In.	889.00
Vase, Blue & Green, White Flowers, Bulbous Stick, Gold Handles, Pierced, Signed, 12 In.	316.00
Vase, Cover, Agate, Gilded Handles, Leaves, Wedgwood & Bentley, c.1775, 12 ¼ In. *illus*	4148.00
Vase, Cover, Fairyland Luster, Lahore Pattern, Mother-Of-Pearl, Animals, Figures, Gilt, 8 ½ In. *illus*	15525.00
Vase, Cover, Jasper Dip, Black, Yellow Border, White Festoons, Urn Shape, 1800s, 9 In.	2370.00
Vase, Cover, Jasper Dip, Tricolor, Applied White Relief Figures, Marked, c.1890, 11 In., Pair *illus*	3851.00
Vase, Cover, Jasper Dip, White, Green, Lilac, Pedestal Base, Flower Garland, 1800s, 14 In.	1422.00
Vase, Cover, Jasperware, Blue, White, Leaf Border, Dancing Hours, Handles, 1800s, 10 In., Pair *illus*	1896.00
Vase, Cover, Queen's Ware, Gilt, Bronze, 2 Handles, Leaf Borders, Vines, c.1880, 10 In., Pair	3081.00
Vase, Cover, Urn Finial, Upturned Loop Handles, Greek Key, Pandora, 1800s, 18 In.	13035.00
Vase, Dragon Luster, Gilt Dragon, Pearl, c.1920, 8 ¾ In.	440.00
Vase, Fairyland Luster, Candelmas Pattern, Baluster, England, c.1910, 8 ½ In.	1121.00
Vase, Fairyland Luster, Jewel Tree, Castle, Boat, Fairy, Bronze, Baluster, Flare Rim, Signed, 8 In.	6900.00
Vase, Fairyland Luster, Maidens & Candles, Marked, Wedgwood Made In England, 9 x 6 In. *illus*	5580.00
Vase, Faryland Luster, Trumpet, Blue, Gilt Dragon, Daisy Makeig-Jones, 6 In. *illus*	465.00
Vase, Gray Glaze, Wide Ribs, Impressed Mark, Keith Murray, Blue Ink Stamp, 8 ⅜ In. *illus*	518.00
Vase, Jasper Dip, Baluster, 2 Handles, Blue & White, Relief Design, 1800s, 7 In., Pair	472.00
Vase, Jasper Dip, Figures, Tree, Cupid, 2 Handles, Flared Rim, Dark Blue, White, 1800s, 10 In.	2015.00
Vase, Jasper Dip, White, Green, Lilac, Flower Festoons, 2 Loop Handles, 1800s, 10 In.	1541.00
Vase, Jasper Dip, Yellow, Black Fruiting Grapevine, Round Foot, Rolled Rim, c.1930, 6 In., Pair	1304.00
Vase, Jasperware, Light Blue & White, Flowers, Octagonal Base, c.1800, 5 In., Pair	735.00
Vase, Jasperware, Tricolor Relief, Medallions, Lion Masks, Rings, Marked, c.1900, 6 ¾ In. *illus*	490.00
Vase, Moonstone, Open Shoulder, Tapered, 1930s, 9 ½ In.	560.00
Vase, Sponged, Bacchus Head Mask Handles, Wedgwood & Bentley, c.1775, 13 ¼ In. *illus*	2844.00
Vase, Stand, Jasper Dip, Leaves, Figures, Grapevine, Ram's Heads, Griffins, 1800s, 20 In.	4740.00
Vase, Trumpet, Luster, Butterfly, Mottled Orange, Mother-Of-Pearl, Marked, c.1920, 8 ⅜ In. *illus*	711.00

WELLER pottery was first made in 1872 in Fultonham, Ohio. The firm moved to Zanesville, Ohio, in 1882. Artwares were introduced in 1893. Hundreds of lines of pottery were produced, including Louwelsa, Eocean, Dickens Ware, and Sicardo, before the pottery closed in 1948.

LOUWELSA WELLER

Alvin, Vase, Cherries On Branches, Lavender Glaze, Ruffled Rim, 4 Branch Handles, 9 In.	81.00
Ardsley, Jardiniere, Green Leaves, Blue & Pink Butterflies, 7 x 8 ½ In.	459.00
Ardsley, Vase, Flared, Striated Green, Base Daisy, Orange Inclusions, 19 ½ In.	202.00
Ardsley, Wall Pocket, Iris, Cone Shape, 8 ½ In.	67.00
Ashtray, 3 Pigs On Rim, White Glaze, 4 x 5 In.	140.00
Aurelian, Jardiniere, Virginia Adams, Marked, 10 ¾ x 7 ¼ In.	46.00
Aurelian, Jug, Loop Handle, Blackberries, Brown, Green, Orange, 5 In.	127.00
Aurelian, Jug, Signed Frank Ferrell, Mark, 5 x 5 ½ In.	184.00

Aurelian, Tankard, Ear Of Corn, Brown Glaze, Hattie Mitchell, 12 In.		1026.00
Aurelian, Vase, Bulbous, Narrow Rim, Flowers, Yellow, Orange, Brown, 10 ¾ In.		748.00
Aurelian, Vase, Friar, Marked, 7 In.		124.00
Aurora, Candlestick, Flowers, Blue Ground, Marked, 5 x 9 In., Pair		468.00
Aurora, Candlestick, Painted Flowers, Blue Ground, Signed, 5 x 9 In.		510.00
Baldin, Jardiniere & Pedestal, Apples, Signed, 40 In.		417.00
Baldin, Vase, Apples, Blue Ground, Marked, 12 ¾ In.		258.00
Baldin, Vase, Squat, Green, 5 ½ x 7 In.		75.00
Bank, Dime, Log Cabin, Glazed, 4 ⅝ In.		1150.00
Barcelona, Vase, Stylized Flower, Urn Shape, Ribbed, 2 Handles, Stamped Mark, 6 ½ In.		108.00
Bedford, Urn, Green Matte, Arts & Crafts, Footed, 8 ½ In.		295.00
Blossom, Bowl, Lid, Smokestack, Round Foot, Wave Shape Finial, Blue, Pink, 6 ⅛ In.		58.00
Blue Drapery, Wall Pocket, 8 ¼ In.		59.00
Bonito, Bowl, Flower Frog, 16 ¾ In.	*illus*	153.00
Bonito, Vase, Flowers, Waist Handles, Signed LM, 7 ¼ In.		50.00
Brighton, Figurine, Rooster, White, Red Cock, 9 ½ x 11 In.		935.00
Brighton, Flower Frog, Bluebird On Tree Stump, 8 ¼ x 7 ½ In.		567.00
Brighton, Flower Frog, Kingfisher, Marked, 7 x 9 In.		420.00
Bronze Ware, Vase, Curdled Purple Iridescent Glaze, Oval, 13 ½ In.		594.00
Burnt Wood, Vase, 3 Bulls, Scrolled Finger Base, Flared Black Neck, 7 ½ In.		270.00
Burnt Wood, Vase, Griffins, Tapered, Bulbous Rim, 6 ½ x 5 ½ In.		119.00
Burnt Wood, Vase, Incised Grapes & Vines, Tan, Black Base & Rim, 12 In.		76.00
Cactus, Vase, Boy With Bag, Green Glaze, 5 x 3 x 3 ¾ In.		49.00
Cactus, Vase, Figural, Fish, Open Mouth, Yellow, 3 ½ x 4 In.		27.00
Cameo Jewel, Mug, Woman's Profile, Pale Yellow, To Purple, Marked, 6 ½ In.		374.00
Cameo, Candlestick, Creamware, 8 In.		35.00
Chase, Vase, Hunter On Horse, Dog, Ivory, Cobalt Blue Ground, Cylindrical, 9 In.		59.00
Chengtu, Vase, Mottled Chrome Red Glaze, 3 Lobes, Asymmetric Handles, 8 In.		59.00
Claywood Assyrian, Vase, Tapered Footed, Cream, Brown, 13 ½ x 6 In.		155.00
Claywood, Bowl, Incised Mice, 3 ½ x 2 In.		29.00
Claywood, Jardiniere, Grapevine, Black, Gray, 8 ¾ x 11 ½ In.		106.00
Claywood, Vase, Butterflies, 3 In.		28.00
Cloudburst, Basket, Luster, 5 In.		24.00
Coppertone, Bowl, Frog, Lotus Bloom, Flower, Marked, 15 ½ In.		259.00
Coppertone, Bowl, Frog, Water Lily Shape, 10 x 15 ½ In.		523.00
Coppertone, Frog, Seated, Round Base, Green & Yellow, Stamped 12, 5 In.		259.00
Coppertone, Garden Ornament, Frog, Holding, Banjo, Green, Brown, Yellow, 16 x 14 In.		2530.00
Coppertone, Garden Sprinkler, Frog, Marked, 10 x 8 In.		1140.00
Coppertone, Pitcher, Bulbous, Ruffled Rim & Spout, Fish Shape Handle, 7 In.	690.00 to	748.00
Coppertone, Vase, 2 Fish, Opened Mouths, Signed M.D., 7 ½ x 8 ½ In.		770.00
Coppertone, Vase, Fish, Water Lily, Green, Marked, 4 x 8 In.		605.00
Coppertone, Vase, Green & Black, Bulbous, 2 Handles, 7 x 8 In.		216.00
Coppertone, Vase, Mottled Green & Brown, 2 Frog Handles, Signed M.D., 9 x 8 In.		660.00
Coppertone, Vase, Swollen Shape, Neck Rings, Rolled Rim, 9 In.		891.00
Copra, Basket, Pansies, Green Glaze, Flared, Elongated Handle, 12 x 8 In.		184.00
Copra, Vase, Flared, Footed, c.1910, 11 ¼ In.		180.00
Cornish, Ginger Jar, Lid, Green Leaf, Berries, Brown Ground, Lug Handles, Marked, 8 In.		73.00
Cretone, Vase, Running Gazelles, Flowers, White, Black Ground, Globular, 7 In.		590.00
Cretone, Vase, White, Black Designs, Mae Timberlake, Marked, 6 x 6 ½ In.		575.00
Dickens Ware I, Vase, Chrysanthemums, Art Nouveau Style, 10 ⅝ In.	*illus*	403.00
Dickens Ware II, Jug, Hollowhorn Bear, American Indian Chief, E.L. Pickens, 6 ½ x 12 In.		523.00
Dickens Ware II, Jug, Monk's Head, Brown, Green, Ball Shape, 6 In.		259.00
Dickens Ware II, Mug, Man & Woman Golfers, Stamped, 5 ½ x 5 ¼ In.		527.00
Dickens Ware II, Mug, Monk, Signed E. Pickens, Marked, 5 ¼ In.		63.00
Dickens Ware II, Tobacco Jar, Turk's Head, 7 x 7 In.		227.00
Dickens Ware II, Vase, Cavalier, Feathered Hat, White Ground, 12 x 5 In.		567.00
Dickens Ware II, Vase, Ghost Bull, Native American Chief, A. Daugherty, 5 x 8 ½ In.	770.00 to	840.00
Dickens Ware II, Vase, Golfer At Play, Tall, Slender, Marked, 3 x 12 ½ In.		770.00
Dickens Ware II, Vase, Monk, Green, Tan, Pillow Form, Squared Feet, 5 x 6 ½ In.		259.00
Dickens Ware II, Vase, Water Lilies, Incised, Footed, Flared Rim, Stamped, 15 x 6 In.		682.00
Dickens Ware III, Mug, Man, Monocle, Bowtie, Light Blue Glaze, 2 Handles, 3 x 6 In.		70.00
Dickens Ware III, Vase, Dombey & Son, Marked, 8 ¾ In.		345.00
Dresden, Vase, Blue Green Windmill Landscape, Bulbous, Paint, 5 x 6 ½ In.		275.00
Eocean, Candlestick, Marked, 7 In., Pair		173.00
Eocean, Vase, Flared Foot, Narrow Base, Bulbous Top, Narrow Rim, Pansies, Blue, Pink, Green, 7 In.		288.00
Eocean, Vase, Flowers, Gray Blue Ground, Signed Levi J. Burgess, Marked, 12 In.		776.00

A Standish

A *standish* is an inkstand. Most are figural with inkwells and containers for pens, blotting material, sealing wax, or other things needed to write a letter in the ninteenth century.

Wedgwood, Potpourri, Cover, Jasper Dip, Classical Figures, Loop Handles, Marked, c.1850, 9 ½ In. $184.00

Skinner, Inc.

Wedgwood, Vase, Cover, Agate, Gilded Handles, Leaves, Wedgwood & Bentley, c.1775, 12 ¼ In. $4148.00

Skinner, Inc.

W

TIP
Store photographs flat, in acid-free albums.

Wedgwood, Vase, Cover, Fairyland Luster, Lahore Pattern, Mother-Of-Pearl, Animals, Figures, Gilt, 8 ½ In. $15525.00

James D. Julia Inc.

Wedgwood, Vase, Cover, Jasper Dip, Tricolor, Applied White Relief Figures, Marked, c.1890, 11 In., Pair $3851.00

Skinner, Inc.

Wedgwood, Vase, Cover, Jasperware, Blue, White, Leaf Border, Dancing Hours, Handles, 1800s, 10 In., Pair $1896.00

Skinner, Inc.

Eocean, Vase, Lily Of The Valley, Footed, Marked, 8 ½ In.	58.00
Eocean, Vase, Pink Virginia Creeper, Black Ground, Marked, 6 ¼ In.	213.00
Eocean, Vase, White & Purple Iris, Green, Elongated Oval, Rolled Narrow Rim, 10 In.	230.00
Eocean, Vase, Wisteria, Gray, Green Ground, Marked, 9 In.	336.00
Ethel, Vase, Portrait, 2-Sided, Marked, 8 ¾ In.	196.00
Etna, Jardiniere, Roses, Marked, 11 x 8 ¼ In.	52.00
Etna, Mug, Pink, Hydrangeas, Blue & White Glaze, Straight-Sided, 5 ¼ In.	27.00
Etna, Mug, Yellow Mums, Marked, 5 ¼ In.	69.00
Etna, Pitcher, Red Carnations, White & Gray Ground, 10 ¼ In.	69.00
Etna, Vase, Bold Rose Design, Marked, 12 ½ In.	104.00
Etna, Vase, Flowers To Shoulder, Pink Ground, Marked, 10 ¼ In.	109.00
Etna, Vase, Violets, Flared, 6 In.	173.00
Fairfield, Wall Pocket, Green Shaded To Brown, 10 In.	70.00
Figurine, Dog, Pop-Eye, Black, Tan, Cream, Seated, Smiling, 3 ¾ In.	316.00
Figurine, Dog, Pop-Eye, Garden Ornament, Brown, White, Mark, 8 x 10 In.	1760.00
Figurine, Gnome, Yellow, Blue, 15 x 9 ½ In.	868.00
Flemish, Jardiniere Stand, Bird On Branch, Flowers, Multicolor, Flared Rim, 22 In.	215.00
Flemish, Jardiniere, Flowers, Green, 11 x 8 ¾ In.	84.00
Flemish, Umbrella Stand, Pheasants, Bluebirds, Flowers, 22 ¾ In.	825.00
Flemish, Umbrella Stand, Pink Roses, 4 Panels, 20 In.	345.00
Flemish, Vase, Flowers, Beige Ground, 10 In.	144.00
Flemish, Vase, Green Flower Band, Brown Glaze, 3-Footed, 5 x 6 ½ In.	103.00
Floretta, Mug, Flowers, Green Ground, Marked, 5 In.	45.00
Floretta, Vase, 2-Tone Brown, Handles, Impressed, 4 ½ In.	28.00
Floretta, Vase, Purple Flower, Tan Ground, Impressed Seal, c.1900, 18 In.	316.00
Flower Frog, Frog In Lily, Green Glaze, Round Base, 4 ½ x 5 In.	65.00
Flower Frog, Lobster, Seaweed, Marked, 6 In.	138.00
Flower Frog, Mushroom Shape, Green, Brown, 2 ¾ In.	50.00
Flower Frog, Pheasant, Blue, Yellow, 6 ½ x 5 In.	275.00
Flower Frog, Woodpecker, 4 x 6 In.	138.00
Forest, Jardiniere, 9 x 11 In., Pedestal 18 In.	546.00
Forest, Jardiniere, Pedestal, 26 x 10 In.	864.00
Forest, Planter, Landscape Scene, Trees, 5 ⅜ x 15 In.	633.00
Forest, Teapot, High Gloss Glaze, 5 ¼ x 7 In.	97.00
Fru Russet, Vase, Buckeye, Multicolor Matte Glaze, 7 x 9 ½ In.	495.00
Fru Russet, Vase, Daisies, Green, Squat, 3 ¼ x 5 ¼ In.	168.00
Fru Russet, Vase, Flowers, Reticulated Neck, Blue Ground, Marked, 10 In.	504.00
Fru Russet, Vase, Mushroom, Purple Ground, 2 Handles, Matte Glaze, 5 ¼ x 6 ¼ In.	518.00
Fru Russet, Vase, Oak Leaf, 5 x 3 In.	73.00
Fru Russet, Vase, Organic Design, Maroon Glaze, Green Highlights, 6 x 8 ½ In.	825.00
Fudzi, Vase, Bottle Shape, Rolled Narrow Rim, Geometric Design, Long Leaves, Green, 9 In.	460.00
Garden Ornament, Cat, White, Blue Eyes, 14 x 8 ½ In.	1430.00
Garden Ornament, Dog, Pop-Eye, Tan, Cream, Blue Eyes, 4 x 4 In.	390.00
Garden Ornament, Hen, Chicks, Painted, 7 ½ x 8 In.	1920.00
Garden Ornament, Squirrel, Eating, Brown, Marked, 11 x 12 In.	1210.00
Gardenware, Duck, Cracked Egg, Yellow, White, Marked, 5 x 10 In.	5225.00
Glendale, Vase, Bird Flying, Grasses, Sky Blue Ground, Swollen Cylinder, 7 In.	351.00
Glendale, Vase, Bird, Nest, Marsh, Blue Ground, 6 ¼ In.	364.00
Glendale, Vase, Birds, Butterflies, Thistles, Daisies, Multicolor, 11 ¾ In.	575.00
Glendale, Vase, Bud, Double, Bird, Berries, Nest, 5 x 8 In.	243.00
Glendale, Vase, Bud, Double, Brown, Blue, 7 x 7 ¾ In.	299.00
Glendale, Wall Pocket, Birds, Blue Flower Ground, 6 ½ x 12 ½ In., Pair	523.00
Glendale, Wall Pocket, Painted, Birds, Marked, 6 ½ x 12 ½ In., Pair	570.00
Green Matte, Planter, Round, Square Feet, Grapes, Leaves, 11 In.	147.00
Greenaway, Jardiniere, House, Windmill, Rectangular Handles, Wide Rim, Marked, 8 ⅞ In.	345.00
Greora, Vase, Brown, Green, Handles, 8 x 7 ½ In.	259.00
Greora, Vase, Green, Orange, 8 ¾ In.	201.00
Hobart, Flower Frog, Kingfisher On Branch, Light Blue Glaze, 7 x 5 In.	86.00
Hudson, Parrot, Painted, Double Handles, Signed, Timberlake, Marked, 9 ½ x 13 ½ In.	6300.00
Hudson, Vase, Apple Blossom, Swollen, Round Foot, Marked, 11 In.	431.00
Hudson, Vase, Bengal Tiger, Palm Tree, Cylinder, Marked, 4 ½ x 13 ½ In.	7700.00
Hudson, Vase, Dogwood, Green Ground, Tapered, Signed, 5 x 9 In.	275.00
Hudson, Vase, Dogwood, Pink, Gray Ground, Hester Pillsbury, 10 ½ In.	392.00
Hudson, Vase, Elongated Oval, Irises, Blues, White, Marked KKT, 7 In.	575.00
Hudson, Vase, Fish, Aquatic Plants, Cream Matte Ground, Raised Rim, 7 x 6 ½ In.	1620.00
Hudson, Vase, Flower Branch, Shaded Blue To Green, 2 Handles, Ink Mark, 6 ¾ In. *illus*	295.00

W

Hudson, Vase, Flowers, 2 Panels, Silvertone Colors, Sarah Reid McLaughlin, 8 ¼ In. ......*illus*	1380.00
Hudson, Vase, Flowers, Blue Ground, Signed Kennedy, 8 In.	336.00
Hudson, Vase, Flowers, Green Ground, Marked, E. Hood, 8 ½ x 5 In.	434.00
Hudson, Vase, Grapes, Leaves, Vines, Floor, 22 ⅛ In.	575.00
Hudson, Vase, Milkweed, Blue Ground, Signed Hester Pillsbury, 12 x 6 ½ In.	434.00
Hudson, Vase, Parrot, Flowering Branch, Bulbous, Handles, Signed Timberlake, 9 x 13 ½ In.	5780.00
Hudson, Vase, Peacock, Feathers Spread, Blue, Green, Flowering Vines, 13 In.	6325.00
Hudson, Vase, Perfecto, Flowers, Blue, Cream, Oval, Hester Pillsbury, 5 ¾ In.	243.00
Hudson, Vase, Perfecto, Pink Flower, Green & Cream Ground, Tapered, 7 In.	205.00
Hudson, Vase, Pink Flower, Blue Ground, Bottle Shape, Marked, 9 ½ In.	168.00
Hudson, Vase, Pink Flowers, Blue Shaded To Green, Bulbous, 2 Handles, D. England, 8 In.	648.00
Hudson, Vase, Pink Flowers, Cream Ground, Octagonal, Marked, 7 ¼ In.	123.00
Hudson, Vase, Prunus Blossoms, Branch, Rolled Rim, 12 In.	1035.00
Hudson, Vase, Red, Signed Timberlake, Marked, 6 ¼ In.	518.00
Hudson, Vase, Rolled Rim, Flowers, Blue Ground, Marked, 7 ¼ In.	324.00
Hudson, Vase, Roses, Blue Ground, Marked, Signed, 5 ⅝ In.	265.00
Hudson, Vase, Slip Painted Roses, White & Yellow, Shouldered, Flared Rim, 15 In.	513.00
Hudson, Vase, Tapered, Painted White Roses, 4 ½ x 9 In.	150.00
Hudson, Vase, White Flower, Blue, Pink Ground, Ruth Axline, Marked, 9 In.	308.00
Hudson, Vase, White Roses, Tapered, 4 ½ x 9 In.	138.00
Iris, Vase, Shaded Pink & Green Ground, Cylindrical, Tapered, H. Pillsbury, 9 ¾ In.	398.00
Ivory, Jardiniere, Poppies, Art Nouveau Style, 11 x 9 ½ In. .... 55.00 to	60.00
Ivory, Jardiniere, Stand, Cylindrical, Flowers, 26 In.	102.00
Ivory, Umbrella Stand, Impressed Scrolls, Cylindrical, Marked, 19 ¾ In.	67.00
Ivory, Umbrella Stand, Scroll Design, Leafy, Cylindrical, 20 In.	230.00
Jap Birdimal, Jar, Yellow Sail Ship, Blue Ground, Round, Marked, 4 x 2 In.	67.00
Jap Birdimal, Jardiniere, Trees, Shades Of Blue, 7 ½ x 9 ½ In.	76.00
Jap Birdimal, Pitcher, Band Of Flowers, Turquoise, Green, Smokestack, Handle, 7 ¾ In. ..	460.00
Jardinere, Flared Rim, Yellow, Painted, Leaves, Marked, FF, 6 In.	69.00
Jardiniere, Grapevine, Majolica, Green Matte Glaze, Marked, 9 x 11 ½ In.	78.00
Jardiniere, Majolica Glaze, Green & Brown, 9 x 11 ½ In.	86.00
Jardiniere, Pinecones, Green Blend Glaze, Brown Rim Band, Marked, 7 x 8 ¾ In.	179.00
Jardiniere, Stand, Cream & Tan, Circles Design, Flowers, 25 In.	113.00
Jardiniere, Stand, Goblet Shape, Rose Colored Flower Design, 28 In.	339.00
Jardiniere, Stand, Oak Leaf, Blended Glaze, 28 ¾ In.	173.00
Kenova, Vase, Grapes, Vine, Green Matte Glaze, 12 In. ....*illus*	1265.00
Knifewood, Bowl, Swans, Water, Grasses, High Gloss Glaze, 3 ½ x 5 In.	324.00
Knifewood, Vase, Birds, Glossy, Marked, 5 In.	403.00
Knifewood, Vase, Butterfly & Daisy, Gloss, Marked, 4 ⅜ x 4 ⅝ In.	150.00
Knifewood, Vase, Daisies, Brown, Swollen Cylinder, 7 x 5 In.	243.00
Lamar, Vase, Landscape, Red, Black, 11 ½ In.	84.00
Lamar, Vase, Mountain Landscape, Trees, Red Glossy Glaze, Tapered, 8 ½ In.	86.00
Lasa, Vase, 3 Trees, Hill, River, Marked, 3 ⅝ In. ....*illus*	161.00
Lasa, Vase, Cylindrical, Swollen Top, Rolled Rim, Palm Trees, Seashore, Multicolor, 7 In.	316.00
Lasa, Vase, Globular Form, Copper Design With Tropical Scene Of Palm Trees, 4 In.	375.00
Lasa, Vase, Scenic Red, Gold Green Iridescent, Signed, 5 ¾ In.	269.00
Lasa, Vase, Smokestack Shape, Iridescent, Purple To Gold, Trees, 13 In.	267.00
Lasa, Vase, Tapered, Cylindrical, Lake, Pine Trees, Clouse, Gold, Pink, Green Iridescent, 7 In.	431.00
Lasa, Vase, Trees, Gold, Maroon, Blue, Metallic, 16 x 7 In. ....*illus*	992.00
Lasa, Vase, Trees, Mountains, Egg Shape, 4 ¼ In.	354.00
Lavonia, Wall Pocket, Woman, Holding Up Dress, Pink, White, Art Nouveau, 8 In.	230.00
Lorbeek, Flower Frog, Gazelle, Yellow, 7 x 4 ½ In.	140.00
Lorbeek, Flower Frog, Light Blue, Fluted Spiral, 5 ½ x 6 In.	77.00
Lotus, Flower Frog, Bloom & Bud, 2 x 4 In.	72.00
Louwelsa, Ewer, Trefoil Glaze, Clover Design, Marked, 4 In.	75.00
Louwelsa, Jardiniere, Ruffled Rim, Footed, Squat, Spider Mums, Brown, Orange, 8 x 12 In.	115.00
Louwelsa, Jardiniere, Yellow Flowers, Black Ground, 11 ½ x 9 In.	35.00
Louwelsa, Jardiniere, Yellow Poppies, Shaded Green & Brown Ground, 11 x 13 In.	237.00
Louwelsa, Jug, Native American Portrait, Brown Glaze, Handle, Signed, E. Sulcer, 5 x 6 In.	495.00
Louwelsa, Jug, Portrait African Man, Brown Glaze, 5 ½ x 6 ¾ In.	358.00
Louwelsa, Mug, Berries, Brown Ground, Marked, 5 In.	50.00
Louwelsa, Pedestal, Twin, Green, Orange, Twisted Shape, Signed C. Dibowski, Marked, 21 ¾ In.	127.00
Louwelsa, Stein, Ears Of Corn, Slip Decorated, Brown Glaze, Tapered, 6 In.	675.00
Louwelsa, Vase, Dog, St. Bernard, Painted, Brown Glaze, Bulbous, Signed E. Blake, 8 x 9 ½ In.	715.00
Louwelsa, Vase, Elongated Oval, Shouldered, Narrow Rim, Lilies, Brown, Glazed, Signed, 19 In.	259.00
Louwelsa, Vase, Fish, Green Brown Glaze, Bulbous, Footed, Abel, 8 x 10 ½ In.	1045.00

Wedgwood, Vase, Fairyland Luster, Maidens & Candles, Marked, Wedgwood Made In England, 9 x 6 In. $5580.00

Rago Arts & Auction Center

Wedgwood, Vase, Faryland Luster, Trumpet, Blue, Gilt Dragon, Daisy Makeig-Jones, 6 In. $465.00

Leslie Hindman Auctioneers

Wedgwood, Vase, Gray Glaze, Wide Ribs, Impressed Mark, Keith Murray, Blue Ink Stamp, 8 ⅜ In. $518.00

Humler & Nolan

W

Wedgwood, Vase, Jasperware, Tricolor Relief, Medallions, Lion Masks, Rings, Marked, c.1900, 6 ¾ In.
$490.00

Skinner, Inc.

Wedgwood, Vase, Sponged, Bacchus Head Mask Handles, Wedgwood & Bentley, c.1775, 13 ¼ In.
$2844.00

Skinner, Inc.

Wedgwood, Vase, Trumpet, Luster, Butterfly, Mottled Orange, Mother-Of-Pearl, Marked, c.1920, 8 ⅜ In.
$711.00

Skinner, Inc.

W

Louwelsa, Vase, Fish, Oval, Signed, 9 ¼ x 5 ½ In.	868.00
Louwelsa, Vase, Grapes & Leaves, Signed, c.1895, 50 In. *illus*	4444.00
Louwelsa, Vase, Green Matte Glaze, 6 ¾ In.	776.00
Louwelsa, Vase, Indian, Marked, 11 ½ x 6 ½ In.	1364.00
Louwelsa, Vase, Pansies, 3 Handles, Yellow, Green, Marked, 5 ½ x 6 ½ In.	127.00
Luster, Basket, Yellow, 6 ½ In.	28.00
Marbleized, Vase, Overlapping Ikat Design, Cylindrical, Marked, 7 ¼ In.	78.00
Matte Ware, Vase, Blue, Frosted, 4 ½ x 9 In.	110.00
Matte Ware, Vase, Frosted, Pillar Shape, Blue, 4 ½ x 9 In.	120.00
Matte Ware, Vase, Green, 4-Buttress Shape, Stylized Designs, 6 x 10 In.	420.00
Matte Ware, Vase, Green, Geometric Indian Design, 9 ¾ In.	138.00
Matte Ware, Vase, Holly, Green, Marked, 3 ¾ In.	146.00
Matte Ware, Vase, Poppies, Incised, Shouldered, 6 ½ x 14 In.	2860.00
Muskota, Bowl, Floating Swan Shape, Backward Glancing, 5 x 9 In.	345.00
Muskota, Figurine, Hen & Chicks, Multicolor, Signed, 8 x 7 In.	806.00
Muskota, Flower Frog, 2 Swans, Open Wings, Stamped, 6 ¼ In.	480.00
Muskota, Flower Frog, Boy, Seated, Fishing, Marked, 7 In.	56.00
Muskota, Flower Frog, Crab Green, Yellow, Marked, 5 In.	184.00
Muskota, Flower Frog, Fisher Boy, Marked, 6 ½ In.	161.00
Muskota, Flower Frog, Frog, In Lotus Blossom, 4 ¼ In.	108.00
Muskota, Flower Frog, Nude, On Rocks, Marked, 8 In.	345.00
Muskota, Flower Frog, Starfish Shape, 6 Holes, Yellow, Orange, 5 In. Diam.	150.00
Muskota, Vase, Swan Shape, White, High Gloss, 5 In.	67.00
Nasturtium, Vase, Shouldered, Cylindrical, Narrow Rim, Signed, 11 In.	1955.00
Oak Leaf, Vase, Double, 7 In.	237.00
Oak Leaf, Vase, Shaped Mouth, 11 In.	62.00
Oak Leaf, Wall Pocket, 8 ½ In. *illus*	115.00
Perfecto, Vase, Centurion, White Horse, Tiger, 10 ¾ In. *illus*	2300.00
Perfecto, Vase, Flowers, Blue, Yellow, Cream, Hester Pillsbury, 5 ¾ In.	243.00
Pheasant, Flower Frog, Painted, Multicolor, 6 ½ x 5 In.	300.00
Plaque, Abe Lincoln, White, c.1904, 4 ½ In.	50.00
Ragenda, Vase, Drapery, Burgundy, Oval, 13 ¼ x 10 In.	162.00
Rhead Faience, Jardiniere, Pedestal, Squeezebag, 10 x 12 ½ In.	3596.00
Rhead Faience, Lamp, Geishas, Oil, Square Footed Base, 15 ½ x 9 ½ In.	806.00
Rhead Faience, Mug, Geisha, Butterfly, Bees, 5 ¼ In.	265.00
Roma, Jardiniere, Applied Multicolor Fruits, Masks, Black Gloss Ground, Marked, 4 ¾ In.	45.00
Roma, Jardiniere, Green Vertical Stripes & Rim, 7 x 9 In.	86.00
Roma, Jardiniere, Tan, Flower Garland, Pedestal, 12 ½ x 15 ½ In.	184.00
Roma, Vase, Dupont, Cylindrical, Marked, 9 ¼ In.	161.00
Rosemont, Jardiniere, Birds, Cherry Blossom Branches, Dark Blue Ground, 7 x 9 In.	243.00
Rosemont, Vase, Blue Birds, Butterflies, Black Ground, 10 ½ In.	316.00
Rudlor, Bowl, Mint Green, 4 ½ In.	35.00
Sabrinian, Ewer, Pink, Green, Seahorse Handle, 9 In.	194.00
Sicardo, Jardiniere Stand, S-Shaped Body, Spread Top, Eye, Lion's Head, Brown, Yellow, Green, 22 In.	113.00
Sicardo, Vase, Cotton Plants, Etched, Cylindrical, Metallic Glaze, Signed, 2 ¼ x 8 In.	1210.00
Sicardo, Vase, Cover, Etched Designs, Round, Metallic Glaze, 4 ½ x 4 In.	715.00
Sicardo, Vase, Double Gourd, Metallic Glaze, Etched Leaves, Berries, 3 ¼ x 4 ½ In.	420.00
Sicardo, Vase, Etched Organic Design, Shouldered, Tapered, Metallic Glaze, 3 ½ x 9 ¾ In.	440.00
Sicardo, Vase, Flowers, Berries, Leaves, Blue, Green & Blue Iridescent, Cylindrical, 5 ¾ In.	504.00
Sicardo, Vase, Flowers, Blue, Green, Purple, Marked, 4 ½ In.	489.00
Sicardo, Vase, Flowers, Iridescent Ground, Marked, 5 In.	236.00
Sicardo, Vase, Green, Purple Metallic Glaze, Signed, 3 ½ x 4 In.	341.00
Sicardo, Vase, Leaf & Berry Design, Multicolor, 4 ⅛ In.	431.00
Sicardo, Vase, Leaf & Berry, Purple Metallic, Double Gourd Shape, Signed, 3 x 4 ½ In.	385.00
Sicardo, Vase, Metallic Glaze, Etched Stylized Cotton Plants, Cylindrical, Signed, 2 ½ x 8 In.	1320.00
Sicardo, Vase, Oval, Green Design With Iridescent Gold & Platinum Leaves, 4 In.	315.00
Sicardo, Vase, Tapered, Multicolor Metallic Glaze, Etched Flowers, 3 ½ x 9 ½ In., Pair	1560.00
Tea Set, Teapot, Creamer, Sugar, Crocus, Standard Glaze, Wicker Handle, Markland, 1894, 7 x 5 In.	523.00
Toothpick Holder, Bucket Shape, 2 Handles, 3 In., Pair	144.00
Trial Glaze, Vase, 2 Handles, Footed, Brown To Green, 7 In.	201.00
Turkis, Vase, Red, Green Drip, 2 High Handles, 9 ½ In.	297.00
Tutone, Vase, Green, Over Plum, 4 High Handles, 12 ½ In.	157.00
Vase, 3 Base Loops, Ivory, Pink Flowers, Green Leaves, 5 ⅜ x 7 ¼ In.	129.00
Vase, Arts & Crafts, Yellow, Green Flower, Vine Painted Band, Cream Ground, Cylindrical, 12 ¾ In.	431.00
Vase, Cherry Blossoms, Brown, Blue, Lavender Ground, Bulbous, 7 x 8 ¼ In.	303.00
Vase, Flowers, Butterflies, Handles, Silvertone, Ruffled Rim, 12 In.	383.00

Vase, Green, Scalloped Rim, Footed, 11 ¼ In.	68.00
Vase, Nude, On Sea Lion, Seahorse, Dark Beige, Bulbous, 7 ½ x 8 In.	978.00
Vase, Oak Leaf, Creamware, Triangular, Footed, 8 In.	39.00
Vase, Pink Shading To Blue, Long Stemmed Iris, Cylindrical, Signed, 10 In.	600.00
Vase, Roses, Gray, White Ground, 6 ½ In.	115.00
Velva, Ginger Jar, Lid, Dark Orange, Green Tones, Mark, 8 ¼ In.	374.00
Velvetone, Pitcher, Purple, Mauve, Marked, 8 In.	40.00
Voile, Vase, Cream Ground, 9 In.	253.00
Wild Rose, Vase, Tan, Handles, 7 ¾ In.	23.00
Woodcraft, Ashtray, Match Holder, Mottled Green, Marked, 6 x 3 In.	50.00
Woodcraft, Bowl, Squirrels, Shaped Rim, Footed, 3 x 5 ¾ In.	92.00
Woodcraft, Bowl, Woodpecker Perched On 1 Side, Mushroom On Other, 6 x 12 In.	403.00
Woodcraft, Box, Cover, Acorn Shape, Squirrel Finial, Orange, Yellow, Green, 9 In.	345.00
Woodcraft, Boy, Fishing, Fish Bowl Base, Marked, 12 In.	354.00
Woodcraft, Jardiniere, Cylindrical, Downy Woodpecker Handle, 6 ¼ x 8 ½ In.	243.00
Woodcraft, Jardiniere, Figural Woodpecker & Squirrel Handles, 9 ½ x 14 In.	945.00
Woodcraft, Nut Dish, Squirrel, Figural, On Leafy Rim, Marked, Label, 5 ¼ x 6 ½ In.	216.00
Woodcraft, Smoker's Set, Match & Cigarette Holder, Ashtray, Marked, 5 x 7 ¾ In.	115.00
Woodcraft, Vase, Allover Flowers, Green, Pink, Marked, 15 ¾ In.	190.00
Woodcraft, Vase, Bud, Double, Tree Stumps, 7 ½ x 7 In.	86.00
Woodcraft, Vase, Oak Tree Trunk, Owl Looking Out, Squirrel Climbing Down, Flared Foot, 18 In.	690.00
Woodcraft, Vase, Plums, Yellow Ground, Marked, 12 In.	190.00
Woodcraft, Vase, Squirrel & Owl, Tree Hole, Marked, 18 In.	633.00
Woodcraft, Wall Pocket, Owl, Peering Out From Hollow Tree, Marked, 10 ½ In.	184.00
Xenia, Vase, Flowers, Swollen Bottom, Marked, 11 ¼ In.	472.00
Xenia, Vase, Red Flowers, Purple Ground, Green Highlights, Marked, 12 In.	633.00
Zona, Pitcher, Ducks, Puddles, Marked, 7 In.	161.00
Zona, Pitcher, Kingfisher, Brown Handle, 8 ½ x 8 ½ In.	162.00
Zona, Pitcher, Pink Gloss, 7 ½ In.	62.00

WEMYSS ware was first made in 1882 by Robert Heron, the owner of Fife Pottery in Kirkaldy, Scotland. Large colorful flowers, hearts, and other symbols were hand painted on figurines, inkstands, jardinieres, candlesticks, buttons, pots, and other items. Fife Pottery closed in 1932. The molds and designs were used by a series of potteries until 1957. In 1985 the Wemyss name and designs were obtained by Griselda Hill. The Wemyss Ware trademark was registered in 1994. Modern Wemyss Ware in old styles is still being made.

Figurine, Pig, Pink Roses, Unmarked, 16 In. ....*illus*	71.00

WESTMORELAND GLASS was made by the Westmoreland Glass Company of Grapeville, Pennsylvania, from 1890 to 1984. The company made clear and colored glass of many varieties, such as milk glass, pressed glass, and slag glass.

Argonaut Shell, Candy Dish, Blue Milk Glass, Cover, Dolphin Feet, c.1950, 6 In.	79.00
Ashburton, Candy Dish, Ruby Flash, Footed, Lid, 7 In.	95.00
Beaded Rope Panel, Toothpick Holder, Clear	45.00
Bird On Nest Cover, Candy Dish, Tree, Pink, 6 In.	75.00
Blue Satin Glass, Compote, Painted Daisies, 1940s, 6 x 5 ¼ In.	65.00
Dogwood, Basket, Cranberry, Split Handle, c.1950, 4 x 4 ½ In.	29.00
Figurine, Bulldog, Orange	16.00
Figurine, Owl, On Stack Of Books, Amber, 3 ½ In.	14.00
Hen On Nest Cover, Salt, White, Red	18.00
Lovebirds Cover, Candy Dish, Yellow Mist, 5 ¾ x 4 ½ In.	45.00
Milk Glass, Bride's Box, Purple Ribbon, Leaves, Rosebuds, Pedestal, Lid, Finial, 8 x 4 In.	59.00
Pillow & Sunburst, Toothpick Holder, Clear	20.00
Powder Box, Cover, Woman Shape, Hoop Skirt, c.1960, 5 x 3 ¾ In.	60.00
Wakefield, Centerpiece, Pedestal, Square Base, Ruby, c.1960, 10 x 5 In.	95.00

WHEATLEY POTTERY was established in 1880. Thomas J. Wheatley had worked in Cincinnati, Ohio, with the founders of the art pottery movement, including M. Louise McLaughlin of the Rookwood Pottery. Wheatley Pottery was purchased by the Cambridge Tile Manufacturing Company in 1927.

Plate, 2 Lily Stalks, Mottled Blue, White Barbotine Ground, 1880, 11 In.	1200.00
Tile, 3 Wave Shapes, Pink, Yellow, Gray Matte Glaze, c.1920, 4 In.	245.00
Tile, Blue Matte Glaze, Yellow, Gold, c.1916, 4 ⅛ In.	135.00
Tile, Circles, Curdled Green Matte Glaze, Brown Matte Glaze Self-Framed, c.1925, 4 ¼ In.	300.00
Tile, Fruit Tree, Mountains, Lake, Square, Arts & Crafts Oak Frame, 6 In.	165.00

TIP
Rearrange your furniture so valuable silver or paintings can't be seen from the street.

Weller, Bonito, Bowl, Flower Frog, 16 ¾ In.
$153.00
Conestoga Auction Co., Inc.

Weller, Dickens Ware, Vase, Chrysanthemums, Art Nouveau Style, 10 ⅝ In.
$403.00
Humler & Nolan

Weller, Hudson, Vase, Flower Branch, Shaded Blue To Green, 2 Handles, Ink Mark, 6 ¾ In.
$295.00
Morphy Auctions

W

Weller, Hudson, Vase, Flowers, 2 Panels, Silvertone Colors, Sarah Reid McLaughlin, 8 ¼ In. $1380.00

Humler & Nolan

Weller, Kenova, Vase, Grapes, Vine, Green Matte Glaze, 12 In. $1265.00

Humler & Nolan

Weller, Lasa, Vase, 3 Trees, Hill, River, Marked, 3 ⅝ In. $161.00

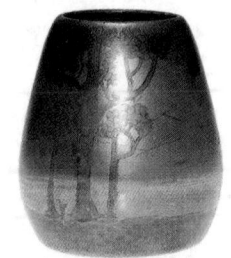

Humler & Nolan

Tile, Fruit Tree, Mountains, Multicolor, Arts & Crafts Style Frame, 6 x 6 In.	180.00
Tile, Geometric, Flower Center, Blue, Yellow, Orange Matte Glaze, c.1910, 6 In.	395.00
Tile, Pink, Orange Stylized Cross, Wood Frame, 9 In.	78.00
Tile, Shield Shape, 4 Heraldic Squares, Black, Gold, Green, Beige, c.1925, 4 ¼ In.	230.00
Tile, Stylized Flower, Cranberry Edge, Black, Mottled Green, 4 ⅛ In.	185.00
Tile, Swastika Cross, Gray, Turquoise Matte Glaze, c.1918, 4 ⅛ In.	150.00
Tile, Swimming Fish, Bubbles, Turquoise, Tan, Arts & Crafts Style Frame, 6 ¼ x 6 ¼ In.	270.00
Tile, Textured Cranberry Fleur-De-Lis, Muted Blue Ground, c.1915, 6 ⅛ In.	345.00
Tile, Yellow Fish, White Bubbles, Green Waves, Arts & Crafts Oak Frame, 6 ¼ In.	248.00
Vase, Vertical Leaves, Buds, Green Matte Glaze, 5 ½ x 4 ¼ In.	523.00 to 570.00
Wall Pocket, Green Matte Glaze, Bulbous, 7 x 7 ¼ In.	138.00 to 150.00

WHIELDON was an English potter who worked alone and with Josiah Wedgwood in eighteenth-century England. Whieldon made many pieces in natural shapes, like cauliflowers or cabbages, and they are almost always unmarked. Do not confuse it with F. Winkle & Co., which made a dinnerware pattern marked *Whieldon Ware.*

Bowl, Green, Yellow, Shell Shape, Tortoiseshell Glaze, 8 x 8 In.	250.00
Plate, Creamware, Mottled Green, Black, Tortoiseshell Glaze, 9 ½ In.	285.00
Plate, Creamware, Scalloped Rim, Tortoiseshell Glaze, 18th Century, 9 ½ In.	147.00
Plate, Creamware, Scalloped Rim, Tortoiseshell Glaze, Black Ground, c.1750, 7 In.	176.00
Plate, Creamware, Tortoiseshell Glaze, Molded Rim, c.1775, 9 ½ In.	382.00
Plate, Green, Brown, Tortoiseshell Glaze, Scalloped Rim, 1750, 9 In.	650.00

WILLETS MANUFACTURING COMPANY of Trenton, New Jersey, began work in 1879. The company made belleek in the late 1880s and 1890s in shapes similar to those used by the Irish Belleek factory. It stopped working about 1912. A variety of marks were used, all including the name Willets.

Bowl, Green, Water Lilies, Ruffled Edge, Belleek, Signed, 1904, 4 x 11 In.	330.00
Candlestick, White, Gilt, 3-Footed, c.1900, 3 ½ x 4 ½ In.	18.00
Cup & Saucer, Demitasse, Flowers, Gold Snowflake, Ribbed, c.1890, 2 ½ x 4 ¾ In.	115.00
Loving Cup, Green & Flower Panel, Gold Handles, Footed, Marked, c.1900, 7 ½ In.	2250.00
Mug, Floral Silver Overlay, 2 Women Musicians, 5 ½ In.	300.00
Mug, Indian Portrait, Cream Ground, 16-In. Gold Grotesque Handle, 5 ¾ In.	110.00
Pitcher, Bamboo Shape, White, Tan, Angular Handle, 6 ¾ In.	94.00
Pitcher, Cider, Green, Brown, Falstaff Portrait, Belleek, 6 ¼ In.	125.00
Pitcher, Faux Bamboo, Gold, White, c.1895, 6 ½ x 4 In.	285.00
Salt, Dark Pink Roses, Hand Painted, Footed, 2 ½ In.	22.00
Soap Dish, Fuchsia Pink Band, Gilt Trim, Opaque, Oval, c.1885, 5 ¾ x 3 ¾ In.	10.00
Tankard, Blackberries, Rose Ground, Hand Painted, c.1900, 14 In.	1495.00
Tankard, Flowers, Green Ground, Dragon Handle, Hand Painted, c.1900, 15 x 8 In.	799.00
Tankard, Gold Handle, Drinker Portrait, Green Ground, c.1890, 14 ½ In.	1100.00
Vase, Art Deco, Pink Flowers, Blue Band, Gilt, c.1885, 13 x 7 ½ In.	975.00
Vase, Feathery Yellow Poppies, Cylindrical, c.1900, 10 In.	379.00
Vase, Roses, Lilacs, Hand Painted, 16 x 24 In.	2495.00

WILLOW pattern has been made in England since 1780. The pattern has been copied by factories in many countries, including Germany, Japan, and the United States. It is still being made. Willow was named for a pattern that pictures a bridge, birds, willow trees, and a Chinese landscape. Most pieces are blue and white.

Chop Plate, Green, Brown Pagoda, Gold Trim, Narumi China, Japan, 12 In.	29.00
Cruet Set, Carrier, Japan, c.1930, 7 ½ x 7 ½ In., 5 Piece	149.00
Cruet, Oil & Vinegar, White Handle, 5 ¾ x 3 ½ In., Pair	70.00
Cup, Coffee, Marked Japan, c.1950	4.00
Cup, Handleless, Homer Laughlin	10.00
Mug, Irish Coffee, Churchill England, 4 x 2 ½ In., Pair	12.00
Mug, Ironstone, Wood & Sons, England, 1950s, 3 ¼ x 3 ¼ In.	10.00
Mug, Marked USA, 3 ½ x 3 ½ In.	16.00
Pitcher, Applied Handle, Acanthus Leaf Relief, Spur, 8 In.	71.00
Plate, John Steventon & Sons, c.1930, 9 In.	10.00
Plate, Old Willow Blue, Gilt Scalloped Rim, Booths, 10 ¼ In.	25.00
Plate, Olde Altonware, England, 6 ¾ In.	5.00
Plate, Royal China Ironstone, 10 In.	13.00
Plate, Royal China, 9 In.	8.00
Platter, 18 x 14 In. ....*illus*	12.00
Platter, Blue & White, Oblong, Pearlware, 15 x 19 In., Pair	123.00

W

Platter, Green, Brown Pagoda, Gold Trim, Oval, Narumi China, Japan, 17 x 12 ¼ In.	44.00
Platter, Old Willow Blue, Scalloped Rim, Oval, Booths, 14 x 11 In.	125.00
Platter, Transfer, Joseph Twigg, England, c.1805, 18 x 14 In.	200.00
Platter, Transfer, Staffordshire, 18 ¾ x 14 ¼ In.	200.00
Saltshaker, Pepper, House Of Blue Willow, Japan, 3 ¼ x 1 ½ In.	18.00
Saucer, Johnson Bros., 5 ½ In.	4.00
Server, 7 Compartments, Pierced Wood Handle, Booths, 16 ¾ x 11 ¾ In.	144.00
Serving Bowl, Royal China, 8 ½ In.	12.00
Soup, Dish, Homer Laughlin., 8 In.	5.00
Teapot, Droop Spout, Pink Willow, Royal China	125.00
Teapot, Flat, Royal China	90.00
Toaster, Porcelain, Electric, c.1928, 6 ½ x 7 ½ In.	403.00
Tureen, Cover, Rosa, Transfer, Churchill China	60.00

WINDOW glass that was stained and beveled was popular for houses during the late nineteenth and early twentieth centuries. The old windows became popular with collectors in the 1970s; today, old and new examples are seen.

Beveled, Sidelight, Faceted, 18 x 15 ½ In., Pair	1200.00
Crest, Wrought Iron, S-Scroll, 7 Spikes, Stand, 1800s, 14 x 15 ½ In., Pair	805.00
Leaded, 2 Figures Relaxing In Parlor, Flowers, Red Roses, Swirling Filigree, 78 x 46 In.	6490.00
Leaded, Archangel Gabriel, Lily, Shield, c.1900, 60 x 36 In.	3000.00
Leaded, Art Nouveau, Garlands, Geometric, Painted Frame, c.1900, 89 ½ In., Pair	2124.00
Leaded, Jeweled Design, Scrolling Flowers, Vines, 7 Ft. 10 In. x 4 Ft. 4 In.	3540.00
Leaded, Landscape, Frame, Panel, 23 ½ x 68 In.	806.00
Leaded, Portrait, Beethoven, Circle Center, Wreath, Flowers, Wooden Frame, 43 x 23 In.	978.00
Leaded, Stained, 3 Parrots, Beveled, Frame, 79 x 50 In.	690.00
Leaded, Stained, 3 Women, Placing Clock On Child, 29 x 15 ½ In.	750.00
Leaded, Stained, Angel, Holding Censor, Blue & Pink, Yellow Ground, 1800s, 52 ½ x 25 In.	360.00
Leaded, Stained, Art Deco, Asymmetric, Yellow, Blue Arrow Border, c.1930, 83 x 51 In.	5000.00
Leaded, Stained, Art Deco, Jeweled, Multicolor Border, 83 x 45 In.	10500.00
Leaded, Stained, Diamond Shape Beveled Glass Sides, Jewels, Victorian, 49 x 26 In.	575.00
Leaded, Stained, Flowers, Rondels, Mahogany Frame, 20 x 32 In.	138.00
Leaded, Stained, Geometric, Gothic Arch, Multicolor, 66 x 20 In., Pair	767.00
Leaded, Stained, Landscape, Sunset, River, Painted Leaf Border, c.1890, 47 x 21 ½ In.	1093.00
Leaded, Stained, Pelican Plucking Breast, Church, Symbol, Tondo, Black, White, Gold, 1800s, 27 In.	3600.00
Leaded, Stained, Pink, Green Medallion, Bull's-Eye Border, 33 ½ x 24 In.	2100.00
Leaded, Stained, Square, Urn, White Flowers, Leaves, Amber Ground, 42 x 42 In.	604.00
Leaded, Stained, St. Francis, Germany, c.1890, 28 x 18 In.	1400.00
Leaded, Stained, St. Ignatius Of Loyola, Book, Gothic Style, 1800s, 60 x 16 In., 2 Panels	3120.00
Leaded, Stained, Thalia, Mask & Staff, Victorian, Signed, A.L. Moore, Frame, 44 x 30 In. ....*illus*	1708.00
Leaded, Stained, Wood Frame, Circular Design, Early 1900s, 40 ½ In.	144.00
Leaded, Urn, Sitting Doves, Flowers, Butterflies, c.1925, 73 x 84 In.	9500.00
Mercury Glass, Light Green, Iron Frame, Round, 51 In.	2200.00
Stained, Aesthetic Movement, Grapevine, Multicolor, Arched, Frame, 28 x 18 In.	360.00
Stained, Arched Design, Yellow, Green, 53 x 27 In.	178.00
Stained, California Mission, Landscape, Green, Mauve, Oak Frame, c.1915, 29 ½ x 17 ½ In.	5000.00
Stained, Central Urn, Flowers, Fruits, Yellow Ground, Sweden, c.1900, 23 x 44 In.	15.00
Stained, Double Roman Arch Design, Cobalt Blue, Lilies, 1900s, 36 x 58 In.	316.00
Stained, Geometrics & Flowers, Metal Frame, England, c.1880, 43 ½ x 18 ½ In. ....*illus*	2370.00
Stained, Green Linear Border, Arched, Philadelphia, 28 x 28 In.	750.00
Stained, Jeweled, Flowers, Multicolor Ripples, 15 x 45 In.	1500.00
Stained, Knight, 3 Squires Praying, Metal Frame, 1700s, 25 x 18 In. ....*illus*	1035.00
Stained, Mauve, Green, Blue, Clear Textured Center, 14 Tile Border, 24 x 30 In.	550.00
Stained, Mosaic, Woman, Reading Book, Geometric Cane, Crimped, Frame, c.1900, 35 x 28 In. *.illus*	2015.00
Transom, Stained, Arch Shape, Central Flower, c.1900, 24 ½ x 52 In.	356.00
Transom, Stained, Flower, Garland, Wood Frame, Green Ground, 58 x 12 In.	975.00
Transom, Stained, Green, Brown Scrolls, Wood Sash, c.1895, 36 x 22 In.	350.00
Wood, Open Lattice Work, Chinese, 42 x 45 In., Pair	531.00

WOOD CARVINGS and wooden pieces are listed separately in this book. Many of the wood carvings are figurines or statues. There are also wooden pieces found in other categories, such as Kitchen.

Adam & Eve, Garden Of Eden, Trees & Leaves, Unto Jarvi, 1900s	1500.00
American Coot, Signed, 11 In.	59.00
American Eagle, Spread Wings, Pine, Gilt, Early 1900s, 16 x 46 In.	1093.00

Weller, Lasa, Vase, Trees, Gold, Maroon, Blue, Metallic, 16 x 7 In.
$992.00

Rago Arts & Auction Center

Weller, Louwelsa, Vase, Grapes & Leaves, Signed, c.1895, 50 In.
$4444.00

Skinner, Inc.

Weller, Oak Leaf, Wall Pocket, 8 ½ In.
$115.00

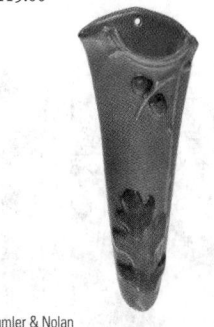

Humler & Nolan

W

As always, the edited listings in *Kovels' Antiques & Collectibles Price Guide* aren't available on any website, but readers should visit Kovels.com for information on trends, tips, reproductions, marks, old prices, and more!

WOOD CARVING

Weller, Perfecto, Vase, Centurion, White Horse, Tiger, 10 ¾ In.
$2300.00

Humler & Nolan

Wemyss, Figurine, Pig, Pink Roses, Unmarked, 16 In.
$71.00

DuMouchelles Art Gallery

Willow, Platter, 18 x 14 In.
$12.00

Conestoga Auction Co., Inc.

Window, Leaded, Stained, Thalia, Mask & Staff, Victorian, Signed, A.L. Moore, Frame, 44 x 30 In.
$1708.00

Leslie Hindman Auctioneers

American Goldeneye Drake, Signed, 16 In.	165.00
Angel, Cornucopia Pricket, Flowers, Gesso, Gilt, Painted, c.1800, 34 x 32 In.	3577.00
Angel, Draped, Kneeling, Holding Cornucopia Sconce, Germany, 1700s, 18 ¾ In.	459.00
Angel, Kneeling, Outstretched Hands, Giltwood, Naples, Italy, c.1895, 31 In.	6518.00
Angel, Wings, Feathers, Back Brace, Giltwood, 1900s, 52 x 56 In.	295.00
Arlechinno, Gilt Mask, Bicorn Hat, Red, White Check Suit, Gilt, 30 ½ In., Pair	1287.00
Asian Man, Rope Draped Over Shoulder, Multicolor, Japan, 21 In.	240.00
Attendant, Standing, Robes, Hand Up, Square Base, Gilt, Burma, 19 In.	717.00
Bald Eagle, On Rock, Round Base, Black Walnut, Signed, 1974	13800.00
Baltimore Oriole, Life Size, Mounted On Weathered Wood, Signed, 8 ½ In.	142.00
Bear, Black Forest, Glass Eyes, Germany, c.1900, 10 x 5 In.	1200.00
Bear, Black Forest, Standing, Tree, Rockwork Plinth, Ring, Walnut, Tabletop, 11 ½ In.	177.00
Bear, Black Forest, Walking, Glass Eyes, Switzerland, 6 ¾ In.	195.00
Bear, Standing Upright, Holding Goblet, Smoking Pipe, Painted, 12 In.	551.00
Beast, Human Head, Lion Shape Double Body, 10 In., Pair	275.00
Bird Tree, 3 Birds, Tack Eyes, Driftwood, c.1875, 17 In.	241.00
Bird, On Twig, Tack Eyed, Wire, 5 In.	106.00
Bird, Spread Wings, Pine, 6 In.	85.00
Bison, Mahogany, Base, c.1900, 5 In.	294.00
Black Bear Cub, Signed, 13 x 7 ½ In.	59.00
Blackamoor, Rowing Gondola, Holding Torch, Gesso, Venice, 1800s, 34 In.	3900.00
Blue-Winged Green Parrot, On Perch, Signed, 21 ½ In.	53.00
Boar's Head, Black Forest, Glass Eyes, Bristle Body, Plaque Mounted, 18 In.	1135.00
Bottle, Snuff, Bamboo, Bats, Lotus, Flattened Peach Shape, Dome Stopper, Chinese, 2 ½ In.	711.00
Bowl, Burl, Thin Walls, Scalloped Rim, Handles, 1800s, 6 ½ In. *illus*	4406.00
Bowl, Para Kingwood, Turned, Boat Shape, Round Foot, Signed, Brazil, c.1968, 3 x 6 In.	750.00
Bowl, Water, Zitan, Incised Poems, Round, Chinese, Seal, 3 x 5 In.	1107.00
Boy, Classical, Arms Out, Gesso, Square Base, Italy, 1800s, 53 x 23 In.	836.00
Buddha, Enlarged Cranium, Flowing Robe, Dog, 8 ¾ In.	1159.00
Buddha, Seated, Multicolor Glass Insets, Double Lotus Blossom Base, 29 In.	458.00
Buddha, Seated, Pedestal Throne, Inlaid Mosaic Glasses, Giltwood, Burma, 1800s, 23 In.	858.00
Buddha, Seated, Robe, Mandrola, 19th Century, Japan, 10 In.	675.00
Buddha, Standing, Spread Hands, Open Robes, Lotus Blossom, Red Paint, Gilt, 44 In.	430.00
Buddha, Traveling, Gilt, Lotus Form Base, Burmese, c.1900, 14 In.	288.00
Buddhist Nun, Natabori Style, Japan, 20th Century, 16 ¼ x 5 In.	300.00
Bull Head, Walnut, Folksy, Real Horns, c.1875, 12 ½ In.	999.00
Burmese Angel, Glass Accents, Standing, Headdress, Round Base, 39 In.	1500.00
Bust, American Indian, 24 x 13 In.	688.00
Bust, Bishop Saint, Miter, Scarf, Multicolor, 16 ½ x 22 ½ In.	1287.00
Bust, Buddha, Jeweled Headpiece, Giltwood, 1900s, 23 ½ In.	360.00
Bust, Farmer, Wife, Walnut, 9 In., Pair	114.00
Bust, Gentleman, Maple, c.1825, 11 In.	588.00
Bust, J.F. Kennedy, Painted, Phil Wright, 26 x 14 In.	518.00
Bust, Man, Wrinkled Brow, Moustache, African American, Signed, Zimbabwe, 1900s, 19 In.	671.00
Bust, Native American, Facing Upward, Square Base, Signed Armaza, 14 ½ x 4 In., Pair	60.00
Bust, St. Joseph, Bearded, Gesso, Paint, Robes, Italy, 17th Century, 20 In.	1750.00
California Quail, Standing, Signed, 11 ½ x 12 In.	53.00
Canada Goose, Scolding, Swimming, Signed, 31 In.	77.00
Canada Goose, Signed, 24 In.	71.00
Carolina Wren, On Branch Stub, Signed, 4 x 6 ½ In.	94.00
Caryatid, Female Figure, Standing, Holding Flower, Art Nouveau, Cherry, D. Hurd, 61 In.	177.00
Caryatid, Maiden's Bust, Ionic Capital, Mahogany, 21 x 7 In., Pair	55.00
Cat, Reclining, White, Black, Brown, Leather Ears, Glass Eyes, Whiskers, 4 x 20 In.	23.00
Cherub, Head, Parcel Gilt, Painted, 4 x 15 In., Pair	876.00
Cherub, On Plinth, Gilt, Mounted As Lamp, Continental, 24 ½ In., Pair	826.00
Christ At The Pillar, Thorn Crown, Tied Hands, Half Length, 19 x 10 In.	936.00
Common Merganser, Hen, Signed, 16 ½ In.	911.00
Corpus, Christi, Gesso, Paint, South America, c.1750, 13 x 11 In.	431.00
Coupe, Gnarled Pine Branches Into Well, 4 ¾ x 3 In.	10073.00
Crest, Neoclassical, Eagle, Fruit & Leaf Garland, Giltwood, Italy, c.1800, 41 x 22 In.	2375.00
Dancer, Straw Hat, Slung On Back, Flowing Ribbons, Dog, 14 ½ In.	496.00
Deer, 2 Deer, Rocky Base, Black Forest, 14 x 10 In.	220.00
Dionysius, Infant Bacchante, Oak, Standing, Nude, Grapes, Holding Child, 1800s, 31 ½ In.	1960.00
Dog, Pointing, Pine, Inset Bead Eyes, Base, c.1875, 7 x 11 ½ In.	392.00
Dog, Rosewood, Chinese, 1800s, 7 ½ x 4 In.	83.00
Dog, Spaniel, Standing, Walnut, 12 In.	565.00

W

Downy Woodpecker, Mounted On Branch, Signed, 6 ¾ In.	71.00
Dragon, Guardian, Standing, Chain From Nose, Painted, Chinese, 40 x 40 In.	717.00
Duck, Pintail, White Cheeked, Pink Bill, Signed, 18 ¼ In.	35.00
Duck, Red-Necked Grebe, Signed, 13 ½ In.	106.00
Eagle, Banner, Open Beak, Spread Wings, Shield, Gilt, Painted, 1920s, 48 In. ....*illus*	2585.00
Eagle, Catching Fish, Spread Wings, Round Base, Stained, 72 x 39 x 25 In.	270.00
Eagle, Head Bent, Spread Wings, Carved Shield, Bellamy Style, 1800s, 6 x 26 In.	460.00
Eagle, Head To Left, On Rocks, Giltwood, 12 ¾ x 29 In.	1872.00
Eagle, On Rock, Extended Claw, Spread, Wings, Gilt, 12 ½ x 19 In.	420.00
Eagle, Perched, Pine, Carl Snavely, Penn., 1972, 7 ¼ In.	334.00
Eagle, Pilot House, Spread Wings, On Rock, Gilt, Wood Base, 1800s, 27 x 37 In.	5975.00
Eagle, Pine, Spread Wings, Head Turned, Perched On Branch, 1800s, 22 In.	940.00
Eagle, Spread Wings, Clutching 2 Arrows, From Ship's Stern, c.1900, 27 x 48 In.	329.00
Eagle, Spread Wings, Gold Paint, Wall Mount, c.1900, 14 x 18 In.	403.00
Eagle, Spread Wings, Holding Branch, Gilt, 1800s, 15 ½ x 26 In.	1000.00
Eagle, Spread Wings, Holding Ring In Talons, Parcel Gilt, Sweden, 38 x 46 In.	1673.00
Eagle, Spread Wings, Sideward Glancing, 15 x 44 In.	1116.00
Eagle, Spread Wings, Walnut, On Rockery, Inscribed, Wengen, 1913, 19 x 22 In.	4444.00
Eagle, Wall Plaque, Spread Wings, Clutching Shield, Arrows, c.1900, 15 x 44 In.	1725.00
Elephant, Mahout, 2 Riders, India, 1800s, 11 x 8 In.	237.00
Fairy, Wings, Dragonfly Woman's Head, Heart Shaped Leaves, Mahogany, c.1880, 16 x 28 In..	920.00
Family Of 4, J.W. Michel, Haiti, 16 ¼ In.	115.00
Fish, Miro Wood, Pitcairn Island, John Christian, c.1920, 16 In.	598.00
Fish, Painted White, Ribbed Fin & Tail, 6 x 18 In.	460.00
Flamingo, Painted On Both Sides, 36 ½ & 38 ½ In., Pair	113.00
Flower Swag, 3 Bows, Cascading Ribbon, Giltwood, France, 74 x 22 In.	268.00
Foo Dog, Gilt Lacquer High Scrolled Base, Chinese, 1800s, 42 ½ In., Pair	4029.00
Foo Dog, Leaping, Head Turned Back, Rock Base, Chinese, 14 ½ In.	674.00
Frieze Panel, Giltwood, Horses, Riders, Pavilion Scenes, Chinese, 25 x 6 ¾ In.	2478.00
Geisha, Ivory Accents, Standing, Kimono, Inset Roundels, Holding Scroll, Japan, 8 In.	538.00
Gentleman, Holding Book, Long Coat, Pine, 1900s, 10 ½ In.	118.00
Gentleman, Playing Flute, 1800s, 26 ¾ In.	474.00
Goddess, Guanyin, Peach, Rocky Base, Chinese, c.1800, 15 x 4 In.	275.00
Goddess, Guanyin, Seated, Ebony, 7 ¾ In.	115.00
Goldfish, Protruding Glass Eyes, Fan Tails, Signed, 1900s, 2 x 6 In., Pair	173.00
Great Blue Heron, Mounted On Single Leg, Signed, 38 ½ In.	130.00
Great Blue Heron, Perched On Driftwood Base, Signed, Peter Peltz, 1982, 16 ¾ In.	345.00
Greek Muse, Holding Torch, Lyre, Scroll, Gilt, 79 x 21 In.	230.00
Group, Releasing Christ From Cross, Italy, 1800s, 12 x 8 In.	1035.00
Guanyin, Goddess, Seated, On Rocks, Above The Sea, Hardwood, Chinese, c.1890, 11 ½ In.	245.00
Guanyin, Seated, Red Lacquer, Gilt, Chinese, 1800s, 27 ½ In.	5629.00
Guanyin, Standing, Loose Robes, Tiara, Chignon, Hand In Mudra, c.1900, 21 In.	430.00
Hand Foot, Mexican Mahogany, Signed Pedro Friedberg, 7 x 2 In.	682.00
Horse Head, Ring In Mount, Pine, Carved, Painted, Hitching Post, c.1890, 13 x 16 In.	770.00
Horse, Chinese Style, White, Multicolor Saddle, Paint, Gilt, 44 x 13 In.	305.00
Horse, Multicolor, Standing, Circles, Dots, Swirls, Sweden, Early 1900s, 8 In.	403.00
Horse, Stylized, Hardwood, Glass Eyes, Horsehair Tail & Mane, c.1875, 23 In.	362.00
Horse, With Sulky, Metal, Leather, c.1870, 19 In.	6750.00
Immortal, Monkeys, Peach Tree, Rootwood, Chinese, c.1890, 58 In.	119.00
Immortal, Rosewood, Chinese, c.1900, 14 ½ In.	472.00
Indian Warrior, Waist Cloth, Feathers, Headdress, Bow & Spear, Gesso, Pedestal, c.1800, 19 In....	5750.00
Inro, Organic Designs, Brown, Green, Ivory Bead, Scenes, Japan, c.1840, 2 x 3 ½ In.	605.00
Jester Head, From Circus Wagon, Painted, c.1910, 19 ½ In. ....*illus*	3750.00
John The Baptist, Camel Hair Cloak, Cross In Hand, Blue, Yellow Base, Paint, 18 ¾ In.	652.00
Killer Whale, Black & White Paint, Signed, Peter Thompson, 24 In.	345.00
Kuan Ti, Seated, God Of War, Chinese, 1700s, 16 In.	326.00
Lazybones, Man, Resting Against Stump, Pine, Wade Martin, c.1950, 8 x 6 ¾ In.	1180.00
Leda & The Swan, Giltwood, 17 ½ x 26 In.	240.00
Lion, Dying, c.1825, 3 x 2 In.	123.00
Little Navigator, Standing, Painted, Gilt Accents, Square Base, 1900s, 24 In.	230.00
Lohan, Seated, Red Belt, Painted, Japan, 19 In.	488.00
Long-Billed Curlew, Mounted On Burl Wood, Signed, 16 In.	94.00
Lumberjack, Axe Over Shoulder, Kendall Wayne Martin, 9 ¼ In.	118.00
Luohan, Robes, Bald, Hands In Prayer, Paint & Gesso, 14 ¾ In.	400.00
Madonna & Child, Mary Standing, Gilt, Painted, 27 In.	1470.00
Madonna & Child, Plaque, Italy, 1800s, 20 x 13 In.	345.00

Ford Charcoal

Henry Ford invented charcoal briquettes. They were made from leftover scraps of wood from Model T car manufacturing.

Window, Stained, Geometrics & Flowers, Metal Frame, England, c.1880, 43 ½ x 18 ½ In. $2370.00

Skinner, Inc.

Window, Stained, Knight, 3 Squires Praying, Metal Frame, 1700s, 25 x 18 In. $1035.00

Early Auction Co.

WOOD CARVING

Window, Stained, Mosaic, Woman, Reading Book, Geometric Cane, Crimped, Frame, c.1900, 35 x 28 In. $2015.00

Skinner, Inc.

Wood Carving, Bowl, Burl, Thin Walls, Scalloped Rim, Handles, 1800s, 6 ½ In. $4406.00

Garth's Auctions, Inc.

Wood Carving, Eagle, Banner, Open Beak, Spread Wings, Shield, Gilt, Painted, 1920s, 48 In. $2585.00

Cowan's Auctions

Wood Carving, Jester Head, From Circus Wagon, Painted, c.1910, 19 ½ In. $3750.00

Bonhams & Butterfields

Madonna & Child, Red Robe, Giltwood, Italy, c.1500, 34 In.	9480.00
Madonna & Child, Seated, Crown, Red Robe, Giltwood, 17 In.	711.00
Maiden, Robed, Looking Upward, Hands In Prayer, Fruitwood, 56 In.	984.00
Man, African Tribal, Brown & Orange, Hanging, 46 x 8 In.	180.00
Man, Armless, No Ears, Metal Nose, Paint, c.1910, 60 In.	1610.00
Man, Kicking Ball, Minimally Dressed, Barefoot, Pedestal Base, 10 In.	79.00
Man, Kneeling, Bowed Head, Chip Carved, Signed R.G., 1946, 25 x 15 In.	246.00
Man, Seated, Crossed Legs, Eyes Closed, Headpiece, Round Base, 17 In.	281.00
Man, Seated, Holding Mask, Ivory Face, Hands, Lacquer, Paint, 3 x 4 ½ In.	1100.00
Man, Seminude, Hands Tethered To Branch, White Stain, Gadrooned Bracket, 29 x 9 In.	1053.00
Man, Standing, Carrying Hat On Back, Gilt Lacquered, Chinese, 35 ¼ In.	123.00
Man, Top Hat, Smoking Pipe, Mahogany, c.1900, 26 In.	2370.00
Mannequin, Artist's Model, Ball & Dowel-Jointed, Articulated Muscles, 1860s, 26 In.	798.00
Mask, Feathers, African, 17 x 10 In.	295.00
Medallion, Classical, Leaf, Berry Streamer, Gilt, Paint, Italy, 1900s, 24 x 20 In., Pair	540.00
Model, Arcaded Loggia, Fruitwood, Mahogany, Paved Floor, Stenciled, Italy, 9 ½ x 16 In.	553.00
Model, Bus, Chicago City, Aluminum Bumpers, Paint, c.1960, 5 x 19 ½ In.	330.00
Model, Chapel, Dome Roof, Arched Windows, Cupola, Fruitwood, Mahogany, Octagonal, 24 ½ x 10 In.	615.00
Model, Church, Spires, Openwork Base, Gray Paint, 38 x 21 In.	1580.00
Model, Printing Press, Handmade, 7 ¾ x 10 In.	153.00
Monk, Pensive, Signed Hermann Steiner, Poland, c.1945, 8 ¼ In.	180.00
Monk, Praying, c.1900, 21 x 8 ¼ In.	434.00
Monkey, Black Forest, Seated, Arms Begging, Brass Cap, 1900s, 14 In.	295.00
Mother & Child, Standing Woman, Nude, Holding Child's Hand, Black Walnut, 1950, 65 In.	9375.00
Mother & Child, Woman, Standing, Arms Wrapped Around Boy, J. Ingraham, 34 In.	575.00
Naval Officer, Standing, Hand In Jacket, Cap, Mutton Chops, Bow Tie, Paint, Stand, c.1850, 63 In.	4600.00
Northern Oriole, Life Size, On Weathered Wood, Signed, 7 x 8 ½ In.	142.00
Nutcracker, Bear Head, Glass Eyes .... *illus*	138.00
Old Man, Seated, Holding Basket, Bamboo, Chinese, c.1800, 6 ½ In.	10073.00
Oldsquaw Drake, Signed, 17 ¼ In.	94.00
Our Lady Of Guadalupe, On Winged Snake, Gesso, Multicolor Paint, 63 x 23 In.	2875.00
Ox Team, Cart, Drover, Painted, Red, Blue, 8 & 19 ½ & 6 ¼ In.	153.00
Palm Tree, Textured Trunk, Downcurved Leaves, Semicircle Wood Base, Giltwood, 39 In.	1007.00
Panel, Dancing Couple, Fruitwood, Signed Sinaz Gabloner, Austria, c.1950, 12 x 8 In.	510.00
Panel, Walnut, Mythical Figures, Scrolling Leaves, Painted, Gilt, Frame, 27 x 10 In., 4 Piece	2032.00
Pegasus, Rocks, 60 ½ x 39 ½ In.	575.00
Penguin, Applied Tack Eyes, Mounted On Rock, 1930s, 9 ½ In.	652.00
Penguin, Painted, Standing, Square Base, c.1900, 5 ¾ In.	403.00
Penguin, Standing On Rocks, Tack Eyes, Painted, c.1905, 10 In.	652.00
Peregrine Falcon, Perched On Fence Post, Signed, 21 ½ In.	118.00
Plaque, 2 Shaking Hands, Maple, Unfinished Patina, c.1875, 18 In. .... *illus*	6463.00
Plaque, Armorial, Spanish Oak, Leaves, Shield, 1700s, 17 x 14 & 16 x 15 In.	584.00
Plaque, Boar Hunt, Gone Bad, Attacking Dogs, Hunter, Signed, 1800s, 21 x 27 In.	805.00
Plaque, Cupid Riding Lioness, One Sad, One Frightened, Oak, c.1880, 20 x 25 ½ In., Pair	1035.00
Plaque, Dragons, Gilt, Chinese, 19th Century, 10 x 10 In., Pair	100.00
Plaque, Eagle, Handles, 14 x 8 In.	248.00
Plaque, Eagle, Spread Wings, Banner, Live & Let Live, Shield, c.1950, 73 x 24 In.	4720.00
Plaque, Game Bird, Hanging, Flower Swag, Carved, 1800s, 40 x 15 In., Pair	2185.00
Plaque, Horn, Tambourine, Leaf Branches, Parcel Gilt, Canted Corners, 19 x 17 In.	276.00
Plaque, Horseracing, 4 Horses, Jockeys, Stretching For Finish, Signed CK, 7 ½ x 26 In.	1534.00
Plaque, Hunt Symbols, Black Forest, Leaves, 38 x 24 In., Pair	3159.00
Plaque, Kindom Of Granada, Pomegranate, Crown, Gilt, Spain, c.1950, 28 x 19 In. ....*illus*	4428.00
Plaque, Lion Flanked By Scrolls & Tassels, Walnut, 26 x 19 In.	826.00
Plaque, Lion's Face, White Eyes & Teeth, Oak, c.1900, 19 x 17 In. ....*illus*	940.00
Plaque, Setter, Relief Profile, Signed, H. Newhouse, Hardwood, 15 x 25 In.	265.00
Polar Bear, White, Painted, 9 ¾ In.	158.00
Prophet, Bearded, Cloak, Staff, Parcel Gilt, 19 x 22 ½ In.	1053.00
Punch, From Punch & Judy, Painted, Multicolor, c.1960, 72 x 24 In.	431.00
Pyrrhuloxia, Mounted On Tree Branch, Signed, 8 ¼ In.	47.00
Red-Tailed Hawk, On Driftwood, 18 ¼ x 23 In.	201.00
Rooster, Base, Painted, Wilfrid Richard, Canada, 20 In.	1012.00
Rooster, Multicolor, D.M. 1941, 15 In.	452.00
Ruffed Grouse, Mounted On Burl Wood, Signed, 10 ½ In.	130.00
Ruyi Scepter, Bamboo, Peach, Precious Object, Bat, Chinese, 13 In.	239.00
Ruyi Scepter, Jade Plaque Insert, Cranes, Pine Tree, 14 In.	380.00
Saint Holding Book, Painted, 18th Century, 47 In.	1001.00

W

Saint, Arm Raised, Roman Costume, Italy, 1600s, 33 In.	660.00
Saint, Woman, Painted, Gilt, Book In Right Hand, Molded Base, France, 34 ½ x 23 In.	2450.00
Saint, Woman, Robes Flowing, Italy, 49 In.	1416.00
Salome, Nude Female, Spear, Severed Head, John The Baptist, Maple, D. Hurd, 69 In.	354.00
Santo, Michael, Archangel, Glass Eyes, Plume, Plaid Skirt, Gesso, Painted, 1800s, 34 x 13 In.	1955.00
Santo, Our Lady Of Guadalupe, Paint, 1 ½ x 7 ½ In.	173.00
Scholar, Standing, Holding Staff, Dead Tree Trunk, Burl, Chinese, 21 In.	304.00
Seal, On Front Flippers, Upturned Real Flipper, Painted, c.1900, 21 x 34 In.	6900.00
Shrine, St. Francis Of Assisi, Saints, Tin Glazed Tiles, Brass Plaque, c.1850, 22 x 15 In.	584.00
St. Anthony Of Padua, Spanish Colonial, Multicolor, c.1810, 14 x 7 In.	480.00
St. Anthony, Abbot, Full Figure, Glass Eyes, Paint, Giltwood, 1800s, 13 ¾ In.	240.00
St. Catherine, Crown, Bible Sword, Oak, 16 ½ x 7 ½ In.	1521.00
St. Ignatius, Standing, Cape, Holding Book, Spain, 1700s, 29 In.	652.00
St. Lawrence, Raised Arm, Parcel Gilt Trim, Red, Black Paint, 33 x 16 In.	702.00
St. Ulrich, Bishop's Miter, Croiser, Book In Hand, Germany, c.1900, 20 ½ In.	600.00
Star, 5-Point, Painted Green, Wire Mounted, Black Base, 10 In.	325.00
State Seal, Maine, Painted, Pine, Round, 24 ½ In. Diam.	1955.00
Steer Head, Polished, 20 x 22 In., Pair	295.00
Swordfish, Ironwood, Wood Base, Dark Finish, 17 ½ x 10 In.	144.00
Taverner, Balanced On 1 Leg, Holding Mug, Rectangular Base, 27 In.	1126.00
Teak Tree, Arch, Fighting Dragons, Phoenix, 87 x 72 In.	259.00
Totemic Figure, Man, Arms At Chest, Red & Black Eyes, Square Base, c.1890, 15 In.	230.00
Tundra Swan, Realistic Head, Signed, 33 ½ In.	153.00
Ventriloquist Head, Movable Mouth, Applied Ears, Painted, Mounted On Base, c.1890, 12 In. *illus*	3055.00
Viking, Winged Helmet, Cloak, Holding Sword Handle, Painted, Stand, c.1900, 46 In. *illus*	920.00
Wall Pocket, Leaf, Victorian, Black Paint Highlights, Late 1800s, 23 ½ In., Pair	46.00
Warrior, Leaning On Cat, Facing A Staff, Coiled Snake, Round Base, 17 In.	119.00
Water Buffalo, Looking Backwards, Rider, Holding Spear, Barrel On Back, Asia, 24 x 20 In.	119.00
Whip Hook, Alpine Climber, 11 In. *illus*	316.00
Wolf, Painted, c.1950, 63 In.	237.00
Woman & Child, Kneeling On Base, Baby In Arms, Republic Of Congo, Africa, 16 In.	227.00
Woman, Fertility, Hands On Waist, Painted Face Mask, Metal Base, Africa, 30 In.	81.00
Woman, On Stool, Milking Cow, Horns, Cat, Pine, Rectangular Base, Early 1900s, 7 In.	115.00
Woman, Seated, On Stool, Holding Box, Headpiece, Africa, 31 In.	299.00

WOODEN wares were used in all parts of the home. Wood was used for many containers and tools. Small wooden pieces are called *treenware* in England, but the term *woodenware* is more common in the United States. Additional pieces may be found in the Advertising, Kitchen, and Tool categories.

Artist's Model, Articulated, Hinged, Pine, c.1820, 16 In.	1121.00
Barrel, Flour, Oak, Reed Wrapped Sides, 1800s, 9 In.	69.00
Barrel, Red Stain, 22 ¾ In.	296.00
Barrel, Storage, Sycamore Log, Bark Remnants, Carved Bottom Plank, 18 x 15 In.	165.00
Barrel, Strap, Iron, Weathered, c.1900, 53 x 32 In.	246.00
Barrel, Wine, Spout, Base, Stand, c.1880, 11 x 8 In.	230.00
Bin, Grain, Lift Top, 4 Sections, Metal Hinges, 1800s, 50 x 24 In.	201.00
Bowl, Ash Burl, Oblong, 19th Century, 4 x 14 In.	1998.00
Bowl, Ash Burl, Rim, Footed, 1800s, 8 In.	294.00
Bowl, Ash Burl, Turned, Wide Rim, Varnished, 6 ¼ x 15 ½ In.	823.00
Bowl, Ash Burl, Woodlands, c.1810, 17 ¼ In.	3525.00
Bowl, Ash, Turned, Red Paint, Carved Pouring Notch, 1800s, 7 x 20 In.	1363.00
Bowl, Blue, c.1850, 4 ½ x 16 In.	470.00
Bowl, Burl, 1800s, 4 ½ x 9 ¾ In.	516.00
Bowl, Burl, Elm, Carved Handles, 1700s, 9 x 24 In.	1116.00
Bowl, Burl, Elm, Turned, c.1800, 3 ¼ x 8 ½ In.	2147.00
Bowl, Burl, Shouldered Rim, 7 ½ In.	1130.00
Bowl, Burl, Turned Rim, 1800s, 5 x 14 In.	840.00
Bowl, Burl, Turned Rim, 19th Century, 4 ½ x 12 In.	1438.00
Bowl, Burl, Turned, Painted, Banded Rim, New England, 5 ¼ x 18 ¾ In.	1659.00
Bowl, Burl, Turned, Round, Incised Collar Lines, Early 1800s, 17 ½ In.	2133.00
Bowl, Gray Paint, 1800s, 19 x 6 ½ In.	69.00
Bowl, Maple, Ash, Squat, Bulbous, Narrow Rim, Signed, c.1970, 8 x 13 In.	1250.00
Bowl, Maple, Painted Red, c.1850, 2 ½ x 11 In.	353.00
Bowl, Maple, Turned, Beveled Rim, Hanger Hole, 17 x 18 In.	161.00
Bowl, Maple, Turned, Painted, Hanger Hole, Painted Blue, c.1875, 18 x 19 In.	150.00

Twin Beds

Twin beds were designed by Thomas Sheraton in England in the eighteenth century. They did not become popular or even acceptable until the twentieth century. The Hays Code covering morals in movies ruled in 1934 that married couples could only be pictured in twin beds about a foot apart. It became stylish.

Wood Carving, Nutcracker, Bear Head, Glass Eyes
$138.00

Fox Auctions

Wood Carving, Plaque, 2 Shaking Hands, Maple, Unfinished Patina, c.1875, 18 In.
$6463.00

Garth's Auctions, Inc.

TIP

Don't wash wooden spoons, bowls, cutting boards, or anything with a wooden handle in the dishwasher. The hot water will make the wood swell. When dry the wood will shrink but sometimes leaves the piece with gaps or wobbly bases.

W

Wood Carving, Plaque, Kindom Of Granada, Pomegranate, Crown, Gilt, Spain, c.1950, 28 x 19 In. $4428.00

New Orleans Auction Galleries, Inc.

Wood Carving, Plaque, Lion's Face, White Eyes & Teeth, Oak, c.1900, 19 x 17 In. $940.00

Garth's Auctions, Inc.

Wood Carving, Ventriloquist Head, Movable Mouth, Applied Ears, Painted, Mounted On Base, c.1890, 12 In. $3055.00

Garth's Auctions, Inc.

TIP

Rattan and wicker furniture will pick up the smell of cigarette smoke. If you want to remove it, put the piece outside to air.

W

Bowl, Pine, Turned, Hanging Hole, Painted, 4 x 14 In.	102.00
Bowl, Tapered Side, Carved Handle, Pierced, Red Paint, Round, 1800s, 16 In.	652.00
Bowl, Tiger Maple, Oval, c.1800, 23 In.	650.00
Bowl, Turned, Painted Robin's-Egg Blue, c.1880, 4 ¼ x 14 In.	588.00
Bowl, Turned, Painted, Green Exterior, Dogwood Interior, Beveled Rim, 12 x 12 In.	104.00
Bowl, Turned, Pennsylvania, 1800s, 7 ¼ x 21 ¾ In.	563.00
Bowl, White Paint, Round 1800s, 18 In.	288.00
Bowl, Yellow Paint, Wide Rim, c.1850, 19 In.	241.00
Brush Holder, Rosewood, Bird & Flower, Square Shape, 8 In.	747.00
Brush Holder, Zitan, Elephant, Scrolling Leaves, Coins, Chinese, 5 ¼ In.	896.00
Brushpot, 7 Sages, Scholars, Pavilion, Bamboo, Cylindrical, Chinese, 7 x 4 ½ In.	248.00
Brushpot, Bamboo, Rosewood, Leaf Border, Seated Sages, 6 ½ x 6 ⅜ In.	2460.00
Brushpot, Burl, Dense, Graining, Chinese, c.1800, 9 ½ In.	613.00
Brushpot, Cranes, Pine Tree & Lotus, Bamboo, Cylindrical, Chinese, 6 In.	598.00
Brushpot, Huanghuali, Yellow Rosewood, Square, Footed, 1800s, 3 ½ x 3 ½ In.	2460.00
Brushpot, Sage, Seated, Rocky Ledge, Teapot & Stove, Tree, Stream, Tree Trunk, Oval, 7 ½ In.	1599.00
Brushpot, Tree Trunk Shape, Pine Branches, Chinese, 5 ¼ In.	3318.00
Bucket, Banded, Bentwood Swing Handle, Stave Construction, Blue Paint, 11 ½ In.	558.00
Bucket, Berry, Carved Staves, 2 Iron Hoops, Ears, Bail Handle, Wood Grip, Painted, 4 x 5 In.	1074.00
Bucket, George III, Mahogany, Brass Bound, Loop Handle, 1800s, 16 In.	406.00
Bucket, Green Paint, Bent Wood Handle, Stave Construction, 1800s, 13 ½ x 15 In.	323.00
Bucket, Ice, Handle, Teak, Jens Quistgaard, Dansk, 20 In.	420.00
Bucket, Iron Bands, Bail Handle, Wood Grip, Painted, 9 x 12 In.	136.00
Bucket, Mahogany, Elm, Brass Band, Ebonized Ring Bowl, Vertical Staves, Liner, Victorian, 13 x 12 In.	702.00
Bucket, Mixed Woods, Iron Bands, Gray, Stave, 19th Century, 6 ½ x 9 In.	59.00
Bucket, Pine, Mustard Yellow, Swing Handle, 1800s, 6 ½ x 9 In.	1541.00
Bucket, Pine, Tin, Painted Graining Over Ivory, Bail Handle, Stave Construction, c.1890, 7 x 8 In.	151.00
Bucket, Sugar, Finger Bands, Bentwood, Swing Handle, Stave Construction, 13 x 13 In.	1058.00
Bucket, Sugar, Vine Design, Iron Band, Vertical Staves, Lehnware, Lid, 8 ¾ In.	283.00
Bucket, Tin Bands, Green Paint, Penciled Notation, Bail Handle, c.1880, 9 ½ x 12 In.	382.00
Cage, Squirrel, Hinged, Pin Lock, Slatted, Oval, 11 ½ x 20 In.	106.00
Carrier, Utensil, Nailed Joints, Painted, Pinwheel Design, 4 x 14 x 7 In.	2034.00
Carrier, Wine Bottle, Rosewood, Brass Mounts, Tapered, Hinged Lids, Swing Handle, 10 x 14 In.	88.00
Case, Carrying, Walnut Butter, 5 Compartment, Double Slide Lids, Finger Holes, Iron Bail, 19 x 21 In.	94.00
Charger, Georgia Pine, Turned, Branded, Ed Moulthrop, c.1980, 22 x 2 ½ In. *illus*	1736.00
Cigar Case, Flamed Maple, Rolled Edges, Match Striker On Side, 7 x 4 ½ x 2 In.	283.00
Coffee Tree Trunk, Gnarled, Twisted Branches, Root Base, Silver Leaf Overlay, 89 In.	1045.00
Cup, Libation, Rosewood, Friends Of Winter, Pine, Bamboo, Prunus, 1 ½ x 2 In., Pair	461.00
Cup, Libation, Zitan, Mythical Creature, Head, Vipor Handle, Bulging Eyes, Open Mouth, 6 ½ In.	799.00
Cup, Maple, Black & White Smoke Decoration, Footed, c.1875, 2 ½ In.	59.00
Cup, Multicolor Flower, Salmon Ground, Lehnware, 3 In.	1422.00
Cutlery Urn, Mahogany, Satinwood Inlay, Telescoping Lid, Fitted Interior, 27 x 10 In., Pair	2868.00
Farrier's Box, Pine, Handle, Footed, Early American, 20 x 19 x 10 In.	118.00
Firkin, Brown Paint, Handle, 1800s, 7 ½ In.	288.00
Firkin, Cover, 3-Finger, Staved, Tapered, Painted Blue, Wood Strip Bail Handle, 12 x 12 ½ In.	325.00
Firkin, Cover, Tapered, Lapped Bands, Swing Handle, Stained, Stamped Saratoga, 12 x 12 ¼ In.	201.00
Firkin, Finger Lapped Lid Band, Nail & Wood Pins, Painted, 6 ¼ In.	735.00
Firkin, Tapered Lap Jointed Bands, Copper Nails, Wood Pins, Handle, 9 x 9 In.	283.00
Foot Warmer, Turned Spindles, Punched Tin Sides, Metal Bail, 5 ¾ x 8 ¾ In.	66.00
Foot Warmer, Walnut Case, Brass Bail, Pierced Vents, Sheet Iron Cover, 6-Sided, 8 x 12 In.	94.00
Ice Bucket, Rosewood, High Handle, Tapered, Jens Quistgaard, Dansk, 18 x 8 ½ In.	403.00
Manhole Cover, Poplar, Painted Black, Rochester Water Works, c.1918, 21 In., 2 Piece	413.00
Mold, Shoe, Adjustable, Egg Shape Heel, Push Button Mechanism, 12 ½ In.	11.00
Mold, Western Hat, 2 Section, 11 ½ x 4 ½ x 13 In.	28.00
Mug, Walnut, Stirrup Handle, Round Foot, Relief Carving, Stars, Leaves, 5 ⅜ x 4 ¾ In.	118.00
Pail, Copper Swing Handle, 1800s, 19 x 12 In.	115.00
Piggin, Round, Banded, Blue Paint, Shaped Hanger, 19th Century, 13 x 8 In.	863.00
Plate Pail, George III, Mahogany, Brass Liner, Pierced, Swing Handle, Octagonal, 25 ¼ x 11 In.	702.00
Plate, Arts & Crafts, Winter Troika Scene, Landscape, Paint, Signed B. Kavalevskiy, Russia, 16 In.	540.00
Platter, Provincial, Round, Raised Edge, Triangular Handles, 21 In., 4 Piece	215.00
Propeller, Laminated, c.1920, 66 In. *illus*	267.00
Rack, Drying, Cherry, Square Beveled Base, Octagonal Shape Post, 2 Cross Arms, 35 In.	215.00
Rack, Shoe Drying, Walnut, Footed, 1800s, 28 x 36 In.	69.00
Saffron Cup, Pomegranates, Multicolor, Lid, Finial, 4 ⅜ In.	678.00
Salt, Blue, Green Red, Pomegranates, Lehnware, 3 In.	1582.00
Tankard, Pine, Staved, Wood Banding, New England, c.1780, 11 ½ x 8 ¼ In.	1062.00

Tray, Apple, Pine, Chestnut, Canted Sides, Painted Green, 9 ¾ x 13 ¼ In.	353.00
Tray, Leaf Shape, Chinese, 7 In.	239.00
Tray, Mahogany, Inlay, Scrolling Leaf Design, Molded Gallery, Brass Handles, 25 In.	207.00
Tray, Mahogany, Oval, Galleried, Inlaid Shell, England, 1800s, 12 x 8 In.	148.00
Tray, Olivewood, Inlay, Oval, c.1876, 18 x 24 In.	600.00
Tray, Utensil, Divided, Walnut, Pierced Handle, Splayed Sides, 5 x 11 In.	51.00
Trencher, Carved, Oblong, 5 x 19 In.	165.00
Trencher, Cream Color, Inscribed Anna Osgood, 8 In. Diam.	1659.00
Trencher, Pine, Painted, 4 ¼ x 15 ¼ In.	147.00
Trough, Feed, Oval, 42 In.	431.00
Urn, Cutlery, Regency, Mahogany, Parcel Gilt, Acorn Finial, c.1900, 37 x 14 In., Pair	1830.00
Urn, Lamp Base, Swags, Tassels, Giltwood, 1900s, 17 ½ x 33 In.	531.00
Urn, Treen, Ribbed, 9 ½ x 4 ½ In., Pair	235.00
Vase, Bamboo Books, Ear Shaped Rosewood Handles, Chinese, 1700s, 31 In., Pair	3308.00
Vase, Gnarled Plum Tree, Branches, Cranes, Roots, Feet, Rosewood, Chinese, 9 In.	307.00
Vase, Red Lacquer, Chinese, 1800s, 5 ½ x 7 In.	550.00
Vase, Water & Warrior Scenes, Red, Brown, Cylindrical, Chinese, 1700s, 6 x 14 ½ In.	1210.00
Wall Pocket, Double, Painted, Gold Pinstripes, Applied Shapes, 16 x 8 In. ......*illus*	189.00
Wall Pocket, Pierced, Welcome Banker, Leaves, Walnut, Impressed 51, 24 x 13 ½ In. ....*illus*	94.00

WORCESTER porcelains were made in Worcester, England, from 1751. The firm went through many name changes and eventually, in 1862, became The Royal Worcester Porcelain Company Ltd. Collectors often refer to Dr. Wall, Barr, Flight, and other names that indicate time periods or artists at the factory. It became part of Royal Worcester Spode Ltd. in 1976. The company was bought by the Portmeirion Group in 2009. Related pieces may be found in the Royal Worcester category.

Bowl, Painted, Flowers, Vining, Grainger Lee & Co., 1800s, 4 x 9 In.	270.00
Coffeepot, Cover, Dignitary, Woman, Fan, Child, Leaf Tip Rim, Flower Knop, c.1770, 9 In.	826.00
Cup & Saucer, Flowers, Leaves, Blue, White, Crescent Mark, 18th Century, 4 ½ In. ......*illus*	305.00
Cup, Long Eliza Figure, Umbrella, Peonies, Birds, Lobed Bell Shape, Scroll Handle, c.1753, 2 ½ In.	8007.00
Dish, Dessert, Gilt Fan Shape Panels, Roundels, Flowers, Leaves, Blue Ground, c.1770, 7 In.	354.00
Dish, Dessert, Square, Wavy Rim, Lord Henry Thynne, Flowers, Birds, Leaves, c.1782, 9 In.	885.00
Dish, Shaped Rim, Hexagonal Medallions Border, Chinese Warrior, Serpent, 1800s, 15 In.	119.00
Dish, Sweetmeat, Blind Earl, Leaves, Chinese Figures, Boat, Pagoda, Stem Handle, c.1767, 6 In.	1888.00
Dish, Sweetmeat, Square, Gilt Gadroon Sides, Green Border, Bird Center, FBB Mark, 9 ¾ In., Pair	1075.00
Jug, Cabbage Leaf, Fluted Neck, Milking Scene, Milkmaids, Yellow, Roses, Leaves, c.1765, 9 In.	3776.00
Jug, Gold, Blue, Red, Chamberlain, c.1807, 7 In., Pair	345.00
Jug, Milk, Exotic Birds, Insects, Panels, Cobalt Blue Ground, Gilt, Loop Handle, c.1772, 5 In.	354.00
Plate, Armorial, Dejeuney, Scallops, Flower Band, Gilt, Ironstone, Chamberlain, c.1825, 9 ½ In., Pair	246.00
Plate, Medallion, Birds In Flight, Cartouches, Birds, Insects, Scalloped Rim, Gilt, Blue, 1770, 7 ½ In.	902.00
Platter, Canted Corners, Basket Weave Sides, Flower Sprays, Blue & White, 15 x 11 In.	345.00
Sauceboat, Wavy Vines & Leaves, Chinese Woman, Holding Fan, Garden, 1755-57, 9 In.	1534.00
Soup, Dish, Rimmed, Blue & White, Flowers, Dr. Wall, 9 ¼ In., Pair	413.00
Stand, Sweetmeat, Scallop Shell, Scroll Handles, Shells, Moss, Gilt, Pedestal, c.1840, 6 In.	590.00
Tea Caddy, Cover, Dragon, Fluted Oval, Diaper Border, Flowers, Flower Sprig Knop, c.1770, 6 In.	595.00
Teapot, Cover, Double Cylinder, Blue Chinese Motif, c.1875, 5 In.	326.00
Teapot, Cover, Spherical, Woman Holding Vase, Boy, Basket, Spade, Tree, 1768, 70, 6 In.	944.00
Vase, Banded Hedges, Trees, Bamboo, Kakiemon Style, Lobed, Chinese Handles, c.1753, 4 In.	21018.00
Vase, Bisque, Dragon Entwined, White Ground, Gilt, c.1883, 15 x 8 In.	480.00
Vase, Cobalt Blue Ground, Gold Leaves Design, Japanese Style, c.1877, 8 In., Pair	153.00
Vase, Figural, Hand, Holding Cup, Parian, Gold, Turquoise Bands, c.1864, 6 In.	316.00
Vase, Gilded, Enameled, Leaves, Nuts, Scrolled Handles, Grainger, c.1895, 11 In. ......*illus*	796.00
Vase, Honeycomb Design, Ivory Beading, Double Walled, Gilt Flowers, Butterfly Cartouches, 3 ¼ In.	633.00
Vase, Persian Style, Flowers & Leaves, Pierced Handles, Gilt, c.1887, 14 In.	245.00
Vase, Raised Bird, Branches, Scrolled Feet, Multicolor, c.1883, 15 In., Pair	633.00

WORLD WAR I and World War II souvenirs are collected today. Be careful not to store anything that includes live ammunition. Your local police will tell you how to dispose of the explosives. See also Sword and Trench Art.

WORLD WAR I

Andirons, Brass, 75 Mm Casings, 22 x 19 In.	875.00
Artillery Round, American, 75 Mm Round, Brass Case, Copper Band, 25 In.	250.00
Badge, Private 1st Class Infantry, Wool, Chevron, Crossed Rifles, 2 ½ In.	50.00
Book, Liberty's Victorious Conflict, Photographic History Of The World War, 1918, 128 Pages.	55.00
Book, World War For Liberty, F. Rolt-Wheeler, 1919, 551 Pages, 9 x 7 In.	45.00

Wood Carving, Viking, Winged Helmet, Cloak, Holding Sword Handle, Painted, Stand, c.1900, 46 In.
$920.00

James D. Julia Inc.

Wood Carving, Whip Hook, Alpine Climber, 11 In.
$316.00

Fox Auctions

Wooden, Charger, Georgia Pine, Turned, Branded, Ed Moulthrop, c.1980, 22 x 2 ½ In.
$1736.00

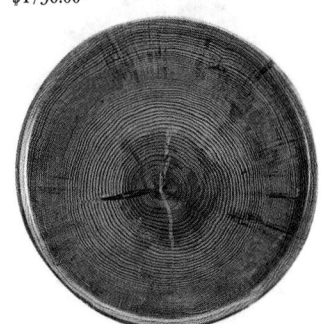

Rago Arts & Auction Center

W

Wooden, Propeller, Laminated, c.1920, 66 In.
$267.00

Auction Team Breker

Wooden, Wall Pocket, Double, Painted, Gold Pinstripes, Applied Shapes, 16 x 8 In.
$189.00

Conestoga Auction Co., Inc.

Wooden, Wall Pocket, Pierced, Welcome Banker, Leaves, Walnut, Impressed 51, 24 x 13 ½ In.
$94.00

Conestoga Auction Co., Inc.

Bowl, 5 Country Flags, 1914-1918, Gold Rim, 6 x 1 ½ In.	10.00
Box, Presentation, Gilt Brass, Embossed, Princess Mary Gift To Troops, 1914, 5 x 3 ¼ In.	145.00
Button, Uniform, United States Eagle Insignia, Scovill Mfg., ⅝ In., Pair	15.00
Button, Watch Wilson Wallop Wilhelm, Celluloid, 2 ¼ In.	1450.00
Doll, Soldier, Composition, Painted Face, Hair, Cloth Uniform, Hat, Jointed, 1914-18, 17 In.	99.00
Helmet, German Cavalry Officer's, Picklehaub, Eagle, Sceptor, Orb, C.E. Junker, 1916	565.00
Helmet, Leather, Sheep Skin Interior, Snap Closure, U.S. Pilot, Berlin Tanning Co., Wisc.	355.00
Helmet, Spiked, Prussian, Marked Berlin, 1916	714.00
Ladle, Commemorative, Royal Engineers On The Western Front, Wood, c.1917, 33 In.	478.00
Newspaper, CookBook, March 17, 1918, San Francisco Examiner, Recipes, 8 Pages	45.00
Paper, Army Regulations, Underwear, Frame, 8 ¼ x 5 ¾ In.	45.00
Plate, Gen. Lord Kitchener, Sec. Of War, Portrait, Transfer, Shaped, Scalloped, 5 In.	35.00
Plate, Nurse, Soldier, Walking, End Of War Commemorative, Royal Doulton, 1919, 4 ½ In.	495.00
Postcard, Photograph, 2 Uniformed Buddies, c.1918, 5 ½ x 3 ½ In.	10.00
Postcard, Soldier, Sweetheart, If Wishes Came True, Signed Archie Gun, c.1914	14.00
Poster, All For One, One For All, Vive La France, Soldiers, Liberty, 1917, 28 x 40 In.	384.00
Poster, Colored Man Is No Slacker, Black Couple, Cavalry Uniform, Paper, Frame, 1918, 17 x 20 In.	350.00
Poster, Destroy This Mad Brute, Enlist, Ape, German Helmet, Carrying Woman, 42 In.	3500.00
Poster, Fight Or Buy Bonds, Lady Liberty, Holding Flag, Soldiers, c.1918, 40 x 30 In.	460.00
Poster, Forward To Victory, Enlist Now, Cavalryman, Saber, Horse, Lucy Kemp-Welch, 28 x 19 In.	1003.00
Poster, Keep 'Em Smiling, 3 Servicemen, Frame, Bracker M. Leone, 1918, 41 x 28 In.	450.00
Poster, Put The Pennant Beside The Flag, 56 x 40 In.	633.00
Poster, Societe Centrale, Soldier, Gun, Linen, Signed Jean Droit, France, 31 x 40 In.	550.00
Poster, Uncle Sam Says Enlist For College, 2 Soldiers, M.M. Petersham, 28 x 21 In.	288.00
Poster, Victory Garden, Boy & Girl Garden Scene, Paper Lithograph, c.1917, 30 x 19 ⅞ In. *illus*	275.00
Poster, Victory Loan, W.P. No. 9, Frame, Canada, 1918, 26 x 39 In. *illus*	33.00
Poster, Women!, Help America's Sons, Older Woman, Hands Out, Linen Backed, 20 x 30 In.	600.00
Poster, Your War Savings Pledge, Uncle Sam, Savings Bonds, Linen Backed, 20 x 30 In.	480.00
Sewing Roll Up, Khaki Cotton, Compartments, Buttons, Needles, Wool, 20 ½ x 9 ½ In.	58.00
Sheet Music, End Of A Perfect Day, Peace Edition, Statue Of Liberty, Carrie Bond, 1918, 14 x 11 In.	12.00
Teapot, Victorious Peace Signed 1919, Portraits, Flags Of Allies, Porcelain	200.00

WORLD WAR II

Armband, Aircraft Warning Service, Felt, Gold Wings, Blue Ground, c.1942, 17 x 4 In.	10.00
Bank, Dime Register, Keep 'Em Rolling, Tank, Red, Tin Lithograph, 1940s, 2 ½ In.	202.00
Bank, Dime Register, Keep 'Em Sailing, Battleship, Tin Lithograph, 1940s, 2 ½ In.	230.00
Beaker, Pottery, RAF Wings, British War Relief Society, Copeland Spode, 1945, 4 ¼ In.	55.00
Book, All Yours Uncle Sam, 2 Girls Join Service, Barisis, 1943	25.00
Book, Brief History Of 131st Infantry, 1943, 5 ¼ x 7 ¼ In.	50.00
Bowl, For Right & Liberty, Canada, English Insignia, Paragon Patriotic Series, 1941, 3 ½ In.	55.00
Box, Metal, Bell's Vestas, Waterproof Matches, Green, Black Tin, 2 ¾ x 1 ½ In.	35.00
Bracelet, Sailor ID, Engraved Fred Herrington, 250-45-45, Sterling Silver Links	65.00
Button, I Didn't Raise My Boy To Be A Soldier, Eli Radish, Blue, Red, White, Celluloid, 1 In.	7.84
Button, Uncle Sam Hanging Hitler, Mechanical, Tin Lithograph, Evans Novelty *illus*	127.00
Buttons, Uniform, Eagle Symbol & E Pluribus Unum, Brass, Waterbury Co., 4 Piece	55.00
Can, Oil, Green, Lid Chain, 5 x 2 ¾ In.	13.00
Cap, Captain's, Poland Army Infantry, 3 Stars, Eagle Badge, Buttons, Leather, Locke & Co., c.1939	1380.00
Clock, Bulkhead, Navy, 24 Hour, Bakelite Case, Cheslsea Clock Co., 7 ½ In.	475.00
Compact, M.V. Warwick Castle, English Ship, Multicolor, Well, Mirror, Silvertone, 2 x 2 In.	120.00
Cribbage Set, U.S. Eagle Emblem, Cards, Board, Wood, Plastic	35.00
Doll, Mussolini Youth Group, Felt Swivel Head, Googly, Eyes, Jointed, Italy, 1930s, 14 In.	6325.00
Envelope, Not So Fast Adolf, 1942, 6 ½ In.	5.00
Equipment Roll, Guns, Tools, Canvas, Straps, 23 x 34 In.	25.00
Field Dressing, Unopened, Johnson & Johnson, 4 x 2 ¼ In., Pair	20.00
Flag, Nazi, 33 ½ x 24 In.	156.00
Flag, Third Reich, Battle, 76 x 126 In.	299.00
Gloves, Green, Wool, Lining, Size Medium	9.00
Helmet, Medic, Navy, D-Day Invasion, LCI Landing Craft, Red Cross, Blue Paint, 6 ½ x 9 In.	345.00
Lighter, B-17, Blue, White Lettering	12.00
Medical Kit, Pocket, Dental, Surgical Tools, Canvas, USN Inscribed, 7 x 3 In.	120.00
Patch, Shoulder, Army, Phillipine American, Black, Gold, Round, 1942, 3 ¼ In.	20.00
Patch, 6th Army, Red, White Star, Green Ground, Cotton, Round, 2 ¾ In.	16.00
Pennant, Third Reich, Triangular, 14 x 21 In.	184.00
Pin, Bomb Shape, Remember Pearl Harbor, Sterling Silver, 2 ⅛ In.	316.00
Pin, Eagle, Brass, Red, White & Blue Enamel, Remember Pearl Harbor, 2 In.	191.00
Pin, Greek Soldier, Flag, Euzonas Mountain Unit, Enamel, Metal, Victor Silson, 2 x 1 In.	99.00

Pin, I Am A Filipino, Remember Manila, Pearl Harbor, Red V, 1 In.	348.00
Pin, I Do Not Buy Japanese, German Or Italian Goods, Canada, 1 ¼ In.	138.00
Pin, Remember Pearl Harbor, Gold Metal, Red, White, Blue Enamel, ¾ In.	22.00
Pin, Remember Pearl Harbor, White, Blue Letters, 3 ½ In.	75.00
Pin, Save Your Bull For Your Victory Garden, Happy Cartoon Bull, 3 ½ In.	127.00
Pin, U.S. Will Take The Nip Out Of Nipponese, Celluloid, Blue Ground, Red Rim, White	17.00
Pin, Uncle Sam With Bayoneted Rifle, Remember Pearl Harbor, Blue, White, 1 ¼ In.	173.00
Pin, V For Victory, Celluloid, White Ground, Red Rim, Blue V, 1 In.	12.00
Pocket Watch, Military, England, 15 Jewel, Metal Dial, Arrow Hands	250.00
Postcard, Comic, You Better Go Maybel, They Put The Lights Out At 9:30, Technor Bros.	4.00
Postcard, Photograph, Adolf Hitler, Posed, Unused	22.00
Poster, American Flag, Give It Your Best!, 1942, 14 x 20 In.	345.00
Poster, Americans Will Always Fight For Liberty, 1778-1943, 22 ¼ x 28 In. ....*illus*	170.00
Poster, America's Answer!, Gloved Hand, Wrench, Jean Carlu, U.S. Gov. Printing, 1941, 30 x 40 In. ..*illus*	1725.00
Poster, Armed Forces Insignias, Disney Cartoon Characters, 1942, 21 x 25 In.	49.00
Poster, Buy That Invasion Bond, Soldiers, On Beach, Explosions, Planes, 28 x 20 In.	259.00
Poster, Buy War Bonds, Doing All You Can, Brother?, Soldier, Bandaged Head, 1943, 29 x 40 In.	167.00
Poster, Buy War Bonds, Uncle Sam, American Flag, Bombers Overhead, 30 x 40 In.	1265.00
Poster, Careless Talk, Got There First, Marine Dropping Rifle, Bleeding Face, 29 x 40 In.	460.00
Poster, Death On Subs!, Do Your Part, Make Your Part, On Time, c.1944, 40 x 30 In.	316.00
Poster, Enlistment, Sub Spotted, Let 'Em Have It, 1942, 28 x 42 In.	611.00
Poster, Fore!, Let's Put Everything Into This Drive, Golfer, Hitler On Ball, 40 x 30 In.	443.00
Poster, Frenchmen With Hands In Air, We French Workers Warn You, 1942, 28 ½ x 40 In.	345.00
Poster, G.I., Save Gas, Harold Von Schmidt, U.S. Gov. Printing Office, 1944, 40 x 28 ½ In. ..*illus*	288.00
Poster, I'm Counting On You, Uncle Sam, Frame, c.1943, 20 x 28 In.	1140.00
Poster, Keep Faith With Them, Mother Son, Navy Relief Society, 12 x 17 In.	45.00
Poster, Lend As They Fight, Shooting Soldier, Injured Soldier, 20 x 30 In.	288.00
Poster, Let's Give Him Enough & On Time, Tattered Soldier, Gun, N. Rockwell, 40 x 29 In.	1150.00
Poster, Nazi Dagger, Holy Bible, Swastika, This Is The Enemy, 1943, 28 x 20 In.	345.00
Poster, Next Of Kin Notified, Your Work Will Save Lives, Mother & Child Grieving, 1942, 29 x 40 In.	173.00
Poster, Sailor Looking Out Porthole, This Man May Die If You Talk Too Much, 1943, 28 x 22 In.	230.00
Poster, Save Rubber, Check Your Tires Now, Jeep Full Of Soldiers, 1942, 29 x 40 In.	230.00
Poster, Soldier Throwing Grenade, Let 'Em Have It, Buy Extra Bonds, 1943, 28 x 20 In.	259.00
Poster, Soldier With Head Wound, Have You Really Tried To Save Gas?, 1944, 40 x 28 ½ In.	288.00
Poster, Tattered American Flag, Smoke, Remember Dec. 7th, 1943, 28 x 22 In.	374.00
Poster, Together To Victory, Soldiers & Factory Workers Form V, 1942, 34 x 22 In.	144.00
Poster, United We Are Strong, United We Will Win, Flags, Cannon Barrel, 1943, 56 In.	144.00
Poster, War Bond, Ring It Again, Liberty Bell, 34 x 26 In.	124.00
Poster, War Bonds, Attack, Attack, Attack, Armed Soldiers, Advancing, 1942, 28 x 40 In.	388.00
Poster, War Bonds, To Have & To Hold, Soldier, Waving Big Flag, 1944, 29 x 40 In.	388.00
Poster, Work On A Farm This Summer, Join The U.S. Crop Corps., Farming Couple, 29 x 21 In.	173.00
Pouch, Mask Waterproofing Kit, Snap Closure, U.S., 5 x 5 In.	8.00
Ration Book, Office Of Price Administration, Enes Cole Issue, Stamps Inside	24.00
Rucksack, U.S. Mountain, Canvas, Leather Straps, Morrow & Douglas, 1943	45.00
Salt & Pepper, Figural, Aviator, Girl, Chalkware, 2 ½ In.	25.00
Scarf, Camp Shelby, Miss, Red, White, Fringe, Envelope, 24 x 24 In.	20.00
Sword, Brass Guard, Wire Wrapped Sharkskin Grip, Nickel Plated Scabbard, Japan, 31 In.	411.00
Tumbler, Eisenhower, Laurel Leaves, 4 ¼ In.	35.00
Tumbler, Ike, In Uniform, Etched Image, 5 ½ In.	67.00
Tumbler, Stalin, Laurel Leaves, 1941, 4 ¼ x 2 ¾ In.	45.00
Yearbook, U.S. Navy, Blue Cover, 1945	80.00

WORLD'S FAIR souvenirs from all of the fairs are collected. The first fair was the Great Exhibition of 1851 in London. Some other important exhibitions and fairs include Philadelphia, 1876 (Centennial); Chicago, 1893 (World's Columbian); Buffalo, 1901 (Pan-American); St. Louis, 1904 (Louisiana Purchase); Portland, 1905 (Lewis & Clark Centennial Exposition); San Francisco, 1915 (Panama-Pacific); Philadelphia, 1926 (Sesquicentennial); Chicago, 1933 (Century of Progress); Cleveland, 1936 (Great Lakes); San Francisco, 1939 (Golden Gate International); New York, 1939 (World of Tomorrow); Seattle, 1962 (Century 21); New York, 1964; Montreal, 1967; Knoxville (Energy Turns the World) 1982; New Orleans, 1984; Tsukuba, Japan, 1985; Vancouver, Canada, 1986; Brisbane, Australia, 1988; Seville, Spain, 1992; Genoa, Italy, 1992; Seoul, South Korea, 1993; Lisbon, Portugal, 1998; Hanover, Germany, 2000; and Aichi, Japan, 2005. Memorabilia of fairs include directories, pictures, fabrics, ceramics, etc. Memorabilia from other similar celebrations may be listed in the Souvenir category.

Ashtray, 1962, Seattle, Space Needle, Monorail, Science Pavilion Scenes, Round, Metal, 4 ¼ In.	30.00

Worcester, Cup & Saucer, Flowers, Leaves, Blue, White, Crescent Mark, 18th Century, 4 ½ In.
$305.00

Worcester, Vase, Gilded, Enameled, Leaves, Nuts, Scrolled Handles, Grainger, c.1895, 11 In.
$796.00

World War I, Poster, Victory Garden, Boy & Girl Garden Scene, Paper Lithograph, c.1917, 30 x 19 ⅞ In.
$275.00

HELPING HOOVER IN OUR U.S. SCHOOL GARDEN

World War I, Poster, Victory Loan, W.P. No. 9, Frame, Canada, 1918, 26 x 39 In. $33.00

Old Barn Auction

World War II, Button, Uncle Sam Hanging Hitler, Mechanical, Tin Lithograph, Evans Novelty $127.00

Hake's Americana & Collectibles

World War II, Poster, Americans Will Always Fight For Liberty, 1778-1943, 22 ¼ x 28 In. $170.00

Showtime Auction Services

Badge, 1909, Seattle, Chief Seattle, Welcome To The World, Gold Nugget Form, 2 In.	75.00
Ballad Book, 1939, New York, From Ballantine Inn, 11 x 7 In.	25.00
Bank, 1893, Chicago, Columbus Raises Arm, Indian Arises, Cast Iron, J. & E. Stevens, 7 x 8 In.	633.00
Bell, 1982, Knoxville, Top Emblem, Ringer, Metal, 4 x 2 In.	14.00
Bottle, Vinegar, 1939, New York, Globe Base, Continents Embossed, Milk Glass, 9 ¼ In.	55.00
Bracelet, 1939, Golden Gate International Exposition, California Building, Metal, 1 x 7 In.	35.00
Button, 1904, St. Louis, Paper, Any State Button Mailed For 10 Cents, Mercantile Novelty, 1 ¼ In. *illus*	221.00
Candy Box, 1939, New York, Scenes Of The Fair, Blue & Orange, 2 ⅞ x 6 ¾ In.	65.00
Candy Tin, 1939, New York, Exhibit Scenes, Bagatelle Chocolates, Blue, Orange, Metal, 2 ⅞ x 6 ¾ In.	65.00
Casket, 1893, Chicago, Columbian Exposition, Beveled Glass, 2 x 2 x 2 In.	175.00
Chamber Pot, Cover, 1893, Chicago, Columbian Exposition, Anna Pottery, Inscribed, 1 ½ x 2 ½ In.	2875.00
Clock, 1939, New York Trylon & Perisphere, Yellow, 4 In. Diam.	362.00
Coloring Book, 1963, New York, Panoramas, Spertus Publishing, Unused, 14 x 11 In.	65.00
Compact, 1939, New York, Trylon & Perisphere Lid, Black Silver Rim, Round, Metal, 2 ¾ x 2 In.	70.00
Creamer, 1893, Chicago, Victor Carlsbad, White Porcelain, Gilt Letters, 7 ¼ x 4 In.	45.00
Cuff Links, 1964, New York, Unisphere, Silver Metal, Black Enamel, Rope Rim, 1 In.	45.00
Cup & Saucer, 1962, Seattle, Lusterware	20.00
Cup, 1904, St. Louis, Black Building Sketches, White Porcelain, Gilt Rims, 3¾ x 2 ½ In., 3 Piece	55.00
Doll, 1939, New York, Native South African, Celluloid, Box, 8 In.	150.00
Fair Trade Dollar, 1962, Seattle, Exhibit Scenes, Embossed, Brass, 1 ½ In.	20.00
Fan, 1939, New York, Front Advertises Nation Transportation Co., Limonene, 10 x 11 In.	65.00
Figurine, 1933, Chicago, Dogs On Seesaw, Made In Japan, 1 ½ x 1 In.	12.00
Figurine, 1933, Chicago, Elephant, Blue, Moriage Design, Porcelain, 4 ½ x 3 ¾ In.	35.00
Flag, 1940, New York, Trylon & Perisphere, Blue & Gold, 24 x 25 In.	237.00
Flask, 1893, Chicago, Columbus Portrait, Molded, Clear, Frosted, 6 ¼ In.	225.00
Guard Badge, 1893, Chicago, 6-Point Star, Brass, Eagle, Ring, 3 In.	195.00
Guidebook, 1964, New York, Vatican Pavilion	8.00
Hot Pad, 1933, Chicago, Panel Scenes, Federal Building, Silver, Copper, 6 ½ x 9 ¾ In.	13.00
Keychain, 1964, New York, Oklahoma At The World's Fair, Round, Metal, 1 ½ In.	12.00
Letter Opener, 1904, St. Louis, Figural Indian, Louisiana Purchase Expo, Bronze, 11 In.	375.00
Liberty Bell, 1904, St. Louis Exposition, Philadelphia's Souvenir, Celluloid, 1 ¼ In.	20.00
Mirror, 1933, Chicago World's Fair, Netherlands Day, Queen Wilhelmina, Celluloid, 1 ¾ In.	35.00
Mug, 1974, Spokane, Pavilion Scenes, Porcelain, Footed, 4 In.	15.00
Panorama, 1939, New York, Scenes, Folded Paper, Multicolor, 5 ½ x 4 ½ In.	195.00
Parasol, 1933, Chicago, Red, Teal, Cream, Paper, Wood Handle, Box, 29 x 24 In.	75.00
Patch, 1940, New York, Blue Trylon & Perisphere, Orange Ground, 3 x 3 In.	28.00
Pear, 1893, Chicago, Peachblow, New England Glass Works Exhibit, Hand Blown, Pink, 5 In.	125.00
Pencil Sharpener, 1982, Knoxville, Sunsphere, Die Cast Metal, 4 In.	17.00
Pennant, 1939, New York, I Was There Closing Day, Trylon & Perisphere, Yellow, 9 In.	57.00
Perfume Bottle, 1893, Chicago, Columbian Exposition Scene, Enameled Glass, Brass Lid, 2 ¾ In.	350.00
Pin, 1901, Buffalo, Pan-American Exposition, Windrath Back Paper, Celluloid, 1 ¼ In.	59.00
Pin, 1904, St. Louis, Chinese Village, Dragon, Black On Yellow, 1 ½ In.	75.00
Pin, 1904, St. Louis, Palace Of Machinery, Sepia, Celluloid, 3 ½ In.	86.00
Pin, 1939, New York, Deutsche Tag, June 2, Gerhartdt Hoffmann, Celluloid, Swastika, 2 ¼ In.	178.00
Pin, 1964, New York, New York State Exhibit, Star Of The Fair, Viewing Tower, 3 ½ In.	62.00
Pitcher, 1893, Chicago, Blue, White Relief Scenes, Fort Dearborn, Fire, Copeland, 8 In.	475.00
Plate, 1897, Brussels Exposition Internationale, Glass, Lacy Edge, 5 ¼ In.	22.00
Plate, 1904, St. Louis, Louisiana Purchase, Marked Weller, 5 In.	138.00
Plate, 1939, New York, Art Deco Graphics, Blue, J & G Meakins, Eng., 10 ½ In.	125.00
Plate, 1939, New York, Cobalt Blue, J & G Meakins, England, 10 In.	125.00
Plate, 1939, New York, Trylon & Perisphere, Wooden, Flowers	34.00
Platter, 1876, Philadelphia, Ironstone, Give Us This Day Our Daily Bread, Open Handles, Oval	275.00
Postcard, 1939, New York, Trylon & Perisphere, Linen	90.00
Poster, 1926, Philadelphia, Miss Liberty Holding Flags, Linen Back, Dan Smith, 17 x 26 ¾ In. *illus*	518.00
Poster, 1929, New York, Uniformed Tour Guide, Perisphere, Fireworks, 30 x 20 In.	509.00
Poster, 1937, Paris, Face, Silhouette, Flags, Lithograph, Jean Carlu, 63 x 47 In.	735.00
Poster, 1964-65, New York, Family, Unisphere, Bob Peak, Linen Mount, 43 x 28 In.	345.00
Powder Box, 1900, St. Louis, Glass Liner, Mirror, Embossed Scrolls, Brass, 4 ½ In.	85.00
Print, 1893, Chicago, Columbian, Ferris Wheel, 10 x 12 In.	12.00
Puzzle Set, 1876, Philadelphia, Centennial, Exhibition, Wood, Chromolithograph, 22 x 12 In., 5 Piece	502.00
Ring, 1939, New York, Brass, Trylon & Perisphere Buildings, Adjustable *illus*	153.00
Salt & Pepper, 1962, Seattle, Space Needle Shape, Pewter, Box, 1 ½ x 4 ½ In.	60.00
Scarf, 1939, New York, Boy Scouts, Service Camps, Purple, Orange, 30 x 30 In.	85.00
Seat, 1939, New York, Walking Stick, Chair, Cane, Wood, 36 In.	195.00
Spoon, 1893, Chicago, 16 Palmer Cox Brownies At Ferris Wheel, Silver, 6 In.	158.00
Spoon, 1893, Chicago, Flared Handle, Columbus Bust, Coin Silver, 4 ½ In.	10.00

Spoon, 1962, Seattle, Space Needle, Embossed, Silver, 4 In.	12.00
Teapot, Lid, 1939, New York, Cobalt Blue, Gold, Trylon & Perisphere, 1939, 10 x 6 In.	204.00
Tie Bar, 1939, New York, Trylon & Perisphere, 2 Chains, Blue, Silver, Black, Round, Metal, 2 In.	31.00
Tip Tray, 1904, St. Louis, Antikamnia Pharmacy Co., Sick Woman, Pills, 3 ¼ x 4 ¾ In.	275.00
Toy, 1939, New York, Tractor Train, Cast Iron, Tin Lithograph Canopies, Arcade, 15 ¾ In. .... *illus*	920.00
Toy, 1964, New York, Fairground Greyhound Transporter, Tin, Rubber Wheels, Japan, 6 x 3 ½ In.	220.00
Toy, Tractor Tram, 1939, New York, Decals, Cast Iron, Arcade, 7 In.	497.00
Tray, 1964, New York, Red Plastic, Exhibit Scenes, Round, United States Steel, 10 ½ In.	25.00
Tumbler, 1904, St. Louis, Louisiana Purchase Exposition, Scenes, Pressed Glass, Gold Band, 5 In..	20.00
Tumbler, 1964, New York, Pool Of Industry Water Display, Plastic, 2 ¾ x 6 ½ In.	22.00
Vase, 1904, St. Louis, Baseball Player, Handles, Weller, Marked, 3 ½ x 1 ¾ In. ....*illus*	633.00
Vase, 1939, New York, White Trylon & Perisphere, Pink Ground, Lenox, 7 x 4 In.	650.00
Vase, 1940, New York, Ruby Flash, Clear, Gilt Rim Bands, Footed, 4 In.	18.00
Vest, 1909, Alaska-Yukon-Pacific Expo, Good Luck, Symbols, Embroidery, Beads, Seattle, Men's M.	431.00

WPA is the abbreviation for Works Progress Administration, a program created by executive order in 1935 to provide jobs for millions of unemployed Americans. Artists were hired to create murals, paintings, drawings, and sculptures for public buildings. Pieces are marked *WPA* and may have the artist's name on them.

Book, America Eats, Ethnic Food History, Illinois Writers' Project, Nelson Algren, c.1938	15.00
Book, History Of Farmers On Relief & Rehabilitation, WPA Progress, 1937, 10 In.	18.00
Book, Writer's Project, History, Westfield State Teachers College, Mass., 1941, 141 Pages	34.00
Bust, Black Soldier, Plaster, c.1940, 14 ½ In.	2500.00
Doll, Cloth, Girl, Light Brown Clothes, Hat, Shoes, Painted Face, String Hair, 22 In.	748.00
Figurine, Alice In Wonderland With Ugly Duchess, Edris Eckhardt, Pottery, c.1935, 5 ⅞ In. ...*illus*	460.00
Figurine, Dog's Head, Black, High Gloss, New Jersey Work Project, 4 ¾ In.	123.00
Folk Art, Pig's Head, Papier-Mache, Macbeth Drama Group, Southern Program, 1930s, 16 x 12 In.	65.00
Postcard, Photograph, Basket Weavers, Sally Cathey Instructing, Tyron, N.C., 1930s	100.00
Print, Charcoal On Paper, Figures, Hills, Ernest W. Scanes, Michigan Regionalist, c.1938, 17 x 22 In.	250.00
Watercolor, New York City, Cityscape, David Burliuk, 11 ½ x 15 ¾ In.	3200.00
Watercolor, On Paper, Family, House, David Levine, California Regionalist, 14 x 20 ¾ In.	350.00

WRISTWATCHES came into use during World War I. Wristwatches are listed here by manufacturer or as advertising or character watches. Wristwatches may also be listed in other categories. Pocket watches are listed in the Watch category.

Art Deco, 14K White Gold Case, Accent Diamonds, Silvertone Dial, Woman's, 1 In.	63.00
Art Deco, Diamond, Sapphire, Platinum, 18K Gold, Embossed Flowers, Woman's, ¾ x ½ In.	242.00
Art Deco, Link Set, Diamonds, Platinum, c.1925, 6 ½ In.	3000.00
Baume & Mercier, 14K Yellow Gold, Round Dial, Square Case, Mesh Bracelet, Woman's, 7 In.	1298.00
Baume & Mercier, 18K Yellow Gold, Round Opal Dial, 36 Round Diamonds, Woman's, 6 ½ In.	2360.00
Baume & Mercier, Stainless Steel, Diamonds, Purple Satin Dial, 1 ½ x 1 In.	834.00
Blancpain, Aqua Lung, Stainless Steel, Black Dial, Arabic & Baton Numerals	2963.00
Breitling, Navitimer World, Stainless Steel, Chronograph Movement, Gold Bezel	3245.00
Bulova, Diamonds, Mother-Of-Pearl Dial, 14K Yellow Gold Band, Quartz, Woman's	805.00
Burberry, Copper Colored Dial, Leather Band, Man's	148.00
C.H. Meylan, Platinum, 71 Diamonds, Art Deco, Tiffany & Co., Marked, Woman's	3450.00
Cartier, Panthere, 18K Gold, Ivory Dial, Roman Numerals, Date, Quartz, Gold Links	5925.00
Cartier, Pasha, Chronograph, Stainless Steel, Diamond, Roman & Dot Numerals	5819.00
Cartier, Stainless, Santos Quartz Calendar	1093.00
Cartier, Tank, 18K Yellow Gold, Leather Band	4720.00
Cartier, Tank, Stainless Steel, White Dial, Roman Numerals, Quartz Movement, Papers, Box ...*illus*	2844.00
Cartier, Tank, White Dial, Diamond Mellee Sides, Roman Numerals, Pink Band, Woman's	3555.00
Cartier, Tank, White Dial, Square, Roman Numerals, Blue Leather Band, Quartz	3555.00
Cartier, Trinity, 18K Yellow Gold, 98 Round Diamonds, 6 Extra Leather Bands, Box	12980.00
Cartier, Vermeil Case, Square Dial, Black Leather Band, Blue Cabochon, Box	805.00
Chopard, Happy Sport, Stainless Steel Brickwork Link, White Dial, Diamonds, Woman's	3851.00
Coach, Stainless Steel, 6 Multicolor Interchangeable Bezels	118.00
Croton, 14K Yellow Gold, Open Links, White Gold Diamond Set Links, Woman's, 7 ¼ In.	649.00
Ebel, 1911 Series, Round, Stainless Steel, Rubies, Diamonds, Wave Bracelet, Woman's	1006.00
Eberhard & Co., Chrono 4, 18K Rose Gold, White Dial, 4 Subsidiary Dials, Date, Box ....*illus*	2489.00
Eloga, 14K White Gold, Diamonds, Silver Tone, Gold Plated Stretch Band, Woman's	184.00
Franck Muller, 18K Rose Gold, Rectangular Dial, Leather Band	7670.00
Geneve, Diamond, 14K Yellow Gold, Oval Dial, Woman's, 6 ⅞ In.	708.00
Girard Perregaux, 14K White Gold, 24 Round Diamonds, Bracelet, Woman's, 7 In.	633.00
Gruen, Diamond, Platinum, 14K White Gold Bracelet, Quartz, Art Deco, Woman's	1062.00

World War II, Poster, America's Answer!, Gloved Hand, Wrench, Jean Carlu, U.S. Gov. Printing, 1941, 30 x 40 In. $1725.00

Humler & Nolan

World War II, Poster, G.I., Save Gas, Harold Von Schmidt, U.S. Government Printing Office, 1944, 40 x 28 ½ In. $288.00

Humler & Nolan

World's Fair, Button, 1904, St. Louis, Paper, Any State Button Mailed For 10 Cents, Mercantile Novelty, 1 ¼ In. $221.00

Hake's Americana & Collectibles

TIP

Scratches can be rubbed off the glass in a mirror by using a piece of felt and polishing rouge from a paint store.

W

World's Fair, Poster, 1926, Philadelphia, Miss Liberty Holding Flags, Linen Back, Dan Smith, 17 x 26 ¾ In. $518.00

World's Fair, Ring, 1939, New York, Brass, Trylon & Perisphere Buildings, Adjustable $153.00

World's Fair, Toy, 1939, New York, Tractor Train, Cast Iron, Tin Lithograph Canopies, Arcade, 15 ¾ In. $920.00

World's Fair, Vase, 1904, St. Louis, Baseball Player, Handles, Weller, Marked, 3 ½ x 1 ¾ In. $633.00

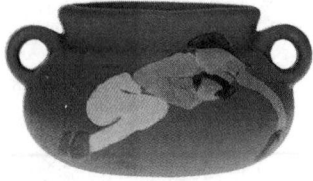

Gruen, Edwardian, Platinum, Diamond, Oval Matte Dial, Emerald, Onyx, Woman's	15535.00
Hamilton, 14K Rose Gold, 12 Diamonds, Garnets, Snake Chain Bracelet, Woman's, 6 ¾ In.	413.00
Hamilton, 14K White Gold, Diamond Bracelet, Monogram, 1959, Woman's	460.00
Hamilton, 14K White Gold, Diamonds, Cushion Shape Dial, Woman's, 7 In.	472.00
Hamilton, 6 Diamonds, 14K White Gold, Black Cord Band, Woman's	266.00
Hamilton, Cushion Shape, 17 Jewel Diamonds, 14K White Gold, Woman's	1404.00
Hamilton, Diamond, 14K White Gold, Oval Dial & Case, 68 Diamond Bracelet, Woman's, 6 ½ In.	590.00
Hamilton, Platinum, 34 Round Diamonds, Black Cord Bracelet, Women's, 6 In.	1093.00
Hamilton, Platinum, Diamond, Black Cord, Woman's, 6 In.	1093.00
Hamilton, Platinum, Diamonds, Barrel Shape Case, Woman's, c.1940	3585.00
Hermes, Stainless Steel, Rectangular Case, White Dial, Quartz, Brown Leather Band	600.00
IWC Schaffhausen, 18K Gold, Strap Buckle, 33 Mm Case, 1941	2875.00
Kaltron, 14K Gold, Yellow, Bracelet, Braided Mesh & Rope, Pear Shape Cover, Tassel, 6 ½ In.	805.00
Longines, 14K Gold, 16 Diamonds, Woman's, 7 In.	506.00
Lord Elgin, Gold Filled, Retro, Fluted Case, Manual Wind Movement, Leather Band	266.00
Lucien Piccard, 14K Gold, Yellow, Guilloche Dial, Diamond, Calendar, Signed, Leather Strap, Quartz	330.00
Lucien Piccard, 14K Yellow Gold, Mesh, Rope Chain, Hinged Clasp, 11 Diamonds, Woman's, 9 In.	2124.00
Lucien Piccard, Goldtone Dial, Roman Numerals, Diamond Melee, Woven Link Strap	1422.00
Mothey Tissot, 14K Yellow Gold, Rectangular, Cream Dial, Engraved, Woman's, 6 In.	541.00
Omega, 14K Yellow Gold, Diamonds, Tapered Bracelet, Oval, Woman's, 6 In.	690.00
Omega, 14K Yellow Gold, Manual Wind, Silver Satin Dial, Stretch Band, 1 ⅓ In.	426.00
Omega, 14K Yellow Gold, Rectangular Dial, Mesh Bracelet, Women's, 6 ¾ In.	649.00
Omega, Texture Square Case, Brushed Steel Dial, 14K Gold, Black Suede Band, Box, c.1960	508.00
Panerai Luminor Marina, Stainless Steel, Automatic, Black Dial, Stainless Bracelet, Case	3540.00
Patek Philippe, Round Dial, Baton Hour Markers, 18 Jewel, 14K Yellow Gold	7605.00
Platinum, 14K White Gold, Diamonds, Silvertone Dial, Woman's, 1 ¼ In.	529.00
Rolex, 14K Yellow Gold, Cushion Shape Dial, Mesh Bracelet, Woman's, 7 ¼ In.	767.00
Rolex, 18K Gold Case & Band, Round Dial, Date Window, Box	4600.00
Rolex, 18K Yellow Gold, Oyster, Perpetual, Woven Mesh Band, Foldover Clasp	5378.00
Rolex, Celini, 18K Gold, Manual Wind, Leather Band, Box, Papers, Woman's	2400.00
Rolex, Cellini, White, Rose Gold, Leather Band, Geneva, Case	5175.00
Rolex, Oyster Perpetual Datejust, Champagne Dial, 28 Jewel, c.1983	1210.00
Rolex, Oyster Perpetual, 18K Gold, 2-Tone, Sapphire Crystal, Bracelet Band, 1989	2990.00
Rolex, Oyster, Perpetual, 14K Gold Case, c.1970	1547.00
Rolex, Platinum, Round Dial, Hinged Cover, Diamonds, Woman's, 7 ¼ In.	4366.00
Rolex, Stainless Steel, Oyster Chronometer, Grosgrain Strap, Bubbleback, 1930s	2124.00
Rolex, Submariner, 18K Gold, Stainless Steel, Blue Dial, Sapphire Crystal, c.1995	4485.00
Rolex, Submariner, Stainless Steel, Stretch Bracelet, Black Dial, Box, 1960s	13570.00
Sheffield, 14K Yellow Gold, Polished Zigzag Design, 6 ¾ In.	767.00
South Bend, Tricolor, 14K Gold, Floral & Scroll Base, Gilt, Monogram, Marked, Woman's, 1 ¼ In.	531.00
Tiffany & Co., Black Case & Dial, Silver Color Numbers, Black Band, Quartz, Stamped, Box	384.00
Tiffany, 14K Yellow Gold, Black Leather Band, Alarm, c.1956	1035.00
Tiffany, 18K White Gold, Diamonds, Reptile Band, Woman's, 7 ¼ In.	1888.00
Tissot, Silver, Wind, Round Edged Frame, Woman's, 1950s	400.00
Van Cleef & Appels, Clover Leaf Face, Mother-Of-Pearl Dial, 18K Gold, Woman's, 1999, 7 ¾ In.	4313.00
Wittnauer, Bracelet, 14K Gold, Woman's	476.00

YELLOWWARE is a heavy earthenware made of a yellowish clay. It varies in color from light yellow to orange-yellow. Many nineteenth- and twentieth-century kitchen bowls and jugs were made of yellowware. It was made in England and in the United States. Another form of pottery that is sometimes classed as yellowware is listed in this book in the Mocha category.

Bank, Coin, Barrel Shaped, Drip Design, 3 ½ In.	106.00
Batter Bowl, Brown & White Lines, Lipped Rim, Raised Foot, 6 x 12 In. ....*illus*	71.00
Batter Bowl, Pouring Lip, Lobed, Scalloped, Orton Plantation, 1840s, 8 x 17 In.	230.00
Bowl, 3 White Lines, 5 x 7 In.	34.00
Canister, Lid, White Stripes, Round, 4 x 6 In.	68.00
Coffeepot, Footed, Handle	356.00
Colander, 9 ½ In. ....*illus*	45.00
Crock, Butter, Cover, Impressed, Butter, Abstract Designs, Iron Bail Handle, 4 x 7 In.	57.00
Figure, Lion, Lying Down, Base, c.1875, 6 x 9 In.	235.00
Figure, Spaniel, Seated, c.1875, 10 ½ In.	264.00
Loving Cup, Salamander, Frog, Cylindrical, Rounded Foot, 2 Loop Handles, 1800s, 5 x 5 In.	288.00
Match Holder, Castle Shape, Sand Finish, 19th Century, 5 x 7 x 5 In.	87.00
Mixing Bowl, Applied Skillet Handle, Spout & Relief Design Around Rim, 3 ½ x 6 In.	18.00
Mold, Ear Of Corn, Arched Sides, 2 ¾ x 9 In.	34.00

W

Mold, Frog Design, Spread Legged, Grass & Leaves, Oval, 1800s, 5 ½ In.	86.00
Mold, Grape Bunch, Arched Paneled Sides, Raised Foot, 4 x 9 In.	28.00
Mold, Impressed, John Bell, Waynesboro, Pennsylvania, 3 ¾ x 7 ¼ In.	504.00
Mold, Rabbit, 8 ¼ In.	79.00
Mold, Turk's Head, Manganese Splotches, 8 In.	51.00
Mug, Bulbous, Flared Top, Applied Loop Handle, Pad Foot, 3 ½ x 4 In.	35.00
Pitcher, Oval, Applied Molded Handle, 8 ¾ In.	40.00
Pitcher, Straight-Sided, Molded Handle, 6 ¾ In.	68.00
Teapot, Lid, Rotund Shape, Pouring Spout, Spurred Handle, c.1900, 6 In.	23.00

ZANE Pottery was founded in 1921 by Adam Reed and Harry McClelland in South Zanesville, Ohio, at the old Peters and Reed Building. Zane pottery is very similar to Peters and Reed pottery, but it is usually marked. The factory was sold in 1941 to Lawton Gonder.

ZP B ZANE WARE MADE U.S.A

Bowl, Green Matte Glaze, Ribbed, Wavy Rim, Marked, 6 ½ x 3 In.	55.00
Candlestick, Green Matte Glaze, Hexagonal Base, Flared Crown, Marked, c.1930, 9 x 4 ¾ In.	28.00
Flower Frog, Round, Incised Mark, 1920s, 3 ¾ In.	89.00
Vase, Watery Green Matte Glaze, Marked, c.1923, 8 ¾ x 4 ¼ In.	375.00

ZANESVILLE Art Pottery was founded in 1900 by David Schmidt in Zanesville, Ohio. The firm made faience umbrella stands, jardinieres, and pedestals. The company closed in 1962. Many pieces are marked with just the words *La Moro*.

LA MORO

Bean Pot, Brown Glaze, Blue Lid, Handle, 6 ¼ In.	50.00
Bowl, Aqua Gloss, Ruffled Rim, 8 x 3 ¼ In.	75.00
Bowl, Delph Blue Gloss, Flared, Pinched Shape, 10 ⅓ x 5 ½ In.	65.00
Bowl, Stardew Blue, Footed, Flared, Long Opening, 10 ¼ x 5 ½ In.	75.00
Bowl, White Gloss, Drips, Round, 5 In.	40.00
Jardiniere, White, High Gloss, Embossed Bands, Lug Handles, 7 In.	95.00
Jug, Rose Gloss, High Handle, 6 In.	35.00
Mug, Beer, Brown Gloss, 4 In.	35.00
Oil Jar, Yellow, Neck Twist Handles, 15 In.	495.00
Pitcher, Blue Gloss, Wheel Thrown, 5 ¾ In.	125.00
Pitcher, Delph Blue Gloss, Concentric Bands, 5 ¼ In.	60.00
Pitcher, Delph Blue, Duotone, White Interior, 6 ⅞ In.	75.00
Planter, Green, Figural, Duck, 5 ½ x 4 In.	36.00
Sugar, Cover, 3 x 3 In.	16.00
Teapot, Lid, Rose Matte Glaze, 7 ½ In.	100.00
Vase, Aqua Gloss, 6 x 6 In.	28.00
Vase, Aqua Gloss, Handles, 12 In.	185.00
Vase, Blue Gloss, 8 ½ In.	50.00
Vase, Blue Gloss, Triangular, 4 x 6 In.	30.00
Vase, Blue Matte Glaze, 8 ¼ In.	125.00
Vase, Blue Matte Glaze, Bulbous, 4 In.	50.00
Vase, Blue Matte Glaze, Embossed Rim, c.1920, 6 ¾ x 3 ½ In.	85.00
Vase, Brown, Ring, Cylindrical, 10 In.	50.00
Vase, Bud, Aqua, Shouldered, Footed, c.1951, 6 x 3 ½ In.	28.00
Vase, Cobalt Blue Gloss, 5 ¾ x 5 In.	30.00
Vase, Cylindrical, Pale Green Matte Drip, 5 ½ x 3 ½ In.	30.00
Vase, Delph Tobacco Leaf, Curved Rim, 8 In.	150.00
Vase, Gold Homespun, Cylindrical, Rings, 1960s, 10 x 4 In.	48.00
Vase, Green Embossed Flower, c.1930, 8 ¼ x 4 ½ In.	85.00
Vase, Green Gloss, 4 In.	50.00
Vase, Green Gloss, Lobed, Bulbous, Squat, 6 In.	40.00
Vase, Green Gloss, Wavy Rim, 4 ½ In.	70.00
Vase, Green Matte Glaze, Arts & Crafts, Marked, 7 ¼ In.	81.00
Vase, Lavender Matte Glaze, Tapered, 10 ½ In.	150.00
Vase, Mottled Olive Brown Glaze, Handles, 6 In.	150.00
Vase, Oil Jar, White Drip, 24 In.	995.00
Vase, Pillow, Lobed, Rectangular, c.1945, 5 ¾ x 4 ¼ In.	35.00
Vase, Rose Matte Glaze, Embossed Panels, 8 ½ x 4 In.	130.00
Vase, Seacrest Green, Embossed Flower, 4 x 4 ½ In.	48.00
Vase, Seacrest Green, Stubby Handles, 6 x 4 ½ In.	35.00
Vase, Tan Glaze, Green Mottled & White Drip, Double Handles, 16 x 17 In.	240.00
Vase, Trumpet, Seacrest Green, c.1920, 11 ¾ x 6 ¼ In.	285.00
Vase, White, High Gloss, Triangular, Folded Rim, 4 In.	40.00

WPA, Figurine, Alice In Wonderland With Ugly Duchess, Edris Eckhardt, Pottery, c.1935, 5 ⅞ In.
$460.00

Humler & Nolan

Wristwatch, Cartier, Tank, Stainless Steel, White Dial, Roman Numerals, Quartz Movement, Papers, Box
$2844.00

Skinner, Inc.

Wristwatch, Eberhard & Co., Chrono 4, 18K Rose Gold, White Dial, 4 Subsidiary Dials, Date, Box
$2489.00

Skinner, Inc.

X Y Z

Yellowware, Batter Bowl, Brown &
White Lines, Lipped Rim, Raised Foot,
6 x 12 In.
$71.00

Conestoga Auction Co., Inc.

Yellowware, Colander, 9 ½ In.
$45.00

Conestoga Auction Co., Inc.

Zsolnay, Jardiniere, Panels, Reticulated
Grillwork, Openwork Foot, Marked,
5 Churches, 7 In.
$230.00

Humler & Nolan

Zsolnay, Vase, Flowers, Dragons, Winged
Beasts, Ink Stamp, Hungary, 12 ⅝ In.
$1150.00

Humler & Nolan

ZSOLNAY pottery was made in Hungary after 1853 and was characterized by Persian, Art Nouveau, or Hungarian motifs. A series of new Zsolnay figurines with green-gold luster finish is available in many shops today. Early Zsolnay was not marked, but by 1878 the tower trademark was used.

Basket, Openwork, Pink, Green Flowers, Ivory Glaze Body, c.1890, 6 x 4 ½ In.	250.00
Bowl, Flowers, Butterflies, Scalloped Rim, 4 ¾ In.	22.00
Bowl, Folded Sides, Crescent Shape, Reticulated, Pink, Yellow, Blue, Gilt Trim, c.1890, 10 x 6 ¾ In.	850.00
Bowl, Mottled Iridescent Glaze, c.1900, 3 ½ x 2 ¾ In.	165.00
Box, Lid, Flowers, Butterflies, White Ground, 2 x 3 In.	36.00
Canister, Lid, Green Iridescent, Relief Decoration, 3 ½ x 5 In.	236.00
Card Holder, Green Eosin, Shell Shape	155.00
Centerpiece, Bowl, Boat Shape, Dragon Handles, Gilded, c.1890, 7 ½ x 15 ½ In.	9500.00
Ewer, Reticulated, 3 Flower Medallion, Moorish, c.1880, 7 In.	74.00
Ewer, Woman, Applied, To Side, Pushing, Eosin Green, 6 x 4 In.	159.00
Figurine, Child, Ball, Signed Andras Sinko, c.1930, 5 ½ x 4 In.	130.00
Figurine, Deer, Resting, Entwined, Green Eosin, c.1930, 6 ¼ x 3 ¼ In.	250.00
Figurine, Doe, Fawn, Eosin, 3 ½ x 2 ⅓ In.	125.00
Figurine, Dog, Dachshund, Long Hair, Brown, 3 x 5 In.	75.00
Figurine, Dog, German Shepherd, Green, High Gloss, 4 ½ x 6 In.	500.00
Figurine, Dog, Terrier, Seated, Eosin, 1930, 3 x 5 In.	225.00
Figurine, Geese, Brown, White, 7 x 7 In.	240.00
Figurine, Girl, Feeding Chick, Eosin Green Glaze, 3 ½ x 1 ¾ In.	65.00
Figurine, Girl, Seated, Scarf Cap, Blue Flower Band, 3 In.	75.00
Figurine, Group, 2 Polar Bears, Walking, White, c.1920, 7 ¾ x 4 ½ In.	350.00
Figurine, Man, Playing Flute, 10 ½ x 4 ¼ In.	250.00
Figurine, Nude Woman, Kneeling, Green Iridescent, 9 ¼ In.	108.00
Figurine, Shepherdess, Dog, Multicolor, 1935, 13 In.	750.00
Figurine, Woman, Dog, Arriving Home, Multicolor, Signed Sinko, 13 In.	450.00
Figurine, Woman, Nude, Crouching, 8 ½ x 6 In.	236.00
Figurine, Woman, Nude, Kneeling, Brown Hair, White, 8 ½ x 3 ½ In.	300.00
Figurine, Woman, Playing Harp, Green Eosin Glaze, Stamped, 12 ⅝ In.	288.00
Humidor, Cover, Persian Style, Flowers, Blue, Ivory, Reticulated, Pierced Appliques, 1870s, 11 x 7 In.	1250.00
Inkwell, Cover, Ivory, Relief Figures, Cantered Corners, Brass Collar, c.1895, 8 x 5 In.	887.00
Inkwell, Octagonal Profile, Classical Historical Scenes, 1880-1900, 8 x 5 In.	877.00
Jardiniere, Louis XV Style, Applied Flowers, Yellow Body, Pierced, 1879, 6 x 9 ¼ In.	650.00
Jardiniere, Panels, Reticulated Grillwork, Openwork Foot, Marked, 5 Churches, 7 In. ....*illus*	230.00
Jardiniere, Pierced, Reticulated, Multicolor, Gilt, Double Skin, c.1885, 4 ½ In.	220.00
Pitcher, Eosin, Stripe, c.1930, 7 ½ x 4 In.	1250.00
Pitcher, Old Ivory, White Rose, Gold, Beaded Handle, 1889, 7 ½ x 9 In.	450.00
Puzzle Jug, Pecs Art Pottery, Stylized Flower, Scrolling, 1800, 7 ½ In.	354.00
Tankard, Old Ivory Pattern, Hunt Scenes, Pink, Burgundy, Gold, c.1887, 10 ½ x 6 ⅝ In.	750.00
Tile, Green Eosin Glaze, Embossed Flowers, Square, 9 ⅛ x 9 ½ In.	125.00
Vase, 3 Folded Corners, Double Skin, Pierced, Flowers, Pastels, c.1900, 7 ½ x 5 ½ In.	450.00
Vase, Art Deco, Silver, Black, Red, 17 In.	3300.00
Vase, Cream, Caramel, Reticulated, Bulbous, c.1895, 8 x 6 In.	750.00
Vase, Double Wall Pierce, Reticulated, Blue, Cream, 8 In.	275.00
Vase, Egyptian Figures, Circles Inside Band, Spear Heads, Stamped, Horvath, 11 In.	431.00
Vase, Figurine, Dove, Eosin Glaze, c.1930, 4 ¼ x 4 In.	375.00
Vase, Flowers, Dragons, Winged Beasts, Ink Stamp, Hungary, 12 ⅝ In. ....*illus*	1150.00
Vase, Flowers, Multicolor, Ivory Ground, c.1880, 2 ¼ x 2 In., Pair	180.00
Vase, Gray & Peach Glaze, Narrow Neck, 3 Applied Handles, 8 In.	150.00
Vase, Green Eosin Glaze, Long Neck, 6 x 5 In.	365.00
Vase, Harvest Pattern, 4 Women Holding Cup, Grapes, Green Eosin Glaze, 6 x 3 In.	70.00
Vase, Jazz Dancer, Red, Green, Janos Torok, c.1960, 16 ¼ In.	495.00
Vase, Leaves, Flowers, Yellow, Reticulated Applied Handles, Rim, Moorish, c.1870, 14 ½ x 8 In..	1099.00
Vase, Lobed, Fluted, Green Eosin, 3 x 4 ½ In.	200.00
Vase, Nude Woman Handle, Eosin Green Glaze, 2 ½ x 5 In.	175.00
Vase, Orange, Ivory, Reticulated, Angled Handles, c.1890, 8 ½ x 5 In.	750.00
Vase, Persian Style, Flowers, Yellow, Brown, Olive, Red, Blue, Gilt, Reticulated Rim, c.1878, 11 In.	495.00
Vase, Persian Style, Ivory Body, Flowers, Multicolor, Reticulated Hearts, 1878, 8 ⅛ In.	550.00
Vase, Pink Dahlias, Ivory Ground, Tankard Shape, Reticulated Handle, c.1885, 9 ¾ In.	850.00
Vase, Pitcher, Old Ivory, Greek Figures, Mauve Glaze, c.1890, 6 In.	400.00
Vase, Reticulated, Petal Rim, Moorish, Pink, Green, 1880, 6 ¼ x 2 In.	550.00
Vase, Scalloped, Pierced, Reticulated, Footed, Cream, Blue Band, c.1880, 5 ¼ x 4 In.	265.00
Vase, Wave Shape, Flowers, Multicolor, Pierced Appliques, Reticulated Rim, Base, c.1878, 10 x 4 In.	550.00

X
Y
Z

PHOTO CREDITS

This is a list of the auction houses that provided photographs used in this book. Every dealer or auction house has to buy antiques to have items to sell. Call or email if you want to discuss buying or selling. If you need an appraisal or advice, remember that it is a part of their business and there is a charge.

Aleph-Bet Books
85 Old Mill River Rd.
Pound Ridge, NY 10576
www.alephbet.com
914-764-7410

Allard Auctions
PO Box 1030
St. Ignatius, MT 59865
www.allardauctions.com
406-745-0500

American Bottle Auctions
2523 J St., Ste. 203
Sacramento, CA 95816
www.americanbottle.com
800-806-7722

American Glass Gallery
PO Box 227
New Hudson, MI 48165
www.americanglassgallery.com
248-486-0530

Anderson Americana
PO Box 644
Troy, OH 45373
www.anderson-auction.com
937-339-0850

Auction Team Breker
Otto-Hahn St. 10
50997 Cologne, Germany
breker@thebestthings.com
703-796-5544 (U.S.)

Bertoia Auctions
2141 DeMarco Dr.
Vineland, NJ 08360
www.bertoiaauctions.com
856-692-1881

Bob Courtney Auctions
Route 122A
12 Providence St.
Millbury, MA 01527
www.bobcourtneyauctions.com
508-865-1009

Bonhams & Butterfields
7601 W. Sunset Blvd.
Los Angeles, CA 90046
www.bonhams.com
323-850-7500

Brunk Auctions
PO Box 2135
Asheville, NC 28802
www.brunkauctions.com
828-254-6846

Conestoga Auction Co.
PO Box 1
Manheim, PA 17545
www.conestogaauction.com
717-898-7284

Cottone Auctions
120 Court St.
Geneseo, NY 14454
www.cottoneauctions.com
585-243-3100

Cowan's Auctions
6270 Este Ave.
Cincinnati, OH 45232
www.cowanauctions.com
513-871-1670

DuMouchelles Art Gallery
409 East Jefferson Ave.
Detroit, MI 48226
www.dumouchelles.com
313-963-6255

Early American History Auctions
PO Box 3507
Rancho Santa Fe, CA 92067
www.earlyamerican.com
858-759-3290

Early Auction Co.
123 Main St.
Milford, OH 45150
www.earlyauctionco.com
513-831-4833

Fontaine's Auction Gallery
1485 W. Housatonic St.
Pittsfield, MA 01201
www.fontainesauction.net
413-448-8922

Fox Auctions
PO Box 4069
Vallejo, CA 94590
www.foxauctionsonline.com
631-553-3841

Garth's Auctions
PO Box 369
Delaware, OH 43015
www.garths.com
740-362-4771

Glass Works Auctions
102 Jefferson St.
East Greenville, PA 18041
www.glswrk-auction.com
215-679-5849

Gray's Auctioneers
10717 Detroit Ave.
Cleveland, OH 44102
www.graysauctioneers.com
216-458-7695

Hake's Americana & Collectibles
PO Box 12001
York, PA 17402
www.hakes.com
717-434-1600

Humler & Nolan
28 W. Fourth St.
Cincinnati, OH 45202
www.humlernolan.com
513-381-2041

Ivey-Selkirk Auctioneers
7447 Forsyth Blvd.
St. Louis, MO 63105
www.iveyselkirk.com
314-726-5515

James D. Julia, Inc.
203 Skowhegan Rd.
Fairfield, Maine 04937
www.jamesdjulia.com
207-453-7125

Jeffrey S. Evans & Assoc.
PO Box 2638
Harrisonburg, VA 22801
www.jeffreysevans.com
540-434-3939

Lang's Sporting Collectibles
663 Pleasant Valley Rd.
Waterville, NY 13480
www.langsauction.com
315-841-4623

Leighton Galleries
6 Pearl Court, Ste. C
Allendale, NJ 07401
www.leightongalleries.com
201-327-8800

Leland Little Auction
620 Cornerstone Ct.
Hillsborough, NC 27278
www.llauctions.com
919-644-1243

Leslie Hindman Auctioneers
1338 West Lake St.
Chicago, IL 60607
www.lesliehindman.com
312-280-1212

Los Angeles Modern Auctions (LAMA)
16145 Hart St.
Van Nuys, CA 91406
www.lamodern.com
323-904-1950

Marbeth Schon Gallery
415 Main St.
Natchez, MS 39120
www.mschon.com
228-424-7274

Martin Auction Company
PO Box 2
100 Lick Creek Rd.
Anna, IL 62906
www.martinauctionco.com
618-833-3589

Morphy Auctions
2000 North Reading Rd.
Denver, PA 17517
www.morphyauctions.com
717-335-3435

Neal Auction Co.
4038 Magazine St.
New Orleans, LA 70115
www.nealauction.com
800-467-5329

New Orleans Auction Galleries
801 Magazine St.
New Orleans, LA 70130
www.neworleansauction.com
800-501-0277

Noel Barrett Antiques & Auctions
PO Box 300
Carversville, PA 18913
www.noelbarrett.com
215-297-5109

Norman C. Heckler & Company
79 Bradford Corner Rd.
Woodstock Valley, CT 06282
www.hecklerauction.com
860-974-1634

Northeast Auctions
93 Pleasant St.
Portsmouth, NH 03801
www.northeastauctions.com
603-433-8400

Old Barn Auction
10040 St. Route 224
Findlay, OH 45840
www.oldbarn.com
419-422-8531

Past Tyme Pleasures
5424 Sunol Blvd., #10-242
Pleasanton, CA 94566
www.pasttyme1.com
925-484-6442

Philip Weiss Auctions
1 Neil Court
Oceanside, NY 11572
www.weissauctions.com
516-594-0731

Potteries Specialist Auctions
271 Waterloo Rd
Cobridge, Stoke On Trent,
England
ST6 3HR
www.potteriesauctions.com
+44(0)1782 286622

Rago Arts and Auction Center
333 North Main St.
Lambertville, NJ 08530
www.ragoarts.com
609-397-9374

Rock Island Auction Co.
7819 42nd St. West
Rock Island, IL 61201
www.rockislandauction.com
800-238-8022

Seeck Auctions
PO Box 377
Mason City, IA 50402
www.seeckauction.com
641-424-1116

Serious Toyz
1 Baltic Place
Croton on Hudson, NY 10520
www.serioustoyz.com
866-653-8699

Showtime Auction Services
22619 Monterey Dr.
Woodhaven, MI 48183
www.showtimeauctions.com
951-453-2415

Skinner, Inc.
274 Cedar Hill St.
Marlborough, MA 01752
www.skinnerinc.com
508-970-3000

Sloans & Kenyon
7034 Wisconsin Ave.
Chevy Chase, MD 20815
www.sloansandkenyon.com
301-634-2330

Stein Auction Company
PO Box 136
Palatine, IL 60078
www.garykirsnerauctions.com
847-991-5927

Strawser Auction Group
PO Box 332
200 North Main
Wolcottville, IN 46795
www.strawserauctions.com
260-854-2859

Theriault's
PO Box 151
Annapolis, MD 21404
www.theriaults.com
800-638-0422

Tom Harris Auctions
203 South 18th Ave.
Marshalltown, IA 50108
www.tomharrisauctions.com
641-754-4890

Treadway Toomey Galleries
2029 Madison Rd.
Cincinnati, OH 45208
www.treadwaygallery.com
513-321-6742

Victorian Casino Antiques
4520 Arville St. #1
Las Vegas, NV 89103
www.vcaauction.com
702-382-2466

William H. Bunch Auctions
1 Hillman Dr.
Chadds Ford, PA 19317
www.williambunchauctions.com
610-558-1800

William Morford Antiques
RD #2
Cazenovia, NY 13035
www.morfauction.com
315-662-7625

Willis Henry Auctions
22 Main St.
Marshfield, MA 02050
www.willishenry.com
781-834-7774